SAMSAD BENGALI-ENGLISH DICTIONARY

SAMSAD
BENGALI-ENGLISH DICTIONARY

[REVISED & ENLARGED THIRD EDITION]

Compiled by

Late SAILENDRA BISWAS M.A.

Second Edition Edited by

Late BIRENDRAMOHAN DASGUPTA M.A.

Revised by

Late SUBODHCHANDRA SENGUPTA M.A, Ph.D.

Third Edition Revised by

Sri SUBHAS BHATTACHARYA M.A.

SAHITYA SAMSAD

ISBN 978-81-86806-86-5

First Edition	:	May 1968
Reprint	:	1972, 1976, 1979, 1980
Second Edition	:	May 1982
Reprint	:	1983, 1984, 1985, 1986, 1987, 1988, 1989, 1990, 1991, 1992, 1993, 1994, 1995, 1996, 1997, 1998, 1999
Revised & Enlarged Third Edition	:	July 2000
Reprint	:	2000, 2001, 2002, 2003, 2004, 2005, 2006, 2007, 2008, 2009, 2010, 2011, 2012
Twentysecond Impression	:	March 2013

Published by : DEBAJYOTI DATTA, SHISHU SAHITYA SAMSAD PVT LTD
32A Acharya Prafullachandra Road, Kolkata 700 009

Printed at : DAS PRINTERS
61 Surya Sen Stree, Kolkata 700 009

Distributor : INDIAN BOOK DISTRIBUTING CO.
65/2 Mahatma Gandhi Road, Kolkata 700 009

₹ 270.00

তৃতীয় সংস্করণ সম্পর্কে প্রকাশকের নিবেদন

সংসদের Bengali-English Dictionary-র দ্বিতীয় সংস্করণ প্রকাশের আঠারো বছর পর এই তৃতীয় সংস্করণ প্রকাশিত হল। কয়েকটি বিষয়ে পূর্ববর্তী সংস্করণ থেকে তৃতীয় সংস্করণের পার্থক্য বিশেষ লক্ষণীয়। প্রথমত, বহু নতুন শব্দ এই সংস্করণে সংযোজিত হয়েছে। অর্থ ও প্রতিশব্দের বিবৃতিতে যেসব ত্রুটি ও অসম্পূর্ণতা ছিল তা বহুলাংশে সংশোধিত হয়েছে। এমনকী, পরিশিষ্টে কতকগুলি বিষয় সন্নিবিষ্ট হওয়ায় গ্রন্থখানির ব্যবহারযোগ্যতা নিঃসন্দেহে বেড়েছে।

এই অভিধানের সংশোধিত ও পরিবর্ধিত সংস্করণটি প্রস্তুত করেছেন সাহিত্য সংসদের সম্পাদকমণ্ডলীর অন্যতম সদস্য শ্রীসুভাষ ভট্টাচার্য। তাঁকে যথাবিধি সাহায্য করেছেন শ্রীরমেন ভট্টাচার্য। উভয়েই আমাদের কৃতজ্ঞতাভাজন। অভিধানের কলেবর বৃদ্ধি সত্ত্বেও এবং প্রকাশনব্যয়ের আধিক্য সত্ত্বেও কেবল পাঠকদের কথা বিবেচনা করেই গ্রন্থের মূল্য যথাসম্ভব কম ধার্য করা হয়েছে।

কলকাতা
জুলাই ২০০০

দেবজ্যোতি দত্ত

তৃতীয় সংস্করণের ভূমিকা

সংসদ Bengali-English Dictionary-র তৃতীয় সংশোধিত ও পরিবর্ধিত সংস্করণ প্রকাশিত হল। ইতিপূর্বে ১৯৮২ সালে দ্বিতীয় সংস্করণ প্রকাশিত হওয়ার পরে বারবার পুনর্মুদ্রিত হয়েছে এই অভিধান এবং প্রায় প্রতিবারই পুনর্মুদ্রণকালে কিছু সংশোধনও সাধিত হয়েছে। এই তৃতীয় সংস্করণে অবশ্য অভিধানখানি আদ্যন্ত সংশোধিত হয়েছে, বহু নতুন শব্দ সংযোজিত হয়েছে।

নতুন শব্দের অন্তর্ভুক্তি এই সংস্করণের একটি উল্লেখযোগ্য বৈশিষ্ট্য বটে। ভাষায় প্রতিনিয়ত নতুন নতুন শব্দ এবং নতুন নতুন প্রয়োগ অনুপ্রবিষ্ট হচ্ছে। সেসবের অন্তর্ভুক্তি একান্তই আবশ্যক। এই সংস্করণে সেকাজ যত্নের সঙ্গে করা হয়েছে। বাংলা-ইংরেজি অভিধান প্রায়ই বাংলা ভাষা থেকে ইংরেজি ভাষায় অনুবাদে পাঠককে সাহায্য করবে এটাই অভিপ্রেত। সেইজন্য প্রতিশব্দের প্রতি বিশেষ নজর রাখা হয়েছে। উদ্ভিদের ক্ষেত্রে প্রায়ই বৈজ্ঞানিক নাম সংযোজিত হয়েছে।

এই সংস্করণের পরিশিষ্টটিকে বিশেষভাবে সমৃদ্ধ করা হয়েছে। ভারতীয় পশুপাখি ও উদ্ভিদের বৈজ্ঞানিক নাম, অ্যাপ্রোপ্রিয়েট প্রিপজিশন, শব্দের সংক্ষিপ্ত রূপের তালিকা প্রভৃতি এই প্রথম এই অভিধানে সংযোজিত হয়েছে। পাঠক ও লেখকদের পক্ষে তা বিশেষভাবে সহায়ক হবে আশা করা যায়।

এই সংস্করণটি প্রস্তুত করার সময় সাহিত্য সংসদের সর্বাধ্যক্ষ শ্রীদেবজ্যোতি দত্তের পরামর্শ প্রতিপদে আমাকে সাহায্য করেছে। শ্রীরমেন ভট্টাচার্য প্রতিবারের মতো এখানেও আমাকে প্রভূত সাহায্য করেছেন। তাঁর সহৃদয়তার তুলনা নেই। সাহিত্য সংসদের কর্মী শ্রীবাসুদেব গঙ্গোপাধ্যায়ের নিরলস শ্রম ও নিষ্ঠার কথা ভোলা সম্ভব নয়। এই সংস্করণটিকে ত্রুটিমুক্ত ও আকর্ষক করে তুলতে তাঁর উদ্যম বিশেষ প্রশংসনীয়।

কলকাতা
জুলাই ২০০০

সুভাষ ভট্টাচার্য

দ্বিতীয় সংস্করণ সম্পর্কে প্রকাশকের নিবেদন

বাঙ্গালা-ইংরেজি অভিধান-এর দ্বিতীয় সংস্করণ প্রকাশিত হইল। শ্রীবীরেন্দ্রমোহন দাশগুপ্ত, এম.এ. অশেষ যত্নে ইহার সম্পাদনা করিয়াছেন। প্রথম সংস্করণ আদ্যোপান্ত সংশোধন করিয়া এবং নূতন শব্দের বিন্যাস সংযোজন করিয়া এই অভিধানের গুণগত মান বৃদ্ধিতে তিনি চেষ্টার কার্পণ্য করেন নাই। ইংরেজি সাহিত্যে পাণ্ডিত্যের জন্য বিখ্যাত ডঃ সুবোধচন্দ্র সেনগুপ্ত মহাশয় বীরেন্দ্রমোহনবাবুর সম্পাদনাকার্য তদারক করিয়া দিয়াছেন। উভয়ের কাছেই আমরা আন্তরিক কৃতজ্ঞতা জ্ঞাপন করি। প্রথম সংস্করণের ক্রাউন অক্টেভো আকার পরিবর্তন করিয়া ডিমাই অক্টেভো আকারে অভিধানখানি গ্রন্থিত করায় ব্যবহারকারীদের সুবিধা হইবে আশা করি। প্রকাশন-ব্যয়বৃদ্ধির আধিক্য সত্ত্বেও অভিধানের যথাসাধ্য কম মূল্য ধার্য করা হইয়াছে।

১৫ এপ্রিল ১৯৮২ — মহেন্দ্রনাথ দত্ত

প্রকাশকের নিবেদন

বর্তমান বাঙ্গালা-ইংরেজি অভিধানটি সাধারণের হাতে তুলিয়া দিতে পারিয়া আমরা আনন্দিত হইয়াছি। ভরসা করি, আমাদের অন্যান্য অভিধানগুলির মতো এটিও সাধারণ্যে সমাদৃত হইবে। অপরিহার্য কারণে অভিধানটি প্রকাশে অনেক বিলম্ব হইল—এই ত্রুটির জন্য আমরা সাধারণের নিকট ক্ষমা প্রার্থনা করিতেছি। পাণ্ডুলিপি প্রণয়নের দুরূহতাই ইহার মুখ্য কারণ।

শ্রীশৈলেন্দ্র বিশ্বাস অশেষ পরিশ্রম ও অধ্যবসায় সহকারে অভিধানটি সংকলন করিয়া দিয়াছেন এবং সুপণ্ডিত ড. সুবোধচন্দ্র সেনগুপ্ত অতি যত্নসহকারে পাণ্ডুলিপি সংশোধন করিয়া দিয়াছেন। আমরা ইঁহাদের নিকট কৃতজ্ঞ।

বর্তমান দুর্মূল্যের দিনে অভিধানটির দাম যথাসম্ভব কম ধার্য করা হইয়াছে।

২০ মে ১৯৬৮

দ্বিতীয় সংস্করণের ভূমিকা

সংসদ বাঙ্গালা-ইংরেজি অভিধানের দ্বিতীয় সংস্করণ প্রকাশিত হইল। প্রথম সংস্করণের তৃতীয় পুনর্মুদ্রণকালে পরিশিষ্টে যে-সকল নূতন শব্দ এবং প্রয়োগবিধির দৃষ্টান্ত সংযোজন করিয়াছিলাম বর্তমান সংস্করণে তাহা মূল অভিধানে সন্নিবেশিত হইয়াছে। ইহা ছাড়া, প্রায় পাঁচ হাজার নূতন শব্দ, নির্দিষ্ট ভাবপ্রকাশক শব্দসমষ্টি (phrases), বাগ্‌ধারা (idioms) এবং পারিভাষিক শব্দ ইহাতে সংযোজিত হইয়াছে।

সম্পাদনকালে শব্দাদির অর্থবৈচিত্র্যের প্রতি বিশেষ লক্ষ রাখা হইয়াছে এবং অনেক স্থানে শব্দার্থ বিস্তৃততর করা হইয়াছে। অভিধানোক্ত শব্দসমূহের অর্থাদি পুঙ্খানুপুঙ্খভাবে পুনর্বিচার করা হইয়াছে এবং প্রয়োজন অনুযায়ী সংশোধন অথবা পরিমার্জন করা হইয়াছে। জীবন্ত ভাষার শব্দার্থে ও প্রয়োগবিধিতে নিরন্তর পরিবর্তন ঘটে। এই পরিবর্তনশীলতা আভিধানিকের কাজ দুরূহ করিয়া তোলে। এই বিষয়ের প্রতি লক্ষ রাখিয়া নিজ কর্তব্য পালন করিতে চেষ্টার ত্রুটি করি নাই। যাহাতে অভিধানখানির উপযোগিতা এবং জনপ্রিয়তা সর্বাংশে বৃদ্ধি পায় তৎপ্রতিও বিশেষ মনোযোগী হইয়াছি। সাফল্যের বিচার সহৃদয় পাঠকমণ্ডলী করিবেন। তাঁহাদের নিকট একান্ত অনুরোধ যে কোনো ভুলত্রুটি লক্ষ করিলে তাঁহারা যেন উহা আমাদের গোচরে আনয়ন করেন।

সাহিত্য সংসদের সর্বাধ্যক্ষ শ্রীযুক্ত মহেন্দ্রনাথ দত্ত এবং কৃতী ও সুযোগ্য পরিচালক শ্রীযুক্ত দেবজ্যোতি দত্ত বর্তমান সংস্করণ সম্পাদনার ভার আমার উপরে ন্যস্ত করিয়া এবং সম্পাদনকার্যে নানাভাবে উপদেশ দিয়া আমাকে অপরিশোধনীয় ঋণপাশে আবদ্ধ করিয়াছেন। তাঁহাদের সহৃদয়তা কৃতজ্ঞতার সহিত স্মরণ করি।

স্বনামধন্য শ্রদ্ধেয় পণ্ডিতপ্রবর ডক্টর সুবোধচন্দ্র সেনগুপ্তের নিকট আমার ঋণ সমধিক। তাঁহার অমূল্য উপদেশ এবং সংশোধন অভিধানখানির উৎকর্ষসাধনে সাতিশয় সহায়তা করিয়াছে। তাঁহার অপরিশোধ্য ঋণ কৃতজ্ঞচিত্তে স্মরণ করি।

এই প্রসঙ্গে সাহিত্য সংসদের সুযোগ্য ম্যানেজার শ্রীযুক্ত গোলোকেন্দু ঘোষ মহাশয়ের নাম বিশেষভাবে উল্লেখযোগ্য। তাঁহার নিরলস সহযোগিতা ও নানা মূল্যবান উপদেশ আমার অমূল্য পাথেয় হইয়াছে। মুদ্রণকালে আর যাঁহাদের সহায়তা লাভ করিয়াছি তাঁহাদের মধ্যে শ্রীযুক্ত রমেন ভট্টাচার্য সর্বাগ্রগণ্য। শ্রীযুক্ত মনোমোহন চক্রবর্তী এবং শ্রীযুক্ত কৃষ্ণ সেনগুপ্ত অত্যন্ত দক্ষতার সহিত প্রুফ-সংশোধন-কার্যে সহায়তা করিয়াছেন। ইঁহারা সকলেই নান ত্রুটিবিচ্যুতির প্রতি আমার দৃষ্টি আকর্ষণ করিয়াছেন। ইঁহাদের নিকট আমার কৃতজ্ঞতা অপরিসীম। পরিশেষে, অকুণ্ঠ সহযোগিতার জন্য সাহিত্য সংসদের সহকর্মীবৃন্দের প্রতি আন্তরিক ধন্যবাদ জানাই।

১৯ মার্চ ১৯৮২ — বীরেন্দ্রমোহন দাশগুপ্ত

প্রথম সংস্করণের ভূমিকা

'সংসদ্ বাঙ্গালা অভিধান' এবং 'Samsad English-Bengali Dictionary' প্রকাশিত হইবার পর শুভানুধ্যায়ী সুধী-সমাজের নিকট হইতে প্রায়ই একটি অনুরোধ পাইতে থাকি ; অনুরোধটি হইল এমন একখানি Bengali-English Dictionary রচনা করিবার জন্য যাহা বাঙ্গালা হইতে ইংরেজিতে অনুবাদকার্যে এবং বঙ্গভাষাধ্যায়ী বিদেশীদের পাঠকার্যে সহায়তা করিতে পারিবে। 'সাহিত্য সংসদ্'-এর ম্যানেজিং ডিরেক্টর শ্রীযুক্ত মহেন্দ্রনাথ দত্তকে এই কথা জানাইলে, তিনি উক্ত অভিধান মুদ্রণ ও প্রকাশের দায়িত্ব গ্রহণ করিতে এবং ব্যয়ভার বহন করিতে সম্মত হন। সে আজ চার বৎসরেরও আগের কথা। এই দীর্ঘকাল প্রায় সর্বকর্ম পরিত্যাগ করিয়া উক্ত অভিধান রচনায় ব্যাপৃত থাকি। এই অভিধান রচনায় সুধীজনের নির্দেশ কতটা সাফল্যের সঙ্গে পালন করিতে পারিয়াছি, তাহা তাঁহাদেরই বিচার্য। ভ্রমপ্রমাদ নিশ্চয়ই ঘটিয়াছে, এবং সে সম্বন্ধে যদি তাঁহাদের মন্তব্য জানিতে পাই, তাহা হইলে তাঁহাদের নিকট কৃতজ্ঞ থাকিব।

প্রত্যেক জীবন্ত ভাষার শব্দসম্ভারে, শব্দার্থে, প্রয়োগবিধিতে নিরন্তর পরিবর্তন ঘটিতেছে। এই পরিবর্তনশীলতার ফলে আভিধানিকের কাজ বিষম কঠিন হইয়া উঠে। অধিকন্তু, ইতিপূর্বে যে তিনখানি অভিধান রচনা করিয়াছি ('সংসদ বাঙ্গালা অভিধান', 'Samsad English-Bengali Dictionary' এবং 'Samsad Little English-Bengali Dictionary'), সে কয়খানির ক্ষেত্রে পূর্বগামীদের রচিত গ্রন্থাবলী হইতে প্রচুর সাহায্য পাইয়াছি ; কিন্তু বর্তমান বাঙ্গালা-ইংরেজি অভিধানখানির রচনাকার্যে সেরূপ কোনো সাহায্য পাই নাই বলিলেই চলে। সেই অভাব বহুলাংশে পূরণ করিয়াছেন এই গ্রন্থের সংশোধক ডক্টর সুবোধচন্দ্র সেনগুপ্ত। তাঁহার সঙ্গে কাজ করিয়া এই কথাটি স্পষ্টই হৃদয়ঙ্গম হইয়াছে যে, তিনি কেবল বর্তমান ভারতের অন্যতম অগ্রগণ্য সাহিত্যপণ্ডিতই নহেন, জ্ঞানের বিভিন্ন রাজ্যেও তাঁহার বিশেষাধিকার আছে। সর্বোপরি, অভিধান রচনার কার্যে যে সর্বরসে রসিক মন থাকার প্রয়োজন, তেমন একটি মনের তিনি অধিকারী। কিন্তু দুঃখের বিষয়, তাঁহার নির্দেশাবলী সর্বক্ষেত্রে যথাযথভাবে পালন করিতে পারি নাই, কারণ তাহা করিতে হইলে অভিধানখানির কলেবর অনেক বড়ো হইয়া পড়িত। আমি নিজেও যে পাণ্ডুলিপি রচনা করিয়াছিলাম, তাহা সম্পূর্ণ বজায় রাখিতে গেলে এই গ্রন্থখানির আয়তন প্রায় দ্বিগুণ বৃদ্ধি পাইত। বর্তমান অবস্থায় তাহা করা সম্ভব ছিল না। ফলে, নির্মমভাবে পাণ্ডুলিপির অঙ্গহানি করিতে হইয়াছে। তবে, বর্তমান গ্রন্থখানি যদি পাঠকসমাজে সমাদর লাভ করে

এবং পাঠকবর্গ যদি দাবি করেন, তাহা হইলে ভবিষ্যতে একখানি বড়ো আকারের বাঙ্গালা-ইংরেজি অভিধান প্রণয়নের ইচ্ছা রহিল।

বর্তমান গ্রন্থখানির প্রুফ-সংশোধনের দায়িত্ব যাঁহারা যোগ্যতার সঙ্গে পালন করিয়াছেন, তাঁহারা হইলেন শ্রীযুক্ত আশুতোষ ভট্টাচার্য বি.এ., শ্রীযুক্ত পূর্ণেন্দু সেনগুপ্ত, শ্রীযুক্ত রজত নন্দী বি.এ.। গ্রন্থের রচনা, মুদ্রণ ও প্রকাশনার কার্যে সর্বক্ষণ যথোচিত তত্ত্বাবধান করিয়াছেন 'সাহিত্য সংসদ'-এর সুযোগ্য কর্মসচিব সুসাহিত্যিক শ্রীযুক্ত গোলোকেন্দু ঘোষ বি.কম.। সংযোগরক্ষার দায়িত্ব নিয়মিতভাবে পালন করিয়াছেন শ্রীযুক্ত মাধবচন্দ্র দাস। ইঁহারা সকলেই আমার আন্তরিক ধন্যবাদের পাত্র। সর্বোপরি, এতগুলি সুধী ব্যক্তি ও কর্মীকে একত্র করিয়া এবং বিগত চার বৎসর ধরিয়া এই অভিধান রচনার কার্যে নানা সাহায্য করিয়া ও প্রেরণা দিয়া শ্রীযুক্ত মহেন্দ্রনাথ দত্ত যে মনোবৃত্তি ও নিষ্ঠার পরিচয় দিয়াছেন, তাহা প্রকৃত সাধকের মধ্যেই দৃষ্ট হয়। তাঁহার মনোবৃত্তি ও নিষ্ঠা আমাকে মুগ্ধ করিয়াছে।

পরিশেষে, পাঠকবর্গের নিকট পুনরায় সবিনয় নিবেদন করিতেছি যে, তাঁহারা যেন অনুগ্রহ করিয়া বিনা দ্বিধায় তাঁহাদের মতামত আমাকে জ্ঞাপন করেন, তাঁহাদের মন্তব্য গ্রন্থখানির ভবিষ্যৎ সংস্করণের সংশোধন-কার্যে প্রচুর সহায়তা করিবে বলিয়া বিশ্বাস করি। ইতি—

রবীন্দ্র-জন্মতিথি, ১৩৭৫ — শৈলেন্দ্র বিশ্বাস

বেলঘরিয়া

অভিধানে ব্যবহৃত সংকেতাবলির অর্থ

a.	adjective
aban.	abandoned
abbre.	abbreviation
accts.	accounts
adv.	adverb
affect.	affectionate
alg.	algebra
alt.	alternative
anat.	anatomy
approx.	approximately
arch.	archaic
arith.	arithmetic
art.	article
astr.	astronomy
astrol.	astrology
Beng.	Bengali
bot.	botany
chem.	chemistry
christ.	christianity
coll.	colloquial
collect.	collective
com.	common
comm.	commerce
comp.	compound
compar.	comparative
con.	conjunction
contemp.	contemptuous
contr.	contraction
cp.	compare
correl.	correlative
corrup.	corruption, corrupted
def.	definite
deg.	degree
dero.	derogatory
dial.	dialectal
dim	diminutive
distr.	distributive
econ.	economics
e.g.	exempli gratia (for example)
elec.	electricity
Eng.	English
erron.	erroneous
esp.	especially
etc.	et cetera
ety.	etymologically
euph.	euphemism
exclam.	exclamatory
facet.	facetious
fem.	feminine
fig.	figurative
for.	formal
gen.	gender
geog.	geography
geol.	geology
geom.	geometry
gr.	grammar
High.	High Bengali
hist.	history
hon.	honorific
hum.	humorous
idiom.	idiomatic
i.e.	id est (that is)
imi.	imitative
imperat.	imperative
imperf.	imperfect
imprec.	imprecatory
ind.	indecent
inf.	informal
infe.	inferior
infi.	infinitive
int.	interjection
interro.	interrogative
joc.	jocular
leg.	legal
ling.	linguistics
lit.	literary
log.	logic
loos.	loosely, loose

masc.	masculine	post.	post position
math.	mathematics	*p. pt.*	past participle
mech.	mechanics	*pr.*	present
med.	medical	*prep.*	preposition
metaph.	metaphysics	print.	printing
mil.	military	*pro.*	pronoun
mod.	modern	pros.	prosody
Mus.	Muslim		
mus.	music	rare	rarely
myth.	mythology	rej.	rejected
		relat.	relative
n.	noun	rhet.	rhetoric
naut.	nautical	ridi.	in ridicule
neut.	neuter		
		Sans.	Sanskrit
obs.	obsolete	sarcas.	sarcastic
obsc.	obscene	sc.	science
ori.	original	*sfx.*	suffix
		sing.	singular
p.	past	sl.	slang
part.	participle	spell.	spelling
perf.	perfect	*super.*	superlative
pfx.	prefix		
ph.	phrase	*trans.*	transitive
phil.	philosophy	theol.	theology
phon.	phonetics	theos.	theosophy
pl.	plural	usu.	usually
poet.	poetic use		
pol.	politics	*v.*	verb
pop.	popular	*var.*	variant
pos.	positive	voc.	vocative
poss.	possessive	vul.	vulgar

SAMSAD BENGALI–ENGLISH DICTIONARY

অ১ *n.* the first vowel of the Bengali alphabet. **অ আ** (বা **অ আ ক খ**) elementary knowledge; rudiments of any subject (সংগীতের অ আ ক খ) ; the alphabet (অ আ শিখছে) ; A B C.

অ২ *pfx.* indicating : negation, contradiction, contrariety, absence, want, non-, un-, il-, im-, in, ir-, dis-, mis-, a-, an-, less; other than or inferior (অব্রাহ্মণ).

অঋণী *a.* without any debts; not indebted.

অংশ *n.* a portion or part; a share; a region or locality (দেশের উত্তর অংশ = the northern region of the country) ; (astrol.) $^1/_{30}$ of the zodiac; (geog.) $^1/_{360}$ of earth's circumference; degree; concern, respect (কোনো অংশে মহৎ নয় = noble in no respect) ; divine incarnation (বিষ্ণুর অংশ = an incarnation of Vishnu). **~ক** *n.*(alg.) a mantissa. **অংশ করা** *v.* to divide into parts or shares; apportion (food, property, task etc.) among others. **~গত** *a.* included in a part or share; relating to part(s) or share(s). **~গ্রাহী** *a.* taking a share , participating. ☐ *n.* a sharer, a shareholder; a participant, a party. **~ত** *adv.* partly, in part; partially; to some extent. **~ন** *n.* dividing; sharing; apportionment, distribution. **অংশনীয়** *a.* divisible into parts or shares; to be divided into parts. **~প্রেষ** *n.* (sc.) partial pressure. **~ভাক্**, **~ভাগী** *a.* enjoying a share; having a claim to a share. ☐ *n.* a share, a shareholder; a claimant to a share; one who is responsible for a part, a partner. **(কিছুতে) অংশ নেওয়া** *v.* to take part (in), to participate (in). **অংশাংশ** *n.* fraction of fraction; minute fraction; tiny part; bit.

অংশাংশি *n.* division into respective shares. ☐ *a.* & *adv.* according to or dividing into respective shares.

অংশাঙ্কন *n.* graduation, marking (a scale).

অংশাঙ্কিত *a.* (of a measuring scale, thermometer etc.) marked with measured distance or degrees, graduated.

অংশানো *v.* to descend as an inheritance, to devolve on.

অংশাবতার *n.* demi-god, partial incarnation (of a god.)

অংশিত *a.* divided into parts or shares; partitioned.

অংশী *a.* entitled to a share. ☐ *n.* a partner or shareholder; co-sharer; participant.

অংশীদার *n.* a partner or shareholder. **অংশীদারি** *n.* partnership. ☐ *a.* relating to partnership. **অংশীদারি** (বা **অংশীদার**) **চুক্তি** partnership agreement. **অংশীদারিত্ব** *n.* same as **অংশীদারি** ।

অংশু *n.* ray, a narrow beam of light (from a small or distant source). **~ক** *n.* fine cotton fabric; silk cloth. **~মান**, **~মতী** *a.* luminous; radiant. **~মালা** *n.* a stream of rays. **~মালী** *n.* the sun; the sun-god. **~ল** *a.* having rays; full of rays; radiant.

অংশ্যমান *a.* that which is in the process of being divided or partitioned.

অংস *n.* shoulder. **~কূট**, **~কূট** *n.* a bull's hump. **~ফলক**, **~ফলকাস্থি** *n.* shoulder-blade, the scapula. **অংসল** *a.* . bull-necked; robust, strong.

অকচ *a.* alopecoid; having no hair, bald, baldheaded.

অকঞ্চুক *a.* (of fruits) skinless; (of lizards) achlamydeous.

অকটু *a.* (of smell or taste) not acrid or bitter or pungent.

অকঠিন *a.* not hard or difficult; not severe.

অকঠোর *a.* not rigorous or strict; not rude or severe.

অকণ্টক *a.* thornless; (fig.) free from trouble and difficulty; safe and peaceful. **অকণ্টকে** *adv.* in peace and safety; with nothing standing in the way; untroubled; freely.

অকথন *n.* bad or abusive language; obscene words. ☐ *a.* unspeakable; indescribable.

অকথনীয় same as **অকথ্য** ।

অকথা *n.* abusive or filthy or obscene language (also **অকথা-কুকথা**).

অকথিত *a.* untold; unspoken; undisclosed; unrevealed; secret.

অকথ্য *a.* unspeakable, unutterable; obscene, filthy. **~কথন** utterance of undesirable or bad language; uttering foul or filthy language.

অকপট *a.* frank, candid, sincere, aboveboard; straightforward; unreserved. **~তা** *n.* frankness; candour, sincerity, **~চিত্তে, অকপটে** *adv.* open-heartedly, frankly, sincerely, candidly.

অকম্প, অকম্পিত, অকম্প্র *a.* not trembling or trembled, not tremulous; undaunted; unmoved, unshaken, unperturbed; steady.

অকরণী *n.* (math.) a rational quantity or number.

অকরণীয় *a.* that which should not be done. **অকরণীয় ঘর** a family or house not acceptable for matrimonial alliance.

অকরুণ *a.* merciless; unkind; cruel; unsympathetic.

অকরোটি, অকরোটী *n.* (zoo.) the acrania.

অকর্ণ *a.* earless; deaf. ☐ *n.* an earless or deaf person.

অকর্তব্য *a.* that which should not be done; improper.

অকর্তৃত্ব *n.* lack of ruling or controlling power; lack of authority.

অকর্ম *n.* a misdeed, a mischief; a useless act; inaction, absence of work.

অকর্মক *a.* (gr. of a verb) intransitive. **অকর্মক ক্রিয়া** intransitive verb.

অকর্মণ্য *a.* disabled; inefficient; not in working order, unserviceable. **~তা** *n.* incompetence, inefficiency; uselessness.

অকর্মা *a.* having no employment or occupation; grossly inefficient; idling. **অকর্মার ধাড়ি** an inveterate bungler, an arch-bungler, a muff; a good-for-nothing or worthless fellow; a great idler.

অকর্ষিত *a.* (of land) unploughed, uncultivated; fallow.

অকলঙ্ক, অকলঙ্কী *a.* spotless, taintless, unblemished, immaculate; clean, pure.

অকলঙ্ক চরিত্র unblemished character.

অকলঙ্কিত *a.* unstained, unsullied, unblemished; undefiled, unpolluted. **অকলঙ্কিত চরিত্র** same as **অকলঙ্ক চরিত্র** ।

অকলুষ *n.* absence of corruption or blemish or sin. ☐ *a.* uncorrupted; unblemished; sinless.

অকলুষিত *a.* undefiled, unpolluted; uncorrupted; pure, clean.

অকল্পিত *a.* not imaginary or fanciful; real; unthought-of, unimagined. **~পূর্ব** *a.* unpremeditated; unthought-of not thought-of before.

অকল্যাণ *n.* harm, injury; spiritual or moral harm; misfortune; woe. **~কর** *a.* harmful, injurious; inauspicious; woeful.

অকষ্টকল্পনা *n.* spontaneous (and not forced or far-fetched) imagination or (literary) composition. **অকষ্টকল্পিত** *a.* not forced or far-fetched, spontaneous, facile, easy-going.

অকস্মাৎ *adv.* all at once, suddenly, all of / on (arch.) a sudden; unexpectedly, unawares; without cause, unwarrantedly.

অকাজ *n.* a useless act; a mischief; a wrong-doing. **অকাজের কাজি** a mischief-maker, wrongdoer.

অকাট var. of **আকাট** ।

অকাট্য *a.* irrefutable. **অকাট্য প্রমাণ** a conclusive evidence. **অকাট্য যুক্তি** incontrovertible or irrefutable argument.

অকাতর *a.* (in suffering, danger etc.) unperturbed, undistressed; unflinching; patient, calm; (in toil, fighting etc.) untiring; (of gift, charity etc.) ungrudging, bountiful. **অকাতরে** *adv.*

unperturbedly; feeling no distress, unflinchingly; patiently, calmly; soundly, deeply (অকাতরে ঘুমানো) ; untiringly; ungrudgingly; bountifully.

অকাম্য *a.* undesirable, unwanted.

অকায় *a.* bodiless, incorporeal, disembodied; formless, shapeless; (poet.) unbodied.

অকার *n.* the letter and the vowel sound অ ; **অকারাদি** *a.* (of words) beginning with the letter অ. □ *n.* অ and other vowels. **অকারাদিক্রমে** *adv.* in the alphabetical order. **অকারান্ত** *a.* (of words) ending with the vowel sound অ.

অকারণ *a.* unnecessary; purposeless, causeless; baseless; unaccountable; aimless (অকারণ ভ্রমণ) ; (of quarrel, war, attack etc.) without provocation, unprovoked (অকারণ আক্রমণ). □ *adv.* without cause; unnecessarily, for nothing; groundlessly; unaccountably; aimlessly; without provocation.

অকারণে *adv.* same as **অকারণ** (*adv.*).

অকারাদি, অকারান্ত see **অকার।**

অকার্য *n.* a misdeed; a useless act; a mischief; a wrong-doing; a bungle. **~কর** *a.* impractiable; ineffectual, futile, serving no purpose, useless; unpractical. **~কারিতা, ~করতা** *n.* ineffectiveness. **~কারী** *a.* ineffective, inffectual, useless.

অকাল *n.* an inauspicious time ; hard times; an unusual time (অকালের বর্ষা) ; premature time (অকালপক্ব) ; inappropriate time; (loos.) scarcity, famine. **~কুষ্মাণ্ড** *n.* a gourd grown at an unusual time; (fig.) a useless or stupid person. **~জ, ~জাত** *a.* born at an unusual time; untimely or prematurely born. **~জলদোদয়** untimely gathering of clouds. **~পক্ব** *a.* (of fruits) prematurely ripened; (of persons) precocious, pert. **~পক্বতা** *n.* premature ripeness; precocity, pertness. **~বর্ষণ** *n.* untimely rain. **~বার্ধক্য** *n.* premature ageing. **~বৃদ্ধ** *a.* gone old prematurely. **~বোধন** *n.* (myth.) untimely awakening of Goddess Durga by Ramachandra; (fig.) any untimely performance. **~মরণ, ~মৃত্যু** *n.* premature death.

অকালি *n.* a member of a militant sect of Shikhs, an Akali.

অকালে *adv.* at an inauspicious time; at an unusual time; aforetime, prematurely; inopportunely.

অকিঞ্চন *a.* indigent, extremely poor; distressed, miserable; insignificant; lowly; humble and modest. □ *n.* such a person. **~তা** *n.* indigence, extreme poverty; distressed condition, misery; insignificance, lowliness; stupidity.

অকিঞ্চিৎ, অকিঞ্চিৎকর *a.* trifling, insignificant, paltry; negligible.

অকীক *n.* agate.

অকীর্তি *n.* ill-repute, infamy; disgrace; a disgraceful or disreputable act. **~কর** *a.* infamous, disreputable, disgraceful.

অকীর্তিত *a.* unsung; not preached or announced publicly, unpublicized; uncelebrated, unhonoured.

অকু *n.* an incident; an event; a criminal offence. **~স্থল** *n.* the place of occurrence (esp. of a crime).

অকুটিল *a.* not crooked; frank.

অকুণ্ঠ, অকুণ্ঠিত *a.* unhesitating; unabashed; ungrudging, without reserve, liberal (অকুণ্ঠ দান বা প্রশংসা). **অকুণ্ঠচিত্তে, অকুণ্ঠিতচিত্তে** *adv.* with no hesitation (in the mind), with an open mind; unhesitatingly; ungrudgingly, liberally, freely.

অকুতোভয় *a.* not stricken with fear from any quarter; undaunted. **~তা** *n.* fearlessness.

অকুল *a.* (of families) unrespectable, lowly, unfit for matrimonial alliance.

অকুলন, অকুলান *n.* deficiency, deficit, shortage; insufficiency.

অকুলীন *a.* not born of a high family; not a high-born; not a man of noble birth (opp. কুলীন) ; (facet.) of mixed breed, hybrid (অকুলীন কুকুর).

অকুশল *n.* indisposition. □ *a* not adroit or skilful, inexpert.

অকূল *a.* shoreless; (fig.) boundless, endless. □ *n.* a shoreless sea, a vast ocean; (fig.) an overwhelming or extreme danger. **~ পাথার** *n.* boundless or shoreless sea; (fig.) great danger, extreme jeopardy; dire straits, hopeless situation. অকূলে কূল পাওয়া (fig.) to find a rescue in a sea of danger. অকূলে ডোবা (fig.) to sink in a sea of danger. অকূলে পড়া (fig.) to fall in or run into a sea of danger. অকূলে ভাসা (fig.) to get into a great danger; to be in extreme danger.

অকৃত *a.* not done or performed or executed; undone, unaccomplished.

অকৃতকার্য *a.* unsuccessful. ~**তা** *n.* failure.

অকৃতজ্ঞ *a.* ungrateful. ~**তা** *n.* ingratitude; ungratefulness.

অকৃতদার *a. mas.* unmarried; celibate.

অকৃতাপরাধ *a.* not guilty; guiltless.

অকৃতার্থ *a.* unsuccessful in attempt; disappointed.

অকৃতিত্ব *n.* unsuccess, failure; want of skill, inefficiency, incapacity.

অকৃতী *a.* unsuccessful; unskilled; inefficient; incapable; worthless or unworthy (অকৃতী সন্তান).

অকৃতোদ্বাহ *a. mas.* unmarried.

অকৃত্য *a.* of that which should not be done. ☐ *n.* an improper act, a wrong-doing, a misdeed.

অকৃত্রিম *a.* not artificial; natural; not feigned, sincere; not faked or forged; genuine, pure, true. ~**তা** *n.* sincerity.

অকৃপণ *a.* not niggardly or miserly; liberal, generous; without reserve (অকৃপণ প্রশংসা). ~**তা** *n.* generousness.

অকৃষ্ট *a.* untilled, uncultivated. **অকৃষ্য** *a.* uncultivable.

অকেজো *a.* having no ability for any work; not in working order, unserviceable; useless.

অকেশর পরাগকোষ *n.* (bot.) sessile anther.

অকৈতব *a.* not false; not deceitful.

অকোমল *a.* not soft or tender; not fragile.

অকৌশল *n.* lack of skill or adroitness; want of tact; want of diplomacy.

অক্কা পাওয়া *v.* (sl.) to die.

অক্ত[1] *a.* smeared with (তৈলাক্ত, রক্তাক্ত); mixed with, containing, full of (লবণাক্ত, বিষাক্ত).

অক্ত[2] *n.* time, one of a number of instances (পাঁচ অক্ত নামাজ).

অক্রম *n.* absence of serial order; disorder. **অক্রমিক** *a.* without serial order; disorderly; unofficial. **অক্রমিক জিজ্ঞাসা** an unofficial reference.

অক্রিয় *a.* without work; inactive; lacking in enthusiasm, lethargic.

অক্রিয়া *n.* absence of work; inaction; an improper act, a wrong-doing. ~**ন্বিত,** ~**সক্ত** *a.* given to improper acts or wrong-doings.

অক্রূর *a.* not crooked; not cruel or merciless; simple, straightforward. ☐ *n.* (myth.) uncle of Krishna.

অক্রেয়, আক্রা *a.* unpurchasable; costly or dear or expensive.

অক্রোধ *n.* absence of anger. ☐ *a.* free from anger. **অক্রোধন** *a.* not angered or wrought up easily.

অক্লান্ত *a.* untired, unwearied; untiring, tireless; indefatigable; persisting, assiduous (অক্লান্ত চেষ্টা). ~**কর্মা** *a.* indefatigable; indefatigably laborious or hard-working, extremely assiduous.

অক্লিষ্ট *a.* not feeling any tiredness, untiring; indomitable (অক্লিষ্ট যত্ন); untired, calm (অক্লিষ্টকান্তি). ~**কর্মা** *a.* working untiringly, indefatigable.

অক্লেশে *adv. & a.* without difficulty or trouble; without much effort; easily, effortlessly.

অক্ষ *n.* any of the three long cubes marked with dots thrown at dice-playing; a die; a kind of seed used as bead; (geog.) the axis of the equator; (geog.) latitude; (astr.) the angular distance of any star or planet from the solar orbit, the orbit of a heavenly body; (astrol.) the shape of the zodiac; (zoo.) the second vertebra of the neck; an axle; a sense-organ (অধোক্ষজ). ~**ক** *n.* the collar-bone, the clavicle; a dice player. ~**কর্ণ** *n.* (geom.) a hypotenuse. ~**ক্রীড়া** *n.* game of dice; diceplay. ~**দণ্ড** *n.* (geog.) the axis of the equator, the minor axis. ~**ধুরা** *n.* the front portion of a wheel, an axis; the pole of a cart. ~**ধূর্ত** *n.* an expert or clever dice-player. ~**পাটি** *n.* any of the long cubes marked with dots thrown at dice-playing. ~**বাট** *n.* dice-board; arena for wrestling; wrestling ground; gymnasium. ~**বিচলন** *n.* (astr.)

nutation. ~বিৎ, ~বিদ, ~বেত্তা *a.* versed in law or diplomacy; clever at dice-game. □ *n.* a lawyer; a diplomat; an expert dice-player. ~বৃত্ত, ~সমান্তরাল *n.* (geog.) the parallels of latitude. ~মালা, ~সূত্র *n.* a string of beads, a rosary. ~শক্তি *n.* the Axis Powers in the World War II.

অক্ষটি *n.* hunter.

অক্ষণ *n.* an inauspicious moment or time (ক্ষণ-অক্ষণ বিচার).

অক্ষত *a.* unhurt or unwounded; unimpaired; unblemished; unreserved. ~দেহ, ~শরীর *a.* of a person bearing no wound; unhurt or uninjured or unwounded. ~যোনি *a. fem.* having had no experience of sexual union; possessing true virginity.

অক্ষম *a.* powerless; weak; incapable; ineffective (অক্ষম চেষ্টা).

অক্ষমা *n.* lack of forgiveness or mercy; intolerance.

অক্ষয় *a.* undecaying; inexhaustible; unfailing; imperishable; undying; endless. ~কীর্তি *n.* undying or immortal fame. ~তূণ *n.* a quiver having an inexhaustible stock of arrows. ~তৃতীয়া *n.* the third day of the lunar waxing fortnight of the month of Baisakh (বৈশাখ). ~বট *n.* any of the very old banyan trees found at different holy places of the Hindus; (fig.) an immortal or deathless person. ~লোক *n.* the abode of the blessed; heaven. ~স্বর্গ *n.* the right to dwell permanently in heaven. ~স্বর্গবাস *n.* dwelling permanently in heaven.

অক্ষর *n.* any of the letters of the alphabet; a syllable; (fig.) a symbolic letter . ~জীবী, ~জীবক *n.* a scribe; a copyist; a printer or compositor, a writer. ~পরিচয় *n.* acquaintance with the alphabet; commencement of education; literacy; (fig.) elementary knowledge. ~বিন্যাস *n.* the characteristic style of handwriting. ~বৃত্ত *n.* (pros.) a system of versification in which the number of letters and not the sounds in a line is taken into account. ~মালা *n.* the alphabet. ~যোজক *n.* a compositor. **অক্ষরীকরণ** *n.* transliteration. **অক্ষরে অক্ষরে** to the letter, word for word. verbatim; (fig.) with strict exactitude, rigorously.

অক্ষাংশ *n.* (geog.) degrees of latitude, latitude.

অক্ষারলবণ *n.* rock-salt.

অক্ষি *n.* the eye. ~কাচ *n.* lens. ~কোটর *n.* the socket of the eye. ~গত *a.* lying within the range of vision; visible. ~গোলক *n.* the eyeball. ~তারকা, ~তারা, ~কূট *n.* the pupil of the eye, the apple of the eye. ~পক্ষ্ম *n.* eyelash, cilium. ~পট *n.* the retina. ~পটল *n.* cataract of the eye. ~পুট *n.* the eyelid. ~বিকূর্ণন *n.* casting of a sidelong glance; squinting. ~বিভ্রম *n.* optical illusion. ~শালাক্য *n.* ophthalmic surgery.

অক্ষীণ *a.* not lean or emaciated; not weakened or debilitated.

অক্ষীয় *a.* axial, pertaining to an axis; angular.

অক্ষুণ্ণ *a.* unimpaired or unaffected (অক্ষুণ্ণ স্বাস্থ্য বা মর্যাদা) ; unoffended (অক্ষুণ্ণচিত্ত) ; unhindered, unchecked (অক্ষুণ্ণ গতি) ; unabated (অক্ষুণ্ণ তেজ) ; undamaged or untarnished (অক্ষুণ্ণ সতীত্ব) ; unquestioned, untrammelled, unhampered, supreme, sovereign (অক্ষুণ্ণ প্রতিপত্তি) ; still in force, intact (অক্ষুণ্ণ অধিকার বা স্বার্থ) ; unused, not at all used (অক্ষুণ্ণ মূলধন) ।

অক্ষুধা *n.* lack, absence or loss of appetite.

অক্ষুব্ধ unperturbed, unruffled, unagitated; not mortified or aggrieved.

অক্ষোভ *a.* not agitated or perturbed; not disgruntled; placid. □ *n.* absence of agitation, grudge or regret.

অক্ষৌহিণী *n.* a division of army in ancient India, comprising 109350 foot-soldiers, 65610 cavalrymen, 21870 fighters on elephant-back and 21870 charioteers.

অক্সিজেন *n.* oxygen.

অখণ্ড *a.* not divided into parts, undivided; (math.) integral (অখণ্ড সংখ্যা) ; unabated; uncurbed, undisputed, supreme, sovereign (অখণ্ড প্রতাপ) ; not watery, thickened, curdled ('অখণ্ড পীযূষধারা') ; compact, dense (অখণ্ড অন্ধকার), ~তা *n.* integrality, wholeness;

indivisibility; oneness, unity. ~নীয়, **অখণ্ড্য** *a.* irrefutable, indisputable; unanswerable. **অখণ্ড-মণ্ডলাকার** *a.* completely spherical. **অখণ্ডিত** *a.* unsevered; undivided; unrefuted (অখণ্ডিত যুক্তি বা মত)।

অখদ্যে *a.* (coll.) not fit to be eaten; unfit for work, grossly inefficient; unserviceable. **অখদ্যে-অবদ্যে** *a.* good-for-nothing, worthless; trashy.

অখল *a.* artless, guileless, naive.

অখাত *a.* (of channels etc.) undug or not made by digging; natural.

অখাদ্য *a.* not fit to be eaten; inedible; forbidden to be eaten; (of food) unwholesome; (facet.) worthless (অখাদ্য লোক). □ *n.* inedible or forbidden or unwholesome food.

অখিল *a.* entire, whole. □ *n.* the world; the universe; the sky. **অখিল আত্মা** *n.* the Supreme Spirit. **~প্রিয়** *a.* loved or adored by all. **~বিশ্ব** *n.* the entire world; the universe.

অখুশি *a.* dissatisfied, displeased. □ *n.* dissatisfaction, displeasure.

অখ্যাত *a.* not famous; undistinguished; obscure. **~নামা** *a.* not famous, one whose name is not famous, obscure.

অখ্যাতি *n.* disrepute; notoriety; disgrace; infamy; scandal. **~জনক** *a.* disgraceful; infamous, scandalous, notorious .

অগণন, অগণনীয় *a.* uncountable; countless, innumerable.

অগণিত *a.* (ori.) uncounted; (loos.) countless, innumerable, numberless.

অগণ্য *a.* uncountable; countless, innumerable.

অগতি *a.* motionless; immobile, static; helpless, resourceless. □ *n.* a helpless or resourceless person; the unperformed state of a dead person's obsequies. **অগতির গতি** the resort of the helpless; (loos.) the way-out.

অগত্যা *adv.* having no other course to follow or means to adopt; being compelled; perforce, of necessity, necessarily; as a necessary or unavoidable consequence. **অগত্যা রাজি হওয়া** to agree to follow or adopt a course as a last resort or having no alternative.

অগদ *a.* free from disease or poison, not ill; healthy. □ *n.* a medicine; an antidote (esp. to poison). **~তন্ত্র** *n.* toxicology.

অগনতি, অগুনতি *a.* (coll.) countless, innumerable.

অগন্তব্য *a.* (of places, etc.) not fit to be visited; out of bounds.

অগভীর *a.* not deep; shallow; superficial, not profound (অগভীর জ্ঞান). **অগভীর জলে সফরী ফরফরায়তে** (lit.) a small fry bustles in shallow water; (fig.) an empty vessel sounds much. **~তা** *n.* shallowness.

অগম *a.* not moving, motionless; static; unfathomable, bottomless; inaccessible; incomprehensible.

অগম্য *a.* inaccessible; impassable; incomprehensible, beyond the compass or range or reach of (বুদ্ধির অগম্য). **~গামিনী** *fem.* of **অগম্যাগামী, অগম্যা** *a. fem.* one with whom cohabitation or sexual union is prohibited. **অগম্যাগমন** *n.* incest. **অগম্যাগামী** *a. mas.* incestuous. □ *n.* an incestuous man.

অগস্ত্য *n.* a mythological sage of India; (astrol.) the Canopus. **~যাত্রা** *n.* the first day of the month of Bhadra (ভাদ্র) when the sage Agastya asked the bending Vindhyas to wait till he came back and he never came back (this day has since been regarded by the Hindus as extremely inauspicious to set out on a journey; (cp. a corbie messenger). **অগস্ত্যোদয়** *n.* rise of the star Agastya or Canopus (about the 17th or 18th day of Bhadra).

অগা, অগাকান্ত, অগাচণ্ডী *a.* (coll.) grossly stupid or ignorant; good-for-nothing. □ *n.* such a person.

অগাধ *a.* unfathomable, bottomless; very deep and extensive (অগাধ সমুদ্র) ; unlimited, unbounded (অগাধ আকাশ) ; profound; immeasurable, immense (অগাধ শান্তি).

অগামারা, অগারাম same as **অগা**।

অগুণ *n.* harm, injury; offence, fault. □ *a.* deprived of good qualities; worthless; unqualified. **অগুণ করা** *v.* to do harm, to do mischief.

অগুনতি, অগুন্তি variants of **অগনতি**।

অগুরু *n.* a kind of fragrant wood (mostly used as incense). **~চন্দন** *n.* a fragrant and cool paste of this wood used as an ointment.

অগোচর *a.* beyond the reach of comprehension or of sense-organs; beyond one's knowledge; invisible. **অগোচরে** *adv.* without or beyond one's knowledge; behind one's back; unobservedly; stealthily.

অগোছাল, অগোছালো *a.* of a disorderly kind; unsystematic, unmethodical; slovenly, careless, messy, irregular.

অগোপন *a.* not concealed or secret, unconcealed; open. □ *n.* absence of secrecy or concealment. **অগোপনীয়** *a.* not to be concealed.

অগৌণ *n.* absence of delay; promptness; celerity; hurry. □ *a.* not minor or secondary; primary; chief, principal. **অগৌণে** *adv.* without delay; immediately; quickly. **অগৌণ-পত্রী** *n.* immediate slip.

অগৌরব *n.* dishonour, disgrace; discredit, disrepute.

অগ্নি *n.* fire; the fire-god; digestive power; hunger; burning; affliction (শোকাগ্নি). **~কণা** *n.* a spark. **~কর্তা** *n.& a.* one who performs the rite of singeing the mouth of the deceased at cremation. **~কর্ম** *n.* the rite of agnihotra (অগ্নিহোত্র) ; cremation of the dead. **~কল্প** *a.* fire-like; fiery; extremely hot; extremely severe or violent; terribly angry, furious. **~কাণ্ড** *n.* a great fire, a conflagration. **~কুণ্ড** *n.* a pit in which a fire is made or a pit full of fire, a fire-pit; a furnace. **~কোণ** *n.* the south-east. **~ক্রিয়া** same as **~কর্ম**। **~গর্ভ** *a.* impregnated with fire, containing fire; fiery; impetuous (অগ্নিগর্ভ বক্তৃতা). **~চূর্ণ, ~চূর্ণক** *n.* gun-powder, explosive substance. **~জিতা** *n. fem.* a woman who has passed successfully through an ordeal by fire. **~তপ্ত** *a.* heated with fire; as hot as fire. **~তুল্য** *a.* fire-like; fiery; furious. **~দগ্ধ** *a.* burnt; consumed by fire. **~দাতা** *n. & a.* one who sets fire to anything; one who singes the mouth of the dead at cremation. *fem.* **~দাত্রী**। **~দান** *n.* act of setting fire to; act of singeing the mouth of the dead at cremation. **~দাহ** *n.* a conflagration, combustion, the heat of fire. **~দাহ্য** *a.* combustible. **~দীপক** *a.* causing or promoting fire or hunger or digestion. **~দীপ্ত** *a.* illuminated or brightened with fire. **~দেব, ~দেবতা** *n.* the god of fire, the firegod. **~পক্ক** *a.* cooked with fire; hardened in fire (অগ্নিপক্ক ইট). **~পরীক্ষা** *n.* an ordeal by fire (esp. the one which Sita of the Ramayana passed through); (fig.) a crucial test, an extremely dangerous or unsafe test (cp. baptism of fire). **~প্রবেশ** *n.* act of mounting or falling on a burning pyre. **~প্রভ** *a.* glowing as fire. **~প্রভা** *n.* glow of fire. **~প্রস্তর** *n.* flint. **~বর্ণ** *a.* red as fire; crimson. **~বর্ধক** *a.* promoting fire or hunger or digestion. **~বাণ** *n.* a fire-emitting mythical arrow. **~বৃদ্ধি** *n.* promotion or stimulation of appetite or digestion. **~বৃষ্টি** *n.* a shower of fire (esp. from the sky, instead of rain); a spell of scorching heat; discharge or firing of gun. **~মন্ত্র** *n.* any formula of words or spell that makes one determined to achieve an extremely difficult or dangerous end; the doctrine of revolution or terrorism. **~মন্ত্রে দীক্ষা** initiation in the cult of armed agitation or revolution. **~ময়** *a.* full of fire. **~মান্দ্য** *n.* loss of appetite; indigestion. **~মূর্তি** *a.* extremely angry or haughty, furious. □ *n.* furious appearance or state. **~মূল্য** *a.* extremely costly; unpurchasably dear. **~যুগ** *n.* the age or times of revolution. **~শর্মা** *a.* extremely angry, furious, livid with rage. □ *n.* a furious person, a spitfire. **~শিখা** *n.* the flame of fire, the flame. **~শুদ্ধ** *a.* purified by burning in fire; sanctified by undergoing rigorous penance. **~শুদ্ধি** *n.* purification by burning in fire; sanctification by undergoing rigorous penance. **~সংস্কার** *n.* cremation by burning the dead. **~সখ** *n.* the wind. **~সৎকার** *n.* cremation by burning the dead. **~সহ** *a.* fire-proof. **~সহ ইট** fire-brick. **~সহ**

মৃত্তিকা fire-clay. ~সাৎ *a.* completely consumed by fire. ~সেবন *n.* act of warming up oneself in the heat of fire. ~স্ফুলিঙ্গ *n.* a spark. ~হোত্র *n.* the Hindu rite of maintaining the sacred fire perpetually. ~হোত্রী *n.* one who maintains the sacred fire perpetually and worships with it.

অগ্ন্যস্ত্র *n.* firearm.

অগ্ন্যাশয় *n.* the pancreas. **অগ্ন্যাশয় রস** pancreatic juice.

অগ্ন্যুৎপাত *n.* emission of fire from a volcano, volcanic eruption; raining of fire from the sky; the fall of a meteor; the crash of a thunder.

অগ্ন্যুদ্গম, অগ্ন্যুদ্গার *n.* emission of fire (esp. from the crater of a volcano).

অগ্ন্যুৎসব *n.* display of fire at merrymaking, a bonfire.

অগ্র *n.* the top, the summit; an apex; an end or extremity; the front; the front portion; the surface or the portion at the surface (দধির অগ্র) ; an aim, a purpose (একাগ্র). □ *a.* first, foremost, primary, leading; chief; anterior. ~ক্রয়াধিকার *n.* the right of pre-emption. ~গণ্য *a.* deserving first preference or consideration or mention; foremost; best; principal. ~গতি, ~গমন *n.* forward movement, advancement; progress, promotion, development, increase; (astr.) progressive motion, progression. ~গামী *a.* moving forward or to the front; leading; progressive. *fem.* ~গামিনী। ~জ *a.* born earlier, senior in age, elder, older. □ *n.* the eldest or an elder brother. ~জিহ্বা *n.* the uvula, the epiglottis. ~জ্ঞান *n.* foreknowledge; anticipation. ~ণী *a.* leading, chief, best. □ *n.* a leader; an inaugurator or initiator; a pioneer. ~দণ্ড *n.* impress money. ~দানী *n.* a Brahmin (ব্রাহ্মণ) who receives offerings on behalf of a dead person's soul and consequently is socially degraded. ~দূত *n.* (mil.) a pioneer; an escort, a guide; a leader; (loos.) a forerunner, a precursor, a harbinger. ~নেতা *n.* a leader; an army commander. ~পশ্চাৎ *adv.* considering what is before and after; having foresight and hindsight; pro and con; comprehensively. ~বর্তী *a.* situated in the front; leading; advanced. *fem.* ~বর্তিনী। ~ভাগ *n.* the first part or share; top peak; an extremity or end. ~মহিষী *n.* the queen-consort. ~সর, ~সার *a.* going first or commencing, leading; moving forward, advancing. ~সরণ *n.* advancement. **অগ্রসর হওয়া** *v.* to move forward, to advance; to progress. ~স্থ, ~স্থিত *a.* situated in the front, on the top or at end, apical.

অগ্রহণীয় *a.* unacceptable, not to be taken.

অগ্রহায়ণ *n.* the eighth month of the Hindu calendar (from the middle of November to the middle of December).

অগ্রাধিকার *n.* priority.

অগ্রাহ্য *a.* unacceptable; fit to be ignored; rejected. **অগ্রাহ্য করা** *v.* to ignore; to slight; to refuse, to reject, (in law) to void. **অগ্রাহ্য হওয়া** *v.* to be ignored; to be rejected, (in law) to be voided.

অগ্রিম *a.* first; eldest; chief; (of money) payable or paid in advance. ~ক *n.* the part of cost or charge paid in advance, an advance, earnest money. **অগ্রিম চুক্তি** *a.* forward contract. **অগ্রিম মূল্য** *n.* a price paid in advance.

অগ্রিয়, অগ্রীয় *a.* first; eldest; chief; relating to the front or top.~ **প্রদান** payment on account or as earnest money.

অগ্রে *adv.* at first; at the front; at the outset, in the beginning, before, formerly; beforehand; in the presence of, approaching (বিচারকের অগ্রে আবেদন).

অগ্র্য *a.* first; foremost; chief.

অঘ *n.* sin. ~মর্ষণ *n.* that which (esp. an incantation) dispels sin.

অঘটন *n.* an awkward or unexpected incident; non-occurrence. ~ঘটন *n.* unusual occurrence. **অঘটনঘটন-পটীয়সী** *a. fem.* skilled in bringing about what is impossible.

অঘটনীয় *a.* not likely to happen.

অঘমর্ষণ see **অঘ**।

অঘর *a.* (of families) having no social dignity, unrespectable , base, lowly, unfit for matrimonial alliance.

অঘা var. of **অগা**।

অঘাট, আঘাট *n.* a sea-coast or a riverbank unfit for disembarkment; a bad place.

অঘোর[1] *a.* terrible (অঘোর বাদল) ; unconscious; fainted. **অঘোরে** *adv.* deeply, profoundly. **অঘোর ঘুম** deep or sound sleep.

অঘোর[2] *a.* not terrible; calm. ☐ *n.* God Shiva (শিব). **~পন্থী** *n.* one of a religious community practsing dreadful and abominable rites. **~মন্ত্র** *n.* incantation to invoke Shiva.

অঘোষ *a.* (phon.) voiceless. **~বর্ণ** *n.* a voiceless consonant (e. g. ক খ চ ছ ট ঠ ত থ প ফ).

অঘ্রাত *a.* not smelled; untasted.

অঙ্ক *n.* a mark or sign; a line; a stripe; a spot; a blemish; (math.) a digit, a number, a figure; an arithmetical problem, a sum; a counting, calculation; the lap; (of a drama) an act; (zoo) the belly; (bot.) the venter. **অঙ্ক করা, অঙ্ক কষা** *v.* to do sums; to calculate or count. **~গত** *a.* lying on or in the lap (of); (fig.) under thorough control of. **~গর্ভ** *a.* (zoo.) marsupial (of an animal, e. g. kangaroo). **~তল** *n.* (zoo.) ventral surface. **~দেশ** *n.* the lap; (zoo.) the belly. **~পাত** *n.* act of placing figures; act of marking. **~পাতন** *n.* (math.) notation. **~বাচক** *a.* (math.) cardinal. **~বিদ্যা, ~শাস্ত্র** *n.* mathematics. **~বিদ্যাবিৎ, ~শাস্ত্রবিৎ** *n.* a mathematician. **~লক্ষ্মী** *n.* wife. **~শায়ী** *a.* lying on the lap (of); (fig.) enamoured of. *fem.* **~শায়িনী**। **~স্থিত** *a.* situated or placed on the lap; (fig.) beloved.

অঙ্কন *n.* drawing; painting; marking; writing figures; (geom.) act of plotting; construction. **অঙ্কন করা** *v.* to mark; to draw or paint; (geom.) to plot; to construct. **অঙ্কনী** *n.* pencil, chalk, brush, etc. for drawing or painting. **অঙ্কনীয়** *a.* to be or fit to be marked or drawn or painted or (geom.) plotted or constructed.

অঙ্কিত *a.* marked; drawn or painted; (geom.) plotted; bedecked, decorated; carved; delineated, described, portrayed (অঙ্কিত চরিত্র) ; imprinted (মানসপটে অঙ্কিত). **অঙ্কিত করা** *v.* to mark; to draw; to paint; (geom.) to plot; to bedeck, to decorate; to carve; to delineate, to describe, to portray; to imprint.

অঙ্কীয় *a.* (chiefly bot. & zoo.) ventral.

অঙ্কুর *n.* a sprout, a shoot; a sapling; blossom (চূতাঙ্কুর) ; germ; origination, birth, germination (ভাবের অঙ্কুর) ; anything newly born or commenced; a beginning; an end or tip (তৃণাঙ্কুর, ভগ্নাঙ্কুর). **অঙ্কুরে বিনাশ করা** *v.* to nip in the bud. **অঙ্কুরিত** *a.* sprouted; germinated; published, revealed. **অঙ্কুরিত হওয়া** *v.* to sprout; to germinate. **অঙ্কুরোদয়, অঙ্কুরোদ্গম** *n.* germination, sprouting, blossoming; commencement, beginning.

অঙ্কুশ *n.* an iron goad used in driving an elephant; any iron rod for striking with; a hook with a long handle.

অঙ্কুশগ্রহ *n.* an elephant-driver.

অঙ্কোপরি *a. adv. & prep.* on the lap.

অঙ্গ *n.* a limb; the body; shape or form; a feature; a part; an essential part; an ingredient, a component, an element; an item (নৈবেদ্যের অঙ্গ) ; (esp. bot.) an organ; the ancient name of Bihar or of Bhagalpur and adjoining places. **~গ্রহ** *n.* convulsion of or pain in the body or any part of it, spasm; tetanus. **~গ্লানি** *n.* wearisome or painful physical exertion, tiredness; dirt or soil of the body. **~চালন** *n.* the movement of the body or limbs; physical exercise. **~চ্ছেদ, ~চ্ছেদন** *n.* amputation or cutting off of a limb; deduction of a part; mutilation. **~জ, ~জনু** *a.* born of one's body. ☐ *n.* offspring; a son. **~জা** *a.* daughter. **~ত্র, ~ত্রাণ** *n.* armour, a coat of mail. **~ন্যাস** *n.* touching different parts of the body as one recites (usu. mentally) different incantations. **~প্রত্যঙ্গ** *n.* different limbs and appendages of the body. **~প্রায়শ্চিত্ত** *n.* expiatory rite of removing the taint of the body. **~বিকৃতি** *n.* deformity; apoplexy. **~বিক্ষেপ** *n.* making gestures, posing; a gesture, a pose ; convulsion of a limb or the body, spasm. **~বিন্যাস** *n.* posing; posture. **~বিহীন** *a.* wanting in one or more limbs, crippled; deformed; bodiless, formless, incorporeal. *fem.* **~বিহীনা**।

~ভঙ্গ, ~ভঙ্গি *n.* a pose or posture; a gesture; secret communication of one's intention by means of a physical gesture. ~বৈকল্য *n.* same as ~বিকৃতি। ~মর্দক *n.* masseur. ~মর্দিকা *n. fem.* masseuse. ~মর্দন *n.* massage. ~মোটন *n.* stretching and straightening the body for removing lassitude and sloth. ~রাগ *n.* beautifying the body with cosmetics; any article of cosmetic or toilet. ~রাজ *n.* the king of Anga. ~রাজ্য *n.* a state of a federation. ~রুহ *n.* hair; wool; fur; feather, a gown. ~শুদ্ধি *n.* purification of the body (by ablution or by ceremonial washing). ~সংবাহন *n.* massage. ~শোভা *n.* beauty of the body. ~সংস্থান *n.* morphology. ~সজ্জা *n.* beautifying the body (with dress or cosmetics). ~সঞ্চালন same as ~চালন। ~সৌষ্ঠব *n.* physical grace or beauty or symmetry. ~হানি *n.* loss of a limb; partial omission or curtailment of anything; mutilation; a defect. ~হীন *a.* deformed; lacking one or more limbs; (of a work) lacking in perfection, defective; bodiless, formless, incorporeal.

অঙ্গাদ *n.* an ornamental armlet, bracelet, etc.; son of Bali, the monkey-king of Kishkindhya (Ramayana).

অঙ্গন *n.* a courtyard, the compound of a house.

অঙ্গনা *n.* a woman of graceful physique, a beautiful woman; a woman.

অঙ্গাঙ্গি *n.* mutual attraction of different limbs of a body; correlation; preferential treatment of or partiality towards a member of one's own party. ~ভাব, ~সম্বন্ধ *n.* intimate friendship; inseparable relation; (phil.) the relation between the whole and its parts; interdependence of parts, relation between form and content; the relation between what is primary and what is secondary. ~ভাবে *adv.* in the relation of the part to the whole or of what is secondary to what is primary; inseparably.

অঙ্গাবরণ *n.* covering for the body; a garment.

অঙ্গার *n.* coal; carbon; cinder, charcoal; (fig.) a person or thing causing shame or disgrace (কুলের অঙ্গার বা কলঙ্ক). ~ময় *a.* carbonaceous. ~কৃষ্ণ *a.* black as coal, very black. ~ধানী *n.* an incense-pot, censer. ~ক *n.* carbon. অঙ্গারককমণি *n.* coral. অঙ্গারক রসায়ন *n.* organic chemistry. ~ যৌগিক *n.* carbon compounds. অঙ্গারঃ শতধৌতেন মলিনত্বং ন মুঞ্চতি coal never changes its hue however well it may be washed; black will take no other hue. অঙ্গারাম্ল *n.* carbonic acid.

অঙ্গিরা *n.* (astr.) one of the stars in the constellation of Ursa Major.

অঙ্গী *a.* having a body or form, corporeal; whole; fitted with limbs.

অঙ্গীকরণ *n.* promising.

অঙ্গীকার *n.* promise or undertaking; promising; acceptance. অঙ্গীকার করা *v.* to promise; to give an undertaking; to accept.

অঙ্গীকৃত *a.* promised; accepted.

অঙ্গীভূত *a.* embodied; included. অঙ্গীভূত করা *v.* to embody; to include.

অঙ্গুরি, অঙ্গুরী, অঙ্গুরীয়, অঙ্গুরীয়ক *n.* an ornamental ring for the finger, a ring.

অঙ্গুলাঙ্ক *n.* finger-print. অঙ্গুলাঙ্ক-বিশারদ *n.* a finger-print expert.

অঙ্গুলি, অঙ্গুল *n.* a finger or a toe, a digit. অঙ্গুলি-গ্রন্থি *n.* finger-joint, knuckle. অঙ্গুলিত্র, অঙ্গুলিত্রাণ *n.* a thimble; a metal cap to protect finger in sewing; a metal hook worn on the tip of a finger by musicians whilst playing on stringed instruments; a covernig for the finger-tip, made of leather or iron, worn by archers. অঙ্গুলিনির্দেশ, অঙ্গুলিহেলন *n.* act of beckoning or pointing with the finger, a beck. অঙ্গুলিনির্দেশ করা, অঙ্গুলিসঙ্কেত করা *v.* to beckon or point with the finger, to beck. অঙ্গুলিমেয় *a.* that which can be counted on the finger; (fig.) very few in number. অঙ্গুলিসংকেত *n.* sign or hint made by the finger. অঙ্গুলিমোটন *n.* snapping of the finger. অঙ্গুলিহেলনে চালিত করা to dictate or direct with the movement of the finger. অঙ্গুলীয়ক *n.* an ornamental ring for the finger, a ring.

অঙ্গুষ্ঠ *n.* the thumb. ~প্রদর্শন, অঙ্গুষ্ঠ দেখানো

n. showing one's thumb; (fig.) awkward or point-blank refusal; depriving unpleasantly.

অঙ্গুষ্ঠানা, অঙ্গুস্তানা *n.* a thimble, a thumbstall.

অচকিত *a.* not frightened or alarmed.

অচক্ষু *a.* eyeless, blind.

অচঞ্চল *a.* not restless or bustling or fickle or playful or impatient; lasting; unwavering; firm, steady; unworried, unconcerned; calm, even-minded. *fem.* **অচঞ্চলা।**

অচতুর *a.* not adroit; inefficient; guileless; simple. *fem.* **অচতুরা।**

অচপল *a.* not bustling or fickle or playful or wanton; steady; firm; demure.

অচর *a.* motionless, immobile; stationary, static.

অচরিতার্থ *a.* ungratified, unfulfilled, unsatisfied.

অচর্চিত *a.* not practised or studied; not anointed, unsmeared.

অচর্বিত *a.* not chewed or masticated. **অচর্ব্য** *a.* not fit to be chewed, unchewable.

অচল *a.* motionless, immobile; stationary, static (অচল তড়িৎ); unwavering; firm, steady; gone out of practice, not current, obsolete (অচল প্রথা); counterfeit or forged (অচল টাকা বা নোট); that which cannot be kept going, unmaintainable (অচল সংসার); invalid; untenable (অচল যুক্তি); unserviceable (অচল ঘড়ি); impracticable (অচল প্রস্তাব); (of persons) cast off (সমাজে অচল). ☐ *n.* a mountain, a hill. **অচল অবস্থা, অচলাবস্থা** lack of progress; a deadlock, an impasse, a stalemate, standstill. **~ন** *n.* state of being out of practice or currency, obsoleteness. **~নীয়** *a.* incapable of being introduced or circulated.

অচলতড়িৎ *n.* (sc.) static electricity.

অচলা *a. fem.* not fickle; steady, firm, constant (অচলা ভক্তি). ☐ *n. fem.* the earth.

অচলায়তন *n.* an incorrigibly reactionary or conservative institution.

অচলিত *a.* not in vogue or practice, not current; obsolete.

অচলিষ্ণু *a.* motionless, immobile.

অচাঞ্চল্য *n.* absence of restlessness, calm; firmness; steadiness.

অচালনীয়, অচাল্য *a.* incapable of being conducted or transferred.

অচিকিৎসক *n.* a quack doctor, an ignorant medicine man, a charlatan.

অচিকিৎসনীয়, অচিকিৎস্য *a.* incurable, irremediable; incapable of being redressed; hard to cure.

অচিকিৎসা *n.* lack of medical treatment; bad or faulty medical treatment.

অচিকিৎসিত *a.* not treated medically.

অচিকীর্ষু *a.* unwilling or reluctant (to do); indolent, lazy.

অচিন, অচিনা dial. corrups. of **অচেনা।**

অচিন্তনীয় *a.* unthinkable; unimaginable; inconceivable.

অচিন্তিত, অচিন্তিতপূর্ব *a.* unthought of; unpremeditated; unexpected.

অচিন্ত্য same as **অচিন্তনীয়।**

অচির *a.* of short duration, brief. **~কারী** *a.* prompt. **~কাল** *n.* a very short time. **~কালে** *adv.* soon, shortly; without much delay. **~ক্রিয়** *a.* prompt in action or execution; not dilatory. **~জীবী** *a.* short-lived; impermanent, transient; not lasting long; not immortal. **~স্থায়ী** *a.* not permanent; transitory; perishable, frail, mortal (অচিরস্থায়ী দেহ), **অচিরাৎ, অচিরে** *adv.* soon; without delay; immediately.

অচিরপ্রভা *n.* a lightning.

অচিরাৎ see **অচির।**

অচিহ্নিত *a.* unmarked; undistinguished; uncovenanted (অচিহ্নিত কর্মচারী).

অচূর্ণ, অচূর্ণিত *a.* not pulverized; unbroken; undestroyed; whole, entire.

অচেতন *a.* unconscious; swooned, fainted; ignorant, foolish; stupefied; inanimate; insensate. **অচেতন হওয়া** *v.* to faint, to lose one's consciousness, to fall into a swoon.

অচেনা *a.* unknown; unfamiliar.

অচেষ্ট *a.* unendeavouring, effortless; not zealous; inactive; (rare) insensible, benumbed. **অচেষ্টিত** *a.* unattempted; untried.

অচৈতন্য *a.* unconscious; swooned,

fainted; ignorant, foolish; stupefied; inanimate; insensate. □ *n.* unconsciousness; ignorance; stupefaction; loss or absence of sense. **অচৈতন্য হওয়া** same as **অচেতন হওয়া**।

অচ্ছ *a.* transparent; without impurities; crystalline. □ *n.* crystal.

অচ্ছদ *a.* uncovered; open; roofless; (bot.) leafless.

অচ্ছিদ্র *a.* having no hole or opening; free from defect or loophole; perfect, flawless.

অচ্ছিন্ন *a.* not torn or cut; not split up or divided, unsevered. **~ত্বক** *a.* uncircumcised.

অচ্ছুৎ, অচ্ছুত *a.* (of persons) untouchable; unclean.

অচ্ছেদ্য *a.* incapable of being cleft or split, uncleavable; inseparable.

অচ্ছোদ *a.* having crystalline water ('অচ্ছোদ-সরসীনীরে'). □ *n.* a lake in the Himalayan region. **~পটল** *n.* the cornea.

অচ্যুত *n.* Krishna (কৃষ্ণ) ; Vishnu (বিষ্ণু). □ *a.* undislocated; firm, steady; imperishable, immortal.

অছি *n.* a guardian, a custodian; a trustee; an administrator.

অছিয়তনামা *n.* written document by which a person makes arrangements for his effects on death, a will.

অছিলা *n.* a pretext or plea (usu. a false one); an excuse; a pretence.

অছুৎ, অছুত variants of **অচ্ছুৎ**।

অজ[১] *a.* without birth; existing without being born, self-born. □ *n.* the governing soul of any individual creature (cp. **জীবাত্মা**).

অজ[২] *n.* the ram; the billy-goat, (astrol.) the Ram. *fem.* **অজা** the ewe; the nanny-goat.

অজ[৩] *a.* (dero.) downright, thorough (অজমুর্খ, অজ পাড়াগাঁ) ; entire (অজ পুকুরটা). **অজ পাড়াগাঁ** *n.* a backward and remote village, a grossly backward village, devoid of modern amenities.

অজগর *n.* a python or the boa constrictor.

অজন্ত *a.* (gr. of words) ending with a vowel sound. cf. opp. **হলন্ত** ending with a consonant sound.

অজন্মা *n.* (ori.) spiritual salvation; failure of crops; scarcity. □ *a.* (ori.) existing without being born.

অজপা *n.* (*fem.*) incantations that can be recited without strain (that is 'হং সঃ' etc.); vital breath ('অজপা হতেছে শেষ') ; a goddess of the tantrists.

অজবীথি *n.* (rare) a chariot for gods; the Milky Way, the Galaxy.

অজমূর্খ *a. n.* a perfect fool, a perfect dunce.

অজয় *n.* absence of victory; defeat. □ *a.* unconquerable.

অজর *a.* not subject to decrepitude; never aging, ageless. □ *n.* a god. **অজরামর** *a.* never aging or dying; ever young and immortal. **অজরামরবৎ** *a.* like one who is ageless and immortal.

অজল-অস্থল *n.* (fig.) helpless condition, shelterless state.

অজস্র *a.* innumerable; immeasurable; abundant; profuse; ceaseless. □ *adv.* incessantly; always.

অজহল্লিঙ্গ *n.* (gr.) a noun never changing its gender when used as an adjective.

অজা see **অজ**[২] ।

অজাত *a.* not yet born; unborn; existing without being born; (dial.) socially degraded, born illegitimately, bastard. **~শত্রু** *a.* one whose enemy is not yet born; having no enemy. **~শ্মশ্রু** *a.* one whose beard has not yet grown; beardless; (fig.) not yet grown to manhood; very young, minor.

অজানতে *adv.* unknowingly; unconsciously; unintentionally; secretly, stealthily, surreptitiously.

অজানা *a.* unknown; unfamiliar; strange. □ *n.* an unknown person or place ('কত অজানারে', 'কোন অজানায়').

অজানিত *a.* unknown. **~ভাবে** *adv.* unknowingly, unwittingly; unawares.

অজান্তে alt. spell. of **অজানতে**।

অজিজ্ঞাসিত *a.* unasked; without being questioned.

অজিজ্ঞাস্য *a.* not to be asked or inquired.

অজিত *a.* unconquered, undefeated; unsubjugated.

অজিতেন্দ্রিয় *a.* (lit.) having no control over

one's senses; of unbridled lust, lascivious.

অজিন *n.* deer-skin; hide.

অজিহ্ব *a.* having no tongue, tongueless. □ *n.* a frog.

অজীবজনি *n.* abiogenesis, spontaneous generation.

অজীর্ণ *a.* undigested. □ *n.* indigestion; dyspepsia.

অজু *n.* (Mus.) act of washing hands and feet before prayer; ablution.

অজুরদার *n.* a labourer; a day-labourer.

অজুরা *n.* salary; wages for labour, esp. day-labour.

অজুহাত *n.* a cause (usu. a false one); a pretext, a pretence, a plea.

অজেয়, অজেতব্য *a.* unconquerable, invincible; indomitable.

অজৈব *a.* inorganic (অজৈব খাদ্য, অজৈব রসায়ন) ; mineral (অজৈব লবণ, অজৈব সার).

অজ্ঞ *a.* having no knowledge, unknowing, ignorant, uninformed; stupid; foolish; uneducated. **~তা** *n.* lack of knowledge, ignorance; stupidity; foolishness; want of education. **~তামূলক, ~তাপ্রসূত** *a.* caused by ignorance; relating to ignorance.

অজ্ঞাত *a.* unknown; unpublished, unrevealed; secret, hidden; obscure; mysterious. **~কুলশীল** *a.* one whose family and behaviour are unknown; of unknown identity. **~নামা** *a.* one whose name is not known; (of persons) not famous, obscure. **~পরিচয়** *a.* one whose identity is not known. **~পূর্ব** *a.* not known before; hitherto unknown. **~বাস** *n.* act or period of living incognito. **~রাশি** *n.* (math.) an unknown quantity. **~সারে, অজ্ঞাতে** *adv.* not to one's knowledge, unknowingly; secretly, stealthily.

অজ্ঞান *a.* lacking in knowledge; ignorant; foolish; uneducated; unconscious, fainted; infatuated. □ *n.* lack of knowledge; ignorance; (phil.) illusion, maya. **~কৃত** *a.* done by mistake or owing to ignorance. **~জনিত** *a.* caused by ignorance, owing to ignorance. **~তা** *n.* lack of knowledge, ignorance. **~তিমির** *n.* gloom of ignorance, infatuated condition. **~বাদ, অজ্ঞাবাদ** *n.* (phil.) agnosticism. **~বাদী, অজ্ঞাবাদী** *a* agnostic. □ *n.* an agnostic. **অজ্ঞানী** *a.* unwise; lacking in knowledge, ignorant. **অজ্ঞানে** *adv.* unknowingly; unconsciously; owing to ignorance or foolishness.

অজ্ঞাপন *n.* lack or absence of communication.

অজ্ঞাপনীয় *a.* not to be communicated; not to be made public, secret.

অজ্ঞাবাদ same as **অজ্ঞানবাদ** (see **অজ্ঞান**).

অজ্ঞেয় *a.* unknowable; unintelligible; incognizable; incomprehensible.

অঝোর, (rare) **অঝর** *a.* incessant (অঝোর বাদল), ceaselessly raining; shedding tears ceaselessly (অঝোর নয়ন). **অঝোরে, অঝরে** *adv.* incessantly falling or raining ceaselessly, profusely.

অঞ্চল *a.* the marginal portion of a sari hanging loosely; border, brim ('নয়নক অঞ্চল') ; a region or locality (মেরু অঞ্চল). **~নিধি** *n.* (lit.) dear one clinging to the border of the mother's sari; dear one, (usu) very dear child. **~প্রভাব** *n.* domination of wife; influence of the harem.

অঞ্চিত *a.* worshipped (বিরিঞ্চিঅঞ্চিত) ; raised (রোমাঞ্চিত).

অঞ্জন *n.* an eye-salve; collyrium; antimony; lamp-black; a sty.

অঞ্জনিকা, অঞ্জনি *n.* inflamed swelling on the edge of the eyelid, a sty.

অঞ্জলি *n.* palms of hands folded or cupped together; a present given (esp. to deities) with cupped palms; act of worshipping or serving ('দেবগণ যারে করেন অঞ্জলি') ; the amount that may be held in cupped palms, a handful. **অঞ্জলি দেওয়া** *v.* to offer a present to a deity with folded palms. **~পুট** *n.* palms of hands cupped together. **~বদ্ধ** *a.* having palms of hands folded or cupped together. **~বন্ধ** *n.* act of folding or cupping the palms of hands.

অঞ্জিষ্ণু *n.* the sun; an exceptionally bright object.

অটবী, অটবি *n.* a forest; (loos.) a large tree.

অটল *a.* (lit.) not reeling; unwavering, unflinching; firm, steady; unmoved;

unshaken, constant; unperturbed; stolid, resolute. ~তা *n.* firmness, steadiness; stolidness; constancy. ~ভাবে *adv.* unwaveringly, firmly, resolutely, steadily.

অটুট *a.* unbroken; intact, whole; unimpaired, sound (অটুট স্বাস্থ্য) ; flawless.

অট্ট *a.* excessive or loud. **অট্ট-অট্ট** *n.* a very loud or roaring laughter. ☐ *a.* loud and horrible. **~নাদ, ~নিনাদ, ~রব, ~রোল** *n.* a very loud noise; an uproar. **~হাস, ~হাসি, ~হাস্য** *n.* a very loud or roaring laughter.

অট্টালিকা *n.* a building; a palace; an edifice.

অড়হর *n.* a kind of pulse, a variety of pigeon-pea.

অঢেল *a.* plentiful, immense; profuse; innumerable; inexhaustible.

অণিমা *n.* tenuity, subtlety, extreme thinness or fineness or transparency (which is almost invisible); the supernal power of assuming an extremely thin (and almost invisible) form by means of which gods and demi-gods can move everywhere invisibly.

অণু *a.* very small, minute (অণু পরিমাণ) ; a little, a bit. ☐ *n.* the subtlest or smallest part of anything; just a little amount or portion; a molecule. **~বীক্ষণ** *n.* a microscope. **~ভা** *n.* a lightning. **~মঞ্জরি** *n.* (bot.) spikelet. **~মাত্র** *a.* just a little; infinitesimal; least (অণুমাত্র সন্দেহ).

অণ্ড *n.* egg; either of the two scrotal glands, a testicle; anything round or oval-shaped. **~কোষ** *n.* the scrotum. **~কোষ বৃদ্ধি, ~বৃদ্ধি** *n.* the swelling of the scrotum, hydrocele. **অণ্ডজ** *a.* born of an egg, oviparous. ☐ *n.* an oviparous creature. **~লালা** *n.* the white of an egg; albumen. **অণ্ডাকার, অণ্ডাকৃতি** *a.* egg-shaped, oval; round. **অণ্ডাশয়** *n.* the ovary of any oviparous creature.

অত *a.* & *adv.* so much or so many; that much. ☐ *pro.* so or that much amount of anything; such a large number of anything; so much, so many.

অতএব *con.* & *adv.* hence, so, therefore.

অতঃপর *adv.* henceforth, henceforward, after this, hereafter, then.

অতট *n.* a precipice; a steep bank of a river rising very high above the water-level.

অতথ্য, অতথা *a.* untrue, false.

অতনু *a.* not slender or delicate; gigantic; bodiless, incorporeal. ☐ *n.* Madan (মদন), the Hindu god of love.

অতন্দ্র, অতন্দ্রিত *a.* sleepless; not sleeping, awake; watchful, vigilant, alert; continually active; untiring; incessant.

অতর্ক *n.* unfair or useless argument, sophistry; casuistry.

অতর্কিত *a.* unthought of; unanticipated, unnoticed, unexpected. **অতর্কিত আক্রমণ** sudden or surprise attack. **~ভাবে, অতর্কিতে** *adv.* in an unguarded state; suddenly; unawares, unexpectedly.

অতল *n.* (myth.) the first of the seven underworlds. ☐ *a.* bottomless, abysmal; unfathomable; extremely deep. **~স্পর্শ** *a.* abysmal; unfathomable; extremely deep.

অতলান্তিক *n.* the Atlantic Ocean.

অতশত *n.* so many varieties; so many different things or subjects or details, so much of it, all of it. ☐ *a.* so varied; so many; so much.

অতসী *n.* a variety of golden-coloured flower, rattle wort; linseed; flax.

অতি *adv.* & *prep.* too; over; beyond; improperly; going beyond; excessively; beyond the compass or range (of), outside. ☐ *a.* very improper or unbecoming; excessive; excellent (অতি নাগর). ☐ *n.* an improper or excessive amount (কিছুরই অতি ভালো নয়)। ☐ *pfx.* ex-, extra-, hyper-, out-, over-, super-, sur-, trans-, ultra-. **~ কথা** *n.* exaggerated or useless talk; a myth. **~কায়** *a.* of immense size; gigantic. **~ কোমল** *a.* too soft, too tender; very tender or soft. **~চার** *n.* quick passage (from one place to another); passage or forward movement of a planet from one zodiacal sign to another in a shorter period than usual. **~চালাক** *a.* over-clever, too clever by half; oversmart. **~চালাকের গলায় দড়ি** an over-clever person hangs himself;

the fox must pay his skin to the furrier. ~জন n. the majority. ~তপ্ত a. superheated. ~তর a. very much excessive. ~দর্প n. excessive pride or vanity. ~দর্পে হতা (বা হত) লঙ্কা (lit.) the fall of Lanka was caused by (King Ravana's) excessive vanity; (fig.) pride will have a fall.~নাটকীয় a. melodramatic; unnecessarily over-dramatic. ~নাটকীয়তা n. melodrama. ~দূর a. far-away; remote. □ n. a great distance. ~দৈন্য n. utmost poverty. ~নৈতিকতা n. puritanism, rigid adherence to moral principle or behaviour. ~পাতক n. any of the most heinous sins, a deadly sin. ~পাতকী n. a great sinner. ~পান n. (habitual) overindulgence in intoxicating liquor, intemperance. ~প্রজতা n. overpopulation. ~প্রাকৃত a. supernatural; supernal. ~বড় a. too big; too much. ~বল a. extremely strong or mighty. ~বাড় n. overgrowth; unnatural growth or development; excessive haughtiness or pride; extreme immoderation or excess. ~বাড় বাড়া v. to grow extremely haughty or arrogant. অতিবাড় বেড়ো নাকো ঝড়ে পড়ে যাবে (lit.) don't grow too high lest a storm makes you tumble down; (fig.) pride will have a fall. ~বাদ n. exaggeration. ~বুদ্ধি same as অতিচালাক। ~বৃদ্ধ a. very old; decrepit. ~বৃদ্ধি n. overgrowth. ~বৃষ্টি n. excessive or heavy rainfall. ~বেগনি, ~বেগুনি a. ultraviolet. ~ব্যয় n. extravagance. ~ব্যস্ত a. (usu. dero.) very busy; very anxious; fussy. ~ভক্তি n. excessive devotion or reverence (usu. insincere). অতিভক্তি চোরের লক্ষণ too much courtesy, too much craft. ~ভুজ a. (geom.) a hypotenuse. ~ভোজন n. over-eating, surfeit; gluttony. অতিভোজন করা v. to overeat; to gourmandize, to gormandise. ~ভোজী a. voracious, gourmand. □ n. a gourmand, a glutton. ~মন্দা n. (comm.) slump. ~মাত্র, ~মাত্রায় adv. beyond measure; extremely. ~মান n. excessive vanity. ~মানব n. a great man or a man of exceptional uqalities and powers, a superman; a greatly wise man. ~মানবিক, ~মানুষিক a. superhuman; supernal; spiritual; divine. ~রঞ্জন n. exaggeration. ~রঞ্জিত a. exaggerated. ~রথ n. a great warrior capable of fighting innumerable enemies simultaneously. ~রাষ্ট্রিক a. extra-territorial. ~লোভ n. too much greed, overgreediness.

অতিক্রম, অতিক্রমণ n. going beyond; passing over; crossing; transgression; nonobservance, violation; excelling or exceeding, surpassing or going beyond. অতিক্রম করা v. to go beyond; to pass over; to transgress; to exceed; to excel; to surpass or outdo. অতিক্রমণীয়, অতিক্রম্য a. that which can be or is to be passed beyond or crossed or transgressed or overcome; violable; surpassable.

অতিক্রান্ত a. passed beyond; crossed; transgressed; violated; surpassed, outdone; passed away, elapsed; past (অতিক্রান্ত দিন). অতিক্রান্ত হওয়া v. to be passed beyond or transgressed or violated or overcome or surpassed or outdone; to pass away, to elapse.

অতিথি n. a guest. ~ বৎসল a. hospitable. ~শালা n. a guest-house. ~ সৎকার, ~সেবা n. hospitality. ~সেবক n. a hospitable man; a host.

অতিপত্তি n. lapse.

অতিপন্ন a. lapsed. অতিপন্ন হওয়া v. to lapse.

অতিপাত n. passing; spending. অতিপাত করা v. to spend or pass (time, life, term etc.)

অতিবাহন n. spending or passing (time, life, term etc.) অতিবাহন করা v. to spend or pass.

অতিবাহিত a. (of time, life, term etc.) spent. অতিবাহিত করা v. to spend or pass.

অতিরিক্ত a. more than what is needed, redundant; supernumerary; supererogatory; additional; surplus; extra, superfluous; excessive; exceeding (তদতিরিক্ত কিছু) ; (bot.) accessory.

অতিরেক n. abundance; superfluity; excess; surplus.

অতিরোমশ a. (zool.) villose; very hairy.

অতিশয় a. too many or too much; great, excessive (অতিশয় তাপ) ; large (অতিশয় ভিড়). □ adv. very; exceedingly, excessively. অতিশয়োক্তি n. (rhet.) a figure of speech, hyperbole; exaggeration.

অতিষ্ঠ *a.* unable to stay or keep steady; unsettled; restless; uneasy; irritated. (অতিষ্ঠ হওয়া). **অতিষ্ঠ করা** *v.* to make unsteady; to unsettle; to make restless or uneasy; to make unbearable; to annoy or irritate.

অতিসার *n.* diarrhoea; dysentery.

অতীত *a.* elapsed, passed away, gone by; dead; past; former, existed or occurred in the past. □ *prep.* past, beyond. □ *n.* past times or days; ancient times; the past; (gr.) the past tense. **~কাল** *n.* same as **অতীত** (*n.*). **~বেত্তা** *n.* one who knows things or incidents of the past. **অতীত হওয়া** *v.* to pass away, to elapse, to become a thing of the past.

অতীন্দ্রিয় *a.* beyond the range of the senses; imperceptible; impalpable; subtle; (loos.) transcendental. **~তা** *n.* impalpability; subtlety; (loos.) transcendentalism.

অতীব *adv.* very; very much; extremely; exceedingly, excessively.

অতীসার alt. spell. of **অতিসার**।

অতুল, অতুলন, অতুলনীয়, অতুল্য *a.* beyond compare; incomparable; matchless; peerless; unequalled; unparalleled. *fem.* **অতুলনীয়া**।

অতুষ্ট *a.* unsatisfied; not pleased or gratified; unappeased; discontented.

অতুষ্টি *n.* dissatisfaction; displeasure, lack of gratification; discontent.

অতৃপ্ত *a.* insatiate, ungratified; unsatisfied; unappeased. **অতৃপ্তি** *n.* lack of satiation or gratification, dissatisfaction; lack of appeasement. **অতৃপ্তিকর** *n.* dissatisfactory, causing dissatisfaction or displeasure.

অত্যধিক *adv.* very much, too much; exceedingly, in a great degree, extremely. □ *a.* excessive, great.

অত্যন্ত *adv.* very much, too much; exceedingly, extremely. □ *a.* excessive, extreme, great. **~গামী** *a.* expeditious; extremely swift or speedy. **~সংযোগ** *n.* uninterrupted extension or expansion. **অত্যন্তাভাব** *n.* negation; (phil.) complete non-existence or absence.

অত্যভিমানী *a.* touchy; over-sensitive.

অত্যম্ল *a.* very sour.

অত্যয় *n.* death; destruction, annihilation (দেহাত্যয়); passing away or elapsing (কালাত্যয়) ; waste; fault; crime; vice, sin; danger or hazard; an unexpected danger, emergency. **অত্যয় প্রমাণপত্র** *n.* an emergency certificate. **অত্যয় সংচিতি** *n.* emergency reserve.

অত্যল্প *a.* very little or very few, scanty, meagre, inadequate.

অত্যাশন *n.* over-eating; gluttony.

অত্যহিত *n.* great harm or injury.

অত্যাচার *n.* oppression; outrage; tyranny; strain (চোখের উপর অত্যাচার) ; intemperate and irregular habits; taking undue advantage (স্নেহের বা আতিথ্যের উপর অত্যাচার). **অত্যাচার করা** *v.* to oppress; to outrage; to tyrannize over; to strain; to be of intemperate and irregular habits. **অত্যাচারিত** *a.* oppressed, harassed; persecuted, victimized. **অত্যাচারী** *a.* oppressing; oppressive; outrageous; tyrannizing; tyrannical; of intemperate and irregular habits. □ *n.* an oppressor; a tyrant; a man of profligate habits.

অত্যাজ্য *a.* incapable of being given up or away; not to be abandoned or deserted or relinquished or disowned; indissoluble.

অত্যাদর *n.* over-indulgence.

অত্যাধুনিক *a.* most up-to-date; very modern; up to the minute; recent-most.

অত্যাবশ্যক *a.* essential; urgently or absolutely necessary; very urgent or important.

অত্যাশ্চর্য *a.* most astonishing; very wonderful; amazing; miraculous.

অত্যাসক্ত *a.* very much addicted (to); strongly or too much attached (to). **অত্যাসক্তি** *n.* extreme addiction; strong attachment.

অত্যাসন্ন *a.* imminent; very near; impending; about to happen.

অত্যাহিত *n.* harm, injury; great fear.

অত্যুক্তি *n.* exaggeration.

অত্যুগ্র *a.* violent; unrelenting; extremely haughty or indignant; exceedingly bright or hot; very harsh; excessively austere; very strong (অত্যুগ্র বাসনা).

অত্যুচ্চ *a.* too high, very high.

অত্যুজ্জ্বল *a.* extremely bright or radiant or shining; extremely brilliant (অত্যুজ্জ্বলচরিত্র).

অত্যুৎকট *a.* most severe or terrible; extremely violent; most uncouth; bizarre.

অত্যুৎকৃষ্ট, অত্যুত্তম *a.* superexcellent; exquisite.

অত্যুৎপাদন *n.* (of agricultural produces and factory products) over-production.

অত্যুষ্ণ *a.* very hot, too hot; excessively heated.

অত্র *adv.* in or to or of this place, here. **~ত্য, ~স্থ** *a.* of this place.

অথ *adv.* thereafter, then.

অথই *a.* unfathomable, bottomless, very deep.

অথচ *con.* & *adv.* yet, still; notwithstanding, nevertheless, nonetheless, in spite of, even then; (usually) but.

অথবা *con.* or.

অথর্ব *n.* the last of the four Vedas. □ *a.* weak and infirm (esp. with age), deprived of the power of movement (esp. owing to age); decrepit; disabled.

অথান্তর *n.* (lit.) change of fortune for the worse; distress , worry, anxiety; danger or hazard; difficulty.

অথৈ alt. spell. of **অথই**।

অদক্ষ *a.* unskilled; inexpert. **~তা** *n.* lack of skill, unskilfulness. **~শ্রমিক** an unskilled labour or worker.

অদগ্ধ *a.* unburnt, not consumed by fire.

অদণ্ডনীয় *a.* not to be punished; unpunishable.

অদত্ত *a.* not given, undisbursed.

অদন *n.* eating; any edible article; food.

অদন্ত *a.* toothless, edentate.

অদমনীয়, অদম্য *a.* indomitable, unyielding; pertinacious; unconquerable; turbulent.

অদমিত *a.* unresisted; unrepressed; undefeated; unsubdued.

অদরকারি *a.* unnecessary; unimportant; inessential; dispensable.

অদর্শন *n.* invisibility; absence from the range of sight; disappearance. **অদর্শন হওয়া** *v.* to go out of sight; to become invisible; to disappear.

অদলবদল *n.* interchange; alternation; exchange; mutual transfer; modification. **অদলবদল করা** *v.* to interchange; to alter; to exchange; to transfer mutually; to modify.

অদহনীয়, অদাহ্য *a.* incombustible. **অদহনীয়তা, অদাহ্যতা** *n.* incombustibility.

অদিতি *n.* (myth.) the mother of gods. **~নন্দন** *n.* a son of Aditi; a god.

অদিন *n.* an inauspicious day; hard times, difficult days. **অদিনে পড়া** to fall on evil times or days.

অদীক্ষিত *a.* unconsecrated; uninitiated.

অদীপ *a.* when or where lamps have not yet been lighted (অদীপ সন্ধ্যা) ; without light; dark.

অদূর *a.* not distant, not far; near, close, yonder. **~দর্শিতা** *n.* absence or lack of foresight; imprudence. **~দর্শী** *a.* bereft of foresight; imprudent. *fem.* **~দর্শিনী**। **~বর্তিতা** *n.* state of being not at a distance; nearness, proximity. **~বর্তী** *a.* not in a distant position; proximate; near, yonder. *fem.* **~বর্তিনী, ~বদ্ধ** *a.* having a short or limited range. **~বদ্ধ দৃষ্টি** shortsightedness. **~ ভবিষ্যৎ** *n.* near future. **~স্থ** same as **~বর্তী**। **অদূরে** *adv.* not far; near, close by.

অদূষিত *a.* not corrupted; not defiled; (of water, air, etc.) not polluted.

অদৃঢ় *a.* not firm or strong; not steady; wavering; loose. **~তা** *n.* infirmity, unsteadiness; looseness.

অদৃশ্য *a.* invisible; imperceptible. **অদৃশ্য হওয়া** *v.* to go out of sight; to disappear or vanish; to become invisible or imperceptible.

অদৃষ্ট *a.* not seen, unseen. □ *n.* fate, luck, fortune; destiny. **~ক্রমে** *adv.* as ordained by destiny; as luck would have it; by chance; fortunately. **~দোষে** *adv.* unluckily, unfortunately, as bad luck would have it. **~পরীক্ষা** *n.* act of telling or learning one's fortune by means of divination, palmistry, etc., act of trying one's luck (esp. in a game of chance). **অদৃষ্ট পরীক্ষা করা** *v.* to tell one's fortune; to try one's luck. **অদৃষ্ট পরীক্ষা করানো** *v.* to have one's fortune told. **~পুরুষ** *n. masc.*

Destiny; God. ~পূর্ব *a.* not seen before; novel, new. ~বশত *adv.* as luck would have it; by chance. ~বাদ *n.* fatalism. ~বাদী *n.* a fatalist. □ *a.* fatalistic. ~লিপি *n.* the unseen writing of one's fate; one's destiny. **অদৃষ্টের পরিহাস** irony of fate.

অদেখা *a.* unseen.

অদেয় *a.* incapable of being given, unofferable, that which cannot be given.

অদ্বয় *n.* Brahma (ব্রহ্ম) ; Buddha. □ *a.* having no second or parallel, absolute. ~বাদ *n.* monism; Buddhism. ~বাদী *n.* a monist; a Buddhist. □ *a.* monistic; Buddhistic.

অদ্বিতীয় *a.* having no second or parallel; absolute; matchless; singualr, unique; supreme.

অদ্বৈত *a.* (theo.) having no second or diversity, monistical; unitarian, nondual, absolute. □ *n.* Brahma (ব্রহ্ম) ; God. ~বাদ *n.* non-dualism, monism, monotheism, unitarianism. ~বাদী *n.* a nondualist, a monist, a monotheist, a unitarian.

অদ্ভুত *a.* strange, queer, quaint, odd; uncouth; extraordinary; astonishing. □ *n.* (rhet.) a description that strikes the reader with its extraordinary strangeness or queerness (also **অদ্ভুতরস**). ~কর্মা *a.* endowed with extraordinary capabilities; one who is capable of performing miraculous deeds. ~দর্শন *a.* odd-looking.

অদ্য *n.* & *adv.* today. **অদ্যকার, অদ্যতন** *a.* of today, today's. **অদ্যভক্ষ্যোধনুর্গুণঃ** *n.* (fig.) over-optimistic calculation; (inc. but pop.) state of having nothing to eat today, abject poverty. **অদ্যাপি** *adv.* even today; even now; even at present; as yet. **অদ্যাবধি** *adv.* from today; hereafter; till today; till now.

অদ্রব *a.* insoluble, undissolved.

অদ্রাব্য *a.* insoluble.

অদ্রিজ *a.* born of or produced from a mountain. □ *n.* bitumen; red ochre.

অদ্রিশৃঙ্গ *n.* the peak or summit of a mountain.

অদ্রিসার *n.* iron.

অদ্রোহ *n.* absence of malignity or malice or envy; amicability; absence of quarrel.

অধঃ *adv.* & *prep.* down, below, beneath, under; in or to the underworld. ~কৃত *a.* cast or thrown downwards; felled; vanquished, defeated; lowered. ~ক্রম *n.* descending order. ~ক্ষিপ্ত thrown down, cast or hurled down. ~পতন, ~পাত *n.* falling down; downfall; degradation; degeneration; moral downfall; abandoned state. ~পতিত *a.* fallen down; downfallen; degraded; degenerated; morally degenerate, abandoned. **অধঃপাতে যাওয়া** *v.* to be ruined morally or otherwise, to go to the dogs, to reach a state of ruin. ~স্থ *a.* lying or situated or placed under; lower; subordinate.

অধম *a.* lowest; inferior; vile; mean; despicable, abominable, hateful; insignificant; worthless (অধম ভক্ত). **অধমর্ণ** *n.* a debtor. **অধমাঙ্গ** *n.* the part of the body from the waist downwards; (usu.) the foot or the leg. **অধমাধম** *a.* worse than the worst; vilest of the vile; most insignificant or worthless.

অধর *n.* (ori.) the lower lip; (loos.) any of the two lips or both the lips. ~কোণ *n.* the corner of the lips. ~দল *n.* (bot.) a labellum. ~পল্লব *n.* a lip or lips as tender as tree-leaves. ~প্রান্ত the end or extremity of the lips. **অধরমধু পান, অধরসুধা পান** *n.* (lit.) act of kissing greedily. **অধরমধু বা অধরসুধা পান করা** *v.* to kiss greedily.

অধরা *a.* incapable of being caught hold of; intangible; elusive. **অধরা মাধুরী** elusive charm or beauty.

অধরামৃত পান same as **অধরসুধা পান** (see **অধর**).

অধরিক *a.* inferior. **অধরিক কৃত্যক** inferior service.

অধরোষ্ঠ *n.* upper and lower lips, lips.

অধর্ম *n.* any act in contravention of scriptural or moral laws; a sinful act, a sin; irreligiousness; an unrighteous act; unrighteousness. □ *a.* sinful; unrighteous. **অধর্ম করা** to do or commit an unrighteous or sinful act, to do an immoral act. **~চারী, অধর্মাচারী** *a.* irreligious; ungodly. **~পরায়ণ** *a.* unrighteous; sinful. **অধর্মাচরণ** *n.* committing sins; sinful practice; unrighteous practice. **অধর্মী** *a.* sinful; unrighteous; unreligious; impious; (loos.) treacherous.

অধস্তক *n.* hypodermis.

অধস্তন *a.* lying or situated or placed under; born or grown on a lower stratum; lower; inferior; lower subordinate (অধস্তন কর্মচারী)। **অধস্তন পুরুষ** *n.* a later generation; posterity.

অধাতু *n.* non-metal. **অধাতব** *a.* non-metallic.

অধার্মিক *a.* irreligious; impious; unrighteous; sinful; vicious. **~তা** *n.* irreligiousness; immorality; impiety; unrighteqousness. sinfulness.

অধি *pfx.* used in the senses of above, on, over, upon, higher, greater, more, superior, ruling, dominating, etc., over-, super-, sur-, ad-, etc.

অধিক *a.* many, much; more; exceeding, more than (পাঁচের অধিক) ; additional; superfluous, too many, too much. *compar.* **~তর ;** *super.* **~তম**। **~স্তু** *con. & adv.* moreover; over and above; further, besides, in addition.

অধিকম্প *n.* a beat or beating (নাড়ির অধিকম্প).

অধিকর *n.* super-tax.

অধিকরণ *n.* anything that holds or contains; a container; a place; a vehicle or medium; proximity; a court of justice (ধর্মাধিকরণ) ; domination; possession or occupation; (gr.) the locative case.

অধিকর্তা *n.* director in charge of a (government) department.

অধিকল্প *n.* an era.

অধিকাংশ *a.* almost all, most; greater number or portion of. **অধিকাংশ ক্ষেত্রে বা স্থলে** in most cases, mostly.

অধিকার *n.* ownership; possession, occupation; right, title; claim; domination, control; overlordship; authority; experience, knowledge (গণিতশাস্ত্রে অধিকার) ; jurisdiction; a public directorate (শিক্ষাধিকার) ; ablity, competency or claim (রাজ্যশাসনে অধিকার). **অধিকার করা** *v.* to occupy, to possess. **~ক্ষেত্র** *n.* jurisdiction. **~গত** *a.* in one's possession; concerning one's possession or rights or claim or office; titular. **~চ্যুত, ~ভ্রষ্ট** *a.* dispossessed. **অধিকারী** *a.* having ownership or right or claim or title or possession or competency or authority. ☐ *n.* an owner, a proprietor (who is also the motion-master) of an opera-party, orchestra-party, etc. (যাত্রাদলের অধিকারী) ; any venerable person of the Vaishnava (বৈষ্ণব) community. **অধিকারী হওয়া** *v.* be entitled to. **অধিকারিণী** *a. fem.* of **অধিকারী** *n.* a proprietress, a mistress.

অধিকৃত *a.* that which has been taken possession of; occupied, possessed; brought under control; obtained.

অধিকেশ *n.* periwig.

অধিকোষ *n.* a banking establishment, a bank. **~স্থিতি** *n.* bank balance.

অধিক্রমণ *n.* act of overlapping.

অধিক্ষিপ্ত *a.* rebuked, scolded, reproached; ignored; neglected; censured; placed; thrown.

অধিক্ষেত্র see **অধি**।

অধিক্ষেপ *n.* rebuke, reproach, scolding; neglect; censure; placing.

অধিগত *a.* attained, obtained, acquired, earned; learned, known; studied; brought under control, mastered.

অধিগম্য *a.* accessible, attainable, acquirable; capable of being learnt or known, knowable, comprehensible; capable of being studied; capable of being mastered. **অধিগম, অধিগমন** *n.* attainment; acquisition of knowledge, comprehension.

অধিচাপ *n.* (geom.) a major arc.

অধিজন *n.* the majority. **অধিজন-প্রতিবেদন** *n.* the majority report. **অধিজন-সম্প্রদায়** *n.* the majority community.

অধিজনন *n.* birth; procreation; production.

অধিত্বক *n.* (zool.) exodermis; the outermost layer of an animal's skin.

অধিত্যকা *n.* a plateau, a tableland.

অধিদেব, অধিদেবতা, অধিদৈবত *n.* a guardian deity, a presiding or controlling deity.

অধিদেয় *n.* an allowance of money.
অধিনায়ক *n.* a leader; a chief; the captain or skipper of a playing team; an army commander. **~তা, ~ত্ব** *n.* leadership; captaincy; command.
অধিনিয়ম *n.* a legislative act. **~ন** *n.* enactment; legislation.
অধিপ, অধিপতি *n.* a master, a lord; an owner; a proprietor; a king, a prince.
অধিপাদীয় *a.* epibasal.
অধিপাল *n.* a vice-chancellor (of a university).
অধিপুরুষ *n.* a rector.
অধিপ্রাণবাদ *n.* (phil.) the vitalistic theory.
অধিবক্তা *n.* a legal advocate.
অধিবর্ধন *n.* overgrowth.
অধিবর্ষ *n.* a leap-year.
অধিবাস[1] *n.* a dwelling-place, a home, an abode.
অধিবাস[2]**, অধিবাসন** *n.* ceremonial purification of a person on the eve of a solemn function (বরের অধিবাস) ; any performance preliminary to any solemn ceremony (পূজার অধিবাস) ; invocation.
অধিবাসিত *a.* (of a person) purified ceremonially; invocated; established in a residence; placed.
অধিবাসী *n.* an inhabitant; a native; a resident.
অধিবাস্তববাদ *n.* surrealism. **অধিবাস্তববাদী** *n.* a surrealist.
অধিবিদ্য *a.* erudite, learned.
অধিবিদ্যক *a.* metaphysical.
অধিবিদ্যা *n.* metaphysics.
অধিবিষ *n.* toxin.
অধিবৃত্ত *n.* (math.) a parabola.
অধিবৃত্তি *n.* a bonus.
অধিবেত্তা *n.* a man who marries a second time with first wife still living.
অধিবেদন *n.* marrying a second time when one's first wife is still living.
অধিবেশন *n.* a meeting; a sitting; a session.
অধিভার *n.* a surcharge.
অধিভূ *n.* a master, a lord.
অধিমাংস *n.* an abscess; a tumour; an eye-disease.
অধিমাস *n.* an intercalary month.
অধিমূল্য *n.* a price above par. **অধিমূল্যে** *adv.* above par.
অধিযন্ত্রবাদ *n.* (phil.) the mechanistic theory.
অধিযান্ত্রিক *n.* a mechanical foreman, a machine foreman.
অধিযাচন *n.* requisition. **~পত্রী** *n.* a requisition slip.
অধিযুগ *n.* an epoch.
অধিরথ *n.* chariot-driver, a charioteer; a warrior on chariot who can fight innumerable enemies simultaneously.
অধিরাজ *n.* an emperor; a suzerain, an overlord, a sovereign prince.
অধিরাজ্ঞী *n.* an empress; a sovereign queen.
অধিরাজ্য *n.* a dominion of an empire.
অধিরূঢ় *a.* mounted, seated upon; riding on; ascended. **অধিরূঢ় হওয়া** *v.* to mount; to sit upon; to ride; to ascend.
অধিরোপণ *n.* making one mount or ride or ascend; placing (upon); charging a bow with an arrow. **অধিরোপণ করা** *v.* to make one mount or ride or ascend; to place (upon); to charge (a bow) with (an arrow.) **অধিরোপিত** *a.* placed (upon).
অধিরোহ *n.* an ascent; an elevation. **~ণ** *n.* mounting or ascending or climbing or riding. **অধিরোহণী** *n.* a flight of steps; a ladder; a staircase. **অধিরোহিণী** var. of **অধিরোহণী ;** *fem.* of **অধিরোহী। অধিরোহী** *a.* mounting; ascending; climbing; riding. □ *n.* a mounter; a climber; a rider.
অধিশয়িত, অধিশয়ান *a.* placed or lying upon or over; established over or upon.
অধিশায়িত *a.* placed or laid upon or over.
অধিশ্রয় *n.* (phys.) focus; a receptacle; shelter. **অধিশ্রিত** *a.* placed; sheltered.
অধিষ্ঠাতা *a.* dwelling or living or existing ; present; governing, directing, controlling; presiding; holding (an office or a post); possessing, occupying. □ *n.* a dweller; a governor; a director; a controller; a president; one who is present; one who holds (an office or a post); a possessor, an occupier. *fem.* **অধিষ্ঠাত্রী। অধিষ্ঠাত্রী দেবী** *n.* a presiding deity.
অধিষ্ঠান living or dwelling or existing; presence or appearance; being seated

or placed; presence to guide and control; a dwelling-place, a resort (দেবতার অধিষ্ঠানে) ; state of being situated; holding (an office or a post); (psy.) inherence; taking possession of. **অধিষ্ঠান করা** *v.* to live or dwell or stay in; to exist in; to be present in; to be seated or placed in or upon; to be present to guide and control; to be situated; to hold (an office or a post); (psy.) to inhere; to take possession of, to occupy.

অধিষ্ঠিত *a.* dwelling or living or staying; existent; present; settled; seated; present to guide and control; situated; holding (an office or a post); possessing, occupying; dwelt, inhabited; possessed, occupied. **অধিষ্ঠিত হওয়া** *v.* to live or dwell (in), to inhabit; to exist (in); to be present (in); to appear (in); to be present (in) to guide and control; to be seated or placed (in or upon); to be situated (in); to be established (in an office or a post); to be in possession or occupation of; (psy.) to inhere.

অধিসঞ্চার *n.* atavism. **অধিসঞ্চারী** *a.* atavistic.

অধিহার *n.* a rate above par. **অধিহারে** *adv.* above par; at a premium.

অধীক্ষক *n.* a superintendent; a supervisor, an overseer.

অধীক্ষা *n.* overseeing, superintendence, supervision.

অধীত *a.* read, studied, perused. **অধীত বিষয়** *n.* a subject that has been studied. **অধীতি** *n.* study, act of reading, perusal. **অধীতী** *a.* engaged in studying or reading or perusing; learned, erudite, well-studied.

অধীন *a.* brought under control, subjugated; tamed; dependent; dependent for maintenance or subsistence; bound by obligation (to); included; dominated, governed or ruled (by); subordinate (অধীন কর্মচারী) ; subservient (to), subject (to). *fem.* **অধীনা,** (inc.) **অধিনী।** **অধীনতা, অধীনত্ব** *n.* subjugation; tamed condition; dependence; dependence for maintenance or subsistence; obligation; domination; subordination; subserviency, subjection.

অধীয়মান *a.* that which is being read or studied. □ *n.* a student.

অধীর *a.* restless; fidgety; impatient; eager; anxious; worried; alarmed, concerned; uneasy; excited , agitated; beside oneself. *fem.* **অধীরা।** **অধীরতা** *n.* restlessness; fidgetiness; impatience; eagerness; anxiety , worry; alarm, fear; excitement, agitation. **~চিত্ত** *a.* of a restless turn of mind; scatter-brained. **অধীর হওয়া** *v.* to become restless or impatient or eager or anxious or alarmed or excited or agitated; to fidget; to worry; to be beside oneself.

অধীশ, অধীশ্বর *n.* a great king; an emperor; a sovereign ruler; an owner; a master; a lord; a ruler or director; a chief. *fem.* **অধীশ্বরী।**

অধুনা *adv.* in recent times, at present, nowadays. **~তন** *a.* of recent times, present-day; modern. **~লুপ্ত** *a.* now-extinct.

অধৃত *a.* unshivering , not trembling; steady and still.

অধৃষ্য *a.* difficult to vanquish, unconquerable; indomitable, turbulent.

অধৈর্য *a.* impatient; eager; restless, uneasy; fidgety; anxious, worried. □ *n.* impatience; eagerness; restlessness, uneasiness; fidgetiness; anxiety, worry.

অধোগত *a.* gone downwards, descended; subsided; downfallen; deteriorated; depraved; stricken with misery, distressed; condemned to hell.

অধোগতি, অধোগমন *n.* going downwards, descent; subsidence; downfall, deterioration; depravity; misery, distress; domination.

অধোগামিনী *fem.* of **অধোগামী।**

অধোগামী *a.* going downwards, descending; subsiding; downfallen, deteriorating; depraved; miserable, distressed; condemned to hell.

অধোদৃষ্টি *a.* looking downwards; having looks fixed at the tip of one's nose whilst practising yoga. **অধোদৃষ্টিতে** *adv.* with downcast looks.

অধোদেশ *n.* the lower portion or part; posteriors, buttocks; downward direction.

অধোনমন *n.* degradation; going down; getting down. **অধোনমিত** *a.* brought down; degraded.

অধোবদন *a.* having one's face or head hanging down. *fem.* **অধোবদনা** । **অধোবদন হওয়া** *v.* to hang one's face or head down. **অধোবদনে** *adv.* with one's face or head hanging down.

অধোবায়ু *n.* downward wind; fart.

অধোবাস, অধোবস্ত্র *n.* clothes for the lower part of the body.

অধোবিন্দু *n.* the nadir.

অধোভাগ same as **অধোদেশ** ।

অধোভুবন *n.* the netherworld, the underworld; the Hades.

অধোমুখ same as **অধোবদন** । *fem.* **অধোমুখী** ।

অধোলোক *n.* same as **অধোভুবন** ।

অধৌত *a.* unwashed; uncleaned.

অধ্বগ *n.* a traveller, a wayfarer.

অধ্বর *n.* an ecclesiastical sacrifice (esp. in accordance with the যজুর্বেদ).

অধ্বর্যু *n.* a priest who is versed in the যজুর্বেদ ।

অধ্যক্ষ *a.* manager; a chief executive; a superintendent, an officer in charge; a principal (of a college or institution); a lord or a master (দুর্গাধ্যক্ষ) ; a president or speaker (of a legislative assembly). **~তা** *n.* the post or office or function of a chief executive; superintendentship; superintendence; overlordship or mastership; principalship; presidentship; presidency; speakership.

অধ্যবসায় *n.* perseverance; sustained effort. **~শীল, অধ্যবসায়ী** *a.* persevering.

অধ্যয়ন *n.* reading; study; perusal. **~রত, ~নিরত** *a.* engaged in studying or reading (esp. absorbedly). **~শীল** *a.* studious; studying or reading (esp. absorbedly). **~শীলতা** *n.* studiousness. **অধ্যয়নীয়** *a.* readable; worth reading.

অধ্যশন *n.* over-eating, surfeit; act of eating a second time before the food taken previously has been digested.

অধ্যাত্ম *a.* pertaining to the Supreme Being; pertaining to the individual soul; spiritual; metaphysical; physical. **~চেতনা** *n.* spirituality; spiritualism. **~তত্ত্ব** *n.* knowledge about God; knowledge about the soul; metaphysics. **~তত্ত্ববিৎ** *n.* one who has knowledge about God or the soul; a metaphysician. **~বাদ** *n.* subjectivism; spiritualism. **~বাদী** *a.* subjectivistic; spiritualistic. □ *n.* a subjectivist; a spiritualist. **অধ্যাত্মিক** var. of **আধ্যাত্মিক** । **অধ্যাত্মীয়** *a.* subjective.

অধ্যাদেশ *n.* an ordinance.

অধ্যাপক *n.* a teacher; an instructor; an advisor; (usu.) a professor or lecturer (of a college etc.). *fem.* **অধ্যাপিকা** ।

অধ্যাপন, অধ্যাপনা *n.* act of teaching, or advising or instructing; readership. **অধ্যাপনা করা** *v.* to teach, to instruct, to advise; (usu.) to work as a professor or lecturer (in a college etc.). **অধ্যাপিত** *a.* taught, instructed.

অধ্যাপয়িতা same as **অধ্যাপক** । *fem.* **অধ্যাপয়িত্রী** ।

অধ্যায় *n.* a chapter, a section, a canto, etc. (of a book).

অধ্যারূঢ় *a.* mounted (on).

অধ্যারোপ *n.* (rhet.) transference of epithet; (phil.) imaginary ascription of foreign qualities to a person or a thing; illusion.

অধ্যাস[১] *n.* ascription, attribution; (phil.) imaginary ascription of foreign qualities to a person or a thing, illusion.

অধ্যাস[২]**, অধ্যাসন** *n.* placed or seated upon or over; sitting; being seated; domination; (of deities) invisible presence.

অধ্যাসিত, অধ্যাসীন *a.* placed or seated upon or over; mounted; in possession of; (of deities) present invisibly.

অধ্যাহার, অধ্যাহরণ *n.* (gr.) act of making a word or words elliptic; (gr.) an ellipsis; quotation. **অধ্যাহার্য** *a.* that which can be or should be omitted.

অধ্যাহৃত *a.* (gr.) left out as an ellipsis; quoted.

অধ্যুষিত *a.* inhabited; colonized.

অধ্যেতা *a.* engaged in study. □ *n.* a student; a reader. **অধ্যেতব্য** *a.* to be read or studied; fit to be read.

অধ্রুব *a.* inconstant; unstable; transitory; changeable, variable; uncertain, doubtful.

অন্ var. of অ-[২] to be prefixed to words

beginning with a vowel (e. g. অনধ্যায় < অধ্যায়, অনৈতিহাসিক < ঐতিহাসিক).

অনক্ষ *a.* having no wheel.

অনক্ষর *a.* illiterate, unlettered; ignorant.

অনগ্ন *a.* not naked; not without a cover.

অনগ্রসর *a.* not developed or advanced; backward. **~তা** *n.* lack or absence of progress; backwardness; retardation.

অনঘ *a.* sinless; pure, holy; innocent; free from danger; safe, secure; pleasant; sorrowless; happy.

অনঙ্কুরিত *a.* not yet sprouted or germinated, unsprouted, ungerminated; (poet.) unrealized.

অনঙ্গ *a.* bodiless, unembodied, incorporeal. ☐ *n.* Madan (মদন) the god of love. **~মোহন** *n.* Krishna (কৃষ্ণ). **~শর** *n.* a shaft or shafts of the god of love; pangs of love, love-sickness. **অনঙ্গারি** *n.* Shiva (শিব).

অনচ্ছ *a.* not transparent; opaque; muddy, turbid, dirty. **~তা** *n.* opacity; turbidity; (fig.) obscurity.

অনটন *n.* want; shortage, deficiency; poverty; pecuniary distress or stringency; penury.

অনড্বান *n.* ox, bull.

অনড় *a.* motionless, immobile; still; fixed, firm, stolid, never to be retracted, irrevocable (আমার কথা অনড়).

অনতি *a.* (chiefly used as a *pfx.*) not much or many; not excessive or superfluous; moderate; middling.

অনতিকাল *n.* not a long time; a short time. **~মধ্যে** *adv.* ere or before long; in a short time, shortly.

অনতিক্রম, অনতিক্রমণ *n.* not passing beyond or over; not crossing; not transgressing or infringing or violating. **অনতিক্রমণীয়, অনতিক্রম্য** *a.* incapable of being passed beyond or over; incapable of being crossed; impassable; inviolable; incapable of being overcome (অনতিক্রম্য বাধা) ; insuperable. **অনতিক্রান্ত** *a.* that has not been passed beyond or over; not crossed; not transgressed or violated or infringed; not overcome; not surmounted; unbeaten.

অনতিদীর্ঘ *a.* not very long (অনতিদীর্ঘ পথ বা রাত্রি) ; not very tall (অনতিদীর্ঘ দেহ). **অনতিদীর্ঘ কাল** *n.* not a very long time.

অনতিদূরবর্তী *a.* situated at not a great distance.

অনতিদূরে *adv.* not at or to a great distance, not very far.

অনতিপূর্বে *adv.* not long before; a short while ago.

অনতিবিলম্বে *adv.* not long after, without much delay, before long; shortly, soon.

অনতিবিস্তৃত *a.* not very extensive or broad or wide or spacious.

অনতীত *a.* not yet gone by or past.

অনতীতবাল্য *a.* of one who has not yet passed his childhood or boyhood.

অনধিক *a.* not exceeding, not more than.

অনধিকার *n.* absence of right or claim or possession. ☐ *a.* unrightful; without authority or claim or possession; ultra vires, unwarranted. **~চর্চা** *n.* unauthorized interference, meddling; officiousness; interference without competence or qualification. **অনধিকারচর্চা করা** *v.* to interfere without authority, to meddle, to butt in, to thrust one's nose in; to act officiously; to interfere without competence or qualification. **~প্রবেশ** *n.* trespass, intrusion. **অনধিকারপ্রবেশ করা** *v.* to trespass, to intrude, to encroach; to transgress, to infringe. **অনধিকারী** *a.* without any right or claim or authority or competence; having no right or claim; unrightful; unauthorized; incompetent; not entitled; ineligible.

অনধিকৃত *a.* not taken possession of; not captured or seized; unoccupied; unconquered.

অনধিগত *a.* unearned; unlearnt; unstudied, unread; unattained; not acquired; not reached or gone through.

অনধিগম্য *a.* unknowable, incomprehensible; incapable of being learnt (অনধিগম্য বিষয়) ; inaccessible, unapproachable (অনধিগম্য স্থান) ; uncome-at-able.

অনধিষ্ঠিত *a.* not placed upon or over; not present, absent, inexistent; not established (in a place etc.); not appointed (to a post, office etc.); not seated upon or over.

অনধীত *a.* that which has not been read or studied; unread or unstudied; not gone through.

অনধীন *a.* not depending on; not controlled or dominated by; not subject or subservient to; not subordinate to. **~তা** *n.* state of being not dependent or controlled or dominated or subservient or subordinate; independence, freedom.

অনধ্যবসায় *n.* lack or absence or perseverence.

অনধ্যায়, অনধ্যয়ন *n.* rest from study; a day of rest from study; a school holiday.

অননুকরণীয় *a.* incapable of being imitated; inimitable.

অননুকূল *a.* adverse; unfavourable.

অননুগত *a.* not obedient, disobedient.

অননুভবনীয় *a.* incapable of being felt, unperceivable.

অননুভূত *a.* unfelt; not perceived.

অননুমত *a.* unpermitted; unsanctioned; unapproved; disallowed; not agreeable to.

অননুমেয় *a.* incapale of being guessed, not conjecturable; unimaginable.

অননুমোদন *n.* absence of permission or sanction; disapproval; rejection, absence of consent. **অননুমোদিত** *a.* unpermitted; unapproved (অননুমোদিত পাঠ্যপুস্তক) ; unsanctioned; not assented to; disapproved; disagreed; rejected, prohibited (অননুমোদিত এলাকা) ; unauthorized (অননুমোদিত ব্যয়) ; unaffiliated (অননুমোদিত বিদ্যালয়).

অননুশীলন *n.* lack or absence of systematic practice or training. **অননুশীলিত** *a.* not practised; without systematic training; uncultivated.

অননুষ্ঠিত *a.* unperformed, unexecuted; unaccomplished; outstanding.

অনন্ত *a.* endless; boundless; unlimited; inexhaustible; everlasting, eternal; imperishable. □ *n.* Vishnu (বিষ্ণু) ; Shesha (শেষ) the thousand-headed king of snakes; an ornament, an armlet. **~কাল** *n.* eternity. **~কালব্যাপী, ~কালস্থায়ী** *a.* eternal, everlasting. **অনন্তকাল ধরে** *adv.* for ever. **~চতুর্দশী** *n.* the fourteenth day of the lunar fortnight of the month of Bhadra (ভাদ্র) ; a religious penance observed on this day. **~দেব** *n.* Shesha (শেষ) the king of snakes. **~নিদ্রা** *n.* Vishnu's sleep on the person of Ananta (অনন্ত) the snake-king; everlasting or eternal sleep; (fig.) death. **~নিদ্রায় নিদ্রিত** sleeping the sleep that knows no breaking, sleeping eternal sleep, dead. **~প্রকার** *a.* of endless or countless varieties. **~বীর্য** *a.* of endless or inexhaustible strength or virility. **~প্রভাব** *n.* incessant or endless current or flow. **~মূল** *n.* a medicinal root. **~রূপ, ~রূপী** *a.* of endless forms or shapes; of endless manifestations. **~শয়ন, ~শয্যা** *n.* use of the person of Anantadeva (অনন্তদেব) by Vishnu as his bed; (fig.) death. **~শীর্ষ** *a.* hydra-headed.

অনন্তর *a. & con.* hereafter or thereafter, afterwards, then.

অনন্তরূপ, অনন্তরূপী, অনন্তশয়ন, অনন্তশয্যা, অনন্তশীর্ষ see **অনন্ত** ।

অনন্বয়ী অব্যয় *n.* (gr.) an interjection.

অনন্য *n.* no other than; having no other; intent; resolute; sole, singular, unique; supreme; unparalleled; solely or absorbedly engaged. *fem.* **অনন্যা** । **~কর্মা** *a.* doing no work other than; not attending to any work other than; solely engaged or absorbed in. **~গতি** *a.* having no way or means or alternative other than; compelled by absence of any alternative. **~চিত্ত** *a.* having nothing in the mind other than; fixed with close attention to nothing other than, intent on. **~চিত্তে** *adv.* with undivided attention, intently. **~দৃষ্টি** *a.* looking at nothing other than; gazing steadfastly. **~পরায়ণ** *a.* not devoted to anything other than; solely engaged in. **~বৃত্তি** *a.* engaged in no occupation or endeavour other than; solely occupied in. **~ব্রত** *a.* engaged in or performing no task other than. **অনন্যমনা** same as **~চিত্ত** । **~শরণ, ~সহায়** *a.* having no help or resort or patron or protector other than. **~সাধারণ, ~সুলভ** *a.* not to be found in anybody else; singular, unique; extraordinary, uncommon.

~সাপেক্ষ *a.* not depending on or subject to anything; absolutely independent.

অনন্যোপায় *a.* having no means or resource other than; having no alternative; desperate.

অনন্বিত *a.* (gr.) lacking in sequence or agreement; (phil.) not governed by the law of causation; not related, detached; irrelevant, incoherent.

অনপকারক, অনপকারী *a.* not injurious or harmful, harmless, doing no harm or injury.

অনপগত *a.* not removed, not dispelled; not gone.

অনপচয় *n.* absence of waste or wastefulness or improvidence.

অনপত্য *a.* childless, issueless.

অনপনেয় *a.* indelible, ineffaceable; irremediable (অনপনেয় দুঃখ) ; irremovable (অনপনেয় উৎপাত) ; irredeemable (অনপনেয় কলঙ্ক).

অনপরাধ *n.* absence of sin or crime; impeccability; innocence. □ *a.* impeccable; innocent. **অনপরাধী** *a.* same as **অনপরাধ** (*a*). *fem.* **অনপরাধিনী** ।

অনপেক্ষ *a.* not depending on or subject to; independent; impartial, unbiased.

অনপেক্ষিত *a.* not awaited; unexpected; unanticipated.

অনপেত same as **অনপগত** ।

অনবকাশ *n.* want of leisure or respite or break; lack of time for doing some particular work.

অনবগত *a.* unaware, uninformed; ignorant; unknown.

অনবগুণ্ঠিত *a.* not veiled; unveiled. *fem.* **অনবগুণ্ঠিতা** ।

অনবচ্ছিন্ন *a.* without intermission or respite, non-stop; incessant; continuous.

অনবচ্ছেদ *n.* absence of intermission or respite; continuity.

অনবদ্য *a.* blameless; flawless; faultless; impeccable; unimpeachable; innocent (অনবদ্য কৌতুক) ; beautiful; splendid. **~তা** *n.* blamelessness; flawlessness; faultlessness; innocence; impeccability; unimpeachability. **অনবদ্যাঙ্গী** *a. fem.* of unimpeachable beauty.

অনবধান *n.* inattention; carelessness; inadvertence. □ *a.* inattentive; careless; negligent; inadvertent. **~তা** *n.* inattention; carelessness; negligency; inadvertence. **অনবধানতাবশত** *adv.* inadvertently; unintentionally.

অনবরত *a.* ceaseless, unremitting; continuous. □ *adv.* incessantly, unremittingly; continually; always, ever.

অনবরুদ্ধ *a.* unconfined, not shut up; unbolted; not barricaded or blockaded; not besieged; unrestricted, unhindered (অনবরুদ্ধ স্রোত).

অনবরোধ *n.* freedom from confinement or siege or restriction.

অনবলম্ব, অনবলম্বন *a.* having no prop or support; having nothing to fall back on; having no refuge.

অনবসর *n.* absence of leisure or respite; want of opportunity. □ *a.* having no leisure or respite; (continuously) busy.

অনবসিত *a.* not finished or completed, unfinished or incomplete.

অনবস্থ same as **অনবস্থিত** ।

অনবস্থা *n.* lack of order, disorder; unsettled state, restlessness; (log.) a defect in argument caused by working back from one thing to another especially from effect to cause, a regress.

অনবস্থিত *a.* restless; unsettled; fickle or unsteady; unstable; wavering. **~চিত্ত** *a.* of unsettled mind; unresolved in purpose; mentally wavering; changing one's mind every moment; fickle-minded. **~চিত্ততা** *n.* fickle-mindedness.

অনবহিত *a.* inattentive, unmindful; heedless; careless, neglectful; not on the alert, unguarded, unwary.

অনভিজাত *a.* not born of a good family; not high-born, not aristocratic; low-born; not having a good pedigree.

অনভিজ্ঞ *a.* inexperienced; inexpert; *fem.* **অনভিজ্ঞা** । **~তা** *n.* inexperience; lack of skill.

অনভিপ্রায় *n.* lack of desire or intention; disapproval; contrariety to one's desire or liking or intention.

অনভিপ্রেত *a.* disapproved; disagreed; undesired; not to one's liking; contrary to one's desire or intention.

অনভিব্যক্ত *a.* not expressed; not manifest; not evolved; implicit.

অনভিভবনীয় *a.* unconquerable; indomitable; not to be confounded or overwhelmed.

অনভিভূত *a.* unconquered; not confounded or overwhelmed; unembarrassed.

অনভিমত *a.* disapproved; unsanctioned; contrary to one's opinion.

অনভিলষণীয় *a.* undesirable.

অনভিলষিত *a.* undesired.

অনভিলাষ *n.* unwillingness; contrariety to one's desire; absence of desire. **অনভিলাষী** *a.* unwilling; not desirous of; disapproving; having no desire for.

অনভীষ্ট *a.* not desired; undesired, unwanted.

অনভ্যস্ত *a.* unaccustomed, unwonted; inexperienced; unpractised; inexpert; unfamiliar.

অনভ্যাস *n.* lack of practice or training; unwontedness.

অনমনীয় *a.* unbending, inflexible; unyielding; indomitable; tough, hard, rigid; obstinate. **~তা** *n.* inflexibility; unbendingness; rigidity.

অনম্বর *a.* having no cover; bare; naked. □ *n.* the sky; a Buddhist community.

অনর্গল *a.* unbolted; unrestrained, unhindered; free; profuse, abundant; fluent. □ *adv.* incessantly; excessively; fluently.

অনর্থ *n.* harm, mischief, injury; reverse, peril, danger; ruin; mishap; trouble or unhappy occurrence (অনর্থ ঘটানো).

অনর্থক *a.* futile, useless; unprovoked or unreasonable (অনর্থক কলহ) ; unnecessary. □ *adv.* in vain; without provocation or reason; unnecessarily.

অনর্থকর *a.* injurious, full of mischief , harmful; causing reverse or ruin; devastating.

অনর্থদর্শী *a.* & *n.* pessimist.

অনর্থপাত *n.* occurrence of an accident; befalling of danger or reverse or ruin.

অনর্হ *n.* unfit; unsuitable; not adorable.

অনল *n.* fire. **~প্রভ** *a.* as radiant or lustrous as fire. **~বর্ষণ** *n.* raining of fire; showering or emitting of fire. **~বর্ষী** *a.* raining fire; showering or emitting fire. **~শিলা** *n.* a meteor.

অনলংকৃত *a.* not decorated or ornamented; unadorned.

অনলস *a.* not lazy or indolent; diligent, industrious; untiring; given to action, active; lively and energetic.

অনল্প *a.* not small in number or amount; many or much; considerably large in number or amount.

অনশন *n.* abstinence from food, fasting; starvation. **~ক্লিষ্ট** *a.* stricken with starvation; famished. **অনশন ধর্মঘট** *n.* hunger-strike. **~ব্রত** *n.* abstinence from food (till one's death) under a solemn vow; (loos.) hunger-strike.

অনশ্বর *a.* imperishable; indestructible; immortal. **~তা** *n.* imperishability; indestructibility; immortality.

অনসূয় *a.* free from malice or envy. *fem.* অনসূয়া।

অনস্তগ *a.* (astr.) circumpolar.

অনস্তমিত *a.* not set; not disappeared or declined.

অনস্বীকার্য *a.* undeniable; that which cannot but be admitted.

অনহংকৃত *a.* not proud; not conceited or arrogant, not stuck-up.

অনাকর্ষণীয় *a.* uninviting, unattractive.

অনাকাঙ্ক্ষা *n.* lack or absence of desire; absence of longing.

অনাক্রমণ *n.* non-aggression. **অনাক্রমণ চুক্তি** *n.* a non-aggression pact.

অনাক্রম্য *a.* incapable of being attacked; (hyg.) immune. **~তা** *n.* immunity.

অনাক্রান্ত *a.* unassailed, unattacked.

অনাগত *a.* not yet come or arrived; not yet happened; still to come or happen, future. **~বিধাতা** *n.* one who makes provision for the future; one having foresight.

অনাঘ্রাত *a.* unsmelt; pure and untouched. *fem.* অনাঘ্রাতা।

অনাচার *n.* unscriptural or unholy practice; uncultured or indecent practice; an immoral or abominable practice. **অনাচারী** *a.* abandoned; given to unscriptural or indecent or abominable practice. ☐ *n.* such a man.

অনাচ্ছাদিত *a.* uncovered; having no roof, unthatched; bare.

অনাড়ম্বর *a.* unostentatious, unceremonious; simple.

অনাত্মজ্ঞ *a.* ignorant of one's own self, lacking in self-knowledge; not moving or acting in accordance with one's status or power or circumstances.

অনাত্মীয় *a.* having no blood-relation or matrimonial relation (with), unrelated; unfriendly; having no kindred or relations. *fem.* **অনাত্মীয়া** ।

অনাথ *a.* having none to help or protect, helpless; orphan. *fem.* **অনাথা,** (pop.) **অনাথিনী** । **~নাথ** *n.* one who helps or protects the helpless; God. **~শালা, অনাথাশ্রম** *n.* charitable home or refuge for the helpless; an orphanage.

অনাদর *n.* lack of cordiality or care or attention; neglect; slight; disrespect. **অনাদর করা** *v.* to treat with neglect or disrespect. **অনাদরণীয়** *a.* unworthy of being treated with cordiality or care or attention.

অনাদায় *n.* (of dues, money, revenue, claims, etc.) non-realization or non-recovery. **অনাদায়ী** *a.* unrealized; outstanding.

অনাদি *a.* having no beginning or cause or origin; self-born. ☐ *n.* God.

অনাদিকাল *n.* time immemorial, very old or ancient time.

অনাদিষ্ট *a.* not ordered or commanded.

অনাদৃত *a.* not received with cordiality or care or attention; neglected; slighted.

অনাদেয় *a.* (inc. of dues, money, revenue, claim, etc.) unrealizable.

অনাদ্য *a.* having no beginning; without origin.

অনাদ্যন্ত *a.* having neither beginning nor end, having neither origin nor destruction; self-born and immortal.

অনাপ্য *a.* not obtainable; rare.

অনাবশ্যক *a.* unnecessary; needless ; redundant; superfluous. **~তা** *n.* needlessness.

অনাবাদি *a.* uncultivated, fallow; uncultivable , non-arable.

অনাবাসিক, অনাবাসী *a.* non-resident; non-residential.

অনাবিল *a.* not dirty or muddy, not turbid; limpid, clear, clean; pure; unmixed, unadulterated (অনাবিল সুখ).

অনাবিষ্কৃত *a.* undiscovered; not yet invented; not found out, untraced; unknown.

অনাবিষ্ট *a.* inattentive; absent-minded.

অনাবৃত *a.* uncovered; unconcealed; bare; naked; open; discovered; revealed.

অনাবৃষ্টি *n.* shortage or absence of rain; drought.

অনাব্য *a.* not navigable.

অনাময় *n.* absence of illness; physical soundness; recovery from illness. ☐ *a.* free from illness; recovered from illness and difficulties; peaceful.

অনামা[1] *a.* nameless; one whose name is not known or famous; obscure.

অনামা[2]**, অনামিকা** *n.* the ring-finger.

অনামুখ, অনামুখো *a.* having a face so inauspicious that one should not look at it, one whose face is an ill-omen; sinister-looking. ☐ *n.* such a man. *fem.* **অনামুখী** ।

অনাম্নী *fem.* of **অনামা**[1] ।

অনায়ত *a.* not wide or large; not extended.

অনায়ত্ত *a.* not brought under control; unmastered; beyond one's reach or power; uncome-at-able.

অনায়াস *n.* a state demanding no exertion or offering no difficulty; easiness. ☐ *a.* demanding no exertion or offering no difficulty; effortless, easy; facile, spontaneous. **~কৃত** *a.* done without effort or strain or difficulty; accomplished easily. **~দক্ষতা** *n.* easy skill or gift; gift of doing spontaneously. **~লব্ধ** *a.* obtained or earned without effort or strain or difficulty; got easily. **~লভ্য** *a.* obtainable without effort or difficulty; easily obtainable. **~সাধ্য** *a.* capable of being done or performed or attained or obtained without effort or difficulty; easy. **~সিদ্ধ** *a.* done or accomplished or attained or obtained easily. **অনায়াসে** *adv.* without strain or exertion or difficulty; effortlessly; easily; spontaneously.

অনারব্ধ *a.* not (yet) begun or commenced; not (yet) undertaken.

অনারম্ভ *n.* non-commencement.

অনারোগ্য *n.* state of ill-health; lack of cure. □ *a.* incurable; irremediable.

অনার্তবা *a. fem.* not yet attained puberty.

অনার্দ্র *a.* not wet; dry;(chem.) anhy- drous.

অনার্য *a.* non-Aryan; uncivilized; uncultured; discourteous; low-born. □ *n.* such a man. **অনার্যোচিত** *a.* befitting a non-Aryan; barbarian; uncivilized; uncultured; rudely discourteous; dishonest; impious; low-born.

অনালোকিত *a.* not lighted, unlit; not bright; not enlightened.

অনালোচনীয় *a.* that which should not be or will not be discussed; not fit to be discussed or considered.

অনালোচিত *a.* undiscussed; not discussed or talked about.

অনালোচ্য var. of **অনালোচনীয়** ।

অনাশ্রয় *a.* having no shelter or refuge; shelterless; helpless. □ *n.* helplessness. **অনাশ্রিত** *n.* not sheltered; shelterless; helpless.

অনাসক্ত *a.* having no attachment for or interest in; indifferent, unconcerned. **অনাসক্তি** *n.* absence of attachment or interest; indifference; unconcernedness.

অনাসন্ন *a.* not near or approaching; not imminent or impending.

অনাসৃষ্টি *a.* outside the created world, unnatural; disorderly; queer, strange, bizarre. □ *n.* such a thing or incident or state.

অনাস্থা *n.* lack of trust or faith; no-confidence; unreliability. **~প্রস্তাব** *n.* a no-confidence motion. **~ভাজন** *a.* untrustworthy; unreliable. **অনাস্থাসূচক মত** vote of no-confidence.

অনাস্বাদিত *a.* untasted; unenjoyed. **~পূর্ব** *a.* not tasted or enjoyed previously.

অনাহত *a.* unhurt, unwounded; (of stringed instruments) unstruck, unplayed ('অনাহত মোর বীণা').

অনাহার *n.* state of going without food; fasting, starvation. **অনাহারী** *a.* going without food; fasting. **অনাহারে** *adv.* going without food; on fast. **অনাহারে থাকা** *v.* to go without food; to starve, to fast.

অনাহিত *a.* (phys.) uncharged.

অনাহূত *a.* uncalled; uninvited; unbidden; uncalled-for; unwanted.

অনিঃশেষ *a.* inexhaustible; endless or impersihable (অনিঃশেষ প্রাণ).

অনিঃসৃত *a.* not secreted, not drained out.

অনিকেত, অনিকেতন *a.* homeless.

অনিচ্ছা *n.* unwillingness, reluctance; lack of consent; indifference, disinterestedness. **~কৃত** *a.* done or performed reluctantly or unknowingly; not deliberate, unintentional, undesigned. **~পূর্বক** *adv.* unwillingly, reluctantly; without consent or agreement; indifferently, disinterestedly. **অনিচ্ছা প্রকাশ করা** *v.* to express unwillingness or reluctance; to express disrelish; to disagree, to refuse to consent. **~ভরে, অনিচ্ছায়** same as **~পূর্বক** । **~সত্ত্বেও** *adv.* notwithstanding unwillingness or reluctance or lack of consent or disagreement or lack of interest. **~সহকারে** same as **অনিচ্ছাপূর্বক** ।

অনিচ্ছুক *a.* unwilling, reluctant; refusing consent, disagreeing; indifferent, disinterested.

অনিত্য *a.* not permanent or eternal or everlasting; transient, transitory; temporal (অনিত্য সংসার) ; perishable, frail, mortal (অনিত্য দেহ). **~তা** *n.* impermanence; transience, transitoriness; temporality.

অনিদান *a.* having no cause or ground, causeless, groundless.

অনিদ্র *a.* sleepless; vigilant.

অনিদ্রা, অনিদ্রারোগ *n.* sleeplessness; insomnia; wakefulness.

অনিন্দনীয়, অনিন্দ্য *a.* unblamable; irreproachable; faultless, flawless; praiseworthy. **অনিন্দ্যসুন্দর** *a.*beautiful, beyond reproach; exquisitely beautiful.

অনিন্দিত *a.* (ori.) unreproached; unblemished; not indecent; beautiful; blameless. **~চরিত্র** *a.* possessing an irreproachable or unimpeachable or immaculate character.

অনিপুণ *a.* lacking in dexterity, unskilful; unskilled; ungainly. **~তা** *n.* lack of dexterity or skill; ungainliness.

অনিবদ্ধ *a.* not arranged or laid properly.

অনিবন্ধী *a.* (chem.) amorphous.

অনিবার *a.* unpreventable; irresistible; incessant, non-stop, continuous. ☐ *adv.* incessantly; continually; always.

অনিবারণীয় *a.* unpreventable; irresistible, inevitable. **অনিবারিত** *a.* unprevented; not resisted.

অনিবার্য *a.* unpreventable; irresistible (অনিবার্য বেগ) ; inevitable, ineluctable, inexorable; unavoidable (অনিবার্য কারণে).

অনিমন্ত্রিত *a.* uninvited, unbidden.

অনিমিখ *a.* (poet.) not winking (অনিমিখ আঁখি) ; steadfast ('অনিমিখ দিঠি'). ☐ *adv.* with no winking; with a steadfast gaze.

অনিমিষ, অনিমেষ *a.* not winking; motionless; steadfast. **অনিমেষনেত্রে** *adv.* with eyes not winking; with a steadfast gaze.

অনিয়ত *a.* not regulated; irregular; unsystematic; uncontrolled, unrestrained; not steady; changeful; uncertain. **অনিয়তাকার** *a.* amorphous; shapeless.

অনিয়ন্ত্রণ *n.* lack or absence of control.

অনিয়ন্ত্রিত *a.* not regulated; uncontrolled; unrestrained, loose.

অনিয়ম *n.* lack of rule or system or discipline; irregularity; indiscipline; disorderliness; disorder; want of control or restraint. **অনিয়ম করা** *v.* to violate rule; to be given to irregularity; to behave fitfully or in a disorderly manner. **অনিয়মিত** *a.* uncontrolled; lacking in restraint or discipline; unregulated, unsystematized; irregular, unsystematic.

অনিরুদ্ধ *a.* unobstructed; unhindered; unchecked; free. ☐ *n.* (myth.) grandson of Krishna. **অনিরুদ্ধ পথ** passage without any impediment or obstacle; the sky.

অনিরূপণীয় *a.* indeterminable.

অনিরূপিত *a.* undiscerned; not ascertained or determined; not assessed, unfixed (অনিরূপিত মূল্য).

অনির্ণীত *a.* undiscerned; undefined; not determined; unassessed; unfixed.

অনির্ণেয় *a.* indiscernible; undefinable; indeterminate; unassessable; incapable of being fixed; (math.) indeterminate.

অনির্দিষ্ট *a.* not fixed or settled; uncertain; indefinite. **অনির্দিষ্ট কালের জন্য** *sine die*; for an indefinite period.

অনির্দেশ *n.* absence of direction or directive; uncertain state. **অনির্দেশ্য** *a.* indeterminable, that cannot be ascertained.

অনির্ধারিত *a.* not ascertained; unassessed; unfixed; not settled or decided.

অনির্বচনীয় *a.* indescribable; ineffable, inexpressible. **~তা** *n.* indescribability; ineffability. **অনির্বাচ্য** same as **অনির্বচনীয়**।

অনির্বাচিত *a.* not elected; not selected; not chosen.

অনির্বাণ *a.* (theo.) deprived of salvation; inextinguishable; blazing (for ever).

অনির্বাপিত *a.* not put out, unextinguished.

অনির্ভর *n.* non-reliance, non-dependence. **~তা** *n.* same as **অনির্ভর**। **~যোগ্য** *a.* not reliable, unreliable, not dependable.

অনিল *n.* wind, air, breeze. **~সখ** *n.* fire.

অনিশ্চয় *n.* uncertainty; doubt; doubtfulness; dubiousness. **~তা** *n.* uncertainty; doubt; dubiousness, doubtfulness.

অনিশ্চিত *a.* uncertain; indeterminate; unsettled; unfixed; indefinite; doubtful; dubious. **~ভাবে** *adv.* without certainty; indeterminately; settled or fixed condition; doubtful; hesitatingly.

অনিশ্চিতি same as **অনিশ্চয়তা**।

অনিষিদ্ধ *a.* unprohibited.

অনিষ্ট *n.* harm, injury; mischief; anything harmful or injurious. **~কর** *a.* harmful, injurious; mischievous. **অনিষ্ট করা** *v.* to harm; to do mischief. **~কারী** *a.* & *n.* one who causes harm or mischief, an evildoer, a wrongdoer. **~চিন্তা** *n.* mental act or thought of devising harm (to.), malevolence. **~চিন্তা করা** *v.* to devise harm (to). **~জনক, ~দায়ক** same as **অনিষ্টকর**। **~পাত** *n.* occurrence of harm or injury. **~সাধন** *n.* act of causing harm. **অনিষ্টসাধন করা** *v.* to cause harm (to), to harm. **অনিষ্ট হওয়া** *v.* to be harmed. **অনিষ্টাচরণ** same as **অনিষ্টসাধন**। **অনিষ্টাশঙ্কা** *n.* apprehension of harm, premonition or presentiment (of evil); foreboding.

অনিষ্ঠা *n.* lack of devoutness or faith or trust; lack of sincerity; absence of regard or reverence; non-observance.

অনিষ্পন্ন *a.* not accomplished or done, unexecuted; unfinished; outstanding.

অনীক *n.* army, armed force , troops; a soldier; war , battle.

অনীকিনী *n.* a division of the army (=1/10th of an **অক্ষৌহিণী**).

অনীতি *n.* lack or absence of principle or morality; immorality.

অনীতিজ্ঞ *n.* ignorant of moral principles or ethics.

অনীপ্সিত *a.* undesired , unwanted , not craved or longed for; unexpected.

অনীশ্বর *a.* godless, atheistic. **~বাদ** *n.* atheism. **~বাদী** *n.* an atheist, an unbeliever. ☐ *a.* atheistic.

অনীহ *a.* lacking in energy or effort; apathetic. **অনীহা** *n.* lack of energy or effort, apathy.

অনু *pfx.* denoting: behind in time or position, following, after, imitating, younger, every, duration, expansion, etc.

অনুকম্পা *n.* compassion; sympathy; kindness.

অনুকরণ *n.* imitation, act of copying; act of pursuing or following after; mimicry. **অনুকরণ করা** *v.* to imitate, to copy; to follow after. **~কারী** *a.* & *n.* same as **অনুকারী**। **~পটু** *a.* clever at imitating. **~প্রিয়** *a.* fond of imitating or mimicking. **~বৃত্তি** *n.* faculty of imitation. **~শীল** *a.* given to imitating, habitually imitative. **অনুকরণীয়** *a.* imitable; worthy of being imitated; exemplary. **হীন অনুকরণ** *n.* aping, apery. **হীন অনুকরণ করা** *v.* to ape; to mimic.

অনুকল্প *n.* a secondary injunction; an alternative; a substitute, a deputy. **~ন** *n.* substitution. **~বিধি** *n.* theory of substitution.

অনুকার *n.* imitation; making similar (to). **অনুকার শব্দ** *n.* an onomatopoeic word, an onomatopoeia. **অনুকারী** *a.* imitating, mimicking; imitative; making similar; similar; following after. ☐ *n.* an imitator, a mimic; a follower.

অনুকীর্ণ *a.* scattered, spread about, strewn; diffused.

অনুকীর্তন *n.* publicity or eulogy or praise or glorification at a subsequent time.

অনুকূল *a.* helpful, conducive, opportune; favourable; benign; propitious. **~তা** *n.* helpfulness; help; favourableness; benignity; favour; good grace, propitiousness. **অনুকূল হওয়া** *v.* to be helpful; to help; to be favourable; to become propitious.

অনুকৃত *a.* imitated, copied, mimicked; followed (after). **অনুকৃতি** *n.* imitation, mimicry; travesty; working after the example of.

অনুক্ত *a.* unspoken, untold, unuttered, unpronounced; not mentioned; not expressed, understood. **~কর্তা** *n.* (gr.) subject having third case-ending in the passive voice. **~পূরণ** *n.* act of supplying word or words in blank spaces, act of filling up gaps.

অনুক্রম *n.* serial order; sequence; systematic succession; a programme. **~ণ** *n.* going or coming after, following; recurrence, repetition. **~ণিকা, ~ণী** *n.* (of a book) a preface, a foreword, a list of contents. **অনুক্রমিক** *a.* following the serial order; sequential. **অনুক্রমে** *adv.* in regular order of; sequentially, seriatim.

অনুক্ষণ *adv.* at every moment; always, continually, ever.

অনুগ *a.* going or coming after, following; obeying; according to (নিয়মানুগ) ; conforming to.

অনুগত *a.* obedient, following faithfully, devoted, complying; dependent. **অনুগত হওয়া** *v.* to obey; to follow faithfully; to be devoted to; to depend on.

অনুগমন *n.* going or coming after, following or pursuing.

অনুগামী *a.* & *n.* one who or that which follows or obeys or conforms to, adherent. *fem.* **অনুগামিনী**। **অনুগামী হওয়া** *v.* to follow; to be obedient to; to adhere to, to be in conformity with.

অনুগৃহীত *a.* received in favour or grace; favoured; obliged. *fem.* **অনুগৃহীতা**।

অনুগ্র *a.* not harsh or severe; mild; not

haughty; polite, gentle; (of scent, flavour, taste, etc.) not strong, not pungent; weak, light.

অনুগ্রহ *n.* grace or favour; help; propitiousness; kindness, mercy; preferential treatment, partiality. **অনুগ্রহ করা** *v.* to favour; to help; to treat gracefully or propitiously; to treat with kindness or mercy; to accord preferential treatment to. **~পাত্র** *n.* a favourite, a minion. **~ভাজন** *a.* enjoying favour (of), favoured. **~পূর্বক** *adv.* graciously, kindly, benignantly. **~প্রার্থী** *a.* & *n.* one who curries favour, one who solicits favour.

অনুগ্রাহক, অনুগ্রাহী *a.* conducive, helpful; graceful; favourable; propitious; kind, merciful; treating preferentially; patronizing. ☐ *n. mas.* such a person; a patron.

অনুঘটক *n.* (chem.) a catalyser, a catalyst. **অনুঘটন** *n.* catalysis.

অনুচর *a.* accompanying; attending, attendant; following. ☐ *n.* a companion; an attendant; a follower. *fem.* **অনুচরী**। **~বর্গ** *n. pl.* retinue, a suite or train of companions or attendants.

অনুচারী *a.* following; attending. ☐ *n.* a follower, an attendant, a servant.

অনুচিকীর্ষা *n.* desire to imitate; imitativeness. **অনুচিকীর্ষু** *a.* desirous of imitating.

অনুচিত *a.* improper; unbecoming; unjust; unjustifiable, not allowable; undeserving; inappropriate (অনুচিত শব্দ).

অনুচিন্তন, অনুচিন্তা *n.* mental reproduction of past incidents etc., reflection, recollection , afterthought; recapitulation.

অনুচ্চ *a.* not tall, high or elevated; low; not loud; soft, quiet. **~কণ্ঠে, ~স্বরে** *adv.* in soft or low voice, under (one's) breath. **~তা** *n.* lowness; shortness.

অনুচ্চারণীয় *a.* not proper to be pronounced; unutterable; unspeakable; inexplicable.

অনুচ্চারিত *a.* unpronounced; unuttered, unspoken, untold.

অনুচ্চার্য same as **অনুচ্চারণীয়**।

অনুচ্ছেদ *n.* a paragraph; (of an act, deed, etc.) an article, a section.

অনুজ *a.* younger. ☐ *n.* a younger brother. *fem.* **অনুজা**। **অনুজন্মা, অনুজাত** *a.* younger, born later.

অনুজঙ্ঘাস্থি *n.* (physio.) tibia; (zoo.) fibula.

অনুজাত see **অনুজ**।

অনুজীবী *a.* one who attends on or serves; dependent for maintenance, shelter etc., obeying or following. ☐ *n.* an attendant, a servant; a follower, a dependent.

অনুজীব্য *a.* worthy of being resorted to or served.

অনুজ্জ্বল *a.* not bright; dim; dull.

অনুজ্ঞা *n.* an order, a command, an injunction; permission, consent, sanction; commission, employment. **~ত** *a.* ordered, commanded, enjoined; permitted, allowed; licensed. **~ধারী** *n.* a licensee. **~পত্র** *n.* a permit, a licence. **~পত্র আধিকারিক** licensing officer. **~সূচক ক্রিয়াভাব** (gr.) the imperative mood.

অনুৎকর্ষ *n.* absence of excellence or amelioration or improvement or development or increase.

অনুৎপন্ন *a.* unborn; not grown or produced.

অনুৎপাদী *a.* unproductive.

অনুতপ্ত *a.* repentant, penitent, contrite; pricked by conscience, compunctious.

অনুৎসাহ *n.* want of enthusiasm or energy or encouragement; lack of drive and initiative.

অনুতাপ *n.* repentance, penitence, contrition; remorse; regret. **অনুতাপ করা** *v.* to repent. **অনুতাপী** *a.* repentant, penitent, contrite. ☐ *n.* a penitent, a repenter.

অনুত্তম *a.* (ori.) not best or excellent or superb; not good; bad, inferior.

অনুত্তর *a.* that which or one who has nothing or none to follow, final; supreme, best; not responding or answering, unresponsive; silent; not northern.

অনুত্তীর্ণ *a.* unexpired (অনুত্তীর্ণ কাল) ; not traversed the whole length (অনুত্তীর্ণ পথ) ; uncrossed (অনুত্তীর্ণ সমুদ্র) ; unsurmounted, unconquered (অনুত্তীর্ণ বিপদ) ; failed, plucked, unsuccessful (অনুত্তীর্ণ ছাত্র). **পরীক্ষায় অনুত্তীর্ণ হওয়া** to fail in the examination. অনুত্তীর্ণতা *n.* failure; unsuccess.

অনুত্তেজিত *a.* unimpassioned, unexcited; calm.

অনুত্রিকাস্থি *n.* (anat.) coccyx.

অনুদাত্ত *a.* not loud-voiced; low and grave-toned. (cp.) bass. ☐ *n.* low and grave tone, bass; a Vedic hymn or incantation.

অনুদান *n.* a (government or official) grant.

অনুদার *a.* illiberal; ungenerous; narrow-minded; niggardly. **~তা** *n.* narrow-mindedness; illiberality.

অনুদিত[1] *a.* (of the sun, moon, etc.) not risen; not come or sprung out of, unmanifested; unrevealed.

অনুদিত[2] *a.* unmentioned; unspoken, untold.

অনুদিন *adv.* day after day, everyday.

অনুদৈর্ঘ্য *a.* longitudinal (অনুদৈর্ঘ্য তরঙ্গ) ; lengthwise.

অনুদ্গত *a.* not come or sprung or grown out of, not bulbed, not protuberated; not projecting. **অনুদ্গম** *n.* not growing or springing, lack or absence of springing or sprouting.

অনুদ্ঘাটিত *a.* unopened (as a door, lid etc.) unrevealed or undiscovered (অনুদ্ঘাটিত রহস্য).

অনুদ্ঘাতী *a.* level, plain, not uneven.

অনুদ্দিষ্ট *a.* of unknown whereabouts; missing, lost; not aimed at.

অনুদ্দেশ *n.* absence of trace. ☐ *a.* of unknown wherebouts; missing, lost.

অনুদ্ধত *a.* not arrogant or rude, not insolent or haughty; not proud or vainglorious; polite, modest, humble.

অনুদ্ধৃত *a.* not raised or lifted; not rescued; not cited or quoted.

অনুদ্বায়ী *a.* (chem.) non-volatile.

অনুদ্বিগ্ন *a.* not worried, unworried; not concerned. **অনুদ্বেগ** *n.* absence of worry or anxiety.

অনুদ্ভিন্ন *a.* (of bulbaceous plants) not come or grown out of the soil , not bulbed; unsprouted; unprotuberant; unprotuberated. **~পক্ষ** *a.* unfledged. **~যৌবনা** *a. fem.* one who has not yet attained full lustre of youth, not yet grown to womanhood; adolescent.

অনুদ্ভূত *a.* not grown or born; not issued or resulted (from); not (yet) appeared.

অনুদ্যম *n.* lack or absence of enterprise or effort or perseverence. **অনুদ্যত** *a.* not enterprising or perseverent, lazy , indolent.

অনুদ্যোগী *a.* unenterprising, lacking in drive and initiative; unenthusiastic.

অনুধাবন *n.* running after; pursuit, chase; search; ascertaining; giving attention to; reflection; deliberation, consideration. **অনুধাবন করা** *v.* to run after, to follow hotly; to pursue, to chase; to seek, to search; to ascertain; to attend to; to reflect; to deliberate, to consider. **অনুধাবনীয়** *a.* that which is to be considered or deliberated on; that which should be considered.

অনুধাবিত *a.* run after, pursued, chased; sought, ascertained; attended to; reflected on; deliberated, considered.

অনুধ্বনি *n.* echo; resonance.

অনুধ্যান *n.* continuous thinking or reflection or recollection; wishing well, well-wishing.

অনুধ্যায়ী *a.* thinking or reflecting or recollecting continuously; well-wishing.

অনুধ্যেয় *a.* worthy of being thought of or reflected on or recollected continuously; that which or one who deserves well-wishing.

অনুনয় *n.* entreaty, earnest request, solicitation; beseeching. **অনুনয় করা** *v.* to entreat, to request earnestly, to solicit, to beseech, to implore. **~ -বিনয়** *n.* humble (and repeated) entreaties, importunate solicitation. **অনুনয় -বিনয় করা** *v.* to entreat humbly (and repeatedly), to solicit importunately, to supplicate. **অনুনয়ী** *a.* suppliant; entreating, requesting earnestly, solicitious, beseeching, imploring.

অনুনাদ *n.* an echo; a sympathetic vibration, resonance; a similar sound. **~ক** *n.* a resonating device, a resonator; a sound-box. **অনুনাদিত** *a.* echoed; resonated, reverberated; resounded; having a similar sound; sounding simultaneously. **অনুনাদী** *a.* echoing; resonant, reverberant; resounding; having a similar sound; sounding simultaneously.

অনুনাসিক *a.* speaking through the nose; nasal. ☐ *n.* (gr.) a nasal sound or a letter representing this sound (e.g. ঙ্, ঞ্, ণ্, ন্, ম্, ং). **অনুনাসিক সুরে** in a nasal tone or voice.

অনুনেয় *a.* worthy of being entreated; worthy of being the subject of solicitation, worth imploring or beseeching or supplicating.

অনুন্নত *a.* not high or tall or upgraded or elevated; low; undeveloped, lacking in progress; backward. **অনুন্নত সম্প্রদায়** the depressed or backward class.

অনুন্মীলন *n.* (bot.) cleistogamy.

অনুন্মীলিত *a.* (bot.) cleistogamous.

অনুপ *a.* incomparable, unparalleled, matchless.

অনুপকার *n.* harm; injury, mischief; disservice. **~ক** *a.* harmful, injurious. **অনুপকার করা** *v.* to harm, to injure; to do (one) an ill turn. **অনুপকারিতা** *n.* harmfulness. **অনুপকারী** *a.* harmful, injurious.

অনুপকৃত *a.* not benefited.

অনুপদ *adv.* at every step; immediately following; in the wake of; hereafter, afterwards, later on, then. ☐ *a.* following, pursuing.

অনুপদিষ্ট *a.* unadvised, not instructed or briefed; untaught; untutored.

অনুপদী *a.* following, pursuing; seeking, searching for.

অনুপপত্তি *n.* inconsistency, irrelevance; (of a problem etc.) absence of solution, indecision; want, need.

অনুপম *a.* incomparable, peerless, unequalled; best, excellent. *fem.* **অনুপমা**।

অনুপমেয় *a.* incomparable.

অনুপযুক্ত, অনুপযোগী *a.* unfit, incompetent; unworthy; unsuitable, unbecoming, insufficient (অনুপযুক্ত সংগতি) ; undeserving; undeserved; unjust (অনুপযুক্ত বিচার) ; inappropriate (অনুপযুক্ত শব্দ). **অনুপযুক্ততা, অনুপযোগিতা** *n.* unfitness, incompetence; unworthiness; unsuitability, unbecomingness; insufficiency; unjustness; inappropriateness.

অনুপল *n.* a measure of time (= 1/60 বিপল = 1/150 part of a second); an instant, a jiffy, a trice.

অনুপলক্ষিত *a.* unnoticed, unseen.

অনুপলব্ধ *a.* not realized or comprehended; unfelt; not experienced or suffered or undergone; unacquired. **অনুপলব্ধি** *n.* lack of realization, incomprehension; insensibility, anaesthesia; absence of experience; absence of acquirement.

অনুপশমনীয় *a.* not possible to alleviate or assuage, unrelievable, unmitigable; incurable.

অনুপস্থিত *a.* not present, absent; non-existent, inexistent; wanting, lacking. **অনুপস্থিত থাকা** *v.* to absent oneself; to be non-existent or inexistent in. **অনুপস্থিতি** *n.* absence; non-existence, inexistence.

অনুপাত *n.* (math.) ratio; (geog.) proportion; rate. **অনুপাতে** *adv.* in the ratio of; in proportion to; at the rate of.

অনুপান *n.* anything to be taken along with a medicine to make it effective.

অনুপায় *n.* want of means or resource; helplessness. ☐ *a.* resourceless; helpless.

অনুপাসিত *a.* unworshipped, unadored.

অনুপূরক *a.* complementary; supplementary. ☐ *n.* a complement; a supplement.

অনুপূর্ব *n.* due order or succession, serial order. ☐ *a.* following due order or succession.

অনুপ্ত *a.* unsown; unplanted.

অনুপ্রবিষ্ট *a.* entered or gone into; infiltrated; penetrated, pierced into; gone into the depth or heart (of); one who has realized the inner significance of.

অনুপ্রবেশ *n.* going into; infiltration; entrance; penetration, piercing into, going into the depth or heart (of); realization of the inner significance of. **অনুপ্রবেশ করা** *v.* to infiltrate. **~কারী** *n.* infiltrator.

অনুপ্রভ *a.* phosphorescent. **অনুপ্রভা** *n.* phosphorescence.

অনুপ্রস্থ *a.* crosswise, latitudinal, transverse. □ *adv.* across, crosswise, latitudinally, transversely. ~ **ছেদ** (geom.) a transverse section.

অনুপ্রাণন *n.* invigorating or inspiring. **অনুপ্রাণনা** *n.* invigoration; a stimulus, a fillip, an incentive; an inspiration. **অনুপ্রাণনা দেওয়া** *v.* to invigorate, to stimulate; to inspire.

অনুপ্রাণিত *a.* invigorated, stimulated; inspired. **অনুপ্রাণিত করা** *v.* to invigorate, to imbue with, to stimulate; to inspire. **অনুপ্রাণিত হওয়া** *v.* to be inspired.

অনুপ্রাস *n.* (rhet.) an alliteration.

অনুপ্রেরণা *n.* invigoration; a stimulus; an inspiration; enthusiasm; encouragement.

অনুবদ্ধ ব্যাস *n.* (geom.) a conjugate diameter.

অনুবন্ধ *n.* start; outset; (of a question, point, motion etc.) moving or raising, introduction; relation; resolution; endeavour, effort, attempt; context, contextual connection; request; occasion; correlation; (gr.) any of the letters (esp. of suffixes) which are lost or dropped when added to words. **অনুবন্ধী** *a.* related, connected; (gr.) syntactically connected; inseparable; (geom.) conjugate; consequential; relevant.

অনুবর্তন *n.* coming or going after, following or pursuing; pursuit; succession; leaving for a new place; removal; imitation, repetition; of attending on or serving. **অনুবর্তন করা** *v.* to follow; to pursue; to succeed; to remove to a new place; to imitate; to repeat; to serve, to attend on.

অনুবর্তী *a.* following; attending, accompanying; subservient, obeying, complying; compliant, submissive. □ *n.* a follower. *fem.* **অনুবর্তিনী**। **অনুবর্তিতা** *n.* following or attending or accompanying; subserviency, obedience, compliance, acquiescence. **অনুবর্তী হওয়া** *v.* to follow; to pursue; to succeed; to be the imitation or repetition of; to be subservient to; to obey, to comply with, to acquiesce in, to toe the line.

অনুবল *n.* grace, favour, countenance ('ধর্ম অনুবলে') ; one who aids or renders assistance, a patron ('কেবা মোর হবে অনুবল').; power, strength, dint ('তপের অনুবলে'). □ *a.* as much as one's strength or power or capabilities or competency may permit.

অনুবাত *a.* leeward. **অনুবাতে** *adv.* leewards, before the wind.

অনুবাদ *n.* translation; interpretation; traduction. **অনুবাদক** *n.* a translator; one who speaks of or narrates a thing repeatedly; an imitator; a traducer, a scandal-monger. **অনুবাদিত** inc. var. of **অনূদিত**। **অনুবাদী** *a.* translating; (given to) telling or narrating a thing repeatedly; (given to) imitating, imitative; (given to) traducing; corresponding, similar; (mus. of a note) having no direct or essential connection with the chief note (i. e. বাদী) or its essentially subsidiary parts (i. e. সংবাদী and বিবাদী) of a musical composition.

অনুবাসন *n.* perfuming; fumigation.

অনুবাসিত *a.* perfumed; fumigated. **অনুবাসিত করা** *v.* to perfume; to fumigate.

অনুবিদ্ধ *a.* joined, attached; strong; set in, embedded.

অনুবিধি *n.* a proviso; a clause.

অনুবিভাগ *n.* a section; a sub-section.

অনুবৃত্তি *n.* coming or going after, following or pursuing; pursuit; succession; removal to a new place; imitation; repetition; attending on or serving; about to be started; outset; (of a question, point, motion etc.) moving or raising, introduction; relation; resolution, endeavour, context, contextual connection.

অনুবেদন *n.* imparting knowledge of, enlightenment, instruction, intimation. information, sympathy, compassion.

অনুবেল *adv.* near the shore; in the coastal or littoral region; unceasing, without stopping, incessant.

অনুব্রত *adv.* unceasing, constantly.

অনুভব *n.* knowledge; realization, perception; feeling. **অনুভব করা** *v.* to learn; to realize, to perceive; to feel. **অনুভবনীয়** *a.* perceivable; perceptible; that which can be or should be perceived or felt.

অনুভাব *n.* influence, governing power; unction; feeling of happiness; (rhet.) physical expression of permanent emotions (such as, tears, frowning, sighs, goose-flesh etc.).

অনুভূ *n.* (astro.) perigee.

অনুভূত *a.* realized; felt; perceived by sense. **অনুভূতি** *n.* realization; feeling; intuition; sense-perception. **~হীন** *a.* unthinking, not feeling, without intuition or sense.

অনুভূমিক *a.* horizontal.

অনুমত *a.* agreed, accepted; permitted, approved, sanctioned; ordered, commissioned.

অনুমতি *n.* premission, leave; approval, sanction; acquiescence, consent; order, command, commission; authorization. **অনুমতি দেওয়া** *v.* to permit, to grant leave to; to approve, to sanction, to grant; to acquiesce, to consent, to order, to commission; to authorize. **অনুমতি নেওয়া** *v.* to take permission, to take leave. **~পত্র** *n.* a letter of authority, a permit, permissive note, a pass; letters-patent. **~সূচক** *a.* permissive; indicative of approval or consent. **অনুমত্যনুসারে** *adv.* according to or by order.

অনুমরণ *n.* voluntarily burning oneself to death (on the funeral pyre of a deceased husband). **অনুমৃতা** *a. fem.* embracing death in the aforesaid manner (esp. applicable to a widow following her husband to death). *mas.* **অনুমৃত**।

অনুমস্তিষ্ক *n.* (anat.) the cerebellum.

অনুমান *n.* supposition; guessing, conjecture; a guess, a hypothesis; deduction; (log.) inference; (geom.) a corollary; (rhet.) a Sanskrit figure based on guessing akin to prosopopoeia or vision. **অনুমান করা** *v.* to suppose; to guess; to conjecture; to deduce; (log.) to infer.

অনুমানবাক্য *n.* (log.) a syllogism.

অনুমানসিদ্ধ *a.* inferential.

অনুমাপক *a.* serving as a ground for supposition or conjecture or inference; serving as criterion. □ *n.* a criterion.

অনুমিত *a.* supposed; guessed, conjectured; taken as a hypothesis; deduced; (log.) inferred. **অনুমিত হওয়া** *v.* to seem to appear. **অনুমিতি** same as **অনুমান**।

অনুমেয় *a.* capable of being supposed, conjecturable; deducible; inferable.

অনুমোদন *n.* consent; approval, sanction, confirmation; authorization. **অনুমোদন করা** *v.* to give consent to; to agree to; to approve, to sanction, to confirm; to authorize. **~সাপেক্ষ** *a.* subject to approval or authorization or sanction. **অনুমোদক** *n.* one who approves or sanctions; one who authorizes.

অনুমোদিত *a.* permitted; consented, agreed, approved; sanctioned, confirmed; supported; ordered, commissioned; authorized.

অনুযাত *a.* gone after or followed after; consequent upon, subsequent to, successive; according (to); following faithfully; done after the example of, imitated; subsidiary, subordinate; secondary.

অনুযাত্র, অনুযাত্রিক *a.* going after, following; attending on, serving; consequent; accompanying. □ *n. a.* follower; a servant, an attendant; a consequence; an accompaniment; a companion, (in *pl.*) retinue; a fellow-traveller.

অনুযায়ী *a.* going after, following; consequent upon; according (to); after the example of; similar. □ *adv.* according to.

অনুযুক্ত *a.* blamed; censured; reproached; accused.

অনুযোক্তা *n.* one who blames; a complainant; an accuser. *fem.* **অনুযোক্ত্রী**।

অনুযোগ *n.* blaming; censure; reproof, reproach, admonition; complaint; accusation. **অনুযোগ করা** *v.* to blame; to censure, to reprove, to reproach, to admonish; to complain. **অনুযোগী** *a.* & *n.* one who blames or censures or reproves or reproaches or admonishes or complains or accuses. *fem.* **অনুযোগিনী**।

অনুযোগ্য *a.* blamable; censurable, warranting reproof or reproach; warranting complaint; accusable.

অনুরক্ত *a.* inclined or attracted (to); preferring; attached (to); devoted (to); addicted (to); having affection (for), affectionate, loving; following faithfully or with fidelity. *fem.* **অনুরক্তা** । **অনুরক্তি** *n.* inclination, proneness; preference; attraction; attachment; devotion; addiction; affection, love; fidelity.

অনুরঞ্জক *a.* & *n.* pleasing; delightful; one who dyes or applies colour; one who gives delight or pleasure.

অনুরঞ্জন *n.* giving satisfaction, delight or pleasure (প্রজানুরঞ্জন) ; dyeing or colouring (usu. in one colour).

অনুরঞ্জিত *a.* delighted, pleased; dyed or coloured (usu. in one colour); nourishing affection or love or attachment (towards), inclined (to).

অনুরণন *n.* resonance, sympathetic vibration, reverberation; an echo.

অনুরণিত *a.* resonated, resounded, reverberated; echoed.

অনুরত *a.* devoted (to); attached (to); addicted (to); doting (on); following faithfully or with fidelity, loyal ; engaged or occupied earnestly (in). **অনুরতি** *n.* devotion; attachment; addiction; faithful following; state of being occupied or engaged earnestly.

অনুরথ্যা *n.* a lane, a narrow lane or alley.

অনুরাগ *n.* attachment; affection; love; amour; devotion; addiction; liking; attraction. **অনুরাগী** *a.* & *n.* one who is attached or devoted, or addicted or attracted (to); one who has affection or a liking (for). *fem.* **অনুরাগিণী** । **~বশে** *adv.* out of attachment or devotion or love.

অনুরাধা *n.* the seventeenth of the twenty-seven zodiacal stars in Hindu astronomy.

অনুরুদ্ধ *a.* one who has been requested; requested for; implored.

অনুরূপ *a.* similar, like, resembling, cast in the same mould; corresponding; according (to); agreeable (to); in keeping (with). **অনুরূপে, ~ভাবে** *adv.* accordingly, similarly.

অনুরোধ *n.* a request; a prayer; solicitation, entreaty, imploration; a thing asked for; sake, account. **অনুরোধ করা** *v.* to request, to solicit, to entreat, to implore. **অনুরোধে** *adv.* at the request of; at the instance of; for the sake of, on account of (কার্যানুরোধে).

অনুর্বর *a.* not fertile, infertile; barren, arid.

অনুলম্ব *a.* altitudinal; vertical.

অনুলাপ *n.* telling repeatedly; repeated recitation; tautology.

অনুলিখন *n.* similar writing; copying a writing, transcription; transliteration; taking down dictation; a piece of similar writing; a reproduction of written matter, a copy, a transcript; a piece of transliterated or dictated writing.

অনুলিপি *n.* a piece of similar writing, a facsimile or duplicate copy of written matter, a transcript, a copy; a piece of transliterated or dictated writing.

অনুলিপ্ত *a.* dyed; coloured; daubed, besmeared; engaged or employed or occupied (in).

অনুলেখ *n.* same as **অনুলিপি** । **~ক** *n.* an amanuensis; a copyist; a scribe.

অনুলেপ, অনুলেখন *n.* dyeing or colouring or daubing or besmearing or perfuming; a dye, a colour, an anointment, an unguent, a perfume.

অনুলেহ *n.* (poet.) attachment, attraction; affection, fondness; love.

অনুলোম *n.* serial order; due or regular succession. □ *a.* favourable, conducive, helpful, propitious. □ *adv.* according to serial order, serially; in due or regular succession. **অনুলোম বিবাহ** marriage of a man with a bride of a lower caste (cp. morganatic marriage).

অনুল্লঙ্ঘনীয়, অনুল্লঙ্ঘ্য *a.* impassable; (of obstacles etc.) insurmountable; not to be transgressed or violated.

অনুল্লিখিত *a.* not referred to or mentioned, not alluded to.

অনুল্লেখ *n.* absence of mention or reference; omission; supression.

অনুশাসন *n.* instruction; teaching; advice; an order, a command, an injunction, an edict, a canon.

অনুশিষ্য *n.* a disciple's disciple.

অনুশীর্ষ *n.* (chiefly in book-keeping) a minor head or heading; a sub-heading.

অনুশীলন *n.* repeated study or practice or training or cultivation; exercise. **অনুশীলন করা** *v.* to study or practise or undergo training or cultivate repeatedly. **~সাপেক্ষ** *a.* subject to or requiring repeated study or practice or training or cultivation or exercise. **অনুশীলনী** *n.* a set of problems to be worked out by students; a set of exercises. **অনুশীলনীয়** *a.* that which should be or is to be studied or practised or cultivated repeatedly. **অনুশীলিত** *a.* that which has been or is being studied or practised or cultivated; cultured.

অনুশোচন, অনুশোচনা *n.* regret or penitence, repentance; contrition , compunction, remorse. **অনুশোচনা করা** *v.* to regret, to repent, to remorse. **অনুশোচনীয়** *a.* regrettable. **অনুশোচিত** *a.* repented; regretted.

অনুষঙ্গ *n.* love, amour; kindness; affection; connection; context; attachment, adherence; relation; association, company. **অনুষঙ্গী** *a.* connected; related; associated; accompained.

অনুষ্টুপ, অনুষ্টুভ *n.* (pros.) a Sanskrit metre (e. g. 'মা নিষাদ প্রতিষ্ঠাং ত্বমগমঃ শাশ্বতীঃ সমাঃ').

অনুষ্ঠাতা *a.* one who introduces, or initiates or begins; one who does or performs or executes or renders a work, ceremony etc. ☐ *n.* an introducer or initiator, a commencer; a doer, a performer; an organizer. *fem.* **অনুষ্ঠাত্রী**।

অনুষ্ঠান *n.* commencement, beginning, introduction, initiation, performance, execution, celebration; function or ceremony; a ritual. **অনুষ্ঠান করা** *v.* to arrange for; to perform, to hold, to execute, to organize, to celebrate, to render; to observe (a rite etc.). **~সূচি** *n.* agenda.

অনুষ্ঠিত *a.* done, performed, executed; rendered, celebrated; (of rites etc.) observed.

অনুষ্ঠেয় *a.* that which is to be or should be done or performed; worth doing or performing.

অনুষ্ণ *a.* not warm or hot, cold; (fig.) lazy, indolent; frigid; sluggish, lethargic, inactive.

অনুসন্ধান *n.* search; inquiry; investigation; research, examination. **অনুসন্ধান করা** *v.* to search; to examine; to investigate. **অনুসন্ধানী** *a.* efficient in or engaged in searching or examining or investigating; having the acumen to delve into; well-informed. ☐ *n.* such a person.

অনুসন্ধায়ক, অনুসন্ধায়ী *a.* searching; researching, examining, inquiring, investigating. ☐ *n.* a searcher; a researcher, an examiner; an inquirer; an investigator.

অনুসন্ধিৎসা *n.* inquisitiveness, curiosity. **অনুসন্ধিৎসু** *a.* eager to search or learn; inquisitive, curious.

অনুসন্ধেয় *a.* that which is to be or should be searched or researched or examined or inquired after or investigated.

অনুসরণ *n.* following, pursuit; pursuance; repetition; imitation; similar shape or appearance or behaviour or qualities. **অনুসরণ করা** *v.* to go or come after, to follow or succeed, to pursue; to imitate; to come after in similar shape or appearance or with similar behaviour or qualities. **~কারী** *a.* & *n.* one who follows, comes after, pursues or imitates. *fem.* **~কারিণী**। **অনুসরণীয়** *a.* to be followed or imitated.

অনুসার *n.* accordance, conformity, consequence; pursuance; imitation. **অনুসারী** *a.* conforming, consequent; pursuant, following; imitating. *fem.* **অনুসারিণী**। **অনুসারে** *adv.* accordingly, according to, in accordance with, in conformity with, consequent upon; pursuant of, following; in imitation of.

অনুসিদ্ধান্ত *n.* (geom.) a corollary.

অনুসূচক *a.* signifying, having a meaning; indicating.

অনুসূচি, অনুসূচী *n.* a schedule.

অনুসূর *n.* (astr.) perihelion.

অনুসৃত *a.* followed, pursued; succeeded; imitated; succeeded by another in similar shape or appearance or with similar behaviour or qualities. **অনুসৃতি** *n.* following, pursuit, pursuance; succession; imitation; succession in similar shape or appearance or with similar behaviour or qualities.

অনুস্বর, অনুস্বার *n.* one of the nasal sounds or the letter representing it (ং).

অনুস্মরণ *n.* recollection. **অনুস্মরণ করা** *v.* to recollect.

অনুস্মারক *n.* a reminder; a memento.

অনুস্মৃতি *n.* recollection; that which is recollected.

অনুস্যূত *a.* ever attached, attached inseparably; sewn or strewn together.

অনুস্রবণ *n.* (chem.) percolation.

অনূক *n.* (anat.) urinal bladder.

অনূঢ় *a.* unmarried. *fem.* **অনূঢ়া** ।

অনূদিত *a.* (ori. but rare) said or mentioned afterwards; (loos. but pop.) translated.

অনূপ *n.* a marsh, a swamp, a bog. **অনূপ দেশ** marshy land; a country with many rivers, canals etc. flowing through it.

অনূর্ধ্ব *a.* (of numbers, amount, etc.) not more than, under.

অনৃত *a.* untrue, false. **~বাদিতা** *n.* untruthfulness. **~বাদী, ~ভাষী** *a.* untruthful. □ *n.* a liar. *fem.* **~বাদিনী, ~ভাষিণী** ।

অনেক *a.* more than one; many, numerous; various; much, too much; very much; great; most. □ *pro.* many persons; many a one; excess. □ *n.* (obs.) the universe ('অনেকের পতি' the lord of the universe). **~ত্ব** *n.* plurality. **~ধা** *adv.* & *prep.* in many ways; in various directions. **~প্রকার, ~বিধ, ~রূপ** *a.* of numerous and various kinds or types or sorts; manifold. **অনেক রাত্রিতে** *adv.* late at night. **অনেকাংশে** *adv.* largely, to a great extent; in many respects. **অনেকানেক** *a.* numerous and various, mainfold. **অনেকে** *pro.* many persons; many a one.

অনৈক্য *n.* lack of unity or agreement; discord; disagreement; difference (esp. of opinion), dissension; dissimilarity; inconsistency, incongruity; (loos.) animosity or opposition.

অনৈচ্ছিক *a.* involuntary, compulsory.

অনৈতিক *a.* immoral; dissolute. **~তা** *n.* immorality.

অনৈতিহাসিক *a.* unhistoric, unhistorical.

অনৈপুণ্য *n.* lack of skill or dexterity or proficiency, incompetence.

অনৈসর্গিক *a.* unnatural; supernatural.

অনৌচিত্য *n.* impropriety; unbecomingness; indecorousness, inelegance; unjustness.

-অন্ত *sfx.* to form present participial adjectives (e. g. ঘুমন্ত < ঘুম্, চলন্ত < চল্).

অন্ত *n.* death, destruction; end; break-up; termination; a terminus; a border or limit (বনান্ত, সীমান্ত) ; duration or expanse (পক্ষান্ত) ; intention or intrinsic nature (অন্ত পাওয়া ভার) ; depth or bottom (মনের অন্ত) ; the life beyond death or the next world ('অন্তে দিও গো পদাশ্রয়'). **অন্ত পাওয়া ভার** too deep for comprehension; one whose intention or intrinsic nature can hardly be ascertained; difficult to fathom or gauge.

অন্তঃ *pfx.* denoting : the heart, depth, within, inside, etc.

অন্তঃকরণ *n* the heart; the mind.

অন্তঃকর্ণ *n.* (anat.) an inner ear.

অন্তঃকেন্দ্র *n.* (geom.) in-centre.

অন্তঃকোণ *n.* (geom.) an interior angle.

অন্তঃকোষীয় *a.* intracellular.

অন্তঃপাতী *a.* lying or situated within; lying in.

অন্তঃপুর *n.* a zenana. a gynaeceum, a harem; the inner portion of a dwelling-house. **~চারী** *a.* & *n.* one who keeps to the zenana. *fem.* **~চারিণী** । **~রক্ষক** *n.* a guard of the zenana. (cp.) Lord of the bed-chamber. **অন্তঃপুরিকা** *n.* a woman who keeps to the zenana. **~বাসিনী** *a.* *fem.* keeping constantly to the zenana. *mas.* **~বাসী** ।

অন্তঃপ্রকোষ্ঠাস্থি *n.* (anat.) an ulna.

অন্তঃপ্রবিষ্ট *a.* infused; self-absorbed. **অন্তঃপ্রবেশন** *n.* literary interpolation.

অন্তঃশত্রু *a.* any of the sense-organs (these

are regarded as veritable enemies of man); one who is culpable of treason, a quisling; one who is inimical to or rises against (esp. secretly) his own country or party or family; a traitor.

অন্তঃশীল *a.* lying in the depth or heart of a person or thing; unrevealed; hidden; secret. *fem.* **অন্তঃশীলা।**

অন্তঃশুল্ক *n.* excise.

অন্তঃশ্বসন, অন্তঃশ্বাস *n.* inhalation.

অন্তঃসত্ত্বা *a. fem.* pregnant, (coll.)in the family way, enceinte.

অন্তঃসলিল *a.* containing water within (esp. hidden from the view), *fem.* **অন্তঃসলিলা। অন্তঃসলিলা নদী** *a.* subterranean river.

অন্তঃসাগরীয় *a.* submarine, undersea.

অন্তঃসার *n.* essential core or kernel of anything; useful substance of anything. **~শূন্য** *a.* having no essential core or useful substance; inane, empty, hollow; insincere (অন্তঃসারশূন্য কথা); worthless, useless.

অন্তঃসীমা *n.* inner lines.

অন্তঃস্তর *n.* a substratum (pl. substrata.)

অন্তঃস্থ, অন্তস্থ *a.* lying within or in-between. **অন্তঃস্থ বর্ণ** — য র ল ব হ : any of these letters.

অন্তঃস্রাবী *a.* endocrine. **অন্তঃস্রাবী গ্রন্থি** endocrine gland (also **অন্তর্গ্রন্থি**).

অন্তক *n.* Yama (যম) the god of death and Hades. ☐ *a.* destroying; destructive; causing the end of.

অন্তকাল *n.* the time of death or termination.

অন্তত, অন্ততপক্ষে *adv.* at least.

অন্তর *n.* the heart; the mind; interior, depth; distance; intervening distance; end, termination; limit; difference; contrariety. ☐ *a.* different; other; intimate (অন্তরতম). **~জ্ঞ** *n.* one who knows the mind; God.

অন্তরক *a.* (phys.) insulating. ☐ *n.* an insulator.

অন্তরকলন *n.* (math.) differential calculus.

অন্তরঙ্গ *a.* having blood relation or friendship; very intimate, hand in glove. ☐ *n.* an internal limb or part. **~তা** *n.* close intimacy.

অন্তরটিপুনি *n.* a secret pinching of the heart of a person which is only known to the pincher and the pinched and nobody else, a surreptitious prodding or pinching, blow or thrust.

অন্তরণ *n.* internment; insulation.

অন্তরস্থ, অন্তরস্থিত *a.* lying in the depth of one's heart.

অন্তরা *n.* (mus.) the intermediary part between the refrain and the final development of the music of a song.

অন্তরাত্মা *n.* (phil.) the invisible immortal and guiding soul that every individual possesses, the indwelling spirit; the depth of one's heart.

অন্তরায় *n.* an obstacle, a barrier, a bar, a hindrance, an impediment.

অন্তরায়ণ *n.* internment. **অন্তরায়িত** *a.* interned.

অন্তরাল *n.* a place screened from the view; a hiding; concealment; distance; a point beyond the range of (দৃষ্টির অন্তরালে). **~বর্তী** *a.* stationed or lying or living behind the screen or in a hiding; hidden from the view. *fem.* **~বর্তিনী।**

অন্তরিক্ষ alt. spell of. **অন্তরীক্ষ।**

অন্তরিত *a.* disappeared, vanished; overcast; (thoroughly) covered; overwhelmed, begone; removed, driven away; confined within fixed bounds under government order, interned.

অন্তরিন, অন্তরায়িত *n.* an internee. ☐ *a.* interned.

অন্তরিন্দ্রিয় *n.* the mind.

অন্তরীক্ষ *n.* the intervening region between any two planets or stars; the sky. **~চারী** *a.* (capable of or used to) moving or dwelling in the sky; aerial. ☐ *n.* moving or dwelling in the sky. *fem.* **~চারিণী। ~বাসী** *a.* dwelling in the sky; aerial, ethereal. ☐ *n.* such a person or creature who dwells in the sky. *fem.* **~বাসিনী। ~মণ্ডল** *n.* the atmosphere.

অন্তরীণ obs. form of **অন্তরিন।**

অন্তরীপ *n.* (geog.) a cape, a promontory, a headland. **উত্তমাশা অন্তরীপ** the Cape of Good Hope. **কুমারিকা অন্তরীপ** Cape Comorin.

অন্তরীয়, অন্তরীয়ক *n.* any garment for the lower part of the body; a loin-cloth.

অন্তরে *adv.* at heart; inside; within; in the depth of, in the heart of; amidst, amongst, between; at a distance, removed or screened from; at an interval of.

অন্তর্গত *a.* lying or situated within or in between; included (in); comprised (in); inward.

অন্তর্গূঢ় *a.* concealed within or in the mind or in the heart; unrevealed; secret.

অন্তর্গৃহ *n.* a small room within a larger one; the inside of a room; indoor.

অন্তর্গ্রন্থি *n.* see **অন্তঃস্রাবী**।

অন্তর্গ্লানি *n.* mental agony, heartburning; mortification.

অন্তর্ঘাত *n.* sabotage. **~ক** *n.* a saboteur. **অন্তর্ঘাতী** *a.* pertaining to or causing sabotage; sabotaging.

অন্তর্জগৎ *n.* the realm of the mind; the realm of ideas or thoughts.

অন্তর্জলি *n.* the Hindu rite of keeping immersed the lower part of the body of a dying person in a holy river etc.

অন্তর্জাতীয় *a.* international.

অন্তর্জ্ঞান *n.* (psy.) subconsciousness. **অন্তর্জ্ঞানীয়** *a.* subconscious.

অন্তর্জ্বালা *n.* mental agony.

অন্তর্দর্শন *n.* (psy.) introspection. **অন্তর্দর্শী** *a.* introspective.

অন্তর্দশা *n.* secondary influence of different planets.

অন্তর্দাহ, অন্তর্দাহন *n.* extreme mental agony; heart-burning; envy. **অন্তর্দাহী** *a.* causing extreme mental agony or heart-burning.

অন্তর্দীপন *n.* enlightenment of the mind; development of mental powers and qualities; improvement of the mind.

অন্তর্দৃষ্টি *n.* intuition; insight; (psy.) introspection. **~সম্পন্ন** *a.* having intuition or insight or introspection; intuitive or introspective.

অন্তর্দেশ *n.* the inner part or region; the heart; the interior; the inland; a valley. **অন্তর্দেশীয়** *a.* inland. **অন্তর্দেশীয় পরিবহণ** inland transport.

অন্তর্দ্বন্দ্ব *n.* inner strife; mental reaction; internal quarrel.

অন্তর্দ্বার *n.* a secret door.

অন্তর্ধান *n.* disapperance; vanishing away, evanescence, death. **অন্তর্ধান করা, অন্তর্ধান হওয়া** *v.* to disappear; to vanish, to melt into thin air; to die.

অন্তর্নিবিষ্ট, অন্তর্নিহিত *a.* placed or lying (usu. imperceptibly) within or in the heart; deep-rooted, deep-seated; innate, inherent; latent, dormant (অন্তর্নিহিত শক্তি).

অন্তর্বর্গ *n.* a sub-order.

অন্তর্বর্তী *a.* lying or situated within or in between; included or comprised in; intermediate; interim (অন্তর্বর্তী সরকার).

অন্তর্বাণিজ্য *n.* inland trade.

অন্তর্বাষ্প *n.* suppressed tears.

অন্তর্বাস *n.* an undergarment; a short loin-cloth usually worn by Hindu ascetics.

অন্তর্বাহ, অন্তর্বাহী *a.* afferent.

অন্তর্বিগ্রহ, অন্তর্বিপ্লব *n.* an internal feud; a domestic quarrel; a civil war.

অন্তর্বিবাদ *n.* same as **অন্তর্বিরোধ**।

অন্তর্বিবাহ *n.* marriage within one's own group, endogamy.

অন্তর্বিভাগীয় *a.* inter-departmental.

অন্তর্বিরোধ *n.* internal feud or dissension, domestic quarrel or strife.

অন্তর্বীজ *n.* kernel.

অন্তর্বৃত *a.* introvert. **অন্তর্বৃতি** *n.* introversion.

অন্তর্বৃত্ত *n.* (geom.) an in-circle.

অন্তর্বেদনা *n.* suppressed feeling of pain or agony.

অন্তর্বেদি, অন্তর্বেদী *n.* a strip of land between two rivers.

অন্তর্ভুক্ত, অন্তর্ভূত *a.* included or comprised (in); lying within or in between. **অন্তর্ভূত কোণ** (geom.) an included angle.

অন্তর্ভূমি *n.* (geol.) sub-soil.

অন্তর্ভৌম *a.* underground; subterranean.

অন্তর্মাধুর্য *n.* sweetness of the heart or soul; inward sweetness.

অন্তর্মুখ *a.* introspective; spiritual; (psy.) afferent. **~তা, অন্তর্মুখিতা** *n.* introspection; introversion.

অন্তর্যামী *a.* aware of or competent to know other's mind. □ *n.* such a person God.

অন্তর্লিখিত *a.* (geom.) inscribed; engraved.

অন্তর্হিত *a.* departed; lost to view. **অন্তর্হিত হওয়া** *v.* to disappear; to vanish.

অন্তশ্চর্ম *n.* dermis.

অন্তস্তর *n.* (geol.) a substratum (pl. substrata).

অন্তস্তল *n.* the bottom or the interior of anything; the depth of one's heart.

অন্তস্ত্বক *n.* dermis.

অন্তিক *a.* adjacent; proximate; near; close. ☐ *n.* adjacency; proximity; nearness; the extreme; extremity. **অন্তিকতা** *n.* nearness, proximity.

অন্তিম *a.* final; last, ultimate; of the time of death or termination. **~কাল** *n.* the time of death or termination; last moments. **~দশা** *n.* dying state. **~শয়ন, ~শয্যা** *n.* death-bed.

অন্তেবাসী *n.* a pupil or student or disciple (esp. one who boards at his master's house) ; one of a low-caste Hindu community known as the Chandalas (চণ্ডাল) who in former days burned dead bodies professionally and dwelt in the outskirts of villages for they were regarded as untouchables.

অন্ত্য *a.* last, ultimate; final; extreme; inferior, base, low; remaining; born of a Shudra (শূদ্র) family. **~জ** *a.* low-born; base; mean. ☐ *n.* a low-born person; a low caste, a depressed class; one of the Shudra (শূদ্র) or the Chandala (চণ্ডাল) community. **~বর্ণ** *n.* the last letter of a word.

অন্ত্যেষ্টি, অন্ত্যেষ্টিক্রিয়া *n.* funeral rites, obsequies; last honours.

অন্ত্র *n.* bowels; intestines. **~জ্বর** *n.* enteric fever. **~প্রদাহ** *n.* enteritis. **~বৃদ্ধি** *n.* hernia.

অন্দর, অন্দরমহল *n.* the inner parts (esp. of a dwelling-house); the interior; the apartments of a house in which women are secluded, a zenana, a gynaecium.

অন্ধ *a.* blind, sightless; extremely dark or gloomy. ('অন্ধ তামস') ; utterly ignorant. ☐ *n.* a blind person. **~কূপ** *n.* a dark pit; a black hole. **~কূপহত্যা** *n.* (hist.) the Blackhole Tragedy. **~তম** *a.* darkest; extremely dark. **~তমস** *n.* utter darkness; blinding darkness. **~তা, ~ত্ব** *n.* blindness; utter ignorance. **~তামিস্র** *n.* utter darkness. ☐ *a.* utterly dark. **~প্রায়** *a.* almost blind; like a blind; like a blind person. **~বিশ্বাস** *n.* blind faith. **~ভাবে** *adv.* blindly; rashly; heedlessly, indiscreetly. **অন্ধের কিবা দিন কিবা রাত** a blind person cannot distinguish between day and night or between brightness and gloom. **অন্ধের নড়ি** বা **যষ্টি** (lit.) a stick by the help of which a blind person moves; a blind man's prop; (fig.) a prop for a helpless or incapable person.

অন্ধকার *n.* darkness, gloom; absence of light. ☐ *a.* dark, gloomy; darkened with gloom, dejection etc. (অন্ধকার মুখ) ; deprived of hope, delight, etc. (অন্ধকার জীবন). **অন্ধকার করা** *v.* to make (something) dark, to darken. **অন্ধকার দেখা** *v.* (fig.) to be at one's wit's end to find a means of escape from danger; to be stunned. **অন্ধকার দেখানো** *v.* (fig.) to overwhelm or bewilder (a person), to knock senseless. **অন্ধকার হওয়া** *v.* to become dark, to darken. **অন্ধকারে ঢিল মারা** (fig.) to make a stray or random attempt to hit, to take an off-chance; to beat about the bush. **অন্ধকারে থাকা** *v.* (fig.) to be quite ignorant (of), to be in the dark (about). **অন্ধকারে হাতড়ানো** *v.* (lit. & fig.) to grope in the dark. **~ময়** *a.* full of darkness or gloom; completely dark. **অন্ধকারাচ্ছন্ন, অন্ধকারাবৃত** *a.* enveloped in or overcast with darkness; utterly dark; (fig.) utterly ignorant, distressed, depressed or obsessed.

অন্ধিসন্ধি *n.* creek and corner, ins and outs; secrets; secret intention, design, etc. (মনের অন্ধিসন্ধি).

অন্ন *n.* boiled rice; rice; food. **~কষ্ট** *n.* distress caused by scarcity of food; famine; (fig.) sufferance caused by extreme poverty, indigent circumstances. **~কূট** *n.* a stupendous heap of boiled rice. **~ক্ষেত্র** var. of **অন্নসত্র**। **~গতপ্রাণ** *a.* (absolutely) depending on food or boiled rice for subsistence; (loos.) rice-eating. **~চিন্তা** *n.* thinking out means of procuring food or earning one's livelihood; food-problem, bread-problem.

~চিন্তা চমৎকারা the effort to earn one's livelihood is all-absorbing; bread-problem is the chief problem; thought of one's daily bread preys heavily on the mind or weighs heavily on the spirits. ~জল *n.* food and drink; the Hindu rite of providing food and drink for the soul of the dead. ~দা *a. fem.* one who supplies or gives food. □ *n.* Goddess Durga (দুর্গা). ~দাতা *a.* & *n.* one who supplies or gives food; one who maintains. *fem.* ~দাত্রী। ~দান *n.* charitable or gratuitous supply of food. ~দাস *n.* one who has enslaved himself to another for one's food or maintenance. ~নালী *n.* the aesophagus, the gullet, the food passage. ~পূর্ণা *a. fem.* full of food or rice. □ *n.* Goddess Durga (দুর্গা). ~পথ্য *n.* rice-meal as diet. ~পান *n.* food and drink. ~প্রাশন *n.* the Hindu rite of a child's tasting rice for the first time. ~বস্ত্র *n.* food and clothing. ~ব্যঞ্জন *n.* rice and curry. ~ভোজী *a.* rice-eating. □ *n.* rice-eater. ~ময় *a.* full of food; built up or nourished by food (অন্নময় কোষ). ~রস *n.* chyle. ~সংস্থান *n.* provision for maintenance; procuring food or earning one's livelihood. ~সত্র *n.* a place or institution for charitable supply of rice or food. ~সমস্যা *n.* food-problem, bread-problem. ~হীন *a.* without food; foodless; starving.

অন্নাভাব *n.* want or shortage of food or rice; scarcity; famine.

অন্বয় *n.* succession; (gr.) sequence, syntax, word-order; family; relation; order, serial order; agreement, concord. অন্বয়ী *a.* related, connected; relating, connecting, agreeing, concordant.

অন্বর্থ *a.* real, actual; significant; appropriate. ~নামা *a.* having a name appropriate to one's qualities or nature or properties.

অন্বিত *a.* possessing or endowed with (গুণান্বিত) ; (gr.) having proper correlation or sequence, syntactic (অন্বিত বাক্য).

অন্বীক্ষা *n.* discussion about the teachings of the Vedas after studying them; logical inference.

অন্বেষক *a.* engaged in search or research or investigation. □ *n.* a searcher, a seeker; a researcher; an investigator.

অন্বেষণ *n.* search, research; investigation, inquiry. অন্বেষণ করা *v.* to search; to research; to investigate; to inquire, to look for. অন্বেষণীয় *a.* that which is to be searched or sought or researched or investigated. অন্বেষণে থাকা *v.* to be engaged in search or research or investigation; to be on the look-out for.

অন্বেষিত, অন্বিষ্ট *a.* searched, sought after; researched; investigated.

অন্বেষী same as অন্বেষক।

অন্য *a.* & *pro.* other; some other; any other. □ *a.* different. ~কৃত *a.* done by some other person. অন্য কেউ somebody else. ~ত *a. adv.* & *con.* from or by the other or others or another; in a different way. ~তম *a.* & *pro.* one or any one of several persons, things, etc. ~তর *a.* & *pro.* one or any one of the two; the other. ~ত্র *adv.* at or in or to a different place or topic or subject. ~থা *adv.* & *con.* in a different manner, otherwise, elsewise, or; contrarywise. □ *a.* contrary. □ *n.* violation, infringement; exception; the contrary. অন্যথাকরণ *a.* doing otherwise; disobeying. অন্যথা করা *v.* to do or act otherwise; to violate, to infringe, to disobey. অন্যথা হওয়া *v.* to be contrary to; to be in violation of. অন্যথাচরণ *n.* acting or doing otherwise; violation, infringement, disobedience. অন্যথাচরণ করা *v.* same as অন্যথা করা। ~পূর্বা *a. fem.* formerly betrothed or married to somebody else. *mas.* ~পূর্ব। ~প্রকার, ~বিধ *a.* of a different or other kind(s). ~প্রকারে *adv.* same as অন্যভাবে। ~ভাব *n.* a different or another state or attitude or manner; change of state or attitude or manner. ~ভাবে *adv.* in a different or other way. ~ভৃৎ *a.* bringing up another (esp. one not belonging to one's kind). □ *n.* such a person or creature; the crow. ~ভৃত, ~পুষ্ট *a.* brought up by another (esp. by one belonging to a different kind). □ *n.* such a person or creature; the cuckoo. ~মত *n.* a different opinion; disagreement; a different manner or way. ☐ *a.* holding a different opinion; disagreeing; in or of a different manner or way. **~মতে** *adv.* in a different way or manner; according to a different view. **~মনস্ক, ~মনা** *a.* preoccupied by some other thought; absent-minded; inattentive. **~মনে** *adv.* absentmindedly, inattentively. **~মনস্কতা** *n.* preoccupied state; absent-mindedness; inattentiveness, inattention. **~সাপেক্ষ** *a.* relative. **~রূপ** *a.* same as **অন্যপ্রকার, অন্যবিধ।**

অন্যপুষ্ট *a.* & *n.* see **অন্য।**

অন্যান্য *a. pl.* other; several and various; sundry; the others.

অন্যায় *n.* impropriety; injustice; an unjust act; a wrong; a misdeed; an unreasonable act. ☐ *a.* unjust; improper; unreasonable (অন্যায় অনুরোধ) ; wrongful. **অন্যায় করা** *v.* to do injustice; to act improperly or unjustly or unreasonably or wrongfully; to do a wrong. **~ত** *adv.* improperly; injustly; unreasonably; wrongfully. **অন্যায়াচরণ** *n.* an unjust or improper or unreasonable or wrongful act; a wrong; a wrong-doing. **অন্যায়াচারী** *a.* acting unjustly or improperly or unreasonably or wrongfully. ☐ *n.* a wrong-doer. **অন্যায়োপজীবী** *a.* & *n.* one who lives by unfair means or wrong-doing.

অন্যায্য *a.* improper, unseemly, unjust; wrongful; unreasonable; unbecoming. **~তা** *n.* impropriety; unjustness; wrongfulness; unreasonableness; unbecomingness.

অন্যার্থ *n.* another meaning, a different meaning. **অন্যার্থক** *a.* having another or a different meaning.

অন্যাসক্ত *a.* (of a husband) attached to some woman not one's wife; adulterous; unfaithful. *fem.* **অন্যাসক্তা।** **অন্যাসক্তি** *n.* attachment to some man or woman other than one's husband or wife; adultery; unfaithfulness.

অন্যূন *a.* not less than; at least, in the least.

অন্যোন্য *n.* mutual, reciprocal. **~জীবী** *n.* (bot.) a symbion, a symbiont. ☐ *a.* symbiotic. **~জীবিত্ব** *n.* symbiosis. **~তা** *n.* mutuality, reciprocity. **~বিরুদ্ধ, ~বিরোধী** *a.* opposed to each other or one another; contradictory, antagonistic. **~সাপেক্ষ** *a.* depending on one another or each other. interdependent; correlative; reciprocal. **অন্যোন্যাভাব** *n.* relative difference, reciprocal absence or negation. **অন্যোন্যাশ্রয়** *n.* interdependence, mutual dependence.

অপ *pfx.* off, away, from, under, down, bad, undesirable, unnatural, distorted, base, ugly, opposite to, against, etc.; apo-, a-, ab-, abs-, an-, anti-, contra-, counter-, dis-, dys-, ex-, i-, mal(e)-, non-, out-, etc.

অপকর্ম *n.* a misdeed; a mischief; a wrongful or harmful act; a scandalous act; a crime. **অপকর্ম করা** *v.* to do a misdeed; to make some mischief; to commit a crime. **অপকর্মা** *a.* doing mischiefs or wrongful acts. ☐ *n.* a misdoer; a mischief-maker; a wrong-doer; a criminal, a miscreant.

অপকর্ষ *n.* (ori.) downward attraction; deterioration, decline, downfall, degeneration; baseness, inferiority.

অপকলঙ্ক *n.* a false imputation, slander, calumny.

অপকার *n.* harm, injury, disservice. **~ক, অপকারী** *a.* harmful, injurious. ☐ *n.* a wrong-doer, a malefactor. **অপকার করা** *v.* to harm, to injure, to do disservice (to).

অপকীর্তি *n.* disrepute, ill-fame; notoriety; a wrongful or disgraceful act, a misdeed; a mischief; a crime.

অপকৃত *a.* harmed, injured. **অপকৃতি** *n.* harm, injury.

অপকৃষ্ট *a.* base, inferior; bad; degenerated; mean; wretched.

অপকেন্দ্র *n.* (sc.) centrifugal. **অপকেন্দ্র বল** centrifugal force.

অপক্ব *a.* unripe, immature; unboiled; not thoroughly boiled, parboiled; uncooked. **~তা** *n.* unripeness, immaturity, unboiled or parboiled or uncooked state.

অপক্রিয়া *n.* a misdeed; a harmful or

wrongful act; a foul or malignant act; a crime.

অপক্ষপাত *n.* impartiality; neutrality, non-alignment; freedom from prejudice or bias; justness; even-handed justice. □ *a.* impartial; neutral, non-aligned; unprejudiced, unbiased; just. অপক্ষপাতী *a.* same as অপক্ষপাত (*a.*). অপক্ষপাতিতা, অপক্ষপাতিত্ব *n.* same as অপক্ষপাত (*n.*).

অপগত *a.* gone away; departed; passed away; fled away; removed, dispelled; subsided; repealed; withdrawn.

অপগম্, অপগমন *n.* flying away, flight; departure; removal; subsidence; withdrawal.

অপগা *a.* going downwards or seawards. □ *n.* a river.

অপগুণ *n.* demerit, defect; vice; guilt; blemish.

অপগ্রহ *n.* (astrol.) an unfavourable or malignant planet (or star).

অপঘাত *n.* death by accident; unnatural death; accidental hurt or injury to one's person. ~ক, অপঘাতী *a.* & *n.* one who or that which causes unnatural death. অপঘাত-মৃত্যু *n.* death by accident.

অপচয় *n.* loss; waste; wastage; state of being wasted or squandered away; decrease; decay; misuse. অপচয় করা *v.* to waste; to squander away, to fritter away, to throw away; to misuse.

অপচয়িত *a.* ill-spent; wasted; squandered away; misused.

অপচার *n.* straying from one's own religion; taking bad or faulty or prohibited diet; pernicious conduct or behaviour; a fault; corruption. ~-নিরোধ *n.* curbing corruption. ~-নিরোধ বিভাগ the anti-corruption department.

অপচিকীর্ষা *n.* malignity, malevolence, ill-will. অপচিকীর্ষু *a.* malignant, malevolent, desirous of evil (to others).

অপচিত *a.* decayed; ill-spent; wasted; squandered away, decreased, diminished; slowed down; weakened. অপচিতি *n.* katabolism; decay; waste; squandering away; decrease; diminished state; emaciation; enfeeblement; dimness, weakness.

অপচীয়মান *a.* that which is being decayed or ill-spent or wasted or diminished; on the wane; waning.

অপচেষ্টা *n.* endeavour to do a wrongful or harmful act; a vile or blamable or disgraceful move; a vicious or mischievous move.

অপচ্ছায়া *n.* a phantom; an apparition; a ghost; a ghastly illusion.

অপজাত *a.* degenerate; base-born. অপজাতি *n.* a degenerated or base race or community.

অপঞ্জরী *n.* an invertebrate.

অপজ্ঞান *n.* slight, contempt; disrespect, disregard; neglect.

অপটু *a.* inexpert, unskilful; unskilled; incapable; incompetent, unfit; indisposed, stricken with illness. ~তা, ~ত্ব *n.* lack of dexterity or skill; incapability, incompetence, unfitness; indisposition, illness.

অপঠিত *a.* not perused, unread; that which has not been gone through; unstudied.

অপণ্ডিত *a.* lacking in erudition or learning; unlearned; not versed in scriptures etc.; not specialized in, inexpert; uneducated; unlettered.

অপণ্য *a.* not marketable or fit to be sold, unsaleable.

অপত্নীক *a.* one whose wife is dead; one who has not yet taken a wife, unmarried.

অপত্য *n.* a son or a daughter; a child; a young of any creature. ~নির্বিশেষে *adv.* making no discrimination between one's own children and those of other people, not treating differently from one's son, just like one's own children. ~স্নেহ *n.* love for one's children, parental affection, philoprogenitiveness. ~হীন *a.* childless.

অপথ *n.* a wrong or bad or improper path; improper means or conduct.

অপথ্য *n.* diet that is injurious for a patient, bad or faulty or prohibited or injurious or unwholesome diet.

অপদ *a.* having no feet or legs, apod.

অপদস্থ *a.* (of posts or positions) not of a

high rank; insulted, humiliated, disgraced; out of countenance; embarrassed. **অপদস্থ করা** *v.* to insult or humiliate or disgrace; to put to shame; to offend one's dignity; to embarrass. **অপদস্থ হওয়া** *v.* to be insulted or humiliated or disgraced; to be embarrassed.

অপদার্থ *a.* worthless, useless; trashy; incompetent, unfit; good-for-nothing. **~তা** *n.* worthlessness; incompetence; uselessness.

অপদূরক *a.* (astr.) apsides.

অপদেবতা *n.* an evil spirit; a demon; a ghost.

অপনয়, অপনয়ন *n.* removal; elimination; deletion; revocation.

অপনীত *a.* removed; eliminated; deleted; dispelled; allayed.

অপনেয় *a.* removable, effaceable; eliminable; revocable.

অপনোদন *n.* removal; elimination; deletion; dispelling or allaying; refutation. **অপনোদন করা** *v.* to remove; to wipe out; to eliminate; to delete; to dispel; to allay; to alleviate; to refute. **অপনোদিত** *a.* removed; wiped out; eliminated; deleted; dispelled; allayed; refuted.

অপপাঠ *n.* wrong or distorted reading, misreading.

অপপ্রয়োগ *n.* misapplication; abuse; misuse. **অপপ্রয়োগ করা** *v.* to misapply.

অপবর্গ *n.* salvation; liberation.

অপবর্তন *n.* (alg.) division by a common measure; alteration, change; transfer; removal; difraction. **অপবর্তিত** *a.* divided by a common measure.

অপবাদ *n.* ill-repute, bad name; defamation; slander, calumny. **অপবাদ দেওয়া** *v.* to blame, to give a bad name, to defame; to slander, to calumniate.

অপবারণ *n.* concealment; avoidance, staving off. **অপবারিত** *a.* concealed; avoided; staved off.

অপবাহিত *a.* removed to a different place, shifted; transferred; driven or chased away, beaten off.

অপবিত্র *a.* unholy, profane; unhallowed; impure; unclean; unchaste. **অপবিত্র করা** *v.* to spoil the holiness or purity of, to profane, to desecrate; to make unclean; to outrage , to ravish. **~তা** *n.* unholiness, profanity; impurity; unclean state; unchasteness.

অপব্যবহার *n.* misuse, abuse; misbehaviour, misconduct. **অপব্যবহার করা** *v.* to misuse, to abuse; to spend wrongfully or imprudently, to waste. **অপব্যবহার হওয়া** *v.* to be misused or abused; to be spent wrongfully or imprudently, to be wasted.

অপব্যয় *n.* wrongful or imprudent spending, misuse; waste; wastage; extravagance; squandering away. **অপব্যয় করা** *v.* to spend ill, to misspend; to misuse; to waste; to spend money imprudently; to squander away. **অপব্যয়িত** *a.* ill-spent, misspent; misused; wasted; (of money etc.) squandered away. **অপব্যয়ী** *a.* given to ill-spending or squandering away or misuse; wasteful; prodigal, extravagant; spendthrift. **অপব্যয়িতা** *n.* practice of ill-spending or misusing or squandering away; wastefulness; prodigality, extravagance; misuse; waste.

অপভাষ *n.* ill-repute, infamy ('শুনিলে হইবে অপভাষ').

অপভাষা *n.* obscene or slang or vulgar language.

অপভূ *n.* apogee.

অপভ্রংশ *n.* corrupted or incorrect form of a word; vulgar dialects descended from a classical language, incorrectness; corruption; perversion; vulgarization.

অপভ্রষ্ট *a.* fallen; dislodged; degenerated; corrupt or incorrect (অপভ্রষ্ট শব্দ).

অপমান *n.* insult, dishonour; affront; indignity; disgrace; defamation. **~ কর, ~জনক** *a.* same as **অপমানসূচক**। **অপমান করা** *v.* to insult, to dishonour; to affront; to disgrace; to defame. **~গ্রস্ত** *a.* same as **অপমানিত**। **~সূচক** *a.* insulting, insolent. **অপমান হওয়া** *v.* (coll.) to be insulted or dishonoured or affronted or disgraced or defamed; to be treated with insolence. **অপমানিত** *a.* insulted, dishonoured; affronted; disgraced; defamed.

অপমিশ্রণ *n.* adulteration.

অপমৃত্যু *n.* death by accident; unnatural death.

অপযশ *n.* ill-repute, bad name, infamy; disgrace. **~স্কর** *a.* disgraceful; scandalous; discreditable.

অপয়া, অপেয়ে *a. fem.* (also used in masc.) ill-omened, ominous; unlucky; inauspicious (usu. attributed to the appearance or presence of a person, creature or thing).

অপর *a.* other, another (অপর ব্যক্তি) ; opposite (নদীর অপর তীর) ; later, coming after (পূর্বাপর বিষয়) ; last, terminating (অপরাহ্ন). ☐ *pro.* somebody else (অপরের শক্তিতে). **অপরঞ্চ** *con. & adv.* moreover, further, in addition. **অপরত্র** *adv. & con.* elsewhere; on the other hand. **অপরন্তু** var. of **অপরঞ্চ**। **~পক্ষে** *adv.* on the other side; on the other hand.

অপরা *a. & pro. fem.* of **অপর**। ☐ *a. fem.* (phil.) other than the absolute or supreme; illusory; worldly, mundane.

অপরাঙ্মুখ *a.* not averse (to), not turning away (from); not disinclined.

অপরাজিত *a.* undefeated, unbeaten, unconquered. **অপরাজিতা** *a. fem.* of **অপরাজিত**। ☐ *n.* a creeper of the clitoria genus or its flower; (pros.) a Sanskrit metre; an appellation of Goddess Durga (দুর্গা).

অপরাজেয় *a.* unconquerable; unbeatable; invincible; unparalleled, matchless (অপরাজেয় কথাশিল্পী)।

অপরাধ *n.* a fault, a defect; a sin; a guilt, an offence, a crime. **অপরাধ করা** *v.* to commit a fault; to sin; to commit an offence or crime. **~জনক, ~মূলক** *a.* criminal; sinful. **~বোধ** *n.* consciousness or sense of guilt; feeling of guiltiness; guilty conscience; guilt complex. **অপরাধী** *a.* one who commits a fault; sinful; guilty, offending, criminal. ☐ *n.* such a person; a sinner; an offender, a criminal. *fem.* **অপরাধিনী**।

অপরাধীন *a.* not dominated by other; not subjugated.

অপরাপর *a.* all other.

অপরার্ধ *n.* the other half.

অপরাহ্ন *n.* afternoon. **অপরাহ্নে** in the afternoon. **আজ অপরাহ্নে** this afternoon. **কাল বা আগামীকাল অপরাহ্নে** tomorrow afternoon. **কাল বা গতকাল অপরাহ্নে** yesterday afternoon.

অপরিকল্পিত *a.* not planned or designed; undeliberate. **~পূর্ব** *a.* not planned or designed beforehand; unpremeditated. **~ভাবে** *adv.* in an unplanned or unpremeditated manner or way.

অপরিক্লিষ্ট *a.* unwearied, untired, not fatigued; untroubled.

অপরিগৃহীত *a.* unaccepted; refused, rejected, turned down.

অপরিগ্রহ *n.* non-acceptance; refusal, rejection.

অপরিচয় *n.* non-acquaintance; incognizance; lack of knowledge (in or of).

অপরিচিত *a.* not familiar; unacquainted, unknown; unfamiliar; strange. *fem.* **অপরিচিতা**। **অপরিচিত ব্যক্তি** an unknown person; a stranger. **অপরিচিতি** *n.* non-acquaintance; incognizance; lack of knowledge (in or of), ignorance; unfamiliarity; strangeness.

অপরিচ্ছন্ন *a.* untidy, dirty; dingy; slovenly; unclean; (fig.) impure (অপরিচ্ছন্ন মন). **~তা** *n.* untidiness, dirtiness; dinginess; slovenliness; uncleanliness, impurity.

অপরিচ্ছিন্ন *a.* undivided; entire; incessant, non-stop, uninterrupted; continuous.

অপরিজ্ঞাত *a.* unknown; unacquainted; unfamiliar; uninformed, unlearned, unstudied; strange.

অপরিজ্ঞেয় *a.* unknowable; incognizable, unrecognizable.

অপরিণত *a.* not fully grown-up or developed, immature; embryonic; young, tender, green, raw, verdant. **~বয়স্ক** *a.* tender-aged, young; under-age, minor. *fem.* **~বয়স্কা**। **~বুদ্ধি** *a.* one whose intelligence or judgement has not yet attained maturity; childish, puerile, frivolous. **~বুদ্ধি যুবক** a greenhorn, a callow youth.

অপরিণামদর্শী *a.* lacking in foresight, improvident, unforeseeing; imprudent; rash. **অপরিণামদর্শিতা** *n.* want of foresight, improvidence; imprudence; rashness.

অপরিণীত *a.* unmarried; unwedded. *fem.* অপরিণীতা।

অপরিতুষ্ট, অপরিতৃপ্ত *a.* not thoroughly satisfied or gratified; unsatisfied; insatiate; ungratified, unfulfilled. **অপরিতৃপ্তি** *n.* absence of full satisfaction or pleasure.

অপরিত্যাজ্য *a.* incapable of being forsaken or deserted given up or avoided or disowned.

অপরিপক্ব *a.* not fully ripe; unripe; not thoroughly experienced or skilled; immature; inexperienced; unskilled; inexpert. **~তা** *n.* unripeness; immaturity; greenness; inexperience; lack of skill.

অপরিপাক *n.* indigestion.

অপরিপূর্ণ *a.* not thoroughly filled or fulfilled; unsatisfied, ungratified. **~তা** *n.* incompleteness.

অপরিপৃক্ত *a.* (phys.) unsaturated.

অপরিবর্তন *n.* absence or lack of change or alteration or modification; constancy; fixity; firmness. **অপরিবর্তনীয়** *a.* unchangeable , unalterable, immutable, invariable; unchanging; constant; fixed; firm. **অপরিবর্তনীয়তা** *n.* unchangeability, immutability; unchanging state; constancy; fixity; firmness.

অপরিবর্তিত *a.* unchanged, unaltered, unvaried.

অপরিবাহী *a.* non-conducting. ☐ *n.* nonconductor.

অপরিবেষ্টিত *a.* not surrounded or encircled; not enclosed; unenclosed.

অপরিমাণ *a.* immeasurable; innumerable; profuse, plentiful; excessive.

অপরিমার্জিত *a.* not refined or revised or cleaned.

অপরিমিত *a.* immeasurable; innumerable, countless; unlimited, boundless, profuse, too many or too much, plentiful; immoderate; more than enough; excessive (অপরিমিত আদর) ; unrestricted, unrestrained, unbridled. **অপরিমিত ভোজন** over-eating, surfeit. **অপরিমিতাচার** *n.* intemperance, lack of moderation, overindulgence.

অপরিমেয় *a.* immeasurable; countless; innumerable. **~তা** *n.* immensity; immeasurableness.

অপরিম্লান *a.* fadeless, never-fading; amaranthine; unfaded; tireless; untiring; unwearied; unfatigued; cheerful; lively.

অপরিশীলন *n.* lack of study or practice, non-cultivation. **অপরিশীলিত** *a.* uncultivated, uncultured, unrefined; unsophisticated.

অপরিশুদ্ধ *a.* impure; unholy; unclean; incorrect.

অপরিশোধনীয় *a.* unrepayable; unreturnable.

অপরিশোধিত *a.* unrepaid, outstanding, owed (pop.); unrefined.

অপরিশোধ্য var. of **অপরিশোধনীয়**।

অপরিশ্রান্ত *a.* not tired out or wearied or fatigued.

অপরিষ্কার *n.* uncleanliness, untidiness; impurity. ☐ *a.* unclean, untidy; impure; (fig.) not perspicuous or lucid or explicit.

অপরিষ্কৃত *a.* uncleaned; unclean, untidy; unpurified, unrefined; impure.

অপরিসর *a.* not wide, narrow; not spacious.

অপরিসীম *a.* limitless, boundless; unbounded; endless.

অপরিস্ফুট *a.* not fully perceptible or expressed; not manifest or apparent; indistinct; dim.

অপরিস্রুত *a.* not filtered, unfiltered.

অপরিহার্য, অপরিহরণীয় *a.* unavoidable; indispensable; inevitable.

অপরীক্ষিত *a.* unexamined, untested; unexperimented, untried.

অপরূপ *a.* unprecedented, incomparably beautiful; wonderful, amazing; strange, queer, odd; ugly.

অপরোক্ষ *a.* perceptible; visible; within one's reach; not roundabout, direct; without any intervening agency, immediate. **অপরোক্ষ অনুভূতি** (phil.) direct or immediate perception. **অপরোক্ষ উক্তি** (gr.) direct speech or narration.

অপর্ণ *a.* leafless, apetalous.

অপর্ণা *n. fem.* a woman who has not eaten even a tree-leaf during her penance; an appellation of Goddess Durga (দুর্গা).

অপর্যাপ্ত *a.* more than sufficient, excessive; too much or too many; profuse, plentiful, abundant; (rare) insufficient inadequate.

অপলক *a.* (of eyes) unwinking; (of look) steadfast. **অপলক চোখে, অপলক দৃষ্টিতে** *adv.* with eyes unwinking; looking steadfastly; with steadfast gaze.

অপলকা *a.* extremely brittle or fragile.

অপলাপ *n.* suppression or concealment (তথ্যের অপলাপ) ; denial (সত্যের বা উক্তির অপলাপ) ; a false statement, *suggestio falsi*.

অপশব্দ *n.* a grammatically incorrect word; a corrupt word; an obscene or vulgar word; a cant phrase; vulgar speech.

অপশাসন *n.* misrule; bad government.

অপশ্রুতি *n.* (gr.) ablaut.

অপসংস্কৃতি *n.* degenerate culture; perverted or corrupt taste, mentality etc.

অপসরণ *n.* leaving for a different place; removal, movement; withdrawal, retreat; going out, exit. **অপসরণ করা** *v.* to move to a different place; to move away, to shift, to remove; to withdraw, to retreat; to go out; (phys.) to diverge.

অপসারণ *n.* taking away to a different place; transfer, removal; withdrawal; dismissal (কর্মচারীর অপসারণ) ; (phys.) divergence. **অপসারণ করা** *v.* to take away to a different place; to shift, to transfer, to remove; to withdraw; to dismiss; to dispel or expel (অন্ধকার অপসারণ করা) ; (phys.) to diverge. **অপসারণ কোণ** angle of divergence.

অপসারি (poet.) *pr. pt.* of **অপসারণ করা** (see **অপসারণ**).

অপসারিত *a.* shifted, gone away; removed, transferred; withdrawn; dismissed; dispelled or expelled. **অপসারিত করা** same as **অপসারণ করা** (see **অপসারণ**). **অপসারিত হওয়া** *v.* to move to a different place; to move away; to shift; to remove; to withdraw, to retreat; to go back, to recede; to go away; to be dispelled or expelled; (phys.) to diverge.

অপসারী *a.* (phys.) divergent.

অপসিদ্ধান্ত *n.* wrong conclusion, fallacious inference.

অপসূর *n.* (astr.) aphelion.

অপসৃত var. of **অপসারিত ।**

অপস্মার *n.* epilepsy.

অপস্রিয়মাণ *a.* receding, retreating; withdrawing.

অপহত *a.* killed, slain; murdered; destroyed; perished.

অপহন্তা *n.* a killer, a slayer; a murderer; a destroyer.

অপহরণ *n.* stealing, theft; pilferage, filching; plunder, loot; robbery; misappropriation; abduction; carrying off or lifting. **অপহরণ করা** *v.* to steal; to pilfer; to plunder, to loot; to rob; to misappropriate; to abduct; to carry off, to lift.

অপহর্তা *n.* a thief; a pilferer; a plunderer; a looter; a robber; one who misappropriates; an abductor; a lifter.

অপহসিত *a.* laughed at, ridiculed, mocked at; laughed to scorn; derided.

অপহারক, অপহারী *a.* & *n.* a thief, a robber; one who steals or plunders or robs or abducts or carries off. □ *a.* thievish; plunderous.

অপহাস *n.* derisive or scornful laughter or smile; simper.

অপহৃত *a.* stolen; pilfered; plundered; looted; robbed, snatched; misappropriated; abducted; carried off, lifted.

অপহ্নব, অপহ্নুতি *n.* concealment (of truth); denial; theft; (rhet.) a figure of speech in which the object of comparison is concealed under the analogy ('এ তো মালা নয় গো, এ যে তোমার তরবারি').

অপাক *n.* indigestion.

অপাঙ্‌ক্তেয় *a.* debarred from dining together with the members of one's own caste; socially cast out; outcaste.

অপাঙ্গ *n.* the outer corner of the eye; squint. **~দৃষ্ট** *n.* a glance from the outer corner of the eye; a side-glance; a stolen glance; an ogling or leering glance.

অপাচ্য *a.* indigestible; (fig.-of teaching, writing, books etc.) unintelligible.

অপাটব *n.* lack of skill or dexterity; ungainliness, awkwardness.

অপাঠ্য *a.* (of books etc.) not suitable for

reading; not worth reading; hard-reading; indecent, obscene.

অপাত্র *n.* an unfit or undeserving or incompetent or improper or base or vile person or thing; a man unfit or not worth consideration for matrimonial alliance.

অপাদান *n.* (gr.) the ablative case.

অপান *n.* the wind of the lower space; the wind that prevails within the lower part of the body; wind that passes through the anus. **~ বায়ু** *n.* wind passed through the anus, fart.

অপাপ *a.* sinless; guiltless; **~বিদ্ধ** *a.* one who or that which has never committed any sin; not affected by sin, taintless; not vitiated.

অপাবরণ *n.* unveiling or uncovering; opening the door (of).

অপাবৃত *a.* unveiled; uncovered, opened.

অপায় *n.* destruction, ruin; harm, loss; injury; a disaster, a mishap; a hazard, a danger; an impediment, a hindrance.

অপার *a.* shoreless (অপার সমুদ্র) ; unlimited, boundless, endless, vast, immense.

অপারক *a.* incapable, unable.

অপারগ *a.* not going or moving to or towards the coast; incapable, unable.

অপার্থিব *a.* unearthly; preternatural, extramundane, celestial; supernatural.

অপার্যমানে *adv.* in case of failure owing to inability or incapability.

অপালন *n.* bad government, maladministration, misrule.

অপিচ *con.* moreover, also, besides, in addition, further; on the other hand, conversely.

অপিতৃক *a.* fatherless, one who has lost one's father or is without one's father.

অপিনিহিতি *n.* (phon.) epenthesis.

অপুচ্ছ *a.* tailless; anurous.

অপুণ্য *n.* lack of virtue.

অপুত্র, অপুত্রক *a.* sonless; (loos.) childless.

অপুরুষ, অপুরুষোচিত *a.* unmanly; cowardly.

অপুষ্ট *a.* undeveloped; undernourished; lean, thin. **অপুষ্টি** *n.* lack of nourishment; malnutrition.

অপুষ্প, অপুষ্পক *a.* unflowering, flowerless; (bot.) cryptogamous.

অপুষ্যি *n.* (coll.) an undesirable or unwanted dependent for maintenance.

অপূত *a.* not sacred, unhallowed, unsanctified, unholy; defiled, impure.

অপূপ *n.* a cake.

অপূরণ *n.* non-fulfilment; shortage, want.

অপূর্ণ *a.* not full or filled; imcomplete; imperfect; unfinished; undone, outstanding (অপূর্ণ কার্য) ; ungratified, unfulfilled, unsatisfied (অপূর্ণ বাসনা). **~তা, ~ত্ব** *n.* incompletion; non-completion; imcompleteness; imperfection; unfinished state; non-fulfilment.

অপূর্ব *a.* that which has no previous existence; unprecedented; novel; new and strange; uncommon, unusual; wonderful; excellent, grand; original. **~তা** *n.* unprecedentedness; novelty; uncommonness, unusualness; wonderfulness; excellence, originality.

অপেক্ষ *a.* depending on (মুখাপেক্ষ) ; conditional. **অপেক্ষ সংখ্যা** quorum.

অপেক্ষক *a.* waiting, waiting for, awaiting; expectant, anticipant; dependent. □ *n.* (alg.) a function.

অপেক্ষণীয় *a.* one who or that which is or should be awaited; one who or that which is or should be expected or anticipated; desirable; desired.

অপেক্ষবাদ *n.* the theory of relativity.

অপেক্ষমাণ *a.* in the state of waiting or awaiting.

অপেক্ষা *n.* await; waiting (for) or tarrying; expectation, expectancy, anticipation (সুদিনের বা সাহায্যলাভের অপেক্ষা) ; reliance (দৈবের অপেক্ষা) ; caring for or depending on (কারও অপেক্ষা না রাখা). □ *con.* than, of, in comparison to or with. **অপেক্ষা করা** *v.* to await; to wait for; to tarry; to expect, to anticipate; to rely on; to care for. **~কৃত** *adv.* comparatively; relatively.

অপেক্ষিত *a.* awaited, waited for; expected, anticipated.

অপেক্ষী *a.* var. of **অপেক্ষক** (*a.*).

অপেয় *a.* that which is not fit to drink, undrinkable.

অপেরণ *n.* (astr.) aberration.

অপেশাদার, অপেশাদারি *a.* non-professional.

অপোগণ্ড *a.* good-for-nothing; infant; minor; underage. □ *n.* an infant, a baby, a child; a boy or girl; a lad or lass; a minor; a good-for-nothing fellow.

অপোহ *n.* (log.) a counter-argument; removal (of doubt etc.), refutation.

অপৌরুষ *n.* unmanliness; cowardice; infamy; discredit; shame.

অপৌরুষেয় *a.* not man-made; unspoken by man (বেদ অপৌরুষেয়) ; supernatural, preternatural; divine.

অপ্রকট *a.* unrevealed, concealed; disappeared, vanished; dead. **অপ্রকট লীলা** (Vaishnava lit.) solemn or divine activities in an incorporeal or non-manifest existence, (cp.) miracles.

অপ্রকাশ *n.* non-revelation; non-manifestation; non-disclosure; non-appearance; concealment. □ *a.* unrevealed; unmanifested; undisclosed; concealed; unpublished. **অপ্রকাশিত** *a.* same as **অপ্রকাশ** (*a.*). **অপ্রকাশ্য** *a.* that which should not be revealed or manifested or disclosed or published; secret; private (অপ্রকাশ্য স্থান).

অপ্রকৃত *a.*not genuine, spurious; untrue; false; unreal; immaterial; incorrect, wrong. **অপ্রকৃত ভগ্নাঙ্ক বা ভগ্নাংশ** (math.) improper fraction (with numerator greater than denominator).

অপ্রকৃতিস্থ *a.* off one's natural state; deprived of one's self-control; excited; fuddled (esp. with drink); drunk; mentally upset or deranged, not in the proper frame of mind; crazy. **~তা** *n.* drunkenness; craziness.

অপ্রকৃষ্ট *a.* not good; inferior; bad; base, mean; inadvisable, inexpedient.

অপ্রখর *a.* not sharp or strong; dull; mild; not very hot or scorching.

অপ্রগল্ভ *a.* not proud or haughty or untowardly; polite, modest; not brazenfaced or shameless, not saucy or pert; coy; not garrulous; tongue-shy.

অপ্রচলন *n.* obsolescence, going out of use; obsoleteness; state of being not current; state of not being in current use.

অপ্রচলিত *a.* gone out of use; obsolete; antiquated; not in vogue; not current. **অপ্রচলিত হওয়া** *v.* to go out of use; to become obsolete or antiquated; to go out of fashion or currency.

অপ্রচারিত *a.* not made public; unpublished; unannounced; uncirculated; unrevealed, undisclosed; not preached or propagated.

অপ্রচুর *a.* insufficient; not ample or profuse; scanty.

অপ্রণয় *n.* lack or loss of love or friendliness or attachment; unfriendliness; quarrel, bad blood. **অপ্রণয়ী** *a.* & *n.* one who has no room for love in one's heart; unloving.

অপ্রণিধান *n.* inattention; neglect; carelessness.

অপ্রতর্ক্য *a.* that which cannot be settled by discussion or debate; beyond logic and reason; not to be disputed or called in question; undiscussable, undebatable.

অপ্রতিকরণীয় var. of **অপ্রতিকার্য**।

অপ্রতিকার *n.* absence of redress, non-remedy, non-prevention.

অপ্রতিকার্য *a.* that which cannot be redressed, irremediable; unpreventible.

অপ্রতিকূল *a.* not unfavourable or antagonistic; favourable; friendly; helpful.

অপ্রতিদ্বন্দ্ব, অপ্রতিদ্বন্দ্বী *a.* unrivalled, matchless, peerless, unparalleled.

অপ্রতিপত্তি *n.* lack of influence or power.

অপ্রতিপন্ন *a.* unproved, not vindicated or justified; unfounded.

অপ্রতিবন্ধ *a.* unobstructed; uninterrupted; unconditional.

অপ্রতিবিধান *n.* absence of remedy or redress.

অপ্রতিবিধেয় *a.* that which cannot be redressed, irremediable, irrecoverable, incurable, unpreventible.

অপ্রতিভ *a.* embarrassed, abashed, nonplussed, out of countenance; lacking in presence of mind; dull-witted. **অপ্রতিভ হওয়া** *v.* to become embarrassed or abashed, to be put out of countenance.

অপ্রতিম *a.* incomparable, unparalleled, matchless; unique.

অপ্রতিরথ *n.* a matchless warrior. ☐ *a.* matchless in combat.

অপ্রতিরুদ্ধ *a.* unresisted, unprevented, unobstructed, unopposed, unhindered.

অপ্রতিরূপ *a.* without equal, matchless, incomparable, unique.

অপ্রতিরোধ্য *a.* irresistible; unavoidable, inevitable.

অপ্রতিষেধ্য *a.* that which cannot be prevented.

অপ্রতিষ্ঠ *a.* not setttled or established; one who or that which is in an uncertain state or position; one who could not yet assert himself or come into the limelight; not renowned; obscure. **অপ্রতিষ্ঠা** *n.* uncertain state or position; obscurity. **অপ্রতিষ্ঠিত** same as **অপ্রতিষ্ঠ** and—(of institutions etc.) unfounded, unestablished.

অপ্রতিসম *a.* asymmetric, asymmetrical.

অপ্রতিসাম্য *n.* asymmetry.

অপ্রতিহত *a.* unresisted, unobstructed, unprevented, unopposed; unhindered; irresistible (অপ্রতিহত প্রভাব বা বেগ).

অপ্রতীক *a.* without a symbol; intangible.

অপ্রতীতি *n.* incredulity; doubt; lack of belief or conviction; non-comprehension, non-perception, non-realization. **অপ্রতীত** *a.* not believed, disbelieved; doubted.

অপ্রতীয়মান *a.* not revealed or disclosed; not expressed.

অপ্রতুল *n.* lack of abundance or plenty; shortage, dearth; insufficiency; want, need, indigence.

অপ্রত্যক্ষ *a.* transcendental; not perceptible by sense-organs; imperceptible; invisible; indirect.

অপ্রত্যয় *n.* lack of belief or conviction; disbelief; diffidence; incredulity; doubt. **অপ্রত্যয়ী** *a.*disbelieving; unconvinced; different; incredulous; doubting.

অপ্রত্যাশা *n.* lack or absence of expectation.

অপ্রত্যাশিত *a.* unexpected; not anticipated; unhoped-for; unlooked-for; unthought-of; sudden, accidental. **~ভাবে** *adv.* unexpectedly; suddenly, accidentally, by chance.

অপ্রথিত *a.* not celebrated or distinguished, not famous, not well-known.

অপ্রদীপ *n.* black-out. ☐ *a.* having no lamps burning; destitute of light or lamps.

অপ্রধান *a.* not principal or chief; secondary; subordinate; unimportant; non-essential; minor. **অপ্রধান কর্ম** (gr.) an indirect object.

অপ্রবল *a.* not strong or stout.

অপ্রবাসী *a.* not living in a foreign country; not living abroad.

অপ্রবৃত্ত *a.* not engaged or employed; disengaged.

অপ্রবৃত্তি *n.* disinclination; distaste; unwillingness; apathy.

অপ্রবেশ্য *a.* impermeable; impervious; impenetrable. **অপ্রবেশ্য শিলা** (geol.) an impervious rock.

অপ্রমত্ত *a.* not maddened; not drunk or intoxicated; one who has not lost one's self-control; sober, calm, placid; unruffled, composed.

অপ্রমাণ *n.* lack of proof or evidence or justification; disproof, refutation.

অপ্রমাণিত *a.* unproved; not established or substantiated.

অপ্রমাদ *n.* absence of mistake; correctness, rightfulness; sobriety; carefulness, vigilance. **অপ্রমাদী** *a.*unerring; careful, vigilant.

অপ্রমিত *a.* unmeasured; uncounted; unlimited; immense; profuse, copious.

অপ্রমেয় *a.* immeasurable; uncountable; countless; unlimited, boundless; immense, profuse; innumerable; incomprehensible (অপ্রমেয় ব্রহ্ম).

অপ্রযত্ন *n.* lack of effort or endeavour or enthusiasm or assiduity; laxity; neglect.

অপ্রযুক্ত *a.* inapplicable, unsuitable, inapposite, inapt (অপ্রযুক্ত শব্দ) ; (loos.) misapplied; (loos.) unused. **~তা** *n.* inapplicability, inappositeness, inaptness, inaptitude.

অপ্রযোজ্য *a.* not applicable, inapplicable.

অপ্রয়োগ *n.* non-application; lack of use;

non-currency, abeyance; misapplication, misuse.

অপ্রয়োজন *n.* needlessness, absence of necessity. **অপ্রয়োজনীয়** *a.* unnecessary, needless; redundant, superfluous; useless. **অপ্রয়োজনীয়তা** *n.* unnecessariness, needlessness; uselessness; redundance, superfluity.

অপ্রশংসনীয় *a.* not praiseworthy or commendable, not laudable; disreputable; censurable. **অপ্রশংসা** *n.* lack of praise; disrepute, bad name. **অপ্রশংসিত** *a.* not praised or eulogized; censured.

অপ্রশমিত *a.* not subdued or neutralized or pacified; not allayed.

অপ্রশস্ত *a.* not wide or spacious, narrow; not respectable; disreputable; inauspicious, unfavourable, unsuitable, improper (অপ্রশস্ত সময়).

অপ্রসন্ন *a.* displeased, dissatisfied; unfavourable, antagonistic (অপ্রসন্ন ভাগ্য) ; gloomy, morose, melancholy, saddened, sad, offended, vexed. **~তা** *n.* displeasure, dissatisfaction; antagonism; gloom, melancholy, sadness; offended state. **অপ্রসন্ন হয়ে** *adv.* with a bad grace. **অপ্রসন্ন চিত্তে** *adv.* with a discontented or heavy heart.

অপ্রসিদ্ধ *a.* not famous or renowned or well-known; obscure; unknown, not current. **অপ্রসিদ্ধি** *n.* lack of fame or reputation or renown; absence of currency.

অপ্রস্তুত *a.* not made or prepared; unready, unprepared; embarrassed, out of countenance; inexistent, absent; not related to the subject-matter, irrelevant (অপ্রস্তুত বিষয়ের বর্ণনা). **অপ্রস্তুত প্রশংসা** *n.* (rhet.) allegory. **অপ্রস্তুত হওয়া** *v.* to become embarrassed, to be disconcerted; to be put out of countenance. **অপ্রস্তুতি** *n.* lack of preparation or readiness.

অপ্রাকৃত *n.* unnatural; supernatural; uncommon; artificial.

অপ্রাচীন *a.* not old or ancient.

অপ্রাচুর্য *n.* lack (of); shortage (of); dearth; insufficiency, inadequacy; rareness.

অপ্রাপ্ত *a.* that which has not come into possession of; one who has not obtained or received or earned or acquired or realized or attained. **~বয়স্ক** *a.* one who has not yet come of age, underage, minor; below the age of legal majority. *fem.* **অপ্রাপ্তবয়স্কা।** **~যৌবন** *a.* one who has not yet attained youth; underage, minor. *fem.* **অপ্রাপ্তযৌবনা।** **~ব্যবহার** *a.* same as **অপ্রাপ্তবয়স্ক।**

অপ্রাপ্তি *n.* non-availability; non-receipt; non-acquisition; non-procurement; non-realization, non-attainment.

অপ্রাপ্য *a.* unavailable; unattainable; unacquirable, unprocurable; rare, scarce.

অপ্রামাণিক *a.* not proved or vindicated; unauthentic; unacceptable.

অপ্রামাণ্য *a.* not provable; unproved.

অপ্রাসঙ্গিক *a.* unconnected; unrelated; irrelevant; not relating or pertaining to the matter at hand. **~তা** *n.* lack of connection or relation; irrelevance.

অপ্রিয় *a.* disagreeable, unpleasant; undesired, disliked; disgusting. **~কারী** *a.* & *n.* one who does disagreeable or unpleasant deeds. *fem.* **~কারিণী।** **~বাদী, ~ভাষী** *a.* & *n.* one who speaks harshly or disagreeably or unpleasantly; one who is rude in speech. *fem.* **~বাদিনী, ~ভাষিণী।** **অপ্রিয় হওয়া** *v.* to be disagreeable (to); to fall from grace (of); to be disliked by.

অপ্রীতি *n.* lack of affection; displeasure; distaste; disagreeableness; unpleasantness; malice, bad blood. **~কর, ~জনক, ~প্রদ** *a.* displeasing; unpleasant; distasteful; disagreeable; disgusting; unfriendly; malicious. **~ভাজন** *n.* & *a.* one who deserves no love or affection; one who is an object of dislike or hatred.

অপ্সরা, (pop.) **অপ্সরী** *n. fem.* (myth.) a voluptuously beautiful nymph of Paradise with exceptional gifts in music and dancing.

অফলন *n.* lack or absence of fruition; lack or absence of harvest; bad harvest.

অফলা *a.* unfructiferous, unfruitful; unproductive; barren; infructuous.

অফুটন্ত *a.* not boiling; not blooming.

অফুরন্ত, অফুরান *a.* unending, endless (অফুরন্ত পথ বা অবসর) ; inexhaustible (অফুরন্ত ভাণ্ডার).

অব[1] *pfx.* indicating : certainty, inferiority, baseness, expanse, downwards, inward, encircling, absence, contrariety, middle etc., ab-, apo-, de-, i-, ob-.

অব[2] *adv.* (obs. & poet.) now ('সখি অব কি করব উপদেশ').

অবকাশ *n.* leisure; respite, vacation (গ্রীষ্মাবকাশ) ; necessary time for (কাজের অবকাশ) ; cessation; time or space between, interval; scope, room, opportunity (সন্দেহের অবকাশ).

অবক্তব্য *a.* that which cannot or should not be uttered; unspeakable.

অবক্রম *n.* grade (*term.*).

অবক্ষয় *n.* depreciation; dilapidation; decadence; ruin; loss; erosion, waste.

অবক্ষিপ্ত *a.* scattered; cast downwards, deposited; ridiculed, jeered at, bantered, taunted.

অবক্ষেপ, অবক্ষেপণ *n.* scattering; casting downwards; depositing, deposition; ridicule, jeer, taunt.

অবগত *a.* informed, aware, acquainted; *au fait*; known, learnt. **অবগত করানো** *v.* to inform, to intimate, to acquaint, to apprise of. **অবগত থাকা** *v.* to know, to be aware of, to be acquainted with. **অবগত হওয়া** *v.* to learn, to come to know, to become acquainted with or apprised of, to receive information or intimation of. **অবগতি** *n.* knowledge; awareness; information.

অবগাঢ় *a.* immersed, sunk; one who or that which has penetrated; bathed; (fig.) deeply involved, engrossed.

অবগাহ, অবগাহন *n.* bathing by immersing one's body in a river, tank, etc.; bath. **অবগাহন করা** *v.* to have a bath, to take a bath.

অবগুণ *n.* absence of virtue or good qualities; a fault or a blemish; a defect.

অবগুণ্ঠন *n.* a cover for the head and face (used by women), a veil; a hood. **~বতী** *a. fem.* veiled; concealed. *fem.* **অবগুণ্ঠিতা** ।

অবঘাত *n.* a fatal blow; unnatural death. **~ন** *n.* dealing one a fatal blow; (arith.) evolution. **অবঘাতী** *a.* one who or that which deals one a fatal blow or causes unnatural death.

অবচয় *n.* plucking or picking or gathering flowers etc.; wasting, waste; (of properties etc.) depreciation. **অবচয় সংচিতি** depreciation reserve.

অবচিত *a.* (of flowers etc.) plucked, picked, gathered; ill-spent, wasted; depreciated.

অবচূর্ণন *n.* reducing to powder or grinding into dust, pulverization; powder, dust; dusting with medicinal powder. **অবচূর্ণিত** *a.* reduced to powder, ground into dust, pulverized.

অবচেতন *a.* subconscious (অবচেতন মন).

অবচ্ছিন্ন *a.* possessing, full of (মেঘাবচ্ছিন্ন) ; separated, parted, having an interval (নিরবচ্ছিন্ন) ; mixed, adulterated (দুঃখাবচ্ছিন্ন সুখ) ; (phil.) limited by, bounded by (দেহাবচ্ছিন্ন প্রাণ).

অবচ্ছেদ *n.* cutting off, section; separation; detachment; (usu. temporary) cessation; interval; (of books etc.) a chapter or section; a portion, a part, a fragment; a division; a limit or boundary. **~ক** *a.* & *n.* one who or that which cuts off or separates or detaches or divides; causing temporary cessation or interval; limiting. **অবচ্ছেদে** *adv.* in all; on the whole; without exception.

অবজ্ঞা *n.* slight; contempt; scorn; disrespect; disregard; neglect. **অবজ্ঞা করা** *v.* to neglect, to disregard, to slight; to ignore, to pay no regard to. **অবজ্ঞাত** *a.* slighted; scorned; disrespected; disregarded; neglected; obscure. **~জনিত, ~প্রসূত** *a.* arising out of contempt or neglect; caused by disregard or contempt; contemptuous. **~ভরে** *adv.* contemptuously, disrespectfully. **অবজ্ঞেয়** *a.* contemptible; despicable; negligible; trifling.

অবতংস *n.* an ornament; (fig.) one who adds to the glory of or brings credit to (বংশাবতংস).

অবতরণ *n.* going or coming downwards, descending, descent; alighting or climbing down or dismounting; getting out of a vehicle; disembarkment; (of birds etc.) flying down to or towards the ground; stepping down (from position etc.); relegation to a lower class, position, status etc.; degradation. **অবতরণ করা** *v.* to come or go downwards, to get down, to descend; to alight, to climb down, to dismount; to get out of any vehicle, to disembark; (of birds etc.) to fly down to or towards the ground; to step down (from a position, etc.); to be relegated to a lower class. **অবতরণিকা** *n.* (of books etc.) a preface, an introduction, a preamble, a prologue, a prelude; a flight of steps, a staircase; a ladder, an escalator.

অবতল *a.* concave. **~ভঙ্গ** *n.* (geol.) a syncline.

অবতার *n.* incarnation; an incarnation, an avatar; a personation (শয়তানের অবতার = Satan personated); a personification (দয়ার অবতার = kindness personified); (pop.) an ugly and odd-looking person, an antic. **~বাদ** *n.* the doctrine of incarnation.

অবতারণ *n.* bringing down; putting up a proposal or raising a question for consideration; introduction. **অবতারণা** *n.* putting up a proposal or raising a question for consideration, introduction etc.; an introduction, a preface. **অবতারণা করা** *v.* to put up (a proposal) or raise (a question), to introduce. **অবতারণী** *n.* a flight of steps, a staircase; a ladder, an escalator.

অবতীর্ণ *a.* one who or that which has come down or gone down or descended or alighted or climbed down or dismounted; flown down to or towards the ground; one who has got out of any vehicle, disembarked; (of a celestial being) incarnated ('অবতীর্ণ এ ধরায়') ; one who or that which has appeared or arrived. **অবতীর্ণ হওয়া** *v.* to come or go down, to get down, to descend, to alight, to climb down, to dismount; to get out of any vehicle, to disembark; (of birds etc.) to fly down to or towards the ground; to step down (from a position etc.); (of a celestial being) to become incarnated, to take one's birth upon the earth; to appear or arrive; (rare) to pass over or come through. **ভূমিকায় অবতীর্ণ হওয়া** to appear in the role of, to act as (in a play).

অবদংশ *n.* any pungent food that excites thirst (chiefly taken with drinks); an appetizer; a stimulant.

অবদমন *n.* repression. **অবদমন করা** *v.* to repress. **অবদমনীয়** *a.* repressible. **অবদমিত** *a.* repressed.

অবদাত *a.* white; pure, free from impurities.

অবদান *n.* an act performed, a performance; a feat, an exploit, an achievement; a great or commendable deed.

অবদারণী *n.* a digging instrument such as a spade, a crowbar etc.

অবদ্ধ *a.* untied, unfastened, unbound; unbolted, unlocked; unconfirmed; unobstructed, unprevented; unrestrained; loose.

অবদ্য *a.* unspeakable, unutterable; unfit for utterance; disgraceful, base; (of words, expression etc.) in bad taste, vulgar.

অবধান *n.* careful attention, weighing in mind; deliberation, consideration; hearing attentively. □ *v. imp.* o hear, please hear ('অবধান মহীপতি'). **অবধান করা** *v.* to pay attention or heed to; to deliberate, to consider; to hear attentively.

অবধায়ক *n.* a caretaker.

অবধারণ, অবধারণা *n.* determining, fixing or settling; determination, fixation, settlement; discernment; cognition. **অবধারণ করা** *v.* to determine, to fix, to settle, to appoint; to discern; to cognize. **অবধারণীয়** *a.* same as **অবধার্য**।

অবধারিত *a.* determined, fixed, settled, appointed; discerned; cognized; sure, certain, inevitable (জয় অবধারিত).

অবধার্য *a.* determinable, fixable; discernible; cognizable; determined, fixed, settled, appointed; discerned; cognized; sure, certain, inevitable.

অবধি *prep.* from, since ('জনম অবধি হাম') ; up to, till (মৃত্যু অবধি). □ *n.* limit; end; termination. **~বাধিত** *a.* (in law) barred by limitation.

অবধূত[১] *n.* one of a class of anchorites who worship Shiva (শিব).

অবধৃত[২] *a.* determined, fixed, settled, appointed; discerned; cognized.

অবধেয় *a.* warranting attention or deliberation or careful hearing.

অবধৌত[১] *a.* washed or cleansed (carefully).

অবধৌত[২], **অবধৌতিক** *a.* pertaining to anchorites (অবধূত) individually or collectively.

অবধ্য *a.* one who or that which should not or cannot be killed or slain. *fem.* **অবধ্যা**।

অবনত *a.* bent down, stooping; downfallen, depressed (অবনত জাতি) ; low (অবনত স্থান) ; base, depraved (অবনতচরিত্র). **অবনত মস্তকে** *adv.* with one's head bending down; humbly, meekly. **অবনতি** *n.* bent or stooping state; downfall, depression; fall; lowness; deterioration; baseness, depravity.

অবনমন, অবনয়ন *n.* bending or bringing down; state of being bent or brought down; degradation; depression.

অবনমিত *a.* bent down; brought down; humbled; humiliated, degraded; put out of countenance; depressed.

অবনিবনা *n.* lack of amity; disagreement; bad blood; ill-feeling.

অবনি, অবনী *n.* the earth, the world; land. **~তল** *n.* the surface of the earth; the earth; ground. **~পতি** *n.* a king; an emperor. **~মণ্ডল** *n.* the whole of the earth; the world; (loos.) the universe. **অবনীশ, অবনীশ্বর** *n.* a king; an emperor.

অবপতন *n.* falling down; decline, downfall. **অবপাত** same as **অবপতন**।

অবপতন-কোণ *n.* angle of diffraction.

অববাহিকা *n.* the basin of a river.

অববুদ্ধ *a.* enlightened; awakened; perceived.

অববোধ[১] *n.* special or specialized or esoteric knowledge; enlightenment; awakening; state of being awakened.

অববোধ[২] *n.* inauguration; initiation; information.

অবভাস *n.* manifestation, exposition; illusion; (usu. false) ascription; a pretence.

অবম *a.* deficient, short, insufficient; inferior; base, low. □ *n.* (alg.) the minimum.

অবমত *a.* slighted; neglected; unreckoned. **অবমতি** *n.* slight; neglect.

অবমন্তা *a.* & *n.* one who slights or neglects; one who refuses to reckon.

অবমর্দ, অবমর্দন *n.* oppression; eradication; extermination, extirpation.

অবমর্শ, অবমর্শন *n.* realization, consideration; taking counsel.

অবমর্ষ, অবমর্ষণ *n.* extinction, destruction, obliteration.

অবমান, অবমানন, অবমাননা variants of **অপমান**।

অবমানিত var. of **অপমানিত**।

অবমোচন *n.* releasing (as of an arrow from a bow); liberation (from trouble, sorrow, duty, restrictions or fixed position); acquittal. **অবমোচন করা** *v.* to release; to unloose.

অবয়ব *n.* body; a limb; a part, a portion; a constituent; a figure, a form. **~হীন** *a.* bodiless; without a shape or form. **অবয়বী** *a.* having a body, corporeal.

অবর *a.* inferior; younger, junior; assistant, subordinate, subservient. **~ধাতু** *n.* a base metal. **~ ন্যায়াধিকরণ** *n.* a small causes court. **~ন্যায়াধীশ** *n.* a subordinate judge. **~পরিদর্শক** a sub-inspector. **~বর্গ** *n.* the lower division.

অবরা *a. fem.* most excellent, supreme, superb. □ *n.* an appellation of Goddess Durga.

অবরার্ধ *n.* latter part.

অবরুদ্ধ *a.* shut, closed; blockaded, barricaded; confined; imprisoned; checked, frustrated (অবরুদ্ধ বাসনা) ; besieged (অবরুদ্ধ নগর) ; obstructed (অবরুদ্ধ পথ) ; choked (অবরুদ্ধ স্বর). **অবরুদ্ধ করা** *v.* to shut, to close; to block or blockade; to confine; to imprison; to check, to frustrate; to besiege; to obstruct; to choke.

অবরূঢ় *a.* alighted, descended.

অবরেণ্য *a.* unworthy of cordial reception, unwelcome; unacceptable; dishonourable; inferior.

অবরে-সবরে *adv.* (coll.) at times; occasionally; seldom, rarely.

অবরোধ *n.* obstruction, hindrance; blockade; a siege; a prison; a covering; a container or case; imprisonment; detention; zenana (অবরোধবাসিনী). **~ক** *a.* & *n.* one who or that which obstructs or hinders or blockades or besieges or imprisons or detains. **অবরোধ করা** *v.* to obstruct, to hinder; to blockade; to besiege; to imprison; to detain. **~প্রথা** *n.* the practice of keeping women confined in the zenana so that they cannot be seen by outsiders, the purdah system. **~বাসিনী** *a. fem.* secluded in the zenana. □ *n.* woman living in the zenana.

অবরোপণ *n.* implantation; transplantation.

অবরোহ *n.* getting down, descent; (log.) deduction. **~ণ** *n.* descent. **অবরোহণ করা** *v.* to get down, to descend. **~ণী** *n.* a flight of steps or stairs; a ladder; an escalator. **অবরোহ প্রণালী** *n.* deductive method. **অবরোহী** *a.* (log.) deductive. **~পত্র** *n.* a landing permit.

অবর্জনীয়, অবর্জ্য *a.* that which cannot be rejected or discarded; unavoidable; inevitable.

অবর্ণনীয় *a.* indescribable; ineffable, beyond expression.

অবর্তমান *a.* inexistent, non-existent; absent; dead; departed; past. **অবর্তমানে** *adv.* during (one's) absence; after (one's) death or departure.

অবর্ষিত *a.* unshed ('অবর্ষিত অশ্রু') ; not cast or thrown (অবর্ষিত শর).

অবল *a.* weak, feeble; infirm; frail.

অবলম্ব *n.* a support, a prop. □ *a.* hanging or suspended vertically. **~ন** *n.* having recourse to for support, maintenance, help, shelter etc.; accepting or adopting (সন্ন্যাসাবলম্বন) ; holding oneself in (ধৈর্যাবলম্বন) ; acceptance, adoption; a support; a prop; a help; a means for maintenance or accomplishing something. **অবলম্বন করা** *v.* to have recourse to for support, maintenance, help, shelter etc.; to resort to; to accept, to take, to take upon; to adopt. **~হীন** *a.* without a shelter or help; without a means for maintenance. **অবলম্বিত** *a.* resorted to for support, maintenance, help, shelter etc., accepted, adopted; hanging or suspended vertically. **অবলম্বী** *a.* resorting to (something or somebody) for support, maintenance, help, shelter etc.; one who has accepted or taken upon oneself or adopted; hanging or suspended vertically.

অবলা *a. fem.* deprived of strength, powerless; weak. □ *n.* a woman.**~জাতি** *n.* women as a class.

অবলিপ্ত *a.* bedaubed, smeared with, bespattered.

অবলীঢ় *a.* licked; tasted.

অবলীলা *n.* dalliance; absence of strain or effort; carefree manner or state; ease; absence of hesitation; promptness, readiness. **~ক্রমে, ~ভরে, ~য়** *adv.* playfully; without strain or effort, without toil and trouble, effortlessly; easily; in a carefree manner; unhesitatingly, promptly, readily.

অবলুণ্ঠন *n.* falling flat (esp. on the ground), wallowing. **অবলুণ্ঠিত** *a.* rolling or rolled to and fro (on); falling flat (on); wallowing. *fem.* **অবলুণ্ঠিতা**। **অবলুণ্ঠিত হওয়া** *v.* to roll to and fro (on); to fall flat (on); to wallow (in).

অবলুপ্ত *a.* extinct; completely destroyed; lost to view; concealed or screened off ('ঘন মেঘে অবলুপ্ত'). **অবলুপ্ত হওয়া** *v.* to become extinct; to be destroyed completely; to disappear; to be concealed or screened off. **অবলুপ্তি** *n.* extinction.

অবলেপ *n.* smearing or daubing or anointing; a paint, an ointment, an unguent; pride; vanity; vainglory. **~ন** *n.* smearing or daubing or anointing. **অবলেপন করা** *v.* to smear, to daub, to anoint.

অবলেহ *n.* licking or lapping; any article of food or medicine which is to be taken by licking. **~ন** *n.* licking. **অবলেহন করা** *v.* to lick or lap. **অবলেহ্য** *a.* that which can or should be licked.

অবলোকন *n.* looking at; seeing or observing. **অবলোকন করা** *v.* to look at; to see, to observe, to view. **অবলোকনীয়** *a.* fit to be seen, worth seeing; observable, noticeable. **অবলোকিত** *a.* looked at; seen, viewed. **অবলোকিত হওয়া** *v.* to come within or into view, to become visible; to be seen or observed.

অবলোপন *n.* writing off; state of being written off.

অবলোহিত *a.* & *n.* (phys.) infrared.

অবশ *a.* benumbed; paralysed; intractable, indocile, unruly, unmanageable, refractory, beyond control, disobedient; untamed, uncontrolled, unrestrained, unsubdued; torpid, benumbed. insensitive; weak; nerveless. **অবশ করা** *v.* to benumb; to paralyse; to make insensitive.

অবশিষ্ট *a.* remaining, residual, surplus; outstanding. ☐ *n.* a remainder or residue, a surplus; the rest and others; an outstanding portion or thing.

অবশিষ্টাংশ *n.* remainder, remnant, residue.

অবশীকৃত *a.* one who or that which has not been tamed or brought under control; unsubdued, unsubjugated.

অবশীভূত *a.* one who or that which has not yielded or submitted; unsubdued, unsubjugated, untamed, uncontrolled; unyielding, disobedient.

অবশেষ *n.* a remainder, a residue, a surplus; termination, the last stage, end (দিনের বা দুঃখের অবশেষ) ; a portion left out, leavings (খাদ্যাবশেষ). **অবশেষে** *adv.* at last, at length, ultimately; in the end.

অবশ্য[1] *a.* intractable; untamable; unruly, disobedient; uncontrollable, ungovernable; one who or that which cannot be disciplined or subdued.

অবশ্য[2] *adv.* surely, certainly; unavoidably, inevitably (অবশ্য ঘটবে) ; by all means (অবশ্য পরিত্যাজ্য) ; compulsorily (অবশ্যপাঠ্য) ; undoubtedly, needless to say, of course. ☐ *con.* but. ☐ *int.* of course. **অবশ্য অবশ্য** without fail, by all means. **~কর্তব্য, ~করণীয়** *a.* that which must be done, obligatory. **~পাঠ্য** *a.* that which has to be studied compulsorily. **~পাঠ্য বিষয়** *n.* compulsory subject for study. **~পালনীয়** *a.* (of work or duty) enforced; compulsory; obligatory; mandatory. **~ভাবী** *a.* inevitable. **~ভাবিতা** *n.* inevitability.

অবসন্ন *a.* tired, exhausted, fatigued; bereft of sprightliness or enthusiasm (owing to exhaustion), wearied, weary. **অবসন্ন করা** *v.* to exhaust, to fatigue; to weary. **~তা** *n.* extreme tiredness, exhaustion, fatigue; weariness.

অবসর *n.* leisure; respite; opportunity; retirement (চাকরি থেকে অবসর নেওয়া) ; time or space between. **~ক্রমে** *adv.* at one's leisure. **~গ্রহণ** *n.* retirement. **অবসরপূর্ব অবকাশ বা ছুটি** leave preparatory to retirement. **~প্রাপ্ত** *a.* retired (from an employment or office). **~বিনোদন** *n.* recreation; relaxation. **অবসর নেওয়া** *v.* to retire (from).

অবসহন *n.* sufferance; suffering.

অবসাদ *n.* tiredness, exhaustion, fatigue; weariness; languor, lassitude; loss of spirit or enthusiasm (owing to exhaustion); ennui. **~কর, ~জনক** *a.* tiresome, wearisome, irksome; fatiguing, exhausting; languorous. **~গ্রস্ত** *a.* tired, exhausted, fatigued; deprived of spirit or enthusiasm (owing to exhaustion), wearied; weary.

অবসান *n.* termination, conclusion, close, finis, end; death. **অবসান হওয়া** *v.* to terminate, to end, to come to an end. **~স্থিতি** *n.* closing balance.

অবসায়ক *n.* liquidator. **অবসায়ন** *n.* liquidation.

অবসিত *a.* terminated, concluded, closed, finished, ended; past; dead. **অবসান হওয়া** *v.* to terminate, to end, to come to an end; to meet with death.

অবসৃত *a.* removed; retired. **অবসৃত হওয়া** *v.* to be removed, to move away; to retire.

অবস্তু *a.* unsubstantial, immaterial, sapless; worthless. ☐ *n.* any worthless or unsubstantial thing; matter without essence or existence; (phil.) the universe considered without having relation to God, that which is not a reality; illusion.

অবস্থা *n.* state, condition; temperament, mood (মনের অবস্থা) ; circumstances (অবস্থা বুঝে ব্যবস্থা) ; financial condition; position (সংকটাবস্থা). **~গতিকে** *adv.* being compelled by circumstances; in the circumstances. ~ঘটিত *a.* dependent on circumstances; circumstantial, incidental. ~ন্তর *n.* a different state or condition; change of fortune. ~পন্ন *a.* well-to-do; wealthy, rich, in affluent circumstances. ~প্রাপ্ত *a.* reduced to a state. ~প্রাপ্ত হওয়া *v.* to be reduced to a state, to fall into a state. অবস্থা ফেরানো *v.* to better one's fortune or circumstances. ~ভেদে *adv.* in a different or changed condition, in different or changed circumstances. ~সংকট *n.* a critical position, tight corner. ~হীন *a.* indigent, poor, impecunious, badly off.

অবস্থান *n.* stay, residence; a dwelling place; a position, situation, location; a site.

অবস্থান-ধর্মঘট *n.* stay-in-strike.

অবস্থাপন *n.* placing or laying (esp. in an orderly manner or for display); establishing (সিংহাসনে অবস্থাপন).

অবস্থাপন্ন, অবস্থাপ্রাপ্ত see **অবস্থা**।

অবস্থাপিত *a.* placed, laid; established.

অবস্থাভেদে see **অবস্থা**।

অবস্থায়ী a staying, reading; settled; stable, permanent.

অবস্থা সঙ্কট, অবস্থাহীন see **অবস্থা**।

অবস্থিত *a.* situated, located; residing, living, dwelling; stationed; placed, laid; established. ~চিত্ত *a.* even-minded; composed; self-possessed; unwavering. **অবস্থিতি** *n.* a situation, location; presence; residence, dwelling; state of being stationed or placed or laid or established; position. **অবস্থিতিকাল** *n.* period of stay.

অবহনীয় *a.* that which cannot be carried or borne.

অবহসিত *a.* ridiculed, mocked, laughed at, taunted.

অবহার *n.* theft; armistice; cease-fire; transfer or removal or withdrawal of soldiers from the front to the camp; conversion to another religion, apostasy; (comm.) a discount.

অবহি, অবহুঁ, অবহু *adv.* (obs.) presently, at once, just now; at present, now.

অবহিত *a.* attentive, heedful; entirely occupied, absorbed; careful, watchful, alert; aware. ~চিত্তে *adv.* attentively; absorbedly.

অবহেলা *n.* neglect; disrespect, disregard; slight; heedlessness, inattention. **অবহেলনীয়** *a.* negligible, trifling; worthless; unimportant. **অবহেলা করা** *v.* to neglect; to disrespect, to disregard; to slight; to pay no attention or heed to; to attach no importance to. ~ভরে *adv.* neglectfully; slightingly; carelessly, coldly; heedlessly, inattentively; easily, without effort or strain.

অবহেলিত *a.* neglected; ignored; disregarded, slighted; despised.

অবহেলে *adv.* (poet.) without effort or strain; with ease, easily.

অবাক *a.* stunned or made speechless with amazement, stupefied, dumbfounded; amazed, astonished; amazing, astonishing; stupefying, dumbfounding. ~-জলপান a kind of savoury snack. **অবাক হওয়া** *v.* to wonder, to be struck dumb. **অবাক কাণ্ড** *n.* wonderful or strange event.

অবাক[২] *a.* speechless; mute; silent.

অবাঙ্মুখ *a.* having one's face or head hanging down. *fem.* **অবাঙ্মুখী**।

অবাঙালি *n. & a.* a non-Bengali; contrary to customs or characteristics or practices of the Bengali.

অবাচী *n.* the south; the lower region or part. **অবাচী উষা** aurora australis.

অবাচ্য *a.* unutterable, unspeakable; inexplicable; obscene, indecent. □ *n.* anything unutterable or unspeakable or inexplicable; obscene or indecent words; rude or vulgar speech.

অবাধ *a.* unobstructed, unrestrained, unrestricted; unopposed; unimpeded; uninterrupted; unbridled; free; facile. **অবাধ কল্পনা** unbridled or facile imagination. **অবাধ নীতি** laissez faire. **অবাধ বাণিজ্য** free trade. **অবাধ ভ্রমণ** unrestricted travel; travel as you like. **অবাধে** *adv.* without obstruction or restraint or restriction; without let or hindrance; without opposition or impediment; freely; facilely.

অবাধ্য *a.* (ori.) irresistible, inevitable; obstinantely disobedient, refractory, recalcitrant; untoward, indocile, unruly; unyielding; unmanageable; uncontrollable; turbulent; obstinate, wayward; untamed. **~তা** *n.* disobedience, recalcitrance; untowardness; indocility; obstinacy, waywardness.

অবান্তর *a.* irrelevant, digressing, beside the mark, extraneous; not primary or chief, secondary.

অবান্ধব *a.* having no friends or relations, friendless.

অবায়ুজীবী, অবায়ুভুক *a.* (bot.) anaerobic.

অবার *a.* irresistible; unpreventible; indomitable; unrestrainable; inevitable.

অবারণীয়, অবার্য *a.* irresistible; inevitable; unpreventible.

অবারিত *a.* unresisted, unprevented; unrestrained; unchecked, unrestricted; unbarred; open (অবারিত দ্বার); free (অবারিত ভ্রমণ) **~দ্বার** *n.* open door; free access; unbounded or liberal hospitality.

অবার্ণ *a.* (phys.) achromatic. **~তা** *n.* achromatism.

অবাস্তব, অবাস্তবিক *a.* unreal, immaterial; untrue, false; fanciful (অবাস্তব কল্পনা); unpractical, impracticable (অবাস্তব পরিকল্পনা); non-existent; inexistent; illusory. **~তা** *n.* unreality, immateriality; untrueness, falseness; fancifulness; impracticability; non-existence; inexistence; illusoriness.

অবিকল *a.* (ori.) not defective or crippled; unimpaired, undamaged, undistorted; perfect, whole, complete, entire; exact, precise; resembling in all respects, true to the model (অবিকল চিত্র). □ *adv.* exactly, precisely; faithfully to the model. **অবিকল প্রতিরূপ** *a.* facsimile, a true or exact copy.

অবিকল্প *a.* having no alternative or substitute.

অবিকার *a.* that which or one who is in the natural or original state; unchanged, unaltered; unchanging; undistorted, uncorrupted; unperverted; unmixed; unputrefied; unmoved, unshaken, unperturbed; unwavering; unimpassioned; dispassionate; having no distaste or allergy or apathy towards. □ *n.* such a state.

অবিকৃত *a.* that which is in the natural or original state; unchanged, unaltered; undistorted, uncorrupted, unperverted; unmixed; pure; unputrefied. **অবিকৃতি** *n.* unchanged or unaltered state; freedom from putrefaction.

অবিক্রান্ত *a.* lacking in prowess or valour; weak; cowardly, timid.

অবিক্রীত *a.* unsold, undisposed of.

অবিক্রেয় *a.* unsaleable, unvendible.

অবিক্ষত *a.* unhurt; undamaged; entire, intact, whole.

অবিক্ষিপ্ত *a.* not scattered; not distracted; not restless; composed, calm.

অবিক্ষুব্ধ *a.* unperturbed, unruffled, unagitated; calm, composed, collected.

অবিখ্যাত *a.* not famous; not celebrated.

অবিচক্ষণ *a.* imprudent, unwise; indiscreet. **~তা** *n.* imprudence; indiscretion.

অবিচল, অবিচলিত *a.* unmoved, unshaken; unperturbed; unmoved; stolid, calm; not vacillating, unwavering; faithful, firm (অবিচল ভক্তি). **~কণ্ঠে** *adv.* in an unshaken voice, unfalteringly. **~চিত্তে** *adv.* unperturbedly; unfalteringly; calmly.

অবিচার *n.* injustice; misjudgment; unfair or wrong decision or assessment. **অবিচার করা** *v.* to do injustice; to judge unfairly or incorrectly or with partiality, to misjudge; to assess unfairly or incorrectly or with prejudice. **~ক, অবিচারী** *a.* & *n.* one who does injustice or misjudges or misconceives; one who assesses improperly or incorrectly. **অবিচারে** *adv.* unjustly.

অবিচ্ছিন্ন *a.* unseparated; unsevered, undivided, whole; united; incessant, uninterrupted; continuous; not desultory or discursive. **~তা** *n.* inseparation; inseparability; unsevered or undivided condition; ceaselessness; compactness.

অবিচ্ছেদ *n.* inseparation; inseparability; unity; entirety; no cessation or interruption, ceaselessness; continuity, continuousness. □ *a.* unseparated; inseparable; incessant; uninterrupted;

continuous. অবিচ্ছেদে *adv.* incessantly; uninterruptedly; continually; continuously. অবিচ্ছেদ্য *a.* inseparable; unseverable; undetachable; inalienable.

অবিচ্যুত *a.* undetached; unseparated; unstrayed; undeviated; not violating, conforming to, abiding; firm.

অবিজ্ঞ *a.* unwise, imprudent; inexperienced; foolish. ~তা *n.* lack of wisdom, imprudence; inexperience; foolishness.

অবিজ্ঞাত *a.* unknown; unaware, uninformed; not well-known, obscure.

অবিজ্ঞেয় *a.* unknowable; incognizable.

অবিতথ *a.* true; truthful.

অবিতর্কিত *a.* undebatable, unquestioned, undisputed.

অবিদিত *a.* unknown, unaware, uninformed; not famous or well-known.

অবিদ্যমান *a.* not present, absent; not existing, inexistent. ~তা *n.* absence; inexistence.

অবিদ্বান *a.* not learned; uneducated; ignorant.

অবিদ্যা *n.* ignorance; (phil.) illusion.

অবিধান *n.* an unjust regulation, a black ordinance; an unscriptural direction.

অবিধি *n.* an irregularity; a bad rule; an act or direction contrary to scriptural instructions.

অবিধেয় *a.* not conforming to the rules or scriptures; unjust; improper; inadvisable.

অবিনয় *n.* lack of modesty or politeness or civility; immodesty, discourteousness, incivility; haughtiness, impertinence; impudence. অবিনয়ী *a.* impolite, immodest, discourteous; haughty, impertinent; impudent, cheeky, saucy.

অবিনশ্বর, অবিনাশী *a.* imperishable, indestructible; everlasting, immortal; undecaying; eternal. অবিনশ্বরতা, অবিনাশিতা *n.* indestructibility; imperishableness.

অবিনাশ *a.* not subjected to decay; nondestructible; non-perishable. □ *n.* one who is not subject to decay or destruction.

অবিনীত *a.* impolite; immodest, discourteous, disrespectful; haughty, impertinent; impudent. *fem.* অবিনীতা ।

অবিন্যস্ত *a.* not laid or placed in an orderly manner; in disarray, ill-arranged, disarranged, confused. অবিন্যাস *n.* lack of order; disorder.

অবিবাহিত *a.* unmarried; unwedded. □ *n.* a bachelor. *fem.* অবিবাহিতা *n.* a spinster.

অবিবেক *n.* lack of conscientiousness; indiscretion; unscrupulousness; ignorance. □ *a.* lacking in conscientiousness; unscrupulous; ignorant. অবিবেকিতা *n.* lack of conscientiousness; indiscreetness; unscrupulousness; ignorance. অবিবেকী *a.* lacking in conscientiousness; indiscreet, unscrupulous; ignorant.

অবিবেচক *a.* injudicious; inconsiderate; indiscreet; imprudent; thoughtless.

অবিবেচনা *n.* injudiciousness; inconsiderateness, lack of consideration; indiscretion; imprudence; thoughtlessness. ~প্রসূত *a.* indiscreet; imprudent; unthinking; অবিবেচ্য *a.* not to be considered.

অবিভক্ত *a.* undivided; not partitioned; not separated or severed.

অবিভাজ্য *a.* indivisible. ~তা *n.* indivisibility.

অবিমিশ্র *a.* unmixed; unadulterated; pure.

অবিমুক্ত *a.* not freed; unliberated.

অবিমৃশ্য *a.* indiscreet, injudicious, imprudent; thoughtless, rash; (dero.) undoubting, over-sure. ~কারী *a.* & *n.* one who acts indiscreetly or injudiciously or imprudently or rashly; one who is (indiscreetly) undoubting. ~কারিতা *n.* indiscretion. injudiciousness, imprudence; thoughtlessness.

অবিযুক্ত *a.* not separated or severed; not detached or disconnected.

অবিরত *a.* ceaseless, incessant, unremitting, non-stop; continual; continuous; constant. □ *adv.* ceaselessly, incessantly, unremittingly, without stopping; continually; continuously; constantly; always.

অবিরল *a.* compact, dense; incessant, nonstop; continual; continuous; profuse, adundant. ☐ *adv.* incessantly; continually; continuously; profusely, abundantly. ~**ধারে** *adv.* in a ceaseless or endless stream; incessantly.

অবিরাম *a.* non-stop, ceaseless, incessant, having no respite or pause, unremitting; continuous, continual; remittent (অবিরাম জ্বর). ☐ *adv.* incessantly; without respite or pause, unremittingly; continuously; continually; always.

অবিরুদ্ধ *a.* unopposed; not contrary or hostile or antagonistic; compatible, congruous, conforming, accordant; favourable, friendly.

অবিরোধ *n.* absence of opposition or hostility; accord, agreement, harmony; friendliness, amicability, amity; peace. **অবিরোধী** *a.* unopposed; unopposing; not hostile or antagonistic or contrary; compatible, congruous, conforming, accordant; favourable, friendly; peace-loving; peaceful. **অবিরোধে** *adv.* without opposition or hostility or dispute; in a friendly manner; in peace, peacefully.

অবিলম্ব *n.* absence of delay; promptness, briskness, alacrity, quickness. ☐ *a.* prompt, brisk, quick, immediate. **অবিলম্বিত** *a.* not delayed, undelayed; not deferred; done promptly. **অবিলম্বে** *adv.* without delay; promptly, quickly, in no time; immediately.

অবিশঙ্কিত *a.* not afraid or scared; undaunted; not alarmed.

অবিশুদ্ধ *a.* impure, unclean; unholy; incorrect, erroneous; corrupted; mixed, adulterated, not genuine.

অবিশেষ *n.* absence of distinction or discrimination; uniformity, equality. ☐ *a.* not differentiated or distinguished, indiscriminate; uniform, equal. **অবিশেষে** *adv.* without differentiation, indiscriminately; uniformly, equally.

অবিশ্বস্ত *a.* untrustworthy, unfaithful, unreliable; perfidious. ~**তা** *n.* untrustworthiness, unreliability; perfidiousness; perfidy.

অবিশ্বাস *n.* distrust, mistrust; incredulity; disbelief; want of conviction or faith; no-confidence; suspicion. **অবিশ্বাস করা** *v.* to distrust, to look on with distrust; to disbelieve; to have no faith or confidence in; to treat with suspicion, to suspect. **অবিশ্বাসী** *a.* untrustworthy, unfaithful, unreliable; perfidious; distrustful; incredulous; disbelieving; lacking in conviction or faith; suspicious; (esp. in phil.) sceptical. ☐ *n.* a doubter, a disbeliever; (phil.) a sceptic. *fem.* **অবিশ্বাসিনী**। **অবিশ্বাস্য** *a.* incredible, unbelievable.

অবিশ্বাসযোগ্য *a.* incredible, unbelievable, unworthy of credit, untrustworthy.

অবিশ্যি dial. corrup. of **অবশ্য**[২] ।

অবিশ্রান্ত, অবিশ্রাম *a.* untiring, tireless; incessant, non-stop, unremitting; continuous. ☐ *adv.* untiringly; without rest; incessantly, without break, unremittingly; continuously. **অবিশ্রান্তভাবে** *adv.* same as **অবিশ্রান্ত** (*adv.*).

অবিশ্রুত *a.* not famous or well-known; not much heard of; obscure.

অবিষয়ী *a.* indifferent to secular interests; extra-mundane; not mindful of worldly interests; unpractical.

অবিষহ্য *a.* unbearable; insufferable; intolerable; hard to bear or suffer or tolerate.

অবিসংবাদ *n.* absence of hostility or opposition or dispute; amity; amicability; unanimity, unity. **অবিসংবাদিত** *a.* undisputed, unchallenged; unquestionable; unanimous. **অবিসংবাদিতরূপে** *adv.* undisputedly; unanimously. **অবিসংবাদিত সত্য** undisputed truth; universal truth. **অবিসংবাদী** *a.* not opposing or contrary; indisputable. **অবিসংবাদে** *adv.* unopposedly; without dispute or hostility; amicably; unanimously; peacefully.

অবিস্তীর্ণ *a.* not spacious or wide or extensive; narrow; small.

অবিস্তৃত *a.* not spread out; composed; compact; concise; precise, brief.

অবিস্ময় *n.* absence of astonishment. **অবিস্মিত** *a.* not astonished or surprised, not taken by surprise.

অবিস্মরণীয় *a.* unforgettable; memorable.

অবিস্মৃত *a.* unforgotten.

অবিহিত *a.* unscriptural, unlawful; improper; unjust; inadvisable.

অবীক্ষিত *a.* unseen; unobserved; unnoticed.

অবীজপত্রী *n.* (bot.) acotyledon.

অবীর *a.* destitute of heroism or valour; cowardly; destitute of heroes and heroines (অবীর নগর). *fem.* **অবীরা** । **অবীরোচিত** *a.* not befitting a hero; unheroic.

অবুঝ *a.* inconsolable; not amenable to reason, unreasonable; obstinate; stupid; foolish.

অবৃন্ত, অবৃন্তক *a.* attached directly by the base without stalk, stalkless, sessile.

অবৃষ্টি *n.* scanty rainfall, absence of rain, drought.

অবেক্ষক *a.* one who views or observes or discusses or investigates. ☐ *n.* a viewer, an observer; a reviewer; a judge; an investigator.

অবেক্ষণ, অবেক্ষা *n.* viewing, observation; review, discussion; investigation. **অবেক্ষণীয়** *a.* that which is to be or should be viewed or observed or reviewed or discussed or investigated; observable; discussible; open to investigation.

অবেক্ষমাণ *a.* engaged in viewing or observation or reviewing or judging *fem.* **অবেক্ষমাণা** ।

অবেক্ষা var. of **অবেক্ষণ** । **~ধীন** *a.* on probation, probationary.

অবেক্ষিত *a.* viewed, observed, reviewed, discussed; investigated.

অবেক্ষ্যমাণ *a.* in the process of being viewed or observed or reviewed or discussed or judged or investigated. *fem.* **অবেক্ষ্যমাণা** ।

অবেণীবদ্ধ, অবেণীসংবদ্ধ *a.* unplaited, untressed (অবেণীবদ্ধ কেশ).

অবেদন *n.* anaesthesia. ☐ *a.* pain-killing; lenitive.

অবেদনিক *a.* anaesthetic. ☐ *n.* an anaesthetic.

অবেদনীয়, অবেদ্য *n.* unknowable, incognizable.

অবেলা *n.* unsuitable or inconvenient hour or time; improper hour or time; inauspicious hour or time; late afternoon.

অবৈতনিক *a.* not drawing any pay in lieu of service, unpaid, honorary (অবৈতনিক পদ) ; demanding no fees, free (অবৈতনিক বিদ্যালয় = a free school, a charity school).

অবৈদ্য *n.* an inefficient physician, a quack-doctor.

অবৈধ *a.* unlawful, illegal; unauthorized, *ultra vires*; improper; prohibited; illicit (অবৈধ প্রণয়) ; illegitimate (অবৈধ সন্তান) ; unfair (অবৈধ উপায়). **~তা** *n.* unlawfulness, illegality; lack of authority; scriptural opposition; impropriety; prohibitedness; illicitness; illegitimacy; unfairness.

অবোধ *a.* without the sense of understanding, slow-witted, insensible; dullheaded, stupid, foolish; imprudent; inconsolable (অবোধ হৃদয়).

অবোধগম্য, অবোধ্য *a.* unintelligible, incomprehensible; unknowable, mysterious.

অবোলা *a.* dumb, mute; unable to speak; uncomplaining or innocent (অবোলা জীব).

অব্জ *n.* the lotus.

অব্দ *n.* an era; a year.

অব্ধি *n.* a sea; an ocean.

অব্যক্ত *a.* undisclosed, unexpressed; inexpressible; indistinct; unknown; unknowable; unspeakable; indescribable (অব্যক্ত বেদনা) ; unspoken; (phil.) latent. ☐ *n.* the Absolute Being, God; nature. **~গণিত** *n.* algebra. **~পুষ্পক** *a.* (bot.) cryptogamous, flowerless. ☐ *n.* a cryptogam. **~রাশি** *n.* unknown quantity.

অব্যক্তিক *a.* impersonal.

অব্যগ্র *a.* not eager, not ardent or enthusiastic.

অব্যবধান *n.* absence of intervening space or time, absence of interval; contiguity, immediacy; adjacency; compactness. **অব্যবধানে** *adv.* not away from.

অব্যবসায় *n.* lack of practice or training; lack of enterprise; incompetence. **অব্যবসায়ী** *a.* lacking knack in business enterprise; unpractical, unbusinesslike; not having any practice or training; unenterprising; inexperienced; incompetent.

অব্যবস্থ *a.* disordered; disorderly; lacking in arrangement; lacking in composure or decision; unsteady, fickle, hesitant.

অব্যবস্থা *n.* disorder; want of arrangement; mismanagement.

অব্যবস্থিত *a.* lacking in decision; unsteady, wavering; changeable, unsettled or unprincipled in action. **~চিত্ত** *a.* fickle-minded. **~চিত্ততা** *n.* fickle-mindedness.

অব্যবহার *n.* non-use; non-application; disuse, desuetude.

অব্যবহার্য *a.* not fit to be used; out of order; useless; inapplicable; out of use; unused; unuseful; unserviceable. **~তা** *n.* uselessness.

অব্যবহিত *a.* contiguous; adjoining, anjacent; immediate; next. **অব্যবহিত পরে** immediately afterwards. **অব্যবহিত পূর্বে** *adv.* immediately before, just before.

অব্যবহৃত *a.* unused, fallen out of use, fallen into desuetude or disuse.

অব্যভিচার *n.* absence of laxity or straying; absence of depravity; absence of exception; absence of change; constancy, steadiness. **অব্যভিচারী** *a.* not lax or straying; undepraved; without exception; unchanging; constant, steady.

অব্যয় *a.* not expendable; inexhaustible; undecaying; imperishable; immortal; changeless, unchanging. ☐ *n.* the Absolute Being, God; (gr.) an indeclinable word (i. e. a preposition, conjunction or interjection). **অব্যয়ীভাব** *n.* (gr.) a system of forming a compound word by adding a noun to an indeclinable word.

অব্যর্থ *a.* unfailing, sure to succeed, infallible. **~তা** *n.* unfailingness, infailibility. **~লক্ষ্য** *n.* sure aim, unfailing marksmanship. **~সন্ধান** *a.* surefire, sharp-shooting. ☐ *n.* good or unfailing marksmanship; a sure aim. **~সন্ধানী** *a.* sharp-shooting. ☐ *n.* a sharp-shooter, an unfailing marksman, a dead shot.

অব্যাকুল *a.* unperturbed; unworried, not stricken with anxiety; not anxious or eager; calm, composed, cool and collected. **~তা** *n.* absence of worry or anxiety or eagerness; calmness, composure.

অব্যাখ্যাত *a.* unexplained.

অব্যাজে *adv.* not hypocritically, sincerely; immediately, without delay, at once.

অব্যাপক *a.* not extensive, inextensive.

অব্যাপকতা *n.* absence of extensiveness or extensive circulation; inextension.

অব্যাপার *n.* a useless work; an uncalled-for piece of business.

অব্যাপ্ত *a.* not spread or pervaded or diffused or circulated extensively; inextended. **অব্যাপ্তি** *n.* state of not being spread or pervaded or diffused or circulated extensively; inextension.

অব্যাহত *a.* unhindered, undeterred, unimpeded; uninterrupted; unfrustrated; unprevented, unopposed; unfailing; unimpaired. **~গতি** *a.* one who or that which moves without hindrance or impediment or interruption or frustration or prevention or opposition.

অব্যাহতি *n.* escape; exemption; release; acquittal, absolution; relief. **অব্যাহতি দেওয়া** *v.* to exempt; to release; to acquit; to relieve. **অব্যাহতি পাওয়া** *v.* to escape; to be exempted; to be released or acquitted or relieved.

অব্যুৎপন্ন *a.* not erudite; not versed or adept in; incompetent, inefficient; not properly or correctly derived; not derived from.

অব্যূঢ় *a.* unmarried. *fem.* **অব্যূঢ়া** ।

অব্রাহ্মণ *n.* a non-Brahman; a degenerated Brahman; (rare) a non-Brahman endowed with the qualities of a Brahman. ☐ *a.* destitute of the qualities or status of a Brahman; non-Brahman.

অভক্ত *a.* not devoted; irreverent; having no faith or confidence; not having a liking or fondness or attachment for.

অভক্তি *n.* absence of devotion; irreverence; want of faith or confidence; distaste; apathy; abhorrence.

অভক্ষিত *a.* uneaten.

অভক্ষ্য, অভক্ষণীয় *a.* unfit or prohibited to be eaten; inedible, uneatable; unfit for human consumption.

অভক্ষ্যভক্ষণ *n.* eating or consumption of forbidden food.

অভগ্ন *a.* not broken, unbroken; unsevered;

whole. ~রাশি (arith.) a whole number, an integer.

অভঙ্গ *a.* unsevered, undivided; uninterrupted; united.

অভঙ্গুর *a.* not brittle or breakable, unbreakable, infrangible; not subject to decay or destruction.

অভদ্র *a.* discourteous, uncivil; ungentlemanly; unmannerly. **~জনোচিত, অভদ্রোচিত** *a.* ungentlemanly; unmannerly. **~তা** *n.* discourtesy, incivility; ungentlemanliness; unmannerliness.

অভদ্রা *n.* (dial.) hindrance or an ill omen.

অভব্য *a.* unmannerly, ill-mannered; unpolished, unrefined, rude; discourteous; vulgar. **~তা** *n.* unmannerliness; lack of polish, rudeness; discourtesy; vulgarity; slanginess.

অভয় *n.* fearlessness; courage; assurance that no harm shall be done. ☐ *a.* fearless, dauntless; courageous; that which removes fear. **অভয় দেওয়া** *v.* to assure that no harm shall come. **~বাক্য, ~বাণী** *n.* assurance or pledge of safety or security. **অভয়া** *n. fem.* an appellation of Goddess Durga (দুর্গা).

অভয়ারণ্য *n.* a sanctuary, esp. for birds and animals.

অভাগা *a.* luckless, unlucky, unfortunate; pitiable. ☐ *n.* a luckless or unlucky person. *fem.* **অভাগী, অভাগিনী** ।

অভাগ্য *a.* luckless, unlucky, unfortunate. ☐ *n.* a luckless person; ill luck.

অভাজন *n.* an unworthy person; an unfit or incompetent or worthless person; a distressed or destitute person; a wretch.

অভাব *n.* non-existence, absence; want, lack; need; dearth, shortage, scarcity; financial want; indigence; deficiency; deficit. **~গ্রস্ত** *a.* stricken with want, needy; indigent; poverty-stricken, destitute. **~পূরণ** *n.* meeting or supplying wants or needs; making up for deficiency or deficit. **~মুক্ত** *a.* relieved of want or poverty. **অভাব মেটানো** *n. v.* removing or to remove want. **~মোচন** *n.* removal of want or need or poverty; making up for deficiency or deficit. **~মোচন করা** *v.* to remove a want or wants or a need or needs; to make up for deficiency or deficit; to free from poverty or indigence. **অভাবে স্বভাব নষ্ট** want is at the root of corruption, (cp) necessity knows no law.

অভাবগ্রস্ত see **অভাব** ।

অভাবনীয়, অভাব্য *a.* incapable of being thought of beforehand; incapable of being anticipated or expected; unthinkable, unimaginable, inconceivable; unexpected; amazingly novel.

অভাবপূরণ, অভাবমুক্ত, অভাবমোচন see **অভাব** ।

অভাবিত, অভাবিতপূর্ব *a.* unthought of (before); not anticipated, unforeseen; unexpected; unpremeditated.

অভাবী *a.* needy; indigent, poor.

অভাব্য var. of **অভাবনীয়** ।

অভি *pfx.* denoting : front, approach, proximity, onward direction, spaciousness, ambi-, circum-, peri-, pro-, towards, to-.

অভিকর *n.* a municipal rate or tax.

অভিকর্ষ *n.* (mech.) gravitational attraction, gravity.

অভিকেন্দ্র *a.* (mech.) centripetal. **অভিকেন্দ্র বল** centripetal force.

অভিক্রমণ *n.* going forwards or setting out (esp. to face an enemy); an expedition; an attack; ascension.

অভিক্রিয়া *n.* an experiment; an analysis.

অভিক্ষিপ্ত *a.* projected.

অভিক্ষেপ, অভিক্ষেপণ *n.* a projection (শাঙ্কব অভিক্ষেপ = a conical projection). **~তল** *n.* a plane or projection. **অভিক্ষেপাক্ষ** *n.* axis of projection.

অভিগ *a.* (math.) positive.

অভিগত *a.* gone towards or forward or near; one who or that which has approached; one who or that which has approached for the purpose of sexual intercourse; one who or that which has had sexual intercourse with; obtained, earned; one who or that which has found a shelter or refuge in, sheltered.

অভিগম, অভিগমন *n.* going towards or forward or near; approaching, accession; approach; approaching for the purpose of sexual intercourse; sexual intercourse; going forward (after leaving one's seat) to receive a visitor; obtainment, receipt; approaching for shelter or refuge; a shelter or refuge. **অভিগমন করা** *v.* to go towards or forward or near; to approach; to approach for the purpose of sexual intercourse; to have sexual intercourse with; to (leave one's seat and) go forward to receive a visitor; to approach for shelters or refuge; to take shelter or refuge in. **অভিগম্য** *a.* approachable for the purpose of taking shelter or refuge in; accessible, approachable. **অভিগম্যতা** *n.* accessibility.

অভিগামী *a.* one who or that which is going towards or forward or near. *fem.* **অভিগামিনী** ।

অভিগ্রস্ত *a.* attacked; seized; swallowed; plundered, looted.

অভিগ্রহ, অভিগ্রহণ *n.* an attack; going forward for the purpose of fighting; an onset; an expedition; a challenge to a fight or a duel; plunder, loot, sack.

অভিঘাত *n.* a stroke, a blow, a hit, a hitting or striking back, a return blow; (gr.) a mark of emphasis on words. **অভিঘাতী** *a.* one who or that which strikes or hits or kills. □ *n.* a striker, an assailant; a killer; an enemy, an adversary, an antagonist.

অভিচার *n.* rites performed according to the prescriptions of the Tantra in order to harm others; incantation, black art. **অভিচারী** *a.* one who performs these rites.

অভিজন *n.* aristocracy; (rare) a family; a high or noble family.

অভিজাত *a.* high-born, of noble birth; aristocrat; learned; wise; gentlemanly, mannerly; aristocratic. **~তন্ত্র** *n.* government by the aristocracy. **অভিজাত সম্প্রদায়** *n.* the aristocratic class, the aristocracy.

অভিজিৎ *n.* (astr.) the star Vega.

অভিজ্ঞ *a.* (vastly) experienced, veteran; seasoned; specialized, expert, *au fait*, well versed (in); wise. **অভিজ্ঞতা** *n.* (vast) experience; specialized or expert knowledge; wisdom.

অভিজ্ঞা *n.* final knowledge, profound knowledge.

অভিজ্ঞাত *a.* known by sign or mark or investigation; identified.

অভিজ্ঞান *n.* an identifying token; a keepsake. **~পত্র** *n.* an identity card; a letter of introduction.

অভিতপ্ত *a.* burnt in fire; mortified; afflicted.

অভিতাপ *n.* intense heat; affliction, sorrow.

অভিধা *n.* an appellation, a name; a title; (gr.) the primary meaning of a word; (log.) the denotation of a word. **~বৃত্তি** *n.* the primary meaning or property of a word.

অভিধান *n.* a dictionary, a lexicon. **~কার** *n.* the compiler of a dictionary, a lexicographer.

অভিধেয় *a.* one who or that which is to be named as; appellative; naming; (log.) denotative. □ *n.* an appellation, a name, a title; (gr.) the primary meaning of a word; (log.) the denotation of a word; the meaning (of a word) to be established or proved or verified.

অভিনন্দন *n.* felicitation, congratulation; expression of happiness by eulogy; felicitous eulogy; a welcome. **অভিনন্দন জানানো** *v.* to felicitate, to congratulate; to welcome. **~পত্র** *n.* a letter of congratulatory or welcome address, an address.

অভিনন্দিত *a.* congratulated; felicitated; acclaimed; welcomed; honoured; received with honour. **অভিনন্দিত করা** *v.* to acclaim, to felicitate, to congratulate.

অভিনব *a.* new and strange, novel; unprecedented; new and amazing; new-fashioned, new-fangled. **~ত্ব** *n.* novelty.

অভিনয় *n.* a dramatic performance; acting of the role of a dramatic character; simulation, feigning, affectation. **অভিনয় করা** *v.* to play one's part; to feign or simulate.

অভিনিবিষ্ট *a.* intently attentive, intent, absorbed, deeply engrossed. *fem.* **অভিনিবিষ্টা** ।

অভিনিবেশ *n.* close attention; diligent application of mind (to), intentness; absorption. **~সহকারে** *adv.* attentively; with close or rapt attention, intently, absorbedly.

অভিনীত *a.* (of a drama or dramatic role) played, acted, enacted; performed (on the stage), staged.

অভিনেতা *n.* (in a film or drama) an actor.

অভিনেতৃ *a.* & *n.* one who acts or plays.

অভিনেত্রী *fem.* of **অভিনেতৃ**। □ *n. fem.* an actress.

অভিনেয় *a.* that which is to be or can be acted or played; worthy of being played or acted, fit to be staged.

অভিন্ন *a.* not separate or different or dissimilar; identical, one and the same, one and undivided, same; not detached or severed; uniform; similar. **অভিন্ন পরিবার** same as **যৌথ পরিবার**। **অভিন্নতা** *n.* identicalness, sameness; wholeness, entirety; uniformity; similarity. **~হৃদয়** *a.* (of two persons) inseparably united (in feeling, thought etc.); intimate. **~হৃদয় বন্ধু** a very close and dear friend; a bosom friend.

অভিপন্ন *a.* fallen in danger, faced with hazard; one who has come for refuge or shelter.

অভিপ্রায় *n.* desire; intention, design, purpose, object, aim; significance, purport, meaning; opinion.

অভিপ্রেত *a.* desired; intended, designed, aimed; signified, purported, meant; approved.

অভিবন্দনা *n.* welcome and worship, adoration ('চিরসুন্দরের অভিবন্দনা').

অভিবাদক *a.* one who greets or salutes or courtesies or makes obeisance. *fem.* **অভিবাদিকা**।

অভিবাদন *n.* salutation, greeting, courtesy, obeisance, a bow. **অভিবাদন করা** *v.* to salute, to curtsey, to do obeisance to, to bow.

অভিবাদ্য *a.* one who or that which is to be or should be saluted or greeted or paid obeisance; venerable.

অভিবাসন *n.* immigration.

অভিবাসী *a.* immigrant. □ *n.* an immigrant.

অভিব্যক্ত *a.* thoroughly manifested or expressed or developed; evolved. **অভিব্যক্ত করা** *v.* to manifest or express or develop thoroughly; to evolve.

অভিব্যক্তি *n.* thorough manifestation or expression or development; gradual manifestation or development, evolution. **~বাদ** *n.* the theory of evolution.

অভিব্যাপ্ত *a.* thoroughly extended or scattered; spread or scattered all over; diffused. **অভিব্যাপ্ত হওয়া** *v.* to extend or be scattered or be spread thoroughly or all over; to be diffused.

অভিব্যাপ্তি *n.* state of being extended or scattered or spread thoroughly or all over; diffusion.

অভিভব, অভিভাব *n.* (thorough) defeat; disgrace, dishonour, insult; ecstatic trance, ecstasy, transport; embarrassment, the confused state of the mind, bewilderment.

অভিভাবক *n.* a guardian; a custodian; a caretaker, a curator; a superintendent; a trustee; a regent; one who gives shelter or refuge. *fem.* **অভিভাবিকা**। **~তা, ~ত্ব** *n.* guardianship; custody, care, superintendence; trusteeship; regency; protectorate. **অভিভাবকতা করা** *v.* to be the guardian or custodian or caretaker or curator or trustee or regent of; to look after, to superintend; to protect.

অভিভাষণ *n.* a public speech or a platform speech, an address.

অভিভূত *a.* (thoroughly) overcome with emotion; stricken; begone (দুঃখাভিভূত = woe-begone); embarrassed, nonplussed, bewildered. **অভিভূত করা** *v.* to defeat or overcome (thoroughly), to trounce; to attack, to beset, to overwhelm; to embarrass, to bewilder.

অভিমত *n.* desire; choice; intention; opinion. □ *a.* approved; nominated, chosen; intended. **অভিমত দেওয়া** *v.* to pronounce or pass an opinion, to desire or choose.

অভিমন্থ *n.* ophthalmia.

অভিমান *n.* pride, vanity; self-respect, self-esteem, dignity, amour propre; egotism; huff; tiff; state of one's feeling being hurt; offended state of mind; sensitiveness. **অভিমানী** *a.* proud; vain;

(excessively) self-respecting, self-conceited; dignified, exalted, noble; egotistic; one whose feelings are hurt, offended; in a huff; sensitive; (loos.) maudlin; touchy, thin-skinned, easily stung. ☐ *n.* such a person. *fem.* **অভিমানিনী।**

অভিমুখ *n.* the direction leading to, approach (গৃহাভিমুখ). ☐ *a.* facing; moving towards; bound for. *fem.* **অভিমুখী।** **অভিমুখীন** *a.* var. of **অভিমুখ**(*a.*). **অভিমুখে** *adv.* in the direction of, towards, to.

অভিযাচন *n.* a prayer for grant of something; a request; solicitation.

অভিযাচিত *a.* prayed for; requested; solicited.

অভিযাত্রা *n.* expedition.

অভিযাত্রী *n.* & *a.* adventurer, one who sets out on an expedition or an adventuresome exploration. **অভিযাত্রিক** *a.* expeditionary. ☐ *n.* & *a.* (loos.) var.of **অভিযাত্রী।**

অভিযান *n.* an expedition; (setting out on) an adventuresome exploration.

অভিযুক্ত *a.* accused; charged; prosecuted in a (civil or criminal) law-suit. **অভিযুক্ত করা** *v.* to accuse; to charge; to bring an action against, to prosecute before a court.

অভিযোক্তা *n.* an accuser; a complainant; a plaintiff. ☐ *a.* accusing or pursuing by law. *fem.* **অভিযোক্ত্রী।**

অভিযোগ *n.* accusation, charge; a complaint; allegation, imputation; legal prosecution. **অভিযোগ করা** *v.* to complain, to lodge a complaint; to bring a charge, to accuse; to prosecute in a court of law, to bring an action; to allege. **~কারী** *n.* & *a.* var. of **অভিযোক্তা।** *fem.* **~কারিণী।** **অভিযোগ্য** *a.* actionable. **~পত্র** *n.* a charge-sheet.

অভিযোজন *n.* adaptation. **অভিযোজন করা** *v.* to adapt. **অভিযোজিত** *a.* adapted. **অভিযোজ্য** *a.* adaptable. **অভিযোজ্যতা** *n.* adaptability.

অভিরত *a.* excessively attached or addicted (to); very fond of; **অভিরত থাকা বা হওয়া** *v.* to be excessively attached or addicted (to); to be very fond (of);

অভিরতি *n.* excessive attachment or addiction; over-fondness.

অভিরাম *a.* pleasing, pleasant; beautiful, handsome; entertaining, gratifying (নয়নাভিরাম).

অভিরুচি *n.* desire, liking, pleasure; wish; (arch.) purpose, intention, design. **তোমার যেমন অভিরুচি (হয়)** as you please.

অভিরূপ *a.* similar, like; pleasing, pleasant; dear, beloved.

অভিলক্ষ্য *a.*(phys.) objective.

অভিলম্ব *a.* (phys.) normal.

অভিলষণীয় *a.* desirable, covetable.

অভিলষিত *a.* desired; wished for; intended; coveted.

অভিলাষ *n.* desire; wish; pleasure, intention. **অভিলাষ করা** *v.* to desire, to wish (for); to intend. **অভিলাষী** *a.* desirous; wishful; intending; covetous. *fem.* **অভিলাষিণী।** **অভিলাষী হওয়া** to be desirous of; to wish (for); to intend; to covet.

অভিশংসক *n.* a public prosecutor.

অভিশংসন *n.* impeachment.

অভিশঙ্কা *n.* apprehension, fear; doubt. **অভিশঙ্কী** *a.* apprehending, apprehensive, fearful; doubting, doubtful.

অভিশপ্ত *a.* subjected to a curse, accursed, cursed; doomed.

অভিশাপ *n.* a curse, malediction, imprecation. **অভিশাপ দেওয়া** *v.* to curse, to imprecate.

অভিশ্রুতি *n.* (phon.) vowel-change, vowel-mutation, umlaut.

অভিষঙ্গ *n.* embrace; attachment; envy; calumny, scandal, disparagement, vilification, defamation; misfortune, disaster; grief.

অভিষব, অভিষবণ *n.* distillation (of wine etc.); bathing; ablution (after a sacrificial rite).

অভিষিক্ত *a.* one (usu. a king, queen, bridegroom, bride, idol, convert etc.) whose person has been washed as a part of a ceremonial; installed; immersed, bathed; appointed, employed, initiated.

অভিষেক *n.* ceremonial washing of the person of a king, queen, bridegroom, bride, idol, convert etc. on the eve of their installation or initiation, ablution;

installation; act of bathing, bath; appointment; induction, employment, initiation; enthronement, coronation. **অভিষেক করা** *v.* to wash ceremonially; to install; to immerse, to bathe; to appoint, to induct, to employ, to initiate; to enthrone. **অভিষেকোৎসব** *n.* the ceremony of crowning, coronation.

অভিষেচন *n.* drenching; ablution, ceremonial washing; immersion, bathing.

অভিষ্যন্দ alt. spell. of **অভিস্যন্দ**।

অভিসন্তপ্ত *a.* stricken with remorse, mortified.

অভিসন্তাপ *n.* mortification, remorse.

অভিসন্ধান, অভিসন্ধি *n.* (chiefly evil) intention, purpose, motive, design.

অভিসম্পাত *n.* a curse, imprecation, malediction. **অভিসম্পাত দেওয়া** *v.* to curse, to imprecate.

অভিসরণ *n.* act of following; a lover's journey to the place of assignation or to the trysting place.

অভিসার *n.* lover's appointed meeting, a love tryst. **অভিসারক, অভিসারী** *a.* (of a lover) going to assignation; convergent. ☐ *n.* a lover going to the place of assignation. *fem.* **অভিসারিকা, অভিসারিণী**।

অভিসৃতি *n.* convergence.

অভিস্যন্দ *n.* exudation, oozing; flow, stream (as of water); abundance, excess, overgrowth. **অভিস্যন্দী** *a.* exuding, oozing; flowing, streaming, running; (of eyes) weeping; overgrown.

অভিস্রবণ *n.* osmosis.

অভিহত *a.* struck, hurt, wounded; driven back, driven away, warded off; defeated, beaten, perished, ruined.

অভিহিত *a.* named, called; entitled; mentioned, referred to. **অভিহিত মূল্য** face value.

অভী, অভীক[1] *a.* fearless, dauntless; brave.

অভীক[2] *a.* lustful; greedy.

অভীক্ষণ *n.* (chem.) testing, a test.

অভীক্ষা *n.* a test.

অভীপ্সা *n.* earnest desire, longing (for); aspiration.

অভীপ্সিত *a.* earnestly desired, longed for; aspired to.

অভীপ্সু *a.* earnestly desirous, longing for. ☐ *n.* an aspirant.

অভীষ্ট *a.* desired, wished for, longed for, cherished; aimed at, intended. ☐ *n.* a desired object; an objective; an intention, a purpose. **~পূরণ** *n.* gratification or fulfilment of one's desire; attainment of one's objective, the accomplishment of (one's) aims. **~প্রদ** *a.* that which gratifies or fulfils. **~লাভ, ~সিদ্ধি** *n.* same as **অভীষ্টপূরণ**।

অভুক্ত *a.* that which has not been eaten, uneaten, unconsumed, untasted; one who has not eaten, unfed, fasting. **অভুক্ত থাকা** *v.* to go without food, to remain unfed, to abstain from eating, to keep fasting.

অভূত *a.* that which or one who has not (ever) come into being, unborn, never born; that which has not happened; (of time) not gone by or passed. **~পূর্ব** *a.* unprecedented; novel.

অভেদ *n.* absence of difference or distinction or dissimilarity or discrimination; identity, oneness; similarity; unity. ☐ *a.* identical; similar, like. **অভেদাত্মা** *a.* (of two persons) inseparably united, intimate. **অভেদী** *a.* making up discrimination; one who or that which accepts philosophical identity. **অভেদ্য** *a.* undetachable, inseparable; impenetrable; impervious; impregnable. **অভেদ্যতা** *n.* impenetrability; imperviousness.

অভোক্তব্য *a.* not eatable; unfit for consumption, inedible.

অভোক্তা *n.* an abstemious or temperate eater.

অভোগ্য *a.* that which or one who cannot be or should not be enjoyed or used. *fem.* **অভোগ্যা**।

অভোজ্য *a.* that which cannot be or should not be eaten; uneatable, inedible.

অভ্যগ্র *a.* impending; near; new.

অভ্যঙ্গ, অভ্যঞ্জন *n.* rubbing the body with oil or any oily substance, unction; applying collyrium to the eyelashes. **অভ্যঙ্গস্নান** *n.* bathing after having one's body rubbed with oil or any oily substance.

অভ্যন্তর *n.* the inside, the interior. **অভ্যন্তরীণ** *a.* internal. **অভ্যন্তরে** *adv.* within; inside; into, in.

অভ্যর্থন, অভ্যর্থনা *n.* greeting or hailing; a greeting, a hail; welcome, reception. **অভ্যর্থনা সভা, অভ্যর্থনা সমিতি** *n.* a reception committee.

অভ্যর্থিত *a.* greeted, hailed; one who or that which has been accorded a reception or welcome; received cordially.

অভ্যর্হিত *a.* received with honour; honoured; adored; worshipped.

অভ্যস্ত *a.* practised, regularly studied; accustomed, wont; used to; habituated; familiar; acclimatized.

অভ্যাগত, অভ্যাগতজন *n.* a guest; a visitor, a caller. **অভ্যাগতসমাগম** *n.* arrival or assemblage or gathering of guests or visitors.

অভ্যাগম, অভ্যাগমন *n.* approach; presence; arrival; coming; calling on or at, a visit; advent.

অভ্যাস *n.* practice regular study or exercise; habit; accustoming, acclimatization. **~গত** *a.* habitual. **অভ্যাসাধীন** *a.* (to be) mastered by constant practice. **অভ্যাসী** *a.* & *n.* one who practises or studies or learns regularly. *fem.* **অভ্যাসিনী**।

অভ্যাহার *n.* robbing, plundering, snatching; robbery; attack; eating.

অভ্যুত্থান *n.* getting up from sitting or recumbent position; thriving or prospering or flourishing; coming into prominence or power; rise; insurgence, a revolt. **অভ্যুত্থান করা বা ঘটানো** *v.* to get up; to thrive, to prosper, to flourish; to come into prominence or power; to rise; to rise in revolt, to revolt.

অভ্যুত্থিত *a.* risen from sitting or recumbent position; prosperous, flourishing; one who or that which has come into prominence or power; eminent; insurgent.

অভ্যুদয় *n.* rise; coming into prominence or power; thriving or prospering or flourishing; prosperity; (sudden) appearance, advent.

অভ্যুদাহরণ *n.* a counter-instance or counter-example; a counter; a counter-evidence.

অভ্যুদিত *a.* risen; one who or that which has come into prominence or power; prosperous, flourishing; one who or that which has appeared or surfaced (suddenly). **অভ্যুদিত হওয়া** *v.* to rise; to come into prominence or power; to thrive, to prosper, to flourish; to appear (suddenly).

অভ্যুপগত *a.* approached, come near; pledged, committed.

অভ্যুপেত *a.* promised; attained, acquired, earned.

অভ্র *n.* cloud; the sky; mica. **অভ্রংলিহ** *a.* sky-kissing, cloud-kissing; skyhigh; very lofty, towering. **অভ্রংলিহ অট্টালিকা** a sky-scraper. **~ভেদী** *a.* shooting through the sky; piercing the clouds; very lofty, soaring, towering.

অভ্রক *n.* talc; mica; the sky.

অভ্রাতৃক *a.* brotherless.

অভ্রান্ত *a.* not incorrect, correct, right; unerring; unfailing (অভ্রান্ত লক্ষ্য) ; infallible.

অভ্রান্তচিত্তে *adv.* confidently; unmistakeably, unerringly.

অমঙ্গল *n.* absence of welfare or well-being, evil; harm, danger, misfortune. **~চিহ্ন** *n.* an evil omen. **~কর, ~জনক, ~সূচক, অমঙ্গল্য** *a.* boding ill (for), sinister, ominous.

অমত *n.* absence of approval or consent; disapproval. **অমতে** *adv.* without approval or consent; against one's approval or consent.

অমৎসর *a.* not stricken with envy or malice; unenvious.

অমত্ত *a.* not drunk, not intoxicated about, not beside oneself.

অমন *a.* & *adv.* like that, such. **~ই** *a.* & *adv.* just like that, just so.

অমনি *a.* like that, such (অমনি রূপ) ; causeless, unwarranted (অমনি কাঁদে). □ *adv.* like that, such, so; without cause, unwarrantedly, for nothing; without employment, vacantly; empty-handed(ly); without covering; without accompaniment, condiment, support etc.; without price or payment, gratis; without effort; instantly, at once, just. **অমনি অমনি** *adv.* without cause; without guilt or offence; for nothing. **অমনি একরকম** fairly good or well, middling, so so.

অমনুষ্য *a.* (of a human being) devoid of human qualities; inhuman; unworthy of being called a human being; good-for-nothing. ☐ *n.* such a man. **~ত্ব** *v.* lack of human qualities; inhumanity; unmanliness; worthlessness.

অমনোনয়ন *n.* refusal to nominate or select or choose; non-acceptance; rejection; disapproval.

অমনোনীত *a.* not nominated or selected or chosen; unaccepted; rejected; disapproved. **অমনোনীত করা** *v.* to refuse to nominate or select or choose; to reject; to disapprove.

অমনোযোগ *n.* inattention; unmindfulness, inadvertence; heedlessness, carelessness; neglect; negligence; indifference. **অমনোযোগী** *a.* inattentive; unmindful, inadvertent; heedless, careless; negligent; indifferent. **অমনোযোগী হওয়া** *v.* to pay no attention (to); to take no heed (of); to take no care of; to neglect; to treat with indifference; to be inattentive or unmindful or inadvertent or heedless or negligent or indifferent.

অমন্থর *a.* not slow; speedy, quick.

অমন্দ *a.* not bad; not slow or gently moving.

অমর *a.* immortal, undying, deathless; imperishable, undecaying, eternal; celestial, heavenly (অমর জীবন). ☐ *n.* a god; a celestial or heavenly or divine being; a deathless creature. **~তরু** *n.* a celestial tree; an imperishable tree. **~তা, ~ত্ব** *n.* immmortality; immortalization; imperishability; divinity, godhead. **~ধাম, ~পুরী** *n.* the abode of gods, heaven. **~লোক** *n.* same as **অমরধাম**। **অমর হওয়া, অমরতা লাভ করা** *v.* to become immortal; to be everlasting; to be blessed with immortal or celestial life.

অমরা[১] *n.* the placenta.

অমরা[২] *n.* the abode of gods, heaven; realm of Indra (ইন্দ্র) the king of gods.

অমরাত্মা *a.* endowed with immortal soul; celestial, divine.

অমরাধিপ, অমরাধীশ *n.* Indra (ইন্দ্র) the king of gods.

অমরাবতী, অমরাপুরী, অমরালয় *n.* same as **অমরা[২]**।

অমরাবিন্যাস *n.* placentation.

অমরেশ, অমরেশ্বর *n.* same as **অমরাধিপ**।

অমর্ত্য *a.* unearthly; extra-mundane; heavenly, celestial, divine. ☐ *n.* an immortal being; a god. **~লোক** *n.* the abode of gods, heaven.

অমর্দিত *a.* not trampled, untrodden; not thrashed, unmolested.

অমর্যাদা *n.* lack of cordial treatment; neglect; disrespect; indignity, disgrace; slight; non-observance, violation (শর্তের অমর্যাদা). **অমর্যাদা করা** *v.* not to accord cordial treatment; to neglect; to show disrespect (to); to cause indignity (to); to slight; to violate.

অমর্ষ, অমর্ষণ *n.* anger; lack of forgiveness or mercy; intolerance. ☐ *a.* angry; wrathful; irritable; unforgiving, merciless; inclement; intolerant, impatient. **অমর্ষপরায়ণ** *a.* same as **অমর্ষ** (*a.*). **অমর্ষিত, অমর্ষী** *a.*angered; angry, wrathful; irascible; merciless.

অমল *a.* free from dirt or stain; clear; unblemished.

অমলক same as **আমলকি**।

অমলধবল *a.* exquisitely white, impeccably white, flawlessly white; (cp.) milk-white, snow-white.

অমলা *fem.* of **অমল**।

অমলিন *a.* free from dirt, untarnished, unstained; free from gloom; undecayed or undecaying (অমলিন খ্যাতি) ; unblemished; unfaded or unfading, (cp.) amaranthine (অমলিন পুষ্প).

অমসৃণ *a.* unsmooth, uneven, rough; (fig.) not easy-going, full of difficulties and hazards, full of ups and downs. **~তা** *n.* absence of smoothness, unevenness, roughness.

অমা same as **অমাবস্যা**।

অমাংসল *a.* not fleshy.

অমাতৃক *a.* motherless.

অমাত্য *n.* a minister; a cabinet minister; a councillor of the state; a high government official; (loos.) a courtier. **~বর্গ** *n.* the body of ministers or officials; the cabinet; (loos.) the body of courtiers.

অমাননা *n.* disrespect, neglect; non-observance, disregard, violation, infringement; non-acceptance, disobedience.

অমানব *a.* (of a place, house etc.) not inhabited or frequented by human beings, uninhabited, depopulated, deserted; (of a creature) not human, superhuman, sub-human, non-human, inhuman; (of a human being) unworthly of being regarded as a human being.

অমানিশা *n.* the night of the new moon.

অমানুষ *a.* superhuman; (of a human being) deprived of humanity, inhuman, beastly. ☐ *n.* an inhuman or beastly human being, a brute; a base fellow. **অমানুষিক** *a.* not expected of a human being, superhuman (অমানুষিক শক্তি বা প্রচেষ্টা) ; inhuman, brutal (অমানুষিক অত্যাচার).

অমান্য *a.* not warranting respect or obedience. **অমান্য করা** *v.* to refuse to treat with respect or honour, to disregard, to neglect; to deny to accept or comply with, to disobey, to violate. **~কারী** *a.* disobeying, disrespecting; violating. ☐ *n.* one who disobeys or violates.

অমাবস্যা *n.* the new moon.

অমায়িক *a.* candid, open-hearted, frank, ingenuous, guileless; affectionate, loving; unpretentious, unassuming, modest; polite, courteous, genial, amiable. **~তা** *n.* candour, open-heartedness, frankness, modesty; ingenuousness; affectionateness; politeness, geniality, amiability; bonhomie.

অমার্জনীয় *a.* unpardonable, unforgivable.

অমার্জিত *a.* unpolished, unrefined; uncouth; crude; rough, coarse; impolite, uncivil, indecorous, vulgar, unmannerly.

অমিত *a.* unmeasured; immeasurable; unlimited, boundless; excessive, too much, immense; intemperate, immoderate. **~তেজা** *a.* immensely spirited or powerful. **~বল** *a.* immensely powerful. **~ব্যয়** *n.* extravagance, wasteful expenditure. **~ব্যয়িতা** *n.* extravagance, prodigality. **~ব্যয়ী** *a.* extravagant, prodigal, lavish in expenditure. **~ব্যয়ী লোক** *n.* spendthrift. **~ভাষী** *a.* excessively talkative or garrulous; unrestrained in speech, free-spoken. **~ভোজন** *n.* intemperance in eating, overeating; surfeit. **~ভোজী** *a.* given to excessive or intemperate eating; garrulous. ☐ *n.* a glutton, a guzzler, a gourmand.

অমিতাচার *n.* intemperance in food, drink, practice and conduct. **অমিতাচারী** *a.* intemperate, immoderate, over-indulgent.

অমিতাভ *n.* one with boundless splendour or glory; an appellation of Lord Buddha.

অমিত্র *n.* one who is not a friend, an adversary, an enemy, a foe.

অমিত্রাক্ষর *a.* unrhymed. **অমিত্রাক্ষর ছন্দ** blank verse.

অমিয়, অমিয়া *n.* (poet.) nectar, ambrosia. ☐ *a.* as sweet or delicious as nectar, ambrosial (অমিয় বাণী).

অমিল *n.* dissimilarity; disagreement; discord; dissension; scarcity, non-availability (খাদ্যের অমিল). ☐ *a.* scarce, unavailable.

অমিশুক *a.* shy of society, coy, (of one) avoiding or shunning company; unamiable.

অমিশ্র *a.* unmixed; unadulterated; pure; genuine; (math.) simple (অমিশ্র যোগ বিয়োগ প্রভৃতি) ; (math.) whole (অমিশ্র রাশি =a whole number). **~ণীয়** *a.* immiscible. **অমিশ্রিত** *a.* unmixed; unadulterated; pure; genuine.

অমীমাংসিত *a.* undecided. **অমীমাংসিত খেলা** a drawn game, a drawn match. **অমীমাংসিত প্রশ্ন** an unresolved question.

অমুক *a.* a certain, one not definite, such. ☐ *n.* & *pron.* a certain person. **অমুক অমুক** *pron. pl.* such and such.

অমুক্ত *a.* in bondage, unliberated; unfreed; bolted; restricted. **~হস্ত** *a.* close-fisted, niggardly, stingy.

অমুণ্ডিত *a.* unshaven.

অমুদ্রণীয় *a.* unprintable, not to be or not fit to be printed.

অমূর্ত *a.* incorporeal, formless, unembodied.

অমূল, অমূলক *a.* rootless; baseless, groundless; unfounded; false; fantastic.

অমূলদ *a.* (alg.) irrational.

অমূলপ্রত্যক্ষ *n.* (psy.) hallucination.

অমূল্য *a.* priceless, invaluable; too costly to be purchased.

অমৃত *n.* nectar, ambrosia, amrita; extremely sweet or delicious or invigorating food; a god (অমৃতের পুত্র) ; the abode of gods, heaven. ☐ *a.* nectarlike; extremely sweet or delicious or invigorating; ambrosial; immortal. **~কল্প** *a.* nectarlike, nectarine; ambrosial. **~কুণ্ড** *n.* the spring or well of nectar; a container of life-giving or invigorating element. **~কুম্ভ** *n.* the pitcher containing nectar. **~তুল্য** *a.* same as **~কল্প**। **~ধারা** *n.* a stream of nectar; an ambrosial stream. **~নিস্যন্দী, ~নিষ্যন্দী** *a.* exuding or oozing nectar. **~ফল** *n.* the mango. **~বর্ষী** *a.* that which showers nectar. **~বল্লী** *n.* a medicinal plant. **~বিন্দু** *n.* a drop of nectar. **~ভাষী** *a.* one whose words are as sweet or delicious or invigorating as nectar; fair-spoken. **~ময়** *a.* full of nectar; extremely sweet or delicious or invigorating. **~লোক** *n.* the abode of the immortals, heaven. **~স্রাবী** *a.* same as **~নিস্যন্দী**।

অমৃতাংশু *n.* the moon.

অমৃতি *n.* a kind of sweetmeat.

অমৃতোপম *a.* comparable with nectar; nectar-like; extremely sweet or delicious or invigorating.

অমেধাবী *a.* lacking in intelligence, unintelligent; dull-headed.

অমেধ্য *a.* unholy; impure; unfit for use in a scriptural sacrifice or as altarage. ☐ *n.* impurities; excrement.

অমেয় *a.* immeasurable; immense; (psy.) infinite.

অমেরুদণ্ডী *a.* (zoo.) invertebrate; (fig.) lacking firmness of character.

অমোঘ *a.* infallible, unfailing; imperative, compulsive, peremptory (অমোঘ আদেশ). **~তা** *n.* infallibility.

অমোচনীয়, অমোচ্য *a.* that which cannot be dispelled or removed.

অম্বর *n.* the sky, the firmament; cloth, loincloth (পীতাম্বর) ; ambergris. **অম্বরী** *n.* a piece of loincloth to be worn by women, a sari; tobacco perfumed with ambergris. ☐ *a.* perfumed with ambergris.

অম্বল *n.* a kind of sour broth taken as table-delicacy; (path.) acidity caused by indigestion, waterbrash.

অম্বা, অম্বালিকা, অম্বিকা *n.* mother; mother Goddess Durga. **অম্বিকানাথ** *n.* God Shiva.

অম্বু *n.* water. **~জ** *a.* water-born. ☐ *n.* the lotus; conch. **~জা** *n. fem.* Goddess Lakshmi. **~দ** *a.* that which gives or supplies water. ☐ *n.* the cloud. **~ধি, ~নিধি** *n.* the ocean; the sea. **~বাচি, ~বাচী** *n.* three consecutive days usually of Ashara (আষাঢ়) for Hindu widows to fast as religious observance. **~বাহ, ~বাহী** *a.* that which or one who carries water, water-carrying. ☐ *n.* the cloud. **~বিম্ব** *n.* bubble of water.

অম্বুরী var. of **অম্বরী**।

অম্ভঃ *n.* water.

অম্ভোজ *a.* water-born. ☐ *n.* the lotus; conch; the moon.

অম্ভোদ *n.* the cloud.

অম্ভোধি, অম্ভোনিধি *n.* the ocean, the sea.

অম্রাত, অম্রাতক variants of **আম্রাত** and **আম্রাতক**।

অম্ল *n.* the sour taste; anything tasting sour; (path.) acidity caused by indigestion, waterbrash, heart-burn; (chem.) an acid. ☐ *a.* sour. **~তা** *n.* acidity; sourness. **~পিত্ত** *n.* acidity caused by biliary disturbance, acidity of the stomach, acidosis. **~ফল, ~বীজ** *n.* the tamarind. **~মধুর** *a.* possessing a mixed taste of sour and sweet; (rhet. of words) sweet but acid and biting, sweet sounding but caustic. **~মতি** *n.* acidimetry. **~রস** *n.* the sour taste.

অম্লজান *n.* oxygen.

অম্লরাজ *n.* aqua regia.

অম্লাক্ত *a.* mixed or dyed with acid; sour.

অম্লান *a.* unfaded; unfading; not withered (অম্লানকুসুম) ; not soiled or tarnished; not saddened or gloomy; unhesitating, unperturbed, expressionless (অম্লানমুখ, অম্লানবদন). **~বদনে** *adv.* glibly, without hesitation.

অম্লীকরণ *n.* acidification.

অম্লীকৃত *a.* acidulated; acidified.

অম্লোদগার *n.* sour eructation, waterbrash.

অযত্ন *n.* lack of care or effort or attention or interest or cordiality; carelessness; neglect; indifference; slight. **অযত্ন করা** *v.* to neglect; to treat with indifference or slight. **~কৃত** *a.* done without care or effort; done with ease or spontaneity. **~জাত** *a.* born or grown spontaneously. **~পালিত, ~লালিত** *a.* reared in neglect. **~বিন্যস্ত** *a.* placed indecorously or haphazardly. **~রক্ষিত** *a.* kept or maintained in neglect. **~লব্ধ** *a.* earned or attained without effort. **~শীল** *a.* effortless; neglectful. **~সম্ভূত** *a.* same as **~জাত**। **অযত্নে** *adv.* carelessly; negligently.

অযথা *a.* baseless, groundless; false (অযথা নিন্দা) ; inappropriate (অযথা প্রয়োগ) ; unnecessary; unwarranted (অযথা কলহ) ; fruitless, wasteful, extravagant (অযথা খরচ) ; exaggerated (অযথা প্রশংসা). □ *adv.* without cause, unwarrantedly, for nothing; unjustly.

অযথাযথ *a.* inaccurate, inexact; inappropriate, not proper.

অযথার্থ *a.* untrue, unreal; false; feigned, unjust. **~তা** *n.* untruth, unreal.

অযাচক *a.* not asking or soliciting.

অযাচনীয় *a.* unworthy of being asked for.

অযাচিত *a.* uncalled for, not asked for, unasked, unsolicited; gratuitous, voluntary. **অযাচিত উপদেশ** advice gratis. **~ভাবে** *adv.* gratuitously; voluntarily.

অযাচ্য *a.* var. of **অযাচনীয়**।

অযাজনীয়, অযাজ্য *a.* debarred from offering religious sacrifice; debarred from calling for the services of a priest to perform religious rites on one's behalf; (cp.) excommunicated. **অযাজ্যযাজন** *n.* act of conducting religious rites as a priest on behalf of an অযাজনীয় person.

অযাজ্যযাজী *a.* (of a priest) guilty of conducting religious rites on behalf of an অযাজনীয় person. □ *n.* such a priest.

অযাত্রা *n.* occurrence or object considered portending evil for one setting out on a journey; an ill omen for a journey; inauspicious journey.

অযুক্ত *a.* not joined or connected or attached; disjointed, disconnected, unattached, detached, separated. **অযুক্তি** *n.* disunion, disconnection, separation; unreasonableness, unjustness; illogicality; a wrong or fallacious argument; a fallacy; bad or mischievous advice; sophistry; impropriety. **অযুক্তিযুক্ত** *a.* untenable by reason, unreasonable, illogical.

অযুগ্ম *a.* not even, odd, unpaired, separate. **~সংখ্যা** *n.* odd number.

অযুত *a.* & *n.* ten thousand.

অযোগ *n.* lack of contact or relation or union; disunion, separation; unsuitability; (astr.) any inauspicious conjunction of stars, an inauspicious time.

অযোগবাহ, অযোগবাহ বর্ণ *n.* 'ং' and 'ঃ' of the Bengali alphabet; the letter that cannot stand alone.

অযোগ্য *a.* unsuitable, unfit, unworthy, undeserving; unmerited; incompetent; disabled; improper. *fem.* **অযোগ্যা**। **~তা** *n.* unsuitability, unfitness, unworthiness; incompetence; disability; impropriety.

অযোধ্য *a.* not combatable; too strong to be fought with; unconquerable.

অযোনি *a.* one who has no birth, agenetic. **~জ, ~সম্ভব, ~সম্ভূত** *a.* not born of a womb; born spontaneously. (cp.) abiogenetic. *fem.* **~জা, ~সম্ভবা, ~সম্ভূতা**।

অযৌক্তিক *a.* untenable by reason or contrary to reason; unreasonable; illogical. **~তা** *n.* unreasonableness; illogicality.

অযৌন *a.* asexual. **অযৌন প্রজনন, অযৌন জনন** asexual reproduction.

অয়ন *n.* a path, a route, a course; a passage through a military array or a battle order; scriptures; the ground; the earth; a homestead, a dwelling; (astr.)

the sun's movement or course. ~কাল *n.* (astr.) the interval between the two solstices. ~চলন *n.* (astr.) precession. ~বৃত্ত, ~মণ্ডল *n.* the ecliptic. অয়নাংশ *n.* (astr.) a part or measure thereof of the ecliptic esp. the distance between the vernal equinoctial point and the first point in the Aries. অয়নান্ত *n.* (astr.) solstice. অয়নান্তবৃত্ত *n.* any of the two tropics of Cancer and Capricorn.

অযশ *n.* disrepute; discredit. **অযশস্কর** *a.* disreputable; discreditable; damaging; disgraceful; inglorious. **অযশস্বী** *a.* not famous. *fem.* **অযশস্বিনী** ।

অয়স *n.* iron.

অয়স্কঠিন *a.* as hard as iron; extremely hard.

অয়স্কর্ষণী *a.* magnetic. □ *n.* magnetic power.

অয়স্কান্ত *n.* magnet; loadstone.

অয়ি *int.* (poet.) (used in addressing a female) O, oh.

অয়োমল *n.* rust on iron.

অয়োমুখ *a.* iron-headed, iron-tipped. □ *n.* an iron-tipped arrow.

অর *n.* the spoke of a wheel; (geom.) a radius.

অরক্ষণ *n.* not keeping or maintaining or guarding or protecting or defending. **অরক্ষণীয়** *a.* not fit to be kept or maintained or guarded or protected or defended. **অরক্ষণীয়া** *a. fem.* of **অরক্ষণীয়** । □ *a.* & *n.* a Hindu girl who is too old to have her marriage deferred any longer; an unmarried girl who has just reached her puberty.

অরক্ষিত *a.* unprotected; unguarded; defenceless; (of promises, requests, orders, injunctions etc.) not complied with, not observed, not obeyed, not kept properly or safely or securely; uncared for; not kept. **অরক্ষিত নগর** an open city. **অরক্ষিত বাড়ি** a deserted house.

অরগুণ *n.* good quality, merit, virtue, **অরগুণ নেই বরগুণ আছে** having none of the virtues but only lots of vices, having more bad qualities than good.

অরঘট্ট *n.* a draw-well; an apparatus for drawing water from a well.

অরজস্ক, অরজা, অরজাঃ *a.* (of a girl) whose menstruation has not yet started; who has not yet attained her puberty.

অরণি *n.* matchwood, flintwood; flint.

অরণ্য *n.* wood, forest, jungle. ~জ, ~জাত *a.* grown in the forest. ~জাত দ্রব্য forest products. ~পাল *n.* ranger. ~বাসী *a.* living in a wood. □ *n.* such a person; a forester, a bushman. ~ময়, ~সংকুল *a.* woody. **অরণ্যানী** *n.* a vast or extensive forest. **অরণ্যায়ন** *n.* afforestation. **অরণ্যে রোদন করা** *v.* to cry in the wilderness, to cry in vain.

অরতি *n.* absence of amorous or sexual desire; absence of attachment or affection; apathy.

অরন্ধন *n.* the Hindu festival of abstaining from cooking observed on the last day of Bhadra (ভাদ্র) ; abstaining from cooking.

অরব *a.* noiseless; silent, still. **অরবে** *adv.* noiselessly; silently.

অরবিন্দ *n.* a lotus.

অরমণীয়, অরম্য *a.* not pleasing or attractive or beautiful, not lovely.

অররু *n.* an enemy. □ *a.* cruel, ferocious.

অরসজ্ঞ, অরসিক *a.* incapable of appreciating, lacking in power of appreciation; devoid of the sense of humour. *fem.* **অরসজ্ঞা, অরসিকা** । **অরসিকেষু রসস্য নিবেদনম্** wit is meant for the witty alone; a witty remark that falls flat on a person devoid of humour.

অরাজক *a.* anarchical; divested of law and order, lawless; disorderly. ~তা *n.* absence of government in a society; anarchy; lawlessness and disorder; political or social disorder; turmoil.

অরাতি, অরি *n.* an enemy, an adversary, a foe. **অরিঘ্ন** *a.* destroying or liquidating the enemy. **অরাতিদমন, অরিজিৎ, অরিন্দম, অরিমর্দন** *a.* & *n.* one who subdues or conquers or has subdued or has conquered one's enemies.

অরিত্র *n.* (নৌকার হাল) helm, rudder.

অরিষ্ট *n.* fermented wine, alcohol; any medicinal sublimate; good luck. ~চূর্ণ *n.* powder of any medicinal sublimate.

অরীতি *n.* improper practice or usage; bad custom.

অরুগ্ণ *a.* not sickly; not diseased.

অরুচি *n.* loss of appetite; strong aversion (chiefly to food and pleasure); distaste, disinclination, disrelish; apathy. **~কর** *a.* causing aversion to food and pleasure; unpalatable; distasteful, disagreeable.

অরুণ *n.* the sun; (myth.) the name of the charioteer of the sun; the newly-risen sun, the morning sun; glow of the morning sun; purple or crimson colour. ☐ *a.* purple, crimson; sanguine, florid. **~নয়ন, ~লোচন** *a.* purple-eyed, crimson-eyed. **অরুণিত** *a.* crimsoned, purpled; reddened. **অরুণিম** *a.* having a purple or crimson glow; rosy. **অরুণিমা** *n.* crimson or purple glow; rosiness. **অরুণোদয়** *n.* sunrise; dawn, daybreak. **অরুণোপল** *n.* the ruby.

অরুদ্ধ *a.* not closed or barred; not restrained or obstructed; unchecked, unimpeded.

অরুন্তুদ *a.* heart-rending, cutting to the quick; extremely agonizing; very painful.

অরুন্ধতী *n.* (astr.) a dim star in the Ursa Major; (myth.) the devoted wife of sage Vasistha (বশিষ্ঠ).

অরুষ্ট *a.* not angry; not annoyed, not displeased.

অরূপ *a.* shapeless, formless, amorphous, unembodied; bereft of beauty, ugly. **~রতন** *n.* an unbodied gem.

অরোগী *a.* free from illness; hale.

অর্ক *n.* the sun; crystal; a ray or beam of light; sunrays; light; the sun-plant, the swallow-wort (অর্কপত্র). **~প্রিয়া** *n.* a kind of china rose. **~বর্ষ** *n.* the solar year. **~বৃক্ষ** *n.* the margosa-tree.

অর্গল *n.* a bolt, a bar; a hindrance, an obstacle, a barrier.

অর্ঘ ১ *n.* price, cost, value.

অর্ঘ ২ *n.* worship; offerings.

অর্ঘ্য *n.* offerings, sacrifice, altarage; presents and address with which an honourable person is received; anything offered in homage (to).

অর্চক *n.* a worshipper; a priest; a communicant.

অর্চন, অর্চনা *n.* worship; cult; adoration; homage. **অর্চনা করা** *v.* to worship; to adore; to pay homage to. **অর্চনীয়** *a.* one who or that which should be or is to be worshipped; worshipful; adorable; honourable; venerable, reverend.

অর্চা *n.* an idol; worship (used as a correlative of পূজা as in পূজাঅর্চা). ☐ *v.* (poet.) to worship.

অর্চি, অর্চিঃ *n.* a flame; glow; heat.

অর্চিত *a.* worshipped; adored; honoured.

অর্চিষ্মান *a.* glowing, beaming. ☐ *n.* the sun.

অর্চ্য *a.* var. of **অর্চনীয়**।

অর্জক *a.* & *n.* one who earns or acquires or attains.

অর্জন *n.* earning or acquiring or attaining; that which is earned or acquired or attained; acquisition, attainment; gain. **অর্জন করা** *v.* to earn, to acquire, to attain; to gain.

অর্জয়িতা *n.* var. of **অর্জক**।

অর্জিত *a.* earned, acquired; attained.

অর্জুন *n.* a stye on the eyelid; a kind of tree (the juice of its bark is used as a cordial medicine;— cp. foxglove, digitalis).

অর্ণব *n.* an ocean, a sea. **~পোত, ~যান** *n.* a sea-going vessel or ship.

অর্ডারি *a.* ordered for, indented; made to order; sent in accordance with order or indent.

অর্থ ১ *n.* meaning, import, significance; interpretation. **অর্থ করা** *v.* to give the meaning of; to interpret; to explain, to expound. **~গৌরব** *n.* weight or weightiness of significance; richness of import. **~পূর্ণ** *a.* meaningful, significant; signifying. **~প্রদ** *a.* conveying meaning; signifying. **~বহ** *a.* bearing some meaning, significant; suggestive. **~বিচার** *n.* consideration or determination of meaning. **~বিদ** *a.* conversant with the meaning of words; one who has insight into reality. ☐ *n.* such a person; a metaphysician, a philosopher. **~বোধ** *n.* realization of meaning. **~ভেদ** *n.*

difference in interpretations; different interpretations; interpretation or explanation ('কৃপার শাস্ত্রের অর্থভেদ'). ~**শূন্য** *a.* meaningless, nonsense. **অর্থশূন্য দৃষ্টি** *n.* vacant look. ~**সংগতি** *n.* consistency in meanings; appropriateness of meaning. ~**হানি** *n.* misinterpretation; meaninglessness. ~**হীন** *a.* same as **অর্থশূন্য**।

অর্থ ২ *n.* money, wealth; purpose, end in view, object; behalf (পরার্থে) ; earthly or secular prosperity, comfort and happiness (ধর্ম-অর্থ-কাম-মোক্ষ) ; politics; political economy, economics; purpose (মোক্ষার্থে তপস্যা) ; any branch or subject of learning (সর্বার্থতত্ত্ব) ; the thing desired (পুরুষার্থ). **অর্থ আধিকারিক** *n.* finance officer. ~**কর** *a.* helpful in earning money, money-earning, money-making. *fem.* ~**করী**। ~**করী বিদ্যা** learning or training conducive to earning money; professional training. ~**কষ্ট** *n.* pecuniary hardship or trouble; want or shortage of money. ~**কামী** *a.* (eagerly) desirous of earning or acquiring money or wealth; avaricious. ~**কৃচ্ছ্র** *n.* same as ~**কষ্ট**। ~**গৃধ্নু** *a.* avaricious, mammonish. ~**চিন্তা** *n.* pecuniary worry; devising means of earning money. ~**চেষ্টা** *n.* effort to earn or procure money. ~**তত্ত্ব** *n.* political economy; economics. ~**দণ্ড** *n.* a fine; pecuniary loss. ~**নীতি** *n.* political economy, economics; principles of economics. ~**নীতিজ্ঞ**, ~**নীতিবিদ** *n.* an economist. ~**নৈতিক** same as **আর্থনীতিক**। ~**পর**, ~**পরায়ণ** *a.* avaricious, mammonish; miserly. ~**পাল** *n.* a treasurer. ~**পিপাসা** *n.* thirst for money. ~**পিপাসু** *a.* thirsty for money. ~**পিশাচ** *n.* one who is unscrupulously greedy of money; one having an inordinate lust for money; a Mammon-worshipper. ~**প্রদ** *a.* that which fetches money, money-earning. ~**প্রাপ্তি** *n.* act of obtaining or earning money. ~**বল** *n.* financial strength or competency; power of wealth. ~**বান** *a.* rich, wealthy. ~**বিদ্যা** *n.* same as **অর্থতত্ত্ব**। ~**বিনিয়োগ** *n.* investment of money. ~**বিজ্ঞান** *n.* same as **অর্থতত্ত্ব**। ~**বিজ্ঞানী** *n.* an economist. ~**ব্যয়** *n.* act of spending money; expenditure, expense, cost. ~**ভাণ্ডার** *n.* treasury; fund. ~**মন্ত্রক** *n.* the ministry of finance. ~**লাভ** *n.* same as **অর্থপ্রাপ্তি**। ~**লালসা**, ~**লিপ্সা**, ~**লোভ** *n.* (chiefly morbid) desire for money; avarice, cupidity. ~**লিপ্সু**, ~**লোভী** *a.* avaricious. ~**শালী** *a.* rich, wealthy. ~**শাস্ত্র** *n.* political economy, economics; political science, politics (কৌটিল্যের অর্থশাস্ত্র). ~**শূন্য** *a.* unprovided with money; grossly short of money; penniless, insolvent. ~**শূন্যতা** *n.* lack of money; gross shortage of money; insolvency, pauperism. ~**সংকট** *n.* financial crisis. ~**সংগ্রহ** *n.* procurement or collection or acquisition or earning of money. ~**সংগ্রহ করা** *v.* to procure or collect or acquire or raise or earn money. ~**সংস্থান** *n.* provision or procurement of money. ~**সংস্থান করা** *v.* to provide or procure money (for). ~**সংগতি** *n.* provision or possession of money; solvency. ~**সংগতি থাকা** *v.* to possess money or funds (for); to be well-to-do or solvent. ~**সচিব** *n.* finance secretary. ~**সঞ্চয়** *n.* saving or hoarding or accumulating money or wealth. ~**সঞ্চয়ী** *a.* money-saving. ~**সাহায্য** *n.* monetary aid or grant; donation. ~**সাহায্য করা** *v.* to grant monetary aid; to help with money. ~**হানি** *n.* loss of money. ~**হীন** *n.* same as **অর্থশূন্য**।

অর্থাগম *n.* inflow or influx of money; income.

অর্থাৎ *con.* that is to say, that is, signifying that.

অর্থান্তর *n.* difference in interpretation; a different interpretation; another or a different meaning or significance. ~**ন্যাস** *n.* (rhet.) a figure of speech which corroborates the general by the particular or the particular by the general or the cause by the effect or the effect by the cause, corroboration.

অর্থাপত্তি *n.* (log.) a circumstantial source of proof, a kind of inference; presumption; (rhet.) a figure of speech akin to metonymy.

অর্থাভাব *n.* lack or want of money; paucity of fund.

অর্থিত *a.* one of whom anything is asked or begged; that which is asked for or begged.

অর্থি-প্রত্যর্থী *n.* the accuser and the accused, the plaintiff and the defendant.

অর্থী *a.* one who is asking or praying for, solicitous (ধনার্থী); desirous of (বিদ্যার্থী); one who accuses or complains; rich, wealthy. ☐ *n.* such a person; a petitioner, an applicant; a candidate, a desirer; an accuser, a complainant, a plaintiff; a rich man.

অর্থে *prep.* for, on account of. **কী অর্থে** in what sense.

অর্থোপার্জন *n.* earning money. **অর্থোপার্জন করা** *v.* to earn money.

অর্থোদ্ভেদ *n.* exploring the meaning of.

অর্দন *n.* killing; a killer.

অর্দিত *a.* killed.

অর্ধ *n.* any of two unequal parts (অসম অর্ধ); a half, a moiety. ☐ *a.* half; divided into two parts (অর্ধ বঙ্গ); incomplete, partial (অর্ধাশন). ☐ *adv.* half; incompletely, partially, in part. **~কথিত** *a.* told in part, half-told. **~কৃত** *a.* halved; divided into two parts; half-done, partially done, inompletely done. **~গ্রাস** *n.* (astr.) partial eclipse. **~ঘণ্টা** *n.* half an hour. **~চন্দ্র** *n.* the crescent moon; (facet.) act of driving out by pushing by the neck, act of beating in this manner. **~চন্দ্র দেওয়া** *v.* (facet.) to seize (a person) by the neck and drive out by pushing, to beat or thrash in this manner. **~চন্দ্রাকার, ~চন্দ্রাকৃতি** *a.* crescent, crescent-shaped. **~দগ্ধ** *a.* half-burnt. **~দণ্ড** *n.* twelve minutes (see দণ্ড). **~নারীশ্বর** *n.* a deity the right half of whose body is that of God Shiva (শিব) whilst the left half is that of Durga (দুর্গা). **~নমিত** *a.* (of a flag) at half-mast. **~নিমীলিত** *a.* partially closed, half-shut. **~পথ** *n.* half the way; the middle of the way. **~পরিস্ফুট** *a.* half-articulate; indistinct. **~বয়স্ক** *a.* middle-aged. **~বৃত্ত** *n.* a semicircle. **~বৃত্তাকার** *a.* semicircular. **~ব্যক্ত** *a.* half-revealed, half-disclosed; half-expressed. **~ভাগ** *n.* a half part or share; half, a moiety. **~ভূমণ্ডল** *n.* a hemisphere. **~মাত্রা** *n.* the half of a quantity or dose or musical metre. **~মৃত** *a.* half dead; almost dead; more dead than alive; dying. **~রাত্রি** *n.* one half of the night; midnight. **~শত** *n.* & *a.* fifty. **~শয়ান** *a.* recumbent, reclining. **~শিক্ষিত** *a.* (usu. dero.) half-educated. **~সত্য** *n.* half-truth. **~স্ফুট** *a.* half-articulate; indistinct; babbling.

অর্ধাংশ *n.* one of two equal parts, a share, half, a moiety.

অর্ধাঙ্গ *n.* half of the body; (facet.) a husband. **অর্ধাঙ্গী, অর্ধাঙ্গিনী** *n. fem.* wife, better half.

অর্ধাধিক *a.* (of moon or planet) gibbous.

অর্ধার্ধ *n.* a quarter. ☐ *a.* sharing or dividing equally in halves.

অর্ধাশন *n.* underfeeding; imperfect nutrition or feeding, a starvation diet or meal.

অর্ধেক same as **অর্ধ**।

অর্ধেন্দু *n.* the crescent moon; the half-risen moon. **~শেখর, ~মৌলি** *n.* one who has the crescent moon on one's forehead; appellations of Shiva (শিব).

অর্ধোক্তি *n.* inarticulate or suppressed utterance; incomplete utterance.

অর্ধোচ্চারিত *a.* uttered inarticulately or in a suppressed manner, mumbled; half-pronounced.

অর্ধোদয় *n.* an auspicious annual conjunction of stars in Paus (পৌষ) or Magh (মাঘ) considered a holy occasion for the Hindus for ceremonial bathing in the Ganges.

অর্ধোদিত *a.* (of the sun, moon and stars) half-risen.

অর্পণ *n.* giving or offering; placing or depositing; handing over or making over; committal; bestowal; award; investment. **অর্পণ করা** *v.* to give, to offer; to place, to deposit; to hand over, to make over; to commit (to); to bestow; to award; to invest (with). **অর্পণীয়** *a.* that which is to be or should be given or offered or placed or deposited or handed over or made over or committed to or bestowed or awarded or invested (with).

অর্পয়িতা *a.* & *n.* one who gives or offers or places or deposits or hands over or makes over or commits (to) or bestows or awards or invests (with). *fem.* **অর্পয়িত্রী**।

অর্পিত *a.* given, offered; placed, deposited; handed over, made over, committed, bestowed, awarded, invested. *fem.* **অর্পিতা**।

অর্বাচীন *a.*(often dero.) one who or that which is coming after; backward; younger; new; modern; immature; one whose intelligence and knowledge have not matured; inexperienced; unwise; foolish, an ignoramus. **~তা** *n.* backwardness; state of being younger or new or modern; immaturity in age or intelligence and knowledge; inexperience; lack of wisdom; foolishness.

অর্বুদ *a.* & *n.* one hundred million. ☐ *n.* a tumour; (bot.) a node. **~যুক্ত** *a.* (bot.) nodulous.

অর্শ *n.* piles, haemorrhoids.

অর্শানো *v.* to devolve on; to come upon or influence or make responsible by way of contact, association etc.; to contaminate.

অর্হ *a.* worthy, deserving, -able (সম্মানার্হ). ☐ *n.* cost, price, value (মহার্হ).

অর্হণ, অর্হণা *n.* worthiness, ability; worship; adoration. **অর্হণীয়** *a.* worshipful; adorable.

অর্হৎ *n.* a Buddhist or Jain anchorite who has attained salvation or is worthy of attaining it; Lord Buddha.

অর্হা *fem.* of **অর্হ**।

অল *n.* a sting (esp. of a scorpion).

অলংকরণ *n.* ornamentation; adornment, decoration; act of painting or dressing; artistic works or touches; (in lit.) use of rhetoric. **অলংকরণ করা** *v.* to ornament; to adorn, to decorate; to dress, to paint; to deck; (in lit.) to use rhetorical language.

অলংকর্তা *n.* one who ornaments or adorns, a decorator, a painter, a dresser. *fem.* **অলংকর্ত্রী**।

অলংকার *n.* an ornament; act of dressing or painting; an ornamental dress; anything worn to display physical grace and beauty; a mark of honour, beauty; (fig.) pride, glory; (in lit.) rhetoric. **~বর্জিত** *a.* (in lit.) simple; unrhetorical; bald. **~বহুল** *a.* (ভাষা-সম্বন্ধে) florid. **অলংকারবহুল ভাষা** ornate language. **~শাস্ত্র** *n.* the art of rhetoric.

অলংকৃত *a.* ornamented; adorned, decorated; painted, dressed; furnished with artistic workmanship; decorated with a badge or mark of honour; (in lit.) rhetorical, full of figures of speech. **অলংকৃত করা** *v.* to ornament; to adorn, to decorate; to paint; to dress; to deck; to decorate with a badge or mark of honour; (in lit.) to make rhetorical; (fig.) to bring pride or glory to (বীরত্বের দ্বারা দেশকে অলংকৃত করা).

অলংকৃতি var. of **অলংকরণ**।

অলক *n.* a forelock, a ringlet, a fringe; a curling tress of hair ('অলকে কুসুম না দিয়ো') ; cirrus, goat's hair. **~দাম** *n.* tresses of forelocks or curling hair.

অলকমেঘ *n.* cirrus, goat's hair.

অলকা *n.* the kingdom of Kuvera (কুবের) the god of riches. **~ধিপ** *n.* king of Alaka, Kuvera.

অলকাতিলক, অলকাতিলকা *n.* painting on one's face with sandal-paste.

অলকানন্দা *n.* a celestial river; an Indian river which is actually a part of the Ganges.

অলকাপুরী *n.* the palace of Kuvera (কুবের) the god of riches.

অলক্ত, অলক্তক *n.* lac; the liquid dye of lac. **অলক্তরঞ্জিত** *a.* dyed with liquefied lac. **অলক্তরাগ** *n.* the colour or tint of lac.

অলক্ষণ *n.* an ill omen; an inauspicious sign. ☐ *a.* ill-omened; inauspicious; sinister. *fem.* **অলক্ষণা**।

অলক্ষণে, অলক্ষুনে *a.* ill-omened; inauspicious; sinister; portending evil.

অলক্ষিত *a.* unnoticed, unobserved; unseen; unperceived; furtive, stealthy. **অলক্ষিতে** *adv.* unnoticed; unnoticeably, unobservedly; without being seen; imperceptibly; furtively; stealthily; suddenly; in an unguarded moment or state.

অলক্ষুনে var. of **অলক্ষণে**।

অলক্ষ্মী *n.* the goddess of misfortune and misery; a woman or girl who brings misfortune and misery; a sinister woman or girl. **অলক্ষ্মীতে পাওয়া** *v.* to get under the evil influence of the goddess of misfortune and misery; to be stricken with misfortune and misery; to become addicted to such practices as may bring misfortune and misery. **অলক্ষ্মীর দশা** *n.* influence of the goddess of misfortune and misery; (state of being constantly in) misfortune and misery; utter poverty, indigence. **অলক্ষ্মীর দৃষ্টি** *n.* the sinister look of the goddess of misfortune and misery; (the state of being in) misfortune and misery.

অলক্ষ্য *a.* invisible; unseen; undiscernible; imperceptible. ☐ *n.* a place screened from the view, an invisible place (অলক্ষ্য থেকে) ; the sky or heaven ('অলক্ষ্যের পানে'). **অলক্ষ্যে** *adv.* invisibly, unseen; undiscernibly; imperceptibly; furtively, stealthily.

অলখ poet. form of **অলক্ষ্য** (*a.*) ('অলখ আলোকে'). **অলখিতে** *adv.* (poet.) invisibly, unseen; undiscernibly, imperceptibly; furtively, stealthily.

অলগ্ন *a.* not attached or joined; disconnected; separated; not an auspicious moment.

অলঙ্করণ, অলঙ্কার, অলঙ্কৃত, অলঙ্কৃতি alt. spellings of **অলংকরণ, অলংকার, অলংকৃত** and **অলংকৃতি** respectively.

অলঙ্ঘন *n.* act of refraining from overstepping or disobeying; non-transgression, non-violation, non-infringement. **অলঙ্ঘনীয়, অলঙ্ঘ্য** *a.* that which cannot be or should not be overstepped, disobeyed, transgressed, violated or infringed; inviolable; that which must be complied with (অলঙ্ঘনীয় আদেশ) ; that which cannot be crossed over by leaping, impassable. **অলঙ্ঘনীয়তা** *n.* inviolability; impassability. **অলঙ্ঘিত** *a.* not overstepped, not disobeyed; not violated.

অলজ্জ *a.* unabashed; shameless; brazen-faced. **অলজ্জিত** *a.* unabashed.

অলপ্পেয়ে *a.* (in raillery) one who is not to live long.

অলবড্ডে *a.* (dial. & vul.) disorderly, ungainly, gawky; careless; dull-headed.

অলব্ধ *a.* not obtained or got or earned or attained or gained or found. **~প্রবেশ** *a.* having not obtained entry; not yet accepted.

অলভ্য *a.* that which cannot be obtained or got or earned or attained or gained or found; unobtainable, unattainable.

অলয় *a.* without decay or destruction; eternal; existing for ever.

অলস *a.* idle, lazy, slothful, indolent; effortless; dull-headed. **~তা** *n.* idleness, laziness, sloth, indolence; effortlessness; dull-headedness. **~প্রকৃতি** *a.* idle or indolent by nature; habitually idle or indolent; sluggish.

অলাত *n.* a piece of live coal or wood; a firebrand; embers. **~চক্র** *n.* the transitory fire-red curve produced by whirling a piece of live coal or wood; a circle of fire.

অলাবু *n.* a gourd.

অলাভ *n.* absence of profit or gain; loss. **~জনক** *a.* unprofitable; profitless.

অলি[১] *n.* the bumble-bee; the scorpion; wine (অলিপান).

অলি[২] *n.* a guardian; a custodian; a trustee.

অলি-অছি *n.* the guardian of a minor person and the trustee of his or her property (usu. the mother or an elder brother).

অলিকুল *n.* a swarm of bees.

অলিখিত *a.* unwritten.

অলিগলি *n.* lanes and bye-lanes; an extremely narrow path; nook and corner.

অলিজিহ্বা *n.* the uvula.

অলিঞ্জর *n.* a large earthen cask or jar; a pitcher.

অলিন্দ *n.* a balcony, a verandah; an aisle; a terrace in the front part of a building.

অলিপান *n.* drinking wine; a drinking bout.

অলীক *n.* untruth; falsehood. ☐ *a.* untrue, false; baseless; vain, empty (অলীক স্বপ্ন).

অলুক *n.* not subject to elision. ☐ *n.* absence of elision. **~সমাস** *n.* (gr.) a compound of words in which the first word does not drop its case-ending.

অলুব্ধ *a.* untempted; not greedy.

অলোকদৃষ্টি *n.* clairvoyance. ☐ *a.* clairvoyant.

অলোকসাধারণ, অলোকসামান্য *a.* not common or easily available in the world; uncommon, out of the ordinary, extraordinary or rare or superhuman. *fem.* **অলোকসামান্যা।**

অলোকসুন্দর *a.* of unearthly or superhuman beauty; of rare or uncommon beauty.

অলোল, অলোলিত *a.* not loose, not loosely moving; tight, steady.

অলৌকিক *a.* superhuman; not possible or available in the world; extra-mundane; unworldly; supernatural.

অল্প *a.* small in number or amount; a few; a little, a bit; short; of short duration, short-lived (অল্পজীবী) ; (gr.) unaspirated (অল্পপ্রাণ) ; illiberal, narrow (অল্পমতি) ; delicate (অল্পতনু) ; less than what is necessary or usual, insufficient, inadequate, scanty, poor. ☐ *pro.* a small number of persons or things. **~ই** *adv.* only a few, a little; but little; rarely, scarcely, seldom; insufficiently. **অল্প অল্প করে** *adv.* little by little, bit by bit; by degrees; gradually; slowly. **~কাল, ~ক্ষণ** *n.* a short time, a short while. **~কাল পরে, ~কাল মধ্যে** *adv.* shortly after, in a short time; before long. **~চেতা** *a.* narrow-minded; illiberal. **~জীবী** *a.* short lived. **~জ্ঞ** *a.* imperfectly educated, not knowledgeable; not erudite. **~তম** *a.* minimum. **~তা, ~ত্ব** *n.* smallness in number or quantity; shortness; shortness of duration; illiberality, narrowness; insufficiency, inadequacy, shortage. **~দর্শী** *a.* lacking in foresight, short-sighted; imprudent; lacking in experience, inexperienced; narrow in outlook. **~দর্শিতা** *n.* want of foresight, short-sightedness; imprudence; want of experience,; narrowness of outlook. **~ধী** *a.* dull-witted, unintelligent. **~প্রাণ** *a.* short-lived; narrow-minded, illiberal, mean-minded; (gr.) unaspirated. **~বয়সী, ~বয়স্ক** *a.* of tender age, young, minor. **~বিদ্য** *a.* possessing but a little learning; imperfectly educated. **~বিদ্যা** *n.* a little learning; imperfect education. **অল্পবিদ্যা ভয়ংকরী** a little learning is a dangerous thing. **~বিস্তর** *adv.* & *a.* more or less. **~বুদ্ধি** same as **অল্পধী।** **~ভাষী** *a.* of few words; reserved in speech; taciturn; reticent. **~ভাষিতা** *n.* taciturnity; reticence. **~মতি** *a.* mean-minded. **~মাত্র** *a.* just a little. **~মাত্রা** *n.* a small dose or quantity. **~মূল্য** *a.* cheap. **~মূল্যে** *adv.* at a low price, cheaply. **~শ** *adv.* same as **অল্প অল্প করে।** **~সংখ্যক** *a.* a few, small in number. **~স্বল্প** *a.* a little, a bit; a few; not much or many; not frequent; temperate; moderate.

অল্পাধিক *a.* more or less.

অল্পায়ু *a.* shortlived; doomed to die early.

অল্পাশয় *a.*mean-minded; craving for trifles.

অল্পাহার *n.* temperance in eating; restricted diet; light repast. **অল্পাহারী** *a.* restrained or temperate or moderate in eating; one who eats less.

অল্পে *adv.* not involving much; without much trouble or expense. **অল্পে অল্পে** *adv.* little by little, bit by bit; by degrees; gradually; slowly; not involving much; without much trouble or expense. **অল্পের উপর দিয়ে** *adv.* lightly; not involving much or giving much trouble.

অশক্ত *a.* unable; incapable; disabled; imcompetent; powerless; doddering; decrepit. **অশক্তি** *n.* inability; incapability, disability; incompetency; powerlessness.

অশক্য *a.* that which cannot be accomplished; impracticable; lying beyond the reach of one's power.

অশঙ্ক *a.* fearless; undaunted; brave; intrepid; unshaken, unworried. **অশঙ্কনীয়** *a.* that which or one who is not to be feared, not alarming. **অশঙ্কিত** *a.* unafraid, fearless, undaunted; intrepid; unshaken, unworried.

অশথ coll. form of **অশ্বত্থ।**

অশন *n.* act of eating; an article of food;

food, victuals; a meal, a repast. ~নালি *n.* alimentary canal, gullet, oesophagus. ~বসন *n.* food and clothing.

অশনি *n.* thunderbolt; thunder; lightning. ~গর্জন, ~পতন, ~পাত, ~সম্পাত *n.* a crash of thunder, thunderclap.

অশব্দ *a.* noiseless, still.

অশরণ *a.* unsheltered, resortless, homeless, helpless. □ *n.* such a person.

অশরীরী *a.* bodiless, incorporeal; formless; unembodied; intangible, uncome-at-able; supernatural. **অশরীরী আত্মা** a supernatural spirit; a ghost. **অশরীরী বাণী** a supernatural voice; a voice from heaven; an oracle.

অশাখ *a.* branchless.

অশান্ত *a.* not calm or tranquil; disquieted; untamed, wild (অশান্ত অশ্ব) ; not gentle, restless, naughty (অশান্ত বালক) ; rough, troubled, ruffled (অশান্ত সমুদ্র) ; ceaseless (অশান্ত গর্জন) ; worried, anxious, ill at ease; unconsoled, inconsolable, disconsolate. **অশান্তি** *n.* absence of calm or tranquillity, agitation, unrest, disquiet; worry, anxiety; disturbed state.

অশালীন *a.* indecorous, indecent; in bad taste; not courteous. ~তা *n.* indecency, indecorum, lack of decorum or decency.

অশাশ্বত *a.* not eternal or ever-lasting, transient.

অশাসন *n.* absence of rule or government; lack of discipline or control; indiscipline. **অশাসনীয়, অশাস্য** *a.* ungovernable; uncontrollable; unruly; grossly disobedient or recalcitrant. **অশাসিত** *a.* ungoverned; uncontrolled; not disciplined.

অশাসিত, অশাস্য see **অশাসন**।

অশাস্ত্র *n.* any book other than the scriptures; any book containing unscriptural teaching; a harmful book. □ *a.* unscriptural; imparting unscriptural or harmful teaching. **অশাস্ত্রীয়** *a.* contrary to or not included in the scriptures, not in conformity with scriptural decrees, unscriptural; improper, unconventional.

অশিক্ষা *n.* lack of education or training or instruction; bad or improper or harmful education or training or instruction; (loos.) ill-breeding. **অশিক্ষিত** *a.* uneducated; untrained; uninstructed; illiterate. *fem.* **অশিক্ষিতা**।

অশিথিল *a.* not loose, firm, tight.

অশিব *n.* evil, bale; an unhappy incident or misfortune, contretemps. □ *a.* evil, sinister; baleful.

অশিষ্ট *a.* uncivil, impolite, discourteous; ill-mannered; impolite; impertinent; impudent, pert, saucy. ~তা *n.* incivility, impoliteness; discourtesy; ungentleness; impertinence; impudence; sauciness; rudeness, harshness; haughtiness; arrogance; undignifiedness; naughtiness. **অশিষ্টাচরণ, অশিষ্টাচার** *n.* rude behaviour; incivility, discourtesy; impertinence, impudence, sauciness; arrogance; naughtiness.

অশীতি *n.* eighty. ~তম *a.* eightieth. *fem.* ~তমী। ~পর *a.* octogenarian. **অশীতিপর ব্যক্তি** *n.* an octogenarian.

অশুচি *a.* desecrated, profane; unholy; impure; unclean, foul. **অশুচিতা** *n.* desecration, profanity; unholiness. impurity; uncleanness, foulness.

অশুদ্ধ *a.* unholy; unsanctified; impure; unclean; unpurified; unrefined; unrectified; unamended; incorrect, erroneous, wrong. ~তা, **অশুদ্ধি** *n.* unholiness; unsanctified state; impurity; uncleanness; impure or unrefined state; incorrectness, erroneousness; an error. **অশুদ্ধিপত্র** *n.* a list of errata or corrigenda (esp. one attached to a book). **অশুদ্ধিশোধন** *n.* purging impurities, purification; rectification, amendment, correction.

অশুভ *n.* a harm or bale; an evil; a contretemps; a sin. □ *a.* harmful, baleful, evil, sinister; imauspicious; ominous. ~কর, **অশুভংকর** *a.* doing harm (to); evil, sinister. ~কামনা *n.* illwishing. ~ক্ষণ *n.* an inauspicious moment or time. ~সূচক *a.* foreboding evil, ominous, portentous; sinister. ~সূচনা *n.* a bad start.

অশেষ *a.* endless, unending; infinite, eternal; unlimited, boundless; numerous and various. ~জ্ঞ, ~তত্ত্বজ্ঞ *a.* all-knowing, omniscient. ~প্রকার, ~বিধ *a.* numerous and various; numerous and various kinds of; adopting numerous and various ways. ~প্রকারে, ~রূপে *adv.* in numerous and various ways, in thousand and one ways.

অশোক *a.* free from grief. □ *n.* a kind of flower or its tree, the flamboyant; the great Maurya emperor of India. ~কানন *n.* a flamboyant-grove (esp. one in which Sita in the Ramayana was kept as a captive). ~চক্র *n.* the symbolic wheel introduced by King Ashoka illustrating the stages of birth prior to salvation (it is the emblem of the official flag of India). ~বন *n.* same as ~কানন। ~লিপি *n.* any of the religious and moral edicts of Ashoka inscribed on stone-pillars, an inscription of Ashoka. ~স্তম্ভ *n.* any of the stone-pillars of Ashoka on which his edicts are inscribed, an Ashoka pillar (it is the official emblem of India).

অশোচনীয়, অশোচ্য *a.* that which or one who is not to be grieved for, unlamentable, not to be lamented.

অশোচিত *a.* unlamented.

অশোচ্য var.of অশোচনীয়।

অশোধন *n.* lack of purification or sanctification or refinement or reclamation or rectification or correction; (rare) non-repayment, non-requital. অশোধনীয়, অশোধ্য *a.* incapable of being purified or sanctified or refined or reclaimed or rectified or corrected or repaid or requited; incorrigible; unrepayable. অশোধিত *a.* not purified; unsanctified, unrefined; unreclaimed; unrectified; unrepaid, unrequited.

অশোভন *a.* unbecoming; unbefitting; improper; lacking in decorum, indecorous; indecent. *fem.* অশোভনা। ~তা *n.* unbecomingness; unbefittingness; impropriety; indecorousness; indecency. অশোভিত *a.* unadorned, undecorated.

অশোষণীয়, অশোষ্য *a.* not absorbable.

অশৌচ *n.* uncleanness; impurity; profanity; (scriptural) impurity of one's person owing to the birth or death of a relative, the period of duration of this personal impurity. অশৌচান্ত *n.* termination or end of the period of personal impurity.

অশ্ব *n.* the horse. *fem.* অশ্বা। অশ্বী a mare. ~কোবিদ *a.* experienced about horses; skilled in horse-breaking or horse training. □ *n.* one experienced about horses; a horse-breaker; a horse-trainer; a skilled horesman, an equestrian. ~খুর *n.* a horse's hoof; a plant used as perfume. ~খুরা *n.* a creeper of the clitoria genus; its flower. ~গতি *n.* the pace (usu. galloping) of a horse. ~গন্ধা *n.* a medicinal plant, withania somnifera. ~গ্রীব *n.* having a neck curved like that of a horse, horse-necked. ~চক্র *n.* a move in chess in which the two knights are placed in a position where the opponent's king is checkmated. ~চালনা *n.* driving or riding a horse. ~চালনা করা *v.* to drive or ride a horse. ~চিকিৎসক *n.* a horse-doctor, a farrier; a veterinary surgeon. ~চিকিৎসা *n.* farriery. ~ডিম্ব *n.* a mere nothing, a hoax, (cp.) fiddlesticks! (*int.*), (cp.) a mare's nest. ~তর *n.*the mule. *fem.* ~তরী। ~তুল্য *a.* like a horse, equine. ~পাল, ~পালক *n.* a professional caretaker of horses; an equerry; a groom. ~পৃষ্ঠে *adv.* on horseback. ~বিদ *a.* same as অশ্বকোবিদ। ~বৈদ্য *n.* same as অশ্বচিকিৎসক। ~মেধ (যজ্ঞ) *n.* a solemn ritual performed by the princes of ancient India to have their sins condoned : in this ritual a horse was given in sacrifice, the horse-sacrifice. ~যান *n.* a horse-drawn carriage; a horse-cart. ~রক্ষক *n.* same as অশ্বপাল। ~রজ্জু, *n.* a horse's rein or bridle. ~শক্তি *n.* (mech.) horsepower, about 745 watts. ~শাবক *n.* a colt, a foal (*fem.* filly). ~শালা *n.* a stable. ~সংক্রান্ত *a.* relating to the horse, equine.

অশ্বত্থ *n.* an Indian fig-tree, a peepul-tree, *ficus religiosa*.

অশ্বা see অশ্ব।

অশ্বারূঢ় *a.* mounted on a horse, equestrian.

অশ্বারোহ, অশ্বারোহণ *n.* horse-riding; horsemanship. **অশ্বারোহী** *a.* mounted on a horse, equestrian, fighting on horseback. ☐ *n.* a horseman, a rider; a horse-soldier. **অশ্বারোহী বাহিনী** *n.* the cavalry.

অশ্বিনী *n.* the first of the twenty-seven stars according to Hindu astronomy; (myth.) the horse-shaped wife of the sun-god; (pop.) the mare. **~কুমার, ~নন্দন** *n.* either of the twin brothers who are physicians of heaven.

অশ্বী see **অশ্ব**।

অশ্বেতকায় *a.* not white-skinned.

অশ্ম *n.* stone, rock, bitumen; fossil. **~পুষ্প** *n.* benzoin. **~মণ্ডল** *n.* (geol.) lithosphere. **~ময়, ~র** *a.* full of stones or rocks, rocky. **~রী** *n.* (path.) concretion. **অশ্মীভবন** *n.* fossilization. **অশ্মীভূত** *a.* fossilized. **অশ্মীভূত হওয়া** *v.* to fossilize.

অশ্রদ্ধ *a.* without faith or confidence in; irreverent; apathetic, disgusted. **অশ্রদ্ধা** *n.* want or loss of faith or confidence; irreverence; apathy, disgust. **অশ্রদ্ধা করা** *v.* to treat with contempt; to despise; to refuse to put faith or confidence in; to attach no importance to. **অশ্রদ্ধেয়** *a.* not reverend or venerable; not worthy of faith or confidence. **অশ্রদ্ধাজনক** *a.* dishonourable; blasphemous.

অশ্রবণীয় *a.* same as **অশ্রাব্য**।

অশ্রান্ত *a.* untired; untiring; tireless; incessant. ☐ *adv.* incessantly. **~ভাবে** *adv.* untiringly, unweariedly, indefatigably. **অশ্রান্তি** *n.* tirelessness; ceaselessness.

অশ্রাব্য *a.* (of words etc.) unworthy of being heard, obscene; indecent; (rare) inaudible. **অশ্রাব্য ভাষা** vulgar or filthy language.

অশ্রু *n.* tear, tears. **~গদগদকণ্ঠে** *adv.* in a voice choked with tears, in a sobbing voice. **~জল** *n.* tears. **~ধারা** *n.* the flow of tears. **~পাত** *n.* shedding tears, weeping. **~পাত করা** *n.* to shed tears, to weep. **~পূর্ণ** *a.* tearful. **অশ্রুপূর্ণ চোখে** *adv.* with tearful eyes; tearfully. **~প্লাবিত, ~প্লুত** *a.* suffused or flooded with tears. **~বর্ষণ** *n.* same as **অশ্রুপাত**। **~বারি** *n.* same as **অশ্রুজল**। **~বিগলিত** *a.* moistened with tears, blubbering; blubbered. **~বিন্দু** *n.* a tear-drop, a tear. **~বিমোচন, ~বিসর্জন** *n.* same as **অশ্রুপাত**। **~ভরা** *a.* full of tears, tearful. **~ভারাক্রান্ত** *a.* (of voice) choked with tears. **~ময়** *a.* full of tears. **~মুখ** *a.* having a blubbered face. *fem.* **~মুখী**। **~মোচন** *n.* same as **অশ্রুপাত**। **~রুদ্ধ** *a.* choked with tears. **অশ্রুসংবরণ করা** *v.* to check tears, to stop weeping. **~সিক্ত** *a.* drenched or moistened with tears; moist; blubbering; blubbered.

অশ্রুত *a.* unheard; unheard-of; obscure; unheard-of before. **~চর, ~পূর্ব** *a.* unheard-of-before.

অশ্রেয় *a.* harmful, baleful,evil; inauspicious, unfavourable, not congenial. ☐ *n.* harm, bale, evil; disservice; contretemps. **~স্কর** as **অশ্রেয়** (*a.*).

অশ্রোতব্য var. of **অশ্রাব্য**।

অশ্রোত্রিয় *n.* a Brahman who has not studied the Vedas. ☐ *a.* having no knowledge of the Vedas.

অশ্লাঘনীয় *a.* not praiseworthy or commendable; discreditable.

অশ্লীল *a.* obscene; abominable; indecent; lascivious, wanton. **অশ্লীল বাক্য** obscene or filthy words or talk; bawdy talk. **অশ্লীল সাহিত্য** obscene or blue literature, pornography. **~তা** *n.* obscenity; abomination; indecency; lasciviousness, wantonness. **~ভাষী** *a.* & *n.* one who indulges in obscene or bawdy talk.

অশ্লেষা *n.* (astr.) the ninth of the zodiacal stars, a star considered inauspicious by astrologers.

অষ্ট *n.* & *a.* eight. **~ক** *n.* any collection of eight, an octave; a book containing eight chapters; a verse containing eight couplets. ☐ *a.* eight. **~আশি** see **অষ্টাশি**। **~কোণ** *n.* (geom.) an octagon. ☐ *a.* octagonal. **~কোণী** *a.* octagonal. **~গুণ** *a.* multiplied by eight, eightfold. ☐ *n.* eight times. **~চত্বারিংশ** *a.* forty-eighth. **~চত্বারিংশৎ** *n.* & *a.* forty-eight. **~চত্বারিংশত্তম** *a.* forty-eighth. *fem.* **~চত্বারিংশত্তমী**। **~দিকপাল** *n.* the eight guardian deities of the eight points of the earth. **~ধা** *adv.* & *a.* eight times; eightfold; in eight ways. **~ধাতু** *n.* the eight metals; gold, silver, copper, bronze, bell-metal, zinc, lead and iron. ~নবতি *n.* & *a.* ninety-eight. ~নবতিতম *a.* ninety-eighth. *fem.* ~নবতিতমী। ~নাগ *n.* (myth.) the eight chief snakes. ~নায়িকা *n.* the eight minor goddesses; the eight manifestations of Goddess Durga (দুর্গা) ; (lit.) eight moods of the heroine or the sweetheart (namely, going to assignation, expecting her lover to come to her bed-chamber, worried owing to sudden absence of her lover, deceived by her lover, stricken with anger and jealousy on observing on the person of her lover signs indicating that he had been to another woman, feeling miserable for having quarrelled with and sent back her lover, enjoying domineering control over her lover, and separated from her lover as he has gone abroad). ~পঞ্চাশৎ *n.* & *a.* fifty-eight. ~পঞ্চাশত্তম *a.* fifty-eighth. *fem.* ~পঞ্চাশত্তমী। ~পাদ *a.* octopod. □ *n.* an octopod; the spider; a mythological octopod said to be even stronger than the lion (cp. octopus, শরভ). ~প্রহর *n.* a whole day and night, twenty-four hours, a form of collective religious chanting by the Hindus continuing for twenty-four hours at a stretch. □ *adv.* throughout the whole day and night; always; ceaselessly. ~বজ্র *n.* the eight infallible weapons of the eight principal gods. ~বজ্রমিলন *n.* simultaneous hurling of **অষ্টবজ্র,** which causes the destruction of the universe; precipitation of a highly explosive condition. ~বসু *n.* the eight demi-gods (see বসু). ~বিধ *a.* of eight kinds. ~ভুজ *a.* eight-handed, octagonal. □ *n.* an octagon. ~ভুজা *a.* & *n. fem.* of **অষ্টভুজ**। □ *n.* a manifestation of Goddess Durga (দুর্গা). ~ভৈরব *n.* the eight terrible manifestations of Shiva (শিব). **অষ্টম** *a.* eighth. ~মঙ্গলা *n.* a manifestation of Durga (দুর্গা); the custom according to which the newly-wed groom comes back to the father-in-law's house with his wife on the eighth day of marriage. **অষ্টমবর্ষীয়** *a.* of or in the eighth year; eight years old. **অষ্টমবাৎসরিক, অষ্টমবার্ষিক** *a.*of the eighth year. ~মাংশ *n.* one-eighth; the eighth part. ~মী *n. fem.* the eighth day of either fortnight of a lunar month. □ *a. fem.* eighth; eight years old. ~মূর্তি *n.* the eight manifestations of Shiva (শিব). ~রম্ভা *n.* (pop.) a mere nothing, a hoax, a mare's nest; a fiasco. ~ষষ্টি *n.* & *a.* sixty-eight. ~ষষ্টিতম *a.* sixty-eighth. ~সপ্ততি *n.* & *a.* seventy-eight. ~সপ্ততিতম *a.* seventy-eighth. ~সিদ্ধি *n.* the eight superhuman qualities attainable by ascetical or austere practice.

অষ্টাংশিত *a.* divided into eight; (of a sheet of paper) octavo.

অষ্টাঙ্গ *n.* the eight limbs of the body (namely, two hands, the breast or bosom, the forehead, two eyes, the throat or speech, and the backbone; or alternatively, two great toes, two knees, two hands, the breast and the nose); the eight systems of yoga. □ *a.* having eight branches or departments (অষ্টাঙ্গ আয়ুর্বেদ).

অষ্টাত্রিংশ *n.* & *a.* thirty-eight. **অষ্টাত্রিংশৎ** *n.* & *a.* thirty-eight. ~ত্তম *a.* thirty-eighth. *fem.* ~ত্তমী।

অষ্টাদশ *n.* & *a.* eighteen. **অষ্টাদশী** *a. fem.* eighteen years old.

অষ্টাধিক *a.* more than eight; exceeding by eight.

অষ্টাপদ *n.* (obs.) gold.

অষ্টাবক্র *n.* an ancient sage whose body was ridiculously misshapen at eight places; (facet.) a ridiculously deformed person.

অষ্টাবিংশ *a.* twenty-eighth. ~তি *n.* & *a.* twenty-eight. **অষ্টাবিংশতিতম** *a.* twenty-eighth. *fem.* **অষ্টাবিংশতিতমী**।

অষ্টাশি, অষ্টআশি, অষ্টাশীতি *n.* & *a.* eighty-eight. **অষ্টাশীতিতম** *a.* eighty-eighth. *fem.* **অষ্টাশীতিতমী**।

অষ্টাশ্র *a.* octagonal. □ *n.* an octagon.

অষ্টাশ্রি *a.* octagonal; eight-angled.

অষ্টাহ *n.* eight days.

অষ্টেপৃষ্ঠে var. of **আষ্টেপৃষ্ঠে**।

অষ্টোত্তরশত *a.* one hundred and eight.

অসংকীর্ণ *a.* not narrow, wide; not lacking in breadth.

অসংকুচিত *a.* unhesitating; free; open; frank; liberal; not contracted.

অসংকোচ *a.* absence of hesitation; openness; frankness; liberality; absence of contraction. **অসংকোচে** *adv.* unhesitatingly; freely; frankly; liberally.

অসংখ্য, অসংখ্যক *a.* innumerable, numberless; countless; infinite. **অসংখ্যাত** *a.* unnumbered; uncounted. **অসংখ্যেয়** *a.* innumerable, countless.

অসংগত *a.* unreasonable, unjustifiable; irrelevant; incoherent; impertinent; improper; unjust, unfair. **অসংগতি** *n.* unreasonableness; unjustifiability; irrelevance; incoherence; impertinence; impropriety; unjustness.

অসংনম্য *a.* (phys.) incompressible. **~তা** *n.* incompressibility.

অসংবদ্ধ alt. spell. of **অসম্বদ্ধ** ।

অসংবৃত *a.* not covered, uncovered; divested of clothing, undressed; bare; one whose garments are about to fall off one's body. *fem.* **অসংবৃতা** ।

অসংযত *a.* unrestrained, unbridled, uncontrolled; uncontrollable; wild.

অসংযম *n.* lack of self-control; wantonness; sensual indulgence, sensualism, incontinence; lack of restraint; intemperance. **অসংযমী** *a.* lacking in self-control; abandoned; indulging in sensual enjoyment, sensual, incontinent; lacking in restraint; intemperate.

অসংযুক্ত *a.* unattached; disjointed; detached; disconnected; not united or joined. **অসংযুক্ত বর্ণ** *n.* not a conjunct letter.

অসংযোগ *n.* absence of union or connection or relation or communication or contact.

অসংলগ্ন *a.* disjointed; unconnected, unattached; detached; incoherent; irrelevant, inconsistent, rambling (অসংলগ্ন বাক্য, অসংলগ্ন বিষয়). **~তা** *n.* irrelevance, incoherence, inconsistency.

অসংশয় *a.* undoubting; confident; doubtless. □ *n.* freedom from or absence of doubt; confidence. **অসংশয়িত** *a.* undoubted or undoubting; confident; sure. **অসংশয়ে** *adv.* without doubt, doubtlessly; confidently; surely.

অসংশোধিত *a.* unrectified; uncorrected; unamended.

অসংশ্লিষ্ট *a.* unattached; unrelated; unconcerned.

অসংসক্ত *a.* unattached, unconnected, unassociated; separate.

অসংস্কার *n.* want of reform, repair or conditioning.

অসংস্কৃত *a.* unconsecrated; unrefined; vulgar; inelegant; not dressed or tended, loose (অসংস্কৃত কেশপাশ) ; (of languages etc.) non-Sanskritic. **অসংস্কৃত বাক্য** a speech in a language other than Sanskrit; vulgar language; obscene language.

অসংস্থান *n.* non-provision.

অসংহত *a.* not concentrated or united; sporadic; scattered; uncoordinated.

অসকাল *n.* inopportune time; end, termination; evening, nightfall ('বেলি অসকাল').

অসকৃৎ *adv.* more than once; time and again, again and again; many times.

অসঙ্কীর্ণ alt. spell. of **অসংকীর্ণ** ।

অসঙ্কুচিত, অসঙ্কোচ, অসঙ্কোচে alt. spellings of **অসংকুচিত, অসংকোচ** and **অসংকোচে** respectively.

অসঙ্গ *a.* companionless; unaccompanied; lonely, solitary. □ *n.* solitariness; renunciation of worldly ties and interests; the Supreme Being.

অসঙ্গত alt. spell. of **অসংগত** ।

অসচ্চরিত্র *a.* unchaste; incontinent, licentious, profligate; immoral. *fem.* **অসচ্চরিত্রা** । **~তা** *n.* unchasteness; incontinence, licentiousness, profligacy; immorality.

অসচ্ছল *a.* financially uneasy; hard-up, ill-off, tight, indigent, poor. **~তা** *n.* financial uneasiness, hardship or difficulty; indigence, poverty.

অসজ্জন *n.* a dishonest or wicked man; a man lacking in propriety.

অসৎ *a.* dishonest; bad, evil (অসৎ সঙ্গ) ; wicked; unchaste, immoral; depraved; obscene (অসৎ বাক্য) ; rude (অসদাচরণ) ; (phil.) inexistent, non-existent; (phys.)

virtual (অসৎ ফোকাস). □ *n.* inexistence, non-existence, virtual nonentity.

অসৎকর্মা *a.* given to doing wicked or dishonest acts; wrongdoing.

অসৎকৃত *a.* not accorded cordial reception, not treated with hospitality; neglected, ignored.

অসততা *n.* same as **অসাধুতা** ।

অসৎপথাবলম্বী *a.* one who has taken to evil ways and means; wicked; dishonest.

অসতর্ক *a.* inadvertent; careless; unguarded; incautious. **~তা** *n.* carelessness; unguardedness; lack of caution. **অসতর্ক মুহূর্তে** *adv.* in an unguarded moment.

অসৎসঙ্গ *n.* evil company.

অসতী *a. fem.* unchaste; unfaithful to one's husband. □ *n.* such a woman.

অসত্তা *n.* non-existence.

অসত্য *a.* untrue; false. □ *n.* untruth; falsehood; a lie. **~বাদী, ~ভাষী** *a.* untruthful; indulging in telling lies. **~বাদী বা ~ভাষী ব্যক্তি** an untruthful person, a liar. **~বাদিতা, ~ভাষিতা** *n.* act or habit of telling lies; untruthfulness. **~সন্ধ** *a.* one who does not keep one's promise or word.

অসদ্গ্রাহী *a.* one who accepts improper or unlawful gifts; given to accepting unlawful gratification. **অসদ্গ্রাহিতা** *n.* acceptance of improper or unlawful gifts; practice of accepting unlawful gratification; practice of accepting bribes.

অসদ্বিম্ব *n.* (phys.) a virtual image.

অসদ্বৃত্তি *n.* dishonest or evil practice or occupation; bad conduct.

অসদাচরণ *n.* rude behaviour or treatment; wickedness. **অসদাচরণ করা** *v.* to behave or treat rudely; to indulge in wickedness.

অসদাচার *n.* indecent or dishonest or evil practice; wickedness. □ *a.* given to indecent or dishonest or evil practice; indulging in wickedness. **অসদাচারী** *a.* same as **অসদাচার** (*a.*).

অসদুদ্দেশ্য *n.* bad intentions; evil designs.

অসদুপদেশ *n.* mischievous or harmful counsel or advice.

অসদুপায় *n.* unfair means.

অসদৃশ *a.* dissimilar, unlike; incongruous; different; unbecoming, improper.

অসদ্ব্যবহার *n.* discourteous or rude behaviour; ill-treatment; misuse, abuse.

অসদ্ভাব *n.* inexistence, absence; want of amity, unfriendliness; ill-feeling, bad blood; quarrel.

অসন্তুষ্ট *a.* displeased; dissatisfied; discontented; ill-disposed; aggrieved. **অসন্তুষ্ট করা** *v.* to displease; to dissatisfy; to make discontented or ill-disposed; to aggrieve.

অসন্তুষ্টি, অসন্তোষ *n.* displeasure; dissatisfaction; discontent; ill disposition; aggrieved state; grievance. **অসন্তোষজনক** *a.* unsatisfactory; unsatisfied; dissatisfied; displeased.

অসন্দিগ্ধ *a.* unsuspicious, undoubting; unhesitating; doubtless, sure, certain. **~চরিত্র** *a.* unsuspecting; credulous. □ *n.* a character above suspicion. **~চিত্তে** *adv.* with mind free from suspicion or doubt or hesitation; unsuspiciously; unhesitatingly.

অসন্দিহান *a.* unsuspicious, not doubting, free from misgivings.

অসম্বিত *a.* not joined or tied (together); disjointed, united; detached; unfermented.

অসন্নিধান *n.* distance; absence of proximity or nearness.

অসপত্ন *a.* one who has no enemy.

অসফল *a.* unsuccessful; abortive.

অসবর্ণ *a.* not belonging to the same caste. **অসবর্ণ বিবাহ** intercaste marriage.

অসভ্য *a.* uncivil, discourteous, uncultured, unpolished, rude; unsocial; uncivilized, wild; aboriginal, primitive. **~জাতি** *n.* a wild or aboriginal race. **~তা** *n.* incivility, discourtesy; lack of culture or refinement or polish; rudeness; unsocialness; lack of civilization. **অসভ্যতা করা, অসভ্য হওয়া** *v.* to behave discourteously or rudely or unculturedly; to behave ill-manneredly or indecorously.

অসম *a.* unequal; dissimilar; incongruous; different; uneven, rugged, undulating.

অসমকক্ষ *a.* unequal (esp. in strength); no match for.

অসমক্ষে *adv.* at the back of, in one's absence.

অসমজননকোষী *a.* heterogamous.

অসমঞ্জস *a.* asymmetrical; disproportionate, dissimilar, varying; irrelevant; unjust, undue; unbefitting, unbecoming.

অসমতল *a.* not smooth or plain, uneven, rough.

অসমতা *n.* inequality; dissimilarity; incongruity; difference; unevenness; ruggedness.

অসমদর্শী *a.* not taking an impartial view; viewing or judging with partiality, partial. **অসমদর্শিতা** *n.* partiality; partial view or judgment.

অসমনিয়ত *a.* asynchronous.

অসমপুংদণ্ড *n.* heterostyly.

অসমবর্তিত *a.* (astr.) unpolarized.

অসমবেগ *n.* (mech.) variable velocity. □ *a.* endowed with variable velocity.

অসময় *n.* inopportune or unsuitable time; inauspicious time; hard times; time of stress. **অসময়ে** *adv.* at an inopportune or unsuitable time; at an inauspicious time; during or in hard times, in time of need; unseasonably. **অসময়ের ফল** an unseasonal fruit. **অসময়ের বন্ধু** a friend in need. **অসময়ের বৃষ্টি** unseasonal or untimely rain.

অসমিয়া *n.* an Assamese; the Assamese language. □ *a.* of or about Assam or its people or their language; born or produced in Assam; Assamese.

অসমরূপতা *n.* absence of uniformity; dissimilarity; difference.

অসমরেণু-প্রসূ *a.* heterosporous.

অসমর্থ *a.* incapable, unable, incompetent; disabled. *fem.* **অসমর্থা**। **অসমর্থতা** *n.* incapability, inability; incompetence; disability.

অসমর্থন *n.* want of support or sanction or confirmation; disapproval; want of consent.

অসমর্থিত *a.* unsupported; unsanctioned; unconfirmed (অসমর্থিত সংবাদ) ; disapproved, unapproved; not consented to.

অসমর্পিত *a.* not given or handed over; not bestowed.

অসমসত্ত্ব *a.* (psy.) heterogeneous.

অসমসাহস *n.* a rare feat of daring; complete fearlessness; rashness. □ *a.* endowed with rare daring; completely fearless; over-daring, over-bold; daredevil; rash. **অসমসাহসিক, অসমসাহসী** *a.* same as **অসমসাহস** (*a.*). **অসমসাহসী ব্যক্তি** a very brave person, a man of rare courage.

অসমাংশক (bot.) heteromerous.

অসমাঙ্গ *a.* lacking in physical proportion or symmetry; deformed; disproportionate, asymmetrical.

অসমাদর *n.* absence of cordial reception or acceptance; slight; neglect, disregard, **অসমাদর করা** *v.* to deny cordial reception or acceptance, to receive or accept coldly; to slight; to neglect, to disregard.

অসমাদৃত *a.* received or accepted coldly, treated coldly; slighted; neglected, disregarded.

অসমান *a.* unequal; dissimilar; uneven, rugged, undulating; not straight, curved.

অসমাপিকা *a. fem.* not completing. **অসমাপিকা ক্রিয়া** (gr.) an infinite verb; a verb in its participial form.

অসমাপিত, অসমাপ্ত *a.* unfinished; not ended or concluded or terminated; not over; not completed, incomplete. **অসমাপ্তি** *n.* state of being not finished or ended or concluded or terminated or completed, incompletion.

অসমিয়া *n.* an Assamese; the Assamese language. □ *a.* of or about Assam or its people or their language; born or produced in Assam; Assamese.

অসমীক্ষ্যকারী *a.* lacking in due consideration; rash, impetuous; reckless. **অসমীক্ষ্যকারিতা** *n.* absence of due consideration; rashness, impetuosity; recklessness.

অসমীচীন *a.* indiscreet, injudicious, unjust, wrongful, improper, unbecoming.

অসমৃদ্ধ *a.* not prosperous; not affluent or wealthy.

অসমৃদ্ধি *n.* lack of prosperity or affluence.

অসম্পন্ন *a.* unfinished, unaccomplished; unexecuted, unperformed, undone; outstanding; not well-to-do, ill-off.

অসম্পর্ক *n.* absence of connection or relation. **অসম্পর্কিত, অসম্পর্কীয়** *a.* unconnected, unrelated.

অসম্পাদন *n.* not performing or accomplishing. **অসম্পাদিত** *a.* unfinished, uncompleted, unaccomplished.

অসম্পূর্ণ *a.* incomplete,unfinished; outstanding; not full; imperfect. **~তা** *n.* incompletion, incompleteness, unfinished state, state of not being full; imperfection.

অসম্পৃক্ত *a.* unrelated; unconnected; unattached; disjointed, detached; unconcerned. **অসম্পৃক্তি** *n.* absence of relation or connection; absence of attachment; disjointed or detached state; unconcern.

অসম্প্রীতি *n.* absence or lack of amity or friendliness.

অসম্বদ্ধ *a.* (rare) not tied together; incoherent, desultory, rambling, incoherent and nonsensical, irrelevant (অসম্বদ্ধ প্রলাপ) ; unconnected, unrelated, unattached, unaffiliated. **~তা** *n.* (rare) state of not being tied together; incoherence, desultoriness; state of being incoherent and nonsensical, irrelevance; absence of connection or relation or attachment or affiliation.

অসম্বন্ধ *a.* unrelated; incoherent; irrelevant; inappropriate; unjust.

অসম্বাধ *a.* unobstructed, unimpeded, unopposed; free from collision.

অসম্ভব *a.* impossible; unlikely, improbable; absurd; uncommon and astonishing. ☐ *n.* an impossible or uncommon incident, the impossible. **~পর** *a.* same as **অসম্ভব** (*a.*).

অসম্ভাবনা *n.* impossibility; unlikelihood, improbability; absurdity. **অসম্ভাবনীয়, অসম্ভাব্য** *a.* unlikely to occur, improbable.

অসম্ভাবিত *a.* unexpected, unanticipated.

অসম্ভাব্য see **অসম্ভাবনা।**

অসম্ভোগ *n.* non-enjoyment.

অসম্ভ্রম *n.* indignity, dishonour, disrespect; insult.

অসম্ভ্রান্ত *a.* not respectable or honourable; not aristocratic; not nobly born; undignified.

অসম্মত *a.* unwilling, reluctant, dissenting, disagreeing, declining. **অসম্মত হওয়া** *v.* to be unwilling or reluctant; to disagree; to refuse to give consent, to dissent; to decline. **অসম্মতি** *n.* unwillingness, reluctance, dissent, act of disagreeing or declining. **অসম্মতিসূচক** *a.* dissentient; dissident.

অসম্মান *n.* dishonour, disrespect, indignity; insult, affront; slight, neglect; ignominy, disgrace. **~কর** *a.* dishonourable, undignified, disgraceful, ignominious; disrespectful; insulting; slighting. **অসম্মান করা** *v.* to dishonour, to disrespect; to insult; to slight, to neglect. **~জনক** *a.* dishonourable, undignified; disgraceful, ignominious. **~সূচক** *a.* disrespectful; insulting; slighting. **অসম্মানিত** *a.* insulted; disrespected; slighted.

অসরল *a.* (of lines etc.) not straight, curved; (of human nature etc.) not frank or candid or forthright; tortuous; (of plans, proposals etc.) crooked, deceptive; fishy. **~তা** *n.* curvedness; tortuosity; crookedness; fishiness.

অসহ *a.* (ori.) intolerent,unforbearing, unforgiving; intolerable, insufferable, unbearable. **অসহন** *n.* intolerance; non-forbearance; unforgivingness. ☐ *a.* same as **অসহ। অসহনশীল** *a.* intolerant; impatient. **~নীয়** *a.* intolerable, insufferable, unbearable. **অসহমান** *a.* incapable of toleration or forgiveness, intolerant, unforgiving.

অসহযোগ, অসহযোগিতা *n.* non-cooperation; (rare) indifference. **অসহযোগ আন্দোলন** *n.* the Non-cooperation Movement of India. **অসহযোগী** *a.* non-cooperating; noncooperative.

অসহায় *a.* helpless; lonely, solitary; companionless; defenceless, weak. **~তা** *n.* helplessness; defencelessness. *fem.* **অসহায়া।**

অসহিষ্ণু *a.* impatient, incapable of enduring; restless; fretful. **~তা** *n.* impatience; restlessness, fretfulness.

অসহ্য *a.* unendurable, insufferable, unberarable, intolerable.

অসাংবিধানিক *a.* unconstitutional, not sanctioned by the constitution.

অসাক্ষাৎ *n.* the state of being out of sight or view. **অসাক্ষাতে** *adv.* in one's absence, at one's back; stealthily, unobservedly, secretly. **অসাক্ষাতে নিন্দা করা** *v.* to backbite, to speak ill of or slander a person behind his back.

অসাড় *a.* bereft of sensation or feeling or consciousness; insensate; benumbed, torpid; bereft of sensibility, insensible. **~তা** *n.* loss of sensation or feeling or consciousness; insensateness, unconsciousness; torpidity; insensibility. **অসাড়ে** *adv.* insensately, unconsciously; unknowingly, unawares.

অসাদৃশ্য *n.* dissimilarity, unlikeness.

অসাধ *n.* unwillingness; disinclination; aversion, apathy. **আমার কি অসাধ** do I not feel the urge for it, do I not conceive a desire for it, am I unwilling ?

অসাধারণ *a.* uncommon, unusual, extraordinary; rare; distinguishing, distinctive; (log.) not general, particular, specific. **~ত্ব** *n.* uncommonness, unusualness, extraordinariness; rareness; peculiarity, distinctiveness; a rarity; (log.) particularity.

অসাধিত *a.* unaccomplished, unexecuted; unrealized.

অসাধু *a.* evil, bad, wicked, dishonest; corrupt. **অসাধুতা** *n.* badness, wickedness; dishonesty; corruptness; corruption.

অসাধ্য *a.* incapable of being done or accomplished or attained or realized; unperformable, impracticable, unattainable, unrealizable, unachievable through meditation, asceticism etc. (অসাধ্য সাধনা) ; irremediable, incurable (অসাধ্য রোগ). **~সাধন** *n.* making the impossible possible; realization of the unrealizable, attainment of the unattainable; (loos.) accomplishment of a seemingly impossible task (esp. through extraordinary efforts). **শিবের অসাধ্য** even gods cannot do, even beyond the power of gods.

অসাফল্য *n.* failure, lack of success.

অসাবধান, অসাবধানী *a.* uncareful, careless; incautious; unguarded; inattentive, inadvertent, unheeding. **~তা** *n.* carelessness; incaution; unguarded state; inattention, inadvertence. **অসাবধানতাবশত** *adv.* through carelessness or inadvertence, inadvertently.

অসামঞ্জস্য *n.* lack of proportion or symmetry, disproportionateness, asymmetry; incongruity; irrelevance, incoherence; unlikeness, difference, disagreement; lack of compromise.

অসাময়িক *a.* untimely; unseasonal; inopportune.

অসামরিক *a.* non-military; civil.

অসামর্থ্য *n.* lack of strength or power or competence; inability; incapability; incompetence; disability.

অসামাজিক *a.* not pertaining to the society, not in keeping with the rules, formalities and traditions of the (or chiefly a particular) society; unsocial; unsociable, coy, shy; unmannerly.

অসামান্য *a.* uncommon, unusual, extraordinary; not negligible; considerable; very deep (অসামান্য দুঃখ) ; profound (অসামান্য জ্ঞান) ; superhuman. **অসামান্যতা** *n.* uncommonness, unusualness, extraordinariness; considerableness; considerable depth; profundity; superhuman state.

অসামাল *a.* off one's balance, unsteady; embarrassed; uncareful, off one's guard; (vul.) unable to restrain natural discharges or evacuations, incontinent. see also **বেসামাল। অসামাল হওয়া** *v.* to be unsteady, to lose one's grip on oneself, to be off one's balance.

অসাম্প্রদায়িক *a.* non-sectarian; non-communal; cosmopolitan, universal; open to all; free from prejudice etc., liberal. **~তা** *n.* non-sectarianism; non-communalism; cosmopolitanism, universality; openness to all; freedom from prejudice etc., liberality.

অসাম্য *n.* dissimilarity, incongruity; difference; inequality; disunity; disagreement.

অসার *a.* unsubstantial, vapoury; negligible; worthless; false; pithless, marrowless, sapless (অসার কাঠ) ; futile, pointless (অসার যুক্তি). **~তা, ~ত্ব** *n.* unsubstantiality; vaporiness; negligibility; worthlessness; falseness, falsity; lack of pith or marrow or sap; futility; pointlessness. **অসার সংসার** the inane and unmeaning world, the insubstantial world.

অসার্থক *a.* unsuccessful; failed; unrealized, unfulfilled.

অসি *n.* a sword. **~ক্রীড়া** *n.* a sword-play; a sword-fight. **~চর্ম** *n.* the sword and the buckler. **~চর্মসহযোগে দ্বন্দ্ব** *a* sword-and-buckler duel. **~চর্যা, ~চালনা** *n.* learning or practising swordcraft; wielding the sword in a fight; swordcraft, swordsmanship, fencing. **~চালনা করা** *v.* to wield the sword in a fight. **~ধারা** *n.* the edge of a sword. **~ধারী** *n.* one armed with a sword, a swordsman. **~নৃত্য** *n.* a sword-dance. **~পত্র** *n.* the sugar-cane (for its leaves resemble swordblades); the scabbard of a sword. **~পুচ্ছ** *n.* a dolphin, a porpoise. **~ফলক** *n.* the blade of a sword. **~ফলকাকার** *a.* (bot.) ensiform. **~যুদ্ধ** *n.* a sword-fight, a sword-play. **~যোদ্ধা** *n.* a swordsman; a sword-player.

অসিত *n.* the black colour. □ *a.* black; sky-coloured, deep blue. *fem.* **অসিতা** । **~পক্ষ** *n.* the dark fortnight of a lunar month. **~বর্ণ, ~বরন** *a.* black; deep-blue; dark-complexioned. □ *n.* the black colour. **অসিতাঙ্গ** *a.* dark-complexioned. **অসিতোপল** *n.* sapphire.

অসিদ্ধ *a.* unboiled, uncooked; half-baked; incomplete; unaccomplished; unsuccessful, futile, unfulfilled; (of arguments etc.) untenable. **অসিদ্ধি** *n.* lack of success or fulfilment; failure.

অসীম *a.* unlimited, unbounded; infinite; endless; vast; immense; profound. □ *n.* the sky, the heaven (অসীমের পানে) ; the eternal world or life, the beyond (অসীমের যাত্রী). **~কাল** *n.* time infinite.

অসীমপথ *n.* (math.) asymptote.

অসু *n.* life; the five constituent elements of the temporal body.

অসুখ *n.* unhappiness; distress, grief; uneasiness, discomfort; displeasure; illness, ailment; a disease. **~কর, ~দায়ক, অসুখাবহ** *a.* causing unhappiness, unhappy; distressing, oppressive; causing discomfort, uncomfortable. **অসুখী** *a.* distressed, unhappy; sorrowful; displeased.

অসুন্দর *a.* not beautiful; ugly; ungraceful; ungainly; uncouth.

অসুপ্ত *a.* not asleep, awake.

অসুবিধা *n.* inconvenience, disadvantage; incommodiousness; discomfort; difficutly, trouble; hindrance; impediment. **~জনক** *a.* inconvenient, disadvantageous; incommodious; difficult; troublesome.

অসুর *n.* (myth.) one of a superhuman race hostile to gods, (cp.) a Titan; a demon; a giant; a monster; (fig.) a man of gigantic appearance or superhuman strength, a monster of a man. *fem.* **অসুরী** ।

অসুলভ *a.* not easily available, rare; not cheap; dear.

অসুষ্ঠু *a.* ungraceful; ungainly.

অসুস্থ *a.* unwell, indisposed; sick; ill; diseased, ailing; uneasy, troubled, distressed. **~তা** *n.* indisposition, sickness; illness; ailment, uneasiness, distress.

অসূক্ষ্ম *a.* not fine or refined or subtle; crude; coarse; gross; thick; blunt. **~তা** *n.* crudity; coarseness; grossness; thickness; bluntness. **~দর্শী** *a.* lacking in keen perception or acumen; short-sighted. **~দর্শিতা** *n.* lack of keen perception or acumen; short-sightedness.

অসূচিত *a.* unindicated; not expressed or signified or said; unmarked, unspecified.

অসূয়ক *a.* slandering; malicious; cynical. □ *n.* a slanderer; a malicious person; a cynic.

অসূয়া *n.* malice; envy; grudge; jealousy; cynicism. **~পর, ~পরতন্ত্র, ~পরবশ, ~পরায়ণ** *a.* malicious; envious; jealous; cynical.

অসূর্যম্পশ্যা *a. fem.* not ever sighted by

the sun; living in the gynaeceum; living in the harem; never seeing the light of day; never coming out in the public.

অসৃক *n.* blood.

অসৃক্কর *n.* (med.) serum.

অসৃষ্ট *a.* not created; of spontaneous origin.

অসেব্য, অসেবনীয় *a.* (of medicine etc.) not to be taken.

অসৈরণ *a.* incapable of being brooked; unbearable; intolerable.

অসোয়াস্তি same as **অস্বস্তি**।

অসৌজন্য *n.* discourtesy, impoliteness; lack of cordiality; incivility, unbecoming conduct.

অসৌম্য *a.* unlovely; ungentle; not calm or placid; not sedate or sober.

অসৌষ্ঠব *n.* lack of grace or beauty; ungainliness, disorderliness, clumsiness; indecorousness, indecency.

অসৌহার্দ, অসৌহার্দ্য *n.* lack of amity or friendliness.

অস্খলন *n.* lack or absence of the guilt or a lapse or mistake; lack or absence of felling or shedding.

অস্ট্রেলয়েড *n.* one ethnically belonging to the Australoid group.

অস্ট্রেলিয়ান, অস্ট্রেলীয় *a.* Australian. ☐ *n.* an Australian; the language of Australia.

অস্ট্রেলেশীয় *a.* Australasian. ☐ *n.* an Australasian; any of the languages of Australasia.

অস্ত *n.* (myth.) an imaginary mountain behind which the sun goes down whilst setting (also **অস্তগিরি, অস্তাচল**); the setting of the sun, moon etc., going below the horizon; decline; end; fall. **~গত, ~মিত** *a.* (of the sun, moon etc.) that which has set or gone below the horizon, declined. **~গমন, ~মন** *n.* setting or going below the horizon, decline. **~গামী, অস্তাচলগামী** *a.* going to set, setting. **অস্তোদয়** *n.* the rising and setting (of the sun). ☐ *adv.* throughout the day; from dawn to dusk.

অস্তর[১] coll, corrup. of **অস্ত্র**।

অস্তর[২] *n.* a mixture of slaked lime, sand etc. used for coating walls, ceilings; plaster; material sewn to the inner surface of a garment, lining.

অ-স্তরীভূত *a.* unstratified.

অস্তাচল see **অস্ত**।

অস্তি *v.* is. ☐ *n.* existence; presence; esse. **~ত্ব** *n.* existence; presence; esse. **অস্তিত্বশীল** same as **~মান**। **অস্তিত্বহীন** *a.* inexistent; absent; false; illusory, vapoury. **~নাস্তি** *n.* existence and inexistence, presence and absence; theism and atheism; (phil.) dialectics. **~বাচক** *a.* denoting presence or existence. **~মান** *a.* existent; present; in esse.

অস্তু *v.* (*imp.*) let there be, may there be, let it be, may it be.

অস্তেব্যস্তে *adv.* in haste, in a great hurry, in a flurry.

অস্তোদয় see **অস্ত**।

অস্তোন্মুখ *a.* about to go down below the horizon, about to set; setting.

অস্ত্যর্থ *n.* implication of existence or presence. **~ক** *a.* containing implication or implying of existence or presence.

অস্ত্র *n.* a missile; a weapon; arms (অস্ত্রহীন) ; a tool or instrument for cutting, boring etc. (ডাক্তারি অস্ত্র) ; (fig.) one who or that which is used as an instrument (সে তোমার অস্ত্র). **অস্ত্র করা** *v.* to operate (upon) surgically, to lance (a boil etc.), to cut open with a lancet. **~ক্ষত** *n.* a wound caused by a weapon. **~ক্ষেপ, ~ক্ষেপণ** *n.* the discharge of a missile; act of striking with a weapon. **~ক্ষেপণ করা** *v.* to discharge or hurl a missile; to strike with a weapon. **~গ্রহণ** *n.* same as **অস্ত্রধারণ**। **~চালনা** *n.* use of arms. **~চিকিৎসক** *n.* a surgeon. **~চিকিৎসা** *n.* surgery. **~চিকিৎসা করা** *v.* to operate (upon); to practise surgery. **~ত্যাগ** *n.* the discharge of a missile; act of relinquishing or giving up one's arms. **~ত্যাগ করা** *v.* to discharge or hurl a missile; to relinquish or give up one's arms, to lay down one's arms; to surrender. **~ধারণ** *n.* act of arming oneself; act of taking up arms; act of encountering in an armed fight. **~ধারণ করা** *v.* to arm oneself; to take up arms; to encounter in a battle. **~ধারী** *a.* armed (অস্ত্রধারী প্রহরী). ☐

n. an armed person. ~নিবারণ *n.* act of warding off or counteracting a missile thrown. ~নিবারণ করা *v.* to ward off or counteract a missile thrown. ~বর্ষণ *n.* throwing missiles; shower of missiles. ~বল *n.* military power; power of the arms. ~বিদ *a.* & *n.* one who is skilled in using weapons. ~বিদ্যা *n.* the art and science of using weapons; surgery. ~বৃষ্টি *n.* a shower of missiles. ~লেখা *n.* a wound caused by a weapon; mark of such a wound. ~শস্ত্র *n.* (collec.) weapons, arms, armoury. ~শালা same as অস্ত্রাগার। ~সংবরণ *n.* act of laying down arms; cease-fire; act of refraining from using weapons; act of withdrawing a missile thrown. ~সংবরণ করা *v.* to lay down arms; to refrain from using weapons; to withdraw a missile thrown. ~হীন *a.*unarmed; disarmed. ~হীন করা *v.* to unarm; to disarm.

অস্ত্রাগার *n.* an armoury.

অস্ত্রাঘাত *n.* the blow of a weapon.

অস্ত্রাহত *a.* struck or wounded or hurt with a weapon.

অস্ত্রী *a.* armed. □ *n.* an armed person.

অস্ত্রোপচার *n.* surgical operation. অস্ত্রোপচার করা *v.* to operate (upon). অস্ত্রোপচার বিভাগ the surgical ward.

অস্থান *n.* a vicious or miserable place; an evil place; a wrong or improper or unsuitable place. অস্থানে রাখা *v.* to misplace.

অস্থান-কুস্থান *n.* a foul or filthy place, a bad place; a place to be avoided or not to be visited.

অস্থানিক *a.* not native or local; foreign, extraneous, alien; (bot.) adventitious.

অস্থাবর *a.* (of property etc.) movable. অস্থাবর সম্পত্তি *n.* movable property.

অস্থায়ী *a.* impermanent; temporary; transient; unstable; not durable; floating, passing (অস্থায়ী ভাব); perishable (অস্থায়ী জীবন). অস্থায়িত্ব, অস্থায়িতা *n.* impermanence; temporariness; transience; instability; want of durability; perishability.

অস্থি *n.* bone; skeleton. ~চর্মসার *a.* lean, skinny, skin-and-bone, gaunt. অস্থি দেওয়া *v.* to deposit in or commit to the Ganges (or other holy waters) the bone or bone-ash of a deceased person (as the final part of the obsequies). ~পঞ্জর *n.* bones and ribs; skeleton. ~বৎ *a.* bone-like, bony. ~বিজ্ঞান, ~বিদ্যা *n.* osteology. ~বিজ্ঞানী *n.* an osteologist. ~বিদ্যাগত *a.* osteological. ~সার *a.* having little flesh; bony, lean, gaunt.

অস্থিতপঞ্চ, অস্থিতপঞ্চক, অস্থিতপঞ্চম *n.* arithmetic of infinites; (arith.) the double rule of three or unitary method; a difficult or intricate problem; a puzzle; bewilderment.

অস্থিতি *n.* movement; unstableness; change.

অস্থিতিস্থাপক *a.* inelastic. ~তা *n.* inelasticity.

অস্থির *a.* restless; unsteady; unstable; agitated; excited; perturbed; impatient; fretting, fretful; uneasy; fickle; frivolous; changeful; uncertain. ~চিত্ত, ~প্রকৃতি, ~বুদ্ধি, ~মতি *a.* fickle-minded; frivolous; batty, barmy; impetuous. ~চিত্ততা *n.* fickle-mindedness; restlessness; impatience. ~তা *n.* restlessness; unsteadiness; instability; excitement; agitated or perturbed state; impatience; fretting, fretfulness, uneasiness; frivolity; changefulness; uncertainty. ~সংকল্প *a.* irresolute; undecided (in action or purpose). ~সংকল্পতা *n.* irresolution; indecision.

অস্থিরপঞ্চক, অস্থিরপঞ্চম variants of অস্থিতপঞ্চ।

অস্থূল *a.* not fat or thick, thin, delicate, slim; not gross or coarse; fine; subtle; transcendental.

অস্থৈর্য *n.* impatience; restlessness.

অস্নাত *a.* unbathed.

অস্নাতক *a.* undergraduate. □ *n.* a non-graduate; an undergraduate.

অস্নেহ *n.* unfriendliness; lack of affection; neglect.

অস্পন্দ *a.* not throbbing; motionless; stiff; still. অস্পন্দিত *a.* of suspended throbbing; not throbbing; not vibrating.

অস্পর্শনীয়, অস্পর্শ variants of অস্পৃশ্য।

অস্পষ্ট *a.* indistinct; not clear; obscure; hazy; vague; dim (অস্পষ্ট আলো); inarticulate (অস্পষ্ট বুলি); illegible (অস্পষ্ট

লেখা). **~তা** *n.* indistinctness; obscurity; haziness; vagueness; lack of clarity (of thought, expression etc.), dimness; inarticulateness; illegibility. **~ভাবে** *adv.* indistinctly, vaguely; inarticulately.

অস্পৃশ্য *a.* that should not be touched; untouchable; profane, unclean; abominable; dirty; intangible. **~তা** *n.* untouchability; dirtiness; profanity; abominableness; intangibility.

অস্পৃষ্ট *a.* untouched; untasted (অস্পৃষ্ট খাদ্য).

অস্পৃহ *a.* having no desire or longing, not desirous; not covetous or avaricious; indifferent. **অস্পৃহা** *n.* absence of desire or longing; indifference or unconcern.

অস্ফীত *a.* not swollen or inflated.

অস্ফুট *a.* unbloomed; inarticulate (অস্ফুট বুলি) ; unexpressed, unrevealed; indistinct (অস্ফুট রেখা) ; obscure, translucent (অস্ফুট আলোক) ; low and indistinct (অস্ফুট কণ্ঠ) ; undertoned (অস্ফুট স্বর). **~কণ্ঠে** *adv.* in an undertone; whisperingly. **~বাক** *a.* of inarticulate speech, babbling, mumbling.

অস্বচ্ছ *a.* not transparent, opaque; not clear; turbid. **~তা** *n.* lack of transparency, opacity, opaqueness; turbidity.

অস্বচ্ছন্দ *a.* uneasy; uncomfortable; not facile; faltering, halting; not in easy circumstances. **~তা, অস্বাচ্ছন্দ্য** *n.* uneasiness, discomfort; absence of facileness; stringency.

অস্বভাবী *a.* abnormal; unnatural.

অস্বস্তি *n.* uneasiness; discomfort; trouble. **~কর** *a.* uneasy; uncomfortable.

অস্বাচ্ছন্দ্য see **অস্বচ্ছন্দ**।

অস্বাভাবিক *a.* unusual; unnatural; abnormal; rare. **~তা** *n.* unusualness; unnaturalness; abnormalcy; rarity.

অস্বামিক *a.* without an owner; ownerless. **অস্বামিক সম্পত্তি** unclaimed property.

অস্বাস্থ্য *n.* ill-health; illness; ailment. **~কর** *a.* detrimental or unfavourable to health; unhealthy; unhygienic.

অস্বীকার *n.* refusal; denial; non-acceptance; rejection; repudiation; dissent; non-compliance. **অস্বীকার করা** *v.* to refuse; to gainsay, to deny; to disavow; to reject; to disown, to repudiate; to dissent; to decline.

অস্বীকার্য *a.* unacceptable; inadmissible.

অস্বীকৃত *a.* refused; gainsaid, denied; disavowed; repudiated; rejected; disowned; dissented; not complied (with); declined. **অস্বীকৃত হওয়া** *v.* to decline; to refuse; to deny. **অস্বীকৃতি** *n.* same as **অস্বীকার**।

অস্মদীয় *a.* (rare) to ours, ours.

অস্মদ্দেশীয় *a.* of or relating to our country.

অস্মদ্দেশে *adv.* in our country.

অস্মরণ *n.* non-remembrance; oblivion; forgetfulness. **অস্মরণীয়** *a.* not worth remembering, not memorable.

অস্মার *n.* amnesia.

অস্মিতা *n.* egotism; vanity; conceit.

অস্র *n.* an angle; a side, an arm.

অস্রোত *n.* lack or absence of flow; lack of movement.

অহং *pro.* I. ☐ *n.* self, the ego; egotism; self-conceit, vanity; arrogance. **~বুদ্ধি** *n.* self-conceit, vanity; egotism; (loos.) selfishness.

অহংকার *n.* self-conceit; vanity, pride; haughtiness, arrogance; vainglory. **অহংকার করা** *v.* to take pride in; to boast, to brag. **~বিহীন** *a.* unpretentious; modest. **অহংকারী** *a.* self-conceited; proud; haughty, arrogant; vainglorious. **অহংকারে মত্ত** maddened with pride.

অহংকৃত *a.* self-conceited; proud; haughty, arrogant, insolent; vainglorious.

অহনা *n.* the dawn.

অহম্ var. of **অহং**।

অহমিকা *n.* (psy.) egoism, egotism, pride; self-conceit, vanity.

অহমিয়া correct form of **অসমিয়া**।

অহরহ *adv.* every day, daily; day in and day out; always; incessantly.

অহর্নিশ, অহর্নিশি *adv.* day and night; all the time; always; incessantly.

অহল্যা *a.* (of land) not yet cultivated or ploughed or tilled (অহল্যা ভূমি) ; (in the Puranas) name of Gautama's wife whom Ramachandra freed or redeemed from a curse.

অহি *n.* the snake, the serpent. **~তুণ্ডিক** *n.* a

snake-charmer. ~নকুলসম্পর্ক *n.* perpetual enmity as that existing between the snake and the mongoose. ~ভূষণ *n.* one who is ornamented with snakes; an appellation of Shiva (শিব). ~রাজ *n.* king of snakes.

অহিংস *a.* free from malice; nonmalignant; non-violent; inoffensive; harmless. **অহিংস অসহযোগ** (pol.) non-violent non-cooperation. ~ক *a.* free from malice or ferocity; inoffensive; harmless; innocent. **অহিংসা** *n.* freedom from malice; (phil.) ahimsa; non-violence.

অহিংস্র same as **অহিংসক** (see **অহিংস**).

অহিত *n.* harm; injury. ~কর *a.* harmful; injurious; malignant; unwholesome. ~কামী *a.* desirous of doing harm, evil-minded, evil-intentioned; malevolent, maleficent. ~কারী *a.* & *n.* one who causes harm or injury; one who maligns. **অহিতাচরণ, অহিতাচার** *n.* harmful practice, prejudicial practice; harm.

অহিতুণ্ডিক, অহিনকুল সম্পর্ক see **অহি**।

অহিন্দু *n.* a non-Hindu, one who is not a Hindu.

অহিফেন *n.* opium; the poppy-plant. ~সেবী *n.* an opium-eater.

অহিভূষণ see **অহি**।

অহৃষ্ট *a.* not pleased or glad, not delighted or happy.

অহেতুক *a.* causeless, reasonless; groundless, unjustified; unreasonable; unaccountable; without provocation; for nothing. □ *adv.* without cause or provocation; for nothing.

অহৈতুক *a.* causeless; unjustified; unaccountable; spontaneous. *fem.* **অহৈতুকী**। **অহৈতুকী ভক্তি** disinterested or selfless devotion.

অহো *int.* oh, O, alas, alack, ah.

অহোরাত্র, অহোরাত্রি *adv.* day and night; always.

অহ্ন *n.* (used as a *sfx.*) day; the fixed part of a day (usu. three hours পূর্বাহ্ণ, মধ্যাহ্ন).

অ্যাঁ *int.* expressing : surprise, is it so ?

অ্যাটলাস *a.* an atlas.

অ্যারোরুট *n.* arrowroot.

অ্যাসিড *n.* acid.

আ[1] *n.* the second vowel of the Bengali alphabet.

আ[2] *int.* expressing : surprise, bewilderment, delight, relief, regret, vexation, aversion, anxiety, suspense, fright, consternation; ah, oh.

আ[3] *pfx.* denoting : a little, slight (আকম্প) ; thorough (আক্ষিপ্ত) ; starting from (আজন্ম, আসমুদ্র) ; up to (আকণ্ঠ, আমরণ) ; during the whole of, throughout (আজীবন) ; including (আচণ্ডাল) ; contrary to (আগমন) ; implying negation, up-, non- (আকাটা) ; perverted, vile (আকথা) ; bad, disagreeable, unsuitable, difficult, hard (আঘাট, আকাল) etc.

আই *n.* mother; one's mother's mother or aunt.

আইও alt. spell. of **আইয়ো**।

আইডিন var. of **আইয়োডিন**।

আইঢাই *adv.* feeling extreme uneasiness (owing to excess of anything). □ *a.* extremely uneasy. **আইঢাই করা** *v.* to feel or become extremely uneasy.

আইন *n.* a law; an act; a regulation; an ordinance; a statute; a rule; a system; the whole code of laws, the law. **আইন করা** *v.* to enact a law; to pass a bill; to legislate; to make a rule. **দেওয়ানি আইন** civil law. **ফৌজদারি আইন** criminal law. **সামরিক আইন** martial law. **আইন-উপদেষ্টা** *n.* one who advises on legal points, a legal adviser; counsel. **~-কানুন** *n. pl.* rules and regulations. **~গত** *a.* legal; statutory. **~গ্রন্থ** *n.* a law-book. **~জীবী, ~-ব্যবসায়ী** *n.* a legal practitioner; a pleader, an advocate, a barrister, an attorney, a solicitor, etc., a lawyer. **~জ্ঞ** *a.* versed in law. □ *n.* a jurist. **~ত** *adv.* according to or in keeping with the law or laws, legally or lawfully. **~-পরিষদ** *n.* a legislative council; a legislature. **~-প্রণয়ন** *n.* enactment; legislation. **~-প্রণেতা** *n.* a legislator; a lawgiver. **~মন্ত্রক** *n.* the ministry of law. **~মন্ত্রী, ~সচিব** *n.* a law-minister. **~মাফিক** *a.* & *adv.* same as **আইনানুযায়ী**। **~শাস্ত্র** *n.* jurisprudence; the whole code of laws, the law; a law-book. **~সংগত, ~সম্মত** *a.* lawful; legitimate. **~-সভা** *n.* a legislative assembly; a legislature. **আইনানুগ** *a.* law-abiding; lawful; legitimate. **আইনানুযায়ী** *adv.* according to or in keeping with the law, legally or lawfully. □ *a.* legal; lawful. **আইনানুসারে** same as **আইনানুযায়ী** (*adv.*)

আইবড়, আইবুড়ো *a.* unmarried. **আইবুড়োভাত** *n.* the ceremony of taking the last meal by a Hindu bride or bridegroom on the night immediately preceding their wedding-day. **আইবুড়ো মেয়ে** a woman who remains single after the conventional age for marrying, a spinster.

আইমা *n.* one's mother's mother or aunt.

আইয়ো *n.* a woman whose husband is alive.

আইয়োডিন *n.* tincture of iodine.

আইল[1] (pronun. : আইল্) corrup.of **আলি**।

আইল[2] (pronun. : আইলো)—currup. of **আসিল**।

আইস obs. form of **এসো**। **আইসে** obs. form of **আসে**।

আউওল *a.* first; chief; best.

আউট *adv.* & *a.* out; incorrigibly depraved or abandoned, gone to the dogs.

আউটানো *v.* to stir (milk) whilst boiling.

আউরত var. of **আওরত**।

আউল[1] (pronun. : আউল্) *n.* a religious mendicant sect of India following a very easy course of worship; a person possessing supernatural powers. **আউলিয়া** *a.* of the আউল sect.

আউল[2] (pronun. : আউলো), **আউলা** *a.* dishevelled. **আউলা-ঝাউলা** *a.* dishevelled and untidy. **আউলানো** *v.* to dishevel. □ *a.* dishevelled.

আউলিয়া see **আউল**[1] ।

আউশ, আউস *a.* (chiefly of paddy) ripening in the rainy season or in autumn; (loos.) ripening or growing early.

আওটানো var. of **আউটানো**।

আওড় *n.* a whirlpool.

আওড়ানো *v.* (chiefly facet.) to pronounce or recite (usu. repeatedly). ☐ *n.* (repeated) pronouncement or recitation.

আওতা *n.* (rare) shade, sunshade; care; guardianship, custody; control; reach; jurisdiction; purview. (কারও) **আওতায়** under one's power or tutelage or guardianship.

আওয়াজ *n.* sound; noise; voice.

আওয়াজি *n.* a small window in the upper part of the wall, (cp.) a bay-window, (cp.) a skylight.

আওরত *n.* a woman; one's wife.

আওরানো *v.* (of boils etc.) to swell and become painful, to inflame.

আওল[১] var. of **আউওল**।

আওল[২] arch. form of **আসিল**।

আওলাত, আওলাদ *n.* fruit-trees and other immovable property; offspring, progeny.

আওসত *n.* a large holding of land held in fee under a landowner, (cp.) a fief.

আংটা *n.* a ring; a ring-like handle.

আংটি *n.* a finger-ring.

আংরা *n.* burning coal, live coal; charcoal; cinder.

আংরাখা *n.* a jacket; a coat; a cloak.

আংশিক *a.* of a part or parts or a share or shares; partial; incomplete. **~ভাবে** *adv.* in part, partially.

আঃ emphatic form of **আ[২]**।

আঁ *int.* expressing : dismay, pain etc.

আঁইশ corrup. of **আঁশ**।

আঁক *n.* a mark or line; (arith. & alg.) a problem, a sum. **আঁক কষা** *v.* to do a sum. **আঁক কাটা** *v.* to draw a line; to scratch.

আঁকড়া *n.* a hook; a tendril; a ring. **আঁকড়া-আঁকড়ি** *n.* act of holding fast as in an embrace, grappling. **~নো** *v.* to grapple (doggedly); to embrace (tightly); to grasp, to gripe. **আঁকড়ে ধরা** to hold in a tight grasp or embrace.

আঁকড়ি *n.* any hook-shaped object or sign; any of such signs affixed to alphabetical letters.

আঁকন *n.* act or manner of painting; a painted picture.

আঁকশি *n.* a pole with a hook fixed to one of its ends, used for plucking fruits, flowers etc. or for other purposes.

আঁকা *v.* to draw, to trace, to paint; to mark; to write; to describe, to delineate. ☐ *n.* act of drawing or tracing or painting or marking or writing or describing or delineating. ☐ *a.* drawn, traced, painted; marked; written; described, delineated. **~নো** *v.* to cause to draw or trace or paint or mark or write or describe or delineate. **আঁকার হাত** *n.* ability to draw.

আঁকিবুকি *n.* a scribble, drawing or writing carelessly or unmindfully.

আঁকাবাঁকা *a.* zigzag, winding, meandering; tortuous.

আঁকুপাঁকু, আঁকুবাঁকু *n.* fidget. **আঁকুপাঁকু করা** *v.* to fidget.

আঁকুশি var. of **আঁকশি**।

আঁখ corrup. of **আঁখি**।

আঁখর *n.* a letter of the alphabet.

আঁখি *n.* an eye. **~জল** *n.* tear. **আঁখি ঠারা** *v.* to ogle; to wink or blink (at). **~পাত** *n.* an eyelid.

আঁচ *n.* the ignited state of an oven, ignition; degree of ignition; heat; glow; surmise, guess, conjecture, a hint; anticipation; a presage. **আঁচ ওঠা** *v.* to ignite, to take fire. **আঁচ করা** *v.* to surmise, to sense, to guess, to conjecture, to anticipate. **আঁচ দেওয়া** *v.* to ignite, to enkindle, to set on fire; to hint; to presage. **আঁচ ধরা** *v.* to take fire, to ignite. **আঁচ পাওয়া** *v.* to get a hint (of). **আঁচ লাগা** *v.* to be affected with slight stress or burden (of).

আঁচড় *n.* an instance of scraping or digging with the finger-nails or claws, a scratch; a thin mark or line; (fig.) a cursory or slight examination or effort (এক আঁচড়ে বুঝে নেওয়া). **এক আঁচড়ে** upon a cursory or slight examination.

আঁচড়কামড় *n.* act of scratching and biting; bites and scratches.

আঁচড়া-আঁচড়ি *n.* act of mutual scratching with finger-nails or claws in a fight.

আঁচড়ানো *v.* to scratch or dig with finger-nails or claws; to comb (hair). ☐ *a.* scratched or dug with the finger-nails or claws; combed, kempt.

আঁচর poet. corrup. of **আঁচল**।

আঁচল *n.* an expanse of a part or an end of a loin-cloth (esp. one worn by women). **~-ধরা** *a.* (said of a man) very obedient to women or to one's wife; henpecked; (of a boy) very much dependent on his mother.

আঁচলা *n.* an ornamented border of a woman's loin-cloth.

আঁচা *v.* to surmise, to sense, to guess, to conjecture; to anticipate.

আঁচানো *v.* to wash one's mouth, esp. by rinsing after a meal. **না আঁচালে বিশ্বাস নেই** there's many a slip betwixt the cup and the lip.

আঁচিল *n.* a wart, a mole, a blotch.

আঁজনাই *n.* a sty, a stye; a very small kind of lizard akin to the iguana.

আঁজলা, আঁজল *n.* palms of one's hands cupped together; the amount that a cup thus contains, a handful.

আঁট *n.* tightness, tension; compactness (কথার আঁট), restraint, reserve (মুখের আঁট). □ *a.* tight; close-fitting; tense. **আঁট করা** *v.* to make tight, to tighten.

আঁটকুড়, আঁটকুড়া, আঁটকুড়িয়া, আঁটকুড়ে *a.* childess. *fem.* **আঁটকুড়ি**। **আঁটকুড়ের বেটা** a barren woman's son, a monstrosity (a term of absue). *fem.* **আঁটকুড়ের বেটি**।

আঁটনি var. of **আঁটুনি**।

আঁটসাঁট *a.* tight, not loose. **আঁটসাঁট পোশাক** tight-fitting clothes, close-fitting garment. **আঁটসাঁট বেঁধে কাজ করা** to start (work etc.) with due preparation and precaution and by providing against probable contingency.

আঁটা *v.* to fasten tightly, to tighten; to wear, to put on (পাগড়ি আঁটা) ; to bolt (দরজায় খিল আঁটা) ; to fix (স্ক্রু আঁটা) ; to affix (খামে টিকিট আঁটা) ; to shut, to close (দরজা আঁটা, লেফাফা আঁটা) ; to (be able to) contain or hold, to have capacity or room for (বালতিতে দুধ আঁটা), to contend with (usu. equally); to be equal to; to contrive (ফন্দি আঁটা) ; to be equal to, to cope with (বুদ্ধিতে আঁটা). □ *a.* closed, shut. **আঁটাআঁটি, আঁটিসাঁটি** *n.* excessive tightness; excessive strictness or rigour; firmness; higgling; excessive attention to (usu. one's own) interests (নিজের বেলা আঁটিসাঁটি). **~নো** *v.* to cause or force to contain or hold.

আঁটি[1] *n.* a bundle. **বোঝার উপর শাকের আঁটি** the last straw that breaks the camel's back.

আঁটি[2] *n.* the stone of a fruit.

আঁটিসাঁটি see **আঁটা**।

আঁটুনি *n.* tightness, tension; tight fastening or fixation; strictness, rigour; (of speech etc.) compactness.

আঁটুবাঁটু *n.* effort in spite of incapability, fumbling. □ *adv.* fumblingly.

আঁটো *a.* tight; close-fitting.

আঁটোসাঁটো var. of **আঁটসাঁট**।

আঁত *n.* intestines, entrails; catgut; vital or inmost part (আঁতে ঘা লাগা) ; one's secret intention or design or mental disposition (আঁত বোঝা). **আঁতে ঘা দেওয়া** to grieve or hurt a person by pricking his or her weak point, to cut to the quick.

আঁতকানো *v.* to feel sudden alarm, to startle. **আঁতকে ওঠা** same as **আঁতকানো**। **আঁতকানি** *n.* startle.

আঁতড়ি *n.* entrails, intestines.

আঁতরস *n.* gastric juice.

আঁতাঁত *n. entente*; alliance in politics.

আঁতিপাঁতি *adv.* at the head and at the foot of a bed; everywhere.

আঁতুড় *n.* a lying-in room, a labour-room (আঁতুড় ঘর) ; confinement of a woman at childbirth.

আঁদরু-পেঁদরু *n.* (facet. & derog.) an Indian Christian ludicrously imitating the Europeans in his daily life.

আঁদিসাঁদি *n. pl.* loopholes; tricks and stratagems; (*sing.*) due arrangement, order, system.

আঁধার *n.* darkness, gloom; absence of light. □ *a.* dark, gloomy; deprived of light. **আঁধার ঘরের মানিক** an object of precious hope and consolation amidst utter misery; silver-lining. **মনের আঁধার** ignorance; extreme sorrow or dejection. **আঁধারি** same as **আঁধার**।

আঁধি *n.* stormy wind, strong wind; a storm; a danger; mental suffering; agony; a cause of disturbing something ('ঘুম ভাঙাবার আঁধি').

আঁধিসাধি var. of **আঁদিসাদি।**

আঁব dial. corrup. of **আম।**

আঁশ *n.* fibre; scales of a fish; (any) thin membranous excrescence on some insects, seeds, fruits etc; nap of cloth; grain of wood; (any of the) threadlike membranes in some fruits.

আঁশটে *a.* smelling of scales of fish; smelling of fish.

আঁশফল *n.* a kind of small fruit having similarity to litchi; longan, *Euphoria longana.*

আঁশানো *v.* to harden by boiling in liquefied sugar, molasses, treacle, etc. □ *a.* thus boiled.

আঁশালো *a.* fibrous.

আঁষ *n.* any article of non-vegetarian food such as fish or meat. □ *a.* used in cutting or dressing or cooking articles of non-vegetarian food. (আঁষবটি). **~টে** *a.* smelling of fish or meat.

আঁস্তাকুড়, আস্তাকুঁড় *n.* a place for depositing household and other rubbish, a dump, a dustbin. **আঁস্তাকুড়ের পাতা বা পাত** any large tree-leaf used for a dinner-plate and then thrown into the dustbin; (fig.) an ignoble or base person. **আঁস্তাকুড়ের পাত কখনো স্বর্গে যায় না** an ignoble person can never continue in a noble company.

আক dial. corrup. of **আখ।**

আককুটে, আকখুটে *a.* (of a person) wasteful, squandering, prodigal, spendthrift.

আকচা-আকচি *n.* mutual envy or jealousy; unhealthy competition (over trifling things).

আকছার, আকচার *adv.* frequently, every now and then, often; always.

আকজ, আখজ *n.* grudge, malice, animosity, spite.

আকড়িয়া *a.* penniless, very poor; worthless. □ *n.* a penniless person, a pauper. **আকড়ে** coll. var. of **আকড়িয়া।**

আকণ্ঠ *adv.* (filling) up to one's throat; (fig.) almost completely submerged or sunk (আকণ্ঠ নিমজ্জিত). **ঋণে আকণ্ঠ নিমজ্জিত হওয়া** to be over head and ears in debt. **আকণ্ঠ ভোজন করা** *v.* to eat and drink to excess, to overfeed, to surfeit.

আকথা coll. var. of **অকথা।**

আকনি var. of **আখনি।**

আকন্দ *n.* a kind of tree, the sunplant, *Calotropis gigantia,* the swallow wort.

আকপিল, আকপিশ *a.* greyish, of light ash colour.

আকবরি, আকব্বরি *a.* of Emperor Akbar or his reign.

আকম্প, আকম্পন *n.* a slight trembling or thrill or throbbing or vibration.

আকম্পিত, আকম্প্র *a.* trembling or throbbing or vibrating slightly.

আকর *n.* a mine, a quarry; a source or origin; a store or repertory. **আকরিক** *a.* of mines, mineral. □ *n.* a mineral ore. **আকরীয়** *a.* of mines, mineral.

আকর্ণ *adv.* (stretched or drawn) up to the ear. **~পূরিত** *a.* (of a string of a bow) drawn up to the ear of the shooter whilst taking aim. **~বিস্তৃত** *a.* (of one's eyes etc.) stretched up to the ears.

আকর্ষ *n.* attraction; pull; any object by which something is drawn or pulled; magnet; a tendril. **আকর্ষক, আকর্ষিক, আকর্ষী** *a.* that which attracts or draws or pulls. □ *n.* lodestone.

আকর্ষণ *n.* attraction; pull; affection, love. **আকর্ষণী** *a.* attracting.

আকর্ষিক, আকর্ষী see **আকর্ষ।**

আকলন *n.* calculation; (accts.) credit. **~স্থিতি** *n.* credit balance.

আকলপত্র *n.* a letter of credit.

আকসার var. of **আকছার।**

আকস্মিক *a.* sudden; unexpected. **আকস্মিক ঘটনা** unexpected or chance occurrence. **~তা** *n.* suddenness, unexpectedness; abruptness.

আকাঁড়া *a.* (of rice etc.) unhusked; not thoroughly husked; unrefined.

আকাঙ্ক্ষণীয় *a.* desirable; worthy of being desired or wished for.

আকাঙ্ক্ষা *n.* a desire; a wish, a longing; (gr.) necessity for a word to complete a sentence. **আকাঙ্ক্ষা করা** *v.* to desire; to wish, to long for.

আকাঙ্ক্ষিত *a.* desired; wished for.

আকাঙ্ক্ষী *a.* desirous; wishing for. *fem.* **আকাঙ্ক্ষিণী।**

আকাট[1] var. of **আকাঠ।**

আকাট২ *a.* downright, out-and-out, thorough, arrant (আকাট মূর্খ) ; foolish (আকাট লোক).

আকাটা *a.* uncut. **আকাটা হীরা** rough diamond.

আকাঠ, আকাঠা *n.* inferior or worthless timber.

আকাম *n.* bad or unworthy work.

আকামানো *a.* unshaved; (rare) unearned (আকামানো কড়ি).

আকার১ *n.* shape, form; figure; appearance.

আকার২ *n.* the vowel আ or its sound; addition of the vowel-sound আ or the vowel itself to consonants; the post-consonantal symbol of আ।

আকার-ইঙ্গিত *n.* gestures and postures.

আকার-পরিমাপ *n.* contour survey.

আকার-প্রকার *n.* appearance and bearing.

আকারমাত্রিক *a.* (of musical notation) using the post-consonantal আ-কার as the measure in notation.

আকারান্ত *a.* (of words) ending with the vowel or the vowel-sound আ।

আকারিক *n.* a summons bailiff.

আকাল *n.* famine; scarcity; hard times.

আকালিক *a.* grown or ripened out of season, untimely; short-lived, transient.

আকাশ *n.* the sky, the firmament; the heavens. **আকাশকুসুম** *n.* a visionary project, a day-dream; a fool's paradise. **~কুসুম কল্পনা করা** *v.* (fig.) to build castles in the air. **~গঙ্গা** *n.* the Milky Way, the Galaxy. **~চর** *a.* living or moving in the sky or ether, aerial, ethereal, aery; celestial. **~চিত্র** *n.* a picture or photograph of the sky or any part of it. **~চুম্বী** *a.* touching the sky; sky-scraping, sky-kissing; very lofty. **~চুম্বী অট্টালিকা** a sky-scraper. **~ছোঁয়া** *a.* touching the sky; (fig.) very lofty. **~জাত** *a.* born or grown in the sky or ether, aerial, ethereal, aery; celestial. **~তার** *n.* (radio.) an aerial. **আকাশ থেকে পড়া** *n. v.* (fig.) to drop from the blue; to be struck with amazement. **~দীপ** same as **আকাশপ্রদীপ**। **~দুহিতা, ~নন্দিনী** *n.* an echo. **~পট** *n.* the canvas or the expanse of the sky. **~পথ** *n.* an air route; an ethereal route. **আকাশ পাতাল** *adv.* everywhere; from heaven to the underworld; including everything. □ *a.* in a large degree, maximum, extreme (আকাশপাতাল প্রভেদ). **আকাশ পাতাল ভাবা** to be worried with numberless puzzling thoughts crowding pell-mell into one's mind. **আকাশ পাতাল ভেবে না পাওয়া** to be at a loss to think out. **~প্রদীপ** *n.* a light suspended from the top of a pole set up every evening by the Hindus during the month of Kartik (কার্তিক) in reverence to their deceased forefathers or gods. **~প্রান্ত** *n.* the border of the sky; the skyline; the horizon. **~বাণী** *n.* a celestial voice; a supernatural or divine voice from the sky; an oracle; radio broadcast; radio. **~বিহার** *n.* flying in the sky. **~বৃত্তি** *n.* the practice of somehow making both ends meet, casual subsistence; the state of having no ostensible means of living; fending for oneself in a resourceless condition. **~ভ্রমণ** same as **আকাশবিহার**। **~মণ্ডল** *n.* the (whole) expanse of the heavens, the sky, the firmament, the celestial sphere; the atmosphere. **~যান** *n.* an aircraft, an aeroplane, an airship; a balloon. **~স্থ, ~স্থিত** *a.* of or in the sky, ethereal, aerial; heavenly, celestial; divine. **আকাশে তোলা** *v. fig.* to extol in disingenuous advertisement, to puff; to flatter with praise.

আকিঞ্চন *n.* indigence, utter poverty; humble prayer or desire, craving; zeal, earnestness; endeavour, effort.

আকীর্ণ *a.* strewn, bestrewn; scattered, bespattered.

আকুঞ্চন *n.* slight contraction or shrivelling or wrinkle or curl or contortion.

আকুঞ্চিত *a.* slightly contracted or shrivelled or wrinkled or curled or contorted.

আকুতি, আকূতি *n.* ardour; fervidity; a fervent prayer, eager solicitation; entreaty.

আকুল *a.* extremely distressed or anxious or worried or uneasy; ardent, fervent, eager; nonplussed; overflowing. **~কুন্তল** unarranged or dishevelled or tousled hair. ~তা *n.* extreme distress or anxiety or worry; ardency, fervidity, eagerness; nonplus; perplexity; restlessness; overflow.

আকুলা[১] *v.* (poet.) to become or make distressed or anxious or worried or eager or nonplussed or overflowing.

আকুলা[২] *fem.* of **আকুল।**

আকুলি *imperf.* form of **আকুলা।**

আকুলিত *a.* struck with extreme distress or anxiety or perplexity.

আকুলিবিকুলি *n.* restlessness owing to worry or anxiety; extreme distress or anxiety or worry; ardency, fervidity; eagerness. □ *adv.* very anxiously or worriedly; ardently, fervently, eagerly.

আকুলীকৃত *a.* worried or perplexed; perturbed; overflowed.

আকৃতি *n.* appearance; shape, form. **~গত** *a.* pertaining to appearance or shape or form; formal; outward. **~প্রকৃতি** *n.* appearance and nature; demeanour, bearing. **~বিশিষ্ট** *a.* having a definite or specific form or shape; shaped.

আকৃষ্ট *a.* attracted;charmed, enticed; drawn, pulled; (rare) ploughed, tilled.

আকৃষ্যমাণ *a.* that which is being attracted or drawn or pulled.

আক্কেল *n.* understanding, intelligence, wit; common sense; faculty of judgment; considerateness. **আক্কেল গুড়ুম** *n.* nonplus, bewilderment, confusion. **আক্কেল গুড়ুম হওয়া** to be struck with bewilderment or confusion, to be nonplussed, to be at one's wit's end. **~দাঁত** *n.* the wisdom tooth. **~পছন্দ** *n.* ability to appraise or assess, the sense of proportion; aptitude or talent for selection and rejection; good practical sense. **~মন্ত** *a.* considerate; wise. **~সেলামি** *n.* the penalty paid or the loss suffered on account of folly.

আক্রম *n.* a forcible passage; inroad; prowess; invasion; defeat; rise, appearance.

আক্রমণ *n.* an attack; an invasion; an inroad. **আক্রমণ করা** *v.* to attack, to invade; to fall upon. **~কারী** *n.* one who attacks, an attacker, an assailant; an aggressor, an invader. **আক্রমণীয়** *a.* that which can be or is to be attacked or invaded.

আক্রা *a.* high in price, dear; costly. **আক্রাগণ্ডার দিন বা কাল** period of high prices or expensive living, hard times.

আক্রান্ত *a.* attacked; invaded; oppressed; stricken (শোকে আক্রান্ত) ; affected.

আক্রামক *n.* same as **আক্রমণকারী।**

আক্রোশ *n.* grudge; malice; anger, wrath. **~বশে** *adv.* maliciously or grudgingly, owing to malice or grudge.

আক্লান্ত *a.* extremely tired or fatigued.

আক্ষরিক *a.* relating to a letter or letters of the alphabet; literal (আক্ষরিক অর্থ) ; accurately faithful; to the letter or literal (আক্ষরিক অনুবাদ).

আক্ষিপ্ত *a.*cast, flung; scattered; affected with convulsion (usu. physical); agitated with sorrow; extremely aggrieved or distressed.

আক্ষেপ *n.* convulsion (esp. muscular); fits; grief; sorrow; lamentation.

আক্ষোট same as **আখরোট** and **আখোট।**

আখ *n.* sugarcane.

আখছার var. of **আকছার।**

আখজ see **আকজ।**

আখড়া *n.* a gymnasium; a place or institution where people assemble to practise anything esp. music, play-acting, etc.; a place where the Vaishnavas assemble for religious worship; (facet.) a club or society; (dero.) a haunt of vice, a den. **~ই** *n.* dramatic rehearsal. **~ধারী** *n.* the headman or the keeper of a place where the Vaishnavas assemble for religious worship.

আখনি *n.* stew, esp. of meat; a solution prepared by boiling water with spices for cooking some dishes.

আখর *n.* a letter of the alphabet; refrain of a song.

আখরোট *n.* the walnut.

আখা *n.* an oven; a stove; hearth; fireplace.

আখাম্বা *n.* uncouthly tall and thick as a pillar.

আখির var. of **আখের।**

আখুটি *n.* capricious and obstinate insistence or demand (as of a child). **আখুটে**

a. capriciously and obstinately insisting or demanding.

আখেটক, আখেটিক *n.* a hunter (esp. by profession or birth).

আখের *n.* consequence; the future; the end, termination. **আখেরি** *a.* last; terminal; concluding. **আখেরে ভালো হওয়া** to be paying or profitable in the long run.

আখোট same as **আখরোট**।

আখোলা *a.* not open, shut, closed; fastened, tied.

আখ্যা *n.* an appellation, a name; a title, a designation; a denomination. **~ত** *a.* named, called; entitled, designated; denominated; spoken, mentioned, said; known, renowned, celebrated. **~ন** *n.* history; a legend; a tale (esp. historical or legendary); a narrative; a story; a fable; narration, naming; act of designating or denominating. **~বস্তু** *n.* a theme. **~পত্র** *n.* a title-page (of a book). **~য়ক** *n.* a narrator; a story-teller. **~য়িকা** *n.* a tale, a story, a narrative.

আখ্যেয় *a.* having a specific appellation, named, entitled, designated, denominated; to be narrated.

আগ *n.* the forepart. □ *a.* foremost; topmost. **~ডাল** *n.* the topmost branch of a tree. **~দুয়ার** *n.* the frontdoor of a house; an outhouse. **~পাছ** *adv.* before and after, pros and cons.**আগ বাড়া** *v.* to step forward, to march forward.

আগড় *n.* an unfixed door usually made of straw, bamboo, wattles etc.; a hurdle.

আগড়ম-বাগড়ম *n.* rapid and big but idle talk, chatter. **আগড়ম-বাগড়ম বকা** *v.* to chatter.

আগত *a.* one who or that which has come, arrived. **~প্রায়** *a.* about to arrive shortly; imminent, impending.

আগন্তুক *n.* a visitor; a guest; a caller; a newcomer, a stranger. □ *a.* adventitious.

আগম *n.* the esoteric scriptures of the Hindus (viz. বেদ, তন্ত্র etc); arrival, coming (শরদাগম) ; income; earning (ধনাগম, সুখাগম) ; (bio.) an inhaling organ, an inhalant; (gr.) insertion of an extra letter or syllable in the middle of a derivative word; (phil.) any of the sources of knowledge; (comm.) import. **~নিবন্ধ** *n.* incoming or inward register. **~নিয়ামক** *n.* the controller of imports. **আগম বাণিজ্য নিয়ামক** *n.* import trade controller. **~শুল্ক** *n.* import duty.

আগমন *n.* coming; arrival. **আগমনী** *n.* any of the songs about the coming of Uma (উমা), Shiva's (শিব) wife, to her father's house as told in the Hindu legend. □ *a.* relating to coming or arrival.

আগমিত *a.* (rare) imported.

আগম্য *a.* fit to come, due to come.

আগর *n.* carpenter's boring or drilling tool, auger, perforator, borer.

আগল *n.* a door; a bolt for the door; an unfixed door (usu. made of wattles, straw, bamboo etc.); a hurdle; a barrier.

আগলা[১] *a.* uncovered, bare; unbolted, unfastened; open.

আগলা[২], **আগলানো** *v.* to restrain; to guard; to keep watch over; to manage or protect (সম্পত্তি আগলানো).

আগলি[১] *imperf.* form of **আগলা**[২]।

আগলি[২] *n.* (obs.) a house, a store, a repertory ('বুদ্ধির আগলি').

আগা[১] *n.* top (গাছের আগা) ; tip (আঙুলের আগা) ; end, extremity (লাঠির আগা).

আগা[২] *n.* a title of honour applied to a Musalman, esp. an Afghan.

আগাগোড়া *adv.* from beginning to end; alpha and omega; from head to foot, from top to bottom.

আগাছা *n.* weed.

আগানো *v.* to proceed, to go forward; to go ahead; to progress.

আগাপাছতলা, আগাপাসতলা, আগাপাস্তলা *adv.* from head to foot, cap-a-pie.

আগাম *a.* advance. □ *adv.* in advance.

আগামিক *a.* incoming.

আগামী *a.* that which is to come or happen in future; future; coming; next. **আগামী-কাল** tomorrow. **আগামীপরশু** day after tomorrow.

আগার *n.* a house; a room; a store; (rare) a container.

আগি *n.* (obs. & poet.) fire.

আগিলা *a.* (obs. & poet.) situated in the front.

আগু *n.* the first, the beginning; the past; advance. ☐ *a.* first; preceding; advance; forward. ☐ *adv. a.* first of all. ~তে *adv.* at first; in the past. ~পাছু, ~পিছু *adv. n.* from beginning to end, alpha and omega; the past and the future. ~পাছু করা, ~পিছু করা *v.* to hesitate. ~পাছু ভাবা *v.* to look before and after, to consider the pros and cons of a thing. ~য়ান, ~সার *a.* going or coming forward, advancing; proceeding; leading. আগুয়ান বা আগুসার হওয়া *v.* to go or come forward, to advance; to proceed; to take the lead.

আগুন *n.* fire. আগুন ধরা বা লাগা *v.* to take or catch fire. আগুন ধরানো বা লাগানো *v.* to set fire to. আগুন হওয়া *v.* to become inflamed; (fig.) to be heated or enraged. কপালে আগুন (fig.) extremely unfortunate, wretched; extremely scarce (মাছের কপালে আগুন). পেটে আগুন intolerable hunger. (তার) মুখে আগুন (in imprecation) may the Devil take (him). রেগে আগুন burning with rage, in a towering rage, furiously angry.

আগুনখাকি *n.* a woman of fiery temper, a highly irritable or irascible woman, virago, a shrew.

আগুনদর *n.* exorbitant or extortionate price.

আগুনে *a.* fiery. আগুনে বোমা an incendiary bomb.

আগুলফ *adv.* as far as the ankle.

আগে *adv.* at first, in the beginning; in the past; in front; before. ~কার *a.* of the beginning; of the past; of the front; preceding. আগে আগে *adv.* continuously or always in front. ~পাছে *adv.* in front and at the back; before and after. আগে পাছে করা *v.* to hesitate. ~ভাগে *adv.* first of all; at first; in advance.

আগ্নেয় *a.* of fire; impregnated with fire; emitting or producing fire; produced by fire; igneous, fiery. ~গিরি, ~পর্বত *n.* a volcano. জীবন্ত আগ্নেয়গিরি an active volcano. মৃত আগ্নেয়গিরি an extinct volcano. সুপ্ত আগ্নেয়গিরি a dormant volcano. আগ্নেয়গিরির অগ্ন্যুৎপাত volcanic eruption. আগ্নেয়গিরির মুখ a crater. ~প্রস্তর, ~শিলা *n.* igneous rock. আগ্নেয়াস্ত্র *n.* fire-arm(s).

আগ্রহ *n.* eagerness; zeal, earnestness, intentness, an intent desire; an inclination; wistfulness. আগ্রহাতিশয় *n.* excessive eagerness or zeal or affection or wistfulness. আগ্রহান্বিত *a.* eager; zealous; intent; intently desirous; inclined (to); wistful.

আগ্রাসন *n.* aggresssion, aggressive or imperialistic policy; aggrandizement; invasion. আগ্রাসী *a.* aggressive; aggrandizing.

আঘাট, আঘাটা *n.* an unused or improper place (usu. on a river-bank) for landing, mooring, bathing etc.

আঘাত *n.* a blow, a stroke, a hit; a shock; a wound, an injury; act of beating. ~ক *a.* & *n.* one who or that which deals a blow or strikes or hits or gives a shock or wounds or injures or beats. ~ন *n.* act of dealing a blow or striking or hitting or giving a shock or wounding or injuring or beating. ~সহ *a.* capable of withstanding or resisting. আঘাত করা *v.* to deal a blow, to strike, to hit; to give a shock, to shock; to wound, to injure; to beat. আঘাত পাওয়া *v.* to receive or sustain a blow, to be struck or hit; to receive or sustain a shock, to be shocked; to be wounded or injured; to be beaten.

আঘূর্ণন *n.* act of being turned or rolled or whirled round; circling or whirling; revolving. আঘূর্ণিত *a.* turned; whirled round; rolling.

আঘ্রাণ *n.* smelling or sniffing.

আঘ্রাত *a.* smelled.

আঙটা, আঙটি, আঙন, আঙরা, আঙরাখা alt. spellings of আংটা, আংটি, আঙ্গন, আংরা and আংরাখা respectively.

আঙিনা, (arch.) আঙ্গিনা *n.* a courtyard, a compound.

আঙিয়া, আঙ্গিয়া *n.* a woman's bodice, a bra.

আঙুর *n.* grape. ~খেত *n.* a vineyard grapery. আঙুর গাছ, আঙুর লতা *n.* vine আঙুরের রস *n.* grape-juice.

আঙুল *n.* a finger or a toe. আঙুল দিয়ে

দেখানো *n. v.* to point or pointing with fingers. **আঙুল ফুলে কলা গাছ** (fig.) a sudden increase in wealth or power or importance. **আঙুলের গাঁট** *n.* a knuckle. **আঙুল মটকানো** *v. n.* cracking or to crack the knuckles. **~হাড়া** *n.* whitlow. **হাতের আঙুল** a finger. **পায়ের আঙুল** a toe. **বুড়ো আঙুল** the thumb. **কড়ে আঙুল** the little finger. **আঙুলের ছাপ** fingerprint.

আঙ্কিক *a.* relating to mathematics; mathematical or arithmetical; relating to calculation.

আঙ্গন poet. corrup. of **অঙ্গন**।

আঙ্গার *n.* cinder, charcoal; coal (esp. burnt); burnt wood.

আঙ্গিক *a.* relating to the body or a limb or limbs; produced or done by the body; done or executed or acted by gestures and postures. □ *n.* gestures and postures as parts of dramatic acting; dramatic motion; form, structure; (pop.) artistry.

আঙ্গিনা arch. spell. of **আঙিনা**।

আঙ্গিয়া arch. spell. of **আঙিয়া**।

আঙ্গুর arch. spell. of **আঙুর**।

আঙ্গুল arch. spell. of **আঙুল**।

আঙ্গোট *n.* a ring for the toe.

আচকা *a.* not measured or counted. □ *adv.* suddenly, unexpectedly.

আচকান *n.* a kind of long coat or gown for men (orig. Persian).

আচঞ্চল *a.* slightly stirred up or agitated or excited.

আচমকা *adv.* suddenly; unexpectedly; unawares; causing surprise.

আচমন *n.* washing one's mouth and hands (esp. after meals); formal purification of one's body with water before religious worship as prescribed in the Hindu scriptures. **আচমন করা** *v.* to rinse and wash. **আচমনীয়** *n.* water for such washing or purification.

আচম্বিতে *adv.* suddenly; unexpectedly; unawares; surprisingly.

আচরণ *n.* conduct, behaviour; dealing, treatment; practice, observance. **আচরণ করা** *v.* to behave; to deal (with), to act (towards); to practise. **~বিধি** *n.* code of conduct, rules for conduct or behaviour or dealing. **আচরণীয়** *a.* fit for use; that which is to be practised or observed.

আচরিত *a.* practised, observed, followed, obeyed; treated; habitual.

আচষা *a.* uncultivated, unploughed.

আচাভুয়া *a.* very strange, queer; queerly shaped.

আচার[১] *n.* sauce; pickle. **আমের আচার** pickled slices of mango, mango pickles or preserves.

আচার[২] *n.* religious or scriptural rules or prescriptions, rites; observance of these rules and prescriptions; conduct, behaviour; custom, practice (দেশাচার) ; good manners or conduct. **~চ্যুত** *a.* same as **~ভ্রষ্ট**। **~নিষ্ঠ, ~পরায়ণ, ~বান** *a.* observant of religious or scriptural rules and prescriptions; well-mannered; observant of the rules of conduct. **আচারনিষ্ঠ ব্যক্তি** a person with due regard for rituals and religious practices; a ritualist. **~বিরুদ্ধ** *a.* contrary to custom or practice. **~ব্যবহার, ~বিচার** *n.* established customs and practices; conduct and behaviour. **~ভ্রষ্ট** *a.* one who has failed to observe or does not observe prescribed religious or scriptural rites. **~হীন** *a.* not observing religious or scriptural rites; impious. **আচারী** same as **~নিষ্ঠ**।

আচার্য *n.* one who teaches the Vedas; a scriptural teachers; a teacher; a tutor. *fem.* **আচার্যা** a woman teacher of the Vedas or scriptures; a woman teacher, a tutoress. *fem.* **আচার্যানী** the wife of an acharya (আচার্য).

আচালা *a.* (of wheat, rice, pulses etc.) unsifted.

আচোট *a.* uncultivated, unploughed; fallow.

আচ্ছন্ন *a.* covered; overcast; concealed; pervaded; comatose; drowsy; overwhelmed; dumbfounded.

আচ্ছা *int.* well; yes; fine; that's right. □ *a.* good, excellent; (iron.) fine (আচ্ছা বুদ্ধি) ; perfect (আচ্ছা সাধু) □ *adv.* thoroughly (usu. **আচ্ছামতো**). **আচ্ছা ঘা কতক দেওয়া** to give a good or sound drubbing, to give a good licking, to beat soundly.

আচ্ছাদক *a.* & *n.* that which or one who covers or roofs or conceals.

আচ্ছাদন *n.* covering or roofing or clothing or concealing; a covering or roofing, a cover, a lid; clothing, garment, clothes. **আচ্ছাদনীয়, আচ্ছাদ্য** *a.* that which is to be covered or roofed or clothed or concealed. **আচ্ছাদিত** *a.* covered; roofed; clothed; concealed.

আচ্ছাদিত, আচ্ছাদ্য see **আচ্ছাদন**।

আছ *v.* (*2nd. per.*) are.

আছড়া *n.* a spell of sprinking. **এক আছড়া বৃষ্টি** a spell of light shower.

আ-ছড়া *a.* unflayed; unscratched.

আছড়া-আছড়ি *n.* throwing continuously to the ground with force; mutual knocking to the ground as in wrestling.

আছড়ানো *v.* to throw or dash to the ground violently (esp. when washing clothes).

আছাঁকা *a.* unstrained, unfiltrated.

আছাঁটা *a.* unhusked (আছাঁটা চাল) ; uncut (আছাঁটা চুল বা লোম).

আছাড় *n.* a throw or fall to the ground with force. **আছাড় খাওয়া** *v.* to fall to the ground with force; to tumble. **আছাড় দেওয়া, আছাড় মারা** *v.* to throw or fling to the ground violently.

আছাড়ি-পিছাড়ি *n.* writhing or wriggling violently (in pain or grief); flouncing.

আছি *v.* (*sing.*) am; (*pl.*) are.

আছিনু *v.* (poet.) *1st per.* (*sing.*) was; (*pl.*) were.

আছিল *v.* (poet.) *3rd. per.* (*sing.*) was; (*pl.*) were.

আছিলে *v.* (poet.) *2nd. per.* were.

আছে, আছেন *v.* *3rd. per.* (*sing.*) is; (*pl.*) are.

আছোলা *a.* unskinned; unscraped.

আজ *adv.* today; at present, now. ☐ *n.* today; this day; the present time. **~কার,** (coll.) **~কের** *a.* of today, today's; of the present time. **~কাল** *adv.* at present, nowadays. **আজ-কাল করা** *v.* to procrastinate, to temporize. **~কে** *adv.* today. **আজকের দিনে** today; nowadays. **আজ নয় কাল** procrastination. **আজ পর্যন্ত** *adv.* till today, to this day. **আজ বাদে কাল** shortly in future.

আজগুবি *a.* incredible and impossible; queer; fantastic; cock-and-bull.

আজড়ানো *v.* to uncover; to open.

আজনাই var. of **আঁজনাই**।

আজন্ম *adv.* & *a.* since one's birth; ever since one's birth. **~কাল** *adv.* during the whole of one's life, for life.

আজব *a.* queer, strange; wonder-inspiring. **আজব কাণ্ড** a strange or queer incident. **আজব দেশ** a wonderland. **আজব দুনিয়া** the strange world.

আজল, আজলি, আজুল *a.* open; uncovered.

আজা *n.* the father of one's mother, maternal grandfather.

আজাড় var. of **উজাড়**।

আজাদ *a.* free, independent. **আজাদ হিন্দ** Free India. **আজাদ হিন্দ ফৌজ** Indian National Army. **আজাদি** *n.* freedom, independence.

আজান *n.* a call to Muslims to attend prayer-meeting in a mosque. **আজান দেওয়া** *v.* to announce this call formally.

আজানু *adv.* down to the knees. **~লম্বিত** *a.* reaching down to the knees. **~লম্বিতবাহু** *a.* possessing arms that are long enough to reach down to the knees. ☐ *n.* such long arms.

আজি poet. var. of **আজ**।

আজি, আজিমা *fem.* of **আজা**।

আজীবন *adv.* & *a.* throughout the whole of one's life; for life; till death.

আজু obs. poet. form of **আজ**।

আজুরা var. of **অজুরা**।

আজেবাজে *a.* of little or no value, trash worthless, useless, not worth a straw meaningless, nonsensical. **আজেবাজে কথা বলা** *v.* to talk nonsense.

আজ্জানো *v.* to sow, to plant. ☐ *a.* sown planted.

আজ্ঞপ্তি *n.* an order; a decree.

আজ্ঞা *n.* an order; a command; a decree; an injunction; permission. ☐ *int.* indicating : response; willingness, consent etc (whilst talking to superiors), yes sir right sir. **আজ্ঞা করা** *v.* to order, to command; to permit. **আজ্ঞা দেওয়া** *v.* to give an order or command or permission. **~কারী** *a.* & *n.* one who orders or commands or permits. *fem.* **~কারিণী**। **~কারী হওয়া** *v.* to carry out or obey an order or command. **~ক্রমে, আজ্ঞানুক্রমে** *adv.* in obedience to or in accordance with an order. **~ধীন, আজ্ঞানুবর্তী** *n.* subservient; subordinate, bound to carry out one's orders; subject to one's orders, obedient. **আজ্ঞানুবর্তিতা** *n.* subordination, subjection; obedience. **আজ্ঞানুযায়ী, আজ্ঞানুসারে** same as **আজ্ঞাক্রমে**। **~পক** *a.* & *n.* one who orders or commands. **~পত্র** *n.* a writ of command, a written order; a permit. **~পন** *n.* act of ordering or commanding. **~পালক** *a.* (also *n.*) one who carries out or obeys an order or command; subservient or subordinate (person). **~পালন** *n.* act of carrying out or complying with an order; obedience. **~পিত** *a.* ordered, commanded. **~বহ** same as **আজ্ঞাধীন**। **~মতো** same as **আজ্ঞাক্রমে**। **~লঙ্ঘন** *n.* act of disobeying an order. **~লিপি** same as **আজ্ঞাপত্র**। **~লেখ** *n.* a writ.

আজ্ঞে *int.* indicating : a polite response, acknowledgment, inquiry etc. (whilst talking to superiors); yes, sir; what's your pleasure, sir ? **যে আজ্ঞে** as you please, sir.

আজ্য *n.* ghee as offered in religious sacrifice.

আঝালা *a.* not pungent, not mixed with capsicums or chillies.

আঝোড়া *a.* not clipped or pared down, not sheared or pruned.

আঞ্চলিক *a.* local; regional. **~তা** *n.* regionalism. **আঞ্চলিক ভাষা** *n.* a regional language.

আঞ্জনি *n.* a sty or stye on the eyelid; a small lizard akin to the iguana.

আঞ্জা *n.* the interim period between the delivery of a child and the next conception.

আঞ্জাম *n.* execution, performance; supply (টাকার আঞ্জাম) ; arrangement, provision; (pop.) income and expenditure.

আঞ্জিনেয়, আঞ্জনি variants of **আঞ্জনি**।

আঞ্জুমান, আঞ্জুমন *n.* an association, a society, a club; a meeting.

আট *a.* & *n.* eight. **আটই, আটুই** *n.* the eighth day of a month. □ *a.* (of the days of a month) eighth. **~কড়াই, ~কৌড়ে** *n.* the Hindu ceremony of distributing eight kinds of fried snacks on the eighth day of a child's birth. **~খানা করা** *v.* to break or tear into pieces. **~খানা হওয়া** *v.* to be beside oneself (with joy). **~চল্লিশ** *a.&n.* forty-eight. **~চালা** *n.* a thatched room with eight roofs and no wall. **~ত্রিশ** *a.* & *n.* thirty-eight. **~পহর,** (dial.) **~পর** *n.& adv.* whole day and night. **~পৌরে** *a.* worn or used all day round or ordinarily; (fig.) commonplace, hackneyed. **~ষট্টি** *a.& n.* sixty-eight.

আটক *n.* a bar, obstruction, hindrance; detention, confinement; restraint. □ *a.* confined, detained; imprisoned; enclosed. **আটক করা** *v.* to obstruct or confine or detain. **আটক পড়া বা হওয়া** *v.* to become obstructed or confined or detained. **আটকবন্দি** *n.* a detenu.

আটকপালিয়া, (coll.) **আটকপালে** *a.* extremely unfortunate. *fem.* **আটকপালি**।

আটকা *n.* obstruction, hindrance; a bar. □ *a.* confined; enclosed; obstructed. **আটকা-আটকি** *n.* restriction; stricture. **আটকা পড়া** *v.* to be detained or confined or obstructed. **আটকে যাওয়া** *v.* to become blocked or clogged.

আটকানো *v.* to confine; to obstruct, to impede; to restrain, to check; to prevent; to detain; to imprison; to fix (দেওয়ালে পেরেক আটকানো). □ *a.* confined; obstructed; impeded; restrained, checked; prevented; detained; affixed.

আটকে, আটকিয়া *n.* a fixed quantity of food offered daily to Lord Jagannath at Puri and then distributed amongst his votaries. **আটকে বাঁধা** *v.* to contribute such an amount of money to the temple of Jagannath at Puri as will be sufficient to provide food for one votary.

আটঘাট *n.* all sides; ins and outs. **আটঘাট বাঁধা** *v.* to arrange for safeguarding all sides.

আটপিঠে, আটপিটে *a.* efficient in everything; very clever.

আটা[1] coll. var. of **আঠা**।

আটা[2] *n.* coarse flour, meal. **আটা মাখা** *v.* to knead flour.

আটাইশ arch. spell. of **আটাশ** ।

আটাত্তর *a.* & *n.* seventy-eight.

আটানব্বই *a.* & *n.* ninety-eight.

আটান্ন *a.* & *n.* fifty-eight.

আটাশ, আঠাশ *a.*& *n.* twenty-eight. **আটাশে** *v.* the twenty-eighth day of a month. □ *a.* (of the days of a month) twenty-eighth; (of a child) born in the eighth month of conception; very weak, rickety.

আটি var. of **আঁটি**[১,২] ।

আটুই coll. corrup. of **আটই** (see **আট**).

আঠা *n.* any glutinous or adhesive or viscid substance; gum, glue, paste.

আঠারো *a.* & *n.* eighteen. **~ই** *n.* the eighteenth day of a month. □ *a.* (of the days of a month) eighteenth. **আঠারো মাসে বছর** intolerable procrastination.

আঠালো *a.* glutinous, viscid, gluey, adhesive, sticky; clayey (আঠালো মাটি).

আঠাশ see **আটাশ** ।

আঠি var. of **আঁটি**[২] ।

আড়[১] *a.* a device or a thing that intercepts the view, a screen; a cover; a position or place which is intercepted from the view; a hiding, concealment.

আড়[২] *n.* a kind of salt-water fish.

আড়[৩] *a.* other, opposite (আড়পার).

আড়[৪] *n.*, width, breadth; (in utterance) a stutter, uneasiness; a horizontal pole suspended from the ceiling etc. of a room for hanging clothes; a perch for birds. **আড় ভাঙা** *v.* to remove stutter from utterance. **~কাঠ** *n.* a cross-beam. **আড়ে-দিঘে** *adv.* in length and breadth. **আড়ে-হাতে** *adv.* up-and-doing; with might and main; with full force.

আড়[৫] *a.* squint, oblique (আড় চোখ) ; half (আড়পাগলা). **আড় ভাঙা** *v.* to straighten. **আড় হওয়া** *v.* to lie down obliquely; to recline. **~চোখে চাহনি, ~চাহনি** sidelong look or glance. **~বাঁশি** *n.* a kind of flute usu. made of bamboo or reed. **~ভাবে** *adv.* crosswise; obliquely. **~মোড়া, আড়ামোড়া** *n.* straightening or stretching one's body and removing inertia or lethargy or weariness.

আড়ং *n.* a central market-place; a wholesale market; a storehouse, an entrepot; a fair. **~ঘাটা** *n.* a place on the river-bank for getting into or alighting from a boat. **~ছাঁটা** *a.* (of rice etc.) imperfectly husked. **আড়ং ধোলাই** *n.* thorough washing and bleaching of clothes; (coll.) beating someone black and blue.

আড়কাটি, আড়কাঠি *n.* a recruiter; a pilot; a weaver's shuttle.

আড়ত *n.* a warehouse or godown of a wholesale dealer; an entrepot, a storehouse, a depot. **~দার** *n.* the owner or keeper of a warehouse; a wholesale merchant.**~দারি** *n.* wholesale business; the commission of a wholesale merchant.

আড়ম্বর *n.* pomp, eclat, grandeur, splendour, pompous display; roar of clouds; sound of war-trumpet; pride, vanity. **~শূন্য, ~হীন** *a.* not pompous or showy, simple; devoid of pomp and grandeur.

আড়ষ্ট *a.* benumbed; inert; hesitant. **~তা** *n.* inertness, sluggishness; hesitation due to shyness.

আড়া[১] *n.* form, shape; mould; size; type.

আড়া[২] *n.* a measure of grain (= about 75 kgs).

আড়া[৩] *n.* a river-bank; a crossbeam; a horizontal pole suspended from the ceiling etc. of a room for hanging clothes and other things.

আড়াআড়ি *adv.* crosswise; across; diagonally. □ *n.* mutual ill-feeling or rivalry.

আড়াই *a.* & *n.* two and a half times.

আড়াঠেকা *n.* a measure of Indian music.

আড়ানা *n.* an Indian musical mode.

আড়ানি *n.* a large umbrella; a large fan.

আড়ামোড়া see **আড়**[৫] ।

আড়াল *n.* a device or a thing that intercepts the view; a screen, a cover; a position or place intercepted from the view, hiding, concealment. **আড়াল কর** *v.* to put out of view; to hide, to conceal. **আড়াল হওয়া** *v.* to go out of view; to go behind the screen; to go in hiding, to hide. **আড়াল আবডাল** *n.* secrecy, cover; hiding. **আড়ালে আবডালে** *adv.* secretly, confidentially, in camera; in a hidden place, in concealment.

আড়ি[১] var. of **আড়া**[২] ।

আড়ি[২] *n.* a hiding; concealment; termination of friendship; quarrel; envy, malice, grudge; rivalry; obstinacy. **আড়ি করা** *v.* to terminate friendship with; to be obstinate in one's resolution. **আড়ি পাতা, আড়ি মারা** *v.* to go in hiding for overhearing, to eavesdrop.

আড়ে-দিঘে, আড়ে-হাতে see **আড়**[৪] ।

আড্ডা *n.* a dwelling-place, a habitat; a haunt; a (fixed or permanent) meeting-place, a rendezvous; a place or institution for practising anything (গানের আড্ডা) ; a club; a company of informal and friendly talkers, their meeting-place or talk; a place for assemblage, a station or stand (গাড়ির আড্ডা). **আড্ডা গাড়া** *v.* to take up abode (usu. permanently) to settle. **আড্ডা দেওয়া, আড্ডা মারা** *v.* to join in an assembly of idle talkers; to indulge in informal and friendly talk with others. **~ধারী** *n.* the keeper or the chief person of a club; a regular club-goer. **~বাজ** *a.* fond of indulging in idle talk with others or of haunting clubs where such talk is indulged in.

আঢাকা *a.* not covered, uncovered; exposed, open.

আঢ্য *a.* wealthy, rich, affluent; in possession of, rich in (ধনাঢ্য).

আণব, আণবিক *a.* molecular.

আণুবীক্ষণিক *a.* microscopic.

আণ্ডা, আণ্ডাবাচ্ছা, আণ্ডিল see **আন্ডা, আন্ডাবাচ্চা** & **আন্ডিল** respectively.

আতঙ্ক *n.* terror, great fear, dread; panic. **~গ্রস্ত, আতঙ্কিত** *a.* frightened, terrified; panicstricken; panicky.

আতত *a.* spread out, extended, stretched out.

আততায়ী *a.* one who assails; one who is about to kill. □ *n.* an assailant; an assassin. **আততায়িতা** *n.* act of assailing.

আতপ *n.* sunshine, sunlight, the sun. **~চাল** rice obtained by sunning paddy and not by boiling it. **~দগ্ধ** *a.* sunburnt.

আতপত্র *n.* a sunshade; an umbrella; a parasol.

আতপ্ত *a.* slightly hot; tepid.

আতর *n.* attar, otto. **~দান** *n.* a container for otto, an otto-pot.

আতশ, আতস *n.* fire; heat. **~বাজি** *n.* fireworks.

আতশিকাচ *n.* flint-glass, burning-glass.

আতা *n.* custard-apple.

আতান্তর *n.* distress, misery; danger. **আতান্তরে পড়া** *v.* to get into or to be in distress.

আতাম্র *a.* slightly copper-coloured; slightly dull red.

আতালিপাতালি *adv.* everywhere; all about.

আতিক্ত *a.* slightly bitter.

আতিথেয় *a.* hospitable. **~তা** *n.* hospitality; hospitableness.

আতিথ্য *n.* hospitality; that with which a host entertains a guest. **~গ্রহণ, ~স্বীকার** *n.* acceptance of one's hospitality as a guest. **আতিথ্য গ্রহণ করা, আতিথ্য স্বীকার করা** *v.* to become a guest (of).

আতিশয্য *n.* state of being overmuch or too many; excess; too much abundance or intensity.

আতুর *a.* sick; afflicted, distressed; agonized. □ *n.* a lying-in room (also **আতুরঘর**). **আতুরাশ্রম** *n.* a refuge for the sick and the distressed.**আতুরে নিয়মো নাস্তি** necessity knows no law.

আত্তি *n.* display of kindredship or affection.

আত্তীকরণ *n.* (esp. in bio.) assimilation.

আত্ম *a.* own; belonging to or related to one's own self. **আত্ম** *pfx.* self-, by or of one's own self, mutual etc. **~কলহ** *n.* internal discord or dissension; domestic discord; civil strife. **~কৃত** *a.* done or performed by one's own self. **~কেন্দ্রিক** *a.* self-centred; one who thinks only about himself. **~গত** *a.* kept to one's own self; aside; absorbed in one's own self, self-possessed. **~গরজি** *a.* preoccupied with self-interest; self-interested. **~গরিমা** same as **আত্মগর্ব**। **~গরুজে** dial. corrup. of **আত্মগরজি**। **~গর্ব** *n.* self-conceit, vanity. **~গর্বী** *a.* self-conceited, bloated or puffed up with pride. **~গোপন** *n.* concealment or disguise of one's own self or identity. **~গোপন করা** *v.* to go into hiding, to hide, to conceal one's own identity. **~গৌরব** *n.* self-glorification; self-conceit; self-praise. **~গ্লানি** *n.*

self-reproach; remorse. ~ঘাত *n.* suicide. ~ঘাতী *a.* one who kills himself, self-killing, suicidal. *fem.* ~ঘাতিনী। ~চিন্তা *n.* meditation about atman or God; spiritual meditation; thinking about one's own interest or welfare. ~চেতনা *n.* self-consciousness. ~জ *n.* a son *fem.* আত্মজা a daughter. ~জীবনী *n.* an autobiography. ~জ্ঞ *a.* possessing self-knowledge; possessing spiritual or metaphysical knowledge or wisdom. ~জ্ঞান *n.* spiritual or metaphysical knowledge or wisdom. ~জ্ঞানী *a.* in possession of spiritual or metaphysical knowledge. □ *n.* a spiritualist; a metaphysician. ~তত্ত্ব *n.* spiritual or metaphysical knowledge. ~তত্ত্বজ্ঞ *a.* in possession of spiritual or metaphysical knowledge. ~তুষ্ট, ~তৃপ্ত *a.* self-complacent. ~তুষ্টি, ~তৃপ্তি *n.* self-complacency, self-content. ~তুল্য *a.* like one's own self, self-like. *fem.* ~তুল্যা। ~ত্যাগ *n.* self-abnegation, self-denial; self-sacrifice. ~ত্যাগী *a.* self-denying; self-sacrificing. ~ত্রাণ *n.* rescue or salvation of one's own self. ~দমন *n.* self-restraint, self-control. ~দর্শন *n.* self-examination, introspection; self-realization. ~দর্শিতা *n.* practice or capacity of self-examination or introspection or self-realization. ~দর্শী *a.* self-examining, introspecting; self-realizing. ~দান *n.* self-sacrifice. ~দোষ *n.* one's own fault. ~দোষক্ষালন *n.* act of clearing oneself of a charge; act of justifying one's own conduct; clean-up of one's own self. ~দ্রোহ *n.* self-torment, self-torture; internal discord. ~দ্রোহী *a.* self-tormenting, self-torturing; indulging in or involved in internal strife. □ *n.* a self-tormentor, a self-torturer; one who indulges in or is involved in internal strife. *fem.* ~দ্রোহিণী। ~নিগ্রহ *n.* self-torture, self-repression, self-inflicted pain; masochism. ~নিন্দা *n.* self-condemnation, self-accusation. ~নিবিষ্ট *a.* self-absorbed, egocentric, self-centred, wrapped up in oneself. ~নিবেদন *n.* offering one's own self, self-dedication; self-sacrifice. ~নিয়ন্ত্রণ *n.* self-control; self-government, self-discipline. ~নিয়োগ *n.* engaging one's own self; self-appointment. ~নির্ধারণ *n.* self-determination. ~নির্ভর *n.* self-help; self-reliance. □ *a.* working for oneself, independent of external aid, self-reliant, self-supporting. ~নির্ভরশীল *a.* self-reliant. ~নিষ্ঠ *a.* devoted to God or atman; devout; self-devoted; subjective; introspective. ~নিষ্ঠা *n.* devotion to God or atman; devoutness; self-devotion; subjectivity; introspection. ~নেপদ *n.* (Sans. gr.) a mode of conjugating verbs. ~নেপদী *a.* of or in or according to this mode. ~পক্ষ *n.* one's own side or party or team or supporters or people etc. ~পক্ষসমর্থন *n.* self-defence. ~পক্ষ সমর্থন করা *v.* to defend oneself. ~পর *n.* oneself and others; near and far ones; friend and foe. □ *a.* selfish, self-devoted. ~পরতা *n.* selfishness; self-love, self-devotion. ~পরায়ণ *a.* (phil.) devoted to God or atman; devout; selfish, self-devoted. ~পরিচয় *n.* introduction of one's own self. আত্মপরিচয় গোপন করা *v.* to conceal one's own identity. আত্মপরিচয় দেওয়া *v.* to introduce oneself. ~পরীক্ষা *n.* self-examination, self-scrutiny; introspection. ~পীড়ন *n.* self-torture. ~প্রকাশ *n.* public appearance; self-revelation; self-assertion. ~প্রচার *n.* self-advertisement. ~প্রতারণা *n.* self-deception. ~প্রত্যয় *n.* self-confidence; (rare) conviction. ~প্রত্যয়শীল *a.* self-confident, self-assured. ~প্রবঞ্চনা same as আত্মপ্রতারণা। ~প্রশংসা *n.* self-praise. আত্মপ্রশংসা করা *v.* to praise one's own self, to blow one's own trumpet. ~প্রসাদ *n.* self-satisfaction, self-complacency. ~বঞ্চনা *n.* self-deception. ~বৎ *adv.* like one's own self. □ *a.* self-like. ~বলি,~বলিদান *n.* self-immolation, self-sacrifice. আত্মবলি দেওয়া *v.* to sacrifice oneself. ~বশ *a.* independent; self-directed; self-restrained; (rare) self-devoted. *n.* self-restraint. ~বিকাশ *n.* manifestation or development of one's own self. ~বিক্রয় *n.* undesirable and servile submission to somebody or something for some gain;

selling out oneself; selling one's soul. ~বিগ্রহ, ~বিচ্ছেদ *n.* internal discord; civil strife; domestic quarrel. ~বিৎ, ~বিদ same as আত্মজ্ঞ। ~বিদ্যা *n.* knowledge about God and atman; theology; spiritual knowledge. ~বিনাশ same as আত্মবিলোপ। ~বিরোধ *n.* self-contradiction; self-repugnance; internal discord; civil strife; domestic quarrel. ~বিরোধী *a.* self-contradictory; self-repugnant; given to or involved in internal discord or civil strife or domestic quarrel. ~বিলোপ *n.* self-effacement. ~বিশ্বাস *n.* self-confidence. ~বিশ্বাসী *a.* self-confident. ~বিসর্জন *n.* self-sacrifice, self-abnegation, self-denial. ~বিস্মরণ, ~বিস্মৃতি *n.* self-forgetfulness, self-oblivion; absent-mindedness. ~বিস্মৃত *a.* self-oblivious; absent-minded. ~বিস্মৃত হওয়া *v.* to forget oneself. ~বুদ্ধি *n.* one's own thinking power or intellect or knowledge; knowledge about one's own self-consciousness. ~বেদী same as আত্মজ্ঞ। ~বোধ *n.* knowledge about one's own self, self-consciousness; self-realization. ~মগ্ন *a.* self-absorbed. ~মগ্ন সংলাপ *n.* soliloquy. ~মর্যাদা *n.* self-respect, self-esteem. ~মর্যাদাজ্ঞান, ~মর্যাদাবোধ *n.* sense of self-respect or self-esteem. ~মর্যাদাপূর্ণ, ~মর্যাদাশালী *a.* full of self-respect or self-esteem. ~মর্যাদাশূন্য, ~মর্যাদাহীন *a.* devoid of self-respect or self-esteem. আত্মম্ভরি *a.* overwhelmingly self-interested, selfish; self-conceited, egotistical, vain. আত্মম্ভরিতা *n.* extreme self-interest, selfishness; self-conceitedness, vanity. ~রক্ষা *n.* self-protection, self-preservation; self-defence. আত্মরক্ষা করা *v.* to protect or preserve oneself; to defend oneself. ~রতি *n.* auto-erotism, sexual excitement generated by one's own body. ~রূপ *n.* selfhood. ☐ *adv.* like one's own self. ~লোপ *n.* same as আত্মবিলোপ। ~শক্তি *n.* one's own power; power of the spirit. ~শাসন *n.* self-government; self-control, self-discipline. ~শাসিত *a.* self-governed; self-governing. ~শিক্ষিত *a.* self-taught, self-educated. ~শুদ্ধি, ~শোধন *n.* self-purification. ~শ্লাঘা *n.* self-praise, boasting, self-applause. ~শ্লাঘাপরায়ণ *a.* given to self-praise or boasting, boastful. ~শ্লাঘাপূর্ণ *a.* boastful. ~সংবরণ *n.* checking oneself, self-restraint. আত্মসংবরণ করা *v.* to check or restrain oneself. ~সংযম *n.* continence; self-restraint, collectedness. ~সংযমী *a.* self-continent; self-restrained. ~সংশোধন *n.* self-correction. আত্মসংশোধন করা *v.* to rectify oneself. ~সমর্থন *n.* self-defence. আত্মসমর্থন করা *v.* to defend oneself or plead for oneself. ~সমর্পণ *n.* surrender; capitulation, self-dedication. আত্মসমর্পণ করা *v.* to surrender, to yield or give up oneself; to capitulate; to dedicate oneself. ~সমাহিত *a.* self-absorbed. ~সমীক্ষা *n.* self-assessment. ~সম্পর্কীয়, ~সম্বন্ধীয় *a.* related to or connected with one's own self. ~সম্ভ্রম, ~সম্মান *n.* self-respect, self-esteem. ~সর্বস্ব *a.* extremely self-centred or self-loving or selfish. ~সাৎ *n.* appropriating to one's own use (usu. unlawfully); misappropriation; filching. ☐ *a.* appropriated to one's own use; misappropriated; filched. আত্মসাৎ করা *v.* to appropriate to one's own use; to misappropriate; to filch. ~সার *a.* self-centred; extremely selfish. ~সিদ্ধি *n.* attainment of one's own desires; salvation of one's own soul. ~সুখ *n.* one's own happiness. ~সুখপরায়ণ, ~সুখী *a.* happy only to attain one's own desires; extremely selfish. আত্মসুখী পরবৈরাগি highly concerned about one's own interest whilst apathetic to that of others. ~স্থ *a.* self-possessed; absorbed; self-absorbed. ~হত্যা *n.* self-killing, suicide. আত্মহত্যা করা *v.* to commit suicide. ~হত্যাকারী, ~হন্তা *a.* killing oneself, committing suicide. ☐ *n.* a self-murderer. *fem.* ~হত্যাকারিণী, ~হন্ত্রী। ~হনন *n.* same as আত্মহত্যা। ~হারা *a.* one who has lost self-possession, beside oneself. আত্মহারা হওয়া *v.* to lose self-possession; to be beside oneself. ~হিত *n.* one's own good or welfare.

আত্মা *n.* (Hindu theol.) the conscious immortal independent and active guide of every being which is present in the body but is not an inseparable part of it; the soul, the atman; the Superme Being, God; a guardian deity; one's own likeness, self-identity, selfhood, the body; the heart, the mind; natural disposition, nature.

আত্মাদর *n.* self-esteem, self-respect.

আত্মাদর্শ *n.* self-example.

আত্মাধীন *a.* working for oneself independently of external aid, self-reliant; independent.

আত্মানুসন্ধান, আত্মান্বেষণ *n.* an endeavour to acquire theological or spiritual knowledge; self-examination. **আত্মানুসন্ধায়ী, আত্মান্বেষী** *a.* endeavouring to acquire theological or spiritual knowledge; self-criticizing.

আত্মাপরাধ *n.* one's own fault or crime.

আত্মাপহারক, আত্মাপহারী *a.* guilty of false personification; dissimulating.

আত্মাপুরুষ (pop.) *n.* soul; life. **আত্মাপুরুষ খাঁচাছাড়া হওয়া** to die. **আত্মাপুরুষ শুকিয়ে যাওয়া** to cower, to show extreme fear, to be numb with fear.

আত্মাভিমান *n.* self-conceit, vanity, egotism, amour-propre. **আত্মাভিমানী** *a.* self-conceited, vain, egotistic. *fem.* **আত্মাভিমানিনী** ।

আত্মারাম *n.* the soul; life; the mind; life as imagined as a bird enclosed by the prison of a body; a term of endearment with which a pet parrot, or parakeet, or magpie is addressed (বলো বাবা আত্মারাম). **আত্মারাম খাঁচাছাড়া হওয়া** *v.* to die. **আত্মারাম শুকিয়ে যাওয়া** *v.* to cower.

আত্মাশ্রয়ী *a.* working by oneself without external aid, self-reliant, independent.

আত্মাহুতি *n.* self-immolation, self-sacrifice.

আত্মীকরণ *n.* assimilation.

আত্মীয় *a.* one's own; related by blood; belonging to one's own family or clan. ☐ *n.* a blood-relation, a relative, a kinsman; a friend; a supporter, one's own man. **~তা** *n.* kinship; blood relationship; relationship; friendship. sharing common characteristics. *fem.* **আত্মীয়া** । **~বন্ধু, ~স্বজন** *n.* friends and relations; one's own people, kith and kin.

আত্মোৎকর্ষ *n.* elevation of one's own self or soul, self-elevation; self-advancement.

আত্মোৎসর্গ *n.* self-sacrifice; self-dedication. **আত্মোৎসর্গ করা** *v.* to dedicate one's life, to sacrifice oneself.

আত্মোন্নতি same as **আত্মোৎকর্ষ** ।

আত্মোপম *a.* like one's own self, equal to one's own-self, selflike.

আত্যন্তিক *a.* excessive; endless; extreme.

আত্যয়িক *a.* signalling death or danger; of pressing necessity, emergent. **আত্যয়িক ক্ষমতা** emergency power. **আত্যয়িক বল** emergency force.

আথান্তর var. of **আতান্তর** ।

আথাল *n.* a cowshed, a cowhouse.

আথালপাতাল, আথালিপাথালি var. of **আতালিপাতালি** ।

আথিবিথি, আথেবেথে, আথেব্যথে *adv.* in a confused hurry, helter-skelter.

আদত *a.* whole, entire, total, full, unbroken; real, actual, true; genuine, unadulterated, pure. ☐ *n.* conduct, nature; behaviour, practice; custom. **আদতে** *adv.* as a matter of fact, in fact; in reality, really; in truth.

আদপে *adv.* in reality, really; in truth; in fact, as a matter of fact; at all, in the least.

আদব *n.*etiquette, courtesy. **~কায়দা** *n.* forms of ceremony or decorum, etiquette; conventional laws of courtesy; good manners. **~কায়দাদোরস্ত, ~কায়দাদুরস্ত** *a.* conversant with or observant of forms of ceremony or decorum; courteous; smart; fashionable; correct in demeanour.

আদম *n.* (according to the Bible and the Quran) the name of the first man, Adam.

আদমশুমার, আদমশুমারি *n.* census.

আদমি *n.* a man; a person; husband. **কালা আদমি** (dero. or facet.) a dark-skinned man, a coloured man, a blackie.

আদর *n.* caress; cordiality; cordial reception; appreciation; fondness; love, affection; respect, honour, esteem. **আদর করা** *v.* to caress, to fondle; to receive cordially; to treat with cordiality; to appreciate; to respect, to honour, to esteem. ~-অভ্যর্থনা, ~-আপ্যায়ন, ~যত্ন *n.* hearty reception and kind attention (to guests, invitees and others); warm welcome. **আদরণীয়** *a.* worthy of being received cordially or appreciated or esteemed.

আদরা *n.* a rough or preliminary sketch; an outline; a profile.

আদরিণী *a. fem.* beloved; treated with too much indulgence, petted.

আদর্শ *n.* a pattern of excellence, a person or thing to be copied, an ideal; an imitation of something usu. on a smaller scale, a model, a role model, a specimen; a prototype. ☐ *a.* ideal. **~চরিত্র** *a.* having an exemplary character. **আদর্শ পুরুষ** an ideal man. **আদর্শ পুস্তক** a model book. **আদর্শ বিদ্যালয়** a model school. **~লিপি** *n.* a copy-book. **~স্থানীয়** exemplary, ideal. **~স্বভাব** *a.* of an ideal character. **~স্বরূপ** *a.* of the nature of a model, model; ideal, exemplary.

আদল *n.* similarity (esp. of appearance); a faint appearance or shadow.

আদা *n.* ginger. **আদাজল খেয়ে লাগা** *v.* to engage in something doggedly. **আদায় কাঁচকলায়** *adv.* at daggers drawn. **আদার ব্যাপারীর জাহাজের খবরে কাজ কী** an ordinary man should not meddle in big affairs.

আদাড় *n.* a place for depositing household and other rubbish; a dump; a dustbin. **আদাড়ে** *a.* extremely dirty, filthy.

আদান *n.* receiving or accepting or taking. **~প্রদান** *n.* giving and taking; exchange; commerce; social communication or relation; matrimonial relation.

আদাব *n.* (Muslim) greeting with gesture, obeisance.

আদায় *n.* realization or collection (of bills, taxes etc.); winning or earning (সম্মান আদায়) ; payment or repayment. **আদায় করা** *v.* to realize; to collect. **আদায় দেওয়া** *v.* to pay; to repay. **~পত্র** *n.* realization; collection. **আদায়পত্র করা** *v.* to realize; to collect.

আদালত *n.* a court of justice. **আদালতি** *a.* pertaining or relating to a court of justice; judicial.

আদি *n.* beginning; origin; source; birth. ☐ *a.* first; original, fundamental, primary. ☐ *in comp.* (used as a *sfx.*) and the like, et cetera (সুখদুঃখাদি). **~কবি** *n.* the first poet; Valmiki. **~কলা** *n.* the fundamental tissue. **~কলাতন্ত্র** *n.* the fundamental tissue system. **~কাব্য** *n.* the first epic. **~কারণ** *n.* the first cause; the Supreme Being; the fundamental cause; the primary cause. **~কাল** *n.* ancient times. **~কোষ** *n.* embryonic cell. **~দেব** *n.* the Supreme Being; any one of the three principal Hindu gods : Brahma (ব্রহ্মা), Vishnu (বিষ্ণু) and Maheswara (মহেশ্বর). **~নাথ** *n.* the Supreme Being; Shiva (শিব). **~পুরুষ** *n.* the first progenitor or ancestor of a clan or family. **~বাসী** *n.* the aborigines. **~বৃত্ত** *n.* equinoctial colure. **~ভূত** *a.* born or created first, primordial; primary (আদিভূত কারণ). *fem.* **আদিভূতা** । **~রস** *n.* (rhet.) the emotion of love; sex-passion; eroticism. **~রূপ** *n.* a prototype, an archetype.

আদিখ্যেতা *n.* simulation; feigning ignorance; petty ostentatious activity, fuss; intolerable excess.

আদিগন্ত *a.* extending up to the horizon; vast; immense.

আদিতেয় *n.* a son of Aditi (অদিতি) the mother of gods, a god.

আদিত্য *n.* the name of the sungod (cp. Apollo, Sol); the sun.

আদিত্যমণ্ডল *n.* the orb of the sun; the solar region.

আদিম *a.* first; aboriginal; primordial; primitive; original. **আদিম অধিকার** (law) Original Jurisdiction. **~তা** *n.* primitiveness; primordiality.

আদিষ্ট *n.* ordered, commanded; decreed; directed; ordained.

আদুড় *a.* uncovered bare; naked, unclothed; undressed; untied. **~-গা** *n.* bare body. **~চুলি** *a. fem.* one whose hair is undressed or untied or dishevelled; a woman having no veil over her head.

আদুরি *fem.* of **আদুরে** ।

আদুরে *a.* treated with or brought up with excessive indulgence; petted. **আদুরে গোপাল** a child spoilt with excessive indulgence; a pampered child; the pet child of over-indulgent parents.

আদুল var. of আদুড় ।

আদৃত *a.* received cordially, well-received; treated with cordiality, welcome; well-appreciated; esteemed, honoured.

আদেখলা, আদেখলে *a.* inordinately covetous about some object as if he or she has not seen anything like it before; inordinately greedy. ~পনা *n.* greediness; indecently or indecorously greedy.

আদেখা var. of অদেখা ।

আদেয়ক *n.* a bill.

আদেশ *n.* an order, a command; a decree; an ordinance; an injunction; a directive; direction; permission; (gr.) substitution of a letter or word for another. আদেশ করা, আদেশ দেওয়া *v.* to order, to command; to decree; to enjoin; to direct; to permit. আদেশ হওয়া *v.* to be ordered or decreed or permitted; to be decreed by an oracle; (gr. of a letter or word) to be substituted for another letter or word. ~ক *a.* & *n.* one who orders or commands or decrees or directs or permits. ~ক্রমে *adv.* in obedience to or in accordance with an order or decree. ~পত্র *n.* a writ of command or decree; a directive; a permit. ~পালক *a.* & *n.* one who obeys or executes an order or decree. ~পালন *n.* carrying out an order or decree. আদেশানুবর্তী *a.* obedient to an order, decree, injunction or direction. আদেশানুযায়ী same as আদেশক্রমে ।

আদেষ্টা *a.* & *n.* one who orders or commands or decrees or enjoins or directs or permits.

আদৌ *adv.* (ori. & lit.) in the beginning, at first; (pop. and current) at all, in the least.

আদ্য *a.* first, prime; primeval; primitive; primordial; chief; best; primary. ~কৃত্য *n.* the work to be done first (also see আদ্যশ্রাদ্ধ). ~প্রাণী *n.* the protozoa. ~প্রান্ত *adv.* from beginning to end; from top to bottom. ~শ্রাদ্ধ, ~কৃত্য *n.* solemn obsequies performed in memory of the deceased on the day following the period of mourning.

আদ্যন্ত *n.* beginning and end. □ *adv.* from beginning to end; from first to last.

আদ্যা *a. fem.* born or created or originated first, primordial. □ *n. fem.* Nature; (Hindu theol.) the Supreme Goddess associated with God in the work of creation, Goddes Durga (দুর্গা). ~শক্তি same as আদ্যা (*n.*).

আদ্যিকাল *n.* very ancient times; remote days. আদ্যিকালের বুড়ি (usu. facet.) a very old-fashioned aged woman.

আদ্যোপান্ত *adv.* from beginning to end, from first to last; from top to bottom; all over; all through.

আদ্রক *n.* ginger.

আদ্রিয়মাণ *a.* in the state of being received or treated cordially or with respect.

আধ, আধা *n.* & *a.* half. আধকপালি, আধকপালে *n.* hemicrania, migraine, megrim. আধখেঁচড়া *a.* half-done; done perfunctorily; disordered; bungled. আধথালা *a.* half-plate. আধপাকা *a.* half-ripe; partly ripe. আধপাগলা *a.* crack-brained, cranky, having a screw loose, mentally defective, crazy. □ *n.* one with a screw loose, a crack-brain, a crank. আধপেটা *a.* sufficient to satisfy only half the hunger; half-fed. □ *adv.* to the extent of being half-fed. আধপোড়া *a.* half-burned; half-roasted; half-baked. আধবয়সী, আধবুড়ো *a.* middle-aged. *fem.* আধবুড়ি । আধমনি *a.* containing half a maund (of things). আধমনি কৈলাস a gluttonous person, one who eats too much; one who is capable of eating too much. আধমরা *a.* half-dead; almost dead, more dead than alive. আধসিদ্ধ *a.* parboiled. আধসের *n.* (now obs.) half a seer. আধহাতি *a.* half a cubit long.

আধর্ষপত্র *n.* a writ for arresting a person, a warrant.

আধলা *a.* half; halved. □ *n.* a half-piece; a half-piece of brick; brickbat.

আধলি var. of আধুলি ।

আধা see আধ । আধাআধি *a.* half; fifty-fifty; almost half. □ *adv.* half-and-half; fifty-fifty; by halves. ~খেঁচড়া same as আধখেঁচড়া (see আধা). ~-দর, ~-দাম *n.*

half-price. ~বয়সী same as আধবয়সী (see আধ). ~সরকারি *a.* demi-official. আধাসরকারি প্রতিষ্ঠান semi-government institution.

আধান *n.* placing or depositing; installation; infusion, instillation; (phy.) charge; receiving or taking; putting on. বদ্ধ আধান bound charge. মুক্ত আধান free charge.

আধার[১] *n.* a container; a receptacle; a vessel, a case; a store; a haunt, a dwelling-place, a source; a cause.

আধার[২] *n.* food (esp. of birds); a nest.

আধি *n.* anxiety; worry. ~ক্লিষ্ট *a.* suffering from worries and anxieties, mentally distressed or afflicted. ~ব্যাধি *n.* mental and physical ailments.

আধিকারিক *n.* an officer (esp. a high-ranking officer).

আধিক্য *n.* excess; abundance; intemperance; predominance; rifeness.

আধিখ্যেতা var. of আদিখ্যেতা।

আধিদৈবিক *a.* supernatural; fortuitous; pertaining to natural disasters such as flood, famine etc.; elemental.

আধিপত্য *n.* mastery; overlordship; predominance; supremacy; rule, government; suzerainty. আধিপত্য করা *v.* to dominate; to lord (it) over; to rule, to govern.

আধিবিদ্যক *a.* metaphysical.

আধিব্যাধি see আধি।

আধিভৌতিক *a.* originating from the four (or five) elements, elemental; effected or produced by living organism, biological; pertaining to organic life, organic.

আধিরাজ্য *n.* imperiality; overlordship; suzerainty.

আধুত *a.* slightly trembling or vibrant.

আধুনিক *a.* of present times, modern, current; new. *fem.* আধুনিকী। (inc. but current) আধুনিকা। ~তা *n.* modernism, modernity.

আধুনিকীকরণ *n.* modernization.

আধুলি *n.* a coin of the value of half a rupee, a half-rupee. ব্যাঙের আধুলি an insignificant amount hoarded very cautiously and proudly by an extremely poor person, an ewe-lamb.

আধূত alt. spell. of আধুত।

আধৃত *a.* caught hold of; held; taken, received; arrested; seized, captured; accepted.

আধৃতি (phy.) capacitance.

আধেক *a.* & *adv.* half.

আধেয় *a.* & *n.* that which is worthy of being placed or deposited or produced. ☐ *n.* content.

আধো *a.* half; partial; indistinct. আধো-আধো *a.* babbling; mumbling; indistinct.

আধোয়া *a.* unwashed; unbleached.

আধ্যাত্মিক *a.* originating in the soul; spiritual; theological; relating to God or the Supreme Being; psychic; metaphysical; intellectual, mental. ~তা *n.* spiritualism.

আধ্যান *n.* recollection; meditation; anxiety.

আন *a.* & *adv.* (obs. & poet.) another, of another kind.

আনক *n.* a large drum; a wardrum; thunder-cloud. ☐ *a.* thunderous; sounding.

আনকা, আনকো *a.* queer, strange; new; unfamiliar; unknown.

আনকোরা *a.* quite new, brand-new; fresh; untarnished; unsoiled; not yet used, untried.

আনখা var. of আনকা।

আনচান *a.* anxious; restless; uneasy.

আনত *a.* stooped, bent down; inclined; stooping in obeisance; obeisant. আনত হওয়া *v.* to stoop, to bend down, to incline; to stoop in obeisance, to bow down. ~তল *n.* inclined plane. ~শির *a.* with the head bending or stooping low. আনতি *n.* act or state of bending down or stooping; inclination; act or state of stooping in obeisance; obeisance.

আনদ্ধ *n.* any instrument of percussion. ☐ *a.* (of musical instruments etc.) having the mouth covered with hide, percussive (আনদ্ধ যন্ত্র) ; dressed up, tied up, arranged (আনদ্ধ কেশপাশ) ; clothed.

আনন *n.* face; (loos.) mouth.

আনন্তর্য *n.* immediacy; adjacency; proximity; contiguity.

আনন্ত্য *n.* infiniteness, infinitude; endlessness; interminableness.

আনন্দ *n.* joy, delight; happiness; gladness, cheerfulness; pleasure; merriment. **আনন্দ করা** *v.* to rejoice; to make merry. **~কর** *a.* delightful; pleasant; gladdening. **~কানন** *n.* a delightful woodland or grove; a pleasure-grove. **~জনক, ~দায়ক** *a.* causing joy; delightful; pleasant. **~ন** *n.* producing joy, delight etc. **~বিহ্বল** *a.* beside oneself with joy, overwhelmed with joy. **~ময়** *a.* full of joy, joyful; delightful; happy; cheerful; pleasant; merry. **~ময়ী** *a. fem.* of **আনন্দময়** । □ *n.* Goddess Durga (দুর্গা). **~লহরী** *n.* a wave of delight; a musical instrument with one string held in one hand and played with a plectrum by the other.

আনন্দাশ্রু *n.* tears of joy.

আনন্দিত *a.* delighted; happy; glad; pleased; merry. **আনন্দিত করা** *v.* to delight; to gladden. **আনন্দিত হওয়া** *v.* to be delighted or pleased; to be happy.

আনন্দোচ্ছ্বাস *n.* an outburst of joy, an ecstasy of delight.

আনমন[1] *n.* bending down; bending down or curving slightly.

আনমন[2] *a.* unmindful, absentminded.

আনমনা *a.* unmindful; absentminded, listless; abstracted, unconcerned, uninterested.

আনমনে *adv.* listlessly, unmindfully, absent-mindedly, lackadaisically.

আনমিত *a.* bent down, inclined.

আনম্য *a.* pliant, flexible; capable of being bent or bent down; deserving obeisance or respect.

আনম্র *a.* gentle, courteous, polite; slightly bent or stooping.

আনয়ন *n.* bringing or fetching. **আনয়ন করা** *v.* to bring, to fetch.

আনর্থ, আনর্থ্য, আনর্থক্য *n.* futility; ineffectualness.

আনা[1] *n.* an anna, four pice; one-sixteenth part or share.

আনা[2] *v.* to fetch, to bring.

আনাগোনা *n.* coming and going (esp. frequently); frequenting; come-and-go; prying. **আনাগোনা করা** *v.* to come and go (esp. frequently). to frequent; to pry.

আনাচ-কানাচ *n.* the outlying and usually neglected parts of a house etc.; the eaves and like parts; nook and corner. **আনাচে-কানাচে** *adv.* in nooks and byways; in nooks and eaves.

আনাজ *n.* vegetables (usu. green.) **~পত্র** *n.* spinach and vegetables.

আনাড়ি *a.* inexpert, unskilled, inefficient; inexperienced; untrained; ignorant; foolish. **~পনা** *n.* inefficiency; lack of experience or skill; awkward behaviour.

আনানো *v.* to cause to be brought or fetched.

আনায় *n.* a snare, a mesh; a trap.

আনার *n.* pomegranate.

আনারস *n.* ananas, pineapple.

আনি var. of **আনা[1]** ।

আনীত *a.* brought; fetched.

আনীল *a.* slightly blue, bluish.

আনুকূল্য *n.* aid, help; assistance; support; patronage; favour; a good turn. **আনুকূল্য করা** *v.* to aid, to help; to assist; to support; to patronize; to do (one) a favour; to do (one) a good turn.

আনুগত্য *n.* allegiance; fidelity; obedience; fealty; faithful adherence. **আনুগত্য স্বীকার করা** *v.* to own allegiance (to); to submit (to). **আনুগত্যের শপথ** oath of allegiance.

আনুতোষিক *n.* a gratuity.

আনুনাসিক var. of **অনুনাসিক** ।

আনুপদিক *a.* coming or going after, following.

আনুপাতিক *a.* proportional.

আনুপূর্ব, আনুপূর্ব্য *n.* sequence, serial succession, due succession. **আনুপূর্বিক** *adv.* in due succession, serially; from beginning to end. □ *a.* serial, in due succession; from beginning to end; entire, complete, overall.

আনুমানিক *a.* inferential; probable; (loos.) approximate.

আনুরক্তি *n.* attachment; affection, love, fondness.

আনুরূপ্য *n.* similar state or appearance, similarity, likeness; agreement, congruity; resemblance.

আনুশাসনিক *a.* (pol.) concerning an order or ordinance or edict; scriptural.

আনুষঙ্গিক *a.* accompanying, concomitant; incidental; secondary; associated.

আনুষ্ঠানিক *a.* ritual, ceremonial; formal.

আনূপ *a.* watery; marshy. ☐ *n.* any of the terrestrial animals fond of bathing in water such as the buffalo, the rhinoceros etc.

আনৃশংস্য *n.* lack or absence of cruelty; mercifulness; kindness; severe cruelty.

আনেতা *a.* & *n.* one who brings or fetches.

আন্ডা *n.* an egg. **আন্ডাবাচ্চা** *n.* (facet. or dero.) one's all children, kiddies.

আন্ডিল *a.* very rich. ☐ *n.* a heap; a bundle.

আন্তঃপ্রাদেশিক *a.* inter-provincial; (in a federal state like India) inter-state.

আন্তর *a.* mental; inherent.

আন্তরযন্ত্র *n.* (anat.) viscera. **আন্তরযন্ত্রীয়** *a.* visceral.

আন্তরিক *a.* cherished or lying in the heart; entertained in the mind; mental; candid; sincere; genuine; hearty; heartfelt; cordial; inward, inner; (rare) hidden. **~তা** *n.* candour; sincerity; heartiness; cordiality.

আন্তরিক্ষ *a.* of or in the sky, skyey; atmospherical, aerial; ethereal; heavenly. ☐ *n.* the sky; the cloud.

আন্তর্জাতিক, অন্তর্জাতীয় *a.* international.

আন্তর্বিদ্যালয় *a.* inter-school.

আন্ত্রিক *a.* intestinal; duodenal; enteric. ☐ *n.* (loos.) gastro-enteritis. **আন্ত্রিক জ্বর** *n.* enteric fever, typhoid (fever).

আন্দাজ *n.* guess, conjecture. ☐ *a.* approximate or conjectural. ☐ *adv.* more or less, approximately (আন্দাজ একশো গ্রাম). **আন্দাজি** *a.* depending on or deduced by guessing; uncertain. **আন্দাজে** *adv.* by guess, by surmise or conjecture.

আন্দোলন *n.* agitation; movement; stir; swinging, oscillation; vibration; cogitation, discussion. **রাজনীতিক আন্দোলন** political agitation or movement. **আন্দোলন করা** *v.* to agitate; to stir; to swing, to oscillate; to vibrate; to cogitate, to discuss. **মনে আন্দোলন হওয়া** *v.* to have a thing cogitated in one's mind.

আন্দোলিত *a.* swung, oscillated; stirred; vibrated; cogitated, discussed.

আন্ধি var. of **আঁধি** ।

আন্বয়িক *a.* relating to concord or syntax, relating to agreement.

আন্বীক্ষিকী *n.* the science and art of reasoning, logic.

আন্যত্রিকতা *n.* alibi.

আপ *n.* one's own self. ☐ *a.* one's own. **আপ ভালা তো জগৎ ভালা** to a good soul all are good; to the pure all things are pure. **আপ রুচি খানা পর রুচি পরনা** eat according to your own taste but dress according to the taste of others; eat to please yourself but dress to please others.

আপকাওয়াস্তে *adv.* for one's own self. ☐ *a.* self-seeking, selfish.

আপক্ব *a.* imperfectly ripened, half-ripe; half-cooked, half-baked, half-roasted, half-boiled.

আপখোরাকি *a.* in the state when one has to pay for one's own food.

আপগা *n.* a stream flowing into a sea, a river.

আপজাত্য *n.* privation or lack or absence of national or racial or familial good qualities; degeneration, degeneracy.

আ-পড়া *a.* unread; uneducated.

আপণ *n.* a shop; a market. **আপণিক** *a.* of a shop or shops, of a market or markets; commercial. ☐ *n.* a shopkeeper; a trader.

আপৎকাল *n.* time of danger or distress or calamity or emergency.

আপতন *n.* falling; a fall; occurrence; a happening, an incident; an accident; (chiefly in math.) incidence; coming; an arrival; alighting; descent. **আপতন কোণ** *n.* angle of incidence. **আপতন বিন্দু** *n.* (math.) the point of incidence.

আপতিক *a.* accidental; incidental.

আপতিত *a.* arrived or come by chance or accident; fallen (down); alighted. **আপতিত রশ্মি** (phys.) an incident ray.

আপত্তি *n.* objection; dissent; protest, expostulation, remonstrance. **~কর, ~জনক** *a.* objectionable, open to exception. **আপত্তি করা** *v.* to object; to dissent; to protest, to expostulate, to remonstrate. **আপত্তি তোলা** *v.* to raise an objection.

আপদ *n.* danger; distress; misery; calamity; any unpleasant person or thing.

~গ্রস্ত *a.* involved in danger, endangered, imperilled; involved in difficulty or distress; troubled or distressed. ~ধর্ম, আপদ্ধর্ম *n.* a course or measure (usu. not thoroughly honest) that may be adopted in time of danger or disaster or emergency. ~বালাই *n. pl.* dangers and harms. ~-বিপদ *n.* dangers and difficulties.

আপন *a.* one's own, own. ~জন *n.* one's own man, a friend or relative. ~পর *a.* one's near and far ones. □ *n.* friend and foe. ~ভোলা *a.* careless about one's own interests; absent-minded, absorbed.

আপনা *n.* one's own self. □ *a.* one's own. আপনা-আপনি *adv.* by or of one's own self; on one's own; without any outward aid; spontaneously. □ *n. pl.* one's own people, friends and relatives. আপনা-আপনির মধ্যে among one's own people; among friends and relations. আপনার var. of আপন। আপনা থেকে of or by one's own self; on one's own; of its own; spontaneously. আপনার পায়ে কুড়ল মারা (fig.) to dig one's own grave.

আপনি[১] *pro.* the honorific form of তুমি।

আপনি[২] *n.* one's own self. আপনি বাঁচলে বাপের নাম self-preservation is the first law of nature.

আপন্ন *a.* endangered, imperilled; (chiefly used as a *sfx.*) affected with, involved in (বিপদাপন্ন). seeking refuge in (শরণাপন্ন).

আপন্নসত্ত্বা *a.* pregnant. □ *n.* a pregnant woman.

আপরাহ্লিক *a.* of or in or during the afternoon.

আপশোস *n.* regret; chagrin; repentance. আপশোস করা *v.* to regret; to become chagrined; to repent.

আপস[১] corrup. of ওয়াপস।

আপস[২] var. of আপোশ।

আপসানো var. of আফসানো।

আপসে[১] alt. spell. of আপোশে।

আপসে[২], আপ্‌সে *adv.* of one's own, spontaneously.

আপাং *n.* a medicinal plant, *Achyranthus aspera.*

আপাকা *a.* unripe, raw; not thoroughly ripened.

আপাণ্ডুর *a.* palish, paly.

আপাত *n.* the present or the actual time in question, the time being; incidence; occurrence. ~কঠিন *a.* appearing as hard or difficult at first or for the time being (but not actually so); apparently or seemingly hard or difficult. ~গতি *n.* apparent motion. ~ত *adv.* at the present time or actual time in question, for the time being, for the nonce. ~দৃষ্টিতে *adv.* at the first sight; to the cursory view or consideration; seemingly. ~প্রসারণ *n.* apparent expansion. ~মধুর *a.* seemingly sweet or sweet for the time being only. ~রমণীয় *a.* agreeable or pleasant for the time being; seemingly alluring or fascinating.

আপাদমস্তক *adv.* from head to foot, cap-a-pie; from top to bottom.

আপান *n.* a place for drinking (wine esp. in a party); a public-house, a bar; a wineshop, an alehouse.

আপামর *adv.* including even the meanest or the lowest. ~ জনগণ *n.* high and low; one and all; everybody.

আপিঙ্গল *a.* brownish, slightly copper-coloured.

আপিল *n.* (in law) a prayer for retrial; an appeal. আপিল করা *v.* to prefer an appeal, to appeal. ~-আদালত *n.* an appellate court. ~কারী *n.* an appellant. আপিলে খালাস acquitted or released on appeal.

আপিস *n.* a place where work or business is carried out, an office. আপিস করা *v.* to go to one's office (daily or regularly), to attend office.

আপীড়ন *n.* pressing or squeezing or hugging or oppressing thoroughly. আপীড়িত *a.* pressed or squeezed or hugged or oppressed thoroughly.

আপীত[১] *a.* yellowish.

আপীত[২] *a.* that which has been drunk thoroughly, drunk to the dregs; drained.

আপীন *n.* an udder, a dug, a teat.

আপেক্ষিক *a.* comparative; (esp. in science) relative. ~তা *n.* comparativeness; relativity. আপেক্ষিক আর্দ্রতা *n.* relative humidity. আপেক্ষিক গুরুত্ব *n.* specific gravity. **আপেক্ষিক ঘনত্ব** *n.* relative density. **~তত্ত্ব** *n.* the theory of relativity. **আপেক্ষিক বেগ** *n.* relative velocity.

আপেল *n.* the apple.

আপোশ *n.* compromise. **আপোশ করা** *v.* to compromise, to strike out a compromise; to settle amicably. **~রফা, ~মীমাংসা** *n.* amicable settlement, compromise. **আপোশে** *adv.* amicably; by arrangement.

আপ্ত[1] *a.* obtained, attained, realized, gratified (আপ্তকাম) ; free from errors; authoritative (আপ্তবাক্য) ; closely related as friends and relatives (আপ্তজন). **~করণিক** *n.* confidential clerk. **~কাম** *a.* one whose desires have been gratified. **~কারী** *a.* reliable; trustworthy. **~জন** *n.* one's own relative or friend. **~বচন** same as **আপ্তবাক্য**। **~বন্ধু** same as **আপ্তজন**। **~বাক্য** *n.* a revealed truth, revelation; (phil.) a source of knowledge; advice of one's own friends and relatives; a presumptive truth, an a priori truth.

আপ্ত[2] *a.* (used as a *pfx.*) own, self-, **~গরজি, ~গরুজে** *a.* preoccupied with self-interest; extremely self-seeking.

আপ্যায়ন *n.* hospitable reception and treatment, entertainment; act of felicitating; entertaining with amusements. **আপ্যায়ন করা** *v.* to receive and treat hospitably, to entertain, to felicitate.

আপ্যায়িত *a.* received and treated hospitably, entertained; felicitated. **আপ্যায়িত করা** same as **আপ্যায়ন করা**।

আপ্রাণ *adv.* & *a.* as long as one lives, till death, to the last breath; even at the risk of one's life; to the extent of one's utmost power and abilities, tooth and nail. **আপ্রাণ করা** *v.* to do one's utmost. **আপ্রাণ চেষ্টা** utmost effort.

আপ্লব, আপ্লাব, আপ্লাবন *n.* a flood; a deluge; inundation; bathing. **আপ্লাবিত** *a.* flooded; inundated; bathed; drenched.

আপ্লুত *a.* flooded; inundated; bathed; drenched; (fig.) overwhelmed or begone (ভাবে আপ্লুত).

আফখোরা var. of **আবখোরা**।

আফগান *n.* an Afghan. ☐ *a.* of Afghanistan or Afghans. **আফগানি** *a.* of Afghanistan.

আফলা var. of **অফলা**।

আফলোদয় *a.* & *adv.* till fructuation; till attainment or realization (of aim, desires etc.). **~কর্মা** *n.* a worker who works till he succeeds.

আফশোস var. of **আপশোস**।

আফসানো *v.* to bluster, to brag; to fret or chafe or express chagrin on account of failure; to tear one's hair. **আফসানি** *n.* blustering or bragging; fretting or chafing or an expression of chagrin at failure.

আফিং *n.* opium. **~খোর, আফিমখোর** *n.* an opiumeater.

আফিম var. of **আফিং**।

আফুটন্ত, আফোটা *a.* not yet bloomed, unblown; not clearly visible; indistinct; (in the process of being boiled but) not yet boiling; parboiled.

আফ্রিকান *n.* an African; an African Negro. ☐ *a.* African.

আব *n.* an excrescence (usu. spherical) on the skin, a tumour.

আবওয়াব *n.* any of the conventional and usually illegal payments exacted by landowners from tenants.

আবকার, আবকারি ori. but obs. forms of **আবগার** and **আবগারি** respectively.

আবখোরা *n.* a large drinking-glass or tall cup, a tumbler.

আবগার *n.* a manufacturer of or dealer in alcoholic spirits and other intoxicating drugs; a distiller. **আবগারি** *n.* sale or manufacture of alcoholic spirits and other intoxicating drugs; a tax or duty imposed on this manufacture or sale, excise duty (also **আবগারি কর, আবগারি শুল্ক**) ; the public department entrusted with the charge of collecting this tax or duty, the excise department (also **আবগারি বিভাগ**). ☐ *a.* relating to alcoholic spirits and other intoxicating drugs or to their manufacture and sale; relating to excise tax or the excise department.

আবছায়া, (coll.) **আবছা** *n.* a shadowy or indistinct figure. ☐ *a.* shadowy; indistinct.

আবডাল see **আড়াল**।

আবণ্টন *n.* allotment.

আবদার *n.* a childish or capricious insistence on having or doing something; an unreasonable demand or claim; a fanciful claim preferred to an affectionate person. **আবদার করা** *v.* to insist childishly or capriciously on having or doing something; to demand or claim unreasonably. **আবদারে, আবদেরে** *a.* insisting childishly or capriciously on having or doing something.

আবদ্ধ *a.* bound, tied; shut; confined; besieged; enclosed (আবদ্ধ স্থান) ; involved; beset; mortgaged, pawned. **আবদ্ধ করা** *v.* to bind, to tie; to shut; to confine; to besiege; to enclose; to involve; to beset; to mortgage, to pawn.

আবপন same as **বপন** ।

আবরক *a.* that which covers or screens or veils. ☐ *n.* a cover; a covering; a screen; a lid; a veil.

আবরণ *n.* covering or screening or veiling; a cover or covering; a lid; a screen, a veil. **আবরণী** *n.* a cover or covering; a lid; a screen; a veil.

আবরিত *a.* (poet.) covered; screened; veiled.

আবরু *n.* (usu. a woman's) dignity, honour; chastity, modesty; a screen; a veil, a yashmak.

আবর্জন *n.* casting off or giving up thoroughly; forcing to bend down; controlling or regulating.

আবর্জনা *n.* things thrown away or left as worthless, cast-off, refuse; sweepings; (fig.) an undesirable or mean person; an outcast.

আবর্জিত *a.* cast-off; bent down; controlled or regulated.

আবর্ত *n.* a whirling motion or shape; a whirl; a vortex; a whirlpool, an eddy; whirling or revolving or rotating. ☐ *a.* whirling; revolving; rotating. **আবর্ত ঘর্ষণ** *n.* rolling friction. **~ন** *n.* whirling or revolving or rolling; a whirl, revolution; rotation; gyration; return; stirring or churning; repetition. **আবর্তন দণ্ড, আবর্তনী** *n.* a pestle for churning. **~মান** *a.* whirling or revolving or gyrating or returning. **আবর্তিত** *a.* revolved; rotated; gyrated; returned; repeated. **আবর্তিত হওয়া** *v.* to whirl; to revolve; to rotate; to gyrate; to eddy; to return; to be repeated.

আবলি *n.* a row or line (বৃক্ষাবলি) ; a group or series (প্রশ্নাবলি, বংশাবলি) ; a collection (গ্রন্থাবলি).

আবলুস *n.* ebony, ebon. **আবলুস-কালো** *a.* ebon-coloured, black as ebony.

আবল্য *n.* weakness; fatigue; lethargy, torpidity; drowsiness caused by fatigue.

আবশ্যক *a.* necessary; essential. ☐ *n.* necessity, need. **~তা** *n.* necessity, need. **~বোধে** *adv.* having considered or considering it necessary. **আবশ্যকীয়** *a.* necessary; essential.

আবশ্যিক *a.* compulsory.

আবহ *a.* (chiefly used in *comp.*) carrying, conducting, producing (শোকাবহ). ☐ *n.* the air that pervades the world; atmosphere. **~চিত্র** *n.* a weather-chart. **~বিজ্ঞান** *n.* meteorology. **~বিদ, ~বিৎ** *n.* meteorologist. **~বিদ্যা** *n.* meteorology. **~মণ্ডল** *n.* the atmosphere. **~সংবাদ** *n.* weather report. **~সংগীত** *n.* background music. **~সূচনা** *n.* weather forecast.

আবহমান *a.* existing or continuing since the beginning; traditional and ever-existent. **~কাল** *adv.* continuing or existing from time immemorial; ever since the beginning.

আবহাওয়া *n.* climate; weather.

আ-বাঁধা *a.* untied, unfastened; (esp. of books etc.) unbound; (of hair) not done up; disorderly (আ-বাঁধা সংসার).

আবাগা, আবাগে *a.* ill-fated, unfortunate. *fem.* **আবাগি** ।

আবাদ *n.* cultivation, tillage; cultivated land; land developed for agriculture; a human habitation; a settlement. **আবাদি** *a.* arable; fit for or developed for cultivation; cultivated.

আবাপন *n.* the art of weaving cloth.

আবাপনিক *n.* reeler.

আবার *adv.* again, once more; moreover, and also (গরিব আবার বদখেয়ালি). ☐ *int.* expressing uncertainty or distrust or negation (কালো মেয়ের আবার বিয়ে,

গরিবের আবার সুখ, নিত্য-ভিখারিকে কী আবার দেবে).

আবাল *n.* a boy or a child or an underage person (esp. one who is foolish or helpless); an ignorant or dull-headed person. **~বৃদ্ধবনিতা** *n.* one and all; men women and children.

আবাল্য *adv.* from childhood or infancy; ever since one's childhood.

আবাস *n.* a dwelling-place, a habitation, a home, an abode; a residence; a house. **আবাসিক** *n.* a caretaker (chiefly of a Buddhist monastery). □ *a.* resident (আবাসিক শল্য-চিকিৎসক) ; (of a student) living in a students' hostel. **আবাসিক বিদ্যালয়** residential school.

আবাহন *n.* invocation; invitation; a call. **আবাহন করা** *v.*to invoke; to invite; to call. **আবাহনী** *n.* a gesture made with one's palms and fingers for invoking a god or goddess. □ *a.* invocatory; relating to invitation or call.

আবির *n.* a kind of perfumed and coloured powder that the Hindus sprinkle over one another esp. during the Holi (হোলি) festival.

আবির্ভাব *n.* coming into view (esp. for the first time or from hiding); apperarance (esp. sudden); advent; arrival; birth; coming into existence; (of a deity) installing oneself somewhere; (of authors, painters, actors etc.) first appearance before the public; (of flowers etc.) coming out or being revealed, manifestation.

আবির্ভূত *a.* one who or that which has come into view or appeared or arrived; born; one who or that which has come into existence; (of a deity) one who has installed oneself; (of authors, painters, actors, musicians) who have appeared before the public for the first time; (of flowers etc.) that which has come out, revealed; manifested. **আবির্ভূত হওয়া** *v.* to come into view (esp. for the first time or from hiding); to appear; to come; to arrive; to take birth; to install oneself; to appear before the public for the first time; to come out; to be revealed or manifested.

আবিল *a.* defiled; turbid, muddy; filthy, foul. **~তা** *a.* defilement; turbidity; filthiness, foulness.

আবিষ্করণ, আবিষ্করণীয়, আবিষ্কর্তা see **আবিষ্কার**।

আবিষ্কার, আবিষ্করণ, আবিষ্ক্রিয়া *n.* discovering; a discovery; invention; the thing invented. **আবিষ্কার করা** *v.* to discover; to invent. **আবিষ্করণীয়** *a.* that which is to be discovered or invented; well worth discovering or inventing. **আবিষ্কর্তা, আবিষ্কারক** *n.* a discoverer; an inventor.

আবিষ্কৃত *a.* discovered; invented.

আবিষ্ট *a.* thoroughly engrossed or absorbed (in) (পাঠাবিষ্ট) ; rapt in (মোহাবিষ্ট) ; possessed (by) (ভূতাবিষ্ট) ; overwhelmed (with) (বিস্ময়াবিষ্ট) ; begone (শোকাবিষ্ট) ; overcast or pervaded with (মেঘাবিষ্ট) ; nonplussed, confounded; (phy.) induced.

আবীর arch. spell. of **আবির**।

আবৃত *a.* covered; encircled, surrounded (মেখলাবৃত) ; overcast or pervaded with (মেঘাবৃত). **আবৃত করা** *v.* to cover; to encircle, to surround; to overcast; to pervade. **আবৃতি** *n.* state of being covered or encircled or pervaded; covering; a cover; encirclement; pervasion; a wall; a fence; an enclosure.

আবৃত্ত *a.* read or studied over and over again; repeated; recited; that which has returned or recurred; revolved; (esp. in arith.) recurring. **~চক্ষু** *a.* one who has turned one's eyes inwards; introspective. **আবৃত্ত দশমিক** (airth.) recurring decimal. **আবৃত্তি** *n.* reading or studying over and over again; repetition; recital, recitation; return, recurrence; revolving or being revolved, revolution. **আবৃত্তি করা** *v.* to read or study over and over again; to repeat; to recite; to return; to recur; to revolve.

আবেগ *n.* tremendous or extraordinary velocity or force (বেগের আবেগ) ; outburst of passion or emotion (আবেগে বলা) ; passion (স্বরে আবেগ আছে) ; anxiety; state of suspense; mental uneasiness; troubled state of the mind; mental suffering (শোকাবেগ). **~পূর্ণ** *a.* impassioned;

passionate. ~শূন্য, ~হীন *a.* devoid of passion; dispassionate. আবেগোচ্ছ্বাস *n.* an outburst of passion; a passionate or impassioned outburst.

আবেদক *a.* one who submits an application. □ *n.* an applicant; a petitioner; a plaintiff.

আবেদন *n.* representation, prayer, solicitation; an application; a petition; a plaint; appeal (কবিতার আবেদন হৃদয়ের কাছে) আবেদন করা *v.* to represent, to pray, to solicit; to put in an application, to apply; to petition; to lodge a complaint; to appeal. ~কারী same as আবেদক। *fem.* ~কারিণী। ~পত্র *n.* an application; a petition. আবেদনীয় *a.* fit to be solicited or entreated.

আবেশ *n.* confounded state of mind; mental confusion, perplexity; tremendous excitement of passion ('আবেশে হিয়ার মাঝারে লই') ; attachment, love ('আবেশে অবশ তনু') ; entrance; infiltration, taking possession (ভূতাবেশ) ; rapt attention; trance; engrossment; rapture; obsession.

আবেশ-কুণ্ডলী *n.* (phy.) induction coil.

আবেশ্যতা *n.* (phy.) inductive capacity.

আবেষ্টক *a.* surrounding, enclosing. □ *n.* a fence, a wall; that which encloses, an enclosure.

আবেষ্টন *n.* surrounding or enclosing; a fence; a wall; that which encloses, an enclosure; surroundings, environment. আবেষ্টনী *n.* a fence; a wall; that which encloses, an enclosure; a circurmference; environment, surroundings.

আবেষ্টিত *a.* surrounded, enclosed, encircled.

আবোলতাবোল *n.* incoherent talk; nonsense; delirium; nonsense rhymes. □ *a.* incoherent and nonsensical.

আব্বা *n.* (Mus.) father; dad.

আব্রহ্ম *adv.* starting with or from Brahma (ব্রহ্ম). ~স্তম্ব *n.* all creatures and objects starting with Brahma (ব্রহ্ম) or the Supreme Consciousness down to the inanimate straw.

আভরণ *n.* anything worn for personal embellishment, an ornament. কলঙ্ক তার অঙ্গের আভরণ scandal she wears as a jewel on her person.

আভা *n.* glow; shine; lustre, glaze; beam; flash; tinge. ~ময় *a.* full of glow, glowing; beaming; shining.

আভাং *n.* rubbing the body with oil etc; anointment.

আভাঙা *a.* not broken, unbroken (আভাঙা ডাল) ; not ground, unground (আভাঙা গম).

আভাষ *n.* a preface, a prologue, a prefatory note, an introduction; an introductory talk; a conversation. ~ণ *n.* addressing and talking to; conversation; an address, a speech, a talk. আভাষিত *a.* delivered as or mentioned in a speech.

আভাস *n.* faint or indistinct presence ('আভাসে দাও দেখা') ; a shadow; a hint (আভাসে জানানো) ; glow. আভাস দেওয়া *v.* to appear faintly or indistinctly; to give a hint, to hint. ~ইঙ্গিত *n.* hints; slight or indirect suggestion. আভাসে ইঙ্গিতে *adv.* by indirect suggestion, by hints.

আভাসা *v.* (poet.) to blaze up, to glow; (poet.) to be revealed.

আভাসিত *a.* indicated, suggested.

আভিজন *n.* noble birth; aristocracy; surname.

আভিজাতিক *a.* of aristocrat or aristocracy or noble birth; aristocratic; pertaining to or indicative of the family; familial. আভিজাতিক চিহ্ন *n.* heraldry.

আভিজাত্য *n.* noble birth; aristocracy.

আভিধানিক *a.* lexicographical. □ *n.* the compiler of a dictionary, a lexicographer.

আভিমুখ্য *n.* state of being towards; state of being in front or face to face of; confrontation; assistance, help.

আভীর *n.* a member of the cowherd class; a cowherd. *fem.* আভীরী। ~পল্লি *n.* a locality or village where cowherds live.

আভূমি *adv.* down to the ground; having prostrated oneself (আভূমি প্রণত হওয়া).

আভোগ *n.* a kind of concluding note in the Indian musical modes; act of enjoying; completeness, fullness; expansion; expanse.

আভ্যন্তর, আভ্যন্তরিক, (inc. but pop.) **আভ্যন্তরীণ** *a.* internal, inner.

আভ্যুদয়িক *a.* pertaining to progress or promotion in life; pertaining to or causing well-being; causing prosperity. ☐ *n.* a ceremony performed on the eve of wedding etc. praying to the spirits of one's forefathers to bless the present occasion.

আম[১] *n.* mucus; cyst; dysentery. **~বাত** *n.* nettlerash, urticaria. **~রক্ত** *n.* blood coming out with the stool of a dysentery patient. **~রোগ** *n.* dysentery.

আম[২] *n.*the common people. ☐ *a.* of or for the common people. **~দরবার** *n.* a place for public audience. **~মোক্তার** *n.* a legally appointed representative, an attorney. **~মোক্তারনামা** *n.* power-of-attorney.

আম[৩] *a.* uncooked, raw (আমমাংস) ; unburnt, unbaked (আমসরা, আমহাঁড়ি). **~গন্ধি** *a.* (of food) cooked but somewhat raw.

আম[৪] *n.* the mango. **~আদা** *n.* the mango ginger, a variety of ginger smelling like the mango. **~চুর, ~শি** *n.* dried slices of green mango preserved in salt or in salt and mustard. **মুখ শুকিয়ে আমশি হওয়া** to look haggard, to have a shrivelled look, to have an emaciated and wizened face. **~সত্ত্ব** *n.* a thin cake made of the sweet juice of ripe mango by drying it in the sun (used as food), preserved essence of ripe mango. **~হলুদ** same as **আম-আদা। বর্ণচোরা আম** a variety of mango that looks green and should be sour but is actually ripe and sweet; (fig.) a person concealing his or her merits.

আমড়া *n.* the hog-plum. **~গাছি** *n.* flattering with some end in view, coaxing, cajolement. **আমড়াগাছি করা** *v.* to flatter with some motive or design, to coax, to cajole.

আমতা, (usu.) **আমতা-আমতা** *n.* hesitating in speech as if taken aback or not ready to speak, faltering. **আমতা-আমতা করা** *v.* to falter; to hesitate to say.

আমদানি *n.* (comm.) import; income; gathering (লোকের আমদানি) ; onrush, assemblage (বহুলোকের আমদানি) ; attack (রোগের আমদানি). **আমদানি করা** *v.* (comm.) to import; (in other cases) to bring. **আমদানি বাণিজ্য** *n.* import trade. **আমদানি শুল্ক** *n.* import duty.

আমধুর *a.* slightly sweet, sweetish; not excessively sweet, pleasantly sweet.

আমন *a.* late autumnal. ☐ *n.* late autumnal crop of paddy; autumn rice (also **আমন ধান**).

আমন্ত্রণ *n.* invitation; a call to come; a greeting. **আমন্ত্রণ করা** *v.* to invite; to call; to greet.

আমন্ত্রয়িতা *n.* an inviter; a host; one who gives a call to come; one who greets.

আমন্ত্রিত *a.* invited; called to come; greeted.

আমবাত see **আম**[১] ।

আমমোক্তার see **আম**[২] ।

আময় *n.* disease, ailment.

আময়দা *a.* plentiful, abundant; excessive.

আ মর *int.* indicating : light imprecation, bashfulness, shame, reproach, censure etc.; Devil take thee, go to hell, beshrew me.

আমরণ *adv.* & *a.* till death; all through one's life. **~স্থায়ী** *a.* lasting till death, continuing till the end of one's life.

আমরা *pro.* we.

আমরি, আ মরি *int.* indicating : praise, taunt, ridicule, sorrow etc.; now I'II die happily; I'II rather die.

আমরুল *n.* a variety of spinach having sour taste, sorrel.

আমর্শ, আমর্শন *n.* touch, contact; counsel, advice, consultation; weighing something in the mind, deliberation.

আমর্ষ *n.* mercilessness; anger.

আমল *n.* region, rule, regime; possession, control; age, time, period; attention, heed, indulgence (আমল দেওয়া). **আমল না দেওয়া** to attach no importance to, to pay no heed to, to refuse to consider; to overlook. **মান্ধাতার আমল** see **মান্ধাতা।**

আমলক, আমলকি, আমলকী *n.* emblica, the emblic myrobalan.

আমলা *n.* an office-clerk; a government office. **~তন্ত্র** *n.* bureaucracy. **~তান্ত্রিক** *a.* bureaucratic.

আমলানো *v.* to become painful gradually.

আমা[1] *a.* half-burnt, not perfectly burnt (আমা-ইট).

আমা[2] *pro.* (poet.) I myself; myself; I; me; to me.

আমাকে, আমায় *pro.* me; to me.

আমাতিসার *n.* dysentery; amoebic dysentery; (loos.) bacillary or biliary dysentery.

আমাদিগকে (obs.) *pro.* us; to us.

আমাদিগের (obs.) *pro.* our, of us, ours.

আমাদের *pro.* our, of us, ours; us; to us.

আমানত *a.* deposited; credited; placed in one's custody. ☐ *n.* the thing or money deposited or credited, deposit, credit. **আমানত করা, আমানত দেওয়া, আমানত রাখা** *v.* to deposit; to credit; to place in the custody of. **আমানতি** *a.* pertaining to deposit or credit; deposited; credited.

আমানি *n.* the water in which cooked rice has been soaked overnight.

আমান্ন *n.* uncooked rice.

আমার *pro.* my, mine.

আমাশয় *n.* dysentery; the part of the belly in which mucus collects.

আমাশা *n.*(coll.) dysentery.

আমি *pro.* I. ☐ *n.* self-knowledge; the soul, the ego; egoism, pride, vanity, self-importance. **~ত্ব** *n.* egoism, vanity.

আমিন *n.* a land surveyor; a supervising officer. **আমিনি** *a.* relating to a surveyor.

আমির *n.* (Mus.) a wealthy nobleman or high-born person; a title of some Muslim kings, an Amir, an Ameer. **~-ওমরাহ্** *n. pl.* princes and courtiers or noblemen; men of high and wealthy class. **আমিরি** *n.* amirate; high style of living or ostentatious show of wealth; pomp and grandeur. ☐ *a.* of an Amir or emirate; living in a high style or making an ostentatious show of wealth; full of pomp and grandeur.

আমিষ *n.* meat; non-vegetarian food or diet. **~ভোজী, আমিষাশী** *a.* carnivorous; non-vegetarian.

আমীক্ষা *n.* posset.

আমীন arch. spell. of **আমিন** ।

আমীর arch. spell. of **আমির** ।

আমুদে, আমোদপ্রিয় *a.* given to merriment; sportive, merry; gay, cheerful, jolly; vivacious, sprightly; witty, humorous.

আমূল *adv.* to the root; radically; thoroughly, completely, root-and-branch. ☐ *a.* extended to the root; radical (আমূল সংস্কার) ; thorough.

আমৃত্যু *adv.* till death; till the end of one's life.

আমেজ *n.* subtle presence or slight trace, a touch; a touch of similarity; the ultimate part of anything passing away, after-image, after-taste (সুরের আমেজ, নেশার আমেজ) ; pleasant drowsiness or rapt attention (গানে আমেজ আসা).

আমোদ *n.* delight; joy; gladness; merriment, amusement; festivity; fun; (rare) far-reaching fragrance, extremely sweet fragrance. **~আহ্লাদ** *n. pl.* rejoicings. **আমোদআহ্লাদ করা** *v.* to rejoice. **আমোদ করা** *v.* to express delight or joy; to make merry; to indulge in or enjoy amusement; to be festive; to make fun; to poke fun (at); to fill with fragrance. **~জনক** *a.* delightful; merry; amusing; funny. **~ন** *n.* amusing, amusement, recreation; perfuming. **~প্রমোদ** *n. pl.* amusements, recreations. **আমোদপ্রমোদ করা** *v.* to indulge in amusements. **~প্রিয়** see **আমুদে** । **আমোদিত** *a.* delighted; perfumed, scented. **আমোদী** *a.* delighted; jolly, sportive; sweet-scented. *fem.* **আমোদিনী** ।

আম্বা *n.* audacity, effrontery, impudence, (coll.) cheek; bragging, boast, vaunt; audacious ambition.

আম্মা *n.* mother.

আম্র *n.* (for. High.) the mango. **~কানন, ~কুঞ্জ, ~বন** *n.* a mango-grove.

আম্রাত, আম্রাতক *n.* the hog plum.

আম্ল *a.* acid, sour. **আম্লা** *n. fem.* the tamarind-tree. **আম্লিক** *a.* acid, sour; acidic (আম্লিক অকসাইড). **আম্লিক সন্ধান** acid fermentation. **আম্লিকা, আম্লীকা** *n. fem.* the tamarind-tree.

আয়ুক্ত *a.* in-charge. **~ক** *n.* an officer-in-charge. **আয়ুক্ত মন্ত্রী** minister-in-charge.

আয়[1] *v.* 2nd pers. imp. of **আসা** । **আয়, খেলি** come, let us play.

আয়² *n.* income; earnings; profit; revenue. **~কর** *n.* income-tax. ☐ *a.* profitable. **~ব্যয়** *n.* income and expenditure; (accts.) debit and credit. **~ব্যয় পরীক্ষা** *n.* audit. **~ব্যয় পরীক্ষক** *n.* auditor. **~ব্যয়ক** *n.* budget. **~ব্যয়ক শীর্ষ** *n.* budget-head. **~ব্যয়ক সত্র** *n.* budget session. **আয় বুঝে ব্যয় করা** to live within one's means; (cp.) to cut one's coat according to one's cloth. **আয়ের অধিক ব্যয় করা** to spend beyond one's means or income. **আয়ের ঘর** (accts.) credit side.

আয়ত *a.* extensive, wide; expanded; very large; (geom.) rectangular but having unequal sides, oblong. **~ক্ষেত্র** *n.* (geom.) an oblong, a rectangle. **~চক্ষু, ~লোচন** *a.* wide-eyed or large-eyed. *fem.* **~লোচনা** ।

আয়তন *n.* area or its measure; volume or its measure; extension; breadth; width; a house, an abode; an institution (অচলায়তন) ; an altar. **~স্থাপকতা** *n.* bulk-elasticity. **আয়তনাঙ্ক** *n.* bulk-modulus.

আয়তি¹ *n.* state of a married woman whose husband is alive; any of the symbols (usu. borne on the person of the wife) indicating this marital state.

আয়তি² *n.* length; width, breadth; extension; the future; time for bearing fruit.

আয়তী *n. fem.* a married woman whose husband is alive.

আয়ত্ত *a.* brought under control or taken possession of; controlled; subjugated; subject; dominated; mastered; tamed; seized. **আয়ত্ত করা, আয়ত্তে আনা** *v.* to bring under control; to control; to take possession of; to subjugate; to dominate; to master; to tame; to seize. **বন্য ঘোড়াকে আয়ত্তে আনা** to break a wild horse. **আয়ত্তের বাইরে** out of control; beyond control, out of hand. **আয়ত্তি** *n.* control, hold; possession; subjugation; subjection; domination; mastery; seizure.

আয়ন বায়ু *n.* trade wind.

আয়না *n.* a mirror, a looking-glass, a speculum.

আয়মা *n.* a grant of rent-free land made by Muslim princes to religious preachers and to learned people. **~মহল** *n.* an estate of land held under this grant.

আয়স *a.* of or made of or caused by iron; ferrous. ☐ *n.* iron. **আয়সী** *n. fem.* a coat-mail made of iron, an iron armour.

আয়া *n.* a nurse-maid or waiting-maid, an ayah.

আয়াম¹ *n.* width, breadth; length.

আয়াম² *n.* season; suitable time; right time.

আয়াস *n.* pain, trouble; exhaustion, fatigue; an exertion of strength or power, labour, strain; an endeavour, an effort. **~সাধ্য** *a.* involving effort, strenuous, laborious, arduous, toilsome, uphill.

আয়ি alt. spellings of **আই** ।

আয়ু *n.* the span of one's life, longevity; lifetime; life. **~প্রদ, ~বর্ধক** *a.* that which prolongs life; rejuvenating; that which bestows long life. **~বর্ধন** *n.* prolonging life; prolongation of life; rejuvenation. **~বৃদ্ধি** *n.* prolongation of life; rejuvenation. **~স্কর** same as **আয়ুপ্রদ** । **~স্কাল** *n.* the span of one's life, lifetime. **~স্মান** *a.* long-lived. *fem.* **আয়ুস্মতী** । **আয়ুষ্য** same as **আয়ুপ্রদ** ।

আয়ুধ *n.* weapon, arms.

আয়ুধশালা *n.* armoury, arsenal.

আয়ুর্বৃদ্ধি, আয়ুস্কর, আয়ুস্কাল, আয়ুস্মতী, আয়ুস্মান, see **আয়ু** ।

আয়ুর্বেদ *n.* the traditional Hindu science of medicine as taught in the Atharva Veda. **আয়ুর্বেদীয়** *a.* relating or pertaining to this science; according to this science.

আয়েন্দা *a.* coming; ensuing, next; future, later.

আয়েশ, আয়েস *n.* ease; comfort; luxury. **আয়েশ করা** *v.* to take one's ease; to relax; to take rest. **আয়েশি, আয়েসি** *a.* ease-loving; easy-going; brought up amidst ease and luxury; easy.

আয়োগ *n.* a committee (esp. a public one) set up for investigation etc., a commission.

আয়োজক *a.* & *n.* one who makes preparation for or collects the things necessary for a purpose; one who organises or makes preparation for a function.

আয়োজন *n.* preparation; collection of things necessary to serve a purpose;

things so collected; making or becoming ready. **আয়োজন করা** *v.* to make preparations (for).

আয়োজিত *a.* that for which necessary things have been collected or preparation has been made; that which has been made ready.

আয়োডিন var. of **আইয়োডিন**।

আর *conj.* and, and also (রাম আর শ্যাম); or (বাঁচা আর মরা), or not. □ *adv.* else, more (আর কী বলব); enough (আর কেন); no more (আর কান্না নয়); at the same time, simultaneously, but (শক্তের ভক্ত আর নরমের যম); on the other hand, yet in return (সে তোমার উপকার করে আর তুমি তার নিন্দা কর); in future, again (আর যেন এমন না হয়); still now, still then (আর কেন আশা কর); at present, now (আর সেদিন নেই); moreover, besides, in addition to that (আর দেখ); ever (বিড়ালে কি আর মাছ খাওয়া ছাড়ে); ever before or after (এমন আর দেখিনি বা দেখব না); since then (সেই গেল আর ফিরল না); of course, certainly (তুমি তো আর বোকা নও). □ *a.* other, another, different (আর লোকেরা, আর কেউ); past, last (আর বছর সে এসেছিল); coming, next (আর সপ্তাহে যাব). □ *pro.* another person or thing, the other person or thing, a different person or thing (আরটি কোথায়, আরে কী বলে). **আর আর** all other. **আরও** *a.* more. □ *adv.* still more; further, moreover. **আর বার** on the other occasion; another time; once again, once more. **আর সব** and others.

আরক *n.* extract, essence; juice; spirit; arrack; tincture.

আরক্ত, আরক্তিম *a.* slightly red, reddish; blood-red; deep red, scarlet, crimson. **আরক্তনয়ন, আরক্তনেত্র, আরক্তলোচন** *a.* with reddened or blood-shot eyes; angry. □ *n.* such eyes. **আরক্তবদন, আরক্তমুখ** *a.* with face (or cheeks) flushed on account of shame or anger. □ *n.* such a face.

আরক্ষ *n.* police or military station; an outpost; defence force, homeguard. □ *a.* engaged in defence. **আরক্ষা** *n.* the police. **আরক্ষাবাহিনী** *n.* the police force. **আরক্ষিক, আরক্ষী** *n.* a policeman; a guardsman. **আরক্ষিদল** *n.* a police picket.

আরজি, আর্জি *n.* a prayer, request; a petition; a plaint. **আরজি করা** বা **দাখিল করা** *v.* to file or submit a petition or plaint.

আরণি *n.* whirlpool; eddy.

আরণ্য *a.* of or relating to a forest or forests; wild; sylvan; born or grown or living in forests. **~ক** *a.* wild; forest-grown; living in forests; sylvan. □ *n.* concluding section of the Brahmanas (ব্রাহ্মণ) which are parts of the Vedas; a person (esp. a saint of ancient India) living in forests; a forester, a forest-dweller.

আরতি[1] *n.* end; subjugation; deep attachment.

আরতি[2] *n.* greeting a deity by waving a lamp, thurible, incenser etc. before his or her face.

আরদালি *n.* an orderly; an office bearer.

আরব[1] var. of **আরাব**।

আরব[2] *n.* an Arab, an Arabian; the Arabian nation, the Arabs. **আরবি** *a.* Arabian. □ *n.* the language of Arabia, Arabic; an Arabian; an Arab; the Arabs. **আরবি গঁদ** gum arabic.

আরব্ধ *a.* that which has been undertaken or begun. **আরব্ধ কার্য** *n.* a task undertaken or commenced.

আরভমাণ *a.* in a state of being commenced or undertaken; about to commence.

আরমানি *n.* an Armenian; the language of Armenia; Armenian. □ *a.* Armenian.

আরম্ভ *n.* commencement, inception, beginning, start; origin, birth; introduction; a prologue. **আরম্ভ করা** *v.* to commence, to begin, to start; to introduce. **আরম্ভ হওয়া** *v.* to commence; to begin, to start; to originate; to take birth; to be introduced. **~ক** *a.* & *n.* one who commences or introduces. **আরম্ভিক** *a.* relating to inception or beginning; starting; introductory.

আরশ *n.* a throne.

আরশি *n.* a mirror, a looking glass; a speculum.

আরশুলা var. of **আরশোলা**।

আরশোলা *n.* the cockroach, the black-beetle.

আরাত্রিক *n.* (act of) greeting a deity by waving a lamp, thurible, incenser etc. before his or her face.

আরাধক *a.* one who worships. □ *n.* a worshipper, a devotee.

আরাধনা, আরাধন *n.* worship; service; prayer. **আরাধনা করা** *v.* to worship; to pray to. **আরাধনীয়** same as **আরাধ্য** ।

আরাধিত *a.* worshipped; adored.

আরাধ্য *a.* worshipped; deserving to be worshipped; worshipful; adorable. **~মান** *a.* being worshipped or in the state of being worshipped.

আরাব *n.* a (high) sound or note; a (great) noise; tumult; a roar.

আরাম[১] *a.* recovered from illness, cured; relieved. **আরাম করা** *v.* to cure. **আরাম হওয়া** *v.* to be cured or soothed.

আরাম[২] *n.* ease, comfort; pleasure; happiness; relaxation; rest; a garden (সংঘারাম). **~কেদারা** *n.* an easy-chair. **আরাম করা** *v.* to take rest; to lie down; to recline; to relax; to enjoy ease and comfort; to enjoy pleasures. **আরাম দেওয়া** *v.* to give ease and comfort; to give relief. **আরাম পাওয়া** *v.* to enjoy ease and comfort; to get relief. **~প্রিয়, আরামি** *a.* ease-loving, fond of ease.

আরূঢ় *a.* mounted; seated on. **আরূঢ় হওয়া** *v.* to mount; to sit on.

আরে *int.* expressing : fear, shame, astonishment, hate, disgust, anger etc. used in addressing or hailing, ah, oh, eh, hi, holla.

আরোগ্য *n.* recovery from ailment or illness, cure; restoration to health; sound health, health. **আরোগ্য করা** *v.* to cure, to bring round. **আরোগ্য হওয়া** *v.* to be cured, to recover, to come round. **~নিকেতন, ~শালা** *n.* a hospital, an infirmary. **~লাভ** *n.* coming round, recovery. **~লাভ করা বা হওয়া** *v.* same as **আরোগ্য হওয়া** ।

আরোপ *n.* ascription or attribution of a quality of one thing to another; imputation; imposition; assignment; bestowal. **আরোপ করা** *v.* to ascribe, to attribute; to impute; to impose; to assign; to bestow. **~ক** *a.* attributing, ascribing; imputing; imposing; assigning; bestowing; placing; implanting. □ *n.* an imputer; an imposer; one who assigns; one who bestows or places; one who strings (a bow); a planter. **~ণ** *n.* attribution, ascription; imputation; imposition; assignment; bestowal; placing, emplacement; mounting a thing or person upon something; stringing a bow; act of planting; implantation. **আরোপণ করা** *v.* to attribute, to ascribe; to impute; to impose; to assign; to bestow; to place; to mount; to string (a bow); to plant; to implant. **আরোপিত** *a.* attributed, ascribed; imputed; imposed; assigned; bestowed; placed; mounted; (of a bow) strung; planted; implanted.

আরোপপত্র *n.* a charge-sheet.

আরোহ *n.* height, altitude; ascent; boarding (a ship, railway train etc.) entrainment, embarkation; buttock esp. of a woman (বরারোহা) ; grade; (log.) induction. **~ণ** *n.* mounting or climbing or riding or placing oneself upon; ascent, ascension, boarding a carriage. **আরোহণ করা** *v.* to mount, to climb, to scale; to ascend; to ride; to place oneself upon; to board (a ship, railway train etc.) to embark, to entrain. **~ণী** *n.* a flight of steps, a stair, a stair-case; a ladder; an escalator. **~পত্র** *n.* an embarkation permit. **~প্রণালী** *n.* inductive method. **~স্থান** *n.* a remount depot. **আরোহী** *a.* mounting; climbing; scaling; riding; boarding, embarking; mounted; emplaced; boarded; ascended; (log.) inductive; (mus. of notes) gradually increasing in pitch. □ *n.* a climber; a rider; a passenger; (mus.) a note which increases gradually in pitch. *fem.* **আরোহিণী** ।

আর্ক *a.* solar. **~ফলা** (৴) *n.* this sign over Bengali consonant letters to indicate a preceding '-r' sound; sun-ray; (facet.) a tuft of long hair maintained by a conservative Brahman on his crown.

আর্জব *n.* straightness; upright or vertical position; straightforwardness; candour; uprightness; honesty.

আর্জি alt. spell. of **আরজি** ।

আর্ট *n.* art; (loos.) an artistic posture or affectation.

আর্টিস্ট *n.* an artist; a painter.

আর্ত *a.* sick; distressed, stricken with grief or sorrow; aggrieved; afflicted; oppressed; involved in danger. **~ত্রাণ** *n.* relief of the distressed or afflicted or oppressed or endangered persons. **~সেবা** *n.* helping the distressed or afflicted, relief work. **~স্বর** *n.* a piteous cry or wailing, an outcry of grief or pain or affliction. **~স্বরে** *adv.* in a piteous tone or voice, piteously.

আর্তনাদ *n.* groaning; cry of pain or grief or affliction etc.

আর্তব *n.* menstruation. □ *a.* menstrual; seasonal. **~কাল** *n.* the time or duration of menses.

আর্তি *n.* illness, ailment; pain; distress; grief, sorrow; affliction; state of being oppressed; state of being involved in danger; (poet.) intense mental agitation or urge.

আর্থ same as **আর্থিক** ।

আর্থনীতিক *a.* pertaining to economics, economic; pertaining to financial policy.

আর্থিক *a.* financial; pecuniary; monetary. **আর্থিক ক্লেশ** pecuniary difficulties, financial distress or straits. **আর্থিক ক্ষমতা** financial powers. **আর্থিক বৎসর** financial year. **আর্থিক সাহায্য** pecuniary help, financial aid.

আর্দালি alt. spell. of **আরদালি** ।

আর্দ্র *a.* wet; moist; damp, humid; soft; softened with affection tears etc. **~কণ্ঠে, ~স্বরে** *adv.* in a doleful or mournful voice. **~তা** *n.* wetness; moistness; moisture; dampness, humidity; softness; softened state. **~ভূমিজ** *a.* hygrophyte.

আর্দ্রক *n.* ginger.

আর্দ্রকণ্ঠে, আর্দ্রতা, আর্দ্রস্বরে see **আর্দ্র** ।

আর্দ্রা *n.* the sixth of the twenty-seven zodiacal stars according to Hindu astronomy.

আর্মানি alt. spell. of **আরমানি** ।

আর্মেচার *n.* an armature.

আর্য *n.* the Aryan race; an Aryan; the people who spoke the Aryan language; a venerable person. □ *a.* Aryan; venerable; best; of noble birth; civilized. **~তা** *n.* Aryanism; civilized conduct and behaviour. **~পুত্র** *n.* a son of the father-in-law, (usu.) husband. **~সমাজ** *n.* a Vedic community founded by Dayananda Saraswati. **~সমাজী** *a.* of or belonging to the Arya Samaj (আর্যসমাজ).

আর্যা[1] *fem.* of **আর্য** ।

আর্যা[2] *n.* a kind of metre used in Sanskrit verse; any of the rhymed arithmetical formulae.

আর্যাবর্ত *n.* upper or northern India where the ancient Aryans settled.

আর্যামি *n.* (facet. & dero.) Aryanism.

আর্শি alt. spell. of **আরশি** ।

আর্ষ *a.* relating to (Hindu) sages (esp. of ancient India); (chiefly of words and their meanings) ungrammatical but current being used by the sages esp. of ancient India. (cp.) archaic. **~প্রয়োগ** *n.* a use which is ungrammatical but considered correct, being used by ancient sages.

আল[1] *n.* the sting of insects etc.; an antenna; sharp point of anything such as the barb of an arrow; an awl; (fig.) prick (কথার আল).

আল[2] *n.* a ridge of earth set up around a piece of agricultural land; a dyke; a dam. **আল বাঁধা** *v.* to set up a ridge of earth around a piece of agricultural land; to build a dyke, to dam.

আলংকারিক *a.* figurative; rhetorical; relating to ornament; decorative. □ *n.* a rhetorician; an author of a treatise on rhetoric or poetics.

আলকাটা *a.* barbed; grooved.

আলকাতরা *n.* tar, pitch, coal-tar.

আলকুশি *n.* cowhage, cowage, cowitch.

আলখাল্লা *n.* a loose cloak or gown, a gaberdine.

আলগা *a.* unbound, untied, unfastened; open; unbolted; loose; lax; detached; avoiding company, isolated (আলগা থাকা) ; uncovered; bare; naked; uncontrolled (আলগা জিভ) ; insincere or uncalled-for (আলগা সোহাগ) ; uncareful, unmindful (আলগা লোক). **আলগা দেওয়া** *v.* to relax, to become lax; to give indulgence. **মুখ-আলগা** *a.* loose-tongued; outspoken.

আলগুচি *n.* first efforts of a child to stand on its feet (আলগুচি দেওয়া).

আলগোছ *a.* detached, not touching. **আলগোছে** *adv.* (of hands, eating and drinking vessels etc.) not bringing into contact with the mouth (whilst eating or drinking); not touching, avoiding contact (আলগোছে ডিঙানো); aloof (আলগোছে থাকা); carefully and softly (আলগোছে যাওয়া); lightly (আলগোছে মারা).

আলঙ্কারিক alt. spell. of **আলংকারিক**।

আলজিহ্বা, আলজিভ, আলজিব *n.* the uvula, the epiglottis.

আলটপকা *adv.* suddenly, unexpectedly; suddenly and thoughtlessly.

আলটাকরা *n.* the uvula, the epiglottis.

আলতা *n.* lac-dye esp. as used by Hindu women to paint the borders of their feet.

আলতারাফ, আলতারাপ *n.* stapler, fastener.

আলতো *a.* not forceful or firm, light (আলতো হাতে, আলতো মার); incoherent or insincere (আলতো কথা).

আলনা *n.* a rack or stand for clothes, hats etc.

আলপনা *n.* painting on the floors or walls of a house or temple usu. with liquefied pigment of rice-powder, zinc oxide etc.

আলপাকা *n.* the alpaca; cloth made of its wool.

আলপিন *n.* a pin.

আলবত, আলবাত *adv.* of course, certainly, (coll.) definitely.

আলবাল *n.* a ridge of earth raised round the root of a tree for the purpose of watering.

আলবোলা *n.* hubble-bubble with a long flexible smoking-tube.

আলমারি *n.* an almirah; a cupboard.

আলম্ব *n.* a support, a prop; a shelter; (mech.) fulcrum. **~ন** *n.* a prop, a shelter; (rhet.) the person that is the object of a sentiment. **আলম্বিত** *a.* held; propped, supported; suspended, hung. **আলম্বী** *a.* supported; sheltered; hanging, pendant.

আলয় *n.* (for. & High.)a home; an abode, a dwelling house, a residence; a dwelling place; a house, a building; a place, a resort; a store, a repertory, a repository.

আলস poet. corrup. of **আলস্য**।

আলসে[1] *n.* a parapet around the roof of a building.

আলসে[2] *a.* idle, lazy, slothful, sluggish, indolent. **আলসেমি** *n.* idleness, sloth; procrastination.

আলস্য *n.* idleness, laziness, sloth; procrastination; dilatoriness; lethargy, indolence. **আলস্য ত্যাগ করা** *v.* to give up idleness; to be up and doing; to shake off lethargy by moving one's limbs; to yawn. **~পরায়ণ** *a.* lazy; lethargic; given to idleness; slothful. **আলস্য ভাঙা** *v.* to shake off lethargy by moving or stretching one's limbs; to yawn.

আলা[1] var. of **ওয়ালা**।

আলা[2] *a.* & *sfx.* first; highest; best.

আলা[3] *a.* illuminated; brightened up. □ *n.* light ('আলার ভিতরে কালাটি').

আলাই-বালাই *n.* all sorts of misfortune or harm; evils.

আলাং তালাং *a.* (coll.) (of talks) meaningless; high-sounding; pompous but without basis.

আলাত var. of **অলাত**।

আলাদা *a.* (also *adv.*) different; separate; detached.

আলান *n.* a pillar or post to which an elephant is tethered; a peg or stake to which domestic animals are tethered.

আলানো *n.* to dishevel or spread out (as hair); to ruffle; to spread out (as paddy etc. whilst sunning); to unloose or untie; to open (বই বা পাঁজি আলানো).

আলাপ *n.* conversation; talk, conference, discussion; greeting; acquaintance; (mus.) introductory singing or playing of a tune (esp. a conventional one in Indian classical music) in detail. **আলাপ করা** *v.* to converse; to talk, to confer, to discuss; to greet; to make one's acquaintance (with); to cultivate acquaintance (with); (mus.) to sing or play a tune in detail. ~ন *n.* conversation, talk, conference. ~নীয় *a.* conferrable, discussable. ~পরিচয়, ~সালাপ *n.* (coll.) acquaintance and speaking terms; familiarity, intimacy; discussion.

আলাপচারি *n.* conversation, talk, discussion; a friendly chat.

আলাপিত *a.* talked or spoken to; greeted; acquainted. *fem.* আলাপিতা।

আলাপী *a.* given to cultivating acquaintances; sociable; acquainted.

আলাভোলা *a.* simple, plain; artless, guileless.

আলাল *n.* a wealthy man. *fem.* আলালী। আলালের ঘরের দুলাল a pampered boy or young man of a rich family spoilt by over-indulgence.

আলাহিদা obs. var. of আলাদা।

আলি[1] *n.* a ridge of earth set up around a piece of agricultural land, a dyke, a dam.

আলি[2] (obs.) *n.* a woman's female friend or confidante or maid.

আলিঙ্গন *n.* embracing or hugging; an embrace; a hug. আলিঙ্গন করা *v.* to embrace; to hug.

আলিঙ্গিত *a.* embraced; hugged.

আলিঞ্জর *n.* an earthen jar for water.

আলিবন্ধন *n.* setting up a ridge of earth around a piece of agricultural land; building a dyke; damming. আলিবন্ধন করা *v.* to set up a ridge of earth around a piece of agricultural land; to build a dyke; to dam.

আলিম *n.* (Mus.) a learned man.

আলিম্পন, আলিম্পনা variants of আলপনা।

আলিসা obs. var. of আলসে[1]।

আলী rej. spell. of আলি[1,2]।

আলীঢ় *a.* licked; tasted. □ *n.* a posture (adopted esp. whilst shooting an arrow) with a knee folded in the front and the other stretched out behind, (cp.) a crouchant position.

আলীন *a.* passed out of existence; extinct; diffused.

-আলু[1] *sfx.* denoting nature, tendency, propensity etc. (নিদ্রালু, কৃপালু).

আলু[2] *n.* potato. গোল আলু potato, মিঠে আলু, রাঙা আলু sweet potato, yam, batata.

আলুথালু *a.* (of hair) unkempt, dishevelled, tousled; (of dress etc.) lacking in trimness, blowsy, disorderly.

আলুনি *a.* (of cooked food) deficient in salt; salt-free;(fig.) insipid, tasteless.

আলুফা *a.* obtained for nothing or without payment. □ *adv.* for nothing, gratis.

আলুবোখরা *n.* a variety of plum or prune of which jelly is prepared.

আলুলায়িত, আলুলিত *a.* (of hair) loosened and spread out, dishevelled, unkempt. আলুলায়িত করা *v.* to untie and spread out, to dishevel, to ruffle.

আলেকুম *n.* (Mus.) a word forming a part of the return salute.

আলেখ্য *n.* a painting; a painted portrait; depiction; portrait.

আলেপ, আলেপন *n.* smearing or painting (with); any substance to smear with (such as ointment, grease oil etc.); a paint, a wash.

আলেম var. of আলিম।

আলেয়া *n.* ignus fatuus, will-o'-the-wisp; (fig.) delusion. আলেয়ার আলো the light of will-o'-the-wisp; (fig.) a ray of false hope or delusion, golden dreams; insubstantial thing, optical illusion.

আলো *n.* light; a beam, a ray; effulgence; lustre, splendour; a flash of light; a lamp, a lantern. আলো করা *v.* to brighten; to light up; to lighten; to illuminate; to glorify. আলো দেখানো *v.* to show light to; (fig.) to give hope, to promise good.

আলো-আঁধারি *n.* a mixture of light and shade; chiaroscuro. আলো-আঁধারের খেলা interplay of light-and-shade.

আলোক *n.* light; a beam, a ray; effulgence; lustre, splendour; a flash of light. ~গৃহ *n.* a lighthouse. ~চিত্র *n.* a photograph; photography. ~চিত্রকর *n.* a photographer. ~চিত্রবিদ্যা *n.* photography. ~চ্ছটা *n.* a flash of light. ~তড়িৎ *n.* photo-electricity. ~তাড়িত *a.* photo-electric. ~বিজ্ঞান, ~বিদ্যা *n.* optics. ~বিহীন *a.* lightless; dark; gloomy. ~ময় *a.* full of light; flooded with light; lightsome. ~লতা *n.* a parasitic creeper. ~শক্তি *n.* light as an energy. ~শূন্য same as আলোকবিহীন। ~সংকেত *n.* a beacon. ~সজ্জা *n.* decoration of a stage etc. with light; illumination. ~স্তম্ভ *n.* a light-house. আলোকিত *a.* lighted, illuminated. আলোকোজ্জ্বল *a.* illuminated; bright with light; lighted.

আলোকন *n.* seeing; casting a glance; observation; showing, demonstration. আলোকনীয় *a.* worth seeing; sightly.

আলোকিত *a.* illuminated; glowing; brightened. আলোকিত করা *v.* to illuminate; to brighten up. আলোকিত হওয়া *v.* to become illuminated; to brighten up.

আলোচনা, আলোচন *n.* discussion; deliberation, consideration. আলোচনা করা *v.* to discuss; to deliberate, to consider. আলোচনা হওয়া *v.* to be discussed or deliberated or considered.

আলোচনী *n.* a subject or subjects for discussion; a place or an institution where discussions are held.

আলোচনীয় *a.* submitted or placed for discussion; worthy of discussion; discussible.

আলোচাল *a.* rice obtained by sunning paddy and not by boiling it, sunned rice.

আলোচিত *a.* discussed; deliberated, considered.

আলোচ্য *a.* same as আলোচনীয়।

আলোচ্যমান *a.* what is being discussed, (of a subject) under discussion.

আলো-ছায়া *n.* a mixture of light and shade, chiaroscuro. আলো-ছায়ার খেলা light -and-shade play.

আলোড়ক *n.* one who or that which stirs or churns; an exciter; an agitator; one who recollects; a deliberator; a pestle for churning with.

আলোড়ন *n.* stirring or churning; excitation; agitation; recollection; deliberation. আলোড়ন করা *v.* to stir; to churn; to excite; to agitate; to revolve in mind; to ponder; to deliberate.

আলোড়িত *a.* stirred; churned; excited; agitated; pondered; deliberated.

আলোময় *a.* full of light, lightsome; illuminated; brightened up.

আলোয় আলোয় *adv.* whilst there is light or daylight, by light or day-light.

আলোয়ান *n.* a woollen wrapper for the body, a shawl; a wrapper.

আলোল *a.* slightly excited or agitated; moving or rolling or lolling with greed (আলোলরসনা).

আলোহিত *a.* slightly red, reddish.

আল্লাহ্, আল্লা *n.* (Mus.) God, Allah.

আশ[1] coll. & poet. corrup. of আশা। আশ মিটানো *v.* to satisfy or gratify one's desire to the full.

আশ[2] *n.* food (প্রাতরাশ).

আশংসন, আশংসা *n.* hoping, expectation; a hope, an expectation; desiring; a desire; possibility, prospect; praise, reception. আশংসিত *a.* hoped for; expected; desired; praised; received.

আশক *n. mas.* a lover, a suitor, a sweetheart.

আশকারা *n.* indulgence; over-indulgence. আশকারা দেওয়া *v.* to treat with indulgence or over-indulgence.

আশঙ্কনীয় *a.* dreadful, frightening, alarming; suspicious; doubtful.

আশঙ্কা *n.* fear, dread, fright, alarm; a misgiving, apprehension, suspicion; doubt. আশঙ্কা করা *v.* to fear, to dread; to apprehend; to suspect; to doubt. ~স্থল *n.* an object of dread or suspicion or doubt.

আশঙ্কিত *a.* feared, dreaded; apprehended; suspected; doubted.

আশনাই *n.* illicit love, an affair, an affaire de coer; a love-affair; love.

আশপাশ *n.* surroundings; environs; outskirts; neighbourhood. আশপাশে, আশেপাশে *adv.* hither and thither; around; on all sides; in the outskirts; in the neighbourhood.

আশমান *n.* the sky, the firmament; the heavens. ~-জমিন ফারাক *n.* great difference. □ *a.* pole apart; vastly different. আশমানি *n.* the sky colour. □ *a.* of the sky; of sky-blue colour, sky-blue; azure.

আশয় *n.* (mostly used as a *sfx.*) a receptacle, a container (জলাশয়) ; a heart or character; an intention, a purpose, an aim.

আশরফি *n.* a gold coin.

আশা[1] alt. spell. of আসা[1]।

আশা[2] *n.* hope, expectation; assurance; confidence, reliance, trust (চাকরির উপর আশা, ছেলের উপর আশা) ; a part of the horizon (পূর্বাশা). **আশা করা, আশা রাখা** *v.* to hope, to expect; to place confidence (upon), to rely (upon), to trust. **~তিরিক্ত, ~তীত** *a.* beyond expectation, unhoped-for; unexpected. **~নুরূপ** *a.* up to expectation. **~ন্বিত** *a.* hopeful, cherishing hope; expectant. **~পথ চেয়ে থাকা** to wait in expectation, to look forward to. **আশা পোষণ করা** *v.* to cherish hopes. **~প্রদ** *a.* that which excites or inspires hope, hopeful. **~বাদ** *n.* optimism. **~বাদী** *a.* optimistic. ☐ *n.* an optimist. **~ভঙ্গ** *n.* disappointment, frustration. **~ভরসা** *n.* hopes and confidence. **~শূন্য, ~হীন** *a.* hopeless; disappointed. **~হত** *a.* disappointed, frustrated.

আশান alt. spell. of আসান।

আশানড়ি alt. spell. of আসানড়ি।

আশাবরদার alt. spell. of আসাবরদার (See আশা[2]).

আশাবরি *n.* an Indian musical mode.

আশাবাহী alt. spell. of আসাবাহী।

আশাসোঁটা alt. spell. of আসাসোঁটা।

আশি *n.* & *a.* eighty.

আশিস *n.* blessing, benediction, benison.

আশী[1] rej. spell. of আশি।

আশী[2] *n.* a serpent's fang. **~বিষ** *n.* that which has venom in its fang; a venomous snake; the snake.

আশীর্বচন, আশীর্বাদ *n.* blessing, benediction, benison. **আশীর্বাদক** *a.* & *n.* one who blesses. *fem.* **আশীর্বাদিকা**। **আশীর্বাদী** *a.* benedictory. ☐ *n.* an emblem of benediction.

আশীষ rej. spell. of আশিস।

আশু[1] var. of আউস।

আশু[2] *adv.* early; quickly, speedily; without delay, immediately. ☐ *a.* early; quick, speedy (আশু প্রতিকার) ; immediate (আশু সমস্যা). **~গ, ~গতি, ~গামী** *a.* quick-moving; swiftfoot, swift-footed, fleet-footed. **~তোষ** *a.* one who is easily or quickly pleased or appeased. ☐ *n.* an appellation of Shiva (শিব). **~পাতি** *a.* readily shed or fallen, fugacious.

আশেপাশে see আশপাশ।

আশৈশব *adv.* since infancy or childhood or boyhood.

আশ্চর্য *a.* astonishing, surprising, wonderful, marvellous; queer. ☐ *n.* a wonder or marvel; a surprise; a queer object. **আশ্চর্য করা** *v.* to strike with astonishment or wonder; to surprise, to astonish; to take a person by surprise. **আশ্চর্য হওয়া** *v.* to be astonished. **~জনক** *a.* wonderful, astonishing; surprising; amazing, astounding; queer. **আশ্চর্যান্বিত** *a.* wonder-struck, astonished; amazed, astounded. **আশ্চর্যান্বিত করা** same as **আশ্চর্য করা**। **আশ্চর্যান্বিত হওয়া** same as **আশ্চর্য হওয়া**।

আশ্বস্ত *a.* assured; heartened with hope or promise or assurance or consolation or confidence etc. **আশ্বস্ত করা** *v.* to assure; to hearten with hope or assurance.

আশ্বাস *n.* heartening with hope or promise or assurance or consolation or confidence etc. **~ন** *n.* heartening with hope or promise or assurance or consolation or confidence etc. **~বাণী** *n.* words that hearten with hope or promise or assurance or consolation or confidence etc.

আশ্বাসিত var. of আশ্বস্ত।

আশ্বিন *n.* the sixth month of the Bengali calendar (from the middle of September to the middle of October). **আশ্বিনে** *a.* of or grown or produced in Aswin (আশ্বিন), occurring in Aswin (আশ্বিনে ঝড়).

আশ্রম *n.* a hermitage; a residence (usu. a small one), a cottage (পুণ্যাশ্রম) ; an asylum or refuge (আতুরাশ্রম, অনাথাশ্রম) ; a residential institution (esp. an educational or religious one) (বিদ্যাশ্রম) ; a stage of life (গার্হস্থ্যাশ্রম). **~ধর্ম** *n.* duties or rites to be performed by inmates of a hermitage or asylum or refuge or residential institution; duties to be performed in each of the stages of life. **~বাসী** *a.* & *n.* one who lives in a hermitage or asylum or refuge or residential institution. *fem.* **~বাসিনী**। **~ভ্রষ্ট** *a.*

fallen from one's religious order. **আশ্রমিক, আশ্রমী** *a.* of or living in a hermitage or asylum or refuge or residential institution, or pertaining to the life in it; adopting any of the stages of life. □ *n.* an inmate of a hermitage or asylum or refuge or residential institution; one in any of the stages of life.

আশ্রয় *n.* adoption; shelter, aid, help, support, protection (দীনের আশ্রয়) ; a container, a store; a resort, a possessor, an embodiment (of) (সর্বগুণের আশ্রয়) ; a dwelling house, a residence (আশ্রয়হীন). **আশ্রয় করা** *v.* to adopt; to take shelter (in); to go or resort to for shelter or aid or support or protection. **আশ্রয় দেওয়া** *v.* to shelter, to give shelter; to give protection. **আশ্রয় নেওয়া** same as **আশ্রয় করা**। **~গ্রহণ** same as **আশ্রয়ণ**। **আশ্রয়গ্রহণ করা** same as **আশ্রয় করা**। **~ণ** *n.* adoption; taking shelter (in); going or resorting to for shelter or aid or support or protection. **~ণীয়** *a.* worthy of being adopted; worthy of being resorted to for shelter or aid or support or protection. **~দাতা** *n.* & *a.* one who gives shelter or protection. **~দান** *n.* sheltering. **আশ্রয়দান করা** same as **আশ্রয় দেওয়া**। **~পুষ্ট** *a.* nourished or flourished in shelter or support or protection (of); (bot.) endotropic. **~প্রার্থী** same as **আশ্রয়ার্থী**। **~শূন্য, ~হীন** *a.* shelterless; deprived of shelter, supportless.

আশ্রয়ার্থী *a.* seeking shelter. □ *n.* one who seeks shelter; a refugee. *fem.* **আশ্রয়ার্থিনী**।

আশ্রয়ী *a.* one who adopts or takes shelter; sheltered.

আশ্রিত *a.* adopted, resorted to; sheltered, supported, protected; dependent (esp. for maintenance). *fem.* **আশ্রিতা**। □ **আশ্রিত ব্যক্তি** a person who has been given help and protection, a protege. **~পালক, ~রক্ষক** *n.* & *a.* one who maintains or protects those who ask for maintenance or shelter or aid or support or protection. **~বৎসল** *a.* affectionate and kind to those who seek shelter and protection. **~ বাৎসল্য** *n.* kindness and affection to a dependant or a person under one's protection. **~রাজ্য** *n.* a protectorate.

আশ্রুত *a.* promised; heard.

আশ্লিষ্ট *a.* embraced; pervaded; permeated; attached; amalgamated; united; sarcastic; sardonic.

আশ্লেষ *n.* an embrace; pervasion, diffusion; attachment; amalgamation; union; a sarcasm, a pun.

আষাঢ় *n.* the third month of the Bengali calendar (from the middle of June to the middle of July); (poet. & fig.) the monsoon. **আষাঢ়ে** *a.* of or in or during the month or Ashara (আষাঢ়) ; produced or growing or occurring in Ashara (আষাঢ়) ; false, fantastic. **আষাঢ়ে গল্প** a queer or fantastic tale, a cock-and-bull story.

আষ্টেপৃষ্ঠে *adv.* all over the body; all over; thoroughly.

আসক *n.* (obs.) love, attachment, devotion (পিরীতি আসকে).

আসকে *n.* a variety of pancake made of a thin paste of liquefied rice-powder.

আসক্ত *a.* greatly enamoured (of); addicted to; having a deep love (for); devoted (to); attached (to); deeply or profoundly attached to (worldly) pleasures and interests. **আসক্তি** *n.* deep love; attention; addiction; devotion; attachment; attachment to (worldly) pleasures and interests; (worldly) pleasures and interests; cohabitation.

আসঙ্গ *n.* sexual intercourse; company, fellowship, social intercourse; union; desire to enjoy; love, attachment; profound attention. **~লিপ্সা** *n.* desire for sexual intercourse; desire for company or union. **~লিপ্সু** *a.* desirous of sexual intercourse or of company or union.

আসছে *a.* coming, next, ensuing. **আসছে কাল** *n.* & *adv.* tomorrow.

আসঞ্জন *n.* adhesion.

আসঞ্জিত *a.* adhered or adhering to.

আসত্তি *n.* union, amalgamation; proximity, adjacency; acquisition, acquirement; profit; (gr.) proximity of related words within a sentence (cp. collocation).

আসন *n.* anything used for or intended for

sitting upon, a seat; an office or post (সদস্যদের আসন) ; a place for sitting or placing (দেবীর আসন) ; a posture of sitting (বীরাসন) ; reception with honour (বিদ্বানের আসন সর্বত্র). **~গ্রহণ** *n.* sitting. **আসন গ্রহণ করা** *v.* to take one's seat. **~পিঁড়ি** *n.* the posture of squatting. **আসনপিঁড়ি হয়ে বসা** *v.* to squat.

আসনাই alt. spell. of **আশনাই**।

আসন্ন *a.* imminent, approaching, impending, coming; proximate; last, final; (esp. in math.) approximate. **আসন্ন কাল** *n.* the time of death; the time of danger, critical time; the eleventh hour, the last moment. **~প্রসবা** *a. fem.* parturient; in an advanced stage of pregnancy, nearing delivery. **আসন্ন বিপদ** *n.* impending or imminent danger. **আসন্ন মান** *n.* approximate value or standard. **~মৃত্যু** *a.* about to die, dying.

আসব *n.* distilled spirit; alcoholic beverage, wine. **আসবিক** *a.* alcoholic.

আসবাব *n.* furniture. **~পত্র** *n.* furniture and fittings and all other movable goods, goods and chattels. **~পত্র দিয়ে সাজানো** to furnish.

আসমান rej. spell. of **আশমান**।

আসমুদ্র *a.* & *adv.* extending up to the ocean. **~হিমাচল** *a.* & *adv.* extending from the ocean to the Himalayas.

আসর *n.* a gathering, a meeting, a sitting; a party (চায়ের আসর) ; a function (গানের আসর) ; a match, a tournament, a competition (খেলার আসর) ; a field; a society, a club. **আসর গরম করা, আসর সরগরম করা** *v.* to brighten up a party. **আসর জমেছে** *v.* the party warms up or becomes interesting; the party becomes crowded. **আসর জমানো, আসর জাঁকানো** same as **আসর গরম করা**। **আসর মাতানো** *v.* to brighten up a party; to make a party ripple with interest. **আসরে অবতীর্ণ হওয়া, আসরে নামা** *v.* to make one's appearance before the public or in society; to take the field; to make one's debut.

আসল *a.* genuine; pure; authentic; unadulterated; true, real; actual; original (আসল দলিল) ; nett (আসল লাভ) ; principal or capital (আসল দেনা) ; primary (আসল উদ্দেশ্য). □ *n.* principal or capital money or amount. **আসলি** *a.* genuine, pure, unadulterated (আসলি চিজ). **আসলে** *adv.* in actuality, in truth; in fact.

আসশেওড়া *n.* a kind of wild herb, *Glycomis pentaphylla.*

আসা[১] *n.* a stick (usu. a thick one), a staff; a mace; a sceptre.

আসা[২] *v.* to come; to appear; to come up; to arrive (ট্রেন আসা) ; to reach, to come up to (মুখ পর্যন্ত আসা) ; to commence, to begin (জ্বর আসা) ; to set in (শরৎ আসা) ; to be excited with (আবেগ আসা) ; to rise, to crop up (মনে আসা) ; to enter (ঘরে আসা) ; to attack, to come upon (ঢুলুনি আসা) ; to be struck with (ভয় আসা) ; to be supplied with (কথা আসা) ; to be filled with (চোখে জল আসা) ; to take place, to occur, to come about (বিপদ আসা) ; to be earned, to accrue (টাকা আসা) ; to be on the point of (ফুরিয়ে আসা). □ *a.* that which has come (কাছে আসা). □ *n.* act of coming; arrival. **এগিয়ে আসা** *v.* to come up, to advance. **আসা-যাওয়া** *n.* come-and-go. **উঠে আসা** *v.* to come up; to get up; to remove; to get loose, to be detached, to come off (ছাল উঠে আসা). **কথা আসা** *v.* to be able to speak. **কাছে আসা** *v.* to come or draw near, to come by; to approach. **কাজে আসা, ব্যবহারে আসা** *v.* to be of use, to be useful, to be serviceable. **কান্না আসা** *v.* to feel like crying or weeping. **নেমে আসা** *v.* to come down; to get down; to alight; to descend; to dismount. **নিভে আসা** *v.* to get dimmer and dimmer. **নিয়ে আসা** *v.* to bring along, bring with oneself; to fetch. **ফিরে আসা** *v.* to come back, to return. **ফুরিয়ে আসা** *v.* to be about to be exhausted; to be about to end. **ফেলে আসা** *v.* to leave behind. **বহে আসা** *v.* to flow down, to stream down; to come along. **বেয়ে আসা** *v.* to come steering along. **বাইরে আসা** *v.* to come out, to emerge. **ভিতরে আসা** *v.* to come in, to enter. **রেখে আসা** same as **ফেলে আসা**।

আসাদন *n.* obtaining; attainment, acquirement; receipt; income; arrival; performance or execution (of a work).

আসাদিত *a.* obtained; attained, acquired; received; arrived within reach; arrived; performed; executed.

আসান *n.* termination, end, subsidence, relief, mitigation (দুঃখের আসান, রোগের আসান) ; inflow, easy supply (পয়সার আসান).

আসানড়ি *n.* a thick stick; a staff.

আসাবরদার *n.* a mace-bearer, a beadle.

আসামি *n.* a defendant in a criminal case, an accused.

আসার *n.* torrential rain, a heavy shower; water-drop(s) (নয়নাসার).

আসাসোঁটা *n.* a sceptre; (loos.) staffs and maces.

আসিক্ত *a.* slightly wet; thoroughly wet, drenched.

আসিদ্ধ *a.* half-boiled; not thoroughly or properly boiled, parboiled; unboiled.

আসীন *a.* seated, sitting; placed; present; situated.

আসুর, আসুরিক *a.* of or like the mythological demons, (cp.) Titanic; of or like a demon, demoniac; giant-like, gigantic, titanic; terrible; vile; unholy. *fem.* **আসুরী, আসুরিকী। আসুর বিবাহ, আসুরিক বিবাহ** a form of marriage in which the bridegroom purchases the bride from her parents in exchange of money.

আসেচন *n.* watering or wetting thoroughly.

আসেধ *n.* (personal) restraint; restriction; an injunction; limitation (কালাসেধ). **আসেধক** *n.* a bailiff. **আসেধাজ্ঞা** *n.* an injunction.

আসোয়ার, আসোবার *a.* mounted on an elephant, horse etc. ☐ *n.* one who is thus mounted, a rider.

আস্কন্দিত *n.* the gallop of a horse.

আস্কারা rej. spell. of **আশকারা।**

আস্কে rej. spell. of **আসকে।**

আস্ত *a.* whole; entire; unbroken, uncut; downright (আস্ত চোর) ; thorough; stark (আস্ত পাগল) ; real (আস্ত কেউটে). **আস্ত না রাখা** (fig.) to beat severely, to beat up.

আস্তর[1] var. of **অস্তর।**

আস্তর[2]**, আস্তরণ** *n.* bed; a bedcover, a coverlet; a bedsheet; a carpet or any similar article (esp. to sit upon); an ornamental cloth placed on the back of an elephant for the rider to sit upon. **আস্তর মেঘ** stratus.

আস্তানা *n.* a haunt; an abode, a dwelling-place; a hermitage. **আস্তানা গাড়া** *v.* to set up an abode (esp. a temporary one); to take shelter (temporarily). **আস্তানা গোটানো** *v.* to depart for good; to strike the tent.

আস্তাবল *n.* a stable (for horses, elephants etc.).

আস্তিক *a.* having faith in God and in life beyond death and in the scriptures, theistic. ☐ *n.* a person having such faith, a theist. **~তা, আস্তিক্য** *n.* theism.

আস্তিন *n.* a sleeve. **আস্তিন গোটানো** *v.* to prepare oneself for a duel, to be ready for a fight; to throw down the gauntlet, to challenge.

আস্তীর্ণ, আস্তৃত *a.* spread out; stretched out; extending; pervaded with, covered by, strewn with (কুসুমাস্তীর্ণ).

আস্তে *adv.* slowly; carefully; lightly, mildly, gently (আস্তে মারা) ; stepping lightly or noiselessly (আস্তে আসা) ; in an undertone (আস্তে কথা বলো) ; noiselessly.

আস্তেব্যস্তে *adv.* in a great hurry; helter-skelter; fussily (see also **অস্তেব্যস্তে**).

আস্তেসুস্থে *adv.* leisurely; with no haste or flutter.

আস্থা *n.* confidence; reliance; faith, trust; regard, reverence, respect; devotion. **আস্থা রাখা** *v.* to have confidence (in); to rely (on); to have faith (in); to trust; to have regard (for); to be devoted (to.). **ধর্মে আস্থা থাকা** to have faith in religion.

আস্থান *n.* confidence; faith, trust; stay; presence; a shelter; a meeting.

আস্থাবান *a.* confident; faithful; devoted.

আস্থায়ী *n.* the first line of a song or its music.

আস্পদ *n.* one who or that which contains or holds or deserves; one who is an object (of) (শ্রদ্ধাস্পদ).

আস্পর্ধা *n.* effrontery, impudence, impertinence, audacity; arrogance, haughtiness; boasting.

আস্ফালন *n.* brandishing; moving violently (বাহু আস্ফালন) ; bragging or boasting or vaunting. **আস্ফালন করা** *v.* to brandish; to move violently; to brag, to bluster, to boast, to vaunt.

আস্ফালিত *a.* brandished; moved violently.

আস্ফোট, আস্ফোটন *n.* collision, clash; sound of clashing or thrashing; (in wrestling) slapping on one's own arms etc. as an indication of preparing to attack.

আস্বাদ *n.* taste; savour; relish; tasting. **~ন** *n.* tasting; enjoying, enjoyment; experiencing. **~নীয়, আস্বাদ্য** *a.* fit to be tasted; enjoyable. **আস্বাদিত** *a.* tasted; enjoyed; relished; experienced.

আস্য *n.* the face; the mouth.

আস্রাবণ *n.* decantation. **আস্রাবিত** *a.* decanted.

আহত *a.* hurt, struck; beaten, smitten; wounded; injured; thrashed, treaded (পদাহত) ; (of stringed musical instruments) played or sounded. **আহতি** *n.* a blow, a stroke; a beating; a hurt, a wound; injury; thrashing; playing or sounding.

আহব[1] *n.* a war; a battle; a fight.

আহব[2] *n.* a place for oblation; an oblation. **~নীয়** *a.* fit to be sacrificed as burnt-offering. ☐ *n.* sacrificial fire.

আহরণ *n.* procurement; collection; amassing, accumulation; compilation; earning; preparation. **আহরণী** *n.* an anthology. **আহরণীয়, আহর্তব্য** *a.* fit to be procured or collected or amassed or accumulated or earned or prepared. **আহর্তা** *a.* one who procures or collects or accumulates or earns or prepares. ☐ *n.* a procurer; a collector; an accumulator; a compiler; one who earns; one who prepares.

আহরিৎ *a.* slightly green, greenish.

আহরিত *inc.* but *pop.* form of **আহৃত**।

আহর্তব্য, আহর্তা see **আহরণ**।

আহা *int.* expressing sorrow, bereavement, sympathy etc,; alas, ha, ah, oh. **~মরি** *int.* expressing : praise or ridicule. ☐ *a.* (chiefly dero. or facet.) astonishing, wonderful.

আহাম্মক, (dial.) **আহাম্মুক** *a.* lacking in common sense; extremely foolish. ☐ *n.* one who lacks common sense; a fool, a dunce.

আহার *n.* eating; food; a meal. **আহার ও বাসস্থান** food and lodging, bed and board. **আহার করা** *v.* to eat; to eat a meal, to dine. **আহার দেওয়া** *v.* to give food; to feed. **~দাতা** *n.* one who gives food; a feeder; (fig.) a maintainer. *fem.* **~দাত্রী**। **আহারনিদ্রা ত্যাগ করা** to give up eating and sleeping (when one is troubled with anxiety or misgiving). **~বিহার** *n.* dinner or food and enjoyment. **আহারান্ত** *n.* termination of dinner or eating. **আহারাভাব** *n.* want of food; starvation; shortage or scarcity of food. **আহারার্থ** *adv.* for dining or eating. **আহারার্থী** *a.* seeking food or dinner. **আহারী** *a.* one who eats, eating; voracious.

আহার্য *a.* fit to be procured or collected; requiring labour; eatable, edible. ☐ *n.* food; victuals. **~দ্রব্য, ~সামগ্রী** *n.* an article of food.

আহিক *n.* a snake-charmer.

আহিত *a.* deposited; placed; founded, established; given, handed over. **আহিতাগ্নি** *n.* a Brahman who keeps the holy sacrificial fire burning always.

আহিতুণ্ডিক *n.* same as **আহিক**।

আহির *n.* a member of the cowherd class; a cowherd. *fem.* **আহিরি, আহিরিনি**।

আহুত *a.* sacrificed as burnt-offering. **আহুতি** *n.* a burnt-offering; an oblation.

আহূত *a.* invited; called; asked to come; summoned; invoked. **আহুতি** *n.* invitation; a call; a summons; invocation.

আহৃত *a.* procured; collected; accumulated, amassed; compiled; earned; obtained; prepared.

আহেরিয়া, আহেড়িয়া *n.*(amongst the Rajputs) the ceremony of hunting in the forest on the first day of spring; a hunting clan.

আহেল, আহেলি *a.* pure; genuine; unadulterated; of high and pure origin; new raw; inexperienced.

আহ্নিক *a.* daily, diurnal. ☐ *n.* prescribed daily prayer of God. **আহ্নিক করা** *v.* to say the prescribed daily prayer to God **~গতি** diurnal rotation of the earth

আহ্নিকে বসা *v.* to sit for saying the prescribed daily prayer to God.

আহ্বান *n.* invitation; a call; a summons; address; invocation. **আহ্বান করা** *v.* to invite; to call; to summon; to ask to come; to address; to invoke.

আহ্বায়ক *a.* one who invites or calls or summons or addresses or invokes. ☐ *n.* an inviter; a caller; a summoner; an addresser; convener; an invocator. *fem.* **আহ্বায়িকা।**

আহ্লাদ *n.* delight, gladness, joy, coddling; indulgence. **আহ্লাদ করা** *v.* to express delight; to rejoice; to coddle, to fondle. **আহ্লাদ দেওয়া** *v.* to give indulgence. **আহ্লাদিত** *a.* delight, gladdened. **আহ্লাদি** *a. fem.* one who is spoilt by coddling and over-indulgence; one who likes to be coddled and indulged and feigns innocence. ☐ *n.* such a girl or woman. *masc.* **আহ্লাদে।** **আহ্লাদে আটখানা** beside oneself with joy. **আহ্লাদে মাথায় চড়া** to become impudent as a result of over-indulgence.

ই *n.* the third vowel of the Bengali alphabet.

-ই *sfx.* denoting : certainty (আমি যাবই), emphasis (অবশ্যই) ; only (তোমাকেই দেব), at all (যদি বৃষ্টি হয়ই).

ইউনানি *a.* Greek; pertaining to conventional Muslim therapy.

ইউনিয়ন *n.* a union. **ইউনিয়ন বোর্ড** a Union Board.

ইউরেশীয় *a.* Eurasian. ☐ *n.* a Eurasian.

ইউরোপীয়, ইয়োরোপীয় *a.* European. ☐ *n.* a European.

ইংরেজ, ইংরাজ *n.* an Englishman; the English. **ইংরেজ জাতি** *n.* the English. **~প্রীতি** *n.* excessive admiration of English customs and ways, Anglophilia, Anglomania. **ইংরেজ-ভীতি** *n.* Anglophobia. **ইংরেজিয়ানা** *n.* Anglomania; Anglicism; Englishness. **ইংরেজি, ইংরাজি** *n.* the English language, English. ☐ *a.* English.

ইংল্যান্ড *n.* England. **ইংল্যান্ডীয়** *a.* of England; English.

ইঃ *int.* expressing : anger, sorrow, grief, suffering etc.; eh.

ইঁচড় *n.* an unripe jackfruit (cooked as food). **ইঁচড়েপাকা** *a.* precocious; prematurely clever. **ইঁচড়ে পাকা** *v.* to become precocious; to become prematurely clever.

ইঁট pop. spell. of **ইট** ।

ইঁদারা *n.* a draw-well.

ইঁদুর *n.* the rat; the mouse.

ইকড়ি-মিকড়ি *n.* an indoor game of children.

ইকার *n.* the symbol ি affixed to consonants whilst adding the ই-sound to it; post-consonantal ি symbol. **ইকারাদি** *a.* (of words) beginning with ই or ই sound. **ইকারান্ত** *a.* (of words) ending in ই or ই-sound.

ইকেবানা *n.* the Japanese art of flower decoration, ikebana.

ইক্ষু *n.* the sugar-cane. **~চিনি** *n.* cane-sugar. **~দণ্ড** *n.* the sugar-cane plant. **~রস** *n.* juice of sugar-cane. **~সার** *n.* molasses (obtained from sugar-cane juice).

ইগল *n.* the eagle.

ইঙ্কার alt. spell. of **ইনকার** ।

ইঙ্গবঙ্গ *a.* (of the Bengali language as used by Bengali Anglomaniacs) having a ridiculous mixture of English and Bengali words, phrases, sentences etc.; (of the Bengali society or the people of Bengal) having a ridiculous mixture of what is English and what is Bengali in style, manner, language etc.; (of the people of Bengal) one who has visited England and has become an Anglomaniac.

ইঙ্গ-ভারতীয় *a.* Anglo-Indian. ☐ *n.* an Anglo-Indian.

ইঙ্গিত *n.* a sign, a hint, a gesture, a beckoning; gesticulation; a wink; a signal (ঝড়ের ইঙ্গিত). **ইঙ্গিত করা** *v.* to gesticulate; to beckon, to make a sign; to wink (at); to signal. **ইঙ্গিত দেওয়া** *v.* to give a hint; to signal. **ইঙ্গিতে জানানো, ইঙ্গিতে বলা** *v.* to hint at. **~পূর্ণ** *a.* suggestive, significant, meaningful; allusive.

ইঙ্গুদি, ইঙ্গুদ *n.* a species of thorny plant. **ইঙ্গুদি-তেল** *n.* oil produced from the seed of this plant.

ইচ্ছা *n.* will, volition; intention; wish; pleasure; desire; liking; choice, option; inclination. **ইচ্ছা করা** *v.* to intend; to wish; to desire; to like; to choose or please. **~কৃত** *a.* intentional, wilful. **~ক্রমে** *adv.* according to one's desire or pleasure; willingly, voluntarily. **~ধীন** *a.* subject to one's will or desire; optional; dependent on one's pleasure. **ইচ্ছানুযায়ী, ইচ্ছানুসারে** *adv.* according to one's will or pleasure; at pleasure. **ইচ্ছানুরূপ, ~মতো** *a.* & *adv.* to one's liking; as one pleases. **~পত্র** *n.* a document containg a person's last wishes. **~পূর্বক** *adv.* wilfully; voluntarily; willingly. **~বসন্ত** *n.* small-pox. **~ময়** *n.* one whose will is law; an appellation of God. *fem.*

~ময়ী। ~মরণ, ~মৃত্যু *n*. power to prevent one's death till one desires to die. ~যত্ত same as ইচ্ছাধীন। ~শক্তি *n*. will-force, will-power. ইচ্ছায় হোক আর অনিচ্ছায় হোক willy-nilly, *nolens volens*. যা ইচ্ছা whatever one pleases.

ইচ্ছু, ইচ্ছুক *a*. willing; ready; consenting, agreeing; desirous; intending; having a liking for, inclining (to).

ইজার *n*. shorts; short trousers.

ইজারদার var. of ইজারাদার (see ইজারা).

ইজারা *n*. lease; leasehold. ~দার *n*. a leasehold, a lessee. ইজারা দেওয়া বা নেওয়া *v*. to lease. ~পাট্টা *n*. a lease-deed.

ইজের coll. var. of ইজার।

ইজ্জত *n*. prestige, dignity; honour; chastity. ইজ্জত নষ্ট করা *v*. to spoil or lose one's prestige; to dishonour or to lose honour; to violate one's chastity or to have one's chastity violated. ~নাশ, ~হানি *n*. loss of prestige; dishonour; violation of chastity; (loos.) rape.

ইঞ্চি *n*. an inch; 2.54 cm.

ইঞ্জিন *n*. an engine.

ইঞ্জিনিয়ার *n*. an engineer. ইঞ্জিনিয়ারি, ইঞ্জিনিয়ারিং *n*. engineering. ☐ *a*. pertaining to engineering.

ইট *n*. brick; (loos.) brickbat. ইট ছোড়া *v*. to throw bricks and brickbats. ইট মারা, ইটানো *v*. to pelt with bricks and brickbats, to throw stones at. ~খোলা *n*. a brick-field. ~পাটকেল *n*. bricks and brickbats. ~পাতন *n*. brick-laying. ইটের পাঁজা বা ভাটি *a*. brick-kiln. ইটটি মারলে পাটকেলটি খেতে হয় tit for tat, a tip for a tap.

ইটা *n*. a small scaleless riverfish.

ইটানো see ইট।

ইড়া *n*. an artery on the left side of the spine.

ইৎ *n*. (gr.) a letter used to indicate some inflections but not actually pronounced when any of the said inflections is added to a word; omission.

ইতঃপূর্বে *adv*. hereinbefore, heretofore, before this, ere now.

ইতর *a*. (ori.) other, other than (বামেতর) ; (pop.) base or mean, caddish (ইতর লোক), inferior or lower in status (ইতর জীব), ordinary or common (ইতরজন), ungenerous or narrow (ইতর নজর), vulgar (ইতর ভাষা). ~তা, ~পনা *n*. baseness, meanness, caddishness; lack of generosity; narrowness, paltriness, pettiness; vulgarity, ignoble conduct. ইতরতা করা *v*. to behave basely or meanly or narrow-mindedly; to behave or speak vulgarly. ~বিশেষ *n*. (little) difference. ইতরামো, ইতরামি same as ইতরতা। ইতরেতর *a*. mutual, reciprocal.

ইতস্তত *adv*. here and there, hither and thither; thinly; irregularly; in diverse directions or places; on all sides, in all places, everywhere, all over. ☐ *n*. hesitation; stammering. ইতস্তত করা *v*. to hesitate (to do something); to stammer; to procrastinate, to dilly-dally.

ইতি *n*. end, termination, conclusion; completion; settlement; all this; such and such-like. ☐ *adv*. (chiefly used at the end of a correspondence) this is all (that the writer has got to say or write), here ends. ইতি করা *v*. to put an end to, to complete, to finish, to conclude, to settle up. ~উতি *adv*. on this side and that, in this direction and that; on all sides, in all directions. ~কর্তব্য, ~কর্তব্যতা, ~কর্তব্য জ্ঞান *n*. the decision that this is the right thing to do, decision about what is to be done. ~কর্তব্যবিমূঢ়তা *n*. nonplus, bewilderment, confusion, quandary. ~পূর্বে inc. but pop. form of ইতঃপূর্বে। ~মধ্যে inc. but pop. form of ইতোমধ্যে।

ইতিকথা *n*. a tale; a legend; a chronicle; history. ইতিকাহিনী *n*. same as ইতিকথা।

ইতিবৃত্ত *n*. history; a chronice. ~কার *n*. a historian; a chronicler.

ইতিহাস *n*. history. ~বেত্তা *n*. & *a*. one who is conversant with history or well-versed in history. ~লেখক *n*. a historian.

ইতু *n*. the sun-god (esp. as worshipped by Hindu women in the month of Agrahayana (অগ্রহায়ণ).

ইতো নষ্টস্ততো ভ্রষ্ট deprived of both the chances by wavering between this and that.

ইতোমধ্যে *adv*. meanwhile, in the meantime.

ইত্তিলা, ইত্তেলা var. of **এত্তেলা** and **এত্তেলা** respectively.

ইত্যনুসারে *adv*. according to this, accordingly; in this way or manner.

ইত্যবসরে *adv*. seizing the interim opportunity; during the interval, in the meantime, meanwhile.

ইত্যাকার *a*. such.

ইত্যাদি *adv*. and so on, and so forth, and such others, et cetera.

ইথার *n*. ether.

ইথে (obs.) *adv*. in this; for this. □ *pro*. (obs.) this. □ *a*. (obs.) of this.

ইদ, ঈদ *n*. one of the chief Muslim festivals, Id. **ইদগা, ঈদগা** *n*. the place or building where Muslims assemble to say prayer, esp. on the occasion of Id.

ইদানীং *adv*. at present, nowadays; of late. **ইদানীন্তন** *a*. recent; present-day; of modern times.

ইনকার *n*. denial (esp. of a charge). **ইনকার করা** *v*. to deny; refuse.

ইনসপেকটর, ইনস্পেক্টর *n*. an inspector.

ইনসাফ *n*. justice; equity; correct or right decision.

ইনাম *n*. a reward; a tip.

ইনামেল *n*. enamel. **ইনামেল করা** *v*. to enamel. **ইনামেল-করা** *a*. enamelled.

ইনি *pro*. (applied to persons deserving respect) he or she, this person.

ইনিয়ে-বিনিয়ে *adv*. (dero.) exaggerating to a great extent, in elaborate detail; with numberless humble entreaties.

ইন্তাকাল *n*. death.

ইন্তাজার *n*. waiting for eagerly, eager expectation.

ইন্তিজাম *n*. good arrangement. **ইন্তিজাম করা** *v*. to arrange.

ইন্দারা *n*. a draw-well.

ইন্দিবর *n*. the blue lotus.

ইন্দিরা *n*. a name of Goddess Lakshmi (লক্ষ্মী).

ইন্দীবর alt. spell. of **ইন্দিবর**।

ইন্দু *n*. the moon. **~নিভানন** *a*. one whose face resembles the moon (in beauty), possessing a moonlike face. *fem*. **~নিভাননা, ~নিভাননী**। **~ভূষণ** *n*. one who has the moon for his ornament; an appellation of God Shiva (শিব). **~মতী** *n*. *fem*. the full moon (personified). **~মুখী** *n*. *fem*. a woman whose face resembles the moon (in beauty). **~মৌলি, ~শেখর** *n*. one who has the moon for an ornament on his forehead; an appellation of Shiva (শিব). **~লেখা** *n*. a digit of the moon; the digit of the moon on the forehead of Shiva (শিব) ; a creeper from the extract of which the legendary celestial wine was made, wormwood.

ইন্দুর, ইন্দূর for. variants of **ইঁদুর**।

ইন্দো *pfx*. Indo-. **~চীন** *n*. Indo-China. **~চৈনিক** *a*. Indo-Chinese. **~নেশীয়** *a*. Indonesian. □ *n*. an Indonesian.

ইন্দ্র *n*. the king of gods and goddesses (cp. Jupiter, Zeus, Jove). **~কল্প** *a*. like Indra (in might or status or wealth). **~চাপ** same as **~ধনু**। **~জিৎ** *a*. & *n*. one who has defeated Indra (ইন্দ্র). **~ত্ব** *n*. the office or status of Indra (ইন্দ্র) ; an office or status as mighty or wealthy as that of Indra (ইন্দ্র). **~ধনু** *n*. the rainbow; (lit.) the bow of Indra (ইন্দ্র). **~পতন, ~পাত** *n*. (lit.) fall of Indra, the king of gods; (fig.) death of a great man. **~পুরী, ~লোক, ইন্দ্রালয়** *n*. the abode or city of Indra (ইন্দ্র) ; Paradise; Heaven. **~সভা** *n*. the court of Indra (ইন্দ্র). **~সুত** *n*. a son of Indra (ইন্দ্র). **~সেন** *n*. one whose army is as large and powerful as that of Indra (ইন্দ্র).

ইন্দ্রগোপ *n*. a species of insect of red velvety colour.

ইন্দ্রজাল *n*. magic, conjuring; jugglery; a spell. **ইন্দ্রজালিক, ঐন্দ্রজালিক** *n*. magician. □ *a*. magical.

ইন্দ্রনীল, ইন্দ্রনীলক, ইন্দ্রমণি *n*. the sapphire, the emerald, the beryl.

ইন্দ্রবজ্রা *n*. a Sanskrit metre.

ইন্দ্রলুপ্ত *n*. a bald, baldness.

ইন্দ্রাগার *n*. a draw-well.

ইন্দ্রাণী *n*. the wife and consort of Indra (ইন্দ্র).

ইন্দ্রায়ুধ *n*. the rainbow; the bow of Indra (ইন্দ্র).

ইন্দ্রিয় *n*. a sense-organ. **~গম্য, ~গোচর, ~গ্রাহ্য** *a*. perceptible by the senses. **~গম্যতা, ~গোচরতা, ~গ্রাহ্যতা** *n*. state of being within sense perception. **~গ্রাম** *n*. *pl*. sense-organs collectively. **~জয়, ~দমন** *n*. self-control or self-restraint of sensual appetites; continence. ~জয়ী *a.* continent. ~তৃপ্তি *n.* gratification of the senses. ~দোষ *n.* licentiousness, lewdness; libidinousness. ~নিচয় same as ইন্দ্রিয়গ্রাম। ~নিগ্রহ *n.* austere self-restraint, repression of sensual appetites. ~পরতন্ত্র, ~পরবশ, ~পরায়ণ *a.* given to indulgence of sensual appetites; voluptuous, lewd, concupiscent. ~বৃত্তি *n.* the function or power of sense-organs. ~লালসা *n.* sensual desires, concupiscence. ~সংযম same as ~জয়। ~সুখ *n.* sensual pleasures. ~সেবী same as ~পরতন্ত্র। ইন্দ্রিয়াতীত *a.* beyond sense perception; that cannot be perceived by the sense organs.

ইন্ধন *n.* fuel. ইন্ধন দেওয়া, ইন্ধন জোগানো *v.* to feed with fuel, to fuel, to stoke; (fig.) to intensify the severity of, to encourage; to enkindle or inflame with passion, etc. ইন্ধনিক টিন্ডাল *a.* stoker tindal.

ইবাদতখানা *n.* a room or house of worship (esp. a private one).

ইমন *n.* a mode of Indian classical music.

ইমান *n.* religious faith; piety; fidelity; honesty; conscience; conscientiousness. ~খোর *a.* faithless, treacherous, perfidious. ~দার *a.* faithful (in religion); devout, pious; having fidelity; honest; conscientious. ~দারি *n.* faithfulness (in religion); devoutness, piety; fidelity; honesty; conscientiousness.

ইমাম *n.* the religious head or chief priest of Muslims, an Imam. ~বাড়া *n.* a house built for observing the Muharram.

ইমারত *n.* a building; an edifice.

ইয়ত্তা *n.* (reckoning or) number or quantity; reckoning; limit.

ইয়াংকি, ইয়াঙ্কি *n.* (dero.) a Yankee, an American. □ *a.* Yankee.

ইয়াদ *n.* remembrance; recollection; heed, attention. ইয়াদ করা *v.* to remember; to recollect; to pay heed to. ইয়াদ রাখা *v.* to bear in mind, to remember; to be heedful of.

ইয়ার *n.* (usu. dero.) a friend, a companion; a witty or pert person. ইয়ারকি *n.* waggery. ইয়ারকি করা, ইয়ারকি দেওয়া, ইয়ারকি মারা *v.* to practise waggery (upon), to wag; to crack or make a joke. ~বকসি, ~বন্ধু *n.* (collec.) friends and companions and associates.

ইয়ারিং *n.* an earring.

ইয়ুনানি alt. spell. of ইউনানি।

ইয়ে *int.* indicating : failure to remember something, what-do-you-call-it.

ইরম্মদ *n.* the flash of lightning; a natural fire rising out of the sea, sea-fire; the elephant.

ইরা *n.* the goddess of speech; power of speech personified; the earth; wine; water; food.

ইরাদা *n.* determination, resolution, will; desire.

ইরানি *a.* Iranian, Persian. □ *n.* an Iranian, a Persian; the language of Iran or Persia, Iranian, Persian.

ইরাবতী *n.* the river Ravi in the Punjab.

ইরাবান *n.* the sea.

ইললি, ইল্লি *int.* exclamatory word indicating distrust or disbelief.

ইলশাগুঁড়ি, ইলশেগুঁড়ি coll. variants of ইলিশগুঁড়ি (see ইলিশ).

ইলশে coll. var. of ইলিশ।

ইলা *n.* the earth; the cow; speech (esp. when personified); wine; water.

ইলাকা var. of এলাকা।

ইলাহি *n.* (Mus.) God. □ *a.* great (ইলাহি পুরুষ) ; grand, pompous (ইলাহি কাণ্ড). ইলাহি গজ *n.* a yard-measure about 33 inches or 84 cms in length.

ইলিশ *n.* a variety of freshwater river fish, the hilsa. ~গুঁড়ি, ইলশেগুঁড়ি *n.* drizzle, serein.

ইলেক *n.* any one of the arithmetical symbols affixed to numerical figures to indicate money or weight.

ইলেকট্রিক *a.* electric, electrical. □ *n.* electricity.

ইল্লত *n.* filthiness, dirtiness; meanness, baseness. ইল্লত যায় না ধুলে the leopard cannot change its spots.

ইশকাপন *n.* (of playing-cards) spades.

ইশতিহার var. of ইস্তাহার।

ইশারা *n.* beckoning; gesture. ইশারা করা *v.* to beckon; to gesticulate; to make a sign.

ইশীকা, ইষিকা, ইষীকা alt. spellings of ঈষিকা।

ইষু *n*. an arrow.
ইষুধি *n*. a quiver.
ইষের মূল *n*. a medicinal herb.
ইষ্ট[1] *n*. an oblation.
ইষ্ট[2] *a*. intended, desired; cherished; beneficial; one who or that which is worshipped; worshipful; related by blood, of the same family (ইষ্টকুটুম্ব) ; dear, beloved. ☐ *n*. an intended or desired or cherished thing (ইষ্টলাভ) ; dear or beloved person. **~কবচ** *n*. a holy amulet safeguarding the person who puts it on. **~কর্ম** *n*. an intended work. **~কুটুম্ব** *n. pl.* one's kinsmen both from father's side and mother's side. **~চিন্তা** *n*. thoughts about one's welfare. **~জন** *n*. a dear or beloved person. **~দেব** *n*. a spiritual teacher and guide, a guru. **~দেবতা** *n*. a deity of one's worship, a tutelary god; (cp.) a guardian angel. **~নাম** *n*. the name of one's deity of worship. **~বিয়োগ** *n*. death of one's kinsman or beloved person. **~মন্ত্র** *n*.. mystical incantations which are recited when worshipping one's deity. **~লাভ, ~সাধন, ~সিদ্ধি** *n*. realization of one's desire, attainment of one's object.
ইষ্টক *n*. brick; (loos.) brickbat. **~খণ্ড** *n*. a piece of brick or brickbat. **~নির্মিত, ~ময়** *a*. brick-built.
ইষ্টানিষ্ট *n*. benefit and harm, weal and woe.
ইষ্টাপত্তি *n*. realization or attainment of one's desire; profit; benefit.
ইষ্টাপূর্ত *n*. digging of wells or building of temples and similar works for public welfare, public works; sacrifice for public welfare.
ইষ্টি[1] *n*. an oblation, a sacrifice.
ইষ্টি[2] *n*. desire. **~পত্র** *n*. a written document directing the disposal of one's effects at death, a will. **ইষ্টিপত্র-প্রমাণক** *n*. probate.
ইষ্টিকা *n*. brick-dust, powdered brick.
ইস *int*. expressing : amazement, pain, sorrow etc., ah.
ইসদন্ত *n*. a molar tooth.
ইসবগুল *n*. a medicinal seed, *Plantago ovata* usually taken for clearing of bowels.
ইসলাম *n*. Islam; the Islamic race, Muslim. **ইসলামি** *a*. Islamic.
ইস্কাপন alt. spell. of **ইশকাপন** ।
ইস্কুল coll. var. of **স্কুল** ।
ইস্ক্রুপ *n*. a screw.
ইস্তক *adv*. & *prep*. from; up to; till. ☐ *n*. (in card-playing) the king and the queen of trumps. **~নাগাদ** *adv*. from start to finish, from beginning to end.
ইস্তফা *n*. end, termination; cessation; resignation, relinquishment; giving up, abandonment. **ইস্তফা দেওয়া** *v*. to resign, to relinquish; to give up, to abandon; to cease (from).
ইস্তামাল *n*. use; practice. **ইস্তামাল করা** *v*. to practise. **ইস্তামাল হওয়া** *v*. to be used; to be practised.
ইস্তাহার *n*. a circular, a notice; a communiqué; a pamphlet; a handbill.
ইস্তিরি[1] vul. corrup. of **স্ত্রী** ।
ইস্তিরি[2] *n*. a smoothing-iron, calender; ironing. **ইস্তিরি করা** *v*. to iron (clothes).
ইস্তেমাল var. of **ইস্তামাল** ।
ইস্ত্রি var. of **ইস্তিরি**[1,2] ।
ইস্পাত *n*. steel. **ইস্পাতি** *a*. of steel; made of steel.
ইহ *adv*. in this place or time; in this world. ☐ *a*. this ('ইহ বাত') ; present (ইহজীবন). **~কাল, ~জন্ম, ~জীবন** *n*. the earthly or mortal life; its duration. **~কালীন** *a*. temporal. **~জগৎ, ~লোক, ~সংসার** *n*. the world, the earth.
ইহা *pro*. this (thing or animal); it. **ইহারা** *pro. pl.* these, they. **ইহার** *pro. a.* its. **ইহাদের** *pro. a. pl.* their, theirs.
ইহুদি *n*. a Jew. ☐ *a*. Jewish. **ইহুদি পাড়া** *n*. the Jewry.

ঈ *n.* the fourth vowel of the Bengali alphabet.

ঈকার *n.* the symbol ' ী ' affixed to consonants whilst adding the ঈ-sound to it. **ঈকারাদি** *a.* (of words) beginning with ঈ or ঈ-sound. **ঈকারান্ত** *a.* (of words) ending in ঈ or ঈ-sound.

ঈক্ষণ *n.* sight; seeing or sighting; observation; an eye.

ঈক্ষিত *a.* seen; sighted, noticed; observed.

ঈগল alt. spell. of **ইগল**।

ঈদ alt. spell. of **ইদ**।

ঈদৃক্, ঈদৃশ *a.* like this or like him, similar to this or similar to him. *fem.* **ঈদৃশী**।

ঈপ্সা *n.* desire to obtain; desire, longing.

ঈপ্সিত *a.* desired, longed for. *fem.* **ঈপ্সিতা**।

ঈপ্সু *a.* desirous of obtaining; desirous.

ঈর্ষা *n.* envy; malice, spite. **ঈর্ষানল** *n.* fire or heat of envy or malice. **ঈর্ষান্বিত, ~পরতন্ত্র** *a.* envious, malicious, spiteful. **~বশে** *adv.* being impelled or directed by envy or malice, out of ill-will or spite. **~মূলক** *a.* caused by envy or malice. **~যুক্ত, ~লু** same as **ঈর্ষান্বিত**।

ঈশ *n.* God; a god, a deity; God Shiva; a master or lord; a husband; an overlord, a king.

ঈশা[১] *fem.* of **ঈশ** ; Goddess Durga.

ঈশা[২] *n.* a plough-stilt, a plough-tree.

ঈশা[৩] *n.* Jesus Christ.

ঈশান *n.* a name of Shiva (শিব) ; the north-east. **ঈশানী** *n.* a name of Goddess Durga (দুর্গা), the wife of Shiva.

ঈশিতা, ঈশিত্ব *n.* godhead; divinity; supremacy; domination.

ঈশ্বর *n.* God; the Creator; a god; a creator; a lord, a master, an owner; an overlord, a king; the head of an order etc. (যোগীশ্বর) ; an appellation added to the name of a deceased person; its symbol is ৺(৺ভূদেব মুখোপাধ্যায়). **ঈশ্বর না করুন** God forbid, far be it. **~কৃপা** *n.* God's mercy; God's grace. **~চিন্তা** *n.* divine meditation. **~ত্ব** *n.* godhead; divinity. **~দত্ত** *a.* God-given. **~নিষ্ঠ, ~পরায়ণ** *a.* devoted to God, faithful to god; devout, pious. **~নিষ্ঠা, ~পরায়ণতা** *n.* devotion to God; faith in God; piety; godliness. **~পূজা** *n.* worship of God. **~প্রণোদিত** *a.* inspired by God. **~প্রসাদ** *n.* God's grace. **~প্রসাদে** *adv.* through God's grace; by the grace of God. **~প্রাপ্তি** *n.* spiritual union with God; death. **~প্রীতি, ~প্রেম** *n.* love of or towards God. **~প্রেমিক** *a.* & *n.* one who loves God. **~প্রেরিত** *a.* God-sent, divinely inspired. **~বাদ** *n.* theism. **~বাদী** *a.* theistic. □ *n.* a theist. **~বিরোধী** *a.* atheistic. □ *n.* an atheist. **~বিষয়ক** *a.* relating to God. **~ভক্ত** *a.* devoted to God; devout; pious. **~ভক্তি** *n.* devotion to God; devoutness; piety. **~ভাব** *n.* godhead; divinity; godliness. **~ভীরু** *a.* God-fearing. **~সাধনা** *n.* austerities and meditations leading to communion with God. **~সৃষ্ট** *a.* created by God. **~সেবা** *n.* worship of God.

ঈশ্বরাজ্ঞা, ঈশ্বরাদেশ *n.* God's commandment, a divine commandment.

ঈশ্বরাধীন *a.* dependent on the will of God; divine.

ঈশ্বরী *fem.* of **ঈশ্বর** ; Goddess.

ঈশ্বরেচ্ছা *n.* the will of God; divine will. **ঈশ্বরেচ্ছায়** *adv.* by the will of God, God willing.

ঈশ্বরোপাসক *n.* a worshipper or devotee of God.

ঈশ্বরোপাসনা *a.* worship of God, divine service; devotion to God.

ঈষ *n.* a ploughshare.

ঈষৎ *a.* & *adv.* a little, a bit, slight or slightly.

ঈষৎবক্র *a.* slightly bent or curved.

ঈষদচ্ছ *a.* translucent.

ঈষদুষ্ণ *a.* moderately warm, tepid, lukewarm. **ঈষদুষ্ণতা** *n.* moderate warmth, tepidity, lukewarmness.

ঈষদূন *a.* a little less than, a little short of.

ঈষদ্বিকশিত *a.* in partial bloom; not fully open.

ঈষদ্ভিন্ন *a.* in partial bloom; partially or slightly separated.

ঈষন্মাত্র *a.* just a little, very little.

ঈষা *n.* a plough-stilt, a plough-tree; a furrow; a ploughshare. **~দণ্ড** *n.* the handle of a plough.

ঈষিকা, ঈষীকা *n.* an eyeball of an elephant; a painter's brush; a tall species of grass of which mats are made.

ঈহা *n.* effort, attempt, endeavour; desire.

উ *n.* the fifth vowel of the Bengali alphabet.

উই *n.* white ant, termite (also **উই পোকা**). **~চারা, ~ঢিপি, ~ঢিবি** *n.* an ant-hill. **উই লাগা** *v.* to get attacked with white ants. **~ধরা, ~লাগা** *a.* attacked with or eaten up by white ants.

উইচিংড়া var. of **উচ্চিংড়া**।

উইল *n.* a written document directing the disposal of one's effects at death, a will, a testament. **উইল করা** *v.* to draw up a will, to will, to bequeath.

উঃ *int.* expressing : pain, amazement, impatience, derision, disgust etc.

উঁকি *n.* a peep; a prying; a furtive glance. **~ঝুঁকি** *n.* (frequent or repeated) peeping and prying. **উঁকিঝুঁকি মারা** *v.* to peep and pry (frequently or repeatedly), to look and peer about inquisitively. **উঁকি দেওয়া, উঁকি মারা** *v.* to peep; to look shyly or furtively or surreptitiously; to begin to appear; to put in first appearance shyly or furtively.

উঁচকপালে *a.* having a protuberant or bulging or convex forehead (such a forehead indicates luck in case of men, but ill-luck in case of women); fortunate (in case of women : unfortunate). *fem.* **উঁচকপালি**।

উঁচু *a.* high, elevated, tall, lofty; exalted, noble (উঁচু মন) ; loud; rough (উঁচু কথা). **উঁচু করা** *v.* to raise; to elevate. **উঁচানো** *v.* to raise, to elevate. □ *n.* raising. □ *a.* raised. **উঁচু-নিচু** *a.* high and low; undulating, uneven.

উঁহুঁ *int.* expressing : unwillingness, non-acceptance, bashfulness, slight pain.

উকড়া *n.* parched paddy coated or sweetened with sugar or molasses.

উকা var. of **উখা**।

উকার *n.* the symbol '্ু' affixed to a consonant whilst adding the উ-sound to it. **উকারাদি** *a.* (of words) beginning with উ or উ-sound. **উকারান্ত** *a.* (of words) ending in উ or উ-sound.

উকি[1] var. of **উঁকি**।

উকি[2] *n.* a hiccup; retching. **উকি তোলা** *v.* to hiccup; to retch.

উকিল *n.* a pleader, an advocate; a lawful or legal representative; (facet. or derog.) a supporter. **উকিল দেওয়া, উকিল লাগানো** *v.* to engage a pleader. **উকিল হওয়া** *v.* to take up the profession of a pleader; to be a pleader; to act as a pleader for, to plead for; to advocate; to support. **উকিলি** *a.* of or like a pleader (উকিলি বুদ্ধি).

উকুন *n.* the louse (*pl.* lice).

উকো coll. var. of **উখা**[2]।

উক্ত *a.* said, mentioned; aforesaid, aforementioned. **উক্ত থাকা, উক্ত হওয়া** *v.* to be said or mentioned.

উক্তি *n.* speech; a saying, an apophthegm; a statement; a pronouncement. **~-প্রত্যুক্তি** *n.* statement and counter-statement, bandying of words; mutual recrimination.

উখড়ানো *v.* to uproot, to extirpate. □ *n.* extirpation. □ *a.* uprooted.

উখা[1] *n.* a dixie or cooking-pail usually with a concave bottom; an oven.

উখা[2] *n.* a file, a rasp. **উখা দিয়ে ঘষা** *v.* to file; to rasp.

উখি *n.* dandruff, scurf.

উগরানো *v.* to disgorge, to belch out, to eruct, to vomit, to spew; (fig.) to be compelled to confess or give back. □ *n.* disgorgement, belching out, eructation, vomiting or spewing. □ *a.* disgorged, belched out, eructed, vomited, spewed. **চোরাই মাল উগরানো** to be compelled to give back stolen goods. **পরীক্ষার খাতায় উগরানো** to write down mechanically in an answer-paper what has been crammed. **পেটের কথা উগরানো** to be compelled to give out or confess secrets.

উগ্র *a.* violent; cruel; rough, harsh (উগ্র কথা) ; haughty; angry, wrathful, hot (উগ্র স্বভাব) ; severe, fierce (উগ্র তেজ) ; sharp, pungent, strong (উগ্র শব্দ, উগ্র

গন্ধ, উগ্র বিষ). **~কণ্ঠ, ~স্বর** *a.* harsh-and-angry-voiced, raucous. **~কণ্ঠে, ~স্বরে** *adv.* in a harsh and angry voice, in a rough or rude voice, raucously. **~কর্মা** *a.* one who performs terrible or cruel deeds. **~ক্ষত্রিয়** *n.* the Aguri. **~চণ্ডা, ~চণ্ডী** *n. fem.* an appellation of Goddess Durga (দুর্গা) when conceived as the goddess of wrath; a termagant woman, a termagant, a shrew. **~গন্ধী** *a.* strong-scented. **~তপা** *a.* practising severe penance or asceticism. **~তা** *n.* violence; cruelty; roughness, harshness; haughtiness; anger, wrath, heat; severity, fierceness; sharpness. **~দর্শন** *a.* angry-looking, of fierce looks, of a stern and forbidding appearance. *fem.* **উগ্রদর্শনা**। **~পন্থী** *a.* & *n.* extremist; terrorist. **~প্রকৃতি** *a.* hot-tempered; quick-tempered; irascible, choleric. **~বীর্য** *a.* high-spirited. **~মূর্তি** *a.* angry-looking; fierce-looking. **~স্বভাব** same as **উগ্রপ্রকৃতি**।

উচক্কা *a.* in the state of growing up or attaining maturity, adolescent (উচক্কা বয়স) ; sudden (উচক্কা ভয়). □ *adv.* suddenly.

উচল *a.* (poet. & obs.) high.

উচাটন *n.* anxiety; restlessness; over-eagerness. □ *a.* anxious; restless; over-eager.

উচিত *a.* just, equitable; reasonable; proper, right; worthy, becoming, suitable. **~বক্তা** *a.* outspoken. **উচিত ব্যবহার** just and equitable treatment, a square deal.

উচোট dial. var. of **হোঁচট**।

উচ্চ *a.* (for. High.) high, tall; elevated (উচ্চ ভূমি) ; socially high (উচ্চ বংশ) ; noble, exalted (উচ্চ মন) ; dignified or pompous (উচ্চ চালচলন) ; upper (উচ্চ শ্রেণি) ; high-pitched, loud (উচ্চ স্বর) ; dear, costly (উচ্চ মূল্য) ; superior, senior (উচ্চ পদ, উচ্চ কর্মচারী). **~কুলজাত** *a.* born of a high family, highborn, nobly born. **~তম** *a.* super; highest; loftiest. **~তর** *a. compar.* higher; loftier. **~তা** *n.* height, altitude; tallness; elevation; state of being socially high; nobleness, exaltedness; loudness. **~নাদ** *a.* high-sounding, making a loud noise; loud. □ *n.* a loud noise or sound. **~নীচ** *a.* & *n.* high and low. **~পাত** *n.* (astr.) the ascending node. **~বাচ্য** *n.* response; anything in favour or opposition; commenting. **~বাচ্য না করা** *v.* not to respond; not to say anything in favour or opposition; not to pass any comments; to keep quiet, to remain silent. **~বিত্ত** *n.* upper class. □ *a.* belonging to the upper class. **উচ্চ বিদ্যালয়** a high school. **~বেতন** *n.* high or handsome or fat or big salary. **~ভাষী** *a.* harsh-tongued; bragging. **~মধ্যবিত্ত** *n.* upper middle-class. **~মূল্য** *n.* high price. **~রোল** *n.* loud noise, clamour. **~শিক্ষা** *n.* high or higher education. **~হার** *n.* high rate. **~হারে** *adv.* at a high rate. **~হাসি** *n.* a loud laugh, a guffaw, laughter. **~হৃদয়** *a.* large-hearted, high-minded, magnanimous, generous.

উচ্চকিত *a.* anxious, worried; on tenterhooks; agitated; restless; on the tiptoe of expectation.

উচ্চণ্ড *a.* violent; terrible, fierce; indomitable; very angry or hot-tempered; severe.

উচ্চয় *n.* act of plucking or collecting (পুষ্পোচ্চয়) ; collection; multitude, heap.

উচ্চস্বর *n.* a loud voice. **উচ্চস্বরে** *adv.* in a loud voice. See also **উচ্চৈঃস্বর**।

উচ্চাকাঙ্ক্ষা *n.* ambition, aspiration. **উচ্চাকাঙ্ক্ষী** *a.* ambitious, aspiring. *fem.* **উচ্চাকাঙ্ক্ষিণী**।

উচ্চাটন *n.* eradication, extirpation; act of agitating; agitation; act of tormenting, oppression, persecution; anxiety, state of suspense; a kind of pseudo-spiritual practice undertaken to persecute an enemy.

উচ্চাবচ *a.* uneven, undulating.

উচ্চাভিলাষ *n.* ambition, aspiration. **উচ্চাভিলাষী** *a.* ambitious, aspiring. *fem.* **উচ্চাভিলাষিণী**।

উচ্চায় var. of **উচ্চয়**।

উচ্চার *n.* excrement, faeces, stool, dung; utterance.

উচ্চারণ *n.* act of speaking; elocution, articulation, utterance; mode of speaking; pronunciation. **উচ্চারণ করা** *v.* to speak out; to elocute; to articulate; to utter, to say; to pronounce. ~স্থান *n.* (gr.) any of the parts of the mouth that becomes most active whilst pronouncing a particular letter of the alphabet; place of articulation.

উচ্চারণীয়, উচ্চার্য *a.* that which should be or can be said or uttered or pronounced, utterable. **উচ্চার্যমাণ** *a.* that which is in the process of being said or uttered or pronounced.

উচ্চারিত *a.* spoken; elocuted; uttered; pronounced.

উচ্চাশয় *a.* noble-minded, high-souled.

উচ্চাশা *n.* high-hope; ambition, aspiration. **উচ্চাশা করা** *v.* to aspire.

উচ্চিংড়া, উচ্চিংড়ে *n.* a kind of insect akin to the cricket.

উচ্চৈঃশ্রবা *n.* (myth.) the horse owned by Indra (ইন্দ্র) the king of gods.

উচ্চৈঃস্বর *n.* a loud voice; a shout. **উচ্চৈঃস্বরে** *adv.* in a loud voice; with a shout. **উচ্চৈঃস্বরে ডাকা বা বলা** *v.* to call or say loudly; to shout.

উচ্ছল, উচ্ছলিত *a.* all-pervading; surging; lively; thrown up, disgorged; bulged out; swelled. **উচ্ছল হওয়া, উচ্ছলিত হওয়া** *v.* to be all-pervading; to be lively; to swell up; to bulge out, to swell. **উচ্ছলন** *n.* state of being all-pervading; state of being thrown up or disgorged; act of swelling up or bulging out.

উচ্ছিত্তি *n.* eradication, extirpation; ejectment, eviction; extermination; destruction, abolition.

উচ্ছিদ্যমান *a.* in the state of being eradicated or extirpated or ejected or evicted or exterminated or destroyed or abolished.

উচ্ছিন্ন *a.* eradicated, extirpated; ejected, evicted; exterminated; destroyed, abolished. **উচ্ছিন্ন করা** *v.* to eradicate, to extirpate; to eject; to exterminate; to destroy, to abolish.

উচ্ছিষ্ট *a.* (of food) left or remaining in the plate after eating; not washed after eating (উচ্ছিষ্ট মুখ) ; that which has come in contact with cooked food (উচ্ছিষ্ট হাঁড়ি). □ *n.* orts; leavings of food in the plate after eating (also **উচ্ছিষ্টান্ন**) ; scraps of food. ~ভোজন *n.* feeding of left-overs in another person's plate. ~ভোজী *a.* one who eats the scraps of food left in another person's plate. □ *n.* a cringing dependant.

উচ্ছৃঙ্খল *a.* disorderly; not disciplined; self-willed, wayward; uncontrolled, unregulated; lawless, dissolute, wild; Bohemian. **উচ্ছৃঙ্খলতা** *n.* disorderliness; indiscipline; waywardness; want of control or regularity; lawlessness; dissoluteness; Bohemianism.

উচ্ছে *n.* bitter gourd, a variety of kitchen vegetable having bitter taste.

উচ্ছেদ *n.* eradication, extirpation; ejectment, eviction; destruction, abolition. **উচ্ছেদ করা** *v.* to eradicate, to extirpate; to eject, to evict; to destroy, to abolish. **ভিটেমাটি উচ্ছেদ করা** *v.* to eject or evict from hereditary homestead. **সমূলে উচ্ছেদ করা** to uproot, to extirpate; (fig.) to destroy root and branch. **উচ্ছেদক** *a.* one who or that which eradicates or extirpates or ejects or evicts or destroys. □ *n.* an eradicator, an extirpator; an ejector, an evictor; a destroyer, an abolisher; an abolitionist (as of slavery). **উচ্ছেদন** same as **উচ্ছেদ। উচ্ছেদনীয়, উচ্ছেদ্য** *a.* eradicable, extirpable; fit to be ejected or evicted, fit to be destroyed or abolished. ~সাধন *n.* act of eradicating or extirpating or ejecting or evicting or destroying or abolishing; eradication, extirpation; ejection, eviction; destruction, abolition. ~সাধন করা same as **উচ্ছেদ করা।**

উচ্ছোষণ *n.* act of sucking up; act of afflicting. □ *a.* that which sucks up or afflicts.

উচ্ছোষিত *a.* sucked up; afflicted.

উচ্ছ্বসন *n.* act of bursting out; act of swelling or welling up; act of overflowing or filling; respiration; motional imbalance.

উচ্ছ্বসিত *a.* swollen, swelled; welled up; swelling; overflowed; overflowing; filled to the brim; overfull; full of ardour; impassioned; seized with overmastering emotion.

উচ্ছ্বাস *n.* strong emotion or passion; an emotional or passionate outburst; great delight; a bursting forth; manifestation; a swelling; breathing; breath; a chapter of a book. **উচ্ছ্বাসিত** *a.* swollen, swelled; welled up; swelling; overflowed; overflowing; filled to the brim, overfull; seized with emotion; impassioned; bursting forth; opened; manifested.

উচ্ছয়, উচ্ছায়, উচ্ছিতি *n.* height, altitude; elevation, gradual rise or ascent, elation, development. **উচ্ছায়ী** *a.* ascending; rising gradually; in the process of being elated or developed. **উচ্ছিত** *a.* heightened; swelled; developed. **উচ্ছা** *v.*(poet.) to rise upwards, to swell ('উচ্ছিয়া উঠিবে বিশ্ব').

উছল *a.* swelling up; swelled up; overflowing. **উছলানো** *v.* to swell up; to overflow. ☐ *n.* swelling up; overflow. ☐ *a.* swollen, overflowing, swelled up.

উজবুক *a.* stupid; ignorant; uneducated; uncouth.

উজবেক, উজবেগ *n.* an Uzbeg; an inhabitant of Uzbekistan.

উজর, উজল poet. corruptions of **উজ্জ্বল**।

উজাগর *a.* sleepless.

উজাড় *a.* empty, exhausted; depopulated; desolate (ঠক বাছতে দেশ উজাড়).

উজান *n.* a course against the current, an upstream course. **উজান-ভাটি** *n.* flow-tide and ebb-tide, flow and ebb. **উজানি-বেলা** *n.* forenoon. **উজানে** *adv.* upstream, against the current.

উজানো *v.* to go upstream. ☐ *a.* going or moving upstream; upstream.

উজির *n.* a minister of state esp. the prime minister (usu. in Muslim rule). **উজিরি, উজিরালি** *n.* office of the prime minister; premiership. **রাজাউজির মারা** *v.* to try to establish one's importance by fabricating stories about one's familiarity with big persons.

উজু *n.* (amongst Muslims) formal washing of one's person before praying and other religious services; washing one's person.

উজোর poet. corrup. of **উজ্জ্বল**।

উজ্জীবন *n.* infusion of a new life, regeneration; bringing back or coming back to life or consciousness, resuscitation; act of being predominant again from a state of extinction, revival.

উজ্জীবিত *a.* infused with a new life, regenerated; brought back or returned to life or consciousness, resuscitated; returned to predominance from a state of extinction, revived. **উজ্জীবিত করা** *v.* to infuse a new life into, to regenerate; to bring back to life or consciousness, to breathe fresh life into, to resuscitate; to revive.

উজ্জৃম্ভণ *n.* manifestation; development; evolution; change.

উজ্জ্বল *a.* illuminated; bright; luminous; lustrous; radiant; splendent; resplendent; splendorous; splendid; shining; dazzling; beautiful; glorious; vivid. **উজ্জ্বল করা** *v.* to illuminate, to illumine; to brighten; to glorify (মুখ উজ্জ্বল করা, বংশ উজ্জ্বল করা) ; to make vivid, to vivify. **উজ্জ্বল হওয়া** *v.* to become illuminated; to brighten (up); to become glorified; to become vivid. **উজ্জ্বল রস** (rhet.) effect (on the reader's mind) produced by the (final) union of lovers. **উজ্জ্বলতা** *n.* brightness; luminousness; lustre; radiance; splendour; shine; dazzle; beauty; glory; vividness. **উজ্জ্বল শ্যামবর্ণ** *a.* of a complexion more fair than dark, of a glossy light dark complexion. **উজ্জ্বলিত** *a.* illuminated; lighted, enkindled; shining; brightened; radiated; beautified; glorified; vivified. **উজ্জ্বলীকরণ** *n.* illumination; act of brightening (up); glorification. **উজ্জ্বলীভবন** *n.* act of becoming illuminated or brightened (up) or glorified or vivid.

উঞ্ছ *n.* act of gleaning as a means of one's livelihood; a mean livelihood. **~জীবী** *a.* subsistent on gleaning. **~বৃত্তি** *n.* the practice of subsisting on gleaning; practice or act of somehow making both ends meet; earning a living by shifts. ☐ *a.* subsistent on gleaning. **~শীল** same as **উঞ্ছজীবী**।

উট *n.* the camel.

উটকপালে var. of **উঁচকপালে**।

উটকো *a.* unknown (উটকো লোক) ; unbelievable, preposterous, queer (উটকো গল্প) ; unexpected (উটকো ব্যাপার) ; incidental (উটকো খরচা) ; unnecessary, causeless (উটকো ঝামেলা) ; insincere (উটকো সোহাগ) ; frivolous, flippant (উটকো মেয়ে) ; given to slipping away frequently from one's husband's house (উটকো বউ).

উটজ *n.* a hut thatched with straw, tree-leaves etc; a thatched hut. **~শিল্প** *n.* cottage-industry.

উটতি coll. var. of **উঠতি**।

উটপাখি *n.* the ostrich.

উঠতি *n.* rise, growth, development, flourish, increase. □ *a.* rising, growing, developing, flourishing, thriving, increasing. **উঠতি অবস্থা** flourishing stage. **উঠতি পড়তি** *n.* rise and fall; (comm.) boom and slump, fluctuation. **উঠতি বয়স** adolescence. **উঠতির মুখ** the first stage or beginning of rise or flourish or prosperity.

উঠন *n.* act of swelling; act of getting up or climbing or ascending or rising.

উঠন্ত *a.* rising; growing. **উঠন্ত মুলো পত্তনে চেনা যায়** (fig.) morning shows the day.

উঠবন্দি *n.* a temporary or periodical lease of agricultural land. **~চাষ** *n.* shifting cultivation.

উঠা, (coll.) **ওঠা** *v.* to ascend, to climb, to rise (সূর্য উঠছে) ; to get up from a place; to ride, to mount, to get in, to board (গাড়িতে ওঠা) ; to get up from bed; to wake; to awake, to arise; to grow; to cut (দাঁত উঠছে) ; to come out (মাটি ফুঁড়ে ওঠা) ; to have a rise (জ্বর উঠছে) ; to be promoted (ক্লাসে ওঠা) ; to be raised (জাতে ওঠা) ; to be available (বাজারে ওঠা) ; to be built or constructed (বাড়ি ওঠা) ; to fall (চুল ওঠা) ; to come off (রং উঠবে) ; to be collected (চাঁদা ওঠা) ; to enter (কানে ওঠা, মুখে ওঠা) ; to be current (ঢং ওঠা) ; to be abolished, to go out of practice (পূজাপাট ওঠা, নিয়ম ওঠা) ; to be closed down (দোকান ওঠা) ; to come to an end (আড্ডা উঠেছে) ; to be mentioned (নাম ওঠা) ; to be drawn (লটারিতে নাম ওঠা). **অন্ন ওঠা** *v.* to be deprived of subsistence (from). **উঠিয়ে দেওয়া** same as **উঠানো**। **ওঠা-উঠি** *n.* act of getting up frequently; (amongst school-boys in a classroom) change of rooms or class-promotion. **ওঠা-নামা** *n.* act of ascending and descending (usu. at regular intervals); rise and fall; elevation and depression; undulation; promotion and demotion; (comm.—of markets) boom and slump, fluctuation. **উঠি-পড়ি করে ছোটা** to run in hot haste or at a breakneck speed. **উঠে যাওয়া** *v.* to get up (from a place); to remove (from a place); to fade or to go off (রং উঠে যাওয়া) ; to be closed down; to be abolished, to go out of practice. **উঠে পড়ে লাগা** *v.* to be up and doing; to engage doggedly in.

উঠান (pronun. উঠান্) *n.* a courtyard.

উঠানো *v.* to cause to ascend or climb; to lift; to heave, to haul up; to pick up; to raise; to cause to mount or ride; to extract or cause to be extracted (দাঁত উঠানো) ; to pluck or cause to be plucked; to promote (ক্লাসে উঠানো) ; to build or construct; to remove (রং উঠানো) ; to collect (চাঁদা উঠানো) ; to cause to enter (কানে উঠানো) ; to abolish (পূজাপাট উঠানো) ; to close down (দোকান উঠানো) ; to bring to an end (আড্ডা উঠানো) ; to include (তালিকায় উঠানো) ; to mention (নাম উঠানো) ; to evict, to eject (প্রজা বা ভাড়াটে উঠানো).

উঠিত *a.* (of land) developed for agriculture or habitation.

উঠতে বসতে *adv.* every now and then, frequently, at every step.

উঠোন coll. var. of **উঠান**।

উড়কি same as **উড়িধান**।

উড়তি *a.* flying; (of rumour, news etc. esp. such as are untrue) passing from man to man, current.

উড়নচণ্ডী, উড়নচণ্ডে *a.* possessing the habit of a spendthrift, wasteful, extravagant, squandering. □ *n.* a spendthrift, an extravagant man, a squanderer.

উড়নি coll. var. of **উড়ানি**।

উড়ন্ত *a.* moving through or in the air, flying, fluttering (উড়ন্ত নিশান).

উড়া, (coll.) **ওড়া** *v.* to move through or in the air, to fly; to flutter; to go up in the air; to aviate; to run rapidly, to dart; to flaunt one's wealth and squander it in dissoluteness, to dissipate (বড়লোকের ছেলেটা উড়ে বেড়াচ্ছে) ; to abound (কলকাতায় টাকা উড়ছে). □ *n.* act of flying or fluttering; act of going up in the air; aviation; dissipation; abundance. □ *a.* flown; flying, capable of flying; not coming from any definite or reliable source (ওড়া খবর). **উড়িয়ে দেওয়া** *v.* to let fly (esp. by setting free); to cause to vanish, to vanish (জাদুকর তাসখানি উড়িয়ে দিল) ; to squander (money etc.); to pay no heed to, to attach no importance to. **উড়ে যাওয়া** *v.* to fly away; (of birds) to escape from bondage and fly away; to disappear, to vanish (ঘুড়িটা উড়ে গেছে) ; to be spent rapidly (পয়সা উড়ে যাওয়া) ; to be blown away (বাতাসে মেঘ উড়ে যাওয়া). **উড়ে এসে জুড়ে বসা** to come uncalled for and take possession without right, to drop from the moon and settle down permanently, to usurp. **উড়ানো** *v.* to fly (ঘুড়ি উড়ানো) ; to cause to vanish (তাস উড়ানো) ; to squander (টাকা উড়ানো) ; to attach no importance (to), to pay no heed to (কথা উড়ানো).

উড়ানি *n.* a scarf; a modesty scarf.

উড়ি, উড়িধান *n.* paddy grown in uncultivated land from seeds driven by wind.

উড়িয়া var. of **ওড়িয়া**।

উড়িষ্যা var. of **ওড়িশা**।

উড়ী, উড়ীধান rej. spellings of **উড়ি** and **উড়িধান** respectively.

উড়ু-উড়ু *a.* extremely eager to fly in the air; extremely eager to go away; very restless or impatient (মন উড়ু উড়ু).

উড়ুক্কু *a.* flying; capable of or given to flying; very restless or impatient. **উড়ুক্কু মাছ** *n.* flying fish.

উড়ুনি coll. var. of **উড়ানি**।

উড়ুনে *a.* extravagant, spendthrift.

উড়ুপ *n.* a raft, a float; the moon.

উড়ুম্বর var. of **উদুম্বর**।

উড়ো pop. var. of **উড়া** (*a.*). **~খবর** *n.* unconfirmed news or report; rumour; hearsay. **~চিঠি** *n.* an anonymous letter. **~জাহাজ** *n.* an aircraft, an aeroplane, an airship.

উড্ডয়ন *n.* going up or moving in the air, soaring or flying, flight.

উড্ডীন, উড্ডীয়মান, (rare) **উড্ডয়মান** *a.* flying or moving in the air; soaring; going upwards.

উৎ *pfx.* denoting : above, excessive, contrary, going beyond etc.; a-, supra-, super-, up-, ultra-, extra-, anti-, in-, non-, out-, preter-, trans-, etc.

উৎকট *a.* severe; terrible, hideous; monstrous; queer, odd (উৎকট আবদার). **উৎকট ব্যাধি** *n.* an unusual and severe disease which is difficult to cure.

উৎকণ্ঠ *a.* having one's neck craned in inquisitiveness, eagerness, anxiety etc.; anxious; worried; in grim suspense or in extreme eagerness.

উৎকণ্ঠা *n.* state of having one's neck craned in inquisitiveness, eagerness, anxiety etc.; anxiety; worry; suspense; extreme eagerness.

উৎকণ্ঠিত same as **উৎকণ্ঠ**। *fem.* **উৎকণ্ঠিতা**।

উৎকর্ণ *a.* all ears, very eager to hear. **উৎকর্ণ হওয়া** *v.* to be all ears.

উৎকর্ষ *n.* excellence; superiority; improvement; development; amelioration; increase. **~সাধন** *n.* act of improving or developing or ameliorating or increasing. **উৎকর্ষ সাধন করা** *v.* to improve, to develop, to ameliorate; to increase.

উৎকল *n.* Orissa, a state in the Indian Union.

উৎকলিকা *n.* a wave; a bud; anxiety, worry; suspense; extreme eagerness.

উৎকলিত *a.* anxious, worried; in suspense; wavy, billowy, undulating; quoted or extracted from, taken from.

উৎকিরণ *n.* engraving; carving.

উৎকীর্ণ *a.* engraved; carved; painted, drawn; pierced, perforated; raised; thrown up. **উৎকীর্ণ লিপি** inscription.

উৎকীর্তন *n.* proclamation; publicity; announcement; laudation. **উৎকীর্তন করা** *v.* to proclaim; to make public; to announce; to laud.

উৎকীর্তিত *a.* proclaimed; made public; announced; lauded.

উৎকুন *n.* the louse (*pl.* lice).

উৎকূলিত *a.* brought up or hauled up ashore; thrown up ashore.

উৎকৃষ্ট *a.* excellent, best; elevated. **~তা** *n.* excellence; elevatedness.

উৎকেন্দ্র *a.* (chiefly in math.) eccentric. **~তা** *n.* eccentricity.

উৎকোচ *n.* a bribe. **উৎকোচ দেওয়া** *v.* to bribe. **~গ্রাহী** *a.* & *n.* one who accepts a bribe. **~দাতা** *n.* a briber. **~দান, ~প্রদান** *n.* bribery.

উৎক্রম *n.* an inverse or reverse order; a move against or departure from the order; an inverse course; inversion, reversion; infringement, violation; an exception; a going upwards; a going out; death. **~ণ** *n.* an inverse or reverse movement, inversion, reversion; reversion of order, disorder; a leaping over; death; (gr.) transpostition (esp. disorderly transposition) of words within a sentence.

উৎক্রান্ত *a.* that which has been crossed by leaping over; leapt over; shot up or come up (from); dead. **উৎক্রান্তি** *n.* crossing by leaping over; leaping over; shooting up or coming up (from); gradual development or heightening; a going out; death.

উৎক্রোশ *n.* a species of bird akin to the eagle or osprey.

উৎক্ষিপ্ত *a.* thrown up; lifted; uprooted.

উৎক্ষেপ, উৎক্ষেপণ *n.* throwing up, launching or sending up, casting or tossing up.

উৎক্ষেপক *a.* (of a thing) throwing up or launching something; of means used to launch or toss up an aircraft or spacecraft or to give it a higher speed or range. □ *n.* the thing which throws up or launches a rocket, a means of throwing or tossing up missiles etc. into the air, a projecting or hurling device.

উৎখনন *n.* digging. **উৎখনিত** *a.* dug up.

উৎখাত *a.* dug up; uprooted, eradicated, extirpated; destroyed; cleft; (fig.) evicted, ejected. □ *n.* digging up; eradication, extirpation; destruction; cleaving; eviction, ejectment, ejection. **উৎখাত করা** *v.* to dig up; to root out, to eradicate, to extirpate; to destroy; to cleave; to evict, to eject, to oust.

উৎত্রসন, উৎত্রাস *n.* great fear or dread; alarm, dismay. **উৎত্রাসন** *n.* intimidation.

উৎপতন *n.* origination; rising or coming into view, appearance; going or rising upwards, ascension; going up in the air, flight. **~শীল** *a.* flying, in flight.

উৎপতিত *a.* originated; risen; one who or that which has got up; ascended; gone up in the air, flown.

উৎপত্তি *n.* origin, origination; creation; birth; production; coming into view, appearance; flourish. **~মূল, ~স্থান** *n.* the source; place of origin.

উৎপথ *n.* a contrary way; a wrong path; an evil way. **~গামী** *a.* following a contrary way, diverging; taking to or taken to a wrong path, erratic, off the track, deviated, gone astray; erratic; eccentric; taken to an evil way, depraved.

উৎপদ্যমান *a.* in the state of being born or being produced.

উৎপন্ন *a.* born; created; grown; made; produced; originated; sprung (from). **উৎপন্ন হওয়া** *v.* to be born; to be created; to grow; to be made; to be produced; to originate; to result (from). **~দ্রব্য** *n.* produce, product. **মোট উৎপন্ন দ্রব্য** total produce, output. **~মতি** *a.* having presence of mind, ready-witted. **~মতিত্ব** *n.* ready-wittedness.

উৎপল *n.* the water-lily, the lotus, the blue lotus. **উৎপলাক্ষ** *a.* lotus-eyed; blue-eyed. *fem.* **উৎপলাক্ষী।**

উৎপাটক *a.* & *n.* one who or that which uproots or extirpates or eradicates; one who extracts; (fig.) one who evicts or displaces or removes or destroys.

উৎপাটন *n.* act of uprooting, extirpation, eradication; extraction; (fig.) eviction, displacement, removal, destruction. **উৎপাটন করা** *v.* to uproot, to extirpate, to eradicate; to extract; (fig.) to evict, to displace, to remove, to destroy.

উৎপাটনীয় *a.* that which is to be or can be extirpated or extracted; eradicable; extractable.

উৎপাটিত *a.* uprooted, extirpated, eradicated; extracted; (fig.) evicted, displaced, removed, destroyed.

উৎপাত *n.* a disturbance; a nuisance; an annoyance, irritation; a mischief; a natural calamity; a pest. **উৎপাত করা** *v.* to disturb; to trouble; to annoy, to tease; to pester; to make mischief.

উৎপাদ[1] *a.* having heels over head.

উৎপাদ[2] *n.* output.

উৎপাদক *a.* one who or that which creates or begets or generates or produces or manufactures. □ *n.* a creator; a begetter, a generator; a producer; a manufacturer; that which helps to produce; (math.) a factor.

উৎপাদন *n.* creation; act of begetting, generation; production; manufacture; produce; manufactured goods. **উৎপাদন করা** *v.* to create; to beget, to generate; to produce; to manufacture. **~ক্ষম** *a.* capable of producing or generating. **উৎপাদনী** *a.* (*fem.*) creative, generative, productive (উৎপাদনী শক্তি). **উৎপাদনীয়** same as **উৎপাদ্য** ।

উৎপাদয়িতা same as **উৎপাদক**। *fem.* **উৎপাদয়িত্রী**।

উৎপাদিত *a.* created; begotten, generated; produced; manufactured.

উৎপাদিকা *fem.* of **উৎপাদক**। **উৎপাদিকা শক্তি** *n.* productivity; capability of producing.

উৎপাদী *a.* that which is created or begotten or generated or produced or manufactured; creative, generative, productive.

উৎপাদ্য *a.* that which is to be or can be created or begotten or generated or produced or manufactured. **~মান** *a.* in the process of being created or begotten or generated or produced or manufactured.

উৎপিঞ্জর *a.* freed from a cage; freed from bondage.

উৎপিপাসু *a.* extremely thirsty; anxious; stricken with suspense.

উৎপীড়ক *a.* persecuting; oppressive; harassing; annoying, vexatious; pestering. □ *n.* a persecutor; an oppressor; one who or that which distresses or harasses or annoys or vexes or pesters.

উৎপীড়ন *n.* persecution; oppression; distress; harassment; annoyance, vexation; pesterment. **উৎপীড়ন করা** *v.* to persecute; to oppress; to distress; to harass; to annoy, to vex; to pester.

উৎপীড়িত *a.* (also used as *n.*) persecuted; oppressed; distressed; harassed; annoyed, vexed; pestered. *fem.* **উৎপীড়িতা**। **উৎপীড়িত করা** same as **উৎপীড়ন করা**।

উৎপেতে *a.* troublesome; annoying; bothersome; mischievous.

উৎপ্রেক্ষা *n.* (rhet.) a figure of speech akin to simile and sustained metaphor in which it seems as if one thing has been transposed to another, a comparison introduced by 'as if', 'as though' etc.; guess, surmise; supposition; doubt.

উৎফুল্ল *a.* blooming; highly delighted or exultant.

উতরাই *n.* a descent of a mountain or hill, a slope, a mountain-side, a hill-side.

উতরানো *v.* to come down, to descend; to reach, to arrive at; to become successful, to shape, to pass a test (পরীক্ষায় উতরানো, রান্না উতরানো) ; to pass through or spend or pass (দিন উতরানো) ; to traverse (পথ বা নদী উতরানো).

উতরোল *n.* tumult, uproar, hullabaloo. □ *a.* restless, anxious ('চিত উতরোল').

উতল, উতলা *a.* anxious; worried; excited; impatient, restless (উতলা বাতাস).

উৎস *n.* a fountain, a spring; a cascade, a fall; a source. **~কূপ** *n.* an artesian well. **~মুখ** *n.* a fountain-head; a source.

উৎসঙ্গ *n.* the fold of the body of a person sitting, lap; a tableland, a plateau.

উৎসন্ন *a.* perished; destroyed; ruined; utterly depraved, gone to the bad, gone to the dogs; evicted. **উৎসন্ন করা** *v.* to destroy; to ruin; to evict. **উৎসন্নে দেওয়া** *v.* to ruin; to deprave; to evict. **উৎসন্নে যাওয়া** *v.* to be ruined; to go to the dogs, to go to the bad.

উৎসব *n.* a festival; a fête; a fiesta; festivity; ceremony. **উৎসব করা, উৎসব পালন**

করা *v.* to hold a festival. ~মুখর *a.* festive and gay.

উৎসর্গ *n.* ritual or religious offering; sacrifice; dedication; gift or foundation for public welfare; ejection, relieving oneself of, letting out (পুরীষোৎসর্গ). **জীবন উৎসর্গ করা** *v.* to sacrifice or dedicate one's life. **পুকুর উৎসর্গ করা** *v.* to dig a tank for public welfare. **পুস্তক উৎসর্গ করা** *v.* to dedicate a book. **উৎসর্গীকৃত** *a.* offered; sacrificed; dedicated; given or founded for public welfare.

উৎসর্জক *a.* & *n.* one who relinquishes or sacrifices or dedicates or gives in charity.

উৎসর্জন *n.* relinquishment; sacrifice; dedication; act of giving in charity; charitable gift. **উৎসর্জন করা** *v.* to relinquish; to sacrifice; to dedicate; to give in charity. ~**মূলক** *a.* dedicatory.

উৎসাদন *n.* extirpation, eradication; destruction; eviction, ejection; removal. **উৎসাদন করা** *v.* to uproot, to extirpate, to eradicate; to destroy; to evict, to eject; to remove. **উৎসাদনীয়** *a.* that which or one who is to be or can be eradicated or destroyed or evicted or ejected or removed.

উৎসাদিত *a.* uprooted, extirpated, eradicated; destroyed; evicted, ejected; removed.

উৎসার, উৎসারণ *n.* removal; act of throwing up or driving upwards. **উৎসারণীয়** *a.* that which or one who is to be or can be removed; that which is to be or can be thrown up or driven upwards.

উৎসারিত *a.* removed; thrown up; driven upwards. *fem.* **উৎসারিতা** ৷

উৎসাহ *n.* zeal, ardour, enthusiasm; impetus; encouragement; perseverance; interest. **উৎসাহ দেওয়া** *v.* to encourage; to enthuse. ~**ক**, ~**দায়ক** *a.* one who encourages or inspires; encouraging; enthusiastic. *fem.* ~**দায়িনী** ৷ ~**দাতা** *n.* an encourager. *fem.* ~**দাত্রী** ৷ ~**ন** *n.* encouragement; act of enthusing. **উৎসাহনীয়** *a.* worthy of being encouraged, deserving encouragement. ~**বৃদ্ধি** *n.* increase of enthusiasm or energy. ~**ভঙ্গ** *n.* loss of enthusiasm; callousness. ~**সহকারে** *adv.* enthusiastically, zealously. **উৎসাহিত** *a.* encouraged; enthused. *fem.* **উৎসাহিতা** ৷ **উৎসাহী** *a.* zealous, enthusiastic; persevering; energetic.

উৎসিক্ত *a.* besprinkled with water; proud; arrogant, haughty.

উৎসুক *a.* eager.

উৎসৃষ্ট *a.* forsaken, abandoned; sacrificed; dedicated; given; given as a present, presented; applied.

উৎসেক, উৎসেচন *n.* act of besprinkling with water; incitation, incitement, excitation, excitement. **উৎসেচন করা** *v.* to besprinkle with water; to incite, to excite. **উৎসেচনক্রিয়া** *n.* fermentation.

উৎসেচক *n.* enzyme.

উৎসেধ *n.* altitude, height.

উত্তপ্ত *a.* extremely hot or heated; excited; extremely angry or enraged.

উত্তম *a.* (also *adv.*) very good; excellent; best; fine; delicious. ~**পুরুষ** *n.* (gr.) the first person. ~**মধ্যম** *n.* (facet.) a sound drubbing. **উত্তমমধ্যম দেওয়া** *v.* to beat or drub soundly, to give a sound drubbing, to larrup or whack.

উত্তমর্ণ *n.* a creditor; a money-lender.

উত্তমা *fem.* of **উত্তম** ৷

উত্তমাঙ্গ *n.* the principal part of the body; the head; the part of the body from the head to the waist, the upper part of the body.

উত্তমাশা অন্তরীপ *n.* the Cape of Good Hope.

উত্তর *n.* an answer, a reply; a retort, a counter; response; reaction; a rejoinder, refutation or objection; solution; conclusion; the north. ☐ *a.* future, later, post- (উত্তরপুরুষ, উত্তরকাল, যুদ্ধোত্তর) ; upper (উত্তরচ্ছদ) ; northern. **উত্তর করা** *v.* to retort; to answer; to respond, to react; to come to a solution. **উত্তর দেওয়া** *v.* to answer, to reply; to respond. **উত্তর অয়নান্ত** *n.* summer solstice. ~**কাল** *n.* the future; posterity; the coming age or ages. ~**ক্রিয়া** *n.* annual obsequies; act of answering or responding or reacting. **উত্তরচ্ছদ** *n.* a covering; a bedsheet, a bedcover; a scarf; a garment of the upper part of the body. ~দান *n.* act of answering or responding or retorting. ~দায়ক *a.* & *n.* one who answers or responds or retorts. ~পক্ষ *n.* a solution of a problem; an answer to a question. ~পত্র *n.* a book containing an examinee's written answers, answer scripts. ~পশ্চিম *n.* & *a.* north-west. □ *a.* north-western. ~পুরুষ *n.* posterity; successor. ~পূর্ব *n.* & *a.* north-east. ~প্রত্যুত্তর *n.* bandying of words, argument and counter-argument. ~ফল্গুনী, ~ফাল্গুনী *n.* the twelfth of the twenty-seven zodiacal stars according to Hindu astronomy. ~বিচার *n.* (law) an appeal. ~ভাদ্রপদ *n.* the twenty-sixth of the twenty-seven zodiacal stars according to Hindu astronomy, the Andromeda. ~মালা *n.* a list of answers or solutions. ~মীমাংসা *n.* Vedanta (বেদান্ত). ~মেরু see মেরু। ~যোগ্য *a.* fit to be answered, answerable. ~সাধক *a.* assisting (esp. in the religious practices) according to the Tantras (তন্ত্র). □ *n.* a chief assistant; poets or scholars of a late age. *fem.* উত্তরসাধিকা। ~সূরি *n.* wise men or scholars of a later age; people of a later age. ~হিমমণ্ডল *n.* north frigid zone.

উত্তরঙ্গ *a.* full of waves, billowy.

উত্তরণ *n.* crossing or passing over; arrival; going upwards or climbing, ascension; promotion; (loos.) landing or alighting. ~স্থান *n.* a landing place, a landing ground.

উত্তরাখণ্ড var. of **উত্তরাপথ**।

উত্তরাধিকার *n.* right of succession, inheritance. ~পত্র *n.* a succession certificate. ~সূত্রে *adv.* by way of inheritance, as a hereditary right. **উত্তরাধিকারী** *n.* a successor, an heir, an inheritor. *fem.* **উত্তরাধিকারিণী**।

উত্তরাপথ *n.* the part of India lying between the Himalayas and the Vindhyas; Northern India, Upper India.

উত্তরায়ণ *n.* (astr. & geog.) the summer solstice. **উত্তরায়ণান্তবৃত্ত** *n.* the Tropic of Cancer.

উত্তরাশা[1] *n.* the north.

উত্তরাশা[2] *n.* hope of receiving a reply or response.

উত্তরাষাঢ়া *n.* the twenty-first of the twenty-seven zodiacal stars according to Hindu astronomy.

উত্তরাস্য *a.* facing the north.

উত্তরীয় *n.* a scarf, a modesty scarf, (cp.) a stole.

উত্তরোত্তর *adv.* successively; one after another; gradually, by degrees; more and more.

উত্তল *a.* convex. ~তা *n.* convexity. ~দর্পণ a convex mirror.

উত্তান *a.* lying or sitting or situated with the face upturned; lying flat on one's back, supine.

উত্তাপ *n.* heat; warmth; ardour, zeal; excitement; anger. **উত্তাপিত** *a.* heated; warmed-up; excited; angered. **উত্তাপিত করা** *v.* to heat; to warm up; to excite; to anger. ~সহ *a.* heatproof.

উত্তাল *a.* very high (উত্তাল তরঙ্গ) ; billowy (উত্তাল সমুদ্র) ; monstrous; extremely agitated (উত্তাল হৃদয়).

উত্তিষ্ঠমান *a.* endeavouring to rise, rising; enterprising; flourishing, prospering.

উত্তীর্ণ *a.* one who has passed over or crossed or got over or spent; that which has been passed over or crossed or elapsed; successful (উত্তীর্ণ পরীক্ষার্থী) ; escaped (বিপদ থেকে উত্তীর্ণ). **উত্তীর্ণ করা** *v.* to spend (সময় উত্তীর্ণ করা). **উত্তীর্ণ হওয়া** *v.* to pass over, to cross; to get over, to elapse, to be over or up (সময় উত্তীর্ণ হওয়া) ; to be successful (in), to pass (পরীক্ষায় উত্তীর্ণ হওয়া) ; to escape, to get rid of.

উত্তুঙ্গ *a.* very high or tall, lofty.

উত্তুরে *a.* in or of or coming from the north; northerly (উত্তুরে হাওয়া) ; northern.

উত্তেজক *a.* encouraging; inciting, exciting; instigating; provocative; agitating; stimulating, stimulant; developing, accelerating; quickening.

উত্তেজন, উত্তেজনা *n.* encouragement, incitation, incitement, excitation, excitement; instigation; provocation; agitation, stimulation, development, acceleration; quickening. **চাপা উত্তেজনা** tension. **উত্তেজনা-সৃষ্টিকারী** *n.* one who incites or stirs up discontent or trouble, a trouble-maker.

উত্তেজিত *a.* encouraged, incited, excited; instigated; provoked, wrought-up; agitated; stimulated; developed; accelerated; quickened. **উত্তেজিত করা** *v.* to encourage, to incite, to excite; to instigate; to provoke; to agitate; to stimulate; to develop, to accelerate; to quicken. **উত্তেজিত হওয়া** *v.* to be excited or incited.

উত্তোলক *a.* one who or that which raises or lifts or hauls or heaves. **~যন্ত্র** *n.* a lever.

উত্তোলন *n.* act of raising or lifting or hauling or heaving. **উত্তোলন করা** *v.* to raise, to lift, to haul, to heave.

উত্তোলিত *a.* raised, lifted, hauled, heaved. **উত্তোলিত করা** same as **উত্তোলন করা।**

উত্ত্যক্ত *a.* extremely annoyed or vexed or disgusted or harassed or made restless.

উত্থ *a.* risen (from) (সমুদ্রোত্থ) ; produced (from), born (of) (কুলোত্থ).

উত্থান *n.* getting up; rise; flourishing; appearing (esp. suddenly and for the first time); emergence; insurgence, a rebellion. **~পতন** *n.* rise and fall; flourishing and downfall; undulation; increase and decrease; (comm.—of markets) boom and slump, fluctuation.

উত্থানশক্তিরহিত, উত্থানশক্তিহীন *a.* having no strength to get up or rise; unable to rise; bed-ridden.

উত্থাপক *a.* & *n.* one who raises; one who brings forward or moves or proposes; mover; one who mentions.

উত্থাপন *n.* raising; bringing forward or moving or proposing; mention. **উত্থাপন করা** *v.* to raise; to bring forward, to move; to propose; to mention. **উত্থাপন হওয়া** *v.* to be raised; to be brought forward or moved or proposed; to be mentioned. **উত্থাপনীয়** *a.* that which is to be or can be raised or moved or brought forward or proposed or mentioned.

উত্থাপিত *a.* raised; moved, brought forward; proposed; mentioned.

উত্থিত *a.* one who has got up; risen; raised; rising; rising out (of); grown; produced; born; elevated; flourished; risen in rebellion; opposing. **উত্থিত হওয়া** *v.* to get up; to rise; to rise out (of); to grow; to be produced; to be born; to be elevated; to flourish; to rise in rebellion, to revolt; to stand in opposition, to oppose. **উত্থিতি** *n.* getting up; rising; rising out (of) or growing or being produced or being born; state of being elevated, elevation; flourish; rising in rebellion; standing in opposition.

উথল, উথাল *a.* surging up, swelling up; overflowing; very high (উথল ঢেউ) ; billowy (উথল সমুদ্র). **উথলানো** *v.* to surge up, to swell up; to overflow. **উথালপাথাল** *a.* topsy-turvy, rising and falling rapidly. **উথলিত** *a.* surged up, swollen; surging up, swelling up; overflowing; overflowed.

উদ[1] *n.* the otter.

উদ্[2] var. of **উৎ।**

উদক, উদ[3] *n.* water. **উদকুম্ভ** *n.* a pitcher full of water, a water-jar.

উদক *n.* the north; northern part of country. □ *a.* northern; northward.

উদগ্র *a.* severe; very strong (উদগ্র বাসনা) ; monstrous; extreme (উদগ্র রাজনীতি) ; facing upwards; upturned; very tall or high or elevated; arrogant, haughty.

উদ্‌গ্রীব *a.* extremely eager; full of curiosity; in suspense; anxious.

উদজ *a.* water-born, aquatic.

উদজান *n.* hydrogen.

উদধি *n.* an ocean; a sea; a bay.

উদ্‌ভ্রান্ত *a.* agitated; confused, embarrassed, perplexed; distracted; demented, maddened; mad; stupefied; loitering aimlessly or in a disorderly manner. **~চিত্ত, ~হৃদয়** *a.* one whose mind or heart is agitated or embarrassed or distracted. **~ভাবে** *adv.* in a confused state; distractedly; wildly, in a bewildered manner.

উদম var. of **উদোম।**

উদ্‌যাপন *n.* observance (of a rite, ceremony, etc.), execution or accomplishment (of a task etc.) **উদ্‌যাপন করা** *v.* to observe; to execute, to accomplish. **উদ্‌যাপিত** *a.* observed; executed; accomplished.

উদয় *n.* dawn; rise (সূর্যোদয়) ; sunrise (উদয়াস্ত) ; flourishing; (first) appearance or coming into view (মেঘোদয়) ; a debut; coming into existence; stirring, first sensation (ক্ষুধার উদয়) ; dawning (আশার উদয়) ; awakening (জাতির উদয়). **~কাল** *n.* the time of sunrise. **~গিরি, উদয়াচল** *n.* (myth.) a mountain from the top of which the sun rises every morning; a hill in Orissa. **উদয়াস্ত** *n.* the time from sunrise to sunset; the whole day; sunrise and sunset; (fig.) rise and fall. □ *adv.* from sunrise to sunset; all day long. **উদয়োন্মুখ** *a.* on the point of rising; on the point of flourishing.

উদর *n.* the belly; (loos.) the stomach; the abdomen; womb; the inside (পর্বতোদরে). **~পরায়ণ, ~সর্বস্ব** *a.* given to too much eating or interested in eating only; voracious, gluttonous. **~পরায়ণতা** *n.* gluttony, voracity. **~পূর্তি** *n.* filling the stomach with foodstuff. **~সর্বস্ব ব্যক্তি** a belly-god. **~পীড়া** *n.* diarrhoea; disorder or ailment of the stomach. **~ভঙ্গ** *n.* strong diarrhoea. **~সাৎ** *a.* eaten; swallowed; appropriated; consumed. **উদরসাৎ করা** *v.* to eat up. **~স্থ** *a.* received in the belly or stomach; eaten; swallowed; lying in the belly or stomach. **উদরস্থ করা** *v.* to swallow. **উদরস্থ থাকা** *v.* to lie or remain in the belly or stomach; to be accepted by the stomach. **উদরান্ন** *n.* food; indispensable food; a living, livelihood. **উদরান্ন জোগাড় করা, উদরান্নের সংস্থান করা** to find food; to earn a living; to earn (one's) bread. **উদরাময়** *n.* diarrhoea. **উদরী** *n.* dropsy.

উদলা *a.* uncovered, bare; naked.

উদস্থিতিবিদ্যা *n.* hydrostatics.

উদাত্ত *n.* (esp. in music) a high and deep tone, (cp.) baritone. □ *a.* in or using this tone; high, noble (উদাত্ত চরিত্র).

উদান *n.* one of the five vital winds prevalent within the human body (উদান lies in the throat).

উদাবর্ত *n.* inversion of one portion of intestine within another, intussusception.

উদাম *a.* uncontrollable, indomitable; violent; unrestrained; unbounded; free; open; reckless; wayward; uncovered, bare; naked; very naughty.

উদার *a.* high, lofty; noble; liberal; charitable, generous, munificent; magnanimous; kind; open-hearted; free from narrowness. **উদার আকাশ** the high (and open or free) sky. **~চরিত্র, ~প্রকৃতি, ~স্বভাব** *a.* noble-charactered, noble-natured; noble; liberal; magnanimous; lofty. **~চেতা, ~মতি, ~মনা, ~হৃদয়** *a.* noble-minded, high-souled, noble-hearted; noble; liberal; magnanimous; open-hearted. **~তা** *n.* loftiness; nobleness; liberality; charitableness, generosity, munificence; magnanimity; kindness; freedom from narrowness. **~নীতি** *n.* (chiefly pol.) liberalism. **~নীতিক, ~নৈতিক** *a.* liberal. **~পন্থী** same as **উদারনৈতিক**।

উদারা *n.* (mus.) the scale of deepest tone, (cp.) bass.

উদাস *n.* indifference, disinterestedness, unconcern, callousness, stoicism; (rare) indifference to worldly interests. □ *a.* indifferent to worldly interests; indifferent, disinterested, callous; languid, spiritless; stoical, distracted; seedy or listless (উদাস মূর্তি). **উদাসিনী** *fem.* of **উদাসী** and **উদাসীন**। **উদাসী** *a.* indifferent to worldly interests; callous, stoical; pococurante. □ *n.* one belonging to an order of ascetics who are indifferent to worldly interests or practise stoicism; a pococurante. **উদাসীন** *a.* disinterested, unattached; unaffected, unperturbed; callous; stoical; indifferent to worldly interests; pococurante; practising stoical asceticism. **উদাসীনতা** *n.* disinterestedness, aloofness; freedom from affection or perturbation; callousness; stoicism; indifference to worldly interests; pococurantism; practice of stoical asceticism.

উদাহরণ *n.* an example, an instance; a precedent; an illustration. **উদাহরণ দেওয়া** *v.* to cite an example, to exemplify; to give an instance; to quote a precedent; to illustrate. ~স্বরূপ *adv.* (as)for example, (as) for instance. ☐ *a.* exemplary; precedential; illustrative.

উদাহৃত *a.* cited as an example, mentioned (esp. as a precedent).

উদিত *a.* risen; risen up; ascended; grown, born; revealed; flourished; appeared (esp. suddenly and for the first time). **উদিত হওয়া** *v.* to rise; to rise up, to come up; to ascend; to grow, to be born; to be revealed; to flourish; to appear.

উদীচী *n.* the north. **উদীচী উষা** the aurora borealis. **উদীচীন, উদীচ্য** *a.* northern; lying in the north.

উদীয়মান *a.* rising, ascending; flourishing; up and coming.

উদীরণ *n.* pronouncing, speaking. **উদীরিত** *a.* pronounced, spoken, uttered.

উদীর্ণ *a.* risen; emanated.

উদুম্বর *n.* the wild fig or its tree.

উদূখল *n.* a mortar for grinding or husking corn.

উদো *a.* dull-witted, stupid. ☐ *n.* a dullard, a booby. **উদোর পিণ্ডি বুধোর ঘাড়ে** one doth the scath and another hath the scorn, penalization or condemnation of a wrong man, making a scapegoat of.

উদোম *a.* naked; open; uncovered.

উদোমাদা *a.* stupid and careless.

উদ্গত *a.* born, produced, grown; emanated; issued; risen; risen up; sprouted. **উদ্গত হওয়া** *v.* to be born or produced, to grow; to emanate; to issue; to rise, to rise up, to come out or up; to sprout.

উদ্গম *n.* birth, production, growth; emanation; issue; rise; a rising up; sprouting.

উদ্গাতা *n.* a singer of the Sama Veda; (fig.) an exponent. ☐ *a.* singing in a loud voice; (fig.) announcing or preaching in a loud voice, exponent (of) (মুক্তিমন্ত্রের উদ্গাতা). *fem.* **উদ্গাত্রী** ।

উদ্গার *n.* a belch, eructation; a hiccup; vomiting; ejection (ধূম্রোদ্গার). **উদ্গার তোলা** *v.* to belch, to eruct, to eructate; to hiccup; to vomit; to eject.

উদ্গিরণ *n.* eructation, belching; vomiting; disgorgement; ejection; (usu. facet.) utterance. **উদ্গিরণ করা** to eruct, to eructate, to belch; to vomit; to disgorge; to eject; (usu. facet.) to utter.

উদ্গীত *a.* sung in a loud voice; (fig.) announced or preached in a loud voice. **উদ্গীতি** *n.* singing in a loud voice; (fig.) announcement or preaching in a loud voice.

উদ্গীথ *n.* a part of the Sama Veda containing hymns and songs; chanting of the Sama Veda.

উদ্গীর্ণ *a.* eructed, eructated, belched out; vomited; disgorged; ejected; (facet.) uttered.

উদ্ঘাটক *a.* one who or that which uncovers or opens or unbolts or unlocks or reveals or discovers.

উদ্ঘাটন *n.* uncovering or opening or unbolting or unlocking; revelation; discovery. **উদ্ঘাটন করা** *v.* to uncover; to open; to unbolt, to unlock; to reveal; to discover; to bring to light.

উদ্ঘাটিত *a.* uncovered; laid bare; opened; unbolted, unlocked; revealed; discovered; brought to light.

উদ্ঘাত *n.* undulation, ruggedness; a blow, a stroke; a mallet; a device for drawing water from a well, a pulley; a chapter or section of a book; allusion, reference.

উদ্ঘাতন *n.* (arith.) involution.

উদ্ঘোষণা *n.* proclamation.

উদ্দংশ *n.* a louse; a gadfly; a species of mosquito.

উদ্দণ্ড *n.* a raised staff; a raised sceptre; a punishment about to be inflicted, (cp.) the sword of Damocles. ☐ *a.* holding a raised staff or sceptre; holding a hideous staff or sceptre; ready to punish; uncontrollable; powerful.

উদ্দাম *a.* indomitable; uncontrollable, intractable; violent; lacking in discipline; impetuous; unrestrained, unbounded, uncontrolled; self-willed, wayward; reckless. ~তা *n.* indomitableness; violence; indiscipline; impetuosity; lack of restraint or control, intractableness; waywardness; recklessness.

উদ্দিষ্ট *a.* alluded (to); directed (towards); aimed (at); intended, desired; addressed (to); traced, found out. **উদ্দিষ্ট অর্থ** *n.* the desired meaning. **উদ্দিষ্ট স্থান** *n.* the desired place.

উদ্দীপক *a.* enkindling; inciting; inspiring; incentive; encouraging; animating; manifesting; developing; provoking (হাস্যোদ্দীপক). **উদ্দীপক বস্তু** an incentive.

উদ্দীপন *n.* act of enkindling; incitation; act of inspiring or encouragement; animation; manifestation; development.

উদ্দীপনা *n.* incitement; an inspiration; an incentive; encouragement; animus; impetus; enthusiasm, exuberance. **উদ্দীপনীয়** *a.* that which should be or can be enkindled or incited or inspired or given an incentive or encouraged or animated or manifested or developed.

উদ্দীপিত *a.* enkindled, incited, excited; animated; manifested; developed. **উদ্দীপিত করা** *v.* to enkindle; to incite or excite; to animate; to manifest; to develop.

উদ্দীপ্ত *a.* inflamed, blazing, flared up; enkindled; illuminated; incited, excited; animated; made or become violent; impassioned; manifested. **উদ্দীপ্ত করা** *v.* to inflame, to flare up; to enkindle; to illumine or illuminate; to incite or excite; to animate; to make violent or impassioned; to manifest.

উদ্দেশ *n.* aim, direction (উদ্দেশে বলা) ; search for (উদ্দেশ করা) ; trace (উদ্দেশ পাওয়া) ; intention, purpose (কী উদ্দেশে) ; information, news (উদ্দেশ নেওয়া) ; whereabouts or address (উদ্দেশ জানা নেই). **উদ্দেশক** *a.* aiming; directing; searching; intending; inquiring.

উদ্দেশ্য *a.* aimed (at); searched; intended; addressed, spoken to. □ *n.* an intention or purpose; a design; an object or end; a motive (বিনা উদ্দেশ্যে) ; (gr—to a sentence) a subject. **~মূলক** *a.* (chiefly dero.) motivated. **~হীন** *a.* motiveless; purposeless; aimless.

উদ্ধত *a.* rude; insolent; impudent; saucy; haughty, arrogant, bumptious, high and mighty; formidable; proud, vainglorious, stuck-up; obstinate, headstrong.

উদ্ধরণ *n.* act of rescuing; act of lifting or reclaiming; quotation from a writing etc. **~চিহ্ন** *n.* quotation-marks (" ").

উদ্ধার *n.* rescue, deliverance (উদ্ধারলাভ) ; uplift, emancipation (পতিতোদ্ধার) ; reclamation, development (লুপ্তোদ্ধার) ; recovery (স্বাস্থ্যোদ্ধার) ; removal esp. by extracting or lifting (কণ্টকোদ্ধার, পঙ্কোদ্ধার) ; a quotation from a writing etc. **উদ্ধার করা** *v.* to rescue, to deliver; to uplift, to emancipate; to reclaim, to develop; to recover; to remove (esp. by extracting or lifting); to quote from a writing etc.). **~ক, ~কর্তা, ~কারী** *n.* a rescuer, a deliverer, a saviour ; an uplifter, an emancipator; a reclaimer; a recoverer; a remover; one who quotes. **~কার্য** *n.* rescue work; rescue operation. **~চিহ্ন** *n.* (gr.) quotation marks, inverted commas (" " or ' '). **উদ্ধার পাওয়া, উদ্ধার লাভ করা** *v.* to be rid of an awkward or difficult situation; to be rescued; to be saved. **~ভবন** *n.* a rescue-home. **উদ্ধারাশ্রম** *n.* a home or camp for homeless or rescued persons; a rescue-home.

উদ্ধৃত *a.* quoted (from a writing etc.). **উদ্ধৃতাংশ** *n.* a passage quoted from a writing etc., an excerpt, an extract. **উদ্ধৃতি** *n.* that which is quoted; a quotation (from a writing etc.)

উদ্ধৃতিচিহ্ন *n.* quotation marks.

উদ্বন্ধন *n.* hanging by the halter (for killing or self-killing). **~রজ্জু** *n.* a halter for hanging, a hangmans's rope. **উদ্বন্ধনে মরা** *v.* to die by hanging.

উদ্বমন *n.* vomiting or retching; disgorgement, ejection.

উদ্বর্ত *n.* & *a.* surplus, excess.

উদ্বর্তন[1] *n.* upliftment, uplift; development; progress; survival. **যোগ্যতমের উদ্বর্তন** survival of the fittest.

উদ্বর্তন[2] *n.* act of anointing with perfumes; perfume for anointing; massage.

উদ্বর্তিত *a.* uplifted; developed; survived; anointed with perfumes; (of muscles, joints etc.) rubbed or kneaded.

উদ্বায়ী *a.* volatile. **উদ্বায়িতা** *n.* volatileness or volatility; the property of evaporating rapidly.

উদ্বাসন *n.* abandonment; abandoning one's country; evacuation; banishment.

উদ্বাস্তু *n.* a refugee, an evacuee; a piece of adjoining land in front of a homestead; a deserted or evacuated homestead. □ *a.* one who has evacuated. **উদ্বাস্তু পুনর্বাসন** *n.* refugee rehabilitation. **উদ্বাস্তু সমস্যা** *n.* refugee problem.

উদ্বাহ *n.* marriage, wedding, bridal. **~ন** *n.* act of giving in marriage. **উদ্বাহিত** *a.* married, wedded. **উদ্বাহী** *a.* one who marries, marrying; one who wishes to or is going to marry.

উদ্বাহু *a.* one who has raised one's arms upwards; one with arms raised upwards.

উদ্বিগ্ন *a.* worried; concerned, anxious.

উদ্বিড়াল *n.* the otter.

উদ্বিন্দু *n.* ascending node.

উদ্বুদ্ধ *a.* made wise, enlightened; awakened; inspired; reanimated.

উদ্বৃত্ত *a.* surplus; excess.

উদ্বেগ *n.* worry, concern; anxiety; suspense. **~হীন, ~শূন্য** *a.* unworried, without anxiety.

উদ্বেজক *a.* causing anxiety or concern; worrying.

উদ্বেজন *n.* act of causing anxiety or concern; act of worrying; worry, concern; anxiety; suspense.

উদ্বেজিত *a.* worried; harried; stricken with anxiety.

উদ্বেল, উদ্বেলিত *a.* washing or inundating the bank or shore; overflowing; swollen; overwhelmed; seized with (anxiety); brimming with (emotion).

উদ্বোধ *n.* awakening of knowledge in one's mind, enlightenment; recollection. **~ক** *a.* & *n.* (of) one who or that which enlightens or awakens knowledge (in); (of) one who or that which incites or excites or inspires; (of) one who or that which enkindles; (of) one who or that which brings back to mind. **~ন** *n.* act of awakening knowledge (in), enlightenment; awakening; commencement or inauguration or opening. **উদ্বোধন বা উদ্বোধনী সংগীত** an opening song.

উদ্ব্যক্ত *a.* expressed with an emphasis, emphatic. **উদ্ব্যক্তি** *n.* emphasis.

উদ্ভট *a.* good and popular or traditional but of unknown authorship (উদ্ভট কবিতা) ; not included in any book, unwritten (উদ্ভট শ্লোক) ; (pop.) queer, odd, quaint (উদ্ভট কাণ্ড) ; bizarre, fantastic (উদ্ভট কল্পনা). **উদ্ভুট্টি, উদ্ভুট্টি** *a.* queer, odd, quaint, grotesque, fantastic; unheard-of; strange, outlandish. □ *n.* a strange or quaint thing.

উদ্ভব *n.* origination, origin; birth; act of coming into existence or being. □ *a.* originating (from);born (of or in) (উচ্চ কুলোদ্ভব).

উদ্ভাবক *a.* inventing, inventive; creating; creative; devising or designing. □ *n.* an inventor; a creator; a deviser, a contriver.

উদ্ভাবন *n.* invention; creation; act of devising or designing, excogitation. **উদ্ভাবন করা** *v.* to invent; to create; to devise or design, (often humorously) to excogitate. **উদ্ভাবনী** *a.* inventive; imaginative. **উদ্ভাবনীয়** same as **উদ্ভাব্য** ।

উদ্ভাবিত *a.* invented; created; devised or designed, excogitated.

উদ্ভাব্য *a.* (of) that which can be or is to be invented or created or devised or designed or excogitated.

উদ্ভাস *a.* manifestation, exposition; glow; shine; beautiful appearance or show. **~ক** *a.* illuminant, illuminative, illuminating; brightening; manifesting, expressing. **~ন** *n.* illumination; act of brightening (up); manifestation, exposition. **উদ্ভাসিত** *a.* illumined, illuminated; brightened (up); manifested, exposed; expounded. **উদ্ভাসিত করা** *v.* to illuminate; to brighten up; to manifest, to expose; to expound.

উদ্ভিজ্জ *n.* that which grows up from under the surface of the ground, a plant or vegetable. □ *a.* produced or derived from a plant, vegetable. **উদ্ভিজ্জ তেল** *n.* vegetable oil. **উদ্ভিজ্জাণু** *n.* a plant or vegetable that cannot be discerned with the naked eye, a microscopic plant or vegetable, a micro-organism. উদ্ভিজ্জাশী *a.* vegetarian. □ *n.* a vegetarian.

উদ্ভিদ *n.* a plant or tree or vegetable or herb etc. that grows up from under the surface of the ground. **~কুল** *n.* the flora. **~তত্ত্ব, ~বিজ্ঞান, ~বিদ্যা** *n.* botany. **~তাত্ত্বিক, ~বিজ্ঞানী, ~বিৎ** *n.* a botanist. **~ভোজী** *n.* herbivorous. **~সর্গ** *n.* the plant kingdom. **উদ্ভিদণু,** (inc.) **উদ্ভিদাণু** same as **উদ্ভিজ্জাণু** (see **উদ্ভিজ্জ**) ।

উদ্ভিন্ন *a.* germinated or germinating; sprouted or sprouting; manifested or becoming manifest; grown up or growing up from under the surface of the ground. **উদ্ভিন্ন হওয়া** *v.* to germinate; to sprout; to become manifest; to grow up from under the surface of the ground. **~যৌবনা** *a. fem.* (of a girl) in the bloom of youth, in the first flush or glow of youth.

উদ্ভূত *a.* produced, born; manifested, revealed, appearing to the view; risen; evolved. *fem.* **উদ্ভূতা** । **উদ্ভূত হওয়া** *v.* to be produced or born; to come into existence; to be manifested or revealed, to come into view; to rise; to evolve.

উদ্ভেদ *n.* manifestation, revelation, exposition (অর্থোদ্ভেদ) ; act of coming into view; act of blooming (পুষ্পোদ্ভেদ) ; act of sprouting (অঙ্কুরোদ্ভেদ) ; union, confluence (গঙ্গোদ্ভেদ). **উদ্ভেদী** *a.* growing up from under the surface (of the ground etc.).

উদ্যত *a.* about to, on the point of; ready, prepared; enterprising ('উদ্যত কর, জাগ্রত কর') ; raised (উদ্যত দণ্ড). *fem.* **উদ্যতা** । **উদ্যত করা** *v.* to raise; to make enterprising or energetic or active, to energize, to activize. **উদ্যত হওয়া** *v.* to be on the point of, to be about to, to be ready or prepared. **উদ্যতি** *n.* readiness, preparedness; preparations.

উদ্যম *n.* enthusiasm, earnestness; perseverance; enterprise; endeavour, effort; preparation; readiness. **~নাশ, ~ভঙ্গ** *n.* failure of enterprise or effort; waste of energy. **~শীল** *a.* enthusiastic, earnest; persevering; enterprising; energetic; preparing oneself, in the state of getting ready. **~শীলতা** *n.* enthusiasm, elan; earnestness; perseverance; drive and initiative, push and thrust. **~হানি** same as **উদ্যমনাশ** । **~হীন, নিরুদ্যম** *a.* lacking in enterprise, unenterprising; unenthusiastic; lethargic; unpersevering.

উদ্যমী *a.* enthusiastic, persevering; enterprising. **উদ্যমী হওয়া** *v.* to make an enterprise or effort; to persevere.

উদ্যান *n.* a garden; a grove; a greenhouse; a park. **~পাল, ~পালক** *n.* a keeper or caretaker of a garden, a gardener; a horticulturist. **~পালন** *n.* gardening; horticulture. **~বাটি, ~বাটিকা** *n.* a gardenhouse; a villa. **~বিদ্যা** *n.* horticulture; gardening. **~বীথি** *n.* a garden-path. **~রক্ষক** *n.* one who looks after a garden, a gardener. **~সম্মেলন** *n.* a garden party.

উদ্যুক্ত *a.* enterprising; endeavouring; persevering; making preparations.

উদ্যোক্তা *a.* & *n.* one who makes preparations for or gets ready for; one who undertakes an enterprise; one who is on the point of undertaking or is about to undertake.

উদ্যোগ *n.* act or state of being on the point of; preparation; endeavour, effort; enterprise; assiduity; industry. **উদ্যোগ করা বা নেওয়া** *v.* to be on the point of; to make preparations, to get ready; to endeavour; to (be about to) undertake an enterprise. **উদ্যোগী** *a.* enterprising; endeavouring; assiduous; on the point of, ready (for). **উদ্যোগী হওয়া** *v.* to be on the point of, to get ready for; to undertake an enterprise; to endeavour; to be assiduous; to come forward; to take the initiative.

উদ্র *n.* the otter.

উদ্রথ *n.* the pin of the axle of a chariot or carriage; a cock.

উদ্রাব *n.* loud noise or report.

উদ্রিক্ত *a.* incited, excited; roused.

উদ্রেক *n.* incitement, excitement; rousing. **উদ্রিক্ত করা** *v.* to incite, to excite, to rouse. **উদ্রিক্ত হওয়া** *v.* to be incited or excited or roused. **ক্ষুধার উদ্রেক হওয়া** to feel hungry.

উধাও *n.* act of flying through the air, flight. □ *a.* vanished; missing; passed out of sight ('উধাও উধাও সুদূর আকাশে পক্ষিরাজ'). **উধাও হওয়া** *v.* to disappear, to vanish; to be missing; to pass out of sight.

উধো var. of **উদো**।

উন alt. spell. of **ঊন**।

উনচল্লিশ, উনত্রিশ see **ঊন**।

উনন dial. var. of **উনান**।

উননব্বই see **ঊন**।

উনপাঁজুরে *a.* unfortunate, wretched; extremely weak, rickety.

উনবিংশ see **ঊন**।

উনা var. of **ঊন**।

উনাশি *a.* & *n.* (coll.) seventy-nine.

উনি *pro.* (hon.) that person, he or she.

উনিশ *a.* & *n.* nineteen. **উনিশ-বিশ** *n.* slight or negligible or insignificant difference; hair-splitting difference; partiality. **উনিশ-বিশ করা** *v.* to treat with partiality; to make a slight difference. **উনিশ-বিশ হওয়া** *v.* to differ slightly. **উনিশে** *n.* the nineteenth day of a month. □ *a.* (of days of a month) nineteenth.

উনুন, উনান *n.* an oven, a furnace; a stove. **উনুনে আঁচ দেওয়া, উনুন ধরানো** *v.* to light the oven, to make a fire.

উনো বর্ষা দুনো শীত the less rain, the more cold; the year in which rainfall is insufficient is doubly cold. **উনো ভাতে দুনো বল** eat less and gain more strength.

উন্নত *a.* prosperous, wealthy, well-to-do (উন্নত অবস্থা) ; fortunate; flourishing; ameliorated, improved; advanced, progressed; uplifted; high, tall, lofty; elevated; raised; great; noble. **উন্নত করা** *v.* to raise, to elevate; to develop, to uplift. **~চরিত্র** *a.* possessing a noble character. **~দেহ** *a.* possessing a tall body. **~মনা** *a.* high-minded, high-souled. **~মস্তক** *a.* holding one's head high; unbending, unyielding; dignified. **~শির** *a.* same as **উন্নতমস্তক**। **উন্নত সমাজ** high society, the upper class; cultured society; progressive society; the well-to-do class. **উন্নত সম্প্রদায়** an advanced community. **~হৃদয়** same as **উন্নতমনা**।

উন্নতি *n.* prosperity; good fortune; flourish; amelioration, improvement, advancement; progress; uplift; promotion; development; tallness; loftiness; elevatedness; (geom. geol.) rise, height, altitude, elevation; greatness, nobleness. **উন্নতি করা, ~সাধন করা** *v.* to prosper or cause to prosper; to flourish or cause to flourish; to improve; to advance or cause to advance, to progress or cause to progress; to get promotion; to be uplifted or to uplift; to be developed or to develop; to rise or cause to rise. **উন্নতি লাভ করা** *v.* to prosper; to flourish; to improve; to advance or progress; to be uplifted or developed, to rise. **~শীল** *a.* prospering; prosperous; flourishing; improving; progressing; progressive.

উন্নদ্ধ *a.* tied and hung up, put up (উন্নদ্ধ বেণী) ; swollen.

উন্নমন *n.* act of raising or lifting up; act of bringing forward or moving (a proposal etc.); uplift, upliftment; advancement, progress; development; improvement.

উন্নমিত *a.* raised, lifted up; elevated; brought up, moved; uplifted; advanced, progressed; developed; improved.

উন্নয়ন *n.* act of raising or lifting; elevation; prosperity; flourish; amelioration; improvement; advancement, progress; uplift; development. **~-পরিকল্পনা** *n.* development plan, plan for development. **~শীল** *a.* developing. **~সাধন করা** *v.* to raise, to lift; to elevate; to cause to prosper or flourish; to ameliorate; to improve; to uplift; to develop.

উন্নাসিক *a.* treating everything and everybody disdainfully, supercilious, highbrow.

উন্নিদ্র *a.* sleepless; watchful, alert, vigilant. **উন্নিদ্রা** *n.* sleeplessness; watchfulness, alertness, vigilance.

উন্নীত *a.* raised, lifted, elevated, flourished, prospered; ameliorated; improved; advanced, promoted, progressed, uplifted; developed. **উন্নীত করা** *v.* to raise, to lift, to elevate; to cause to flourish or prosper; to ameliorate; to improve; to cause to advance or progress; to uplift, to make better, to upgrade.

উন্নেতা *a.* & *n.* one who raises or lifts or elevates; one who causes to flourish or prosper; one who ameliorates or improves; one who causes to advance or progress; one who uplifts.

উন্মগ্ন *a.* risen from underwater etc.; floating.

উন্মজ্জন *n.* act of rising from underwater etc.; act of floating.

উন্মত্ত *a.* insane, mad; crazy; maddened, demented, frenzied; excited; impassioned; frantic; furious; unreasonably attached or addicted (to); drunken, extremely intoxicated; bereft of self-possession, beside oneself; delirious. *fem.* **উন্মত্তা**। **~তা** *n.* insanity, madness; craziness; craze; dementia; frenzy; excitement; fury; furiousness; unreasonable attachment or addiction; drunkenness; extreme intoxication; loss of self-possession; deliriousness. **~প্রায়, ~বৎ** *a.* almost insane. □ *adv.* frantically; furiously.

উন্মথন *n.* thorough stir or churning; thorough kneading or thrashing or massaging; act of killing, slaughter; rout. **উন্মথন করা** *v.* to stir or churn or knead or thrash or massage thoroughly; to kill, to slay; to rout, to mop up. **উন্মথিত** *a.* stirred or churned or kneaded or thrashed or massaged thoroughly; in turmoil; killed, slain; routed; mopped up; swelling up or agitated owing to external attraction.

উন্মদ *a.* mad, insane; lunatic; maddened; frenzied. *fem.* **উন্মদা**।

উন্মনা, (poet.) **উন্মন** *a.* mentally agitated or restless; worried, anxious; absent-minded, preoccupied; listless.

উন্মন্থন, উন্মন্থ *n.* thorough stir or churning; act of killing, slaughter, rout. **উন্মন্থন করা** *v.* to stir or churn thoroughly; to kill, to slay; to rout; to mop up.

উন্মাদ *n.* insanity, madness, lunacy; dementia. □ *a.* mad, insane, lunatic, demented; frantic; violent (উন্মাদ বেগ). **উন্মাদ করা** *v.* to madden; to enrage; to excite; to divest of self-possession; to intoxicate. **উন্মাদ হওয়া** *v.* to become insane, to go mad; to become enraged; or become excited or frantic; to lose self-possession, to be beside oneself; to be intoxicated. **উন্মাদ আশ্রম** *n.* a lunatic asylum; a mental hospital. **~ক** *a.* making insane; maddening, enraging; exciting, intoxicating. **~গ্রস্ত** *a.* mad, insane. **~ন** *n.* act of making mad or insane; act of enraging or exciting; act of depriving of self possession; intoxication. □ *a.* making insane; maddening ('উন্মাদন-রূপরাশি') ; enraging; exciting; depriving of self-possession; intoxicating. **উন্মাদনা** *n.* violent excitement or agitation; great enthusiasm; mental distress. **উন্মাদাগার** same as **উন্মাদ আশ্রম**। **উন্মাদিত** *a.* maddened; enraged; excited; divested of self-possession; intoxicated, mad, insane. **উন্মাদী** *a.* mad, insane; enraged; excited; divested of self-possession; intoxicated; maddening (চিত্তোন্মাদী রূপ). *fem.* **উন্মাদিনী**।

উন্মার্গ *n.* an evil or prohibited path, a wrong course; misconduct; wrong-doing, act of committing sin(s). □ *a.* addicted to an evil or prohibited course; misbehaving; given to wrong-doing, sinning. **~গামী** same as **উন্মার্গ** (*a.*).

উন্মিষিত same as **উন্মেষিত** (see **উন্মেষ**).

উন্মীলন *n.* opening of eyes; eye-opening; opening; unfolding; blooming; exposition, manifestation. **উন্মীলন করা** *v.* to open eyes; to open; to unfold; to expose, to manifest.

উন্মীলিত *a.* open-eyed; opened; unfolded; blooming; exposed, manifested. **উন্মীলিত করা** same as **উন্মীলন করা**।

উন্মুক্ত *a.* unbolted or uncovered, open; unsheathed; released, liberated, set free; at liberty, unrestrained; unbounded; frank, candid. **উন্মুক্ত করা** *v.* to open; to unsheathe; to release, to set free. **~তা** *n.* opening, uncovering; openness. **হৃদয় উন্মুক্ত করা** *v.* to open one's heart.

উন্মুখ *a.* craned in eagerness; eagerly expectant, looking forward; anxious; on the point of, about to (গমনোন্মুখ); ready, prepared. ~তা *n.* craning (one's neck) in eagerness; eager expectancy; anxiety; state of being on the point of; readiness.

উন্মূলন *n.* extirpation, uprooting, eradication; eviction, ejection, removal; destruction, extermination. **উন্মূলন করা** *v.* to extirpate, to uproot, to eradicate; to evict, to eject, to remove; to destroy, to exterminate. **উন্মূলনীয়** *a.* eradicable; destroyable.

উন্মূলয়িতা *n.* an extirpator, an eradicator; an evictor, an ejector, a remover; a destroyer; an exterminator. *fem.* **উন্মূলয়িত্রী**।

উন্মূলিত *a.* extirpated, uprooted, eradicated; evicted, ejected, removed; destroyed, exterminated. **উন্মূলিত করা** same as **উন্মূলন করা**।

উন্মেষ, উন্মেষণ *n.* opening or unfolding; bloom; incitation, incitement; slight exposition or manifestation; rousing or state of being roused, awakening; birth (esp. embryonic). **উন্মেষিত** *a.* opened; unfolded; blooming; slightly exposed or manifested; roused, awakened; born (esp. in embryonic form). **উন্মেষিত করা** *v.* to open; to unfold; to cause to bloom; to incite, to expose or manifest slightly; to rouse, to awaken; to cause to be born (esp. in embryonic form).

উন্মোচক *n.* & *a.* one who unveils or unfolds.

উন্মোচন *n.* act of untying or uncovering or unveiling; act of setting free, release. **উন্মোচন করা** *v.* to untie; to uncover or unveil; to set free, to release.

উন্মোচিত *a.* untied, freed from bondage; uncovered or unveiled; unfolded; set free, released, liberated. **উন্মোচিত করা** same as **উন্মোচন করা**।

উপ *pfx.* expressing : nearness, adjacency, excellence, similarity, shortcoming, shortage, subordination, subjection, incompleteness, sub-, under-, etc.

উপকণ্ঠ *n.* outskirts; neighhourhood, vicinity.

উপকথা *n.* a tale; a legend; a folk tale.

উপকন্দ *n.* pseudo-bulb.

উপকর *n.* a cess.

উপকরণ *n.* an ingredient; an elemental or constituting material (esp. a raw one); an equipment; an implement; an apparatus; an accessory; an article (esp. of food and clothing) offered in religious worship.

উপকর্তা *a.* doing good (to); benignant; benevolent; helpful; useful. □ *n.* a benefactor; a helper; *fem.* **উপকর্ত্রী**।

উপকার *n.* a good turn, benefaction; benevolence; good service; help; favour. **উপকার করা** *v.* to do good (to), to do a good turn (to); to benefit; to help. **~ক, উপকারী** *a.* doing good (to), benignant; beneficent; (not used of persons) efficacious; benevolent; helpful; useful. *fem.* **উপকারিকা, উপকারিণী**। **উপকারিতা** *n.* active goodness; good; use; helpfulness; usefulness; benefit; beneficence. **উপকারে আসা** to come of use, to be useful some time or other, to come in handy. **উপকার্য** *a.* deserving help or favour.

উপকূল *n.* coast; shore, beach; bank. **~বর্তী** *a.* littoral; orarian, coastal. **~বাণিজ্য** *n.* coasting-trade; coastal trade. **~বাসী** *a.* orarian. □ *n.* an orarian.

উপকৃত *a.* benefited; helped. **উপকৃতি** same as **উপকার**।

উপকেন্দ্র *n.* epicentre.

উপকেশ *n.* false hair, wig.

উপক্রম *n.* state or being on the point of or about to; endeavour, effort; beginning, commencement, start, outset. **উপক্রম করা** *v.* to be about to or on the point of; to endeavour; to be about to commence. **উপক্রম হওয়া** *v.* to be about to be or on the point of being; to be about to be commenced. **~ণিকা** *n.* beginning, commencement, outset; an introduction, a preface, a prelude. **~ণীয়** *a.* that which should be begun or undertaken.

উপক্রান্ত *a.* begun; commenced; started, undertaken.

উপক্রিয়া same as **উপকার**।

উপক্ষয় *n.* damage or waste (esp. due to long use); wear and tear; depreciation.

উপক্ষার *n.* an alkaloid.

উপগত *a.* present; arrived; near, adjacent; having attachment to or attraction for; having enjoyed sexual intercourse (with); mated; obtained, attained; learnt.

উপগম, উপগমন *n.* presence; arrival, approach, act of going near; a happening, an occurrence, an incident; attachment; sexual intercourse, mating; act of obtaining or attaining; what is obtained or attained; knowledge. **উপগম্য** *a.* approachable; worthy of being sexually united or mated; obtainable, attainable; knowable.

উপগিরি *n.* a small hill, a hillock; an artificial hill.

উপগীত *a.* sung; extolled; celebrated.

উপগুরু *n.* a venerable person (who is not a preceptor or teacher); one who deputizes or assists a preceptor or teacher.

উপগ্রহ *n.* a satellite; a minor planet; a moon; (coll.) an undesirable dependant or companion; (coll.) a source of trouble.

উপঘাত *n.* a blow; harm; injury; destruction; extermination; extinction.

উপচক্ষু *n.* spectacles; glasses.

উপচয় *n.* a collection, an assemblage, a multitude; prosperity; improvement; nourishment; increase of value (of property), appreciation; (astrol.) the third, sixth, tenth and eleventh houses of the astrological zodiac.

উপচরিত *a.* (esp. of deities) entertained with offerings or presents; worshipped or served; (rhet.) metaphorically signified.

উপচর্যা *n.* act of waiting on, attendance; nursing; medical treatment.

উপচানো *v.* to overflow. □ *a.* overflowing; overflowed.

উপচার *n.* any of the articles given in religious offering; things or materials necessary for worship or used in worship; religious service or ceremony; medical treatment; surgical operation; figurative expression or its explanation. **~শালা** *n.* (med.) an operation theatre.

উপচিকীর্ষা *n.* disposition to do good, benevolence; the will to do good to others.

উপচিকীর্ষু *a.* benevolent.

উপচিত *a.* amassed, accumulated, collected; nourished; developed; prospered, flourished; (of property etc.) increased in value; appreciated. **উপচিতি** *n.* amassment, accumulation; collection; nourishment; development; flourish; increase in value, appreciation; (bio.) anabolism.

উপচীয়মান *a.* in the process of being amassed or accumulated or collected; in the process of being nourished or developed; prospering; prosperous, flourishing; (of property etc.) increasing in value.

উপচ্ছায়া *n.* a ghost; a phantom; (astr.) a penumbra.

উপজনন *n.* origin, birth; a coming into existence; production.

উপজা *v.* (poet.) to be born or produced or to generate.

উপজাত *a.* originated, born; produced. □ *n.* a by-product.

উপজাতি *n.* a metre used in Sanskrit versification; a sub-caste, a subclass; a tribe or tribal; a backward tribe; an aboriginal tribe. **উপজাতীয়** *a.* tribal.

উপজিল *v.* (in poet.) was or were produced or generated.

উপজিহ্বা *n.* the uvula, the epiglottis.

উপজীবিকা *n.* livelihood; a profession, a trade.

উপজীবী *a.* living upon; taken to a particular profession or trade.

উপজীব্য *a.* acceptable as a livelihood or profession or trade; acceptable as a means to satisfy one's demand; to be depended on. □ *n.* livelihood; a profession; a trade; a means to satisfy one's demand; a shelter; a prop; leit-motif, basic idea (কবিতার উপজীব্য).

উপজ্ঞা *n.* an instinct.

উপড়ানো *v.* to uproot, to extirpate, to eradicate, to pull up; to exterminate. □ *a.* uprooted, extirpated, eradicated; exterminated.

উপঢৌকন *n.* a gift or present given to express respect or amity.

উপতপ্ত *a.* heated; distressed, aggrieved.

উপতারা *n.* the iris; the pupil of the eye.

উপত্যকা *n.* a valley. **গ্রংস-উপত্যকা** a rift valley.

উপদংশ *n.* syphillis.

উপদর্শক *n.* an overseer; door-keeper, an usher.

উপদল *n.* a faction; a faction within a party.

উপদিশ্যমান *a.* one who is being advised or instructed; one who is the object of advice or instruction.

উপদিষ্ট *a.* of one who has been advised or instructed, of that which has been said by way of advice or instruction, advised, instructed, taught, counselled, directed.

উপদেবতা, উপদেব *n.* a demi-god; an apparition, a ghost; an evil spirit.

উপদেশ *n.* counsel, advice; instruction, teaching; precept; admonition. **উপদেশ দেওয়া** *v.* to counsel, to advise; to instruct, to teach; to admonish. **~ক** same as **উপদেষ্টা**। **~নীয়** *a.* worthy of receiving advice or instruction or teaching. **~মূলক** *a.* giving or containing advice or teaching, didactic, instructive, instructional. **উপদেশ্য** same as **উপদেশনীয়**।

উপদেষ্টা *a.* imparting advice or instruction. □ *n.* a counsellor; an adviser; an instructor, a teacher; a preceptor.

উপদ্বীপ *n.* a peninsula. **উপদ্বীপীয়** *a.* peninsular.

উপদ্রব *n.* a disturbance, a trouble; annoyance, irritation, pesterment; oppression; a raid; a danger, a mishap, calamity. **উপদ্রব করা** *v.* to disturb, to trouble; to pester; to oppress; to raid. **~কারী** *a.* & *n.* one who disturbs or gives trouble to or pesters or annoys or oppresses or raids.

উপদ্রষ্টা *n.* same as **উদর্শক**।

উপদ্রুত *a.* disturbed (উপদ্রুত অঞ্চল) ; troubled; pestered; oppressed; raided; laid waste.

উপধর্ম *n.* an irrational or false faith or religion; a superstition believed to be a part of religious worship; a fetish; an unscriptural but traditional religious practice.

উপধা *n.* (gr.) the penultimate letter of a word; a trick; a means; a test or testing of courtiers' honesty.

উপধাতু *n.* a metalloid; a sulphate of metal; an excrescence or secretion of the body (e. g. hair tooth sweat lymph milk menses etc.)

উপধান *n.* a pillow; act of holding; act of placing or depositing.

উপধারা *n.* sub-section.

উপধূপন *n.* fumigation.

উপনগর *n.* outskirts of a town, a suburb; a small town, a township.

উপনদ, উপনদী *n.* a stream that runs into another, a tributary, an affluent.

উপনয়ন *n.* the ritual ceremony of investing a Brahmin or Kshatriya or Vaishya with the holy or sacred thread.

উপনাম *n.* a nickname, an alias; a surname; an appellation.

উপনায়ক *n.* (in novels, plays etc.) a character second in importance only to the hero; the subordinate or secondary hero or leader.

উপনিধি *n.* a thing committed to somebody's care; or valuable thing kept or deposited in one's care.

উপনিবিষ্ট same as **উপনিবেশিত** (see **উপনিবেশ**).

উপনিবেশ *n.* a colony. **উপনিবেশ স্থাপন করা** *v.* to colonize, to set up a colony. **উপনিবেশিত** *a.* set up as or set up in a colony, colonized.

উপনির্বাচন *n.* a by-election.

উপনিষদ, উপনিষৎ *n.* the Upanishads; the philosophical portion of the Vedas, the Vedantic philosophy; Sanskrit philosophical treatises giving an exposition of the Vedas.

উপনিমিত্ত নিধি contingency fund.

উপনিহিত *a.* deposited on trust, entrusted.

উপনীত *a.* brought; ushered; arrived; attained; (of Brahmins, Kshatriyas or Vaishyas) invested with the holy thread. **উপনীত হওয়া** *v.* to be brought or ushered; to arrive, to attain; to be invested with the holy thread.

উপনেতা[১] *n.* a bringer; an usher.
উপনেতা[২] *n.* a deputy leader, an assistant leader.
উপনেত্র *n. pl.* spectacles, eyeglasses.
উপন্যস্ত *a.* placed, deposited; pledged; arranged.
উপন্যাস *n.* a novel, a book of fiction; a long story; a romantic tale, a romance; a preface or introduction; a proposal. **~কার, ~রচয়িতা, ~লেখক** *n.* a novelist.
উপপতি *n.* (*masc.*) a paramour, a gallant.
উপপত্তি *n.* argument, reasoning, inference; proof, demonstration, justification; knowledge; solution; accomplishment, execution; origination, origin; attainment; provision.
উপপত্নী *n. fem.* a concubine.
উপপত্র *n.* (bot.) a stipule. **উপপত্রিক** *a.* stipulate. ☐ *n.* a stipulate leaf. **উপপত্রিকা** *n.* a stipel.
উপপথ *n.* a by-way, by path.
উপপদ *n.* (gr.) the first of two words compounded into one; (gr.) a system of forming compound words by adding a suffix denoting an agent (usu. **উপপদ তৎপুরুষ**).
উপপাতক *n.* a venial sin, a minor sin.
উপপাদক *a.* & *n.* one who or that which decides or solves or accomplishes or executes or proves or justifies or demonstrates.
উপপাদন *n.* decision, solution; accomplishment, execution; proving, justification, demonstration. **উপপাদন করা** *v.* to decide, to solve; to accomplish, to execute; to prove, to justify, to demonstrate. **উপপাদনীয়** same as **উপপাদ্য** (*a.*).
উপপাদ্য *a.* that which is to be or can be decided or solved or accomplished or executed or proved or justified or demonstrated. ☐ *n.* (geom.) a proposition to be proved, a theorem. **এটিই উপপাদ্য বিষয়** quod erat demonstrandum (Q.E.D.).
উপপুর *n.* outskirts of a town, a suburb; a township. **উপপৌর** *a.* suburban.
উপপুরাণ *n.* a minor or secondary Purana.
উপ-প্রকরণ *n.* a sub-clause.
উপপ্লব *n.* a natural calamity or disaster; a danger; a pest; an insurrection or insurgence; a coup d'état.
উপপ্লুত *a.* stricken with natural calamity or disaster; encompassed with danger, endangered; pestered; torn with insurrection; trouble-infested.
উপবন *n.* a garden, a park; a grove; an artificial forest.
উপবাস *n.* abstinence from food, fast; starvation; a fast enjoined by religion. **উপবাস করা** *v.* to go without food; to abstain from food, to fast; to go hungry, to starve; to observe a religious fast. **উপবাসী** *a.* abstaining from food, fasting; starving; observing a religious fast.
উপবিধি *n.* a by-law.
উপবিষ *n.* subsidiary poison; a toxin; an artificial poison.
উপবিষ্ট *a.* seated, sitting. **উপবিষ্ট থাকা** *v.* to remain seated; to be in office; to occupy a seat; to be sitting. **উপবিষ্ট হওয়া** *v.* to sit, to take one's seat.
উপবীত *n.* the holy thread of a Brahmin or Kshatriya or Vaishya.
উপবৃত্ত *n.* an ellipse. **উপবৃত্তাকার** *a.* elliptical in shape.
উপবেদ *n.* any of the four minor or subsidiary Vedas : they deal with (1) the art of healing, (2) archery, (3) music and aesthetics and (4) architecture or masonry.
উপবেশন *n.* act of sitting, act of taking one's seat. **উপবেশন করা** *v.* to sit, to take one's seat.
উপবেশয়িতা *a.* & *n.* one who sits or causes to sit.
উপবেশিত *a.* seated.
উপভাষা *n.* a dialect.
উপভুক্ত *a.* enjoyed; eaten or drunk; used.
উপভোক্তা *a.* & *n.* one who enjoys or eats and drinks or uses.
উপভোগ *n.* enjoying, enjoyment; eating or drinking; using. **উপভোগ্য** *a.* enjoyable; eatable or drinkable; usable; that which is to be enjoyed or eaten and drunk or used.
উপম *a.* (*in comp.*) like, similar, identical etc. (দেবোপম).

উপমক্ষিকা *n.* flea.
উপমন্ত্রী *n.* deputy minister.
উপমহাদেশ *n.* sub-continent.
উপমা *n.* likeness, similarity, comparison, equal (উপমা দেওয়া, উপমা নেই) ; (rhet.) a simile. **উপমা দেওয়া** *v.* to liken, to compare. **~রহিত** *a.* having no equal or parallel; without comparison; unparalleled.
উপমাংস *n.* a wart, a mole.
উপমাতা *n. fem.* a woman as venerable as one's mother; foster-mother; wet-nurse.
উপমান *n.* the object with which something is compared; (log.) analogy.
উপমিত *a.* compared, likened.
উপমিতি *n.* a simile, an analogy; (log.) knowledge obtained with the help of analogy, analogical knowledge.
উপমেয় *a.* comparable; compared. ☐ *n.* that which has been compared, an object of comparison.
উপমেরু *n.* consequent poles.
উপযাচক *a.* asking for or soliciting personally; volunteering; unsolicited; too ready or prompt, forward. ☐ *n.* one who asks for or solicits personally; a volunteer; one who is too ready or prompt. **উপযাচক হয়ে** *adv.* unsolicitedly.
উপযাচন *n.* act of asking for or soliciting personally; act of volunteering; act of being too ready or prompt.
উপযাচিকা *a.* & *n. fem.* of **উপযাচক** । *n. fem.* a woman who comes forward to ask for love or sexual intercourse.
উপযাচিত *a.* asked for or solicited personally, volunteered.
উপযুক্ত *a.* suitable, deserving, worthy (উপযুক্ত পাত্র) ; fitting; befitting; becoming; proper (উপযুক্ত সময়) ; right, appropriate, just; adequate, sufficient; fit, competent; expedient; evenly balanced, equal. **উপযুক্ত হওয়া** *v.* to suit, to deserve, to be worthy; to be fitting, to become, to fit; to be proper or right or appropriate or just; to be adequate, to suffice; to be competent; to be expedient; to be evenly balanced; to equal. **~তা, উপযুক্তি** *n.* suitableness, suitability, deservingness, worthiness; fitness, becomingness; propriety, rightness, appropriateness, justness; eligibility; adequacy, sufficiency; competency, competence; expediency; state of being evenly balanced, equalness.
উপযোগ *n.* good, benefit; necessity; service; use, usefulness, utility; assistance, support; eating, enjoyment; application; suitableness. **~বাদ** *n.* utilitarianism. **~বাদী** *a.* utilitarian. ☐ *n.* a utilitarian.
উপযোগিতা see **উপযোগী** ।
উপযোগী *a.* suitable, fitting; fit, competent; deserving, worthy; becoming; serviceable, useful; proper; adequate, sufficient; expedient, applicable; favourable, helpful. **উপযোগিতা** *n.* suitableness, suitability; fitness, competency, competence; deservingness; becomingness; serviceability; usefulness; propriety; adequacy; sufficiency; expedience, applicability; use; favourableness, helpfulness.
উপযোজন *n.* act of making suitable; act of accommodating, accommodation, adjustment, adaptation. **উপযোজন করা** *v.* to render suitable; to render accommodating, to accommodate, to adjust, to adapt.
উপর *n.* the top of anything; the upper portion of anything; surface; roof; overhead space. ☐ *a.* upper; upward; extra. ☐ *prep.* up, on, upon, above, over, overhead, upwards. **~আলা, ~ওয়ালা** *a.* superior. ☐ *n.* a superior officer; a boss; (fig.) God. **উপর-উপর** *a.* superficial, cursory; shallow, not deep; consecutive (উপর-উপর তিন দিন). ☐ *adv.* superficially or cursorily. **~কার** *a.* of or on the top or surface; upper. **~চড়া** *a.* disposed to kick up a row, quarrelsome; aggressive, intruding, obtrusive; assaulting on person. **~চড়াও** *adv.* coming forward to quarrel or assault (esp. without provocation), aggressively, obtrusively. **~চাল** *n.* (in chess.) a move suggested by a non-playing spectator; a counter-move; (fig.) an action to foil

another. ~চালাক *a.* superficially (and usu. officiously) cunning, act of parading one's cunning (esp. precociously). ~তলা *n.* a higher or upper storey of a building; (fig.) the higher or wealthier or nobler stratum of the society, the upper class. ~তলায় *adv.* upstairs; to or in the upper class. ~তলার *a.* of or in the upper storey; (fig.) of the upper class. ~তলার লোক *n.* the high-ups; man of the upper class. ~পড়া *a.* officious, obtrusive, intruding; aggressive. ~পিঠ *n.* the opposite face of a thing; antipodes.

উপরত *a.* abstained or abstaining (from), refrained, ceased, given up; (of wordly interest) renounced; dead, deceased; gone by, passed. **উপরতি** *n.* renunciation, renouncement; abstinence, cessation, act of giving up; death.

উপরত্ন *n.* a thing as bright as a gem; a cheap gem; an imitation gem.

উপরন্তু *adv.* in addition, moreover, over and above, besides; into the bargain.

উপরাজ *n.* a viceroy.

উপরাষ্ট্রপতি *n.* vice-president.

উপরি[1] *adv.* & *prep.* & *a.* on, upon, above, over, overhead, upwards, upper; surfacial; superficial; then, thereafter. **উপরি-উপরি** *a.* consecutive. □ *adv.* superficially, cursorily; one upon another; one after another; consecutively. ~ক *a.* superior. **উপরিক কৃত্যক** superior service. **উপরিউল্লিখিত** *a.* above-mentioned, referred to above. ~গত *a.* situated or placed upon; situated above; surfacial; ascended; superficial. ~চর *a.* flying or moving in the air, aerial. ~তন *a.* superior; higher. ~তল *n.* surface; the upper face of a thing; (loos.) the upper storey or deck. ~দৃষ্টি *n.* (astrol.) malignant influence. ~ন্যস্ত *a.* super-imposed. ~পন্ন *a.* superposed. ~পাত *n.* superposition. ~ভাগ *n.* the top; the surface; the upper part; the space above. ~ভাগে *adv.* on the top of; on the surface of; in or on the upper part; over, on. ~লিখিত *a.* written above. ~স্থ, ~স্থিত *a.* placed or situated above, lying or standing above.

উপরি[2] *a.* (used as a *pfx.*) extra, irregular, additional, super-, sur-, by way of illegal gratification (উপরি আয়). □ *n.* a perquisite; a tip; a bribe; an illegal or irregular gratification. **উপরি আয়** *n.* an extra income; a perquisite; an illegal extra income, a bribe; a tip. **উপরি কর** *n.* a surtax. **উপরি খরচ, উপরি ব্যয়** *n.* extra expenses; overhead charges. ~পাওনা same as **উপরি আয়**। ~লাভ *n.* an extra profit or excess profit; an extra income; a bribe; a tip.

উপরুদ্ধ *a.* requested; solicited; asked for.

উপরে *adv.* & *prep.* on, upon, over, up, above, upwards, overhead, high up, in the sky, upstairs.

উপরোক্ত pop. var. of **উপর্যুক্ত**।

উপরোধ *n.* an earnest request; importunity, solicitation; recommendation; sake (কাজের উপরোধে). **উপরোধে ঢেঁকি গেলা** *v.* to swallow the (bitter) pill reluctantly in order to comply with a request.

উপর্যুক্ত *a.* above-mentioned; mentioned above or earlier.

উপর্যুপরি *adv.* one after another; one upon another. □ *a.* coming or occurring one after another; placed one upon another; consecutive (উপর্যুপরি তিন দিন).

উপল *n.* a pebble; a stone; a gem, a jewel.

উপলক্ষ, উপলক্ষ্য *n.* an end in view, a purpose; an aim; an occasion; an opportunity, a pretext, an excuse.

উপলক্ষণ *n.* a presage; an omen; an ominous sign; a prelude; state of being at the point of commencement; an incidental (as opposed to an essential) characteristic or feature.

উপলক্ষণা *n.* (rhet.) a figure of speech akin to metonymy or synecdoche.

উপলক্ষিত *a.* purposed; aimed at; presaged; taken as an occasion or opportunity; advanced as a pretext or excuse; inferred or deduced (from).

উপলক্ষ্য alt. spell of **উপলক্ষ**।

উপলব্ধ *a.* felt, perceived; understood, realized, learnt; attained, obtained, acquired; (loos.) appreciated.

উপলব্ধি *n.* feeling, perception; understanding, realization, cognition; attainment, acquirement; (loos.) appreciation; (psy.) sense-perception. **উপলব্ধি করা** *v.* to feel, to perceive; to understand, to realize, to cognize, to learn; to attain, to obtain, to acquire; (loos.) to appreciate.

উপলভ্য *a.* knowable, cognizable; attainable; capable of being accomplished; that which is to be learnt or attained or accomplished.

উপলিপ্ত *a.* besmeared, bedaubed; anointed; plastered; (bot. & bio.) accreted.

উপলেপ *n.* smearing or anointing or plastering; an ointment; a plaster; (bot. & bio.) accretion. **~ন** *n.* smearing or anointing or plastering.

উপশম *n.* relief; alleviation; abatement, subsidence; cessation; intermission; repression of one's own senses. **উপশম করা** *v.* to relieve; to alleviate, to allay; to mitigate; to abate, to cause to subside or cease or intermit; to repress one's own senses. **উপশম হওয়া** *v.* to be relieved; to be alleviated or mitigated; to abate, to subside; to cease; to intermit; (of one's senses) to be repressed. **~ক** *a.* relieving; alleviating, allaying, mitigating; causing abatement or subsidence or cessation or intermission; causing repression of one's senses. **~নীয়** *a.* that which is to be or can be relieved or alleviated or allayed or mitigated or abated or made to cease or made to imtermit or repressed. **উপশমিত** *a.* relieved; alleviated, mitigated, allayed; abated, subsided; ceased; intermitted; (of one's senses) repressed.

উপশয় *n.* lying down.

উপশাখা *n.* a sub-branch; a section.

উপশান্ত same as **উপশমিত** (see **উপশম**). **উপশান্তি** same as **উপশম**।

উপশিরা *n.* a thin or delicate vein; a subsidiary vein.

উপশিষ্য *n.* a minor disciple; a disciple of a disciple.

উপশুল্ক *n.* a toll. **উপশুল্ক সংগ্রাহক** *n.* a toll collector.

উপশোভিত *a.* adorned, beautified, decked.

উপশ্রেণি *n.* a sub-class.

উপসংহার *n.* conclusion; termination, close, end; concluding part or remarks; closing part. **উপসংহার করা** *v.* to conclude; to terminate, to close, to end.

উপসংহৃত *a.* concluded; terminated, closed, ended. **উপসংহৃতি** *n.* conclusion; termination.

উপ-সচিব *n.* deputy secretary.

উপ-সভাপতি *n.* vice-chairman.

উপসমিতি *n.* a sub-committee.

উপসর্গ *n.* any of the accompanying complaints of a disease; morbidity; a symptom (esp. of a disease); a trouble, a disturbance; an impediment, an obstacle; a calamity; (gr.) a prefix.

উপসাগর *n.* a bay, a gulf. **উপসাগরীয় স্রোত** *n.* a gulf-stream.

উপসুন্দ see **সুন্দ**।

উপসেক *n.* act of alleviating or abating by sprinkling with water.

উপসেচন *n.* act of sprinkling water upon; act of wetting.

উপসেবক *a.* in the practice of enjoying or worshipping; having attachment (to); addicted (to); given to adultery, adulterous. □ *n.* an enjoyer; a worshipper; one who has attachment (to); an addict; an adulterer.

উপসেবন *n.* act of enjoying, enjoyment; worship; attachment; addiction.

উপসেবা *n.* enjoying, enjoyment; attachment; worshipping; worship; addiction; occupation of a servant or employee, service.

উপসেবিত *a.* enjoyed; worshipped; treated with attachment, fawned upon; taken or tasted as an addiction; (of a wife) enjoyed by a man other than one's husband; served.

উপসেবী *a.* in the practice of enjoying or worshipping; having attachment (to); addicted (to); given to adultery, adulterous; serving, in the service (of); attending upon.

উপস্কার *n.* materials; positing of some new quality; care; cleansing; (gr.) introduction of words in order to complete the sense of an incomplete sentence.

উপস্কৃত *a.* supplemented; collected; beautified; embellished, decorated; dressed, toileted.

উপস্ত্রী *n.* a concubine, a mistress.

উপস্থ *a.* proximate, in the vicinity of; neared; situated or lying on the top (of). □ *n.* the male or female genitals, the penis or the vagina. **~নিগ্রহ** *n.* control of sex appetite or sexual desire; continence.

উপস্থাপক *a.* bringing in, ushering; proposing, moving, introducing; submitting (a petition etc.). □ *n.* an usher; a proposer, a mover, an introducer; one who submits (a petition etc.).

উপস্থাপন *n.* bringing in or ushering; proposing or moving or introducing; act of submitting, submission. **উপস্থাপন করা** *v.* to bring in, to usher; to propose, to move, to raise, to introduce; to submit. **উপস্থাপিত** *n.* brought in; proposed or moved; introduced; placed; submitted.

উপস্থাপয়িতা same as **উপস্থাপক।** *fem.* **উপস্থাপয়িত্রী।**

উপস্থাপিকা *fem.* of **উপস্থাপক।**

উপস্থিত *a.* arrived or assembled in the place in question; present; now existing, current; impending. **উপস্থিত করা** *v.* to bring in, to usher; to propose or introduce. **উপস্থিত থাকা** *v.* to be present; to exist, to be current. **উপস্থিত হওয়া** *v.* to put in or make an appearance, to appear, to come, to arrive; to assemble; to be present; to be current. **~বক্তা** *n.* one who can deliver an extempore speech, an extemporizer. **~বুদ্ধি** *n.* presence of mind, ready wit. □ *a.* ready-witted. **উপস্থিতি** *n.* arrival; assemblage; presence; attendance; existence at present, currency. **উপস্থিতি-নিবন্ধ** *n.* an attendance register.

উপস্পর্শক *n.* a sub-tangent.

উপস্বত্ব *n.* income or profit from landed property, business firm etc.; revenue.

উপহত *a.* hurt; wounded; attacked; overwhelmed.

উপহসিত *a.* ridiculed, taunted, laughed at, mocked.

উপহার *n.* a presentation; a complimentary gift, a present. **উপহার দেওয়া** *v.* to offer as a present.

উপহাস *n.* ridicule, taunt; a joke; contempt. **উপহাস করা** *v.* to ridicule or taunt, to laugh at, to mock, to jeer; to crack a joke; to treat with contempt. **উপহাসাস্পদ** *n.* an object of ridicule or taunt, a ridiculous person; a laughing-stock; a laughable person; a contemptible person. **উপহাস্য** *a.* ridiculous, fit to be taunted or jeered at; laughable; contemptible.

উপহৃত *n.* given or offered as present, presented; given or offered; collected.

উপহ্রদ *n.* a lagoon.

উপা var. of **উবা।**

উপাংশু *a.* lonely; deserted.

উপাক্ষ *n.* (geog.) a minor axis; spectacles.

উপাখ্যান *n.* a story; a tale; a fable; a fairy tale; a narrative; an episode; an anecdote.

উপাগত *a.* arrived within the approaches of, neared; present; current; existing; one who has or that which has been obtained or attained.

উপাগম *n.* approaching or nearing, approach; presence; act of obtaining, obtainment; attainment.

উপাঙ্গ *n.* an accessory limb; a part of a limb; an excrescence; a text regarded as a part of or accessory of the Vedas; an epilogue or appendix. **উপাঙ্গ-প্রদাহ** *n.* appendicitis.

উপাচার্য *n.* (of a university) a vice-chancellor.

উপাত্ত *a.* accepted; admitted, supposed (for the sake of argument), earned, obtained. □ *n.* (log. etc.) a datum.

উপাদান *n.* a (raw) material, an ingredient; a constituent. **উপাদান কারণ** the material cause.

উপাদেয় *a.* pleasant, delightful; enjoyable; tasteful, delicious, dainty, pleasant to eat. **~তা** *n.* pleasantness, delightfulness; enjoyableness; tastefulness, deliciousness, daintiness.

উপাধান *n.* a pillow.

উপাধি *n.* a title; an academic degree or appellation given to the recipient of a degree; a designation; a surname; a quality or property that distinguishes an individual from the class, a denotation. ~ক, ~ধারী *a.* titled; a degree-holder. ~পত্র *n.* a diploma, an academic certificate.

উপাধ্যক্ষ *n.* a vice-principal.

উপাধ্যায় *n.* surname or title of an upcountry Brahmin; a professor or reader; a teacher; an instructor; a professional teacher or reader of the Vedas. **উপাধ্যায়া, উপাধ্যায়ী** *n. fem.* a female professor or reader; a lady-teacher; an instructress. **উপাধ্যায়ী, উপাধ্যায়ানী** *n. fem.* the wife of a professor or reader or instructor or of a professional teacher of the Vedas.

উপানৎ *n.* (rarely in use) shoe, boot, slipper. **~কার** *n.* a shoe-maker.

উপান্ত *n.* outskirts; an approach; vicinity; border, extremity; any penultimate or post-ultimate object. **উপান্ত্য** *a.* lying in the outskirts; penultimate. **উপান্ত্য টীকা** *n.* marginal note. **উপান্ত্য বর্ণ** (gr.) the penultimate letter of a word.

উপাবর্তন *n.* returning or retreating; a turning round; rotation, act of whirling.

উপাবৃত্ত *a.* returned, retreated; turned round; rotated, whirled.

উপায় *n.* a means, a way, an expedient; a method (অঙ্ক কষার উপায়) ; a contrivance, a device; income, earnings (উপায় কত ?) ; a remedy (রোগের উপায়) ; a measure; a means to relieve or help, support (বিধবার উপায়). **উপায় করা** *v.* to devise means or method; to earn; to remedy; to devise means to relieve or help, to find a support for.

উপায়-উপকরণ *n. pl.* ways and means.

উপায়ক্ষম *a.* capable of earning.

উপায়জ্ঞ *a.* able to find out means; resourceful.

উপায়ন *n.* a present, a complimentary gift; a reward.

উপায়বিহীন, উপায়হীন *a.* resourceless; having no means; helpless.

উপায়ান্তর *n.* an alternative means; an alternative. **~হীন** *a.* left without an alternative, having no alternative.

উপায়ী *n.* one who earns (esp. money), earning.

উপারম্ভ *n.* beginning; outset; start.

উপার্জক *a.* one who earns (esp. money). □ *n.* a money-earner; an earner.

উপার্জন *n.* earning (esp. money); winning; gaining or obtaining; acquirement; earning, income (উপার্জন কত ?). **উপার্জন করা** *v.* to earn; to win; to gain, to obtain. **~ক্ষম** *a.* capable of earning. **~রত, ~শীল** *a.* engaged in earning.

উপার্জিত *a.* earned; won; gained, obtained, acquired.

উপার্থন *n.* canvassing votes; canvassing.

উপালম্ভ *n.* reproof, reproach; censure, reprimand. **উপালব্ধ** *a.* reproved, reproached, censured.

উপাশ্রয় *a.* fit to be a shelter. □ *n.* one who takes shelter; a refugee; taking shelter; resorting to. **উপাশ্রিত** *a.* taken or given shelter; protected.

উপাসক *a.* engaged in worshipping or adoring or praying; devoted (to); engaged in religious meditation; engaged in serving or flattering a person in the hope of getting some benefit in return; admiring. □ *n.* a worshipper, an adorer; one who prays; a devotee; one who meditates; a servant, a flatterer; an admirer.

উপাসঙ্গ *n.* a thing or an object always ready to hand; a quiver.

উপাসন, উপাসনা *n.* worship; adoration; prayer; devotion; religious meditation; act of serving or flattering a person in the hope of getting some benefit in return; admiration; solicitation. **উপাসনা করা** *v.* to worship; to adore; to pray; to be devoted to; to be engaged in religious meditation, to meditate.

উপাসিকা *fem.* of **উপাসক** ।

উপাসিত *a.* worshipped; adored; meditated; served in the hope of getting some benefit in return; admired; solicited.

উপাস্থি *n.* a cartilage.

উপাস্য *a.* worthy of being worshipped, adorable; warranting devotion; worthy of being meditated upon; worthy of being served or flattered; warranting admiration or deep attachment or addiction.

উপাহার *n.* a light repast, tiffin, snack.

উপাহৃত *a.* collected; brought; imagined; fancied.

উপুড় *a.* lying with face on the ground, prostrate. **উপুড় হওয়া** *v.* to prostrate; to turn turtle.

উপুড়হস্ত *a.* open-handed, munificent, generous; ready to pay off (debts etc.). **উপুড়হস্ত না করা** *v.* to be reluctant to pay or (esp.) to repay; not to pay off a debt.

উপেক্ষক *a.* & *n.* one who disregards or rejects or neglects; one who attaches no importance to; one who treats with contempt or indifference or inattention; one who ignores or overlooks.

উপেক্ষা, উপেক্ষণ *n.* disregard; rejection; neglect; contempt; indifference, heedlessness, inattention. **উপেক্ষা করা** *v.* to disregard; to reject; to neglect; to attach no importance to; to treat with indifference or inattention; to pay no attention or heed to, to take no care of; to ignore; to overlook. **উপেক্ষণীয়** *a.* negligible; contemptible; not deserving any notice; ignorable.

উপেক্ষিত *a.* disregarded; rejected; neglected; treated with indifference or inattention; unheeded; uncared for; ignored; overlooked. *fem.* **উপেক্ষিতা** ।

উপেত *a.* endowed with, invested with, possessed of (e. g. **গুণোপেত** having or possessing qualities, qualified).

উপোদ্ঘাত *n.* beginning, start; a presage; a preface; a prologue, an introduction.

উপোস *n.* abstinence from food, fasting, fast. **উপোস করা** *v.* to fast; to go without food. **উপোসি** *a.* fasting, going or gone without food; hungry. **উপোসিত** *a.* going without food, fasting.

উপ্ত *a.* (of seeds) sown, sowed. **উপ্তি** *n.* act of sowing.

উবরানো *v.* to be surplus.

উবা *v.* to evaporate; to vanish; to disappear.

উবু *a.* seated on one's heels, squatted; high, elevated. **উবু হওয়া** *v.* to sit on one's heels, to squat.

উবুড় dial. var. of **উপুড়** ।

উবে যাওয়া same as **উবা** ।

উভ[১] *pro.* both. **~চর** *a.* amphibious, amphibian. **উভচর প্রাণী** an amphibian. **উভচর প্রাণীবর্গ** the amphibia. **~বল** *n.* ambivalence. ☐ *a.* ambivalent. **~লিঙ্গ** *a.* (bio. & zoo.) androgynous, bisexual; (gr.) of common gender. ☐ *n.* an androgynous creature; (gr.) common gender or a word in this gender.

উভ[২] *a.* high; loud; upturned (উভলেজ). **~রড়ে** *adv.* (obs.) at a high speed, with breakneck speed. **~রায়** *adv.* at the top of one's voice. **~রোল** *n.* tumultuous noise. **~লেজ** *a.* having one's tail turned up.

উভয় *pro.* two persons or things, two; both. ☐ *a.* both. **~ত** *adv.* on or from or for both or either directions or sides or parties. **উভয়তোমুখ** *a.* facing or looking both ways; double-faced. *fem.* **উভয়তোমুখী** । **~ত্র** *adv.* on or from or for both persons or parties or sides or directions. **~থা** *adv.* in both ways or methods. **~পার্শ্ব** *n.* both sides. **~লিঙ্গ** *a.* (zoo. & bio.) hermaphroditi (al). ☐ *n.* a hermaphrodite. **~সংকট** *n.* a dilemma.

উভয়ার্থ *a.* ambiguous, equivocal, having both or dual meanings.

উমদা *a.* wealthy, rich; excellent; brilliant.

উমর *n.* age.

উমরাহ, উমরা *n.* (Mus.) a very rich man; a nobleman.

উমা *n.* the name of the wife of Shiva (শিব).

উমানো *v.* to heat; to agitate. ☐ *n.* measure, weight; quantity.

উমাপতি, উমাশংকর *n.* Shiva (শিব) the husband of Uma (উমা).

উমেদ *n.* hope, desire; expectation. **উমেদার** *a.* cherishing a hope, desirous, expectant. ☐ *n.* a candidate (for a job etc.). **উমেদারি** *n.* soliciting for a job etc.; offering oneself as a candidate; candidature.

উমেশ same as **উমাপতি** ।

উর, উরঃ *n.* the bosom, the breast; the

chest. **উরঃফলক** *n.* a sternum, a breast-bone.

উরগ, উরঙ্গ, উরঙ্গম *n.* a reptile; a serpent; a snake. *fem.* **উরগী, উরঙ্গী, উরঙ্গমী** ।

উরজ *n.* either of the two mammary glands in a woman, the female breast.

উরত var. of **উরুত** ।

উরমাল *n.* a handkerchief; a thigh-plate (esp. of a horse).

উরশ্ছদ *n.* a piece of armour for the breast, a breastplate.

উরস *n.* the breast, the bosom; the chest.

উরসিজ same as **উরজ** ।

উরস্ত্র, উরস্ত্রাণ same as **উরশ্ছদ** ।

উরা alt. spell. of **উরা** ।

উরুত *n.* thigh.

উরুমাল var. of **উরমাল** ।

উরোগামী *a.* crawling.

উরোজ *a.* born of or produced from the breast. ☐ *n.* either of the two mammary glands in women, the female breast.

উর্ণনাভ alt. spell. of **উর্ণনাভ** ।

উর্ণা alt. spell. of **উর্ণা** ।

উর্দি *n.* a distinctive garb for members of a body; a uniform.

উর্দু *n.* the Urdu language, Urdu. **~নবিশ** *n.* one who is proficient in or professes to know Urdu.

উর্বর *a.* fertile, productive; prolific. *fem.* **উর্বরা** । **উর্বর করা** *v.* to make fertile, to fertilize. **~তা** *n.* fertility, productivity. **~তাসাধন** *n.* fertilization.

উর্বরমস্তিষ্ক *a.* fertile-brained, ingenious. **উর্বর মস্তিষ্ক** *n.* fertile brain, resourcefulness, ingenuity.

উর্বশী *n.* the name of the chief dancer of heaven celebrated for her ageless youth and undying beauty.

উর্বী *n.* the earth (esp. when personified as the mother of all created beings), Mother Earth. **~ধর** *n.* a mountain. **~রুহ** *n.* a tree; a plant.

উল *n.* wool.

উলকি *n.* a design marked on the skin by puncturing with a needle and inserting pigment; tattoo, a tatu. **উলকি আঁকা** *v.* to tattoo, to tatu. **~-আঁকা** *a.* tattooed.

উলঙ্গ *n.* naked, nude; bare; uncovered; unsheathed (উলঙ্গ অসি) ; candid, frank (উলঙ্গ পরান). *fem.* **উলঙ্গা, উলঙ্গিনী** ।

উলটকম্বল *n.* a medicinal herb, abroma angusta.

উলটা, (coll.) **উলটো** *a.* turned upside down; lying or bent with face on the ground, prostrate; opposite; reverse; contrary; contradictory (উলটো কথা). **উলটো বোঝা** *v.* to misunderstand; to misinterpret; to get hold of the wrong end of the stick; to be in the wrong; to take amiss, to take (it) ill. **উলটো বোঝানো** *v.* to explain or represent in a wrong way; to try to give a false notion by distorting facts. **উলট-পালট, উলটোপালটা** *a.* topsy-turvy; confused; disorderly; contradictory (উলটোপালটা কথা) ; completely chaotic. **উলটানো** *v.* to reverse or be reversed; to turn over or cause to turn over, to turn turtle or cause to turn turtle, to overturn, to capsize, to turn or cause to turn upside down; to tumble or cause to tumble; to make null and void, to annul, to revoke (রায় উলটানো, আইন উলটানো) ; to withdraw or deny (কথা উলটানো) ; to change esp. radically, to alter, to abolish (ধারা উলটানো). ☐ *a.* reversed; turned over, overturned, turned turtle; turned upside down; made null and void, annulled; withdrawn, denied; changed, altered, abolished. **উলটি** *n.* vomit, vomiting, ejecting things from the stomach through the mouth. **উলটে-পালটে** *adv.* turning round and round; doing over and over again; getting topsy-turvy or confused; rolling about, wallowing. **উলটা বুঝলি রাম** (lit.) God misinterprets prayers; one asks for a mare but gets the scare; you've misunderstood completely. **উলটো রথ** see **রথ** ।

উলটি[1] *n.* see **উলটা** ।

উলটি[2] *adv.* (poet.) having turned upside down.

উলটো see **উলটা** ।

উলস *n.* (poet.) delight, joy; gladness; hilarity; merriment.

উলসা *v.* to be delighted or gladdened.

উলসিত *a.* (poet.) delighted, gladdened.

উলু[1] *n.* a sound made by Hindu women

by moving their tongues within their mouths on any festive occasion. (also উলু উলু, উলুধ্বনি)।

উলু[2] *n.* a kind of reedy grass (usu. উলুখড়). ~খাগড়া *n.* a variety of reed;(fig.) an insignificant or indigent person; (fig.) an innocent or common person or citizen. উলুবনে মুক্তো ছড়ানো (fig.) to cast pearls before a swine. রাজায় রাজায় যুদ্ধ হয় উলুখাগড়ার (বা উলুখড়ের) প্রাণ যায় (fig.) kings with one another vie and the innocent people die.

উলুক *n.* the owl. *fem.* উলুকী।

উলেমা *n.* a Muslim scholar or learned man, an ulema.

উল্কা *n.* an aerolite or aerolith, a shooting star, a meteor; a spark, a scintilla; a torch. ~পাত *n.* the fall of a meteor to the earth. ~পিণ্ড *n.* meteorite; a meteor. ~মুখী *n.* the fox; ignis-fatuus, will-o'-the-wisp; a woman whose face is ever ruddy with anger; a fire-vomiting female ghoul.

উল্কি alt. spell. of উলকি।

উল্টা alt. spell. of উলটা।

উল্লঙ্ঘন *n.* act of crossing by leaping or vaulting over, act of leaping or vaulting over; transgression, violation, infringement, disobedience. উল্লঙ্ঘন করা *v.* to cross by leaping or vaulting over, to leap or vault over; to transgress, to violate, to infringe, to disobey. উল্লঙ্ঘনীয় same as উল্লঙ্ঘ্য।

উল্লঙ্ঘিত *a.* crossed by leaping or vaulting over; transgressed, violated, infringed, disobeyed.

উল্লঙ্ঘ্য *a.* that which can be or is to be leapt over or transgressed or violated or infringed or disobeyed.

উল্লম্ফন, উল্লম্ফ *n.* act of jumping or leaping or springing or bounding or skipping; a jump, a leap, a spring; a spell of skipping or frisking.

উল্লম্ব *a.* vertical. ~চ্ছেদ, ~ছেদ *n.* (geom.) a vertical section. ~তল *n.* (geom.) a vertical plane. ~ভাবে *adv.* vertically.

উল্লসিত *a.* delighted, gladdened; exulted; exultant; jovial, jubilant, hilarious, *fem.* উল্লসিতা।

উল্লাস *n.* delight, gladness; exultation; joy, joviality, jubilation, hilarity; (of books) a chapter. উল্লাস করা *v.* to express joy, to exult, to jubilate. উল্লাসী same as উল্লসিত। *fem.* উল্লাসিনী।

উল্লিখিত *a.* written above; above-mentioned; alluded to.

উল্লুক *n.* the gibbon, a south-east Asian anthropoid ape; a term of abuse.

উল্লেখ *n.* mention; reference; (rhet.) allusion. উল্লেখ করা *v.* to mention; to refer to; to allude to. ~ন *a.* act of mentioning; act of referring to or alluding to. ~নীয়, উল্লেখ্য *a.* mentionable, worth mention; that which is to be mentioned. ~যোগ্য *n.* mentionable, worth mention.

উল্লোল *n.* a billow; a breaker. □ *a.* dangling.

উশখুশ *n. int.* expression of or expressing restlessness or fidgetiness. উশখুশ করা *v.* to become restless with eagerness or inquisitiveness; to fidget. উশখ্শানি *n.* fidgetiness, fidgets.

উশীর *n.* aromatic root of a variety of grass, cuscus.

উশুল *n.* requited; avengement; realisation (of a claim, bill, dues etc.). উশুল করা *v.* to avenge (a wrong); to realize (a claim or a bill or dues).

উশো *n.* a mason's wooden tool for plaining or smoothing.

উষসী[1] *a. fem.* of the morning or dawn; glowing in the light of dawn; extremely beautiful. □ *n.* dawn (esp. when personified).

উষসী[2] *n.* close of the day; evening.

উষা the Vedic spell. of ঊষা।

উষীর alt. spell. of উশীর।

উস্কখুস্ক rej. spell. of উসকোখুসকো।

উষ্ট্র *n.* the camel. *fem.* উষ্ট্রী। ~চালক *n.* a camel-drive, a cameleer.

উষ্ণ *n.* heat; warmth; the sun or the summer (উষ্ণপ্রধান, উষ্ণকাল) ; anger, passion. □ *a.* hot; warm; heated; passionate, angry. ~কাল *n.* summer, hot or warm weather. ~তা, ~ত্ব *n.* heat, warmth; bad temper; temperature. ~প্রকৃতি, ~স্বভাব *a.* ill-tempered, irritable, irascible, easily provoked to anger. ☐ *n.* hot temper. ~প্রধান *a.* torrid; tropical. ~প্রধান অঞ্চল same as উষ্ণাঞ্চল। ~প্রস্রবণ *n.* a hot spring, a geyser. ~বীর্য *a.* invigorating, stimulating; excitative, excitatory. ~মণ্ডল same as উষ্ণাঞ্চল। ~স্নান *n.* hotbath.

উষ্ণাঞ্চল *n.* (geog.) the torrid zone.

উষ্ণীষ *n.* a turban, a headgear; a coronet, a diadem. ~কমল *n.* the lotus on the scalp according to the Buddhist scriptures. ~ধারী *a.* turbaned; coroneted, diademed.

উষ্ণোদক *n.* hot or warm water.

উষ্ম, উষ্মা *n.* heat; warmth; anger, rage, passion; huff; excitement; summer; temperature. উষ্ম হওয়া *v.* to become heated or warm; to get angry or huffy. উষ্মা প্রকাশ করা *v.* to vent one's anger or huff. উষ্মবর্ণ *n.* (gr.) any of the aspirates. উষ্মমাপক *n.* a thermometer. উষ্মস্বেদ *n.* vapour bath. উষ্মাগম *n.* the hot season, summer. উষ্মান্বিত *a.* angered, angry.

উসকানো *v.* to raise or draw up (the wick of a lamp); (usu. dero.) to excite, to instigate; to open (a boil etc.) by piercing. উসকানি *n.* excitation, instigation.

উসকোখুসকো *a.* dry and lean; untrimmed; untidy and slovenly; dishevelled; (of hair) ungreased and unkempt.

উসখুস alt. spell. of উশখুশ।

উসুল rej. spell. of উশুল।

উস্তম-পুস্তম, উস্তম-ফুস্তম *n.* extreme annoyance. উস্তম-পুস্তম করা, উস্তম-ফুস্তম করা *v.* to tease or annoy beyond measure.

উহা *pro.* that (person or thing); it. উহার *a.* its. উহারা *pro. pl.* they. উহাদের *a.* their, theirs.

উহু *int.* expressing pain etc., oh.

উহ্যমান *a.* in the state of being pulled or drawn or brought or borne.

উ *n.* the sixth vowel of the Bengali alphabet. **উকার** *n.* the symbol affixed to a consonant whilst adding the **উ**-sound to it. **উকারাদি** *a.* (of words) beginning with **উ** or **উ** -sound. **উকারান্ত** *a.* (of words) ending in **উ** or **উ** -sound.

উঢ় *a* married, wedded (নবোঢ়). *fem.* **উঢ়া**। **উঢ়ি** *n.* marriage, wedding.

উন *a.* less, lesser; short; inferior; deficient; imperfect; weak. **~আশি** *a.* & *n.* seventy-nine. **~চত্বারিংশ, ~চত্বারিংশত্তম** *a.* thirty-ninth. **~চত্বারিংশৎ, ~চল্লিশ** *a.* & *n.* thirty-nine. **~জন** *n.* the minority. **~তা** *n.* shortage; insufficiency; deficiency; inferiority; imperfection. **~ত্রিংশ, ~ত্রিংশত্তম** *a.* twenty-ninth. **~ত্রিংশৎ, ~ত্রিশ** *a.* & *n.* twenty-nine. **~নবতি, ~নব্বই,** *a.* & *n.* eighty-nine. **~নবতিতম** *a.* eighty-ninth. **~পঞ্চাশ, ~পঞ্চাশৎ** *a.* & *n.* forty-nine. **~পঞ্চাশত্তম** *a.* forty-ninth. **~বিংশ, ~বিংশতিতম** *a.* nineteenth. **~বিংশতি** *a.* & *n.* nineteen. **~মূল্যে** *adv.* below par. **~ষাট** *a.* & *n.* fifty-nine. **~ষষ্টিতম** *a.* fifty-ninth. **~সত্তর, ~সপ্ততি** *a.* & *n.* sixty-nine. **~হার** *a.* below par. **~হারে** *adv.* below par.

উনিশ alt, spell. of **উনিশ**।

উরা *v.* to descend from heaven (esp. upon the earth); to appear.

উরু *n.* the thigh. **~পর্ব** *n.* knee-joint. **~ভঙ্গ** *a.* fracture or splitting of the thigh-bone or femur. **~স্তম্ভ** *n.* a morbid inflammatory boil on the thigh.

উর্জস্বল, উর্জস্বী *a.* very strong, powerful; vigorous, spirited, mettlesome.

উর্ণনাভ, উর্ণনাভি *n.* the spider.

উর্ণসূত্র *n.* a thread of wool; spider's web or net, cobweb.

উর্ণা *n.* wool; cobweb. **~ময়** *a.* made of wool; woollen; full of wool, woolly.

ঊর্ধ্ব *n.* the upward direction or space; height; altitude. ☐ *a.* high; tall; loud (ঊর্ধ্বকণ্ঠ); upper (ঊর্ধ্বাংশ); most (ঊর্ধ্বপক্ষে); raised; lofty; noble; upturned (ঊর্ধ্বনেত্র). **~কায়** *a.* having a tall body; tall. ☐ *n.* the upper part of the body. **~ক্রম** *n.* ascending order. **~গ** *a.* going or moving upwards; ascending; soaring; moving upwards gradually; in the state of being heightened or elevated gradually; increasing; rising. **~গত** *a.* gone or moved upwards; ascended; soared; heightened, elevated; increased; risen. **~গতি** *n.* an upward movement; ascent; a gradual movement upwards; gradual heightening or elevation; increase; rise; rising. **~গামী** same as **ঊর্ধ্বগ**। **~চারী** *a.* moving in the sky or air; aspiring, ambitious; highly imaginative; full of sublime imagination. **~তন** *a.* upper; higher; superior; former. **ঊর্ধ্বতন পুরুষ** an ancestor. **~তল** *n.* surface. **~ত্ব, ~তা** *n.* height, altitude; elevation. **~দৃষ্টি, ~নেত্র** *a.* looking with upturned eyes; having eyes upturned and fixed as in the case of a dying person; looking upwards fixedly as in sublime meditation; looking with indifference or superciliousness. ☐ *n.* any of such looks. **~দেহ** *n.* the subtle body (esp. that one obtains at death). **~পাতন** *n.* (chem.) sublimation. **~পাদ** *a.* having heels upturned, headlong. **~বাহু** *a.* having an arm or both arms turned upwards or lifted up. **~ভাগ** *n.* the upper part; surface; top. **~মুখ** *a.* having the face upturned. **~রেতা** *a.* & *n.* one who has preserved his semen in full by abstaining from sexual pleasures. ☐ *n.* an appellation of Shiva (শিব). **~লোক** *n.* the heaven. **~শায়ী** *a.* lying on one's back. **~শ্বাস** *n.* state of catching the breath; breathlessness; state of panting. ☐ *a.* in the state of catching the breath; breathless, out of breath; panting. **~শ্বাসে** *adv.* catching the breath; out of breath, breathlessly; pantingly. **~সংখ্যা** *n.* highest or maximum number. **~সীমা** *n.* highest or furthest limit; upper limit. **~স্থ, ~স্থিত** *a.* lying or placed above or on high; upper; higher; senior; superior; heavenly.

উর্ধ্বাধঃ, (pop.) **উর্ধ্বাধ** *a.* vertical. **উর্ধ্বাধছেদ** *n.* (geom.) a vertical section.

উর্ধ্বে *adv.* on high, on or in the upper portion; aloft; above; upwards; in heaven; at a (certain) height.

উর্ধ্বোত্থিত *a.* ascended; moved or risen upwards; upturned; raised.

উর্বর *a.* alt. spell. of **উর্বর**।

উর্বস্থি *n.* the thigh-bone, the femur.

উর্মি *n.* a wave; a surge; a billow. **~ভঙ্গ** *n.* a wave broken on rocks or shore, a breaker. **~মান, ~ল** *a.* billowy, full of waves. **~মালা** *n.* a row of waves. **~মালী** *n.* an ocean; a sea.

উষর *a.* (of soil) salty; full of salty soil; barren; desert.

উষসী alt. spell. of **উষসী**।

উষা *n.* dawn, daybreak; early morning. **~কাল** *n.* the time of the dawn. **~কালীন** *a.* pertaining to the dawn. **~কালীন প্রার্থনা** morning prayer. **~কালে** *adv.* at dawn. **~পান** *n.* the practice of drinking a glassful of water just after getting up from bed in the morning (this practice is considered a good remedy for stomach-ailments). **~সমাগম** *n.* the setting in of the day, daybreak. **~সমাগমে** *adv.* at break of day, at dawn.

উষ্মা alt. spell. of **উষ্মা**।

উহ *n.* reasoning based on a supposition or hypothesis, one of the eight exercises of the intellect.

উহিনী *n.* a collection (অক্ষৌহিণী).

উহ্য *n.* not expressed or used but understood, implied; elliptical.

ঋ *n.* the seventh vowel of the Bengali alphabet. ঋকার *n.* the symbol affixed to a consonant whilst adding the ঋ-sound to it. ঋকারাদি *a.* (of words) beginning with ঋ or ঋ-sound. ঋকারান্ত *a.* (of words) ending in ঋ or ঋ-sound.

ঋক্ *n.* the Rig Veda; a Vedic hymn in verse; the esoteric prayer that one says to oneself whilst telling beads.

ঋক্থ, রিক্থ *n.* (*for.*) wealth; inherited wealth and property, heritage; property left by a person at death, assets of a deceased person. ~ভাগ *n.* a share in wealth or property. ~হীন *a.* poor; impecunious.

ঋক্ষ *n.* (*for.*) the bear; a star; a constellation. ~মণ্ডল *n.* (astr.) The Saptarshi, the Great Bear. ~রাজ, ঋক্ষেশ *n.* the moon (when personified).

ঋক্‌সংহিতা *n.* the collection of hymns and prayers of the Rig Veda.

ঋগ্বেদ *n.* the Rig Veda. ~-সংহিতা same as ঋক্‌সংহিতা। ঋগ্বেদী *a.* versed in or obedient to the Rig Veda.

ঋজু *a.* straight; erect; upright; uncurved, unbent; unyielding; candid, frank; sincere; easy; easy to understand or learn or read. ~কায় *a.* erect-bodied, upright. ~তা *n.* straightness, erectness; uprightness; honesty; sincerity; simplicity. ~প্রকৃতি same as ঋজুস্বভাব। ~রেখ *a.* (geom.) rectilinear. ~রেখ ক্ষেত্র (geom.) a rectilinear figure. ~রেখা *n.* a straight line. ~স্বভাব *a.* frank or sincere by nature.

ঋণ *n.* a debt; a loan; liability, (math.) the minus sign. ঋণ করা, ঋণ নেওয়া *v.* to borrow. ঋণ দেওয়া *v.* to lend. ~গ্রস্ত *a.* steeped in or run into debt; indebted. ~গ্রস্ত থাকা *v.* to be indebted (to), to owe. ~গ্রস্ত হওয়া *v.* to run into debt, to incur debt. ~গ্রহণ *n.* act of borrowing (esp. money). ~গ্রহণ করা *v.* to borrow (esp. money). ~গ্রাহী, ~গ্রহীতা *n.* a borrower, a debtor. ~চিহ্ন *n.* (math.) the minus sign (—). ~জাল *n.* the meshes of debt. ~জালে জড়ানো *v.* to enmesh or be enmeshed in debt, to involve or be involved in debt. ~দাতা *n.* a lender; a money-lender; creditor. ~দান *n.* act of lending (esp. money). ঋণদান করা *v.* to lend (esp. money). ~দায় *n.* burden of debt; liability, indebtedness. ~দাস *n.* one who serves as a slave to repay a debt, a bondsman. ~পত্র *n.* a written bond of debt; a note of hand; a debenture. ~পরিশোধ same as ঋণশোধ। ~ভার *n.* the burden of debt. ~ভারে পীড়িত *a.* encumbered with debt. ~মুক্ত *a.* relieved of debt, free from debts. ~মুক্ত করা *v.* to free from a debt or debts. ~মুক্তি *n.* release from a debt or debts; freedom from debts. ~শোধ *n.* act of paying off a debt; repayment. ~শোধ করা *v.* to pay off a debt; to repay.

ঋণাত্মক *a.* (alg.) negative.

ঋণিতা *n.* indebtedness.

ঋণী *a.* involved in debts, indebted. ঋণী থাকা *v.* to be indebted; to owe. ঋণী হওয়া *v.* to be indebted; to run into a debt.

ঋত *n.* the Supreme Being, God; (the) truth. □ *a.* worshipped; adored; ailing, sick (শীতার্ত); true; shining, luminous. ঋতানৃত *a.* true and false. □ *n.* truth and falsehood.

ঋতি *n.* act of going or moving; gait; motion.

ঋতু *n.* season, a tide or time; menstruation, the menses. ~কাল *n.* the period or time of a season, a tide; the period of menstruation, the menstrual period. ~নাথ, ~পতি *n.* the king of seasons; the spring. ~পরিবর্তন *n.* change of season. ~পর্যায় *n.* succession or revolution of the seasons. ~মতী *a.* (of a woman) menstruating, in the menses. ~মতী হওয়া *v.* to menstruate, to be in the menses; to menstruate for the first time. ~রক্ষা *n.* act of copulating with a woman on the fourth day of her menstrual period. ~রক্ষা করা *v.* to copulate with a woman on the fourth day of her menstrual period. ~রাজ same as ঋতুনাথ। ~স্নাতা *a. fem.* bathed on the fourth day of one's menstrual period. ~স্নান *n.* act of bathing on the fourth day of one's menstrual period.

ঋত্বিক *n.* a family priest; an assistant priest; a priest.

ঋদ্ধ *a.* prosperous, flourishing; affluent, well-to-do; fortunate. **ঋদ্ধি** *n.* all-round prosperity; flourishing state; affluence; fortune; property, wealth. **ঋদ্ধিমান** same as **ঋদ্ধ** ; *fem.* **ঋদ্ধিমতী**। **ঋদ্ধিলাভ** *a.* attainment of prosperity.

ঋভু *n.* a god; one of a species of deified man; a superman.

ঋষভ *n.* the ox; a mythological mountain; (mus.) the second note in the natural scale; (as a *sfx.*) the best one (মনুষ্যর্ষভ).

ঋষি *n.* a very wise ascetic, a sage; a saint; a composer of Vedic hymns. ~কল্প, ~তুল্য *a.* equal to or comparable with a saint; saint-like; saintly. ~প্রোক্ত *a.* told by a saint; (gr.—of words etc.) used by a saint but not in accordance with grammatical rules (cp. archaic). ~লোক *n.* the abode of the spirits of saints.

ঋষ্ট *a.* (astrol.) under the evil influence of a star; inauspicious. **ঋষ্টি** *n.* (astrol.) evil influence of a star; an inauspicious thing, an evil.

ঋষ্য *n.* a species of deer, white-footed or dappled antelope.

এ[1] *n.* the eighth vowel of the Bengali alphabet.

এ[2] *int.* expressing a vocative sound ('এ সখি হামারি দুখের নাহি ওর'). □ *pro.* this person or animal or thing, he, she, it. □ *a.* this.

এই *a.* this. □ *pro.* this, it. □ *int.* expressing : a vocative sound (এই ছেলে শোন্) ; displeasure, fear, wonder etc. (এই গেল যা, এই মরল, এই রে). □ *adv.* just (এই এখনি), just this (এই কেবল). **এই অজুহাতে** on this plea or pretext or excuse or ruse. **এই কতক্ষণ** just a little while ago. **এই কারণে, ~জন্য** for this reason, on account of this. **~ক্ষণে** *adv.* this instant, now, this very moment. **এই প্রকারে** in this manner, in this way, thus. **এই বেলা** now that there is time, while this opportunity lasts, meanwhile. **এই মর্মে** to this effect. **এই কেবল, ~তো, ~মাত্র** this much; just this; just now. **~বার** *adv.* this time; now; on this occasion. **~রূপ** *a.* suchlike, similar; such. **~রূপে** *adv.* in this way or manner, in the fashion, thus. **এই হেতু** same as **এই কারণে**।

এইতো, এইবার, এইরূপ see **এই**।

এইসা, অ্যায়সা *a.* suchlike, similar; such; too much; too great or big; tremendous. □ *adv.* in such a manner or amount, such a manner or amount, such; too much; too big; tremendously.

এউজি see **এওজ**।

এওজ, এওয়াজ *a.* exchange, barter. **এওজি, এওয়াজি, এউজি** *a.* obtained by exchange or barter (এওজি জমি).

এঃ *int.* expressing : detestation, displeasure, aversion etc.

এঁকেবেঁকে *adv.* in a winding manner, in a meandering manner; in a zigzag way.

এঁচড় coll. form of **ইঁচড়**। **এঁচড়ে পাকা** see **ইঁচড়**।

এঁটুলি, এঁটুল *n.* a variety of Diptera, a tick.

এঁটে coll. form of **আঁটিয়া** (see **আঁটা**). **এঁটে ওঠা** *v.* to cope with, to be equal to, to be a match for.

এঁটেল *a.* sticky, adhesive; hard in dry state but soft and slippery when wet (এঁটেল মাটি). **এঁটেল পোকা** a variety of Diptera, a tick. **এঁটেল মাটি** clayey soil.

এঁটো, (rare) **এঁঠো** *a.* (of food and drink) left over after eating, left over on the plate after eating; orts; (of things other than food) that which has come in contact with the leavings of one's meal or with cooked food; not washed after eating (এঁটো মুখ). □ *n.* scraps or leavings of one's meal; orts. **এঁটোকাঁটা** *n.* leavings or scraps of a meal. **এঁটোখেকো** *a.* (fig.) cringing. **এঁটো পাত কখনো স্বর্গে যায় না** (fig.) an unworthy person can never accommodate himself or herself in a high position, a swine is never allowed to sit on a sofa. **এঁটো পাড়া** *v.* to remove plates when the dinner is over, to clear the table.

এঁড়িগেঁড়ি *n. pl.* spawn; (contemp.) a large number of offspring, kiddies.

এঁড়ে[1] *n.* an ox, a bull; a bullcalf. □ *a.* male (এঁড়ে বাছুর) ; resembling the roar of an ox,bellowing (এঁড়ে গলা) ; indomitable or obstinate like an angry bull (এঁড়ে লোক).

এঁড়ে[2] *n.* (of infants) constitutional indigestion or dyspepsia or rickets. **এঁড়ে লাগা** *v.* to suffer from constitutional indigestion or dyspepsia or from rickets.

এঁদের coll. form of **ইঁহাদের** (see **ইহারা**).

এঁদো, (dial.) **এঁধো** *a.* full of darkness, gloomy; giving no access to light (এঁদো বাড়ি) ; dark narrow dirty and blind (এঁদো গলি) ; covered with hyacinth etc.; muddy (এঁদো পুকুর) ; damp or marshy, abominable (এঁদো জায়গা).

এক *a.* & *n.* one. □ *n.* & *pro.* one or single person or individual (দেশোদ্ধার একের কাজ নয়). □ *a.* only one; a certain (একসময়) ; completely full or filled or packed or covered (একবাড়ি লোক, একমুখ দাড়ি) ; same, one and the same (এক মায়ের সন্তান) ; united ('যত ভাই বোন এক

হউক') ; amalgamated; joined (দুই হাত এক করা) ; mixed (চালেডালে এক করা) ; one and only one (ঈশ্বর এক ও অভিন্ন) ; one of a number, a (রবীন্দ্রনাথ বিশ্বের এক শ্রেষ্ঠ কবি) ; unchanging, fixed (সেই এক গোঁ, ভদ্রলোকের এক কথা) ; concentrated (একমনে). **~আধ** *a.* a few; sparse; scanty; rare. **এক আঁচড়ে** see **আঁচড়** । **একই** *a.* same; very same, one and the same. **এক-এক** *a.* some, one by one (এক-এক করে), certain (এক-এক দিন). **একক** *a.* alone, unaccompanied. □ *n.* the first figure from the right of an arithmetical number; (math.) a unit. **এককড়া** see **কড়া** । **~কণা** *n.* very little, a very small amount. **~কথায়** in a word. **~কলমী** *n.* a columnist who writes only one column of a newspaper. **~কাটা, ~কাট্টা** pop. var. of **একাট্টা** । **~কালীন** *a.* done or to be done only once, given or to be given only once, at a time; simultaneous; contemporary. **এককালীন অনুদান** a lump grant, non-recurring grant. **~কালে** *adv.* at one time, once upon a time; at one and the same time, simultaneously. **~কাঁড়ি** *a.* a lot of, a heap of. **~কেন্দ্রিক, ~কেন্দ্রী, ~কেন্দ্রীয়** *a.* concentric. **~গঙ্গা** *a.* filled or full to the brim, full, replete (একগঙ্গা জল). **~গর্ভপত্রী** *n.* monocarpellary. **~গলা** *a.* up to the throat or chin. **~-গা** *a.* covering the whole of the body (এক-গা গয়না, এক-গা খোস). **~গাদা** *a.* a heap of; a great number or collection of (একগাদা লোক). **~গাল** *a.* a mouthful of. □ *n.* a mouthful. **~গুঁয়ে** *a.* obstinate, obdurate, stubborn; wilful, wayward; disobedient, indocile; indomitable. **~গুঁয়েমি** *n.* obstinacy; wilfulness, waywardness; disobedience, indocility, stubbornness, indomitableness. **~ঘরে** *a.* ostracized; cast out of society. **একঘরে ব্যক্তি** an outcast. **~ঘাত** *a.* linear. **~ঘাত সমীকরণ** a linear equation. **~ঘেয়ে** *a.* monotonous; hackneyed. **~ঘেয়েমি** *n.* monotony; hackneyedness. **~চত্বারিংশ** *a.* forty-first. **~চত্বারিংশৎ** *a.* & *n.* forty-one. **~চত্বারিংশত্তম** *a.* forty-first. *fem.* **~চত্বারিংশত্তমী** । **~চর** *a.* moving alone (cp. segregarious); shunning company. **~চল্লিশ** *a.* & *n.* forty-one. **~চালা** *a.* having only one slanting roof. □ *n.* such a hut or shed. **~চিত্ত** *a.* absorbedly attentive, intent, concentrated. **~চুল** *a.* hairbreadth, very slight, negligible (একচুল ব্যবধান). □ *adv.* in the least. **~চেটিয়া,** (coll.) **~চেটে** *a.* monopolistic. **একচেটিয়া অধিকার** monopoly. **~চোখো** *a.* one-eyed, single-eyed; looking in one direction only; partial; prejudiced, biased; preferential. **~চোখোমি** *n.* partiality; prejudice; bias; preferential treatment. **~চোট** *adv.* enough or too much at a stroke or at one time. **~চোটে** *adv.* without break or respite (একচোটে বলা বা করা) ; with one stroke or attempt (একচোটে জিতে নেওয়া) ; simultaneously (একচোটে সবাইকে বকা). **~চ্ছত্র** *a.* paramount, sovereign; brought under one rule ('একচ্ছত্র করিবে ধরণী'). **~ছুটে** *adv.* at a single run. **~জাই** *adv.* repeatedly, over and over again, incessantly, continuously, without stop (একজাই বলা). □ *a.* united; assembled, collected. □ *n.* sum total (বাৎসরিক আয়ব্যয়ের একজাই). **একজাই করা** *v.* to unite; to assemble, to collect. **~জিদ্দি** *a.* same as **একগুঁয়ে** । **~জোট** *a.* united; assembled. **~জোটে** *adv.* in a body, in concert, unitedly. **~জ্বরি** *n.* remittent fever. □ *a.* suffering from remittent fever. **~টা, ~টি** *a.* one; only one, not more than one; one particular (একটা পরামর্শ আছে). □ *n. pro.* any one (একটা হলেই হল). **একটা-কিছু, একটা-কোনো** *a.* existent but not known or determinate, some (একটা-কিছু খুঁত আছে). □ *pro* & *n.* something (একটা-কিছু চাই). **একটা-দুটো** *a.* only a few, of a negligible number. **~টানা** *a.* pointed or moving in one direction only; continually onward; continuous, continual; incessant, nonstop (একটানা বৃষ্টি) ; monotonous. □ *adv.* in one direction only; continually onward; continuously; continually; incessantly, without break; monotonously. **একটিমাত্র** *a.* only one; one and one only. **~টু, ~টুকু** *a.* & *adv.* only a little; just a little; a little. **একটু একটু করে** *adv.* little by little, bit by bit; slowly but gradually. ~টেরে *a.* curved a little; leaning to one side, slanting; (of judgment etc.) one-sided, partial, ex parte. □ *a.* & *adv.* lying apart; keeping aloof. ~তন্ত্রী *a.* (of musical instruments) one stringed; unanimous; under one and the same rule. □ *n.* a one-stringed musical instrument, a monochord. ~তম *a.* (*super.*) one of or amongst more than two. ~তর *a.* (*compar.*) one of two, either. ~তরফা *a.* ex parte; partial; one-sided. ~তলা *n.* the ground floor (of a building or a multi-decked vehicle). □ *a.* one-storeyed; one-decked, single-decked. **একতলা গাড়ি** a single decker. ~তলীয় *a.* coplanar. ~তান *n.* a harmonious note; harmony; concert. □ *a.* harmonious; concerted; closely atttentive, concentrated. ~তানমনা *a.* closely attentive, rapt in attention; intent. ~তারা *n.* a variety of monochord (chiefly used by the Vaishnava singers). ~তালা[১] var. of একতলা। ~তালা[২] ~তাল *n.* an Indian musical measure. ~তিল see তিল। ~ত্রিংশ *a.* thirty-first. ~ত্রিংশৎ *a.* & *n.* thirty-one. ~ত্রিংশত্তম *a.* thirty-first. *fem.* ~ত্রিংশত্তমী। ~ত্রিশ *a.* & *n.* thirty-one. ~দন্ত *a.* having but one tooth, one-toothed, single-toothed. ~দম *adv.* at all; in the least; completely, thoroughly, utterly. ~দমে *adv.* in one breath; without stop. ~দল *a.* monocotyledonous. ~দিন *adv.* one day, someday; one day or other (একদিন না একদিন) ; once, once upon a time; at one time in the past; in the past. □ *n.* a glorious time or period (esp. one that has passed away). **একদিন অন্তর একদিন** every other day, every alternate day. ~দৃষ্টি, (poet.) ~দিঠি *a.* looking fixedly, gazing. ~দৃষ্টে *adv.* with a fixed look, gazingly. ~দেশ *n.* a part or portion or division (esp. of a country); a region. ~দেশদর্শিতা *n.* act of viewing partially; partiality; narrow-mindedness, illiberality; bias; prejudice; want of foresight. ~দেশদর্শী *a.* viewing partially; partial; narrow-minded, illiberal; biased; prejudiced; lacking in foresight. ~দেশীয় *a.* of or living in the same country. ~দৌড়ে *adv.* at a run. ~ধাতুমান *n.* (econ.) monometallism. ~নবতি *a.* & *n.* ninety-one. ~নবতিতম *a.* ninety-first. *fem.* ~নবতিতমী। ~নলা, ~নলি *a.* (chiefly of a gun) single-barrelled, one-barrelled. ~নাগাড়ে *adv.* at a stretch, continuously. ~নায়ক *n.* (pol.) an autocrat or a dictator. ~নায়কতন্ত্র *n.* autocracy or dictatorship. ~নায়কতান্ত্রিক *a.* autocratic or dictatorial. ~নিষ্ঠ *a.* devoted to or engaged in only one thing, single-minded or single-acting; absorbedly attentive, intent. *fem.* ~নিষ্ঠা। ~নিষ্ঠতা *n.* devotion to or engagement in only one thing, single-mindedness. **এক পক্ষে** *adv.* viewing from one angle; in a way; somewhat. ~পঞ্চাশ, ~পঞ্চাশৎ *a.* & *n.* fifty-one. ~পঞ্চাশত্তম *a.* fifty-first. *fem.* একপঞ্চাশত্তমী। **একপত্নীক** *a. mas.* having one wife (at a time), monogamous. ~পদীকরণ *n.* (gr.) unification of several words into a compound word, formation of a compound word. ~পাটি *n.* one of a pair; one set of (teeth). ~পাদ *n.* a fourth part, a quarter. □ *a.* one-fourth. ~পার্শ্বিক, ~পার্শ্বীয় *a.* one-sided; partial; (bot.) unilateral. ~পেট *n.* a bellyful, one's fill. □ *a.* bellyful of. □ *adv.* to one's fill. ~পেশে *a.* leaning or stooping to one side; aslant; one-sided; partial. ~প্রকার *adv.* of a sort, in a way, somewhat. □ *a.* of a type; of some sort or other. ~প্রতিসম *a.* zygomorphic. ~প্রস্থ *a.* severe; sufficient, of considerable amount. ~প্রাণ *a.* inseparably united. ~বংশীয়, ~বংশোদ্ভব *a.* descended from the same ancestor, consanguine, consanguineous. একবগ্‌গা coll. corrup. of একবর্গা। ~বচন see বচন। ~বর্গা *a.* obstinate; stubborn, dogged. ~বয়সী *a.* of the same age. ~বর্ণ see বর্ণ। ~বস্ত্র *a.* wearing only a single piece of cloth. ~বস্ত্রে *adv.* wearing only a single piece of cloth and taking nothing along. ~বাক্যে *adv.* with one voice; with one accord, unanimously. ~বার *n.* one time. □ *adv.* at one time; once. একবারে *adv.* at a time; at a stroke; thoroughly. ~বাস same as একবস্ত্র। ~বিংশ *a.* twenty-first.

~বিংশতি *a.* & *n.* twenty-one. ~বিংশতিতম *a.* twenty-first. *fem.* ~বিংশতিতমী। ~বীজপত্রী *a.* (bot.) monocotyledonous. ~বুক *a.* chest-high; breast-deep. ~ভাব *n.* uniformity of state or quality or disposition. ~ভাবাপন্ন *a.* uniform in state or quality or disposition; of one mind. ~ভাবে *adv.* uniformly ; in the same way; without change, unchangingly. ~ভিতে *adv.* in one direction; to one side; apart. ~মত, ~মতাবলম্বী *a.* holding the same opinion; agreed; unanimous; holding the same religious faith. ~মনা *a.* absorbed; single-minded. ~মনে with rapt attention; single-mindedly. ~মাতৃক *a.* born of one and the same mother, uterine. ~মাত্র *a.* only. ~মাত্রা *n.* one dose; one musical or metrical syllable. ~মুখীকরণ *n.* (phys.) rectification. ~মুখো *a.* having one direction, one way. ~মুষ্টি *a.* a handful of. ~মেটে, ~মেটিয়া *a.* (esp. of a mould or cast or an idol) primed; rough-cast; (fig.) rough-wrought. একমেটে করা *v.* to prime; to rough-cast; (fig.) to do in a preliminary manner, to rough out. ~যোগে *adv.* in a body; unitedly. ~রকম *a.* of the same kind, type, nature, appearance etc.; same; similar. □ *adv.* in a way, of a sort, somewhat, moderately; on the whole, somehow. ~রতি, ~রত্তি *a.* (lit.) amounting to a rati (রতি[1]) or 0·121 grams or 1·875 grains; only a little, a bit of; very small, tiny. ~রব, ~ রা *n.* one voice. ~রূপ same as একরকম। ~রেখীয় *a.* (geom.) collinear. ~রোখা *a.* obstinate; self-willed, wilful; hot-tempered, quick-tempered, irascible; having designs on one side only (একরোখা চাদর). ~লহমা *n.* an instant, a moment; jiffy. ~লহমায় *adv.* in an instant, in a moment, in a jiffy. ~লিঙ্গ *n.* Shiva (শিব). □ *a.* unisexual; (bot.) declinous. ~লিঙ্গতা *n.* unisexuality; (bot.) declinism. ~শিরা *n.* hydrocele; orchitis. ~শিরাল *a.* unicostate. ~শিলা *a.* monolithic. ~শেষ *n.* excessiveness, overmuchness; (gr.) a system of forming compound words in which only one word is chosen from amongst a group and is modified to represent the whole group. কষ্টের একশেষ trouble beyond measure. নাকালের একশেষ harassed beyond measure. ~ষট্টি, ~ষষ্টি *a.* & *n.* sixty-one. ~ষষ্টিতম *a.* sixty-first. *fem.* একষষ্টিতমী। ~সঙ্গে *a.* in a body, all together; at the same time, simultaneously. ~সপ্ততি *a.* & *n.* seventy-one. ~সপ্ততিতম *a.* seventy-first. *fem.* একসপ্ততিতমী। ~সূত্রে *adv.* in one string. ~স্থানে *adv.* in or at the same place; in a certain place, somewhere. ~হাঁটু *a.* knee-deep. ~হাত *a.* measuring one cubit. □ *adv.* enough for one time. একহাত নেওয়া *v.* to pay one out or back, to retaliate ; to teach one a lesson. ~হারা *a.* slim; of a delicate structure.

একজামিন *n.* an examination; a test; a trial; an experiment. একজামিন করা *v.* to examine. একজামিন দেওয়া *v.* to appear at or to sit for an examination.

একজিবিশন *n.* an exhibition.

একতা *n.* unity, union; sameness, oneness, identity. একতাই বল unity is strength.

একতান, একতারা see এক।

একত্ব *n.* oneness, sameness, identity; (rare) unity.

একত্র *adv.* in or at one place; unitedly; in a body, en bloc. □ *a.* assembled or lying in one and the same place; united. একত্রিত same as একত্র (*a.*).

একদা *adv.* once upon a time; once, at one time, one day.

একর *n.* an acre.

একরার *n.* confession; promise; agreement; statement. ~নামা *n.* written promise or statement; bond; deed of agreement.

একলসেঁড়ে, একলষেঁড়ে, (coll.) **একলাসেঁড়ে.** *a.* fond of living alone; self-centred; grossly selfish.

একলা *a.* lone; unaccompanied; helpless. □ *adv.* alone; helplessly. একলাই একশো (to be) a host in oneself. also একাই একশো।

একশা *a.* mixed up together or confusedly, in a state of confusion and disorder, in a muddle.

একশেষ see **এক**।

একা *a.* unaccompanied; lone; solitary. ☐ *adv.* alone. **একা-একা** *adv.* by oneself, single-handed.

একাংশ *n.* one part or portion, aliquot part.

একাকার *a.* (lit.) same or similar in shape or appearance; mixed up or conglomerated into a confused mass; mixed up confusedly.

একাকী *a.* & *adv.* alone; unaccompanied; by oneself, single-handed (সে একাকী খাটে). *fem.* **একাকিনী**। **একাকিত্ব** *n.* loneliness; solitariness.

একাক্ষ *n.* one-eyed; (phys.) uniaxial.

একাক্ষর *a.* (of words etc.) of one syllable; one-lettered, single-lettered. *fem.* **একাক্ষরা**।

একাগ্র *a.* intent; single-minded, concentrated; single-acting; absorbedly attentive. **~তা** *n.* intentness; single-mindedness, concentration; rapt attention. **~চিত্ত** same as **একাগ্র**। **~চিত্তে** *adv.* intently; single-mindedly, concentratedly; with rapt attention.

একাঘ্নী *n.* (myth.) a missile which was sure to kill only one person aimed at.

একাঙ্ক নাটক *n.* one-act play.

একাট্টা *a.* assembled, collected, combined, united; concerted.

একাত্তর *a.* & *n.* seventy-one.

একাত্ম *a.* having one and the same soul; inseparably united, closely intimate.

একাত্মতা *n.* (of more than one person) state of having but one and the same soul; inseparable unity; close intimacy and agreement.

একাত্মবাদ *n.* (phil.) there is nothing but God— this Vedantic doctrine, pantheism, monism. **একাত্মবাদী** *a.* monistic. ☐ *n.* a monist.

একাত্মা *a.* (of two or more persons) having but one and the same soul; inseparably united; having close intimacy and agreement.

একাদশ *a.* & *n.* eleven. ☐ *a.* eleventh. **একাদশী** *a. fem.* eleven years old. ☐ *n.* the eleventh day of the lunar fortnight; the fast observed by Hindus on this day.

একাদিক্রমে *adv.* serially from the first; continuously, without break; consecutively, in an uninterrupted sequence, successively.

একাধার *n.* one and the same receptacle or vessel. **একাধারে** *adv.* in one and the same person or thing , in one; simultaneously, at the same time.

একাধিক *a.* more than one. **~বার** *a.* more than once.

একাধিকার *n.* monopoly; exclusive rights.

একাধিপতি *n.* the sole ruler or master; a sovereign or paramount ruler; one who is all in all. **একাধিপত্য** *n.* sole exclusive rule or overlordship; sovereignty, paramountcy; state of being all in all.

একানব্বই, (coll.) **একানব্বুই** *a.* & *n.* ninety-one.

একান্ত *a.* excessive; thorough; downright; overwhelming (একান্ত বিপদ) ; earnest (একান্ত মিনতি) ; sure; certain; solitary, lonely; secluded; private; personal. ☐ *adv.* very, much; thoroughly; earnestly; at all. **একান্ত কক্ষ** a private chamber; (loos.) an ante-chamber. **~ই**, **~পক্ষে** *adv.* if at all. **~সচিব** *n.* a private secretary. **একান্তে** *adv.* in private, confidentially; aside.

একান্তর *a.* alternate. **একান্তর কোণ** *n.* alternate angle.

একান্তরক্রিয়া *n.* alternando.

একান্ন[1] *a.* & *n.* fifty-one.

একান্ন[2], **একান্নবর্তী**, **একান্নভুক্ত** *a.* living and messing jointly; living in a joint family. **একান্নবর্তী পরিবার** a joint family.

একাবয়ব *a.* similar, alike; uniform.

একাবলী *n.* a one-stringed necklace; (pros.) a variety of Bengali metrical foot.

একার[1] *n.* the symbol 'ে' affixed to a consonant whilst adding the এ-sound to it. **একারাদি** *a.* (of words) beginning with এ or এ-sound. **একারান্ত** *a.* ending in এ or এ-sound.

একার[2] *a.* of one's own, belonging to oneself.

একার্থ *a.* having one and the same meaning, synonymous (also **একার্থবোধক**, **একার্থসূচক**) ; having one and the same purpose.

একাল *n.* present times, modern times.

একাশি, একাশীতি *a.* & *n.* eighty-one. **একাশিতম** *a.* eighty-first. *fem.* **একাশিতমী**।

একাশ্রয়, একাশ্রিত *a.* depending on only one for help; deprived of any alternative. **একাশ্রিত গুণ** a simple attribute or predicate; a quality subsisting in one person.

একাসন *n.* one and the same seat. ☐ *a.* sitting on one and the same seat; having no seat but one.

একাহ *n.* a period of one day.

একাহার *n.* only one meal daily. **একাহারী** *a.* taking but one meal daily.

একাহিক *a.* to be accomplished within a day; happening or appearing daily; quotidian (একাহিক জ্বর) ; born or produced daily; living for a day only.

একি, একী *int.* expressing : surprise, what's this, what.

একীকরণ *n.* act of levelling or equalizing; equalization; unification, amalgamation; act of mixing up together, mixture; fusion.

একীকৃত *a.* levelled, equalized; unified, amalgamated; mixed up together; fused.

একীভবন *n.* act of being levelled or equalized or unified or amalgamated or mixed up together, equalization, unification, amalgamation, mixture; fusion.

একীভাব *n.* unity; unification; state of being levelled or equalized; fusion.

একীভূত *a.* levelled, equalized, unified, amalgamated; mixed up together; fused.

একুন *n.* sum total. **একুনে** *adv.* in total; in all, altogether.

একুল-ওকুল *n.* (both.) the house of the husband and the house of the father (of a married woman); (both) the mortal world of life and world or life after death; this world and the next; both the courses; both the alternatives.

একুশ *a.* & *n.* twenty-one. **একুশে** *n.* the twenty-first day of a month. ☐ *a.* (of days of a month) twenty-first.

একে *pro.* one person (একে চায়, আরে পায়) ; one thing ('ভাবে একে আর') ; one. ☐ *adv.* on the one hand, in the first place (একে মূর্খ তায় অহংকারী).

একে-একে *adv.* one by one; one after another; gradually (সে একে-একে সব ভুলেছে).

একেবারে *adv.* thoroughly, out and out. ☐ *a.* downright, thorough.

একেলা var. of **একলা**।

একেশ্বর *n.* only one God; the sole master. **~বাদ** *n.* (theol.) monotheism. **~বাদী** *a.* monotheistic. ☐ *n.* a monotheist.

একোদ্দিষ্ট *n.* the annual obsequial rites in respect of only one deceased person.

একোন *a.* short of or less by one. **~চত্বারিংশ** *a.* thirty-ninth. **~চত্বারিংশৎ** *a.* & *n.* thirty-nine. **~চত্বারিংশত্তম** *a.* thirty-ninth. *fem.* **একোনচত্বারিংশত্তমী**। **~নবতি** *a.* & *n.* eighty-nine. **~নবতিতম** *a.* eighty-ninth. *fem.* **একোননবতিতমী**। **~পঞ্চাশ** *a.* forty-ninth. **~পঞ্চাশৎ** *a.* & *n.* forty-nine. **~পঞ্চাশত্তম** *a.* forty-ninth. *fem.* **একোনপঞ্চাশত্তমী**। **~ষষ্টি** *a.* & *n.* fifty-nine. **~ষষ্টিতম** *a.* fifty-ninth. *fem.* **একোনষষ্টিতমী**। **~সপ্ততি** *a.* & *n.* seventy-nine. *fem.* **একোনসপ্ততিতমী**। **একোনাশীতি** *a.* & *n.* seventy-nine. **একোনাশীতিতম** *n.* seventy-ninth. *fem.* **একোনাশীতিতমী**।

এক্কা *n.* a light two-wheeled vehicle drawn by one horse (resembling a dog-cart).

এক্তিয়ার var. of **এখতিয়ার**।

এক্ষণ *n.* this moment. **এক্ষণে** *adv.* at this moment; at the present time, now; just now, immediately, at once.

এখতিয়ার *n.* jurisdiction; purview; range; authority; right; control.

এখন *adv.* at this time, at this instant; now; at present; in modern times, nowadays; recently, currently; at last, after so long (এত বলার পর এখন খেয়াল হল) ; at some later time (আরে রাখ না, খাব এখন) ; (used in introducing a sentence) and now (এখন সে ছিল ডাকাত). ☐ *n.* this time; present times. **~ই, এখনি** *adv.* at once. **~ও, এখনো** *adv.* till now; even in this state; even after this; notwithstanding this; still. **~কার** *a.* of this time; of the present times; current, recent. **এখন-তখন** *a.* & *adv.* very critical; on the point of death (এখন-তখন অবস্থা). **এখন থেকে** from now on. **এখন পর্যন্ত** till now.

এখান *n.* this place; this world, this mortal

world. ~কার *a.* of this place or world. এখানে *adv.* in or at this place, here.

এগজামিন var. of **একজামিন।**

এগজিবিশন var.of **একজিবিশন।**

এগনো *v.* to advance, to go forward; to proceed, to go on ; to progress; to approach. **এগনো-পিছনো** *n.* (lit.) going forward and retreating; vacillation; irresolution; indecision.

এগারো *a.* & *n.* eleven. **~ই** *n.* the eleventh day of month. ☐ *a.* (of days of a month) eleventh.

এগিয়ে দেওয়া *v.* to go along with somebody; to accompany up to a distance; to see off; push somebody forward (সামনে এগিয়ে দেওয়া).

এগুনো, এগোনো variants of **এগনো।**

এজন্য, (coll.) **এজন্যে** *adv.* for this; for this reason.

এজমালি *a.* (of property) held by more than one; shared jointly; joint (এজমালি সম্পত্তি).

এজলাস *n.* a sitting of a judicial court,the bench. **~খানা** *n.* court-room.

এজাহার *n.* a statement about a crime given to the police; (loos.) deposition.

এজেন্ট *n.* a commercial representative, an authorized delegate, an agent.

এজেন্সি *n.* agency.

এঞ্জিন var. of **ইনজিন।**

এঞ্জিনিয়ার var. of **ইনজিনিয়ার।**

এটর্নি *n.* an attorney-at-law, an attorney.

এটা *pro.* (dero.) this thing or creature or person, it, this.

এটি *pro.* (affectionately) this thing or creature or person, it, this.

এডভোকেট alt. spell. of **অ্যাডভোকেট।**

এডিটর, এডিটার *n.* an editor of a newspaper, periodical etc. **এডিটরি, এডিটারি** *n.* act of editing, editorship.

এড়া *v.* (arch.) to shoot or throw.

এড়ানো *v.* to avoid, to shun; to get rid of; to pass over, to omit; to disobey. **এড়িয়ে যাওয়া** same as **এড়ানো ;** (of tongue) to fail to utter properly, to stutter, to stammer.

এড়ি *n.* heel. **~তোলা জুতো** high-heeled shoes.

এড়িগেড়ি var. of **এঁড়িগেঁড়ি।**

এড়ো *a.* slanting, leaning; crosswise.

এত *adv.* so much or so many; to such a great extent (এত করে) ; in such a great number. **~ক্ষণ** *adv.* so long; by this time. **~গুলি** *a.* so many; so much. **এত তাড়াতাড়ি বা শীঘ্র** so soon. **এতদিকে** in so many directions. **এতবার** so many times. **এত রাতে** so late at night.

এতৎ *pro.* this person or creature or thing, it. ☐ *a.* this. **~কালীন** *a.* of present times.

এতদতিরিক্ত *a.* besides this; more than this, in addition to this; over and above this.

এতদপেক্ষা *a* & *adv.* than this.

এতদর্থে *adv.* for this; for this reason; to this effect; implying this meaning.

এতদিন *adv.* for or during or in so many days, so long. ☐ *n.* so many days. **এতদিনে** *adv.* after so many days, after so long.

এতদীয় *pro. a.* of this person or creature or thing, of this, its.

এতদুত্তরে *adv.* in reply to this, in answer to this.

এতদুদ্দেশ্যে *adv.* for this purpose, with this end in view.

এতদূর *adv.* so far. ☐ *con.* as far. ☐ *int.* what an audacity.

এতদ্দেশীয় *a.* of or belonging to this place or country.

এতদ্দেশে *adv.* in this country.

এতদ্ব্যতীত, এতদ্ভিন্ন *adv.* besides this, in addition to this; apart from this.

এতদ্রূপ *a.* like this; similar to this.

এতন্মধ্যে *adv.* in the midst of it or these; in it or these; amongst these; in the meantime, meanwhile.

এতাদৃশ *a.* like this; similar to this.

এতাবৎ *a.* & *adv.* so much or so many; thus far. **এতাবৎ কাল** so long.

এতিম *a.* having no means of livelihood, helpless; orphan. **~খানা** *n.* a refuge; an orphanage.

এতে coll. form of **ইহাতে।**

এতেক *a.* (chiefly poet.) so much or so many.

এতেলা, এত্তেলা *n.* news; information; notice (বিনা এতেলায়). **এতেলা করা** to inform; to report.

এদানীং corrup. of **ইদানীং।**

এদিক *n.* this side; this country or region

or place; this party. **এদিক-ওদিক, এদিক-সেদিক** *n.* this side and that; all quarters, all sides, all regions or places. ☐ *adv.* (to) this side and that; all around; here and there. **এদিক-ওদিক করা, এদিক-সেদিক করা** *v.* to vacillate, to waver; to misrepresent; to soften (an account) unduly, to mince matters; to defalcate; to balance (an account) by manipulation. **এদিকে** *adv.* in or to this side of country or region or place or party; in the meantime, meanwhile.

এদের *pro. a. pl.* their; of them or these.

এদ্দিন coll. corrup. of **এতদিন**।

এধার *n.* this side. **এধার-ওধার** *n.* this side and that; all sides, all quarters. ☐ *adv.* (to) this side and that; all around; here and there. **এধার-ওধার করা** *v.* to vacillate, to waver; to misrepresent; to mince matters; to defalcate; to balance (an account) by manipulation.

এনকোর *n.* & *int.* encore; applause. **এনকোর দেওয়া** *v.* to applaud, to encore.

এনামেল pop. var. of **ইনামেল**।

এনট্রানস, এনট্রান্স *n.* entrance examination.

এনতার *a.* innumerable, multitudinous, countless; profuse; endless; continuous, continual, incessant. ☐ *adv.* innumerably, without number; immeasurably, profusely; without end or break, incessantly, continuously.

এনভেলাপ *n.* an envelope.

এন্ডা corrup. of **আন্ডা**। **এন্ডায়-গন্ডায় মেলানো** to balance (an account) by manipulation.

এন্ডি *n.* a variety of silk (chiefly produced in Assam).

এন্তাকাল var. of **ইন্তাকাল**।

এন্তাজার var. of **ইন্তাজার**।

এন্তার alt. spell. of **এনতার**।

এন্তেকাল var. of **ইন্তাকাল**।

এন্তেজার corrup, of **ইন্তাজার**।

এ পর্যন্ত *adv.* till now; thus far.

এপার *n.* this bank or shore; this side or extremity. **এপার-ওপার করা** *v.* to go across and come back; ferry over or across.

এপাশ *n.* this side or edge. **এপাশ-ওপাশ করা** *v.* to toss or turn about restlessly and continuously (esp. in bed).

এপ্রিল *n.* April.

এফ এ *n.* the First Arts examination of a university, F.A. (no longer in vogue now).

এফিডেভিট *n.* an affidavit.

এফোঁড়-ওফোঁড় see **ফোঁড়**।

এবং *in comp.* like this, suchlike, such (এবংবিধ). *con.* and.

এবংবিধ *a.* like this kind; of this kind; like this, suchlike, such.

এবমস্তু *int.* be it so, amen.

এবম্প্রকার, এবম্বিধ same as **এবংবিধ**।

এবড়ো-খেবড়ো *a.* rugged, rough; uneven.

এবাদত *n.* worship. **~খানা** *n.* a house of worship.

এবার *n.* this time; this year; this life. ☐ *adv.* on this occasion, at this time, this time; now; in this year, this year; in this life. ☐ *int.* how can you escape now ? **~কার** *a.* of this time or year or life; present, current, this.

এবে *adv.* (poet. obs.) this time; now; nowadays.

এবেলা *n.* this part of the day; forenoon. ☐ *adv.* in this part of the day. **এবেলা-ওবেলা** *adv.* twice daily, in the forenoon and afternoon.

এম এ *n.* the Master of Arts examination of a university, M.A.; one who has passed the M.A. examination, an M.A.

এম এল এ *n.* a Member of the Legislative Assembly, an MLA.

এম পি *n.* a Member of Parliament, an MP.

এমত, (obs. & poet.) **এমতি** *a.* like this; suchlike; such; similar.

এমন *a.* like this; suchlike; such; similar. ☐ *pro.* such a one (এমনটি আর পাবে না). ☐ *adv.* in such a way, to such an extent (এমন করে বলল, এমন বলল). **~কী** *adv.* even. **~তরো** *a.* like this; suchlike; such; similar. **এমন সময়ে** at this time; at such a time; then.

এমনি *a.* & *n.* same as **এমন**। ☐ *adv.* in such a way, to such an extent; without any particular purpose (এমনি এলাম) ; empty-handed (কুটুমের বাড়ি এমনি যাওয়া) ; without cause (কেউ কাউকে এমনি মারে না, অসুখ এমনি হয় না) ; spontaneously (এমনি ফসল ফলে না).

এমনি-এমনি *adv.* without cause; spontaneously.

এম বি *n.* (formerly) the degree examination in medicine (of a university), M.B.; one who holds this degree, an M.B. **এম বি বি এস** *n.* the bachelor's degree in medicine.

এমুড়ো *n.* this end. **এমুড়ো ওমুড়ো** *adv.* from this end to that; throughout the length of; from the beginning to the end; from head to foot; thoroughly.

এ যাত্রা *adv.* this time.

এযাবৎ, এযাবৎকাল *adv.* till now. hitherto.

এয়ার var. of **ইয়ার** ৷

এয়ো, এয়ো-স্ত্রী *n. fem.* a woman whose husband is alive. **এয়োতি** *n.* a woman whose husband is alive; a mark or marks borne on the person of a woman to indicate that her husband is alive. □ *a. fem.* having one's husband alive.

এর *pro. a.* his; its; of this.

এরকা *n.* a variety of reed.

এরণ্ড *n.* the castor-oil plant. **এরণ্ড-তেল** *n.* castor-oil. **এরণ্ডা** *n.* a variety of tree, the peepul.

এরা *pl.* of **এ** ৷

এরারুট var. of **অ্যারোরুট** ৷

এরূপ *a.* like this; suchlike; such; similar. □ *pro.* such a one (এরূপটি). □ *adv.* in such a manner, to such an extent (এরূপ ধমকাল). **এরূপে** *adv.* in this way or manner, in such a way or manner, thus.

এরোপ্লেন *n.* an aeroplane.

এলা *n.* cardamom or its plant.

এলাকা *n.* area; jurisdiction; limit.

এলাচ *n.* cardamom or its plant.

এলানো *v.* to dishevel or be dishevelled, to loosen; to slacken; to relax; to lounge, to recline; (of paddy) to turn over and spread out. □ *a.* dishevelled, hanging loose; relaxing; lounging; reclining.

এলাহি *a.* great, grand; pompous (এলাহিব্যাপার). □ *n.* (Mus.) God.

এলিয়ে দেওয়া *v.* to make dishevelled or disorderly.

এলুমিনিয়াম var. of **অ্যালুমিনিয়াম** ৷

এলেবেলে *a.* loose and unconnected; (fig.) incoherent; insignificant.

এলেম *n.* knowledge; learning; training; cleverness; craft; efficiency. **~বাজ** *a.* learned; clever; crafty; efficient.

এলো *a.* dishevelled, ruffed (এলো চুল) ; hanging loosely (এলো খোঁপা) ; incoherent or irrelevant, haphazard (এলো কথা) ; unrestrained (এলো রাশ) ; disorderly (এলো বাতাস). **~কেশী** *n. fem.* a woman with unkempt hair; an appellation of Goddess Kali (কালী). **~থেলো** *a.* untied, untrimmed; unkempt, undressed; dishevelled. **~পাতাড়ি, ~ধাবাড়ি** *a.* without measure; unrestrained; unsystematic; haphazard; disorderly; continuous. □ *adv.* without measure; without restraint; unsystematically; haphazardly; in a disorderly manner; continuously. **এলোপাতাড়ি মার** a beating or drubbing without measure, a thrashing. **এলাপাতাড়ি লড়াই** a scuffle, a confused fight. **~মেলো** *a.* dishevelled, ruffled; incoherent or irrelevant; disorderly; desultory. **এলোমেলো বলা** *v.* to talk incoherently or irrelevantly.

এলোপাতাড়ি, এলোধাবাড়ি, এলোমেলো see **এলো** ৷

এলোপ্যাথি *n.* allopathy.

এশীয় *a.* Asian. □ *n.* an Asian.

এষণা, এষণ *n.* search; exploration; desire; longing. **এষণীয়** *a.* desirable; searchable; explorable.

এষণী *n.* a goldsmith's balance; (surg.) a probe.

এষা *n.* same as **এষণা** ৷

এস খেলা করি come, let us play.

এসপার-ওসপার *n.* a final decision or settlement (usu. ending in some loss); either good or bad consequence; either (complete) success or (utter) failure; either this or that.

এসরাজ, এসরার *n.* the esraj, a kind of stringed musical instrument having four principal strings and played with a bow.

এসেন্স *n.* essence.

এসে যাওয়া *v.* to matter (much or little).

এস্টেট *n.* estate, landed property.

এস্তেহার var. of **ইশতিহার** ৷

এস্তেমাল var. of **ইস্তামাল** ৷

এহেন *a.* like this; such; suchlike; similar.

ঐ[১] *n* the ninth vowel of the Bengali alphabet.

ঐ[২] same as **অই**।

ঐকতান *n*. concert; a common chord.

ঐকবাক্য *n*. similarity in utterance or statement; concurrence; one voice, unanimity.

ঐকমত্য *n*. agreement in opinion; concord; unanimity; consensus.

ঐকাগ্র্য *n*. same as **একাগ্রতা** (see **একাগ্র**).

ঐকাত্ম্য *n*. oneness; identity; unity.

ঐকান্তিক *a*. profound, intense; earnest (ঐকান্তিক চেষ্টা) ; absorbedly employed, single-minded. *fem*. **ঐকান্তিকী**। **ঐকান্তিকতা** *n*. profundity, intensity; earnestness; sincerity; absorbing employment; single-mindedness. **ঐকান্তিকে** *adv*. in private.

ঐকার *n*. the symbol 'ৈ' affixed to a consonant whilst adding ঐ-sound to it. **ঐকারাদি** *a*. (of words) beginning with ঐ or ঐ -sound. **ঐকারান্ত** *a*. (of words) ending in ঐ or ঐ-sound.

ঐকাহিক *a*. ephemeral; (of fever) tertian.

ঐকিক নিয়ম *n*. (arith.) the unitary method.

ঐক্য *n*. unity, union; concord; agreement. **~বদ্ধ** *a*. united, combined. **~সাধন** *n*. act of establishing unity or concord or agreement (between or amongst). **ঐক্যসাধন করা** *v*. to establish unity or concord or agreement (between or amongst.) **ঐক্যাভাব** *n*. lack of unity or integration.

ঐক্ষব *a*. of or produced from sugarcane.

ঐচ্ছিক *a*. optional; elective; voluntary; volitional; arbitrary.

ঐছন alt. spell. of **অইছন**।

ঐতরেয় *n*. a branch of the Rig Veda.

ঐতিহাসিক *a*. historical, historic; versed in history. ☐ *n*. historian. **~তা** *n*. historicity.

ঐতিহ্য *n*. a tale or belief or custom or practice transmitted orally or handed down from generation to generation, tradition; cultural heritage; hereditary culture. **~গত, ঐতিহ্যিক** *a*. traditional. **ঐতিহ্যাগত** *a*. handed down by tradition.

ঐন্দ্র *a*. of or relating to Indra (ইন্দ্র) the king of gods.

ঐন্দ্রজালিক *a*. of or like or wrought by magic, magical; skilled in magic. ☐ *n*. a magician, a conjuror, a juggler.

ঐন্দ্রিয়, ঐন্দ্রিয়ক *a*. of sense organs; directly perceptible by senses; perceptible; sensuous; sensual.

ঐন্দ্রিলা *n*. wife of demon Vritra.

ঐরাবত *n*.(myth.) an elephant on which Indra (ইন্দ্র) rides.

ঐরূপ *a*. & *adv*. like that. ☐ *n*. one like that.

ঐশ, ঐশিক, ঐশ্বর, ঐশ্বরিক *a*. pertaining to or done by God; divine; heavenly. *fem*. **ঐশী**।

ঐশ্বর্য *n*. wealth, riches; splendour; magnificence; glory; Godhead; godhead; divinity; supremacy; overlordship, majesty; supernatural power obtained through asceticism; divine grace; unction. **~গর্ব, ~মদ** *n*. purse-pride; insolence from wealth. **~গর্বিত, ~মত্ত, ~মদোন্মত্ত** *a*. purse-proud; insolent from wealth, arrogant through wealth. *fem*. **~গর্বিতা, ~মত্তা, ~মদোন্মত্তা**। **~বান, ~মণ্ডিত, ~শালী** *a*. wealthy, opulent, affluent, rich; full of glory, glorious; majestic; possessed of supernatural power obtained through asceticism; bestowed with divine grace. *fem*. **~বতী, ~মণ্ডিতা, ~শালিনী**।

ঐষ্টিক *a*. relating to oblation or sacrifice, ceremonial.

ঐহলৌকিক, ঐহিক *a*. of this world or life; temporal; worldly (ঐহিক সুখ).

ও১ *n.* the tenth vowel of the Bengali alphabet.

ও২ *pro.* that or yonder person or creature or thing, a person or creature or thing in question, he, she, it. □ *a.* that immediately preceding, last (ও মাসে). □ *adv.* too, also, moreover (সে খাবেও) ; even (নামও শুনিনি). □ *con.* and. □ *int.* expressing : a call, recollection, amazement, pity etc.; holla, ho; ah, oh.

ওআড় alt. spell. of ওয়াড় ।

ওই *a.* that; yonder. □ *adv.* there. □ *int.* expressing mild regret for negligence, lapse of memory etc.; ah, ah me (ওই যা).

ওঁ *n.* the mystic sound denoting the Hindu trinity; the origin or root of all sounds; the symbol representing the Supreme Being. ওঁকার, ওঙ্কার, ওংকার *n.* the sound ওঁ (cp. chest-note).

ওঁচলা *n.* skin of fruits and vegetables; refuse. ~কুড় *n.* a dustbin, place where garbage is deposited. Same as আঁস্তাকুড় ।

ওঁচা, ওঁছা *a.* (chiefly coll.) worthless or bad; inferior; contemptible; base, mean; good-for-nothing.

ওঁচানো var. of উঁচানো (see উঁচা) ।

ওঁছা var. of ওঁচা ।

ওঁত var. of ওত ।

ওঁরা *pro.* (hon.) they.

ওক var. of ওয়াক ।

ওকড়া *n.* a variety of herb or its fruit or leaf (when this is rubbed on the skin one gets a terrible itching sensation).

ওকার *n.* the post-consonantal symbol 'ে া' affixed to a consonant whilst adding the ও-sound to it. ওকারাদি *a.* (of words) beginning with ও or ও-sound. ওকারান্ত *a.* (of words) ending in ও or ও-sound.

ওকালতনামা *n.* power of attorney.

ওকালতি *n.* the profession of a pleader, legal profession or practice, pleadership; pleading, advocacy, defence. □ *a.* pertaining to pleaders or pleadership or pleading. ওকালতি করা *v.* to practise as a pleader; to plead for.

ওকি, ওকী *int.* expressing : inquisitiveness, amazement, fright etc., what's that.

ওকে *pro.* to him, him.

ও কে *pro.* who is he or she.

ওক্ত, ওয়াক্ত pop. variants. of অক্ত ।

ওখড়ানো pop. var. of উখড়ানো ।

ওখান *n.* that or yonder place or region.

ওখানকার *a.* of that place or region. ওখানে *adv.* there.

ওগরা *n.* a variety of food cooked by boiling rice and pulse together, hotchpotch.

ওগরানো, ওগলানো pop. variants of উগরানো ।

ওগো *int.* used in affectionate or respectful addressing or apostrophizing (chiefly applied by husband and wife to each other); a form of address applied also to God or a deity.

ওঙ্কার see ওঁ ।

ওচলানো *v.* to winnow, to fan (grain etc.) free of husks and chaff.

ওছিয়তনামা var. of অছিয়তনামা ।

ওজঃ *n.* vigour, strength; lustre; (rhet.) ornateness and vigour of style.

ওজন *n.* act of weighing; weight; a unit of weight, a measure; importance, impressiveness; power, strength (নিজের ওজন বুঝে কাজ করা). ওজন করা *v.* to weigh. ~করা *a.* measured (ওজন-করা কথা). ~দর *n.* price according to or determined by weight (and not according to or determined by number). ~দার *n.* a weighman, a measurer.

ওজর *n.* a plea, an excuse; a pretext. বাজে ওজর a lame excuse. মিথ্যা ওজর a false plea.

ওজস্বল *a.* vigorous, full of strength.

ওজস্বী *a.* strong; vigorous; (rhet.) ornate and vigorous. *fem.* ওজস্বিনী । ওজস্বিতা *n.* strength; vigour; (rhet.) ornateness and vigour of style.

ওজু pop. var. of অজু ।

ওজোগুণ *n.* (rhet.) ornateness and vigour of style.

ওজোন *n.* ozone.

ওঝা *n.* a quack professing to have (supernatural) power of curing snakebites and other morbidities; an exorcist.

ওটকানো, উটকানো *v.* search clumsily and hastily; look for something hurriedly; rummage.

ওটকিশতি, ওটকিস্তি *n.* (in chess) a position in which if a particular piece or chessman is moved, the player in question gets a check, and if not moved, that piece or chessman is taken by the adversary.

ওটা *pro.* (coll. & dero.) that, it, he, she.

ওঠবন্দি pop. var. of **উঠবন্দি**।

ওঠবস, ওঠবোস *n.* act of sitting down and standing up alternately and repeatedly (as a punishment or physical exercise).

ওঠা *v.* to rise; to get up; to climb or ascend (গাছে ওঠা, পাহাড়ে ওঠা) ; to get in (গাড়িতে ওঠা). See also the older form **উঠা**।

ওডিকোলন *n.* eau-de-cologne, a perfume made from water and alcohol.

ওড্র *n.* old name of Orissa.

ওড়না *n.* a piece of thin cloth worn usually as a modesty scarf by women.

ওড়ব *n.* an Indian musical mode which is expressed by five principal notes.

ওড়ম্বা *n.* a spendthrift.

ওড়া *v.* to fly, to move through or in the air; to flutter; to go up in the air. For other uses see **উড়া**।

ওড়িয়া *n.* a native of Orissa; the language of Orissa. □ *a.* of Orissa or its people.

ওড়িশা *n.* Orissa. **ওড়িশি** *a.* of or pertaining to Orissa. □ *n.* an Indian style of classical dance that originated in Orissa.

ওত *n.* lying in wait to attack by surprise, an ambush, an ambuscade. **ওত পাতা, ওত পেতে থাকা** *v.* to lie in wait, to ambush, to ambuscade.

ওতপ্রোত *a.* diffused, pervading; inseparably mixed up; thorough. **~ভাবে** *adv.* inseparably, inextricably.

ওতরানো pop. var. of **উতরানো**।

ওথলানো pop. var. of **উথলানো**।

ওদন *n.* food; meal; rice; boiled rice.

ওধার *n.* that side or extremity or region.

ওপড়ানো pop. var. of **উপড়ানো**।

ওপর coll. form of **উপর**।

ওপার *n.* the other side or bank (of a river, etc.).

ওফ *int.* expressing amazement, anger, regret, pain, disgust etc.; oh.

ওবা pop. corrup. of **উবা**।

ওম্ var. of **ওঁ**।

ওমরাহ, ওমরা variants of **উমরাহ**।

ওমা *int.* expressing : surprise; fear etc.

ওয়াক *int.* expressing an involuntary sound made whilst vomiting. **ওয়াক তোলা** *v.* to make this sound; to expectorate; to hiccup, to retch.

ওয়াকফ *n.* charitable grant for Muslim religious purpose or in service of God. **~নামা** *n.* a grant providing for this gift.

ওয়াকিফ, ওয়াকিব *a.* conversant, familiar, acquainted, knowing; informed; experienced. **ওয়াকিফহাল, ওয়াকিবহাল** *a.* conversant with the situation; well-informed of the situation.

ওয়াজিব *a.* just, proper, right; necessary, essential.

ওয়াড় *n.* a slip for a pillow or bolster; a pillow-case, a pillow-slip; a slip for quilt etc.

ওয়াদা *n.* a point of time by or within which something is promised to be paid or given or done; promise. **ওয়াদা দেওয়া** *v.* to set a time-limit.

ওয়াপস *n.* act of giving back, return. **ওয়াপস করা** *v.* to give back, to return.

ওয়ারিশ *n.* an heir or heiress. **ওয়ারিশান** *n. pl.* heirs or heiresses.

ওয়ারেন্ট *n.* warrant, a written order giving official authority for arrest etc.

-ওয়ালা[1] var. of **আলা[2]**।

-ওয়ালা[2] *sfx.* denoting : a trader, a seller, a practitioner, an owner, one in possession of or endowed with etc., -er, -or, -ist. *fem.* **ওয়ালি, উলি**।

ওয়াসিল var. of **উশুল**। **ওয়াসিল-জমা** *n.* credit deposit. **ওয়াসিল-বাকি** *n.* credit balance.

ওয়াস্তা *n.* act of attaching importance; serious attention, heed, care; dependence; sake (কীসের ওয়াস্তে). **ওয়াস্তা করা, ওয়াস্তা রাখা** *v.* to care (for), to heed, to pay attention (to); to attach importance (to); to depend (upon).

ওয়াহাবি *n.* a follower of Abdul Wahab; a Muslim religious reformer; a group of Muslim socio-religious reformers.

ওর[1] *n.* end, limit ('দুঃখের নাহি ওর').

ওর[2] *pro. a.* his; its.

ওরফে *adv.* & *n.* called otherwise, alias.

ওরসা *a.* wet, moist.

ওরাং ওটাং, ওরাং উটাং *n.* orang-utan (orang-outang), an ape originally of Sumatra and Borneo.

ওরে *pro.* coll. & poet. form of ওকে। *int.* used in addressing or apostrophizing.

ওল *n.* an edible bulbous plant akin to arum or turnip. যেমন বুনো ওল তেমনি বাঘা তেঁতুল (fig.) measure for meaure.

ওলকপি *n.* a kohlrabi; (loos.) a turnip.

ওলটপালট, ওলটানো coll. variants of উলটপালট and উলটানো respectively (see উলটা).

ওলন[1] *n.* a coming down, descent.

ওলন[2] *n.* a plumb-line, a plummet (also ওলনদড়ি). □ *a.* vertical.

ওলন্দাজ *a.* Dutch. □ *a.* a Hollander, a Dutch; the Dutch language.

-ওলা[1] var. of -ওয়ালা[1,2]।

ওলা[2], ওলানো[1] *v.* (dial.) to take down, to bring down.

ওলাইচণ্ডী *n.* the goddess of cholera.

ওলাইবিবি *n.* the name given by the Muslims to ওলাইচণ্ডী।

ওলাওঠা *n.* cholera.

ওলান *n.* udder (of cattle etc.)

ওলানো see ওলা[2]।

ওলো *int.* used by (usu. village) women in addressing one another, hullo.

ওল্টানো alt. spell. of ওলটানো।

ওষধি, ওষধী *n.* a plant that dies after bearing fruit but for once.

ওষধিনাথ, ওষধিপতি *n.* the moon.

ওষধিশালা *n.* herbarium.

ওষুধ pop. and coll. form of ঔষধ। ওষুধ খাওয়া *v.* to take medicine. ওষুধ ধরা *v.* (fig.) to take effect, to bear result.

ওষ্ঠ *n.* (lit.) the upper lip; any of the lips. ~পল্লব *n.* lips as attractive and soft as young shoots. ~পুট *n.* a cavity formed by contracting both the lips. ~ব্রণ *n.* a boil on the lip. ওষ্ঠাকার *a.* shaped like lips; (bot.) labiate. ওষ্ঠাগত *a.* that which has neared the lips in order to come out. ওষ্ঠাগতপ্রাণ *a.* about to die; extremely embarrassed or peeved or irritated. ওষ্ঠাধর *n. pl.* the two lips—upper and lower. ওষ্ঠ্য *a.* (gr.) pronounced by the lips, labial. □ *n.* (gr.) a labial letter.

ওস *n.* dew.

ওসকানো pop. var. of উসকানো।

ওসার *n.* breadth, width; also dial. variant of ওয়াড়।

ওস্তাগর *n.* a very efficient or chief artisan or tailor, a master artisan or tailor.

ওস্তাদ *n.* a trainer, a music-master or music-teacher; a master artist or artisan. □ *a.* skilled, expert. ওস্তাদি *n.* efficiency, skill, mastery; cleverness; an attempt to parade one's skill or mastery, bravado; uncalled-for act of coming forward to help; officiousness. □ *a.* pertaining to a trainer or music-master or master artist or master artisan. ওস্তাদি করা *v.* to try to parade one's skill or mastery; to come forward uncalled-for to help; to be officious.

ওহাবি alt. spell. of ওয়াহাবি।

ওহে *int.* used in addressing or apostrophizing, hullo, hey.

ওহো *int.* expressing : recollection, amazement, regret etc., ah.

ঔ *n.* the fourteenth vowel of the Bengali alphabet.

ঔকার *n.* the post-consonantal symbol 'ৌ' affixed to a consonant whilst adding the ঔ-sound to it. **ঔকারাদি** *a.* (of words) beginning with ঔ or ঔ-sound. **ঔকারান্ত** *a.* (of words) ending in ঔ or ঔ-sound.

ঔচিত্য *n.* propriety, fitness; appropriateness; decorum.

ঔজ্জ্বল্য *n.* brightness, lustre, splendour, brilliance, brilliancy.

ঔড়ব *n.* (mus.) the singing of any mode consisting of five notes.

ঔৎসর্গিক *a.* relating to religious offering, sacrificial; dedicatory.

ঔৎসুক্য *n.* inquisitiveness; eagerness; earnestness; (rare) worry, anxiety.

ঔদনিক *n.* a cook.

ঔদরিক *a.* gluttonous; voracious; abdominal. □ *n.* a glutton, a gourmand, an excessively greedy eater. **ঔদরিকতা** *n.* gluttony; voracity, voraciousness.

ঔদার্য *n.* liberality; magnanimity, greatness; generosity, largeness, munificence.

ঔদাসীন্য, ঔদাস্য *n.* indifference; listlessness; callousness; apathy.

ঔদ্ধত্য *n.* haughtiness, arrogance; insolence, impertinence; vanity, vainglory.

ঔদ্বাহিক *a.* obtained through marriage (as dowry); of marriage, matrimonial, bridal.

ঔপনিবেশিক *n.* colonial; settling in or settling up a colony, colonizing. □ *n.* a settler or an inhabitant of a colony.

ঔপনিষদ *a.* of or according to the Upanishads. **ঔপনিষদিক** *a.* relating to or versed in the Upanishads.

ঔপন্যাসিক *a.* relating to novels or a work of fiction. □ *n.* a novelist.

ঔপপত্তিক *a.* relating to deductive reasoning and arguments; proved, vindicated; authenticated; authentic; authoritative.

ঔপমিক *a.* of or described by a simile or comparison.

ঔপম্য *n.* similitude; similarity; comparability.

ঔপসর্গিক *a.* symptomatic; (gr.) relating to the prefix.

ঔপাধিক *a.* pertaining to title or in title only, titular; nominal; temporary.

ঔরস, ঔরস্য *a.* (of children) legitimate. □ *n.* a legitimate child; (loos & pop.) semen. **ঔরসজাত** *a.* (lit.) legitimately born; (loos. & pop.) born of one's semen.

ঔর্ণ, ঔর্ণিক *a.* woollen; cobwebby.

ঔর্ধ্বদেহিক, ঔর্ধ্বদৈহিক *a.* funeral; obsequial. □ *n.* funeral rite; obsequial rite, obsequies.

ঔর্ব[1] *a.* earthly; pertaining to the Earth.

ঔর্ব[2], **ঔর্বাগ্নি** *n.* a fire coming out from under water (esp. of a sea); a submarine fire.

ঔষধ, (coll.) **ওষুধ** *n.* medicine; a drug; a remedy. **ঔষধ খাওয়া** *v.* to take medicine. **ঔষধবিক্রেতা, ঔষধাজীব** *n.* a druggist. **ঔষধালয়** *n.* a drug-store, a druggist's shop, a chemist's shop, a pharmacy, a dispensary. **ঔষধি** *n.* a medicinal plant, a medicine. **ঔষধীয়** *a.* medicinal.

ঔষ্ম, ঔষ্ম্য *n.* heat, warmth.

ক১ the first consonant of the Bengali alphabet. **ক অক্ষর গোমাংস** an illiterate person, a complete ignoramus, (literally) a person to whom the letter ক or the alphabet is as impure and abominable as beef to an orthodox Hindu.

ক২ coll. corrup. of **কও** or **কহ** and **কয়** or **কত।**

ক৩ *sfx.* added to না, নাই, নি etc. to make them sound sweet.

কই১ *adv.* where. □ *int.* denoting: disappointment, dejection, denial, amazement, cordiality etc.

কই২ *n.* the walking fish, the anabas.

কই৩ coll. corrup. of **কহি।**

কইয়ে *a.* one who has the gift of the gab; one who speaks with flippant ease; fluent in talk. **কইয়ে লোক** a fluent or gifted speaker.

কইলা, (dial.) **কইলে** *n.* a newly born calf (usu. কইলা বাছুর).

কইসন *adv.* (obs. & poet.) of what description, how.

কওন coll. corrup. of **কহন।**

কওয়া coll. corrup. of **কহা।**

কংগ্রেস *n.* an assembly of delegates, specialists etc. for discussion or settlement of problems; a congress; the legislature of the United States and some other American-type republics, the Congress; the Indian National Congress party, the Congress. **কংগ্রেসি** *a.* of or belonging to or following the Indian National Congress. □ *n.* a Congressman, a Congress worker.

কংস, কংশ *n.* bell metal—an alloy of copper and tin, pewter; a vessel of bell metal.

কংসক *n.* copperas, green vitriol.

কংসকার *n.* a worker in bell metal (by trade or caste).

কংসবণিক *n.* a dealer in bell metal products.

কংসারি *n.* (myth.) the slayer of the notorious king Kamsa (কংস) ; an appellation of Krishna (কৃষ্ণ).

ককানো *v.* (chiefly of children) to sob; to groan; to implore with much humble submission. **ককানি** *n.* act of sobbing, sob; groan; imploration, humble submission. **কেঁদে ককিয়ে** *adv.* having made a lot of entreaties or earnest requests.

ককুদ, ককুৎ *n.* the hump on the shoulder of a bull.

ককুভ *n.* a metre of Vedic poetry; an Indian musical mode; a direction, a side.

ককেশীয় *a.* Caucasian. □ *n.* a Caucasian.

কক্ষ *n.* a room, an apartment, a chamber; either of the points at which an arm is joined with the body, an arm-joint (also **কক্ষমূল**) ; an armpit (also **কক্ষপুট**) ; the waist; (astr.) an orbit; (bot.) an axil. **~চ্যুত, ~ভ্রষ্ট** *a.* slipped from the armpit; (astr.—of stars, planets etc.) deviated or fallen from one's orbit. **~তল** *n.* the floor of a room, floor. **~প্রাচীর** *n.* the wall of a room.

কক্ষনো, কক্‌খনো *adv.* at any time, ever; for any reason; in any state or condition, under any circumstances.

কক্ষান্তর *n.* another room.

ক-খ *n.* the alphabet; elementary knowledge, ABC.

কখন *adv.* at what time; when; long ago (সে তো কখন চলে গেছে). **কখনও, কখনো** *adv.* at any time, ever; for any reason; in any condition; under any circumstances. **কখনো কখনো,** (coll.) **কখনো-সখনো** *adv.* sometimes, now and then, now and again; at times. **আর কখনো** ever afterwards. **আর কখনো না** never afterwards.

কঙ্ক, কাঁক *n.* the heron.

কঙ্কণ *n.* a bangle for the wrist, a bracelet.

কঙ্কত *n.* a comb; the gill (of the fish). **কঙ্কতিকা, কঙ্কতী** *n.* a comb.

কঙ্কপত্র *n.* an arrow, a dart, a shaft.

কঙ্কর, কাঁকর *n.* gravel, a coarse grain of sand, a very small particle of stone, grit. □ *a.* coarse; harsh.

কঙ্কাল *n.* a skeleton; a bone. **~মালী** *n.* one

who wears a garland of bones; an appellation of Shiva (শিব). ~মালিনী *n. fem.* one who wears a garland of bones; an appellation of Goddess Kali (কালী). ~সার *a.* reduced to bones or to a skeleton, one who is only skin and bone, (cp.) a bag of bones.

কচ[১] *n.* hair; the pointed end of a quillpen; a nib; a curved projection of a piece of land or a building.

কচ[২] *int.* denoting: a sound like the one made in cutting off or biting off something at one stroke. **কচকচ** *int.* denoting: the sound of hashing or munching or crunching repeatedly. **কচকচ করা** *v.* to give out a munching or crunching sound repeatedly (as on biting an unripe fruit); to grumble; to scold frequently or repeatedly without rhyme or reason; to indulge in intolerably long and dull arguments or talk, to prattle. **কচকচানি** *n.* act of hashing or munching or crunching repeatedly; act of grumbling, grumble; act of scolding repeatedly or frequently without rhyme or reason; intolerably long and dull argument or talk, prattle. **কচকচি** *n.* quarrel; wrangling; peevishness; unnecessary and inconsequential wrangling (তত্ত্বের কচকচি). **কচকচে** *a.* (of unripe fruits) giving out a munching sound when eaten; given to scolding repeatedly or frequently without rhyme or reason; indulging in long dull arguments or talk, prattling.

কচটানো *v.* to knead. **কচটানি** *n.* act of kneading.

কচড়া *n.* thick rope, cable.

কচরমচর *int* denoting: a sound as of munching; confused noise as of hot discussion or incessant prattling. **কচরমচর করা** *v.* to munch noisily; to discuss noisily; to prattle rapidly.

কচলাকচলি *n.* act of wringing or squeezing repeatedly; act of rubbing; act of higgling (অনেক কচলাকচলির পর দাম কমাল). **কচলাকচলি করা** *v.* to wring or squeeze repeatedly; to rub; to higgle.

কচলানো *v.* to wring, to squeeze; to rub; (rare.) to higgle.

কচাৎ *int.* denoting: a sound like the one made in cutting off something at one stroke.

কচাল *a.* irritating discussion or debate or dispute. **কচালে** *a.* indulging in irritating discussion or debate or dispute.

কচি *a.* (of fruits etc.) fresh and soft; green; (of children, plants etc.) very young and delicate; (of youth etc.) new and tender. **কচি আম** a green mango the pulp of which has not yet developed. **কচিকাঁচা** *n. pl.* small children, kiddies. **কচি খোকা বা খুকি, কচি ছেলে বা মেয়ে** a baby, a child, an infant. **কচি পাতা** *n.* young shoot; a new leaf.

কচি কলাপাতা রং *n.* foliage green; light green colour like that of the plantain leaves.

কচু *n.* an esculant edible root; (contem.) a mere trifle, nothing. **কচু করা** *v.* to be able to do nothing; to be able to do no harm. **কচু খাওয়া** *v.* (contem.) to eat or get nothing, to be disappointed. **কচু বোঝা** *v.* to fail utterly to understand or comprehend. ~কাটা *a.* chopped easily at will; chopped fine; hashed. **কচুকাটা করা** *v.* to chop or hash with ease and at will, to chop fine. ~ঘেচু *n. pl.* worthless vegetables; vegetables not normally edible; trifles. ~পোড়া *n.* anything inedible; nothing. **দুঃখ না কচু** no genuine sorrow but a mere show of it.

কচুরি *n.* a kind of pancake made of kneaded flour and pulped pulses.

কচুরিপানা *n.* water hyacinth.

কচ্ছ *n.* a shore; a coastal region; a marshy place; Kutch; (facet.) the part of the loincloth which the wearer tucks behind him between his legs.

কচ্ছটি *n.* the part of the loincloth which the wearer tucks behind him between his legs; loincloth as tucked up by the wearer; loincloth worn as a suspensor as by Indian ascetics and wrestlers.

কচ্ছপ *n.* the tortoise, the turtle, the chelonian. *fem.* **কচ্ছপী। কচ্ছপের খোলা** tortoise-shell, carapace.

কছু *n.* & *adv.* (obs. & poet.) anything.

কজ্জল *n.* eye-wash, eye-salve, collyrium; lampblack; cloud; dark cloud.

কজ্জলী *n.* mercurous sulphate (as used in medicine).

কজ্জ্বল *n.* eye-wash, eye-salve, collyrium.

কঞ্চি *n.* a bamboo twig; a slip of bamboo.

কঞ্চুক, কঞ্চু *n.* armour, a coat of mail; a modesty vest, bodice, brassiere; a slough or cast skin of a snake.

কঞ্চুকী *n.* a Brahmin (ব্রাহ্মণ) supervisor of a royal household, (cp.) the Lord of the Bed-chamber; a eunuch guarding a harem; a man in armour; the snake.

কঞ্চুল *n.* an ornament for women's breast.

কঞ্চুলিকা, কঞ্চুলী *n.* bodice, brassiere, a modesty vest.

কঞ্জুস *a.* niggardly, miserly, close-fisted. ☐ *n.* a close-fisted man, a niggard, a miser. **~পনা** *n.* miserliness, niggardliness.

কট১ *int.* denoting: the sound of cutting or biting a hard thing as a nut. **~কটানি** *n.* croaking; painful throbbing or drumming; harsh reproaches. **কট কট** *int.* denoting: repeated sounds of cutting or biting a hard thing; a croaking sound; repeated painful throbbing or drumming sound (কান কটকট) ; a harsh or blunt sound (কটকট করে বলা). **কট কট করা** *v.* to throb or drum painfully; to reproach harshly; (chiefly of frogs) to croak. **~কটে** *a.* giving out the sound as of cutting or biting a hard thing; throbbing or drumming painfully; given to reproaching harshly; croaking; heart-rending or blunt (কটকটে কথা) ; frowning or terror-striking (কটকটে চাহনি). **~মট** *int.* expressing: anger, threat, frown (কটমট করে তাকানো). **~মটে** *a.* angry, frowning, sinister, terror-striking.

কট২ *a.* hypothecated, mortgaged; conditional, stipulated. ☐ *n.* a mortgage deed; a deed of conditional sale.

কটক *n.* an army, armed forces; encampment (of an army); tented accommodation (esp. of an army); the ridge of a hill; a bangle or an armlet.

কটকবালা *n.* a deed of conditional sale; a mortgage deed.

কটকি *a.* of or relating to Cuttack in Orissa.

কটকিনা *n.* stringency of rule or order; a conditional or periodical lease; resolve, determination, a promise.

কটকেনা var. of **কটকিনা** ।

কটমট see **কট১** ।

কটরকটর, কটরমটর *int.* denoting: a sound produced whilst munching hard things such as nuts.

কটলেট var. of **কাটলেট** ।

কটা১ coll. var. of **কয়টা** ।

কটা২ *a.* brownish; having a white complexion with a tinge of red; tawny; (usu. dero.) fair-complexioned.

কটাক্ষ *n.* a side-glance, a sidelong look, an oblique look; significant or meaningful look; reflection, insinuation. **কটাক্ষ করা** *v.* to cast a side-glance, to look obliquely or askew; to cast a significant or meaningful look; to insinuate, to reflect on. **~পাত** *n.* casting a sidelong glance; a sidelong or oblique look; act of casting a significant look; a significant or meaningful look; insinuation, reflection. **~পাত করা** same as **কটাক্ষ করা** । **কটাক্ষে** *adv.* at or by or with a sidelong or meaningful look; by way of insinuation or reflection; in a moment, at once.

কটা-চোখ *n.* a brownish eye as of a cat. ☐ *a.* possessing catlike brownish eyes, cat-eyed.

কটাৎ var. of **কটাস্** ।

কটাল *n.* spring tide; flood-tide. **ভরাকটাল** *n.* spring tide; flood-tide. **মরাকটাল** *n.* neap tide; ebb-tide.

কটাস্ *int.* denoting: the sound of biting off or cutting off (esp. suddenly) a portion of a hard thing at one stroke; a snapping sound; an imaginary sound made by an ant when it pricks. **কটাস্ কটাস্** *int.* denoting: repetition of any of these sounds.

কটাসে *a.* slightly brownish or tawny.

কটাহ *n.* a cauldron; a large tumblerlike cooking utensil; a dixie.

কটি১ coll. corrup. of **কয়টি** ।

কটি২ *n.* the waist; the loin; the hip. **~তট, ~দেশ** same as **কটি** । **~ত্র, ~বন্ধ** *n.* a waistband, a belt, a girdle. **~ভূষণ** *n.* an ornament worn as a girdle by women. ~শূল, ~বাত *n.* lumbago; sciatica.

কটু *a.* bitter; acrid, pungent (কটুরস) ; tasting hot (কটু তেল) ; harsh, acrimonious (কটুবাক্য). **কটু হয়ে যাওয়া** *v.* to have the taste or flavour spoilt or fouled, to grow or to run rancid. **কটু কথা** *n.* same as **কটূক্তি**। ~**কাটব্য** *n. pl.* bitter reproaches. ~**তা**, ~**ত্ব** *n.* bitterness; pungency; hot taste; harshness, acrimony. **কটু তেল** *n.* mustard oil. ~**ভাষী** *a.* rude or impolite in speech, foul-spoken, foul-mouthed.

কটূক্তি *n.* a bitter or acrimonious or sharp remark.

কটূত্তর *n.* caustic or sharp reply.

কটোরা *n.* a goblet.

কট্টর *a.* uncompromising; inveterate; obstinate; bigoted; ultra-conservative.

কঠিন *a.* hard, firm; stiff; stern, strict; severe; difficult; cruel, merciless (কঠিন হৃদয়) ; tremendous, intense; solid (কঠিন পদার্থ) ; serious (কঠিন রোগ). *fem.* **কঠিনা**। ~**তা**, ~**ত্ব** *n.* hardness, firmness; stiffness; sternness, strictness, severity; difficulty; cruelty, mercilessness; tremendousness, intensity; solidity; seriousness.

কঠিনী, কঠিনিকা *n.* chalk.

কঠিনীভূত *a.* hardened; stiffened.

কঠোপনিষৎ, কঠোপনিষদ্ *n.* Katha, the name of one of the major Upanishads.

কঠোর *a.* hard; stern, harsh; firm, steady, unflinching; merciless, cruel, heartless (কঠোর শাসক) ; strict, severe; difficult; intense; serious (কঠোর ব্যাধি) ; dull; rough (কঠোর অবয়ব). ~**তা** *n.* hardness; sternness, harshness; firmness, steadiness; mercilessness, cruelty, heartlessness; strictness, severity; difficulty; intensity; seriousness; dullness; roughness.

কড় *n.* an iron ring for the wrist to be worn by married women, a lac-bracelet.

কড়ক, কড়কচ *n.* sea salt.

কড়কড় *int.* denoting: the sound of munching hard or of a loud rumbling noise (as of a clap of thunder); imaginary sound produced by the stiffening of anything glutinous (ভাত শুকিয়ে কড়কড় করছে). **কড়কড়ানি** *n.* any of the aforesaid sounds. **কড়কড়ে** *a.* giving out a sound that is caused by the stiffening of anything glutinous; hard and glutinous.

কড়কানো *v.* (coll. & inf.) to rebuke, to reprimand; to check, to pull up.

কড়ঙ্গা *n.* a beggar's bowl or drinking bowl made of coconut shell.

কড়চা *n.* a chronicle, a biography, a narrative; an account book containing details of rent payable by tenants, a descriptive rent-roll.

কড়তা *n.* tare.

কড়মড় var. of **কড়কড়**।

কড়া[1] *n.* a metal ring; such a ring affixed to a thing as a handle.

কড়া[2] *n.* a coin of smallest value (usu. denominated by cowries or small conch-shells), a cowrie. **এক কড়া** (to the) smallest amount or degree; an iota. ~**কিয়া** *n.* a table for counting cowries from 1 to 100. ~**ক্রান্তি** see **ক্রান্তি**। **কড়ায় গণ্ডায়** *adv.* to the last farthing; completely, thoroughly.

কড়া[3] *a.* hard; stiff; difficult; severe; tremendous, intense; angry; haughty; harsh, rude (কড়া কথা) ; strict; rough. □ *n.* a corn on the skin. ~**কড়ি**, ~**ক্কড়**, ~**ক্কড়ি** *n.* strictness; stringency. **কড়া আইন** a strict or stringent law. **কড়া মনিব** an exacting master; a hard or strict task-master. **কড়া লোক** a strict man or disciplinarian.

কড়া[4], **কড়াই** *n.* a large tumblerlike cooking utensil, (cp.) a vat.

কড়াৎ *int.* denoting: the sound of the clapping of thunder or fracture of a bone.

কড়ার *n.* a condition, a stipulation; a promise. **কড়ারি** *a.* conditional.

কড়ি[1] *n.* a snail-like gastropod resembling a miniature conch, a cowrie; a cowrie-shell (formerly) used as a coin of the smallest denomination; a coin of the smallest denomination (cp. a stiver); money. **কানাকড়ি** a coin of the smallest denomination which is useless as a medium of exchange; (fig.) of no value, quite ineffective.

কড়ি২ *n.* a joist.

কড়ি৩ *n.* (mus.) any of the notes in the natural major scale. (cp. sharp).

কড়িআল alt. spell. of **কড়িয়াল**।

কড়িকপালে *a.* lucky in making money, fortunate.

কড়িকাঠ *n.* a joist.

কড়িমধ্যম *n.* (mus.) a higher variation of the fourth note in the Indian musical gamut; a subdued variation of the fourth note in the natural major scale.

কড়িয়াল১ *a.* wealthy, opulent, rich.

কড়িয়াল২, কড়িয়ালি *n.* a horse's bit.

কড়ুয়া *a.* rancid (কড়ুয়া গন্ধ) ; pungent or hot (কড়ুয়া স্বাদ) ; strong (কড়ুয়া তামাক) ; made of mustard. **কড়ুয়া তেল** mustard-oil.

কড়ে *a.* youngest, smallest; little; young. **কড়ে আঙুল** the little finger (of the hand or foot.) **কড়ে রাঁড়ি** a woman widowed in childhood or at an early age, a childwidow.

কণা, কণিকা *n.* a very small or fine particle; a grain of dust or powder; a grain of corn. **কণাকার** *a.* granular.

কণিকাবাদ *n.* corpuscular theory.

কণ্টক *n.* a thorn; a thistle; the spine of a fish; (fig.) an obstacle (সুখের কণ্টক) ; disgrace (কুলের কণ্টক) ; an insignificant adversary; a horripilation or goose-flesh. **~ফল** *n.* the jack-fruit or its tree. **~ময়** *a.* full of thorns; thorny. **~যুক্ত** *a.* thorny. **~লতা** *n.* a thorny creeper. **কণ্টকে কণ্টকোদ্ধার করা** to set a thief to catch a thief. **~শয্যা** *n.* a bed of thorns; (fig.) unbearable torment or anguish, extreme discomfort.

কণ্টকাকীর্ণ *a.* thorny, strewn with thorns or thistles.

কণ্টকিত *a.* full of thorns, thorny; pricking as thorns, prickly; horripilated.

কণ্টকিফল *n.* the jack-fruit or its tree.

কণ্টকী *a.* thorny; prickly. □ *n.* any thorny plant such as dates; a fish with too many (thin) spines or bones.

কণ্টকীফল *n.* alt. spell. of **কণ্টকিফল**।

কণ্টকোদ্ধার *n.* extraction of a thorn; removal of thorns; removal of an obstacle or difficulty; destruction of an enemy.

কণ্টিকারী *n.* a prickly nightshade used in medicine.

কন্ট্রাক্টর, কন্ট্রাক্টার variants of **কনট্রাকটর**।

কণ্ঠ *n.* the throat; (bio.) the windpipe; the oesophagus; voice. **~গত** same as **কণ্ঠাগত**। **~নালী, ~নালি** *n.* the windpipe; the oesophagus, the gullet. **~বদ্ধ** *a.* clinging to the throat. **~ভূষণ** *n.* lace, chain etc. worn round the neck; (fig.) an object of pride or affection. **~মণি** *n.* jewel worn at or round the throat; the Adam's apple; (fig.) an object of affection or pride. **~রোধ** *n.* act or an instance of choking or stifling or throttling; deprivation of the power of speaking or making any (adverse) comment. **~রোধ করা** *v.* to choke, to stifle, to throttle; to silence, to gag, to deprive of the power of speaking or making any (adverse) comment. **~রোধ হওয়া** *v.* to be choked or stifled or throttled; to be deprived of the power of speaking or criticizing (esp. adversely). **~লগ্ন, ~লীন** same as **কণ্ঠবদ্ধ**। **~সংগীত** *n.* vocal music. **~স্থ** *a.* of the throat; lying in or at the throat; stored in memory; memorized. **~স্থ করা** *v.* to commit to memory, to memorize, to learn by heart. **~স্বর** *n.* voice; tone of voice. **~হার** *n.* a necklace.

কণ্ঠা *n.* the clavicle, the collarbone.

কণ্ঠাগত *a.* that which has come up to the throat; about to get out of the mouth. **~প্রাণ** *a.* about to breathe one's last; about to die. **~প্রায়** *a.* that which has come up almost to the throat; about to spill.

কণ্ঠাভরণ *n.* an ornament for the throat; a necklace.

কণ্ঠাস্থি same as **কণ্ঠা**।

কণ্ঠি *n.* a necklace of the twigs of holy basil worn by Vaishnavas. **কণ্ঠি ছেঁড়া** to cast out a person from the Vaishnava sect. **~ধারণ** *n.* initiation into Vaishnavism; act of wearing the holy basil-necklace. **~ধারী** *a.* wearing a holy basil-necklace. ☐ *n.* a Vaishnava. **~বদল** *n.* the Vaishnava system of marriage in which the bridegroom and the bride exchange the holy basil-necklaces.

কণ্ঠী *n.* a one-stringed necklace; the holy basil-necklace of Vaishnavas.

কণ্ঠৌষ্ঠ্য *a.* (gr.) both guttural and labial, gutturo-labial.

কণ্ঠ্য *a.* (gr.) guttural. **~বর্ণ** *n.* (gr.) a guttural letter, a guttural.

কণ্ডন *n.* husking. **কণ্ডন করা** *v.* to husk. **কণ্ডনী** *n.* a pestle (for husking).

কণ্ডু, কণ্ডূ *n.* itch, scabies; ringworm; act of scratching as an itch. **কণ্ডূতি** *n.* itch, scabies, ringworm; (fig.) eager desire or urge (হস্তকণ্ডূতি). **কণ্ডূয়ন** *n.* act of scratching to relieve itching; (fig.) eager desire or urge. **কণ্ডূয়ন করা** *v.* to scratch. **কণ্ডূয়মান** *a.* in the act of scratching where it itches.

কণ্ডোল *n.* a large basket or container for storing grains or cereals.

কত *a.* how much, how many; much, many. ☐ *adv.* to a great extent, much. ☐ *n.* a great number or amount (কত এল, কত গেল). ☐ *pro.* how much or how many of it or them. **কত করে** at what price (কত করে কিনলে) ; with much solicitation or entreaty (কত করে বললাম) ; after or with a great effort (কত করে পাশ করেছি). **~ক** *a.* some; somewhat. ☐ *adv.* to some extent; partially. ☐ *pro.* some of it or them. ☐ *n.* some people (দেশের কতক অর্ধাশনে থাকে). **কতক কতক** to a certain extent; somewhat; partially. **কতকটা** *a.* some. ☐ *adv.* partially; somewhat. ☐ *pro.* some of it. ☐ *n.* some amount. **কতক পরিমাণে** *adv.* to some extent; partially. **~কাল** *adv.* how long; for a long time (কতকাল বসে আছি). ☐ *n.* a long time. **কত কী, কত কিছু** various; various things; various and unknown (things); a large number of (things.) **~ক্ষণ** *adv.* how long; for a long time. ☐ *n.* a long time. **~দিন** *adv.* how many days; for many days; for a long time. ☐ *n.* many days; a long time. **কত না** *adv.* countlessly; immeasurably. **~বার** *adv.* how many times; many times. **~মতো** *a.* of numerous and various kinds. ☐ *adv.* in numerous and various ways. **~শত** *a.* countless. **~হুঁ** *a.* (poet. & obs.) numerous and various.

কৎ *n.* the pointed end of a quill-pen, a nib.

কতবেল var. of **কয়েতবেল।**

কতল *n.* beheading, decapitation. **কতল করা** *v.* to behead, to decapitate.

কতিপয় *a.* several, some, a number of.

কতেক *a.* some; several; much; how much. ☐ *pro.* some, a few of them, a little or a part of it.

কত্থক *n.* an Indian classical dance form.

কথক *n.* a professional narrator of scriptural and mythological stories (usu. **কথকঠাকুর**) ; a speaker. **~তা** *n.* professional practice of narrating scriptural and mythological stories.

কথঞ্চন, কথঞ্চিৎ *adv.* somehow; (loos.) somewhat. ☐ *a.* (pop.) a small amount of.

কথন *n.* act or mode of speaking; utterance; words spoken; a saying; a statement; a speech. **কথনীয়** *a.* worthy of being spoken or told, speakable, utterable; that which is to be spoken or told.

কথা *n.* a word or words spoken; a saying; an utterance; a statement; mode of speaking, pronunciation (তার কথা আড়ষ্ট) ; voice (তার কথা শুনতে পেলাম) ; a dialect (বর্ধমানের কথা) ; a tale, a story; a chronicle or history (ভারত-কথা) ; news (গ্রামের কথা) ; a word (সে নিজের কথা রাখে) ; an opinion (এ বিষয়ে আমার কথা হল যে) ; professional narration of scriptural and mythological stories (জমিদার বাড়িতে কথা হবে) ; a topic, a discourse (এ কথার অবতারণা) ; conversation; speaking terms (তার সঙ্গে আমার কথা নেই) ; consultation, discussion (ডাক্তারের সঙ্গে কথা হয়েছে) ; counsel, advice; instigation; comparison (তার সঙ্গে কার কথা) ; an incident, an affair (যে সে কথা নয়) ; a request (সে আমার কথা রেখেছে) ; order, direction (ছেলেটা কথা শোনে না) ; necessity, need, compulsion (এ কাজ করতেই হবে, এমন কথা আছে?) ; plea (ভুল হলে কোনো কথা শুনব না) ; a proverb (কথায় বলে). **কথা কওয়া** v. to speak; to talk. **কথা কাটা** *v.* to refute; to protest. **কথা দেওয়া** *v.* to give one's word, to promise. **কথা চালা** *v.* to tell one's secrets to another; to indulge in scandal-mongering, to talk scandal, to gossip. **কথা পাড়া** *v.* to raise a topic; to propose. **কথা না থাকা** not to be on speaking terms with; not to be promised or decided beforehand. **কথা রাখা** to keep a promise; to be true to one's word. **কথায় কথায়** in course of conversation; incidentally during conversation, by the by, by the way; whilst talking (কথায় কথায় রাত হল). **কথায় থাকা** to involve oneself in. **কথায় না থাকা** to have nothing to do with. **কথার কথা** a word for word's sake; worth serious consideration (এ কি একটা কথার কথা হল ?). **কথার খেলাপ** breaking a promise. **কথার ঝুড়ি** (of a person) a chatterbox. **কথার ধার** sting of words. **কথার নড়চড়** deviation from one's promise. **কথার ফের, কথার মারপ্যাঁচ** a sly turn of speech; verbal trickery; jugglery of words; quibble. **কথার শ্রাদ্ধ** too much or unnecessary talking, words and words. **~কলি** *n.* Indian dance depicting ancient wartales. **কথা কাটাকাটি** *n.* arguments and counter-arguments; bandying of words; altercation; hot exchange. **কথা কাটাকাটি করা** *v.* to advance arguments and counter-arguments; to bandy words; to altercate; to be engaged in a hot exchange. **কথা চালাচালি** *n.* act of telling one's secrets to another; scandal-mongering; gossiping. **কথা চালাচালি করা** same as **কথা চালা**। **~চ্ছলে** same as **কথাপ্রসঙ্গে**। **~ন্তর** *n.* altercation; bandying of words; another topic; interval in course of conversation; a breach of promise. **~প্রসঙ্গ** *n.* conversation, talk; act of raising a topic; a topic; a context. **~প্রসঙ্গে** *adv.* in course of conversation; incidentally during conversation, by the way. **~বার্তা** *n.* conversation; a talk; a chat. **~বার্তা বলা** *v.* to talk; to chat. **~মতো** *adv.* in keeping with one's words or promise; in obedience to one's order or direction. **~মাত্র** *n.* mere words (having no genuine worth). **~মাত্রসার** mere words having no genuine worth, words or promises ending in smoke; false promise. **~মুখ** *n.* a preface. **~রম্ভ** *n.* the beginning of a story or conversation. **~শিল্প** *n.* creative literary works written in prose such as novels, stories etc. **~শিল্পী** *n.* an author of prose fiction, stories etc. **~শেষ** *n.* the end of a story or conversation. **~সাহিত্য** same as **কথাশিল্প**। **~সাহিত্যিক** same as **কথাশিল্পী**।

কথিকা *n.* a story in a sketchy shape; a talk.

কথিত *a.* uttered, pronounced; said, told; narrated, described; mentioned, spoken of. **কথিত আছে যে** it is said that.

কথোপকথন *n.* a conversation; a talk, a chat; a dialogue. **কথোপকথন করা** *v.* to talk. **কথোপকথনের ভাষা** colloquial or spoken language.

কথ্য *a.* worthy of being spoken or told, speakable, utterable; that which is to be spoken or told; colloquial (কথ্য ভাষা).

কদক্ষর *n.* a letter (of the alphabet) written badly; bad handwriting. □ *a.* (of a letter) badly writtten; one who writes a bad hand.

কদন্ন *n.* bad food; abominable food; food unfit for human consumption.

কদভ্যাস *n.* a bad habit.

কদম[1] *n.* coll. var. of **কদম্ব**।

কদম[2] *n.* a foot; a leg; a step; (of horses) trot. **কদমে চলা** *v.* to trot.

কদমা *n.* a round and hard sweetmeat shaped like a kadam (কদম) flower.

কদম্ব *n. the Nauclea kadamba*, the kadamba flower (কদম) or its tree.

কদর *n.* respect, honour; regard; importance; appreciation; cordial reception; value, worth. **কদর করা** *v.* to respect, to honour; to have regard for; to attach importance to; to appreciate; to receive cordially; to deem valuable.

কদর্থ *n.* a distorted meaning; a misinterpretation; a perverted meaning. **কদর্থ করা** *v.* to distort or pervert the meaning (of); to misinterpret. **~ন, ~না** *n.* distortion or perversion of meaning; misinterpretation; censure. **কদর্থিত** *a.* having the meaning distorted or perverted; misinterpreted.

কদর্য *a.* extremely ugly; detestable; abominable, hateful; base; miserly, niggardly. **~তা** *n.* extreme ugliness; detestableness, abomination, hatefulness; baseness; miserliness, niggardliness.

কদলী *n.* the banana or plantain (fruit or tree).

কদাকার *a.* unshapely, ungainly, ugly-looking; deformed.

কদাচ, কদাচন, কদাচিৎ *adv.* at any time, ever; rarely, seldom. **কদাচ না** never.

কদাচার, কদাচরণ *n.* an abominable habit or practice; malpractice. ☐ *a.* given to abominable or loathsome habits or practice. **কদাচারী** same as **কদাচার** (*a.*).

কদাপি *adv.* same as **কদাচ** ।

কদিন coll. corrup. of **কতদিন** or **কয়দিন** (see **কয়**২).

কদু *n.* the gourd.

কদুক্তি *n.* obscene utterance or words; harsh words; filthy or foul language, abusive words; malicious words.

কদুত্তর *n.* an insolent or impertinent reply; an ungracious or unseemly answer; a retort.

কদুষ্ণ same as **কবোষ্ণ** ।

কদ্দিন var. of **কদিন** ।

কদ্দুর coll. corrup. of **কত দূর** ।

কনক *n.* gold. ☐ *a.* in comp. (used as a *pfx.*) golden, made of gold (কনকমুকুট) ; auriferous. **~ক্ষার** *n.* borax. **~চাঁপা** *n.* a golden-coloured sweet-scented flower or its plant. **~চূড়** *n.* a variety of paddy. ☐ *a.* golden-crested (কনকচূড় মুকুট). **~ ধুতুরা** *n.* a species of Datura, its plant or flower. **~দীপ** *n.* a lamp made of gold, a gold lamp. **~পুরী** *n.* a city full of architectural works made of gold; a city of gold; (fig.) a beautiful city or dwelling-house. **~প্রভ** *a.*bright or shining as gold. **~প্রভা** *n.* the lustre of gold. **~বরণ** *a.* golden-coloured. **~ময়** *a.* made of gold, full of gold, golden. **~মুকুট** *n.* a gold crown. **~রঞ্জিত** *a.* gold-gilt. **~লতা** *n.* a golden creeper, (cp.) golden rod.

কনকন *int.* denoting a twinging or painful sensation; smarting; shivering with cold. **কনকন করা, কনকনানো** *v.* to twinge; to ache, to smart; to feel smarting pain; to shiver with cold. **কনকনানি** *n.* twinge; aching; the bite of cold; shivering caused by cold. **কনকনে** *a.* (of pain) twinging, smarting; (of cold) biting or piercing.

কনকাচল *n.* (myth.) a mountain of gold or as bright as gold.

কনকাঞ্জলি *n.* a ceremonial gift of gold made at wedding or just before the immersion of an idol.

কনকানটে *n.* a dark-red variety of edible spinach, the golden spinach.

কনট্রাকটর *n.* a contractor. **কনট্রাকটরি** *n.* the profession of a contractor, esp. of a building-contractor; a contract (বাড়ির কনট্রাকটরি তাকে দিয়ো).

কনস্টবল, কনস্টেবল *n.* a constable.

কনিষ্ঠ *a.* smallest; youngest; (loos. but pop.) younger (সহদেব কনিষ্ঠ পাণ্ডব). ☐ *n.* a younger or the youngest brother or son. **কনিষ্ঠা** *a.* & *n. fem.* of **কনিষ্ঠ** । ☐ *n.* the little finger or toe.

কনীনিকা *n.* the apple of the eye, the pupil.

কনীয়ান *a.* smaller; younger; (loos.) very small, little, puny. *fem.* **কনীয়সী** ।

কনুই *a.* the elbow. **কনুই দিয়ে গুঁতানো** *v.* to elbow, to jostle.

কনে *n.* a bride; a virgin of marriageable age; a newly-married wife. **~বউ** *n.* a newly-married wife; a child-wife; the youngest wife of a family.

কনস্টেবল var. of **কনস্টবল** ।

কন্ট্রাক্টর, কন্ট্রাক্টার variants of **কনট্রাকটর** ।

কন্ট্রোল *n.* control; a shop or place where controlled or specified goods are sold at a scheduled price (কনট্রোলে যাওয়া).

কন্থা *n.* a cotton covering made of patch-work.

কন্দ *n.* any of the bulbous or tuberous plants, a bulb or tuber.

কন্দমূল *n.* radish.

কন্দর *n.* a. mountain-cave, a cavern.

কন্দর্প *n.* the name of Hindu love god (cp. Cupid, Eros).

কন্দল১ *a.* bulbous, tuberous.

কন্দল২ *n.* a quarrel, an altercation; a

strife, a fight, a war. **কন্দলিয়া** *a.* quarrelsome; wrangling; shrewish; belligerent.

কন্দু *n.* a cooking pan made of iron.

কন্দুক, কন্দূক *n.* a spherical shot for putting; a ball for playing with. **~ক্রীড়া** *n.* a game with a ball; the game of putting the shot.

কন্ধ *n.* the shoulder; the head; the body; the trunk, torso. **~কাটা** *a.* headless; truncated. □ *n.* a headless being or spirit.

কন্ধর *n.* the throat; the neck; the shoulder.

কন্না coll. corrup. of **করনা**।

কন্যকা *n.* a ten year old virgin; a daughter.

কন্যা *n.* a daughter; a virgin; a marriageable girl; a bride; (astrol.) the Virgo. **~কর্তা** *n.* (in a wedding) the chief man amongst the bride's people. **~কাল** *n.* maidenhood. **~গ্রহণ** *n.* act of taking a girl as wife; act of receiving a girl in marriage in one's family. **~দান** *n.* act of giving away a girl esp. a daughter in marriage; the ceremony of committing the bride into the hands of the bridegroom. **~দায়** *n.* the responsibility of arranging for the marriage of one's daughter; the state of being burdened with a marriageable daughter for whom a husband has not yet been found. **~দায়গ্রস্ত** *a.* of one who is yet to marry off his daughter, burdened with the responsibility of arranging for the marriage of one's daughter. **~পক্ষ** *n.* (in a wedding) the bride's people or party. **~প্রণিধি** *n.* a girl guide. **~যাত্রী** *n.* a wedding-guest invited by the bride's people. **~রাশি** *n.* (astrol.) the Virgo. **~সম্প্রদান** same as **কন্যাদান**।

কপ *int.* expressing : the sound of gulping or swallowing quickly. **কপকপ** *int.* expressing : repetition of this sound. **কপাকপ** *adv.* with this repeated sound.

কপচানো *v.* (of or like talking birds) to utter or reproduce by rote, to say what is hackneyed or stock by rote; to indulge in empty talk in order to parade one's learning; to prattle, to talk bunkum; to cut or shear (চুল কপচানো). **কপচানি** *n.* act of roting or prattling.

কপট *n.* a chicane, a trick; chicanery, trickery; deceit. □ *a* deceitful; hypocritical, feigning, insincere (কপট বন্ধু) ; dissimulating, assumed (কপট বেশ). **~তা** *n.* chicanery; deceitfulness; hypocrisy, feigning, insincerity; dissimulation. **~তাময়** same as **কপট** (*a.*). **~প্রবন্ধ** *n.* a deceitful trick or design, a chicane, a stratagem. **~বন্ধু** a false friend. **~বেশ** a disguise. **~বেশী** *a.* disguised. **কপটাচরণ, কপটাচার, কপটচারিতা** *n.* chicanery; act of deceiving, deceit; feigning; hypocrisy, insincerity; dissimulation. **কপটাচরণ করা** *v.* to chicane, to deceive, to doublecross; to feign; to dissimulate. **কপটাচারী, কপটচারী, কপটী** *a.* practising chicanery, tricky; deceitful; hypocritical, feigning, insincere; dissimulating; disguising. *fem.* **কপটাচারিণী, কপটচারিণী, কপটিনী**। **কপটালাপ** *n.* hypocritical or insincere talk.

কপনি *n.* a small piece of loincloth worn after the fashion of a suspensor by Indian ascetics; a very small and cheap loincloth.

কপর্দক *n.* a snail-like gastropod resembling a miniature conch, a cowrie; a cowrie-shell used as a coin or medium of exchange of the smallest denomination; a coin of the smallest denomination, (cp.) a stiver. **~বিহীন ~শূন্য, ~হীন** *a.* penniless, (coll.) broke extremely poor.

কপর্দী *n.* Lord Shiva (ref. to his ringlets).

কপাকপ see **কপ**।

কপাট *n.* a door; a door-panel; a lid; a shutting or concealing device (মনের কপাট). **কপাটক** *n.* (anat.) a valve.

কপাটি *n.* an Indian outdoor game; lock jaw, trismus (usu. **দাঁতকপাটি**).

কপাৎ same as **কপ**।

কপাল *n.* the skull, the cranium; the forehead; a beggar's bowl; a shred of an earthen pitcher. **কপাল চাপড়ানো** *v.* to beat one's forehead in despair; to complain bitterly against bad luck. **কপাল ঠোকা** *v.* to strike one's forehead against something (in order to express grief, complaint etc.); to try one's luck; to undertake a venture abandoning oneself into the hands of destiny. **কপাল পোড়া** *v.* to lose the favour of fortune, to be down on one's luck; (coll.) to become a widow, (of women) to be widowed. **কপাল ফেরা** *v.* to win the favour of fortune; to improve one's state and position; to begin to flourish; to be on the rise. **কপাল ভাঙা** same as **কপাল পোড়া**। **কপালের লিখন** decree of fate or providence. **~ক্রমে** *adv.* luckily, fortunately; by luck; as luck would have it; unfortunately, unluckily (কপালক্রমে সুযোগ হারানো). **~জোর, জোর কপাল** *n.* good luck, good fortune. **~গুণে, ~জোরে** *adv.* by good luck (and esp. by chance). **~পোড়া** *a.* luckless, down on one's luck, unfortunate. **~ভৃৎ, ~মালী, কপালী** *n.* appellations of Shiva (শিব). **~মালিনী, কপালিনী** *n. fem.* appellations of Goddess Kali (কালী). **কপালিয়া, কপালে** *a.* fortunate, lucky, favoured by fortune. **হায় কপাল** *int.* oh dear! dear me !

কপি১ *n.* the monkey.

কপি২ *n.* cabbage or cauliflower. **ওলকপি** *n.* kohlrabi. **ফুলকপি** *n.* cauliflower. **বাঁধাকপি** *n.* cabbage.

কপি৩ *n.* matter for printing; a transcript; a copy. **কপি করা** *v.* to transcribe, to make a duplicate of; (by a student) to look on a fellow-student's work and filch the result; to copy unfairly from a fellow-student's answer-script in the examination hall; to copy; to duplicate. **কপি-করা** *a.* copied.

কপিকল *n.* a pulley.

কপিকেতন *n.* a chariot on the top of which sits a monkey; Arjuna (অর্জুন) of the Mahabharata for he had such a chariot.

কপিঞ্জল *n.* the Indian swallow; the chatak; the sandpiper, the lapwing.

কপিত্থ *n.* a shelled fruit with sour pulp akin to the wood-apple; its tree.

কপিধ্বজ same as **কপিকেতন**।

কপিল *a.* brown, tawny. ☐ *n.* the brown colour. **কপিলা** *a. fem.* of **কপিল ;** (of cows) female. ☐ *n.* a brown cow; a wishing cow; a cowcalf.

কপিশ *n.* pale yellowish colour, mud-colour. ☐ *a.* pale yellow, mud-coloured.

কপোত *n.* the pigeon. *fem.* **কপোতী, ~পালী, ~পালিকা** *n.* a pigeonry, a pigeon-house; a dovecot. **~বৃত্তি** *n.* behaviour of or like a pigeon; a livelihood in which there is no means of providing for the future. ☐ *a.* behaving like a pigeon or dove; living from hand to mouth without any means to provide for the future. **কপোতাভ** *a.* of the colour of a pigeon; grey. **কপোতারি** *n.* the hawk, the falcon. **কপোতেশ্বর** *n.* an appellation of Shiva (শিব).

কপোল *n.* the cheek. **~কল্পনা** *n.* false fancy; fanciful imagery or talk or depiction, figments of the imagination. **~কল্পিত** *a.* imaginary; fictitious. **~দেশ** *n.* the region of the cheek; the cheek. **~রাগ** *n.* a glow or flush of the cheek.

কফ *n.* phlegm; catarrh; rheum; mucus.

কফঘ্ন *a.* counteracting or removing phlegm or catarrh.

কফজ *a.* phlegmatic; catarrhal; mucous.

কফণি, কফোণি *n.* the elbow.

কফনিঃসারক *n.* & *a.* (an) expectorant.

কফি *n.* coffee.

কফিন *n.* a coffin.

কফোণি var. of **কফণি**।

কবচ *n.* an armour, a coat of mail; a metrical form of words believed to possess occult power, a spell, a charm; an amulet, a trinket, a talisman. **কবচ করা** *v.* to protect or guard with a spell; to give an amulet for protection. **কবচ ধারণ করা** *v.* to wear an amulet for protection. **~ধারী** *a.* wearing a coat of mail, armour-clad; wearing an amulet.

কবচকুণ্ডল *n.* armour and earrings.

কবচী *a.* armour-clad; wearing an amulet; crustacean. ☐ *n.* a crustacean.

কবজ১ *n.* a receipt (esp. for the rent paid); a note of hand, a bond.

কবজ২ *n.* a charm, a spell; an amulet, a trinket, a talisman.

কবজা *n.* a hinge; grip; control.

কবজি *n.* the wrist; grip; control; (fig.) the pulse.

কবন্ধ *n.* a headless or truncated body; a headless or truncated goblin; the ascending node, the descending node; a comet.

কবয়ী *n.* the walking or climbing fish, the anabas.

কবর *n.* a grave; a tomb. **কবর দেওয়া** *v.* to bury; to inter; to entomb. **~খানা** *n.* a burial-ground, a cemetery, a graveyard.

কবরী *n.* hair in the state of being plaited, a chignon; a pigtail; a braid or plait of hair; braiding of hair; hairdessing. **~বন্ধন** *n.*braiding or plaiting of hair, hairdressing, hairdo. **~ভূষণ** *n.* any ornament for hair or chignon such as a hairpin or a hairnet.

কবর্গ *n.* ক্ খ্ গ্ ঘ্ ঙ্ ; these five consonants collectively.

কবল *n.* gape; gulp; act of gurgling or rinsing the mouth; forceful occupation; seizure; grip.

কবলানো *v.* to confess; to promise; to offer; to claim. ☐ *n.* confession; act of promising; act of offering.

কবলিত, কবলীকৃত *a.* taken into the mouth; gulped, swallowed, eaten; forcefully occupied; seized; gripped; possessed.

কবহু কবহুঁ *adv.* (poet.) at any time; ever.

কবাট var. of **কপাট**।

কবাডি *n.* an Indian outdoor game.

কবালা *n.* a deed of sale or transfer, a conveyance, a bill of sale. **কবালা করে দেওয়া** *v.* to sell or convey by a deed.

কবি *n.* a poet; a scholar; a philosopher; a kind of song-tournament, this song (cp. strophe and antistrophe), its composer or singer. **~ওয়ালা** *n.* a composer of songs for a song-tournament; a singer of these songs; the leader of a party competing in a song-tournament. **~কল্পনা** *n.* a visionary thing; fanciful imagination; a baseless and unreal conception; (rare) poetic imagination. **~কল্পিত** *a.* visionary; fanciful; baseless and unreal; imagined or invented by a poet. **~গান** *n.* a kind of song-tournament or duel; a song for this tournament. **~গুরু** *n.* the first poet; the chief of poets. **~জনোচিত** *a.* befitting a poet, poetical. **কবির লড়াই** a kind of song-tournament; a contest of poets. **কবিতা** *n.* a poem; a verse; a couplet; poetry. **কবিত্ব** *n.* poetical imagination or talent, poetry; poetic quality. **কবিত্বপূর্ণ, কবিত্বময়** *a.* full of poetry; full of poetic quality; endowed with a talent for composing poems. **কবিত্ব শক্তি** *n.* poetical talent or genius. **~প্রসিদ্ধি** *n.* any imaginative description of nature originally made by a poet and afterwards repeated by other poets, a poetical convention. **~বর** *n.* a great poet, a master poet. **কবি সম্মেলন** *n.* an assembly or conference of poets. **কবীশ** *n.* the chief among poets.

কবিরপন্থী *a.* of the religious order established by Kabir. ☐ *n.* one belonging to this order.

কবিরাজ *n.* a physician who follows the Ayurvedic (আয়ুর্বেদীয়) system of treatment; (euphem.) a prince among poets. **কবিরাজি** *n.* the Ayurvedic system of treatment; the profession of an Ayurvedic physician. ☐ *a.* pertaining to an Ayurvedic physician or according to Ayurvedic system of treatment, Ayurvedic.

কবুতর *n.* the pigeon. *fem.* **কবুতরী**।

কবুল *n.* confessions; acknowledgement; promise. ☐ *a.* categorical, explicit; accepting the responsibility or consequence (কবুল জবাব) ; based on the defendant's admission of the plaintiff's claims (কবুল ডিক্রি) ; admitted; accepted; bound by promise. **কবুল করা** *v.* to confess; to admit, to acknowledge; to promise. **কবুল হওয়া** *v.* to be accepted; to be bound by promise.

কবুলতি, কবুলিয়ত *n.* a deed of agreement in which a tenant undertakes to pay the landowner rents regularly, a counter-lease; a note of acknowledgement.

কবে *adv.* on what day; when; long ago (সে কি আর বেঁচে আছে, কবে মরেছে !).

কবোষ্ণ *a.* lukewarm, tepid.

কব্য *n.* an oblation of food offered to the manes of deceased ancestors.

কব্যবাহ *n.* fire believed to carry the food offered to deceased ancestors.

কব্জা alt. spell. of **কবজা**।

কব্জি alt. spell. of **কবজি**।

কভু (poet. & High) *adv.* ever, at any time. **কভু নহে** *adv.* never.

কম[1] *a.* lovely, graceful; pleasant; charming; desirable.

কম[2] *a.* deficient, short; less; small (in amount or degree); a few, not many; a little, not much; inadequate; inefficient, inexpert, inferior (লাঠিবাজিতেও কম নয়). **কম করা** *v.* to lessen, to curtail, to reduce, to decrease, to abate. **কম পড়া** *v.* to fall short (of); to run short (of); to be inadequate; to decrease. **~জোর** *a.* weak; weakened. **~জোরি** *a.* weak. ☐ *n.* weakness. **~তি** *n.* deficiency, shortage; smallness; fewness; inadequacy; inefficiency, inferiority. ☐ *a.* inefficient, inexpert, inferior (সে কমতি কীসে ?). **~পোক্ত** *a.* not very strong, somewhat frail or weak. **~বেশি** *a.* & *adv.* more or less. **~সম** *a.* not many or much; restrained; moderate. **~পক্ষে, কমসে কম** *adv.* at least.

কমঠ *n.* the tortoise, the turtle; a waterpot used by Hindu ascetics.

কমণ্ডলু *n.* a water-pot used for religious purposes and also by Hindu ascetics.

কমনীয় *a.* lovely, graceful; pleasant; charming; desirable. *fem.* **কমনীয়া**। **কমনীয়তা** *n.* loveliness, gracefulness; grace; pleasantness; charm; desirability.

কমনে *adv.* (dial.) where, whither; in or by which way; how.

কমবক্ত, কমবখত *a.* wretched, miserable; down on one's luck, ill-fated.

কমল *n.* the water lily, the lotus. **~-আঁখি** *n.* an eye as beautiful as a lotus; a lotus-eyed man. ☐ *a.* lotus-eyed. **~কলি, ~কোরক, ~কোষ** *n.* a lotus-bud. **~দল** *n.* a lotus-petal. **~নয়ন** same as **কমল-আঁখি**। *fem.* **কমলনয়না**। **~যোনি** *n.* an appellation of God Brahma (ব্রহ্মা). **~লোচন** same as **কমল-আঁখি**। *fem.* **কমললোচনা**।

কমলা[1] *n.* an appellation of Goddess Lakshmi (লক্ষ্মী).

কমলা[2] *n.* an orange (also **কমলালেবু**).

কমলাগুঁড়ি *n.* an orange-coloured fruitdust used to dye cloth.

কমলাপতি *n.* an appellation of Vishnu (বিষ্ণু).

কমলালয়া *n.* an appellation of Goddess Lakshmi (লক্ষ্মী).

কমলাসন *n.* an appellation of God Brahma (**ব্রহ্মা**).

কমলাসনা *n.* an appellation of Goddess Lakshmi (লক্ষ্মী).

কমলিনী *n.* a lotus clump; lotuses collectively.

কমলেকামিনী *n.* a female deity, described as sitting on a lotus floating in the sea and gorging and disgorging an elephant continuously.

কমসম, কমসে কম see **কম**[2]।

কমা[1] *n.* (gr.) a comma (,).

কমা[2] *v.* to fall short; to decrease; to abate; to grow less; to diminish; to fall, to come down (দাম কমেছে).

কমানো *v.* to shorten, to curtail, to reduce; to cause to decrease or abate or diminish, to abate, to diminish. ☐ *n.* act of shortening or cutting down, curtailment, reduction; act of decreasing or abating or diminishing. ☐ *a.* shortened, cut down., curtailed, reduced; decreased, abated; diminished.

কমিটি *n.* a committee.

কমিশন *n.* a percentage paid to an agent, commission; (loos.) discount; a body of persons appointed to perform certain duties, a commission.

কমিশনার *n.* designation of several high public officials (such as, the Divisional Commissioner, the Food Commissioner etc.); a member of a municipal board, a commissioner.

কম্প, কম্পন *n.* tremor, quake, shiver, tremble, shudder; ague; quiver; throb, vibration. **কম্প হওয়া** *v.* to be stricken with tremor, to quake; to shiver, to tremble, to shudder; to be stricken with ague; to throb. **কম্পক** *n.* vibrator. **কম্পজ্বর** *n.* a fever marked by shivering; an ague; malaria. **কম্পমান** *a.* quaking; shivering, trembling, tremulous, shuddering; stricken with ague; quivering; throbbing; vibrating.

কম্পাউন্ডার *n.* one who prepares medicines according to a doctor's prescription; a pharmacist.

কম্পাঙ্ক *n.* frequency of vibration.

কম্পানি var. of **কোম্পানি**।

কম্পান্বিত *a.* trembling, tremulous; shivering, shuddering; throbbing; quivering. *fem.* **কম্পান্বিতা**। **কম্পান্বিত-কলেবর** *a.* trembling all over (esp. being stricken with fear).

কম্পাস *n.* an instrument with a magnetized needle used in finding directions, a compass; an instrument with a pair of jointed legs used for describing circles etc., a pair of compasses.

কম্পিত *a.* trembling, tremulous; shivering, shuddering; throbbing; quivering; stricken with ague. **কম্পিত স্বরে, কম্পিত কণ্ঠে** *adv.* in a trembling voice. **কম্পিত হওয়া** *v.* to tremble; to shiver; to shudder; to throb; to quiver; to vibrate.

কম্পোজ *n.* (print.) act of composing. **কম্পোজ করা** *v.* to compose. **কম্পোজিটর, কম্পোজিটার** *n.* a compositor. **কম্পোজিটরি, কম্পোজিটারি** *n.* the profession or work of a compositor.

কম্প্র *a.* trembling, tremulous.

কম্ফর্টার *n.* a long narrow woollen scarf (usu. worn round the neck), a comforter.

কম্বল *n.* a blanket, a rug. **~সম্বল** *a.* (lit.) one whose whole earthly possession consists of only a blanket; extremely poor, indigent; taken to asceticism.

কম্বু *n.* a conch. **~কণ্ঠ** *n.* a neck striated like a conch; a voice as grave and loud as the sound made by the blowing of a conch. □ *a.* possessing such a neck or voice. *fem.* **কম্বুকণ্ঠী**। **~গ্রীব** *a.* possessing a neck striated like a conch. **~গ্রীবা** *n.* a neck striated like a conch. **~নাদ** *n.* sound as grave and loud as the sound made by the blowing of a conch; the sound made by blowing a conch. **~রেখা** *n.* a stria or thin line or linear mark as on a conch.

কম্র *a.* desirous, lustful; desirable; attractive, charming; beautiful.

কয়¹ coll. var. of **কহে**।

কয়² *a.* how many; a few, several.

কয়লা *n.* coal. **কাঠকয়লা** *n.* charcoal. **কোককয়লা** *n.* coke. **পাথুরে কয়লা** *n.* coal. **~ওয়ালা** *n.* a seller of coal, a coal-dealer. **~খনি** *n.* a coalmine, a coal-pit. **কয়লাখনি অঞ্চল** *n.* a coalfield.

কয়াল *n.* one whose profession is to weigh goods, esp. cereals, at the time of transaction; a professional weighing man, a weighman, a weigher. **কয়ালি** *n.* the profession of a weigher; weighage.

কয়েক *a.* a small number of, a few, several.

কয়েতবেল *n.* a shelled fruit with sour pulp akin to the wood-apple.

কয়েদ *n.* a prison, a gaol, a jail (কয়েদে থাকা) ; imprisonment, duress, confinement (কয়েদ হওয়া). □ *a.* imprisoned, jailed, confined. **কয়েদ করা** *v.* to imprison; to confine. **কয়েদ থাকা** *v.* to be in duress; to be in prison or in confinement. **কয়েদ হওয়া** *v.* to be sentenced to imprisonment. **~খানা** *n.* a guard-room, a guard-house, lock-up, prison. **কয়েদি** *n.* a prisoner, a convict. □ *n.* imprisoned; confined.

কর¹ *n.* a ray or beam (of light.)

কর² *n.* a tax; customs, a duty; revenue; a toll; a cess; tribute; rent; a rate. **~গ্রহ, ~গ্রহণ** *n.* collection of taxes, customs, revenues etc. **~গ্রাহক, ~গ্রাহী** *a.* one who collects taxes, revenue etc. □ *n.* a tax-collector, a revenue officer etc. (also see **কর³**). **~দাতা** *n.* a taxpayer, a ratepayer, one who pays revenue, rent, tribute etc. **~নির্ধার** *n.* taxation. **~নির্ধারণ** *n.* assessment (of taxes). **~পীড়িত** *a.* chafing or fretting under the burden of high taxation. **~মুক্ত** rent-free, exempt from taxes, duty-free, etc. (also see **কর⁴**). **~যোগ্য** *a.* taxable.

কর³ *n.* the hand; the trunk of an elephant. **~কণ্টক** *n.* a finger-nail. **~কণ্ডূয়ন** *n.* itching of the palm; intense or burning desire to do something. **~কবলিত** *a.* held or seized firmly with the hand, grasped; (fig.) occupied or taken possession of or brought under control esp. by force (and usu. unlawfully).

~কমল *n*. a hand conceived as a lotus; a hand as beautiful as a lotus. ~কোষ্ঠী *n*. lines of the palm from which fortune is told; the readings of a palmist. ~কোষ্ঠী বিদ্যা *n*. palmistry. ~গ্রহ, ~গ্রহণ *n*. act of wedding (by a bridegroom), marriage. ~গ্রাহ, ~গ্রাহক *a*. *mas*. marrying (a girl). □ *n*. a husband. ~জোড়ে *adv*. with folded hands (indicating submission and humility). ~তল *n*. the palm of a hand; (fig.) full control or possession, easy reach. ~তলগত *a*. (lit.) lying or held in the palm; taken firm hold of; taken complete possession of;brought or kept under full control or easy reach; thoroughly mastered over or learned; conquered or dominated or subjugated. ~তলধৃত *a*. held in one's palm or palms. ~তলন্যস্ত *a*. placed or put or lying in one's palm. ~তলস্থ *a*. grasped, lying in the palm; of the palm. ~তলাকার *a*. palmate. ~তাল *n*. (usu. in *pl*.) a cymbal. ~তালি *n*. clapping of the hands. ~তালি দেওয়া *v*. to clap hands. ~ধৃত *a*. held in or seized with the hand or hands. ~ন্যাস *n*. a typical system of gesticulation with fingers at the time of prayer. ~পদ্ম *n*. a hand conceived as a lily; a hand as beautiful as a lily. ~পল্লব *n*. a hand as delicate and beautiful as a young twig. ~পীড়ন same as করগ্রহণ। ~পুট *n*. palms joined to form a cup. ~পুটে *adv*. in or with cupped hands. ~ভূষণ *n*. a bracelet, a wristlet; a bangle. ~মর্দন *n*. handshake. ~মর্দন করা *v*. to shake hands. ~মুক্ত *a*. released from grasp or grip. ~স্পর্শ *n*. a touch of or with the hand.

করকচ *n*. sea salt.

করকচি *a*. soft and not yet filled with pulp (করকচি ডাব). □ *n*. such a green coconut.

করকর *int*. expressing: the sound of crushing or rubbing grits or of chewing hard and crisp things; the sound of scraping (as the pulp of a coconut); scratching sensation; restlessness; pain; burning sensation. **করকরা, করকরানো** *v*. to give a sensation of scratching or paining or burning. **করকরানি** *n*. scratching or paining or burning sensation. **করকরে** *a*. gritty; giving out a sound of or as of crushing or rubbing grits; brand new (করকরে নোট).

করকা *n*. a grain of ice falling from the clouds, hailstone. ~পাত *n*. sleet, hailstorm.

করকুর্চাস্থি *n*. the carpal bone, the carpal.

করগেট, করুগেট see **করোগেট**।

কঙ্ক, কড়ঙ্ক *n*. a small portable waterpot used for holy purposes and by ascetics; a beggar's bowl; a coconut-shell or a fragment of it esp. when used as a pot; a pot, a vessel, a box; the skull.

করচা var. of **কড়চা**।

করঞ্জ, করঞ্জক, করঞ্জা *n*. a variety of sour fruit (it becomes crimson when ripe).

করণ *n*. doing or working or performing; accomplishment, execution, action; a work done, a deed, an act; a cause or motive; any of the sense organs; body; physique; a place, a field; a place where business is carried on, an office; (gr.) the instrumental case. ~কারক *n*. (gr.) the instrumental case. ~কারণ *n*. exchange of gifts at a wedding.

করণিক *n*. an office-clerk, a clerk.

করণী *n*. (math.) √ this sign, surd. **করণী নিরসন** *n*. (alg.) rationalization.

করণীয় *a*. that which can be or is to be done; practicable; worthy; fit for matrimonial alliance (করণীয় ঘর).

করণ্ড *n*. a bee-hive; a flower-basket; a basket, a wickerwork.

করতা var. of **কড়তা**।

করদ *a*. tributary. ~রাজ্য *n*. a tributary state, a tributary.

করনা *n*. (chiefly used as a correl.) duties, tasks (ঘরকরনা).

করপত্র *n*. a hand-saw; a saw.

করপাল, করবাল *n*. a sword, a scimitar.

করবী, করবীর *n*. the oleander tree or its flower, *nerium odorum*. **রক্তকরবী** *n*. the red oleander. **শ্বেতকরবী** *n*. the white oleander.

করভ *n*. the young of an elephant; the camel or its young; the mule. *fem*. **করভী**।

করম poet. corrup. of **কর্ম**।

করমচা *n.* a variety of sour fruit (it becomes crimson when ripe).

করলা *n.* a variety of kitchen vegetable having a bitter taste, the larger variety of bitter gourd.

করহ *v. imperat.* (obs.) do.

করা *v.* to do, to perform, to accomplish, to execute (কাজ করা) ; to build (বাড়ি করা) ; to make; to earn, to come into possession of, to save (টাকা করা) ; to invent, to devise (বুদ্ধি করা, কৌশল করা) ; to apply (জোর করা) ; to shoot (গুলি করা) ; to be stricken with (রাগ করা, স্নেহ করা, দ্বিধা করা) ; to visit (তীর্থ করা) ; to hire or rent (গাড়ি ভাড়া করা) ; to attend (আপিস করা) ; to manage (সংসার করা) ; to found, to establish (স্কুল করা) ; to cook, bake, roast, etc. (তরকারি করা, রুটি করা) ; to reduce to (সরল করা) ; to render into (গদ্য করা) ; to translate (ইংরেজি করা) ; to work out (অঙ্ক করা) ; to lay (বিছানা করা, আসন করা) ; to practise (ওকালতি করা) ; to accumulate (মেঘ করা) ; to take (হাতে করা, ভাড়া করা). □ *a.* that which makes (বাড়ি-আলো-করা ছেলে) ; that which is done (করা কাজ).

করাঘাত *n.* a blow with the palm or hand, a slap, a cuff. **করাঘাত করা** *v.* to strike with the palm or hand, to slap, to cuff.

করাত *n.* a saw. **করাত দিয়ে কাটা বা চেরা** *v.* to saw. **~কল** *n.* a saw-mill. **করাতি** *n.* a sawyer.

করাধান *n.* imposition of a tax or taxes, taxation.

করানো *v.* to cause to do or perform or accomplish or execute or build or make or earn or invent or devise or apply or shoot or be stricken with or move or visit or hire or rent or attend or manage or found or establish or cook or bake or roast or reduce to or render into or translate or work out or lay or practise or accumulate or take.

করায়ত্ত *a.* gripped, grasped; taken firm hold or possession of; brought under one's control or power; usurped; learned thoroughly.

করাল *a.* having large teeth; rodent; having a frightful appearance; terrible, awful; very high or turbulent (করাল ঢেউ, করাল সমুদ্র) ; extremely severe and cruel. **~বদনা** *a. fem.* having a frightful aspect. □ *n.* an appellation of Goddess Kali (কালী). *masc. a.* **করালবদন**। **করালী** *n.* an appellation of Goddess Kali (কালী).

করিতকর্মা *a.* efficient and industrious; go-getting; smart.

করিষ্ণু *a.* engaged in doing, in the state of doing.

করী *n.* the elephant. *fem.* **করিণী**। **করিকর** *n.* the proboscis of an elephant, a trunk. **করিকুম্ভ** *n.* the frontal globe or sinus of an elephant. **করিদন্ত** *n.* the tooth of an elephant, a tusk; ivory. **করিশাবক** *n.* a calf of an elephant. **করিশুণ্ড** same as **করিকর**।

করীষ *n.* dried cow-dung; a cake of dried cow-dung used as fuel.

করুগেট var. of **করোগেট**।

করুণ *a.* pathetic, sad; doleful; compassionate (করুণহৃদয়). **করুণ স্বরে** *adv.* in a doleful or piteous or plaintive voice, in a mournful or sorrowful tone.

করুণা *n.* compassion; kindness. **~নিদান, ~নিধান, ~নিধি, ~নিলয়, ~ময়** *a.* compassionate; kind. *fem.* **করুণাময়ী**। **~সাগর, ~সিন্ধু** *a.* & *n.* one who is an ocean of compassion or kindness. **~র্দ্র** *a.* compassionate; tender.

করে *prep.* as the result of, resulting from, caused by, due to, for (তাতে করে). **করে-কর্মে নেওয়া** *v.* to assist in the management or execution of.

করেণু *n.* the elephant. *fem.* **করেণু, করেণুকা**।

করোগেট *n.* a corrugated sheet.

করোট, করোটি, করোটিকা, করোটী *n.* the skull, the cranium. **করোটিক** *a.* cranial.

কর্ক *n.* a stopper made of cork, a cork.

কর্কট *n.* the crab; (astrol.) the Crab. **~ক্রান্তি, ~কান্তিবৃত্ত** *n.* the Tropic of Cancer. **~রাশি** *n.* (astrol.) the Crab. **~রোগ** *n.* cancer.

কর্কটি, কর্কটী *n.* a kitchen vegetable akin to cucumber, its plant.

কর্কটীয় শান্তবলয় *n.* the Calms of Cancer.

কর্কশ *a.* rough; harsh; gruff, hoarse,

husky; rude; cruel. ~তা *n.* roughness; harshness; hoarseness, huskiness; rudeness; cruelty. ~ভাবে *adv.* harshly, roughly, rudely.

কর্জ *n.* debt, loan. **কর্জ করা** *v.* to borrow. **কর্জ দেওয়া** *v.* to lend. ~পত্র *n.* a bond, a promissory note. ~শোধ *n.* repayment of debt.

কর্ণ *n.* the ear; (of boats and ships) a helm, a rudder ; (of violins etc.) a key; (geom.) a diagonal. ~কুহর, ~কূপ *n.* the ear-hole. ~কীট *n.* an earwig. ~গোচর *a.* heard; within the range of hearing; audible. ~গোচর করা *v.* to make one hear; to inform; to tell. **কর্ণগোচর হওয়া** *v.* to be heard; to come to know; to hear. ~ধার *n.* a helmsman, a steersman; a pilot; (fig.) a leader. ~পট, ~পটহ *n.* the ear-drum, the tympanum. ~পাত *n.* act of listening (to). **কর্ণপাত করা** *v.* to listen (to); to pay heed to. ~বিবর *n.* the ear-hole. ~বেধ *n.* act or ceremony of boring one's ears (usu. for wearing ear-rings). ~ভূষণ *n.* any ornament for the ear. ~মল *n.* ear-wax. ~মূল *n.* root of the ear. ~মূলস্ফীতি *n.* inflammation of the auricular glands, mumps. ~রন্ধ্র *n.* the ear-hole. ~শূল *n.* earache.

কর্ণান্তর *n.* act of telling another (esp. undesirably); act of passing a piece of information to others.

কর্ণিক rej. spell of **কর্নিক**।

কর্ণিকা *n.* an ornament for the ear, an ear-ring; a seed-vessel of lotus; a stalk, a stem; a pen.

কর্ণিকার *n.* a plant bearing yellow flowers or its flower, the Indian marigold (?).

কর্তন *n.* act of cutting or chopping or trimming or lopping or amputating or shearing etc.; act of severing; act of spinning; refutation (যুক্তি-কর্তন). **কর্তন করা** *v.* to cut, to chop, to trim, to lop, to amputate, to shear; to sever; to spin; to refute; to pass or spend. **কর্তনী** *n.* any instrument for cutting, chopping, trimming etc.; a pair of scissors.

কর্তব্য *a.* that which is proper or ought to be done; proper. □ *n.* duty. **কর্তব্য করা** *v.* to do one's duty. ~কর্ম *n.* duty; an obligation. ~চ্যুত *a.* failed in one's duty. ~চ্যুতি *n.* failure in one's duty, dereliction of duty. ~জ্ঞান *n.* sense of duty. ~তা *n.* propriety. ~নিষ্ঠ, ~পরায়ণ *a.* dutiful, duteous. ~নিষ্ঠা, ~পরায়ণতা *n.* dutifulness, duteousness, devotion to duty; (loos.) fidelity. ~পালন *n.* act of doing one's duty. **কর্তব্যপালন করা** *v.* to do one's duty. ~প্রিয় same as **কর্তব্যপরায়ণ**। ~বিমুখ *a.* undutiful. ~বিমুখতা *n.* undutifulness. ~বিমূঢ় *a.* at a loss to determine one's duty; bewildered. ~বিমূঢ়তা *n.* bewilderment, failure to discern what to do. ~বুদ্ধি *n.* sense of duty. ~ভ্রষ্ট same as **কর্তব্যচ্যুত**। ~ভ্রষ্টতা same as **কর্তব্যচ্যুতি**। **কর্তব্যাকর্তব্য বোধ** *n.* power of discriminating between what ought to be done and what ought not to be done. **কর্তব্যানুরাগ** same as **কর্তব্যপরায়ণতা**। **কর্তব্যানুরাগী** same as **কর্তব্যপরায়ণ**। **কর্তব্যানুরোধে** *adv.* for the sake of duty or obligation.

কর্তরি, কর্তরী, কর্তরিকা *n.* a cutting or paring instrument.

কর্তা *a.* one who does or performs or works or produces or builds or creates etc. □ *n.* a doer; a performer; a worker; an employee; a producer; an agent; an author; a builder; a creator; the master of a house or family, a householder; a master; a chief, a boss; a husband; (gr.) a nominative, a subject. ~গিন্নি *n.* the master of a household and his wife; the husband and the wife. ~ব্যক্তি *n.* an important or influential person; a man with authority. ~ভজা *n.* a religious sect of Bengal devoted to Sri Gauranga (গৌরাঙ্গ) ; (sarcas.) a yes-man, a flatterer of a powerful or leading person. ~মি, ~লি *n.* (coll.) act of bossing or controlling; interfering; officiousness, meddlesomeness. **কর্তামি করা** v. to boss; to interfere. **কর্তার ইচ্ছায় কর্ম** doing things according to the master's will; submission to the master's dictates.

কর্তিত *a.* cut, chopped, trimmed, lopped, amputated, shorn, severed; spun; refuted.

কর্তুকাম *a.* willing to do; about to do.

কর্তৃক *prep.* by.

কর্তৃকারক *n.* (gr.) the nominative case.

কর্তৃত্ব *n.* authority, rule; domination; act of bossing; state of being a boss. **কর্তৃত্ব করা** *v.* to rule; to control; to dominate; to boss. **কর্তৃত্ব ফলানো** *v.* to boss; to make other people feel one's authority. **~ভার** *n.* the burden of rule or management. **কর্তৃত্বাধীন** *a.* under one's rule or management.

কর্তৃপক্ষ *n. pl.* the authorities.

কর্তৃপদ *n.* (gr.) the nominative.

কর্তৃবর্গ *n. pl.* the authorities.

কর্তৃবাচ্য *n.* (gr.) the active voice.

কর্ত্রী *fem.* of **কর্তা**।

কর্দম *n.* gluey mud, slime; mire; sin. **কর্দমাক্ত** *a.* full of gluey mud, slimy; miry; turbid; sinful.

কর্নিক *n.* a trowel.

কর্পর var. of **খর্পর**।

কর্পূর *n.* camphor. **কর্পূরের আরক** spirit of camphor.

কর্বুর, কর্বূর *n.*(myth.) one of an anthropophagous race, a rakshas; an anthropophagite, a cannibal; sin. ☐ *a.* many-coloured, variegated with colours. **~পতি** *n.* Ravana (রাবণ) as mentioned in the Ramayana (রামায়ণ). **কর্বুরিত, কর্বূরিত** *n.* variegated with colours, many-coloured.

কর্ম *n.* a work, an action, a deed, an activity; a duty, a task; use, service (এ ঘড়ি কোনো কর্মের নয়) ; ceremony, a rite (ক্রিয়াকর্ম, শ্রাদ্ধকর্ম) ; profession; function; a purpose (কোন কর্মে এসেছ) ; effect; good result (এতে কর্ম হবে না) ; (gr.) an object. **~কর্তা** *n.* a supervisor or manager of an affair. **~কর্তৃবাচ্য** *n.* (gr.) the quasi-passive voice. **~কাণ্ড** *n.* a part of the Vedas dealing with rituals; actions; functions; ceremonies. **~কারক** *n.* a doer, a worker, a performer; (gr.) the objective or accusative case. **~কারী** *a.* of one who does or works or performs. ☐ *n.* a doer, a worker, a performer. **~কুণ্ঠ** *a.* averse to work, unwilling to work, lazy. **~কুশল** *a.* efficient, expert; adroit. **~ক্লান্ত** *a.* tired with work, fatigued. **~ক্ষম** *a.* capable of working; able; active. **~ক্ষমতা** *n.* ability to work; working power. **~ক্ষেত্র** *n.* a field or sphere of activity; a place of work. **~খালি** *n.* situation vacant. **~চারী** *n.* an employee; an officer. **~চ্যুত** *a.* dismissed or removed from service; cashiered. **~চ্যুতি** *n.* dismissal or removal from service; cashierment. **~জীবন** *n.* the period of life during which a person works, active part of one's life; service life; practical life. **~জ্ঞ** *a.* conversant with religious rites and duties. **~ঠ** *a.* active; hard-working; industrious. **~ণ্য** *a.* capable of working; able; active; serviceable. **~ত্যাগ** *n.* act of giving up a job, resignation; act of leaving or abandoning a work; retirement from service. **কর্ম ত্যাগ করা** *v.* to give up a job, to resign; (rare) to retire from service. **~দক্ষ** *a.* efficient, expert; adroit. **~দোষ** crime or sin of evil-doing or wrong-doing; a sin; misfortune (esp. which is caused by one's evil doing or wrong-doing in this life or in a previous life). **~ধারা** *n.* same as **কর্মপ্রণালী**। **~নাশা** *a.* & *n.* one who or that which spoils or bungles a work or works. **~নিয়োগ কেন্দ্র** *n.* employment exchange. **~নিষ্ঠ** *a.* devoted to one's work; dutiful; industrious. **~নিষ্ঠা** *n.* devotion to work. **~নীতি** *n.* policy of action. **~পঞ্জি, ~পঞ্জী** *n.* a case-book. **~পথ** *n.* path or field of work; line of action; active life. **~পদ্ধতি, ~প্রণালী** *n.* method or system of working. **~পন্থা** *n.* course of action. **~ফল** *n.* consequences of one's actions (esp. of a previous life) that governs one's weal or woe. **~বশত** *adv.* on business. **~বাচ্য** *n.* (gr.) the passive voice. **~বাদ** *n.* the doctrine that action is the chief end of life or that for the final liberation of one's soul one has to resort to action (and not to thought or meditation alone), the doctrine of action. **~বাদী** *a.* preaching or obeying or inspired by the doctrine of action. ☐ *n.* one who preaches or obeys the doctrine of action. **~বিধি** *n.* rules of action. **~বিপাক** *n.* consequences (now usu. evil ones) of one's action (esp. those governing one's weal or woe). ~বীর *n.* an untiring worker; an uncommonly active person; a performer of great deeds; a great worker. ~ভূমি *n.* the scene or field of one's action; the earthly life. ~ভোগ *n.* enjoyment of pleasures or (more generally) suffering from the unpleasant consequences of one's actions; fruitless suffering or labour. ~ময় *a.* full of actions; extremely active. ~যোগ *n.* the system of purifying one's soul by means of action. ~যোগী *a.* & *n.* one who practises this system; (fig.) one who works most sincerely; one who works sincerely and relentlessly. ~রত *a.* engaged in work. ~শালা *n.* a workshop; a smithy; an atelier; a studio; a place of work or business. ~শীল *a.* possessing active habits; engaged in work; active; devoted to work. ~শীলতা *n.* active habits; engagement in work; fullness of activity; devotion to work. ~সচিব *n.* a (chief) executive officer; a secretary. ~সাক্ষী *n.* any of the natural elements who witness all actions; a witness of an act. ~সাধন *n.* execution of a work or task, performance or accomplishment of a deed. **কর্ম সাধন করা** *v.* to execute a work or task, to perform or accomplish a deed. ~সাপেক্ষ *a.* depending on work or action. ~সিদ্ধি *n.* success in or accomplishment of an undertaking. ~সূচি *n.* programme of work; programme to be undertaken. ~সূত্র *a.* the bond of action; the course of business. ~সূত্রে *adv.* on business or in course of business. ~স্থল, ~স্থান same as **কর্মক্ষেত্র। যেমন কর্ম তেমন ফল** as you brew so you drink, as you sow so you reap. ~হীন *a.* devoid of work; with no work on hand; without employment.

কর্মকার *n.* a blacksmith, an ironsmith; (rare) an ironmonger.

কর্মধারয় *n.* (gr.) a system of forming a compound word with an adjective and a noun.

কর্মপ্রবচনীয় *a.* & *n.* (gr.) prepositional.

কর্মাকর্ম *n. pl.* works useful and useless; deeds, and misdeeds.

কর্মাধীন *a.* subject to the consequences of one's deeds (esp. those done in a previous existence).

কর্মাধ্যক্ষ *n.* a superintendent; a supervisor; an overseer; a workmaster.

কর্মানুবন্ধ *n.* the course of business; necessity caused by business.

কর্মানুরাগ, কর্মানুরক্তি *n.* devotion to work; love of work; diligence. **কর্মানুরাগী, কর্মানুরক্ত** *a.* devoted to work; diligent.

কর্মানুষ্ঠান *n.* performance of a work or ceremony. **কর্মানুষ্ঠান করা** *v.* to perform a work or ceremony.

কর্মানুসারে *adv.* according to one's deeds or works (esp. those done in a previous existence).

কর্মান্তর *n.* another work or job; change of work or job.

কর্মাবসান *n.* the end of the work. **কর্মাবসানে** *adv.* at the end of the work.

কর্মার var. of **কর্মকার।**

কর্মারম্ভ *n.* beginning of a work or ceremony, beginning of activities; beginning of daily activities.

কর্মার্হ *a.* suitable for (beginning) a work; serviceable; fit for work.

কর্মিষ্ঠ *a.* very active; very much devoted to work; hard-working.

কর্মিসঙ্ঘ *n.* trade union.

কর্মী *a.* able to work; efficient; employed (in a service or work); hard-working or full of activities (কর্মী পুরুষ) ; performing great deeds. □ *n.* a worker; an employee.

কর্মেন্দ্রিয় *n.* any of the organs to work with (such as hands, legs, tongue etc.).

কর্মোদ্যম *n.* enterprise; enthusiasm; effort, effortfulness.

কর্মোপলক্ষ্যে *adv.* on business, for the sake of business.

কর্ষ১ *n.* a measure of weight (=·8 oz or 227 gms).

কর্ষ২, কর্ষণ *n.* act of tilling; cultivation; act of drawing or attracting; attraction (বিপ্রকর্ষণ) ; act of pressing, pressure; act of rubbing (নিকষে কর্ষণ). **কর্ষণ করা** *v.* to till, to plough, to cultivate; to draw, to attract; to press; to rub. **কর্ষক** *a.* & *n.* one who or that which tills or attracts or presses or rubs. কর্ষণীয় *a.* ploughable, arable; attractable; that which can be pressed or rubbed; that which is to be ploughed or cultivated or drawn or attracted or pressed or rubbed. কর্ষিকা *n.* a tentacle. কর্ষিত *a.* ploughed, tilled, cultivated; drawn, attracted; pressed; rubbed. কর্ষী *a.* attracting; attractive.

কল[১] *n.* a sprout. **কল হওয়া বা গজানো** *v.* to germinate, to sprout.

কল[২] *n.* a call. **কল দেওয়া** *v.* to call in (as a doctor). **কলে যাওয়া** *v.* to attend a call.

কল[৩] *n.* a machine; an engine; a device, a contrivance, an artifice; a lock (বাক্সের কল) ; (of a gun) a trigger or lock; a factory, a mill; a workshop, a means, a way (পরিত্রাণের কল জানা) ; a trap (ইঁদুরকল) ; a tactic, a stratagem. **~কাঠি নাড়া** *v.* to pull the string or wire, to exert hidden influence. **~কৌশল** *n.* a device. **কল খাটানো** *v.* to set a trap; to have recourse to a ploy or artifice. **কল টেপা** *v.* to advise or instigate secretly; to pull the wires, to intrigue. **কল পাতা** *v.* to set a trap. **কলে-কৌশলে** *adv.* by hook or crook; tactfully. **কলে তৈরি** *a.* mill-made; machine-made. **কলের গাড়ি** a steam-engine; a railway train; an automobile. **কলের গান** a gramophone. **কলের জল** tap-water. **কলের জাহাজ** a steamship, a steamer. **কলের পুতুল** a spring-doll, a marionette, a puppet; (fig.) a person who acts just as one directs him. **কলের মানুষ** (fig.) a person who acts just as one directs him, a puppet; a person without free will or personality. **কলের মজুর** a mill-hand.

কল[৪] *n.* a low sweet and indistinct sound, a sweet murmur; warble (of birds); babble (of streams). ☐ *a.* (of sound) sweet low and indistinct. **~কণ্ঠ** *a.* making a sweet low and indistinct sound; sweetly murmuring; warbling; babbling; sweet-voiced, sweet-toned; (fig.) composing sweet poems (কলকণ্ঠ কবি). *fem.* **কলকণ্ঠী** । **~কল, ~কলানি** *n.* repeated sweet murmur or babble or warble, (usu. coll.) rapid loud talk. **~কল করা, ~কলানো** *v.* to murmur or babble or warble sweetly or repeatedly; (usu. coll.) to talk rapidly and loudly. **~ঘোষ** *n.* the cuckoo. **~তান** *n.* a sweet note. **~ধ্বনি, ~নাদ** same as **কল**[৪] (*n.*). **~নাদী** *a.* making a low sweet and indistinct sound, murmuring or babbling or warbling sweetly. *fem.* **কলনাদিনী** । **~রব, ~রোল** *n.* confused loud noise as made by a multitude of people shouting and talking at a time, an uproar, a hullabaloo, tumult. **~স্বন, ~স্বর** *n.* a low sweet and indistinct sound or voice, a sweet murmur or babble. ☐ *a.* murmuring or babbling sweetly.*fem.* **কলস্বনা** । **~হংস** *n.* the swan, the gander (*fem.* the goose); a small aquatic bird akin to the sandpiper. *fem.* **কলহংসী** । **~হাস, ~হাস্য** *n.* a gentle articulate smile with a sweet cackling noise. *n. fem.* **~হাসিনী** one who smiles gently with a sweet cackling noise. **~হাস্য করা** *v.* to laugh cacklingly.

কলকবজা *n. pl.* machinery.

কলকা *n.* leafy decoration; decorative embroidery in the borders of a sari, shawl etc. **~দার** *a.* decorated with leafy designs; embroidered. **~পাড়, ~পেড়ে** *a.* having an embroidered border.

কলকারখানা *n. pl.* mills and workshops.

কলকি, (coll.) **কলকে** *n.* the bowl of a hookah which holds tobacco and cinder, a chillum. **কলকে না পাওয়া** not to receive recognition, not to gain any importance or prominence; to be ignored.

কলগি, কলগা *n.* a head-dress, a headgear; a turban; a cock on the top of a head-dress.

কলঘর *n.* a machine-room (of a factory); a bathroom.

কলঙ্ক *n.* a spot, a mark; a stain; a sullying mark, tarnish; rust, verdigris; disrepute, disgrace; a taint; a stigma; a disgraceful incident, a scandal. **~কর, ~জনক** *a.* disgraceful; seandalous. **~ভঞ্জন** *n.* act of clearing a person of disrepute, restoration of one's good repute. **কলঙ্ক ভঞ্জন করা** *v.* to clear a person of disrepute. **~ভয়** *n.* fear of scandal or ill fame. **কলঙ্ক রটানো** *v.* to traduce. **কলঙ্কিত, কলঙ্কী** *a.*

sullied, tainted; tarnished; rusted; of ill-repute, disreputable, stigmatized; unchaste. *fem.* **কলঙ্কিতা, কলঙ্কিনী।**

কলতান, কলরব, কলরোল see **কল[৪]**।

কলতানি *n.* morbid watery secretion from a wound or sepsis.

কলত্র *n.* wife.

কলধৌত *n.* gold; silver.

কলন *n.* calculation (ব্যবকলন, সমাকলন) ; compilation (সংকলন) ; act of receiving, receipt.

কলপ *n.* a dye for grey hair; starch.

কলভ *n.* a young elephant.

কলম[১] *n.* a column of a newspaper, a book etc.

কলম[২] *n.* a plant grown by grafting; a prism (বাতি-ঝাড়ের কলম). **কলম করা** *v.* to grow a plant by grafting, to graft.

কলম[৩] *n.* a pen. **কলম কাটা, কলম বাড়া** *v.* to mend a pen. **কলম চালানো** *v.* to wield a pen; to write. **~দান, ~দানি** *n.* a small tray or stand for keeping pens, a pen-case, a pen-stand. **কলম পেশা** *v.* (dero.) to work as a clerk. **কলমপেশা** *n.* clerkship; quill-driving, pen-pushing. ☐ *a.* clerical. **~বাজ** *n.* (dero.) an expert writer. **~বাজি** *n.* (dero.) useless writing. **কলমের এক খোঁচায়** with a stroke of the pen.

কলমচি *n.* an amanuensis; a scribe, a copyist.

কলমা *n.* any of the principal words of an Islamic prayer. **কলমা পড়া** *v.* to pray according to the Islamic scriptures.

কলমি *n.* an edible aquatic plant (cp. Kalmia).

কলম্ব *n.* an arrow; a variety of flower or its tree; a stalk of spinach. **~পত্রাকার** *a.* hastate; triangular like the head of a spear.

কলম্বী, কলম্বিকা same as **কলম্ব**।

কলস, কলসি *n.* a pitcher made of earth or metal. **কলসাকার** *a.* urceolate, pitcher-shaped.

কলহ *n.* a quarrel, a brawl; a dispute, a contention; a strife. **কলহ বাধানো** *v.* to engage or cause to engage in quarrel; to kick up a row; to set (persons) by the ears. **কলহ করা** *v.* to quarrel; to dispute, to contend; to strive, to conflict. **~প্রিয়** *a.* fond of quarrels, quarrelsome. *fem.* **~প্রিয়া। কলহান্তরিতা** *n.* a woman who dismisses her lover after a quarrel and suffers severe mental pain.

কলা[১] *n.* the plantain, the banana; (coll.) nothing, a mare's nest (তুমি আমার কলা করবে). **কলা করা** *v.* (coll.) to be able to do nothing or to be able to do no harm. **কলা খাওয়া** *v.* (lit.) to eat a banana; (coll.) to fail in an attempt. **~গাছ** *n.* a banana tree. **কলা দেখানো** *v.* (lit.) to show a plantain; to raise and show one's thumb defiantly or disdainfully; to deceive, to cheat, to befool, to hoodwink; to bite the thumb, to defy. **কলাপোড়া খাওয়া** *v.* (lit.) to eat a burnt banana; (coll.) to fail or be disappointed utterly. **কলাবউ, কলাবৌ** *n.* a young banana-plant dressed as a married lady and conceived as a female deity worshipped by Hindus; (loos.) wife of God Ganesha (গণেশ) ; (euph.) a woman with a long veil or an awkwardly bashful woman. **কলার কাঁদি** a cluster of plantains. **কলার খোলা** the curved bark of a banana-tree. **কলার ছড়া** a bunch of bananas, a row of plantains. **কলার বাসনা** the dried-up bark of a banana-tree.

কলা[২] *n.* one-sixteenth part of the moon, a lunar digit; (astro.) any of the minutest divisions of the zodiac, (of the circumference of a circle) a minute; a measure of time (=8 seconds); a very small point of time, a moment; a whit, a bit; (anat.) a tissue; an art; a fine art; the sixty-four varieties of fine arts taken collectively; efficiency in fine arts; skill, adroitness; tact. **~কার** *n.* an artist; an artisan. **~কুশল** *a.* versed in all the sixty-four varieties of fine arts; skilled in fine arts. **~কৌশল** *n.* artistic skill; artifice. **~তন্ত্র** *n.* (anat.) the tissue-system. **~ধর, ~নিধি** *n.* an appellation of Shiva (শিব) ; the moon. **~বৎ** *a.* & *n.* one who is versed in the classical vocal music. *fem.* **কলাবতী। ~বিদ্যা** *n.* arts; fine arts. **~বিভাগ** *n.* the department of arts

(e. g. in a university). ~ভবন *n.* a building or room for the culture of arts and crafts; a picture gallery; an opera-house; a studio. ~ভৃৎ *n.* an appellation of Shiva (শিব) ; the moon; an artist; an artiste. ~স্থান *n.* histology.

কলাই[১] *n.* enamel; enamelling; tinning; plating. **কলাই-করা** *a.* enamelled; tinned; plated. **কলাই করা** *v.* to enamel; to tin; to plate. **কলাইয়ের বাসনকোসন** enamelware. **কলাই চটে যাওয়া** (of utensils) to lose one's enamel.

কলাই[২] *n.* any of the varieties of leguminous seeds yielding pigeon-pea or pulses; bean. ~শুঁটি *n.* pea-legume.

কলাদ *n.* a goldsmith.

কলাপ *n.* an ornament esp. one worn round the waist; a peacock's tail; a collection, a multitude (ক্রিয়াকলাপ). **কলাপী** *n.* the peacock. *fem.* **কলাপিনী** the peahen.

কলার *n.* a collar. **কলার তোলা** v. to turn up one's collar.

কলালাপ[১] *n.* a sweet low and indistinct sound; a pleasant (and usu. amorous) tete-a-tete; a bumble-bee.

কলালাপ[২] *n.* a discussion about fine arts.

কলি[১] *n.* the fourth or last age of creation according to Hindu scriptures (কলিযুগ, কলিকাল) ; the presiding deity of this age (also **কলিদেব, কলিদেবতা**). **ঘোর কলি** an age full of sins, an .infernal age. **কলির সন্ধ্যা, কলির শেষ** creation approaching final annihilation; (fig.) utter peril.

কলি[২] *n.* a bud; a shingling style of hairdressing, shingle; the Vaishnavic (বৈষ্ণবীয়) style of painting one's face with sandal-paste (রসকলি) ; a line of a verse or a song.

কলি[৩] *n.* whitewash, limewash. **কলি করা, কলি ধরানো, কলি ফেরানো** *v.* to whitewash.

কলিকা[১] *n.* a bud.

কলিকা[২] pedantic form of **কলকি** ।

কলিকাল see **কলি**[১] ।

কলিঙ্গ *n.* Orissa including the Dravidian region on its south.

কলিচুন *n.* unslaked lime, quicklime.

কলিজা, (coll.) **কলজে** *n.* liver; lungs; bosom; heart; courage.

কলিত *a.* calculated; computed; received.

কলিদেব, কলিযুগ see **কলি** ।

কলিল *a.* dense; mixed, compounded; adulterated.

কলু *n.* an oil-man (esp. by caste). *fem.* **কলুনি** । **কলুর বলদ** (fig.) a person who blindly and mechanically drudges and undergoes extreme hardships for others but without any profit for himself.

কলুষ *n.* a sin or guilt; a fault; defilement; soil, sully. ~নাশন *a.* washing away or purifying a sin or guilt or fault. ~নাশিনী *a. fem.* of **কলুষনাশন** । *n.* an appellation of Goddess Kali (কালী). **কলুষিত** *a.* sinful, guilty, defiled; soiled; vitiated.

কলেকটর, কলেক্টর variants of **কালেকটার** ।

কলেজ *n.* a college. **কলেজি শিক্ষা** *n.* college education.

কলেবর *n.* the body; the shape or form.

কলেরা *n.* cholera.

কল্ক *n.* deposit of any liquid, dregs, sediment; a sin.

কল্কা alt. spell. of **কলকা** ।

কল্কি[১] *n.* the tenth and the last incarnation of Vishnu (বিষ্ণু) expected to take place in the Kaliyuga (কলিযুগ). ~পুরাণ *n.* the name of the scripture announcing and giving an account of this incarnation.

কল্কি[২], (coll.) **কল্কে** alt. spellings of **কলকি** and **কলকে** respectively.

কল্প[১] *sfx.* almost, resembling (**মৃতকল্প**).

কল্প[২] *n.* one of the principal and most ancient Hindu scriptures forming a part of the Vedic literature (also **কল্পসূত্র**) ; one whole day of Brahma (ব্রহ্মা) amounting to 43200,00000 years (কল্পান্তে) ; universal annihilation; a scriptural direction (নবম্যাদি কল্প) ; a ritual rule or a holy time (কল্পারম্ভ) ; object, aim (রক্ষাকল্পে) ; resolution (দৃঢ়কল্প) ; a side or party (মুখ্যকল্প). ~তরু, ~দ্রুম, ~বৃক্ষ *n.* a (mythological) wishing-tree; (fig.) an extremely liberal and generous person. ~লতা *n.* a paradisiacal creeper. ~লোক *n.* a fancied land where everything is good and available, a dreamland, a Utopia, Elysium. **কল্পান্ত** *n.* end or termination of one whole day of Brahma (ব্রহ্মা) ; universal annihilation. **কল্পান্তর** *n.* another whole day and night of Brahma (ব্রহ্মা). **কল্পান্তস্থায়ী** *a.* everlasting, eternal. **কল্পারম্ভ** *n.* beginning or commencement of a day of Brahma (ব্রহ্মা) ; commencement of a holy tide.

কল্পক *a.* one who or that which imagines or composes or plans or ascribes.

কল্পন *n.* act of inventing or imagining or fancying or ascribing or resolving or thinking or supposing. **কল্পনা** *n.* invention; imagination; fancy; ascription; resolve; thought; supposition. **কল্পনা করা** *v.* to invent; to devise; to imagine; to fancy; to ascribe; to resolve; to think; to suppose. **কল্পনাকারী** *a.* inventing or devising; imagining; fancying; ascribing; resolving; thinking; supposing. ☐ *n.* an inventor, a deviser; one who imagines; a fancier; one who ascribes; one who resolves, a thinker; one who supposes. **কল্পনাচিত্র** *n.* picturesque imagination; an imaginary portrait. **কল্পনাত্মক** *a.* actuated by or existing in imagination, imaginative, imaginary. **কল্পনাপ্রবণ** *a.* given to imagination. **কল্পনাপ্রবণ ব্যক্তি** an imaginative person. **কল্পনাপ্রসূত** *a.* imaginary; fancied. **কল্পনাবিলাসী** *a.* overindulging in imagination; vapoury. **কল্পনাশক্তি** *n.* imaginative power, faculty of imagination. **কল্পনীয়** *a.* devisable; imaginable; that which can be fancied; ascribable; thinkable; supposable.

কল্পান্ত, কল্পান্তর, কল্পারম্ভ see **কল্প**[2] ।

কল্পিত *a.* invented, contrived, devised; imagined, fancied; ascribed; resolved; thought (out); supposed; created, composed; fanciful; imaginary.

কল্পী *a.* (chiefly used as a *sfx.*) inventing, contriving, devising; imagining, fancying; ascribing; resolving; thinking; supposing; creating; composing.

কল্প্য *a.* contrivable, devisable; imaginable; that which can be fancied; ascribable; thinkable; supposable; prescribable; proper.

কল্মষ *n.* filth, dirt; sin, guilt. ☐ *a.* filthy, dirty; sinful, guilty.

কল্মা, কল্‌মা alt. spellings of **কলমা** ।

কল্য (for.) *n.* & *adv.* tomorrow; yesterday; (fig.) future or in future. **~কার** *a.* of tomorrow; of yesterday. **কল্য রজনী** *n.* yester-night, last night; coming night. **আগামীকল্য** *n.* & *adv.* tomorrow. **গতকল্য** *n.* & *adv.* yesterday.

কল্যাণ *n.* welfare, good, benefit; well-being; prosperity; an Indian musical mode. ☐ *a.* happy; doing good, beneficial benefactory; giving prosperity; favourable. **কল্যাণী** *a.* & *n. fem.* of **কল্যাণ** । **কল্যাণীয়** *a.* one (usu. a junior fellow) whose well-being is or should be wished. *fem.* **কল্যাণীয়া** । **~কর, ~প্রদ** *a.* doing good, beneficial, benefactory; giving prosperity. **~বর, ~বরেষু** to you or him who deserves (my) good wishes; a form of address in a letter, a younger person deserving affection. *fem.* **কল্যাণীয়াসু** । **~ময়** *a.* beneficent, altruistic; benevolent; benignant, gracious. *fem.* **কল্যাণময়ী** ।

কল্লোল *n.* a roaring wave; a billow; great joy or delight; a loud confused noise, an uproar. **কল্লোলিত** *a.* full of roaring waves; billowy; full of great joy or delight; full of loud confused noise. **কল্লোলিনী** *n. fem.* a river.

কশ *n.* the corner of the mouth; the jaw; the corresponding part of the jaw inside the mouth. **কশের দাঁত** a molar tooth, a molar.

কশা *n.* a whip, a lash. ☐ *v.* to whip, to lash; to strike. **~ঘাত** *n.* whipping, lashing. **কশাঘাত করা** *v.* to whip, to lash, to flog.

কশাড় *n.* a very tall species of grass.

কশানো *v.* to whip, to slash, to flog; to beat. **আচ্ছা দু ঘা কশানো** to give a sound thrashing or drubbing, to drub.

কশি alt. spell. of **কষি** ।

কশিদা *n.* embroidery.

কশেরু *n.* the backbone, the spine, the vertebral column. **কশেরুক** *a.* vertebrate. ☐

n. vertebral bone, the backbone. **কশেরুকা** *n.* the vertebral bone, the backbone; a vertebra.

কশ্চিৎ same as **কোনো এক**।

কষ *n.* a kind of astringent juice of some plants (কলার কষ) ; stain caused by this juice (কষ লাগা) ; tannin; touchstone.

কষটে *a.* same as **কষাটে**। see **কষা**[২]।

কষন[১] *n.* act of rubbing or itching; act of trying gold and other metals on a touchstone; tanning.

কষন[২] *n.* tightening; act of fastening tightly; act of singeing (meat, fish etc.) in oil or fat and with spices; tanning; act of working out a mathematical sum.

কষা[১] obs. spell. of **কশা**।

কষা[২] *a.* astringent; tight; strict, severe; niggardly, close-fisted; constipative (কষা ধাত) ; (of meat, fish etc.) singed in oil or fat and with spices. □ *v.* to try (gold etc.) on a streak-plate; to work out (a mathematical sum); to calculate (price etc.); to singe (meat, fish etc.) in oil or fat and with spices; to tighten; to bind tightly; to tan (hides); to make astringent. **~কষি** *n.* unswerving enforcement of rule, law etc.; rigour, strictness; act of tightening; tugging and counter-tugging; higgling (দরকষাকষি) ; strained state, estrangement (মনকষাকষি). **কষাকষি করা** *v.* to enforce strictness or rigour; to tighten; to contest or try laboriously. **দর কষাকষি করা** *v.* to higgle, to chaffer. **মন কষাকষি করা** *v.* to estrange oneself (from); to quarrel (with). **কষানো** *v.* to singe meat; to tan (hides). **কষাটে** *a.* slightly astringent; (fig.) divested of taste or flavour; (fig.) loathsome, disgusting. **কষা মাংস** *n.* singed meat; meat cooked with oil and spices.

কষায় *n.* bitter or astringent juice or taste; tannic taste; tannin; decoction; dull red colour. □ *a.* of bitter or astringent taste; or tannic taste; dull red; reddish; dyed (esp. in red.) **কষায়িত** *a.* slightly reddened (রোষকষায়িত) ; dyed.

কষি *n.* a straight line drawn with a pen or pencil; a punctuation mark used in Bengali in place of a full stop; the part of the loincloth which is tied round the waist; a tender stone of green mango.

কষিত *n.* tried on a streak-plate; tried on a streak-plate and found perfectly pure (কষিত কাঞ্চন).

কষুটে *a.* same as **কষাটে**।

কষে বাঁধা *v.* & *n.* to fasten or fastening very tightly.

কষ্ট *n.* grief, sorrow; trouble, difficulty; pain, suffering; labour, hard effort, toil (কষ্টার্জিত) ; hardship; want, privation. **কষ্ট করা** *v.* to labour hard, to endeavour laboriously, to toil; to take trouble, to take pains; to undergo hardships; to suffer. **কষ্ট দেওয়া** *v.* to give trouble, to put to difficulty; to put to inconvenience; to oppress, to cause suffering (to), to distress; to pain; to grieve. **কষ্ট পাওয়া** *v.* to get into trouble, to be in difficulty; to suffer (from); to be oppressed or distressed; to feel pain; to grieve (for, at); to be moved with pity or sympathy. **~কর** *a.* difficult, hard; troublesome; laborious, toilsome; painful; distressing; oppressive, vexatious. **~কল্পনা** *n.* a far-fetched or forced or laboured concept or thought. **~কল্পিত** *a.* far-fetched, forced. **~দায়ক** same as **কষ্টকর**। **~ভোগ** *n.* suffering. **কষ্টভোগ করা** *v.* to suffer. **~সহ, ~সহিষ্ণু** *a.* painstaking; able to undergo hardships, inured to hardships. **~সাধ্য** same as **কষ্টকর**।

কষ্টার্জিত *a.* hard-earned (কষ্টার্জিত অর্থ).

কষ্টি *n.* act of trying or testing (gold etc.) on a touchstone; a touchstone. **~পাথর** *n.* touchstone. **কষ্টিপাথরে যাচাই করা** *v.* to try or test the purity (of gold etc.) by rubbing on a touchstone; to assay (metals).

কষ্টেসৃষ্টে *adv.* with considerable or great difficulty. **কষ্টেসৃষ্টে চালানো** *v.* to manage with difficulty; to contrive to live on a small income.

কস alt. spell. of **কশ** and **কষ**।

কসবা *n.* a large and prosperous village with many advantages of a town (cp. township); a suburb.

কসবি *n.* a harlot, a prostitute, a woman of the town; a demirep.

কসম *n.* an oath, a swear. **কসম খাওয়া** *v.* to swear, to take an oath. **খোদার কসম** *int.* in God's name.

কসরত *n.* a physical or athletic feat; an acrobatic feat; a trick; a great effort (পরীক্ষায় পাস করার জন্য কসরত) ; a show or display of skill; exercise; drill.

কসা obs. spell. of **কশা**।

কসাই *n.* a butcher; (fig.) an extremely cruel or unfeeling or hard-hearted person. **~খানা** *n.* a slaughter-house, a butchery, a shambles; (fig.) a place of merciless oppression. **~গিরি** *n.* the profession of a butcher; (fig.) extremely hard-hearted behaviour.

কসাড় alt. spell. of **কশাড়**।

কসি alt. spell. of **কষি**।

কসুর *n.* a fault, an offence; a defect, a shortcoming; want or lack; an omission; neglect; a failing. **কসুর করা** *v.* to commit an offence; to fail or neglect to do.

কসেরু alt. spell. of **কশেরু**।

কস্তা *a.* scarlet-coloured, scarlet. **~পেড়ে** *a.* (of loincloth) having a scarlet border.

কস্তাকস্তি *n.* mutual wrestling or struggling, a scuffle. **কস্তাকস্তি করা** *v.* to wrestle or struggle (with each other).

কস্তুর *n.* the musk-deer; musk. **কস্তুরী, কস্তুরিকা, কস্তূরী, কস্তূরিকা** *n.* musk.

কস্মিন্ কালে *adv.* at any time, ever; at no time, never.

কস্য *pron.* a (used chiefly as a legal term) whose.

কহই *v.* (obs. & poet) says, say. **কহই না পারে** cannot say.

কহতব্য *a.* speakable, utterable; expressible; explicable; worth mentioning.

কহন *n.* act of saying or telling; utterance; act of speaking; narration or relation. **~সাধ্য** same as **কহতব্য**। **কহনীয়** *a.* expressible; utterable; worth mentioning.

কহা *v.* to say, to tell; to utter; to speak; to narrate; to relate. **~নো** *v.* to make one say or tell or utter or speak or narrate or relate. **~য়সি** *v. imper.* make one say or tell.

কহিয়ে pseudo-elegant form of **কইয়ে**।

কহ্লার *n.* the white water-lily.

কাই *n.* glue; paste; starch. **কাই কাই** *a.* gluey; pasty; starchy.

কাইট *n.* dregs or dross or lees of any liquid.

কাউকে *pro.* whom; to anybody; to none (কাউকে দেব না).

কাউর *n.* eczema.

কাওয়াজ *n.* training in the use of guns; parade.

কাওয়ালি *n.* an Indian light musical mode or measure.

কাওরা *n.* one of a very low social caste amongst Hindus.

কাংস্য, কাংস, কাংস্যক, কাংসক *n.* bell metal, alloy of copper and tin; a dish of bell metal used as a musical instrument. **কাংস্যকার, কাংসকর** *n.* a brazier.

কাঁইবীচি, কাঁইবিচি *n.* a seed or stone of tamarind.

কাঁইয়া pseudo-elegant form of **কেঁয়ে**।

কাঁক[১] *n.* the heron.

কাঁক[২] *n.* the armpit, the flank; the hip; the waist.

কাঁকই *n.* a large comb with thick teeth.

কাঁকড়া *n.* the crab. **~বিছে** *n.* the scorpion.**কাঁকড়ার খোল** carapace.

কাঁকন *n.* a bangle; a bracelet.

কাঁকবিড়ালি, কাঁকবেড়ালি *n.* a painful boil in the armpit.

কাঁকর *n.* a very small particle of stone, a coarse grain of sand, gravel, grit. **কাঁকর দিয়ে ছাওয়া** *v.* to gravel, to cobble. **কাঁকরে ছাওয়া পথ** *n.* a gravel-walk; a cobbled road. **কাঁকরের খাদ** *n.* a gravel-pit.

কাঁকরোল *n.* a kind of cucurbitaceous kitchen vegetable.

কাঁকলাস *n.* the chameleon; (fig.) a person who is reduced to skeleton, a very lean person, one who is only skin and bone.

কাঁকাল *n.* the waist; the hip; the flank.

কাঁকুই var. of **কাঁকই**।

কাঁকুড় *n.* the green melon.

কাঁকুরে *a.* gravelly, gritty; full of or mixed with stones.

কাঁখ var. of **কাঁক**।

কাঁচ illogical but pop. var. of **কাচ**।

কাঁচকড়া *n.* tortoise-shell; whale-bone; vulcanite.

কাঁচকলা *n.* a species of plantain which is chiefly used in its green state; (joc.) nothing. **আদায় কাঁচকলায়** *adv.* & *a.* at loggerheads with, at daggers drawn.

কাঁচপোকা *n.* a species of green beetle a bit of whose hard wing is used by women to adorn their foreheads.

কাঁচল, কাঁচলা, কাঁচুলি *n.* a bodice, a corsage, a corset, a modesty-vest, brassiere.

কাঁচা *a.* unripe, green (কাঁচা ফল) ; uncooked (কাঁচা মাংস) ; imperfectly boiled; raw (কাঁচা মাল) ; unburned (কাঁচা ইট) ; made of mud, not brick-built, cutcha (কাঁচা গাঁথনি) ; unmetalled (কাঁচা রাস্তা) ; tender, fresh, verdant (কাঁচা ঘাস) ; young (কাঁচা বয়স) ; immature (কাঁচা বুদ্ধি) ; unpractised (কাঁচা লেখা) ; faulty, defective, unskilful, unwise, bungling (কাঁচা কাজ) ; inexpert, unskilled (কাঁচা লোক) ; deficient, weak (অঙ্কে কাঁচা) ; uncertain, provisional, unreliable (কাঁচা রসিদ, কাঁচা কথা) ; primary, rough (কাঁচা খাতা) ; not fast, liable to fade or run (কাঁচা রং) ; pure, unadulterated (কাঁচা সোনা) ; black, not grey (কাঁচা চুল) ; untanned, raw (কাঁচা চামড়া) ; undried, unsunned, unseasoned (কাঁচা কাঠ) ; not according to or below the standard (কাঁচা ওজন) ; easy or cash (কাঁচা টাকা) ; not deep or sound, in the primary stage (কাঁচা ঘুম) ; that which has not yet been moved to the right place (কাঁচা ঘুঁটি). **~গোল্লা** *n.* a soft drop or round sweetmeat made of posset. **~টে** *n.* not thoroughly ripe or mature; rawish. **~নো** *v.* to undo (all that has been done); to undo all progress; to unsettle a settled thing (design, plan, scheme, work etc.); to send back to the original stage. **~পাকা** *a.* (of hair) partly black and partly grey, greying. **~মাথা** a greehorn's head; (fig.) immature judgment or intellect. **~মাল** raw material (for production of industrial goods); greengrocery (**কাঁচামালের ব্যাপারী** = greengrocer). **~মিঠে** *a.* sweet in the unripe state (কাঁচামিঠে আম).

কাঁচাহলুদ *n.* undried turmeric.

কাঁচি[1] *a.* short; below the standard (কাঁচি ওজন) ; closely woven, close-grained (কাঁচি ধুতি) ; unsweetened curd made of unboiled milk (কাঁচা দই).

কাঁচি[2] *n.* scissors.

কাঁচিয়া older form of **কেঁচে**।

কাঁচিয়া যাওয়া older form of **কেঁচে যাওয়া**।

কাঁচী rej. spell. of **কাঁচি**[1]।

কাঁচুমাচু *a.* embarrassed; shrunken (esp. with fear); scared out of one's wits.

কাঁচুয়া, কাঁচুলি same as **কাঁচল**।

কাঁচ্চা *n.* a measure of weight (= ·51oz. or 14 gms.).

কাঁজি *n.* the water in which boiled rice has been kept steeped overnight (this water tastes sour).

কাঁটা *n.* a thorn, a prickle; any longish thing or instrument with a pointed end or ends (চুলের কাঁটা) ; a pointer (কম্পাসের কাঁটা, দাঁড়িপাল্লার কাঁটা) ; a fork (used in eating meals); a hand (ঘড়ির কাঁটা) ; a fishbone; gooseflesh (শীতে বা ভয়ে কাঁটা দেওয়া). **কাঁটা দিয়ে কাঁটা তোলা** *v.* (fig.) to set a thief to catch a thief. **গায়ে কাঁটা দেওয়া** to have gooseflesh; to have shivering, to shiver. **পথের কাঁটা** (fig.) an obstacle or snag. **পথে কাঁটা দেওয়া** (fig.) *v.* to prevent. **~তার** *n.* barbed wire. **~নটে** *n.* a variety of spinach. **~বন** *n.* a hedge full of prickly shrubs. **~ময়** *a.* thorny. **কাঁটায় কাঁটায়** *adv.* punctually; just at.

কাঁটাচুয়া n. the hedgehog.

কাঁটাল, কাঁঠাল *n.* the jackfruit. **~গাছ** *n.* the jack-tree, the jack. **~চাঁপা** *n.* a yellow flower smelling like a ripe jackfruit. **কাঁটালের আমসত্ত্ব** (fig.) an impossible thing; a mare's nest. **পরের মাথায় কাঁটাল ভাঙা** *v.* (fig.) to make a cat's-paw of another.

কাঁটালি কলা, কাঁঠালি কলা *n.* a superior variety of plantain.

কাঁড়া *v.* to husk. □ *a.* husked. **কাঁড়ানো** *v.* to cause to husk. □ *a.* husked; husky. □ *n.* husking.

কাঁড়াদাস *n.* a foolish but very obstinate fellow.

কাঁড়ি *n.* a heap.

কাঁথা *n.* a cotton wrapper or patched cloth or bedsheet made of patchwork.

কাঁদকাঁদ see **কাঁদোকাঁদো**।

কাঁদন, কাঁদনি *n.* (usu. dero.) act or a spell of weeping; (usu. dero.) lamentation or complaint; humble and importunate solicitation. **কাঁদুনি গাওয়া** *v.* to solicit humbly and importunately; to lament or complain.

কাঁদা *v.* to weep, to shed tears. **~কাটি, ~কাটা** *n.* repeated or continuous weeping; lamentation; humble and importunate solicitation. **কাঁদাকাটি করা** *v.* to weep bitterly; to lament; to solicit humbly and importunately. **কাঁদানে** same as **কাঁদানো** (*a.*). **কাঁদানো** *v.* to cause to weep. **কেঁদে হাট করা, কেঁদেকেটে হাট করা** *v.* to attract a crowd of people by loud lamentation or wailing.

কাঁদানো *v.* to make lachrymose, to make one weep. ☐ *a.* making lachrymose, one who or that which makes one weeping. **কাঁদানো গ্যাস** tear-gas.

কাঁদি *n.* a cluster (কলার কাঁদি). **কাঁদি-কাঁদি কলা** *v.* to grow in cluster.

কাঁদুনি var. of **কাঁদনি**।

কাঁদুনে *a.* given to weeping, lachrymose; causing tears. **কাঁদুনে সুর** a mournful or piteous note.

কাঁদোকাঁদো *a.* about to weep; about to shed tears; tearful.

কাঁধ *n.* the shoulder; the neck. **কাঁধ ঝাঁকানো** *v.* to shrug, to shrug one's shoulder. **কাঁধ দেওয়া, কাঁধ লাগানো** *v.* to volunteer to shoulder a burden; to come forward to assist or cooperate. **কাঁধ বদলানো** *v.* to transfer a burden to another's shoulder or to one's other shoulder when feeling fatigued. **কাঁধে করা, কাঁধে নেওয়া** *v.* to place and carry upon one's shoulder, to bear upon one's shoulder, to shoulder. **কাঁধের হাড়** *n.* the scapula. **কার কাঁধে দশটা মাথা** who has the rashness to risk his head ? who'll dare? **কাঁধাকাঁধি** *n.* state of being carried or borne on shoulders of more than one person at a time. ☐ *adv.* being borne upon the shoulders of more than one person at a time; side by side, cheek by jowl.

কাঁপ var. of **কাঁপন**।

কাঁপই *v.* (poet. & obs.) tremble or trembles, shudder or shudders, shiver or shivers, shake or shakes, quake or quakes.

কাঁপন *n.* trembling, tremble; shudder; shiver; shake; quake, tremor; vibration; palpitation. **কাঁপন ধরা** *v.* to be stricken with trembling or shudder or shiver.

কাঁপয়ে var. of **কাঁপই**।

কাঁপা *v.* to tremble; to shudder; to shiver; to shake; to quake; to quiver; to vibrate; to palpitate (হৃদয় কাঁপা). **কাঁপানো** *v.* to set trembling, to send trembling, to tremble; to cause to shudder, to shiver; to shake; to quake; to cause to quiver; to vibrate; to set palpitating, to palpitate. ☐ *a.* tremulour (কাঁপানো স্বর). **কেঁপে ওঠা** *v.* to start (as in fear); to be startled.

কাঁপুনি var. of **কাঁপন**।

কাঁসর *n.* a dish of bell metal (alloy of copper and tin) used as a musical instrument.

কাঁসা *n.* bell metal. **কাঁসারি** *n.* a brazier.

কাঁসি *n.* a dish of bell metal used as a kitchen utensil or a musical instrument.

কাঁহা (coll.) *adv.* (interro.) where ? **~তক** *adv.* how far ? how long ? to what extent ?

কাক *n.* the crow. *fem.* **কাকী** the female crow. **~চক্ষু** *a.* as transparent as a crow's eyes, (cp.) crystal-clear. **~জ্যোৎস্না** *n.* dim or faint moonlight. **~তন্দ্রা, ~নিদ্রা** *n.* wary nap or slumber. **~তাড়ুয়া** *n.* the scarecrow. **~তালীয়** *a.* (of two or more incidents) coincidental and seemingly related to one another as cause and effect; coincidental; successive but not causally connected. **কাকতালীয় ন্যায়** *post hoc ergo propter hoc* (after it, so because of it—a fallacious reasoning). **~পক্ষ** *n.* a lovelock. **~পদ** *n.* quotation-marks (“ ”); a caret (^). **~পুচ্ছ** *n.* the cuckoo. **~ফল** *n.* the margosa-tree, the nim. **~বন্ধ্যা** *n.* a woman who becomes pregnant but once. **~ভেজা** *n.* &*v.* getting or to get completely drenched (usu. in rainwater). ~ভোর *n.* very early morning. ~শীর্ষ *n.* a species of flower-tree yielding flowers looking like ducks. ~স্নান *n.* brief and careless bath. **কাকের ছা বকের ছা** extremely bad and illegible handwriting.

কাকলি, কাকলী *n.* a low sweet and indistinct murmur or chirping.

কা-কা *n.* & *int.* caw. **কা-কা করা** *v.* to caw.

কাকা *n.* younger brother of one's father, an uncle. *fem.* **কাকি** the wife of an uncle, an aunt. **~সংক্রান্ত, ~বিষয়ক** *a.* avuncular; of an uncle.

কাকাতুয়া *n.* the cockatoo.

কাকিনী *n. fem.* (facet.) the female crow.

কাকী rej. spell. of **কাকি**।

কাকু[১] (coll.) an affectionate form of **কাকা**।

কাকু[২] *n.* voice turned hoarse; supplication; regret; request; solicitation; (rhet.) a figure of speech depending on the tone of voice akin to erotesis; emphasis of tone.

কাকুতি *n.* anything uttered in supplication or regret; importunate request or solicitation. **কাকুতি-মিনতি** *n.* earnest entreaty, supplication; repeated importunate request or solicitation. **কাকুতি-মিনতি করা** *v.* to request or solicit importunately and repeatedly.

কাকুৎস্থ, কাকুৎস্থ্য *n.* a descendant of King Kakootstha (ককুৎস্থ) or Puranjaya (পুরঞ্জয়). ☐ *a.* descending from Kakootstha or Puranjaya.

কাকুবাদ *n.* importunate request or solicitation, supplication or humble prayer.

কাকূতি alt. spell. of **কাকুতি**।

কাকূক্তি *n.* anything said in supplication; (rhet.) a figure of speech depending on the tone of voice akin to erotesis.

কাকে coll. form. of **কাহাকে**।

কাকোদর *a.* the snake.

কাক্ষিক *a.* intrapetiolar.

কাগ corrup. of **কাক**।

কাগজ *n.* paper; newspaper; records; a document; a promissory bond. **কোম্পানির কাগজ** stocks, government securities or bonds. **খবরের কাগজ** a newspaper. **স্বচ্ছ কাগজ** tracing paper. **কাগজে-কলমে** *adv.* in writing or in print, in black and white; only theoretically, on paper. **~চাপা** *n.* a paper-weight. **~পত্র** *n. pl.* documents, papers. **কাগজি** *a.* of paper; of newspaper; having a papery or very thin covering. ☐ *n.* a paper-manufacturer; a paper dealer. **কাগজি মুদ্রা** paper money. **কাগজের মণ্ড** paper pulp.

কাগজি লেবু a small variety of lime with a thin, papery skin.

কাগাবগা *a.* destitute, wretched, abandoned; inconsistent, haphazard. ☐ *n.* such a person or thing.

কাঙাল *a.* poor, indigent; destitute; humbly praying for; meanly hankering after, piteously eager to have (যশের কাঙাল, সন্তানের কাঙাল) ; wistful (কাঙাল নয়ন) ; suffering, miserable; earning one's livelihood by begging. ☐ *n.* an indigent man; a humble petitioner; a suffering or miserable man; a begger. *fem.* **কাঙালিনি**। **~পনা** *n.* (usu. dero.) beggary; supplication. **কাঙালি** same as **কাঙাল**। **কাঙালি বিদায়** *n.* distribution of alms to the poor or beggars. **কাঙালি বিদায় করা** *v.* to distribute alms to the poor or beggars. **কাঙালি ভোজন** *n.* feeding of the poor or beggars.

কাচ *n.* glass; crystal, quartz; pebble, a lens (চশমার কাচ). **কাচিক** *a.* glassy, hyaline.

কাচকড়া var. of **কাঁচকড়া**।

কাচকুপি *n.* a funnel made of glass, a glass funnel.

কাচঘর *n.* a glass-house.

কাচতুল্য *a.* glasslike, hyaline; transparent.

কাচদণ্ড *n.* a glass-rod.

কাচন *n.* act of washing clothes etc. by rinsing and thrashing.

কাচনল *n.* glass cylinder, glass tube.

কাচপাত্র *n.* glass bowl, glass vessel.

কাচপোকা var. of **কাঁচপোকা**।

কাচমণি *n.* quartz, crystal.

কাচা *v.* to wash by rinsing and thrashing (as clothes etc.). ☐ *a.* thus washed. **কাচানো** *v.* to cause to wash by rinsing and thrashing; to get thus washed. ☐ *a.* thus washed.

কাচ্চাবাচ্চা *n. pl.* infants, young children, little ones, (sl.)kiddies.

কাছ *n.* proximity, nearness; vicinity, neighbourhood; approach, presence; reach. **~ছাড়া** *a.* away from one; separated.

কাছটি *n.* a loincloth worn as tightly as a suspensor. **কাছটি করা** *v.* to pull up one's loin-cloth, (cp.) to pull up one's socks.

কাছা[১] *n.* a piece of new and unbleached cloth worn round the neck by a Hindu mourning the loss of any of his parents or a similar person.

কাছা[২] *n.* the part of the loincloth which the wearer tucks behind him at the waist. **~আলগা, ~খোলা** *a.* uncareful, neglectful, careless, heedless. **~ধরা** *a.* cringing; parasitical. **কাছা ধরা** *v.* to cringe; to hang on as a parasite.

কাছাকাছি *adv.* near, close to; nearly, approximately; about; almost . □ *a.* adjacent, situated or placed near.

কাছানো *v.* to draw near; to approach; to step up; to impend, to become imminent.

কাছারি *n.* a court of justice, a law court; a magistrate's court, a kachhari, a cutcherry; an office; a zamindar's (জমিদারের) or a feudal lord's court and office.

কাছি *n.* cable, hawser; thick rope or cord.

কাছিম *n.* the tortoise, the turtle. **কাছিমের খোলা** *n.* tortoise-shell.

কাছুটি var. of **কাছটি**।

কাছে *adv.* & *prep.* near to, in the vicinity of, in the neighbourhood of, beside; in presence of; within the reach of (হাতের কাছে). **কাছে-কাছে** *adv.* keeping always or mostly close to. **কাছে-পিঠে** same as **কাছাকাছি**।

কাজ *n.* work, action; a deed, an act; a job, an employment, a service (কাজ থেকে বরখাস্ত) ; occupation, profession, trade; duty, task (রাজার কাজ প্রজাপালন) ; practice, habit (আড্ডা দেওয়াই তার কাজ) ; need, necessity, use (কথায় কাজ কী) ; motive, business (কী কাজে এসেছ) ; outcome, result, good result, success (ওষুধে কাজ হয়েছে) ; artistry (ছবিতে রঙের কাজ). **কাজ আদায় করা** *v.* to see that one works properly, to make one work properly; to get a work or task done; to wheedle a thing out of another, to wangle (by persuasion, trickery etc.). **কাজও নেই কামাইও নেই** always busy with nothing, ever busy with nothing; ever busy with trifles or with useless work; fussy. **কাজ করা** *v.* to work; to serve; to be effective. **কাজ চলা, কাজ চলে যাওয়া** *v.* & *n.* to be worth working, to be workable; to do (এতে তোমার কাজ চলবে ? will it do ?). **কাজ দেওয়া** *v.* to give employment; to entrust with a work or job, to allocate or allot duties to; to be effective (ওষুধটায় কাজ দিয়েছে) ; to give service (ঘড়িটা ভালো কাজ দিচ্ছে). **কাজ দেখা** *v.* to examine a work done; to supervise a work; to look for an employment or job; (coll.) to be effective (এতে কাজ দেখবে). **কাজ দেখানো** *v.* to try to display ostentatiously that one is busy, to be fussily active; to show off; to prove one's worth through work. **কাজ বাগানো** *v.* to manage to achieve one's end, to manage to obtain. **কাজ বাঁচানো** *v.* to see that one does not lose one's job. **কাজ বাজানো** *v.* (usu. dero.—by an insincere worker) to be on duty neglectfully. **কাজ হাসিল করা** *v.* to have one's object fulfilled; to have one's object achieved. **কাজের কথা** useful talk; the main point of a talk; talk about work. **কাজের কাজি** the right man for a work. **কাজের জিনিস** useful or valuable thing. **কাজের বার** useless, out of order; worthless; disabled. **কাজের বেলায় কাজি কাজ ফুরোলে পাজি** (fig.) ingratitude is the law of the world. **কাজের লোক** *n.* an employee; a servant, an active or useful or competent person.

কাজকর্ম *n. pl.* activities; occupations.

কাজর poet. corrup. of **কাজল**।

কাজরি *n.* an Indian folk-dance or its accompanying music.

কাজল *n.* lamp-black; collyrium. □ *a.* as black as collyrium. **~লতা** *n.* a vessel shaped like a pair of hollow scissors for preparing collyrium. **চোখের কাজল চুরি করা** (fig.) to steal something under one's very nose; to bamboozle, to fox.

কাজলা[1] *a. fem.* as black as collyrium.

কাজলা[2], **কাজলি** *n.* a reddish variety of sugarcane.

কাজি *a.* a Muslim judge or interpreter of laws.

কাজিয়া *n.* quarrel; brawl, wrangle.

কাজুবাদাম *n.* cashew-nut.

কাজেই, কাজেকাজেই *adv.* resultantly, consequently, so, therefore.

কাঞ্চন *n.* gold; wealth, riches (কামিনীকাঞ্চন) ; a variety of golden flower; a variety of paddy. □ *a.* of golden colour (কাঞ্চনকান্তি) ; made of gold (কাঞ্চনমুদ্রা) ; auriferous. **~প্রভ** *a.* having a golden lustre or radiance. **~বর্ণ** *a.* golden, golden-yellow.

কাঞ্চি *n.* an ornament worn round the waist, a girdle, a sash (কাঞ্চিদাম).

কাঞ্জি, কাঞ্জিক, কাঞ্জিকা, কাঞ্জী, কাঞ্জীক *n.* the water in which boiled rice has been kept steeped overnight (this water tastes sour).

কাট[1] pop. var.of **কাঠ** ।

কাট[2] *n.* shape, cut (মুখের কাট).

কাটকুট *n.* making alterations in several places of a manuscript etc. by penning through it; correction; shortening, abridgement; reduction; (usu. minor) surgical operations. **কাটকুট করা** *v.* to pen through and alter at places; to correct; to shorten, to abridge; to reduce; to operate upon.

কাটখোট্টা *a.* tough and obstinate; stiff; humourless; unfeeling, unsympathetic; hard-hearted, merciless; uncouth and ill-mannered; rough, outspoken (কাটখোট্টা কথাবার্তা).

কাটখোলা *n.* a frying-pan without oil or sand.

কাটগোঁয়ার *a.* extremely obstinate, intransigent; obdurate.

কাটছাঁট *n.* (chiefly of garments) cut, shape, alteration; make, make-up; reduction.

কাটতি *n.* power or opportunity of selling; sale; public demand; demand.

কাটন *n.* act of cutting or hewing or cleaving or chopping or carving or mowing or lopping or trimming or paring or amputating or incising or operating or biting or eating or penning through or striking off or deducting or digging or sinking or drawing or painting or writing out or mending or sharpening or refuting or protesting or constructing or capping or reciting or picking or pinching or passing or dispelling or dispersing or lifting or giving the slip to or being sold or selling or being in demand or having recognition or flowing or coming out or being in the act of doing etc. (see **কাটা** *v.*).

কাটনা *n.* act of spinning; a spinning wheel; a spinning-jenny; a spinning spindle or top.

কাটনি[1] *n.* the charge for spinning.

কাটনি[2] *n.* (usu. *fem.*) a spinner.

কাটব্য *n.* (chiefly used as a correl. of কটু) harshness, rudeness.

কাটমোল্লা *n.* an uneducated ignorant and fanatical Muslim priest.

কাটরা *n.* a wooden room or stall; a small wooden enclosure, a box, a dock (সাক্ষীর কাটরা) ; a mart, a market-place.

কাটলেট *n.* a cutlet.

কাটা *v.* to cut; to hew, to cleave; to chop; to carve (মাংস কাটা) ; to mow (ঘাস কাটা) ; to lop (গাছের ডাল কাটা) ; to trim; to pare (নখ কাটা) ; to amputate; to incise, to operate, to lance (ফোড়া কাটা) ; to bite (জিভ কাটা) ; to eat (পোকায় কাটা) ; to pen through, to strike off (লেখা কাটা, নাম কাটা) ; to deduct (পাওনা কাটা) ; to dig (পুকুর কাটা) ; to sink (কুয়ো কাটা) ; to draw (লাইন কাটা, দাগ কাটা) ; to write (আঁক কাটা) ; to write out (চেক কাটা) ; to paint (তিলক কাটা) ; to mend or sharpen (কলম বা পেনসিল কাটা) ; to refute (যুক্তি কাটা) ; to say in retort, to protest (কথা কাটা) ; to construct (পথ কাটা) ; to compose, to recite, to cap (ছড়া কাটা) ; to pinch or pick (পকেট কাটা) ; to pass (সময় কাটা) ; to disperse (মেঘ কাটা) ; to lift (কুয়াশা কাটা) ; to be dispelled (ভয় কাটা) ; to make a slip in (তাল কাটা, সুর কাটা) ; to be sold, to sell, to be in demand (বাজারে মাল কাটা) ; to be in the act of doing, to do (সাঁতার কাটা). □ *a.*

cut; hewn, cleft, cloven; chopped; carved; moved, mown; lopped; amputated; incised, operated, lanced; eaten; penned through, struck off; mended, sharpened; used in cutting or chopping (পেনসিল-কাটা ছুরি, মাংস-কাটা ছুরি). ☐ *n.* cutting; hewing; cleaving; chopping; carving; mowing; lopping; trimming; paring; amputation; incision, operation; a mark of cutting or incision or operation; biting; eating; penning through, striking off; deduction; digging; sinking; drawing; writing, writing out; painting; mending or sharpening. **কথা কাটা** *v.* to answer in retaliation, to retort. **কাটা কাপড়** textile fabrics for making garments, piecegoods. **কাটা ঘায়ে নুনের ছিটা দেওয়া** to add insult to injury. **ঘাস কাটা** *v.* to mow grass; (sarcas.) (to be able) to do nothing. **ছড়া কাটা** *v.* to cap or recite a rhyme. **জিভ কাটা** *v.* to show the tip of one's tongue and press it with the teeth, to bite one's tongue (as a mark of bashfulness or in apology.) **ট্রেনেকাটা** *a.* run-over by a railway train. **ফাঁড়া কাটা** *v.* to avoid or escape a possible or impending calamity. **ফুট কাটা** *v.* to let fall in drops; (pop.) to interpose, to chip in. **ফোঁটা কাটা** *v.* to let fall in drops; to put a holy mark between the eyebrows or on the forehead; (pop.) to interpose, to chip in. **ভারে কাটা** *v.* to pull one's weight. **সাঁতার কাটা** *v.* to swim. **সিঁথি কাটা** *v.* to part hair. **সিঁধ কাটা** *v.* to break stealthily into a mud house, to burgle; to crack a crib. **সুতো কাটা** *v.* to spin.

কাটাই *n.* charges for cutting, hewing, lopping, mowing, spinning etc. ☐ *a.* charged for cutting, hewing, lopping, mowing, spinning etc. (কাটাই খরচ).

কাটাকাটি *n.* mutual killing or slaughter; a skirmish; a fight; a quarrel; act of disfiguring with corrections. **কাটাকাটি করা** *v.* to kill or slay one another; to take part in a skirmish; to fight one another; to quarrel; to make corrections, to disfigure with corrections.

কাটাকুটি var. of **কাটকুট**।

কাটাখাল *n.* an excavated watercourse or canal for irrigation or for inland navigation.

কাটা-ঘা *n.* wound or injury caused by a cut.

কাটাছেঁড়া *n.* minor wound or injury.

কাটানি var. of **কাটাই**।

কাটান (pronun. কাটান্) *n.* escape; anything esp. an incantation that counteracts an evil, an antidote (বিষের বা মন্ত্রের কাটান) ; repayment (দেনার কাটান) ; a clearing up; an explanation.

কাটানো *v.* to cause to be cut or hewn or cleft or chopped or carved or mown or lopped or trimmed or pared or amputated or incised or operated or dug or sunk or written out or painted or constructed or capped or recited or flowed or done; to refute (যুক্তি কাটানো) ; to clear up (দোষ কাটানো) ; to pass or spend (সময় কাটানো) ; to sell (বাজারে মাল কাটানো) ; to get over, to overcome (দুঃখ কাটানো, বিপদ কাটানো). **দোষ কাটানো** *v.* to absolve, to exculpate, to exonerate. **কাটিয়ে ওঠা** *v.* to get over, to overcome.

কাটারি *n.* a large thick and heavy household knife shaped almost like a falchion with a wooden handle; a chopper.

কাটি pop. var. of **কাঠি**।

কাটিম *n.* a bobbin; a reel; a spool.

কাটুনি pop. var.of **কাটনি**।

কাটুরকুটুর *int.* denoting: the sound of cutting or scratching with teeth as by mice.

কাট্য *a.* refutable.

কাঠ *n.* wood; timber; firewood; (fig.) skeleton (রোগে দেহের কাঠ বেরিয়ে পড়েছে). ☐ *a.* motionless like a log (ভয়ে কাঠ হওয়া) ; stiffened (মরে কাঠ হওয়া) ; juiceless, sapless (শুকিয়ে কাঠ) ; dumbfounded. **~কয়লা** *n.* charcoal. **কাঠ কাঠ** *a.* hard and dry and rough. **~কুড়ানি** *n.* an extremely poor woman who lives by collecting twigs and leaves of trees to be burnt as firewood. **~খোলা** *n.* a frying pot in which sand is not used. **~গড়া** *n.* a small wooden enclosure, a box, a dock (সাক্ষীর বা আসামির কাঠগড়া). **~গোলা**

n. a timberyard. ~গোলাপ *n.* a variety of scentless wild rose, the sweet-brier, the eglantine. ~ঠোকরা *n.* the woodpecker. ~পিঁপড়ে *n.* a variety of large and black ant living on trees. ~ফড়িং *n.* a variety of very thin grasshopper. ~ফাটা *a.* scorching, blazing, burning. **কাঠফাটা রোদ** scorching rays of the sun. ~বমি *n.* dry vomit. ~বিড়াল, (coll.) ~বেড়াল, (coll.) ~বেরাল *n.* the squirrel. *fem.* ~বিড়ালী, (coll.) ~বেড়ালী। ~মল্লিকা *n.* a variety of very sweet-scented wild flower belonging to the species of the jasmine. ~রা var. of **কাটরা**। ~রিয়া var. of **কাঠুরিয়া**। **কাঠে কাঠে** *adv.* & *a.* exactly fitting to all grooves or points (কাঠে কাঠে মেলা) ; exactly coinciding; evenly matched; diamond cuts diamond, when Greek meets Greek (কাঠে কাঠে লড়াই). **কাঠের** *a.* of wood, made of wood, wooden. **অনেক কাঠখড় পোড়ানো** to work laboriously (for), to toil hard, to make every endeavour. **কাঠের মিস্তিরি** *n.* a carpenter.

কাঠা *n.* cottah, a measure of land (=720 sq. ft.); a dry measure of grain or a receptacle for this measuring. ~কালি *n.* (arith.) square-measure. ~কিয়া *n.* the table of cottahs (কাঠা).

কাঠাম, কাঠামো *n.* a framework (usu. composed of bamboo, wood, hay etc.), a frame; a structure; a preliminary sketch.

কাঠি *n.* a small chip of wood, bamboo, metal etc. (used as a match-stick, toothpick etc.) **কাঠি-কাঠি** *a.* composed of very thin bones; very thin. **কাঠি দেওয়া** *v.* (vul.) to try to irritate or harm or foil, to baffle or frustrate.

কাঠিন্য *n.* hardness, solidity; inflexibility; firmness; harshness; hard-handedness, severity; hard-heartedness, mercilessness, cruelty. ~প্রাপ্ত *a.* hardened; thickened; solidified.

কাঠিম var. of **কাটিম**।

কাঠিসার *a.* very lean and thin.

কাঠুয়া dial. var. of **কেঠো**[1]।

কাঠুরিয়া, (coll.) **কাঠুরে** *n.* a woodcutter, a woodman.

কাঠে কাঠে see **কাঠ**।

কাড়ন *n.* (now obs.) act of snatching away; act of seizing by force or tactics; act of lifting or grabbing; act of attracting or enticing (মন কাড়ন) ; act of uttering or pronouncing (রা কাড়ন).

কাড়া[1] *n.* a tumbler-shaped instrument of percussion, a drum (chiefly used as a correlative of a **নাকারা** or **নাকাড়া** which is a smaller **কাড়া**).

কাড়া[2] *v.* to snatch away; to seize by force or tactics; to lift; to grab; to attract or entice; to utter or pronounce. ~কাড়ি *n.* mutual attempt to snatch away from one another; scrambling. **কাড়াকাড়ি করা** *v.* to try to snatch away from one another; to scramble. ~নো *v.* to cause to snatch away; to cause to seize by force or tactics; to make one admit or confess or utter (রা কাড়ানো) ; to draw, to warrant (আদর কাড়া).

কাণ্ড *n.* (of a tree) a stalk, a stem, a trunk, a caulis; (of a book) a chapter or canto; an event, an incident, an affair; a deed or exploit (ভীমের বিষম কাণ্ড). ~কারখানা *n.* (as *pl.*) deeds, workings, activities, exploits; (as *sing.*) an affair or matter (usually serious or strange). ~জ *a.* (bot.) cauline, caulinary. ~জ্ঞান *n.* common sense, gumption. ~জ্ঞানশূন্য *a.* devoid of or wanting in common sense. ~জ্ঞানবিহীন same as **কাণ্ডজ্ঞানশূন্য**। ~হীন *a.* without a stem or stalk or trunk. **কাণ্ড বাধানো** *v.* to throw up a row; to create a funny or serious or curious affair; to make a scene.

কাণ্ডাকাণ্ডজ্ঞান *n.* power of discriminating between good and bad or between propriety and impropriety.

কাণ্ডারী, (obs.) **কাণ্ডার** a streersman, a helmsman, a pilot; (fig.) a leader (ভবের কাণ্ডারী) ; (fig.) a rescuer or saviour (বিপদের কাণ্ডারী). **ভবের কাণ্ডারী** God (imagined as a steersman).

কাত *n.* side (কোন কাতে). ☐ *a.* slanted or slanting; tilted or tilting; laid or lying on one side; knocked to the ground, floored, defeated, taken aback, fatigued; bedridden (এক চড়ে কাত, ভয়ে

কাত, খাটুনির চোটে কাত, রোগে কাত). **কাত করা** *v.* to slant; to tilt; to lean; to lay or turn on one side; to knock to the ground, to floor; to defeat, to cause to be taken aback, to fatigue, to put to bed. **কাত হওয়া** *v.* to slant; to tilt; to lean; to lie or turn on one side; to be thrown to the ground, to be floored, to be vanquished, to be taken aback, to be fatigued, to be bedridden.

কাতর *a.* distressed, afflicted; aggrieved, stricken with grief, sorrowful; intent, extremely solicitous (কাতর প্রাণের ডাক) ; grudging, reluctant (ব্যয়কাতর, পরিশ্রম করতে কাতর). **~কণ্ঠ** *n.* a sad voice, a plaintive tone. ☐ *a.* speaking in a doleful voice. **~তা** *n.* distress, affliction; aggrieved state; solicitude; rancour; reluctance. **~হৃদয়** *n.* an afflicted or aggrieved heart; an extremely sensitive or feeling heart. ☐ *a.* having such a heart. **~স্বর** same as **কাতরকণ্ঠ।**

কাতরানি *n.* groaning or moaning; groan or moan; fidgeting; fidget.

কাতরানো *v.* to groan; to moan; to fidget.

কাতরোক্তি *n.* an expression of pain or sorrow, a doleful utterance; supplication.

কাতর্য var. of **কাতরতা** (see **কাতর**).

কাতলা *n.* a variety of fresh-water flat fish, *Catla buchamani*; (sarcas.) an extremely wealthy or influential or important man.

কাতা *n.* coir.

কাতান *n.* a large knife or bill-hook (esp. for cutting metal-plates), a shearing tool.

কাতার *n.* a large crowd (কাতারে কাতারে লোক) ; a long row or line or file (কাতার দিয়ে দাঁড়ানো).

কাতারি var. of **কাতুরি।**

কাতি *n.* a knife or saw for cutting conchs and shells, a conch-cutter, a shell-cutter.

কাতুকুতু *n.* tickling (with the hand esp. in the arm-pit); titillation. **কাতুকুতু দেওয়া** *v.* to tickle; to titillate.

কাতুরি *n.* a tool or knife for paring metal-plates, a metal-cutter.

কাত্যায়নী *n.* a name of Goddess Durga (দুর্গা).

কাদম্ব *a.* pertaining to the kadam (কদম) flower. ☐ *n.* kadam flowers collectively; an arrow; the teal. **কাদম্বা** *n. fem.* the female teal; a kadam (কদম) tree.

কাদম্বর *n.* the cream of curd; a kind of wine akin to rum.

কাদম্বরী[1] *n.* a name of Goddess Saraswati (সরস্বতী) ; the female cuckoo; the female parrot.

কাদম্বরী[2] *n.* a variety of wine akin to rum.

কাদম্বিনী *n.* a collection of clouds.

কাদা *n.* gluey mud, slime. ☐ *a.* full of gluey mud, slimy (পথ কাদা হয়েছে). **কাদা করা** *v.* to make muddy or slimy, to muddy; to make turbid. **~খোঁচা** *n.* the snipe. **~টে** *a.* slimy; viscous; full of gluey mud; muddy. **~ময়** *a.* full of mud, muddy; covered all over with mud. **~মাখা** *a.* smeared with mud; covered all over with mud.

কান *n.* the ear; sense or power of hearing; audition; heed (কথায় কান দেওয়া) ; an ear-like key of a violin or similar instruments; anything resembling an ear. **কান কাটা** *v.* (fig.) to defeat or supersede outright. **কান কাটা যাওয়া** *v.* to suffer deep humiliation. **কান খাড়া করা** *v.* (fig.)to prick up one's ears, to be all ears. **কান ঝালাপালা করা** *v.* to vex or annoy by deafening or discordant noise. **কান দেওয়া** *v.* to give attention or ear (to), to listen to, to pay heed (to), to lend an ear (to). **কান ধরা** *v.* to pull one's ears (as a mark of chastisement, rebuke or insult). **কান না দেওয়া** *v.* to turn a deaf ear (to), to refuse to hear, to pay no heed (to). **কান পাকা** *v.* to have pus formed within one's ear-holes. **~পাটা** *n.* the cluster or lock of hair hanging by the side of ears, sideburns; flap of the ear, lobe of the ear. **কান পাতা** *v.* to give ear (to); to pay heed (to). **কান ফুটানো, কান বিঁধানো** *v.* to get the lobe of the ear pierced, esp. for wearing earrings. **কান ভাঙানো, কান ভারী করা** *v.* to speak to a person secretly in order to prejudice him against another, to earwig. **কান**

মলা *v.* to pull one's ear, to pull one by the ear; (fig.) to put out of countenance or defeat utterly, to discomfit. কানে আঙুল দেওয়া *v.* to put one's fingers into one's ears (as a mark of refusal to hear). কানে ওঠা *v.* to reach the ears or to come to hear. কানে খাটো *a.* short of hearing, hard of hearing. কানে তালা লাগা *v.* to have one's ears deafened by loud or ear-splitting noise etc.) কানে তোলা *v.* to inform (against); to pay heed to. কানে ধরে বলা *v.* to draw one's attention with rebuke. কানে লাগা *v.* to sound plausible or acceptable or sweet. ~-কাটা *a.* shameless, brazenfaced, unblushing; thick-skinned, unperturbed by ridicule or derision. ~কুয়া, (coll.) ~কো *n.* the gill of a fish etc., the branchia. ~খুশকি *n.* an ear-pick. ~পাতলা *a.* apt to believe (evil reports about others) without sufficient evidence, credulous. ~ফাটা[1], ~ফাটানো *a.* (of sounds etc.) deafening, stunning. ~ফাটা[2] *a.* of a class of monks with their external ears split (কানফাটা যোগী). ~বালা *n.* an earring. ~ভাঙানি *n.* speaking secretly to a person in order to prejudice him or her against another, earwigging.

কানন *n.* a forest, a garden; a grove. ~কুসুম *n.* a wild flower.

কানা[1] *n.* border, edge; brim, rim. কানায় কানায় *adv.* to the brim. কানায় কানায় ভরা full to the brim, brimful. ~ভাঙা *a.* with broken brim.

কানা[2] *a.* blind of one eye, one-eyed; blind; having a hole, useless, valueless (কানাকড়ি). ~কড়ি *n.* (lit.) a cowrie (কড়ি) with a hole; a cowrie which is not convertible, a useless or valueless cowrie; (fig.) minimum wealth (কানাকড়িও সম্বল নেই). ~খোঁড়া *n.* (as *pl.*) the blind and the lame; (as *sing.*) a blind and lame person. কানাখোঁড়ার একগুণ বাড়া (fig.) a worthless person is often full of troublesome vanity or mischief. ~গলি a blind alley, a cul-de-sac, an impasse. কানা গোরুর ভিন্ন পথ (lit.) a one-eyed cow often goes astray from the right way; (fig.) a fool or an ignorant person often strays away from the safe route. কানা ছেলের নাম পদ্মলোচন (fig.) a ridiculous affair such as adorning an ugly person gaudily, a cur put in fur. ~মাছি *n.* blindman's buff.

কানাই corrup. of কৃষ্ণ।

কানাকানি, কানাঘুষা, (coll.) কানাঘুষো *n.* whispering; secret discussion; secret rumour; secret scandal-mongering. কানাকানি করা, কানাঘুষো করা *v.* to whisper together; to discuss secretly; to spread rumour secretly; to carry scandal secretly.

কানাচ *n.* outlying part at the back of a house (esp. where refuse and soil are deposited); the space under the eaves at the back of a house.

কানাচি পাতা *v.* to eavesdrop; to hear secretly.

কানাড়া *n.* an Indian musical mode sung at night.

কানাত *n.* a tent; a curtain or screen (round a tent for a sort of wall).

কানামাছি see কানা[2]।

কানি *n.* a rag.

কানীন *a.* born of an unmarried woman's womb. □ *n.* one so born. *fem.* কানীনী।

কানু corrup. of কৃষ্ণ।

কানুন *n.* a law; a regulation; a rule. কালাকানুন a notorious act; a black act.

কানুনগো an accounts officer of the revenue department; a public surveyor, a settlement officer.

কানে কানে *adv.*(talking) in whispers, in one's ear; (saying a word) in private or privately.

কানেস্তারা *n.* a canister.

কান্ত *n.* (chiefly used as a *sfx.*) a husband (কমলাকান্ত) ; a gem or a precious stone (অয়স্কান্ত). □ *a.* lovely, beautiful; beloved, dear; charming.

কান্তলোহা *n.* a precious stone; lodestone; magnet; pig iron; steel; cast iron.

কান্তা *n. fem.* wife; a lady-love, a mistress.

কান্তায়স var. of কান্তলোহা।

কান্তার *n.* a deep forest; a road not easily accessible, an impassable road.

কান্তি *n.* grace; charm; beauty; splendour; brightness; radiance. **কান্তিক, ~লোহা** same as **কান্তলোহা**। **~বিদ্যা** *n.* aesthetics. **~মান** *a.* graceful; charming; beautiful; splendid; bright; radiant. *fem.* **~মতী**।

কান্না *n.* act or a spell of weeping. **~কাটি** n. effusive weeping, blubbering; continuous weeping; lamentation; (fig.) earnest request; solicitation. **কান্নাকাটি করা** *v.* to weep effusively, to blubber, to blub; to weep continuously; to lament; to request earnestly; to solicit; to pester with earnest request or solicitation. **কান্না-হাসি** *n.* sorrow and joy, tears and smiles.

কাপ[১] *n.* a cup.

কাপ[২] *n.* one of a section of the Brahmans (ব্রাহ্মণ) ; dissimulation, pretence, feigning. ☐ *a.* dissimulating, disguised; pretending, feigning; hypocritical; funny, mirth-provoking. **কাপ করা** *v.* to pretend, to feign.

কাপটিক *a.* deceitful, fraudulent; hypocritical; sly.

কাপট্য *n.* chicanery; trickishness; deceit; deception; act of feigning, pretence, make-believe; hypocrisy; insincerity; dissimulation.

কাপড় *n.* cloth-fabric; loincloth; dress, garment. **কাপড় ছাড়া** *v.* to change the loincloth, to change; to undress. **কাপড় পরা** *v.* to put on clothes or the loincloth; to dress. **কাপড়-চোপড়** *n. pl.* clothes, garments, wearing apparel; dress. **কাপড়-চোপড় ছাড়া** *v.* to undress; to change. **কাপড়-চোপড় পরা** *v.* to dress. **কাপড়ের দোকান** a cloth-shop; a clothier's shop; a textile-shop.

কাপালিক *n.* an ascetic worshipping the cult of Kali or Shiva using the human skull for drinking and sitting on human skulls.

কাপাস *n.* cotton. **কাপাস গাছ** *n.* the cotton-plant. See also **কার্পাস**।

কাপুড়ে, কাপুড়িয়া *a.* of cloth; made of cloth; dealing in cloth. ☐ *n.* a cloth-merchant; a clothier or a cloth-dealer.

কাপুরুষ *n.* a coward, a poltroon; a faint-hearted or hen-hearted person. ☐ *a.* cowardly, poltroon; faint-hearted, hen-hearted. **~তা, ~ত্ব** *n.* cowardice; cowardliness; faint-heartedness. **কাপুরুষোচিত** *a.* cowardly, befitting a coward or a chicken-hearted person.

কাপে কাপে *adv.* to a nicety; exactly; to a T.

কাপ্তেন, কাপ্তান *n.* the captain of a ship; a military officer holding the rank of a captain; a leader or captain of a team of players or sportsmen; a captain; (sl.) a fop who spends money prodigally in order to play the boss amongst his companions in vulgar amusements. **কাপ্তানি** *n.* captaincy; captainship; (sl.) act of spending money foppishly and prodigally in order to play the boss amongst one's companions in vulgar amusements. **কাপ্তানি করা** *v.* to captain; to lead; (sl.) to spend money foppishly and prodigally in order to play the boss amongst one's companions in vulgar amusements.

কাফন *n.* a winding-sheet, a shroud.

কাফরি *n.* an African negro; an African.

কাফি *n.* an Indian musical mode.

কাফির, কাফের *n.* a Kafir; an infidel (according to Muslims).

কাফিল, কাফেলা *n.* a company of pilgrims travelling together; a company travelling together, a caravan.

কাফ্রি alt. spell. of **কাফরি**।

কাবলি coll. corrup. of **কাবুলি**।

কাবা *n.* a kind of a very long and loose-fitting shirt; a quadrangular mosque in Mecca where Muslim Haj pilgrims gather to say their prayers before the holy Black Stone.

কাবাড়ি *n.* persons who buy in an auction-mart for resale; a class of fishermen.

কাবাব *n.* roasted meat.

কাবাবচিনি *n.* cubeb.

কাবার *n.* end, termination, winding-up (দিন কাবার, কাজ কাবার) ; the last day (মাসকাবার). **কাবার করা** *v.* to finish; to complete; to wind up; to spend; to do to death, to do in. **কাবার হওয়া** *v.* to end, to terminate, to be over; to be finished; to be spent.

কাবিল *a.* competent, fit; grown up, of age.

কাবিলনামা *n.* marriage settlement for a wife.

কাবু *a.* weak, feeble; subdued; enfeebled. **কাবু করা** *v.* to weaken; to subdue, to defeat by superior strength, to overpower, to enfeeble. **কাবু হওয়া** *v.* to become weak, to weaken; to be subdued or enfeebled.

কাবুলি *a.* of Kabul or Afghanistan. ☐ *n.* a native of Kabul or Afghanistan, an Afghan. **~ওয়ালা** *n.* same as **কাবুলি** *(n.)*.

কাব্য *n.* a poetic saying or utterance; poetry; poetic composition; a poetical work; a book of verse. **~কলা** *n.* poetics; the poetical art. **~কুঞ্জ** *n.* the grove of the Muses of poetry. **~গ্রন্থ** *n.* a poetical work; a book of verse. **~চর্চা** *n.* exercise in poetry, writing poetry; study of poetry. **~জগৎ** *n.* the realm of poetry; poets of the world collectively; the realm of imagination. **~নাটক** *n.* a poetic drama. **~বিশারদ** *a.* skilled in poetry. ☐ *n.* one who is skilled in poetry; (dero. & sarcas.) a poetaster. **~রস** *n.* the beauty of poetry, the aesthetic value of poetry; political beauty. **~রসিক** *n.* one who can appreciate poetry, one who finds pleasure in reading poetry. **কাব্যিক** *a.* poetic; unduly poetic.

কাব্যানুশীলন *n.* same as **কাব্যচর্চা**।

কাব্যালোচনা *n.* a discussion on poetry.

কাম[1] dial. corrup. of **কর্ম**।

কাম[2] *n.* the god of love and lust (cp. Cupid, Eros); desire; passion; love; lust, eroticism; sex-urge. **~কলা** *n.* the erotic science, the sexual science; the science of love. **~কেলি** *n.* sexual intercourse; an amorous sport. **~গন্ধ** *n.* trace of lust; trace of sex. **~চর** *a.* one who can travel at will; self-willed. **~চার** *n.* self-will. ☐ *a.* self-willed. **~চারী** *a.* one who can travel at will; self-willed; wanton, lascivious, profligate; lustful. *fem.* **~চারিণী**। **~জ** *a.* born of lust, produced by lust, erotogenic, erotogenous. **~জ্বর** *n.* a terrible fit of sex hunger. **~দ** *a.* granting or having the power of granting whatever one desires. **~দা** *a. fem.* of **কামদ**। ☐ *n.* a (mythological) wishing-cow. **~দুঘা** same as **কামধেনু**। **~দূতী** *n.* a female go-between in an amour or love affair; (dero.) procuress, a bawd. **~দেব, ~দেবতা** *n.* the god of love and lust (cp. Cupid, Eros). **~ধেনু** *n.* a (mythological) wishing-cow. **~পত্নী** *n.* the wife of the god of love and lust. **~পীড়িত** *a.* stricken with the desire for sexual intercourse; love-sick. *fem.* **~পীড়িতা**। **~প্রদ** same as **কামদ**। **~প্রবৃত্তি** *n.* sexual desire or appetite, sex urge. **~বল্লভ** *n.* the spring. **~বাই** *n.* a maddening sex urge. **~বাণ** *n.* any of the five arrows of the god of love and lust, any one of Cupid's arrows. **কামবাণে জর্জরিত** smitten with carnal desires. **~মোহিত** *a.* overwhelmed with sexual desire. *fem.* **কামমোহিতা**। **~রূপ, ~রূপী** *a.* capable of assuming shapes at will; extremely beautiful or good-looking. **~শর** same as **কামবাণ**। **~শাস্ত্র** *n.* the the erotic science, the sexual science; the science of love. **~সখ** *n.* the Spring (personified). **~সূত্র** same as **কামশাস্ত্র**।

কামঠ *a.* of or pertaining to the tortoise. ☐ *n.* tortoise meat; (dial.) the tortoise.

কামড় *n.* a bite; act of seizing with the teeth; grip, seizure (মরণকামড়) ; exorbitant or merciless demand (মহাজনের সুদের কামড়) ; pain (পেটের কামড়) ; strong desire (কামের কামড়). **কামড় দেওয়া** same as **কামড়ানো**। **কামড়া** *v.* (poet.) to bite, to seize with the teeth, to gripe, to seize. **কামড়ানি** *n.*biting; griping pain; strong desire. **কামড়ানো** *v.* to bite; to seize with the teeth, to gripe, to seize; to demand exorbitantly or mercilessly; to pain; to feel pain; to stick firmly to (মাটি কামড়ে পড়া থাকা) ; to be stricken with strong desire. **কামড়াকামড়ি** *n.* mutual biting; mutual biting at or scrambling.

কামদানি *n.* embroidery; an embroidered piece of cloth.

কামদার *a.* embroidered.

কামনা *n.* a desire, a wish; a wishing; a prayer. **কামনা করা** *v.* to desire; to wish;

to pray for. ~নাশ *n.* annihilation or destruction or extinction of desire. ~সিদ্ধি *n.* fulfilment of a desire.

কামরা *n.* a compartment, a room, a chamber, a cubicle.

কামরাঙা *n.* an edible sour fruit, *averrhoa carambola*.

কামরূপ *a.* assuming any shape or form at will; beautiful, handsome, comely. ☐ *n.* a district in Assam.

কামলা *n.* jaundice.

কামাই[1] *n.* earnings, income. **কামাই করা** *v.* to earn.

কামাই[2] *n.* absence; cessation (বকবকানির কামাই নেই). **কামাই করা** *v.* to absent oneself from.

কামাক্ষী *n.* an appellation of Goddess Kamakhya (কামাখ্যা) so called because of her beautiful eyes.

কামাখ্যা *n.* the presiding goddess of Kamakhya (কামাখ্যা) ; a holy place in Assam.

কামাগ্নি *n.* fire of lust, burning desire for sexual pleasure or intercourse; fire of love.

কামাতুর *a.* stricken with desire for sexual gratification or intercourse; love-sick. *fem.* **কামাতুরা** ।

কামান *n.* a great gun, a cannon. **কামান ছোড়া, কামান দাগা** *v.* to fire a cannon, to bombard with a cannon. **কামান দেগে আক্রমণ করা বা চূর্ণবিচূর্ণ করা** *v.* to cannonade. **কামানগর্জন** *n.* the roar or report of a cannon. **কামানগোলা** *n.* a cannon-ball.

কামানল same as **কামাগ্নি** ।

কামানি *n.* wage.

কামানো *v.* to earn; to shave. ☐ *n.* earning; shaving. ☐ *a.* earned; shaved.

কামান্ধ *a.* blinded with lust or love. **কামান্ধতা** *n.* inordinate or intense sex impulses.

কামাবশায়িতা, কামাবসায়িতা *n.* power of fulfilling one's desires at will; power of restraining one's sexual appetite; continence.

কামার *n.* a blacksmith (by trade or caste). *fem.* **কামারনি** the wife of a blacksmith. ~**শালা** *n.* a smithy, a forge; a blacksmith's workshop.

কামার্ত *a.* stricken with lust; inordinately love-sick; love-lorn.

কামাল *n.* a unique performance or deed. **কামাল করা** *v.* to do a unique work.

কামাসক্ত *a.* libidinous, lustful, voluptuous; lewd, lecherous, lascivious. **কামাসক্তি** *n.* lust, violent or strong desire for sexual pleasure.

কামিজ *n.* a loose-fitting shirt.

কামিন *n.* a woman labourer, a female labourer.

কামিনী *n.* a (charming) woman; wife; a variety of sweet-scented flower. ~**কাঞ্চন** *n.* woman and gold; desire for woman and gold, i.e.; wealth. ~**সুলভ** *a.* womanly; effeminate.

কামী *a.* lustful; (chiefly used as a *sfx.*) desirous of, loving (শান্তিকামী).

কামুক *a.* lustful, lascivious, libidinous, lewd. *fem.* **কামুকা, কামুকী** ।

কামেচ্ছা *n.* sexual desire or appetite.

কামোদ *n.* an Indian musical mode. **কামোদা** *n. fem.* an Indian musical mode subservient to Kamod (কামোদ).

কামোদ্রেক *n.* sexual excitement.

কাম্য *a.* desirable; desired (কাম্য ফল) ; that which should be or is to be performed for realization of one's desire (কাম্য কর্ম).

কায় *n.* the body. ~**কল্প** *n.* an Ayurvedic (আয়ুর্বেদীয়) system of therapy for rejuvenation or prolongation of life. ~**ক্লেশ** *n.* physical labour. ~**ক্লেশে** *adv.* by physical labour; (loos.) with much difficulty and toil. ~**মনোবাক্যে** *adv.* (lit.) in or with body and mind and words; with undivided attention and concentration; whole-heartedly.

কায়দা *n.* artistic workmanship, artistry; an artifice, a trick; a contrivance, a device; a style or fashion; a means, a mode, a manner; skill; demeanour, deportment, manners (আদবকায়দা) ; control (কায়দায় পাওয়া).

কায়স্থ *n.* a caste amongst the Hindus; one belonging to this caste. *fem.* **কায়স্থা,** (অশু.) **কায়স্থিনী** a woman or a girl of the Kayastha (কায়স্থ) caste; a wife of a Kayastha.

কায়া *n.* the body.
কায়িক *a.* bodily, physical (কায়িক শ্রম). **কায়িক শ্রম** *n.* physical or manual labour.
কায়েত coll. corrup. of **কায়স্থ**।
কায়েম *a.* firm, steady, durable, permanent (কায়েম হওয়া) ; firmly established (রাজ্য কায়েম হওয়া) ; intact, in force (কায়েম থাকা). **কায়েমি** *a.* firm; durable; permanent (কায়েমি বন্দোবস্ত). **কায়েমি স্বার্থ বা কায়েমি স্বার্থবাদী লোকজন** vested interests.
কার[1] coll. form of **কাহার** (whose).
কার[2] *n.* a cord (esp. one made of silk).
কার[3] *n.* trouble, difficulty; a fix. **কারে পড়া, কারে আটকানো** *v.* to get into trouble, to be in the soup; to be in a fix. **কারে পড়ে সাধুতা দেখানো** to make a virtue of necessity.
কার[4] *in comp.* used as a *sfx.* indicating: a doer, a maker, a performer, an author, an artist, an artisan etc. (কুম্ভকার, সূপকার, গ্রন্থকার, রূপকার, স্বর্ণকার) ; utterance (জয়জয়কার, ধিক্কার) ; an act (নমস্কার, বহিষ্কার) ; any of the post-consonantal symbols (আ-কার, এ-কার) ; indicative of the genitive case (অদ্যকার, বৎসরকার).
কারক *a.* (chiefly used as a *sfx.*) one who or that which does or performs or brings about (ক্ষতিকারক). □ *n.* (gr.) the case.
কারকিত *a.* thoroughly equipped or made fit. □ *n.* cultivation. **কারকিত করা** *v.* to equip thoroughly; to undertake all necessary arrangements to make (anything) fit; to cultivate or dress (land).
কারকুন *n.* a steward or caretaker of a landed estate.
কারখানা *n.* a workshop, a factory, a mill.
কারখানা-পরিদর্শক *n.* inspector of factories.
কারচুপি *n.* a tricky device; shrewdness.
কারণ *n.* the instrument (of a work), a means; the body; any of the sense organs; cause, reason; motive, purpose; root; seed; the cause or agent or instrument (of an action); origin; wine (when consecrated or considered sacred). □ *con.* because, since, for, as. **~জল, ~বারি** *n.* the water that existed everywhere before the creation of the universe; wine (when consecrated or considered holy). **কারণ দর্শানো** *v.* to show cause. □ *n.* a show-cause or a show-cause notice. **~শরীর** *n.* the body as conceived in the Vedanta. **~সম্বন্ধ** *n.* causal relation. **কারণে** *adv.* due to, owing to; with a view; for the purpose of.
কারণাভাব *n.* absence of cause; (loos.) absence of (adequate) evidence.
কারণিক *a.* pertaining to cause, causal; examining, judging. □ *n.* an examiner; a judge; a clerk.
কারণীভূত *a.* one who or that which has become the cause of; causing; supposed to be or appeared as the cause of.
কারণ্ডব *n.* a species of duck.
কারদানি *n.* a feat; skill; an ostentatious display of skill; bravado.
কারপরদাজ, কারপরদার *n.* an armed attendant or follower.
কারবার *n.* business, trade; profession; calling; working, action; commerce; a business concern, a mercantile concern; (usu. dero.) an affair. **কারবার করা** *v.* to engage in a trade or business; to deal in, to trade in; to trade with; to have commercial transactions (with). **কারবারি** *a.* pertaining to business, trading; commercial. **কারবারি লোক** a businessman, a trader; (dero.) a trafficker.
কারয়িতা *a.* one who or that which makes another do something, causing to do. *fem.* **কারয়িত্রী**।
কারসাজি *n.* trickery, a tricky device; deception; shrewdness; fraud.
কারা[1] *pro. pl.* who, which persons, which people.
কারা[2]**, কারাগার, কারাগৃহ** *n.* a prison, a gaol, a jail. **কারাকক্ষ** *n.* a prison-cell, a prisoner's cell. **কারাদণ্ড** *n.* a sentence of imprisonment, incarceration. **কারাদণ্ড দেওয়া** *v.* to sentence to imprisonment. **বিনাশ্রম কারাদণ্ড** simple imprisonment. **সশ্রম কারাদণ্ড** rigorous imprisonment. **কারাপাল** *n.* a gaoler, a jailor. **কারাবরণ** *n.* imprisonment. **কারাবাস** *n.* duress, imprisonment; prison-life. **কারাবাসী** *a.* imprisoned. □ *n.* a prisoner. **কারামুক্ত** *a.*

released from prison. **কারামুক্তি** *n.* release from prison. **কারারুদ্ধ** *a.* imprisoned. **কারারোধ** *n.* imprisonment.

কারাবা var. of **কার্বা**।

কারি *n.* a spiced soup of vegetables or fish or meat, a curry.

কারিকর var. of **কারিগর**।

কারিকা *n.* any treatise, esp. chronological and other than literary (কায়স্থ-কুলকারিকা) ; a short couplet having various meanings; an artistic work; artistry; workmanship. ☐ *a. fem.* of **কারক**।

কারিকুরি *n.* workmanship; artistry; artistic skill; deftness.

কারিগর *n.* a workman; a worker; an artisan; a handicraftsman; a mechanic; an artist. **কারিগরি** *n.* workmanship; mechanical skill; artistry; artistic skill. ☐ *a.* pertaining to workmanship, or mechanical skill or artistry or artistic skill; pertaining to handicrafts.

কারিত *a.* caused to be done.

কারী *sfx.* indicating: working, causing, doing etc. (হিতকারী). *fem.* **কারিণী**।

কারু *n.* an artisan; a craftsman. ☐ *a.* making, doing, causing. **~কর্ম, ~কলা, ~শিল্প** *n.* crafts, handicraft; artistry; handiwork. **~কর্মী, ~শিল্পী** *n.* a craftsman, an artisan. **~কার্য** *n.* artistic design; artistry. **~সমবায়** *n.* a guild-organization.

কারুণিক *a.* kind; merciful; compassionate.

কারুণ্য *n.* kindness; mercy; compassion.

কার্কশ্য *n.* roughness; harshness; rudeness; cruelty.

কার্টিজ *var.* of **কার্তুজ**।

কার্ড *n.* a card.

কার্তিক *n.* the seventh month of the Bengali calendar (from the middle of October to the middle of November); the name of the god who is the commander-in-chief of heavenly forces; an extremely goodlooking (young) man. **কেলেকার্তিক, নবকার্তিক, লোহার কার্তিক** *n.* (sarcas. or dero.) an extremely ugly man. **কার্তিকী** *a.* of the month of Kartik (কার্তিকী পূর্ণিমা). **কার্তিকেয়** *n.* name of the god who is the commander-in-chief of heavenly forces.

কার্তুজ, কার্তুস *n.* cartridge, cartouche.

কার্নিশ, কার্নিস *n.* a cornice.

কার্পণ্য *n.* niggardliness, miserliness, parsimony.

কার্পাস *n.* cotton; a cotton plant. **কার্পাস বীজ** *n.* cotton seed.

কার্পেট *n.* carpet.

কার্বা *n.* a rose-water spray.

কার্মিক *a.* embroidered; variegated; made, composed.

কার্মুক *n.* a bow. **কার্মুকী** *n.* an archer.

কার্য *n.* (for.) a work, an action; a deed; a duty; a task; a job; an occupation; use, service; ceremony, rite (শ্রাদ্ধকার্য) ; profession, function; a purpose, an object, a motive (কোন কার্যে এসেছ) ; effect, good result, benefit (এতে কোনো কার্য দর্শাবে না). **~কর** *a.* effective; feasible; serviceable. *fem.* **কার্যকরী**। **কার্যকরী সমিতি** *n.* working committee. **~করতা** *n.* effectiveness; feasibility; serviceability. **~কলাপ** *n.* acts and deeds, doings, actions. **~কারণ ভাব** *n.* causality. **~কারণসম্বন্ধ** *n.* causal connection or relation. **~কারিতা** same as **কার্যকরতা**। **~কারী** same as **কার্যকর**। *fem.* **কার্যকারিণী**। **~কাল** *n.* the period during which a work is done; working period, working hours; the period or term of service. **~কুশল** *a.* expert; skilful, adroit; clever. **~ক্রম** *n.* a programme. **~ক্রমে** *adv.* in course of business. **~ক্ষম** *a.* competent; capable or fit for work. **~ক্ষেত্র** *n.* the field of action; the sphere of activities. **~গতিকে** *adv.* on business; by way of business; in course of business. **~চ্যুত** *a.* removed from office, dismissed (from service); cashiered. **~চ্যুতি** *n.* removal from office, dismissal (from service); cashierment. **~তাগে** *adv.* to begin with (used often unnecessarily, in the beginning of the reading matter of a letter or legal deed). **~ত** *adv.* actually, indeed; as a matter of fact. **~দক্ষ** same as **কার্যকুশল**। **~ধারা** *n.* same as **কার্যপদ্ধতি**। **~নির্বাহ** *n.* execution of a work. **~নির্বাহী, ~নির্বাহক** *a.* executing, executive; working (কার্যনির্বাহক সভাপতি). **~নিয়ম** *n.* rules of business. **~নির্বাহী সমিতি** *n.* an executive committee. **~পঞ্জি** *n.* the calendar.

~পদ্ধতি, ~প্রণালী *n.* the mode or process of work, procedure, *modus operandi.* ~পরম্পরা *n.* a regular succession of work. ~বশত *adv.* for the sake of work or business; on business. ~বাহ *n.* proceedings. ~বিবরণ, ~বিবরণী *n.* the report of a work or proceedings. ~বৃত্ত *n.* minutes (of a meeting). ~ব্যপদেশে same as কার্যগতিকে and কার্যবশত। ~ভার *n.* the charge of a task; the burden or pressure of work. ~সমাধা *n.* completion of work. ~সম্পাদন *n.* performance or completion of work. ~সিদ্ধি *n.* accomplishment of a work or task; realization of an end. ~স্থান *n.* a place of work or business. কার্যাকার্য *n.* what ought to be done and what ought not to be done; proper and improper work. কার্যাকার্য বিচার *n.* discrimination between proper and improper work or between right and wrong. কার্যাধ্যক্ষ *n.* a superintendent, a supervisor, an overseer, a manager. কার্যানুরোধে same as কার্যবশত। কার্যান্তর *n.* another work; a different work. কার্যার্থ same as কার্যবশত। কার্যারম্ভ *n.* the beginning of a work; commencement of work or working hours; inauguration of an institution or firm or any similar establishment. কার্যালয় *n.* an office. কার্যোদ্ধার same as কার্যসিদ্ধি।

কার্শ্য *n.* thinness; slimness; leanness.

কার্ষাপণ *n.* ancient value in silver equal to 1280 cowries (কড়ি).

কার্ষ্ণ *a.* pertaining to Lord Krishna (কৃষ্ণ). কার্ষ্ণি *n.* a son of Lord Krishna. কার্ষ্ণ্য *n.* blackness.

কাল[1] *n.* & *adv.* next day; tomorrow; last day; yesterday.

কাল[2] *a.* (dial.) very cold. □ *n.* too much coldness.

কাল[3] *n.* time, period (নিশাকাল, শাসনকাল) ; season (বর্ষাকাল) ; proper time; time, age (একাল) ; leisure (কালাভাব) ; any of the stages of human life (শৈশবকাল, যৌবনকাল, প্রৌঢ়কাল, বৃদ্ধকাল) ; lifetime, span of life, time of existence (কাল পূর্ণ হওয়া) ; Yama (যম) the god of death; death (কালের কবল) ; ruination, ruin, the cause of ruin (মোকদ্দমাই তার কাল হল) ; (gr.) the tense (অতীত কাল = the past tense, বর্তমান কাল = the present tense, ভবিষ্যৎ কাল = the future tense). কাল কাটানো *v.* to pass time. কাল হওয়া *n.* to meet with one's death, to die; to be the ruin of.

কালকবল *n.* the jaws of death. কালকবলিত *a.* (lit.) taken or seized by death; dead. কালকবলিত হওয়া *v.* (lit.) to be taken away or seized by death; to die.

কালকিষ্টি *a.* (coll.) extremely black and dirty or soiled.

কালকূট *n.* a deadly poison (cp. hemlock).

কালকৃত *a.* done in (proper) time; worked or done by time.

কালকে *adv.* & *n.* (coll.) tomorrow; yesterday. কালকের *a.* tomorrow's; yesterday's.

কালক্রমে *adv.* in course of time; after some time.

কালক্ষেপ, কালক্ষেপণ *n.* act of passing time. কালক্ষেপ করা, কালক্ষেপণ করা *v.* to pass time.

কালগঙ্গা *n.* the river Yamuna (যমুনা).

কালগ্রাস *n.* the jaws of death. কালগ্রাসে পতিত হওয়া *v.* to fall or be led into the jaws of death, to die or be killed.

কালঘাম *n.* perspiration at the time of death; perspiration owing to excessive toil. কালঘাম ছোটা *v.* to perspire as if dying; to perspire as at death; to perspire owing to excessive labour.

কালচক্র *n.* the wheel of time; the cycle of season.

কালচিটে, কালচিটা *n.* black or dark stain.

কালচিন্তক *n.* an astrologer.

কালচিহ্ন *n.* sign or symptom of death.

কালচে *a.* blackish; darkish.

কালজ্ঞ *a.* having the power (usu. astrological) to know which is the right or opportune moment for doing anything. □ *n.* such a man; an astrologer. কালজ্ঞান *n.* (astrol.) knowledge that enables one to determine or divine the right or opportune moment for doing anything; astrology.

কালত্রয় *n.* the three ages past, present and future.

কালদণ্ড *n.* the staff of Yama (যম) the god of death; the scourge of death.

কালদৃক *n.* a chronoscope.
কালদ্রষ্টা *n.* one who knows everything about the three ages; omniscient.
কালধর্ম *n.* the spirit or trend of an age, zeitgeist (time-spirit); death as the inevitable final stage of life.
কালনাগ *n.* the black cobra, the cobra. *fem.* **কালনাগিনি**।
কালনিদ্রা *n.* the sleep that never ends, death.
কালনেমি *n.* the name of the maternal uncle of Ravana (রাবণ) of the Ramayana. **কালনেমি মামা** (fig.) a venerable man who is an abettor in wicked deeds, a Devil's counsel. **কালনেমির লঙ্কাভাগ** (fig.) to count the chickens before they are hatched, to build castles in the air.
কালপুরুষ *n.* (myth.) an attendant or envoy of Yama, the god of death; (astr.) the Orion.
কাল পূর্ণ *a.* having one's span of life or existence completed. **কাল পূর্ণ হয়েছে** one's time is up, one's days are numbered, one has not long to live.
কালপেঁচা, কালপ্যাঁচা *n.* the screech-owl; the barn owl; (dero.) an extremely ugly person.
কালপ্রবাহ *n.* efflux of time; influence of an age; (loos.) trend of an age.
কালপ্রভাব *n.* influence of an age.
কালপ্রেরিত *a.* sent by death.
কালফণী same as **কালনাগ**।
কালবিলম্ব *n.* delay; delay for a moment. **কালবিলম্ব না করা** *v.* to refrain from delaying or losing time. **কালবিলম্ব না করে** without delay, without loss of time.
কালবুদ *n.* a boot-last, a boot-tree; a culvert; a mould for constructing an arch, an arch.
কালবেলা *n.* (astro.) an inauspicious part of the day.
কালবৈশাখী *n.* a storm or strong wind that rises in the afternoons of April and May, a nor'wester.
কালবোস *n.* a species of large fresh-water flat fish with blackish scales and reddish eyes, (cp.) the rudd or roach.
কালভৈরব *n.* a furious deity born of Shiva (শিব).
কালমহিমা same as **কালমাহাত্ম্য**।
কালমান *n.* a measure or measurement of time, a chronometer or chronometry.
কালমাহাত্ম্য *n.* influence of the age or time; the distinctive quality of an age.
কালমেঘ *n.* a bitter medicinal plant, *Andrographis paniculata.*
কালযাপন same as **কালক্ষেপ**।
কালরাত্রি *n.* a night on which one's death or danger comes; (astrol.) an inauspicious part of the night.
কালশিরা, কালশিটা, (coll.) **কালশিটে** *n.* lividity of the skin caused by a bruise or hard beating. **মেরে কালশিটে ফেলা** *v.* to beat black and blue.
কালশুদ্ধি *n.* (astrol.) determination of the auspicious parts of the year for doing anything.
কালশোধন *n.* equation of time.
কালসমুদ্র same as **কালসিন্ধু**।
কালসর্প, কালসাপ same as **কালনাগ**।
কালসদৃশ *a.* death-like; deadly.
কালসহ *a.* capable of or resisting wear and tear caused by time, durable, lasting, enduring.
কালসিটে alt. spell. of **কালশিটে**।
কালসিন্ধু *n.* the ocean of time; eternity.
কালসীমা *n.* time limit.
কালস্রোত *n.* the current of time; everflowing time.
কালা[১] *a.* deaf; hard of hearing.
কালা[২] *a.* black; defaced, soiled, dirty, in disrepute, stigmatized (কালা মুখ). □ *n.* an appellation of Krishna (কৃষ্ণ). **~কানুন** a black act. **~বাজার** the black market. **~মুখ** *a.* shamefaced; brazen-faced. □ *n.* a shamefaced man; a brazen-face; a shameful face. **~মুখো** *a.* shamefaced; brazen-faced. □ *n.* a shamefaced man; a brazen-face; a man of soiled reputation. *fem.* **কালামুখী**।
কালাকাল *n.* proper and improper time; auspicious and inauspicious time.
কালাগুরু *n.* dark-coloured sandal.
কালাগ্নি, কালানল *n.* (myth.) the expected divine conflagration which will annihilate the universe, the fire of universal annihilation.
কালাচাঁদ *n.* an appellation of Lord Krishna (কৃষ্ণ).

কালাজ্বর *n.* kala-azar.

কালাতিক্রম, কালাতিক্রমণ, কালাতিপাত same as **কালক্ষেপ।**

কালাতীত *a.* transcending time; perpetual, eternal.

কালাত্যয় *n.* waste or loss or lapse of time.

কালানুগ, কালানুবর্তী, কালানুসারী *a.* timely; in keeping with the spirit of time; drifting with the time. **কালানুগতা, কালানুবর্তিতা, কালানুসারিতা** *n.* timeliness; opportuneness.

কালানো v. (dial.) to get or become extremely cold; to chill. □ *a.* that which has got or become extremely cold; chilled.

কালান্তক *a.* causing universal dissolution; bringing about the end of an age; deadly. □ *n.* an appellation of Yama (যম), the god of death.

কালান্তর *n.* another or a different time or age; transition from one age to another.

কালাপানি *n.* the dark-coloured waters of an ocean or a sea esp. of the Indian Ocean; an ocean, a sea; the Andaman and the Nicobar islands; Port Blair; sentence of transportation from India in the British regime. **কালাপানি ঘুরে আসা** *v.* to have served a sentence of transportation from India. **কালাপানি পার হওয়া** *v.* to go across a sea or an ocean.

কালাপাহাড় *n.* (hist.) a Brahmin who after embracing Islam was turned into a notorious iconoclast; (fig.) an awful religious renegade, a decrier of current beliefs, a turbulent heretic. **কালাপাহাড়ি** *a.* of or like an awful religious renegade or a decrier of current beliefs; heretical. □ *n.* iconoclasm; heresy.

কালাবাজার, কালামুখ see **কালা**[২] ।

কালাশুদ্ধি *n.* (astrol.) the unpropitious part of a year (esp. for religious purposes); an inauspicious time or moment.

কালাশৌচ *n.* the period of mourning that lasts for a year due to the death of any of one's parents or an equally respected kinsman.

কালি[১] obs. & poet. form of **কাল**[১] ।

কালি[২] *n.* ink; darkness, gloom (মনের কালি) ; a dark spot, discoloration (চোখের কালি). □ *a.* stigma, disgrace (কুলের কালি) ; soot, smut (ঝুলকালি). **চোখের কালি** black eye, a black in the eye. **জুতোর কালি** shoe polish. **প্রদীপের কালি** lamp-black. **কালির আঁচড়** (fig.) minimum education or learning. **পেটে কালির আঁচড়ও না থাকা** not to have even the minimum education or learning, to be completely illiterate.

কালি[৩] *n.* summation or addition; measurement (কাঠাকালি, বিঘাকালি) ; cubic measure, square measure, area measure. **কালি করা, কালি কষা** *v.* to find the square measure or cubic measure or area measure of.

কালিক *a.* pertaining to time; of a time; temporal; temporary; timely.

কালিকা *n.* a name of goddess Kali (কালী). **~পুরাণ** *n.* the scripture that narrates the feats of Kalika (কালিকা).

কালিদহ *n.* (myth.) the deep river described as the abode of Kaliya (কালিয় or কালীয়) the serpent in the Yamuna.

কালিঝুলি *n.* soot, smut.

কালিনী[১] *a.* (poet. & obs.) woe-stricken.

কালিনী[২] *n.* poet. & obs. form of **কালিন্দী** ।

কালিন্দী *n.* the river Yamuna (যমুনা).

কালিমা *n.* blackness; darkness, gloom (মনের কালিমা) ; blemish; disrepute, a stigma (চরিত্রের কালিমা). **~ময়** *a.* dark, darkened with stigma; stigmatized; disgraceful, defamed.

কালিয় *n.* (myth.) a terrible serpent living in the river Yamuna. **~দমন** *n.* (myth.) subdual of Kaliya (কালিয়) by Lord Krishna (কৃষ্ণ) ; Lord Krishna.

কালিয়া[১] *n.* a rich curry usu. of fish or meat.

কালিয়া[২] *n.* (poet.) Lord Krishna (কৃষ্ণ).

কালী *n.* an awe-inspiring manifestation of Goddess Durga (দুর্গা) ; (sarcas.) an extremely dark-skinned girl or woman. **~তলা** *n.* a place of worshipping Goddess Kali (কালী) esp. in congregation. **~বাড়ি** *n.* the temple of Goddess Kali.

কালীন, কালীয়[১] *a.* (used as a *sfx.*) of a particular time.

কালীয়[২] alt. spell. of **কালিয়** ।

কালে, কালে কালে *adv.* in course of time, with the passage of time. **কালে ধরা** *v.* to approach one's death, to be in the jaws of death.

কালেকটর, কালেক্টর *n.* the official in charge of the administration and revenue collection of a district, a collector. **কালেকটরি, কালেক্টরি** *n.* collectorate; collectorship.

কালে ভদ্রে *adv.* rarely; seldom, once in a while, once in a blue moon; occasionally, now and then.

কালো *n.* the black colour. ☐ *a.* black. **কালো করা** *v.* to make black, to blacken; to make dark, to darken; to pollute; to defame. **কালো হওয়া** *v.* to become black; to blacken; to become dark, to darken; to become polluted or to be defamed. **কালো পতাকা** *n.* a black flag (usually shown to somebody, as a mark of protest or disapproval). **~বাজার** the black market. **~বাজারি** *n.* a black marketeer.

কালোচিত *a.* befitting the time or age or occasion; timely, opportune; seasonal.

কালোজাম *n.* a kind of small juicy fruit akin to blackberry; a kind of sweetmeat made from curd or posset.

কালোজিরে *n.* black cummin.

কালোমানিক *n.* (attributed endearingly or sarcastically to a very dark-skinned person) a black jewel; Lord Krishna.

কালোয়াত *n.* a man proficient in Indian classical music. **কালোয়াতি** *n.* proficiency in the Indian classical music; (sarcas.) act of parading one's superior knowledge or skill in classical music. **কালোয়াতি করা** *v.* (sarcas.) to parade one's superior knowledge or skill in anything. **কালোয়াতি** *a.* pertaining to Indian classical music or musicians.

কাল্পনিক *a.* imaginary; fanciful; fabricated; fictitious; false.

কাশ[১] *n.* (dial.) cough; expectoration of mucus by coughing, expectoration.

কাশ[২] *n.* a tall species of grass of which mats are made. **~পুষ্প, ~ফুল** *n.* white flower of this grass; catkin.

কাশা *v.* to cough. **কেশে তোলা** *v.* to expectorate by coughing, to expectorate.

কাশি *n.* cough; expectoration of mucus by coughing.

কাশী *n.* Banaras or Varanasi (a holy place of Hindus). **~প্রাপ্তি, ~লাভ** *n.* death at Kashi; attainment of heaven after death. **~বাস** *n.* living in Kashi or Banaras. **~বাসী হওয়া** *v.* become a resident of Kashi; to go to Kashi to live there permanently. **~শ, ~শ্বর** *n.* the lord of Kashi; an appellation of Shiva (শিব), the king of Kashi.

কাশ্মীরি *a.* of Kashmir. ☐ *n.* an inhabitant of Kashmir; a shawl made in Kashmir.

কাশ্যপেয় *n.* a son or descendant of the great sage Kashyapa (কশ্যপ) ; the sun personified; Garuda (গরুড়).

কাষায় *a.* of the colour of red ochre.

কাষ্ঠ *n.* wood; timber. **~কীট** *n.* termite, white ant. **~খণ্ড** *n.* a piece of wood or log. **~পাদুকা** *n.* a (pair of) wooden sandals, a (pair of) clogs. **~পুত্তলিকা** *n.* a wooden doll or puppet; (fig.) a powerless man, a person with no real authority, a figurehead. **~ফলক** *n.* a board; a wooden tablet; a plank of wood. **~বৎ** *a.* (hard and insipid) like wood. **~মঞ্চ** *n.* a wooden platform. **~মণ্ড** *n.* wood-pulp. **~ময়** *a.* wooden; woody. **~মার্জার** *n.* a squirrel. **~ল** *a.* wooden. **~হাসি** *n.* an affected smile (esp. for the sake of courtesy), a simper.

কাষ্ঠাসন *n.* a wooden seat (such as a chair, a stool, a bench etc.).

কাষ্ঠিকা *n.* a slender or thin piece of wood.

কাস alt. spell. of **কাশ**[২] ।

কাসুন *n.* a soup made of mustard-powder.

কাসন্দ var. of **কাসুন্দি** ।

কাসি alt. spell. of **কাশি** ।

কাসীস *n.* sulphate of iron, green vitriol.

কাসুন্দি *n.* a pickle (usu. made of dried slices of green mango) preserved in mustard and salt.

কাস্তে *n.* a sickle, a scythe.

কাহন *n.* a unit or measure of counting (= 1280 pieces).

কাহাকে *pro.* (interro.) whom.

কাহার[১] *pro.* (genit.) whose.

কাহার[২] *n.* palanquin bearers; one of the backward castes amongst the Hindus; one of this caste. *fem.* **কাহারনি** ।

কাহারবা *n.* an Indian musical measure.

কাহিনি, (rej.) **কাহিনী** *n.* a history, a chronicle, annals; an account; an episode; an anecdote; a tale; a story. **~কার** *n.* a story-writer. **~চিত্র** *n.* a feature film.

কাহিল *a.* thin, lean; weak, feeble; weakened, enfeebled.

কি *con. interro.* (used as an auxiliary interrogative word. (তুমি কি যাবে ? = will you go ?); whether (কি বালক কি বৃদ্ধ).

কিংকর alt. spell. of **কিঙ্কর**।

কিংকর্তব্যবিমূঢ় *a.* at a loss to determine what to do, nonplussed, bewildered, perplexed, confounded, at fault. **কিংকর্তব্যবিমূঢ়তা** *n.* nonplus, bewilderment, perplexity, confounded state, quandary.

কিংকিণি, কিংকিণী alt. spellings of **কিঙ্কিণি**।

কিংখাপ, কিংখাব *n.* brocade.

কিংবদন্তি, কিংবদন্তী *n.* a traditional or familiar report or rumour; hearsay.

কিংবা *conj.* or; on the other hand; or, alternatively.

কিংশুক *n.* a variety of very beautiful but scentless red flower (cp. guelder-rose).

কিঙ্কর *n.* a servant; a slave; an attendant, a follower, *fem.* **কিঙ্করী**।

কিঙ্কিণি, কিঙ্কিণী *n.* a girdle or an anklet set with small bells jingling sweetly at every movement.

কিচকিচ[1], **কিচমিচ**[1] *int.* expressing: presence of abundant grit; a grating noise caused as if by chewing grit.

কিচকিচ[2], **কিচমিচ**[2], **কিচিরমিচির** *int.* & *n.* the tweeting or chirping noise of birds etc., loud prattling or babble. **কিচকিচ করা, কিচমিচ করা, কিচিরমিচির করা** *v.* to tweet; to chirp; to prattle or babble noisily.

কিচ্ছু an emphatic form of **কিছু**।

কিছু *a.* a small number or amount of, some. ☐ *pro.* anything (আমি কিছুর মধ্যে নেই). ☐ *adv.* of course (সে এখনই কিছু যাচ্ছে না). **একটা কিছু** *pro.* anything; a certain thing, something. ☐ *a.* a certain, some. **কিছু কিছু** *a.* a small number or amount of, some. ☐ *pro.* & *n.* a portion. ☐ *adv.* to some extent. **কিছুতে** *adv.* in any way, by any means, anyhow. ☐ *pro.* (in or by) anything (কিছুতে অভাব মিটবে না) ; to anything. **কিছুতেই না** by no means. **কিছু না** nothing. **কিছু না কিছু** something or other; at least something. **কিছু পরিমাণ** *n.* some amount (of).

কিঞ্চিৎ *a.* small amount of, a little. **কিঞ্চিদধিক** *a.* a little more than. **কিঞ্চিদপি** *adv.* only a little. **কিঞ্চিদুষ্ণ** *a.* lukewarm; tepid. **কিঞ্চিদূন** *adv.* a little less than. **কিঞ্চিন্মাত্র** *a.* & *n.* only a little; even a little; a little. ☐ *adv.* to the least degree; at all.

কিঞ্জল, কিঞ্জলক *n.* the stamen or the filament of a flower; pollen.

কিটকিট *n.* see **খিটখিট**।

কিট্ট *n.* dregs; excrement.

কিড়মিড়, কিড়িমিড়ি *int* expressing: the sound of grinding or gnashing one's teeth. **দাঁত কিড়মিড় করা** to grind or gnash one's teeth.

কিণ *n.* a grazing mark; a hardness in an area of the skin caused by (frequent) friction, a corn; a dried-up pimple. **কিণাঙ্কিত** *a.* containing a grazing mark or a corn or a dried-up pimple.

কিণ্ব *n.* leaven, ferment; sin.

কিতব *n.* a deceiver, a cheat, a chicaner; a swindler, a gambler; a gamester.

কিতা *n.* a piece (এক কিতা জমি বা কাগজ) ; a volume (এক কিতা বই) ; a bundle (এক কিতা নোট) ; a packet; a lot (এক কিতা মাল) ; (now rare) manner, custom (মুসলমানি কিতা) ; fashion, etiquette.

কিতাব var. of **কেতাব**।

কিনা[1] older var. of **কেনা**।

কিনা[2], **কি না** *adv.* whether or not, if (সে যাবে কি না ঠিক নেই) ; a meaningless word, used to emphasize or sweeten one's speech (বুঝলে কিনা).

কিনার *n.* border, edge (চোখের কিনার) ; a bank or shore; outskirts (গ্রামের কিনার, শহরের কিনার, বাড়ির কিনার). **নদীর কিনার** riverside, river-bank. **পথের কিনার** roadside. **সমুদ্রের কিনার** seaside, sea-shore, coast.

কিনারা *n.* border; edge (চোখের কিনারা) ; a bank or shore; outskirts (গ্রামের কিনারা, শহরের কিনারা, বাড়ির কিনারা) ; arrangements; remedy, measure, redress, removal, reparation (দুঃখের কিনারা, বিপদের

কিনারা) ; solution (সমস্যার কিনারা) ; trace (হারানো টাকার কিনারা) ; solution or discovery or detection by investigation (চুরির কিনারা) ; decision, settlement (মোকদ্দমার কিনারা). **কিনারা করা** *v.* to arrange for; to make arrangements for the provision of; to remedy, to redress, to remove, to repair; to solve; to trace; to solve or discover or detect by investigation; to decide; to settle. **নদীর কিনারা** riverside, river-bank. **পথের কিনারা** roadside. **মনের কিনারা** depth of one's mind. **সমুদ্রের কিনারা** seaside, sea shore, coast.

কিন্তু *con.* & *adv.* but; notwithstanding; nevertheless; however; still; on the other hand. ☐ *a.* hesitating, hesitant (কিন্তু ভাব). **কিন্তু করা** *v.* to hesitate; to demur; to cherish doubt; to be shy of. **কিন্তু কিন্তু** *n.* hesitation. ☐ *a.* hesitating, hesitant. **কিন্তু ভাব** *n.* hesitating attitude or state, hesitancy.

কিন্নর *n.* (myth.) one of a class of demigods expert in music and dance. *fem.* **কিন্নরী** ।

কিপটা, (coll.) **কিপটে** *a.* close-fisted, niggardly, miserly. **কিপটেমি** *n.* close-fistedness, niggardliness, miserliness.

কিফায়ত *n.* a cut in expenditure; reduction of expenditure; cheapness; profit, gain.

কিবা *con.* or *adv.* how (কিবা মনোহর). ☐ *a.* how beautiful; (dero.) how awkward, how ugly (কিবা ভঙ্গি). ☐ *n.* what else (কিবা তুমি বলবে).

কিমত pop. var. of **কিম্মত** ।

কিমা *n.* minced meat.

কিমাকার *a.* (lit.) of what shape or form; (used as a correlative of কিম্ভূত) of ugly or hereto unseen shape or form.

কিমিতি, কিমিয়া *n.* chemistry; alchemy.

কিম্পুরুষ *n.* a Kinnar (কিন্নর) ; (myth.) a province of ancient India or a country in the neighbourhood of India.

কিম্বা inc. spell. of **কিংবা** ।

কিম্ভূত *a.* (lit.) of what form or shape, (pop.) queer, strange, odd, grotesque, antic. **~কিমাকার** *a.* of strange and ugly form or shape, grotesquely shaped or formed, monstrous. **~কিমাকার প্রাণী বা বস্তু** an antic; a monstrosity.

কিম্মত *n.* price; worth, value.

কিয়ৎ *a.* a small amount or number of, a little, a few. **~কাল** *n.* a short while.

কিয়দ্দিন *n.* a few days. ☐ *adv.* for a few days.

কিয়দ্দূর *n.* a short distance. ☐ *adv.* to a short distance. **কিয়দ্দূরে** *adv.* a short distance away, not far off.

কিয়ামত var. of **কেয়ামত** ।

কিরকির a milder form of **করকর** ।

কিরকিরা, কিরকিরে *a.* full of grains of sand, gritty.

কিরণ *n.* a ray or beam or gleam (of light). **কিরণ দেওয়া** *v.* to emit rays, to send forth rays; to radiate, to shine. **~চ্ছটা** *n.* the glow of rays. **~জাল** *n.* the mesh of rays. **~পাত, ~বর্ষণ** *n.* shedding of rays, radiation. **~পাত করা, ~বর্ষণ করা** *v.* to shed or emit rays, to radiate. **কিরণ বিকিরণ** *n.* radiation. **কিরণ বিকিরণ করা** *v.* to radiate. **~ময়,** (inc.) **কিরণ্ময়** *a.* full of rays, emitting rays, radiant. *fem.* **কিরণময়ী,** (inc.) **কিরণ্ময়ী** । **~মালী** *n.* the sun (for it is garlanded with rays). **~সম্পাত** same as **কিরণপাত** ।

কিরবানি *n.* a mode of Indian classical music.

কিরা *n.* an oath, a swearing. **কিরা দেওয়া** *v.* to enjoin by uttering an oath.

কিরাত *n.* one of an uncivilized race of ancient India who lived by hunting; the province of ancient India inhabited by the Kiratas (কিরাত), the land of Kiratas. *fem.* **কিরাতিনী** ।

কিরিচ *n.* a kris, a falchion.

কিরীট n. a crown, a coronet, a diadem. **কিরীটী** *a.* wearing a crown or diadem, coroneted; crested. ☐ *n.* an appellation of Arjuna (অর্জুন) of the Mahabharata. *fem. a.* **কিরীটিনী** ।

কিরূপ, কীরূপ *a.* of what sort. **কিরূপে, কীরূপে** *adv.* in what manner or way, by what means, how.

কিরে coll. corrup. of **কিরা** ।

কি রে *int.* used in addressing or questioning a person (কি রে কী খবর ? কি রে খাবি নাকি ?).

কিল *n.* a fist; a blow with the fist esp. with the side of the fist, **কিল খেয়ে কিল**

চুরি করা to take a beating or insult silently and without retaliation, to endure humiliation or affront without protest, to pocket an insult. **কিল মারা** *v.* to strike with the fist, to fist. **কিলাকিলি** *n.* fighting with fists; fisticuffs, blows and counterblows. **কিলানো** same as **কিল মারা**। **কিলিয়ে কাঁঠাল পাকানো** to make a futile attempt at correcting or subduing a person by overmuch beating or chastisement; to spoil a person or hinder his natural development by excessive interference; to try to do the impossible by injudicious or rash means. **কিল মারার গোঁসাই** an over-assertive person or master who has no competence to maintain his dependents.

কিলকিল, কিলবিল *int.* expressing: movement in a swarm (of fish esp. small ones, worms etc.). **কিলকিল করা, কিলবিল করা** *v.* to move in a swarm, to swarm; swimming to and fro (of fish) in shoals.

কিলো *n.* a unit of weight, kilogram.

কিশতি, কিস্তি *n.* a boat, a barge; (in chess) a check; an instalment (for payment etc.); a time, an occasion. **কিস্তি দেওয়া** *v.* (in chess) to check. **~বন্দি** *n.* arrangement of payment by instalments. **~মাত** *n.* (in chess) a complete check, (inc.) checkmate.

কিশমিশ *n.* raisin, currant.

কিশলয় *n.* a green and tender leaf of a tree; a young shoot with such leaves.

কিশোর *a.* adolescent; teenaged. □ *n.* an adolescent boy, an adolescent; a teenager; a lad. *fem.* **কিশোরী**। **~বয়স্ক** *a.* adolescent; teenaged.

কিষান var. of **কৃষান**। **কিষান সংগঠন** a peasant organization.

কিষ্কিন্ধ্যা, কিষ্কিন্ধা *n.* the land of the monkeys as described in the Ramayana.

কিসম *n.* variety, kind, type.

কিসমত *n.* luck, lot; destiny.

কিসমিস alt. spell. of **কিশমিশ**।

কিসলয় alt. spell. of **কিশলয়**।

কিসিম var. of **কিসম**।

কিসে, কীসে *pro.* (in Eng. *adv.*) from what; what for, why; by what or which; in which way or manner, how; by what or which means; in what or which. **কীসে আর কীসে** what a comparison to draw or make; comparing things opposed in character.

কিসের, কীসের *pro.* (genit.) of or for what or which; in what respect (implying: in no respect or at all) (কীসের গরিব সে?) ; causeless, useless, pointless (কীসের দুঃখ, কীসের দৈন্য)

কিস্তি alt. spell. of **কিশতি**।

কী *pro.* (interrogative) what, which (কী খাবে ?) ; nothing (ও আবার কী বলবে ?) ; a thing or an amount (জীবনে কত কী ঘটবে, কত কী দেখলাম). **কী করে ?** *adv.* how, in what way. **কীজন্য ?** *adv.* why, what for. **কী প্রকারে, কীভাবে** same as **কী করে**। *exclam.* how (কী সুন্দর ! how beautiful!)

কীচক *n.* a variety of hollow bamboo which whistles with the wind; the name of the giantlike brother-in-law and commander-in-chief of Virata (বিরাট) who was killed by Bhima (ভীম) and turned into a rounded heap as described in the Mahabharata. **কীচক বধ** *n.* killing of or like Keechaka (কীচক), beating to a mummy.

কীট *n.* a worm; an insect. **~ঘ্ন** *a.* insecticidal. **~ঘ্ন পদার্থ** an insecticide. **~জ** *a.* born of worms; spun by worms. **~তত্ত্ব, ~বিদ্যা** *n.* entomology. **~তাত্ত্বিক, ~বিদ** *n.* an entomologist. **~দষ্ট** *a.* worm-eaten; moth-eaten. **~ভুক** *a.* insectivorous, entomophagous. **~ভুক প্রাণী** an insectivore. **~পতঙ্গ** *n. pl.* worms and insects. **কীটাণু** *n.* a microscopic worm or insect, a microbe. **কীটাণুকীট** *n.* a worm or insect even smaller than a microbe; (fig.) a very insignificant person.

কীদৃক্, কীদৃশ *a.* like or resembling what; of what sort or variety. *fem.* **কীদৃশী**।

কীর্ণ *a.* scattered or strewn here and there; pervaded; extended or spread over.

কীর্তক *n.* a narrator; a celebrator, a celebrant; a singer of the names of God; a singer of songs about Radha (রাধা) and Krishna (কৃষ্ণ).

কীর্তন *n.* narration (যশঃকীর্তন) ; glorification; celebration, extolment; act of singing in praise; a song in praise; act of singing the names of God; any of the songs about Radha (রাধা) and Krishna (কৃষ্ণ) or act of singing these songs. **কীর্তন করা, কীর্তন গাওয়া** *v.* to sing songs about Radha (রাধা) and Krishna (কৃষ্ণ) ; to narrate; to glorify; to celebrate, to extol; to sing in praise; to sing the names of God. **কীর্তনাঙ্গ** *n.* any of the modes of singing songs about Radha (রাধা) and Krishna (কৃষ্ণ). **কীর্তনীয়** *a.* worthy of being narrated or celebrated; praiseworthy. **কীর্তনীয়া,** (coll.) **কীর্তনে** *n.* a singer of songs about Radha (রাধা) and Krishna (কৃষ্ণ). ☐ *a.* singing those songs.

কীর্তি *n.* fame, renown, celebrity; a glorious performance or achievement or deed or feat. **~কলাপ** *n. pl.* glorious deeds or achievements; exploits; activities. **~ধ্বজা** *n.* the standard of fame. **~বাস, ~মান** *a.* famous, renowned, celebrated, glorified. **~স্তম্ভ** *n.* a monument.

কীর্তিত *a.* narrated; celebrated, extolled; glorified; sung.

কীর্যমাণ *a.* (that which is) being thrown or hurled.

কীল, কীলক *n.* a bolt; a peg; a stake; a wedge; a nail; a probe. **কীলকাকার** *a.* wedge-shaped, cuneal, cuneate; (of alphabetical letters) cuneiform, cuneatic. **কীলকলিপি** *n.* cuneiform writing.

কু *n.* a sin; a guilt; a fault; an evil; the earth; exposition of the scriptures ('কু-কথায় পঞ্চমুখ'). ☐ *a.* (chiefly used as a *pfx.*) bad, evil, indecent (কুকথা) ; ill-omened; wicked (কুমন্ত্রণা) ; unattainable (কু-আশা) ; southern (কুমেরু).

কুইনিন, কুইনাইন *n.* quinine.

কুংফু *n.* a chinese style of karate, kung fu.

কুঁইকুঁই *int.* expressing: the suppressed groaning sound of distress caused by hunger, cold, pain etc. **কুঁইকুঁই করা** *v.* to utter this sound, to groan.

কুঁকড়া, (coll.) **কুঁকড়ো** ☐ *n.* the cock; (loos.) the hen or the cock. *fem.* **কুঁকড়ি** the hen.

কুঁকড়ানো *v.* to shrink or cause to shrink; to shrivel or cause to shrivel; to recoil or cause to recoil. *a.* shrunk; shrivelled; recoiled.

কুঁকড়ি-সুকড়ি *a.* shrunk or contracted into a circular shape (chiefly due to cold). **কুঁকড়ি-সুকড়ি হওয়া** *v.* to shrink or contract as though into a lump or into a circular shape.

কুঁকড়ি, কুঁকড়ো see **কুঁকড়া।**

কুঁচ *n.* a very small and red-coloured stony fruit with a black patch on the top, *Abrus precalorius*; this is used as a measure of weight esp. by jewellers.

কুঁচকানো *v.* to contract, to shrink; to shrivel. ☐ *a* contracted; shrunk; shrivelled. **ভুরু কুঁচকানো** *v.* to contract one's eyebrows; to knit one's brows; to frown.

কুঁচকি *n.* the groin.

কুঁচানো *v.* to crimp; to rumple. ☐ *a.* crimp; rumpled.

কুঁচি *n.* a small broom or besom; a brush; a bristle.

কুঁচিয়া older var. of **কুঁচে।**

কুঁচিলা var. of **কুচিলা।**

কুঁচে *n.* a variety of fish akin to the eel.

কুঁজ *n.* a hunch, a hump. **কুঁজো** *a.* hunch-backed, humpbacked. ☐ *n.* a hunchback, a humpback. *fem.* **কুঁজি।**

কুঁজড়া, (coll.) **কুঁজড়ো** *a.* quarrelsome; wrangling; crooked; spiteful. **কুঁজড়োপনা, কুঁজড়ামি** *n.* quarrelsomeness; wrangling disposition; crookedness; spitefulness.

কুঁজি see **কুঁজ।**

কুঁজুড়িয়া older var. of **কুঁজড়া।**

কুঁজো see **কুঁজ** amd **কুজো।**

কুঁড়া *n.* the powdery crust of rice beneath the husk, bran, rice-dust.

কুঁড়াজালি *n.* a small fishing-net; a small pouch made of cloth for holding a Vaishnava's rosary.

কুঁড়ি[১] *n.* correlative of **হাঁড়ি** indicating plurality and variety (হাঁড়িকুঁড়ি).

কুঁড়ি[২] *n.* a bud.

কুঁড়িয়া obs. var. of **কুঁড়ে।**

কুঁড়ে[১] *n.* a (usu. small) thatched hut; a poorly made hut, a hovel, a shanty.

কুঁড়ে[2] *a.* idle, lazy, slothful. ~মি *n.* idleness, laziness, sloth.

কুঁড়ো coll. form of কুঁড়া।

কুঁড়োজালি pop. form of কুঁড়াজালি।

কুঁতা, কুঁথা *v.* to strain oneself for evacuating one's bowels; to strain oneself to collect one's strength; to groan. □ *n.* act of straining for evacuating one's bowels, tenesmus; act of straining oneself to collect one's strength; act of groaning. কুঁতানো, কুঁথানো *v.* to strain or cause to strain for evacuating one's bowels; to strain or cause to strain oneself to collect one's strength; to groan or cause to groan.

কুঁদ *n.* a (turner's) lathe; a variety of multi-petalled jasmine.

কুঁদন, কোঁদন *n.* act of turning (a thing) on a lathe; act of carving; act of rushing forward to attack or beat; act of skipping or frisking; act of bragging.

কুঁদ[1] *v.* to turn (a thing) on a lathe, to shape by turning on a lathe; to carve; to rush forward to attack or beat; to skip, to frisk; to brag.

কুঁদ[2] *n.* a stock or butt (of a gun); a stump or trunk (of a tree); a log (of wood); a lump (of sugar etc.).

কুঁদুলি *a. fem.* quarrelsome; spiteful. □ *n. fem.* a quarrelsome or spiteful woman or girl. *masc.* কুঁদুলে।

কুকথা *n.* foul or abusive words, indecent or filthy language, obscene talk, ribaldry; (rare) philosophical truths or discussion about the earth; (rare) exposition or explanation of scriptures esp. of the esoteric text of the scriptures.

কুকরি *n.* a short dagger, a stiletto.

কুকর্ম, কুকার্য *n.* a wicked act; a sinful act; a blameable act; a mischief. ~কারী, কুকর্মা *a.* given to doing wicked or sinful or blameable act; given to mischief-making. □ *n.* a performer of a wicked or blameable act; a sinner; a mischief-maker, an evil-doer. কুকর্মান্বিত, কুকর্মাসক্ত *a.* given to doing wicked or sinful or blameable act. কুকর্মী *a.* same as কুকর্মকারী। □ *n.* a performer of a wicked or blameable act; a sinner; a mischief-maker; a bungler; a botcher.

কুকাজ coll. form of কুকর্ম and কুকার্য।

কুকীর্তি *n.* misdeed; immoral act; a wicked act; a mischief.

কুকুর *n.* the dog. *fem.* কুকুরী the bitch. ~কুণ্ডলী *n.* the manner of lying down in a coil as a dog. ~কুণ্ডলী হওয়া *v.* to crouch or lie like a dog. ~ছানা *n.* the puppy (of a dog), the pup. কুকুরে-গোঁ *n.* doggedness. কুকুরে-দাঁত *n.* the canine tooth (of a human being). কুকুরের ঘর বা বাসা *a.* kennel. যেমন কুকুর তেমনি মুগুর (fig.) the right whip for the right dog, condign punishment.

কুক্কুট *n.* the cock. *fem.* কুক্কুটী the hen. ~ধ্বনি *n.* a cock's crow.

কুক্রিয় *a.* given to evil deeds or bad practices; wrong-doing; depraved. কুক্রিয়া *n.* an evil deed; a bad practice; depravity. কুক্রিয়ান্বিত, কুক্রিয়াসক্ত *a.* given to evil ways.

কুক্ষণ *n.* an inauspicious point of time, an evil hour, a bad or unfortunate moment.

কুক্ষি *n.* the pit of the belly or abdomen; the womb; a cave; the interior. ~গত *a.* entered into the belly; lying in the belly or the womb or a cave; lying inside, interior; (fig.) completely seized or appropriated, under absolute control.

কুখাদ্য *n.* uneatable or forbidden food; food that is not fit for human consumption.

কুখ্যাত *a.* notorious; infamous. কুখ্যাতি *n.* notoriety; infamy.

কুগঠন *n.* a misshaped or uncouth figure. □ *a.* misshaped; uncouth; shabby.

কু গাওয়া *n.* foreboding, presaging an omen or a portent. □ *v.* to forebode an evil omen or a portent.

কুগ্রহ *n.* (astrol.) an unfavourable star, an evil star; (fig.) an object of trouble, a pest, a plague.

কুঙ্কুম *n.* saffron; the safflower.

কুচ[1] *n.* either of the mammary glands in a woman, (either of) a woman's breasts.

কুচ[2] *n.* military march. ~কাওয়াজ *n.* military parade.

কুচ৩ expressing : the sound of cutting off with one stroke of a very sharp implement; the sound of piercing suddenly with the very pointed edge of an implement.

কুচকুচ১ *int.* expressing: glaze or brightness of the black colour. **কুচকুচে** *a.* (of the black colour) glazy or bright and deep. **কুচকুচে কালো করা** *v.* to make glazily or brightly black, to japan.

কুচকুচ২ a milder sound than **কচকচ**।

কুচক্কুরে coll. corrup. of **কুচক্রী**।

কুচক্র *n.* conspiracy, a plot; a ring of conspirators or bad men. **কুচক্রী** *a.* conspiring, plotting. □ *n.* a conspirator, a plotter, an intriguer, a schemer.

কুচনি *n. fem.* of **কোচ ;** a prostitute, a harlot.

কুচন্দন *n.* red sandal.

কুচফল *n.* the pomegranate.

কুচমুখ *n.* same as **কুচাগ্র**।

কুচরিত্র *n.* bad or vile character or conduct; immorality. □ *a.* possessing bad or vile character or conduct, wicked; immoral. *fem.* **কুচরিত্রা**।

কুচর্যা *n.* abominable behaviour; an evil practice; an evil custom.

কুচা *n.* a small piece or fragment, a chip, a slice, a slip. coll. **কুচো**।

কুচাগ্র *n.* a nipple, a pap, a teat.

কুচানো *v.* to cut into minute pieces, to chop fine. □ *a.* cut into minute pieces, chopped fine, minced.

কুচাল *n.* bad conduct or manners; an astute or shrewd or wicked move.

কুচি১ var. of **কুঁচি**।

কুচি২ *n.* a very small piece or fragment, a chip.

কুচিকিৎসক *n.* an unskilled or inexperienced physician, a bad physician; a medical quack, a quacksalver.

কুচিকিৎসা *n.* bad or faulty medical treatment; medical quackery.

কুচিন্তা *n.* worry; an evil thought or design.

কুচিলা *n.* nux vomica.

কুচুক্করে coll. form of **কুচক্রী**।

কুচুটে, (obs.) **কুচুটিয়া** *a.* malicious; spiteful; jealous; having angularity in character, crooked; intriguing.

কুচুৎ a milder form of **কচাৎ**।

কুচুরমুচুর a milder form of **কচরমচর**।

কুচেষ্টা *n.* a bad or futile attempt; an evil attempt or design.

কুচোকাচা *n. pl.* odds and ends; kiddies.

কুচোচিংড়ি *n.* a shrimp.

কুচোনো coll. form of **কুচানো**।

কুচ্ছা, কুচ্ছ coll. corruptions of **কুৎসা**।

কুচ্ছিত coll. corrup. of **কুৎসিত**।

কুজ *n.* (astro.) the Mars.

কুজড়া, কুজড়ো variants of **কুঁজড়া** and **কুঁজড়ো** respectively.

কুজন *n.* a bad man, a wicked fellow.

কুজা, কুঁজা older variants of **কুজো** and **কুঁজো**।

কুজুড়িয়া var. of **কুঁজুড়িয়া**।

কুজো, (pop.) **কুঁজো** *n.* a pitcher with a long and narrow neck.

কুজ্ঝটি, কুজ্ঝটিকা, কুজ্ঝটী *n.* fog, mist. **কুজ্ঝটিকাময়** *a.* overcast with fog or mist, foggy, misty. **কুজ্ঝটিকাচ্ছন্ন** *a.* enveloped in fog or mist, foggy, misty.

কুজ্ঞান *n.* harmful thought or design; craftiness; evil intention.

কুঞ্চন *n.* curling; shrinking; wrinkling, shrivelling, wizening; contraction; curving, curvature; a curl; shrinkage; a wrinkling; a curve.

কুঞ্চি *n.* a measure of grains (= 8 handfuls).

কুঞ্চিকা *n.* a very red-coloured stony fruit with a black patch on the top; a thin twig of bamboo; a slip of bamboo; a key; an index, a table or list of contents; a variety of fish akin to the eel.

কুঞ্চিত *a.* curled, curling (কুঞ্চিত কেশ) ; shrunk; wrinkled, shrivelled, wizen; contracted; curved. **কুঞ্চিত করা, কুঞ্চিত হওয়া** *v.* to curl; to shrink; to wrinkle, to shrivel, to wizen ; to contract; to curve.

কুঞ্জ১ *n.* an arbour, a grove, a bower; (loos.) a garden thick with trees and plants; a boscage (also **কুঞ্জকানন, কুঞ্জবন**) ; a garden house where a Vaishnava resides and worships (also **কুঞ্জবাটিকা, কুঞ্জবাটী**).

কুঞ্জ২ *n.* decorative embroidery in the borders of a sari (শাড়ি), shawl etc. **~দার** *a.* embroidered.

কুঞ্জর *n.* the elephant; (as a *sfx.*) the best one (নরকুঞ্জর = the best of men,). *fem.* **কুঞ্জরা, কুঞ্জরী** ।

কুঞ্জি *n.* a key.

কুট[1] *int.* expressing the imaginary sound of a small bite as by an ant.

কুট[2] *n.* a fort, a fortress; a hill; a tree.

কুটকুট *int.* expressing repeated inflammatory itching sensation. **কুটকুট করা** *v.* to feel or cause to feel repeated itching sensation. **কুটকুটানি, কুটকুটুনি** *n.* repeated inflammatory itching sensation, tingling sensation. **কুটকুটে** *a.* causing or full of repeated inflammatory itching or tingling sensation.

কুটজ *n.* a medicinal flower-plant usu. grown on hillsides.

কুটনা *n.* vegetable chopped or to be chopped into pieces for cooking. **কুটনা কোটা** *v.* to cut or chop vegetables into pieces for cooking, to dress vegetables.

কুটনী *n. fem.* a female pander; a procuress, a pimp, a bawd. **~গিরি** *n.* the profession of the female pander or procuress, bawdry.

কুটনো coll. form of **কুটনা** ।

কুট্‌মল *n.* a bud.

কুটা[1] older form of **কুটো** ।

কুটা[2] older var. of **কোটা**[1] ।

কুটি *n.* straw chopped fine; a bit of this straw, a small chip of straw. **~কুটি** *a.* cut into very small bits; minced; torn into shreds; beside oneself (হেসে কুটিকুটি হওয়া). **কুটিকুটি করা** *v.* to cut into very small bits; to mince; to tear into shreds. **হেসে কুটিকুটি (কুটিপাটি) হওয়া** *v.* to be beside oneself with laughter, to be convulsed with laughter; to split one's sides (with laughter).

কুটিনী falsely elegant form of **কুটনী** ।

কুটির *n.* a hut, a cottage; (usu. in politeness) a humble abode. **~বাসী** *n.* a cottager. *fem.* **~বাসিনী** । **~শিল্প** *n.* cottage industry.

কুটিল *a.* bent, curved; tortuous, zigzag; crooked; insincere, hypocritical, deceitful, dissimulating (কুটিলচরিত্র, কুটিলচিত্ত, কুটিলস্বভাব) ; complicated (কুটিল প্রশ্ন). *fem.* **কুটিলা** । **~গামী** *a.* going tortuously or in a zigzag manner; following a crooked path. **~তা** *n.* the bent state, curvedness, tortuosity, tortuousness; crookedness; angularity (চরিত্রের কুটিলতা) ; insincerity, hypocrisy, deceitfulness, dissimulation. **~রেখা** *n.* a curved line, a curve. **কুটিলান্তঃকরণ** *a.* crooked at heart, having a crooked heart.

কুটুম্ব, (coll.) **কুটুম** *n.* a kinsman, a kindred; a relative (esp. allied by matrimony); one's dependants; one's family. **কুটুম্বী** *a.* having kinsmen and relatives; having dependants or a family. □ *n.* a house-holder. **কুটুম্বিনী** *a. fem.* of **কুটুম্ব** । □ *n. fem.* a housewife esp. one having her husband and children; a kinswoman; a female relative. **কুটুম্বিতা** *n.* kinship; relationship; matrimonial alliance; formalities required to be exhibited where matrimonial alliance exists.

কুটুর a milder form of **কুট** । **কুটুর কুটুর** *int.* repeated sounds of a small animal (like the rat or the squirrel) biting and cutting things with its tiny teeth.

কুটো *n.* (a piece of) straw, a bit of straw.

কুট্টন *n.* act of cutting or chopping esp. into pieces; act of digging; act of pounding or squeezing; act of censuring or blaming or abusing.

কুট্টনী *n.* a female pander; a procuress, a bawd, a pimp.

কুট্টিত *a.* cut or chopped esp. into pieces; pounded; squeezed; censured; blamed; abused.

কুট্টিম *n.* a terrace; a paved or cemented floor (গৃহকুট্টিম) ; a mine of precious stones.

কুষ্ঠ *n.* leprosy. **কুষ্ঠে** (coll.) *a.* (of a person) suffering from leprosy. □ *n.* a leper.

কুঠরি *n.* a small room, a chamber, a compartment, a cabin, a cubicle.

কুঠার *n.* an axe, a hatchet. **কুঠারিকা** *n.* a small axe.

কুঠি *n.* an office or the head office of a business organization (নীলকুঠি) ; a house, a building; a bungalow; an official residence of a high-ranking government officer (ম্যাজিসট্রেটের কুঠি). **কুঠিয়াল** *n.* the owner or the manager of a factory or a business organization; a factor; a merchant.

কুঠিয়া *a.* leprous. ☐ *n.* a leper.

কুঠুরি var. of **কুঠরি**।

কু ডাকা same as **কু গাওয়া**।

কুড় *n.* a medicinal plant; a measure of land (= ·33 acre or ·13 hectare approx.) a heap (পাঁশকুড়) ; a slit, a hole; a place for depositing, a depository (আঁস্তাকুড়).

কুড়কুড় *int.* expressing the sound of chewing crisp things. **কুড়কুড় করা** *v.* to give out or make this sound.

কুড়চি *n.* a medicinal flower-plant usu. grown on hillsides.

কুড়বা *n.* an obsolete measure of land (=·33 acre or ·13 hectare approx.).

কুড়মুড় var. of **কুড়কুড়**।

কুড়ানি *n. fem.* one who draws together and picks up what is lying scattered (পাতাকুড়ানি).

কুড়ানো *v.* to draw together (what is lying scattered), to gather, to collect; to glean; to pick up; to sweep (ঘর কুড়ানো). ☐ *a.* drawn together, gathered, collected; gleaned; picked up; swept. **কুড়ানো শিশু, কুড়িয়ে পাওয়া শিশু** a foundling.

কুড়াল, কুড়ালি *n.* an axe.

কুড়ি *n.* & *a.* twenty.

কুড়ুনি corrup. of **কুড়ানি**।

কুড়ুল coll. corrup. of **কুড়াল**।

কুড়ে var. of **কুঁড়ে**।

কুড্মল alt. spell. of **কুট্মল**।

কুণ্ঠ *n.* (chiefly used as a *sfx.*) disinclined to, unwilling, reluctant, afraid of, shy, recoiling (কর্মকুণ্ঠ, শ্রমকুণ্ঠ, ব্যয়কুণ্ঠ) ; hesitating; different; feeling delicacy. **কুণ্ঠা** *n.* hesitation, hesitancy; diffidence; feeling of delicacy; shyness; fear; recoil. **কুণ্ঠাবোধ করা** *v.* to feel delicacy; to feel shy; to hesitate. **কুণ্ঠিত** *a.* stricken with hesitation or diffidence; hesitating; feeling delicacy; feeling shy; shy; abashed; disinclined to, unwilling; reluctant, afraid of; recoiling from. *fem.* **কুণ্ঠিতা**। **কুণ্ঠিত হওয়া** *v.* to be stricken with hesitation or diffidence; to hesitate; to feel delicacy; to feel shy; to be abashed; to be disinclined to, to be unwilling or reluctant, to be afraid of; to recoil from.

কুণ্ড *n.* a hole, a cavity (নাভিকুণ্ড, হোমকুণ্ড) ; a tank or lake or basin etc. (সীতাকুণ্ড) ; a round and shallow receptacle (তাম্রকুণ্ড).

কুণ্ডল *n.* an ornament for the ear, an earring; a bangle; an annular ornament or knot; a collection. **কুণ্ডলিত** *a.* rolled or twisted into a coil, coiled. **কুণ্ডলিত নীহারিকা** spiral nebula. **কুণ্ডলিনী** *n.* the female vital force latent in a creature according to scriptures; the female snake. **কুণ্ডলী** *a.* wearing an earring. ☐ *n.* any annular object. **কুণ্ডলী পাকানো** *v.* to twist into a coil.

কুত *n.* toll. **~ঘর** *n.* a toll-house on a waterway. **~ঘাট, ~ঘাটা** *n.* a toll station on a waterway.

কুতন্ত্র *n.* bad advice or counsel; bad policy or measure.

কুতর্ক *n.* sophistry; unreasonable or useless argument, false but clever argument (intended mainly to outwit), quibbling.

কুৎসা *n.* calumny, slander; scandal. **কুৎসা করা** *v.* to calumniate, to slander; to scandalize. **~কারী** *n.* a calumniator, a slanderer; a scandal-monger. **~জনক** *a.* calumniatory, calumnious, slanderous; scandalous.

কুৎসিত *a.* ugly; ill-shaped; abominable, hateful; nasty (কুৎসিত ব্যবহার) ; indecent; obscene; filthy, gross.

কুতুকুতু var. of **কাতুকুতু**।

কুতূহল *n.* inquisitiveness, curiosity; delight, pleasure; sport. **কুতূহলী** *a.* inquisitive, curious; delighted; sportive. **কুতূহলে** *adv.* (poet.) delightedly; sportively; owing to delight.

কুত্তা, (dial.) **কুত্তো** *n.* the dog. *fem.* **কুত্তি** the bitch.

কুত্রাপি *adv.* anywhere.

কুদন var. of **কুঁদন**।

কুদরত *n.* glory (আল্লার কুদরত) ; a creditable performance, a feat; bravado;

power, strength, skill. কুদরতি *a.* glorious; creditable; powerful, skilful.

কুদর্শন *a.* ugly-looking, revolting to the sight; ugly; ill-shaped.

কুদা var. of কুঁদা[1] and কুঁদা[2] ।

কুদাল, কুদালি obs. variants of কোদাল ।

কুদিন *n.* hard times; an inauspicious day. Same as দুর্দিন ।

কুদৃশ্য *n.* an ugly or indecent or hateful or abominable sight, a repulsive spectacle.

কুদৃষ্টি *n.* an evil eye, a sinister look; (esp. in astrol.) an evil or unfavourable aspect or influence. কুদৃষ্টি দেওয়া *v.* to cast an evil eye (on); to influence unfavourably.

কুদেতা *n.* coup d'état, a sudden stroke of state policy; a sudden political or military uprise.

কুধারা *n.* a bad custom, an unwholesome tradition.

কুনকি *n.* a female elephant tamed and trained by elephant-catchers to allure wild elephants into the trap.

কুনকে coll. corrup. of কুনকি and কুনিকা ।

কুনখ *n.* morbidity of the nails of hands and feet, felon; whitlow. কুনখী *a.* having morbid nails, suffering from felon or whitlow.

কুনজর same as কুদৃষ্টি ।

কুনাম *n.* a bad name; ill fame, notoriety, ill repute.

কুনি *n.* a morbid inward turning of the end of a nail causing pain, a painful ingrowing nail; inflammation of the end of a nail.

কুনিকা *n.* a unit of dry measure of rice, pigeon-pulses etc.; a vessel for measuring this amount.

কুনীতি *n.* bad or perverted morals; evil conduct; corruption; a bad or unwise policy. ~পরায়ণ *a.* having bad or perverted morals; having an evil conduct; corrupted; adopting bad or unwise policies.

কুনো *a.* pertaining to a corner; home-keeping, domestic; shy of company, unsociable; shy, bashful. কুনো ব্যাং a species of frog which seldom comes out of its hole; (fig.) a home-keeping or domestic person. ~মি *n.* habit of home-keeping; unsociableness; shyness.

কুন্তল *n.* hair (of human head); tresses.

কুন্থন *n.* act of straining to evacuate one's bowels; act of groaning (esp. when one strains to apply all one's strength). see কোঁথ ।

কুন্দ *n.* a variety of multi-petalled jasmine; a (turner's) lathe. ~কার *n.* a turner. ~শুভ্র *a.* as white as a jasmine.

কুপথ *n.* a bad or wrong or evil way. ~গামী *a.* gone astray; off the fairway. কুপথে যাওয়া *v.* to go astray.

কুপথ্য *n.* harmful diet (esp. for a patient). কুপথ্য করা *v.* to take harmful or unwholesome diet or food.

কুপন্থা *n.* a bad or wrong or evil means or policy or way.

কুপরামর্শ *n.* unwholesome advice; bad or evil counsel.

কুপা, কুপো *n.* a narrow-necked earthen or leather vessel; (sarcas.) a potbellied person. কুপোকাত *a.* utterly defeated, vanquished; knocked down.

কুপাত্র *n.* an undeserving or undesirable or bad man; a man who cannot make a good husband, an unworthy husband or bridegroom. *fem.* কুপাত্রী ।

কুপানো same as কোপানো ।

কুপি *n.* a small oil-lamp; a small oil-bottle.

কুপিত *a.* enraged, angered; angry; provoked; (med.) increased, developed, aggravated. কুপিত বায়ু (med.) flatulence, flatulency.

কুপিতা[1] *fem.* of কুপিত ।

কুপিতা[2] *n.* a bad father, an unworthy father.

কুপুত্র *n.* a bad or wicked or disobedient son, an unworthy son.

কুপুরুষ *n.* an unmanly man; a cowardly man, a coward; an ugly-looking man; a man of bad character. □ *a. masc.* bereft of manly qualities, unmanly; cowardly; ugly-looking; bad-charactered, immoral.

কুপুষ্যি coll. var. of কুপোষ্য ।

কুপো, কুপোকাত see **কুপা।**

কুপোষ্য *a.* one who has to be maintained though reluctantly. □ *n.* an undesirable dependant.

কুপ্য *n.* any of the base metals.

কুপ্রবৃত্তি *n.* evil propensity, wicked inclination; evil or unwholesome mentality.

কুফল *n.* a bad result or consequence or effect; harmful effect.

কুবক্তা *n.* a bad speaker.

কুবচন same as **কুবাক্য।**

কুবলয় *n.* the blue lotus.

কুবাক্য *n.* rude or harsh words, abusive language.

কুবিচার *n.* a wrong decision; an unfair or wrong judgment or verdict; miscarriage or perversion of justice.

কুবিন্দু *n.* (geog. & astr.) the nadir.

কুবুদ্ধি *n.* an evil or harmful design or inclination or counsel. □ *a.* having evil or harmful design or inclination. **কুবুদ্ধি দেওয়া** *v.* to give evil or harmful counsel.

কুবের *n.* the Hindu god of wealth (cp. Pluto, Mammon). **~পুরী** *n.* the abode or city of Kuvera (কুবের) which is full of wealth and pomp and grandeur. **~সদৃশ, ~তুল্য** *a.* as rich as Kuvera (কুবের) ; extremely wealthy, very rich.

কুবৈদ্য *n.* a bad or inept physician; a quack.

কুব্জ *a.* humpbacked, hunchbacked. *fem.* **কুব্জা, কুব্জী। কুব্জ লোক** a hunchback.

কুভোজন *n.* act of eating bad or harmful food; bad or harmful food.

কুমকুম *n.* a ball filled with red powder and scented water for sprinkling; a red paste made from saffron juice used by women as a cosmetic.

কুমড়া, (coll.) **কুমড়ো** *n.* the pumpkin. **গুড়-কুমড়ো, মিঠে কুমড়া, বিলাতি কুমড়ো** *n.* the sweet pumpkin, the ordinary pumpkin. **চালকুমড়ো, ছাঁচিকুমড়ো, দেশি কুমড়ো** *n.* the evergreen variety of the pumpkin.

কুমতলব *n.* an evil plan; an evil or mischievous plan or design.

কুমতি *n.* a wicked or harmful inclination or thought or design; evil design; evil counsel. □ *a.* having such inclination or thought or design.

কুমন্ত্রণা *n.* bad or evil counsel.

কুমন্ত্রী *n.* one who gives bad or wicked counsel, a bad or wicked counsel, a bad or wicked counsellor or minister; a wicked-natured counsellor or minister.

কুমরে পোকা see **পোকা।**

কুমাতা *n.* a bad or unworthy mother; a mother lacking in affection.

কুমার[1] obs. var. of **কুমোর।**

কুমার[2] *n.* a young boy; a son; a prince; a crown price; a prince-royal; Kartikeya (কার্তিকেয়) the commander-in-chief of the heavenly hosts; an unmarried or celibate man, a bachelor. **~ব্রত** *n.* the vow of celibacy.

কুমারিকা *n.* the Cape Comorin; (rare) a twelve years old girl; (rare) an unmarried girl or woman, a maid, a virgin, a spinster.

কুমারী *n.* an unmarried girl or woman, a maid, a maiden; a virgin, a spinster; a feme sole, a daughter; a princess. **কুমারীত্ব** *n.* virginity; maidenhood. **কুমারী নাম** *n.* a patronym.

কুমির *n.* the crocodile; the alligator. **কুমির-কুমির খেলা** push in the corner. **জলে কুমির ডাঙায় বাঘ** (fig.) between Scylla and Charybdis, between two great dangers.

কুমিরেপোকা *n.* the weevil.

কুমুদ *n.* the red or the white lotus; stalk of a lotus. **~নাথ** *n.* the lord of lotuses; the moon. **~বতী, কুমুদ্বতী** *n.* a cluster or collection of red or white lotuses; red or white lotuses. □ *a.* full of red or white lotuses. **কুমুদিনী** *n.* a cluster of red or white lotuses; a pond full of red and white lotuses. **কুমুদিনীকান্ত, কুমুদিনীনাথ** *n.* the beloved or lord of lotuses; the moon. **কুমুদী** *n.* a stalk of a lotus. **কুমুদ্বান** *a.* (of a place) abounding in red or white lotuses.

কুমেরু *n.* the South Pole, the Antarctic. **~জ্যোতি, ~প্রভা** *n.* Aurora Australis. **~বৃত্ত** *n.* (geog.) the Antarctic Circle.

কুমোর *n.* a potter, a claymodeller. **~শালা** *n.* a potter's workshop. **কুমোরের চাক** the potter's wheel. **কুমোরের মাটি** potter's clay.

কুম্ভ *n.* a pitcher; a roundish pot; the

frontal globe at the side of an elephant's head; (astrol.) the Aquarius.

কুম্ভক *n.* a physio-religious practice of controlling or suspending one's breath.

কুম্ভকর্ণ *n.* the monstrous second brother of Ravana (রাবণ) as described in the Ramayana (he used to keep awake only for a day after sleeping for six months at a stretch); (hence—fig.) a man who sleeps overmuch.

কুম্ভকার *n.* a potter; a person who makes clay pots by hand.

কুম্ভমেলা *n.* a duodecennial religious gathering of ascetics at one of the 4 holy places— Haridwar, Ujjaini, Nasik, Allahabad (Prayag).

কুম্ভরাশি *n.* (astrol.) the Aquarius.

কুম্ভশালা, কুম্ভশাল *n.* a potter's or claymodeller's workshop; a pottery.

কুম্ভিল, কুম্ভিলক *n.* a thief; a plagiarist.

কুম্ভীপাক *n.* a terrible cell of the hell.

কুম্ভীর *n.* (for.) the crocodile; the alligator. **কুম্ভীরাশ্রু** *n.* crocodile tears, insincere sorrow or sympathy.

কুম্ভীলক alt. spell. of **কুম্ভিলক**।

কুযশ *n.* ill-repute, disrepute; notoriety.

কুযাত্রা same as **অযাত্রা**।

কুযুক্তি *n.* evil or harmful counsel, bad advice, useless or fallacious reasoning; unsubstantial and ill-motived argument, a false but clever argument with intention to deceive or outwit.

কুয়াশা, কুয়াসা *n.* fog, mist.

কুয়ো *n.* a draw-well, a well. **কুয়োর ব্যাং** a frog that lives in a well and seldom comes out of it; (fig.) a narrow-minded person with limited knowledge; (fig.) a person of limited vision; (fig.) a home-keeping person.

কুরকুর a milder form of **করকর**।

কুরঙ্গ, কুরঙ্গক, কুরঙ্গম *n.* the male deer, the stag, the buck. *fem.* **কুরঙ্গী,** (inc.) **কুরঙ্গিনী** the female deer, the hind, the doe. **কুরঙ্গীনয়না** *a. fem.* having fine eyes like a deer's.

কুরচিনামা *n.* a genealogical table.

কুরণ্ড *n.* hydrocele.

কুরনি coll. var. of **কুরানি**।

কুরনিশ alt. spell. of **কুর্নিশ**।

কুরব *n.* an ugly or harsh voice or sound; a disgraceful report, a scandal; obscene language or words. □ *a.* having an ugly or harsh voice or sound.

কুরবক var. of **কুরুবক**।

কুরবানি var. of **কোরবানি**।

কুরর *n.* the osprey. *fem.* **কুররী** the female osprey.

কুরল *n.* a larger variety of the osprey; the eagle, a lock of hair.

কুরসি *n.* a chair.

কুরা, কুরানো, কোরা, কোরানো *v.* to scrape (as the pulp of a coconut); to gnaw; to eat into (কুরে কুরে খাওয়া).

কুরানি, কোরানি *n.* a notched tool for grating or scraping coconut, a coconut-scraper.

কুরীতি *n.* a bad or harmful custom or usage or practice or deportment.

কুরু *n.* a mythological king of India; his descendants or line; a mythological kingdom (কুরুবর্ষ, কুরুদেশ).

কুরুক্ষেত্র *n.* a place near New Delhi where the Kauravas (কৌরব) and the Pandavas (পাণ্ডব) of the Mahabharata fought each other; (fig.) a terrible fight or noisy quarrel or brawl (কুরুক্ষেত্র বেধেছে). **কুরুক্ষেত্র ব্যাপার** (fig.—often facet.) an affair as terrible as the fight of Kurukshetra (কুরুক্ষেত্র).

কুরুচি *n.* bad or perverted taste. **~পূর্ণ** *a.* in bad taste; gross, indecent, vulgar. **~সম্পন্ন** *a.* having bad or perverted taste.

কুরুণ্ড coll. corrup. of **কুরণ্ড**।

কুরুণ্ডিয়া, (coll.) **কুরুণ্ডে** *a.* having hydrocele. □ *n.* a person having hydrocele.

কুরুনি coll. var. of **কুরানি**।

কুরুবক *n.* a flower-plant or its flower, the red amaranth.

কুরুবিন্দ *n.* the corundum; (loos.) the ruby.

কুরুবৃদ্ধ *n.* an ancient of the Kuru (কুরু) family.

কুরুশ-কাঠি var. of **ক্রুশ-কাঠি**।

কুরূপ *a.* having an ugly or uncomely appearance, ugly; ill-shaped and deformed. □ *n.* ugliness. *fem.* **কুরূপা**।

কুর্তা *n.* a small jacket or coat or shirt.

লালকুর্তা *n.* the Red Shirts; patriotic and social welfare organization of North-West Frontier formed by Khan Abdul Gaffar Khan in India's pre-independence days.

কুর্তি dim. of **কুর্তা**।

কুর্দন *n.* act of skipping; act of bragging; act of rushing forward to attack or beat.

কুর্নিশ, কুরনিশ *n.* (Mus.) a mode of salutation in accordance with official etiquette. **কুর্নিশ করা** *v.* to salute.

কুর্পর *n.* the knee; the elbow. ☐ *a.* dependent.

কুর্মি *n.* a backward caste amongst Hindus; a member of this caste.

কুর্সি alt. spell. of **কুরসি**।

কুল[১] *n.* the jujube.

কুল[২] *n.* a religious sect amongst Hindus practising a very severe form of Tantric worship (কুলমার্গ).

কুল[৩] *n.* family; a clan; lineage, pedigree; good pedigree or lineage, a kulin (কুলীন) family (সে কুলের ছেলে) ; purity of blood; dignity of one's family, family prestige, aristocracy, high or noble birth (কুলগর্ব) ; descendants, line (তার কুল আজও টিকে আছে) ; one's own house or family or society (কুলত্যাগ) ; family religion or cult; residence (গুরুকুল) ; a race, a tribe (রক্ষঃকুল) ; a species or kind or class (নরকুল) ; a collection, a herd, a flock, a swarm (শিবাকুল). **কুল করা** *v.* to enter into a matrimonial alliance with a kulin (কুলীন) family. **কুল মজানো** *v.* (fig.) to bring disgrace upon one's family. **কুল রাখি কি শ্যাম রাখি** (fig.) on the horns of a dilemma. **কুলে কালি দেওয়া** (fig.) to bring disgrace upon one's (own) family, to tarnish the good name of one's (own) family. **কুলের বার হওয়া** same as **কুলত্যাগ করা**। **একুল-ওকুল দুকুল খাওয়া বা হারানো** (lit.—of a married woman) to lose shelter and support of both one's husband and parents; (fig.) to reject one alternative and lose the other; to be utterly ruined, to leave one's friends and be ill-treated by one's foes. **~কণ্টক** *n.* one who is a disgrace to or a pest of one's family. **~কন্যা** *n.* a girl born of a high (kulin) family. **~কর্ম** same as **কুলক্রিয়া**। **~কলঙ্ক** *n.* one who is a disgrace to his family. *fem.* **কুলকলঙ্কিনী**। **~কলঙ্কী** *a. masc.* bringing disgrace on one's family. **~কামিনী** *n.* a wife of a good family; a girl born of a good family; (loos.) a family woman (esp. one living in a zenana.) **~কুণ্ডলিনী** same as **কুণ্ডলিনী**। **~ক্রিয়া, ~কার্য** *n.* traditional customs and practices of a family or befitting a family; act of entering into a matrimonial alliance with a kulin (কুলীন) family. **~ক্ষয়** *n.* destruction or decay of a family or line. **~ক্ষয়কর** *a.* causing decay or destruction of a family or line. **~গত** *a.* pertaining to a family. **~গরিমা, ~গর্ব** *n.* dignity of a family, family prestige; pride of birth. **~গুরু** *n.* a family preceptor; the hereditary religious guide of a family. **~গৌরব** same as **কুলগরিমা**। **~ঘ্ন** *a.* destroying a family, causing destruction of a family. **~চ্যুত** *a.* expelled from one's family, interdicted, ostracized; one who has lost his family prestige or status. **~জ, ~জাত** *a.* born of a good family; born of a kulin (কুলীন) family. **~জি** *n.* a (descriptive) genealogy (often composed in verse). **~জিনামা** *n.* a genealogical table. **~জ্ঞ** *a.* acquainted with the genealogy of a family. ☐ *n.* a herald. **~জ্ঞতা** *n.* knowledge of heraldic lore. **~টা** *n.* a woman who has brought disgrace upon her family (usu. by leaving it for good); a woman of bad moral character. ☐ *a.* of or like such a woman. **কুলটার স্বামী** the husband of such a woman, (cp.) a cuckold. **~তিলক** *n.* (one who is) the glory or pride of one's family. ☐ *a.* glorifying one's family. **~ত্যাগ** *n.* (of women) leaving one's home for good for immoral purposes; (of men) abandoning one's family, giving up the customs and practices of one's family. **কুলত্যাগ করা** *v.* (of women) to leave one's home for good for immoral purposes or to elope with her paramour; (of men)to abandon one's family, to repudiate the customs and practices of one's family. ~ত্যাগী *a. masc.* one who has abandoned one's family or has repudiated the customs and practices of one's family. ~ত্যাগিনী *a. fem.* one who has left her home for good for immoral purposes or eloped with one's paramour. ~দূষক, ~দূষণ *a.* bringing disgrace upon one's family. □ *n.* (one who is) the disgrace to one's family. ~দেবতা *n.* the hereditary or tutelary or guardian deity of a family. ~ধর্ম *n.* the traditional customs and practices of a family. ~নারী same as কুলকামিনী। ~নাশন same as কুলঘ্ন। ~নাশা *a.* bringing disgrace upon one's family. ~নিন্দা *n.* family scandal. ~পঞ্জি, ~পঞ্জী same as কুলজি। ~পতি *n.* the headman or chief of a clan; a patriarch; an arch-sage. ~পাংশুলা *n.* an unchaste woman; a woman who is a disgrace to the family. ~পুরোহিত *n.* a family priest. ~প্রথা *n.* a family custom or practice. ~প্রদীপ *n.* (fig.) one who glorifies one's family. ~বতী, ~বধূ *n.* a virtuous wife; (loos.) a family woman (esp. one living in a zenana). ~বালা same as কুলকামিনী। ~ভঙ্গ *n.* loss of one's family prestige or status (esp. due to matrimonial alliance with a family of inferior prestige or status). ~ভূষণ, ~মণি *n.* one who glorifies one's family, the ornament of one's family. ~ভ্রষ্ট same as কুলচ্যুত। ~মজানে *a.* bringing disgrace upon a family. ~মর্যাদা *n.* the dignity of a family, family prestige; the heraldic sign or mark of a family. ~মান *n.* the dignity of a family, family prestige. ~লক্ষণ *n.* any of the nine good qualities of a kulin (কুলীন) namely; (1) observance of rites, (2) politeness, (3) education, (4) good or reputable social position, (5) pilgrimage, (6) constancy or firm devotion, (7) honourable profession, (8) penance, and (9) benevolence or charity. ~লক্ষ্মী *n. fem.* the guardian goddess of a family; the guardian goddess of fortune of a family; a housewife who brings prosperity to a family. ~শীল *n.* lineage and character. ~শীলমান *n.* lineage, character and dignity. ~শ্রেষ্ঠ *n.* the best or most distinguished person in a family or line. ~সম্ভব *a.* born of a particular family; born of a good family. ~স্ত্রী same as কুলবধূ।

কুলকুচা, (coll.) **কুলকুচো** *n.* taking water into one's mouth and shaking it for the purpose of washing, act of rinsing or swilling one's mouth with water; gurgling. **কুলকুচো করা** *v.* to gurgle, to rinse or swill one's mouth with water.

কুলকুল *int.* expressing: the babbling noise as of a flowing river. **কুলকুল করা** *v.* to babble (like a river).

কুলক্ষণ *n.* an inauspicious sign or mark; a bad omen. □ *a.* having an inauspicious sign or mark (esp. on one's person); ill-omened. *fem.* **কুলক্ষণা**। **কুলক্ষণ দেখানো** *v.* to forebode or presage ill.

কুলগ্ন *n.* (chiefly astrol.) an inauspicious point of time.

কুলঙ্গি *n.* a recess or small shelf in a wall, a niche.

কুলথ *n.* a kind of pulse or vetch.

কুলপি *n.* a small conical container for freezing ice cream. ~বরফ *n.* ice cream made in this container. ~মালাই *n.* ice cream made of milk frozen in this container.

কুলা, (coll.) **কুলো** *n.* a flat and light vessel made of bamboo slips for winnowing grains etc., a winnowing platter or tray.

কুলাঙ্গার *n.* one who tarnishes the good name of one's family, a black sheep of a family.

কুলাচার *n.* the traditional usage or custom of a family.

কুলাচার্য *n.* the hereditary religious guide or preceptor of a family; a matrimonial match-maker versed in genealogy.

কুলানো *v.* to be sufficient for meeting the demand of, to suffice, to be adequate. **কুলিয়ে যাওয়া** *v.* to suffice, to be enough or adequate.

কুলাভিমান *n.* family pride or dignity; pride of birth; pride of high birth. **কুলাভিমানী** *a.* conscious of or sensitive about one's family pride or dignity;

proud of one's birth; proud of one's high birth. *fem.* **কুলাভিমানিনী** ।

কুলায় *n.* a bird's nest; (fig.) a cosy abode.

কুলাল *n.* a potter; a maker of ceramic vessels. **~চক্র** *n.* the potter's wheel.

কুলি[১] same as **কুলকুচো** ।

কুলি[২] *n.* a porter; a labourer. **~ কামিন** *n. pl.* male and female labourers; a labourer and his wife. **~ধাওড়া** *n.* the labourers' lines or quarters.

কুলির, কুলিরক *n.* the crab.

কুলিশ *n.* a thunderbolt.

কুলীন *n.* one belonging to any of the families on whom an order of honour was conferred by King Ballal Sen of ancient Bengal. □ *a.* belonging to any of these families or enjoying this order of honour; of a noble caste; high-born; honourable.

কুলীর, কুলীরক alt. spellings of **কুলির** and **কুলিরক** respectively.

কুলীশ alt. spell. of **কুলিশ** ।

কুলুঙ্গি var. of **কুলঙ্গি** ।

কুলুজি coll. form of **কুলজি** (see **কুল**[৩]).

কুলুপ *n.* a lock, a padlock. **কুলুপ-আঁটা** *a.* locked. **কুলুপ আঁটা** *v.* to lock.

কুলো coll. form of **কুলা** ।

কুলোক *n.* a bad man, a knave, a rogue.

কুল্যে *adv.* altogether, in all; only.

কুল্লে alt. spell. of **কুল্যে** ।

কুশ *n.* a kind of holy grass; Rama's son in the Ramayana; a mythological island. **~পুত্তলি, ~পুত্তলী, ~পুত্তলিকা** *n.* an effigy of a dead or living person made of this grass, a jackstraw. **কুশপুত্তলি দাহ করা** *v.* to burn an effigy (in order to express dislike against a person or to consummate cremation scripturally of a person who is believed to be dead but whose body has not been found). **কুশ-পেয়ে** *a.* having the tip of one's feet turned inside, suffering from knock-feet or pedis valgum. **কুশাগ্র** *n.* the tip of a blade of kusha (কুশ) grass. □ *a.* as pointed or sharp as the tip of a blade of kusha grass. **কুশাগ্রধী, কুশাগ্রবুদ্ধি** *a.* very sharp-witted, having very keen intelligence. **কুশাগ্রীয়** same as **কুশাগ্র** (*a*). **কুশাঙ্কুর** *n.* a sharp-pointed young shoot or blade of kusha (কুশ) grass. **কুশাঙ্গুরী, কুশাঙ্গুরীয়** *n.* a ring for the finger made of kusha grass (worn during the performance of a holy rite). **কুশাসন** *n.* a small mat made of kusha (কুশ) grass (used for sitting upon by holy persons or during the performance of a holy rite).

কুশণ্ডিকা *n.* a scriptural sacrifice to be performed at marriage etc.

কুশতি var. of **কুস্তি** ।

কুশল[১] *n.* well-being, weal. □ *a.* being well, in weal. **কুশলী** *a.* being well, in weal. **কুশল জিজ্ঞাসা, কুশল প্রশ্ন** *n.* inquiries about well-being or weal; cordial greeting; good wishes. **কুশল হোক** may you be in weal, may peace and happiness be with you.

কুশল[২] *a.* expert, skilled, proficient, dexterous. adroit. **~তা** *n.* expertness, skill, skilfulness, proficiency, dexterity, adroitness. **কুশলী** inc. var. of **কুশল**[২] ।

কুশলী see **কুশল**[১,২] ।

কুশাগ্র, কুশাঙ্কুর see **কুশ** ।

কুশাসক *n.* a bad or unjust ruler or administrator.

কুশাসন[১] see **কুশ** ।

কুশাসন[২], **কু-শাসন** *n.* misgovernment, misrule, maladministration.

কুশি[১] var. of **কোষী** ।

কুশি[২] *n.* the mango or any other fruit in green and undeveloped state.

কুশীলব *n.* (as *pl.*) the characters of a drama or play, dramatis personae; (as *sing.*) an actor, a singer, a dancer, an artiste; (as *pl.*) Kusha (কুশ) and Laba (লব) of the Ramayana; (hence) twins.

কুশ্রী *a.* same as **কুরূপ** ।

কুষি alt. spell. of **কুশি**[১,২] ।

কুষ্ঠ *n.* leprosy. **~ঘ্ন** *a.* curing leprosy. **~ময়** *a.* leprous. **কুষ্ঠাশ্রম** *n.* a hospital or asylum for lepers.

কুষ্ঠি coll. form of **কোষ্ঠী** ।

কুষ্ঠী *n.* a leper.

কুষ্মাণ্ড *n.* the evergreen variety of the pumpkin; the pumpkin; (fig.) a worthless person.

কুসংসর্গ *n.* evil company, bad association. **কুসংসর্গী** *a.* keeping evil company, associating with undesirable persons.

কুসংস্কার *n.* superstition. **~গ্রস্ত, কুসংস্কারাচ্ছন্ন** *a.* superstition-ridden, superstitious. **~মূলক** a. caused by superstition, superstitious.

কুসঙ্গ *n.* bad or evil company. **কুসঙ্গী** *n.* a bad or wicked companion or friend.

কুসন্তান *n.* a bad or wicked child; an unworthy son or daughter.

কুসম-কুসম *a.* lukewarm, tepid. **কুসম-কুসম গরম করা** to make lukewarm or tepid, to take the chill off.

কুসিম্বী *n.* the kidney bean or its plant.

কুসীদ *n.* interest on loan; the money-lending business or interest, usury. **~জীবী** *n.* a usurer, a money-lender on interest. **~ব্যবহার** *n.* usury; calculation of interest on loan.

কুসুম[1] coll. form of **কুসুম্ভ**।

কুসুম[2] *n.* a flower; menstruation, menses; a disease of the eye, the yolk of an egg. **~কলি, ~কলিকা, ~কোরক** *n.* a flower-bud. **~কার্মুক, ~চাপ, ~ধনু, ~ধন্বা** *n.* appellation of Madana (মদন) the Hindu god of love whose bow is made of flowers. **~কোমল, ~পেলব** *a.* as soft as a flower. **~দাম** *n.* a flower-wreath, a garland of flowers. **~বাস** *n.* the scent or perfume of a flower. **~মালিকা** *n.* a small flower-wreath, a chaplet or small garland of flowers. **~শয়ন, ~শয্যা** *n.* a bed of flowers; a very soft bed; (fig.) ease and comfort. **~স্তবক** *n.* a bunch of flowers, a bouquet, a nosegay. **কুসুমাকর, কুসুমাগম** *n.* the season of flowers, the spring, the vernal season. **কুসুমায়ুধ** same as **কুসুমকার্মুক**। **কুসুমাসব** *n.* the juice or honey of flowers, the nectar of flowers. **কুসুমাস্তীর্ণ** *a.* strewn with flowers; (fig.) (of life) easy going, smooth.

কুসুম-কুসুম var. of **কুসম-কুসম**।

কুসুমিত *a.* in blossom, blossomed, flowered; budded.

কুসুমেষু *n.* same as **কুসুমকার্মুক**।

কুসুম্ভ *n.* the safflower the juice of which is used in dyeing cloth etc.

কুস্তি *n.* wrestling; (fig.) struggling, vying. **কুস্তি করা, কুস্তি লড়া** *v.* to wrestle; (fig.) to struggle. **~গির** *n.* a wrestler.

কুস্বপ্ন *n.* a bad dream; an ill-omened dream, a nightmare.

কুস্বভাব *n.*bad nature or conduct or character. □ *a.* ill-natured; of bad conduct or character. *fem.* a **কুস্বভাবা**।

কুহক *n.* sorcery, witchcraft, black magic; magic; deception, delusion. **কুহকী** *a.* skilled in sorcery or magic; magical; deceiving, deluding. □ *n.* a sorcerer, a wizard; a magician, a juggler; a deceiver, a deluder. **কুহকিনী** *a. fem.* of **কুহকী**। □ *n. fem.* a sorceress, a witch; a female magician or juggler; a woman who deceives or deludes.

কুহর *n.* a hole, a cavity (কর্ণকুহর) ; voice.

কুহরণ *n.* act of cooing; the note of a cuckoo.

কুহরই *v. imperf.* (obs. & poet.) cooing.

কুহরা *v.* (poet.) (of a cuckoo) to coo.

কুহরিত *a.* resounded with the cooings of a cuckoo or cuckoos.

কুহরিল *v.* (of cuckoo) cooed.

কুহু, কুহূ *n.* the cooing of a cuckoo. **~ কণ্ঠ** *n.* the cuckoo. **~তান** *n.* the dulcet note of the cuckoo, a cuckoo's sweet and soothing song. **~রব** *n.* the cooing of a cuckoo; the cuckoo.

কুহেলিকা, কুহেলি, কুহেলী *n.* fog, mist. **কুহেলিকাময়, কুহেলিকাচ্ছন্ন** *a.* foggy, misty, enveloped in fog or mist; (fig.) mysterious, obscure, dark.

কূচিকা *n.* a small brush; a painter's brush, a hair-pencil.

কূজন *n.* a sweet note or call of a bird, cooing, warbling, chirping; (fig.—esp. of lovers) whispering. **কূজন করা** *v.* (of birds) to call, to coo, to warble, to chirp; (fig.—esp. of lovers) to whisper. **কূজিত** *a.* resounded or resounding with a bird's call or cooing or warbling or chirping.

কূট *a.* shrewd, subtle (কূটবুদ্ধি) ; complicated, intricate (কূটপ্রশ্ন) ; tricky, deceptive (কূটচাল) ; false, fabricated (কূটসাক্ষ্য) ; cooked up, got-up, framed up (কূট মোকদ্দমা) ; crooked (কূটচরিত্র) ; diplomatic, politic (কূটনীতি). □ *n.* an incomprehensible or unexpoundable couplet or saying (ব্যাসকূট) ; a mountain-peak (চিত্রকূট) ; the top of anything (প্রাসাদকূট) ; a heap (অন্নকূট) ; a trap; a trick; (rhet.) a paradox. **~চাল** *n.* obstacles and hindrances; intricacies; useless arguments; sophistry. **~কচালে** *a.* intricate; incomprehensible; full of obstacles and hindrances; given to useless arguments or sophistry. **~কর্ম** *n.* forgery; swindling; fraud. **~কৌশল** *n.* shrewd tricky or crafty policy; tricky or shrewd contrivance or device. **~ঘাত** *n.* sabotage. **~ঘাতী** *a.* pertaining to or of the nature of sabotage. ☐ *n.* a saboteur. **~জ** *n.* a medicinal plant usu. grown on hillsides. **~তর্ক** *n.* scholastic but useless arguments, sophistry. **~তার্কিক** *n.* one given to sophistry, a sophist. **~তুলা** *n.* a false scale or balance (esp. made to deceive buyers). **~নীতি** *n.* diplomacy; shrewd politics; shrewdness; politics. **~নীতিক** *a.* diplomatic; shrewd; political. ☐ *n.* a diplomat. **~নীতিজ্ঞ** *a.* shrewd; versed in diplomacy. ☐ *n.* a diplomat. **~নৈতিক** same as **কূটনীতিক**। **~প্রশ্ন** *n.* an intricate question, a poser; a riddle, a puzzle. **~বন্ধ** *n.* a trap, a snare. **~বুদ্ধি** *a.* crooked, wily, guileful, crafty. ☐ *n.* crookedness, wile, guile, craftiness. **~ভাষী** *a.* given to speaking in riddles; given to lying. **~যন্ত্র** *n.* a trapping device, a trap. **~যুদ্ধ** *n.* a diplomatic fight, manoeuvring and counter-manoeuvring in diplomacy. **~সাক্ষী** *n.* a false witness; a tutored or got-up witness. **~সাক্ষ্য** *n.* false evidence, perjury. **~স্থ** *a.* (phil.) eternally uniform or unchanging (যেমন— ঈশ্বর, আকাশ) ; occult, latent (কূটস্থ চৈতন্য). **কূটাভাস** *n.* (rhet.) a paradox. **কূটার্থ** *n.* far-fetched meaning; an implied or implicit meaning, implication; a distorted meaning.

কূপ *n.* a draw-well, a well; a hole, a cavity (লোমকূপ, কর্ণকূপ). **~মণ্ডূক** *n.* (lit.) a frog that dwells in a well and seldom comes out of it; (fig.) a narrow-minded person with limited knowledge or vision; (fig.) a home-keeping person.

কূপোদক *n.* water of a well.

কূর্চ, কূর্চা *n.* a small brush, a painter's brush, a hair-pencil; the space between the eyebrows; bristly hair of one's beard; a bristle. **কূর্চিকা** *n.* a small brush, a painter's brush, a hair-pencil; a tuft of grass; a needle.

কূর্পর alt. spell. of **কুর্পর**।

কূর্ম *n.* the tortoise, the turtle; the second of the ten incarnations of Vishnu (বিষ্ণু). **~পুরাণ** *n.* the name of the Purana (পুরাণ) narrating the exploits of the second incarnation of Vishnu (বিষ্ণু). **~পৃষ্ঠ** *n.* the back of a tortoise, a tortoise-shell. ☐ *a.* convex.

কূর্মাকার *a.* shaped like (the back of) a tortoise.

কূর্মাবতার *n.* the second of the ten incarnations of Vishnu (বিষ্ণু) assuming the form of a tortoise.

কূর্মী *fem.* of **কূর্ম**।

কূল *n.* a bank (of a river); a shore, a coast, a beach; a border, an edge (চোখের কূলে জল) ; (fig.) a shelter or help (অকূলে কূল পাওয়া) ; end, limit (দুঃখের কূল নেই). **~কিনারা** *n.* (fig.) a way or means of escape (কূলকিনারা না পাওয়া) ; end, limit (চিন্তার কূলকিনারা). **~কিনারাহীন** *a.* endless; at sea. **~প্লাবী** *a.* overflowing or inundating the bank or shore. **কূলে কূলে** to the brim.

কৃকলাস, কৃকলাশ *n.* the chameleon; (fig.) a very lean person.

কৃচ্ছ্র *n.* physical hardship, hard labour; austerity; austere vow or (religious) meditation or penance (কৃচ্ছ্র করা). ☐ *a.* austere (কৃচ্ছ্র ব্রত). **~লব্ধ** *a.* hard-earned. **~সাধন** *n.* a very austere vow or (religious) meditation or penance; extremely hard labour; practice of austerities, self-castigation. **~সাধ্য** *a.* requiring hard labour or practice or adoption of austerities.

কৃৎ[১] *sfx.* indicating one who does or performs or works (পথিকৃৎ).

কৃৎ[২] (gr.) *n.* a system of adding suffixes to words (কৃৎপ্রত্যয়).

কৃত *a.* done, made, performed (কৃতকর্ম) ; instituted, committed (কৃত অপরাধ) ; composed (ব্যাসকৃত মহাভারত) ; built, learnt, earned (কৃতবিদ্য) ; taken, accepted (কৃতদার) ; appointed, employed, engaged (কৃতদাস) ; fixed, settled

(কৃতবেতন). ~কর্ম *n.* a work done, a deed. ~কর্মা *n.* one who has done a work or performed a feat. ~কাম, ~কার্য *a.* one who has succeeded in performing a task undertaken, one who has achieved one's end, successful. ~কার্যতা *n.* success. ~কৃত্য *a.* one who has been able to accomplish one's duty or task; a person who has had his education completed; well-educated, learned. ~তীর্থ *a.* one who has done one's pilgrimage. ~দার *a. masc.* one who has taken a wife, married. ~দাস *n.* one who has been made a slave for a term, a bond-slave. *fem.* ~দাসী। ~ধী *a.* having firm resolve; having one's intellect sharpened; having intellectual sharpness or accomplishments. ~নিশ্চয় *a.* thoroughly convinced; having firm resolve; thoroughly convinced of success. ~নিশ্চয়তা *n.* thorough conviction; firm resolve; thorough conviction about success. ~পূর্ব *a.* already done or accomplished. ~বিদ্য *a.* one who has had his education completed; well-educated, learned. ~বিদ্যতা *n.* (successful) completion of one's education; state of being well-educated or learned. ~সংকল্প *a.* one who has resolved, determined; bent or intent upon. ~সংকল্প হওয়া *v.* to resolve, to determine, to make up one's mind.

কৃৎকৌশল *n.* technique; technicality; technical devices or methods.

কৃতঘ্ন *a.* one who harms one's benefactor; ungrateful, unthankful. ~তা *n.* act of harming one's benefactor; ingratitude, thanklessness, ungratefulness.

কৃতজ্ঞ *a.* grateful, obliged, thankful. ~চিত্তে *adv.* with a grateful or thankful heart; with feelings of gratitude. ~তা *n.* gratitude, thankfulness.

কৃৎস্ন *a.* (obs.) all; entire, whole.

কৃতাঞ্জলি *a.* having one's hands folded; in folded hands; having cupped one's palms. ~পুটে *adv.* with one's palms formed into a cup, having cupped one's palms. ~পূর্বক *adv.* with folded hands; having cupped one's palms (in supplication etc.).

কৃতান্ত *n.* a name of Yama (যম) the Hindu God of death.

কৃতাপরাধ *a.* one who has committed an offence, guilty, criminal.

কৃতাভিষেক *a.* anointed for installation or enthronement; installed, enthroned.

কৃতাভ্যাস *a.* one who has practised or received training, practised, trained.

কৃতার্থ *a.* one who has achieved one's goal, successful; gratified. ~ম্মন্য *a.* one who thinks oneself gratified.

কৃতাহ্নিক *a.* one who has performed one's daily religious services or prayer.

কৃতি *n.* performance, execution, action, achievement, construction; contribution (কৃতির পুরস্কার) ; authorship (কৃতিস্বত্ব) ; an act, a deed, a work. সুকৃতি *n.* a deed of piety; a virtuous act.

কৃতিত্ব *n.* proficiency, skill; credit; achievement.

কৃতিস্বত্ব *n.* patent; copyright.

কৃতী *a.* proficient; successful; one who has accomplished a great task or has been successful in a great effort; successful in life; well-educated, erudite, learned.

কৃতোদ্বাহ *a.* married.

কৃতোপকার *a.* one who benefits, benevolent; benefited.

কৃত্তি *n.* skin or hide of beasts; skin of human beings, epidermis, cutis. ~ক *n.* cuticle. ~কা *n.* (astro.) the Pleiads, the Pleiades; (myth.) any of the six nymphs who nursed Kartikeya (কার্তিকেয়). ~বাস *n.* a name of Shiva (শিব) who wears a tiger's skin. ~বাসী *a.* composed by Krittibas (কৃত্তিবাস) who rendered the Sanskrit Ramayana into Bengali.

কৃত্য *a.* that which ought to be or is to be done. □ *n.* a duty, a task (নিত্যকৃত্য, প্রাতঃকৃত্য) ; (gr.) a system of adding suffixes to words. ~ক *n.* a public department, public service (শিক্ষণ-কৃত্যক = the educational service). কৃত্যকবই *n.* a service-book. কৃত্যক সূচি *n.* service-roll. ~সূচি *a.* agenda. কৃত্যা *n. fem.* enchantment, witchery; an act or deed. কৃত্যাকৃত্য *n.* what ought to be and ought not to be done.

কৃত্রিম *a.* artificial (কৃত্রিম হ্রদ) ; imitated (কৃত্রিম হিরা = an imitation diamond); synthetic (কৃত্রিম রেশম) ; counterfeit (কৃত্রিম মুদ্রা) ; faked, forged (কৃত্রিম দলিল) ; simulated (কৃত্রিম বেশ) ; pretended, make-believe (কৃত্রিম আচরণ) ; false, sham (কৃত্রিম স্নেহ). **~তা** *n.* artificiality; imitation; state of being synthetic or counterfeit or faked or forged; simulation; pretension, make-believe; falseness, shamness.

কৃদন্ত *a.* (gr.—of a word) having a suffix added in accordance with the **কৃৎ** system. ☐ *n.* such a word.

কৃন্তক *a.* incising; incisive; incisory. ☐ *n.* an incisor. **কৃন্তন** *n.* cutting. **কৃন্তনিকা** *n.* a cutting instrument.

কৃপণ *a.* miserly, niggardly, close-fisted, parsimonious, stingy, illiberal, narrow-minded. *fem.* **কৃপণা, কৃপণী**। **~তা** *n.* miserliness, niggardliness, close-fistedness, parsimony, stinginess, narrow-mindedness. **~স্বভাব** *a.* miserly or niggardly by nature; illiberal or narrow-minded by nature. *fem.* **কৃপণস্বভাবা**।

কৃপা *n.* kindness, mercy (কৃপানিধি) ; compassion, pity (কৃপার পাত্র) ; grace, favour, benignancy (কৃপাদৃষ্টি). **কৃপা করা** *v.* to be kind or merciful to; to be compassionate to, to pity; to be gracious or benignant to, to favour. **~কটাক্ষ, ~দৃষ্টি** *n.* a look of favour, a favourable look. **কৃপাকটাক্ষ করা, কৃপাদৃষ্টি করা** *v.* to cast a favourable glance. **~নিধি** *n.* an extremely kind or merciful person; (lit.) a store of mercy or kindness. **~নেত্রে** *adv.* with a kind or kindly look. **~পাত্র** *n.* one who deserves pity, an object of pity. *fem.* **কৃপাপাত্রী**। **~প্রার্থী** *a.* one who longs for mercy. **~বলোকন** same as **কৃপাদৃষ্টি**। **~ময়, ~লু** *a.* kind, merciful; compassionate; gracious, benignant. **কৃপার্থী** same as **কৃপাপ্রার্থী**। **~লেশ** *n.* an iota of pity or mercy. **~সিন্ধু** *n.* (fig.) an extremely kind or merciful person; (lit.) an ocean of kindness or mercy. **~হীন** *a.* merciless, unkind.

কৃপাণ *n.* a sword; a scimitar; a dagger. **~পাণি** *a.* holding a sword or a scimitar or a dagger in one's hand.

কৃমি *n.* a worm (esp. that is found in the intestines of a human being). **গোল কৃমি** *n.* a round-worm. **ফিতাকৃমি** *n.* a tape-worm. **সুতাকৃমি** *n.* a thread-worn. **হুককৃমি** *n.* a hook-worm. **~ঘ্ন** *a.* anthelmintic. ☐ *n.* an anthelmintic. **~জ** *a.* produced by worms. ☐ *n.* lac. **~শৈল** *n.* an anthill.

কৃশ *a.* lean, thin; slender, slim; weak, feeble; weakened, enfeebled. **~কায়, ~তনু** *a.* of a slender frame, lean, thin. **~তা** *n.* leanness, thinness; weakness, feebleness.

কৃশর, কৃশরান্ন *n.* kedgeree; a kind of edible hotchpotch (usu. made of rice, pigeon-pulse, spices and sometimes vegetables).

কৃশাঙ্গ *a.* slender-bodied, slim; thin-bodied, lean; feeble-bodied, weak. *fem.* **কৃশাঙ্গী**।

কৃশানু *n.* fire.

কৃশোদর a. having a slender waist. *fem.* **কৃশোদরী**।

কৃশ্চান, কৃশ্চিয়ান variants of **খ্রিস্টান**।

কৃষক *n.* a peasant, a husbandman, ploughman, a cultivator, a farmer. **~সম্প্রদায়** *n.* the peasantry.

কৃষান *n.* a peasant; a farm-hand, a farm-labourer. *fem.* **কৃষানি**।

কৃষানি[1] *n.* agriculture, cultivation, farming; wages of a farm-hand. ☐ *a.* agricultural.

কৃষানি[2] *n. fem.* of **কৃষান**।

কৃষি *n.* agriculture, cultivation, husbandry, farming. **~কর্ম, ~কার্য** *n.* cultivation. **~জ, ~জাত** *a.* produced by agriculture. **~জাত দ্রব্য** agricultural produce. **~জীবী** *a.* living by agriculture. ☐ *n.* a peasant, a cultivator, a farmer. **~বিদ** *n.* an agronomist. **~ভূমি** *n.* agricultural land.

কৃষ্ট *a.* ploughed, tilled, cultivated; attracted. **কৃষ্টি** *n.* ploughing, tillage, cultivaton; culture.

কৃষ্ণ *n.* (myth.) an incarnation of God Vishnu or Narayana (নারায়ণ), Krishna who was one of the chief characters of the Mahabharata. ☐ *a.* black or deep-blue or dark-complexioned (কৃষ্ণকায়, কৃষ্ণমেঘ) ; dark, gloomy (কৃষ্ণরাত্রি). **কৃষ্ণ পাওয়া** *v.* (usu. sarcas.) to have access to the eternal and celestial company of Krishna (কৃষ্ণ) after one's death; to die. **~কলি** *n.* a flower-plant; its flower. **~কায়** *a.* dark-complexioned. **~চন্দন** *n.* the white Sandalwood, *Santalum album*. **~চূড়া** *n.* a flowering shrub; its red-coloured flower. **~জীরে, ~জীরক** *n.* the black cummin. **~তা** *n.* blackness. **~তিথি** *n.* any of the lunar days of the dark fortnight. **~পক্ষ** *n.* the dark fortnight. **~পক্ষীয়** *a.* of the dark fortnight. **~প্রাপ্তি** *n.* access to the eternal and celestial company of Krishna (কৃষ্ণ) ; death. **~বর্ণ** *a.* black, dark-coloured. □ *n.* black or dark colour. **~বর্ত্মা** *n.* fire; (myth. & astro.) the dragon's head, the ascending node. **~ভক্ত** *a.* devoted to Lord Krishna. □ *n.* a devotee of Lord Krishna. **~মুগ** *n.* a black variety of pigeon-pulse. **~যাত্রা** *n.* any of the open-air dramatic performances enacting the life and activities of Krishna (কৃষ্ণ). **~লোহিত** *a.* & *n.* purple. **~লৌহ** *n.* a magnet. **~সর্প** *n.* a venomous black snake, the krait. **~সার, ~শার** *n.* the antelope. **~সারথি** *n.* Arjuna (অর্জুন) of whom Krishna (কৃষ্ণ) is the charioteer as told in the Mahabharata. **~সীস** *n.* graphite, black lead. **কৃষ্ণা** *a. fem.* dark complexioned. □ *n.* a name of Draupadi (দ্রৌপদী) of the Mahabharata. **কৃষ্ণাঙ্গ** *n.* the black-skinned; the black people. □ *a.* black-skinned. opp. **শ্বেতাঙ্গ**। **কৃষ্ণাগুরু** same as **কৃষ্ণচন্দন**। **কৃষ্ণাজিন** *n.* skin of an antelope. **কৃষ্ণাভ** *a.* blackish; bluish; darkish. **কৃষ্ণাষ্টমী** *n.* the birth-day of Krishna (কৃষ্ণ) ; the eighth lunar day of the dark fortnight of the month of Bhadra (ভাদ্র).

কৃষ্য *a.* ploughable; arable; cultivable.

কে *pro.* who; which (ওদের মধ্যে কে বড় ?) ; how related, what (সে তোমার কে ?) ; a certain, a (কে এক সাহেব). **কে কে** *pro. pl.* who or which (distributively). **কেবা** *pro.* whoever, whichever.

কেউ *pro.* someone, somebody; anyone; one belonging to or related to (সে আমার কেউ নয়). **কেউ কেউ** some people; some. **কেউ না** none, nobody. **কেউ না কেউ** one or the other. **আর কেউ, অন্য কেউ** someone else, somebody else.

কেউকেটা *n.* a person of distinction, a big gun. □ *a.* of high standing, distinguished.

কেউটে, কেউটিয়া *n.* the krait.

কেওট *n.* one of the lowest castes amongst the Hindus (their original profession was fishing). *fem.* **কেওটনি**।

কেওড়া *n.* the screwpine flower or its plant; the essence of the screwpine flower. **কেওড়া-দেওয়া জল** drinking water perfumed with the essence of the screwpine flower.

কেঁউকেঁউ *int.* expressing the whining of a dog in distress. **কেঁউকেঁউ করা** *v.* (of a dog in distress) to whine; (of a person in trouble) to groan piteously; (sarcas.) to whine complainingly like a dog.

কেঁচ alt. spell. of **ক্যাঁচ**।

কেঁচে *inf.* & pop. var. of **কাঁচিয়া**। **কেঁচে যাওয়া** *v.* (of a thing that has been done or nearly done) to become undone, to revert to the original position.

কেঁচো *n.* the earthworm. **(ভয়ে) কেঁচো** cowering (in fear). **ভয়ে কেঁচো হওয়া** v. to cower in fear.

কেঁড়ে *n.* (usu.) an earthen pail (for holding milk etc.).

কেঁদে-ককিয়ে *adv.* with importunate entreaty.

কেঁদো *a.* very fat, corpulent; very large, gigantic (কেঁদো বাঘ).

কেঁয়ে *n.* a Marwari (মারওয়াড়ি) trader. □ *a.* captious; miserly, close-fisted, parsimonious; selfish.

কেক *n.* a cake.

কেকর *a.* squint-eyed.

কেকা *n.* a peacock's call. **কেকী** *n.* the peacock.

কে কে see **কে**।

কেঙ্গারু rej. spell. of **ক্যাঙারু**।

কেচ্ছা *n.* a scandal; malicious gossip; a story.

কেজো *a.* efficient; active; useful, serviceable.

কেটলি, কেতলি *n.* a kettle.

কেঠো¹ *n.* a large species of the tortoise.

কেঠো[২] *n.* a wooden vessel or trough. ☐ *a.* made of wood, wooden; (fig.) rough (কেঠো চেহারা).

কেডস *n.* keds (trade name of the canvas shoes by US Rubber Co.) plimsoll, a rubber-soled sports shoe made of canvas.

কেড়ি, কেড়িপোকা *n.* a small insect usu. found in long-stored rice.

কেতক, কেতকী *n.* the screwpine flower or its tree.

কেতন *n.* a flag, a banner, a standard; colours.

কেতলি *a.* var of **কেটলি** ৷

কেতা *n.* a bundle (এক কেতা কাগজ) ; a lot (এক কেতা মাল) ; manner, custom (আধুনিক কেতা) ; fashion (কেতাদুরস্ত) ৷

কেতাদুরস্ত, কেতাদোরস্ত *a.* fashionable; one who is conversant with and observes rules of etiquette and fashion.

কেতাব *n.* a book. **~কীট** *n.* (lit. & fig.) a book-worm. **কেতাবি** *a.* bookish. **কেতাবি বিদ্যা** bookishness; learning acquired from books only; book learning.

কেতু *n.* (astrol. & myth.) the descending node, the dragon's tail; a flag, a banner, a standard.

কেৎলি rej. var. of **কেটলি** ৷

কেদার *n.* a holy place for Hindus on the Himalayas; a name of Shiva (শিব) ; a piece of agricultural land, a field, a garden; a ridge round a piece of agricultural land; a ridge round the foot of a tree for watering. **~নাথ** *n.* Shiva (শিব).

কেদারা[১] *n.* a chair.

কেদারা[২] *n.* an Indian musical mode.

কেন *adv.* why. ☐ *n.* one of the books of the Upanishads. **~না** *conj.* because, since.

কেনা *v.* to buy, to purchase. ☐ *a.* bought, purchased. ☐ *n.* buying, purchase. **~কাটা** *n.* purchases, marketing, shopping. **কেনাকাটা করা** *v.* to make purchases, to shop. **কেনা দর** cost price. **~গোলাম** a slave. **~নো** *v.* to cause to buy. **~-বেচা** *n.* buying and selling; trading; brokery. **কেনা-বেচা করা** *v.* to buy and sell; to trade (in); to act as a (professional) broker.

কেনেস্তারা rej. form of **কানেস্তারা** and **ক্যানেস্তারা** ৷

কেন্দু same as **তিন্দু** and **তিন্দুক** ৷

কেন্দ্র *n.* the centre (of or as of a circle); the principal place or station; (astrol.) the fourth or the seventh or the tenth house from the birth-house in the zodiac. **~গত** *a.* lying in or entered into the centre; central; (phys.) centric. **~বিন্দু** *n.* the centre; the central place; the headquarters. **~বিমুখ, কেন্দ্রাতিগ, কেন্দ্রাপসারী** *a.* (sc.) centrifugal. **~শাসিত** *a.* centrally administered. **~স্থল** *n.* the centre; the principal place or station, the headquarters. **কেন্দ্রাভিগ, কেন্দ্রাভিগামী, কেন্দ্রাভিকর্ষী, কেন্দ্রাভিমুখ** *a.* (sc.) centripetal. **কেন্দ্রিত** *a.* lying or placed or drawn in the centre; (sc.) centric. **কেন্দ্রী** *a.* central; (sc.) centric. **কেন্দ্রীয়** *a.* central (কেন্দ্রীয় সরকার). **কেন্দ্রীভূত** *a.* centralized; lying in or brought into the centre; reduced to the centre.

কেন্নো, কেন্নুই, কেন্নাই *n.* a centipede, an earwig.

কেবট the elegant var. of **কেওট** ৷

কেবল *a.* (theo. & phil.) sole, without a second, absolute, one and only one (কেবলপুরুষ) ; pure, unpolluted (কেবলাত্মা) ; only (ঈশ্বরই কেবল সহায়) ; unchanging, just (কেবল একই কথা) ; incessant; unmixed. ☐ *adv.* just, just now (কেবল এসেছি) ; incessantly (কেবল হাসছে). **~ই** *adv.* continuously, incessantly; only.

কেবলরাম *n.* a dull-witted man, a dunce; a clumsy fellow; a weakling.

কেবল-হাসি *a.* given to laughing overmuch or always.

কেবলা alt. spell. of **ক্যাবলা** ৷

কেবলা-চৈতন্য, কেবলা-চৈতন *a.* dull-witted.

কেবলাত্মা *a.* pure-souled. ☐ *n.* God.

কেবা see **কে** ৷

কেবিন *n.* a cabin.

কেমন *adv.* how, of or in what sort or manner. ☐ *a.* of a sort (কেমন বোকার মতো) ; anxious, perturbed (মন কেমন করা) ; excellent, fine (কেমন মজা). **কেমন করে** how. **কেমন-কেমন** *a.* suspicious; (of health or mind) inexplicable; dubious; doubtful. **কেমন-কেমন করা** *v.* not to feel well or all right, to feel sick (শরীর

কেমন-কেমন করা) ; to be in an alarming or dying condition (রোগী কেমন-কেমন করছে) ; to become anxious or perturbed (মন কেমন-কেমন করছে). **কেমন-কেমন ঠেকা** *v.* to appear as suspicious or dubious or doubtful; to smell of something sinister. **~তরো** *a.* peculiar; of what sort. **কেমন যেন** *a.* not appearing to be quite well; suspicious, dubious, doubtful; to some extent, somewhat. **কেমনে** (poet.) *adv.* how.

কেমবিস *n.* canvas.

কেমব্রিক *n.* cambric, a kind of white cotton fabric.

কেমিকেল, কেমিক্যাল *n.* a chemical. □ *a.* made of chemicals, chemical.

কেয়া[১] *n.* the screwpine flower or its tree.

কেয়া[২] *a.* how fine, excellent (কেয়া মজা).

কেয়াকাঁদি *n.* a cluster of screwpine flowers.

কেয়াবাত *int.* bravo.

কেয়ামত *n.* the Day of (final) Resurrection or Judgment (according to the Islamic faith).

কেয়ার *n.* care. **কেয়ার করা** *v.* to care. **কেয়ারে** *adv.* in or under the care of.

কেয়ারি *n.* a well-laid flower-bed or pleasure garden encircled with a ridge; careful dressing (চুলের কেয়ারি). **কেয়ারি-করা** *a.* well-laid and encircled with a ridge (কেয়ারি-করা বাগান) ; carefully parted or dressed (কেয়ারি-করা চুল). **কেয়ারি করা** *v.* to beautify (a garden) by careful maintenance; to dress (hair) carefully.

কেয়ূর *n.* an ornament for the arm, an armlet.

কেরদানি var. of **ক্যারদানি** ।

কেরল *n.* Kerala, a south-Indian state; an inhabitant of Kerala (কেরল).

কেরাঞ্চি *n.* a kind of covered bullock cart for carrying passengers, a hackery; an inferior kind of horse-carriage for passengers.

কেরানি *n.* an office-clerk, a clerk. **~গিরি** *n.* clerkship. **মাছিমারা কেরানি** *a.* clerk or copyist who does his routine business or daily score or duty without using his discretion; an incompetent or unintelligent worker.

কেরামতি *n.* skill, efficiency; power; a glorious feat.

কেরায়া *n.* the price paid for use of anything, hire; freight; rent.

কেরাসিন, কেরোসিন *n.* kerosene.

কেলানো *v.* (vul. & dero.) to exhibit, to show, to display (দাঁত কেলানো) ; (sl.) to take off the skin. **দাঁত কেলানো** *v.* (vul. & dero.) to simper.

কেলাস[১] vul. corrup. of **ক্লাস** ।

কেলাস[২] *n.* crystal. **কেলাসন** *n.* crystallization. **কেলাসিত** *a.* crystallized. **কেলাসিত করা** *v.* to crystallize. **~বিদ্যা** *n.* crystallography. **কেলাসিত শিলা** *n.* crystalline rock.

কেলি *n.* amorous sport (কেলিকুঞ্জ) ; sport; amusement. **~কদম্ব** *n.* (myth.) the kadamba (কদম্ব) tree under which the amorous sports of Krishna (কৃষ্ণ) were held. **~গৃহ** *n.* a house for pleasure and pastime.

কেলে *a.* (vul.) dark-skinned; dark-complexioned. black; blackened. **কেলে কার্তিক** see **কার্তিক** । **কেলে ভূত** see **ভূত** । **কেলে হাঁড়ি** see **হাঁড়ি** ।

কেলেঙ্কারি *n.* a scandal; infamy; disgrace, disrepute; a scandalous affair or act. **~জনক** *a.* scandalous; disgraceful; infamous.

কেলেন্ডার rej. spell. of **ক্যালেন্ডার** ।

কেল্লা *n.* a fortress, a fort, a stronghold; a castle. **~দার** *n.* the governor or master of a fort or fortress; a castellan. **কেল্লা ফতে করা** *v.* to capture or take a fort or fortress; (fig.) to realize one's end, to achieve one's goal. **কেল্লা মাত করা** *v.* to capture a fort or fortress; (in chess) to kill the opponent's castle or to checkmate the opponent by moving one's castle(s); (fig.) to realize one's end, to achieve one's goal, to carry the day.

কেশ *n.* hair. **~কর্তন** *n.* haircut. **কেশকর্তন করা** *v.* to cut one's hair; to have a haircut. **~কলাপ, ~গুচ্ছ, ~দাম, ~পাশ** *n.* a lock or tuft of hair; a tress. **~কীট** *n.* a louse. **~গ্রহ, ~গ্রহণ** *n.* act of seizing by the hair. **~তৈল** *n.* hair-oil. **~প্রসাধন, ~বিন্যাস** *n.* hairdressing; act of combing and plaiting hair; tressing hair; act of putting up hair. **কেশপ্রসাধন করা, কেশবিন্যাস করা** *v.* to dress one's hair; to comb and plait one's hair; to tress one's hair; to put up one's hair. **~বতী** *a. fem.* one with long and beautiful hair. ☐ *n.* a woman having long and beautiful hair. **~বন্ধ, ~বন্ধনী** *n.* hair-band. **~বর্ধন** *n.* the growth of one's hair. **~মুণ্ডন** *n.* act of shaving one's head; tonsuring. **কেশমুণ্ডন করা** *v.* to shave one's head; to tonsure. **~সংস্কার** same as **কেশপ্রসাধন**। **~স্পর্শ** *n.* touching one's hair; (fig.) act of doing the least harm to. **কেশস্পর্শ করা** *v.* to touch one's hair; (fig.) to do one the least harm, to harm in the least. **~হীন** *a.* with the scalp wholly hairless, bald.

কেশব *n.* a name of Krishna (কৃষ্ণ).

কেশর *n.* (bot.) a pollen-tube, a stamen; mane (of lions, horses). **কেশরী** *n.* the lion. ☐ *in comp.* (used as a *sfx.*) the chief or best one (**বীরকেশরী** = the chief amongst the heroes, a lion of heroes etc.).

কেশাকর্ষণ *n.* pulling one by the hair, pulling one's hair. **কেশাকর্ষণ করা** *v.* to pull one's hair; to pull one by the hair.

কেশাকেশি *n.* pulling each other by the hair in a scuffle. **কেশাকেশি করা** *v.* to pull each other by the hair in a scuffle.

কেশাগ্র *n.* the tip of the hair. **কেশাগ্র স্পর্শ করা** *v.* to touch the tip of one's hair. **কেশাগ্র স্পর্শ করতে না পারা** *v.* to fail to touch the tip of one's hair; (fig.) to fail to do even the least harm (to).

কেশী *a.* possessing long or fine or dense hair; hairy. ☐ *n.* (myth.) a giant killed by Krishna (কৃষ্ণ). *fem. a.* **কেশিনী**।

কেশুর *n.* a kind of bulbous plant.

কেষ্ট coll. corrup. of **কৃষ্ণ**। **কেষ্ট পাওয়া** same as **কৃষ্ণ পাওয়া** (see **কৃষ্ণ**). **কেষ্ট-বিষ্টু** *n.* (sarcas.) a man of importance, a notable, a notability; anybody who is somebody.

কেস *n.* a law-suit; an incident (মজার কেস) ; a patient (টাইফয়েড কেস) ; a client or a brief (উকিলটি কেস পান না) ; a chest or a packing-box (এক কেস মদ), a case.

কেসর, কেসরী alt. spellings of **কেশর** and **কেশরী** respectively.

কেহ older form of **কেউ**।

কৈ alt. spell. of **কই**[১],[২]।

কৈছন alt. spell. of **কইসন**।

কৈছে *adv.* (poet. & obs.) how.

কৈতব *n.* chicane, deceit, dissimulation; falsehood; flattery; gambling; fraud. **~বাদ** *n.* act of telling lies; lying; flattery. **~বাদী** *a.* given to telling lies.

কৈন্দ্রিক *a.* central; centric.

কৈফিয়ত *n.* what is said to account for something, a cause shown, an explanation. **কৈফিয়ত কাটা** *v.* to try to clear up a charge rather impertinently; (bookkeeping) to explain the difference between the debit and the credit side of an accounts book. **কৈফিয়ত চাওয়া** *v.* to bring to account, to call to account, to demand an explanation, to take to task. **কৈফিয়ত দেওয়া** *v.* to give an explanation.

কৈবর্ত *n.* a caste amongst the Hindus (originally they were fishermen and peasants); a member of this caste.

কৈবল্য *n.* (phil. & theo.) soleness, state of being one and only one, absoluteness; identification of one's soul with the Absolute, merging of one's soul with the Absolute; salvation of the soul; release from the world or the influence of nature, eternal emancipation, nirvana. **~দায়িনী** *a. & n. fem.* one who emancipates or redeems the soul eternally, one who gives salvation. ☐ *n.* an appellation of Goddess Durga (দুর্গা) or Kali (কালী)।

কৈলাসনাথ *n.* the lord of the Kailasa mountain; an appellation of Shiva (শিব)।

কৈলাসবাসিনী *a. & n. fem.* one who resides on the Kailasa mountain. ☐ *n. fem.* an appellation of the Goddess Durga (দুর্গা)।

কৈলাসেশ্বর same as **কৈলাসনাথ**।

কৈশিক *a.* capillary. **~তা** *n.* capillarity.

কৈশোর *n.* early youth; adolescence. **~ক** *a.* of early youth, relating to adolescence. **কৈশোর-প্রেম** *n.* calf-love; romantic love or attachment or infatuation among adolescents.

কৈসে var. of **কৈছে**।

কো[1] alt. spell. of **ক**[3] ।
কো[2] *pro.* who.
কোই (obs. & poet.) *pro.* anybody, anyone; somebody, someone.
কোং abbr. of **কোম্পানি,** Co.
কোঁ *int.* expressing a groaning sound.
কোঁক *n.* the abdomen, the belly; one of the sides of the belly; the womb.
কোঁকড়া *a.* curled, curling, curly, wavy.
কোঁকড়ানো same as **কোঁকড়া** ।
কোঁকানো var. of **ককানো** ।
কোঁচ[1] var. of **কোচ** ।
কোঁচ[2] *n.* a wrinkle, a fold.
কোঁচ[3] *n.* a kind of small harpoon for catching fish.
কোঁচকানো pop. var. of **কুঁচকানো** ।
কোঁচড় *n.* the lap of one's loincloth. **কোঁচড় পাতা** *v.* to hold out the lap of one's loincloth (in order to receive something).
কোঁচবক *n.* the little heron.
কোঁচা *n.* the plaited end of the loincloth tucked at the front of the wearer. **কোঁচা দুলিয়ে বেড়ানো** to pass time idly shunning responsibility; to indulge in ludicrous foppishness. **বাইরে কোঁচার পত্তন ভিতরে ছুঁচোর কেত্তন** the ludicrous attempt of dressing oneself elegantly when one has no means of obtaining one's livelihood; a tawdry outside is the badge of poverty.
কোঁচানো pop. var. **কুঁচানো** ।
কোঁড়, কোঁড়া *n.* a young shoot of a plant esp. of bamboo, cane etc.
কোঁত, কোঁথ *n.* act of straining esp. to evacuate one's bowels, straining oneself as during defecation, tenesmus. **কোঁত পাড়া** *v.* same as **কোঁথা** ।
কোঁতকা *n.* a cudgel, a club.
কোঁতা pop. var. of **কোঁথা** ।
কোঁথা *v.* to strain oneself as during defecation.
কোঁদন *n.* coll. form of **কুঁদন** ।
কোঁদল coll. form of **কোন্দল** ।
কোঁদা pop. var. of **কুঁদা**[1,2] ।
কোঁস্তা *n.* a scrubbing brush.
কোক *n.* coke.
কোকনদ *n.* the red lotus.
কোকিল *n.* the cuckoo. *fem.* **কোকিলা** । **~কণ্ঠ** *a.* as sweet-voiced as the cuckoo. *fem.* **~কণ্ঠী** । **কোকিলাসন** *n.* a sitting posture according to the yoga (যোগ) system. **কোকিলেক্ষু** *n.* a reddish variety of sugarcane.
কোকেন *n.* cocaine.
কোকো *n.* cocoa.
কোঙর, কোঙার *n.* (obs.) a son.
কোচ *n.* a caste amongst Hindus (originally they were fishermen); a member of this caste; an aboriginal tribe of Cochbehar; one of this tribe.
কোচওয়ান *n.* a coachman.
কোচবাক্স *n.* a coach-box.
কোচমান, কোচম্যান, কোচোয়ান variants of **কোচওয়ান** ।
কোচিনী *fem.* of **কোচ** ।
কোজাগর *n.* the day of the fullmoon in the month of Ashwin-Kartik (আশ্বিন-কার্তিক) when goddess Lakshmi is worshipped. **কোজাগরী** *a.* of or on or during this day; performed on this day.
কোট[1] *n.* a coat.
কোট[2] *n.* a fort, a fortress (রাজকোট) ; a town, a city (পাঠানকোট) ; control, power, jurisdiction (কোটে পাওয়া) ; one's area (নিজের কোটে থাকা) ; bounds (কোটের বাইরে যাওয়া) ; position, resolve, claim (কোট বজায় রাখা) ।
কোটন pop. var. of **কুটন** ।
কোটনা[1] pop. var. of **কুটনা** ।
কোটনা[2] *n.* (masc. of **কুটনী**) a procurer, a pander. **~গিরি, ~মি** *n.* the profession of a pander, procuring; act of whispering malicious reports against a person.
কোটর *n.* a crevice or hollow (বৃক্ষকোটর) ; a socket (অক্ষিকোটর) ; a hole; a very small (and usu. dark) room. **~গত** *a.* hollow, sunken.
কোটা[1] *v.* to cut into pieces (as fish or vegetables), to dress; to grind, to pound; to husk or make flat by thrashing under a foot-driven molar (চাল কোটা, চিঁড়ে কোটা). **~নো** v. to cause to cut into pieces, to cause to dress; to cause to grind or pound; to cause to husk.
কোটা[2] v. to strike (against), to dash (against) (দেওয়ালে মাথা কোটা).
কোটাল pop. *var.* of **কটাল** and **কোতোয়াল** ।

কোটি *n.* ten million, a crore; the point or end of a sword or a bow or any similar object; a side, an edge; an end or extremity, a tip. ☐ *a.* ten million; innumerable, countless; (math.) ordinate. **~কল্প** *n.* a crore of days of Brahma (ব্রহ্মা) which is equal to 432000000000000000 years of man; eternity. **কোটিপতি, কোটীশ্বর** *n.* a billionaire, a multimillionaire; an extremely wealthy man.

কোটেশন *a.* a quoted saying or excerpt, a quotation; (gr.) quotation-mark (" "); a price quoted, a quotation.

কোঠা *n.* a room; a brick-built room (also **কোঠাঘর**) ; a brick-built house, a building (also **কোঠাবাড়ি**) ; a stage (জীবনের শেষ কোঠা), a column or space (জমার কোঠা).

কোঠি var. of **কুঠি**।

কোড়া *n.* a whip, a scourge, a lash.

কোণ *n.* an angle; a corner; a bay (কোণ নেওয়া) ; the inside or interior (গৃহকোণ) ; edge, border (আঁখিকোণ) ; the point (ছুরির কোণ) ; the interior of a house where women live, a gynaeceum, zenana (সন্ধ্যা হতেই বাবুটি কোণে ঢোকেন). **~ঠাসা** *a.* driven into a corner, held or kept at bay, subdued. **~মাপক** *n.* a protractor. **প্রবৃদ্ধকোণ** *n.* (geom.) a reflex angle. **সন্নিহিত কোণ** *n.* (geom.) an adjacent angle. **সমকোণ** *n.* (geom.) a right angle. **সমকোণী** *a.* (geom.) right-angled. **সরলকোণ** *n.* (geom.) a straight angle. **সরলকোণী** *a.* (geom.) straight-angled. **সূক্ষ্মকোণ** *n.* (geom.) an acute angle. **সূক্ষ্মকোণী** *a.* (geom.) acute-angled. **স্থূলকোণ** *n.* (geom.) an obtuse angle. **স্থূলকোণী** *a.* (geom.) obtuse-angled. **কোণানুপাত** *n.* trigonometrical ratios.

কোণা, কোণাকুণি, কোণাকোণি, কোণাচে rej. spellings of **কোনা, কোনাকুনি, কোনাকোনি** and **কোনাচে** respectively.

কোতওয়াল alt. spell. of **কোতোয়াল**।

কোতরা *n.* a loose or thin treacle or molasses of blackish colour and slightly bitter taste.

কোতোয়াল *n.* a policeman; a constable; the chief of a police station; a police chief. **কোতোয়ালি** *n.* a police station; the profession of a policeman or a constable or that of the chief of a police station or a police chief.

কোথা *adv.* & *n.* where. **~ও** *adv.* at or in any place, anywhere. **কোথাও কোথাও** at or in some places. **~কার** *a.* of or from which or what place; (in contempt.) of or from an unknown or contemptible place. **~য়** *adv.* & *n.* where. **কোথা থেকে** from where, whence, wherefrom.

কোদণ্ড *n.* a bow; an eyebrow. **~টংকার** *n.* a twang of a bow.

কোদলানো *v.* to dig or to dig up with a spade.

কোদাল, কোদালি *n.* a broad-bladed digging tool, a spade **কোদালিয়া** *a.* one who digs with a spade. **কোদাল দিয়ে খনন** spadework. **কোদাল পাড়া** *v.* to dig with a spade.

কোন, কোন্ *pro.* & *a.* which, what (chiefly interro.) a certain, some (কোন দিন হয়তো শুনব). ☐ *adv.* in what respect, how (তুমিই কোন সাধু) ; why (আমিই কোন না বলি). **কোন কোন** *pro.* & *a. pl.* which ones.

কোনা *n.* a corner; a bay; the narrow inside of a room; a nook. **~কুনি, ~কোনি** *adv.* diagonally; slantwise, athwart. ☐ *a.* diagonal; slantwise; athwart. **~চে** *a.* aslant; awry.

কোনো, কোনও *pro.* & *a.* any; a certain, some (কোনো লোক বলেছিল) ; anyone (কোনোটি চাই না). **কোনো এক** someone, somebody; a certain. **কোনোকালে** *adv.* at one time; long ago; at any time. **কোনো কালে নয়** at no time, never. **কোনো কোনো** *pro. pl.* some, a certain. **কোনোই** emphatic form of **কোনো**। **কোনোক্রমে** *adv.* anyhow, somehow, by any means. **কোনোক্রমে নয়** by no means. **কোনোমতে** *adv.* same as **কোনোক্রমে**। **কোনোরূপে** *adv.* somehow, any how, by some means.

কোন্দল, (pop.) **কোঁদল** *n.* a quarrel; a wrangle, a brawl. **কোন্দল করা** *v.* to quarrel, to wrangle, to brawl. **কোন্দলিয়া,** (pop.) **কুঁদুলে** *a.* (*mas.* & *fem.*) quarrelsome; peevish.

কোপ[1] *n.* a blow with a sharp cutting

implement such as a sword. **কোপ মারা, কোপ দেওয়া** *v.* to deal a blow with a sharp cutting implement.

কোপ[২] *n.* anger, indignation, wrath, fury, rage. **কোপ করা** *v.* to express anger, to be angry (with). **কোপে পড়া** *v.* to incur one's anger or displeasure. **~কটাক্ষ, ~দৃষ্টি** *n.* an angry look. **কোপকটাক্ষ করা** *v.* to cast an angry glance. **~ন** *a.* given to anger, easily angered or irritable, irascible, wrathful; peevish. *fem.* **কোপনা।** **কোপনস্বভাব, কোপনপ্রকৃতি** *a.* easily irritable or angered by nature. *fem.* **কোপনস্বভাবা।** **~পরবশ, ~পরায়ণ** same as **কোপন।** **~যুক্ত** *a.* angry, wrathful; angered.

কোপানল, কোপাগ্নি *n.* the fire of anger or wrath or fury; fit of violent anger.

কোপানো *v.* to chop or strike with a sharp cutting implement as a sword; to dig with a spade. □ *a.* thus struck or chopped or dug.

কোপ্তা *n.* a kind of fried chop of meat.

কোফতা alt. spell. of **কোপ্তা।**

কোবালা var. of **কবালা।**

কোবিদ *a.* (chiefly used as a *sfx.*) versed in, wise, learned, expert, skilled in (অশ্বকোবিদ = *n.* an expert on the breed and excellence of horses and also on how to train and manage them. সংস্কৃতকোবিদ = well-versed or erudite in Sanskrit).

কোমর *n.* the waist, the middle. **কোমর বাঁধা** *v.* (fig.) to gird up the loins. **~বন্ধ** *n.* a waist belt, a girdle. **~ভর, ~সমান** *a.* & *adv.* up to the waist, waist-high, waist-deep. **কোমরের বাত** lumbago.

কোমল *a.* soft; mild, gentle; suave, bland (কোমল ভাষা) ; sweet; tender, delicate; kind; weak (কোমল হৃদয়) ; (mus.) flat. □ *n.* (mus.) any of the notes in the subdued scale, a flat. *fem.* **কোমলা। কোমল করা, কোমল হওয়া** *v.* to soften. **~চিত্ত** *a.* soft-hearted, tender-hearted; kind; weak-hearted. **~তা, ~ত্ব** *n.* softness; mildness, gentleness; suavity, blandness; sweetness; tenderness; delicacy; kindliness; weakness. **~প্রকৃতি** *a.* softnatured, tender-hearted, of a mild disposition; kindly-natured; weak-hearted, weak-natured. **~প্রাণ, ~মতি** same as **কোমলচিত্ত। ~স্বভাব** same as **কোমলপ্রকৃতি।** *fem.* **কোমলস্বভাবা। ~হৃদয়** same as **কোমলচিত্ত। কোমলাঙ্গ** *a.* having a soft or delicate or tender body or limbs, of a delicate frame. *fem.* **কোমলাঙ্গী। কোমলায়ন** *n.* annealing. **কোমলায়ন করা** *v.* to anneal. **কোমলাস্থি** *n.* a cartilage.

কোম্পানি *n.* a number of persons trading together; a mercantile firm, a company; the East India Company; the (Indian) government (during the rule of the East India Company). **কোম্পানির আমল** the regime or times of the East India Company. **কোম্পানির কাগজ** the Company's securities or papers. **কোম্পানির মুলুক** the realm or dominion of the East India Company. **কোম্পানির লোক** (joc.) a government officer, a public servant. **কোম্পানির শাসন** the rule of the East India Company.

কোয় *pro.* (poet. & obs.) whomsoever, to anybody.

কোয়া *n.* any of the juicy divisions or sections of a fruit containing the seed, a replum, a legume, a pod (কাঁটালের কোয়া, কমলালেবুর কোয়া).

কোয়াসিয়া, কোয়াশিয়া *n.* quassia.

কোয়েল *n.* (poet.) the cuckoo. *fem.* **কেয়েলা।**

কোর *n.* (poet.) the fold of the body of a person sitting, one's lap.

কোরক *n.* a bud (of a flower). **কোরকোদ্গম** *n.* budding.

কোরণ্ড pop. var. of **কুরণ্ড।**

কোরফা alt. spell. of **কোর্ফা।**

কোরবানি *n.* (according to Islamic scriptures) immolation of a beast on a religious occasion.

কোরমা alt. spell. of **কোর্মা।**

কোরা[১] pop. var. of **কুরা।**

কোরা[২] *a.* brand-new; unbleached (কোরা কাপড়).

কোরান, কোরানশরিফ *n.* the Quran or Koran.

কোরানো, কোরানি pop. variants of **কুরানো** and **কুরানি** respectively.

কোর্ট *n.* a law-court, a court.

কোর্তা var. of **কুর্তা**।

কোর্ফা *a.* subleased, held by an undertenant. **কোর্ফা জমি** subleased land, the holding of an undertenant. **কোর্ফা প্রজা, কোর্ফা রায়ত** an undertenant, a subtenant. **কোর্ফা স্বত্ব** undertenancy.

কোর্মা *n.* a kind of highly-spiced grilled curry of meat or fish or eggs.

কোল[১] *n.* an aboriginal tribe of India; a member of this tribe.

কোল[২] *n.* the fold of the body of a person sitting, the lap (কোলে বসা) ; the flank of a person standing; the middle (মাছের কোল) ; flank or side or brink or middle (নদীর কোলে) ; foot, vicinity or neighbourhood (পাহাড়ের কোল) ; bosom, heart, the inside (সমুদ্রের কোল) ; an embrace (কোল দেওয়া). **কোল জুড়ানো** *v.* (of a child) to give delight to one (usu. the mother) who takes it up on one's lap. **কোল দেওয়া** *v.* to embrace; (fig.) to welcome or give shelter. **কোলে ওঠা** *v.* to climb up to one's lap or flank. **কোলে করা** same as **কোলে তোলা**। **কোলে চড়া** same as **কোলে ওঠা**। **কোলে তোলা** *v.* to take up in one's arms or to lift to one's flank; to take (up) on one's lap. **কোলে বসা** *v.* to sit upon one's lap. **কোলে নেওয়া** same as **কোলে তোলা**। **কোলে-পিঠে করে মানুষ করা** *v.* to bring up with care and affection (as by the mother or nurse). **কোলের সন্তান** one's youngest child; a suckling, an infant, a nursling. **~আঁকড়া** *a.* tied to the mother's apron-strings, too much attached to or dependent on mother. **~কুঁজো** *a.* stooping sideways. **~জুড়ানো** a. (of a child) causing delight to one (usu. the mother)who takes it on one's lap. **কোলজুড়ানো সন্তান** a darling child. **~পোঁছা** *a.* (of a child) last-born. **~বালিশ** *n.* a bolster. **~মোছা** same as **কোলপোঁছা**।

কোলন *n.* (gr.) the colon (:).

কোলা *n.* a large barrel or cask bulging in the middle; (dial.) a large field or meadow (কোলায় কোলায় চরা). □ *a.* corpulent, fat, pot-bellied. **কোলা-ব্যাং** *n.* a large species of frog dwelling chiefly in a field.

কোলাকুলি *n.* mutual embracing; warm greeting; (fig.—usu. iron.) alliance or mutual understanding (সেয়ানে সেয়ানে কোলাকুলি). **কোলাকুলি করা** *v.* to embrace mutually; to greet (each other) warmly; (fig.—usu. iron.) to enter into an alliance. **সেয়ানে সেয়ানে কোলাকুলি** two shrewd persons read or try to read each other's mind well; close and even contest or competition between two shrewd persons.

কোলা-ব্যাং see **কোলা**।

কোলাহল *n.* a loud confused noise or shout (as of many persons speaking loudly at the same time), an uproar, a tumult, din and bustle. **কোলাহল করা** *v.* to make a loud and confused noise. **~পূর্ণ** *a.* tumultuous, uproarious; clamorous; full of din and bustle.

কোশ[১] alt. spell. of **কোষ**।

কোশ[২] coll. corrup. of **ক্রোশ**।

কোশা alt. spell. of **কোষা**।

কোশী alt. spell. of **কোষী**।

কোষ *n.* a cover, a jacket, a sac (অণ্ডকোষ) ; a case, a sheath, a scabbard; a bladder (পিত্তকোষ) ; a store, a repertory, a fund, a treasury (রাজকোষ) ; a juicy division or section of a fruit containing the seed, a replum, a legume, a pod (কাঁঠালের কোষ) ; a receptacle, a container, a box, a chest; a water-container (usu. made of copper) shaped like a canoe used in religious worship by Hindus; a silk-cocoon; (bio.) a cell; (phil.& theo.) any of the stages of existence of a created being (অন্নময় কোষ) ; a dictionary, a lexicon, a glossary; the scrotum, the bag containing testicles; the palm of hand formed into a cup (এক কোষ জল). **~কলা** *n.* (bio.) a cellular tissue. **~কাব্য** *n.* an anthology of poems. **~কার** *n.* a lexicographer; a silk worm. **~গঠন** *n.* (bio.) cell-formation. **~গ্রন্থ** *n.* an encyclopedia; a dictionary. **~পাল** *n.* a treasurer. **~প্রাকার** *n.* (bot.) a cellplate. **~প্রাচীর** *n.* (bio.) a cell-wall. **~বদ্ধ** *a.* sheathed. **~বদ্ধ করা** *v.* to sheathe (one's sword etc.). **~বৃদ্ধি** *n.* hydrocele. **~মুক্ত** *a.* unsheathed, drawn.

কোষমুক্ত করা *v.* to unsheathe or draw (one's sword etc.). **কোষের একীকরণ** (bot.) cell-fusion.

কোষা *n.* a small water-container (usu. made of copper) shaped like a canoe used in worship by Hindus; a small canoe-shaped boat. **কোষাকুষি** *n.* a canoe-shaped water container and a small canoe-shaped spoon for taking water from a কোষা ।

কোষাগার *n.* a treasury.

কোষাধ্যক্ষ *n.* a treasurer; a cashier.

কোষী *n.* a small canoe-shaped spoon (usu. made of copper) for taking up water out of a কোষা ।

কোষীয় *a.* cellular.

কোষ্টা *n.* jute.

কোষ্ঠ *n.* a room, a compartment; the inner part of a (dwelling) house; a granary; the large bowel, the colon (কোষ্ঠ পরিষ্কার করা). **কোষ্ঠ কঠিন হওয়া** *v.* to have costiveness. **কোষ্ঠ পরিষ্কার করা** v. to evacuate thoroughly. **কোষ্ঠ পরিষ্কার হওয়া** *v.* to have bowels cleared; to have an easy or regular evacuation of one's bowels. **~কাঠিন্য** *n.* constipation, costiveness. **~বদ্ধ** *a.* constipated. **কোষ্ঠবদ্ধ হওয়া** *v.* to get constipated; to suffer from constipation. **~বদ্ধতা** *n.* constipation. **~শুদ্ধি** *n.* thorough or easy evacuation or purging of one's bowels.

কোষ্ঠী *n.* a horoscope, a nativity. **কোষ্ঠী করা** *v.* to cast one's horoscope. **কোষ্ঠী গণনা করা** *v.* to predict the future of one's life from one's horoscope. **নষ্ট কোষ্ঠী উদ্ধার করা** *v.* to cast one's horoscope from hypotheses or insufficient or uncertain data. **~গত** *a.* horoscopic. **~গণক** *n.* a horoscopist, an astrologer. **~গণনা** *n.* horoscopy.

কোহল *n.* alcohol.

কোহিনুর *n.* the famous diamond called kohinoor; (fig.) a very costly thing; (fig.) one's most valuable treasure; (fig.) the best specimen or person.

কৌঁসুলি, কৌঁসিলি *n.* a counsel; a barrister or lawyer.

কৌচ *n.* a couch.

কৌটা, (coll.) **কৌটো** *n.* a small container or box with a lid.

কৌটো coll. form of **কৌটা** ।

কৌড়ি arch. var. of **কড়ি** ।

কৌণিক *a.* pertaining to an angle; angular; diagonal; aslant. **~তা** *n.* angularity. **কৌণিক অবনতি** (astr.) the angle of inclination. **কৌণিক ভরবেগ** (mech.) the moment of momentum; (phys.) angular momentum.

কৌতুক *n.* a fun; a joke, a jest; inquisitiveness; curiosity. **কৌতুক করা** *v.* to make fun (of), to crack a joke; to jest. **~জনক** *a.* funny; jocular; curious, queer; interesting. **~প্রিয়** *a.* fond of fun or jokes. **কৌতুকাবহ** same as **কৌতুকজনক** । **কৌতুকাবিষ্ট** *a.* amused; curious. **কৌতুকী** *a.* funny, amusing; given to making fun or jokes; fond of amusements.

কৌতূহল *n.* inquisitiveness, curiosity. **~জনক** *a.* awakening curiosity, curious. **~নিবৃত্তি** *n.* satisfaction of curiosity. **কৌতূহলী, কৌতূহলাক্রান্ত, কৌতূহলাবিষ্ট** *a.* seized with curiosity; inspiring curiosity; curious. **কৌতূহলোদ্দীপক** *a.* that which rouses curiosity, inspiring or rousing curiosity.

কৌন্তেয় *n.* a son of Kunti (কুন্তী) of the Mahabharata.

কৌন্সিলি, কৌন্সুলি variants of **কৌঁসুলি** ।

কৌপ *a.* of a draw-well. ☐ *n.* water of a well.

কৌপীন *n.* a small piece of loincloth worn after the fashion of a suspensor by Indian ascetics. **~ধারী** *a.* one who is wearing the loincloth. ☐ *n.* an ascetic.

কৌমার *n.* boyhood; bachelorhood, bachelordom; celibacy; virginity; an unmarried son. ☐ *a.* relating to a boy or a bachelor. **~ব্রত** *n.* the vow of celibacy. **~ভৃত্য, ~ভৃত্যতন্ত্র** *n.* (the Ayurvedic system of) midwifery and treatment of children's diseases. **কৌমারী** *n. fem.* an unmarried daughter; one's first wife; (myth.) one of the six nymphs who nursed Kartikeya (কার্তিকেয়).

কৌমার্য *n.* bachelorhood or virginity; celibacy.

কৌমুদী *n.* moonlight, moonshine. **~পতি** *n.* the lord of moonlight; the moon.

কৌরব *n*. a descendant of King Kuru (কুরু) ; any of the one hundred sons of King Dhritarashtra (ধৃতরাষ্ট্র) of the Mahabharata. **কৌরব্য, কৌরব্যেয়** *a*. descended from King Kuru (কুরু) ; relating to the one hundred sons of King Dhritarashtra (ধৃতরাষ্ট্র).

কৌর্ম *a*. of the tortoise. ☐ *n*. the name of the Purana narrating the history of the second incarnation of Vishnu (বিষ্ণু) in the shape of a tortoise (কূর্ম) ।

কৌল *a*. born of good family; nobly born; born of a kulin (কুলীন) family; pertaining to a family or a clan or lineage, lineal; ancestral, hereditary.

কৌলিক *a*. pertaining to a family or a clan or lineage, lineal; ancestral, hereditary; in accordance with the tradition and usage peculiar to a family or line. ☐ *n*. a weaver by caste.

কৌলীন্য *n*. high birth or descent; state of being born in a kulin (কুলীন) family; state of being a kulin; the honorarium to be paid to a kulin. **~গর্ব** *n*. pride of high birth; pride for being born a kulin. **~প্রথা** *n*. the custom or practice of a kulin family; the kulin system.

কৌশল *n*. dexterity, skill, artistry; an artifice, a device, an expedient; a trick, a deceptive artifice or make-believe, a stratagem. **কৌশল করা** *v*. to devise means; to devise; to play a trick (with or upon); to deceive cleverly or artfully. **কৌশলে, ~ক্রমে** *adv*. artfully; tactfully; by means of a trick or a stratagem, craftily. **কৌশলী** *a*. dexterous, skilful; crafty, wily, artful, tricky.

কৌশিক *a*. made of silk, silken, silk.

কৌশিকী *n*. (in Hindu mythology) a form of the primordial Female Energy.

কৌশেয়, কৌষিক variants of **কৌশিক** ।

কৌষিকী alt. spell. of **কৌশিকী** ।

কৌষেয় var. of **কৌশিক** ।

কৌস্তুভ *n*. (myth.) a precious stone that Narayana (নারায়ণ) wears on his bosom.

ক্কচিৎ *adv*. at any place, anywhere; at any time, ever; rarely, seldom. **ক্কচিৎ কখনো** *adv*. rarely, seldom; sometimes. **ক্কচিৎ ক্কচিৎ** few and far between; sometimes.

ক্বণ *n*. the jingling sound of a stringed musical instrument when played on or of metals (esp. metal ornaments) clashing together. **ক্বণন** *n*. act of making this sound; jingle; jingling. **ক্বণিত** *a*. jingled; jingling. **ক্বণিত করা** *v*. to jingle.

ক্বাথ *n*. decoction. **ক্বাথ করা** *v*. to decoct.

ক্যাঁক *int*. expressing the sound of kicking or striking or of excitement or pain or a surly utterance. **ক্যাঁক-ক্যাঁক করা** *v*. to grumble or rebuke (usu. repeatedly) in a surly manner; to whine.

ক্যাঁচ *int*. expressing a creaking noise or the sound of chopping. **ক্যাঁচক্যাঁচ** frequentative **ক্যাঁচ** sound. **ক্যাঁচক্যাঁচ করা** *v*. to make a creaking sound, to creak.

ক্যাঁচকেঁচে *a*. creaky.

ক্যাঁচক্যাচানি *n*. the confused noise by many talking together; an intolerable noise.

ক্যাঁচরক্যাঁচর, ক্যাঁচরম্যাচর *int*. expressing the confused noise made by talking together; a harsh and unpleasant noise. **ক্যাঁচরক্যাঁচর করা, ক্যাঁচরম্যাচর করা** *v*. to talk together making a confused noise; to make a harsh and upleasant noise.

ক্যাঁট *int*. expressing peevishness. **ক্যাঁটক্যাঁট করা** *v*. to be given to peevish rebuking, to constantly express peevishness, to carp or nag (at); to look over bright or gaudy. **ক্যাঁটক্যাঁট করে বলা** *v*. to say with harsh outspokeness. **ক্যাঁটকেঁটে** *a*. harsh; peevish; carping; gaudy.

ক্যাঁত *int*. expressing the sound of kicking.

ক্যাঙারু *n*. the kangaroo.

ক্যানকেনে *a*. (of voice) thin and effeminate.

ক্যানসার *n*. cancer.

ক্যানেস্তারা var. of **কানেস্তারা** ।

ক্যাবলা *a*. dull-witted, unsmart, awkwardly unsmart. ☐ *n*. an unsmart fellow.

ক্যামেরা *n*. a camera.

ক্যাম্বিস *n*. canvas.

ক্যারদানি coll. var. of **কারদানি** ।

ক্যালেনডার, ক্যালেন্ডার *n*. a calendar, a chart showing days, weeks and months of the year.

ক্যাশবাক্স *n*. money-box, (loos.) a cash-box.

ক্যাস্টর অয়েল *n.* castor oil.

ক্রকচ *n.* a saw.

ক্রতু *n.* a holy sacrifice or oblation at which a fire is enkindled or a burnt-offering is given; the name of a Vedic sage or rishi (ঋষি) supposed to have been transformed into one of the group of stars forming the Great Bear of Ursa Major. **~পুরুষ** *n.* an appellation of Vishnu; the Kratu appellation of Vishnu.

ক্রন্দন *n.* weeping. **~রোল** *n.* a loud noise of weeping or wailing.

ক্রন্দসী *n.* the sky and the earth, heaven and earth.

ক্রন্দিত *a.* weeping; tearful. ☐ *n.* weeping; a call, a summons.

ক্রব্য *n.* meat. **ক্রব্যাদ** *n.* a cannibal; a carnivore.

ক্রম *n.* one of a series, a grade, order, sequence; procedure, a method, a form; a rule, a law, a directive; a syllabus (পাঠক্রম) ; succession (পর্যায়ক্রমে) ; a step or pace; course (কালক্রমে) ; a dilution (esp. of a Homoeopathic medicine). **ক্রমণ** *n.* act of pacing; act of walking, ambulation; act of going. **~নিম্ন** *a.* sloping downwards; declining or decreasing gradually; gradually lower or inferior. **~নিম্নতা** *n.* downward slope, declivity; gradual decline or decrease or descent; gradual lowness or inferiority. **~পরিবর্তন** *n.* gradual change. **~পর্যায়** *n.* grade or gradation. **~বর্ধন** *n.* gradual increase or development. **~বর্ধমান** *a.* increasing or developing gradually. **~বর্ধিত** *a.* increased or developed gradually. **~বিকাশ** *n.* gradual development, evolution. **~বৃদ্ধি** same as **ক্রমবর্ধন** । **~ভঙ্গ** *n.* break of continuity or serial order; disorder, confusion, jumble. **~মাণ** *a.* pacing or ambulating in a leisurely manner. **~শ** *adv.* gradually; seriatim. **~সূক্ষ্ম** *a.* getting gradually thinner or subtler; tapering. **~হ্রাসমান** *a.* gradually decreasing or declining or waning; on the wave. **ক্রমে ক্রমে** same as **ক্রমশ** ।

ক্রমাগত *a.* coming serially or gradually; serial, gradual; succeeding gradually; successive; continuous, incessant. ☐ *adv.* incessantly, continuously; always.

ক্রমাঙ্ক *n.* (phys.) calibre or its measurement. **ক্রমাঙ্ক নির্ণয় করা** *v.* to calibrate. **ক্রমাঙ্কন** *n.* calibration.

ক্রমানুযায়ী *a.* serial; gradual; successive. ☐ *adv.* serially; gradually; successively.

ক্রমানুসারে *adv.* according to the serial order, seriatim; gradually; successively.

ক্রমান্বয় *n.* a serial order or succession; gradualness. **ক্রমান্বয়ে** *adv.* serially, seriatim; one after another; gradually.

ক্রমায়াত *a.* succeeding serially, successive.

ক্রমিক *a.* serial, gradual. **ক্রমিক গুণফল** continued product. **ক্রমিক সংখ্যা** *a* serial number.

ক্রমেল, ক্রমেলক *n.* the camel.

ক্রমোচ্চ *a.* gradually higher; in the ascending order, ascending.

ক্রমোৎকর্ষ *n.* gradual progress or development, evolution.

ক্রমোন্নত *a.* gradually higher; inclining or sloping upwards; gradually increasing or developing or evolving. **ক্রমোন্নতি** *n.* gradual rise; upwards inclination or slope, acclivity; gradual increase or development; evolution. **ক্রমোন্নতিশীল** *a.* developing or evolving gradually; progressing; progressive.

ক্রয় *n.* buying, purchase. **ক্রয় করা** *v.* to buy, to purchase. **ক্রয়-বিক্রয়** *n.* buying and selling; commercial transaction; trading. **~মূল্য** *n.* cost price. **~যোগ্য** *a.* fit for buying, that which can be bought, purchasable. **~সাধ্য** *a.* same as **ক্রয়যোগ্য** । **~সীমা** *n.* purchasing power.

ক্রস *n.* two lines or other objects lying transversely to each other; a cross. **ক্রস করা** *v.* to go across; to cross out; to draw a line or lines transversely or vertically; cross. **ক্রসিং** *n.* act of crossing; a crossing; a cross-road.

ক্রান্ত *a.* of **ক্রান্তি** ; spread, covered, pervaded, surrounded.

ক্রান্তি *n.* transition, transit; attack; gait, change of state or condition; (astr.) the ecliptic; (astrol.) the zodiac; an obsolete Indian coin of the lowest value

(=1/3 কড়া). **~কোণ** *n*. (astr.) the obliquity of the ecliptic. **~পাত** *n*. (astr.) an equinoctial point; (geog.) the equinox. **~বিন্দু** *n*. (astr.) an equinoctial point. **~বৃত্ত, ~বলয়, ~মণ্ডল** *n*. (astr.) the ecliptic; (geog.) the tropics. **~বিশ্ব** *n*. (astr.) the celestial latitude. **ক্রান্তীয়** *a*. tropical (ক্রান্তীয় মরু) ; ecliptical. **ক্রান্ত্যংশ** *n*. (astr.) the celestial longitude.

ক্রিকেট *n*. (the game of) cricket. **ক্রিকেট খেলোয়াড়** *n*. a cricketer.

ক্রিমি alt. spell. of **কৃমি**।

ক্রিয়মাণ *a*. in the state of being done.

ক্রিয়া *n*. function; action; an act, a work; a ceremony or performance; a scriptural rite (অন্ত্যেষ্টিক্রিয়া) ; performance or observance of a scriptural rite, ritual; worship; (gr.) a verb. **~কর্ম** *n. pl*. scriptural rites; performance or observance of scriptural rites; rituals. **~কলাপ, ~কাণ্ড** *n. pl*. actions; functions; workings; activities, deeds; performances; scriptural rites collectively; performance or observance of scriptural rites; rituals. **~কুশল** *a*. efficient, expert. **~তৎপর** *a*. active, prompt. **~ন্বিত** *a*. observant of scriptural rites; ritualistic; (gr.) construed with a verb. **~পদ** *n*. (gr.) a verb. **~ফল** *n*. the result of an action; the consequence of an act. **~বাচক** *a*. (gr.) verbal; gerundial; participial. **~বিশেষণ** *n*. (gr.) an adverb. **~রত** *a*. engaged in work; active. **~শক্তি** *n*. capacity for work or exertion; energy, vigour. **~শীল** *a*. given to performance or observance of scriptural rites, ritualistic; given to holding functions (esp. pompous ones); active; operative; of active habits. **~সক্ত** *a*. having enthusiasm or passion for work, devoted to work. **~সক্তি** *n*. fondness or passion for work, devotion to work. **~হীন** *a*. inactive, without work or occupation; inoperative; (gram.) verbless, without the verb.

ক্রিশ্চান var. of **খ্রিস্টান**।

ক্রীড়ক *a*. one who plays; one who exhibits a show. ☐ *n*. a player; a sportsman; a showman.

ক্রীড়ন *n*. act of playing; exhibition. **~ক** *n*. a toy; one who is made the tool of another, a cat's-paw. **ক্রীড়নীয়** *a*. playable.

ক্রীড়মান *a*. engaged in playing or in exhibiting a show.

ক্রীড়া *n*. a play, a game, a sport; a pastime; a show, an exhibition; an amusement, an entertainment; fun. **ক্রীড়া করা** *v*. to play; to sport, to frolic. **~কন্দুক** *n*. a ball to play with. **~কৌতুক** *n. pl*. sports and pastimes, games and frolics. **~কৌতুক করা** *v*. to sport and jest. **~ঙ্গন** same as **ক্রীড়াভূমি**। **~চ্ছলে** *adv*. under pretence of sport; playfully; jestingly; whilst playing with. **~প্রতিযোগিতা** *n*. a competition of games or sports. **~ভূমি, ~স্থান** *n*. a playground, a playing field; an arena; a venue of a game or sport. **~মোদী** *n*. a lover of games, one who loves and enjoys games. **~রত, ~শীল** *a*. engaged in games, engaged in playing; playing. **ক্রীড়াসক্ত** *a*. attached (overmuch) to games or sports; frolicsome. **ক্রীড়াসক্তি** *n*. (overmuch) attachment to games and sports. **~সামগ্রী** *n*. sports goods.

ক্রীড়োদ্যান *n*. a pleasure garden.

ক্রীত *a*. bought, purchased. **~দাস** *n*. one who has been purchased to be the slave of the buyer for life, a slave. see also **দাস**। *fem*. **~দাসী** *a*. slave-woman; a slave-girl. **~দাসত্ব** *n*. slavery. **~দাসবৎ** *a*. slavish. **~দাস-ব্যবসায়** *n*. slave-trade. **~দাস-ব্যবসায়ী** *n*. a slave-trader, a slaver.

ক্রুজার *n*. a cruiser.

ক্রুদ্ধ *a*. angry; angered; enraged; wrathful; indignant. *fem*. **ক্রুদ্ধা**। **~দৃষ্টি** *n*. an angry look. ☐ *a*. with an angry look, looking angrily.

ক্রুশ *n*. a cross; a cruciform gibbet on which the ancient Romans executed malefactors; the gibbet on which Jesus Christ was crucified, the Cross. **~বিদ্ধ** *a*. crucified. **ক্রুশবিদ্ধ করা** *v*. to crucify. **ক্রুশাকার** *a*. cruciform.

ক্রুশকাঠি, ক্রুশকাটি *n*. a crochet.

ক্রুশবিদ্ধ, ক্রুশাকার see **ক্রুশ**।

ক্রূর *a*. merciless, unkind, hard-hearted; cruel, envious, malicious, spiteful; crooked; wicked; malignant. **~কর্মা** *a*.

one who performs horrible or cruel deeds; merciless. ~তা *n.* mercilessness, unkindness, hard-heartedness; cruelty; envy, malice, spite; crookedness; wickedness; malignance, malignancy. ~মতি *a.* crooked-minded, malevolent.

ক্রেংকার *n.* the call of a duck or swan.

ক্রেতব্য *a.* worth buying, that which can be or is to be bought, buyable, purchasable.

ক্রেতা *n.* a buyer, a purchaser, a customer. *fem.* ক্রেত্রী।

ক্রেয় same as ক্রেতব্য।

ক্রোক *n.* legal seizure or attachment of goods or property, seizure, distraint. **ক্রোক করা** *v.* to seize, to attach, to distrain. **ক্রোক হওয়া** *v.* to be seized, to be in distraint. **ক্রোকি** *a.* pertaining to distraint. **ক্রোকি পরওয়ানা** a warrant of distraint. **ক্রোকি সম্পত্তি** *a.* property of distraint. **মালক্রোক** distraint of movables.

ক্রোড়[1] *n.* a ten million, a crore. □ *a.* ten million, crore. ~পতি *n.* a multi-millionaire, a billionaire; an extremely wealthy man.

ক্রোড়[2] *n.* the fold of the body of a person sitting, the lap (ক্রোড়ে বসা) ; the flank of a person standing (ক্রোড়ে তোলা) ; flank or side or brink (নদীর ক্রোড়) ; foot or vicinity or neighbourhood (বৃক্ষ-ক্রোড়ে) ; bosom, heart, the inside (সমুদ্রের ক্রোড়). **ক্রোড়ে ওঠা** *v.* to get upon one's lap or to one's flank. **ক্রোড়ে করা, ক্রোড়ে তোলা, ক্রোড়ে নেওয়া** (now obs.) *v.* to take on one's lap; to lift to one's flank, to take in arms. See কোল[2] । **ক্রোড় অঙ্ক, ক্রোড়াঙ্ক** *n.* an epilogue of a drama. ~চ্যুত *a.* fallen or removed from one's lap; separated; estranged; out of control. ~পত্র *n.* a supplement (of a magazine, deed etc.); a codicil (of a will); an appendix (of a book).

ক্রোধ *n.* anger, wrath, rage, fury; indignation. ~ন, ~পরায়ণ, ~প্রবণ, ~পরবশ *a.* easily angered; hot-tempered; sulky, wrathful. ~বহ্নি, **ক্রোধাগ্নি, ক্রোধানল** *n.* the fire of anger or rage; terrible anger or fury. ~শান্তি *n.* appeasement of anger. ~ভরে *adv.* angrily, in a fit of ill-temper, in a huff. **ক্রোধান্ধ** *a.* blind with rage. **ক্রোধান্বিত, ক্রোধাবিষ্ট** *a.* angered, furious, enraged. *fem.* **ক্রোধান্বিতা, ক্রোধাবিষ্টা।** **ক্রোধাবেশ** *n.* incitement of anger. **ক্রোধী** *a.* hot-tempered; sulky by nature. **ক্রোধোদ্দীপক** *a.* exciting anger. **ক্রোধোদ্দীপন, ক্রোধোদ্রেক** *n.* excitement of anger. **ক্রোধোন্মত্ত** *a.* mad or maddened with rage, furiously angry, livid with rage. **ক্রোধোপশম** same as **ক্রোধশান্তি।**

ক্রোর var. of ক্রোড়[1] ।

ক্রোশ *n.* a measure of length or distance equal to 8000 cubits or a little more than two miles or three kilometres.

ক্রৌঞ্চ *n.* a species of the heron or the curlew, the stork. *fem.* ক্রৌঞ্চী। ~মিথুন *n. pl.* a couple or pair (one male and one female) of this bird.

ক্রৌর্য same as ক্রূরতা (see ক্রূর).

ক্লম *n.* extreme weariness, fatigue, exhaustion.

ক্লান্ত *a.* extremely tired, wearied, fatigued, exhausted.

ক্লান্তি *n.* extreme tiredness, weariness, fatigue, exhaustion. ~কর, ~জনক *a.* tiresome, wearisome, fatiguing, exhausting. ~নাশক, ~হর *a.* removing tiredness or weariness or fatigue; refreshing.

ক্লাব *n.* a club, an association, a society.

ক্লাস *n.* a class. **ক্লাসে ওঠা** *v.* to move to or to be promoted to a higher class. **ক্লাসে তোলা** *v.* to promote to a higher class.

ক্লিন্ন *a.* besmeared with liquid filth; besmeared with any morbid matter secreted from within one's body such as sweat, pus, slaver etc.; soiled; wet, moist.

ক্লিশিত same as ক্লিষ্ট।

ক্লিশ্যমান *a.* suffering; in sorrow or misery; in trouble; suffering from pain.

ক্লিষ্ট *a.* troubled; stricken with sorrow or misery; suffering; pained; painful; wearied, fatigued.

ক্লীব *n.* a man divested of manliness; a sexually impotent man; an asexual or neuter human being. □ *a.* unmanly; cowardly; sexually impotent; asexual or neuter. ~ত্ব *n.* lack of manliness;

cowardliness, cowardice; sexual impotency (in man); asexuality. ~লিঙ্গ *n.* (gr.) the neuter gender.

ক্লেদ *n.* liquid filth or soil; foul water; any morbid matter secreted from within one's body such as pus, sweat, saliva etc.; humidity, moisture. **ক্লেদাক্ত** *a.* besmeared with liquid filth; besmeared with any morbid matter secreted from within one's body; soiled, dirty.

ক্লেশ *n.* trouble; sorrow; misery; pain. **ক্লেশ দেওয়া** *v.* to trouble; to distress; to inflict sorrow or misery (on); to pain. **ক্লেশ পাওয়া** to be distressed or afflicted; to suffer. **~কর, ~জনক, ~দায়ক** *a.* troublesome; distressing; painful; difficult. **ক্লেশাবহ** same as **ক্লেশদায়ক। ক্লেশার্জিত** *a.* hard-earned. **ক্লেশিত** *a.* one who is being troubled or distressed or pained; troubled; sorrowful; in misery; afflicted, distressed; pained.

ক্লৈব্য same as **ক্লীবত্ব** (see **ক্লীব**).

ক্লোম *n.* (anat.) the gall-bladder; the kidney; the lung. **~নালিকা** *n.* (anat.) the wind-pipe. **~শাখা** *n.* (anat.) the bronchus.

ক্লোরিন *n.* a poisonous gaseous element of greenish yellow colour (used for purifying water), chlorine.

ক্ষওয়া alt. spell. of **খওয়া।**

ক্ষণ *n.* a measure of time equal to about four minutes; a very small point of time, a moment, an instant, a while (ক্ষণমাত্র) ; a point of time (এক্ষণ) ; a length of time (বহুক্ষণ) ; a particular point of time (শুভক্ষণ). **অশুভক্ষণ** *n.* an evil hour, an inauspicious moment. **কিছুক্ষণ** *n.* some time; a short time. □ *adv.* for or during some time; for or during a short time. **কুক্ষণ** same as **অশুভক্ষণ। প্রতিক্ষণ** *adv.* every moment, always; ceaselessly. **বহুক্ষণ** *n.* a long time. □ *adv.* for or over or during a long time. **শুভক্ষণ** *n.* an auspicious moment. **সর্বক্ষণ, সারাক্ষণ** *adv.* always. **~কাল** *n.* a moment, an instant; a very short time. □ *adv.* for a moment, for an instant; for or during a very short time. **ক্ষণকাল পরে** shortly after; a little later; before long, ere long. **ক্ষণকাল পূর্বে** shortly before. **~চর** *a.* roaming or existing for a very short time; fleeting, evanescent; short-lived; ephemeral; transient. **~জন্মা** *a.* (astrol. & pop.) born at an uncommonly auspicious moment; very fortunate; (loos.) endowed with rare qualities; highly gifted. **~দা** *n.* the night. **~দ্যুতি** same as **ক্ষণপ্রভা। ~ধ্বংসী** *a.* perishing in a moment; transitory; most frail. **~পরে** *adv.* shortly after; a little later; ere long, before long. **~পূর্বে** *adv.* a little while ago, shortly before. **~প্রভ** *a.* flashing or gleaming only for a moment. **~প্রভা** *n.* the lightning. **~ভঙ্গুর** *a.* breaking or perishing in a moment; transitory; most fragile. **~মাত্র** *adv.* only for a moment. **~স্থায়িত্ব** *n.* momentariness; transitoriness; existence for a very short period. **~স্থায়ী** *a.* lasting for a moment, momentary; transitory; continuing for a very short period (ক্ষণস্থায়ী সুখ).

ক্ষণিক *a.* lasting for a moment, momentary; lasting for a very short time, transitory. □ *adv.* for or during a moment only; for or during a very short time. □ *n.* a moment, a shortest point of time (ক্ষণিকের অতিথি).

ক্ষণে *adv.* in a moment, at one moment, at one time ('ক্ষণে হাতে দড়ি ক্ষণে চাঁদ'). **ক্ষণেক্ষণে** *adv.* frequently; repeatedly; at short intervals, every now and then; spasmodically.

ক্ষণেক *n.* the shortest point of time, a moment; a short time. □ *adv.* for a while; for a short time, a little. **ক্ষণেক দাঁড়াও** tarry a little or while; wait for a moment.

ক্ষত *n.* a wound; an ulcer; a morbid boil; a sore part of the body, a sore. □ *a.* wounded; ulcerated; sore. **~চিহ্ন** *n.* a scar. **~জ** *a.* coming out or born of a sore or wound. □ *n.* blood; pus. **~নাশক** *a.* removing or wiping out or healing up injury or wound. **~বিক্ষত** *a.* wounded at several parts of one's body, covered all over with wounds. **~যোনি** *a.* (of a woman) one whose virginity has been violated, ravished, deflowered. ~স্থান *n.* the wound; the injury; the injured or wounded part.

ক্ষতাশৌচ *n.* impurity of the body on account of a wound or sore or haemorrhage.

ক্ষতি *n.* injury, harm; damage, detriment; depreciation; loss. **ক্ষতি করা** *v.* to injure, to harm; to damage; to depreciate; to cause a loss (to). **~কর, ~কারক, ~জনক** *a.* injurious, harmful; damaging, detrimental; depreciatory; causing a loss (to), losing. **~গ্রস্ত** *a.* damaged; depreciated; one who has sustained a loss; injured, harmed. **ক্ষতিগ্রস্ত করা** same as **ক্ষতি করা।** **ক্ষতিগ্রস্ত হওয়া** *v.* to sustain a loss; to be harmed or injured; to be damaged or depreciated. **~পূরণ** *n.* compensation; indemnity. **ক্ষতিপূরণ করা** *v.* to compensate; to indemnify. **ক্ষতিপূরণ হওয়া** *v.* to be compensated; to be indemnified. **~বৃদ্ধি** *n.* loss or gain. **ক্ষতিবৃদ্ধি না হওয়া** *v.* to have nothing to lose or gain. **~সাধন** *n.* doing damage or harm. **ক্ষতিসাধন করা** same as **ক্ষতি করা।**

ক্ষত্তা *n.* a man born of a sudra (শূদ্র) father and Kshatriya (ক্ষত্রিয়) or Vaisya (বৈশ্য) mother; one's (esp. a king's) son born of his maid-servant.

ক্ষত্র *n.* the Kshatriya (ক্ষত্রিয়) caste; a member of this caste. **~কর্ম** *n.* an action or activities becoming a Kshatra (ক্ষত্র). **~জাতি** *n.* the Kshatriya caste. **~ধর্ম** *n.* the traditional obligations and duties of a Kshatriya (ক্ষত্রিয়) ; chivalry. **~নারী** *n. fem.* Kshatriya (ক্ষত্রিয়) woman. *masc.* **~পুরুষ।**

ক্ষত্রিয় *n.* the second caste amongst Hindus according to the scriptural order; they were chiefly entrusted with the administration and defence of the realm; a member of this caste; a caste amongst up-country Hindus, a member of this caste, a Kshetri (ক্ষেত্রি). *fem.* **ক্ষত্রিয়া।** **ক্ষত্রিয়াণী** *n.* Kshatriya (ক্ষত্রিয়) woman. *fem.* **ক্ষত্রিয়ী** *n.* wife of a Kshatriya (ক্ষত্রিয়) who may not necessarily be a Kshatriya woman herself. **~জাতি** *n.* the Kshatriyas (ক্ষত্রিয়). **ক্ষত্রিয়োচিত** *a.* becoming a Kshatriya (ক্ষত্রিয়).

ক্ষত্রোচিত *a.* becoming or befitting a Kshatra (ক্ষত্র).

ক্ষত্রী *n.* a Kshatra (ক্ষত্র) or Kshatriya (ক্ষত্রিয়) ; a caste amongst up-country Hindus or a member of this caste.

ক্ষন্তব্য *a.* pardonable, forgivable, excusable.

ক্ষন্তা *a.* & *n.* one who forgives.

ক্ষপণক *n.* an ancient Buddhist or (also) Jaina Digambar (nude) mendicant or ascetic.

ক্ষপা *n.* the night.

ক্ষম *a.* (used as a *sfx.*) able (কর্মক্ষম) ; deserving (মার্জনক্ষম) ; -able, -ible.

ক্ষমতা *n.* power, strength, might; ability, capacity; efficiency, proficiency, dexterity, skill; influence, control. **ক্ষমতা অভিযোজন** *n.* delegation of power. **~চ্যুত** *a.* devoid or deprived of power. **~প্রিয়** *a.* power-loving. **~প্রিয়তা** *n.* love of power. **~বান, ~শালী, ~সম্পন্ন** *a.* powerful, strong, mighty; influential; able, capable; proficient, skilful. *fem.* **~বতী, ~শালিনী।** **~শূন্য, ~হীন** *a.* powerless; lacking in influence; unable, incapable; inefficient, unskilled. **ক্ষমতাসীন** *a.* ruling; wielding power; possessed of power or authority, possessing or holding power.

ক্ষমা *n.* forgiveness; pardon; forbearance; tolerance. **ক্ষমা করা** *v.* to forgive; to pardon; to forbear; to excuse; to tolerate to brook. **ক্ষমা চাওয়া** same as **ক্ষমা প্রার্থনা করা।** **ক্ষমা দেওয়া** *v.* to forbear; to desist (from). **~গুণ** *n.* the quality of forgiveness or forbearance or tolerance in man. **~ধর্ম** *n.* the doctrine of forgiveness or pardon or forbearance or tolerance (as enjoined for man). **~পর ~পরায়ণ** *a.* forgiving, tolerant, given to forgiveness or tolerance. *fem.* **~পরায়ণা** **~প্রার্থনা** *n.* asking for forgiveness; begging pardon; an apology. **~প্রার্থনা করা** *v.* to ask for forgiveness, to beg pardon to apologize. **~প্রার্থী** *a.* (one who is asking for forgiveness or begging pardon or apologizing. **~বান** same as **~পর।** *fem.* **~বতী।** **~ভিক্ষা** same as

~প্রার্থনা। ~শীল same as ~পর। *fem.* ~শীলা। ~হীন *a.* unforgiving; unrelenting. **ক্ষমার্হ** same as **ক্ষম্য**।

ক্ষমী *a.* given to forgiveness or tolerance, forgiving, forbearing, tolerating, enduring; able; capable.

ক্ষম্য *a.* forgivable, pardonable; excusable.

ক্ষয় *n.* destruction (শত্রুক্ষয়) ; defeat (অধর্মের ক্ষয়) ; waste, loss (অর্থক্ষয়) ; erosion (কুলক্ষয়) ; depreciation (মুদ্রাক্ষয়) ; decay, waning (চন্দ্রের ক্ষয়) ; consumption, phthisis, tuberculosis (ক্ষয়রোগ). **ক্ষয় করা** *v.* to destroy; to defeat, to vanquish; to waste, to lose; to erode, to eat into or away; to depreciate; to decrease. **ক্ষয় পাওয়া, ক্ষয় হওয়া** *v.* to be destroyed; to be defeated or vanquished; to be wasted or lost; to be eroded, to be eaten into or away; to be depreciated; to decay; to decrease. **~কর, ~কারক, ~জনক** *a.* destroying; defeating; causing waste or loss; erosive; depreciating; causing decay or decrease; consuming. **~কাশ** *n.* consumption, phthisis, tuberculosis. **~ক্ষতি** *n.* wear and tear. **~জাত পর্বত** *n.* residual mountain. **~পক্ষ** *n.* the fortnight of the waning moon. **~প্রাপ্ত** *a.* destroyed; defeated; wasted, lost; eroded, eaten into or away; depreciated; decayed; decreased; dilapidated (ক্ষয়প্রাপ্ত অট্টালিকা) ; consumed. **~রোগ** same as **~কাশ**। **~রোগী** *n.* a person suffering from phthisis, a consumptive or tubercular patient. **~শীল** same as **ক্ষয়িষ্ণু**। **~হীন** *a.* undecaying, uneroding; that which does not erode or decay.

ক্ষয়া alt. spell. of **খয়া**।

ক্ষয়িত *a.* destroyed; defeated; wasted, lost; eroded, eaten into or away; decayed; decreased; dilapidated.

ক্ষয়িষ্ণু, ক্ষয়ী *a.* tending to decay or wear away or decrease; consumptive; perishable. **ক্ষয়িষ্ণুতা** *n.* tendency towards decaying or wearing away or decreasing; consumptiveness; perishability.

ক্ষর *n.* an ooze or oozing; exudation; dripping. □ *a.* oozy; exuding; dripping; perishable, fragile. **ক্ষরণ** *n.* oozing; exudation; dripping; destruction. **ক্ষরিত** *a.* oozed; exuded. **ক্ষরণ হওয়া, ক্ষরিত হওয়া, ক্ষরা** *v.* to ooze; to exude; to drip. **ক্ষরী** *a.* oozy; oozing; exuding; dripping.

ক্ষাত্র *a.* pertaining to kshartiyas (ক্ষত্রিয়) ; becoming a kshartiya. □ *n.* the traditional obligations and duties or might of a kshatriya; chivalry; the state of being a kshatriya. **~ধর্ম** *n.* the duties and obligations of a kshatriya.

ক্ষান্ত *a.* tolerant; forbearing; forgiving; desisted, stopped. **ক্ষান্ত করা** *v.* to cause to forbear or desist (from); to stop or terminate. **ক্ষান্ত দেওয়া** *v.* to forbear; to desist (from), to leave off. **ক্ষান্ত হওয়া** *v.* to forbear; to desist (from), to leave off (যুদ্ধে ক্ষান্ত হওয়া) ; to stop, to be over (যুদ্ধ ক্ষান্ত হওয়া). **ক্ষান্তি** *n.* tolerance; forbearance; forgiveness; desistance; a stop, termination. **ক্ষান্তি দেওয়া** same as **ক্ষান্ত দেওয়া**।

ক্ষার *n.* alkali; a basic salt. **ক্ষারক** *n.* a chemical base; alkali; a washerman. *fem.* **ক্ষারিকা**। **ক্ষারকীয়** *a.* (chem.) basic, alkaline. **~জল** *n.* alkali water, alkaline water; salt water. **~ধাতু** *n.* alkali metal. **~মিতি** *n.* alkalimetry. **~মৃত্তিকা** *n.* alkaline earth, fuller's earth.

ক্ষারণ *n.* act of causing to ooze or drip; melting; liquefaction; slandering, stigmatization; corruption.

ক্ষারিত *a.* caused to ooze or drip; melted; liquefied; slandered, stigmatized; corrupted.

ক্ষারীয় *a.* alkaline. **ক্ষারীয় সন্ধান** alkaline fermentation.

ক্ষালন *n.* washing (বস্ত্রক্ষালন) ; cleansing; exoneration (দোষক্ষালন, পাপক্ষালন) ; removal; purification. **ক্ষালন করা** *v.* to wash; to cleanse; to exonerate; to remove; to purify.

ক্ষালিত *a.* washed; cleansed; exonerated; removed; purified.

ক্ষিতি *n.* the ground (ক্ষিতিতল) ; clay; the earth, the world; (ক্ষিতি অপ্‌ তেজঃ মরুৎ ব্যোম). **~জ** *a.* earthborn; growing on the ground, earth-grown. □ *n.* Mars; the horizon. **~জ রেখা** *n.* a horizontal line, a horizontal. ~জ লম্বন *n.* horizontal parallax. ~তল *n.* the surface of the earth, the ground. ~ধর *n.* a mountain. ~নাথ, ~প, ~পতি, ~পাল *n.* a king. ~ভৃৎ *n.* a mountain. ~রুহ *n.* a tree (usu. a large one).

ক্ষিতীশ *n.* a king.

ক্ষিদা, ক্ষিদে *rej.* spellings of **খিদা** and **খিদে** respectively.

ক্ষিপ্ত *a.* (ety.) thrown, ejected; distracted; maddened, frenzied, mad; (of animals) must, musty; frantic; furious. *fem.* **ক্ষিপ্তা**। **ক্ষিপ্ত করা** *v.* to madden; to make musty; to make frantic or furious. **ক্ষিপ্ত হওয়া** to go mad; to madden, to become frenzied; to become musty; to get frantic or furious. ~তা *n.* mental distraction; madness, frenzy; (of animals) must; furiousness, fury. ~বৎ *adv.* like one gone mad, in a fit of madness; madly; frantically; furiously. □ *a.* mad, madding; frantic; furious.

ক্ষিপ্যমাণ *a.* in the state of being thrown or ejected.

ক্ষিপ্র *a.* swift, quick; prompt; rapid. □ *adv.* swiftly, quickly; promptly; rapidly. ~কারী *a.* ready in action, prompt. ~কারিতা *n.* promptness, promptitude. ~গতি *a.* swift-moving, swift, fast, nimble. □ *n.* a swift motion. ~গামী *a.* swift-moving, fast-going, swift, fast, nimble. *fem.* ~গামিনী। ~তা *n.* swiftness, quickness, promptitude; rapidity. ~বেগে *adv.* swiftly, quickly; fast; rapidly. ~হস্ত *a.* swift-handed. ~হস্তে *adv.* swift-handedly; quickly.

ক্ষীণ *a.* decayed (ক্ষীণ চন্দ্র) ; lean, thin (ক্ষীণ দেহ) ; slender (ক্ষীণ কটি) ; meagre; insufficient (ক্ষীণ আলোক) ; subdued (ক্ষীণ কণ্ঠ) ; feeble, weak (ক্ষীণ দৃষ্টি). *fem.* **ক্ষীণা**। **ক্ষীণ করা** *v.* to decay; to emaciate; to attenuate; to make slender; to lessen (আলো ক্ষীণ করা) ; to subdue; to enfeeble, to weaken. **ক্ষীণ হওয়া** *v.* to decay; to be emaciated; to become slender; to lessen; to become subdued; to become feeble, to weaken. ~কণ্ঠ *n.* a feeble or subdued voice, a faint or low voice. □ *a.* feeble-voiced; having a subdued voice. ~কণ্ঠে *adv.* in a faint or feeble voice; in an undertone. ~কায় *a.* leanbodied; emaciated; thin, small (ক্ষীণকায় বই). ~চন্দ্র *n.* the waning moon or the moon in wane (that is, the moon of the dark fortnight). ~চেতা *a.* feeble-hearted, weak-minded. ~জীবী *a.* having low vitality; short-lived; frail. ~তা, ~ত্ব *n.* decayed state; leanness, thinness; emaciation; slenderness; meagreness, insufficiency; subdued state; feebleness, weakness. ~দৃষ্টি *a.* weak-sighted. ~দেহ same as ~কায়। ~প্রাণ same as ~জীবী। ~বল *a.* weak; weakened; weak in military strength (ক্ষীণবল রাষ্ট্র). ~বুদ্ধি *a.* dull-witted. ~মতি *a.* weak-minded. ~মধ্যা *a. fem.* having a slender waist. *masc.* ~মধ্য। ~শক্তি same as ~বল। ~শ্বাস *a.* having one's breath failing; dying; completely deprived of vigour; enfeebled; short-lived (ক্ষীণশ্বাস প্রাণ). ~স্বর *n.* & *a.* same as ~কণ্ঠ। ~স্বরে *adv.* same as ~কণ্ঠে। **ক্ষীণাঙ্গী** *a.* (*fem.*) having a slim body.

ক্ষীণালোক *n.* dim light.

ক্ষীয়মাণ *a.* decaying; waning.

ক্ষীর *n.* milk (গো-ক্ষীর) ; juice; latex; milk condensed and sweetened by boiling (taken as a sweetmeat). ~পুলি *n.* a sweetmeat made from sweetened and condensed milk. ~মোহন *n.* a kind of sweetmeat. ~সমুদ্র, ~সাগর *n.* (myth.) a sea containing milk instead of water, the Milk Sea.

ক্ষীরা, (dial.) **ক্ষীরই** *n.* variants of **খিরা** and **খিরই** respectively.

ক্ষীরাব্ধি var. of **ক্ষীরোদ**।

ক্ষীরিকা var. of **ক্ষীরা**।

ক্ষীরোদ *n.* (myth.) a sea containing milk, The Milk Sea. ~তনয়, ~নন্দন *n.* the Moon (personified). ~তনয়া *n. fem.* Goddess Lakshmi.

ক্ষুঁয়া *n.* silk; jute; cloth made of silk or jute. ~তাঁতি *n.* a jute-weaver; a weaver of coarse cloth.

ক্ষুণ্ণ *a.* saddened; mortified; offended; restricted, restrained, frustrated, curbed, hindered; pulverized. ~মনা *a.* (mentally) distressed or mortified or aggrieved.

ক্ষুৎ *n.* hunger. **~কাতর, ~পীড়িত** *a.* distressed or afflicted with or suffering from hunger. **~পিপাসা** *n.* hunger and thirst.

ক্ষুদ, ক্ষুদি, ক্ষুদে alt. spellings of **খুদ, খুদি** and **খুদে** respectively.

ক্ষুদ্র *a.* small, little (ক্ষুদ্রকায়, ক্ষুদ্র বালক) ; base, mean (ক্ষুদ্রমতি) ; narrow; illiberal (ক্ষুদ্রাশয়) ; niggardly (ক্ষুদ্র দান) ; contemptible, insignificant (ক্ষুদ্র লোক) ; trifling (ক্ষুদ্র ব্যাপার) ; poor (ক্ষুদ্র অবস্থা) ; short, short-lived (ক্ষুদ্রপ্রাণ). *fem.* **ক্ষুদ্রা**। **~কায়** *a.* having a short and thin body, little, tiny (ক্ষুদ্রকায় প্রাণী) ; small and not voluminous (ক্ষুদ্রকায় গ্রন্থ) ; small (ক্ষুদ্রকায় বাহিনী, ক্ষুদ্রকায় অট্টালিকা). **~চেতা** same as **ক্ষুদ্রাশয়**। **~তম** *a.* smallest. **~তর** *a.* smaller. **~তা, ~ত্ব** *n.* smallness, littleness; baseness, meanness; narrowness, illiberality; niggardliness; contemptibleness; insignificance; triviality; poorness, poverty; shortness; short duration. **~দৃষ্টি** *a.* narrow in outlook; miserly. **~প্রাণ** *a.* having low vitality or short span of life, short-lived; mean-minded; miserly. **~বুদ্ধি, ~মতি** *a.* of limited intelligence, dull-witted; (inc.) mean-minded. ☐ *n.* dull-wittedness; humble opinion (আমার ক্ষুদ্রবুদ্ধিতে). **ক্ষুদ্রাকার** *a.* of small size or structure; small, little. **ক্ষুদ্রান্ত্র** *n.* the small intestine. **ক্ষুদ্রায়তন** *a.* small in size or magnitude; small-scale; small. **ক্ষুদ্রাশয়** *a.* mean-minded. **ক্ষুদ্রাশয়তা** *n.* mean-mindedness, meanness.

ক্ষুধা *n.* hunger; desire for food, appetite; desire; inclination; greed, avidity; a longing or craving. **ক্ষুধা বাড়ানো** *v.* to improve or increase one's appetite. **ক্ষুধা বোধ হওয়া** *v.* to feel hungry. **ক্ষুধা হওয়া** *v.* to feel hungry; to strike with hunger, to whet one's appetite (এ ওষুধে ক্ষুধা হবে). **~কর** same as **~বর্ধক**। **~কাতর, ~তুর** *a.* hunger-stricken, extremely hungry, famished; hungry. **~তৃষ্ণা** *n.* hunger and thirst. **~নাশ** *n.* loss of appetite. **ক্ষুধা নাশ করা** *v.* to still or dull one's appetite. **~নিবৃত্তি** *n.* appeasement or satisfaction of hunger. **~ন্বিত** *a.* hungry. **~বর্ধক** *a.* appetizing. **ক্ষুধাবর্ধক ওষুধ বা বস্তু** an appetizer. **~বর্ধন** *n.* appetizement. **~মান্দ্য** *n.* loss of appetite; (inc.) indigestion. **~র্ত** same as **~কাতর**। **~শান্তি** same as **~নিবৃত্তি**। **~সঞ্চার** *n.* feeling of hunger; appetizement. **দুষ্টক্ষুধা** see **দুষ্ট**। **দৃষ্টিক্ষুধা** see **দৃষ্টি**। **ক্ষুধা মানুষকে পাগল করে** (fig.) hunger drives the wolf out of woods.

ক্ষুধিত *a.* hungry; desirous; inclined (to); greedy, avid; longing or craving (for). *fem.* **ক্ষুধিতা**।

ক্ষুন্নিবারণ, ক্ষুন্নিবৃত্তি *n.* appeasement or satisfaction of hunger. **ক্ষুন্নিবৃত্ত** *a.* one whose hunger has been appeased or satisfied.

ক্ষুপ *n.* a shrub, a bush.

ক্ষুব্ধ, ক্ষুভিত *a.* perturbed; distracted; agitated; distressed; offended; mortified, aggrieved, sorrowed, pained; sorrowful, sorry. *fem.* **ক্ষুব্ধা, ক্ষুভিতা**। **ক্ষুব্ধ করা** *v.* to perturb; to distract; to agitate; to distress; to offend; to mortify, to strike with grief or sorrow, to pain.

ক্ষুমা *n.* silk, linseed, hemp; jute.

ক্ষুর *n.* a razor; a razor-blade; (of articles of furniture) a leg or foot or castor.

ক্ষুরধার *a.* (of intellect etc.) as sharp as a razor, very sharp or keen.

ক্ষুরপ্র *n.* (myth.) a kind of arrow shaped like a crescent moon; a crescent-shaped digging tool.

ক্ষুরা rej. spell.of **খুরা**।

ক্ষুরী *n.* a barber; a hoofed animal.

ক্ষেউরি rej. spell. of **খেউরি**।

ক্ষেত, ক্ষেতি *rej.* spellings of **খেত** and **খেতি** respectively.

ক্ষেত্র *n.* an agricultural land, a field (ক্ষেত্রজাত ফসল) ; an area, a place, a field (কাজের বিস্তীর্ণ ক্ষেত্র) ; a venue (যুদ্ধক্ষেত্র) ; jurisdiction, bounds (ক্ষেত্রবহির্ভূত) ; a holy place (কুরুক্ষেত্র, তীর্থক্ষেত্র) ; (phil.) the body, a sense organ, the mind; (geom.) a figure (চতুষ্কোণ ক্ষেত্র) ; (geom.) surface; one's wife (ক্ষেত্রজাত সন্তান) ; circumstances, condition, state (এ ক্ষেত্রে তুমিই দোষী). **~কর্ম** *n.* cultivation, agriculture, husbandry; action according to the circumstances. **~গণিত** *n.* geometry. **~জ** *a.*

grown on an agricultural field, produced by agriculture, agricultural; (of a child) born of one's wife by another man (usu. appointed by the husband). □ *n*. a son thus born. *fem*. *n*. ~জা। ~জীবী *n*. a peasant, a cultivator, a husbandman, a farmer, an agriculturist. □ *a*. one who earns one's livelihood by agriculture; depending on cultivation for one's livelihood. ~জ্ঞ *n*. (phil. & theol.) the immortal soul that is inherent in every individual creature. □ *a*. conversant with the circumstances or condition, au fait; one who knows what should be done in the circumstances; learned; dexterous, adroit; versed in or engaged in agriculture. ~পতি, ~পাল *n*. a land-owner, a landlord. ~ফল *n*. measurement of an area, area measure; measure of an area, area. ~বর্ধক লেন্স *n*. a field lens. ~মিতি *n*. geometry; mensuration. ~স্বামী, ক্ষেত্রাধিকারী, ক্ষেত্রাধিপতি same as ~পতি and ~পাল।

ক্ষেত্রী১ rej. spell. of খেত্রি।

ক্ষেত্রী২ *a*. land-owning. □ *n*. a husband (of a wife); a husbandman, a peasant, a cultivator.

ক্ষেপ১ rej. spell. of খেপ।

ক্ষেপ২, ক্ষেপণ *n*. casting, a throw (শরক্ষেপ, দৃষ্টিক্ষেপ) ; hurling or casting down; putting forth or placing (পদক্ষেপ) ; passing or spending (কালক্ষেপ) ; infringement, non-compliance (বিধিক্ষেপ). ক্ষেপণ করা *v*. to cast, to throw; to hurl down; to put forth, to place; to pass, to spend; to infringe, to disobey. ক্ষেপক *a*. one who or that which throws or hurls down or puts forth or places or passes or spends or infringes or disobeys. □ *n*. (of a book) an interpolated portion, an interpolation. ক্ষেপণাস্ত্র *n*. a missile. ক্ষেপণি, ক্ষেপণী *n*. a spoon-shaped oar, a scull; an oar; a casting-net. ক্ষেপণিক *n*. a sculler; an oarsman. ক্ষেপণীয় *a*. that which is to be or should be cast or hurled down or put forth or placed or spent or infringed or disobeyed; suitable for throwing or discharging. □ *n*. a missile.

ক্ষেপলা rej. spell. of খেপলা।

ক্ষেপা rej. spell. of খেপা।

ক্ষেপ্তা *a*. var. of ক্ষেপক (see ক্ষেপ২)।

ক্ষেম *n*. weal, welfare, well-being, benefit, good; preservation of a (valuable) thing obtained (যোগক্ষেম). ক্ষেমঙ্কর, ক্ষেমংকর *a*. benignant, benign. ক্ষেমঙ্করী, ক্ষেমংকরী *a*. *fem*. of ক্ষেমঙ্কর। *n*. an appellation of Goddess Durga (দুর্গা). ~বান *a*. well-off, prosperous. *fem*. ~বতী।

ক্ষোণি, ক্ষোণী variants of ক্ষৌণি।

ক্ষোদক *a*. one who or that which pulverizes or engraves or carves. □ *n*. a pulverizer; an engraver, a carver.

ক্ষোদন *n*. pulverization; engraving, carving. ক্ষোদন করা *v*. to pulverize; to engrave, to carve.

ক্ষোদা rej. spell. of খোদা।

ক্ষোদিত *a*. pulverized; engraved, carved.

ক্ষোভ *n*. grudge; perturbation; distraction; agitation; distress; offended state, huff; mortification, grief, sorrow, pain. ~শূন্য, ~হীন *a*. having nothing to complain against, ungrudging, unaggrieved.

ক্ষোভিত var. of ক্ষুব্ধ। *fem*. ক্ষোভিতা।

ক্ষৌণি, ক্ষৌণী *n*. the earth, the world. ক্ষৌণীশ *n*. an emperor; a king.

ক্ষৌম *n*. linen-cloth, linen (also ক্ষৌমবস্ত্র) ; linen-thread; flax. □ *a*. made of linen or linen-thread.

ক্ষৌর *n*. shaving; tonsuring (also ক্ষৌরকর্ম). □ *a*. pertaining to the razor. ~কার *n*. a barber; a tonsor. ক্ষৌরি rej. spell. of খৌরি। ক্ষৌরিক *n*. a barber. ক্ষৌরী *n*. a razor, a razor-blade.

খ[1] *n.* the second consonant of the Bengali alphabet.

খ[2] *n.* the sky, the air (খগোল, খপোত).

খই *n.* a very light food prepared by frying paddy in sand heated on oven, parched rice. **খই ফোটা** *v.* (fig.) to talk or prattle rapidly or volubly (just like grains of paddy bursting open noisily whilst being fried), to speak unusually verbosely and fast. **খই ভাজা** *v.* to fry paddy to prepare parched rice. **~চুর** *n.* a ball-shaped sweetmeat prepared by boiling coarsely-powdered parched rice in sugar malt, a sweet blob of parched rice. **~ঢেঁকুর** *n.* eructation tasting of bile (caused by indigestion), bilious eructation. **~য়া,** (coll.) **~য়ে** *a.* having the colour or shape of parched rice, grey or tiny.

খইনি *n.* a quid (of tobacco).

খইল *n.* oil-cake; earwax.

খওয়া *v.* to wear away or out, to be eaten away or in. ☐ *a.* worn away or out, eaten away or in. **~নো** *v.* to cause to wear away or wear out or eaten away or eaten in; to eat away or in. ☐ *a.* worn away or out, eaten away or in.

খক *int.* expressing the sound of a cough or a hawking sound. **খক করা** *v.* to make this sound; to cough or hawk. **খকখক** *int.* expressing the sound of coughing or hawking or laughing with such a sound continuously. **খকখক করা** *v.* to cough or hawk continuously. **খকখক করে তোলা** *v.* to hawk up or out. **খকখকানি** *n.* a fit of loud and continued coughing or hawking or laughter. **খকখকে** *a.* (of cough) attended with a hawking noise.

খগ *n.* the bird.

খগপতি, খগরাজ, খগেন্দ্র, খগেশ্বর *n.* the king of birds; (myth.) different appellations of Garuda (গরুড়).

খগোল *n.* the sky, the heavens, the firmament; a globe representing the sky, a celestial globe. **~বিদ, ~বিৎ, ~বেত্তা** *n.* an astronomer. **~বিদ্যা** *n.* astronomy.

খচ *int.* expressing the imaginary sound of chopping at one stroke or piercing suddenly; a pricking sensation. **খচখচ** *int.* repeated খচ sound. **খচখচ করা** *v.* to carp, to give a pricking sensation. **খচখচানি** *n.* carping. **খচখচে** *a.* that which carps.

খচমচ *int.* expressing a harsh clamorous noise (as of beating cymbals or of continuous carping). ☐ *n.* this sound; a troublesome affair, botheration (রাজসেবা কত খচমচ) ; hullaballoo, dissension and quarrel (খচমচ লেগেই আছে)।

খচরখচর, খচরমচর *int.* expressing a harsh rustling sound.

খচাখচ *int.* same as **খচখচ** (see **খচ**). *adv.* ☐ quickly and noisily (খচাখচ কাটা).

খচিত *a.* interwoven; enwreathed, strung; inlaid; inset, embedded; pervaded, diffused; bedecked, adorned. **খচিত করা** *v.* to interweave; to enwreathe; to string; to inlay, to inset, to embed; to pervade, to diffuse; to bedeck, to adorn.

খচোমচো alt. spell. of **খচমচ**।

খচ্চর *n.* the mule; (in abuse) a bastard, a rogue or scoundrel or scapegrace. **তিলে খচ্চর** *n.* (in abuse) an incorrigible scoundrel or scapegrace.

খঞ্চা *n.* a large dish or tray.

খঞ্চিপোশ *n.* a cover for a tray or a large dish.

খঞ্জ *a.* lame. **খঞ্জ হওয়া** *v.* to be lame, to become lame. **~তা, ~ত্ব** *n.* lameness.

খঞ্জন *n.* the wagtail. **খঞ্জন-গঞ্জন** *a.* putting the wagtail to shame in restlessness (খঞ্জন-গঞ্জন আঁখি).

খঞ্জনা *fem.* of **খঞ্জন**।

খঞ্জনি *n.* the tambourine.

খঞ্জনিকা *fem.* of **খঞ্জন**।

খঞ্জনী alt. spell. of **খঞ্জনি**।

খঞ্জর *n.* a kind of short dagger or scimitar, a han(d)jar.

খট *int.* expressing the sound made by

striking on or at something hard (as of knocking the door or of striking or stamping the hoof on stony ground). **খটখট, খটাখট** *int.* expressing repetition of this sound; thorough dryness. **খটখট করা** *v.* to strike noisily and repeatedly on or at something hard; to look hard and dry (রোদে খটখট করা). **খটখটে** *a.* thoroughly hard and dry.

খটকা *n.* a (sudden) doubt or suspicion, a misgiving; hesitation; a hitch (কাজে খটকা বেধেছে) ; a trouble or difficulty (খটকার অঙ্ক). **খটকা লাগা** to have a doubt or misgiving.

খটমট *a.* complicated, intricate, difficult (also **খটমটে**).

খটাং same as **খটাৎ**।

খটাখট *int.* expressing the sound made by striking repeatedly on or at something hard.

খটাৎ *int.* expressing a noise louder than **খট**। **খটাৎ খটাৎ** *int.* expressing repetition of this noise.

খটাশ, খটাস[1] same as **খট্টাশ**।

খটাস[2] *int.* expressing a noise louder than **খটাৎ**। **খটাস খটাস** *int.* expressing repetition of this noise.

খটিকা, খটিনী, খটী *n.* chalk.

খটোমটো var. of **খটমট**।

খট্টাশ, খট্টাশ same as **খট্টাশ**।

খট্টি *n.* an improvised cot for carrying the dead to the crematorium; a bier.

খট্টা *n.* a cot, a bedstead.

খট্টাঙ্গ *n.* a leg or foot of a cot.

খট্টারূঢ় *a.* mounted or lying on a cot; lazy; foolish; wicked.

খট্টাশ *n.* the polecat; the civet cat.

খড var. of খদ।

খড় *n.* hay; straw. **~কুটো** *n.* dry straw, grass, twigs etc. collectively.

খড়কে *n.* a toothpick; a small species (খড়কে পুঁটি, খড়কে বাটা).

খড়খড় *int.* expressing a rustling noise as of treading dry leaves; a grating noise or sensation. **খড়খড়ে** *a.* giving out or making this noise or sensation.

খড়খড়ি *n.* a venetian blind.

খড়ম *n.* a wooden sandal, a clog, (cp.) a sabot. **~পেয়ে** *a.* (esp. of a girl or woman) one with convex-shaped soles.

খড়রা *n.* a curry-comb.

খড়ি *n.* chalk (also **চা-খড়ি, ফুলখড়ি**) ; silt or alluvial clay (with which the forehead is painted); a cardinal number or a figure (খড়ি পাতা) ; dry dirt in the form of a crust on the skin (খড়ি ওড়া). **খড়ি ওড়া, খড়ি ওঠা** *v.* (of skin or body) to give off dry dirt (esp. when rubbed). **খড়ি পাতা** *v.* to divine or foretell by means of writing down numbers or drawing figures. **হাতে-খড়ি** see **হাত**।

খড়িকা older var. of **খড়কে**।

খড়িমাটি *n.* same as **খড়ি**।

খড়ো *a.* made of straw (খড়ো চাল) ; thatched with straw (খড়ো বাড়ি).

খড়্গ *n.* a large falchion for immolating beasts; a large falchion; a scimitar; the horny appendage on the nose of the rhinoceros. **~কোষ** *n.* the sheath of a sword. **~চর্ম** *n.* sword and shield, sword and buckler. **~পাণি** *a.* holding or carrying a falchion in one's hand, armed with a falchion. **~হস্ত** *a.* (ety.—rare) holding or carrying a falchion in one's hand; (fig.) extremely angry with, about to strike. **খড়্গাঘাত** *n.* the stroke of a falchion. **খড়্গাঘাত করা** *v.* to strike with a scimitar or a falchion. **খড়্গী** *a.* armed with a scimitar or sword. □ *n.* a swordsman; a rhinoceros.

খণ্ড *n.* a part; a fragment; a portion, a region (ভূখণ্ড) ; a piece (প্রস্তরখণ্ড, বস্ত্রখণ্ড) ; a slice (একখণ্ড পাউরুটি) ; a section (of a story, poem etc.); a volume, a copy (বইয়ের প্রথম খণ্ড). **~কাব্য** *n.* (rhet.) a minor epic or a short poem; an imperfect epic. **~কাল** *n.* a portion of a particular time, a part of a period. **খণ্ড খণ্ড** *a.* cut or broken or separated into pieces. **খণ্ড খণ্ড করা** *v.* to cut or break or separate into pieces. **~গ্রাস** *n.* (astr.) a partial eclipse. **~প্রলয়** *n.* a partial destruction of the universe; a tremendous upheaval or affray (resembling universal annihilation). **~বাক্য** *n.* (gr.) a clause. **~বিখণ্ড** same as **খণ্ড খণ্ড**। **~যুদ্ধ** *n.* a strife, a skirmish, an affray. **খণ্ডশ, খণ্ডে খণ্ডে**

adv. part by part, in parts; piece by piece, piecemeal.

খণ্ডন *n.* cutting or cleaving or breaking or dividing or separating into parts or pieces; cutting or severing; refutation (যুক্তিখণ্ডন) ; freeing from, vindication, absolution (দোষখণ্ডন, পাপখণ্ডন) ; annulment, rescission (বিধিলিপি-খণ্ডন). **খণ্ডন করা** *v.* to cut or cleave; to break; to divide, to separate; to sever; to refute; to free from, to vindicate, to absolve; to contradict; to confute, to reverse, to annul, to rescind. **খণ্ডনীয়** *a.* that which is to be or can be cut or cleft or severed; breakable; dividable, separable; refutable; vindicable, that which can be absolved; reversible, that which can be rescinded.

খণ্ডা *n.* a sword. **খণ্ডাতি** *n.* a swordsman.

খণ্ডাখণ্ডি *n.* severe brawl or fighting; quarrel.

খণ্ডানো *v.* to refute or cause to refute; to vindicate or cause to vindicate, to absolve or cause to absolve; to reverse or cause to reverse, to annul or cause to annul, to rescind or cause to rescind; (cty.—not in use) to cut or break, to cause to cut or break.

খণ্ডিত *a.* that which has been cut or cleft; cloven (খণ্ডিত খুর) ; sliced; broken, divided, separated; severed; refuted; freed from, vindicated, absolved; reversed, annulled, rescinded; cut short (খণ্ডিত আলোচনা, খণ্ডিত জীবন) ; imcomplete, obstructed, frustrated; partial (খণ্ডিত দৃষ্টি). **খণ্ডিত করা** *v.* to cut or cleave; to slice; to break, to divide, to separate; to sever; to refute; to free from, to vindicate, to absolve; to reverse, to annul, to rescind; to cut short, to impede completion (of), to obstruct, to frustrate. **খণ্ডিত বর্তনী** open circuit. **খণ্ডিতব্য** *a.* that which should be cut or cleft apart; refutable. **খণ্ডিতা** *n. fem.* (poetics) a heroine angered and made jealous at the sight of marks of cohabitation with another on the person of her lover. **খণ্ডিতাংশ** *n.* broken or sliced part. **খণ্ডীকরণ** *n.* dividing, slicing, cleaving. **খণ্ডীকৃত** *a.* divided, sliced, cleft.

খত *n.* a letter or a chit, a note; a note of hand, a promissory note, a debenture, a loan-bond; a written undertaking (দাসখত) ; act of rubbing esp. on the ground (নাকে খত). **নাকে খত দেওয়া** *v.* to rub one's nose on the ground (as a mark of undergoing punishment).

খতনা *n.* the Muslim custom of circumcision.

খতবা *n.* a Mohammedan public prayer delivered in mosques every Friday in the name of Mohammed or his heir or in that of a Muslim prince, khutba.

খতম *n.* end, termination; completion; removal; slaughter, murder. **খতম করা** *v.* to finish; to complete; to terminate; to accomplish; to put an end to; to remove; to kill, to slay, to murder, (sl.) to do in, to do to death. **খতম হওয়া** *v.* to be finished or completed or terminated or accomplished; to end; to be removed; to be killed or slain, or murdered, (sl.) to be done in, to be done to death.

খতরা *n.* fright, fear; danger; difficulty; a hitch.

খতানো *v.* to examine closely; to calculate; to reckon; to estimate.

খতিয়ান *n.* a book of accounts, a ledger.

খতিয়ে দেখা same as **খতানো**।

খদ *n.* a cavern, a mountain fault, a crevice; a very low valley.

খদির same as **খয়ের**।

খদ্দর *n.* a hand-woven coarse cotton cloth, khadi. **~ধারী** *a.* dressed in khadi, in khadi.

খদ্দের coll. form of **খরিদদার** (see **খরিদ**).

খদ্যোত *n.* the glow-worm, the firefly. *fem.* **খদ্যোতিকা**। **~মালা** *n.* a string of glow-worms, a multitude of glow-worms.

খনক *n.* a digger, an excavator. □ *a.* employed in or used in digging, digging.

খনখন *int.* expressing the sound as made by striking on bell-metal. **খনখন করা** *v.* to give out this sound; to speak loudly and with this sound in the voice. **খনখনে** *a.* giving out this sound.

খনন *n*. digging; excavation. **খনন করা** *v*. to dig; to excavate. **~যন্ত্র** *n*. a digging tool. **খননীয়** *a*. that which can be or is to be dug or excavated.

খনি *n*. a mine, a quarry.

খনিজ *a*. mineral. **খনিজ লবণ** rock salt. **খনিজ সম্পদ** mineral resources.

খনিত *a*. dug, excavated.

খনিত্র *n*. a spud; a small weeding tool; a pick-axe; a crowbar.

খন্তা *n*. a spud.

খন্তি var. of **খুন্তি**।

খন্দ[১] *n*. a ditch; a pit; a piece of low land.

খন্দ[২] *n*. crop (রবিখন্দ). **~কার, খোন্দকার** *n*. a producer of crops, a farmer; a (Muslim) title of honour awarded to wealthy farmers.

খন্য same as **খননীয়** (see **খনন**).

খপ *int*. expressing quickness, haste, suddenness (খপ করে). **খপ খপ** *int*. expressing quickly or suddenly one after another; quickly, hastily.

খপরা var. of **খাপরা**।

খপাখপ same as **খপখপ** (see **খপ**).

খপাৎ *int*. expressing quickness or suddenness.

খপুষ্প *n*. a mare's nest, a fiddlestick; moonshine.

খপোত *n*. an aeroplane, an airship.

খপ্পর *n*. clutches, grip; a trap; pantile; a roof of pantile, a pantile shed. **খপ্পরে পড়া** *v*. to get into the clutches or snares of.

খবর *n*. news, tidings; report, information; intelligence. **খবর করা** *v*. to inquire about; to communicate with (either personally or through letters). **খবর জানা** *v*. to have information; to be in the know; to get intelligence or news. **খবর নেওয়া** same as **খবর করা**। **খবর পাওয়া** *v*. to get news (of); to be informed (of); to come to know or learn. **খবর রাখা** same as **খবর জানা**। **খবরের কাগজ** a newspaper. **খবরাখবর** *n. pl*. all sorts of news or information. **খবরাখবর করা** *v*. to keep oneself in intimate contact with, to keep oneself well-informed about, to keep in constant touch with, to enquire after a person etc. off and on.

খবরদার *int*. expressing: take care, beware, be on guard, watch out, halt for safety. **খবরদারি** *n*. caution; cautiousness; act of looking after; careful attendance; care, custody, guardianship (ছেলেটি তার খবরদারিতে আছে) ; management (তার খবরদারিতে সংসার চলে).

খবিশ *a*. unholy; dirty, nasty. □ *n*. an evil spirit, a ghost; a dirty or slovenly person.

খমধ্য *n*. (astr. & geog.) the zenith.

খমির var. of **খামির**।

খয়রা[১] var. of **খয়েরি**।

খয়রা[২] *n*. a species of very small fish.

খয়রাত *n*. bounty; charity, almsgiving; alms, a charitable gift or donation. **খয়রাত করা** *v*. to give in charity; to give as alms. **খয়রাতি** *a*. charitable; gratuitous.

খয়া var. of **খওয়া** (*a*.).

খয়ের *n*. catechu.

খয়ের খাঁ *n*. (also *a*.) a yes-man, a flatterer, a bootlicker.

খয়েরি *a*. of the colour of catechu, dark brown, dark tan.

খর *a*. sharp, keen (খর তরবারি) ; severe, fierce (খর রৌদ্র) ; strong, violent (খরবায়ু) ; very quick or fast (খর বেগ) ; harsh, rough (খর বাক্য) ; (of water) saltish, salty, saline, hard. **খর জল** hard water. **~জালি** *n*. salt obtained by sunning something instead of boiling it. **~তর** *compar*. of **খর**। **~দশন** *a*. sharp-toothed. **~দৃষ্টি** *a*. keen-sighted, hawk-eyed. **~ধার, ~শান** *a*. very sharp. **~স্রোত** *a*. having a strong current. □ *n*. a strong current. *fem*. **খরস্রোতা**। **~স্পর্শ** *a*. rough to the touch.

খরখর *int*. expressing a grating noise or sensation (খরখর করে ঘষা) ; quickness or celerity (খরখর করে চলা). **খরখর করা** *v*. to make a grating noise, to grate; to give a grating sensation; to move or talk rapidly; to move fussily. **খরখরে** *a*. that which makes a grating noise or gives a grating sensation; rough, not smooth; restless; moving fussily.

খরগোশ *n*. the hare; the rabbit.

খরচ, (coll.) **খরচা** *n*. expenditure, expense; allowance (রাহাখরচ, খাইখরচ) ;

cost (মামলাখরচ) ; act of spending (সময় খরচ) ; consumption (স্টোভে তেল খরচ) ; debit (জমাখরচ). **খরচ করা** *v.* to spend; to consume. **খরচ লেখা** *v.* (book-keeping) to debit. **খরচ হওয়া** *v.* to be spent or expended; to cost; to be consumed; (hum.) to die, to go to one's account. **খরচের অঙ্ক** any of the entries on the debit side of an account, a debit entry; the total of the debit side, total debit; (loos.) an expenditure. **খাইখরচ** *n.* eating expenses; expenses for food. **টিফিন-খরচ** *n.* tiffin money, tiffin allowance. **পকেট-খরচ** *n.* pocket-money. **পথখরচ, রাহাখরচ** *n.* travelling allowance or expenses. **বাজে খরচ** incidental expenditure. **বিবিধ খরচ** miscellaneous expenditure. **হাতখরচ** *n.* pocket-money. **খরচখরচা, খরচপত্র** *n. pl.* expenses (collectively). **খরচপত্র করা** *v.* to make expenses; to bear the expenditure. **খরচান্ত** *a.* one whose purse has been exhausted by heavy expenditure (খরচান্ত হওয়া). □ *n.* termination of expenditure (খরচান্তে). **খরচে** *a.* lavish, extravagant, prodigal, spendthrift.

খরচের খাতায় (hum.) written off, corsidered to be lost or of no more use.

খরজ *n.* (mus.) the first note of the gamut. See **ষড়্জ**।

খরমুজ, খরমুজা, খরবুজ, খরবুজা *n.* the melon, the musk-melon.

খররা *n.* alt. spell. of **খড়রা**।

খরশুলা, খরশোলা *n.* a kind of small fish.

খরা *n.* sunshine, the sun; summer; drought. □ *a.* strongly fried; over-fried. **~নো** *v.* to fry hard; to overfry; to overbake.

খরিদ *n.* buying, purchase. **খরিদ করা** *v.* to buy, to purchase. **~দার, খরিদ্দার** *n.* a buyer, a purchaser, a customer. **~বিক্রি** *n.* buying and selling. **~মূল্য** *n.* cost price. **খরিদা** *a.* obtained by purchase; bought; purchased.

খরিফ *n.* autumnal harvest or crop.

খরোষ্ঠী *n.* an ancient language of the north-west frontier of India; its script or style of writing, Kharosthi.

খর্জুর *n.* the date-palm; its fruit, the date.

খর্পর *n.* a piece of broken earthenware, a potsherd; a skull of a dead person; the skull; an almsdish, a beggar's bowl; a thief; a sly rogue, a knave; a sharper, a cheat.

খর্ব[1] *a.* short, not tall (খর্বকায়) ; reduced, decreased, diminished (তেজ খর্ব হওয়া) ; thwarted, curved, restrained, foiled (গতি খর্ব করা) ; lowered, humbled (গর্ব খর্ব হওয়া). **খর্ব করা** *v.* to reduce, to decrease, to diminish; to thwart, to curve, to restrain, to foil; to lower, to humble. **~কায়** *a.* of short stature, short, small, diminutive. **~তা** *n.* shortness. **খর্বাকৃতি** same as **খর্বকায়**। **খর্বীকৃত** *a.* reduced, decreased, diminished; thwarted, curved, restrained, foiled; lowered, humbled.

খর্ব[2] *n. & a.* ten thousand million or ten billion.

খর্সুলা var. of **খরশোলা**।

খল[1] *n.* a small boat-shaped gallipot for pounding medicine, mortar. **~নুড়ি, ~নোড়া** *n. pl.* this gallipot or mortar and a pestle.

খল[2] *a.* malicious, envious; dissimulating, hypocritical; crooked; cruel; base, mean. **~তা** *n.* malice, envy; maliciousness; dissimulation, hypocrisy; crookedness; cruelty; baseness, meanness. **~নায়ক** *n.* a villain. **~প্রকৃতি, ~স্বভাব** *a.* of a malicious or crooked nature. **খলোক্তি** *n.* a crooked or insidious utterance.

খলখল *int.* expressing the metallic noise of sweet laughter. **খলখল করা** *v.* to laugh loudly with a sweet metallic noise. **খলখলে** *a.* loud and giving out a sweet metallic noise.

খলপা *n.* a coarse bamboo mat; a granary made of bamboo mats. **খলপা দিয়ে মোড়া** *v.* to cover with coarse bamboo matting. **খলপার বেড়া** a fencing of bamboo mats.

খলশে coll. form of **খলিশা**।

খলি *n.* oilcake; earwax, cerumen.

খলিত *a.* bald.

খলিন *n.* a bridle; rein; curb-bit of a bridle.

খলিফা *n.* a caliph, a khalif; a master artisan, master tailor; a tailor; (dero.) one who plays the big boss. **~গিরি** *n.* caliphate; the profession of an artisan or a tailor. **খলিফার রাজ্য** বা **শাসন** বা **আমল** বা **পদ** caliphate.

খলিশা *n.* a species of fish akin to but smaller than the anabas.

খলোক্তি see **খল**[২] ৷

খসখস[১], **খশখশ** *n.* a species of grass used in making fans; cuscus, khuskhus.

খসখস[২] *int.* expressing a rustling sound.

খসখসে *a.* not smooth, rough (to the touch).

খসড়া *n.* a preliminary sketch, a draft; a manuscript. **খসড়া করা** *v.* to make a draft.

খসম *n.* (mus.) husband.

খসা *v.* to become detached, to come away (খিল খসা) ; to come off (দেওয়াল থেকে চুনবালি খসা) ; to fall off, to be shed (গাছ থেকে পাতা খসা) ; to become loose (কোমরের কাপড় খসা) ; to become dishevelled (খোঁপা খসা) ; to drop off (মালা থেকে ফুল খসা) ; to get out of position accidentally, to slip (হাত থেকে খসে পড়া) ; to come out, to be uttered (মুখ থেকে কথা খসা) ; to be spent esp. unnecessarily, to be spent or lost (টাকা খসা) ; (sarcas.) to die (বুড়ো এবার খসবে) ; to flee, to escape (চোরটা খসেছে) ; to depart immediately (অনেক জ্বালিয়েছ, এখন খসে পড়ো). **~নো** *v.* to detach, to cause to come away; to cause to come off; to cause to fall off, to shed; to loosen; to dishevel; to cause to drop off; to cause to slip (away or out); to cause to come out, to cause to utter; to cause to be spent or lost.

খাই[১] *n.* a hole, a pit; a ditch, a trench (গড়খাই) ; a moat; depth (গর্তটার দু-হাত খাই).

খাই[২] *v.* (*pr.& 1st. per.*) eat. □ *n.* eating (খাই-খরচ) ; desire for food, appetite (যতই খাক, ওর খাই মেটে না) ৷ **খাই-খরচ** see **খরচ** ৷ **খাই-খাই** *n.* constant or strong desire for food. **খাই-খাই করা** *v.* to feel or express a strong desire for food; to be extremely hungry; to feel strong hunger constantly; to be insatiably hungry. **খাই-খালাসি** *a.* usufructuary. **খাইখালাসি সম্পত্তি** *n.* property in usufructuary mortgage. **খাইয়ে** *a.* able to eat much, voracious, gourmand, gluttonous; given to or fond of eating well, fond of choice dishes. **খাইয়ে লোক** a gourmand, a glutton; a gourmet, an epicure; a belly-god, a voracious eater.

খাওন *n.* act or manner of eating.

খাওয়া *v.* to eat; to drink (জল খাওয়া) ; to take or enjoy (চা খাওয়া, ওষুধ খাওয়া, হাওয়া খাওয়া) ; to smoke (সিগারেট খাওয়া) ; to chew (পান খাওয়া) ; to accept or take (ঘুষ খাওয়া) ; to take or receive, to suffer (মার খাওয়া, কিল খাওয়া) ; to cause to lose, to cause to be dismissed from (চাকরি খাওয়া) ; to spoil or ruin (মাথা খাওয়া) ; to consume or absorb (লণ্ঠনটা খুব তেল খায়) ; to eat away, to wear away, to corrode. □ *a.* eaten or drunk or taken or smoked or chewed completely or incompletely (পাখিতে-খাওয়া ফল); used by one whilst eating or drinking and yet unwashed (খাওয়া থালা) ; partly eaten away or worn away or corroded. **কিল খাওয়া** *v.* to receive a blow; to be buffeted. **কুরে খাওয়া** *v.* to scrape or gnaw away, to eat away. **গালি খাওয়া** *v.* to be rebuked or rated. **চরিত্র খাওয়া** *n.* character-assassination. **বকুনি খাওয়া** *v.* to be rebuked or abused or reprimanded, to be taken to task. **খাওয়া-খাওয়ি** *n.* mutual entertainment at tables; mutual feasting; (idiom.) mutual quarrelling (খাওয়া-খাওয়ি করা). **খাওয়া-দাওয়া** *n.* eating and drinking. **খাওয়া-দাওয়া করা** *v.* to eat and drink. **খাওয়ানো** *v.* to feed; to cause to eat or drink or take or smoke or chew; to cause to accept (ঘুষ খাওয়ানো) ; to cause to receive or suffer (মার খাওয়ানো) ; to cause to spoil or ruin (মাথা খাওয়ানো) ; to cause to consume or absorb (তেল খাওয়ানো) ; to cause to be eaten or worn away; to cause to be corroded.

খাঁই *n.* desire, craving; avidity, greed; demand (বরের বাপের বেজায় খাঁই).

খাঁকতি *n.* want; shortage; (pop.) avidity, greed, demand.

খাঁকার, খাঁকারি, খাঁকরি *n.* the noise of clearing one's throat, a hawking noise. **খাঁকার দেওয়া** *v.* to hawk.

খাঁ-খাঁ *int.* expressing: emptiness or loneliness (বাড়ি খাঁ-খাঁ করছে) ; suffering due to estrangement or bereavement (মন খাঁ-খাঁ করা) ; state of being extremely stricken or scorched with heat (রোদে মাঠ খাঁ-খাঁ করছে).

খাঁচা *n.* a cage; a frame (বুকের খাঁচা). **খাঁচার পাখি** a bird in a cage; (fig.) one under restraint or in bondage. **খাঁচায় ভরা** বা **পোরা** বা **আটকানো** *v.* to encage. **খাঁচায় বন্দি** caged, encaged.

খাঁজ *n.* a notch, an indent; a groove; a hollow, an aperture (দেওয়ালের খাঁজ) ; a line, a wrinkle, a furrow (কপালের খাঁজ) ; a fold (পেটের খাঁজ). **~কাটা** *a.* notched, serrated. **খাঁজ কাটা** *v.* to notch, to indent. **খাঁজ পড়া** *v.* to contract into wrinkles or furrows or folds; to become hollow. **খাঁজে খাঁজে** *adv.* to a T; fitting to the dovetail(s). **খাঁজে খাঁজে আটকানো** বা **জোড়া** *v.* to dovetail.

খাঁটি[1] *n.* (sl.) country-made or homebrewed wine, country wine, grog.

খাঁটি[2] *a.* pure, unadulterated (খাঁটি ঘি) ; genuine; real; honest, pure-souled, dependable (খাঁটি লোক) ; weighty, right, important, judicious (খাঁটি কথা).

খাঁড় *n.* molasses condensed into granular form.

খাঁড়া *n.* a large falchion used in immolating beasts; a large falchion; a scimitar; the horny appendage on the nose of the rhinoceros.

খাঁড়ি[1] *n.* an estuary; an inlet, a creek.

খাঁড়ি[2] *a.* husked but unbroken. **~মুসুরি** *n.* husked but unbroken lentil.

খাঁদা, (coll.) **খ্যাঁদা** *a.* snub-nosed. *fem.* **খাঁদি,** (coll.) **খেঁদি।** **খাঁদানাক** a snub-nose.

খাক *n.* ashes. **পুড়ে খাক হওয়া** *v.* to be burnt to ashes.

খাকসার *n.* a humble servant.

খাকি[1] *a.* dust-coloured, of light brown colour, khaki. ☐ *n.* a light drab cloth used esp. for military uniforms.

খাকি[2], **খাগি** *sfx. fem.* indicating: one who eats up, consuming, devouring (ভাতারখাকি, গতরখাকি).

খাকী rej. spell. of **খাকি।**

খাগ *n.* a kind of reed used as a pen.

খাগড়া *n.* a species of tall reed.

খাগড়াই *a.* made at Khagra (খাগড়া) in Bengal (খাগড়াই বাসন).

খাগী ref. spell. of **খাগি।**

খাজনা *n.* revenue; rent; **~খানা** *n.* a treasury. **খাজনা আদায়** *n.* realization of rent or revenue.

খাজা *n.* a kind of crispy sweetmeat made of flour and sugar. ☐ *a.* (of fruits) slightly hard (খাজা কাঁঠাল) ; (coll.) lacking in intelligence, stupid, good-for-nothing (খাজা লোক).

খাজাঞ্চি *n.* a treasurer; a cashier; a paymaster. **~খানা** *n.* a treasury; a cashroom; a paymaster's office.

খাজানা obs. form of **খাজনা।**

খাঞ্জাখাঁ *n.* (dero.) one who tries (ridiculously) to live in a princely style; a fop.

খাট *n.* a cot, a bedstead.

খাটনি var. of **খাটুনি।**

খাটলি var. of **খাটুলি।**

খাটা *v.* to toil, to labour (পরীক্ষার জন্য খাটা) ; to work (বাড়িতে রাজমিস্ত্রি খাটছে, এ রোগে ওষুধ খাটে না) ; to fit, to suit, to match, to become (হলদের পাশে কালো খাটে না, তোমার এ আচরণ খাটে না) ; to be laid out, to be invested in (ব্যবসায়ে বা সুদে টাকা খাটা) ; to come true (তার ভবিষ্যদ্বাণী খেটে গেছে) ; (usu. in neg.) to be of value, to be of (no) avail (পাপীর কাছে ধর্মের কথা খাটে না) ; to hold good (এখানে এ নিয়ম খাটে না). **জেল খাটা** *v.* to undergo a term of imprisonment, to serve a sentence. **খাটা পায়খানা** *n.* a service-latrine. **~নো** *v.* to cause to toil or serve or work; to supervise others at work; to lay out, to invest; to pitch (তাঁবু খাটানো) ; to hang (দেয়ালে আলনা খাটানো) ; to hoist, to ring up, to set (পাল খাটানো) ; to set (ফ্রেমের ছবি খাটানো).

খাটাল *n.* a large cattle-shed.

খাটিয়া *n.* an improvised cot usu. of coir rope.

খাটিয়ে *a.* industrious, laborious, hardworking.

খাটুনি *n.* labour, toil; effort; a (hard) task.

খাটুলি *n.* an improvised cot; an improvised cot for carrying the dead to the crematorium, a bier.

খাটো *a.* not long or tall, short (খাটো দড়ি, খাটো গড়ন) ; of short width (খাটো কাপড়) ; not loud, low (খাটো গলা) ; backward (পড়াশোনায় খাটো) ; inefficient (কাজে খাটো) ; lacking, short, weak (বুদ্ধিতে খাটো). **খাটো করা** *v.* to shorten, to reduce; to shorten the width of; to lower; to humble (কাউকে খাটো করা, কারও মান খাটো করা) ; to disparage, to belittle. **খাটো হওয়া** *v.* to become short; to become less wide or long than what is necessary, to be of short measure (জামাটা খাটো হয়েছে) ; to be inferior to (কারও চেয়ে খাটো হওয়া) ; to prove oneself inefficient; to be humiliated, to look small (লোকের কাছে খাটো হওয়া). **খাটো গলা** a low voice. **খাটো নজর** (lit.) shortsightedness; (fig.) narrow-mindedness, mean-mindedness. **কানে খাটো** hard of hearing. **বুদ্ধিতে খাটো** lacking in intelligence or understanding.

খাট্টা *n.* any sour substance, an acid. □ *a.* sour. **মেজাজ খাট্টা** out of humour.

খাড়ব *n.* any of the musical modes that are expressed in six notes.

খাড়া *a.* erect, upright; vertical; perpendicular; precipitous, steep; full, at a stretch, without break (খাড়া দু-মাইল, খাড়া দু-ঘণ্টা) ; standing (খাড়া পাহারা). □ *n.* a stem or stalk (শজনের খাড়া). **খাড়া করা** *v.* to cause to stand up; to set erect; to put up (দাবিদার খাড়া করা) ; to present; to bring into existence; to draw up (খসড়া খাড়া করা) to set up, to found, to establish (স্কুল খাড়া করা, যুক্তি খাড়া করা) ; to bring round (রোগীকে খাড়া করা). **খাড়া হওয়া** *v.* to stand up; to stand erect; to keep standing; to come round. **খাড়াই** *n.* height, altitude; upward slope, a steep gradient or rise. **~খাড়ি** *adv.* lengthwise.

খাড়ি var. of **খাঁড়ি**।

খাড়ু, (obs.) **খাড়ুয়া** *n.* a scalloped bangle or anklet (usu. worn by a woman whose husband is alive).

খাণ্ডিক *n.* a confectioner.

খাত *n.* a pit; a hole; a ditch; a pond, a tank; a creek; an inlet; a mine; a moat. □ *a.* dug.

খাতক *n.* a debtor.

খাতা *n.* a book for writing or scribbling; an account-book, a ledger; a register. **খাতা লেখা** *v.* to maintain an account-book or ledger. **~পত্র** *n. pl.* books for writing or scribbling; different account-books or ledgers; records; registers. **হালখাতা** *n.* a fresh account-book or ledger opened (usu. on the Bengáli/Indian New Year's Day) for the coming year; a (religious) festival on the occasion of ceremonial opening of the new account-book or ledger.

খাতির *n.* cordial treatment or reception (খাতির পাওয়া) ; respect, honour (বিদ্বানের খাতির সর্বত্র) ; influence (মুরুব্বির খাতিরে চাকরি পাওয়া) ; amity, good terms, intimacy (দুই বন্ধুতে খুব খাতির) ; interest, sake, account (চাকরির খাতিরে). **খাতির করা** *v.* to receive cordially; to treat respectfully; to care for (কারও খাতির করা) ; to comply with a friendly request of; to comply with. **খাতির পাওয়া** *v.* to receive or enjoy cordial reception; to receive cordial treatment; to be treated respectfully. **খাতির রাখা** *v.* to comply with a friendly request of; to comply with; to care for. **~জমা** *n.* certainty, asssuredness, assurance. □ *a.* assured. **খাতির-নাদারত, খাতির-নাদারদ** *a.* outspoken. □ *n.* slight, contempt; disregard. **~যত্ন** *n.* respect; polite regard; flattering attention.

খাতুন *n.* (Mus.) a title suffixed to the names of (unmarried) Muslim women.

খাদ[1] *n.* alloy; base metal. **~হীন, নিখাদ** *a.* unalloyed; unmixed.

খাদ[2] *n.* (mus.) the bass; a quarry; a pit; a hole; a ditch; a mine.

খাদক *a.* one who eats or consumes. □ *n.* an eater; a consumer.

খাদন *n.* eating; consumption.

খাদি var. of **খদ্দর**।

খাদিত *a.* eaten; consumed.

খাদিম *n.* a servant, an attendant; a caretaker or warden of a mosque.

খাদী *sfx.* indicating: one who eats, eating (নরখাদী).

খাদেম var. of **খাদিম**।

খাদ্য *n.* food. □ *a.* eatable, edible. **খাদ্য-খাদক-সম্বন্ধ** *n.* (lit.) the relation between food and its consumer; the relation resembling that between the hare and the hunter. **~গ্রহণ** *n.* taking food. **~নালি** *n.* (*anat.*) the food canal, the alimentary canal, the gullet, the oesophagus or esophagus. **~প্রাণ** *n.* vitamin. **~ভাণ্ডার** *n.* a food store, a grain store. **~মন্ত্রক** *n.* the food ministry. **~মন্ত্রী** *n.* the food minister. **~মূল্য** *n.* food price; food value. **~শস্য** *n.* food grains. **খাদ্যাখাদ্য** *n.* edible and inedible things; good and bad food. **খাদ্যাভাব** *n.* scarcity of food, paucity of food-supply, want of food.

খান১ dial. corrup. of **খানা৪**। **ভেঙে খান খান করা** to break to pieces, to smash into smithereens.

খান২ *n.* (used as a *sfx.*) a place (এইখান, সেখান).

খানকি *n.* a prostitute, a harlot, a whore. **~গিরি** *n.* prostitution, harlotry. **~পনা** *n.* act of behaving like a wanton, wantonness, whorishness. **~বাড়ি** *n.* a brothel.

খানদান *n.* a high or aristocratic family; aristocracy. **খানদানি** *a.* speaking of or becoming a high family, aristocratic; distinguished.

খানসামা *n.* a table servant, a khidmutgar. **~গিরি** *n.* the profession of a table servant; the occupation of a butler.

খানা১ *n.* a hole; a pit; a ditch. **~খোঁদল, ~খন্দর** *n. pl.* holes or pits or ditches. **~ডোবা** *n.* pits and ditches.

খানা২ *n.* place (পিলখানা) ; a house or abode (দৌলতখানা) ; a room (বৈঠকখানা). **~তল্লাশ, ~তল্লাশি** *n.* a search (usu.) made by the police. **খানাতল্লাশের পরওয়ানা** a. search-warrant.

খানা৩ *n.* cooked food; meal. (খানা খাওয়া) ; a feast (খানা দেওয়া). **~পিনা** *n.* eating and drinking.

খানা৪ *sfx.* indicating : a number, a piece, a fragment (দুখানা, চারখানা) ; used as the article 'the' (বইখানা, বাড়িখানা).

খানাবাড়ি *n.* a dwelling-house; a dwelling-house and land (usu. leased out) within the precincts of a countryhouse.

খানি *a.* milder form of **খানা৪**।

খানিক *adv.* for a little while (খানিক দাঁড়াও). □ *a.* a little, only a little, a bit. **~ক্ষণ** *adv.* for a little while. □ *n.* a little while.

খানুম var. of **খাতুন**।

খানেক *a.* (used as a *sfx.*) one, about one, one approximately (সেরখানেক, ঘণ্টাখানেক) ; nearly, approximately.

খান্ডার *a.* qurrelsome; termagant. *fem.* **~নি, খান্ডারি** *a.* termagant, shrewish.

খাপ *n.* a scabbard, a sheath (তরোয়ালের খাপ) ; a holster (রিভলভারের খাপ) ; a case (চশমার খাপ) ; agreement, congruity, suitability; closeness or density of texture, texture. **খাপ খাওয়া** *v.* to agree with, to be congruent with; to be in keeping or harmony with, to suit; to adjust oneself to. **খাপে রাখা** *v.* to sheathe; to put in the case. **খাপ থেকে খোলা** *v.* to unsheathe; to take out of the case. **খাপ-খোলা** *a.* unsheathed, bare. **খাপ-ছাড়া** *a.* unsuitable, unbecoming, inconsistent, irrelevant, incoherent, disjointed; casual, stray; queer, quaint (খাপছাড়া লোক বা স্বভাব).

খাপরা *n.* a potsherd; tile or pantile. **খাপরেল** *n.* a small hut with pantile shed.

খাপা১ var. of **খাপ্পা**।

খাপা২ *v.* to agree, to be congruent; (of textiles) to shrink. □ *a.* agreed; shrunk. **খাপানো** *v.* to cause to agree, to bring to agreement; to cause to shrink, to shrink. See also **খাপ খাওয়া**।

খাপি *a.* (of textiles) closely woven, close-grained.

খাপ্পা *a.* enraged; furious or angry. **খাপ্পা হওয়া** *v.* to get angry, to be out of temper, to get or fly into a rage.

খাবল, খাবলা *n.* the palm of the hand; a handful (এক খাবলা) ; the paw; a seizure or a stroke (usu. a sudden one) with the palm or the paw; a bite. **খাবলা মারা** *v.* to seize or strike or scratch (usu. suddenly) with the palm or the paw, to paw. to bite; (*fig.*) to (try to) appropriate to oneself a part of. **খাবলানো** *v.* same as **খাবল মারা**। □ *a.* seized or struck or scratched with the palm or the paw, pawed, bitten. **খাবলে নেওয়া** *v.* to snatch with the hand or paw, to grab.

খাবার *n.* food; meal; tiffin, snacks. □ *a.* edible, meant for eating or drinking (খাবার জিনিস, খাবার জল). **~ওয়ালা** *n.* a seller of snacks. **খাবার ঘর** dining room. **খাবার জল** drinking water.

খাবি *n.* an instance of obstructed breathing, a gasp. **খাবি খাওয়া** *v.* to gasp (as a drowning person does); (fig.) to be on the point of death, to have the last gasp; (fig.) to fumble.

খাম[১] *n.* an envelope, a cover. **খাম আঁটা, খামের মুখ বন্ধ করা** *v.* to close an envelope. **খামে আঁটা, খামে ভরা** *v.* to enclose in an envelope.

খাম[২] *n.* a pillar, a post. **খাম-আলু** *n.* a variety of yam.

খামকা, খামখা, খামোকা *adv.* variants of **খামাকা**।

খামখেয়াল *n.* eccentricity; whimsicality; vagary; a whim, a caprice, a freak. **খামখেয়ালি** *a.* eccentric; whimsical; capricious, freakish. **খামখেয়ালিপনা** *n.* freakishness, whimsicality; capriciousness.

খামচ, খামচা same as **খাবল, খাবলা**।

খামচানো *v.* to tweak or scratch with all the nails of a hand or a paw. □ *a.* tweaked or scratched thus.

খামচি *n.* act of tweaking with several (usu. five or four) fingernails. **খামচি মারা** *v.* to tweak thus.

খামাকা *adv.* without cause or provocation, for nothing, unnecessarily.

খামার *n.* a threshing-floor, a farmyard; a granary. **~বাড়ি** *n.* a granary, a farm; a granary-building, a farmhouse; a dwelling-house with a granary within its precinct.

খামি *n.* ferment, yeast; a joint or loop of a piece of ornament (such as a necklace).

খামির *n.* ferment, yeast, leaven.

খামিরা *n.* perfumed tobacco.

খামোকা, খামোখা pop. variants of **খামাকা**।

খাম্বা *n.* a pillar; a large post.

খাম্বাজ *n.* an Indian musical mode.

খাম্বিরা var. of **খামিরা**।

খারাপ *a.* bad, evil, ill, harmful (খারাপ অভ্যাস, খারাপ আবহাওয়া) ; inferior (খারাপ কাপড়) ; wicked (খারাপ স্বভাব) ; discourteous, uncivil, haughty, rude (খারাপ আচরণ) ; obscene, filthy (খারাপ কথা) ; bad, rotten, unwholesome (খারাপ খাবার) ; out of humour or rude (খারাপ মেজাজ) ; distressed, sad (মন খারাপ) ; unwell, indisposed (শরীর খারাপ) ; out of order, unserviceable (ঘড়িটা খারাপ হয়েছে) ; miserable, indigent (খারাপ আর্থিক অবস্থা) ; deteriorated, worsened, alarming (রোগীর অবস্থা খারাপ হওয়া) ; hard to cure or infectious (খারাপ রোগ বা রোগী) ; infected (খারাপ রক্ত) ; ominous, inauspicious (খারাপ দিন) ; ugly (খারাপ চেহারা) ; deranged (মাথা খারাপ) ; soiled, dirty (কাদা লেগে জামাটা খারাপ হয়েছে) ; evil or difficult (খারাপ পথ). **খারাপ করা** *v.* to make bad; to spoil, to bungle (কাজ খারাপ করা) ; to pollute (চরিত্র খারাপ করা) ; to soil (জামা খারাপ করা) ; to make or become unwell (শরীর খারাপ করা) ; to ruin (স্বাস্থ্য খারাপ করা) ; to distress or feel distressed (মন খারাপ করা) ; to cause a decline (আর্থিক অবস্থা খারাপ করা) ; to make or grow worse, to worsen, to deteriorate (রোগীর অবস্থা খারাপ করা) ; to put out of order, to damage (সে ঘড়িটাকে খারাপ করেছে) ; to soil or deface (সে বইখানাকে খারাপ করেছে) ; to ruffle (চুল খারাপ করা) ; to derange (মাথা খারাপ করা) ; to upset (পেট খারাপ করা). **মন খারাপ করা** *v.* to feel distressed, to become glum or morose. **মাথা খারাপ করা** *v.* to get crazy; to worry. **মুখ খারাপ করা** *v.* to utter or use filthy words. **মেজাজ খারাপ করা** *v.* to lose one's temper; to get out of humour. **শরীর খারাপ করা** *v.* to feel indisposed; to be indisposed; to spoil or ruin one's health.

খারাবি *n.* harm; ruin, utter ruin, disaster; villainy, wickedness.

খারিজ *a.* rejected, dismissed, set aside; cast away, forsaken; discarded; revised; substituted. □ *n.* annulment; rejection, dismissal; act of casting away or forsaking, discarding; revision, substitution. **খারিজ করা** *v.* to reject, to dismiss, to set aside; to cast away, to forsake, to discard; to revise, to substitute.

খারিজা *a.* same as **খারিজ** (*a.*). **খারিজ-দাখিল** *n.* substitution of names in the rent-roll, mutation (also **দাখিল-খারিজ**).

খাল *n.* a canal; a strait; a channel; a quagmire; a pit; lowland (also **খালিজমি**) ; (dial.) cramp; (dial.) skin, hide. **খাল কাটা** *v.* to dig a canal or a channel. **খাল তোলা** *v.* to flay. **খাল ধরা** *v.* to have a cramp; to cramp. **খাল কেটে কুমির (বা বেনো জল) আনা** *v.* to invite evil, to ask or look for trouble, to allow room to an evil-doer through indiscreet act; to dig one's grave.

খালই var. of **খালুই**।

খালা *n.* (Mus.) the husband of one's mother's sister, an uncle. *fem.* **খালু** one's mother's sister, an aunt. **~তো** *a.* born of one's mother's sister; related through an aunt.

খালাস *n.* release (of a prisoner); acquittal (of an accused); delivery (of a woman in travail); relief, riddance (দায় থেকে খালাস) ; (of a consignment) act of taking delivery (of); unloading; (of a thing pawned or mortgaged) redeeming. □ *a.* released; acquitted; delivered (of a child); relieved, rid; that which has been taken delivery of; unloaded; redeemed. **খালাস করা** *v.* to release; to obtain the acquittal of; to deliver (a woman in travail) of a child; to relieve, to rid; to take delivery of; to unload; to redeem. **খালাস দেওয়া** *v.* to release; to acquit; to relieve, to rid; to give delivery of. **খালাস পাওয়া** *v.* to be released or acquitted; to be delivered of a child; to be relieved. **~পত্র** *n.* a passport; an order for acquittal or release.

খালাসি[1] *a.* released; acquitted; that which has been taken delivery of; unloaded; redeemed. **খাইখালাসি** *a.* usufructuary.

খালাসি[2] *n.* a shipmate, a mate; (rare) an ordinary soldier or sailor without rank.

খালি[1] *a.* empty (খালি কলসি) ; vacant (খালি পদ) ; void; bare (খালি গা) ; incessant, continuous (খালি কান্না) ; mere (খালি ধাপ্পা). □ *adv.* only (খালি একটু বসল) ; always (খালি কাঁদে). **~হাত** *a.* penniless, moneyless. □ *n.* empty-handedness. **~হাতে** *adv.* empty-handed, carrying nothing. **~পেট** *n.* empty stomach.

খালি-খালি *adv.* & *a.* for nothing (আমাকে খালি-খালি বকছ) ; rather empty (ঘরখানা খালি-খালি ঠেকছে).

খালিজুলি *n.* a very small stream, a streamlet.

খালিত্য *n.* baldness.

খালু see **খালা**।

খালুই *n.* a small portable creel; a fishcreel; fisherman's wicker-basket.

খাস *a.* especial, special (খাসদরবার) ; personal, private, own (খাসকামরা) ; under direct ownership or control of the proprietor (খাসসম্পত্তি). **~কামরা** *n.* a private chamber. **~খামার** *n.* agricultural land not let out to the tenants but cultivated directly by the owner; a demesne, a demain. **~নবিশ, ~মুনশি** *n.* a private secretary; a personal assistant. **~বরদার** *n.* a mace-bearer. **~মহল, ~মহাল, ~সম্পত্তি** *n.* an estate directly under the landlord; a demesne, a demain. **খাসে আনা, খাস করা** *n.* to bring under direct control, to take away from tenancy.

খাসগেলাস *n.* cutglass; a chandelier made of cutglass.

খাসা *a.* of superior quality; excellent, fine; delicious.

খাসি *n.* a castrated goat; (in mild rebuke) a fool, a nincompoop. □ *a.* castrated (খাসি ভেড়া, খাসি মোরগ). **খাসি করা** *v.* to castrate.

খাস্তা[1] *a.* corrupted, spoilt. **সাত (*বা* পাঁচ) নকলে আসল খাস্তা** frequent imitations spoil (or corrupt the original), (cp.) Religion hides her face when her clergymen preach.

খাস্তা[2] *a.* (of food) crisp (খাস্তা বিস্কুট, খাস্তা কচুরি). □ *n.* a kind of crisp sweetmeat.

খিঁচ *n.* a grit; a slight defect or omission or trouble or difficulty; discord or disagreement, a hitch; a pull or sprain or cramp; a debate or argument. **খিঁচ ধরা** *v.* to have a sprain or cramp. **খিঁচ পড়া** *v.* to have a slight defect or omission. **খিঁচ মারা** *v.* to give a pull. **খিঁচ মিটানো** *v.* to settle a dispute, to end a quarrel or misunderstanding. **খিঁচ লাগা** *v.* to have a sprain or cramp; to be stricken with discord or disagreement; to have a slight trouble or difficulty.

খিঁচা var. of **খেঁচা**।

খিঁচানো *v.* to make an ugly or angry movement of (মুখ খিঁচানো, দাঁত খিঁচানো); to make faces (at); to move spasmodically (হাত খিঁচানো); to scold. **দাঁত খিঁচানো** *v.* to make an ugly movement of one's teeth in anger or scolding, to grin in anger or scolding; to snap at (a person). **মুখ খিঁচানো** *v.* to make faces (at), to mouth; to scold. **খিঁচানি,** (pop.) **খিঁচুনি** *n.* an ugly or angry movement (of teeth or mouth); a grimace; convulsion, a spasm; scolding.

খিচখিচ, খিচমিচি, খিচমিচ variants of **খিচিমিচি**।

খিচড়ি var. of **খিচুড়ি**।

খিচিমিচি *n.* frequent scolding; frequent tiffs or petty quarrels; peevishness; mutual quarrel. □ *a.* peevish (খিচিমিচি লোক). **খিচিমিচি করা** *v.* to scold frequently, to worry and annoy by scolding, to find fault (with) continuously, to nag at; to quarrel mutually.

খিচুড়ি *n.* a food prepared by boiling rice and pigeon-pea together with spices and fat, kedgeree, hotchpotch. **খিচুড়ি পাকানো** *v.* to cook hotchpotch; (fig.) to make a mess of, to jumble up; to bungle.

খিটিমিটি, খিটখিট, খিটমিট *n.* displeasure or quarrel or discord on negligible account. **খিটিমিটি করা, খিটখিট করা, খিটমিট করা** *v.* to scold or quarrel peevishly. **খিটখিটে** *n.* peevish, pettish, petulant. **খিটখিটে স্বভাব** petulance.

খিড়কি *n.* a back-door, a postern gate.

খিদমত, খিদমদ *n.* act of waiting on or serving, attendance. **খিদমত করা** *v.* to wait on, to attend upon, to serve. **~গার** *n.* a waiter, an attendant; a servant.

খিদা, খিদে coll. corruptions of **ক্ষুধা**।

খিদ্যমান *a.* grieving (for), sorrowing; lamenting.

খিন্ন *a.* aggrieved, distressed; sad; tired; fatigued. **~মনে** *adv.* in an aggrieved state of mind.

খিমচানো same as **খিমচি কাটা**।

খিমচি *n.* a light tweaking (usu. with two finger-nails), a tweak; a pinch. **খিমচি কাটা** *v.* to tweak; to pinch.

খিরা, (dial.) **খিরাই** *n.* a variety of small cucumber.

খিল১ *a.* uncultivated, fallow (খিল জমি); serving as an appendix of a book, appendicular (খিল হরিবংশ).

খিল২ *n.* a bolt (of a door); a pin or a peg or a nail (for fastening or fixing anything); cramp (পেটে খিল লাগা). **খিল খোলা** *v.* to unbolt. **খিল দেওয়া** *v.* to bolt. **খিল লাগা, খিল ধরা** *v.* to have a cramp; to cramp.

খিলখিল *int.* expressing a giggling sound. **খিলখিল করা** *v.* to giggle, to titter.

খিলাত *n.* a robe of honour awarded by a prince; (loos.) a title or a gift of honour awarded by a prince.

খিলান *n.* (arch.) an arch; a vault, a dome. **খিলান-করা** *a.* arched; vaulted.

খিলি *n.* betel-leaf rolled into a cup having lime, catechu, betel-nut etc. within it.

খিলেন coll. form of **খিলান**।

খিলোদ্ধার *n.* development of fallow land, land development.

খিস্তি *n.* utterance of obscene language; obscene revilings, an instance of railing, raillery; obscenity. **খিস্তি করা, মুখ-খিস্তি করা** *v.* to utter obscene or filthy words; to rail (at or against), to revile.

খুঁচি *n.* a vessel for measuring rice paddy and other grains weighing $2^1/_2$ seers.

খুঁজা older var. of. **খোঁজা**।

খুঁঞা alt. spell. of **খুঁয়া**।

খুঁট *n.* the corner of a piece of cloth; a pinch (এক খুঁট খাবার).

খুঁট-আখরিয়া, খুঁট-আখুরে *n.* one who has little or no education; one who makes a fuss over trifles; a stickler (for perfection).

খুঁটন *n.* taking a small amount or portion with the tips of one's fingers or beaks, nibbling; pinching or nipping.

খুঁটা১ var. of **খোঁটা২**।

খুঁটা২, খোঁটা *v.* to take a small amount or portion with the tips of one's fingers or beaks, to nibble; to pinch or nip (ঘামাচি খুঁটছে). ☐ *a.* taken slightly with the tips of one's fingers or beaks, nibbled; pinched or nipped. **খুঁটানো, খোঁটানো** *v.* to cause to pinch or nip; to cause to be pinched or nipped.

খুঁটি *n.* a wooden post or pillar; a post or pillar made of bamboo; a peg, a stake (গোরু বাঁধার খুঁটি) ; (fig.) a patron, an upholder (খুঁটির জোর). **খুঁটি গাড়া** *v.* to set up or fix a post or pillar; (fig.) to settle down at a place permanently.

খুঁটিনাটি *n. pl.* trifling offences and omissions; trifles; details; niceties. ☐ *a.* trifling (খুঁটিনাটি ব্যাপার).

খুঁটিয়ে *adv.* minutely, closely, meticulously scrutinizingly; in a thorough-going manner; making an oversubtle distinction, in a hair-splitting manner. **খুঁটিয়ে দেখা** *v.* to judge or scrutinize minutely, to make a thorough and detailed examination, to scan carefully, to split hairs.

খুঁড়া, খোঁড়া *v.* to dig, to excavate; to knock or strike (মাথা খুঁড়ছে) ; to cause harm to a person by taking excessive notice of or praising him or her; to cast an evil eye on. ☐ *a.* dug, excavated. **খুঁড়ানো, খোঁড়ানো** *v.* to cause to dig or excavate; to cause to be dug or excavated. ☐ *a.* dug, excavated.

খুঁড়ি *n.* (of a woman) lame. ☐ *n.* a lame woman.

খুঁত *n.* a scar; an ugly mark; a defect in the shape or appearance; a defect; a flaw, a fault; an omission; a blemish. **খুঁত ধরা** *v.* to find fault with, to cavil, to carp at.

খুঁতখুঁত, খুঁতখুঁতানি, খুঁতখুঁতুনি *n.* carping, peevishness, pettishness; fastidiousness. **খুঁতখুঁত করা** *v.* to carp at, to cavil; to grumble mildly for a trifling omission or defect.

খুঁতখুঁতে *a.* peevish, pettish; fastidious, hard to please.

খুঁতি *n.* a small hand-bag or purse woven with thread.

খুঁতে¹ dial. var. of **খুঁতখুঁতে**।

খুঁতে², খুঁতেল *a.* scarred; possessing an ugly mark; defective in shape or appearance; defective, faulty; having a blemish.

খুঁয়া *n.* silk; jute; fabric made of silk or jute; a kind of coarse fabric.

খুঁয়ে *a.* one who weaves coarse fabric (খুঁয়ে তাঁতি).

খুক, খুকখুক, খুকখুকানি milder forms of **খক, খকখক** and **খকখকানি** respectively.

খুকি *n.* an infant girl; a little girl; a daughter. ☐ *int.* (voc.) my daughter, my girl. **~পনা** *n.* simulating the behaviour of a little girl, affected girlishness. **খুকু** affectionate form of **খুকি**। **খুকুমণি** *n.* (in endearment) dear girl.

খুঙ্গি, খুঙি *n.* a portable wicker-bag for carrying books, (cp.) a satchel. **~-পুঁথি** *n.* a satchel and the books in it.

খুচরা, (coll.) **খুচরো** *a.* miscellaneous and small, casual (খুচরো কাজ, খুচরো খরচ) ; converted into small coins (খুচরো টাকা) ; retail (খুচরো বিক্রি). ☐ *n. (sing. & pl.)* small coin(s), change. **খুচরো করা** *v.* to convert a currency note etc. into small coins, to change money. **খুচরো কারবার** *n.* retail business; petty or small business.

খুজলি *n.* itch, scabies.

খুঞা var. of **খুঁয়া**।

খুঞ্চি *n.* a small tray. **~পোশ** *n.* a cover for a tray.

খুট, খুট খুট milder forms of **খট** and **খট খট** respectively.

খুড়তুতো *a.* born of a younger brother of one's father or father-in-law, avuncular.

খুড়শ্বশুর see **খুড়ো**।

খুড়ো *n.* a younger brother of one's father, an uncle. *fem.* **খুড়ি** the wife of one's father's younger brother, an aunt. **খুড়শ্বশুর** *n.* a younger brother of one's father-in-law, an uncle-in-law. **খুড়শাশুড়ি** *n. fem.* an aunt-in-law.

খুদ¹ var. of **খোদ**।

খুদ² *n.* a particle or fragment of a grain of rice; a particle or fragment of any grain. **~কণা** *n.* a single such fragment or particle. **~কুঁড়া,** (coll.) **~কুঁড়ো** *n.* (lit.) huskings and particles of grains; (fig.)

very humble or meagre food; (fig.) paltry things or acquisitions.

খুদা[১] var. of **খোদা[২]** ।

খুদা[২] *v.* to engrave; to carve.

খুদাই, খুদানো older variants of **খোদাই** and **খোদানো** respectively.

খুদি[১], খুদে *a.* very small, tiny. *fem.* **খুদি[২]** । **খুদে রাক্ষস** one as gluttonous as the mythical anthropophagi, (fig.) an extremely voracious eater.

খুন *n.* blood; a murder, an act of homicide. □ *a.* exhausted (কেঁদে কেঁদে খুন) ; beside oneself (হেসে খুন). **খুন করা** *v.* to murder, to do (one) to death, to do (one) in. **খুন চড়া, খুন চাপানো, খুন চাপা** *v.* to become possessed with a murderous frenzy, to have murder in one's eyes; to grow furious, to fly into a towering rage, to see red. **খুন হওয়া** *v.* to be murdered; to be beside oneself; to become exhausted. **খুন কখনো চাপা দেওয়া যায় না** murder will out.

খুনখারাব, খুনখারাবি, খুনখারাপি *n.* a bloody affray or riot; an extensive bloodshed.

খুনসুটি *n.* a bickering for pleasure; an amorous bickering for pleasure.

খুনি, (coll.) **খুনে** *a.* murderous; one who has committed murder (খুনি আসামি) ; extremely cruel; blood-red (খুনে-রং). □ *n.* a murderer; an extremely cruel man.

খুনোখুনি *n.* mutual killing; a violent affray; a tumultuous brawl or bloodshed. **খুনোখুনি করা** *বা* **হওয়া** *v.* to be engaged in mutual killing or a violent affray or a tumultuous brawl.

খুন্তি *n.* a cooking tool resembling a spud, a cooking spud.

খুপরি n. a small house, a hovel, a small (and usu. dingy) room, a shack; a hole (পায়রার খুপরি); a cell; a recess, a niche. **খুপরি-করা** *a.* divided into small rooms or holes or cells. **খুপরি-কাটা** *a.* recessed (খুপরি-কাটা দেওয়াল).

খুপসুরত var. of **খুবসুরত** ।

খুপি[১] *n.* a small (usu. square) cell.

খুপি[২] *a.* (chiefly used as a *sfx.*) cellular, having square cells (চৌখুপি).

খুব *adv.* very (খুব সুন্দর) ; very much, too much (খুব খায়) ; excellently (খুব বলেছে) ; surely (খুব পারবে). □ *int.* enough, surely. **খুব করা** *v.* to do the right thing; to serve right; to do much; (sarcas.) to do nothing, to bungle.

খুবলানো same as **খাবলানো** । see **খাবল** ।

খুবরি var. of **খুপরি** ।

খুবসুরত *a.* very handsome or beautiful.

খুবানি *n.* apricot.

খুয়া, খুয়ানো older variants of **খোয়া** and **খোয়ানো** respectively.

খুর *n.* hoof of an animal.

খুরপা, খুরপি, (dial.) **খুরপো** *n.* a small spud.

খুরলি *n.* exercise; practice of archery; practice ('মুরলী খুরলি') ; a prank.

খুরা *n.* a leg or heel or castor of an article or furniture.

খুরি *n.* a small earthen cup without handle.

খুরো coll. form of **খুরা** ।

খুর্মা rej. spell. of **খুরমা** ।

খুলি *n.* the skull, the cranium; a small earthen cup without handle.

খুল্লতাত *n.* (for.) a younger brother of one's father, an uncle.

খুশ var. of **খোশ** ।

খুশকি *n.* dandruff, scurf.

খুশবু *n.* good smell, fragrance; perfume.

খুশামদ var. of **খোশামোদ** ।

খুশি *n.* happiness, joy, delight; cheerfulness, jollity; pleasure, desire, volition, will (আমার খুশি আমি যাব না) ; satisfaction. □ *a.* happy, joyful, delighted, cheerful, glad, jovial, jolly; pleased; willing; satisfied. **খুশি করা** *v.* to satisfy, to please. **~মতো** *adv.* at one's pleasure, as one wishes or pleases. **~মনে** *adv.* happily; gladly; willingly.

খুসকি, খুস্কি alt. spellings of **খুশকি** ।

খৃষ্ট, খৃস্ট alt. spellings of **খ্রিস্ট** । **খৃষ্টান, খৃস্টান** alt. spellings of **খ্রিস্টান** । **খৃষ্টাব্দ, খৃস্টাব্দ** alt. spellings of **খ্রিস্টাব্দ** । **খৃষ্টীয়, খৃস্টীয়** alt. spellings of **খ্রিস্টীয়** ।

খেই *n.* an end of a thread; the number of threads or cords (পাঁচ খেই সুতো) ; a clue or trail (খেই পাওয়া). **খেই হারানো** *v.* to lose a clue or trail; (fig.) to be at a loss to find one's way; (fig.) to be confused or perplexed; to lose the thread of a story or an argument.

খেউড় *n.* a kind of scurrilous song or poem; an instance of railing; ribald abuse.

খেউরি *n.* shaving. **খেউরি করা বা হওয়া** *v.* to shave.

খেংরা alt. spell. of **খ্যাংরা**।

খেঁক, খ্যাঁক *int.* expressing a snarling sound of a dog or a vixen or of one in anger. **খ্যাঁক (খেঁক) করা** *v.* to snarl; to shout fretfully. **খেঁক খেঁক, খ্যাঁক খ্যাঁক** *int.* expressing repeated snarling or fretting noise. **খেঁকখেঁক করা, খেঁকানো, খ্যাঁকানো** *v.* to snarl repeatedly; to rebuke fretfully and repeatedly in a loud voice. **খেঁকানি, খ্যাঁকানি, খ্যাঁকখ্যাঁকানি** *n.* repeated and fretful rebuke in a loud voice. **খেঁকিয়ে ওঠা** same as **খ্যাঁকানো**।

খেঁকশিয়াল *n.* the fox. *fem.* **খেঁকশিয়ালি** *n.* the vixen.

খেঁকানি, খেঁকানো see **খেঁক**।

খেঁকারি var. of **খাঁকারি**।

খেঁকি *a.* ill-tempered, peevish; snarling. **খেঁকি কুত্তা** a snarling dog; (loos.) a cur, a tyke.

খেঁচড়া *a.* wayward, indocile, obstinate; unmannerly, ill-mannered.

খেঁচা *v.* to pull or tug or snatch (esp. forcefully and suddenly); to have a spasm, to convulse; to have a cramp, to cramp. □ *n.* a pull or tug or snatch (esp. a forceful and sudden one); a spasm, convulsion; a cramp.

খেঁচাখেঁচি *n.* mutual quarrelling (usu. noisy and frequent one); mutual ill-feeling.

খেঁচাখেঁচি করা *v.* to fall out or quarrel (usu. noisily and frequently).

খেঁচুনি var. of **খিঁচুনি**।

খেঁট alt. spell. of **খ্যাঁট**।

খেঁকো[1] *sfx.* indicating : eaten (by) (পোকায় খেকো) = moth-eaten).

খেকো[2], **খেগো** *masc.* of **খাকি**[2] and **খাগি** respectively.

খেঙরা *rej.* spell. of **খেংরা** and **খ্যাংরা**।

খেচর *a.* moving in the air; capable of moving in the air; flying. □ *n.* a flying creature; a bird (esp. one capable of flying).

খেচরান্ন *n.* a food prepared by boiling rice and pigeon-pea together with spices and fat, hotchpotch, kedgeree.

খেচরী *fem.* of **খেচর**।

খেচামেচি same as **খেঁচাখেঁচি**।

খেজুর *n.* persimmon, date; the date-palm. □ *a.* made of the juice or sap of the date-palm (খেজুর গুড়). **~ছড়ি** *n.* cluster of persimmon or date; a border of loincloth etc. patterned as a collection of date-leaves; a superior variety of paddy. **~রস** *n.* juice or sap of the date-palm. **খেজুরে, খেজুরিয়া** *a.* made of dates or of the juice or sap of the date-palm. **খেজুরে আলাপ** *n.* useless or idle talk. **খেজুরে গুড়** molasses prepared from the sap of the date-palm.

খেটক *n.* a shield.

খেটে[1] *n.* a small club or cudgel. □ *a.* dumpy (বেঁটে-খেটে লোক).

খেটে[2] coll. corrup of **খাটিয়া** (see **খাটা**).

খেটেল *n.* a labourer; a servant; a menial worker.

খেত *n.* (a piece of) agricultural land. **~খামার** *n.* an agricultural farm, the cultivator's place of work. **~মজুর** *n.* an agricultural labourer, a farm worker, a farmhand.

খেতাব *n.* a title or honour (esp. one awarded officially). **~ধারী** *a.* titled; enjoying or holding a title.

খেতি[1] corrup. of **ক্ষতি**।

খেতি[2] *n.* agriculture, husbandry. □ *a.* pertaining to agricultural land. **~মজুর** a husbandman; a farmhand on hire.

খেত্রি *n.* an upcountry caste of India (believed to be Kshatriyas).

খেদ *n.* lamentation, lament; regret, grief. **খেদ করা** *v.* to lament; to regret.

খেদজনক *a.* lamentable; regrettable.

খেদমত var. of **খিদমত**।

খেদা *n.* an enclosure for catching wild elephants, a kheda, a keddah.

খেদানো *v.* to drive away, to chase away, to expel; to scare away; to tend (গোরু খেদানো) ; (sarcas.) to teach (ছাত্র খেদানো). □ *a.* driven away, expelled (বাপে-তাড়ানো মায়ে খেদানো ছেলে). **খেদানিয়া, খেদানে** *a.* one who or that which drives away or expels or scares away or tends.

খেদোক্তি *n.* what is said by way of lamentation or regret. **খেদোক্তি করা** *v.* to say by way of lamentation or regret; to lament; to regret.

খেপ[১] *n.* a round of action or occupation, a round (এক খেপ দাঁড় টানা).

খেপ[২] *n.* an instance of casting (জালের প্রথম খেপে).

খেপলা, খেপলা-জাল *n.* a cast net.

খেপা *v.* to go mad; to madden; to get angry; to rave; to be in a frenzy; to run amok or amuck; to be greatly irritated or excited, to rage, to become violent (বাতাস খেপেছে) ; to become uncontrollable (শিশু খেপেছে). ☐ *a.* maddened; mad; nutty; angered; angry; raving; frenzied; raging; uncontrollable. ☐ *n.* a lunatic; a madman; a nutty man; a madcap; an inspired man; one maddened or fired with some great idea, feeling, ambition etc.; (in endearment) a naughty or wild man or boy. ☐ *n. fem.* **খেপি** । **খেপা কুকুর** a rabid dog, a mad dog. **খেপানো** *v.* to provoke, to irritate; to incite; to madden.

খেমটা *n.* an Indian musical measure; a kind of dance. **~ওয়ালি** *n.* a professional khemta (খেমটা) dancing-girl; a professional dancing-girl.

খেয়া *n.* a ferry-boat; a ferry; act of ferrying. **খেয়া দেওয়া, খেয়া বাওয়া, খেয়াপার করা, খেয়াপার হওয়া** *v.* to ferry. **খেয়াতরী, খেয়ানৌকা** *n.* a ferry-boat. **খেয়া-পারাপার** *n.* act of ferrying. **খেয়া-পারাপার করা** *v.* to ferry (esp. professionally). **খেয়ামাঝি, খেয়ারি** *n.* a ferryman.

খেয়াল[১] *n.* a fancy; a dream, a daydream; consciousness, carefulness, attention; wariness (ভবিষ্যৎ সম্বন্ধে খেয়াল) ; remembrance, recollection (কথাটা খেয়াল ছিল না) ; inclination, predisposition, propensity (বদখেয়াল) ; a caprice, a whim, a whimsical fancy, a vagary, a fad, a crotchet (বড়লোকের খেয়াল, প্রকৃতির খেয়াল). **খেয়াল করা** *v.* to notice; to pay heed to, to be attentive to; to mind; to try to recollect. **খেয়াল থাকা** *v.* to have an eye to, to be conscious about; to have in remembrance or consciousness. **খেয়াল হওয়া** *v.* to remember or recollect (suddenly); **~খাতা** *n.* a notebook of the kind of a diary in which one notes down whatever occasionally occurs to him. **~খুশি** *n.* a fancy, a caprice, a whim. **~খুশিমতো** *adv.* whimsically, capriciously. **খেয়ালি** *a.* fanciful; extravagantly imaginative; whimsical, capricious, crotchety.

খেয়াল[২] *n.* kind or system of Indian classical vocal music. **খেয়ালি** *n.* singer of kheyal songs. **খেয়ালিয়া** *n.* one who sings the kheyal.

খেয়োখেয়ি *n.* mutual quarrel or fighting; a feud.

খেরাজ *n.* rent, revenue, tax. (**তু. নাখেরাজ, লাখেরাজ** rent-free). **খেরাজি** *a.* taxable; rent-bearing.

খেরুয়া, খেরো *n.* a thick coarse cloth dyed red (used in wrapping books). **খেরোখাতা, খেরোর খাতা** *n.* an all-purpose notebook; a notebook for writing down all sorts of accounts.

খেল *n.* sport, game; trick, jugglery. **এক খেল খেলা** to make a clever or deceptive move; to play a trick.

খেলনা *n.* a toy, a plaything.

খেলা *n.* a play, a game, a sport; a recreational match or contest; a pastime; a diversion; an amusement; a show of an entertaining trick or feat (সাপখেলা, জাদুখেলা, লাঠিখেলা, সার্কাসের খেলা) ; artistry, artistic display (ছবিতে রঙের খেলা, আকাশে মেঘের খেলা) ; act of trifling (পড়াশোনা নিয়ে খেলা, বিপদ নিয়ে খেলা) ; act of fondling. ☐ *v.* to play; to work (বুদ্ধি খেলা, অঙ্কে মাথা খেলা) ; to trifle; to fondle. **খেলা কথা নয়** something not to be trifled with or taken lightly. **খেলা করা** *v.* same as **খেলা** (*v*). **~ঘর** *n.* (rare.) a room or hall for indoor games; a miniature house built by children at play with sand or mud or straw, a doll's house; (fig.) domestic life or earthly life. **~ধুলা** *n.* games and sports; sports and pastime. **~নো** *v.* to cause to play; to supervise at play; to control and lead at pleasure, to make a person do everything one wishes him to do, to lead by the nose (বণিকরা সরকারকে খেলায়) ; (in football, hockey etc.) to pass the ball frequently in the course of a game to a player of one's own side to play (উইংকে দিয়ে খেলানো). **খেলার ছলে** *adv*. playfully. **খেলার মাঠ** *n*. a playground. **খেলার সঙ্গী, খেলার সাথি** *n*. a playmate. **খেলার সরঞ্জাম** *n*. sports goods.

খেলাত var. of **খিলাত**।

খেলাপ *n*. (of a promise, rule etc.) breach, infringement, violation (কথার খেলাপ). **খেলাপ করা** *v*. to breach, to break, to infringe, to violate. **আইনের খেলাপ** violation of (a) law. **কথার (বা প্রতিশ্রুতির) খেলাপ** break or breach of promise. **কিস্তি-খেলাপ** *n*. failure to pay an instalment or to meet pecuniary or other obligation. **নিয়মের খেলাপ** infringement or breach of (a) rule. **বিশ্বাসের খেলাপ** breach of trust.

খেলুড়িয়া obs. var. of **খেলুড়ে**।

খেলুড়ি *fem*. of **খেলুড়ে**।

খেলুড়ে *n*. a player; a playmate.

খেলো *a*. of inferior quality, inferior (খেলো কাপড়) ; unimportant, trivial, unreliable, unthoughtful (খেলো কথা, খেলো লোক) ; base, mean, worthless; humiliated (খেলো হওয়া). **খেলো করা** *v*. to humiliate; to belittle; to offend one's dignity.

খেলোয়াড় *n*. a player; an expert player; an expert diplomat; a cunning person, a wily man; a swindler; a conspirator. **সাপ-খেলোয়াড়** *n*. a snake-charmer. **সার্কাসের খেলোয়াড়** a showman.

খেলোয়াড়ি *a*. sportsmanlike. **খেলোয়াড়ি মনোভাব** sportsmanlike spirit.

খেসারত *n*. compensation; cost (বোকামির খেসারত, মামলার খেসারত). **খেসারত দেওয়া** *v*. to compensate; to pay cost (of).

খেসারি *n*. a variety of pigeon-pea.

খৈ rej. spell. of **খই**।

খৈল rej. spell. of **খইল**।

খোঁচ *n*. a thorn; a sharp pointed end (as of a needle); a sharp corner; a hitch or slight difficulty.

খোঁচা *n*. a prick, a poke; injury or wound caused by the poking or prick of a sharp and pointed instrument or weapon; taunt, jeer. **খোঁচা দেওয়া** *v*. to prick or poke; to taunt or jeer. **খোঁচা মারা** same as **খোঁচা দেওয়া**। **খোঁচা-খোঁচা** *a*. upright and sharp-pointed, bristly (খোঁচা-খোঁচা দাড়ি). **~খুচি** *n*. mutual pricking; pricking or poking or jabbing; repeated or continuous pricking or poking or instigating. **~নো** *v*. to prick; to thrust; to poke; to jab; to goad; to annoy; to instigate.

খোঁজ *n*. search; act of seeking; investigation; inquiry; trace, trail. **খোঁজ করা** *v*. to search; to look for; to inquire (after); to investigate; to try to trace. **খোঁজ নেওয়া** *v*. to inquire (about or after); to make inquiries about. **খোঁজ পাওয়া** *v*. to find trace of; to track out; to detect; to discover. **খোঁজ-খবর** *n*. information, news; trace; inquiry. **খোঁজ-খবর নেওয়া** *v*. to make enquiries; to remain in close touch with. **খোঁজা** *v*. to search, to seek; to trace. **খোঁজাখুঁজি** *n*. continuous search. **খোঁজাখুঁজি করা** *v*. to search continuously, to hunt for, to hunt high and low. **খোঁজানো** pop. var. of **খুঁজানো**।

খোঁট var. of **খুঁট**।

খোঁটন[১] pop. var. of **খুঁটন**।

খোঁটন[২] *n*. act of taking a small amount or portion with the tips of one's fingers or beaks; act of nibbling; act of pinching or nipping.

খোঁটা[১] *n*. spiteful and stinging reference; caustic comment. **খোঁটা খাওয়া, খোঁটা শোনা** *v*. to hear galling, spiteful, stinging accusation ; to be sarcastically reminded (of something unpleasant or uncomplimentary). **খোঁটা দেওয়া** *v*. to make stinging or biting insinuations.

খোঁটা[২] *n*. a small pillar of wood or bamboo, a pale, a stake; a peg, a wedge. **খোঁটার জোর** strong or large backing or support. **খোঁটার বেড়া** *n*. a paling, a palisade.

খোঁটা[৩]**. খোঁটানো** pop. variants of **খুঁটা**[২] and **খুঁটানো** respectively.

খোঁড়ল *n*. a hole, a cavity, a hollow, a crevice.

খোঁড়া[১] *a*. lame. □ *n*. a lame person. **খোঁড়া করা** *v*. to make lame, to lame.

খোঁড়া[২]**, খোঁড়ানো**[১] pop. variants of **খুঁড়া** and **খুঁড়ানো** respectively.

খোঁড়ানো[2] *v.* to limp, to hobble.

খোঁদল var. of **খোঁড়ল**।

খোঁপা *n.* hair dressed in a rounded mass, a bun, chignon. **খোঁপা খোলা** *v.* to unloose or undress a bun, to undo or unfasten a coiffure; to cause dishevelment. **খোঁপা বাঁধা** *v.* to dress or put up hair in a bun. **আলগা খোঁপা** a hanging bun; a loose bun, a bun not tied with cords.

খোঁয়াড় *n.* a cattle-shed, a cowshed, a cowhouse; a sheepfold; a pound for stray cattle, a pinfold. **খোঁয়াড়ে আটকানো, খোঁয়াড়ে পোরা** *v.* to put into or enclose in a cattleshed; to pound, to impound; to pinfold.

খোকা, (in endearment) **খোকন** *n.* a little boy; an infant boy; a son; (sarcas.) a grown-up man behaving boyishly. □ *int.* (voc.) my boy; my son. **খোকাপনা, খোকামি** *n.* boyish behaviour or boyishness of a grown-up man; puerility.

খোক্কস *n.* (in fairy tales) a terrible anthropophagous demon.

খোজা *n.* (*mas. & fem.*) a eunuch; a sexually powerless person, an impotent person. □ *a.* castrated; gelded; impotent; **খোজা-করা পশু** a gelding. **খোজা-প্রহরী** *n.* a eunuch guarding a harem. **খোজা করা** *v.* to castrate, to emasculate; to geld.

খোট্টা *n.* (contem. or ridi.) a Hindustani, an upcountry man (of India). *fem.* **খোট্টানি**।

খোতবা var. of **খতবা**।

খোদ *a.* in person (সে খোদ) ; real, actual (খোদ-কর্তা). **খোদ-কর্তা** *n.* the real master; the master himself, the master in person.

খোদকার *n.* an engraver; a carver. **খোদকারি** *n.* engraving; carving; interference in other's work.

খোদা[1] pop. var. of **খুদা**[2]।

খোদা[2] *n.* (Mus.) God. **খোদার উপর খোদকারি** (fig. & sarcas.) an attempt to teach God how to create; to overdo. **খোদার খাসি** (ridi.) a corpulent man, a roly-poly.

খোদাই *n.* engraving; carving. **খোদাই করা** *v.* to engrave; to carve. **খোদানো** *v. & n.* engraving; carving.

খোদা-ই-খিদ্‌মদ্‌গার *n.* (self-dedicated) servant of God., freedom-fighter under 'Frontier Gandhi' Abdul Gaffur Khan.

খোদানো see **খোদাই**।

খোদাবন্দ *n.* (voc.) My Lord; Your Majesty; Sire; Master; Sir.

খোদিত *a.* engraved.

খোনা *a.* pronounced or spoken with breath passing through the nose, nasal. □ *n.* a person speaking through the nose. **খোনা সুরে বলা** to speak through the nose.

খোন্দল var. of **খোঁড়ল**।

খোপ, খোপর *n.* a small hole (পায়রার খোপ), a cell; a recess, a niche.

খোপা var. of **খোঁপা**।

খোবানি var. of **খুবানি**।

খোয়া[1] *n.* solidified milk or cream (also **খোয়া-ক্ষীর**) ; a broken stone, macadam. **খোয়া দিয়ে বাঁধানো** *v.* to macadamize, to pave with stone chips, to cobble. **খোয়া বাঁধানো রাস্তা** cobbled streets.

খোয়া[2] *a.* lost; wasted; stolen. **খোয়া যাওয়া** *v.* to be lost or wasted or stolen. **খোয়ানো** *v.* to lose; to waste.

খোয়াব *n.* a dream; a daydream; (fig.) a false fancy, an illusion.

খোয়ার *n.* misery; distress; harm; humiliation; insult; punishment; condemnation; reproof; blame. **খোয়ার হওয়া** *v.* to be stricken with misery or distress; to suffer harm or humiliation or insult; to be punished or condemned or reproved or blamed.

খোয়ারি *n.* tiredness or depression that strikes in when drunkenness is over. **খোয়ারি ভাঙা** *v.* to drink a little in order to remove post-drunken depression.

খোর *sfx.* indicating: one who eats (মছলিখোর) ; one who is addicted to (গাঁজাখোর, নেশাখোর).

খোরপোশ, (rej.) **খোরপোষ** *n.* food and clothing (খোরপোশের বিনিময়ে চাকরগিরি) ; maintenance (খোরপোশের ভার নেওয়া) ; alimony (খোরপোশের মামলা). **বিবাহ-বিচ্ছেদকারিণী স্ত্রীকে স্বামী কর্তৃক আইনত প্রদত্ত খোরপোশ** alimony.

খোরশোলা, খোরসোলা variants of **খরশোলা**।

খোরা, খোরাই *n.* a large cup without a handle, a goblet without a stem.

খোরাক *n.* food, provision; capacity for eating (তার খোরাক বেশি), appetite; ration of food. **খোরাক-পোশাক** *n.* food and clothing. **খোরাকি** *n.* cost of food (খোরাকি লাগে না) ; rations or ration-money (এ চাকরিতে খোরাকি মিলবে).

খোরাসানি *a.* of Khorasan (খোরাসান). ☐ *n.* a native of Khorasan.

খোর্মা var. of **খুরমা**।

খোল[1] coll. var. of **খইল**।

খোল[2] *n.* a cover; a case (বালিশের খোল) ; a shell (কচ্ছপের খোল) ; a skin (লাউয়ের খোল) ; a calabash; bark or spathe of trees (নারিকেল-সুপারির খোল) ; a hole, a hollow, a cavity, a crevice, a socket (চোখের খোল), a pit or fold (পেটের বা বুকের খোল), a hold (জাহাজের বা নৌকোর খোল) ; a musical instrument of percussion resembling a longish tomtom; the water-containing vase of a hookah. **~করতাল** *n.* the tomtom and cymbals. **খুলি** *a.* one who beats the afore-mentioned musical instrument of percussion.

খোলক *n.* a hood for covering the whole body, a yashmak; a shell (of the crustacean). **খোলকী** *a.* crustacean. ☐ *n.* a crustacean.

খোলতাই *n.* beautiful show, beauty; brightness. ☐ *a.* having a good show, showy; beautiful; bright.

খোলনলচে *n.* the bowl of burning tobacco and the pipe of a hookah. **খোলনলচে বদলানো** (fig.) to change something so completely and thoroughly as to give it a new look.

খোলস *n.* an outer covering; a slough, a fell (সাপের খোলস) ; (sarcas.) garment. **খোলস ছাড়া** *v.* (of snakes) to cast or slough off (its) skin, to moult.

খোলসা *a.* clear, clean; plain; frank, candid; free (খোলসা মন) ; emptied, vacated. **খোলসা করা** *v.* to open (মন খোলসা করা) to evacuate thoroughly (পেট খোলসা করা). **খোলসা করে বলা** *v.* to speak clearly or point-blank or leaving no room for doubt; to be outspoken; to speak out without reserve, to open one's heart; to make a clean breast of. **দিল খোলসা** *a.* open-hearted, frank, candid; above-board.

খোলা[1] *n.* (of fruits) skin (মোচার খোলা) ; an outer covering or a shell, a carapace (কাঁকড়ার খোলা, কচ্ছপের খোলা) ; (of trees) bark or spathe (কলাগাছের খোলা) ; a kind of frying-pan (ভাজনা-খোলা), pantile (খোলার চাল) ; a field (ধানখোলা) ; a place (হাটখোলা) ; an open place for manufacturing, a yard (ইটখোলা). **খোলার ঘর** a hut with a pantile shed.

খোলা[2] *v.* to open (দরজা খোলা) ; to expose or reveal, to open (মন খোলা) ; to unfasten (গোরুর দড়ি খোলা) ; to set on a voyage or journey, to leave; to start or found (নতুন স্কুল খোলা) ; to open for day's work (এ দোকান বেলা দশটায় খুলবে) ; to resume work, to re-open (ছুটির পর আদালত খুলবে) ; to untie or undress (খোঁপা খোলা, চুল খোলা) ; to put off, to take off (জামা খোলা). ☐ *a.* open, unfastened; untied or undressed; unobstructed, unhindered (খোলা পথ) ; frank, without reserve (খোলা মন). **খোলা বাজার** (comm.) open market. **খোলাখুলি** *a.* frank, categorical, candid, outspoken, unreserved (খোলাখুলি কথা). ☐ *adv.* frankly, categorically, point-blank, outspokenly, unreservedly. **খোলানো** *v.* to cause to open or unfasten; to cause to leave; to cause to start or found; to cause to open for day's work; to cause to re-open; to cause to untie or undress; to cause to take off or put off.

খোলামকুচি *n.* a broken piece of ceramic material potsherd; (fig.) a trifling object.

খোশ *a.* delightful, pleasant (খোশখবর) ; happy, cheerful (খোশমেজাজ) ; done by one's own self, voluntary. **~কবালা** *n.* (law) a deed of conveyance executed voluntarily by the proprietor himself. **~খবর** *n.* glad tidings; agreeable or pleasing news. **~খেয়াল** *n.* a fad, a crotchet; a caprice, a whim. **~খোরাক** *n.* dainty food, delicate dishes, table delicacies. ~খোরাকি *a.* fond of dainty food; accustomed to taking dainty food. ~গল্প *n.* a pleasant chat; an amusing tale or story. ~নবিশ *n.* a calligrapher; a good writer. ~নাম *n.* reputation; fame; goodwill. ~পোশাক *n.* fine dress; fancy dress. ~পোশাকি *a.* fond of fine dress; foppish. খোশবু same as খুশবু। ~মেজাজ *n.* cheerful or merry or self-complacent mood.

খোশামোদ *n.* flattery, adulation. খোশামোদ করা *v.* to flatter, to adulate. খোশামোদে ভোলা *v.* to be moved with flattery. খোশামুদি, খোশামোদি *n.* flattery, adulation. খোশামুদে *a.* flattering, adulatory. খোশামুদে লোক a flatterer, a sycophant.

খোস *n.* itches, scabies.

খোসা *n.* skin (of fruits).

খ্যাংরা *n.* a broom or broomstick, a besom.~পেটা করা *v.* to beat or thrash with a broom, to strike with a broom.

খ্যাঁক্ alt. spell. of খেঁক্। খ্যাঁকানো *v.* to snarl, to rebuke fretfully and harshly.

খ্যাঁট *n.* (hum.) a feast.

খ্যাত *a.* famous (খ্যাতনামা) ; called, named designated or known as (আর্যনামে খ্যাত জাতি). ~নামা *a.* one whose name is well-known, famous, renowned, celebrated.

খ্যাতি *n.* fame, renown; celebrity; (rare) a name or designation. খ্যাতিলাভ করা *v.* to be famous, to earn fame.

খ্যাপক *a.* & *n.* one who or that which announces or proclaims or gives publicity.

খ্যাপন *n.* announcement; proclamation; publicity.

খ্যাপলা alt. spell. of খেপলা।

খ্রিস্ট *a.* Christ. ~ধর্ম *n.* Christianity.~পূর্ব *a.* B.C., Before Christ. খ্রিস্টান *a.* Christian. □ *n.* a Christian. খ্রিস্টানি *n.* manners and customs of Christians; (dero.) imitation of Christians; (dero.) Europeanism; (vul.) Christianism or Christianity; (arch.) a Christian. খ্রিস্টাব্দ *n.* A. D., of the Christian era. খ্রিস্টীয় *a.* of Christ or of the Christian era; Christian.

গ১ *n.* the third consonant of the Bengali alphabet.

গ২ *sfx.* indicating: going; going towards (নিম্নগ).

গইবি alt. spell. of গৈবি।

গং abbr. of **গয়রহ** = etc.

গঁদ *n.* gum (also **গঁদের আঠা**).

গগন *n.* the sky, the heavens, the firmament, free space overhead; the blue. **~চর, ~চারী** *a.* (capable of) flying or moving in the sky, aerial, ethereal. **~চুম্বী** *a.* sky-kissing, sky-high; very lofty. **গগনচুম্বী অট্টালিকা** a sky-scraper. **~চ্যুত, ~ভ্রষ্ট** *a.* fallen from the sky. **~তল** *n.* the floor of the sky, the vault of the heavens, the firmament. **~পট** *n.* the canvas of the sky, the vault of the heavens, the firmament; skyscape. **~পথ** *n.* the celestial path; an aerial route. **~প্রান্ত** *n.* a corner of the sky, the sky-line, the horizon. **~বিহারী** *a.* (capable of) flying or moving in the sky, aerial, ethereal; (fig.) imbued with lofty ideas or plans, aspiring. **~মণ্ডল** *n.* the sky; the dome of the sky; the heavens. **~স্পর্শী** *a.* touching or reaching the sky; sky-high; very lofty; very high, soaring (গগনস্পর্শী মূল্য) ; (fig.) highly aspiring or ambitious. **গগনস্পর্শী অট্টালিকা** a sky-scraper. **গগনাঙ্গন** *n.* the courtyard of the heavens, the sky. **গগনাম্বু** *n.* rain-water.

গঙ্গা *n.* the Ganges, the Ganġa; a river; a wife of Shiva (শিব). (poet.) **গঙ্গা, গঙ্গজ** *a.* Gangetic; riverine. **গঙ্গাজলি১** *n.* act of putting the water of the Ganges into the mouth of a dying person; act of swearing by taking the water of the Ganges in one's palm. **গঙ্গাজলি২** *a.* having the colour of the water of the Ganges, of a brownish cream colour. **~তীর** *n.* bank of the Ganges. **~ধর** *n.* an appellation of Shiva (শিব). **~পুত্র** *n.* (in the Mahabharata) Bhishma; one belonging to a Hindu caste whose business is to cremate or to help cremation, (cp.) an undertaker by caste. **~প্রাপ্ত** *a.* (lit.) one whose mortal remains have been thrown in the Ganges; dead. **গঙ্গাপ্রাপ্ত হওয়া** *v.* to die (esp. holily). **~প্রাপ্তি** *n.* death (esp. in a holy manner). **~ফড়িং** *n.* the grasshopper (of the green and large variety). **~বাসী** *a.* living near or on the bank of the Ganges; riverine. **~মাহাত্ম্য** *n.* the glory of the Ganges; a hymn glorifying the Ganges. **~যমুনা** *n.* the Ganges and the Jumna or their confluence. ☐ *a.* black-and-white; mixed with gold and silver, bimetallic. **~যাত্রা** *n.* act of carrying a dying person to the bank of the Ganges. **গঙ্গাযাত্রা করা** *v.* to be carried to the bank of the Ganges on the eve of one's death. **গঙ্গাযাত্রা করানো** *v.* to carry (a dying person) to the bank of the Ganges. **~যাত্রী** *n.* a person who is being carried to the bank of the Ganges on the eve of his death; a dying man; a pilgrim to the mouth of the Ganges esp. on a holy occasion. *fem.* **~যাত্রিণী**। **~লাভ** same as **গঙ্গাপ্রাপ্তি**। **~সংগম, ~সাগর** *n.* the confluence of the Ganges and the Bay of Bengal, the mouth of the Ganges. **~স্নান** *n.* bathing in the Ganges. **গঙ্গাস্নান করা** *v.* to bathe in the Ganges; (fig.) to cleanse oneself of guilt, sin etc. to make oneself pure.

গঙ্গোত্রী, গঙ্গোত্তরী *n.* a holy place of the Hindus in Garhwal (flowing through this place the Ganges comes down to the plains).

গঙ্গোদক *n.* the water of the Ganges.

গচ্চা, গচ্ছা *n.* (ori.) a compensation; a loss for nothing; penalty for one's folly, carelessness etc. **গচ্চা দেওয়া** *v.* to compensate; to lose for nothing; to pay penalty (for). **গচ্চা যাওয়া** *v.* to have to lose or suffer loss for nothing; to be paid by way of penalty or compensation. (for).

গচ্ছিত *a.* placed in the custody of; entrusted; deposited. **গচ্ছিত দেওয়া** *v.* to place in the custody (of); entrust (with); to deposit. **গচ্ছিত রাখা** *v.* to place or receive in the custody (of); to entrust or be entrusted with; to give or receive as a deposit. **গচ্ছিত নেওয়া** *v.* to have in the custody (of); to be entrusted (with); to take as a deposit. **গচ্ছিত ধন** money deposited; trust money. **গচ্ছিত সম্পত্তি** a trust property. **সম্পত্তি গচ্ছিত রাখার দলিল** *a.* trust deed.

গছানো *v.* to cause to accept a thing or a responsibility (esp. craftily), to persuade to accept. ☐ *a.* that has been caused to be accepted (esp. craftily.) **গছিয়ে দেওয়া** same as **গছানো** (*v.*).

গজ[1] *n.* gauze (ঘায়ের মধ্যে গজ ঢোকানো) **গজ ঢোকানো** *v.* to put a piece of gauze into.

গজ[2] *n.* a protuberance, a swelling (মাথায় গজ বেরিয়েছে) ; a sprout (ঝুনো নারকেলটার গজ বেরিয়েছে). **গজ বার হওয়া** *v.* to protuberate, to have a swelling; to sprout.

গজ[3] *n.* a measure of length equal to 3 feet, a yard, 91.5 cm or 0.9144 m. ☐ *a.* measuring a yard (একগজ কাপড়, পাঁচগজ লম্বা). **~কাঠি** *n.* a yardstick. **গজি** same as **গজ**[3] (*a*).

গজ[4] *n.* the elephant; (in chess) the bishop; a very small variety of worm (গজভুক্ত কপিত্থ). **~কচ্ছপ** *n.* (myth.) two brothers, who contended with each other for the possession of their paternal wealth, were turned into a huge elephant and a huge tortoise, in their new shapes too they went on fighting frightfully and relentlessly; (fig.) two terrible contestants; (hum.) a man of elephantine build. **গজকচ্ছপের যুদ্ধ** (fig.) a relentless encounter between equals; Greek meeting Greek. **~কুম্ভ** *n.* a globular appendage on the forehead of the elephant **~গতি, ~গমন** *n.* slow and majestic or stately gait (of a well-built person) resembling that of an elephant. ☐ *a.* moving majestically like an elephant. **~গামিনী** *a. fem.* mounted on an elephant; moving majestically like an elephant. ☐ *n.* such a woman or girl. *masc.* (*a.* & *n.*). **~গামী।** **~ঘণ্টা** *n.* a bell tied round an elephant's neck to warn the passers-by from a distance. **~চক্ষু** *n.* a very small and squint eye. ☐ *a.* one with such an eye. **~দন্ত**[1] *n.* ivory. **~দন্ত**[2] *n.* an extra tooth (of a man) growing in front of another. **~ন্দর** *a.* very big; fat; pot-bellied. **~পতি** *n.* a leader amongst the wild elephants. **~বীথি** *n.* an orderly line of elephants. **~ভুক্ত** *a.* eaten by an elephant; eaten by a small worm called গজ (see above). **~ভুক্তকপিত্থবৎ** *a.* & *adv.* like a sour wood-apple eaten up by worms (a **গজ** worm enters unnoticeably into a sour wood-apple and eats up the whole of its kernel); (fig.) utterly hollow though looking full. **~মোতি,** (inc.) **~মতি, ~মুক্তা** *n.* any of the costly pearls which, according to fables, are shed from an elephant's head. **~যূথ** *n.* a herd of elephants. **~রাজ** same as **গজপতি।**

গজকাঠি see **গজ**[3] ।

গজগজ *int.* expressing: low grumbling (usu. to one's own self) in anger, annoyance, discontent, dissatisfaction etc, (চাকরটা রাগে গজগজ করছে) ; restless desire for coming out (পেটে কথা গজগজ করছে) ; overcrowding (পেটে খাবারগুলো গজগজ করছে). **গজগজ করা** *v.* to grumble; to try restlessly to come out; to overcrowd. **গজগজানি** *n.* grumbling; (rare) restless desire for coming out; (rare) overcrowding.

গজগির, গজগিরি *n.* the pavement round a draw-well etc., (cp.) a well-curb; (archi.) a work of decorative plastering.

গজব *n.* oppression, tyranny, outrage, violence, high-handedness; injustice.

গজরগজর var. of **গজগজ।**

গজরানো *v.* to rumble; to grumble surlily, to growl. **গজরানি** *n.* a rumbling; a rumbling noise; a growl.

গজল *n.* a Persian musical mode (chiefly used in singing love-songs); a love-song; a love-lyric.

গজা *n.* a kind of sweetmeat made of flour.

গজানন *n.* a person who has on his shoulders an elephant's head instead of his own; an appellation of Ganesha (গণেশ).

জানীক *n.* a warrior mounted on an elephant.

জানো *v.* to sprout; to originate; to evolve; to grow. ☐ *a.* sprouted; originated; evolved, grown.

জারি *n.* an enemy of the elephant; the ion.

জারূঢ় same as গজারোহী। *fem.* গজারূঢ়া।

জারোহী *a.* mounted on an elephant. ☐ *n.* a man or soldier mounted on an elephant. *fem.* গজারোহিণী।

জাল *n.* a large and thick nail, a peg, a rivet; a variety of freshwater fish shaped almost like a cylinder.

জি see গজ[৩]।

জেন্দ্র *n.* a leader of a herd of wild elephants; the best elephant; a superb elephant. ~গমন *n.* majestic or stately gait of a well-built person) resembling that of an elephant. ☐ *a.* moving majestically like an elephant. *fem.* ~গমনা, ~গামিনী।

n. a granary, a store; a central market esp. which is a centre for import and xport); a stock exchange, (cp.) Rialto; large market-place, a large grain market.

ন *n.* act of scolding or chiding or upraiding; act of insulting; act of putting o shame or reproaching (by displaying uperior excellence). ☐ *a.* one who or hat which scolds or insults; one who r that which puts to shame or reroaches ('খঞ্জনগঞ্জন আঁখি'). গঞ্জনা *n.* scolding, chiding, upbraiding; insult; utting to shame; reproach. গঞ্জনা দেওয়া to scold, to chide; to upbraid; to insult; to reproach; to put to shame.

v. (poet.) same as গঞ্জনা দেওয়া।

dial. corrup. of গেঞ্জি।

কা *n.* the female flowering tops of Indian hemp, ganja; (loos.) hemp. ~সেবী given to smoking ganja. ☐ *n.* a (habitual) smoker of hemp.

ত *a.* scolded, chid; insulted; put to hame, reproached.

var. of গ্যাঁট।

টি, গটমট *int.* expressing: the sound of walking or marching firmly and arrogantly. গটগট বা গটমট করে চলা *v.* to walk or march firmly and arrogantly; to walk with firm and quick steps.

গঠন *n.* building or modelling or shaping, construction, formation (স্বাস্থ্যগঠন, মূর্তিগঠন, শব্দগঠন, দলগঠন) ; build, shape, form, appearance, structure. গঠন করা *v.* to build, to model, to shape, to construct, to form, to make, to create. ~প্রণালী, ~ভঙ্গি, ~শৈলী *n.* the style or manner of building or modelling or shaping or constructing or forming. ~সৌষ্ঠব *n.* the beauty or grace of a thing built or modelled or shaped or constructed or formed; beauty or elegance of form. গঠিত *a.* built, modelled, shaped, constructed, formed, made, created.

গড্ডল, গড্ডর *n.* the ram; (fig.) a stupid man.

গড্ডলিকা, গড্ডরিকা *n. fem.* the ewe leading a flock, a bell-wether; a flock following a bell-wether. গড্ডলিকাপ্রবাহ *n.* (lit.) the movement of a flock of sheep blindly following the bell-wether; (fig.) a multitude of blind followers or their act of following en masse; a continuous flow.

গড়[১] *n.* shape, build.

গড়[২] *n.* genuflexion, genuflection. গড় করা *v.* to genuflect, to bow in salutation (to a person or deity). গড় হওয়া *v.* to genuflect.

গড়[৩] *n.* an average, a mean; an approximate amount. ~পড়তা see below. গড়ে *adv.* on an average.

গড়[৪] *n.* a fort; a fortress; a moat; a hollow into which the mouth of a husking pedal falls to thrash grains. গড়ের প্রাচীর the rampart. গড়ের বাদ্যি the military band of a fort; the music of this band. গড়ের মাঠ the esplanade.

গড়খাই *n.* a moat; (cp.) a ravelin.

গড়গড় *int.* expressing: a rumbling sound (as of thunder), a rattling sound (as of a running hackney-carriage), a continuous rattle. গড়গড় করা *v.* to rumble; to speak with flippant ease, to rattle; to grumble surlily. গড়গড় করে বলা *v.* to say or utter unobstructedly and rapidly, to speak unfalteringly or glibly.

গড়গড়া *n.* a hubble-bubble.

গড়ন *n.* act of making or creating or building or shaping or moulding or forming (see also **গড়**[1]) ; build, shape, mould, formation, structure; grace or beauty of build, shape etc. **~পিটন, ~পেটন** *n.* shape and appearance. **~দার** *n.* one who makes things by casting metals; a moulder.

গড়পড়তা *a.* average; approximate. ☐ *adv.* on an average; approximately.

গড়বড় *n.* confusion, disorder, mess, muddle, disarray.

গড়া[1] *n.* a kind of very coarse white loin-cloth without any border.

গড়া[2] *n.* an enclosure of stakes etc. set in a stream as a trap for fish, weir.

গড়া[3] *v.* to make (পিঠে গড়া) ; to shape, to mould, to model (পুতুল গড়া) ; to create; to build, to construct (বাড়ি গড়া) ; to form (দল গড়া) ; to found (স্কুল গড়া, রাজ্য গড়া) ; to bring up (ছেলে গড়া) ; to develop (দেশ গড়া). ☐ *a.* made; shaped, moulded, modelled; created; built, constructed; formed; founded; brought up; developed; made up, fabricated (গড়া সাক্ষী).

গড়াগড়ি *n.* state of weltering; a scattered and unclaimed state (টাকাপয়সার গড়াগড়ি). **গড়াগড়ি খাওয়া, গড়াগড়ি দেওয়া** *v.* to welter, to roll about, to wallow. **গড়াগড়ি যাওয়া** *v.* to welter (ছেলেটা ধুলোয় গড়াগড়ি যাচ্ছে) ; to roll about; to be scattered here and there (টাকাপয়সা গড়াগড়ি যাচ্ছে).

গড়ানে *a.* rolling, that which is rolling; rolling on the ground; (in football etc.) that runs all the way along the grass, touching the grass.

গড়ানো[1] *v.* to roll; to cause to roll, to send rolling; to pour (কলসি থেকে জল গড়ানো) ; to welter; to be beside oneself (আহ্লাদে গড়ানো) ; to flow (তেল গড়ানো) ; to go, to reach, to develop into (ব্যাপারটা বহুদূর গড়াল). ☐ *n.* act of rolling or pouring or weltering or being beside oneself or flowing or reaching. **গড়িয়ে দেওয়া** *n.* to send rolling; to pour somebody (আমাকে একটু জল গড়িয়ে দা **গড়িয়ে পড়া** *v.* to roll down; to come pouring; to lie down and roll; to f down and welter; to flow down. **গড়ি যাওয়া** *v.* to go rolling; to flow on; reach, to roll down; to develop into.

গড়াপেটা *v.* to give definite form or sha to, to hammer or knock into (rig shape. ☐ *a.* that which is decided b forehand (esp. by way of comp mise); got-up.

গড়ায় গড়ায় *adv.* side by side; snug (গড়ায় গড়ায় পড়ে থাকা).

গড়িমসি *n.* wilful or habitual delay, pr crastination, dilatoriness. **গড়িমসি করা** to delay wilfully or habitually, to pr crastinate, dilly-dally; to be dilatory.

গড়ু *n.* any morbid protuberance or e crescence on the body (such as hunc goitre, wart etc.) *a.* hunch-backed.

গণ *n.* a collection, a multitude; a numb more than one (used as *a sfx.* to in cate plurality, e.g. বালকগণ = bo পুরুষগণ = men); a community, a cla a group; a genus; a species; the co mon people, the masses; the attenda of Shiva (শিব) ; a clan, a race, a fa ily; a classification of persons acco ing to the stars predominant at th birth (দেবগণ, নরগণ, রাক্ষসগণ) ; Sanskrit gr.) a classification of ve (ভ্বাদিগণ). **~অভ্যুত্থান** *n.* mass rising, m upheaval, mass revolt. **~আদালত** people's court. **~আন্দোলন** *n.* ma movement. **~চেতনা** *n.* popular awa ness; awakening of the people. **~তন্ত্র** a form of government in which the preme power is vested in the elect representatives of the people; dem racy; a republic. **~তন্ত্রী, ~তান্ত্রিক** *a.* publican; democratic. **~দেব** *n.* appellation of Ganesha (গণেশ). **~দে** *n.* one of a class of subordinate deiti the people conceived as a deity. **~** *n.* people's theatre. **~নায়ক** *n.* a leader the people. **~নাথ, ~পতি** *n.* the lord the host; an appellation of Ganes (গণেশ) and also Shiva (শিব). **~পরিষদ**

a constituent assembly. **~বিক্ষোভ** *n.* popular unrest, people's agitation. **~ভোট** *n.* plebiscite. **~মাধ্যম** *n.* mass media. **~যুদ্ধ** *n.* people's war. **~শক্তি** *n.* power of the people, the united strength of the people; the people collectively; the sovereignty of the people. **~সংগীত** *n.* folk song; group music; song of the masses. **~সংগ্রাম** *n.* mass struggle. **~হত্যা** *n.* genocide.

ইতে *v. inf.* (poet.—obs.) counting; going to count, to count.

ক *n.* an astrologer, a soothsayer; a palmist; a calculator. ☐ *a.* one who or that which calculates, calculating.

তি rej. spelling of **গনতি** ।

ৎকার rej. spelling of **গনতকার** ।

ন, গণনা *n.* act of reckoning or counting, enumeration (সংখ্যাগণনা) ; act of doing a mathematical sum; act of deciding or judging (as); decision, judgment (দোষী বলে গণনা করা) ; act of considering or regarding (as), consideration (মানুষ বলে গণনা) ; act of pointing out (as), mention (শত্রু বলে গণনা) ; (astrol.) prediction, foretelling, divination. **গণনা করা** *v.* to reckon, to count, to enumerate; to calculate, to compute; to do (a mathematical sum), to work out; to judge; to consider, to regard (as); to point out, to mention; (astrol.) to predict, to foretell, to divine. **গণনাকারী** *n.* an enumerator. **~যন্ত্র** a counting instrument, a calculator. **গণনার্হ** *a.* worthy of being reckoned or counted; worth considering or counting. **গণনীয়** *a.* countable; calculable; worth considering or mentioning.

alt. spell. of **গনা** ।

ধিপ *n.* same as **গণনাথ** (see **গণ**).

কা *n.* a prostitute, a harlot, a whore.

গৃহ, ~লয় *n.* a brothel, a bawdy-house.

ত *a.* reckoned, counted; enumerated; calculated, computed; (rare—of a mathematical sum) worked out; decided, adjudged; considered, regarded (as); pointed out, mentioned; (astrol.) predicted, divined. ☐ *n.* mathematics.

ক *n.* accounts. **গণিতকবিদ্যা** *n.* accountancy. **~জ্ঞ** *a.* versed in mathematics. ☐ *n.* a mathematician. **~বিদ্যা** *n.* (the science of) mathematics. **~বিষয়ক** *a.* mathematical. **~শাস্ত্র** same as **গণিতবিদ্যা** ।

গণীভূত *a.* belonging to a race or tribe, racial, tribal, belonging to a genus, generic; belonging to a community, communal; belonging to a party.

গণেশ *n.* the lord of the hosts; the name of the eldest son of Shiva (শিব) and Durga (দুর্গা) who is the presiding deity of success.

গণ্ড *n.* the cheek; any morbid fleshy growth on the body, a tumour, a boil (গলগণ্ড) ; a gland (গণ্ডমালা) ; any massive thing (গণ্ডশৈল). ☐ *a.* large and important. **~কূপ** *n.* a dimple on the cheek; a valley. **~গ্রাম** *n.* a large populous village; a remote village. **~দেশ, ~ফলক** *n.* the cheek. **~মালা** *n.* mumps; scrofula. **~মূর্খ** *a.* utterly ignorant or illiterate; utterly stupid. **গণ্ডশিলা** *n.* a boulder. **গণ্ডশৈল** *n.* a volcanic rock. **~স্থল** *n.* the cheek.

গণ্ডক *n.* the rhinoceros; an obstacle; a unit of counting in fours; a river of that name.

গণ্ডকীশিলা *n.* a kind of black stone found in the river Gandaki.

গণ্ডি, গণ্ডী *n.* an encircling line, a boundary-line; bounds, limit; a (circular) part of land immunized by means of a charm. **গণ্ডি দেওয়া** *v.* to draw a (circular) line along the boundary; to draw a line encircling a plot of land and immunize it by means of a charm.

গণ্ডু *n.* a pillow; a knot.

গণ্ডূষ *n.* a mouthful or handful of water; the cavity or capacity of a cupped palm; act of taking water in the cup of one's palm by uttering some sacred incantation and drinking it.

গণ্য *a.* countable, calculable, estimable; worth regarding as; considered, regarded as (পূজনীয় বলে গণ্য) ; deserving attention, important (গণ্যমান্য). **গণ্য করা** *v.* to consider or to reckon as; to attach importance to, to care. **~মান্য** *a.* important and respectable.

গৎ *n*. the (cardinal) notes of a musical air; an utterance, a slogan (সব নেতারই এক গৎ) ; a code of laws or rules, routine (বাঁধা গৎ). **বাঁধা (বা বাঁধি) গৎ** set words or speech; a catchword; rigid rules or routine.

গত *a*. departed; finished; bygone, past; last (গত সোমবার) ; dead (তার পিতা গত হয়েছেন) ; obtained, held (হস্তগত) ; entered, lying (রন্ধ্রগত, মনোগত). **গত হওয়া** *v*. to go by, to depart; to be finished; to pass away; to die. **গতস্য শোচনা নাস্তি** let bygones be bygones, it's no use crying over past things, let the dead past bury its dead. **~কল্য, ~কাল** *n*. & *adv*. yesterday. **~ক্লম** *a*. refreshed. **~চেতন** *a*. unconscious; fainted, swooned. **~জীব, ~জীবন** *a*. dead. **~দিন, ~দিবস** *n*. & *adv*. yesterday. **~নিদ্র** *a*. sleepless; wakeful; awake. **~পরশু** *n*. & *adv*. (the) day before yesterday. **~প্রাণ** *a*. dead. **~প্রায়** *a*. nearly gone. **~বৎসর** *n*. & *adv*. (the) last year. **~ব্যথ** *a*. relieved of pain. **~ভর্তৃকা** *a*. *fem*. widowed. **~যৌবন** *a*. past one's prime of life, past one's youth; middle-aged; aged, old. *fem*. **~যৌবনা**। **~রাত্রি** *adv*. last night. **~শোক** *a*. one who has conquered grief and sorrow. **~শোচনা** *n*. grief for the past. **~সঙ্গ** *a*. having no attachment to anything worldly. **~স্পৃহ** *a*. disinterested; apathetic.

গতর *n*. body; health; physical strength or ability. **~খাকি, ~খাগি** *a*. *fem*. (abusively) physically strong yet averse to work; extremely lazy. *masc*. **~খেকো, ~খেগো**। **গতর খাটানো** *v*. to undergo physical toil; to work as a manual labourer.

গতাগত, গতাগতি *n*. going and coming; frequenting; advent and departure;birth and death ('করম বিপাকে গতাগতি পুন পুন').

গতানুগতিক *a*. routine; customary; usual; conventional; traditional; trite, hackneyed, commonplace; monotonous. **~তা** *n*. state of being customary; traditionalism; subservience to routine; triteness; lack or absence of variety; monotony. **~ভাবে** *adv*. in a customary or hackneyed fashion, by keeping the beaten track.

গতানুশোচনা, গতানুশোচন *n*. regret or gri for the past or for one's past actior **গতানুশোচনা করা** *v*. to lament for the pa to lament for one's past actions; to pent.

গতায়তি, গতায়াত variants of **গতাগতি** a **গতাগত** respectively.

গতায়ু *a*. one whose days are numbere about to die, dying.

গতাসু *a*. dead. **গতাসু হওয়া** *v*. to die, to e pire.

গতি *n*. going, passage, movement; ga motion, velocity; a way, a means (অ গতি নেই) ; a refuge or shelter, one w shelters or aids, a helper, a protector patron (দীনের গতি) ; a remedy; cons quence; the state into which one has pass after one's death (নরকগতি) ; means or way of rescue or salvati (পাপিষ্ঠের গতি) ; obsequies (মৃতের গ করা) ; end (মৃত্যুই জীবনের গতি) ; con tion, state (দুর্গতি, আকাশের গতি) ; গ **করা** *v*. to make necessary arrangeme for; to remedy; to take necessary a tion; to provide for; to perform fune rites of. **আহ্নিক গতি** (astr.) diurnal m tion. **কৌণিক গতি** (phys.) angular m tion. **বার্ষিক গতি** (astr.) annual motic **গতিক** *n*. state, condition (মনের গতিক a means or stratagem (কোনো গতিকে **কার্যগতিকে** *adv*. in course of business work; on business. **~ক্রিয়া** *n*. procras nation. **~দায়িনী** *a*. *fem*. one who giv spiritual salvation. **~প্রকৃতি** same **গতিবিধি**। **~বিজ্ঞান, ~বিদ্যা** *n*. kineti dynamics. **~বিধি** *n*. movement, activ (শত্রুর গতিবিধি) ; regular access or int course (রাজবাড়িতে তার গতিবিধি আছে (arch.) a means of spiritual salvation মা, কর গতিবিধি'). **~বেগ** *n*. speed, pa velocity. **~বেগমাপন যন্ত্র** *n*. an instrum for measuring speed, a speedometer tachometer. **~ভঙ্গ, ~রোধ** *n*. stoppage arrest of movement in the midway. ~ **করা** *v*. to stop in the midway; to br journey. **~ময়** *a*. moving, mobile; h ing movement. **~ময়তা** *a*. mobil movement; the state of having movement. **~রোধক** *a.* that which checks the movement. ☐ *n.* a break. **~রোধ করা** *v.* to cause to stop in the midway, to stop in the midway. **~হীন** *a.* motionless, immobile, still, having nothing to fall back on, resourceless.

তীয় *a.* kinetic, dynamic.

ত্যন্তর *n.* another means or way, an alternative means or way, an alternative. **~হীন** *a.* without an alternative, without any other means, left without an alternative.

দ *n.* poison; disease; morbid presence of undigested food in the stomach (পেটে গদ জমেছে).

গদ *n.* a voice made indistinct with excessive emotion. ☐ *a.* overwhelmed with emotion, ecstatic (গদগদচিত্ত) ; one whose voice has been choked with emotion (গদগদ হওয়া) ; choked or confused with excessive emotion (গদগদ ভাষা).

দা *n.* a mace, a club. **~ঘাত** *n.* a blow with a club, a stroke of a club. **গদাঘাত করা** *v.* to strike with a club, to club. **~ধর, ~পাণি** *a.* holding a club. ☐ *n.* an appellation of Vishnu (বিষ্ণু). **~যুদ্ধ** *n.* fight with clubs.

দাইলশকরি, গদাইলস্করি *a.* extremely sluggish. **গদাইলশকরি চাল** *n.* sluggishness; the habit of doing things in a very slow and tardy manner.

দাঘাত, গদাধর, গদাপাণি see **গদা**।

দি *n.* a mattress, a cushion; a mercantile office (মারোয়াড়ির গদি) ; a king's seat, a throne, a gadi (গদিতে আরোহণ করা) ; the seat of a zemindar or landlord or of an ecclesiastical chief, an abbot etc. (গদি পাওয়া). **গদিয়ান** *a.* seated; ruling; holding a post.

দ্য *n.* & *a.* prose. **~কবিতা** *n.* a prose-poem. **~ছন্দ** *n.* prose rhythm; the unversified language of poetry (গদ্যছন্দে লেখা কবিতা). **~ময়** *a.* prosaic. **~লেখক** *n.* a prose-writer.

গনগন *int.* expressing the blazing state. **গনগন করা** *v.* (of fire) to burn blazingly, to blaze. **গনগনে** *a.* blazing.

গনতি var. of **গুনতি**।

গনতকার *n.* a foreteller, an astrologer, a palmist; a soothsayer.

গনা *v.* to count. to enumerate; to calculate, to compute; to consider; to regard as (মানুষ বলে গনা) ; to anticipate, to apprehend (বিপদ গনা) ; to foretell, to divine; to read as a palmist. ☐ *a.* counted, enumerated; calculated; considered, reckoned; anticipated; exactly just (গনা দশ বৎসর). **~গনতি, ~গুনতি** *a.* neither more nor less, exact, just.

গনাগোষ্ঠী *n.* the whole race or family.

গনানো *v.* to cause to count or enumerate or calculate or compute; to cause to anticipate; to cause to foretell or divine; to cause to read (one's palm, horoscope etc.) as by an astrologer.

গন্ডগোল *n.* tumult, uproar; disturbance; disorder; complication; difficulty; hitch. **গন্ডগোল করা** *v.* to make a noise; to kick up a row; to create disorder.

গন্ডা *n.* a set of four; a unit in fours; one's due or share (আপন গন্ডা) **~কিয়া** *n.* the table of counting by fours.

গন্ডায় গন্ডায় *adv.* in a large number.

গন্ডার *n.* the rhinoceros.

গন্ডেপিন্ডে *adv* & *a.* stuffing or gorging oneself to the full.

গন্ডেপিন্ডে খাওয়া *v* . to stuff or gorge oneself with food to the full; to gormandize.

গন্তব্য *a.* where one is to go, destined. ☐ *n.* destination. **~পথ** *n.* the destined route or way. **~স্থল** *n.* destination.

গন্তা *a.* one who goes or journeys, going, travelling. ☐ *n.* a goer, a traveller. *fem.* **গন্ত্রী**।

গন্ধ *n.* a scent, an odour, an aroma, a smell; a perfume (গন্ধ মাখা) ; spices (গন্ধবণিক) ; faint mention or touch or presence or trace (নামগন্ধ) ; connection (এতে টাকার গন্ধ আছে). **গন্ধ ছড়ানো** *v.* to give out smell, to smell. **গন্ধ পাওয়া** *v.* to smell, to get the smell of; to get an inkling of, to be on the scent. **গন্ধ নেওয়া, গন্ধ শোঁকা** *v.* to smell. **~কাষ্ঠ** *n.* sandalwood, aloe-wood. **~গোকুল, ~গোকুলা** *n.* a variety of pole-cat or civet. **~জল** *n.*

perfumed or scented water. ~তেল *n.* perfumed oil, scented oil. ~দ্রব্য *n.* an aromatic substance, a perfume; a kind of flower plant. ~পুষ্প *n.* a fragrant flower; a flower besmeared with or soaked in sandal-paste. ~বণিক *n.* a Hindu caste dealing in spices; a member of this caste. ~বহ, ~বাহ *n.* the wind. ~বিহীন *a.* same as **গন্ধহীন**। ~বেনে coll. corrup. of **গন্ধবণিক**। ~ভাদাল, ~ভাদুলি *n.* a kind of (medicinal) creeper with a strong scent, Paederia foetida. ~মূষিক *n.* the musk-rat, the mole. ~মৃগ *n.* the musk-deer. ~রাজ *n.* a kind of fragrant flower or its tree, the Gardenia. ~হীন *a.* scentless. **গন্ধে গন্ধে** *adv.* trailing the scent of.

গন্ধক *n.* sulphur, brimstone. ~কাঠি *n.* sulphur match for lighting a lamp. ~চূর্ণ *n.* sulphur powder; gunpowder. ~দ্রাবক, **গন্ধকাম্ল** *n.* sulphuric acid.

গন্ধরস *n.* myrrh.

গন্ধর্ব *n.* (myth.) one belonging to a class of demi-gods proficient in music and war; (rare) a natural musician, a born musician. ~বিদ্যা *n.* the science and art of music, music. ~বিবাহ *n.* secret marriage of lovers (usu. by exchange of garlands) without any formal ceremony. ~বেদ *n.* the treatise on music; the science of music. ~লোক *n.* the land or abode of the Gandharvas (গন্ধর্ব).

গন্ধলি lit. var. of **গাঁদা**।

গন্ধসার *n.* sandal tree.

গন্ধাধিবাস, গন্ধাধিবাসন *n.* a ceremonial perfuming prior to a marriage or a holy rite.

গন্ধী *a.* (chiefly used as a *sfx.*) having a specific scent, scented. □ *n.* a dealer in spices (by caste); a kind of beetle with an abominable odour or offensive smell, a flying bug.

গন্ধেন্দ্রিয় *n.* the organ of smell, the nose.

গন্ধেশ্বরী *n.* the tutelary deity of dealers in spices.

গন্ধোপজীবী *n.* a dealer in spices (by caste). □ *a.* dealing in spices.

গন্নাকাটা *a.* hare-lipped.

গপ গপ *int.* expressing: the sound of eating rapidly or voraciously in larg morsels. **গপাগপ** *adv.* rapidly or vor. ciously in large morsels (গপাগপ গেলা).

গপাগপ see **গপ গপ**।

গপ্পো, গপ্পো *n.* (coll.) gossip, chit-cha prate. **গপ্পো করা** *v.* to talk idly, to cha ter; to blab. ~বাজ, **গপ্পে** *a.* given to id or too much talk, talkative, gossip able to talk or chat flippantly. □ *n.* a idle talker; a flippant talker.

গবচন্দ্র *n.* the name of a ludicrously stup minister of folk tales; an utter fool.

গবদা *a.* corpulent, bulky, plump, fa fleshy, chubby.

গবয় *n.* a kind of (wild) cow having r dewlap (chiefly found in the Him layan region).

গবা *n.* a fatty and stupid person. □ fatty and foolish.

গবাক্ষ *n.* a ventilator in the shape of bull's eye; an eyelet; a bay-window.

গবাগব var. of **গপাগপ**।

গবাদি *n.* the cow and similar other (do mestic) animals; the cattle group.

গবুচন্দ্র var. of **গবচন্দ্র**।

গবেট *n.* fool, idiot, simpleton, do blockhead, dunce, booby.

গবেষক *n.* one who researches, researc ing. □ *n.* a research-worker; a r searcher.

গবেষণা, গবেষণ *n.* research. **গবেষণা করা** to research. **গবেষণাগার** *n.* a laboratory, lab.

গবেষিত *a.* researched.

গব্য *a.* relating to the cow; produced the cow or cow-milk. □ *n.* anythi produced of the cow or cow-mi (such as milk, ghee, curd, cowdu and cow's urine: these five collective are called **পঞ্চগব্য**) ; milk-product.

গব্যোৎপাদন *n.* dairy farming.

গভর্নমেন্ট *n.* (pol.) government.

গভর্নর *n.* (pol.) a governor (of a state).

গভীর *a.* deep; hollow (গভীর পাত্র) ; den (গভীর বন) ; intense; thick (গভী অন্ধকার) ; profound (গভীর পাণ্ডিত্য) ; fa reaching, intricate, secret, esote (গভীর তত্ত্ব) ; far-advanced (গভীর রাত্রি low-pitched, grave (গভীর স্বর). □ *n.* t inmost or deepest part, depth (মনের গভীরে). **গভীরতা, গভীরত্ব** *n.* depth; hollowness; density; intensity, thickness; profundity; intricacy; far advanced state; gravity, graveness. **গভীর জলের মাছ** *n.* a deep-water fish; (fig.) a very cunning and secretive person, a person whose designs or motives are too deep for divination. **গভীর রাত্রে** in the dead of night. **গভীর শ্বসন** deep breathing.

ম *n.* wheat.

মক *n.* (mus.) a kind of artistic trill.

মগম *int.* expressing: the state of being resounded with deep or grave sound; the state of being filled (esp. solemnly). **গমগম করা** *v.* to resound with deep or grave sound; to be full (esp. solemnly). **গমগমে** *a.* (of sound or voice) resounding, deeply resounding.

মন *n.* act of going, departure; movement; motion; gait; sexual intercourse, coition (পরদারগমন). **গমন করা** *v.* to go; to depart, to leave; to move. **~পথ** *n.* a route; a way. **~শীল** *a.* going, moving. **গমনাগমন** *n.* going and coming; departure and arrival; frequentation. **গমনাগমন করা** *v.* to go and come; to depart and arrive; to frequent. **গমনার্হ, গমনীয়** *a.* where one may go to; that which can be traversed, passable, accessible; where one is to go, destined. **গমনোদ্যত** *a.* about to go or depart or move. **গমনোন্মুখ** *a.* eager or about to go or depart or move.

জ var. of **গুম্বজ**।

ীর *a.* grave, solemn (গম্ভীর স্বর); affecting or expressing importance (গম্ভীর চাল, গম্ভীর আকৃতি); serious, glum, sullen (গম্ভীর মুখ); sparing in speech, reserved. **~তা** *n.* gravity, solemnity; affectation or expression of importance; seriousness; glumness; sullenness; reticence in speech, reservedness. **গম্ভীর নাদ** a grave or resounding sound; a deep roar. **~নাদী** *a.* resounding; emitting a deep or resounding sound; roaring deeply. **~প্রকৃতি** *a.* reserved and grave. **গম্ভীর স্বর** a grave or serious voice. **গম্ভীরাকৃতি** *a.* looking or appearing grave and solemn.

গম্ভীরা *n.* a form of worshipping Shiva (শিব) in the month of Chaitra (চৈত্র); a kind of folk-song sung esp. in the Malda district on this occasion; the music of these songs; a form of decoration with tinsels; the inner part of a temple.

গম্য *a.* where one may go; fit to be visited; that which can be traversed, passable, accessible; where one is to go, destined; obtainable; comprehensible; enjoyable; fit for sexual intercourse. **~তা** *n.* visitability; accessibility; motion. *fem.* **গম্যা**।

গয়ংগচ্ছ *n.* dilatoriness, procrastination; laziness.

গয়না coll. corrup. of **গহনা**।

গয়বি *a.* secret, concealed, undisclosed (গয়বি খুন); cock-and-bull, fantastic (গয়বি কথা); providential, divine (গয়বি আদেশ). **গয়বি চাল** (in chess) a move conducted or directed from a distance and without looking at the chess-board; (fig.) a direction for action without knowing the state of affairs. **গয়বি চিঠি** an anonymous or unsigned letter.

গয়রহ *con.* (in law) and the rest, and others, etcetera, et al.

গয়লা, গয়লানি coll. corruptions of **গোয়ালা** and **গোয়ালিনি** respectively.

গয়ার, গয়ের *n.* phlegm. **গয়ের তোলা** *v.* to expectorate, to eject phlegm.

গয়ালি *n.* a priest and guide for the pilgrims to the temple of Gaya.

গর *pfx.* denoting: negation (গরহাজির); disparity, want (গরমিল); non-, dis- etc.

গরগর¹ *a.* overwhelmed (ভাবে গরগর); beside oneself, esp. with delight ('রাইরূপ হেরি অন্তর গরগর'); deeply reddened (চক্ষু গরগর). **গরগরে** *a.* overwhelming; deep; very hot or strong (গরগরে ঝাল).

গরগর² *int.* expressing: sign of anger or angry muttering; low roaring sound; deep colour effect. **গরগর করা** *v.* to betray or give out signs of anger; to mutter angrily; to roar suppressedly; to betray repressed anger or irritation; to fret and fume (রাগে গরগর করা) ; to redden deeply (চক্ষু গরগর করা). **গরগরে** *a.* flushed with anger; muttering angrily; roaring suppressedly; deep red; (of any colour) deep.

গরজ *n.* necessity or interest (আপন গরজে) ; attention, devotion (পড়াশোনায় গরজ). **গরজ করা** *v.* to feel eagerness to do, to be up and doing, to be active; to pay attention to. **গরজি** *a.* (chiefly used as a *sfx.*) interested (আপ্তগরজি). **গরজ বড় বালাই** (fig.) necessity is the most exacting taskmaster; (fig.) necessity knows no law.

গরজনি poet. corrup. of **গর্জন**।

গরজানি, গরজানো poet. corruptions of **গর্জানি** and **গর্জানো** respectively.

গরঠিকানা *n.* a wrong address, an incorrect address. **গরঠিকানিয়া** *a.* one whose address is not known; without an address.

গরদ *n.* a kind of silk fabric.

গরদা alt. spell. of **গর্দা**।

গরব poet. corrup. of **গর্ব**।

গরবা *n.* a kind of dance accompanied with songs current in Gujarat.

গরবিত poet. corrup of **গর্বিত**।

গরবিনি, (rej.) **গরবিনী** *a. fem.* glorious, honoured, proud ('তোমার গরবে গরবিনী হাম').

গরম *n.* heat (গ্রীষ্মের গরম) ; summer (গরমের সময়) ; arrogant, haughtiness (কথার গরম) ; vanity, pride (টাকার গরম) ; morbidity, illness (পেট গরম). ☐ *a.* hot (গরম জল, গরম কাল) ; warm, woollen (গরম জামা) ; arrogant, haughty (গরম মেজাজ) ; angry (গরম কথা) ; characterized by high price, dear (গরম বাজার) ; excited, belligerent (গরম পরিস্থিতি) ; fresh and exciting (গরম খবর). **গরম মশলা** cardamom cloves and cinnamon taken together as used in cooking to make food rich. **গরম গরম, গরমাগরম** *a.* (of food) hot; (fig.—of news etc.) fresh and exciting.

গরমি *n.* heat; summer; anger; syphilis.

গরমিল *n.* disparity; disagreement; disharmony.

গররাজি *a.* unwilling, reluctant, loth, not consenting. **গররাজি হওয়া** *v.* to expres one's reluctance or unwillingness; no to agree.

গরল *n.* poison.

গরহাজির *a.* absent. **গরহাজির থাকা** *v.* to ab sent oneself.

গরাদ *n.* a bar (as of a window).

গরান *n.* the mangrove or its timber.

গরাস dial. corrup. of **গ্রাস**।

গরিব *a.* poor. **~খানা** *n.* (in polite speech the speaker's dwelling-house which i supposed to be poor, (my) poor o humble residence. **~গুরবো** *n. pl.* th poorer classes; the proletariat. **গরিবান গরিবি** *n.* poverty; a poor man's state poor arrangement. ☐ *a.* poor; poorly.

গরিমা *n.* glory; pride; vanity; importance spiritual glory earned by yoga or austere religious practice.

গরিলা *n.* the gorilla.

গরিষ্ঠ *a.* weightiest; most important; larg est; greatest; maximum; most vener able or honourable; richest; chief. **গরি সাধারণ গুণনীয়ক,** (সংক্ষেপে) **গ সা গু** (i arith.) greatest common measure G.C.M.; (in alg.) highest common fac tor, H.C.F. **গরিষ্ঠ সম্প্রদায়** the majorit community.

গরীব rej. spell. of **গরিব**।

গরীয়ান *a.* weightier; more importan larger; more venerable or honourabl richer. *fem.* **গরীয়সী**।

গরু alt. spell. of **গোরু**।

গরুজে coll. corrup. of **গরজি** (see **গরজ**)।

গরুড় *n.* (myth.) the name of the prince c the birds on whom Vishnu (বিষ্ণু) ride. **~ধ্বজ, ~বাহন** *n.* Vishnu (বিষ্ণু). **গরুড়াস** *n.* a posture of sitting in yoga after th manner of Garuda (গরুড়).

গরুৎ *n.* a wing (as of a bird); a feather.

গরুত্মান *n.* Garuda (গরুড়) ; a bird. ☐ winged; feathered. **গরুত্মতী** *n. fem.* a fe male bird. ☐ *a. fem.* winged; feathere having a sail or sails (গরুত্মতী তরী).

গর্জক *a.* one who or that which roar roaring.

গর্জন[1] *n.* roar, rumble, howl, thunderin sound. **গর্জন করা** *v.* to roar, to rumbl to howl, to thunder.

গর্জন[২] *n.* a species of tall tree, *Dipterocarpus turbinatus*, the garjan. **~তেল** *n.* juice of garjan used in varnishing idols etc.

গর্জমান *a.* engaged in or in a state of roaring, roaring, rumbling, howling, thundering.

গর্জানো *v.* to roar, to rumble, to howl, to thunder. **গর্জানি** *n.* roaring, rumbling, howling, thundering.

গর্জিত *a.* sounded or resounded loudly.

গর্ত *n.* a hole, a slot, a cavity, a crevice, a cavern, a pit, a cave. **গর্ত করা** *v.* to make a hole; to dig a hole. **গর্ত ভরাট করা** to fill a hole.

গর্দভ *n.* the ass; (in reproof or taunts) an utter fool. *fem.* **গর্দভী**। **গর্দভ রাগিণী** *n.* (ridi.) the intolerably harsh voice of a bad singer.

গর্দা *n.* soil, dirt, filth.

গর্দান *n.* the neck or the throat; the part of the body above the shoulders; the head. **গর্দান দেওয়া** *v.* to sentence to death by beheading; to behead; to sacrifice one's own head. **গর্দান নেওয়া** *v.* to behead. **গর্দানি** *n.* holding by the neck and pushing one out.

গর্ব *n.* pride; conceit; vanity; boasting, bragging; an object of pride or glory (রবীন্দ্রনাথ ভারতের গর্ব, এই ছবিখানি তার গর্ব). **গর্ব করা** *v.* to pride (in); to boast, to brag. **~শূন্য** *a.* free from pride; modest; unpretentious. **গর্বিত, গর্বী** *a.* proud; conceited; vain, vainglorious; boastful, braggart. *fem.* **গর্বিতা, গর্বিণী**। **গর্বোজ্জ্বল** *a.* radiant with pride or glory. **গর্বোদ্ধত** *a.* arrogant and vainglorious.

গর্ভ *n.* inner part; interior, inside (নারকেলের গর্ভ, ভূগর্ভ) ; bed, bottom (নদীগর্ভ) ; hollow, pit (খনিগর্ভ) ; womb (গর্ভে ধারণ) ; a spathe (of a plant); embryo, foetus (গর্ভধারণ) ; pregnancy, conception (গর্ভলক্ষণ) ; belly (পেয়ারাগুলো সব ছেলেদের গর্ভে গেছে) ; (fig.) undue appropriation (এ টাকা মহাজনের গর্ভে যাবে). **গর্ভ হওয়া** *v.* to be in the family way; to become pregnant. **~কটি** *a.* perigynous. **~কাল** *n.* gestation. **~কেশর** *n.* the pistil (of a flower). **গর্ভকেশরের অগ্রভাগ** a stigma. **~কোষ** *n.* the uterus, seed-vessel. **~গৃহ** *n.* a lying-in room; a small room or compartment within a larger one often in a temple to house the idol (cp. an anteroom). **~চ্যুত** *a.* miscarried (in birth); fallen from the womb. **~চ্যুতি** *n.* miscarriage. **~জ, ~জাত** *a.* born of the womb (of). **~তন্তু, ~দণ্ড** *n.* (bot.) a style. **~দাস** *n.* a son of a slave woman (such a son is bound to slavery by birth); one's son by one's slave-woman. **~ধারণ** *n.* conception. **গর্ভধারণ করা** *v.* to conceive, to become pregnant, to be with child or in the family way. **গর্ভে ধারণ** act of bearing in one's womb; gestation. **~ধারিণী** *n.* mother. **~নাড়ি** *n.* umbilical cord. **~নাশ** *n.* same as **গর্ভপাত**। **~নিঃসৃত** *a.* one who or that which has come out of the womb (of); extricated from the womb (of). **গর্ভনিঃসৃত হওয়া** *v.* to come out of the womb (of). **~পত্র** *n.* (bot.) a carpel. **~পরিস্রব, ~ফুল** *n.* placenta. **~পাত** *n.* miscarriage, abortion. **~পাত করা** *v.* to cause abortion (esp. illegally). **গর্ভপাত হওয়া** *v.* to have abortion, to miscarry. **~বতী** *a.* pregnant, with child, in the family way. **গর্ভবতী হওয়া** *v.* (of women) to become pregnant, to conceive; (of beasts) to be gravid or big with young. **~বাস** *a.* the period of gestation or act of living in one's mother's womb. **গর্ভবাস করা** *v.* to be in one's mother's womb, to live in one's mother's womb. **~বেদনা, ~ব্যথা** same as **গর্ভযন্ত্রণা**। **~মাস** *n.* the first month of conception. **~মুণ্ড** *n.* (bot.) a stigma. **~মোচন** *n.* delivery of a child. **গর্ভমোচন করা** *v.* to be delivered of a child. **~যন্ত্রণা, ~যাতনা** *n.* throes of labour, travail, labour-pain; (fig.) excessive pain or labour. **গর্ভযন্ত্রণা ভোগ করা** *v.* (lit. & fig.) to be in travail, to be in labour. **~লক্ষণ** *n.* sign of pregnancy. **~শীর্ষ** *a.* (bot.) epigynous. **~সংক্রমণ, ~সঞ্চার** *n.* appearance of the embryo in the womb; conception. **গর্ভসঞ্চার হওয়া** *v.* to become pregnant, to be with child. **~স্থ** *a.* lying in the womb; of the womb. **~স্থলী** *n.* the womb; the uterus. **~স্রাব** *n.*

miscarriage in childbirth, abortion; (vul.—in abuse or contempt) a bastard, a wastrel, a good-for-nothing fellow. **গর্ভস্রাব হওয়া** *v.* to miscarry.

গর্ভাগার *n.* a lying-in room; a small room or compartment within a larger one (cp. ante-room).

গর্ভাঙ্ক *n.* a scene (of a drama).

গর্ভাধান *n.* a ceremony on attainment of puberty by a married girl; act of making one pregnant, impregnation or fertilization (of the womb).

গর্ভাশয় *n.* the uterus, the ovary. **গর্ভাশয় প্রদাহ** *n.* ovaritis.

গর্ভিণী *a.* pregnant. □ *n.* a pregnant woman.

গর্ভোৎপাদন *n.* making one pregnant, impregnation or fertilization (of the womb.)

গর্মি alt. spell. of **গরমি** I

গর্হণ, গর্হণা, গর্হা *n.* condemnation, censure, blame, accusation; reproach, reproof.

গর্হিত *a.* utterly condemned or censured; abominable, detestable; vile. **গর্হিত কাজ** an atrocious or odious or heinous act.

গর্হ্য *a.* condemnable, blameworthy; reproachable; detestable.

গল *n.* the throat; the neck. **~কম্বল** *n.* a dewlap. **~গণ্ড** *n.* goitre. **~গ্রহ** *n.* an undesirable burden hanging from one's throat; (fig.) an undesirable dependant who willy-nilly has to be supported and cannot be got rid of. **~দাহ** *n.* inflammation of the throat, sore-throat, laryngitis, quinsy. **~দেশ** *n.* the region of the throat, the throat. **~নালি** *n.* the gullet, the oesophagus, the larynx, the wind-pipe. **~বন্ধ** *n.* a neckerchief, a muffler; a neckband, a collar (of a dog etc.). **~বস্ত্র** *a.* having a piece of cloth round one's neck (to indicate humility). **~বস্ত্র হওয়া** *v.* to put a piece of cloth round one's neck (in humble submission). **~ভঙ্গ** *n.* morbid hoarseness of voice, sore-throat. **~ভঙ্গ হওয়া** *v.* to become hoarse of voice. **~রন্ধ্র** *n.* the cavity of the throat. **~রজ্জু** *n.* a halter. **~রসগ্রন্থি** *n.* the adenoids. **~লগ্ন** *a.* clung to one's neck. **~লগ্নীকৃতবাস** same as **গলবস্ত্র** (*a*). **~হস্ত** *n.* act of holding by the neck or throat and pushing one out. **গলহস্ত দেওয়া** *v.* to hold by the neck or throat and push one out.

গলই var. of **গলুই** I

গলগল *int.* expressing the sound of quick and profuse pouring out or coming out of liquid matter.

গলৎ, গলতি[১] *a.* in a melting state; dripping; secreting morbid matter (গলৎকুষ্ঠ). **গলৎকুষ্ঠ** *n.* ulcerous leprosy secreting morbid matter.

গলতি[২] *n.* a mistake, an error; a shortcoming, a defect.

গলদ *n.* an error; a defect; a failing, an omission; a fault. **গলদ থাকা** *v.* to be erroneous or defective or faulty. **গলদ হওয়া** *v.* to commit an error or fault; to be faulty or erroneous through inadvertence or incapacity.

গলদঘর্ম *a.* perspiring copiously, weltering in sweat, (lit.) melting in sweat. **গলদঘর্ম হওয়া** *v.* to perspire copiously, to welter in sweat.

গলদশ্রু *a.* with tears flowing from the eyes or rolling down the cheeks (গলদশ্রুলোচন). **গলদশ্রুলোচনে** *adv.* with tearful eyes.

গলদা, গলদা-চিংড়ি *n.* the lobster.

গলন *n.* act of being melted, melting; act of passing through; act of being overwhelmed; softening; act of bursting open and secreting morbid matter. **গলনাঙ্ক** *n.* melting-point.

গলা[১] *v.* to melt (বরফ গলা) ; to pass or slip through; (fig.) to be tight-fisted (হাত দিয়ে জল গলে না) ; to pass through or enter (ঘরের মধ্যে গলে যাওয়া) ; to soften (মন গলা) ; to be overwhelmed (স্নেহে গলা) ; to burst open and secrete morbid matter (ফোঁড়া গলা) ; to decompose (মৃতদেহটা গলে গেছে, পচে গলে যাওয়া). □ *a.* melted; worn out; softened overmuch; that which has burst open and is secreting morbid matter; decomposed; rotten. **গলানো** *v.* to (cause to) melt; to (cause to) pass through; to (cause to) soften; to overwhelm; to put on easily or lightly (জুতোটা পায়ে গলিয়ে

নাও) ; to cause to burst open and secrete morbid matter; to decompose. ☐ *a.* melted. **গলা গলা** *a.* excessively softened or soft (গলা গলা ভাত).

গলা² *n.* the throat; the neck; the Adam's apple; voice (তার গলা পাচ্ছি, গানের গলা) ; strength of voice (খেয়াল গাইতে হলে গলা থাকা চাই). **গলা কাটা** *v.* to cut one's throat. **গলা চাপা** *v.* to restrain one's voice; to throttle. **গলা ছাড়া** *v.* to remove restraint from one's voice (whilst singing, lamenting, calling etc.) **গলা টেপা** *v.* to throttle. **গলা টিপলে দুধ বেরোয়** (lit.—of a person) so young that milk comes out of the mouth when the throat is pressed; (fig.) very young or inexperienced (cp. greenhorn). **গলা ধরা, গলা বসা, গলা ভাঙা** *v.* to be hoarse. **গলায় গাঁথা** same as **গলায় পড়া**। **গলায় দড়ি** (in curses) damn! hang! **গলায় পড়া** *v.* to come upon one as an undesirable burden. **গলায় লাগা** *v.* to feel an uneasy sensation or pain in the throat, to have choking in the throat preventing easy passage of food; to cause irritation or inflammation of the larynx. **গলার কাঁটা** a fishbone stuck in one's throat; (fig.) a bothersome burden. **গলার জোর** strength of voice. **গলার থলি** (anat.) the pouch in the gullet or the crop. **গলার ব্যথা** throat-pain, inflammation of the throat, throatsore, quinsy. **একগলা, গলা পর্যন্ত** *a.* reaching up to the neck, reaching up to the chin. **ভারী গলা** grave or deep voice. **~কাটা** *a.* exorbitant, cut-throat (price etc.) (গলাকাটা দাম). ☐ *n.* one who demands an exorbitant price (cp. a cut-throat). **~খাঁকারি** *n.* act of clearing one's throat noisily, act of hawking. **গলাখাঁকারি দেওয়া** *v.* to hawk. **গলা খুসখুসুনি** *n.* itching sensation in the throat. **~গলি** *a.* very intimate; close; matey; bosom; side by side. ☐ *adv.* very intimately; closely; cheek by jowl. ☐ *n.* close intimacy; closeness. **~গলি করা** *v.* to be intimate with; to make free with; to hug. **গলাধঃকরণ** *n.* act of swallowing or gulping; act of eating or drinking. **গলাধঃকরণ করা** *v.* to swallow, to gulp; to eat or drink; (fig.) to brook, to endure (অপমান গলাধঃকরণ করা). **~ধাক্কা** *n.* catching by the neck and driving one out. **গলাধাক্কা দেওয়া** *v.* to catch by the neck and drive one out. **~বন্ধ** *n.* a neckerchief; a comforter; muffler. **~বাজি** *n.* shouting (usu. continuous); (ridi.) oration; bragging; bullying. **গলাবাজি করা** *v.* to shout (usu. continuously); (ridi.) to deliver a lecture, to harangue; to brag; to bully. **গলাবাজি করে জেতা** to shout others down. **গলায় গলায়** *a.* very close, intimate, hand in glove (গলায় গলায় ভাব). ☐ *adv.* neck and neck, side by side; up to the throat; up to the brim; very closely, intimately.

গলাসি *n.* the neck-rope of an animal.

গলি *n.* a narrow street, a lane; a corridor. **কানা গলি** a blind alley, a cul-de-sac. **~ঘুঁজি** *n. pl.* different narrow passages and concealed corners; lanes and by-lanes; (fig.) secret regions or parts nook and corner (মনের গলিঘুঁজি).

গলিজ *a.* extremely dirty or filthy; full of stench; rotten; decomposed; abominable (গলিজ ব্যাপার).

গলিত *a.* melted (গলিত লোহা) ; liquid, liquefied (গলিত অশ্রু) ; worn out, decrepit, old and infirm (গলিতনখদন্ত) ; decomposed (গলিত শবদেহ) ; secreting morbid matter (গলিত কুষ্ঠ). **গলিত কুষ্ঠ** same as **গলৎকুষ্ঠ** (see **গলৎ**).

গলুই *n.* either of the tapering parts at the front and the back of a boat or ship, the prow or the stern.

গল্প *n.* a story; a tale; a fable; an anecdote; a fantastic or fictitious narrative, a fib; gossip; chit-chat. **গল্প করা** *v.* to gossip; to chat; to speak of (সে বিলাতের সম্বন্ধে গল্প করছে) ; to tell fantastic or fictitious tales about (নে আর তোর বাহাদুরির গল্প করিস না). **গল্প পড়া** *v.* to read out a story or anecdote. **গল্প ফাঁদা** *v.* to spin or invent or fabricate a story. **গল্প বলা** *v.* to tell a tale. **গল্প লেখা** *v.* to write stories or tales. **গল্প শোনা** *v.* to hear a tale or anecdote. **~কার** *n.* a storywriter; a story-teller. **~গুজব করা** *v.* to gossip, to chat. **গল্প বলিয়ে** *n.* a tale-teller; a raconteur (*fem.* a raconteuse). **গল্প-সল্প** same as **গল্পগুজব**। **গল্পে** *a.* gossipy; talkative.

গ সা গু see **গরিষ্ঠ**।

গস্ত *n.* act of walking or travelling, ambulation; act of purchasing goods (esp. for a retail shop) by ambulating in a (wholesale) market, shopping. **গস্ত করা** *v.* to purchase goods (esp. for a retail shop) by ambulating in a (wholesale) market, to shop.

গস্তানি *n.* a harlot, a prostitute, a whore.

গহন *a.* dense; not easily accessible; difficult to comprehend. ☐ *n.* a part or region not easily accessible (মনের গহনে).

গহনা[1] *n.* (formal) an ornament. **~গাটি, ~পত্র** *n. pl.* ornaments and other valuables.

গহনা[2], **গহনার নৌকা** *n.* a boat that runs regularly with passengers from stage to stage, a stage-boat.

গহিন *a.* deep; not easily accessible; far advanced (গহিন রাতে = at dead of the night).

গহ্বর *n.* a hole; a cavity; a pit.

-গা[1] *fem.* of **গ**[2] (নিম্নগা).

গা[2] *int.* a meaningless term or expletive used in conversation (হ্যাঁ গা মেয়ে, বল কি গা).

গা[3] *n.* (mus.) the third note in the natural scale, E.

গা[4] *n.* the body (গায়ের জোর) ; the surface of the body, the skin (খসখসে গা) ; sensibility, sensitiveness (অপমান গায়ে না লাগা) ; attention, heed, interest, willingness (কাজে গা নেই). **গা করা** *v.* to set one's mind (to); to pay heed (to); to take interest (in). **গা কাঁপা** *v.* to shudder in fear; to shiver. **গা কেমন করা, গা কেমন-কেমন করা** *v.* to be stricken with nausea, to feel uneasy or have nausea; to feel indisposed; to be stricken with fear. **~-গতর** *n.* the whole body. **~-গরম** *n.* state of having or running a temperature. **গা গরম হওয়া** *v.* to have one's body warmed up; to have a temperature, to run a temperature; to become feverish. **গা গুলানো** *v.* to be stricken with nausea, to have nausea, to feel queasy. **গা ঘামানো** *v.* to toil (esp. earnestly); (of an athlete, performer, etc.) prepare for a contest, performance, etc. by practising, warm up. **গা ঘেঁষা** *v.* to get very close to; to try to be intimate with. **গা জুড়ানো** *v.* to soothe, to gratify, to please; to refresh. **~-জুড়ানো** *a.* soothing; pleasant; refreshing (গা-জুড়ানো বাতাস). **~-জোরি** *n.* application or showing of undue force. **গা জ্বালা করা** *v.* to have burning sensation in the body; (fig.) to be malicious or spiteful; to be jealous; to grudge; to be displeased; to get angry. **গা ঝাড়া দেওয়া** *v.* to shake one's body. **গা ঝাড়া দিয়ে ওঠা** *v.* (lit.) to get up after shaking one's body; (fig.) to become active again with an effort, to shake off inertia. **গা ঝিমঝিম করা** *v.* to feel dizzy. **গা ঢাকা দেওয়া** *v.* to go into hiding, to abscond. **গা ঢেলে দেওয়া** *v.* to lie down; to relax one's efforts and let things have their own course; to join (in a work) wholeheartedly. **গা তোলা** *v.* to get up. **গা দেওয়া** same as **গা করা**। **গা পেতে নেওয়া** *v.* to invite (punishment, insult etc.) upon oneself. **গা বমি-বমি করা** same as **গা গুলানো**। **গা মাটি-মাটি করা** *v.* to feel like lying down in idleness. **গা ম্যাজম্যাজ করা** *v.* to feel uneasy, to feel out of sorts; to feel sluggish. **গায়ে কাঁটা দেওয়া** *v.* to have horripilation; to have one's hair stand on end, to have goose-flesh. **গায়ে গায়ে** very close, closely situated, standing very close; side by side; clinging together. **গায়ে থুতু দেওয়া** *v.* to spit upon one's face; (fig.) to detest extremely, to abhor, to abominate. **গায়ে দেওয়া** *v.* to wear, to put on. **গায়ে পড়ে** officiously; uninvitedly. **গায়ে ফুঁ দিয়ে বেড়ানো** *v.* (fig.) to move about avoiding toil and responsibility. **গায়ে ফোসকা পড়া** *v.*(fig.) to fret with pain or malice or jealousy; to be over-sensitive. **গায়ে মাংস (বা মাস) লাগা** *v.* to grow fat, to gain flesh, to put on flesh or weight. **গায়ে-পড়া** *a.* officious; talking or doing something unsolicitedly. **গায়ে মাখা** *v.* (fig.) to pay heed to, to care for. **গায়ে-হলুদ** *n.* the Hindu ceremony of besmearing the bridegroom and the bride with a paste of turmeric and then bathing them on the eve of their wedding. **গায়ে হাত তোলা** *v.* to beat, to lay hands on. **গায়ের জোরে** by brute force, by physical force. **গায়ের জ্বালা** burning sensation of the body; (fig.) malice, spite, jealousy, hatred, anger, displeasure. **গায়ের ঝাল ঝাড়া বা মেটানো** *v.* to vent one's grudge (against another), to vent one's spleen. **গা জ্বালা** same as **গায়ের জ্বালা**। **গা-সওয়া, গা-সহা** *a.* accustomed (to an evil) by repeated suffering (from it).

গাই, গাইগোরু *n.* the cow.

গাইয়ে *a.* one who is adept in singing; one who sings. □ *n.* a singer.

গাওন *n.* act of singing. **গাওনা** *n.* the singing or a call for singing of a professional singer; a demonstration of singing by a professional singer. **গাওনা দেওয়া** *v.* to arrange for demonstration of a professional singer's singing.

গাওয়া[1] *n.* a witness.

গাওয়া[2] *a.* made of cowmilk (গাওয়া ঘি).

গাওয়া[3] *v.* to sing; to chant; to sing in praise; to praise. □ *a.* that has been sung (গাওয়া গান). **~নো** *v.* to cause to sing.

গাং *n.* (coll.) a river, a stream. **~চিল** *n.* a river-gull, seagull. **~শালিক** *n.* the bank myna.

গাঁ *n.* a village; a hamlet. **গাঁয়ে মানে না আপনি মোড়ল** a self-styled leader.

গাঁই *n.* a classification of Brahmins according to their original village home.

গাঁইগুঁই *int.* expressing imaginary sound of indirect unwillingness. **গাঁইগুঁই করা** *v.* to show or express one's unwillingness usu. by gestures or suggestion, to demur.

গাঁইট var. of **গাঁট**।

গাঁইতি *n.* a pickaxe.

গাঁইয়া var. of **গেঁয়ো**।

গাঁক-গাঁক, গাঁ-গাঁ *int.* expressing the bellowing sound as of an angry bull. **গাঁক-গাঁক করা, গাঁ-গাঁ করা** *v.* to bellow.

গাঁজ, গাঁজলা *n.* froth, scum; yeast, leaven. **গাঁজন** *n.* fermentation; putrefaction.

গাঁজা[1] *v.* to be fermented; to come up in froth, to be frothy; to be putrefied.

গাঁজা[2] *n.* the female flowering tops of Indian hemp, *Cannabis sativa*, ganja; (loos.) hemp, marijuana (coll.) a cock-and-bull story. **গাঁজা খাওয়া** *v.* to smoke ganja.

গাঁজাখুরি *a.* absurd, incredible, cock-and-bull (গাঁজাখুরি গল্প).

গাঁজাখোর *a.* given to smoking ganja. □ *n.* a ganja-smoker, a ganja addict.

গাঁজানো *v.* to ferment, to leaven; to putrefy. □ *a.* fermented, leavened, putrefied. **গেঁজে ওঠা** same as **গাঁজানো**।

গাঁট *n.* a knot; a joint (esp. of bones); a knuckle; a knob; a node; a large bundle, a bale; a rim of the loincloth round one's waist where money is kept concealed. **গাঁট কাটা** *v.* (fig.) to cut the rim of one's loincloth and steal one's money, to pick one's pocket. **~কাটা** *n.* a cutpurse, a pickpocket. **~ছড়া** *n.* the Hindu custom of tying a corner of the bride's sari (শাড়ি) with a corner of the bridegroom's scarf at wedding. **গাঁটছড়া বাঁধা** *v.* (lit.) to tie a corner of the bride's sari (শাড়ি) with a corner of the bridegroom's scarf at wedding; (fig.) to marry; (fig.) to unite inseparably. **~বন্দি** *a.* baled, packed in a bale, made into a bale. **গাঁট বাঁধা** *v.* to tie up in a bale or in a large bundle. **গাঁটে বাঁধা** *v.* to keep (esp. money) concealed in the rim of one's loincloth. **গাঁটের কড়ি** (fig.) one's own money.

গাঁটরি, গাঁটুরি *n.* a bundle.

গাঁট্টা var. of **গাট্টা**।

গাঁট্টাগোঁট্টা alt. form of **গাট্টাগোট্টা**। see **গাট্টা**।

গাঁতি[1] *n.* a small holding to tenanted land.

গাঁতি[2] *n.* a pickaxe.

গাঁথন *n.* act of stringing (as a garland); composition (ছন্দে গাঁথন) ; construction; act of laying (bricks, stones etc. for constructing a building).

গাঁথনি *n.* manner of laying bricks, stones, etc. in construction of buildings; brickwork, stonework, mudwork; construction; stringing together (ফুলের গাঁথনি) ; (fig.) structure of sentences or verse. **কাঁচা গাঁথনি** mudwork. **পাকা গাঁথনি** brickwork or stonework, masonry.

গাঁথা *v.* to lay (as bricks, stones etc. in construction of buildings); to construct, to build; to string (as garland); compose, to set (ছন্দে গাঁথা) ; to cling or stick steadfastly (হৃদয়ে গেঁথে থাকা). ☐ *a.* laid; constructed; built; strung; composed, set; clung, stuck.

গাঁথুনি var. of **গাঁথনি। কথার গাঁথুনি** fine effective and attractive use of words; a clever and dexterous way of talking.

গাঁদা *n.* the Indian marigold.

গাঁধাল, গাঁদাল *n.* a kind of medicinal creeper (see **গন্ধভাদাল**).

গাঁধি var. of **গান্ধি**।

গাগরি *n.* a pitcher.

গাঙ alt. spell. of **গাং**।

গাঙ্গ *a.* of the Ganges, Gangetic; born of the Ganges; riverine.

গাঙ্গেয় *n.* the son of the Ganges. ☐ *a.* of the Ganges; Gangetic; born of the Ganges.

গাছ[1] var. of **গাছা**।

গাছ[2] *n.* a tree, a plant; a tree-like object (ঘানিগাছ) ; a creeper, a herb (লাউগাছ). **গাছকোমর বাঁধা** *v.* (of girls and women) to tie the loose end of the sari tightly round the waist, (cp.) to tuck up one's clothes. **~ড়া** *n.* a herb; a medicinal herb. **~গাছড়া** *n.* herbs or medicinal herbs collectively. **~গাছালি** same as **গাছগাছড়া**। **~তলা** *n.* the bottom or underneath part of a tree. **~পাকা** naturally ripe. **~পালা** *n. pl.* trees and plants collectively; vegetation. **~মরিচ** *n.* red pepper. **গাছে কাঁঠাল গোঁপে তেল বা গাছে না উঠতেই এক কাঁদি** (fig.—ridi.) to count one's chickens before they are hatched. **গাছে চড়ানো** *v.* (fig.—ridi.) to inflate one with overpraise or flattery, to heap hyperbolical or excessive praise upon a person. **গাছে তুলে (দিয়ে) মই কেড়ে নেওয়া** (fig.—ridi.) to induce a person to run into a hazard by promising help and then abandon him.

গাছা[1] *n.* a lampstick (cp. a candlestick); a lampstand.

গাছা[2], **গাছি** *a.* (art.) the, a, an (একগাছা লাঠি).

গাজন *n.* the festival of worshipping Shiva (শিব) in the month of Chaitra (চৈত্র) ; any of the songs sung on this occasion; the music of these songs. **অনেক সন্ন্যাসীতে গাজন নষ্ট** (fig.) too many cooks spoil the broth.

গাজর *n.* carrot.

গাজি *n.* a Muslim warrior fighting for the cause of religion (cp. a crusader).

গাটাপার্চা *n.* a strong plastic substance obtained from latex; gutta-percha.

গাট্টা *n.* a blow on the head with the knuckles of the fist. **গাট্টা মারা, গাট্টা দেওয়া, গাট্টা লাগানো** *v.* to strike another's head with the knuckles of one's fist. **~গোট্টা** *a.* strongly built, short but robust; thick-set; dumpy.

গাড্ডা *n.* a pit, a hole; (fig.) trouble, difficulty or distress; (coll. and inf.) failure esp. in an examination (গাড্ডা মারা).

গাড়ওয়ান alt. spelling of **গাড়োয়ান**।

গাড়ল, গাড়র *n.* the ram; (in mild rebuke or taunts) a stupid man.

গাড়া *v.* to plant, to drive in (খুঁটি গাড়া) ; to spread firmly, to strike (শিকড় গাড়া) ; to establish, to set up (আস্তানা গাড়া) ; to fold (হাঁটু গাড়া). **শিকড় গাড়া** *v.* to strike root; (fig.) to settle down firmly or permanently. **হাঁটু গাড়া** *v.* to kneel down.

গাড়ি *n.* a vehicle, a cart, a coach, a carriage, a car; a hackney-carriage, a hackney-coach, a cab, a taxi-cab. **গাড়ি করা** *v.* to hire or take a hackney-carriage or a taxi; to purchase a coach and horse or a motor car for one's own use. **গাড়ি চাপা পড়া** to be run over by a car. **গাড়ি ডাকা** *v.* to call or get a hackney-carriage or a taxi. **~বারান্দা** *n.* a covered porch for parking cars and carriages, (cp.) a vestibule.

গাড়ু *n.* a pitcher or a tankard, with a spout (and often with a handle), a vase.

গাড়োয়ান *n.* a carter, a coachman, a waggoner, a carman. **গাড়োয়ানি** *n.* the profession of a carter or a coachman or a waggoner or a carman; vulgar behaviour and talk, vulgarity.

গাঢ় *a.* solidified, condensed, thickened, thick (গাঢ় দুধ) ; sound (গাঢ় নিদ্রা) ; cumulated (গাঢ় মেঘ) ; intense (গাঢ়

অন্ধকার) ; severe, strong (গাঢ় দুঃখ) ; deep (গাঢ় স্বর) ; concentrated (গাঢ় মনোযোগ) ; close (গাঢ় আলিঙ্গন) ; clenched (গাঢ় মুষ্টি). **গাঢ় করা** *v.* to solidify, to condense, to thicken; to make sounder; to deepen, to intensify; to make severe; to choke; to concentrate; to make close or closer. **~তা, ~ত্ব** *n.* solidity, condensedness, thickness; soundness; cumulation; deepness, intensity; severity; concentration; closeness.

গাণনিক *n.* an accountant.

গাণনিক্য *n.* book-keeping.

গাণপত্য *a.* relating to Ganesha (গণেশ). □ *n.* a sect worshipping Ganesha.

গাণিতিক *a.* versed in mathematics; relating to mathematics, mathematical. □ *n.* a mathematician.

গাণ্ডিব, গাণ্ডীব *n.* (myth.) Arjuna's bow, the Gandib. **গাণ্ডীবী** *n.* an archer with this bow; (specifically) Arjuna.

গাণ্ডেপিণ্ডে var. of **গণ্ডেপিণ্ডে** ।

গাত *n.* (poet. & obs.) the body.

গাতা *a.* one who (or that which) sings.

গাত্র (for.) *n.* the body; the surface of the body (গাত্রাবরণ) ; the surface (পর্বতগাত্র). **~জ্বালা, ~দাহ** *n.* the burning sensation of the body or the skin; (fig.) jealousy, malice, anger, displeasure, grudge. **গাত্রজ্বালা করা, গাত্রদাহ করা** same as **গা জ্বালা করা** । **~বেদনা, ~শূল** *n.* pain of the body; muscular pain. **~মার্জনী** *n.* a napkin, a towel. **~রুহ** *n.* hair (growing on one's body). **~হরিদ্রা** same as **গায়ে-হলুদ** ।

গাত্রানুলেপনী *n.* a brush to paint the body.

গাত্রাবরণ, গাত্রাবরণী *n.* a cover or wrapper for the body; a cloak; an armour, a coat of mail.

গাত্রোত্থান, গাত্রোৎপাটন *n.* getting up; rising from the bed. **গাত্রোত্থান করা** *v.* to get up; to rise from the bed.

গাথা *n.* a poem; a couplet, a distich; a verse; a ditty, a song; a ballad; narration (গুণগাথা).

গাদ *n.* scum, dross; dregs, sediment, leas.

গাদন *n.* (act of) stuffing or cramming; (act of) loading or ramming (as a gun); beating soundly, thrashing.

গাদনি *n.* loading (a gun); ramming; stuffing or cramming.

গাদা[১] *n.* a slice from the back of a flat-fish.

গাদা[২], **গাদানো** *v.* to stuff, to cram; to load or ram (a gun). **~বন্দুক** *n.* a gun in which powder is to be crammed with hand, a blunderbuss, a musket, a muzzle-loader.

গাদা[৩], **গাদি** *n.* a heap, a pile; a stack (খড়ের গাদা) ; a crowd, a swarm. **গাদা গাদা** *a.* in heaps, heaps of, in large quantities. **গাদাগাদি** *n.* (act of) crowding or huddling; state of being crowded. **গাদাগাদি করা** *v.* to crowd; to huddle. **গাদানো** *v.* to pile, to heap, to crowd.

গাধা *n.* the ass; (in mild reproof or ridicule) a stupid fellow, a dunderhead. **~বোট** *n.* a very heavy and slow-moving boat or ship carrying cargo, barge; (ridi.) any slow-moving vehicle, a sluggard. **~মি** *n.* folly, silliness. **গাধামি করা** *v.* to make an ass of oneself, to behave in a crassly stupid fashion. **গাধার খাটুনি** dull and excessive toil not calling for exercise of intelligence; drudgery.

গাধেয় *n.* a son of Gadhi the sage.

গান *n.* a song; a lyric; a poem; a musical play; an opera (esp. an open-air one); sweet note. (পাখির গান). **~বাজনা** *n.* music; musical soiree; entertainment with music. **ওস্তাদি গান** classical song. **চুটকি গান** a light tripping song with a dancing rhythm. **গানের দল** *n.* a musical party; a party of professional singers.

গান্ধর্ব *a.* of Gandharvas (গন্ধর্ব) ; of a system of marriage which is secretly gone through by a willing couple usually by exchange of garlands without the knowledge of their guardians and without observance of customary rites.

গান্ধার *n.* an ancient name of Kāndahar; (mus.) the third note in the natural scale. □ *a.* of or living in Kandahar.

গান্ধি, গান্ধিপোকা *n.* a kind of cornfly; a flying bug, a beetle giving out very offensive odour. See also **গন্ধী** ।

গান্ধিবাদ *n.* the (philosophical and sociopolitical) doctrine of Mahatma Gandhi, Gandhism.

গাপ *a.* concealed, hidden; invisible; unduly and secretly appropriated to oneself, misappropriated. **গাপ করা** *v.* to appropriate to oneself unduly and secretly, to misappropriate; to conceal, to hide. **গাপ হওয়া** *v.* to go into hiding or concealment; to be concealed; to become invisible; to be misappropriated.

গাফিলি, গাফিলতি *n.* negligence, neglect; inattention, heedlessness; dilatoriness, laziness. **গাফিলতি করা** *v.* to treat with negligence or heedlessness; to procrastinate.

গাব *n.* a kind of tree Diospyros *embryopteris*; its fruit (its juice is used in coating the strings of a net), the mangosteen; a coating of resin on the skin that covers an instrument of percussion.

গাবগুবাগুব *n.* a kind of monochord. □ *int.* expressing the sound of dealing one severe and repeated fisticuffs on the back.

গাবদা *a.* fat or thick; uncouthly fat or thick. **গাবদা-গোবদা** *a.* healthy and fatty; plump, roly-poly (গাবদা-গোবদা ছেলে).

গাবানো[1] *v.* to smear (a boat or ship) with the juice of mangosteen (see **গাব**) ; to tar.

গাবানো[2] *v.* to go about parading or bragging or gossiping. also **গাবিয়ে বেড়ানো**।

গাবানো[3] *v.* to stir thoroughly (the water of a pond etc.)

গাভিন *a.* (of beasts, esp. the cow) big with young; gravid. **গাভিন হওয়া** *v.* to be big with young.

গাভী *n.* the cow.

গাভীন alt. spell. of **গাভিন**।

গামছা *n.* a napkin.

গামলা *n.* a basin.

গামা-রশ্মি *n.* (phys.) Gamma rays (X-rays of very short wave-length).

গামোছা obs. var. of **গামছা**।

-গামী *sfx.* indicating : going, moving (ধীরগামী) ; going or moving towards (উত্তরগামী). *fem.* **গামিনী**।

গাম্ভারি *n.* a kind of decorative tree.

গাম্ভীর্য *n.* gravity; solemnity; reserve, sobriety; affected importance.

গায়ক *n.* a singer, a songster. *fem.* **গায়িকা**। **গায়কি** *n.* style of singing.

গায়ত্রী *n.* the personified female energy worshipped in the Vedas; Brahma's wife; Goddess Durga; a Vedic incantation which is recited musingly by a Brahman at prayers; a Vedic metre of versification. **গায়ত্রী জপ করা** *v.* to recite musingly the prescribed Vedic incantation at prayer.

গায়িকা see **গায়ক**।

গায়েন *a.* one who sings. □ *n.* a singer. **মূল গায়েন** a leader or leading singer of a chorus.

গায়েব *a.* concealed, hidden; invisible; absconding; unduly and secretly appropriated to oneself, misappropriated. **গায়েব করা** *v.* to conceal, to hide; to send out of sight; to appropriate to oneself unduly and secretly, to misappropriate. **গায়েব হওয়া** *v.* to go into hiding; to be concealed; to be sent out of sight; to be misappropriated. **গায়েবি** *a.* concealed, hidden, secret.

গারদ *n.* a gaol, a jail, a prison; a lockup; a guard-room, a guard-house; confinement; imprisonment. **গারদ হওয়া** *v.* to be sentenced to imprisonment; to be jailed.

গারুড় *a.* of Garuda (গরুড়). □ *n.* a very precious stone; a mythological missile; an ancient method of arraying soldiers in a battle; mysterious words that are uttered in order to dispel snake-poison. **গারুড়িক** *n.* a doctor who heals snake-bites.

গার্জিয়ান, গার্জেন *n.* a guardian.

গার্হপত্য *n.* holy fire; the holy fire which a householder keeps burning day and night all his life. □ *a.* of such a householder.

গার্হস্থ্য, গার্হস্থ *n.* the life of a householder (the second stage of man's life according to the Hindu scriptures), domestic life. □ *a.* of the householder.

গাল[1] *n.* abuse, rebuke, reproach. **গাল খাওয়া** *v.* to be abused or rebuked or reviled or reproached. **গাল দেওয়া, গাল পাড়া** *v.* to revile; to reproach, to rebuke, to abuse.

গাল[2] *n.* the cheek; the mouth (গালের মধ্যে

নিয়ে চিবানো). **গালে চড় মারা** to slap on the face, to give a slap in the face. **গালে লাগা** *v.* to have a burning and itching sensation within one's mouth (caused by eating edible roots akin to arum). **গালে হাত দেওয়া** *v.* to place the palm of one's hand on one's cheek as a mark of astonishment; (fig.) to be astonished. **~গল্প** *n.* a fanciful or idle tale, gossip, chit-chat. **গালগল্প করা** *v.* to tell fanciful tales (esp. about one's own importance); to gossip, to chat. **~পাট্টা** *n.* thick or massive beard all over cheeks and the chin; side-whisker, a lovelock. **~বাদ্য** *n.* a peculiar sound made by inflating cheeks and striking them with fingers. **গালবাদ্য করা** *v.* to make this sound. **গালভরা** *a.* mouth-filling; tumid, bombastic. **~মন্দ** *n.* reviling. **গালমন্দ করা, গালমন্দ দেওয়া** *v.* to revile.

গালচে coll. form of **গালিচা**।

গালন *n.* act of squeezing out or pressing out; act of causing to flow out; act of straining; act of melting.

গালা[1] *n.* lac, shellac.

গালা[2] *v.* to melt; to press out or squeeze out the matter (usu. morbid matter) of something (ফোঁড়া গালা) ; to cause to flow out (ভাতের ফেন গালা) ; to strain; to utter (দিব্যি গালা).

গালাগাল, গালাগালি *n.* revilings; rebuke; abuse. **গালাগালি করা, গালাগালি দেওয়া** *v.* to revile; to rebuke; to abuse, to call (a person) names.

গালানো *v.* to melt. ☐ *a.* melted.

গালি *n.* an abusive word, revile; reproach; rebuke; an obscene word. **গালি খাওয়া** *v.* to be reproached or rebuked or abused. **গালি দেওয়া** *v.* to revile; to reproach; to rebuke; to abuse; to utter an obscene word. **~গালাজ** *n. pl.* revilings; reproach; rebuke; obscene or filthy words or language; abuses.

গালিচা *n.* carpet; mattress-like thick cover usu. spread on the floor.

গাহ, গাহন[1] *n.* act of bathing by dipping the whole body in the water of a pond, river, sea etc.; immersion. **গাহন করা** *v.* to bathe.

গাহন[2] *n.* act of singing.

গাহা, গাহানো obs. variants of **গাওয়া** and **গাওয়ানো** resp.

গিঁট, গিঁঠ *n.* a knot; a joint (esp. of bones); a knuckle; a knob; a node. **গিঁট দেওয়া** *v.* to tie in a knot, to knot.

গিজ গিজ *int.* expressing : a state of crowding or swarming (সভায় লোক গিজ গিজ করছে).

গিটকিরি *n.* (mus.) quick utterance of notes to make a song sound sweeter.

গিদ্ধড়, গিধড় *n.* the jackal. ☐ *a.* (dial.) dirty, filthy.

গিনি *n.* a guinea. **~সোনা** *n.* twenty-two parts pure gold and two parts copper alloy mixed together, gold that is eleven-twelfths fine (22 carat), (loos.) guinea gold.

গিন্নি *n.* the mistress of a house, a housewife; a wife. **~পনা** *n.* duties and department of a housewife, housewifery, (ridi.) a young girl's mimicry of a housewife. **~বান্নি** *n.* an elderly and experienced housewife.

গিমা *n.* a kind of edible bitter spinach.

গিয়া, (coll.) **গিয়ে** *v.* having gone.

গিরগিটি *n.* the chameleon.

গিরা[1] *n.* a knot.

গিরা[2] *n.* (obs.) a measure of length esp. of cloth (=1/16 yard or 5.7 cms).

-গিরি[1] *sfx.* meaning : being so and so, status, office, honour, tenure of office, skill in certain capacity, -ship (বাবুগিরি, রাজাগিরি, কেরানিগিরি).

গিরি[2] *n.* a mountain; a hill; one of a particular order of ascetics. **~কন্দর, ~গহ্বর, ~গুহা, ~দরী** *n.* a mountain-cave. **~খাত** *n.* a ravine, a gorge. **~কুমারী, ~জা** *n.* a daughter of a mountain (esp. of the Himalayas); appellations of Goddess Durga (দুর্গা). **~তল** *n.* the surface of a mountain. **~তরঙ্গিণী** *n.* a mountain-stream. **~দুর্গ** *n.* a hill-fort; a hill serving as a fort. **~দ্বার** *n.* a mountain-pass, a pass. **~নন্দিনী** same as **~কুমারী**। **~পথ, ~বর্ত্ম** *n.* a mountain-defile, a ravine, a gorge; a col. **~বাসী** *n.* living in the mountains. ☐ *n.* a mountain dweller. **~মল্লিকা** *n.* a medicinal herb grown on the hills. ~মাটি, ~মৃত্তিকা *n* red ochre. ~রাজ *n.* the king of mountains; an appellation of the Himalayas. ~রানি *n.* (myth.) the wife of the Himalayas. ~শ *n.* one who lies down or sleeps upon a mountain; an appellation of Shiva (শিব). ~শৃঙ্গ, ~শিখর *n.* a mountain-peak. ~শ্রেণি *n.* a mountain-range. ~সংকট *n.* a mountain-defile, a gorge. ~সুতা *n.* the daughter of the Himalayas; an appellation of Goddess Durga.

গিরীন্দ্র *n.* the chief of mountains; an appellation of the Himalayas.

গিরে coll. form of গিরা[1],[2] ।

গির্জা *n.* a church.

গির্দা *n.* a short and fat bolster, a dumpy bolster.

গিলটি *n.* gilding. □ *a.* gilt. **গিলটি করা** *v.* to gild. **গিলটি-করা** *a.* gilt. **গিলটি সোনা** *n.* rolled gold.

গিলা[1], **গিলে** *n.* a seed of mimosa scandens. **গিলে করা** *v.* to frill cloth by pressing and rubbing with a seed of mimosa scandens. **গিলে-করা** *a.* thus frilled, or finely creased.

গিলা[2] var. of গেলা ।

গিলিত *a.* swallowed; eaten or drunk; devoured. ~চর্বণ *n.* rumination. **গিলিত-চর্বণ করা** *v.* to chew the cud, to ruminate. ~চর্বণকারী *n.* a ruminant.

গিলে coll. form of গিলা[1] ।

গিল্টি alt. spell. of গিলটি ।

গিসগিস var. of গিজ গিজ ।

গীঃ *n.* speech (গীষ্পতি) ।

গীত *a.* sung; chanted. □ *n.* a song. **গীত গাওয়া** *v.* to sing a song, to sing, ~জ্ঞ *a.* skilled or versed in the art of singing. ~বাদ্য *n.* vocal and instrumental music. ~ল *a.* lyrical. ~লতা *n.* lyricism.

গীতা *n.* the (Shrimadbhagavad) Gita; a famous Hindu scripture.

গীতি *n.* a song; a hymn. ~কবিতা *n.* a lyric poem, a lyric. ~কা *n.* a short lyric poem; a song; a ballad. ~কাব্য *n.* lyric poetry; a lyric poem. ~নাট্য *n.* a musical drama; a lyrical drama.

গীর্ণ *a.* uttered; said, told; narrated; praised, eulogized; swallowed, devoured.

গীর্দেবী *n.* Saraswati (সরস্বতী) the presiding goddess of speech.

গীর্পতি var. of গীষ্পতি ।

গীর্বাণ *n.* one who can use one's speech as an arrow; a god.

গীষ্পতি *n.* the lord or the presiding deity of speech; an appellation of Brihaspati (বৃহস্পতি).

গু *n.* faeces, ordure, stool; dung, droppings. ~খোরি, ~খুরি *n.* an abominable deed; an inexcusable folly; a glaring or gross mistake, a blunder.

গুঁজা, গোঁজা *v.* to drive into, to plant into, to thrust into, to insert; to bend downwards or hide (মুখ গোঁজা). □ *n.* act of driving or planting or thrusting into, insertion; act of bending downwards or hiding; a thing inserted into, an insertion; a wisp of straw inserted into an old thatch for repairing it; an undue insertion to balance up an account. (হিসেবে গোঁজা দেওয়া). □ *a.* inserted into; bent downwards or concealed.

গুঁজামিল obs. var. of গোঁজামিল ।

গুঁজি *n.* a short stake or pale; a wedge; a hair-pin; a device containing several straps of cloth tied at one end in a thick knot used in a woman's hair-dressing to give the bun a massive appearance, a chignon. **গুঁজি দেওয়া** *v.* to plug up a leak in an old thatch by inserting new straw.

গুঁড়া, (coll.) **গুঁড়ো** *n.* powder (হলুদগুঁড়ো). □ *a.* reduced to powder, powdered, pulverized (গুঁড়ো মশলা). **গুঁড়ো করা** *v.* to reduce to powder, to powder; to pulverize, to pound. **গুঁড়ানো** *v.* same as **গুঁড়ো করা** । □ *a.* pulverized, pounded, powdered.

গুঁড়ি[1] *n.* a stock of a tree, a bole, a stump.

গুঁড়ি[2] *n.* a powder (দাঁতের গুঁড়ি) ; an extremely small drop (গুঁড়ি গুঁড়ি বৃষ্টি). **ইলশেগুঁড়ি** *n.* serein. **গুঁড়ি গুঁড়ি বৃষ্টি হওয়া** to drizzle.

গুঁড়ো see গুঁড়া ।

গুঁতা, (coll.) **গুঁতো** *n.* a shove, a push, a thrust; a butt; a beating. **গুঁতানো** *v.* to shove, to push, to thrust; to butt, to gore; to beat. **গুঁতোগুঁতি** *n.* goring and counter-goring.

গুঁতুনে *a.* given to shoving or pushing or thrusting or butting or beating. **গুঁতুনে গাই** a cow ready to gore.

গুঁফো, গুঁপো *a.* moustached.

গুখুরি, গুখোরি see **গু** ।

গুগলি *n.* oyster, shell-fish.

গুগগুল, গুগগুলু *n.* bdellium.

গুচ্চের dial. var. of **গুচ্ছের** ।

গুচ্ছ *n.* a cluster, a bunch, a fascicle (পুষ্প-গুচ্ছ) ; a bundle (পত্রগুচ্ছ) ; a tuft (কেশগুচ্ছ).

গুচ্ছের *a.* undesirably numerous or countless, too many.

গুছানো, গোছানো *v.* to set in due order, to arrange properly; to provide for or to supply (ভাত-কাপড় গুছানো) ; to manage (কাজ গুছানো). ☐ *a.* set in due order, properly arranged; economically managed; managed with domestic economy; orderly; thrifty. **গোছানে** *a.* orderly; thrifty; having capacity for managing one's own affairs. **গোছালো** same as **গোছানো** (*a.*).

গুছি *n.* a device containing several straps of cloth tied at one end in a thick knot used in woman's hairdressing to give the bun a massive appearance, a chignon.

গুজগুজ *int.* expressing muttering or whispering. **গুজগুজ করা** *v.* to whisper; to confer secretly. **গুজগুজানি** *n.* whispering, talking in whispers; act of conferring secretly. **গুজগুজে** *a.* one who does not speak out one's mind frankly; whispering.

গুজব *n.* a rumour; hearsay. **গুজব ছড়ানো, গুজব রটানো** *v.* to spread rumour. **গুজব আছে (যে)** there is a rumour (that), a rumour goes. **গুজব রটনাকারী** *n.* a rumour-monger.

গুজরত *prep.* through, by. **গুজরত খোদ** through one's own self, personally.

গুজরতি *n.* a smaller variety of cardamom.

গুজরাটি, গুজরাতি *n.* a native of Gujarat (গুজরাত) ; the language of Gujarat. ☐ *a.* of Gujarat.

গুজরান act of spending or passing.

গুজরানো *v.* to spend or pass. ☐ *n.* spending or passing.

গুঁজিয়া *n.* a kind of small ring-shaped sweetmeat made of congealed milk and sugar.

গুঞ্জ *n.* a cluster, a bunch; a bouquet, a nosegay; humming; humming sound.

গুঞ্জন *n.* act of humming, a humming sound; lilting or lilt; (fig. & dero.) whispering. **গুঞ্জন করা** *v.* to hum; to lilt; to whisper. **~ধ্বনি** *n.* a humming sound.

গুঞ্জরন *n.* a humming sound; (loos.) act of humming; musing; (fig. & dero.) whispering. **গুঞ্জরন করা** *v.* to hum, to muse; to whisper.

গুঞ্জরা *v.* (poet.) to hum.

গুঞ্জরিত *a.* resounding with; filled with a humming noise; whispered.

গুঞ্জা, গুঞ্জিকা *n.* an extremely small red-and-black seed; the shrub bearing this seed.

গুটলি, (coll.) **গুটলে** *n.* a small hard and roundish ball of anything.

গুটানো *v.* to roll up, to wind up, to ravel in (সুতো গুটানো) ; to contract, to draw in, to fold, to double up (পা গুটানো) ; to compose (ডানা গুটানো) ; to close down (কারবার গুটানো) ; to pull up, to haul up (জাল গুটানো). ☐ *a.* rolled up, wound up, ravelled in; contracted, drawn in, folded, doubled up; closed down; pulled up, hauled up.

গুটি[1] *a.* a (small) number of. **~কত, ~কতক** *a.* a small number of, a few.

গুটি[2]**, গুটিকা** *n.* a pill, a pilule, a globule (ওষুধের গুটিকা) ; any small globular or granular object; (in chess and similar games) a piece, a man, a pawn; any fruit in its early stage of growth (আমের গুটি) ; a vesicle, a blister (বসন্তরোগের গুটি) ; a cocoon; a chrysalis (গুটিপোকা). **গুটিকাপাত করা** *v.* to decide by means of lots, to cast lots.

গুটিগুটি *adv.* pacing or moving very slowly (like a silk-worm).

গুটিপোকা *n.* the silk-worm.

গুটিশুটি *adv.* coweringly; crouchingly.

গুড় *n.* molasses, treacle. **গুড়কুমড়ো** see **কুমড়ো** । **গুড়ে বালি** (fig.) a fly in the ointment; disappointment.

গুড়গুড় *int.* expressing a mild rumbling or

rattling sound; a sound of movement in the stomach.

গুড়গুড়ি *n.* a hubble-bubble.

গুড়া *n.* a plank of wood placed sideways in a boat to sit upon.

গুড়াকেশ *n.* (lit.) one who has won over sleep, an appellation of Shiva (শিব) and of Arjuna (অর্জুন) of the Mahabharata.

গুড়ি *n.* cowering or crouching movement or position. **গুড়ি মারা** *v.* to cower, to crouch; to lie in ambush.

গুড়িগুড়ি var. of **গুটিগুটি**।

গুড়ুক *n.* a preparation of tobacco mixed with an inferior quality of treacle for smoking in a hubble-bubble or hookah. **গুড়ুক খাওয়া, গুড়ুক টানা** *v.* to smoke a hookah or hubble-bubble.

গুড়ুম *n & int.* a booming noise (as of a gun), a loud report, sound of an explosion; any similar sound.

গুড়ুচি, গুড়ুচী *n.* a medicinal plant.

গুণ[1] *rej.* spell. of **গুন**।

গুণ[2] *n.* a quality, a property, a characteristic দ্রব্যগুণ) ; a good quality, a virtue, a merit, excellence (গুণমুগ্ধ) ; (ridi.) a bad or mischievous quality or practice, a vice, a demerit (গুণে ঘাট নেই) ; a good effect or action (শিক্ষার গুণ, ওষুধের গুণ) ; an effect or action; (ridi.) an evil result or action (মিথ্যার গুণ) ; an influence (সঙ্গগুণ) ; an evil influence; power, competency, efficacy (লোক বশ করার গুণ) ; (sc.) a natural quality or property; (phil.) any of the three primordial qualities in living beings (**সত্ত্বগুণ** = goodness; **রজোগুণ** = passion or spiritedness; **তমোগুণ** = darkness); occult power, charm, sorcery, exorcism (ওঝা গুণ জানে) ; (rhet.) any of the qualities constituting the excellence of a literary composition (**ওজঃগুণ** = vigour, **মাধুর্যগুণ** = elegance, **প্রসাদগুণ** = lucidity); (math.) multiplication; (math.) one of a number of multiplied instances, so many times (পাঁচ-দু-গুণে দশ) ; a bowstring; a string, a thread ('গাঁথে বিদ্যা গুণে') ; a towline, a towrope. **গুণ করা** *v.* to multiply; to allure or charm or influence or control by sorcery, to bewitch, to cast a spell over. **গুণ গাওয়া** *v.* to sing in praise of; to praise, to laud, to eulogize, to speak highly of. **গুণ টানা** *v.* to tow. **গুণ পাওয়া** *v.* to be benefited by the good action or influence (of); to find a virtue (in). **~ক** *n.* a multiplier, multiplicator; a factor. ☐ *a.* that which multiplies, multiplying, multiplicating. **গুণকনির্ণয়** *n.* factorization. **~কারক** *a.* that which multiplies, multiplying, multiplicating; beneficial; productive of good, efficacious. **~কীর্তন, ~গান** *n.* act of singing in praise of; act of praising, laudation; publicity of one's good qualities. **গুণকীর্তন করা, গুণগান করা** *v.* to sing in praise of; to praise, to laud; to circulate the good qualities of. **~গরিমা, ~গৌরব** *n.* value or glory of one's good qualities or virtues. **~গ্রহণ** *n.* appreciation of one's good qualities or virtues. **গুণগ্রহণ করা** *v.* to appreciate the good qualities or virtues of. **~গ্রাম** *n. pl.* good qualities or virtues. **~গ্রাহিতা** *n.* appreciation of others' good qualities or virtues. **~গ্রাহী** *a.* one who appreciates the good qualities or virtues of others. *fem.* **~গ্রাহিণী**। **~জ্ঞ** *a.* conscious or appreciative of the good qualities or virtues of others. **~জ্ঞতা** *n.* consciousness about or appreciation of the good qualities or virtues of others. **~ত্রয়** *n. pl.* (phil.) the three primordial qualities in living beings (namely, সত্ত্বগুণ, রজোগুণ, তমোগুণ). **~ধর** *a.* full of good qualities or parts; (ridi.) full of vices or demerits. **~ধাম, ~নিধি** *n.* a man richly endowed with good qualities or parts. **~ন** *n.* (math.) multiplication. **~নীয়** *a.* (math.) that which is to be or may be multiplied (by). ☐ *n.* a multiplicand. **~নীয়ক** *n.* (math.) a factor, a measure; (math.) a multiplicand. **গরিষ্ঠ সাধারণ গুণনীয়ক** see **গরিষ্ঠ**। **~পনা** *n.* skill; good qualities; attainment, accomplishment. **~ফল** *n.* (math.) a product (of multiplication). **~বত্তা** *n.* possession of good qualities or parts or merits. **~বর্ণন, ~বর্ণনা** *n.* description or account of one's good qualities or merits. **গুণ বর্ণনা করা** *v.* to describe the good qualities or merits (of), to give an account of one's good qualities or merits. **~বাচক** *a.* expressing the good qualities or merits of; (fig.) adjectival, attributive; (log.) connotative. **~বাদ** *n.* praise, laudation. **~বাদ করা** *v.* to praise, to laud. **~বান** *a.* possessing good qualities or parts. *fem.* **~বতী**। **~বান পুরুষ** a man of qualities or parts. **~বৃক্ষ** *n.* a mast. **~বৈষম্য** *n.* dissimilarity or disparity of qualities or virtues or properties; combination or mixture of contrary qualities or virtues or properties. **~মণি** *n.* a man possesed of the noblest qualities or the highest excellence. **~ময়** same as **~বান**। *fem.* **~ময়ী**। **~মুগ্ধ** *a.* fascinated by one's good qualities or virtues or merits. *fem.* **~মুগ্ধা**। **~মুগ্ধ ব্যক্তি** *n.* (*masc.* & *fem.*) an admirer. **~যুক্ত** *a.* having good qualities or virtues or merits; having a (particular) quality or property. **~শালী** same as **~বান**। *fem.* **~শালিনী**। **~শালিতা** same as **~বত্তা**। **~শূন্য** *a.* having no good quality or virtue or merit; lacking in a (particular) quality or property. **~সম্পন্ন** same as **~যুক্ত**। *fem.* **~সম্পন্না**। **~সাগর** same as **~নিধি**। **~হীন** *a.* destitute of good qualities or merits or parts. *fem.* **~হীনা**।

গুণতি rej. spell. of **গুনতি**।

গুণাকর *n.* (lit.) a mine of virtues or good qualities; (fig.) a man endowed with countless virtues or good qualities.

গুণাগুণ *n. pl.* merits and demerits.

গুণাঙ্ক *n.* (phys.) a coefficient.

গুণাঢ্য *a.* rich in good qualities or merits; endowed with qualities or virtues.

গুণাতীত *a.* (phil.) beyond the reach of three primordial qualities (see **গুণত্রয়** under **গুণ**[২]), absolute. ☐ *n.* the Absolute Being, God.

গুণাধার *n.* (lit.) a repository of good qualities or parts; a man of qualities or parts.

গুণানুবাদ *n.* act of praising, laudation. **গুণানুবাদ করা** *v.* to praise, to laud, to extol, to eulogize.

গুণানুরাগ *n.* love for virtues or good qualities; attraction or admiration for others' good qualities or virtues. **গুণানুরাগী** having love for virtues or good qualities; attracted by or admiring others' good qualities or virtues. *fem.* **গুণানুরাগিণী**। **গুণানুরাগী ব্যক্তি** an admirer.

গুণান্তর *n.* another quality or property, a different quality or virtue.

গুণান্বিত *a.* having good qualities or virtues or merits; having a (particular) quality or property. *fem.* **গুণান্বিতা**।

গুণাপকর্ষ *n.* depreciation.

গুণাপকর্ষক *a.* depreciative.

গুণাবলি *n. pl.* virtues or qualities or properties collectively.

গুণাভাস *n.* a false notion that a person or a thing has a good quality or merit; semblance of good qualities or merits.

গুণালংকৃত *a.* adorned or endowed with good qualities or virtues.

গুণাশ্রয় *a.* same as **গুণাধার**।

গুণিত *a.* (math.) multiplied; multiplicated.

গুণিতক *n.* (math.) a multiple. **লঘিষ্ঠ সাধারণ গুণিতক** see **লঘিষ্ঠ**।

গুণিন alt. spell. of **গুনিন**।

গুণী *a.* having good qualities or parts or merits, talented, meritorious; having sound skill or knowledge in some pursuit esp. an artistic one; versed in exorcism or sorcery, having an occult power. **গুণী লোক** a man of qualities or parts; an adept.

গুণীভূতব্যঙ্গ্য *n.* (rhet.) a figure of speech in which the apparent or surface meaning is more beautiful than the inner or underlying or true meaning.

গুণোৎকর্ষ *n.* abundance of good qualities or merits; excellence owing to possession of good qualities.

গুণোত্তর-শ্রেণি (পরি.) *n.* geometric series.

গুণোপেত same as **গুণান্বিত**।

গুণ্ঠন *n.* a veil; a hood; a cover, a covering; a skin or bark.

গুণ্ঠিত *a.* veiled; hooded; covered.

গুণ্ডা rej. spell. of **গুন্ডা**।

গুণ্ডিত *a.* pulverized, powdered, pounded.

গুণ্য *a.* & *n.* same as **গুণনীয়** (see **গুণ**[২]).

গুদাম, (dial.) **গুদম** *n.* a godown, a warehouse; a storehosue, a storeroom, a store. **গুদামজাত** *a.* stored. **গুদামজাত করা** *v.* to store in a warehouse; to store.

গুদার, গুদারা *n.* a landing for a ferry, a ferry.

গুন *n.* gunny. **~চট** *n.* sackcloth. **~থলি** *n.* a gunny-bag. **~সুচ,** (coll.) **~ছুঁচ** *n.* a packing-needle.

গুনগুন *int.* expressing : humming or lilting; whispering; complaining in an undertone. **গুনগুন করা** *v.* to hum; to lilt; to whisper; to complain in an undertone.

গুনতি *n.* act of counting; computation. **গুনতি করা** *v.* to count; to compute. **গুনতি হওয়া** *v.* to be counted or computed.

গুনা১ *n.* a metal string or thread, wire, funicle; screw-thread.

গুনা২, গুনাহ *n.* a fault; an offence; a sin. **গুনা করা** *v.* to commit a fault or offence or sin. **গুনা হওয়া** *v.* to be in fault. **গুনাগার, গুনাগারি** *n.* penalty or punishment for a fault or offence or folly. **গুনাগার দেওয়া, গুনাগারি দেওয়া** *v.* to pay for one's fault or folly.

গুনা, গুনানো variants of **গনা** and **গনানো।**

গুনাহ see **গুনা২।**

গুনিন *n.* a man with an occult power; an exorciser; a sorcerer.

গুনো dial. corrup. of **গুনা১, ২।**

গুন্ডা *n.* a rogue, a hooligan, a rowdy, a gangster, a ruffian. **~মি** *n.* hooliganism, rowdyism, gangsterism; ruffianism. **গুন্ডামি করা** *v.* to act as a hooligan, to practise hooliganism.

গুপ্ত *a.* protected or guarded by (মন্ত্রগুপ্ত) ; hidden; unknown, unseen, invisible; unrevealed (গুপ্ত তত্ত্ব) ; concealed; mysterious, esoteric (গুপ্ত রহস্য). *fem.* **গুপ্তা।** **গুপ্ত কথা** *n.* a secret; a mystery. **গুপ্ত কথা ফাঁস করা** to divulge or let out a secret. **গুপ্ত গুহাশ্রয়, গুপ্ত গর্তাশ্রয়** *a.* burrow. **~ঘাতক** *n.* an assassin. **~চর** *n.* a spy; a detective, a sleuth. **~চরবৃত্তি** *n.* espionage, spying. **~তত্ত্ব** *n.* mysteries. **~তথ্য** *n.* secret information. **~ধন** *n.* hidden treasure. **~বেশ** *n.* a disguise. **~বেশে** *adv.* in disguise. **~ব্যাধি** *n.* a vicious disease kept concealed; a venereal disease; (fig.) a vice kept concealed. **~ভাব** *n.* secrecy or a concealed or unrevealed state; a stealthy or clandestine manner. **~ভাবে** *adv.* secretly; stealthily. **~ভোট, ~মত** *n.* a secret vote or voting, ballot. **~মন্ত্র** *n.* a secret or mysterious word; a password; (lit.) an esoteric mantra or sacred word. **~মন্ত্রণা** *n.* secret counsel or conference. **গুপ্তমন্ত্রণা সমিতি** *n.* a secret council, a close assembly. **~রহস্য** *n.* a mystery, a secret. **~সভা, ~সমিতি** *n.* a secret council, a close assembly; a secret society. **~হত্যা** *n.* assassination; a secret murder. **গুপ্তহত্যা করা** *v.* to assassinate; to commit a murder in secret. **গুপ্তহত্যা প্রকাশ পাবেই** murder will out. **~হত্যাকারী** *n.* an assassin.

গুপ্তি *n.* act of keeping or guarding in secret; act of keeping secrets (মন্ত্রগুপ্তি) ; a sword-stick.

গুফা *n.* a mountain-cave.

গুবরেপোকা *n.* the dung-beetle, the dor-beetle, the dor-fly, the dor, the dorr.

গুবাক *n.* the betel-nut or its tree.

গুম১ *a.* secret, unrevealed, concealed (গুমখুন) ; carried off and kept concealed (লাশ গুম করা) ; gone in hiding or absconding (গুম হওয়া) ; missing; speechless and motionless (গুম হয়ে বসে থাকা). **গুম করা** *v.* to carry off and keep concealed. **~খুন** *n.* a secret murder or assassination. **গুম হওয়া** *v.* to be carried off and kept concealed; to abscond, to go into hiding; to be missing; to become speechless and motionless.

গুম২ *int.* expressing : a thudding noise as of a blow of the fist on the back. **গুম করে** *inf. v.* with a thud. **গুমগুম, গুমাগুম** *int.* expressing : repeated thudding noise. □ *adv.* with thuds, thuddingly.

গুমট *n.* sultry atmosphere or weather, sultriness, stuffiness, fustiness.

গুমটি *n.* a sentry-box; a shed or enclosure (বাসের গুমটি, ট্রামের গুমটি).

গুমর *n.* vanity, pride. **গুমর করা, গুমর দেখানো** *v.* to be proud of, to brag, to boast. **গুমর ভাঙা** *v.* to shed or cause to shed one's pride.

গুমরানো *v.* to suffer from suppressed

grief, sorrow, pain etc. গুমরানি *n.* such suffering.

গুমসা, (coll.) **গুমসো** *a.* sultry, stuffy, fusty; rancid. **গুমসানো** *v.* to become sultry or rancid. **গুমসানি** *n.* sultriness, stuffiness, fustiness, rancidity.

গুমাগুম see **গুম।**

গুম্ফ *n.* moustache; a bunch.

গুম্ফন *n.* act of stringing (together); composition.

গুম্ফা var. of **গুফা।**

গুম্ফিত *a.* strung; composed.

গুম্বজ *n.* a dome, a vault, a cupola.

গুয়া *n.* the betel-nut or its tree.

গুরমুখি coll. corrup. of **গুরুমুখি** (see **গুরু**).

গুরু *n.* a spiritual teacher or guide, a preceptor, a master, a guru; a priest; a teacher; an adviser; a venerable person; Brihaspati (বৃহস্পতি) the priest of gods; (astrol.) the Jupiter. □ *a.* heavy, weighty (গুরুভার) ; very responsible or difficult or important or serious (গুরুরাজকার্য, গুরুদায়িত্ব, গুরুকর্তব্য) ; excessive (গুরুভোজন) ; venerable (গুরুজন) ; great, glorious ('গুরু-কাছে লব গুরু দুখ') ; (gr.—of vowels or vowel-sounds) long. **~কল্প** *a.* like a spiritual guide, like a preceptor or teacher; (of a person) conceived as a spiritual guide. **~কৃপা** *n.* kindness or benevolence or gracious behaviour such as one receives from one's teacher, spiritual guide or guru. **~কুল** *n.* the abode or the family of one's guru or teacher. **~গম্ভীর** *a.* serious and grave. **~গিরি** *n.* the profession of a guru or teacher or priest, priesthood or teachership. **~গৃহ** *n.* the abode of one's teacher or guru. **~চণ্ডালী** *n.* an instance of using undersirably Sanskrit and non-Sanskrit words or elegant and inelegant words side by side. **~জন** *n.* a venerable person; an elder. **~ঠাকুর** *n.* a spiritual teacher or guide, a preceptor, a guru. **~তর** *a.* heavier, weightier; more responsible or difficult or important or serious; very serious (গুরুতর অপরাধ). **~তা, ~ত্ব** *n.* weight, heaviness; gravity (আপেক্ষিক গুরুত্ব = specific gravity); importance; seriousness. **গুরুত্বহীন** *a.* divested of or wanting in weight or seriousness, unimportant; negligible. **~দক্ষিণা** *n.* a fee paid or payable to a guru or a teacher when teaching is completed or on completion of education. **~দণ্ড** *n.* heavy punishment. **লঘুপাপে গুরুদণ্ড** heavy punishment for a light offence. **~দশা** *n.* the period of mourning on the death of one's father or mother; (astrol.) the period of domination by the planet Jupiter. **~দেব** same as **~ঠাকুর।** **~দ্বার** *n.* a temple of the Sikhs, Gurudwara. **~নিন্দা** *n.* upbraiding of one's guru or teacher. **~পত্নী** *n.* the wife of one's guru or teacher. **~পত্নী গমন** *n.* sexual intercourse with the wife of one's guru or teacher. **~পত্নী-হরণ** *n.* act of abducting the wife of one's guru or teacher for immoral purpose. **~পাক** *a.* hard to digest. **~পাপ** a deadly sin, felony. **~পূর্ণিমা** *n.* the full-moon of the month of Ashara, the third month of the Bengali calendar. **~বরণ** *n.* the ceremony of appointing one as one's guru or of receiving a guru usually accompanied with offer of presents. **~বল** *n.* occult power conferred upon by one's benignant guru; grace of the guru. **~বাক্য** n. words or advices of a guru. **~বার** *n.* Thursday. **~বৃত্ত** *n.* a great circle. **~ভক্ত** *a.* devoted to one's guru or teacher. **~ভক্তি** *n.* devotion to one's guru or teacher. **~ভাই** *n.* a codisciple, a brother disciple. **~ভার** *a.* very heavy; unbearably heavy. □ *n.* heavy burden. **~মণ্ডল** *n.* (geog.) barysphere. **~মহাশয়,** (coll.) **~মশাই** *n.* a teacher; a primary teacher. **~মস্তিষ্ক** *n.* (anat.) cerebrum. **~মা** *n.* the wife of a teacher or guru; a preceptress; a woman teacher, a lady teacher. **~মারা-বিদ্যা** *n.* art or learning in which the student excels the teacher in course of time; (ridi.) art or learning which the student uses against the teacher to discomfit him. **~মুখি** *n.* the script or (loos.) the language used by the Sikhs. **~লঘুজ্ঞান** *n.* due sense of respect for superiors; sense of proportion; capacity for making distinction between the high and the low. ~শিষ্য-সংবাদ *n.* a report of the conversation or discussion between a guru and his disciple or between a teacher and his student. ~সেবা *n.* attendance on a guru or a teacher. ~স্ফীতি *n.* (astro.) springtide. ~স্থানীয় *a.* as venerable as a guru or a teacher. ~হত্যা *n.* murder of one's guru or teacher by oneself; parricide. ~হন্তা *n.* one who murders one's guru or teacher, a parricide. *fem.* ~হন্ত্রী। **যেমন গুরু তেমনি চেলা** like master like man.

গুরু গুরু *int.* expressing rumbling sound. □ *adv.* with a rumbling sound ('গুরু গুরু দেয়া ডাকে')।

গুরূপদেশ *n.* teachings or advice of a guru.

গুর্খা corrup. of **গোর্খা**।

গুর্জর *a.* Gujarat; a native of Gujarat. *fem.* **গুর্জরী** a female native of Gujarat; an Indian musical mode.

গুর্বিণী *a.* pregnant, in the family way, (of inferior creatures) big with young.

গুর্বী *n.* a guru's wife. □ *a. fem.* pregnant; great, glorious.

গুল[1] *n.* powder of burnt tobacco (this is applied to teeth and the gum or used as a dentifrice); a kind of small balls prepared by mixing and drying cowdung, mud and coal-powder together (used as fuel). **গুল দেওয়া** *v.* to make small balls of cowdung, mud and coal-powder mixed together and dry them in the sun; to apply powder of burnt tobacco (to one's teeth and gum).

গুল[2] *n.* a fib. **গুল দেওয়া, গুল মারা** *v.* to fib. **গুলপট্টি** same as **গুল**[2]।

গুল[3] *n.* the rose; a fancy-work, a diaper. ~দার *a.* diapered. ~বদন *a.* having a body as soft or delicate as the rosepetal, tender-bodied. *fem.* ~বদনী। ~বাগ *n.* a rose-garden. ~বাহার *n.* a piece of diapered sari (শাড়ি).

গুলজার *a.* splendid; packed or crowded and noisy (সভা গুলজার, নরক গুলজার). **গুলজার করা** *v.* to brighten; to crowd and fill with warmth and noise.

গুলঞ্চ *n.* a medicinal plant, menispermum glabrum.

গুলতানি *n.* assemblage in a small party or crowd and indulgence in useless talk. **গুলতানি করা, গুলতানি পাকানো, গুলতানি মারা** *v.* to assemble in a small group and indulge in useless talk or discussion.

গুলতি *n.* a catapult.

গুলফ *n.* the ankle or the heel. ~সন্ধি *n.* the ankle-joint.

গুলবাঘ *n.* the leopard.

-গুলা[1] (obs. & dial.) *sfx.* indicating plurality (মানুষগুলা).

গুলা[2] *v.* to dissolve in or blend with water by pressing and rubbing. see also **গোলা**[3]।

গুলানো, (coll.) **গুলোনো** *v.* to confuse, to make a mess of (সে কাজ গুলিয়ে ফেলে) ; to fail to recollect (সে পথ গুলিয়ে ফেলে, সে পড়া গুলিয়ে ফেলে) ; to be confused or disordered (এতে কাজ গুলিয়ে যায়) ; to be spoiled, to be reduced to a fiasco (সব পরিকল্পনা গুলিয়ে গেল) ; to be agitated morbidly (পেট গুলানো) ; to be stricken with nausea (শরীর গুলোচ্ছে).

গুলাব, গুলাবি variants of **গোলাপ** and **গোলাপি** respectively.

গুলাল *n.* a red powder which Hindus sprinkle over one another during the Holi (হোলি) festival.

-গুলি[1] var. of **-গুলা**[1]।

গুলি[2] *n.* any small round ball; a globule; a pill (as of medicine); either of the biceps or triceps or either of the hough muscles; a pill or preparation of opium for smoking; a bullet, ammunition. **গুলি করা** *v.* to shoot, to fire. **গুলি খাওয়া** *v.* to be shot (with a bullet); to smoke opium. ~খোর *a.* addicted to smoking opium. □ *n.* one who smokes opium, an opium-addict; an opium-smoker. **গুলিখোরি (গুলিখুরি) গল্প** fantastic or wholly incredible story, cock-and-bull story. ~ডাণ্ডা *n.* tip-cat. ~বিদ্ধ *a.* pierced by a bullet, wounded by a bullet, hit by a bullet.

গুলিকা *n.* a small globule or pill; a bullet.

গুলিন dial. var. of **গুলি**[1]।

গুলো *sfx.* indicating plurality (**গাছগুলো**)।

গুল্ম *n.* a bush, a shrub; the spleen; morbid enlargement of the spleen (also **গুল্মরোগ**) ; a military station or assemblage; a small division of an army (consisting of 9 elephant-riders, 9 charioteers, 27 horsemen and 45 foot-soldiers).

গুষ্টি, গুষ্টি (coll.) form of **গোষ্ঠী**। **গুষ্টির পিণ্ডি, গুষ্টির মাথা** (abusively) an extremely loathsome thing; nothing.

গুহ *n*. God Kartik (কার্তিক) ; Vishnu (বিষ্ণু). **~ষষ্ঠী** *n*. sixth day of the lunar fortnight of the month of Agrahayana (অগ্রহায়ণ).

গুহা *n*. a cave; a mountain-cave; a den (সিংহের গুহা) ; (fig.) the inmost region or recess (মনের গুহায়). **~বাসী** *a*. one who or that which lives in a cave or den, cave-dwelling; troglodyte. **গুহাবাসী প্রাণী** a troglodyte. **গুহাবাসী লোক** a cave-man. **~শয়** *a*. dwelling in a cave. □ *n*. the lion, the tiger and similar beasts that sleep in caves.

গুহ্য *a*. confidential, private; secret, concealed, hidden; mysterious; esoteric; occult; lonely. *n*. the anus. **~দ্বার** *n*. the anus. **~সংবাদ** *n*. a secret news.

গুহ্যক *n*. one of the demigods attending on Kuvera (কুবের).

গূঢ় *a*. secret, hidden, concealed, surreptitious (গূঢ় অভিসন্ধি) ; unknown, unrevealed, deep (গূঢ় তত্ত্ব) ; invisible, inaccessible, incomprehensible (গূঢ় মায়া) ; intricate (গূঢ় ব্যাপার) ; profound (গূঢ় বুদ্ধি, গূঢ় অর্থ) ; mysterious, occult, esoteric (গূঢ় বিদ্যা) ; lonely. **~তা, ~ত্ব** *n*. secrecy, concealment; invisibility, inaccessibility, incomprehensibility; intricacy; profundity; mysteriousness; loneliness. **~পথ** *n*. a secret path or route; a lonely path. **~পাদ** *n*. the tortoise. **~পুরুষ** *n*. a spy, a secret emissary. **~মার্গ** *n*. a secret path; a secret tunnel. **~সাক্ষী** *n*. a witness employed by the plaintiff or by the accuser to overhear what the defendant or the accused has to say. **গূঢ়ার্থ** *n*. the inner meaning; underlying implication.

গূঢ়ৈষণা *n*. (phil.) a complex.

গৃধ্নু *a*. greedy, covetous. **~তা** *n*. greed, greediness, avarice.

গৃধিনী illogical but pop. *fem*. of **গৃধ্র**।

গৃধ্র *n*. the vulture.

গৃহ *n*. a room, a chamber; a house; a home, an abode, a dwelling; (astrol.) any of the signs of the zodiac. **~কপোত** *n*. a tame pigeon. **~কর্তা** same as **গৃহস্বামী**। *fem*. **~কর্ত্রী**। **~কর্ম, ~কার্য** *n*. housework, domestic work or chores. **~কলহ** same as **গৃহবিবাদ**। **~কোণ** *n*. the inside of one's home; the corner of a house; household. **~গোধিকা, ~গোধা** *n*. the lizard. **~ছিদ্র** *n*. a secret defect or blemish of a family; a (secret) discord in a family; the weak point of a family. **~চ্যুত** *a*. ejected or displaced or ousted from one's homestead; homeless. **গৃহচ্যুত করা** *v*. to oust or evict one from one's homestead; to render one homeless. **~জাত** *a*. home-made; home-grown; stored in a house esp. in a dwelling-house. **~তল** *n*. the floor of a room. **~ত্যাগ** *n*. quitting a house or one's home; adoption of asceticism; renunciation of worldly life. **গৃহত্যাগ করা** *v*. to quit a house; to quit home; to adopt asceticism; to renounce worldly life. **~ত্যাগী** *n*. one who has quitted a house or home; one who has adopted asceticism. **~দাহ** *n*. arson; (fig.) complete destruction of one's family happiness and peace. **~দেবতা** *n*. a tutelar deity, a household god. **~ধর্ম** *n*. the family life, household duties. **~পতি** same as **গৃহস্বামী**। **~পালিত** *a*. domestic; (joc.) tame. **~প্রবেশ** *n*. the ceremony of first entrance into a newly-built house; house-warming. **~প্রাঙ্গণ** *n*. a courtyard. **~বাটিকা** *n*. a garden within the precincts of a dwelling-house; a garden-house. **~বাসী** *a*. leading the life of a family man; living in a dwelling-house or in a family. □ *n*. a family man; a male member of a family; an inmate of a dwelling-house. *fem*. **~বাসিনী**। **~বিচ্ছেদ** *n*. dissension in a family; dissension amongst the people of a state; civil dissension. **~বিবাদ** *n*. dissension in a family; family strife, family feud; vendetta; internal strife; civil dissension; civil strife, civil war. **~ভেদী** *a*. sowing dissension in a family or a party;

betraying secrets of one's own family or party. গৃহভেদী বিভীষণ one who betrays the secrets of one's own family or party, a quisling, a fifth-columnist, a traitor (after the character of Bibhishana of the Ramayana). ~মণি *n.* lamp; the lamp of a house. ~মার্জন *n.* cleaning the house. গৃহমার্জন করা *v.* to scrub and clean the house. ~মৃগ *n.* a domestic dog. ~মেধী same as গৃহস্থ। ~যুদ্ধ same as গৃহবিবাদ। গৃহলক্ষ্মী *n.* a housewife whose suave and judicious dealings bring peace and prosperity to her family; (loos. & often facet.) a wife. ~শত্রু *n.* an enemy of one's own family or party, a quisling. ~শিক্ষক *n.* a private tutor; a guardian tutor. ~শূন্য *a.* homeless. ~সজ্জা *n.* fittings and furniture. ~স্থ *n.* a family man; a middle-class man. □ *a.* of or in a house. ~স্থধর্ম *n.* the practice of a householder (the second stage of life according to Hindu scriptures); family life. ~স্থালি, ~স্থালী *n.* housework, domestic work; domestic science, domestic economy; household duties. ~স্থাশ্রম same as ~স্থধর্ম। ~স্বামী *n.* the master of a house, a householder. *fem.* গৃহস্বামিনী the mistress of a house, a house-wife. ~হারা, ~হীন *a.* homeless, shelterless.

গৃহাগত *a.* one who has come to a house; one who has come back home. □ *n.* a guest; a visitor.

গৃহান্তর *n.* another room or house or home.

গৃহাভিমুখী *a.* walking or going towards one's home or house; returning home, home-coming.

গৃহাভ্যন্তর *n.* the inside of the house, the inner part of the house.

গৃহাশ্রম same as গৃহস্থাশ্রম (see under গৃহ).

গৃহাসক্ত *a.* extremely home-keeping; over-devoted to one's own family.

গৃহিণী *n.* a housewife, a house-mother; one's wife; a wife. ~পনা *n.* housewifery.

গৃহী *n.* a household, a family man; a married man.

গৃহীত *a.* received; accepted; held; obtained; passed (সিদ্ধান্ত গৃহীত হওয়া); sheltered.

গৃহোপকরণ *n.* a domestic utensil; furniture.

গৃহ্য[1] *a.* acceptable; brought under control.

গৃহ্য[2] *a.* relating to home; homely; domestic; home-bred; home-made. ~সূত্র *n.* a Hindu scripture prescribing ceremonies to be performed at birth, marriage etc.

গে dial. corrup. of গিয়া and গিয়ে।

গেঁইয়া alt. form of গাঁইয়া and গেঁয়ো।

গেঁজ *n.* a sprout, a plumule, a tumour, a node; (inc.) a wedge (গেঁজ ঠোকা).

গেঁজলা, গেঁজা coll. variants of গাঁজলা।

গেঁজানো[1] coll. var. of গাঁজানো।

গেঁজানো[2] alt. spell. of গ্যাঁজানো।

গেঁজে *n.* a tubular purse made of cloth.

গেঁজেল *a.* addicted to smoking ganja; (fig.) given to telling lies or cock-and-bull stories. □ *n.* a ganja-smoker, a ganja-addict; (fig.) one who is given to telling lies or cock-and-bull stories.

গেঁটা *a.* short and fat and stout, dumpy.

গেঁটে *a.* nodose, knotty (গেঁটে বাঁশ, গেঁটে লাঠি); of or in or occurring in knuckles (গেঁটে বাত = gout).

গেঁড়াগাঁড়া, গেঁড়াগোঁড়া variants of গাঁড়াগোঁড়া।

গেঁড় *n.* a tuberous root, a tuber; a rhizome.

গেঁড়া *n.* (sl.) act of stealing or misappropriating or swindling. গেঁড়া দেওয়া, গেঁড়া মারা *v.* to steal; to misappropriate; to swindle.

গেঁড়াকল *n.* a dishonest way of achieving one's end by deceiving or threatening people; a racket.

গেঁড়ি *n.* the snail.

গেঁড়ু, গেঁড়ুয়া *n.* a ball or a disc for throwing and catching; bunch; a wreath, a garland ('ফুলের গেঁড়ুয়া লুকিয়া ধরয়ে').

গেঁতো *a.* indolent, slothful, lazy, of extremely dilatory habit.

গেঁদা *rej.* form of গাঁদা।

গেঁয়ো, গেঁয়ে *a.* rural; rustic; uneducated; unpolished, vulgar. গেঁয়ো লোক *n.* rustic; (dero.) a clodhopper.

গেছো *a.* of trees and plants; living in

trees or given to climbing trees (গেছো ব্যাং, গেছো পেতনি) ; (of women) of undesirable masculine habit. **গেছো ব্যাং** a tree-frog. **গেছো মেয়ে** a tomboy.

গেজেট *n*. a gazette.

গেঞ্জি *n*. a vest; a guernsey.

গেট *n*. a gate.

গেন্ডু, গেন্ডুক, গেন্ডুয়া variants of **গেঁড়ু**।

গেনু *v. 1st per. sing.* (obs.—poet. & dial.) went.

গেন্দুক var. of **গেন্ডুক**।

গেয় *a*. worth singing, singable; that which is sung or is to be sung.

গেয়ান poet. & dial. coll. corrup. of **জ্ঞান**।

গেরস্ত corrup. of **গৃহস্থ**।

গেরি *a*. (dial.) of the colour of red ochre (গেরিমাটি).

গেরিলা *n*. a member of a political group engaged in irregular fighting esp. against larger and regular forces, the guerrilla. **~যুদ্ধ** *n*. guerrilla warfare, irregular fighting of the guerrilla.

গেরুয়া *a*. having the colour of red ochre ; dyed with red ochre (গেরুয়া কাপড়). ☐ *n*. a piece of loincloth dyed with red ochre (গেরুয়াধারী).

গেরো[১] pop. var. of **গিরা[১]**।

গেরো[২] *n*. a scrape, a difficulty; the influence of an evil star. **কপালের গেরো** bad luck; predestined misfortune.

গের্দ *n*. circumvention, encircling; confinement; a region; a certain area; jurisdiction.

গেল[১] *v*. has or have gone; went. (see **যাওয়া**).

গেল[২] *a*. immediately preceding, last (গেল মাসে, গেলবার).

গেল[৩] *int*. expressing astonishment (এই গেল যা).

গেলা *v*. to swallow (ঢোক গেলা, ভাত গেলা) ; to devour; (in anger or taunts) eat or drink (কাঁড়ি কাঁড়ি ভাত গেলে) ; eat or drink greedily. ☐ *n*. drinking or swallowing. ☐ *a*. swallowed; devoured. **~নো** *v*. to cause to swallow, make someone swallow.

গেলাপ *n*. a cover, a case, a slip (as of a pillow).

গেলাস *n*. a drinking glass, a tumbler. **একগেলাস জল** a glass of water. **একগেলাস পরিমাণ** a tumblerful.

গেহ, গেহা *n*. (poet.) a house; a dwelling house; an abode, a residence, a home. **গেহী** *n*. a householder, a family man. *fem*. **গেহিনী** a housewife.

গৈবি var. of **গয়বি**।

গৈরিক *n*. red ochre; gold-dust or gold; powder or dye of red ochre ('অলক সিঞ্চিত গৈরিক স্বর্ণে') ; a piece of loincloth dyed with red ochre (গৈরিকধারী). ☐ *a*. born of or produced in mountain; of the colour of red ochre (গৈরিক আকাশ) ; dyed with red ochre (গৈরিক পতাকা).

গৈরেয় *n*. red ochre; any object produced or grown in or on a mountain.

গো[১] sweeter var of **গা[২]**।

গো[২] *n*. the cow; the ox; any of the sense-organs (গোচর) ; the earth (গোপতি).

গোই *v. imp*. (poet. & obs.) concealing ('মরমহি গোই').

গোঁ *n*. obstinate insistence, obstinacy; dogged perseverance, doggedness. **গোঁ ধরা** *v*. to insist on obstinately. **গোঁ বজায় রাখা** *v*.to persevere doggedly.

গোঁ-গোঁ *int*. expressing a groaning sound. **গোঁ-গোঁ করা** *v*. to groan.

গোঁজ *n*. a peg, a stake, a wedge. ☐ *a*. silent and glum with discontent (মুখ গোঁজ করে থাকা). **গোঁজ গাড়া** to drive a peg.

গোঁজা pop. var. of **গুঁজা**।

গোঁজামিল *n*. act of balancing up an account by means of undue insertion(s). **গোঁজামিল দেওয়া** *v*. to balance up an account by means of undue insertion(s); somehow to balance accounts; to manipulate or cook up accounts.

গোঁড় *n*. a roundish exterior protuberance of the umbilical cord; a tumorous growth.

গোঁড়া[১] *a*. having a roundish exterior protuberance of the umbilical cord; roundish.

গোঁড়া[২] *a*. bigoted; fanatic; orthodox; extremely conservative; extremely biased; following blindly, blind (গোঁড়া ভক্ত).

গোঁড়ামি, (coll.) **গোঁড়ামো** *n* bigotry; fanaticism; orthodoxy; extreme conservativeness; an extremely strong bias; act of following blindly.

গোঁড়ালেবু, (dial.) **গোঁড়ানেবু** *n.* the citron.

গোঁফ, গোঁপ *n.* moustache; whiskers. **গোঁফে তা দেওয়া** *v.* to trim the ends of one's moustache (figuratively this indicates great delight or ease or nonchalance). **~খেজুর** *a.* extremely lazy (from the story of a person who lay hungry under a date-tree and yet refused to move his hand to reach the date that fell upon his moustache but hoped that a date would fall straight into his mouth).

গোঁয়ানো *v.* (mainly poet.) to pass or spend ('ভেবেছিনু দিন মিছে গোঁয়ালেম') ; to elapse, to pass by ('মিছে খেলায় দিন গোঁয়াল') ; to follow, to go after ('সকল লোক পশ্চাতে গোঁয়ায়') ; to co-exist peacefully (তার সঙ্গে গোঁয়ানো শক্ত).

গোঁয়ার *a.* obstinate, unyielding, stubborn; headstrong, foolhardy, foolishly rash. **~গোবিন্দ** *a.* very rash or reckless, devil-may-care. ☐ *n.* a very rash or head-strong person, a devil-may-care sort of fellow. **~তুমি, ~তমি, গোঁয়ার্তুমি** *n.* obstinacy, stubbornness; foolhardiness.

গোঁয়ারা *n.* the artificial coffin of Hasan and Hussain carried in procession during the festival of Moharram (cp. a feretory); the festival of Moharram.

গোঁসাই, গোঁসাঞি alt. spellings of **গোসাই।**

গোকর্ণ *n.* the reach of the thumb and the ring-finger outstretched; the cavity or capacity of a cupped palm of hand.

গোকুল *n.* a herd of cows (and also of oxen); a cowhouse; a grazing ground for cows and oxen, a pasture or pasturage; a village of India originally inhabited by milkmen ('তোমারে বধিবে যে, গোকুলে বাড়িছে সে'). **গোকুলের ষাঁড়** (ridi.) a wayward or wilful man, a self-willed person.

গোক্ষীর *n.* cow-milk.

গোক্ষুর *n.* (lit.) a cow's hoof; a thorny plant, Tribulus terrestris, the thistle; the cobra de capello, the cobra.

গোখরো (coll.) var. of **গোখুরা।**

গো-খাদক *a.* beef-eating. ☐ *n.* a beef-eater.

গোখুরা *n.* cobra, a hooded and poisonous snake.

গোগৃহ *n.* a cowhouse (usu. a large one), a byre.

গোগ্রহ *n.* forceful carrying off of another's cattle; abaction.

গোগ্রাস *n.* an offering of sanctified grass to a cow at the end of one's penitence; a large morsel. **গোগ্রাসে খাওয়া বা গেলা** *v.* to eat hastily in large morsels, to gobble; to eat ravenously or wolfishly.

গোঘাতক *n.* a cow-slaughterer.

গোঘ্ন *a.* one who or that which kills a cow or cows; a guest (for whom a cow was killed or slaughtered by the host).

গোঙরানি, গোঙরানো variants of **গোঙানি** and **গোঙানো** respectively.

গোঙা *a.* unable to speak, dumb. ☐ *n.* a dumb man, one having no power of speech.

গোঙানো[1] var. of **গোঁয়ানো।**

গোঙানো[2] *v.* to whimper; to moan; to groan or whine. **গোঙানি** *n.* act or noise of whimpering or moaning or groaning or whining.

গোচ dial. corrup. of **গোছ।**

গোচন্দন *n.* a bright yellow pigment secreted from the kidney of a cow.

গোচর *n.* the reach or range of sense-organs, sense-perception; anything perceptible by the senses; (astrol.) jurisdiction or range of influence (শনির গোচর) ; cognition, knowledge, perception (গোচরে আনা, অগোচরে) ; a grazing ground, a pasture or pasturage. ☐ *a.* perceptible by or within the range of (নয়নগোচর, শ্রুতিগোচর) ; used as a grazing ground (গোচর জমি). **গোচরে আনা** *v.* to bring to one's knowledge or notice. **গোচরীভূত** *a.* brought to one's knowledge or notice.

গোচর্ম *n.* cowhide.

গোচারক *n.* a cowherd.

গোচারণ *n.* act of tending or grazing cows, pasturage. **গোচারণ ভূমি** *n.* grazing ground. **গোচারণে যাওয়া** *v.* to go to graze or tend cows or beeves.

গো-চিকিৎসক *n.* a cow-leech, a cow-doctor.

গো-চিকিৎসা *n.* treatment of cows and cattle.

গোছ *n.* a bunch, a bundle, a sheaf; (due) order or arrangement, orderliness (কাজের গোছ) ; a type (সাধারণ গোছের বাড়ি) ; the hough. **গোছ করা** *v.* to put in due order; to arrange into bunches or sheaves. **পায়ের গোছ** the hough, fleshy part of the back of the human leg between the knee and the ankle, the calf. **~গাছ** *n.* due order or arrangement; act of packing up. **গোছগাছ করা** *v.* to put in due order; to make necessary arrangement (for); to pack up.

গোছা *n.* a bunch, a bundle, a sheaf; the hough.

গোছানে, গোছানো, গোছাল pop. variants of **গুছানে, গুছানো** and **গুছাল** respectively.

গোট *n.* an ornamental metal girdle worn by women.

গোটা *a.* whole, full, entire, undivided, unbroken (গোটা মানুষটা, গোটা দেশ). **গোটাকতক, গোটাকয়েক** a few, a small number of. **গোটা গোটা** *a.* & *adv.* whole and in unbroken form.

গোটানো pop. var. of **গুটানো**।

গোঠ[১] var. of **গোট**।

গোঠ[২] *n.* a grazing ground, a pasture or pasturage.

গোড় *n.* the base, the root; the foot. **~তোলা, ঘোড়তোলা** *a.* high-heeled. **গোড়ে গোড় দেওয়া** *v.* to follow in one's footsteps; to support blindly; to say ditto to.

গোড়া *n.* the root, the base, the bottom (গাছের গোড়া, দাঁতের গোড়া, থামের গোড়া) ; reach (হাতের গোড়ায়) ; foundation (গোড়াপত্তন) ; the beginning or start, inception (সৃষ্টির গোড়া থেকে) ; the root cause (নষ্টের গোড়া). **~গুড়ি** *adv.* in the beginning, at first. ☐ *n.* the beginning, inception (গোড়াগুড়ি থেকে). **~পত্তন** *n.* act of laying the foundation; start. **গোড়াপত্তন করা** *v.* to lay the foundation of; to start. **গোড়া কেটে আগায় জল** (lit.) ridiculous act of cutting off a tree from its bottom and then watering its branches to rejuvenate it; (fig.) mending a thing after ending it; an attempt to mend something when it is too late.

গোড়ালি *n.* the ankle; the heel.

গোড়ে *n.* a thick wreath of flower.

গোণা rej. spell. of **গোনা**।

গোতম *n.* a sage who wrote a famous treatise on logic; Gautama Buddha.

গোতা, গোত্তা *n.* a sudden and quick headlong fall. **গোতা বা গোত্তা খাওয়া** *v.* to make a sudden and quick headlong movement. **গোতা খেয়ে বা গোত্তা খেয়ে পড়া** *v.* to fall (down) headlong suddenly and quickly.

গোত্র[১] *n.* a mountain. **~প্রধান** *n.* the Himalayas.

গোত্র[২] *n.* a family, a line; classification of families in accordance with the names of the saints who founded them; descent, lineage (কাশ্যপ গোত্র). **~জ** *a.* having common descent or lineage, belonging to the same family, kindred.

গোত্রীয় *a.* of or belonging to a family or clan; familial.

গোদ *n.* elephantiasis; a leg swelled in elephantiasis, an elephantiac leg. **গোদের উপর বিষফোড়া** (fig.) an extra trouble; a trouble upon trouble.

গোদা *a.* suffering from elephantiasis; very fat; corpulent, bulky, very thick (গোদা লাঠি). ☐ *n.* an elephantiac patient; a leader, a ring-leader (পালের গোদা).

গোদান *n.* the ceremony of giving away a cow or cows.

গোদুগ্ধ *n.* cowmilk.

গোদোহন, গোদোহ *n.* act of milking a cow or cows. **গোদোহন করা** *v.* to milk a cow or cows. **গোদোহিনী, গোদোহনী** *n.* a milk-pail.

গোদ্রব *n.* cow's urine.

গোধন *n.* a herd of cows regarded as property, cattle-wealth; a herd of cows.

গোধা, গোধিকা *n.* the iguana.

গোধূম *n.* wheat. **~কীট** the Hessian fly. **~চূর্ণ** *n.* flour, farina; coarse flour, atta.

গোধূলি *n.* twilight. **~লগ্ন** *n.* the hour of twilight esp. the evening twilight; the hour of gloaming or dusk.

গোনা variant of **গনা**। *v.* to count, to enumerate, to compute; to consider, to regard as (মানুষ বলে গোনা) ; to anticipate or apprehend (বিপদ গোনা). ☐ *a.* counted, enumerated, computed (গোনা

জিনিস). ~গুনতি *a.* neither more nor fewer.

গোপ *n.* a milkman (by caste or profession); a cowherd; a king; a landowner; a feudal lord. **~কন্যা** *n.* the daughter of a milkman, a (young) milkmaid, (cp.) a milk-girl. **~নারী** *n.* the wife or a daughter of a milkman, a milkmaid, (cp.) a milk-woman. **~বধূ** *n.* wife of a milkman, (cp.) a milk-wife. **~বালক** *n.* a boy of the milk-man class; a cowboy.

গোপন *n.* hiding, concealment; secrecy. □ *a.* hidden, concealed, confidential, private, secret, unrevealed, mysterious. **গোপন করা** *v.* to hide, to conceal; to keep secret; to keep back (সত্য গোপন করা). **গোপন থাকা** *v.* to remain hidden or concealed or unrevealed; to remain secret. **গোপন রাখা** *v.* to keep secret or unrevealed; to keep one's own or another's counsel. **গোপন আলোচনা** a confidential conference; a close-door conference, a conference in camera. **গোপন কথা** a secret; a mystery; a confidential matter or report; a private or confidential talk; a close-door conference, a conference in camera. **~তা** *n.* secrecy; privacy. **গোপনীয়** *a.* that which should be kept secret or kept back; confidential, private; secret. **গোপনে** *adv.* secretly; privately, confidentially; in concealment. **গোপনে থাকা** *v.* to be in hiding or concealment; to hide; to be in secret. **গোপনে রাখা** *v.* to keep hidden or concealed; to hide; to keep in hiding.

গোপা same as **গোপিকা**।

গোপাঙ্গনা *n.* the wife of a milkman, a milkmaid. (cp.) a milk-woman.

গোপাল[1] *n.* a herd of cows.

গোপাল[2] *n.* a milkman (by caste or profession); a cowherd; a name of Krishna (কৃষ্ণ) ; a king; a son (নন্দগোপাল, আদুরে গোপাল). **আদুরে গোপাল** an over-indulged son; a pampered child; a son spoilt by over-indulgence.

গোপালক *n.* one who keeps and tends cows; a cowherd.

গোপালন *n.* act of tending and looking after cows; cattle-farming.

গোপালভোগ *n.* a species of very sweet and large mango.

গোপাষ্টমী *n.* the eighth lunar day in the moonlit fortnight of the month of Kartika (কার্তিক) when Krishna (কৃষ্ণ) began to act as a cowboy.

গোপিকা *n.* the wife or daughter of a milkman, a milkmaid, (cp.) a milkwoman. **~মোহন** *n.* one who has charmed the milkmaids, an appellation of Krishna.

গোপিত *a.* concealed, hidden; kept concealed or hidden; kept in custody; guarded; kept.

গোপিনী, গোপী same as **গোপিকা**। **গোপিনীবল্লভ, গোপীজনবল্লভ, গোপীনাথ** *n.* appellations of Krishna (কৃষ্ণ). **গোপীচন্দন** *n.* a kind of whitish clay with which Vaishnavas paint their faces and limbs. **গোপীমৃত্তিকা** *n.* a kind of yellowish clay found in Brindaban which is regarded by Vaishnavas as holy and is used by them in painting their faces and limbs. **গোপীযন্ত্র** *n.* a kind of monochord used by Vaishnavas to support a voice.

গোপুচ্ছ *n.* the tail of a cow, ox, bull etc.

গোপুর *n.* a gate (usu. an ornamental one) of a temple; a portal of a city, an ornamental city-gate.

গোপুরম *n.* the high ornamental gate of a South Indian temple.

গোপুরীষ *n.* cow-dung.

গোপ্তব্য same as **গোপনীয়** (see under **গোপন**).

গোপ্তা[1] var. of **গোতা**।

গোপ্তা[2] *a.* one who guards or protects. □ *n.* a guard; a custodian.

গোপ্য same as **গোপনীয়** (see under **গোপন**).

গোবৎস *n.* the young of a cow, a bullock or a heifer, a calf.

গোবদা *a.* uncouthly fatty or plum (গোবদা চেহারা).

গোবধ *n.* cow-slaughter.

গোবর *n.* cow-dung, muck. **~গণেশ** *a.* soft-headed corpulent lazy and good-for-nothing. □ *n.* such a man or boy. **~গাদা** *n.* a dung-heap, a dung-hill, a muck-heap. **গোবর গ্যাস** *n.* gas (usu. cooking gas) obtained from cow-dung. **গোবরভরা** *a.* (ridi.) full of stupidity (গোবরভরা মাথা = a stupid head). **গোবরে পদ্মফুল** (lit.) a lotus in a dung-hill; (fig.) a solitary instance of beauty or talent in the midst of ugly or stupid environment, a Venus amongst hags, a Socrates amongst fools.

গোবরাট *n.* a door sill or a window sill.

গোবর্ধন *n.* a hillock in Brindaban (বৃন্দাবন). **~ধারী** *n.* one who held high গোবর্ধন, an appellation of Krishna (কৃষ্ণ).

গোবসন্ত *n.* cowpox.

গোবাঘ, গোবাঘা *n.* one of a class of tigers given to preying upon cows, the wolf (?).

গোবিন্দ *n.* a name of Krishna (কৃষ্ণ) or Vishnu (বিষ্ণু).

গোবিষ্ঠা same as **গোবর**।

গোবীজ *n.* the serum taken from cowpox. **গোবীজের টিকা** vaccination or inoculation by administering the serum taken from cowpox.

গোবুচন্দ্র var. of **গবচন্দ্র**।

গোবেচারা, গোবেচারি *a.* as harmless and gentle as a cow; an artless or guileless person.

গোবেড়েন *n.* act of belabouring (one) with a stick like a cow; severe beating (esp. with a stick). **গোবেড়েন দেওয়া** *v.* to belabour severely with a stick; to beat severely.

গোবৈদ্য *n.* a cow leech, a cow's doctor; (contem. or ridi.) a medical quack.

গোভাগাড় *n.* a place for depositing the carcasses of cows; (fig.) a filthy place.

গোমড়া *a.* sullen and silent, glum and grave; darkened with huff.

গোময় *n.* cow-dung.

গোমশতা, গোমস্তা *n.* a rent-collector or bill-collector or steward (of a landlord, a businessman, a mercantile firm etc.).

গোমসূরিকা *n.* same as **গোবসন্ত**।

গোমাংস *n.* beef. **গোমাংসভোজী** *a.* beef-eating. **গোমাংসভোজী লোক** a beef-eater. **ক-অক্ষর গোমাংস** (fig.) utterly illiterate.

গো-মাছি *n.* the gadfly.

গোমুখ *n.* the mouth or the face of a cow; a musical instrument shaped like a cow's mouth or face; a small bag for holding the rosary, rosary-bag. ☐ *a.* having a face or mouth like that of a cow. **গোমুখী** *n.* a holy cave in the Himalayas shaped like a cow's face or mouth; a rosary bag.

গোমূর্খ *a.* utterly ignorant or illiterate or stupid.

গোমূত্র *n.* cow's urine.

গোমেদ *n.* chrysolite; zircon; jacinth.

গোমেধ *n.* ceremonial sacrifice of a cow or cows, cow-sacrifice.

গোযান *n.* a bullock-cart, a hackery.

গোয়াল *n.* a cowshed.

গোয়ালা *n.* a milkman (by caste or profession); a cowherd. *fem.* **গোয়ালিনি** a wife or a daughter of a milkman, a milkmaid, a milk-woman. **নামে গোয়ালা কাঁজি ভক্ষণ** (fig.) a nobleman whose meagre income forces him to eat more beef than mutton.

গোয়েন্দা *n.* a spy, a sleuth; a detective. **~কাহিনি** *n.* a detective story. **~গিরি** *n.* espionage, spying. **গোয়েন্দা পুলিস** *n.* the detective police.

গোর *n.* a grave, a tomb. **গোর দেওয়া** *v.* to bury, to inter, entomb. **গোরে যাওয়া** *v.* to lie in one's grave; to die.

গোরক্ষক *n.* one who keeps or tends a cow or cows; a cowherd.

গোরক্ষণ, গোরক্ষা *n.* keeping of cows, protection of cows.

গোরখা alt. spell. of **গোর্খা**।

গোরস *n.* cowmilk; any cowmilk product (e.g. butter, curd etc.).

গোরস্থান *n.* a burial ground, a cemetery, a graveyard.

গোরা *a.* having a complexion of cream-colour tinged with red; (loos.) fair-complexioned; English or European (গোরা সৈন্য). ☐ *n.* a pet name of Chaitanya ('কৃষ্ণ কৃষ্ণ বলি গোরা কাঁদে') ; an Englishman or a European; an English or a European soldier. **~চাঁদ** *n.* a name of Chaitanya. **গোরার বাদ্য** *n.* English or European military band.

গোরু *n.* the cow; the ox; beeves; (in reproof or ridicule) a stupid person. **~খোঁজা** *n.* (fig.) thorough and minute searching, searching everywhere and at every nook. **~চুরি** *n.* act or an instance of stealing cows; cattle-lifting; an extremely shameful deed or act. ~চোর *n.* one who steals cows, a cattle-lifter, an abactor; one who has done an extremely shameful deed. গোরু মেরে জুতা দান (lit.) the ridiculous or false attempt to compensate one with a pair of shoes after killing one's cow; (fig.) foolishly making amends after doing wrong or harm. গোরুর গাড়ি a bullock-cart, a hackery. গোরুর পাল a herd of cattle.

গোরোচনা *n.* a bright yellow pigment secreted from a cow's kidney.

গোর্খা *n.* one of the dominant people of Nepal, a Gurkha.

গোল[১] *n.* (in football, hockey, water polo etc.) a goal; a goal-post. গোল করা, গোল দেওয়া *v.* to score a goal. ~দাতা *n.* a scorer. ~রক্ষক *n.* a goal-keeper, (coll.) a goalie.

গোল[২] *a.* round; roundish; globular; spherical; circular. ☐ *n.* a round or roundish or spherical thing; a circle; a ball. ~ক *n.* a round or roundish or spherical object (ভূগোলক) ; a ball; a globe; a sphere. ~কায় same as গোলাকার। ~গাল *a.* almost round; roly-poly; chubby, plump, corpulent; fleshy and rounded. ~মরিচ *n.* black pepper.

গোল[৩] *n.* a loud and confused noise, an uproar, a row, a hubbub, disturbance (ক্লাসে গোল কোরো না) ; crookedness, angularity, distrust, doubt, suspicion (মনের গোল) ; confusion, a difficulty, a complication, a hitch (গোল বাধানো) ; an error, a mistake; confusion (গোল করে ফেলা). ~মাল, ~যোগ *n.* confusion, disturbance, chaos; din and bustle. ~মেলে *a.* confusing; disturbing; subject to suspicion, suspicious; crooked. গোল পাকানো *v.* to make a mess of, to muddle; to give rise to complication, to complicate. গোলে হরিবোল দেওয়া to evade one's duty by a false show of doing it in a noisy crowd.

গোলক see গোল[২]।

গোলকধাঁধা *n.* a labyrinth, a maze; an intricate problem.

গোলদার *n.* an owner of a warehouse; a wholesaler. গোলদারি *n.* ownership of a warehouse; wholesale trade or trading. ☐ *a.* of an owner of a warehouse; of wholesale trade; wholesale. গোলদারি কারবার wholesale business or trade.

গোলন্দাজ *n.* a gunner, an artilleryman. ~বাহিনী *n.* artillery. গোলন্দাজি *n.* gunnery, artillery. ☐ *a.* relating to the gunner or gunnery.

গোলপাতা *n.* a leaf of a small tree akin to the fanpalm (these leaves are used in thatching, Nipa fruticans).

গোলা[১] *a.* untrained, uneducated, inexperienced, ordinary, one without a refinement of taste (গোলা পায়রা, গোলা লোক).

গোলা[২] *n.* a ball; a cannon-ball. ~গুলি *n. pl.* cannon-balls and bullets. গোলা ছোড়া *v.* to cannonade. ~বারুদ *n.* ammunition.

গোলা[৩] *v.* to dissolve in or blend with water esp. by pressing and rubbing. ☐ *n.* dissolution in or blending with water by pressing and rubbing; a thin paste made by such dissolution or blending (চুনগোলা, গোবরগোলা). ☐ *a.* dissolved in or blended with water by pressing and rubbing. ~হাঁড়ি *n.* an earthen pot in which cow-dung is blended with water for plastering a mudbuilt house.

গোলা[৪] *n.* a wicker corn-bin, a granary, a barn; a warehouse (কাঠগোলা) ; a central market. ~জাত *a.* garnered; stored or stocked in a warehouse. ~জাত করা *v.* to garner, to store or stock in a warehouse. ~বাড়ি *n.* a grange; a barn, a farm-building.

গোলাকার, গোলাকৃতি *a.* round, spherical; circular, roundish.

গো-লাঙুল *n.* a cow's tail.

গোলাপ *n.* the rose; rose-water (গোলাপপাশ). ~গাছ *n.* the rose-plant. ~গোত্র *n.* the Rosaceae. ~গোত্রীয় *a.* rosaceous. ~জল *n.* rose-water. ~জাম *n.* the rose-apple. ~পাশ *n.* a vessel fitted with a device for spraying rose-water. ~বাগ *n.* a rose-garden, a rosary. গোলাপি *a.* scented like the rose; rose-coloured, rose-hued, rosed-red, rosy; slight, mild (গোলাপি নেশা).

গোলাম *n.* a bond-slave, a slave; a servant;

(of playing-cards) the knave. **কেনা গোলাম** one who has been purchased to act as a slave, a bondsman, a bondman (*fem.* a bondswoman, a bondwoman). **~খানা** *n.* quarters for slaves, slavequarters; (fig.) a manufactory for imbuing people with slave-mentality. **গোলামি** *n.* slavery; (fig.) drudgery; slave-mentality.

গোলার্ধ *n.* (geog.) a hemisphere; (geom.) a semi-circle.

গোলালো *a.* roundish.

গোলীয় *a.* spherical; globular.

গোলোক *n.* (myth.) the part of the heaven which is the abode of Narayana (নারায়ণ) or Vishnu (বিষ্ণু). **~ধাম** *n.* the abode of Narayana (নারায়ণ) or Vishnu in heaven; a kind of indoor game. **~নাথ, ~পতি, ~বিহারী** *n.* appellations of Narayana (নারায়ণ) or Vishnu (বিষ্ণু). **~প্রাপ্তি** *n.* divine permission to live in Goloka (গোলোক) after one's death.

গোল্লা *n.* a globular sweetmeat (রসগোল্লা, কাঁচাগোল্লা) ; a cipher, zero (পরীক্ষায় গোল্লা পাওয়া) ; ruin, spoilt state (গোল্লায় যাওয়া). **গোল্লায় যাওয়া** *v.* to be ruined morally, to go to the bad; to be ruined or lost, to go to the dogs.

গোশত alt. spell of **গোস্ত**।

গোশালা *n.* a cowshed; a cow-house, a byre.

গোশৃঙ্গ *n.* a cow's horn.

গোষ্ঠ *n.* a grazing ground, a pasture or pasturage; a meeting-place, an assembly, an association, a society, a club (গোষ্ঠাগার). **~গৃহ, গোষ্ঠাগার** *n.* a cowshed; a cow-house, a byre; an association-hall, a society hall, a club-house, a club-room. **~বিহারী** *n.* an appellation of Krishna (কৃষ্ণ). **~লীলা** *n.* the pastoral activities and sports of Krishna (কৃষ্ণ). **গোষ্ঠাধ্যক্ষ** *n.* the chief of an assembly or society.

গোষ্ঠাগার, গোষ্ঠাধ্যক্ষ see **গোষ্ঠ**।

গোষ্ঠী *n.* a family; a kindred; a clan; a race; a tribe; a class, a kind; a collection or body (শিষ্যগোষ্ঠী) ; a team; a group; a society, an association. **~পতি** *n.* the chief of a tribe or clan or family; a president; a leader. **~বর্গ** *n. pl.* members of the family and kinsfolk. **~ভুক্ত** *a.* belonging to or included in a family, race, group etc.; incorporated within a group.

গোষ্পদ *n.* a cow's footprint. **~তুল্য** *a.* as small in area as a cow's footprint.

গোসল *n.* bathing, bath. **গোসল করা** *v.* to take one's bath; to bathe. **~খানা** *n.* a bathroom; a bathing establishment, a hammam, a bathhouse.

গোসা *n.* anger; huff or mortification. **গোসা করা** *v.* to get angry; to be in a huff.

গোসাঘর *n.* a room or apartment to which a lady in a huff retires (cp. a boudoir).

গোসাঁই *n.* a master; God, Lord; a title of Vaishnava gurus.

গোসাঞি var. of **গোসাঁই**।

গোসাপ *n.* the iguana.

গোসেবা *n.* feeding and care of a cow or cows.

গোস্ত *n.* meat; beef.

গোস্তন *n.* a cow's udder.

গোস্তাকি *n.* insolence, impertinence, audacity.

গোস্বামী *n.* the lord or the protector of cows or of the earth; a master; God; a religious teacher, a preceptor, a guru; a title of Vaishnava gurus.

গোহত্যা *n.* cow-slaughter, cow-killing. **গোহত্যা করা** *v.* to slay a cow or cows. **~কারী** *n.* a cow-slaughterer. **~নিরোধ** *n.* prevention of cow-slaughter.

গোহাল falsely elegant var. of **গোয়াল**।

গৌড় *n.* an ancient name of modern Bengal (controversial opinions exist as to the actual area or Gauda). **~জন** *n.* the people of Bengal, Bengalis. **গৌড়ী** *n.* an Indian musical mode; a kind of poetical diction; a kind of rum prepared from molasses. **গৌড়ীয়** *a.* of or living in or produced in Gauda (গৌড়).

গৌড়সারং *n.* a morning raga or classical musical mode of the Sarang class.

গৌণ *a.* minor, unimportant, secondary. □ *n.* delay. **গৌণ করা** *v.* (arch.) to make delay. **~কর্ম** *v.* minor duty; (gr.) an indirect object. **~তা** *n.* secondariness; less importance; inferiority. **গৌণার্থ** *n.* (rhet.) secondary significance, figurative meaning.

গৌণিক *a.* factorial.

গৌর *a.* cream-coloured tinged with red; (loos.) fair-complexioned. □ *n.* a name of Chaitanya. **~চন্দ্র** *n.* a name of Chaitanya. **~চন্দ্রিকা** *n.* a song in praise of Chaitanya before beginning the scheduled song; prefatory remarks, a prologue, a preamble, a preface.

গৌরব *n.* importance; glory; majesty; dignity; honour; cordial reception; pride; excellence; worth. **গৌরব করা** *v.* to be proud of, to pride in. **~গাথা** *n.* tales of glory; song, poem etc. composed in praise of a person or one's country. **~রবি** *n.* the sun of glory. **গৌরবান্বিত, গৌরবিত, ~মণ্ডিত** *a.* important, glorious; majestic; dignified; honoured; proud. **গৌরবের বিষয়** a creditable or highly praiseworthy affair or thing, a glory, a glorious achievement.

গৌরাঙ্গ *a.* having a cream-coloured complexion tinged with red; (loos.) fair-complexioned. □ *n.* a name of Chaitanya. *fem.* **গৌরাঙ্গা, গৌরাঙ্গী** ৷

গৌরী *a. fem.* having a cream-coloured complexion tinged with red; (loos.) fair-complexioned. □ *n.* a woman or a girl having a cream-coloured complexion tinged with red; Goddess Durga (দুর্গা) ; an unmarried girl of eight years. **~কান্ত** *n.* an appellation of Shiva (শিব). **~দান** *n.* giving away in marriage an under-age girl; giving away in marriage an eight-year old Hindu girl. **~পট্ট** *n.* the pedestal symbolizing Gauri (গৌরী) or Durga on which the symbol of Shiva is placed. **~শঙ্কর** *n.* Goddess Durga (দুর্গা) and Shiva (শিব) ; Mount Everest.

গৌরী সেন a proverbially rich bountiful and lavish Bengali gentleman who never kept account of his expenses and never said no to anybody who applied to him for monetary help. **গৌরী সেনের টাকা** money which may be squandered freely and for which no account is required to be submitted; (sarcas.) public funds. **লাগে টাকা দেবে গৌরী সেন** (sarcas.) it matters little if wasteful or extravagant expenses are incurred because this will be paid out of public exchequer or funds, the people will bear the brunt of official wastefulness.

গ্যাঁজ var. of **গেঁজ** ৷

গ্যাঁজলা pop. var. of **গাঁজলা** ৷

গ্যাঁজা coll. var. of **গাঁজা** ৷

গ্যাঁজানো *v.* to gossip uselessly, to go on gossiping without any purpose.

গ্যাঁট *int.* expressing firmly motionless or immobile state (গ্যাঁট হয়ে বসে থাকা = to sit tight, to stick firmly to one's purpose, opinions etc.).

গ্যাঁটগ্যাঁট, গ্যাটগ্যাট variants of **গটগট** ৷

গ্যাঁদা pop. var. of **গাঁদা** ৷

গ্যাস *n.* gas; (inf. and sl.) a bluff, a fib. **গ্যাসীয়** *a.* gaseous.

গ্রথন *n.* act of stringing (as flowers in a wreath); composition (as of an essay or a book). **গ্রথিত** *a.* strung; composed. **গ্রথিত করা** *v.* to string; to compose.

গ্রন্থ *n.* a book. **~কার, ~কর্তা** *n.* an author; a writer. *fem.* **~কর্ত্রী** an authoress. **~কীট** *n.* a bookworm. **~ন, ~না** same as **গ্রথন** ৷ **গ্রন্থিত** same as **গ্রথিত** ৷ **~স্বত্ব** *n.* copyright.

গ্রন্থাগার *n.* a library. **গ্রন্থাগারিক** *n.* a librarian.

গ্রন্থানুরাগ *n.* love for books, fondness for books. **গ্রন্থানুরাগী** *a.* & *n.* (a person) fond of books, a book-lover, a bibliophile.

গ্রন্থাবলি *n.* books; works of a particular author or authoress.

গ্রন্থালয় *n.* a library; a bookshop.

গ্রন্থি *n.* a knot, a joint (of bones), a knuckle; a node, a gland. **~কলা** *n.* glandular tissue. **~রস** *n.* glandular secretion. **~সম্বন্ধীয়** *a.*glandular. **শিরাগ্রন্থি** *n.* varicose veins.

গ্রন্থিক *n.* a soothsayer, an astrologer, a fortune-teller.

গ্রন্থিচ্ছেদক, গ্রন্থিভেদক *n.* pickpocket, a cut-purse.

গ্রন্থিবদ্ধ *a.* knotted, tied together.

গ্রন্থিবন্ধন *n.* act of tying into a knot, knotting; the Hindu practice of tying a corner of the bride's sari with a corner of the bridegroom's scarf at wedding. **গ্রন্থিবন্ধন করা** *v.* to tie into a knot, to knot; to tie a corner of the bride's sari with a corner of the bridegroom's scarf at wedding.

গ্রন্থিল *a.* knotty.

গ্রসন *n.* act of swallowing or devouring or gulping; act of eclipsing.

গ্রসমান *a.* engaged in swallowing or devouring or gulping or eclipsing.

গ্রস্ত *a.* swallowed, devoured, gulped; eclipsed; attacked; seized; affected with; involved in; overwhelmed. **গ্রস্ত উপত্যকা** *n.* a rift valley. **গ্রস্তোদয়** *n.* rising of the sun or the moon after eclipse.

গ্রহ *n.* (astr. & astrol.) a planet; (astrol.) an evil planet, (loos.) an evil star (গ্রহের ফের) ; eclipse; act of taking; act of assuming (রূপগ্রহ) ; realization, comprehension (অর্থগ্রহ) ; misfortune. **~কোপ** *n.* the antagonism or opposition or evil influence of a planet. **~জগৎ** *n.* the planetary world. **~তত্ত্ব** *n.* astronomy. **~দশা** *n.* (astrol.) the period of direct influence of a planet esp. an evil planet. **~দৃষ্টি** *n.* (astrol.) planetary influence (direct or indirect), esp. evil influence. **~দেবতা** *n.* (astrol.) the guardian or presiding deity of a planet. **~দোষ** *n.* (astrol.) the evil influence of a planet. **~পতি** *n.* the sun. **~পীড়া** *n.* (astrol.) the suffering owing to the evil influence of a planet. **~পূজা** *n.* worship of the sun and other planets in order to propitiate them. **~বিপ্র** *n.* a Brahmin astrologer. **~বৈগুণ্য, ~বিপাক** *n.* (astrol.) antagonism or hostility or opposition of a planet. **~মণ্ডল** *n.* (astr. & astrol.) the planetary system. **~রাজ** *n.* the sun. **~শান্তি** *n.* (astrol.) propitiation of planets. **~স্ফুট** *n.* a zodiacal sign indicating the position of a planet.

গ্রহণ[১] *n.* taking or receiving (ভিক্ষাগ্রহণ) ; holding (হস্তগ্রহণ) ; assuming (ছদ্মবেশ গ্রহণ) ; adoption (সন্ন্যাস গ্রহণ) ; reception (অতিথিকে সাদরে গ্রহণ) ; acceptance (নিমন্ত্রণ গ্রহণ) ; comprehension, realization (রচনার অর্থগ্রহণ) ; drinking or eating (জলগ্রহণ, অন্নগ্রহণ) ; taking in (শ্বাসগ্রহণ) ; act of inhaling (গন্ধগ্রহণ). **গ্রহণ করা** *v.* to take, to receive; to hold; to assume; to adopt; to accept; to comprehend, to realize; to drink or eat; to take in; to inhale. **~ক্ষম** *a.* receptive. **~ক্ষমতা, ~শক্তি** *n.* receptive power or capacity.

গ্রহণ[২] *n.* an eclipse. **গ্রহণ ছাড়ে** *v.* an eclipse ends. **গ্রহণ লাগে** *v.* an eclipse begins or starts. **গ্রহণ হয়** *v.* an eclipse takes place or occurs. **~মোক্ষ** *n.* end of an eclipse. **~স্থিতি** *n.* duration of an eclipse. **~স্পর্শ** *n.* commencement of an eclipse. **পূর্ণগ্রহণ** *n.* total eclipse. **খণ্ডগ্রহণ** *n.* partial eclipse.

গ্রহণি, গ্রহণী *n.* chronic diarrhoea; the duodenum.

গ্রহণীয় *a.* acceptable.

গ্রহাচার্য *n.* a soothsayer, an astrologer.

গ্রহাণু *n.* (astr.) an asteroid. **~পুঞ্জ** *n. pl.* asteroids.

গ্রহান্তর *n.* another planet.

গ্রহান্তর্বর্তী *a.* inter-planetary.

গ্রহাবিষ্ট *a.* (astrol.) influenced by an evil planet; possessed.

গ্রহীতা *n.* a recipient.

গ্রাবরেখা *n.* (geog.) moraine.

গ্রাবু *n.* a kind of card-game.

গ্রাম *n.* a hamlet, a village; a small settlement; (as a *sfx.*) a collection (গুণগ্রাম, স্বরগ্রাম) ; (mus.) a scale (উচ্চগ্রাম). **~খরচা** same as **গ্রামভাটি**। **~জ, ~জাত** *a.* produced in a village, rural. **~ণী** *n.* (hist.) a village headman. **~ধর্ম** *n.* sexual intercourse (esp. with one's wife). **~বাসী** *n.* a villager, a village-dweller. **~ভাটি** *n.* a monetary contribution to be given for village welfare at the time of wedding etc. **~মৃগ** *n.* a (village) dog. **~সম্পর্ক, ~সুবাদ** *n.* the relation that arises owing to living in the same village. **~সম্পর্কীয়** *a.* rural; pertaining to co-villagers. **~স্থ** *a.* of or in or living in a village; rural.

গ্রামাধ্যক্ষ *n.* a village headman.

গ্রামান্ত *n.* outskirts of a village; the border of a village.

গ্রামান্তর *n.* another village.

গ্রামিক *a.* & *n.* one who owns or rules or guards a village.

গ্রামী *a.* one who lives in or rules a village; rural; rustic; consisting of or containing villages or musical scales.

গ্রামীণ *a.* produced in a village; in or of or dwelling in a village; rural; rustic.

গ্রামোফোন *n.* a gramophone, a record-player.

গ্রাম্য *a.* of or relating to a village; born or

produced in a village; found or available in a village; living in a village; rural; rustic; (esp. of words and speech) vulgar. ~তা *n.* rusticity; (esp. of words and speech) vulgarity. ~ধর্ম *n.* sexual intercourse (esp.) with one's wife. ~মৃগ *n.* a (village) dog.

গ্রাস *n.* a mouthful, a morsel; the inner cavity of an opened mouth, a gape; a handful (as at snatching); a grip, a hold, seizure; appropriation; act of swallowing or devouring or eating or drinking; feed; food; an eclipse. **গ্রাস করা** *v.* to swallow or devour; to eat or drink; to seize; to grip; to appropriate to oneself; to eclipse. **গ্রাস হওয়া** *v.* to be eclipsed. ~কারী *a.* & *n.* one who or that which swallows or devours or eats or drinks or seizes or appropriates or eclipses. ~নালি *n.* the gullet, the oesophagus. **গ্রাসাচ্ছাদন** *n.* food and clothing; subsistence; bare subsistence.

গ্রাহ *n.* act of taking or receiving; seizure; appropriation; enlightenment; knowledge; cognition; comprehension; understanding; intelligence; solicitation or insistence; earnestness, zeal; the crocodile, the alligator, the shark etc. **গ্রাহক** *a.* one who takes or receives; one who buys or subscribes. ☐ *n.* a recipient; a buyer, subscriber. *fem.* **গ্রাহিকা**। **গ্রাহকশ্রেণিভুক্ত করা** *v.* to enlist or enrol as a subscriber. **গ্রাহিতা** *n.* practice of taking or receiving or seizing; (phys.) susceptibility (চৌম্বক গ্রাহিতা). **গ্রাহী** *a.* & *n.* one who or that which takes or receives; one who or that which seizes or appropriates; one who or that which comprehends or appreciates or acknowledges (গুণগ্রাহী) ; one who or that which attracts (চিত্তগ্রাহী) ; astringent. **গ্রাহী সেল** (phys.) a secondary cell.

গ্রাহ্য *a.* acceptable; perceptible (ইন্দ্রিয়গ্রাহ্য) ; admissible; worthy of consideration; reckonable. **গ্রাহ্য করা** *v.* to accept; to pay heed to, to care. **গ্রাহ্য না করা** *v.* to reject, to dismiss, not to accept, to pay no heed to, not to care. **গ্রাহ্য হওয়া** *v.* to be accepted; to be considered; to be heeded.

গ্রিক *a.* Greek. ☐ *n.* a Greek; the Greek language, Greek.

গ্রিসীয় *a.* Grecian, Greek.

গ্রীবা *n.* the throat; the neck; the nape of the neck. ~দেশ *n.* the nape of the neck; (loos.) the neck or the throat. ~ভঙ্গি *n.* a (beautiful) gesture of the neck or the throat.

গ্রীষ্ম *n.* summer; heat. ☐ *a.* hot; torrid (গ্রীষ্মমণ্ডল). ~কাল *n.* summer, the hot season. ~কালীন *a.* of summer, of the hot season, summer. ~ক্লিষ্ট *a.* same as ~পীড়িত। ~তাপিত *a.* oppressed by the heat of summer; heated by summer. ~পীড়িত *a.* oppressed with heat or by summer. ~প্রধান tropical. ~প্রধান দেশ a tropical country, a hot country. ~বলয়, ~মণ্ডল *n.* (geog.) the torrid zone. **গ্রীষ্মাতিশয়, গ্রীষ্মাতিশয্য** *n.* excess of heat; extreme heat. **গ্রীষ্মাবকাশ** *n.* the summer vacation or recess.

গ্রেন *n.* a grain (a unit of weight).

গ্রেপ্তার, গ্রেফতার *n.* arrest, apprehension, seizure. ☐ *a.* arrested, apprehended, seized (গ্রেপ্তার হওয়া). **গ্রেপ্তার করা** *v.* to arrest, to apprehend, to seize. **গ্রেপ্তারি, গ্রেফতারি** *a.* empowering or directing to arrest. **গ্রেপ্তারি পরওয়ানা** a warrant of arrest.

গ্রৈব, গ্রৈবেয় *a.* of the neck or the throat; of the nape of the neck.

গ্রৈষ্মিক *a.* of summer; of summer heat.

গ্লান *a.* wearied, tired; exhausted, fatigued; unhealthy; filthy, dirty; disreputed, disreputable, shameful; upbraided, slandered, accused (falsely); mortified. ~যান *n.* an ambulance car.

গ্লানি *n.* weariness, tiredness; exhaustion, fatigue; unhealthiness, filth, dirt (ঘামের গ্লানি) ; disgrace, disrepute, shame (বীরকুলগ্লানি) ; upbraiding, slander, (false) accusation; mortification (মনের গ্লানি). ~কর, ~জনক *a.* filthy; disgraceful, shameful; slanderous; mortifying.

গ্লাস *n.* a tumbler, a glass.

ঘ *n.* the fourth consonant of the Bengali alphabet.

ঘচ same as **খচ** । **ঘচ ঘচ** same as **খচ খচ** । **ঘচাঘচ** same as **খচাখচ** ।

ঘট *n.* a small earthen or metal pitcher or pot; a receptacle, a container, a place, a sphere (সর্ব ঘটে) ; the brain or head (ঘটে বুদ্ধি নেই) ; the body, the frame (ঘটের মধ্যে সাঁই বিরাজে). **সর্বঘটে** *adv.* (usu. dero.) everywhere, at every place (সে সর্বঘটেই থাকে).

ঘটক *n.* one who brings about or causes to occur (an event); a match-maker. *fem.* **ঘটকী** a female match-maker. **ঘটকালি** *n.* match-making.

ঘটকর্পর *n.* (a piece of) potsherd.

ঘটকার *n.* a potter.

ঘটকালি, ঘটকী see **ঘটক** ।

ঘট ঘট same as **ঘটর ঘটর** ।

ঘটন *n.* occurrence, happening; act of joining; a chance happening.

ঘটনা *n.* an event, an occurrence; an instance of joining; a chance happening or occurrence. **ঘটনাক্রমে** *adv.* by chance, accidentally, it so happened that; in course of events (ঘটনাক্রমে দেখা হয়ে গেল) ; in course of circumstances (ঘটনাক্রমে তাকে বাড়ি বেচতে হল). **ঘটনাচক্র** *n.* (lit.) the wheel of events, (fig.) the course of events. **ঘটনাচক্রে** same as **ঘটনাক্রমে** । **ঘটনাধীন** *a.* dependent on force of events; subject to the course of events or circumstances. **ঘটনাপরম্পরা** *n.* due succession of events. **ঘটনাপূর্ণ, ঘটনাবহুল** *a.* eventful. **ঘটনাবলি** *n.* (a collection of) events. **ঘটনাস্রোত** *n.* (lit.) the stream of events, (fig.) the course of events. **ঘটনাস্থল** *n.* the place or scene of occurrence, a venue.

ঘটনীয় *a.* likely to occur; probable.

ঘটমান *a.* still occurring or happening; (gr.) progressive, continuous. **ঘটমান অতীত** (gr.) past continuous or progressive (tense).

ঘটরঘটর *int.* expressing a rolling noise as of a pestle moving in a mortar or on a paved floor. **ঘটরমটর** *int.* this and similar noise.

ঘটস্থাপন, ঘটস্থাপনা *n.* ceremonial placing of a pitcher full of holy water on the altar making the commencement of worship.

ঘটা *n.* occurrence; pomp, grandeur, eclat; a collection or multitude (ঘনঘটা). □ *v.* to occur, to happen, to come to pass; to be possible (যাওয়া ঘটে উঠল না) ; to originate, to arise, to spring from (কী থেকে কী ঘটল). **ঘটা করে** *adv.* with a spectacular display, with pomp and grandeur, ceremoniously, ostentatiously. **ঘটানো** *v.* to cause to occur or happen or come about, to bring to pass, to bring about; to originate, to give rise to.

ঘটাটোপ *n.* a covering with side-screens for a carriage (such as palanquins, litters, etc.) a yashmak.

ঘটি *n.* a small pitcher-shaped metal water-pot.

ঘটিকা *n.* an hour; a moment; a bell, a gong; any machine for measuring time; a timepiece, a clock (also **ঘটিকা-যন্ত্র**) ; time of the clock (সাড়ে তিন ঘটিকায়) ; a small pitcher-shaped earthen or metal water-pot. **ঘটিকায়** *adv.* o'clock (সাড়ে ছয় ঘটিকায় = at six o'clock).

ঘটিত *a.* caused to occur by, caused by, due to (দুর্বলতাঘটিত ভয়) ; concerning, involving (নারীঘটিত, অর্থঘটিত) ; mixed or blended with, containing. **ঘটিতব্য** *a.* that which is to happen; that which shall happen.

ঘটিরাম *n.* a stupid or worthless officer or worker. □ *a.* stupid or worthless (ঘটিরাম ডেপুটি).

ঘটী same as **ঘটিকা** । **~যন্ত্র** *n.* a pulley or a device for drawing water from a well.

ঘট্ট *n.* a landing stair at the bank of a river, tank etc. **~জীবী** *n.* a ferryman.

ঘট্টন *n.* act of abrading, abrasion; act of

pounding; act of stirring; act of causing to occur, act of bringing about; act of forming; formation. **ঘট্টনী** *n.* a pestle.

ঘট্টিত *a.* brought about, caused to occur; made; formed; pounded; stirred.

ঘড় ঘড় *int.* expressing a rattling sound as of a wheeled car moving or of the breathing of a bronchial patient.

ঘড়া *n.* a vase without a handle, a jar, a pitcher.

ঘড়াঞ্চি *n.* a step-ladder.

ঘড়ি *n.* a clock, a watch, a wristwatch, a timepiece; an hour. **ঘড়ি-ঘড়ি** *adv.* at every hour; at every moment; repeatedly; frequently; often. **অ্যালার্মঘড়ি** *n.* an alarm clock. **ট্যাঁকঘড়ি** *n.* a pocket watch. **টেবলঘড়ি** *n.* a table clock, a time-piece. **দেওয়ালঘড়ি** *n.* a wall clock. **পকেটঘড়ি** *n.* a pocket watch. **পেটাঘড়ি** *n.* a gong. **বালিঘড়ি** *n.* a sand-glass, hourglass. **বিরামঘড়ি** *n.* (phys.) a stop-watch. **সূর্যঘড়ি** *n.* a sundial. **হাতঘড়ি** *n.* a wrist-watch.

ঘড়িয়াল[১] *n.* one who is employed to strike a gong to indicate hours, (cp.) a bellman.

ঘড়িয়াল[২] *n.* a crocodile with a very long muzzle, a gavial, Gavialis gangeticus; (fig.) an extremely sly and self-seeking person.

ঘড়েল coll. corrup. of **ঘড়িয়াল**[১,২] ।

ঘণ্ট *n.* a dish of minced and spiced vegetables cooked almost dry; (fig.) reckless waste (টাকার ঘণ্ট). **ঘণ্ট করা** *v.* to cook a dish of minced and spiced vegetables; (fig.) to waste or squander recklessly.

ঘণ্টা *n.* a bell; a gong; an hour; (sarcas.) nothing of any value (ঘণ্টা করবে). **ঘণ্টা করা** *v.* to fail to do anything, to do nothing. **~ধ্বনি, ~রব** *n.* the sound of a bell or a gong. **ঘণ্টা পড়ে** *v.* the bell goes. **ঘণ্টা বাজানো** *v.* to ring a bell; to sound a gong; to tintinnabulate. **~বাদন** *n.* ringing of a bell; act of sounding a gong; tintinnabulation. **ঘণ্টায়-ঘণ্টায়** *adv.* at every hour; repeatedly and frequently. **বিড়ালের গলায় ঘণ্টা বাঁধা** *v.* to bell the cat.

ঘণ্টাকর্ণ *n.* the bell-flower, the campanula, (cp.) the tulip; a traditional deity presiding over skin-diseases.

ঘণ্টাগার *n.* a belfry.

ঘণ্টাধ্বনি, ঘণ্টাবাদন see **ঘণ্টা** ।

ঘণ্টিকা, ঘণ্টী *n.* a small bell; the uvula.

ঘণ্টেশ্বর *n.* a traditional deity presiding over skin-diseases (regarded as the son of Mars).

ঘন *n.* cloud (ঘনঘটা) ; (arith. & alg.) a cube (ঘনফল) ; (geom.) a solid. ☐ *a.* dense (ঘন বন); thick, condensed (ঘন মেঘ, ঘন দুধ) ; frequent (ঘন ঘন গর্জন) ; deep (ঘন আঁধার) ; close (ঘন বৃক্ষসারি, ঘন বুনুনি) ; coarse (ঘন কাপড়) ; severe (ঘন বরষা) ; (geom. & sc.) solid (ঘন পদার্থ, ঘনক্ষেত্র). **ঘন করা** *v.* to thicken; to condense. **ঘন হওয়া** *v.* to thicken; to become condensed; to draw close together; to draw close (to). **~কাল** *n.* the rainy season, the rains. **ঘন কালো** deep black. **~কৃষ্ণ** *a.* as black or dark as a cloud; deep black, jet black. **~ক্ষেত্র** *n.* (geom.) a solid figure, a cube. **~গর্জন** *n.* the roar or rumbling of clouds; a peal of thunder. **~ঘটা** *n.* a thick and extensive cumulation of (dark) clouds, the cumulus. **~ঘটাচ্ছন্ন** *a.* overcast with clouds. **~ঘন** *adv.* repeatedly and frequently, every now and then, often. **~ঘোর** *a.* overcast with thick clouds; (loos.) darkened with clouds. **~জ্যামিতি** *n.* solid geometry. **~তা, ~ত্ব** *n.* density; thickness; closeness; solidity; (geom. & sc.) dimension, volume. **~ফল** *n.* (math.) cubic measure. **~ফুট** *n.* cubic foot. **~বর্ত্ম** *n.* the path of the cloud across the sky; the sky. **~বসতি** *n.* thick or dense cluster of habitations, thick population. **~বসতিপূর্ণ** *a.* crowded with habitations; thickly populated, congested. **~বস্তু** *n.* a solid thing; (phys.) a solid body. **~বিন্যস্ত** *a.* thickly set. **~বিন্যাস** *n.* thick setting. **~বীথি** *n.* the region of clouds; air route. **~মান** *n.* (phys.) volume. **~মিটার** *n.* cubic metre. **~মূল** *n.* (math.) a cube root. **~শ্যাম** *a.* as black or dark as a cloud, deep black; dark-complexioned; bottle-green. ☐ *n.* an appellation of Krishna (কৃষ্ণ).

~সন্নিবিষ্ট same as ~বিন্যস্ত। ~সন্নিবেশ same as ~বিন্যাস। ~সার *n.* camphor.

ঘনাগম *n.* (lit.) arrival of clouds; the rainy season, the rains.

ঘনাঙ্ক *n.* density. **পরম ঘনাঙ্ক** (phys.) absolute density.

ঘনাচ্ছন্ন *a.* same as **ঘনাবৃত**।

ঘনাত্যয়, ঘনান্ত *n.* (lit.) removal or end of clouds; the autumn season.

ঘনানো *v.* to draw close or closer, to near; to make thick, to thicken. **তার দিন ঘনিয়েছে** his or her time is up; his or her days are numbered.

ঘনান্ধকার *n.* deep darkness. □ *a.* deep dark.

ঘনাবৃত *a.* overcast with clouds.

ঘনায়মান *a.* in the state of being thickened, thickening; drawing near, approaching.

ঘনায়িত *a.* drawn near; thickened.

ঘনিমা *n.* density; thickness; closeness; solidity.

ঘনিষ্ঠ *a.* close, near (ঘনিষ্ঠ সম্পর্ক, ঘনিষ্ঠ হয়ে বসা) ; hand in glove (with), intimate (ঘনিষ্ঠ বন্ধু = an intimate or close friend, a bosom friend). *fem.* **ঘনিষ্ঠা**। **~তা** *n.* closeness, nearness; intimacy.

ঘনীকরণ *n.* act of making thick, thickening; condensation; act of bringing near.

ঘনীকৃত *a.* thickened; condensed; brought near.

ঘনীভবন *n.* act of getting thick, thickening; condensation; act of drawing near.

ঘনীভূত *a.* thickened; condensed; drawn near.

ঘনোপল *n.* hail.

ঘর *n.* a house, a building; a dwelling, a residence, an abode, a home; a shrine, a temple (ঠাকুরঘর) ; a room, a compartment, an apartment (পড়ার ঘর) ; one's own family (ঘরের লোক) ; a family (দুশো ঘরের বাস) ; descent, lineage (স্বঘর, হাঘর) ; a groove, a pocket (ছাপার টাইপের ঘর) ; a hole (বোতামের ঘর = a button-hole); (of machines etc.) a button, a reed (হারমোনিয়ামে 'সা'-এর ঘর) ; a rectangle or a square (ঘর কাটা) ; a place, a space, a side, a division, a column etc. (খরচের ঘর). **ঘর আলো করা** *v.* to beautify or edify a house (esp. with one's personal charm); to bring joy or glory or pride to a family. **~করনা, ~কন্না** *n.* (usu. of a woman) housekeeping, household duties; domestic science; the life and duties of a housewife; housewifery. **ঘরকরনা করা, ঘরকন্না করা** *v.* (usu. of a woman) to keep a house for, to act as a housewife (সে শান্তিতে ঘরকন্না করছে) ; to perform household duties; to be a housewife. **ঘর করা** *v.* to build a house; to act as a wife or mistress to (স্বামী নিয়ে ঘর করা) ; to act as a housewife, to do housekeeping (সে দেওরদের ঘর করছে) ; to lead the life of a housewife (কীসের জন্য আর ঘর করা) ; (of men) to live as a householder, to live as a family man (স্ত্রীপুত্র নিয়ে ঘর করা). **ঘর কাটা** *v.* to divide into or draw separate spaces, columns, squares, rectangles etc. **~কাটা** *a.* divided into separate spaces, columns, squares, rectangles etc. **~কুনো** *a.* homekeeping, shy of company. □ *n.* a home-bird. **~কুনোমি** *n.* home-keeping nature. **ঘর গড়া** *v.* to build one's house or home, to set up one's residence; to establish one's family. **ঘর-ঘর** *adv.* to or at every door, from door to door; to every family or house (বঙ্গের ঘর-ঘর). **~ছাড়া** *a.* one who has renounced hearth and home or has taken to asceticism (ঘরছাড়া সন্ন্যাসী) ; away from home, living abroad (ঘরছাড়া জীবন) ; revolting against the domestic life (ঘরছাড়া মন). **~জামাই** *n.* a man who lives in his father-in-law's family at the latter's cost. **~জোড়া** *a.* occupying the whole space of a room; crowding or over-crowding a room; making a family or house charming and delightful by one's presence (ঘরজোড়া নাতি-নাতনি). **ঘর জ্বালানো** *v.* to set fire to a house or dwelling, to commit arson; (fig.) to destroy the peace and happiness of a family; (fig.) to ruin a family. **~জ্বালানে** *a.* (fig.) one who or that which destroys the peace and happiness of a family; (fig.) one who or that which ruins a family. *fem.* **ঘরজ্বালানি**। **ঘর তোলা** *v.* to build a house or room (esp. a residential one). **ঘর-পর** *n.* one's own people and others. **ঘর পাতা** *v.* to settle down to a married life. **~পোড়া** *a.* one whose house or dwelling has been burnt down; that which burns down a house or dwelling. □ *n.* an appellation of Hanuman (হনুমান) who set fire to Lanka (লঙ্কা) ; an incendiary or saboteur. **ঘরপোড়া গোরু সিঁদুরে মেঘ দেখে ডরায়** a burnt child dreads the fire. **ঘরপোড়া বুদ্ধি** a thought or plan that harms oneself or one's own family or side. **~পোষা** *a.* domestic, tame. **~বর** *n.* one's husband and his house or family. **~বসত** *n.* act of dwelling or residing (ঘরবসত করা) ; a dwelling, a homestead; act of going to live with the husband permanently (generally said of childwives). **ঘর বাঁধা** *v.* to build a house or dwelling; to settle, to colonize. **~বার করা** *v.* to go out of doors and come indoors alternately and repeatedly (esp. in anxiety). **ঘর ভাঙা** *v.* to pull down or demolish a house or room (esp. a residential one); to cause internal strife through instigation; to cause to lose one's aristocracy through matrimonial alliance with an inferior family. **ঘর ভাঙানো** *v.* to cause to pull down or demolish a house or room; to cause internal strife through instigation; to cause to lose one's purity of blood through matrimonial alliance with an inferior family. **ঘর-ভাঙানে** *a.* one who or that which causes internal strife through instigation. *fem.* **ঘর-ভাঙানি**। **~মুখো** *a.* homeward; homing. **ঘরসংসার** same as **ঘরকরনা**। **~সন্ধান** *n.* act of prying into a family or party to find out any of its weak points by means of which internal dissension may be caused. **~সন্ধানী** *a.* prying into a family or party to find out any of its weak points by means of which internal dissension may be caused. **ঘরে আগুন দেওয়া** same as **ঘর জ্বালানো**। **ঘরে-পরে, ঘরে-বাইরে** *adv.* out of doors and within; at home and abroad. **ঘরের কথা** the secret of a family or a party. **ঘরের শত্রু** one who is an enemy to his own family or party, one who betrays his own family or party. **ঘরের শত্রু বিভীষণ** one whose activities and behaviour do a lot of harm to the family; a quisling (see **গৃহশত্রু বিভীষণ**).

ঘরনি *n.* a housewife; a wife.

ঘরাঘরি *a.* mutual; between two houses; inter-domestic; among the members of a family.

ঘরানা *a.* born of or belonging to or relating to a family or a high family. □ *n.* (in Indian music) a typical tradition or style set up by a famous composer or singer of a place or family (আগ্রা ঘরানা, কিরানা ঘরানা).

ঘরামি *n.* a thatcher, one who builds huts professionally. **~গিরি** *n.* the occupation of building huts; the occupation of a thatcher.

ঘরোয়া *a.* pertaining to a family (and usu. confidential) (ঘরোয়া ব্যাপার = family matter); internal (ঘরোয়া বিবাদ) ; homely (ঘরোয়া ব্যবহার) ; domestic (ঘরোয়া কাজকর্ম) ; non-official, informal (ঘরোয়া বৈঠক) ; intimate, one's own (ঘরোয়া লোক).

ঘর্ঘর *int.* expressing a rattling sound as of a tyreless wheeled vehicle moving on a stony road. **ঘর্ঘর করা** *v.* to rattle. **ঘর্ঘর শব্দে** with a rattling noise. **ঘর্ঘরিত** *a.* rattling; resounded or filled with a rattling noise.

ঘর্ম *n.* sweat, perspiration. **~সিক্ত, ঘর্মাক্ত, ঘর্মাপ্লুত** *a.* drenched or wet with perspiration. **ঘর্মাক্তকলেবর** *a.* one whose body is wet with perspiration, one who is sweating all over.

ঘর্ষণ, ঘর্ষ *n.* act of rubbing or grazing, abrasion; act of scouring; (esp. in sc.) friction. **ঘর্ষণ করা** *v.* to rub; to graze; to abrade; to scour. **ঘর্ষণাঙ্ক** *n.* (sc.) coefficient of friction. **ঘর্ষণীয়** *a.* that which is to be or can be rubbed or scoured. **ঘর্ষবিদ্যুৎ** *n.* (phys.) frictional electricity. **ঘর্ষিত** *a.* rubbed; grazed; abraded; scoured.

ঘষটানো, ঘষড়ানো *v.* to drag along something hard; to graze; to abrade; (fig.) to practise or read or try repeatedly or continuously **ঘষটানি, ঘষড়ানি** *n.* an instance or act of dragging along something hard; an instance or act of grazing; abrasion; (fig.) repeated or continuous practice or reading or effort.

ঘষা *v.* to rub; to graze; to abrade; to scour. □ *a.* rubbed; grazed, abraded; scoured. **ঘষা ঘষা** *a.* appearing as grazed or abraded; slightly grazed or abraded. **~ঘষি** *n.* act of repeated or mutual rubbing or grazing or abrading or scouring; repeated or mutual friction; (fig.) repeated or continuous practice or training or coaching; (fig.) repeated solicitation or endeavour. **~মাজা** *n.* (of writings) correction and brushing up; act of scouring; (fig.) act of assiduous coaching or training; (fig.) assiduous attempt at improvement. **~মাজা করা** *v.* to scour; (fig.) to coach or train assiduously; (fig.) to endeavour to improve assiduously; to brush up. **ঘষেমেজে রূপ** made-up or toileted beauty or glamour, painted beauty or glamour.

ঘা *n.* a stroke, a blow, a shock (লাঠির ঘা) ; a wound, a sore, an ulcer (পচা ঘা) ; a bite (সাপের ঘা) ; heart-sore, grief, insult (অপমানের ঘা) ; a loss (ব্যাবসায় ঘা খাওয়া). **ঘা করা** v. to cause a wound or sore, to ulcerate. **খুঁচিয়ে ঘা করা** (lit.) to cause a wound by unnecessary probing; (fig.) to open up or rub an old sore. **ঘা খাওয়া** *v.* to receive a blow or shock; to be struck; to be bitten; to be stricken or wounded at heart; to suffer a loss (ব্যাবসায় ঘা খাওয়া) ; to be harmed (লোকসানে ঘা খাওয়া). **ঘা দেওয়া** *v.* to deal (one) or inflict a blow; to shock; to strike; (of snakes) to bite; to wound one's heart; to cause a loss (to); to harm; to knock, to rap (at) (দরজায় ঘা দেওয়া). **ঘা মারা** *v.* to deal (one) or inflict a blow; to strike; (of snakes) to bite; to wound one's heart. **ঘা-মুখ** *n.* the opening of a sore or ulcer. **ঘা শুকিয়েছে** *v.* a wound or ulcer has healed. **ঘা সওয়া** *v.* to bear or endure or sustain a blow or shock or a loss or harm. **ঘা হওয়া** *v.* to be ulcerated. **~কতক** *n.* a good number of blows. **~কতক খাওয়া** *v.* to sustain a sound beating or a good number of blows. **~কতক বসিয়ে দেওয়া** *v.* to deal (one) a good number of blows; to give a sound beating. **~-ঘো'** (coll.) *n.* wounds, injuries; cuts and blows. **ঘা-ঘো দেওয়া** *v.* to deal or administer a blow or two, to deal a few blows.

ঘাই *n.* a (heavy) stroke or blow; a noisy stroke on the surface of water made by a large fish with its tail.

ঘাঁটা১ *n.* a hard growth on the foot or toe or hand, a corn.

ঘাঁটা২ *v.* to stir; to beat, to whisk away, to move about; to rummage (কাগজপত্র ঘাঁটা) ; to mix up (সুতোগুলো বা মশলাগুলো সে ঘেঁটে ফেলেছে). □ *a.* stirred; moved about, handled; mixed up. **~ঘাঁটি** *n.* act of stirring or rummaging or handling repeatedly or continuously. **~ঘাঁটি করা** *v.* to stir or handle repeatedly or confusedly. **~নো** *v.* to cause to stir; to vex, to irritate, to annoy; to disturb; to agitate.

ঘাঁটি *n.* a watch-post; an outpost (পুলিশের ঘাঁটি) ; a station, a depot (বিমানঘাঁটি = an airport, জাহাজঘাঁটি = a dock); a military outpost or station; a haunt or rendezvous (বদমাশের ঘাঁটি) ; a gateway or a junction of several ways (ঘাঁটি জুড়ে থাকা). **ঘাঁটি আগলানো** *v.* to guard a camp or post. **~য়াল** *n.* one who guards or keeps a post.

ঘাঁতঘোঁত *n.* secret means or methods, artifice, contrivances, devices; tricks or wiles; ins and outs.

ঘাগরা *n.* a skirt usually worn by an upcountry woman.

ঘাগি *a.* hardened by long practice, inveterate (ঘাগি বদমাশ) ; veteran, long-experienced (ঘাগি খেলোয়াড়, ঘাগি কেরানি) ; punished or convicted repeatedly; confirmed (ঘাগি চোর). **ঘাগি হওয়া** *v.* to be hardened or made callous by long practice or experience. **ঘাগু** same as **ঘাগি**।

ঘাঘর *n.* a pair of cymbals.

ঘাট১ *n.* a fault, a slight offence, a failing, a shortcoming; shortage, want (গুণে ঘাট

নেই). ঘাট মানা *v.* to own or acknowledge a fault or failing; to apologize for a fault or failing. ঘাট হওয়া *v.* to be in fault.

ঘাট[২] *n.* a landing-stage (as on the bank of a river, pond etc.) a ghat, a quay, a wharf, a moorage, a mooring; (of a harmonium) a reed, (of a stringed musical instrument) a bridge; a mountain or mountain range (পূর্বঘাট, পশ্চিমঘাট) ; a mountain-pass, a gorge, a ghat. ~ওয়াল var. of ঘাটোয়াল। ~লা *n.* a brick-built or stone-built landing-stair (as on the bank of a pond). ~কামান *n.* the practice (among Hindus) of shaving head, chin etc. of sons when their period of mourning is over. ঘাটের মড়া (lit.) a corpse for cremation or burial; a person having one-foot in the grave; (as an abuse) a haggard and ghostly-looking person. সাত ঘাটের জল খাওয়া (fig.) to knock at every door only to be disappointed or harassed.

ঘাটখরচ *n.* funeral expenses.

ঘাটতি *n.* shortage, shortfall, deficit; fault, flaw, defect (কাজে ঘাটতি).

ঘাটমাঝি *n.* a ferryman.

ঘাটা *n.* (used as a *sfx.*) a quay, a wharf, a moorage (জাহাজঘাটা).

ঘাটি var. of ঘাঁটি।

ঘাটোয়াল *n.* a wharfinger; a guard of an outpost; a collector of toll from pilgrims. *fem.* ঘাটোয়ালি[১]। ঘাটোয়ালি[২] *n.* the profession or post of a wharfinger; land held on condition of service as a wharfinger; *fem.* of ঘাটোয়াল।

ঘাড় *n.* the nape of the neck; the neck; the shoulder. ঘাড় ঝাঁকানো *v.* to shrug. ঘাড় ধরা *v.* to seize by the neck. ঘাড় ধরে করানো *v.* to compel or force (a person) to do. ঘাড় নাড়া *v.* to nod (to indicate acquiescence or refusal or affirmation or negation). ঘাড় ভাঙা *v.* to cause to spend for oneself (through fraudulence, cajolement etc.). ঘাড়ে করা *v.* to take upon the shoulder, to shoulder. ঘাড়ে-গর্দানে এক stubbily built; short-necked. ঘাড়ে চাপা, ঘাড়ে পড়া *v.* to come or fall upon the shoulder as a burden. ঘাড়ে চাপানো *v.* to place upon the shoulder of another, to impose a burden on another. ঘাড়ে নেওয়া same as ঘাড়ে করা। ~ধাক্কা *n.* a push out by the neck; expulsion. ঘাড়ধাক্কা দেওয়া v. to push out by the neck; to expel.

ঘাত *n.* a stroke, a blow; a beating; a wound, a sore, an ulcer; malice; slaughter; killing; murder; (math.) a power. ~ক *n.* a slayer, a killer; a murderer; an executioner. ~চিহ্ন *n.* (math.) an index. ~ন *n.* act of causing to kill or murder or beat; an implement for beating or killing with; a weapon; slaughter; murder; sacrificial slaughter; immolation; a stroke, a blow. □ *a.* one who or that which slays or murders, slaying or murdering. ~-প্রতিঘাত *n.* action and reaction; striking and restriking, blows and counterblows. ~বল *n.* (sc.) impulsive force. ~শ্রেণি *n.* (sc.) power series. ~সহ *a.* capable of bearing strokes and strains; malleable. ~স্থান *n.* a place of execution, an execution dock; a gallows-lee; a slaughter-house.

ঘাতী *a.* (used as a *sfx.*) one who or that which slays or murders (পিতৃঘাতী = patricidal, মাতৃঘাতী = matricidal, ভ্রাতৃঘাতী = fratricidal, নরঘাতী = homicidal, আত্মঘাতী = suicidal).

ঘাতুক *a.* cruel; merciless; destroying or killing. □ *n.* an executioner.

ঘাত্য *a.* fit to be killed or beaten; (math.) multipliable.

ঘানি *n.* a large block of wood used in grinding oil-seeds to express oil from them, a grinding tree (also ঘানিগাছ) ; an oil-mill (also ঘানিকল). ঘানি টানা, ঘানি ঠেলা *v.* to move or operate a grinding tree; (fig.) to do an extremely laborious and dull job, to drudge; (fig.) to serve a term of rigorous imprisonment, to serve time. ঘানিতে জোড়া, ঘানিতে জোতা *v.* to yoke to a grinding tree; (fig.) to put to drudgery. ঘানিতে পড়া *v.* to be yoked to a grinding tree; (fig.) to be put to drudgery.

ঘাপটি *n.* a lying in wait, an ambush, an ambuscade; feigned sleep. ঘাপটি মারা,

ঘাপটি মেরে থাকা *v.* to lie in wait, to ambush, to ambuscade; to feign sleep.

ঘাবড়ানো *v.* to lose or cause to lose one's balance, to upset mentally; to get nervous; to be or to cause to be panicky, to be afraid or to frighten; to be taken aback or cause to be taken aback. **ঘাবড়ানি** *n.* panic; fright; state of being taken aback.

ঘাম *n.* sweat, perspiration. **ঘাম দিয়ে জ্বর ছাড়া** (lit.) to perspire on the eve of being relieved of fever; (fig.) to be relieved of anxiety or danger. **মাথার ঘাম পায়ে ফেলে** with the sweat of one's brow.

ঘামা *v.* to sweat, to perspire.

ঘামাচি *n.* prickly-heat.

ঘামানো *v.* to cause to perspire. **মাথা ঘামানো** *v.* to think hard on a difficult problem, to strain one's brains, to cudgel one's brains.

ঘায়েল *a.* wounded; killed; defeated. **ঘায়েল করা** *v.* to wound; to overpower; to kill; to defeat.

ঘাস *n.* grass. **ঘাস কাটা** *v.* to mow grass; (dero.) to do practically little or no work; to work to no purpose. **ঘাস-কাটা কল** a mowing machine, a grass-cutter.

ঘাসি *a.* relating to grass, like grass, grassy. ☐ *n.* a dealer in grass; one who cuts grass, a grass-cutter. **ঘাসি-নৌকো** a long and narrow boat for carrying chiefly grass, hay etc. and also goods and passengers.

ঘাসুড়িয়া falsely elegant form of **ঘেসেড়া**।

ঘাসুয়া falsely elegant form of **ঘেসো**।

ঘি *n.* clarified butter (of cow's or buffalo's milk), ghee. **ঘিয়ে ভাজা** *a.* fried in ghee; (joc.) very weak, sickly and emaciated (ঘিয়ে ভাজা কুকুর). **মাথার ঘি** the soft or grey matter within the skull, brains.

ঘিচিঘিচি *a.* closely placed in an inelegant or indecent manner.

ঘিঞ্জি *a.* dense; very closely placed; stuffy; narrow; thickly populated; overcrowded, congested.

ঘিনঘিন *int.* expressing a feeling of loathing or detestation. **ঘিনঘিন করা** *v.* to be stricken with a feeling of loathing or detestation. **ঘিনঘিনে** *a.* that which creates a feeling of detestation.

ঘিরা, ঘেরা *v.* to enclose; to shut in; to surround; to overcast or pervade ('আকাশ ঘিরে মেঘ জমেছে') ; to besiege. ☐ *n.* an enclosed place or an enclosing device, an enclosure. ☐ *a.* enclosed; shut in; surrounded; besieged. **ঘিরে ফেলা** *v.* to encircle; to besiege.

ঘিলু *n.* the soft or grey matter within the skull, brains; (fig.) intelligence.

ঘুংড়িকাশি *n.* hooping-cough, whooping-cough.

ঘুঁজি *n.* a narrow lane or place or corner; a dirty place or corner (গলিঘুঁজি).

ঘুঁটা, ঘোঁটা *v.* to stir with a pestle in a mortar; to beat up; to agitate; to search or traverse thoroughly, to rifle, to ransack. ☐ *a.* stirred with a pestle in a mortar; beaten up; agitated; thoroughly searched or traversed, rifled, ransacked. **ঘুঁটানো, ঘোঁটানো** *v.* to cause to stir with a pestle in a mortar; to cause to beat up; to cause to agitate; to cause to search or traverse or be searched or be traversed thoroughly, to cause to rifle or ransack or be rifled or be ransacked.

ঘুঁটি *n.* a piece or pawn in chess and similar other games. **ঘুঁটি চালা** *v.* to move a piece or pawn.

ঘুঁটে *n.* a cake of dried dung used as fuel, a dungcake.

ঘুঁটেকুড়ানি, ঘুঁটেকুড়ুনি *n.* (lit.) a woman engaged in collecting dungcakes; (fig.) a poor and humble woman.

ঘুগনি, ঘুগনিদানা *n.* a kind of food prepared with pigeon-peas, potato, coconut-kernel, spices etc. all boiled together.

ঘুঘু *n.* the dove; (fig.) a sly and wily person (লোকটি একটি ঘুঘু) ; (fig.) a wily and harmful person (বাস্তু ঘুঘু) ; (fig.) a veteran (জেলঘুঘু). **ঘুঘুর বাসা** a dovecot(e); a dove's nest; (fig.) a nasty or dirty place (তার মাথাটা ঘুঘুর বাসা) ; a den. **ঘুঘু দেখেছ, ফাঁদ দেখনি** (fig.) you are after the honeycomb but have forgotten the bees. **(কারও) ভিটায় ঘুঘু চরানো** to raze someone's homestead to the ground;

(fig.) render a person homeless or to ruin him utterly.

ঘুঙুর *n.* a string of bells worn at the ankle.

ঘুচা, ঘোচা *v.* to be destroyed or lost; to cease to exist (শান্তি ঘোচা, আরাম ঘুচে যাওয়া) ; to pass, to elapse, to come to an end (সুখের দিন ঘোচা) ; to be removed or dispelled, to lift (আঁধার ঘোচা). **ঘুচানো** *v.* to destroy or cause to pass or elapse; to remove or dispel; to cause to remove or dispel.

ঘুটঘুট *int.* expressing deep blackness or darkness. **ঘুটঘুট করা** *v.* to be darkening deep. **ঘুটঘুটে** *a.* deep; deeply darkening.

ঘুটিং *n.* calcined lime.

ঘুড়ি[১] *n.* a paper-kite or a cloth-kite, a kite.

ঘুড়ি[২] *n.* the mare.

ঘুড্ডি dial. var. of **ঘুড়ি।**

ঘুণ *n.* a kind of wood-mite or wood-worm, termite. □ *a.* expert or well-experienced; engaged steadfastly (ঘুণ হয়ে আমার পিছনে লেগেছে). **~-ধরা** *a.* affected with wood-mite; (fig.) in the process of decaying; worn out. **ঘুণ ধরা** *v.* to be affected with wood-mite. **ঘুণে ধরা** *v.* to be affected with wood-mite; to decay. **ঘুণাক্ষর** *n.* a small mark on timber made by wood-mite; (fig.) a slight hint. **ঘুণাক্ষরে** *adv.* even slightly, to the slightest extent.

ঘুন্টি *n.* a button usu. made of cloth; a very small bell.

ঘুনশি *n.* a coloured thread worn round the waist (cp. a girdle).

ঘুনি *n.* a kind of box-like wickertrap used in catching fish.

ঘুপচি var. of **ঘুপসি।**

ঘুপটি var. of **ঘাপটি।**

ঘুপসি *a.* dark and narrow; crouching (ঘুপসি মেরে থাকা). □ *n.* a dark and narrow place.

ঘুম *n.* sleep, slumber. **ঘুম চটে যাওয়া** *v.* to have one's sleep spoiled. **ঘুম দেওয়া, ঘুম লাগানো** *v.* to go to sleep, to sleep. **ঘুম পাড়ানো** *v.* to lull to sleep. **ঘুম ভাঙা** *v.* to wake up, to awake. **ঘুম ভাঙানো** *v.* to rouse from sleep. **কাঁচা ঘুম** incomplete sleep. **~কাতুরে** *a.* prone to sleeping overmuch; sleepy; drowsy. **~ঘোর** *n.* sound sleep; drowsiness. **ঘুমানো** *v.* to sleep. □ *a.* sleeping. **ঘুমন্ত** *a.* sleeping, asleep. **~পাড়ানি** *a.* soporific; lulling. **~পাড়ানি গান** a lullaby.

ঘুর *n.* an instance or act of revolving or reeling; reeling sensation (ঘুর লাগা). □ *a.* winding, sinuous, circuitous; roundabout, devious (ঘুরপথ) ; deep (**ঘুরঘুট্টি** = deep dark). **~পথ** *n.* a roundabout route. **~পাক** *n.* whirling, revolving, circular motion. **ঘুরপাক খাওয়া, ঘুরপাক দেওয়া** *v.* to revolve or reel, to turn about; to wander about aimlessly. **~প্যাঁচ, ঘোরপ্যাঁচ** *n.* intricacy, complication; crookedness, angularity (মনের ঘোরপ্যাঁচ).

ঘুরঘুর[১] *int.* expressing (continuous) prying movement or act of prying (continuously). **ঘুরঘুর করা** *v.* to snoop about, to move about constantly trying to get at or pry into something.

ঘুরঘুর[২], **ঘুরঘুরিয়া, ঘুরঘুরে** *n.* a kind of noisy beetle belonging to the family of Cystocirca Gregaria.

ঘুরা, ঘোরা *v.* to turn about, to revolve, to spin round; to reel; to ramble, to travel; to grope. □ *a.* roundabout; circuitous, indirect (ঘোরাপথ). **~ঘুরি** *n.* continuous rambling or travelling; frequentation, continuous coming and going. **ঘোরাঘুরি করা** *v.* to ramble or travel continuously; to frequent. **ঘুরানো** *v.* to cause to turn about, to revolve, to spin; to cause to reel, to reel; to cause to ramble or travel unnecessarily; to harass. □ *a.* revolving; roundabout, circuitous, indirect.

ঘুরুনি same as **ঘুর** (*n.*).

ঘুলঘুলি *n.* a bay-window.

ঘুলানো var. of **ঘোলানো** (see **ঘোলা**).

ঘুষ, ঘুস *n.* a bribe, illegal gratification. **ঘুষ খাওয়া, ঘুষ নেওয়া** *v.* to take or accept a bribe. **ঘুষ দেওয়া, ঘুস দেওয়া** *v.* to bribe, to grease one's palm.

ঘুষখোর, ঘুসখোর *n.* one who is given to taking bribes.

ঘুসঘুস *int.* expressing secrecy or whispering. **ঘুসঘুস করা** *v.* to move stealthily; to whisper. **ঘুসঘুসে** *a.* secret (ঘুসঘুসে ব্যাপার) ; whispering (ঘুসঘুসে আলোচনা) ; low (ঘুসঘুসে জ্বর) ; suppressed (ঘুসঘুসে ব্যথা).

ঘুষা[1], ঘুসা[1], ঘুসি[1], ঘুসো[1] *n.* the smallest variety of the shrimp (also **ঘুষো-চিংড়ি, ঘুসো-চিংড়ি**).

ঘুষা[2], ঘুষি, ঘুসা[2], ঘুসি[2], (coll.) **ঘুষো,** (coll.) **ঘুসো[2]** *n.* a fisticuff, a box, a buffet, a blow. **ঘুসি খাওয়া** *v.* to be boxed or fisticuffed. **ঘুসি মারা** *v.* to box, to fisticuff, to buffet. **ঘুসি লড়া** *v.* to engage in boxing; to take part in a boxing contest. **ঘুসাঘুসি,** (coll.) **ঘুসোঘুসি** *n.* boxing or fisticuffing each other, blows and counterblows.

ঘুসকি, ঘুস্কি *n. fem.* a prostitute without a licence; a demirep.

ঘুৎকার *n.* the note of the owl, hoot.

ঘূর্ণ *n.* a circular movement; a turning about; whirling, revolution, spinning, reeling. □ *a.* circling, turning about, whirling, spinning, reeling. **~ন** *n.* act of circling or revolving or whirling or reeling continuously. **~বাত, ~বায়ু** *n.* a cyclone, a whirlwind. **~মান** *a.* that which is revolving or reeling.

ঘূর্ণাবর্ত *n.* a whirlpool, an eddy.

ঘূর্ণায়মান *a.* that which is revolving or reeling or rolling; that which is being revolved; that which reels or rolls; engaged in travelling.

ঘূর্ণি *n.* an instance or act of circling or turning about or revolving or reeling or rolling; a whirlpool, an eddy; a cyclone. **~জল** *n.* a whirlpool, an eddy. **~ঝড়** *n.* cyclone, hurricane, tornado. **~বৃষ্টি** *n.* rain accompanied by cyclone. **~ত** *a.* that which is being turned about or revolved or reeled or rolled; turned about, revolved, reeled, rolled. **ঘূর্ণিতনয়ন** *n.* rolling eyes (indicating anger). **~মস্তক** *n.* giddiness; vertigo; confusion, perplexity. **~পাক** *n.* a turning about, revolution; a whirlpool, an eddy. **~বাত, ~বাত্যা, ~বায়ু** *n.* a cyclone, a whirlwind. **~রোগ** *n.* giddiness, vertigo.

ঘূর্ণ্যমান *a.* that which is being turned about or revolved or rolled.

ঘৃণা *n.* hate, hatred; aversion, abhorrence, detestation; dislike; contempt, scorn, repugnance; feeling of shame, self-mortification (এত তিরস্কারেও তার ঘৃণা হয় না). **ঘৃণা করা** *v.* to hate; to abhor, to detest; to dislike; to despise, to scorn, to look down upon. **ঘৃণা হওয়া** *v.* to have a feeling of hate or abhorrence or dislike or repugnance or scorn; to feel shame, to be mortified. **ঘৃণার্হ, ঘৃণাস্পদ** *a.* hateful, detestable; contemptible, despicable; base, low.

ঘৃণিত *a.* hated or hateful; abhorred, detested or detestable; disliked; contemptible, despicable; base, low. **ঘৃণিত জীবন** wretched or repulsively filthy or squalid life.

ঘৃণী *a.* one who hates or abhors or detests or dislikes or despises or scorns or looks down upon; (rare) one who takes pity, kind.

ঘৃণ্য same as **ঘৃণার্হ** (see **ঘৃণা**).

ঘৃত *n.* clarified butter (of cow's or buffalo's milk), ghee. **~কুমারী** *n.* the aloe. **~পক্ব** *a.* cooked with butter or ghee. **ঘৃতাক্ত** *a.* smeared with ghee. **ঘৃতান্ন** *n.* rice boiled in clarified butter, pilau. **ঘৃতার্চি** *n.* fire. **ঘৃতাহুতি** *n.* pouring of ghee in the sacrificial fire, burnt offering of ghee. **অগ্নিতে ঘৃতাহুতি দেওয়া** (fig.) to add fuel to the fire or the flames.

ঘৃষ্ট *a.* pounded; trampled on, treaded on; grazed, rubbed; scoured; caused by rubbing or grazing or scouring; (gr.) affricate.

ঘেউ, ঘেউ ঘেউ *int.* expressing a barking noise. □ *n.* the bark of a dog. **ঘেউ ঘেউ করা** *v.* to bark.

ঘেঁচড়া *n.* callosity of skin caused by frequent rubbing (ঘেঁচড়া পড়া). □ *a.* affected with callosity; disobedient and obstinate (ঘেঁচড়া ছেলে) ; unfeeling, hardened, callous (মারঘেঁচড়া).

ঘেঁচু *n.* a small and wild esculent root (কচুঘেঁচু) ; (coll.) nothing, figs (ঘেঁচু করবে).

ঘেঁষ[1] *n.* touch, contact (ঘেঁষে থাকা) ; indulgence or liberty (ঘেঁষ দেওয়া). □ *a.* touching, close (ঘেঁষ হয়ে বসা).

ঘেঁষ², **ঘেঁস** *n.* the dust of coal; dust of broken brick or stone; coal ash.

ঘেঁষা *n.* to stay touching; to come in contact with; to draw close (to); to approach. **ঘেঁষাঘেঁষি** *adv.* closely; crowdingly. □ *n.* closeness or crowding state (ঘেঁষাঘেঁষির জন্য অসুবিধা).

ঘেঁস see **ঘেঁষ**।

ঘেঙানো *v.* to whine, to whimper. **ঘেঙানি** *n.* whining; a whine, a whimper.

ঘেটেল *n.* a ferryman.

ঘেনঘেন rej. spell. of **ঘ্যানঘ্যান**।

ঘেন্না coll. form of **ঘৃণা**।

ঘেমো *a.* sweaty (ঘেমো গা, ঘোমো জামা).

ঘেয়ো *a.* having an ulcer or sore or wound, ulcerous; ulcerated; (of a dog) mangy (ঘেয়ো কুকুর).

ঘের *n.* perimeter, circumference; girth (শায়ার ঘের) ; an enclosing frame or an enclosed place, an enclosure. **ঘের দেওয়া** *v.* to enclose.

ঘেরা pop. var. of **ঘিরা**।

ঘেরাও *n.* act of enclosing or shutting in or surrounding; gherao, encircling employers or authorities to coerce them to accept demands; besiegement. □ *a.* enclosed; shut in; surrounded; gheraoed; besieged.

ঘেরাটোপ same as **ঘটাটোপ**।

ঘেরানো pop. var. of **ঘিরানো**।

ঘেসেড়া, (dial.) **ঘেসুড়ে** *n.* one who deals in or cuts grass professionally, a grass-cutter. *fem.* **ঘেসেড়ানি**।

ঘেসো *a.* full of grass, grass-grown (ঘেসোজমি = a grass-plot); grass-like, grassy (ঘেসো গন্ধ) ; having a disagreeable smell, bad-smelling; made of grass (ঘেসো কাগজ).

ঘোঁজ *n.* a curve; a bend or bent, a turn; a bend of a furrow-line or of the side of a field; a nook; a corner. **ঘোঁজ-ঘাঁজ** *n.* nook and corner; (fig.) secret wiles, trick or device (esp. to deceive).

ঘোঁট *n.* a conference (esp. of conspirators); gossip; a rumour; a faction; an idle crowd. **ঘোঁট করা, ঘোঁট পাকানো** *v.* to hatch a conspiracy; (dero.) to engage in conference, to spread a malicious rumour; to form a faction; to form an idle crowd.

ঘোঁটন *n.* act of stirring with a pestle in a mortar; act of beating up; act of agitating, agitation; act of searching or travelling thoroughly, act of rifling or ransacking. **ঘোঁটনা** *n.* a pestle.

ঘোঁটা, ঘোঁটানো pop. variants of **ঘুঁটা** and **ঘুঁটানো** respectively.

ঘোঁতঘোঁত *int.* expressing : the grunting of the boar; angry grumbling. **ঘোঁতঘোঁত করা** *v.* to grunt; to grumble angrily. **ঘোঁতঘোঁতানি** *n.* the grunting of the boar; angry grumbling.

ঘোগ *n.* a kind of beast having resemblance to the wolf and the dog, the tigerwolf; the wild dog, the hyena-dog.

ঘোঙ্গট *n.* (obs. & poet.) a veil.

ঘোচা, ঘোচানো pop. variants of **ঘুচা** and **ঘুচানো** respectively.

ঘোটক *n.* the male horse, the stallion; the horse. *fem.* **ঘোটকী** the mare. **ঘোটকারূঢ়** *a.* mounted or seated on a horse.

ঘোটন, ঘোটনা, ঘোটা alt. spellings of **ঘোঁটন, ঘোঁটনা** and **ঘোঁটা** respectively.

ঘোড়তোলা var. of **গোড়তোলা**।

ঘোড়দৌড় *n.* a horse-race; (fig.) fatiguing harassment or running about. **ঘোড়দৌড় করা** *v.* (fig.) to run about out of breath. **ঘোড়দৌড় করানো** *v.* (fig.) to fatigue with harassment; (fig.) to cause to run about out of breath. **ঘোড়দৌড়ের মাঠ** a race-course.

ঘোড়শাল same as **ঘোড়াশাল** see **ঘোড়া**।

ঘোড়সওয়ার *n.* a horseman; a horse-soldier, a cavalryman.

ঘোড়া¹ *n.* the horse; (in chess) a knight. **ঘোড়া জোতা** *v.* to yoke a horse, to fasten a horse to a cart, plough etc. **ঘোড়া ডিঙিয়ে ঘাস খাওয়া** (fig.) to ignore or bypass the proper channel. **ঘোড়া দেখে খোঁড়া হওয়া** (fig.) to get idle when there is somebody to do a job. **ঘোড়ায় চড়া** *v.* to ride a horse. **ঘোড়ার গাড়ি** same as **ঘোড়াগাড়ি**। **ঘোড়ার ডাক¹** neigh. **ঘোড়ার ডাক²** the horse mail, the mail carried by the horse. **ঘোড়ার ডিম** (fig.) a mare's nest. **ঘোড়ার সাজ** harness. **ঘোড়ার সাজ পরানো** *v.* to harness a horse. **খেলনা ঘোড়া** *n.* a hobby-horse; a rocking horse. **গাড়ির ঘোড়া** a carriage-horse. **চড়বার ঘোড়া**

a riding horse. **ভারবাহী ঘোড়া, মাল-টানা ঘোড়া** a pack-horse, a draught-horse. **যুদ্ধের ঘোড়া** a war-horse, a charger. **~ওয়ালা** *n.* a horse-dealer. **~গাড়ি** *n.* a horse-drawn carriage, a carriage. **ঘোড়া ঘোড়া খেলা** *n.* a children's game in which one player acts as a horse whilst another as a rider (cp. horse-play). **~মুগ** *n.* an inferior kind of pigeon-pea chiefly used as food for horses, gram. **~রোগ** *n.* an extremely harmful or expensive hobby or craze. **ঘোড়ায় টানা** *a.* horse-drawn. **ঘোড়াশাল** *n.* a stable. **ভাড়াটে ঘোড়ার গাড়ি** *a.* a hackney carriage.

ঘোড়া[২] *n.* the trigger of a pistol or a revolver or a gun. **ঘোড়া টেপা** *v.* to pull the trigger.

ঘোণা *n.* the nose of the horse; (sarcas.) a human nose.

ঘোপ *n.* a small hole or pocket; a secret or invisible place. **~ঘাপ** *n.*a narrow hiding-place.

ঘোমটা *n.* a veil. **ঘোমটা খোলা** *v.* to unveil. **ঘোমটা দেওয়া** *v.* to cover with a veil, to veil. **ঘোমটার ভিতর খেমটা নাচ** (fig.) debauchery under the veil of chastity, wickedness under the veil of goodness.

ঘোর *a.* dreadful, frightful, awful (ঘোর বিপদ) ; severe (ঘোর যুদ্ধ) ; excessive, extreme, intensive (ঘোর নেশা) ; beside oneself, dead (ঘোর মাতাল) ; dense and dark (ঘোর অরণ্য) ; deep (ঘোর অন্ধকার, ঘোর লাল) ; sound (ঘোর নিদ্রা) ; dark (ঘোর সন্ধ্যা). ☐ *n.* obsession (নেশার ঘোর, সুখের ঘোর) ; illusion (চোখের ঘোর) ; darkness (সন্ধ্যার ঘোর). **ঘোর করা** *v.* to become dark, to darken. **ঘোর কাটা** *v.* to be freed from obsession or illusion. **ঘোর হওয়া** *v.* to become dark, to darken; to become deep, to deepen. **ঘোর-ঘোর** *n.* slight darkness, darkishness, duskiness; slight deepness. ☐ *a.* darkish; slightly deep. **~তর** *compar.* of **ঘোর** ৷ *a.* (pos. deg.) extremely terrible or severe. **~দর্শন** *a.* horrid-looking, having a frightful appearance, hideous looking. *fem.* **~দর্শনা** ৷ **~প্যাঁচ** *n.* intricacy or complication; crookedness; angularity. **ঘোরে** *adv.* under the influence or spell of.

ঘোরা[১] *fem.* of **ঘোর** ৷

ঘোরা[২], ঘোরাঘুরি, ঘোরানো pop. variants of **ঘুরা, ঘুরাঘুরি** and **ঘুরানো** respectively.

ঘোরাকৃতি *a.* having a frightful or terrible appearance.

ঘোরাফেরা *n.* walking or wandering or sauntering here and there.

ঘোরালো *a.* extremely dark, deep dark (ঘোরালো রাত্রি) ; deep (ঘোরালো রং) ; grave or glum (ঘোরালো মুখ) ; terrible (ঘোরালো বিপদ) ; very complicated or intricate (ঘোরালো ব্যাপার).

ঘোল *n.* whey, buttermilk. **ঘোল করা** *v.* to make whey. **ঘোল খাওয়া** *v.* (fig.) to be put out of countenance, to be put to shame, to be bewildered or harassed. **ঘোল খাওয়ানো** *v.* (fig.) to bewilder or harass. **ঘোল মওয়া** *v.* to churn butter. **মাথায় ঘোল ঢালা** to pour whey on one's shaven head (as a mark of public disgrace); (fig.) to disgrace publicly. **ঘোল-মউনি** *n.* a churning-stick. **ঘোলের শরবত** a beverage or drink prepared with whey.

ঘোলা *a.* turbid, muddy (ঘোলা জল) ; opaque, dull (ঘোলা চোখ) ; dim, hazy (ঘোলা দৃষ্টি). **~টে** *a.* slightly turbid or muddy; slightly opaque or dull; slightly dim or hazy. **~নো** *v.* to make turbid or dull esp. by beating up or stirring; to make or become opaque or dull or dim or hazy; (fig.) to complicate matters, to rake up old quarrels.

ঘোষ *n.* a grave sound; a sound, a noise, a note; an announcement, a loud declaration, a proclamation; a milkman by profession or caste (ঘোষপাড়া) ; a milkman's hamlet (ঘোষযাত্রা). ☐ *a.* (gr.) voiced **(ঘোষধ্বনি). ~ক** *n.* an announcer, a proclaimer, a crier. **~ণ, ~ণা** *n.* announcement, proclamation. **ঘোষণাপত্র** *n.* a written announcement or proclamation, a bulletin, a notice. **ঘোষণীয়** *a.* that which can be or to be announced or proclaimed. **~পল্লি, ~পাড়া** *n.* a milkman's hamlet. **~বর্ণ** *n.* (gr.) a voiced consonant. **~যাত্রা** *n.* a visit in state by a prince to a hamlet of milkmen where his cattle are kept.

ঘোষা *v*. to announce, to proclaim; to recite or recapitulate aloud (নামতা ঘোষা).

ঘোষিত *a*. announced, proclaimed, declared.

ঘ্যাঁচ *int*. expressing : the sound of chopping or cutting a soft object with a sharp weapon. **ঘ্যাঁচঘ্যাঁচ** *int*. repeated sound of chopping or cutting with a sharp weapon.

ঘ্যাঁট *n*. a mixed dish of vegetables.

ঘ্যাগ *n*. goitre.

ঘ্যানঘ্যান expressing : whining; importunate solicitation. □ *n*. whining, whimpering; whimper. **ঘ্যানঘ্যান করা** *v*. to whine or whimper, to solicit importunately. **ঘ্যানরঘ্যানর** same as **ঘ্যানঘ্যান**। **ঘ্যানঘ্যানানি** same as **ঘ্যানঘ্যান**।

ঘ্রাণ *n*. smell, scent, odour; act of smelling; power of smelling (also **ঘ্রাণশক্তি**) ; the olfactory organ, the nose (also **ঘ্রাণেন্দ্রিয়**). **ঘ্রাণ নেওয়া** *v*. to smell. **ঘ্রাণ পাওয়া** *v*. to get the smell or scent (of).

ঘ্রাত *a*. smelled; sniffed.

ঘ্রাতব্য *a*. worthy of being smelled; that which is to be smelled.

ঘ্রাতা *n*. a smeller.

ঘ্রেয় same as **ঘ্রাতব্য**।

ঙ

ঙ *n*. the fifth consonant of the Bengali alphabet.

চ *n.* the sixth consonant of the Bengali alphabet.

চই *n.* a creeper or its pungent root.

চওড়া *a.* broad, wide. ☐ *n.* breadth, width (চওড়ায় দু-মিটার). **চওড়াই** *n.* measure of breadth or width, breadth or width. **চওড়া বুক** a large or wide chest; (fig.) a courageous or generous or liberal heart.

চক[1] *n.* chalk.

চক[2] *n.* a square or rectangle; a square or rectangular piece of land; a piece of open land (usu. square or rectangular) in the centre of a city or village (মোল্লার চক); a series of buildings round a square or rectangular courtyard (চক-মিলানো বাড়ি); a square-shaped or rectangular market-place; a taluk or tahsil. **~বন্দি** *n.* settlement of boundaries of a plot or agricultural land or village; a parcel of ground or agricultural land, a lot. **~বন্দ** *a.* (of agricultural land or village) that of which boundaries have been settled; settled; settling boundaries of such land; (of buildings) built around a square or rectangular courtyard. **~-মিলানো** *a.* (of buildings) built around a square or rectangular courtyard.

চকচক[1] *int.* expressing : brightness or glaze or shine. **চকচক করা, চকচকানো** *v.* to glaze or glitter, to shine, to glisten. **চকচকানি** *n.* brightness, glitter. **চকচকে** *a.* bright, glittering, shining, glistening.

চকচক[2] *int.* expressing the noise of licking liquids like water, milk etc.

চকমক milder var. of **ঝকমক**।

চকমকি *n.* flint. **চকমকি-বাক্স** *n.* a tinder-box. **চকমকি-পাথর** *n.* flint-stone, flint.

চকা *n.* the curlew or heron.

চকি *fem.* of **চকা**।

চকিত *a.* startled, started up; taken aback; timid (চকিত চাহনি). ☐ *n.* a moment, an instant (চকিতের মধ্যে). **চকিতে** *adv.* in an instant or moment, in a trice, in a jiffy.

চকিতনয়ন *a.* timid-eyed, timorous or bewildered looking, looking startled, awe-struck or panicky. ☐ *n.* timid eye, timorous or frightened look. *fem. a.* **চকিতনয়না**। **চকিত নয়নে** *adv.* with a startled and timid eye, with a startled and timorous look.

চকী alt. spell. of **চকি**।

চকোর *n.* a kind of bird said to enjoy drinking moonbeam, the red-legged or Himalayan partridge or curlew or bartavelle, Caccabis chucar. *fem.* **চকোরী**।

চক্কর *n.* a wheel; (a spell of) rotation or revolution; anything circular or wheel-shaped, a circle (ঘোড়দৌড়ের চক্কর); a round or circular mark (as on the hood of a snake); the hood of a snake (কুলোপানা চক্কর); a course or a spell of rambling or walking, going round (সে পার্কে চক্কর দিচ্ছে); circling (বিমানখানি অবতরণক্ষেত্রের উপর চক্কর দিচ্ছে = the aircraft is circling over the landing field); (in games and tournaments) a round, a stage; (in polo) a chukker; reeling (মাথা চক্কর দেওয়া). **বিষ নেই তার কুলোপানা চক্কর** (fig.) futile rage of an impotent person.

চক্র *n.* a wheel; a ring; a wheel-shaped or circular thing or course (কুম্ভকারের চক্র); anything rotating like a wheel (কালচক্র); an ancient wheel-shaped missile or discus (সুদর্শন চক্র); a wheel-shaped battle-order (চক্রব্যূহ); (astr. & astrol.) the zodiac; a halo; a collection or block of neighbouring villages; an extensive state or kingdom or land (চক্রবর্তী); a circular mark (as on the hood of a snake); the hood of a snake; a conspiracy, an intrigue (দশচক্র); a cycle, a group, a faction, an association. **~গতি** *n.* circular motion, rotation, revolution. **~চর** *a.* vagrant. **~ধর** *n.* an appellation of God Vishnu (বিষ্ণু) or a king or a snake. **~ধারী** same as **চক্রপাণি**। **~নাভি** *n.* the hub of a wheel. **~নায়ক** *n.* leader of a group of men; commander of an army. ~নেমি *a.* the rim of a wheel. ~পাণি *n.* an appellation of Vishnu (বিষ্ণু) or Krishna (কৃষ্ণ). ~বৎ *a.* wheel-like, circular. □ *adv.* like a wheel; in a circular motion. ~বর্তী *n.* the ruler of an extensive kingdom; an emperor; a sovereign ruler. ~বাক *n.* the curlew or partridge or heron. *fem.* ~বাকী। ~বাত *n.* a cyclone. ~বাল *n.* the horizon. ~বৃদ্ধি *n.* (arith.) compound interest. ~ব্যূহ *n.* a wheel-shaped battle-order. ~যান *n.* a wheeled vehicle. চক্ররেল *n.* a circular railway. দশচক্রে ভগবান ভূত (fig.) a brute majority may guillotine even God.

চক্রাকার, চক্রাকৃতি *a.* wheel-shaped; circular, annular, round; (bot.) rotate, discoid.

চক্রান্ত *n.* a conspiracy, an intrigue, a plot; an evil design. **চক্রান্ত করা** *v.* to conspire, to intrigue, to plot (against.) ~কারী *a.* conspiring, intriguing. □ *n.* a conspirator, an intriguer, a plotter.

চক্রাবর্ত *n.* rotation; rotatory motion.

চক্রায়ুধ *n.* same as **চক্রপাণি** (see **চক্র**).

চক্রিকা *n.* the knee-pan, the patella; the knee.

চক্রী *a.* armed with a wheel-shaped missile; conspiring, intriguing; crooked; deceitful. □ *n.* an appellation of Vishnu (বিষ্ণু) ; the snake.

চক্ষু *n.* (for.) the eye; sight (তার চক্ষু খারাপ) ; a look or glance; attention (এদিকে তার চক্ষু নেই) ; covetous look or glance (আমার খাবারের দিকে চক্ষু দিয়ো না) ; a part of some plants and fruits out of which a new plant grows, a leaf bud (আনারসের চক্ষু). **চক্ষু ওঠা** *v.* to be affected with conjunctivitis or ophthalmia. **চক্ষুকর্ণের বিবাদ ভঞ্জন করা** *v.* to be freed from doubt about what has been heard by visualizing or witnessing it. **চক্ষু কাটানো** *v.* to undergo ophthalmic surgery or an eye operation. **চক্ষু খুলে দেওয়া** *v.* (fig.) to open one's eyes, to make wise; (fig.) to disillusion. **চক্ষু খুলে যাওয়া** *v.* (fig.) to have one's eyes opened, to be made wise; (fig.) to be disillusioned. **চক্ষু টেপা** *v.* to wink. **চক্ষু ছলছল করা** *v.* to have tears gathering in one's eyes; to be about to shed tears; to be tearful. **চক্ষু দেওয়া** *v.* to cast an evil eye (at); to cast a greedy glance (at); to envy; to have attention or care (for), to attend (to); to keep an eye on, to be watchful about; to look (at). ~পীড়া *n.* eye-disease; inflammation of the eye. **চক্ষু ফোটা** same as **চক্ষু খুলে যাওয়া**। **চক্ষু ফোটানো** same as **চক্ষু খুলে দেওয়া**। **চক্ষু বোজা, চক্ষু মোদা** *v.* to shut one's eyes. **চক্ষু রাখা** *v.* (fig.) to keep an eye on, to be watchful about, to be vigilant. **চক্ষু লাগা** *v.* to be subject to another's evil look, to be envied. **চক্ষুর পলক** a wink. **চক্ষুর পাতা** the eyelid. **চক্ষুর লোম** the eyelash. ~কোটর *n.* the socket of the eye. ~গোচর *a.* lying or coming within the range of sight, perceptible by the eye, visible. **চক্ষু-চিকিৎসক** *n.* an eye-specialist or an ophthalmologist. **চক্ষু-চিকিৎসা** *n.* treatment of the eye. ~তারকা, ~তারা *n.* the pupil of the eye. ~দান pop. var. of **চক্ষুর্দান**। ~পীড়া *n.* eye-disease. ~রুন্মীলন *n.* act of opening the eyes; (fig.) getting or making wise; (fig.) disillusioment. **চক্ষুরুন্মীলন করা** *v.* to open one's eyes. (fig.) to make wise; (fig.) to disillusion. **চক্ষুরুন্মীলন হওয়া** *v.* to have one's eyes opened; (fig.) to become wise; (fig.) to be disillusioned. ~রোগ *n.* eye-disease. ~র্দান *n.* act of investing with sight; donation of one's eye (usu. to an eye-bank for the benefit of a sightless person); the ceremony of investing an idol with sight; the act of investing an ignorant person with wisdom; (sarcas.) stealing, filching. **চক্ষুর্দান করা** *v.* (sarcas.) to have an eye or cast a glance with a view to stealing, to steal; to filch. ~লজ্জা *n.* a feeling of delicacy in doing openly something undesirable or unseemly. ~শূল *n.* an eyesore. ~শ্রবা *n.* a snake (from the belief that it perceives sounds etc. with its eyes). ~ষ্মত্তা *n.* possession of sight; possession of insight; power of perceiving truth. ~ষ্মান *a.* possessing sight; possessing insight; capable of perceiving truth.

fem. ~ষ্মতী। ~স্থির *a.* state of being dazed or bewildered or astounded. **চক্ষুস্থির হওয়া** *v.* to be dazed or bewildered or astounded. **লোকচক্ষে** in the eyes of the public.

চঙ্ক্রমণ *n.* repeated or continuous rambling or walking, perambulation.

চচ্চড় var. of **চড়চড়**।

চচ্চড়ি *n.* a dry dish of spiced vegetables cooked in oil and often with fish-bones.

চঞ্চরীক *n.* a repeated or continuous walker or rambler; perambulator; the bee. *fem.* **চঞ্চরীকা, চঞ্চরী**।

চঞ্চল *a.* moving, mobile; moving briskly, brisk; restless; trembling; oscillating, throbbing; throbbing fast (নাড়ি বা হৃদয় চঞ্চল হওয়া) ; agitated, wavering, vacillating; fickle (চঞ্চলমতি) ; perturbed; anxious. **চঞ্চলা** *a. fem.* of **চঞ্চল**। *n.* an appellation of goddess Lakshmi (লক্ষ্মী) or lightning. **চঞ্চল করা** *v.* to agitate; to cause to waver or vacillate; to perturb; to affect with anxiety. **চঞ্চল হওয়া** *v.* to throb fast; to be restless or agitated; to waver or vacillate; to become perturbed or anxious. ~**চিত্ত** *a.* with a restless mind; affected with anxiety; agitated; fickle-minded. ~**তা** *n.* mobility; brisk movement;briskness; restlessness; throbbing; quick throbbing; agitation; wavering, vacillation; fickleness; perturbation; anxiety. **চঞ্চলিত** *a.* caused to move; caused to move briskly; made restless; caused to tremble or oscillate or throb; caused to throb fast; agitated; caused to waver or vacillate; perturbed; stricken with anxiety. **চঞ্চলিয়া** *a.* (obs. & poet.) restless. ☐ *n.* a restless person or creature or thing ('যত চপলতা করে চঞ্চলিয়া'). ☐ *v. inf.* being restless.

চঞ্চা *n.* a bamboo or wicker mat; a rattan stool; a scarecrow.

চঞ্চু *n.* a beak or bill (of a bird). ~**পুট** *n.* the cavity formed within the beaks when shut.

চট[1] *int.* expressing quickness, promptness (চট করে নিয়ে এসো). **চট করে** *adv.* promptly, quickly.

চট[2] *n.* a coarse cloth made of jute, gunny, sackcloth, hessian; (loos.) jute (চটকল). **চটের থলি** a gunny-bag.

চটক[1] *n.* the sparrow.

চটক[2] *n.* fascinating or spectacular show (বিজ্ঞাপনের চটক) ; glamour (রূপের চটক) ; attractiveness (রঙের চটক). ~**দার** *a.* having a fascinating show; gaudy; apparently or falsely fascinating; showy; glamorous; attractive or spectacular.

চটকা[1] *n. fem.* the hen-sparrow (see **চটক**[1]).

চটকা[2] *n.* drowsiness; mental abstraction, reverie. **চটকা ভাঙা** *v.* to shake off drowsiness suddenly; to have one's light sleep or drowsiness disturbed suddenly; to awake suddenly; to shake off one's reverie suddenly; to be suddenly disturbed in one's reverie; to come to one's senses suddenly.

চটকানো *v.* to knead; to handle roughly; (sl.) to manhandle; to fondle vigorously. ☐ *a.* kneaded; roughly handled; (sl.) manhandled; vigorously fondled. **চটকানি** *n.* kneading; rough handling, (sl.) manhandling; vigorous fondling.

চটচট[1] *int.* expressing the repeated noise of splitting, slapping etc. **চটচট করা** *v.* to split noisily and repeatedly.

চটচট[2] *int.* expressing adhesiveness, stickiness. **চটচট করা** *v.* to feel sticky.

চটচটে *a.* adhesive, sticky, gluey.

চটপট *adv.* quickly, promptly. **চটপটে** *a.* prompt; quick; swift.

চটা[1] *n.* a thin slip of bamboo-wood, tin etc.; a lath, a splinter.

চটা[2] *v.* to break into a chink or chinks, to crack, to split; to be broken or spoiled (ঘুম চটা, বন্ধুত্ব চটা). **চটানো** *v.* to cause to break into a chink or chinks, to crack, to split; to cause to break or be spoiled, to break or spoil.

চটা[3] *v.* to get angry; to be offended. **চটানো** *v.* to make angry; to offend.

চটাচটি *n.* a bickering; a tiff; rancour, bad blood, bitter feelings; quarrel; severance or estrangement owing to a quarrel. **চটাচটি করা** *v.* to quarrel (with); to quarrel (with) and sever (from).

চটানো see **চটা**[2] and **চটা**[3]।

চটাপট var. of **চটপট**।

চটি১ *n.* a tavern, an inn.

চটি২ *a.* thin (চটি বই).

চটি৩ *n.* a kind of slippers open at heels (also **চটিজুতো**).

চটু *n.* flattery; cajolement; adulatory words.

চটুকে *a.* showy, glamorous, apparently attractive.

চটুল *a.* moving frequently or swiftly, not calm, restless, nimble, brisk, swift-moving (চটুল চাহনি, চটুল চরণ) ; fascinating, captivating (চটুল ভঙ্গি). *fem.* **চটুলা**। **~তা** *n.* restlessness, nimbleness, briskness; (rare) fascination, grace. **~নয়না** *a.* having swift-moving eyes, possessing eyes capable of quick glances; having charming or fascinating eyes.

চড় *n.* a blow with the open palm of the hand, a cuff, a slap, a buffet. **চড় খাওয়া** *v.* to be cuffed or slapped or buffeted. **চড় দেওয়া, চড় মারা** *v.* to cuff, to slap, to buffet.

চড়ই dial. corrup. of **চড়াই**।

চড়ক *n.* the festival of worshipping God Shiva (শিব) on the last day of the Bengali year (also **চড়ক-পূজা**) ; the ceremonial swinging from a tall pole by worshippers of Shiva (শিব) on this occasion. **~গাছ** *n.* a tall pole from which a worshipper of Shiva (শিব) swings on the day of chadaka (চড়ক) festival. **চক্ষু চড়কগাছ হওয়া** to be dazed or stupefied. **চড়ক সংক্রান্তি** *n.* the last day of the Bengali year i. e. the last day of the month of Chaitra (চৈত্র).

চড়চড় *int.* expressing the onomatopoeic sound as of itching, pricking etc.; expressing the sound of splitting or cracking; the sound of extreme dryness or parchedness.

চড়চড়ি var. of **চচ্চড়ি**।

চড়তি *n.* act of mounting or ascending or riding; rise, increase (দামের চড়তি) ; boom in the market. □ *a.* soaring, rising, increasing (চড়তি দর). **চড়তি বাজার** a market in which there has been a boom; a market with soaring prices.

চড়ন *n.* act of mounting or climbing up or ascending or riding; act of boarding (a vehicle); rise, increase. **~দার** *a.* one who mounts or rides; one who boards (a vehicle). □ *n.* a climber; a rider; a passenger.

চড়বড় *int.* expressing : an onomatopoeic sound as of bursting of grains of corn when singed or fried; rapid movement or prattling. **চড়বড় করা** *v.* to make a repeated sound as of bursting of grains of corn when singed or fried, to fritter; to move or prattle rapidly. **চড়বড়ে** *a.* moving or talking rapidly.

চড়া১ *n.* a piece of land; (usu. a sandy one) rising out of the river-bed, a silted piece of land. **চড়া পড়েছে** a piece of land has risen out of the river-bed. **মগ্ন চড়া** *n.* a shoal.

চড়া২ *a.* haughty, arrogant, angry (চড়া কথা) ; severe, strong (চড়া রোদ) ; high (চড়া সুর, চড়া দাম).

চড়া৩ *v.* to climb (up), to ascend, to mount, to ride; to increase, to go up (দাম চড়া) ; to become louder (সুর চড়েছে) ; to become stronger (রোদ চড়া) ; to attack (শত্রুর উপরে চড়া) ; (of cooking utensils) to be placed on the oven (হাঁড়ি চড়া).

চড়াই১ *n.* an ascent, acclivity, upward slope; act of mounting or climbing up; upward movement; altitude. **চড়াই-উতরাই** acclivity and declivity, upward and downward movement.

চড়াই২ *n.* the sparrow.

চড়াইভাতি *n.* picnic.

চড়াও *n.* an attack, a raid, an assault. □ *a.* one who has attacked or fallen upon; attacked. **চড়াও হওয়া** *v.* to fall upon, to attack, to raid, to assault, to assail.

চড়াৎ *int.* expressing : the noise of bursting or splitting or slapping.

চড়ানো১ *v.* to cause to mount or ride or board, to mount or board; to increase (দাম চড়ানো) ; to make louder or deeper (গলা চড়ানো) ; to fix, to adjust (ধনুকে ছিলা চড়ানো, বেহালায় সুর চড়ানো) ; to place upon; to load (গাড়িতে মাল চড়ানো) ; to put on, to wear (গায়ে জামা চড়ানো) ; (of cooking utensils) to place upon the oven (ভাতের হাঁড়ি চড়ানো).

চড়ানো[২] *v.* to strike with the open palm of the hand, to slap.

চড়িভাতি dial. corrup. of **চড়াইভাতি**।

চড়ুই dial. var. of **চড়াই**[২]।

চড়ুইভাতি pop. var. of **চড়াইভাতি**।

চণক *n.* chick-pea, gram.

চণ্ড *a.* furious, tremendous, violent (চণ্ডবিক্রম) ; very angry, fierce, ferocious (চণ্ডপ্রকৃতি) ; severe, strong (চণ্ডরশ্মি). □ *n.* (myth.) the name of a furious demon.

চণ্ডা *a. fem.* of **চণ্ড.** (*a.*).

চণ্ডাল *n.* one of the lowest castes amongst Hindus (usu. entrusted with the burning of the dead or execution of criminals); a member of this caste; (fig.) a ferocious or merciless man.

চণ্ডালিকা *n.* a kind of lute; a name of Goddess Durga (দুর্গা).

চণ্ডালী, চণ্ডালিনী *fem.* of **চণ্ডাল**।

চণ্ডিকা var. of **চণ্ডী** (*n.*).

চণ্ডী *a. fem.* of **চণ্ড**। *n.* a manifestation of Goddess Durga (দুর্গা) ; the name of a Hindu scriptural book narrating the activities and glory or Chandi (চণ্ডী) ; (fig.) a furious or turbulent woman, a termagant. **~পাঠ** *n.* recital of the Chandi (চণ্ডী) a Hindu scriptural book. **~মণ্ডপ** *n.* a shrine including its raised vestibule, of Goddess Chandi (চণ্ডী). **উগ্রচণ্ডী** *n. fem.* (often *masc.*) a termagant. **মঙ্গলচণ্ডী** *n.* the benignant form of Goddess Chandi (চণ্ডী). **রণচণ্ডী** *n.* goddess Chandi (চণ্ডী) esp. when engaged in fighting demons; (fig.) a violent and bad-tempered woman, a termagant, a shrew; (fig.) an Amazon. □ *a.* termagant, shrewish; Amazonian.

চণ্ডু *n.* an intoxicating preparation from opium. **চণ্ডু খাওয়া** *v.* to smoke opium. **~খোর** *a.* & *n.* one who is addicted to smoking opium.

চতুঃ *n.* & *a.* four. **~পঞ্চাশৎ** *n.* & *a.* fifty-four. **~পঞ্চাশত্তম** *a.* fifty-fourth. *fem.* **~পঞ্চাশত্তমী**। **~পার্শ্ব** *n.* four sides; all the four sides; all sides. **~শত** *n.* & *a.* four hundred. **~শততম** *a.* four-hundredth. *fem.* **~শততমী**। **~শাল, ~শালা** *n.* a building or a group of buildings around a square courtyard. **~ষষ্টি** *n.* & *a.* sixty-four. **~ষষ্টিতম** *a.* sixty-fourth. *fem.* **~ষষ্টিতমী**। **~সপ্ততি** *n.* & *a.* seventy-four. **~সপ্ততিতম** *a.* seventy-fourth. *fem.* **~সপ্ততিতমী**। **~সীমা** *n.* perimeter; boundary. **~সীমাবচ্ছিন্ন** *a.* bounded on all sides.

চতুর *a.* intelligent; clever; dexterous, skilful, ingenious, artful; cunning, crafty, sly.

চতুরংশ *n.* four shares or parts. □ *a.* divided into four shares or parts, quadripartite. **চতুরংশিত** *a.* divided into four parts, quadripartite; (of books) quarto.

চতুরঙ্গ *a.* (of an army) comprising four parts such as elephants, cavalry, chariots and infantry; four-limbed; having all limbs; complete, thorough. □ *n.* an army complete in all the four parts such as elephants, cavalry, chariots, and infantry; a form of (Indian) music; chess.

চতুরতা *n.* intelligence; dexterity, skill, ingenuity, cleverness; astuteness; artfulness; cunning; slyness.

চতুরশীতি *n.* & *a.* eighty-four. **চতুরশীতিতম** *a.* eighty-fourth. *fem.* **চতুরশীতিতমী**।

চতুরশ্ব *n.* four horses. □ *a.* drawn by or having four horses, four-horsed.

চতুরস্র *a.* square; quadrangular; rectangular, rectilinear; level (চতুরস্র জমি). □ *n.* a square; a rectangle.

চতুরা *fem.* of **চতুর**।

চতুরানন *n.* one who has four faces; an appellation of God Brahma (ব্রহ্মা).

চতুরালি *n.* cleverness, slyness, trickiness; deception; an instance or act of cleverness or trickiness or deception.

চতুরাশ্রম *n.* the four stages of human life according to Hindus, such as the celibate student-life, the life of a householder, the life of a hermit and the life of an ascetic.

চতুর্গুণ *a.* fourfold, four times; excessive; much more (than). **চতুর্গুণ করা** *v.* to multiply by four, to quadruple. **চতুর্গুণ বাড়া** *v.* to increase fourfold; to increase many times over. **চতুর্গুণিত** *a.* multiplied by four, quadrupled.

চতুর্ঘাত *a.* & *n.* (math.) biquadratic raised to a fourth power, square of a square.

চতুর্থ *a.* fourth. **চতুর্থাংশ** *n.* one-fourth, a fourth part. **চতুর্থী** *a. fem.* of **চতুর্থ** । □ *n.* (astr.) the fourth day of a lunar fortnight, obsequial rites performed by a married daughter on the fourth day of the death of either of her parents; (gr.) the fourth case-ending.

চতুর্দশ *n.* & *a.* fourteen. □ *a.* fourteenth. **~পদী** *a.* consisting of fourteen lines. **চতুর্দশপদী কবিতা** a quatorzain; a sonnet. **চতুর্দশ পুরুষ** fourteen generations in the ascending order such as the father, the grandfather etc.; the fourteenth generation. **চতুর্দশ বিদ্যা** the four Vedas, the six Vedangas (বেদাঙ্গ), the Mimamsas (মীমাংসা), logic, history and mythologies; all these collectively. **চতুর্দশ ভুবন** the seven heavens and the seven underworlds. **চতুর্দশী** *n. fem.* the fourteenth day of a lunar fortnight; a girl of fourteen. □ *a. fem.* fourteen years old.

চতুর্দিক *n.* the four quarters of the compass, namely north, south, east and west; four sides; all the four sides; all sides or places; all affairs or things. **চতুর্দিকে** *adv.* on all sides; in all directions.

চতুর্দোল, চতুর্দোলা *n.* a kind of litter carried by four bearers.

চতুর্ধা *adv.* in four ways; on four sides; fourfold, four times; in four parts.

চতুর্নবতি *n.* & *a.* ninety-four. **~তম** *a.* ninety-fourth. *fem.* **~তমী** ।

চতুর্বক্ত্র same as **চতুর্মুখ** ।

চতুর্বর্গ *n.* Dharma, Artha, Kama & Moksha, or virtue, wealth, love and final salvation : these four goals or pursuits of human life.

চতুর্বর্ণ *n.* the brahmanas, the Kshartiyas, the Vaishyas, and the Shudras : these four castes or orders of the Hindu society.

চতুর্বিংশ *a.* twenty-four. **~তি** *n.* & *a.* twenty-four. **~তিতম** *a.* twenty-fourth. *fem.* **~তিতমী** ।

চতুর্বিধ *a.* of four sorts or kinds. *fem.* **চতুর্বিধা** ।

চতুর্বেদ *n.* the four Vedas, namely Rik, Yajus, Sama and Atharva. **চতুর্বেদী** *a.* versed in all the four Vedas.

চতুর্ভুজ *a.* having four hands or arms; (geom.) rectilineal, quadrilateral. □ *n.* an appellation of Narayana (নারায়ণ) or Vishnu (বিষ্ণু) ; (geom.) a rectilineal or quadrilateral figure.

চতুর্মাস *n.* the four monsoon months.

চতুর্মুখ *a.* having four mouths or faces, four-faced. □ *n.* an appellation of God Brahma (ব্রহ্মা).

চতুশ্চত্বারিংশ *a.* forty-four. **~ৎ** *n.* & *a.* forty-four. **~ত্তম** *a.* forty-fourth. *fem.* **~ত্তমী** ।

চতুষ্ক *n.* a square; a rectangle; a square or rectangular courtyard or portico or vestibule; a four-pillared square or rectangular courtyard or platform.

চতুষ্কোণ *a.* square; rectangular. □ *n.* a square; a rectangle.

চতুষ্টয় *a.* having four limbs or divisions; of four kinds (আশ্রমচতুষ্টয়). □ *n.* an aggregate of four, quartet (নীতিচতুষ্টয়).

চতুষ্পথ *n.* a junction of four roads or an intersection of two roads.

চতুষ্পদ *n.* a quadruped animal; a beast. □ *a.* quadruped, four-footed; (fig.) as foolish as a beast. **চতুষ্পদী** *n. fem.* a four-lined or four-footed stanza, a quatrain.

চতুষ্পাঠী *n.* a school for teaching Sanskrit, esp. the four Vedas or grammar, poetry, law and philosophy.

চতুষ্পাদ *a.* four-footed or four-lined (চতুষ্পাদ শ্লোক) ; complete; entire; having all the parts; having four parts (চতুষ্পাদ ধর্ম). □ *n.* a quadruped.

চতুষ্পার্শ্ব *n.* four sides; all the four sides; all sides; neighbourhood. **চতুষ্পার্শ্বে** *adv.* on all sides.

চতুস্তল *a.* (of a building etc.) four-storied; (of a vehicle etc.) four-decked; (geom.) tetrahedral. **~ক** *n.* a tetrahedron.

চতুস্ত্রিংশ *a.* thirty-four. **~ৎ** *n.* & *a.* thirty-four. **~ত্তম** *a.* thirty-fourth. *fem.* **~ত্তমী** ।

চত্বর *n.* a courtyard; a portico, a vestibule; vicinity (এই চত্বরে কোনো কাঁচা বাড়ি নেই).

চত্বারিংশ *a.* forty. **~ৎ** *n.* & *a.* forty. **~ত্তম** *a.* forty-fourth. *fem.* **~ত্তমী** ।

চত্বাল *n.* same as **চাতাল** ।

চনচন *int.* expressing smarting sensation or pain. **চনচনে** *a.* smarting.

চনমন *int.* expressing vivacity or liveliness. **চনমনে** *a.* vivacious, lively, sprightly.

চন্দক *n.* a round-shaped silvery white river-fish, the moon-fish, the opah.

চন্দ obs. & poetic form of **চন্দ্র** ।

চন্দন *n.* sandal, sandalwood; sandalpaste. **রক্তচন্দন, কুচন্দন** *n.* red sandalwood. **শ্বেতচন্দন, হরিচন্দন** *n.* white sandalwood, *Santalum album*. **~চর্চিত** *a.* smeared or painted with sandalpaste. **~তিলক** *n.* mark of sandalpaste on the forehead. **~পঙ্ক** *n.* sandalpaste. **~পিঁড়ি** *n.* a stone mortar on which sandalwood is rubbed to make sandal-paste. **~পুষ্প** *n.* clove. **~শাল** *n.* a kind of paddy.

চন্দনা *n.* Chandana, the name of an Indian river; a kind of parrot having red streaks round its throat, *Paloeornis nepalensis;* a species of hilsa fish.

চন্দ্রা *n.* (obs. & poet.) the moon.

চন্দ্র *n.* the moon; (in comp.—used as a *sfx.*) a superior member or specimen (কুলচন্দ্র). **~ক** *n.* the crescent spot on the peacock's tail. **~কর** *n.* moonlight. **~করোজ্জ্বল** *a.* brightened by moonlight, moonlit. **~কলা** *n.* 1/16th part of the moon's orb, a digit or phase of the moon. **~কলাশৃঙ্গ** *n.* (geog.) the horns of the moon. **~কান্ত** *n.* the moonstone (also **চন্দ্রকান্তমণি**). □ *a.* as beautiful as the moon. **~কান্তি** *a.* as beautiful as the moon. □ *n.* silver. **~কিরণ** *n.* moonbeam, moonlight. **~কিরণোদ্ভাসিত** *a.* same as **~করোজ্জ্বল** । **~গ্রহণ** *n.* a lunar eclipse. **~চূড়** *n.* one who wears the moon as his crown; an appellation of Shiva (শিব). **~নিভ** *a.* resembling the moon; as bright as the moon. **~পুলি** *n.* a sweet pastry made of coconut-kernel and sugar. **~প্রভ** *a.* as shining or bright as the moon; of pleasing appearance. **~প্রভা** *n.* moonlight, moonbeam. □ *a.* *fem.* as shining or beautiful as the moon. **~বংশ** *n.* a family originating from the moon or from a sage named Chandra (চন্দ্র). **~বংশীয়** *a.* of this family. **~বদন** *a.* having a face as shining or beautiful as the moon, moon-faced; (sarcas.) ugly-faced; (sarcas.) having a round and stupid face. *fem.* **~বদনা** । **~বিন্দু** *n.* ँ this nasal sign in the Bengali alphabet. **~বোড়া** *n.* the Russell's viper. **~ভাগা** *n.* the Chenab in the Punjab. **~মণি** *n.* the moonstone. **~মণ্ডল** *n.* the orb or disc of the moon; the halo round the moon; the lunar region. **~মল্লিকা** *n.* the Chrysanthemum. **~মা** *n.* the moon. **~মুখ** same as **~বদন** । *fem.* **~মুখী** । **~মৌলি** same as **~চূড়** । **~রশ্মি** *n.* moonlight. **~রেখা, ~লেখা** *n.* 1/16th part of the moon's orb, a digit of the moon; a metre used in Sanskrit poetry. **~রেণু** *n.* a plagiarist. **~লোক** *n.* the region of the moon, the lunar region or heaven. **~শালা, ~শালিকা** *n.* an attic. **~শেখর** same as **~চূড়** । **~সম্ভব** *n.* a son of the moon; (astr.) Mercury. **~সুধা** *n.* moonlight. **~হার** *n.* a kind of ornamental girdle or necklace. **~হাস** *n.* a bright or shining falchion.

চন্দ্রাংশু *n.* a ray of the moon.

চন্দ্রাতপ *n.* a canopy, an awning; moonlight.

চন্দ্রানন *a.* having a face as shining or beautiful as the moon, moon-faced. *fem.* **চন্দ্রাননা, চন্দ্রাননী** ।

চন্দ্রাপীড় *n.* an appellation of Shiva (শিব).

চন্দ্রাবলী *n.* moonlight.

চন্দ্রালোক *n.* moonlight. **চন্দ্রালোকিত** a. moonlit.

চন্দ্রিকা *n.* moonlight; the pupil of the eye; a round-shaped silvery white river-fish, the moon-fish, the opah; a metre used in Sanskrit poetry.

চন্দ্রিমা *n.* (inc.) moonlight.

চন্দ্রোদয় *n.* moonrise, the rising of the moon.

চপ *n.* a round-shaped fried preparation usu. of vegatables or meat.

চপচপ *int.* expressing drenched or slushy state. **চপচপ করা** *v.* to be drenched or slushy or sloppy. **চপচপে** *a.* excessively drenched or slushy or sloppy, dripping wet.

চপল *a.* restless; fick'e; vivacious, lively; wanton; impudent, saucy; talkative; full of levity; flippant; fleeting, momentary. **চপলা** *a. fem.* of **চপল** । ☐ *n. fem.* Goddess Lakshmi (লক্ষ্মী) ; the lightning. **~তা** *n.* restlessness; fickleness; vivacity, liveliness; wantonness; impudence, sauciness; talkativeness; levity; flippancy; fleetingness.

চপেট, চপেটা, চপেটিকা *n.* a blow with the open palm of the hand, a slap. **চপেটাঘাত** *n.* a slap. **চপেটাঘাত করা** *v.* to slap.

চপ্পল *n.* a kind of sandals.

চবর্গ *n.* চ ছ জ ঝ ঞ : these five letters of the Bengali alphabet.

চবুতর, চবুতরা *n.* a courtyard; a portico, a vestibule.

চব্বিশ *n.* & *a.* twenty-four. **চব্বিশ ঘণ্টা** *n.* & *adv.* twenty-four hours; all day; whole day; always. **চব্বিশে** *n.* the twenty-fourth day of a month, the twenty-fourth. ☐ *a.* (of days of a month) twenty-fourth.

চমক *n.* flash (বিদ্যুতের চমক) ; amazement (চমক লাগা) ; alarm, fright; consciousness. **চমক দেওয়া** *v.* to flash; to strike with amazement. **চমক ভাঙা** *v.* to regain consciousness or come back to sense suddenly, to be suddenly freed from a rapt state of mind. **চমক লাগা** *v.* to be stricken with amazement; to be dazed.

চমকদার *a.* sparkling, glittering, glaring, scintillating.

চমকপ্রদ *a.* startling; thrilling; amazing; too good to be true.

চমকানো *v.* to flash; to startle, to give a jolt or cause to startle, or to be taken by surprise. **চমকানি** *n.* a flash or flashing; startle, a start or surprise or jolt.

চমকিত *a.* flashed; startled. *fem.* **চমকিতা** ।

চমচম *n.* a kind of juicy sweetmeat made of posset.

চমৎকরণ *n.* act of striking with amazement; act of causing wonder.

চমৎকার *a.* amazingly beautiful or good; amazing. ☐ *adv.* well, nicely (চমৎকার বুঝতে পারা, চমৎকার বোঝানো)। ☐ *int.* fine, excellent; marvellous. **চমৎকারক, চমৎকারী** *a.* amazing. *fem.* **চমৎকারিণী** । **চমৎকারিতা, চমৎকারিত্ব** *n.* marvellousness; excellence.

চমৎকৃত *a.* amazed. **চমৎকৃত করা** *v.* to amaze, to strike with marvel. **চমৎকৃত হওয়া** *v.* to be amazed, to marvel (at).

চমর *n.* the yak; a kind of fan or a brush for fanning made of the hair of a yak's tail; a fly-whisk. *fem.* **চমরি** the she-yak.

চমস *n.* a spoon; a spatula; a ladle. **চমসাকার** *a.* spoon-shaped or ladle-shaped; (bot.) spatulate.

চমূ *n.* 1/30th part of an **অক্ষৌহিণী** ; a company of troops; an army.

চম্পক *n.* a flower or its tree of the magnolia family, the *Michelia champaca*, the champak. **~দাম** *n.* a wreath or garland of champak flowers.

চম্পট *n.* decampment, escapade; escape, flight. **চম্পট দেওয়া** v. to decamp; to escape, to flee away, to run off, to show a clean pair of heels, to give the slip (to).

চম্পা[১] *n.* the name of an ancient Indian city.

চম্পা[২] same as **চম্পক** ।

চম্পূ *n.* a literary composition in which both prose and verse are used.

চয় *n.*(chiefly used as a *sfx.*) a collection, an assemblage, a multitude, a heap (অরাতিচয়) ; act of collecting or gathering, amassing.

চয়ন *n.* act of collecting or plucking, collection (পুষ্পচয়ন) ; a number collected or plucked, a collection, an anthology (কবিতাচয়ন, গল্পচয়ন). **চয়ন করা** *v.* to collect or cull or gather or pick or pluck. **চয়নিকা** *n. fem.* a small collection; a collection of poems or other literary works, an anthology. **চয়নীয়, চেয়** *a.* worthy of being collected; that which is to be collected.

চয়িত inc. but pop. var. of **চিত** ।

-চর[১] *a.* (used as a *sfx.*) moving in (গগনচর, বনচর) ; dwelling in, inhabiting (জলচর) ; mobile (চরাচর).

চর[২] *n.* a strip of sandy land rising out of the bed of a river or a sea above the water-level.

চর[৩] *n.* a secret emissary; a spy; (astrol.) Mars.

চরকসংহিতা *n.* a treatise on medicine written by Charaka the sage.

চরকা, (rare) **চরখা** *n.* a spinning-wheel, a spinning-jenny. **চরকা কাটা** *v.* to spin. **নিজের চরকায় তেল দেওয়া** (fig.) to oil one's own machine, to mind one's own business. (usu. imp.).

চরকি *n.* a rotating firework, a Catherine-wheel; a Ferris wheel; (mech.) a windlass. **চরকির মতো ঘোরা** *v.* to turn round and round like a wheel; (fig.) to gad about.

চরণ *n.* a foot, a leg, a foot or line of a verse; ambulation, walking, travelling, wandering, moving; observance, practice. **~কমল** *n.* a foot fancied as a lotus; a beautiful or divine foot. **~চারণ** *n.* ambulation, walking; perambulation; peregrination. **~চারী** *a.* (also *n.*) pedestrian. **~তরী, ~তরি** *n.* a foot regarded as a boat esp. to cross the river Baitarani (বৈতরণী) after one's death. **~তল** *n.* the sole; the foot. **চরণতলে থাকা** *v.* to lie under the foot or sole of; (fig.) to act as one's bond-slave for attainment of final salvation; (fig.) to depend cringingly on. **চরণতলে পড়া** *v.* to fall at the feet of (esp. in order to win favour). **~দাসী** *n.* a devoted wife; one belonging to a sect of Vaishnavas founded by Charandas; (sarcas.) a female companion or associate of a Vaishnava. **~ধূলি, ~ধুলা** *n.* the dust of one's feet. **~পদ্ম** same as **~কমল**। **~প্রান্ত** *n.* the border or end of one's feet. **~প্রান্তে** *adv.* at one's feet. **~বন্দনা** *n.* act of worshipping one's feet; act of bowing down at one's feet in obeisance, genuflection. **~যুগল** *n.* both the feet, the two feet; a pair of feet. **~রেণু** same as **~ধূলি**। **~সেবক** *n.* a devotee. **~সেবা** *n.* act of worshipping one's feet; act of massaging one's legs and feet. **~স্পর্শ** *n.* contact of one's feet; act of touching one's feet. **চরণ স্পর্শ করা** *v.* to touch one's feet. **~স্পর্শে** *adv.* at the contact or touch of one's feet. **চরণাঙ্কিত** *a.* marked with the footprint (of). **চরণাঙ্গুলি** *n.* a toe. **চরণামৃত** *n.* the water with which the feet of a deity or revered person has been washed. **চরণাম্বুজ, চরণারবিন্দ** same as **চরণকমল**। **চরণোপান্তে** *adv.* at one's feet.

চরম *n.* end, termination (কিছুর চরম দেখা) ; ultimate or last or final stage, most critical stage (চরমে ওঠা) ; highest stage, greatest height, climax, culmination, maximum (দুঃখের চরম). □ *a.* ultimate or final (চরমপত্র, চরম সিদ্ধান্ত) ; last (চরমকাল) ; extreme (চরমসীমা, চরম জলবায়ু) ; highest, maximum (চরমোৎকর্ষ), pertaining to death or the time of death, dying (চরম দশা). **~কাল** *n.* the dying moment. **~গতি** *n.* last resort, only prop and support. **চরম জলবায়ু** extreme climate. **~পত্র** *n.* a document containing the disposition of one's effects at death, a will; an ultimatum. **~সীমা** *n.* utmost limit. **চরমাদর্শ** *n.* highest ideal. **চরমাবস্থা** *n.* last or final stage, ultimate stage, most critical stage. **চরমোৎকর্ষ, চরমোন্নতি** *n.* highest excellence or improvement.

চরস *n.* an intoxicant narcotic prepared from the exudation of hashish; hemp, charas. **চরস খাওয়া** *v.* to smoke charas.

চরা *v.* to wander, to rove, to travel; (of cattle) to graze; (of other beasts, birds, anthropophagies etc.) to go about for food; (sarcas.) to go about one's business; (of fish) to nibble at bait. **চরে খাওয়া** *v.* to graze; to go about for food; (sarcas.) to shift or fend for oneself.

চরাচর *n.* mobile and immobile objects; (as sing.) the world, the universe, the whole creation.

চরানো *v.* to cause to graze, to tend or feed (cattle); (derog.) to direct or govern, to make a person do everything one wishes him to do, to lead a person by the nose; (derog.) to teach (ছেলে চরানো).

চরিত *n.* character; deportment, behaviour, manners, conduct; activities; custom, usage; biography, life. □ *a.* observed, performed, executed, accomplished; invested with. **চরিতকার, চরিতাখ্যায়ক** *n.* a biographer. **চরিতাবলি** *n. pl.* biographies, lives; collections of biographies. **চরিতাভিধান** *n.* a biographical dictionary.

চরিতার্থ *a.* one whose desires have been

fulfilled; successful; satisfied, gratified. চরিতার্থ করা *v.* to fulfil one's desire; to satisfy, to gratify. ~তা fulfilment of one's desire, success; satisfaction, gratification.

চরিত্র *n.* character; conduct; manner, behaviour, deportment; disposition; nature; custom, usage; function; activities; good character or behaviour, a biography; a character in a drama; a role. **চরিত্র খোয়ানো, চরিত্র হারানো** *v.* to lose one's character or morals, to have one's character or moral corrupted, to become depraved, to go to the bad. ~গত *a.* relating to the character; natural (চরিত্রগত দোষ). ~গুণ *n.* the excellence of one's character; a characteristic quality (good or bad). ~চিত্র *n.* a character-sketch. ~চিত্রণ *n.* delineation or portrayal of characters, characterisation, character-painting. ~দোষ *n.* moral corruption; a vice or defect in one's character; dissoluteness, debauchery. ~বান *a.* good-charactered; virtuous; chaste. *fem.* ~বতী। ~হনন *n.* character assassination. ~হীন *a.* morally corrupt or ruined, characterless, depraved, dissolute, debauched, profligate. *fem.* ~হীনা। **চরিত্রহীন ব্যক্তি** a debauchee, a libertine. **চরিত্রাভিনয়** *n.* (in drama or film) acting in a certain role.

চরিত্রাঙ্কন *n.* delineation or portrayal of one's character. **চরিত্রাঙ্কন করা** *v.* to delineate one's character.

চরিষ্ণু *a.* mobile, moving.

চরু *n.* an oblation of sunned rice boiled in milk with sugar and ghee.

চর্চরী *n.* a kind of musical instrument; an ancient folk-music; a ceremony observed on the eve on the holi (হোলি) festival.

চর্চা discussion; criticism (পরচর্চা); culture, cultivation, practice, study (বিদ্যাচর্চা, সংগীতচর্চা); meditation, thought ('চক্রপাণিচর্চা যার চিত্তে'); act of smearing or painting, anointment (তিলকচর্চা). **চর্চা করা** *v.* to discuss; to criticize; to cultivate, to practise, to study; to meditate, to think; to smear, to paint, to anoint. **চর্চিত** *a.* discussed; cultivated, practised, studied; meditated, thought; smeared, painted, anointed.

চর্পট *n.* a blow with the open palm of the hand, a slap.

চর্পটী *n.* a kind of bread shaped like a thin disc prepared by the hand.

চর্বণ *n.* act of chewing, mastication. **চর্বণ করা** *v.* to chew, to masticate.

চর্বি *n.* fat; animal fat; lard, tallow.

চর্বিত *a.* chewed, masticated. ~চর্বণ *n.* act of chewing the cud, rumination; (fig.) discussion of an old topic or repeated discussion of the same topic. **চর্বিতচর্বণ করা** *v.* to chew the cud, to ruminate; (fig.) to discuss an old topic or to discuss the same topic repeatedly.

চর্ব্য *a.* (of food) that which has to be chewed; masticable. ~চূষ্য *a.* that which has to be chewed and that which has to be sucked; (fig.) of or pertaining to different delicious varieties. □ *n. pl.* articles of food comprising that which has to be chewed and that which has to be sucked; (fig.) articles of food of different delicious varieties, rich and costly dishes. **চর্ব্য-চূষ্য-লেহ্য-পেয়** *a.* those which have to be chewed and sucked and licked and drunk; (fig.) of different delicious varieties, delicious and costly. □ *n.* (lit. & fig.) delicious food or dishes, delicacies of all descriptions.

চর্ম *n.* skin, cutis; the true skin, derm; cuticle; hide; leather; bark (of plants), rind; a shield. ~কার *n.* a shoemaker or a tanner or currier (by profession or caste). ~কীল *n.* a wart, a mole, a small bump on human skin. ~চক্ষু *n.* the physical eye. **~চটকা, ~চটিকা, ~চটী** *n.* the titmouse; the bat; the vampire. ~জ *a.* leathern, made of leather. ~দল *n.* impetigo. ~ধারী *a.* armed with a shield; one who bears a shield. ~নির্মিত *a.* made of leather; leathern. ~পাদুকা *n.* a leather shoe or boot or slipper, a leather footwear. **~পেটিকা, ~পেটী** *n.* a leather bag or suitcase; a leather belt.

~বন্ধ *n*. a leather-band. ~ব্যবসায়ী *n*. a dealer in hide or leather; a tanner. ~ময় *a*. leathern; leathery; hide-bound. ~রোগ *n*. skin disease. ~সার *n*. serum, lymph. □ *a*. hide-bound; very lean or emaciated. ~স্থলী *n*. a leather-bag; a container for leather.

চর্মাবরণ *n*. a leathern cover or jacket.

চর্মার *n*. a shoemaker or a tanner or currier (by caste or trade).

চর্মাসন *n*. a seat made of skin (of deer, tiger etc.).

চর্য *a*. that which is to be practised or observed. **চর্যা** *n*. practice or observance (ধর্মচর্যা, ব্রতচর্যা) ; observance of rules or routine (দিনচর্যা) ; culture (দেহচর্যা, সাহিত্যচর্যা) ; act of looking after (রোগীচর্যা). **চর্যাপদ** *n*. any of the lyrics composed by a sect of Buddhists about their religion and religious practice, supposed to be the earliest specimen of Bengali literature.

চল *a*. unsteady, restless, fickle (চলচিত্ত). □ *n*. currency, vogue, fashion (চল থাকা) ; (math.) variable.

চলকানো *v*. to run out of a vessel owing to a push or jerk, to spill.

চলচিত্ত *a*. fickle-minded, mentally unsteady. ~তা *n*. fickle-mindedness.

চলচ্চিত্র *n*. cinematograph, cinema; a cinematograph film, (pop.) movie. ~বিদ্যা *n*. cinematography.

চলচ্ছক্তি inc. form of **চলনশক্তি** (see **চলন**). ~হীন *a*. having no power of motion, unable to move, paralysed.

চলৎ *a*. moving; mobile; current; in vogue.

চলতি *a*. moving, going, running, rolling, passing (চলতি গাড়ি) ; in activity, going (চলতি ব্যাবসা) ; colloquial (চলতি ভাষা) ; current, present (চলতি বছর, চলতি বাজার) ; usual, customary (চলতি কথা, চলতি রীতি) ; fit for social intercourse, fit for matrimonial alliance (চলতি ঘর). **চলতি আমানত** current deposit.

চলন *n*. act of going or moving or travelling (চলনশীল) ; gait (চলন বাঁকা) ; motion; currency, vogue, custom (চলন থাকা) ; behaviour, deportment (চালচলন) ; usage, practice, fashion, style (সাবেকি চলন). **চলন থাকা** *v*. to be current, to be in vogue. ~যোগ্য *a*. workable; passable, tolerable. ~শক্তি *n*. power of moving, motion. ~শীল *a*. going, moving, travelling; mobile. ~সই *a*. passable, tolerable.

চলমান inc. but pop. form of **চলৎ** and **চলন্ত। চলমান জীবন** passing or moving life, life in motion.

চলন্ত *a*. moving, going, passing, running, in motion, on the move.

চলরেণু *n*. zoospore.

চলা *v*. to go, to move, to walk (লোক চলা) ; to run, to ply (ট্রামবাস চলা) ; to depart; to set for (দেশে চলা) ; to proceed (তুমি চলো, আমিও যাচ্ছি) ; to get on, to run (কারবার চলা) ; to pass away, to elapse (সময় চলে যাওয়া) ; to be maintained (সংসার চলা) ; to suffice, to cover as expenses, to defray (খরচ চলা) ; to be getting on (জীবন চলা) ; to work, to operate (ঘড়ি চলা, মেশিন চলা) ; to begin to work or operate; to circulate (রক্ত চলা) ; to pass current, to be introduced (ফ্যাশন চলা) ; to be accepted (সমাজে চলা) ; to behave or act (খুশিমতো চলা) ; to be permitted or allowed (ফাঁকি চলবে না) ; to continue (সারারাত গান চলল) ; to begin, to start (এবার গল্প চলবে) ; to extend (দৃষ্টি চলা) ; to be used (হাত চলা) ; to be fired or shot (বন্দুক চলা). **চলে আসা** *v*. to come; to come away from; to come quickly. **চলে যাওয়া** *v*. to go away. **কথামতো চলা** *v*. to act or behave in obedience to; to obey. ~চল *n*. passage, travelling (চলাচলের পথ) ; movement, traffic (লোক-চলাচল) ; circulation (রক্ত-চলাচল, বায়ু চলাচল). **চলাচল করা** *v*. to travel; to move; to circulate. ~নো *v*. to cause to walk or move; to cause to pass current; to cause to be accepted. ~ফেরা *n*. act of walking or moving (চলাফেরার ক্ষমতা) ; movement; gait; behaviour, deportment. **শন-শন শব্দে চলা** to whiz past.

চলিত *a*. current; customary; usual; colloquial (চলিত ভাষা). **চলিত নিয়ম** *n*. (arith.) practice.

চলিষ্ণু *a*. moving, mobile; restless, unsteady; about to go away or depart.

চলোর্মি *n.* a dancing or restless wave, a rushing wave.

চল্লিশ *n.* & *a.* forty.

চশমখোর *n.* brazen-faced, shameless.

চশমা *n.* (a pair of) spectacles; an eyeglass; (coll.) specs. **~ওয়ালা** *a.* spectacled. □ *n.* a spectacled man; a dealer in spectacles and other optical goods. **~ধারী, ~-পরা** *a.* spectacled; bespectacled.

চষক *n.* a wine-cup; honey; wine, alcohol.

চষা *v.* to plough, to till; to cultivate. □ *a.* ploughed, tilled; cultivated. **~নো** *v.* to cause to plough or till or cultivate.

চা *n.* tea. **চা খাওয়া** *v.* to take tea, to drink tea. **চা-কর** *a.* planting or producing tea. □ *n.* a tea-planter. **চা খাওয়ার সময়** tea-time. **চা-দানি** *n.* a tea-tray. **চা-বাগান** *n.* a tea-garden, a tea-plantation. **চায়ের দোকান** a tea-shop. **চায়ের পাত্র** tea-pot. **চায়ের পেটি** a tea-chest. **চায়ের বাসনকোসন** tea-service, tea-set.

চাই, চাও, চায় *v.* (pr. t.) forms of **চাওয়া**[1] & **চাওয়া**[2] । **কী চাই, কী চাও** what do you want ? **চাই-কি** *adv.* even; probably. **চাইলেই** for the asking.

চাইতে *post.* than.

চাউনি coll. form of **চাহনি** ।

চাউর *a.* publicized, circulated; current.

চাউল *n.* rice. **আতপ চাউল** sunned rice. **সিদ্ধ চাউল** parboiled rice.

চাউলমুগরা *n.* a medicinal plant of the family Flacourtiaceae, chaulmoogra.

চাওয়া[1] *v.* to want; to ask for, to request for (ভিক্ষা চাওয়া, সময় চাওয়া) ; to desire (মরতে চাওয়া) ; to be ready to. **চাওয়া-চাওয়ি** *n.* act of wanting or asking for or desiring repeatedly. **~নো** *v.* to cause to want; to cause to ask for or request for; to cause to desire; to cause to consent. **~মাত্র** *adv.* for the asking.

চাওয়া[2] *v.* to look at; to open (চোখ চাওয়া) ; to cast an evil eye (on or at). **চাওয়া-চাওয়ি** *n.* act of looking at one another; act of coming to an agreement by favouring one another. **~নো** *v.* to cause to look at; to cause to open. **মুখ তুলে চাওয়া** *v.* to look favourably on; to be favourably inclined towards.

চাওয়া-চাওয়ি, চাওয়ানো see **চাওয়া**[1] & **চাওয়া**[2] ।

চাঁই[1] *n.* (dero.) a leader; a chief; a ring-leader; a veteran person; a somebody.

চাঁই[2] *n.* a clod; a device made of bamboo slips for catching fish.

চাঁচ[1] *n.* a kind of mat made of date-leaves or bambo slips.

চাঁচ[2] *n.* a piece of lac beaten into a leaf.

চাঁচর[1] *n.* a ceremony observed on the eve of the holi (হোলি) festival.

চাঁচর[2] *a.* curly ('চাঁচর চিকুর') ।

চাঁচা *v.* to scrape, to shave. □ *a.* scraped; shaved. **চাঁচা-ছোলা** *a.* (lit.) thoroughly scraped or shaved; (fig.) rude and out-spoken, curt. **চাঁচনি, চাঁচুনি** *n.* act of scraping; a scraper. **~নো** *v.* to cause to scrape or shave.

চাঁচা-ছোলা see **চাঁচা** ।

চাঁচাড়ি var. of **চেঁচাড়ি** ।

চাঁচি *n.* the scrapings of calcined milk or of some milk products or of sticky dross of other foods.

চাঁছা, চাঁছানো variants of **চাঁচা** and **চাঁচানো** respectively. **চাঁছনি, চাঁছুনি** *n.* same as **চাঁচুনি** ।

চাঁছি variant of **চাঁচি** ।

চাঁট variant of **চাট** ।

চাঁটা, চাঁটি variants of **চাটা**[1] and **চাটি**[2] respectively.

চাঁড়াল coll. form of **চণ্ডাল** ।

চাঁদ *n.* the moon; the most beautiful or glorious person (নদিয়ার চাঁদ) ; (sarcas.) an ugly person; (inf. & coll.) a friend (এসো দেখি চাঁদ). **~কুড়া, ~কুড়ো** *n.* a variety of small silvery-white fish, the moon-fish, the opah. **~নি** *n.* moonlight; a canopy, an awning; a vestibule, a spacious corridor, □ *a.* moonlit (চাঁদনি রাত). **~পানা** *a.* like the moon, moonlike, resembling the moon. **~বদন** *a.* having a face as beautiful as the moon, moon-faced; (sarcas.) ugly-faced. □ *n.* a face as beautiful as the moon; a moon-faced man or boy; (sarcas.) an ugly-faced man or boy. *fem.* **~বদনি** । **~মারি** *n.* a target, a range; target-practice. **~মালা, ~হার** *n.* a necklace designed in the likeness of the moon. **~মুখ** *n.* a face as beautiful as the moon. **চাঁদের কণা** (lit.) a small fragment of the moon; (fig.) an extremely beautiful or delightful person esp. such a baby, a charming little child. **চাঁদের হাট** a company of beautiful charming young women; a gathering of pretty faces.

চাঁদনি see **চাঁদ**।

চাঁদা[1] var. of **চাঁদি[2]**।

চাঁদা[2] *n.* the moon (চাঁদামামা) ; a variety of small silvery-white fish, the moon-fish, the opah; (geom.) a protractor.

চাঁদা[3] *n.* subscription; contribution; quota. **চাঁদা দেওয়া** *v.* to pay subscription; to subscribe. **চাঁদা তোলা** *v.* to raise subscription. **চাঁদা ধরা** *v.* to allot one's quota.

চাঁদি[1] *n.* pure silver; silver. □ *a.* pure (চাঁদি রুপো).

চাঁদি[2] *n.* the crown of the head.

চাঁদিনি *a.* moonlit (চাঁদিনি রাত). □ *n.* moonlight; a moonlit night.

চাঁদিমা *n.* moonlight.

চাঁদোয়া *n.* a canopy, an awning.

চাঁপা *n.* a kind of flower or its tree belonging to the magnolia family, the champak **~কলা** *n.* a kind of small banana. **~নটে** *n.* a variety of pot-herb.

চাক *n.* a wheel (কুমোরের চাক) ; anything wheel-shaped (ছোলার চাক) ; hive (মৌচাক).

চাকচিক্য *n.* lustre, glaze; polish, showy glitter; glamour. **~পূর্ণ, ~ময়** *a.* lustrous, glazing; glittering; glamorous.

চাকতি *n.* a wafer; a disc; a discus. **রুপোর চাকতি** (fig. & usu. dero.) a silver coin; money.

চা-কর[1] see **চা**।

চাকর[2] *n.* a man-servant, a servant; a menial, an attendant; a follower; an officer or employee (সরকারের চাকর). *fem.* **চাকরানি** a maid-servant, a maid. **~বাকর** *n. pl.* (*com.gen.*) servants or menials or followers collectively.

চাকরান *n.* a grant of land to a servant in lieu of salary. □ *a.* thus granted (চাকরান জমি).

চাকরি *n.* employment, service; a situation, a job. **চাকরি করা** *v.* to serve, to work. **চাকরি খালি** situation vacant. **চাকরি খালি নেই** (there is) no vacancy. **চাকরি খোঁজা** *v.* to seek or look or hunt for employment, to seek a job. **চাকরি খোয়ানো** *v.* to lose a job, to be dismissed. **চাকরি চাই** a job or situation (is) wanted. **চাকরি ছাড়া** *v.* to resign from service. **চাকরিতে ঢোকা** *v.* to enter service. **চাকরি থেকে অবসর বা বিদায় নেওয়া** *v.* to retire from service. **চাকরি পাওয়া** *v.* to get employment, to get or secure a job. **চাকরি বজায় রাখা** *v.* to be able to continue in service. **চাকরি মেলা** same as **চাকরি পাওয়া**। **চাকরি যাওয়া, চাকরি হারানো** same as **চাকরি খোয়ানো**। **সরকারি চাকরি** public service, government service. **চাকরিজীবী** same as **চাকুরে**। *fem.* **চাকরিজীবিনী**।

চাকলা[1] *n.* a slice or slip (আমের চাকলা).

চাকলা[2] *n.* a district; a county, a shire. **চাকলাদার** *n.* the governor or the owner of a district or shire.

চাকা[1] dial. corrup. of **চাখা**।

চাকা[2] *n.* a wheel (গাড়ির চাকা) ; anything round or wheel-shaped; a round piece (মাছের চাকা). □ *a.* wheel-shaped, discoid, round (চাকা দাগ).

চাকি *n.* a disc; a discoid piece of wood or stone for making bread and similar other things (চাকি-বেলুন) ; a grinding-stone, a mill (আটার চাকি).

চাকু *n.* a clasp-knife; a pen-knife; a knife. **চাকু মারা** *v.* to stab, to knife, to knive.

চাকুরি var. of **চাকরি**।

চাকুরিয়া variant of **চাকুরে**।

চাকুরে *a.* working (চাকুরে মেয়ে = a working girl). □ *n.* an employee, a worker, a servant. **বড় চাকুরে** an officer (usu. a high-ranking one). **সরকারি চাকুরে** a public servant.

চাক্ষুষ *a.* ocular; visual; visible, evident. **চাক্ষুষ জ্ঞান** visual knowledge or perception. **চাক্ষুষ প্রত্যক্ষ** visual perception; a visual percept. **চাক্ষুষ প্রমাণ** an ocular demonstration. **চাক্ষুষ সাক্ষী** an eye-witness.

চা-খড়ি *n.* chalk.

চাখন *n.* tasting; tasting the quality of dish or food or something. **~দার** *n.* a taster.

চাখা *v.* to taste; (fig.) to enjoy (জীবনকে চাখা). **চাখানো** *v.* to cause to taste or enjoy. □ *a.* caused to taste or enjoy.

চাগা *v.* to become vigorous, to gain strength; to become acute or more acute, to increase (ব্যথা চেগেছে) ; to rise, to spring up (মনে চেগেছে) ; to come into consciousness, to originate (বুদ্ধি চেগেছে). **চাগানো** *v.* to become or make vigorous, to gain or cause to gain strength; to become or make acute or more acute, to increase; to spring up or cause to spring up; to rise or cause to rise, raise; to come or bring into consciousness, to originate.

চাগাড় *n.* agitation; act or state of becoming acute or more acute. **চাগাড় দিয়ে ওঠা** *v.* to become agitated; to get incited or excited; to become acute or more acute.

চাঙ, চাং *n.* an improvised platform (usu. made of timber, bamboo, twigs etc.).

চাঙড়, চাঙড়া *n.* a large lump; a large clod.

চাঙারি, চাঙাড়ি *n.* a large wicker basket; a big creel.

চাঙ্গা, চাঙা *a.* restored to health; invigorated; reinforced; refreshed. **চাঙ্গা করা** *v.* to restore to health; to reinvigorate; to reinforce; to refresh. **চাঙ্গা হওয়া** *v.* to gain strength; to come round. **মন চাঙ্গা তো দুনিয়া চাঙ্গা** (fig.) when the mind is happy, all is well.

চাঙ্গাড়ি, চাঙ্গারি alt. spells. of **চাঙাড়ি** and **চাঙারি**।

চাচা *n.* a father's brother or cousin, an uncle. *fem.* **চাচি** an aunt. **চাচাতো** *a.* avuncular. **চাচাতো ভাই বা বোন** *n.* a cousin.

চাঞ্চল্য *n.* restlessness; agitation, perturbation (মানসিক চাঞ্চল্য) ; fretful activity; rapid movement, rapidity. (নাড়ির চাঞ্চল্য), bustle; anxiety. **~কর** *a.* thrilling, sensational. **~হীন** *a.* unperturbed; calm; steady.

চাট[1] *n.* the kick of an animal (as of a cow or horse). **চাট খাওয়া** *v.* to be kicked (as by an animal). **চাট মারা** *v.* to kick.

চাট[2] *n.* a food that is to be taken by licking; any snack which is to be taken with an intoxicant.

চাটনি *n.* a condiment, chutney, sauce.

চাটা[1] var. of **চাটি[2]**।

চাটা[2] *v.* to lick. □ *a.* licked; given to or engaged in licking. **~চাটি** *n.* repeated or continuous licking; act of licking each other; (iron.) intimacy or mutual laudation or compliment or adulation. **~নো** *v.* to cause to lick.

চাটাই *n.* a coarse mat made of date leaves or palm-leaves or bamboo slips.

চাটাচাটি, চাটানো see **চাটা[2]**।

চাটি[1] *a.* razed to the ground (ভিটেমাটি চাটি).

চাটি[2] *n.* a blow or a stroke with the open palm of the hand, a slap. **চাটি মারা** *v.* to slap.

চাটিম *n.* a kind of banana.

চাটু[1] *n.* a frying-pan.

চাটু[2], চাটুবাদ, চাটূক্তি *n.* adulatory words, flattery, sycophancy. **চাটুকার, চাটুবাদী, চাটুভাষী** *a.* flattering. □ *n.* a flatterer, an adulator, a sycophant. *fem.* **চাটুবাদিনী, চাটুভাষিণী**।

চাট্টি coll. corrup. of **চারটি**।

চাড়, চাড়া[1] *n.* an instance or act of shoving up something forcefully, a forceful upward shove (চাড় দিয়ে তোলা) ; enthusiasm, earnestness, zeal (লেখাপড়ায় চাড়) ; pressure or urgency (কাজের চাড়). **চাড় থাকা** *v.* to have keenness or zeal. **চাড় দেওয়া** *v.* to give an upward shove with force. **চাড় দিয়ে খোলা** to prize or prise up, to force open. **চাড় দিয়ে তোলা** *v.* to shove up forcefully.

চাড়া[2] *n.* an instance or act of twirling or twisting up (গোঁফে চাড়া) ; a support, a prop. **চাড়া দেওয়া** *v.* to twist up; to prop up.

চাড়ি *n.* (dial.) a large earthen manger.

চাতক *n.* a bird of the rainy reason, the pied crested cuckoo (wrongly believed to be a swallow). *fem.* **চাতকী,** (inc. but pop.) **চাতকিনী**।

চাতাল *n.* a vestibule, a terrace.

চাতুরি coll. var. of **চাতুর্য**।

চাতুর্বর্ণ্য *n.* the hierarchy of four principal castes amongst Hindus, namely, the brahmanas, the kshatriyas, the vaishyas and the shudras; prescribed practices of these castes. □ *a.* pertaining to these castes or their practices.

চাতুর্মাস্য *n.* a vow that is to be observed for four months at a stretch.

চাতুর্য *n.* intelligence; dexterity, skill, cleverness; artfulness; cunning, slyness.

চাদর *n.* a sheet of cloth worn over the body; a cover made of cloth; a bedsheet; a thin sheet of metal or other things.

চান dial. corrup. of **স্নান**।

চানকানো *v.* to excite into activity or to speed up, to make active or prompt (চাকরকে চানকানো, শরীর চানকানো) ; to brighten, to brush up, to polish (আসবাবপত্র চানকানো) ; to heat or fry slightly (মশলা চানকানো).

চানা *n.* a kind of gram or chick-pea fried crisp. **~চুর** *n.* a crisp snack prepared by frying chick-pea, monkey-nuts and other things with salt and spices.

চান্দ্র *a.* lunar (চান্দ্রগতি, চান্দ্রমাস). **~মাস** *n.* a lunar month.

চান্দ্রায়ণ *n.* a kind of expiatory penance.

চান্দ্রেয় same as **চান্দ্র**।

চাপ১ *n.* a bow; (geom.) an arc.

চাপ২ *n.* pressure (কাজের চাপ, বায়ুর চাপ, রক্তের চাপ) ; weight, influence, request, importunity etc. (মায়ের চাপে পড়ে সে বিয়ে করল) ; a layer (বরফের চাপে চাপে). □ *a.* clotted, coagulated (চাপরক্ত, চাপদই) ; thick, close-set (চাপ-বুনন) ; massive and extensive. **চাপ খাওয়া** *v.* to be pressed; to coagulate, to thicken. **চাপ দেওয়া** *v.* to press. **~দণ্ড** *n.* a piston; a pump. **~দাড়ি** *n.* massive or thick-set beard extending all over the cheeks and chin. **~মান (যন্ত্র)** *n.* a barometer.

চাপকান *n.* a loose and long robe (chiefly used as a part of official dress).

চাপটি *n.* the posture of squatting or sitting on one's haunches with legs folded. **চাপটি খেয়ে বসা** *v.* to sit upon one's haunches with legs folded, to squat; to sit tight or immovably; to remain seated obstinately.

চাপড় *n.* a blow or stroke with the open palm of the hand, a slap. **চাপড় খাওয়া** *v.* to be slapped. **চাপড় দেওয়া, চাপড় মারা** v. to slap.

চাপড়া *n.* a flat piece of clod or turf.

চাপড়ানো *v.* to strike (chiefly repeatedly) with the open palm of one's hand, to slap or pat (chiefly repeatedly).

চাপদণ্ড, চাপদাড়ি, চাপমান see **চাপ২**।

চাপরাস, চাপরাশ *n.* the distinctive dress of the servants of a person or office or institution, a livery. **~ধারী** *a.* liveried. **চাপরাসি** *n.* a liveried servant; an office messenger, an orderly, a chaprasi.

চাপল্য *n.* restlessness; fickleness; vivacity, liveliness; fluidity; wantonness; impudence, sauciness; talkativeness; levity; fleetingness; momentariness; rashness, imprudence.

চাপা *v.* to press; to compress; to suppress, to conceal, to hide (কথা চাপা) ; to restrain, to check (উন্নতি চাপা) ; to extend, to cover ('পঞ্চগৌড় চাপিয়া গৌড়েশ্বর রাজা', 'কুরুকুল চাপি') ; to ride or mount (ঘোড়ায় চাপা) ; to board or get into (গাড়িতে চাপা) ; to come upon as a load or weight, to burden (ঘাড়ে চাপা). □ *n.* act of pressing; compression; suppression, concealment; act of restraining; act of extending or covering; act of riding or mounting; act of boarding or getting into; a cover or lid (ঘটের চাপা, গর্তের চাপা) ; a weight (কাগজ-চাপা). □ *a.* pressing or compressing (বুক-চাপা ব্যথা) ; subdued, low, not clearly audible (চাপা গলা, চাপা সুর) ; not prominent, dull (চাপা রং) ; covered (কাঁটাঝোপে চাপা) ; restrained, obstructed, frustrated (চাপা বরাত) ; sunk or depressed to a lower level (পৃথিবী উত্তর-দক্ষিণে কিঞ্চিৎ চাপা) ; secretly circulated, private (চাপা গুজব) ; secret, concealed, suppressed (চাপা দুঃখ) ; uncommunicative, reserved (চাপা লোক). **~কান্না** *n.* mute or suppressed weeping, inarticulate crying. **চাপা গলায়** in an undertone. **~চাপি,** (coll.) **~চুপি** *n.* continuous pressing or thrusting or stuffing; mutual pressing; continuous solicitation; suppression, concealment; an attempt to suppress or conceal. **চাপাচাপি করা** *v.* to press or thrust or stuff continuously; to press mutually; to solicit or pester continuously; to suppress, to conceal; to endeavour to suppress or conceal. **চাপা দেওয়া** *v.* to cover; to suppress, to conceal, to hush up;; (as by a vehicle) to run over. **চাপা পড়া** *v.* to be covered; to be suppressed, to be concealed or hushed up; to be run over (by a train, a vehicle etc.). **চাপা স্বরে** in an undertone. **চেপে ধরা** *v.* to hold tight or pressed; to press. **চেপে বসা** *v.* to sit upon one's buttock; to sit tight; to sit firmly; to settle firmly; to be fixed tightly or firmly. **চেপে যাওয়া** *v.* to avoid disclosing; to desist from mentioning. **চেপে রাখা** *v.* to keep pressed; to keep restrained; to keep concealed or undisclosed. **(ঘাড়ে) শয়তান চাপা** to be possessed by a devil.

চাপাটি *n.* a piece of disc-shaped thin bread made by hand, chapati, chapattie, chapatty.

চাপান (pronoun : চাপান্) *n.* a problematic charge in verse set to music, thrown by a party of singers at the opposite party for answering.

চাপানো *v.* to place upon (উনুনে হাঁড়ি চাপানো) ; to load (গাড়িতে মাল চাপানো) ; to burden (ঘাড়ে চাপানো) ; to cause to ride or mount (ঘোড়ায় চাপানো) ; to cause to board or get into (যাত্রীদের জাহাজে চাপানো) ; to impute or ascribe (to) (দোষ চাপানো).

চাবকানো *v.* to whip, to lash, to flog, to flagellate, to scourge. **চাবকানি** *n.* whipping, lashing, flogging, scourging, flagellation.

চাবড়া *n.* alt. of **চাপড়া**।

চা-বাগান see **চা**।

চাবি, চাবিকাটি, চাবিকাঠি *n.* a key. **চাবি দেওয়া, চাবি বন্ধ করা** *v.* to key; to lock; to keep confined (ছেলেটাকে চাবি দিয়ে রেখেছে) ; to keep shut (মুখে চাবি দেওয়া).

চাবুক *n.* a whip, a lash, a scourge, a flagellum. **চাবুক খাওয়া** *v.* to be whipped or flogged or scourged or flagellated. **চাবুক মারা** *v.* to whip, to flog, to scourge, to flagellate.

চাম same as **চামড়া**।

চামচ *n.* a spoon; a ladle. **চামচ দিয়ে কাটা বা তোলা বা দেওয়া** *v.* to spoon or ladle (out).

চামচা *n.* a lackey, a servile follower.

চামচিকা, (coll.) **চামচিকে** *n.* the titmouse.

চামচে coll. corrup. of **চামচ**।

চামড়া *n.* skin; derm; (of larger animals & also dero.) hide; leather (চামড়ার জুতো). **কাঁচা চামড়া** hide. **পাকা চামড়া** leather. **চামড়া ছাড়ানো, চামড়া তোলা** *v.* to flay, to skin.

চামর *n.* a kind of fan or a brush for fanning made of the hair of a yak's tail; a fly-whisk. **~ধারিণী** *a.* & *n. fem.* one who fans with the aforesaid fan or brush or fly-whisk. **চামরী** *a.* having this brush of fan. ☐ *n.* the horse.

চামসা, (dial.) **চামসে** *a.* shrunk or smelling like dried hide.

চামাটি, চামাতি *n.* a strip of leather; a strop.

চামার *n.* a shoemaker or tanner or currier (by caste or trade); (fig.) a merciless or base man; (fig.) a skinflint. *fem.* **চামারনি**।

চামুণ্ডা *n.* a manifestation of Goddess Durga (দুর্গা) when she killed two giants—Chanda (চণ্ড) and Moonda (মুণ্ড).

চামেলি *n.* a kind of sweet-scented white jessamine, Catalonian or Spanish Jasmine.

চার১ var. of **চারা১** and **চারা২**।

চার২ *n.* bait (used to entice or catch fish (পুকুরে চার ফেলা) ; the part of a pond where bait has been dropped (চারে মাছ আসছে).

চার৩ *n.* & *a.* four. **চার-আনা** *n.* a fouth part, one-fourth, a quarter; four annas; a four-anna piece. *a.* one-fourth (চার-আনা অংশ). **চার-আনি** *n.* a four-anna piece. **~ইয়ারি** *a.* elicited out of the meeting of four friends. **~কোনা** *a.* square; qudrangular. **~খানা** *n.* four pieces or bits or units. **~গুণ** *a.* four-times. **~চালা** *a.* having a thatched roof consisting of four parts. ☐ *n.* a house having such a roof. **~চোখের মিলন** the meeting of the eyes of two persons (usu. two lovers). **~চৌকো** *a.* square. **~টা,** (coll.) **~টে** *a.* four. ☐ *n.* four o'clock. **~টি** *a.* four; a few or a little. ☐ *n.* four **~টিখানি** *a.* a little. **~দিক** *n.* four directions or sides or quarters; all directions or sides or quarters or places. **~পায়া,** (dial. corrup.) **~পাই** *n.* a kind of four-legged cot (usu. made of bamboo and coconutcoir). **চার পায়ে** on all fours. **~পেয়ে** *a.* four-legged, four-footed, quadruped. **~পোয়া,** (dial.) **~পো** *a.* complete, full. **~ভিত** same as **চারদিক**। **~সন্ধ্যা** four evenings; four parts or points of the day, namely, the morning, the noon, the evening and the midnight. **চার-হাত এক করা** *v.* to get a couple married, to marry. **চার হাতে পায়ে** on all fours.

চারক *a.* & *n.* one who tends or grazes (cattle).

চারণ[1] *n.* act of tending or grazing cattle; a pasture, a grazing ground. **~ভূমি** *n.* pasture; pasture land.

চারণ[2] *n.* a holy minstrel who sings the glory of a country or race or family. *fem.* **চারণী** । **~গান, ~গীতি** *n.* song of the minstrel.

চারণ[3], **চারণা** *n.* act of moving (পদচারণ).

চারা[1] *n.* fragrant things thrown into a fishing area to allure fish; a fishing area into which fragrant things have been thrown to allure fish; a bait.

চারা[2] *n.* a remedy; a means of reparation or redress (এ দুর্গতির চারা নেই).

চারা[3] *n.* a young plant, a sapling; a young fish, a spawn. ☐ *a.* newly-grown, newly-born, young (চারাগাছ, চারামাছ).

চারানো *v.* to spread out, to scatter, to be or to make widespread.

চারি older var. of **চার**[4] ।

-চারিণী *a. fem.* of **-চারী** ।

চারিত *a.* tended, grazed; infused; conducted, led, driven.

চারিত্র, চারিত্র্য *n.* character; conduct; good character; good conduct. **চারিত্রপূজা** *n.* hero-worship. **চারিত্রিক** *a.* relating to character or conduct; characteristic.

চারিদিক see **চার**[3] ।

-চারী *in comp.* (used as *sfx.*) plying, moving (আকাশচারী) ; observing or adopting (ব্রতচারী, মিথ্যাচারী).

চারু *a.* beautiful, pleasant, charming, good-looking (চারুদর্শন, চারুনেত্র) ; fine, polite. **~কলা** *n.* fine art(s). **~তা** *n.* charm, handsomeness, loveliness; elegance, grace. **~শীলা** *a. fem.* having pleasing manners. **~হাসিনী** *a. fem.* having a charming smile.

চারুত্ব same as **চারুতা** ।

চার্ম *a.* pertaining to skin, dermal, cutaneous; pertaining to hide; cuticular; pertaining to a shield.

চাল[1] *n.* rice. see also **চাউল** ।

চাল[2] *n.* a thatched roof or covering, a thatch (ঘরের চাল, নৌকার চাল) ; a circular canvas of mat containing paintings of heavenly scenes placed at the back of an idol (usu. **চালচিত্র**). **~কুমড়ো** *n.* a kind of pumpkin the plant of which is allowed to creep up on a thatched roof. **~চুলা,** (coll.) **~চুলো** *n.* (lit.) a thatched roof overhead and an oven to cook; (fig.) food and shelter. **চাল কেটে ওঠানো** *v.* to evict (one) from one's homestead.

চাল[3] *n.* mode of living, practice, style (বনেদি চাল) ; behaviour, manners (চালচলন, হালচাল) ; fashion (সেকেলে চাল) ; gait, movement (গদাইলশকরি চাল) ; a deceitful device or move, a trick (চাল ফসকানো) ; (in chess etc.) a move; affectation of superiority, airs (চাল মারা). **চাল কমানো** *v.* to forgo or cut down costly style of living. **~চলন** *n.* bearing, demeanour; deportment. **চাল চালা** *v.* to play a trick (upon); to talk boastfully; (in chess) to make a move. **চাল দেওয়া** *v.* to give airs; to try to hoodwink; (in chess) to make a move. **চাল বদলানো** *v.* to change one's style of living, to adopt a new style of living; to change a trick; (in chess) to change a move. **~বাজ** *a.* one who is accustomed to giving airs; a braggart. **~বাজি** *n.* the practice of giving airs; bragging. **চাল বাড়ানো** *v.* to go in for a better style of living incurring thereby more expenses. **চাল মারা** *v.* to give airs; to speak boastfully.

চালক *a.* one who or that which drives or leads or manages or rules or commands. ☐ *n.* a driver; leader; a manager; a ruler; a commander.

চালতা, (coll.) **চালতে** *n.* an edible acid fruit or its tree, Dillenia speciosa.

চালন, চালনা *n.* act of moving (হস্তচালনা), act of wielding (অসিচালনা) ; exercise (মস্তিষ্কচালনা, দেহচালনা) ; application (বুদ্ধিচালনা) ; management, defraying expenses of (সংসারচালনা) ; ruling, governing (রাজ্যচালনা) ; act of guiding, guidance (সুপথে চালনা) ; act of leading or commanding (সৈন্যচালনা) ; act of directing (দৃষ্টিচালনা) ; act of driving

(পোতচালনা). **চালনা করা** *v.* to move; to wield; to direct; to exercise; to apply; to manage; to rule, to govern; to guide, to lead, to command; to drive.

চালনি *n.* a sieve; a strainer. **চালনি বলে সুঁচকে তোর কেন ছেঁদা** (lit.) a sieve laughs at the eye of a needle; (fig.) a man with countless defects laughs at a small defect in another, the pot calling the kettle black.

চালনীয় *a.* that which or one who can be or is to be moved or wielded or exercised or applied or managed or ruled or guided or led or commanded or driven.

চালপড়া *n.* a handful of rice charmed so as to detect criminals.

চালশে coll. corrup. of **চালিশা**।

চালা[১] *a.* having a thatched roof, thatched (চালাঘর). □ *n.* a thatched house, a thatch; a hut.

চালা[২] *v.* to move (ঘুঁটি চালা) ; to wield (অস্ত্র চালা) ; to exercise (মাথা চালা) ; to make a move; to apply (বুদ্ধি চালা, চাল চালা) ; to lead, to deploy (সৈন্য চালা) ; to cause to move by means of occult power (বাটি চালা) ; to circulate (কথা চালা).

চালাক *a.* clever; intelligent; sly; shrewd. **চালাকি** *n.* cleverness; intelligence; slyness; shrewdness. **চালাকি করা** *v.* to try to outwit or hoodwink; to try to prove one's cleverness.

চালাঘর *n.* a thatched house or room, a thatch; a hut.

চালাচালি *n.* act of moving or circulating about (ঘুঁটি-চালাচালি, কথা-চালাচালি).

চালান (pronun. : চালান্) *n.* consignment (মাল চালান) ; despatch (লোক চালান) ; export (বিদেশে মাল চালান) ; an invoice or a bill of lading; act of sending up for trial (আসামিকে চালান). **চালান দেওয়া** *v.* to consign; to despatch; to export; to send up for trial; to commit to sessions.

চালানো *v.* to conduct, to manage, to run, to carry on (প্রতিষ্ঠান চালানো, সংসার চালানো, কাজ চালানো) ; to drive, to steer, to pilot (গাড়ি চালানো, নৌকা চালানো, এরোপ্লেন চালানো) ; to wield, to use (অস্ত্র চালানো) ; to discharge or fire (গুলি চালানো) ; to circulate (নোতুন টাকা চালানো) ; to introduce (নোতুন নিয়ম চালানো) ; to cause to accept (সমাজে চালানো) ; to find market for (বই চালানো, পণ্যদ্রব্য চালানো) ; to utter or put into circulation esp. unlawfully (জাল টাকা চালানো) ; to cause to move by means of occult power (বাটি চালানো) ; to guide, to lead (ছেলেকে বিপথে চালানো) ; to continue (গান চালানো) ; to defray (খরচ চালানো) ; to cause to move or operate (মেশিন চালানো, ইলেকট্রিক পাখা চালানো). **পা চালানো** *v.* to move one's foot; to kick; to walk quickly or more quickly; to quicken one's steps; to paddle esp. more quickly. **মুখ চালানো** *v.* to talk or eat (esp. voraciously); to scold; to complain, to grumble. **হাত চালানো** *v.* to move one's hands esp. more quickly; to eat or work with the hand esp. quickly or more quickly; to beat.

চালানি *a.* relating to export; exported; exportable; consigned. **চালানি কারবার** export trade. **চালানি মাল** export goods; consigned goods, consignment; not locally produced or fresh. **চালানি শুল্ক** export duty.

চালিত *a.* moved; wielded; exercised; applied; managed; ruled, governed; guided; led or commanded; directed; driven. **চালিত করা** to move; to wield; to exercise; to apply; to manage; to rule, to govern; to guide; to lead or command; to direct; to drive.

চালিতা older var. of **চালতা**।

চালিশা, (coll.) **চালশে** *n.* old-sightedness, long-sightedness, presbyopia. **চালশে ধরা** *v.* to be attacked or affected with presbyopia.

চালু *a.* current, in vogue (চালু মত) ; that which sells in the market, selling, salable (চালু মাল) ; running (চালু কারবার) ; (iron.) social and smart, unscrupulously clever (চালু ছেলে). **চালু করা** *v.* to introduce; to give a start to; to make accepted or acceptable. **চালু থাকা** *v.* to be current, to be in vogue; to be running. **চালু মাল** a marketable or salable commodity; (iron.) a crafty and clever person.

চালুনি pop. var. of **চালনি**।

চাষ[1] *n.* a species of the roller bird.

চাষ[2] *n.* tilling, ploughing, cultivation (জমিচাষ, ধানের চাষ) ; agriculture; culture (মাছের চাষ) ; endeavour or practice for promotion, cultivation (বুদ্ধির চাষ). **চাষ করা** *v.* to till, to plough, to grow (আলু আখ মাছ ইত্যাদির চাষ করা) ; to cultivate. **~বাস** *n.* agriculture.

চাষা, চাষি *n.* a ploughman, a husbandman, a cultivator, a farmer; (dero.) a rude or vulgar person, a boor; (dero.) a clodhopper. **চাষাড়ে** *a.* (rare) like a cultivator; vulgar; uncultured; uneducated; obstinate; rustic. **চাষাভুষা,** (coll.) **চাষাভুষো, চাষিভুষি** *n.* (also *a.*) agriculturists; poor rustic people living by agriculture; uncultured or uneducated rustic people. **গেঁয়ো চাষা** (dero.) a clodhopper; a rustic.

চাহন[1] obs. form of **চাওন**[1]।

চাহন[2] *n.* act of looking at; act of opening one's eyes.

চাহনি *n.* a look, a glance.

চাহিদা *n.* need; demand. **চাহিদা মেটা** *v.* get one's demand fulfilled.

চিংড়ি *n.* the prawn or the shrimp. **কুচো চিংড়ি, ঘুসো চিংড়ি** the shrimp. **গলদা চিংড়ি** the lobster. **বাগদা চিংড়ি** the crayfish or crawfish. **মোচা চিংড়ি, শলা চিংড়ি** the prawn.

চিঁ, চিঁ চিঁ *int.* expressing : a low creeking sound of pain (as made by a small bird).

চিঁড়া older var. of **চিঁড়ে**।

চিঁড়ে *n.* paddy moulded into flattened rice by boiling and then thrashing, flattened rice; (of playing-cards) the club. **চিঁড়ে কোটা** *v.* to thrash boiled paddy into flattened rice. **চিঁড়েচ্যাপটা** *a.* (lit.) flattened as a grain of flattened rice; pressed hard.

চিঁহি, চিঁহিঁহিঁ *int.* expressing a neighing sound. **চিঁহিঁহিঁ করা** *v.* to neigh; (iron.) to speak with a neighing voice.

চিক *n.* a kind of tight-fitting necklace looking like a laced object; a hanging door-screen or sun-blind of laced bamboo-slips etc., a chick.

চিকচিক, চিকমিক *int.* expressing : glitter, glisten, sparkle. **চিকচিক করা** *v.* to sparkle, to glisten. **চিকচিকে, চিকমিকে** *a.* glistening, sparkling.

চিকণ, চিকণিয়া rej. spellings of **চিকন**[2] and **চিকনিয়া**[1] & **চিকনিয়া**[2] respectively.

চিকন[1] *n.* fine embroidery work or needlework on cloth etc. (চিকনের কাজ). ☐ *a.* fine (চিকন কাপড়).

চিকন[2] *a.* glossy, glazing, lustrous; unctuous; beautiful.

চিকনাই, চেকনাই *n.* brightness; glow; glaze, gloss, lustre.

চিকন-কালা *n.* a man having a beautifully dark complexion; an appellation of Krishna (কৃষ্ণ) ; beautiful Krishna.

চিকনিয়া[1] *a.* (in poet.) glossy, lustrous; unctuous; beautiful ('চূড়া চিকণিয়া').

চিকনিয়া[2] *infi. v.* (used as *adv.*) making (it) fine. ('চিকণিয়া গাঁথিনু ফুলমালা').

চিকারি *n.* shorter extra strings of a sitar.

চিকিচ্ছে dial. corrup. of **চিকিৎসা**।

চিকিৎসক *n.* a physician, a doctor, a medical practitioner; a medical officer (আবাসিক চিকিৎসক = a resident medical officer).

চিকিৎসনীয় *a.* that which or one who is to be treated medically; curable, remediable.

চিকিৎসা *n.* the art or act of healing, (medical) treatment; a remedy, a medicine, cure (এ রোগের চিকিৎসা নেই). **চিকিৎসা করা** *v.* to treat medically; to practise medicine. **চিকিৎসায় থাকা** to be under treatment. **~কৃত্যক** *n.* the medical service. **~গার** same as **~লয়**। **~ধীন** *a.* under (medical) treatment. **~বিদ্যা** *n.* the art and science of healing, medical science, medicine. **চিকিৎসা বিভ্রাট** *n.* mis carriage of treatment on account of being wrongly treated or being treated by many physicians simultaneously. **~লয়** *n.* a place where patients are treated, a healing institution, a clinic; a hospital, a nursing home. **~শাস্ত্র** *n.* the science of healing, medical science; a medical treatise; medical treatises collectively; pathology.

চিকিৎসিত *a.* treated medically, under treatment.

চিকিৎস্য *a.* same as **চিকিৎসনীয়**।

চিকীর্ষা *n.* desire for doing. **চিকীর্ষু** *a.* desirous of doing.

চিকুর *n.* hair ('চিকুর ফুরিছে বসন উড়িছে') ; lightning ('চিকুর ঝিকিমিকে'). **~জাল** *n.* (long and luxurant) tresses; a lock of hair.

চিক্কণ *a.* smooth and bright; glossy; glazing, lustrous.

চিক্কুর১ *n.* a thunderbolt; a flash of lightning. **চিক্কুর ঝন্‌ঝনা** thunderclap. **চিক্কুর হানছে** *v.* there is a thunderclap or a flash of lightning.

চিক্কুর২ *n.* (dial.) shrill and loud cry. **চিক্কুর দেওয়া, চিক্কুর মারা** *v.* to utter a shrill and loud cry, to scream, to shriek.

চিঙ্গট *n.* the prawn or the shrimp. *fem.* **চিঙ্গটি** *n.* the shrimp.

চিচিংফাঁক *int.* & *n.*. open sesame.

চিচিঙ্গা, চিচিঙা, (coll.) **চিচিঙে** *n.* a kind of green kitchen vegetable looking like a long tube tapering at both ends, snake gourd, Trichos anthes anguina.

চিচ্ছক্তি *n.* (phil. & theol.) inherent or spiritual cognition or perception.

চিজ১ *n.* (inf & coll.) a thing, an article; a valuable thing; (iron.) a shrewd or wicked or queer person or character (সে একটি চিজ).

চিজ২ *n.* cheese.

চিট১, *n.* a small piece of paper, a slip; a small letter usu. sent by hand, a note; a chit, a memorandum.

চিট২ *n.* viscosity, adhesiveness (চিট ধরা). **~চিটে** *a.* viscous, adhesive, sticky.

চিটা১, (coll.) **চিটে** *a.* dried; having no substance within. □ *n.* a grain of paddy having no substance within.

চিটা২, (coll.) **চিটে** *a.* viscous, adhesive. □ *n.* a kind of course treacle tasting slightly bitter (usu. **চিটাগুড়, চিটেগুড়**).

চিঠি *n.* a letter; an epistle; a memorandum; a missive. **~চাপাটি** *n.* correspondence. **~পত্র** *n.* letter or letters; correspondence.

চিড় *n.* a split, a crack, a rent, a slit; a crevasse; (fig.) dissension, estrangement, separation. **চিড় খাওয়া, চিড় ধরা** *v.* to split, to crack.

চিড়চিড় milder form of **চড়চড়**।

চিড়বিড় *int.* expressing : continuous itching and irritation. **চিড়বিড় করা** *v.* to itch and irritate continuously.

চিড়া var. of **চিঁড়া**।

চিড়িক্ *int.* expressing : the feeling of smarting pain. **চিড়িক মারা** *v.* to smart.

চিড়িতন *n.* (of playing-cards) the club.

চিড়িয়া *n.* the bird. **~খানা** *n.* an aviary; (loos. & pop.) a zoo.

চিড়ে var. of **চিঁড়ে**।

চিত১ poet. corrup. of **চিত্ত**।

চিত২ *a.* lying or laid on one's back or in a dorsal position, (fig.) killed or defeated (তোমার শত্রুরা রণক্ষেত্রে চিত). **চিত করা** *v.* to lay on one's back; (chiefly med.) to cause to turn to a dorsal position; to cause to turn turtle; (fig.) to defeat. **চিত হওয়া** *v.* to lie on one's back; (chiefly med.) to turn to a dorsal position; to turn turtle; (fig.) to be defeated. **~পটাং, ~পাত** *a.* lying fully or flat on one's back. **চিতপটাং বা চিতপাত হওয়া** *v.* to lie or be laid fully on one's back; to be thrown to the ground on one's back. **~সাঁতার** *n.* a style of swimming by floating on one's back.

চিত৩ *a.* culled, collected, plucked; stored, saved up; composed.

চিৎ *n.* (esp. in phil. & theol.) inherent or spiritual cognition or perception.

চিৎকার *n.* a shout; a scream; a yell. **চিৎকার করা** *v.* to shout; to scream; to yell.

চিতল *n.* a variety of flat-fish, the chital.

চিতা১ *n.* a kind of herb (রাংচিতা, শ্বেতচিতা) ; musty spot on cloth caused by damp; mould, mildew; freckles, lentigo. **চিতা-পড়া** *v.* to become mouldy.

চিতা২ *n.* the Indian leopard, the cheetah.

চিতা৩ *n.* a funeral pyre. **~রোহণ** *n.* act of mounting one's funeral pyre for the purpose of being burnt. **চিতারোহণ করা** *v.* to mount one's funeral pyre willingly for the purpose of being burnt; to die (cp. to lie in one's grave). **~ভস্ম** *n.* the ashes of a funeral pile. **রাবণের চিতা** the funeral pyre of Ravana of the Ramayana, said to be burning for ever; (fig.) an everlasting grief or torment.

চিতান falsely elegant var. of **চিতেন**।

চিতানো *v.* to lie or lay flat on one's back,

(med.) to lie or lay in a dorsal position; to swell or expand (বুক চিতানো) ; to awake.

চিতাবাঘ *n.* the leopard.

চিতি, চিতিসাপ *n.* a kind of variegated snake with stripes.

চিতি-কাঁকড়া *n.* a variety of small crab, the fiddler.

চিতে coll. corrup. of চিতা ১,২,৩ ।

চিতেন *n.* the tenor portion of a musical composition.

চিত্ত *n.* the mind; the heart. **~ক্ষোভ** *n.* mental depression; dejection; grief; sorrow. **~গ্রাহী** *a.* captivating; attractive; pleasant. **~চাঞ্চল্য** *n.* mental agitation or perturbation; anxiety, worriedness; unsteadiness of mind; lack or loss of attention. **~চোর** *n.* a captivator of the mind or heart. **~জয়** *n.* winning somebody's heart. **~দমন** *n.* control of the mind; self-restraint. **~দাহ** *n.* anguish; mortification; envy. **~নিরোধ** *n.* absolute concentration of the mind to one and only one point; absolute inward concentration of the mind. **~প্রসাদ** *n.* mental contentment or pleasure, complacency. **~বিকার** *n.* perversion or change of mental state or mood. **~বিক্ষেপ** *n.* distraction of the mind; loss of concentration or attention. **~বিচলন** *n.* perturbation; disquiet; mental agitation. **~বিনোদন** *n.* recreation, amusement, entertainment. **~বিনোদন করা** *v.* to amuse. **~বিভ্রম** *n.* beguilement of the mind; bewilderment. **~বৃত্তি** *n.* the faculty of the mind; feelings and inclinations. **~বেদনা** *n.* affliction, heartache. **~বৈকল্য** same as ~বিভ্রম । **~ভ্রংশ** *n.* loss of mental powers, dementia. **~রঞ্জন** *n.* amusement, recreation, entertainment. ☐ *a.* amusing or pleasing to the heart, pleasant. **~রঞ্জিনী বৃত্তি** aesthetic faculty of the mind. **~শুদ্ধি** *n.* purification of the mind. **~সংযম** *n.* control of the mind; self-restraint. **~স্থৈর্য** *n.* serenity of the mind, mental composure, self-possession. **~হারী, চিত্তাকর্ষক** *a.* captivating, fascinating. *fem.* **চিত্তহারিণী** । **চিত্তোদ্বেগ** *n.* anxiety, worry. **চিত্তোন্নতি** *n.* elevation of the mind.

চিত্র *n.* a picture, a painting, a drawing; a portrait; (esp. in geom.) a figure; a sketch; an illustration; a film or cinema; a description. ☐ *a.* amazing, wonderful; variegated. **~ক** *n.* the Indian leopard, the cheetah; a painter. **~কর, ~কার, ~কৃৎ** *n.* a painter. **~কলা** *n.* (the art of) painting. **~কাব্য** *n.* an acrostic. **~গন্ধ** *n.* sweet fragrance; the yellow orpiment. **~গুপ্ত** *n.* (myth.) the name of the secretary or clerk of Yama (যম) the god of death. **~ণ** *n.* act of painting or drawing or sketching; illustration; decoration; description; delineation, portrayal. **~তারকা** *n.* a film star. **~নাট্য** *n.* a cinematic adaptation of a drama or story or fiction, scenario. **~নাট্যকার** *n.* a scenarist, a writer of scenarios. **~নিপুণ** *a.* skilled in painting. **~নৈপুণ্য** *n.* skill in painting. **~পট** *n.* a (painter's) canvas; a plate or canvas. **~পুত্তলিকা** *n.* a painted image or puppet. **~ফলক** *n.* a plate with a painting; a plate for painting; an easel. **~বৎ** *adv.* like a picture. **~বিচিত্র** *a.* particoloured, motley, variegated; decorated with various paintings, mottled. **~বিদ্যা** *n.* the art and science of painting, painting. **~ভানু** *n.* fire; the sun. **~ময়** *a.* full of pictures or painting; picturesque; described or illustrated by pictures or drawings. *fem.* **~ময়ী** । **~মৃগ** *n.* the spotted deer. **~ল** *a.* same as ~ময় । **~লিপি** *n.* ideogram; pictogram, pictorial symbol or writing. **~শালা** *n.* a painter's studio, an atelier; a picture-gallery. **~শিল্প** *n.* the art of painting. **~শোভিত** *a.* decorated with pictures. **~সমালোচনা** *n.* art criticism; film criticism. **~শিল্পী** *n.* a painter, an artist. **~সূচি** *n.* list of illustrations (in a book).

চিত্রা *n.* the fourteenth of the twenty-seven stars according to Hindu astronomy.

চিত্রাক্ষ *a.* having beautiful eyes.

চিত্রাঙ্কন *n.* drawing or painting pictures.

চিত্রানুগ *a.* picturesque; vivid.

চিত্রাভিনেতা *n.* a filmstar, an actor of a film.

চিত্রায়ণ *n.* drawing pictures, painting pictures; making of a film. **চিত্রায়িত** *a.* (of a picture) drawn; painted; (of a film) made, produced; cinematised.

চিত্রার্পিত *a.* drawn in a picture, painted; motionless like a painted figure. **~বৎ** *adv.* as motionless as a painted figure.

চিত্রালংকার *n.* (rhet.) a kind of writing in the shape of painting.

চিত্রিণী *n.* a woman of the second order of physical excellence.

চিত্রিত *a.* drawn in picture, painted; described; written; decorated; picturesque. **~বৎ** *adv.* like one painted; (dumb) like a picture.

চিদাকাশ *n.* the Supreme Being conceived as unperturbed or indifferent as the sky or conceived as identical or coinciding with the mind; God as conceived from the idealistic and introspective viewpoint; (loos. but pop.) the canvas of the mind conceived as the sky, the firmament of the mind (চিদাকাশে উদয় হল).

চিদাত্মা *n.* the conscious mind or spirit; the knowing or cognitive self; the thinking principle.

চিদানন্দ *n.* the Supreme Being conceived as the source of (spiritual) consciousness or cognition and delight of bliss.

চিদাভাস *n.* manifestation or introduction of (spiritual) consciousness or knowledge; the soul of a living being, the individual soul, (cp. Latin) animus.

চিদ্রূপ *n.* the Soul or the Supreme Soul identified with (spiritual) consciousness and knowledge, the Supreme Being.

চিন[1] poet. corrup. of **চিহ্ন** (লেজের চিন)

চিন[2] *n.* & *a.* coll. corrup. of **চিনা** (চিন-পরিচয়, অচিন).

চিনচিন *int.* expressing very mild inflammation or pain.

চিনা[1], **চেনা** *v.* to recognize; to be acquainted with; to know; to identify (লাশ চেনা) ; to choose or differentiate (ভালোমন্দ চেনা) ; to learn (অক্ষর চেনা). □ *a.* acquainted;known; learnt; familiar. **~নো, ~নো** *v.* to make one acquainted with, to introduce; to cause to know; to enable to chose or differentiate; to teach. **চেনাচিনি** act of being acquainted. **চেনাপরিচয়, চেনাশুনা** *n.* acquaintance.

চিনা[2] pop. var. of **চীনা**।

চিনা[3] *a.* small. **~হাঁস** *n.* a small species of duck.

চিনি *n.* sugar. **~পাতা** *a.* sweetened with sugar in course of processing. **চিনিপাতা দই** sweetened or sugared curd. **চিনির বলদ** (fig.) one who labours hard for another's profit but cannot share it; a drudge. **যে খায় চিনি জোগায় চিন্তামণি** (fig.) the cost of one's good habit is always met by Providence.

চিন্তক *a.* one who thinks, thinking.

চিন্তন *n.* thinking; consideration, cogitation, pondering; meditation; recollection. **চিন্তনীয়** *a.* subject to or requiring thought or consideration or cogitation or meditation; thinkable, cogitable.

চিন্তা *n.* thought, cogitation; meditation; consideration; recollection; imagination; fancy (উদ্ভট চিন্তা) ; anxiety worry (চিন্তায় পড়া, চিন্তাকুল) ; concern, fear (বৃদ্ধ বয়সের আঘাত— চিন্তার কথা). **চিন্তা করা** *v.* to think; to cogitate; to meditate; to consider, to judge; to recollect; to imagine; to fancy; to devise; to be stricken with anxiety, to worry; to be stricken with fear. **চিন্তা নেই** never mind, don't worry; never fear. **চিন্তা হওয়া** *v.* to be worried; to be stricken with fear. **চিন্তাকারী** *a.* one who thinks or cogitates or meditates or considers or judges or recollects or imagines or fancies or devises; anxious, worried; stricken with fear. **~কুল, ~কুলিত** *a.* extremely worried or perturbed or anxious or frightened or alarmed or concerned. **~জনক** *a.* causing anxiety or worry or fear of concern. **~জ্বর** *n.* morbidity caused by anxiety or worry or fear or concern. **~নিমগ্ন, ~ন্বিত, ~ভিভূত, ~মগ্ন** *a.* (extremely) worried; (greatly) stricken with fear or concern; drowned in or overwhelmed with or lost in thought; thoughtful. **~মণি** *n.* a mythological wishing gem; a philosopher's stone; God Narayana (নারায়ণ) ; God. **~শীল** *a.* thoughtful, meditative, musing; pensive; wise.

চিন্তিত *a.* engaged in thinking; thoughtful;

worried, anxious; stricken with fear or anxiety; recollected; considered; devised; meditated. **~পূর্ব** *a.* premeditated. **~ভাবে** *adv.* anxiously; in a pensive mood, thoughtfully. **চিন্ত্য** *a.* requiring consideration, considerable; thinkable; cogitable.

চিন্ময় *a.* personifying (true) consciousness or knowledge (often used as an epithet of the Supreme Being). *fem.* **চিন্ময়ী**।

চিপটান, (coll. & pop.) **চিপটেন** *n.* a heart-rending insinuating remark uttered calmly.

চিপটানো *v.* flatten by squeezing or pressing.

চিপসানো var. of **চুপসানো**।

চিপিটক *n.* paddy moulded into flattened rice by boiling and then thrashing, flattened rice.

চিবনো, চিবানো *v.* to chew, to masticate. ☐ *a.* chewed, masticated. **কড়্মড়্ করে চিবানো** *v.* to crunch. **হামহাম করে চিবানো** *v.* to munch.

চিবুক *n.* the chin.

চিবুনি *n.* chewing, mastication.

চিবোনো alt. spell. of **চিবনো**।

চিমটা *n.* tongs; pincers; forceps. **~নি** *n.* act of pinching. **~নো** *v.* to pinch.

চিমটি *n.* an instance of pinching, a pinch. **চিমটি কাটা** *v.* to pinch.

চিমটে coll. form of **চিমটা**।

চিমড়ে *a.* tough like dried hide (চিমড়ে লুচি) ; very lean and dry (চিমড়ে গড়ন) ; obstinate or disobedient (চিমড়ে স্বভাব).

চিমনি *n.* a chimney.

চিমসা, (coll.) **চিমসে** variants of **চামসা** and **চামসে** respectively.

চির১ (pronun. চির্) *n.* a crack, a slit.

চির২ (pronun. চিরো) *a.* relating to all times, everlasting (চিরসত্য) ; never-ending, endless, perpetual (চিরদুঃখ) ; long-continuing ('সুচিরশবরী') ; all, whole, entire (চিরজীবন, চিরকাল). **চির অন্ধকার** *a.* perpetually dark. ☐ *n.* perpetual darkness. **চির অম্লান** *a.* never-fading, unfading, amaranthine. **~ঋণী** *a.* indebted for ever. **~কর্মা, ~কারী** *a.* sluggish, slow, slothful, dilatory, procrastinating. **~কাঙ্ক্ষিত** *a.* (of a desire) long-cherished. **~কারিতা** *n.* sluggishness, sloth, dilatoriness, procrastination. **~কাল** *n.* all times; eternity. ☐ *adv.* always, ever, for ever; continually, incessantly, perpetually, endlessly; eternally. **~কালীন,** (coll.) **~কেলে** *a.* lasting for or covering all times; very ancient; inveterate. **চিরকালের জন্য** for ever. **~কুমার** *a.* celibate. ☐ *n.* a celibate. *fem.* **~কুমারী**। **~কৌমার্য** *n.* celibacy. **~ক্রিয়** same as **~কর্মা**। **~ক্রীত** *a.* (of slaves etc.) bought or bounded for life-long servitude; obliged or grateful for ever. **~জীবন** *n.* one's whole life. ☐ *adv.* for the whole of one's life, for life. **~জীবিতা** *n.* long life; immortality; everlastingness. **~জীবী, ~ঞ্জীব** *a.* long-lived, immortal; undying, imperishable; everlasting. *fem.* **~জীবিনী**। **চিরজীবী হওয়া** *v.* to live long; to become immortal. **~জ্যোতি** *a.* unfading; full of eternal light or halo. **~তরে** *adv.* for ever. **~তুষার** *n.* the state of being always covered with snow. **~তুষার রেখা** *n.* the snow-line. **~ত্ব** *n.* perpetuity. **~দারিদ্র** *n.* perpetual poverty. **~দাসত্ব** *n.* life-long slavery or servitude or dependence; perpetual or long-continued dependence. **~দিন** same as **~কাল**। **~দুঃখ** *n.* perpetual or long-continued affliction or sorrow. **~দুঃখী** *a.* aggrieved or afflicted or distressed for ever or for a long time. *fem.* **~দুঃখিনী**। **~নবীন** same as **~নূতন**। **~নিদ্রা** *n.* eternal sleep; death. **~নিদ্রিত, ~নিদ্রাভিভূত** *a.* succumbed to eternal sleep; dead. **চিরনিদ্রিত** বা **চিরনিদ্রাভিভূত হওয়া** *v.* to succumb to eternal sleep; to die. **~নির্বাসন** *n.* banishment or transportation for life. **চিরনির্বাসিত করা** *v.* to banish or transport for life. **~নির্ভর** *n.* (a source of) never-failing help or support. ☐ *a.* always offering help or support; (inc.) always depending on for help or support. **~নির্ভরতা** *n.* act of depending for ever for help or support. **~নীহার** same as **~তুষার**। **~নূতন** *a.* ever new, fresh for ever. **~ন্তন** *a.* existing or continuing for ever; perpetual, eternal; endless; of long standing (চিরন্তন প্রথা). *n.* **~ন্তনতা** eternity; perpetuity. *fem.*

~স্তনী। ~পরিচিত *a.* known for ever; known for long. ~প্রচলিত *a.* prevailing for ever or for a long time. ~প্রবাস *n.* act of living abroad or away from one's home for ever or for a pretty long time. ~প্রবাসী *a.* living abroad or away from one's home for ever or for a pretty long time. ~প্রবাহিত *a.* ever-flowing. ~প্রসিদ্ধ *a.* famous or well-known for ever or for a pretty long time. ~প্রসিদ্ধি *n.* state of being famous or well-known for ever or for a pretty long time. ~বাঞ্ছিত *a.* ever-desired; long-desired. ~বিচ্ছেদ *n.* separation or estrangement for ever. ~বিদায় *n.* adieu for ever; last or final parting or separation. **চিরবিদায় গ্রহণ করা** *v.* to bid farewell for ever; to be separated for ever. ~বিদ্বেষ *n.* perpetual or long-existing malice. ~বিদ্বেষী *a.* malicious for ever or for a long time. ~বৈরি, ~শত্রুতা *n.* perpetual or long-lasting enmity or feud. ~বৈরী, ~শত্রু *n.* a perpetual or old enemy. ~রিপু *n.* same as ~বৈরী। ~রুগ্ণ *a.* ailing for ever. ~শরণ *n.* (a source of) never-failing help or support. ~শ্যামল *a.* evergreen. ~সখা *n.* a constant friend, a friend for ever. ~সঙ্গী *n.* a constant companion. ~সহচর *n.* same as ~সঙ্গী। ~সুখী *a.* happy for ever. ~সুহৃৎ *n.* a constant friend; an old friend. ~স্থায়িত্ব *n.* permanence; durability, stability; immutability. ~স্থায়ী *a.* everlasting, perpetual; long-lasting; constant; permanent. **চিরস্থায়ী বন্দোবস্ত** Permanent Settlement. ~স্থির *a.* unmoved or steady or calm or unperturbed for ever. ~স্মরণীয় *a.* worthy of being remembered for ever, unforgettable. ~হরিৎ *a.* evergreen.

চিরকুট *n.* a small piece of paper, a slip; a short letter, a memorandum, a note; a piece of rag; a piece of dirty and ragged loincloth.

চিরণী, চিরণি rej. spellings of **চিরনি**।

চিরতা *n.* a bitter-tasting medicinal herb, Swertia chirata.

চিরনদাঁতি *a. fem.* having sparsely set teeth, having spaced teeth.

চিরনি var. of **চিরুনি**।

চিরা, চেরা *v.* to cleave, to split; to hew, to saw (কাঠি চেরা) ; to slice; to scratch (আমার গা চিরেছে) ; to incise, to gash, to cut; to cut open, to operate (পেট চিরে বার করা). □ *a.* cloven, cleft, split; sliced; scratched; incised, gashed; cut open, operated.

চিরাই, চেরাই *n.* act of hewing or sawing; charge or cost of hewing or sawing.

চিরাগ var. of **চেরাগ**।

চিরাগত *a.* prevailing for ever; conventional, of long usage.

চিরাচরিত *a.* practised for ever; practised through the ages; traditional.

চিরানো *v.* to cause to cleave or split or hew or saw or slice or scratch or incise or gash or cut open or operate.

চিরাভ্যস্ত *a.* practised or habituated for a long time or for ever.

চিরাভ্যাস *n.* a long or permanent practice or habit.

চিরায়ত *a.* pervading or pervaded for ever; all-pervading; eternal and universal. **চিরায়ত সাহিত্য** classical literature, classics.

চিরায়মানা *a. fem.* existing or living for ever; immortal; long-lived.

চিরায়ু, চিরায়ুষ্মান *a.* living for ever, immortal; long-lived. *fem.* **চিরায়ুষ্মতী** immortal; long-lived; never-widowed.

চিরাশ্রিত *a.* of one who is for ever sheltered or protected.

চিরুনি *n.* a comb; an instrument for combing or carding wool etc., a card; a heckle.

চিল *n.* a kind of rapacious bird, the kite.

চিলতা, (coll.) **চিলতে** *n.* a thin or small slice or slip (এক চিলতে মাছ, এক চিলতে কাগজ).

চিলমচি *n.* a basin for washing hands and mouth, a wash-basin.

চিলে কোঠা *n.* an attic, a garret.

চিল্লাচিল্লি *n.* a hue and cry, an uproar, a hullabaloo, an outcry. **চিল্লাচিল্লি করা** *v.* to make a hullabaloo, to raise an uproar.

চিল্লানো *v.* to shout, to give a loud or sharp cry; to make a hullabaloo, to raise an uproar.

চিহ্ন *n.* a stain, a stigma, a spot (কালির চিহ্ন, ক্ষতচিহ্ন) ; a mark, a line (সীমাচিহ্ন) ; an impression, a print (পদচিহ্ন) ; a sign

(মৃত্যুর চিহ্ন, দুঃখের চিহ্ন) ; an insignia, a symbol (রাজচিহ্ন) ; a token (প্রণয়চিহ্ন) ; a hint, a beck, a beacon; a notation. **ক্ষতচিহ্ন** *n.* a cicatrice, a scar left by a healed wound. **স্মৃতিচিহ্ন** *n.* a memento, a keepsake. **চিহ্নিত** *a.* stained, stigmatized, branded, stamped; marked; marked off; printed; bearing a sign.

চীজ[১] rej. spell. of **চিজ[১]** ।

চীজ[২] rej. spell. of **চিজ[২]** ।

চীৎকার rej. spell. of **চিৎকার** ।

চীন *n.* China. **চীন সাধারণতন্ত্র** *n.* the Chinese Republic.

চীনা *n.* a Chinaman, a Chinese. ☐ *a.* Chinese. **চীনাংশুক** *n.* Chinese silk. **~ঘাস** China grass. **~বাদাম** *n.* ground-nut, peanut, monkey-nut. **~মাটি** *n.* porcelain, chinaclay, kaolin. **~মাটির বাসন** chinaware, china, porcelain. **~সিঁদুর** *n.* the Chinese vermilion or red lead.

চীবর *n.* a piece of scanty loincloth as worn by an ascetic; a piece of rag.

চীর *n.* a piece of rag; bark of a tree; a slip of paper.

চীর্ণ *a.* torn; cleaved; split; cracked.

চুঁইচুঁই *int.* expressing : a mild singing sound caused by boiling; an uneasy feeling caused by extreme hunger or contraction.

চুঁচি *n.* (vul.) the breasts of a woman.

চুঁয়া, চোঁয়া *a.* giving out a bad smell as of the smoke of coal (চোঁয়া দুধ) ; tasting of bile, bilious (চোঁয়া ঢেকুর = bilious eructation). **চুঁয়ানো** *v.* to calcine slightly or partly. ☐ *a.* calcined slightly or partly.

চুক *n.* (used as a correl. of ভুল) a fault, a defect, a failing.

চুকচুক *int.* expressing : mild sound of licking or sipping liquids; sound of sucking or lisping.

চুকলি *n.* act of informing against maliciously (and usu. falsely), tale-bearing; backbiting. **চুকলি খাওয়া** *v.* to inform against maliciously (and usu. falsely); to backbite. **~খোর** *a.* given to tale-bearing or backbiting. ☐ *n.* a tale-bearer; a backbiter.

চুকা[১] *a.* (dial.) sour, acid. **চুকা পালং** a variety of sorrel.

চুকা[২], চোকা *v.* to be finished, to end, to terminate (কাজ চোকা) ; to be decided or settled (মামলা চুকেছে) ; to be solved (সমস্যা চুকে যাবে) ; to be repaid (দেনা চোকা).

চুকানো *v.* to finish, to end, to complete; to decide or settle; to solve; to repay.

চুক্তি *n.* a term, a condition, a stipulation (দলিলের চুক্তি) ; a contract, an agreement (চুক্তি করা) ; a settlement (মামলার চুক্তি হওয়া) ; completion or termination (এতক্ষণে খাটুনির চুক্তি). **চুক্তি করা** *v.* to make a condition, to stipulate; to enter into an agreement, to contract. **~নামা** *n.* a deed of agreement, a contract. **~ভঙ্গ** *n.* breach of contract.

চুঙ্গি, চুঙি *n.* a narrow and small pipe or tube; duty on exports and imports; octroi or duty levied on goods entering a town for sale (also **চুঙ্গিকর**).

চুচুক *n.* the nipple, the teat, the pap.

চুচুকৃতি *n.* a mild noise of licking or sipping or sucking or lisping or kissing; the nipple, the teat, the pap.

-চুঞ্চু *a.* (used as a *sfx.*) famed for proficiency in (ন্যায়চুঞ্চু ; বিদ্যাচুঞ্চু).

চুটকি[১] *n.*(sl.) a tuft of uncut hair kept at the back of the head by some Brahmins.

চুটকি[২] *n.* a ring with small bells worn by women on their toes; a sound made by rubbing the thumb and the middle finger (cp. fillip, flip); a pinch; easy familiar talk or writing gossip. ☐ *a.* light; flippant; short light and humorous or sarcastic (চুটকি সাহিত্য).

চুটানো *v.* to do one's utmost, to employ or exert utmost strength or power, to apply one's energies to the full (চুটিয়ে কাজ করা).

চুড় *n.* a bracelet.

চুড়ি *n.* a variety of thin bangle. **~দার** *a.* (of garments) plaited. ☐ *n.* the Indian woman's pyjama-like dress plaited at the fringes, the salwar.

চুড়ো coll. var. of **চূড়া** ।

চুণ, চুণা rej. spellings of **চুন** and **চুনা** respectively.

চুণি, চুণী rej. spellings of **চুনি** ।

চুন *n.* lime; calcium. □ *a.* pale (মুখ চুন হওয়া). **চুন ফোটানো** *v.* to slake lime. **চুনের জল** limewater. **চুনের ভাটি** a lime-kiln.

চুনকাম *n.* whitewash, limewash. **চুনকাম করা** *v.* to whitewash, to limewash.

চুনকালি *n.* (fig.) disrepute, disgrace, infamy. **মুখে চুনকালি দেওয়া** (lit.) to besmear one's face with lime-paste and soot as a mark of disgrace; (fig.) to put to shame, to disgrace.

চুনট *n.* a pucker, a wrinkle; contraction, shrinking; (of garments) a frill. □ *a.* puckered, wrinkled; contracted, shrivelled; frilled.

চুনবালি *n.* mixture of sand, lime and water (so prepared or mixed for plastering walls etc.), mortar. (দেওয়াল প্রভৃতিতে) **চুনবালি ধরানো** *v.* to plaster (walls etc.) with the mixture of sand and lime or mortar.

চুনরি var. of **চুনুরি** ।

চুনা[1] *a.* limy, calcareous, calciferous. **~পাথর** limestone.

চুনা[2], (coll.) **চুনো** *n.* any variety of the smallest fish. □ *a.* very small (চুনো মাছ) ; very narrow (চুনোগলি).

চুনাট var. of **চুনট** ।

চুনারি[1] var. of **চুনুরি**[1] ।

চুনারি[2] *n.* a lime-manufacturer by caste or trade.

চুনি *n.* a ruby; an emerald.

চুনুরি[1] *n.* a piece of coloured or dyed loincloth or cloth. □ *a.* coloured, dyed.

চুনুরি[2] var. of **চুনারি**[2] ।

চুনো pop. var. of **চুনা**[1] and **চুনা**[2] ।

চুনোপুঁটি *n.* very small fish; (sarcas.) a negligible person, a small fry.

চুপ *a.* silent, hushed; speechless. □ *int.* silence, hush. **চুপ করা** *v.* to become silent; to keep quiet, to keep mum; to hush. **চুপ করানো** *v.* to silence, to hush. **চুপ থাকা** *v.* to remain silent; to keep quiet. **চুপ মারা, চুপ হওয়া** *v.* to become silent; to stop talking; to stop, to cease (গোলমাল চুপ হওয়া).

চুপচাপ *a.* silent; noiseless; speechless; inactive (বিপ্লবীরা চুপচাপ হয়ে গেছে) ; ceased, discontinued (আন্দোলন চুপচাপ হওয়া). □ *adv.* noiselessly, without noise (চুপচাপ কাজ করে যায়). **চুপচাপ স্বভাবের** by nature calm and secretive.

চুপটি *a.* perfectly silent or noiseless or speechless. **চুপটি করে, চুপটি মেরে** quite silently or noiselessly or speechlessly.

চুপড়ি *n.* a wicker-basket.

চুপসা, চুপসানো[1] *a.* depressed, sunk, fallen, shrunken (চুপসা গাল) ; shrunk esp. because of the coming out of the inside matter (চুপসা ফোড়া). □ *v.* to become depressed, to sink, to fall; to shrink.

চুপসানো[2] *v.* to soak, to absorb, to smudge (ব্লটিং কাগজে কালি চুপসানো).

চুপিচুপি, চুপিসারে, চুপেচুপে *adv.* noiselessly; unobservedly; stealthily, lurkingly; secretly; whisperingly.

চুবড়ি dial. var. of **চুপড়ি** ।

চুবানি, চুবুনি *n.* a spell or act of dipping, immersion.

চুবানো *v.* to immerse thoroughly for a time, to immerse. □ *a.* dipped, immersed.

চুমকি *n.* a spangle, a foil, a tinsel. **~বসানো** *a.* spangled, tinselled.

চুমকুড়ি *n.* the sound of noisy kissing; any similar sound. **চুমকুড়ি দেওয়া** *v.* to kiss noisily; to sip or suck noisily.

চুমরানো *v.* to adulate or cajole into doing something; to twist the end(s) of (গোঁপ চুমরানো).

চুমরি *n.* the spathe of the coconut, date etc.

চুমা, (coll.) **চুমু** *n.* a kiss. **চুমু খাওয়া, চুমু দেওয়া** *v.* to give a kiss, to kiss. **চুমাচুমি,** (coll.) **চুমোচুমি** *n.* mutual kissing.

চুমুক *n.* a draught, a sip. **চুমুক দেওয়া** *v.* to take a draught, to sip. **এক চুমুকে** in one sip, at a draught.

চুমো coll. var. of **চুমা** ।

চুম্ব var. of **চুম্বন** ।

চুম্বই *v.* (poet.) kisses, kiss. □ *v. imp.* (poet.) kissing.

চুম্বক *n.* magnet, lodestone, loadstone (also **চুম্বক-পাথর**) ; an abstract, a gist, a summary (ন্যায়শাস্ত্রের চুম্বক). **তাড়িত-চুম্বক** *n.* electro-magnet. **~ক্ষেত্র** *n.* a magnetic field. **~ত্ব** *n.* magnetic force or power; magnetism. **~ত্বহরণ** *n.* demagnetization. **~ন** *n.* magnetization. **~শলাকা** *n.* a magnetic needle. **চুম্বকিত** *a.* magnetized. **চুম্বকীয়** *a.* magnetic.

চুম্বন *n.* kissing; a kiss. **চুম্বন করা** *v.* to kiss.

চুম্বিত *a.* kissed; touched; contiguous.

চুম্বী *a.* (*sfx.*) kissing; touching; contiguous; scraping (গগনচুম্বী).

চুয়া *n.* a kind of condensed perfume.

চুয়াত্তর *n.* & *a.* seventy-four.

চুয়ানো *v.* to fall in drops, to exude, to ooze; to distil. ☐ *a.* fallen or falling in drops, exuded or exuding, oozed or oozing; distilled. **চুয়ানি** *n.* oozing; exudation.

চুয়ান্ন *n.* & *a.* fifty-four.

চুয়াল্লিশ *n.* & *a.* forty-four.

চুর *n.* powder, dust (লোহাচুর). ☐ *a.* stupefied, dazed (নেশায় চুর) ; pulverized; crumbled; destroyed ('যশ অর্থ মান স্বার্থ সকলি করেছ চুর').

চুরট var. of **চুরুট**।

চুরমার *a.* broken or crumbled or shattered to pieces; utterly destroyed.

চুরানব্বই, (coll.) **চুরানব্বুই** *n.* & *a.* ninety-four.

চুরাশি *n.* & *a.* eighty-four.

চুরি *n.* an instance or act of stealing, pilferage, theft. **চুরি করা** *v.* to steal, to pilfer; to lift. **চুরি হওয়া** *v.* to be stolen. **~চামারি** *n.* pilferage, filching; unfair and shameful act or means; stealth. **চুরি করে** by means of stealing; by stealth, stealthily.

চুরুট *n.* a cigar not pointed at either end, a cheroot; a cigar. **চুরুট খাওয়া** *v.* to smoke a cheroot or cigar. **চুরুটিকা** *n.* a small cheroot or cigar, cigarette.

চুল *n.* hair (of the head). **চুল এলানো** *v.* to dishevel hair. **চুল খোলা** *v.* to undo or undress hair. **চুল বাঁধা** *v.* to dress hair; to do up or put up hair. **চুলের গোছা** a tuft of hair. **চুলের গোড়া** the root of hair. **একচুল** *a.* amounting to the turning of a hair; hair's breadth. ☐ *adv.* by a hair's breadth. **~চেরা** *a.* hair-splitting. **চুল-চেরা বিচারে** by judgement resting on subtle arguments and fine distinctions. **চুল-চেরা বিচার করা** বা **প্রভেদ করা** *v.* to split hair. **~পরিমাণ** *a.* hair-breadth.

চুলকনা, চুলকনি *n.* itches, scabbies; an itching sensation, itching; (sarcas.) undue curiosity, or interest.

চুলকানো *v.* to itch; to be stricken with a desire for scratching. **পিঠ চুলকানো** *v.* (sarcas.) to be desirous of being beaten or flogged. **মুখ চুলকানো, জিভ চুলকানো** *v.* (hum.) to be desirous of speaking or of opening one's mouth. **হাত চুলকানো** *v.* (hum.) to be desirous of beating or flogging.

চুলকানি, চুলকুনি variants of **চুলকনা**।

চুলচেরা, চুলপরিমাণ see **চুল**।

চুলবুল *int.* expressing restlessness. **চুলবুল করা** *v.* (sarcas.) to be restless. **পিঠ চুলবুল করা** *v.* to itch for having a beating or flogging. **মুখ চুলবুল করা** *v.* (hum.) to itch for opening one's mouth, to itch for talking. **হাত চুলবুল করা** *v.* (hum.) to have an itch to beat or flog. **চুলবুলে** *a.* restless. **চুলবুলানি** *n.* restlessness.

চুলা, (coll.) **চুলো** *n.* an oven, a furnace; a stove; a pyre. **চুলো জ্বালানো, চুলো ধরানো** *v.* to ignite an oven or furnace or stove or pyre, to make a fire in an oven etc. **চুলোয় যা** (*imprec.*) go to hell. **চুলোর দোরে যা** (*imprec.*) go to death's door.

চুলাচুলি, (coll.) **চুলোচুলি** *n.* act of pulling one another by the hair; (fig.) a terrible quarrel or scramble. **চুলোচুলি করা** *v.* to pull one another by the hair; (fig.) to quarrel or scramble (together) terribly.

চুল্লি *n.* an oven; a furnace; a stove; a pyre.

চুষা, চোষা *v.* to suck. ☐ *a.* sucked (বাদুড়েচোষা ফল) ; sucking (রক্তচোষা).

চুষানো, চোষানো *a.* to cause to suck.

চুষি *n.* an artificial nipple or pap. (also **চুষিকাঠি**). **~পিঠে** *n.* a kind of semi-liquid dish of sweetmeat.

চূড়া *n.* top, summit (বৃক্ষচূড়া, পর্বতচূড়া) ; a peak; a pinnacle (মন্দিরের চূড়া) ; a diadem, a crown, a coronet; the solemn ceremony of shaving one's head leaving a tuft of hair uncut; (cp.) tonsuring (also **চূড়াকরণ, চূড়াকর্ম**) ; a tuft of hair thus left out uncut (চূড়া বাঁধা). **চূড়ান্ত** *n.* the acme or extreme; conclusion, decision; finality. ☐ *a.* extreme; conclusive, decisive; final. **~মণি** *n.* a jewel for a diadem or crown; a title awarded to some scholars; (fig.) the best or chief man. ~মণিযোগ *n.* a conjunction of planets regarded as holy by Hindus.

চূত *n.* (*for.*) the mango tree; the mango. ~**মঞ্জরি** *n.* mango-bud.

চূর্ণ *n.* powder, dust; lime; coloured powder thrown at one another on the holi (হোলি) festival. ☐ *a.* pulverized, powdered; broken; fractured (অস্থি চূর্ণ হওয়া) ; utterly destroyed (আশা চূর্ণ হওয়া). ~**কার** *n.* a manufacturer of lime (by trade or caste). ~**কুন্তল** *n.* forelock; a ringlet. ~**ন** *n.* pulverization; act of breaking; act of fracturing; utter destruction. ~**নীয়** *a.* pulverizable; breakable; frangible; easily fractured; destructible; that which is to be pulverized or broken or destroyed. ~**বিচূর্ণ** *a.* broken to pieces, broken to smithereens; utterly pulverized; utterly destroyed. **চূর্ণিত, চূর্ণীকৃত, চূর্ণীভূত** *a.* pulverized, powdered; broken; fractured; utterly destroyed.

চূষণীয় *a.* that which is to be or can be sucked.

চূষিত *a.* sucked.

চূষ্য var. of **চূষণীয়** ।

চেং rej. spell. of **চ্যাং** ।

চেংড়া alt. spell. of **চ্যাংড়া** ।

চেঁচাড়ি *n.* a slip or lath of bamboo.

চেঁচানি *n.* same as **চেঁচামেচি** ।

চেঁচানো *v.* to shout; to scream; to yell; (dero.) to talk or read or sing or lecture loudly. **চেঁচিয়ে** *adv.* loudly, in a loud voice.

চেঁচামেচি *n.* a confused loud noise, hullabaloo, hue and cry. **চেঁচামেচি করা** *v.* to make a hullabaloo; to clamour, to raise a hue and cry.

চেঁচেপুঁছে *adv.* by licking a plate or dish or any similar object dry; by licking up entirely.

চেক[1] *n.* a pattern of cross lines forming small squares, a check; a piece of checked cloth. ☐ *a.* checked, checkered, chequered. **চেক-কাটা** *a.* checked, checkered, chequered.

চেক[2] *n.* a bank-cheque, a cheque. **চেক কাটা** *v.* to write out a cheque, to draw a cheque. **চেক ভাঙানো** *v.* to cash a cheque. (ব্যাঙ্ক কর্তৃক) **চেকে টাকা না দেওয়া** *v.* to dishonour a cheque, to bounce. ~**দাখিলা** *n.* a descriptive rent-receipt (given by a landowner containing the particulars about the land and its tenancy). ~**বই** *n.* a cheque-book. ~**মুড়ি** *n.* the counterfoil of a descriptive rent receipt.

চেকনাই pop. var. of **চিকনাই** ।

চেঙ্গমুড়ী, চেঙ্গমুড়ি *a.* (usu. *fem.*) having an extremely small head (চেঙ্গমুড়ী কাণী).

চেঙ্গারি, চেঙারি variants of **চাঙাড়ি** ।

চেট, চেটক see **চেটী** ।

চেটাং চেটাং alt. spell. of **চ্যাটাং চ্যাটাং** ।

চেটালো alt. spell. of **চ্যাটালো** ।

চেটী, চেটিকা, চেড়ী *n. fem.* a maid-servant; a female attendant or follower; (myth.) a female guard of Lanka, a female guard, a guardswoman. *masc.* **চেট, চেটক, চেড়** a man-servant, a servant; a follower or attendant; a guard, a guardsman.

চেটো *n.* the palm (of the hand); the sole (of the foot).

চেড়, চেড়ী see **চেটী** ।

চেতঃ *n.* the mind; the heart; mental powers, cognition; mental attitude, mentality; animus.

চেতক *a.* one who or that which gives consciousness or knowledge; enlightening; animating.

চেতন *a.* conscious; sensible; having knowledge, knowing, enlightened; animated; living. ☐ *n.* consciousness; sensibility; conscience; knowledge, enlightenment, light; animation; a living being, an animate creature; the soul (cp. Latin anima or animus). **চেতন পদার্থ** an animate object.

চেতনা *n.* consciousness; sensibility; sensation; feeling; perception; conscience; knowledge; cognition; good sense (পাপিষ্ঠের চেতনা হওয়া) ; animation, life. **চেতনা থাকা** *v.* to have consciousness or sensibility or sensation; to be conscious or aware of; to have animation. **চেতনা জাগানো** *v.* to instil consciousness or awaken sensation; to give knowledge; to make one conscious of a fault etc. **চেতনা পাওয়া** *v.* to regain consciousness;

to come back to senses; to become conscious of a fault etc. ~শূন্য, ~হীন *a*. unconscious, insensible; impercipient, insensitive. চেতনা হারানো *v*. to lose consciousness; to swoon, to faint.

চেতা *v*. to regain consciousness; to become conscious; to become active. চেতানো *v*. to bring to consciousness; to make conscious; to warn; to make active, to animate, to stimulate; to tease, to irritate.

চেতাবনি *n*. a warning.

চেন *n*. a chain.

চেনা pop. var. of চিনা। ~জানা *a*. known and familiar (চেনাজানা লোক). ~নো, চিনিয়ে দেওয়া *v*. to introduce, to make known.

চেপটা *a*. flat (চেপটা নাক) ; flattened (usu. by pressure.) ~নো *v*. to make flat, to flatten. ☐ *a*. flattened.

চেপে ধরা, চেপে যাওয়া see চাপা।

চেয় *a*. that which is to be or should be plucked or culled or collected.

চেয়ার *n*. a chair. ~ম্যান *n*. a chairman.

চেয়ে *con*. than.

চেরা, চেরাই pop. variants of চিরা and চিরাই respectively.

চেরাগ *n*. (Mus.) a lamp (usu. a small and cheap one). চেরাগি *n*. a piece of rentfree land granted for bearing the cost of burning lamps regularly in the tomb of a Muslim saint.

চেরানো pop. var. of চিরানো।

চেল *n*. loincloth; garment, raiment.

চেলা[১] *n*. a kind of very small silvery fish.

চেলা[২] *n*. a disciple, a follower, a chela. ~গিরি *n*. discipleship. যেমন গুরু তেমনি চেলা like master, like man.

চেলা[৩], **চেলাকাঠ** *n*. a chopped log of wood.

চেলানো *v*. to chop or cause to chop (as with an axe).

চেলি, চেলিকা *n*. a kind of silk cloth or loincloth usu. worn in religious festivals.

চেলো *n*. a violincello, a cello.

চেল্লাচিল্লি var. of চিল্লাচিল্লি।

চেল্লানো var. of চিল্লানো।

চেষ্টক *a*. one who endeavours, endeavouring, trying; one who seeks; enterprising.

চেষ্টন *n*. act of endeavouring or trying; act of seeking.

চেষ্টমান *a*. engaged in endeavouring or seeking or procuring.

চেষ্টা *n*. an instance or act of trying, an endeavour, an attempt; an effort; an enterprise; act of seeking. চেষ্টা করা, চেষ্টা পাওয়া *v*. to try, to endeavour; to attempt; to seek. ~চরিত্র *n*. continuous or careful effort or efforts. ~ন্বিত same as চেষ্টমান। ~শূন্য, ~হীন *a*. effortless; unenterprising; inactive; idle.

চেষ্টিত same as চেষ্টমান।

চেষ্টিতব্য *a*. worth attempting, endeavouring.

চেহারা *n*. appearance; countenance; form, figure, shape. চেহারা দেখানো *v*. to show oneself in, to present oneself, to appear; to appear as, to seem (to be), to look.

চৈ rej. spell. of চই।

চৈত poet. corrup. of চৈত্র।

চৈতন *n*. a tuft of uncut hair on the head maintained esp. by a Brahmin.

চৈতন্য *n*. consciousness; sensibility; sensation; feeling; perception; conscience; knowledge; cognition; good sense; animation, life; awakening; watchfulness; (chiefly sarcas.) a tuft of uncut hair on the head maintained by Hindus esp. by a Brahmin. চৈতন্য থাকা *v*. to have consciousness or sensibility or sensation; to be conscious or aware (of); to have animation. চৈতন্য জাগানো *v*. to instil with consciousness or sensation; to give knowledge; to make one conscious of a fault etc. চৈতন্য পাওয়া *v*. to regain consciousness; to come back to one's senses; to become conscious of a fault etc.; to earn knowledge. চৈতন্য হারানো *v*. to lose consciousness; to swoon, to faint.

চৈতন্যোদয় *n*. dawning of consciousness; spiritual awakening; coming to one's senses, regaining consciousness.

চৈতালি *n*. the crop of the month of Chaitra (চৈত্র) ; rent or revenue to be paid in the month of Chaitra (চৈত্র) ; vernal breeze; emotion or passion experienced during the spring, vernal emotion or passion. □ *a.* grown in or relating to the month of চৈত্র।

চৈতি *a.* of the month of Chaitra (চৈত্র).

চৈত্ত, চৈত্তিক *a.* mental.

চৈত্য[1] *n.* a place of worship or sacrifice; a Buddhist monastery or shrine or monument esp. one containing one or more relics of Gautama Buddha.

চৈত্য[2] *a.* relating to a (funeral) pyre. □ *n.* a tree near a cemetery to be worshipped by Jainas (জৈন).

চৈত্র *n.* the last month of the Bengali year (from the middle of March to the middle of April.) **~সংক্রান্তি** *n.* the last day of the month of Chaitra.

চৈন, চৈনিক *a.* Chinese (চৈনিক সংস্কৃতি).

চোঁ *int.* expressing : the noise of swishing movement or of sucking quickly in one breath. **চোঁ করে** *adv.* very quickly; with a swishing movement, boltingly; in one breath. **চোঁচা** *adv.* (also *a.*) straight ahead and with utmost speed. **চোঁচা দৌড় মারা** *v.* to dart or bolt straight ahead, to scamper off. **চোঁ চোঁ করে** *adv.* very quickly; swishingly; quickly and breathlessly (চোঁ চোঁ করে দুধ খাওয়া).

চোঁচ *n.* slender but finely pointed fibre of wood,bamboo etc.

চোঁয়া, চোঁয়ানো pop. variants of **চুঁয়া** and **চুঁয়ানো** respectively.

চোক *n.* (obs.) one-fourth of a kahan (কাহন) ; one-fourth of anything; a symbol indicating one-fourth.

চোকলা *n.* rind or skin of fruits and vegetables; husk of corn; a flake or slice.

চোকা, চোকানো pop. variants of **চুকা**[2] and **চুকানো** respectively.

চোখ *n.* the eye. **চোখ ওঠা** *v.* to be afflicted with ophthalmia or inflammation of the eye. **চোখ গালা** *v.* to force out the eyeballs with fingers, to gouge. **চোখ ঝলসানো** *v.* to dazzle the eye, to dazzle; to be dazzled. **চোখ টাটানো** *v.* to have pain in one's eyes; (fig.) to be stricken with jealousy, to envy. **চোখ টেপা, চোখ ঠারা** *v.* to nictitate, to wink (at); to wink significantly. **চোখ দেওয়া** *v.* to cast an evil eye on. **চোখ ধাঁধানো** same as **চোখ ঝলসানো।** **চোখ পাকানো** *v.* to goggle in anger, to roll one's eyes; to frown. **চোখ পিটপিট করা** *v.* to blink; to wink. **চোখ ফোটা** *v.* (of young birds) to have eyes opened for the first time; (fig.) to be enlightened (esp. suddenly). **চোখ বুজে থাকা** *v.* (fig.) to refuse to take notice of, to close eyes to, to connive at. **চোখ বোজা** *v.* to close or shut eyes; (fig.) to die. **চোখ রাঙানো, চোখ লাল করা** *v.* (lit.) to redden one's eyes; (fig.) to look with angry eyes. **চোখ রাখা** *v.* to keep a watch (on), to keep an eye (on). **চোখে আঙুল দিয়ে দেখানো** *v.* to show or demonstrate or prove beyond doubt. **চোখে চোখে রাখা** *v.* to keep always an eye on; to keep under continuous observation or constant watch or surveillance. **চোখে জল আসা** *v.* to have tears in one's eyes, to feel like weeping. **চোখে ধুলো দেওয়া** *v.* (fig.) to throw dust in one's eyes, to hoodwink. **চোখে-মুখে কথা বলা** *v.* to talk smartly and cleverly; to display one's gift of the gab; to talk overmuch in order to conceal something; to talk too much; to prattle. **চোখের আড়ালে** out of sight; unobservedly; at one's back. **চোখের উপরে** before ones eyes. **চোখের জল** a tear-drop, tear. **চোখের জল ফেলা** *v.* to weep, to shed tears. **চোখের তারা** pupil of the eye. **চোখের দেখা** act of seeing only and nothing else; seeing only for a moment. **চোখের নেশা** a fascination of the eye, a strong desire of seeing only and nothing else. **চোখের পাতা** eyelid. **চোখের বালি** a mote in one's eye; (fig.) an eyesore. **চোখের ভুল** illusion; optical illusion. **চোখের মণি** *n.* the pupil of the eye; (fig.) a darling, a very dear person. **চোখের মাথা খাওয়া** (in abuses) to be lacking in ability to see, to fail to take notice (of), to be unobservant. **চোখে সরষে ফুল দেখা** (fig.) to be dazed (esp. being stricken with fear); to find everything falling to ruin. **কটা চোখ** brown eyes (as those of a cat). **রাঙা চোখ, লাল চোখ** eyes reddened with anger or intoxication. **সাদা চোখ** natural (that is not intoxicated or otherwise affected) vision, plain eyes. **চোখখাকি, চোখখাগি** *a. fem.* (in abuses) blind.

চোখল *a.* having eyes; clever and smart.

চোখা *a.* cutting or piercing or pointed, sharp (চোখা বাণ) ; severe, pungent, cutting (চোখা কথা) ; clever and smart, intelligent, all-round (চোখা লোক) ; genuine, pure (চোখা মাল).

চোখাচোখি, চোখাচুখি *n.* act of seeing or meeting or facing one another.

চোখালো *a.* tasting rich (চোখালো রান্না) ; clever and smart, all-round (চোখালো লোক) ; sharp (চোখালো বাণ) ; pungent (চোখালো কথা).

চোখো *a. comp.* having an eye or eyes or vision, -eyed, -sighted (একচোখো).

চোগা *n.* a loose outer garment (resembling a surplice)

চোঙ, চোঙা *n.* a tube or pipe (usu. a fat one); a barrel; a spout.

চোট *n.* a stroke, a blow, a shock (লাঠির চোট) ; a wound; force, strength, strain, virtue (কথার চোট, হাসির চোট) ; anger, rage (চোট দেখানো) ; stretch, time (একচোটে). **চোট করা** *v.* to bully, to bluster, to threaten noisily, to thunder; to express anger (often futile anger) noisily. **চোট খাওয়া** *v.* to receive a shock or wound or bite; (coll.) to be cheated. **চোট দেওয়া** *v.* to give a shock; to hurt; to wound; to bite; (coll.) to cheat, to deceive. **চোট হওয়া** *v.* to be robbed, to lose. **এক চোটে** *adv.* at one stroke, at one and the same time, simultaneously.

চোটপাট *n.* an instance or act of scolding, bullying or blustering. **চোটপাট করা** *v.* to bluster, to bully; to browbeat, to reprove, to scold.

চোটা *n.* a system of lending money at an exorbitant interest, usury. **চোটায় খাটানো** to lay out (money) under this system.

চোটানো *v.* to strike; to strike or cleave or cut off with an axe or any similar tool; to cause to be bitten.

চোট্টা (coll.) *n.* a thief; a cheat, a swindler. **~মি** *n.* cheating, deceiving; deception.

চোণা *rej.* spell. of **চোনা**।

চোত coll. corrup. of **চৈত্র**।

চোতা *a.* worthless, useless (চোতা লোক, চোতা কাগজ).

চোদ্দো, চোদ্দুই coll. variants of **চৌদ্দ** and **চৌদ্দই** respectively. **চোদ্দো পুরুষ** *n.* fourteen forefathers; fourteen generations.

চোনা *n.* urine of cattle esp. of the cow. **চোনানো** *v.* (of the cow etc.) to pass urine, to urinate. **এক গামলা দুধে একফোঁটা চোনা** a fly in the ointment; a small defect that spoils the total substance.

চোপ[১] *int.* hush ! silence !

চোপ[২] *n.* a stroke of a weapon (esp. of a heavy and sharp weapon). **এক চোপে** with one stroke.

চোপদার *n.* a mace-bearer; an usher.

চোপরও *int.* hush ! silence ! keep quiet ! shut up!

চোপরা var. of **চোপা**।

চোপরাও var. of **চোপরও**।

চোপসা, চোপসানো pop. variants of **চুপসা** and **চুপসানো** respectively.

চোপা *n.* (dero.) the face (পোড়াচোপা) ; severe scolding (চোপা করা) ; a rude reply, a repartee or retort. **চোপা করা** *v.* to scold severely; to reply rudely, to retort. **চোপা ভাঙা** *v.* to thrash one's face. **পোড়াচোপা** (lit.) a burnt face; (fig.) an ugly or ill-omened face; (fig.) the face of a disgraceful person, a disgraceful face.

চোপানো *v.* to strike or chop with a weapon (esp. with a heavy weapon). ☐ *a.* struck or chopped thus.

চোবদার var. of **চোপদার**।

চোবানো, চোবানি variants of **চুবানো** and **চুবানি** respectively.

চোবে corrup. of **চৌবে**।

চোয়াড় *n.* an unmannerly or rude person; a rough, a rowdy. ☐ *a.* unmannerly; rude; rough (চোয়াড় লোক, চোয়াড় চেহারা). **চোয়াড়ে** same as **চোয়াড়** (*a.*).

চোয়ানি, চোয়ানো pop. variants of **চুয়ানি** and **চুয়ানো** respectively.

চোয়াল *n.* the jawbone; the jaw, the chap. **চোয়াল-ধরা রোগ** *n.* lockjaw. **চোয়াল-বসা** *a.* chap-fallen, jaw-fallen. **চোয়াল-ভাঙা** *a.* (fig.) hard to pronounce, jaw-breaking. **চোয়াল-ভাঙা শব্দ** a jaw-breaker.

চোর *n.* a thief; a pilferer; a stealthy man. **~কাঁটা** *n.* a kind of prickly thistle that sticks fast to the clothes of a passer-by, bur, burr. **~কুঠুরি** *n.* a secret chamber; a secret recess or cupboard in the wall of a room. **চোর-চোর খেলা** a game of hide-and-seek in which some children act as policemen and the rest as thieves. **চোরছ্যাঁচড়** *n. pl.* thieves and swindlers. **চোরে চোরে মাসতুতো ভাই** (fig.—dero.) birds of the same feather (flock together). **চোরের ধন বাটপাড়ে খায়** (fig.) ill-earned money has to be lost for nothing. **চোরের মার বড় গলা** (fig.) an inveterate sinner is always the loudest in denunciation.

চোরা[১] *n.* a thief; a deceiver. **চোরা না শোনে ধর্মের কাহিনি** (fig.) Satan turns a deaf ear to the teachings of scriptures, good counsel to a rógue bears no fruit.

চোরা[২] *a.* stolen (চোরা টাকা) ; secret, hidden, concealed (চোরা গর্ত) ; furtive (চোরা চাহনি) ; unlawful, black (চোরা কারবার, চোরাবাজার) ; secret, unseen (চোরা আঘাত). **~ই** *a.* stolen (চোরাই মাল) ; unlawful, black (চোরাই কারবার). **~গর্ত** a pitfall. **~গলি** a narrow (and usu. blind) lane. **~গোপ্তা** *a.* clandestine. **~চালান** *n.* smuggling. **~চালানদার** *n.* a smuggler. **~চাহনি, ~চাউনি** *n.* a furtive or secret or stealthy look. **~দরজা** *n.* a secret door. **~পথ** *n.* a secret path or way. **~বাজার** black market. **~বালি** *n.* quicksand. **~মার** a stealthy or surreptitious blow.

চোরিত *a.* stolen.

চোল[১] *n.* a dynasty in ancient India; the kingdom of the Cholas (চোল).

চোল[২] *n.* a bodice, a corset, a modesty vest, a skirt.

চোলক *n.* a shield.

চোলাই *n.* (now rare) act of falling or letting fall in drops, oozing, exudation; distillation; (loos.) act of brewing (মদ চোলাই) ; anything (esp. wine) distilled or brewed (চোলাই খাওয়া). **চোলাই করা** *v.* to distil; (loos.) to brew.

চোষ, চোষন *n.* suction. **চোষক** *a.* sucking. **চোষ-কাগজ** *n.* blotting-paper. **চোষনীয়, চোষ্য** *a.* that which can be or is to be sucked.

চোষা, চোষানো pop. variants of **চুষা** and **চুষানো** respectively.

চোষ্য see **চোষ**।

চোস্ত *a.* level, even; smooth; straight; fine, elegant (চোস্ত ইংরেজি) ; scrupulously correct and smart (চোস্ত আদবকায়দা) ; tight-fitting (চোস্ত পাজামা) ; decent (চোস্ত পোশাক-পরিচ্ছদ).

চৌ *a.* (used as *pfx.*) four, quadri-. **চৌকাঠ** *n.* a rectilineal doorframe; a door-sill. **~কোনা** *a.* quadrangular; square. **~খুন্তি** *n.* a fourlegged cot or stool. **~খুপি** *n.* a square; a check. □ *a.* containing squares or checks, check. **~গুণ, ~গুণা** *a.* quadruple, fourfold. **~ঘুড়ি** *n.* a carriage or chaise and four. **~চাকা, ~চাক্কা** *a.* four-wheeled. **~চালা** *n.* a hut (usu. a thatch) with a roof having four distinct parts. **~চির** *a.* split in four; split in smithereens; split in pieces. **~ঠা** *n.* the fourth day of a month. □ *a.* (of days of a month) fourth. **~তালা** *a.* four-storeyed. □ *n.* the third floor. **~তারা** *n.* a kind of four-stringed musical instrument, a tetrachord. **~তাল** *n.* an Indian musical measure. **~তালা** *n.* same as **চৌতাল**। *a.* four-storeyed. **চৌত্রিশ** *n.* & *a.* thirty-four. **~দিক,** (poet.) **~দিশ** *n.* the four quarters or sides; all sides. **~দিকে** *adv.* on all sides. **~দোল, ~দোলা** *n.* a kind of litter carried by four bearers. **~পদী** *n.* a variety of four-footed versification, (cp.) tetrameter; a quatrain. □ *a.* four-footed, tetrametrical. **~পর** *n.* whole day or night, twelve hours. □ *a.* incessant, continuing always; entire, whole (চৌপর দিন). **~পল** *a.* quadrangular; square. **~পায়া** *n.* a four-legged cot or stool. □ *a.* four-legged. **~মাথা, ~রাস্তা** *n.* a junction of four roads or a point where two roads intersect, a crossroad. **~ষট্টি** *n.* & *a.* sixty-four. **~ষট্টি কলা** sixty-four branches of fine arts.

চৌকস *a.* expert in everything, having all-round proficiency; expert, dexterous, dextrous; careful; clever; cunning.

চৌকি *n.* a four-legged wooden cot or stool; a watch-box or outpost (esp. one situated at a crossroad); act of guarding, watch (চৌকি দেওয়া) ; an outpost for collecting revenue and taxes, a toll-station, a toll-booth, a toll-house, a choky. **চৌকি দেওয়া** *v.* to guard, to watch. **~দার** *n.* a watchman, a guard, a sentinel; a village watchman, a chowkidar; a bailiff who collects revenue. **~দারি** *n.* the office or pay of a watchman or chowkidar or revenue bailiff. ☐ *a.* relating to a watchman or chowkidar or revenue bailiff.

চৌকো *a.* rectangular, rectilineal; square. ☐ *n.* a playing-card with four pips.

চৌখস var. of **চৌকস**।

চৌগোঁপ্পা *a.* having one's beard parted in two at the middle of the chin and turned up.

চৌচাপট, চৌচাপড় *n.* the surrounding expanse or land. **চৌচাপটে, চৌচাপড়ে** *adv.* exerting one's utmost strength or power; in full swing.

চৌথ *n.* one-fourth; (hist.) one-fourth of the total annual crop or the value thereof exacted as revenue by Maratha rulers from their subjects or from states subjugated by them.

চৌদ্দ (for.) *n.* & *a.* fourteen. **~ই** *n.* the fourteenth day of a month. ☐ *a.* (of days of a month) fourteenth. **~পুরুষ** *n.* past fourteen generations; fourteen generations to come; past seven generations and seven generations to come. **চৌদ্দপুরুষ উদ্ধার করা** (fig.) to abuse in the filthiest language.

চৌধুরানি *fem.* of **চৌধুরী**।

চৌধুরী *n.* a feudatory prince; one of a class of generals; the chief merchant of a city or of a central market, a merchant-prince; a village headman; a foreman of labourers, a gangsman; a title of honour; a surname.

চৌপট *a.* level, flat; destroyed; baffled, foiled.

চৌপাটি, চৌপাঠী coll. forms of **চতুষ্পাঠী**।

চৌপালা *n.* a large-sized palanquin.

চৌবাচ্চা *n.* a rectangular water-reservoir, a storage tank for water etc.

চৌবে *n.* one of a class of upcountry brahmins (descended from those who were versed in all the four Vedas); (dero.) a porter, a doorkeeper, a janitor.

চৌম্বক *a.* capable of attracting; relating to magnet or magnetism; magnetic. **চৌম্বক আকর্ষণ** (phys.) magnetic attraction. **চৌম্বক উত্তর** (phys.) magnetic north. **~গ্রাহিতা** *n.* (phys.) magnetic susceptibility. **চৌম্বক পর্বত** a magnetic rock. **চৌম্বক প্রস্তর** magnet, lodestone. **চৌম্বক শলাকা** (phys.) a magnetic needle.

চৌর older var. of **চোর**।

চৌরস *a.* spacious, roomy; wide; level, flat; levelled, flattened; rectangular.

চৌর্য *n.* act or an instance of stealing, theft. **~বৃত্তি** *n.* the profession or practice of stealing. **চৌর্যোন্মাদ** *n.* (med.) kleptomania. **চৌর্যোন্মাদগ্রস্ত ব্যক্তি** a kleptomaniac.

চৌহদ্দি *n.* (lit.) boundary lines on four sides; (pop.) boundary, periphery, perimeter; a specified area; jurisdiction. **চৌহদ্দি করা, চৌহদ্দি ঠিক করা** *v.* to delimit.

চ্যাং *n.* a species of small river fish with very soft flesh.

চ্যাংড়া *a.* young and flippant; flippant. ☐ *n.* a flippant youth. **~মি** *n.* flippancy; sauciness.

চ্যাংদোলা *n.* carrying as a dead body (by grasping one's arms and legs). **চ্যাংমুড়ি** *a.* (usu. *fem.*) having an extremely small head.

চ্যাটাং চ্যাটাং *a.* (of words) insolent and rude; high-flying and rude.

চ্যাঙারি, চ্যাঙ্গারি coll. variants of **চাঙারি**।

চ্যাটালো *a.* flat (চ্যাটালো পা). **চ্যাটালো করা** বা **হওয়া** *v.* to make or become flat; to flatten.

চ্যাপটা *a.* flat; flattened; (of a nose) snub.

চ্যুত *a.* got detached, dislocated, dislodged, come away, shed (বৃক্ষচ্যুত) ; fallen or slipped (হস্তচ্যুত) ; dismissed or removed (পদচ্যুত, রাজ্যচ্যুত) ; strayed (পথচ্যুত) ; (bot.) deviated; off the fairway; failing; fallen, false to one's vow or religion (ব্রতচ্যুত, ধর্মচ্যুত). **চ্যুতি** *n.* detachment, dislocation, dislodgment, coming away, shedding; fall or slip; dismissal or removal; straying; (bot.) deviation; failing; (geog.) a fault. **চ্যুতিভ্রম** *n.* (bot.) deviation-error.

ছ[1] *n.* the seventh consonant of the Bengali alphabet.

ছ[2] coll. corrup. of **ছয়** ।

ছই *n.* a portable covering made of straw for a boat or hackery.

ছউই *n.* the sixth day of a month. □ *a.* (of the days of a month) sixth.

ছক *n.* a check of a checker-board; a checker-board; a descriptive form (আবেদনের ছক) ; a plan usu. a detailed one (আক্রমণের ছক) ; a rough sketch, a roughcast plan or outline (গল্পের ছক) ; a prescribed or traditional shape; a pattern (উপন্যাসের ছকে ফেলা). **~কাগজ** *n.* squared paper; graph paper. **~কাটা** *a.* marked with squares; checkered; marked with descriptive columns. **ছক কাটা** *v.* to draw squares; (fig.) to roughcast; (fig.) to make a preliminary plan; (fig.) to draft.

ছকড়া-নকড়া *n.* utter disregard or neglect, utter disorder; utter waste or wastefulness. □ *a.* lying at sixes and sevens, lying pell-mell; utterly neglected or wasted. **ছকড়া-নকড়া করা** *v.* to waste by utter disregard or neglect; to waste utterly; to throw at sixes and sevens.

ছকা *v.* to sketch or draft; to roughcast; to make a preliminary or draft plan; to chalk out, to draw.

ছক্কা[1] *n.* a spiced dish of vegetables cooked almost dry.

ছক্কা[2] *n.* a playing card marked with six pips.

ছক্কাই-পাঞ্জাই *n.* tall talk. **ছক্কাই-পাঞ্জাই করা** *v.* to boast; to brag.

ছটকানো dial. corrup. of **ছিটকানো** ।

ছটফট *int.* expressing restlessness, anxiety etc. **ছটফট করা** *v.* to become restless; to fidget; to be impatient with eagerness; to be troubled with anxiety; to toss about. **ছটফটানি** *n.* restlessness; fidgetiness; impatience. **ছটফটে** *a.* restless.

ছটরা *n.* a small bullet; a grapeshot.

ছটা *n.* glow, shine, lustre; light; beauty, glamour, splendour (রূপের ছটা) ; sequence, serial, succession (শ্লোকের ছটা) ; a series.

ছটাক *n.* a measure of weight (= ১/১৬ সের) ; a little over 58 grams; a measure of area (4.18 square-metre).

ছড়[1] *n.* hide, skin (হরিণের ছড়).

ছড়[2] *n.* a long slender bar of metal or other material, a rod; a stick; a bow of a musical instrument (বেহালার ছড়) ; a long scratching mark, a long scratch (গায়ে ছড় লাগা).

ছড়রা var. of **ছটরা** ।

ছড়া[1] *v.* to get scratched or grazed or bruised or flayed; to strip the skin or bark from.

ছড়া[2] *n.* a rhyme (**ছেলে-ভোলানো ছড়া** = a nursery rhyme; **গ্রাম্য-ছড়া** = a folk-rhyme); a set of things threaded together or arranged as if threaded, a string (গোটছড়া) ; a bunch, a cluster (একছড়া কলা) ; a spell of sprinkling or a solution for sprinking (গোবর ছড়া). **ছড়া কাটা** *v.* to cap verses, to quote apt verses.

ছড়াছড়ি *n.* scattering about negligently and profusely; state of being scattered about negligently and profusely; profusion, abundance. **ছড়াছড়ি যাওয়া** *v.* to lie scattered about neglectedly and abundantly; to go a-begging.

ছড়ানো *v.* to scatter about in a disorderly manner, to strew; to scatter (বীজ ছড়ানো) ; to sprinkle (জল ছড়ানো) ; to give out, to emit (গন্ধ ছড়ানো) ; to spread (রোগ ছড়ানো).

ছড়ি *n.* a slender stick; a stick; a bow of a musical instrument; a walking-stick; (bot.) a spike (খেজুর ছড়ি). **ছড়ি ঘোরানো** *v.* to brandish one's stick; (fig.) to lord it over (a person), domineer, command undesirably.

ছড়িদার *n.* a person who helps and leads pilgrims (usu.) on an uphill journey.

ছতরি *n.* roof (esp. of a carriage); a wicker covering (as of a boat); a frame on a cot for rigging up a mosquito-net.

ছত্র[1] coll. corrup. of **সত্র** ।

ছত্র[2] *n.* a line of writing (দু-ছত্র লেখা) ; a foot of a verse.

ছত্র[3] *n.* an umbrella; a sunshade, a parasol. **~ছায়ায়** *adv.* (fig.) under the shelter or protection of.

ছত্রক *n.* fungus; mushroom; a kingfisher.

ছত্রখান *a.* scattered about in a disorderly manner, all over the shop; scattered about, strewn here and there; scattered to pieces.

ছত্রদণ্ড *n.* a royal parasol and sceptre.

ছত্রধর, ছত্রধারী *a.* & *n.* one who holds an open umbrella (as a regalia) over the head of a monarch or a person of importance.

ছত্রপতি *n.* a king; an emperor; a title of the Maratha king Shivaji.

ছত্রভঙ্গ *n.* stampede, debacle; confusion and disorder; (rare) anarchy. ☐ *a.* stampeded; confused and disordered. **ছত্রভঙ্গ করা** *v.* to stampede, to dispel or disperse; to rout.

ছত্রাক pop. var. of **ছত্রক** । **~দেহ** *n.* mycelium.

ছত্রাকার *a.* shaped like an open umbrella; scattered about; scattered about in a disorderly (and usu. wasteful) manner, all over the shop.

ছত্রি[1] *n.* a wicker covering as of a boat.

ছত্রি[2] *n.* an Indian upcountry caste of Kshatriya origin; a member of this caste.

ছত্রী *a.* umbrella-bearing; one who bears an open umbrella (as a regalia) over the head of a monarch or a person of importance or high status.

ছদ *n.* a leaf of a tree (সপ্তচ্ছদ) ; a covering, a mantle (পরিচ্ছদ). **ছদন** *n.* the act of covering; a cover.

ছদ্ম *a.* feigned, disguised, assumed, pretended; counterfeit, faked. **~নাম** *n.* assumed name, pen-name, pseudonym. **~বেশ** *n.* a disguise. **ছদ্মবেশ ধারণ করা** *v.* to disguise oneself, to assume a disguise. **~বেশী** *a.* disguised. *fem.* **~বেশিনী** । **ছদ্মবেশী লোক** an imposter; a person incognito. **~বেশে** *adv.* in disguise, incognito.

ছনছন, ছন্‌ছন্‌ *int.* expressing a feeling of physical indisposition. **শরীর ছন্‌ছন্‌ করা** to feel indisposed or out of sorts.

ছন্দ[1] *n.* inclination, liking, proneness, desire (ছন্দানুগমন) ; control (স্বচ্ছন্দে) ; manner, way, fashion (বিবিধ ছন্দে). **ছন্দানুগমন** *n.* act of moving or working at will; wilfulness. **ছন্দানুগামী** *a.* moving or working at will; wilful. **ছন্দানুবর্তন** *n.* act of moving or working at another's will; act of complying with another's will. **ছন্দানুবর্তী** *a.* moving or working at another's will, complying. **ছন্দানুবৃত্তি** same as **ছন্দানুবর্তন** । **ছন্দানুসরণ** same as **ছন্দানুগমন** । **ছন্দানুসারী** same as **ছন্দানুগামী** ।

ছন্দ[2], **ছন্দঃ** *n.* poetical metre; prosody. **ছন্দপতন, ছন্দপাত, ছন্দোভঙ্গ** *n.* an instance of defect or break in the poetical metre (cp. catalectic); (fig.) disturbance (জীবনের ছন্দপতন). **ছন্দবিশ্লেষণ** *n.* scansion. **ছন্দঃশাস্ত্র, ছন্দশাস্ত্র** *n.* prosody.

ছন্দানুগমন, ছন্দানুগামী, ছন্দানুবর্তন, ছন্দানুবর্তী, ছন্দানুবৃত্তি, ছন্দানুসরণ, ছন্দানুসারী see **ছন্দ**[1] ।

ছন্দেবন্দে *adv.* by means fair or foul, by hook or by crook.

ছন্দোবদ্ধ *a.* versified. **ছন্দোবদ্ধ পদ** metrical composition.

ছন্দোবন্ধ *n.* versification; metrical rhythm.

ছন্দোভঙ্গ see **ছন্দ**[2] ।

ছন্ন *a.* covered; overcast; obscured; disappeared, removed ('পাপতাপ হবে ছন্ন') ; lost. **~ছাড়া** *a.* ruined, homeless; Bohemian, vagabond, roving. **~মতি** *a.* out of one's senses, out of one's right wits, not in the proper frame of mind.

ছপ *int.* expressing a splashing noise. **ছপছপ** *int.* expressing repeated or continuous splashing noise.

ছপ্পর var. of **ছাপর** ।

ছবি[1] *n.* glow, lustre (রবিচ্ছবি) ; beauty, show (মুখচ্ছবি).

ছবি[2] *n.* a painting, a picture; a portrait. **ছবি তোলা** to take a photograph or snapshot, to photograph. **ছবি আঁকা** to draw or paint a picture.

ছমছম *int.* expressing an uncanny or eerie

sensation. **ছমছমে** *a.* uncanny, eerie, weird.

ছয় *n.* & *a.* six.

ছয়লাপ *a.* overfull; overflowing; flooded; strewn with (ঘরখানা কাগজপত্রে ছয়লাপ) ; extravagantly wasted, squandered (জিনিসপত্রের বা টাকাপয়সার ছয়লাপ). **ছয়লাপ করা** *v.* to fill to excess; to flood; to strew; to waste extravagantly, to squander.

ছরকট, ছরকোট *n.* mess; mismanagement.

ছররা var. of **ছটরা** ।

ছল *n.* deception, deceit, fraud; dissimulation; a hoax, a deceptive trick, a stratagem; course (কথাচ্ছলে) ; form, shape ('বৃষ্টিছলে মেঘ কাঁদে') ; a beck ('কথা কয় ছলে') ; a pretext, a pretence, a plea (প্রণামের ছলে, ক্রীড়াচ্ছলে) ; a fault or failing, a defect (ছল ধরা). **ছল করা** *v.* to hide one's real feelings, thoughts etc. to give a wrong idea of them, to feign. **ছল ধরা** *v.* to find fault with, to cavil. **ছল পাতা** *v.* to lay a trap. **~চাতুরি** *n.* fraud and deceit. **~গ্রাহী** *a.* fault-finding, cavilling. □ *n.* a faultfinder, a caviller. **~ছুতো** *n.* faults and pretexts, pretexts and pretences; a negligible fault or defect; excuses (to explain or defend one's conduct etc.) **ছলেবলে** *adv.* by force or fraud, by hook or by crook.

ছলচ্ছল *int.* expressing rippling noise. □ *a.* making a rippling noise, rippling ('ছলচ্ছল...তরঙ্গ').

ছলছল *int.* expressing the noise made by running water (ছলছল করে বয়ে চলা) ; tearfulness (চক্ষু ছলছল করা). □ *a.* tearful, lachrymose, moist (ছলছল চোখে). **ছলছল করা** *v.* to become tearful.

ছলনা, ছলন *n.* deception, deceit, fraud; dissimulation; beguilement, double-dealing; hoaxing. **ছলনা করা** *v.* to deceive; to beguile; to hoax; to play (a person) false.

ছলা *v.* to deceive; to beguile; to hoax.

ছলাকলা *n.* tricks and posturings; false gestures.

ছলাৎ *int.* expressing the sound of dashing any liquid against a hard substance.

ছলিত *a.* deceived, cheated; beguiled; hoaxed.

ছা *n.* a young one of a bird and also of small animals (পাখির ছা) ; an infant, a child, an offspring (ছাপোষা). **~পোষা** *a.* burdened or encumbered with the responsibility of rearing several or many children on a small income; (fig.) meek and timid; fearful.

ছাই *n.* ashes; a negligible or worthless thing; trash, rubbish; nothing (ছাই জানে). **~পাঁশ, ~ভস্ম** *n. pl.* (fig.) trash, rubbish; nonsensical talk, stuff and nonsense. **ছাইচাপা আগুন** (lit.) fire smouldering under ashes; (fig.) a latent quality or a suppressed feeling. **~দান, ~দানি** *n.* an ashtray. **ছাই ফেলতে ভাঙা কুলো** a neglected person of a family who is made to do all unpleasant and unimportant jobs. **~রং** *n.* ash colour, dull grey colour. **~রঙা** *a.* ash, grey.

ছাঁইচ older var. of **ছাঁচ**[1] ।

ছাউনি[1] *n.* roofing, roof (খোলার বা খড়ের ছাউনি) ; an awning.

ছাউনি[2] *n.* a cantonment; a military encampment or base.

ছাও dial. corrup. of **ছা** ।

ছাওয়া *v.* to cover; to roof, to thatch; to spread; to overcast; to pervade; to beset. □ *a.* covered; roofed, thatched; spread; overcast; shaded; shady; pervaded; beset. □ *n.* act of covering or roofing or thatching; shade, a shaded place. **ছাওয়ানো** *v.* to cause to cover or roof or thatch.

ছাওয়াল *n.* (dial.) a son, a child, offspring.

ছাঁকনি, ছাঁকনা *n.* a sieve, a strainer.

ছাঁকা *v.* to sieve, to sift, to strain; to filtrate. □ *a.* sieved, sifted, strained; filtered; true or clear (ছাঁকা কথা) ; especially selected or chosen, select (ছাঁকা ছাঁকা প্রশ্ন বা মানুষ) ; unmixed, unadulterated, pure (ছাঁকা গঙ্গাজল) ; easily available (ছাঁকা পয়সা) ; used in sifting or filtration (আটা-ছাঁকা চালুনি, চা-ছাঁকা ন্যাকড়া). **ছাঁকা তেলে ভাজা** to fry in so much oil or fat as to necessitate straining. **ছেঁকে ধরা** *v.* to beset, to encircle, to hem in; to besiege; to surround from all sides.

ছাঁকি জাল *n.* a scoop-net, a dipping-net.

ছাঁচ১ *n.* eaves (of a roof or thatch); a pent-house. **~তলা** *n.* the space below the overhanging roof or thatch.

ছাঁচ২ *n.* a mould (সন্দেশের ছাঁচ) ; any food shaped in a mould (ক্ষীরের ছাঁচ) ; a matrix; likeness, similarity, image (একই ছাঁচে গড়া).

ছাঁচকার *n.* a moulder.

ছাঁচি *a.* pure, genuine; indigenous (ছাঁচি কুমড়ো). **ছাঁচি কুমড়ো, ছাঁচি পান, ছাঁচি বেত** see **কুমড়ো, পান** and **বেত** respectively.

ছাঁট *n.* clippings, loppings, cuttings, scrap of anything; style of cutting or cropping, cut (জামার ছাঁট, চুলের ছাঁট). □ *a.* scrap (ছাঁট কাগজ).

ছাঁটা *v.* to cut, to cut off, to clip, to trim, to crop, to lop, to prune; (rare) to husk; to exclude (দল থেকে ছাঁটা) ; to retrench; to cut short, to reduce (খরচ ছাঁটা, গল্প ছাঁটা). □ *a.* clipped, trimmed, cropped, lopped, pruned; husked, husking; excluded; retrenched; reduced. **~ই** *n.* cutting off or clipping or trimming or cropping or pruning; exclusion; retrenchment; reduction; scrap. **ছাঁটাই করা** *v.* to cut off, to clip, to trim, to prune; to exclude; to retrench; to reduce. **~প্রস্তাব** *n.* a cut motion. **~নো** *v.* to cause to cut off or clip or trim or prune; to cause to be cut off or clipped or trimmed or pruned. **ছেঁটে ফেলা** *v.* to cut off, to clip, to trim, to lop; to exclude.

ছাঁৎ *int.* expressing the sound caused by casting something in hot oil or fat; sudden and sharp sensation of something alarming or disturbing (বুকের মধ্যে ছাঁৎ করে ওঠা).

ছাঁদ *n.* shape, form, cut (মুখের ছাঁদ) ; type, style, manner (অক্ষরের ছাঁদ, কথার ছাঁদ, নানান ছাঁদ).

ছাঁদন *n.* act of encircling or tying round; act of binding the hind feet of a cow at the time of milking. **~দড়ি** *n.* the string or cord or rope with which the hind feet of a cow are tied at the time of milking.

ছাঁদনাতলা *n.* a canopied place in the open where a Hindu marriage ceremony is held.

ছাঁদা *v.* to pack or wrap (chiefly used as a correl. of **বাঁধা**) ; to bind, to tie, to tether the hind feet of a cow at the time of milking; to commence (গল্প ছাঁদা, বাড়ি ছাঁদা) ; to design, to plan, to contrive, to contemplate (ফন্দি ছাঁদা). □ *a.* designed, planned, contrived, contemplated; commenced, started. □ *n.* a packet of food that a guest takes or manages to obtain from his host to carry home.

ছাগ, ছাগল *n.* the he-goat; the goat. *fem.* **ছাগী, ছাগলী** the she-goat. **ছাগলদাড়ি** *n.* a goatee. **ছাগদুগ্ধ** *n.* goat's milk. **ছাগলনাদি,** *n.* dung-pellets of a goat. **ছাগশিশু, ছাগলছানা** *n.* the young of a goat, a yeanling, a kid. **ছাগলাদ্য ঘৃত** an Ayurvedic (আয়ুর্বেদীয়) medicine prepared from the fat of a castrated goat.

ছাট *n.* a beating in of rain driven by wind; a spray or sprinkle (জলের ছাট, বৃষ্টির ছাট).

ছাড় *n.* omission (লেখার ছাড়) ; release (হাজত থেকে ছাড়) ; escape (বিপদ থেকে ছাড় নেই) ; exemption (দায় থেকে ছাড়) ; allowance, discount, rebates, commission (ছাড় বাদ দেওয়া) ; permission (ছাড়পত্র) ; a permit for unloading a ship. **~ছোড়** *n.* rebate, discount; escape. **~পত্র** *n.* a passport; a permit for movement.

ছাড়া *v.* to quit, to forsake (সংসার ছাড়া) ; to put or take off or leave or change (কাপড় ছাড়া, বাড়ি ছাড়া) ; to give up (নেশা ছাড়া) ; to begin to move off or leave, to depart (গাড়ি ছাড়া) ; to release, to set free (চোরকে ছেড়ে দিয়েছে) ; to undergo remission, to subside (জ্বর ছাড়া) ; to exempt, to overlook (ছেড়ে কথা বলা) ; to get detached or disentangled, to come off, to loosen (জোড় ছাড়া, জট ছাড়া) ; to make louder, to raise, to open out (গলা ছাড়া) ; to post (চিঠি ছাড়া) ; to stop beating, to sink (নাড়ি ছাড়া) ; to bring forth, to lay (ডিম ছাড়া) ; to throw, to shoot (বাণ ছাড়া) ; to cast or slough off (খোলস ছাড়া). □ *a.* deserted (গ্রামছাড়া) ; bereft of, deprived of, separated from, evicted from (মা-ছাড়া, ভিটেছাড়া) ; set free, let loose (ছাড়া গোরু) ; abandoned by, forsaken by (লক্ষ্মীছাড়া) ; excluded from (সৃষ্টিছাড়া). □ *n.* release or exemption (ছাড়া পাওয়া). □ *prep.* except, without, but (তোমাকে ছাড়া চলবে না) **ছাড়া-ছাড়া** *a.* not thickly set, sparse; incoherent (ছাড়া-ছাড়া কথা). **~ছাড়ি** *n.* separation; parting; estrangement. **~নো** *v.* to cause to quit or forsake or put off or change or give up; to obtain release (আসামিকে ছাড়ানো) ; to cause remission; to detach or disentangle, to cause to come off, to loosen; to cause to make louder or open out; to cause to cast off. **ছাড়া পাওয়া** *v.* to get released; to get or enjoy an exemption.

ছাড়ান *n.* (pron. ছাড়ান্) release or exemption.

ছাত *n.* roof; ceiling.

ছাতলা *n.* a fine woolly or pasty growth usually caused by damp and dirt, mould, mildew; fungus; (of teeth) tartar; (of tongue etc.) a morbid or dirty coating; rust.

ছাতা[1] *n.* umbrella; (coll.) brolly; parasol.

ছাতা[2] *n.* a fungus; a mushroom; mould, a dirty or morbid coating, rust, tartar. **ছাতা-ধরা, ছাতা-পড়া** *a.* mouldy, musty, having a dirty or morbid coating, rusted, having tartar. **ব্যাঙের ছাতা** a mushroom; a fungus.

ছাতার, (coll.) **ছাতারে** *n.* a small grey bird of the sparrow kind given to chattering overmuch, the babbler or seven sisters.

ছাতি[1] var. of **ছাতা[1]** ।

ছাতি[2] *n.* the width of the chest (বুকের ছাতি) ; chest; (fig.) courage. **ছাতি ফাটা** *v.* to feel as if one's chest will split (in thirst, sorrow etc.); to feel like dying. **ছাতি ফোলানো** *v.* to expand one's chest; to make an exhibition of one's strength; to vaunt, to brag, to rattle the sabre.

ছাতিম *n.* a large tree with digitate leaves.

ছাতিয়া *n.* (poet. & obs.) chest.

ছাতু *n.* flour made of barley, pigeonpea, maize etc.; farina. **~খোর** *n.* (*sl.*) an upcountry Indian whose staple food is barley or maize.

ছাত্র *n.* a student, a pupil; a learner; a disciple. *fem.* **ছাত্রী** । **~জীবন, ছাত্রাবস্থা** *n.* student-life. **~নায়ক** *n.* a class monitor. **~নিবাস, ছাত্রাগার, ছাত্রাবাস** *n.* a students' boarding-house, a hostel. **~বৃত্তি** *n.* a scholarship; a middle school examination held formerly in Bengal. **~সংসদ** *n.* a students' union or association.

ছাৎলা rej. spell. of **ছাতলা** ।

ছাদ *n.* roof; ceiling. **ছাদের ঘর** an attic. **~ক** *a.* & *n.* one who or that which covers; one who builds a roof or thatches. **~ন** *n.* act of covering or roofing or thatching; a roofing or thatching material.

ছাদিত *a.* covered; roofed; thatched.

ছানতা *n.* a perforated ladle, a strainer ladle.

ছানা[1] *v.* to knead; to make into a paste by pressing with hands, to soften by kneading (কাদা ছেনে পুতুল গড়া). □ *a.* kneaded; made into a paste by pressing with hands, softened by kneading.

ছানা[2] *n.* posset. **ছানা কাটা** *v.* (of milk) to turn or be turned into posset; to curdle. **ছানার জল** whey. **~বড়া** see **ছানাবড়া** ।

ছানা[3] *n.* a young of a bird or beast. **~পোনা** *n.* young ones collectively of a bird or beast; (hum.—of men) little ones. **ছানা বিয়ানো** *v.* to bring forth young ones. **কুকুরছানা** *n.* a pup, a puppy. **ছাগলছানা** *n.* a kid. **বিড়ালছানা** *n.* a kitten. **মুরগির ছানা** *n.* a chick or a chicken. **শিয়ালছানা** *n.* a cub. **শূকরছানা** *n.* a pig. **হরিণছানা** *n.* a fawn. **হাঁসের ছানা** *n.* (পাতিহাঁসের) a duckling; (রাজহাঁসের) a gosling.

ছানাবড়া *n.* posset cake. **চোখ ছানাবড়া হওয়া** (fig.) to be dumbfounded or flabbergasted; to look aghast, to be awestruck.

ছানি[1] *n.* an opaque condition of the cornea, cataract. **ছানি কাটা, ছানি তোলা** *v.* to remove a cataract by ophthalmic surgery. **ছানি পড়া** *v.* to be affected with cataract.

ছানি[2] *n.* (law) a review of judgment.

ছানি[3] *n.* a beck, a signal (হাতছানি).

ছানি[4] *n.* hay or fodder for cattle.

ছান্দ[1] *n.* (poet. obs.) a bond or tie ('মায়া ছান্দে বিশ্ব পড়ি কাঁদে').

ছান্দ[2] *n.* (poet. obs.) manner, style, fashion ('বিনাইয়া নানা ছান্দে').

ছান্দস *n.* a Vedic scholar or teacher. ☐ *a.* originating from the Vedas, Vedic; relating to poetical metre, metrical.

ছান্দসিক *a.* versed in prosody or poetic metre. ☐ *n.* one who is versed in prosody.

ছাপ *n.* a seal, a stamp; a print, an impression; a mark, a stain. **ছাপ দেওয়া, ছাপ মারা** *v.* to seal, to stamp; to print; to mark.

ছাপর *n.* a covering, a roof, a thatch. **~খাট** *n.* a bedstead fitted with rods for hanging a mosquito-net.

ছাপয়ল *v.* (obs. & poet.) covered, veiled, concealed, hid.

ছাপরা var. of **খাপরা**।

ছাপল var. of **ছাপয়ল**।

ছাপা[১] *v.* to print. ☐ *a.* printed. ☐ *n.* print (ছাপার অক্ষর). **~ই** *n.* printing; cost of printing, printing charges. **~খরচ** *n.* cost of printing. **~খানা** *n.* a printing house, a letter-press, a press. **~নো** *v.* to cause to print; to get printed. ☐ *a.* printed.

ছাপা[২] *v.* to lie or become covered or suppressed or concealed. ☐ *a.* covered, suppressed; concealed. **~ছাপি** *n.* concealment; act of keeping secret from one another; act of overflowing or going beyond bounds. ☐ *a.* overflowing (পুকুরে জল ছাপাছাপি হয়েছে). **~নো** *v.* to conceal, to hide; to overflow or go beyond bounds. ☐ *a.* concealed; overflowing (কূল-ছাপানো জল).

ছাপ্পর coll. var. of **ছাপর**।

ছাপ্পান্ন *n.* & *a.* fifty-six.

ছাব্বিশ *n.* & *a.* twenty-six. **ছাব্বিশে** *n.* the twenty-sixth day of a month. ☐ *a.* (of days of a month) twenty-sixth.

ছায়া *n.* a reflection, a shadow; shade, umbra (ছায়ায় বসা) ; semblance, resemblance, likeness (ছেলেটি বাপেরই ছায়া) ; slight influence (এ কবিতায় রবীন্দ্রনাথের ছায়া আছে) ; a faint shadow (এ উৎসবে আনন্দের ছায়াও নেই) ; a constant companion (ছায়া হয়ে সঙ্গে থাকা) ; a spectre, an apparition, a ghost (ছায়াশরীর) ; darkness (রাতের ছায়া, সন্ধ্যার ছায়া) ; glow, shine, lustre (রত্নচ্ছায়া) ; shelter or protection ('দেহ পদচ্ছায়া') ; the name of the wife of the Hindu sungod. **ছায়া না মাড়ানো** to keep one's distance, to stand or keep aloof. **~চিত্র** *n.* a cinematographic film; a cinema. **~তরু** *n.* a large tree giving shade. **~ত্মজ, ~সুত** *n.* Saturn, the son of the sungod. **~দেহ, ~শরীর** *n.* a spectre, an apparition, a phantom, a ghost. **~নট** *n.* an Indian musical mode. **~পথ** *n.* galaxy, the. Milky Way. **~বাজি** *n.* magic; magic lantern. **~ভিনয়** *n.* shadow-play. **~মণ্ডপ** *n.* a canopied place in the open (esp. where a Hindu wedding-ceremony is held). **~ময়** *a.* shady, umbrageous, shadowy, bowery (ছায়াময় স্থান) ; spectral, apparitional, ghostly (ছায়াময় দেহ). **~মূর্তি** *n.* an apparition, a phantom, a spectre, a ghost.

ছার *n.* ashes; (fig.) a contemptible thing, rubbish (কী ছার বলছ) ; (fig.) a contemptible person (সে কোন ছার) ; (fig.) the mortal body ('রাগ দ্বেষ মোহ লইয়া ছার'). ☐ *a.* base; contemptible. **~কপালে** *n.* (vul. in abuses) an unfortunate or ill-starred man. ☐ *a.* unfortunate or ill-starred. *fem.* **~কপালী**। **~খার** *n.* ruin, downfall (ছারখারে যাওয়া). ☐ *a.* ruined, downfallen (ছারখার হওয়া). **আমি কোন ছার** not to speak of a humble man like me.

ছারপোকা *n.* the bug.

ছাল *n.* epidermis, scarf-skin; scarf; skin; hide; leather; bark (of trees). **ছাল ছাড়ানো, ছাল তোলা** *v.* to flay, to skin.

ছালট *n.* bark (of trees).

ছালটি *n.* cloth woven with the yarn of jute, hemp etc.

ছালন *n.* spicy curry.

ছালা *n.* a sack, a gunny-bag.

ছালুন var. of **ছালন**।

ছি *int.* fie. **ছি-ছি** *n.* reproach, upbraiding, abuse, condemnation. **ছি-ছি করা** *v.* to reproach, to upbraid, to look down upon, to condemn.

ছিঁচকা[১], (coll.) **ছিঁচকে**[১] *n.* a skewer for cleansing the pipe of a hookah.

ছিঁচকা[২], (coll.) **ছিঁচকে**[২] *a.* given to pilfering. **~চুরি** *n.* pilferage; petty larceny. **ছিঁচকেচুরি করা** *v.* to pilfer. **ছিঁচকেচোর** *n.* a pilferer.

ছিঁচকাদুনে *a.* lachrymose, prone to be tearful; maudlin. *fem*; **ছিঁচকাদুনি**।

ছিঁচকে coll. form of **ছিঁচকা**[১],[২] ।

ছিঁড়া, (coll.) **ছেঁড়া** *v.* to tear, to rend; to rip open, to detach, to tear off (মুণ্ডু ছেঁড়া) ; to pluck (ফুল ছেঁড়া) ; to uproot (ঘাস ছেঁড়া) ; to pull up, to tear off (চুল ছেঁড়া) ; to get decomposed, to rot, to curdle (দুধ ছেঁড়া). □ *a.* torn, rent; of no importance, airy (ছেঁড়া কথা). **ছেঁড়াছিঁড়ি** *n.* a spell of continuous tearing; act of mutual tearing. **ছেঁড়ানো** *v.* to cause to tear or rend.

ছিট[১] *n.* a drop, a blob (কালির ছিট) ; chintz; a faint sign (পাগলামির ছিট) ; slight mental derangement, eccentricity, a fad or caprice.

ছিট[২] *n.* a fragment, a piece or portion. □ *a.* detached, separate (ছিটমহল).

ছিটকানো *v.* to spatter (both *t.* & *i.*); to rebound, to fly off (only *i*). □ *a.* spattered; rebounded, flown off.

ছিটকিনি *n.* a bolt or cleat.

ছিটগ্রস্ত *a.* capricious, eccentric; a bit touched.

ছিটমহল *n.* land or holding lying detached from the parent estate; an enclave.

ছিটা, (coll.) **ছিটে** *n.* a particle sprinkled or scattered (বৃষ্টির ছিটে) ; a drop, a blob, a pinch (এক ছিটে চিনি) ; grapeshot; a globular preparation of opium taken as a drug. **কাটা ঘায়ে নুনের ছিটে দেওয়া** (fig.) to add insult to injury, to tread over a soft spot. **ছিটেগুলি** *n.* grapeshot. **ছিটাছিটি** *n.* act of sprinkling at one another. **ছিটানো** *v.* to sprinkle, to spray; to scatter. **ছিটে-ফোঁটা** *n.* a small or negligible drop or amount. □ *a.* of negligible amount. **ছিটে-বেড়া** *n.* a wall made of mud-plastered bamboo laths (ছিটা-বেড়ার ঘর).

ছিদ্যমান *a.* in the process of being cut up or hewed.

ছিদ্র *n.* a hole; a slot; a pore; a perforation; an opening; a fault, a defect, a shortcoming (পরের ছিদ্র খোঁজা) ; a weak point. (শত্রুর ছিদ্রে ঘা দেওয়া). **~দর্শী** *a.* fault-finding. □ *n.* a fault-finder. **~যুক্ত** *a.* porous, perforated; leaky. **ছিদ্রানুসন্ধান, ছিদ্রান্বেষণ** *n.* act of looking for others' fault. **ছিদ্রানুসন্ধায়ী, ছিদ্রান্বেষী** *a.* fault-finding. **ছিদ্রিত** *a.* holed; perforated; bored; pierced; having a hole or holes.

ছিনতাই *n.* theft or appropriation by snatching.

ছিনা[১] dial. var. of **সিনা** ।

ছিনা[২], (coll.) **ছিনে** *a.* very thin. **ছিনেজোঁক** *n.* a very thin species of leech that sticks fast to the object it sucks; (fig.) a dogged or pertinacious person.

ছিনানো *v.* to snatch; to seize; to wrest. □ *a.* appropriated by snatching or seizure.

ছিনাল *n.* an unchaste or lewd woman, an adulteress; a strumpet, a whore; a coquette, a flirt. **ছিনালি** *n.* coquetry, flirtation. **ছিনালি করা** *v.* to coquette, to flirt.

ছিনিমিনি *n.* act of playing ducks and drakes; (fig.) reckless use or expenditure, squandering. **ছিনিমিনি খেলা** *v.* to play ducks and drakes; (fig.) to use or spend recklessly, to squander, to fritter away.

ছিনে coll. var. of **ছিনা**[১],[২] ।

ছিন্ন *a.* torn, rent; split, cloven; cut down (ছিন্ন বৃক্ষ) ; uprooted; detached, separated; removed (ছিন্নসংশয়). **ছিন্না** *a. fem.* of **ছিন্ন** । *n.* a prostitute, a harlot. **~দ্বৈধ** *a.* freed from hesitation. **~নাস** *a.* one whose nose has been cut off or amputated. **~পক্ষ** *a.* one whose wings have been clipped off; (fig.) rendered powerless, frustrated. **~পত্র** *n.* a fragment of a letter. **~বাস** *a.* one whose clothes are torn; wearing ragged clothes, in tatters, out at elbows. □ *n.* torn or tattered clothes. **~বিচ্ছিন্ন, ~ভিন্ন** *a.* torn or cut or broken to pieces; fragmented; torn asunder; ruined by dissensions or factions. **~মস্তক, ~শির, ~শীর্ষ** *a.* truncated: decapitated; lopped. **~মস্তা** *n.* a truncated manifestation of Goddess Durga (দুর্গা). **~মূল** *a.* uprooted, weeded out. **ছিন্নমূল জনগণ** uprooted or homeless people; refugees, displaced persons. **~মুষ্ক, ছিন্নাণ্ড** *a.* castrated.

ছিপ[১] *n.* a very fast-moving lightweight and long boat.

ছিপ[২] *n.* a fishing-rod, an angle, **ছিপে মাছ ধরা** *v.* to angle.

ছিপছিপে *a.* slim; slender; lean.

ছিপানো *v.* to slip, to give (one) the slip, to hide; to keep in hiding, to lie concealed. □ *a.* slipped away, hidden; concealed.

ছিপি *n.* a cork, a stopper. **ছিপি আঁটা** *v.* to cork, to stopple.

ছিবড়া, (coll.) **ছিবড়ে** *n.* the dry refuse of anything the juice of which has been extracted.

ছিমছাম *a.* smart and tidy, spruce, spick and span.

ছিয়াত্তর *a.* & *n.* seventy-six. **ছিয়াত্তরের মন্বন্তর** the famine that occurred in Bengal and also in several other provinces of India in the Bengali era 1176 (1769 A.D.).

ছিয়ানব্বই, (coll.) **ছিয়ানব্বুই** *n.* & *a.* ninety-six.

ছিয়াশি *n.* & *a.* eighty-six.

ছিয়ে *int.* (obs. & poet.) fie.

ছিরি coll. corrup. of **শ্রী**। **ছিরিছাঁদ** *n.* (coll.) charm or grace and shape.

ছিল *p.* of the verb-root **আছ** or **থাকা**।

ছিলকা, (coll.) **ছিলকে** *n.* a thin slip of wood, a thin lath; the bark of a tree, the skin of a fruit, a shred of tobacco etc.

ছিলমচি *n.* the rod of the hookah on which the chillum is placed, the chillum-holder.

ছিলা *n.* a bowstring; fringe of a piece of cloth, fringe of the sari worn by the Indian women.

ছিলিম *n.* the bowl of a hookah, a chillum; a quantity of tobacco that may be smoked in a chillum at one time, chillumful (এক ছিলিম তামাক).

ছিলে coll. var. of **ছিলা**।

ছিষ্টি dial. corrup. of **সৃষ্টি**।

ছুঁচ dial. form of **সূচ**।

ছুঁচো *n.* the mole, the musk-rat; (fig. & dero.) a mean person. **~মি** *n.* meanness, baseness, rascality; pettiness, little-mindedness. **ছুঁচো মেরে হাত গন্ধ করা** (fig.) to sue a beggar and get a louse. **ছুঁচোর কেত্তন** (fig.) disgusting noise, hullabaloo, a state of noisy confusion, bedlam let loose.

ছুঁচোলো dial. var. of **সূচালো**।

ছুঁচোবাজি *n.* a squib.

ছুঁড়া inc. form of **ছুড়া**।

ছুঁড়ি *n.* (dero.) a young woman, a lass. **ওঠ্ ছুঁড়ি তোর বিয়ে** (fig.) a sudden call for an action esp. an important one, feverish haste.

ছুঁত *n.* touch, contagion, contact impurity caused by touching what is untouchable, contactile impurity; a defect, a fault. **~মার্গ** *n.* the Hindu system of untouchability; fear of being defiled by contact with so-called 'low-caste' people.

ছুঁয়া var. of **ছোঁয়া**।

ছুকরি *n.* (usu. dero.) a young woman or maid, a lass.

ছুচুন্দরী *n.* the female musk-rat, the she-mole.

ছুট[1] *n.* a string for dressing hair; a fillet; a wearing cloth.

ছুট[2] *n.* recess; leisure; escape, exemption; release; relief.

ছুট[3] *n.* a commercial discount (ছুট বাদ দেওয়া) ; an omission (ছুট যাওয়া) ; a run (এক ছুটে). **ছুট দেওয়া, ছুট মারা** *v.* to run off, to spurt off, to bolt; to run away, to scamper off. **এক ছুটে** *adv.* in a run; in a breath.

ছুটকা, (coll.) **ছুটকো** *a.* stray. **ছুটকোছাটকা** *a.* stray and minor, trifling.

ছুটন্ত *a.* running, on the run; racing.

ছুটা, ছোটা *v.* to run; to flow speedily (স্রোত ছোটা) ; to flow out profusely or rapidly (ঘাম ছোটা) ; to come or go out (আগুন ছুটছে) ; to pour down profusely or rapidly ('বাদল ছুটেছে') ; to fly, to go off (তির ছোটা) ; to come off flying (খিল ছোটা) ; to release from influence, to relax influence (নেশা ছোটা) ; to come off, to fade (রং ছোটা) ; to break (ঘুম ছোটা). to stream out (মুখ ছোটা) ; **ঘুম ছোটা** *v.* to awake. **নেশা ছোটা** *v.* to get sober. **মুখ ছোটা** *v.* to vituperate; to be vociferous. **ছুটাছুটি, ছোটাছুটি** *n.* act or spell of running about; bustle. **ছুটানো** *v.* to cause to run or to flow speedily; to cause to flow out profusely or rapidly; to expel; to cause to come off flying; to remove the influence of; to break (ঘুম ছুটানো) ; to cause to stream out (মুখ ছুটানো).

ছুটি *n.* leisure, recess; break; break-up; a holiday; a vacation (গ্রীষ্মের ছুটি, পূজার ছুটি) ; a leave of absence; retirement; relief; release. **ছুটির দিন** a holiday. **লম্বা ছুটি** a furlough, long leave.

ছুড়া, ছোড়া *v.* to throw, to hurl; to cast, to fling; to shoot (তির ছোড়া, গুলি ছোড়া) ; to fire (বন্দুক ছোড়া). **পাথর ছুড়ে মারা** to pelt (one) with stones. **ছোড়াছুড়ি** *n.* act of throwing at one another; act of throwing continuously. **ছোড়ানো** *v.* to cause to throw or cast or fling or shoot or fire.

ছুৎ rej. spell. of **ছুঁত**।

ছুত var. of **ছুঁত**।

ছুতা, (coll.) **ছুতো** *n.* a pretext, an excuse; a plea (ছুতো পাওয়া) ; a small or negligible fault (ছুতো ধরা). **ছুতোনাতা** *n.* a shallow pretext, a thin excuse.

ছুতার, (coll.) **ছুতোর** *n.* a carpenter; a joiner. **~গিরি** *n.* carpentry.

ছুপানো see **ছোপ**।

ছুবলানো see **ছোবল**।

ছুবানো var. of **ছুপানো**।

ছুমন্তর *n.* charms and incantations; magic.

ছুরত var. of **সুরত**।

ছুরি, ছুরিকা *n.* a knife; a pen-knife (usu. **পেনসিল-কাটা ছুরি**) ; a clasp-knife; a dagger; a dirk. **ছুরি মারা** *v.* to knife, to knive, to stab. **গলায় ছুরি মারা** (lit.) to cut one's throat, to assassinate, to kill; (usu. fig.) to ruin esp. by exacting a heavy payment. **ছুরিকাঘাত** *n.* a stab, stabbing.

ছুরিত *a.* besmeared, coated; entangled; inlaid, beset; bedecked; pervaded; involved.

ছুলা, ছোলা *v.* to peel (নারকেল ছোলা) ; to scrape (জিভ ছোলা). ☐ *n.* act of peeling or scraping; something to scrape with (জিভ ছুলছে). **ছোলানো** *v.* to cause to peel or scrape.

ছুলি *n.* nettle-rash, urticaria; a skin disease akin to ringworm.

ছে *n.* (dial.) a slice; (dial.) recess or suspension, interval, stoppage (বৃষ্টির ছে নেই).

ছেঁক[1] dial. form of **সেক**।

ছেঁক[2] rej. spell. of **ছ্যাঁক**।

ছেঁকা alt. spell. of **ছ্যাঁকা**।

ছেঁচকি *n.* a dry dish of vegetables cooked in a little oil.

ছেঁচড়া[1], (coll.) **ছেঁচড়** *a.* given to cheating or swindling; knavish; unwilling to repay debts. ☐ *n.* a cheat, a swindler; a knave; one who is unwilling to repay debts; a bad paymaster.

ছেঁচড়া[2] *n.* a dry dish of vegetables and fish-bones cooked in a little oil.

ছেঁচড়ানো *v.* to drag along the ground esp. forcibly.

ছেঁচড়ামি *n.* swindling, cheating; knavery; unwillingness to repay debts.

ছেঁচা[1] coll. form of **সেচা**।

ছেঁচা[2] *v.* to pound, to thrash. **~নো** *v.* to cause to pound or thrash or be pounded or be thrashed.

ছেঁচোড় alt. spell. of **ছেঁচড়**।

ছেঁড়া, ছেঁড়াছিঁড়ি, ছেঁড়ানো pop. variants of **ছিঁড়া, ছিঁড়াছিঁড়ি** and **ছিঁড়ানো** respectively.

ছেঁড়াখোড়া *a.* torn and worn-out, torn and ragged.

ছেঁদা *n.* a hole, a cavity, a slot, a rent. **ছেঁদা করা** *v.* to make a hole, to bore, to perforate.

ছেঁদো *a.* of no importance, airy, evasive (ছোঁদো কথা). **ছেঁদো কথা** *n.* meaningless, worthless or useless talk.

ছেক[1] *n.* stoppage, remission, cessation, suspension.

ছেক[2] (rhet.) alliteration of more than one consonant.

ছেকড়া alt. spell. of **ছ্যাকড়া**।

ছেচল্লিশ *n.* & *a.* forty-six.

ছেত্তা *a.* one who cuts or cleaves or severs. **ছেত্তব্য** *a.* to be cut or split, to be cleft or fit to be cleft or cut.

ছেত্রি coll. corrup. of **ক্ষেত্রী**।

ছেদ *n.* act of cutting or severing (শিরশ্ছেদ) ; a section (দীর্ঘচ্ছেদ) ; cessation, suspension (বৃষ্টিতে বা কথায় ছেদ পড়া) ; a part, a chapter (পরিচ্ছেদ) ; (gr.) any of the punctuation marks (also **ছেদচিহ্ন**). **ছেদ পড়া** *v.* to cease. **~ক** *a.* one who or that which cuts or cleaves or severs. ☐ *n.* a cutter; (geom.) a section, a sector. **~ক-দন্ত** *n.* a canine tooth. **~ন** *n.* act of cutting or cleaving or severing. **ছেদনী** *n.* a cutting tool, a cutter.

ছেদনীয়, ছেদ্য *a.* that which is to be or can be cut or cleaved or severed. **~হীন** *a.* unceasing, ceaseless; incessant. **ছেদিত** *a.* cut, cleft, severed.

ছেদচিহ্ন see **ছেদ**।

ছেদবিন্দু *n.* point of intersection.

ছেনাল, ছেনালি coll. corruptions of **ছিনাল** and **ছিনালি** respectively.

ছেনি *n.* a chisel esp. a small one.

ছেবলা *rej.* spell. of **ছ্যাবলা**।

ছেলে *n.* a boy; a lad; a male child; a son; (vul.) a person (মেয়েছেলে). **~খেলা** *n.* a boy's or child's play; a very easy task; act of trifling with; dalliance. **ছেলেখেলা করা** *v.* to trifle with, to play with. **~ছোকরা** *n. pl.* young men or chaps or fellows; lads. **~ধরা** *n.* a child-lifter, a kidnapper of children. **~পিলে, ~পুলে** *n. pl.* children, kiddies; one's sons and daughters collectively (not necessarily minor ones). **~বেলা** *n.* childhood; infancy. **ছেলেভুলানো খেলনা** *n.* the child's toys. **ছেলেভুলানো গান** *n.* lullaby. **ছেলেভুলানো ছড়া** *n.* nursery rhyme. **~মানুষ** *a.* tenderaged; inexperienced; childish; young and inexperienced (cp. a greenhorn). **~মানুষি, ~মি** *n.* frivolity; silliness; immaturity; childishness. **ছেলেমেয়ে** boys and girls; children; sons and daughters.

ছেষট্টি *n.* & *a.* sixty-six.

ছৈ alt. spell. of **ছই**।

ছোঁ *n.* a sudden swoop or spring with an attempt to seize or bite, a pounce. **ছোঁ মারা** *v.* to pounce (upon), to swoop down on.

ছোঁকছোঁক *int.* expressing the watering state of the mouth in greed. **ছোঁকছোঁক করা** *v.* to fret in suppressed greed.

ছোঁচা *a.* ludicrously greedy of food; given to ludicrous thieving of food. **~মি** *n.* ludicrous greed for food; practice of ludicrous thieving of food. **ছোঁচামি করা** *v.* to indulge in ludicrous greed for food or in ludicrous thieving of food.

ছোঁচানো *v.* to wash the posterior after evacuation.

ছোঁড়া[1] var. of **ছোড়া**।

ছোঁড়া[2] *n.* (dero.) a young man, a lad.

ছোঁয়া *v.* to touch. ☐ *n.* touch (ছোঁয়া লাগা). ☐ *a.* touched, contacted; touching (আকাশছোঁয়া). **~চ** *n.* (usu. dero.) touch, contact, contagion, influence. **~চে** *a.* contagious. **~ছুঁয়ি** *n.* mutual touch or contact; impurity caused by touch or contact. **~নো** *v.* to cause to touch or be touched. **~লেপা** *n.* act of touching the untouchable; impurity caused by the touch of the so-called untouchable.

ছোকরা *n.* (usu. dero.) a young man; a lad; a boy; a greenhorn; a boy servant; a serving-boy; a page; an underage employee. ☐ *a.* tender-aged, young; young and inexperienced.

ছোট *a.* small, little, tiny (ছোট ছেলেমেয়ে, ছোট কুকুর, ছোট গাছ, ছোট পুকুর) ; short (ছোট গল্প, ছোট দড়ি) ; trifling (ছোট ব্যাপার) ; mean, base, low (ছোট মন, ছোট নজর, ছোটলোক) ; lower, subordinate, concerned with small causes (ছোট আদালত) ; junior (ছোট সাহেব) ; younger (ছোট ভাই) ; youngest (ছোট ছেলে, ছোট বউ) ; socially depressed (ছোট জাত) ; holding lesser amount of shares, junior (ছোট তরফ) ; belittled (লোকের চোখে ছোট হওয়া) ; modest ('বড় যদি হতে চাও, ছোট হও তবে'). **~খাটো** *a.* (very) trifling (ছোটখাটো ব্যাপার) ; (very) small (ছোটখাটো ঘর বা গাছ) ; (very) short (ছোটখাটো গল্প). **~জজ** a puisne judge. **~লোক** *n.* a base or mean-minded person; a rude or uncivil person; a person belonging to a socially depressed class. **~হাজরি** see **হাজরি**।

ছোটা[1] pop. var. of **ছুটা**।

ছোটা[2] *n.* a piece of dried bark of banana or dried straw used as a string.

ছোটো alt. spell. of **ছোট**।

ছোট্ট *a.* (very) small, little, tiny; (very) short; (very) trifling; young.

ছোড় *n.* separation; act of leaving or giving up (নাছোড়). ☐ *a.* separated, detached, parted (ছোড় হওয়া). **~ই** *v.* (obs. & poet.) leave(s), give(s) up; discontinue(s). **~ন** *n.* act of leaving or giving up or discontinuing. **~ব** *v.* 3rd per. (obs. & poet.) will leave, will give up, will discontinue. **~বি** 2nd per. (obs. & poet.) of **ছোড়ব**। **~ভঙ্গ** *a.* stampeded;

confused and disorderly; separated or detached from the bunch.

ছোড়া pop. var. of **ছুড়া**।

ছোপ *n.* stain (ছোপ লাগা) ; tint (লালের ছোপ) ; a paint (রঙের ছোপ). **ছোপানো, ছুপানো** *v.* to dye. ☐ *a.* dyed.

ছোবড়া *n.* the inedible outer portion or skin of fruits; coconut-coir; refuse of anything the juice of which has been extracted (ছোবড়া করা).

ছোবল *n.* a sudden stroke with nails or fangs or teeth or tongue. **ছোবল মারা, ছোবলানো, ছুবলানো** *v.* to strike suddenly with nails or fangs or teeth or tongue, to snap.

ছোবানো dial. corrup. of **ছোপানো** (see **ছোপ**).

ছোয়ারা var. of **ছোহারা**।

ছোরা *n.* a dagger, a dirk. **ছোরা মারা** *v.* to stab, to knife.

ছোলঙ্গ *n.* the shaddock.

ছোলদারি *n.* a small triangular tent (esp. one used in the army).

ছোলা[১] *n.* vetch, gram, chick-pea.

ছোলা[২] pop. var. of **ছুলা**।

ছোহারা *n.* dried date, currant.

ছ্যা emphatic form of **ছি**।

ছ্যাঁক *int.* expressing the sound of anything falling into hot oil or fat. **ছ্যাঁকছ্যাঁক** *adv.* expressing or indicating a slight temperature (গা ছ্যাঁক ছ্যাঁক করছে). **ছ্যাঁকছেঁকে** *a.* expressing or indicating a slight temperature.

ছ্যাঁকা *n.* a slight burn caused by contact with anything hot or burning; a spell of cauterization or searing. ☐ *v.* to singe lightly in oil or fat. **ছ্যাঁকা দেওয়া** *v.* to cauterize; to sear.

ছ্যাঁচড় alt. spell. of **ছেঁচড়**।

ছ্যাঁচড়া alt. spell. of **ছেঁচড়া**।

ছ্যাঁচোড় alt. spell. of **ছেঁচড়**।

ছ্যাঁদা alt. spell. of **ছেঁদা**।

ছ্যাকড়া, ছ্যাকড়াগাড়ি *n.* a hackney carriage.

ছ্যাতলা var. of **ছাতলা**।

ছ্যাবলা *a.* frivolous, babbling awkwardly, puerile. **~মি** *n.* frivolity, levity; undignified prattle.

জ১ *n.* the eighth consonant of the Bengali alphabet.
জ২ *n.* a measure of length equal to $^1/_4$ inch. or 6.35 millimetres.
জ৩ *sfx.* born of, produced by or in (জলজ, পঙ্কজ, দুঃখজ).
জই *n.* oat.
জউ *n.* lac. **~ঘর** *n.* a house built with lac.
জওয়ান *n.* a soldier, an armyman.
জওয়ার alt. spell. of **জোয়ার২** ।
জং *n.* rust. **জং ধরা** *v.* to rust. **জং-ধরা** *a.* rusty. **জং ধরানো** *v.* to rust.
জংলা, জংলি see **জঙ্গল** ।
জক alt. spell. of. **যক** ।
জখম *n.* wound, injury. □ *a.* wounded, injured, hurt. **জখম করা** *v.* to wound, to injure, to hurt. **জখমি** *a.* wounded, injured, hurt; relating to wounds, or wounding.
জগ১ *in comp.* the world (জগজন, জগমোহন).
জগ২ *n.* a jug.
জগজগ *int.* expressing : sparkling or dazzling state. **জগজগা** *n.* a sparkling or dazzling tinfoil. **জগজগে** *a.* sparkling, dazzling, shining.
জগজ্জন, (poet.) **জগজন** *n. pl.*(poet.) the people of the whole world, mankind.
জগজ্জননী *n.* the mother of the world : an appellation of Goddess Durga (দুর্গা).
জগজ্জয়ী *a.* world-conquering. □ *n.* a conqueror of the whole world, a world-conqueror.
জগঝম্প *n.* a war-drum; a kettle-drum.
জগৎ *n.* the world, the earth, the universe; society (পশুজগৎ) ; sphere (শিল্পজগৎ) ; field (ধাতুজগৎ, কাব্যজগৎ). **~কর্তা** *n.* God, the Lord of the universe. **~কারণ** *n.* the First Cause, God. **~জোড়া** *a.* world-wide; all-pervading; universal. **~পতি, ~পাতা, ~পিতা** same as **~স্রষ্টা** । **~ময়** *adv.* throughout the world. **~স্রষ্টা** *n.* the Creator, God. **~সংসার** *n.* the whole world.
জগতী *n. fem.* the mother earth, the earth, the world; *(pl.)* the people of the world. **~তল** *n.* the face or surface of the earth.
জগদ্‌গুরু *n.* the teacher of the world; God.
জগদ্‌গৌরী *n.* an appellation of Goddess Manasa (মনসা).
জগদম্বা *n.* the mother of the world : an appellation of Goddess Durga (দুর্গা).
জগদীশ, জগদীশ্বর *n.* the Supreme Lord, God.
জগদীশ্বরী *n. fem.* of **জগদীশ্বর** ।
জগদ্দল *a.* that which presses down the universe; too heavy to be moved, immovably heavy. □ *n.* an immovably heavy stone.
জগদ্ধাত্রী *n. fem.* the mother or protector of the world.
জগদ্বন্ধু *n.* the friend or benefactor of all; God.
জগদ্বাসী *a.* inhabiting the world. □ *n.* an inhabitant of the world. *fem.* **জগদ্বাসিনী** ।
জগদ্বিখ্যাত *a.* of worldwide fame or reputation, celebrated, renowned, famous.
জগদ্ব্যাপী *a.* spread over the world, worldwide.
জগন্নাথ *n.* the Supreme Lord of the world, God; an appellation of Krishna (কৃষ্ণ) ; the presiding deity of the temple at Puri, Jagannath. **~ ক্ষেত্র** *n.* the domain of Jagannath, Puri.
জগন্নিবাস *n.* the container of the universe : an appellation of Vishnu (বিষ্ণু) or Krishna (কৃষ্ণ) ; God.
জগন্ময়ী *n. fem.* the Female Spirit or Mother Spirit pervading all through the universe. *masc.* **জগন্ময়** God.
জগন্মণ্ডল *n.* the (whole) world; the whole universe.
জগন্মাতা *n. fem.* the Mother of the world, the Supreme Being viewed as the Mother, the great Mother.
জগন্মোহন, জগমোহন *a.* & *n.* one who or that which captivates the world or the universe.
জগাখিচড়ি, জগাখিচুড়ি *n.* hotchpotch; a confused medley, farrago, mess.

জগাতি *n.* a tax-collector; an obstacle.
জগ্ধ *a.* eaten, consumed.
জঘন *n.* the lower region of a woman's abdomen; the loins (usu. of a woman).
জঘন্য *a.* abominable, hateful, detestable; repugnant; filthy; hated; vile; base, mean; contemptible. **~তা** *n.* abomination, hatefulness, detestation; repugnance; filthiness; vileness, baseness, meanness; contemptibility. **~বৃত্তি** *n.* hateful or loathsome or odious pursuit.
জঙ, জঙ্গ১ alt. spellings of **জং**।
জঙ্গ২ *n.* a war, a battle. **~ডিঙ্গা** *n.* a battleship, a man-of-war.
জঙ্গম *a.* mobile; movable; having power of locomotion; living, animate.
জঙ্গল *n.* a bush, a thicket, a jungle; a forest; wild plants and herbs, weed. **জঙ্গলা, জংলা** *a.* wild; bushy. **জংলি, জঙ্গুলে** *a.* wild; bushy; living in a jungle; uncivilized; rude; uncultured; unpolished; unrefined. **জঙ্গলি লোক, জংলি লোক** *n.* a woodman, a bushman; an ill-mannered or uncultured person.
জঙ্গাল *n.* an embankment, a dam.
জঙ্গি *a.* military (জঙ্গি লাট) ; fighting (জঙ্গি বিমান) ; armoured (জঙ্গি গাড়ি) ; belligerent (জঙ্গি মনোভাব) warlike (জঙ্গি লোক). **জঙ্গি বিমান** *n.* a fighter-plane, a fighter-aeroplane, a fighter.
জঙ্গুলে see **জঙ্গল**।
জঙ্ঘা *n.* (of men) the shank; (of beasts) the ham or hough. **~ত্রাণ** *n.* greaves. **~স্থি** *n.* the tibia.
জজ *n.* a judge; a justice. **জজিয়তি** *n.* judgeship.
জঞ্জাল *n.* refuse, sweepings, rubbish, garbage; (fig.) a trouble, a fix; (fig.) an unwanted or burdensome person or thing.
জঞ্জির *n.* chains.
জট *n.* matted hair; a tangle, a complication; entanglement; confusion; an aerial or hanging root of a tree; (psy.) complex. **জট পাকা, জট বাঁধা** *v.* to get matted, to mat; to become complicated, to tangle; to form into a tangle or complex. **জট পাকানো, জট বাঁধানো** *v.* to cause to get matted, to mat; to complicate, to tangle; to give rise to a tangle; to involve or to get involved.
জটলা *n.* an irregular assemblage of persons debating about or discussing something; an assemblage; a crowd, a multitude; (loos.) hullabaloo. **জটলা করা** *v.* to form an assembly, to make a clique.
জটা *n.* matted hair; mane; an aerial or hanging root (বটের জটা). **~জাল, ~জুট** *n.* a mass of matted hair. **~ধর, ~ধারী** *a.* having matted hair; □ *n.* an appellation of Shiva (শিব). **~বল্কল** *n. pl.* matted hair and the bark of a tree (as worn by an ascetic). **~ভার** *n.* the load of matted hair. **~মাংসী** *n.* the Indian spikenard. **~ল** *a.* having matted hair; having aerial or hanging roots.
জটিবুড়ি var. of **জোটেবুড়ি**।
জটিয়া *a.* having matted hair (জটিয়াবাবা).
জটিল *a.* (rare) having matted hair or mane or aerial roots; tangled; confused; entangled; inscrutable; complicated; difficult; complex; (arith.) compound (জটিল ভগ্নাংশ). **জটিলা** *a. fem.* of **জটিল** ; and also mischievously shrewd; quarrelsome; tyrannizing over or oppressing the daughters-in-law. **জটিল বাক্য** a complex sentence.
জটিলতা *n.* complexity, intricacy; (fig.) confused state, tangle, tangled skein.
জটী *a.* having matted hair or mane or aerial roots.
জটুল ori. form of **জড়ুল**।
জটে coll. form of **জটিয়া**।
জটেবুড়ি var of **জুজুবুড়ি**।
জঠর *n.* the belly; the stomach; the womb; the interior. **~জ্বালা** *n.* hunger-pain, the pang of hunger; hunger. **~বাস** *n.* stay in the mother's womb (between conception and birth), remaining in the mother's womb. **~যন্ত্রণা** *n.* birth-pangs; labour-pain; the suffering of the baby during its stay in its mother's womb ('দিবি পুনঃ জঠরযন্ত্রণা'). **~স্থ** *a.* lying or staying in the belly or stomach or womb.
জঠরাগ্নি, জঠরানল *n.* terrible hunger; digestive power, digestion; gastric juice.

জঠরানল জ্বলে ওঠা to be stricken with terrible hunger, to be terribly hungry. **জঠরানল নিবৃত্ত হওয়া** to have one's hunger satisfied or stilled.

জড়[1] rej. spell. of **জড়ো**।

জড়[2] *n.* root; the root cause (রোগের জড় মারা). **জড় মারা** *v.* to uproot, to eradicate; to expel or remove the root cause (of).

জড়[3] *a.* inanimate; insensate; perceptible by the senses; worldly, earthly; material (জড়বাদ) ; inactive, inert; stupid, imbecile; ignorant. □ *n.* an imbecile; something inanimate or insensate (জড়ের তিন অবস্থা). **~ক্রিয়** *a.* sluggish. **~জগৎ** *n.* the inanimate world; the physical world; the material world. **~তা, ~ত্ব** *n.* inanimateness, insensateness; state of being perceptible by the senses; worldliness, earthliness; materiality; inactivity, intertia; uneasiness (শরীরের জড়তা) ; stupidity, imbecility; ignorance; sluggishness. **~পদার্থ** *n.* any inanimate substance; inanimate matter; (fig.) an extremely inactive or immobile person, a person bereft of all sensation. **~পিণ্ড** *n.* a mass of anything insensate, a conglomerated mass of things. **~পুত্তলি** *n.* a puppet; (fig.) a person rendered inactive or a person without any freedom of action. **~বাদ** *n.* materialism. **~বাদী** *a.* materialistic. □ *n.* a materialist. **~বিজ্ঞান** *n.* physical or natural science. **~বুদ্ধি** *a.* imbecile, fatuous, oafish. **~ভরত** *n.* (myth.) King Bharata who lost his salvation because of his over-attachment to a fawn and when reborn he remembered the incidents of his former life and so refrained from speaking and all voluntary activities; (fig.) an imbecile or inactive person, a clodhopper. □ *a.* imbecile or inactive. **~সড়** *a.* cowering or cowered. **জড়সড় হওয়া** *v.* to flinch or shrink as through fear or shyness.

জড়াজড়ি *n.* mutual hugging; intertwining. □ *a.* hugged mutually; intertwined. **জড়াজড়ি করা** *v.* to hug mutually; to intertwine.

জড়ানে *a.* too close, interwoven (জড়ানে লেখা).

জড়ানো *v.* to embrace; to hug; to grasp or grapple (as in a scuffle); to wrap (কাগজ দিয়ে জড়ানো) ; to surround; to roll up (লাটাইয়ে সুতো জড়ানো) ; to intertwine; to form into a tangle; to entangle; to mess up or be messed up; to become confused (কথা জড়ানো) ; to involve or to be involved, to implicate or be implicated. □ *a.* embraced; hugged; grasped; grappled; wrapped; surrounded; rolled up; intertwined; formed into a tangle; messed up; confused; involved or implicated in.

জড়িত *a.* connected, related; attached; involved or implicated in; engaged in; inlaid, studded with; affected with; confused (জড়িত কণ্ঠে). **জড়িত করা** *v.* to involve or entangle. **জড়িত হওয়া** *v.* to be involved or implicated.

জড়িবুটি *n.* empiric medicine or cure, medicinal herbs, drugs.

জড়িমা *n.* inactivity, inertia; lethargy, langour, lassitude, fatigue; uneasiness; confusion; a confusing influence (স্বপ্নজড়িমা).

জড়ীভূত *a.* rendered inanimate or insensate; stupefied; rendered inactive or motionless; involved in, implicated in; beset with; affected with. **জড়ীভূত করা** *v.* to render inanimate or insensate or inactive or motionless; to stupefy; to involve in; to beset with; to affect.

জড়ুল *n.* a naevus, a sharply defined mark on skin, a birth-mark like an urticarial spot.

জড়ো *a.* collected, assembled; amassed. **জড়ো করা** *v.* to bring together, to assemble, to collect; to amass. **জড়ো হওয়া** *v.* to meet together, to assemble, to gather.

জড়োপাসক *a.* worshipping inanimate or natural objects; naturistic; animistic. □ *n.* a worshipper of inanimate or natural objects; a naturist; an animist. **জড়োপাসনা** *n.* worship of inanimate objects; nature-worship, naturism, animism.

জড়োয়া *n.* a piece of bejewelled ornament. □ *a.* bejewelled (জড়োয়া গয়না).

জতু *n.* lac; lac-dye (as used by Hindu women to paint their feet). **~গৃহ** *n.* a house built with lac; (fig.) an extremely dangerous abode. **~রস** *n.* lac-dye.

জত্রু *n.* the collar-bone, the clavicle.

জন *n.* a person, a man (শতজন) ; a labourer (জন খাটানো) ; the common people, the masses, demos (জননেতা). □ *in comp.* a person, a head (দশজন, দুজন). **জনকল্যাণ** *n.* welfare of the people, masses etc. **জন খাটা** *v.* to work as a labourer. **জন খাটানো** *v.* to supervise labourers at work, to requisition the service of a labourer. **~গণ** same as **~সাধারণ**। **~গণনা** *n.* census. **~গণেশ** *n.* the presiding god of the common people or the proletariat. **জনগণের দাবি** public demand. **~গোষ্ঠী** *n.* a clan; a tribe. **~তা** *n.* an assembly or crowd of persons; a mob; the rabble; (pol.) the proletariat. **অবৈধ জনতা** an unlawful assembly. **~নায়ক, ~নেতা** *n.* a leader of the people; a demagogue. **~পদ** *n.* any human habitation with distinct boundary lines such as a village or a town, a settlement, a township. **~পদবধূ** *n.* a prostitute, a whore. **জনপালন কৃত্যক** civil service. **~প্রবাদ** *n.* hearsay, a rumour. **~প্রাণী** *n.* a single person or creature. **~প্রিয়** *a.* popular. **~প্রিয়তা** *n.* popularity. **~বল** same as **লোকবল**। **~বসতি** *n.* human habitation, habitation. **~বহুল** *a.* populous, numerously inhabited, thickly populated, congested, crowded. **~বিরল** *a.* sparsely inhabited or populated; almost desolate. **~মজুর** *n.* a labourer (chiefly a temporarily hired one). **~মত** *n.* popular opinion or verdict, public opinion. **~মানব** *n.* (even) a single human being. **~মানবহীন** *a.* desolate, totally desolate; lonely, deserted. **~মুখী** *a.* aimed at the benefit of the people. **~যুদ্ধ** *n.* people's war. **~রব** *n.* hearsay; a rumour. **~লোক** *n.* (myth.) the fifth of the seven heavens which is the abode of pious people after their death. **~শূন্য** *a.* desolate. **~শ্রুতি** *n.* hearsay, a rumour. **~সংখ্যা** *n.* population. **~সংঘ** *n.* a people's society; a society for public welfare, a social service or welfare institution. **~সংভরণ** *n.* civil supply. **~সভা** *n.* mass meeting, public meeting. **~সমক্ষে** *adv.* publicly, before everybody's eyes, openly. **~সমষ্টি** *n.* same as **জনগণ** and **জনসাধারণ**। **~সমাজ** *n.* the human society. **~সমাবেশ** *n.* a gathering (of people, crowds etc.), an assembly, an assemblage of people. **~সমুদ্র** *n.* (lit.) a sea of people; a great multitude of people, a vast concourse of people. **~সাধারণ** *n.* the common people; the masses; the public; (pol.) the proletariat. **~স্বাস্থ্য** *n.* public health. **~স্রোত** *n.* a stream of people. **~হিতকর** *a.* beneficial to the public, doing good to the people; philanthropic. **~হীন** *a.* desolate. **জনে জনে** one after another; one by one; individually; severally.

জনক *n.* father, a progenitor; a producer. □ *a.* producing or causing (সুখজনক).

জনন *n.* the act of begetting, progenition, procreation; birth; origination; production; reproduction. **~কোষ** *n.* a reproductive cell, a gamete, a germ-cell. **~কোষাধার** *n.* gametangium. **~যন্ত্র** *n.* the reproductive organ. **~শক্তি** *n.* generative or procreative power. **~শক্তিহীন** *a.* sterile, barren; impotent; unproductive.

জননাশৌচ *n.* impurities or unholy state, as enjoined by Hindu scriptures, consequent on the birth of a baby in a family.

জননী *n.* mother, a progenitrix. □ *a. fem.* producing or causing.

জননীয় *a.* to be begotten; producible.

জননেন্দ্রিয় *n.* a reproductive (male) organ, the penis.

জনম poet, corrup. of **জন্ম**।

জনয়িতা *n.* a begetter, a progenitor, a father; a producer; an originator. *fem.* **জনয়িত্রী** a progenitrix, a mother.

জনা *n.* (chiefly coll. & poet.) a person, a head (দশজনা). **~জাত** *adv.* individually.

জনাকীর্ণ *a.* thickly or densely populated; overcrowded, teeming with people.

জনান্তিক *a.* (in a drama) aside. **জনান্তিকে** *adv.* aside.

জনপ্রবাদ *n.* a scandal; ill-repute.

জনাব *n.* (Mus.) sir, Mr.

জনার *n.* an inferior variety of cereal, mealie.

জনার্দন *n.* the vanquisher of Jana (জন) the demon: an appellation of Vishnu (বিষ্ণু).

জনি[১] *n.* origination; birth; a mother; a woman; a wife; a daughter-in-law.

জনি[২] *con.* & *adv.* (poet. & obs.) if, nowise; let not; perhaps.

জনিত *a.* born of, begotten by; originating from, resulting from, caused or produced by.

জনিতা[১] *fem.* of **জনিত**।

জনিতা[২] *n.* father, a progenitor, a begetter; a producer; a cause.

জনিত্র *n.* a producing machine, a plant (গ্যাসজনিত্র = a gas plant).

জনিত্রী *fem.* of **জনিতা**[২]।

জনী alt. spell. of **জনি**[১]।

জনু[১] *adv.* (poet. & obs.) as if or in that case.

জনু[২] var. of **জনি**[২]।

জনেক var. of **জনৈক**।

জনৈক *a.* a certain, some, one. *fem.* **জনৈকা**।

জন্তু *n.* an animal, a creature; a beast.

জন্ম *n.* birth, nativity; generation; origination; production; life (জন্ম কাটা); life-time. **জন্ম দেওয়া** *v.* to give birth (to), to beget; to procreate, to originate; to generate; to produce. **জন্ম নেওয়া** *v.* to take one's birth, to be born; to originate; to come into existence; to be produced; to evolve. **~-এয়স্ত্রী, ~-এয়তি** *n.* & *a. fem.* one who is outlived by her husband. **~কুণ্ডলী** *n.* (astrol.) a horoscope; nativity. **~গত** *a.* pertaining to birth or birthtime, natal, innate, bred in the bone; congenital. **~গ্রহণ** *n.* taking one's birth; nativity; origination. **জন্মগ্রহণ করা** same as **জন্ম নেওয়া**। **~ঘটিত** *a.* caused by or pertaining to one's birth; natal. **~-জন্মান্তর** *n.* the present life and the lives following (and also preceding). **~তিথি** *n.* one's lunar birthday; (loos. & pop.) birthday. **~তিথি-পালন, ~তিথি-উৎসব** *n.* birth-anniversary. **~দ, ~দাতা** *n.* a father, a begetter, a progenitor; an originator; a producer. *fem.* **~দা, ~দাত্রী** *a.* mother, a progenitrix; an originator; a producer. **~দান** *n.* procreation; origination; production. **জন্মদান করা** *v.* to procreate, to beget; to give birth to; to generate, to produce. **~দিন, ~দিবস** *n.* birthday. **~দুঃখী** *a.* ever miserable, ever distressed, suffering for ever, born to suffer. **~নক্ষত্র** *n.* the star or planet under which a person is born, the natal star. **~নিয়ন্ত্রণ** *n.* birth-control. **~পত্র, ~পত্রিকা** *n.* a horoscope. **~পরিগ্রহ** same as **~গ্রহণ**। **~বৃত্তান্ত** *n.* an account of one's birth. **~ভূমি** *n.* native land, fatherland, motherland : birth-place. **~মাস** *n.* the month in which one is born, the month of one's birth. **~রাশি** *n.* (astrol.) the zodiacal sign of nativity. **~শোধ** *adv.* for the last time in one's life, once for all. **~সংক্রান্ত** *a.* relating to birth or nativity, natal. **~স্থান** *n.* place of one's birth. **জন্মে জন্মে** at every birth; for ever. **জন্মের মতো** same as **~শোধ**।

জন্মা *v.* to take one's birth, to be born; to come into existence, to originate; to spring up; to be produced, to grow; to occur; to evolve; to accrue.

জন্মাধিকার *n.* birthright.

জন্মানো *v.* to take one's birth, to be born; to come or bring into existence, to originate; to grow or cause to grow, to be produced or to produce; to occur or cause to occur; to evolve or cause to evolve.

জন্মান্তর *n.* another life or existence; physical regeneration after death, rebirth. **~বাদ** *n.* the doctrine of rebirth. **জন্মান্তরে** *adv.* in another birth or life or existence.

জন্মান্ধ *a.* born blind.

জন্মাবচ্ছিন্ন *a.* lifelong.

জন্মাবধি *adv.* since one's birth; throughout one's life.

জন্মাষ্টমী *n.* the eighth lunar day of the dark fortnight of the month of Bhadra (ভাদ্র) when (in Hindu myth.) Krishna (কৃষ্ণ) was born.

জন্মিত *a.* born (of); produced (by) : originating (in, from); evolved (out of).

জন্মোৎসব, জন্মজয়ন্তী *n.* birthday celebration.

জন্য[১] (for. & little used in mod. Bengali) *a.* born of, growing out of (দারিদ্রজন্য দুঃখ) ; that which or one who is to be given birth to, that which is to be grown; that which or one who procreates or produces, procreative. **~জনক-সম্বন্ধ** *n.* the relation between the progenitor and the progeny, the patri-filial relation; the relation between grower and the grown or between the cause and the effect.

জন্য[২], (coll.) **জন্যে** *prep.* for; because of, owing to; in consequence of, as the result of; for the sake of; on behalf of.

জপ *n.* praying silently; silent and repeated recitation of prayers or names esp. as enjoined by scriptures or by a guru; act of telling one's beads; a rosary. **জপ করা** same as **জপা। জপের মন্ত্র** esoteric words to be recited silently in prayers. **~তপ** *n.* (practice of) silent prayers and religious austerities. **~ন** *n.* praying silently; silent and repeated recitation of prayers or names esp. as enjoined by scriptures or by a guru; act of telling one's beads. **~নীয়** *a.* that which is to be or should be recited silently and repeatedly esp. in prayers. **~মালা** *n.* a rosary; (fig.) an object of constant or frequent thought.

জপা *v.* to say one's prayers silently; to recite silently and repeatedly prayers or names esp. as enjoined by scriptures or by a guru; to tell one's beads; (fig.) to think of constantly or frequently. **জপানো** *v.* to cause to recite silently and repeatedly prayers or names esp. as enjoined by scriptures; to make one memorize; (coll. & pop.) to cajole, to win over by cajolery, to persuade by flattery, deceit etc., to coax (into doing something).

জপিত *a.* recited silently and repeatedly; uttered in silent prayers; (fig.) thought of constantly or frequently.

জপ্য *a.* that which is to be or should be recited silently and repeatedly esp. in prayers.

জবজব *int.* expressing : the state of being drenched or moist thoroughly. **জবজব করা** *v.* to be drenched or soaked or moist all over or thoroughly. **জবজবে** *a.* thoroughly drenched or moist with watery or oily substance.

জবর *a.* grand, pompous (জবর উৎসব, জবর আয়োজন) ; excellent (জবর জিনিস) ; hard, grievous, powerful (জবর আঘাত) ; strong (জবর পালোয়ান) ; pertinacious, dogged (জবর লোক, জবর আক্রমণ) ; urgent, of considerable importance, tremendous (জবর সংবাদ) ; attractive, interesting, first-rate (জবর খেলা) ; heavy (জবর শাস্তি). **~দখল** *n.* forcible occupation. **জবরদখল করা** *v.* to occupy by force. **~দস্ত** *a.* indomitable; forceful, imperious, autocratic; very powerful; formidable; violent; forcible; very pertinacious; oppressive; high-handed; tyrannous. **~দস্তি** *n.* application of force, violence; pertinacity; oppression. □ *adv.* forcibly. **জবরদস্তি করা** *v.* to force; to oppress, to behave in a high-handed manner.

জবরজং, জবড়জং *a.* clumsy; unwieldy; odd-looking, ill-shaped, uncouth, (জবরজং পোশাক).

জবা *n.* a red species of the Chinarose, *hibiscus rosa sinensis.*

জবাই *n.* sacrificial slaughter of an animal or the method of slaying an animal in slaughter; slaughter. **জবাই করা** *v.* to slay an animal in sacrifice or in the sacrificial manner; to sacrifice; to kill or murder.

জবান *n.* language (হিন্দি জবান) : speech or word (বদ জবান) ; a promise (জবানের ঠিক নেই) ; the tongue (জবান দোরস্ত করা). **~বন্দি** *n.* attestation, deposition. **~বন্দি দেওয়া** *v.* to depose. **জবানি** *n.* a statement. □ *a.* relating to an answer or rejoinder. □ *adv.* verbally from. **অপরের জবানিতে** through another person's lips.

জবাব *n.* an answer, a reply, a response;

an explanation; (in law) a rejoinder (সওয়াল-জবাব), a retort (মুখের মতো জবাব) ; dismissal (চাকরি থেকে জবাব). **জবাব করা** *v.* to reply, to respond; to retort, to answer back. **জবাব চাওয়া** *v.* to call for an explanation; to ask for a reply. **জবাব দেওয়া** *v.* to answer, to reply, to respond; to explain, to submit an explanation; to rejoin, to submit a rejoinder; to retort; to dismiss. **~দিহি** *n.* an explanation; liability to explain. **জবাবদিহি করা** *v.* to give an explanation; to account for. **জবাবি** *a.* said in reply; said or done in reply (জবাবি হামলা).

জবুথবু *a.* lacking in agility or easy movements; ungainly; decrepit; inert due to old age or disease.

জব্দ *a.* discomfited, put to shame; harassed (ঘুরে ঘুরে জব্দ) ; put out of countenance (জাঁক করতে গিয়ে জব্দ) ; defeated, subdued (শত্রু জব্দ) ; forfeited, confiscated, foreclosed (জমানত জব্দ, ভিটেমাটি জব্দ). **জব্দ করা** *v.* to harass; to put out of countenance; to defeat, to subdue; to forfeit, to confiscate, to foreclose. **কেমন জব্দ** completely befooled or outwitted.

জমক *n.* pomp, grandeur (chiefly used in জাঁকজমক). **জমকালো** *a.* pompous, splendid; showy, spectacular; gaudy, gorgeous.

জমজম *int.* expressing : splendour, pomp, richness, crowded or overcrowded state.

জমজমা *n.* grandeur, pomp; eclat.

জমজমাট *a.* full of grandeur, attractiveness and crowd; in full swing; in full glory; (of celebration, soiree etc.) at its height.

জমা *n.* (rare) capital or principal money; savings; (book-keeping) deposit; credit or income (জমাখরচ) ; revenue or the rate of revenue (বার্ষিক তিন টাকা জমা) ; rented land (তাঁর কাছে আমার কিছু জমা আছে). □ *v.* to be saved or accumulated (টাকা জমা) ; to accrue (সুদ জমা) ; to collect (ময়লা জমা) ; to gather, to assemble (লোক জমা) ; to settle (পলি জমা) ; to congeal or coagulate, to freeze (দুধ জমা, রক্ত জমা) ; to become attractive or captivating (আসর বা গান জমা) ; to be filled with crowd and enthusiasm (সভা জমা). □ *a.* accumulated, saved up; accrued; collected; settled or deposited; congealed, coagulated, frozen; that which has become attractive; filled with crowd and enthusiasm. **জমা করা** *v.* to accumulate; to amass; to cause to assemble, to collect; to deposit; (book-keeping) to credit. **জমা দেওয়া** *v.* to deposit. **জমা নেওয়া** *v.* to take as a deposit. **জমার দিক** (in a book of accounts) the credit side. **~-ওয়াসিলবাকি** *n.* an account or a statement of accounts of realized and unrealized revenue. **~খরচ** *n.* (book-keeping) credit and debit, income and expenditure, receipts and payment or disbursements. **~নবিশ** *n.* an accounts clerk in the receipts branch. **~বন্দি** *n.* a descriptive rent-roll (usu. drawn up annually).

জমাট *a.* congealed, frozen, coagulated (জমাট দুধ, জমাট রক্ত) ; thick (জমাট গাঁথনি, জমাট অন্ধকার) ; inseparable, intimate (জমাট বন্ধুত্ব) ; deep (জমাট আনন্দ) ; thoroughly interesting or delightful (জমাট গান) ; full of crowd and enthusiasm (জমাট সভা). **জমাট বাঁধা** *v.* to coagulate, to congeal; to thicken. **~বাঁধা** *a.* coagulated; frozen; hardened.

জমাটি same as **জমাট**।

জমাদার *n.* an Indian Army officer holding the lowest commissioned rank; a head constable; a head sweeper; a police constable or a sweeper; a foreman or a gangsman. *fem.* **জমাদারনি**।

জমানত *n.* a security, a surety. **জমানত জব্দ বা বাজেয়াপ্ত করা** *v.* to forfeit a security.

জমানো *v.* to lay or put by, to save up; to hoard; to amass, to accumulate; to cause to assemble, to gather; to freeze, to congeal, to coagulate; to crowd and fill with enthusiasm (সভা জমানো) ; to make interesting, to arrest attention (গান জমানো). □ *a.* saved up; amassed, accumulated; frozen, congealed, coagulated.

জমায়েত *n.* an assemblage, a gathering.

জমায়েত হওয়া *v.* to assemble, to gather. **অবৈধ জমায়েত** an unlawful assembly.

জমি, জমিন *n.* ground; land; field; landed property; (of cloth) texture. **জমিজমা** *n.* landed property, real estate. **জমিজায়গা** same as **জমিজমা**। **জমিজিরাত,** (coll.) **জমিজিরেত** *n.* agricultural or arable land. **জমিদার** *n.* a landowner, a zemindar, a landlord. **জমিদারি** *n.* the jurisdiction or property of a zemindar, zemindary, a real estate; the office of a zemindar. □ *a.* pertaining to a zemindary or zemindar. **কাপড়ের জমিন** texture of textile material or fabric or cloth.

জম্পতি, জম্পতী *n.* a married couple; a husband and a wife.

জম্বির *n.* the lime; the citron.

জম্বু *n.* the rose-apple, the jambu; (myth.) one of the seven islands or divisions of the world; Asia; India.

জম্বুক, জম্বূক *n.* the jackal. *fem.* **জম্বুকী, জম্বূকী**।

জয় *n.* act of defeating or conquering; victory, triumph, win, conquest; ovation, applause (জয়ধ্বনি). □ *int.* victory (জয় ভগবান). **জয় করা** *v.* to win; to defeat; to conquer; to succeed. **জয় হওয়া** *v.* to be won or conquered; to be crowned with victory or success (তোমার জয় হবে). **~গান** *n.* a song of praise; singing in praise. **~জয়কার** *n.* (popular) praise of a victorious person; huzza; (loos.) great or repeated victory. **জয়জয়কার করা** *v.* to receive with an ovation, to huzza; **জয়জয়কার হওয়া** *v.* to be received with an ovation, to be acclaimed. **~জয়ন্তী** *n.* an Indian musical mode. **~ঢাক** *n.* a war-drum. **~তু** *v.* be victorious, let victory attend you (জয়তু শিবাজি) ; glory be. **~দুর্গা** *n.* a manifestation of Goddess Durga (দুর্গা). **~ধ্বনি** *n.* peals of victory; noise of ovation with which a triumphant or famous person is received, huzza. **জয়ধ্বনি করা** *v.* to receive with an ovation, to huzza. **~ধ্বজ, ~পতাকা** *n.* a flag or standard of victory or triumph. **~পত্র** *n.* a written certificate or declaration of success or triumph. **~-পরাজয়** *n.* victory and defeat; success and failure. **~ভেরি** *n.* a war-drum. **~মাল্য** *n.* a wreath or laurel of victory. **~যুক্ত** *a.* victorious, triumphant; successful. **~লক্ষ্মী** same as **~শ্রী**। **~লাভ** *n.* attainment of victory. **~লেখ** same as **~পত্র**। **জয়শঙ্খ** *n.* a conch that is blown by a person to announce his or her victory. **~শ্রী** *n.* the presiding goddess of victory. **~সাধ্য** *a.* conquerable, vincible. **~স্তম্ভ** *n.* a pillar or monument of victory.

জয়ত্রী *n.* the aril of the nutmeg, mace.

জয়ন্তী *n.* a flag, a standard; a name of Goddess Durga (দুর্গা) ; a birthday celebration (রবীন্দ্রজয়ন্তী) ; an anniversary, a jubilee; a kind of tree. **রৌপ্যজয়ন্তী** *n.* the silver jubilee. **সুবর্ণজয়ন্তী** *n.* the golden jubilee. **হীরকজয়ন্তী** *n.* the diamond jubilee.

জয়পাল *n.* the croton.

জয়া *n.* a name of Goddess Durga (দুর্গা) or one of her female attendants.

জয়িত্রী, জয়িত্রি variants of **জয়ত্রী**।

জয়ী *a.* victorious, triumphant, successful.

জয়োৎসব *n.* victory celebration.

জয়োন্মত্ত *a.* flushed or beaming with victory, maddened by victory.

জয়োল্লাস *n.* rejoicings and celebrations after victory or signal success.

জয়োস্তু *v.* be victorious, let victory attend you.

জরজর *a.* very much oppressed or stricken with (দুঃখে জরজর) ; worn out; saturated with (নুনে জরজর) ; beside oneself.

জরতী *a. fem.* decrepit; very old; very old and without any novelty (জরতী পৃথিবী). *masc.* **জরৎ**।

জরদ *a.* yellow.

জরদ্গব *n.* a decrepit bull; (fig.) a decrepit man who can do no work; a stupid, good-for-nothing fellow.

জরদা *n.* a preparation of tobacco to be taken or chewed with betel-leaves. □ *a* yellow. **জরদা-পোলাও** *n.* a kind of sweet pilau coloured with saffron.

জরা[1] *n.* old age; decrepitude, infirmity; senility. **~রহিত** *a.* not subject to old age or decay, not subject to senile decay; undecaying and immortal.

জরা[২] *v.* to be smeared with esp. for preservation (লবণে জরা); to be pickled. see also **জরানো**।

জরাগ্রস্ত *a.* seized with infirmities of old age, decrepit and infirm, worn-out, senile.

জরাজীর্ণ *a.* worn-out, dilapidated and decayed through age.

জরানো *v.* to smear with esp. for preservation (লবণে আম জরানো); to pickle. □ *a.* smeared with; pickled.

জরায়ু *n.* the uterus; the womb. **~জ** *a.* viviparous. (*cp.* oviparous).

জরি *n.* thread of gold or silver. **~দার** *a.* woven or fringed or embroidered with thread of gold or silver.

জরিপ *n.* measurement of an area of land, land-survey. **জরিপ করা** *v.* to measure or survey land. **জরিপ-আমিন** *n.* a land-surveyor. **~কারী** *a.* surveying (land). □ *n.* a land-surveyor.

জরিমানা *n.* a money penalty, a fine, a mulct. **জরিমানা করা** *v.* to impose a fine, to fine, to mulct.

জরিষ্ণু *a.* decaying.

জরু alt. spell. of **জোরু**।

জরুর *adv.* surely, certainly; perforce; by all means. **জরুরত** *n.* necessity, need. **জরুরি** *a.* urgent; necessary; important. **জরুরি তার** an express or urgent telegram.

জরোজরো alt. spell. of **জরজর**।

জর্জর, জর্জরিত *a.* very much oppressed or stricken with (দুঃখে জর্জর); worn out; deeply engrossed or involved in (ঋণে জর্জর).

জর্দা alt. spell. of **জরদা**।

জল *n.* water; aqua : rain (জল হচ্ছে); a stream ('যেতেছে জলের মত'); (fig.) a light repast, refreshment, snack, tiffin (জলখাবার). □ *a.* cooled, comforted, refreshed (প্রাণ জল হওয়া); liquefied (গলে জল); rendered watery, thinned (রক্ত জল); mixed or adulterated with water (জল দুধ); wasted (টাকা জল হওয়া); exhausted, ruined (দেহ বা রক্ত জল হওয়া); very easy (জল অঙ্ক). **খর জল** hard water. **চোখের জল** tears. **নারকেলের জল** milk of coconut. **বৃষ্টির জল** rain-water. **ভারী জল** (phys.) heavy water. **মিঠে জল** fresh water. **মৃদু জল** soft water. **জল করা** *v.* to waste (টাকা জল করা); to ruin, to exhaust (দেহ বা রক্ত জল করা); to cool or comfort (প্রাণ জল করা). **জল খাওয়া** *v.* to drink water; to take light repast, to take tiffin, (coll.) to refresh; to take or require water (ইঞ্জিনটা খুব জল খায়). **জল ঝরা** *v.* to drip. **জল দেওয়া** *v.* to give water; to give a dying person water to drink; to offer drinking water to the manes; to water (গাছে জল দেওয়া). **জল পড়া** *v.* to rain; to leak water (কলসিটা থেকে জল পড়ে); to stream with tears. **জল মরা** *v.* to dry up. **জল নেওয়া** *v.* to take water; (of an engine etc.) to water. **জল সওয়া** *v.* to fetch water from a river or pond on the eve of a festival. **জল সরা** *v.* to pass out water; to use the water of a pond esp. for purposes other than drinking; (of a pregnant woman) pass fluid (esp. immediately before childbirth). **জল হওয়া** *v.* to rain; to become liquid, to liquefy, to melt (গলে জল হওয়া); to cool or be comforted (প্রাণ জল হওয়া); to cool or calm down (রাগ জল হওয়া); to become cold (চা জল হওয়া). **জলে দেওয়া** *v.* (fig.) to give to an undeserving person; (fig.) to waste. **জলে পড়া** *v.* (fig.) to arrive at a bad place; (fig.) to fall in a danger; (fig.) to fall to an undeserving person; (fig.) to be wasted. **জলে ফেলা** same as **জলে দেওয়া**। **জলে যাওয়া** *v.* to go to a river or pond; (fig.) to be wasted (টাকাটা জলে গেল). **জলের কল** *a.* water-tap. **কলের জল** tap-water. **জলের গাড়ি** a water-cart. **জলের দামে** (fig.) at a throw-away price. **জলের স্রোত** a stream of water. **~কণা** *n.* a little or small drop of water. **~কন্যা** *n.* a water-nymph, a naiad, a mermaid. **~কপাট** *n.* a watergate, a sluicegate, a sluice. **~কর** *n.* a tax imposed on ponds, water reservoirs etc.; a water toll; a tax on fishery. **~কল্লোল** *n.* noise (usu. loud) made by a running stream or wave; a noisy wave; a roaring wave. **~কষ্ট** *n.* scarcity of water.

~কাচা *a.* (of textile goods) washed in water only (that is, without using soap or other washing materials). ~কাদা *n.* rain-water and mud; slush. ~কুক্কুট *n.* the water-fowl; the gull. ~কুণ্ড *n.* a water-font; a water-reservoir. ~কূট *n.* (phys.) a water-trap. ~ক্রিয়া *n.* drink-offering to the deceased, water libation, offering drinking water to the manes. ~ক্রীড়া, ~কেলি *n.* aquatic sports, watersports; bathing in rivers or ponds for amusement. ~খাবার *n.* a light repast, refreshment, tiffin, snack. ~গাহ *n.* waterbath. জলগ্রহণ না করা *v.* not to drink water; not to take even the slightest food, refuse to take any food. ~গ্রাহী *a.* (bot.) hygroscopic. ~চক্র *n.* (phys.) a water-mill. ~চর *a.* living or growing in water, aquatic. □ *n.* an aquatic animal. ~চল *a.* belonging to a caste whose touch does not pollute water to be used by high-caste people. ~চাষ বিদ্যা hydroponics, art of growing plants in water impregnated with nutrients. ~চিকিৎসক *n.* a hydropathist. ~চিকিৎসা *n.* hydropathy. ~চিহ্ন *n.* manufacturer's design on some kinds of paper—seen when the paper is held against light, watermark. ~চুড়ি *n.* a watermark in the shape of a thin streak. ~চৌকি *n.* a low and small wooden stool. ~ছত্র coll. corrup. of ~সত্র। ~ছবি *n.* a transfer picture. ~ছাপ *n.* a watermark. ~জ *a.* born in or of water, ponds, rivers, seas etc.; aquatic. □ *n.* the water-lily, the lotus. ~জন্তু *n.* an aquatic animal. ~জীয়ন্ত, ~জিয়ন্ত, (coll.) ~জ্যান্ত *a.* perfectly alive (just like a fish in water); (fig.) quite obvious, downright (জলজ্যান্ত মিথ্যা). ~ঝড় *n.* rain and storm. ~টুঙি *n.* a raised hut built in the midst of a pond, marsh, river etc. ~ঢোঁড়া *n.* a species of non-venomous water-snake. ~তরঙ্গ *n.* a wave; a ripple; a kind of musical instrument consisting of seven bowls which are filled with water and are struck with one or more sticks in order to produce musical sounds. ~দস্যু *n.* a pirate; a buccaneer. ~দস্যুতা *n.* piracy. ~তা করা *v.* to act as a pirate; to buccaneer. ~দেবতা *n.* a watergod; Neptune; Varuna (বরুণ). ~দোষ *n.* morbid collection of water in the abdomen, dropsy. ~দ্রোণী *n.* a water-cask, a water-barrel; a water-bucket; a trough. ~ধর *a.* containing water; full of water. □ *n.* the cloud; the sea. ~ধারা *n.* a stream of water. ~নকুল *n.* the otter. ~নালী *n.* a water-passage; an aqueduct; a drain. ~নিকাশ *n.* draining out water, drainage. ~নিকাশের পথ a drain, an outlet for water. ~নিধি *n.* an ocean; a sea. ~নিরোধক *a.* waterproof. ~নির্গম *n.* passage of water, drainage. ~নির্গমপথ *n.* an outlet for water; a drain. ~নির্গম প্রণালী *n.* drainage system; an outlet for water, a conduit; a drain. ~পটি *n.* a strip of cloth soaked in water and placed on a wounded limb or on the forehead. ~পড়া *n.* water into which curative or supernatural power is believed to have been infused by means of mysterious words uttered by a sorcerer or magician. ~পথ *n.* a waterway; an outlet for water. ~পথে *adv.* by water. ~পরাগী *a.* hydrophilous. ~পরি *n.* a water-nymph; a water fairy, mermaid. ~পাত্র *n.* a water-vessel, a water-pot; a drinking cup or glass. ~পান *n.* a light repast, snacks; act of drinking water. জলপান করা *v.* to take a light repast; to drink water. ~পানি *n.* a scholarship, a studentship, student's stipend; pocket-money (আশুতোষ তাঁর বাবার কাছ থেকে নিত্য এক টাকা করে জলপানি পেতেন). ~ পিপাসা *n.* thirst. ~পিপি *n.* a small species of wading bird, the jacana, Metopidius indicus. ~পিঁড়ি *n.* a low wooden pedestal on which pitchers are placed. ~পুলিশ *a.* water police; marine police. ~পৃষ্ঠ *n.* water level, surface of water. ~প্রণালী *n.* an outlet for water; a drain; a water-course; a strait. ~প্রপাত *n.* a waterfall, a cataract, a cascade, a fall. ~প্লাবন *n.* a flood; a deluge. ~প্লাবিত *a.* overflooded; flooded with water. ~বৎ *a.* (fig.) clear as water, perspicuous, very easy to understand. ~বসন্ত *n.* chicken-pox.

~বাতাস, ~বায়ু *n.* climate. **~বাহক** *n.* a water-carrier. **~বাহিত** *a.* (of goods or diseases) water-borne. **~বিছুটি** *n.* nettle drenched in water (which, when rubbed on any part of the body, causes a terrible irritation). **~বিজ্ঞান** *n.* hydrostatics. **~বিদ্যুৎ** *n.* hydro-electricity, hydro-electric power. **~বিন্দু** *n.* a drop of water. **~বিম্ব** *n.* a bubble. **~বিভাজিকা** *n.* watershed. **~বিযুক্ত করা** *v.* to dehydrate. **~বিয়োজন** *n.* dehydration. **~বিষুব** *n.* the autumnal equinox. **~বিশ্লেষণ** *n.* hydrolyzation. **জলবিশ্লেষণ করা** *v.* to hydrolize. **~বিহার** same as **~ক্রীড়া।** **~বোমা** *n.* a depth charge, a bomb used against a submarine for explosion under water. **জল ভাঙা** *v.* to proceed or walk through water with difficulty. **~ভ্রমি** *n.* a whirlpool. **~মগ্ন** *a.* immersed or sunk in water; drowned; flooded or submerged. **জলমগ্ন হওয়া** *v.* to sink; to drown; to be submerged. **~ময়** *a.* full of water; watery; flooded with water; full of ponds, rivers etc. (জলময় দেশ). **~মার্জার** *n.* the otter. **~মুক** *n.* the cloud. **~যন্ত্র** *n.* a machine or pulley for hauling up water; a water-clock, a clepsydra; a spraying instrument, a spray. **~যাত্রা** *n.* a sea voyage. **~যাত্রী** *n.* a voyager. □ *a.* voyaging. **~যান** *n.* a ship or a boat, a vessel. **~যুদ্ধ** *n.* a fight on water, a naval fight; a naval war; naval warfare. **~যোদ্ধা** *n.* a naval soldier, a navy-man. **~যোগ** *n.* tiffin or a light repast. **জলযোগ করা** *v.* to take tiffin or a light repast. **~রং** *n.* water colour. **~রাশি** *n.* a mass of water. **~রেখা** *n.* a water-line. **~রোধী** *a.* waterproof; watertight. **~শক্তি** *n.* hydro-electricity, power obtained from flowing or falling water capable of generating electric current etc., waterpower. **~শূন্য** *a.* waterless; dry. **~শৌচ** *n.* act of washing the posteriors (and also other parts of the body) with water after purging. **~সত্র** *n.* a place for charitable distribution of drinking water to the public. **~সম** *a.* level with water. **~সমতল** *n.* water-level. **~সিক্ত** *a.* soaked in or drenched with water, wet; moist. **~সিঞ্চন, ~সেচন** *n.* act of sprinkling water; act of watering (trees etc.) **জলসিঞ্চন করা, জলসেচন করা** *v.* to sprinkle water (upon); to water. **~সেক** *n.* act of sprinkling water; act of sprinkling; act of fomenting with a piece of cloth dipped in hot water. **~স্তম্ভ** *n.* a waterspout. **~স্ফীতি** *n.* spate. **~স্রোত** *n.* a stream of water. **~হস্তী** *n.* the hippopotamus. **~হাওয়া** *n.* climate.

জলদ[১] *a.* that which gives water. □ *n.* the cloud. **~কাল** *n.* the rainy season. **~ক্ষয়** *n.* autumn. **~গম্ভীর** *a.* as grave or deep as the rumbling of the cloud. **জলদাগম** *n.* the break of monsoon; the rainy season, the rains.

জলদ[২] *a.* quick, rapid (জলদ লয়ে বাজানো) □ *adv.* quickly, rapidly.

জলদি *adv.* quickly; rapidly.

জলধি *n.* the sea; the ocean.

জলপাই *n.* the olive. **জলপাই রং** *n.* olive colour. **জলপাই রংয়ের** *a.* olive-green, olivaceous. **জলপাইয়ের তেল** olive-oil.

জলসা *n.* a majlis or assembly for musical demonstration, a musical soiree.

জলা *n.* a marsh, a bog. □ *a.* marshy. **~জমি** *n.* wetlands, a marshy or swampy land, a swamp.

জলাচরণীয় *a.* pertaining to a caste whose touch does not pollute water or render it unfit for use by people of higher castes.

জলাঞ্জলি *n.* act of taking water in cupped palms of hands and offering it to the deceased when the cremation is over; (fig.) act of giving up, abandonment (লেখাপড়ায় জলাঞ্জলি) ; (fig.) waste (টাকা জলাঞ্জলি). **জলাঞ্জলি দেওয়া** *v.* to take water in cupped palms of hands and offer it to the deceased at the end of cremation; (fig) to give up, to abandon; (fig.) to waste.

জলাতঙ্ক *n.* hydrophobia; rabies.

জলাত্যয় *n.* the end of the monsoon; autumn.

জলাধার *n.* a receptacle of water, a water-vessel, a reservoir of water.

জলাধিপ, জলাধিপতি *n.* a sea; an ocean; Varuna (বরুণ) the presiding deity of water.

জলাবর্ত *n.* a whirlpool, an eddy.

জলাভাব *n.* scarcity of water.

জলাভূমি *n.* a marsh, a swamp, a bog.

জলাভেদ্য *a.* waterproof.

জলাশয় *n.* a water-reservoir; a pond, a tank, a pool, a lake, a river etc.

জলীয় *a.* of water, aqueous. **জলীয় বাষ্প** aqueous vapour, water vapour.

জলুনি pop. spell. of **জ্বলুনি**।

জলুস *n.* lustre; brightness; splendour; glamour.

জলেশ, জলেশ্বর same as **জলাধিপ**।

জলো *a.* adulterated or mixed with water (জলো দুধ) ; wet (জলো বাতাস) ; full of water (জলো মাঠ) ; marshy (জলো জায়গা) ; watery, thin (জলো রং).

জলোচ্ছ্বাস *n.* spate; high tide, high water; a bore; a tidal wave.

জলোদ্ভব *a.* aquatic.

জলৌকা *n.* the leech.

জলৌষধি *n.* medicinal water-plants or water-cresses.

জল্প *n.* (log.) establishment of one's own opinion by refuting another's; discussion (usu. of no importance); garrulity; prating. **~ক** *a.* garrulous. **~ন, ~না** *n.* utterance; discussion; talk; speculation; a proposal. **জল্পিত** *a.* uttered; discussed; speculated; proposed.

জল্লাদ *n.* an executioner, a hangman, a fierce and ugly man; (fig.) an extremely merciless or heartless person.

জহর[1] *n.* poison.

জহর[2] *n.* a precious stone, a gem, a jewel.

জহরত *n.* jewels collectively, jewellery.

জহরব্রত *n.* a rite practised by Rajput women of old by burning themselves alive on funeral pyres to escape shame and insult.

জহরি, জহুরি *n.* a jeweller; a lapidary. **জহুরি জহর চেনে** (fig.) a shepherd knows his ewe.

জা[1] *n. fem.* a wife of one's husband's brother, a woman's sister-in-law.

জা[2] *sfx.* son (বোসজা) = a son of Mr Bose, a son of a Bose family).

জাইগির var. of **জায়গির**।

জাউ *n.* gruel; porridge.

জাং *n.* the thigh.

জাঁক *n.* vaunt, brag, boast; parade; pomp, éclat. **জাঁক করা** *v.* to vaunt, to brag, to boast. **জাঁক দেখানো** *v.* to show off, to display ostentatiously; to parade one's importance. **~জমক** *n.* pomp and grandeur; great éclat. **জাঁকজমক করা** *v.* to ostentatiously parade pomp and grandeur; to arrange with a display of pomp and grandeur.

জাঁকড় *n.* purchase on condition that if not approved, the article will be returned.

জাঁকা *v.* to be filled with splendour; to sit or settle firmly upon (জেঁকে বসা) ; to be flourishing; to hold or seize fast.

জাঁকানো *v.*. to fill with splendour. □ *a.* redolent of splendour, flourishing.

জাঁকালো *a.* pompous; showy, ostentatious; splendid.

জাঁতা[1] *n.* mill-stone, grindstone; bellows.

জাঁতা[2] *v.* to press down firmly; to massage ('চরণ জাঁতিছে').

জাঁতানো *v.* to load. □ *a.* loaded.

জাঁতি *n.* a nut-cracker. **~কল** *n.* a mechanism to catch rats, a toothed or serrated rat-trap. **জাঁতিকলে পড়া** (fig.) to be in a difficult situation or tight corner.

জাঁদরেল *a.* ostentatious, pompous; grand; overbearing; very strong or powerful; gigantic; great.

জাঁহাপনা var. **জাহাঁপনা**।

জাঁহাবাজ var. of **জাহাঁবাজ**।

জাগ *n.* artificial warmth produced by heaping straw or tree-leaves etc. upon something (in order to ripen or soften or decompose it); to ret (পাট জাগ দেওয়া). **জাগ দিয়ে পাকানো** to ripen artificially or prematurely.

জাগ-গান *n.* a kind of folk-song sung at night in some parts of Bengal.

জাগতিক *a.* worldly, earthly, of this world.

জাগন্ত *a.* awake; wakeful.

জাগর *n.* awakening; awakened state; wakeful or sleepless state ('রজনী জাগরক্লান্ত') ; (dial.) a kind of awakening song. **~স্বপ্ন** *n.* a day-dream; a reverie.

জাগরণ *n.* act of waking; sleeplessness; wakefulness; (fig.) coming back to activity or consciousness, awakening, rise (জাতির জাগরণ). **জাগরণী** *n.* an awakening song; the period of waking. □ *a.* relating to waking.

জাগরিত *a.* awakened, risen from sleep; sleepless, wakeful; (fig.) come back to one's senses or consciousness. **জাগরিত করা** *v.* to rouse from sleep, to awake or awaken; (fig.) to bring one to one's senses. **জাগরিত হওয়া** *v.* to rise from sleep, to wake; (fig.) to come back to one's senses, to regain one's consciousness.

জাগরী *a.* one who keeps awake; wakeful; sleepless.

জাগরূক *a.* awake; wakeful; watchful; careful; still unforgotten or existent (হৃদয়ে জাগরূক).

জাগা *v.* to rise from sleep, to wake (ভোরে জাগা) ; to rise (ঘুম ভেঙে জাগা) ; to be without sleep (সারারাত জেগেছে) ; to be inspired ('জাগিয়া উঠেছে প্রাণ') ; to occur to, to strike (মনে জাগা). □ *a.* awake. **জাগানো** *v.* to rouse from sleep, to awake; to rouse; to keep awake; to inspire; to cause to wake; to remind.

জাগুয়ার *n.* the jaguar.

জাগ্রৎ, জাগ্রত *a.* awake; wakeful; watchful; conscious.

জাঙ, জাঙ্গ alt. spellings of **জাং**।

জাঙ্গাল, জাঙাল *n.* a dam, a weir; an embankment, a dyke; a bridge; a ridge; an elevated road; a highway; fallow land; verdigris; unending line (পিঁপড়ের জাঙাল).

জাঙ্গি *a.* unripe, green (জাঙ্গি হরীতকী).

জাঙ্গিয়া, জাঙিয়া *n.* drawers, shorts.

জাজিম *n.* a cloth-sheet (esp. a richly decorated one) to cover a bed or a seat; (loos.) a mattress.

জাজ্বল্যমান *a.* refulgent, shining; very bright or vivid; flaming; glaring.

জাট, জাঠ *n.* a race inhabiting Rajputana, Haryana etc.; a member of this race.

জাঠর *a.* relating to the belly or womb; abdominal.

জাঠা[1] *n.* an iron cudgel used as a weapon in war in ancient times.

জাঠা[2] *n.* a moving assembly of men; a procession.

জাড় *n.* a spell of cold weather, cold; chill; winter.

জাড্য *n.* inactiveness, sloth, idleness; inertia, stupor; imbecility, fatuity; ignorance; frigidity.

জাত[1] (pronun. : জাতো) *a.* born (সদ্যোজাত) ; grown, produced (ক্ষেত্রজাত) ; evolved, resulted from, caused by (শ্রমজাত) ; made of (দুগ্ধজাত). □ *n.* birth (জাতকর্ম) ; collection, assemblage (দ্রব্যজাত). **~ক** *a.* one who takes one's birth; born. □ *n.* a newly born baby; a horoscope; rites to be performed at birth; a book narrating the incidents of the former lives of Gautama Buddha; a Buddhist friar. **~কর্ম, ~কৃত্য, ~ক্রিয়া** *n.* rites to be performed at birth. **~ক্রোধ** *a.* angered, enraged. □ *n.* anger against a particular person or thing existing since one's birth (cp. vendetta, bloodfeud). **~দ্রব্য** *n.* products or produces collectively. **~পক্ষ, ~পক্ষ্ম** *a.* fledged. □ *n.* a fledgling. **~পত্র** *n.* a horoscope. **~পুত্র** *a.* one to whom a son is born, one who has a son. **~প্রত্যয়** *a.* convinced. **~বেদা** *n.* one who knows all that is created : an appellation of Agni (অগ্নি), the god of fire. **~ব্যবহার** *a.* one who has come of age. □ *n.* such a person, a major. **~মাত্র** *adv.* as soon as one is born. □ *a.* just born. **~শত্রু** *a.* one who has many enemies. □ *n.* a born enemy.

জাত[2] (pronun. : জাত্) *n.* caste (কায়েত জাত) ; kind, sort, class (ভালো জাতের আম) ; breed (সেরা জাতের কুকুর). □ *a.* by or since birth (জাতবোষ্টম) ; belonging to the same caste (জাতভাই) ; hereditary (জাত-ব্যাবসা). **জাত খোয়ানো, জাত দেওয়া** *v.* to lose one's claim to remain in the fold of one's caste, to lose one's caste; to get oneself declassed. **জাত মারা** *v.* to deprive one of the claim of remaining in the fold of one's caste, to expel one from one's caste, to outcaste; to declass. **জাত যাওয়া** *v.* to be outcasted. **জাত হারানো** same as **জাত খোয়ানো**। **জাতে ওঠা** *v.* to be reclaimed into the fold of one's caste; to have one's status uplifted. ~গোত্রহীন *a.* having no good or respectable lineage or parentage. **জাতে তোলা** *v.* to reclaim into the fold of one's caste; to uplift the status of. ~**নাশা** *a.* causing expulsion from one's caste (জাতনাশা লোক, জাতনাশা কাণ্ড) ; abominable. ~**পাত** *n.* distinction of caste; casteism. ~**পেশা,** ~**ব্যবসায়,** ~**ব্যাবসা** *n.* hereditary occupation or trade. ~**ভাই** *n.* a kinsman.

জাত৩ (pronun : জাত্) *a.* best, chief, real (জাত কেউটে). ~**সাপ** *n.* the cobra.

জাত৪ (pronun : জাতো) *sfx.* stored or kept in (গুদামজাত).

জাতাঙ্কুর *a.* germinated, sprouted.

জাতান্ধ *a.* born blind.

জাতাশৌচ *n.* (personal) impurity or unholy state caused by child-birth.

জাতি১ *n.* birth, origin (জাতিতে হিন্দু) ; kind, sort, class (নানা জাতির ফুল) ; breed or pedigree (নানা জাতির কুকুর) ; a race, a tribe (নানা জাতির মানুষ) ; a genus or species (মানবজাতি, সর্পজাতি, স্ত্রীজাতি) ; caste (কায়স্থজাতি) ; a nation (হিন্দুজাতি, ইংরেজজাতি) ; a community; lineage (শ্রেষ্ঠ জাতির ব্রাহ্মণ). **জাতি খোয়ানো** *v.* to lose one's claim to remain in the fold of one's caste, to be outcasted. **জাতি দেওয়া** *v.* to forgo one's claim to remain in the fold of one's caste. **জাতি মারা** same as **জাতি খাওয়া**। **জাতি যাওয়া, জাতি হারানো** same as **জাতি খোয়ানো**। **জাতিতে ওঠা** *v.* to be reclaimed into the fold of one's caste; to have one's status uplifted. **জাতিতে তোলা** *v.* to reclaim into the fold of one's caste; to uplift the status of. ~**কর্ম** *n.* a hereditary trade or occupation. ~**গত** *a.* pertaining to the race, nation, caste, class, community etc.; racial, national, generic; phylogenetic. ~**চ্যুত** *a.* expelled from one's caste, outcasted. ~**জনি** *n.* phylogenesis, phylogeny. ~**তত্ত্ব** *n.* ethnology. ~**তত্ত্বীয়** *a.* ethnological. ~**তাত্ত্বিক** *a.* ethnological. □ *n.* an ethnologist. **একজাতিতত্ত্ব** *n.* the one-nation theory. ~**ধর্ম** *n.* duties and practices pertaining to one's caste or race, racial duties and practices; racial character. ~**ধর্মনির্বিশেষে** *adv.* without distinction of caste and creed. ~**নাশ** *n.* expulsion from one's caste. ~**নাশা** *a.* causing one to be outcasted; extremely disgraceful. ~**বর্ণ-নির্বিশেষে** *adv.* without distinction of caste and colour. ~**বাচক** *a.* generic; (gr.) denoting the class. ~**বিচার** *n.* act of distinguishing the castes, caste-distinction; distinction of class. ~**বিদ্বেষ** *n.* race-hatred. ~**বিদ্যা** *n.* ethnology. ~**বিদ্যাগত** *a.* ethnological. ~**বিদ্যাবিৎ** *n.* an ethnologist. ~**বৈর** *n.* racial enmity; vendetta, bloodfeud. ~**ব্যবসায়** same as ~**কর্ম**। ~**ভেদ** *n.* caste-distinction. ~**ভেদপ্রথা** *n.* caste-system. ~**ভ্রংশ** *n.* loss of one's claim to remain in the fold of one's caste. ~**ভ্রষ্ট** same as ~**চ্যুত**। ~**রূপ** *n.* national or racial type. ~**লক্ষণ** *n.* distinctive mark of a caste or race, typical mark. ~**সংঘ** *n.* (the) League of Nations. ~**স্বভাব** *n.* the racial character. ~**স্মর** *a.* one who remembers the incidents of one's former lives. ~**হীন** *a.* outcasted; casteless; declassed. **সম্মিলিত জাতিপুঞ্জ, রাষ্ট্রসংঘ** the United Nations Organization.

জাতি২, জাতী *n.* a variety of white flower.

জাতিপত্র, জাতিপত্রী, জাতীপত্র, জাতীপত্রী *n.* the aril of the nutmeg, mace.

জাতিফল *n.* the nutmeg.

জাতীয় *a.* of a nation, tribe, community, class, species, type or variety; national, racial, typical. *fem.* **জাতীয়া**। ~**তা** *n.* nationalism. ~**তাবাদী** *a.* & *n.* nationalist. **জাতীয় গর্ব** national pride. **জাতীয় চরিত্র** national or racial character. **জাতীয় মহাসভা** National Congress. **নানাজাতীয়** of different kinds or varieties.

জাতেষ্টি *n.* rites to be performed at birth.

জাত্য *a.* well-born, nobly-born; of a high lineage; legitimate; noble; best.

জাত্যংশ *n.* lineage, descent, family.

জাত্যন্ধ *a.* born blind.

জাত্যভিমান *n.* pride in one's lineage or family; race-consciousness. **জাত্যভিমানী** *a.* proud of one's lineage or family; race-conscious. *fem.* **জাত্যভিমানিনী**।

জাত্যর্থ *n.* connotation.

-জাদা *sfx.* son (শাহজাদা = the son of a king). *fem.* **-জাদি** daughter.

জাদু[1] *n.* (chiefly used in addressing a baby affectionately) darling, dearie.

জাদু[2] *n.* magic, jugglery; sorcery, witchcraft, enchantment; engrossing charm (রূপের জাদু). **জাদু করা** *v.* to enchant, to bewitch; to charm. **~কর,** (rare) **~গর** *a.* a magician, a juggler; a sorcerer, a wizard; an enchanter, a charmer. *fem.* **~করী,** (rare) **~গরী** a female magician or juggler; a sorceress, a witch; an enchantress. **~ঘর** *n.* a museum (of curiosities). **~বল** *n.* magical power—good or bad, force of charm or enchantment. **~বিদ্যা** *n.* magic, jugglery; black art, sorcery, witchcraft; enchantment.

জান[1] *n.* a soothsayer, a diviner; an all-knowing person; a person possessing occult power to know things; (erron.) a wizard or a witch.

জান[2] *n.* life.

জানপদ *a.* of a human settlement; produced in or dwelling in a village or country, rural, rustic.

জানলা alt. form of **জানালা**।

জানা *v.* to know, to come to know, to learn; to be cognizant of; to have knwoledge (of or in); to feel, to perceive, to realize (জানছি কষ্ট হবে) ; to be acquainted with (তাকে জানি). □ *a.* known (জানা কথা) ; learnt. **~জানি** *a.* made public, circulated. □ *n.* circulation, publicity. **জানান দেওয়া** *v.* to announce or proclaim or notify beforehand; to announce oneself. **~নো** *v.* to acquaint with; to inform; to make known.

জানানা *n.* a woman, a female; a woman living in a zenana; a wife; apartments in which women are secluded, a zenana, a gynaeceum.

জানালা *n.* a window.

জানাশোনা *n.* acquaintance; familiarity. □ *a.* acquainted.

জানিত *a.* known, familiar.

জানু *n.* the knee. **জানু-কাপালিক** *n.* the knee-cap, the patella. **~ত্রাণ** *n.* protective covering for the knee, knee-cap. **~সন্ধি** *n.* knee-joint.

জানুয়ারি *n.* January.

জানোয়ার *n.* a beast, an animal; a brute.

জান্তব *a.* of or like a beast or animal; beastly. **জান্তব চর্বি** animal fat. **জান্তব চিৎকার** (lit.) the cry of an animal; (fig.) a horrid, fierce or alarming cry.

জান্নাত *n.* the heavenly garden.

জাপক *a.* & *n.* one who says one's prayers or tells one's beads silently; one who recollects silently.

জাপটাজাপটি *n.* mutual hugging or embracing or clasping. **জাপটাজাপটি করা** *v.* to try to hug or embrace or clasp one another; to be locked in embrace.

জাপটানো *v.* to hug, to embrace; to clasp.

জাপানি *a.* Japanese. □ *n.* a native of Japan; the language of Japan, Japanese.

জাফরান *n.* saffron. **জাফরানি** *n.* saffron yellow. □ *a.* saffron yellow.

জাফরি *n.* lattice, trellis. **~-কাটা** *a.* latticed, trellised.

জাব, জাবনা *n.* a mixture of chopped straw, oil-cake, water etc. given to cattle as their food, fodder. **জাবনাভান্ড, জাবপাত্র** *n.* a manger. **ভিজে জাব** thoroughly wet or drenched or soaked (like জাব).

জাবড়া *a.* wet or drenched like জাব ; thoroughly wet or drenched; disorderly, messy; thick and ugly; smudgy. **জাবড়ানো** *v.* to wet or drench thoroughly; to make a mess of; (dial.) to hug, to clasp. □ *a.* thoroughly wet or drenched; messy; clasped.

জাবদা var. of **জাবেদা**।

জাবনা see **জাব**।

জাবর *n.* cud. **জাবর কাটা** *v.* to chew the cud, to ruminate; (fig.) to meditate on or discuss the same thing over and over again.

জাবেদা, জাবদা *n.* daily accounts; a book of daily accounts, a journal. **জাবদা খাতা** *n.* a (usu. thick and big) book of daily accounts.

জাম *n.* the rose-apple, the jambu.

জামড়া *n.* a corn or callosity.

জামদগ্নেয়, জামদগ্ন্য *n.* the son of Jamadagni (জমদগ্নি) the sage.

জামদানি *n.* a variety of muslin woven in design of flowers, a jamdani. □ *a.* woven in design of flowers (জামদানি কাপড়).

জামবাটি *n.* a large bowl or cup without handle made of bell metal, a big bowl.

জামরুল *n.* a variety of greenish white juicy fruit, the star-apple (?).

জামা *n.* any garment for the upper body such as a coat, a shirt, a blouse, a jacket, a vest etc.

জামাই, জামাতা *n.* a son-in-law. **জামাইষষ্ঠী** *n.* the sixth day of the waxing moon in the month of Jaistha (জ্যৈষ্ঠ) when a son-in-law is received and blessed by his parents-in-law, the son-in-law's day; this rite.

জামানত var. of **জমানত**।

জামিন *n.* one who becomes or stands a security or surety for another or the thing given as security, a bail. **জামিন দেওয়া** *v.* to grant bail. **~দার** *n.* a bailsman; a surety. **~নামা** *n.* a bail-bond. **জামিনের যোগ্য** bailable. **জামিনের অযোগ্য** non-bailable.

জামিয়ার *n.* a richly embroidered shawl.

জামির *n.* the citron, the lime.

জাম্বীর same as **জামির**।

জায় *n.* a detailed statement of accounts; an estimate; a list, a catalogue, an inventory; exchange (সুদের জায়ে ভিটেমাটি নেওয়া, টাকার জায়ে খাটা).

জায়গা *n.* a place (এ জায়গায় থাকা) ; land (জায়গা কেনা) ; a site (বাড়ি করার জায়গা) ; room, accommodation (এখানে তার জায়গা নেই) ; abode, haunt (সাপের জায়গা) ; a place of frequent occurrence (এটা বৃষ্টির জায়গা) ; a suitable place (এটা গানের জায়গা) ; a fixed place or seat (এটা তার জায়গা) ; a receptacle, a container (ঘিয়ের জায়গা) ; circumstance, situation (এ জায়গায় তর্ক বৃথা) ; stead, position, post, place, exchange (রামের জায়গায় শ্যাম).

জায়গির *n.* a piece of land assigned by the State to a person with power to administer, a jagir (cp. a feoff). **জায়গির দেওয়া** *v.* to assign a jagir. **~দার** *n.* a holder of a jagir, a jagirdar (cp. a feoffee).

জায়দাদ *n.* landed property or the right to it by virtue of occupation.

জায়ফল *n.* the nutmeg.

জায়মান *a.* nascent.

জায়া *n.* a wife. **জায়াজীব, জায়াজীবী** *n.* a man who lives on the income of his wife; the husband of a professional actress or dancing-girl.

জায়াপতি *n.* see **দম্পতি**।

জার *n.* a secret and unlawful lover of a woman esp. of a married woman, a paramour.

জারক *a.* digestive, promoting or aiding digestion; corrosive; used in pickling. **জারক-লেবু** *n.* a pickled lemon meant for aiding digestion.

জারক-শিখা *n.* oxidizing flame.

জারজ *a.* misbegotten, bastard, illegitimate. □ *n.* a bastard.

জারণ *n.* digestion; corrosion; act of pickling.

জারব *v.* (poet & obs.) wears out or withers, will wear out or wither.

জারা *v.* to corrode, to cause to wear out; to digest; to pickle. □ *n.* corrosion; digestion; a thing pickled; a thing corroded. **~নো** *v.* to cause to corrode or wear out or digest or pickle. □ *a.* corroded, worn-out, digested; pickled.

জারি[1], জারিগান *n.* a kind of folk-song of Bengal (composed in memory of the martyrs at Karbala and sung usually in East Bengal, now Bangladesh, on the occasion of Mohurrum).

জারি[2] *a.* instituted, introduced, enforced, passed (নিয়ম বা আইন জারি) ; served (সমন জারি). □ *n.* institution, introduction, enforcement, enactment; act of serving, service. **জারি করা** *v.* to institute, to introduce, to enforce, to enact, to pass; to serve. **~জোরি, ~জুরি** *n.* tactics and pressure (জারিজুরি খাটানো).

জারিত *a.* corroded; worn-out; digested; pickled; (of metals etc.) reduced (জারিত স্বর্ণ).

জারুল *n.* a kind of tree yielding an inferior variety of timber (used in making furniture etc.), Lagerstroemia flosreginae.

জাল[1] *n.* a net (মাছ-ধরা জাল) ; web (মাকড়সার জাল) ; a mesh, a snare, a trap; a network (রশ্মিজাল) ; a lace with network; a thin and fine covering with network (মুখঢাকা জাল) ; (fig.) allurement, illusion, enchantment, charm (সৌন্দর্যের জাল) ; a collection or mass (জটাজাল). **জাল পাতা** *v.* to lay or set a trap. **জাল ফেলা** *v.* to cast a net. **জাল বাওয়া** *v.* to practise casting a net. **খেপলা-জাল** *n.* a cast net. **ছাঁকি জাল** *n.* a scoop-net, a dipping net. **টানা-জাল** *n.* a draw-net.

জাল২ *a.* counterfeit, forged, fake (জাল টাকা, জাল দলিল) ; disguised, dissembling, dissimulating, false (জাল সন্ন্যাসী). **জাল করা** *v.* to forge, to counterfeit, to fake (দলিল বা টাকা জাল করা) ; to dissimulate; to impersonate falsely.

জালক *n.* a flower-bud; a net; a very young and tender gourd or any other similar fruit; a capillaire.

জালতি *n.* a small net; netting (লোহার জালতি) ; a long staff with a net fixed to one of its ends used in plucking fruits.

জালজীবী *n.* a fisherman.

জালপাদ *a.* web-footed.

জালবদ্ধ *a.* ensnared.

জালবাজি *n.* forgery.

জালা১ pop. var. of **জ্বালা২** ।

জালা২ *n.* a large fat-bellied earthen jar, an earthen barrel.

জালাকার *a.* netted; reticulate.

জালাতন, জ্বালাতন *n.* irritation, vexation; annoyance; pestering; harassment; a pest. □ *a.* irritated, vexed, pestered; harassed. **জালাতন করা** *v.* to irritate, to vex, to annoy, to pester; to harass.

জালাতুনে *a.* (coll.) irritating, annoying, vexatious, pestering; harassing.

জালানি, জালানে, জালানো pop. variants of **জ্বালানি, জ্বালানে** and **জ্বালানো** respectively.

জালি১ *n.* a very young and tender gourd or any other similar fruit. □ *a.* very young and tender.

জালি২ *n.* a small net; anything reticular; lattice, trellis. □ *a.* woven like a net, reticular (জালি গেঞ্জি).

জালিক *a.* deceiving, deceitful. □ *n.* a fisherman; a hunter, a fowler; a spider; a cheat.

জালিবোট *n.* a jolly-boat.

জালিম *a.* oppressing, oppressive.

জালিয়া *n.* a fisherman; (rare) a hunter, a fowler.

জালিয়াত *n.* a forger, a faker, a counterfeiter. **জালিয়াতি** *n.* forgery. **জালিয়াতি করা** *v.* to forge; to practise forgery.

জাল্ম *n.* a vulgar or base or vile person, a rascal. □ *a.* ignorant; illiterate; vulgar; base; vile, wicked.

জাসু *a.* knavish; (dero.) veteran or leading. □ *n.* a knave; (dero.) a veteran or leading person; a ring-leader.

জাস্তি *n.* excess; abundance, plenty. □ *a.* excessive.

জাহাঁপনা *n.* the refuge or shelter of the world : used whilst addressing a prince (cp. Your Majesty).

জাহাঁবাজ *a.* (dero.) very shrewd or vastly experienced; uncontrollable; dominating; terrible.

জাহাজ *n.* a ship, a vessel; a steamer. **উড়োজাহাজ** an airship, an aeroplane. **কলের জাহাজ** a steamship, a steamer. **ডুবোজাহাজ** a submarine. **বিদ্যার জাহাজ** a prodigy of learning, a vastly learned or omniscient person. **যুদ্ধজাহাজ** *n.* a warship, a battleship, a man-of-war. **সওদাগরি জাহাজ, বাণিজ্য জাহাজ** *n.* a merchantman, a merchant ship, a trading ship. **এক-জাহাজ মাল** *a.* shipload of goods or cargo. **জাহাজ চালানো** *v.* to steer or pilot a ship. **জাহাজ ভাসানো** *v.* to launch a ship; to set sail; to sail. **জাহাজে ওঠা** বা **চড়া** *v.* to board a ship, to embark. **জাহাজ থেকে নামা** *v.* to disembark. **~ঘাটা** *n.* a dock, a wharf, a pier, a jetty. **~ডুবি** *n.* shipwreck. **জাহাজি** *a.* relating to ships; ship-borne; working on board a ship; marine, naval. **জাহাজি মাল** cargo; imported goods.

জাহান *n.* the world (মুসলিম জাহান).

জাহান্নম, জাহান্নাম *n.* (Mus.) hell, Inferno. **জাহান্নামে দেওয়া** *v.* (lit.) to condemn to hell; (fig.) to deprave or ruin beyond repair. **জাহান্নমে যাওয়া** *v.* (lit.) to be damned or condemned to hell; (fig.) to be depraved or ruined beyond repair or redemption, to go to the dogs. **জাহান্নমি** *a.* deserving to be condemned to hell; hellish.

জাহির *a.* ostentatiously made public; asserted; displayed ostentatiously. **জাহির**

করা *v.* to make public or announce ostentatiously; to assert; to display ostentatiously.

জাহ্নবী *n.* the daughter of Jahnoo (জহ্নু) the Puranic sage : an appellation of the Ganges.

জি *n. (masc. & fem.)* a title of courtesy affixed at the end of a person's name (নেতাজি, মাতাজি, গুরুজি) ; Sir, or Madam (হাঁ জি).

জিউ *v.* (in blessing etc.) may you be alive, may you live long.

জিওল *a.* (of fish) that which, if kept in a vessel full of water, can be kept alive for a long time; (of trees etc.) long-lived. □ *n.* such a fish or tree. **~গাছ** *n.* a kind of tree that lives long, *Odina wadier*. **~মাছ** *n.* the anabas, the barbed fish, the catfish etc.

জিগ্গেস, জিগ্যেস coll. forms of **জিজ্ঞাসা**।

জিগির *n.* emphasis; a refrain; loud outcry or clamour, a slogan; a public announcement; a shout of triumph.

জিগীষা *n.* desire for victory or conquest. **জিগীষু** *a.* desirous of victory or conquest.

জিঘাংসা *n.* desire to murder. **~বৃত্তি** *n.* murderous instinct, blood-thirstiness, propensity to murder. **জিঘাংসু** *a.* desirous of murdering, murderous.

জিজিয়া *n.* a tax imposed by Muslim rulers on non-Muslim pilgrims or non-Muslim subjects.

জিজীবিষা *n.* desire to remain alive. **জিজীবিষু** *a.* desirous of remaining alive.

জিজ্ঞাসক *a.* one who asks or questions or inquires.

জিজ্ঞাসন *n.* act of questioning, interrogation; inquiry. **জিজ্ঞাসনীয়** same as **জিজ্ঞাস্য**।

জিজ্ঞাসা *n.* a question, an interrogation; inquiry. **জিজ্ঞাসা করা** *v.* to ask, to question, to interrogate; to inquire. **জিজ্ঞাসার চিহ্ন** (gr.) the note of interrogation, the question-mark (?). **~বাদ** *n.* interrogation; a talk or discussion. **জিজ্ঞাসাবাদ করা** *v.* same as **জিজ্ঞাসা করা**।

জিজ্ঞাসিত *a.* one who or that which has been asked or questioned, interrogated; inquired of or about.

জিজ্ঞাসু *a.* one who asks, questioning; inquiring; inquisitive, curious.

জিজ্ঞাস্য *a.* that which is to be asked or questioned or inquired about. **আমার জিজ্ঞাস্য যে** I want to know that; my question is.

জিঞ্জির *n.* chain, shackles, fetters; (rare) imprisonment or deportation.

জিত *a.* (pronun : জিতো) conquered (জিতরাজ) ; vanquished, defeated (জিতশত্রু) ; subdued, brought under control (জিতক্রোধ). □ *n.* (pron. জিৎ) victory (হারজিত).

জিতা *v.* to win; to be victorious; to conquer. □ *a.* that which has been won; conquered. **জিতানো,** (coll.) **জেতানো** *v.* to cause to win or conquer; to declare victorious, to declare one a winner.

জিতেন্দ্রিয় *a.* (lit.) one who has subdued or mastered passions; continent. **~তা** *n.* subjugation or restraining of one's passions; continence, self-control, self-restraint.

জিৎ *sfx.* conquering (বিশ্বজিৎ = a conqueror of the world, world-conquering).

জিদ, জেদ *n.* insistence; importunity; tenacity, pertinacity, doggedness. **জিদ ধরা** *v.* to insist (on). **জেদাজেদি** *n.* continual or mutual insistence. **জেদি** *a.* insistent, importunate; tenacious, pertinacious, obstinate, dogged: insisting, given to pertinacity or doggedness.

জিন[1] *a.* victorious. □ *n.* Buddha; a Buddhist or Jaina friar; Vishnu (বিষ্ণু).

জিন[2] *n.* a demon, a giant.

জিন[3] *n.* a saddle, a harness.

জিন[4] *n.* twilled cotton cloth, jeans.

জিনা *v.* to win, to conquer, to vanquish, to defeat.

জিনিস, (rej.) **জিনিষ** *n.* a thing, an article; substance (এতে জিনিস কিছু নেই). **~পত্র** *n. pl.* things, articles.

জিন্দা *a.* alive, living (জিন্দা থাকা). **~বাদ** *int.* long live! vive!

জিন্দিগি, জিন্দেগি *n.* life, life-time.

জিব, জিভ *n.* the tongue. **~ছোলা** *n.* a tongue-scraper. **জিব কাটা** *v.* to put out the tip of one's tongue and press it between the teeth as a mark of abashment, or shamefacedness. **জিব বার হওয়া** *v.* to pant for breath (owing to exhaustion). **জিবে** *a.* tongue-shaped (জিবে গজা). **জিবে জল আসা** to make one's mouth water.

জিমনাস্টিক *n.* gymnastics. □ *a.* gymnastic.

জিম্মা *n.* custody, charge, care. **জিম্মা করে দেওয়া, জিম্মায় দেওয়া** *v.* to commit to the custody or charge of, to put under care of. **~দার** *n.* a custodian. **~দারি** *n.* custodianship; charge.

জিয়ন্ত *a.* alive, living.

জিয়ল var. of **জিওল**।

জিয়া *v.* same as **জিয়ানো**।

জিয়াদা var. of **জেয়াদা**।

জিয়ানো *v.* to keep (fish etc.) alive by preserving in a vessel full of water (কইমাছ জিয়ানো); to bring back to life (লক্ষ্মীন্দরকে জিয়ানো). □ *a.* preserved in a vessel full of water in order to keep (fish etc.) alive; brought back to life. **জিইয়ে রাখা** *v.* to keep alive, to preserve; (fig.) to keep in force; to nurse.

জিরজিরে *a.* very thin or slender; rickety; skin-and-bone.

জিরা *n.* cummin, cumin.

জিরাত *n.* (chiefly used as a correl. of জমি) land.

জিরান *n.* rest; respite; leisure. **জিরান কাট** the first day of the renewed incision into a date-tree for its juice after a respite of three days.

জিরানো *v.* to rest, to take rest.

জিরাফ *n.* the giraffe.

জিরে coll. form of **জিরা**।

জিরেন coll. form of **জিরান**।

জিল্দ, জিল *n.* the cover of a book; a method of book-binding in which each form is sewn separately.

জিলা old. var. of **জেলা**।

জিলাপি, (coll.) **জিলিপি** *n.* a kind of wheel-shapped sweetmeat. **জিলিপির পাক, জিলাপির প্যাঁচ** (lit.) the tortuous shape of this sweetmeat; (fig.) tortuosity, crookedness, angularity.

জিল্লা rej. var. of **জেল্লা**।

জিষ্ণু *a.* victorious.

জিহাদ var. of **জেহাদ**।

জিহীর্ষা *n.* desire to steal; kleptomania. **জিহীর্ষু** *a.* desirous of stealing.

জিহ্বা *n.* the tongue; power of tasting, palate (চেখে দেখার মতো জিহ্বা নেই). **~গ্র** *n.* the tip of one's tongue. **~গ্রে** *adv.* at the tip of one's tongue, in readiness for utterance. **~মূল** *n.* the root of the tongue. **~মূলীয়** *a.* pertaining to the root of the tongue; (phon.) guttural.

জী rej. spell. of **-জি**।

জীব[1], **জীউ** rej. spellings of **জিউ**।

জীব[2] *n.* an animal, a creature, an organism; life; a corporeal or embodied soul; a living being; the soul of a living or dead being; (sc. & phil.) anything animate. **কৃষ্ণের জীব** (hum.) an extremely harmless or pitiable person. **~জগৎ** *n.* the animal kingdom, the animal world; the animate world. **~জনি** *n.* biogenesis. **~জন্তু** *n.* animals or creatures. **~তত্ত্ব** *n.* biology, life science. **~তত্ত্বীয়** *a.* biological. **~তাত্ত্বিক** *a.* biological. □ *n.* a biologist. **~বলি** *n.* animal sacrifice. **~বিদ্যা** same as **~তত্ত্ব**। **~লোক** *n.* the animate world; the world, the earth. **~সংক্রমণ** *n.* metempsychosis, transmigration. **~হত্যা** *n.* killing of animals, killing a living being, animal slaughter. **~হিংসা** *n.* animal slaughter.

জীবক *n.* a snake-charmer; a servant; a usurer, a money-lender; a beggar, a mendicant; a physician; the physician of Buddha.

জীবৎ *a.* alive, living; animate. **~কাল** *n.* lifetime.

জীবদ *a.* life-giving; animating.

জীবদ্দশা *n.* lifetime; state of being alive, living state.

জীবন *n.* life; existence; lifetime (আজীবন); duration of life (জীবন ফুরানো); a living or livelihood (চাষই তার জীবন); a person or thing as dear or valuable as (one's) life (ছেলেটি তার জীবন); water. **জীবন দেওয়া** *v.* to sacrifice or lay down one's life, to die for; to give life to. **জীবন পাওয়া** *v.* to come to life; to come back to life. **জীবন যাওয়া, জীবন হারানো** *v.* to lose one's life, to die. **জীবন নেওয়া** *v.*

to take one's life, to kill. **~কথা, ~কাহিনি, ~চরিত** *n.* biography. **~চরিতকার** *n.* a biographer. **~জিজ্ঞাসা** *n.* quest or inquiry into life's meaning. **~দর্শন** *n.* philosophy of life. **~দান** *n.* act of giving life to. **জীবনদান করা** same as **জীবন দেওয়া**। **~দায়ক** *a.* life-giving, life-saving. **~ধারণ** *n.* act of living; existence; act of leading one's life. **জীবনধারণ করা** *v.* to live; to exist; to lead one's life. **~নাশ** *n.* destruction of life; death. **জীবননাশ করা** *v.* to destroy the life (of); to kill. **জীবননাশ হওয়া** *v.* to have one's life destroyed; to lose one's life; to die. **~প্রবাহ** *n.* the cycle or flow of life. **~বল্লভ** *n.* husband; a lover. **~বিমা** *n.* life insurance, life assurance. **জীবনবিমা করা** *v.* to insure one's life. **~বিহীন** same as **~শূন্য**। **~বৃত্তান্ত** *n.* biography. **~বেদ** *n.* the view of life, philosophy of life, *Weltans-chauung*. **~ভোর, ~ভর** *adv.* throughout one's life. **~মরণ** *n.* life and death □ *a.* life-and-death (জীবনমরণ সমস্যা). **~যাত্রা** *n.* livelihood. **~যাপন** *n.* leading one's life; living. **জীবনযাপন করা** *v.* to lead one's life; to live. **~শূন্য** *a.* lifeless; dead; inanimate. **~সংগ্রাম** *n.* the stru-ggle for existence. **~সংশয়** *n.* a critical or precarious condition. **~সঙ্গিনী** *n.* a wife; a female life-companion. *masc.* **~সঙ্গী** a male life-companion; a husband. **~সঞ্চার** *n.* infusion of life, resuscitation. **~সর্বস্ব** *n.* everything in or of one's life; all that one lives for. **~হীন** same as **~শূন্য**। **~স্মৃতি** *n.* an autobiographical memoir.

জীবনাধিক *a.* more important or valuable or dearer than (one's) life.

জীবনান্ত, জীবনাবসান *n.* end or termination of life; death. **জীবনান্তে** *adv.* after death.

জীবনী *a.* life-giving. □ *n.* a biography. **~কার** *n.* a biographer. **~শক্তি** *n.* vitality.

জীবনীয় *a.* necessary for the protection or sustenance of life. □ *n.* water.

জীবনোৎসর্গ *n.* sacrifice of one's life.

জীবনোপায় *n.* means of livelihood or subsistence.

জীবন্ত *a.* living alive; full of life, vivacious; obvious or vivid (জীবন্ত সত্য); active (জীবন্ত আগ্নেয়গিরি).

জীবন্মুক্ত *a.* freed from earthly attachment even whilst living in this world; one who has attained salvation even whilst living in this world; freed in the living state. **জীবন্মুক্তি** *n.* freedom from earthly attachment or attainment of salvation even whilst living in this world; freedom (of the spirit) in the living state.

জীবন্মৃত *a.* almost dead although living; more dead than alive.

জীবাণু *n.* the microbe. **রোগজীবাণু** *n.* the bacillus (*pl.* bacilli).

জীবাত্মা *n.* the sentient or embodied soul; the Supreme Soul as existent in different individual creatures.

জীবাধান *n.* preservation of life.

জীবাধার *n.* the world; the body.

জীবান্তক *a.* destroying life, life-taking, killing. □ *n.* a hunter.

জীবাশ্ম *n.* a fossil.

জীবিকা *n.* livelihood; a profession, a calling, a trade. **জীবিকার্জন করা, জীবিকানির্বাহ করা** *v.* to earn one's livelihood, to earn a living.

জীবিত *a.* living, alive. □ *n.* life (জীবিতনাথ). **~কাল** *n.* same as **জীবিতাবস্থা**। **~নাথ, জীবিতেশ্বর** *n.* □ the lord of (one's) life; a husband. **জীবিতাবস্থা** *n.* life-time.

-জীবী *a.* living, existing (দীর্ঘজীবী); practising for livelihood (ব্যবহারজীবী).

জীমূত *n.* the cloud; the mountain. **~নাদ, ~মন্দ্র** *n.* the rumbling of the cloud. **~বাহন** *n.* one who is borne by clouds : an appellation of Indra (ইন্দ্র) the king of gods.

জীয়ন্ত alt. spell. of **জিয়ন্ত**।

জীয়ল alt. spell. of **জিয়ল**।

জীয়ানো alt. spell. of **জিয়ানো**।

জীরক, জীর *n.* cummin, cumin.

জীরে rej. spell. of **জিরে**।

জীর্ণ *a.* worn out, decayed, dilapidated (জীর্ণ গ্রন্থ, জীর্ণ অট্টালিকা); impoverished (জীর্ণ দশা); emaciated (জীর্ণ দেহ); eaten away, corroded (জীর্ণ লোহা); digested (জীর্ণ অন্ন); ragged (জীর্ণ বস্ত্র). **জীর্ণ করা** *v.* to digest. **~জ্বর** chronic fever. **~তা** *n.* worn-out state; dilapidated or impoverished or emaciated state; eaten-away or corroded state; digested state; raggedness. **~শীর্ণ** *a.* emaciated and shrivelled, lean and thin; haggard. **~সংস্কার** *n.* repair. **জীর্ণসংস্কার করা** *v.* to repair.

জীর্ণা *fem.* of **জীর্ণ**।

জীর্ণোদ্ধার *n.* repair; reclamation.

জীর্ণোদ্ধার করা *v.* to repair; to reclaim.

জুঁই *n.* the jessamine or jasmine.

জুখা rej. var. of **জোখা**।

জুগুপ্সা *n.* upbraiding, censure, abuse, blame; defamation; scorn. **জুগুপ্সিত** *a.* upbraided, censured, abused, blamed; defamed, scorned.

জুজ *n.* (in book-binding) a form of a book. **~সেলাই** *n.* a method of book-binding in which each format is sewn separately.

জুজু *n.* bugbear, a bug.

জুজুৎসু *n.* the Japanese system of wrestling, ju-jitsu.

জুজুবুড়ি same as **জুজু**।

জুঝা *v.* to vie, to compete, to fight, to contend. **~নো** *v.* to cause to vie or compete or fight or contend.

জুটা, জোটা *v.* to be available or acquired (অন্ন জুটবে না, টাকা জোটা) ; to collect, to gather, to assemble (বহু লোক জুটেছে) ; to appear, to put in one's appearance (সময়মতো জুটব). **জুটানো, জোটানো** *v.* to get, to acquire; to cause to collect or assemble, to assemble; to cause to appear, to bring.

জুড়া, জোড়া *v.* to join; to add; to affix, to attach; to cement or plaster (ফাটল জোড়া) ; to yoke or harness (লাঙলে বলদ জোড়া, গাড়িতে ঘোড়া জুড়ল) ; to begin, to commence (গল্প জোড়া) ; to spread over, to pervade, to cover (দেশ জোড়া).

জুড়ানো[১], জোড়ানো *v.* to cause to join or add or affix or attach or cement or yoke or harness or begin; to join or add or affix.

জুড়ানো[২] *v.* to cause to cool or to cool (দুধ জুড়ানো) ; to allay or be allayed (জ্বালা জুড়ানো) ; to console or be consoled, to satisfy or be satisfied (হৃদয় জুড়ানো). □ *a.* cooled; allayed, consoled, satisfied. **কোলজুড়ানো ছেলে** a bonny or handsome baby (that delights its mother).

জুড়ি *n.* a pair, a couple; one of a pair or couple, a doublet; an equal, a parallel; an associate; an accessory, an accomplice; a coach drawn by a pair of horses (also **জুড়িগাড়ি**) ; singers singing in a concert (জুড়ির গান) ; a particular string of the সেতার। **~দার** *n.* match, a peer; an associate; an accessory, an accomplice; a singer of a concert.

জুত[১] *n.* lustre, shine, light (চোখের জুত) ; energy, vigour, ability, fitness (দেহের জুত).

জুত[২] *n.* suitability, fitting, an opportunity or advantage. **~সই** *a.* suitable, fitting, opportune, advantageous.

জুৎ rej. spell. of **জুত[১]** & **জুত[২]**।

জুতা, জোতা *v.* to yoke or harness (লাঙলে বলদ জুতছে, গাড়িতে ঘোড়া জোতা).

জুতো *n.* shoe, boot. **জুতানো, জুতো মারা** *v.* to beat with a shoe; (fig.) to insult grossly. **জুতো শেলাই থেকে চণ্ডীপাঠ** all kinds of jobs or chores from the lowest to the highest.

জুদা *a.* separated, differing. **জুদা করা** *v.* to distinguish between, to separate.

জুন *n.* June, the sixth month of the English calendar.

জুবিলি *n.* jubilee. **রৌপ্যজুবিলি** silver jubilee (on completion of twenty-five years of existence). **স্বর্ণজুবিলি** golden jubilee (on completion of fifty years). **হীরক জুবিলি** diamond jubilee (on completion of sixty years).

জুব্বা var. of **জোব্বা**।

জুমা, জুম্মা *n.* (Mus.) Friday, the weekly day of prayer. **জুম্মাবার** Friday.

জুয়া *n.* gambling; gambling at dice-play. **জুয়া খেলা** *v.* to gamble. **জুয়ার আড্ডা** a gambling-house, a gambling-hell, a gambling-den.

জুয়াচুরি *n.* swindling; deception; fraud. **জুয়াচুরি করা** *v.* to swindle; to deceive; to defraud; to have recourse to fraud.

জুয়াচোর *n.* a sharper; a swindler; a cheat.

জুয়াড়ি *n.* a gambler, a gamester.

জুয়ানো *v.* (obs.) to get a supply of ('কথা না জুয়ায়') ; to be proper ('ছাড়িতে না জুয়ায়').

জুয়ারি var. of **জুয়াড়ি**।

জুরি *n.* jury; a juror. **জুরির রায়** the verdict of the jury. **জুরির প্রধান** the foreman of the jury.

জুলজুল *int.* expressing : winking repeatedly and sparklingly as with small restless eyes.

জুলফি, জুলপি *n.* a lovelock, sideburns.

জুলাই *n.* July, the seventh month of the English calendar.

জুলি *n.* a narrow outlet for water, a narrow drain or ditch. **নয়নজুলি** *n.* a narrow roadside ditch or an outlet for water.

জুলু *n.* a Zulu; the Zulu tribe of Africa.

জুলুম *n.* application of unlawful force, violence, outrage, oppression.

জুলুম করা *v.* to force, to practise violence upon, to oppress, to resort to force or coercion. **~বাজ** *a.* given to practising violence, outrageous, oppressive. **~বাজি** *n.* practice of violence, oppression.

জুষ্ট *a.* served, worshipped ('দেবগণজুষ্ট').

জুস[১] var. of **জুজ** ।

জুস[২] *n.* juice; curry; broth.

জূট *n.* (chiefly used as a *sfx.*) a collection, a mass, a cluster (জটাজূট).

জুষ rej. spell. of **জুস**[১], **জুস**[২] ।

জৃম্ভণ, জৃম্ভ *n.* act of yawning or gaping; a yawn; a gape; act of opening or blooming or bursting out. **জৃম্ভক** *a.* producing sleep, soporific (জৃম্ভক অস্ত্র). **জৃম্ভমান** *a.* yawning; gaping; opening; blooming; bursting out. **জৃম্ভিত** *a.* yawned; gaped; opened; bloomed; burst out.

জেঁকো *n.* (dial.) bragging; boastful; ostentatious.

জেটি *n.* a jetty.

জেঠ *pfx.* related through an elder brother of one's father or father-in-law. **~তুতো** *a.* related through an elder brother of one's father. **~তুতো ভাই** a son of an elder brother of one's father, a cousin. **~তুতো বোন** a daughter of an elder brother of one's father, a cousin. **~শ্বশুর** *n.* an elder brother of one's father-in-law. *fem.* **~শাশুড়ি** the wife of one's **~শ্বশুর** ।

জেঠা *n.* an elder brother of one's father, an uncle. *a.* (hum. or in rebuke) precocious; impertinent. *fem.* **জেঠাইমা, জেঠি, জেঠিমা** the wife of an elder brother of one's father, an aunt. **~তো** same as **জেঠতুতো** (see **জেঠ-**). **~মি,** (dial.) **~মো** *n.* precocity; impertinence.

জেঠি, জেঠী[১] *n.* the common lizard found in dwelling-houses.

জেঠী[২], **জেঠীমা** rej. spellings of **জেঠি** & **জেঠিমা** respectively.

জেতব্য same as **জেয়** ।

জেতা[১] pop. var. of **জিতা** ।

জেতা[২] *a.* one who has conquered or defeated or won, conquering, victorious, winning. **~নো** *v.* to help or enable someone to conquer.

জেদ pop. var. of **জিদ** ।

জেনানা pop. var. of **জানানা** ।

জেন্দ *n.* an ancient language in which the Avesta of Zoroaster was written.

জেব *n.* a pocket; a purse.

জেব্রা *n.* the zebra.

জেয় *a.* worth winning or conquering; that which can be or is to be won or conquered, conquerable.

জেয়াদা *a.* too much, excessive.

জের *n.* (book-keeping) the balance; (fig.) the smouldering continuity (ঝগড়ার জের). **জের টানা** *v.* (book-keeping) to carry over, to bring forward; (fig.) to keep up or drag on. **জের মেটানো** *v.* (book-keeping) to balance (account); to pay up arrears; to complete arrears of work; to put out the smouldering embers; to suffer the consequences.

জেরবার *a.* harassed; bewildered (জেরার চোটে জেরবার) ; ruined (মোকদ্দমায় জেরবার).

জেরা *n.* (chiefly legal) cross-examination. **জেরা করা** *v.* to cross-examine.

জেল *n.* a jail, a gaol, a prison : imprisonment or sentence of imprisonment, incarceration (জেল হওয়া). **জেল খাটা** *v.* to undergo a term of imprisonment, to serve term. **জেল হওয়া** *v.* to be sentenced to imprisonment; to be jailed or gaoled. **জেলে দেওয়া, জেলে পাঠানো** *v.* to commit to prison; to jail, to gaol. **জেলে যাওয়া** *v.* to be jailed or gaoled or imprisoned. **জেলঘুঘু** *n.* a seasoned prisoner or convict; a jail-bird, a gaol-bird. **জেলদারোগা** *n.* a jailer, a jailor, a gaoler. **জেল-ভাঙা কয়েদি** *a.* prison-breaker.

জেলজেল, জেলজেলে alt. spellings of **জ্যালজ্যাল** & **জ্যালজেলে** respectively.

জেলা *n.* a district; a county; a shire. **~দার** *n.* (hist.) the administrator of a district. **~শাসক** *n.* the district magistrate.

জেলার *n.* a jailor, a jailer, a gaoler.

জেলি *n.* jelly.

জেলে, জেলিয়া *n.* a fisherman, a fisher (by caste or trade). *fem.* **~নি** *a.* fish-wife, a fish-woman. **~ডিঙি** *n.* a longish open fishing boat. **~পাড়া** *n.* fishermen's quarters or colony or parts in a village or town.

জেল্লা *n.* lustre, shine, brightness, brilliance, glossiness. **জেল্লা ধরানো** *v.* to put a shine on.

জেহাদ *n.* (Mus.) a fight for the cause of religion and also for any other pious object, a holy war, crusade.

জৈত্রি coll. form of **জয়ত্রী**।

জৈন *n.* an adherent of Jainism, a Jain. **~ধর্ম** *n.* Jainism.

জৈব *a.* organic; of or obtained from a creature or animal. **~রসায়ন** *n.* organic chemistry, biochemistry. **~সার** *n.* compost.

জো *n.* an opportunity (ঘুমোবার জো নেই) ; (rare) a suitable time or condition for sowing (জমিতে জো হওয়া).

জোঁক *n.* the leech. **ছিনেজোঁক** a variety of leech that clings pertinaciously to a person or creature whose blood it sucks; (fig.) a pertinacious or insistent or die-hard person.

জোখ, জোক *n.* comparative measurement of a thing by placing it side by side with another object (মাপজোক). **জোখ নেওয়া, জোখা, জোকা** *v.* to take a comparative measurement of a thing by placing it side by side with another object.

জোকার *n.* a sound made by women by moving their tongues rapidly within their mouths in order to accord cordial reception to a person or deity. **জোকার দেওয়া** *v.* to make this sound.

জোগাড় *n.* procurement; obtaining, securing; collection; preparation, arrangement. **জোগাড় করা** *v.* to procure; to secure; to collect to make preparations for, to arrange for. **জোগাড় করে দেওয়া** *v.* to procure for another, to find for. **~যন্ত্র** *n.* preparations including procurement of necessary things; securing or procurement esp. by manipulation of resources (চাকরির জোগাড়যন্ত্র), preparations and arrangements. **জোগাড়িয়া,** (pop.) **জোগাড়ে** *a.* & *n.* one adept in procurement or in getting things; one adept in or employed in making preparations and arrangements; one acting as an assistant; a hodman or hodcarrier.

জোগান *n.* supply, purveyance; finding, supply (কথার জোগান) ; assistance, help (কাজে জোগান). **~দার** *n.* a supplier, a purveyor; an assistant, a helper; a hodman or hodcarrier. **জোগানো** *v.* to supply, to purvey; to be found, to be supplied with (কথা জোগানো) ; to adulate, to flatter, to humour (মন জোগানো).

জোচ্চোর coll. form of **জুয়াচোর**।

জোছনা coll. & poet. form of **জ্যোৎস্না**।

জোঝা, জোঝানো pop. variants of **জুঝা** and **জুঝানো** respectively.

জোট *n.* assemblage, collection, union (জোট বাঁধা) ; a group, a party, a caucus, (dero.) a faction (জোট পাকানো) ; a knot or tangle (জোট পড়া). **জোট করা** *v.* to assemble; to unite. **জোট পাকানো** *v.* to form together a party or faction or caucus; to group together; to form or cause to form into a knot or tangle. **জোট বাঁধা** *v.* to be united; to assemble; to form together a party or faction, to group together; to form into a knot or tangle. **একজোটে, জোট বেঁধে** *adv.* in a body, all together.

জোটা, জোটানো pop. variants of **জুটা** and **জুটানো** respectively.

জোটেবুড়ি variant of **জুজুবুড়ি**।

জোড় *n.* a joint (জোড়ের মুখ) ; joining, union (জোড় বাঁধা) ; a pair, a couple (মানিকজোড়) ; a married couple (জোড়ে আসা) one of a pair (জোড় মেলানো) ; a piece of loincloth and a scarf (চেলির জোড়). □ *a.* joined, folded (জোড়হাতে) ; grafted (জোড়কলম) ; even (জোড়সংখ্যা). **জোড় করা** *v.* to fold (as one's hands). **জোড় বাঁধা** *v.* to unite; to join; to pair. **জোড় বাঁধানো** *v.* to cause to unite or join or pair. **জোড় মেলানো** *v.* to find one to pair with; to pair. **জোড়ে আসা** *v.* (chiefly of a married couple) to come in pair. **~সংখ্যা** an even number. **~কলম** *n.* a graft. **করজোড়ে, ~হাতে** *adv.* with folded hands. **জোড়ে জোড়ে** *adv.* by or in pair.

জোড়া[১] pop. var. of **জুড়া**।

জোড়া[২] *a.* two (জোড়া পাঁঠা). □ *n.* a pair, a couple; one of a pair or couple; an equal; a joint or joining (জোড়া খুলে গেছে). **জোড়া দেওয়া** *v.* to join.

জোড়াতালি *n.* a patchwork. **জোড়াতালি দেওয়া** *v.* to mend clumsily, to patch; (fig.) to patch up; to make up temporarily. **জোড়াতালি দিয়ে কাজ চালানো** to manage somehow with whatever comes ready to hand.

জোত *n.* agricultural land or property; an agricultural farm held on proprietary basis, a farm; a rope for binding a bull or a yoke or plough etc., a halter. **~জমা** *n.* landed property, pieces or parcels of land for cultivation. **~দড়ি** *n.* ropes or straps that fasten a bullock or a draught-animal to the yoke. **~দার** *n.* the owner of a proprietary agricultural farm; a big and rich farmer; a landlord.

জোতা pop. var. of **জুতা[১]**।

জোত্র, (coll.) **জোত্তর** *n.* an opportunity (রোজগারের জোত্র মিলেছে) ; an expedient, a means (খাওয়ার জোত্র করা).

জোনাকি *n.* the firefly, the glow-worm.

জোবড়া dial. var. of **জাবড়া**।

জোব্বা *n.* (Mus.) a kind of long and loose-fitting outer garment for males.

জোয়ান[১] *n.* caraway, ptychotis.

জোয়ান[২] *n.* a young man, a strong or stout man, (pol.) a soldier. □ *a.* young; strong, stout.

জোয়ানো coll. & pop. var. of **জুয়ানো**।

জোয়ার[১] *n.* high tide, flow tide, flow. **জোয়ার-ভাটা** *n.* ebb and flow, high and low tides.

জোয়ার[২] *n.* durra, millet, jowar. **জোয়ারি** *a.* made of jowar, jowari.

জোয়াল *n.* a yoke. **জোয়ালে বাঁধা** *v.* to yoke.

জোর *n.* strength, power, might, force; violence (রোদের জোর) ; severity; loudness (গলার জোর). firmness; keenness (চোখের জোর) ; emphasis (কথার জোর) ; claim or right (মাতৃস্নেহের উপর সন্তানের জোর). □ *a.* forceful, strong, violent; severe; urgent (জোর তলব) ; unexpectedly fortunate or good (জোর বরাত) ; quick, swift (জোর কদম). **জোর করা, জোর খাটানো** *v.* to force; to insist (on). **~জবরদস্তি** same as **জবরদস্তি**। **~জুলুম** *n.* violence; pressure; pressurizing; pertinacity; oppression. **জোর তলব** *n.* an urgent call. **জোর দেওয়া** *v.* to put an emphasis on, to emphasize; to strengthen. **জোর বরাত** *n.* a very good luck. **জোর বলা** *v.* to say or use just the word for; to make the most appropriate comment. **জোর হওয়া** *v.* to become strong or severe or keen or emphatic. **জোরে জোরে** *adv.* quickly; forcefully. **~সে** *adv.* forcibly; with force; using force; violently.

জোরাজুরি, জোরাজোরি *n.* display or use of force, violence; insistence.

জোরালো *a.* strong, powerful, forceful; forcible.

জোরু *a.* a wife.

জোল, জোলা[১] *n.* a narrow and long outlet for water, a narrow ditch.

জোলা[২] *n.* a Mohammedan weaver. *fem.* **জোলানি**।

জোলাপ, জোলাব *n.* a purgative, a cathartic; (loos) a laxative.

জোলি var. of **জুলি**।

জোলো alt. spell. of **জলো**।

জৌ alt. spell. of **জউ**।

-জ্ঞ *sfx.* knowing, conversant, versed (শাস্ত্রজ্ঞ, বিশেষজ্ঞ, সময়জ্ঞ).

জ্ঞাত *a.* conversant, versed; aware of, informed; known.

জ্ঞাতব্য *a.* that which is to be learnt or known; worth knowing or learning.

জ্ঞাতসারে *adv.* to one's knowledge; knowingly, deliberately.

জ্ঞাতা *a.* conversant, au fait, informed, aware of; experienced.

জ্ঞাতি *n.* a kinsman (*fem* : a kinswoman). **~কুটুম্ব** *n. pl.* kinsfolk and other relations. **~গোষ্ঠী** *n. pl.* kinsmen, kinsfolk, kith and kin; near relations. **~ত্ব** *n.* kinship; relationship. **~বৈর** *n.* blood-feud, vendetta; (also) internecine quarrel or enmity. **~ভাই** *n.* a cousin; a kinsman.

জ্ঞান *n.* wisdom; knowledge, enlightenment, light; intelligence, information; understanding, cognition; consciousness (জ্বরের ঘোরে জ্ঞান হারানো) ; feeling, sense, sensation (ক্ষুধাতৃষ্ণাজ্ঞান) ; consideration, judgement (তৃণসম জ্ঞান) ; discretion (ভালোমন্দ জ্ঞান) ; learning, experience; philosophical knowledge, realization; command of fundamentals (তত্ত্বজ্ঞান) ; (theol. & phil.) gnosis. **জ্ঞান করা** *v.* to regard, to count; to consider; to feel; to conceive; to resuscitate. **জ্ঞান দেওয়া** *v.* to impart knowledge, to enlighten; to make wise; (fig.) to open one's eyes; (coll.) to put one wise, to wise up; to teach. **জ্ঞান পাওয়া** *v.* to earn knowledge, to be enlightened; to become wise; (fig.) to have one's eyes opened; (coll.) to wise up, to be taught; to regain one's consciousness. **জ্ঞান হওয়া** *v.* to regain one's consciousness; to be wise; to grow in wisdom. **জ্ঞান হারানো** *v.* to swoon; to lose one's sense, to be beside oneself (ক্রোধে জ্ঞান হারানো). **~কাণ্ড** *n.* the philosophical or epistemological portion of the Vedas; (coll.) intelligence and discretion, common sense. **~কৃত** *a.* deliberate, wilful. **~গম্য** *a.* cognizable, knowable. **~গম্যি** *n.* (coll.) intelligence and discretion, common sense. **~গর্ভ** *a.* full of knowledge and wisdom; imparting knowledge and wisdom, enlightening, instructive. **~গোচর** *a.* lying within the range of knowledge, knowable. **জ্ঞানগোচর হওয়া** *v.* to come within the range of knowledge, to become knowable or cognizable. **~চক্ষু** *n.* knowledge conceived as sight, enlightened eyes; awareness; enlightenment. **~জগৎ** *n.* the realm of knowledge. **~ত** *adv.* knowingly. **~তৃষ্ণা, ~তৃষা** *n.* thirst for knowledge. **~তৃষ্ণার্ত** *a.* thirsty for knowledge. **~দ** *a.* imparting knowledge, enlightening. **~পবন** *n.* (coll.) intelligence and discretion, common sense. **~পাপী** *a.* & *n.* one who commits sins wilfully or consciously. **~পিপাসা** same as **~তৃষ্ণা**। **~পিপাসু** same as **~তৃষ্ণার্ত**। **~বতী** *fem.* of **~বান**। **~বাদ** *n.* the doctrine that knowledge is the (only) way to salvation, Gnosticism. **~বাদী** *a.* & *n.* one who adheres to this doctrine, Gnostic. **~বান** *a.* wise; knowing; learned. **~বিজ্ঞান** *a.* knowledge and science, knowledge general and scientific, (cp.) arts and science; knowledge spiritual and temporal. **~বিরুদ্ধ** *a.* contrary to (one's) knowledge or information. **~বৃদ্ধ** *a.* as venerable as an old man because of one's profound wisdom or knowledge; wise and experienced. **~ব্রত** *n.* ardent search for knowledge. **~ব্রতী** *a.* & *n.* one who seeks knowledge ardently, deeply devoted to the pursuit of knowledge. *fem.* **~ব্রতিনী**। **~ভাণ্ডার** *n.* a repertory of knowledge and wisdom. **~ময়** *a.* full of knowledge and wisdom (জ্ঞানময় পুরুষ) ; imparting knowledge and wisdom, enlightening (জ্ঞানময় জগৎ). **~মার্গ** *n.* knowledge considered as the way to salvation. **~যোগ** *n.* austere search for knowledge in order to attain salvation. **~যোগী** *a.* & *n.* one who searches for knowledge austerely in order to attain salvation. **~রহিত** *a.* devoid of knowledge; ignorant; foolish; unconscious, swooned. **~লাভ** *n.* attainment of knowledge; regaining of consciousness: (coll.) state of being wised up. **জ্ঞানলাভ করা** same as **জ্ঞান পাওয়া**। **~লিপ্সা** *n.* ardent desire for attaining knowledge. **~লিপ্সু** *a.* ardently desirous of attaining knowledge. **~শালী** same as **~বান**। *fem.* **~শালিনী**। **~শূন্য** same as **~রহিত**। **~সঞ্চার** *n.* act of bringing back to consciousness; act of regaining consciousness; infusion of knowledge, enlightenment, resuscitation. **~হারা** same as **~রহিত**। **~হীন** same as **~রহিত**।

জ্ঞানাঙ্কুর *n.* (lit.) the sprout of knowledge; (fig.) the first infusion of knowledge, the dawning of knowledge.

জ্ঞানাঞ্জন *n.* knowledge conceived as collyrium or an eye-opener; enlightenment.

জ্ঞানাত্মক *a.* pertaining to or consisting of knowledge.

জ্ঞানানুশীলন, জ্ঞানাভ্যাস *n.* cultivation of knowledge. **জ্ঞানানুশীলন করা, জ্ঞানাভ্যাস করা** *v.* to cultivate knowledge.

জ্ঞানার্জন *n.* acquirement or acquisition of knowledge. **জ্ঞানার্জন করা** *v.* to acquire knowledge. **~স্পৃহা** *n.* desire to acquire knowledge.

জ্ঞানী *a.* wise; learned; experienced.

জ্ঞানেন্দ্রিয় *n.* sense-organ (that is, eyes, ears, the nose, the tongue and the skin).

জ্ঞানোদয় *n.* the first infusion of knowledge, the dawning of knowledge.

জ্ঞানোন্নতি *n.* the development or progress of knowledge.

জ্ঞাপক *a.* intimating; informing; expressing, indicative, signifying (অর্থজ্ঞাপক), দুঃখজ্ঞাপক) ; announcing, notifying (আজ্ঞাজ্ঞাপক) ; communicating, circulating (সংবাদজ্ঞাপক).

জ্ঞাপন *n.* act of informing or intimating, information, intimation; act of expressing or indicating or signifying, expression, indication, signification; announcement, notification : communication, circulation. **জ্ঞাপন করা** *v.* to inform, to intimate; to express, to indicate, to signify, to mean; to announce, to notify, to apprise; to communicate, to circulate. **~পত্র** *n.* a bulletin. **~যোগ্য** *a.* that which is fit for communication, to be communicated. **জ্ঞাপনীয়** *a.* that which is to be or can be informed or intimated or indicated or expressed or signified or meant or announced or notified or apprised or communicated or circulated.

জ্ঞাপয়িতা *a. & n.* one who or (rare) that which informs or intimates or indicates or expresses or signifies or announces or notifies or apprises or communicates or circulates. *fem.* **জ্ঞাপয়িত্রী** ।

জ্ঞাপিত *a.* that which has been informed or intimated or indicated or expressed or signified or announced or notified or apprised or communicated or circulated or made known.

জ্ঞেয় same as **জ্ঞাতব্য** ।

জ্বর *n.* fever; temperature (জ্বর কত ?) ; affected or feverish state. **জ্বর ছাড়া** *v.* to have a remission of fever. **জ্বর জ্বর ভাব** feverishness. **জ্বর দেখা** *v.* to take temperature. **জ্বর হওয়া** *v.* to get fever; to run a temperature. **জ্বরে পড়া** *v.* to be stricken with fever, to be laid up with fever. **জ্বরে ভোগা** *v.* to suffer from fever. **~ঘ্ন, ~নাশক** *a.* febrifugal, antipyretic. **~জ্বালা** *n.* fever and other allied ailments, fever and attendant symptoms. **~ঠুটো** *n.* feverblister. **~বিকার** *n.* high fever attended with delirium; (loos.) typhoid fever. **~বোধ, ~ভাব** *n.* same as **জ্বরজ্বর ভাব** ।

জ্বরাতিসার *n.* fever attended with acute diarrhœa or dysentery.

জ্বরান্তক *a.* febrifugal, antipyretic.

জ্বরিত *a.* stricken with fever; running a temperature.

জ্বরোজ্বরো *a.* febrile, feverish.

জ্বলজ্বল *int.* expressing : shining or glaring or blazing or sparkling state. **জ্বলজ্বল করা** *v.* to shine, to glare, to blaze; to sparkle. **জ্বলজ্বলে** *a.* shining, glaring, blazing; sparkling.

জ্বলৎ *a.* burning, flaming, blazing, glowing; sparkling.

জ্বলতহিঁ *v.* (poet. & obs.) is or are burning or flaming or (fig.) suffering extremely.

জ্বলদগ্নি *n.* blazing fire.

জ্বলদর্চি *a.* having the glow and radiance of blazing fire, glowing, radiant, incandescent. □ *n.* blazing fire, burning flame.

জ্বলন *n.* act or state of burning or flaming or blazing or glaring or glowing or sparkling or (fig.) extreme suffering or smarting. **জ্বলনাঙ্ক** *n.* flash-point, ignition temperature.

জ্বলন্ত same as **জ্বলৎ** । **জ্বলন্ত অক্ষরে** in glowing letters, vividly.

জ্বলা *v.* to be enkindled (বাতি জ্বলা) ; to take fire, to fire up (উনুন জ্বলা) ; to burn, to be in flame, to flame up; to shine; to glow; to blaze, to flare; to sparkle (চোখ জ্বলা) ; to give or feel a burning sensation, to smart (ঘা জ্বলা, হৃদয় জ্বলা). **ক্রোধে জ্বলে ওঠা** to fly into a towering rage, to flare up.

জ্বলানো *v.* to kindle or ignite.

জ্বলিত *a.* enkindled, ignited; burning;

burnt up; (fig.) enlightened; (fig.) exposed, revealed.

জ্বলুনি same as **জ্বলন**। **জ্বলুনি-পুড়ুনি** *n.* extreme suffering, smart, mortification.

জ্বাল *n.* heat of fire; flame; act of boiling on fire (দুধের জ্বাল) ; firewood, fuel (জ্বাল ঠেলা). **জ্বাল দেওয়া** *v.* to boil on fire; to put firewood or fuel (into a burning oven).

জ্বালা[1] *n.* a flame, a blaze; burning sensation or pain (জ্বালা করা). **জ্বালা দেওয়া** *v.* to give trouble to, to bother; to torture. **সংসারের জ্বালাযন্ত্রণা** trials and tribulations of life, irritants of workaday world, annoyances and vexations of life. **সব জ্বালাযন্ত্রণার অবসান হওয়া** to get rid of all troubles and worries (esp. by dying).

জ্বালা[2] *v.* to light, to kindle, to ignite.

জ্বালানি *n.* firewood, fuel. □ *a.* used as or fit for use as fuel.

জ্বালানিয়া var. of **জ্বালানে**।

জ্বালানী[1] alt. spell. of **জ্বালানি**।

জ্বালানী[2] *fem.* of **জ্বালানে**।

জ্বালানে *a.* irritating, annoying, pestering; vexatious; smarting, mortifying; one who or that which burns or sets fire to; (fig.) quarrelsome, factious (ঘরজ্বালানে).

জ্বালানো *v.* to kindle, to ignite, to light (উনুন জ্বালানো, বাতি জ্বালানো) ; to set fire to, to set on fire (ঘর জ্বালানো) ; to burn (মড়া জ্বালানো) ; to irriate, to vex, to pester, to annoy (দুষ্টু ছেলেটা মাকে জ্বালায়) ; to smart, to mortify (হৃদয় জ্বালানো) ; (rare) to enlighten.

জ্বালামালিনী *n.* a manifestation of Goddess Durga (দুর্গা).

জ্বালামুখ *n.* the mouth of a volcano, a crater.

জ্বালিত *a.* ignited, enkindled, lighted; inflamed; mortified.

জ্যা *n.* a bowstring; (geom.) a chord, a sine; the earth. **ধনুকে জ্যা পরানো** to string a bow.

জ্যাকেট *n.* a jacket.

জ্যাঠা alt. spell. of **জেঠা**।

জ্যানির্ঘোষ *n.* the twang of a bow.

জ্যান্ত coll. corrup. of **জিয়ন্ত**।

জ্যামিতি *n.* geometry. **জ্যামিতিক** *a.* geometrical. **জ্যামিতিবিদ** *a.* versed in geometry. □ *n.* a geometrician.

জ্যামুক্ত *a.* loosened or flung from the bow.

জ্যারোপণ *n.* act of stringing a bow.

জ্যালজ্যাল *int.* expressing : the loose weave of fabric. **জ্যালজ্যাল করা** *v.* to look to be with loose weave. **জ্যালজেলে** *a.* loosely woven (জ্যালজেলে কাপড়).

জ্যেষ্ঠ *a.* eldest (জ্যেষ্ঠ পুত্র) ; elder (ওই ভাইটি আমার জ্যেষ্ঠ) ; older, senior (বয়োজ্যেষ্ঠ) ; highest (জ্যেষ্ঠবর্ণ). □ *n.* eldest brother or the elder brother. **~তাত** *n.* an elder brother of one's father. **জ্যেষ্ঠা** *a. fem.* of **জ্যেষ্ঠ**। □ *n.* the eighteenth of the twenty-seven zodiacal stars according to Hindu astronomy. **জ্যেষ্ঠাধিকার** *n.* primogeniture. **জ্যেষ্ঠাশ্রম** *v.* the second stage of human life as enjoined by Hindu scriptures; the life of a householder.

জ্যেষ্ঠী *n.* the common lizard found frequently in dwelling-houses.

জ্যৈষ্ঠ *n.* second month of the Bengali calendar (from the middle of May to the middle of June).

জ্যোৎস্না *n.* moonlight. **~ময়** *a.* moonlit. *fem.* **~ময়ী**। **~রাত্রি** *n.* a moonlit night.

জ্যোতি *n.* light; lustre, glow; a star or planet; the sun; sight (চোখের জ্যোতি হারানো). **জ্যোতির্বিদ্যা, জ্যোতির্বিজ্ঞান** *n.* astronomy; astrology. **জ্যোতির্বিদ, জ্যোতির্বেত্তা** *a.* versed in astronomy or astrology. □ *n.* an astronomer; an astrologer. **জ্যোতির্মণ্ডল** *n.* the luminous or celestial sphere, the (astronomical) zodiac; stars and planets collectively. **জ্যোতির্ময়** *a.* luminous, radiant, bright. *fem.* **জ্যোতির্ময়ী**। **জ্যোতিঃশাস্ত্র** *n.* astronomy. **জ্যোতিশ্চক্র** *n.* the (astronomical or astrological) zodiac; a halo. **জ্যোতিঃস্রোত** *n.* a stream of (heavenly or divine) light.

জ্যোতিষ *n.* astronomy; astrology. **জ্যোতিষিক** *a.* astronomical; astrological. **জ্যোতিষী** *a.* versed in astronomy or astrology. □ *n.* an astronomer; an astrologer.

জ্যোতিষ্ক *n.* any of the stars or planets, a luminary. **~মণ্ডল** *n.* the celestial sphere, the zodiac, luminaries collectively.

জ্যোতিষ্মতী *fem.* of **জ্যোতিষ্মান**।

জ্যোতিষ্মত্তা *n.* luminosity, brightness.

জ্যোতিষ্মান *a.* luminous, shining, lustrous, bright. *fem.* **জ্যোতিষ্মতী**।

ঝ *n.* the ninth consonant of the Bengali alphabet.

ঝংকার *n.* a jingling sound (as of the strings of a harp); a clattering sound (as of weapons); a humming sound (as of bees); (mus.) a sharp and loud sound, a blaze; a loud and sudden brawling or bullying sound. **ঝংকার দেওয়া,** (poet.) **ঝংকারা** *v.* to jingle; to clatter; to hum; (mus.) to twist into a sharp and loud sound, to blaze up; to burst out into brawling or bullying.

ঝংকৃত *a.* jingled; clattered; (mus.) twisted into a sharp and loud sound; burst into brawling or bullying. **ঝংকৃতি** *n.* jingle; clatter; hum; (mus.) a twisting into a sharp and loud sound.

ঝকঝক, ঝকমক *int.* expressing : sparkling or glistening state. **ঝকঝক করা, ঝকমক করা, ঝকঝকানো, ঝকমকানো** *v.* to sparkle, to glisten, to glitter; to shine brightly. **ঝকঝকানি, ঝকমকানি** *n.* sparkling or glistening or glittering state. **ঝকঝকে, ঝকমকে** *a.* sparkling, glistening, glittering, brightly shining.

ঝকমারি *n.* a folly (ঝকমারি করা) ; a mistake, a bloomer; a fault, an offence; a trouble (ঝকমারি সওয়া). **ঝকমারির মাশুল দেওয়া** to pay for one's mistake or folly.

ঝক্কি *n.* a risk; troublesome burden or charge.

ঝগড়া *n.* a quarrel, a brawl, a row; an altercation; a dispute. **ঝগড়া করা** *v.* to quarrel; to altercate, to wrangle. **ঝগড়া বাধানো** *v.* to kick up a row, to pick a quarrel; have a dispute with, to set by the ears. **ঝগড়া মেটানো** *v.* to make up a quarrel, to settle a dispute. **~ঝাঁটি** *n.* (usu. *pl.*) trifling or peevish quarrel or altercation or dissension; quarrels. **~টে** *a.* quarrelsome, cantankerous; wrangling.

ঝঞ্ঝট var. of **ঝঞ্ঝাট**।

ঝঞ্ঝনা *n.* a clattering sound (অস্ত্রঝঞ্ঝনা) ; a clap of thunder; thunder ('ঝঞ্ঝনা পড়ুক তার মাথার উপর').

ঝঞ্ঝা *n.* a rainstorm. **~ক্ষুব্ধ, ~পীড়িত** *a.* stricken by a rainstorm. **~তাড়িত** *a.* driven or blown by a rainstorm. **~বর্ত** *n.* a cyclone. **~বাত, ~বায়ু** *n.* a stormy wind, a strong gale.

ঝঞ্ঝাট *n.* a trouble; a fix; a disturbance; a troublesome burden or worry or charge (ঝঞ্ঝাট পোহানো). **ঝঞ্ঝাটে পড়া** *v.* to be in a trouble, to get into a scrape; to get into a mess; to be in a fix. **ঝঞ্ঝাট বাধানো, ঝঞ্ঝাট করা** *v.* to create trouble or disturbance. **ঝঞ্ঝাট পোহানো, ঝঞ্ঝাট সহা** *v.* to bear a trouble or the stress or strain of a crisis.

ঝঞ্ঝাটে *a.* troublesome; disturbing.

ঝট, ঝটপট[1] same as **চট** and **চটপট** respectively.

ঝটপট[2] *int.* expressing : flapping or the noise of flapping. **ঝটপট করা, ঝটপটানো** *v.* to flap. **ঝটপটানি** *n.* act or noise of flapping.

ঝটকা, ঝটকানি *n.* a sudden and forceful snatch or pull or jerk. **ঝটকা মারা** *v.* to snatch or pull or jerk or snatch suddenly and forcefully; to cut or kill by a blow or with one stroke.

ঝটাপটি *n.* mutual hugging and clasping; fluttering or flapping of wings; scuffle, disorderly fight.

ঝটিকা *n.* a storm; a strong gale. **~বর্ত** *n.* a whirlwind.

ঝটিতি *adv.* quickly, hastily, hurriedly.

ঝড় *n.* a storm; a strong gale. **~ঝাপটা** *n.* the press or stress of a storm; (fig.) the press or stress of a danger or dangers. **~তুফান** *n.* tempest and high waves. **~জল, ~বৃষ্টি** *n.* a rainstorm.

ঝড়তি-পড়তি *n.* clippings or other waste matters; remnants, scraps.

ঝড়ো *a.* stormy, tempestuous (ঝড়ো হাওয়া) ; storm-beaten (ঝড়ো কাক).

ঝন *int.* expressing : a clattering sound as of weapons or of striking a thin metal plate; the chink of coins. **ঝনঝন** *int.* expressing : repeated or continuous clattering sound or chinking; jingle (as of coins); a strong dizzy sensation (মাথা ঝনঝন করা). **ঝনঝনানো, ঝনঝন করা** *v.* to clatter or cause to clatter; to chink or cause to chink; to be afflicted or to afflict with a strong dizzy sensation. **ঝনঝনানি** *n.* clatter; chink; a strong dizzy sensation.

ঝনকাঠ *n.* the lintel; the upper wooden bar of the frame of a door.

ঝনৎকার *n.* a clattering sound as of weapons; the chink of coins.

ঝনাৎ *int.* expressing a sound louder than **ঝন**।

ঝপ *int.* expressing the sound of diving or falling into water or air suddenly; a sudden splashing sound; quickness (ঝপ করে খাওয়া). **ঝপঝপ** *int.* expressing : the repeated or continuous sound of diving or falling into water or air or of sudden splashing; incessant pouring (ঝপঝপ বৃষ্টি) ; quickness (ঝপঝপ করে খাওয়া). **ঝপাঝপ** *adv.* very quickly (ঝপাঝপ খাওয়া) ; quickly one after another (ঝপাঝপ ডুব দেওয়া).

ঝপাং same as **ঝপাৎ**।

ঝপাঝপ see **ঝপ**।

ঝপাৎ *int.* expressing the sound of diving or springing into water or of flinging down a heavy object.

ঝমঝম *int.* expressing a loud jingling sound as of anklets; a loud pattering sound as of rain falling in torrents. **ঝমঝম করা** *v.* to jingle. **ঝমরঝমর** *int.* expressing a very loud jingling noise as of anklets. **ঝমাঝম** *adv.* with a loud jingling noise (ঝমাঝম মল বাজে) ; noisily in torrents (ঝমাঝম বৃষ্টি পড়ছে).

ঝমরঝমর, ঝমাঝম see **ঝমঝম**।

ঝম্প *n.* a jump, a spring, a dive, a plunge. **ঝম্প দেওয়া** *v.* to jump, to spring, to plunge, to dive. **~দান, ~প্রদান** *n.* act of jumping or springing or plunging or diving.

ঝরই *v.* (poet. & obs.) falls or fall, is or are shed, drops or drop, exudes or exude.

ঝরকা alt. spell. of **ঝরোকা**।

ঝরঝর *int.* expressing the state or sound of rapid and continuous falling in small drops of minute particles (ঝরঝর করে বৃষ্টি বা বালি পড়া, ঝরঝর করে কাঁদা). □ *adv.* in incessant flow or falling ('ঝরঝর বরিষে বারিধারা'). **ঝরঝরে** *a.* neat and clean (ঝরঝরে ঘর) ; neat (ঝরঝরে কাজ) ; neat and legible (ঝরঝরে ছাপা, ঝরঝরে লেখা) ; refreshed or freed from morbidity (দেহটা ঝরঝরে লাগছে) ; freed from moisture (ঝরঝরে ভাত) ; dilapidated (বাড়িখানার ঝরঝরে অবস্থা) ; in utter ruin. **পরকাল ঝরঝরে করা** *v.* to spoil one's life, to spoil one's future; to deprave utterly.

ঝরণা rej. spell. of **ঝরনা**।

ঝরতি *n.* any negligible portion of things fallen out of a heap and passed over at the time of loading or carrying.

ঝরনা *n.* a fountain, a waterfall, a cascade, a spring. **~কলম** *n.* a fountain-pen.

ঝরা *v.* to fall in drops; to ooze, to exude; to fall; to be shed (গাছের পাতা ঝরা) ; to cast off or moult (পাখির পালক ঝরা) ; to run (সর্দিতে নাক ঝরা). **ঝরানো** *v.* to cause to fall in drops; to cause to ooze or exude; to cause to fall; to shed; to cast off, to moult; to cause to run.

ঝরিত *a.* fallen in drops; oozed; exuded; fallen, shed; cast off, moulted; flowing ('নির্ঝরঝরিত বারিরাশি').

ঝরোকা *n.* a small window; a bay window; a latticed window.

ঝর্ঝর *n.* the sound of rapid fall as of a stream of water; a sieve, a colander; a cymbal, cymbals.

ঝর্ঝরিত *a.* full of the noise of rapid fall as of a stream of water; perforated in several places.

ঝর্ণা, ঝর্না rej. spellings of **ঝরনা**।

ঝলক, (coll.) **ঝলকা** *n.* a gush (রক্তের ঝলক) ; a spray (আলোর ঝলক) ; a dazzling flash (রূপের ঝলক) ; a spell of outpouring or outburst (সুরের ঝলক) ; a spell. **ঝলকানি** *n.* coruscation; sparkling, flashing. **ঝলকানো** *v.* to scatter in gushes; to coruscate; to flash. **ঝলকে ঝলকে** in gushes.

ঝলকিত *a.* coruscated; flashed.

ঝলঝল *int.* expressing the state of hanging loosely. **ঝলমলানি** *n.* the glitter, the sparkle.

ঝলঝলে *a.* loosely hanging.

ঝলমল *int.* expressing coruscation. **ঝলমলানো, ঝলমল করা** *v.* to coruscate; to sparkle, to glitter. **ঝলমলে** *a.* coruscating.

ঝলসানো *v.* to daze or be dazed (চোখ ঝলসানো) ; to dazzle (হীরেখানা ঝলসাচ্ছে) ; to scorch or be scorched, to singe or become singed (আগুনে ঝলসানো) ; to brown (রোদে গাছপালা ঝলসানো). □ *a.* dazed; dazzling; scorched, singed; browned. **ঝলসানি** *n.* daze or dazing; dazzle or dazzling; scorched or singed state; act of scorching or singeing; browned state or browning.

ঝলসিত *a.* dazed; dazzled; scorched, singed; browned.

ঝলা v. (chiefly poet.) to dazzle or shine ('পিঙ্গল জটাজাল ঝলিছে').

ঝল্লক, ঝল্লরী *n.* a dish-shaped musical instrument made of bell metal played at the time of worshipping; a cymbal or cymbals.

ঝাউ *n.* the tamarisk tree.

ঝাঁ *int.* expressing great swiftness. **ঝাঁ করে** very swiftly, in a jiffy, in a moment.

ঝাঁক *n.* a flock (পাখির ঝাঁক) ; a swarm (মৌমাছির ঝাঁক) ; a shoal (মাছের ঝাঁক) ; a collection, a crowd, an assemblage (বদমাশের ঝাঁক). **ঝাঁকে ঝাঁকে** in flocks; in swarms; in shoals; in smart showers (ঝাঁকে ঝাঁকে বৃষ্টি).

ঝাঁকড়া *a.* long and clustering.

ঝাঁকড়া-মাকড়া *a.* shaggy.

ঝাঁকনি var. of **ঝাঁকুনি**।

ঝাঁকরানি var. of **ঝাঁকুনি**। **ঝাঁকরানো** var. of **ঝাঁকানো**।

ঝাঁকা[১] *n.* a large wicker-basket.

ঝাঁকা[২] *v.* to shake (ঝাঁকানো, ঝেঁকে ওঠা). □ *n.* a shake (ঝাঁকা খাওয়া).

ঝাঁকানো *v.* to shake. □ *a.* shaken.

ঝাঁকা-মুটে *n.* a porter who carries his load in a wicker-basket on his head.

ঝাঁকি *n.* a shake.

ঝাঁকিদর্শন *n.* visiting a place etc. for a moment; stopping on the way for a moment to see someone or something.

ঝাঁকুনি *n.* shake; act of shaking.

ঝাঁগুড়গুড় *int.* expressing the noise of beating a drum.

ঝাঁজ[১] *n.* strong heat (রোদের ঝাঁজ) ; a strong pungent aroma or taste (ওষুধের ঝাঁজ) ; severity or harshness (কথার ঝাঁজ).

ঝাঁজ[২], **ঝাঁজর**[১] *n.* a dish-shaped musical instrument played at the time of worshipping a deity.

ঝাঁজর[২] *a.* full of holes, porous; alveolar, honeycombed; perforated in many places; extremely worn out. □ *n.* a colander, a sieve, a strainer.

ঝাঁজরা *a.* full of holes, porous, alveolar, honeycombed.

ঝাঁজরি *n.* a colander, a sieve, a strainer; a porous cover or lid (as on the mouth of a drain); a spray; a porous water-pot for watering trees.

ঝাঁ-ঝাঁ *int.* expressing severe heat (রোদ ঝাঁ-ঝাঁ করা) ; burning sensation (চোখমুখ ঝাঁ-ঝাঁ করা) ; great swiftness (ঝাঁ-ঝাঁ করে কাজ শেষ করা).

ঝাঁজালো, ঝাঁঝালো *a.* very hot; pungently aromatic; severe, harsh.

ঝাঁজি *n.* a kind of shaggy fibrous rush or sedge growing in water.

ঝাঁঝ var. of **ঝাঁজ**[১,২] and **ঝাঁজি**।

ঝাঁঝালো var. of **ঝাঁজালো**।

ঝাঁঝর var. of **ঝাঁজর**[১]।

ঝাঁঝরা var. of **ঝাঁজরা**।

ঝাঁঝরি var. of **ঝাঁজরি**।

ঝাঁট *n.* sweeping; a sweep. **ঝাঁট দেওয়া** v. to sweep, to broom.

ঝাঁটা *n.* a broom; a besom. **~খেকো** *a.* (in abuses) accustomed to be flogged with a broom; contemptible. **~নো** *v.* to sweep. **~পেটা** *n.* a flogging with a broom, a stroke with a broom. **ঝাঁটা মারা** *v.* to flog with a broom. **ঝাঁটার বাড়ি** *n.* a stroke with or of a broom.

ঝাঁটি *n.* a flowering shrub, the amaranth (?).

ঝাঁপ[১] *n.* an improvised door or lid made of wicker.

ঝাঁপ[২] *n.* a jump, a spring, a dive, a plunge. **ঝাঁপ দেওয়া, ঝাঁপানো** *v.* to spring, to dive, to plunge; to rush to (কোলের মধ্যে বা বুকের মধ্যে বা বুকের উপর ঝাঁপানো).

ঝাঁপটা *n.* an ornament for the woman's head, a tiara.

ঝাঁপতাল *n.* an Indian musical measure.

ঝাঁপা[1] var. of **ঝাঁপটা**।

ঝাঁপা[2] *v.* (obs.) to rush to, to jump into; (obs.) to rise, to come up ('রূপ সদা মনে ঝাঁপে') ; to cast, to fling ('জাল তুরিতে ঝাঁপায়') ; (obs.) to cover, to screen ('বদন ঝাপিব বাসে').

ঝাঁপান *n.* a playful handling and control of snakes (মনসাপূজার ঝাঁপান) ; a litter used for carrying people on hills.

ঝাঁপানো see **ঝাঁপ**[2] ।

ঝাঁপি *n.* a wicker-basket esp. a small one with a lid.

ঝাট *adv.* quickly; at once.

ঝাড় *n.* a bush, a thicket (ঝোপঝাড়) ; a cluster, a clump (বাঁশঝাড়, গোলাপঝাড়) ; a race or family (শয়তানের ঝাড়) ; a chandelier (বেলোয়ারি ঝাড়). **~বাঁধা** *a.* growing in clusters bunches or dumps. **ঝাড়ে-বংশে** *adv.* to the last member of the family, not excluding a single member of the family, one and all of the family. **ঝাড়ে-মূলে** *adv.* root and branch.

ঝাড়লণ্ঠন, ঝাড়বাতি *n.* a chandelier.

ঝাড়া *v.* to thresh or beat out grain from (corn etc.), to separate chaff from grain, to winnow (চাল ঝাড়া) ; to dust, to brush, to remove dust or dirt by shaking or with a piece of cloth or some sort of duster; to empty or remove contents of (bags etc.), to shake out contents of vessels, bags etc. (ঝুলি ঝাড়া) ; to throw brickbats or other missiles (মাথার ইট ঝাড়া) ; to show ill-temper, to vent one's spleen (গায়ের ঝাল ঝাড়া) ; to exorcise (ভূত ঝাড়া). □ *a.* threshed or winnowed or cleaned (ঝাড়া চাল). □ *n.* threshing or winnowing; dusting and cleaning, brushing; emptying contents of. **ঝাড়া দুই ঘণ্টা** for full two hours, for two hours at a stretch. **ঝাড়পোঁছ** *n.* sweeping and cleaning. **ঝাড়াপোঁছা** same as **ঝাড়পোঁছ**। **ঝাড়ফুঁক** *n.* exorcising of evil spirit by uttering charms and incantations. **ঝাড়ানো** *v.* to cause to thresh and winnow, to expel evil spirit etc., to exorcise.

ঝাড়ন[1] *n.* dusting and cleaning, cloth for dusting furniture etc., a duster; winnowing or fanning grains etc.

ঝাড়ন[2] *n.* act of expelling or exorcising evil spirit out of a person by reciting charms and incantations or by invocation of holy names, exorcism.

ঝাড়পোঁছ, ঝাড়ফুঁক see **ঝাড়া**।

ঝাড়াই *n.* sweeping and cleaning; threshing and beating (ধান ঝাড়াই) ; winnowing (চাল ঝাড়াই). **ঝাড়াই-বাছাই** *n.* sweeping and cleaning; eliminating and selecting.

ঝাড়ু *n.* broom. **ঝাড়ু দেওয়া** to sweep. **ঝাড়ু মারা** *v.* to beat with a broom. **~দার** *n.* a sweeper, a scavenger, a dustman, a person who takes away dirt, garbage and rubbish from streets, buildings etc.

ঝানু *a.* veteran, experienced; sly, cunning.

ঝান্ডা *n.* a flag, a banner, a standard.

ঝাপট, ঝাপটা[1] *n.* (of wind or storm) a gust; (of rain) a spray; (of wings) a flap; (of tails) a violent stroke.

ঝাপটা[2] var. of **ঝাঁপটা**।

ঝাপসা *a.* obscure; hazy; murky; blurred. **ঝাপসা দৃষ্টি বা নজর** dim vision; blurred vision.

ঝামটা, (rare) **ঝামট** *n.* angry movement, spouting. **মুখঝামটা** *n.* angry movement of the face attended with scolding. **মুখঝামটা দেওয়া** *v.* to scold with a wry face, to mouth.

ঝামর, ঝামরু, (rare) **ঝামরি** *a.* browned or pale ('হেমকান্তি ঝামরু হইল'). **ঝামরানো** *v.* to become browned or pale; to look flushed (as with cold); to be overcast with rainy clouds (আকাশ ঝামরানো). □ *a.* browned, turned pale, paled; flushed; rainy.

ঝামা *n.* a piece of over-burnt brick.

ঝামেলা *n.* a trouble; a fix; a disturbance; a row; a troublesome burden or charge. **ঝামেলা করা, ঝামেলা বাধানো** *v.* to create a trouble or disturbance; to quarrel, to kick up a row. **ঝামেলা পোহানো, ঝামেলা সহা** *v.* to bear a trouble or disturbance. **ঝামেলায় পড়া** *v.* to be in a trouble; to get into trouble; to be in a scrape; to be in a fix.

ঝারা *n.* a porous device to spray water etc. on a plant.

ঝারি *n.* a water-can with a porous spout.

ঝাল[১] *n.* solder. **ঝাল দেওয়া** *v.* to solder.

ঝাল[২] *a.* acrid, biting; pungent, hot. ☐ *n.* an acrimony or grudge (গায়ের ঝাল) ; pungency, hotness (লংকার ঝাল) ; chilli (তরকারিতে ঝাল দেওয়া) ; a variety of hot curry or gravy (মাছের ঝাল). **ঝাল ঝাড়া, ঝাল মেটানো** *v.* (coll.) to feed one's grudge (esp. by flogging or scolding severely). **ঝালে-ঝোলে-অম্বলে** *adv.* in all affairs or places.

ঝালর *n.* a fringe, a valance; tatting. **~ওয়ালা** *a.* fringed, valanced.

ঝালা[১] *v.* (mus.) to twist up a sharp and loud sound on string instruments, to blaze up. ☐ *n.* a spell or act of blazing up.

ঝালা[২] *v.* to solder; to dredge (পুকুর ঝালা).

ঝালানো *v.* to cause to solder; to dredge (পুকুর ঝালানো) ; (fig.) to refresh (বন্ধুত্ব ঝালানো, স্মৃতি ঝালানো) ; to recapitulate or revise (পড়া ঝালানো). ☐ *a.* soldered; dredged; (fig.) refreshed or recapitulated or revised.

ঝালাপালা *a.* almost deafened or stunned or extremely vexed with a loud and unbearable noise (কান ঝালাপালা হওয়া) ; extremely afflicted (রোদে শরীর ঝালাপালা হওয়া).

ঝালি *n.* the festival of ঝুলন or swinging; a pit dug at the mouth of a gutter; a bag; a basket; a wicker-basket.

ঝি *n.* a daughter (রাজার ঝি, ঘোষের ঝি) ; a maid-servant. **ঝিকে মেরে বউকে শেখানো** (fig.) to flog or punish one's own innocent people to teach others a lesson.

ঝিউড়ি *n.* a daughter; an unmarried daughter.

ঝিঁক *n.* a raised construction on an oven upon which cooking utensils are placed; any removable metal device to serve the same purpose.

ঝিঁকড়া *n.* a kind of small bushy plant.

ঝিঁকা, (coll.) **ঝিঁকে** *n.* a jerk. **ঝিঁকা দেওয়া** *v.* to give a jerk, to jerk; to shrug (কাঁধ ঝিঁকে দেওয়া).

ঝিঁঝি[১] *n.* a species of insect, the cricket. **ঝিঁঝির শব্দ** বা **ডাক** the drone or chirping of the cricket.

ঝিঁ ঝিঁ[২] *int.* indicating : a dizzy or buzzing or twinging sensation (মাথা ঝিঁ ঝিঁ করা, পায়ে ঝিঁ ঝিঁ ধরা). **ঝিঁ ঝিঁ করা** *v.* to feel dizzy, to be stricken with a buzzing sensation. **ঝিঁ ঝিঁ ধরা** *v.* to be stricken with a twinging sensation, to have pins and needles.

ঝিঁঝিট *n.* an Indian musical mode.

ঝিকমিক *int.* expressing : sparkling or glittering or twinkling. **ঝিকমিক করা** *v.* to sparkle, to glitter, to twinkle.

ঝিকিমিকি same as **ঝিকমিক** ।

ঝিকুট, (rare) **ঝিকুর** *n.* the brain, the encephalon. **ঝিকুট নড়া** *v.* to be off one's head.

ঝিঙে *n.* a kind of vegetable, a cucurbitaceous plant and its fruit.

ঝিনঝিন same as **ঝিঁ ঝিঁ**[২] । **ঝিনঝিনি** *n.* a dizzy or buzzing or twinging sensation; the sensation of having pins and needles.

ঝিনিঝিনি, ঝিনিকিঝিনি *int.* expressing a sweet and musical jingling sound (as of a dancer's anklets).

ঝিনুক *n.* a bivalve mollusc, the cockle, the oyster; an ear-shell; an abalone; a metal spoon shaped almost as a valve of the cockle (chiefly used in feeding babies).

ঝিন্টি *n.* a flowering shrub, the amaranth (?).

ঝিম *n.* drowsiness or langour (ঝিম ধরা). ☐ *a.* stricken with drowsiness or langour, drowsy, languid (ঝিম হয়ে বসা).

ঝিমঝিম *int.* expressing a dizzy or fainting sensation. **ঝিমঝিম করা** *v.* to feel dizzy; to feel like swooning (গা ঝিমঝিম করা).

ঝিমানি, ঝিমুনি *n.* dozing; a doze; slackening, abatement, flagging; inaction; lethargy.

ঝিমানো *v.* to drowse, to doze; slacken, to abate, to flag (আন্দোলন ঝিমিয়ে পড়েছে) ; to become inactive (সন্ত্রাসবাদীরা ঝিমিয়ে পড়ল).

ঝিয়ারি *n.* a daughter; an unmarried daughter; one who is like a daughter, e.g. a son-in-law's sister.

ঝিরঝির *int.* expressing the sound of wind or breeze blowing gently or of drizzling rain. **ঝিরঝিরে** *a.* (of the wind) gently blowing; (of the rain) drizzling.

ঝিল *n.* a very large pond.

ঝিলমিল[1] *int.* expressing gentle sparkle or fine coruscation or sparkle. **ঝিলমিল করা** *v.* to coruscate or sparkle gently. **ঝিলমিলি** *n.* fine coruscation or sparkle. **ঝিলমিলে** *a.* finely coruscating or sparkling.

ঝিলমিল[2], **ঝিলমিলি**[1] *n.* a shutter, a venetian blind.

ঝিলমিলি[2], **ঝিলমিলে** see **ঝিলমিল**[1] ।

ঝিলিক *n.* a sudden but mild or light flash. **ঝিলিক দেওয়া, ঝিলিক মারা** *v.* to flash mildly or lightly.

ঝিলিমিলি *a.* coruscating, sparkling, glittering. □ *n.* fine and gentle flash or coruscation (রোদের ঝিলিমিলি).

ঝিল্লি *n.* a species of insect, the cricket; membrane.

ঝুঁকা, ঝোঁকা *v.* to incline, to stoop, to lean; to tilt; to have slight desire or liking (for), to be disposed or drawn (খেলার দিকে ঝুঁকছে, ছেলের দিকে মায়ের মন ঝোঁকে). **ঝুঁকানো, ঝোঁকানো** *v.* to cause to incline or stoop or lean; to rouse slight desire or liking in, to dispose or draw.

ঝুঁকি *n.* a risk, a hazard; a risky responsibility. **ঝুঁকি নেওয়া** *v.* to risk, to hazard. **বড় রকমের ঝুঁকি** a great risk.

ঝুঁটি, ঝুঁট, ঝুট[1] *n.* a tuft of long hair on the head kept tied in a bun; a bun; a bird's crest (কাকাতুয়ার মাথায় ঝুটি) ; (of bulls, camels, etc.) a hump.

ঝুট[2] *a.* false. **~মুট** *adv.* for nothing.

ঝুটা *a.* (of articles of food) partly eaten; (of dinner-plates etc.) not yet washed after being used in dining; defiled, ravished; false (ঝুটা কথা) ; counterfeit or forged (ঝুটা দলিল) ; artificial, sham, imitation (ঝুটা হীরা) ; dissembling (ঝুটা লোক).

ঝুটাপুটি *n.* a scuffle (chiefly a playful one.) **ঝুটাপুটি করা** *v.* to scuffle.

ঝুটি var. of **ঝুঁটি** ।

ঝুটো coll. var. of **ঝুটা** (ঝুটো গয়না).

ঝুটোপুটি coll. var. of **ঝুটাপুটি** ।

ঝুড়ি *n.* a wicker basket, a scuttle, a hamper. **ঝুড়ি ঝুড়ি** basketfuls of, a large number or amount of.

ঝুনঝুন same as **ঝুনুঝুনু** (often used to express a quicker sound).

ঝুনা older and for. var. of **ঝুনো** ।

ঝুনুঝুনু, ঝুনুর-ঝুনুর *int.* expressing a musical jingling sound as of anklets of a dancer. **ঝুনুঝুনু করা, ঝুনুর ঝুনুর করা** *v.* to jingle musically.

ঝুনো *a.* ripe and hardened (ঝুনো নারকেল) ; veteran and experienced (ঝুনো উকিল) ; shrewd and sly. cp. ঝানু ।

ঝুপ *int.* expressing the noise (milder than **ঝপ**) of diving or falling into water or air suddenly; a sudden splashing sound; suddenness. **ঝুপঝুপ, ঝুপঝাপ** *int.* expressing this noise repeatedly; quick succession.

ঝুপড়ি *n.* a low hut built with tree-leaves, wicker, bamboo etc.

ঝুপুরঝুপুর milder var. of **ঝপঝাপ** and **ঝুপঝুপ** (see **ঝপ** and **ঝুপ**).

ঝুম same as **নিঝুম** ।

ঝুমকা, (coll.) **ঝুমকো** *n.* the bellflower, the campanula; a bell-shaped earring.

ঝুমঝুম milder var. of **ঝমঝম** ।

ঝুমঝুমি *n.* a rattle for children.

ঝুমুর *n.* a kind of love-song accompanied with dance.

ঝুরঝুর *int.* expressing the state or sound (milder than **ঝরঝর**) of rapid and profuse falling in drizzles or in minute particles (ঝুরঝুর করে বৃষ্টি বা বালি পড়া) ; the state or sound of blowing gently (ঝুরঝুর করে বাতাস বওয়া). **ঝুরঝুরে** *a.* drizzling (ঝুরঝুরে বৃষ্টি) ; freed from moisture (ঝুরঝুরে বালি, ঝুরঝুরে ভাত) ; gently blowing (ঝুরঝুরে বাতাস).

ঝুরা[1] *v.* (poet.) to stream with tears ('রূপ লাগি আঁখি ঝুরে').

ঝুরা[2] *a.* pulverized; freed from moisture (ঝুরা ভাত) ; granular and dry (ঝুরা বালি). **ঝুরাঝুরা** *a.* freed from moisture; granular and dry.

ঝুরি *n.* an aerial root of a tree. **ঝুরিভাজা** *n.* a kind of crisp snack made of pulverized pigeon-pea.

ঝুরুঝুরু milder and sweeter var. of **ঝরঝর** ।

ঝুরো coll. var. of **ঝুরা**[2] ।

ঝুল *n.* act of stooping, inclination (অত ঝুল দিলে পড়ে যাবে) ; vertical or downward length (জামার ঝুল) ; soot or dirt caught in cobweb (ঝুলকালি) ; lamp-black, soot (হারিকেনের ঝুল) ; (coll. & sl.) trash, worthless.

ঝুলন *n.* act of swinging; suspension in the air; the Hindu festival of swinging (also **ঝুলনযাত্রা**).

ঝুলনা *n.* a rocking cradle.

ঝুলপি var. of **জুলপি** ।

ঝুলা, ঝোলা *v.* to be hung, to hang, to be suspended in the air; (hum.) to be hanged; to swing; to incline towards, to lean to, to tend to; to be still in action, still hanging fire (মামলা ঝুলছে). **ঝুলা-ঝুলি, ঝুলোঝুলি** *n.* (rare) repeated or continuous swinging; earnest solicitation (for some length of time). **ঝুলানো** *v.* to hang, to suspend in the air; (hum.) to hang by the neck; to suspend or adjourn; to keep in suspense.

ঝুলি *n.* a small cloth-bag (esp. one that can be carried by hanging it from one's shoulder)

ঝুলোঝুলি coll. var. of **ঝুলাঝুলি** (see **ঝুলা**).

ঝেঁটা coll. corrup. of **ঝাঁটা** ।

ঝেঁপে দেওয়া *v.* (coll. & sl.) to cheat, to grab unfairly.

ঝোঁক *n.* a stooping state; inclination, propensity, a tendency; liking; earnest interest (রাজনীতিতে ঝোঁক) ; a whim, a caprice, a leaning, a penchant (দেশভ্রমণের ঝোঁক) ; overwhelming or besotting influence (নেশার ঝোঁক). **~মাত্র** *n.* velleity.

ঝোঁকা pop. var. of **ঝুঁকা** ।

ঝোঁটন *n.* a crest (as of a bird). □ *a.* crested (ঝোঁটন বুলবুলি).

ঝোড়া[1] *n.* a large wicker-basket, a scuttle, a hamper.

ঝোড়া[2] *v.* to lop off the unnecessary or overgrown branches. **~নো** *v.* to cause to lop off the unnecessary or overgrown branches of.

ঝোড়ো alt. spell. of **ঝড়ো** ।

ঝোপ *n.* an underwood; a bush, a thicket, a copse, a coppice. **~জঙ্গল** *n.* a thicket, a bushy undergrowth, underwood.

ঝোরা *n.* a cascade, a waterfall, a fountain (পাগলাঝোরা).

ঝোল *n.* broth, juice, soup.

ঝোলা[1] pop. var. of **ঝুলা** ।

ঝোলা[2] *a.* (of garments) hanging loosely (ঝোলা আস্তিন).

ঝোলা[3] *a.* as thin as broth.

ঝোলা[4] *n.* a (comparatively large) cloth-bag esp. one that can be carried by hanging it from one's shoulder.

ঝোলাগুড় *n.* thin molasses, treacle.

ঝোলাঝুলি[1] pop. var. of **ঝুলাঝুলি** (see **ঝুলা**).

ঝোলাঝুলি[2] *n. pl.* belongings or luggage collectively, baggage. **ঝোলাঝুলিসমেত** *adv.* bag and baggage.

ঝোলানো pop. var. of **ঝুলানো** (see **ঝুলা**).

ঞ

ঞ *n.* the tenth consonant of the Bengali alphabet.

ট *n.* the eleventh consonant of the Bengali alphabet.

টইটম্বুর *a.* swollen to the extreme; full to the brim; brimming, overfull, overflowing.

টং[১] *n.* a high platform for living or shooting from, a machan.

টং[২] *a.* about to burst (রেগে টং) ; thoroughly besotted, dead drunk (মদে টং).

টং[৩] *int.* expressing : twang as of a bowstring. **টংটং** *int.* expressing : repeated twangs. **টংটং করে বেড়ানো** to tramp idly; to while away time.

টংকার alt. spell. of **টঙ্কার** ।

টক[১] *a.* sour, acrid. ☐ *n.* sour taste, acridity; any sour-tasting pickle. **টক লাগা** to taste sour.

টক[২] *int.* expressing : haste, quickness, promptness.

টক[৩] *int.* expressing : a light noise of rapping or drumming.

টকটক[১] *a.* sourish, acidulous.

টকটক[২] *int.* expressing : deepness or brightness or gorgeousness or brilliance (লাল টকটক করছে). **টকটকে** *a.* & *adv.* deep, bright, gorgeous (টকটকে লাল, টকটকে চেহারা).

টকটক[৩] *int.* expressing : the ticking sound of a clock; the sound made by a carter in order to speed up the horse or ox, gee-gee.

টকা *v.* to turn sour; to become acid; to rot, to putrefy; to become irritated by being acidified (দাঁত টকা).

টকাটক[১] *int.* & *adv.* very quickly or promptly.

টকাটক[২] *int.* expressing a very light sound of rapping or drumming repeatedly. ☐ *adv.* making this sound.

টকানো *v.* to cause to turn sour, to turn sour; to acidify; to cause to rot, to putrefy; to irritate by acidifying (দাঁত টকানো).

টকাস *int.* expressing a light sound made by impact of two hard things (টকাস করে গাট্টা মারা) ; promptness or suddenness (টকাস করে বলে ফেলা).

টকো *a.* sour, acrid; sourish; acidulous.

টক্কর *n.* a jolt; friction; collision, impact; competition, vying. **টক্কর খাওয়া** *v.* to stumble (against); to collide (with). **টক্কর দেওয়া** *v.* to compete or vie (with). **টক্কর বাধানো** *v.* to collide (with); to compete (with); to set at strife (with), to set by the ears; to be in competition or strife (with). **টক্কর লাগা** *v.* to stumble (against); to come in collision (with); to be faced with competition (with), to be vying (with); to be in strife (with).

টগর *n.* a kind of small flower (usu. white), *Tabernamontana coronaria.*

টগবগ, টগবগাবগ *int.* expressing : bubbling noise made by water or any other liquid when being boiled (টগবগ করে ফোটা) ; noise made by or as by hoofs of a horse when running (টগবগ করে চলা) ; fretting and fuming state (রাগে টগবগ করা = to seethe in anger); to boil with indignation.

টঙ alt. spell. of **টং**[১] ।

টঙ্ক[১] *n.* any weapon for cutting or hewing such as an axe or a sword or a scimitar; any tool for digging such as a spud; anger or bragging or arrogance (রোগা লোকের মুখে টঙ্ক).

টঙ্ক[২] *n.* a coin; a rupee. **~পতি** *n.* (obs.) the superintendent of a mint, a mint-master. **~বিজ্ঞান** *n.* numismatics. **~শালা** *n.* a mint.

টঙ্ক[৩] *a.* (dial.) strong, firm.

টঙ্কন *n.* borax.

টঙ্কপতি, টঙ্কবিজ্ঞান, টঙ্কশালা see **টঙ্ক**[২] ।

টঙ্কা *n.* a rupee.

টঙ্কার *n.* the twang of a bowstring; any similar sound (টাকার টঙ্কার).

টঙ্গ[১] var. of **টঙ্ক**[১] ।

টঙ্গ[২], **টঙ্গি** variants of **টং** ।

টন *int.* expressing a sharp metallic sound.

টনক *n.* the seat of memory; remembrance, recollection. **টনক নড়া** *v.* to come to remember or recollect; to be aware of; to be alerted; to be ruffled; to see the gravity of.

টনটন *int.* expressing: severe irritation or pain caused by tightness or tension or strain or overfulness or sharpness. **টনটন করা** *v.* to smart, to twinge, to feel acute or sharp pain. **টনটনানি** *n.* this irritation or pain; throbbing pain (as of an abscess). **টনটনে** *v.* very sharp or sensitive; keenly alive, very much alive (টনটনে জ্ঞান).

টপ[1] *int.* expressing the noise of falling of a drop of liquid. **টপটপ** *int.* expressing repetition of this noise.

টপ[2] *int.* expressing quickness or promptness (টপ করে খেয়ে নাও). **টপাটপ** *adv.* promptly, quickly.

টপ[3] *n.* a small concave mound.

টপকানো *v.* to leap over, to cross by leaping over.

টপতোলা *a.* shaped as a small concave mound.

টপাটপ see **টপ**[2] ।

টপাস *int.* expressing the noise of falling of a large drop of liquid.

টপ্পা *n.* a light classical variety of amorous songs sung in a particular or special or typical mode.

টব *n.* a tub.

টবর্গ *n.* ট্ ঠ্ ড্ ঢ্ ণ্ : these five consonants respectively, the ট-pentad.

টমটম *n.* a tandem.

টম্যাটো *n.* the tomato.

টরেটক্কা *n.* the code of the telegram; the peculiar noise of the telegraph.

টর্চ, টর্চলাইট *n.* a torch. **টর্চের আলো** torch-light.

টর্নি *n.* one who supervises the legal affairs of others; an attorney.

টল var. of **টলন** ।

টলটল *int.* expressing : crystal clearness or slight movement of any liquid. **টলটলানি** *n.* state of being or looking crystal clear; slight stir or movement; stagger; state of being on the verge of downfall or a crash. **টলটলানো** *v.* to look crystal clear; to move or stir slightly; to stagger; to be on the verge of downfall or a crash. **টলটলায়মান** *a.* staggering; on the verge of downfall or crash (টলটলায়মান সিংহাসন) ; (rare) looking crystal clear or stirring slightly. **টলটলে** *a.* (of a liquid) crystal clear.

টলন *n.* dislocation; fall; stagger; bewilderment.

টলমল *int.* expressing : restlessness or agitation, state of being on the verge of tumbling (সিংহাসন টলমল) ; shaking state ('ধরণী টলমল বীরদাপে'). overflowing state ('নদীজল টলমল'). **টলমলানি** *n.* restlessness of agitation; state of being on the verge of tumbling; state of being shaken or quaking; overflowing state, overflow. **টলমলানো** *v.* to become restless or agitated; to be on the verge of tumbling; to be shaking, to quake; to be overflowing.

টলা *v.* to waver, to vacillate (মন টলা) ; to stagger, to totter (পা টলা) ; to shake, to quake (পৃথিবী টলা) ; to tumble, to be dislocated or displaced (সিংহাসন টলা, টলে পড়া) ; to be otherwise; to be retracted (কথা টলা) ; to tend to defect (দলের লোক টলা). □ *n.* wavering, vacillation; stagger, tottering; shake, quake, tumble, dislocation, displacement; change or retraction or non-compliance; flinching. **টলানো** *v.* to cause to waver or vacillate; to cause to stagger or totter; to shake or quake; to cause to tumble, to dislocate or displace; to cause to retract, to cause to go back upon; to cause to flinch or defect.

টসকানো *v.* to be impaired or weakened or damaged (শরীর টসকানো) ; to be run down in health; to die (লোকটা টসকেছে) ; would bend rather than break (টসকায় তো মচকায় না). **টসকানোর লোক নয়** not the person to flinch or defect.

টসটস *int.* expressing : the noise of repeated fall of liquid drops (টসটস করে জল ঝরা) ; state of being overfull with (রসে টসটস) ; state of being flushed with cold (চোখ-মুখ টসটস করছে). **টসটসে** *a.* (over) filled with juice, juicy; flushed with cold or fever.

টহল *n.* ambulation; act of begging by

wandering and singing; a round or beat (as of a watchman); act of going on one's round. **টহল দেওয়া** *v.* to ambulate, to tramp; to beg wandering and singing; to go on one's round, to patrol. **~দার** *n.* an ambulator, a tramper; an ambulating watchman. **~দারি** *n.* ambulation; act of keeping watch by ambulation.

-টা *sfx.* used in Bengali to serve the purpose of the definite article, the (ছেলেটা, দুধটা).

টাইট *a.* tight, fast; strict; close-fisted. **টাইট দেওয়া** *v.* (coll.) to tighten; (sl.) to take one to task.

টাইপ *n.* a printing type, a type; a model or pattern, a kind, a type (নানা টাইপের লোক) ; a typical specimen, a type (নাটকের টাইপচরিত্র) ; typewriting (সে টাইপ জানে). **টাইপ করা** *v.* to typewrite, to type. **টাইপ-করা** *a.* typewritten, typed.

টাইম *n.* time. **টাইম-বাঁধা, টাইম-ধরা** *a.* regulated by fixed intervals of time, punctual; routine.

টাঁক *n.* an aim; a greedy gaze; act of awaiting. **টাঁক করা** *v.* to aim at; to gaze greedily (at); to await.

টাঁকশাল *n.* a mint.

টাঁকা[১] *v.* to stitch, to tack, to sew (বোতাম টাঁকা) ; to put a tuck in, to tuck.

টাঁকা[২] *v.* to aim at; to prophesy or anticipate or guess beforehand or estimate; (now rare) to imprecate (মরণ টাঁকা).

টাঁসা *v.* to stiffen owing to the suspension of blood-circulation; (sl.) to be stone-dead; (sl.) to die (বুড়োটা টেঁসেছে).

টাক[১] *n.* baldness; a bald patch. □ *a.* bald, glabrous (টাক মাথা). **টাক পড়া** to become bald.

টাক[২] *sfx.* about, nearly, approximately (সেরটাক, মাইলটাক).

টাকরা *n.* the palate.

টাকা *n.* a rupee; money (টাকা করা) ; wealth (টাকার মানুষ). **টাকা ওড়ানো** *v.* to squander or fritter away money. **টাকা করা** *v.* to make money, to acquire money; to amass wealth. **টাকা খাওয়া** *v.* to accept bribe. **টাকা ঢালা** *v.* to spend or invest money. **টাকা ভাঙানো** *v.* to change a coin or a currency note. **টাকা মারা** *v.* to misappropriate money; to defalcate or embezzle. **টাকার কুমির** (dero.) a very rich man, a moneyed man. **টাকার গরম** pride of wealth. **টাকার মুখ দেখা** *v.* to begin to earn or obtain money, to come to money; to begin to be solvent; to see good days. **টাকার বাজার** money market. **টাকার মানুষ** a moneyed man, a wealthy man. **~ওয়ালা** *a.* moneyed; wealthy, rich. **~কড়ি, ~পয়সা** *n.* money; wealth. **টাকার শ্রাদ্ধ** squandering of money, pouring money down the drain.

টাকু, টাকুয়া *n.* a spindle, a reel.

টাঙা, টাঙ্গা *n.* a light two-wheeled carriage drawn by a pony, (cp.) a gig.

টাঙানো *v.* to hang up; to rig up (পাল টাঙানো, মশারি টাঙানো). □ *a.* hanging.

টাঙি, টাঙ্গি *n.* a battle-axe.

টাট[১] var. of **টাটি[২]** ।

টাট[২] *n.* a copper plate used in worship and prayer.

টাটকা *a.* fresh, newly grown (টাটকা মাছ বা সবজি) ; not stale (টাটকা খাবার) ; new, recent (টাটকা খবর).

টা-টা *int. n.* goodbye (usu. to children).

টাটানো *v.* to be inflamed. **টাটানি** *n.* inflammation. **চোখ টাটানো** *v.* to be stricken with eyesore; (fig.) to be envious of.

টাটি[১] *n.* a low and small earthen cup.

টাটি[২] *n.* hempen matting, tat; a wall or roof or door made of tat.

টাট্টি *n.* excrement, stool, faeces; latrine, a privy.

টাট্টু *n.* the pony.

টাড়স var. of **তাড়স** ।

টান *n.* a pull or tug (জোর টান) ; attraction (স্নেহের টান) ; attachment, affection (ছেলের প্রতি টান) ; a drawing in, a pull (সিগারেটের টান) ; tightness, tension (গেরোটায় বেশ টান আছে) ; want, need, shortage, scarcity (পয়সার টান) ; demand (বাজারে ভালো বইয়ের টান) ; difficult breathing, spasm (হাঁপানির টান) ; style of writing or painting, flourish (লেখায় সুন্দর টান) ; quick and rather interwoven style of writing as of a veteran writer (টানের লেখা) ; manner of speaking or pronouncing (কথার টান) ; provincialism or typical intonation

(উচ্চারণে যশুরে টান) ; consumption (পোলাওতে খুব টান) ; stretch (এক টানে) ; current (নদীতে খুব টান) ; force (স্রোতের টান) ; contraction (শিরার টান) ; (math. & phys.) tension, strain. **টান দেওয়া** *v.* to pull, to tug; to give a pull; to draw in (as smoke); to snatch; to flourish; to pronounce or speak with provincial accent or intonation or in a peculiar manner. **টান ধরা** *v.* to be in short supply, to run short (পয়সার টান ধরা) ; to contract (শিরায় টান ধরা) ; to have fits of spasm (হাঁপানির টান ধরা) ; to commence to dry up (ঘায়ে টান ধরা). **টানটান** *a.* fully stretched out (টানটান হয়ে শোওয়া) ; very tight or tense; full of vanity or arrogance (টানটান কথা). **টান-টোন** *n. pl.* strokes and flourishes (as in calligraphy or drawing). **একটানে** *adv.* in a single tug or pull; at a stretch.

টানা[১] *n.* (in weaving) a warp; (of a chest or cabinet) a drawer. **~পড়েন** *n.* (lit. & fig.) warp and woof; (fig.) continuous coming and going; the inconvenience or trouble for continuously going back and forth.

টানা[২] *v.* to pull, to tug; to drag (পা টেনে টেনে চলা) ; to draw (রেখা টানা) ; to attract (মন টানা) ; to carry (মাল টানা) ; to move quickly (পা টেনে চলা) ; to be partial to (ছেলের দিকে টানা) ; to stretch out (সুর টানা) ; to cut down expenditure (আয় কম হলে টেনে চলা) ; to smoke or drink (গাঁজা টানা, মদ টানা) ; to extract (রস টানা) ; to consume (খাইয়েরা খুব মিষ্টি টানছে) ; to sell (বাজারে মাল টানা). □ *a.* borne or drawn (ঘোড়ায়-টানা গাড়ি) ; operated by pulling or dragging (টানা পাখা, টানা জাল) ; straight (টানা পথ) ; continuous (টানা তিন ঘণ্টা) ; skimmed (টানা দুধ) ; wide, broad, large, big (টানা চোখ) ; drawn (কালি দিয়ে টানা রেখা) ; quick and somewhat interwoven (টানা লেখা). **গুণ টানা** v. to tow. **বইঠা টানা, দাঁড় টানা** *v.* to row, to scull. **টানা-জাল** *n.* a drag-net. **টানাটানা** *a.* broad, wide, large (টানাটানা চোখ) ; smelling of arrogance or vanity (টানাটানা কথা) ; quick and somewhat interwoven (টানাটানা লেখা). **টানাটানি** *n.* mutual or continuous pulling or tugging or dragging; mutual or continuous attraction; act of dragging forcibly; act of forcing; want, shortage, hardship (টানাটানির সংসার). **টানাটানি করা** *v.* to pull or tug or drag or attract mutually or continuously; to drag forcibly; to force; to cut down expenditure (টানাটানি করে সংসার চালানো). **দড়ি-টানাটানি** *n.* tug-of-war. **টানা-হ্যাঁচড়া** *n.* act of dragging forcibly; act of forcing; continuing or running on with difficulty; coming and going frequently. **একটানা** *a.* continuous; lying at a stretch. **দোটানা** *n.* vacillation, wavering.

টাপুর-টুপুর *int.* expressing a pattering noise as of rain falling.

টাবা *n.* a kind of lime, the citron.

টায়টায়, (coll.) **টায়টোয়** *adv.* just sufficient or enough and no more, barely.

টায়রা *n.* an ornament for the head, a tiara.

টাল[১] *n.* a heap (কাঠের টাল). **টাল করা, টাল দেওয়া** v. to heap.

টাল[২] *n.* curvature (অস্ত্রখানায় একটু টাল আছে) ; inclination (ঘুড়িখানায় টাল আছে) dodge or stagger (টাল খেয়ে পড়া) ; impact, collision, danger, crisis (টাল কাটানো) ; a difficult charge or task or crisis (টাল সামলানো) ; adulation or quibble (টাল দেওয়া) ; a capricious demand (টাল করা). **টাল করা** *v.* to make a capricious demand. **টাল কাটানো** *v.* to get over a crisis. **টাল খাওয়া** *v.* to have a curvature or inclination; to dodge or stagger; to be faced with a crisis; (dial.) to worsen (রোগটা আবার টাল খেল). **টাল দেওয়া** *v.* to put in danger or in a crisis; to try to evade by means of adulation or quibble. **টাল যাওয়া** *v.* to pass through danger or a crisis. **টাল সামলানো** *v.* to get over or steer through a crisis or danger; to manage a difficult charge or task. **টাল হওয়া** *v.* to have a curvature or inclination, to bend or incline. **~বাহানা** *n.* quibble and false pretext. **~মাটাল** *n.* great danger or crisis or turmoil.

টালনি *n.* inclination, bending ('চূড়ার টাল বামে').

টালবাহানা, টালমাটাল see **টাল**[২] ।

টালা *v.* to neglect or waste; to pass ('মনুষ্য দুর্লভ জন্ম বৃথা কেন টাল') ; to evade, to dodge ('সত্য কথা মিথ্যা করি টালে') ; to pay no heed to; to sift (আটা টালা) ; to take back (প্রতিজ্ঞা টালা) ; to circulate (কথা টালা). **~টালি** *n.* repeated or continuous transfer (জিনিসপত্রের টালাটালি) ; circulation (কথা টালাটালি).

টালি *n.* tile. **টালি দিয়ে ছাওয়া** *v.* to tile. **টালি-ছাওয়া** *a.* tiled.

-টি milder var. of **-টা**।

টিউশনি, টিউশানি *n.* tuition; the profession of a private tutor. **টিউশনি করা** *v.* to teach as a private tutor.

টিক *n.* light sound (esp. of a clock or watch), tick; a small mark (✓) put against names, figures etc. **~টিক** *n.* ticking sound (of a clock etc.), tick-tock. **টিকটিক করা** *v.* to make ticks, to tick. **টিক দেওয়া** *v.* to put a small mark or tick against, to tick (off).

টিকটিক *int.* expressing : ticking or tick-tock as of a clock.

টিকটিকি *n.* the common lizard found frequently in dwelling houses; (sarcas.) a detective; (cp.) a sleuth, a nark.

টিকলি *n.* a small piece (আখের টিকলি) ; an ornament for the head, a tiara, an aigrette.

টিকলো *a.* (esp. of features, nose etc.) sharp, pointed.

টিকসই, টিকসহি obs. variants of **টেকসই**।

টিকা১ *n.* a small cake of charcoal dust used as fuel.

টিকা২ *n.* a holy mark or dot on the forehead with sandal-paste etc.

টিকা৩ *n.* vaccination, inoculation. **টিকা দেওয়া** *v.* to vaccinate, to inoculate. **টিকা নেওয়া** to be vaccinated or inoculated.

টিকা৪, টেকা *v.* to stay (ঘরে টেকা) ; to last (ঘড়িটা টিকবে) ; to endure or survive (ধোপে টেকা) ; to stand test or scrutiny (যুক্তি টেকা) ; to remain alive or continue to live (এ রোগী টিকবে না).

টিকাদার *n.* a vaccinator, an inoculator.

টিকানো *v.* to cause to stay or last or endure or survive; to keep alive.

টিকারা *n.* a kind of small kettledrum.

টিকালো older var. of **টিকলো**।

টিকি *n.* a tuft of never-cut hair kept on the back of the head to maintain personal holiness. **টিকির দেখা নেই** not to have even a glimpse of, to find no sign or trace of.

টিকিট *n.* a ticket; a postal stamp, a postage-stamp (usu. **ডাকটিকিট**) ; nomination of a political party for election. **টিকিট কাটা** *v.* to purchase or buy a ticket, to book; to punch a ticket. **টিকিট কেনা** *v.* to purchase a ticket, to book; to purchase postage stamps. **~ঘর** *n.* a booking-office. **~পরীক্ষক** *n.* a ticket-examiner. **~বাবু, ~মাস্টার** *n.* a booking-clerk. **~সংগ্রাহক** *n.* a ticket-collector. **বিনা টিকিটে ভ্রমণ** travelling without tickets.

টিকিন *n.* ticking.

টিকে coll. form of **টিকা১** & **টিকা৩**।

টিটকারি *n.* sneer, ridicule; hooting. **টিটকারি দেওয়া** *v.* to sneer, to ridicule, to hoot.

টিটিভ, টিটির, টিট্টিভ *n.* the partridge; the lapwing.

টিন *n.* tin; a cannister; tinfoil; a tinshed (টিনের বাড়ি). **~মিস্ত্রি** *n.* a tinsmith.

টিনচার আইয়োডিন *n.* tincture iodine.

টিনটিন *int.* expressing : extreme thinness. **টিনটিনে** *a.* very thin.

টিপ *n.* a fingertip; a thumb impression; a quantity taken up between the index finger and the thumb; a dotted mark with sandal paste etc. put on the forehead as a mark of sanctity (টিপ পরা) ; a piece of tinsel or a dotted mark with vermilion, saffron etc. put on the forehead for personal decoration; aim (বন্দুকের টিপ) ; a squeeze or pinch (তার পিঠে একটা টিপ দাও). **এক টিপ নস্যি** a pinch of snuff. **টিপ দেওয়া** *v.* to squeeze, to pinch, to press with fingertips. **~কল** *n.* a device that may be opened and shut or operated by means of pressing. **~বোতাম** *n.* a pair of buttons that may be fixed to one another by pressing them with fingertips, a press-button. **~সই, ~সহি** *n.* thumb impression.

টিপ টিপ *int.* expressing : the noise made by the fall of very small drops (smaller and milder than **টপটপ**), the noise of drizzling; burning or flaming faintly

(টিপটিপ করে জ্বলছে) ; subdued palpitation caused by fear (বুক টিপটিপ করা). **টিপটিপানি** *n.* subdued palpitation caused by fear.

টিপনি, টিপন *n.* act of pressing or massaging or pinching or squeezing or winking; act of cautioning or warning furtively.

টিপা, টেপা *v.* to press; to massage; to pinch; to squeeze; to wink (চোখ টিপছে) ; to caution or warn furtively (তাকে টিপে দিয়ো যেন টাকা না দেয়) ; to place or put noiselessly or cautiously (পা টিপে চলা). □ *a.* that which is to be opened and shut or operated by means of pressing (টেপা কল). **কল টেপা** *v.* (fig.) to direct others from behind the curtain. **চোখ টেপা** *v.* to wink; to give a hint or warn by winking. **নাড়ি টেপা** *v.* to feel (one's) pulse. **টিপে চলা** *v.* (fig.) to spend cautiously.

টিপাই *n.* a teapoy, a tripod.

টিপাটিপি, (coll.) **টেপাটিপি** *n.* mutual pressing or pinching; mutual consultation conducted furtively.

টিপানো *v.* to cause to press or massage or pinch or squeeze.

টিপিটিপি *adv.* stealthily, furtively; in drizzles. □ *a.* stealthy, furtive, drizzling.

টিপুনি pop. var. of **টিপনি** ।

টিপ্পনী *n.* a comment, a gloss; a commentary, a glossary (টীকা-টিপ্পনি) ; a sarcastic comment. **টিপ্পনী কাটা** *v.* to make a sarcastic comment.

টিফিন *n.* a light repast, tiffin; a recess or break in a school or office or factory for taking tiffin, tiffin break.

টিমটিম *int.* expressing : dimness of light or glory; hardly perceptible existence. **টিমটিম করা** *v.* (of a lamp etc.) to burn dimly; (of a glorious object) to be in the last stage of decline, to be at the fag-end of one's glory; (of an institution etc.) to keep up one's existence with great difficulty. **টিমটিমে** *a.* dimly burning; declining, at the fag-end of one's glory; almost passed out of existence.

টিয়া *n.* a species of parrot, the popinjay, the parakeet.

টিলা *n.* a mound, a hillock, a knoll, a hummock.

-টী rej. spell. of **-টি** ।

টীকা *n.* a key, a note; a commentary. **~কার** *n.* a commentator. **~কারে** *adv.* in the form of a commentary.

টীট *a.* (obs. & poet.) shameless, brazen-faced; (obs. & poet.) knavish. **~পনা** *v.* shamelessness, brazen-facedness; knavery.

টুইল *n.* twill.

টুং same as **টুন** ।

টুঁ *n.* the sound : 'toon'; the feeblest possible noise (কোথাও টুঁ শোনা যায় না) ; very feeble protest (তার কথার বিরুদ্ধে কেউ টুঁ করে না).

টুঁটি *n.* the throat, the gullet. **টুঁটি ছেঁড়া** *v.* to tear off or asunder the throat; to kill. **টুঁটি টেপা** *v.* to press the throat; to choke. **টুঁটি টিপে মারা** *v.* to throttle.

টুক *int.* expressing the milder var. of **টক** ।

টুকটাক *a.* small and paltry (টুকটাক জিনিস) ; brief and casual (টুকটাক কাজ বা কথা). □ *adv.* silently but quickly and one after another (টুকটাক করে কাজ করা) ; not affluently yet smoothly (টুকটাক করে সংসার চলা).

টুকটুক *int.* expressing the milder var. of **টকটক** ।

টুকনি *n.* a small beggar's bowl.

টুকরি *n.* a small wicker basket.

টুকরো *n.* a piece, a bit, a fragment, a slip. □ *a.* cut up into pieces. **টুকরো করা** *v.* to cut into pieces; to break into fragments. **টুকরো কাপড়** a small piece of cloth. **টুকরো জমি** a fragment or small parcel of land. **টুকরো টুকরো** in pieces or fragments; cut up into pieces; all to pieces (টুকরো টুকরো হয়ে যাওয়া).

টুকা[1] older var. of **টোকা**[1] ।

টুকা[2] *v.* to sew up, to stitch up.

টুকিটাকি *a.* light and paltry (টুকিটাকি কাজ বা জিনিস বা খাবার). □ *n.* a light and paltry object (টুকিটাকিগুলো সারানো) ; tit-bits, odds and ends.

-টুকু, -টুকুন *sfx.* indicating : smallness or paltriness (খাবারটুকু, কাজটুকু, ব্যথাটুকু).

টুঙি, টুঙ্গি *n.* a high platform; a house or building on a high platform.

টুটই *v.* (poet. & obs.) breaks or break tears or tear, shatters or shatter reduces or reduce, removes or remove.

টুটত *v.* (poet. & obs.) get or gets broken or torn or shattered; are or is reduced or removed.

টুটব *v.* (poet. & obs.) will be broken or torn or shattered or reduced or removed.

টুটা *v.* to be broken or torn or shattered or reduced or removed. □ *a.* broken, torn, shattered. **~নো** *v.* to (cause to) break or tear or shatter; to reduce; to remove. **~যব** *v.* (obs. & poet.) will break or tear or shatter or reduce or remove.

টুন milder or lighter var. of **টন** ।

টুনটুনি *n.* a species of small warbling bird, the tailor-bird.

টুনি[1] affec. var. of **টুনটুনি** ।

টুনি[2] *a.* tiny, very small (টুনিবালব).

টুপ milder or lighter var. of **টপ**[1] ।

টুপি *n.* a cap, a hat. **~ওয়ালা** *a. n.* one wearing a cap or a hat. **টুপি পরানো** *v.* (coll. fig.) to cajole, to coax into taking a responsibility; to deceive, to spoof.

টুল *n.* a stool (usu. a small and low one); (loos.) a bench.

টুলি *n.* (used as a *sfx.*) a locality, a colony or quarters, a town (কুমোরটুলি).

টুলো *a.* taught in a Sanskrit (grammar) school; of a (Sanskrit) school.

টুস milder or lighter var. of **টস** ।

টুসু *n.* a kind of folk song of Bengal.

টুসি, টুসকি *n.* a flip, to fillip.

টুস্কি alt. spell. of **টুসকি** ।

-টে coll. var. of **-টা** ।

টেংরা alt. spell. of **ট্যাংরা** ।

টেংরি *n.* the shin-bone of an animal esp. a sheep or goat; (chiefly hum.) the tibia or the shank. **টেংরির সুপ বা জুস** bone-marrow soup.

টেঁক *n.* (rare) the waist; the fold of the loincloth tied at the waist; (fig.) money in possession (টেঁক খালি). **টেঁক খালি** out of pocket, penniless, broke, stricken with penury. **টেঁকে গোঁজা** *v.* to keep in the fold on the loincloth tied at the waist; to appropriate to oneself firmly; to misappropriate; to keep exclusively to oneself (ছেলেকে টেঁকে গুঁজে রেখো).

টেঁকঘড়ি *n.* a pocket-watch (formerly used to be kept by Indians in the fold of their loincloth).

টেঁকশাল dial. corrup. of **টাঁকশাল** ।

টেঁকা var. of **টিকা**[4] and **টেকা**[4] ।

টেঁটরা *n.* a small drum which is beaten to announce something; announcement by the beat of a drum. **টেঁটরা দেওয়া** *v.* to announce by beating a drum.

টেঁসা, টেঁসে যাওয়া *v.* (sl.) to die.

টেকটেক *int.* expressing : the state of being outspoken and stinging (টেকটেক করে বলা) ; act of bragging or boasting or nagging (টেকটেক করা). **টেকটেকে** *a.* outspoken and stinging.

টেকসই *a.* lasting, durable.

টেকা pop. var. of **টিকা**[4] ।

টেকো[1] dial. corrup. of **টাকু** ।

টেকো[2] *a.* bald, glabrous.

টেক্কা *n.* (of playing cards) an ace; competition, vying; excellence, superiority; triumph. **টেক্কা মারা, টেক্কা দেওয়া** *v.* (lit.) to play an ace; (fig.) to compete or vie with; (fig.) to establish one's superiority or excellence (over another), to triumph over, to outplay, to outvie.

টেক্স rej. spell.of **ট্যাক্স** ।

টেঙরা, টেঙ্গরা rej. spelling of **ট্যাংরা** ।

টেঙরি alt. spell. of **টেংরি** ।

টেটন *n.* a trickster, a knave; a swindler, a cheat; a precocious or pert man. *fem.* **টেটনি** ।

টেটা *n.* a fishing-spear, a harpoon; a spear.

টেড়া *a.* squint-eyed; oblique, awry, sidelong (কাঠখানা টেড়া) ; rude or insinuating (টেড়া কথা) ; haughty or peevish (টেড়া মেজাজ). **~ব্যাঁকা** *a.* not uniform or straight, with many curves, sinuous; distorted, zigzag.

টেড়ি *n.* a parting of hair at one side or on the top of the head. **টেড়ি কাটা** *v.* to dress hair by parting it at one side or on the top of the head.

টেনা, ট্যানা *n.* a piece of rag. **টেনা-পরা** *a.* ragged.

টেনেটুনে *adv.* (fig.) with great difficulty. **টেনেমেনে** same as **টেনেটুনে** ।

টেন্ডাই-মেন্ডাই see **ট্যান্ডাই-ম্যান্ডাই**

টেপা see **টিপা** ।

টেপারি *n.* a species of small juicy fruit

akin to the gooseberry tasting slightly sweet and slightly sour.

টেবিল *n.* a table, a desk.

টেবো *a.* plump or chubby like a lime (টেবো গাল).

টেমি *n.* (dial.) a small oil-lamp.

টের[1] *n.* feeling, sensation; awareness; intimation. **টের পাওয়া** *v.* to feel (ব্যথা টের পাওয়া, মনে টের পাওয়া) ; to sense; to be aware of (বিপদ টের পাওয়া).

টের[2] *n.* a bend; a side, an extremity; a corner; a position removed from company (একটেরে পড়ে থাকা).

টেরছা, টেরচা variants of **তেরছা** ।

টেরা[1] pop. var. of **টেড়া** ।

টেরা[2], **ট্যারা** *a.* squint-eyed, cross-eyed.

টেরি pop. var. of **টেড়ি** ।

টেলিগ্রাফ *n.* telegraph; a telegraphic message, a telegram. **টেলিগ্রাফ করা** *v.* to telegraph, to wire, to cable (also **টেলিগ্রাম করা**).

টেলিফোন *n.* telephone. **টেলিফোন করা** *v.* to telephone, to ring up.

টোকা[1] v. to write down, to take down; to write after, to copy; to copy by adopting unfair means; to point out the faults of; to reprove. **~টুকি** *n.* copying (by an examinee) unfairly from books or scripts in the examination hall; adopting of unfair means.

টোকা[2] *n.* a flip, a fillip; a tap. **টোকা মারা, টোকা দেওয়া** *v.* to flip, to fillip; to tap.

টোকা[3] *n.* a farmer's field-hat, a large straw-made covering for the head to protect it from the sun and rain, a covering for the head made of palm leaves or straw and shaped like a slouch-hat.

টোঙা, টোঙ্গা variants of **টাঙা** ।

টোটকা *n.* an empiric medicine or cure. □ *a.* empiric, empirical; paltry.

টোটা *n.* a cartridge.

টোটো *int.* expressing : continuous or frequent wandering without any aim. **টোটো করা** *v.* to wander continuously or frequently without any aim, to gad about. **টোটো কোম্পানি** a group of idlers or vagrants. **টোটো কোম্পানির ম্যানেজার** (fig.) an inveterate gadabout.

টোড়ি *n.* an Indian musical mode.

টোন *n.* a twisted chord, twine.

টোপ[1] *n.* (dial.) a top-hat or a conical hat.

টোপ[2] *n.* a bait; (fig.) an allurement. **টোপ গেলা** *v.* to swallow a bait. **টোপ ঠোকরানো** *v.* to nibble at the bait. **টোপ ফেলা** *v.* to bait; (fig.) to allure.

টোপ[3] *n.* any diapered fancy-work raised (usu. concavely) from the ground; a drop, a blob.

টোপর *n.* a conical sola hat; a crown or coronet.

টোপা *a.* concave; globate, globular, round; roundish. **~কুল** *n.* the roundish variety of jujube.

টোপানো *v.* to fall or let fall in drops or drop by drop; to distil.

টোয়ানো var. of **তোয়ানো** ।

টোরা *n.* (dial) an ornamental metal girdle for children.

টোল[1] *n.* a Sanskrit (grammar) school.

টোল[2] *n.* a kind of tax, a toll.

টোল[3] *n.* a small depression or hollow; a dimple. **টোল-খাওয়া, টোলপড়া** *a.* slightly depressed or hollowed; dented; dimpled; dimply. **টোল খাওয়া, টোল পড়া** *v.* to have a slight depression; to dimple.

টোলা var. of **টুলি** ।

টৌড়ি var. of **টোড়ি** ।

ট্যাঁ *int.* expressing : cry or scream of an infant (esp. a newborn one); cry of pang. **ট্যাঁট্যাঁ** *int.* expressing : repeated cry of an infant; repeated cry of pang. **ট্যাঁফো** *n.* slightest protest or complaint or adverse comment.

ট্যাঁক alt. spell. of **টেঁক** ।

ট্যাঁপারি var. of **টেপারি** ।

ট্যাংরা *n.* a species of small scaleless river fish.

ট্যাঁস, ট্যাঁশ *n.* (dero.) Eurasian.

ট্যাকস, ট্যাক্স *n.* a tax, a duty.

ট্যাকসি, ট্যাক্সি *n.* a taxi, a taxicab.

ট্যাটন see **টেটন** ।

ট্যাটা alt. spell. of **টেটা** ।

ট্যাভাই-ম্যাভাই *n.* bragging and blustering.

ট্রাঙ্ক *n.* a travelling box or chest (made esp. of steel), a trunk.

ট্রাম *n.* a tramcar, a tram. **~রাস্তা** *n.* a tramroad, a tramway. **ট্রাম-লাইন** *n.* a tramline.

ট্রেন *n.* a railway-carriage, a railway-train.

ঠ *n.* the twelfth consonant of the Bengali alphabet.

ঠং *int.* expressing : a light noise caused by the concussion of a metallic object against a hard thing. **ঠং ঠং** *int.* expressing : this noise made repeatedly or continuously.

ঠক[১] *a.* deceitful; swindling; knavish. □ *n.* a deceiver, a cheat; a swindler; a knave; a trickster. **~বাজ** same as **ঠক** (*a.* & *n.*). **~বাজি** *n.* cheating, swindling; knavery.

ঠক[২] *int.* expressing a rapping noise as of a stick on the floor. **ঠকঠক, ঠকাঠক** *int.* expressing this noise made repeatedly and quickly. **ঠকঠকানো** *v.* to make this noise repeatedly and quickly; to shiver violently (in cold, fear, anger etc.). **ঠকঠকানি** *n.* a spell of rapping noise made repeatedly and quickly; a spell of violent shiver.

ঠকঠকি *n.* a kind of loom, a fly-shuttle loom.

ঠকা *v.* to be cheated or swindled; to lose (to) (আমি তোমার কাছে দু-টাকা ঠকে গেলাম) ; to be defeated or outwitted; to be beguiled. **ঠকানো** *v.* to cheat or swindle; to cause to lose; to defeat or outwit; to beguile. **ঠকানে** *a.* puzzling, confusing, perplexing; misleading (ঠকানে প্রশ্ন).

ঠকাঠক see **ঠক**।

ঠক্কর var. of **ঠোকর**।

ঠগ *a.* given to deception or cheating or swindling; knavish. □ *n.* a trickster; a cheat; a swindler; a knave; a member of a murdering band or robbers once prevalent in India, a thug. **ঠগি** *n.* a murderous band of robbers once prevalent in India, the thug or thuggee.

ঠন *int.* expressing a light, clattering noise as of the concussion of a thin metallic object. **ঠন ঠন** *int.* expressing this noise made repeatedly; nothingness or vacuity or emptiness (পকেট ঠনঠন). **ঠনঠনে** *a.* empty.

ঠমক, ঠসক *n.* style; glamour; affectedly artistic bearing; coquetry; conceit.

ঠাওর coll. & pop. form of **ঠাহর**।

ঠাঁই[১] *int.* expressing the noise as of slapping strongly. **ঠাঁই ঠাঁই** *int.* expressing this noise made repeatedly and quickly.

ঠাঁই[২] *n.* a place; a seat on which one sits to take one's meal (অতিথির জন্য ঠাঁই করা) ; shelter (চোরকে বাড়িতে ঠাঁই দিয়ো না) ; accommodation, room, space ('ঠাঁই নাই ঠাঁই নাই, ছোট সে তরী') ; bottom (নদীর ঠাঁই পাওয়া) ; possession or source. **ঠাঁই-ঠাঁই** *a.* living apart from one another (ভাই-ভাই ঠাঁই-ঠাঁই) ; separated, disunited, disintegrated. **~নাড়া, ~বদল** *n.* change of place.

ঠাকরুন coll. var. of **ঠাকুরানি** (see **ঠাকুর**).

ঠাকুমা coll. var. of **ঠাকুরমা**।

ঠাকুর *n.* a god, a deity; an idol; God; an overlord; a lord; a master; a man deserving respect or reverence (পিতাঠাকুর) ; an elder (সমাজের ঠাকুর হয়ে বসা) ; a spiritual guide, a guru; a priest; a teacher; a Brahman; a Brahman employed as a cook (রান্নার ঠাকুর) ; a father or a forefather; (of a woman) a father-in-law (শ্বশুরঠাকুর). *fem.* **ঠাকুরানি**। **ঠাকুর কাত** (hum.) the patron divine or human has forsaken; (hum.) displeased. **~ঘর** *n.* a room in a dwelling house set apart for worship and prayer. **ঠাকুর ঘরে কে—আমি তো কলা খাইনি** (fig.) an offender often betrays himself unconsciously. **~জামাই** *n.* the husband of a sister of one's husband, a brother-in-law. **~ঝি** *n.* a sister of one's husband, a sister-in-law. **~দাদা** *n.* a (paternal) grandfather or granduncle. **~দালান** *n.* a hall or building attached to or within the precincts of a dwelling house set apart for worship and prayer. **~পূজা** *n.* the daily worship of the guardian deity of a family. **~পো** *n.* a younger brother of one's husband, a brother-in-law. **~মা** *n.* a (paternal) grandmother or grandaunt. **~সেবা** same as ~পূজা। **ঠাকুরালি,** (chiefly poet.) **ঠাকুরাল** *n.* authority, rule; supremacy, predominance; godhead, godhood; godlike deceit or fun or assumption ('ছাড় তোমার ঠাকুরালি').

ঠাঞ্রি obs. spell. of **ঠাঁই**।

ঠাট[১] *n.* (now obs.) a column of troops ('নাদিল ঠাট') ; a party or multitude ('বরাতির ঠাট').

ঠাট[২] *n.* outward look or show, appearance (ঠাট বজায় রাখা) ; a framework (কাঠামোর ঠাট) ; glamour; tricks and artifices (কত ঠাট জানো) ; style or fashion (এ এক নোতুন ঠাট).

ঠাট-ঠমক *n.* outward show of glamour; deceptive show; false gestures; pretences; affectation; parade.

ঠাট-বাট *n.* outward show; grandeur; decoration.

ঠাট্টা *n.* joke; banter, persiflage, waggery. **~ইয়ার্কি** *n.* light raillery, fun, a good-humoured teasing. **ঠাট্টা করা** *v.* to joke; to cut a joke; to poke fun at; to banter. **~বাজ** *n.* a merry person full of amusing sayings and fond of practical jokes, a wag.

ঠাঠা রোদ, ঠাঠাপড়া রোদ *n.* scorching sun.

ঠাড় *a.* erect, upright, vertical.

ঠান *n.* (used in comp. & coll.) a respectable woman, a lady (মাঠান, বউঠান). □ *in comp.* (used as a *pfx.*) of the second degree of parentage, grand (ঠানদিদি). **~দিদি,** (coll.) **~দি** *n.* a (paternal and maternal) grandmother or grandaunt, (arch.) a grandam, a grandma.

ঠান্ডা *a.* cold; chilly; mild, sweet (ঠান্ডা কথা) ; cooled (প্রাণ ঠান্ডা). □ *n.* cold (মাঘের ঠান্ডা) ; chill (ঠান্ডা লাগা). **ঠান্ডা করা** *v.* to cool; to cool down; to console or comfort or pacify or appease (মন ঠান্ডা করা, রাগ ঠান্ডা করা) ; to refresh (দেহ ঠান্ডা করা) ; to subdue, to bring under control (বদমাশ ঠান্ডা করা) ; to put down, to quell (বিদ্রোহ ঠান্ডা করা) ; to put to silence, to kill, to do to death (মেরে ঠান্ডা করা). **ঠান্ডা লাগা** *v.* to catch cold.

ঠান্ডা-লড়াই *n.* cold war.

ঠাম *n.* a place, a resort ('রহল কোন ঠাম') ; possession or company (রাধার ঠাম) ; shape, form, figure (বঙ্কিম ঠাম, সুঠাম দেহ) ; beauty ('কিবা সে ঠাম') ; style, manner, fashion, posture ('চূড়ার টালনি বামে মউর-চন্দ্রিকা ঠামে').

ঠায় *adv.* without moving, motionlessly, fixedly (ঠায় বসে থাকা) ; incessantly or at a stretch (ঠায় উপবাস করা, ঠায় জ্বলছে). □ *a.* incessant or consecutive (ঠায় দুদিন).

ঠার *n.* a beck, a gesticulation. **ঠারা** *v.* to make a sign with, to gesticulate with (চোখ ঠারা). **ঠারে-ঠোরে** *adv.* (coll.) by means of signs and gestures, by hints and insinuations.

ঠাস[১] *int.* expressing the sound as of a violent slap. **ঠাস ঠাস** *int.* expressing quick and repeated sound of such slapping. □ *adv.* making this noise repeatedly and in quick succession.

ঠাস[২] *a.* close, thick, compact, crowded (ঠাস বুননি, ঠাস হয়ে বসা).

ঠাসা *v.* to cram, to stuff; to load; to press, to press down; to knead (ময়দা ঠাসা) ; to beat soundly, to thrash; to reprimand. □ *a.* thoroughly crammed or stuffed or loaded. **~ঠাসি** *n.* act of pressing repeatedly to stuff a thing; overcrowding.

ঠাহর *n.* act of seeing or noticing; visualization; vision, sight; attention, care (ঠাহর করে দেখা) ; recognition; cognition; realization; discernment, act of finding; determination. **ঠাহর করা** *v.* to see, to notice; to visualize; to treat with attention (ঠাহর করা) ; to recognize (তোমাকে তো ঠাহর করতে পারছি না) ; to cognize; to realize; to discern, to find, to think out, to devise, to determine (পথ বা উপায় ঠাহর করা) ; to invent (বুদ্ধি ঠাহর করা) ; to anticipate (এ বিপদের কথা তো ঠাহর করিনি). **ঠাহর পাওয়া** *v.* to come to or be able to see or notice or visualize or recognize or to cognize or realize or discern or find or determine or anticipate. **ঠাহর হওয়া** *v.* to be seen or noticed; to be visible; to be recognized or cognized or realized or discerned or found or determined or anticipated. **ঠাহরানো** same as **ঠাহর করা**।

ঠিক *a.* fixed, settled (এখনও কিছু ঠিক হয়নি) ; appointed, specified (ঠিক দিনে) ; right (ঠিক কথা) ; correct (অঙ্কের ফলটা ঠিক) ; exact, precise (ঠিক) ; just (ঠিক দু-দিন) ; proper, right (ঠিক কাজ, ঠিক লোক) ; in working order (ঘড়িটা ঠিক নেই) ; suitable, fit, fitting (এ জামা তোমার গায়ে ঠিক) ; corrected or cured (মেরে বা ওষুধ দিয়ে ঠিক করা) ; arranged (চুলটা ঠিক নেই) ; regarded, decided, judged, diagnosed (পাগল বলে ঠিক হওয়া). □ *n.* fixity (তারিখের ঠিক নেই) ; firmness (কথার ঠিক) ; regularity or certainty (বৃষ্টির ঠিক নেই) ; natural healthy state (মাথার ঠিক নেই) ; total, sum, addition (ঠিক দেওয়া) ; estimate, estimation (ঠিকে ভুল) ; discernment or determination (পথ বা উপায় ঠিক পাওয়া). □ *adv.* certainly, surely (ঠিক যাব) ; for certain (ঠিক জানি) ; exactly, just (ঠিক তেমনি). □ *int.* exactly, right, that's it. **ঠিক করা** *v.* to fix, to settle; to appoint, to specify; to correct or cure; to repair or regulate or adjust (ঘড়ি ঠিক করা) ; to set to rights; to determine or resolve (মনে মনে ঠিক করা) ; to regard or decide or adjudge (পাগল বলে ঠিক করা) ; to discern or find (পথ ঠিক করা). **ঠিক দেওয়া** *v.* to add, to tot up. **ঠিক পাওয়া** *v.* to be able to discern or find (পথ ঠিক পাওয়া). **ঠিকে ভুল** an error in adding; (fig.) a wrong decision; an error of judgement. **ঠিক যেন** (just) as if, as though, as it were.

ঠিকঠাক *a.* exact, precise, just; firmly fixed or settled.

ঠিকঠিকানা *n.* certainty; fixity; trace; whereabouts; fixed abode or address.

ঠিকরা *n.* a small (and usu. globular) ball of stone or clay used in the bowl of a hookah; an inferior species of pigeon-pea.

ঠিকরানো *v.* to rebound; to scatter or disperse (মালা থেকে মুক্তোগুলো ঠিকরে পড়ল) ; to issue in rays, to radiate (আলো ঠিকরানো) ; to shine or dazzle (হিরেখানা আলোতে ঠিকরাচ্ছে) ; to be dazed (চোখ ঠিকরানো).

ঠিকরে coll. var. of **ঠিকরা** ।

ঠিকা *a.* employed for part-time or casual service, hired, part-time (ঠিকা ঝি) ; temporary (ঠিকা চাকরি) ; holding possession temporarily for a fixed period (ঠিকা প্রজা) ; hired, hackney (ঠিকা গাড়ি) ; that which is done on contract or on piece-system (ঠিকা কাজ). □ *n.* a work done by contract, a contract (ঠিকা পাওয়া) ; a sub-contract; lease (জমি ঠিকা নেওয়া). **ঠিকা কাজ** a piece-work; a temporary job; a part-time job. **ঠিকা গাড়ি** a hackney-coach, a hackney-carriage. **ঠিকা চাকর** a hired servant; a hireling. **ঠিকা ঝি** a hired maidservant, a charwoman. **ঠিকা প্রজা** a temporary tenant. **ঠিকা মজুর** a hired or casual labour or a hireling.

ঠিকাদার *n.* a contractor. **ঠিকাদারি** *n.* contractorship. □ *a.* relating to contract work.

ঠিকানা *n.* an address (as given in a letter); one's fixed residence; trace, direction or location (পথের ঠিকানা) ; a clue or solution (চুরির ঠিকানা) ; fixity or limit (আয়ের ঠিকানা).

ঠিকুজি *n.* a brief horoscope.

ঠিকে coll. var. of **ঠিকা** ।

ঠুং milder or lighter var. of **ঠং** । **ঠুং ঠুং** milder or lighter var. of **ঠং ঠং** ।

ঠুংরি *n.* a mode and measure of a light classical Indian music.

ঠুঁটা, (coll.) **ঠুঁটো** *a.* handless; (fig.) powerless, incapable. **ঠুঁটো জগন্নাথ** (lit.) the handless deity of Puri, Juggernaut; (fig.) one in office but rendered powerless, one in a high position but with no power, a puppet.

ঠুক *int.* expressing the noise of a gentle stroke or rap (ঠুক করে আওয়াজ হল). **ঠুকঠাক** *int. n.* repeated noise of gentle stroke or rap. **ঠুক ঠুক** *int. n.* same as **ঠুকঠাক** ; the noise of a gentle rap; a word denoting (usu.) the carpenter's or blacksmith's gentle manner of work.

ঠুকরানো *v.* to peck, to nibble; to nibble at a bait. □ *a.* pecked; nibbled at.

ঠুকা, ঠোকা *v.* to hit esp. on the head (হাতুড়ি ঠোকা) ; to hammer; to drive in by hitting on the head (পেরেক ঠুকছে) ; to strike against, to knock, to rap (মাথা ঠোকা, গোড়ালি ঠোকা, লাঠি ঠোকা) ; to slap noisily (তাল ঠোকা) ; to beat or thrash, to scold or reprimand (লোকটাকে ঠুকে দিয়ো). □ *n.* a knock or impact; beating or thrashing, scolding or reprimanding. **ঠুকাঠুকি, ঠোকাঠুকি** *n.* repeated striking (on the head); repeated (slight) collision or quarrel; mutual bantering.

ঠুঙ্গি, ঠুঙি *n.* a small container or carton (chiefly bowl-shaped) made of tree-leaves or paper, a cornet.

ঠুন milder or lighter var. of **ঠন**। **ঠুন ঠুন** milder or lighter var. of **ঠন ঠন**।

ঠুনকো[১] *n.* milk fever (also ঠুনকো জ্বর).

ঠুনকো[২] *a.* brittle, fragile; (fig.) unstable or trivial (ঠুনকো দেমাক, ঠুনকো কথা).

ঠুমকি *n.* a mode or posture of dancing.

ঠুলি *n.* a flap to prevent an animal from seeing, a blinker; a blind.

ঠুস milder or lighter var. of **ঠাস**। **ঠুসঠাস** *int.* expressing : repeated noise of **ঠুস** and **ঠাস** alternatingly; act of beating or acting mildly and violently in alternation.

ঠুসা var. of **ঠাসা**।

ঠেং rej. spell. of **ঠ্যাং**।

ঠেঁটা *a.* shameless, brazen-faced; knavish; deceitful; impertinent, impudent, saucy; outspoken; disobedient, arrogant, obstinate, refractory.

ঠেঁটামি, ঠেঁটামো *n.* shamelessness; rude disrespect, impudence, sauciness; impertinence, brazen-facedness; arrogance, obstinacy, refractoriness.

ঠেঁটি *n.* a small loincloth without any decorated border.

ঠেক, ঠেকনা, (coll.) **ঠেকনো** *n.* a prop, a support, a lean-to; (fig.) temporary or interim support or lease of life. **ঠেক দেওয়া, ঠেকনা দেওয়া** *v.* to prop; (fig.) to give a temporary or interim support or lease of life.

ঠেকা *v.* to touch (আকাশে ঠেকা, পায়ে ঠেকা) ; to reach, to reach and stop at (তিরটা গিয়ে গাছে ঠেকল) ; to come down to (আয় শূন্যে ঠেকেছে) ; to strike or dash against (বলটা দেওয়ালে ঠেকে ফিরে এল) ; to be obstructed or impeded or prevented, to be at a dead end or at a knotty point (অঙ্কটা ঠেকছে কীসে) ; to be involved in (দায়ে ঠেকা, বিপদে ঠেকা) ; to be involved in difficulty or danger, to be in a fix (ঠেকে শেখা) ; to be felt or considered (খারাপ ঠেকা). □ *n.* a difficulty, a fix (ঠেকায় পড়া) ; financial difficulty or want (ঠেকার কাজ চালানো) ; touch, contact (ঠেকা লাগা) ; act of accompanying a piece of music by beating 'tabla' (তবলা) (ঠেকা ছাড়া ঠুংরি জমে না) ; a prop, a support, a lean-to (ঘরের চালে ঠেকা দেওয়া). □ *a.* touching (আকাশে ঠেকা মাথা). **চোখে ঠেকা** *v.* to look bad or uncomely. **ঠেকে ঠেকে বলা** to speak haltingly. **ঠেকাঠেকি** *n.* mutual touching or contact. **ঠেকানো** *v.* to cause to touch, to bring into contact; to cause to reach; to cause to reach and stop; to bring to; to cause to strike or dash against; to obstruct, to impede, to prevent; to stave off; to involve; to involve in difficulty or danger.

ঠেকাঠেকি, ঠেকানো see **ঠেকা**।

ঠেকার *n.* false vanity, vainglory; fastidiousness; superciliousness; snobbery. **ঠেকারে** *a.* vainglorious; fastidious; supercilious; snobbish. *fem* **ঠেকারি**।

ঠেকো var. of **ঠেক**।

ঠেঙা *n.* a staff, a stave, a wooden pole, a heavy stick, a lathi; a wooden rod (esp. one used for bolting a door). **ঠেঙাঠেঙি** *n.* act of exchanging blows with lathis, a fight with lathis; fighting. **ঠেঙাড়ে** *n.* a community of Indian robbers who used to kill pedestrians by beating them with lathis; one of these robbers. **ঠেঙানি** *n.* act of flogging with a lathi; flogging. **ঠেঙানো** *v.* to flog with a lathi or rod; to bastinado; to flog, to birch.

ঠেঙে *a.* (used *in comp.*) legged (একঠেঙে = one-legged).

ঠেঞে (obs. poet.) *prep.* from.

ঠেলা *n.* a shove, a push (ঠেলা দেওয়া) ; a difficulty or a difficult task (ঠেলা সামলানো) ; a hand-cart or a hand-barrow. □ *a.* that which is driven by pushing with hands (ঠেলাগাড়ি). □ *v.* to push, to shove; to ignore or disobey (কথা ঠেলা) ; to avoid or desert ('না ঠেলহ ছলে অবলা অখলে') ; to expel (জাতে ঠেলা).

জাতে ঠেলা, সমাজে ঠেলা *v.* to outcaste, to excommunicate, to boycott socially. **ঠেলার নাম বাবাজি** (fig.) a cat in a mesh calls the mouse its brother. **~গাড়ি** *n.* a push-cart, a hand-barrow. **~ঠেলি** *n.* mutual or repeated shoving or pushing.

ঠেস *n.* act of leaning; recumbence; anything to lean against (চেয়ারের ঠেস) ; a prop or support; an insinuating remark (ঠেস মারা). **ঠেস দেওয়া** *v.* to lean against; to provide with a prop, to prop; to make an insinuation against. **ঠেস মারা** *v.* to insinuate against.

ঠেসা var. of **ঠাসা** ।

ঠেসান *n.* act of leaning; recumbence; the back (of a chair or bench). **ঠেসান দেওয়া** *v.* to lean (against).

ঠোঁট *n.* the lip; the beak (of a bird). **ঠোঁট ওলটানো, ঠোঁট বাঁকানো** *v.* to pout lips in derision or contempt. **ঠোঁট ফোলানো** *v.* to pout lips in displeasure. **ঠোঁট-কাটা** *a.* outspoken; (lit. & rare) harelipped.

ঠোকন, ঠোকনি *n.* (coll.) reprimanding or flogging.

ঠোকর *n.* act of pecking or nibbling; a light kick with the tip of one's toes or shoe; act of stumbling (against); reprimand; act of interposing a speaker with a small sharp cutting remark. **ঠোকর খাওয়া** *v.* to stumble (against); to be reprimanded. **ঠোকর দেওয়া, ঠোকর মারা** *v.* to peck or nibble; to kick lightly with the tip of one's toes or shoe; to reprimand; to interpose (a speaker) or to chip in with a small sharp cutting remark.

ঠোকরানো pop. var. of **ঠুকরানো** ।

ঠোকা pop. var. of **ঠুকা** ।

ঠোক্কর var. of **ঠোকর** ।

ঠোঙা *n.* a container or carton (chiefly bowl-shaped) made of tree-leaves or paper, a cornet.

ঠোনা *n.* a light box on the chin. **ঠোনা মারা** *v.* to box one's chin lightly.

ঠোস *n.* (dial.) fullness, overfullness, fill (পেট ঠোস হয়েছে) ; (dial.) a swelling; (dial.) a blister (নোতুন জুতোয় পায়ে ঠোস পড়েছে).

ঠোসা pop. var. of **ঠুসা** ।

ঠ্যাং *n.* leg; shank.

ঠ্যাঁটা alt. spell. of **ঠেঁটা** ।

ঠ্যাঁটামি, ঠ্যাঁটামো alt. spellings of **ঠেঁটামি, ঠেঁটামো** ।

ঠ্যাকার alt. spell. of **ঠেকার** ।

ঠ্যাঙা alt. spell. of **ঠেঙা** ।

ঠ্যাঙানো alt. spell. **ঠেঙানো** ।

ড *n.* the thirteenth consonant of the Bengali alphabet.

ডওর coll. var. of **ডহর**।

ডক *n.* a dock.

ডগ dial. var. of **ডগা**।

ডগডগ *int.* expressing deepness or brightness. **ডগডগে** *a.* very deep or bright (ডগডগে লাল, ডগডগে রং).

ডগমগ *a.* overflowing with, brimming over with (আহ্লাদে ডগমগ). **ডগমগ করা** *v.* to overflow with, to brim over with.

ডগরা *a.* (dial.) huge, very big, outsize.

ডগা *n.* tip or top or extremity or point (আঙুলের ডগা, গাছের ডগা, সুতোর ডগা, তরোয়ালের ডগা).

ডঙ্কা *n.* a large kettle-drum, a trumpet, a drum. **ডঙ্কা দেওয়া, ডঙ্কা মারা** *v.* to announce by drum-beat; to beat a drum; to announce proudly in public. **ডঙ্কা মেরে চলে যাওয়া** (fig.) to meet death triumphantly, to pass away defying death; (lit.) to pass away triumphantly.

ডজন *n.* a dozen. **ডজন-ডজন** *a.* dozens of. **ডজনে ডজনে** *adv.* dozens of; in or by dozens.

ডন *n.* a system of free-hand exercise by waving the diaphragm on fours.

ডবকা *a.* (usu. *fem.*) one who or that which attained youth recently, adolescent, juvenescent (ডবকা মেয়ে) ; blooming (ডবকা বয়স).

ডবডব *int.* expressing : tearfulness or largeness; widened state. **ডবডবে** *a.* tearful or large (ডবডবে চোখ) ; widened.

ডবল *a.* double. **ডবল করা** *v.* to double. **ডবল দেওয়া** *v.* (in card-playing) to double.

ডমরু *n.* a kind of small tabour shaped like an hour-glass and played by shaking it with one hand. **~মধ্য** *a.* having a waist as slender as the middle of the aforesaid tabour.

ডম্ফ[1] *n.* (obs.) a kind of small drum.

ডম্ফ[2] *n.* (obs.) boast. **ডম্ফ করা** *v.* to boast, to vaunt.

ডম্বর *n.* an ostentatious show or a great crowd (মেঘডম্বর, মধুকর-ডম্বর).

ডম্বরু, ডম্বুরু, ডম্বুর variants of **ডমরু**।

ডর *n.* (poet. & dial.) fear, fright, dread. **ডর করা** *v.* to fear; to be frightened. **ডর লাগা** *v.* to be frightened.

ডরা, ডরানো *v.* to fear, to dread.

ডলন *n.* rubbing; massaging; act of pressing or kneading (তামাক ডলন) ; (rare) rolling into a thin cake; a roller for shaping thin cakes, bread etc.

ডলা *v.* to rub; to massage; to press or knead (তামাক ডলা). **ডলাই-মলাই** *n.* massage. **ডলানো** *v.* to cause to rub or massage or press or knead.

ডহর *a.* deep or fathomless (ডহর পানি). □ *n.* a deep lake or channel or watercourse; an extremely deep pit, an abyss; the hold of a ship or boat.

ডাইন[1], (কথ্য) **ডান**[1] *n.* the right-side. □ *a.* lying on or to the right, right. **ডাইনে আনতে বাঁয়ে কুলায় না** earning less than what one requires to spend, failing to make both ends meet. **ডান হাত** (lit.) the right hand; (fig.) the principal helper or aid. **ডান হাত বাঁ-হাত করা** to give and take, to exchange; to transfer; to misappropriate. **ডান হাতের ব্যাপার** act of eating.

ডাইন[2], **ডাইনি,** (coll.) **ডান**[2] *n. fem.* a witch.

ডাইল obs. form of **ডাল**[1]।

ডাংগুলি *n.* tipcat.

ডাঁই *n.* a heap, a pile. **ডাঁই করা** *v.* to heap (up), to pile (up).

ডাঁট[1] *n.* a handle; a haft.

ডাঁট[2] *n.* (coll.) firmness; spiritedness, vigour; (coll.) vanity or arrogance. **ডাঁট করা, ডাঁট দেখানো, ডাঁট মারা** *v.* (coll.) to assume an air of firmness or spiritedness or superiority or vanity or arrogance; to parade.

ডাঁটা[1] *n.* a stalk or stem (of a plant); the point at which a fruit is fixed to the bough of a tree.

ডাঁটা[2] *v.* to rebuke, to reprimand, to pull up.

ডাঁটি *n.* a small handle; a small haft; a small pestle.

ডাঁটো *a.* hard, difficult; unripe or incompletely ripened (ডাঁটো ফল) ; (chiefly of aged persons) still strong or robust or able-bodied (ডাঁটো লোক) ; incompletely boiled, parboiled (ডাঁটো ভাত).

ডাঁশ *n.* the gadfly; the gnat.

ডাঁসা, ডাঁশা *a.* half-ripe; incompletely ripened. □ *v.* to ripen, (fig.) to become experienced. **ডাঁসানো, ডাঁশানো** *v.* to cause to ripen; (fig.) to make experienced.

ডাক[1] *n.* the gallinule; the waterfowl.

ডাক[2] *n.* ornaments of sola, tinsel etc. used to decorate an idol (ডাকের সাজ).

ডাক[3] *n.* an ancient milkman famous for his wisdom (ডাকের বচন).

ডাক[4] *n.* a goblin attending upon Shiva (শিব). **~সাইটে** *a.* famous and formidable (ডাকসাইটে জমিদার) ; (often hum.) widely famous (ডাকসাইটে কবি). **~সিদ্ধ** *a.* one who has brought 'Dak' (ডাক) the goblin under one's control.

ডাক[5] *n.* the call or invitation or summons (মায়ের ডাক, ভোজনের ডাক, যুদ্ধের ডাক) ; a note, a call, chirping, a cry, a roar (পাখির ডাক, পশুর ডাক) ; a shout, a scream (ডাক পাড়া) ; a rumbling noise (মেঘের ডাক) ; a professional invitation to attend a patient etc., a call (ডাক্তার ডাকে গেছেন) ; an offer of price at a sale, a bid (নিলামের ডাক) ; fame, celebrity (নামডাক). **ডাক-নাম** *n.* a nickname; a pet name. **ডাকের সুন্দরী** a woman widely famous for her beauty. **এক-ডাকে চেনা** to recognize one at the first mention (as one's name is known to all). **ইঁদুরের ডাক** squeak. **কাকের ডাক** caw. **কুকুরের ডাক** bark; howl. **গাধার ডাক** bray. **গোরুর ডাক** low. **ঘুঘুর ডাক** coo. **ঘোড়ার ডাক** neigh. **নেকড়ের ডাক** bark, howl. **পাতিহাঁসের ডাক** cackle. **পায়রার ডাক** coo. **প্যাঁচার ডাক** hoot, screech. **বাঘের ডাক** growl. **বাঁদরের ডাক** chatter. **বিড়ালের ডাক** mew. **ব্যাঙের ডাক** croak. **ভালুকের ডাক** growl. **ভেড়ার ডাক** bleat. **মউমাছির ডাক** hum, buzz. **মেঘের ডাক** roar, rumble. **মোরগের ডাক** crow, cluck, cackle. **রাজহাঁসের ডাক** hiss, cackle. **শকুনের ডাক** scream. **শিয়ালের ডাক** yelp, howl. **শুয়োরের ডাক** grunt. **ষাঁড়ের ডাক** bellow. **সিংহের ডাক** roar. **হাতির ডাক** trumpet.

ডাক[6] *n.* an established system of conveying letters, post (ডাকবিভাগ) ; a batch of letters, mail, dak (বিলাতের ডাক). □ *in comp.* postal, post-mail (ডাকবাক্স, ডাকগাড়ি). **ডাকে** *adv.* by post. **~খরচা** *n.* postal charge, postage. **ডাকের ঘোড়া** a horse employed to carry mails. **ডাকের থলি** a mailbag. **~খানা, ~ঘর** *n.* a post-office. **~গাড়ি** *n.* a mailcoach; a mail van; a mail train. **~টিকিট** *n.* a postal stamp. **~পিওন, ~পিয়ন** *n.* a postman (*fem.* a postwoman). **~বাংলা, ~বাংলো** *n.* a house for travellers, a dak bungalow. **~বাক্স** *n.* a pillar-box, a letter-box. **~বিভাগ** *n.* the postal department. **~মাশুল** *n.* postage. **~হরকরা** *n.* a postman; a mail-runner. **~যোগে** *adv.* by post. **ফেরত ডাক** next return mail. **ফেরত ডাকে** by return of post, by return mail.

ডাকা *v.* to call (পাখি ডাকে) ; to summon, to ask to come (দরবারে ডাকা) ; to invite (খেতে ডাকা) ; to address (নাম ধরে ডাকা) ; to pray to or invoke (ভগবানকে ডাকা) ; to offer a price at a sale, to bid (নিলাম ডাকা) ; to bid or call in card games; to roar or rumble (মেঘ ডাকে) ; to attract (পথ আমাকে ডাকে) ; to make undesirable or morbid noise (নাক ডাকা, পেট ডাকা) ; to apprehend (বিপদ ডাকা). **ডেকে বলা** *v.* to call one by name and then announce; to announce loudly.

ডাকাডাকি *n.* repeated calling esp. with a great noise.

ডাকাত *n.* a gangster, a dacoit, a robber, a brigand, a bandit. **ডাকাত পড়া** *v.* to be raided by dacoits or brigands. **ডাকাতি** *n.* banditry, brigandage, robbery. **ডাকাতি করা** *v.* to commit a dacoity or robbery. **ডাকাতে** *a.* of dacoits; relating to dacoity. **ডাকাতে কালী** Goddess Kali (কালী) as worshipped by dacoits.

ডাকানো *v.* to send for; to cause to call.

ডাকাবুকো *a.* uncommonly daring, daredevil; fearless.

ডাকিনী *n.* a female goblin attending upon Shiva (শিব) or Durga (দুর্গা) ; a witch.

ডাকু coll. form of **ডাকাত**।

ডাক্তার *n.* a physician, a doctor; (now rarely) a holder of a doctorate degree. **~খানা** *n.* a doctor's chamber; a dispensary; a pharmacy; a drug-store, chemist's shop. **ডাক্তারি** *n.* medical science (ডাক্তারি পড়া) ; medical profession or practice (ডাক্তারি করা). □ *a.* relating to the medical science or profession or practice; relating to a physician; medical. **ডাক্তারি করা** *v.* to practise medicine; (chiefly hum.) to treat or examine medically, to show off one's medical skill. **ডাক্তারি পড়া** *v.* to study medicine. **ডাক্তারি বিদ্যা** *n.* medical science; (often hum.) knowledge of medical science.

ডাগর *a.* large, big, wide ('ডাগর আঁখি যদি দিয়েছিলে') ; grown-up, full-grown (ডাগর মেয়ে) ; costly or excellent ('সাগরের মত নারী ডাগর জিনিস').

ডাঙশ *n.* a goad.

ডাঙা *n.* land; upland; high and dry land (ডাঙা জমি) ; coast, shore, bank (জল থেকে ডাঙায় ওঠা) ; a habitual place of production or birth or multiplication (ফরাসডাঙা, নারকেলডাঙা) ; an abode (কালিডাঙা). **~পথ** *n.* overland route. **ডাঙায় বাঘ জলে কুমির** (fig.) between Scylla and Charybdis, between the horns of a dilemma, between the devil and the deep sea.

ডান see **ডাইন**[1] & **ডাইন**[2]।

ডানপিটে *a.* uncommonly daring, daredevil; (rare) indomitable or obstinate. **~গিরি, ~মি** *n.* daredevil activities.

ডানা *n.* a wing (as of birds); a fin (as of fish). **ডানাকাটা পরি** a woman or girl as beautiful as a fairy. **ডানা গজানো** *v.* (fig. usu. iron.) to begin to be precociously independent; to grow up enough to act independently.

ডান্ডা *n.* a thick rod of iron, wood etc., a staff, a cudgel. **ডান্ডা মারা** *v.* to strike or hit with a rod. **~গুলি** *n.* tipcat.

ডান্ডি *n.* a kind of roofed litter used in carrying passengers along mountain-paths.

ডাব *n.* the green coconut.

ডাবর *n.* a small metal basin.

ডাবা[1], **ডাব্বা** *n.* a large earthen trough or tub; a kind of hookah with a large water-container made of coconut-shell. □ *a.* having a large water-container (ডাবা হুকা).

ডাবুহাতা *n.* a big spoon, a ladle.

ডামাডোল *n.* widespread and disorderly turmoil; widespread and tumultuous confusion; hurly-burly.

ডাম্বেল *n.* a dumb-bell. **ডাম্বেল করা, ডাম্বেল ভাঁজা** *v.* to take exercise with dumb-bells.

ডায়মন *n.* bevel-work as is done on a piece of diamond. **ডায়মন-কাটা** *a.* bevelled as a piece of diamond (ডায়মন-কাটা চুড়ি) ; (often sarcas.) as beautiful as a piece of bevelled diamond (ডায়মন-কাটা মুখ).

ডারা *v.* (poet.) to sacrifice or pour down ('জীবন দিনু ডারি', 'বক্ষ-শোণিত ডারি দিব তব পায়ে').

ডাল[1] *n.* pigeon-pea, dal; soup of pigeon-pea. **~পুরি** *n.* a thin round cakelike food of flour and pasted dal or pigeon-pea.

ডাল[2] *n.* a bough, a branch; a twig.

ডালকুত্তা *n.* the greyhound.

ডালচিনি dial. corrup. of **দারচিনি**।

ডালনা *n.* a kind of rich curry or gravy.

ডালপালা *n. pl.* branches twigs and leaves of a tree; (fig.) offshoots.

ডালমুট *n.* a tasty and spicy mixture of fried gram, salt and monkey-nuts.

ডালা *n.* a small open wicker-basket shaped like a high-rimmed tray; such a basket containing offerings to a deity (কালীবাড়ির ডালা) ; (fig.) a container or depository or store (রূপের ডালা) ; a lid (বাক্সের ডালা).

ডালি *n.* (dim. of **ডালা**) a small high-rimmed wicker-tray; such a tray containing offerings to a deity (পূজার ডালি) ; any basket containing presents usu. given to one's superior or boss (বড়দিনে বড়সাহেবকে ডালি দেওয়া) ; (fig.) a container or repository (রূপের ডালি).

ডালিম *n.* the pomegranate.

ডাহা *a.* out and out, downright (ডাহা মিথ্যা) ; thorough; absolute (ডাহা নকল).

ডাহিন elegant but now rarely used form of **ডাইন**[1] ।

ডাহুক *n.* the gallinule; the waterfowl.

ডিক্রি *n.* a decree. **ডিক্রি জারি করা** *v.* to execute a decree. **ডিক্রি দেওয়া** *v.* to decree. **ডিক্রি পাওয়া** *v.* to obtain a decree. **~দার** *n.* a decree-holder.

ডিগডিগ *int.* expressing extreme leanness. **ডিগডিগে** *a.* extremely lean.

ডিগবাজি *n.* a tumble, a somersault, a vault. **ডিগবাজি খাওয়া, ডিগবাজি দেওয়া** *v.* to tumble, to somersault, to vault.

ডিগ্রি *n.* a degree signifying : unit of measurement for angles; unit of measurement for temperature; academic title given by a university; one of the three forms of comparison of an adjective or adverb.

ডিঙা[1], **ডিঙ্গা**[1] *n.* a boat, a vessel; a sailing-ship.

ডিঙা[2], **ডিঙ্গা**[2] *n.* act or state of standing tiptoe. **ডিঙা মারা** *v.* to stand or skip tiptoe. **ডিঙা মেরে চলা** *v.* to skip along on tiptoe.

ডিঙানো *v.* to cross by leaping, to leap over (সাগর ডিঙানো) ; to cover by leaping (সাত মিটার ডিঙানো).

ডিঙি[1], **ডিঙ্গি**[1] variants of **ডিঙা**[2] ।

ডিঙি[2], **ডিঙ্গি**[2] *n.* a small boat.

ডিণ্ডিম *n.* a musical instrument of percussion.

ডিপো *n.* a depot; (fig.) a birth-place or habitat (রোগের বা মশার ডিপো).

ডিবা, (coll.) **ডিবে** *n.* a small box or container (পানের বা নস্যির ডিবে) ; a small lamp with no cover or chimney for the flame (কোরোসিনের ডিবে).

ডিম *n.* an egg (of ducks, hens, geese, birds, snakes, ants etc.); spawn (of fish); the calf of the leg. **ডিম ছাড়া** *v.* to lay an egg; to spawn. **ডিম পাড়া** *v.* to lay an egg. **ডিম ফোটানো, ডিমে তা দেওয়া** *v.* to hatch. **ডিমের কুসুম** yolk. **ডিমের খোলা** an eggshell. **ডিমের শ্বেতাংশ** the white of an egg, glair. **ঘোড়ার ডিম** (fig.) an absurd or fantastic thing, a mare's nest. **ডিম-ডিম** *a.* globular, granular.

ডিমাই *n.* demy, a size of paper (56.4 × 44.4 cm.).

ডিমিডিমি *int.* expressing the low sound of an instrument of percussion, thud.

ডিম্ব *n.* (*High*) an egg (of birds, ducks, hens, geese, snakes etc.) spawn (of fish etc.) **ডিম্বক** *n.* ovule. **ডিম্বকত্বক** *n.* integument. **ডিম্বকনাড়ী** *n.* funiculus. **ডিম্বকনাভি** *n.* hilum. **~কোষ** *n.* (bot.) ovary; egg-cell; ovum. **ডিম্বজ** *a.* oviparous. **ডিম্বাকার** *a.* egg-shaped, oval. **ডিম্বাণু** *n.* an egg-cell, ovum. **ডিম্বাশয়** *n.* ovary.

ডিশ *n.* a dish.

ডিসমিস *a.* dismissed. **ডিসমিস করা** *v.* to dismiss.

ডিহি *n.* a collection or group or union of villages.

ডুকরানো *v.* to weep or wail aloud. **ডুকরে ওঠা, ডুকরে কাঁদা** same as **ডুকরানো** ।

ডুগডুগি *n.* a small tabor played by moving it with one hand.

ডুগি *n.* the smaller one of the pair of a musical instrument of percussion (see **তবলা**).

ডুণ্ডুভ *n.* a species of non-venomous water-snake.

ডুব *n.* a plunge into water, liquid, air etc.; a dive, a dip; immersion; ablution. **ডুব দেওয়া, ডুব মারা** *v.* to dive, to dip, to plunge; to sink; to go in hiding (চোরটা ডুব দিয়েছে). **ডুব পাড়া** *v.* to dive or dip repeatedly. **ডুবন** *n.* act of diving or dipping; immersion; ablution; submersion; act of sinking. **~জল** *n.* a mass of water as will drown a person standing erect on his feet. **~ন্ত** *a.* one who or that which is sinking or setting; drowning, sinking. **ডুবরি** var. of **ডুবুরি** ।

ডুবা *v.* to sink; to be submerged; to be drowned; to be ruined (ব্যাঙ্ক ফেল হওয়ায় সে ডুবেছে) ; to fail (কারবার ডুবেছে) ; to set (চাঁদ ডুবেছে). □ *a.* sunk; submerged; drowned; ruined; that which has failed, in liquidation; that which has set, sunken. **ডুবানো** *v.* to cause to sink; to submerge; to drown; to ruin; to cause to fail, to liquidate. **ডুবারি** var. of **ডুবুরি** । **ডুবে ডুবে জল খায়, শিবের বাবাও টের পায় না** (fig.) practises a vice or vices so secretly that even God is not aware of it.

ডুবি *n.* an instance of sinking (নৌকাডুবি).

ডুবুডুবু *a.* almost sunk or submerged or drowned or ruined or failed or set; on the point of sinking, about to sink, on the point of being submerged or drowned or ruined, on the point of failing or setting.

ডুবুরি *n.* a diver. **ডুবুরি-পাখি** *n.* a diving bird.

ডুবো *a.* submarine, underwater, submerged, drowned, sinking. **~জাহাজ** *n.* a submarine. **~ পাহাড়** a hill under water, a submarine mountain.

ডুম *n.* an electric bulb.

ডুমনি see **ডোম** ।

ডুমা *n.* a cube-shaped piece or slice. **ডুমাডুমা** *a.* cut into cube-shaped pieces; cube-shaped and numerous.

ডুমুর *n.* the fig. **ডুমুরের ফুল** (fig.) an almost invisible object (like figflowers which lie invisibly within the fruits); (fig.) a rare object, rara avis.

ডুমো coll. var. of **ডুমা** ।

ডুরি *n.* a thin rope or cord or string; bondage, bonds.

ডুরে *a.* with horizontal stripes, striped (ডুরে শাড়ি).

ডুলি *n.* a small covered litter, an improvised palanquin, a doolie.

ডেউয়া, ডেও[1] *n.* the coral tree or its fruit.

ডেও[2] *n.* a large and black species of ant.

ডেঁড়েমুষে *adv.* (coll.) licking up or consuming thoroughly; thoroughly, completely.

ডেঁপো *a.* precocious; saucy, pert. **~মি** *n.* precociousness, precocity; sauciness, pertness.

ডেক[1] *n.* a large metallic cooking utensil, a large dixie.

ডেক[2] *n.* a deck (of a ship or omnibus).

ডেকচি *n.* a metallic cooking pail, a dixie.

ডেকরা *n.* (dial.) a knave, a rascal; a sly fellow; a cheat; a saucy fellow; a discourteous fellow; a lewd fellow. □ *a.* knavish, rascally; sly; given to cheating; saucy; discourteous; lewd. **ডেকরামি, ডেকরামো** *n.* knavishness, rascality, sauciness.

ডেগ var. of **ডেক**[1] ।

ডেঙ্গু *n.* dengue.

ডেপুটি *a.* acting or employed as a deputy. □ *n.* a deputy magistrate. **~গিরি** *n.* the profession of a deputy magistrate. **~বাবু** *n.* a deputy magistrate.

ডেবরা *a.* left-handed.

ডেমি *n.* demy-paper, prescribed paper used in writing legal deeds etc.

ডেয়ে, ডেয়ো variants of **ডেও**[1] & **ডেও**[2] ।

ডেরা *n.* a temporary abode, a modest lodging; a hutment, tented accommodation. **ডেরা গাড়া, ডেরা বাঁধা** *v.* to come to lodge or to commence to lodge, to take up one's lodging; to build a temporary hut, to pitch a tent. **ডেরা তোলা** *v.* to cease to lodge, to remove from a lodging; to demolish one's hutment; to strike the tent. **~ডাণ্ডা** *n.* a lodging and furniture; a tent and its equipage or accessories.

ডেলা *n.* a lump; a clotted mass. **ডেলা পাকানো** *v.* to gather in a lump, to lump; to clot.

ডেসক, ডেস্ক *n.* a desk, a writing table.

ডোকরা *a.* naughty, wicked; depraved; unfortunate.

ডোকলা □ wasteful; spendthrift.

ডোঙা, ডোঙ্গা *n.* a small boat; a canoe; a canoe (usu.) made of the trunk of a sal tree.

ডোজ *n.* a dose; a potion of medicine.

ডোবা[1] *n.* a pit full of water; a small pool of water.

ডোবা[2] pop. var. of **ডুবা** ।

ডোম *n.* a Hindu caste whose duty is to burn the dead and look after the crematorium; a member of this caste (cp. an undertaker). *fem.* **ডোমনি, ডুমনি** ।

ডোমকাক *n.* the raven, the rook, the jackdaw.

ডোর *n.* a thread (esp. a holy one) to bind (the wrist etc.); (fig.) a tie or bondage (প্রণয়ডোর). **~কৌপীন** *n.* a kind of scanty loin-cloth worn by Vaishnava (বৈষ্ণব) ascetics; the dress of an ascetic.

ডোরা *n.* a stripe, a streak. **ডোরা-কাটা, ডোরা-ডোরা** *a.* striped, streaky; having stripes or streaks of different colours.

ডোরি var. of **ডুরি** ।

ডোল dial. corrup.of **ডৌল** ।

ডোল[২], **ডোলা**[১] *n.* a large corn-bin made of straw, bamboo slips etc.

ডোলা[২] *n.* a small litter or palanquin.

ডৌল *n.* shape, form, cut (মুখের ডৌল).

ড্যাং ড্যাং *int.* expressing : the (joyful) sound of drum-beating; joyfulness (ড্যাংড্যাং করে চলে গেল).

ড্যাকরা alt. spell. of **ডেকরা** ।

ড্যাব ড্যাব pop. var. of **ডব ডব** ।

ড্যাবডেবে var. of **ডবডবে** ।

ড্যাবরা alt. spell. of **ডেবরা** ।

ড্যাশ *n.* (gr.) a dash (–).

ড্রাম[১] *n.* a drachm, a dram.

ড্রাম[২] *n.* cylindrical barrel, a drum.

ড্রিল *n.* training exercise, drill. **ড্রিল করা** *v.* to undergo training exercise.

ড্রেন *n.* a sewer, a drain.

ঢ *n.* the fourteenth consonant of the Bengali alphabet.

ঢং[১] *n.* affected or coquettish bearing or pose; dissimulation; affectation; shape, form, cut, fashion, style, manner. **ঢঙি** *a. fem.* given to affectation; coquettish; dissimulating. □ *n.* such a woman, a poseuse.

ঢং[২] var. of **ঢন**।

ঢক[১] *n.* shape, form, cut; pattern; style (কথা বলার ঢক).

ঢক[২] *int.* expressing : the noise of swallowing or gulping any liquid; the noise of heavy movement of any liquid within a container. **~ঢক** *int.* expressing : repetition of these noises; the noise of swallowing or gulping repeatedly and quickly (ঢকঢক করে জল খাওয়া).

ঢক্কা *n.* a large drum. **~ধ্বনি, ~নিনাদ** *n.* the sound of such a drum.

ঢঙ alt. spell. of **ঢং**[১]।

ঢন *int.* expressing : a metallic sound as of a bell ringing or an empty vessel sounding. **~ঢন** *int.* expressing : repetition of this sound, ding-dong; absolute emptiness (হাঁড়ি ঢনঢন, পকেট ঢনঢন). **~ঢনে** *a.* empty.

ঢপ[১] *n.* shape, form,cut, fashion; a kind of song attended with slow dance current in Bengal.

ঢপ[২] *int.* expressing : a thudding noise as of a heavy body falling softly; the dull noise of striking a soft and empty swelling or a flatulent belly.

ঢপ ঢপ, ঢব ঢব *int.* expressing : repeated and quick thudding noise; the dull noise of repeatedly striking a soft and empty swelling or a flatulent belly.

ঢল *n.* a slope, an incline; declivity; stream of water running down along the slope of a mountain, a rapid (ঢল নেমেছে) ; flood-water (esp. that puts a river in spate).

ঢলকো *a.* loose, slack.

ঢলঢল *int.* expressing : excessive looseness (জামাটা ঢলঢল করছে) ; loveliness (মুখখানা ঢলঢল করছে) ; wideness or largeness (আঁখি ঢলঢল) ; engrossed or rapt state (ভাবে ঢলঢল). □ *a.* large or wide and expressive (ঢলঢল আঁখি) ; full of beauty or charm. ('ঢলঢল কাঁচা অঙ্গের লাবনি'). **ঢলঢলে** *a.* very loose-fitting (ঢলঢলে জামা) ; full of loveliness (ঢলঢলে মুখ).

ঢলতা *n.* extra quantity of any commodity added to the accurately weighed amount (perhaps to ensure customer-satisfaction).

ঢলা *v.* to incline forwards or backwards or sideways; to go down (সূর্য পশ্চিমে ঢলেছে) ; to incline towards, to dote on (ছেলের দিকে ঢলা). **~ঢলি** *n.* scandalous behaviour (esp. in love); objectionable familiarity or mixing; a scandalous affair. **ঢলানে** *a.* given to scandalous behaviour. *fem.* **ঢলানি**। **ঢলানো** *v.* to cause to incline; to behave scandalously. **ঢলে পড়া** *v.* to droop, to collapse (from loss of muscular strength etc.).

ঢাউস *a.* very large or big, enormous, monstrous, huge.

ঢাঁই *n.* a species of large fish without scale, (cp.) the trout.

ঢাক[১] *n.* a drum. **ঢাক পেটা, ঢাক বাজানো** *v.* to beat a drum; (fig.) to make public or announce publicly. **ঢাকের কাঠি** a drumstick; (fig.) an instigator. **ঢাকের বাঁয়া** useless appurtenances or paraphernalia; something merely decorative. **ঢাকের বাদ্যি** drum-beat. **ঢাকের দায়ে মনসা বিকানো** (fig.) to run insolvent in attempting to keep up appearances, to sell one's homestead to grease one's car.

ঢাক[২] (usu. hum. or dero.) cover, concealment, act or instrument of countenancing or hushing up.

ঢাকঢাক, ঢাকঢাক-গুড়গুড় *n.* an attempt to conceal or hush up; hush-hush state.

ঢাকনা *n.* a cover; a lid; a veil; a blinker.

ঢাকনি *n.* a cover, a lid.

ঢাকা *v.* to cover; to veil; to screen; to envelop; to overcast (মেঘে ঢাকা) ; to conceal, to hide; to hush up; (usu. dero.) to countenance or to connive at. □ *n.* a lid; a cover; a veil; (usu. dero.) connivance. □ *a.* covered; veiled; screened; enveloped; overcast.

ঢাকাই *a.* made or manufactured at Dacca (a district of Bangladesh).

ঢাকি *n.* a drummer. **ঢাকি সুদ্ধ বিসর্জন** (lit.) to throw away or immerse the drummer with the idol; (fig.) to lose or sarcifice everything; to let go the rope after the bucket, to throw the baby out with the bathwater.

ঢামালি *n.* pleasantries, drolleries, jokes.

ঢাল[১] *n.* a shield; a buckler.

ঢাল[২] *n.* a slope, a declivity, a descent. cp. **ঢল**।

ঢালা *v.* to pour (দুধ ঢালা) ; to cast, to mould (ছাঁচে ঢালা) ; to invest or spend esp. lavishly (ব্যাবসাতে টাকা ঢালা, ছেলের পড়াশোনার পিছনে টাকা ঢালা) ; to confer (স্নেহ ঢালা) ; to cause to flow out (দেশের জন্য রক্ত ঢালা). □ *a.* that which is poured (ঢালা জল) ; cast, moulded; extensively outspread, large, spacious (ঢালা বিছানা, ঢালা ফরাশ) ; lavishly distributed (ঢালা খাবার) ; permanent, standing (ঢালা হুকুম). **ঢালাই** *n.* act of casting or moulding. □ *a.* moulded, cast (ঢালাই লোহা). **ঢালাই করা** *v.* to mould, to cast. **ঢালাইকর** *n.* a caster. **ঢালাই-কারখানা** *n.* an iron-foundry; a foundry.

ঢালাও *a.* extensively outspread, spacious (ঢালাও ফরাশ, ঢালাও জায়গা) ; distributed lavishly (ঢালাও খাবার) ; permanent, standing (ঢালাও হুকুম).

ঢালাঢালি *n.* act of transferring a liquid repeatedly from one container to another by pouring it; act of pouring and repouring a liquid into a container. **ঢেলে সাজা** *v.* to undo a thing and then to do it afresh, to fashion anew, to recast.

ঢালী *n.* a shield-bearer; a soldier bearing a shield or buckler.

ঢালু *a.* sloping or slanting downwards, declining.

ঢিট, (obs.) **ঢীট** *a.* saucy, pert; shameless, brazen-faced ('ঢীট কানাই') ; thoroughly subdued or rectified or corrected (মারের চোটে ঢিট). **ঢিট করা** *v.* to subdue or correct or rectify thoroughly. **~পনা** (obs.) *n.* sauciness, pertness; shamelessness.

ঢিঢি *n.* (usu. of disrepute, censure, scandal) loud noise or discussion, extensive publicity and reproach (ঢিঢি পড়ে গেছে). □ *a.* (usu. dero.) given extensive public reproach (ঢিঢিরব). **~কার, ~ক্কার, ~রব** *n.* extensive public censure and hooting; loud noise (of anything).

ঢিপ *int.* expressing : a mild thudding noise as of a heavy body falling softly. **ঢিপ করে প্রণাম করা** to genuflect suddenly or quickly. **ঢিপ ঢিপ** *int.* expressing : repeated mild thudding noise; palpitation or throbbing esp. in fear (বুক ঢিপ ঢিপ করছে).

ঢিপি *n.* a mound; a hillock; an artificial hill; a heap, a pile (কাপড়চোপড়ের ঢিপি) ; a hill (উইয়ের ঢিপি).

ঢিবি var. of **ঢিপি**।

ঢিমা, (coll.) **ঢিমে** *a.* mild, low (ঢিমে আওয়াজ) ; slow, slow-moving (ঢিমে তাল, ঢিমে কাজ) ; sluggish, lazy, dilatory, spiritless (ঢিমে লোক, ঢিমে স্বভাব). **~তেতালা** *n.* an Indian musical measure; slowness, sluggishness, dilatoriness, procrastination; lack of enthusiasm or spiritedness.

ঢিল[১] *n.* a hard roundish lump esp. of stone or brick or clay. **ঢিল মারা** *v.* to pelt with these lumps, to throw stones or brickbats.

ঢিলা, (coll.) **ঢিলে,** (dial.) **ঢিল**[২] *a.* loose, not tight, slack (ঢিলা বাঁধন) ; not strict, lax (ঢিলা শাসন) ; not eager or diligent or attentive, slack, lazy, dilatory, careless (ঢিলে লোক) ; slow (ঢিলে কাজ). □ *n.* slackness, sluggishness, lack of enthusiasm or spiritedness (কাজে ঢিলা দেওয়া). **ঢিলেঢালা** *a.* slow and unmethodical in action, careless, sloppy.

ঢিলানো same as **ঢিল মারা** (see **ঢিল**[১]).

ঢিলামি, (কথ্য) **ঢিলেমি** *n.* slackness, sluggishness, lack of enthusiasm or spiritedness.

ঢীট see **ঢিট**।

ঢু, ঢুঁ *n.* act of butting (as by a goat etc.). **ঢু মারা, ঢুঁ মারা** *v.* to butt; to put in appearance, to knock (চাকরির জন্য সর্বত্র ঢুঁ মারা).

ঢুঁড়া *n.* to search; to traverse (দেশে দেশে ঢুঁড়ছে).

ঢু ঢু var. of **ঢুঢু**।

ঢুঢু *int.* (also *n.*) expressing nothingness. **কাজের বেলায় ঢুঢু** found wanting when called upon to prove (one's) worth; of no worth or value at the time of work or crucial test.

ঢুল *n.* an instance or act of nodding or stooping in drowsiness or intoxication; drowsy stupor, drowsiness (চোখে ঢুল নামা). **ঢুলঢুলে, ঢুলঢুল, ঢুলুঢুলু** *a.* heavy with drowsiness or intoxication (ঢুলঢুলে চোখ) ; smitten with passion ('সুখে আঁখি ঢুলুঢুলু'). **ঢুলনি, ঢুলুনি** same as **ঢুলু**।

ঢুলা *v.* (dial.) to nod or stoop in drowsiness or intoxication.

ঢুলানো *v.* (obs.) to wave (চামর ঢুলানো) ; to rock or dangle (মা শিশুটিকে ঢুলাচ্ছে).

ঢুলঢুল, ঢুলুঢুলু, ঢুলুনি see **ঢুল**।

ঢুসানো *v.* to butt (as by a goat). **ঢুসাঢুসি** *n.* act of butting one another; a crowded state in which heads knock against one another. coll. **ঢুসোঢুসি**।

ঢেউ *n.* a wave; a billow, a surge; a ripple; **ঢেউ ওঠা** *v.* to rise in waves or surges or ripples; to wave, to surge, to ripple; **ঢেউ কাটানো** *v.* to dodge waves. **ঢেউ খেলা** *v.* to move in waves or ripples, to wave, to ripple. **ঢেউ তোলা** *v.* to cause to rise in waves or surges or ripples, to surge, to ripple; to swell up in waves or surges or ripples, to surge up. **ঢেউ-খেলানো, ঢেউ-তোলা** *a.* wavy; undulating; corrugated.

ঢেঁকি *n.* a kind of husking pedal operated in a seesaw manner. **ঢেঁকির আঁকশালি** the fulcrum of a husking pedal. **~কল** *n.* a seesaw. **~শাক** *n.* an edible fern. **~শাল, ~শালা** *n.* a room (usu. a cutcha one) where the husking pedal is fixed. **ঢেঁকি স্বর্গে গেলেও ধান ভানে** (fig.) an expert worker has to work even in heaven; a drudge will drudge even in heaven.

ঢেঁকুর var. of **ঢেকুর**।

ঢেঁটরা var. of **ঢেঁড়া**।

ঢেঁড়স *n.* the lady's finger, the kidney-vetch; (fig.) a good-for-nothing fellow; a worthless or do-nothing fellow.

ঢেঁড়া, ঢেঁড়ি[1] *n.* a drum, a tympan (ঢেঁড়া পেটা) ; a proclamation by drum-beat (ঢেঁড়া দেওয়া).

ঢেঁড়ি[2] *n.* a kind of earring; a poppy-seed; a poppy pod or seed-vessel.

ঢেকুর *n.* a belch, an eructation. **ঢেকুর তোলা** *v.* to belch, to eructate.

ঢেঙা alt. spell. of **ঢ্যাঙা**।

ঢেপসা *a.* shaped like a mound; bulky or fatty but not strong and stout, flaccid (ঢেপসা শরীর).

ঢেমনা *a.* lewd, libertine, profligate; a species of non-poisonous snake.

ঢের *a.* profuse, numerous; lavish; plentiful, abundant; enough, sufficient; too much or too many.

ঢেরা *n.* a cross-mark; a bobbin. **~সই** *n.* a cross-mark put instead of signature by an illiterate person.

ঢেরি *n.* a heap, a pile, a stack. **ঢেরি করা** *v.* to heap, to pile.

ঢেলা *n.* a small lump or clod esp. of earth; a small brickbat. **ঢেলা মারা** *v.* to pelt with a small clod of earth or with a small brickbat.

ঢোঁড়ন *n.* act of searching or traversing.

ঢোঁড়া[1] pop. var. of **ঢুঁড়া**।

ঢোঁড়া[2] *n.* a non-venomous water-snake; (sarcas.) a person without personality and power.

ঢোক *n.* a gulp; gulping. **ঢোক গেলা** *v.* to gulp; to make a movement as of gulping something (esp. to express hesitation).

ঢোকা *v.* to go or come in or into, to enter (ঘরে ঢুকবে, গর্তে ঢোকা) ; to be admitted into (কলেজে ঢোকা, দলে ঢোকা) ; to be taken in or employed, to enter (চাকরিতে ঢুকেছে) ; to be driven in (পেরেক ঢুকানো) ; to be comprehended by (মাথায় ঢোকা) ; to be put in or interpolated (লেখায় ঢোকা). **ঢুকানো** *v.* to cause to go or come in or into, to enter; to admit into; to cause to be taken in or employed; to drive in or penetrate; to fix or let into (আঙটি আঙুলে ঢোকানো) ; to implant (in);

to make one understand or comprehend, to hammer in (মাথায় ঢুকানো) ; to put in or interpolate.

ঢোল *n.* a tom-tom. **ঢোল দেওয়া** *v.* to announce or circulate by beating a tom-tom. **ঢোল পেটা** *v.* (dero.) to beat a tom-tom; (dero.) to make a loud noise (কথা বলছে যেন ঢোল পিটছে) ; to announce or circulate by beating a tom-tom; (usu. dero.) to make public. **ঢোল হওয়া** *v.* to be swollen in the shape as of a tom-tom. **নিজের ঢোল নিজে পেটা** to beat one's own trumpet, to advertise oneself. **ঢোলক** *n.* a small variety of tom-tom. **~শোহরত** *n.* announcement or circulation by beating a tom-tom.

ঢোলা[১] pop. var. of **ঢুলা** ।

ঢোলা[২] *a.* very loose-fitting (ঢোলা জামা).

ঢোসকা *a.* fat and flabby, flaccid.

ঢ্যাঁড়স, ঢ্যাঁড়শ alt. spellings of **ঢেঁড়স** ।

ঢ্যাঁড়া alt. spell. of **ঢেঁড়া** ।

ঢ্যাঙা *a.* lanky.

ঢ্যাপসা alt. spell. of **ঢেপসা** ।

ঢ্যামনা alt. spell. of **ঢেমনা** ।

ণ

ণ *n.* the fifteenth consonant of the Bengali alphabet.

ণত্ববিধান, ণত্ববিধি *n.* (gr.) the rules governing the change of ন into ণ ।

ণত্ব-ষত্ব জ্ঞান *n.* (lit.) knowledge as to where ণ and ষ should be used; (fig.) gumption, nous, common sense.

ণ-ফলা *n.* the system of adding ণ to other letters.

ণিচ্ *n.* (gr.) a causative inflection of verbs (e.g. দৃশ্, to see + ণিচ্ = দর্শি, to show).

ণিজন্ত *a.* (gr.) inflected with ণিচ্ (ণিজন্ত ধাতু).

ত১ *n.* the sixteenth consonant of the Bengali alphabet.
ত২ alt. spell. of **তো**১ ।
ত৩ dial. & coll. corrup.of **তত** ।
তই *n.* a kind of cooking pan without handle.
তইখন *adv.* & *con.*(poet. & obs.) by that time, at once, at that time, then.
তঁহি *adv.* (poet. & obs.) there; in that, in him, in her, in them. □ *pro.* (poet. & obs.) he, she, it, they.
তক *prep.* (used chiefly as a *sfx.*) up to, till (শেষতক), as soon as (যাহাতক).
তকতক *int.* expressing : tidiness (ঘরখানা তকতক করছে) ; transparence (জল তকতক করছে) ; brightness or freshness (রংটা তকতক করছে). **তকতকে** *a.* tidy, neat and clean; transparent; bright or fresh; in mint condition.
তকদির, (rej.) **তকদীর** *n.* luck, fate.
তকমা *n.* a distinctive dress or badge, livery; a medal. **তকমা-আঁটা, তকমা-পরা** *a.* wearing a livery or medal, liveried or medalled.
তকরার *n.* an argument, a debate; an altercation.
তকলি *n.* a spindle or distaff (esp. a small or improvised one). **তকলি কাটা** *v.* to spin yarn.
তকলিফ *n.* trouble; hardship; pain; suffering; difficulty.
তক্ক coll. corrup. of **তর্ক** ।
তক্কেতক্কে *adv.* cautiously and secretly, surreptitiously; in ambush, in wait.
তক্ত, তক্ততাউস pop. corruptions of **তখ্‌ত** and **তখ্‌ত-তাউস** respectively.
তক্তপোশ *n.* a plain rectangular cot without any arrangement for hanging curtains.
তক্তা *n.* a plank of wood; a piece of board; a flat and hard sheet of anything. **মেরে তক্তা বানানো** (sl.) to flatten by beating or thrashing, to beat or thrash severely.
তক্তানামা pop. corrup. of **তখতনামা** ।
তক্তাপোশ var. of **তক্তপোশ** ।
তক্তি *n.* a small plank of wood, a tablet; a small piece of board; a small flat and hard sheet of anything; a hard and flat sweetmeat shaped like a tablet.
তক্র *n.* whey. **~পিণ্ড** *n.* posset.
তক্ষক *n.* a carpenter; a joiner; (myth.) a kind of strongly venomous winged snake; a kind of venomous chameleon.
তক্ষণ *n.* act of planing or carving wood; woodwork; carpentry; a (carpenter's) plane or vice. **~শিল্প** *n.* the art or craft of carpentry.
তক্ষণি, তক্ষুণি rej. spellings of **তক্ষনি** & **তক্ষুনি** respectively.
তক্ষণী *n.* carpenter's tool for shaping or trimming wood, a chisel, a plane.
তক্ষনি coll. var. of **তখনই** ।
তখ্‌ত *n.* throne (রাজতখ্‌ত). **তখ্‌ত-তাউস** *n.* peacock throne.
তখতনামা *a.* a kind of conveyance carried by men; a litter for use in marriage processions (cp. a palanquin).
তখন *adv.* (also *conj.*) at that time; in that age (তখন কলকাতায় ট্রাম ছিল না) ; then; and then; so; after that time; at last (চোর পালালে তখন গৃহস্থ সাবধান হল). □ *n.* that time or age (তখন থেকে). **~ই, তখনি** *adv.* just then; immediately, forthwith, at once, **~ও** *adv.* still then. **~কার** *a.* of that time or age. **তখন থেকে** *adv.* since then.
তখমা var. of **তকমা** ।
ত-খরচ *n.* incidental expenses.
তগর obs. var. of **টগর** ।
তঙ্কা var. of **টঙ্কা** ।
তচনচ alt. spell. of **তছনছ** ।
তছনছ *a.* upset; destroyed; utterly spoiled; messed up; squandered.
তছরুপ *n.* embezzlement, defalcation. **তছরুপ করা** *v.* to embezzle, to defalcate. **তহবিল তছরুপ করা** *v.* to embezzle, to defalcate a fund.
তছু *pro. a.* (poet. & obs.) his or her.
তজ্জনিত *a.* caused by that; arising or

arisen from that; grown or evolved out of that.

তজ্জন্য *adv.* for that; for that reason; because of that ; for the sake of that.

তজ্জাত *a.* born of him or that; grown or arisen or evolved out of that; caused by that.

তজ্জাতীয় *a.* of that class or kind or race.

তঞ্চক *a.* & *n.* one who or that which cheats or deceives or swindles. **~তা** *n.* cheating, deception, swindling, trickery.

তঞ্চন *n.* contraction; clotting; (chem.) coagulation.

তঞ্চিত *a.* contracted; clotted; coagulated, congealed.

তট *n.* beach, shore, coast, bank; land (তটভাগ) ; region (কটিতট) ; a tract of level ground on the top of a mountain. **~রেখা** *n.* coastline.

তটস্থ[1] *a.* confusedly worried and bustling; very much frightened and eager to please; extremely perturbed.

তটস্থ[2] *a.* lying on the shore or bank; coastal; disinterested, unbiased, impartial. ('তটস্থ হইয়া বিচারিলে তরতম') *fem.* **তটস্থা**।

তটিনী *n.* a river; a stream.

তড়কা *n.* a spasmodic fit (esp. of children). convulsion, spasm.

তড়প, তরপ *n.* one of a number of smaller strings in a stringed musical instrument which producs resonance.

তড়পানো *v.* to jump; to brag menacingly; to bluster; to fret or fuss; to move violently or restlessly (দিল তড়পাচ্ছে). **তড়পানি** *n.* act of jumping; act of bragging menacingly; act of fretting or fussing; violent or restless movement.

তড়বড় *int.* expressing : excessive hurry or rapidity. **তড়বড়ানি** *n.* excessive hurry, excessively rapid movement or speech. **তড়বড়ানো** *v.* to hurry excessively; to move or speak with excessive rapidity. **তড়বড়ে** *a.* excessively hurried or rapid; given to excessive hurry; given to moving or talking with excessive rapidity.

তড়াক *int.* expressing : suddenness or quickness (তড়াক করে লাফানো).

তড়াগ *n.* a large (and deep) pond.

তড়িঘড়ি *adv.* very quickly or promptly; at once, forthwith.

তড়িচ্চালক *a.* electromotive. **তড়িচ্চালক বল** electromotive force.

তড়িচ্চুম্বক *n.* electromagnet. **তড়িচ্চুম্বকীয়** *a.* electromagnetic.

তড়িৎ *n.* lightning; electricity.

তড়িতালোক *n.* the glow or light of a lightning.

তড়িত্বান, তড়িদ্‌গর্ভ *n.* thunder-cloud; cloud. □ *a.* emitting lightning; containing electricity, charged with electricity.

তড়িদ্দ্বার *n.* an electrode.

তড়িদ্‌বিশ্লেষণ *n.* electrolysis.

তড়িদ্‌বিশ্লেষ্য *a.* electrolyte.

তড়িদ্বীক্ষণ *n.* an electroscope.

তড়িন্ময় *a.* charged with electricity.

তড়িল্লতা *n.* a streak of lightning; lightning; a wave of electricity.

তণ্ডুল *n.* rice. **~কণা** *n.* a grain of rice. **~চূর্ণ** *n.* powdered rice, rice-powder.

তত[1] *a.* extended, outspread; extensive; diffused. □ *n.* a stringed musical instrument. **~যন্ত্র** *n.* a stringed musical instrument.

তত[2] *adv.* & *con.* to that amount or number or extent or degree. □ *adv.* so much, so, up to expectation (বইখানা তত ভালো নয়). □ *con.* so, as. □ *a.* that much or so many (তত সময়, তত লোক). **~ক্ষণ** *adv.* up to or till or during or within that time. **~ক্ষণে** *adv.* by that time. **~দিন** *adv.* for so many days; for those days; up to or till or during so many or those days. **~দিনে** *adv.* same as **ততক্ষণে**। **~হি, ~হিঁ** *adv.* (poet. & obs.) at that.

তৎ *pro.* he, she, it; they; that; those. **~কর্তৃক** *adv.* by him or her or it. **~কাল** *n.* that time or period or age. **~কালীন** *a.* of or for or during that time or period or age; occurring or prevalent at that time or period or age. **~কালে** *adv.* at that time, then. **~কালোচিত** *a.* right or suitable for the occasion. **~কৃত** *a.* done by him or her or it. **~ক্ষণাৎ** *adv.* at once, immediately, forthwith. **~ক্ষণে** *adv.* at that moment; at or by that time. **~পর** *adv.* after that, thereafter. □ *a.* expert;

skilful, adroit; zealous, earnest; eager; enterprising, endeavouring; careful; prompt. **~পরতা** *n.* expertness, skilfulness, adroitness; zeal, earnestness; eagerness; enterprise; endeavour; carefulness, care; promptness, promptitude. **~পরায়ণ** *a.* sincerely or zealously attached to or engaged in that thing or work. **~পরে** same as **তৎপর** (*adv.*). **~পশ্চাৎ** *adv.* after or behind that or him or her or it. **~পুরুষ** *n.* the Supreme Being, God; (gr.) a system of compounding words (by this system the preceding word loses its inflexion and the succeeding word becomes more prominent. e. g. রাজার পুত্র = রাজপুত্র). **~পূর্বে** *adv.* before that, prior to that. **~সংক্রান্ত, ~সম্বন্ধীয়** *a.* relating to that, regarding that. **~সত্ত্বেও** *adv.* in spite of that; even then. **~সদৃশ** *a.* similar to that, like that. **~সম** *a.* same as that. **তৎসম শব্দ** (gr.) a Sanskrit word used in the unchanged form in Bengali. **~স্থলাভিষিক্ত** *a.* installed in his or her or its place. **~স্বরূপ** same as **তৎসদৃশ**।

ততঃ *adv.* thereafter, then. **ততঃ কিম্** what then ? what next ?

ততোধিক *a.* more than that.

তত্তাবৎ *pro.* & *a.* all that.

তত্তুল্য *a.* similar to or equal to or like him or her or it.

তত্ত্ব *n.* real or essential nature, reality, essence, (fundamental) truth (তত্ত্বদর্শী) ; God (তত্ত্বজ্ঞান) ; spiritual or philosophical or ontological knowledge (তত্ত্বকথা) ; knowledge or philosophy, principle (ধর্মতত্ত্ব) ; theory or doctrine; information (তত্ত্ব পাওয়া) ; search, inquiry (তত্ত্ব নেওয়া) ; any of the twenty-four principal constituting elements according to the Sankhya philosophy; a present, a gift (পূজার তত্ত্ব, বিয়ের তত্ত্ব). **তত্ত্ব করা** *v.* to inquire after; to search for or about or out; to send customary gifts to one related matrimonially. **~কথা** *n.* spiritual or philosophical knowledge or discussion. **~চিন্তা** *n.* meditation on God; spiritual meditation; philosophical or theological meditation. **~জিজ্ঞাসা** *n.* theological inquiry; inquiry about God; inquiry about reality or truth, philosophical inquiry. **~জিজ্ঞাসু** *a.* inquisitive about theological knowledge; inquiring about God or reality or truth. **~জ্ঞ** *a.* having knowledge about God or reality of truth; possessing theosophical or philosophical or spiritual knowledge. □ *n.* one who has knowledge about God or reality or truth; the possessor of theological or philosophical or spiritual knowledge. **~জ্ঞান** *n.* knowledge about God; theological or spiritual or philosophical knowledge; knowledge about reality or truth. **~জ্ঞানী** *a.* & *n.* one who has knowledge about God or reality or truth; one who has theological or spiritual or philosophical knowledge. **~তল্লাস, ~তালাশ** *n.* communication and exchange of customary gifts; seeking information about one's condition and whereabouts. **~দর্শী** *a.* & *n.* one who has knowledge about God or reality or truth; one who has theological or spiritual or philosophical knowledge; wise or judicious (man). *fem.* **~দর্শিনী**। **~দর্শিতা** *n.* possession of knowledge about God or reality or truth; possession of theological or spiritual or philosophical knowledge; wisdom or judiciousness. **~নির্ণয়, ~নিরূপণ** *n.* ascertainment of truth; ascertainment of the true nature of a thing. **~বিদ** *a.* & *n.* one who has knowledge about God or reality or truth; one who has theological or spiritual or philosophical knowledge; one who is in the know of things. **~বিদ্যা** *n.* ontology. **~বোধ** *n.* perception of truth.

তত্ত্বানুসন্ধান *n.* search for information; search for truth; search for knowledge about God or reality; investigation; research.

তত্ত্বানুসন্ধানী *a.* & *n.* one who or that which searches for information or truth or for knowledge about God or reality; one who or that which investigates or researches.

তত্ত্বাবধান *n.* act of taking care of or looking after; supervision; guardianship or custody. **তত্ত্ববধান করা** *v.* to take care of, to look after. **তত্ত্বাবধানে রাখা** *v.* to put under care or guardianship or tutelage or custody of.

তত্ত্বাবধায়ক *n.* a caretaker; a curator; a guardian; a custodian. □ *a.* taking care of, looking after; having under one's own guardianship; having in custody.

তত্ত্বাবধারক *a.* & *n.* one who or that which ascertains truth or reality or actual state or information.

তত্ত্বাবধারণ *n.* ascertainment of truth or reality or actual state or information.

তত্ত্বালোচনা *n.* discussion about God or truth or reality; philosophical or ontological or theological or spiritual discussion or discourse.

তত্ত্বীয় *a.* relating to truth or reality; relating to philosophical or ontological or theological or spiritual knowledge; theoretical.

তত্র *adv.* there, at that place. □ *con.* so (যত্র আয় তত্র ব্যয়). **~ত্য, ~স্থ** *a.* of that place.

তত্রাচ, তত্রাপি *adv.* (lit. but rare) even there; even in that case; in spite of that, notwithstanding, nevertheless, withal; still.

তথা *n.* that place. □ *adv.* at or in or to that place, there. □ *adv.* & *con.* so, like (যথা আয় তথা ব্যয়) ; and, and also or for the matter of that (সমগ্র বঙ্গদেশ তথা ভারতবর্ষ) ; moreover, further; even. **~কথিত** *a.* so-called. **~কার** *a.* of that place. **~গত** *a.* come or gone in that way. □ *n.* one who has attained Nirvana (নির্বাণ) ; an appellation of Gautama Buddha. **~চ, ~পি** same as **তত্রাচ**। **~বিধ** *a.* of that kind or nature; such; similar. **~ভূত** *a.* of or in that state; passed into that state; produced or born or grown or evolved in that way. **~য়** *adv.* at or in or to that place, there. **~স্তু** *int.* so be it, amen.

তথি *adv.* (obs.) at or in or to that place, there; in or at or to that. □ *n.* that place (তথিমধ্যে). □ *adv.* & *con.* and; and also.

তথৈব *adv.* even in that manner or way. □ *a.* of that manner or way. □ *n.* that manner or way. **~চ** *adv.* just the same.

তথ্য *n.* actuality; actual state or affair; information; reality; truth; facts or data. □ *a.* real or true or unanimous or universal (তথ্যবচন). **~জ্ঞান** *n.* knowledge of facts. **~নিরূপণ, ~নির্ণয়** *n.* determination of truth; ascertainment of facts. **~বাদী** same as **তথ্যভাষী**। **~বাহী** *a.* informative. **~ভাষী** *a.* truthful. **~ভিত্তিক** *a.* based on facts; documented. **~সমৃদ্ধ** *a.* well-documented; informed; informative.

তথ্যানুসন্ধান *n.* search for truth or reality; search for information; investigation; research.

তদতিরিক্ত *adv.* more than that; beyond that; over and above that; beside that, besides, moreover, further.

তদনন্তর *adv.* after that, thereafter.

তদনুগ, তদনুগামী, তদনুবর্তী *a.* following him or her or that; like him or her or that; according to that.

তদনুপাতে *adv.* in proportion to that, proportionately.

তদনুযায়ী, তদনুরূপ *a.* & *adv.* following or like that; according to that.

তদনুসারী *a.* following or like that; according to that. **তদনুসারে** *adv.* following or like that; according to that.

তদন্ত *n.* investigation, inquiry. **তদন্ত করা** *v.* to investigate. **~কারী** *n.* one who investigates, an investigator.

তদন্য *a.* apart from that; other than that; beside that.

তদবধি *adv.* since then, from then onwards; (rare) till then.

তদবস্থ *a.* in that state or condition or position or posture.

তদবির *n.* act of looking after or taking care of (শরীরের তদবির) ; act of looking after the interst of, act of taking steps so that a thing is properly managed or organized (মামলার তদবির) ; canvassing (চাকরির তদবির). **তদবির করা** *v.* to look after, to take care of; to look after the interest of, to take steps for proper management or organization of; to canvass for.

তদর্থ *adv.* for that; for the sake of that. □ *n.* the meaning of that. **তদর্থক** *a.* ad hoc. **তদর্থে** *adv.* for that; for the sake of that.

তদা *adv. & con.* at that time, in that age, then.

তদাকার *a.* of that shape or form.

তদাত্মা *a.* having the same soul as his or her; identical with him or her.

তদানীং *adv.* at that time; in that age, in those days; then.

তদানীন্তন *a.* of that time or age, the then (তদানীন্তন রাষ্ট্রপতি).

তদারক *n.* investigation (ডাকাতির তদারক) ; act of looking after or taking care of, care, management, superintendence (সম্পত্তির তদারক, স্বাস্থ্যের তদারক, কাজকর্মের তদারক). **তদারক করা** *v.* to investigate; to look after, to take care of, to manage, to superintend.

তদীয় *a.* of him or her or it or that.

তদুপযোগী *a.* suitable to that, well-fitted for that, befitting that, right for that.

তদুপরি *adv.* on or above him or her or it or that.

তদুপলক্ষে, তদুপলক্ষ্যে *adv.* on that occasion; on account of that; with that purpose, with that end in view.

তদুর্ধ্বে *adv.* above him or her or it or that; more than it or that.

তদেক *a.* one identical with him or her or it or, that (তদেকচিত্ত) ; no other (তদেকশরণ).

তদ্গত *a.* absorbed or engrossed in or engaged wholly in him or her or it or that; intently engaged or attentive. **~চিত্ত** *a.* rapt in attention (to) or thought (of).

তদ্দণ্ডে *adv.* at that very moment; immediately, at once, forthwith.

তদ্দরুন *adv.* for that, because of that, on acccount of that, caused by that, for the sake of that, on that account.

তদ্দিন dial. corrup. of **তত দিন**।

তদ্দেশীয় *a.* of or belonging to that country.

তদ্দ্বারা *pro. & adv.* by him or her or it or that.

তদ্ধিত *n.* (gr.) any of the inflexions or suffixes added to nouns, pronouns and adjectives to form derivatives, nominal inflexion.

তদ্বৎ *a. & adv.* like or similar to or comparable to that or it or him or her.

তদ্বাচক *a.* meaning or signifying that; indicating that.

তদ্বিধ *a.* of that sort or kind.

তদ্বিধায় *adv.* on account of that, on that account.

তদ্বির rej. spell. of **তদবির**।

তদ্বিষয়ক *a.* concerning him or her or it or that; concerning that subject. **তদ্বিষয়ে** *adv.* in or about or as regards him or her or it or that or that subject.

তদ্ব্যতিরিক্ত, তদ্ব্যতীত *a. & adv.* beside or other than or without him or her or it or that; more than it or that.

তদ্ভব *a.* born of or descended from or originating from or grown out of or evolved out of him or her or it or that. **তদ্ভব শব্দ** (gr.) a Bengali word derived from Sanskrit but used in a corrupted form.

তদ্ভাব *n.* that or his or her or its state or condition or mental disposition or mood or nature or essential quality etc.; thoughts about him or her or it or that. **তদ্ভাবাপন্ন** *a.* having or in or under that or his or her or its state or condition etc. **তদ্ভাবে** *adv.* in that state or condition; in that way or manner.

তদ্ভিন্ন same as **তদ্ব্যতীত**।

তদ্রূপ *a.* like or similar to that or it or him or her. □ *adv.* in that manner or way. **তদ্রূপে** same as **তদ্রূপ** (*adv.*)

তনখা *n.* wage, salary, remuneration.

তনয় *n.* a son. *fem.* **তনয়া** a daughter.

তনিমা *n.* graceful or delicate slimness (of the body); subtlety.

তনু, তনূ *n.* the body. □ *a.* gracefully or delicately slim and lovely (তনুদেহ) ; rarefied. **~চ্ছদ** *n.* an armour. **~জ** *n.* a son. *fem.* **~জা** *a.* daughter. **~তা** *n.* graceful or delicate slimness and loveliness; delicacy. **~ত্যাগ** *n.* act of dying, death, act of giving up the ghost. **~ত্যাগ করা** *v.* to die, to give up the ghost. **~ত্র, ~ত্রাণ** *n.* an armour. **~বাত** *n.* (geog.) rarefied atmosphere. **~মধ্যা** *n.* a woman with a delicately slender waist. **~রুচি** *n.* physical beauty or grace. **~রুহ** *n.* hair (of the body and not of the head); a feather; a son or a daughter, an offspring. **~করণ** *n.* rarefaction; attenuation; extenuation. **~কৃত** *n.* rarefied; attenuated; extenuated. **তনূদ্ভব** *n.* a son. *fem.* **তনূদ্ভবা** a daughter. **তনূনপাৎ** *n.* fire. **তনূভবন** *n.* act of being rarefied or attenuated or extenuated.

তন্তু *n.* thread, yarn, string; fibre; gut; handloom. **~কীট** *n.* the silkworm; the caterpillar. **~নাভ** *n.* a spider. **~বায়** *n.* a weaver (by trade or caste). **~মূল** *n.* fibrous root. **~শালা** *n.* weaver's workshop. **~সার** *n.* betel-nut tree. □ *a.* very lean and thin, emaciated.

তন্ত্র *n.* a scripture or service book or the system of the religious worship of Shaktas (শাক্ত) ; any scripture or service book or system or cult of religious worship; a religious order (শৈবতন্ত্র, সন্ন্যাসতন্ত্র) ; a section or branch of the Vedas (বেদ) ; a science (চিকিৎসাতন্ত্র) ; a system (সাধনাতন্ত্র) ; a system of government (প্রজাতন্ত্র, রাজতন্ত্র) ; a doctrine (বস্তুতন্ত্র, জড়তন্ত্র) ; a decision; a chapter or section (পঞ্চতন্ত্র) ; any esoteric and mystical charm or means (মন্ত্রতন্ত্র) ; a handloom (তন্ত্রবায়) ; gut (পশুর তন্ত্র) ; a string (বীণাতন্ত্র). **~ধার, ~ধারক** *n.* a Brahman who reads out excerpts from a service book for the priest to recite them. **~বাপ** *n.* a weaver (by trade or caste). **~মন্ত্র** *n.* charms and incantations. **~শাস্ত্র** *n.* scriptures; theory or system contained in the scriptures. **~সার** *n.* a digest of religious service.

তন্ত্রী *n.* the string or gut of a musical instrument; a stringed musical instrument, a vina. □ *a.* stringed or having a gut or guts (তন্ত্রী বাদ্যযন্ত্র) ; belonging or relating to a religious order (শৈবতন্ত্রী).

তন্দুর *n.* a covered oven for baking bread.

তন্দ্রা *n.* drowsiness; light sleep, siesta, nap. **~গত, তন্দ্রাভিভূত** *a.* seized or overwhelmed with drowsiness, affected with drowsiness; sleeping, asleep. **তন্দ্রাগত হওয়া, তন্দ্রাভিভূত হওয়া** *v.* to fall asleep; to sleep; (rare) to drowse. **~বেশ** *n.* drowsiness; sleepiness; cat-nap. **~লু** *a.* drowsy; affected with drowsiness. **~হীন** *a.* sleepless. **তন্দ্রিত** *a.* drowsy; affected with drowsiness; fallen asleep; sleeping.

তন্নতন্ন *a.* thorough (তন্নতন্ন খোঁজ). □ *adv.* searching thoroughly. **তন্নতন্ন করা** *v.* to ransack, to rummage, to comb; to rifle.

তন্নিবন্ধন *adv.* for that; because of that; on account of that; for the sake of that.

তন্নিষ্ঠ *a.* rapt in attention; very attentive and absorbed.

তন্মধ্যে *adv.* in him or her or it or that or them; in the midst of it; between or amongst them.

তন্মন, তন্মনা, তন্মনস্ক, তন্ময় *a.* absorbed in or engaged wholly in him or her or it or that; engrossed, rapt, intently engaged or attentive. **তন্ময়তা** *n.* absorbedness, raptness, intent attention.

তন্মাত্র *adv.* & *n.* only that; only to that extent or in that degree or measure.

তন্বঙ্গী, তন্বী *a. fem.* (of a woman) having a slim body.

তপঃ, (pop.) **তপ** *n.* austere endeavour to achieve an end; practice of ascetic or religious austerities; austere worship of God. **তপঃকৃশ** *a.* physically thinned or shrivelled by ascetic austerities. **তপঃক্লেশ** *n.* austerities of ascetic practice. **তপঃপ্রভাব** *n.* force or power acquired through the practice of ascetic or religious austerities. **তপঃসাধ্য** *a.* obtainable only through austere endeavour or through ascetic or religious austerities. **তপঃসিদ্ধ** *a.* accomplished by means of austere endeavour or through ascetic or religious austerities; one who has attained success by means of austere endeavour or through ascetic or religious austerities.

তপতী *n.* shadow (personified); the [illegible] or the daughter of the sungod; the river Tapti.

তপন *n.* the sun. **~তনয়** *n.* Yama the god of death. **~তনয়া** *n.* the river Jamuna; the shami tree, *Acacia suma*. **~তাপ** *n.* sunrays; (scorching) sunlight.

তপনীয় *a.* worthy of being heated; that which is to be heated. □ *n.* gold.

তপশ্চরণ, তপশ্চর্যা, তপশ্চারণ same as **তপঃ**।

তপসি *n.* the mango-fish.

তপসিল var. of **তফসিল**।

তপসে var. of **তপসি**।

তপস্যা *n.* religious austerities; asceticism or severe self-discipline.

তপস্বী *a.* engaged in austere endeavour to achieve an end; practising ascetic or religious austerities; engaged in worshipping God austerely. □ *n.* such a man; a hermit or ascetic (esp. one who dwells apart from human habitations or in a forest); the mango-fish. *fem.* **তপস্বিনী**।

তপোধন, তপোনিধি *n.* one who is rich in ascetic or religious austerities, a great hermit or ascetic.

তপোবন *n.* a hermitage (esp. one situated in a secluded place or in a forest).

তপোবল *n.* force or power acquired through practice of ascetic or religious austerities.

তপোভঙ্গ *n.* interruption in austere ascetic or religious meditation or in austere devotion of God.

তপোমূর্তি *n.* a body thinned and uncommonly brightened by the practice of ascetic or religious austerities; a hermit practising austerities.

তপোলোক *n.* a mythological world of happiness which may be attained through the practice of ascetic or religious austerities.

তপ্ত *a.* hot; heated; warm; having temperature; burning (রোষতপ্ত) ; angry; enraged (তপ্ত কথা) ; reddened with rage (তপ্ত আঁখি) ; agitated; molten (তপ্তকাঞ্চন). **~কাঞ্চনবর্ণ** *n.* the complexion as bright as molten gold. **~কাঞ্চনসন্নিভ** *a.* as bright and fair as molten gold.

তফসিল *n.* a schedule; a cadastre. **তফসিলি** *a.* scheduled; cadastral. □ *n.* one belonging to the scheduled caste. **তফসিলি সম্প্রদায়** the scheduled caste.

তফাত *n.* intervening space or distance; distance; difference, otherness; aloofness (তফাতে তফাতে থাকা). □ *a.* removed afar; separated; differentiated. □ *int.* avaunt; keep back. **তফাত করা** *v.* to remove; to separate; to alienate, to estrange; to differentiate; to discriminate. **তফাত হওয়া** *v.* to move or go away from; to be separated from; to be alienated or estranged. **তফাতে থাকা** *v.* to keep aloof; to remain at a distance; to keep one's distance.

তফিল dial. corrup. of **তহবিল**।

তব[1] *pro. a.* (used in poetry) your, yours, thy, thine.

তব[2] *adv. & con.* then.

তবক[1] *n.* a leaf of metal esp. of gold or silver, a foil; a layer (তবকে তবকে ভাসন্ত মেঘ).

তবক[2] *n.* (obs.) a gun (তবকের গুলি).

তবকি *n.* a gunman; a soldier armed with a gun.

তবল *n.* an axe. **~দার** *n.* a wood-cutter.

তবলচি *n.* one who plays on tabla (তবলা).

তবলা *n.* a kind of tabour played as musical accompaniment.

তবলিয়া *n.* same as **তবলচি**।

তবহি, তবহিঁ *adv.* (poet. & obs.) immediately, at once, forthwith; only in that case, then and then only.

তবহু, তবহুঁ *adv.* (poet. & obs.) still then, in spite of that, notwithstanding, withal.

তবিয়ত *n.* state of health; mental state, mood, humour.

তবিল coll. corrup. of **তহবিল**।

তবু, তবুও *adv. & con.* still then, in spite of that, nonetheless, nevertheless, notwithstanding, withal.

তবে *con. & adv.* then (যদি খেলা না হয়, তবে যেয়ো না) ; so, now (আসি তবে) ; thereafter or only then, then alone (আগে অভাবে পড় তবে পয়সা চিনবে) ; but, on the other hand (একান্তই যদি যাও, তবে আর আটকাব না). □ *int.* well (তবে রে).

তম[1] *sfx.* forming ordinal numerals, -th (শততম).

তম[2] *sfx.* forming superlative adjectives (প্রিয়তম).

তমঃ, (pop.) **তম**[3] *n.* darkness, gloom; the lowest element or primary quality of human nature and character, marked by ignorance and vice (also see **সত্ত্ব** and **রজঃ**).

তমস *n*. darkness, gloom.

তমসা *n*. the name of the river on the bank of which Valmiki received his first poetical inspiration; (pop.) darkness; (pop.) ignorance and vice.

তমসাচ্ছন্ন, তমসাবৃত *a*. pervaded or overcast with darkness or gloom.

তমসুক *n*. a writing of obligation to pay a sum, a bond; a hand-note. **বন্ধকি তমসুক** a deed of mortgage.

তমস্বিনী *a. fem.* full of darkness; dark, gloomy. □ *n. fem.* a dark night.

-তমা *fem*. of **তম১** and **-তম২** ।

তমাল *n*. a species of dark-coloured tree.

তমিস্র *n*. darkness, gloom. □ *a*. dark, gloomy. **তমিস্রা** *n*. (ori. *fem*.) a dark night. □ *a*. (ori. *fem*.) full of darkness, dark, gloomy.

-তমী *fem*. of **-তম১** and **তম২** ।

তমোগুণ *n*. the lowest element or the lowest primary quality of human nature and character marked by ignorance and vice (see also **সত্ত্বগুণ, রজোগুণ**) ।

তমোঘ্ন, তমোপহ *a*. expelling darkness; removing ignorance and vice. □ *n*. fire; the sun; the moon; a lamp; knowledge.

তমোময় *a*. full of darkness; full of ignorance and vice. *fem*. **তমোময়ী** ।

তমোহর same as **তমোঘ্ন** ।

তম্বি *n*. bluster; act of bullying; oppression. **তম্বি করা** *v*. to bluster; to bully; to oppress.

তম্বুর, তম্বুরা variants of **তানপুরা** ।

তয় *n*. full settlement; conclusion; a fold or plait (তয় করে রাখা).

তয়খানা *n*. an underground room or shelter (esp. one to live in during hot summer days).

তয়ফা *n*. party of professional dancing girls; (inc.) a professional dancing girl.

তয়ের dial. corrup. of **তৈয়ার** ।

-তর১ *sfx*. forming comparative adjectives (মহত্তর).

তর২ *n*. delay (তর সয় না).

তর৩ *a*. stupefied, besotted.

তর৪ *a*. (chiefly used as a *sfx*.) of a sort or kind (এমনতর, কেমনতর).

তর৫ *n*. act of crossing (as a river, a desert etc.).

তরওয়াল alt. spell. of **তরোয়াল** ।

তরকারি *n*. kitchen vegetables, garden stuff; vegetable curry. **তরকারির বাগান** a kitchen garden.

তরক্ষু *n*. the wolf; the hyena.

তরঙ্গ *n*. a wave; a ripple; a wavy or undulating stream, a wave (চিন্তাতরঙ্গ = a thought-wave, বায়ুতরঙ্গ, শব্দতরঙ্গ, বিদ্যুৎ-তরঙ্গ). **উত্তাল তরঙ্গ** *a*. billow, a high wave. **~ক্ষুব্ধ** *a*. lashed into fury by rolling waves; billowy, wavy; convulsed. **~চঞ্চল** *a*. rippling. **~ণ** *n*. undulation. **~দৈর্ঘ্য** *n*. wave-length. **~পাদ** *n*. the trough or hollow of a wave. **~পৃষ্ঠ** *n*. wave-surface. **~বিক্ষুব্ধ** same as **তরঙ্গক্ষুব্ধ** । **~বেগ** *n*. wave velocity. **~ভঙ্গ** *n*. breaking of waves (against rocks or other waves), curling and falling of waves. **~মালা** *n*. a string or series of waves. **~মুখ** *n*. wave front. **~শীর্ষ** *n*. the crest of a wave.

তরঙ্গাকুল *a*. restless on account of unquiet waves; very much disturbed (used of seas or oceans).

তরঙ্গাভিঘাত *n*. the push of a wave or waves.

তরঙ্গায়িত *a*. undulating, wavy, curling (তরঙ্গায়িত পথ বা চুল), (inc.) rippling.

তরঙ্গিণী *n. fem.* a river, a stream.

তরঙ্গিত *a*. wavy; rippling; undulating; curling; full of poses or attitudes.

তরঙ্গোচ্ছ্বাস *n*. swelling up of waves; rise and fall of waves.

তরজমা *n*. rendering into another language, translation. **তরজমা করা** *v*. to translate.

তরজা *n*. a kind of contest in songs composed extempore (cp. a strophe and its antistrophe).

তরণ *n*. act of going over, act of crossing; rescue, act of getting over; any means of crossing (e. g. a boat).

তরণি, তরণী *n*. a boat ; a ship; any means of crossing.

তরতম *n*. quality or quantity more or less; difference; differentiation.

তরতর১ *a*. of various kinds or sorts.

তরতর২ *int*. expressing : quick climbing or the quick running of a stream.

তরতরিয়ে *adv.* climbing quickly; flowing quickly (তরতরিয়ে গাছে ওঠা, তরতরিয়ে বয়ে যাওয়া).

তরতাজা *a.* fully alive (তরতাজা মাছ) ; quite fresh (তরতাজা খবর).

তরতিব *n.* a rule, a system, an order; an order of succession. **~ওয়ারি** *a.* following the order of succession, serial.

তরপণ্য *n.* charge of ferrying, ferriage.

তরফ *n.* a direction, a side, an end or extremity; either of two contesting parties (উভয় তরফ) ; a party; behalf (বাদীর তরফে উকিল) ; a revenue area, a tahsil (তরফ দেবীপুর) ; a partition or a partner of a landed estate. **~দার** *n.* the revenue-collector of an area; a partisan. **তরফা** *a.* relating to or affecting a party (এক তরফা = ex-parte).

তরবার, তরবারি *n.* a sword; a scimitar.

তরবুজ obs. var. of **তরমুজ**।

তরবেতর *a.* of various kinds or sorts; indisposed (শরীর তরবেতর হওয়া).

তরমুজ *n.* the water-melon.

তরল *a.* liquid, fluid, watery (তরল পদার্থ) ; thin (কালিটা বড় তরল) ; liquefied, diluted, thinned; melted, softened (স্নেহে তরল হওয়া) ; fickle, inconstant (তরলমতি). *fem.* **তরলা**। **তরল করা** *v.* to liquefy; to make more fluid or thinner, to dilute; to melt, to soften. **তরল হওয়া** *v.* to become liquefied, to liquefy; to become thinner or diluted; to melt, to soften. **তরল পদার্থ** a liquid, a fluid. **~তা, ~ত্ব** *n.* liquidity, fluidity, wateriness; thinness; softness; fickleness, inconstancy. **~নয়না, ~লোচনা** *a. fem.* giving quick glances, making eyes, having wanton eyes. **~মতি** *a.* fickle-minded, irresolute; of an immature frame of mind, of mind in the incipient stage of growth.

তরলাবস্থা *n.* liquid or fluid state, liquidity, fluidity.

তরলিত *a.* liquefied; dilute; melted, softened.

তরলীকরণ *n.* liquefaction; dilution; melting.

তরলীকৃত *a.* liquefied; diluted; melted.

তরলীভবন *n.* act of being liquefied or diluted or melted, liquefaction or dilution or melting.

তরলীভূত *a.* liquefied; diluted; melted, softened.

তরশু *adv.* three days before or after today.

তরসা *adv.* quickly, soon, promptly.

তরস্থান *n.*a ferry-station; a landing-place, a wharf.

তরস্বান, তরস্বী *a.* speedy; strong, powerful. *fem.* **তরস্বতী, তরস্বিনী**।

-তরা[১] *fem.* of **-তর**[১]।

তরা[২] *v.* to cross, to go across; to get over, to escape from. **তরে যাওয়া** *v.* to get over; to escape.

তরাই *n.* a belt of marshy region full of jungles at the foot of a hill (esp. at the foot of the Himalayas).

তরাজু *n.* balance, a pair of scales.

তরানো *v.* to take across; to rescue.

তরাস *n.* (coll.) fear, fright, alarm. **তরাসে** *a.* easily frightened.

তরি *n.* a vessel that is driven on water or in air (আকাশতরি, সমুদ্রতরি) ; a boat, a ship, a craft.

তরিক *n.* a small boat; a ferryman.

তরিকা *n.* a method, a system, a rule.

তরিত *a.* carried or ferried across.

তরিতরকারি *n.* kitchen vegetables, potherb. **তরিতরকারির বাগান** a kitchen garden.

তরিত্র *n.* any vessel or means for going across (e. g. a boat, a ship).

তরিবত *n.* etiquette; demeanour; education, teaching, training; careful cultivation (গোঁপের তরিবত) ; care. **তরিবত করা** *v.* to cultivate carefully; to look after carefully, to take care of.

তরী alt. spell. of **তরি**।

তরু *n.* a tree; a plant. **~কোটর** *n.* a hollow of a tree. **~ক্ষীর** *n.* latex. **~তল, ~মূল**[১] *n.* the foot of a tree. **~বর, ~রাজ** *n.* a large tree (such as, the banyan tree, the palm-tree etc.). **~বল্লী, ~লতা** *n.* a parasitic creeper; (in pl.) trees and creepers. **~ভুক, ~ভোজী** *a.* herbivorous. **~মূল**[২] *n.* the root of a tree. **~শিখর, ~শির** *n.*the top of a tree. **~সার** *n.* camphor.

তরুণ *a.* young; juvenile; adolescent;

fresh, new (তরুণ জ্বর) ; tender (তরুণাস্থি) ; immature (তরুণ বয়স, তরুণ বুদ্ধি). □ *n.* a young man or lad, a youth, a younker, a youngster. *fem.* **তরুণী** । **~তা, ~ত্ব** *n.* youth; juvenility; adolescence; freshness, newness; tenderness; immaturity. **~বয়স্ক** *a.* tender-aged; young. **তরুণাস্থি** *n.* cartilage, gristle. **তরুণিমা** same as **তরুণতা** ।

তরে *prep.* (dial. & poet.). for, on account of; because of; for the sake of.

-তরো alt. spell. of **-তর**⁴ ।

তরোয়াল *n.* a sword; a scimitar.

তর্ক *n.* a debate, an argument; reasoning; logic (তর্কশাস্ত্র) ; cause; discussion; consideration (মনে মনে তর্ক) ; dispute, controversy; altercation; doubt; assumption. **তর্ক করা** *v.* to debate; to argue; to reason; to discuss, to consider; to dispute; to altercate, to bandy words. **~কারী** *a. & n.* one who debates or argues or reasons or considers or disputes or altercates or bandies words; one who chops logic. **~জাল** *n.* array of arguments; (derog.) cobweb of argument. **~বিজ্ঞান, ~বিদ্যা, ~শাস্ত্র** *n.* logic. **~বিতর্ক** *n.* debate; altercation; arguments; bandying of words. **~যুদ্ধ** *n.* war of words. **~যোগ্য** *a.* arguable; debatable; controversial. **~সাধ্য** *a.* arguable; disputable; debatable. **তর্কাতর্কি** same as **তর্কবিতর্ক** । **তর্কাভাস** *n.* sophistry; a sophism. **তর্কের খাতিরে** *adv.* for the sake of argument.

তর্কিত *a.* debated; argued; discussed, considered; probable; anticipated; assumed.

তর্কী *a.* versed in logic or reasoning, one who debates or argues or bandies words; one who chops logic; given to debating or arguing. □ *n.* a logician.

তর্কু *n.* a spindle, a distaff. **~পিণ্ড** *n.* the ball at the lower end of the spindle.

তর্কেতর্কে *adv.* cautiously and secretly, surreptitiously (তর্কেতর্কে যাওয়া) ; in ambush, in wait (তর্কেতর্কে থাকা). coll. **তক্কেতক্কে** ।

তর্জন *n.* angry roar or shout; reprimand, severe scolding; blustering; bullying; threat; angry and loud bragging. **তর্জন করা** *v.* to roar or shout angrily; to reprimand, to scold severely; to bluster; to bully; to threaten; to brag angrily and loudly. **~গর্জন** *n.* severe scolding and loud shouts; threats and roars; explosion of feeling in angry words, angry outburst.

তর্জনী *n.* the index-finger, the forefinger. **তর্জনী হেলনে** *adv.* by waving one's finger.

তর্জমা alt. spell. of **তরজমা** ।

তর্জা alt. spell. of **তরজা** ।

তর্জানো same as **তর্জন করা** (see **তর্জন**) ।

তর্জিত *a.* blustered; bullied; severely scolded, reprimanded; threatened.

তর্পণ *n.* the sacrament of offering drinking water to the manes or deities. **তর্পণ করা** *v.* to offer drinking water to the manes or deities. **তর্পিত** *a.* (of dead spirits or deities) one to whom drinking water has been offered; satisfied, pleased. **তর্পী** *a.* one who offers drinking water to the manes or deities; one who satisfies. *fem.* **তর্পিণী** ।

তল *n.* the underneath (চরণতল, আকাশতল) ; base, foot, root (বৃক্ষতল) ; bottom, bed (সমুদ্রতল) ; surface (ভূতল) ; a plane (সমতল) ; the palm of the hand (করতল, তলপ্রহার) ; a storey, a floor (অট্টালিকার দ্বিতলে) ; a deck (জাহাজের দ্বিতলে). **~দেশ** *n.* bottom, bed; base, foot; the underneath. **~পেট** *n.* the lower part of the belly, the abdomen. **~প্রহার** *n.* a stroke with the open palm, a slap, a buffet. **তলপ্রহার করা** *v.* to slap, to buffet. **~স্থিত** a. lying at the bottom. **তলে তলে** at bottom; at heart; from behind the curtain, unobservedly, secretly, clandestinely, surreptitiously.

তলতল *int.* expressing : over-softness (chiefly caused by over-mellowness). **তলতলে** *a.* over-soft.

তলতা, তলদা *n.* a variety of thin and pliant bamboo.

তলপ var. of **তলব** ।

তলপি var. of **তল্পি** ।

তলব *n.* an order to come or appear or join; a summons, a call; salary.

তলবানা *n.* the fee of a peon for serving a summons or process.

তলবার rej. var. of **তলোয়ার**।

তলা *n.* the underneath (আকাশের তলা, পায়ের তলা) ; base, foot (গাছতলা) ; bottom, bed (সমুদ্রের তলা) ; a region or locality (ফুল তলা, নিমতলা, রথতলা) ; (of a building etc.) a storey, a floor; (of a ship, omnibus etc.) a deck.

তলাও *n.* a pond, a tank.

তলাতল *n.* the fourth of the seven mythological underworlds.

তলানি *n.* leas, dregs, sediment, deposit.

তলানো *v.* to sink (down), to be drowned (জাহাজখানা সমুদ্রে তলিয়ে গেল) ; to go to the bottom (তলিয়ে বোঝা, তলিয়ে দেখা) ; to be engrossed or absorbed in (চিন্তায় তলানো) ; to go down into, to be digested (পেটে তলানো). **তলিয়ে দেখা** v. to see or judge thoroughly. **তলিয়ে বোঝা** *v.* to realize or understand thoroughly. **পেটে না তলানো** *v.* not to be accepted in the stomach; not to be digested; to be vomited out; (fig.) not to be able to keep a secret.

তলাভিঘাত *n.* a stroke with the open palm of the hand, a slap, a buffet.

তলাশ, তলাস variants of **তল্লাশ**।

তলিত *a.* fried or roasted in oil or clarified butter or fat.

তলি[1] *n.* (chiefly dial.) the underneath or bottom; the sole.

-তলি[2] *sfx.* denoting : outskirts (শহরতলি).

তলোয়ার *n.* a sword, a scimitar.

তল্পি *n.* a bundle of bedding (esp. of a traveller). **~তল্পা** *n.* luggage (তল্পিতল্পা বাঁধা) ; one's household belongings (তল্পিতল্পা গোটানো). **~তল্পা গোটানো** *v.* to pack up one's household belongings; to pack up luggage; (fig.) to get ready for departure or disembarkment; (fig.) to leave a place for good, to clear out bag and baggage. **~দার, ~বাহক** *n.* a servant carrying one's luggage; a porter.

তল্লাট *n.* a region, a locality, a quarter, an area, a province. **এ তল্লাটে** in the neighbouring area, in the neighbourhood or vicinity.

তল্লাশ *n.* search; investigation; trace (তার তল্লাশ নেই). **তল্লাশ করা** *v.* to search; to investigate; to trace. **তল্লাশি** *a.* searching; investigating; tracing; authorizing to search or investigate; of search or investigation. □ *n.* a search. **তল্লাশি পরোয়ানা** *a.* search warrant.

তশরিফ *n.* (one's personal) greatness. **তশরিফ রাখুন** (will your greatness) please be seated.

তসবি *n.* (Mus.) a string of beads, a rosary.

তসবির *n.* a painting, picture or a portrait.

তসর *n.* a fawn-coloured silk from wild Indian silkworms, a coarse variety of Indian silk, tusser.

তসরিফ alt. spell. of **তশরিফ**।

তসরুফ, তসরুপ variants of **তছরুপ**।

তসলিম *n.* (Mus.) obeisance, salutation. **তসলিম করা** *v.* to salute.

তসিল coll. corrup. of **তহসিল**।

তস্কর *n.* a thief. *fem.* **তস্করী**। **~তা** *n.* theft.

তস্য *pro.* a. (now obs.) his.

তহখানা *n.* an underground room or cell.

তহবিল *n.* a fund; cash (in hand); a treasury. **~দার** *n.* one in charge of a fund; a cash-keeper; a cashier; a treasurer. **~দারি** *n.* charge of a fund; cash-keeping; cashiership; treasureship.

তহমত *n.* accusation, complain.

তহরি *n.* fee of a writer or copyist (esp. of a letter or a legal document); an extra payment exacted for themselves by the officers of a landowner from tenants; a discount given by a seller for the personal appropriation of a servant making purchases for his master; a discount given to an agent of purchase.

তহসিল *n.* collected revenue; collection of revenue; a revenue collector's office; a revenue area, a tahsil **~দার** *n.* a revenue collector, a revenue officer, a tahsilder. **~দারি** *n.* the post or office of a revenue collector or tahsilder.

তহি, তহিঁ *adv.* & *con.* (poet. & obs.) there; moreover, further; for that, so, therefore; in it; then.

তহু তহুঁ *pro.* (poet. & obs.) in it; there.

তহুরি var. of **তহরি**।

-তা[1] *sfx.* denoting : -ness, -ship, -ity, etc. (মূর্খতা, কুটিলতা, নির্জনতা).

তা[২] coll. contr. of **তাহা**।

তা[৩] *n.* a sheet (as of paper).

তা[৪] *n.* twist, twirl, trimming (গোঁপে তা). **তা দেওয়া** *v.* to twist, to twirl, to trim.

তা[৫] *n.* act of sitting upon eggs (as by mother-birds), hatch, incubation. **তা দেওয়া** *v.* to sit upon eggs, to hatch, to incubate.

তা[৬] *int.* an expletive inserted chiefly as a breather in a speech (তা কখন আমি যাব ?) ; let it go, well (তা তোমার কী মত ?). □ *con.* but, still (রোজ যাব ভাবি, তা যাওয়া আর হয়ে ওঠে না).

তাই[১] coll. contr. of **তাহাই**।

তাই[২] *n.* clap of hands. **তাই দেওয়া** *v.* to clap one's hands, to clap.

তাই[৩] *adv. & con.* for that, so. **~তো** *adv. & con* and so, because. □ *int.* expressing : certainty, amazement, bewilderment etc. **~তে** *adv. & con.* for that, because of that, on account of that, so; and in reply to that. **তাই নাকি** is it so ? **তাই বলে** *adv. & con.* for that, because of that, on account of that, so.

তাইরে-নাইরে *int. & n.* (chiefly dero.) noise of a song; whiling away one's time in useless things; idling.

তাউই, তাওই variants of **তালুই**।

তাওয়া *n.* a metal baking pan (রুটি সেঁকার তাওয়া) ; an earthen vessel to hold burning husk or chaff or charcoal etc.; a metal plate with which the bowl of a hookah is covered.

তাওয়ানো *v.* to heat; to make red-hot by burning; (fig.) to enrage or agitate; (fig.) to incite.

তাং abbr. of **তারিখ**।

তাংড়ানো *v.* to be spacious enough to hold or contain; to be able to manage.

তাঁকে coll. var. of **তাঁহাকে**।

তাঁত *n.* a loom; a gut; a catgut; a thong. **~ঘর, ~শালা** *n.* a weaver's workshop. **তাঁত বোনা** *v.* to weave cloth, to work at a loom.

তাঁতি *n.* weaver (by trade or caste). *fem.* **তাঁতিনি**। **অতি লোভে তাঁতি নষ্ট** too much greed ruins a person.

তাঁবা dial. corrup. of **তামা**।

তাঁবু *n.* a tent. **তাঁবু খাটানো** *v.* to pitch a tent. **তাঁবু তোলা** *v.* to strike a tent. **তাঁবু পড়েছে** *v.* a tent is pitched.

তাঁবে *n.* control, rule, authority, command. **তাঁবে থাকা** *v.* to be under (a person), to be under control or rule or authority or command of. **~দার** *n.* a dependant; a subordinate; one who carries out orders (of), a servile person; a servant. □ *a.* dependent; subordinate; carrying out orders; servile. **তাঁবেদার রাষ্ট্র** *a.* dependency, a mandatory state. **তাঁবেদার সরকার** a government servile to a foreign power; a puppet government; a satellite government. **~দারি** *n.* subjection, dependence; servility. **তাঁবেদারি করা** *v.* to do a person's bidding or obey his orders obsequiously.

তাক[১] *pro.* (poet. & obs.) him or her.

তাক[২] *n.* a shelf; a recess in a wall, an alcove.

তাক[৩] *n.* a target, an aim, a mark; a guess (অন্ধকারে তাক করা) ; act of lying in wait, ambush, ambuscade (বাঘটা তাক করে আছে) ; bewilderment; amazement (তাক লাগা). **তাক করা** *v.* to aim at; to guess; to lie in wait, to ambush, to ambuscade. **তাক লাগা** *v.* to be stricken with bewilderment, to be bewildered; to be dazed; to be wonder-struck, to be amazed. **তাকে তাকে থাকা** to be on the lookout or watch (for).

তাকত *n.* physical strength.

তাকর *pro. a.* (poet. & obs.) his or her.

তাকা[১] *v.* to imprecate (esp. something evil), to aim at; to guess, to anticipate.

তাকা[২] *v.* to look (at), to gaze (at).

তাকাদা var. of **তাগাদা**।

তাকানো *v.* to look (at).

তাকাবি *n.* an agricultural loan or earnest money.

তাকিদ var. of **তাগাদা**।

তাকিয়া *n.* a dumpy bolster.

তাকে coll. contr. of **তাহাকে**।

তাগ variants of **তাক**[৩]।

তাগড়া, তাগড়াই *a.* tall and robust or massive, stout, gigantic, hefty.

তাগা *n.* an armlet; an amulet to be tied round one's arm or waist or any other part of the body; a ligature put on to stop blood circulation (as in the case of snakebites).

তাগাড় *n.* a (bricklayer's) hod; a piece of ploughed land made clayey by watering for the germination of seeds.

তাগাদা *n.* (repeated) reminder for payment, dunning (বাড়ি ভাড়ার তাগাদা) ; (repeated) demand (লেখার জন্য তাগাদা) ; (repeated) urging (পড়াশোনার জন্য তাগাদা) ; urgency (পৌঁছানোর তাগাদা) ; urge (বাঁচার তাগাদা). **তাগাদা করা, তাগাদা দেওয়া** *v.* to remind (repeatedly) for payment, to dun; to demand (repeatedly); to urge (repeatedly), to press for.

তাগারি *n.* a large trough, a vat.

তাগিদ var. of **তাগাদা** ।

তাগুড়ানো alt. spell. of **তাংড়ানো** ।

তাচ্ছিল্য, (rare) **তাচ্ছল্য** *n.* slight, contempt; disregard; neglect. **তাচ্ছিল্য করা** *v.* to treat with slight or contempt; to disregard; to neglect. **~পূর্ণ** *a.* full of slight, contemptuous; disregardful, neglectful.

তাজ *n.* a crown, a diadem, a coronet; a tiara.

তাজা *a.* fresh (তাজা আনাজ) ; new; alive, living; lively, spirited (তাজা প্রাণ, তাজা মন) ; refreshed, reinvigorated (শরীর তাজা হওয়া). **তাজা কার্তুজ** a live cartridge.

তাজিয়া *n.* (Mus.) a feretory carried in imitation of the coffin of Hasan and Hussain in Moharram processions.

তাজি *n.* an excellent variety or breed of horses, a steed.

তাজ্জব *a.* queer, quaint; amazing; amazed (তাজ্জব বনা, তাজ্জব হওয়া). □ *n.* queerness, quaintness; amazement (তাজ্জবের ব্যাপার).

তাঞ্জাম *n.* an ornamented sedan-chair or palanquin.

তাড় *n.* a kind of armlet.

তাড়কা *n.* the name of a dreadful female rakshasa as mentioned in the Ramayana; (fig.) a vicious woman of monstrous appearance.

তাড়ন, তাড়না *n.* guiding rule or control; beating, chastisement, flogging; act of striking; rebuke, scolding; pressing, urging; goading; urge; oppression. **তাড়না করা** *v.* to rule or control for guidance; to beat, to chastise, to flog; to strike; to rebuke, to scold; to press, to urge, to impel; to goad; to oppress; to vex. **তাড়নী** *n.* any contrivance to flog or goad or urge with, such as a stick, a lash, a cane, a scourge, a goad.

তাড়স *n.* pressure of or suffering caused by pain or inflammation, brunt (ব্যথার তাড়স) ; stupor (জ্বরের তাড়স). **তাড়সের জ্বর** sympathetic fever.

তাড়া[১] *n.* a bundle (চিঠির তাড়া), a sheaf.

তাড়া[২] *v.* to chase (তাড়া করা). □ *n.* chase (পুলিশের তাড়া) ; rebuke, reproof, chastisement (গুরুজনদের তাড়া) ; act of scaring away (তাড়া পেয়ে বাঘটা সরেছে). **তাড়া খাওয়া** *v.* to be chased; to be rebuked or chided; to be snubbed. **তাড়া দেওয়া** *v.* to give one a talking-to, to snub.

তাড়া[৩] *n.* urgent pressure or call, urgency (কাজের তাড়া) ; hurry (আমার তাড়া নেই) ; pressure for hurrying (তাড়া দেওয়া).

তাড়াতাড়ি *adv.* quickly, hurriedly, hastily. □ *n.* hurry, haste (আমার তাড়াতাড়ি নেই). **তাড়াতাড়ি করা** *v.* to make haste.

তাড়ানো *v.* to chase away; to drive away; to shoo away; to expel or banish (বাড়ি বা দেশ থেকে তাড়ানো) ; to ward off, to guard against; to cause to graze, to tend (গোরু তাড়ানো) ; (sarcas. & dero.) to teach and discipline (ছেলে তাড়ানো). □ *a.* chased or driven away; expelled or banished; warded off.

তাড়াহুড়ো *n.* excessive hurry or haste; hurry and bustle, hurry-scurry.

তাড়ি[১] *n.* a small-bundle, a packet, a sheaf (এক তাড়ি খড়).

তাড়ি[২] *n.* arrack, toddy. **~খানা** *n.* an arrack-shop, a toddy-shop.

তাড়িত[১] *a.* beaten, chastised, flogged; rebuked, scolded; struck; pressed; urged, impelled; propelled; goaded; oppressed; driven or chased away; expelled or banished.

তাড়িত[২] *a.* of or produced by or run by electricity, electric, electrical; galvanic. □ *n.* electricity. **~কোষ** *n.* a galvanic pot. **তাড়িত চুম্বক** *n.* an electro-magnet. **তাড়িত প্রবাহ** *n.* electric current.

~বার্তা *n.* a telegraphic message, a telegram, (coll.) a wire. **~বিজ্ঞান, ~বিদ্যা** *n.* the science of electricity, electricity. **~বিজ্ঞানী** *n.* an electrical scientist.

তাড়িতালোক *n.* electric light.

তাড়িতী *n.* an electrician.

তাডু *n.* a wooden or metal ladle with a broad blade used in making sweets.

তাড্যমান *a.* in the state of being rebuked or stricken or hit or chastised or wounded on (in case of a musical instrument) played upon.

তাণ্ডব *n.* an annihilation dance; a frantic or frenzied dance; frantic or frenzied behaviour or affair (বন্যার তাণ্ডব, তাণ্ডব বাধানো). **~লীলা** *n.* the frantic dance of Shiva (শিব) at the time of the annihilation of the world.

তাত[1] *n.* (now obs.) father; used chiefly in addressing one's father or superior or (in affection) a younger person.

তাত[2] *n.* heat (আগুনের তাত) ; (fig.) anger. **তাত সয় তো বাত সয় না** hot weather is bad, but foul weather is worse.

তাৎকালিক *a.* of that time, the then; contemporary.

তাৎক্ষণিক *a.* extemporaneous, off-hand.

তাৎপর্য *n.* purport, significance, meaning (কবিতার তাৎপর্য) ; purpose, object (এ কাজের তাৎপর্য কী) ; ; quickness, sharpness (বুদ্ধির তাৎপর্য). **~হীন** *a.* nonsense, meaningless; purposeless.

তাতল *a.* (poet. & obs.) hot, heated.

তাতা *v.* to be heated; to warm up; (fig.) to get angry or excited.

তাতা-থৈ *n.* symbolical words or sounds guiding the Tandava (তাণ্ডব) dance; symbolical sound of dance.

তাতানো *v.* to make hot, to heat; to warm up; (fig.) to make angry or to excite. □ *a.* heated, warmed up; (fig.) angered or excited.

তাতার *n.* a Tatar. *fem.* তাতারি।

তাতাল *n.* a soldering-iron.

তাত্ত্বিক *a.* relating to or versed in truth or reality; relating to or versed in philosophical or ontological or spiritual knowledge; theoretical. □ *n.* such a person (ভাষাতাত্ত্বিক).

তাথ্যিক *a.* relating to actual state or affair, factual; informative; relating to reality or truth.

তাদর্থ্য *n.* identity of meaning or object or purpose or motive or reason.

তাদাত্ম্য *n.* identity in spirit or soul; identity, unity, sameness.

তাদৃশ *a.* suchlike; such; similar. *fem.* **তাদৃশী**।

তাধিয়া var. of **তাতা-থৈ**।

তান *n.* the key-note of a song; musical note, strain, melody; (pop) very quick recital of musical notes. **তান ছাড়া** *v.* (mus.) to open out one's voice. **তান তোলা** *v.* (mus.) to open out one's voice gradually. **তান ধরা** *v.* to begin to sing a particular melody; to utter a melodious note (পাপিয়া তান ধরেছে).

তানপুরা *n.* a stringed musical instrument (usually of four strings, but sometimes of six strings) that helps a singer to maintain perfect or flawless tune.

তানা-না-না *n.* the prefatory airs of music; (sarcas). waste of time by dilatoriness in making useless preparatory arrangement, act or an instance of saying neither yes nor no.

তান্তব *a.* made of thread or gut; made on loom; of thread or loom or gut; ductile.

তান্ত্রিক[1] *a.* of or according to or versed in or worshipping in accordance with the Tantras (তন্ত্র) of Shaktas (শাক্ত). □ *n.* one who worships in accordance with the Tantras. **~তা** *n.* obedience to the Tantras.

তান্ত্রিক[2] *sfx.* used with nouns to form adjectives (e. g. গণতান্ত্রিক, বস্তুতান্ত্রিক).

তাপ *n.* heat, warmth; anger; sorrow, grief, affliction, suffering. **~ক** *a.* that which or one who heats or excites or grieves or afflicts. **~ক্লিষ্ট** *a.* afflicted with heat; aggrieved. **~গতিবিদ্যা** *n.* thermodynamics. **~গ্রহণ** *n.* (phys.) absorption of heat. **~গ্রাহিতা** *n.* thermal capacity. **~জনক** *a.* producing heat; (sc.) calorific; causing sorrow, afflicting. **~ত্রয়** *n.* the three kinds of affliction: spiritual, supernatural and material.

~ধারকত্ব *n.* thermal capacity. ~ন *n.* generation or application of heat; the sun. □ *a.* producing heat; calorific (তাপন মূল্য) ; causing affliction. ~নীয় *a.* that to which heat is to be applied. ~প্রবাহ *n.* a period of very hot weather; heat wave. ~বীক্ষণ *n.* a thermoscope. ~মাত্রা *n.* temperature. ~মান, ~মান-যন্ত্র *n.* a thermometer. ~রোধিত্ব *n.* heat-resistance; athermancy. ~সহ *a.* heat resistant, heat-proof. ~সেক *n.* fomentation. ~স্থাপক *n.* thermostat.

তাপস *a.* practising ascetic or religious austerities; engaged in worshipping God by means of severe austerities. □ *n.* such a man; a hermit or ascetic. ~তরু *n.* a tree from the berries of which ancient Indian sages used to prepare a medicinal oil.

তাপসিক *a.* ascetic.

তাপসী *fem.* of তাপস।

তাপস্য *n.* state of being a hermit, asceticism.

তাপা *v.* to get heated; to warm up; to bask; to be afflicted. ~নো *v.* to heat; to warm up; to afflict. ~য়ন *v.* (poet. & obs.) to afflict; to heat; to warm up.

তাপাপন *n.* calorescence.

তাপিত *a.* heated, hot; afflicted, stricken with sorrow, aggrieved, *fem.* তাপিতা।

তাপিনী *fem.* of তাপী।

তাপী *a.* (rare) heated, hot; afflicted, sorrow-stricken; mortified, remorseful; (rare) producing heat, calorific; (rare) causing affliction or mortification.

তাপীয় *a.* thermal; calorific, caloric.

তাপ্পি *n.* coll. var. of তালি[৩] ।

তাফতা *n.* taffeta, a silklike fabric.

তাবৎ *a.* & *pro.* all, all those or all that. □ *adv.* & *con.* to that number or quantity or degree or extent; till then; till.

তাবিজ *n.* an amulet usually worn on the arm.

তামড়ি *n.* garnet.

তামরস *n.* the lotus; copper; gold.

তামলি *n.* a Hindu caste selling betel-leaves; a member of this caste.

তামস *a.* full of deep darkness; full of Cimmerian darkness, irrevocably dark; having the lowest of the elements or primal qualities of human nature and character; full of ignorance and vice. ~যজ্ঞ *n.* a ritual performed with vanity and pomp but without reverence. **তামসিক** *a.* having the lowest of the elements or primary qualities of the human nature and character; relating to this quality; full of ignorance and vice; overcast with cloud, cloud-ridden. **তামসী** *a. fem.* of তামস। □ *n.* a dark night; a night of the new moon.

তামা *n.* copper. ~তুলসী *n.* copper and basil (these two are considered very holy by Hindus, and whilst taking an oath, one holds them in one's hand).

তামাক, তামাকু *n.* tobacco. **তামাক খাওয়া, তামাক টানা, তামাক ফোঁকা** *v.* to smoke a hookah or a hubble-bubble or a pipe; to smoke. **তামাক সাজা** *v.* to fill a hookah or a hubble-bubble or a pipe with tobacco for smoking. ~খোর *n.* a tobacco-smoker, a smoker; (facet.) a tobaccanalian. ~বিক্রেতা *n.* a tobacconist.

তামাটে *a.* copper-coloured, coppery, copper, cupreous (তামাটে আকাশ = copper sky).

তামাদি *n.* lapse of limited time; state of being time-barred. □ *a.* time-barred, barred by limitation.

তামাম *a.* all, whole, entire. **তামামি** *n.* end, termination (সালতামামি).

তামাশা *n.* an entertaining or amusing performance, a show, an exhibition; a fun, a joke, a jest. **তামাশা করা** *v.* to make fun (of); to make a song (of); to poke fun (at); to crack a joke (with); to jest. **তামাশা দেখা** *v.* to enjoy a show; to find fun in. **তামাশা দেখানো** *v.* to give a show.

তামিল[১] *n.* a South Indian language; the language of Tamil Nadu; an inhabitant of Tamil Nadu; a speaker of Tamil.

তামিল[২] *n.* compliance, act of carrying out. **তামিল করা** *v.* to comply with, to carry out.

তামুক corrup. of তামাক।

তাম্বু var. of তাঁবু।

তাম্বুরা var. of তম্বুরা।

তাম্বূল *n.* betel-leaf; a preparation of betel-leaves with lime, catechu, areca nut etc. which is chewed as a quid. **~করঙ্ক** *n.* a box to hold the aforesaid preparation of betel-leaves. **~বল্লী** *n.* a betel creeper or plant. **~রাগ** *n.* a red tint on the lips caused by the juice of the aforesaid preparation of betel-leaves as one chews it. **তাম্বূলাকার** *a.* cordate. **তাম্বূলিক, তাম্বূলী** *n.* a Hindu caste selling betel-leaves; a member of this caste.

তাম্র *n.* copper. □ *a.* copper-coloured (তাম্রকেশ) ; made of copper (তাম্রপাত্র) ; like or of copper (তাম্রবর্ণ). **~কার** *n.* a coppersmith, a brazier. **~কুণ্ড** *n.* a copper pot. **~গর্ভ** *n.* sulphate of copper, copperas. **~চূড়** *n.* a cock. **~পট্ট, ~পত্র, ~ফলক** *n.* a copper plate. **~পাত্র** *n.* a copper vessel. **~বর্ণ** *a.* copper-coloured, coppery, copper, cupreous. □ *n.* the colour of copper. **তাম্রবর্ণ আকাশ** copper-coloured sky. **~যুগ** *n.* the Copper Age. **~রুচি** same as **তাম্রবর্ণ** (*a.*) **~লিপি** *n.* an inscription on a copper plate, a copper inscription. **~শাসন** *n.* a royal edict or inscription on a copper plate. **~সার** *n.* red sandalwood.

তাম্রকূট *n.* tobacco. **~সেবন** *n.* act of smoking tobacco. **~সেবী** *a.* tobacco-smoking. □ *n.* a tobacco-smoker, a smoker.

তাম্রাভ *a.* copper-coloured, coppery, copper, cupreous.

তাম্রাশ্ম *n.* ruby.

তায় *pro.* him or her; in him or her. □ *adv. & con.* over and above, on the top of, and moreover (একে রাত্রি তায় ঝড়).

তায়দাদ *n.* description of the confine or boundary of a plot of land.

তার[১] coll. form of **তাহার**।

তার[২] *n.* taste, savour, savouriness.

তার[৩] *n.* act of going across, act of crossing.

তার[৪] *a.* ve y loud (তারস্বর).

তার[৫] *n.* metal string, wire; funicle; a telegram, (coll.) a wire. **তার করা** *v.* to telegraph; (coll.) to wire. **তার খাটানো** *v.* to supply a building etc. with wire; to do wiring. **তার পাওয়া** *v.* to receive a telegram. **তার পাঠানো** *v.* to send a telegram, to telegraph. **তারের জাল** wire netting. **তারের কাজ** filigree work.

তারক *a.* one who rescues or saves. □ *n.* a rescuer, a deliverer; a saviour; a helmsman; a pilot; a boat, a raft. **~নাথ** *n.* a name of Shiva (শিব). **~ব্রহ্ম** *n.* ওঁ শ্রীরামরাম : these holy words.

তারকা[১] *fem.* of **তারক** (*n*).

তারকা[২] *n.* a star; the pupil of the eye; the star-mark, an asterisk *; prominent performer or an actor or actress especially of the film, a film-star (also **চিত্রতারকা**). **~খচিত** star-spangled. **~চিহ্নিত** *a.* marked with an asterisk. **~মণ্ডিত** *a.* star-spangled.

তারকায়িত *a.* starry, bedecked with stars; star-spangled; marked as a star performer or a film-star.

তারকারি *n.* the slayer of Taraka (তারক) the demon; an appellation of Kartikeya (কার্তিকেয়).

তারকিণী *a. fem.* starry. □ *n. fem.* the night.

তারকিত *a.* having a star or stars, marked with a star, starred, starry.

তারকী *a.* having a star or stars, starry.

তারঙ্গ *a.* undulatory. **~বাদ** *n.* undulatory theory.

তারজালি *n.* fine mesh of wire, wire-gauze.

তারণ *a.* one who or that which rescues or takes across. □ *n.* a rescuer, a deliverer, a saviour; one who takes across; a ferryman.

তারণি *n.* a boat, a raft, a vessel.

তারতম্য *n.* state of being more or less; difference; disparity; discrimination: comparison. **তারতম্য করা** *v.* to make more or less; to differentiate; to discriminate; to compare.

তারপর *adv.* after that, thereafter, then.

তারপলিন *n.* tarpaulin.

তারপিন *n.* turpentine, terebinth.

তারবার্তা *n.* a telegram, (coll.) a wire.

তারযন্ত্র *n.* a stringed musical instrument.

তারযোগে *adv.* by telegraph, telegraphically, by wire.

তারল্য *n.* liquidity, fluidity, wateriness; thinness; lack of concentration; melted or softened state; softness; fickleness, inconstancy.

তারসপ্তক *n.* the major E-scale.

তারস্বর *n.* a very loud voice. **তারস্বরে** *adv.* in a very loud voice.

তারা *v.* to rescue, to deliver. □ *n. fem.* one who rescues or delivers from worldly sufferings; a manifestation or name of goddess Durga (দুর্গা) ; (mus.) the major E-scale, (cp.) tenor; a star; an asterisk; the pupil of the eye. **~কার** *a.* stellate. **~চন্দ্র, ~নাথ, ~পতি** *n.* the lord or husband of stars; an appellation of the moon. **~পতন, ~পাত** *n.* the fall of a meteor. **~পথ** *n.* the stellar course; the sky, the welkin. **~বাতি** *n.* a firework that emits starlike sparks. **~মণ্ডল** *n.* the stellar region or orbit; a constellation. **~মাছ** *n.* the starfish. **~সম্বন্ধীয়** *a.* stellar.

তারানা *n.* a vocal style of Indian classical music like the Khayal but sung with meaningless words.

তারিকা *fem.* of **তারক** (*a.*).

তারিখ *n.* a statement of time or a day of a month, a date. **তারিখ দেওয়া** *v.* to date, to give a date. **আগামী মাসের দোসরা তারিখে** on the 2nd of the coming month, on the 2nd proximo. **গত মাসের দোসরা তারিখে** on the 2nd of the last month, on the 2nd ultimo. **বর্তমান বা চলতি মাসের দোসরা তারিখে** on the 2nd of the current month, on the 2nd instant. **~হীন** *a.* undated.

তারিণী *a. fem.* one who rescues or delivers. □ *n. fem.* an appellation of goddess Durga (দুর্গা).

তারিফ *n.* praise, applause, plaudit, admiration; appreciation; bravado. **তারিফ করা** *v.* to praise, to applaud, to admire; to appreciate, to speak highly of.

তারুণ্য *n.* youth; juvenility; adolescence; freshness, newness; tenderness; immaturity.

তারে var. of **তাকে** (now chiefly used in poetry).

তার্কিক *a.* versed in or fond of argumentation or logic; (loos.) sophistical. □ *a.* a logician; one w io is versed in or fond of agrumentati‹ n; (loos.) a sophist.

তার্পিন *n.* turpentine, terebinth.

তাল১ var. of **টাল২** ।

তাল২ *n.* a push or impact, pressure, weight, unexpected difficulty or danger (তাল সামলানো). **তাল সামলানো** *v.* to bear the weight or stand the impact of; to keep up one's composure or evenness of mind under trying circumstances.

তাল৩ *n.* a span or its measure (সপ্ততাল = measuring seven spans).

তাল৪ *n.* an imaginary goblin (তালবেতাল).

তাল৫ *n.* a large lump or ball or clod. **তাল করা** *v.* to collect into a lump, to heap up, to amass. **তালগোল পাকানো, তাল পাকানো** *v.* to form into a confused (round) ball or lump; to make or be made a mess of, to bungle or be bungled. **~গোল** *n.* a confused round ball or lump; confusion. **~তাল** *a.* lumps of; a large amount of.

তাল৬ *n.* the fanpalm or palmyra; its fruit; the juice or any preparation made of the juice of the palmyra-fruit (তাল খাওয়া, তাল দিয়ে ভাত মাখা). **তাল পড়ছে** *v.* palmyra-fruits are falling (from the tree); (facet.) heavy fisticuffs are being rained (upon). **~ক্ষীর** *n.* a sweetmeat prepared of the juice of the palmyra-fruit. **~চোঁচ, ~বাতাসি** *n.* the palm-swift bird. **~নবমী** *n.* the ninth day of the waxing moon of the month of Bhadra (ভাদ্র). **~পাখা** *n.* a fan made of a palmyra-leaf. **~পাতা** *n.* palmyra-leaf (this was formerly used in place of paper to write upon). **তালপাতার সেপাই** (facet.) a cowardly and sickly or thin-built man who introduces himself as a soldier. **~পুকুর** *n.* a pond surrounded on all sides by fanpalm trees. **~বৃন্ত** *n.* a stalk with leaves of a palmyra-tree; a fan made of this. **~শাঁস** *n.* the edible kernel of the stone of a palmyra-fruit.

তাল৭ *n.* musical time or measure (গানের তাল) ; beating or keeping of musical time chiefly by clapping one's hands (তাল দেওয়া) ; act or an instance of slapping one's arms or palms at the time of attacking (তাল ঠোকা). **তাল কাটা** *v.* to fail to maintain musical time or measure (সে বাজনায় বড় তাল কেটে ফেলে) ; to have a breach of musical time or measure (গানে তাল কেটেছে). **~কানা** *a.* lacking in proper sense of musical time or measure; blind to the right way or method. **~জ্ঞান** *n.* sense of time or measure in music; sense of proportion; common sense. **তাল ঠোকা** *v.* (fig.) to give a call to fight (to see who is better), to throw out challenge. **তাল দেওয়া** *v.* (mus.) to beat time; (fig.) to instigate. **তাল রাখা** *v.* to maintain musical time. **তাল রেখে চলা** *v.* to keep pace with; to humour, to flatter; to keep in with a person's tastes and temperament. **~মান** *n.* musical measure and pitch. **~মাফিক** *adv.* at the right moment; in tune with circumstances. **ঢিমা তাল** see **ঢিমা**।

তালই dial. var. of **তালুই**।

তালব্য *a.* palatal. **~বর্ণ** *n.* (gr.) a palatal letter.

তালা[1] *n.* a padlock, a lock. **তালা দেওয়া** *v.* to lock. **তালা লাগানো** *v.* to lock; to fit with a lock.

তালা[2] *n.* a storey or floor (of a building); a deck or tier (of a ship, an omnibus etc.).

তালা[3] *n.* act of deafening temporarily. **তালা লাগা** *v.* to be deafened temporarily. **তালা লাগানো** *v.* to deafen temporarily.

তালাক *n.* (mus.) divorce. **তালাক দেওয়া** *v.* to divorce. **~নামা** *n.* a deed of divorcement.

তালাশ, তালাস variants of **তল্লাস**।

তালি[1] var. of **তালা[3]**।

তালি[2] *n.* act of clapping (esp. one's hands). **তালি দেওয়া** *v.* to clap (esp. one's hands).

তালি[3] *n.* a patch (as on torn clothes). **তালি দেওয়া** *v.* to patch.

তালি[4] *n.* the fanpalm or palmyra; its fruit. **~বন** *n.* a palmyra-grove.

তালিকা *n.* a list, a catalogue, an inventory; a roster; a table.

তালিবন see **তালি[4]**।

তালিম *n.* instruction; teaching; training; education. **তালিম দেওয়া** *v.* to instruct; to teach; to train; to educate.

তালু *n.* the palate (of the mouth); the crown (of the head). **~মূল** *n.* the root of the palate.

তালুই *n.* the father-in-law or an uncle-in-law of one's brother or sister.

তালুক *n.* a tract of proprietary land, a taluk; a landed estate. **~দার** *n.* the owner of a taluk, a talukdar; the owner of a landed estate, a landholder (esp. one who pays revenue not directly to the government. **~দারি** *n.* estate or rule or office of a talukdar or landholder. □ *a.* relating to a talukdar or a taluk.

তালেগোলে *adv.* in the confusion or disorder, in the confused state of things (তালেগোলে কলমটা হারিয়ে গেল).

তালেবর *a.* (chiefly facet.) claiming to be respectable and influential, wealthy and powerful.

তাস *n.* playing card(s). **তাস-খেলা** *n.* card-game. **তাস খেলা, তাস পেটা** *v.* to play cards. **তাস দেওয়া, তাস বাঁটা** *v.* to deal out cards. **তাস ভাঁজা** *v.* to shuffle cards. **তাসের ঘর, তাসের বাড়ি** (fig.) any construction that may tumble down easily at any time; a house of cards. **তাসের পিঠ** a trick.

তাসা[1] **তাসানো** *v.* to shuffle cards. □ *a.* shuffled.

তাসা[2] *n.* a kind of small drum or tabor.

তাস্কর্য *n.* the profession of a thief, stealing, thievery; theft.

তাহা (now obs.) *pro.* that (thing). **তাহাকে,** (rej.) **তাহারে** *pro.* him. *pl.* **তাহাদিগকে,** (rej.) **তাহাদেরকে** them. **তাহাতে** *pro.* in that; in him or her; because of that, on account of that, for that; at that; with him or her or that (তাহাতে আমাতে সদ্ভাব নাই). □ *con & adv.* notwithstanding (that), withal; still (যদি না পার তাহাতে ক্ষতি নাই) ; over and above, on the top of, moreover (একে ধনী তাহাতে উচ্চপদস্থ). **তাহার** *pro. a.* his, her, its; of that. *pl.* **তাহাদের,** (obs.) **তাহাদিগের** their; of those. **তাহারা** see **সে**।

তাহে (poet.) *con. & adv.* over and above, moreover, on the top of ('একে কুহু

যামিনী, তাহে কুলকামিনী'). □ *pro.* (poet. & obs.) him or her or it, in him or her or it.

তিক্ত *n.* bitter taste, bitterness, a bitter substance, bitter. □ *a.* bitter; (fig.) unpleasant or acrimonious. **~তা** *n.* bitterness; (fig.) unpleasantness or acrimoniousness.

তিগ্ম *a.* violent; hot, torrid; keen, sharp. **~কর** *n.* the sun; scorching sunrays.

তিঙন্ত *a.* (Sans. gr.) declinable.

তিজারত var. of **তেজারত** ।

তিজেল *n.* an almost semi-circular large clay dixie for cooking and other purposes.

তিড়বিড় *int.* expressing restlessness. **তিড়বিড়ানি** *n.* restlessness. **তিড়বিড়ে** *a.* restless, fickle.

তিড়িং, তিড়িক *int.* expressing : a sudden skip. **তিড়িংতিড়িং, তিড়িংবিড়িং** *int.* expressing : repeated skipping, **তিড়িংতিড়িং করা** *v.* to skip repeatedly, to cut a caper.

তিত, তিতা[1] coll. corruptions of **তিক্ত** ।

তিতকুটে *a.* slightly bitter in taste.

তিতা[2] *v.* (obs.) to get wet or moistened ('তিতি অশ্রুনীরে') ; to be embittered ('তিতায় তিতিল দে'). □ *a.* wet (স্নানান্তে তিতা বস্ত্র এড়িলেন). **তিতানো** *v.* to make wet, to wet. to moisten; to embitter.

তিতিক্ষা *n.* forbearance, patience; forgiveness. **তিতিক্ষিত** *a.* forborne; forgiven. **তিতিক্ষু** *a.* forbearing, patient; forgiving.

তিতিবিরক্ত see **ত্যক্ত** ।

তিতির, তিত্তির *n.* the Francoline partridge; the lapwing; the titlark.

তিতীর্ষু *a.* desirous of going across or of being rescued.

তিথি *n.* (astr.) a lunar day. **~কৃত্য** *n.* rituals to be performed on a particular lunar day. **~ক্ষয়** *n.* the day on which the conjunction of three lunar days occurs; the newmoon. **~সন্ধি** *n.* the meeting of two lunar days.

তিন *n.* & *a.* three. **~কাল** *n.* infancy youth and middle age. **তিনকাল গিয়ে এককালে ঠেকা** to be in the last quarter of one's life, (cp.) to have one foot in the grave. **~গুণ** *adj.* & *adv.* threefold, three times. **~কুল** one's father's line and mother's line and in-law's line. **~সত্যি** *n.* uttering 'true' or 'promise' three times by way of swearing. **~সন্ধ্যা** same as **ত্রিসন্ধ্যা** ।

তিনি var. of **সে** used in reverence.

তিন্তিড়ী, তিন্তিলী, তিন্তিড়, তিন্তিড়ীক *n.* the tamarind (tree or its fruit).

তিন্দু, তিন্দুক *n.* the mangosteen (tree or its fruit).

তিপ্পান্ন *n.* & *a.* fifty-three.

তিব্বতি, তিব্বতীয় *a.* of Tibet, Tibetan. □ *n.* a Tibetan; the language of Tibet, Tibetan.

তিব্বত *n.* Tibet.

তিমি *n.* the whale (*mas.* the bull-whale, *fem.* the cow-whale). **তিমিংগিল** *n.* an imaginary puranic marine creature that was able to swallow a whale. **~তৈল** *n.* train-oil, train, whale-oil. **তিমিধরা জাহাজ বা নৌকা** *n.* a whale-boat, a whaleman, a whaler. **~শাবক** *n.* a whale-calf, a calf whale. **~শিকার** *n.* whale-fishing, whaling, whalery. **~শিকারি** *a.* whale-fishing, whaling. □ *n.* a whale-fisher, a whaler.

তিমিত *a.* wet, drenched; stand-still, motionless; dim, about to be extinguished.

তিমির *n.* darkness, gloom; cataract of the eye, blindness. **তিমির নাশ করা** *v.* to dispel or disperse darkness or gloom. **~গর্ভ** *n.* the dark interior. **তিমিরাচ্ছন্ন** *a.* beset or overcast with darkness. **তিমিরাবগুণ্ঠিত** *a.* veiled in darkness. **তিমিরাবৃত** *a.* covered with darkness.

তিয়াত্তর *n.* & *a.* seventy-three.

তিয়াষ, তিয়াস, তিয়াসা poet. corruptions of **তৃষা** ।

তির *n.* an arrow, a dart, a shaft. **তির ছোড়া** *v.* to shoot an arrow. **তির মারা** *v.* to shoot with an arrow; to shoot an arrow. **তিরের ডগা** an arrow-head. **~ধনুক** *n.* bow and arrow. **~ন্দাজ** *n.* an archer. **~বেগ** *n.* darting speed. **~বেগে** *adv.* as quickly as an arrow, dartingly. **তিরবেগে যাওয়া** *v.* to dart.

তিরপিত poet. corrup. of **তৃপ্ত** ।

তিরস্করণী, তিরস্করিণী *n.* the art or power of becoming invisible; a screen; (fig.) an obstruction.

তিরস্কার *n.* reproof, rebuke; reprimand; neglect, slight; reproach, censure, blame. **তিরস্কার করা** *v.* to reprove, to rebuke, to take to task; to reprimand; to censure, to reproach, to blame; (rare) to neglect or slight.

তিরস্কারিণী var. of **তিরস্করণী**।

তিরস্কৃত *a.* reproved, rebuked, taken to task; reprimanded; censured, reproached, blamed; neglected, slighted; screened off.

তিরানব্বই, (coll.) **তিরানব্বুই** *n. & a.* ninety-three.

তিরাশি *n. & a.* eighty-three.

তিরি *n.* (of playing-cards) the cards with 'three' marked on it.

তিরিক্ষি, (dial.) **তিরিক্ষে** *a.* irascible, hot-tempered, irritable.

তিরিশ coll. form of **ত্রিশ**।

তিরোধান, তিরোভাব *n.* disappearance, exit; passing away; (of great persons) death. **তিরোধান করা** *v.* to disappear, to vanish; to pass away; to die.

তিরোভূত, তিরোহিত *a.* disappeared, vanished; passed away; (of great persons) passed out of the world, dead. *fem.* **তিরোভূতা, তিরোহিতা**।

তির্যক *a.* oblique, zigzag, mazy (তির্যক রেখা) ; tortuous (তির্যক পথ) ; squint (তির্যক দৃষ্টি) ; sub-human, lower than human beings (তির্যক প্রাণী). **তির্যক কম্পন** transverse vibration. **তির্যক কিরণ** slanting rays. **~দৃষ্টি** *a.* squint-eyed. **~তরঙ্গ** a transverse wave. **~পত্র** *a.* (bot.) decussate. **~পাতন** *n.* distillation. **~ভাবে** *adv.* obliquely; transversely; crookedly; awry. **~সংঘাত** *n.* (mech.) oblique impact.

তির্যক্গতি *a.* moving obliquely or tortuously or awry. □ *n.* oblique movement.

তির্যগ্যোনি *n.* any of the sub-human creatures (such as, birds, beasts, insects etc.).

তিল *n.* sesame, til; a very small blotch on the body (usu. a birth-mark); a very small coin or its value (=1/80 cowrie); an iota (এক তিল পরিমাণ). □ *n.* not even an iota, least ('তিল ঠাঁই আর নাহি রে'). **~কাঞ্চন** *n.* act of performing one's sraddha (শ্রাদ্ধ) ceremony only by offering handfuls of til and an iota of gold. **~কল্ক, ~কিট্ট** *n.* oil-cake of sesamum. **~কুট, ~কুটো** *n.* a sweetmeat or toffee made of powdered til. **তিলকে তাল করা** (fig.) to exaggerate beyond measure, to make a mountain of a mole-hill. **তিল তিল করে** little by little. **~তুলসী** *n.* til and basil (these are considered holy by Hindus, and one holds them in one's hand whilst taking a vow or offers them to a deity etc. as a mark of complete submission). **~তেল** *n.* til-oil. **~মাত্র, তিলার্ধ, একতিল** *n.* even an iota. □ *a.* even an iota of, slightest. □ *adv.* even to the slightest amount or measure or degree, at all (তিলমাত্র বিশ্বাস করা) ; even for a moment (তিলমাত্র অপেক্ষা করা). **তিলে তিলে** same as **তিল তিল**।

তিলক *n.* a sectarian mark painted or impressed on the forehead; an ornament (কুলের তিলক). □ *a.* serving as an ornament, embellishing (কুলতিলক). **তিলক কাটা** *v.* to paint or print a sectarian mark (on one's body, generally on the forehead). **তিলকছাপা,** (dial.) **তিলক-ছাবা** corruptions of **তিলকসেবা**। **তিলক পরা** same as **তিলক কাটা. ~মাটি, ~মৃত্তিকা** *n.* the holy clay of the Ganges and other holy places with which sectarian marks are painted. **~সেবা** *n.* daily painting of sectarian marks on the eight places of the body by Vaishnavas.

তিলকা *n.* an innate mark resembling a sesame blossom on the body ('অলকা-তিলকা ভালে').

তিলকিত, তিলকী *a.* painted or imprinted or decorated with a sectarian mark or marks. *fem.* **তিলকিতা, তিলকিনী**।

তিলা var. of **তিলে**।

তিলাঞ্জলি *n.* act of performing sraddha (শ্রাদ্ধ) ceremony by offering handfuls of sesame and water; (fig.) complete abandonment or estrangement ('তিলাঞ্জলি দিনু কুললাজে').

তিলানো *v.* (ori. & rare) to grow fatty or oily; (sl.) to grow audacious.

তিলার্ধ see **তিল**।

তিলি *n.* Hindu caste (originally dealing in oilseeds); member of this caste.

তিলুয়া *n.* a kind of hard and roundish toffee (originally made of powdered sesame).

তিলে *a.* mixed with or made of sesame powder (তিলে খাজা) ; downright or incorrigible (তিলে খচ্চর = a downright or incorrigible scoundrel or rascal).

তিলেক *n.* even an iota, even the slightest amount or measure or degree; even the shortest duration, even the fraction of a moment. □ *a.* even an iota of, slightest; even of the shortest duration. □ *adv.* even to the slightest amount or measure or degree; even for the fraction of a moment.

তিলোত্তমা *n.* a mythological virgin woman of incomparable beauty whose different limbs were made by Vishwakarma (বিশ্বকর্মা) the heavenly artisan by taking bits from all that were most beautiful in the universe; (fig.) a woman who is a paragon of beauty,

তিলোদক *n.* water mixed with sesame, sesame in water.

তিষ্ঠানো *v.* to stay or dwell; to continue to stay or dwell.

তিষ্য *n.* the name of a star.

তিসি *n.* linseed. **তিসির তেল** linseed-oil.

তিহাই var. of **তেহাই**।

তীক্ষ্ণ *a.* sharp or keen, penetrating (তীক্ষ্ণ ছুরি, তীক্ষ্ণ বুদ্ধি, তীক্ষ্ণ স্মরণশক্তি) ; pointed (তীক্ষ্ণ কাঁটা) ; intense (তীক্ষ্ণ তাপ) ; strong (তীক্ষ্ণ বিষ) ; shrill তীক্ষ্ণ স্বর) ; poignant, acute (তীক্ষ্ণ যন্ত্রণা) ; rude, pungent (তীক্ষ্ণ কথা) ; hot (তীক্ষ্ণ স্বাদ). **~তা, ~ত্ব** *n.* sharpness; keenness; pointedness; intensity; strength; shrillness; acuteness; rudeness; pungency; hotness. **~দ্রংষ্ট্র, ~দ্রংষ্ট্রা** *a.* sharp-toothed; rodent. **~দৃষ্টি** *a.* keensighted, sharp-eyed. **তীক্ষ্ণ দৃষ্টি রাখা** to keep a sharp look-out or watch. **~ধার** *a.* sharp-edged. **~ধী, ~বুদ্ধি** *a.* sharp-witted. **~লৌহ, তীক্ষ্ণায়স** *n.* steel: **তীক্ষ্ণাগ্র** *a.* sharp-pointed.

তীবর *n.* a Hindu caste (originally engaged in hunting); a member of this caste. *fem.* **তীবরী**।

তীব্র *a.* strong, violent, intense (তীব্র রোদ, তীব্র বাতাস) ; very swift (তীব্র বেগ) ; unbearable (তীব্র দুঃখ) ; rude, rough, harsh (তীব্র ভাষা) ; very loud and usually angry (তীব্র স্বর) ; hard, angry, sharp (তীব্র দৃষ্টি) ; deadly, fatal (তীব্র বিষ) ; severe (তীব্র বেদনা). **~তা** *n.* violence, intensity; excessive swiftness; unbearableness; rudeness, roughness, harshness; excessive loudness usu. mixed with anger; hardness, fury, sharpness; deadliness.

তীয়র coll. corrup. of **তীবর**।

তীর১ *n.* shore, coast (of a sea), bank (of a river); margin, edge, border. **তীরে নামা** *v.* to land (on the shore or bank). **~গামী** *a.* going towards the shore, coasting; going towards the bank. **~বর্তী** *a.* riparian; coastal. **~ভূমি** *n.* land on the bank or shore. **~লগ্ন** *a.* attached or brought to the bank or shore. **~স্থ, ~স্থিত** *a.* of or on or situated on the bank or shore. **নদীতীরবাসী** *a.* & *n.* riparian. **সমুদ্রতীরবাসী** *a.* living on the shore. □ *n.* a shoresman.

তীর২ rej. spell. of **তির**।

তীরোপরি *adv.* on the shore, ashore; on the bank.

তীর্ণ *a.* gone across, crossed; got over. *fem.* **তীর্ণা**।

তীর্থ *n.* a holy place; a place for pilgrimage; a river or a sea or a lake etc. containing holy waters (পঞ্চতীর্থ) ; a landing-stair or a landing-place on the bank or the shore of a river or a sea etc. containing holy waters (সাগরতীর্থ) ; a preceptor, a teacher, alma mater (সতীর্থ) ; a title awarded for scholarship in Sanskrit (কাব্যতীর্থ). **তীর্থ করা** *v.* to go on pilgrimage. **তীর্থের কাক** (fig.) one who lives upon and waits expectantly for others' favour (just like the crows of a holy place which live upon the crumbs or leavings of offerings given by pilgrims). **~ক্ষেত্র** *n.* a holy place, a place for pilgrimage. **~দর্শন** *n.* act of visiting a holy place; pilgrimage. **~পর্যটন, ~ভ্রমণ** *n.* act of touring in holy places; pilgrimage, perigrination. **~বাসী** *a.* & *n.* one who lives permanently at a holy place. *fem.* **~বাসিনী**। **তীর্থযাত্রা করা** *v.* to set out on a pilgrimage; to pilgrimage.

~যাত্রী *a.* pilgrimaging, spiritual. □ *n.* a pilgrim, a perigrin(e). *fem.* **~যাত্রিণী**। **~সলিল, তীর্থোদক** *n.* the water of a holy place. **তীর্থংকর, তীর্থঙ্কর** *n.* a Jaina author of scriptures, a Jaina lawgiver; a Jaina or Buddhist monk who has attained spiritual perfection.

তু[1] *int.* expressing : a sound which is uttered to call a dog.

তু[2] poet. & obs. form of **তুই**।

তুঅ *pro. a.* (poet. & obs.) thy, thine, your, yours.

তুই *pro.* (used in familiar or affectionate or disrespectful or solemn address) thou. **~তোকারি** *n.* exhibition of disrespect by using তুই, তোর, তোকে etc. in address; disrespectful address.

তুঁ var. of **তু**[2]।

তুঁত *n.* mulberry. **~পাতা** *n.* mulberry leaf. **~পোকা** *n.* mulberry-worm.

তুঁতিয়া, তুঁতে *n.* copper-sulphate, blue vitriol.

তুঁষ var. of **তুষ**।

তুঁহুঁ var. of **তু**[2]।

তুক *n.* occult method of charming, enchantment (তুক করা) ; a magical incantation of enchatment (তুক জানা). **তুক করা** *v.* to cast a spell over (a person with a view to harming him), to put a spell on. **~তাক** *n.* occult methods and incantations of enchantment.

তুক্ক *n.* an arrow without a barb (used in training of archery), a blunt arrow; (rhet.) the last line of a four-lined stanza; part of a kirtan (কীর্তন) song.

তুখড়, তুখোড় *a.* clever, smart, artful; skilful; adroit, expert; experienced.

তুঘলকি *n.* wayward or whimsical ways and activities (like those of Sultan Muhammad-bin-Tughlaq). □ *a.* wayward and whimsical.

তুঙ্গ *a.* high, elevated; highest, most elevated; (astrol.) ascending. **তুঙ্গী** *a.* (astrol.) ascending, ascendant; high, elevated; highest, most elevated. **তুঙ্গে ওঠা** *v.* to reach the highest point; to come to a head; to culminate (অসন্তোষ তুঙ্গে ওঠা).

তুচ্ছ *a.* insignificant; scanty; contemptible; despicable, banal; trivial, trifling; unsubstantial. **তুচ্ছ করা, তুচ্ছ জ্ঞান করা** *v.* to treat with contempt or neglect; to despise; to disregard, to ignore; to attach no importance to. **~তা** *n.* insignificance; scantiness; worthlessness; contemptibility; contempt; despicability, banality; triflingness; unsubstantiality. **~তাচ্ছিল্য** *n.* contemptuous or neglectful treatment, neglect; contempt; disregard. **তুচ্ছতাচ্ছিল্য করা** *v.* to disregard, to ignore, to look down upon, to hold in light esteem, to slight. **তুচ্ছ বিষয়** a trivial matter.

তুঝ *pro. a.* (poet. & obs.) thy, thine, your, yours. **তুঝে** *pro.* (poet. & obs.) thee, you.

তুড়া[1] *v.* to snub; to rebuff, to retort; to talk big, to boast, to vaunt. **তুড়ে** *adv.* snubbing; with a rebuff or retort; boastfully.

তুড়া[2] *v.* (obs.) to break, to split (হাড় তুড়া) ; (of a cheque, bill etc.) to cash; (of a coin or currency note) to change (into or for small coins). **~নো** *v.* to cause to break or split; to cause to cash or change.

তুড়ি *n.* a sound made by grazing the middle finger and the thumb against each other. **তুড়ি দেওয়া** *v.* to produce a sound by grazing the middle finger and the thumb against each other. **তুড়ি মেরে বা তুড়ি দিয়ে ওড়ানো** to defeat easily. **~লাফ** *n.* a sudden skip in delight.

তুড়ুম var. of **তুরুম**।

তুড়ে see **তুড়া**[1]।

তুণ্ড *n.* mouth (of beasts); snout (of hogs etc.); beak; bill (of birds); lip.

তুত var. of **তুঁত**।

তুতিয়া, তুতে variants of **তুঁতিয়া** and **তুঁতে** respectively.

তুত্থ, তুত্থক *n.* copper sulphate, blue vitriol. **তুত্থাঞ্জন** *n.* eye-salve or collyrium prepared from cropper sulphate.

তুন্দ, তুন্দি *n.* a protuberant belly; the belly. **তুন্দিভ** *a.* pot-bellied.

তুন্নবায় *n.* a tailor.

তুফান *n.* a violent storm; a tempest; high waves caused by a tempest.

তুবড়ানো, তোবড়ানো *v.* to become sunken or hollowed or shrivelled (গাল তোবড়ানো) ; to form a depression (কাঁসার বাসন তুবড়েছে).

তুবড়ি *n.* a kind of fire-work (also **তুবড়ি-বাজি**) ; a snake-charmer's flute made of a gourd-shell fitted with two tubes (also **তুবড়িবাঁশি**). **কথার তুবড়ি** (sarcas. or facet.) a rapid and voluble speaker or rapid and voluble talk. **কথার তুবড়ি ছোটানো** to speak rapidly and volubly.

তুমার *n.* an account-book or a ledger. **~নবিশ** *n.* an accountant or a ledger-keeper.

তুমি *pro.* (*nom.*) you.

তুমুল *a.* terrible or hard or tumultuous (তুমুল যুদ্ধ বা ঝগড়া). □ *n.* a terrible or tumultuous brawl or scrimmage (দুজনে তুমুল হয়ে গেছে). **তুমুল রব** very loud or strident noise.

তুম্ব, তুম্বক, তুম্বি *n.* the gourd; a dried and hollowed shell of a gourd; any musical instrument made of a dried and hollowed gourd-shell.

তুয় var. of **তুঅ**।

তুয়া *pro.* (*nom. accus. dat. & poss.*–poet. & obs.) thou or you, thee or you, thy or your, thine or yours.

তুরক, তুরকি *n.* a Turk; Turks; (now almost obs.) a Mohammedan. **তুরক-সওয়ার** *n.* a Turkish horseman.

তুরগ, তুরঙ্গ, তুরঙ্গম *n.* the horse. *fem.* **তুরগী, তুরঙ্গী, তুরঙ্গামী** the mare.

তুরন্ত *adv.* very quickly or swiftly or hastily.

তুরপুন *n.* a (carpenter's) drill, an auger, a gimlet. **তুরপুন দিয়ে ছেঁদা করা** to bore with a drill.

তুরস্ক *n.* Turkey; bitumen. **~মণি** *n.* turquoise.

তুরি *n.* a (weaver's) shuttle; a horn sounded in war, a bugle-horn.

তুরিত, তুরিতে *adv.* (poet. & obs.) quickly or hastily.

তুরী alt. spell. of **তুরি**।

তুরীয় *a.* fourth; that which or one who has attained supreme (spiritual) excellence; gone beyond the reach of worldly attractions or delusions. □ *n.* the most engrossing state of spiritual trance; the Supreme Being, Brahman, God. **তুরীয় অবস্থা** a hypnotic or (quiescent state; a state of supreme bliss (when one is in communion with the Infinite or Supreme being). **তুরীয়ানন্দ** *n.* the delight found in the most engrossing state of spiritual trance; (sarcas. or facet.) state of being beside oneself.

তুরুক[1] var. of **তুরক**।

তুরুক[2] *a.* immediate or prompt (তুরুক জবাব). □ *adv.* immediately or promptly.

তুরুপ, তুরুফ *n.* act of trumping or ruffing; a trump-card, a trump. **তুরুপ করা** v. to trump, to ruff.

তুরুম *n.* an iron frame into which the hands and the feet of a criminal were formerly put to keep him motionless as a punishment, stocks, (cp.) a pillory. **তুরুম ঠোকা** *v.* to confine or lock in the aforesaid iron frame or stocks; (cp.) to set in the pillory; to pillory; to scold or reprimand or reproach severely.

তুর্ক, তুর্কি *n.* a Turk; Turks; the Turkish language. □ *a.* Turkish. **তুর্কিনাচন** *n.* a wild dance by turning round and round, a whirling dance; (fig.) a fretfully troublesome state.

তুল[1] poet. & coll. corrup.of **তুলনা** and **তুল্য**।

তুল[2] *n.* a weighing machine, a balance, a pair of scales; act of weighing or balancing (তুল করা). **তুল করা** *v.* to weigh; to balance the weight of; to compare. **~পাত্র** *n.* a scale-pan.

তুলক *n.* (phys.) a balancer.

তুলকালাম *n.* a terrible or tumultuous brawl; a great hubbub or commotion; rampage (cp. on the rampage).

তুলট *a.* made of cotton-pulp (তুলট কাগজ). □ *n.* a kind of paper made of cotton-pulp (তুলটে লেখা পুঁথি).

তুলতুল *int.* expressing : (delightful) softness; over-softness. **তুলতুলে** *a.* (delightfully) soft; excessively soft.

তুলনা *n.* comparison; similarity; an equal (বীরত্বে তার তুলনা নেই). **তুলনা করা** *v.* to compare; to liken. **~মূলক** *a.* comparative. **তুলনামূলক সাহিত্য** comparative literature. ~হীন *a.* incomparable, beyond compare; peerless.

তুলনীয় *a.* comparable.

তুলসী *n.* basil.

তুলা[1] *n.* (poet.) an equal ('শারদশশী সে মুখের তুলা').

তুলা[2] *n.* cotton. **~কার্মুক** *n.* a carding bow. **~-গাছ** *n.* the cotton-plant.

তুলা[3] *n.* a weighing machine, a balance, a pair of scales; (astrol.) a zodiacal constellation, the Libra; a measure of weight of gold and silver (=400 তোলা or about 4050 grams). **~দণ্ড** *n.* a beam of balance , a weighing machine, a pair of scales. **~দান** *n.* charitable gift of gold or silver or anything else up to the weight of the person of the donor. **~ধর** *n.* the sun. **~ধারী** *a.* one who weighs or carries on a trade. □ *n.* a weighing man, a weighman; a trader. **~মান** *n.* a measure of weight; act of weighing in the balance. **~যন্ত্র** *n.* a weighing machine. **~রাশি** *n.* (astrol.) the Libra.

তুলি, তুলিকা *n.* a paint-brush; a hair pencil.

তুলিত *a.* compared, likened; weighed.

তুলো coll. form of **তুলা**[3] ।

তুলোট var. of **তুলট** ।

তুল্য *a.* comparable; similar; like, identical; equal; (math. & sc.) equivalent. **~তা** *n.* comparability; similarity; likeness; identity; equality; equivalence, equivalency. **~জলাঙ্ক** *n.* water-equivalent. **~প্রতিযোগিতা** *n.* an evenly balanced contest. **~বল** *a.* equal in strength, equally strong. **~মান** *a.* of equal measure or weight. □ *n.* an equal measure or weight. **~মূল্য** *a.* of equal value or worth; equal. **~রূপ** *a.* of the same class or kind; similar. **তুল্যাকৃতি** *n.* similar appearance or shape. □ *a.* similar in appearance or shape. **তুল্যাঙ্ক** *n.* equivalent.

তুষ *n.* husk, chaff, bran. **তুষ ঝাড়া** *v.* to winnow husk.

তুষা, তোষা *v.* to gratify, to satisfy; to please; to appease, to propitiate; to flatter, to adulate, to gloze.

তুষানল *n.* a fire made with husk or chaff (this fire is not easily extinguished); (fig.) inextinguishable (but not blazing) fire of affliction, an inconsolable affliction.

তুষার *n.* snow; frost; ice. □ *a.* cold or ice-cold (তুষারকর). **তুষার পড়া** *v.* to snow. **~কণা** *n.* a minute particle or crystal of snow; (inc.) frost. **~কর** *n.* camphor; the moon. **~কিরীটী** *a.* snow-capped, snow-capt. **~গিরি** *n.* the Himalayas (as it is always snow-capped). **~ঝড়** *n.* snow-storm, a blizzard. **~ধবল** *a.* snow-white; whitened with snow. **~পাত** *n.* a snowfall. **~পিণ্ড** *n.* a conglomerated mass of snow, a snowball or a snowflake. **~বর্ষ** *n.* sleet. **~ভূমি** *n.* a snowfield. **~মৌল** *a.* snow-capped. **~যুগ** *n.* ice-age. **~রেখা** *n.* snowline. **~শীতল** *a.* as cold as snow. **তুষারাদ্রি** same as **তুষারগিরি** । **তুষারাবৃত** *a.* snow-covered. **তুষারাবৃত ভূমি** a snowfield.

তুষ্ট *a.* gratified, satisfied; pleased; appeased; propitiated; contented. **তুষ্ট করা** *v.* to gratify, to satisfy; to please; to appease, to propitiate; to content.

তুষ্টি *n.* gratification, satisfaction; appeasement, propitiation; contentment. **~কর, ~জনক** *a.* gratifying, satisfactory; pleasing; appeasing, propitiatory. **~বিধান, ~সাধন** *n.* gratification, satisfaction; appeasement, propitiation; contentment. **তুষ্টিবিধান করা** *v.* to appease, to satisfy, to propitiate, to please.

তুস[1] alt. spell. of **তুষ** ।

তুস[2] *n.* a kind of very soft woollen wrapper.

তুহ var. of **তুঁহু** ।

তুহার var. of **তোঁহার** ।

তুহিন *n.* snow; frost; hoar-frost, rime. □ *a.* extremely cold, ice-cold. **~শীতল** *a.* ice-cold, icy. **~শুভ্র** *a.* snow-white.

তুহু, তুহুঁ variants of **তুঁহু** ।

তূণ, তূণীর *n.* a quiver.

তূবর, তূবরক *n.* a beardless man.

তূরী *n.* a horn sounded in war, a buglehorn.

তূর্ণ *adv.* quickly, swiftly; promptly; hastily; soon. □ *a.* quick, swift, prompt; hasty; early. **~পত্র** *n.* an express letter.

তূর্য *n.* a horn sounded in war, a buglehorn; (fig.) fanfare. ~ধ্বনি, ~নাদ, ~নিনাদ *n.* fanfare, blare (of trumpets or horns).

তৃলি, তুলী alt. spellings of তুলি। তুলিকা alt. spell. of তুলিকা।

তূষ্ণীভাব *n.* act or state of keeping mum, refusal to speak, silence, reticence. তূষ্ণীভূত *a.* keeping mum, silent, reticent. তূষ্ণীভূত থাকা বা হওয়া *v.* to keep one's mouth shut, to keep mum, to keep quiet, to remain silent.

তৃণ *n.* grass; straw; herb; any monocotyledonous plant of the *Gramineae* genus (শরতৃণ). ~কাণ্ড *n.* a culm, a haulm. ~কুটির *n.* a hut made of straw. ~ক্ষেত্র *n.* a grassy field, a meadow; a pasture. ~জীবী *a.* same as ~ভোজী। ~জ্ঞান *n.* considering as contemptible or insignificant as a straw; slighting. তৃণজ্ঞান করা *v.* not to care a straw for; to slight. ~দ্রুম *n.* a monocotyledonous tree (such as the coconut, the palm, the date etc.) ~ধান্য *n.* paddy that grows in waste land without cultivation. ~বৎ *a.* strawlike. □ *adv.* like a straw. ~ভোজী *a.* herbivorous. ~ময় *a.* full of grass or straw; grassy. ~শূন্য, ~হীন *a.* destitute of plants and vegetation; arid.

তৃণাদ *a.* herbivorous.

তৃণাসন *n.* a sheet made of straw to sit upon; a mat.

তৃতীয় *a.* third. তৃতীয় ব্যক্তি a third man or person; a neutral or disinterested man. তৃতীয় মূল (arith.) cube root. তৃতীয়া *a. fem.* of তৃতীয়। □ *n.* the third lunar day; (gr.) the third case-ending. তৃতীয়া বিভক্তি third or instrumental case-ending.

তৃপ্ত *a.* gratified, satisfied; satiated; highly pleased. *fem.* তৃপ্তা। তৃপ্ত করা *v.* to gratify, to satisfy; to satiate; to please highly. তৃপ্তি *n.* gratification, satisfaction; satiety; extreme pleasure. তৃপ্তিকর, তৃপ্তিজনক, তৃপ্তিদায়ক *a.* gratifying, satisfactory, satiating; highly pleasing or agreeable. তৃপ্তি পাওয়া *v.* to derive pleasure or satisfaction, to be satisfied or satiated.

তৃষ্ণা, (poet.) তৃষা *n.* thirst; (fig.) earnest desire or greed, longing. তৃষ্ণা নিবারণ করা, তৃষ্ণা মিটানো *v.* to allay or quench (one's) thirst. তৃষ্ণা পাওয়া *v.* to get thirsty, to be or to become thirsty. তৃষ্ণা বোধ করা *v.* to feel thirsty. তৃষাতুর, তৃষ্ণাতুর, তৃষ্ণার্ত *a.* afflicted with thirst; thirsty. *fem.* তৃষাতুরা, তৃষ্ণাতুরা, তৃষ্ণার্তা।

তৃষিত *a.* thirsty. *fem.* তৃষিতা।

তৃষ্য *a.* desirable, attractive; lucrative.

তে[1] *a.* (obs.) that (তেকারণ).

তে[2] *a.* (used as *pfx.*) three, tri-, triple. তেঐঁটে *a.* (of fruits) three-stoned; (of a head) having three mounds; ugly-looking; (fig. & sl.—of persons) crooked and hard to deal with, roguish, knavish. ~কাঁটা, ~কাটা[1] *n.* a kind of three-veined plant. ~কাটা[2], ~কাঠা *n.* a triangular frame made of three pieces or wood. ~কোনা *a.* triangular, three-cornered. ~চোখা, (কথ্য) ~চোখো *a.* three-eyed. ~ঠেঙে *a.* three-legged, three-footed. ~তলা, ~তালা[1] *n.* (of a building) the second floor; (of a vessel) the third deck. □ *a.* three-storeyed; three-decked. ~তালা[2] *n.* a mode of Indian musical measure. ~তাস *n.* a kind of gambling at cards, flush. ~থাক *a.* three-tiered. ~পায়া *a.* three-legged. □ *n.* a tripod, a teapoy. ~মাথা *n.* a meeting-place or junction of three roads; a person appearing to be three-headed, that is a decrepit person who usually sits with his head sunken between his knees, an elder (তেমাথার কাছে বুদ্ধি নিয়ো). ~মেটে *a.* (in sculpture) thrice plastered esp. with clay. ~মোহানা *n.* a junction of the mouths of three streams; (loos.) a junction of three streams. ~শিরা *a.* triple-veined; three-veined. □ *n.* a species of plant. ~হাতি *a.* measuring three cubits or 1.5 metres.

তেই var. of তেঁই।

তেইশ *n. & a.* twenty-three. তেইশে *n.* the twenty-third day of a month. □ *a.* (of days of a month) twenty-third.

তেউড় *n.* a young plant that shoots up from the root of a banana tree.

তেওড়[1] *n.* the pod of a variety of pigeon-pea.

তেওড়², **তেওড়া** *a.* crooked, curved. **তেওড়ানো** *v.* to make or become crooked, to curve.

তেওর *n.* a Hindu caste (engaged in fishing); a member of this caste.

তেঁ¹ *pro.* (obs.) they.

তেঁ², **তেঁই** *adv. & con.* (obs.) because of that, on account of that.

তেঁতুল *n.* tamarind. **তেঁতুলে** *a.* shaped like a pod of tarmarind (তেঁতুলে বিছে) ; as dark-coloured as a ripe tamarind seed (তেঁতুলে নদী) ; very sour; knavish (তেঁতুলে লোক).

তেঁদড় see **ত্যাঁদড়**।

তেজ, **তেজঃ** (-জস্) *n.* light; glow, radiation; shine, lustre; heat; glory; splendour; power, strength; might, force; energy; vigour; valour; prowess; spiritedness; manliness; semen; (coll.) haughtiness or anger (অত তেজ দেখাসনে) ; (rare) spirit, wine (বন্য মধুর তেজ খাওয়া). □ *a.* (comm. & coll.) booming (তেজ বাজার). **তেজঃপুঞ্জ** *n.* an accumulation of (spiritual) lustre. □ *a.* (loos.) having such lustre; full of lustre, with a nimbus of glory (তেজঃপুঞ্জ ঋষি).

তেজই see **তেজা**।

তেজপক্ষ *n.* act of marrying for the third time; one married as the third wife or husband.

তেজপত্র, (coll.) **তেজপাতা**, (dial.) **তেজপাত** *n.* cassia leaf (?).

তেজব see **তেজা**।

তেজবর *n.* a bridegroom who has married twice before; a man who has married for the third time. **তেজবরে** *a.* (of a bridegroom or husband) one who has taken two wives before the present one.

তেজস্কর *a.* invigorating; stimulating; strong, forceful; inspiring; encouraging.

তেজস্ক্রিয় *a.* redioactive. **~তা** *n.* radioactivity.

তেজস্বান, **তেজস্বী** *a.* glorious; lustrous; radiating; shining; vigorous; valorous; powerful, mighty, forceful; spirited. *fem.* **তেজস্বতী**, **তেজস্বিনী**। **তেজস্বিতা** *n.* vigorousness; vigour; valorousness; valour; powerfulness; mightiness, forcefulness; spiritedness; gloriousness; lustrousness; radiation.

তেজলি, **তেজলুঁ**, **তেজলু** see **তেজা**।

তেজা *v.* (poet.) to forsake, to adandon, to give up, to forgo, to relinquish. *pr. 3rd per.* **তেজই** ; *pt. 1st. per.* **তেজলুঁ**, **তেজলু** ; *fut. 1st. per.* **তেজব**।

তেজারত *n.* trade and commerce; money-lending business, usury. **তেজারতি** (rej.) *n.* money-lending business, usury. □ *a.* relating to money-lending business; commercial.

তেজালো *a.* very strong or hot (তেজালো রোদ, তেজালো লঙ্কা) ; haughty or angry or spirited (তেজালো কথা).

তেজি¹ *a.* (comm.) showing a rise in prices, booming. **~মন্দি** *n.* (comm.) boom and slump; (comm.) fluctuation of price(s); upward and downward movement of prices, rise and fall in prices.

তেজি² *a.* spirited, vigorous (তেজি লোক) ; strong; powerful (তেজি ওষুধ).

তেজীয়ান *a.* extremely spirited or valorous or vigorous or powerful.

তেজোগর্ভ *a.* pregnant with spiritedness or power or vigour or valour or force or heat; charged with power or energy.

তেজোময় *a.* luminous, radiating, shining; lustrous; bright; glorious; spirited. *fem.* **তেজোময়ী**।

তেজোমূর্তি, **তেজোরূপ** *n.* a man or being having a luminous or shining or lustrous appearance; lustre or power personified. □ *a.* having a luminous or shining or lustrous appearance.

তেজোহীন *a.* spiritless, lacking in vigour, weak; lacking in lustre or glow or brightness; dim or dull. *fem.* **তেজোহীনা**।

তেড় coll. form of **তেউড়**।

তেড়ছা, **তেড়চা**, **তেড়ছ** variants of **তেরছা**।

তেড়া var. of **টেড়া**।

তেড়ি var. of **টেড়ি**।

তেড়ে • *adv.* chasing offensively (তেড়ে যাওয়া) ; threatening loudly (তেড়ে মারতে যাওয়া) ; forcefully (তেড়ে বল মারা). **~ফুঁড়ে** **~মেড়ে** *adv.* chasing speedily;

chasing and threatening; quickly or headstrongly and forcefully.

তেতাল্লিশ *n.* & *a.* forty-three.

তেতো coll. var. of **তিতা**[1]।

তেত্রিশ *n.* & *a.* thirty-three.

তেনা[1] var. of **টেনা**।

তেনা[2] *pro.* (obs.) he or she. **তেনাকে** pro. (dial. & vul.) him or her. **তেনার** *pro.* (dial. & vul.) his, her or hers. *pl.* **তেনাদের** their, theirs.

তেপান্তর *n.* a desolate and extensive field or wilderness. □ *a.* desolate and extensive (তেপান্তর মাঠ).

তেমত *a.* (obs.) suchlike, like that, such. **তেমতি** *adv.* & *con.* (poet. & obs.) like that; in that way or manner; so.

তেমন *a.* like that, suchlike, such. □ *adv.* (also *con.*) like that; in that or such way or manner; so. **তেমনই** *a.* (also *con.*) just like that, exactly similar; □ *adv.* & *con.* just in that way or manner, just so. **তেমনি** *a.* (also *con.*) like that, just like that; similar; exactly similar; fitting. □ *adv.* at once, forthwith. □ *con.* so; such.

তেয়াগ poet. corrup. of **ত্যাগ**।

তেরছা, তেরচা, (poet.) **তেরছ** *a.* awry, askance, crooked, oblique (তেরছা চাহনি). **তেরছা রেখা** an oblique or crooked line, an oblique stroke.

তেরপল coll. var. of **ত্রিপল**।

তেরস্পর্শ coll. corrup. of **ত্র্যহস্পর্শ**।

তেরাত্তির coll. var. of **ত্রিরাত্রি**।

তেরিজ *n.* (arith. & alg.) addition.

তেরিমেরি *n.* scolding and threats; bullying and abuses. **তেরিমেরি করা** *v.* to scold and threaten; to bully and abuse.

তেরিয়া *a.* haughty; angry; furious; intending to attack or fight, bellicose, inclined to fighting, aggressive.

তেরেট *n.* a kind of tree-leaf used as writing material in place of paper.

তেরো *n* & *a.* thirteen. **~ই** *n.* the thirteenth day of the month. □ *a.* (of the day of a month) thirteenth.

তেল *n.* oil; fat (মাছটায় বেশ তেল) ; a lubricant (মোটরগাড়ির তেল) ; (sarcas. & sl.) strength, power, courage, vanity, audacity (তার বড় তেল বেড়েছে). **তেল দেওয়া** *v.* to oil; to lubricate; to flatter, to butter up, to gloze. **নিজের চরকায় তেল দেওয়া** (fig.) to oil one's own machine, to mind one's own business, to go about one's own business. **পায়ে তেল দেওয়া** (fig.) to flatter servilely. **তেল পড়া** *v.* to infuse charm into oil by incantation. **তেল মাখা** *v.* to smear or massage or rub one's own body with oil. **তেল মাখানো** *v.* to rub or smear with oil; to lubricate; to smear or massage another's body with oil; to flatter or fawn on servilely. **তেলে-বেগুনে জ্বলে ওঠা** to fly out fretfully; to flare up in anger, to blaze with anger or indignation. **~কল** *n.* an oil-mill. **~কাষ্টে গন্ধ** *n.* an unpleasant smell of old oily substances. **~কুচকুচে, ~চুকচুকে** *a.* as glossy as oil; so profusely smeared with oil as to look glossy. **~চিটা, ~চিটে** *a.* thickly soiled (as dregs of oil), sticky and dirty. **~তেলে** *a.* oily, smooth; slippery. **~ধুতি** *n.* a short loin-cloth worn when one smears his body with oil. **~পড়া** *n.* charmed oil (used for curing diseases).

তেলা *a.* oily; lubricious; greasy; smooth; glossy; slippery; bald (তেলা মাথা). **তেলা মাথা** a bald head; a head (thoroughly) smeared with oil. **তেলা মাথায় তেল দেওয়া** (lit.) to rub oil on a head that is already well-oiled or sleek; (fig.) to carry coals to Newcastle.

তেলাকুচা, (coll.) **তেলাকুচো** *n.* a species of a creeping plant; its fruit.

তেলানো *v.* to grow fatty or adipose; to smear with oil; to season by smearing with oil and then sunning; (sl. & sarcas.) to grow powerful or audacious; (sl.) to flatter or to fawn on servilely. **তেলানি** *n.* fatty or adipose state; act of growing fatty or adipose; act of smearing with oil; act of seasoning by smearing with oil and subsequently sunning; (sl. & sarcas.) power or audacity; (sl.) servile flattery.

তেলাপোকা *n.* the cockroach, the oil beetle.

তেলি *n.* a Hindu caste (manufacturing and selling oil); a member of this caste; an oilman. *fem.* **তেলিনি, তেলেনি**।

তেলুগু *n.* a South Indian language. □ *a.* of Andhra, Telengana and Rayalaseema.

তেলেঙ্গা *a.* of Andhra and Telengana. □ *n.* an Indian sepoy in the employ of the East India Company in the early days of its activity.

তেলেনা *n.* a set of nonsensical words or phrases uttered prefatorily before singing a classical song. **তেলেনা ভাঁজা** *v.* to utter the aforesaid words; (fig.) to indulge in a long irrelevant discourse before coming to the actual subject-matter.

তেলেনি see **তেলি**।

তেলেভাজা *n.* any snack or other food fried in oil. □ *a.* fried in oil; (fig.) as dark brown as a snack fried in oil, sunburnt.

তেলো¹ *n.* the crown of the head; the pate.

তেলো² *n.* the palm (of the hand); the sole (of the foot).

তেষট্টি *n.* & *a.* sixty-three.

তেষ্টা *n.* coll. form of **তৃষ্ণা**।

তেসরা *n.* the third day of a month. □ *a.* (of the days of a month) third.

তেহাই¹ *n.* (mus.) a system of striking an instrument of percussion thrice consecutively.

তেহাই² *n.* one-third.

তেহারা *a.* threefold; having three strands or folds.

তৈক্ষ্ণ্য *n.* sharpness; keenness; pointedness; intensity; strength; shrillness; acuteness; rudeness; pungency; hotness. Same as **তীক্ষ্ণতা**।

তৈখন (poet.) *adv.* & *con.* at that time, then; just then.

তৈছন (poet.) *a.* & *con.* like that, such, suchlike.

তৈছে *adv.* & *con.* like that, just like that, so.

তৈজস *a.* relating to light or radiation or luminosity; made of metal, metalled. □ *n.* a metal utensil (esp. one used for household purposes). **~পত্র** *n.* household metal utensils and allied articles.

তৈত্তিরীয় *n.* a section of the Yajurveda. □ *a.* of this section.

তৈরি, (now rare) **তৈয়ারি** *n.* act of making or building or creating etc.; manufacture, construction, production, creation etc.; preparation; training. □ *a.* made, manufactured, built, constructed, produced, created etc.; ready or ripe (তৈরি আম) ; ready-made (তৈরি জামা) ; trained; got up (তৈরি মামলা) ; of age, major, competent; (facet, or sarcas.) over-smart, precocious and wicked (তৈরি ছেলে). **তৈরি করা** *v.* to make; to build or construct; to found (স্কুল তৈরি করা) ; to manufacture; to produce; to create; to draw up (নকশা তৈরি করা) ; to compose (মুখে মুখে ছড়া তৈরি করা) ; to contrive or devise or invent (উপায় তৈরি করা) ; to make ready (যুদ্ধের জন্য বাহিনীকে তৈরি করা) ; to prepare (পড়া তৈরি করা) ; to train or educate (ছেলে তৈরি করা).

তৈল (*for.*) *n.* oil; lubricant; fat (see also **তেল**). **~কল্ক, ~কিট্ট** *n.* oil-cake. **~কার** *n.* an oilman; an oil-manufacturer. **~গ্রন্থি** *n.* an oilgland. **~দ্রোণী** *n.* an oil-pot, an oil-vessel. **~নিষিক্ত** *a.* steeped in oil; smeared with oil, soaked in oil; oiled. **~প, ~পক, ~পা, ~পায়িকা** *n.* the cockroach. **~পক্ব** *a.* fried in oil; cooked in or with oil. **~বীজ** *n.* oil-seed. **~মর্দন** *n.* act of massaging with oil; (facet.) servile flattery. **তৈলমর্দন করা** *v.* to massage with or to rub oil; (facet.) to flatter servilely. **~যন্ত্র** *n.* an oil-press; an oil-mill. **~সিক্ত** *a.* soaked in oil. **~সেক** *n.* act of smearing or anointing with oil. **~স্ফটিক** *n.* amber. **~হীন** *a.* devoid of oil, oil-less.

তৈলাক্ত *a.* oily, greasy; unctuous; smeared or anointed with oil. **তৈলাক্ত কলেবর** body smeared with oil.

তৈলাধার *n.* an oil-can or oil-vessel, a receptacle for oil.

তো¹ *int.* (& *adv.*) expressing : question or inquiry (ভালো তো ?) ; request (একবার আসুন তো) ; worry or surprise (তাই তো) ; uncertainty (যাই তো—তারপর বোঝা যাবে) ; doubt (হয়তো) ; supposing, even if (তুমি তো দিলে) ; but (আমি তো খাব না) ; if, in case (বাঁচতে চাও তো) ; at least (আজ তো বাঁচি) ; sometimes inserted at random in a speech (আমি তো জানি না).

তো২ *n.* a fold (as of cloth). **তো করা** *v.* to fold.
তো৩ *pro.* (nom.) you, thou ('তো বিনে উনমত কান'). □ *pro. a.* your, thy (তো সেবা নাহি জানি). **তোই** *pro.* (*accus. & dat.*) you, thee 'কত পরবধব তোই'.
তোকমারি *n.* the seed of the hollyhock (used in poultices.) **তোকমারি দেওয়া** *v.* to poultice with the seed of the hollyhock.
তোকে *pro.* (*accus. & dat.*) thee.
তোখড় var. of **তুখড়** ।
তোটক *n.* a duodecasyllabic metre of Sanskrit poetry.
তোড় *n.* the speed or the impact of current. **মুখের তোড়** the force of volubility.
তোড়ই *v. 3rd.per.* (obs. & poet.) uproots or uproot; tears or tear; breaks or break; opens or open.
তোড়জোড় *n.* action for getting or making ready, preparation; arrangements. **তোড়জোড় করা** *v.* to make preparation or arrangements for, to take action for getting or making ready.
তোড়া১ pop. var. of **তুড়া** ।
তোড়া২ *n.* a purse (টাকার তোড়া) ; a bunch, a bouquet, a nosegay (ফুলের তোড়া) ; a bundle (নোটের তোড়া) ; a kind of jingling ornament for ankles. **তোড়া বাঁধা** *v.* to enclose in a purse; to string in a bunch; to tie up in a bundle; to put on the aforesaid jingling anklet.
তোড়ি *n.* an Indian musical mode.
তোতলা *a.* given to or marked with stammering, stuttering. **তোতলা লোক** a stammerer, a stutterer. **তোতলানো, তোতলামি করা** *v.* to stammer, to stutter. **তোতলামি** *n.* stammering or stuttering.
তোতা *n.* the parrot, the popinjay.
তোৎলা alt. spell. of **তোতলা** ।
তোপ *n.* a cannon, a big-gun, a gun. **তোপ দাগা** *v.* to fire cannon. **তোপ দেগে আক্রমণ করা বা উড়িয়ে দেওয়া** *v.* to cannonade. **তোপের গোলা** a cannonball, cannon-shot. **তোপের পাল্লা** the range of a cannon, cannon-shot. **~খানা** *n.* a place or establishment where cannon is stored or mounted or manufactured (cp. an arsenal). **~চি** *n.* a cannoneer, a cannonier. **~ধ্বনি** *n.* the boom of a cannon fire.
তোফা *a.* excellent, very delicious, extremely beautiful or good.
তোবড়া *a.* sunken (তোবড়া গাল) ; having a depression or dent (তোবড়া বাসন, তোবড়া জায়গা).
তোবড়ানো pop. var. of **তুবড়ানো** ।
তোবা *int.* (Mus.) expressing : regret; resolve for not doing a particular thing again.
তোমর *n.* an ancient weapon of war resembling almost an iron pike.
তোমরা *pro. pl.* (of **তুমি**) you.
তোমা *pro.* (*nom.*) you. □ *pro.* (*accus. & dat.*) you, to you.
তোমাকে, তোমায় *pro.* (*accus. & dat.*) you, to you.
তোমার *pro. a.* your, yours.
তোয়১ poet. & obs. corrup of **তোমায়** ।
তোয়২ *n.* water. **~দ** *n.* cloud. **~দাগম** *n.* advent of rains; the rainy season. **~নিধি, ~ধি** *n.* a sea; an ocean.
তোয়াক্কা *n.* deference; dependence; fear; care. **তোয়াক্কা করা, তোয়াক্কা রাখা** *v.* to treat with deference; to depend upon; to be afraid of. **তোয়াক্কা না করা** *v.* not to care.
তোয়াজ *n.* entertainment; gratification; flattery, adulation, glozing; looking after carefully, careful attendance; care; comfort. **তোয়াজ করা** *v.* to amuse, to arrange for mental diversion, to entertain; to gratify; to flatter, to adulate, to fawn on, to gloze; to look after carefully, to attend to or upon carefully, to arrange for one's comfort. **তোয়াজে রাখা** *v.* to keep or nurse in comfort; to keep in good humour.
তোয়ানো *v.* to grope (usu. with one's hand); to adulate or cajole.
তোয়ালে *n.* a towel.
তোর poss. form of **তুই** ।
তোরঙ্গ *n.* a large portmanteau usually made of steel, a trunk.
তোরণ *n.* the main gate (usu. decorated); a portal; a gate. **~দ্বার** *n.* the door of a portal. **~পথ** *n.* a gateway.
তোরা *pl.* of **তুই** ।
তোরে (dial. & poet.) var. of **তোকে** ।
তোল, তোলক variants of **তোলা২** ।
তোলন১ *n.* act of weighing.

তোলন২ *n.* act of raising or lifting etc. (see **তুলা**).

তোলপাড় *n.* violent movement or commotion; violent agitation; a terrible brawl or disturbance. □ *a.* violently moved or agitated; ransacked, fished. **তোলপাড় করা** *v.* to move or agitate or disturb violently; to ransack, to fish.

তোলা১ *v.* to raise; to lift; to bring forward into consideration or notice; to raise (প্রসঙ্গ তোলা) ; to rouse, to wake (ঘুমন্ত লোককে তোলা) ; to call to mind, to cause to rise in view, to call up; to admit into or promote (জাতে তোলা, পদে তোলা) ; to exalt or elevate; to pluck, to pick, to cull (শাক তুলছে, ফুল তুলবে) ; to extract (দাঁত তোলা) ; to uproot (পাকা চুল তোলা) ; to embroider (কাপড়ে ফুল তুলছে) ; to collect (চাঁদা তোলা) to remove, to expunge, to wipe out, to obliterate (দাগ তোলা) ; to make keener, to raise (তান তোলা) ; to adapt (গানের সুর তোলা) ; to create or make, to raise, to spread (গুজব তোলা, আওয়াজ তোলা) ; to take (ফোটো তোলা) ; to construct, to build (বাড়ি তোলা) ; to evict or eject (ভাড়াটে তোলা) to cause to board, to help one board (তাকে গাড়িতে তুলে দিয়েছি) ; to vomit, to spew (ছেলেটা দুধ তুলছে) ; to set up, to fix (পাল তোলা) ; to put away esp. in an orderly manner (বিছানা তুলতে হবে) ; to abolish or close (দোকান তোলা) ; to cause to enter (কানে তোলা) ; to mention or refer (নাম তোলা, কথা তোলা) ; to propose formally before a meeting, to move (আইনপরিষদে বিল তোলা) ; to take off, to detach (ছাল তোলা) ; to paint, to engrave, to mould. **ছাল তোলা** *v.* to flay. **ফিলম তোলা** *v.* to make a motion picture of, to film. **মনে তোলা** *v.* to call to mind. **হাই তোলা** *v.* to yawn. **গায়ে হাত তোলা** *v.* to assault. **মাথা তুলে দাঁড়ানো** *v.* (fig.) to flourish, to prosper; (fig.) to face, to brave, to oppose, to rise in opposition or in revolt. **স্বর্গে তোলা** *v.* to praise to the skies.

তোলা২ var. of **তোলো** ।

তোলা৩ *n.* a measure of weight (=180 grains or approx. 12 grams).

তোলা৪ (see **তুলা**৪) *n.* a rate in kind collected by the owner of a market from traders (তোলা আদায় করা). □ *a.* set apart or in reserve (তোলা খাবার) ; raised (আকাশে তোলা নিশান) ; constructed, built (নতুন তোলা বাড়ি) ; set apart for special or festive occasions (তোলা কাপড়) ; lifted and carried from a river or pond etc. (তোলা জল) ; plucked, culled (তোলা ফুল) ; churned (মাখন-তোলা দুধ) ; painted, engraved, moulded (পল-তোলা) ; portable (তোলা উনুন) ; (fig.) stored in memory (সব কথা তোলা আছে).

তোলানো *v.* to cause to raise or lift; to cause to bring forward into consideration or notice; to cause to rouse or wake; to cause to call up; to cause to be admitted into or promoted; to cause to pluck or pick or cull; to cause to extract or uproot; to cause to embroider; to cause to collect or raise; to cause to remove or expunge or wipe out or obliterate; to cause to make keener; to cause to adapt; to cause to create or make; to cause to take; to cause to construct or build; to cause to eject or evict; to cause to set up or fix, to cause to put away esp. in an orderly manner; to cause to mention or refer; to cause to move (as a proposal or bill); to cause to take off or detach; to cause to paint or engrave or mould.

তোলাপাড়া *n.* cogitation; restless weighing in the mind, restless thinking; discussion. **তোলাপাড়া করা** *v.* to cogitate; to discuss.

তোলাহাঁড়ি var. of **তোলোহাঁড়ি** ।

তোলিত *a.* weighed; compared.

তোলো, তোলোহাঁড়ি *n.* a kind of dixie with a convex bottom; sullenness, glumness, angry mood. □ *a.* sullen, glum, angry (তোলোহাঁড়ি মুখ).

তোল্য *a.* that which is to be weighed or compared; weighable; comparable.

তোশক *n.* a mattress for lying upon.

তোশা *n.* valuable things or belongings, valuables. **~খানা** *n.* a room in which the valuables of a house are stored.

তোষ *n.* satisfaction, gratification; propitiation; contentment; pleasure, delight. **তোষণ** *n.* satisfying or gratifying or propitiating or pleasing; flattering or adulation; conciliation; (chiefly *in comp.*) a satisfying or gratifying or propitiating or pleasing or conciliatory object. ☐ *a.* (*in comp.*) satisfying, gratifying, propitiatory, pleasing, delightful, adulatory, conciliatory. *fem.* **তোষিণী**—(only *in comp.*). **তোষণ করা** *v.* to try to please or flatter or conciliate. **~নীতি** *n.* the policy of conciliation or appeasement. **তোষণীয়** *a.* one who can be or is to be satisfied or gratified or propitiated or pleased or conciliated.

তোষা[1] pop. var. of **তুষা** ।

তোষা[2] alt. spell. of **তোশা** ।

তোষামুদে *a.* given to adulation or obsequious flattery; hanging on obsequiously; adulatory, full of flattery.

তোষামোদ *n.* adulation, glozing, flattery, sycophancy; act of hanging on obsequiously, cringing; humble request. **তোষামোদ করা** *v.* to adulate, to gloze, to fawn on, to flatter obsequiously; to hang on obsequiously, to cringe (on); to request humbly. **~প্রিয়** *a.* fond of flattery.

তোষিত *a.* satisfied, gratified; propitiated, conciliated.

তোসদান *n.* a container or bag for gun and bullets; a magazine.

তোহে poet. & obs. corrup. of **তোকে** and **তোমাকে** ।

তৌজি *n.* a descriptive inventory containing the names of tenants with the amounts of their holdings and rents thereof.

তৌর্য *n.* fanfare.

তৌল *n.* weight; weighing; a weighing machine, a balance; (fig.) comparison. **তৌল করা** *v.* to weigh; to compare. **~ন** *n.* act of weighing or comparing. **~নিক** *a.* comparative. **~মান** *n.* (mech.) weight. **~যন্ত্র** *n.* a weighing machine.

তৌলিক[1] *n.* a painter.

তৌলিক[2] *n.* a weigher, a weighman. ☐ *a.* gravimetric.

-ত্ব *sfx.* indicating: ability, state, propensity etc., -ness, -ity, -ality, -ability, -ty etc.

ত্বক *n.* skin, derm, dermis, cuticle; epidermis; hide; bark, rind (বৃক্ষত্বক) ; the organ of touch. **~চ্ছেদ, ~চ্ছেদন** *n.* circumcise. **~তন্ত্র** *n.* epidermal system.

ত্বদীয় *a.* relating to you; your, yours.

ত্বরক *a.* accelerating.

ত্বরণ *n.* acceleration. **ত্বরণ-চিত্র** *n.* hodograph. **ত্বরণ-বল** *n.* effective force.

ত্বরমাণ *a.* hurrying, hastening.

ত্বরস্বান *a.* swift-moving, fast-moving.

ত্বরা *n.* haste, hurry, quickness. **ত্বরা করা** *v.* to make haste, to hurry; to be quick. **ত্বরান্বিত** *a.* hurried; quickened; accelerated. **ত্বরান্বিত করা** to expedite, to hasten. **ত্বরায়** *a.* hastily, hurriedly; quickly.

ত্বরিত *a.* hastened; quickened; accelerated; hurried; quick, swift, prompt. **~গতি, ~গামী** *a.* quick-moving, swift, fast-going.

ত্বষ্টা *n.* a carpenter; an appellation of Vishwakarma (বিশ্বকর্মা).

ত্বষ্টি *n.* carpentry.

ত্বাদৃশ *a.* like you.

ত্বিষাম্পতি *n.* the sun (usu. personified).

ত্যক্ত *a.* given up; abandoned; forsaken; relinquished; cast out; annoyed. **ত্যক্ত করা** *v.* to annoy. **ত্যক্ত-বিরক্ত,** (coll.) **তিতি-বিরক্ত,** (coll.) **তিতবিরক্ত** *a.* annoyed, extremely vexed, irritated, badgered.

ত্যজন *n.* act of giving up; abandonment; act of forsaking; relinquishment; act of casting out; act of leaving.

ত্যজা same as **তেজা** ।

ত্যজ্যমান *a.* that which or one who is being given up or abandoned or forsaken or cast out.

ত্যাঁদড় *a.* obstinate, disobedient; impertinent; brazen-faced, shameless; wicked. **ত্যাঁদড়ামি** *n.* obstinacy, disobedience; impertinence; shamelessness. **ত্যাঁদড়ামি করা** *v.* to show impertinence; to behave impertinently.

ত্যাগ *n.* giving up (দাবিত্যাগ, প্রাণত্যাগ) ; abandonment, act of forsaking, desertion; leaving (দেশত্যাগ) ; relinquishment, resignation (পদত্যাগ, কর্মত্যাগ) ; casting or casting off (শরত্যাগ,

(খোলসত্যাগ) ; renunciation, sacrifice; giving away in charity or benevolence; disavowal (ধর্মত্যাগ) ; divorce (পত্নীত্যাগ) ; act of disowning (পুত্রত্যাগ). **ত্যাগ করা** *v.* to give up; to abandon, to forsake, to desert; to leave; to relinquish, to resign; to cast (off); to renounce, to sacrifice; to give away in charity or benevolence; to disavow; to divorce; to disown. **~পত্র** *n.* a deed of relinquishment (as of a right, interest etc.); a bill of divorcement. **~স্বীকার** *n.* self-denial, self-abnegation. **ত্যাগস্বীকার করা** *v.* to deny oneself, to renounce one's interests. **ত্যাগী** *a.* self-denying, self-abnegating; renouncing one's interests or pleasures. □ *n.* a self-denier or self-abnegator, a renouncer of self-interests or pleasures.

ত্যাজ্য *a.* that which or one who is to be or can be given up or abandoned or forsaken or deserted or left or cast off or sacrificed or given away or disavowed or divorced or disowned; that which is to be or can be relinquished or resigned or renounced. **~পুত্র** *n.* a son disowned and disinherited by his father. **ত্যাজ্যপুত্র করা** *v.* to disown or disinherit a son; to cut off with a shilling.

ত্যাড়া *a.* sidelong; oblique, awry; (of words) oblique and haughty. **~বাঁকা** *a.* having many curves, not straight; distorted.

ত্রপমাণ *a.* in the state of being abashed or ashamed.

ত্রপা *n.* shame. **ত্রপান্বিত** *a.* stricken with shame.

ত্রপিত *a.* ashamed, abashed. *fem.* **ত্রপিতা** ।

ত্রপু *n.* lead; tin; zinc.

ত্রয় *n.* three, a trio or triad. □ *a.* three, triple, threefold, tri-, **ত্রয়ঃপঞ্চাশ, ত্রয়ঃপঞ্চাশৎ** *n.* & *a.* fifty-three. *fem.* **ত্রয়ঃপঞ্চাশী, ~ঃপঞ্চাশতী** । **ত্রয়পঞ্চাশত্তম** *a.* fifty-third. *fem.* **ত্রয়ঃপঞ্চাশত্তমী** । **ত্রয়ঃষষ্টি** *n.* & *a.* sixty-three. **ত্রয়ঃষষ্টিতম** *a.* sixty-third. *fem.* **ত্রয়ঃষষ্টিতমী** । **ত্রয়ঃসপ্ততি** *n.* & *a.* seventy-three. **ত্রয়ঃসপ্ততিতম** *a.* seventy-third. *fem.* **ত্রয়ঃসপ্ততিতমী** । **~শ্চত্বারিংশ** *a.* forty-three. **~শ্চত্বারিংশৎ** *n.* & *a.* forty-three. *fem.* **~শ্চত্বারিংশতী** । **~শ্চত্তারিংশত্তম** *a.* forty-third. *fem.* **~শ্চত্তারিংশত্তমী** । **~স্ত্রিংশ** *a.* thirty-three. **~স্ত্রিংশৎ** *n.* & *a.* thirty-three. *fem.* **~স্ত্রিংশতী** । **~স্ত্রিংশত্তম** *a.* thirty-third. *fem.* **~স্ত্রিংশত্তমী** ।

ত্রয়ী *a. fem.* of **ত্রয়** । □ *n.* Brahma (ব্রহ্মা), Vishnu (বিষ্ণু) and Shiva (শিব): these three manifestations of divinity collectively; Rik (ঋক্), Sama (সাম) ; Yajus (যজুঃ) : these three Vedas collectively.

ত্রয়োদশ *n.* & *a.* thirteen. □ *a.* thirteenth. **ত্রয়োদশী** *a. fem.* thirteenth; thirteen years old. □ *n. fem.* a girl of thirteen; the thirteenth day of a lunar fortnight.

ত্রয়োবিংশ *a.* twenty-third; twenty-three. **~তি** *n.* & *a.* twenty-three. **ত্রয়োবিংশতিতম** *a.* twenty-third. *fem.* **ত্রয়োবিংশতিতমী** ।

ত্রসন *n.* state of being frightened or alarmed or panicked; fright, alarm; panic.

ত্রসর *n.* a (weaver's) shuttle.

ত্রসরেণু *n.* (phys.) any of the minute particles of dust appearing to be floating in a stream of light esp. sunlight; (phil.) a collection of six atoms or three diatoms.

ত্রস্ত *a.* stricken with fear, alarmed, terror-stricken, panicked; fearful, timorous, timid; confusedly bustling.

ত্রাণ *n.* salvation, deliverance, rescue, succour, relief; protection; a protective covering or an armour (অঙ্গুলিত্রাণ, বাহুত্রাণ, উরস্ত্রাণ, শিরস্ত্রাণ). **ত্রাণ করা** *v.* to administer salvation, to save, to deliver, to rescue, to succour, to relieve. **~কর্তা** *n.* a saviour, a deliverer, a rescuer. □ *a.* one who administers salvation or saves or delivers or rescues or succours or relieves. *fem.* **~কর্ত্রী** ।

ত্রাত *a.* saved, delivered, rescued, succoured, relieved.

ত্রাতা same as **ত্রাণকর্তা** (see **ত্রাণ**).

ত্রায়মাণ *a.* one who is being saved or delivered or rescued or succoured or relieved; one who is saving or delivering or rescuing or succouring or relieving.

ত্রাস *n.* alarm, fright; panic; fear, dread, terror. **~কর, ~জনক** *a.* alarming, frightful, fearful, dreadful; terrible, terrifying.

ত্রাসিত *a.* frightened, alarmed, terror-stricken; panicky. *fem.* **ত্রাসিতা** ।

ত্রাহি *v.* please save or deliver or rescue or relieve or protect. **ত্রাহি ত্রাহি** *int.* save ! save! **ত্রাহি ত্রাহি করা** বা **ডাক ছাড়া** *v.* to shout for help to be saved or delivered or rescued or relieved or protected.

ত্রি *n.* three. □ *a. & n. comp.* three, tri-. **~কাল** *n.* the past, the present and the future: these three ages collectively; all times. **~কালজ্ঞ** *a.* acquainted with all the three ages : past present and future; omniscient, all-knowing. **~কালদর্শী** *a.* one who or that which sees all three ages: past, present and future; all-seeing. **~কালবেত্তা** same as **ত্রিকালজ্ঞ** । **~কুল** *n.* the three families or family lines of one's father, mother and in-law. **~কূট** *n.* a three-peaked mountain of the Deccan. **~কেশর** *a.* (bot.) triandrous. **~কোণ** *a.* triangular. □ *n.* a triangle. **~কোণমিতি** *n.* trigonometry. **~কোণাকৃতি** *a.* triangular. **~কোণী** *n.* a set square. **~কোষ্ঠ** *a.* (bot.) tri-locular. **~খণ্ড** *a.* trisected. **~খণ্ডন** *n.* trisection. **~গঙ্গা** *n.* confluence of three streams (esp. that of the Ganges, the Jamuna and the Saraswati at Allahabad). **~গামী** *a.*(phys.) three-way. **~গুণ** *n.* the three characteristic primal qualities of man and other creatures, namely, সত্ত্ব, রজঃ and তমঃ. □ *a.* having the aforesaid qualities; trebled; three times; multiplied by three. **~গুণা** *a. fem.* of **ত্রিগুণ** । □ *n.* an appellation of Goddess Durga (দুর্গা). **~গুণাত্মক** *a.* having the three characteristic primal qualities, namely, সত্ত্ব, রজঃ and তমঃ. *fem.* **~গুণাত্মিকা** । **~গুণিত** *a.* trebled. **~ঘাত** *a.* (arith. & alg.) cubic; (geom.) having three dimensions, solid. **~চক্রযান** *n.* a three-wheeled car or carriage; a tricycle. **~চত্বারিংশ** *a.* forty-three. **~চত্বারিংশৎ** *n. & a.* forty-three. *fem.* **~চত্বারিংশতী** । **~চত্বারিংশত্তম** *a.* forty-third. *fem.* **~চত্বারিংশত্তমী** । **~জগৎ** *n.* the three worlds collectively, namely, heaven earth and the underworld or Hades; the universe. **~তন্ত্রী** *n.* a three-stringed harp. **~তয়** *n.* a triad; a triplet; (phys.) three. **~তল** *a.* (of buildings) three-storeyed; (of ships, omnibuses etc.) three-decked. □ *n.* the second floor; the third deck. **~তাপ** *n.* the three kinds of affliction: spiritual, material and supernatural. **~দণ্ডী** *a.* three-stringed (ত্রিদণ্ডী পইতা). **~দিব** *n.* the sky; the heaven. **~দোষ** *n.* morbidity of the three humours of the body; bile, blood and phlegm. **~দোষজ** *a.* caused by or arising from or relating to the morbidity of the three humours of the body. **~ধা** *adv.* in or from three ways; in or to or from three directions. **~ধার** *a.* (bot.) triangular. **~ধারা** *n.* a river with three streams; a three-pronged river; a river with three streams called the Mandakini that flows in heaven, the Alakananda that flows on earth and the Bhogawati that flows in the underworld; a collection or confluence of three streams. **~নবতি** *n. & a.* ninety-three. **~নবতিতম** *a.* ninety-third. *fem.* **ত্রিনবতিতমী** । **~নয়ন** *a.* three-eyed. □ *n.* an appellation of Shiva (শিব). **~নয়না,** (inc. but pop.) **~নয়নী** *a. fem.* of **ত্রিনয়ন** । □ *n.* an appellation of Goddess Durga (দুর্গা). **~নাথ** *n.* God Shiva (শিব), Brahma (ব্রহ্মা), Vishnu (বিষ্ণু) and Shiva (শিব) : these three divine manifestations taken collectively; the presiding deity of hemp. **~নেত্র** *a.* same as **ত্রিনয়ন** (*a.*). **~পক্ষ, ~পক্ষীয়, ~পাক্ষিক** *a.* tripartite. **~পঞ্চাশৎ** *n. & a.* fifty-three. *fem.* **~পঞ্চাশতী** । **~পঞ্চাশত্তম** *a.* fifty-third. *fem.* **~পঞ্চাশত্তমী** । **~পণ্ড** *a.* one who spoils religious material and spiritual good; rascally. □ *n.* a rascal, a rogue, a knave. **~পত্র** *a.* three-leaved, trifoliate. □ *n.* a trefoil; a leaf of the bel (বেল) tree. **~পথগা, ~পথগামিনী** *n.* an appellation of the river Ganges as it flows in heaven, on earth and in the underworld simultaneously. **~পদ** *n.* (math.) a tripod. **~পদী** *n.* a kind of Bengali and Sanskrit metre of poetry; a tripod, a teapoy. **~পর্ণ** *a.* three-leaved, trifoliate. □ *n.* a trefoil; a kind of flower tree. **~পাদ** *a.* three-legged; three-footed; measuring three human feet (ত্রিপাদ জমি) ; three-quarter (ত্রিপাদ পুণ্য). □ *n.* an incarnation of Vishnu (বিষ্ণু) (see **বামনাবতার**). **~পাপ** *n.* three kinds of sins: mortal sins, punishable sins and venial sins. **ত্রিপিটক** *n.* the name of the Buddhist scripture. **~পুণ্ড্র, ~পুণ্ড্রক** *n.* a trident-shaped sectarian mark painted on the forehead. **~ফলক** *a.* ternate (leaf). **~ফলা** *n.* the three kinds of myrobalans collectively. **~বর্গ** *n.* the three pursuits of the human life: religion, wealth and love collectively; the three characteristic primal qualities of man and other creatures; সত্ত্ব or knowledge, রজঃ or action, and তমঃ or ignorance collectively; income, expenditure and accumulation or multiplication: these three collectively. **~বর্ণ** *n.* Brahmin (ব্রাহ্মণ), Kshatriya (ক্ষত্রিয়) and Vaishya (বৈশ্য): these three castes of Hindus collectively. □ *a.* tricoloured, tricolour. **ত্রিবর্ণ পতাকা** a tricoloured flag, a tricolour. **~বর্ণরঞ্জিত** *a.* dyed or painted in three colours, tricoloured. **~বলি, ~বলী** *n.* the three muscular folds or wrinkles of the belly or the throat. **~বার্ষিক** *a.* triennial. **~বিদ্যা** Rik (ঋক্), Sama (সাম) and Yajus (যজুঃ): these three Vedas. **~বিধ** *a.* of three kinds; threefold. **~বেণি** *n.* a river with three streams; the river Ganges as it flows in heaven under the name of Mandakini, on earth under the name of Alakananda and in the underworld or Hades under the name of Bhogawati; a confluence of three rivers or streams; the confluence of the Ganges, the Jamuna and the Saraswati at Allahabad. **~বেদী** *n.* one esp. a Brahmin conversant with the three Vedas, namely, the Rik (ঋক্), the Sama (সাম) and the Yajus (যজুঃ). **~ভঙ্গ, ~ভঙ্গিম** *a.* bent or crooked in three parts of the body. **ত্রিভঙ্গ-মুরারি** *n.* an appellation of Krishna (কৃষ্ণ) esp. as he piped his flute standing; (sarcas.) a ludicrously ugly person who cannot keep his body erect. **~ভুজ** *n.* a triangle. **~ভুজীয়** *a.* triangular. **~ভুবন** *n.* heaven, earth and the underworld or Hades: these three collectively; the (whole) universe. **~ভুবনখ্যাত, ~ভুবনবিখ্যাত** *a.* reputed or famed all over the three world; having universal reputation or fame. **~ভুবনবিজয়ী** *a.* one who or that which has conquered or can conquer the three worlds, namely, heaven, earth and the underworld; world-conquering. **~মাত্রিক** *a.* (geom.) having three dimensions, solid; (arith. & alg.) cubic. **~মুকুট** *n.* triple-crowns or titles (esp. of victory in athletic sports and games). **~মূর্তি** *n.* the Hindu trinity: Brahma (ব্রহ্মা), Vishnu (বিষ্ণু) and Shiva (শিব) ; (chiefly facet.) a group of three persons or friends who seem to be inseparable; a trio. **~যামা** *n.* night. □ *a.* consisting of or divided into three parts (ত্রিযামা-যামিনী). **~যোজী** *a.* trivalent. **~রত্ন** *n.* Buddha, Buddhism and the Buddhist monastery: these three as considered holy by Buddhists; (chiefly facet. & sarcas.) three precious persons. **~রাত্র** *n.* three consecutive nights and the two days in between them; three nights; a feast or fast continuing for this period. **~লোক** same as **ত্রিভুবন**। **ত্রিলোচন** same as **ত্রিনয়ন**। **~শক্তি** *n.* three powers. □ *a.* tripartite. **~শাখা বিন্যাস** *n.* (bot.) trichasium. **~শির, ~শিরা** *a.* three-headed; three-veined, three-pronged. **ত্রিশূল** *n.* a trident. **~শূলী, ~শূলধারী** *a.* armed with or holding a trident. □ *n.* an appellation of Shiva (শিব). **~শূলিনী, ~শূলধারিণী** *a.* *fem.* of **~শূলী** and **~শূলধারী** respectively. □ *n.* appellations of Goddess Durga (দুর্গা). **~ষষ্টি** *n.* & *a.* sixty-three. **~ষষ্টিতম** *a.* sixty-third. *fem.* **~ষষ্টিতমী**। **~সংসার** same as **~ভুবন**। **ত্রিসংসারে তার কেউ নেই** he has none to call his own in the whole world. **~সত্য** *n.* an oath thrice repeated or affirmed. **~সন্ধ্যা** *n.* morning midday and afternoon: these three parts of one day collectively. **~সপ্ততি** *n.* & *a.* seventy-three. **~সপ্ততিতম** *a.* seventy-third. *fem.* **~সপ্ততিতমী**। **~সীমা, ~সীমানা** *n.* the three boundaries or ends; proximity, neighbourhood. **ত্রিসীমানা না**

মাড়ানো never to come too near, to keep well away from. ~স্রোতা same as ত্রিধারা।

ত্রিংশ *a.* thirtieth; thirty. **ত্রিংশৎ** *n. & a.* thirty. *fem.* **ত্রিংশতী**। **ত্রিংশত্তম** *a.* thirtieth *fem.* **ত্রিশংত্তমী**।

ত্রিক *n.* the loins; three; a three-headed way.

ত্রিকাস্থি *n.* the sacrum.

ত্রিত্ব threeness; trinity; threefold state or condition.

ত্রিদশ *n.* a god, an immortal. **~বধূ, ~বনিতা** *n.* (according to Hindus) a celestial courtesan or prostitute. **ত্রিদশাধিপতি** *n.* Indra (ইন্দ্র) king of the gods. **ত্রিদশারি** *n.* an enemy of gods; a demon. **ত্রিদশালয়** *n.* heaven (which is the abode of gods and goddesses).

ত্রিদিব see ত্রি।

ত্রিপল *n.* tarpaulin. □ *a.* thrice-bevelled (ত্রিপল কাচ).

ত্রিপুরান্তক, ত্রিপুরারি *n.* an appellation of Shiva (শিব) who killed the demon Tripur (ত্রিপুর).

ত্রিশ *n. & a.* thirty.

ত্রিশঙ্কু *n.* a mythological king who was accommodated after his death in the void between heaven and earth; (fig.) a man who catches at the shadow and loses the substance, a man who can have recourse to neither of two alternatives.

ত্রুটি *n.* a shortcoming, a deficiency; a defect; harm; a failing, a lapse; an offence, a fault. **~বিচ্যুতি** *n.* failings and errors, errors and omissions, faults and failings. **~হীন** *a.* free from defects, flawless, faultless, perfect, impeccable.

ত্রেতা *n.* the second age of the world according to Hindus.

ত্রৈকালিক *a.* of or relating to the three ages; past, present and future; of or relating to all times or ages; eternal.

ত্রৈগুণ্য *n.* an aggregate or collection or union or synthesis of the three primal characteristic qualities of man, namely, সত্ত্ব or knowledge, রজঃ or action and তমঃ or ignorance.

ত্রৈবার্ষিক *a.* continuing for three years or occurring every third year, triennial.

ত্রৈমাসিক *a.* continuing for three months or occurring or being published every third month, trimonthly, quarterly; relating to three months. □ *n.* a periodical published every third month, a quarterly.

ত্রৈরাশিক *n.* (arith.) the rule of three.

ত্রৈলঙ্গ, (rare) **ত্রৈলিঙ্গ** *a.* of the province of Tailanga. □ *n.* a native of Tailanga; the language of Tailanga, Telugu.

ত্রৈলোক্য *n.* heaven, earth and the underworld: these three worlds collectively; the universe; creation.

ত্র্যংশ *n.* the third part or share; three parts or shares.

ত্র্যক্ষর *n.* the holy letter ওঁ (অ + উ + ম). □ *a.* containing ওঁ; consisting of three letters. **ত্র্যক্ষরা** *n.* the final knowledge.

ত্র্যঙ্ক *a.* consisting of three acts, three-act (ত্র্যঙ্ক নাটক).

ত্র্যঙ্গুল *a.* measuring three fingers.

ত্র্যম্বক *n.* a name of Shiva (শিব).

ত্র্যস্র *a.* triangular.

ত্র্যহস্পর্শ *n.* a conjunction of three lunar days in one calendar day.

থ১ *n.* the seventeenth letter of the Bengali alphabet.

থ২ *a.* stupefied or dumbfounded and motionless, confounded or amazed or flabbergasted (থ হওয়া).

থই *n.* the bottom (of rivers, ponds, lakes etc.); limit (of sorrow, misery etc.); a shelter. **থই না পাওয়া** to be out of depth.

থইথই *int.* expressing : vast expanse of any liquid (জল থইথই করছে).

থক *int.* expressing : the sound of spitting phlegm (থক করে থুতু ফেলা).

থকথক *int.* expressing : clayeyness or splashed state (কাদা থকথক করছে) ; stickiness (আঠা থকথক করছে) ; a raw wound exposed to view (often filled with morbid matter) (ঘা থকথক করছে) ; compact sliminess (পোকাগুলো থকথক করছে). **থকথকে** *a.* clayey; sticky, viscid, viscous; exposed to view and often containing morbid matter; slimy.

থকা *v.* (owing to hard labour) to be run down or exhausted; to be out of breath, to pant; to come to a stop in a state of exhaustion. **থকিত** *a.* stopped on account of exhaustion (থকিত পায়ের চলা).

থতমত *int.* expressing : embarrassment; stammering with perplexity. **থতমত খাওয়া** *v.* to be embarrassed; to be disconcerted; to stammer with perplexity.

থপ *imt.* expressing : a thudding noise. **থপথপ** *int.* expressing : repeated thudding noise. **থপথপে** *a.* giving out a thudding noise (থপথপে চলন).

থপাস *int.* expressing : a sound louder than **থপ**।

থমকানো *v.* to come to a stop suddenly; to be taken aback.

থমকি *v. imp.* stopping suddenly. **থমকি থমকি** *adv.* stopping at every step.

থমথম *int.* expressing: dreadful depth, silence and darkness (রাত থমথম করছে) ; swollenness with morbid humour or passion or glumness (মুখ থমথম করছে) ; filled with rain or overcast with cloud (আকাশ থমথম করছে) ; filled with dreadful uncertainty or suspense (সারা দেশ থমথম করছে). **থমথমে** *a.* dreadfully gloomy and dark; dreadfully still; swollen with morbid humour or passion or glumness; filled with rain or overcast with cloud; filled with dreadful uncertainty or suspense.

থর *n.* a layer, a stratum, a tier. **থরে-থরে, থরে-বিথরে** *adv.* in layers or strata or tiers one upon another, stratifyingly.

থরথর *int.* expressing violent, trembling or shaking (থরথর দেহ, কাঁপে থরথর). **থরথর করা** *v.* to tremble or quake violently. **থরথরানি** *n.* violent trembling or quaking.

থরহরি *a & adv.* trembling violently esp. with fear.

থল poet. & dial. corrup. of **স্থল**।

থলথল *int.* expressing : lax fleshiness or flabbiness. **থলথল করা** *v.* (usu. of lax flesh of a flabby person) to hang loosely. **থলথলে** *a.* fleshy or flabby but lax.

থলি, থলিয়া, (coll.) **থলে** *n.* a bag, a sack, a pouch; (anat.) a bladder.

থলো *n.* a cluster, a bunch. **থলো থলো** in bunches or clusters; clustering.

থস্‌থস্‌, থসথস *in.* expressing : moistness or wetness and looseness. **থস্‌থস্‌ করা** *v.* to be moist and loose. **থস্‌থসে** *a.* moist or wet and loose.

-থা১ *in. comp.* a place (হেথা, এথা).

-থা২ *in. comp.* a manner or way or means or kind (অন্যথা, সর্বথা).

থাউকা, (coll.) **থাউকো, থাওকা** *a. & adv.* in lump.

থাক *n.* a tier, a layer; a group.

থাকবন্দি *a.* tiered, stacked in layers one above another, stratified; kept in separate groups.

থাকবস্তি *n.* determination of the periphery, boundary etc. of land; cadastral survey.

থাকা *v.* to live, to dwell (ওরা ওখানে থাকে) ; to stay, to be at (ঘরে থাকা) ; to remain, to be in (পালিয়ে থাকা) ; to pass time (কষ্টে থাকা) ; to have (টাকা থাকা) ; to be in possession (টাকা চিরকাল থাকে না) ; to exist (ঈশ্বর চিরকাল আছেন ও থাকবেন) ; to last esp. permanently (এ রং থাকবে না) ; to be alive (বাপ থাকতে তোমার টাকার ভাবনা নেই) ; to be present (আমি সেখানে থাকলে এটা ঘটত না) ; to be saved or preserved (এ যুদ্ধে প্রাণ থাকবে না) ; to be maintained or observed or kept (কথা থাকা) ; to remain unimpaired or intact (জাত থাকা, ধর্ম থাকা, সতীত্ব থাকা) ; to be retained (মনে থাকা) ; to lag behind, to straggle (সবাই যখন গেল, তখন আমি আর থাকি কেন) ; to be involved, to take part in (আমি কিছুতে থাকি না) ; to be accustomed to (সে সকালে চা খেয়ে থাকে) ; to continue (চলতে থাকা) ; to associate with, to accompany (লক্ষ্মণ রামের সঙ্গে সঙ্গে থাকত) ; (vul.) to have illicit connection with; to be left off or out (ও কথা থাক). **থাকাথাকি** *n.* stay; existence; act of staying and not staying.

থাকে-থাকে *adv.* in tiers, in rows.

থান[১] *n.* a holy place (বাবার থান) ; proximity, presence ('ধর্মথানে পাইব মুকতি').

থান[২] *a.* whole, unbroken (থান ইট) ; without coloured border or edge (থান ধুতি). □ *n.* an entire sheet of woven fabric (জামার থান) ; a loincloth without any coloured border or edge.

থানকুনি *n.* variety of edible herb Hydrocotyle asiatica.

থানা *n.* stationing or encamping (থানা দেওয়া) ; assemblage or encampment ('চারিভিতে কটকের থানা') ; a station or outpost (পুলিশের থানা) ; a police station (থানায় পুলিশ নেই). **থানা দেওয়া** *v.* to be stationed for attacking (রামলক্ষ্মণ সসৈন্য লঙ্কাপুরী বেষ্টন করে থানা দিলেন). **~দার** *n.* an officer in charge of a police station or an outpost. **থানা-পুলিশ করা** *v.* to go repeatedly to the police station for obtaining police help.

থাপড়, থাপড়া, থাপ্পড়, থাবড়া *n.* a slap with the open palm of the hand. **থাপড় মারা, থাপড়ানো, থাবড়ানো** *v.* to slap.

থাবড়ি *n.* a squatting posture; an instance or act of squatting. **থাবড়ি খাওয়া, থাবড়ি খেয়ে বসা** *v.* to squat, to sit on one's buttocks.

থাবা *n.* the paw; (facet.) a man's palm; a palmful, a handful (এক থাবা চিনি). **থাবা দেওয়া, থাবা মারা, থাবানো** *v.* to (try to) seize or snatch with the paw; to paw; (facet.) to (try to) seize or snatch with the palm of the hand.

থাম *n.* a pillar, a post, a column.

থামা *v.* to stop; to come to a stop; to halt, to pause; to stop doing or taking (অনেক বলেছ, এবার থামো) ; to forbear or desist; to be calmed or appeased (রাগ থেমেছে, টাকা না পেলে পাওনাদাররা থামবে না) ; to cease (বৃষ্টি থামা) ; to abate, to have remission (জ্বর থামা).

থামানো *v.* to cause to stop, to stop; to stop (one) doing or talking; to cause to forbear or desist; to calm or appease; to cause to cease; to abate; to check or prevent.

থামাল *n.* (arch.) plinth.

থাম্বা dial. form of **থাম** ৷

থারি *n.* (poet.) a small plate or platter, or salver.

থার্মোমিটার, থার্মমিটার *n.* a thermometer.

থালা, (corrup.) **থাল** *n.* a plate, a platter, a salver.

থালি *n.* a small plate or platter or salver.

থাসা *v.* to press down; to knead; to stuff or ram esp. forcibly.

থিকথিক milder var. of **থকথক** ৷

থিতানো *v.* to sink down to the bottom, to settle; to subside; (fig.) to be calmed or quietened or to become weakened (আন্দোলন থিতানো).

থিতু dial. form of **স্থিত** esp. in the sense of: settled down. **থিতু হওয়া** *v.* to settle, to settle down; to get settled.

থিয়েটার *n.* a theatre. **থিয়েটার করা** *v.* to act on the stage; to stage a play. **~ওয়ালা** *n.* a proprietor or manager of a theatre; a stage actor. **~ওয়ালি** *n.* a stage actress. **থিয়েটারি** *a.* stagey; theatrical.

থির poet. & coll. corrup. of **স্থির** ৷

থু, থুঃ *int.* expressing : noise of spitting roughly; fie (তাকে থুঃ).

থুঁতনি, থুঁতি variants of **থুতনি** and **থুতি** respectively.

থুক *int.* expressing : noise of spitting. □ *n.* spittle (থুক ফেলা). **থুকদানি, থুকদান** *n.* a spitoon.

থুক্‌থুক, থুকথুক variants of **থিকথিক** ৷

থুড়থুড় *int.* expressing : constant trembling

or inability to stand steady owing to old age, decrepitude or weakness; decrepitude. **থুড়থুড়ে** *a.* trembling constantly or unable to stand steady owing to old age, decrepitude or weakness; decrepit.

থুড়া *v.* to mince, to chop fine; to thrash or rebuke severely.

থুড়ি *int.* expressing : withdrawal or retraction of a word uttered or of an action done by mistake; sorry.

থুৎকার *n.* act of spitting; act of making the sound of spitting; (fig.) act of crying shame upon.

থুতনি, থুতি *n.* the chin.

থুতু *n.* spittle; saliva. **থুতু দেওয়া** *v.* to spit (upon or at). **থুতু ফেলা** *v.* to spit.

থুথু alt. spell. of **থুতু** ।

থুপ *n.* a heap, a pile, a stack. **থুপ করা** *v.* to heap, to pile, to stack.

থুপি *n.* a small heap or pile or bunch or cluster.

থুবড়া[1] *a.* unmarried though advanced in years. *fem.* **থুবড়ি** । **থুবড়া লোক** an old bachelor. **থুবড়ি** (or **থুবড়া**) **মেয়ে** an old maid or spinster.

থুবড়া[2] *a.* very old; decrepit. *fem.* **থুবড়ি** ।

থুবড়ানো *v.* to fall flat on one's face (মুখ থুবড়ে পড়া).

থুবড়ি see **থুবড়া[1]** & **থুবড়া[2]** ।

থুবড়ো coll. var. of **থুবড়া[1]** & **থুবড়া[2]** ।

থুরথুর var. of **থুড়থুড়** ।

থুরা var. of **থুড়া** ।

থেঁতলানো see **থেঁতো** ।

থেঁতো *a.* pounded; smashed; bruised; mauled. **থেঁতো করা** *v.* to crush to a pulp. **থেঁতা, থেঁতানো, থেঁতলানো** *v.* to pound; to smash; to bruise; to make soft and shapeless by repeated pounding; to maul. □ *a.* pounded; smashed; bruised; mauled.

থেকে *prep.* from (বাড়ি থেকে, তার কাছ থেকে) ; since (সেই সময় থেকে) ; than, of, to (রামের থেকে শ্যাম বড়ো).

থেবড়া *a.* flat; snub. **থেবড়া নাক** a snub-nose. **থেবড়া করা, থেবড়ানো** *v.* to flatten.

থেলো *a.* having a large roundish water container made of a coconut-shell (থেলো হুঁকো).

থৈ alt. spell. of **থই** ।

থৈথৈ alt. spell. of **থইথই** ।

থোওয়া, থোয়া *v.* (dial.) to place, to put, to keep; to lay down; to deposit. □ *a.* placed, put, kept; laid down; deposited. **থোওয়ানো, থোয়ানো** *v.* to cause to place or put or keep or lay down or deposit.

থোঁতা[1] *a.* smashed; rendered toothless or blunt (মুখ থোঁতা করা). **মুখ থোঁতা করে দেওয়া** *v.* (fig.) to render powerless, to take the venom out of, to extract the fang of, to discomfit.

থোঁতা[2] *n.* the chin (থোঁতা ভেঙে দেওয়া). □ *a.* having a chin; heavy and blunt (থোঁতা মুখ). **থোঁতা মুখ ভোঁতা করা** (fig.) to put an end to one's tall talk, to put out of countenance, to discomfit; to humble one's pride, to make one lick the dust.

থোক *n.* a net amount; an aggregate, a total, a lump; an instalment, an item (থোকে থোকে) ; a bundle; a bunch. □ *a.* net, lump, total (থোক লাভ, থোক টাকা).

থোকা *n.* a bunch, a cluster; a bundle. **থোকা বাঁধা** *v.* (*i.* & *t.*) to gather or collect in bunches or bundles. **থোকায় থোকায়** in bunches or bundles.

থোকে *adv.* in a lump. **থোকে বিক্রয়** disposal or sale on a wholesale basis.

থোড় *n.* the spathe of a banana tree before it shoots from the stem; an ear of paddy corn about to be sprouted. **থোড়-বড়ি-খাড়া** hackneyed monotony; monotonous repetition or lack of variety, truism.

থোড়া[1] pop. var. of **থুড়া** ।

থোড়া[2] *a.* a little; a few.

থোড়াই *adv.* not much, but little. **থোড়াই কেয়ার করা** not to care a fig or a straw for; (sl.) not to care a damn.

থোতনা *n.* (dero.) a large and heavy and odd-looking chin.

থোতা alt. spell. of **থোঁতা[2]** ।

থোপ *n.* a bunch, a cluster, a tuft (থোপ থোপ ঘাস = tufts of grass).

থোপনা[1] var. of **থোতনা** ।

থোপনা[2] *n.* a large tuft or bunch or cluster.

থোপা *n.* a bunch, a cluster, a tuft.

থোয়া, থোয়ানো variants of **থোওয়া** and **থোওয়ানো** respectively.

থোর, থোরি *a.* (obs. & poet.) little or few.

থোলো alt. spell. of **থলো** ।

থ্যাতলানো alt. spell. of **থেঁতলানো** (see **থেঁতো**).

থ্যাবড়া alt. spell. of **থেবড়া** ।

দ[1] *n.* the eighteenth consonant of the Bengali alphabet.

দ[2] coll. form of **দহ। দয়ে জমা** *v.* (fig.) to be drowned beyond hope of rescue in an abyss (of danger); to be utterly ruined.

-দ[3] *sfx.* indicating: one who or that which gives (সুখদ, জলদ).

দই *n.* curdled milk, curd. **দই পাতা** *v.* to curdle milk; to keep milk in such a way that it will congeal or freeze into curd. **চিনিপাতা দই** milk curdled with sugar, sweet curd. **সাজা দই** recently curdled milk, fresh curd. **হাতে দই পাতে দই তবু বলে কই কই** (lit.) with curd on the palm of one's hand and on the plate, one still complains that it is not enough; (fig.) there is more than enough, yet complaining of scarcity; (cp.) want is unlimited and insatiable.

দউ *a.* (poet. & obs.) two, both.

দংশ *n.* the gadfly, a large gnat.

দংশক *a.* one who or that which bites or stings. □ *n.* a large gnat, the gadfly.

দংশন *n.* act of biting or stinging; a bite or sting. **দংশন করা** *v.* to bite or sting.

দংশল *v.* (obs. & poet.) bit or stung.

দংশা *v.* (usu. poet.) to bite or sting. **দংশানো** *v.* to cause to bite or sting; to bite or sting; (fig.) to cause grief, pain or suffering, to distress.

দংশিত *a.* bitten; stung.

দংশী *fem.* of **দংশ।**

দংষ্ট্র *n.* a tooth (esp. a large or sharp one). **দ্রংষ্ট্রা** *n.* a claw or prong or fang (as of a crab or a lobster); a large (and usu. sharp) tooth (as of a dog or a fox); a sting (as of a mosquito or a gadfly). **দ্রংষ্ট্রাঘাত** *n.* a bite or a sting. **দংষ্ট্রায়ুধ** *n.* a wild boar. **দ্রংষ্ট্রাল, দ্রংষ্ট্রী** *a.* having a claw or prong or fang or tooth or sting, clawed, pronged, fanged, toothed, stinged.

দক, দঁক *n.* a soft and deep mass of mud, a pool of soft and deep mud, quagmire, slough (দকে পড়া). **দকে পড়া** *v.* (fig.) to run into a great danger suddenly.

দক্ষ[1] *n.* (myth.) the name of a divine being entrusted formerly with the charge of creation of earthly beings; the father of Sati (সতী), the wife of Shiva (শিব). **~কন্যা** *n.* Sati (সতী), the wife of Shiva (শিব). **~যজ্ঞ** *n.* (myth.) a religious feast held by Daksha (দক্ষ) in which Shiva (শিব) was not invited and was publicly abused or censured and Sati (সতী), the wife of Shiva, unable to stand this, died of grief. Shiva came with his followers to the feast, spoilt it and killed Daksha; (fig.) tremendous turmoil; utter confusion, pandemonium.

দক্ষ[2] *a.* expert, skilful, adroit; clever; competent. *fem.* **দক্ষা। ~তা** *n.* expertness, skill, adroitness; cleverness; competence.

দক্ষিণ *n.* the south; the right hand side, the right. □ *a.* southern, south; Antarctic; dexter, right (দক্ষিণ হস্ত); favourable, pleased, graceful (রুদ্রের দক্ষিণ মুখ); (rhet.) a gallant who can love several women equally at the same time. **~অয়নান্ত** *n.* winter solstice. **~কালিকা, দক্ষিণাকালী** *n.* a manifestation of Goddess Kali (কালী). **~পন্থী** *a.* rightist. □ *n.* a rightist in politics. **দক্ষিণ-পশ্চিম** *n. & a.* south-west. □ *a.* south-western. **দক্ষিণ-পূর্ব** *n. & a.* south-east. □ *a.* south-eastern. **~মেরু** *n.* the South Pole. **~মেরু অঞ্চল** the Antarctic. **~হস্ত** *n.* the right hand; (fig.) the principal support or helper, one's right-hand man. **দক্ষিণহস্তের ব্যাপার** the affair or business of taking one's meal, eating.

দক্ষিণরায় *n.* the presiding tiger-deity of the Sundarbans.

দক্ষিণা *n.* a fee or gift given to a priest or a Brahman or a teacher etc.; the south (দক্ষিণাপ্রবণ); (rhet.) a mistress who still retains her attachment towards her former lover. □ *a.* southern, south.

দক্ষিণা-কালী see **দক্ষিণ**।

দক্ষিণাচার *n.* a system of Tantric (তান্ত্রিক) rituals. **দক্ষিণাচারী** *a.* & *n.* one who follows this system.

দক্ষিণাচল *n.* the mythological southern mountain, the Malaya; the Antarctic Mountain.

দক্ষিণান্ত *n.* termination of a religious function by paying the priest his fees. **দক্ষিণান্ত করা** *v.* to conclude or terminate a religious function by paying the priest his fees.

দক্ষিণাপথ *n.* the Deccan.

দক্ষিণাবর্ত *a.* moving or winding clockwise; clockwise, dextral. □ *n.* the Deccan.

দক্ষিণাবহ *n.* the south wind; the vernal breeze.

দক্ষিণায়ন *n.* the winter solstice. **দক্ষিণায়নবৃত্ত** *n.* the Tropic of Capricorn.

দক্ষিনে, (coll.) **দখনে,** (coll.) **দখনো** *a.* southern, south.

দখল *n.* occupation, possession; hold, control; right to hold or possess; mastery, knowledge, skill, aptitude (তার ন্যায়শাস্ত্রে বা গণিতে দখল আছে). **দখল করা** *v.* to occupy (আসন বা জমি দখল করা); to take possession of (শত্রুতে দেশ দখল করল); to appropriate to oneself (সে আমার কলমটা দখল করল). **দখল থাকা** *v.* to have right to hold or possess (জমিতে দখল থাকা); to have possession; to have hold or control (ভাগ্যের উপর দখল থাকা); to have mastery or knowledge or skill or aptitude (শাস্ত্রে বা খেলায় দখল থাকা). **দখলে থাকা** *v.* to be in occupation or possession or control. **~কার, ~দার** *a.* one who is in occupation or possession, occupying. □ *n.* an occupant, an occupier; a possessor. **~চ্যুত** *a.* dispossessed. **~নামা** *n.* a deed or title of possession or occupancy. **দখলি** *a.* relating to occupancy or occupation or possession; occupied, held. **দখলিকার, দখলিদার** same as **দখলকার**। **দখল স্বত্ব** right by occupancy, possessory right.

দখিন coll. & poet. corrup. of **দক্ষিণ**।

দখিনা *a.* southern, south.

দগড় *n.* a kind of war-drum or kettledrum.

দগড়া *n.* a raised streak on the skin caused by lashing, a wale. **দগড়া পড়া** *v.* to be marked with a wale. **দগড়া ফেলা** v. to wale.

দগদগ *int.* expressing : burning sensation; inflammation or extensive openness of a wound (ঘা দগদগ করছে). **দগদগানি, দগদগি** *n.* burning sensation; inflammation. **দগদগে** *a.* giving a burning sensation, burning; inflammatory.

দগ্ধ *a.* burnt; scorched, parched; singed, roasted; very hot or red hot (দগ্ধ লোহা); (fig.) extremely afflicted or distressed (দগ্ধ হৃদয়); (fig.) unfortunate, unlucky, illfated (দগ্ধ কপাল); (fig.) tarnished with shame or disrepute, disgraced (দগ্ধ বদন); (fig.) unkind, ungraceful (দগ্ধ বিধাতা). **দগ্ধা** *n. fem.* an ominous or ill-omened lunar day (মাসদগ্ধা). □ *v.* (chiefly poet.) to burn; to scorch, to parch; to singe, to roast; to make very hot, to heat; (fig.) to afflict, to distress; (fig.) to annoy, to badger, to torment. **দগ্ধানো** *v.* same as **দগ্ধা** (*v.*). □ *a.* same as **দগ্ধ** (*a.*) **~হৃদয়** *a.* having a heart in deep and bitter grief. **দগ্ধাবশেষ** *a.* remaining as residue after burning. □ *n.* residue after burning.

দঙ্গল *n.* a crowd, a swarm; a group (এক দঙ্গল ছেলে); wrestling; a wrestling bout. **দঙ্গল বাঁধা** *v.* to form into a crowd; to crowd, to swarm.

দজ্জাল *a.* (usu. of a woman) hot-tempered, querulous and overbearing, refractory; wayward; wicked; choleric; (dero.) uncontrollable.

দড় *a.* strong, hard, steady; stiff; firm; strong; sharp (মুখে দড়); stronger, harder, stiffer (বাঁশের চেয়ে কঞ্চি দড়); able, competent (কাজে দড়).

দড়কচা, দড়কাঁচা variants of **দরকচা** and **দরকাঁচা** respectively.

দড়বড় *int.* expressing : the noise of a horse's trot. **দড়বড়ি** *adv.* (poet.) trotting(ly).

দড়মা dial. var. of **দরমা**।

দড়া *n.* a thick cord, a rope, a hawser. **~দড়ি** *n.* ropes and cords, cordage. **~বাজি** *n.* rope-dancing, rope-walking, funambulation; acrobatics; acrobatism. **~বাজিকর** *n.* a rope-dancer, a rope-walker, a funambulist, an acrobat. **দড়াবাজি করা** *v.* to funambulate, to perform or exhibit acrobatic feats.

দড়াম *int.* expressing : a banging or slamming or booming or loud thudding noise. **দড়াম করে দরজা ভেজানো** to shut the door with a bang, to slam the door.

দড়ি *n.* a cord, a string; a halter (ফাঁসির দড়ি) ; a fillet (চুল-বাঁধা দড়ি). **দড়ি ছেঁড়া** *v.* to snap a string; to get loose from bonds or bondage; to escape from captivity or control. **~ছেঁড়া** *a.* got loosened from bonds or bondage; (fig.) out of captivity; (fig.) unrestrained. **~দড়া** *n.* strings and ropes, cordage. **দড়ি দেওয়া** *v.* (lit.) to give a piece of string; to put a halter round one's neck; to hang. **দড়ি পাকানো** *v.* to twist ropes and cords, to make ropes and cords. **~কলসি** *n.* a piece of cord and a pitcher: equipment for committing suicide (one may drown oneself by tying a pitcher full of water to one's neck with a piece of cord). **তোমার দড়ি-কলসি জোটে না** (in curses and scolding) go, get yourself drowned. **তোমার গলায় দড়ি** (in curses and scolding) go, hang yourself. **ভেবে ভেবে দড়ি হওয়া** to be reduced to a skeleton or be emaciated through worries and anxieties.

দণ্ড[1] *n.* a measure of time (=24 minutes). **দণ্ডে দণ্ডে** at every moment; every now and then, frequently, often; repeatedly. **একদণ্ডে** *adv.* in a short time; in a trice, in a moment, in a jiffy.

দণ্ড[2] *n.* a rod, a mace, a club, a staff, a stick, a pole, a sceptre; a pestle; a mallet; a churning stick; a maulstick; a ramrod; a rudder; anything resembling a rod; a measure of length (=4 cubits); punishment, penalty; a sentence (প্রাণদণ্ড) ; a fine (অর্থদণ্ড) ; a loss (ব্যবসায়ে টাকা দণ্ড) ; government or statesmanship, any form or policy of government (সামদানভেদদণ্ড) ; a war or battle; an army or column (দণ্ডনায়ক). **~কর্তা** *n.* one who is empowered to punish; a punisher; a governor or ruler; a judge. *fem.* **~কর্ত্রী** । **~কাক** *n.* the god of death or Yama (যম) in the guise of a crow; jackdaw, a raven. **~গ্রহণ** *n.* acceptance of or submission to punishment; act of taking to asceticism. **দণ্ডগ্রহণ করা** *v.* to accept punishment, to submit to punishment, to kiss the rod; to take to asceticism, to renounce the world. **~চুম্বক** *n.* a bar magnet. **~দাতা** *n.* an inflicter of punishment, a scourger. *fem.* **~দাত্রী** । **~দান** *n.* infliction of punishment; an award of a sentence of punishment. **দণ্ডদান করা, দণ্ড দেওয়া** *v.* to punish; to sentence to punishment, to award a sentence of punishment. **~ধর** *n.* a king; a ruler or governor; a name of Yama (যম) the god of death and punisher of sinners. □ *a.* sceptred; armed with or bearing a staff. **~ধারী** *a.* armed with or bearing a staff; sceptred. □ *n.* a king; an ascetic. **~ন** *n.* act of punishing or infliction of punishment, punishment. **~নায়ক** *n.* a commander-in-chief; an army commander; one empowered to punish, a punisher, a scourger. **~নীতি** *n.* principles of government; political economy, politics; principles regulating punishment, penal system. **~নীয়** *a.* punishable. *fem.* **~নীয়া** । **~পাণি** same as **দণ্ডধর** । **~প্রদান** same as **দণ্ডদান** । **~পাল, ~পালক** *n.* a gatekeeper, a porter (*fem.* porteress, portress), a janitor (*fem.* janitrix, janitress). **~বিধাতা** same as **~দাতা** । *fem.* **~বিধাত্রী** । **~বিধান** *n.* award or determination of punishment; the penal code. **~বিধি** *n.* the penal code; the criminal or penal procedure; a criminal or penal law. **~মুণ্ড** *n.* all sorts of punishments ranging from the most lenient ones to capital punishment. **দণ্ডমুণ্ডের কর্তা** one who has the absolute power of punishing; a king; an absolute ruler or master; a judge. **~যোগ্য** *a.* punishable. **~স্বরূপ** *adv.* by way of punishment, as a penalty.

দণ্ডবৎ *int.* expressing : prostration to pay homage or to show reverence. □ *n.* lying prostrate in worship or respect. □ *a.* prostrate in worship or respect. **দণ্ডবৎ করা** *v.* to prostrate oneself in worship or respect (to or before). **দণ্ডবৎ হওয়া** *v.* to lie prostrate in worship or respect. **খুরে খুরে দণ্ডবৎ** I bow down to your or his or her hoofs; a facetious expression to call a person a beast and get rid of him or her.

দণ্ডাঘাত *n.* hitting or striking with a stick, beating up or belabouring with a rod.

দণ্ডাধীন *a.* subject to punishment; liable to be punished; sentenced to punishment; subject to government or rule.

দণ্ডায়মান *a.* in the standing posture, standing up. **দণ্ডায়মান হওয়া** *v.* to stand up.

দণ্ডার্হ *a.* deserving punishment, punishable.

দণ্ডি *n.* a holy or sacrificial thread measuring 4 cubits or about 2 metres in length.

দণ্ডিত *a.* punished, penalized; sentenced to a punishment; subjected to financial loss or fine.

দণ্ডী *a.* armed with or bearing a staff; sceptred. □ *n.* a king; an ascetic; Yama (যম) the god of death and punisher of sinners.

দণ্ড্য same as **দণ্ডার্হ**।

দত্ত *a.* given; given away; awarded; conferred, bestowed; paid. **দত্তা** *n. fem.* of **দত্ত**। □ *a. fem.* given away in marriage; betrothed. **দত্তক, দত্তক পুত্র** *n.* an adopted son. **দত্তহারী, দত্তাপহারক, দত্তাপহারী** *a.* (committing the offence of) taking back what has been given away by oneself. **দত্তাপহরণ** *n.* act of taking back what has been given by oneself; the offence of doing this.

দদ্রু *n.* ringworm. **~নাশন** *n.* a curative medicine for ringworm. □ *a.* curative of ringworm.

দধি *n.* curdled milk, curd. **~ভাণ্ড** *n.* a pail containing curd. **~মঙ্গল** *n.* a ritual of feeding a Hindu bride in the small hours previous to the wedding day. **~মন্থন** *n.* act of churning milk into butter or act of churning curd into whey. **দধিমন্থন করা** *v.* to churn milk into butter or to churn curd into whey. **~মন্থনদণ্ড** *n.* a churning rod or stick. **~সার** *n.* butter or cream.

দধ্যন্ন same as **দম্বল**।

দনুজ *n.* (myth.) a son or descendant of Danu (দনু), a demon (demons were traditional enemies of gods). *fem.* **দনুজা**। **~দলনী** *n. fem.* the destroyer of demons: an appellation of goddess Durga (দুর্গা).

দন্ত *n.* a tooth; a tusk (হস্তিদন্ত) ; a fang (সর্পদন্ত). **~কাষ্ঠ** *n.* a twig used as a toothbrush. **দন্ত কিড়িমিড়ি** *n.* an instance or act of gnashing one's teeth. **~চিকিৎসক** *n.* a dentist. **~চিকিৎসা** *n.* dentistry. **~ধাবন** *n.* act of cleansing or brushing one's teeth; a toothbrush. **~ধাবনী** *n.* a toothbrush, a stick or twig for cleaning teeth. **~পঙ্ক্তি** *n.* a row of teeth. **~পেশি** *n.* gums. **~বিকাশ** *n.* (dero. & facet.) smile or simper. **দন্তবিকাশ করা** *v.* (dero. & facet.) to smile or simper. **~বেষ্ট** *n.* gums. **~মঞ্জন** *n.* act of cleansing or brushing one's teeth; toothpowder or tooth-paste, dentifrice. **~মল** *n.* the tartar of teeth. **~মাংস** *n.* gums. **~মার্জন** *n.* cleaning or brushing one's teeth. **~মূল** *n.* the root of the tooth. **~মূলীয়** *a.* pertaining to the root of the tooth; (gr.) dental. □ *n.* (gr.) a dental letter or sound, a dental. **~রুচি** *n.* the beauty or whiteness of teeth (as seen when one smiles). **~শূল** *n.* toothache, odontalgia. **~স্ফুট** *n.* act of piercing with teeth; act of biting; (fig.) comprehension. **দন্তস্ফুট করা** *v.* to bite; (fig.) to comprehend. **~হীন** *a.* toothless, edentate, edentulous. **দন্তহীন প্রাণী** an edentate. **দন্তহীন প্রাণীবর্গ** the Edentata.

দন্তাগ্র *n.* the point of a tooth.

দন্তাঘাত *n.* a bite.

দন্তাবল *n.* the elephant.

দন্তায়ুধ *n.* the hog, the boar.

দন্তী *a.* toothed, dentate; having a tusk or a dreadful tooth; rodent. □ *n.* the elephant; the hog; a rodent; (collect.) the Rodentia.

দন্তুর *a.* toothed, dentate, having a tusk; having a large or dreadful tooth or teeth; rodent. **দন্তুর প্রাণী** a rodent. **দন্তুর প্রাণীবর্গ** the Rodentia.

দন্তোদ্গম, দন্তোদ্ভেদ *n.* dentition, teething. **দন্তোদ্গম হওয়া, দন্তোদ্ভেদ হওয়া** *v.* to cut one's teeth, to teethe.

দন্তৌষ্ঠ্য *a.* (gr.) labiodental. □ *n.* a lobiodental letter or sound, a labiodental.

দন্ত্য *a.* dental. **~বর্ণ** *n.* a dental letter, a dental.

দপ্, দপ *int.* expressing : a sudden blaze. **দপ্ করে** *adv.* blazing up suddenly. **দপ্ দপ্, দপদপ** *int.* expressing : blazing up repeatedly and rather tremulously; throbbing inflammation (ফোড়া দপ্‌দপ্ করা). **~দপা** *n.* importance and power. **~দপানি** *n.* repeated throbbing pain.

দফতর, দপ্তর *n.* an office; a secretariat; official papers, files, registers, records (দফতর গোছানো) ; definite charge, portfolio (দফতরহীন). **দফতরখানা, দপ্তরখানা** *n.* a record room. **দফতরহীন, দপ্তরহীন** *a.* without portfolio (দফতরহীন মন্ত্রী). **দফতরি, দপ্তরি** *n.* a record keeper; an office-boy in charge of official files, stamps etc. and postage; a book-binder.

দফা *n.* an instalment, a time; an item; a section, a paragraph, a clause, a division; condition, state, affair (তার দফা রফা). **দফায় দফায়** by instalments; again and again. **~রফা** (or **নিকেশ** or **শেষ**) **করা** *v.* to kill; (vul.) to do for; to undo or ruin or discomfit utterly. **দফারফা হওয়া** *v.* to be ruined or undone.

দফাওয়ারি *a.* counted or given or arranged instalment by instalment or item by item; (inc.) piecemeal.

দফাদার *n.* a military or police officer holding a rank equivalent to that of a corporal.

দফে *adv.* item. **দফে দফে** *adv.* by instalments; item by item.

দব্‌দব্, দবদব variants of **দপ্‌দপ্** ।

দবদবা *n.* the height of power, prosperity and prestige; pomp and splendour.

দম[১] *n.* rule, control, control or repression of senses, continence (শমদম).

দম[২] *int.* expressing : a light thudding or banging noise. **দমদম** *int.* expressing : repeated light thudding or banging noise. **দমাদম** *adv.* with repeated thuds.

দম[৩] *n.* respiration, breathing, breath (দম আটকানো) ; a spell of catching the breath (দম ফুরানো) ; the breath of life, life breath (দম বেরোনো) ; a forceful puff (গাঁজায় দম) ; a spell or act of winding a machine (ঘড়িতে দম) ; (chiefly dial.) a winding key (ঘড়ির দমটা বদলাতে হবে) ; a bluff, a fib, a hoax, a bam (দমে ভোলা) ; mild heat (দমে বসানো মাংস) ; a variety of highly seasoned thick curry (আলুর দম). **দম আটকানো** *v.* to catch the breath; to have difficulty in breathing; to cause difficulty in breathing; to be suffocated or choked; to suffocate or choke. **দম ছাড়া** *v.* to recover freedom of breathing, to take breath. **দম ছাড়ার অবকাশ** breathing-space, breathing-time, a breather. **দম দেওয়া** *v.* to wind (as a watch); to hoax, to bamboozle; to have a hard spell of smoking (গাঁজায় দম দেওয়া). **দম ফাটা** *v.* to choke; (fig.) to feel extremely oppressed at heart when forced not to speak out or express something. **~ফাটা** *a.* choking, suffocating, that which causes choking or suffocation (দমফাটা হাসি). **দম ফুরানো** *v.* to be out of breath, to be breathless; to die; (of clocks etc.) to require fresh winding. **দম বন্ধ করা** *v.* to catch one's breath. **দম বন্ধ করানো** *v.* to cause to catch one's breath; to suffocate, to choke. **দম বন্ধ হওয়া** *v.* to be suffocated or choked. **দম বার করা** v. to put out of breath, to take one's breath; to make one breathe one's last. **দম বার হওয়া** *v.* to be out of breath; to breathe one's last. **দম রাখা** *v.* to hold one's breath. **দম নেওয়া** *v.* to take breath, to have a respite. **দম লাগানো** same as **দম দেওয়া**। **একদম** *adv.* at all. **একদমে** *adv.* at one breath; quickly at a stretch. **পুরোদমে** *adv.* in full swing; in full speed; in a downright manner; thoroughly. **বেদম** *a.* that which puts one out of breath; excessive (বেদম প্রহার).

দমক[১] *a.* one who or that which restrains or subdues or represses.

দমক[২] *n.* a sudden blast or flash or burst a gust; a spell.

দমকল *n.* a fire-engine; the fire-brigade (dial.) a pressure pump for raising water and other fluids. **~বাহিনী** *n.* the fire brigade.

দমকা *a.* coming in a sudden blast or flash or burst, gusty, gustful (দমকা বাতাস) ; unforeseen or unexpected (দমকা খরচ).

দমদম see **দম**[২] ।

দমদমা *n.* a raised mound of earth for target practice.

দমন *n.* subdual, quelling (শত্রুদমন) ; restraint, repression (ইন্দ্রিয়দমন) ; suppression, coercion (বিদ্রোহদমন) ; removal or abatement, check, subsidence (রোগদমন). **দমন করা** *v.* to subdue, to quell; to restrain, to repress; to suppress, to coerce; to remove or abate, to check. **~নীতি** *n.* the policy of coercion or repression. **দমনীয়, দম্য** *a.* subduable; restrainable, repressible; suppressible; coercible; removable or abatable, mitigable. **~শীল** *a.* oppressive, coercing.

দমবাজ *n.* a fibber; a braggart; a bamboozler, a hoaxer. **দমবাজি** *n.* bragging; bamboozlement, hoaxing; a hoax, a fib, a bam.

দময়িতা *a.* & *n.* one who subdues or restrains or represses or suppresses or coerces or checks or removes or abates or causes to subside. *fem.* **দময়িত্রী** ।

দমসম *n.* suffocation or spasm caused by surfeit.

দমা *v.* to be subdued or restrained or repressed or suppressed or coerced; (of diseases etc.) to be removed or abated or mitigated, to subside; (of place etc.) to sink to a lower level; to become dejected or depressed or downcast (লোকসান খেয়ে সে বড় দমে গেছে). □ *a.* depressed, sunk, downcast. **দমানো** *v.* to subdue, to restrain, to repress, to suppress, to coerce; to remove, to abate, to mitigate; to depress; to deject. □ *a.* depressed, sunk.

দমিত *a.* subdued, quelled, put down, restrained, repressed, suppressed, coerced; removed, abated, subsided; depressed, sunk to a lower level; dejected, discouraged.

দমী same as **দময়িতা** ।

দম্পতি, দম্পতী *n.* a husband and a wife, a male and a female creature, a couple.

দম্বল *n.* rennet, curdler.

দম্ভ *n.* vanity, conceit; pride; boast, brag, vaunt, tall talk; arrogance, haughtiness. **দম্ভ করা** *v.* to boast, to brag, to vaunt, to talk tall or big; to challenge.

দম্ভী *a.* conceited, vainglorious, proud; boastful, braggart; arrogant, haughty.

দম্ভোক্তি *n.* a boastful utterance, a brag.

দম্ভোলি *n.* the thunderbolt.

দম্য see **দমন** ।

দয়া *n.* kindness, charity; compassion; tender-heartedness; pity; mercy; favour, benignancy, grace; (rare) benevolence, bounty. **দয়া করা** *v.* to be kind to, to be charitable towards; to look at someone in (or with) compassion; to pity; to take pity on; to treat mercifully; to favour, to be gracious towards. **দয়া করে** kindly. **দয়ার পাত্র** an object of pity; a miserable or despicable man. **দয়ার সাগর** (fig.) an ocean of kindness or compassion, an extremely kind or compassionate man. **~দাক্ষিণ্য** *n.* charity, kindness; bounty; benignancy; mercy. **~নিধি** *n.* (fig.) a store of kindness or compassion, an extremely kind or compassionate man. **~ন্বিত, ~পরবশ, ~পরতন্ত্র** *a.* moved or stricken with kindness or compassion or mercy; kind; compassionate; merciful. **~বান, ~ময়** *a.* kind, charitable; compassionate; tender-hearted; merciful; gracious, benignant; (rare) benevolent, bountiful. *fem.* **~বতী, ~ময়ী** । **~মায়া** *n.* pity and love, compassion and affection. **~মায়াহীন** *a.* without mercy or compassion, pitiless. **~র্দ্র** *a.* melted or softened with kindness or compassion or mercy. *fem.* **দয়ার্দ্রা** । **~র্দ্রচিত্ত** *a.* having one's heart softened with kindness or compassion or mercy; kind-hearted. **~ল, ~লু** same as **দয়াবান** । **~শীল** *a.* kind or charitable or compassionate or tenderhearted or merciful or gracious or benignant or benevolent or bountiful (by nature); practising kindness or charity or benevolence. *fem.* **~শীলা** । **~শূন্য, ~হীন** *a.* unkind, uncharitable; uncompassionate, pitiless; merciless; ungracious. *fem.*

~শূন্যা, ~হীনা। দয়া হওয়া *v.* to feel compassion or pity for.

দয়িত *a.* beloved, dear. □ *n.* a lover; a husband. **দয়িতা** *a. fem.* of **দয়িত**। □ *n.* lady-love; a wife.

দয়েল alt. spell. of **দোয়েল**।

দর[1] *n.* hole, a pit; a crevice (of a mountain); fear, dread, terror; a quake, a shake; a stream; an exudation. □ *adv.* a little, slightly.

দর[2] *n.* price; rate; a price quoted, a quotation; value, worth. **দর করা** *v.* to bargain; to haggle or higgle, to chaffer. **দর দেওয়া** *v.* to quote (a price). **দরে বনা** *v.* to agree about terms.

দর[3] *pfx.* indicating: sub-, under-.

দর-ইজারা *n.* sub-lease, under-lease; a sub-leased holding. **দর-ইজারাদার** *n.* a sub-lessee, an under-lessee.

দরওয়াজা var. of **দরজা**।

দরওয়ান var. of **দরোয়ান**।

দরকচা, দরকাঁচা *a.* partly ripe, imperfectly mellowed; (of vegetables, meat etc.) refusing to be thoroughly softened by boiling; (of skin etc.) stricken with callosity.

দর-কষাকষি *n.* bargaining, chaffering or haggling or higgling. **দর-কষাকষি করা** *v.* to chaffer, to haggle or higgle.

দরকার *n.* necessity; need; requirement; use. **তোমার দরকার কত** what is your requirement ? **তোমার দরকার কী** what do you want ? what is your business ? **তাকে তোমার কী দরকার** what do you want him for ? why do you want him ? what do you want to do with him ? **তাতে তোমার দরকার কী** how does it concern you ? **দরকারি** *a.* necessary; useful; important (দরকারি কথা). **তোমার দরকার নেই** it is none of your business or concern. **দরকারমতো** according to necessity, as and when necessary.

দরখাস্ত *n.* a petition, an application. **দরখাস্ত করা** *v.* to put in or submit a petition or application, to apply. **~কারী** *n.* a petitioner, an applicant. □ *a* petitioning, applying. *fem.* **~কারিণী**।

দরগা *n.* (Mus.) a mausoleum of a holy saint.

দরজা *n* a door; a gate; an entrance or doorway; a portico; (police jargon) a constable on duty at the gate of a police station. **দরজা দেওয়া** *v.* to shut or close a door. **দরজায় দরজায়** *adv.* from door to door, at every door.

দরজি *n.* a tailor; a sempster, a seamster; an outfitter. **মেয়েদরজি** *n. fem.* a tailoress; a semptress, a seamstress.

দরদ[1] *a.* frightful, dreadful. □ *n.* an ancient Indian race; the Sanskrit name of Dardishan.

দরদ[2] *n.* sympathy; compassion; affection, attachment; pain, inflammation.

দরদর *int.* expressing : continuous and rapid flow or oozing (দরদর করে ঘাম ঝরা বা চোখের জল পড়া).

দরদস্তুর, দরদাম *n.* the price of an article and the terms and conditions of purchasing it. **দরদস্তুর করা, দরদাম করা** *v.* to bargain; to chaffer, to haggle or higgle.

দরদালান *n.* a covered corridor (of a building).

দরদি, (poet. var.) **দরদিয়া** *a.* sympathetic; compassionate; full of affection or attachment; (lit. criticism) appreciative.

দরপত্তন *n.* sub-lease, under-lease. **দরপত্তন দেওয়া** *v.* to sub-lease, to under-lease. **দরপত্তনি** *n.* a sub-leased or under-leased holding (esp. a permanent one). **দরপত্তনিদার** *n.* a sub-lessee or under-lessee (esp. a permanent one).

দরপন, দরপণ poet. corruptions of **দর্পণ**।

দরবার *n.* an audience-chamber, a levee, a court, a durbar (রাজদরবার) ; a seeking or solicitation (চাকরির জন্য দরবার). **দরবার করা** *v.* to seek or solicit, to canvass; to hold a court or levee; to audience. **দরবার বসা** *v.* the court sits. **দরবার ভাঙা** *v.* the court rises. **দরবারে বসা** *v.* to sit at court. **দরবারি** *a.* one who frequents a royal court (দরবারি লোক) ; befitting a court, according to the regulations of a court (দরবারি ভাষা, দরবারি পোশাক, দরবারি রীতিনীতি). **দরবারি কানাড়া** an Indian musical mode. **দরবারি চালচালন** court-manners. **দরবারি ব্যাপার** a court-affair. **দরবারি ভাষা** court-language. **দরবারি রীতিনীতি**

court-regulations, protocol. **দরবারি লোক** a courtier.

দরবিগলিত *a.* that which has been melted and is oozing or flowing in a stream. **দরবিগলিত ধারায়** *adv.* in an incessant stream, in continuous flow.

দরবেশ *n.* a Mohammedan ascetic or friar, a fakir; a kind of sweetmeat.

দরমা *n.* a mat (used in walling up buildings etc.) made of bamboo slips, tatty.

দরমাহা *n.* monthly wages or salary.

দরশ, দরশন poet. corruptions of **দর্শন**।

দরাজ *a.* spacious, roomy (দরাজ জায়গা) ; generous, liberal (দরাজ হাত, দরাজ দিল, দরাজ লোক) ; unrestrained or unsubdued (দরাজ গলা, দরাজ মুখ). **দরাজ গলা** loud or full-throated voice. **দরাজ মুখ** outspoken utterance; outspokenness.

দরাদরি *n.* haggling or higgling, chaffering. **দরাদরি করা** *v.* to haggle, to chaffer.

দরি *n.* a carpet, a thick cloth used for sitting or as laid under a bed.

দরিদ্র *a.* poor, penurious, indigent; lacking, deficient; wretched. *fem.* **দরিদ্রা**। **~তা** *n.* poverty, penury; indigence; lack, deficiency; wretchedness. **~নারায়ণ** *n.* the poor conceived as God personified; the beggar class. **~নিবাস** *n.* a poorhouse; a workhouse.

দরিদ্রিত *a.* impoverished, reduced to poverty.

দরিয়া *n.* a sea; an ocean; a bay; a river (usu. a large one).

দরী *n.* a cave, a gorge, a rivine; a glen.

দরুদ *n.* an appellation of reverence and obeisance to a Mohammedan saint.

দরুন *prep.* for, because of, owing to, due to, on account of; for the sake of.

দরোয়ান *n.* a porter (*fem.* porteress, portress), a janitor (*fem.* janitress), a door-keeper, a gate-keeper, a gateman. **দরোয়ানের ঘর** a porter's lodge. **দরোয়ানি** *n.* the office or duty of a porter.

দর্গা alt. spell. of **দরগা**।

দর্জি alt. spell. of **দরজি**।

দর্দুর *n.* the frog; the cloud.

দর্প *n.* vanity, conceit, pride;boast, vaunt, arrogance, haughtiness; daring, challenge. **দর্প করা** *v.* to be proud of, to take pride in; to boast, to vaunt; to dare, to challenge. **দর্প চূর্ণ করা, দর্প ভাঙা** *v.* to humble one's pride. **~নাশ** *n.* ruin or destruction of pride; conquest or quelling of pride or vanity. **~হর, ~হারী** *a.* one who or (rarely) that which humbles one's pride or vanity. **দর্পিত, দর্পী** *a.* vain, conceited, proud; boastful; bumptious, arrogant, haughty; daring. **দর্পোক্তি** *n.* proud or arrogant or overbearing or stiff-necked utterance.

দর্পণ *n.* mirror, a looking-glass.

দর্পনাশ, দর্পহর, দর্পহারী, দর্পিত, দর্পী see **দর্প**।

দর্বি, দর্বী *n.* a ladle. **দর্বিকা** *n.* a small ladle, a spoon.

দর্ভ *n.* a generic name for different species of small grass. **~ময়** *a.* grassy; made of grass. **দর্ভাসন** *n.* a grass mat for sitting upon.

দর্শক *a.* one who sees. □ *n.* a seer, an observer, an onlooker; a spectator; (loos.) a member of an audience; (loos.) a visitor.

দর্শন *n.* seeing or noticing or viewing; observation; meeting, interview (দর্শনপ্রার্থী) ; a visit or visitation; seeing or visiting in order to pay homage (দেবদর্শন, তীর্থদর্শন, রাজদর্শন) ; knowledge or experience (ভূয়োদর্শন) ; an eye; sight, the faculty of seeing; vision, perception (দর্শনশক্তি) ; appearance (কুদর্শন) ; philosophy (দর্শনশাস্ত্র) ; science (জীবদর্শন) ; a mirror, a looking-glass. **দর্শন করা** *v.* to see, to behold., to notice, to espy, to view, to look at; to observe; to meet, to interview; to pay a visit; to visit; to see or visit in order to pay homage; to experience; to perceive. **দর্শন দেওয়া** *v.* to put in an appearance; to come into view; to grant an interview; to give audience; to meet. **দর্শন পাওয়া** *v.* to be granted an interview; to be given an interview; to be given an audience; to meet; to catch sight of. **প্রথম দর্শনে** at first sight. **~ক্ষম** *a.* capable of seeing. **~দারি, ~ডালি, ~ডারি** *n.* consideration of outward show or beauty. □ *a.* good-looking. **দর্শনার্থী** *a.*

visitor, a caller. □ *a.* one who has come to visit. **দর্শনী** *n.* a fee or contribution paid on visiting a shrine etc.; a physician's fee; the price of a ticket of a cinema, theatre, circus, exhibition, match, athletic bout etc. **দর্শনীয়** *a.* worth seeing, good-looking; beautiful; conspicuous. **দর্শনেন্দ্রিয়** *n.* the sense of sight; the visual organ; an eye.

দর্শয়িতা *a.* one who exhibits or displays or exposes. □ *n.* an exhibitor, a displayer, an exposer. *fem.* **দর্শয়িত্রী।**

দর্শা *v.* to be seen, to show result (সুফল দর্শে). **দর্শানো** *v.* to show; to exhibit; to cause.

দর্শিত *a.* shown, exhibited, displayed.

-দর্শী *a.* (chiefly used as a *sfx.*) seeing, perceiving (সর্বদর্শী) ; knowing, conversant, versed (তত্ত্বদর্শী) ; scrutinizing (সূক্ষ্মদর্শী).

দল *n.* a leaf (বিল্বদল) ; a petal (পুষ্পদল) ; a blade (তৃণদল) ; a cress or watercress (কলমিদল) ; a piece (মেঘদল) ; a party, a group, a company, a band, a body, a train, a flock, a herd, a swarm, a gang, a team, a side, a party (দুইদলে মামলা) ; a faction, a clique (দল পাকানো) ; a union (দল বাঁধা) ; (dero.) evil company (দলে মিশে উচ্ছন্নে যাওয়া). **দল ছাড়া** *v.* to leave or desert one's flock or party; to give up evil company. **দল পাকানো, দল বাঁধা** *v.* to unite into a body; (dero.) to form a faction or clique. **দল বেঁধে** in a body. **দল ভাঙা** *v.* to disrupt or disintegrate a party; to demobilize a troop. **দল ভেঙে বেরিয়ে আসা** v. to break away from a party; (cp.) to cross the floor; to defect. **দলে দলে** in (different) groups or flocks (দলে দলে লোক যাচ্ছে, দলে দলে পশু চরছে) ; between or amongst parties or factions (দলে দলে বিবাদ). **দলে ভারী** large in number; greater in number, enjoying a majority. **দলে হালকা** small or smaller in number. **খেলার দল, খেলোয়াড়ের দল** a team of players. **দস্যুদল** *n.* a gang of robbers. **নর্তকের দল** a band or group of dancers. **নাচের দল** a dancing party. **নাবিকদল** *n.* a party or band of sailors. **পশুর দল** a herd of beasts. **পাখির দল** a flock of birds. **বদমাশের দল** a gang of ruffians. **যাত্রার দল** an opera party. **রাজনীতিক দল** a political party. **সৈন্যদল** *n.* an army of soldiers. **~কচু** *n.* a kind of edible plant. **~গত** *a.* counted as a group, collective (দলগত শক্তি) ; taken as a group or party (দলগত সংহতি). **~চ্যুত** *a.* separated or expelled from one's flock or party. **~চ্যুতি** *n.* separation or expulsion from one's flock or party. **~ছাড়া** *a.* separated from one's flock or party; (rare) moving alone; solitary, singular; unusual, queer, exceptional. **~ত্যাগ** *n.* leaving or deserting one's party or flock. **দলত্যাগ করা** *v.* to leave or desert one's party or flock. **~ত্যাগী** *a.* one who leaves or deserts one's party or flock. **দলত্যাগী ব্যক্তি** *n.* one who has left his party; a defector; a deserter of his party, a turncoat; a renegade, an apostate. **~পতি** a leader; a headman, a chief, a chieftain; a gangster. **~পরিবর্তন** *n.* change of party or side; transfer from one club or team to another. **~বদ্ধ** *a.* united into a body; united; flocked or herded together; (rare) gregarious (দলবদ্ধ জীবন). **~বদ্ধ ভাবে** *adv.* in a body, en masse; unitedly; in a flock; gregariously. **~বদ্ধ হওয়া** *v.* to unite in a group, to band together. **~বল** *n.* one's followers and forces. **~বাজি** *n.* factionalism, partisanship, cliquism. **~ভ্রষ্ট** same as **দলছাড়া। ~মণ্ডল** *n.* (bot.) a corolla. **~মত নির্বিশেষে** *adv.* irrespective of parties or opinions. **~লগ্ন** *a.* (bot.) epipetalous. **~হীন** *a.* unattached to any party; (pol.) non-party, independent; (bot.) apetalous. **দলে ভেড়া** *v.* to join a party or group, to associate oneself with a body of like-minded people.

দলদল *int.* expressing : excessive softness. **দলদলে** *a.* excessively soft, oversoft.

দলন *n.* act of pressing or kneading; (loos.) act of trampling under foot, act of treading over; chastisement, repression, subdual, coercion, quelling. □ *a.* one who chastises or represses or subdues or coerces or quells. **দলনী** *a. fem.*

of **দলন** (*a.*). **দলন করা** *v.* to press or knead; (loos.) to trample underfoot, to tread over; to chastise, to repress, to subdue, to coerce, to quell. **দলনীয়** *a.* to be trampled or crushed under foot; to be subdued.

দলা[১] *n.* a lump.

দলা[২] *v.* to press or knead; (loos.) to trample under foot, to tread over, to chastise, to repress, to subdue, to coerce, to quell. **পায়ে দলা** *v.* to trample under foot, to tread over.

দলাইমলাই *n.* act of currying (a horse); act of massaging (a human being); (fig.) strenuous and continuous effort. **দলাইমলাই করা** *v.* to curry; to massage; (fig.) to make strenuous and continued effort.

দলাদলি *n.* partisanship, factionalism, fissiparism; formation of factions or cliques; (loos.) dissension, dissidence. **দলাদলি করা** *v.* to indulge in partisanship or factionslism or fissiparism; to form factions or cliques; (loos.) to dissent.

দলিত *a.* pressed or kneaded; (loos.) trampled under foot, trodden, chastised, repressed, coerced, quelled.

দলিল *n.* a deed; a document; an evidential document; a piece of evidence.

দলীয় *a.* relating to a party or community. **দলীয় কোঁদল** *n.* inner-party squabble, inner-party quarrel. **দলীয় প্রতীক** *n.* party symbol.

দলুয়া, দলো *n.* a kind of reddish sugar made of dried molasses.

দশ *n.* ten; (fig.) the people, the public (দেশ ও দশ, দশের কাজ) ; (fig.) several persons united into a body (দশে মিলি করি কাজ). □ *a.* ten; many, several (দশ কথা শোনানো, এক কথা দশবার শোনানো). **দশই** *n.* the tenth day of a month. □ *a.* (of the days of a month) tenth. **দশক** *n.* (arith.) the place of tens; a decade. **~কথা** *n.* many words; much talking; many rude words, much scolding. **~কর্ম** *n.* the ten Hindu sacraments. **~কর্মান্বিত** *a.* one who takes or has taken the ten Hindu sacraments. **~কাহন** *n.* ten kahans (কাহন) ; many words; much talking; exaggeration; many rude words, much scolding. **~কিয়া** *n.* a table of numeration by multiple of ten. **~কোষী,** (dial.) **~কুশি** *n.* a measure of kirtan (কীর্তন) songs. **~গুণ** *a.* & *adv.* ten times. **~চক্র** *n.* a plot or intrigue or bad counsel by ten or many persons. **দশচক্রে ভগবান ভূত** (fig.) even a very intelligent man may be discomfited or cornered or pushed to the wall or endangered by the intrigue or bad counsel of the many. **~তলক** *n.* a decahedron. **~দশা** see **দশা**। **~দিক** see **দিক**। **~নামী** *n.* ten religious communities obeying the doctrines of Shankaracharya. **~পঁচিশ** *n.* an indoor game like dice played with cowries (কড়ি). **~প্রহরণধারিণী** *a. fem.* (also used as *n.*) holding ten weapons esp. in ten hands (an epithet of Goddess Durga). **~বল** see **বল**। **~বিধ** *a.* of ten kinds or varieties. **~বিধ সংস্কার** the ten Hindu sacraments. **~ভুজ** (বা **দশকোণী**) **ক্ষেত্র** *n.* a decagon. **~ভুজা** *a. fem.* (also used as *n.*) ten-handed (an epithet of Goddess Durga). **দশম** *a.* tenth. **~মহাবিদ্যা** see **মহাবিদ্যা**। **দশমাংশ, দশাংশ** *n.* a tenth; the tenth part. **~মাবতার** *n.* (kalki) (কল্কি) the tenth and last incarnation of Vishnu (বিষ্ণু). **~মিক** *a.* (arith.) decimal (দশমিক ভগ্নাংশ). □ *n.* (arith.) decimal fraction. **দশমিক পদ্ধতি** decimal system. **দশমিক-মুদ্রা প্রথা** decimal system of coinage. **দশমিক-মুদ্রা প্রথা চালু করা** বা **হওয়া** to go decimal. **দশমী** *n.* the tenth day of a lunar fortnight. **~মূল** see **মূল**। **~রথ** *n.* one whose chariot can fly in all ten directions; Ramachandra's father (in the Ramayana). **~শত** *n.* & *a.* thousand. **~সহস্র** *n.* & *a.* ten thousand, myriad. **~সালা** *a.* decennial. **দশসালা বন্দোবস্ত** (hist.) the decennial settlement (of land). **~স্কন্ধ** *a.* ten-necked. **~হারা** *n.* the tenth day of the lunar fortnight of the month of Jaistha (জ্যৈষ্ঠ) ; the date of the descent of the Ganges upon earth; on this date a bath in the Ganges relieves one of ten kinds of sin. **~হাত** *n.* ten cubits. □ *a.* measuring ten cubits; (fig.) very much expanded or puffed up (বুক ফুলে দশ হাত). **~হাতি** *a.* measuring ten cubits; (of cloth) having the standard length (=10 cubits).

দশন *n.* tooth; bite. **~পঙ্ক্তি** *n.* a set or row of teeth.

দশা *n.* state, condition (দুর্দশা) ; disposition (মনের দশা) ; a phase, a stage (শেষ দশা) ; one of the ten phases of the human mind, namely, volition, thought, memory, adoration, worry, delirium, madness, illness, infirmity, death (all collectively called **দশদশা**) ; one of the ten stages of human life, namely, staying in the womb, birth, infancy, childhood, adolescence and celibacy, youth, old age, decrepitude, the last gasp, and death (all stages collectivly called **দশদশা**) ; (astrol.) the planetary influence on a person's life (শনির দশা) ; a Hindu obsequial rite observed on the tenth day of death; any of the ten forms of devotion or charity according to Vaishnavas, namely, audition, glorification, recollection or enumeration of qualities and graces, worship, adoration, obeisance or genuflection, attendance or servitude, friendship or attachment, self-sacrifice in love, and unification; (religious) trance or reverie (দশায় পড়া). **দশায় পড়া** *v.* to fall into a state, to run into a condition; to fall into a trance whilst singing or hearing kirtan (কীর্তন) songs.

দশানন *n.* a ten-headed being; one of the names of Ravana of the Ramayana.

দশাবতার *n.* the ten incarnations of Vishnu (বিষ্ণু), namely, the Fish, the Tortoise, the Hog, the Man-Lion (that is,half man and half lion), the Dwarf, Parashuram (or the Axe-man), Rama (the hero of the Ramayana), Balaram or Krishna or Krishna and Balaram together (characters of the Mahabharata), Buddha, and Kalki (কল্কি).

দশাবিপর্যয় *n.* reversal of fortune, a change of fortune for the worse; a reverse, a set-back; misfortune; adversity.

দশাশ্ব *n.* one whose chariot is drawn by ten horses; an appellation of the moon.

দশাশ্বমেধ *n.* ten performances (usu. by one devotee) of the horse-sacrifice.

দশাসই *a.* tall and bulky, tall and hefty (দশাসই চেহারা) ; (often) average.

দশাহ *n.* ten days at a stretch; a feast or festival continuing for ten days. □ *a.* lasting for ten days.

দশি *n.* a thin strip or shred or tatting of cloth usually rolled into a wick of a lamp; a wick thus made.

দশেরা *n.* a feast (held by non-Bengalis) on the day of immersion of the image of Goddess Durga (দুর্গা).

দষ্ট *a.* bitten (সর্পদষ্ট) ; eaten (কীটদষ্ট) ; stung (ভ্রমরদষ্ট).

দস্তক *n.* a summons, a warrant; a permit; a warrant of distress or arrest.

দস্তখত *n.* act of signing; a signature. **দস্তখত করা** *v.* to sign. **দস্তখতি** *a.* signed; (rare) intended to be signed; (rare) relating to signing.

দস্তা *n.* zinc. **দস্তার চাদর** a zinc sheet.

দস্তানা *n.* a glove; a gauntlet. **দস্তানা-পরা** *a.* gloved; gauntleted.

দস্তাবেজ, (rare) **দস্তাবিজ** *n.* a document; a deed.

দস্তুর *n.* a custom or practice, a usage; a convention; a rule. **~মতো, ~মাফিক** *a.* in keeping with custom or convention or rule, customary, conventional. □ *adv.* thoroughly, quite.

দস্তুরি *n.* discount; commission, brokerage.

দস্যি *n.* (in affection) a person (usu. a small boy or girl) as daring and uncontrollable as a robber; a rogue. □ *a.* extremely naughty and dare-devil. **~পনা** *n.* dare-devilry.

দস্যু *n.* a robber, dacoit; (ori.) a non-Aryan race of ancient India or a member of it; (in affection) a person as daring and unmanageable as a robber; a rogue. **জলদস্যু** *n.* a pirate. **~তা, ~বৃত্তি** *n.* robbery, dacoity. **দস্যুতা করা** *v.* to plunder, to take to robbery, to commit robbery. **~দল** *n.* a band of robbers or gangsters, a gang of freebooters. **~পনা** *n.* daredevilry. **~ভয়** *n.* fear of robbers.

দহ *n.* the unfathomable and whirling

part of a river, lake, sea etc.; a whirlpool, an eddy; a lake (usu. a large and natural one); a deep pit, an abyss; (fig.) a terrible danger.

দহই *v.* (poet. & obs.) burns or burn, scorches or scorch, afflicts of afflict.

দহন *n.* act of burning; (phys.) combustion; inflammation; cremation; (fig.) anguish, affliction. □ *a.* that which or one who burns or scorches or inflames or cremates or afflicts (বিশ্বদহন ক্রোধ). **দহন করা** *v.* to burn; to scorch; to inflame; to cremate; to afflict. **দহনীয়** *a.* that which is to be burned or cremated; combustible, inflammable.

দহরম, দহরমমহরম *n.* intimate friendship; intimacy; familiar association or relation; close familiarity.

দহল *v.* (poet. & obs.) burned, scorched, afflicted.

দহলা *n.* the ten of playing cards. **দহলামহলা করা** *v.* (fig.) to hesitate, to vacillate, to be in two minds.

দহা *v.* to burn or be burned; to scorch or be scorched; to inflame or be inflamed; (fig.) to afflict or be afflicted.

দহি obs. var. of **দই**।

দহ্যমান *a.* that which has been or is being burned or scorched or inflamed or (fig.) afflicted.

দা¹ *n.* a heavy knife or chopper with a haft. **দা-কাটা** *a.* (chiefly of tobacco) chopped fine or minced with the aforesaid knife. **দা-কুমড়ো সম্পর্ক** relationship as between a chopper and a pumpkin; (fig.) deadly or inveterate enmity; implacable antagonism.

-দা² coll. contr. of **দাদা** (বড়দা).

-দা³ *fem.* of **-দ³**।

দাই pop. corrup. of **ধাই**।

দাইল obs. form of **ডাল**।

দাউদাউ *adv.* & *int.* expressing : state of burning furiously, bursting into a blaze.

দাও dial. corrup. of **দা¹**।

দাওয়া¹ *n.* a verandah, a gallery; a terrace.

দাওয়া² *n.* (correl. of **দাবি**) title, right, dues (দাবিদাওয়া).

দাওয়াই, দাওয়া³ *n.* medicine; remedy. **~খানা** *n.* a drug-store; a dispensary; a chemist's shop, a pharmacy. **দাওয়াই দেওয়া** *v.* to give or administer a medicine; (fig.) to take action for correction or to remedy a wrong.

দাওয়াত *n.* an invitation; a feast. **দাওয়াত দেওয়া** *v.* to invite.

দাঁও *n.* an opportunity, a chance (দাঁও পাওয়া) ; a fluke; a fat bargain made in a fluke (দাঁও মারা). **দাঁও মারা** *v.* to make a fat bargain in a fluke.

দাঁড় *n.* an oar (of a boat); a rod for a bird to sit on, a perch. □ *a.* standing (দাঁড় হওয়া) ; set upright (দাঁড় করানো) ; well-established (কারবার দাঁড় করানো) ; waiting (গাড়িখানা আর কতক্ষণ দাঁড় করিয়ে রাখব) ; halted (পুলিশ এখানে সব গাড়ি দাঁড় করায়) ; brought or presented (সাক্ষী দাঁড় করানো) ; instituted or filed (মামলা দাঁড় করানো) ; brought to or reduced to (অবস্থা দাঁড় করানো). **দাঁড় করানো** *v.* to cause to stand; to set erect or upright; to build up or establish firmly; to bring or present; to institute or file; to bring to or reduce to. **দাঁড় টানা, দাঁড় বাওয়া** *v.* to ply an oar, to oar, to punt, to row. **দাঁড় হওয়া** *v.* to stand up; to stand erect or upright. **দাঁড়ে বসা** *v.* to perch, to roost.

দাঁড়কাক *n.* the raven, the jackdaw, the rook.

দাঁড়া¹ *n.* spine, backbone; a claw (as of a crab or a lobster).

দাঁড়া² *n.* practice, custom, usage, go (বেদাঁড়া).

দাঁড়ানো *v.* to stand; to stand up; to wait (for), to await (সময় কারও জন্য দাঁড়িয়ে থাকে না) ; to tarry (একটু দাঁড়াও—কাজটা সেরেনি) ; to stop, to halt (এখানে গাড়ি দাঁড়াবে না) ; to collect (রাস্তায় জল দাঁড়ানো) ; to be well-established (কারবারটা দাঁড়াল না) ; to end or terminate (ব্যাপার যে কোথায় গিয়ে দাঁড়াবে) ; to come, to be, to become (অবস্থা খারাপ দাঁড়ানো) ; to stand for (কারও পক্ষে উকিল হয়ে দাঁড়ানো). □ *a.* standing (দাঁড়ানো অবস্থা) ; erect, upright. □ *n.* act or manner or posture of standing; a standing or erect position.

দাঁড়াশ *n.* a species of large non-venomous snake.

দাঁড়ি[1] *n.* a punctuation mark serving the purpose of a full stop (।); a beam of balance, a pair of scales.

দাঁড়ি[2] *n.* an oarsman, a rower.

দাঁড়িপাল্লা *n.* a pair of scales.

দাঁত *n.* a tooth; a tusk (as of an elephant or a hog); a fang (as of a serpent); (fig.) strength or pride (এ পরাজয়ে শত্রুদের দাঁত ভেঙে গেছে). **দাঁত ওঠা** *v.* to cut teeth, to teethe. **দাঁত ওঠানো** *v.* to have a tooth extracted; to extract a tooth. **দাঁত কনকন করা** *v.* to be afflicted with toothache. **দাঁত কিড়মিড় করা** *v.* to gnash or grind one's teeth (esp. in anger). **দাঁত খিঁচানো** *v.* to scold bawlingly and with grimaces, to show one's teeth. **দাঁত তোলা** *v.* to extract a tooth. **দাঁত তোলানো** *v.* to have a tooth extracted. **দাঁত নড়া** *v.* to have a tooth loosened. **দাঁত পড়া** *v.* to have a tooth fallen away. **দাঁত ফেলা** same as **দাঁত ওঠানো।** **দাঁত ফোটানো** *v.* (lit.) to pierce with teeth, to bite; (fig.) to be able to understand or comprehend. **দাঁত বাঁধানো** *v.* to make or have artificial teeth (or tooth); to fit with denture. **দাঁত বিঁধানো** same as **দাঁত ফোটানো।** **দাঁত ভাঙা** *v.* (fig.) to humble one's pride or weaken one's strength. **দাঁত মাজা** *v.* to brush or cleanse one's teeth. **দাঁতে কুটো করা** (fig.) to eat dirt, to eat the humble pie. **দাঁতের গোড়া** the root of a tooth, the gum. **দাঁতের পাথরি** chalk-like substance deposited on the teeth, tarter. **দাঁতের পোকা** caries. **দাঁতে দাঁতে লাগা** same as **দাঁত কপাটি লাগা।** **আক্কেল দাঁত** a wisdom tooth. **কুকুরের দাঁত** a canine tooth (of man), an incisor. **গজ দাঁত** an additional or extra tooth growing out of the root of another tooth, a subsidiary tooth. **দুধে দাঁত** a milk-tooth; milk dentition; a stomach-tooth. **পোকাদাঁত** *n.* a carious tooth. **বাঁধানো দাঁত** an artificial tooth, a false tooth. **মাড়ির দাঁত** a cheek-tooth, a molar tooth, a molar. **শুয়োরের দাঁত** a tusk. **সাপের দাঁত** a fang. **হাতির দাঁত** a tusk. **দাঁত কনকনানি** *n.* toothache. **দাঁত-কপাটি** *n.* state of having one's teeth clenched (esp. in fear or convulsive fits), lockjaw, trismus. **দাঁতকপাটি লাগা** *v.* to have one's teeth clenched, to be affected with lockjaw or trismus. **দাঁত-ভাঙা** *a.* difficult to pronounce or understand, break-jaw. **দাঁতের মাজন** *n.* dentifrice, a tooth-powder or toothpaste. **দাঁত থাকতে দাঁতের মর্যাদা না বোঝা** not to value blessings till they are gone.

দাঁতন *n.* a twig used as a toothbrush (also **দাঁতন-কাঠি**).

দাঁতাল *a.* having large teeth or tusks.

দাক্ষায়ণী *n.* a daughter of Daksha (দক্ষ) ; an appellation of Goddess Durga (দুর্গা) in her previous birth (see **সতী**).

দাক্ষিণাত্য *a.* of the southern part of a country; of the Deccan. □ *n.* (inc. but pop.) the Deccan.

দাক্ষিণ্য *n.* kindness, charity; favour; generosity, liberality; benevolence, bountifulness; benignance; gracefulness; cordiality, amiability; simplicity.

দাখিল *a.* presented for consideration or trial, submitted, filed (দাখিল করা) ; paid; brought (in or before); rendered or reduced almost to (মরার দাখিল). **দাখিল করা** *v.* to present or submit (for consideration) (আইনসভায় তথ্য দাখিল করা) ; to file (মামলা বা দলিল দাখিল করা) ; to deposit (পরীক্ষার ফি দাখিল করা) ; to bring (in or before); to present or produce (অপরাধীকে বিচারকের কাছে দাখিল করা) ; to render or reduce almost to (মরণের দাখিল করা). **দাখিল-খারিজ** *n.* substitution of the name of the new owner in place of the old one in a rent-roll, mutation.

দাখিলা *n.* a rent-receipt (esp. one issued to a tenant by the landowner).

দাখিলি *a.* presented, submitted, filed; paid; relating to presentation or submission or filing or payment.

দাগ *n.* a mark, a spot, a stain (কালির দাগ) ; a macle, a dark spot (চাঁদেও দাগ আছে) ; a scar (পোড়া দাগ) ; rust (লোহায় দাগ ধরা) ; an aspersion, a slur, a blot or blemish (চরিত্রে দাগ দেওয়া) ; a line, a tick (দাগ কাটা) ; a bounded plot of land bearing an official number, this number (জমির দাগ, দাগ নম্বর) ; a distinctive mark, an earmark, a brand (পণ্যদ্রব্যে দাগ দেওয়া) ; (fig.) a morbid or unfavourable impression (মনের দাগ). **দাগ কাটা** *v.* to draw a line, to tick (off); to mark off, to determine (a share, the boundary etc.); to leave a good or bad impression on, to impress upon (মনে দাগ কাটা). **দাগ তোলা** *v.* to remove or erase a mark or spot or stain. **দাগ দেওয়া** *v.* to draw a line, to tick (off); to mark (off); to determine; to cast aspersion, to slur; to earmark, to brand; to produce an unfavourable impression upon. **দাগ ধরা, দাগ পড়া, দাগ লাগা** *v.* to be affected with dark spots; to be discoloured or soiled or stained or macled; to rust; to be affected with a slur; to accept a mark (জলে দাগ পড়ে না) ; to be affected with a morbid or unfavourable impression.

দাগড়া var. of **দগড়া**।

দাগবিলি *n.* an account or description of a land-holding and its tenant.

দাগরাজি *n.* repair works (of a building etc.)

দাগা[1] var. of **গাদা**[2]।

দাগা[2] *v.* to paint (গায়ে হরিনাম দাগা) ; to mark or tick (পড়া দাগা) ; to brand; to write or practise writing by tracing (অক্ষর দাগা) ; to fire, to bombard (কামান দাগা). **দাগানো** *v.* to cause to paint or mark or brand or write or fire or bombard.

দাগা[3] *n.* an emotional shock or distress or affliction (মনে দাগা পাওয়া) ; treachery or deception (দাগাবাজ) ; a specimen script for tracing to practise handwriting. **দাগা বোলানো** *v.* to practise handwriting by tracing on a specimen script. **~দার** *a.* one who harms or shocks; treacherous. **~দারি** *n.* act of harming or giving emotional shocks; treachery. **~বাজ** *a.* treacherous; deceitful; fraudulent. **~বাজি** *n.* treachery; deception; fraudulence. **দাগাবাজি করা** *v.* to practise treachery or deception or fraud.

দাগি *a.* bearing a darkish stain or spot of rottenness (দাগি আম) ; branded (দাগি লোক) ; previously convicted (দাগি আসামি).

দাঙ্গা *n.* an affray, a fracas, a riot; a row. **দাঙ্গা করা** *v.* to be engaged in an affray or fracas, to riot. **~বাজ** *a.* given to rioting or rowdyism; riotous or rowdy. **~বাজি** *n.* act or practice of making a riot; rowdyism. **~হাঙ্গামা** *n.* continuous riot and disturbances.

দাড়া var. of **দাঁড়া**[1]।

দাড়ি *n.* the chin; beard. **চাপদাড়ি** see **চাপ**। **ছাগলদাড়ি** *n.* a goatee.

দাড়িম্ব, দাড়িম *n.* the pomegranate.

দাতব্য *a.* that which is to be or can be given; charitable (দাতব্য চিকিৎসালয় = a charitable dispensary, দাতব্য প্রতিষ্ঠান, দাতব্যখানা = a charitable institution, দাতব্য বিদ্যালয় = a free school). □ *n.* (coll.) charity, munificence (তোমার যে বড় দাতব্য). **দাতব্য করা** v. (coll.) to give (away) in charity.

দাতা *a.* one who or that which gives away in charity or gives or pays or contributes or donates; munificent, charitable. □ *n.* a giver, a payer, a contributor, a donor; a charitable or munificent man. **~কর্ণ** *n.* (fig.) a person as boundlessly charitable or bountiful as Karna of the Mahabharata.

দাতৃত্ব *n.* bounty; charitableness; munificence.

দাত্যূহ *n.* a species of water-fowl, the gallinule.

দাত্র *n.* a heavy knife or chopper with a haft.

দাত্রী *a. fem.* of **দাতা**।

দাদ[1] *n.* ringworm.

দাদ[2] *n.* a grudge. **দাদ তোলা** *v.* to pay off old scores, to quit scores with, to wreak vengeance on.

দাদখানি *n.* a variety of superfine rice.

দাদন *n.* a loan or advance given as earnest money. **~দার** *n.* a money-lender (usu. a professional one) who lends money as earnest money.

দাদরা *n.* an Indian musical measure.

দাদা *n.* an elder brother or cousin brother; (voc.) a (paternal or maternal) grandfather; (voc.) an older or senior man; (in affectionate address) a younger brother, a younger cousin (brother), a grandson, a younger or junior man. **~বাবু** *n.* an employer or master as respectable as one's elder brother; (dial.) an elder sister's or cousin's husband. ~ঠাকুর *n.* a Brahmin (as addressed by a non-Brahmin). ~মশায়, ~মশাই *n.* a maternal (or also paternal) grandfather. ~শ্বশুর *n.* a grandfather-in-law or grand-uncle-in-law.

দাদি *n.* (chiefly Mus.) a paternal grandmother.

দাদু *n.* grandfather.

দাদুপন্থী *n.* a religious sect obeying the liberal doctrine of Dadu.

দাদুর *n.* the frog. *fem.* দাদুরী ।

দাদূপন্থী rej. spell: of দাদুপন্থী ।

-দান[1] *n.* (used. as *sfx.*) a container (আতরদান).

দান[2] *n.* act of giving; act of giving away; bestowal; award; charitable giving or distribution (অন্নদান) ; act of giving in marriage (কন্যাদান) ; offering, sacrifice, dedication (পরার্থে জীবনদান) ; contribution; a gift or a charitable gift (মহামূল্য দান) ; an offering, a sacrifice; a donation; a throw or cast (at dice. etc.); a turn (for doing something). দান করা *v.* to give; to give away; to give or distribute in charity; to donate, to contribute; to bestow; to confer; to award; to give in marriage; to offer, to sacrifice; to dedicate. ~কর্ম, ~কার্য *n.* practice of charity; act or instance of charity. ~কাতর, ~কুণ্ঠ *a.* slow or unwilling to give, not charitable; miserly, parsimonious, stingy, close-fisted, niggardly. ~খয়রাত *n.* bounty, charity; charitable deeds; act or practice of charity. ~ধর্ম *n.* the virtue of charity. ~ধ্যান *n.* charity and religious meditation. ~পত্র *n.* a deed of gift. ~বীর *a.* & *n.* one who is extremely (lit. heroically) bountiful. ~যোগ্য *a.* worthy of being given. ~শীল *a.* bountiful, munificent, charitable, generous. ~শীলতা *n.* bounty, munificence, charity; generosity. ~শৌণ্ড same as দানবীর। ~সজ্জা *n.* (in a wedding) display of gifts given to the bride and the bridegroom. ~সত্র *n.* an almshouse; a charitable institution. ~সাগর *n.* sixteen sets of gifts given in a sraddha (শ্রাদ্ধ) ceremony. ~সামগ্রী *n.* an article of gift (esp. one given to the bride or bridegroom at a wedding). যেমন দান তেমনি দক্ষিণা (fig.) a niggardly master will have a lazy servant.

দানব *n.* (myth.) any one of the giants hostile to gods, (cp.) a Titan; a demon; a monster; an evil spirit, a devil. *fem.* দানবী a giantess, a demoness. ~দলনী *n. fem.* a vanquisher of demons: an appellation of Goddess Durga (দুর্গা). দানবারি *n.* (lit.) an enemy of demons; a god; an appellation of Vishnu (বিষ্ণু). দানবিক, দানবীয় *a.* demoniac(al); devilish, diabolical, gigantic.

দানা[1] coll. corrup. of দানব। দানায় পাওয়া to be possessed by a devil or an evil spirit.

দানা[2] *n.* a pea or grain; a seed or stone or pip (ডালিমের দানা) ; any small granular or pea-shaped thing (সাগুদানা) ; a necklace of pea-shaped beads; food (দানাপানি). দানা বাঁধা *v.* to form into grains, to granulate.

দানাদার *a.* granular, pea-shaped. □ *n.* a kind of granular sweetmeat.

দানাপানি *n.* food and drink.

দানী *a.* bountiful, munificent, generous, charitable.

দানীয় *a.* worth giving; that which is to be given. □ *n.* a recipient of a gift; a gift.

দানো coll. var. of দানব। দানোয় পাওয়া *v.* to be possessed by an evil spirit.

দান্ত[1] *a.* one who has controlled one's sense-organs, continent; subdued, restrained; one who sustains the austerities of religious practices; controlled.

দান্ত[2] *a.* dental; made of tooth or ivory.

দান্তি *n.* continence; restraint, temperance.

দাপ *n.* pride, vanity, haughtiness; authority, power; prowess; rage; passion.

দাপক *a.* & *n.* one who or that which causes to give.

দাপট *n.* force or power; terrible authority or influence.

দাপন[1] *n.* act of causing to give.

দাপন[2] *n.* pressing, pressure; trampling.

দাপদুপ var. of দুপদাপ।

দাপনা var. of দাবনা।

দাপাদাপি *n.* bragging or fretting repeatedly; bustling or fussing or bullying with a show of authority; romping noisily. **দাপাদাপি করা** same as **দাপানো**।

দাপানো *v.* to brag; to fret; to shake, esp. by stamping with one's feet; to fill with uproarious threats or noise; to romp noisily. **দাপানি** same as **দাপাদাপি**।

দাপিত *a.* given; punished.

দাব[1] *n.* pressure; control, restraint, discipline, overbearing authority (দাবে রাখা).

দাব[2] *n.* a forest (দাবানল) ; a forest-fire (দাবদাহ) ; fire, heat.

দাবড়ানো *v.* to bully; to rebuke; to threaten; to snub; to chase.

দাবড়ানি, দাবড়ি *n.* act of bullying; rebuke; threat; snub; act of chasing.

দাবদগ্ধ *a.* burnt in a forest-fire.

দাবদাহ *n.* the heat of a forest-fire; a forest-fire; (inc. but pop.) the scorching heat.

দাবনা *n.* the fleshy part of the thigh; ham (of a beast).

দাবা[1], **দাবানো** *v.* to press down ; to suppress, to curb, to restrain (বিদ্রোহ দাবানো) ; to cow; to massage; to curry (পা দাবানো). **দাবিয়ে রাখা** to hold or keep in check.

দাবা[2] *n.* (the game of) chess; the queen (of chess). **দাবা খেলা** *v.* to play chess. **দাবার ছক** a chess-board. **দাবার ঘুঁটি** a chessman.

দাবাই var. of **দাওয়াই**।

দাবাগ্নি, দাবানল *n.* a forest-fire.

দাবাড়ে, দাবাড়ু *n.* a chess-player.

দাবানো see **দাবা**[1]।

দাবাবোড়ে *n.* (the game of) chess; a chess-board and chessmen.

দাবি *n.* right, title (এ জমিতে তার দাবি নেই) ; demand, claim (দাবি করা) ; a prayer or complaint. **দাবি করা** *v.* to demand, to claim; to pray or complain. **~দাওয়া** *n.* right and claims. **~দার** *n.* a claimant (esp. of title or inheritance); (loos.) a successor or inheritor. **~পত্র** *n.* a charter of demands.

দাম[1] *n.* price, cost, value. **চাওয়া-দাম** *n.* the asking price. **দাম দেওয়া** *v.* (fig.) to pay for (trouble, foolish behaviour etc.). **দাম পড়া, দাম লাগা** *v.* to cost. **দামাদামি** *n.* haggling or higgling, chaffering; bargaining.

দাম[2] *n.* a thread, a cord (দামোদর) ; a string, a garland (কুসুমদাম) ; a bunch, a cluster, a lock (কেশদাম) ; a watercress or an aquatic grass (দামদল).

দামড়া *n.* a castrated ox or bull, a bullock (also **দামড়া গোরু**). **দামড়া-ঘোড়া** *n.* a gelding.

দামামা *n.* an ancient war-trumper or kettle-drum. **~ধ্বনি** *n.* fanfare.

দামাল *a.* (chiefly of a child) unmanageably spirited or naughty or romping, tough and indomitable. **~পনা** *n.* unmanageable spiritedness or naughtiness or toughness.

দামি *a.* costly, expensive, valuable.

দামিনী *n. fem.* lightning.

দাম্পত্য *a.* conjugal, nuptial. □ *n.* conjugal relation, conjugality; conjugal love. **~প্রণয়, ~প্রেম** *n.* mutual love between husband and wife, conjugal love.

দাম্ভিক *a.* vainglorious, braggart, conceited; proud; arrogant, haughty. **দাম্ভিকতা** *n.* vaingloriousness, braggartism, conceit; arrogance, haughtiness.

দায়[1] *n.* wealth or property to be inherited from father or others, patrimony, heritage or inheritance.

দায়[2] *n.* a danger or difficulty (দায়ে ঠেকা) ; necessity or need (কী দায় পড়েছে ?) ; an important duty or responsibility or obligation (মাতৃদায়, কন্যাদায়) ; an encumbrance (দায়গ্রস্ত) ; a debt or mortgage, hypothecation (দায়বদ্ধ) ; a risk, a risky charge (পরের দায় ঘাড়ে নেওয়া) ; a criminal charge (ডাকাতির দায়ে ধরা পড়া = to be arrested on charge of robbery); account, sake (প্রাণের দায়ে). **দায়ে ঠেকা, দায়ে পড়া** *v.* to be in a difficulty or danger, to be in a trying situation from which escape seems all but impossible, to come to trouble or get into a scrape; to be in an awkward predicament; to be compelled (to). **কী দায় পড়েছে** what necessity is there ? **তোমার কী দায় পড়েছে** what necessity do you have ? **প্রাণের দায়ে** on account of one's life, for the sake of one's life.

দায়ক *a.* (used as a *sfx.*) giving, causing etc., -ful (সুখদায়ক).

দায়গ্রস্ত *a.* faced with danger, endangered; trouble-stricken; bound by obligation or duty or responsibility.

দায়বদ্ধ *a.* duty-bound; promise-bound; contract-bound.

দায়ভাগ *n.* an ancient code or book of laws on inheritance and patrimony written by Jimutabahana.

দায়রা *n.* (law) sessions. **দায়রা-আদালত** *n.* a sessions-court. **দায়রা-জজ** *n.* a sessions-judge. **দায়রায় সোপর্দ করা** *v.* to commit to sessions.

দায়াদ *n.* a claimant to an inheritance; an heir; a son; a sharer of one's partimony; a kinsman. **দায়াদি** *n. fem.* a female claimant to inheritance; an heiress; a daughter; a female sharer of one's patrimony; a kinswoman. □ *a.* (in all genders) inherited, obtained by inheritance.

দায়িক *a.* responsible; indebted.

দায়িকা *fem.* of **দায়ক**।

দায়িত্ব *n.* responsibility; liability; charge or risk (নিজের দায়িত্বে at one's own risk). **~জ্ঞান** *n.* sense of responsibility. **~জ্ঞানহীন** *a.* devoid of a sense of responsibility. **~পরায়ণ, ~পূর্ণ, ~শীল** *a.* responsible; liable for carrying out a duty. **~হীন** *a.* without any responsibility, having no responsibility.

দায়ী *a.* responsible; liable; (used as a *sfx.*) giving. **দায়িনী** *a. fem.* (used as a *sfx.*) giving.

দায়ের *a.* submitted or filed for consideration or trial. **দায়ের করা** *v.* to submit or file or institute (for consideration or trial). **মোকদ্দমা দায়ের করা** to file or institute a suit.

দার[১] *n.* (usu. in *comp.*) a wife. **~কর্ম, ~গ্রহণ, ~পরিগ্রহ** *n.* act of taking a wife, marriage or wedding (of a man).

দার[২] *sfx.* implying : furnished or embroidered with (জরিদার) ; causing or producing (মজাদার) ; owning or possessing or having, (cp.) -or, -er (পাওনাদার) ; superintending or controlling (থানাদার) ; employed in, taking to (ব্যাবসাদার, বাজনাদার). **-দারি** *sfx.* implying: -ship (জমিদারি, থানাদারি, ব্যাবসাদারি).

দারক *n.* a son. □ *a.* cleaving, splitting.

দারওয়ান var. of **দরোয়ান**।

দারকর্ম see **দার**[১]।

দারগা rej. spell. of **দারোগা**।

দারগ্রহণ see **দার**[১]।

দারচিনি *n.* cinnamon.

দারপরিগ্রহ see **দার**[১]।

দারা *n.* a wife.

-দারি see **-দার**[২]।

দারিকা *n.* a daughter. □ *a. fem.* cleaving, splitting.

দারিদ্র, দারিদ্র্য *n.* poverty; indigence; penury; lack, want: humbleness. **~ব্যঞ্জক, ~সূচক** *a.* betraying or indicating poverty. **~মোচন** *n.* removal or elimination of poverty, liquidation of poverty. **~সীমা** *n.* poverty level.

দারু[১] *n.* wine, liquor.

দারু[২] wood, timber.

দারুচিনি ori. form of **দারচিনি**।

দারুণ *a.* very great, intense, excessive; terrible (দারুণ ভয়) ; severe (দারুণ শীত) ; very high (দারুণ গাত্রতাপ) ; unbearable ('কান্ত পাহুন কাম দারুণ') ; very hard or difficult (দারুণ সংকল্প) ; cruel (দারুণ অত্যাচার) ; cutting to the quick (দারুণ বাক্য) ; heart-rending (দারুণ শোক). □ *adv.* very (দারুণ ভালো).

দারুব্রহ্ম *n.* the wooden image of Juggernaut (জগন্নাথ) at Puri.

দারুভূত *a.* transformed or changed into a wooden image or entity (দারুভূত মুরারি) ; (fig.). inert or numb (with amazement, grief etc.)

দারুময় *a.* wooden, woody.

দারোগা *n.* an inspector or sub-inspector or assistant sub-inspector of police. **বড় দারোগা** an inspector or sub-inspector in command of a police station, an officer-in-charge of a police station. **ছোট দারোগা** a sub-inspector (or an assistant sub-inspector of police) who is the second in command of a police station.

দারোয়ান var. of **দরোয়ান**।

দার্ঢ্য *n.* firmness; steadiness; unyieldingness; hardness; stiffness; strictness.

দার্শনিক *a.* versed in philosophy; philosophical; metaphysical; thoughtful. □ *n.* a philosopher; a metaphysician; a thoughtful man. **~তা** *n.* philosophical character or quality or attitude; (often sarcas.) thoughtfulness. **~তত্ত্ব** *n.* doctrines or principles or tenets of philosophy.

দাল *n.* pigeon-pea, pulse, lentils, dal.

দালচিনি dial. corrup. of **দারচিনি**।

দালনা var. of **ডালনা**।

দালপুরি *n.* a kind of thin discoid bread fried in clarified butter or oil and stuffed with a paste of pigeon-pea.

দালমুট var. of **ডালমুট**।

দালান *n.* a brick-built or stone-built building; a corridor of a building; a brick-built or stone-built platform or room or hall built permanently (পূজার দালান). **~কোঠা** *n.* a brick-built or stone-built house.

দালাল *n.* a broker, a cambist; an agent; a commission agent; a go-between; a tout; (sarcas.) a supporter or helper (ধনতন্ত্রের দালাল). **দালালি** *n.* brokerage, an agent's commission; brokery, commission agency; the act of business of a go-between or a tout.

দালিম var. of **ডালিম**।

দাশ *n.* a fisherman; one belonging to the fishing caste.

দাশরথি, (rare) **দাশরথ** *n.* a son of Dasharatha (দশরথ): an appellation of Rama and his brothers as narrated in the Ramayana.

দাশী *fem.* of **দাশ**।

দাস *n.* a servant, an attendant; a slave (দাসব্যবসায়); a fisherman by caste (দাসজাতি); a Shudra (শূদ্র); a non-Aryan; a victim or a minion (অবস্থার দাস); a humble man or a dependant (হুজুর দাসের প্রতি দয়া করুন). *fem.* **দাসী**। **~খত** *n.* a written bond of slavery. **~ত্ব** *n.* servitude; slavery; state of being a victim, bondage, dependence. **দাসত্ব করা** *v.* to be slave of, to serve as a slave. **~ত্ব প্রথা** *n.* the institution of ownership of slaves, slavery. **দাসত্ববন্ধন, দাসত্বশৃঙ্খল** *n.* the bonds of slavery. **দাসত্বশৃঙ্খল মোচন** *n.* emancipation or freedom from bondage. **দাসত্ববৃত্তি** *n.* slavery. **দাসত্বে আবদ্ধ** enslaved, in bondage. **~দাসী** *n. pl.* servants male and female, man-servants and maid-servants. **~প্রথা** same as **দাসত্বপ্রথা**। **~ব্যবসায়** *n.* slave-trade. **~মনোবৃত্তি, ~মনোভাব** *n.* slave mentality; servility. **দাসানুদাস** *n.* a slave of one's slave, a very humble servant or dependant. **দাসীপুত্র** *n.* one's son born of his maid-servant; an illegitimate son. **দাসীবৃত্তি, দাসীত্ব** *n.* profession of or service as a maid or maid-servant.

দাসেয় *a.* born of a slave-girl (usu. by her master). □ *n.* a son of a slave-girl and (usu.) her master.

দাস্ত *n.* evacuation of the bowels, motion purgation; faeces, stool; loose motion; diarrhoea.

দাস্য *n.* state of being a servant; servitude; servility; act of considering oneself as the servant of one's god. **~বৃত্তি** *n.* servitude; servility; service.

দাস্যা inc. var. of **দাসী** (see **দাস**) when used as a surname of a Shudra (শূদ্র) widow.

দাহ *n.* burning, conflagration, combustion (গৃহদাহ); cremation (শবদাহ); severe or scorching heat (দিনের দাহ); inflammation (রোগের দাহ); affliction (অন্তর্দাহ). **দাহক** *a.* burning; cremating; scorching; inflammatory; afflicting, distressing. *fem.* **দাহিকা**। **~ক্রিয়া** *n.* cremation. **~ন** *n.* act of burning; cremation; act of scorching; inflammation; affliction. **~ভূমি** *n.* burning or cremation ground. **দাহিকাশক্তি** *n.* the power of burning; burning capacity. **দাহী** same as **দাহক**।

দাহ্য *a.* inflammable; combustible; that which is fit to be burned. **দাহ্য পদার্থ** combustible substance.

দিওয়ানা var. of **দেওয়ানা**।

দিক১, দিকদারি *n.* vexation, annoyance, irritation. **দিক করা, দিকদারি করা** *v.* to vex, to annoy, to irritate; to pester.

দিক২ *n.* any one of the ten quarters of the globe; a point of the compass (উত্তর দিক); a direction (বাড়ির দিক); an end or side (চার দিক); a part or portion

(বাড়ির ভিতরের দিক) ; a region or quarters (এ দিকে কেউ আসেনি) ; an extremity or end or side (ভারতের তিন দিকে সমুদ্র) ; a party or side (তিনি আমার দিকে). **দিকে দিকে** in all directions; everywhere. **দশ দিক** *n.* north, north-east, east, south-east, south, south-west, west, north-west, above, under: these ten quarters of the globe collectively. **~চক্র, ~চক্রবাল** *n.* the horizon. **~পতি, ~পাল** *n.* any one of the deities presiding over the ten quarters of the globe; (fig.) a very powerful and prominent man. **~শূল** *n.* (astrol.) a day extremely unfavourable to a journey in a particular direction. **~স্থিতি** *n.* (bot.) orientation.

দিগংশ *n.* azimuth.

দিগ্গজ *n.* (myth.) any one of the eight celestial elephants guarding the quarters of the globe; (chiefly iron.) a very erudite or prominent or capable man; a portentous idiot. □ *a.* (chiefly iron.) very erudite or vastly learned or prominent or capable (দিগ্গজ পণ্ডিত, দিগ্গজ উকিল, দিগ্গজ ছেলে).

দিগ্জ্ঞান *n.* knowledge of ascertaining the points of the compass; (fig.) minimum knowledge, common sense.

দিগ্দর্শন *n.* visualization or ascertainment of the points of the compass; experience; (act of giving) a general review or hints. **দিগ্দর্শন করা** *v.* to visualize or ascertain a point of the compass; to experience; to give a general review or hints. **দিগ্দর্শন-যন্ত্র** *n.* a compass; a mariner's compass. **দিগ্দর্শী** *a.* capable of or engaged in visualizing or ascertaining the points of the compass; experienced; giving a general review or hints. □ *n.* a compass; a mariner's compass.

দিগ্দিগন্ত *n.* all quarters or directions of the globe; all regions or places. **দিগ্দিগন্তর** *n.* different quarters or directions of the globe; different regions or places. **দিগ্দিগন্তে, দিগ্দিগন্তরে** *adv.* everywhere, far and near, far and wide.

দিগন্ত *n.* the horizon. **~প্রসারী, ~বিস্তৃত, ~ব্যাপী** *a.* extending or stretching to or as far as the horizon; extending or stretching endlessly.

দিগন্তর *n.* the distance or space between two points of the compass or two directions; another direction or another point of the compass. **দিগন্তরে** *adv.* to or in another direction or another point of the compass, beyond this direction or point of the compass; beyond the horizon, in or to another region. **দিগন্তরাল** *n.* the space or distance between two quarters of the globe; the sky. **দিগন্তরালে** *adv.* beyond the horizon.

দিগ্ভ্রম, দিগ্ভ্রান্তি *a.* an error in ascertainment of the right direction; failure in ascertaining the points of the compass. **দিগ্ভ্রান্ত** *a.* one who has failed to ascertain the right direction; gone astray; one who has failed to ascertain the points of the compass; perplexed, puzzled; bewildered.

দিগম্বর *a.* one who has the quarters of the globe as his sole clothing; naked, nude. □ *n.* an appellation of Shiva (শিব) ; quarters of the globe imagined as a loincloth. **দিগম্বরী** a. *fem.* of **দিগম্বর।** □ *n.* an appellation of Goddess Kali (কালী).

দিগ্ধ *a.* smeared (with); steeped (in); mixed (with). *fem.* **দিগ্ধা।**

দিগ্বধূ same as **দিগঙ্গনা।**

দিগ্বলয় *n.* the horizon.

দিগ্বসন same as **দিগম্বর.** *fem.* **দিগ্বসনা।**

দিগ্বালা, দিগ্বালিকা same as **দিগঙ্গনা।**

দিগ্বিজয় *n.* conquest of (all the quarters of) the world (by armed invasion or by any good quality such as learning, literary talent etc.), world-conquest. **দিগ্বিজয় করা** *v.* to conquer the whole world. **দিগ্বিজয়ী** *a.* world conquering. □ *n.* a world-conquerer.

দিগ্বিদিক *n.* all quarters; all regions or places; what is good and what is evil, what is right and what is wrong. **দিগ্বিদিক জ্ঞান** *n.* knowledge of ascertaining the points of the compass; power of discrimination between right and wrong; common sense; mental balance, composure or calmness of mind (আতঙ্কে দিগ্বিদিকজ্ঞানশূন্য).

দিগ্বিন্দু *n.* (geog.) a cardinal point.

দিঘ *n.* (dial.) length (আড়েদিঘে). □ *a.* (obs.) long.

দিঘল *a.* (chiefly poet.) long, tall, large.

দিঘি *n.* a large and deep tank or pond.

দিঙ্নাগ *n.* any one of the eight mythical celestial elephants guarding the quarters of the globe; a famous Buddhist philosopher (also **দিঙ্নাগাচার্য**) ; (sarcas.) a stupid but harsh critique.

দিঙ্নির্ণয়, দিঙ্নিরূপণ *n.* ascertainment of the points of the compass; ascertainment of a particular or the right direction. **দিঙ্নির্ণয় করা** *v.* to ascertain the points of the compass; to ascertain the direction. **দিঙ্নির্ণয়যন্ত্র** *n.* a compass; a mariner's compass.

দিঙ্মণ্ডল *n.* the horizon.

দিঙ্মূঢ় same as **দিগ্ভ্রান্ত** (see **দিগ্ভ্রম**).

দিঠি, (obs.) **দিঠ,** (obs.) **দিট** *n.* (poet.) a glance or look; an eye.

দিতি *n.* (myth.) the first mother of daityas (দৈত্য). **~জ, ~সুত** *n.* a son of Diti (দিতি), any of the mythological demons hostile to gods.

দিৎসা *n.* desire for giving or contributing (esp. in charity). **দিৎসু** *a.* desirous of giving or contributing.

দিদা *n. fem.* (in affection) a grandmother or a granddaughter.

দিদি *n. fem.* an elder sister or cousin (sister); (in courteous or affectionate address) a lady, a woman, a girl; (in affection) a grandmother or granddaughter. **~ঠাকুরানি** *n.* (chiefly joc.) a lady, a woman, a girl (esp. of the Brahmin caste). **~মা** *n.* a maternal (also paternal) grandmother or grand aunt.

দিদৃক্ষা *n.* desire to see. **দিদৃক্ষমাণ, দিদৃক্ষু** *a.* desirous of seeing.

দিধিষু *n.* the second husband of a woman married twice.

দিন১ *n.* a day (in all senses); the time of light from sunrise to sunset; twenty-four hours from one sunrise to the next; a sidereal day; (astr. & astrol.) a lunar day; daily working period or hours; a length of time, a period (দীর্ঘদিন) ; time of existence, duration of life (তার দিন ফুরিয়েছে) ; an age or a point of time (সেদিন আর নেই) ; time (আমার দিন কাটে না) ; an auspicious or favourable time (যদি দিন আসে). **দিন কাটানো** same as **দিন যাপন করা। দিন গোনা** *v.* (fig.) to look forward to eagerly (esp. for a long time). **~কর** *n.* the sun. **~কাল** *n.* present time or times (দিনকাল বড় খারাপ). **~ক্ষণ** *n.* (astrol.) suitability or auspiciousness of a day for doing something. **~ক্ষণ** *n.* a conjunction of three lunar days in one sidereal day. **~ক্ষেপ, ~ক্ষেপণ** same as **দিনযাপন। ~গত** *a.* pertaining to a day; daily, diurnal. **দিনগত পাপক্ষয়** (lit. but rare) sacramental and other purifications prescribed for the daily life; (pop. & dero.) the routine drudgery or monotonous toil of daily life. **~দগ্ধা** *n.* (astrol.) an inauspicious day for doing anything. **দিন দিন** *adv.* day by day; gradually; everyday, daily. **~দুপুরে** *adv.* in broad daylight. **~নাথ, ~পতি** *n.* the sun. **~পঞ্জি** *n.* day-to-day record of events, a diary. **~পঞ্জিকার** *n.* a diarist. **~পত্রী** *n.* a daily journal, a diary. **~পাত** same as **দিনযাপন। ~ভর** *adv.* all day long, throughout the day. **~মজুর** *n.* a day-labourer. **~মণি** *n.* the sun. **~মান** *n.* the time of light from sunrise to sunset, daytime. **দিন মাইনে** *n.* daily wage. **~যাপন** *n.* spending a day. **দিনযাপন করা** *v.* to spend one's days, to pass one's time, to lead a life; to spend a day. **~রাত** *n.* day and night. □ *adv.* at all hours of the day and night, constantly, always. **~লিপি** *n.* a diary. **~শেষ** *n.* close or end of a day, the evening. **দিনাতিপাত করা** *v.* spend days. **দিনে-ডাকাতি** robbery in broad daylight; (fig.) an extremely daring villainy or misdeed. **দিনকে রাত করা** (fig.) to exaggerate beyond recognition; to tell a downright lie. **দিনে দিনে** day by day, gradually. **দিনেদুপুরে** more pop. var. of **দিনদুপুরে। দিনের আলো** the light of the day, daylight. **দিনের নাগাল পাওয়া** to be in sight of better days.

দিন২ *n.* (Mus.) religion, faith. **~দুনিয়ার মালিক** God (or Allah) as the Lord of the (Islamic) faith and of the world.

দিনাত্যয়, দিনান্ত, দিনাবসান *n.* close of a day, the evening. **দিনান্তে** *adv.* at the end of the day, in the evening.

দিনান্ধ *a.* unable to see during daytime or in daylight, day-blind. □ *n.* an owl.

দিনার *n.* dinar, the ancient Arab gold coin.

দিনেমার *n.* a Dane. □ *a.* Danish. **~জাতি** *n.* Danes.

দিনেশ *n.* the sun.

দিবস *n.* a day; the time from sunrise to sunset; twenty-four hours from one sunrise to the next; daytime. **দিবসাত্যয়, দিবসাবসান** *n.* close or end of the day; the evening. **দিবসালোক** *n.* daylight.

দিবা *n.* daytime. □ *a.* & *adv.* of or in daytime. **~কর** *n.* the sun. **~চর** *a.* active during daytime. **~নিদ্রা** *n.* sleep during daytime. **~নিশি,** (poet.) **~নিশ, ~রাত্রি** *adv.* day and night, all the time, always. **~ন্ধ** *a.* day-blind. □ *n.* the owl. **~বসান** *n.* close of the day, the evening. **~বসু** *n.* the sun. **~বিহার** *n.* noon-time rest or sleep; sexual enjoyment in daytime. **~ভাগ** *n.* daytime. **~লোক** *n.* daylight. **স্পষ্ট বা প্রকাশ্য দিবালোক** broad daylight. **~স্বপ্ন** *n.* a day-dream; a brown study; a reverie; (fig.) a false fancy, a waking dream.

দিব্য, (coll.) **দিব্যি** *a.* celestial, heavenly; divine; supernal; miraculous; delightful, pleasant, beautiful. □ *n.* an oath. □ *adv.* quite (দিব্যি ভালো ছেলে) ; well (দিব্যি গান গায়) ; excellently (দিব্য এঁকেছে). **দিব্য করা, দিব্যি পাড়া** *v.* to swear, to affirm solemnly. **দিব্যি দেওয়া** *v.* to adjure. **আমার দিব্যি** a form of asseveration, upon my honour, upon my word. **ঈশ্বরের দিব্যি** by God. **দিব্যগন্ধ** *a.* sweet-scented; having a divine odour. **দিব্যচক্ষু** *a.* having supernal or transcendental vision; having insight; (rare) having beautiful eyes. □ *n.* supernal or transcendental vision; insight; (rare) a beautiful eye. **দিব্যজ্ঞান** *n.* supernal or transcendental or divine or spiritual knowledge or wisdom. **দিব্যদর্শী** *a.* having supernal or transcendental vision; having insight. **দিব্যদৃষ্টি** *a.* having supernal or transcendental vision; having insight. □ *n.* supernal or transcendental vision; insight. **দিব্যদেহ** *n.* a divine or celestial form or body. □ *a.* having a divine or celestial form or body. **দিব্যধাম** *n.* the celestial abode, heaven. **দিব্যনারী** *n.* a courtesan of heaven; a nymph. **দিব্যনেত্র** same as **দিব্যচক্ষু । দিব্যরথ** *n.* a chariot of the gods; a chariot capable of running in the air, an aerochariot; an aeroplane. **দিব্যলোক** *n.* the divine or celestial region, heaven.

দিব্যাঙ্গনা *n.* a courtesan of heaven; a nymph.

দিব্যাস্ত্র *n.* a god's weapon; a divine weapon.

দিব্যি coll. var. of **দিব্য ।**

দিব্যোদক *n.* celestial water; holy water.

দিয়ে, (now. obs.) **দিয়া**[১] *prep.* by, with; by means of, by the instrumentality of, through; mixing with, adding (চিনি দিয়ে ঘোটা) ; in (তেল দিয়ে ভাজা) ; along (এই পথ দিয়ে যাও) ; through (জানালা দিয়ে তাকানো) ; from (মাথা দিয়ে ঝরা).

দিয়া[২] *n.* lamp, light (দিয়া জ্বালাও).

দিয়ালা var. of **দেয়ালা ।**

দিয়ালি var of **দেয়ালি ।**

দিয়াশলাই *n.* a match, matches; safety matches; a match-box. **দিয়াশলাইকাঠি** *n.* a match-stick. **দিয়াশলাই বাক্স** a match-box.

দিল *n.* mind, heart; heartiness or magnanimity, benevolence, charitableness, generosity, kind-heartedness. **~খুশ, ~খোশ** *a.* happy at heart, light-hearted, merry, cheerful; pleasant, delightful. **~খোলসা** *a.* open-hearted, frank, candid; unburdening one's heart. **~দরিয়া** *a.* open-hearted, frank; high-minded, large-souled, magnanimous; large-handed. **~দার** *a.* hearty; open-hearted; high-minded, magnanimous.

দিল্লিকা লাড্ডু *n.* (lit.) a ball-shaped sweetmeat manufactured in Delhi; (fig. & pop.) a thing that causes dejection when not obtained and causes repentance or regret when obtained, (cp.) Hobson's choice.

দিশ *n.* (obs. & poet.) a point of the compass. **~পাশ** *n.* reckoning, estimate, limit (কাজের দিশপাশ নেই).

দিশা *n.* a point of the compass; a quarter

of the globe; trace (পথের দিশা) ; collectedness of one's mind for ascertaining what one should do (দিশাহারা). **দিশা না পাওয়া** *v.* to fail to find out; to be at a loss (to determine, ascertain, devise or find out); to be nonplussed or bewildered. **~হারা** *a.* failing to ascertain the points of the compass; failing to ascertain the right way; (fig.) confused, nonplussed, bewildered, confounded, perplexed to the extreme.

দিশি[1] *adv.* (ori.) to or towards a point of the compass. □ *n.* a point of the compass, a quarter or side. **দিশি দিশি** *n.* all quarters or sides. □ *adv.* to or towards or in all quarters or sides, everywhere.

দিশি[2] dial. var. of **দেশি**।

দিশে coll. corrup. of **দিশা**।

দিস্তা, (coll.) **দিস্তে** *n.* a quire (of paper); a pestle (হামানদিস্তা).

দীক্ষক *a.* one who initiates esp. to a religious practice. □ *n.* an initiator, a preceptor, a guru, a teacher.

দীক্ষণীয় *a.* worthy of being initiated, fit for initiation.

দীক্ষা *n.* admission with rite (as to a religious practice or order, a secret society etc.), initiation; employment in service of some sacred cause (স্বাধীনতার মন্ত্রে দীক্ষা) ; an instruction or teaching; a sacrament; an inspiration; (dero.) an instigation. **দীক্ষা দেওয়া** *v.* to initiate; to convert (মুসলমানধর্মে দীক্ষা দেওয়া) ; to baptize (খ্রিস্টধর্মে দীক্ষা দেওয়া) ; to teach, to indoctrinate (into a subject); to employ. **দীক্ষা পাওয়া, দীক্ষা নেওয়া** *v.* to be initiated; to be converted; to be baptized; to be taught or indoctrinated, to learn; to be employed. **~গুরু** *n.* an initiator; a guru or preceptor who has initiated. **~গ্রহণ** *n.* act of receiving initiation. **দীক্ষা গ্রহণ করা** *v.* to be initiated. **~মন্ত্র** *n.* a mysterious formula that a person is taught at initiation.

দীক্ষিত *a.* initiated; converted (মুসলমানধর্মে দীক্ষিত) ; baptized (খ্রিস্টধর্মে দীক্ষিত) ; indoctrinated (বদমাশিতে দীক্ষিত). **দীক্ষিত করা** *v.* to initiate; to convert; to baptize; to indoctrinate.

দীঘল alt. spell. of **দিঘল**।

দীঘি alt. spell. of **দিঘি**।

দীধিতি *n.* a ray, light; the name of a treatise on logic. **~মান** *n.* the sun.

দীন[1] alt. spell. of **দিন**[2]।

দীন[2] *a.* extremely poor or needy, indigent; afflicted, distressed; humble; wretched, miserable. **~চিত্ত** *a.* having a mind stricken with melancholia or sorrow or with a sense of humiliation; humble in attitude. **~চিত্তে** *adv.* with a melancholy or sorrowful or humiliated mind; humbly. **~তা** *n.* extreme poverty or need; indigence; affliction, distress; humbleness; wretchedness. **~দয়াময়** *a.* kind to the poor. **~দরিদ্র** *a.* extremely humble and poor, downtrodden. **~দুঃখী** *a.* indigent and distressed. **~নাথ** *n.* a refuge or helper or supporter of the poor; God. **~বন্ধু** *n.* a friend of the poor, God. **~ভাবাপন্ন** *a.* humble, modest; affecting humility or poverty. **~শরণ** *n.* a refuge of the poor; God. **~হীন** *a.* poor and lowly.

দীনা *fem.* of **দীন**[2]।

দীনার rej. spell. of **দিনার**।

দীপ *n.* a lamp. **~গৃহ** *n.* the light-house. **~নির্বাণ** *n.* extinguishment of a lamp; lights out; (loos.) a black-out. **দীপ নির্বাণ করা** *v.* to put out a lamp; to extinguish lights. **~পুঞ্জ** *n.* a multitude of lamps (usu. lighted ones). **~প্রজ্বালন** *n.* act of lighting a lamp. **দীপপ্রজ্বালন করা** *v.* to light a lamp. **~বর্তিকা** *n.* wick (of a lamp). **~বৃক্ষ** *n.* a lampstand, a candlestick. **~মালা** *n.* a row or set of lamps (usu. lighted ones). **~শক্তি** *n.* candle power. **~শলাকা** *n.* a match-stick; a match. **~শিখা** *n.* the flame of a lamp.

দীপক *a.* radiating; illuminating, illuminative; inflaming; enkindling; enlightening; inspiring, rousing, exciting, excitant; revealing, displaying, exhibiting; beautifying, embellishing. □ *n.* a lamp ('রঘুকুল দীপক') ; a musical mode (দীপক রাগিণী).

দীপন *n.* radiation; illumination; act of inflaming; act of enkindling or lighting; enlightenment; act of inspiring or rousing, excitation; revelation, display, exhibition; effulgence; beautification, embellishment. □ *a.* same as **দীপক**। **~মাত্রা** *n.* (phys.) intensity of illumination. **~শক্তি** *n.* (phys.) illuminating power.

দীপনীয় *a.* that which is to be illuminated or excited; illuminable; excitable.

দীপাগার *n.* the lighthouse.

দীপাধার *n.* a lampstand, a lampad.

দীপান্বিতা *n. fem.* the day of the new moon in the month of Kartik (কার্তিক) when Goddess Kali (কালী) is worshipped and the dwelling-houses of Hindus are illuminated with rows of lighted lamps. □ *a. fem.* furnished with a (lighted) lamp, lamped; illuminated, radiating. *a. masc.* **দীপান্বিত**।

দীপাবলি, দীপালি *n.* a collection of (lighted) lamps; the festival of **দীপান্বিতা**।

দীপালোক *n.* lamplight. **দীপালোকিত** *a.* illuminated with lamplight.

দীপিকা *n. fem.* moonlight; a lamp; a glossary or commentary (of a text). □ *a. fem.* of **দীপক**।

দীপিত *a.* lighted; lamped; illuminated; enkindled; exhibited, displayed, revealed, brought to light; excited, roused. *fem.* **দীপিতা**।

দীপ্ত *a.* burning; shining; lighted; illuminated; radiant, luminous; blazing; bright; lustrous; revealed, brought to light, exhibited; dazzling, glaring (দীপ্ত তেজ). **~কীর্তি** *a.* one whose fame has spread far and wide, widely famous or renowned. **দীপ্ত হুতাশন** blazing fire.

দীপ্তি *n.* light; shine, radiance, glow, lustre; splendour; brilliance; brightness; high spirit; beauty. **দীপ্তি পাওয়া** *v.* to shine, to glow, to radiate. **~মান** *a.* shining, glowing; radiant, luminous; bright, lustrous; brilliantly revealed; beautifying, embellishing; glowing with high spirit. *fem.* **দীপ্তিমতী**। **~মাপক** *n.* (phys.) a photometer. **~মিতি** *n.* (phys.) photometry.

দীপ্য *a.* worthy of being lighted or enkindled; illuminable; worthy of being revealed. **~মান** *a.* shining, glowing; radiant, luminous; bright, lustrous, sparkling, resplendent; in the state of being revealed; revealed.

দীপ্র *a.* shining, luminous, radiant, glowing; bright.

দীয়মান *a.* in the state of being given or distributed.

দীর্ঘ *a.* long (দীর্ঘ কেশ, দীর্ঘ পথ); tall (দীর্ঘ দেহ); much (দীর্ঘ সময়); prolonged, long-continuing (দীর্ঘ নিদ্রা, দীর্ঘায়ু); lengthy (দীর্ঘ কাহিনি); large; deep (দীর্ঘশ্বাস); (gr.) aspirate; (mus.) slow, protracted, sustained. **দীর্ঘ করা** *v.* to lengthen; to elongate. **~কায়** *a.* tall-bodied, tall. *fem.* **দীর্ঘকায়া**। **~কাল** *n.* a long time. **~কাল ব্যাপী** *a.* continuing for a long time. **~কেশ** *a.* long-haired. *fem.* **দীর্ঘকেশা, দীর্ঘকেশী**। **~গ্রীব** *a.* long-necked. □ *n.* the crane; the heron; the giraffe; the camel. **~চ্ছেদ** *n.* (geom.) a longitudinal section. **~জিহ্ব** *a.* long-tongued. □ *n.* the snake. **~জীবন** *n.* long life. **~জীবিতা** *n.* longevity. **~জীবী** *a.* long-lived. *fem.* **দীর্ঘজীবিনী**। **~তপা** *a.* one who has practised religious austerities for a long time. **~তা, ~ত্ব** *n.* length; lengthiness. **~দর্শী, ~দৃষ্টি** *a.* far-sighted, prudent, wise, sagacious. *fem.* **দীর্ঘদর্শিনী**। **~দিন** *n.* a long day; a long time. **~দেহী** *a.* (usu. of a man) tall (দীর্ঘদেহী পুরুষ). **~নাশ** *a.* long-nosed. **~নিদ্রা** *n.* a long or long-continuing sleep. **~নিঃশ্বাস, ~নিশ্বাস,** same as **দীর্ঘশ্বাস**। **~পথ** *n.* a long way. **~পদ** *n.* a lengthy word. **~পাদ** *a.* long-legged. □ *n.* the crane; the heron; the camel. **~বাহু, ~ভুজ** *a.* long-armed. **~মাত্রা** *n.* (pros.) a long metre; (mus.) a slow or protracted measure; a large amount or dose, a great deal (দীর্ঘমাত্রায় ঘুম). **~মেয়াদি** *a.* long-term (দীর্ঘমেয়াদি পরিকল্পনা, দীর্ঘমেয়াদি ঋণ); on a long-term basis. **~রাত্রি** *n.* a long night. **~রোমা** *a.* long-haired; shaggy. □ *n.* the bear. **~শ্বাস** *n.* a long and deep respiration, a sigh. **দীর্ঘশ্বাস ফেলা** *v.* to heave a sigh, to sigh. **দীর্ঘশ্বাস নেওয়া** *v.* to take a deep breath. **~সূত্র, ~সূত্রী** *a.* dilatory, procrastinating; slothful; sluggish. **~সূত্রতা** *n.* dilatoriness, procrastination; sloth;

sluggishness. **দীর্ঘসূত্রতা করা** *v.* to procrastinate. **~স্থায়ী** *a.* long-standing; long-drawn; existing for a long time. **~স্বর** *n.* (gr.) a long or aspirate vowel; a long note. □ *a.* having a long note.

দীর্ঘাকৃতি, দীর্ঘাকার *a.* tall; large.

দীর্ঘাগ্র *a.* acuminate.

দীর্ঘায়ত *a.* large; wide.

দীর্ঘায়ু *a.* long-lived.

দীর্ঘিকা *n.* a large and deep pond or tank.

দীর্ণ *a.* split, cleft, rent, broken, torn; (fig.) afflicted.

দু *pfx.* contr. of **দুই**। **দু-আনি** alt. spell. of **দুয়ানি**। **দু-এক** alt. spell. of **দুয়েক**। **দুকথা** *n.* a few words; rough or harsh words, rebuke (দুকথা শুনিয়ে দেওয়া). **দুকান করা** *v.* to give out (a secret). **দুকান-কাটা** *a.* (fig.) bare-faced, brazen-faced, shameless. **দুকুল** *n.* the father's family and the in-law's family (of a woman); the paternal and the maternal lines (of any person); (fig.) both alternatives. **দুকুল খাওয়া** (fig.) to lose all means of aid or support. **দুকূল** *n.* both banks of a river; (fig.) earthly life and life after death; (fig.) both alternatives. **দুখানা, দুখানি,** (dial.) **দুখান** *n.* two pieces, two. □ *a.* two pieces of, two; split or torn or broken into two. **দুগুণ** *a.* twice, double. **দুচার** *a.* a few; only a few, very few (দুচার দিন, দুচার কথা). **দুচারটি, দুচারটে, দুচারখানা** *n* & *a.* a few or a few things (দুচারটি বই). **দুচালা** *a.* having two thatched roofs. □ *n.* such a hut. **দু-চোখের বিষ** (fig.) an eyesore. **দু-চোখ যেদিকে যায়** wherever (my) eyes lead (me) to. **দুজন** *pro.* two (persons). □ *a.* two. **দুজনই** *pro.* & *a.* both. **দুটি, দুটো**[1] *pro.* two (objects or things). □ *a.* two. **দুটো**[2] *n.* & *a.* two o'clock. **দুটানা** *n.* simultaneous pulls in two opposite directions; oscillation; a dilemma. **দুটানায় পড়া** to be in a dilemma or quandary, to be in a state of indecision. **দুটোচারটে** *n.* & *a.* a few things or a few; only a few things or only a few. **দু-তরফা** *a.* pertaining to or contested by both the opposite sides, bipartite. **দুতলা, দুতালা** *a.* two-storied; double-decked. □ *n.* the first floor; the upper deck. **দুতারা** *a.* two-stringed. □ *n.* a double-stringed musical instrument. **দুধার** *n.* both sides; two sides. **দুধারী** *a.* pertaining to or inclined to both the sides; two-sided; double-handed. **দুনম্বরি** *n.* dishonesty; doing things in a dishonest manner, the habit or practice of doing dishonest things. □ *a.* dishonest, unfair; unlawful, illegal (দুনম্বরি ব্যাবসা) ; gained by evil or illegal means (দুনম্বরি পয়সা). **দুনলা** *a.* double-barrelled. □ *n.* a double-barrelled gun. **দু-নৌকোয় পা দেওয়া** (fig.) to fall between two stools, to serve God and Mammon simultaneously. **দু-পাক** *n.* act or an instance of enfolding or taking round twice; two coils;a short stroll, a short leisurely walk. **দু-পেয়ে** *a.* two-legged; biped. **দু-ফলা** *a.* (of a knife) having two blades; (of a tree) bearing fruit twice a year. **দুফাঁক** *a.* split asunder into two. **দু-ফালি,** (dial.) **দু-ফাল** *n.* two slices. □ *a.* sliced or parted into two. **দুবার** *n.* two times. □ *adv.* twice. **দুভাষী** *a.* speaking two languages (esp. as one's mother-tongue); bilingual. □ *n.* an interpreter; a bilingual man. **দু-মনা** *a.* of two minds, hesitating, vacillating, wavering. **দু-মুখো** *a.* two-faced; double-faced; two-way (দু-মুখো গলি). **দু-মুখো আচরণ** double-dealing, double-crossing. **দু-মুখো লোক** a double-dealer. **দু-মুঠা, দু-মুঠো** *a.* two handfuls of. **দু-মেটে** *a.* (of clay images etc.) doubly plastered. **দুয়ানি** *n.* a two-anna bit or piece. **দুয়েক** *a.* one or two; a few. **দু-রঙা** *a.* bicoloured. **দু-সন্ধ্যা** *adv.* & *a.* both in the daytime and evening (or at night). **দু-সুতি** *n.* a coarse cloth woven in double thread. **দু-হাত এক করা** *v.* to unite (a bride and a bridegroom) in marriage; to cup one's palms. **দু-হাতি** *a.* measuring two cubits. **দুহাতিয়া** *a.* (of a stroke) dealt with both hands. □ *adv.* with both hands.

দুই *n.* & *a.* two. □ *a.* & *pro.* both (দুই-ই খারাপ). **দুই-এক** *a.* one or two; a few.

দুও alt. spell. of **দুয়ো**[1] ।

দুঃ *pfx.* signifying: vile, wicked, bad, prohibited, inauspicious, distressing, sorrowful etc. (দুঃশীল, দুঃসময়, দুঃসংবাদ).

দুঃখ *n.* sorrow; affliction; grief; distress, suffering, misery (দুঃখে পড়া) ; pain, inflammation; regret (দুঃখ প্রকাশ করা). **দুঃখ করা** *v.* to regret; to rue, to grieve; to suffer pain, to take trouble; to be in distress, to undergo misery. **দুঃখ দেওয়া** *v.* to cause sorrow or regret, to grieve; to afflict; to distress; to pain; to give trouble. **দুঃখ পাওয়া বা ভোগ করা** *v.* to be stricken with sorrow or grief or misery (জীবনে অনেক দুঃখ পেয়েছি); to be afflicted or distressed or pained; to be in trouble, to suffer. **দুঃখে পড়া** *v.* to run into distress or trouble. **দুঃখের কাহিনি** a woeful or pathetic tale. **দুঃখের বিষয়** a matter of regret; a pity; a painful affair. **~কর, ~জনক, ~দ, ~দায়ক, ~দায়ী, ~প্রদ** *a.* painful; troublesome; woeful, distressing, agonizing; sorrowful. *fem.* **দুঃখদায়িনী**। **~দারিদ্র** *n.* distress and poverty, want and suffering or misery. **~প্রদ** same as **দুঃখকর**। **~বাদ** *n.* (phil.) pessimism. **~বাদী** *a.* pessimistic. □ *n.* a pessimist. **~ভাগী** *a.* sharing the sorrow of another. *fem.* **দুঃখভাগিনী**। **~ভোগ** *n.* act of suffering pain or undergoing distress. **~ময়** *a.* full of or abounding in sorrow or suffering. **~মোচন** *n.* act of relieving pain or distress; allaying or alleviation or mitigation of sorrow. **~সহিষ্ণু** *a.* one who patiently endures sorrow or suffering. **~সাগর** *n.* an ocean of sorrow, a sea of distress; endless sorrow or suffering. **~হর, ~হারী** *a.* one who or that which relieves pain or sorrow or suffering. *fem.* **দুঃখহরা, দুঃখহারিণী**।

দুঃখাতীত *a.* past all sorrow or suffering; immune to sorrow or suffering.

দুঃখার্ত, দুঃখান্বিত *a.* stricken with sorrow, rueful; afflicted; distressed; suffering. *fem.* **দুখার্তা, দুঃখান্বিতা**।

দুঃখিত *a.* stricken with sorrow; rueful, sorrowful, woeful, grieved; sad; afflicted, suffering; distressed; pained; regretful, sorry. *fem.* **দুঃখিতা**। **~চিত্ত, ~হৃদয়** *a.* having a sorrowing or regretful mind or heart; pained at heart.

দুঃখী *a.* stricken with sorrow or misery; woe-stricken, afflicted, distressed, miserable, suffering; sad; poor; destitute. *fem.* **দুঃখিনী**। **দুঃখের দুঃখী** a sympathizer.

দুঃখোক্তি *n.* sad or sorrowful utterance.

দুঃশাসন *a.* ungovernable, indomitable; unruly, intractable or refractory; (loos.) misgoverning, tyrannous. □ *n.* misgovernment; tyranny.

দুঃশীল *a.* misbehaved; ill-natured; wicked; depraved or vicious. *fem.* **দুঃশীলা**। **~তা** *n.* misbehaviour; bad nature; wickedness; depravity; viciousness.

দুঃসংবাদ *n.* a bad or evil news.

দুঃসময় *n.* evil days; hard times.

দুঃসহ *a.* hard to bear or endure or suffer, severe; unbearable, insufferable, intolerable. **দুঃসহ যন্ত্রণা** unbearable or severe pain.

দুঃসাধ্য *a.* hard to accomplish, difficult, arduous; hard to cure, incurable. **দুঃসাধ্য কার্জ** an arduous or uphill task. **~তা** *n.* state of being hard to accomplish; incurability.

দুঃসাহস *n.* improper or overmuch daring or boldness, overboldness. **দুঃসাহসিক, দুঃসাহসী** *a.* improperly or excessively bold or daring; warranting overboldness; overbold; overdaring, dare-devil. **দুঃসাহসিকতা** same as **দুঃসাহস**।

দুঃস্থ *a.* poor, needy, indigent; wretched, miserable; distressed, afflicted, woebegone.

দুঃস্থিত *a.* distressed, afflicted, woebegone; (phys.) instability; unstable equilibrium.

দুঃস্পর্শ *a.* difficult to touch.

দুঃস্বপ্ন *n.* a bad or distressing dream; an inauspicious dream; an awful or terrifying or oppressive dream; (loos.) a nightmare.

দুঁদে *a.* militant; difficult to cope or contend with, unyielding; litigious; terrible; experienced and tough; roguish.

দুহঁ, দুঁহা, দুঁহু *pro.* (poet.) both.

দুকূল see **দু**।

দুখ, দুখি, দুখিনি poet. & dial. corruptions of **দুঃখ, দুঃখী** and **দুঃখিনী** respectively.

দুগ্ধ *n.* milk; juice; latex (উদ্ভিজ্জ দুগ্ধ). **~জ, ~জাত** *a.* produced from milk. **দুগ্ধজাত দ্রব্য** a milk-product. **~পাত্র, ~ভাণ্ড** *n.* a milk-pail; a milk-trough. **~পোষ্য** *a.* living on one's mother's milk, suckling; (rare and often hum.) living on milk (esp. on cow's milk). **দুগ্ধপোষ্য শিশু** a child at the breast, a suckling. **~ফেননিভ** *a.* as white and soft as the froth of milk, (cp.) milk-white. **~বতী** *a.* giving milk; milch. **দুগ্ধবতী গাভি** a milch cow. **~বৎ** *a.* milk-like, milky. **~বিক্রেতা** *n.* a milk-man, a milk-seller. **~শর্করা** *n.* lactose.

দুড়দুড়, দুড়দাড় *int.* expressing : noise of heavy and hurried footsteps or of the rumbling of cloud; rapid and audible palpitation of the heart (esp. caused by fright etc.).

দুড়ুম milder form of **দড়াম**।

দুৎ var. of **ধুৎ**।

দুত্তোর pop. var. of **ধুত্তোর**।

দুদ্দাড় corrup. of **দুড়দাড়**।

দুধ *n.* milk; juice (নারকেলের দুধ) ; latex (গাছের দুধ). **দুধ কেটে গেছে** same as **দুধ ছানা হয়ে গেছে। দুধ খাওয়া** *v.* to drink milk; to draw the breast, to suck. **দুধ খাওয়ানো** *v.* to cause to drink milk; to give suck (to), to suckle. **দুধ ছাড়ানো** *v.* to wean (a baby from the habit of sucking or lactation). **দুধ ছানা হয়ে গেছে, দুধ ছিঁড়ে গেছে** *v.* (the) milk has turned sour or curdled. **দুধ তোলা** *v.* to vomit or spew milk after drinking it (as by a child). **দুধ দেওয়া** *v.* to give or yield milk; to give suck (to), to suckle. **দুধ দোওয়া** *v.* to milk. **দুধের ছেলে** an infant boy, a suckling. **দুধের মেয়ে** an infant girl, a suckling. **দুধের সর** a thin layer or film that collects on boiled milk, milk-film. **দুধের সাধ ঘোলে মেটানো** (fig.) to console oneself with a base substitute, to satisfy oneself with a glass of grog when the bottle of champagne is beyond one's reach. **দুধ-কলা দিয়ে কালসাপ পোষা** (fig.) to fatten one's mortal enemy, to nourish a viper in one's breast. **দুধ-কুসুম্ভা** *n.* a kind of milkshake mixed with a paste of hemp-leaves. **দুধ-রুটি** *n.* milk-sop. **দুধে-জলে মেশা** *v.* to get mixed or blended completely; (fig.) to be compromised thoroughly. **দুধে-দাঁত, দুধের দাঁত** *n.* a milk tooth; milk dentition. **দুধে ভাতে থাকা** *v.* to live in affluence, to enjoy loaves and fishes, to have one's bread buttered on both sides.

দুন *n.* (mus.) double quick measure; act of playing a musical instrument or singing doubly quick.

দুনা *a.* double, twice.

দুনি *n.* a long canoe-shaped bucket for bailing out water.

দুনিয়া *n.* the earth, the world; the universe. **~দার** *a.* worldly; worldly-minded; self-seeking; having vested interest. **~দারি** *n.* worldliness; worldly-mindedness; act of seeking self-interest; worldly life.

দুনো pop. var. of **দুনা**।

দুন্দুভি *n.* a large war-trumpet or kettle-drum of ancient India.

দুপ্ *int.* expressing : a thudding noise. **দুপ্ দাপ্, দুপ্ দুপ্** *int.* expressing : repeated thudding noise or romping.

দুপুর *n.* midday, noon. **দুপুর রাত** midnight. **দুপুর রাতে** *adv.* at dead of night, far into the night.

দুম্ *int.* expressing : a banging or booming or thudding noise. **দুম্ করে** with a thud. **দুমদুম্, দুমাদুম** *int.* expressing : repeated banging or booming of thudding noise.

দুমড়ানো *v.* to fold or twist by pressure. □ *a.* thus folded or twisted.

দুমাদুম see **দুম্**।

দুম্বা *n.* a kind of fat sheep having a short tail.

দুয়ার *n.* a door, a gate. **দুয়ারি** *n.* a door-keeper, a gateman. **দুয়ারে বাঁধা হাতি** (lit.) keeping or owning an elephant; (fig.) exceptionally affluent or wealthy.

দুয়ো[১] *int.* fie, boo. **দুয়ো দেওয়া** v. to cry fie upon, to boo, to hoot.

দুয়ো[২] *a.* unfortunate; wretched; (only *fem.*) neglected by one's husband. **~রানি** *n.* a queen neglected by her royal husband who is infatuated by his other wife or wives.

দুরজন poet. corrup. of **দুর্জন**।

দুরতিক্রমণ *n.* act of going across or through with great difficulty. **দুরতিক্রম, দুরতিক্রমণীয়, দুরতিক্রম্য** *a.* very difficult to go across or through.

দুরত্যয় *a.* very difficult to go across or through.

দুরদুর *int.* expressing : palpitation of the heart caused esp. by fear; trembling. **দুরুদুরু** *int.* same as **দুরদুরু**। ☐ *a.* palpitating; trembling; tremulous; fearful.

দুরদৃষ্ট *n.* ill luck, ill fate; misfortune. ☐ *a.* ill-fated, unfortunate; unlucky. **~ক্রমে, ~বশত** *adv.* through misfortune, as ill luck would have it.

দুরধিগম, দুরধিগম্য *a.* difficult to obtain, not easily available; not easily accessible, difficult of access; difficult to comprehend or learn, not easily knowable or cognizable; abstruse. *fem.* **দুরধিগম্যা**।

দুরধ্যয় *a.* hard-reading, difficult or hard to read.

দুরন্ত *a.* unmanageably restless or naughty (দুরন্ত শিশু) ; romping and mischievous; terrible, awful (দুরন্ত ক্রোধ) ; not easily subdued, very powerful and ferocious (দুরন্ত শত্রু) ; extremely galling and hard to cure (দুরন্ত ব্যাধি) ; intolerably hot (দুরন্ত রোদ্দুর) ; severe (দুরন্ত শীত) ; very strong (দুরন্ত ঝড়) ; very steep, difficult to go through or across (দুরন্ত পথ) ; very restless or billowy (দুরন্ত সমুদ্র). **~পনা** *n.* restlessness that is difficult to control; romping and mischievous conduct or behaviour; uncontrollable naughtiness.

দুরন্বয় *n.* a mistake in syntax, a syntactic error.

দুরপনেয় *a.* difficult to remove or efface, not easily delible. **দুরপনেয় কলঙ্ক** indelible stain or blemish or blot.

দুরবগম, দুরবগম্য same as **দুরধিগম** and **দুরধিগম্য**।

দুরবগাহ *a.* difficult to bathe in; difficult to enter; difficult of access; difficult to comprehend.

দুরবস্থ *a.* fallen into a bad state; distressed; miserable, wretched; poverty-stricken, in straitened circumstances, indigent.

দুরবস্থা bad or low state; distress; misery, wretchedness; poverty, indigence.

দুরবিন alt. spell. of **দূরবিন**।

দুরভিগ্রহ *a.* difficult to take or accept or apprehend; difficult to comprehend or know or cognize; abstruse.

দুরভিসন্ধি *n.* an evil design or purpose, a sinister motive. **~মূলক** *a.* stemming from a sinister motive, ill-motivated.

দুরমুশ *n.* a rammer for beating down earth etc.; act of beating down with a rammer; (fig. & sarcas. or hum.) a sound drubbing. **দুরমুশ করা** *v.* to beat down with a rammer; to drub soundly.

দুরস্ত *a.* free of errors, correct; corrected, amended (ভুল দুরস্ত হওয়া) ; well-arranged, orderly, spruce (বেশবাস দুরস্ত থাকা) ; in keeping with (কায়দাদুরস্ত) ; levelled (রাস্তা দুরস্ত হওয়া) ; corrected by drubbing (ছেলে দুরস্ত হওয়া). **দুরস্ত করা** *v.* to correct, to amend; to arrange properly, to put in order; to level; to correct by drubbing.

দুরাকাঙ্ক্ষা *n.* unrealizable longing or desire, a cry for the moon; an ambition or aspiration. **দুরাকাঙ্ক্ষ, দুরাকাঙ্ক্ষী** *a.* having an unrealizable longing or desire, audaciously or inordinately ambitious; ambitious. *fem.* **দুরাকাঙ্ক্ষিণী**।

দুরাক্রম, দুরাক্রম্য *a.* difficult to attack, not easily invaded.

দুরাগ্রহ *n.* desire for or interest in evil or difficult things; a wicked or difficult venture. ☐ *a.* desirous of or interested in evil or difficult things; indulging in or engaged in a wicked or difficult venture.

দুরাচরণীয় *a.* very difficult to perform or accomplish.

দুরাচার *a.* wicked; depraved; sinful; indulging in nasty or foul or abominable practices. ☐ *n.* wickedness; depravity; sinfulness; a nasty or abominable practice. *a. fem.* **দুরাচারিণী**।

দুরাত্মা *a.* sinful; depraved; wicked; roguish or villainous; tyrannous, oppressive.

দুরাধর্ষ *a.* difficult to capture or subdue; unruly; turbulent.

দুরারোগ্য *a.* difficult to cure. **দুরারোগ্য ব্যাধি** an incurable disease.

দুরারোহ *a.* difficult to climb; having a very steep ascent.

দুরাশয় *n.* evil design or purpose. □ *a.* having an evil design or purpose; wicked; evil-minded.

দুরাশা same as **দুরাকাঙ্ক্ষা**।

দুরাসদ *a.* difficult to capture or subdue; turbulent; difficult to obtain or procure, not easily available or attainable; difficult to comprehend or cognize; hard to bear or suffer.

দুরি *n.* the two of playing-cards or dice, the deuce.

দুরিত *n.* a sin; harm. □ *a.* sinning, sinful; wicked.

দুরুক্তি *n.* harsh or rude words; revilement, filthy language, abuse.

দুরুচ্চার, দুরুচ্চার্য *a.* difficult to pronounce or utter, break-jaw; obscene; unspeakable. **দুরুচ্চার শব্দ, দুরুচ্চার্য শব্দ** a word hard to pronounce or utter, (sl.) a jaw-breaker.

দুরুদুরু see **দুরদুর**।

দুরূহ *a.* difficult, hard; stiff; incapable of being solved by arguments; difficult to know or cognize or comprehend; abstruse. **~তা** *n.* difficulty in understanding; stiffness; abstruseness.

দুর্গ *n.* a fort; a fortress; a castle; a stronghold; a tower; a fortification. **~পতি** same as **দুর্গেশ**। **~প্রাকার** *n.* a rampart.

দুর্গত *a.* stricken with adversity or danger; poverty-stricken, indigent; distressed, afflicted; miserable, wretched.

দুর্গতি *n.* adversity; danger, poverty, indigence; distress, affliction; misery, wretchedness; condemnation to hell; hell. **~নাশিনী** *n.* (*fem.*) one who dispels distress, misery etc. (দুর্গতিনাশিনী দুর্গা).

দুর্গন্ধ *n.* an offensive smell, a bad odour. □ *a.* ill-smelling; fetid, smelly, stinking. **দুর্গন্ধী** *a.* ill-smelling; fetid.

দুর্গপতি, দুর্গপ্রাকার see **দুর্গ**।

দুর্গম *a.* difficult of access or approach, not easily passable; inaccessible; impenetrable; difficult to know or cognize or comprehend.

দুর্গস্থ *a.* staying within a fort.

দুর্গা *n.* Goddess Durga also called Shakti (শক্তি) or Force; the wife of Shiva (শিব)—she is the chief of female deities and a slayer of demons, and she presides over prosperity, victory, and fame of mankind.

দুর্গা-টুনটুনি *n.* the sunbird.

দুর্গাধিকারী, দুর্গাধ্যক্ষ same as **দুর্গেশ**।

দুর্গাপূজা *n.* the worship of Goddess Durga (দুর্গা) ; the annual festival of worshipping Durga (it comes off in autumn).

দুর্গেশ *n.* a governor or captain or master or owner of a fort; a castellan. **~নন্দিনী** *n.* a castellan's daughter.

দুর্গোৎসব same as **দুর্গাপূজা**।

দুর্গ্রহ[1] *n.* (astrol.) a malicious or ill-boding star.

দুর্গ্রহ[2] *a.* difficult to take or capture or know or comprehend.

দুর্ঘট *a.* unlikely to happen; of rare occurrence.

দুর্ঘটনা *n.* a mishap; an accident; (loos.) a calamitous incident, a calamity.

দুর্জন *a.* wicked; villainous; roguish. **দুর্জন ব্যক্তি** *n.* a wicked person; a villain; a rogue.

দুর্জয় *a.* difficult to conquer or subdue; invincible; turbulent.

দুর্জ্ঞেয় *a.* difficult to know or learn or cognize or comprehend; abstruse. **~তা** *n.* abstruseness; incomprehensibility, unknowableness.

দুর্দম, দুর্দমনীয়, দুর্দম্য *a.* difficult to subdue or put down or tame; turbulent; unruly.

দুর্দশা *n.* adversity; misery; bad state; dilapidated state. **~গ্রস্ত, ~পন্ন** *a.* stricken with adversity; miserable, wretched; fallen into a bad state; dilapidated.

দুর্দান্ত *a.* hard to subdue or tame; turbulent; unruly; (coll.) severe (দুর্দান্ত গরম) ; terrible, in a great measure; very fine (দুর্দান্ত খেলা, দুর্দান্ত ছবি).

দুর্দিন *n.* a difficult time, hard or troublesome times; a time of danger; evil days, a time of adversity or distress; a day of foul weather. **দুর্দিনের বন্ধু, দুর্দিনের সহায়** a friend or patron in adversity.

দুর্দৈব *n.* ill-luck, misfortune; a mishap.

দুর্ধর্ষ *a.* difficult to vanquish or capture or conquer; difficult to bear or suffer; very powerful or turbulent.

দুর্নাম *n.* disrepute, ill-fame; discredit; a bad name; notoriety.

দুর্নিবার, দুর্নিবার্য *a.* difficult to prevent or check or resist.

দুর্নিমিত্ত *n.* a bad sign; an ill omen.

দুর্নিরীক্ষ্য *a.* hard to look at, difficult to be viewed.

দুর্নীত *a.* morally degenerated; indulging in malpractices; corrupted; perverted; depraved; wicked. □ *n.* moral degeneration; a malpractice; a corruption; perversion; wickedness.

দুর্নীতি *n.* moral degeneration; a malpractice; a corruption; perversion; wickedness. **~পরায়ণ** *a.* same as **দুর্নীত** (*a.*).

দুর্বচন *n.* rude or harsh words; discourteous language or words; a reviling speech, revilement. □ *a.* (given to) speaking rude or harsh words; (given to) using discourteous language; (given to) reviling.

দুর্বৎসর *n.* an inauspicious year; a year of scarcity or famine or hardship; a bad or troublesome year.

দুর্বল *a.* weak; feeble (দুর্বল দৃষ্টি) ; weakened; debilitated. *fem.* **দুর্বলা** I **দুর্বল করা** *v.* to weaken; to enfeeble; to debilitate. **~চিত্ত** *a.* weak-minded, chickenhearted, imbecile. **দুর্বল হওয়া** *v.* to grow or become weak, to be enfeebled or debilitated.

দুর্বলতা *n.* weakness; feebleness; debility.

দুর্বহ *a.* hard to carry or bear; heavy; hard to endure or suffer.

দুর্বাক *a.* harsh-tongued; foul-mouthed; rudely outspoken.

দুর্বাক্য *n.* harsh words; discourteous words or language; revilement.

দুর্বার *a.* difficult to prevent or check or resist; turbulent.

দুর্বাসনা *n.* a desire hard to realize; an evil desire.

দুর্বাসা *a.* dressed in nasty or dirty cloth; shabbily dressed. □ *n.* a mythological saint notorious for his quick temper and harsh words; a quick-tempered and harsh-tongued person, a fire-eater.

দুর্বিনীত *a.* impolite, discourteous; haughty, arrogant, insolent; ill-mannered, unmannerly. *fem.* **দুর্বিনীতা** I

দুর্বিনেয় *a.* untamable; indocile; refractory.

দুর্বিপাক *n.* a disaster; a danger, a hazard; a difficulty, a trouble.

দুর্বিষহ *a.* hard to endure or suffer; unendurable, unbearable, insufferable.

দুর্বুদ্ধি *n.* an evil or mischievous or harmful thought or design; evil-mindedness; folly. □ *a.* evil-minded; foolish.

দুর্বৃত্ত *a.* depraved; wicked, ill-natured, villainous, roguish. **দুর্বৃত্ত ব্যক্তি** a depraved person; a wicked or ill-natured person, a villain, a rogue, a scoundrel. **~তা, দুর্বৃত্তি** *n.* depravity; wickedness, villainy, roguery.

দুর্বোধ, দুর্বোধ্য *a.* hard to understand or comprehend or know or cognize; not easily intelligible.

দুর্ব্যবহার *n.* rude demeanour or harsh treatment, misbehaviour. **দুর্ব্যবহার করা** *v.* to treat (one) rudely or harshly, to misbehave (with).

দুর্ভক্ষ্য *a.* hard to eat, not easily eatable; unfit for eating.

দুর্ভগ *a.* unfortunate, ill-fated. **দুর্ভগা** *a. fem.* unfortunate, ill-fated; estranged from the love of one's husband.

দুর্ভর *a.* hard to bear or carry; very heavy; hard to sustain or endure.

দুর্ভাগা *a.* unfortunate, ill-fated, unlucky; wretched, miserable. *fem.* **দুর্ভাগিনী** I

দুর্ভাগ্য *n.* ill luck, sinister fate; misfortune. □ *a.* unfortunate, unlucky, ill-fated. **~ক্রমে, ~বশত** *adv.* unfortunately, unluckily, as ill luck would have it.

দুর্ভাবনা *n.* a troublesome thought, worry, anxiety; misgiving. **দুর্ভাবনা করা** *v.* to worry. **~গ্রস্ত, ~পীড়িত** *a.* worried, troubled with anxiety or misgiving.

দুর্ভিক্ষ *n.* (lit. & obs.) a time when alms is scarce; (pop.) (a time of) scarcity, famine; extreme want or shortage. **~পীড়িত** *a.* famine-stricken.

দুর্ভেদ, দুর্ভেদ্য *a.* difficult to penetrate or

enter or force one's way into; impervious; difficult to raid or conquer; difficult to comprehend. **দুর্ভেদ-প্রকোষ্ঠ** *n.* strong room. **~তা** *n.* impenetrability, imperviousness.

দুর্ভোগ *n.* suffering; distress; trouble.

দুর্মতি same as **দুর্বুদ্ধি**।

দুর্মদ *a.* terribly intoxicated, maddened with intoxication; frenzied; difficult to subdue or resist; turbulent.

দুর্মনা *a.* worried, stricken with anxiety or misgiving. **দুর্মনায়মান** *a.* worrying.

দুর্মর *a.* inflexible; extremely stiff; rigid; extremely conservative, diehard.

দুর্মুখ same as **দুর্বাক**।

দুর্মূল্য *a.* very costly or dear, highly expensive. **দুর্মূল্য ভাতা** dearness allowance. **~তা** *n.* excessive costliness or dearness.

দুর্মেধা *a.* having a dull memory; dull-witted; evil-minded; foolish.

দুর্যোগ *n.* a time or instance of foul weather; a difficult time, hard times; a time of danger; a danger. **~পূর্ণ** *a.* full of foul weather. **দুর্যোগপূর্ণ আবহাওয়া** a foul or inclement or stormy weather.

দুর্যোধন *a.* hard to cope with in battle. ☐ *n.* the name of the arch-villain of the Mahabharata; (fig.) a rare villain.

দুর্লক্ষণ *n.* an inauspicious omen; a bad sign or symptom. ☐ *a.* having an inauspicious omen or sign; sinister; bearing on one's person an inauspicious mark; unlucky; ill-fated. *fem. a.* **দুর্লক্ষণা**।

দুর্লক্ষ্য *a.* difficult to discern or look at; almost invisible; not noticeable; hard to foresee.

দুর্লঙ্ঘ, দুর্লঙ্ঘ্য *a.* hard to surmount or scale; insurmountable, impassable. **দুর্লঙ্ঘ বাধা** insuperable or insurmountable barriers.

দুর্লভ *a.* difficult to obtain or procure or attain; rare, scarce; extremely costly or dear.

দুল *n.* an ear-drop or earring.

দুলকি *n.* a slow jerking motion as of a palanquin or a horse, trot. **দুলকি চালে চলা** *v.* to trot; (of a person) to walk slowly with an air of self-importance and ease.

দুলদুল *int.* expressing : dangling or swinging loosely.

দুলানো *v.* to cause to swing or rock, to swing or rock or dangle or oscillate.

দুলাল *n.* a darling, a dear, a minion; a darling child who is brought up with much affection and often spoilt by over-indulgence. *fem.* **দুলালি**।

দুলিচা *n.* a piece of small carpet esp. one to sit upon.

দুলুনি *n.* a mild rocking; an instance or act of swinging or rocking. ☐ *a.* one who or that which swings or rocks.

দুলে *n.* one of a backward or depressed caste amongst the Hindus (usually employed as palanquin-carriers). *fem.* **দুলেনি**।

দুশমন *n.* an enemy, a foe, an adversary; a rogue, a scoundrel, a wicked or vile person. **দুশমনি** *n.* enmity, hostility; roguery, wickedness.

দুশ্চর *a.* difficult to traverse (দুশ্চর অরণ্য) ; too austere to undergo or observe, extremely austere (দুশ্চর তপস্যা).

দুশ্চরিত্র *a.* characterless, having a vitiated character; wicked, vile; corrupted; perverted; depraved. ☐ *n.* a vitiated or wicked or corrupted or perverted or depraved character. **দুশ্চরিত্রতা** *n.* moral vitiation; wickedness, vileness; corruption; perversion; depravity.

দুশ্চিকিৎস্য *a.* difficult to cure; irremediable; without remedy.

দুশ্চিন্তা same as **দুর্ভাবনা**।

দুশ্চেষ্টা *n.* an attempt to accomplish an impossible task; a desperate attempt; an impossible or futile or unjustifiable attempt. **দুশ্চেষ্টিত** *a.* attempting to accomplish an impossible task; attempting desperately; making an impossible or futile or unjustifiable attempt.

দুশ্ছেদ্য *a.* difficult to cut off or sever; difficult to tear off or separate.

দুষমন rej. spell. of **দুশমন**।

দুষা *v.* to blame,to impute fault to, to accuse.

দুষ্কর *a.* difficult to do or accomplish or execute; arduous, uphill.

দুষ্কর্ম, দুষ্কার্য *n.* a wicked act, a misdeed; a

mischief; a crime; a sin. **দুষ্কর্মা** *a.* one who has committed a wicked act or a crime or a sin; given to wickedness, evil-doing; mischievous; criminal; sinning, sinful.

দুষ্কাল *n.* an inauspicious or unpropitious time.

দুষ্কুল *n.* a base or dishonest or humble or lowly family or line.

দুষ্কৃত *n.* a wicked act, a misdeed; a mischief; a crime; a sin. □ *a.* done wickedly or mischievously; done in grief. **~কারী, দুষ্কৃতী** *a.* one who has committed a wicked act or a crime or a sin; given to wickedness, evil-doing; mischievous; criminal; sinning, sinful. **দুষ্কৃতি** *n.* a wicked act, a misdeed; a mischief; a crime; a sin; misfortune.

দুষ্ক্রিয়া same as **দুষ্কর্ম**। **দুষ্ক্রিয়, দুষ্ক্রিয়ান্বিত** same as **দুষ্কর্মা**।

দুষ্ট *a.* faulty, defective (দুষ্ট বাচনভঙ্গি) ; malignant, morbid, septic (দুষ্টব্রণ, দুষ্টক্ষত) ; fatal or dangerous (দুষ্টব্যাধি) ; vile, vicious, wicked, depraved or lax in morals (দুষ্ট চরিত্র) ; bad, evil (দুষ্ট সঙ্গী) ; guilty (দুষ্ট মন) ; malicious (দুষ্টগ্রহ) ; naughty. *fem.* **দুষ্টা**। **~ক্ষত** *n.* an ulcer, a septic wound. **~ক্ষুধা** *n.* morbid or unwholesome appetite, false hunger. **~গ্রহ** *n.* (astrol.) a malicious star. **~প্রকৃতি** *a.* ill-natured; bad-charactered; depraved or lax in morals; reprobate; wicked. **~বুদ্ধি, ~মতি** *a.* evil-minded; mischievous. **~ব্রণ** *n.* a malignant or morbid boil; a carbuncle. **দুষ্টামি** *n.* naughtiness; mischievousness; a mischief. **দুষ্টাশয়** *a.* wicked; roguish.

দুষ্টু *a.* (in endearment) naughty; mischievous. **~মি** *n.* naughtiness; mischievousness; a mischief. **দুষ্টুমি করা** *v.* to be naughty; to make a mischief; to play a mischievous trick.

দুষ্পাচ্য, (rare) **দুষ্পচ** *a.* hard to digest.

দুষ্পাঠ্য *a.* hard to read.

দুষ্প্রবৃত্তি *n.* a wicked or evil disposition or inclination or desire.

দুষ্প্রবেশ্য, দুষ্প্রবেশ *a.* difficult to enter or penetrate.

দুষ্প্রাপ্য *a.* difficult to obtain or attain; rare, scarce.

দুস্তর *a.* difficult to go across; difficult to cross, impassable. **~তা** *n.* impassability.

দুস্থ *a.* wretched, distressed, hard-up. **~তা** *n.* distress, wretched condition, poverty.

দুহা older form of **দোয়া**[১]।

দুহিতা *n.* a daughter.

দুহ্য *a.* fit to be milked (as a cow). **~মানা** *a. fem.* one who or that which is being milked.

দূত *n.* a messenger; a courier; an envoy; an ambassador; an emissary; a harbinger, a forerunner; a go-between (esp. in an unlawful love-affair); a pander, a procurer, a male bawd; (now rare) a spy. *fem.* **দূতী, দূতি** (esp. in the sense of a bawd or panderess). **দূতাবাস** *n.* an ambassador's residence (and office), an embassy. **দূতালি** *n.* office of a messenger or courier or envoy or ambassador or emissary; forerunning; office of a go-between; bawdry; panderism; espionage. **দূতিয়ালি, দূতীয়ালি, দূতিগিরি, দূতীগিরি** *n.* office of a bawd or panderess, bawdry.

দূর *n.* distance; a distant place (আর কত দূরে নিয়ে যাবে). □ *a.* distant, far-off (দূর দেশ, দূর ভবিষ্যৎ) ; far-reaching esp. into the future (দূরদৃষ্টি) ; far-reaching; long, extensive (দূর পথ) ; expelled, removed, driven away or out (কাঁটা দূর হওয়া). □ *int.* expressing : contempt, shame, vexation, distrust, disagreement etc., fie, hang it, ah. **দূর করা** *v.* to expel; to banish; to drive away or out; to remove; to dispel; to turn out; to eject; to relieve (ব্যথা দূর করা). **দূর হওয়া** *v.* to go away; to pass out of sight; to be removed; to be expelled. **দূর হোক, দূর হোক ছাই** *int.* hang it, chuck it, damn it. **দূরে থাকা** *v.* to keep a distance, to keep aloof. **দূরের কথা** an affair of distant future; not to speak of (টাকা দেওয়া দূরের কথা). **দূরক** *n.* (astr.) a radius vector. **দূরক ক্ষেত্র** (astr.) a sectional area. **দূরগ, দূরগামী** *a.* far-going, long-distance (দূরগামী ট্রেন) ; (fig.) far-reaching; long, extensive (দূরগামী পথ). *fem.* **দূরগা, দূরগামিনী**। **দূর ছাই করা** *v.* to slight; to treat contemptuously. **দূরত** *adv.* from a distance; from a remote place. **দূরতম** *a.* remotest; longest (দূরতম পথ). **দূরতা, দূরত্ব** *n.* (amount of) distance; (amount of) length; (amount of) difference. **দূরত্ব রক্ষা করা** to keep one's distance. **~দর্শন** *n.* act of seeing from a distance or act of seeing distant things; foresight; farsight; act of seeing into the future; prudence; (sc.) television. **~দর্শী** *a.* far-seeing; farsighted; foresighted; seeing into the future; prudent. *fem.* **~দর্শিনী** । **~দর্শিতা** *n.* farsightedness; foresightedness; foresight; ability to see into the future; prudence. **দূর-দূর** *int.* fie; hang it. **দূর-দূর করা** *v.* to treat contemptuously (like a cur). **~দূরান্তর** *n.* very distant or remote places. **~পাল্লা** *a.* a long distance. **দূর-পাল্লার ক্ষেপণাস্ত্র** a long-range missile. **~প্রসারী** *a.* far-extending; far-reaching; very long. **~বর্তী** *a.* lying or staying at a distance; far-off, distant, remote; (fig.) separated by a large margin or differing to a great extent. *fem.* **~বর্তিনী** । **~বর্তিতা** *n.* state of lying or staying at a distance; remoteness; (fig.) separation by a large margin or great difference. **~বীক্ষণ, ~বিন** *n.* a telescope. **~ব্যাপী** *a.* far-extending; far-reaching. **~ভাষ** *n.* a telephone. **~স্থ, ~স্থিত** *a.* situated or located or lying or staying at a distance; distant, remote. **দূরে** *adv.* at or to a distance.

দূরহি poet. & obs. var. of **দূরে** ।

দূরাগত *a.* one who or that which is coming or has come from a distance.

দূরান্ত *n.* a remote or far-off place.

দূরান্তর *a.* remote or distant place.

দূরীকরণ *n.* expulsion; removal, banishment; act of driving out or away, act of turning out.

দূরীকৃত *a.* expelled; removed; banished; driven away or out; turned out.

দূরীভবন *n.* act of being turned out or driven away; removal; ejectment; expulsion.

দূরীভূত *a.* expelled; removed; ejected; turned out, driven away or out.

দূরেক্ষণ *n.* television.

দূর্বা *n.* grass. **~দল** *n.* a blade of grass. **~দলশ্যাম** *n.* grass-green, verdant green.

দূষক *a.* one who or that which blames or finds fault with, fault-finding; carping, cavilling.

দূষণ *n.* imputation of blame; fault-finding; carping; corruption; defilement; pollution. □ *a.* (chiefly used as a *sfx.*) blaming; fault-finding; carping; defiling; corrupting; polluting.

দূষণীয় *a.* blamable, blameworthy, condemnable; reprehensible.

দূষয়িতা same as **দূষক** । *fem.* **দূষয়িত্রী** ।

দূষিত *a.* corrupted, polluted, defiled, vitiated; befouled; impure. **দূষিত করা** *v.* to corrupt, to pollute, to defile, to vitiate; to befoul.

দূষ্য same as **দূষণীয়** ।

দৃক, দৃক্ *n.* the eye; sight, vision; knowledge; wisdom. **দৃক্‌পাত** *v.* act of casting a glance; act of taking (slightest) notice of or paying (slightest) heed to. **দৃক্‌পাত করা** *v.* to cast a glance (at); to take (any) notice of, to pay (any) heed to.

দৃগক্ষ *n.* visual axis.

দৃঢ় *a.* durable, sound (দৃঢ় ভিত্তি) ; strong (দৃঢ়কায়) ; firm, steady; constant (দৃঢ়প্রতিজ্ঞ) ; strict, severe (দৃঢ় শাসন) ; unwavering (দৃঢ় আনুগত্য) ; tight, taut (দৃঢ় বন্ধন) ; deep (দৃঢ় ভক্তি) ; unfaltering (দৃঢ় স্বর) ; unflinching (দৃঢ় বেগ) ; categorical (দৃঢ় নির্দেশ). **দৃঢ় করা** *v.* to make strong or firm; to tighten, to tauten; to make stronger or more firm. **~কায়** *a.* having a well-built or strong body. **~চিত্ত** *a.* firm in mind; firm in determination. **~জ্ঞান** *n.* firm belief; positive knowledge; conviction. **~তা** *n.* durability, soundness; strongness; firmness, steadiness; tightness; constancy; strictness, severity; unwaveringness; deepness. **দৃঢ়তা সহকারে** *adv.* firmly. **~নিশ্চয়** *a.* convinced; confident; firmly resolved; sanguine; certain. **~প্রতিজ্ঞ** *a.* one who intends firmly to fulfil his promise or vow; firmly resolved or resolute; firm in determination. **~প্রত্যয়, ~বিশ্বাস** *n.* conviction; firm belief, strong faith. **~বদ্ধ** *a.* tightly fastened or closed; tightened, taut. **~বন্ধন** *n.* a strong tie or bondage; tight fastening. **~মুষ্টি** *a.* one who has clenched one's fist; (fig.) tight-fisted, niggardly; (fig.) resolved, determined. □ *n.* a clenched fist. **~মূল** *a.* firmly rooted; deep-rooted; deep-seated. **~সঙ্কল্প** *a.* firmly resolved or determined, resolute. **~সন্ধ** *a.* firm in one's promise or vow; firmly resolved. **~স্বরে** *adv.* in a firm tone, in an unfaltering voice. **~হস্তে** *adv.* with a firm hand, firmly (দৃঢ়হস্তে মোকাবিলা করা).

দৃঢ়ীকরণ *n.* act of making strong or stronger or firm or more firm; tightening or tautening; act of confirming, confirmation; act of establishing firmly; consolidation; congelation.

দৃঢ়ীকৃত *a.* made strong or stronger, strengthened; made firm or more firm; tightened; confirmed; firmly established; congealed.

দৃঢ়ীভবন *n.* act of becoming strong or stronger or firm or more firm; act of being tightened or tautened; act of being confirmed, confirmation; act of being firmly established; act of being congealed, congelation.

দৃঢ়ীভূত *a.* that which has become strong, or stronger, strengthened; that which has become firm or more firm; that which has become tight or taut, tightened or tautened; confirmed; firmly established; congealed.

দৃপ্ত, (rare) **দৃপ্র** *a.* proud, vain; arrogant, haughty; spirited; flaming, blazing, scorching (দৃপ্ত সৌরকর) ; flared up (দৃপ্ত ক্রোধ).

দৃশ্য *n.* scenery, a sight, a spectacle, a view (পূর্ণিমারাত্রে তাজমহলের দৃশ্য) ; (of a drama) a scene. □ *a.* (rare) worth seeing, spectacular; that which is to be enjoyed by seeing (দৃশ্যকাব্য) ; visible, obvious, apparent (দৃশ্যত). **~কাব্য** *n.* a drama, a play. **~ত** *adv.* apparently; manifestly; obviously; visibly. **~দিগন্ত** *n.* (astr.) the visible horizon. **~পট** *n.* a scene that is put up on a stage, scenery. **~মান** *a.* that which is being seen; present to view; visible. **~সংগীত** *n.* dance. **দৃশ্যাদৃশ্য** *a.* visible and invisible. **দৃশ্যান্তর** *n.* another scene or sight.

দৃষ্ট *a.* seen, noticed, observed; visible, manifest. **~চর, ~পূর্ব** *a.* seen or noticed before or in the past. **দৃষ্টত** *adv.* apparently; obviously; visibly; manifestly. **~বৎ** *a.* (as if) visible. **~বাদ** *n.* (phil.) positivism. **~বাদী** *a.* positivistic. □ *n.* a positivist.

দৃষ্টাদৃষ্ট *a.* seen and unseen; partly seen and partly unseen; revealed and unrevealed.

দৃষ্টান্ত *n.* a precedent; an instance; an example; an illustration; (rhet.) a parallel. **দৃষ্টান্ত দেওয়া** *v.* to show a precedent, to cite an example; to exemplify; to illustrate. **~প্রদর্শন** *n.* act of showing a precedent or citing an example; exemplification; illustration; act of setting an example. **দৃষ্টান্ত রাখা, দৃষ্টান্ত স্থাপন করা** *v.* to make a precedent, to set an example; to show or quote a precedent, to cite an example. **~স্থল** *n.* a person or thing worthy of being cited as an example or instance; an exemplary person or thing. **~স্থাপন** *n.* setting an example setting a precedent. **~স্বরূপ** *adv.* for instance, for example. □ *a.* fit to be cited as an example.

দৃষ্টি *n.* act of seeing or viewing; power of seeing; the organ of sight or vision; sight, vision, observation; perception; cognition; knowledge; wisdom; foresight, careful attention or observation (ছেলের দিকে দৃষ্টি রেখো) ; a sinister or malicious look, a covetous or evil glance (আমার খাবারের দিকে দৃষ্টি দিয়ো না) ; an aspect esp. a sinister one (শনির দৃষ্টি). **দৃষ্টি দেওয়া** *v.* to cast a glance, to look at; to keep an eye on; to pay heed to; to cast a sinister or malicious look; (astrol.) to influence esp. unfavourably. **~কৃপণ** *a.* one who grudges any large expenditure, niggardly. **~কোণ** *n.* an angle of vision, a view-point. **~ক্ষেত্র** *n.* (phys.) a field of vision or view. **~ক্ষুধা** *n.* morbid or unwarranted hunger which is roused as soon as one sees an article of food.

~ক্ষেপ same as **দৃষ্টিপাত**। **~গোচর** *a.* visible. **দৃষ্টিগোচর হওয়া** *v.* to be visible, to come into sight or view. **~নন্দন** *a.* beautiful to look at, nice to look at, that gives pleasure to the eye, pleasing. **~নিবন্ধ** *n.* (phys.) persistence of vision. **~পথ** *n.* the range or direction of vision; sight, view. **~পথবর্তী হওয়া** *v.* to come into view, to appear in sight; to become visible. **~পাত** *n.* act of casting a glance; a glance, a look; notice; observation. **দৃষ্টিপাত করা** *v.* to cast a glance, to look at; to notice; to pay heed to. **~বিক্ষেপ** *n.* a side-glance, a leer; a casual or neglectful look. **দৃষ্টিবিক্ষেপ করা** *v.* to cast a side-glance, to leer; to look casually or neglectfully. **~বিজ্ঞান** *n.* optics. **~বিভ্রম** *n.* an optical illusion. **~ভঙ্গি** *n.* attitude of looking at, view-point. **দৃষ্টি রাখা** *v.* to keep an eye on; pay attention to; look after. **~শক্তি** *n.* power of seeing, eye-sight, sight, vision; perception. **~শক্তিহীন** *a.* sightless, blind; deprived of or lacking in perception or foresight. **~হীন, ~শূন্য** *a.* sightless, blind, paying no heed to, careless; lacking in perception or foresight. **~হীনতা** *n.* sightlessness, blindness.

দে১ dial. corrup. of **দিয়ে**।

দে২ *imperat.* form of **দেওয়া** (*v.*) used in familiarity or contempt.

দেইজি *n.* a kinsman, a blood-relation. **দেইজি-শত্রুতা** bloodfeud, vendetta.

দেউটি *n.* a lamp, a light.

দেউড়ি *n.* the main gate; a vestibule; a porch, a portico.

দেউল *n.* a temple, a shrine (দেবদেউল).

দেউলিয়া, (coll.) **দেউলে** *a.* bank insolvent; beggared.

দেওয়া *v.* to give; to confer (on), to bestow (খেতাব দেওয়া) ; to award (পুরস্কার দেওয়া) ; to distribute (বেঁটে দেওয়া) ; to give out of charity (ভিক্ষা বা বর দেওয়া) ; to donate (চাঁদা দেওয়া) ; to provide (ভাতকাপড় দেওয়া) ; to give in marriage, to marry (to), to wed (বড়ো বংশে মেয়ে দেওয়া) ; to impart (উপদেশ দেওয়া) ; to sacrifice (পরার্থে জীবন দেওয়া) ; to sprinkle (গাছে জল দেওয়া) ; to spray (গায়ে রং দেওয়া) ; to add or mix (দুধে জল দেওয়া) ; to administer (রোগে ওষুধ দেওয়া) ; to sell (for) or give in exchange (দশ টাকায় একখানা কাপড় দেওয়া) ; to ascribe (নাম দেওয়া) ; to impute (দোষ দেওয়া) ; to render or extend (ধন্যবাদ দেওয়া) ; to pay (পরীক্ষার ফি দেওয়া) ; to repay (শোধ দেওয়া) ; to spare (সময় দেওয়া) ; to allow (ভাবতে সময় দাও) ; to furnish with (ঠেকনো দেওয়া) ; to lean (ভর বা ঠেস দেওয়া) ; to place (রোদে দেওয়া) ; to build or construct (বেড়া দেওয়া) ; to put on (গায়ে দেওয়া, পায়ে মোজা দেওয়া) ; to hold over (মাথায় ছাতা দেওয়া) ; to offer or dedicate (দেবতাকে নৈবেদ্য দেওয়া) ; to yield or produce (গোরু দুধ দেয়, গাছ ফল দেয়) ; to deal or inflict (ঘা দেওয়া, মার দেওয়া) ; to set (কাজে হাত দেওয়া, বলে পা দেওয়া) ; to shut or close or bolt (ঘরের দরজা দেওয়া) ; to fasten (খিল দেওয়া) ; to give in or arrange for (বিয়ে দেওয়া) ; to execute (ফাঁসি দেওয়া) ; to entrust (ভার দেওয়া), to employ in, to put to (চাকরি দেওয়া, লজ্জা দেওয়া) ; to write (চিঠিতে তারিখ দেওয়া) ; to paint (ফোঁটা দেওয়া) ; to sew or stitch (কাপড়ে তালি দেওয়া) ; to affix (চিঠিতে টিকিট দেওয়া) to post (ডাকে চিঠি দেওয়া) ; to cast (দৃষ্টি দেওয়া) ; to send (ছেলেকে স্কুলে দেওয়া) ; to intimate, to inform, to apprise (সংবাদ দেওয়া) ; to grant or sanction (ছুটি দেওয়া) ; to permit, to allow, to let (যেতে দেওয়া) ; to accord (অনুমোদন দেওয়া) ; to sow or scatter (জমিতে বীজ দেওয়া) ; to thrust into (গলায় আঙুল দেওয়া) ; to pierce with (বুকে ছুরি দেওয়া) ; to keep out (বাদ দেওয়া) ; to strike in unison, to keep time (তাল দেওয়া) ; to set (গানে সুর দেওয়া) ; to pronounce (রায় দেওয়া) ; to pass (মতামত দেওয়া) ; to impose or inflict (শাস্তি দেওয়া) ; to lend (ঋণ বা ধার দেওয়া) ; to sharpen, to whet (ধার দেওয়া) ; to serve (টেবিলে খাবার দেওয়া) ; to supply (হাসপাতালে খাবার দেওয়া) ; to complete as an action (ফেলে দেওয়া). □ *a.* given (দেওয়া জিনিস) ; conferred, bestowed; awarded; distributed; offered; dedicated.

দেওয়ান *n.* a finance minister; a financial

steward (as of a business concern) or of a landowner; a steward; a dewan. **দেওয়ান-ই-আম** a sovereign's court, a royal court, a durbar; a legislative assembly. **দেওয়ান-ই-খাস** *n.* the private council of a sovereign, a privy-council. **দেওয়ানি** *n.* office of a finance minister; stewardship; dewani, diwani. □ *a.* (law) civil. **দেওয়ানি আদালত** civil court. **দেওয়ানি মামলা** *a.* civil suit.

দেওয়ানা *n.* one who has renounced the world for the sake of some particular object; one who is mentally obsessed or deranged. □ *a.* renouncing the world; mentally obsessed or deranged.

দেওয়ানি see **দেওয়ান**।

দেওয়ানো *v.* to cause to give or confer or bestow or award or distribute or provide or impart or sprinkle or add or administer or ascribe or impute or render or extend or pay or repay or furnish or put or place or set up or build or construct or put on or offer or dedicate or yield or produce or deal or inflict or employ or apply or shut or bolt or fasten or accomplish or execute or entrust or write or paint or sew or stitch or affix or put in or cast or send or intimate or inform or grant or sanction or permit or sow or scatter or thrust into or pierce or rub or keep or strike or set or impose upon or take to or pronounce or pass or impose or lend or sharpen or whet or serve or supply or complete.

দেওয়াল *n.* a wall. **দেওয়াল তোলা, দেওয়াল দেওয়া** *v.* to raise or build a wall. **দেওয়াল দিয়ে ঘেরা বা বন্ধ করা** *v.* to wall up. **দেওয়াল ঘড়ি** *n.* a wall-clock. **দেওয়াল-পঞ্জি** *n.* a wall-calendar. **দেওয়াল-লিখন** *n.* writing on the wall.

দেওয়ালি *n.* the day of the new-moon in the month of Kartik (কার্তিক) when Goddess Kali (কালী) is worshipped and the dwelling house of Hindus are illuminated with rows of lighted lamps. **দেওয়ালি-পোকা** *n.* a variety of Lepidoptera that are found in late autumn nights when they scorch themselves by fluttering about a burning substance.

দেওর *n.* a younger brother of one's husband, a brother-in-law. **~ঝি** *n.* a daughter of one's husband's younger brother. **~পো** *n.* a son of one's husband's younger brother.

দেঁতো *a.* large-toothed; tusked; tusky; displaying one's teeth; (fig.) insincere or forced (দেঁতো হাসি).

দেখ *v. int.* I say, mind, take care.

দেখতা *a.* seen; occurring before one's eyes. □ *adv.* before one's eyes; contemporaneously.

দেখন *n.* act of seeing or looking or beholding or viewing. **দেখন-হাসি** *a.* one who smiles at first sight; one who makes one smile in delight at first sight; (dero.) one who always greets with a smile.

দেখভাল *n.* supervision, overseeing; taking care of.

দেখা *v.* to see, to behold, to view, to notice, to espy; to look (at); to visit (চিড়িয়াখানা দেখতে যাব) ; to experience directly (দেখে শেখা) ; to judge or consider (অবস্থা দেখা) ; to examine (পরীক্ষার খাতা দেখা) ; to observe (যুদ্ধের গতি দেখা) ; to inspect (অডিটর হিসাব দেখবেন) ; to feel (নাড়ি দেখা) ; to attend on or nurse (অসুস্থ লোকটিকে দেখা) ; to attend to, to look after (জমিজমা দেখা) ; to treat (এ রোগীকে কোন ডাক্তার দেখছে) ; to witness (থিয়েটার দেখা, খেলা দেখা) ; to search (চাকরি দেখা) ; to come across, to meet (পথে একটা পাগল দেখলাম) ; to read through (বইয়ের শেষ পাতা দেখো) ; to think (ছেলেটা বকে গেছে দেখছি) ; to endeavour, to try (আর দেখে লাভ কী—এ রোগী বাঁচবে না) ; to think over (ভেবে দেখা) ; to take to or follow (নিজের পথ দেখো) ; to wait (আর খানিকক্ষণ দেখি—হয়তো সে আসবে). □ *a.* seen, beheld, viewed, noticed, espied; visited; experienced; examined; inspected; read. **দেখতে কুৎসিত** ugly to look at, ugly-looking. **দেখতে ভালো, দেখতে সুন্দর** good or beautiful to look at, good-looking; beautiful, handsome. **দেখতে-দেখতে** *adv.* very soon; within a short while; in an instant; gradually. **দেখা করা** *v.* to call on, to see. **দেখা যাক** let me or let us try; let us wait.

দেখাদেখি *n.* mutual seeing or meeting or visits (তাদের দেখাদেখি নেই, মুখ দেখাদেখি) ; an act of copying from another's paper by adoption of unfair means (as by examinees). □ *adv.* in imitation of (বাপের দেখাদেখি ছেলেও মদ ধরল). **দেখানো** *v.* to cause to see; to show; to point out; to demonstrate; to exhibit; to display; to cause to experience directly (মজা দেখানো) ; to cause to examine or inspect; to cause to feel; to cause to treat; to take (to) for enjoyment; to bear the expenses of (থিয়েটার দেখানো). **দেখানিয়া, দেখানে** *a.* (chiefly used as a *sfx.*) ostentatiously formal; showy, ostentatious; pretended, affected. **~শোনা, ~শুনা** *n.* act of looking after; attendance; supervision; direct experience (এ জীবনে অনেক দেখাশোনা হল) ; examination or inspection (অনেক দেখা-শোনার পর সে মালটা কিনল) ; a visit esp. for examination or negotiation (পাত্রপক্ষ দেখাশোনা করে গেছে) ; meeting (দুজনে দেখাশোনা নেই). **দেখাশোনা করা** *v.* to look after; to attend to or on; to supervise; to examine or inspect; to visit esp. for examination or negotiation; to meet or visit mutually. **~সাক্ষাৎ** *n.* meeting or visits; continuous or repeated visits; a visit for negotiation of a marriage. **দেখে শুনে** *adv.* from what one has seen or experienced. **দেখে শেখা** *v.* to learn from experience; to learn from example; to learn in imitation of.

দেড় *n.* & *a.* one and a half (of). **~গুণ** *a.* one and a half times (of).

দেড়া *a.* one and a half times (of).

দেড়ে, দেড়েল *a.* having a beard (esp. a long one), (long-) bearded.

দেদার *a.* plentiful, abundant, profuse, a lot of; innumerable; immeasurable.

দেদীপ্যমান *a.* very brightly flaming or blazing; brilliantly shining; effulgent.

দেদো *a.* stricken with ringworm.

দেধান *n.* millet, durra, jowar.

দেনদার see **দেনা**।

দেনমোহর *n.* (Mus.) the marriage portion or dower that a husband has to allot for his wife at wedding.

দেনা *n.* a debt; an outstanding payment or bill, a liability; dues. **দেনা করা** *v.* to borrow; to run into a debt. **দেনা থাকা** *v.* to be indebted. **দেনা দেওয়া** *v.* to repay a debt; to acquit oneself of debts. **দেনায় ডুবু-ডুবু** over head and ears in debt. **দেনায় মাথার চুল বিকানো** (lit.) to have to sell one's hair in order to repay debts; (fig.) to be on one's last legs to pay off one's debts. **~দার, দেনদার** *n.* a debtor; a borrower. □ *a.* indebted. **দেনা-পাওনা** *n.* assets and liabilities.

দেনো *a.* worth giving; given as a present or offering as in a religious ceremony (দেনো গামছা) ; given as a gift or present.

দেব *n.* God; a male deity, a god; (in respectful address) a king, a master, an elder, a father, a husband, a preceptor, a guru, a teacher, a Brahman, any person commanding respect; (as a *sfx.*) the chief or best man (ভূদেব, নরদেব). **~কণ্ঠ** *a.* having a god-like voice. *fem.* **~কণ্ঠী**। **~কন্যা** *n. fem.* a celestial female, a daughter of heaven. **~কল্প** *a.* godly, godlike; perfectly holy or beautiful. **~কার্য** *n.* a divine mission; a task enjoined by God or a god, religious worship. **~কাষ্ঠ** *n.* deodar. **~কুল** *n.* a temple, a shrine; the race of gods. **~কৃপা** *n.* divine grace. **~খাত** *n.* a natural lake or lagoon. **~গুরু** *n.* Brihaspati (বৃহস্পতি) the teacher of gods. **~গৃহ** *n.* a house of worship, a temple, a shrine. **~চরিত্র** *a.* & *n.* (having) a divinely pure or saintly character. **~চিকিৎসক** *n.* the physician of the gods, the heavenly physician. **~তরু** *n.* any of the five celestial trees; mandar (মন্দার), parijat (পারিজাত), santan (সন্তান) ; kalpabriksha (কল্পবৃক্ষ) and harichandan (হরিচন্দন). **~তা** *n.* a goddess; a god; a deity; (fig.) an object of worship or deep reverence (স্বামীই স্ত্রীর দেবতা). **~তুল্য** *a.* godly, godlike. **~ত্ব** *n.* godhead, divinity; godliness. **দেবত্বারোপ** *n.* ascription of divinity, apotheosis. **~ত্র** *n.* a property endowed for defraying the cost of worshipping a deity. **~দত্ত** *a.* godgifted. **~দর্শন** *n.* a visit to pay homage to an idol; a pilgrimage to the seat of a god. **~দারু** *n.* deodar. **~দাসী** *n.* a woman dedicated to the service of an idol of a particular temple. **~দুর্লভ** *a.* even difficult for gods to obtain; rare even amongst gods (দেবদুর্লভ কান্তি). **~দূত** *n.* a heavenly messenger, an angel. *fem.* **~দূতী**। **~দেব** *n.* a god of gods; an appellation of Brahma (ব্রহ্মা), Vishnu (বিষ্ণু) and Shiva (শিব). **~দ্বিজ** *n. pl.* gods and Brahmans (দেবদ্বিজে ভক্তি). **~দ্বেষী** *a.* hostile or inimical to gods; anti-God; godless, atheistic. □ *n.* any one of the mythological demons hostile to gods. **~ধান্য** *n.* millet, durra, jowar. **~ধূপ** *n.* bdellium. **~নাগর, ~নাগরী** *n.* a script in which Sanskrit is written. **~নিষ্ঠা** *n.* devotion to gods. **~পতি** same as **দেবরাজ**। **~পথ** *n.* the celestial path, the sky, the firmament. **~পশু** *n.* a creature earmarked to be immolated at a holy sacrifice. **~পুরী** *n.* the city of gods, Paradise; (fig.) a very beautiful house or residence. **~পূজক** *n.* a votary or worshipper of gods; a priest. **~পূজা** *n.* worship of a deity; religious worship. **~প্রতিম** *a.* godlike; godly. **~প্রতিমা** *n.* an idol; an image of a deity, a holy image. **~প্রতিষ্ঠা** *n.* the ceremony of establishing an idol at a particular place. **~প্রসাদ** *n.* grace or kindness of the gods. **~প্রিয়** *a.* beloved of gods. **~বাক্য, ~বাণী** *n.* the voice of God; a divine or heavenly voice; an oracle. **~বৈদ্য** same as **দেবচিকিৎসক**। **~ভক্ত** *a.* devoted to gods; pious. **~ভক্তি** *n.* devotion to gods; godliness; piety. **~ভাষা** *n.* the Sanskrit language. **~ভূমি** *n.* heaven; paradise; the Himalayas; a place of pilgrimage, a holy place; (fig.) an extremely beautiful place. **~ভোগ্য** *a.* fit to be enjoyed by gods, fit for divine consumption. **~মন্দির** *n.* a temple, a shrine. **~মহিমা** *n.* divine greatness or grandeur or glory or splendour. **~মাতা** *n.* Aditi (অদিতি) the first mother of gods. **~মাতৃক** *a.* (of a country) nursed by rain. **~যান** *n.* a celestial chariot or car; a path which leads the wise to heaven; an aeroplane. **~যোনি** *n.* a ghost, a spirit; a demigod. **~রথ** *n.* a celestial chariot or car; the chariot of the sun-god; a path leading the wise to heaven; an aeroplane. **~রাজ** *n.* Indra (ইন্দ্র) the king of gods, (cp. Zeus, Jove, Jupiter). **~র্ষি** *n.* one who is both a god and a saint, a celestial saint. **~ল** *n.* a priestly Brahman. □ *a.* employed in priestly service (দেবল ব্রাহ্মণ). **~লোক** *n.* the abode of gods, heaven. **~শর্মা** *n.* a general surname used of Brahmans. **~শিল্পী** *n.* Vishwakarma (বিশ্বকর্মা) the celestial artisan and designer, (cp.) Vulcan). **~সভা** *n.* the assembly of gods; the court of Indra (ইন্দ্র) the king of gods. **~সেনা** *n.* the army of gods; the wife of Kartikeya (কার্তিকেয়) the commander of the army of gods. **~সেনাপতি** *n.* Kartikeya (কার্তিকেয়) the commander of the army of gods. **~স্ব** *n.* a property endowed for defraying the cost of worshipping a deity; a god's property; (loos.) a religious endowment.

দেবর *n.* a younger brother of one's husband, a brother-in-law.

দেবা *n.* (dero. & sarcas.) a god or a man (**'যেমন দেবা, তেমনি দেবী'** = like man, like wife).

দেবাঙ্গনা *n.* a celestial woman.

দেবাত্মা *a.* godlike; divine; holy.

দেবাদিদেব *n.* the supreme god, the chief of gods; an appellation of Shiva (শিব), Vishnu (বিষ্ণু) and Brahma (ব্রহ্মা).

দেবাদেশ same as **দৈবাদেশ**।

দেবানুগ্রহ same as **দৈবানুগ্রহ**।

দেবায়তন *n.* a house of a god, a temple, a shrine.

দেবায়ুধ *n.* a god's weapon; a divine or celestial weapon; the rainbow.

দেবারাধনা same as **দেবার্চনা**।

দেবারি *n.* an enemy of gods; a mythological demon; a rakshasa (রাক্ষস).

দেবার্চন, দেবার্চনা *n.* the worship of God or of a god; religious worship.

দেবালয় same as **দেবায়তন**।

দেবাশ্রিত *a.* protected or patronized by a god or gods, under a god's protection or care; in a god's favour or good grace.

দেবাসুর *n.* gods and mythological demons.

দেবী *n.* a goddess; a female deity; Goddess Durga (দুর্গা) or Chandi (চণ্ডী) ; (in respectful addresses and mention) a lady (মাতৃদেবী, সারদাদেবী). **~পক্ষ** *n.* the light fortnight of the Durga worship. **~পুরাণ** *n.* an ancient holy book narrating the glory of Goddess Chandi (চণ্ডী). **~মাহাত্ম্য** *n.* a portion of a holy book, written by Markandeya (মার্কণ্ডেয়) the sage singing of the glory of Goddess Chandi (চণ্ডী).

দবেন্দ্র *n.* the lord or king of gods; an appellation of Indra (ইন্দ্র).

দবেশ *n.* the god of gods; an appellation of Shiva (শিব).

দবোচিত *a.* befitting a god, right and proper for a god; godly; divine.

দবোত্তর coll. corrup. of **দেবত্র** (see **দেব**).

দবোদ্যান *n.* a heavenly garden, (cp. Eden, Paradise); a garden which is the seat of a deity, a holy garden.

বোপম *a.* godlike, godly.

বোপাসক *n.* a votary or worshipper of a god or gods. □ *a.* employed in religious worship.

বোপাসনা *n.* worship of a god or gods; religious worship.

ব্যা *n.* (inc. & obs.) a goddess; used as a surname affixed to the name of a (widowed Brahman) lady.

মাক *n.* self-conceit, vanity, amour-propre; haughtiness, arrogance. **দেমাক করা** *v.* to brag, to boast, to be proud of; to give oneself airs. **দেমাক দেখানো** *v.* to express anger or haughtiness. **দেমাকি** *a.* vain, conceited; arrogant, haughty.

য় *a.* that which is to be given or worth giving; due payable.

য়ক *n.* fee.

য়া[1] pop. contr. of **দেওয়া**।

য়া[2] *n.* the cloud. **দেয়ার ডাক** the roar or rumble of clouds. **গুরুগুরু দেয়া ডাকে** the clouds rumble.

য়াল coll. contr. of **দেওয়াল**।

য়ালা *n.* the smile of a dreaming infant.

য়ালি coll. contr. of **দেওয়ালি**।

য়াসি *n.* a votary.

দেয়াসিনি *n. fem.* a votaress or female worshipper; a nun; a woman versed in mystic incantations.

দেরকো *n.* a wooden lampstand.

দেরাজ *n.* a drawer (as of a cabinet or a desk).

দেরি *n.* delay. **দেরি করা** *v.* to be late; to delay. **দেরি করানো** *v.* to defer, to procrastinate, to delay; to cause to delay. **দেরি হওয়া** *v.* to be late; to be delayed.

দেশ *n.* a country, a land; a state; a province (বঙ্গদেশ, অঙ্গদেশ) ; motherland, native land (কাফ্রিদের দেশ আফ্রিকায়) ; native village (ছেলেটি সবে দেশ থেকে শহরে এসেছে) ; a region (মরুদেশ) ; a place (পৃষ্ঠদেশ) ; a part or portion (মধ্যদেশ) ; a direction or quarter (অধোদেশ) ; a raga or musical mode. **~কাল** *n.* a particular place and a point of time or their nature or condition; a particular circumstance. **~কালজ্ঞ** *a.* conversant with the nature of a particular place and time or with that of different places and points of time. **~কালপাত্র** *n.* a particular place and a point of time and a person or their nature or condition. **~কালাতীত** *a.* transcending space and time, universal and eternal. **~কালোচিত** *a.* befitting and serving the needs of a particular place and a point of time; befitting the circumstances. **~খ্যাত** *a.* same as **দেশপ্রসিদ্ধ**। **~ছাড়া** *a.* away from home; away from one's motherland. **~গৌরব** *n.* pride of a or of one's country. **~জ, ~জাত** *a.* indigenous. **~জোড়া** same as **দেশব্যাপী**। **~ত্যাগ** *n.* leaving a country or one's own country (esp. for good), emigration or migration from one's native land. **দেশত্যাগ করা** *v.* to leave a country or one's own country (esp. for good); to emigrate or migrate. **~ত্যাগী** *a.* (also *n.*) emigrant, migrant. **~দেশান্তর** *n.* one's native land and other countries; countries far and near, different countries. **~দ্রোহ** *n.* treason or treachery against one's own country or state. **~দ্রোহী** *a.* committing treason or treachery against one's own country or state. **~ধর্ম** *n.* customs and practices peculiar to a country. ~পর্যটন same as দেশভ্রমণ। ~প্রথা same as দেশধর্ম। ~প্রসিদ্ধ *a.* famous all over the country. ~প্রিয় *a.* beloved of one's countrymen. ~প্রেম *n.* attachment to or love for one's motherland, patriotism. ~প্রেমিক *n.* a lover of one's motherland, a patriot. ~বন্ধু *n.* a friend of the country; the friend of one's own country. ~বিখ্যাত same as দেশপ্রসিদ্ধ। ~বিদেশ *n.* one's native land and foreign countries, home and abroad. ~বিদেশে *adv.* at home and abroad; all over the world. ~বিশ্রুত same as দেশপ্রসিদ্ধ। ~বিধান *n.* customs and conventions peculiar to a country. ~ব্যাপী *a.* countrywide. ~বিভাগ *n.* the partition of a country. ~ভেদে *adv.* according to the change of countries; in different lands. ~ভ্রমণ *n.* travel in different lands, journeying from country to country; travel in different parts of a country. দেশভ্রমণ করা *v.* to travel in different countries or in different parts of a country. ~ময় *a.* countrywide. □ *adv.* all over the country. ~মাতৃকা *n.* a country conceived or personified as the mother of its inhabitants; motherland. ~রক্ষা *n.* the defence of a country. দেশরক্ষা-মন্ত্রক *n.* the ministry of defence. ~সেবক *n.* a servant of one's motherland. ~সেবা *n.* service to one's motherland. ~স্থ *a.* situated or living in a country; (loos.) of or concerning a country, internal; (loos.) indigenous. ~হিত *n.* welfare of a country. ~হিতকর *a.* beneficial to a country, conducive to a country's welfare. ~হিতব্রত *n.* avowed determination to do good to one's country. □ *a.* same as দেশহিতব্রতী। ~হিতব্রতী *a.* avowedly devoted to the welfare of one's country. ~হিতৈষণা, ~হিতৈষিতা *n.* desire of doing good to one's own country. ~হিতৈষী *a.* desirous of doing good to one's own country.

দেশলাই coll. var. of দিয়াশলাই।

দেশাচার *n.* customs and practices peculiar to a country.

দেশাত্মবোধ *n.* act of identifying oneself with one's country; nationalism.

দেশাধিপতি *n.* the ruler of a country; a king.

দেশান্তর *n.* another country, a different country; a distant land; (geog.) longitude. দেশান্তরিত *a.* gone to another country or a different country; gone to a distant or foreign land; expelled from a country or from one's country; living and settled in a foreign country. দেশান্তরি *a.* gone to a foreign country; emigrant, migrant; living or settled in a foreign country.

দেশি *a.* indigenous. □ *n.* a musical mode. দেশি কাপড় a variety of loincloth produced by the weavers of Bengal on handlooms; cloth manufactured in India (as opp. to বিলাতি). দেশি কুমড়ো see কুমড়ো। দেশি জিনিস, দেশি পণ্য a home product; indigenous goods.

দেশিক *n.* a traveller; one who guides along the right path or shows the way to salvation; a preceptor (দেশিকোত্তম).

দেশী alt. spell. of দেশি।

দেশীয় *a.* concerning a particular country or home affairs; inland, internal; born in a particular country, native; indigenous. ~করণ *n.* naturalization. দেশীয় কলহ an internal strife. দেশীয় বাণিজ্য inland trade. দেশীয় ব্যাপার home affairs. দেশীয় হানাহানি a civil war.

দেশোয়ালি *n.* a rustic; a co-villager; an upcountryman. দেশোয়ালি ভাই (ridi.) a country cousin; a person hailing from the same country or region.

দেশ্য same as দেশীয়।

দেহ *n.* the body; physique; a corpse. দেহ মাটি করা *v.* (fig.) to ruin one's health. ~কোষ *n.* the skin; the cell of the body; (loos.) a blood-cell or blood-vessel. ~ক্ষয় *n.* waste or decay of the body; deterioration or break-down of health; death. দেহক্ষয় করা *v.* to ruin one's health (esp. by hard toil). ~চর্যা *n.* care of the body or physique; physical exercise. ~জ, ~জাত *a.* born or produced out of body; bodily (দেহজ মল). □ *n.* a son. *fem.* ~জা a daughter. ~তত্ত্ব *n.* physiology; anatomy; the doctrine that the body is the seat of all truths. ~তত্ত্বজ্ঞ

versed in physiology or anatomy or in the aforesaid doctrine. ~ত্যাগ *n.* death, act of giving up the ghost. **দেহত্যাগ করা** *v.* to die, to give up the ghost. ~**ধারণ** *n.* act of assuming a body; act of taking one's birth; incarnation; subsistence (দেহধারণের ব্যয়). **দেহধারণ করা** *v.* to assume a body; to take one's birth; to assume an incarnate body or to take one's birth as an incarnation ; to subsist (upon). ~**ধারী** *a.* corporeal; bodied; incarnate. ~**পাত** same as **দেহক্ষয়। দেহপাত করা** *v.* samc as **দেহক্ষয় করা।** ~**পিঞ্জর** *n.* the body conceived as a cage for the spirit. ~**পুষ্টি** *n.* nourishment of the body. ~**ভৃৎ** *n.* an embodied soul; a living being, a creature. ~**যষ্টি** *n.* the body, conceived as an upright stick, the body, the frame. ~**যাত্রা** *n.* subsistence. ~**রক্ষা** *n.* death. **দেহরক্ষা করা** *v.* to die, to breathe one's last, to give up the ghost. ~**রক্ষী** *n.* a body-guard. ~**সার** *n.* marrow. ~**সৌন্দর্য,** ~**সৌষ্ঠব** *n.* the beauty or grace of the body, bodily grace.

হলি *n.* a terrace; a gallery, a verandah; a door-sill; a door-frame.

হা *n.* (poet. & obs.) the body or life.

হাত *n.* a village, countryside.

হাতি *a.* rural; rustic.

হাতীত, দেহাতিরিক্ত *a.* beyond (the reach) of the body, transcending the body, transcendental; not incorporate, unembodied, incorporeal.

হাত্মপ্রত্যয় *n.* the belief in the identity of the body and the soul, the belief that the body is the soul; materialistic belief.

হাত্মবাদ *n.* the doctrine of the identity of the body and the soul (that is, body is the soul); materialism. **দেহাত্মবাদী** *a.* identifying the body and the soul; materialistic. □ *n.* a believer in the identity of the body and the soul; a materialist.

হান্ত *n.* death. **দেহান্ত হওয়া** *v.* to meet one's death, to die.

হান্তর *n.* another body; rebirth; (loos.) death. ~**প্রাপ্তি** *n.* the transmigration of soul, metempsychosis, rebirth. **দেহান্তর লাভ করা** *v.* to migrate into another body; to be born again; (loos. but pop.) to die.

দেহাবসান *n.* death. **দেহাবসান হওয়া** *v.* to meet one's death, to die.

দেহালা obs. var. of **দেয়ালা।**

দেহি *v. imperat.* give.

দেহী *a.* corporeal, bodied; material.

দেহোপজীবিনী *n. fem.* a women who earns by engaging herself in sexual activity, a prostitute, a whore.

দৈ rej. spell. of **দই।**

দৈত্য *n.* a mythological demon hostile to gods; a giant, a monster, an ogre; a gigantic man. ~**কুল** *n.* the race of demons. **দৈত্যকুলে প্রহ্লাদ** (fig.) a saint born in the race of sinners, a Christ amongst Jews. ~**গুরু** *n.* (myth.) Shukracharya the guru or preceptor of demons. ~**নিসূদন** *n.* a slayer of demons. ~**পতি** *n.* a king of demons. ~**মাতা** *n.* (myth.) Diti (দিতি) the first mother of demons. **দৈত্যারি** *n.* an enemy of demons; a god; an appellation of Vishnu (বিষ্ণু), Shiva (শিব), Indra (ইন্দ্র) or Krishna (কৃষ্ণ).

দৈনন্দিন *a.* daily; diurnal; (fig.) routine (দৈনন্দিন কাজকর্ম).

দৈনিক *a.* daily; diurnal. □ *n.* a daily newspaper, a daily. **দৈনিক অধিদেয়** বা **ভাতা** daily allowance. **দৈনিক পত্রিকা** *n.* a daily newspaper, a daily.

দৈন্য *n.* utter poverty or need, indigence; affliction, distress; humbleness; wretchedness, misery; penury. ~**দশা, দৈন্যাবস্থা** *n.* utter poverty, indigent condition; afflicted or distressed or humble or wretched or miserable state. ~**দশাগ্রস্ত,** ~**দশাপন্ন,** ~**পীড়িত** *a.* poverty-stricken, indigent; afflicted, distressed; wretched, miserable; penurious.

দৈব *n.* providence; destiny; luck, fate; a chance occurrence. □ *a.* pertaining to or caused by gods, divine, heavenly; providential; accidental; miraculous. ~**কর্ম** *n.* rites performed to propitiate gods or deities; a religious rite. ~**ক্রমে,** ~**গতিকে** *adv.* by providence; by chance; accidentally, luckily; (rare) miraculously. ~**ঘটনা** *n.* a providential incident;

a chance occurrence; a miraculous incident; an accident. ~জ্ঞ *a.* prescient. □ *n.* a diviner, a prognosticator, a soothsayer; a fortune teller, an astrologer. ~দুর্ঘটনা *n.* a mishap, an accident. ~দুর্বিপাক *n.* a misfortune, an unforeseen calamity or adversity. ~দোষ *n.* misfortune, ill fate, ill luck. ~দোষে *adv.* through ill luck. ~ধন *n.* heaven-sent treasure; a treasure found by chance, a windfall; (loos.) a hidden treasure. ~নির্দিষ্ট *a.* ordained by God; predestined, foreordained. ~প্রেরিত *a.* heaven-sent. ~বল same as দৈবশক্তি। ~বশে same as দৈবক্রমে। ~বাণী *n.* an oracle; a voice from heaven (conveying a divine message), the word of God, a revelation; a prophecy. ~বিড়ম্বনা *n.* irony of fate; antipathy of fortune; misfortune. ~যোগে same as দৈবক্রমে। ~লব্ধ *a.* obtained by chance; god-gifted. ~শক্তি *n.* divine power; god-gifted power. ~শক্তিসম্পন্ন *a.* endowed with god-gifted power.

দৈবাৎ *adv.* by chance; accidentally; suddenly; peradventure.

দৈবাদেশ *n.* a divine command; a commandment; a divine inspiration; (loos.) an oracle.

দৈবাধীন *n.* dependent on fate, controlled by destiny, fateful.

দৈবানুগৃহীত *a.* received in the grace of God; favoured by a god or gods.

দৈবানুগ্রহ *n.* grace of God; divine favour. দৈবানুগ্রহে *adv.* by Gods' grace, through the grace of God.

দৈবায়ত্ত same as দৈবাধীন।

দৈবী *a. fem.* of দৈব। ~শক্তি same as দৈবশক্তি and দৈববল।

দৈর্ঘ্য *n.* length. দৈর্ঘ্য-প্রসারণ *n.* linear expansion.

দৈশিক *a.* concerning a country or a province or a region or a locality, native, provincial, regional, local; concerning a part; partial.

দৈহিক *a.* corporeal (দৈহিক প্রয়োজন); bodily, physical; corporal (দৈহিক শাস্তি). দৈহিক পরিশ্রম physical labour.

দো *a.* (chiefly used as *pfx.*) two, twofold, twice. ~আনি *n.* a two-anna piece. ~আব *n.* a tongue of land between two rivers a doab; (ori.) a confluence of two rivers. ~আঁশ *a.* loamy. দোআঁশ মাটি loamy soil, loam. ~আঁশলা, (rej.) ~আঁসলা *a* hybrid; crossbred; mongrel; loamy. □ *n.* a hybrid; a crossbreed; a mongrel ~কর *a.* two times of, double. □ *adv* twice, two times, doubly. ~কলা, ~কা *a* & *adv.* only two together; in pair; having a companion or second. ~কাটি *n* two sticks; two sticks striking agains each other. ~চালা same as দুচালা (see দু ~ছুট, ~ছোট *n.* a piece of large scar worn loosely on the upper part of th body. ~টানা same as দুটানা (see দু ~তরফা same as দুতরফা (see দু). ~তল দোতালা same as দুতলা (see দু). ~তা same as দুতারা (see দু). ~ধারী same a দুধারী (see দু). ~নলা same as দুনলা (se দু). ~পাট্টা *a.* arranged into two fold folded in two parts; double-folde joined together lengthwise (দোপা চাদর). ~পিয়াজি, ~পিয়াজা, ~পিঁয়াজি ~পিঁয়াজা *n.* a highly seasoned dish meat or fish prepared with too man onions doubly fried. ~পেয়ে same দুপেয়ে (see দু). ~ফলা same as দুফলা (se দু). ~ফাল, ~ফালি same as দুফাল (see দু ~বরা *a.* doubly refined and granul (দোবরা চিনি). □ *adv.* twice over (দোব কাজ করা). ~ভাঁজ *a.* doubly folde folded in two plaits, doubled. ~ভা same as দুভাষী (see দু). ~মনা same দুমনা (see দু). ~মুখো same as দুমুখো (se দু). ~মেটে same as দুমেটে (see দু). ~য়া pop. spell. of দোআনি। ~য়াব pop. spel of দোআব। ~রঙা *a.* bi-coloured. ~রক ~রোকা *a.* embroidered on both side ~রসা *a.* (of fish etc.) partly decon posed or rotten, half-decomposed half-rotten; (of soil) loamy. ~শালা *n.* shawl woven in double plaits, a doub plaited shawl; any one of a pair costly shawls. ~সুতি same as দুসুতি (s দু). ~হাতিয়া, ~হাথিয়া, ~হাত্তা same দুহাতিয়া (see দু).

দোঁহা¹ *n.* a kind of Hindi couplet curre in the mediaeval age.

দোঁহা², দোঁহে *pro.* (poet.) two or bot

দোঁহার, দোঁহাকার *poss. pro.* of two or both.

দোকান *n.* a shop; goods for sale, merchandise (মেলায় দোকান সাজানো). **দোকান করা** *v.* to visit shops for the purpose of buying, to shop; to set up a shop, to start or open a shop; to keep or run a shop; to open a shop for the day's work. **দোকান খোলা** *v.* to set up a shop, to start or open a shop; to open a shop for the day's work. **দোকান তোলা** *v.* to close a shop for the day; to close down or wind up a shop, to shut up a shop. **দোকান দেওয়া** *v.* to set up or open a shop; to arrange goods for sale (as in a fair). **দোকান বন্ধ করা** same as **দোকান তোলা।** **দোকান সাজানো** *v.* to furnish a shop, to display goods for sale. **দোকান-কর্মচারী** *n.* a shop-man. **~দার** *n.* a shopkeeper. **~দারি** *n.* shopkeeping; bargaining; business-dealing; bargain-hunting, shoppiness; shoppy or selfish behaviour. **দোকানদারি করা** *v.* to keep or run a shop; (fig.) to try to clinch a bargain. **দোকানদারি কথাবার্তা** shoppy talk. **দোকানদারি কথাবার্তা বলা** to talk shop. **~পাট** *n.* a shop and its commodities. **দোকান-হাট করা** *v.* to visit shops and markets for the purpose of buying.

দোকানি *n.* a shopkeeper.

দোক্তা, দোক্‌তা *n.* dried tobacco-leaf (often perfumed) for chewing. **দোক্তা খাওয়া** *v.* to take dried tobacco-leaf.

দোগ্ধা *a.* one who milks (as a cow).

দোগ্ধ্রী *a. fem.* of **দোগ্ধা।** □ *n.* a milch cow.

দোজখ *n.* (Mus.) hell, inferno.

দোজবরে, দোজ়বর *a. masc.* married or marrying for a second time.

দোটানা *n.* simultaneous pulls in two opposite directions; indecision, dilemma.

দোদুল *a.* moving to and fro, swinging, oscillating, dangling; wavering. **দোদুল্যমান** *a.* constantly swinging or oscillating; constantly wavering. **দোদুল্যমান হওয়া** *v.* to swing or oscillate constantly; to waver constantly.

দোনা[১] *n.* pocket for holding a roll of betel-leaf.

দোনা[২] *n.* a dug-out, a tub, a canoe.

দোনি *n.* a small dug-out.

দোপাটি *n.* a kind of flower or its plant, a flower of the balsam species.

দোবজা *n.* a kind of large and coarse cotton scarf.

দোমড়ানো pop. var. of **দুমড়ানো।**

দোমালা *a.* (of coconut) half-ripe.

দোয়া[১] *v.* to milk (as a cow); (fig.) to extort (money etc.) from (a person). **~নো** *v.* to cause to milk; to milk.

দোয়া[২] *n.* (Mus.) blessing, grace.

দোয়াত *n.* an ink-pot.

দোয়ার var. of **দোহার।**

দোয়েল *n.* the magpie robin of Bengal.

দোর coll. corrup. of **দ্বার।** **~গোড়া** *n.* door-step, threshold.

দোরমা pop. var. of **দোলমা।**

দোরস্ত coll. corrup. of **দুরস্ত।**

দোর্দণ্ড *n.* the hand conceived as the rod (of punishment). □ *a.* (erron.) terrible (দোর্দণ্ড ক্রোধ বা গরম). **~প্রতাপ** *a.* terribly powerful or mighty. □ *n.* the might of the hand; terrible might.

দোর্মা alt. spell. of **দোরমা।**

দোল *n.* a swing, a dangling movement; oscillation; the Hindu festival of Krishna's (কৃষ্ণ) swinging in a rocking cradle, when dyed powder is sprinkled at one another, the Holi (হোলি) festival. **দোল খাওয়া** *v.* to swing, to dangle, to oscillate. **দোল খাওয়ানো, দোল দেওয়া** *v.* to give a push so as to cause to swing; to cause to swing; to dangle, to oscillate. **দোল-দুর্গোৎসব** *n.* the principal festivals of Hindus such as the swinging feast of Krishna (কৃষ্ণ) and the worship of Durga (দুর্গা). **দোলন** *n.* act of swinging or dangling, oscillation; a swing. **দোলনকাল** *n.* the period of oscillation. **দোলনতল** *n.* the plane of oscillation. **~মঞ্চ** *n.* the altar on which the rocking cradle of Krishna (কৃষ্ণ) and his lady-love Radha (রাধা) is set up. **~যাত্রা** *n.* the feast of Krishna's (কৃষ্ণ) swing, when dyed powder is sprinkled at one another.

দোলক *n.* a pendulum (as of a clock).

দোলনা *n.* a rocking cradle, a swing.

দোলমা *n.* a kind of food prepared by stuffing a পটোল (a kitchen vegetable) with minced fish or meat etc.

দোলা[1] *v.* to swing, to rock, to oscillate, to dangle.

দোলা[2] *n.* a litter (esp. a ceremonial one); an improvised cot to carry a corpse to the crematorium; a rocking cradle.

দোলাই *n.* a kind of wrapper made of plaited cotton cloth.

দোলানো pop. var. of **দুলানো**।

দোলায়মান *a.* swinging; dangling, oscillating; vacillating, wavering; hesitating; wavering with suspicion.

দোলায়িত *a.* caused to swing or dangle or oscillate; hung; caused to vacillate or waver or hesitate. **~চিত্ত** *a.* having a mind wavering with indecision. □ *n.* a vacillating mind.

দোষ *n.* a sin; a vice; a guilt; a crime; an offence; a bad practice or tendency (ওই তার মহা দোষ) ; a weak point (esp. in one's character); a defect, a demerit; morbidity or derangement or weakness (চোখের দোষ, মাথার দোষ, বুকের দোষ) ; a blemish, a flaw, a fault, a lapse (দোষে পাওয়া) ; blame, calumny (দোষ দেওয়া) ; sinister influence (গ্রহের দোষ) ; inauspiciousness (যাত্রাকালে হাঁচি বড় দোষের). **দোষ করা** *v.* to commit a sin or crime or offence; to be in fault. **দোষ খণ্ডানো** *v.* to refute a charge; to free from a charge; (astrol.) to undo the sinister influence of a planet; to counteract inauspiciousness. **~স্খালন** *n.* exculpation; absolution; exoneration. **দোষস্খালন করা** *v.* to exculpate; to absolve; to exonerate. **দোষ খোঁজা** *v.* to try to find fault with. **দোষ ঘোচানো** same as **দোষ খণ্ডানো**। **দোষ দেওয়া** *v.* to accuse; to blame, to lay the blame on, to censure. **দোষ দেখা, দোষ ধরা** *v.* to notice a defect or fault in; to find fault with, to pick holes in; to take a fault into consideration, to count a fault against. **~গ্রাহী** *a.* given to fault-finding; captious. **~জ্ঞ** *a.* able to discern or distinguish merits and demerits. □ *n.* an erudite person; a physician. **~দর্শন** *n.* finding fault with; fault-finding. **~দর্শী** same as **দোষগ্রাহী**। **~স্বীকার** *n.* confession. **দোষ স্বীকার করা** *v.* to confess a fault or guilt or sin, to admit or acknowledge one's guilt.

দোষা *v.* to blame, to put blame on, to accuse, to impute fault to.

দোষাক্রান্ত, দোষান্বিত *a.* defective, faulty stricken with morbidity, morbid, diseased; affected with a vice, vicious.

দোষাদোষ *n.* merits and demerits; vices and virtues.

দোষান্বেষণ *n.* a search for a defect or fault (in); fault-finding. **দোষান্বেষণ করা** *v.* to search for a defect or fault (in); to find fault (with). **দোষান্বেষী** *a.* searching for a defect or fault (in); given to fault-finding; captious.

দোষাবহ *a.* faulty, defective; noxious harmful; vicious; blamable.

দোষারোপ *n.* imputation of a fault; finding fault with, act of blaming; accusation recrimination. **দোষারোপ করা** *v.* to impute a fault to; to find fault with; to blame or to lay blame on; to accuse, to censure, to recriminate.

দোষাশ্রিত *a.* faulty, defective; given to vices.

দোষী *a.* guilty, offending; criminal; sinning. **দোষী সাব্যস্ত হওয়া** to be adjudged a guilty.

দোষৈকদর্শী, দোষৈকদৃক্‌ *a.* given only to counting demerits; cynical.

দোসর *n.* a second; a comrade; a companion; an attendant; an associate; an accomplice. □ *a.* acting as a second or companion or attendant or associate or accomplice; seconding, accompanying attending, associating.

দোসরা *a.* second; another; (of the days of a month) second. □ *n.* (of a month) the second day.

দোস্ত *n.* a friend; (loos.) a comrade. **দোস্তি** *n.* friendship.

দোহ same as **দোহন**। **দোহবর্ধন-আধিকারিক** *n.* dairy development officer.

দোহক *n.* one who or that which milks (fig.) one who exacts or extorts.

দোহদ *n.* the peculiar longing of a pregnant woman; an earnest desire o longing; pregnancy. **~দান** *n.* a ceremony of giving an expectant mother delicacies or highly palatable food she longs to eat. **~বতী** *n.* a pregnant woman longing to have particular delicacies of food. **~লক্ষণ** *n.* signs or symptoms of pregnancy.

দোহন *n.* act of milking, (fig.) extortion, exaction, exploitation. **দোহনী** *n.* a milk-pail, a milk-can; a milk-trough. **দোহনীয়** *a.* fit to be milked.

দোহশালা *n.* a dairy farm, a dairy.

দোহা pop. var. of **দোয়া**[১] ।

দোহাই *int.* meaning: in the name of, by, upon (ঈশ্বরের দোহাই = by God. আমার সম্মানের দোহাই = upon my honour); please (দোহাই মহারাজ = please Your Majesty). □ *n.* an appeal for justice or support (রাজার দোহাই) ; an oath (দোহাই পাড়া ভালো নয়) ; a pretext or plea or excuse (রোগের দোহাই) ; a cause (বৃষ্টির দোহাই) ; swearing by a precedent (অতীতের দোহাই). **দোহাই দেওয়া, দোহাই পাড়া** *v.* to appeal to (for justice or support); to put forward as a pretext; to swear; to swear by a precedent.

দোহার *n.* any one of the members of a chorus song or choir, who repeats the burden or every line after the leader of the party, (cp.) a chorist; (sarcas.) a second or a yes-man. **~কি** *n.* act of singing the burden of a chorus song after the leader; (sarcas.) act of seconding or yes-manship.

দোহারা *a.* double, twice; woven in double threads or in plaits, doubly woven (দোহারা কাপড়) ; doubled (দোহারা সুতো) ; middle-sized, of medium build, neither too thin nor too fat, well-proportioned (দোহারা চেহারা).

দোহাল *a.* yielding milk, milch; one who milks. □ *n.* a milker, a milkman.

দোহ্য same as **দোহনীয়** ।

দৌড় *n.* act of running, a run; a spurt; a race; act of fleeing, flight (চোরটা দৌড় মারল) ; (sarcas.) extent, limit (বিদ্যার দৌড়) ; (sarcas.) ability or strength (ওর দৌড় কত দেখছি). **এক দৌড়ে** at a hasty run. **দৌড় করানো** *v.* to cause to run or race, to run, to race, to rush; to harass by causing to move about repeatedly or constantly. **দৌড় দেওয়া, দৌড় মারা** *v.* to start running; bolt; to spurt; to run off, to take to one's heels. **~ঝাঁপ, ~ধাপ** *n.* act of romping, a romp; boisterous and hard effort attended with repeated or constant hurried movements. **~বাজ** *n.* a runner; a racer; one who is proficient in running (esp. races).

দৌড়াদৌড়ি *n.* act of running about; act of romping or gadding; boisterous and hard effort attended with repeated or constant hurried movements. **দৌড়াদৌড়ি করা** *v.* to run about; to romp; to gad about; to be engaged in a boisterous and hard effort attended with repeated or constant hurried movements.

দৌড়ানো *v.* to run; to flee, to run off.

দৌত্য *n.* office of a messenger or courier or envoy or ambassador or emissary; forerunning; office of a go-between; bawdry, panderism.

দৌবারিক *n.* a gateman, a doorkeeper, a janitor (*fem.* a janitress), a porter (*fem.* a porteress, a portress).

দৌরাত্ম্য *n.* oppression; cruel treatment; tyranny; naughtiness; boisterous mischievousness. **দৌরাত্ম্য করা** *v.* to oppress; to treat cruelly; to tyrannize; to be naughty; to be boisterously mischievous.

দৌর্বল্য *n.* weakness; debility; a weak point. Same as **দুর্বলতা** ।

দৌর্মনস্য *n.* worry, anxiety, concern; grief; dejection, depression; melancholia.

দৌলত *n.* riches, wealth, treasure, fortune (ধনদৌলত) ; aid, help, favour, grace (ঈশ্বরের দৌলতে). **~খানা** *n.* a palatial residence full of riches. **~দার** *a.* rich, wealthy; affluent. **~দারি** *n.* wealthiness, affluence; enjoyment of cakes and ale.

দৌহিত্র *n.* a daughter's son, a grandson. **দৌহিত্রী** *n.* a daughter's daughter, a granddaughter.

দ্বন্দ্ব *n.* a quarrel, a dispute; a conflict; a strife; a fight; a duel; a competition; rivalry; a pair, a couple; a pair of two opposite things ; (gr.) a copulative compound joining together two or more words or equal grammatical status (চখাচখী,স্বর্গ-মর্ত্য-পাতাল). **দ্বন্দ্ব করা** *v.* to quarrel (with); to fight (with); to compete or rival or vie (with). **~প্রিয়** *a.* quarrelsome; fond of fighting duels, pugnacious. **~প্রিয়তা** *n.* quarrelsomeness; pugnacity. **~যুদ্ধ** *n.* a single combat, a duel. **~যোদ্ধা** *n.* a duelist. **দ্বন্দ্বাতীত** *a.* (phil.) transcending all feelings of conflict or opposition; beyond controversy. **দ্বন্দ্বী** *a.* quarrelling; conflicting; fighting (with or against); duelling; competing, vying, rivalling.

দ্বয় *pro.* two; both; two or both of a pair or couple.

দ্বাচত্বারিংশ *a.* forty-two. **দ্বাচত্বারিংশৎ** *n. & a.* forty-two. **দ্বাচত্বারিংশত্তম** *a.* forty-second. *fem.* **দ্বাচত্বারিংশত্তমী** ।

দ্বাত্রিংশ *a.* thirty-two. **দ্বাত্রিংশৎ** *n. & a.* thirty-two. **দ্বাত্রিংশত্তম** *a.* thirty-second. *fem.* **দ্বাত্রিংশত্তমী** ।

দ্বাদশ *a. & n.* twelve. □ *a.* twelfth. **দ্বাদশী** *a. fem.* twelfth; twelve years old; (of the days of a lunar fortnight) twelfth. □ *n.* the twelfth day of a lunar fortnight. **~বর্ষীয়** *a.* of the age of twelve, aged twelve. **~বার্ষিক** *a.* duodecennial. **দ্বাদশিক** *n.* (arith.) duodecimal.

দ্বাপর *n.* the third age of the world according to Hindu scriptures, the brazen age.

দ্বাবিংশ *a.* twenty-two. **~তি** *a. & n.* twenty-two. **দ্বাবিংশতিতম** *a.* twenty-second. *fem.* **দ্বাবিংশতিতমী** ।

দ্বার *n.* a door; a gate; an entrance, a doorway; a gateway; a portico. **~দেশ, ~প্রান্ত** *n.* the proximity of a gate or door; doorway, doorstep, gateway, portal; entrance. **~দেশে, ~প্রান্তে** *adv.* at the door or gate or portal. **~পাল, ~পালক, ~বান, ~রক্ষক, ~রক্ষী** *n.* a doorkeeper, a gateman, a janitor (*fem.* : a janitress), a porter (*fem.* : a porteress, a portress). **দ্বার রোধ করা** *v.* to obstruct the door, to block up the door to make it impossible to pass. **~স্থ** *a.* standing or lying or situated at the gate; (humbly) waiting or begging at another's gate; to supplicate; seeking help from another (অসুবিধেয় পড়ে আপনার দ্বারস্থ হয়েছি). **দ্বারে দ্বারে** from door to door.

দ্বারকানাথ, দ্বারকাপতি, দ্বারকেশ *n.* the lord or ruler of the city of Dwaraka; an appellation of Krishna (কৃষ্ণ).

দ্বারা *prep.* by, with, through, by means of.

দ্বারিক same as **দ্বারপাল** (see **দ্বার**).

দ্বারিকানাথ, দ্বারিকাপতি same as **দ্বারকানাথ** ।

দ্বারী same as **দ্বারপাল** (see **দ্বার**).

দ্বারোদ্ঘাটন *n.* ceremony of opening the gate or door; the inaugural or opening ceremony of an establishment; inauguration.

দ্বাষষ্টি *n. & a.* sixty-two. **~তম** *a.* sixty-second. *fem.* **~তমী** ।

দ্বাসপ্ততি *n. & a.* seventy-two. **~তম** *a.* seventy-second. *fem.* **~তমী** ।

দ্বি *n.* two. □ *a.* two; double. □ *incomp.* bi-, di-, two- etc. **দ্বি-অংশক** *a.* (bot.) bimerous. **দ্বি-আর্ক** *a.* (bot.) di-arch. **দ্বি-কক্ষ** *a.* bicameral. **~কর্মক** *a.* (gr.) having two objects, having double objects. **~কেশর** *a.* (bot.) diandrous. **~কোষ** *a.* (bio.) bivalve, bivalvular. **~কোষ্ঠ** *a.* (bot.) bilocular. **~খণ্ড, ~খণ্ডিত** *a.* cut or divided into two (equal or unequal) pieces; bisected; bifurcated. **দ্বিখণ্ড করা** *v.* to cut or divide into two pieces; to bisect; to bifurcate. **~খণ্ডক** *n.* (geom.) a bisector. **~খণ্ডন** *n.* (geom.) bisection; bifurcation. **~গর্ভ** *a.* (bio. & zoo.) marsupial; (bot.) bicarpellate. **~গুচ্ছ** *a.* (bot.) diadelphous. **~গুণ** *a.* multiplied by two, doubled; two times of; double. **~গুণিত, ~গুণীকৃত** *a.* doubled, multiplied by two. **~ঘাত** *n.* (alg.) quadratic. **~ঘাত সমীকরণ** quadratic equation. **অমিশ্র দ্বিঘাত** (alg.) pure quadratic. **~চক্রযান** *n.* a two-wheeler; a bicycle. **~চত্বারিংশ** *n. & a.* forty-two. **~চত্বারিংশৎ** *a.* forty-two. **~চত্বারিংশত্তম** *a.* forty-second. *fem.* **দ্বিচত্বারিংশত্তমী** । **~চারিণী** *a. fem.* adulterous, unchaste; unfaithful to one's husband; (ori.) sexually attached to two men. **~জাতিতত্ত্ব** *n.* the two-nation theory. **~জিহ্ব** *a.* double-tongued; having a bifurcated or double-pronged tongue; (fig.) given to lying or insincere talk. □ *n.* the snake; a liar. ~তয় *a.* aggregate of two. □ *n.* a couple, a pair; a twin; a couplet. ~তল *a.* (of a building) two-storied; (of a ship or other vessels) double-decked; (sc.) dihedral. □ *n.* (of a building) the first floor; (of a ship etc.) the upper deck. ~তলকোণ *n.* (geom.) dihedral angle. ~ত্ব *n.* doubleness; doubling; reduplication; duplication; repetition. ~দল *n.* bi-petalous. □ *n.* pigeon-pea, dal. ~দৃক *a.* binocular. ~ধাতুক *a.* bi-metallic. ~ধাতুমান *n.* bimetallism. ~নবতি *n.* & *a.* ninety-two. ~নবতিতম *a.* ninety-second. *fem.* ~নবতিতমী। ~নেত্র *a.* two-eyed; binocular. ~নেত্র দৃষ্টি binocular vision. ~পক্ষ *a.* two-winged; bipartite (দ্বিপক্ষ দ্বন্দ্ব) ; having two fortnights; continuing for two fortnights. ~পঞ্চাশৎ *n.* & *a.* fifty-two. ~পঞ্চাশত্তম *a.* fifty-second. *fem.* ~পঞ্চাশত্তমী। ~পত্র বিমান a biplane. ~পথ *a.* two-way. ~পদ *a.* biped, two-footed, two-legged; (alg.) binomial (দ্বিপদ রাশি = binomial expression). □ *n.* a biped. ~পদসমীকরণ *n.* (alg.) equation. ~পদী *n.* a couplet. ~পরমাণুক *a.* (phys.) diatomic. দ্বিপাক্ষিক *a.* bilateral. ~পাদ *a.* same as দ্বিপদ (*a.*). ~পার্শ্ব, ~পার্শ্বীয় *a.* bilateral (দ্বিপার্শ্বীয়-প্রতিসাম্য = bilateral symmetry); biparous. ~প্রহর *n.* noon; midnight. ~বচন *n.* (gr.) the dual number. ~বন্ধ *n.* (chem.) double bond. ~বর্ষজীবী *a.* (bot.) biennial. ~বার্ষিক *a.* biennial; two years old; the second annual. ~বাহু *a.* having two arms, two-armed; two-sided, bilateral; double-handed (দ্বিবাহু আঘাত) ; having two branches, bifurcate (দ্বিবাহু পথ). ~বিধ *a.* of two sorts or kinds. ~বীজপত্রী *a.* (bot.) dicotyledonous. ~ভাব *a.* hypocritical; insincere; deceitful; double-minded; hesitant, wavering; two-way; having two attitudes. □ *n.* hypocrisy; insincerity; duplicity, deceit; double-mindedness; hesitation; wavering; two ways or attitudes. ~ভাষী *a.* speaking two (native or habitual) languages, bilingual. □ *n.* an interpreter; a bilingual person. ~ভুজ *a.* having two arms or hands, two-handed; having two sides, two-sided. ~মত *n.* difference of opinion. দ্বিমত পোষণ করা *v.* to have a difference of opinion. ~মাসিক *a.* bi-monthly. ~মুখ *a.* having two mouths or faces, two-mouthed, double-faced; branching into two directions, bifurcate. দ্বিমুখ টেলিগ্রাফ duplex telegraph. ~মূল *a.* (phys.) binary. দ্বিমূল যৌগিক binary compound. ~মেরু *a.* (phys.) bipolar. ~রদ *n.* the elephant. ~রদরদ *n.* an elephant's tusk; ivory. ~রূপ *a.* having two conflicting forms; (bot.) dimorphic; having two forms (usu. differing from each other); of or having two kinds or sorts. ~রূপতা *n.* (bot.) dimorphism. ~রেফ *n.* the bumble-bee. ~লিঙ্গ *a.* bisexual. ~শত *n.* & *a.* two hundred. ~শিরস্ক, ~শিরা, ~শীর্ষ, ~শীর্ষক *a.* two-headed, bicephalous. ~ষষ্ট *a.* sixty-second. ~ষষ্টি *n.* & *a.* sixty-two. ~ষষ্টিতম *a.* sixty-second. *fem.* দ্বিষষ্টিতমী। ~সপ্ততি *n.* & *a.* seventy-two. ~সপ্ততিতম *a.* seventy-second. *fem.* দ্বিসপ্ততিতমী। ~সমত্রিভুজ *n.* (geom.) an isosceles triangle. ~সূত্র, ~সূত্রী *a.* (bot.) bifilar.

দ্বিগু *n.* (gr.) a system of forming numerative compounds.

দ্বিচর *a.* binary; amphibious.

দ্বিজ *a.* twice-born; having two births (once from mother's womb and then again through religious sacraments or from eggs etc.); regenerated. □ *n.* (pop.) a Brahman; any oviparous creature such as a bird, an ant, a fish etc. *fem.* দ্বিজা। ~পতি, ~বর, ~রাজ, দ্বিজেন্দ্র, দ্বিজোত্তম, ~সত্তম *n.* an excellent or distinguished Brahman.

দ্বিতীয় *a.* second; another. দ্বিতীয়া *a. fem.* second; another; (of the days of a lunar fortnight) second. □ *n.* a second day of a lunar fortnight. দ্বিতীয়ত *adv.* secondly, in the second place. দ্বিতীয় বিশ্বযুদ্ধ *n.* the Second World War. দ্বিতীয়াশ্রম *n.* the domestic or married life which is the second of the four stages of human life according to Hindu scriptures.

দ্বিধা *adv.* in two ways or directions etc.

☐ *a.* divided into two; partitioned. ☐ *n.* hesitation; wavering in the mind caused by indecision; suspicion or doubt. দ্বিধা করা *v.* to hesitate; to waver in the mind; (rare) to divide into two; (rare) to partition. ~করণ *n.* act of dividing into two; act of partitioning; (rare) hesitation. ~কৃত *a.* divided into two; partitioned. ~গ্রস্ত *a.* caught in two minds, hesitating, wavering. ~বিভক্ত *a.* divided or split into two.

দ্বিপ *n.* the elephant.

দ্বিরাগমন *n.* the ceremony of a newly-wed bride's coming for the second time to her husband's house from her paternal abode.

দ্বিরুক্ত *a.* uttered or mentioned twice; reduplicated; repeated; (loos.) tautologic. দ্বিরুক্তি *n.* act of uttering or mentioning twice; reduplication; repetition; (loos.) tautology; a word or saying repeated; (loos.) objection (বিনা দ্বিরুক্তিতে আদেশপালন).

দ্বিষৎ *n.* a malicious person; an antagonist; an enemy.

দ্বিষ্ট *a.* envied; maliced.

দ্বীপ *n.* an island, an isle. ক্ষুদ্র দ্বীপ an islet. দ্বীপপুঞ্জ *n.* a group of islands, an archipelago. ব্রিটিশ দ্বীপপুঞ্জ the British Isles. দ্বীপবাসী *n.* an islander, an islesman, (rare) an isleman. ☐ *a.* living in an island.

দ্বীপান্তর *n.* another island; a different island; banishment of offenders beyond the seas, deportation, transportation, exilement, exile. দ্বীপান্তর হওয়া *v.* to be deported or transported or exiled. দ্বীপান্তরিত *a.* deported, transported, exiled. দ্বীপান্তরিত করা, দ্বীপান্তরে পাঠানো বা দেওয়া *v.* to deport, to transport, to exile.

দ্বীপী *n.* the tiger; the leopard, the cheetah; a sea or an ocean.

দ্বেষ *n.* envy; malice, hatred, grudge; enmity; aversion, antipathy, dislike. দ্বেষ করা *v.* to envy; to malice, to grudge; to be inimical towards, to be averse or antipathetic to, to dislike. দ্বেষণ *n.* act of envying or hating or grudging; act of being inimical to, antagonism; act of being antipathetic to, aversion. দ্বেষী, দ্বেষ্টা *a.* envying; malicious, spiteful, grudging; inimical; averse, antipathetic. *fem.* দ্বেষিণী। দ্বেষ্য *a.* fit to be hated.

দ্বৈত *n* duality, twoness; a dyad (শব্দদ্বৈত). ~বাদ *n.* (phil.) dualism. ~বাদী *a.* (phil.) dualistic. ☐ *n.* a dualist. ~শাসন *n.* dual government, diarchy. ~সংগীত *n.* a duet (song), antiphony. দ্বৈতাদ্বৈত *n.* (phil.) simultaneous diversity and unity of God and the Soul. দ্বৈতী same as দ্বৈতবাদী।

দ্বৈধ *n.* duality, twoness; disagreement, difference; hesitation; a suspicion or doubt.

দ্বৈধীভাব *n.* hesitation, vacillation; double-dealing, duplicity.

দ্বৈপ *a.* relating to or living in an island, insular; relating to the tiger or cheetah, tigrine.

দ্বৈপায়ন *n.* one who is born in an island; an appellation of Vyasa (ব্যাস) the author of the Mahabharata.

দ্বৈপ্য *a.* relating to an island, insular.

দ্বৈবার্ষিক *a.* biennial.

দ্বৈবিধ্য *n.* twofoldness; duality.

দ্বৈভাগিক *a.* (bot.) bifurcate.

দ্বৈমাতৃক *a.* (of countries or lands) irrigated both by river-water and rain-water (and consequently abounding in crops).

দ্বৈমাসিক *a.* bimonthly.

দ্বৈরথ *n.* a single combat between two charioteers. ☐ *a.* involving such a combat (দ্বৈরথ সমর).

দ্বৈরাজ্য *n.* a diarchy.

দ্ব্যক্ষ *a.* (phys.) biaxial.

দ্ব্যক্ষর *a.* consisting of two letters, two-lettered; consisting of two syllables, disyllabic. ☐ *n.* a two-lettered incantation.

দ্ব্যঙ্গুল *a.* measuring two fingers.

দ্ব্যণুক *a.* evolving out of union of two atoms, diatomic.

দ্ব্যর্থ *n.* two meanings, double meanings, ambiguity; equivocation. ☐ *a.* having two or double meanings; ambiguous; equivocal. দ্ব্যর্থক *a.* having two or double meanings; ambiguous; equivocal. দ্ব্যর্থক

কথা a quibble or equivocation. **দ্ব্যর্থক শব্দ** a double entendre. **দ্ব্যর্থকতা, দ্ব্যর্থতা** *n.* ambiguity, equivocalness. **দ্ব্যর্থহীন** *a.* unequivocal, unambiguous.

দ্ব্যশীতি *a.* & *n.* eighty-two. **~তম** *a.* eighty-second. *fem.* **~তমী** ।

দ্ব্যহ *n.* a couple of days.

দ্ব্যাত্মবাদী *a.* (phil.) dualistic. □ *n.* (phil.) a dualist.

দ্ব্যাহিক *a.* continuing for two days; occurring after an interval of two days; (loos.) tertian (দ্ব্যাহিক জ্বর).

দ্যু *n.* heaven; the sky.

দ্যুতি *n.* radiation, glow, effulgence; lustre, shine; brightness; splendour; splendid beauty; a ray. **~মান** *a.* radiating, radiant, glowing, effulgent; lustrous, shining; bright; resplendent; splendidly beautiful. *fem.* **~মতী** ।

দ্যুলোক *n.* heaven; the region of heaven.

দ্যূত, দ্যূতক্রীড়া *n.* dice-playing (esp. with betting); gambling. **দ্যূতকার, দ্যূতকর** *a.* given to playing dice or gambling. □ *n.* a dice-player (esp. one who bets); a gambler.

দ্যোতক *a.* indicating, expressing; expressive or suggestive (of); signifying; inspiring; enlightening, illumining.

দ্যোতন *n.* act of indicating or expressing or signifying or inspiring or enlightening or illumining; indication, expression, inspiration, enlightenment. **দ্যোতনা** *n.* figurative expression; implication; suggestiveness, significance.

দ্রঢ়িমা *n.* hardness; stiffness; toughness; firmness; steadiness.

দ্রঢ়িষ্ঠ *a.* hardest; stiffest; toughest; most firm; steadiest; very hard or stiff or tough or firm or steady. *fem.* **দ্রঢ়িষ্ঠা** ।

দ্রঢীয়সী *fem.* of **দ্রঢীয়ান** ।

দ্রঢীয়ান *a.* harder; stiffer; tougher; more firm; steadier.

দ্রব *a.* liquid, fluid; liquefied, melted. □ *n.* (chem.) a liquid solution, a solution. **গাঢ় দ্রব** concentrated solution. **দ্রব করা** *v.* to liquefy; to melt; to dissolve or solve. **দ্রব হওয়া** *v.* to be liquefied or melted, to liquefy or melt; to be dissolved or solved. **দ্রবণ** *n.* liquefaction; melting; (chem.) dissolution or solution. **দ্রবণশীল** *a.* disposed to be liquefied or melted or solved; liquefiable; (chem.) soluble. **দ্রবণাঙ্ক** *n.* melting-point. **দ্রবণীয়** *a.* liquefiable; (chem.) soluble. **দ্রবণীয়তা** *n.* solubility. **দ্রবীকরণ** same as **দ্রবণ** । **দ্রবীকৃত** *a.* liquefied, melted; (chem.) dissolved or solved. **দ্রবীভবন** *n.* act of melting; act of being liquefied or dissolved or solved. **দ্রবীভূত** *a.* liquefied; melted; (chem.) dissolved or solved.

দ্রব্য *n.* a thing, a substance, an article; (phil. & phys.) matter. **~গুণ** *n.* property present in a thing or substance; medicinal property of a thing or plant. **~জাত** *a.* produced of a material thing. □ *n.* a collection of things. **দ্রব্যজাত বস্তু** a product. **~বাচক** *a.* (gr.) material. **~সামগ্রী** *n. pl.* various things.

দ্রষ্টব্য *a.* worth seeing or visiting (দ্রষ্টব্য স্থান) ; worthy of reference (এই প্রসঙ্গে গীতা দ্রষ্টব্য) ; worthy of note; warranting attention, remarkable; warranting consideration. □ *int.* (erron.) vide, see.

দ্রষ্টা *a.* one who sees or observes or witnesses or judges. □ *n.* a seer; an observer; an onlooker; a witness; a judge; a philosopher; a seer of things to come.

দ্রাক্ষা *n.* grape. **~কুঞ্জ, ~ক্ষেত্র** *n.* a vineyard. **~ফল** *n.* grape. **~রস** *n.* grape-juice. **~রিষ্ট** *n.* a kind of medicinal liquor prepared from grape-juice, *vinum rubrum*, (cp.) vintage. **~লতা** *n.* the vine. **দ্রাক্ষা-শর্করা** *n.* grape-sugar.

দ্রাঘিমা *n.* (geog.) a longitude. **~ন্তর** *n.* longitudinal distance, distance east or west from the prime meridian.

দ্রাঘিষ্ঠ *a.* longest; extremely long.

দ্রাঘীয়সী *fem.* of **দ্রাঘীয়ান** ।

দ্রাঘীয়ান *a.* longer.

দ্রাব *n.* act of melting, liquefaction, dissolution or solution. **দ্রাবক** *a.* solvent; corrosive. □ *n.* a solvent; an acid (গন্ধক দ্রাবক = nitric acid, যবক্ষার দ্রাবক = sulphuric acid). **দ্রাবণ** *n.* melting, liquefaction, dissolution or solution. **দ্রাবিত** *a.* melted, liquefied, dissolved or solved.

দ্রাবিড় *n.* Dravidians; a Dravidian; the

Dravidian language; a region of Southern India inhabited by the Dravidians. □ *a*. Dravidian. **দ্রাবিড়ী** *n. fem.* a Dravidian woman; the Dravidian language.

দ্রাব্য *a.* that which can be melted, liquefiable, dissolvable, soluble, solvent. **~তা** *n.* solubility.

দ্রুত *a.* quick, swift, speedy, fast. □ *adv.* quickly, swiftly, speedily, fast. **~ক্রিয়** *a.* quick in action, prompt; nimble, agile. **~গতি** *a.* swift-moving, quick-paced, swift, speedy; fast. □ *adv.* moving swiftly, with a quick pace; swiftly, speedily, fleetingly; fast. **~গামী** *a.* fast-moving; fast, fleet; swift. **~তা** *n.* quickness, swiftness, speediness, fastness, celerity, nimbleness. **~পদে** *adv.* at a brisk pace; swiftly. **~বিলম্বিত** *n.* a Sanskrit metre or musical measure alternatingly quick and slow. **~বেগে** *adv.* speedily; swiftly, rapidly. **দ্রুতি** *n.* (chiefly in mech.) speed; quickness, swiftness, fastness, speediness, celerity. **দ্রুতিগণক, দ্রুতিমাপক** *n.* a speedometer, a speed-counter. **দ্রুতিজ্ঞাপক, দ্রুতিসূচক** *n.* a speed-indicator. **দ্রুতিলিখ** *n.* a speed-recorder.

দ্রুম *n.* a tree. **~দল** *n.* leaves of trees.

দ্রোণ *n.* a dry measure of thirty-two seers i.e. a little over 29 kilograms for corn etc. or a measuring vessel having this capacity; the raven, the carrion-crow. **~কাক** *n.* the raven, the carrion-crow.

দ্রোণি, দ্রোণী *n.* a small (and usu. improvised) boat; a dugout, a raft; a vessel for baling out water, a bail, a bale; a pitcher; a bucket; a trough; a valley (esp. a narrow one); a gorge.

দ্রোহ *n.* enmity, hostility; malice; malevolence or malefeasance; (loos.) revolt or rebellion. **দ্রোহী** *a.* (chiefly used as a *sfx.*) envious, hostile; malicious; malevolent or malefeasant; (loos.) rebellious; opposing; revolting; causing harm. **দ্রোহিতা** same as **দ্রোহ**। **রাষ্ট্রদ্রোহ** *n.* treason. **রাষ্ট্রদ্রোহী** *a.* guilty of treason.

দ্রৌণি *n.* a son of Drona (দ্রোণ) the master archer of the Mahabharata.

দ্রৌপদী *n.* the name of the heroine of the Mahabharata as she was the daughter of the King Drupada (দ্রুপদ). **রন্ধনে দ্রৌপদী** a female cook of incomparable efficiency.

দ্রৌপদেয় *n.* five sons of Draupadi (দ্রৌপদী) by five Pandavas (they were প্রতিবিন্ধ্য, শ্রুতিসোম, শ্রুতিকর্মা, শতানীক and শ্রুতসেন).

ধ *n.* the nineteenth letter of the Bengali alphabet.

ধক *int.* expressing : sudden blaze or glow (as of fire); sudden throb or jerk (বুকটা ধক করে উঠল). **ধকধক** *int.* expressing : state of blazing or glowing by flashes or repeatedly; throbbing or palpitation. **ধকধক করা** *v.* to glow or blaze by flashes or repeatedly; to dazzle (হিরেখানা ধকধক করছে) ; to palpitate or throb greatly. **~ধকানি** *n.* loud and great throbbing or palpitation.

ধকল *n.* stress, brunt, impact; pressure of work, hard labour, strain (রোগা শরীরে এত ধকল সইবে না) ; manhandling or wear and tear (ঘড়িটা খুব ধকল সয়েছে) ; disturbing or troublesome charge (ছেলেপিলেদের ধকল).

ধঞ্চে dial. corrup. of **ধনিচা**।

ধটি, ধটিকা, ধটী *n.* loincloth; a piece of scanty loincloth (as worn by an ascetic or a wrestler); a piece of old or worn-out cloth, a rag.

ধড় *n.* the body apart from the head and legs or limbs, the trunk, the torso; a truncated body. **ধড়ে প্রাণ আসা** (fig.) to recover or regain mental composure (as after a deadly or severe shock).

ধড়ফড় *int.* expressing : restlessness or palpitation. **ধড়ফড় করা** *v.* to be restless or nervous; to palpitate. **ধড়ফড়ানি** *n.* restlessness, palpitation; trepidation.

ধড়মড় *int.* expressing : sudden bustle or flutter or hurry.

ধড়া *n.* loincloth. **~চূড়া** *n.* loincloth and head-dress (esp. as worn by Krishna); (sarcas. or hum.) official dress (esp. one in European or English style).

ধড়াম same as **দড়াম**।

ধড়াস *int.* expressing : a heavy thudding noise as of a fall, thud; a loud banging noise as of opening or closing a door violently, bang; a sudden impetuous throb (বুকটা ভয়ে ধড়াস করে উঠল). **ধড়াস-ধড়াস** *int.* expressing : repeated thuds or bangs or impetuous throbs. **ধড়াস-ধড়াস করা** *v.* to make thudding or banging noise repeatedly; to throb or palpitate impetuously.

ধড়িবাজ *a.* guileful, deceitful, tricksy, cunning, full of ruses. **ধড়বাজি** *n.* guilefulness, deceitfulness, tricksiness, cunning; guile, deceit, trick, cunning. **ধড়িবাজ লোক** a trickster, a cunning or deceitful or wily fellow.

ধন *n.* money (ধনবিজ্ঞান) ; riches, wealth (ধনসম্পদ) ; treasure (গুপ্তধন) ; a highly valued thing (মাতৃস্নেহ পরম ধন) ; a dearly loved person or thing, a darling (আদরের ধন) ; (math.) the plus sign. **~কুবের** *n.* a man as wealthy as the god of wealth, an extremely or fabulously rich man, a millionaire, a billionaire. **~ক্ষয়** *n.* loss or waste of money; impoverishment. **~গর্ব, ~গৌরব** *n.* insolence from wealth. **~গর্বী** *a.* insolent from wealth, arrogant through wealth, purse-proud. **~চিন্তা** *n.* eagerness or anxiety about how to acquire wealth, concern for acquisition of wealth or property; Mammonism. **~চিহ্ন** *n.* (math.) a plus sign. **~জন** *n.* wealth and one's own people, men and money. **~তন্ত্র, ~তন্ত্রবাদ, ~তান্ত্রিকতা** *n.* capitalism. **~তান্ত্রিক, ~তন্ত্রবাদী** *a.* capitalistic, capitalist. □ *n.* a capitalist. **~তৃষ্ণা, ~তৃষা** *n.* thirst or great desire for wealth; avarice, cupidity. **~দ** *n.* one who or that which gives wealth, money-giving. □ *a.* an appellation of Kuvera (কুবের) the god of wealth, (cp.) Plutus, Mammon. **~দা** *a. fem.* of **ধনদ**। □ *n.* an appellation of Lakshmi (লক্ষ্মী) the presiding goddess of wealth. **~দাতা** *a.* one who gives money or wealth. *fem.* **ধনদাত্রী**। **~দান** *n.* act of giving money or wealth (esp. in charity). **~দাস** *n.* one who is ready to undergo all sorts of humiliation and privation for the sake of money-making; a hateful servant of Mammon: an extremely avaricious man; an inveterate miser. ~দৃপ্ত *a.* arrogant through possession of vast wealth, purseproud. ~দেবতা *n.* the god of wealth; Kuvera (কুবের), (cp.) Plutus, Mammon. ~দৌলত same as ধনসম্পত্তি। ~ধান্য *n.* wealth and crops, abundance of wealth or affluence. ~ধান্যপূর্ণ *a.* full of wealth and food; full of milk and honey; affluent. ~নিয়োগ same as ধনবিনিয়োগ। ~পতি *n.* the god of wealth; Kuvera (কুবের), (cp.) Plutus, Mammon; an extremely rich man. ~পিপাসা same as ধনতৃষ্ণা। ~পিশাচ *n.* one who is ready to do any heinous act for the sake of money; a sordid miser. ~পূর্ণ *a.* replete with wealth. ~বন্টন *n.* distribution or apportionment of wealth. ~বতী *fem.* of ধনবান। ~বত্তা *n.* opulence. ~বান *a.* opulent, wealthy, rich. ~বিজ্ঞান *n.* economics. ~বিনিয়োগ *n.* investment of money. ধনবিনিয়োগ করা *v.* to invest money. ~বিভাগ *n.* divison of money or wealth; distribution or apportionment of property. ~বৃদ্ধি *n.* multiplication or increase or growth of wealth. ~ভাগ্য *n.* (chiefly astrol.) luck for earning money. ~ভাণ্ডার *n.* a treasury; a (public) fund. ~মত্ত same as ধনগর্বী। ~মদ same as ধনগর্ব। ~মান *n.* wealth and honour or dignity. ~রক্ষা *n.* safe keeping or preservation of wealth. ~রত্ন same as ধনদৌলত। ~রাশি *n.* (math.) a positive quantity. ~লক্ষ্মী *n.* the goddess of wealth. ~লালসা, ~লিপ্সা, ~লোভ *n.* greed for wealth, avarice, cupidity. ~লিপ্সু, ~লুব্ধ, ~লোভী *a.* greedy of wealth, avaricious. ~শালী *a.* wealthy, rich, moneyed, affluent, opulent. ~শালিতা *n.* wealthiness, affluence. ~শ্রী *n.* an Indian musical mode. ~সঞ্চয় *n.* accumulation or saving of money or wealth. ~সম্পত্তি, ~সম্পদ *n.* wealth and property, riches and wealth. ~হীন *a.* poor, indigent. *fem.* ধনহীনা।

ধনাকাঙ্ক্ষা same as ধনলালসা।

ধনাগম *n.* income, earning; acquirement or acquisition of wealth.

ধনাগার *n.* a treasury; a (public) fund.

ধনাঢ্য same as ধনশালী।

ধনাত্মক *a.* (phys. & math.) positive.

ধনাধার *n.* a treasury; a treasure-chest.

ধনাধিকারী *a.* possessed of or possessing wealth.

ধনাধিপ, ধনাধিপতি *n.* the lord of wealth; Kuvera (কুবের), (cp.) Plutus, Mammon.

ধনাধ্যক্ষ *n.* a treasurer; a finance minister, a dewan, Chancellor of the Exchequer. ~তা *n.* treasurership; office of the finance minister.

ধনাপহরণ *n.* act of stealing money; misappropriation of money; defalcation, embezzlement; act of depriving one of one's money. ধনাপহরণ করা *v.* to steal or rob money; to misappropriate money, to defalcate; to embezzle; to deprive one of one's money. ধনাপহারী *a.* one who robs or steals or misappropriates money.

ধনার্জন *n.* earning of money; acquisition of wealth.

ধনার্থী *a.* desirous of obtaining or earning money, seeking money.

ধনাশা *n.* desire for wealth, longing or craving for wealth.

ধনি[1] (poet.) *int.* (in addressing a woman esp. a young woman) O thou blessed one.

ধনি[2] *n.* (poet. & obs.) a beautiful young woman or damsel. □ *a.* (poet. & obs.) beautiful and young.

ধনিক *a.* moneyed, wealthy, rich, affluent, opulent; capitalistic, capitalist. □ *n.* one who invests money in a business, an investor, a capitalist; a rich merchant, a merchant prince; a moneylender; a rich man. *fem.* ধনিকা a rich man's wife; a young and beautiful woman. ~গোষ্ঠী, ~সমাজ, ~সম্প্রদায় *n.* the moneyed class, the capitalist class; the capitalist world. ~তন্ত্র *n.* capitalistic or capitalist government; capitalism.

ধনিচা *n.* a jute-like fibrous plant.

ধনিনী *fem.* of ধনী[2] ।

ধনিয়া older form of ধনে।

ধনিষ্ঠা *n.* (astro.) the twenty-third of the twenty-seven stars according to Hindu astronomy.

ধনী[1] alt. spell. of ধনি[2] ।

ধনী[2] *a.* rich, wealthy, moneyed, affluent, opulent. □ *n.* a rich man.

ধনু *n.* a bow; a linear measure equivalent to four cubits; an arc or arch; anything arch-shaped (রামধনু) ; (astrol.) the ninth sign of zodiac, the Sagittarius. **~ক** *n.* bow; a bow-like device for carding and cleaning cotton, (cp.) a cottongin; a bow of a violin or any other musical instrument. **ধনুকধারী** *n.* a bowman, an archer. **ধনুকাকার, ধনুকাকৃতি** *a.* bow-shaped, arched. **~র্গুণ** *n.* a bow-string. **ধনুর্গুণ আরোপণ করা** to string a bow. **অদ্য ভক্ষ্যঃ ধনুর্গুণঃ** state of having nothing to eat (this day); utter poverty. **~র্ধর** *n.* an archer, a bowman; (sarcas. & hum.) a very capable or efficient man (গণিতশাস্ত্রে ধনুর্ধর). **~র্ধারী** *n.* an archer, a bowman. **~র্বন্ধনী** *n.* (math. print, etc.), braces, the second bracket. **~র্বাণ** *n.* bow and arrow. **~র্বিদ্যা** *n.* the art and science of archery; archery. **~র্বেদ** *n.* an ancient treatise on archery written by Viswamitra (বিশ্বামিত্র) the sage; any treatise on archery; the art and science of archery. **~র্ভঙ্গ** *n.* act of splitting a bow into two. **ধনুর্ভঙ্গ পণ** *n.* (fig.) an irrevocable or unalterable determination or resolve, a grim or inflexible resolution. **~ষ্কোটি** *n.* an end or tip of a bow; a Hindu holy place in South India. **~ষ্টঙ্কার, ~ষ্টংকার** *n.* the twang of a bow; (med.) tetanus, convulsion, spasm; lock-jaw.

ধনে *n.* coriander seed, coriander.

ধনেশ *n.* the lord or god of wealth; an appellation of Kuvera (কুবের), (cp.) Plutus, Mammon; a beautiful long-billed bird, the hornbill. □ *a.* very rich or wealthy, affluent, opulent.

ধনোপার্জন *n.* same as **ধনার্জন**।

ধন্দ, ধন্ধ *n.* confusion or dazzlement of eyesight; confusion; bewilderment; suspicion.

ধন্না coll. corrup. of **ধরনা**।

ধন্ব, ধন্বা *n.* (chiefly used in *comp.*) a bow (সুধন্বা).

ধন্বন্তরি *n.* (Hindu myth.) the name of the physician of heaven; (fig.) an unfailing physician.

ধন্বী *a.* carrying a bow; armed with a bow; versed or efficient in archery.

ধন্য *a.* fortunate or gratified (ধন্য করা, ধন্য হওয়া) ; blessed (জগতে সাধুরাই ধন্য) ; praiseworthy or admirable (ধন্য সাহস) ; virtuous or holy. □ *n.* thanks or thanksgiving (ধন্য তোমাকে). *fem.* **ধন্যা**। **~বাদ** *n.* thanksgiving; thanks. **ধন্যবাদ দেওয়া** *v.* to thank, to give thanks.

ধন্যাক, (rare) **ধন্যা** *n.* coriander-seed, coriander.

ধপ ধপ *int.* expressing : brilliant whiteness or tidiness. **ধপ ধপ করা** *v.* to appear brilliantly white or tidy. **ধপধপে** *a.* brilliantly white (ধপধপে কাপড়) ; luminous (ধপধপে জোছনা) ; immaculately tidy (ধপধপে উঠোন) ; brilliant or dazzling (ধপধপে সাদা).

ধপাৎ same as **ধপাস**।

ধপাধপ *int.* expressing : a succession of thudding or thumping noise as of heavy bodies falling one after another. **ধপাধপ করে** with thuds.

ধপাস *int.* expressing : a loud thud or thump as caused by the fall of a heavy body. **ধপাস করে** with a thud.

ধবধব same as **ধপধপ**।

ধবল *a.* white (ধবলগিরি, ধবল আকাশ) ; grey (ধবল কেশ). □ *n.* the white colour; the grey colour; leucoderma. **ধবলা** *a. fem.* of **ধবল**। □ *n.* a white cow. **ধবল-কুষ্ঠ** *n.* leucoderma. **ধবলাকার, ধবলাকৃতি** *a.* looking white; white. **ধবলিত** *a.* made or turned white, whitened; turned grey (ধবলিত কেশ). **ধবলিমা** *n.* whiteness; whitishness. **ধবলী** *n.* a white cow. **ধবলীকৃত** *a.* made white, whitened. **ধবলীভূত** *a.* turned white or grey.

ধমক, ধমকানি *n.* a rebuff, a snub; a scolding, a reprimand; threat, intimidation. **ধমক দেওয়া, ধমকানো** *v.* to rebuff, to snub; to scold, to reprimand; to threaten, to intimidate. **ধমকধামক** *n.* mild reproof, expression of blame or disapproval.

ধমনি, ধমনী *n.* an artery; a vein; the pulsating vein palpable at the wrist. **~স্পন্দন, ~ঘাত** *n.* pulse-beat, pulse; arterial throbbing.

ধম্মিল্ল *n.* (of a human being) a bun; (of a bird etc.) a hairy crest.

-ধর *a.* (used as a *sfx.*) bearing, carrying, holding (ভূধর, শ্রীধর, হলধর).

ধরণ alt. spell. of **ধরন**।

ধরণী, ধরণি *n.* the earth, the world. **~তল** *n.* the surface of the earth. **~ধর** *n.* the lord of the earth; a king; a mountain. **~পতি, ~পাল** *n.* a king. **~পৃষ্ঠ** same as **ধরণীতল**। **~মণ্ডল** *n.* the terrestrial globe; the whole earth.

ধরতা *n.* (comm.) an extra amount given by the seller to the buyer to guard against any possible shortage during weighing; a word or words sung by the leading singer used as a cue for an associate singer or singers of a chorus song.

ধরতাই *a.* that which is generally known to be true, that which is taken for granted; fixed, ascertained.

ধরতি *n.* (comm.) an extra amount given by the seller to the buyer to guard against any possible shortage during weighing.

ধরন *n.* manner, method, way (কাজের ধরন) ; condition, state, (রোগীর ধরন) ; working, behaviour (রোগের ধরন) ; appearance, look, cut (মুখের ধরন) ; the style, fashion (পোশাকের ধরন) ; bearing, deportment (লোকটার ধরন সন্দেহজনক). **ধরন-ধারণ** *n. pl.* or collec. form of **ধরন**।

ধরনা *n.* act of lying obstinately at one's door or at the temple of a deity soliciting or imploring something. **ধরনা দেওয়া** *n.* to lie obstinately at one's door or at the temple of a deity soliciting or imploring something.

ধরপাকড় *n.* extensive or collective arrests (as by the police); insistent solicitation (চাকরির জন্য ধরপাকড়). **ধরপাকড় করা** *v.* to arrest extensively or collectively, to round up; to solicit insistently.

ধরম poet. corrup. of **ধর্ম**।

ধরা¹ *n.* the earth, the world. **~তল** *n.* the surface or floor of the earth; the ground (মূর্ছিত হয়ে ধরাতলে পতন). **~ধর** *n.* a mountain. **~ধাম** *n.* earthly abode; the earth as an abode; the earth, the world. **~পতি** *n.* a king. **~পৃষ্ঠ** same as **ধরাতল**। **~ভৃৎ** *n.* a mountain. **~শয়ন, ~শয্যা** *n.* the ground or the floor of the earth as bed, the bed of the earth or ground. **~শায়ী** *a.* lying prostrate on the ground; floored, knocked down.

ধরা² *v.* to hold with the hand (বইখানা ধরো) ; to catch (বলটা ছুড়ে দিচ্ছি—ধরো) ; to hold, to seize; to take (এই ভিক্ষা দিলাম—ধরো) ; to touch (চোর-চোর খেলায় বুড়ি ধরা, বাচ্ছাটা যেন গরম দুধটা না ধরে) ; to reach (হাত দিয়ে চাঁদ ধরা) ; to overtake (যতই জোরে যাও—তোমাকে ধরব) ; to arrest, to apprehend, to capture (চোর ধরা) ; to entrap, to catch (বাঘ ধরা, মাছ ধরা) ; to restrain, to check; to hold (পাখিটাকে ধরো নইলে পালিয়ে যাবে) ; to contain, to hold, to accommodate (পাত্রে জল ধরা, ঘরে লোক ধরা) ; to bear (গাছে ফল ধরা) ; to carry, to bear (গর্ভে ধরা) ; to cherish (অন্তরে উচ্চাশা ধরা) ; to wear, to put on (বেশ ধরা) ; to assume (মূর্তি ধরা) ; to take to, to resort to (লাঠি ধরা) ; to be obstinate about (গোঁ ধরা) ; to take up (অস্ত্র ধরা) ; to follow (পথ ধরা) ; to give support to (লোকটিকে ধরো নইলে পড়ে যাবে) ; to attack (ডাকাতে ধরা, রোগে ধরা) ; to affect or infect (চোখে চালশে ধরা, যক্ষ্মায় ধরা) ; to ache (মাথা ধরা) ; to be benumbed (দাঁড়িয়ে থেকে থেকে পা ধরা) ; to infest or attack or damage or contact (পোকায় ধরা, মরচে ধরা) ; to accept, to take in (ছবিতে রং ধরা) ; to act upon successfully, to work (ওষুধ ধরা) ; to start practising (জুয়াচুরি ধরা) ; to be accustomed or addicted to (নেশা ধরা) ; to be under the influence of (নেশায় ধরা) ; to be stricken or affected with (শীতে বা ভয়ে ধরা) ; to catch or board or embark (তিনি মুম্বই থেকে জাহাজ ধরবেন) ; to be in time to catch (এখন না গেলে ট্রেন ধরতে পারব না) ; to stop at, to touch (এ স্টেশনে মেল ট্রেন ধরে না) ; to terminate, to cease (বৃষ্টি ধরা) ; to commence, to begin, to start (গান ধরা) ; to find out, to detect (ভুল ধরা) ; to impose or assess (ট্যাক্স ধরা) ; to charge or fix or ascertain (দাম ধরা) ; to pronounce, to utter (ঈশ্বরের নাম ধরা) ; to declare, to stake or bet or bid (বাজি ধরা) ; to insist upon, to beseech (অনেক ধরে-করে) ; to sustain, to preserve, to maintain (প্রাণ ধরা) ; to run hoarse, to choke (ঠান্ডায় গলা ধরা) ; to grasp, to make out, to understand, to comprehend (কথার অর্থ ধরা) ; to determine or discern (কার লেখা ধরা শক্ত) ; to take fire, to ignite (উনুন ধরা) ; to catch fire (আগুনের কাছ থেকে সরে যাও—কাপড় ধরে যাবে) ; to be set on (ঘরে আগুন ধরা) ; to adopt (সেলিম জাহাঙ্গির নাম ধরলেন) ; to test (পড়া ধরা) ; to be pleasing or acceptable to (মনে ধরা) ; to turn (চুলে পাক ধরা) ; to be under, to contact (টান ধরা) ; to count, to consider, to regard (মানুষের মধ্যে ধরা) ; to pay heed to, to listen to (আমার কথা ধরো) ; to be overfried or overdone (তরকারিটা ধরে গেছে) □ *a.* held; caught; seized; arrested, apprehended, captured; entrapped; contained; reserved or kept in a container; aching; terminated, ceased; commenced, started; found out, detected; seen through (চালাকি ধরা পড়েছে) ; declared or bidden; fixed or ascertained; run hoarse or choked; ignited; tested; one who or that which holds or catches (মাছ-ধরা জাল). **ধরা-ছোঁয়া** *n.* proximity; reach; tangibility; (fig.) comprehension or detection. **ধরা-ছোঁয়ার বাইরে** distant; beyond reach; intangible; (fig.) incomprehensible or beyond detection. **ধরা-ছোঁয়ার মধ্যে** proximate;within reach; tangible; (fig.) comprehensible or detectable. **ধরানো** *v.* to cause to hold or catch or seize or arrest or apprehend or entrap or contain or accommodate or wear or assume or take to or resort to or follow or take up or be attacked or ache or be dazed or be benumbed or contact or accept or work successfully or be accustomed to or addicted to or practise or board or embark or be in time to catch or terminate or commence or find out or detect or declare or bid or buy a ticket of or lie obstinately at or charge or fix or ascertain or run hoarse or choke or ignite or be set or adopt or test or be pleasing or acceptable to or turn or be under; to set to (ঘরে আগুন ধরানো). **~ধরি** *n.* persistent request; importunities; insistent solicitation; rounding up, arrests. **~বাঁধা** *a.* rigidly fixed; hard and fast; rigid; fixed.

ধরাকাট *n.* stringency; bindings.

ধরাট *n.* (comm.) discount.

ধরিত্রী *n.* the earth; the world.

ধরিয়ে *a.* & *n.* (used as a *sfx.*) one who holds or catches or captures.

ধর্তব্য *a.* worthy of being taken into consideration, countable.

ধর্ম *n.* religion, faith, creed; piety, virtue (অহিংসা পরম ধর্ম) ; scriptural laws or directions (ধর্মসম্মত) ; a form of worship (তান্ত্রিক ধর্ম) ; theology (ধর্মগ্রন্থ) ; natural quality or behaviour or disposition, property or function (মানবধর্ম, কালধর্ম, আগুনের ধর্ম) ; virtuousness, righteousness, morality (ধর্মহীন আচরণ) ; law (ধর্মপত্নী) ; justice (ধর্মাধিকরণ) ; holiness, sacredness (ধর্মের সংসারে পাপ) ; Yama (যম) the god of piety and death; a popular god of Bengal (ধর্মঠাকুর) ; chastity (স্ত্রীলোকের ধর্মনাশ) ; (astrol.) the ninth house from the house of birth in the zodiac. **ধর্মে সওয়া** *v.* (of a sin, misdeed etc.) to be tolerated by God or the Divine Judge. **ধর্মের কল বাতাসে নড়ে, ধর্মের ঢাক আপনি বাজে** (fig.) truth cannot be kept concealed, truth must come out; the irrevocable rod of Nemesis is sure to strike in course of time. **ধর্মের ষাঁড়** (fig.) a wildly wayward man allowed to move scotfree. **ধর্মের সংসার** a family practising virtue, a pious family. **ধর্ম-অর্থ-কাম-মোক্ষ** *n* the four principal aims of human life: piety, wealth, love or fulfilment of desire, and salvation of the soul. **~কন্যা** *n. fem.* one solemnly accepted as a daughter by a person other than one's parents; (loos.) a god-daughter. **ধর্ম-কর্ম, ~কার্য** *n.* religious practices (esp. as enjoined by scriptures). **~কাম** *a.* desirous of attaining virtue through religious practices. **~কৃত্য, ~ক্রিয়া** same as **ধর্মকর্ম**। **~ক্ষেত্র** *n.* a holy or consecrated place, a place of pilgrimage. **~গত** *a.* pious, virtuous; concerning or pertaining to religion, religious. **~গতপ্রাণ** *a.* having one's life devoted to religion or piety; very religious-minded; profoundly or deeply pious. **~গ্রন্থ** *n.* a holy book or text, a scripture; a religious book; a theological treatise. **~ঘট** *n.* (ori.) a religious practice consisting in giving away pitchers filled with holy water; (pol. & pop.) cessation of work as a means of putting pressure on employers, a strike. **ধর্মঘটকালীন ভাতা** strike-pay. **ধর্মঘটী** *n.* (pol.) a striker. **~চক্র** *n.* the four laws or directives of Buddha conducive to attaining final salvation. **~চর্চা** *n.* religious discussion or practice. **~চর্যা** *n.* observance of religious rules and rites, religious practice; practice of virtue.**~চারী** *a.* observant of religious rules and rites, devoted to religious practices; virtuous, pious. **~চিন্তা** *n.* religious meditation; spiritual meditation; theological meditation; theology. **~চ্যুত** same as **ধর্মভ্রষ্ট**। **~জ** *a.* legitimately born. **~জিজ্ঞাসা** *n.* religious inquiry; spiritual inquiry. **~জিজ্ঞাসু** *a.* seeking after or inquisitive about religious or spiritual truths. **~জীবন** *n.* religious or spiritual life; pious or virtuous life; ecclesiastical life. **~জ্ঞ** *a.* conversant with religious rules and duties; conversant with religion; pious, virtuous, religious. **~জ্ঞান** *n.* religious knowledge; religious-mindedness; deep sense of piety. **~ঠাকুর** *n.* a popular god of Bengal named Dharma (ধর্ম). **~ত** *adv.* in the eye of righteousness or piety; according to or conforming to righteousness, piously. **~তত্ত্ব** *n* the mysteries of religion; theology; theosophy, a religious doctrine. **~তত্ত্ববিদ** *n.* one conversant with the mysteries of religion; a theologian; one conversant with a religious doctrine. **~তত্ত্বীয়** *a.* concerning the mysteries of religion, religious; theological; concerning a religious doctrine. **~ত্যাগ** *n.* abandonment of one's religion, adoption of another religion, apostasy. **ধর্মত্যাগ করা** v. to abandon one's religion, to adopt another religion. □ *n.* an apostate, a renegade. **~দ্বেষী, ~দ্রোহী** *a.* revolting against or hostile to religion; irreligious; impious; ungodly. *fem.* **ধর্মদ্বেষিণী, ধর্মদ্রোহিণী**। **~দ্রোহ, ~দ্রোহিতা** *n.* revolt against or hostility towards religion; irreligion; impiety; ungodliness. **~ধ্বজী** *a.* simulating piety or virtuousness; sanctimonious; hypocritical. □ *n.* one simulating piety or virtuousness, a religious imposter. **~নাশ** *n.* ravishment of a woman's chastity, rape; profanation or defilement of one's religion or idol. **ধর্মনাশ করা** *v.* to ravish or outrage one's chastity, to rape; to profane or defile one's religion or idol. **~নিন্দা** *n.* disparagement of religion; blasphemy. **ধর্মের নিন্দা করা** *v.* to disparage religion; to blaspheme. **~নিরপেক্ষ** *a.* irrespective of creed (ধর্মনিরপেক্ষ বিচার) ; secular (ধর্মনিরপেক্ষ রাষ্ট্র). **~নির্দিষ্ট** *a.* enjoined by religion; enjoined by scriptures, scriptural. **~নিষ্ঠ** *a.* devoted to religion or religious practices; pious, virtuous, righteous. **~নিষ্ঠা** *n.* devotion to religion or religious practices; piety, virtuousness, righteousness. **~নীতি** *n.* a religious principle or principles; a principle or principles of virtue; a moral principle or principles; ethics. **~পত্নী** *n.* a lawful wife; a lawfully married wife. **~পথ** *n.* the path of virtue or piety. **ধর্মপথে থাকা** *v.* to follow the path of virtue or piety, to practise virtue or piety; to walk in the presence of God. **~পর, ~পরায়ণ** same as **ধর্মনিষ্ঠ**। **~পাল** *n.* a defender of religion; (Christ.) a bishop. **~পালক** *n.* one who observes religious rites and practices; a defender of religion or faith. **~পালন** *n.* observance of religious rites and practices; defence of religion. **~পিতা** *n.* one solemnly accepted as father by a person other than one's children; (loos.) a godfather. **~পিপাসা** *n.* a strong desire for learning religious truths, thirst for religion. **~পিপাসু** *a.* desirous of learning religious truths, thirsty of religion. **~পুত্র,** (coll. corrup.) **~পুত্তুর** *n.* (loos.) a godson; a son of Yama (যম) the god of piety; an appellation of Yudhisthira of the Mahabharata; (sarcas.) one who poses to be a profoundly pious or truthful man; sanctimonious. **ধর্মপুত্র যুধিষ্ঠির** (sarcas.) a profoundly pious or truthful man, a sanctimonious person. **~পুস্তক** same as **ধর্মগ্রন্থ।** **~প্রচার** *n.* preaching of religion; religious preaching or propaganda; evangelization; evangelism. **ধর্মপ্রচার করা** *v.* to preach religion; to evangelize. **~প্রচারক** *a.* preaching religion; evangelizing. □ *n.* a religious preacher; an evangelist. **~প্রধান** *a.* chiefly guided by religion or religious principles; religious-minded, devout. **~প্রবক্তা** *n.* a prophet. **~প্রবণ** *a.* having propensity towards religion; religious-minded. **~প্রবণতা** *n.* leaning towards religion; religious-mindednesss. **~প্রবর্তক** *n.* the founder of a religion. **~প্রাণ** *a.* counting or regarding religion as precious as one's life; profoundly devout. **~প্রাণতা** *n.* act of counting religion as precious as one's life; profound devoutness. **~বন্ধন** *n.* the bond of religion; a sacred or solemn bond or tie; the holy bondage of being members of the same religious community. **~বন্ধু** *n.* a friend or servant of religion; a friend or helper in religious matters. **~বল** *n.* force of piety or virtuousness. **~বাণী** *n.* a word or teaching of religion; a holy word; an evangel, a gospel.**~বিধান, ~বিধি** *n.* a religious law or rule; a sacred law; a scriptural injunction or prescription. **~বিপ্লব** *n.* a revolution in the world of religion; a great religious change, a religious revolution. **~বিরুদ্ধ, ~বিরোধী** *a.* hostile to religion or piety; irreligious or impious, ungodly. **~বিশ্বাস** *n.* a religious faith, a creed; faith in religion. **~বিশ্বাসী** *a.* having faith in a particular religion or creed; following a particular creed; having faith in religion; virtuous, pious, godly. **~বুদ্ধি** *n.* virtuous or pious or just thought or intention; conscientiousness, conscionableness; good conscience. **~বৃদ্ধ** *n.* a religious or ecclesiastical elder; a member of a priesthood, a father. **~ভয়** *n.* fear of God; religious qualm. **~ভগিনী** *n.* one solemnly accepted as a sister by a person other than one's brother or sister; a female disciple of the same teacher; a member of a sisterhood, a nun, a sister. **~ভাই** coll. form of **ধর্মভ্রাতা।** **~ভীরু** *a.* God-fearing. **~ভীরুতা** *n.* God-fearing conduct or nature. **~ভ্রষ্ট** *a.* gone astray from the religious or righteous course; fallen from one's religious belief. **~ভ্রাতা** *n.* one solemnly accepted as a brother by a person other than one's brother or sister; a disciple of the same teacher or preceptor; a member of a brotherhood or sect or faith; a brother. **~মঙ্গল** *n.* a long poem narrating the glory of Dharmathakur (ধর্মঠাকুর). **~মত** *n.* a religious tenet or doctrine. **~মন্দির** *n.* a house of worship, a temple, a shrine. **~ময়** *a.* full of piety; devout or pious. **~মা, ~মাতা** *n.* one solemnly accepted as mother by a person other than one's child. **~মূলক** *a.* concerning religion, religious. **~যাজক** *n.* an ecclesiastic; a clergyman; a priest. **~যুদ্ধ** *n.* a war for the cause of religion, (cp.) a crusade, a holy war. **~যোদ্ধা** *n.* one fighting for the cause of religion, (cp.) a crusader; a holy warrior. **~রক্ষা** *n.* defence of religion; preservation of one's religion or piety; preservation of chastity (স্ত্রীলোকের ধর্মরক্ষা). **~রাজ** *n.* the lord of justice; an appellation of Yudhisthira of the Mahabharata or that of Yama (যম) or Dharmathakur (ধর্মঠাকুর) or Buddha. **~রাজ্য** *n.* a state or kingdom administered with scrupulous justice, a realm of justice; a state or kingdom founded on religion or piety, a holy state. **~রাষ্ট্র** *n.* a theocratic state. **~লক্ষণ** *n.* any one of the (ten) characteristic signs of piety or virtuousness. **~লোপ** *n.* destruction or extinction of religion or piety; profanation of one's religion; ravishment of (a woman's) chastity. **~শালা** *n.* a guesthouse where pilgrims and travellers are accommodated temporarily at a low cost or free of cost; (ori.) a court of justice. ~শাসন *n.* a religious or scriptural edict; administration of justice; lawful judgment; rule of the ecclesiastics, theocracy. ~শাস্ত্র *n.* scripture. ~শাস্ত্রব্যবসায়ী *n.* a dealer in religious books and scriptures; an expounder and teacher of scriptures, a scribe. ~শাস্ত্রানুমত *a.* conforming to or as prescribed by scriptures. ~শিক্ষক *n.* a religious teacher or preceptor. ~শিক্ষা *n.* religious education or teaching. ~শীল *a.* pious, virtuous. ~সংস্কার *n.* religious reformation; a holy sacrament. ~সংস্কারক *n.* a religious reformer. ~সংস্থাপন *n.* introduction or founding of a religion; firm establishment of a religion; rejuvenation or reinforcement or restoration of a religion. ~সংহিতা *n.* a religious code, a book of holy laws. ~সংগত same as ধর্মসম্মত। ~সংগীত *n.* a devotional song or hymn, a psalm. ~সভা *n.* a religious gathering or congress or convention or congregation or society. ~সম্প্রদায় *n.* a religious community, a religious group or sect. ~সম্মত *a.* conforming to the rules and prescription of religion or piety; pious, virtuous; rightful; just. ~সাক্ষী *a.* having or claiming the god of piety as witness. □ *n.* an oath in the name of the god of piety. ধর্মসাক্ষী করে বলা to take an oath in the name of God, to take a solemn oath. ~সাধন *n.* practice of virtue or religion. ~হানি same as ধর্মনাশ। ~হীন *a.* godless, ungodly, irreligious, impious; blasphemous. ~হীনতা *n.* ungodliness; impiety.

ধর্মাচরণ same as ধর্মচর্যা (see ধর্ম).

ধর্মাত্মা *a.* profoundly virtuous or pious, godly.

ধর্মাধর্ম *n.* virtue and vice, piety and sin; right and wrong. ~বিচারশূন্য *a.* not discriminating between right and wrong, regardless of right and wrong; (loos.) unscrupulous.

ধর্মাধিকরণ, ধর্মাধিষ্ঠান *n.* a court of justice; a judge.

ধর্মাধিকার *n.* authority to act as a judge; jurisdiction of a judge; judgeship.

ধর্মাধিকারী *n.* a judge.

ধর্মাধ্যক্ষ *n.* an official superintendent of matters concerning religion; a religious head; a chief justice.

ধর্মানুগত, ধর্মানুমোদিত, ধর্মানুযায়ী same as ধর্মসম্মত (see ধর্ম).

ধর্মানুষ্ঠান *n.* performance of a religious or scriptural rite; rituals; practice of virtue; an act of piety. ধর্মানুষ্ঠাতা *n.* a performer of a rite; a ritualist; a virtuous or pious man. *fem.* ধর্মানুষ্ঠাত্রী।

ধর্মান্তর *n.* another religion, a different religion. ~গ্রহণ *n.* adoption of or conversion to a different religion. ধর্মান্তর গ্রহণ করা *v.* to adopt a different religion, to be converted to a different religion. ধর্মান্তরিত *a.* converted to a different religion. *fem.* ধর্মান্তরিতা। ধর্মান্তরিত ব্যক্তি *n.* a religious convert. ধর্মান্তরীকরণ *n.* conversion to a different faith or religion, proselytism.

ধর্মান্দোলন *n.* a religious or theological movement; a religious or theological discussion or consideration; (loos. but pop.) a religious or theological dispute or agitation.

ধর্মান্ধ *a.* fanatical, fanatic; bigoted. ধর্মান্ধ ব্যক্তি a fanatic; a bigot. ~তা *n.* fanaticism; bigotry.

ধর্মাবতার *n.* virtue or piety or justice incarnate (used in addressing a judge, a king, a patron etc.).

ধর্মাবলম্বন *n.* practising a religion; adoption of a religion. ধর্মাবলম্বন করা *v.* to practise or follow a religion or creed; to adopt a religion. ধর্মাবলম্বী *a.* following or practising a religion. *fem.* ধর্মাবলম্বিনী।

ধর্মারণ্য *n.* hermitage.

ধর্মার্জন *n.* acquisition of virtue or piety. ধর্মার্জন করা *v.* to acquire virtue or piety.

ধর্মার্থ *n.* virtue or piety and wealth. □ *adv.* for the sake of religion or faith. ধর্মার্থে same as ধর্মার্থ (*adv.*).

ধর্মালয় *n.* a temple; a place of worship.

ধর্মাসন *n.* a judgment-seat, a seat of justice; the bench.

ধর্মিষ্ঠ *a.* profoundly pious or virtuous or righteous. *fem.* ধর্মিষ্ঠা।

ধর্মী *a.* (chiefly used as a *sfx.*) having a

particular property or quality (ক্ষারধর্মী, হাঁ-ধর্মী) ; (rare) pious, virtuous.

ধর্মীয় *a.* religious, pertaining to, relating to or concerning religion (ধর্মীয় অনুষ্ঠান, ধর্মীয় উপদেশ)।

ধর্মোন্নতি *n.* advancement of religion.

ধর্মোন্মত্ত *a.* having a religious craze; fanatical.

ধর্মোন্মাদ *n.* religious craze; fanaticism; a religious fanatic.

ধর্মোপদেশ *n.* religious instruction; a sermon. **ধর্মোপদেশ দেওয়া** *v.* to impart religious instruction; to sermonize.

ধর্মোপদেশক, ধর্মোপদেষ্টা *a.* imparting religious instruction; sermonizing. □ *n.* a religious instructor; a semonizer.

ধর্মোপাসক *a.* devoted to or following a religion. □ *n.* a devotee (of a religion).

ধর্মোপাসনা *n.* religious worship or prayer. **ধর্মোপাসনা করা** *v.* to observe religious rites; to pray.

ধর্মোপাসিকা *fem.* of **ধর্মোপাসক**।

ধর্ম্য *a.* virtuous, righteous; rightful, just; lawful; rightfully or lawfully obtained.

ধর্ষ, ধর্ষণ *n.* oppression; act of forcing; ravishment, outrage; rape; subdual; act of defeating. **ধর্ষণ করা** *v.* to oppress; to force; to ravish, to outrage; to rape; to subdue; to defeat. **ধর্ষক** *a.* & *n.* one who or that which oppresses or forces or ravishes or outrages or subdues or defeats. **ধর্ষীয়** *a.* fit to be or capable of being oppressed or forced or ravished or outraged or subdued or defeated. *fem.* **ধর্ষণীয়া**।

ধর্ষিত *a.* oppressed; forced; ravished, outraged; raped; subdued; defeated. *fem.* **ধর্ষিতা**।

ধলা *a.* (usu. dial.) white, fair, fair-complexioned.

ধস[১] *int.* expressing a falling sound as of a landslip.

ধস[২] *n.* a landslip.

ধসকা *a.* that which may easily come down, loose (ধসকা মাটি) ; hanging loosely; easily indisposed, unfit for hard work (ধসকা শরীর). **ধসকানো** *v.* to become so loose that it may come down (নদীর পাড় ধসকেছে) ; to become weak or enfeebled (শরীর ধসকানো).

ধসা *v.* to come off and fall down (নদীর পাড় ধসা) ; to collapse (বাড়ির পাঁচিল ধসা) ; to weaken or deteriorate (রোগে শরীর ধসা). □ *a.* that which has come off and fallen down; collapsed; weakened or deteriorated. **ধসানো** *v.* to cause to come off and fall down; to loosen and throw down; to cause to collapse; to make weak or to impair.

ধস্তাধস্তি *n.* a scuffle or tussle or fray; a hard effort or struggle (অনেক ধস্তাধস্তির পর মাইনে বাড়ল). **ধস্তাধস্তি করা** *v.* to scuffle; to try or struggle hard.

ধা[১] *n.* (mus.) the natural B sound; the sixth note in the Indian musical gamut.

ধা[২] *sfx.* meaning : ways, means etc.. fold (শতধা, বহুধা).

ধাই, ধাই-মা *n.* nurse; nurse-mother; a wet-nurse; a midwife; a foster-mother.

ধাউড় *n.* a swindler, a crook, a cheat.

ধাউড়ে *n.* an errand-boy, a fast messenger.

ধাউস var. of **ঢাউস**।

ধাওড়া *n.* an accommodation or mud-built quarters usually for labourers.

ধাওয়া *v.* to run; to run after, to chase hotly. **ধাওয়া করা** same as **ধাওয়া**। **ধাওয়ানো** *v.* to cause to run or chase; to chase away; to give a hot chase.

ধাঁ *int.* expressing: suddenness (ধাঁ করে জ্বলে ওঠা) or quickness (ধাঁ করে কাজ শেষ করা) or noisy abruptness (ধাঁ করে ঝাপ ফেলা). **ধাঁ করে** *adv.* suddenly; quickly; abruptly with a noise; straightway.

ধাঁচ, ধাঁচা *n.* shape, form, cut; type, manner, pattern; semblance of shape.

ধাঁধা *n.* dazzlement of sight; optical illusion; confusion, bewilderment, daze; an intricate problem; a riddle, a puzzle; a maze; a tricky but interesting question or problem, a poser. □ *v.* (usu. in poet.) to dazzle the sight of, to have one's sight dazzled, to daze. **ধাঁধাঁর উত্তর** the solution of a puzzle. **ধাঁধা দেওয়া** *v.* to give a puzzle for solution; to hoodwink; to confound; to bamboozle. **ধাঁধা লাগা** *v.* to have one's sight dazzled; to be dazed; to be confused or puzzled. **ধাঁধা লাগানো** *v.* to daze the sight of; to daze; to confound; to bewilder, to puzzle; to hoodwink; to dazzle. **ধাঁধানো** same as **ধাঁধা লাগানো** ।

ধাক্কা *n.* a push, a shove; a driving force or action (বাতাসের ধাক্কা) ; an impact, a collision (ট্রেনে ট্রেনে ধাক্কা) ; pressure or attack (কাজের ধাক্কা, রোগের ধাক্কা) ; a shock (মনে ধাক্কা লাগা). **ধাক্কা খাওয়া** *v.* to be shocked; to be pushed or shoved; to get or receive a jolt; to be driven on; to collide or dash against; to be impeded or hindered usu. suddenly, to get a set-back (তার ব্যাবসা ধাক্কা খেয়েছে). **ধাক্কা দেওয়া** *v.* to give a push, to push, to shove; to collide or dash against; to shock; to impede or hinder usu. suddenly, to check progress of. **ধাক্কা লাগা** *v.* to have a collision; to dash or collide against; to be shoved or pushed, to be shocked; to get a set-back. **~ধাক্কি** *n.* mutual or continuous pushing or shoving or elbowing. **ধাক্কানো** *v.* to push, to shove; to elbow.

ধাঙড় *n.* a sweeper (by caste or trade).

ধাড়ি *n. fem.* a dam of beasts (ধাড়ি ও বাচ্চা) ; (chiefly hum.) a mother of many children. □ *n.* (usu. masc.) (dero.) a leader or ringleader (চোরের ধাড়ি) ; (dero.) a grown-up person or child (ধাড়ির বায়নাও সইব নাকি ?). □ *a.* grown-up (ধাড়ি ছেলে) ; inveterate (ধাড়ি শয়তান).

ধাত *n.* mettle, temperament, disposition, spirit, nature (লোকের ধাত বুঝে চলা) ; (physiol.) any of the four fluids of the body, humour (সর্দির ধাত) ; pulse (ধাত ছেড়ে যাওয়া) ; semen, seed (ধাতের রোগ). **ধাত ছেড়ে যাওয়া** failing of pulse, stopping of heart beats; to be in a state of collapse. **ধাতের রোগ** spermatorrhoea; (loos.) gonorrhoea. **~সহ** *a.* in accordance or agreement with bodily condition or constitution or temperament or nature. **~স্থ** *a.* one who is enjoying or has regained one's mental calm, in a state of composure; one who is in his humour; one who has come round or recovered; acclimatized, accustomed.

ধাতব *a.* of or made of or caused by metal, metallic; mineral; (rare) concerning semen. **ধাতব দ্যুতি** metallic lustre. **ধাতব প্রস্রবণ** a mineral spring. **ধাতব ব্যাধি** *a.* disease or disorder of semen, spermatorrhoea; (loos.) gonorrhoea.

ধাতসহ, ধাতস্থ see **ধাত** ।

ধাতা *n.* God; Brahma (ব্রহ্মা) ; father. □ *a & n.* one who contains or bears or protects or creates or builds.

ধাতানি *n.* a sound scolding; reprimand. **ধাতানো** *v.* to scold soundly, to reprimand, to take somebody to task severely.

ধাতু *n.* a metal; a mineral; mettle (লোকটি শক্ত ধাতুতে গড়া) ; temperament, disposition (শিল্পীদের ধাতুই আলাদা) ; (physiol.) any one of the four constituent fluids of the body, a humour; semen, sperm (ধাতুদৌর্বল্য) ; any one of the principal constituents of the physical world (namely, earth, water, fire, air, and atmosphere), an element; (gr.) a verbal root. **অবরধাতু** a base metal. **বরধাতু** a noble metal. **~কল্প** *a.* metalloid. **~ক্ষয়** *n.* (passive) loss of seminal fluid, seminal emission; (rare) abrasion of metal. **~গত** *a.* temperamental; constitutional, characteristic; seminal; (rare) metallic. **~গর্ভ** *a.* impregnated with minerals or metals, mineral; (of a Buddhist temple) containing the remains of a holy person's corpse. **~ঘটিত** *a.* of or made of metal, metallic; mineral; (of medicine) having metal as a constituent; concerning semen. **~দৌর্বল্য** *n.* spermatorrhoea. **~দ্রাবক** *n.* borax. **~নিঃস্রব** *n.* a flowing out of molten metal, lava; a flowing out of semen. **~পাত্র** *n.* a metal vessel. **~পোষক** *a.* nourishing, nutritive. **~বল্লভ** *n.* borax. **~বিজ্ঞান, ~বিদ্যা** *n.* metallurgy. **~বিদ** *n.* metallurgist. **~ময়** *a.* full of or made of or impregnated with metal, metallic or mineral. **~মল** *n.* rust. **~মাক্ষিক** *n.* sulphate of iron or pyrite. **~রূপ** *n.* conjugation. **~লেপন** *n.* plating.

ধাত্রী *n.* a progenitrix, a progenitress, a mother; a nurse-mother; a wet-nurse; a foster-mother; a midwife; a nurse; the

Earth (esp. as conceived as mother of all created beings). □ *a. fem.* one who carries in the womb; one who bears. **~পুত্র** *n.* a son of a nurse-mother or wet-nurse. **~বিদ্যা** *n.* midwifery. **ধাত্রীবিদ্যা বিশারদ** *n.* a midwife, a gynaecologist and obstetrician.

ধাত্রীয় *n.* a nurse-mother; a wet-nurse; a foster-mother, a midwife; a nurse.

ধান *n.* paddy, rice (আমন ধান) ; measure of weight (= nearly 1 grain). **আউস ধান** autumn rice. **আমন ধান** winter rice. **বীজ ধান** *n.* paddy-seed. **ধান কাটা** *v.* to reap or harvest paddy-crop. **ধান কাঁড়া** same as **ধান ভানা**। **ধান কাড়ানো** *v.* to plough a paddy-field in order to remove weeds. **ধান ঝাড়া** *v.* to thresh paddy. **ধান দিয়ে লেখাপড়া শেখা** (fig.) to spend little for one's education; (fig.) to receive indifferent or scant education. **ধান নেড়ে দেওয়া** *v.* to re-sow or transplant paddy-shoots in well-arranged lines; to stir paddy when it is husked by a husking pedal. **ধান বোনা** *v.* to sow paddy-seeds. **ধান ভাঙা, ধান ভানা** *v.* to husk paddy. **ধানভাঙা কল** a husking machine. **ধান ভানতে শিবের গীত** (fig.) an irrelevant talk or digression (often a ludicrous one). **ধান মাড়ানো** *v.* to thresh or separate paddy (from straw by making cows walk upon it). **ধান রোয়া** *v.* to transplant paddy-shoots. **কত ধানে কত চাল** (fig.) actual state or correct information, knowledge of what comes out of what; (fig.) consequence. **পাকা ধানে মই দেওয়া** (fig.) to do (one) irreparable harm; (fig.) to blast one's hopes when they are about to be realized. **~খেত** same as **ধানজমি**। **~গাছ** *n.* a paddy-plant. **ধানগাছের তক্তা** (fig.) a plank of grass, an impossible thing. **~চারা** *n.* a paddy-shoot. **~জমি** *n.* a paddy-field, a paddy-land. **~দূর্বা** *n.* paddy-grains and grass (used as auspicious articles in blessing).

ধানশ্রী, ধানশি *n.* an Indian musical mode.

ধানাইপানাই *n.* irrelevant talk or excuse.

ধানি *a.* green as unripe paddy, paddy-green (ধানি রং) ; very small, puny (ধানি লঙ্কা) ; containing or yielding paddy (ধানি জমি). **ধানি মদ** wine of inferior quality distilled from rice.

ধানী *n.* (used chiefly as a *sfx.*) a place or residence or seat (রাজধানী)।

ধানুকি, ধানুষ্ক *n.* a bowman, an archer; a soldier fighting with bow and arrow. □ *a.* versed in archery; armed with bow and arrow.

ধান্দা, ধান্ধা *n.* dazzlement of sight; optical illusion; confusion, dazed condition; search (চাকরির ধান্দা, টাকার ধান্দা) ; cause of demand (পেটের ধান্দা). **~বাজ** *a.* too self-seeking and opportunist. □ *n.* a self-seeker and opportunist.

ধান্য (High Beng.) *n.* paddy. **~কর্তন** same as **ধান্যচ্ছেদন**। **~ক্ষেত্র** *n.* a paddy field, a paddy land. **~চ্ছেদন** *n.* act of reaping or harvesting paddy crop. **~বপন** *n.* act of sowing paddy seeds. **~বীজ** *n.* paddy seed. **~রোপণ** *n.* act of transplanting paddy shoots.

ধান্যক, ধান্যাক *n.* coriander; coriander seed.

ধান্যাম্ল *n.* acetic acid.

ধান্যেশ্বরী *n.* (facet. & dero.) an inferior wine prepared from rice, rice-grog (coll. ধেনো).

ধাপ *n.* a step (as of a staircase); a stratum; a leap (দৌড়ধাপ). **ধাপে ধাপে** at every step; step by step; in a stratified manner; by degrees.

ধাপধাড়া গোবিন্দপুর *n.* (facet. or dero.) an obscure, contemptible and remote place, an out-of-the-way place.

ধাপা *n.* a low and usually marshy land where rubbish and filth are deposited (also **ধাপার মাঠ**).

ধাপ্পা *n.* a bluff, a hoax. **ধাপ্পা দেওয়া** *v.* to bluff, to hoax. **~বাজ** *a.* (given to) bluffing or hoaxing. □ *n.* a bluffer or a hoaxer. **~বাজি** *n.* practice of bluffing or hoaxing. **ধাপ্পাবাজি করা** *v.* to practise bluffing or hoaxing; to bluff or hoax.

ধাবক *a.* one who runs or flies; one who cleanses or washes; used in cleaning or washing (ধাবক পদার্থ) ; carrying a message or letter. □ *n.* a washerman; a runner; a flier; a courier, a postal runner, a messenger.

ধাবড়া *n.* an ugly extensive mark or impression, an ugly patch. □ *a.* patchy and ugly (ধাবড়া দাগ).

ধাবড়ানো *v.* to scatter in an ugly patch; to overlay with an ugly patch. □ *a.* scattered in or overlaid with an ugly patch.

ধাবধাড়া গোবিন্দপুর var. of **ধাপধাড়া গোবিন্দপুর**।

ধাবন *n.* act of running; a run; a race; flight; act of cleansing or washing. **~পথ** *n.* air-strip.

ধাবমান *a.* rushing; running; flying; fleeting.

ধাবিত *a.* running; flying; fleeting; in flight; washed. **ধাবিত করা** *v.* to cause to run or fly; to wash. **ধাবিত হওয়া** *v.* to run or fly; to rush hastily, to take to one's heels; to wash or be washed.

ধাম *n.* (mostly used as a *sfx.*) a dwelling-house, a residence, an abode (নিজধাম) ; an address (নামধাম) ; a place, a seat (শান্তিধাম) ; a holy place; a place of pilgrimage (গয়াধাম) ; a repository (গুণধাম) ; a receptacle, a container.

ধামনিক *a.* arterial; nervous.

ধামসানি *n.* thrashing; kneading with hands and feet.

ধামসানো *v.* to trample; to knead with hands and feet. □ *a.* trampled; kneaded with hands and feet.

ধামা *n.* a hemispherical rattan-basket or wicker-basket or scuttle having no lid. **~চাপা** *a.* (fig.) concealed, hushed up, shelved. **~চাপা দেওয়া** *v.* to conceal, to hush up, to shelve. **ধামা ধরা** *v.* to fawn or cringe (upon). **~ধরা** *a.* cringing, fawning. □ *n.* a servile flatterer or sycophant or toady.

ধামার *n.* an Indian musical measure or mode.

ধামি dim. of **ধামা**।

-ধার[১] *a.* (used as a *sfx.*) holding or gripping (কর্ণধার).

ধার[২] *n.* a stream or flow (অশ্রুধার).

ধার[৩] *n.* an edge, a border, a brim, a brink, a brow (পথের ধার, নদীর ধার, পাহাড়ের ধার) ; a side or face (এধারে, ওধারে) ; proximity, approach, contiguity, vicinity (বাড়ির ধারে, ধারেকাছে) ; sharpness, edge (ছুরির ধার) ; keenness (বুদ্ধির ধার) ; intelligence or wit; debt, loan (বাজারে অনেক ধার) ; credit (ধারে কেনা) ; concern, connection (ধার ধারা). **ধার করা** *v.* to borrow; to sharpen, to whet. **ধার দেওয়া** *v.* to lend; to sharpen, to whet. **ধার ধারা** *v.* to be indebted to, to have any concern with; to care for, to pay heed to. **ধার হওয়া** *v.* to be in debt. **ধারে কেনা বা বেচা** *v.* to buy or sell on credit. **ধারে কেনা-বেচা** buying and selling on credit. **হয় ধারে কাটা নয় ভারে কাটা** (fig.) to pass or be counted highly on account of merit or prestige and position or weight and importance. **ধারে ডোবা** *v.* to be deeply involved in debt, to be over head and ears in debt.

ধারক *a.* & *n.* one who or that which holds or contains or bears or carries; one who assists and corrects a reader of scriptures at a ritual; one who makes another recite mantras, that is scriptural verses; (an) astringent. **~তা** *n.* capacity; astringency. **~ত্ব** *n.* capacity.

ধারণ *n.* act of holding or catching; act of assuming (মূর্তিধারণ, নামধারণ) ; act of putting on or wearing (বেশধারণ) ; act of bearing (শিরে পৃথিবী ধারণ) ; act of carrying, carriage (গর্ভে ধারণ) ; act of carrying in the womb (সন্তানধারণ) ; act of placing (মাথায় প্রসাদ ধারণ) ; act of retaining in mind, remembrance (উপদেশধারণ) ; acceptance; retention or restraint (মলমূত্রের বেগ ধারণ). **ধারণ করা** *v.* to hold, to catch; to assume; to wear, to put on; to bear; to carry; to carry in the womb; to place or put; to retain in the mind, to remember; to accept; to retain or restrain. **~কারী** same as **ধারয়িতা**।

ধারণা *n.* conception; realization or comprehension; feeling or impression; supposition, surmise; a notion; an idea; belief or faith; remembrance or memory; intelligence; rapt attention. **ধারণা করা** *v.* to conceive; to realize or comprehend; to feel, to have an impression (of); to suppose, to guess; to form or have an idea (of); to believe;

to think. ~তীত *a.* inconceivable; incomprehensible; (loos.) unthought of, unexpected. ~শক্তি *n.* ability to conceive an idea, power of comprehension; intelligence; retentive capacity or power.

ধারণীয় *a.* capable of being or fit to be held or caught or assumed or worn or put on or borne or carried or placed or retained in the mind or accepted or retained or restrained.

ধারয়িতা *a.* one who or that which holds or catches or assumes or wears or puts on or bears or carries or places or retains in one's memory or remembers or accepts or retains or restrains. **ধারয়িত্রী** *a. fem.* of **ধারয়িতা** । □ *n.* the earth (esp. when conceived as the progenitrix of all creatures).

ধারয়িষ্ণু *a.* one who or that which holds or bears or carries or wears.

ধারা[1] *v.* to owe (টাকা ধারা) ; to have any connection or concern with (কারও বা কিছুর ধার ধারা).

ধারা[2] *n.* a stream, a flow (রক্তধারা, আলোকধারা) ; a current (স্রোতোধারা) ; a shower (বৃষ্টিধারা) ; a stream or shower of any liquid (জলধারা, নয়নধারা) ; a spring, a fountain, a waterfall, a cascade (সহস্রধারা) ; a system, a method, a way (কাজের ধারা) ; a rule or go (জগতের বা দুনিয়ার ধারা) ; succession, serial, order, train (চিন্তাধারা) ; fashion, manner (অমনধারা) ; (law) a clause or section (আইনের ধারা). **বর্তমানের ধারা** order of the day, prevailing state of things. **~কদম্ব** *n.* a kind of tree yielding beautiful flowers of globular shape. **~কারে** *adv.* in or like a stream, streamingly; profusely in numerous streams. **~ক্রমে** *adv.* according to system or method, systematically or methodically; according to rule; successively, serially. **~গৃহ** *n.* a bathroom fitted with a shower-bath. **~স্কুর** *n.* a drop of water or rain; hail. **~ধর** *n.* the cloud. **~নি** *n.* a stream of water from above (as from a shower bath). **~বর্ণনা** *n.* running commentary of an event or a game. **~বর্ষ, ~বর্ষণ** *n.* heavy and incessant rain or downpour. **~বাহিক, ~বাহী** *a.* continuous; serial; successive. **~বাহিকতা, ~বাহিতা** *n.* continuity; seriality; succession. **~বাহিকক্রমে, ~বাাহিকভাবে** *adv.* continuously; serially; successively. **~বিবরণী, ~ভাষ্য** same as **ধারাবর্ণনা** । **~মতো, ~মতে** *adv.* (law) according to a particular section or clause of an act. **~যন্ত্র** *n.* a fountain; a syringe; a spraying apparatus, a shower-bath, a shower. **~শ্রাবণ** *n.* the month of Shravan (July-August) when there are heavy showers or when it rains heavily. **~সম্পাত, ~সার** *n.* heavy and incessant rain; torrential rain or downpour.

ধারাপাত *n.* heavy and incessant rain; a book of arithmetical enumeration.

ধারালো *a.* sharp, sharp-edged; keen.

ধারি *n.* a narrow verandah or gallery of a mud-built house; a brim, a margin, an edge, a brink.

ধারিণী *a. fem.* of **ধারী**[2] । □ *n. fem.* the earth.

ধারী[1] rej. spell. of **ধারি** ।

ধারী[2] *a.* (chiefly used as a *sfx.*) holding, carrying, bearing, wearing, assuming (অস্ত্রধারী, বস্ত্রধারী).

ধারোষ্ণ *a.* (of milk esp. of bovine animals) lukewarm because of being drawn from the udder.

ধার্তরাষ্ট্র *n.* a son of King Dhritarashtra of the Mahabharata.

ধার্মিক *a.* pious, righteous, virtuous, godly; religious-minded. *fem.* (rare) **ধার্মিকী,** (loos. but pop.) **ধার্মিকা** । **~তা** *n.* piety, righteousness, virtuousness, godliness; religiosity.

ধার্য *a.* (ori. but obs.) worth holding or bearing or putting on; (pop.) fixed, settled; (of taxes etc.) imposed. **কর ধার্য করা** to impose a tax. **দিন ধার্য করা** to fix a date. **~মাণ** *a.* that which is being fixed or settled or imposed.

ধার্ষ্টামি, ধার্ষ্ট্য *n.* impertinence, sauciness, pertness, insolence; knavery. **ধার্ষ্টামি করা** *v.* to behave impertinently; to be saucy or insolent; to behave knavishly.

ধিক *int.* fie.

ধিক্‌কার, ধিক্কার *n.* act of crying fie upon. **ধিক্কার দেওয়া** *v.* to cry fie upon, to hoot.

ধিক্‌কৃত, ধিক্কৃত *a.* hooted.

ধিকধিক rather a harsher var. of **ধিকিধিকি**।

ধিকিধিকি *adv.* suppressedly and continuously (ধিকিধিকি জ্বলা) ; burning continuously in a suppressed manner, shimmeringly (ধিকিধিকি করা). □ *a.* burning continuously in a suppressed manner, shimmering, smouldering (ধিকিধিকি আগুন).

ধিঙ্গি *a. fem.* wayward, self-willed, undisciplined, unruly, romping, unmannerly, immodest. **ধিঙ্গি মেয়ে** a wayward or somewhat wild or romping or unmannerly or immodest girl; a tomboy.

ধিনধিন, ধিন-তা-ধিন *int.* key-words indicating the measure of a dance.

ধিমা var. of **ঢিমা**।

ধী *n.* intellect; intelligence; cognition; comprehension; knowledge; wisdom; talent; aptitude. **~মান** *a.* intelligent; capable of comprehending, capable of quick appreciation; talented; having aptitude; wise. *fem.* **~মতী**। **~শক্তি** same as **ধী**। **~শক্তিসম্পন্ন** same as **ধীমান**।

ধীবর *n.* a fisherman (by trade or caste), a fisher. *fem.* **ধীবরী** *n.* a fisher-woman; a fishwife, a fish-woman.

ধীমতী, ধীমান see **ধী**।

ধীর *a.* slow, tardy (ধীর গতি) ; unperturbed, calm, composed (ধীর মন) ; gentle or modest or mild (ধীরস্বভাব, ধীর বায়ু) ; grave (ধীরকণ্ঠ) ; firm, steady (ধীর চিত্ত) ; judicious or considerate (ধীর ব্যক্তি). **~তা** *n.* slowness; unperturbedness, calmness, composure; gentleness, modesty, mildness; graveness, gravity; firmness, steadiness; judiciousness, considerateness. **~প্রকৃতি** *a.* gentle or modest by nature. **~প্রশান্ত** *n.* (rhet.) a type of hero endowed with various good qualities. **~ভাবে** *adv.* slowly; mildly; gently; calmly. **~ললিত** *n.* (rhet.) a type of hero who is gentle by nature and of calm disposition and proficient in music and dance. **~স্বভাব** same as **ধীরপ্রকৃতি**। **~স্থির** *a.* calm and composed.

ধীরা *a. fem.* of **ধীর**। □ *n. fem.* (rhet.) a type of heroine whose anger is never exhibited. **~ধীরা** *n. fem.* (rhet.) a type of heroine whose anger or resentment is partially exhibited.

ধীরে, ধীরে ধীরে, (poet.) **ধীরি,** (poet.) **ধীরিধীরি** *adv.* slowly, tardily; leisurely; softly; gradually; by degrees. **ধীরেসুস্থে** *adv.* in a leisurely manner.

ধীরোদাত্ত *n.* (rhet.) a type of hero who is calm and modest and is unmoved by reverses of fortune and who protects others.

ধীরোদ্ধত *n.* (rhet.) a type of hero who is resourceful and usually gentle-natured but at times arrogant and vain.

ধীশক্তি see **ধী**।

ধুঁকনি *n.* a spell of panting for breath; palpitation, throbbing.

ধুঁকা *v.* to pant or gasp for breath; to palpitate, to throb (প্রাণ ধুঁকছে).

ধুঁকুনি pop. var. of **ধুঁকনি**।

ধুঁদুল coll. form of **ধুন্দুল**।

ধুকড়ি var. of **ধোঁকড়**।

ধুকধুক, ধুকপুক *int.* expressing: the sound of palpitating or throbbing. **ধুকধুক করা, ধুকপুক করা** *v.* to palpitate, to throb. **ধুকধুকানি** *n.* palpitation, throbbing.

ধুকধুকি *n.* a locket or pendent worn on the bosom in a necklace.

ধুচনি, ধুচুনি *n.* a wicker-basket for washing rice, fish etc. **ধুচনি-টুপি, ধুচুনি-টুপি** *n.* a straw-hat shaped like a wicker-basket.

ধুৎ *int.* a sound expressing: repulsion, aversion, slight mistrust etc; sh, pish, psh, bosh.

ধুত *a.* caused to tremble or quiver, shaken; sounded or played (as a stringed musical instrument); expelled; removed, driven away, scolded, reprimanded.

ধুতরা, ধুতরো *n.* the thorn apple or its fruit or flower, the datura. **ধুতরোর রস বা নির্যাস** *n.* daturine.

ধুতি *n.* a loincloth for men, dhoti, dhooti. **থানধুতি** see **থান**।

ধুতুরা same as **ধুতরা**।

ধুত্তোর stronger var. of **ধুৎ**।

ধু-ধু *int.* expressing: state of burning or flaming strongly (ধু-ধু করে জ্বলা) ; desolateness or voidance (মন ধু-ধু করা) ; vast expanse (ধু-ধু মাঠ).

ধুন *n.* a light classical musical note usually played on an instrument.

ধুনচি *n.* an incense burner, an incenser, a censer, a thurible.

ধুনন *n.* act of shaking; a shake; act of sounding or playing (as a stringed musical instrument); act of cleaning cotton by shredding it with a bow or cotton-gin, ginning and carding (cotton, wool etc.).

ধুনরি pop. var. of **ধুনারি** ।

ধুনা[1] *n.* resin; incense.

ধুনা[2] *v.* to clean cotton by shredding it with a bow or a cotton-gin; (sl.) to give a sound drubbing.

ধুনাচি var. of **ধুনচি** ।

ধুনারি *n.* one who cleans cotton by shredding with a bow or cotton-gin, a cotton-cleaner.

ধুনি[1] *n.* a (sacrificial) fire enkindled by ascetics.

ধুনি[2], **ধুনী** *n.* (chiefly used as a *sfx.*) a river (সুরধুনী).

ধুনুচি var. of **ধুনচি** ।

ধুন্দুল *n.* a kitchen-vegetable cylindrical and tapering at both ends.

ধুন্ধুমার *n.* a mythological king famous for his valour; uproar, tumult; a tumultuous or terrible affair. □ *a.* tumultuous or terrible (ধুন্ধুমার কাণ্ড).

ধুপ[1] *n.* sunlight, the sun.

ধুপ[2] lighter var. of **ধপ** । **ধুপ ধুপ, ধুপ ধাপ** lighter variants of **ধপ ধপ** ।

ধুপচি *n.* an incense-burner, an incenser, a censer, a thurible, an incensory.

ধুপছায়া *n.* a mixture of blue and light violet, peacock-blue; (loos.) light-and-shade colour; (loos.) chiaroscuro. □ *a.* peacock-blue; (loos.) light-and-shade; (loos.) chiaroscuro.

ধুম *n.* overmuchness, abundance, excess, wantonness, redundance, surfeit (গঙ্গাস্নানের ধুম, বিলাসিতার ধুম, বক্তৃতার ধুম) ; éclat, pomp (এবার পুজোয় বড় ধুম). □ *a.* terrible, hard, thick (ধুম মারামারি).

ধুমড়ি *n. fem.* a corpulent (and usu. lazy) woman.

ধুমধাড়াক্কা *n.* great or tumultuous éclat or pomp.

ধুমধাম *n.* thud; tumult; pomp, grand pageantry.

ধুমসা, (pop.) **ধুমসো** *a.* extremely dark-complexioned and corpulent. *fem.* **ধুমসি** ।

ধুম্ব, ধুম্বা *a.* tall and corpulent, hefty. *fem.* **ধুম্বি** ।

ধুয়া[1] var. of **ধোয়া** ।

ধুয়ো, ধুয়া[2] (coll.) *n.* burden of a song, a refrain, a chorus; (fig.) hackneyed talk or comment, a platitude (পুরোনো ধুয়ো) ; an insistent demand or claim; a pretext; a fashion. **ধুয়ো ওঠা** *v.* to be the current talk or demand; to be in vogue; to be introduced as a fashion; to be demanded or claimed. **ধুয়ো তোলা** *v.* to voice a demand insistently; to demand insistently; to introduce as a fashion. **ধুয়ো ধরা** *v.* to repeat or follow up the burden of a song; (fig.) to insist on a demand or claim.

ধুর var. of **ধুরা** ।

ধুরন্ধর *a.* bearing the yoke; very expert or efficient or adroit; leading, chief. □ *n.* such a person.

ধুরা *n.* the shaft of a vehicle, a thill; a yoke; an axle, an axle-tree; (fig.) burden, load.

ধুরীণ same as **ধুরন্ধর** ।

ধুল *n.* a measure of land (= ১/২০ কাঠা) ; (poet. or dial.) dust.

ধুলট *n.* a spell or act of wallowing in the dust in ecstasy caused by singing devotional song, post-hymnic ecstatic wallowing in the dust.

ধুলা, (coll.) **ধুলো** *n.* dust; dirt. **ধুলোর আস্তরণ** *n.* dust or soot deposited on a surface; grime.

ধুস্তুর, ধুস্তূর *n.* the thorn-apple, the datura. **ধুস্তুরী, ধুস্তূরী** *a.* daturic, atropinic.

ধৃত alt. spell. of **ধুত** ।

ধূনন alt. spell. of **ধুনন** ।

ধূপ *n.* resin, incense. **~কাঠি** *n.* incense burner, incense stick. **ধূপচি** alt. spell of **ধুপচি** । **~ধুনো** *n.* incense; incensing. **ধূপন**

n. act of perfuming or fumigating with incense, incensing.

ধূপায়িত, ধূপিত *a.* perfumed or fumigated with incense, incensed.

ধূম *n.* smoke, fume, vapour, steam, gas; (loos.) mist, fog. **~কুণ্ডলী** *n.* a ring or coil of smoke. **~কেতু** *n.* a comet. **~নালী, ~পথ** *n.* a pipe or conduit for the escape of smoke, fume, vapour etc, a chimney; a fumarole. **~নির্গম, ~নির্গমন** *n.* escape of smoke, vapour, gas etc. **~পান** *n.* smoking (cigars, cigarettes etc.). **ধূমপান করা** *v.* to smoke (cigarettes etc.). **~পায়ী** *a.* addicted to smoking. □ *n.* a smoker. **~বিহীন** *a.* same as **ধূমহীন**। **~ময়** *a.* full of or made of smoke, fume, vapour, gas etc.; smoky, fumy, vapoury, gaseous; (loos.) misty, foggy. **ধূমল** *n.* the colour of smoke, the dark purple colour. □ *a.* smoke-coloured, dark purple. **~হীন** *a.* smokeless, free from vapour or smoke. **~হীনতা** *n.* smokelessness.

ধূমাকার *a.* shaped like or looking like smoke, fume, vapour, gas etc.

ধূমাকীর্ণ, ধূমাচ্ছন্ন *a.* covered with or enveloped in smoke, fume, vapour, gas etc.

ধূমাভ same as **ধূমল** (see **ধূম**).

ধূমায়মান *a.* emitting smoke, fume, vapour, gas etc.; fuming; smouldering.

ধূমায়িত, ধূমিত *a.* full of or emitting smoke, fume, vapour, gas etc.; fumigated.

ধূমোদ্গম *n.* discharge or emission of smoke, fume, gas etc.

ধূমোদ্গার, ধূমোদ্গিরণ *n.* emission of smoke, fume, vapour, gas etc., **ধূমোদ্গার করা** *v.* to emit smoke, fume, vapour, gas etc.

ধূম্র *n.* & *a.* same as **ধূমল** (see **ধূম**). □ *n.* (inc.) smoke, fume, vapour, gas. **~বর্ণ** *a.* smoke-coloured, dark purple. **~লোচন** *a.* having dark purple eye.

ধূর্জটি *n.* a name of Shiva (শিব).

ধূর্ত *a.* sly; wily; knavish; deceitful. □ *n.* a trickster; a gamester; a knave; a cheat. **~তা, ধূর্তামি** *n.* slyness; wiliness; knavery; deception, deceit.

ধূলট alt. spell. of **ধুলট**।

ধূলা alt. spell. of **ধুলা**।

ধূলি, (coll.) **ধুলো** *n.* fine particles of dry earth, dust; (of flowers) pollen. **ধূলি ঝাড়া** *v.* to shake off or brush off dust, to dust. **চোখে ধুলো দেওয়া** (fig.) to throw dust in one's eyes, to hoodwink, to deceive. **ধূলিকণা** *n.* a particle of dust. **ধূলিধূসর, ধূলিধূসরিত** *a.* made grey with dust; dusty. **ধূলিপটল** *n.* a cloud of dust. **ধূলিময়** *a.* full of dust; dusty. **ধূলিমলিন** *a.* soiled with dust. **ধূলিমাখা** *a.* coated with dust; dusty. **ধূলিমুষ্টি** *n.* a handful of dust. **ধূলিমুষ্টি স্বর্ণমুষ্টি হওয়া** (lit.) common dust becomes gold-dust; (fig.) to have unexpected success or turn of fortune in everything. **ধূলিলুণ্ঠিত** *a.* wallowing or lying in dust; fallen or knocked to the ground. **ধূলিশয্যা** *n.* lying state or prostration on the bare ground; making the ground one's bed; the bed of bare ground. **ধূলিশায়ী** *a.* lying on the bare ground; fallen or knocked to the ground. **ধূলিসাৎ** *a.* reduced to dust; razed to the ground; (fig.) thorougly shattered or ruined or lost.

ধূল্যবলুণ্ঠিত same as **ধূলিলুণ্ঠিত** (see **ধূলি**).

ধূসর *n.* the grey colour, the ash-colour. □ *a.* grey, ash-coloured, ashen, ashen-grey, ashy. **ধূসরাভ** *a.* greyish. **ধূসরিত** *a.* made grey, greyed. **ধূসরিমা** *n.* greyness; the grey colour; greyishness.

ধূস্তুর, ধূস্তূর alt. spellings of **ধুস্তুর**।

ধৃত *a.* held; caught; arrested; taken; contained (in); assumed; worn; (rare) quoted. **~ব্রত** *a.* one who has (firmly) taken a vow; determined, resolved. **ধৃত হওয়া** *v.* to be caught; to be arrested; to be apprehended.

ধৃতাত্মা *a.* self-possessed, calm and collected, not distracted.

ধৃতাস্ত্র *a.* armed, in arms.

ধৃতি *n.* act of holding, catching, wearing, assuming, bearing or containing; conception; impression; a notion; an idea; patience; self-possession; complacence; satisfaction, content; perseverance, persistence. **~বিন্দু** *n.* a point of support. **~মান** *a.* patient; self-possessed; complacent; content; persevering. **~হোম** *n.* a sacramental sacrifice done at a wedding.

ধৃষ্ট *a.* arrogant, haughty, insolent; impertinent, audacious, saucy, pert, (coll.) cheeky; talkative; garrulous; impudent. shameless; lascivious, lewd. *fem.* **ধৃষ্টা**। **~তা** *n.* arrogance, insolence; impertinence, audacity, sauciness, pertness; (coll.) cheek, talkativeness, garrulity; impudence, shamelessness; lasciviousness; lewdness.

ধৃষ্য *a.* assailable; subduable.

ধেইধেই *n.* the style or cue-words of the 'tandab' (তাণ্ডব) dance, the dance of extensive annihilation; a wild dance or movement.

ধেড়ানো *v.* to soil clothes by failing to retain motion of stool or urine; (fig.) to make a mess of; to bungle.

ধেড়ে[1] *n.* the otter.

ধেড়ে[2] *a.* (use. dero.) grown-up; big.

ধেৎ var. of **ধুৎ**।

ধেনু *n.* a cow that has recently calved; a milch cow. **~পাল** *n.* a herd of cows.

ধেনো *a.* produced from paddy (ধেনো মদ) ; paddy-growing (ধেনো চাষা) ; yielding paddy (ধেনো জমি) ; paddy-like (ধেনো গন্ধ) ; resembling a paddy-growing peasant, boorish, clodhopping (ধেনো বুদ্ধি). □ *n.* an inferior wine prepared from paddy, rice-grog.

ধেবড়া pop. var. of **ধাবড়া**।

ধেয় *a.* worth holding or taking; acceptable, knowable, cognizable.

ধেয়ান, ধেয়ানী corruptions of **ধ্যান** and **ধ্যানী** respectively.

ধেয়ানো *v.* (poet. or coll.) to meditate, to reflect; to recollect.

ধৈবত *n.* (mus.) the sixth note of the gamut.

ধৈরজ poet. corrup. of **ধৈর্য**।

ধৈর্য *n.* patience, fortitude; endurance; forbearance; composure (মনের ধৈর্য) ; (Vaishnava phil.) disinterestedness, indifference, apathy. **ধৈর্য ধরা** *v.* to have patience. **ধৈর্য রক্ষা করা** *v.* to forbear or endure; to contain oneself; to keep calm; to have patience. **অসীম ধৈর্য** endless patience, the patience of Job. **~চ্যুত** *a.* out of patience; impatient; failing to contain oneself. **~চ্যুতি** *n.* loss of patience; impatience. **~ধারণ** *n.* act of keeping patient, act of containing oneself; forbearance. **~বান, ~শালী, ~শীল** *a.* patient; enduring; forbearing. *fem.* **~বতী, ~শালিনী, ~শীলা**। **~শীলতা** *n.* patience; endurance; calmness. **~হারা** same as **~চ্যুত**। **~রহিত, ~হীন** *a.* lacking patience, devoid of patience; impatient; out of patience; fretting; restless. *fem.* **~হীনা**। **~হীনতা** *n.* impatience; impetuosity, restlessness. **ধৈর্যাবলম্বন** same as **ধৈর্যধারণ**।

ধোওয়া var. of **ধোয়া**।

ধোঁকা[1] *v.* to pant or gasp for breath; to palpitate, to throb.

ধোঁকা[2] *n.* a kind of pie-curry prepared with pulped pigeon-pea.

ধোঁকা[3] *n.* doubt, suspicion (ধোঁকায় পড়া) ; bewilderment, puzzle (ধোঁকা লাগা) ; hoax, hoodwink, deception, dodge (ধোঁকা দেওয়া). **ধোঁকা দেওয়া** *v.* to hoax; to hoodwink, to deceive; to dodge. **ধোঁকা লাগা** *v.* to have doubt or hesitancy; to be dazed or bewildered or puzzled. **ধোঁকায় পড়া** *v.* to be in doubt or suspicion, to be in a fix or dilemma; to be non-plussed. **~বাজ** *a.* given to hoaxing or hoodwinking or deceiving or dodging. **~বাজি** *n.* practice of hoaxing or hoodwinking or deceiving or dodging. **ধোঁকাবাজি করা** *v.* to hoax; to hoodwink, to deceive; to dodge; to practise hoaxing or hoodwinking or deception or dodging.

ধোঁয়া *n.* smoke; fume; vapour, steam; gas; (loos.) mist, fog; (fig.) anything intangible or obscure. **ধোঁয়া ওড়ানো** *v.* (facet. or dero.) to smoke tobacco. **ধোঁয়া ছাড়া** *v.* to emit smoke; to puff tobacco-smoke. **বুদ্ধির গোড়ায় ধোঁয়া দেওয়া** *v.* to (try to) awaken one's dormant intelligence or devise plans by means of smoking tobacco. **ধোঁয়াটে** *a.* smoke-like; smoky; vapoury; (loos.) misty, foggy; (fig.) intangible; unintelligible; woolly, confused; obscure.

ধোঁয়াপথ *n.* chimney.

ধোকড় *n.* rag; coarse cloth; a sack. **কথার ধোকড়** a chatter-box. **মাকড় মারলে ধোকড়**

হয় (lit.) a spider when killed becomes a piece of rag; (fig.) what is a mortal sin for others is a venial offence for one's own self.

ধোনা pop. var. of **ধুনা**[2]।

ধোপ, (dial.) **ধোব** *n.* washing and bleaching (as of clothes.) □ *a.* washed and bleached (ধোপ কাপড়). **ধোপ দেওয়া** *v.* to put to washing. **ধোপে টেকা** *v.* to stand wear and tear; to stand a test or trial. **ধোপদুরস্ত** *a.* properly washed and bleached; neat and clean, tidy; (fig.) refined, polished, elegant (ধোপদুরস্ত চালচলন).

ধোপা, (dial.) **ধোবা** *n.* a washerman (by trade or caste). *fem.* **ধোপানি,** (dial.) **ধোবানি** a washerwoman. **ধোপায় দেওয়া, ধোপার বাড়ি দেওয়া** *v.* to send (clothes) to the washerman for washing. **ধোপা-নাপিত বন্ধ করা** *v.* to boycott socially (by depriving a person of the services of the washerman and the barber).

ধোবিখানা *n.* the washerman's house, the laundry.

ধোয়া *v.* to wash; to cleanse or scrub or scour with water; to wash and bleach; (of rivers) to inundate. □ *a.* washed; cleansed or scrubbed or scoured with water; washed and bleached. **ধোয়ানি** *n.* water or other liquids with which something has been washed; alluvial deposit; dregs. **ধোয়ানো** *v.* to cause to wash; to cause to cleanse or scrub or scour with water; to cause to wash and bleach. **ধোয়া-পাকলা** *n.* act of washing and scrubbing or scouring.

ধোলাই *n.* act of washing; act of washing and bleaching; (fig.) sound beating (ধোলাই দেওয়া). □ *a.* washed; washed and bleached.

ধোসা[1] *n.* a kind of coarse woollen wrapper.

ধোসা[2] *n.* a thin chapati-like South Indian food.

ধৌত *a.* washed; cleansed or scrubbed or scoured with water; washed and bleached; inundated. **ধৌত করা** *v.* to wash, to clean.

ধৌতি *n.* washing and cleaning; a method of cleaning entrails or intestines with water (a practice in হঠযোগ).

ধ্বংস *n.* destruction; annihilation; wreck, wreckage; ruin; death; act of killing, slaughter (শত্রুধ্বংস) ; loss; obliteration, effacement (শরীর ধ্বংস) ; waste or squandering (অর্থধ্বংস) ; undeserving consumption (অন্নধ্বংস) ; demolition, devastation (গৃহধ্বংস, রাজ্যধ্বংস, নগরধ্বংস) ; depravation or corruption (চরিত্র ধ্বংস, ধ্বংসের পথ). **স্মৃতি ধ্বংস** *n.* loss of memory; amnesia. **ধ্বংস করা** *v.* to destory; to annihilate; to ruin; to kill, to slay; to obliterate or efface; to impair; to waste, to squander; to consume undeservingly; to demolish or devastate; to deprave, to corrupt. **ধ্বংস হওয়া** *v.* to be destroyed or annihilated, to perish; to be ruined; to die; to be killed or slaughtered; to be lost; to be obliterated or effaced; to be impaired; to be wasted or squandered; to be consumed undeservingly; to be demolished or devastated; to be depraved or corrupted. **ধ্বংসক** *a.* one who or that which destroys or annihilates or ruins or kills or slays or obliterates or effaces or impairs or wastes or squanders or consumes undeservingly or demolishes or devastates or depraves or corrupts. **ধ্বংসন** same as **ধ্বংস** । **~নীয়** *a.* destructible; perishable. **~প্রাপ্ত** *a.* destroyed; annihilated; wrecked, ruined; dead, gone to one's death; killed, slaughtered; obliterated, effaced; lost; impaired; wasted, squandered; demolished, fallen, devastated; depraved, corrupted. **~মুখ** *n.* jaws or verge of destruction or annihilation or wreck or ruin or death or impairment or fall or demolition or devastation or demoralization or corruption. **~লীলা** *n.* the sport of destruction or annihilation or wreckage or ruining or killing or demolition or devastation. **~স্তূপ** *n.* a pile of ruins, wreckage, debris.

ধ্বংসানো, (poet.) **ধ্বংসা** *v.* to destroy or devastate (নগর ধ্বংসানো) ; to cause waste or useless expenditure, to waste (টাকা

ধ্বংসানো) ; to consume undeservingly (অন্ন ধ্বংসানো).

ধ্বংসাবশেষ *n.* ruins; remains; wreckage; relics.

ধ্বংসিত *a.* destroyed; annihilated; perished; wrecked, ruined; killed; impaired; wasted, squandered; undeservingly consumed; demolished, fallen, devastated.

ধ্বংসী *a.* destroying, annihilating; ruining; wrecking; killing, obliterating; impairing; uselessly spending, squandering, wasting, consuming undeservingly; demolishing; devastating; depraving, corrupting; destructible, perishable; decaying.

ধ্বংসোন্মুখ *a.* about to fall into a ruined state, about to go to rack and ruin, on the point of destruction.

ধ্বজ *n.* a flag, a banner, a standard, an ensign; the penis. **~ক** *n.* a flag, a standard. □ *a.* (bot.) vexillary. **~দণ্ড** *n.* a flag-staff. **~পট** *n.* the bunting of a flag. **~-বজ্রাঙ্কুশ** *n.* three marks resembling a flag, a thunder and a goad imprinted on the sole of Vishnu (বিষ্ণু) ; (astrol.) a birth-mark indicating the chance of becoming a king. **~বাহক** *n.* a standard-bearer; (mil.) an ensign. **~বাহী** *a.* carrying a flag or standard. **~ভঙ্গ** *n.* (of males) loss of sexual power, impotence, impotency. □ *n.* an impotent person.

ধ্বজা *n.* a flag, a banner, a standard, an ensign; (sarcas. & dero.) simulacrum; a pretender (বিদ্যার ধ্বজা) ; (bot.) a vexillum. **~ধারী** *a.* bearing a standard; (sarcas.) one who keeps a tuft of hair uncut on one's crown as a mark of one's holiness or piety; (sarcas.) hypocritically upholding or defending (ধর্মের ধ্বজাধারী).

ধ্বজী *a.* bearing a standard; (sarcas.) hypocritically upholding or defending (ধর্মধ্বজী).

ধ্বনন *n.* act of making a suppressed noise (esp. a vocal one); humming; act of sounding or ringing or playing (as a musical instrument etc.); (rhet.) suggestion.

ধ্বনি *n.* sound; noise; report; note, tone; voice; (rhet.) a suggestion. **~কাব্য** *n.* (rhet.) poetry that suggests a meaning beyond the stated meaning. **ধ্বনিত** *a.* sounded; rung or played; voiced; in the process of being sounded or rung or played or voiced; (rhet.) suggested. **ধ্বনিত করা** *v.* to sound; to ring; to play; to voice. **~তত্ত্ব** *n.* phonetics; phonology. **~পরিবর্তন** *n.* change of sound, sound change. **~বিজ্ঞান** *n.* phonetics; phonology; the science of sound. **~বৃত্তি** *n.* (rhet.) onomatopoeia. **~ভোট** *n.* a vote of voice. **~মাধুর্য** *n.*sweetness of sound. **~রেখা** *n.* the mark of sound-wave; sound-line; line of vibration.

ধ্বন্যাত্মক *a.* (rhet.) onomatopoeic.

ধ্বসা inc. var. of **ধসা** ।

ধ্বস্ত *a.* destroyed; annihilated; perished; wrecked, ruined; impaired, run down; devastated; demolished; fallen; vanquished.

ধ্বস্তাধ্বস্তি alt. spell. of **ধস্তাধস্তি** ।

ধ্বান্ত *n.* darkness, gloom. **ধ্বান্তারি** *n.* the sun (esp. when personified), (cp.) Sol.

ধ্যাত *a.* meditated upon; recollected; remembered. **ধ্যাতব্য** *a.* deserving or fit to be meditated upon or recollected or remembered. **ধ্যাতা** *a. & n.* one who meditates or recollects or remembers.

ধ্যান *n.* meditation; absorbing religious meditation; recollection; remembrance. **ধ্যান করা** *v.* to meditate (upon); to be absorbed in religious meditation; to recollect; to remember. **~গম্ভীর** *a.* grave and silent on account of absorption in meditation; consecrated or sanctified with holy meditation; solemnly absorbed in (spiritual) meditation ('ধ্যানগম্ভীর ঐ যে ভূধর'). **~গম্য, ~গোচর** *a.* comprehensible or cognizable or attainable (only) through (deep) meditation. **~জ্ঞান** *n.* meditation and cognition, thought and feeling; (loos.) sole occupation or absorption. **~তৎপর** *a.* given to meditation; capable of being absorbed in meditation. **~ধারণা** *n.* meditation and impression, thought and perception; idea; impression. **~নিষ্ঠ** *a.* meditative. **~ভঙ্গ** *n.*

interruption or break of meditation (esp. a spiritual one). ~মগ্ন *a.* absorbed or engrossed in meditation. ~রত, ~স্থ *a.* engaged in meditation.

ধ্যানী *a.* (also *n.*) one who is engaged in meditation; one who is capable of meditation.

ধ্যাবড়া more proper alt. spell. of **ধেবড়া** ।

ধ্যেয় same as **ধ্যাতব্য** (see **ধ্যাত**).

ধ্রিয়মাণ *a.* that which is being put on or worn or assumed or held or touched or caught.

ধ্রুপদ *n.* a style of Indian classical song. **ধ্রুপদী** *a. & n.* one who sings or is versed in singing dhrupad (ধ্রুপদ) songs. □ *a.* aristocratic; elevated; excellent; first-rate. **ধ্রুপদী সাহিত্য** classical literature.

ধ্রুব *n.* (myth.) a prince famous for his incomparable devotion to God Hari (হরি) ; the Pole Star, the Polaris, the North Star, the cynosure, □ *a.* sure, certain; fixed; firm, deep-seated (ধ্রুববিশ্বাস) ; constant; actual, real (ধ্রুব সত্য). □ *adv.* surely, certainly (সে ধ্রুব আসবে) ; for sure, for certain (ধ্রুব জেনো). ~তা *n.* sureness, surety, certainty; fixity; firmness; constancy; actuality, reality. ~তারা, ~নক্ষত্র *n.* the Pole Star, the North Star, the Polaris, the cynosure; the constant or firm goal or guide (জীবনের ধ্রুবতারা). ~পদ *n.* a style of Indian classical song, dhrupad (ধ্রুপদ) ; a constant note ('যে ধ্রুবপদ দিয়েছ বাঁধি বিশ্বতানে'). ~বিশ্বাস firm faith or belief or conviction. ~রেখা *n.* (geog.) the equator, the equinoctial line. ~লোক *n.* (myth.) a separate heaven created for Dhruba (ধ্রুব) to live in after his ascension to heaven; Paradise. ~সত্য *n.* an absolute truth, a confirmed truth. □ *a.* absolutely true.

ধ্রুবা *n.* burden or refrain (of a song).

ধ্রুবাক্ষ *n.* (astr.) the Polar axis.

ধ্রুবাঙ্ক *n.* (alg.) a constant quantity, a constant.

ন[1] *n.* the twentieth letter of the Bengali alphabet.

ন[2] coll. corrup. of **নয়[2]** ।

ন[3] *a.* (ori. & obs.) new; (pop.) fourth in seniority (নকাকা, নবউ, নবাবু).

-ন[4] *pfx.* indicating: negation, opposition etc. (নগণ্য, নাতিদীর্ঘ).

নই[1] pop. form of **নহি** ।

নই[2] (poet. & obs.) a river ('কালিনী-নই-কূলে').

নই[3] *a.* female. **নই-বাছুর** *n.* a cow-calf.

নইচা, নইচে dial. corruptions of **নলিচা** ।

নই তালিম *n.* neo-education, neo-literacy; a novel method of education, generally applied to Gandhi's Basic Education scheme.

নইলে *con.* otherwise, else. □ *prep.* without, except (সে নইলে কে যাবে ?) ।

নউই *n.* the ninth day of a month. □ *a.* (of the days of a month) ninth (নউই বৈশাখ).

নও pop. form of **নহ** ।

নওজোয়ান *n.* a young hero; a young man; (collect.) youths of a country.

নওবত *n.* an orchestra in which the sanai (সানাই) is the chief instrument. **~খানা** *n.* a room or platform where the aforesaid orchestra is played.

নওরোজ *n.* the Persian New Year's day; a feast held on this day.

নওল *a.* (poet. & obs.) young or tenderaged (নওলকিশোর).

নওলা coll. corrup. of **নহলা** ।

নং abbr. of **নম্বর** No., no.; number; marks; score.

নকড়া-ছকড়া *n.* slight, neglect; (loos.) confusion, disorder; (loos.) squandering. **নকড়া-ছকড়া করা** *v.* to slight or neglect, to play fast and loose; (loos.) to make a mess of, to throw at sixes and sevens; (loos.) to squander, to play ducks and drakes with. **নকড়া-ছকড়া হওয়া** *v.* to be slighted or neglected; (loos.) to be made a mess of; (loos.) to be squandered.

নকল *n.* imitation; mimicry; a copy; a transcript, a reproduction; act of copying from another's answer-paper or script by adopting unfair means (as by an examinee). □ *a.* artificial, sham, imitation (নকল হিরে) ; counterfeit (নকল টাকা) ; forged (নকল দলিল). **নকল করা** *v.* to imitate; to mimic; to copy; to make a copy of, to transcribe; (of an examinee) to copy from another's answer-paper or script by adopting unfair means; to forge. **~নবিশ** *n.* a scribe, a professional copyist or transcriber. **~নবিশি** *n.* professional copying or transcribing. **~দানা** ori. & now obs. form of **নকুলদানা** ।

নকশা *n.* a rough sketch, a sketch; a rough cast; a plan or design in outlines, a plan (বাড়ির নকশা) ; a diagram; an outline map, a map; an artistic design; an engraving; an embroidered design (পাড়ের নকশা) ; a literary burlesque, a skit. **নকশা আঁকা, নকশা করা** *v.* to draw a sketch or a plan or a map in outlines; to sketch or plan. **~-আঁকা, ~-কাটা, ~দার** *a.* having an artistic design (নকশা-আঁকা পাড়) ; having an engraving. **~কার** *n.* a draftsman. **~পাড়** *a.* having an artistically designed border (নকশাপাড় শাড়ি).

নকশাল *n.* an armed revolutionary Marxist movement which originated in Naxalbari in Darjeeling district; a person who believes in such a movement or is a member of it.

নকশি *a.* having an artistic design (নকশিকাঁথা). **~কাঁথা** *n.* a quilt or rag with artistic design.

নকাশি *n.* carving; engraving; painting or designing on metal vessels.

নকিব *n.* one who is employed to announce the glory of one's prince and the advent of a person to the prince's court, (cp.) an usher.

নকুল *n.* the mongoose, the ichneumon; Shiva (শিব).

নকুলদানা *n.* a kind of white and roundish toffee or sweet drop.

নকুলে *a.* given to or expert in copying or mimicry.

নকুলেশ্বর, নকুলেশ্বর ভৈরব *n.* an angry manifestation of Shiva (শিব).

নক্ত *n.* the night. ~চর, ~চারী, ~ঞ্চারী *a.* active by night; wandering by night; nocturnal; nightfaring, noctivagant. □ *n.* the rakshas; the bat; a thief, a burglar; a person active by night, a night-bird. নক্তান্ধ *a.* blind by night, nyctalopic. নক্তান্ধতা *n.* nyctalopia. Also রাত্র্যন্ধতা।

নক্র *n.* the crocodile; the alligator. *fem.* নক্রা। ~রাজ *n.* the shark.

নক্ষত্র *n.* a star. ~খচিত *a.* star-spangled, studded with stars, starry. ~গতি *n.* speed as quick as of a shooting star, meteoric speed; tremendous speed. □ *a.* having such speed. ~নাথ, ~পতি *n.* the moon (esp. when personified). (cp.) Luna. ~পাত *n.* fall of a meteor or meteorite; (fig.) death or downfall of a great man. ~পুঞ্জ *n.* a group of stars, a constellation. ~বিজ্ঞান *n.* the science of stars, astronomy. ~বিজ্ঞানী *n.* an astronomer, a star-gazer. ~বেগ *n.* same as নক্ষত্রগতি (*n.*). ~বেগে *adv.* with the speed of a shooting star, swiftly as a shooting star; with great speed. ~মণ্ডল, ~লোক *n.* the stellar region, the sidereal system, the firmament, the sky. ~মণ্ডিত *a.* same as নক্ষত্রখচিত। নক্ষত্রালোক *n.* star-light. নক্ষত্রালোকিত *a.* starlit.

নক্সা rej. spell. of নকশা।

নখ *n.* a nail (of a finger or a toe); a talon, a claw (of a bird or a beast). নখ কাটা *v.* to cut or pare nails. নখ কাটা ছুরি বা কাঁচি বা নরুন *n.* a nail-cutter. ~কুনি, ~কোনি *n.* a painful ingrowing nail, whitlow. ~দর্পণ *n.* the esoteric power of reflecting unknown or distant things on the face of the nail; (fig.) the range of one's cognition (সমস্ত ব্যাপার তার নখদর্পণে = the whole thing is within his command or grasp; the entire affair is at his finger-tips). নখর *n.* a talon, a claw (of a bird or beast); (facet.) a nail (of a man). ~রঞ্জনী *n.* nail-polish. নখরাগ্র *n.* the tip of the claw. নখরাঘাত *n.* clawing. নখরাঘাত করা *v.* to claw. ~রেখা, ~লেখা *n.* a mark caused by nail. ~শূল *n.* whitlow.

নখাগ্র *n.* the tip of a nail; the tip of the claw; the range of touch; (fig.) the range of perception or cognition. সমস্ত ব্যাপার তার নখাগ্রে আছে same as সমস্ত ব্যাপার তার নখদর্পণে (see নখ).

নখাঘাত *n.* an instance or act of nailing or clawing. নখাঘাত করা *v.* to nail or claw.

নখানখি *n.* mutual nailing or clawing.

নখী[1] *a.* possessing claws, clawed. □ *n.* a clawed creature.

নখী[2] *n.* an aromatic substance that gives out a sweet smell when fried.

নগ *n.* a mountain; a tree. ~নদী *n.* a river issuing from a mountain, a mountain stream.

নগণ্য *a.* negligible, insignificant; worthless, of no importance. নগণ্য মানুষ an insignificant man, a man of straw.

নগদ *n.* cash money or cash price, cash (নগদ দিয়ে কেনা, নগদ কত আছে?). □ *a.* cash (নগদ টাকা বা দাম); (fig.) prompt, immediate, ready (নগদ জবাব). নগদ কারবার a cash transaction. নগদ বিক্রি cash sale. নগদ বিদায় ready payment in cash of wages, charges, fees etc. on execution of the job undertaken; (loos.) ready payment in cash; (fig.) prompt or ready dismissal. নগদা *a.* cash (নগদা দাম); ready (নগদা কারবার); working for ready payment in cash (নগদা মজুর). নগদানগদি *a.* & *adv.* strictly on cash. নগদি *n.* an armed footman of a landowner etc. collecting rents, issuing summons etc., (cp.) a bailiff.

নগনদী sea নগ।

নগনন্দিনী *n.* a daughter of a mountain (esp. of the Himalayas); an appellation of goddess Durga (দুর্গা).

নগর *n.* a city; a town; a metropolis, a capital. *fem.* নগরী। ~কীর্তন *n.* act of singing religious songs in procession through a city (or village); a song sung thus. ~চত্বর *n.* a market-place of a city. ~জীবন *n.* city-life, town-life, urban life. ~দ্বার *n.* a gate of a city, a city gate. ~পাল *n.* the Police chief of a city, the

Commissioner of Police; a city magistrate; a city father, a town-councillor. **~প্রান্ত** same as **নগরোপান্ত**। **~বাসী** *a.* living in a city or town, urban. □ *n.* a townsman (*fem.* a townswoman; *pl.* townsfolk, townspeople), a citizen, a townee. *fem.* **নগরবাসিনী**। **~রক্ষক** *n.* a metropolitan policeman; a city-guard. **~রাষ্ট্র** *n.* a city state. **~সংকীর্তন** same as **নগরকীর্তন**। **~স্থ** *a.* situated in or living in a town or city; of a town or city.

গরাধ্যক্ষ *n.* the governor or mayor or sheriff of a city or town; a city magistrate.

গররাজ same as **নগাধিপ**।

গরিয়া obs. var. of **নগুরে**।

গরী see **নগর**।

গরীয় *a.* of a town or city, urban; civic.

গরোপান্ত *n.* the outskirts or suburbs of a city or town.

গাধিপ, নগাধিরাজ, নগেন্দ্র *n.* the lord or king of mountains; appellations of the Himalayas.

গুরে *n.* a townman, one who lives in a town or a city; a townee. □ *a.* of one living in a town or a city.

গ্ন *a.* without clothes, unclad, nude, naked (নগ্নদেহ); uncovered, bare (নগ্নপদ, নগ্নশির); without spectacles, naked (নগ্নচক্ষু); without ornaments, bare (নগ্ন বাহু); clear, cloudless (নগ্ন আকাশ); unsheathed, naked (নগ্ন তরবারি = naked steel); obvious or unvarnished or plain or simple (নগ্ন সত্য). *fem.* **নগ্না**। **নগ্ন সত্য** naked truth, stark reality. **~ক** *a.* without clothes, naked, nude. □ *n.* one of a class of Buddhist friars moving naked or very insufficiently clothed. **~তা** *n.* nakedness, nudity; bareness; obviousness. **নগ্নিকা** *a. fem.* without clothes, naked, nude. □ *n. fem.* a girl whose menses have not yet started; an infant girl. **নগ্নীকরণ** *n.* act of making naked, denudation; uncovering. **নগ্নীকৃত** *a.* made naked, denuded; uncovered. **নগ্নীভবন** *n.* act of becoming naked, denudation; act of becoming uncovered.

গর, নঙর older variants. of **নোঙর**।

নচেৎ *con.* otherwise, else.

নচ্ছার *a.* abominable, hateful; wicked; nefarious; depraved; (in endearment or mild imprecations) naughty. □ *n.* such a person.

নজর *n.* sight, vision (নজর খারাপ হওয়া); view (নজরে আসা); a look or glance (কুনজর); a malicious or evil look, evil eye or greedy eye (খাবারে নজর দেওয়া); ambition or aim (উঁচু নজর); outlook or mentality (ছোট নজর); attention, care (পড়াশোনায় নজর); act of looking after (ছেলেটার দিকে নজর রেখো); malicious observation or watch or surveillance (পুলিশের নজরে পড়া); opinion, notion (নেকনজর); good opinion or notion (কেরানিটি বড়কর্তার নজরে পড়েছে); (rare) a present or extra payment made to a dignitary or a superior at an interview (জমিদারের জন্য নজর); (rare) a bribe (দারোগাকে নজর দেওয়া). **নজর করা** *v.* to observe or mark closely; to catch sight of, to notice, to espy; to keep watch on; to strain one's eyes to see (নজর করে দেখা). **নজর দেওয়া** *v.* to cast an evil eye at, to look maliciously at; to keep one's eye on, to watch (ছেলের দিকে নজর দিয়ো); to give an eye to, to attend to (এদিকে নজর দাও). **নজর পড়া** *v.* to have one's glance directed towards, to come to see. **নজর রাখা** *v.* to keep one's eye on, to watch. **নজর লাগা** *v.* to be affected with the evil eye (of). **নজরে থাকা** *v.* to be under observation or watch; to be in view. **নজরে পড়া** *v.* to catch sight of; to attract notice of; to win favour of, to be in the good books of, to be in good graces of. **নজরে রাখা** *v.* to keep under observation; to watch, to have one's eye on. **নজরের দোষ** defect of vision; malicious look; an evil eye. **উঁচু নজর** a lofty aim; noble outlook; magnanimity. **কুনজর** *n.* a malicious or lustful look, evil eye; disfavour; a base aim. **ছোট নজর, নিচু নজর** a base aim; narrow-mindedness, pettiness. **বড় নজর** same as **উঁচু নজর**। **সুনজর** *n.* a favourable or kindly look or glance; favour. **নজরবন্দি** *a.* kept under observation and restraint by the police, kept under house-arrest, (loos.) home-interned.

নজরানা *n.* a present or extra payment made to a dignitary or superior for a favour or grace; tribute.

নজির *n.* a precedent, an example; a case-law. **নজির দেখানো** *v.* to cite a case-law or a precedent. **নজির রাখা** *v.* to set an example. **নজির হওয়া** *v.* to be a precedent (of). **~স্বরূপ** *a.* exemplary; precedental. **~হীন, ~বিহীন** *a.* without a precedent; unexampled.

নঞ্‌তৎপুরুষ *n.* (gr.) a system of forming compound words indicating dissimilarity, absence, negation etc. **নঞর্থক** *a.* bearing a negative meaning, negative.

নট[১] *n.* one of a race of mixed blood. **নটী** *fem.* a female member of this race; a prostitute, a whore.

নট[২] *n.* a professional dancer, a ballet-dancer; an actor. **নটী** *fem.* a dancing-girl, a ballerina; an actress.

নট[৩] *a.* profligate, lewd, licentious; morally perverted; wicked, vile.

নটকান *n.* the anatto.

নটখট, নটখটি *n.* a slight trouble; a petty quarrel. **নটখটে** *a.* slightly troublesome; quarrelsome; difficult to deal with.

নটঘট, নটঘটি *n.* an amourette of petty love affair (esp. a scandalous one); a scandalous affair. **নটঘটে** *a.* consisting of an amourette or a scandalous affair.

নটনারায়ণ *n.* an Indian musical mode.

নটবর[১] *n.* an appellation of Krishna (কৃষ্ণ).

নটবর[২] *n.* the best or chief dancer or actor.

নটরাজ *n.* the best dancer; Shiva (শিব) esp. in a dancing state.

নটিনী *n. fem.* a dancing-girl, a ballerina; a prostitute, a whore.

নটী see **নট**[১] and **নট**[২] ।

নটে *n.* a kind of pot-herb or spinach having different species.

নড়চড় *n.* movement; non-adherence; non-observance, non-compliance; deviation, violation; failing, omission, modification, alteration. **কথার নড়চড়** breach or nonfulfilment of promise or pledge.

নড়ন *n.* movement; shaking or stirring; shifting, removal; act of getting loose; distortion, deviation, alteration (কথার নড়ন). **নড়নচড়ন** same as **নড়চড়** । **নট নড়নচড়ন নট কিচ্ছু** childern's catch-phrase in a game with small marble or glass balls meaning no deviation from or alteration of the position of a ball (before it is hit and sent into the intended hole).

নড়নড়, নড়বড়, নড়নড়ে, নড়বড়ে *a.* flaccid limp; hanging very loose; tottering; unsteady; unstable. **নড়নড় করা, নড়বড় করা** *v.* to be flaccid or limp; to hang very loosely (দাঁত নড়নড় করছে) ; to totter; to be unsteady or unstable.

নড়া[১] *n.* (dero.& vul.) the hand or the arm

নড়া[২] *v.* to move; to shake, to stir; to shift, to remove; to get loose; to become otherwise, to deviate, to be altered. □ *a.* one who or that which has moved; shaken; shifted, removed loosened; altered.

নড়াচড়া *n.* moving about; (casual) movement; act of walking or pacing up and down, a stroll.

নড়ানো *v.* to (cause to) move or shake or stir or shift or remove or loosen or alter

নড়ি *n.* a stick; (fig.) a support or prop (অন্ধের নড়ি).

নত *a.* stooping, bent; bowed down genuflected; directed downwards (নত দৃষ্টি) ; low, depressed (নত স্থান) ; lowered (উঁচু মাথা নত হওয়া) ; inclined humble, meek (নতকণ্ঠে) ; yielding, submissive (বিজয়ীর কাছে নত). **নত করা** *v.* to stoop, to bend; to bow; to cause to genuflect; to direct downwards; to lower; to incline; to humble, to cause to yield or submit. **নত হওয়া** *v.* to stoop to bend; to bow down, to genuflect; to be directed downwards; to incline; to become humble; to yield or submit (to). **~জানু** *a.* knelt down, genuflected **~তল** *n.* (geom.) the plane of inclination. **~নাস, ~নাসিক** *a.* flat-nosed, snub nosed, snub-nose. **~মস্তক, ~শির** *a.* having one's head bowed esp. in obeisance; stooping forward; having th head hanging down; (fig.) downcast or submissive or defeated or discomfited. ~মুখ *a*. having one's face turned downwards, looking down; (fig.) abashed. *fem*. ~মুখী।

নতি *n*. act or state of stooping or bowing or bending down; genuflection; act or state of being directed downwards; depression; (esp. in geom.) inclination; (mech.) slope; (astr.) the dip of the horizon; humbleness, meekness; humbling, yielding, submission. **নতি স্বীকার করা** *v*. to bow down, to yield, to submit.

নতুন *a*. new; novel; fresh; young; at the onset; new-born; newly bloomed; changed, transformed (সে এখন একেবারে নতুন লোক)। **নতুনত্ব** *n*. newness; novelty; freshness, the state or quality of being young or fresh. see also **নূতন**।

নতুবা *con*. else, otherwise, or.

নতোদর *a*. concave.

নতোন্নত *a*. undulating.

নত্তা *n*. a sacrament observed on the ninth day from birth of a baby.

নথ *n*. a nose-ring. **নথ নাড়া দেওয়া** *v*. (fig.) to scold or snub (usu. of a husband by a wife).

নথি *n*. a collection of papers arranged for reference, a file; a record or document; a list, a roll; (in law) documents or a plaint (মোকদ্দমার নথি). ~পট্ট *n*. file board. ~পত্র *n. pl*. records and papers collectively. ~ভুক্ত *a*. accepted as a document or included in the records, filed, recorded, on the record. **নথিভুক্ত করা** *v*. to file. ~নিবন্ধ *n*. a file-register. ~নিবন্ধক *n*. a file-registrar. ~নিষ্পত্তি পত্রী *n*. a file disposal slip. ~প্রাপক *n*. a record-finder. ~রক্ষক *n*. a record-keeper.

নদ *n*. (used rather arbitrarily as *masc*. of নদী) a large river (সিন্ধুনদ). ~নদী *n. pl*. rivers and streams of all descriptions large and small.

নদী *n*. a stream, a river. **নদীর বাঁক** the bend of a river. **ছোট নদী** a rivulet. ~কূল same as **নদীতীর**। ~গর্ভ *n*. the bottom of a river; a river-bed. ~তট, ~তীর *n*. riverbank, riverside. ~তীরবর্তী, ~তীরস্থ *a*. riparian, riverain. ~তীরবাসী *a*. & *n*. riverain. *fem*. ~তীরবাসিনী। ~পথ *n*. river-way. ~পথে *adv*. by river. ~প্রবাহ same as **নদীস্রোত**। ~বক্ষ *n*. the bosom or surface of a river. ~বক্ষে *adv*. on or upon the river. ~বন্দর *n*. a river port. ~বহুল *a*. abounding in rivers, rivery. ~মাতৃক *a*. irrigated or watered by rivers. ~মুখ *n*. a river-mouth, an estuary. ~স্রোত *n*. river-tide; the flowing stream of a river.

নদ্ধ *a*. fastened, tied, bound.

নধর *a*. succulent, juicy, delicious; lovely; plum, rolypoly; buxom; well-shaped, shapely, well-proportioned; fresh.

নন coll. form of **নহেন**।

ননদ, (obs.) **ননন্দা**, (poet.) **ননদিনি**, (poet.) **ননদি** *n. fem*. a sister of one's husband, a sister-in-law. **ননদাই** *n*. the husband of a sister of one's husband, a brother-in-law.

ননি, **ননী** *n*. cream (of milk). **ননির পুতুল** (lit.) a puppet made of cream; (fig. & usu. sarcas.) one who is physically too delicate to stand any toil. ~চোর, ~চোরা *n*. one who steals (and eats) cream; an appellation of (infant) Krishna (কৃষ্ণ).

নন্দদুলাল *n*. a beloved son of Nanda (নন্দ); an appellation of Krishna (কৃষ্ণ); (sarcas.) an over-indulged worthless son.

নন্দন *n*. a son; Paradise, Eden. □ *a*. delightful, pleasing (নয়ননন্দন). ~কানন *n*. Paradise, Eden. **নন্দনন্দন** *n*. son of Nanda, an appellation of Krishna (কৃষ্ণ).

নন্দা[1] *n*. Goddess Durga (দুর্গা); (astr. & astrol.) the first, the sixth and the eleventh lunar day of either fortnight.

নন্দা[2], **নন্দাই** same as **ননদ** and **ননদাই** respectively.

নন্দি[1] *a*. delightful, pleasant.

নন্দি[2], **নন্দিকেশ্বর** *n*. the chief attendant of Shiva (শিব).

নন্দিত *a*. delighted, pleased; congratulated, felicitated. *fem*. **নন্দিতা**।

নন্দিনী *n. fem*. a daughter; a mythological wishing-cow. □ *a. fem*. delightsome, giving delight; pleasing, charming.

নন্দিভৃঙ্গি *n. pl.* Nandi (নন্দি) and Bhringi (ভৃঙ্গি), the two chief attendants of Shiva (শিব) ; (sarcas.) mischievous flatterers, undesirable lieutenants or associates.

নন্দী *n.* same as **নন্দি**[২] । □ *a.* delighted. **নন্দীভৃঙ্গী** same as **নন্দিভৃঙ্গি.**

নন্দোৎসব *n.* the festival to celebrate lord Krishna's birth.

নন্দ্য *a.* worth rejoicing; deserving felicitation.

নপুংসক *n.* a eunuch; a hermaphrodite; a castrated man or animal. □ *a.* hermaphroditic; castrated; neuter; (fig.) impotent or futile (নপুংসক ক্রোধ).

নফর *n.* a man-servant; a menial; a tenant-at-will. **নফরালি** *n.* office or state of a menial.

নব[১] *a.* new; novel; young; modern, recent; new-born; newly grown; early; fresh. **~কারিকা** *n.* a newly-married wife. **~কার্তিক** *n.* infant Kartikeya (কার্তিকেয়) ; (sarcas.) a very ugly man; (hum.) a foppish gallant. **~কুমার** *n.* a new-born son. **~গঠিত** *a.* newly-formed, newly-constructed or composed. **~জলধর** *n.* a newly-formed cloud, a fresh cloud. **~জলধরপটল** *n.* a heap of fresh clouds, cumulus. **~জলধরশ্যাম** *a.* as charmingly dark as a fresh rain-bearing cloud. **~জাগরণ, ~জাগৃতি** *n.* resurgence, new awakening; rebirth, regeneration, renaissance. **~জাত** *a.* new-born; newly-grown or produced. **~জাতক** *n.* a new-born baby. **~জীবন** *n.* a new life; young life; a fresh lease of life; (fig.) rejuvenation or renascence. **~ত্ব** *n.* newness; novelty; modernity; freshness; novelty. **~দম্পতি, ~দম্পতী** *n.* a newly married couple. **~দল** *n.* a fresh or new or tender leaf of a lotus. **~নিযুক্ত** *a.* newly appointed. **~পল্লব** *n.* a young leaf or twig or shoot or sprout. **~বধূ** *n.* a newly-married wife or bride. **~বর্ষ** *n.* New Year. **~বসন্ত** *n.* early spring; a new spring. **~বিধান** *n.* a new law or system; a new order of the Brahma Samaj founded by Keshabchandra Sen; (Christ.) the New Testament. **~মল্লিকা, ~মালিকা** *n.* a variety of jasmine. **~যুবক** *n.* a young man; (cp.) a greenhorn. *fem.* **~যুবতী** a young woman. **~যৌবন** *n.* early youth, the first flush of youth, the prime of youth; a fresh lease of youth; rejuvenation, rejuvenescence. **~যৌবনসম্পন্ন** *a.* in the prime of one's youth. *fem.* **নবযৌবনসম্পন্না, নবযৌবনা** ।

নব[২] *a. & n.* nine. □ *a.* ninth. **~গুণ** same as **নবলক্ষণ** । **~গ্রহ** *n.* (astr. & astrol.) the nine planets (collectively), namely the sun, the moon, Mars, Mercury, Jupiter, Venus, Saturn, the Dragon's head or ascending node, and the Dragon's tail or descending node. **~চত্বারিংশ** *a.* forty-nine. **~চত্বারিংশৎ** *n. & a.* forty-nine. **~চত্বারিংশত্তম** *a.* forty-ninth. *fem.* **~চত্বারিংশত্তমী** । **~দুর্গা** *n.* the nine manifestations collectively of Goddess Durga (দুর্গা). **~দ্বার** *n.* nine vents or inlets or outlets in the human body. **~ধা** *a.* nine times, ninefold; of nine kinds. □ *adv.* by nine times; in nine ways. **~নবতি** *n. & a.* ninty-nine. **~নবতিতম** *a.* ninety-ninth. *fem.* **~নবতিতমী** । **~পত্রিকা** *n.* the image of a female deity formed with leaves of nine plants. **~বিংশতি** *n. & a.* twenty-nine. *fem.* **~বিংশতিতমী** । **~রত্ন** *n.* the nine most precious gems, namely pearl, ruby, chrysoberyl or cat's eye, zircon or jacinth, diamond, (red) coral, beryl, emerald, and sapphire; (hist.) the nine courtiers of King Vikramaditya famous for their learning, wisdom and mastery in arts and letters. **~রত্নসভা** *n.* the court of King Vikramaditya consisting of the aforesaid nine courtiers. **~রস** *n.* the nine poetical flavours or reactions, namely love, heroism, pathos, amazement, anger, fright, comicality, disgust and quietude. **~শায়ক,** (coll.) **~শাক,** (coll.) **~শাখ** *n.* the spicedealer, the garland-maker, the weaver, the milkman, the barber, the grower of betel-leaves, the black-smith, the potter and the confectioner: these nine Hindu communities collectively.

নবতি *n. & a.* ninety. **~তম** *a.* ninetieth *fem.* **~তমী** ।

নবনী, নবনীত *n.* cream (of milk). **নবনীতুল্য** *a.* soft and white like cream, creamlike.

নবম *a.* ninth. **নবমী** *a. fem.* of **নবম**। □ *n.* the ninth day of a lunar fortnight.

নবাংশ *n.* (astrol.) the ninth part.

নবাগত *a.* newly arrived.

নবান্ন *n.* the festival of eating newly grown autumnal rice in the month of Agrahayan (অগ্রহায়ণ).

নবাব *n.* (Mus.) a feudal prince or viceroy, a nawab; (sarcas.) a haughty, ease-loving and luxurious man. **~জাদা** *n.* a nawab's son. *fem.* **~জাদি** a nawab's daughter. **~নাজিম** *n.* a provincial governor and judge. **~পুত্র,** (coll. corrup.) **~পুত্তুর** *n.* a nawab's son; (sarcas.) a haughty, ease-loving and luxurious man. *fem.* **~পুত্রী** a nawab's daughter. **নবাবি** *n.* the office or state of a nawab; position or charge of a nawab; haughty ease-loving and luxurious or extravagant style of living. □ *a.* of or concerning a nawab.

নবার্জিত *a.* newly earned or acquired.

নবি, (rej.) **নবী** *n.* (Mus.) God's messenger, a prophet.

নবিশ[১] *n.* (used as a *sfx.*) a writer, a scribe, a clerk (খাসনবিশ).

নবিশ[২] *n.* a probationer, a novice.

নবিশি *n.* novicehood, noviceship, noviciate, novitiate.

নবীকরণ *n.* renewing, renovation, renewal; mending, repair.

নবীকৃত *a.* renovated, renewed; mended, repaired.

নবীন *a.* new; novel; young, tenderaged; modern; fresh. *fem.* **নবীনা**। **~তা, ~ত্ব** *n.* newness; novelty; state of being young; modernity; freshness.

নবীভবন *n.* state of being renewed, renovation, renewal; state of being mended or repaired.

নবীভাব *n.* renewed or renovated state; mended or repaired state.

নবীভূত *a.* renovated, renewed; mended, repaired.

-নবীশ, -নবীস rej. spellings of **-নবিশ**।

নবোঢ়া *a. fem.* newly or recently married, newly-wed.

নবোৎসাহ *n.* new or fresh energy or vigour or enthusiasm or zeal; a fresh attempt.

নবোদয় *n.* recent rise; new appearance or revelation.

নবোদিত *a.* a recently risen, newly risen; newly appeared or revealed.

নবোদ্গত *a.* (of a plant etc.) newly grown or sprouted; newly cut (নবোদগত দন্ত) ; newly arisen (নবোদগত সমস্যা).

নবোদ্ভাসিত *a.* newly devised or contrived or designed.

নবোদ্যম same as **নবোৎসাহ**।

নবোপলীয় *a.* neolithic.

নব্বই, (coll.) **নব্বুই** *n. & a.* ninety.

নব্য *a.* new, novel; recent; modern; young. **~বঙ্গ** *n.* (hist.) Young Bengal. **~ভারত** *n.* new or modern India.

নভঃ, (pop.) **নভ** *n.* the sky, the firmament, heaven. **নভঃস্থ** same as **নভস্থ**। **নভঃস্থিত** same as **নভস্থিত**। **নভচিত্র, নভদৃশ্য** *n.* skyscape. **নভশ্চক্ষু** *n.* the sun. **নভশ্চর** *a.* moving in the air, aerial; aviating. □ *n.* a bird; air or wind; the cloud; a star; the sun; the moon; a planet; an aerial or celestial being. **নভস্তল, নভস্থল** *n.* the floor of the sky; the skyey region or expanses; the sky. **নভস্থ, নভস্থিত** *a.* situated in the sky, aerial, celestial, heavenly, skyey. **নভস্পর্শী, নভস্পৃক** *a.* touching or reaching or kissing the sky, skyhigh; very lofty. **নভস্বান** *n.* air or wind.

নভেম্বর *n.* November.

নভেল *n.* a book of fiction, a novel. **~লেখক** *n.* a fictionist, a novelist. **নভেলিয়ানা** *n.* act of behaving like a character in a novel.

নভোনীল *n. & a.* azure, skyblue.

নভোবস্তুবিদ্যা *n.* astrophysics.

নভোবীক্ষণ *n.* astronomical telescope.

নভোযোগ্য *a.* air-worthy. **নভোযোগ্যতা** *n.* air-worthiness. **নভোযোগ্যতা-পত্র** *n.* certificate of air-worthiness.

নভোমণ্ডল *n.* the heavenly dome or region; the atmosphere.

নমঃ, (pop.) **নম** *n.* act of bending or prostrating the body in saluting, a bow, an obeisance. **নম করা** *v.* (vul. or childish) to bow, to make an obeisance, to genuflect, to salute. **নম-নম করে সারা** *v.* to deal with summarily; to hurry through; to execute perfunctorily.

নমঃশূদ্র alt. spell. of **নমশূদ্র**।

নমন *n.* act of bending, flexion; act of bowing down; genuflection; a bow or obeisance; submission, yielding; subdual. **নমন বল** (phys.) bending force. **নমনাঙ্ক** *n.* (phys.) bending moment. **নমনীয়** *a.* capable of being bent; flexible, pliable; capable of being bent in obeisance; submissive, yielding; subduable. **নমনীয়তা** *n.* flexibility, pliability, pliancy; submissiveness.

নমশূদ্র *n.* a Hindu community placed low in the social order.

নমস্কর্তা *n.* one who bows or salutes or makes an obeisance. *fem.* **নমস্কর্ত্রী**।

নমস্কার *n.* a bow, an obeisance; a salute; genuflection. **নমস্কার করা** *v.* to bow, to make a bow or obeisance; to salute; to genuflect. **নমস্কারি** *n.* a present (usu. a cloth or money) given in obeisance to respectable relatives by a bride or a bridegroom at a Hindu wedding.

নমস্কার্য same as **নমস্য**।

নমস্কৃত *a.* greeted with a bow or obeisance, saluted.

নমস্য *a.* worthy of being greeted with a bow or obeisance or genuflection, worthy of being saluted; venerable or adorable. *fem.* **নমস্যা**।

নমা *v.* (poet.) to bow, to make obeisance, to genuflect, to salute.

নমাজ *n.* the Muslim system of saying one's prayer. **নমাজ পড়া** *v.* to say one's prayer or namaj, to pray. **নমাজি** *a.* one who says one's namaj regularly, prayerful; devout.

নমাসে-ছমাসে *adv.* once in a blue moon; rarely.

নমিত *a.* bent or bowed down in obeisance; bent, arched; subdued. *fem.* **নমিতা**।

নমুনা *n.* a sample; a specimen; a model; a pattern; an example.

নম্বর *n.* a number; a serial number; marks (in an examination). **নম্বরি** *a.* bearing a number; numbered; marked (as of one whose conduct is watched with suspicion).

নম্য same as **নমনীয়** (see **নমন**).

নম্র *a.* gentle, polite; meek; humble; modest; bland; suave; flexible, pliable; soft, tender (নম্রকণ্ঠে) ; bent down, turned or cast downwards (নম্রমুখ, নম্রনয়ন). **~কণ্ঠ** *a.* soft-voiced; speaking blandly or meekly or humbly. **~তা** *n.* gentleness, politeness; meekness; humbleness; humility; modesty; blandness, suavity; flexibility, pliability; softness, tenderness. **~নয়ন, ~নেত্র** *a.* having looks cast downwards. **~প্রকৃতি** *a.* same as **নম্রস্বভাব**। **~ভাবে** *a.* gently, politely; meekly; humbly; modestly; blandly, suavely; softly, tenderly. **~মুখ** *a.* having face turned downwards. **~স্বভাব** *a.* gentle-natured.

ন যযৌ ন তস্থৌ *a.* motionless; unable to move; unable to go this way or that.

নয়১ *n. & a.* nine. **নয়-ছয়** *a.* scattered at sixes and sevens; squandered away. **নয়-ছয় করা** *v.* to squander away.

নয়২ *n.* a political or sociological or theological or moral principle; politics; sociology; theology; ethics. **~জ্ঞ** *a.* versed in politics, sociology, theology or ethics. □ *n.* such a person. **~জ্ঞান** *n.* knowledge of politics, sociology, theology or ethics. **~শাস্ত্র** *n.* politics, sociology, theology and ethics collectively or separately.

নয়৩ *v.* pop. form of **নহে** (see **নহা**). □ *n.* not-being, no, impossibility (নয়কে হয় করা). □ *con.* or, nor, else, otherwise. **নয়কো** *v.* is not, are not. **নয়তো** *con.* or, else, otherwise. □ *int.* meaning: certainly not, of course not (আমি নয়তো).

নয়ন১ *n.* act of taking or carrying or leading or conveying away.

নয়ন২ *n.* the eye. **~কোণ** *n.* the corner of an eye. **~গোচর** *a.* lying within the range of vision, visible; seen, noticed. **নয়নগোচর হওয়া** *v.* to come into view, to become visible. **~জল** *n.* tears. **~ঠার** *n.* a sign made by a surreptitious look or wink; an ogle; a leer. **~তারা** *n.* the pupil of the eye, the apple of the eye; (fig.) something or someone especially dear. **~নন্দন** *a.* pleasing or agreeable to the eye; very beautiful or handsome. ~নীর *n.* tears. ~পথ *n.* the range of vision. ~পল্লব *n.* an eyelid conceived as a tender and young leaf of a tree. ~প্রীতিকর, ~রঞ্জন same as নয়ননন্দন। ~বাণ *n.* a darting glance esp. an amorous or lustful one; an ogle. ~বারি *n.* tears. ~মণি same as নয়নতারা। ~যুগল *n.* a pair of eyes, the two eyes.

নয়নজুলি *n.* a trench esp. for carrying off filthy water, a gutter.

নয়নসুখ, নয়নসুক *n.* a kind of very fine muslin or cambric.

নয়না *n.* (the poet.) the eye; a side-glance.

নয়নানন্দ *n.* the delight of the eye; one who or that which delights the eye. □ *a.* delightful to the eye.

নয়নাভিরাম same as নয়ননন্দন (see নয়ন).

নয়নী *n.* the pupil of the eye, the apple of the eye.

নয়নোন্মীলন *n.* the act of opening one's eyes.

নয়নোপান্ত *n.* the corner of the eye.

নয়া *a.* new; fresh; recent; modern. নয়া পয়সা naya paisa (*pl.* naye paise).

নয়ান poet. corrup. of নয়ন।

নয়ানজুলি dial. corrup. of নয়নজুলি।

নর[1] *n.* a row, a line.

নর[2] *n.* a human being, man; a male person, a male. □ *a.* (chiefly in *comp.*) male (নরহরিণ). *fem.* see নারী। ~কঙ্কাল *n.* a human skeleton. ~কপাল *n.* a dead person's skull. ~কেশরী *n.* a lion amongst men; a man of great prowess. ~খাদক *a.* man-eating, eating human flesh. □ *n.* a man-eater; a cannibal. ~ঘাতক *n.* a homicide. □ *a.* homicidal. ~ঘাতী *a.* homicidal. ~ত্ব *n.* manhood, humanity; virility. ~ত্বারোপ *n.* anthropomorphism. ~নারায়ণ *n.* the two great mythological sages: Nara (নর) and Narayana (নারায়ণ) who were born as Arjuna (অর্জুন) and Krishna (কৃষ্ণ) of the Mahabharata. ~নারী *n.* men and women. ~পতি *n.* a king. ~পশু *n.* a beast of a man, a brute. ~পাল *n.* a king. ~পিশাচ *n.* a man with instincts as abominable as those of necrophagous goblins. ~পুঙ্গব *n.* (fig.) a great man; (lit.) a bull of a man. ~বর *n.* the best man; a great man. ~বলি *n.* immolation of human beings; human sacrifice. ~ব্যাঘ্র same as নরশার্দূল। ~ভুক *a.* anthropophagous, feeding on human flesh, man-eating. নরভুক প্রাণী an anthropophagite, a man-eater. ~ভুক মানুষ a cannibal. ~মাংস *n.* human flesh (esp. when eaten). ~মাংসভোজন *n.* cannibalism. ~মাংসভোজী *a.* cannibalistic. □ *n.* a cannibal. ~মালিনী *n.* a woman wearing a necklace or garland of human skulls; an appellation of goddess Kali (কালী). ~মেধ same as নরবলি। ~রূপী *a.* having the form or shape of a human being, man-shaped. ~রূপে *adv.* in the form or shape of a human being. ~লীলা *n.* activities (of a god) in a human existence or incarnation. নরলীলা সংবরণ করা *v.* (joc. or for.) to die. ~লোক *n.* the abode of human beings or mortals, the world, the earth. ~শার্দূল *n.* a tiger of a man; (fig.) a man of great prowess. ~শ্রেষ্ঠ *n.* the greatest or best amongst men. ~সিংহ *n.* (lit.) a lion of a man; (fig.) a great or valiant man; (myth.) same as নৃসিংহ। ~সুন্দর *n.* a barber; (cp.) a coiffeur (*fem.* coiffeuse). ~হত্যা *n.* homicide, murder. নরহত্যা করা *v.* to commit a murder or homicide, to murder. ~হত্যাকারী same as নরহন্তা। ~হত্যাঘটিত *a.* homicidal. ~হন্তা *n.* a homicide, a murderer. *fem.* ~হন্ত্রী a murderess. ~হরি same as নৃসিংহ।

নরক *n.* hell, inferno; pandemonium; (fig.) an abominable place, a hellish or infernal place; a mythological asura (অসুর). নরক গুলজার (lit. & fig.) the whole of pandemonium is here! নরক গুলজার করা *v.* to assemble in a group somewhere and make the place warm and noisy with wild talk and tattle. ~কুণ্ড *n.* a pit or well in hell (full of fire or abominable filth) into which sinners are put or thrown for punishment; a hell-pit; (fig.) a vicious or abominable or filthy or extremely disorderly place. ~গামী *a.* condemned to hell, damned. ~বাস, ~ভোগ, ~যন্ত্রণা *n.* condemnation to hell, damnation, perdition; (fig.) extreme suffering. ~স্থ *a.* condemned to hell, damned.

নরদমা, নরদামা alt. spellings or **নর্দমা** and **নর্দামা** respectively.

নরম *a.* soft (নরম শরীর) ; malleable, plastic, easily cut; sleek (নরম চুল) ; low (নরম সুর); bland (নরম স্বর) ; mild, gentle (নরম মেজাজ) ; tender or delicate (নরম মন); softened or appeased or moved with pity (মন নরম হওয়া) ; slack, loose (নরম বাঁধন) ; slackened, loosened (বাঁধন নরম হওয়া) ; not hardened (নরম পাকের সন্দেশ) ; deprived of crispness (বিস্কুটগুলো নরম হয়ে গেছে) ; weak (নরম লোক) ; abated (জ্বর নরম হওয়া) ; pleasant, cool (নরম আলো) ; that which has undergone slump or general drop in prices (নরম বাজার) ; almost rotten (ফলগুলো নরম হয়ে গেছে). **নরম হওয়া** *v.* to soften; to be appeased; to slacken or loosen; to abate; to slump; to come down. **নরম মাটি** soft clay; loamy soil; (fig.) one who is easily pliable; a weak person. **নরম-গরম** *a.* partly angry or rude and partly tender or soft; rather harsh; blandly harsh. □ *n.* harsh words spoken in a bland voice (নরম-গরম শোনানো).

নরা corrup. of **নর**[২] (নরা গজা বিশে শয়).

নরাকার, নরাকৃতি *a.* human-shaped, man-shaped. **নরাকার পশু** a beast in human shape or form; a beastly person, a brute.

নরাধম *n.* a base man, a mean rascal, a wretch.

নরাধিপ *n.* a king.

নরান্তক *n.* a man-killer; an appellation of Yama (যম) the god of death. □ *a.* killing or murdering (man).

নরি *a.* (chiefly used as a *sfx.*) having a row or rows (সাতনরি হার).

নরুন *n.* a nail-cutter shaped like a small and thin chisel. **নরুন-পেড়ে** *a.* (of loin-cloths) having a thin coloured border.

নরেন্দ্র, নরেশ, নরেশ্বর *n.* a king; the greatest or best amongst men.

নরোত্তম *n.* the best amongst men; Narayana (নারায়ণ) or Krishna (কৃষ্ণ).

নর্তক *a.* engaged in or taken to or given to dancing; dancing. □ *n.* a dancer; a professional dancer. **নর্তকী** *a. fem.* of **নর্তক**। □ *n. fem.* a dancer, a dancing-girl, a ballerina.

নর্তন *n.* dancing; a dance. **~কুর্দন** *n.* dancing and jumping about; (fig.) bragging and blustering. **~প্রিয়** *a.* fond of dancing. **~শালা** *n.* a dance-hall, a dancing-salon.

নর্দন *n.* (of bulls) bellow; (of cows) low, moo.

নর্দমা, নর্দামা *n.* a drain; a gutter; a sewer.

নর্দিত *a.* sounded.

নর্ম *n.* play, sport, pastime; amusement, diversion; fun, merry-making; enjoyment, pleasure; luxury. **~সখা, ~সচিব, ~সহচর** *n.* a playmate; a jester, a clown, a fool; a courtier; a flatterer. **~সখী, ~সহচরী** *n. fem.* a girl playmate; a woman partner in enjoyment; a lady-love, an inamorata; a concubine.

নল *n.* a cylinder, a tube, a pipe, a barrel, a rod; a measure of length; a measuring rod; a kind of reed.

নলকূপ *n.* a tube-well. **নলকূপ বসানো** *v.* to sink a tube-well.

নলখাগড়া *n.* a reed.

নলচালা *n.* an artful trick of setting a rod on move (feigned to be done by occult incantation) to detect a thief. **নল চালা** *v.* to set a rod on move to detect a thief by means of occult incantation.

নলচে coll. corrup. of **নলিচা**।

নলবন *n.* a thicket of reeds; a clump of reeds.

-নলা[১] *a.* (used as a *sfx.*) having one or more tubes or barrels (দোনলা = double-barrelled).

নলা[২] *n.* a tubular bone (esp. of hands or legs).

নলাকার *a.* tubular, cylindrical.

নলি *n.* a small tube or pipe or cylinder (সুতোর নলি) ; a tubular bone (হাতের নলি) ; a tubular talon or claw.

নলিকা *n.* a stem or stalk (of a plant); a reed; a pipe, a cylinder; an artery.

নলিচা *n.* the pipe of a hookah (the bowl of burning tabacco is placed on the top of this pipe).

নলিন *n.* the lotus, the lily. **নলিনাক্ষ** *a.* lotus-eyed. **নলিনী** *n. fem.* lotuses or lilies collectively; a clump or bed of the lotus or lily; a place where the lotus or lily grows abundantly; (loos.) the lotus, the lily. **নলিনীরুহ** *n.* a stalk of the lotus or lily.

নলী rej. var. of **নলি** and **নলিকা** ।

নলেন *a.* prepared from new date-juice (নলেন গুড়).

নশ্বর *a.* perishable; mortal; transitory, transient; frail. **নশ্বরতা** *n.* perishability; mortality; transitoriness, transience; frailty.

নষ্ট lifeless (নষ্ট প্রাণ) ; destroyed, ruined (নষ্ট রাজ্য, নষ্ট স্বাস্থ্য) ; lost (নষ্ট চেতনা) ; wasted (নষ্ট ধন বা সম্পদ) ; futile (নষ্ট পরিশ্রম) ; misspent (নষ্ট যৌবন = misspent youth); spoiled, undone (নষ্ট কাজ) ; decomposed; rotten, putrefied, turned (নষ্ট মাছ, নষ্ট দুধ) ; corrupted, depraved, unchaste (নষ্ট মেয়ে, নষ্ট লোক, নষ্ট চরিত্র) ; wicked (নষ্ট বুদ্ধি). **নষ্ট করা** *v.* to destroy, to ruin; to waste; to misspend; to render futile or useless, to foil; to spoil, to undo; to rot, to turn; to corrupt, to deprave; to blunt (বুদ্ধি নষ্ট করা). **নষ্ট হওয়া** *v.* to perish; to be destroyed or ruined; to be wasted; to be lost; to become futile or useless, to be foiled; to be spoiled or undone; to decompose, to rot, to turn; to become corrupted or depraved; to blunt. **~কোষ্ঠী** *n.* a missing or lost horoscope. **নষ্টকোষ্ঠী উদ্ধার করা** to recast one's nativity from assumed data. **~চন্দ্র** *n.* the moon of the fourth lunation of either fortnight in the month of Bhadra (ভাদ্র) ; it is said that one who sees this moon invites calumny upon oneself. **~চেতন** *a.* unconscious, swooned, fainted. **~মতি** *a.* evil-minded, wicked; depraved, unchaste; (affect.) mischievous. **নষ্টা** *a. fem.* given to adultery, unchaste; wicked, vile. □ *n. fem.* an adulteress, an unchaste woman; a wicked or vile woman. **নষ্টামি,** (dial.) **নষ্টামো** *n.* mischievousness; a mischief; knavery, roguery, villainy; peccadillo and delinquency. **নষ্টামি করা** *v.* to make mischief; to commit roguery. **নষ্টেন্দুকলা** *n.* the day of a new moon. **নষ্টোদ্ধার** *n.* recovery or reclamation of a lost thing.

নস coll. corrup. of **নহিস** ।

নসিব *n.* fate, luck; fortune, destiny. **নসিবের দোষ** ill-luck. **নসিবের দোষে** *adv.* through ill-luck, as ill-luck would have it.

নস্য, (coll.) **নস্যি** *n.* snuff; (fig.) an iota. **নস্যি দেওয়া** *v.* to put snuff (to or in). **নস্যি নেওয়া** *v.* to take snuff. **নস্যদান, নস্যদানি, নস্যির কৌটো বা ডিবে** *n.* a snuff-box.

নস্যাৎ *a. & adv.* thoroughly neglected or rejected or flouted; rendered thoroughly ineffective or null and void.

নস্যি coll. corrup. of **নস্য** ।

নহবত falsely elegant form of **নওবত** ।

নহর *n.* a channel or canal; a drain.

নহলি, (rej.) **নহলী** *a.* new or young (নহলি যৌবন)

নহা (obs.) *v.* to be not. 1st. per. **নহি** ; 2nd per. **নহ,** (in slight or familiarity) **নহিস** ; 3rd per. **নহে,** (in respect) **নহেন** ।

নহি see **নহা** ।

নহিলে (now obs. or only poet.) *con.* or, else, otherwise. □ *prep.* without, except, but, other than (সে নহিলে কে যাইবে ?).

নহিস, নহে, নহেন see **নহা** ।

না[১] *pfx.* indicating: negation, absence, opposition etc. (নামঞ্জুর).

না[২] *n.* a boat; a canoe, a dug-out.

না[৩] *adv.* not; no; nay. □ *int.* expressing: question (পড়তে বসবে না ?) ; request or insistence, please (দুটো টাকা দাও না) ; doubt or uncertainty, will it or will it not, will there be or will there not be (বৃষ্টি হবে, না ?) ; want or excess, how much or how many, what a (সংসারে কত না জ্বালা) ; amazement (আগুনেও সে পোড়ে না) ; sorrow or exception or complaint (যাও—আমায় দিলে না তো) ; contempt or ridicule (পারলে না তো). □ *con.* or, nor (না রাম না গঙ্গা). □ *prep.* without (না বুঝে). □ *in comp.* no, not, non-, un- (না-ধর্মী). **না রাম না গঙ্গা** (fig.) neither fish nor fowl.

নাই[১] pop. corrup. of **নাহি**[১] (see **নাহা**).

নাই[২] *n.* (rare) a barber.

নাই৩ *n.* the navel; (of a wheel) a nave, a hub; a wedge; an anvil.

নাই৪ *n.* indulgence, pampering. **কুকুর নাই পেলে মাথায় চড়ে** (lit.) fondle a mongrel and it will jump up on your head, (fig.) a saucy scamp scandalizes his patron.

নাই৫ *adv.* not (যাই নাই, আসে নাই).

নাই৬ pop. corrup. of **নাহি**১ । □ *a.* non-existent (নাই-মামা) ; full of want (নাই ঘরে খাই). **নাই ঘরে খাই** (fig.) the poor have greater hunger; the lesser the supply, the greater the hunger; hungriness grows apace in a destitute person's family. **নাই মামার (নেই মামার) চেয়ে কানা মামা ভালো** (fig.) something is better than nothing, half a loaf is better than no loaf, a live ass is better than a dead lion.

নাই-আঁকড়া *a.* dogged, obstinate, tenacious, persistent.

নাইয়া *n.* a boatman; a sailor.

নাউ coll. corrup. of **লাউ** ।

নাও var. of **না**২ ।

নাওয়া *v.* to bathe, to have a bath or washing. □ *n.* bathing, washing, bath, ablution. **নাওয়ানো** *v.* to cause to bathe, to bath, to wash; to dip (idol etc.) in water.

নাঃ emphatic form of **না**৩ ।

নাক *n.* the nose, the olfactory organ; the sense of smell; the power to distinguish smell, smelling power (তোমার নাক তো খুব). **নাক উঁচানো** *v.* (fig.) to turn up one's nose (at), to show disdain (at). **নাক ঝাড়া** *v.* to blow one's nose. **নাক টেপা** *v.* to press one's nose; (ridi.). to say one's prayers silently. **নাক ডাকা** *v.* to snore. **নাক ফোঁড়া, নাক বেঁধানো** *v.* to perforate the septum of one's nose. **~বরাবর** *adv.* straight, straightaway, in the direction of one's nose. **নাক বাঁকানো** same as **নাক উঁচানো** । **নাক মলা** *v.* to pull or twist one's own nose as a mark of regret for a mistake or fault. **নাক সিঁটকানো** same as **নাক উঁচানো** । **নাকে খত** see **খত** । **নাকে-মুখে গোঁজা** *v.* to eat very hurriedly; to gulp down. **নাকের ছেঁদা** a nostril. **নাকের জলে চোখের জলে হওয়া** (fig.) to be embarrassed, to be in deep waters or quagmire. **নিজের নাক কেটে পরের যাত্রাভঙ্গ করা** (fig.) to do a greater harm to oneself in an attempt to put somebody into trouble.

নাক-কাটা *a.* one who has one's nose cut off; (fig.) shameless, brazen-faced. **নাককান-কাটা** same as **নাক-কাটা** (fig.).

নাক-খত see **খত** ।

নাক-খাঁদা *a.* snub-nosed.

নাকচ *a.* set-aside; cancelled; rejected; annulled, repealed. **নাকচ করা** *v.* to set aside; to cancel; to reject; to annul, to repeal, to rescind.

নাকছাবি *n.* an ornament for the nose, a nose-pin.

নাকা same as **নাকি**২ ।

নাকাড়া var. of **নাকারা** ।

নাকানিচুবানি, নাকানিচোবানি *n.* continuous ducking in water as made by a drowning person; (fig.) continuous harassment or distress or embarrassment. **নাকানিচোবানি খাওয়া** *v.* to have to duck in water continuously (as by a drowning person); (fig.) to be harassed or distressed or embarrassed continuously.

নাকারা *n.* a kind of small kettledrum or war-trumpet.

নাকাল *a.* embarrassed, put out of countenance; put to shame; harassed; fatigued. □ *n.* embarrassment; harassment; fatigue; discomfiture; humiliation; adequate or sound punishment. **নাকাল করা** *v.* to embarrass, to put out of countenance; to harass; to fatigue; to put to shame; to discomfit; to punish adequately or soundly. **নাকাল হওয়া** *v.* to be embarrassed or discomfited, to be put out of countenance; to be humiliated.

না কি *int.* expressing: question, doubt, supposition etc. (যাবে না কি, সত্য না কি, is it ? do you think so ? if it be.

নাকি *a.* spoken through the nose, nasal (নাকি সুর). **নাকি কান্না, নাকে কান্না** *n.* whimper; (sarcas.) crocodile tears.

নাকুয়া, নাকু *a.* given to speaking through one's nose (নাকুয়া লোক) ; spoken through the nose (নাকুয়া কথা) ; long-nosed, nosy (নাকুয়া লোক).

নাকে-কাঁদুনে *a.* given to crying at trifles, whimpering.

নাকে-কান্না see **নাকি**।

নাক্ষত্র, নাক্ষত্রিক *a.* stellar, astral, sidereal *fem.* **নাক্ষত্রিকী**। **নাক্ষত্র কাল** sidereal time. **নাক্ষত্র দিন** a sidereal day. **নাক্ষত্র বৎসর** a sidereal year. **নাক্ষত্র মাস** a stellar or sidereal month. **নাক্ষত্র লম্বন** (astr.) secular parallax.

নাখোদা, নাখুদা *n.* a captain of a ship; a merchant exporting and importing by sea; a Muslim community consisting of merchants (নাখোদা মসজিদ).

নাখোশ, নাখুশ *a.* displeased; dissatisfied.

নাগ *n.* the snake, the serpent; the elephant (দিঙ্‌নাগ). **অষ্টনাগ** *n.* (myth.) the eight chief snakes collectively. **~কেশর** *n.* a kind of flower or its plant. **~দন্ত** *n.* a tusk of an elephant; ivory. **~পঞ্চমী** *n.* the fifth lunar day of the dark fortnight of the month of Shravan (শ্রাবণ) when Goddess Manasa (মনসা) is worshipped. **~পাশ** *n.* an ancient missile said to be capable of producing snakes that bound the victim (as with a noose). **~ফণী** *n.* cactus. **~মাতা** *n.* (myth.) Kadru (কদ্রু) the first mother of snakes. **~রাজ** *n.* the king of snakes; Vasuki (বাসুকী) or Ananta (অনন্ত). **~লোক** *n.* the region inhabited by the snakes; Hades or the nether world.

নাগর *n.* a gallant, a philanderer, an illicit lover, a paramour; lewd man. □ *a.* same as **নাগরিক** (*a.*).

নাগরঙ্গ *n.* the orange.

নাগরদোলা *n.* a merry-go-round revolving from above downwards, a whirlgig.

নাগরা *n.* a kind of loose and usually gaudy shoe or slipper.

নাগরালি *n.* gallantry, philandering; lewdness.

নাগরি *n.* an earthen pitcher (usu. to hold molasses).

নাগরিক *a.* of or living in a city or town; urban; metropolitan; civic. □ *n.* a citizen; a subject or national (ভারতের নাগরিক). **নাগরিকা** *a. fem.* living in a city or town. □ *n. fem.* of **নাগরিক** (*n.*). **নাগরিকতা** *n.* citizenship. **নাগরিকী** *a. fem.* of **নাগরিক** (*a.*).

নাগরী[1] *n.* the Devanagari script.

নাগরী[2] *n. fem.* a flirt, a coquette; a concubine; a lewd woman. □ *a. fem.* living in a town or city.

নাগা *n.* one of a community of ascetics who move about naked; one of an aboriginal tribe of Naga hills.

নাগাড় *a.* continuous, incessant, ceaseless (নাগাড় তিনমাস). **নাগাড়ে** *adv.* continuously, incessantly, ceaselessly. **একনাগাড়ে** *adv.* without break, at a stretch.

নাগাদ *prep.* up to, until, till (শেষ নাগাদ) ; about, nearly; by (কাল নাগাদ).

নাগাল *n.* proximity or range (চোখের নাগাল) ; approach or access (নাগালে যাওয়া) ; reach (নাগাল পাওয়া) ; comprehension (মনের নাগাল). **নাগাল পাওয়া** *v.* to reach; to overtake; to catch up with; to comprehend, to have an access to (মনের নাগাল পাওয়া). **নাগালে থাকা** *v.* to be within the range or reach or access or approach of.

নাগিনী, নাগী *fem.* forms of **নাগ**।

নাগেন্দ্র, নাগেশ *n.* the king of elephants: an appellation of Airavat (ঐরাবত) ; the king of snakes: an appellation of Ananta (অনন্ত) or Vasuki (বাসুকি) ; a phallus of Shiva (শিব).

নাগেশ্বর same as **নাগকেশর**।

নাঙ্গা *a.* naked, nude; uncovered, bare.

নাচ *n.* dancing; capering; a dance; a caper (ছাগলের নাচ, বাঁদরের নাচ) ; (sarcas.) ludicrous gesticulations or fretting. **~উলি, ~ওয়ালি** *n.* a professional dancing girl or dancing-woman, a ballerina. **~ঘর** *n.* a dancing-hall; a ball-room; a theatre. **নাচন, নাচনি**[1], **নাচুনি**[1] *n.* dancing; (sarcas.) ludicrous gesticulations or fretting. **নাচনি**[2], **নাচুনি**[2], **নাচুনে** *n.* a dancing-girl or dancing-woman; a ballerina. □ *a.* engaged in or given to or expert in dancing (নাচুনি মেয়ে) ; having rhythmic beats, dancing, rhythmic (নাচুনে ছন্দ).

নাচা *v.* to dance; to caper (ছাগল নাচে) ; (of eyes) to blink or twinkle; to leap in joy ('হৃদয় আমার নাচে রে') ; to be moved or excited (পরের কথায় নাচা). **নাচ নাচা** to dance a dance; (arch.) to tread a measure. **নাচতে এসে ঘোমটা** (fig.) hypocritical or sham bashfulness, a harlot veils her face when she takes in customers. **নাচতে না জানলে উঠোনের দোষ** a bad workman quarrels with his tools.

নাচাকোঁদা *n.* (lit.) dancing and capering about; (sarcas.) ludicrous gesticulations; (sarcas.) vain bragging or fretting.

নাচানো *v.* to cause to dance; to cause to caper; to cause to leap in joy; to move or excite.

নাচার *a.* having no means; helpless; resourceless.

নাচি *n.* a rivet. **~নাচি করা** *v.* to rivet.

নাচিয়ে *a.* given to or skilled in dancing. □ *n.* a dancer.

নাচুনি, নাচুনে see **নাচ**।

নাছদুয়ার *n.* a back door.

নাছোড় *a.* refusing to give up, unyielding, pertinacious, obstinate, dogged. **~বান্দা** *n.* an unyielding or pertinacious or obstinate person.

নাজিম *n.* (Mus.) a governor (নবাব নাজিম).

নাজির *n.* a head clerk of a lawcourt. **নাজিরি** *n.* office or post or work of the head clerk of a law-court.

নাজেহাল *a.* persecuted; pestered; harassed; fatigued. **নাজেহাল করা** *v.* to persecute; to pester; to harass; to fatigue.

নাট *n.* a dance; dramatic performance, acting; a fun; a stage (for dramatic performance). **নাটের গুরু** a director of a performance; (sarcas.) a wirepuller, a ringleader; an arch-intriguer.

নাটক *n.* a drama, a play. **নাটকীয়** *a.* full of dramatic elements, dramatic, theatrical; histrionic.

নাটমন্দির *n.* a hall within or in front of a temple for devotional dancing and musical performances; a dancing-hall, a ball-room; a theatre, an opera-house.

নাটা *a.* dwarfish, small in height, short.

নাটাই *n.* a reel; a spool; a bobbin.

নাটিকা *n.* a playlet, a short drama or play.

নাটুকে *a.* dramatic; theatrical; histrionic (নাটুকে কথাবার্তা) ; writing dramas (নাটুকে রামনারায়ণ) ; dramaturgic. **~পনা** *n.* theatricality.

নাটুয়া *n.* a dancer; an actor.

নাট্য *n.* the science and art of dancing, singing and music; dances and songs and music; acting; dancing; a drama, a play. **~কলা** *n.* the science and art of dancing, singing and music; art of acting, dramaturgy. **~কার** *n.* a playwright, a dramatist, a dramaturge. **~গৃহ** same as **নাট্যশালা**। **~মন্দির, ~শালা** *n.* a music-hall, a dancing-hall, a ball-room; a theatre, an opera-house. **~সমিতি** *n.* a theatrical party; an opera party; a dramatic club. **নাট্যাচার্য** *n.* a dancing-master; a motion-master; (loos.) a great actor. **নাট্যাভিনয়** *n.* a dramatic performance. **নাট্যাভিনেতা** *n.* the actor of a drama. **নাট্যামোদী** a lover of the drama, one who is interested in the drama. **নাট্যালয়** *n.* a theatre, an opera-house. **নাট্যোক্তি** *n.* dramatic dialogue.

নাড়া[1] *n.* a stubble.

নাড়া[2] *v.* to move; to put in motion; to oscillate; to shake; to give a jerk, to push (নেড়ো না—লেখা বেঁকে যাবে) ; to wave (হাত নাড়া) ; to wag (লেজ নাড়া) ; to stir (চামচ দিয়ে নাড়া) ; to ring or sound by moving with the hand (ঘণ্টা নাড়া) ; to remove or shift (এ রোগীকে নাড়বে কী করে ?) ; to handle (টাকা-পয়সা নাড়া) ; to displace or mess up (কাগজপত্র নাড়া) ; to study (শাস্ত্র নাড়া) ; to inquire of or test esp. cautiously or artfully, to sound (লোকটাকে নেড়ে দেখো) ; to loosen (গোড়ার মাটি নেড়ে দাও).

নাড়াচাড়া *n.* stirring or moving or handling (esp. roughly) or displacing or shifting; casual study (শাস্ত্র নাড়াচাড়া) ; thinking or considering (তথ্য নিয়ে নাড়াচাড়া) ; discussion esp. wide and popular (পরের কলঙ্ক নিয়ে নাড়াচাড়া). **নাড়াচাড়া করা** *v.* to stir or move or handle (esp. roughly); to displace or shift; to study casually; to think or consider; to discuss esp. publicly; to test or sound (ছেলেটিকে একটু নেড়েচেড়ে দেখব).

নাড়ানাড়ি *n.* act of stirring or moving or handling or displacing or shifting repeatedly or continuously; act of discussing publicly. **নাড়ানাড়ি করা** *v.* to stir or move or handle or displace or shift repeatedly or continuously; to discuss publicly.

নাড়ানো *v.* to move; to put in action; to cause to oscillate; to shake; to give a jerk, to push; to wave; to wag; to remove or shift.

নাড়াবুনে *n.* a cultivator; a rustic, a clodhopper; (fig.) a fool, a dunce. **যত ছিল নাড়াবুনে, হল সব কেত্তুনে** (fig.) clodhoppers have turned artists, fools have turned leaders.

নাড়ি, নাড়ী *n.* an artery or vein; the pulse (নাড়ি টেপা) ; the placenta (নাড়ি কাটা) ; the intestines (নাড়ি জ্বলা) ; (loos.) the uterus (নাড়ির দোষ). **নাড়ি কাটা** *v.* to cut the umbilical cord or detach the placenta. **নাড়ির গতি** regular or rhythmical beat of arteries as felt at the wrist. **~ঘাত** *n.* pulse-beat. **(প্রতি মিনিটে) নাড়িঘাতের হার** pulse-rate. **নাড়ি ছেঁড়া** same as **নাড়ি জ্বলা**। **নাড়িছেঁড়া ধন** a child (of a mother). **নাড়ি জ্বলা** *v.* (fig.) to have agonizing pain in the stomach (খিদেয় নাড়ি জ্বলা = to be famished with hunger). **নাড়ি টেপা** *v.* (usu. sarcas.) to feel one's pulse. **~টেপা ডাক্তার** a quack, a charlatan. **নাড়ি দেখা** *v.* to feel one's pulse. **নাড়ি মরা** *v.* to lose power to eat sufficiently (usu. due to continuous underfeeding); to lose appetite or power of digesting. **~মরা** *a.* having a poor or weak digestion; able to consume only a meagre fare; feeble, weak. **~জ্ঞান** *n.* ability for or knowledge of feeling one's (esp. a patient's) pulse (in order to determine one's state of health); (fig.) ability to determine the state of a thing. **~নক্ষত্র** *n.* (ori. & obs.) the star in the ascendant at one's nativity; (pop.) all information about one since one's birth; all or detailed information about anything; ins and outs. **~ব্রণ** *n.* see **নালীব্রণ (নালী)**। **~ভুঁড়ি** *n.* intestines; entrails.

নাড়ু *n.* a sweet drop, a ball of sweetmeat usu. made of coconut, sugar or molasses etc.

নাতজামাই, নাতনি, নাতবউ see **নাতি²**।

নাতি¹ *adv.* (used as a *pfx.*) not much, moderately. **~খর্ব** *a.* not very short or dwarfish. **~দীর্ঘ** *a.* not very long. **~বৃহৎ** *a.* not very big; of moderate or medium size. **~শীতল** *a.* not very cold; moderately cold. **~শীতোষ্ণ** *a.* of mild temperature, temperate. **নাতিশীতোষ্ণ মণ্ডল** (geog.) the temperate zone. **~স্থূল** *a.* not very fat or bulky. **~হ্রস্ব** *a.* not very short.

নাতি² *n.* a grandson. *fem.* **নাতনি, নাতিনি** a grand-daughter. **নাতজামাই** *n.* the husband of a grand-daughter. **~পুতি** *n.* children of one's sons and daughters collectively, grandchildren. **নাতবউ** *n.* the wife of one's grandson.

নাথ *n.* a master, a lord; a husband; a ruler (জগন্নাথ) ; a guardian, a maintainer, a protector, a custodian (নরনাথ, দীননাথ). **~বতী** *a. fem.* one whose husband is alive.

নাদ¹ *n.* sound, noise, report, roar.

নাদ² *n.* excrements (esp. of cattle), droppings, dung.

নাদন *n.* a thick pillar or column; a thick stick, a cudgel, a club. **~বাড়ি** *n.* a heavy cudgel or club. **~পেটা** *a.* cudgelled. **~পেটা করা** *v.* to cudgel.

নাদা¹ *v.* to void excrements (esp. by cattle), to dung, to excrete; (sarcas.) to make dirty work of.

নাদা² *v.* (poet.) to sound; to roar.

নাদা³ *n.* a large earthen trough or vat.

নাদাপেটা *a.* pot-bellied; (loos.) corpulent.

নাদি *n.* a pellet of dung (esp. of a small creature as a rat).

নাদিত *a.* sounded, blown; resounded.

নাদিনী *a.* (chiefly used as a *sfx.*) giving out a sound, sounding, roaring (কলনাদী).

নাদুসনুদুস *a.* roly-poly, podgy, plump, buxom; fleshy, full of flesh.

নাদেয়, নাদ্য *a.* of or born of or grown in a river, riverine.

নানকপন্থী *n.* a Sikh; a Nanakite.

নানা¹ *n.* a maternal grandfather, a grandfather.

নানা², নানান *a.* many and diverse. **নানাজাতীয়** *a.* of (many and) diverse kinds. **নানা দিক** different or various sides or angles or aspects. **নানাদেশীয়** of different or various countries. **নানাপ্রকার** *a.* of various kinds or descriptions.

নানাপ্রকারে *adv.* in various ways or means. **নানাবিধ** same as **নানাপ্রকার**। **নানা মত** *n.* different opinions or views (নানা মুনির নানা মত = many men, many minds; opinions differ or vary). **নানামতে** same as **নানাপ্রকারে**। **নানা রঙের** *a.* of many or various colours, of many hues, multi-coloured; variegated; pied. **নানারূপ** *a.* of various forms or descriptions or kinds. **নানার্থ** *a.* containing or conveying many or diverse meanings; homonymous. **নানার্থ শব্দ** a homonym.

নানি, (rej.) **নানী** *n.* a maternal grandmother, a grandmother.

নান্দী *n.* an invocation at the opening of a drama. **~কর** *n.* one who recites the invocation at the opening of a drama. **~পাঠ** *n.* recital of the invocation at the opening of a drama. **~মুখ** *n.* an obsequial rite performed at the start of a happy ceremony, such as marriage.

না-পছন্দ, না-পসন্দ *a.* not chosen, disapproved; disliked; unaccepted, rejected. **না-পছন্দ করা** *v.* to disapprove; to dislike; to reject.

নাপতে, নাপতিনি see **নাপিত**।

নাপাক *a.* unholy, profane.

নাপিত, (coll. & vul.) **নাপতে** *n.* (of) a barber (by caste or trade). *fem.* **নাপিতানি,** (coll.) **নাপতিনি**।

নাফা *n.* profit, gain; benefit; good.

নাবা, নাবানো dial. corruption of **নামা**[3] and **নামানো** respectively.

নাবাল pop. var. of **নামাল** (brought down).

নাবালক *a.* under-age; (fig.) inexperienced, raw. □ *n.* a minor. *fem.* **নাবালিকা**।

নাবি *a.* (of agricultural produce or crops) late in growing, late (নাবিধান).

নাবিক *n.* a sailor; a boatman; a navigator. **~বিদ্যা** *n.* (the art and science of) navigation.

নাব্য *a.* navigable. **~তা** *n.* navigability.

নাভি *n.* the navel, the umbilicus, (coll.) belly-button; (of a wheel) a hub, a nave. **~কুণ্ডল, ~কূপ** *n.* the umbilical cavity. **~চ্ছেদন** *n.* cutting off of the umbilical cord or the navel string. **~দেশ** *n.* the umbilical region. **~পদ্ম** *n.* a lotus-like navel; (rel.) a lotus in a navel. **~লম্ব** *n.* (conics.) latus rectum. **~শ্বাস** *n.* the last gasp; the dying state or stage; the pangs of death.

নাম *n.* a name, an appellation, a designation, an epithet; reputation, fame, celebrity, renown (নামডাক) ; identity (নামগোত্রহীন) ; mention or reputation (দেশের সর্বত্র তার নাম) ; the name of a deity (নামজপ) ; a name esp. that of a deity or religion invoked or called to witness (ভগবানের নামে, ধর্মের নামে) ; a roll (নাম ডাকা) ; a plea or pretext or pretence (কাজের নাম করে পালানো) ; actual execution or performance (কাজের নামে ঢুঁ ঢুঁ) ; merely nominal or titular existence or possession (নামেই তালপুকুর) ; a very small amount, an iota (নামমাত্র) ; (gr.) a root-word other than verbs, a noun, a substantive. **ছদ্মনাম** *n.* a pseudonym. **ডাকনাম** *n.* a nickname. **ভালো নাম** *n.* proper or Christian or formal first name; the name by which one is known to the outside public. **ভুল নাম** a misnomer. **নাম করা** *v.* to mention one's name; to name; to make a plea (সে বিপদের নাম আর করে না) ; to utter the name of; to utter or recite the name of one's idol (বৈষ্ণবেরা নাম করছেন) ; to earn fame, to become conspicuous, to come into prominence, to cut a figure (সে নাচে নাম করেছে). **নাম কাটা** *v.* to remove one's name (from a register, roll etc.); to strike off one's name, to strike one off. **নাম গাওয়া** same as **নামকীর্তন করা**। **নাম জপা** same as **নামজপ করা**। **নাম ডাকা** *v.* to summon one loudly by one's name (সাক্ষীর নাম ডাকছে) ; to call the roll. **নাম ডোবানো** *v.* to destroy one's reputation; to bring disgrace upon, to drag one's name through the mire. **নাম দেওয়া** same as **নামকরণ করা**। **নাম ধরা** *v.* to tell one's name; to assume a name or designation. **নাম ধরে ডাকা** *v.* to call or summon one by one's name. **নাম বলা** *v.* to tell one's name; to name or mention. **নাম ভাঁড়ানো** *v.* to commit forgery by concealing one's name and assuming a false one. **নাম রটা** *v.* to become famous or notorious. **নাম রাখা** *v.* to give a name to, to christen, to designate, to name; to act up to the reputation of (বংশের নাম রাখা) ; to leave behind a lasting fame (পৃথিবীতে নাম রাখা). **নাম নেওয়া** *v.* to utter the name of; to utter or recite in devotion the name of; to remember or worship. **নাম লেখানো** *v.* to have oneself enlisted or enrolled or registered. **নাম শোনানো** *v.* to sing to one the name of (esp. of a deity). **নাম হওয়া** *v.* to become famous, to earn reputation. **নাম হারানো** *v.* to lose one's reputation. **নামক** *a.* named, by name, called, designated. **~করণ** *n.* act of giving a name to, act of naming; the sacrament of giving a name to, christening; nomenclature. **নামকরণ করা** *v.* to give a name to, to name; to designate; to christen. **~করা** *a.* reputed, renowned, famous; (dero.) notorious (নামকরা চোর). **~কীর্তন** *n.* devotional recitation or singing of the name of one's idol; act of celebrating one's name; act of praising esp. publicly. **নামকীর্তন করা** *v.* to recite or sing in devotion the name of; to celebrate one's name; to praise esp. publicly. **~গন্ধ** *n.* slightest mention or sign or trace. **নামগান** same as **নামকীর্তন**। **~গোত্রহীন** *a.* (fig.) having no established (social) position or credentials. **~জপ** *n.* act of uttering inwardly and continuously the name of one's idol. **নামজপ করা** *v.* to utter in devotion the name of one's idol inwardly and continuously. **~জাদা** *a.* famous, renowned, celebrated, reputed. **~জারি** *n.* mutation or substitution of a name in an official register esp. in the landlord's records; publication or upholding of one's name. **নামজারি করা** *v.* to alter or substitute a name in an official register; to publish or uphold a name. **~ডাক** *n.* fame and influence, prominence in public life. **~ডাকওয়ালা** *a.* famous and influential, prominent in public life. **নাম ডাকা** *v.* to call the rolls; to call one's name. **নামত** *adv.* in name only; nominally. □ *a.* nominal, titular. **~ধর** *a.* named. **~ধাতু** *n.* (gr.) a verbal root derived from a noun, a nominal verb. **~ধাম** *n.* name and address. **~ধারণ** *n.* act of assuming or bearing a name or designation. **নামধারণ করা** *v.* to assume or bear a name or designation. **~ধারী** same as **নামধর**। **~ধেয়** *n.* a name, an appellation, a designation. □ *a.* named, designated. **~পত্র** *n.* the title page of a book; the paper or document bearing one's title. **~পদ** *n.* (gr.) a noun. **নাম প্রত্যাহার** *n.* withdrawal of one's name or candidature (from a contest, election etc.) **~ফলক** *n.* a nameplate. **~বাচক** *a.* expressing or denoting a name; (gr.) proper. **নামবাচক বিশেষ্য** (gr.) a proper noun. **~বিহীন** *a.* nameless; unknown; having no reputation or fame; obscure; anonymous. **~বিহীনতা, ~হীনতা** *n.* namelessness; anonymity. **~ভূমিকা** *n.* the title-role, the name-part. **~মাত্র** *a.* nominal; titular; only a little or only a few. □ *adv.* nominally, in name only; only a little or only a few. □ *n.* (even) the mere name; slightest mention or hint; slightest amount. **~মুদ্রা** *n.* a seal bearing one's name. **~মুদ্রাঙ্কিত** *a.* sealed, with a seal bearing one's name. **~যশ** same as **নামডাক**। **~সংকীর্তন** same as **নামকীর্তন**। **~সর্বস্ব** *n.* a thing or person that is nothing but a mere name. □ *a.* existing merely in name. **~হারা, ~হীন** same as **নামবিহীন**। **নামে** *a.* by name, named, designated; in name only; nominal, titular. □ *adv.* in name only. **নামে গোয়ালা কাঁজি ভক্ষণ** (fig.) one who is reputed as a millionaire but cannot afford to eat more mutton than beef. **নামে নামে** *adv.* separately by or in or under individual names.

না-মঞ্জুর *a.* not sanctioned or allowed or accepted, turned down, rejected. **না-মঞ্জুর করা** *v.* to disallow, to turn down, to reject.

নামতা *n.* (arith.) the multiplication table.

-নামা১ *in comp.* (used as a *sfx.*) bearing a particular name, named, designated. **অজ্ঞাতনামা** *a.* nameless; unknown.

-নামা২ *n.* (used as a *sfx.*) a letter; a deed

(চুক্তিনামা) ; a written authorization (ওকালতনামা) ; a narrative, a chronicle, a history (শাহ্‌নামা).

নামা³ *v.* to come or go down, to get down, to descent, to alight; to climb down; to dismount (ঘোড়া থেকে নামা) ; to disembark, to get out of (জাহাজ বা গাড়ি থেকে নামা) ; to go down into (জলে নামা) ; to stoop, to incline, to slope, to become lower or depressed, to sink (ঘরের ছাদ নেমে গেছে, পথ নেমে গেছে) ; to decrease, to abate, to fall (জ্বর নামা, দর নামা) ; to go down, to set (সূর্য পশ্চিমে নেমেছে) ; to set in, to ensue, to commence (বৃষ্টি নেমেছে) ; to appear in (আসরে নামা) ; to come out in (পথে নামা) ; to take part, to join (তর্কে নামা) ; to flow out, to ooze, to stream (ঘাম নামা, চোখের জল নামা) ; to be degraded or demoted (উঁচু পদ থেকে নামা, ক্লাস থেকে নামা) ; to be depraved (ছেলেটা অনেক দূর নেমে গেছে) ; to quote a lower price or easier terms (সে আর নামবে না তা লেন-দেন হোক আর না হোক) ; to have loose motions or diarrhoea (পেট নামা). □ *a.* depressed, sunk (নামা জায়গা).

নামাঙ্কিত *a.* carved or engraved with a name; with a name carved or engraved on something; containing a name; bearing a signature, signed.

নামাজ pop. var. of **নমাজ** ।

নামানো *v.* to cause to get down, to bring down; to cause to set in (বৃষ্টি নামানো) ; to bring or lay down upon the ground (মাথার বস্তা নামানো) ; to unload (গাড়ি থেকে মাল নামানো) ; to cause to appear in (আসরে নামানো) ; to cause to come out in (পথে নামানো) ; to cause to flow out or stream or ooze (চোখের জল নামানো) ; to degrade or demote; to deprave; to cause to go down or fall, to decrease, to abate; to cause to quote a lower price or easier terms; to cause to have loose motions or diarrhoea; to purge or evacuate strongly (এ ওষুধে পেট নামাবে) ; to have loose motions or diarrhoea (রোগীর পেট নামাচ্ছে).

নামান্তর *n.* another or a different name; difference only in name and not in any other respects (নামান্তরমাত্র).

নামাবলি, (rej.) **নামাবলী** *n.* a piece of scarf with the names of deities printed on it; a list of names; nomenclature.

নামাল *a.* (of land) low-lying, low, depressed.

নামী *a.* renowned, famous.

নামোচ্চারণ *n.* utterance of a name; (slightest) mention. **নামোচ্চারণ করা** *v.* to utter the name of; to mention (slightly).

নামোল্লেখ *n.* mention of a name. **নামোল্লেখ করা** *v.* to mention the name of.

-নাম্নী *fem.* of **নামা¹** ।

নায়ক *a.* leading, guiding, commanding, chief, principal. □ *n.* a leader, a guide, a commander, a captain; a chief; a hero (of a drama, fiction etc.); a (habitual) lover, an amorous man, a gallant.

নায়িকা *a.* & *n. fem.* of **নায়ক** । □ *n. fem.* any one of the eight manifestations of Goddess Durga (দুর্গা).

নায়েক *n.* a soldier holding the lowest non-commissioned rank in the Indian Army, a naik; a surname of south-west Bengali Hindus.

নায়েব *n.* an administrator and rent collector of a rent-collecting unit of a landlord's estate. **নায়েবি** *n.* the post of this official. □ *a.* relating to this official.

নারক *a.* of or condemmed to or condemnable to hell, hellish, infernal; sinning, reprobate. □ *n.* hell, Inferno.

নারকী¹ *a. fem.* of **নারক** (*a.*).

নারকী² *a.* same as **নারক** (*a.*).

নারকীয় *a.* worthy only of hell, hellish, infernal; diabolical.

নারকেল, নারকোল *n.* the coconut. **নারকেল গাছ** *n.* the coconut tree. **নারকেল তেল** coconut oil. **নারকেল দড়ি** coir-rope. **নারকেলের ছোবড়া** coir. **নারকেলের জল** coconut-water, coconut-milk. **নারকেলের শাঁস** kernel of coconut. **নারকেলের শুকনো শাঁস** copra. **নারকেলি, নারকোলি** *a.* of the shape of a coconut, shaped like a cocount; tasting like a coconut copra; containing kernal like that of a coconut. **নারকেলি কুল** a kind of sweet jujube.

নারঙ্গা, নারঙ্গি *n.* the orange.

নারদ *n.* a mythological sage given to

setting gods by the ears. **নারদ নারদ** *int.* let them or may they engage in a quarrel with one another. **নারদীয়** *a.* of Narada (নারদ) the sage.

নারা *v.* (poet. or dial.) cannot, to be unable to, to fail to.

নারাঙ্গা *n.* the orange; erysipelas.

নারাঙ্গি *n.* the orange.

নারাচ *n.* a kind of arrow made of iron, an iron-shaft.

নারাজ *a.* unwilling, disagreeing; displeased; discontented.

নারায়ণ *n.* a manifestation of Vishnu (বিষ্ণু). **~ক্ষেত্র** *n.* a plot of land on the bank of the Ganges stretching four cubits from the watermark or any plot of land conceived as this (a dying Hindu is laid down on this plot). **নারায়ণী** *n. fem.* Goddess Lakshmi (লক্ষ্মী) the wife of Narayana (নারায়ণ). □ *a.* of or evolved from Narayana. **নারায়ণী সেনা** *n.* a band of indefatigable warriors said to be born out of the person of Narayana or Krishna (কৃষ্ণ).

নারিকেল for. & obsolete from of **নারকেল**।

নারী *n.* a woman; womankind (নরনারী) ; a wife (পরনারী). **~চরিত্র** *n.* the character or nature of a woman; the female character or characters of a literary work or play etc. **~জাতি** *n.* womankind. **~ত্ব** *n.* womanhood, femininity. **~ধর্ম** *n.* functions or characteristic qualities of a woman; womanliness. **~ধর্ষণ** *n.* ravishment of a woman; rape. **~নিগ্রহ, ~নির্যাতন** *n.* persecution of a woman; molestation; rape. **~রত্ন** *n.* a jewel of a woman. **~সমাজ** *n.* womenfolk; the community of women. **~স্বভাব** *n.* womanly nature, womanliness, femininity. □ *a.* (of a man) effeminate. **~স্বভাবসুলভ** *a.* womanly, having qualities befitting a woman; womanish; (of a man) effeminate. **~হরণ** *n.* abduction of a woman.

নার্ভ *n.* a nerve.

নার্ভতন্ত্র *n.* the nervous system.

নাল[১] *n.* a horse-shoe. **নাল পরানো, নাল বাঁধানো** *v.* to shoe (a horse). **নাল-পরা, নাল-বাঁধা, নাল-বাঁধানো** *a.* shod. **নালবন্দ, নালবন্ধ** *n.* the smith who shoes horses, a farrier. **নালবন্দি** *n.* farriery.

নাল[২] *n.* saliva, slaver. **নাল ঝরা, নাল পড়া** *v.* to water (তার মুখ থেকে নাল ঝরছে = his mouth waters). **নাল ঝরানো, নাল ফেলা** *v.* to drivel, to slaver.

নাল[৩] *n.* a vein; a tube; a hollow culm or stalk esp. of the lotus.

নালতে coll. corrup. of **নালিতা**।

নাল-পরা see **নাল**[১]।

নালফুল *n.* the white water-lily, the lotus.

নাল-বাঁধা, নাল-বাঁধানো see **নাল**[১]।

নালা *n.* a duct; a drain; a canal; a wayside gutter.

নালায়েক *a.* unfit, incompetent, incapable; under-age, minor.

নালি, নালী *n.* a small duct or drain; a small and thin tube; a vein; a fissure; **নালি ঘা, নালি ব্রণ** *n.* sinus.

নালিকা বান্ডিল *n.* (anat.) vascular bundle.

নালিতা *n.* edible leaves of a jute-plant.

নালিশ *n.* a complaint; a lawsuit, a legal action; an appeal or prayer for redress. **নালিশ করা** *v.* to complain; to bring or file a lawsuit; to sue or prosecute. **নালিশি** *a.* concerning a complaint or lawsuit; in suit (নালিশি সম্পত্তি = a property in suit).

নালী alt. spell. of **নালি**।

নাশ *n.* destruction, annihilation; extinction; spoiling (কর্মনাশ) ; loss or waste (অর্থনাশ) ; ruin (স্বাস্থ্যনাশ) ; removal (দুঃখনাশ) ; act of killing, extermination (কীটনাশ) ; death. **নাশ করা** *v.* to destory, to annihilate; to spoil; to waste; to ruin; to remove; to kill, to exterminate. **নাশ পাওয়া, নাশ হওয়া** *v.* to be destroyed, to perish; to become extinct; to be spoiled or lost or wasted or ruined or removed or killed or exterminated; to die.

নাশক *a.* destructive; destroying; wasting; causing ruin; removing; killing, exterminating. **নাশকতা** *n.* destructiveness; sabotage.

নাশতা same as **নাস্তা**।

নাশন *n.* act of destroying or spoiling or wasting or ruining or removing or killing or exterminating. □ *a.* (chiefly used as a *sfx.*) same as **নাশক** (*a*).

নাশপাতি *n.* the pear.

নাশা *v.* (poet.) same as **নাশ করা** (see **নাশ**). □ *a.* (used as a *sfx.*) same as **নাশক** (কর্মনাশা).

নাশিত *a.* destroyed, perished; wasted; ruined; removed; killed, exterminated.

নাশী *a.* (chiefly used as a *sfx.*) perishable; destructive, destroying; killing; wasting; ruining; spoiling; removing. *fem.* **নাশিনী**।

নাস *n.* snuff; anything inhaled or taken in like the snuff (জলের নাস). **নাস নেওয়া** *v.* to inhale, to take or draw in. **~দান, ~দানি** *n.* the snuffbox.

নাসত্য *n.* the twin gods acting as the physicians of heaven.

নাসা *n.* the nose; a nasal polypus. **নাসাগ্র** *n.* the tip of the nose. **~পথ** *n.* the nasal passage. **~রন্ধ্র** *n.* the nostril.

নাসিকা *n.* the nose. **~গ্র** *n.* the tip of the nose.

নাসিক্য *a.* (chiefly gr.) nasal; nasalized (নাসিক্য ধ্বনি).

নাস্তা *n.* a light repast taken in the morning, a morning tiffin or meal; breakfast.

নাস্তানাবুদ *a.* utterly harried; harassed in the extreme; routed; utterly defeated; thoroughly upset; utterly embarrassed or discomfited; put to shame; put out of countenance.

নাস্তি *v.* is not, are not. □ *n.* inexistence, non-existence; absence.

নাস্তিক *a.* disbelieving in the existence of God, atheistical; disbelieving in the Vedas or scriptures. □ *n.* an atheist; an infidel. **~তা, নাস্তিক্য** *n.* atheism; infidelity.

নাহক *adv.* for nothing (নাহক কষ্ট দেওয়া) ; in vain; uselessly; unjustly; unreasonably.

নাহয়, না হয় *adv.* what if (নাহয় তুমি এলে) ; all right (আমি নাহয় যাব) ; at best or at the worst (নাহয় দশ টাকা লাগবে). □ *con.* or (হয় তুমি নাহয় সে) ; or else (কর নাহয় মর). □ *int.* well (নাহয় মানলামই).

নাহা (for. & poet.) *v.* to bathe, to take a bath.

নাহি (for. & poet.) *v.* is not, are not (ক্ষুধায় অন্ন নাহি). □ *adv.* (rare.) not (বলে নাহি).

নি[1] *pfx.* denoting: proximity, extensiveness, overmuchness, want, similarity, certainty, inferiority etc. (নিকট, নিখাকি, নিখুঁত)।

নি[2] *n.* (mus.) the major sixth of the C-scale, A.

নি[3] coll. corrup. of **নাই**[2]।

নিউমোনিয়া *n.* pneumonia.

নিংড়ানো *v.* to squeeze out or wring out (as water from clothes); to squeeze or wring (as clothes); (fig.) to extort (chiefly money). □ *a.* squeezed out, wrung out; squeezed, wrung; extorted.

নিঃ *pfx.* denoting: want, absence, certainty, overmuchness, completeness, direction towards outside etc. -less, un-, non-, over-, de-, dis-, out- etc. **নিঃক্ষত্র, নিঃক্ষত্রিয়** *a.* devoid of Kshatriyas (ক্ষত্রিয়). **নিঃশঙ্ক** *a.* fearless, intrepid; undaunted. **নিঃশঙ্কচিত্ত** *a.* having a dauntless heart. **নিঃশঙ্কচিত্তে** *adv.* without any fear at heart; with a dauntless heart. **নিঃশত্রু** *a.* without an enemy. **নিঃশব্দ** *a.* noiseless, silent. **নিঃশব্দপদসঞ্চারে** *adv.* stepping silently or noiselessly, in or with stealthy footsteps. **নিঃশব্দে** *adv.* noiselessly, silently. **নিঃশর্ত** *a.* unconditional (নিঃশর্ত আত্মসমর্পণ). **নিঃশেষ** *a.* leaving no remainder (সমস্ত টাকা নিঃশেষ) ; thoroughly exhausted or consumed; utterly impoverished (দান করেই সে নিঃশেষ) ; utterly ruined (সে মামলাতে নিঃশেষ) ; complete, thorough, full (নিঃশেষ অধিকার). **নিঃশেষিত** *a.* thoroughly spent up or exhausted or consumed. **নিঃশ্বসন** *n.* breathing; respiration; exhalation. **নিঃশ্বসিত** *a.* breathed in or out; exhaled. **নিঃশ্বাস** *n.* exhalation; breathing; breath; sigh. **নিঃশ্বাস ছাড়া, নিঃশ্বাস ফেলা** *v.* to exhale; to breathe; to sigh. **নিঃশ্বাস ফেলার অবসর** least respite, a breathing-interval, time to breathe, breathing space. **নিঃশ্বাস বন্ধ বা রোধ করা** *v.* to hold one's breath. **নিঃশ্বাস রোধ করে হত্যা করা** to strangle or throttle (one) to death. **নিঃশ্বাস বন্ধ বা রোধ হওয়া** *v.* to be suffocated (গরমে নিঃশ্বাস বন্ধ হওয়া) ; to be out of breath (খাটুনির চোটে নিঃশ্বাস বন্ধ হওয়া) ; to cease to breathe, to die.

নিঃশ্বাস নেওয়া *v.* to breathe in, to inhale; to breathe, to respire. **এক নিঃশ্বাসে** in a breath. **নিঃশ্বাসপ্রশ্বাস** *n.* breathing in and out, respiration. **নিঃশ্বাসের দুর্গন্ধ** *n.* bad breath, halitosis. **নিঃসংজ্ঞ** *a.* unconscious, fainted, swooned. **নিঃসংশয়** *a.* free or freed from doubt or hesitation, undoubting; unhesitating; convinced; doubtless; certain, sure, positive. **নিঃসংশয়ে** *adv.* unhesitatingly; undoubtedly; certainly, surely, positively. **নিঃসঙ্কোচ** *a.* unhesitating. **নিঃসঙ্কোচে** *adv.* unhesitatingly, without hesitation. **নিঃসঙ্গ** *a.* companionless, unattended, lonely; disinterested, callous; detached, unrelated. **নিঃসত্ত্ব** *a.* having no substance or esse, unsubstantial; inexistent; weak, feeble; lifeless; inanimate; devoid of living creatures. **নিঃসন্তান** *a.* childless. **নিঃসন্দিগ্ধ** *a.* same as **নিঃসন্দেহ**। **নিঃসন্দেহ** *a.* free from doubt, undoubting, unsuspecting; convinced; undoubted; sure, positive. **নিঃসন্দেহে** *adv.* undoubtingly; undoubtedly, doubtlessly; surely, positively. **নিঃসপত্ন** *a.* having no enemy; without any adversary or rival. **নিঃসম্পর্ক** *a.* unrelated, unconnected; not related by blood; detached. **নিঃসম্বল** *a.* resourceless; destitute; indigent; penniless; (coll.) broke. **নিঃসরণ** *n.* act of going or coming out; act of flowing out; ejection, emission, exudation, issue, escape. **নিঃসহায়** *a.* helpless. **নিঃসাড়** *a.* giving no response; silent; unconscious; motionless; noiseless (নিঃসাড়ে চলা). **নিঃসারক** *a.* causing to go or come or flow out; emitting; discharging; purging; ejecting; causing to issue or escape; extracting; expelling. **নিঃসারণ** *n.* act of going or coming or flowing out; emission; discharge; purgation; ejection; issue, escape; extraction; expulsion. **নিঃসারিত** *a.* gone or come or flowed out; emitted; ejected; issued, exuded; expelled. **নিঃসীম** *a.* endless, boundless; infinite. **নিঃসীম শূন্য** *n.* the boundless sky. **নিঃসৃত** same as **নিঃসারিত**। **নিঃস্পৃহ** *a.* having no desire or liking for; unattached; disinterested, callous. **নিঃস্পৃহতা** *n.* absence of desire or liking; disinterestedness, collousness. **নিঃস্ব** *a.* destitute; indigent, utterly poor. **নিঃস্বতা** *n.* destitution; indigence, utter poverty. **নিঃস্বন** *n.* sound, noise; voice; (of birds) a note. **নিঃস্বর** *a.* voiceless; silent. **নিঃস্রব, নিঃস্রাব** *n.* exudation.

নিঁদ poet. corrup. of **নিদ্রা**।

নিকট *a.* imminent, approaching (নিকট মৃত্যু) ; close (নিকট আত্মীয়) ; intimate, bosom (নিকট বন্ধু). □ *prep.* (rare in mod. Beng.) proximate to; near, about (বাড়ির নিকট) ; to, towards, by (আমার নিকট এসো) ; from (পিতার নিকট শুনেছি) ; in possession or in the custody of (তাহার নিকট টাকা আছে). **~বর্তী, ~স্থ** *a.* nearby, neighbouring, proximate, near, close (to); imminent, approaching (মৃত্যু নিকটবর্তী) ; close (নিকটবর্তী স্থান). *fem.* **নিকটবর্তিনী, নিকটস্থা**। **নিকটবর্তী হওয়া** *v.* to draw near, to approach, to close upon. **নিকটবর্তিতা** *n.* nearness, proximity; state of being imminent; closeness. **নিকটে** *adv.* drawing near, approaching, closing upon (মৃত্যু নিকটে). □ *prep.* same as **নিকট** (*prep.*).

নিকড়িয়া, (coll.) **নিকড়ে** *a.* penniless, indigent; without pay ('নিকড়িয়া ছুটি').

নিকনো same as **নিকানো**।

নিকর *n.* a collection, an assemblage, a multitude (নক্ষত্রনিকর).

নিকষ *n.* a streakplate or touchstone; whetstone; whetting; a testing streak of gold. **নিকষণ** *n.* act of rubbing or testing (gold) on a touchstone. **নিকষিত** *a.* rubbed or tested on a touchstone; polished; found to be genuine by testing on a touchstone, pure, sterling ('নিকষিত হেম').

নিকা *n.* (Mus.) widow-marriage; re-marriage of a divorced woman. **নিকা করা** *v.* to marry a widow or a divorced woman. **নিকা বসা** *v.* to re-marry after being widowed or divorced by the husband.

নিকানো *v.* to rub with a swab or mop drenched in a solution of cow-dung (মেটে ঘর নিকানো) ; to swab or mop (এঁটো জায়গা নিকানো). □ *a.* swabbed with a solution of cow-dung; swabbed, mopped.

নিকায় *n.* a collection; a brotherhood; an aim or goal; an abode; God.

নিকারবোকার *n.* a knickerbocker, a loose-fitting garment, usu. worn by children.

নিকারি *n.* a Muslim community of fishermen or butchers.

নিকাশ *n.* act of letting out, drainage (জলনিকাশ); completion, finalization (হিসাবনিকাশ); final accounts or a balance-sheet; destruction or end (দফা নিকাশ). **নিকাশ করা** *v.* to let out, to drain out; to complete, to finalize; to settle up (accounts); to destroy; to put an end to. **নিকাশ হওয়া** *v.* to come or get out (as water); to be completed or finalized; to be settled up; to be destroyed; to come to an end. **নিকাশি** *a.* relating to coming or getting out (**জলনিকাশি ব্যবস্থা**); relating to final accounts or a balance-sheet. **নিকাশি পত্র** *n.* a balance-sheet.

নিকি *n.* a young of a louse; an egg of a louse, a nit.

নিকুচি *n.* (vul.) ruin, destruction. **নিকুচি করা** *v.* to ruin, to destroy, (sl.) to do up.

নিকুঞ্জ *n.* an arbour, a bower (also **নিকুঞ্জকানন, নিকুঞ্জবন**).

নিকুম্ভিলা *n.* (myth.) a sacrificial rite performed by Indrajit (ইন্দ্রজিৎ) to win a victory over his enemy.

নিকৃত *a.* scolded; defeated; humiliated or insulted; oppressed.

নিকৃতি *n.* scolding; poverty; humiliation; oppression.

নিকৃষ্ট *a.* inferior; hateful, vile; low, mean. **~তা** *n.* inferiority; vileness; lowness, meanness.

নিকেতন, নিকেত *n.* a dwelling-house, an abode, a home.

নিক্তি *n.* a balance for minute and accurate weighing (as one used by jewellers). **নিক্তির ওজন** minute or subtle weighing.

নিক্কণ *n.* sweet jingle, sonorous tinkling of bells etc. (নূপুরনিক্কণ).

নিক্ষিপ্ত *a.* thrown; cast, shot, flung, hurled; ejected; scattered; imputed; placed, deposited.

নিক্ষেপ, নিক্ষেপণ *n.* an instance or act of throwing; casting, shooting, flinging, hurling; ejection; scattering; act of giving or conferring or imputing; act of placing or depositing. **নিক্ষেপ করা** *v.* to throw; to cast, to shoot, to fling; to eject; to scatter; to give; to confer; to impute; to place, to deposit. **নিক্ষেপক** *a.* one who or that which throws or casts or shoots or flings or ejects or scatters or gives or confers or imputes or places or deposits; a device for throwing or hurling missiles etc. **নিক্ষেপা** poet. form of **নিক্ষেপ করা**।

নিখরচা, (rare.) **নিখরচ** *adv.* free of cost or charge, gratis; without expense. **নিখরচে** *a.* stingy, parsimonious.

নিখর্ব *n.* a hundred thousand million. ☐ *a.* hundred thousand million.

নিখাকি *a. fem.* (vul.) eating nothing or lacking appetite. ☐ *n. fem.* such a woman.

নিখাত *a.* dug, excavated; thrust into, buried, planted, inserted.

নিখাদ[1] *n.* (mus.) the major sixth of the C-scale.

নিখাদ[2] *a.* unalloyed, unadulterated, pure, genuine (নিখাদ সোনা).

নিখিল *a.* entire, whole (নিখিল সৃষ্টি). ☐ *n.* the whole universe (নিখিলনাথ).

নিখিলভুবন, নিখিলবিশ্ব *n.* the whole universe, the whole world.

নিখুঁত *a.* faultless, flawless, spotless, impeccable, immaculate; perfect.

নিগড় *n.* an iron chain; a shackle for the feet, fetters. **~বদ্ধ** *a.* enchained, chained; fettered.

নিগদ *n.* an utterance, a saying. **নিগদিত** *a.* uttered, spoken.

নিগম *n.* a scripture of the tantra (তন্ত্র) cult; the Vedas; exit; a path, a way or a way out, a city, a town; a marketplace, a Rialto; a corporation, a municipality, a town council; a commercial guild; a chamber of commerce. **~কর** *n.* corporation tax. **~বদ্ধ, নিগমিত** *a.* united in a guild; incorporated. **~বন্ধন** *n.* incorporation.

নিগমন *n.* going out, exit, outflow; issue.

নিগরণ *n.* swallowing or gulping down; eating up.

নিগার *n.* (dero.) a dark-skinned man, a blackie, a negro, a nigger.

নিগীর্ণ *a.* swallowed, gulped down; eaten up.

নিগূঢ় *a.* perfectly concealed; hidden, secret; covert; mystical, occult; extremely abstruse or intricate; mysterious; very profound or deep. **নিগূঢ় অর্থ** same as **নিগূঢ়ার্থ**। **নিগূঢ় তত্ত্ব** a mysterious truth or information, mysteries. **~চ্ছেদ** *n.* a secret cover. **~তা** *n.* perfect concealment; secrecy; occultness; extreme abstruseness or intricacy; mysteriousness; far-reaching profundity or depth. **নিগূঢ়ার্থ** *n.* a hidden or underlying meaning or implication. **নিগূঢ়ার্থক** *a.* having a hidden or underlying meaning.

নিগৃহীত *a.* oppressed, persecuted; afflicted, harried, harassed; repressed, subjected to torture. **নিগৃহীত করা** *v.* to oppress, to persecute; to afflict, to harry, to harrow; to repress, to subject to torture.

নিগ্রহ *n.* coercion, quelling (শত্রুনিগ্রহ) ; oppression, persecution (রাজনিগ্রহ) ; affliction, harrying, harassment (অর্থাভাবজনিত নিগ্রহ) ; repression (ইন্দ্রিয়নিগ্রহ). **নিগ্রহ করা** same as **নিগৃহীত করা** (see **নিগৃহীত**). **নিগ্রহ ভোগ করা** *v.* to suffer coercion, to be coerced or quelled; to be oppressed or persecuted, to be afflicted or harassed or harried; to be repressed or subjected to torture. **নিগ্রাহক** *a. & n.* one who coerces or quells or oppresses or persecutes or afflicts or harries or harasses or represses.

নিঘন্টু *n.* a table of contents, an index; a lexicon; a Vedic glossary or concordance compiled by Yaska (যাস্ক).

নিচ inc. spell. of **নীচ** (*n*).

নিচয় *n.* a collection, an assemblage; increase; development; the greatest height; culmination.

নিচু[1] dial. corrup. of **লিচু**।

নিচু[2] *a.* low (নিচু পাহাড়) ; depressed (নিচু জায়গা) ; low-lying (নিচু জমি) ; bent down, stooping (মাথা নিচু করা) ; sloping (রাস্তা নিচু হয়ে গেছে) ; inferior (নিচু পদ) ; low, depressed (নিচু অবস্থা). □ *n.* a place or position below or underneath (নিচু থেকে) ; a low or depressed position or state.

নিচুল *n.* the rattan-plant; a scarf; a modesty-vest.

নিচে inc. spell. of **নীচে**।

নিচোল *n.* a cover made of cloth; a scarf, a wrapper; a modesty-vest; a skirt; an armour.

নিচ্চিন্দি coll. corrup. of **নিশ্চিন্ত**।

নিচ্ছিদ্র *a.* having no holes; compact; flawless.

নিছক *a.* mere, sheer, undiluted (নিছক কষ্ট). □ *adv.* merely, sheer, absolutely (নিছক বাজে কথা).

নিছনি, (dial.) **নিছুনি** *n.* a conventional rite performed at a wedding ceremony to guard the couple from evils (নিছনি-ডালা) ; a harm, an evil; physical grace; toilet, embellishment of the body; a gift or presentation or offering ('দিতে চাই যৌবন নিছনি') ; comparison.

নিজ *a.* own (নিজ গৃহ). **নিজ নিজ** respective. **নিজ গুণে** *adv.* by virtue of one's own qualities or virtues. **নিজ দোষে** *adv.* by one's own fault. **নিজ মূর্তি ধারণ করা** *v.* to assume one's real form or self.

নিজঝুম var. of **নিঝুম**।

নিজস্ব *n.* one's own property. □ *a.* belonging to or devised by one's own self, own. **নিজস্ব করা** *v.* to appropriate to oneself; to make one's own.

নিজাম *n.* (Mus.) a provincial governor; the Nizam of Hyderabad. **নিজামত, নিজামতি** *n.* the office or rule or property of a Nizam; dispensation of justice in criminal cases. □ *a.* of a Nizam; criminal (নিজামত আদালত = a criminal court).

নিজে *refl. pro.* by one's ownself (নিজে করো = do it yourself). **আমি নিজে** myself or by myself. **আমরা নিজেরা** ourselves or by ourselves. **তুমি নিজে** yourself. **তোমরা নিজেরা** yourselves or by yourselves. **সে নিজে** (*masc.*) himself; (*fem.*) herself. **তারা নিজেরা, এরা নিজেরা** themselves or by themselves. **নিজে নিজে** by one's own self, on one's own, without others' help. **নিজের** *a.* own. **নিজের পায়ে কুড়ুল মারা** (fig.) to dig one's own grave, to work to bring about one's own downfall or ruin.

নিঝর poet. corrup. of **নির্ঝর**।

নিঝুম *a.* perfectly silent; calm; still, motionless.

নিট *a.* remaining after necessary deductions, net (নিট লাভ).

নিটোল *a.* (lit.) having no dimples or depressions; plump; chubby (নিটোল চেহারা) ; perfect (নিটোল স্বাস্থ্য) ; flawless, immaculate (নিটোল সৌন্দর্য).

নিঠুর poet. corrup. of **নিষ্ঠুর** ।

নিড়ানো *v.* to weed out. □ *a.* weeded.

নিড়ানি, নিড়েন *n.* a weeding-tool; act of weeding out.

নিতকনে *n.* a bridesmaid, the best maid.

নিতবর *n.* a groomsman, the best man.

নিতম্ব *n.* the buttocks, the hip (esp. of a woman); (of hills and mountains) a flank or side (গিরিনিতম্ব). **নিতম্বিনী** *a. fem.* having well-shaped or plump buttocks. □ *n.* a woman with well-shaped or plump buttocks; a woman.

নিতল *n.* (myth.) one of the seven regions of the nether world or Hades; (fig.) a very deep or hollow place.

নিতা *n.* (dial.) an invitation at a dinner or feast ('তৃতীয়ায় দিয়া নিতা'). coll. **নিতে** ।

নিতাই corrup. of **নিত্যানন্দ,** the chief religious associate of **শ্রীচৈতন্য** ।

নিতান্ত *a.* extreme (নিতান্ত কষ্ট). thorough or downright (নিতান্ত শয়তান). □ *adv.* extremely (নিতান্ত মন্দ) ; very closely (নিতান্ত ঘনিষ্ঠ) ; thoroughly or downright (নিতান্ত ভালো বা মন্দ) ; perforce or of necessity, even then, still (নিতান্ত যদি যাবে) ; at all (নিতান্তই যদি চাও). **~পক্ষে** *adv.* at least.

নিতি, নিতুই poet. corruptions of **নিত্য** and **নিত্যই** respectively.

নিত্য *adv.* always, ever, for ever, every day, daily. □ *a.* daily (নিত্যকর্ম) ; diurnal (সূর্যের নিত্যগতি) ; immortal (নিত্যলোক) ; perpetual, everlasting; eternal, infinite; (phys.) constant. **~কর্ম, ~কার্য** same as **নিত্যকৃত্য** । **~কাল** *n.* infinite time, eternity. **নিত্যকাল ধরে** for ever; through the eternity. **~কালীন** *a.* eternal; everlasting. **~কৃত্য, ~ক্রিয়া** *n.* daily duties (esp. routine ones); daily religious rites such as prayers. **~তা** *n.* everlastingness; immortality, imperishability; eternity; constancy; (mech.) conservation. **~নৈমিত্তিক** *a.* daily or regular and occasional. **~প্রয়োজনীয়** *a.* of daily use, of everyday use. **~প্রলয়** *n.* sound or deep sleep. **~বৃত্ত** *a.* (gr.) indefinite (নিত্যবৃত্ত বর্তমান, অতীত ইত্যাদি). **~যাত্রী** *n.* daily-passenger, daily commuter. **~লীলা** *n.* daily sports; (of a holy man) daily activities. **~শ** *adv.* constantly, always. **~সঙ্গী** *n.* a constant companion. **~সত্য** *n.* an eternal truth. **~সমাস** *n.* (gr.) a system of forming compound words which cannot be expounded. **~সহচর** same as **নিত্যসঙ্গী** । **~সেবা** *n.* daily (routine) worship. **নিত্যানন্দ** *a.* enjoying perpetual delight, ever delighted. □ *n.* the chief religious associate of **শ্রীচৈতন্য** । **নিত্যানিত্য** *a.* eternal and transitory, perpetual and transient; imperishable and perishable. **নিত্যানিত্য বিচার** *n.* discernment of or discrimination between what is eternal or imperishable and what is transitory or perishable.

নিথর *a.* still, calm, tranquil, motionless.

নিদ poet. corrup. of **নিদ্রা** ।

নিদয় poet. corrup. of **নির্দয়** ।

নিদর্শন *n.* an instance, an example, a precedent; a proof, an evidence, a testimony; a sign; a token; a keepsake; a memento. **~পত্র** *n.* a testimonial, an introduction, a certificate; an identity card. **~স্তম্ভ** *n.* a pillar to fix or mark a boundary. **নিদর্শনা** *n.* (rhet.) transference of attributes.

নিদাঘ *n.* summer; heat. **~কাল** *n.* summertime. **~পীড়িত** *a.* afflicted with summer-heat.

নিদান *n.* the root cause (দুঃখের নিদান) ; the final cause (সৃষ্টির নিদান) ; determination of the cause or symptoms of a disease; (med.) aetiology. □ *a.* final, last, ultimate; dying. **~কাল** *n.* the time of death, the dying moments, the last moments. **~বিদ্যা** *n.* (med.) aetiology; diagnostics; (rare.) the philosophy of causation. **~শালা** *n.* (med.) a clinic. **~শাস্ত্র** same as **নিদানবিদ্যা** । **নিদানিক** *a.* (med.) aetiological or clinical (নিদানিক ভেষজ).

নিদারুণ *a.* extremely terrible; very severe;

thoroughly unbearable; extremely cruel or merciless or relentless (নিদারুণ বিধি).

নিদালি *n.* a handful of dust rendered soporific by occult charm.

নিদিধ্যাস, নিদিধ্যাসন *n.* profound meditation about a meaning or implication that has been learnt (lately); constant consideration.

নির্দিষ্ট *a.* ordered; enjoined; directed; instructed; stated; mentioned.

নিদুটি, নিদুলি coll. corruptions of **নিদালি**।

নিদেন[1] coll. corrup. of **নিদান**।

নিদেন[2]**, নিদেনপক্ষে** *adv.* at least; perforce or still (নিদেন যদি যাবেই).

নিদেশ *n.* an order, a command; an authoritative prescription; a direction; a directive; an instruction. **~কর্তা** *n.* one who gives an order or instruction; one who enjoins; a director. **~পত্র** *n.* a letter containing an order or prescription; a directive. **~বর্তী** *a.* at one's command or beck and call; subordinate; obedient.

নিদেষ্টা *a.* & *n.* one who gives an order or enjoins or directs.

নিদ্রা *n.* sleep. **নিদ্রা আসা** *v.* to feel sleepy; to fall asleep. **নিদ্রা টুটা** same as **নিদ্রা ভাঙা**। **নিদ্রা দেওয়া** *v.* to sleep; to go to sleep. **নিদ্রা পাওয়া** *v.* to feel sleepy. **নিদ্রা ভাঙা** *v.* to rise from sleep, to wake up, to awake; (fig.) to shake off inactivity or sloth or torpor or blind faith. **নিদ্রা ভাঙানো** *v.* to rouse from sleep, to wake (one) up, to awake; (fig.) to shake off (one's) inactivity or sloth or torpor or blind faith. **নিদ্রা যাওয়া** same as **নিদ্রা দেওয়া**। **নিদ্রা হওয়া** *v.* to have sleep. **গভীর নিদ্রা, ঘোর নিদ্রা** deep sleep, sound sleep, profound sleep. **মহানিদ্রা** *n.* sleep that knows no breaking, everlasting or eternal sleep; death. **সুখনিদ্রা** *n.* peaceful sleep. **সুনিদ্রা** *n.* good sleep. **নিদ্রাকর** *a.* soporific, somniferous, narcotic, opiate. **~কর্ষণ** *n.* inducement of sleep, drowsiness. **নিদ্রাকর্ষণ হওয়া** same as **নিদ্রা আসা**। **~কাল** *n.* the hour or time of sleep; bedtime. **নিদ্রাগত** same as **নিদ্রিত**। **~ঘোর** same as **নিদ্রাবেশ**। **~জনক** same as **নিদ্রাকর**। **~তুর** *a.* sleepy; drowsy. **~বিষ্ট** same as **নিদ্রাভিভূত**। **~বেশ** *n.* a sleeping spell; drowsiness. **~বেশে** *adv.* under the spell of sleep; in a sleepy state. **~ভঙ্গ** *n.* break of sleep, awakening. **নিদ্রাভঙ্গ করা** *v.* to rouse from sleep, to awake. **নিদ্রাভঙ্গ হওয়া** *v.* to rise from sleep, to wake up, to awake. **~ভাব**[1] *n.* want of sleep, sleeplessness; insomnia. **~ভাব**[2] *n.* sleepiness, sleeping state. **নিদ্রাভিভূত** *a.* overcome with sleep; lying under the spell of sleep; fast asleep. **নিদ্রাভিভূত করা** *v.* to overcome with sleep; to cause to sleep soundly. **নিদ্রাভিভূত থাকা** *v.* to be sleeping soundly; to be in one's sleep, to remain in sleep. **নিদ্রাভিভূত হওয়া** *v.* to sleep soundly; to be overcome with sleep. **নিদ্রামগ্ন** *a.* fast asleep, sleeping; (fig.) thoroughly inactive or slothful or credulous or unconscious. **নিদ্রামগ্ন থাকা** *v.* to be sleeping; (fig.) to be thoroughly inactive or slothful or credulous or unconscious. **নিদ্রামগ্ন হওয়া** *v.*to fall asleep. **~লস** *a.* indolent from sleepiness; sleepy; drowsy; indolent, lethargic. *fem.* **নিদ্রালসা**। **~লু** *a.* sleepy, drowsy. **~লুতা** *n.* sleepiness, drowsiness. **~হীন** *a.* sleepless; wakeful (নিদ্রাহীন দৃষ্টি বা প্রহরা).

নিদ্রিত *a.* sleeping, asleep; (fig.) thoroughly inactive or indolent or credulous or unconscious *fem.* **নিদ্রিতা**। **নিদ্রিত থাকা** *v.* to be sleeping; (fig.) to be thoroughly inactive or indolent or credulous or unconscious; to be heedless or listless; to be unresponsive or unmoved; to be insensitive or indifferent or impassive. **নিদ্রিত হওয়া** *v.* to fall asleep.

নিদ্রোত্থিত *a.* risen from sleep, awakened; (fig.) to be roused from impassivity or listlessness. *fem.* **নিদ্রোত্থিতা**। **নিদ্রোত্থিত হওয়া** *v.* to get up from sleep, to awake, to wake.

নিধন *n.* destruction; killing; death. **নিধন করা** *v.* to destroy; to kill. **নিধন হওয়া, নিধনপ্রাপ্ত হওয়া** *v.* to be destroyed or killed; to meet with death, to die. **~প্রাপ্তি** *n.* destruction; state of being killed; death.

নিধান *n.* a store, a repertory, a house or abode, a receptacle or treasure-house (করুণানিধান) ; a fund; act of placing or depositing; that which is deposited, deposit; (math.–of logarithm) a base. **নিধানীয়** *a.* (math.–of logarithm) natural.

নিধি *n.* a store, a fount or repertory (গুণনিধি) ; a treasury; wealth, treasure; wealth deposited; a fund; Kuvera's (কুবের) treasure; (fig.) a very rich treasure. **নিধি আবণ্টন** *n.* allotment of funds.

নিধুবন[১] *n.* sexual union, copulation; sports; amusements.

নিধুবন[২] *n.* a garden in Brindaban which was the meeting-place or trysting-place of Radha (রাধা) and Krishna (কৃষ্ণ).

নিধেয় *a.* worthy of being deposited or placed.

নিনাদ *n.* a sound; a noise; a report (esp. a loud one); a roar. **নিনাদ করা** *v.* to roar. **নিনাদিত** *a.* sounded; (of flutes etc.) blown or played or beaten or rung; roared.

নিন্দক correct but obsoelete form of **নিন্দুক**।

নিন্দন *n.* upbraiding, reproaching, blaming, slandering, animadversion, reprehension; reflection; condemnation, vilification.

নিন্দনীয় same as **নিন্দার্হ** (see **নিন্দা**).

নিন্দা *n.* animadversion, upbraiding, reprehension; reflection; reproach, censure, blame, condemnation; slander, calumny, vilification; disrepute, discredit. □ *v.* (poet.) same as নিন্দা করা। **~কর** same as **নিন্দাজনক**। **নিন্দা করা** *v.* to animadvert, to upbraid, to reprehend, to reflect upon, to reproach, to censure, to blame, to condemn, to slander, to calumniate, to vilify, to speak ill of; (poet.) to bring discredit upon, to put to shame. **~কারী** same as **নিন্দুক**। *fem.* **~কারিণী**। **~জনক** *a.* discreditable, disgraceful, slanderous, scandalous, shameful. **~বাদ** *n.* censure, censorious utterance or comments. **~ভাজন** *a.* (of a person) deserving censure or reproach. **~যোগ্য, ~র্হ** *a.* deserving to be censured; condemnable; blamable, blameworthy; discreditable; disreputable. **~সূচক** *a.* condemnatory, slanderous, calumniatory. **নিন্দাসূচক প্রস্তাব** censure motion. **~স্তুতি** *n.* censure and praise.

নিন্দিত *a.* animadverted, reprehended, reproached, blamed, condemned, slandered, calumniated, discredited, disgraced; looked down upon, hated, despicable. □ *in comp.* (used as a *sfx.*) putting to shame, excelling (বীণানিন্দিত). *fem.* **নিন্দিতা**।

নিন্দুক *a.* & *n.* one who upbraids or reprihends or blames or reproaches or animadverts or condemns or vilifies.

নিন্দ্য same as **নিন্দার্হ** (see **নিন্দা**).

নিপট[১] *a.* excessive, overmuch, extreme (নিপট অন্ধকার, নিপট দুঃখ) ; real, genuine, absolute (নিপট সত্য) ; downright (নিপট মিথ্যা).

নিপট[২] *a.* lewd, licentious, dissolute ('নিপট কপট তুয়া শ্যাম'). **নিপট লম্পট** libertine to the backbone.

নিপতন *n.* act of falling down, fall; downfall.

নিপতিত *a.* fallen down; fallen. **নিপতিত হওয়া** *v.* to fall down; to fall.

নিপাট *a.* without a crease or fold; absolute, complete (নিপাট ভদ্রলোক).

নিপাত *n.* death, ruin, destruction. **নিপাত যাওয়া** *v.* to die, to be killed or ruined or destroyed, to go to rack and ruin; to be damned. **নিপাত যাও** to hell with you.

নিপাতন destroying or killing; destruction; throwing down; overthrow; (gr.) irregular but popular use. **নিপাতনে সিদ্ধ** (gr.–of words etc.) accepted because of popularity although irregularly formed or used.

নিপাতিত *a.* destroyed, killed; thrown down; overthrown. **নিপাতিত করা** *v.* to destroy, to kill; to throw down; to overthrow.

নিপীড়ক *a.* & *n.* one who oppresses or persecutes or harries or afflicts or represses or presses or quells.

নিপীড়ন *n.* oppression, persecution; harrying, affliction; repression; act of causing severe suffering, torture; pressing; quelling. **নিপীড়ন করা** *v.* to oppress, to persecute, to tyrannize over, to harry, to afflict; to repress; to press; to quell.

নিপীড়িত *a.* oppressed, persecuted; harried, afflicted; repressed; pressed; quelled. **নিপীড়িত করা** same as **নিপীড়ন করা** (see **নিপীড়ন**).

নিপীত *a.* drunk to the dregs, drunk off or up, drained to the leas.

নিপুণ *a.* skilful, dextrous, adept, adroit, deft, clever (নিপুণ কাজ) ; skilled, expert, efficient (কর্মনিপুণ). *fem.* **নিপুণা**। **~তা** *n.* skilfulness, dexterity, adroitness, deftness; skill; expertness, efficiency.

নিব *n.* a nib.

নিবদ্ধ *a.* bound, tied, fastened; attached, affixed, adhering to; worn, put on; placed or deposited or thrust into; planted; put in, inserted, entered (লিপিনিবদ্ধ) ; fixed, settled, (of a gaze) firm and unchanging (নিবদ্ধদৃষ্টি) ; strung or arrayed (মাল্যনিবদ্ধ) ; registered. **নিবদ্ধীকরণ** *n.* fixation; planting; registration.

নিবন্ত *a.* (of a light etc.) about to be extinguished, about to go out; (fig.) about to be exhausted, about to die out (নিবন্ত উৎসাহ) ; (fig.) exhausted; (fig.) dying; (fig.) dead. see also **নিবুনিবু**।

নিবন্ধ *n.* an essay, a dissertation, a thesis, a literary compostition; a treatise, a book; a means; an arrangement; a system, a rule; fixation, determination; a tie, a bond; a song, a lay. **নিবন্ধক** *n.* a registrar. **নিবন্ধন** *n.* a tie, a bond; fixation, determination. registration. □ *in comp.* (used as a *sfx.*) owing to, due to, because of (নথিনিবন্ধন, কার্যনিবন্ধন). **~ভুক্ত** *a.* entered in a register. **নিবন্ধভুক্ত করা** *v.* to register. **নিবন্ধিত** *a.* composed; written; bound; strung.

নিবর্ত *a.* desisted or refrained; stopped. **নিবর্তক** *a.* & *n.* one who or that which prevents or dissuades or stops; preventive, dissuasive, stopping. **নিবর্তন** *n.* act of giving up, desisting, refraining, cessation, stopping, closing; prevention; supersession; return, recession. **নিবর্তনমূলক** *a.* preventive. **নিবর্তিত** *a.* caused to give up or desist; stopped, ceased; caused to return or recede, returned or receded; prevented.

নিবসই *v.* (obs. poet.) dwells or dwell, lives or live, resides or reside.

নিবসতি, নিবসন *n.* act of dwelling or living, residence; an abode, a dwelling house, a home.

নিবহ *n.* a collection, a multitude ('ম্লেচ্ছনিবহ').

নিবা *v.* (of a light or fire) to go out, to be extinguished or quenched. □ *a.* extinguished; quenched. **নিবানো** *v.* to put out, to extinguish; to quench. □ *a.* extinguished; quenched.

নিবাত *a.* airless; stuffy; not flickering as there is no air (নিবাত প্রদীপ) ; motionless, still, steady (নিবাত নিষ্কম্প).

নিবাপ *n.* an offering of food etc. to the manes (নিবাপ-অঞ্জলি).

নিবারণ, নিবার *n.* prevention; warding off; prohibition; stopping; mitigation, allaying. **নিবারণ করা** *v.* to prevent; to ward off; to prohibit; to stop; to mitigate, to allay. **নিবারণ হওয়া** *v.* to be prevented or warded off; to stop or be stopped; to be mitigated or allayed. **নিবারক** *a.* preventing or preventive; warding off; prohibiting or prohibitory; stopping; mitigating, allaying. □ *n.* a preventer; one who wards off; a prohibitor; one who stops; an allaying agent. **নিবারণীয়** same as **নিবার্য**। **নিবারা** poet. form of **নিবারণ করা**. **নিবারিত** *a.* prevented; warded off; prohibited; mitigated, allayed. **নিবারিত করা** same as **নিবারণ করা**।

নিবার্য *a.* preventible; resistible; mitigable; capable of being warded off or opposed or allayed; avoidable.

নিবাস *n.* a dwelling-place, an abode, a home; a dwelling-house, a residence; act of residing (নিবাস করা). **নিবাসী** *a.* inhabiting. □ *n.* an inhabitant. *fem.* **নিবাসিনী**।

নিবিড় *a.* extremely close (নিবিড় বন্ধুত্ব) ; very dense or thick or deep (নিবিড় বন, নিবিড় অন্ধকার) ; tight (নিবিড় আলিঙ্গন) ; plump, heavy (নিবিড় নিতম্ব). **নিবিড়তা** *n.* extreme closeness, excessive density or thickness or depth; tightness; plumpness, heaviness.

নিবিদ *a.* relating to the ancient sayings about deities.

নিবিষ্ট *a.* deeply engaged, engrossed, absorbed, concentrated; arrayed, placed in an orderly manner; entered. *fem.* **নিবিষ্টা** । **নিবিষ্ট করা** *v.* to engage deeply, to engross, to absorb, to concentrate; to array, to place in an orderly manner; to enter. **~চিত্ত** *a.* having one's mind deeply engaged or engrossed or absorbed or concentrated, intently attentive. **~চিত্তে** *adv.* with close or undivided or rapt attention. **~তা** *n.* engrossment, absorbedness, concentration.

নিবীত *n.* a cotton or linen scarf; a holy thread slung by a Brahmin over the upper part of his body, or round his neck.

নিবুনিবু *a.* (of fire, light etc.) about to go out or be extinguished. **নিবুনিবু হওয়া** *v.* to be on the point of going out or being extinguished.

নিবৃত্ত *a.* desisted, given up, refrained, ceased, stopped; warded off; prevented; returned, receded. **নিবৃত্ত করা** *v.* to cause to desist from or give up or dissuade; to cause to cease, to stop; to ward off; to prevent; to cause to return or recede. **নিবৃত্ত হওয়া** *v.* to desist or refrain from, to give up; to cease, to stop; to be warded off or prevented; to return or recede. **নিবৃত্তি** *n.* desisting, act of going up, refraining; cessation, stoppage; return or recession; renunciation (of earthly pleasures and interests.) **নিবৃত্তিমার্গ** *n.* the path of attaining salvation by renouncing earthly pleasures and interests, the path of renunciation.

নিবেদক *a. & n.* one who narrates and states or represents or submits or informs or petitions humbly or politely; one who dedicates or offers devotedly.

নিবেদন *n.* humble or polite narration or statement or representation or submission or petition; dedication or offering in devotion. **নিবেদন করা** *v.* to narrate or state or represent or submit or petition humbly or politely; to dedicate or offer in devotion. **~পত্র** *n.* a memorandum or memorial, a petition. **নিবেদনীয়** same as **নিবেদ্য** ।

নিবেদিত *a.* narrated or stated or represented or submitted or petitioned humbly or politely; dedicated or offered in devotion.

নিবেদ্য *a.* fit to be or intended to be narrated or stated or represented or submitted or petitioned humbly or politely; fit to be or intended to be dedicated or offered in devotion.

নিবেশ *n.* encampment or a camp (সেনানিবেশ) ; act of placing in an orderly manner; arraying (ব্যূহনিবেশ) ; placing, emplacement; insertion; interpolation; application, engaging (মনোনিবেশ) ; entrance; act of sitting. **নিবেশক** *a. & n.* one who or that which encamps or arrays or places or inserts or interpolates or applies or engages or enters or causes to enter or sits or causes to sit; one who records. □ *n.* a recorder. **নিবেশন** *n.* entrance; act of sitting; placing, emplacement; a dwelling-house, an abode, a house; a place: act of recording (in a book); interpolation. **নিবেশিত** *a.* encamped; placed in an orderly manner, arrayed; placed, put; inserted; interpolated; applied, engaged; entered; seated; recorded; transited; infected; domiciled.

নিবেশী *a. & n.* domiciled; a domiciled person.

-নিভ *sfx.* denoting : similarity or likeness or equality (পদ্মনিভ, দুগ্ধফেননিভ).

নিভন্ত var. of **নিবন্ত** ।

নিভা var. of **নিবা** ।

নিভাঁজ *a.* bearing no crease or foldingline or wrinkle; plane, smooth, unadulterated, pure, genuine.

নিভৃত *a.* secret, private (নিভৃত আলাপ) ; lonely, solitary (নিভৃত স্থান). **~কক্ষ** *n.* a private room; a closet. **~চিন্তা** *n.* meditations in solitude. **~স্থান** *n.* a lonely or solitary place, a lonely retreat, solitude. **নিভৃতে** *adv.* secretly, privately; in a solitary place; in solitude.

নিম১ *pfx.* signifying : half or partly, almost (নিমরাজি, নিমখুন).

নিম২ *n.* the margosa (tree or leaves or fruit).

নিমক *n.* salt, table salt. **নিমক খাওয়া** *v.* to eat one's salt; (fig.) to be indebted to or benefited by. **~দান, ~দানি** *n.* salt-cellar, salt-pot. **~মহল** *n.* an estate consisting of salt-yielding land or salt-pit or salt-marsh. **~হারাম** *a.* ungrateful. **~হারামি** *n.* ingratitude; a treacherous act. **নিমকহারামি করা** *v.* to harm one's benefactor. **~হালাল** *a.* grateful; loyal. **~হালালি** *n.* gratitude; loyalty.

নিমকি *n.* a salted and crisp snack made by frying thin plates of flour dough in clarified butter or oil. □ *a.* salty, salted (নিমকি খাবার).

নিমখুন *a.* almost murdered, half-murdered; (in law) assailed with such a grievous hurt as has or might have amounted to murder. □ *n.* culpable homicide not amounting to murder.

নিমগ্ন, (poet.) **নিমগন** *a.* completely drowned or sunk or plunged or submerged; deeply absorbed or engrossed or overwhelmed (চিন্তানিমগ্ন) ; over head and ears (ঋণনিমগ্ন). *fem.* **নিমগ্না**। **নিমগ্ন হওয়া** *v.* to sink; to be absorbed in.

নিমজ্জন *n.* sinking or drowning; submersion; act of dipping or diving or plunging into; act of bathing by immersing into water (of rivers, ponds etc.) immersion; absorption or engrossment (ধ্যানে বা ঋণে নিমজ্জন).

নিমজ্জমান *a.* in the state of being drowned, sinking; that which is being submerged, immersing; almost engrossed or absorbed or overwhelmed. see also **মজ্জমান**। *fem.* **নিমজ্জমানা**।

নিমজ্জিত *a.* drowned, sunken; submerged; engrossed, absorbed, overwhelmed. *fem.* **নিমজ্জিতা**।

নিমন্ত্রণ *n.* an invitation; an invitation to a dinner or feast; (fig.) a call or summons. **নিমন্ত্রণ করা** *v.* to invite, to ask courteously to come; to invite at a dinner or feast; (fig.) to call or summon; to make a formal and courteous request to do something. **নিমন্ত্রণ গ্রহণ করা** *v.* to accept an invitation. **নিমন্ত্রণ প্রত্যাখ্যান করা** *v.* to refuse or decline an invitation. **নিমন্ত্রণ রক্ষা করা** *v.* to pay a visit to the host in response to his invitation. **বিনা নিমন্ত্রণে** *adv.* without invitation, uninvitedly; unasked. **~পত্র** *n.* an invitation-card, a letter of invitation; (fig.) a writ of summons.

নিমন্ত্রয়িতা *n.* an inviter; a host. *fem.* **নিমন্ত্রয়িত্রী**।

নিমন্ত্রিত *a.* invited; invited to a dinner or feast; (fig.) called or summoned. *fem.* **নিমন্ত্রিতা**। **নিমন্ত্রিত ব্যক্তি** a guest, an invitee.

নিমরাজি *a.* half-willing, half-inclined; reluctantly consenting.

নিমিখ poet. var. of **নিমিষ**।

নিমিত্ত *n.* a cause or reason; a motive, an end in view, an aim; necessity, need; an omen, a prognostic, a presage, a portent (দুর্নিমিত্ত) ; one who acts as an instrument of another, a tool, an agent. □ *prep.* for, because of, on account of, owing to, due to (রোগের নিমিত্ত). **নিমিত্তের ভাগী** responsible only for an action and not for its cause, one held responsible for an action because of one's mere presence although one has taken no part in it. **নিমিত্তের ভাগী হওয়া** to have to share the responsibility and consequence of another person's action. **নিমিত্তজ্ঞ, নিমিত্তবিদ** *n.* an augur, a diviner, a soothsayer. **~মাত্র** *n.* a mere agent or instrument. **নিমিত্তার্থ** *n.* (gr.) the gerundial force or the infinitive mood. □ *a.* gerundial.

নিমিষ *n.* a twinkle of an eye, a wink; the time covered by a wink, a moment, a trice, a triflingly short time (নিমিষের মধ্যে). **এক নিমিষে** in the twinkling of an eye, in a trice, in a jiffy. **~হারা** *a.* (of eyes or glance) steadfast, fixed, unwinking. **নিমিষহারা চোখে চাওয়া** *v.* to look steadfastly, to gaze.

নিমীলন *n.* act of closing or shutting (chiefly eyelids); contraction.

নিমীলিত *a.* closed, shut; contracted. **নিমীলিত করা** *v.* to close or shut; to contract. **নিমীলিত চোখে** *a.* with eyes closed or shut or contracted.

নিমেষ *var.* of **নিমিষ**। **~হারা, ~হীন** *a.* (of eyes or glance) unwinking, winkless; fixed, steadfast.

নিম্ন *a.* low; low-lying or depressed (নিম্নভূমি) ; subordinate, junior (নিম্নপদ) ; lower (নিম্ন আদালত) ; downcast (নিম্নদৃষ্টি) ; base, mean (নিম্নচেতা) ; socially lower or depressed (নিম্ন জাতি). □ *n.* (For.) a place or position underneath or below or low or lower (নিম্ন হইতে). **নিম্ন অক্ষাংশ** (geog.) a low latitude. **নিম্ন আদালত** a lower court. **~গ** *a.* going downwards. **~গা** *a. fem.* of **নিম্নগ**। □ *n. fem.* a river. **~গামী** *a.* going downwards; declining or degenerating; getting debased. *fem.* **~গামিনী**। **~চাপ** *n.* (med.) low pressure; (geog.) downward pressure; a depression. **~তর** *a.* lower. **নিম্নতর কক্ষ** (of legislature) the lower house or chamber. **~তম** *a.* minimum; minimal. **~তল** *n.* a lower deck, downfloor, groundfloor. **~তা** *n.* lowness; depression; depth, baseness, meanness; degeneration. **~তাপ** *n.* a low temperature; an abnormally low temperature. **~দৃষ্টি** *n.* downcast look; a mean outlook or inclination. **~দেশ** *n.* a lower part; a region underneath. **~দেশে** *adv.* in or to a lower part; under, below. **~ধৃত** *a.* undermentioned. **~পদ** *n.* a junior or a lower post. **~পাত** *n.* descending node. **~প্রদেশ** *n.* lowlands; a lower region or part; the part of the body under the waist; the posteriors. **~বিত্ত** *n.* low income; the people with a low income, the low income group. □ *a.* of or pertaining to the low income group. **~মধ্যবিত্ত** *n.* the lower middle class; the low middle class. **~ভূমি** *n.* lowlands; a low or depressed land. **~মুখ** *a.* (bot.) reclinate. **~রেখিত** *a.* underlined, underscored. **~লিখিত** *a.* written below, undermentioned. **~সপ্তক** *n.* (mus.) the low grave octave or gamut of the Indian musical notes. **~সীমা** *n.* the lowest limit. **নিম্নাকর্ষণ** *n.* downward attraction. **নিম্নীভূত** *a.* depressed, sunk. **নিম্নীভূত সমভূমি** (geog.) a sunk plain. **নিম্নোক্ত** *a.* undermentioned. **নিম্নোদ্ধৃত** *a.* quoted below; undermentioned. **নিম্নোন্নত** *a.* uneven, undulating.

নিম্নাংশ *n.* the low or lower part.

নিম্নাঙ্গ *n.* the lower part or limbs.

নিম্নাঞ্চল *n.* the lower region.

নিম্ব, নিম্বক *n.* the margosa (tree or seed).

নিম্বু, নিম্বুক variants of **লেবু**।

নিযুক্ত *a.* employed; engaged; devoted. **নিযুক্ত করা** *v.* to employ; to engage; to devote; to appoint.

নিযুক্তি *n.* same as **নিয়োগ**।

নিযোক্তা *n.* an employer.

নিযোজ্য *a.* fit to be employed or engaged or appointed or applied.

নিয়ত[1] dial. corrup. of **নিয়তি**।

নিয়ত[2] *a.* unchanging; fixed; continuous, perpetual; constant (নিয়ত বায়ু = constant wind); regular; regulated; limited. □ *adv.* always, ever; often. **নিয়ত বৃত্ত** (conics) a director circle.

নিয়তাচার *a.* (of one) who observes or practises religious rites regularly.

নিয়তাত্মা *a.* self-restrained, self-disciplined; continent; abstemious.

নিয়তাহার *a.* abstemious or temperate in food (and also in drink). □ *n.* abstemiousness or temperance.

নিয়তি *n.* predestination; destiny, fate, luck; an inevitable occurrence. **~নির্দিষ্ট** *a.* ordained by fate, decreed by Providence, predestined. **নিয়তিঃ কেন বাধ্যতে** who can oppose or check or restrain destiny.

নিয়ন্তা *a.* & *n.* one who regulates or controls or directs or governs or determines or destines (ভাগ্যনিয়ন্তা).

নিয়ন্ত্রক *a* & *n.* same as **নিয়ন্তা**।

নিয়ন্ত্রণ *n.* regulation; rule; control; restraint; determination. **নিয়ন্ত্রণ করা** *v.* to regulate; to rule; to control; to restrain; to determine; to destine. **~ব্যবস্থা** *n.* control system. **নিয়ন্ত্রণাধীন** *a.* controlled, under control.

নিয়ন্ত্রিত *a.* regulated; ruled; controlled; determined; restrained; destined. **নিয়ন্ত্রিত করা** same as **নিয়ন্ত্রণ করা** (see **নিয়ন্ত্রণ**).

নিয়ন্ত্রী *fem.* of **নিয়ন্তা**।

নিয়ম *n.* a precept, a prescription or direction (শাস্ত্রীয় নিয়ম) ; a law; a rule (সংঘের নিয়ম) ; a system, a method (কাজের নিয়ম) ; a custom (বাঙালির নিয়ম) ; a routine duty; a practice (প্রাতর্ভ্রমণ উত্তম নিয়ম) ; temperance or abstemiousness (অনিয়ম) ; self-discipline, self-control (নিয়ম অভ্যাস) ; a sacrament or an act of scriptural self-mortification (নিয়ম পালন) ; a stipulation or condition; a ruling. **নিয়ম করা** *v.* to lay down a rule; to make (it) a rule; to make a law; to stipulate; to give judicial or authoritative decision, to rule. **~তন্ত্র** *n.* a set or code of laws or constitution (usu. rigid ones); constitutionalism (নিয়মতন্ত্রের যুগ). **~তান্ত্রিক** *a.* constitutional. **~ন** *n.* act of laying down rules or issuing laws; act of regulating; regularization; act of restraining or controlling; act of stipulating; act of issuing a ruling. **~নিষ্ঠ** *a.* ardently obedient to rules and systems; methodical; disciplined; regular; well-regulated; zealously observing scriptural rites; (rare) law-abiding. **~নিষ্ঠা** *n.* ardent obedience to rules and systems; methodicalness; regularity; discipline; zealous observance of scriptural rites. **~পালন** *n.* observance of rules and systems or stipulations; regularity in practice; observance of scriptural rites. **নিয়মপালন করা** *v.* to observe rules and systems; to abide by stipulations and conditions; to observe scriptural rites. **~পূর্বক** *adv.* laying down rules and observing them; making stipulations and observing them; regularly; systematically, methodically; according to fixed rules; in a routine manner. **~বর্জিত, ~বহির্ভূত, ~বিরুদ্ধ** *a.* flouting rules or stipulations; contrary to rules; ultra vires; irregular; informal; unmethodical, unsystematic; undisciplined; unscriptural; (rare) unlawful. **~ভঙ্গ** *n.* infringement or breach or violation of a rule or stipulation; completion or termination of observance of a scriptural rite. **নিয়মভঙ্গ করা** *v.* to infringe or break or violate a rule or stipulation; to complete or terminate observance of a scriptural rite (after a customary period). **~রক্ষা** *n.* observance of rules, rites etc.; formal obedience to rules, customs etc.; **~মতো** same as **নিয়মানুযায়ী**। **~লঙ্ঘন** same as **নিয়মভঙ্গ**। **নিয়মানুগ** *a.* law-abiding, according to or in accordance with law or rules; lawful; regular. **নিয়মাধীন** *a.* bound by or subject to rules or systems; regulated; regular; systematical; constitutional. **নিয়মানুবর্তিতা** same as **নিয়মনিষ্ঠা**। **নিয়মানুবর্তী** same as **নিয়মনিষ্ঠ**। **নিয়মানুযায়ী** *a.* regulated; regular; systematic; methodical; disciplined. □ *adv.* according to prescribed or fixed rules or systems. **নিয়মানুসারে** *adv.* same as **নিয়মানুযায়ী** (*adv.*). **নিয়মাবলি** *n.* a set or code of rules. **নিয়মিত** *a.* regulated; regular. □ *adv.* in a regulated manner; regularly. **নিয়মিত সময়ে** at the appointed time. **নিয়মী** *a.* observant of or adhering to rules or system; constitutional; (rare) law-abiding. **নিয়ম্য** *a.* capable of being or fit to be brought under rigid or fixed rules; capable of being or fit to be regularized.

নিয়ামক *a.* regulating; directing; controlling or systematizing; regularizing.□ *n.* a regulator; a director; a controller; a registrar; a systematizer; (geom.) a directrix.

নিয়োগ *n.* act of employing or engaging or initiating or appointing or applying, employment, initiation, appointment, application. **নিয়োগ করা** *v.* to employ, to engage; to initiate; to appoint; to apply. **~-অধিকর্তা** *n.* the Director of Employment. **~কর্তা** *n.* an employer; an employing or appointing authority; a master (*fem.* a mistress). *fem.* **~কর্ত্রী**। **~পত্র** *n.* an appointment letter. **নিয়োগী** *a.* employed; engaged; appointed; ordered.

নিয়োজক same as **নিযোক্তা**।

নিয়োজন same as **নিয়োগ**।

নিয়োজয়িতা same as **নিযোক্তা**।

নিয়োজিত same as **নিযুক্ত**।

নিয়োজয়িত্রী *fem.* of **নিয়োজয়িতা**।

নিরংশ *n.* (astr.) the first and the last day of the ascendancy of a sign of the zodiac, the transition of the sun from one zodiacal sign to another. □ *a.* not enjoying any share; undivided, whole.

নিরংশু *a.* having no rays; lustreless; having no light; dark.

নিরক্ষ, নিরক্ষ অঞ্চল *n.* (geog.) the equator, the equatorial region. **নিরক্ষরেখা, নিরক্ষবৃত্ত** *n.* the equator.

নিরক্ষর *a.* illiterate. **নিরক্ষরতা** *n.* illiteracy. **নিরক্ষরতা দূরীকরণ** eradication of illiteracy.

নিরক্ষীয় *a.* equatorial. **নিরক্ষীয় তাপরেখা** heat equator. **নিরক্ষীয় শান্তবলয়** doldrums.

নিরখা *v.* (poet.) to see, to look at, to observe, to notice.

নিরগ্নি *a.* having no fire; without heat; a Brahmin who does not keep any sacrificial fire burning (op. **সাগ্নিক**).

নিরঙ্কুশ *a.* unpreventable; inevitable; unhindered; unattached; free from ties of attachment; dispassionate; wayward, wilful. **নিরঙ্কুশ গরিষ্ঠতা** absolute majority.

নিরজন poet. corrup. of **নির্জন**।

নিরঞ্জন *a.* stainless, clean, pure, immaculate. □ *n.* God; Shiva (শিব) ; Dharma (ধর্ম), a popular deity of Bengal; the ceremonial immersion of an idol.

নিরত *a.* engaged, employed; attached, devoted; engrossed, absorbed. *fem.* **নিরতা**।

নিরতিশয় *a.* very great, too much, excessive, extreme.□ *adv.* excessively, exceedingly, extremely, very much.

নিরত্যয় *a.* imperishable; deathless; everlasting; faultless.

নিরন্তর *a.* ceaseless, continuous (নিরন্তর বৃষ্টি) ; having no space between, dense, thick (নিরন্তর বৃক্ষশ্রেণি). □ *adv.* without break, ceaselessly, continuously, always (নিরন্তর খেলা করা). **নিরন্তর পরিবৃত্তি** continuous variation.

নিরন্ন *a.* having no means to procure food; foodless; starving.

নিরপত্য *a.* childless.

নিরপরাধ, (loss.) **নিরপরাধী** *a.* guiltless, innocent. *fem.* **নিরপরাধা,** (loss.) **নিরপরাধিনী**।

নিরপেক্ষ *a.* impartial, unbiased, unprejudiced (নিরপেক্ষ বিচার) ; neutral; independent, disinterested (দলনিরপেক্ষ) ; (phil. & log.) categorical. **নিরপেক্ষতা** *n.* impartiality, freedom from bias or prejudice; neutrality; independence, disinterestedness; (phil. & log.) categoricalness. **নিরপেক্ষ রাষ্ট্র** neutral state; non-aligned state.

নিরবকাশ *a.* leisureless; incessant; continuous.

নিরবচ্ছিন্ন *a.* having no space between, dense, thick (নিরবচ্ছিন্ন তরুশ্রেণি) ; incessant, ceaseless, continuous (নিরবচ্ছিন্ন সুখ) ; uninterrupted (নিরবচ্ছিন্ন বৃষ্টি). **নিরবচ্ছিন্নতা** *n.* continuity.

নিরবধি *a.* unlimited, endless, boundless, infinite, eternal (নিরবধি কাল) ; perpetual, continuous (নিরবধি দুঃখ). □ *adv.* endlessly; continuously; always.

নিরবয়ব *a.* formless, shapeless; unembodied, incorporeal. □ *n.* God.

নিরবলম্ব, নিরবলম্বন *a.* having no support or prop; helpless; destitute; having no shelter, homeless.

নিরবশেষ *a.* leaving no remainder or residue; complete, thorough.

নিরভিমান, (loos.) **নিরভিমানী** *a.* having no amour-propre, not conceited; modest; unassuming. *fem.* **নিরভিমানা,** (loos.) **নিরভিমানিনী**।

নিরভ্র *a.* cloudless; (loos. of the sky) clear (নিরভ্র আকাশ).

নিরমল poet. corrup. of **নির্মল**।

নিরমা var. of **নির্মা**।

নিরমান poet. corrup. of **নির্মাণ**।

নিরম্বু *a.* having no water, waterless. **নিরম্বু উপবাস** fasting in which drinking of even a drop of water is not permitted.

নিরয় *n.* hell, the Inferno. **~গামী** *a.* condemned to hell. **~ভোগ** *n.* suffering in hell.

নিরর্থ *a.* meaningless, nonsense; useless, futile, vain ('নিরর্থ হাহাকারে'). **নিরর্থক** *a.* meaningless, nonsense; unreasonable, unnecessary; purposeless; useless, futile, vain. □ *adv.* in vain; meaninglessly; unreasonably, unwarrantedly; unnecessarily; without purpose.

নিরলংকার *a.* having no ornaments on, unornamented; unadorned; undecorated; unrhetorical; plain, simple, naive.

নিরলস *a.* diligent, industrious; untiring; ceaseless.

নিরসন *n.* removal (দুঃখনিরসন); mitigation (যন্ত্রণানিরসন); refutation; redressing (অন্যায় নিরসন); protection from; covering or concealment (লজ্জা নিরসন); termination (শ্রম নিরসন). **নিরসন করা** *v.* to remove; to mitigate; to refute; to redress; to conceal; to terminate. **নিরসন হওয়া** *v.* to be removed or mitigated or refuted or redressed or concealed or terminated.

নিরস্ত *a.* desisted, refrained, ceased; stopped, prevented; repelled. **নিরস্ত করা** *v.* to cause to desist from or give up; to stop; to prevent; to repel. **নিরস্ত হওয়া** *v.* to desist from, to give up; to stop; to forbear; to be repelled.

নিরস্ত্র *a.* unarmed; disarmed. **নিরস্ত্র করা** *v.* to disarm. **নিরস্ত্রীকরণ** *n.* disarmament; deprival of or curtailment of arms and ammunition.

নিরহংকার, নিরহঙ্কার (loos.) **নিরহংকারী** *a.* not conceited or proud; unassuming; humble, modest, lowly. **নিরহংকারিতা** *n.* humility, modesty, lowliness.

নিরাকরণ *n.* redressing; removal; refutation; mitigation; prevention; repulsion; rejection; (pop.) determination or ascertainment. **নিরাকরণ করা** *v.* to redress; to remove; to refute; to mitigate; to prevent; to repulse, to ward off, to reject; (pop.) to determine or ascertain. **নিরাকরণ হওয়া** *v.* to be redressed or removed or refuted or mitigated or prevented or repulsed or rejected; (pop.) to be determined or ascertained.

নিরাকাঙ্ক্ষ *a.* having no desire; unambitious; having no inclination or greed; disinterested, indifferent.

নিরাকাঙ্ক্ষা *n.* absence of desire; contentment.

নিরাকার *a.* formless, unembodied, incorporeal. □ *n.* the sky; God.

নিরাকুল *a.* very much perturbed or worried or anxious; unperturbed, unworried; calm.

নিরাকৃত *a.* redressed; removed; refuted; mitigated; prevented; repulsed, warded off; rejected; (pop.) determined or ascertained.

নিরাকৃতি[1] same as **নিরাকরণ**।

নিরাকৃতি[2] *a.* same as **নিরাকার** (*a.*).

নিরাতঙ্ক *a.* having no fear, fearless, intrepid, unafraid.

নিরাতপ *a.* without sunshine or without sunlight; dark.

নিরাধার *a.* not held in any container; having no container to be kept in; having no support or shelter, destitute, helpless; homeless.

নিরানন্দ *a.* cheerless, joyless, unhappy; sad, sullen, glum; gloomy (নিরানন্দ গৃহ). □ *n.* cheerlessness, unhappiness; sadness; gloominess.

নিরানব্বই, (coll.) **নিরানব্বুই** *n.* & *a.* ninety-nine.

নিরাপত্তা *n.* safety, security. **নিরাপত্তা পরিষদ** *n.* the Security Council (of the U.N.O.). **নিরাপত্তা রক্ষী** *n.* the security guard.

নিরাপদ *a.* free from danger or mishap, safe, secure. **নিরাপদে** *adv.* safely, securely. **নিরাপৎসু,** (inc. but pop.) **নিরাপদেষু** to one who is safe from dangers (a mode of address in letters).

নিরাবরণ *a.* uncovered, bare.

নিরাভরণ *a.* not wearing any ornaments, unornamented; bare. *fem.* **নিরাভরণা**।

নিরাময় *a.* free from sickness, healthy; cured of or recovered from sickness. □ *n.* act of curing, cure (রোগ নিরাময়ের জন্য). **নিরাময় করা** *v.* to cure; to bring round. **নিরাময় হওয়া** *v.* to be cured; to recover from sickness, to come round.

নিরামিষ *a.* (of food or diet) excluding meat fish and eggs, vegetarian. **~ভোজন** *n.* vegetarianism. **~ভোজী, নিরামিষাশী** *a.* vegetarian. □ *n.* a vegetarian.

নিরাবলম্ব, নিরাবলম্বন *a.* having no support or prop; unaided; helpless, destitute; shelterless, homeless.

নিরায়ুধ *a.* with no weapon, unarmed.

নিরালা *a.* lonely, solitary; secluded; private; secret. □ *n.* a lonely retreat.

নিরালোক *a.* without light, lightless; dark. □ *n.* lightlessness; darkness.

নিরাশ *a.* hopeless; dejected, despondent; despairing; disappointed. **নিরাশ করা** *n.* to disappoint. **নিরাশ হওয়া** *v.* to lose hope; to be dejected, to despair; to despond; to be disappointed. **নিরাশা** *n.* loss of hope; dejection, despondency, despondence; despair; disappointment.

নিরাশ্বাস *a.* despairing, sunk in despair; dejected, despondent.

নিরাশ্রয় *a.* shelterless, homeless; helpless, destitute. *fem.* **নিরাশ্রয়া**।

নিরাসক্ত *a.* indifferent, apathetic; detached; disinterested; without attachment (usu. to worldly or mundane things).

নিরাহার *n.* fasting; starvation. □ *a.* fasting; starving. **নিরাহারে** *adv.* (going) without food, fasting, starving.

নিরিখ *n.* rate of price.

নিরিন্দ্রিয় *a.* having no sense-organ; (fig.) deprived or devoid of sense-perception.

নিরিবিলি *a.* solitary, lonely, secluded. □ *n.* a lonely place. □ *adv.* in or at a lonely place (নিরিবিলি বসা) ; privately (নিরিবিলি কথা বলা).

নিরীক্ষক *a.* observing, seeing; auditing. □ *n.* an observer or onlooker; an auditor.

নিরীক্ষণ *n.* observation, seeing; observing closely; examine carefully; auditing or audit. **নিরীক্ষণ করা** *v.* to observe, to see; to audit.

নিরীক্ষমাণ *a.* engaged in observing or seeing or auditing. *fem.* **নিরীক্ষমাণা**।

নিরীক্ষা same as **নিরীক্ষণ**। **নিরীক্ষাসার** *n.* audit manual.

নিরীক্ষিত *a.* observed, seen; audited.

নিরীক্ষ্যমাণ *a.* that which is being observed or noticed or seen or audited.

নিরীশ্বর *a.* godless; atheistic, atheistical. **~বাদ** *n.* atheism. **~বাদী** *a.* atheistic, atheistical; □ *n.* an atheist.

নিরীহ *a.* unoffending, inoffensive, harmless, innocent; gentle, meek. **~তা** *n.* innocence, harmlessness; gentleness, meekness; disinterestedness.

নিরুক্ত *n.* a Vedic glossary or concordance prepared by Yaska. □ *a.* categorically spoken or stated. **নিরুক্তি** *n.* a categorical speech or statement; an assertion; etymological notes; an enunciation; a Vedic glossary or concordance compiled by Yaska.

নিরুচ্চার *a.* speechless, silent; mute; mum.

নিরুৎসাহ *a.* lacking in or deprived of zeal or enthusiasm; lackadaisical; discouraged; disheartened, dejected. □ *n.* lack or loss of zeal or enthusiasm; discouragement; dejection. **নিরুৎসাহ করা** *v.* to discourage; to dishearten, to deject.

নিরুৎসুক *a.* disinterested, callous; incurious; uninquisitive; (rare) extremely curious or inquisitive.

নিরুত্তর *a.* unanswering, unresponding, irresponsive; silent; unprotesting.

নিরুত্তেজ *a.* unexcited; calm and composed.

নিরুদ *a.* waterless; (chem.) anhydrous; dehydrated. **নিরুদক** *a.* anhydrous. **নিরুদন** *n.* dehydration.

নিরুদ্দিষ্ট *a.* missing, traceless.

নিরুদ্দেশ *a.* having no destination (নিরুদ্দেশ যাত্রা) ; missing, traceless (নিরুদ্দেশ লোক).

নিরুদ্ধ *a.* confined; besieged; bolted, closed (নিরুদ্ধ দ্বার) ; choked (নিরুদ্ধ কণ্ঠ) ; obstructed (নিরুদ্ধ পথ) ; checked, stopped, halted (নিরুদ্ধ গতি).

নিরুদ্বিগ্ন *a.* same as **নিরুদ্বেগ** (*a.*).

নিরুদ্বেগ *a.* unperturbed; unworried; calm. □ *n.* unperturbedness, unworriedness; calmness. **নিরুদ্বেগে** *adv.* without worries and anxieties, calmly.

নিরুদ্যম *a.* unenterprising, effortless; callous; lethargic; slothful; lackadaisical.

নিরুপদ্রব *a.* free from troubles or disturbances or dangers; untroubled, undisturbed; peaceful; safe; secure. **নিরুপদ্রবে** *adv.* without troubles or dangers; undisturbedly; peacefully, safely.

নিরুপম *a.* unparalleled, matchless, peerless, unrivalled, nonpareil; incomparable; unique. *fem.* **নিরুপমা**।

নিরুপাধি, নিরুপাধিক *a.* having no title or surname; diplomaless; having none of the primordial qualities of a created being, namely সত্ত্ব রজঃ and তমঃ (নিরুপাধি ব্রহ্ম).

নিরুপায় *a.* having no means or expedients; resourceless, destitute; helpless.
নিরূপক *a.* ascertaining, determining; fixing; realizing.
নিরূপণ *n.* ascertainment, determination; fixation; realization. **নিরূপণ করা** *v.* to ascertain, to determine; to fix; to realize. **নিরূপণীয়** *a.* that which is to be ascertained or determined or fixed or realized, ascertainable, determinable.
নিরূপিত *a.* ascertained, determined; fixed, appointed; realized. **নিরূপিত মূল্যে** at fixed or settled price. **নিরূপিত সময়ে** at the appointed time or hour.
নিরেট *a.* not hollow or liquid; solid or hard; (sarcas.) dull-headed, doltish, stupid; thorough, utter, downright (নিরেট মূর্খ). ☐ *n.* (coll.) a dunce, a dolt, a blockhead, a numskull (সে একটা নিরেট).
নিরেস *a.* inferior.
নিরোধ, নিরোধন *n.* siege; counteraction, obstruction, opposition, prevention; restraint, control, repression; (phys.) chocking. **নিরোধ করা** *v.* to besiege, to counteract, to obstruct, to oppose, to prevent; to check, to restrain, to control, to repress; (phys.) to choke. **নিরোধক** *a.* besieging; counteracting, obstructing; opposing, preventing; restraining, controlling, repressing; choking.
নির্গত *a.* emerged, issued, ejected, flowed out. **নির্গত করা** *v.* to bring or send out, to emerge, to issue, to eject, to cause to flow out. **নির্গত হওয়া** *v.* to come or go out, to emerge, to issue, to be ejected, to flow out.
নির্গন্ধ *a.* scentless, inodorous, odourless.
নির্গম, নির্গমন *n.* act of coming or going out; emergence, act of issuing out, ejection, outflow. **নির্গমকোণ** *n.* (sc.) an angle of emergence. **নির্গমনিবন্ধ** *n.* outward register. **নির্গমপথ** *n.* an outlet. **নির্গমবাণিজ্য** *n.* export trade. **নির্গমশুল্ক** *n.* export duty.
নির্গলন *n.* melting; exudation; filtration.
নির্গলিত *a.* melted; exuded; filtrated. **নির্গলিত করা** *v.* to melt; to cause to exude; to filtrate. **নির্গলিত হওয়া** *v.* to be melted, to melt; to exude; to be filtrated. **নির্গলিতার্থ** *n.* an obscure implication that has been squeezed out with effort, the real import (got after rejecting verbiage, superfluity etc.); (loos.) the essence, the quintessence; the substance.
নির্গুণ *a.* having no qualities; having no good qualities or qualification (নির্গুণ লোক) ; having none of the primordial qualities of created beings, namely, সত্ত্ব রজঃ and তমঃ (নির্গুণ ব্রহ্ম).
নির্গূঢ় *a.* extremely hidden or secret or mysterious or occult.
নির্গৃহ *a.* shelterless, homeless.
নির্গ্রন্থ *a.* (of string, cloth, mind etc.) having no knot; having no attachment or interest, disinterested, unattached. ☐ *n.* a Jaina or Buddhist friar.
নির্ঘণ্ট *n.* a table of contents, an index; a programme, a bill of fare.
নির্ঘাত *n.* the sound of winds clashing together violently; the violent conflict of two air currents; the sound of a concussion; a thunder-stroke. ☐ *a.* violent, terrible; cruel; heart-rending; unfailing, hitting the mark (নির্ঘাত আঘাত). *adv.* surely (নির্ঘাত করবে).
নির্ঘৃণ *a.* having no aversion or feeling of disgust towards filthy things; shameless, impudent, brazen-faced.
নির্ঘোষ *n.* a loud noise or report.
নির্জন *a.* desolate; lonely, solitary. ☐ *n.* a lonely place; solitude. **~তা** *n.* desolateness, desolation; loneliness; solitude; seclusion.
নির্জর *a.* unageing, not subject to old age or decay. ☐ *n.* an immortal, a god.
নির্জল *a.* waterless; not diluted with water, raw (নির্জল মদ) ; having no permission to drink even a drop of water (নির্জল উপবাস) ; anhydrous; dehydrated. **নির্জল কোহল** absolute alcohol. **নির্জলা** *a. fem.* of **নির্জল**। ☐ *a.* (sarcas.) unmixed, absolute, downright (নির্জলা দুঃখ, নির্জলা মিথ্যা).
নির্জিত *a.* defeated, vanquished, crushed, subdued, subjugated.
নির্জীব *a.* lifeless, dead; inanimate (নির্জীব পদার্থ) ; devitalized, effete; spiritless,

languid, inert; exhausted, fatigued; very feeble, faint; dull. ~তা *n.* lifelessness; inanimation; lack of vitality or vigour; effeteness; languor, inertia, spiritlessness; exhaustion, fatigue; feebleness, faintness; dullness.

নির্ঝঞ্ঝাট *a.* untroubled; unencumbered; unimpeded; peaceful, smooth. **নির্ঝঞ্ঝাটে** *adv.* without trouble or encumbrance or impediment; peacefully, smoothly.

নির্ঝর *n.* a fountain, a spring; a waterfall, a cascade, a cataract; a mountain brook, a rivulet.

নির্ঝরিণী *n. fem.* a river, a stream.

নির্ণয় *n.* discernment; ascertain-ment; determination; decision; resolution. **নির্ণয় করা** *v.* to discern, to descry; to ascertain, to determine; to decide; to resolve.

নির্ণায়ক *a.* discerning; ascertaining; deciding; resolving. □ *n.* a criterion, **নির্ণায়ক মত, নির্ণায়ক ভোট** *n.* a casting vote. **নির্ণায়ক সভা** *n.* a jury. **নির্ণায়ক সভ্য** *n.* a juror.

নির্ণীত *a.* discerned; ascertained, determined; decided; resolved.

নির্ণেতা *a. & n.* one who discerns or ascertains or determines or decides or resolves. *fem.* **নির্ণেত্রী।**

নির্ণেয় *a.* that which is to be or can be discerned or ascertained or decided or resolved; discernible, ascertainable, determinable; decidable.

নির্দয় *a.* merciless, hard-hearted; cruel; extremely severe. ~তা *n.* mercilessness, hard-heartedness; cruelty; extreme severity.

নির্দল *a.* without any party; having no party; (in pol.) unaligned or independent.

নির্দায় *a.* having no liability or responsibility.

নির্দিষ্ট *a.* pointed out, indicated; demonstrated; ascertained, determined; decided; fixed, settled, appointed; particular; definite; defined; ordered; enjoined, directed. **নির্দিষ্ট করা** *v.* to point out, to indicate; to demonstrate; to ascertain, to determine; to decide or resolve; to fix, to settle, to appoint; to particularize; to define; to order, to enjoin, to direct.

নির্দেশ *n.* indication; demonstration; ascertainment, determination; decision; fixation, appointment; definition; an order or directive; direction. **নির্দেশ করা, নির্দেশ দেওয়া** *v.* to point out, to demonstrate; to ascertain, to determine; to decide; to fix, to appoint; to define; to order or enjoin; to direct. **নির্দেশক, নির্দেষ্টা** *a. & n.* one who or that which indicates or demonstrates or ascertains or determines or decides or fixes or defines or orders or directs. ~নামা *n.* a directive. ~পত্র *n.* a written directive or order. ~প্রাপ্ত *a.* in receipt of a directive or order; enjoined; directed.

নির্দেষ্টা see **নির্দেশ।**

নির্দোষ *a.* faultless, guiltless, immaculate (নির্দোষ চরিত্র) ; not guilty, innocent (নির্দোষ ব্যক্তি) ; flawless (নির্দোষ কাজ) ; harmless (নির্দোষ খেলা). **নির্দোষ আমোদ-প্রমোদ** innocent amusements or diversion or pastime. **নির্দোষী** *a.* (pop.) not guilty, innocent. □ *n.* (pop.) an innocent person. **নির্দোষিতা** *n.* innocence; guiltlessness; flawlessness.

নির্দ্বন্দ্ব *a.* free from opposition, free from severity of cold and heat or from anger and malice; free from incompatibility; free from duel or strife; peaceful; amicable.

নির্দ্বিধ *a.* unhesitant, unwavering; without hesitation; certain; sure.

নির্ধন *a.* having no wealth; not rich; poor; indigent. ~তা *n.* poverty; indigence; lack of wealth. **নির্ধনীকৃত** *a.* made a pauper, impoverished.

নির্ধারণ *n.* ascertainment; discernment; determination; fixation; decision; assessment. **নির্ধারণ করা** *v.* to ascertain; to discern; to determine; to fix, to appoint; to decide; to assess. **নির্ধারক** *a. & n.* one who or that which ascertains or discerns or determines or fixes or decides or assesses. **নির্ধারিত** *a.* ascertained; discerned; determined; fixed, appointed; decided; assessed.

নির্ধার্য *a.* that which is to be or can be ascertained or discerned or determined or fixed or decided or assessed; ascertainable; discernible; determinable; fixable; decidable; assessable.

নির্ধর্ম *a.* without a religion; irreligious, impious; sinful.

নির্ধূম *a.* smokeless.

নির্নিমিখ *a.* (poet.) unwinking ('নির্নিমিখ আঁখি') ; (poet.) steadfast (নির্নিমিখ দৃষ্টি). □ *adv.* without winking, steadfastly ('চাহিল নির্নিমিখ').

নির্নিমিত্ত *a.* causeless, groundless; unreasonable, unjustified.

নির্নিমেষ *a.* unwinking ('নির্নিমেষ আঁখি') ; steadfast (নির্নিমেষ দৃষ্টি).

নির্বংশ *a.* having lost all one's descendants; having no descendant, having none to succeed or to continue the line. **নির্বংশে** *a. & n.* (coll.) one whose descendants have all perished; one who has no descendant.

নির্বচন *n.* categorical or emphatic utterance or statement;(of words) derivative explanation; definition; (geom.) enunciation.

নির্বন্ধ *n.* foreordination, ordaining, predestination, prescript, decree (বিধির নির্বন্ধ) ; a law; insistence, repeated solicitation (নির্বন্ধাতিশয্য) ; importunity; contact or communication (নির্বন্ধাভাব) ; a happening (কী দারুণ নির্বন্ধ !). **নির্বন্ধাতিশয়** *n.* (pop.) great importunity.

নির্বর্তন *n.* accomplishment, execution, performance.

নির্বর্তিত *a.* accomplished, executed, performed.

নির্বল *a.* lacking in strength; weak; weakened, debilitated or devitalized.

নির্বর্ষ *a.* rainless; droughty.

নির্বস্ত্র *a.* having no clothes; unclothed, unclad; naked, nude.

নির্বহণ *n.* enforcement.

নির্বাক *a.* speechless; silent, dumbfounded. **নির্বাক করা** *v.* to render speechless; to silence; to dumbfound.

নির্বাচক *a.* elective; voting; selective. □ *n.* an elector (*fem.* electress, electoress), a voter; a selector. **~মণ্ডলী** *n.* electors collectively, the electorate.

নির্বাচন *n.* election; voting; selection (প্রাকৃতিক নির্বাচন = natural selection). **নির্বাচন করা** *v.* to hold an election : to elect, to return; to select. **নির্বাচন-আধিকারিক** *a.* a returning officer. **নির্বাচন কেন্দ্র** *n.* a polling station; a polling-booth. **নির্বাচন ক্ষেত্র** *n.* a constituency. **নির্বাচন নিযুক্তক** *n.* an election agent. **~প্রার্থী** *n.* a candidate for election. □ *a.* seeking election. **~যোগ্য** *a.* worthy of selection or choice; eligible for election. **নির্বাচনী** *a.* of election, electoral. **নির্বাচনী বক্তৃতা** an election speech.

নির্বাচিত *a.* elected, returned (নির্বাচিত সদস্য) ; selected. *fem.* **নির্বাচিতা**। **নির্বাচিত করা** *v.* to elect, to return; to select.

নির্বাণ *n.* extinguishment, extinction, putting out (দীপনির্বাণ) ; annihilation, end; extinction of individuality and absorption into the Supreme Spirit, beatitude, *nirvana*; act of sinking below the horizon, setting. □ *a.* extinguished, extinct (নির্বাণ দীপ) ; one who has attained beatitude (নির্বাণ ঋষি) ; that which has set (নির্বাণ সূর্য). **নির্বাণোন্মুখ** *a.* about to be extinguished, about to go out. **নির্বাণোন্মুখ দীপ** a dying lamp.

নির্বাত *a.* airless; windless; stuffy; motionless, still (নির্বাত নিষ্কম্প).

নির্বাতক *a.* that which makes or renders airless. **নির্বাতক পাম্প** an exhaust pump.

নির্বাধ *a.* unobstructed, unhindered, unrestricted; unopposed; free. **নির্বাধে** *adv.* unobstructedly, without hindrance; unopposedly; freely.

নির্বান্ধব *a.* without a friend; without an acquaintance; (of a place) lonely, desolate (নির্বান্ধব পুরী).

নির্বাপক *a.* extinguishing; allaying or alleviating or mitigating (শোক নির্বাপক). □ *n.* an extinguisher; an allayer, a mitigator. **অগ্নিনির্বাপক-যন্ত্র** *n.* a fire-fighting appliance, a fire-extinguisher.

নির্বাপন *n.* extinguishment, putting out; extinction; allaying, mitigation (শোকনির্বাপণ). **নির্বাপণ করা** *v.* to extinguish, to put out; to allay, to mitigate.

নির্বাপিত *a.* extinguished; extinct; allayed, mitigated.

নির্বাসন *n.* exile, banishment, deportation; (fig.) expulsion or removal. **নির্বাসনে পাঠানো, নির্বাসন দেওয়া** *v.* to send into exile, to exile, to banish. **~দণ্ড** *n.* penal banishment, exile.

নির্বাসিত *a.* exiled, banished, (fig.) expelled or removed. *fem.* **নির্বাসিতা।** **নির্বাসিত করা** *v.* to banish, to exile, (fig.) to expel or remove. **নির্বাসিত ব্যক্তি** an exile.

নির্বাহ *n.* act of carrying out, execution (কার্যনির্বাহ) ; act of carrying on (সংসারযাত্রা নির্বাহ) ; act of passing or spending or leading (সময়নির্বাহ, জীবন-নির্বাহ) ; defraying (ব্যয়নির্বাহ) ; accomplishment (পূজানির্বাহ) ; conclusion. **নির্বাহ করা** *v.* to carry out, to execute; to carry on; to pass or spend or lead; to defray; to accomplish, to perform; to conclude. **নির্বাহ হওয়া** *v.* to be carried out or executed or carried on or passed or spent or led or defrayed or performed or concluded. **নির্বাহক** *a.* & *n.* one who carries out or executes or carries on or passes or spends or leads or defrays or performs or concludes. **নির্বাহিত** *a.* carried out; executed; carried on; passed; spent, led; defrayed; performed; concluded. **নির্বাহী** *a.* executive (নির্বাহী আধিকারিক = an executive officer; নির্বাহী নিযুক্তক = a managing agent; নির্বাহী বাস্তুকার = an executive engineer).

নির্বিকল্প *a.* without an alternative, absolute; untransfigured, without transfiguration; unerring or unhesitating, sure; having no distinction between the cognizer and the cognizable, completely identified with or absorbed into the Infinite. □ *n.* absolute or final knowledge. **নির্বিকল্প সমাধি** a trance or profound meditation in which one is completely identified with or absorbed into the Infinite.

নির্বিকার *a.* having no antipathy to anything; not offended by anything; unchanging, immutable; having no mental perturbation, unperturbed, unruffled, unmoved, not upset or agitated; indifferent, stoical, callous. **~চিত্তে, নির্বিকারে** *adv.* feeling no uneasiness in the mind; calmly.

নির্বিঘ্ন *a.* free from dangers; undisturbed; unimpeded; safe; peaceful. **নির্বিঘ্নে** *adv.* without danger; undisturbedly; unimpeded; safely; peacefully (নির্বিঘ্নে সমাপ্ত).

নির্বিচারে *a.* indiscriminate; promiscuous. **নির্বিচারে** *adv.* indiscriminately; promiscuously.

নির্বিণ্ণ *a.* aggrieved; regretful, repentant; penitent; mortified; sorry.

নির্বিদার *a.* that which cannot be pierced through or rent or cleft; uncleavable ('বর্ম তব নির্বিদার').

নির্বিবাদ *a.* free from strife or quarrel; undisputed; unopposed; peaceful. **নির্বিবাদী** (pop.) *a.* never quarrelling; of peaceful or quiet disposition. **নির্বিবাদে** *adv.* without strife or quarrel or opposition or difficulty; peacefully.

নির্বিরোধ, (pop.) **নির্বিরোধী** *a.* free from strife or quarrel or opposition; quiet, peaceful; never quarrelling; of peaceful or quiet disposition or temperament. **নির্বিরোধে** *adv.* without strife or quarrel; unopposedly; peacefully, amicably.

নির্বিশঙ্ক *a.* fearless, dauntless; free from misgivings.

নির্বিশেষ *a.* irrespective (জাতিধর্মনির্বিশেষে) ; not distinguished from similar, equal (পুত্র নির্বিশেষে). **নির্বিশেষে** *adv.* irrespective or regardless of; not distinguishing from, just like.

নির্বিষ *a.* free or freed from poison (রোগীকে নির্বিষ করা) ; divested of venom ; non-venomous ; (fig.) divested of ability to harm.

নির্বীজ *a.* seedless; (surgically) sterile, aseptic: deprived of generative or procreative power. **নির্বীজ করা** *v.* to divest of seeds; to sterilize, to disinfect; to deprive of generative or procreative power. **নির্বীজন** *n.* sterilization, disinfection. **নির্বীজিত** *a.* sterilized, disinfected.

নির্বীর্য *a.* lacking strength or valour; feeble or timid; impotent.

নির্বুদ্ধি *a.* foolish, stupid. **~তা** *n.* foolishness, stupidity, crassness.

নির্বৃতি *n.* deliverance, rescue, escape; succour.

নির্বেদ *n.* repentance; mortification or remorse; despondence, despondency; dejection; disinterestedness in or callousness towards worldly affairs.

নির্বৈর *a.* having no enemy.

নির্বোধ *a.* dull; stupid, foolish. □ *n.* (pop.) a blockhead.

নির্ব্যাজ *a.* guileless; candid, frank, openhearted.

নির্ব্যূঢ় *a.* proved; conclusive; positive; absolute (নির্ব্যূঢ় অধিকার).

নির্ভয় *a.* fearless, dauntless. **~চিত্ত, ~হৃদয়** *a.* having a fearless heart; having no fear at heart. **নির্ভয়ে** *adv.* fearlessly, dauntlessly, boldly.

নির্ভর *n.* a prop or support; dependence, reliance; confidence. **নির্ভর করা** *v.* to depend (upon), (coll.) to bank (on), to rely (on). **~তা** *n.* (loos.) dependence, reliance. **~যোগ্য** *a.* dependable, reliable. **~যোগ্যতা** *n.* dependability, reliability. **~শীল** *a.* relying on, depending on; dependent.

নির্ভরসা *a.* bereft of trust or confidence or hope.

নির্ভাবনা *n.* freedom from worries and anxieties. □ *a.* free from worries and anxieties (নির্ভাবনা হওয়া).

নির্ভীক *a.* fearless; dauntless. **~তা** *n.* fearlessness.

নির্ভুল *a.* free from mistake or error; correct; unerring; right; just; accurate. **~তা** *n.* (loos.) correctness; accuracy.

নির্ভেজাল *a.* unadulterated, without adulteration. **নির্ভেজাল মিথ্যা** unmixed falsity, unmixed falsehood. **নির্ভেজাল সত্য** unmixed truth.

নির্মক্ষিক *a.* free from flies; desolate; lonely.

নির্মঞ্ছন *n.* articles placed before a deity to accord welcome to it (such as, a waving light, an incenser etc.).

নির্মৎসর *a.* free from envy, unenvious.

নির্মম *a.* merciless; unfeeling; hard-hearted; cruel; relentless. **~তা** *n.* mercilessness; hard-heartedness; cruelty; relentlessness.

নির্মল *a.* free from filth or dirt or stain or anything undesirable; clean (নির্মল পরিচ্ছদ) ; clear, transparent, pellucid (নির্মল জল) ; cloudless, fair (নির্মল আকাশ) ; free from guilt or sin, blameless, spotless, chaste, holy (নির্মল চরিত্র) ; honest, innocent, naive ; unblemished (নির্মল যশ) ; unadulterated, unmixed, pure (নির্মল আনন্দ, নির্মল সুখ). *fem.* **নির্মলা** । **~তা** *n.* freedom from filth or dirt or stain or anything undesirable; clearness, transparence, pellucidity; cloudlessness; chasteness, honesty, innocence, candour, naivety; unblemishedness; purity.

নির্মলি *n.* a kind of fruit that cleanses water.

নির্মা poet. form of **নির্মাণ করা** ।

নির্মাণ *n.* act of making; formation; construction, act of building; manufacture; creating, creation; composition (গ্রন্থনির্মাণ) ; organization (দলনির্মাণ) ; act of setting up, foundation, establishment (রাজ্যনির্মাণ, বিদ্যালয় নির্মাণ). **নির্মাণ করা** *v.* to make; to form; to construct; to build, to manufacture; to create; to compose; to organize; to set up, to found, to establish.

নির্মাল্য *n.* flowers, leaves etc. offered to a deity and subsequently borne upon the head by the votaries as a token of holy grace.

নির্মাতা *a.* making; forming; constructing; building; manufacturing; creating; composing; organizing; setting up, establishing. □ *n.* a maker; a constructor, a builder, an architect; a manufacturer; a creator; a composer; an organizer; a founder.

নির্মিত *a.* made; formed; constructed; built; manufactured; created; composed; organized; founded; established.

নির্মিতি same as **নির্মাণ** ।

নির্মীয়মাণ *a.* in the process of being made or formed or constructed or built or manufactured or created or composed or organized or set up or founded or established.

নির্মুকুল *a.* (of trees) stripped of or destitute of buds ('এখনো ঘুমাও শতরূপা এই কুসুমের মাসে নির্মুকুল').

নির্মুক্ত *a.* completely free from or let loose or liberated.

নির্মূল *a.* uprooted, extirpated, eradicated, exterminated; completely destroyed or expelled; rootless, unfounded, groundless. **নির্মূল করা** *v.* to uproot, to extirpate, to eradicate, to exterminate; to destroy or annihilate or expel completely. **~ন** *n.* uprooting, extirpation, eradication, extermination; thorough destruction or annihilation or expulsion. **নির্মূলিত** *a.* uprooted, exterminated; thoroughly destroyed or expelled.

নির্মেঘ *a.* cloudless; clear (নির্মেঘ আকাশ).

নির্মোক *n.* (of snakes etc.) a slough; (*pl.*) exuviae; an armour; (hum.– of human being) the whole skin.

নির্মোচন *n.* act of removing or taking off or putting off completely; thorough peeling; moulting.

নির্মোচ্য *a.* that which is to be or can be removed or taken off or put off completely.

নির্যাতক *a.* & *n.* oppressor, tormentor.

নির্যাতন *n.* oppression, persecution, tormenting; vengeance. **নির্যাতন করা** *v.* to oppress, to persecute, to torment; to take vengeance (upon). **~কারী** *n.* an oppressor, a persecutor, a tormentor, an avenger. *fem.* **~কারিণী**।

নির্যাতিত *a.* oppressed, persecuted, tormented. *fem.* **নির্যাতিতা**।

নির্যাস *n.* essence; substance; exudation; extract.

নির্লজ্জ *a.* shameless, impudent, brazen-faced. *fem.* **নির্লজ্জা**। **~তা** *n.* shamelessness, impudence.

নির্লিপ্ত *a.* unconcerned; keeping aloof; having no attachment for, disinterested; callous; free from all earthly attachment. **~তা** *n.* disinterestedness; freedom from all earthly attachments; callousness. **নির্লিপ্ত থাকা** *v.* to keep aloof (from).

নির্লোভ *a.* free from greed, not greedy or avaricious.

নির্লোম *a.* hairless; having no fleece or woolly covering.

নিলম্বন *n.* adjournment (of a decision); suspension (as of an employee). **নিলম্বিত** *a.* adjourned; suspended. **নিলম্বিত করা** *v.* to adjourn; to suspend. **নিলম্বিত রাখা** *v.* to adjourn. **নিলম্বিত গণিতক** suspense account.

নিলয় *n.* an abode, a residence, a dwelling-house, a home; a receptacle; a store; (anat.) a ventricle; (rare) complete annihilation.

নিলাজ poet. form of **নির্লজ্জ**।

নিলাম *n.* auction. **নিলাম করা, নিলাম করানো** *v.* to put (a thing) up to auction, to put (a thing) for auction, to sell by auction. **নিলাম ডাকা** *v.* to bid at an auction. **নিলামে কেনা** *v.* to purchase at an auction. **নিলামে তোলা** *v.* to put up to auction, to put up for auction, to auction. **নিলামে বেচা** *v.* to sell at an auction; to sell by auction, to auction. **নিলাম খরিদদার, ~ক্রেতা** *n.* an auction purchaser. **~দার** *n.* an auctioneer. **নিলামের দোকান** an auction-house. **নিলামি** *a.* put up to auction; sold by auction; purchased at an auction; that which is to be auctioned; as cheap as an article sold by auction.

নিলীন *a.* completely sunk or drowned (in); completely fused with; completely lost or absorbed (in); completely disappeared or vanished.

নিলীয়মান *a.* in the state of sinking (in) or being fused (with) or being lost (in) or disappearing or vanishing.

নিশঙ্ক var. of **নিঃশঙ্ক** (see **নিঃ-**).

নিশপিশ *int.* denoting: restlessness to do something; itching or irritation to do something.

নিশা *n.* the night; (Rig Veda) dark daughter of the Day. **~কর** *n.* the moon. **~গম** *n.* nightfall. **~চর** *a.* active by night, nightfaring. □ *n.* an anthropophagite, a rakshasa; any of the nightfaring creatures such as the owl; a burglar. *fem.* **নিশাচরী**। **~জল** *n.* dew; frost. **~ত্যয়** same as **নিশান্ত**। **~নাথ** *n.* the moon. **নিশান্ত** *n.*

the close of night; daybreak. ~পতি *n.* the moon. **নিশাবসান** same as **নিশান্ত**। ~র্ধ *n.* midnight; dead of night. ~সমাগম *n.* nightfall.

নিশান[1] *n.* a flag, an ensign, a standard, a banner.

নিশান[2], **নিশানা,** (dial.) **নিশানি** *n.* a mark, a sign; a badge; a token; an identity; a target; an aim. **নিশান গাড়া** *v.* to set a mark, to mark off. **নিশানা করা** *v.* to aim at. **নিশানদার** *n.* an identifier. **নিশানদিহি** *n.* identification; act of marking off. **নিশানদিহি করা** *v.* to identify; to mark off.

নিশানাথ, নিশান্ত, নিশাপতি, নিশাবসান see **নিশা**।

নিশাস poet. corrup. of **নিঃশ্বাস**।

নিশি *n.* the night (দিবানিশি) ; an evil spirit whose hypnotic call at night makes a sleeping person follow it and meet with his or her death (cp. night-hag). **নিশিতে পাওয়া** *v.* to be hypnotized by this evil spirit.

নিশিত *a.* whetted, sharpened; sharp; keen.

নিশিদিন, নিশিদিশি *adv.* day and night; always, constantly.

নিশিপালন *n.* scriptural fasting or diet control on a full moon or a new moon night. **নিশিপালন করা** *v.* to fast or control one's diet on a full moon or a new moon night.

নিশিযাপন *n.* spending or passing the night; staying for a night. **নিশিযাপন করা** *v.* to pass or spend the night; to stay for a night, to put up for a night.

নিশীথ *n.* midnight; late night; (loos.) the night. **নিশীথিনী** *n. fem.* the night. ~সূর্য *n.* the midnight sun.

নিশুতি *n.* late night, night far advanced. ☐ *a.* late, far advanced (নিশুতি রাত্রি).

নিশ্চয় *n.* firm or sure knowledge, conviction, ascertainment, decision, resolution (কৃতনিশ্চয়). ☐ *a.* free from doubts, convinced, ensured, certain (এ বিষয়ে সে নিশ্চয় হয়েছে) ; firm, sure (নিশ্চয় বাক্য). ☐ *adv.* without doubt, surely, certainly, for certain (নিশ্চয় যাব). ~তা *n.* freedom from doubts certainty; firmness, sureness, surety.

নিশ্চল *a.* stationary; fixed; motionless; immobile, immovable. ~তা *n.* stationariness; fixity; motionlessness; immobility.

নিশ্চায়ক *a.* & *n.* one who or that which convinces or ensures or ascertains or decides.

নিশ্চিত *a.* free from doubts, convinced, ensured (নিশ্চিত হওয়া) ; certain, sure unfailing (নিশ্চিত ঘটনা, নিশ্চিত পদক্ষেপ). ☐ *adv.* certainly, surely, without doubt, for certain, positively (সে নিশ্চিত আসবে). **নিশ্চিত করা** *v.* to make sure, to ensure, to settle. **নিশ্চিত জানা** *v.* to know for certain. ~রূপে *adv.* certainly, definitely.

নিশ্চিতি *n.* same as **নিশ্চয়তা**।

নিশ্চিন্ত, (coll.) **নিশ্চিন্দি** *a.* unworried, unperturbed (নিশ্চিন্ত হওয়া) ; carefree (নিশ্চিন্ত জীবন). **নিশ্চিন্ততা** *n.* unworried-ness; carefreeness, freedom from care. ~মনে *adv.* in a carefree mind, with a mind free from care. **নিশ্চিন্তে** *adv.* in a carefree manner; without care or anxiety.

নিশ্চিহ্ন *a.* without a sign; effaced; obliterated; erased; eradicated. ~করণ *n.* effacing, effacement; obliterating; eradicating. **নিশ্চিহ্ন করা** *v.* to efface; to obliterate; to eradicate.

নিশ্চেষ্ট *a.* making no attempt, effortless; unenterprising; inactive; lazy; immobile. ~তা *n.* effortlessness; lack of enterprise; inactivity; laziness; immobility.

নিশ্ছিদ্র *a.* free from holes, having no hole; compact; flawless.

নিশ্বসন, নিশ্বসিত, নিশ্বাস pop. spellings of **নিঃশ্বসন, নিঃশ্বসিত** and **নিঃশ্বাস** respectively (see **নিঃ-**).

নিষঙ্গ *n.* a container for arrows, a quiver. **নিষঙ্গী** *a.* carrying a quiver.

নিষণ্ণ *a.* situated, located, seated, sitting; lying.

নিষাদ[1] *a.* one of an uncivilized race of ancient India chiefly living on hunting; a swineherd or a fisherman or a fowler (by caste).

নিষাদ[2] *n.*(mus.) the major sixth of the C-scale.

নিষাদী[১] *fem.* of **নিষাদ[১]**।

নিষাদী[২] *n.* an elephant-driver; an elephant-rider.

নিষিক্ত *a.* thoroughly wet or soaked or drenched, soppy; exuded. **নিষিক্ত করা** *v.* to wet or soak or drench thoroughly, to sop; to exude.

নিষিদ্ধ *a.* forbidden (নিষিদ্ধ ফল). prohibited (নিষিদ্ধ কর্ম) ; banned, proscribed (নিষিদ্ধ বই) ; outlawed or interdicted (নিষিদ্ধ ব্যক্তি) ; out of bounds (নিষিদ্ধ এলাকা) ; unlawful. **নিষিদ্ধ করা** *v.* to forbid, to prohibit; to ban, to proscribe; to outlaw or indict; to place (a locality, shop etc.) out of bounds.

নিষুতি *a.* fast asleep, sleeping soundly (নিষুতি নগরী) ; hushed, drowned in silence (নিষুতি রাত্রি).

নিষুপ্ত *a.* fast asleep, sleeping soundly. **নিষুপ্তি** *n.* sound sleep; state of sleeping soundly.

নিষেক *n.* sprinkling or showering; exudation; (bot.) fertilization. **পরনিষেক** *n.* cross-fertilization. **স্বনিষেক** *n.* self-fertilization.

নিষেধ *n.* act of forbidding, prohibition; interdiction; interdict. **নিষেধ করা** *v.* to forbid, to prohibit; to interdict. **~ক** *a.* forbidding, prohibiting, prohibitive, prohibitory; interdictory. **নিষেধাজ্ঞা** *n.* prohibition; a prohibitory order. **নিষেধাজ্ঞা জারি করা** *v.* to prohibit; to issue an order or a decree of prohibition.

নিষেবণ *n.* attending on or serving, attendance, service; worship.

নিষ্ক *n.* gold; a gold coin current in ancient India; a gold coin; a measure for weighing gold.

নিষ্কণ্টক *a.* free from thorns, thornless; free from troubles or dangers or enemies; safe; unhindered; unhampered; peaceful. **নিষ্কণ্টকে** *adv.* without impediment or obstacle or trouble or danger or opposition; safely; peacefully, freely.

নিষ্কম্প *a.* not trembling or vibrating; motionless, still.

নিষ্কর *a.* rent-free, freehold; tax-free. **নিষ্কর সম্পত্তি** *n.* a freehold.

নিষ্করুণ *a.* merciless, pitiless, relentless; cruel; hard-hearted.

নিষ্কর্মা *a.* having no work to do, unemployed; averse to work; lazy; good-for-nothing, worthless.

নিষ্কর্ষ *n.* extract, essence, substance; gist.

নিষ্কর্ষণ *n.* removal; elimination; extraction.

নিষ্কল *a.* not divided into or consisting of or formed of constituent parts; whole; compact; indivisible; stripped of potency or vigour; weakened; aged, old.

নিষ্কলঙ্ক *a.* unblemished, stainless, spotless; immaculate.

নিষ্কলা *fem.* of **নিষ্কল**।

নিষ্কলুষ *a.* free from vice, sinless; pure; free from dirt or stain; clean.

নিষ্কাণ্ড *a.* (bot.) acaulescent.

নিষ্কাম *a.* having no lust or sexual desire, Platonic (নিষ্কাম প্রণয়) ; unconcerned about the effect or consequence, dispassionate, not actuated by any desire or gainful motive (নিষ্কাম কর্ম).

নিষ্কাশ *a.* going or coming out, emergence; an exit; flowing out, outflow; a drain.

নিষ্কাশন, নিষ্কাসন *n.* squeezing out, extraction; expulsion; removal; banishment; drawing out or unsheathing (a sword etc.). **নিষ্কাশন করা** *v.* to extract; to expel, to remove; to banish; to draw out or unsheathe.

নিষ্কাশিত, নিষ্কাসিত *a.* extracted; turned out, expelled; removed; banished; (of a sword etc.) drawn out or unsheathed.

নিষ্কৃত *a.* delivered, rescued, freed; released, set free; exempted.

নিষ্কৃতি *n.* deliverance, rescue; release; exemption. **নিষ্কৃতি দেওয়া** *v.* to deliver, to rescue, to set free, to release, to exempt. **নিষ্কৃতি পাওয়া** *v.* to be delivered or rescued or freed or set free or exempted.

নিষ্কোষণ *n.* drawing out or unsheathing (a sword etc.). **নিষ্কোষণ করা** *v.* to draw out, to unsheathe.

নিষ্কোষিত *a.* (of a sword etc.) drawn out, unsheathed. **নিষ্কোষিত করা** *v.* to draw out, to unsheathe.

নিষ্ক্রম, নিষ্ক্রমণ *n.* going or coming out, emergence, exit; going away or leaving for ever. **নিষ্ক্রমণ করা** *v.* to go or come out, to emerge; to go away or leave or quit for ever. **নিষ্ক্রমণপত্র** *n.* a passport.

নিষ্ক্রয় *n.* price; wages; charge or fee for hiring, hire; that which is paid in exchange; exchanging, exchange; selling, sale. **~ণ** *n.* commutation.

নিষ্ক্রান্ত *a.* gone or come out, emerged; gone away or left or quitted for ever. **নিষ্ক্রান্ত হওয়া** same as **নিষ্ক্রমণ করা** (see **নিষ্ক্রম**).

নিষ্ক্রিয় *a.* not doing any work, inactive; out of order, not working (নিষ্ক্রিয় যন্ত্র) ; inoperative (নিষ্ক্রিয় আইন) ; offering no opposition, passive (নিষ্ক্রিয় প্রতিরোধ = passive resistance); dormant (নিষ্ক্রিয় শক্তি) ; lazy, idle, indolent. **~তা** *n.* inaction, inactivity; inoperativeness; passivity; dormancy; laziness, idleness, indolence.

নিষ্ঠ *a. & in comp.* (used as *sfx.*) well-placed, well-established; fixed; having firm faith or trust (in) (ধর্মনিষ্ঠ) ; having deep attachment (to) or reverence (for) (কর্মনিষ্ঠ) ; greatly devoted or attentive (to) (একনিষ্ঠ) ; very devout.

নিষ্ঠা *n.* firm faith or trust, deep attachment or reverence, great devotion or attention (ধর্মে নিষ্ঠা, কর্মে নিষ্ঠা) ; devoutness (নিষ্ঠাবান উপাসক) ; adherence to the scriptural code of behaviour and observance of religious rites (নিষ্ঠাবান ব্রাহ্মণ). **~বান** *a.* having deep attachment (to) or reverence (for), greatly devoted or attentive (to); devout; punctiliously observant of the scriptural code of behaviour and religious rites. *fem.* **~বতী** । **~ভরে** *adv.* devotedly.

নিষ্ঠীবন, নিষ্ঠীব *n.* spittle. **নিষ্ঠীবন ত্যাগ করা** *v.* to spit.

নিষ্ঠুর *a.* merciless; hard-hearted; cruel; (poet.) fell; ruthless. *fem.* **নিষ্ঠুরা** । **~তা** *n.* mercilessness; cruelty; ruthlessness. **নিষ্ঠুরাচরণ** *n.* a cruel act; merciless or cruel behaviour.

নিষ্ঠ্যূত *a.* vomited, belched out; ejected; thrown out; spat (out).

নিষ্পত্তি *n.* solution (সমস্যার নিষ্পত্তি) ; accomplishment, execution (কার্যনিষ্পত্তি) ; utterance (বাঙ্‌নিষ্পত্তি) ; settlement, decision (মোকদ্দমার নিষ্পত্তি) ; compromise (শরিকদের মধ্যে নিষ্পত্তি). **নিষ্পত্তি করা** *v.* to solve; to accomplish, to execute; to utter; to settle, to decide; to effect a compromise, to compound; to come to terms. **নিষ্পত্তি হওয়া** *v.* to be solved or accomplished or uttered or settled or decided or compromised or compounded.

নিষ্পত্র *a.* leafless, having no leaves (নিষ্পত্র বৃক্ষ).

নিষ্পন্ন *a.* . attained, realized; accomplished, executed, performed (কার্যনিষ্পন্ন, যাত্রানিষ্পন্ন, পূজানিষ্পন্ন) ; evolved (out of); (gr.) formed or derived (from). **নিষ্পন্ন করা** *v.* to attain, to realize; to execute, to perform; to give rise (to); (gr.) to form or derive.

নিষ্পাদক *a.* one who or that which accomplishes or executes or performs, executive.

নিষ্পাদন *n.* accomplishment, execution, performance. **নিষ্পাদন করা** *v.* to accomplish, to execute, to perform. **নিষ্পাদনীয়** same as **নিষ্পাদ্য** ।

নিষ্পাদপ *a.* bereft of trees. **নিষ্পাদপ প্রান্তর** a prairie; a wilderness.

নিষ্পাদিত *a.* accomplished, executed, performed. **নিষ্পাদিত করা** same as **নিষ্পাদন করা** (see **নিষ্পাদন**).

নিষ্পাদ্য *a.* that which is to be or can be accomplished or executed or performed.

নিষ্পাপ *a.* free from sin, sinless; virtuous, pure, holy.

নিষ্পিষ্ট *a.* powdered by beating, pulverized; ground, pounded; crushed; severely thrashed; heavily trodden; trampled on; hard-pressed; severely oppressed; routed, stampeded. **নিষ্পিষ্ট করা** same as **নিষ্পেষণ করা** (see **নিষ্পেষণ**).

নিষ্পেষ, নিষ্পেষণ *n.* beating to powder or grinding or pounding or crushing or thrashing severely or treading heavily or trampling or pressing hard or oppressing severely or routing or stampeding. **নিষ্পেষণ করা** *v.* to beat to powder; to pulverize, to grind, to pound; to crush; to thrash severely; to tread heavily, to trample; to press hard; to rout, to stampede. **নিষ্পেষক** *a.* & *n.* one who or that which beats to powder or grinds or pounds or crushes or thrashes severely or treads heavily or tramples or presses hard or routes or stampedes. **নিষ্পেষিত** same as **নিষ্পিষ্ট**।

নিষ্প্রতিভ *a.* lacking genius; dim; lacking brightness; obscure, dull.

নিষ্প্রদীপ *a.* having no lamp burning; blacked out. □ *n.* state of having no lamp burning; lights out, curfew; blackout.

নিষ্প্রভ *a.* lacking brightness or lustre, lustreless, lacklustre; dim; dull; feckless. **নিষ্প্রভতা** *n.* lack of brightness or lustre; dimness; dullness; fecklessness.

নিষ্প্রয়োজন *a.* unnecessary; needless; purposeless; useless. □ *n.* needlessness, purposelessness. **নিষ্প্রয়োজনে** *adv.* unnecessarily; needlessly; to no purpose, uselessly.

নিষ্প্রাণ *a.* lifeless, dead; inanimate; heartless; lacking vivacity; dull. **~তা** *n.* lifelessness; inanimateness, inanimation; heartlessness; lack of vivacity; dullness.

নিষ্ফল *a.* fruitless; abortive; ineffectual, futile, of no avail, vain; impotent (নিষ্ফল ক্রোধ). **নিষ্ফলা** *a. fem.* of **নিষ্ফল**। □ *a.* (of trees etc.) bearing no fruit, fruitless, acarpous; (of land etc.) unproductive, barren; (of days etc.) yielding no success or benefit (নিষ্ফলা বার). **নিষ্ফল করা** *v.* to frustrate. **নিষ্ফল হওয়া** *v.* to be abortive; to be in vain, to be ineffectual, to be futile; to fail. **~তা** *n.* fruitlessness; ineffectuality; frustration; failure; impotency.

নিষ্যন্দ alt. spell. of **নিস্যন্দ**।

নিসপিস alt. spell. of **নিশপিশ**।

নিসর্গ *n.* the phenomena of the material world as a whole, nature; creation, the cosmos. **~জ** *a.* nature-born; natural. **~বিদ্যা** *n.* natural science; natural study. **~বিদ** *n.* a naturalist. **~শোভা** *n.* the beauty of nature; a scene of natural beauty. **নিসর্গী** *n.* a naturalist.

নিসাড় *a.* benumbed; insensate; not responding or reacting; noiseless, stealthy (নিসাড় পদক্ষেপ).

নিসাড়া *a.* noiseless, stealthy ('নিসাড়া হইয়া আয় লো সজনি').

নিসাদল alt. spell. of **নিশাদল**।

নিসিন্দা *n.* a herbal plant (its leaves are often smoked as tobacco), Vitex negundo.

নিসূদক *a.* one who kills or slays.

নিসূদন *n.* killing or slaying. □ *in comp.* (used as a *sfx.*) one who kills (দৈত্যনিসূদন = giant-killing).

নিসৃষ্ট *a.* entrusted; officially recognized or sent with official recognition, accredited (নিসৃষ্ট প্রতিনিধি).

নিস্তব্ধ *a.* completely motionless or silent or still. **~তা** *n.* complete motionlessness or silence or stillness.

নিস্তরঙ্গ *a.* waveless, having no waves; still, calm.

নিস্তরণ *n.* crossing; rescue, release, deliverance; going or coming out, emergence; exemption.

নিস্তল *a.* bottomless, fathomless; roundish; round; globular.

নিস্তার *n.* rescue, deliverance; release; acquittal (অভিযোগ থেকে নিস্তার) ; exemption (খাজনার দায় থেকে নিস্তার) ; beatitude, salvation. **নিস্তার করা** *v.* to rescue, to deliver, to succour; to let one have one's salvation. **নিস্তার দেওয়া** *v.* to set free; to release; to acquit; to exempt. **নিস্তার পাওয়া** *v.* to be rescued or delivered or set free or released or acquitted or exempted; to have one's salvation. **~কর্তা** *n.* a rescuer, a deliverer; one who lets another enjoy salvation, a saviour. **নিস্তারিণী** *fem.* one who accords salvation; Goddess Durga (দুর্গা).

নিস্তুষ *n.* husked.

নিস্তেজ *a.* lacking vigour, weak, feckless; lacking lustre or brightness, dull, dim; weakened, down in the mouth. **নিস্তেজ হওয়া** *v.* to lose strength and vigour, to be weak.

নিস্পন্দ *a.* (of the pulse or the heart) not beating or throbbing; motionless, still (নিস্পন্দ আঁখি) ; benumbed, stuporous (নিস্পন্দ অঙ্গ).

নিস্পৃহ pop. spell. of **নিঃস্পৃহ** (see **নিঃ**).

নিস্বন *n.* sound, noise; (of wind instruments etc.) note; voice.

নিস্যন্দ *n.* exudation; essence. **নিস্যন্দিত** *a.* exuded, oozed. **নিস্যন্দী** *a.* exuding, oozing.

নিস্রব, নিস্রাব alt. spellings of **নিঃস্রব** and **নিঃস্রাব** respectively (see **নিঃ-**).

নিহত *a.* killed, slain. **নিহত করা** *v.* to kill, to slay.

নিহন্তা *a.* killing or slaying. □ *n.* a slayer, a killer.

নিহাই *n.* an anvil, stithy.

নিহারন *n.* (poet.) seeing or looking at or watching or espying.

নিহারা *v.* (poet.) to see, to look at, to watch, to notice, to espy.

নিহিত *a.* placed, laid, deposited; conferred, bestowed; entrusted; kept; stored; lying hidden; dormant (অন্তরে নিহিত) ; (chiefly in arith.) intrinsic; thrown, flung. **নিহিত ধ্বনি** *n.* (phon.) inherent sound. **নিহিত স্বরধ্বনি** *n.* inherent vowel.

নীচ[1] *n.* a place or position below; a low or depressed position (নীচ থেকে উপরে).

নীচ[2] *a.* low; inferior; base, mean; vile. **নীচ কুল** a family that is socially inferior; a low-caste family. **~কুলজাত, ~কুলোদ্ভব** *a.* of low birth, low-born. *fem.* **~কুলজাতা, ~কুলোদ্ভবা**। **~গামী** same as **নীচাসক্ত**। *fem.* **~গামিনী**। **~চেতা** same as **নীচমনা**। **~জাতীয়** *a.* belonging to or coming of a low caste, low-born. *fem.* **~জাতীয়া**। **~তা, ~ত্ব** *n.* lowness; inferiority; baseness, meanness; vileness. **~প্রকৃতি** *a.* by nature mean; naturally or essentially mean. □ *n.* mean nature. **~প্রবৃত্তি** *a.* having base tendencies or propensities or desire. □ *n.* a base tendency or desire. **~ভাষা** *n.* vulgar language, slang. **~মনা** a small-minded, mean-minded. **~যোনি** *n.* a creature of an inferior (esp. non-human) order; birth in an inferior order of creatures. □ *a.* born as an inferior creature; born of an inferior creature. **~স্বভাব** same as **নীচপ্রকৃতি**। *fem.* **~স্বভাবা**। **~হৃদয়** *a.* same as **নীচমনা**।

নীচান্তঃকরণ, নীচাশয় *a.* small-minded, mean-minded. *fem.* **নীচাশয়া**।

নীচাসক্ত *a.* addicted to or indulging in hateful or vile things; depraved; having sexual connection with a woman of bad repute or low birth. *fem.* **নীচাসক্তা**।

নীচে *adv. prep.* under, below, beneath, underneath (গাছের নীচে) ; in the bottom of (সমুদ্রের নীচে) ; at the foot of (পাহাড়ের নীচে).

নীট rej. spell. of **নিট**[1]।

নীড় *n.* a nest; (fig.) a small or cosy abode.

নীত[1] *n.* a custom or practice; a principle; behaviour, demeanour.

নীত[2] *a.* conducted, led; conveyed, carried, born; received, accepted.

নীতি *n.* morality (নীতিবিরুদ্ধ আচরণ) ; morals (নীতিশাস্ত্র) ; moral science, ethics; a moral teaching, a moral or maxim (গল্পটির নীতি) ; conscience (নীতিতে বাধছে) ; social morality, justice (নীতিসম্মত বিচার) ; politics (নীতিকুশল) ; an edict or prescript (ধর্মের নীতি) ; a principle (অহিংসার নীতি) ; a method or means or policy (কাঁটা দিয়ে কাঁটা তোলার নীতি) ; a custom or practice (সমাজের নীতি) ; a branch of learning, a science (সমাজনীতি, রাজনীতি). **~কথা** *n.* a moral saying or moral advice; a maxim, an aphorism; a moral; a moral tale; a salutary advice. **~কুশল** *a.* proficient in politics or statesmanship or diplomacy or in the rules of morality. **~কুশলতা** *n.* proficiency in politics or statesmanship or diplomacy or moral rules. **~জ্ঞ** *a.* versed in politics or statesmanship or diplomacy or ethics. **~জ্ঞান** *n.* political knowledge; knowledge in statesmanship; diplomatic knowledge; ethical knowledge. **~জ্ঞানবর্জিত, ~জ্ঞানশূন্য, ~জ্ঞানহীন** *a.* divested of ethical knowledge or devoid of moral scruples; immoral; unscrupulous. **~বচন, ~বাক্য** *n.* a moral saying or advice; a maxim, an aphorism; a salutary advice. **~বাগীশ** *a.* one who makes a parade of one's moral sense. **~বিজ্ঞান** *n.* ethics, moral science. **~বিদ** *a.* same as **নীতিজ্ঞ**।

~বিরুদ্ধ, ~বিরোধী *a.* contrary to moral rules or precepts; immoral; unjust; contrary to one's principles. ~মূলক *a.* didactic, moral; concerning a particular principle or principles. ~শাস্ত্র *n.* moral science, moral philosophy, ethics. ~শাস্ত্রবিদ, ~শাস্ত্রবেত্তা *a.* versed in moral science. □ *n.* a moral philosopher. ~শিক্ষা *n.* moral instruction or education; political or judicial education. ~সংগত, ~সম্মত *a.* conforming to morality or justice; righteous or just; conforming to a particular principle or principles. ~হীন *a.* without any principle, unprincipled; lacking moral principles; unscrupulous.

নীপ *n.* (mainly poet.) the kadamba (কদম্ব) flower or its tree.

নীবার *n.* paddy grown from airborne seeds that have fallen on an unploughed field.

নীবি, নীবী *n.* the part of the loincloth fastened round one's (chiefly a woman's) waist; a knot by which the loincloth is fastened at one's waist (usu. নীবিবন্ধ, নীবিবন্ধন) ; (loos.) a waist-band.

নীয়মান *a.* in the state of being conducted or carried or borne or conveyed. *fem.* নীয়মানা।

নীর *n.* water; any liquid; aqua. ~ময় *a.* aqueous, watery, full of water or moisture.

নীরক্ত *a.* bloodless; pale; anaemic.

নীরজ *a.* growing in or born of water, aquatic. □ *n.* the lotus.

নীরজা[১] *fem.* of নীরজ।

নীরজা[২] *a. fem.* free from dirt; (of flowers etc.) having no pollen; (of girls) one whose menstruation has not yet begun to function.

নীরদ *n.* cloud. ~বরণ *a.* dark as a (moisture-bearing) cloud, cloud-coloured.

নীরন্ধ্র *a.* having no hole or opening; compact; dense; closely woven; closed on all sides; stuffy.

নীরব *a.* noiseless; silent; hushed; speechless. নীরব করা *v.* to take off the noise of; to silence; to hush; to render speechless. নীরব হওয়া *v.* to cease to make noise; to become silent; to be hushed; to keep quiet. ~তা *n.* noiselessness; silence; hush; speechlessness. নীরব থাকা *v.* to remain silent or tongue-tied. নীরব সমর্থন silent or tacit support, silent consent. নীরবে *adv.* silently; noiselessly. নীরবে সহ্য করা to bear silently or calmly.

নীরস *a.* not juicy, juiceless; sapless; dry; dull, having no sense of humour, having no power to appreciate finer sentiments and emotions ; insipid, uninteresting, jejune, dull (নীরস কথাবার্তা) ; monotonous, prosaic (নীরস জীবন) ; glum, sullen (নীরস হাসি বা মুখ) ; unpleasant, cheerless (নীরস আবহাওয়া). ~তা *n.* lack of juice or sap; dryness; lack of sense of humour, lack of power to appreciate finer sentiments and emotions; insipidity, lack of interest, dullness, monotony, prosiness, glumness, sullenness; unpleasantness, cheerlessness.

নীরাজন, নীরাজনা *n.* cleaning arms and armour on the eve of going to war; worshipping an idol by waving lamps, fly-whisks etc. before it.

নীরোগ, (pop.) **নীরোগী** *a.* free from disease or sickness; well; hale.

নীল *n.* the blue colour, azure; the indigo plant or the dye made from it; synthetic indigo, azuring; Shiva (শিব) or his worship (নীলের উপোস). □ *a.* blue, azure; azurine. ~কণ্ঠ *a.* blue-necked. □ *n.* a kind of blue-necked bird, the bluebreast, the roller bird; Shiva (শিব). ~কমল *n.* the blue lotus. ~কর *n.* an indigo-planter. ~কান্তমণি *n.* lapis-lazuli, sapphire. ~কুঠি *n.* an indigo-factory. ~গাই *n.* the blue-sheep of Tibet, nilgai, the blue bull, ~পদ্ম *n.* the blue lotus. ~পূজা *n.* the worship of Shiva (শিব) on the penultimate or the last day of the Bengali year. ~প্রভ *a.* having a blue lustre or radiance. ~বর্ণ *n.* & *a.* blue; azure. *a. fem.* ~বর্ণা। নীলবর্ণ শৃগাল (fig.) a pretender. ~বসন *n.* blue clothes or cloth. □ *a.* dressed in blue. *a. fem.* ~বসনা। ~মণি *n.* lapis-lazuli, sapphire;

Krishna (কৃষ্ণ). ~রক্ত *n.* blue blood; (fig.) high birth. ~লোহিত *n.* a colour between crimson and violet, purple; Shiva (শিব). □ *a.* purple. ~ষষ্ঠী *n.* the last or the penultimate day of the Bengali year when Shiva (শিব) is worshipped.

নীলা *n.* lapis-lazuli, sapphire.

নীলাকাশ *n.* the blue sky.

নীলাঞ্জনা *n.* blue-vitriol, antimony.

নীলাব্জ *n.* the blue lotus.

নীলাভ *a.* having a blue tinge or tint, bluish. **নীলাভা** *n.* the blue tinge or tint, bluishness.

নীলাভ্র *n.* a dark cloud.

নীলাম্বর *n.* a piece of blue cloth or loincloth. □ *a.* wearing a blue loincloth. **নীলাম্বরী** *n.* a piece of women's blue loincloth.

নীলাম্বু, নীলাম্বুধি *n.* an ocean or sea; blue water, high sea.

নীলিমা *n.* blueness; bluishness; the blue colour; blue tinge or tint.

নীলোৎপল *n.* the blue lotus.

নীলোপল *n.* sapphire.

নীহার *n.* snow; dew; ice. ~কান্তি *a.* having a snow-white complexion.

নীহারিকা *n.* the nebula. ~বাদ *n.* nebular theory.

নুটি *n.* (of thread, wool, fibre etc.) a ball, a wisp. **নুটি পাকানো** to roll into a ball.

নুড়নুড়ি *n.* the uvula, the epiglottis; a small bell-shaped button.

নুড়া *n.* a faggot, a fagot.

নুড়ি *n.* a pebble; a stone-chip.

নুড়ো coll. form of **নুড়া**।

নুন *n.* salt; table-salt. **নুন খাওয়া** *v.* to take salt; (fig.) to be fed or benefited by another, to eat one's salt. **নুন খাই যার গুণ গাই তার** (fig.) I (should) blindly eulogize my benefactor.

নুনিয়া *n.* a manufacturer of salt by caste, a salter.

নুনুড়ি coll. corrup. of **নুড়নুড়ি**।

নুয়া, নোয়া *v.* to bend forward; to stoop; to bow; (fig.) to submit or yield. **নোয়ানো** *v.* to bend; to cause to bend forward or stoop or bow; (fig.) to cause to submit or yield.

নুর *n.* (Mus.) light (নুরজাহান) ; chin tuft or goatee (chiefly of a Musalman). ~জাহান *n.* the light of the world. ~নবি *n.* the prophet of the light that is Islam; an appellation of Mohammad the Prophet.

নুরি *n.* the lory.

নুলিয়া *n.* one of a community expert in swimming and diving in the sea.

নুলো *a.* with mutilated hands, of one whose forearm has been cut off or amputated. □ *n.* the paw of a cat etc.; (sarcas.) the hand of man.

নূতন *a.* new; novel; young; at the first blush or onset (নূতন যৌবন) ; modern, recent; newly grown or born (নূতন ফল, নূতন শাবক) ; fresh; strange, unknown (নূতন জগৎ, নূতন লোক) ; changed (এখন সে নূতন লোক) ; **নূতন করে** *adv.* anew; over again; afresh. ~ত্ব *n.* newness; novelty; modernity, recency; freshness.

নূপুর *n.* an anklet set with small bells (used by dancers or as an ornament by women). ~নিক্কণ *n.* the jingle of bells in an anklet.

নূর rej. spell. of **নুর**।

নৃ *a.* (chiefly used as a *pfx.*) man or mankind. ~কপাল *n.* a human skull. ~কুলবিৎ, ~কুলবিদ *n.* an ethnologist. ~কুলবিদ্যা *n.* ethnology. ~তত্ত্ব, ~বিদ্যা *n.* anthropology. ~তাত্ত্বিক *a.* anthropological. □ *n.* an anthropologist. ~মণি *n.* a king; a man of greatest or highest worth. ~মুণ্ড *n.* a human head or skull. ~মুণ্ডমালা *n.* a number of human heads strung into a garland or wreath. ~মুণ্ডমালী *a.* wearing a garland of human heads. ~মুণ্ডমালিনী *a. fem.* of ~মুণ্ডমালী। □ *n.* Goddess Kali (কালী). ~লোক *n.* the earth, the world.

নৃত্য *n.* a dance; (sarcas.) a caper; a leap, skipping or frisking. **নৃত্য করা** *v.* to dance; (sarcas.) to cut a caper; to leap, to skip or frisk. ~কলা same as **নৃত্যবিদ্যা**। ~কারী *a.* engaged in or given to or proficient in dancing, dancing; leaping. *fem.* ~কারিণী। ~গীত *n.* dancing and singing. ~গুরু *n.* a dancing-master. ~নাট্য *n.* a dance drama. ~পটীয়সী *a. fem.* proficient in dancing. *masc.* ~পটু।

~পরা *a. fem.* given to dancing. *masc.* ~পর। ~প্রিয় *a.* fond of dancing. ~বিদ্যা *n.* the art and science of dancing. ~শালা *n.* a dancing-hall; a ball-room; a theatre.

নৃপ, নৃপতি *n.* a king, a prince. **নৃপবর, নৃপমণি, নৃপেন্দ্র** *n.* a great king; the greatest king; a king of kings, an emperor. **নৃপাসন** *n.* a royal seat, a throne. **নৃপোচিত** *a.* befitting a king, kingly, princely, royal, regal.

নৃশংস *a.* cruel, ferocious, barbarous, atrocious, heinous, fell. ~তা *n.* cruelty, ferocity, ferociousness, barbarity, atrocity, heinousness.

নৃসিংহ, নৃসিংহাবতার *n.* (myth.) the fourth incarnation of Vishnu (বিষ্ণু) in the form of a being whose upper half of the body was shaped like a man whilst the lower half was shaped like a lion, Man-lion.

নেই, নেই-আঁকড়া coll. var. of **নাই** and **নাই-আঁকড়া** respectively.

নেউটা, নেউটানো *v.* (chiefly dial.) to turn back; to return; to be taken aback; to draw back or be drawn back, to flinch or be flinched (কথা নেউটানো).

নেউল *n.* the ichneumon, the mongoose.

নেওটা, ন্যাওটা *a.* (of a child etc.) extremely fond of or attached to or brought under perfect control by means of affectionate treatment.

নেওয়া *v.* to take; to carry (ছাতা নিয়ে বেড়ানো); to bear; to place; to put; to wear; to assume; to follow (উপদেশ নেওয়া); to accept (নিমন্ত্রণ নেওয়া); to test (পড়া নেওয়া); to borrow (ধার নেওয়া); to inquire (খবর নেওয়া). ~নো *v.* to cause to take or carry or accept or follow; to cause to wear or test; to make one to carry or take or accept or follow.

নেং dial. corrup. of **ল্যাং**।

নেংচানো dial. corrup. of **ল্যাংচানো** (see **ল্যাং**).

নেংটা dial. corrup. of **ল্যাংটা**।

নেংটি[1] the loincloth.

নেংটি[2], (dial.) **নেংটে** *a.* small, tiny. □ *n.* the mouse. **নেংটি ইঁদুর** *n.* the mouse.

নেংড়া dial. corrup. of **ল্যাংড়া**[1], **নেংড়া**[2]।

নেকড়া rej. spell. of **ন্যাকড়া**।

নেকড়ে *n.* the wolf.

নেকনজর *n.* a gracious look; favour, good books; (sarcas.) disfavour, displeasure, anger.

নেকা rej. spell. of **ন্যাকা**।

নেট *n.* a net; a finely reticulated fabric (নেটের মশারি).

নেটা rej. spell. of **ন্যাটা**।

নেড়া *a.* shaven-headed, tonsured (নেড়া লোক); shaven (নেড়া মাথা); bald (চুল উঠে উঠে তার মাথা নেড়া); unornamented, bare (নেড়া হাত); undecorated or scantily decorated (বই-এর মলাটখানা নেড়া); unfurnished or scantily furnished (ঘরখানা বড়ো নেড়া); leafless (নেড়া গাছ); berefit of trees and vegetation (নেড়া মাঠ); not surrounded with walls (নেড়া ছাদ). □ *n.* a tonsured man or boy. **নেড়া গোরু** a hornless cow. *fem.* **নেড়ি**।

নেড়াপোড়া, ন্যাড়াপোড়া *n.* the festival of bonfire on the eve of the holi. see also **চাঁচর**।

নেড়িকুত্তা *n.* a tyke; a cur.

নেত *n.* a kind or very fine muslin (নেতের কাপড়).

নেতা[1] *n.* a leader; a director, a guide; a commander; a headman, a chief; a pioneer.

নেতা[2] rej. spell. of **ন্যাতা**।

নেতানো, ন্যাতানো *v.* to droop or flag; to loose crispness (মুড়িগুলো নেতিয়ে গেছে). **নেতিয়ে যাওয়া** same as **নেতানো, ন্যাতানো**।

নেতিবাচক *a.* negative. **নেতিবাচক উত্তর** negative reply, answer in the negative; denial.

নেতৃত্ব *n.* the lead; leadership; direction; guidance; command; headmanship, pioneering. **নেতৃত্ব করা** *v.* to lead; to direct, to guide; to command; to head; to pioneer.

নেত্র *n.* the eye. ~গোচর *a.* visible. **নেত্রগোচর হওয়া** *v.* to become visible, to come into view. ~গোলক *n.* the eyeball. ~চ্ছদ *n.* the eyelid. ~জল *n.* tears. ~নালি *n.* lachrymal fistula, sinus of the lachrymal duct. ~পল্লব *n.* the eyelid. ~পাত *n.* act of glancing one's eyes (at), act of looking (at). **নেত্রপাত করা** *v.* to glance one's eyes (at), to cast one's glance (at), to look at, to see. **~পীড়া, ~রোগ** *n.* eye-disease, ophthalmia. **~বর্ত্মকলা** *n.* the conjunctiva. **~বর্ত্মকলাপ্রদাহ** *n.* conjunctivitis. **~মল** *n.* sticky or purulent discharge from the eye, viscous or hardened rheum of the eye.

নেত্রী *fem.* of **নেতা**[1] ।

নেপটানো dial. corrup. of **লেপটানো** ।

নেপথ্য *n.* the green-room or dressing-room of a theatre; a place or position behind the stage or screen not visible from the auditorium; costumes and articles used for the make-up of actors and actresses. **~বিধান** *n.* dressing and make-up of actors and actresses. **নেপথ্যে** *adv.* from a place behind the stage or screen and invisible from the auditorium. (fig.) away from the knowledge of the public, secretly.

নেপালি *a.* Nepalese. □ *n.* a Nepalese; the Nepalese language.

নেপো *n.* the name of a sly rogue. **যার ধন তার নয় নেপোয় মারে দই** (fig.) the honest man drudges whilst the idle knave profits by the honest man's labour or toil.

নেবা[1] pop. var. of **নিবা** ।

নেবা[2] rej. spell. of **ন্যাবা** ।

নেবু dial. corrup. of **লেবু** ।

নেভা pop. var. of **নিবা** ।

নেমক dial. corrup. of **নিমক** ।

নেমন্তন্ন coll. corrup. of **নিমন্ত্রণ** ।

নেমি *n.* circumference (of a wheel or any wheel-shaped object).

নেয়া pop. var. of **নেওয়া** ।

নেয়াই coll. corrup. of **নিহাই** ।

নেয়াপাতি *a.* having very thinly grown kernel (নেয়াপাতি ডাব = a green coconut with thin soft jelly-like kernel); (of a pot-belly) soft and mediumsize.

নেয়ামত *n.* grace, God's grace; favour.

নেয়ার, নেয়াড় *n.* a sort of broad tape used to suspend a mosquito-curtain or to strengthen its upper rim or to deck a cot.

নেয়ে coll. corrup. of **নাইয়া** ।

নেলাখেপা rej. spell. of **ন্যালাখ্যাপা** ।

নেশা *n.* any intoxicating drug or liquor (নেশার জিনিস) ; intoxication, (when caused by wine) inebriation (নেশার ঘোর) ; great attraction or attachment or infatuation or propensity (কাজের নেশা, চোখের নেশা) ; a fad, a craze (কবিতা লেখার নেশা) ; stupefaction, besottedness. **নেশা করা** to be a drug-addict or to be addicted to drinking. **~খোর** *a.* addicted to taking an intoxicating drug or addicted to drinking. □ *n.* a drug-addict or a drunkard. **নেশায় বুঁদ** dead drunk, the worse for liquor or drink. **নেশার ঘোরে** under the influence of wine or some other intoxicant. **নেশারি** *a.* intoxicating (নেশারি রূপ).

নেহ[2], **নেহা** *n.* (obs. & poet.) affection; love, fondling; fond indulgence; amorous fondling.

নেহাই pop. var. of **নিহাই** ।

নেহাত *adv.* necessarily, perforce, must (নেহাত যদি যাবেই) ; at all (নেহাত যদি যাই) ; at least (নেহাত পাঁচটা টাকা দাও) ; thoroughly, extremely (নেহাত মন্দ).

নেহারা pop. var. of **নিহারা** ।

নৈকট্য *n.* imminence; proximity; nearness; neighbourhood; closeness; intimacy.

নৈকষেয় *n.* a son of Nikasa (নিকষা) in the Ramayana, Ravana and his brothers.

নৈকষ্য *a.* tested on a streak-plate; pure blooded (নৈকষ্য কুলীন), (of beasts) pedigreed; pure, genuine.

নৈতিক *a.* moral, ethical. **নৈতিক চরিত্র** moral character.

নৈত্যিক *a.* daily. □ *n.* daily work.

নৈদাঘ *a.* of summer or summertime, summer. *fem.* **নৈদাঘী** ।

নৈপুণ্য *n.* skill; dexterity, adroitness; expertness; efficiency.

নৈবচ *adv.* not such, not so, unlike this. **নৈবচ নৈবচ, নৈব নৈবচ** will never be; never; it will never be so (ভিক্ষা চাওয়া নৈবচ নৈবচ).

নৈবেদ্য, (coll. & dial.) **নৈবিদ্যি** *n.* offerings placed on the altar at the time of worship.

নৈমিত্তিক *a.* casual, occasional, incidental, contingent, irregular (নিত্যনৈমিত্তিক) ; versed in reading omens, versed in augury. **নৈমিত্তিক ছুটি** casual leave.

নৈমিষারণ্য *n.* (myth.) a famous forest of

ancient India converted into an extensive hermitage which was a great seat of learning and spiritual meditation.

নৈয়মিক *a.* conforming to or concerning (prescribed) rules; regular (opp. to secular).

নৈয়ায়িক *n.* a logician; a dialectician; a sophist, a debater.

নৈরাকার *a.* (pop.) shapeless, formless; (pop.) messed up, disordered, scattered in a disorderly manner, all over the shop.

নৈরাশ্য, (dial.) **নৈরাশ,** (poet.) **নৈরাশা** same as **নিরাশা।**

নৈর্ঋত *n.* the south-west.

নৈর্গুণ্য *n.* lack of qualities or good qualities or qualifications; absence or lack of primordial qualities of created beings, namely, সত্ত্ব রজঃ and তমঃ।

নৈর্ব্যক্তিক *a.* impersonal (নৈর্ব্যক্তিক ঈশ্বর) ; not man-made, divine (নৈর্ব্যক্তিক শাস্ত্র).

নৈশ *a.* nightly, nocturnal. **~প্রহরী** *n.* a night guard, a night watchman. **নৈশ বিদ্যালয়** night school. **~ভোজ** *n.* dinner.

নৈষধ *a.* of Nishadha (নিষধ) an ancient Indian state. □ *n.* the king of Nishadha; the name of a poetical work by Sriharsha (শ্রীহর্ষ). **নৈষধীয়** *a.* of the king Nishadha.

নৈষ্কর্ম্য *n.* solemn abstention from all work; inaction; inactivity; unemployment; aversion to work; lassitude; idleness; cessation of work; salvation.

নৈষ্ঠিক *a.* greatly devoted or attentive (to); devout; orthodox; of devotion or devoutness.

নৈসর্গিক *n.* natural, physical (নৈসর্গিক শোভা).

নোংরা *a.* dirty, filthy, foul; despicable, hateful, abominable; impure, unclean, unholy; base, mean, vile (নোংরা মন, নোংরা মতলব) ; indecent or obscene (নোংরা ভাষা, নোংরা গল্প). □ *n.* dirt, filth, refuse. **~মি, ~মো** *n.* dirtiness, filthiness, foulness; baseness, meanness, vileness; indecency or obscenity; indulgence in dirtiness or meanness or vileness or indecency or obscenity.

নোকর *n.* a servant, a serving-man; a paid employee, an employee. **নোকরি** *n.* a service, an employment. **নোকরি করা** *v.* to serve; (to) be in the employment (of).

নোঙর *n.* an anchor. **নোঙর করা, নোঙর ফেলা** *v.* to anchor, to cast or set anchor; to lie at anchor. **নোঙর তোলা** *v.* to weigh anchor.

নোট *n.* paper money, a currency note, a bank-note; a memorandum; a short letter (chiefly an official one); a commentary; a note. **নোট করা** *v.* to note down; to make a commentary (of). **নোট দেওয়া** *v.* to dictate notes to be taken down by another. **নোট ভাঙানো** *v.* to cash paper money, to cash a currency note of high denomination in exchange for notes of lower value. **নোট-করা** *a.* noted down. **~খাতা** *n.* a note-book. **~বই** *n.* a note-book; a commentary, a note.

নোটিস *n.* a notice. **নোটিস দেওয়া** *v.* to notify; to serve a notice.

নোড়া *n.* a pestle (esp. one made of stone) a muller.

নোতুন var. of **নতুন।**

নোনতা *a.* saline (নোনতা জল) ; salty (নোনতা স্বাদ) ; salted (নোনতা খাবার). □ *n.* salted snack.

নোনা[1] *n.* the custard-apple.

নোনা[2] *a.* saline, salty. **নোনা জল** saline water, salt-water; sea-water. **নোনা মাছ, নোনা জলের মাছ** salt-water fish.

নোয়া[1] pop. var. of **নুয়া। ~নো** v. to bend; to cause to bend forward or stoop low or bow; (fig.) to cause to or make one submit or yield.

নোয়া[2] *n.* (dial.) iron; an iron wristlet (worn by Hindu women whose husbands are alive). **হাতের নোয়া অক্ষয় হওয়া** to have one's husband living till one's death.

নোলক *n.* a nose-ring set with a pendent, a nose-drop.

নোলা *n.* (hum.) the tongue. **নোলা বড় হওয়া** *v.* to be audaciously greedy. **নোলায় জল আসা** *v.* to become greedy, to have one's mouth watering.

নৌ *n.* (chiefly used as a *pfx.*) a boat, a vessel, a ship (নৌচালনা). **~ঘাঁটি** *n.* a naval base. ~চালন, ~চালনা *n.* rowing; navigation. **নৌচালনা করা** *v.* to row; to navigate. ~চালনবিদ্যা *n.* (the art and science of) navigation. ~দিগ্‌দর্শী *n.* a mariner's compass. ~পরিমাপক *n.* nautical surveyor. ~বল *n.* the naval force, the navy. ~বহর *n.* a fleet of ships or warships, a fleet. ~বাণিজ্য *n.* maritime trade, maritime or sea-borne commerce. ~বাহ *n.* a boatman; an oarsman; a sailor; navigation. ~বাহিনী *n.* the navy; a naval contingent. ~বাহী, ~বাহ্য *a.* navigable. ~বিদ্যা *n.* navigation; ship-building. ~বিভাগ *n.* the navy; the marine department. ~বিমান *n.* a sea-plane. ~বিহার same as **নৌকাবিহার** (see **নৌকা**). ~যুদ্ধ *n.* a naval fight; a sea-fight; naval warfare. ~সম্বন্ধীয় *a.* nautical; naval. ~সারণী *n.* a nautical almanac. ~সেনা *n* the naval force, the navy. ~সেনাপতি *n.* an admiral; a naval officer. ~সেনাবিভাগ *n.* the navy, admiralty. ~সেনা-সম্বন্ধীয় *a.* naval.

নৌকতা *n.* (dial.) social formality, a present or gift given for the sake of formality.

নৌকতা করা *v.* to observe social formality esp. by giving a present or gift.

নৌকা *n.* a boat (esp. one that plies on a river). ~জীবী *n.* a boatman. ~বাহিত *a.* carried or borne by boat. ~ডুবি *n.* the sinking of a boat; the capsizal of a boat. ~বিহার *n.* a pleasure-trip in a boat; a boat-journey. **নৌকাবিহার করা** *v.* to have a pleasure trip in a boat; to journey by boat. ~বিলাস *n.* the sport of rowing; a pleasure-trip in a boat. ~যাত্রা *n.* journey by boat. ~যাত্রী *n.* a boat-passenger. *fem.* ~যাত্রিণী। ~যোগে *adv.* by boat. **নৌকাযোগে ভ্রমণ** journey by boat. ~রোহণ *n.* getting into a boat, embarkation. **নৌকারোহণ করা** *v.* to get into a boat, to embark. ~রোহণে *adv.* by ooat. ~রোহী *a.* boarded on a boat; going by boat; □ *n.* a boat-passenger. *fem.* ~রোহিণী। ~সম্বন্ধীয়, ~সংক্রান্ত *a.* navicular.

ন্যক্কার *n.* vomiting, retching; nausea; disgust; abhorrence. ~জনক *a.* nauseating; disgusting; loathsome, abhorrent, abominable.

ন্যগ্রোধ *n.* the banian tree.

ন্যস্ত *a.* entrusted; given; deposited, put in the custody (of); placed; portrayed (চিত্রে ন্যস্ত) ; flung; fixed (ন্যস্ত দৃষ্টি) ; placed or arranged in order, arrayed. **ন্যস্ত করা** *v.* to entrust; to give; to deposit, to put into the custody (of), to place, to put; to fling; to fix; to place or arrange in order, to array. **ন্যস্ত ধন** trust money. **ন্যস্ত পত্র** *n.* put-up slip.

ন্যাওটা alt. spell. of **নেওটা**।

ন্যাংটা coll. var. of **ল্যাংটা**।

ন্যাকড়া *n.* a torn piece of cloth, a rag or a scrap of cloth; tattered clothes. **ন্যাকড়া-পরা** *a.* dressed in rags; out at elbows.

ন্যাকড়া, ন্যাকরা, ন্যাকা alt. spellings of **নেকড়া, নেকরা** and **নেকা** respectively.

ন্যাকা *a.* & *n.* one who feigns or affects ignorance or honesty. *fem.* **নেকি**। **ন্যাকামি, ন্যাকামো** *n.* affectation of ignorance or honesty.

ন্যাকার coll. corrup. of **ন্যক্কার**।

ন্যাটা *a.* left-handed; one whose left hand works better than the right one.

ন্যাতা *n.* a piece of tattered cloth, a piece of rag, rag; a mop made of rag. **ন্যাতা দেওয়া** *v.* to mop. **ন্যাতা হওয়া** *v.* to droop or flag (ভয়ে ন্যাতা হওয়া) ; to loose crispness (মুড়িগুলো ন্যাতা হয়ে গেছে). see also **নেতানো**।

ন্যাবা *n.* jaundice.

ন্যায় *n.* reasoning; argument; principle; justice, equity; truth; righteousness; honesty; propriety; the science of reasoning, logic; dialectics; a logical and philosophical treatise compiled by Gautama; a syllogism; (rare) a debate. □ *prep.* like, as, similar to, same as. **ন্যায়ের তর্ক, ন্যায়ের বিচার** a logical discussion; (dero.) sophistry. **ন্যায়ের ফাঁকি** a logical fallacy. **ন্যায়ের ভাষ্য** explanation of a logical point. **ন্যায়-অন্যায় যেভাবেই হোক** by fair means or foul. **ন্যায়ত** *adv.* according to or in keeping with justice, justly, rightly, properly. ~তীর্থ *n* a holy bed of logic; a title given to graduates in Sanskrit (or Indian) logic and philosophy. ~নিষ্ঠ *a.* upright; righteous. ~নিষ্ঠতা, ~নিষ্ঠা *n.* uprightness; righteousness; integrity. ~পথ *n.* the path of justice or uprightness; the right or rightful way; the path of righteousness or rectitude; the path of reasoning. **ন্যায়পথ অবলম্বন করা** *v.* to act justly or uprightly; to obey reasoning. **~পথাবলম্বী** *a.* one who follows the path of justice or uprightness; one who follows the right or rightful way; obedient to reasoning. *fem.* **~পথাবলম্বিনী**। **~পর, ~পরায়ণ, ~বান** same as **~নিষ্ঠ**। *fem.* **~পরায়ণা**। **~পরতা, ~পরায়ণতা, ~বত্তা** same as **ন্যায়নিষ্ঠা**। **~বিচার** *n.* justice, equity; judging uprightly. **~বিচারক** *n.* an upright judge. **~বিচারশূন্য** *a.* incapable of judging correctly; contrary to justice or uprightness; devoid of a sense of justice; unjust. **~বিরুদ্ধ** *a.* unjust, unfair; improper; unreasonable, illogical. **~বুদ্ধি** *n.* sense of justice or discernment; conscience; conscientiousness. **~বুদ্ধিসম্পন্ন** *a.* endowed with a sense of justice or discernment; conscientious; *fem.* **~বুদ্ধিসম্পন্না**। **~বুদ্ধিহীন** *a.* deprived of the sense of justice or discernment; unscrupulous. *fem.* **~বুদ্ধিহীনা**। **~বোধ** *n.* sense of justice. **~মার্গ** same as **ন্যায়পথ**। **~রত্ন** *n.* a jewel of a logician or philosopher; a title awarded to some Sanskrit scholars. **~শাসন** *n.* administration or dispensation of justice; just or upright administration or government. **~শাস্ত্র** *n.* the art and science of reasoning, logic; a logical treatise. **~সংগত, ~সম্মত** *a.* lawful; legal; legally sound; just; proper; reasonable; equitable. **~সংহিতা** *n.* a code of civil laws, a civil code. **~সূত্র** *n.* any of the aphorisms contained in Gautama's treatise on logic; a moral precept. **ন্যায়াধিকার** *n.* lawful right or jurisdiction; civil administration; the judiciary. **ন্যায়াধিকরণ** *n.* a law-court, a court of justice; a civil court. **ন্যায়াধীশ** *n.* a judge, a justice. **ন্যায়ালয়** *n.* a court of justice, a law-court. **ন্যায়িক** *a.* judicial. **ন্যায়োপেত** same as **ন্যায্য**।

ন্যায্য *a.* reasonable; logical, logically admissible; just; equitable; upright; right; rightful, lawful, legitimate. **~তা** *n.* reasonableness; logicality; justness; equity; uprightness; rightness; rightfulness, legitimacy.

ন্যালাখ্যাপা *a.* having a screw loose, cranky, touched in the head.

ন্যাস *n.* entrusting or depositing; that which is deposited, deposit; (in law) custody, trust, giving; act of taking care of or looking after, guardianship; a system of yogic (যৌগিক) exercise in which controlling of respiration is practised, breathing-control. **~রক্ষক, ~পাল** *n.* a trustee.

ন্যাসপাতি var. of **নাশপাতি**।

ন্যুব্জ *a.* hunch-backed; bent forward, stooping; bent; curved; upside down; convex. *fem.* **ন্যুব্জা**। **ন্যুব্জ হওয়া** *v.* to bend, to double up; to stoop; to curve; to turn upside down; to become convex. **~তা** *n.* state of being hunch-backed; state or measure of bending forward or bending; curvature; convexity. **~দেহ** *a.* hunch-backed; having one's body stooping forward. **~পৃষ্ঠ** *a.* convex.

ন্যূন *a.* less (than); short of; deficient (in); inferior (to).**ন্যূন হওয়া** *v.* to be less (than); to fall short (of), to be deficient (in); to be inferior (to). **~কল্প** *a.* least, minimum. **~কল্পে** *adv.* at least. **~তা** *n.* state of being smaller in number or amount or degree; shortage; deficiency; inferiority. **~পক্ষে** same as **ন্যূনকল্পে**। **~সংখ্যায়** *adv.* in the least number, at least. **ন্যূনাতিরেক, ন্যূনাধিক্য** *n.* shortage and excess; shortage or excess; disparity. **ন্যূনাধিক** *adv.* more or less.

প১ *n.* the twenty-first consonant of the Bengali alphabet.
প২ *a.* (used as a *sfx.*) breeding or keeping (গোপ), drinking (মধুপ).
পইছা *n.* a kind of bangle or bracelet.
পইঠা *n.* a step or a flight of stairs.
পইতা, (coll.) **পইতে** *n.* the holy thread slung over the shoulder in the fashion of a cross-belt by upper-caste Hindus, especially Brahmans; the sacrament of wearing the holy thread for the first time. **~ধারী** *a.* wearing a holy thread, that is, belonging to any one of the Hindu upper castes, esp. the Brahman community. **পইতে ফেলে দেওয়া** *v.* to discontinue wearing the holy thread, to discard the holy thread. **পইতে নেওয়া** *v.* to put on the holy thread (sacramentally). **পইতে হওয়া** *v.* to pass through the sacrament of putting on the holy thread for the first time.
পইপই *adv.* repeatedly, again and again (usu. পইপই করে বলেছি).
পউষ alt. spell. of **পৌষ**।
পঁইছা alt. spell. of **পইছা**।
পঁইত্রিশ coll. corrup. of **পঁয়ত্রিশ**।
পঁচাত্তর *n.* & *a.* seventy-five.
পঁচানব্বই, (coll.) **পঁচানব্বুই** *n.* & *a.* ninety-five.
পঁচাশি *n.* & *a.* eighty-five.
পঁচিশ *n.* & *a.* twenty-five. **পঁচিশে** *a.* (of the days of a month) twenty-fifth. □ *n.* the twenty-fifth day of a month, the twenty-fifth.
পঁয়তাল্লিশ *n.* & *a.* forty-five.
পঁয়ত্রিশ *n.* & *a.* thirty-five.
পঁয়ষট্টি *n.* & *a.* sixty-five.
পকেট *n.* a pocket. **পকেট কাটা, পকেট মারা** *v.* to pick someone's pocket. **পকেট ভরা, পকেটে পোরা** *v.* to put in the pocket, to pocket. **ঝুল-পকেট** *n.* a side-pocket. **পিছনের পকেট** a hip-pocket. **বুক-পকেট** *n.* a breast-pocket. **ভিতরের পকেট** an inside pocket. **~ ঘড়ি** *n.* a pocket-watch. **~বই** *n.* a pocket-book. **~মার** *n.* a pick-pocket; a cut-purse. **~স্থ** *a.* put or kept in the pocket. **পকেটস্থ করা** *v.* to put or keep (a thing) in the pocket.
পকোড়া, পকৌড়া *n.* a chop of onion fried usu. in oil.
পক্ব *a.* for. form of **পাকা** (*a.*). **~কেশ** *n.* grey hair. □ *a.* grey-haired; aged, old. **~তা** *n.* ripeness; greyness; maturity; precocity; digestion. **~বিম্বাধরোষ্ঠী** *a.* & *n.* (for.) one whose or of one whose lips are beautifylly red. **পক্বাশয়, পাকাশয়** *n.* the stomach.
পক্ষ *n.* a lunar fortnight (কৃষ্ণপক্ষ, শুক্লপক্ষ) ; a period of fifteen days, a fortnight (দুই পক্ষকাল) ; (of birds) a wing, a feather; (of fish) a fin; (of an arrow) a feather; a team, a party, a side (পক্ষভুক্ত) ; a direction or side or hand (পক্ষান্তরে) ; a flank, a side (পক্ষাঘাত) ; question or answer in a debate, support or opposition, a thesis or an antithesis (পূর্বপক্ষ, উত্তরপক্ষ) ; behalf (তার পক্ষে উকিল দাঁড়ায়নি) ; state or condition (পারতপক্ষে) ; (of a person married, more than once) marriage (দ্বিতীয় পক্ষের স্ত্রী) ; a husband or wife, spouse (এটি তার তৃতীয়পক্ষ). **~ক** *n.* (bot.) *a.* a pinule. **~গ্রহণ** same as **পক্ষাবলম্বন**। **~চ্ছেদ, ~চ্ছেদন** *n.* act of cutting off or clipping one's wings; (fig.) act of making powerless; refutation of one's argument. **পক্ষচ্ছেদ করা, পক্ষচ্ছেদন করা** *v.* to cut off or clip one's wings; (fig.) to render powerless. **~ধর** *a.* winged. □ *n.* a bird; the moon. **~পাত, ~পাতিতা, ~পাতিত্ব** *n.* partiality; unreasonable love or fondness (for), favouritism, bias, preference (ছেলের প্রতি মায়ের পক্ষপাত). **~পাতদুষ্ট** *a.* biased, partial; corrupted with partiality or favouritism. **~পাতশূন্য** *a.* impartial, unbiased. **পক্ষপাতী** *a.* partial, prejudicial; biased, prejudiced; inclined to favouring, prone or leaning to. *fem.* **~পাতিনী**। **~পুট** *n.* the inner part or inside of a wing. **~পুটে** *adv.* under cover

of wings, within the wings; (fig.) under one's protection. ~ভুক্ত *a.* included in a side or team. ~ভেদ *n.* act of distinguishing one side from another; (chiefly pol.) disintegration of a party; differentiation of the two opposing sides of an argument. ~ল *a.* winged; having a fin or fins; (bot.) pinnate. ~শিরাবিন্যাস *n.* (bot.) pinnate venation. ~শিরিত *a.* (bot.) pinnately veined. ~সঞ্চালন *n.* act of flapping or moving one's wings (as by a bird). ~সঞ্চালন করা *v.* to flap or move one's wings. ~সমর্থক same as পক্ষাবলম্বী। ~সমর্থন same as পক্ষাবলম্বন। ~সমর্থনকারী same as পক্ষাবলম্বী। *fem.* ~সমর্থনকারিণী।

পক্ষাকার, পক্ষাকৃতি *a.* wing-shaped, feather-shaped; fin-shaped; pinnate.

পক্ষাঘাত *n.* paralysis, palsy. ~গ্রস্ত *a.* paralysed, palsied.

পক্ষান্ত *n.* the end or termination of a lunar fortnight; the full moon or the new moon; (loos.) termination of a fortnight or a period of fifteen days.

পক্ষান্তর *n.* the other side or condition. পক্ষান্তরে *adv.* on the other side, on the other hand, contrary-wise.

পক্ষাপক্ষ *n.* the other fortnight; one's friends and foes or supporters and antagonists. ~বিচার *n.* discrimination between one's friends and enemies. ~বিচারহীন *a.* impartial (পক্ষাপক্ষবিচারহীন মন্তব্য) ; indiscriminate (পক্ষাপক্ষবিচারহীন হত্যা).

পক্ষাবলম্বন *n.* act of siding with or following or standing for or supporting or defending a particular (contending) party or person; partisanship; act of playing for a particular team. পক্ষাবলম্বন করা *v.* to side with; to follow, to adhere to; to stand for, to support, to defend; to play for. পক্ষাবলম্বী *a.* siding with; following, adhering to; standing for, supporting, defending; playing for a particular team. □ *n.* a party-man; a partisan; a follower, an adherent; a supporter, a defender; a player of a particular team. *fem.* পক্ষাবলম্বিনী।

পক্ষিণী *fem.* of পক্ষী।

পক্ষিপালক *a.* employed in aviculture. □ *n.* a bird-fancier, an aviarist.

পক্ষিপালন *n.* aviculture. পক্ষিপালন করা *v.* to collect, keep and breed birds, to be engaged in aviculture. ~শালা *a.* an aviary.

পক্ষিবিদ্যা *n.* ornithology.

পক্ষিরাজ *n.* a king of birds; an appellation of Garuda (গরুড়) ; (myth.) a winged horse.

পক্ষিশাবক *n.* the young ones of a bird; young of a bird (collectively).

পক্ষিশালা *n.* an aviary.

পক্ষিশিকার *n.* killing or shooting of birds, fowling.

পক্ষী *n.* the bird.

পক্ষীমার *n.* a fowler.

পক্ষীয় *a.* of or concerning a side or group or party; belonging to a party.

পক্ষীরাজ alt. and pop. spell. of পক্ষিরাজ।

পক্ষোদ্গম, পক্ষোদ্ভেদ *n.* fledging. পক্ষোদ্গম হওয়া, পক্ষোদ্ভেদ হওয়া *v.* to be fledged.

পক্ষ্ম *n.* eyelash; a feather.

পগার *n.* a ditch or drain marking the boundary of tract or land. পগার পার হওয়া *v.* (lit.) to leap over or cross a ditch; (fig.) to scamper off or to run away beyond reach.

পঙ্ক্তি *n.* a row, a line. ~ভোজন *n.* dining together sitting in a row, dining in company, community-dining; community dinner.

পঙ্ক *n.* soft mud, clay; filth; (geog.) silt; (bio.) protoplasm; a paste (চন্দনপঙ্ক) ; (fig.) vice; (archi.) finial. ~জ *a.* born of or grown in soft mud, clay-born. □ *n.* the lotus, the water-lily. *fem.* ~জা। ~নয়ন, ~নেত্র *a.* lotus-eyed. *fem.* ~নয়না। ~জিনী *n.* a pond in which lotuses grow, a lotus-pool; a clump or cluster of lotuses, a collection of lotuses. ~ময়, পঙ্কিল *a.* full of soft mud, miry, muddy; turbid; filthy; vicious. ~রুহ *n.* lotus. পঙ্কিলতা *n.* muddiness, miriness; turbidity; filthiness; viciousness. পঙ্কোদ্ধার *n.* dredging (as a river) (fig.); cleansing or purification; correction; act of bringing into order out of an intolerable or intricate mess; (fig.) reclamation from vice. পঙ্কোদ্ধার করা *v.* to dredge; (fig.) to bring into order out of an intolerable or intricate mess; (fig.) to reclaim from vice.

পঙ্খ *a.* (dial.—archi.) finial.

পঙ্খী *n.* (vul.) a bird; (vul.) a ganjasmoker and teller of cock-and-bull stories (পঙ্খীর দল). □ *a.* shaped like a bird (ময়ূরপঙ্খী).

পঙ্গপাল *n.* a swarm of locusts; a locust; (fig.) a huge crowd.

পঙ্গু *a.* lame; crippled; deprived of the power of movement; rendered powerless. **~তা** *n.* lameness; crippledom, crippled state or condition; deprivation of the power of movement; deprivation of power.

পচ *n.* putrefaction, rotting. **পচ ধরা** *v.* to begin to rot or putrefy or decay.

পচন *n.* cooking; digesting, digestion; putrefaction, rotting; (med.) sepsis. **~নিবারক** *a.* counteracting putrefaction : (med.) antiseptic. **~শীল** *a.* easily putrefied; putrescent, rotting; (med.) getting septic.

পচা *v.* to rot, to putrefy, to decompose; (med.) to become septic; (fig.) to become too old or hackneyed. □ *a.* rotten, putrefied, decomposed; (med.) that which has become septic; (fig.) too old or hackneyed (পচা খবর). **পচা ভাদ্র (ভাদ্দর)** the humid and sweltering month of Bhadra.

পচাই *n.* a spirituous liquor distilled from rice, arrack.

পচানো *v.* to cause to rot, to rot, to putrefy, to decompose etc.; to ret (jute etc.); (med.) to make septic. □ *a.* that which has been putrefied or decomposed.

পচাল *n.* (dial.) useless garrulous or idle talk or scandal. **পচাল পাড়া** *v.* to indulge in useless garrulous talk or scandal, to be talkative, to have a long tongue.

পচ্য *a.* worth cooking; digestible.

পছন্দ *n.* choice; liking; selection; approbation. □ *a.* chosen; liked; selected; approved. **পছন্দ করা** *v.* to choose; to like; to select; to approve. **~সই** *a.* to one's liking; choice, select.

পঞ্চ *n.* & *a.* five. **~ক** *n.* a set of five, a quintette, a quintet, a pentad (গীতপঞ্চক). **~কোণ, ~কোণী** *a.* pentangular. **~গব্য** *n.* the five articles derived from the cow, namely, curd, milk, clarified butter, cow's urine and cowdung. **~গুণ** *n.* the five qualities or attributes, namely, beauty, exudation or juice, smell, touch and sound. □ *a.* five times, five-fold. **~গৌড়** *n.* a collective name for the ancient regions of Gaud (গৌড়), Mithila (মিথিলা), Utkal (উৎকল), Kanauj (কনৌজ), and the region situated on the bank of the river Saraswati. **~চত্বারিংশ** *a.* forty-five. **~চত্বারিংশৎ** *n.* & *a.* forty-five. **~চত্বারিংশত্তম** *a.* forty-fifth. *fem.* **~চত্বারিংশত্তমী**। **~তপা** *a.* one who practises severe religious austerities with the blazing sun overhead and enkindling four huge fires on four sides. **~ত্রিংশ** *n.* thirty-five. **~ত্রিংশৎ** *n.* & *a.* thirty-five. **~ত্রিংশত্তম** *a.* thirty-fifth. *fem.* **~ত্রিংশত্তমী**। **পঞ্চত্ব** *n.* death. **পঞ্চত্বপ্রাপ্ত** *a.* dead. **পঞ্চত্বপ্রাপ্ত হওয়া** *v.* to meet with death, to give or yield up the ghost, to die. **পঞ্চত্বপ্রাপ্তি** *n.* death. **~দল** *a.* having five petals, quinquepetalous; pentamerous; quinquepartite. **~দল পুষ্প** a cinquefoil. **~দলীয়** *a.* pentamerous; pertaining to or consisting of five parties, quinquepartite. **~দশ** *n.* & *a.* fifteen. □ *a.* fifteenth. **~দশী** *a. fem.* fifteenth; fifteen years old. □ *n.* the ultimate day of a lunar fortnight; the full moon or the new moon; one of the Vedantas (বেদান্ত). **~দেবতা** *n.* five deities or Gods receiving oblation before one's meal. **~নদ** *n.* the Punjab (it is inundated by five rivers). **~পাণ্ডব** *n.* the five Pandava (পাণ্ডব) brothers of the Mahabharata, the Pandava quintette. **~পাত্র** *n.* a vessel used in Hindu religious service: it consists of four small metal cups placed on a metal tray. **~পিতা** *n.* one's progenitor, deliverer from fear, father-in-law, preceptor and maintainer collectively. **~প্রদীপ** *n.* a metal lamp with room for five wicks. **~বটী** *n.* a sacred place with the assemblage of five banyan trees. ~বাণ *n.* the five arrows of Kam (কাম), the god of love, namely, enchantment, excitement, absorption, heating and stupefaction; Kama the god of love. ~বায়ু *n.* the five vital airs (or breaths) that are drawn into or sent out from the body. ~বিংশ *a.* twenty-five. ~বিংশতি *n.* & *a.* twenty-five. ~বিংশতিতম *a.* twenty-fifth. *fem.* ~বিংশতিতমী। ~ভুজ *n.* (geom.) a pentagon. □ *a.* pentagonal. ~ভূত *n.* the five vital elements collectively, namely, earth, water, heat, air and atmosphere or space. **পঞ্চভূতে মেশা** *v.* (lit.) to be dissolved into the five vital elements; (fig.) to die. **পঞ্চম** *a.* fifth. □ *n.* same as **পঞ্চমস্বর**। ~মকার *n.* wine, meat, fish, posture and sexual intercourse collectively, five essential tantric (তান্ত্রিক) practices or rites. **পঞ্চমবাহিনী** *n.* the fifth column; the group of soldiers supporting and working for the enemy within the country. **পঞ্চমস্বর** *n.* (mus.) the major fifth of the C-scale; the cuckoo's note. ~মহাপাতক *n.* the five mortal sins according to Hindu scriptures. **পঞ্চমী** *a. fem.* fifth. □ *n. fem.* the fifth lunar day of either fortnight. ~মুখ *a.* having five faces or mouths, five-faced; eloquent (প্রশংসায় পঞ্চমুখ). □ *n.* an appellation of Shiva (শিব). ~মুখী *a. fem.* five-faced; pentapetalous ; having five surfaces (পঞ্চমুখী নীলা) ; having five bores or holes (পঞ্চমুখী রুদ্রাক্ষ) ; having five parts or sections, pentamerous, five-pronged. ~মুখী পুষ্প a cinquefoil. ~রঙ্গ, ~রং *n.* (in chess) one of the systems of checkmating. ~রত্ন *n.* the five gems collectively, namely, sapphire, diamond, ruby, pearl and coral. ~রাশিক *n.* (arith.) the double rule of three. ~শর same as ~বাণ। ~শস্য *n.* the five principal grains collectively, namely, paddy, kidney-bean or oat, barley, sesame and pigeon-pea.

পঞ্চাঙ্ক *a.* having five acts, five-act (পঞ্চাঙ্ক নাটক).

পঞ্চানন *a.* having five faces. □ *n.* an appellation of Shiva (শিব).

পঞ্চানন্দ *n.* a traditional deity of Bengal; (loos.) Shiva (শিব).

পঞ্চামৃত *n.* the five sweet edible things collectively, namely, curd, milk, clarified butter, sugar and honey; the sacrament of feeding a woman with these five sweet things in the fifth month of her pregnancy.

পঞ্চায়েত *n.* a village council (ori. consisting of five members), a panchayet. **পঞ্চায়েতি** *n.* work or arbitration of a panchayet; councilship of a panchayet. □ *a.* relating to a panchayet.

পঞ্চালিকা, পঞ্চালী *n.* a doll, a puppet.

পঞ্চাশ, পঞ্চাশৎ *n.* & *a.* fifty. **পঞ্চাশত্তম** *a.* fiftieth. *fem.* **পঞ্চাশত্তমী**। **পঞ্চাশবার** *adv.* fifty times; (fig.) many times, (cp.) thousand and one times, times without number.

পঞ্চাশীতি *n.* & *a.* eighty-five. ~তম *a.* eighty-fifth. *fem.* ~তমী।

পঞ্চেন্দ্রিয় *n.* the five sense-organs collectively, namely, the eye(s), the nose, the tongue, the skin.

পঞ্জর *n.* the ribs; the thorax; the skeletal frame of the chest; a flank; a cage. **পঞ্জরাস্থি** *n.* a rib-bone, a rib.

পঞ্জাবি *a.* of or born in the Punjub. □ *n.* a native of the Punjab; the language of the Punjab; a loose-fitting upper-garment with no collar.

পঞ্জি, পঞ্জী, পঞ্জিকা *n.* an almanac, a calendar, an ephemeris; a chronicle, a journal, a diary (ঘটনাপঞ্জি). **পঞ্জিকর, পঞ্জিকাকার** *n.* the maker of an almanac.

পট১ *n.* cloth or canvas (পটমণ্ডপ) ; a canvas for painting on, a canvas with a painting on, a painting (চিত্রপট) ; a painted earthen pot of convex shape; a painted slide as displayed on the stage, a scene (দৃশ্যপট). ~কার *n.* a painter; a weaver.

পট২, পট্ *int.* expressing : crackling noise; noise of bursting, splitting or snapping; suddenness; quickness. **পট করে** *adv.* with a crackling or snapping noise; suddenly; quickly. **পটাপট** *adv.* making such a noise in quick (and often sudden) succession; suddenly; quickly.

পটকা *a.* extremely weak or feeble (রোগাপটকা). □ *n.* a cracker; a squib; the bladder of a fish.

পটকানো *v.* (coll.) to fling to the ground, to knock down; to defeat, to vanquish; to be overpowered.

পটপটি[1] coll. form of **পর্পটি**।

পটপটি[2] *n.* over-fastidiousness about purity; making too much of anything, exaggeration, tall talk, bragging (মুখেই পটপটি) ; a kind of tiny crackling firework; a kind of crackling toy; crackling noise; the air-bladder of fish; a kind of small creeper or its berry.

পটবাস same as **পটাবাস**।

পটভূমি *n.* background.

পটমণ্ডপ *n.* a canopied pavilion.

পটল[1] inc. but pop. spell. of **পটোল**।

পটল[2] *n.* a collection, a multitude ('নবজলধরপটল') ; (of a book) a chapter, a section, a canto; a roof (পটলপ্রান্ত) ; an eye-disease, cataract (অচ্ছোদপটল).

পটহ *n.* a drum, a war-drum, a kettle-drum; a tabor; the ear-drum, the tympanum (usu. **কর্ণপটহ**). **~নিনাদ** *n.* noise of drum-beat, fanfare.

পটা *v.* to be on terms with, to be friendly with (তোমাতে আমাতে পটে) ; to be familiar with or to be in (usu. illicit) love with (মেয়েটা তার সঙ্গে পটেছে) ; to come to terms, to agree, to give in.

পটানো *v.* to bring to terms; to persuade; to cause to agree or give in; to win over; to lure, to seduce (মেয়ে পটানো).

পটাপট see **পট**[2]।

পটাবাস *n.* a tented accommodation; a tent; a canopied pavilion.

পটাশ *n.* potash.

পটাস *int.* expressing : a loud **পট্** sound.

পটি[1] *n.* a small strip or band of cloth, a bandage (জলপটি) ; a pleat of cloth for tucking with, a tuck; a strip of cloth wound round the leg (as by soldier), a puttee, a puttie (বুটপটি). **পটি দেওয়া, পটি লাগানো** *v.* to place a strip of cloth on; to bandage; to tuck with a pleat of cloth. **পটি পরা** *v.* to put on puttees. **পটি মারা** *v.* to tuck with a pleat of cloth.

পটি[2] *n.* a section of a market, a market (সুতাপটি, লোহাপটি) ; a locality or quarters or township (চীনাপটি = a China-town).

পটীয়সী *fem.* of **পটু** & **পটীয়ান**।

পটীয়ান *a.* very expert or adroit; more expert or adroit.

পটু *a.* expert, adroit, skilful, dextrous; efficient, proficient, adept; able; clever; experienced. **~তা, ~ত্ব** *n.* expertness, adroitness, skill, dexterity; efficiency, proficiency; ability; cleverness; experience.

পটুয়া, (coll.) **পটো** *n.* a painter; a painter by caste.

পটোল *n.* a kind of a kitchen-vegetable shaped like a cylinder tapering at both ends. **পটোল-চেরা** *a.* (of eyes) shaped like a longitudinal half of the aforesaid kitchen-vegetable, very wide and beautiful. **পটোল তোলা** *v.* (sarcas.) to die, to kick the bucket. **~লতা** *n.* the bitter-tasting edible creeper bearing the aforesaid kitchen-vegetable.

পট্ট *n.* a plank, a slab; a plate (তাম্রপট্ট) ; a wooden seat for sitting upon squattingly; a seat (রাজপট্ট) ; a throne (পট্টমহিষী) ; jute; silk, linen (পট্টবস্ত্র) ; a town, a city; a village (esp. a large one); a port; a turban; a scarf. **~দেবী** same as **পট্টমহিষী**। **পট্টন** *n.* a city, a town; a port. **~বস্ত্র** *n.* silk-cloth, linen. **~মহিষী, ~রাজ্ঞী** *n.* the chief queen of a king, a queen consort.

পট্টাবাস *n.* a tent.

পট্টি[1] var. of **পটি**[1], **পটি**[2]।

পট্টি[2] *n.* a fib. **পট্টি দেওয়া, পট্টি মারা** *v.* to fib, to spoof. **~বাজ** *n.* a fibster.

পট্টিশ, পট্টিস *n.* a kind of ancient sword used in fighting.

পট্টু *n.* a kind of coarse linen.

পঠদ্দশা *n.* student life, studentship.

পঠন *n.* act of reading, perusal; study; recitation. **পঠনীয়** *a.* that which is to be or can be read or studied or recited; prescribed for reading or study or recitation; readable; recitable. **~শীল** *a.* reading, studying; in the process of reading.

পঠিত *a.* that which has been read; perused; studied; recited.

পঠিতব্য same as **পঠনীয়** (see **পঠন**).

পঠ্যমান *a.* that which is being read or perused or studied or recited.

পড়তা *n.* a continuous succession of winning or lucky throws (as of dice); luck (পড়তা মন্দ) ; favourable time, fortune; good terms, amiability (তার সঙ্গে আমার পড়তা হল না) ; an approximate number or amount, approximation (গড়পড়তা) ; (comm.) cost of production or procurement. **পড়তা পড়া** *v.* (at dice etc.) to be able to make winning or lucky throws in a row; to have a favourable or fortunate time; (comn.) to meet the cost of production or procurement. **পড়তা পোষানো** *v.* to meet or cover the cost of production or procurement.

পড়তি *n.* fall; decline (পড়তির মুখ) ; (comm.) a fall in prices, business etc., slump (উড়তি-পড়তি) ; the portion of materials or ingredient wasted or scattered in course of production of an article (ঝড়তি-পড়তি) ; remainder, remnant. □ *a.* falling, on the decline. **পড়তি বাজার** slump, market with falling prices.

পড়ন¹ *n.* falling, fall; decline.

পড়ন² *n.* (dial.) reading; perusal; study; recitation; recital.

পড়ন্ত *a.* about to fall; declining; about to terminate or end, coming to a close (পড়ন্ত বেলা, পড়ন্ত দিন) ; setting (পড়ন্ত রোদ). **পড়ন্ত বেলা** the closing hours of the day.

পড়পড়, পড়োপড়ো *a.* about to fall or collapse or cave in (মাথার উপরে বাড়ি পড়পড়).

পড়পড়², পড়্‌পড়্‌ *int.* suggesting: the noise of roughly tearing cloth etc.

পড়শি *n.* a neighbour.

পড়া¹ *v.* to fall, to drop (বৃষ্টি পড়া) ; to fall down, to drop down (পড়ে যাওয়া, তাল পড়া) ; to lean to (গায়ে পড়া) ; (as an *aux.*) to perform an action (ঘুমিয়ে পড়া) ; to come to, to fall into (দুঃখে পড়া) ; to be uncultivated (জমি পড়ে থাকা) ; to be vacant or unoccupied (বাড়ি পড়ে থাকা) ; to stay or remain (পিছনে পড়া) ; to be unpaid or unrealized, to get into arrears (অনেক টাকা পড়ে আছে) ; to be outstanding (কাজ পড়ে থাকা) ; to set in, to begin, to ensue (আকাল পড়া) ; to attack, to raid (ডাকাত পড়া) ; to infest (পোকা পড়া) ; to be attacked (রোগে পড়া) ; to be caught (in) (জালে পড়া, দায়ে পড়া) ; to be affected with, to contact, to incur (মরচে পড়া, টাক পড়া, দায়ে পড়া) ; to arrive or appear (গিয়ে পড়া) ; to come across or fall upon (পথে পড়া) ; to set in for a spell (ঠান্ডা পড়া) ; to come upon, to strike, to occur (মনে পড়া = to call to mind); to require or involve or to involve an expenditure (অনেক টাকা পড়বে) ; to exude, to ooze, to flow out (রক্ত পড়া, রস পড়া, লাল পড়া) ; to fall off, to shed or to be shed, to fall (দাঁত পড়া, পাতা পড়া) ; to be placed (পাত পড়া) ; to be served (পাতে খাবার পড়া) ; to be paralyzed (অঙ্গ পড়ে যাওয়া) ; to come to a close, to decline (বেলা পড়া) ; to terminate; to be applied or set (হাত পড়া) ; to be allayed (রাগ পড়া) ; to be abated, to decrease (তেজ পড়া) ; to be directed or cast or set (চোখ পড়া) ; to be attracted (মন পড়া) ; to go into, to take in (পেটে পড়া) ; to be born (পেট থেকে পড়া) ; to be married (মেয়েটি বড় ঘরে পড়েছে). □ *a.* fallen, dropped; fallen down, dropped down; leaning to (গায়ে পড়া) ; hanging loose (ঝুলে-পড়া চামড়া) ; fallen into (বিপদে পড়া লোক) ; uncultivated or fallow; unoccupied, vacant; deserted (পড়া বাড়ি) ; staying, remaining, laid down (বিছানায় পড়া লোক) ; attacked; infested; caught; affected with; lying unclaimed or met with by chance (পড়া টাকা) ; abandoned, derelict (পড়া মাল). **~নো** *v.* to cause to fall or drop or lean to or infest or be attacked or be affected with or require or involve or involve an expenditure of or be turned or be directed or be cast or be set or be attracted or enter. **পড়ে পড়ে কিল** বা **মার খাওয়া** to take constant insult or suffer oppression without retaliation. **পড়ে-পাওয়া** *v.* to come upon something unexpectedly; to get a thing by chance and unexpectedly. **পড়ে-পাওয়া** *a.* got by chance and unexpectedly; that which has been obtained unexpectedly. See also **পাওয়া**। **বাজারে পড়তে না পাওয়া** to have a ready market, to go or sell like hot cakes.

পড়া² *v.* to read, to go through, to peruse; to study; to recite (মন্ত্র পড়া, হলফ পড়া). □ *n.* reading, perusal; study; recital, recitation; an instalment of lesson, lesson, exercise. □ *a.* that which has been read, perused; studied; recited. **পড়া করা** *v.* to learn or prepare one's lessons. **পড়া ধরা, পড়া নেওয়া** *v.* to test whether one can say one's lessons. **পড়া দেওয়া, পড়া বলা** *v.* to say one's lessons. **(কারও) কাছে পড়া** *v.* to read, to take lessons from. **পড়ে শোনানো** *v.* to read to. **বিদ্যালয়ে পড়তে যাওয়া** to go to school. **~নো** *v.* to teach; to cause to read or study or recite; to instruct, prepare by (repeated) instruction, to tutor, to rehearse, to prime (সাক্ষি পড়ান). **পড়ার ঘর** *n.* a study; a reading room. **পড়ার নেশা** *n.* a great liking for or attachment to reading; love of reading. **~শোনা** *n.* study; academic education, schooling. **পড়াশোনা করা** *v.* to study; to have one's schooling; to learn one's lessons. **পড়াশোনায় মন থাকা** to take care of one's lessons or studies, to be mindful of one's lessons or studies.

পড়ানো see **পড়া¹, পড়া²**।

পড়াশোনা see **পড়া²**।

পড়ুয়া *n.* a student, a pupil; a scholar. □ *a.* given to study, studious; scholarly (পড়ুয়া ছেলে); employed in study, studying (পড়ুয়া অবস্থা).

পড়েন¹ *n.* woof, weft.

পড়েন² *n.* a mass of metal, adjusted to a standard and used for finding weight, a weight.

পড়ো¹ coll. form of **পড়ুয়া**।

পড়ো² *a.* uncultivated, fallow (পড়ো জমি); unoccupied, vacant, deserted (পড়ো বাড়ি বা ভিটে); deprived of the power of movement, confined to bed (ঘর-পড়ো, পড়ো লোক).

পণ *n.* a promise, a resolve (পণরক্ষা); a wager, a stake, a bet (পাশাখেলার পণ); price (প্রাণপণ); a condition or term, a stipulation (ধনুকভাঙা পণ); compulsory dowry (esp, what is given to a bridegroom), marriage-money; a commodity; a measure of counting (= 20 গন্ডা). **পণ করা** *v.* to resolve. **পণ দেওয়া** *v.* to pay the dowry, to pay the bridegroom (or the bride) compulsory dowry or marriage-money. **পণ ধরা, পণ রাখা** *v.* to lay a wager, to bet, to stake. **পণ নেওয়া** *v.* to exact compulsory dowry or marriage-money. **কন্যাপণ** *n.* compulsory dowry or marriage-money given to the bride. **বরপণ** compulsory dowry or marriage-money given to the bridegroom. **~কর** *n.* betting tax. **~কিয়া** *n.* a table of reckoning by pans (পণ). **~প্রথা** *n.* the system of exacting dowry or marriage-money; (coll.) dowry system. **~বদ্ধ** *a.* bound by a promise, under pledge of.

পণকিয়া, পণপ্রথা see **পণ**।

পণব *n.* a kind of ancient tomtom.

পণবদ্ধ see **পণ**।

পণ্ড *a.* abortive, futile, vain, useless, fruitless; spoiled, foiled, marred. **পণ্ড করা** *v.* to render abortive, to bring to nothing, to baffle; to spoil, to foil, to mar, to undo. **~শ্রম** *n.* fruitless toil; abortive efforts.

পণ্ডিত *a.* learned, erudite; au fait, versed; wise; experienced; expert, skilled. □ *n.* a teacher of Bengali and Sanskrit literature and language, a pundit. **~চূড়ামণি** *n.* (lit. and fig.) the most precious jewel amongst learned men; the most learned man. **~প্রবর, ~বর** same as **পণ্ডিতশ্রেষ্ঠ**। **~মণ্ডলী** *n.* an assembly of learned people; the learned community, the intelligentsia. **~মূর্খ** *a.* versed in bookish learning but bereft of common sense, learned but unpractical; a wise fool, a wiseacre. □ *n.* such a man, a learned fool, a pedant. **~মানী** same as **পণ্ডিতম্মন্য**। **~শ্রেষ্ঠ** *a.* most learned. □ *n.* the most learned man. **পণ্ডিতম্মন্য, পণ্ডিতাভিমানী** *a.* one who unduly assumes an air of (superior) learning or wisdom. **পণ্ডিতম্মন্য ব্যক্তি** a wiseacre. **পণ্ডিতি** *n.* the post or office of a teacher of Sanskrit and Bengali; (sarcas). wisdom or learning (পণ্ডিতি ফলানো). □ *a.* of or like ancient pundits (পণ্ডিতি চালচলন) ; abounding in Sanskrit words and strictly following rules of Sanskrit grammar (পণ্ডিতি ভাষা).

পণ্য *a.* that which is to be or can be sold, marketable, saleable, salable. □ *n.* a commodity, an article for traffic, (*pl.*) merchandise; price, cost, charge, fare. **~জীবী** *a.* living on or engaged in trade or business. □ *n.* a trader, a tradesman, a merchant, a businessman; a dealer. **~দ্রব্য** *n.* a commodity; (*pl.*) merchandise, wares. **~বীথি, ~বীথী, ~বীথিকা** *n.* a row of shops; a market. **~শালা** *n.* a shop; a departmental store; a market; a manufactory. **~স্ত্রী** *n.* a woman of the street, a prostitute, a harlot. **পণ্যাগার** *n.* a warehouse. **পণ্যাঙ্গনা** same as **~স্ত্রী**। **পণ্যাজীব** same as **~জীবী**।

পতগ *n.* the bird.

পতঙ্গ *n.* the grasshopper; an insect; the fly; the moth; the bird; an arrow; the sun. **~নাশক** *a.* capable of killing insects, insecticidal. **পতঙ্গনাশক পদার্থ** insecticide. **~পরাগণ** *n.* (bot.) entomophily. **~পরাগত** *a.* (bot.) insect-pollinated. **~পরাগী** *a.* (bot.) entomophilous. **~বিজ্ঞান, ~বিদ্যা** *n.* entomology. **~বিজ্ঞানী, ~বিদ** *n.* an entomologist. **~বৃত্ত** *a.* impelled by the insectile desire of killing oneself in the fire of one's pleasure. **~বৃত্তি** *n.* the insectile impulse of killing oneself in the fire of one's pleasure. **~ভুক** *a.* insectivorous. **পতঙ্গভুক প্রাণী** an insectivore. **~ময়** *a.* infested with insects.

পতত্র *n.* a wing (of a bird). **পতত্রি, পতত্রী** *n.* the bird. **পতত্রিরাজ** *n.* Garuda the king of birds (গরুড়).

পতন *n.* act of falling or dropping, a fall; act or state of being shed or showered; a shower; decline, downfall (সাম্রাজ্যের পতন) ; overthrow, defeat (শত্রুর পতন) ; slaughter, death (যুদ্ধে পতন) ; destruction (দেহের পতন) ; capture (দুর্গের পতন) ; depravation, corruption (সাধুর পতন) ; a defect (ছন্দপতন) ; failing, omission ('স্খলন-পতন-ত্রুটি'). **পতন ঘটা** *v.* to have a fall; to fall, to drop; to be shed or showered; to decline, to have a downfall, to be overthrown or defeated or killed or destroyed or captured or depraved or corrupted; to be omitted. **পতন ঘটানো** *v.* to cause a fall; to fell; to drop; to shed or shower; to cause decline or downfall; to overthrow or defeat; to kill; to destroy; to capture; to deprave or corrupt; to cause an omission. **~শীল** *a.* falling, dropping; being shed or showered; declining; on the wane; perishable. **পতনোন্মুখ** *a.* about to fall or drop or decline; tottering.

পতপত, পত্‌পত্‌ *int.* suggesting: a fluttering noise as of a flying flag or a sail moving in air or a flying kite or of the wings of a flying bird.

পতর *n.* a metal hoop. **পতর আঁটা** *v.* to fasten a metal hoop (to).

পতাকা *n.* a banner, a standard, a flag, a pennon. **পতাকা অবনমিত বা অর্ধাবনমিত করা** *v.* to lower or half-mast a flag. **পতাকা উত্তোলন করা** *v.* to hoist of flag. **পতাকা নামিয়ে ফেলা** *v.* to strike a flag. **~দণ্ড** *n.* a flagstaff, a flagpole, a flagstick. **~ধারী, ~বাহী** *a.* carrying or bearing a flag or standard. □ *n.* a standard-bearer; a flag-bearer; an ensign; (fig.) an outstanding leader. **পতাকী** *a.* same as **পতাকাধারী**। □ *n.* (astrol.) a circle drawn for ascertaining the good and evil (usu. **পতাকীচক্র**). *fem. a.* **পতাকিনী**।

পতি *n.* a husband; a master, an employer, a boss; an owner; an overlord, a ruler, a king; a chief; a leader. **~গৃহ** *n.* the husband's house, a woman's husband's house. **পতিংবরা** *a.* & *n. fem.* one who selects or chooses one's husband. **~ঘাতিনী** *a.*& *n. fem.* one who murders or kills one's husband; one who is the cause of one's husband's death. **~ত্ব** *n.* the state of being a husband; state of being a master or employer or boss; ownership; overlordship, rulership, kingship; office or post of a chief; leadership. **পতিত্বে বরণ করা** *v.* to accept or take as one's husband. ~ত্যাগ *n.* act of deserting or divorcing one's husband. ~দেবতা *n.* one's husband regarded as one's deity. ~পরায়ণা *a. fem.* extremely devoted (and faithful) to one's husband. ~-পত্নী *n.* husband and wife. ~-পুত্র *n.* a husband and a son or sons. ~পুত্রহীনা *a.* deprived of both husband and son. ~প্রাণা *a. fem.* one who looks upon one's husband as one's life; one who can hardly live without one's husband, extremely devoted to one's husband. ~বত্নী *a. fem.* having one's husband living. ~বিয়োগ *n.* death of one's husband. ~বিরহ *n.* separation (temporary or permanent) from one's husband. ~বিরহিণী *a. fem.* separated (temporarily or permanently) from one's husband. ~ব্রতা *a. fem.* one who has taken the vow of serving one's husband; extremely devoted to one's husband. ~মতী *a. fem.* having a master or ruler. (পতিমতী পৃথ্বী). ~সেবা *n.* serving one's husband. ~হীনা *a.* widowed. পতিহীনা নারী a widow.

পতিত *a.* fallen, dropped; shed; showered; declined; downfallen; overthrown, defeated; killed, slain; depraved; degenerated; guilty of a failing or lapse; depressed (পতিত জাতি) ; socially cast out, excommunicate (সমাজে পতিত) ; outcasted (জাতে পতিত) ; uncultivated, fallow (পতিত জমি) ; deserted or unoccupied (পতিত ভিটা). পতিত করা *v.* to cast out from the society, to excommunicate; to outcaste. পতিত হওয়া *v.* to fall, to drop; to be shed or showered; to be guilty of a failing or lapse; to be cast out or excommunicated; to be outcasted. ~পাবন *a.* one who delivers sinners from damnation. *fem.* ~পাবনী ।

পতিতা *a. fem.* gone astray from the path of reghteousness and chastity; unchaste; taken to harlotry. □ *n.* a fallen woman; a prostitute, a harlot. ~বাদ *n.* reclamation of fallow land or wastes. ~বৃত্তি *n.* prostitution. পতিতোদ্ধার *n.* redemption or rescue of the sinful.

পত্তন *n.* a city, a town, a port; base, groundwork; construction; foundation, setting up, institution, inauguration; establishment; commencement, beginning, outset; lease or settlement (তালুকের পত্তন নেওয়া) ; length (কোঁচার পত্তন). পত্তন করা *v.* to lay the foundation of; to construct; to found, to institute, to inaugurate; to establish; to commence, to begin. পত্তন দেওয়া *v.* to lease out or settle. পত্তন নেওয়া *v.* to come into possession by dint of a lease or settlement. পত্তন-আরক্ষা *n.* the port-police. ~দার same as পত্তনিদার । ~পাল *n.* port commissioner. পত্তনি *n.* a piece of land leased out, a leasehold; a settlement. □ *a.* leased out, held by dint of a settled tenure. পত্তনিদার *n.* a lease-holder, a lessee, a tenure-holder.

পত্তর coll. corrup. of পত্র ।

পত্তি *n.* a foot-soldier, an infantryman.

পত্নী *n.* a wife. পত্নীত্যাগ করা *v.* to desert or divorce one's wife. ~বিয়োগ *n.* loss or death of one's wife.

পত্র *n.* a leaf (as of a book or a tree); a page (পত্রাঙ্ক) ; a foil or plate (তাম্রপত্র) ; a letter, a missive (পত্রপ্রাপ্তি) ; a piece of paper printed or written (আদেশপত্র) ; a document or deed (বায়নাপত্র) ; a written marriage-contract (usu. পাঁতিপত্র) ; (of a bird) a wing; a correlative of কাগজ, দলিল etc. (চিঠিপত্র, কাগজপত্র, পুঁথিপত্র) ; a collection, and similar things, etcetera (বিছানাপত্র, মালপত্র, খরচপত্র). পত্র করা *v.* to make a marriage-contract in writing. পত্র দেওয়া *v.* to send one a letter, to write a letter to. ~ক *n.* a leaf; (bot.) a pinna. ~কণ্টক *n.* (bot.) a leaf-spine. ~ক্ষত *n.* (bot.) a leaf-scar. ~দারক *n.* a saw. ~পত্রিকা *n. pl.* journals and newspapers. ~পাঠ *n.* act of reading a letter. □ *adv.* as soon as a letter is read; forthwith, at once, immediately. ~পুট *n.* a cup made of tree-leaves. ~বন্ধু *n.* a penfriend. ~বাহ, ~বাহক *n.* a carrier or bearer of a letter; a messenger; a postman. ~বাহী *a.* mail-carrying, mail. ~বিনিময় *n.* act of writing letters to one another; exchange of letters; correspondence. পত্রবিনিময় করা *v.* to write letters to one another; to correspond (with). ~বিন্যাস *n.* (bot.) phyllotaxy. ~মঞ্জরি *n.* (bot.) a leafstalk, a petiole. ~মুকুল *n.* (bot.) a leafbud. ~মূল *n.* (bot.) a leaf-base. ~মোচন *n.* (bot.) leaf-fall, defoliation. ~যোগে *adv.* by letter. ~রচনা *n.* act of writing or composing a letter; (bot.) foliation; (bot.) foliage. ~রন্ধ্র *n.* stoma. ~লেখা *n.* act of writing a letter; decorative paintings on one's person with sandal-paste or similar articles. ~হরিৎ *n.* (bot.) chlorophyl.

পত্রাঙ্ক *n.* (of a book) page-number, page-mark. **পত্রাঙ্কন** *n.* pagination. **পত্রাঙ্কিত** *a.* paginated. **পত্রাঙ্কিত করা, পত্রাঙ্ক দেওয়া** *v.* to paginate, to page.

পত্রাবলি, পত্রাবলী, পত্রালি, পত্রালী *n. pl.* letters collectively, correspondence; (of a tree) leaves collectively, foliage; (of a book) pages collectively; decorative painting on one's person with sandal-paste or similar articles. **পত্রালিকা** *n.* a tiny or concealed decorative painting on one's person with sandal-paste etc.

পত্রাশ্রয়ী *a.* epiphyllous.

পত্রিকা *n.* a letter, a missive, an epistle; a newspaper; a periodical, a magazine (দৈনিক পত্রিকা, মাসিক পত্রিকা) ; a paper containing a writing, a horoscope (জন্মপত্রিকা) ; (rare) a deed, a document; a leaf of young shoot (নবপত্রিকা).

পত্রী *a.* leafed; foliaceous; winged. □ *n.* a tree; a bird; an arrow; a letter, a missive; a newspaper, a periodical.

পত্রোত্তর *n.* the reply of a letter. **পত্রোত্তরে** *adv.* in reply to a letter.

পত্রোদ্গম *n.* (bot.) foliation.

পথ *n.* a passage, a path, a way, a road, a street, a route; doorway, an entrance; a mode or manner (সৎ পথে জীবনযাপন) ; a means, an expedient (মুক্তির পথ) ; range (দৃষ্টিপথ). **অর্ধপথে মিলিত হওয়া** to meet halfway; to compromise. **পথ করা** *v.* to make one's way; to make way. **পথ চলা** *v.* to travel on foot; to walk; to travel; (arch.) to wayfare. **পথ চাওয়া** *v.* to look forward to the coming of, to wait for or expect eagerly the coming of. **পথ ছাড়া** *v.* to get out of the way, to let one pass, to give one way, to make way for; to give up a way or practice (esp. a bad one). **পথ জোড়া** *v.* to block a way; to block one's way; to obstruct. **পথ দেওয়া** *v.* to make way for, to let one pass, to give one way. **পথ দেখা** *v.* to devise (ways and) means; to find a way out; (sarcas.) to go one's way, to depart; to find one's way. **পথ দেখানো** *v.* to show one the way; to guide; to lead the way; (sarcas.) to turn one out, to show one the door. **পথ ধরা** *v.* to follow a (particular) path; to adopt a (particular) method or practice; to set off, to depart, to take the road. **পথ মাড়ানো** *v.* to go or come by a particular way; (fig.) to associate with; (fig.) to come or go in the neighbourhood of. **পথে আসা** *v.* to yield, to submit; to follow the right track (at last). **পথে কাঁটা দেওয়া** *v.* (fig.) to block or obstruct a way. **পথে বসা** *v.* (fig.) to be utterly ruined or to be bankrupt, to have nothing to fall back on or to have none to turn to for support or help. **পথে বসানো** *v.* (fig.) to ruin utterly. **পথের কাঁটা** *n.* a thorn in one's side; (fig.) an obstacle, a hindrance. **পথের কুকুর** (fig.) a street beggar, (cp.) a street Arab. **পথের পথিক** a homeless person. **এক পথের পথিক** a fellow-traveller; (fig.) one who is in the same boat. ~কর *n.* a road-cess. **পথের সাথি** *n.* a companion in travel; a co-passenger. ~খরচ, ~খরচা *n.* travelling expenses; travelling allowance; (chiefly reli.) viaticum. ~চলতি *a.* passing by the way, passing (পথচলতি গাড়ি) ; wayfaring (পথচলতি লোক) ; happening or experienced during wayfaring (পথচলতি ঘটনা). **পথচলতি লোক** same as **পথচারী** । ~চারী *n.* a wayfarer, a pedestrian, a passer-by. *fem.* **পথচারিণী** । ~চ্যুত same as **পথভ্রষ্ট** । ~পার্শ্ব *n.* wayside, roadside. ~পার্শ্বস্থ *a.* wayside, roadside. ~প্রদর্শক *a.* showing one the way, leading the way, guiding or leading. □ *n.* a guide; a leader, a pioneer. ~প্রদর্শন *n.* act of showing one the way, guidance; act of leading the way. **পথপ্রদর্শন করানো** same as **পথ দেখানো** । ~প্রান্ত *n.* wayside, roadside; the end of a road, (cp.) roadhead. **~ভোলা, ~ভ্রষ্ট, ~ভ্রান্ত** *a.* strayed, lost; failing to ascertain the right path; confused, nonplussed; guilty of moral or religious lapse, deviating from the path of righteousness. **~রোধ** *n.* act of blocking a way, road block; act of obstructing (that makes movement difficult or impossible). **~শ্রম, পথের ক্লান্তি** *n.* the exertion or exhaustion from travel, wayweariness. **~শ্রান্ত** *a.* tired with constant walking, wayworn. **~হারা** same as **পথভ্রষ্ট**।

পথিক *n.* a wayfarer, a pedestrian, a passer-by; a traveller.

পথিকৃৎ *a.* preparing the way. □ *n.* a pioneer.

পথিপার্শ্বস্থ *a.* wayside, roadside.

পথিপার্শ্বে, (pop.) **পথপার্শ্বে** *adv.* by the roadside.

পথিমধ্যে *adv.* on the way, on the road, en route.

পথেঘাটে *adv.* anywhere and everywhere, at all places, in all parts; everywhere; here and there.

পথ্য *a.* wholesome. □ *n.* sick-diet; diet for the convalescent. **পথ্য করা** *v.* to take for the first time such diet as is suitable for a convalescent. **~বিচার** *n.* dietetics, dietary. **পথ্যাপথ্য** *n.* proper and improper diet, good and harmful diet.

পথ্যি coll. form of **পথ্য**।

পদ *n.* a leg, a foot; a pace, a footstep, a step; a footprint, a vestige; a line of poetry (ত্রিপদী, চতুর্দশপদী); a distich (চর্যাপদ); a song or lyric (বৈষ্ণব পদাবলি); a post, an office, an employment (পদপ্রার্থী); a position, a station, a rank (রাজপদ); favour, grace, shelter, refuge (as may be granted by a venerable person) (পদে রাখা); a place or habitation (জনপদ); (gr.) an inflected word, a part of speech, a word (নামপদ); a fourth part, a quarter (usu. পাদ); an item (বহু পদ রান্না হয়েছে); (arith. alg. & log.) a term (**বহুপদ** = a polynomial). **পদে থাকা** *v.* to continue somehow in a (particular)post or station, (pop.) to be in a tolerable condition; to be so so. **পদে পদে, প্রতি পদে** at every step. **~কর্তা** *n.* a composer of a distich or song or lyric, a poet. *fem.* **~কর্ত্রী** a poetess. **~ক্ষেপ** *n.* stepping or pacing; a pace, a step, a stride. **প্রতি পদক্ষেপে** at every step. **পদক্ষেপ করা** *v.* to set foot, to tread; to come. **~গর্ব, ~গৌরব** *n.* glory or dignity peculiar to an office, post, position, rank etc., a prerogative, official status. **~চারণ** *n.* pacing; strolling or walking. **পদচারণ করা** *v.* to pace; to stroll, to walk. **~চালনা** *n.* pacing; strolling or walking; kicking; (in football etc.) footwork. **পদচালনা করা** *v.* to pace; to stroll, to walk; to kick; to foot. **~চালিত** *a.* (of a lever or treadle) driven or operated or propelled by foot. **~চিহ্ন** *n.* a footprint, a footmark; a vestige. **~চ্ছায়া,** (loos.) **~ছায়া** *n.* shelter at one's feet; (fig.) favour, grace, gracious protection. **~চ্যুত** *a.* dismissed from office, dismissed, (sl.) sacked; cashiered. **পদচ্যুত করা** *v.* to dismiss, (sl.) to sack; to cashier. **~চ্যুতি** *n.* dismissal; cashierment. **~তল** *n.* the sole (of the foot). **পদতলে** *adv.* under foot (পদতলে পিষ্ট); at one's feet (পদতলে লুটিয়ে পড়া). **পদতলে পতিত হওয়া** *v.* to fall at the feet (in humble submission). **~ত্যাগ** *n.* resignation, relinquishment of a post or position or office, abdication. **পদত্যাগ করা** *v.* to resign, to submit resignation, to relinquish. **~ত্যাগ পত্র** *n.* letter of resignation. **~দলন** *n.* trampling; (fig.) act of disobeying or discarding slightingly. **পদদলন করা** *v.* to trample; (fig.) to disobey or discard slightingly. **~দলিত** *a.* trampled; slightingly disobeyed or discarded; (fig.) downtrodden. *fem.* **পদদলিতা**। **পদদলিত করা** same as **পদদলন করা**। **~ধূলি** *n.* dust of one's feet (placed on head by another in reverence). **~ধ্বনি** same as **পদশব্দ**। **~ন্যাস** *n.* (gr.) syntax. **~পঙ্কজ** *n.* feet conceived as lotuses, lotus-like beautiful feet. **~পরিচয়** *n.* parsing. **~পল্লব** *n.* feet conceived as petals, feet as tender as petals. **~পৃষ্ঠ** *n.* the instep. **~প্রান্ত** *n.* the corner of one's feet. **~প্রান্তে** *adv.* at one's feet. **~প্রার্থী** *a.* offering one's candidature for a post or employment, applying for a post or employment. □ *n.* an applicant, a candidate. *fem.* **~প্রার্থিনী**। **~বিক্ষেপ** *n.* act or manner of stepping (as in a dance or walking); pacing or walking. **~বিন্যাস** *n.* act or manner of stepping (as in a dance or walking); (gr.) syntax. **~বৃদ্ধি** *n.* an advancement in office or rank, promotion. **~ব্রজ** *n.* act of going on foot, act of walking. **~ব্রজে** *adv.* on foot. **~ভরে** *adv.* under the weight of one's feet (esp. when walking haughtily). **~ভ্রষ্ট** *a.* removed or dismissed from a position or office. **~মর্যাদা** *n.* the dignity of a post or position. **~যুগল** *n.* a pair of feet or legs. **~রজ, ~রেণু** same as **পদধূলি**। **~লেহন** *n.* act of licking one's feet; (fig.) act of cringing, footlicking, bootlicking. **~লেহী** *a.* licking one's feet; (fig.) cringing, footlicking, bootlicking. **পদলেহী ব্যক্তি** a cringeling, a footlicker, a bootlicker, a servile person. **~শব্দ** *n.* a footfall. **~সেবা** *n.* massaging one's feet and legs; (fig.) worship; (dero.) act of serving abjectly, cringing, footlicking, bootlicking. **~স্খলন** *n.* a false step; stumbling; (fig.) a moral lapse or slip or aberration. **পদস্খলন হওয়া** same as **পদস্খলিত হওয়া**। **~স্খলিত** *a.* stumbled; (fig.) lapsed, sinful. *fem.* **পদস্খলিতা**। **পদস্খলিত হওয়া** *v.* to stumble; (fig.) to lapse. **~স্থ** *a.* placed in a post or station; (pop.) in high office. **পদাংশ** *n.* (gr.) a syllable or part of a word. **পদাগ্র** *n.* the tip of a foot. **পদাঘাত** *n.* a kick. **পদাঘাত করা** *v.* to kick, to spurn. **পদাঙ্ক** *n.* a footprint, a footmark, a vestige. **পদাঙ্গুল** *n.* a toe. **পদাঙ্গুলাকার** *a.* (bot.) pedate. **পদানত** *a.* prostrate at one's feet; thoroughly subdued or dominated; submissive or dependent (পরের পদানত হয়ে জীবনধারণ). *fem.* **পদানতা**। **পদানুগমন** *n.* act of following one's footprints. **পদানুগমন করা** *v.* same as **পদানুবর্তী হওয়া**। **পদানুবর্তী** *a.* following one's footprints; act of following; (fig.) succeeding. *fem.* **পদানুবর্তিনী**। **পদানুবর্তী হওয়া** to follow one's footprints; to follow; (fig.) to succeed. **পদান্বয়** (gr.) syntax; parsing. **পদান্বয়ী** *a.* (gr.) prepositional. **পদান্বয়ী অব্যয়** (gr.) a preposition **পদাবনত** *a.* prostrate at one's feet; thoroughly subdued or dominated; submissive or dependent; demoted or degraded in rank or office. *fem.* **পদাবনতা** **পদাবনতি** *n.* demotion or degradation in rank or office. **পদাবলি, পদাবলী** *n.* a collection or anthology of songs or lyrics or distichs (বৈষ্ণব পদাবলী). **পদাভিলাষী** *a.* desirous of holding a (particular) post or office. *fem.* **পদাভিলাষিণী**। **পদাম্বুজ, পদারবিন্দ** same as **পদপঙ্কজ**। **পদার্পণ** *n.* (lit.) act of placing one's feet upon; (rare) stepping or pacing; (pop.) act of stepping in or coming. **পদার্পণ করা** *v.* to place or set one's feet upon; to step in, to come. **পদাশ্রয়** *n.* shelter at one's feet; (fig.) favour, grace, gracious protection. **পদাশ্রয় দেওয়া** *v.* to give shelter at one's feet; (fig.) to treat with favour or grace, to protect graciously. **পদাশ্রয়ী, পদাশ্রিত** *a.* sheltered at one's or another's feet; (fig.) enjoying favour or grace (of), favoured, graciously protected (by). *fem.* **পদাশ্রিতা**। **পদাহত** *a.* kicked, spurned; (fig.) grievously insulted.

পদক *n.* a locket; a medal. **~প্রাপ্ত** *a.* one who has won a medal, medalled. **পদকপ্রাপ্ত ব্যক্তি** a medallist.

পদবি *n.* a title, an appellation; a nickname; a family name, a surname.

পদাতি, পদাতিক *n.* a foot-soldier, an infantryman; a footman.

পদাধিকারে, পদাধিকারবলে *adv.* by virtue of one's office or position, ex-officio.

পদার্থ *n.* meaning of a word; connotation of a term; a thing, an article, a material, substance, intrinsic worth (লোকটার আর পদার্থ নেই) ; (log.) category; (phil. & sc.) matter; (sc.) an element. **~বিজ্ঞান, ~বিদ্যা** *n.* physics. **~বিজ্ঞানী, ~বিদ,** *a.* versed in physics. □ *n.* a physicist, a person skilled in physics.

পদোন্নতি *n.* advancement in rank or office, promotion.

পদ্ধতি *n.* a way, a path, a road; a method, a mode, a manner, a system, a rule; a custom, a practice; a row, a stretch, a series; a current; a line. **পদ্ধতি অনুসারে** methodically, systematically.

পদ্ম *n.* the lotus, the lily. □ *n.* & *a.* one thousand million. **~কাঁটা** *n.* a thorn on the stem of a lotus. **~কেশর** *n.* the filament of the lotus. **~গন্ধি** *a.* smelling like a lotus. **~দিঘি** *n.* a large pond full of lotuses, a lotus-pond. **~নাভ** *a.* having a lotus in one's navel. □ *n.* Vishnu (বিষ্ণু). **~নাল** *n.* lotus-stalk. **~নেত্র** *a.* lotus-eyed. **~পত্র** *n.* a leaf of a lotus-plant. **~পলাশ** *n.* a lotus-petal or a leaf of a lotus-plant. **~পলাশলোচন** *a.* having eyes as large as lotus-petals. □ *n.* Vishnu (বিষ্ণু). **~পাণি** *a.* having a lotus in one's hand. □ *n.* Brahma (ব্রহ্মা) ; the sun or Sun-god; Buddha. **~বন** *n.* a clump of lotus. **~বীজ** *n.* lotus-seed. **~মধু** *n.* essence or honey of the lotus. **~মুখী** *a. fem.* having a face as beautiful or sweet as a lotus. **~যোনি** *a.* born out of a lotus. □ *n.* Brahma (ব্রহ্মা). **~রাগ** *n.* ruby; spinel. **~লোচন** *a.* lotus-eyed.

পদ্মা *n.* goddess Lakshmi (লক্ষ্মী) ; Manasa (মনসা) the snake-goddess; a river of Eastern Bengal.

পদ্মাকর *n.* a large pond full of lotuses, a lotus-pond.

পদ্মাক্ষ *a.* lotus-eyed. □ *n.* the lotus-seed.

পদ্মাপুরাণ *n.* a legend in verse narrating the glory of Padma (পদ্ম) or Manasa (মনসা) the snake-goddess.

পদ্মাবতী *n.* Manasa (মনসা) the snake-goddess.

পদ্মালয়া *a.* living in a lotus. □ *n.* goddess Lakshmi (লক্ষ্মী).

পদ্মাসন *n.* a particular posture of yogic sitting; one seated in this posture; an appellation of Brahma (ব্রহ্মা). **পদ্মাসনা** *a.* seated on a lotus. □ *n.* goddess Lakshmi (লক্ষ্মী).

পদ্মাসীনা *a. fem.* seated on a lotus. *masc.* **পদ্মাসীন**।

পদ্মিনী *n.* a collection of lotuses; a clump of lotuses; (inc.) the lotus; a woman belonging to the best of the four physical categories from the sexual point of view. **~কান্ত, ~বল্লভ** *n.* the sun.

পদ্য *n.* a verse, a poem; poetry.

পনরো var. of **পনেরো**।

পনস *n.* the jack-fruit; the jack-tree.

-পনা *sfx.* denoting: showy or feverish practice or imitation, –ness (গিন্নিপনা, গুণপনা).

পনির *n.* cheese.

পনেরো *n.* & *a.* fifteen. **~ই** *a.* (of the days of a month) fifteenth. □ *n.* the fifteenth day of a month, the fifteenth.

পন্থ *n.* (poet. & obs.) a way, a path ('পন্থ বিজন অতি ঘোর').

পন্থা *n.* a way, a path; a means, an expedient (উদ্ধারের পন্থা) ; a system of religious practice (তান্ত্রিক পন্থা) ; a manner or mode or style or school. **~নুসরণ** *n.* act of following a particular path or system or mode.

পন্থানুসারী *a.* following or obeying a particular path or system or mode.

পন্থী *a.* (used as a *sfx.*) belonging to a particular school or religious community (নানকপন্থী), following a particular doctrine (প্রাচীনপন্থী), following a particular style or mode (রবীন্দ্রপন্থী), -ist.

পন্নগ *n.* the snake, the serpent; the reptile; the lizard. *fem.* **পন্নগী**।

পবন *n.* wind, air; the Wind-god (cp. Aeolus, Aiolos) (also **পবনদেবতা**). **~গতি, ~বেগ** *n.* the speed of the wind, the fast pace of the wind. **~নন্দন, পবনাত্মজ** *n.* (myth.) Hanuman (হনুমান) the son of the Wind-god. **~বেগে** *adv.* with the speed of the wind, as fast as wind. **~হিল্লোল** *n.* a gentle undulating current of air.

পবিত্র *a.* sacred, holy; sanctimonious; sanctified; pure, clean; virtuous. *fem.* **পবিত্রা**। **~তা** *n.* sacredness, holiness; sanctity; purity, cleanliness; virtuousness. **পবিত্রিত, পবিত্রীকৃত** *a.* sanctified, consecrated, made holy or sacred; purified, cleaned. **পবিত্রীকরণ** *n.* sanctification; purification, cleansing.

পমেটম *n.* pomatum, pomade.

পয় *n.* auspiciousness, luck; good fortune.

পয়ঃ *n.* milk; water. **~প্রণালী** *n.* a drain, gutter; a watercourse.

পয়গম্বর *n.* (Mus.) a human being accredited as a messenger of God, a prophet.

পয়জার *n.* a loose shoe fixed to the foot only by the vamp, a slipper.

পয়দল rare var. of **পায়দল**।

পয়দা *n.* birth; origination; act of begetting. **পয়দা করা** *v.* to beget. **পয়দা হওয়া** to be born.

পয়নালা, পয়নালি *n.* a drain, a gutter; a watercourse.

পয়মন্ত *a.* auspicious, lucky; having an auspicious or lucky aspect (পয়মন্ত চেহারা) ; bringing in good fortune (পয়মন্ত বউ).

পয়মাল *a.* spoiled; annihilated, destroyed.

পয়রা *a.* thin, watery (পয়রা গুড় = treacle made esp. out of date-palm juice).

পয়লা *n.* the first day of a month; the first. □ *a.* (of days of a month) first (পয়লা আষাঢ়) ; first or best (পয়লা নম্বর). **পয়লা নম্বরের** *a.* the best or the worst (পয়লা নম্বরের চ্যালা, পয়লা নম্বরের শত্রু).

পয়সা *n.* a pice (= 1/100 rupee; formerly 1/64 rupee); money (বাবুগিরির পয়সা) ; wealth. **পয়সা করা** *v.* to acquire or earn wealth, to make money; to amass money or heap up riches. **~ওয়ালা** *a.* moneyed, wealthy, rich. **~কড়ি** *n.* cash money; wealth. **আধ-পয়সা** *n.* half-a-pice. **সিকি পয়সা** a quarter pice. **পয়সার কাজ** work that yields money, profitable work.

পয়স্বিনী *a.* yielding milk, milch (পয়স্বিনী গাভী) ; full of water, yielding water. □ *n.* a milch-cow; a river.

পয়স্য *a.* produced of milk. **পয়স্য দ্রব্য** a milk-product.

পয়া same as **পয়মন্ত**।

পয়ার *n.* a metrical system of Bengali poetry in which each line consists of fourteen letters or syllables; a verse composed in this metre.

পয়োদ *n.* the cloud.

পয়োধর *n.* the cloud; the mammary gland of women; the coconut. **পয়োধরী, পয়োধরা** *n.* a woman (esp. one having well-shaped breasts).

পয়োধি *n.* the ocean, the sea.

পয়োনালি same as **পয়নালা**।

পয়োনিধি same as **পয়োধি**।

পয়োমুক *n.* the cloud.

পয়োমুখ *a.* sweet-tongued.

পর[১], পর contr. of **উপর** ('মাথার পরে দেয়নি তুলে বাস').

পর[২] coll. contr. of প্রহর (তিনপর বেলা).

-পর[৩] *a.* used as a *sfx.* denoting: devoted to, observant of, -ish, -ous, -ly (স্বার্থপর, ন্যায়পর).

পর[৪] *a.* another, other, different; unrelated, not one's relation or kindred (সে আমার পর নয়) ; supreme, chief, best, absolute (পরব্রহ্ম). □ *n.* an enemy, a foe (পরন্তপ) ; a person who is not present on the spot, a third person (পরচর্চা) ; one who is not a kindred, a stranger (পরভৃৎ) ; God. □ *adv.* then, after (অতঃপর, পরবর্তী). **পরের ধনে পোদ্দারি করা** (fig.) to spend another's money as one's own; (fig.) a steward brags of the property he looks after as if it were his own.

পরওয়া alt. spell. of **পরোয়া**।

পরওয়ানা, পরোয়ানা *n.* a warrant, a writ; a summons. **পরওয়ানা জারি করা** to serve or issue a process or writ.

পরক *a.* alien.

পরকলা *n.* glass; a lens; a mirror.

পরকাল *n.* the world beyond death, the beyond, the hereafter, the eternal world; the future (পরকাল ঝরঝরে). **পরকাল খাওয়া, পরকাল ঝরঝরে করা, পরকাল নষ্ট করা** *v.* to ruin one's future; to cause to go to the bad, to deprave; to consign to spiritual damnation. **পরকালের কাজ** an act of piety. **পরকালের চিন্তা** spiritual meditation.

পরকাশ poet. corrup. of **প্রকাশ**।

পরকীকরণ *n.* alienation.

পরকীয় *a.* relating to or belonging to another (opp. to own), foreign, alien. **পরকীয়া** *a. fem.* of **পরকীয়**। □ *n. fem.* a lady-love who is either unmarried or married to somebody else; a concubine. **পরকীয়া প্রেম** *n.* love with a person married to somebody else. **পরকীয়াবাদ** *n.* a doctrine of the Vaishnava (বৈষ্ণব) philosophy of love.

পরক্ষণ *n.* the next moment.

পরখ *n.* test; trial; experiment; examination. **পরখ করা,** (poet.) **পরখা** *v.* to test; to try; to experiment; to examine.

পরগনা *n.* a former administrative division in India, a pargana.

পরগাছা *n.* (bot.) a parasitic plant, a parasite; (fig.) a hanger-on, a sycophant, a parasite.

পরগ্লানি *n.* slandering, backbiting, gossip; scandal.

পরঘরি *a.* (lit.) of a person living in the house of somebody else; (fig.) dependent on others, sheltered by others.

পরচর্চা *n.* discussion about others behind their back; slandering, backbiting, gossip, scandal-mongering. **পরচর্চা করা** *v.* to discuss others; to slander, to gossip about others.

পরচা *n.* a settlement record.

পরচুলা, (coll.) **পরচুলো** *n.* false or artificial hair, a wig, a periwig. **পরচুলা-পরা** *a.* wigged. **পরচুলা পরা** *v.* to put on a wig, to periwig oneself.

পরচ্ছন্দ *n.* another's will or pleasure. □ *a.* guided by or depending on or dominated by another's will or pleasure. **পরচ্ছন্দানুবর্তী** *a.* same as **পরচ্ছন্দ** (*a.*) *fem.* **পরছন্দানুবর্তিনী** ।

পরচ্ছিদ্র *n.* another's fault or weak point. **পরচ্ছিদ্রান্বেষণ** *n.* fault-finding; captiousness. **পরচ্ছিদ্রান্বেষণ করা** *v.* to find fault with others, to seek a hole in another's coat. **পরচ্ছিদ্রান্বেষী** *a.* fault-finding; captious. *fem.* **পরচ্ছিদ্রান্বেষিণী** ।

পরজন্ম *n.* the next birth; life after the present one.

পরজীবী *a.* parasitic, parasitical. □ *n.* a parasitic plant or organism, a parasite. **পরজীবিতা** *n.* parasitism. **পরজীবীয়** *a.* parasitic.

পরটা alt. spell. of **পরোটা** ।

পরত[1] *n.* a layer, a flake, a plait, a fold. **পরতে পরতে** *adv.* in every layer.

পরত[2] *adv.* from or in or by another.

পরতন্ত্র same as **পরবশ** ।

পরতাপ poet. corrup. of **প্রতাপ** ।

পরত্র *adv.* in the world beyond death, in the life beyond; in future.

পরদা *n.* a screen, a curtain; a veil, a zenana, purdah (পরদাপ্রথা) ; a thin skin or membrane, a film (চোখের পরদা) ; a covering; a layer, a strip, a flake (এক পরদা চামড়া) ; (of a musical instrument) a bridge or key; (of voice) a scale (সুরের পরদা). **~নশিন** *a.* (*fem.*) living behind the purdah, living in a zenana. **~প্রথা** *n.* the purdah-system. **চোখের পরদা** (fig.) sense of shame, sense of delicacy.

পরদার *n.* another's wife. **~গমন** *n.* the offence of cohabiting with another's wife; adultery. **পরদার গমন করা** *v.* to cohabit with another's wife, to violate another's marriage-bed, to commit adultery. **~গামী, পারদারিক** *a.* cohabiting with another's wife; adulterous.

পরদিন *adv.* & *n.* next day, the following day.

পরদুঃখ *n.* another's affliction or distress. **~কাতর** *a.* feeling pain at another's affliction, compassionate, commiserated. *fem.* **~কাতরা** । **~কাতরতা** *n.* compassion, commiseration.

পরদেশ *n.* a foreign country, a foreign land. **পরদেশি,** (poet.) **পরদেশিয়া** *a.* inhabiting a foreign land; foreign. □ *n.* a foreigner.

পরদ্বেষ *n.* malice, ill-will, spite. **পরদ্বেষী, পরদ্বেষ্টা** *a.* malicious, bearing ill-will, spiteful. *fem.* **পরদ্বেষিণী** ।

পরদ্রব্য *n.* another's goods or property, what belongs to another.

পরধন *n.* another's money or wealth or property. **পরধন গ্রহণ করা** *v.* to rob another's money or wealth or property; to misappropriate another's money or wealth or property, to defalcate, to embezzle.

পরধর্ম *n.* another's religion; a religion which is not one's own; a calling or profession or job which is not one's own. **~গ্রহণ** *n.* embracing a faith or religion not one's own; apostasy.

পরধর্মদ্বেষী *a.* hostile to others' religion or creed, intolerant of others' religion or of religion not one's own.

পরন *n.* act of putting on or wearing. **পরনের কাপড়** clothing, garments or clothes for wearing.

পরনারী *n.* somebody else's wife, another's wife. **পরনারী হরণ করা** *v.* to abduct another's wife (esp. for immoral purpose).

পরনিন্দা *n.* slander, vilification, animadversion. **পরনিন্দা করা** *v.* to slander, to animadvert.

পরনির্ভর *a.* dependent on others, dependent on somebody else. **~তা** *n.* dependence on others.

পরনিষেক *n.* cross-fertilization; cross-impregnation.

পরন্তপ *a.* one who conquers or vanquishes an enemy, victorious; (fig.) self-restrained.

পরন্তু *conj. & adv.* moreover; on the other hand; but, still, notwithstanding.

পরপতি *n.* another's husband; the Supreme Lord, God ('তোরা পরপতি সনে সদাই গোপনে সতত করিবি লেহা').

পরপত্নী same as **পরদার**।

পরপদ *n.* (fig.) the high place or eminent position (usu. of an enemy); (gr.) the following or latter word. **পরপদ লেহন করা** to lick a person's boots or shoes, to cringe before a person, to be abject or servile, to fawn on.

পরপর *adv.* one after another; successively; consecutively; gradually; side by side.

পরপার *n.* the other or opposite bank or shore; the world beyond death, the next world, the beyond.

পরপালিত *a.* brought up or fostered by others, fostered or brought up, by people other than one's parents.

পরপীড়ক *a.* oppressing others; tyrannous. □ *n.* an oppressor, a tyrant; a bully.

পরপীড়ন *n.* act of oppressing others, tyranny. **পরপীড়ন করা** *v.* to oppress others, to tyrannize; to bully.

পরপুরুষ *n.* a man other than one's husband; the Supreme Being, God; (dial.) the next or future generation. **~গামিনী** *a. fem.* committing adultery; adulterous.

পরপুষ্ট *a.* fostered or brought up or nourished by a stranger. □ *n.* the cuckoo. **পরপুষ্টা** *a. fem.* of **পরপুষ্ট**। □ *n.* a prostitute, a harlot.

পরপূর্বা *a. fem.* one who was married or betrothed to (and subsequently estranged from) another.

পরব *n.* a feast or festival (esp. a holy one); a fiesta.

পরবর্তী *a.* subsequent, next, following, ensuing, succeeding. *fem.* **পরবর্তিনী**।

পরবশ *a.* subject to another; subject; subservient, dependent; affected with, overcome by (ক্রোধপরবশ). **পরবশতা, পরবশত্ব** *n.* subjection to another; subjection, subservience, dependence; the state of being enslaved or overcome by.

পরবাদ[১] poet. corrup. of **প্রবাদ**।

পরবাদ[২] *n.* animadversion, censure; retort; reply, answer.

পরবাস[১] *n.* another's residence or home or abode or homeland.

পরবাস[২], **পরবাসী, পরবেশ** poet. corruptions of **প্রবাস, প্রবাসী** and **প্রবেশ** respectively.

পরব্রহ্ম *n.* the Absolute Being, the Supreme Being, God.

পরভাগ্যোপজীবী *a.* living upon another's destiny or fortune. *fem.* **পরভাগ্যোপজীবিনী**।

পরভাত poet. corrup. of **প্রভাত**।

পরভৃত same as **পরপুষ্ট**।

পরভৃৎ *n.* one who or that which rears others; the crow.

পরভোজী *a.* heterotrophic, parasitical.

পরম *a.* first, primordial, true, real (পরম কারণ) ; best, chief, prime, supreme, principal, highest, greatest, absolute, final (পরম পুরুষ) ; of the highest degree, greatest or worst (পরম সুখ, পরম দুঃখ) ; (sc.) absolute. **পরম আপ্যায়িত** most cordially received; highly gratified or pleased. **পরম একক** (phys.) absolute unit. **পরম কারণ** *n.* Final or Ultimate Cause, God. **পরম কারুণিক** *a.* most merciful or kind, most gracious. **পরম ক্রম** (phys.) absolute scale. **~গতি** *n.* the most blessed state after death, beatitude, heavenly bliss; salvation. **~গুরু** *n.* the supreme or greatest preceptor; the most venerable preceptor; the absolute lord (পতি পরম গুরু). **পরম ঘনত্ব, পরম ঘনাঙ্ক** (phys.) absolute density. **~তত্ত্ব** *n.* final knowledge; (phil.) reality; secrets, mystery; the Absolute Being,

God. ~পদ same as পরমগতি। ~পদার্থ *n.* intrinsic essence; the Final Cause, God. ~পিতা *n.* the Heavenly Father, God. ~পুরুষ *n.* the Absolute Being, God; a divine person, a saint. পরম প্রসার, পরম প্রসারণ (phys.) absolute expansion. ~বিত্ত *n.* a great treasure; an object of the highest value; an object of joy and hope. ~ব্রহ্ম *n.* the Absolute Being, God. পরম মান (phys.) absolute measurement. পরম শূন্য (phys.) absolute zero. ~সুন্দর *a.* most beautiful. *fem.* পরমসুন্দরী। পরম স্পন্দনসংখ্যা (phys.) absolute frequency of vibration. ~হংস *n.* a saint who has attained final knowledge and sanctity.

পরমত *n.* another's or others' view or opinion; a view or opinion not one's own. ~সহিষ্ণু *a.* tolerant of others' views or opinions. ~সহিষ্ণুতা *n.* tolerance or toleration of others' views or opinions. পরমতাবলম্বী *a.* guided by or adopting another's view; having no opinion of one's own. *fem.* পরমতাবলম্বিনী।

পরমা *fem.* of পরম। পরমা গতি same as পরম গতি। পরমা প্রকৃতি same as আদ্যাশক্তি। ~সুন্দরী *n.* & *a. fem.* extremely handsome, very beautiful.

পরমাণু *n.* an atom. পরমাণু-অঙ্ক *n.* (phys.) an atomic number. পরমাণু তত্ত্ব, ~বাদ *n.* the atomic theory; (phil & psy.) atomism. ~তাত্ত্বিক, ~বাদী *n.* an atomist. □ *a.* atomistic. পরমাণু তাপ *n.* (phys.) atomic heat. পরমাণু বোমা *n.* the atom bomb. পরমাণু ভার *n.* (phys.) atomic weight.

পরমাত্মা *n.* the Supreme Being or Spirit or Soul, God.

পরমাত্মীয় *a.* closely related; intimate. □ *n.* a close relative; an intimate friend, a great friend. *fem.* পরমাত্মীয়া। পরমাত্মীয়তা *n.* close relation; intimate friendship.

পরমাদর *n.* great love or attachment; great care or attention; great cordiality; very cordial reception.

পরমাদৃত *a.* greatly loved; highly treasured; punctiliously cared for or attended to; received with great cordiality. *fem.* পরমাদৃতা।

পরমান, পরমাণ poet. corruptions of প্রমাণ।

পরমানন্দ *n.* deepest delight; ecstatic joy, ecstasy; heavenly bliss, beatitude. পরমানন্দিত *a.* extremely or greatly delighted; ecstatically joyful.

পরমান্ন *n.* a sweet dish prepared by boiling rice in milk with sugar and other ingredients, sweet rice-porridge.

পরমায়ু *n.* longevity; life. পরমায়ু ক্ষয় হওয়া *v.* to have one's life-blood running out; to have one's life or longevity (being) cut down; to droop; to approach one's death.

পরমারাধ্য *a.* warranting greatest worship or devotion; most venerable. *fem.* পরমারাধ্যা।

পরমার্থ *n.* the greatest object; the greatest truth, reality; God; religion or spiritual truth. ~চিন্তা *n.* spiritual meditation; meditation about God or reality. ~তত্ত্ব *n.* (phil.). truths about reality; theological truths; spiritual truths.

পরমুখাপেক্ষা, পরমুখাপেক্ষিতা *n.* dependence on another. পরমুখাপেক্ষী *a.* dependent on another. *fem.* পরমুখাপেক্ষিণী।

পরমেশ, পরমেশ্বর *n.* the Supreme Lord, God. পরমেশ্বরী same as আদ্যাশক্তি।

পরমৈশ্বর্য *n.* great wealth; the most valuable treasure or acquisition; a great éclat.

পরমোৎকর্ষ *n.* highest excellence.

পরমোৎকৃষ্ট *a.* most excellent.

পরমোন্নত *a.* elevated or developed or uplifted to the highest degree; advanced to the farthest extent. পরমোন্নতি *n.* highest altitude, zenith; highest elevation; culmination; greatest development or uplift; farthest advancement.

পরম্পর *a.* serial, successive (পরম্পর বিষয়সমূহ). পরম্পরা *n.* a serial succession or sequence; a series. পরম্পরায়, পরম্পরাক্রমে *adv.* serially; seriatim, one after another; in regular succession. পরম্পরীণ *a.* serial, successive.

পররশ্মি *n.* (phys.) a positive ray.

পররাষ্ট্র *n.* a foreign state or country. ~নীতি *n.* (pol.) foreign policy. পররাষ্ট্র দপ্তর *n.* a foreign office. পররাষ্ট্র মন্ত্রক *n.* the ministry of external affairs. ~মন্ত্রী *n.* the minister of external affairs. ~সচিব *n.* a foreign secretary.

পরলোক *n.* the abode of the dead, the world beyond death, the beyond; death. **~গত, ~প্রাপ্ত** *a.* gone to heaven, dead, deceased. **~গমন, ~প্রাপ্তি** *n.* death. **পরলোকগমন করা** *v.* to die.

পরশ, পরশন poet. corruptions of **স্পর্শ** and **স্পর্শন** respectively.

পরশপাথর, পরশমণি *n.* a philosopher's stone.

পরশু[1] *n.* & *adv.* day after tomorrow; day before yesterday.

পরশু[2] *n.* a battle-axe; a scimitar. **~রাম** *n.* the sixth incarnation of Vishnu (বিষ্ণু) who carried a battle-axe with which he exterminated kshatriyas (ক্ষত্রিয়) from the face of the earth for twenty-one times.

পরশ্ব *n.* & *adv.* (for.) day after tomorrow; day before yesterday.

পরশ্রমজীবী *a.* living upon the labour of others; living by exploitation; parasitic.

পরশ্রীকাতর *a.* mortified at another's good or prosperity, pained at another's good fortune or weal, envious. *fem.* **পরশ্রীকাতরা** । **~তা** *n.* envy.

পরসঙ্গ[1] poet. corrup. of **প্রসঙ্গ** ।

পরসঙ্গ[2] *n.* association with others, fellowship, company.

পরসাদ poet. corrup. of **প্রসাদ** ।

পরস্ত্রী same as **পরনারী** ।

পরস্পর *a.* reciprocal, mutual, one another, each other. □ *adv.* reciprocally, mutually, one another, each other. □ *pro.* one another; each other. **~বিরোধ** *n.* mutual opposition; contradiction, antagonism. **~বিরুদ্ধ, ~বিরোধী** *a.* mutually opposed or contradictory, antagonistic. **~বিরোধিতা** *n.* same as **পরস্পরবিরোধ** ।

পরস্ব *n.* another's property or wealth or money, what belongs to another. **~হরণ, পরস্বাপহরণ** *n.* act of robbing what belongs to another; misappropriation of another's property or money. **~হারী, পরস্বাপহারী** *a.* given to or guilty of robbing what belongs to another; given to or guilty of misappropriating another's property or money.

পরস্মৈপদ *n.* (Sans. gr.) any of the verb-inflections used in the active voice; (hum.) another's money or wealth or property. **পরস্মৈপদী** *a.* (Sans. gr.) used in the active voice or having an inflection used in the active voice; (hum.) done for another (পরস্মৈপদী ঝামেলা) ; transferring or transferred to another, entrusted to another belonging to another (পরস্মৈপদী টাকা).

পরহস্তগত *a.* passed into another's possession; possessed by another.

পরহিংসক *a.* malicious, spiteful; envious.

পরহিংসা *n.* malice, spite, envy.

পরহিত *n.* the good of others; (loos. but pop.) public welfare; philanthropy, benevolence. **~কামী** *a.* wishing good to others, doing good to others; philanthropic, benevolent. **~ব্রত** *n.* devotion to the welfare of others, benevolence. **~ব্রতী** *a.* devoted to doing good to others; working for public welfare; altruistic. **~সাধন** *n.* act of doing good to others; social service; philanthropy, benevolence.

পরহিতাকাঙ্ক্ষী same as **পরহিতৈষী** ।

পরহিতৈষণা *n.* an effort to do good to others; an effort for public welfare; altruism.

পরহিতৈষী *a.* willing and endeavouring to do good to others; endeavouring for public welfare; altruistic.

পরা-[1] *pfx.* denoting : excessiveness, contrariety, opposition etc. (পরাজয়).

পরা[2] *fem.* of **-পর**[3] and **পর**[4] ।

পরা[3] *a. fem.* supreme, primordial (পরা প্রকৃতি) ; highest; final (পরা বিদ্যা) ; (elec.) positive.

পরা[4] *v.* to put on, to wear (জামা পরা) ; to put, to paint (টিপ পরা, কাজল পরা) ; to tie (ঘড়ি পরা). □ *a.* wearing, dressed in; bearing, painted with; having tied or fastened (to).

পরাকরণ *n.* act of looking down on, contempt, slight, neglect.

পরাকাষ্ঠা *n.* highest excellence; extreme altitude or limit; acme, zenith; (often iron.) culmination.

পরাকৃত *a.* looked down on, despised, slighted, neglected.

পরাক্রম *n.* strength, power, might; prowess, valour; heroism.

পরাক্রমশালী, পরাক্রমী, পরাক্রান্ত *a.* strong, powerful, mighty; valorous; heroic. *fem.* **পরাক্রমশালিনী, পরাক্রান্তা**।

পরাগ *n.* pollen, farina. **~কেশর** *n.* a stamen. **~কোষ** *n.* anther. **~ধানী** same as **পরাগকোষ**। **~মিলন, ~যোগ** *n.* pollination. **ইতর পরাগযোগ** *n.* cross-pollination. **স্বপরাগযোগ** *n.* self-pollination. **~স্থালী** *n.* a pollen-sac. **পরাগিত** *a.* pollinated. **পরাগিত করা** *v.* to pollinate.

পরাঙ্মুখ *a.* turning away (from); averse (to); disinclined; shunning, opposed; unfavourable; desisting from. **পরাঙ্মুখ হওয়া** *v.* to turn away from; to be averse or disinclined to; to shun, to avoid; to oppose; to disfavour; to desist from.

পরাজয় *n.* defeat. **পরাজয় বরণ করা** *v.* to court defeat. **পরাজয় স্বীকার করা** *v.* to acknowledge or own defeat; to give in, to yield. **পরাজয়ের গ্লানি** disgrace or ignominy or distress or anguish of defeat.

পরাজিত *a.* defeated, vanquished. *fem.* **পরাজিতা**। **পরাজিত করা** *v.* to defeat, to vanquish, to conquer.

পরাজেয় *a.* (of one) who can be defeated or worsted or vanquished.

পরাণুবীক্ষণ *n.* (phys.) an ultra microscope.

পরাত *n.* a large tray or saucer (usu. made of metal).

পরাৎপর *a.* higher than the highest, greater than the greatest; supreme. □ *n.* God.

পরাধিকার *n.* another's right or jurisdiction or domain or holding or property or control or domination. **~চর্চা** *n.* interference or meddling with other's affairs.

পরাধীন *a.* subject; dependent; subordinate; subjugated; subservient; dominated by another. *fem.* **পরাধীনা**। **~তা** *n.* subjection, bondage; dependence; subordination; subjugation; subservience; domination by another.

পরান poet. corrup. of **প্রাণ**।

পরানো *v.* & *n.* to cause to wear or put on, to dress; to harness (ঘোড়ার সাজ পরানো) ; to put, to paint (টিপ বা কাজল পরানো).

পরান্ন *n.* food given in charity by another, unearned or unpaid-for food. **~জীবী** *a.* living on food given by another; eating habitually at another's table; parasitic. □ *n.* a parasite. **~পালিত, ~পুষ্ট** *a.* nourished by food given by another. **~ভোজী** *a.* habitually eating at another's table.

পরাবর্ত *n.* exchange; interchange; transposition; return, retreat. **পরাবর্তক চুল্লী** reverberatory furnace. **পরাবর্তন** *n.* return; reflection. **পরাবর্তিত** *a.* turned back; returned; sent back.

পরাবিদ্যা *n.* knowledge about the Supreme Spirit; spiritual knowledge.

পরাবৃত্ত[1] *n.* (geom.) a hyperbola.

পরাবৃত্ত[2] *a.* returned, receded, retreated; fled. **পরাবৃত্তি** *n.* return, retreat; flight.

পরাভব *n.* defeat.

পরাভূত *a.* defeated, vanquished. *fem.* **পরাভূতা**।

পরামর্শ *n.* counsel; conference; consultation; advice. **পরামর্শ করা** *v.* to confer; to consult. **পরামর্শ দেওয়া** *v.* to counsel; to advise. **পরামর্শ নেওয়া** *v.* to consult; to take advice. **~দাতা** *n.* a counsellor; (in law) a counsel; a conferee; an adviser. **~সভা** *n.* a conference; a council.

পরামর্ষ *n.* tolerance, toleration; forbearance, forgiveness.

পরামানিক *n.* a barber (by caste or trade).

পরায়ণ *a.* (used as a *sfx.*) devoted to, attached to, addicted to, -ous (ঈশ্বরপরায়ণ, উদরপরায়ণ). *fem.* **পরায়ণা**।

পরায়ত্ত *a.* in possession or under control of another (পরায়ত্ত ধন).

পরার্থ *n.* the good or interest or need of others or another. **~পর, ~পরায়ণ** *a.* devoted to doing good to others, devoted to serving the interest or need of others; altruistic. *fem.* **~পরায়ণা**। **~পরতা** *n.* devotion to do good to others, devotion to serve the interest or need of others; benevolence; altruism. **~বাদ, পরার্থিতা** *n.* altruism. **পরার্থে** *adv.* for the sake of others or another.

পরার্ধ *n.* & *a.* hundred thousand million million.

পরাশ্রয় *n.* a house or shelter or refuge other than one's own. **পরাশ্রয়ী** *a.* resorting to another for shelter or refuge; (esp. bot.) parasitic, epiphytal (পরাশ্রয়ী

লতা). **পরাশ্রয়ী উদ্ভিদ** a parasite, an epiphyte. **পরাশ্রিত** *a.* sheltered or protected by another; maintained with food, clothing and shelter by another. *fem.* **পরাশ্রিতা** ।

পরাস্ত *a.* defeated, vanquished, overcome. **পরাস্ত করা** *v.* to defeat, to vanquish, to overcome, to conquer. **পরাস্ত হওয়া** *v.* to be defeated or vanquished or overcome.

পরাহ *n.* the next day.

পরাহত *a.* defeated, vanquished, overcome; obstructed, resisted, prevented; frustrated.

পরাহ্ন *n.* afternoon.

পরি[1] *pfx.* denoting : thoroughness, expensiveness, excessiveness, especiality, opposition, decrial etc.

পরি[2], (rej.) **পরী** *n. fem.* a fairy, a winged fairy.

পরিকর *n.* a companion or assistant; (also used as a *sfx.*) a girdle, a girth (বদ্ধপরিকর).

পরিকর্ম *n.* act of making one's toilet; dressing. **পরিকর্মা** *n.* a servant esp. one attending to toilet and clothes, a valet.

পরিকর্ষ *n.* remarkable improvement; (inc.) culture.

পরিকল্পক *n.* a planner; a deviser; a designer; a planning officer.

পরিকল্পনা, পরিকল্পন *n.* planning, devising, designing a plan, a design. **পরিকল্পনা করা** *v.* to plan, to devise, to contrive, to design. **পরিকল্পনাধিকারিক** *n.* a planning officer.

পরিকল্পিত *a.* planned, devised, contrived, designed; intended.

পরিকীর্ণ *a.* thoroughly or extensively scattered or strewn or spread out or diffused or pervaded.

পরিকীর্তন *n.* act of singing or narrating or praising or glorifying emphatically or in a special manner. **পরিকীর্তিত** *a.* sung or narrated or praised or glorified emphatically or in a special manner.

পরিকেন্দ্র *n.* circumcentre. **পরিকেন্দ্রিক, পরিকেন্দ্রী** *a.* circumcentric.

পরিক্রম, পরিক্রমণ *n.* walking or pacing or strolling, ambulation; travelling or traversing; act of travelling widely or thoroughly, peregrination; act of going round, circumambulation. **পরিক্রমণ করা** *v.* to walk, to pace, to stroll; to ambulate, to travel, to traverse, to travel widely or thoroughly, to peregrinate; to go round, to circumambulate. **পরিক্রমকাল** *n.* periodic time. **পরিক্রমা** *n.* act of going round, rotation (সূর্যপরিক্রমা), circumambulation; wide travelling, peregrination (তীর্থপরিক্রমা) ; (fig.) critical survey (সাহিত্যপরিক্রমা).

পরিক্লিষ্ট *a.* extremely distressed or afflicted or wearied.

পরিক্ষিপ্ত *a.* scattered; abandoned; surrounded.

পরিক্ষীণ *a.* extremely thin or dim or emaciated.

পরিক্ষেপ *n.* scattering; scattered state; abandonment; act or state of being surrounded; that which encloses, such as fencing, railing etc.

পরিখা *n.* a protective ditch around a rampart; a trench, a moat.

পরিগণক *n.* a reckoner, a computer, an enumerator.

পরিগণন, পরিগণনা *n.* thorough reckoning, computation, enumeration; consideration. **পরিগণনা করা** *v.* to reckon thoroughly, to compute, to enumerate; to consider or regard (as).

পরিগণিত *a.* thoroughly reckoned, computed, enumerated; considered or regarded (as). *fem.* **পরিগণিতা** ।

পরিগৃহীত *a.* solemnly taken, accepted; put on ; won; assumed.

পরিগ্রহ *n.* act of taking or accepting solemnly (দারপরিগ্রহ) ; act of putting on or wearing (বেশপরিগ্রহ) ; act of assuming (রূপপরিগ্রহ). **পরিগ্রহ করা** *v.* to take or accept solemnly; to put on, to wear; to assume.

পরিগ্রাহক *n.* one who takes or accepts solemnly; one who puts on or wears; one who assumes. *fem.* **পরিগ্রাহিকা** ।

পরিঘ *n.* a kind of iron cudgel used in war in ancient times.

পরিচয় *n.* acquaintance; familiarity; introduction; identity; particulars about one's identity such as name, address, lineage etc.; experience or practice (এ কাজের সঙ্গে পরিচয়) ; a sign, a token (প্রেমের পরিচয়) ; fame, reputation (সাহিত্যিক হিসাবে পরিচয়) ; love, amour ('নবপরিচয় কালিয়া বঁধুর সনে). **পরিচয় করা** *v.* to make an acquaintance (with), to acquaint oneself (with); to experience. **পরিচয় গোপন করা** *v.* to conceal one's identity; hide one's identity. **পরিচয় দেওয়া** *v.* to introduce, to give one's introduction; to reveal one's identity; to apprise. **পরিচয় নেওয়া** *v.* to ask for one's introduction; to get acquainted; to learn particulars or details (of). **~পত্র** *n.* a letter of introduction; credentials.

পরিচর *n.* a servant, an attendant; a companion; a nurse; a worshipper.

পরিচর্যা *n.* serving, waiting or attending upon; nursing; worship. **পরিচর্যা করা** *v.* to serve, to wait or attend upon; to nurse; to worship.

পরিচলন *n.* (phys.) convection.

পরিচায়ক *a.* introducing, introductory; prefatory; informing; indicative (of.) *fem.* **পরিচায়িকা**।

পরিচারক *n.* a servant, a serving-man, a valet; a varlet. **পরিচারিকা** *n. fem.* a maid-servant; a maid, a female domestic servant.

পরিচালক *a.* one who or that which drives or runs a vehicle etc.; conducting; managing, directing; leading or guiding; administering, ruling. □ *n.* a driver; a conductor; a manager; a director; a leader; an administrator; a ruler; a chief. **পরিচালক সমিতি** *n.* managing committee.

পরিচালন, পরিচালনা *n.* act of driving a vehicle etc.; conduction; management; direction; lead; administration; rule. **পরিচালনা করা** *v.* to drive or run; to conduct; to manage; to direct; to lead; to administer; to rule.

পরিচালিকা *fem.* of **পরিচালক**।

পরিচালিত *a.* driven, run; conducted; managed; directed; led; administrated; ruled.

পরিচিত *n.* acquainted; familiar; known; practised (পরিচিত কর্ম). **পরিচিতি** same as **পরিচয়**। **পরিচিত ব্যক্তি** an acquaintance.

পরিচিন্তন *n.* deep or careful thinking or deliberation; planning.

পরিচিন্তিত *a.* deeply or carefully thought out or deliberated; well-planned.

পরিচ্ছদ *n.* a covering; a dress; clothing; garment.

পরিচ্ছন্ন *a.* clean; tidy; neat, spruce; (of mind etc.) free from impurities or angularity; honest and candid. **~তা** *n.* cleanliness; tidiness; neatness; purity. honesty and candour.

পরিচ্ছিন্ন *a.* divided, parted; separated; severed; detached; limited, bounded; individualized; moderate.

পরিচ্ছেদ *n.* a part, a division; a section; (of books) a chapter; a limit (প্রাণান্তকর পরিচ্ছেদ) ; ascertainment; fixation.

পরিজন *n.* a member of a family; a dependent; a friend; a kinsman; a servant, an attendant. **~বর্গ** *n. pl.* the family circle.

পরিজ্ঞাত *a.* well-known, familiar; well acquainted, thoroughly cognizant or versed, au fait. **পরিজ্ঞাত থাকা** *v.* to know fully, to be fully aware.

পরিজ্ঞান *n.* thorough knowledge or acquaintance; insight.

পরিণত *a.* ripe; full-grown; mature (পরিণত বুদ্ধি) ; resulting in; turned or rendered into; converted to; advanced (পরিণত বয়স) ; arrived at the last stage. **পরিণত করা** *v.* to turn or render into. **পরিণত হওয়া** *v.* to result in or turn into. **পরিণতি** *n.* maturity; ultimate stage or state; conclusion, end; consequence. **পরিণত বয়সে** in old or advanced age. **~বয়স্ক** *a.* advanced in age or years.

পরিণদ্ধ *a.* tied; bound; attached, connected; encircled, girdled, girt.

পরিণয় *n.* marriage, wedding. (কারও) **পরিণয় হওয়া** to be married or wedded to. **~বন্ধন, ~সূত্র** *n.* marriage-tie, wedlock.

পরিণাম *n.* last stage or state; conclusion; consequence; change of state, transformation; future. **~দর্শী** *a.* foreseeing; farsighted. **~দর্শিতা** *n.* foresight; farsightedness. **~বাদ** *n.* the theory of evolution.

পরিণামে *adv.* finally, ultimately, in the end; in the long run; in future.

পরিণাহ *n.* width; contour.

পরিণীত *a.* married, wedded. *fem.* পরিণীতা।

পরিণেতা *n.* one who marries; a husband.

পরিণেয় *a.* marriageable; fit for marrying.

পরিতপ্ত *a.* very much heated; quite warm; extremely afflicted.

পরিতাপ *n.* lament; deep grief or regret; repentance, compunction; remorse. পরিতাপ করা *v.* to lament; to express deep grief. পরিতাপের বিষয় a lamentable affair; a matter of deep regret.

পরিতুষ্ট *a.* well satisfied or gratified; very pleased. *fem.* পরিতুষ্টা। পরিতুষ্ট করা *v.* to satisfy or gratify or please thoroughly. পরিতুষ্টি same as পরিতোষ।

পরিতৃপ্ত *a.* thoroughly satisfied or gratified. পরিতৃপ্ত করা *n.* to satisfy or gratify thoroughly. পরিতৃপ্তি *n.* thorough satisfaction or gratification.

পরিতোষ *n.* thorough satisfaction or gratification; deep pleasure. ~পূর্বক *adv.* with a great or thorough satisfaction; to the point of satiety or to one's heart's content (পরিতোষপূর্বক ভোজন করা). ~জনক *a.* thoroughly or highly satisfactory or gratifying.

পরিত্যক্ত *a.* given up; left off; abandoned; deserted; relinquished; quitted; renounced; omitted. *fem.* পরিত্যক্তা।

পরিত্যাগ, পরিত্যজন *n.* act of giving up or leaving off; abandonment; desertion; relinquishment; quittance; renouncement, renunciation; omission. পরিত্যাগ করা *v.* to give up; to leave off; to abandon; to desert; to relinquish, to quit; to renounce; to leave out, to omit.

পরিত্যাজ্য *a.* fit to be given up or left off or abandoned or deserted or relinquished or quitted or renounced or omitted. *fem.* পরিত্যাজ্যা।

পরিত্রাণ *n.* rescue, deliverance; (theol.) salvation; liberation; relief; exemption; riddance. পরিত্রাণ করা *v.* to rescue, to deliver; (esp. in theol.) to save; to liberate; to relieve. পরিত্রাণ পাওয়া *v.* to be rescued; (esp. in theol.) to be saved; to be liberated or relieved or exempted; to get rid of. ~কর্তা *n.* a deliverer, a liberator, a saviour. পরিত্রাণের পথ বা উপায় path of salvation; way of escape, way out.

পরিত্রাতা *n.* a rescuer, a deliverer; (esp. in theol.) a saviour; a liberator; a reliever.

পরিত্রাহি *v.* (*imperat.*) rescue, deliver, save, relieve. পরিত্রাহি ডাক ছাড়া to call out or cry for help.

পরিদর্শ see পরিদর্শন।

পরিদর্শক *n.* an observer; an inspector; a supervisor; a probation officer (as of juvenile offenders), visitor (of an institution.)

পরিদর্শন, পরিদর্শ *n.* (careful) observation; inspection; supervision. পরিদর্শন করা *v.* to observe (esp. carefully); to inspect; to supervise.

পরিদর্শী *a.* observing (esp. carefully); inspecting; supervising.

পরিদৃশ্যমান *a.* visible all around; thoroughly visible; manifest.

পরিদৃষ্ট *a.* observed, noticed; espied; inspected; supervised.

পরিদেবন, পরিদেবনা *n.* lamentation; wailing; bewailing; repentance.

পরিধান *n.* dress, garment, clothes; act of putting on or wearing. পরিধান করা *v.* to put on, to wear. ~বস্ত্র *n.* garment, colthes.

পরিধি *n.* circumference; periphery; girth. ~মাপক *n.* perimeter.

পরিধেয় *a.* fit to be put on or worn. □ *n.* clothes, garment.

পরিনির্বাণ *n.* the cessation of individual existence, nirvana, salvation, beatitude.

পরিপক্ব *a.* thoroughly ripe; (thoroughly) mature; well-experienced; thoroughly habituated or addicted (নেশায় পরিপক্ব); very precocious (পরিপক্ব ছেলে). ~তা *n.* thorough ripeness; (thorough) maturity; thorough experience; inveterate habit or addiction; precocity.

পরিপত্র *n.* a circular.

পরিপন্থী *a.* unfavourable, adverse; opposing, obstructing, hindering; hostile, inimical.

পরিপাক *n.* digestion; assimilation. পরিপাক করা *v.* to digest; to assimilate. ~দোষ *n.*

digestive trouble. **~যন্ত্র** *n.* the digestive organ, the stomach. **~শক্তি** *n.* digestive power; power of assimilation.

পরিপাটি *n.* orderly arrangement; orderliness; skill. □ *a.* arranged in an orderly manner; orderly; skilful, adroit.

পরিপার্শ্ব *n.* surroundings, entourage.

পরিপালক *n.* one who brings up, a rearer; an administrator.

পরিপালন *n.* act of bringing up or rearing; administration. **পরিপালন করা** *v.* to bring up, to rear, to support; to administrate.

পরিপালিত *a.* brought up, reared; administered.

পরিপুষ্ট *a.* well-developed; plump, robust and muscular; well-nourished; carefully brought up. *fem.* **পরিপুষ্টা**। **~তা, পরিপুষ্টি** *n.* good development; plumpness; robustness and muscularity; sound nourishment; careful bringing up.

পরিপূরক *a.* completing; fulfilling; (chiefly in geom.) complementary (পরিপূরক কোণ).

পরিপূরণ *n.* repletion; act of repleting; fulfilment; completion; act of complementing. **পরিপূরণ করা** *v.* to replete; to fill up; to fulfil; to complete; to complement.

পরিপূরিত, পরিপূর্ণ *a.* replete; teeming; filled up; fulfilled; completed; complemented. *fem.* **পরিপূর্ণা**। **পরিপূর্ণতা** *n.* repleteness, repletion.

পরিপৃক্ত *a.* saturated. **পরিপৃক্ত করা** *v.* to saturate. **পরিপৃক্তি** *n.* saturation. **পরিপৃক্ত দ্রব** saturated solution.

পরিপোষক *a.* nourishing; cherishing; supporting (পরিপোষক মূল্য); protecting, protective.

পরিপোষণ *n.* nourishment; cherishing; support; protection. **পরিপোষণ করা** *v.* to nourish; to cherish; to support; to protect.

পরিপ্রেক্ষিত *n.* perspective.

পরিপ্লব *n.* flooding; flood; submersion; inundation; drenching.

পরিপ্লুত *a.* flooded; submerged; inundated; drenched, soaked, saturated. *fem.* **পরিপ্লুতা**। **পরিপ্লুত করা** *v.* to flood; to submerge; to inundate; to drench; to saturate.

পরিবর্জন *n.* complete abandonment or avoidance or casting off or giving up or renouncement or rejection. **পরিবর্জনীয়** *a.* that which can be or should be abandoned or given up or renounced.

পরিবর্জিত *a.* completely abandoned or avoided or cast off or given up or renounced or rejected.

পরিবর্ত *n.* exchange; barter; a substitute. **পরিবর্ত বিবাহ** marrying a girl into a family and receiving one in marriage from it, inter-marriage. **~ক** *a.* & *n.* one who or that which exchanges or barters or changes or alters or modifies or transforms or effects a change in circumstances or metamorphoses or converts or rotates or recedes or returns. **~মান** *a.* changing.

পরিবর্তন *n.* exchange; barter; change; alteration; modification; transformation; a change in circumstances; metamorphosis; conversion; rotation; recession; return. **পরিবর্তন করা** *v.* to exchange; to barter; to change; to alter; to modify; to transform; to effect a change in circumstances; to metamorphose; to convert; to rotate; to recede; to return. **~বিমুখ** *a.* not ready or willing to change; averse to change, conservatism. **~বিমুখতা** *n.* unwillingness to change; conservatism. **~শীল** *a.* changeful; changing; full of vicissitude or variety; metamorphic. **পরিবর্তনীয়** *a.* exchangeable; that which can be or is to be bartered; changeable; alterable; modifiable; transformable; capable of suffering a change in circumstances; metamorphic; convertible. **পরিবর্তিত** *a.* exchanged; bartered; changed; altered; modified; transformed; metamorphosed; converted; rotated; returned. **পরিবর্তী** *a.* changeful; (sc.) alternating. **পরিবর্তী মোক্ষণ** oscillatory discharge.

পরিবর্তে *adv.* in place of, instead of, in lieu of, in exchange for.

পরিবর্ধক *a.* & *n.* one who or that which develops or improves or extends or magnifies or enlarges or amplifies, promoting or helping development or growth (of). **পরিবর্ধক কাচ** a magnifying glass.

পরিবর্ধন *n.* development; improvement; magnification; enlargement; amplification.

পরিবর্ধিত *a.* developed, magnified; enlarged (পরিবর্ধিত সংস্করণ) ; amplified.

পরিবলন *n.* (bot.) circumnutation.

পরিবহণ *n.* transportation, transport, conveyance; (esp. in elec.) conduction. **পরিবহণ করা** *v.* to transport, to convey; to conduct. **পরিবহণ আধিকারিক** transport officer.

পরিবাদ *n.* disrepute, reproach, blame, slander. **পরিবাদক, পরিবাদী** *a.* reproaching, blaming. **পরিবাদিনী** *a. fem.* of **পরিবাদী** । □ *n.* a seven-stringed musical instrument, a heptachord.

পরিবার *n.* a family; a family circle; a wife. **পরিবার পরিকল্পনা** *n.* family planning.

পরিবাহক্ষেত্র *n.* (geog.) a basin, a catchment area.

পরিবাহণ *n.* conduction.

পরিবাহিত *a.* conducted. **পরিবাহিত মৃত্তিকা** transported soil.

পরিবাহিতা *a. fem.* of **পরিবাহিত** । □ *n.* conductivity.

পরিবাহী *a.* conducting. □ *n.* a conductor.

পরিবৃত *a.* completely surrounded, encircled, beset; completely covered or overcast. **পরিবৃতি** *n.* encirclement, besetment; thorough covering or overcasting.

পরিবৃত্ত *n.* (geom.) a circumcircle.

পরিবৃত্তি *n.* alteration, change; transition; exchange, barter. **~কাল** *n.* (phys.) transition period.

পরিবেত্তা *n.* a younger brother who marries whilst his elder is still unmarried.

পরিবেদন *n.* act of getting married whilst one's elder brother is still unmarried.

পরিবেদনা *n.* great pain or pang or affliction or distress.

পরিবেশ, (rare) **পরিবেষ** *n.* (rare) circumference, periphery; a circle; surroundings; environment; entourage; (pop.) circumstance.

পরিবেশক, পরিবেষক *n.* a distributor, a dealer; one who serves food at table.

পরিবেশন, পরিবেষণ *n.* distribution, act of dealing out; act of serving food at table. **পরিবেশন করা, পরিবেষণ করা** *v.* to distribute, to deal out; to serve (food at table).

পরিবেষ্টক *a.* one who or that which surrounds or goes round or encircles or encloses.

পরিবেষ্টন *n.* an enclosure; act of surrounding or going round or enclosing, encirclement, besetment. **পরিবেষ্টন করা** *v.* to surround, to go round, to encircle; to enclose. **পরিবেষ্টনী** *n.* entourage, surroundings; fencing, railings, enclosure.

পরিবেষ্টিত *a.* surrounded, encircled, beset, engirt; enclosed. *fem.* **পরিবেষ্টিতা** ।

পরিব্যাপ্ত *a.* spread, spread out; extended, expanded. **পরিব্যাপ্তি** *n.* spreading, spreading out; expansion; diffusion; extension.

পরিব্রজ্যা *n.* wandering as a mendicant or wandering asceticism; pilgrimage.

পরিব্রাজক *n.* a travellller; a mendicant or wandering ascetic.

পরিব্রাজন *n.* travelling; wandering.

পরিব্রাজিকা *fem.* of **পরিব্রাজক** ।

পরিভব *n.* defeat; discomfiture.

পরিভাষা *n.* a technical word or term; technical terminology.

পরিভূত *a.* defeated, discomfited.

পরিভৃতি *n.* emolument; wages; salary, pay.

পরিভোগ *n.* thorough enjoyment; sexual intercourse.

পরিভ্রমণ *n.* act of going round, rotation; perigrination; travelling; wandering; roaming; strolling, walking. **পরিভ্রমণ করা** *v.* to go round, to rotate; to perigrinate; to travel; to wander; to stroll, to walk.

পরিভ্রষ্ট *a.* detached and fallen; shed. **পরিভ্রষ্ট হওয়া** *v.* to get detached and fall down; to be shed.

পরিভ্রূণ *n.* perisperm.

পরিমণ্ডল *n.* an orbit; a circle; a circumference; (fig.) a society or sphere; environment; surrounding, encirclement; a globe; any globular object.

পরিমণ্ডিত *a.* well-ornamented, well-decorated, well-adorned; endowed.

পরিমল *n.* fragrance caused by being anointed (with sandal-paste etc.); fragrance, perfume, sweet scent; (pop.) nectar of flowers ('পরিমল লোভে অলি আসিয়া জুটিল').

পরিমাণ *n.* measure, weight, amount, quantity, number, degree; extent. **পরিমাণ করা** *v.* to measure, to weigh; (rare) to count; to survey (as land); to assess (as importance). **পরিমাণে হওয়া** *v.* to measure, to weigh; to be adequate in proportion to. **~ফল** *n.* result of measurement or counting; (arith.) area measure, square measure.

পরিমাত্রা *n.* (mech.) intensity.

পরিমাপ *n.* measurement; weighing; counting; (fig.) assessment (জ্ঞানের পরিমাপ) ; measure, weight, amount, quantity, number, degree; land-measure, survey. **পরিমাপ করা** same as **পরিমাণ করা** (see **পরিমাণ**). **পরিমাপক** *a.* measuring; weighing; counting; surveying; assessing. □ *n.* a measurer; weigher; counter; a surveyor (of land); an assessor; a measuring or weighing or counting or surveying machine. **পরিমাপন** *n.* measuring or weighing or counting or surveying (as land) or (fig.) assessing.

পরিমার্জন *n.* scouring or cleansing; refining or chastening. **পরিমার্জনা** *n.* scouring or cleansing; refining; (of a book, a dictionary etc) correction, editing and making up-to-date.

পরিমার্জিত *a.* scoured; cleansed; refined; corrected and revised; chastened. **পরিমার্জিত করা** *v.* to scour; to cleanse; to refine; to correct and revise; to chasten.

পরিমিত *a.* moderate; temperate, abstemious; measuring or amounting (চারহাত পরিমিত) ; measured; mensurated; (rare) sufficient, adequate. **~ব্যয়ী** *a.* economic, frugal. **পরিমিতাচার** *n.* moderation, temperance. **পরিমিতাচারী** *a.* temperate.

পরিমিতি *n.* measurement; measure; (math.) mensuration.

পরিমেয় *a.* measurable; finite.

পরিমেল *n.* an association. **~নিয়মাবলি** *n.* articles of association. **~বন্ধ** *n.* a memorandum of association.

পরিম্লান *a.* very pale or jaded or worn out; glum or sombre.

পরিযাণ *n.* traffic; migration. **পরিযাণ নির্বাহক, পরিযাণ ব্যবস্থাপক** *n.* a traffic manager. **পরিযাণ আরক্ষী** *n.* traffic police.

পরিযায়ী *a.* trafficking; itinerant; migratory.

পরিরক্ষণ *n.* preservation; protection; guarding; careful custody or guardianship.

পরিরক্ষিত *a.* preserved; protected; guarded; kept under careful custody or guardianship.

পরিরম্ভ, পরিরম্ভণ *n.* close embrace; sexual intercourse.

পরিলক্ষিত *a.* noticed; observed.

পরিলিখিত *a.* (geom.) circumscribed.

পরিলেখ *n.* an outline; an outline sketch.

পরিশিষ্ট *a.* remaining. □ *n.* an appendix, a supplement (as of a book).

পরিশীলন *n.* practice, study, cultivation; an embrace; anointment. **পরিশীলিত** *a.* practised, studied, cultivated; refined; sophisticated; embraced; anointed.

পরিশুদ্ধ *a.* meticulously refined or purified or sanctified. **পরিশুদ্ধ করা** *v.* to refine or purify or sanctify meticulously. **পরিশুদ্ধি** *n.* meticulous refinement or purity or sanctity.

পরিশুষ্ক *a.* very dry; pale; shrivelled.

পরিশেষ *n.* remainder; end; the last stage; conclusion; the concluding part. **পরিশেষে** *adv.* at last, in the end; finally, ultimately; in the long run.

পরিশোধ *n.* repayment (as of a debt); (fig.) revenge or retaliation. **পরিশোধ করা** *v.* to repay, to pay off, to pay back; (fig.) to avenge or retaliate.

পরিশোধন *n.* meticulous refinement or purification or sanctification.

পরিশোধ্য *a.* that which is to be or can be repaid, outstanding or repayable.

পরিশ্রম *n.* labour, toil; diligence, industry; effort, endeavour. **পরিশ্রম করা** *v.* to work hard, to labour, to toil; to work diligently; to endeavour. **~কাতর, ~বিমুখ** *a.* averse to hard work, lazy. **পরিশ্রমী** *a.* hardworking, laborious; diligent, industrious.

পরিশ্রান্ত *a.* fatigued, exhausted; tired; wearied. **পরিশ্রান্তি** *n.* fatigue, exhaustion; tiredness, weariness.

পরিষদ, পরিষৎ *n.* an association, an assembly, a society; a council; (pol.) a legislative council. **পরিষদীয়** *a.* pertaining or relating to or concerning a council or assembly; legislative; parliamentary.

পরিষেবক *n.* a sicknurse, a nurse.

পরিষেবা *n.* care of the sick, nursing.

পরিষেবিকা *fem.* of **পরিষেবক**।

পরিষ্করণ *n.* cleansing or refining.

পরিষ্কার *n.* cleanliness; tidiness; neatness; clarity (as of water). □ *a.* clean; cleansed; clear; tidy; spruce, neat, orderly (পরিষ্কার কাজ) ; legible (পরিষ্কার লেখা) ; clearcut, outspoken, unambiguous, unequivocal (পরিষ্কার কথা) ; beautiful, bright, fair (পরিষ্কার আলো বা আবহাওয়া) ; cloudless (পরিষ্কার আকাশ) ; free from angularity, frank, straightforward, candid, open-hearted, sincere (পরিষ্কার মন) ; intelligent, free from confusion (পরিষ্কার মাথা) ; free from morbidity, healthy (পরিষ্কার বুক) ; musical, sweet (পরিষ্কার গলা) ; keen (পরিষ্কার দৃষ্টি). **পরিষ্কার করা** *v.* to cleanse; to clean; to clear; to tidy; to free from morbidity or angularity; to wash (কাপড় পরিষ্কার করা). **~ক** *a.* cleansing. □ *n.* a cleaner; a cleansing agent. **পরিষ্কার-পরিচ্ছন্ন** *a.* neat and clean, clean and tidy, spick and span.

পরিষ্কৃত *a.* cleansed; cleaned; cleared; tidied; refined; washed (পরিষ্কৃত বস্ত্র).

পরিসংখ্যা *n.* especially enumerated or tabulated number; statistics. **পরিসংখ্যাত** *a.* especially enumerated or tabulated; statistical. **পরিসংখ্যান** *n.* statistics. **পরিসংখ্যায়ক** *n.* statistician.

পরিসমাপ্ত *a.* ended, finished, concluded, completed. **পরিসমাপ্তি** *n.* end, termination; conclusion; completion.

পরিসম্পৎ *n.* assets.

পরিসর *n.* extent; area; limit, boundary, end; width, breadth.

পরিসীমা *n.* limit, bounds; perimeter; end.

পরিস্থিতি *n.* circumstances, situation.

পরিস্ফুট *a.* clearly revealed or expressed; well-developed; manifest, obvious; blossomed, blooming.

পরিস্ফুরণ *n.* vibration; effervescence; manifestation.

পরিস্রব *n.* (biol.) placenta.

পরিস্রাবণ, পরিস্রবণ, পরিস্রুতি *n.* filtration. **পরিস্রুত** *a.* filtered (পরিস্রুত জল).

পরিহরণ same as **পরিহার**। **পরিহরণীয়** same as **পরিহার্য**।

পরিহরা poet. form of **পরিহার করা**।

পরিহর্তব্য same as **পরিহার্য**।

পরিহসনীয় *a.* laughable, ridiculous; fit to be derided or mocked.

পরিহার *n.* giving up; abandonment; avoidance; act of casting off; neglect, disregard; slight. **পরিহার করা** *v.* to give up; to abandon; to avoid, to shun; to cast off; to neglect, to disregard, to slight.

পরিহার্য *a.* avoidable; that which can be given up or renounced or abandoned, renounceable.

পরিহাস *n.* a joke, a jest; ridicule; mockery, derision. **পরিহাস করা** *v.* to poke fun at, to joke; to ridicule; to mock, to deride, to laugh, to scorn. **~চ্ছলে, ~ভরে** *adv.* jokingly. **~প্রিয়** *a.* given to jesting, jestful; witty; fond of joking. **~প্রিয়তা** *n.* jestfulness; jocular; jocoseness; jocosity; playfulness.

পরিহিত *a.* clothed, clad, dressed, wearing; that which is put on or worn (পরিহিত পোশাক). *fem.* **পরিহিতা**।

পরী rej. spell. of **পরি**[2]।

পরীক্ষক *n.* a tester; an examiner; a trier; an investigator; an experimenter; a foreteller, a diviner. **ভাগ্যপরীক্ষক** *n.* a fortune-teller; a soldier of fortune, an adventurer.

পরীক্ষণ *n.* act of testing or examining or trying or investigating or foretelling or divining. **পরীক্ষণীয়** *a.* that which or one who is to be tested or examined or tried or investigated or experimented upon or divined; examinable.

পরীক্ষা *n.* a test; an examination; a trial; an ordeal (অগ্নিপরীক্ষা) ; a cross-examination; an investigation; an experiment; foretelling, divination, reading (হস্তরেখা পরীক্ষা) ; **অদৃষ্টপরীক্ষা, ভাগ্যপরীক্ষা** *n.* fortune-telling; act of seeking fortune. **পরীক্ষা করা** *v.* to test; to examine; to try; to test by an ordeal; to cross examine; to investigate; to experiment; to divine. **পরীক্ষা দেওয়া** *v.* to appear at an examination; to take an examination; to undergo a trial; to submit to an ordeal. **পরীক্ষা নেওয়া** *v.* to examine, to test; to hold an examination; to test by an examination. **পরীক্ষায় উতরে যাওয়া** *v.* to stand a test or scrutiny. **~গার, ~গৃহ, ~ভবন, ~মন্দির, ~শালা** *n.* an examination-hall; a laboratory. **~ধীন** *a.* subject to or under examination or trial or test or investigation or experiment. **~র্থী** *a.* appearing at an examination. □ *n.* an examinee. *fem.* **পরীক্ষার্থিনী** ।

পরীক্ষামূলক *a.* experimental.

পরীক্ষামূলকভাবে *adv.* by way of experiment, experimentally.

পরীক্ষিত *a.* tested; examined; tried; investigated; experimented.

পরীক্ষোত্তীর্ণ *a.* passed at an examination; successful in an examination; one who has come through a test or ordeal successfully; found suitable or good on trial or test. *fem.* **পরীক্ষোত্তীর্ণা** । **পরীক্ষোত্তীর্ণ হওয়া** *v.* to come through or pass an examination or test or ordeal; to stand a test or ordeal; to be found suitable or good on test or trial.

পরুষ *a.* harsh, rough, rude, haughty, arrogant, cruel (পরুষ বচন). **~তা, ~ত্ব** *n.* harshness, rudeness, haughtiness, arrogance, cruelty.

পরে *adv.* & *prep.* after, afterwards (সে পরে আসছে) ; thereafter, then (পরে সেখানে গেলাম) ; in future (পরে কী হয় বলা যায় না) ; after the occurrence of, after that (ট্রেন ছাড়ার পরে স্টেশনে পৌঁছলাম) ; at the back of (রামের পরে শ্যাম যাচ্ছে) ; below (আমার নামের পরেই তার নাম) ; born later (এই ভাইটি আমার পরে). **পরের দিন** *n.* the day after. □ *adv.* on the following day.

পরেশনাথ coll. corrup. of **পার্শ্বনাথ** ।

পরোক্ষ *a.* imperceptible or unseen but known or true, not known directly, circumstantial (পরোক্ষ প্রমাণ) ; indirect (পরোক্ষ উক্তি) ; roundabout (পরোক্ষভাবে). **পরোক্ষ কর** an indirect tax. **পরোক্ষে, ~ভাবে** *adv.* behind one's back , in one's absence. **পরোক্ষে নিন্দা করা** to slander somebody in his absence, to backbite.

পরোটা *n.* a kind of thin bread fried in oil or clarified butter.

পরোপকার *n.* the good of others; philanthropy, benevolence; (loos. but pop.) public welfare. **পরোপকার করা** *v.* to do good to others, to do a good turn (to a person). **~ক, পরোপকারী** *a.* doing good to others; philanthropic, benevolent. *fem.* **পরোপকারিণী** । **পরোপকারিতা** *n.* act of doing good to others; philanthropy, benevolence.

পরোপজীবী, পরোপজীব্য *a.* living on another; depending or hanging on another for subsistence; parasitic.

পরোয়া *n.* heedfulness, care (উপদেশের পরোয়া) ; fear, daunt; concern, anxiety. **পরোয়া করা** *v.* to pay heed to; (esp. in neg.) to care; to be afraid of, to fear; to be concerned or anxious about. **কুছ পরোয়া নেই** no fear; no matter; never mind.

পরোয়ানা alt. spell. of **পরওয়ানা** ।

পর্কটি, পর্কটী *n.* a kind of fig-tree.

পর্চা alt. spell. of **পরচা** ।

পর্জন্য *n.* thunder-cloud, nimbus; Indra (ইন্দ্র) the thunder-god.

পর্ণ *n.* a tree-leaf, a leaf (পর্ণকুটির) ; betel leaf (পর্ণকারী) ; a feather, a plume (সুপর্ণ). **~কারী** *n.* a grower of betel-leaves (by trade or caste). **~কুটির** *n.* a hut thatched with tree-leaves; (loos.) a hut. **~ভোজী** *a.* feeding on tree-leaves; (loos.) graminivorous. **~মোচী** *a.* (bot.) deciduous. **~শয্যা** *n.* a bed made of tree-leaves; (loos.) a pallet. **~শালা** same as **পর্ণকুটির** ।

পর্ণী *a.* leafed, leaved; leafy. □ *n.* a tree.

পর্দা alt. spell. of **পরদা** ।

পপটী *n.* an Ayurvedic (আয়ুর্বেদীয়) drug made from a herbal plant.

পর্ব *n.* a holy day; a fiesta; a feast, a festival; a knuckle, a joint (as of a finger); (bot.) a node; (of books) a canto, a chapter.

পর্বত *n.* a mountain; a hill; a rock; a hillock; a mount. **~কন্দর, ~গুহা** *n.* a mountain-cave, a cave, a cavern. **~চূড়া** *n.* a peak (of a mountain); a hill-top. **~পার্শ্ব** *n.* mountain-side, hillside. **~প্রমাণ** *a.* mountain-high, high as a mountain; mountainous; huge. **~বাসী** *a.* living on hills or mountains; highland. □ *n.* a hillman; a highlander. *fem.* **~বাসিনী**। **~শিখর, ~শৃঙ্গ** same as **~চূড়া**। **~শ্রেণি** *n.* a mountain-range. **~সংকুল** *a.* mountainous, having many mountains; hilly. **পর্বতাকার** *a.* looking like a mountain; mountainous, huge. **পর্বতারোহী** *n.* a mountaineer. □ *a.* climbing a mountain. **পর্বতীয়** *a.* of or grown in or living on mountains or hills; mountainous, highland.

পর্বমধ্য *n.* (bot.) an internode.

পর্বাস্ফোট *n.* act of snapping a knuckle or knuckles of one's finger(s).

পর্বাহ *n.* a day of festival; a holy day; a fiesta; a festival.

পর্যঙ্ক *n.* a costly bedstead or cot; a couch, a divan; (geog.) a basin (of a river).

পর্যটক *n.* a traveller, a perigrinator, a tourist.

পর্যটন *n.* (wide) travel, perigrination, tour. **পর্যটন করা** *v.* to travel (widely), to perigrinate, to tour.

পর্যন্ত *n.* limit, end, extremity. □ *prep.* to (মাথা থেকে পা পর্যন্ত) ; up to (এই সীমা পর্যন্ত) ; till or until (ট্রেন আসা পর্যন্ত, বৃষ্টি না থামা পর্যন্ত). □ *adv.* too, also, even (তিনি পর্যন্ত অনাচারমুক্ত নন).

পর্যবসান *n.* end, close, termination, conclusion; result; reduction. **পর্যবসান হওয়া** *v.* to end, to terminate, to conclude; to result in; to be reduced to.

পর্যবসিত *a.* ended, terminated, concluded; resolved (into); reduced (to); resulting in.

পর্যবেক্ষক *a.* watching; observing. □ *n.* a watcher; an observer.

পর্যবেক্ষণ *n.* watching; observation. **পর্যবেক্ষণ করা** *v.* to watch; to observe. **পর্যবেক্ষণিকা** *n.* an observatory; a watch-tower.

পর্যবেক্ষিত *a.* watched; observed.

পর্যসন *n.* removal; act of throwing all round; scattering.

পর্যস্ত *a.* removed; thrown all round; scattered; turned upside down, overturned; reversed.

পর্যাটক var. of **পর্যটক**।

পর্যাণ *n.* saddle; a panel; a caparison.

পর্যাপ্ত *a.* ample, abundant; sufficient, adequate, enough; moderate, temperate; capable, competent. **পর্যাপ্তি** *n.* amplitude, abundance, plenty; sufficiency, adequacy, moderateness, moderation, temperance; capability, competence, competency.

পর্যাবরণ *n.* environment; surroundings; the environs.

পর্যাবৃত্ত *a.* periodic. **পর্যাবৃত্তি** *n.* periodicity.

পর্যায় *n.* a turn; serial order; succession; state, condition, shape, form, series (নবপর্যায়) ; a generation (আদিপুরুষ থেকে সাতাশের পর্যায়) ; a synonym (usu. **পর্যায়শব্দ**) ; (chiefly in sc.) a period (usu. **পর্যায়কাল**). **~ক্রমে** *adv.* by turns; serially; successively; alternately. **~চ্যুতি, ~ভঙ্গ** *n.* a break in the series, a break in periodicity; inversion. **~শব্দ** *n.* synonymous words; related or cognate words. **~সম** *a.* rhyming alternately. **~সারণি** *n.* (chem.) a periodic table.

পর্যালোচন, পর্যালোচনা *n.* thorough discussion or study or review. **পর্যালোচনা করা** *v.* to discuss or study or review thoroughly.

পর্যালোচিত *a.* thoroughly discussed or studied or reviewed.

পর্যাস *n.* topsyturvy; upset, reverse, a great change; a revolution.

পর্যুদস্ত *a.* utterly defeated, routed, crushed; completely baffled; prevented or repulsed; totally forbidden; foiled, marred. **পর্যুদস্ত করা** *v.* to defeat utterly, to rout, to crush; to baffle completely; to prevent or repulse; to forbid totally; to foil, to mar.

পর্যুদাস *n.* utter defeat, rout, crush; complete frustration; prevention or repulse.

পর্যুষিত *a.* stale (পর্যুষিত অন্ন).

পর্যেষণ, পর্যেষণা *n.* search, investigation; research.

পর্শুকা *n.* a rib, a vertebra.

পর্ষদ, পর্ষৎ *n.* a council, a board.

পল[1] *n.* a measure of time (= 24 seconds); a moment, a while, a very short time; a measure of weight (= 8 তোলা).

পল[2] *n.* a bevel (পল-তোলা).

পলক *n.* wink or blink (of eyes); a very short time, an instant, a moment; an eyelid. **পলক পড়া** *v.* (of eyes) to close, to wink, to blink. **পলক ফেলা** *v.* to wink, to blink. **~পাত** *n.* closing of eyelids. **~শূন্য, ~হীন** *a.* (of eyes) unwinking unblinking; (of sight or look) steadfast, fixed, winkless. **পলকে পলকে** every moment; in very quick succession. **পলকে প্রলয়** instant disaster (with little or no warning). **পলকের মধ্যে, পলকে** *adv.* in an instant, instantly; in the twinkling of an eye.

পলকা *a.* brittle, fragile; frail; delicate; unsubstantial.

পলটন *n.* an armed force; a platoon.

পলটি *v.* (*imperf.*) turning back.

পলতা *n.* the creeper bearing পটোল (this is used as a bitter pot-herb).

পলতে *n.* the wick of a lamp.

পল-তোলা *a.* bevelled.

পলল *n.* meat; silt, slime; alluvium. **পলল ভূমি** *n.* alluvial soil.

পলস্তারা *n.* a plaster (esp. one composed of slaked lime, sand and hair, and used for coating walls etc.). **পলস্তারা দেওয়া** বা **লাগানো** *v.* to plaster.

পলা[1] *n.* coral.

পলা[2] *n.* a kind of tiny ladle or spoon.

পলাগ্নি *n.* bile.

পলাণ্ডু *n.* onion.

পলাতক *a.* fugitive, fleeing; absconding. □ *n.* a fugitive; an absconder. *fem.* **পলাতকা**। **পলাতক হওয়া** *v.* to abscond.

পলানো dial. var. of **পালানো**।

পলান্ন *n.* a highly spiced dish of rice and meat boiled in clarified butter, pilau.

পলায়ন *n.* act of running away or fleeing, flight; escape. **পলায়ন করা** *v.* same as **পালানো** (*v.*). **~পর** *a.* fleeing, fugitive; absconding; escaping. **পলায়নপর সেনাবাহিনী** the retreating army. **পলায়নোদ্যত** *a.* attempting to flee or escape, about to run away.

পলায়মান *a.* fleeing, fugitive; absconding; escaping. *fem.* **পলায়মান**।

পলায়িত *a.* fled; absconded; escaped, *fem.* **পলায়িতা**।

পলাশ *n.* a kind of beautiful red flower having no fragrance; its tree, the dhak, the palas, Butea monosperma.

পলি *n.* silt; alluvium. **পলি পড়া** *v.* to collect alluvial deposit, to silt. **পলি-পড়া** *a.* silted up. **~মাটি** *n.* alluvium, silt; alluvial soil.

পলিজ *a.* alluvial.

পলিত *n.* grey-hairedness, grey-headedness; greyness; grey. □ *a.* grey; aged, old. **~কেশ** *a.* grey-haired; old, aged.

পলিতা for. form of **পলতে**।

পলি-পড়া see **পলি**।

পলীয় *n.* protein.

পলু *n.* a species of silk-worm living on the mulberry tree.

পলেস্তারা var. of **পলস্তারা**।

পলো *n.* a pail-shaped wicker-basket for catching fish.

পল্টন alt. spell. of **পলটন**।

পল্বল *n.* any small pool of water (esp. a shallow one).

পল্যঙ্ক same as **পর্যঙ্ক**।

পল্যয়ন *n.* a saddle; a caparison; a panel, a pack-saddle.

পল্লব *n.* a leaf (বৃক্ষপল্লব, নবপল্লব) ; a lid (অক্ষিপল্লব) ; a new tree-leaf; the forepart of a young shoot or sprout bearing new leaves (আম্রপল্লব). **~গ্রাহিতা** *n.* surface-grazing; dilettantism; eclecticism; smattering acquaintance. **~গ্রাহী** *a.* dilettantish; smattering. **পল্লবগ্রাহী লোক** a dilettante (pl. dilettanti); a smatterer. **পল্লবিত** *a.* containing leaves, leafy; full of new leaves; sprouted; detailed, exhausted; exaggerated (পল্লবিত বর্ণনা).

পল্লি, পল্লী *n.* a small area of human habitation containing a cluster of houses, a locality (গোপপল্লি) ; a hamlet; a village; a municipal division, a ward. ~অঞ্চল *n.* a rural area; countryside. **পল্লি উন্নয়ন** *n.* village development, rural uplift. ~গীতি *n.* folksong, village song. ~গ্রাম *n.* a village. ~জীবন *n.* rural life, countrylife. ~নৃত্য *n.* a country-dance. ~বধূ *n.* a country-woman, a country-wife. ~বালা, ~বালিকা *n.* a country-girl; a country-maid. ~বাস *n.* a village home; a country residence; act of living in a country. ~বাসী *a.* living in a country, rural; (dero.) rustic. □ *n.* a countryman (*fem.* a country-woman), a villager. (dero.) a rustic. *fem.* ~বাসিনী। ~বাসী ভদ্রলোক a country gentleman. ~ভবন *n.* a village home; a country residence; a country-house, a country seat. ~মঙ্গল সমিতি village welfare society. ~সংগঠন *n.* rural organization, rural development. ~সংস্কার *n.* rural reconstruction; village upliftment. ~সমিতি *n.* a village society.

পশতু, পশতো *n.* Pushtu, Pushtoo, Pashto, a language of the Afghans.

পশম *n.* wool; fur. **পশম পরিষ্কার করা** to card or comb wool. **পশমিনা** *n.* a kind of very fine woollen cloth. **পশমি** *a.* woollen; made of fur.

পশরা alt. spell. of **পসরা**।

পশলা *n.* a short spell of fall (as of rain), a shower.

পশা *v.* (poet.) to enter; to penetrate.

পশার, পশারা, পশারি alt. spellings of **পসার, পসারা**[২] and **পসারি** respectively.

পশু *n.* a quadruped animal, a beast, a brute; a beastly or brutal man; an attendant of Shiva (শিব). **গবাদি পশু** cattle. **গৃহপালিত পশু** a domestic animal; (*pl.*) livestock. **বলির পশু** a sacrificial beast. **ভারবাহী পশু** a beast of burden, a draught animal, a pack animal. **শিকারি পশু** a beast of prey. **শিকারের পশু** a game. ~চর্ম *n.* animal skin; hide; pelt. ~চারণ *n.* act of grazing cattle, grazing. **পশুচারণ করা** *v.* to graze or feed cattle. ~চারণ ক্ষেত্র *n.* a pasturage, a grazing-field. ~চারণযোগ্য *a.* pasturable. ~চিকিৎসক *n.* a veterinary surgeon. ~ত্ব *n.* animality; beastliness; brutality. ~ধর্ম *n.* bestiality; sexual intercourse or copulation. ~ধর্মা *a.* bestial; brutal; addicted to excessive sexual intercourse or copulation. ~পতি Shiva (শিব). ~পাল *a.* herd or flock of animals or livestock. ~পাল, ~পালক *n.* a herdsman; a cowherd; a shepherd; a goatherd. ~পালন *n.* act of rearing and tending and raising livestock, livestock farming. ~পালনবিশারদ *n.* a livestock expert. ~বৎ *a.* beast-like, beastly, bestial, brutal. ~বৎ আচরণ bestiality, brutality. ~রাজ *n.* the king of beasts; the lion. ~লোম *n.* wool; fur. ~শক্তি *n.* brute force. ~শালা *n.* a zoological garden, a zoo; a cattleshed; a stable. ~শিকার *n.* game-hunting, hunting. ~শিকারি *n.* a game-hunter, a hunter (*fem.* a huntress). ~সুলভ same as **পশুবৎ**।

পশুরি alt. spell. of **পসুরি**।

পশ্চাৎ *adv.* & *prep.* after, at or to the back of (পশ্চাৎ আসিতেছে). □ *adv.* afterwards, later (পশ্চাৎ বলা) ; in or to the west. □ *a.* living at the back; reverse (পশ্চাৎ দিক). □ *n.* the back; the backside, the rear; the future. **পশ্চাতে** *adv.* behind (গৃহের পশ্চাতে) ; later, afterwards (পশ্চাতে বলব).

পশ্চাৎপদ *a.* retreated; withdrawn; turned back; lagging behind. **পশ্চাৎপদ হওয়া** *v.* to retreat; to withdraw; to turn back; to lag behind.

পশ্চাত্তাপ *n.* repentance, remorse.

পশ্চাদ্‌গতি *n.* retrograde motion, backward movement. **পশ্চাদ্‌গমন** *n.* retrogression, going after, following. **পশ্চাদ্‌গমন করা** *v.* to follow, to go after. **পশ্চাদ্‌গামী** *a.* following, going after. **পশ্চাদ্‌গামী হওয়া** *v.* to follow, to go after. **পশ্চাদ্‌বর্তী** *a.* lying behind; lagging behind; following, coming after or behind. **পশ্চাদ্‌বর্তী হওয়া** *v.* to lie behind; to lag behind; to follow. **পশ্চাদনুসরণ** *n.* act of following; pursuit. **পশ্চাদনুসরণ করা** *v.* to follow; to pursue. **পশ্চাদনুসরণকারী** *a.* following; pursuing. □ *n.* a follower; a pursuer. *fem.* **পশ্চাদনুসরণকারিণী**।

পশ্চাদপসরণ *n.* retreat.

পশ্চাদ্‌ভূমি *n.* the rear; the backgroud; hinterland.

পশ্চাদগতি, পশ্চাদগমন, পশ্চাদগামী alt. spellings of **পশ্চাদ্গতি, পশ্চাদ্গমন** and **পশ্চাদ্গামী** respectively.

পশ্চাদ্ধাবন *n.* act of running after; act of chasing. **পশ্চাদ্ধাবন করা** *v.* to run after; to chase, to pursue.

পশ্চাদ্ধাবিত *a.* running after; chasing, pursuing.

পশ্চাদ্বর্তী alt. spell. of **পশ্চাদ্বর্তী**।

পশ্চাদ্ভাগ *n.* the backside; the rear; the back. **পশ্চাদ্ভাগে** *adv.* in the rear.

পশ্চাদ্ভূমি alt. spell. of **পশ্চাদ্ভূমি**।

পশ্চার্ধ *n.* the lower half of the human body; the lower half; the latter half; the other half.

পশ্চিম *n.* the west; the Occident; the western world, the western hemisphere. □ *a.* final, last, ultimate; subsequent; western. **~দেশীয়** *a.* of a western country; up-country. **~বঙ্গ** *n.* West Bengal. **পশ্চিম বায়ুপ্রবাহ** *n.* westerly winds; the west wind. **পশ্চিম ভারতীয় দ্বীপপুঞ্জ** *n.* the West Indies. **পশ্চিমা** *a.* of the west, western (পশ্চিমা বাতাস) ; up-country (পশ্চিমা লোক) ; □ *n.* an up-country man. **পশ্চিমাঞ্চল** *n.* the western part or region. **পশ্চিমাস্য** *a.* facing westward. **পশ্চিমি** *a.* western; Occidental.

পশ্বাচার *n.* a form of asceticism characterized by self-restraint, continence and abstinence from drinking wine and eating meat; beastly conduct, brutality. **পশ্বাচারী** *a.* practising the aforesaid form of asceticism; bestial, brutal.

পশ্বাধম *a.* even worse than a beast or brute (পশ্বাধম ব্যক্তি).

পষ্ট, পষ্টাপষ্টি coll. corruptions of **স্পষ্ট** and **স্পষ্টাস্পষ্টি** respectively.

পসন্দ var. of **পছন্দ**।

পসরা *n.* a load or heap of articles of traffic, wares, merchandise (পসরা সাজানো) ; a basket containing articles of traffic (পসরা মাথায় করা) ; a load, a heap, a basket (কলঙ্কের পসরা) ; an article of traffic, a commodity.

পসলা older spell. of **পশলা**।

পসার¹ *n.* a market-place, a bazaar; a shop; articles of traffic, wares (দোকানপসার).

পসার² *n.* a professional man's business practice; good practice (এই উকিলটির পসার আছে) ; good reputation, fame (গায়কমণ্ডলীতে পসার করা).

পসারা *v.* (poet.) to stretch out, to extend (বাহু পসারিয়া).

পসারি *n.* a shopkeeper, a seller, a dealer; a pedlar. *fem.* **পসারিনি**।

পসুরি *n.* a measure of weight (about 4.5 kgs.).

পস্তানো *v.* to repent or rue or regret. **পস্তানি** *n.* repentance; regret.

পস্তু alt. spell. of **পশতু**।

পহর coll. corrup. of **প্রহর**।

পহিল *a.* (obs. & poet.) first; early; young. **~হি** *adv.* at first.

পহেলা for. & obs. form of **পয়লা**।

পা¹ *n.* (mus.) the fifth note of the diatonic scale of C major, G.

পা² *n.* a leg; a foot; a paw; a leg of an article of furniture. **পা চাটা** *v.* to toady, to bootlick. **পা চালানো** *v.* to quicken one's steps; to kick, (hum.) to hoof. **পা টিপে, পা টিপে টিপে** *adv.* on tiptoe; stealthily. **পা দেওয়া** *v.* to set foot on; to step in; to come. **পা ধরা** same as **পায়ে ধরা**। **পা ধুতেও না আসা** *v.* to avoid visiting or using (a place) out of sheer disgust or abomination. **পা বাড়ানো** *v.* to step out, to go out, to leave (ঘর থেকে পা বাড়ানো) ; to be on the point of going or setting out or departing; to set out. **পায়ে ঠেলা** *v.* to reject or abandon or shun scornfully, to spurn at (হাতের লক্ষ্মী পায়ে ঠেলা). **পায়ে তেল দেওয়া** *v.* to flatter in a servile manner. **পায়ে দলা** *v.* to trample under foot. **পায়ে ধরা** *v.* to solicit or importune or supplicate humbly. **পায়ে পড়া** *v.* to fall at one's feet in supplication. **পায়ের উপর পা দিয়ে থাকা** *v.* (fig.) to lead a carefree life of ease, comfort and indolence. **পায়ের পাতা** *n.* an instep; a foot. **পায়ে রাখা** *v.* to treat or favour or shelter graciously. **পায়ে হাত দেওয়া** *v.* to touch some one's feet in obeisance. **পা-চাটা** *a.* footlicking, bootlicking. **পা-চাটা লোক** a footlicker, a bootlicker, a toady. **পা-পা করে** *adv.* step by step. **পায়ে পায়ে** *adv.* at every step (পায়ে পায়ে বাধা) ; (of two or more persons or creatures) having one another's legs tied together; (of a single person or creature) having legs tied together (পায়ে পায়ে বাঁধা) ; with slow but steady steps (পায়ে পায়ে এগোনো) ; on the back of, pursuing (সে আমার পায়ে পায়ে আসছে).

পাই *n.* an obsolete Indian coin (= 1/192 rupee), a pie.

পাইক *n.* a foot soldier, an infantryman, a footman; a guard or messenger armed with a staff and also with other weapons (often a liveried one). **পাইক-বরকন্দাজ** *n.* footmen and other followers.

পাইকা *n.* (print.) pica.

পাইকার, (coll.) **পাইকের** *n.* a wholesale buyer or trader, a wholesaler; a pedlar. **পাইকারি** *a.* wholesale (পাইকারি দর) ; collective (পাইকারি জরিমানা).

পাইখানা dial. corrup. of **পায়খানা**।

পাইন obs. var. of **পান**[২]।

পাইপ *n.* a pipe.

পাউডার *n.* powder (esp. cosmetic powder). **পাউডার বোলানো, পাউডার মাখা** *v.* to dust or daub with powder, to powder. **পাউডারের কৌটো** a powder-case, a powder-box. **পাউডারের তুলি** a powder-puff.

পাউন্ড *n.* a unit of weight (= 454 grammes); a unit of money (= 20 shillings).

পাউরুটি *n.* bread baked in the European fashion. **একটা গোটা পাউরুটি** a loaf of bread. **এক টুকরো পাউরুটি** a piece or slice of bread.

পাওনা *a.* that which ought to be paid or done to one, due. □ *n.* due; money due to one; earnings, income (উপরি পাওনা) ; assets or outstanding bills (দেনা-পাওনা). **পাওনা আদায় করা** *v.* to realize what is due; to realize a bill or claim. **পাওনা দেওয়া, পাওনা মেটানো** *v.* to pay what is due; to foot the bill. **~গন্ডা, ~-থোওনা** *n.* due; earnings, income. **~দার** *n.* a creditor.

পাওয়া *v.* to get; to receive (চিঠি পাওয়া) ; to obtain (মুক্তি পাওয়া) ; to find (চাকরি পাওয়া) ; to earn or gain (টাকা পাওয়া) ; to attain, to realize (সিদ্ধি পাওয়া) : to come or happen (দেখতে পাওয়া) ; to have (দেখা পাওয়া) ; to be able (শুনতে পাওয়া) ; to inherit (বাপের স্বভাব পাওয়া) ; to feel or to be stricken with (খিদে পাওয়া) ; to feel like (কান্না পাওয়া) ; to enjoy (আরাম পাওয়া) ; to sense, to be aware of (টের পাওয়া) ; to be possessed by (ভূতে পাওয়া). □ *a.* obtained, earned (পাওয়া জিনিস) ; possessed by (ভূতে-পাওয়া লোক). **পড়ে পাওয়া** to get by chance. **জো পাওয়া** to get an opportunity (for gain etc.) **পাওয়ানো** *v.* to cause to get or obtain or find or earn or gain or attain or inherit or be stricken with or feel like or feel or be possessed by.

পাংশন *a.* bringing disgrace, tarnishing (কুলপাংশন).

পাংশু *n.* ashes; dust; stain, stigma; vice, sin. □ *a.* livid, pale (পাংশুমুখ). **~বর্ণ** *a.* ash-coloured; livid. □ *n.* ash-colour. **~ল** *a.* dusty, dust-ridden; stained; vicious, sinful; libidinous. □ *n.* Shiva (শিব). **~লা** *a. fem.* of **পাংশুল**। □ *n.* the earth.

পাঁইজ obs. var or **পাঁজ**।

পাঁইজর var. of **পাঁয়জোর**।

পাঁইট *n.* a measure of capacity, a pint.

পাঁউরুটি pop. var. of **পাউরুটি**।

পাঁক *n.* slime, silt.

পাঁকাটি pop. var. of **পাকাটি**।

পাঁকাল *n.* a kind of eel. □ *a.* muddy, miry, clayey.

পাঁকুই *n.* chilblain; foot-sore caused by mud.

পাঁচ *n.* & *a.* five. **পাঁচ কথা** a lot of talking; many and varied topics; harsh words; a talking-to; reproof.

পাঁচই *n.* the fifth day of a month, the fifth. □ *a.* (of the days of a month) fifth.

পাঁচজন *n.* (lit.) five persons; (fig.) people at large, others, they.

পাঁচড়া *n.* scabies, itches.

পাঁচন *n.* a medicinal decoction prepared by boiling different herbs.

পাঁচনবাড়ি alt. spell. of **পাচনবাড়ি**।

পাঁচনর *n.* a five-tiered or five-stringed necklace. **পাঁচনরি** *a.* five-stringed or five-tiered (পাঁচনরি হার).

পাঁচনি alt. spell. of **পাচনি**।

পাঁচফোড়ন *n.* cumin-seed, black cumin-seed, fenugreek seed, aniseed and parsley : these five kinds of spices collectively.

পাঁচমিশালি (coll.) **পাঁচমিশেলি** *a.* assorted.

পাঁচহাতি *a.* five cubits long (পাঁচহাতি শাল).

পাঁচালি, (rej.) **পাঁচালী** *n.* a class of Bengali poems celebrating the glory of a deity and often set to music; (loos.) a long-drawnout record or narrative.

পাঁচিল *n.* a wall.

পাঁচুই coll. corrup. of **পাঁচই**।

পাঁজ *n.* a skein or wisp or roll of carded cotton.

পাঁজর, পাঁজরা *n.* the ribs; the thorax; a rib-bone, a rib.

পাঁজা[1] *n.* a birck-kiln, kiln.

পাঁজা[2] *n.* a bundle; a faggot; a pile, a heap. **পাঁজা করা** *v.* to bundle; to pile, to heap.

পাঁজা[3] *n.* outspread hands forming a stretcher.

পাঁজাকোলা *a.* lifted upon hands outspread in the shape of a stretcher. **পাঁজাকোলা করা** *v.* to lift upon hands outspread in the shape of a stretcher.

পাঁজি *n.* a calendar, an almanac, an ephemeris. **~পুথি** *n.* ephemerides and scriptures; books collectively. **হাতে পাঁজি মঙ্গলবার** worrying for ascertaining a date with the almanac in hand; unnecessary groping or search (for a solution that is already there).

পাঁট var. of **পাঁইট**।

পাঁঠা *n.* a he-goat; (dero.) a dunce, a fool. *fem.* **পাঁঠি**। **~বলি** *n.* sacrifice of a goat by chopping off its head. **পাঁঠার মাংস** goat's meat; (pop.) mutton.

পাঁড় *a* ripe (পাঁড় শসা) ; inveterate (পাঁড় মাতাল, পাঁড় বদমাশ). □ *n.* an inveterate drunkard.

পাঁড়ে *n.* the family name of some upcountry Brahmans.

পাঁতি *n.* a row, a line (দাঁতের পাঁতি) ; a line quoted from scriptures as an authority, a scriptural prescription (পাঁতি দেওয়া) ; style, manner ('কথার দেখ পাঁতি') ; a letter, a note ('রতন হারে বাঁধিয়া দিনু পাঁতি') ; information about identity, descriptive particulars (জাতির পাঁতি). **~পত্র** *n.* a solemn marriage-contract drawn up in black and white. **পাঁতিপত্র করা** *v.* to draw up a solemn marriage-contract in black and white.

পাঁদাড় *n.* a dump for sweepings, refuse etc. at the back of a house.

পাঁপর[1] *n.* a snack made of the dough of pigeon-pea rolled into thin roundish saucer and eaten after frying in oil or singeing.

পাঁপর[2] *n.* (law) a pauper.

পাঁয়জোর, (rare) **পাঁয়জর** *n.* an anklet fitted with small jingling bells (as used by a dancer).

পাঁয়তারা *n.* act of pacing to find an opportunity to attack or grapple (as in wrestling); act of bragging before commencing to do something; preliminary preparations. **পাঁয়তারা কষা** *v.* to pace up and down to find a suitable moment to attack or grapple; to brag before commencing to do something; to make preliminary preparations.

পাঁশ *n.* ashes; a worthless or nonsense thing, talk etc. (ছাইপাঁশ). **পাঁশুটে** *a.* ash-coloured; livid, pale.

পাঁশকুড় *n.* dustbin.

পাক[1] a (Mus.) sacred, holy.

পাক[2] *n.* cooking; act of condensing by heat (সন্দেশের পাক) ; digestion (পাকস্থলী) ; consequence (বিপাক) ; greyness (চুলে পাক ধরা). **পাক করা** *v.* to cook. **পাক ধরা** *v.* to begin to be condensed by heat; to begin to turn grey. **~ক্রিয়া** *n.* (function or act of) digestion. **~তেল** *n.* a medicinal oil. **~পাত্র** same as **পাকস্থালী**। **~মণ্ড** *n.* chyme. **~যন্ত্র** *n.* the digestive organ, the stomach. **পাকযন্ত্র-প্রদাহ** *n.* inflammation of the stomach, gastritis. **~শালা** *a.* a kitchen, a cookhouse. **~স্থলী** *n.* the stomach. **~স্থালী** *n.* a cooking pot or utensil. **~স্পর্শ** *n.* the ceremony of a bride's serving out food for the first time to her husband's kinsfolk.

পাক[3] *n.* a mythological demon. **~শাসন** *n.* Indra (ইন্দ্র), the slayer of Paka (পাক) the demon.

পাক[4] *n.* act of going round or winding,

circumambulation, revolution, convolution, circular movement, rotation; a coil or ring (জিলিপির পাক) ; a twirl or spin; a providential or chance occurrence (পাকেচক্রে) ; an intrigue, a conspiracy, a plot, a tangle. **পাক খাওয়া** *v.* to go round; to have a walk; to wind; to circumambulate; to revolve, to convolve, to rotate; to twirl, to spin, to twine; to ravel. **পাক খোলা** *v.* to untwist; to unravel, to puzzle out. **~দণ্ডী** *n.* a circuitous or spiral route that leads to the top of a mountain. **পাক দেওয়া** *v.* to go round; to have a walk; to twist, to spin, to ravel. **পাক পড়া, পাক লাগা** *v.* to become twisted; to become twisted confusedly, to ravel. **পাক লাগানো** same as **পাক দেওয়া। পাকে পড়া** *v.* to be entagled, to be caught in an intrigue; to get into difficulty or trouble. **পাকে ফেলা** *v.* to catch in an intrigue; to drive into difficulty.

পাকড় *n.* arrest, seizure (ধরপাকড়). **পাকড়াও** *a.* seizure, arrest; act of catching with importunity (চাকরির জন্য মন্ত্রীকে পাকড়াও). □ *v. imperat.* arrest, seize; catch. **পাকড়ানো** *v.* to catch; to seize; to arrest.

পাকন *n.* (obs.) ripening or maturing; (dero.) act of being seasoned or experienced; (dero.) becoming precocious or depraved; (of hair etc.) act of turning grey.

পাকলানো *v.* (poet. & obs.) to redden ('চক্ষু পাকলিয়া বলে').

পাকশাট corrup. of **পাখশাট।**

পাকা *v.* to ripen (ফল পাকা) ; to attain maturity, to mature (বুদ্ধি পাকা, বয়স পাকা) ; to turn grey (চুল পাকা) ; to suppurate (ফোঁড়া পাকা) ; to become seasoned (হাড় পাকা) ; to become experienced or skilled (ডাক্তারিতে সে পেকেছে) ; to be hardened (বদমাশিতে পাকা) ; to become depraved or spoilt or precocious (ছেলেটা ভারী পেকেছে). □ *a.* ripe; mature; grey; grey-haired (পাকা মাথা) ; skilled, experienced (পাকা কারিগর) ; inveterate, hardened (পাকা চোর) ; downright, thorough (পাকা বদমাশ) ; precocious, spoilt, depraved; skilful (পাকা হাত) ; set (পাকা লেখা) ; durable, fast (পাকা রং) ; full, nett (পাকা পাঁচ কিলো) ; standard (পাকা ওজন) ; hardened in fire (পাকা ইট) ; brick-built (পাকা বাড়ি) ; permanent (পাকা চাকরি) ; final, settled, fixed (পাকা কথা, পাকা তারিখ) ; pure, genuine, unalloyed (পাকা সোনা) ; seasoned (পাকা হাড়, পাকা কাঠ) ; of a high standard (পাকা রচনা) ; tanned (পাকা চামড়া) ; legally or formally drawn up (পাকা দলিল) ; pucka, pukka. **পাকা ওজন** standard weight esp. in which one seer (সের) is equal to 80 tolas (তোলা). **পাকা কথা** final word; a promise or word. **পাকা করা** *v.* to confirm or finalize. **পাকা খাতা** *n.* finalized book of accounts. **পাকা ধানে মই দেওয়া** (lit.) to harrow and destroy a field of ripened paddy; (fig.) to undo an accomplished piece of work; to do incalculable harm to. **পাকা ঘুঁটি কেঁচে যাওয়া** undoing of what is almost complete. **পাকা চামড়া** leather. **~চুল** *n.* grey hair; an aged and experienced man (পাকাচুলের পরামর্শ নেওয়া). **পাকা দেখা** *v.* to visit formally a prospective bride's house in order to draw up the marriage-contract in black and white. **~দেখা** *n.* a formal visit to a prospective bride's house in order to draw up the marriage-contract in black and white; the final view of a girl by the bridegroom's party before she is accepted in marriage. **~পাকি** *a.* settled, fixed, finalized; sure. **পাকাপাকি করা** *v.* to settle, to fix, to finalize; to make sure. **~পোক্ত** *a.* permanent; settled, fixed, finalized; hardened by long practice (পাকাপোক্ত লোক) ; experienced and seasoned; inveterate (পাকাপোক্ত চোর). **পাকা বাড়ি** a brick-built house, a building. **পাকা মাথা** a grey-headed or grey-haired person; an old or aged person; a wise or experienced person. **পাকা মাথায় সিঁদুর পরা** (for a woman) to have one's husband living even when one becomes hoary-headed. **পাকামি** *n.* precocity. **পাকা রাস্তা** a metalled or cobbled road. **পাকা হাড়ে ভেলকি দেখানো** to show magical or amazing power or proficiency even in one's old age. **পাকা হাত** a set hand; skilled hand; an old hand, an experienced man; an adept. **পাকা হিসাব** final accounts.

পাকাটি *n.* a stalk of the jute-plant used as fuel; (fig.) a lean rickety person.

পাকাটে *a.* wizened.

পাকা দেখা see **পাকা**।

পাকানো *v.* to twist; to twirl; to ravel; to wring, to writhe (শরীর পাকানো) ; to wizen; to complicate (সে ব্যাপারটাকে পাকিয়েছে) ; to organize, to form (দল পাকানো) ; to cook, to ripen; to mature; to cause to turn grey; to cause to suppurate; to season; to make experienced or skilled; to harden; to deprave, to spoil, to make precocious. □ *a.* twisted; twirled; ravelled; wizened.

পাকাপাকি, পাকাপোক্ত, পাকামি see **পাকা**।

পাকাশয় *n.* the stomach. **~প্রদাহ** *n.* inflammation of the stomach, gastritis. **পাকাশয়িক** *a.* stomachal, stomachic; gastric.

পাকি *a.* measured by the standard weight in which one seer (সের) is equal to 80 tolas (তোলা), standard (পাকি ওজন).

পাকিস্তানি *a.* of Pakistan. □ *n.* a citizen of Pakistan, Pakistani.

পাকুড় *n.* a species of fig-tree, *Ficus infectoria*.

পাকেচক্রে, পাকে-প্রকারে *adv.* by this trick or that, through cunning devices; somehow; by hook or by crook.

পাক্কা *a.* emphatical var. of **পাকা** (*a*).

পাক্ষিক *a.* fortnightly. □ *n.* a fortnightly journal.

পাখ var. of **পাখনা**।

পাখওয়াজ alt. spell. of **পাখোয়াজ**।

পাখনা *n.* a wing; a feather; a fin.

পাখলা *n.* rubbing and washing, scouring or rinsing (ধোয়া-পাখলা). **পাখলানো** *v.* to rub and wash; to scour; to rinse.

পাখশাট *n.* a blow or a flap of a bird's wings. **পাখশাট মারা** *v.* (of a bird) to strike with wings, to flap one's wings.

পাখা *n.* a wing; a feather; (rare) a fin; a fan; a propeller; vane or sail (as of a windmill). **টানা পাখা** *n.* a large fan suspended from a pole and moved by pulling; a punkah, a punka. **বিজলি-পাখা** *n.* an electric fan. **হাত-পাখা** *n.* a hand-fan. **পাখা করা** *v.* to fan. **পাখা ঘোরানো** *v.* to set a propeller or vane moving; to switch on an electric fan. **পাখা ঝাপটানো** *v.* (of a bird) to flutter or flap wings. **পাখা টানা** *v.* to pull a punkah.

পাখাওয়ালা *a.* winged; feathered; (rare) finned; having a propeller or vane or sail. □ *n.* a punkah-puller; a dealer in or pedlar of hand-fans; a repairer of electric fans; one who lets out electric fans on hire.

পাখি *n.* the bird; a blind (of a window); a spoke (of a wheel); a step or rung of a ladder. **পাখি পড়ানো** *v.* to teach or get up by rote, to cram. **পাখির প্রাণ** very feeble vitality. **পাখির বাসা** a nest; (fig.) a very disorderly place or thing (মাথাটা যেন পাখির বাসা).

পাখোয়াজ *n.* a musical instrument of percussion shaped almost like a tom-tom. **পাখোয়াজি** *n.* one who can play on this instrument.

পাগড়ি *n.* a turban; a head-cloth. **~ধারী** *n.* turbaned.

পাগল, (coll.) **পাগলা** *a.* mad, lunatic, insane; crazy; frenzied; (of male elephants and camels) musth, mast; (of dogs) rabid; intoxicated (সিদ্ধি খেয়ে পাগল) ; beside oneself (আনন্দে পাগল) ; persistently solicitous (পাবার জন্য পাগল) ; excited or fretting or raving or rabid (ক্রোধে পাগল) ; (in affection) simple, ignorant, foolish. □ *n.* a madman, a maniac, a lunatic; an eccentric man; (in affection) a sinpleton, a fool. *fem.* **পাগলি, পাগলিনি**। **পাগল করা** *v.* to dement; to madden; to enrage, to excite; to strike with extreme eagerness; to intoxicate. **পাগল-করা** *a.* maddening. **পাগল হওয়া** *v.* to become demented; to go mad; to madden; to be enraged or excited; to become extremely eager; to be intoxicated; to be frenzied; to run amok. **পাগল হাওয়া** a very intoxicating or maddening wind, a wind that excites or overwhelms a person; a very strong and wild wind. **পাগলাগারদ** *n.* a lunatic asylum, a bedlam, a madhouse. **পাগলাটে** *a.* crack-brained, cranky, crazy, eccentric. **পাগলাটে লোক** a crack-brain, a crank. **পাগলামি,** (coll.) **পাগলামো** *n.* madness; craziness; craze, eccentricity; (in affection) foolishness, folly.

পা-গাড়ি *n.* a bicycle; (hum.) the foot or the leg (সবচেয়ে ভালো পা-গাড়ি).

পাঙাশ *n.* a large silvery-white fish.

পাঙ্‌ক্তেয় *a.* fit to be included in the same line or row or class; fit to be allowed to sit in a community-dinner (see **পঙ্‌ক্তিভোজন**).

পাঙ্গাশ[1] alt. spell. of **পাঙাশ**।

পাঙ্গাশ[2] *a.* ash-coloured; livid, pale.

পাচক *a.* digestive; gastric; one who cooks. □ *n.* a cook. **~রস** *n.* gastric juice, digestive fluid.

পাচন *a.* digestive; gastric. □ *n.* a medicinal decoction.

পাচনতন্ত্র *n.* digestive system.

পাচনবাড়ি *n.* a truncheon for driving cattle.

পাচনযন্ত্র *n.* the digestive or gastric organ.

পাচনি same as **পাচনবাড়ি**।

পা-চাটা see **পা[2]**।

পাচার *n.* act of finishing or consuming; slaughter, murder; secret removal (and hiding); kidnapping; smuggling; act or removing secretly and doing away. **পাচার করা** *v.* to finish; to consume; to slay, to murder, (coll.) to do in; to remove secretly (and conceal); to kidnap; to smuggle; to remove secretly and do away.

পাচিকা *fem.* of **পাচক**।

পাচ্য *a.* that which can be or is to be cooked; digestive, digestible.

পাছ *n.* the back part, the back.

পাছড়ানো same as **আছড়ানো**।

পাছড়া-পাছড়ি *n.* scuffle, mutual grappling.

পাছদুয়ার *n.* a back-door, a postern gate.

পাছতলা *n.* the lower half of the body; the back part of a dwelling-house.

পাছা *n.* the hip, the buttocks; the loins; the posteriors, the rump.

পাছাড় same as **আছাড়**।

পাছা-পেড়ে *a.* (of a woman's cloth) having a broad lengthwise furbelow in the middle.

পাছু *n.* the back (পাছু থেকে). □ *a.* flinching, retreated. □ *adv.* (dial.) towards one's back, back (পাছু ফেরা) ; from behind (পাছু ডাকা) ; afterwards, later on (পাছু শুনব). □ *prep.* on the back of (আমার পাছু আসবে). **পাছু লাগা** (dial.) *v.* to chase, to pursue; to tease; to watch one closely with mischievous intentions. **পাছু হওয়া** *v.* to flinch, to shrink back; to retreat. **পাছু পাছু** *adv.* & *prep.* on the back of, close behind.

পাছে *prep.* & *adv.* same as **পিছে**। □ *con.* lest. **পাছে পাছে** same as **পিছে পিছে**।

পাজামা var. of **পায়জামা**।

পাজি *a.* mean, vile; wicked; knavish; mischievous; hare-brained. **পাজির পা-ঝাড়া** extremely mean or vile or wicked or knavish or mischievous. **পাজি লোক** a knave, a villain, a rogue, a scoundrel; a scapegrace; a varlet.

পাঞ্চজন্য *n.* (myth.) the conch used to be blown by Krishna (কৃষ্ণ) esp. in battles.

পাঞ্চবার্ষিক *a.* quinquennial.

পাঞ্চভৌতিক *a.* of or composed of the five elements namely the earth, water, fire, air and atmosphere.

পাঞ্চালি *n.* a princess of Panchal (পঞ্চাল) ; Draupadi of the Mahabharata.

পাঞ্জা *n.* the five playing-cards or dice; the palm of a hand; an impression of the palm; a letter or permit marked with the impression of the palm of a king or an official authority. **পাঞ্জা কষা, পাঞ্জা লড়া** *v.* to try the strength of each other's wrist by seizing it and trying to turn it down.

পাঞ্জাবি[1] alt. spell. of **পঞ্জাবি**।

পাঞ্জাবি[2], (rej.) **পাঞ্জাবী[2]** *n.* a kind of loose and long shirt usu. worn by men.

পাট[1] *n.* a well-curb.

পাট[2] *n.* words and actions of a character in a play, a part. **পাট করা** *v.* to act one's part.

পাট[3] *n.* silk, linen; jute; a plank, a board (ধোপার পাট) ; a holy place (শ্রীপাট) ; a seat, an official seat, a throne (পাটে বসা, পাটরানি) ; (myth.) the imaginary mountain behind which the sun goes down whilst setting (সূর্য পাটে নামে) ; a fold, a plait (কাপড়ের পাট, চুলের পাট). □ *a.* royal (পাটহাতি). **পাট করা** *v.* to fold, to plait, to pleat; (fig.) to give a sound drubbing. **পাটে নামা** *v.* (of the sun) to set. **পাটে বসা** *v.* to sit on a throne; to be seated on the official seat; (of the sun) to set. **পাটে পাটে** *adv.* in or by folds; in every fold.

পাট⁴ *n.* routine duties of a household. **পাট তোলা, পাট ওঠানো** *v.* to complete the routine duties of a household; (fig.) to close down. **পাট সারা** *v.* to complete the routine duties of a household; (fig.) to complete a work.

পাটকাটি same as **পাকাটি** ।

পাটকিলে same as **পাটল** ।

পাটকেল *n.* a brickbat.

পাটন *n.* a city, a habitation, a settlement (গৌড় পাটন) ; trade and commerce; sea trade. **পাটনে যাওয়া** *v.* to set out on sea trade.

পাটনাই *a.* grown or produced in Patna; of Patna.

পাটনি *n.* a ferryman; a wharfinger.

পাটব same as **পটুতা** (see **পটু**).

পাটরানি, (rej.) **পাটরাণী** *n.* a prince's chief queen, (cp.) a queen consort.

পাটল *a.* brick-red, pale and pink-coloured.

পাটলা, পাটলি *n.* the trumpet-flower or its plant.

পাটশাক *n.* leaves of the jute-plant used as a pot-herb.

পাটা *n.* (of wood) a plank, a board; (of metals) a plate; a face or surface (বুকের পাটা) ; a document of purchase or leasehold of land. **বুকের পাটা** (fig.) courage or daring.

পাটাতন *n.* a deck or floor (esp. one made of wood).

পাটালি *n.* a discoid solid tablet of molasses.

পাটি[1], পাটী[1] *n.* a finely woven mat of a kind of aquatic grass.

পাটি[2], পাটী[2], *n.* orderliness; order, system, method; a row, a line (দন্তপাটি) ; one of a pair (জুতোর পাটি) ; a plait, a pleat ('মোহন পাটি') ; household duties ('সংসারের পাটি') ; reckoning by figures (পাটীগণিত).

পাটিগণিত, পাটীগণিত *n.* arithmetic.

পাটিসাপটা *n.* a kind of sweet patty or pie.

পাটেশ্বরী same as **পাটরানি** ।

পাটোয়ার *n.* a landowner's or businessman's employee who collects rents and keeps accounts; a manufacturer of haberdashery esp. girdles and strings of beads. □ *a.* very much calculating or cautious about expenditure. **পাটোয়ারি** *n.* same as **পাটোয়ার** (*n.*) □ *a.* relating to the aforesaid landowner's or businessman's employee; relating to haberdashery; very much calculating or cautious about expenditure. **পাটোয়ারি বুদ্ধি** shrewd or keen practical sense, keen consciousness of one's own interest or affairs; circumspection.

পাট্টা *n.* a document of purchase or leasehold of land; a fold, a plait, a pleat (দোপাট্টা) ; a thick layer; massive beard (গালপাট্টা). **পাট্টা দেওয়া** *v.* to sell or to lease out (land.) **পাট্টা নেওয়া** *v.* to purchase or to take on lease (as land). **~দাতা** *n.* a lessor. **~দার** *n.* a leaseholder.

পাঠ *n.* reading, perusal; study; recitation; lesson; a reading of text (পুঁথির মূল পাঠ) ; a text-book. **পাঠ করা** *v.* to read, to peruse; to study; to recite. **পাঠ তৈরি করা** *v.* to learn or prepare one's lesson. **পাঠ দেওয়া** *v.* to give one a lesson. **পাঠ নেওয়া** *v.* to take lessons (from a teacher). **পাঠক** *n.* a reader; one who studies; a student, a pupil; a reciter; one who reads out or recites from scriptures; a professional narrator of mythological stories; a teacher, a reader. **~গৃহ** *n.* a reading-room, a study; a library. **পাঠন** *n.* teaching. **~ক্রম** *n.* a syllabus. **~নিবিষ্ট, ~মগ্ন** *a.* absorbed in reading or study. **~ভবন, ~মন্দির** *n.* a reading-room, a study; a library; a school. **~ভেদ** same as **পাঠান্তর** । **~রত** *a.* engaged in reading or studying. **~শালা** *n.* a primary school. **পাঠানুরাগ** *n.* fondness for reading; devotion to study. **পাঠানুরাগী** *a.* fond of reading; devoted to study. **পাঠান্তর** *n.* another text or a different text or reading or version. **পাঠাভ্যাস করা** *v.* to learn one's lessons.

পাঠার্থী *a.* desirous of reading or studying. □ *n.* a student, a pupil; a prospective student. *fem.* **পাঠার্থিনী** । **পাঠোদ্ধার** *n.* deciphering an obscure piece of writing or passage.

পাঠান *n.* a Pathan, an Afghan.

পাঠানুরাগ, পাঠান্তর, পাঠাভ্যাস, পাঠার্থী see **পাঠ** ।

পাঠিকা *fem.* of **পাঠক** (see **পাঠ**).

পাঠানো *v.* to send, to despatch; to transmit. **ডেকে পাঠানো** *v.* to send for; to summon. **বলে পাঠানো** *v.* to send information to some one through a messenger.

পাঠ্য *a.* to be read; readable; prescribed for reading. **~ক্রম** *n.* a syllabus. **~তালিকা** *n.* a syllabus; a book-list. **পাঠ্যনির্বাচন সমিতি** the Text-Book Committee. **~পুস্তক** *n.* a text-book. **~সূচি** *n.* curriculum. **পাঠ্যাবস্থা** *n.* student life.

পাড়[1] *n.*bank, shore, margin (of a sea, bay, river, lake, pond etc.); a mound of earth raised round a piece of arable land; a well-curb.

পাড়[2] *n.* furbelow, flounce, coloured or decorated border (as of a cloth). **পাড় লাগানো** *v.* to furbelow, to flounce.

পাড়[3] *n.* act of pedalling in an up-and-down manner (as a husking-pestle). **পাড় দেওয়া** *v.* to pedal in an up-and-down manner.

পাড়[4] *n.* a cross-beam.

পাড়ন *n.* bringing down; lowering; causing to come down.

পাড়া[1] *v.* to bring down (নারকেল পাড়া, তাক থেকে পাড়া) ; to pluck (ফুল পাড়া) ; to knock down (ভীম কীচককে পেড়ে ফেললেন) ; to cause to take to one's bed, to prostrate (জ্বরে তাকে পেড়ে ফেলেছে) ; to lay out (**বিছানা পাড়া** = to make a bed); to lay as eggs (**ডিম পাড়া** = to lay an egg); to pronounce loudly (**গাল পাড়া** = to shout abuses at); to invoke as in solemn appeal (**দোহাই পাড়া** = to invoke as in solemn appeal, to call down or upon); to remove, to clear (**এঁটো পাড়া** = to clear the table).

পাড়া[2] *n.* a small area of human habitation containing a cluster of houses, a locality (গোয়ালপাড়া). **পাড়া বেড়ানো** *v.* to stroll about idly in the neighbourhood, to go round the locality.

পাড়া-কুঁদুলি *a. fem.* given to constant and boisterous brawling with neighbours, quarrelsome, cantankerous, (cp.) termagant. □ *n. fem.* such a woman, (cp.) a termagant or fire-eater.

পাড়া-গাঁ *n.* a rural area; countryside; a village.

পাড়াগেঁয়ে *a.* rural; rustic (lit. & fig).

পাড়ানো *v.* to cause to bring down (ফল পাড়ানো) or pluck (ফুল পাড়ানো) ; to induce to (**ঘুম পাড়ানো** = to lull to sleep). **পাড়ানি, পাড়ানিয়া** *a.* inducing to, inducive to (ঘুমপাড়ানি গান). □ *n.* one who brings down fruit esp. from tall trees.

পাড়া-পড়শি *n.* neighbours; a neighbour. □ *a.* dwelling in one's neighbourhood (পাড়া-পড়শি লোক).

পাণি *n.* the hand. **~গ্রহ, ~গ্রহণ, ~পীড়ন** *n.* marriage, wedding. **পাণিগ্রহণ করা, পাণিপীড়ন করা** *v.* to marry, to wed. **~প্রার্থী** *n.* & *a.* one willing to marry somebody.

পাণ্ডব, পাণ্ডবেয় *n.* a son of King Pandu of the Mahabharata. **পঞ্চপাণ্ডব** *n.* the five sons of King Pandu collectively; (fig.) a set of five persons, a quintette. **পাণ্ডববর্জিত** *a.* (of lands and countries) not habitable or worth visiting because avoided even by the Pandavas (পাণ্ডব) during their sojourn; (pop.) uninhabited. **পাণ্ডবসখা** *n.* a friend of the Pandavas; Krishna (কৃষ্ণ).

পাণ্ডা *n.* a Brahman priest acting as a guide to pilgrims at holy places; (dero.) a leader, a ring-leader.

পাণ্ডিত্য *n.* erudition, learning, scholarship; wisdom; expertness, skill; (dero.) pedantry. **~প্রকাশ** *n.* ostentatious display of one's learning by oneself, parade of one's learning; (iron.) act of betraying one's ignorance or folly. **পাণ্ডিত্যাভিমানী** *a.* proud of one's learning. *fem.* **পাণ্ডিত্যাভিমানিনী** ।

পাণ্ডু, পাণ্ডুর *n.* the pale yellow or whitish yellow colour, the mud colour; jaundice; chlorosis, green sickness. □ *a.*

pale yellow, white yellow, mud-coloured; pale; jaundiced; chlorotic, etiolated. **পাণ্ডু রোগ** *n.* jaundice, chlorosis.

পাণ্ডুলিপি, পাণ্ডুলেখ, পাণ্ডুলেখ্য *n.* a hand-written sheet or copy, a manuscript; a draft not yet finalized; a (parliamentary) bill.

পাত¹ *n.* a fall or a shower (বৃষ্টিপাত) ; shedding or dropping (রক্তপাত) ; throwing or casting (দৃষ্টিপাত) ; incidence, occurrence (বিপদ্‌পাত) ; ruin, destruction (দেহপাত) ; (astr.) a node (**উচ্চপাত** = the ascending node. **নিম্নপাত** = the descending node). **পাত করা** *v.* to impair, to ruin, to destroy (শরীর পাত করছে).

পাত² *n.* a leaf (as of a tree or book); a sheet or foil (of metal); a leaf of banana or sal (শাল) used as a dinner-plate. **পাত করা** *v.* to arrange for dinner by laying leaves of banana or sal; to lay the table; to flatten into a sheet (লোহা পিটিয়ে পাত করা). **~কুড়ানি** *n. fem.* one who eats others' leavings; one who stills hunger by eating others' leavings. **পাত কাটা** *v.* to eat off another's table like a beggar; (fig.) to importune cringingly for another's favour, to fawn on. **পাত পাড়া** *v.* (usu. dero.) to enjoy another's hospitality. **~চাটা** *a.* given to eating off another's table; (fig.) cringingly importuning for another's favour, currying favour (with).

পাতক *n.* sin. **পাতকী** *a.* sinful. □ *n.* a sinner. *fem.* **পাতকিনী** ৷

পাতকুয়া, (coll.) **পাতকুয়ো, পাতকো** *n.* a draw-well, a well.

পাতখোলা *n.* a piece of incompletely burnt potsherd.

পাতগালা *n.* sheet-wax.

পাতচাটা see **পাত²** ৷

পাতঞ্জল *a.* of or compiled by Patanjali, the Philosopher of ancient India. **~দর্শন** *n.* the yoga (যোগ) system of philosophy.

পাতড়া *n.* a leaf of banana or sal (শাল) on which food has been taken; a dish of fish or vegetables fried or singed on a banana-leaf. **পাতড়া-চাটা** same as **পাতচাটা** (see **পাত²**).

পাততাড়ি *n.* a bundle of palm-leaves used (instead of paper) in writing by a tyro. **পাততাড়ি গোটানো** *v.* (lit.) to put away the bundle of palm-leaves when the lesson is over; (fig.) to depart or decamp, to quit; to depart lock, stock and barrel; (fig.) to close down or wind up (a business etc.).

পাতন *n.* act of throwing or hurling down; distillation; spreading; overthrowing; killing; writing (অঙ্কপাতন). **~যন্ত্র** *n.* a retort.

পাতনামা *n.* beginning, inception; preface.

পাতলা *a.* diluted (পাতলা দুধ) ; loose (পাতলা দাস্ত) ; thin (পাতলা বই) ; fine (পাতলা কাগজ বা কাপড়) ; slender (পাতলা বেত) ; sparse (পাতলা ঝোপ) ; light (পাতলা ঘুম) ; delicate (পাতলা শরীর).

পাতলুন *n.* pantaloons; trousers; pyjamas.

পাতশাহ, পাতশা *n.* (Mus.) a king or an emperor, a padishah. **পাতশাহি** *a.* royal; imperial.

পাতা¹ *a.* (used as a *sfx.*) one who preserves or protects (বিশ্বপাতা).

পাতা² *n.* a leaf (of a tree or a book); a page (of a book); a leaf of banana or sal (শাল) used as a dinner-plate; a tree-leaf used in writing as a substitute for paper; a pleat, a plait, a braid; a lid (চোখের পাতা) ; the flat surface (পায়ের পাতা). **চোখের পাতা** the eyelid. **পায়ের পাতা** the instep; the foot. **পাতা করা** *v.* to arrange for dinner by laying leaves of banana or sal (শাল) ; to lay the table. **পাতা কাটা** *v.* to plait or braid (hair). **~-কাটা** *a.* plaited, braided. **পাতাচাটা** same as **পাতচাটা** (see **পাত²**). **পাতা-পা** *a.* flat-footed; web-footed. **পাতা পাতা** *v.* same as **পাতা করা** and **পাত পাড়া** (see **পাত²**). **পাতা কুড়ানি,** (coll.) **পাতা-কুড়ুনি** *a. fem.* earning one's livelihood by collecting dried leaves of trees; extremely indigent. □ *n. fem.* such a woman.

পাতা³ *v.* to spread, to lay out (বিছানা পাতা) ; to place ready for use (পাত পাতা) ; to lay (ফাঁদ পাতা) ; to install (পূজার ঘট পাতা) ; to set up, to establish (সংসার পাতা, দোকান পাতা) ; to set, to employ (আড়ি পাতা, কান পাতা) ; to stretch out to catch or hold (হাত পাতা) ; to bend down submissively (পিঠ পাতা) ; to curdle, to congeal, to freeze (দই পাতা).

পাতা কাটা, পাতাকুড়ানি, পাতাকুড়ুনি see **পাতা**[2] ।

পাতানো *v.* to cause to spread or lay out or place ready for use or lay or install or set up or establish or employ or stretch out for catching or bend down submissively or congeal or freeze; to form an alliance, relation etc. where nothing natural exists (বন্ধুত্ব পাতানো, সম্বন্ধ পাতানো). □ *a.* in all the senses of the *v.* and esp. formed by mutual consent only (পাতানো মাসি).

পাতাবাহার *n.* a tropical hedge-plant of the Croton genus, the *Codiaeum variegatum*.

পাতাল *n.* the netherworld, the underworld; Hades; hell. **~পুরী** *n.* the capital city of the netherworld, Hades; the netherworld. **~বাসী** *a.* inhabiting or dwelling in the netherworld. *fem.* **~বাসিনী** ।

পাতালিক *a.* (geog.) sedimentary, plutonic (পাতালিক শিলা).

পাতি[1] *n.* address, whereabouts.

পাতি[2] *n.* a row, a line (বকের পাতি).

পাতি[3] *a.* (used as a *pfx.*) small or inferior. **~কাক** *n.* the common house crow. **~লেবু** *n.* a variety of lemon. **~শিয়াল** *n.* the fox. *fem.* **~শিয়ালি** the vixen. **~হাঁস** *n.* (*fem.*) the duck; (*masc.*) the drake.

পাতিত *a.* felled; flung down; knocked down; brought down, humbled; distilled.

পাতিত্য *n.* the state of being socially cast out; moral or religious fall, degeneration, downfall, depravity.

পাতিপাতি *adv.* line by line; minutely; ransackingly. **পাতিপাতি করা** *v.* to search line by line; to search minutely, to ransack, to rummage, to make a thorough search, to rifle.

পাতিব্রত্য *n.* faithful or loyal devotion of a wife to her husband.

পাতিল *n.* (dial.) a roundish earthen vessel used chiefly for cooking.

পাতী *a.* (used as a *sfx.*) falling (সদ্যঃপাতী) ; falling away; included (অন্তঃপাতী) ; deciduous.

পাত্তা *n.* information, news; trace; address, whereabouts. **পাত্তা করা** same as **পাত্তা লাগানো** । **পাত্তা পাওয়া** *v.* to find trace or wherabouts of; (fig.) to be considered of some value or to be of some account. **পাত্তা না পাওয়া** *v.* to lose trace of; (fig.) to be of small account. **পাত্তা না দেওয়া** *v.* to treat as of little or no importance, to make light of, to take a dim view. **পাত্তা লাগানো** *v.* to try to find trace or whereabouts of.

পাত্র *n.* a pot, a vessel, a utensil, a container; a minister, a counsellor; a deserving man or an object (প্রশংসার পাত্র) ; a man, a fellow (ভবি ভোলার পাত্র নয়) ; a male character in a play; bridegroom; a prospective bridegroom. **পাত্র দেখা** *v.* to interview a prospective bridegroom for selection; to choose a bridegroom. **~পক্ষ** *n.* the bridegroom's people or party. **~মিত্র** *n. pl.* (a monarch's) courtiers and friends. **~স্থ** *a.* lying on or contained in a pot or vessel; (of a girl) wedded, married. **পাত্রস্থ করা** *v.* to give (a girl) in marriage, to marry, to wed. **পাত্রাপাত্র** *n.* deserving and undeserving persons. **পাত্রাপাত্রবিচার** *n.* discrimination between deserving and undeserving persons. **পাত্রী** *n. fem.* a deserving woman or a female object; a female character in a play; a bride; a prospective bride. **পাত্রী দেখা** *v.* to interview a prospective bride for selection; to choose a bride. **পাত্রীপক্ষ** *n.* the bride's people or party. **যোগ্যপাত্র** *n.* a deserving person; a worthy groom. **যোগ্যপাত্রী** *n.* a worthy bride. **সৎপাত্র** *n.* same as **যোগ্যপাত্র** ।

পাথর *n.* stone; a stone-made dinner plate; a precious stone, a gem; (fig.) becoming hardened by grief (দুঃখে পাথর হয়ে যাওয়া) ; a stone-hearted or unfeeling person. **পাথরে পাঁচ কিল** the most formidable good fortune or good time. **~কুচি** *n.* a stone-chip; rubble; an aromatic medicinal herb, stonewort. **~-চাপা** *a.* (fig.) incapable of thriving.

~চুন *n.* lime obtained by calcining calcium carbonate (as limestone). ~বাটি *n.* a stone-cup.

পাথরি *n.* (med.) a stone-like concretion formed within the body, calculus, concretion. **দাঁতের পাথরি** incrustation of saliva, calcium phosphate etc. forming on the teeth, tartar formed on teeth.

পাথার *n.* the sea, the ocean; a vast expanse of water.

পাথুরি pop. var. of **পাথরি** ।

পাথুরিয়া older var. of **পাথুরে** । ।

পাথুরে *a.* of stone; made of stone (পাথুরে গেলাস) ; full of stones (পাথুরে দেশ) ; stone hard (পাথুরে মাটি) ; (fig.) unfeeling or undaunted or impregnable; stony. **পাথুরে কয়লা** stone coal, anthracite.

পাথেয় *n.* travelling expenses; allowance; (chiefly rel.) viaticum.

পাদ[১] *n.* (vul.) a fart.

পাদ[২] *n.* the foot; the leg; a step or pace (সপ্তপাদ পশ্চিমে) ; bottom, foot (পর্বতের পাদদেশ) ; (of a tree) root (পাদপ) ; (of a verse) a line; a quarter (এক পাদ ধর্ম) ; (geom.) a quadrant; a title of honour (প্রভুপাদ). ~ক্ষেপ same as **পদক্ষেপ** (see **পদ**). ~গ্রন্থি *n.* the ankle. ~গ্রহণ *n.* act of touching another's feet in obesiance. ~চারণা, ~চরণ, **পাদাচার** same as **পদচারণা** (see **পদ**). ~চারী *n.* a pedestrian. ~চিহ্ন same as **পদচিহ্ন** (see **পদ**). ~টীকা *n.* a footnote. ~তল *n.* the sole (of the foot). ~ত্রাণ *n.* boot, shoe. ~ত্রিভুজ *n.* (geom.) a pedal triangle. ~দেশ *n.* the region at or around the foot or root or bottom. ~পদ্ম *n.* feet reverentially conceived as a pair of lotuses. ~পীঠ *n.* a foot-stool. ~পূরণ *n.* act of composing the missing line of a verse etc.; an expletive; (journalese) a short poem or quotation printed to fill up the blank space at the bottom of a page of a periodical. **পাদপূরণ করা** *v.* to supply the missing line of a verse; to fill up the blank space. ~পৃষ্ঠ *n.* the instep. **পাদপ্রক্ষালন করা** *v.* to rub and wash one's feet (and also legs). ~প্রদীপ *n.* a footlight; (fig.) limelight. ~প্রহার *n.* a kick. **পাদপ্রহার করা** *v.* to kick. ~বন্দনা *n.* respect shown to a revered person by touching his or her feet. ~বিক *a.* travelling esp. on foot, pedestrian. ~বিক্ষেপ same as **পদবিক্ষেপ** (see **পদ**). ~মূল *n.* the sole (of feet); the heel; the bottom. ~লেহন same as **পদলেহন** (see **পদ**). ~শৈল *n.* a small hill at the foot of a mountain. ~স্ফোট *n.* chilblain; kibe. ~সংস্থান *n.* (astr.) quadrature.

পাদপ *n.* a tree, a plant.

পাদরি, পাদ্রি *n.* a Christian clergyman or ecclesiastical preacher, a padri.

পাদা *v.* (vul.) to fart.

পাদাঙ্গুলি *n.* the toe.

পাদান, পাদানি *n.* a footboard.

পাদুকা *n.* boot, shoe, slipper; footwear. **পাদুকা-পরিহিত** *a.* booted, shoed.

পাদোদক *n.* the water with which the feet of a gracious or reverend person has been washed (a few drops of this water is taken by a devotee).

পাদ্য *n.* water for washing the feet (and also legs.)

পাদ্রি alt. spell. of **পাদরি** ।

পান[১] *n.* betel-leaf. **ছাঁচি পান, বাংলা পান, মিঠা পান** different kinds of betel-leaves. **পান খাওয়া** *v.* to chew betel leaf together with betel-nut, catechu, lime etc. **পান থেকে চুন খসা** *v.* (fig.) to commit a very negligible offence or lapse. **পান সাজা** *v.* to form a small conical cup of betel-leaf after putting betel-nut, catechu, lime etc. within this cup. **পানের বাটা** *n.* a betel-box.

পান[২] *n.* (of iron and baser metals) temper, annealing; (of gold and noble metals) alloy. **পান দেওয়া** *v.* to temper, to anneal; to alloy.

পান[৩] *n.* drinking; act of drinking wine (পানদোষ) ; (fig.) thorough enjoyment (সৌন্দর্যপান). **পান করা** *v.* to drink; to drink wine; (fig.) to enjoy thoroughly.

পানই *n.* (obs.) slipper, (esp.) wooden slipper ('বাঁধা পানই হাতে লইও').

পানক *n.* a drink of sweetened diluted fruit juices, sharbat; water hyacinth.

পানকৌড়ি *n.* a species of a diver; the cormorant.

পানগোষ্ঠী *n.* a den of drunkards; a drinking party.

পানতি *n.* a high-rimmed metal dish (used at dinner, in cooking etc.)

পানতুয়া *n.* a kind of ball-shaped sweetmeat made of posset and soaked in a solution of sugar.

পানদোষ *n.* (unwholesome) drinking habit, addiction to drinking.

পানপাত্র *n.* a drinking-cup; a goblet.

পানফল, পানবসন্ত see **পানি**।

পানভোজন *n.* drinking and eating.

পানমরা *n.* (of gold and noble metals) loss in weight owing to alloying.

পানশৌণ্ড *a.* given to drinking wine; boozy. **পানশৌণ্ড ব্যক্তি** a drunkard; a boozer.

পানসি *n.* a pinnace.

পানসে *a.* tasting like water for not being properly cooked (ঝোলটা পানসে) ; watery in taste; insipid, dull, milk-and-water (পানসে কথাবার্তা বা লেখা) ; lachrymose (পানসে মেয়ে).

পানা[১] *sfx.* like, resembling, seeming to be (চাঁদপানা মুখ).

পানা[২] *n.* a sweet cold drink, sharbat (বেলের পানা).

পানা[৩] *n.* width, breadth.

পানা[৪] *n.* a kind of aquatic algae, waterwort.

পানানো *v.* to make a calf suck the udders of a cow repeatedly before milking; (of baser metals) to temper, to anneal; (of noble metals) to alloy.

পানাপুকুর *n.* a pond covered with or full of algae or waterwort; a pond covered all over with water-hyacinth; a puddle.

পানাসক্ত *a.* addicted to drinking wine, boozy. *fem.* **পানাসক্তা**। **পানাসক্ত ব্যক্তি** a drunkard. **পানাসক্তি** *n.* addiction to drinking.

পানাহার same as **পানভোজন**।

পানি *n.* (usu. among Mus. of Bengal) water. **~পাঁড়ে** *n.* an up-country Brahman selling or supplying drinking water (esp. to railway passengers.) **~ফল,** (dial.) **পানফল** *n.* an aquatic fruit, cress(es), (cp.) water-chestnut. **~বসন্ত,** (pop.) **পানবসন্ত** *n.* chickenpox.

পানীয় *a.* that which is drunk; drinkable. □ *n.* a drink; a sweet drink, sharbat; a cordial; an alcoholic or strong drink; a beverage; a potion. **পানীয় জল** drinking water.

পানে *prep.* in the direction of, towards, to (মুখপানে).

পান্তা *a.* old by more than one night; overnight; cooked overnight and kept steeped in water (পান্তা ভাত) ; stale (পান্তা খবর). □ *n.* rice cooked overnight and kept steeped in water. **পান্তা ভাতে ঘি** (fig.) unnecessary or ludicrous spending of a good or costly thing.

পান্তি alt. spell. of **পানতি**।

পান্তুয়া alt. spell. of **পানতুয়া**।

পান্থ *n.* a traveller, a wayfarer. **~তরু, ~পাদপ** *n.* traveller's tree or palm, the Ravenala. **~নিবাস, ~শালা** *n.* a caravansarai; an inn; a wayside boarding-house; a hotel; (loos.) a boarding-house.

পান্না *n.* emerald.

পান্সি alt. spellings of **পানসি**।

পাপ *n.* sin, vice; a religious or moral lapse; wickedness; a crime; a troublesome person or thing, a pest (পাপ গেলেই বাঁচি). **পাপ করা** *v.* to commit a sin, to sin. **কী পাপ** what a plague or pest! **~কর্ম** *n.* a sinful or wicked act, a crime. **~কর্মা, ~কৃৎ** *a.* committing sins; given to vice or wickedness; sinful , sinning. **~ক্ষালন** *n.* rescue from sins or vice; remission of sins, absolution. **পাপক্ষালন করা** *v.* to rescue from sins or vice; to absolve. **~গ্রহ** *n.* (astrol.) an inauspicious star or planet; (fig.) an unavoidable evil person. **~ঘ্ন** *a.* destroying sins; rescuing from sins. **~জনক** *a.* sinful. **~নাশন** same as **পাপঘ্ন**। **~পঙ্ক** *n.* the mire of sin or vice. **~পুণ্য** *n.* virtue and vice, piety and sin. **~বুদ্ধি** *a.* evil-minded, of sinful or wicked turn of mind or disposition. **~ভাগী** *a.* sinful; sharing another's sin(s). **~মতি** same as **পাপবুদ্ধি**। **~মুক্ত** *a.* freed or absolved from sins or vice. **~মুক্তি** *n.* absolution from sins or vice. **~মোচন** same as **পাপক্ষালন**। **~যোগ** *n.* (astrol.) an inauspicious or unholy planetary conjunction. **~হর** same as **পাপঘ্ন**। **পাপাচার** *a.* same as

পাপকর্মা। □ *n.* a sinful or wicked act. **পাপাচারী** *a.* same as **পাপকর্মা**। *fem.* **পাপাচারিণী**। **পাপাত্মা** same as **পাপিষ্ঠ**। **পাপানুষ্ঠান** *n.* commission of sins, practice of vice. **পাপাশয়** same as **পাপিষ্ঠ**। **পাপাসক্ত** *a.* addicted to sin or vice, sinful; habitually committing sin; wicked. **পাপাসক্তি** *n.* addiction to sin or vice.

পাপড়ি *n.* a petal (of a flower).

পাপিনী *fem.* of **পাপী**।

পাপিয়া *n.* the Indian nightingale, the hawk-cuckoo.

পাপিষ্ঠ *a.* extremely sinful or wicked. *fem.* **পাপিষ্ঠা**।

পাপী *a.* sinful; wicked; criminal; depraved. □ *n.* a sinner; a wicked person; a criminal; a depraved person. **পুরোনো পাপী** an old or hardened or inveterate offender or sinner or criminal.

পাপীয়সী *a. fem.* sinful; wicked; criminal; adulterous. □ *n.* a sinful or wicked woman; a female criminal; an adulteress.

পাপোশ *n.* a doormat.

পাব *n.* a joint; a knuckle (as of a finger); (bot.) a node; the space between two nodes (as of the bamboo).

পাবক *n.* fire. □ *a.* purifying; sanctifying.

পাবদা *n.* a species of fish without scales.

পাবন *a.* (used chiefly as a *sfx.*) purifying or sanctifying (কুলপাবন) ; rescuing or saving (পতিতপাবন). □ *n.* purification or sanctification; fire. **পাবনী** *a. fem.* of **পাবন**।

পামর *a.* most sinful or wicked; vilest; basest; ignorant or low (আপামর). *fem.* **পামরী**।

পাম্প *n.* a pump. **পাম্প করা** *v.* to pump.

পায়খানা *n.* a latrine, a lavatory, a privy, a toilet, a water-closet. **পায়খানা করা** *v.* to ease oneself (of), to defecate, to evacuate.

পায়চারি *n.* act of walking about (esp. at ease), perambulation; a stroll. **পায়চারি করা** *v.* to walk about (at ease), to perambulate, to stroll, to pace up and down, to amble.

পায়জামা *n.* slacks, pyjamas.

পায়দল *adv.* walking, on foot.

পায়রা *a.* the pigeon; the dove. **পায়রার খাঁচা, পায়রার বাসা** a pigeon-house, a dovecot. **পায়রার খোপ** a pigeon-hole.

পায়স, পায়সান্ন *n.* a sweet dish prepared by boiling rice in milk with sugar and other ingredients, sweet rice-porridge, (cp. frumenty).

পায়া *n.* a leg or foot of an article of furniture; a castor, a trundle; (dero. or hum.) position or post or vanity. **~ভারী** *n.* vanity for holding a high post; vanity. □ *a.* vainglorious of one's high position; vain.

পায়ী *a.* (used as a *sfx.*) drinking (স্তন্যপায়ী), taking (ধূমপায়ী).

পায়ু *n.* the anus.

পায়েস coll. form of **পায়স**।

পার *n.* the opposite or the other bank or shore; a bank, a shore, a coast, a margin; a border, an end, bounds; act of crossing or crossing over or passing beyond; rescue, deliverance. **পার করা** *v.* to take or ferry (one) across (a river, a sea etc.); to take (one) to the opposite or the other bank; to conduct one through (a way), to let pass; to deliver, to rescue. **পার হওয়া** *v.* to cross; to cross over to the opposite or the other bank; to pass through; to get through or get over (a difficulty). **পারের কড়ি** same as **পারানি**।

পারংগম *a.* competent, efficient, capable; proficient (সর্বশাস্ত্রপারংগম) ; (rare) crossed over to the other bank or shore or end (of a river etc.).

পারক *a.* capable, competent; dexterous, skilful. **~তা** *n.* capability, competency; dexterity.

পারক্য *n.* alienage. **~যোগ্য** *a.* alienable.

পারগ same as **পারংগম**।

পারঘাট, (dial.) **পারঘাটা** *n.* a wharf, a ferry.

পারঙ্গম alt. spell. of **পারংগম**।

পারণ, পারণা *n.* (act of taking) the first meal after the completion of a fast, breakfast (in the original sense). **পারণ করা, পারণা করা** *v.* to break a fast by taking one's meal.

পারতন্ত্র্য *n.* dependence on another; subservience.

পারতপক্ষে *adv.* if it is possible or if it can be avoided.

পারত্রিক *a.* relating to the other world, extra-mundane; spiritual.

পারদ *n.* quicksilver, mercury. **~মিশ্র** *n.* an amalgam. **~সূত্র** *n.* (chem.) a column of mercury.

পারদর্শী *a.* foresighted; experienced, judicious; expert, adept; competent. *fem.* **পারদর্শিনী** । **পারদর্শিতা** *n.* foresight; experience; judiciousness, expertness, adeptness; competency.

পারদারিক *a.* guilty of violating another's marriage-bed, adulterous. **~তা** *n.* adultery.

পারদার্য *n.* violation of another's marriage-bed, adultery.

পারবশ্য *n.* dependence on another; subservience.

পারমাণব, পারমাণবিক *a.* atomic.

পারমার্থিক *a.* concerning the ultimate Reality or God; theological; spiritual.

পারমিট *n.* a permit.

পারম্পর্য *n.* serial succession or sequence or regular continuity, sequence. **~হীন** *a.* without continuity or regularity; without seriality. **~হীনতা** *n.* absence of continuity or seriality; absence of a regular order.

পারলৌকিক *a.* concerning the next world, extra-mundane; spiritual; conducive to the life in the next world; obsequial. **পারলৌকিক ক্রিয়া** obsequies.

পারশি, পারশিক alt. spellings of **পারসি** and **পারসিক** respectively.

পারশে *n.* a species of small scaled fish.

পারসি *n.* the language of Persia, Persian; a Parsee, a Parasi; a Persian. □ *a.* Persian; of the Parsees (পারসি শাড়ি). **পারসিক** *a.* Persian, Iranian. □ *n.* a Persian, an Iranian.

পারস্পরিক *a.* reciprocal; mutual (পারস্পরিক সম্পর্ক).

পারস্য *n.* Persia, Iran.

পারা[1] *n.* mercury, quicksilver. **~ঘটিত** *a.* containing mercury, mercurial (পারাঘটিত মলম = mercurial ointment).

পারা[2] *prep.* & *a.* (usu. poet.) like, as, resembling (পাগলপারা).

পারা[3] *v.* (*aux.*) to be able, can, may (করতে পারা). □ *v.* to do, to perform, to execute, to manage (সে এ কাজ পারে না) ; to vie with, to compete with (সে তার সঙ্গে পারে না).

পারানি *n.* the fare for ferrying, ferriage.

পারাপার *n.* both banks or shores of a river, sea etc.; crossing or ferrying a sea or a river. **পারাপার করা** *v.* to ferry, to go across, to cross. **পারাপার হওয়া** *v.* to be ferried; to cross.

পারাবত *n.* the pigeon; the dove. **বার্তাবাহী পারাবত** a carrier-pigeon.

পারাবার *n.* an ocean, a sea; both shores or banks of a sea, river etc.

পারায়ণ *n.* completeness, thoroughness; completion; completion of reading a book within the fixed time.

পারিজাত *n.* (myth.) a never-fading heavenly flower or its plant, (cp.) the amarant(h).

পারিতোষিক *n.* a reward; a prize.

পারিপাট্য *n.* orderliness; neatness; tidiness, spruceness.

পারিপার্শ্বিক *a.* surrounding; neighbouring. □ *n.* a courtier; a side-actor assisting the principal one whilst the latter recites the prologue. **পারিপার্শ্বিক অবস্থা** environment, surroundings.

পারিবারিক *a.* pertaining to or restricted to a family; characteristic of a family, familial. **পারিবারিক ব্যাপার** a family affair or matter.

পারিভাষিক *a.* concerning technical terminology; terminological, technical (পারিভাষিক শব্দ = technical term).

পারিশ্রমিক *n.* remuneration, fee.

পারিষদ *n.* a courtier; a councillor; a companion (esp. a cringing one); a toady; a flatterer.

পারিসাংখ্যিক *a.* statistical.

পারুল *n.* a species of trumpet-flower or its plant.

পারুষ্য *n.* haughtiness, arrogance; harshness, rudeness; strong language.

পার্টি *n.* a party.

পার্থক্য *n.* difference; dissimilarity; distinction; (log.) differentia.

পার্থিব *a.* earthly, worldly, mundane; material. □ *n.* a king.

পার্বণ *n.* obsequies to be performed on certain lunar days; (usu. **পার্বণশ্রাদ্ধ**) ; a fast, a festival, a festive day (পৌষপার্বণ). **পার্বণী** *n.* a present or tip given on feast days (esp. to servants and employees).

পার্বত, পার্বত্য *a.* of a mountain or hill; mountainous, hilly; born or living on a mountain or hill or in a hill-district; highland. **পার্বতী** *n.* Goddess Durga (দুর্গা) ; the daughter of the Himalayas. **পার্বত্য অঞ্চল, পার্বত্য প্রদেশ** a hill-district, a hilly region or country. **পার্বত্য উদ্ভিদ** mountain vegetation. **পার্বত্য জাতি** a hilltribe. **পার্বত্য জাতির লোক** a hill-man, a highlander (*pl.* hill-folk).

পার্লামেন্ট *n.* a parliament.

পার্শে alt. spell. of **পারশে** ।

পার্শ্ব *n.* a side, a flank (দক্ষিণপার্শ্ব) ; end, border (নগরপার্শ্ব) ; margin, brink, brim, edge (থালার পার্শ্বে) ; bank or shore (of a river, sea etc.); adjacent space, vicinity (গৃহপার্শ্ব) ; company, presence (স্ত্রীর পার্শ্বে থাকা) ; comparison (সূর্যের পার্শ্বে চন্দ্র ম্লান). **~গত** *a.* close to, very near, adjacent. **~গ্রাবরেখা** *n.* (geog.) a lateral moraine. **~চর** *n.* a companion; an attendant; a follower, a servant; a toady, a sycophant. *fem.* **পার্শ্বচরী** । **~চিত্র** *n.* a profile. **~ত** *adv.* by or from or on or to a side or flank, sidewise, sidewards, edgeways, sideling, flanking. **~দেশ** *n.* a flank, a side. **পার্শ্ব-পরিবর্তন করা** *v.* to turn upon one side. **~বর্তী, ~স্থ** *a.* staying or situated alongside; neighbouring (পার্শ্ববর্তী রাষ্ট্র). *fem.* **~বর্তিনী, ~স্থা** । **~ভাগ** *n.* same as **পার্শ্বদেশ** । **পার্শ্বাভিনেতা** *n.* (in film or theatre) an actor of a minor or supporting role. **পার্শ্বাস্থি** *n.* ribs; skeleton. **পার্শ্বিক, পার্শ্বীয়** *a.* lateral. **পার্শ্বিক উৎক্রম** (phys.) lateral inversion. **পার্শ্বে** *adv.* & *prep.* on or to the side of; sidewise; alongside; by the side of, beside; in company or presence of; in comparison to.

পার্ষদ *n.* a courtier; a councillor; a companion; a toady; a flatterer.

পার্ষ্ণি *n.* the heel; the back; the rear (esp. of an army). **~গ্রাহ** *n.* an attack from the rear.

পার্সি alt. spell. of **পারসি** ।

পার্সেল *n.* a postal parcel. **পার্সেল করা** *v.* to send by parcel post.

-পাল[১] *a.* (used as a *sfx.*) preserving, protecting, defending, keeping (মহীপাল, রাজ্যপাল, ধর্মপাল, গোপাল).

পাল[২] *n.* a sail (as of a boat). **পাল খাটানো, পাল তোলা** *v.* to set sail. **পাল নামানো** *v.* to strike sail. **পাল-তোলা** *a.* under sail. **সমস্ত পাল-তোলা** full sail.

পাল[৩] *n.* mating or coupling (of beasts or birds.) **পাল দেওয়া** *v.* to mate or couple (beasts or birds); (esp. of horses) to sire.

পাল[৪] *n.* (of animals) a flock, a herd, a drove. **একপাল কুকুরছানা** a litter of puppies. **একপাল উট** a drove of camels. **একপাল গোরু-মোষ** a herd of cattle. **একপাল নেকড়ে** a pack of wolves. **একপাল ভেড়া** a flock of sheep. **একপাল মুরগির ছানা** a brood of chickens. **একপাল হরিণ** a herd of deer. **পালের গোদা** the leader of a herd; (dero.) a ring-leader.

পালং *n.* a species of spinach used as a pot-herb.

পালক[১] *n.* (of birds) a wing; a feather.

পালক[২] *a.* one who brings up or rears or nurses or fosters or protects or preserves or defends or breeds or keeps or observes or maintains. □ *n.* an upbringer, a rearer; a fosterer or nurse; a protector, a preserver, a guardian, a defender; a breeder; a fancier, a keeper; an observer, a complier, a fulfiller; a maintainer. **~পিতা** *n.* a foster-father (*fem* : a foster-mother).

পালকি *n.* a palanquin, a palki, palkee. **পালকি-বেহারা** *n.* a palanquin-bearer.

পালখ var. of **পালক**[১] ।

পালঙ[১] alt. spell. of **পালং** ।

পালঙ্ক, পালঙ[২] *n.* a costly bedstead or cot; a divan, a sofa. **~পোষ** *n.* a bed-cover; a cover for a divan; a divan and a bed; a divan.

পালটা *a.* contrary, counteracting, revoking, opposing, counter; return; exchanging. **পালটা অভিযোগ** same as **পালটা নালিশ** । **পালটা আক্রমণ** a counter attack. **পালটা আমন্ত্রণ** a return invitation. **পালটা জবাব**, a retort. **পালটা নালিশ** a countercharge, a counter complaint. **পালটা**

মামলা a counter case. **পালটা হুকুম** a countermand. **পালটানো** *v.* to revoke; to change, to alter. **~পালটি** *n.* exchange; act of changing for or with another. **পালটাপালটি করা** *v.* to exchange, to change for or with another; to swap.

পালটি[1] *a.* (of a family) being on equal social footing with another making thereby matrimonial alliance permissible and possible. **~ঘর** *n.* a family of equal social status or footing.

পালটি[2], **পালটিয়া** *v. imperf.* (poet.) returning or turning back.

পাল-তোলা see **পাল**[2] ।

পালন *n.* upbringing, rearing (সন্তানপালন) ; nursing or fostering (পরের সন্তান পালন) ; maintenance (পোষ্যপালন) ; keeping, breeding, tending (পশুপালন) ; nourishment (শরীরপালন) ; protection, preservation, defence (রাজ্যপালন, ধর্মপালন) ; observance, compliance (নিয়মপালন, আদেশপালন) ; fulfilment (প্রতিশ্রুতিপালন). **পালন করা** *v.* to bring up, to rear; to foster or nurse; to maintain; to keep, to breed, to tend, to fancy; to nourish; to protect, to preserve, to guard, to defend; to observe, to comply (with); to fulfil. **~কর্তা** *n.* same as **পালক**[2] (*n.*). *fem.* **~কর্ত্রী** । **পালনীয়** *a.* to be brought up or reared or nursed or fostered or maintained or kept or bred or nourished or protected or preserved or defended or observed or complied (with) or fulfilled or carried out.

পালপার্বণ *n.* different festivals religious and secular collectively.

পালয়িতা same as **পালক**[2] । *fem.* **পালয়িত্রী** ।

পাললিক *a.* alluvial. **পাললিক শিলা** alluvial rock.

পালা[1] same as **পালন করা** ।

পালা[2] *n.* a turn (এবার তোমার খেলার পালা) ; a period or spell; the story or plot of a drama or a poem (নিমাইসন্ন্যাস পালা). **~ক্রমে** *adv.* by turns. **~গান** *n.* a narrative song or musical play. **~জ্বর** *n.* remittent or periodic fever.

পালান *n.* a panel (of a beast of burden); a packsaddle; a cow's udder or teat.

পালানো *v.* to flee, to run away, to show a clean pair of heels; to play truant, to mooch, to mouch. □ *a.* runaway; fugitive; truant. See also the for. form **পলানো** ।

পালি[1] *n.* the Pali language, Pali.

পালি[2] *n.* a line; a row; a multitude; an end, a margin; a dry measure of grains (over 2 kilograms).

পালিকা *fem.* of **পালক**[2] ।

পালিত *a.* tamed or pet (পালিত পশুপক্ষী) ; brought up, reared; nursed or fostered; maintained, kept, bred; nourished; protected, preserved, defended; observed, complied (with); fulfilled. *fem.* **পালিতা** । **~কন্যা** *n. fem.* a foster-daughter. **~পুত্র** *n.* a foster-son. **~সন্তান** *n.* a foster-child.

পালিনী *a. fem.* (used as a *sfx.*) same as **পালিকা** (জগৎপালিনী).

পালিশ *n.* polish. **উপর পালিশ** apparent polish or refinement. **পালিশ করা** *v.* to polish. **~-করা** *a.* polished.

পালুই *n.* a stack (of paddy or hay).

পালো *n.* starch obtained from zedoary etc.; gruel of this starch.

পালোয়ান *n.* a wrestler; a gymnast; a burly man. □ *a.* burly; adept in gymnastics; heroic. **পালোয়ানি** *n.* burliness; heroism; gymnastics. □ *a.* of a wrestler or wrestling; of a gymnast; gymnastic.

পাল্কি rej. spell. of **পালকি** ।

পাল্টা rej. spell. of **পালটা** ।

পাল্টানো rej. spell. of **পালটানো** ।

পাল্য same as **পালনীয়** (see **পালন**).

পাল্লা *n.* a thin layer, a strip (এক পাল্লা চামড়া) ; either of a pair as a leaf of a door (দরজার পাল্লা) ; a lid or shutter moving on a hinge; a scale-pan (দাঁড়িপাল্লা) ; a beam of balance, a scale; a mass of metal used for finding weight, a weight; competition, distance (দূর পাল্লা) ; speed (পায়ের পাল্লা) ; range, reach (বন্দুকের পাল্লা) ; hold, grasp, clutches, snares, toils (পাল্লায় পড়া) ; company, association (অসৎ সঙ্গীর পাল্লা). **পাল্লা চাপানো** *v.* to put a weight (on a scale-pan). **পাল্লা দেওয়া** *v.* to compete (with), to vie (with). **পাল্লায় পড়া** *v.* to run under the influence of; to get into the clutches of, to be caught in the toils of; to turn into the company of.

পাশ[1] *n.* act of passing an examination; a written permission, a pass (গেটপাশ) a free or complimentary ticket (রেলের বা থিয়েটারের পাশ). □ *a.* got through an examination, passed. **পাশ করা** *v.* to pass (an examination); to sanction or pass. **পাশ করানো** *v.* to help or make one pass an examination; to let (one) pass through (as a gate). **পাশ হওয়া** *v.* to pass an examination; to be passed or sanctioned; to be allowed to pass through. **পাশ নম্বর** *n.* (in examination or test) pass marks.

পাশ[2] *n.* an apparatus for spraying, a spray (গোলাপপাশ).

পাশ[3] *n.* an ancient Indian missile by throwing which an adversary could be fastened (cp. lasso); a tie, a noose, a bond, bondage (ভুজপাশ, স্নেহপাশ) ; a trap, a snare (মায়াপাশ) ; a string, a rope; a bunch or tuft of longish things (কেশপাশ).

পাশ[4] coll. corrup. of **পার্শ্ব**। **পাশ কাটানো** *v.* to turn or move aside, to step aside and avoid; to dodge; to evade. **পাশ দেওয়া** *v.* to move aside to let another pass, to make way (for). **পাশ ফেরা** *v.* to turn on the side.

পাশ[5], **পাশক** *n.* (playing) dice.

পাশক্রীড়া *n.* dice-play.

পাশব *a.* relating to a beast; beastly, bestial, brutal; inhuman. **~তা** *n.* beastliness, bestiality, brutality; inhumanity. **পাশব বল** brute force. **~প্রবৃত্তি** beastly propensity or inclination.

পাশবদ্ধ *a.* entrapped, ensnared.

পাশবালিশ *n.* a bolster.

পাশবিক inc. but pop. var. of **পাশব**। **পাশবিক অত্যাচার করা** *v.* to outrage the modesty or chastity of, to rape.

পাশা[1] *n.* a Turkish title given to governors, officials, and men of importance; Pasha.

পাশা[2] *n.* (playing) dice. **~খেলা** *n.* dice-play. **পাশা খেলা** *v.* to play at dice, to cast or throw dice.

পাশাপাশি *a.* lying or situated side by side; contiguous; adjacent; adjoining (পাশাপাশি বাড়ি) ; neighbouring (পাশাপাশি এলাকা). □ *adv.* side by side; abreast, cheeck by jowl, alongside.

পাশী *a.* armed with the ancient missile for binding an adversary (see **পাশ**[3]). □ *n.* Varuna (বরুণ) the river-god or Yama (যম) the god of death; a hunter, a fowler.

পাশুপত *a.* of Shiva (শিব). □ *n.* the name of Shiva's weapon.

পাশে *adv.* & *prep.* on or to the side of; alongside; beside; by the side of; sidewise; in presence or company of.

পাশ্চাত্য; পাশ্চাত্ত্য *a.* of the west or the western world, western, occidental; hinder; following. □ *n.* the western world (that is Europe, America and Australia); the West, the Occident.

পাষণ্ড *a.* atheistic, godless; heretical; inveterately sinful; extremely wicked and hard-hearted. □ *n.* an atheist, a godless person; a heretic; an inveterate sinner; an extremely wicked and hard-hearted person.

পাষাণ *n.* stone; a weight put on a scale-pan to adjust or equipoise a beam of balance; (fig.) a stone-hearted man (তুমি পাষাণ). □ *a.* (chiefly used as a *sfx.*) made of stone; of stone; stonelike; unfeeling, pitiless; stone-hearted (পাষাণ বাপ) ; callous (শোকে শোকে পাষাণ). **~তুল্য** *a.* stone-like, stony; (fig.) unfeeling, insensate; immobile, unmoved, still. **~প্রাচীর** *n.* a stone-wall. **~-বিদারক** *a.* same as **পাষাণভেদী**। **~ভার** *n.* a weight as heavy as stone. **~ভেদী** *a.* able to pierce even stone; heart-rending. **~মূর্তি** *n.* a stone image, a statue of stone. **~হৃদয়** *a.* stone-hearted; pitiless. **পাষাণী** *n. fem.* a stone-hearted woman.

পাস alt. spell. of **পাশ**[1]।

পাসরন, পাসরণ *n.* (poet.) act of forgetting, oblivion.

পাসরা *v.* (poet.) to forget.

পাহাড় *n.* a hill, a rock; a mountain; a dune; a mound (বালির পাহাড়) ; bank or coast (esp. a steep and high one), upland; (fig.) a heap (টাকার বা মিষ্টির পাহাড়). **~তলি** *n.* a valley, a dale; a level tract of land at the foot of a hill.

পাহাড়ি[1], **পাহাড়ে** *a.* of hills and mountains; hilly; mountainous; lying or growing or dwelling on hills or mountains; hill-born; highland; (fig.) huge (পাহাড়ে ঢেউ), terrible (পাহাড়ে মেয়েমানুষ = a terrible woman; a virago), inveterate (পাহাড়ে বদমাশ). **পাহাড়ি**[2] *n.* a hillman, a highlander; a hill-tribe. **পাহাড়িয়া** same as **পাহাড়ি**[1] and **পাহাড়ি**[2] ।

পাহারা *n.* watching or guarding; a watch, a watchman, a watcher, a sentinel, a sentry, a guard, a guardsman. **পাহারা দেওয়া** *v.* to watch, to guard, to sentinel, to patrol. **~ওয়ালা, ~ওলা** *n.* a watchman; a constable; a policeman.

পাহুন[1] *a.* (poet. & obs.) stone-hearted, cruel ('পুরুষ পাহুন').

পাহুন[2] *n.* (poet & obs.) a visitor, one away from home ('কান্ত পাহুন').

পিউরি *n.* a yellow pigment made from the cow's urine.

পিউপিউ *int.* & *n.* the note or cooing of the hawk-cuckoo.

পিওন alt. spell. of **পিয়ন** ।

পিঁচুটি *n.* mucus or catarrh exuding from eyes. **চোখ দিয়ে পিঁচুটি পড়ছে** eyes are running.

পিঁজরা, (coll.) **পিঁজরে** *n.* a cage. **~পোল** *n.* an institution for keeping disabled cattle, a veterinary asylum.

পিঁজা *v.* to open out the fibres of (cotton, wool etc.), to comb or card (wool, cotton, hemp etc.), to tease; (of cloth) to open out into fibres (চাদরখানা পিঁজে গেছে).

পিঁড়ি, (dial.) **পিঁড়া,** (coll.) **পিঁড়ে** *n.* a low wooden seat to sit upon in a squatting fashion; a stand or altar (লক্ষ্মীর পিঁড়ি).

পিঁপড়ে *n.* the ant.

পিঁপুল same as **পিপ্পল** ।

পিঁয়াজ pop. var. of **পিয়াজ** ।

পিক[1] *n.* the cuckoo.

পিক[2] *n.* spittle; spittle thrown out after chewing betel-leaves. **পিক ফেলা** *v.* to spit; to spit after chewing betel-leaves.

পিকতান *n.* a cuckoo's call or note.

পিকদান, পিকদানি *n.* a spittoon.

পিকধ্বনি same as **পিকতান** ।

পিকনিক *n.* picnic.

পিকরব same as **পিকতান** ।

পিকেটিং *n.* picketing (as by trade-unionists). **পিকেটিং করা** *v.* to picket.

পিঙ্গল *n.* the yellowish brown colour, mud-colour. □ *a.* yellowish brown, mud-coloured. *fem. a.* **পিঙ্গলা** ।

পিচ[1] var. of **পিক**[2] ।

পিচ[2] *n.* a juicy stone-fruit, peach.

পিচ[3] *n.* (in cricket) pitch.

পিচ[4] *n.* a black residue of distillation of tar, pitch. **~ঢালা** *a.* pitched, tarred (পিচ-ঢালা রাস্তা). **পিচ দেওয়া, পিচ ঢালা** *v.* to pitch, to tar.

পিচকারি *n.* a syringe; a squirt; a spray.

পিচবোর্ড *n.* pasteboard; cardboard.

পিচাশ corrup. of **পিশাচ** ।

পিচুটি var. of **পিঁচুটি** ।

পিচ্ছিল, পিচ্ছল *a.* slippery; slabbery.

পিছ, পিছন *n.* the back; the backside, the rear; (fig.) the past. **পিছনে চলা** *v.* to go or move backwards; to retrograde; to return or recede. **পিছনে চাওয়া, পিছনে দেখা** *v.* to look to one's own back; to look back; (fig.) to look to or consider the past. **পিছন পিছন, পিছনে পিছনে** on the back of, at the heels of. **পিছন ফেরা** *v.* to turn back; to look back; (fig.) to look to or consider the past. **পিছটান, পিছনটান** *n.* (lit.) a pull from the back; (fig.) attachment to one's family circle which retards or impedes one's progress. **পিছপা** *a.* taken aback, recoiled; reluctant. **পিছপা হওয়া** *v.* to be taken aback, to recoil, to flinch (in fear, pain etc.); to be reluctant. **পিছমোড়া** *a.* pinioned at the back. **পিছমোড়া করে বাঁধা** to pinion one at one's back. **পিছনে লাগা** *v.* to tease or vex (somebody); to make fun playfully or annoyingly.

পিছটান, পিছনটান, পিছপা, পিছমোড়া see **পিছ** ।

পিছল, পিছলা coll. forms of **পিচ্ছল** । see **পিচ্ছিল** ।

পিছলানো *v.* to slip, to slide, to glide.

পিছানো *v.* to fall back; to recoil, to flinch; to back out; to retreat, to beat a retreat; to move (towards one's) back; to put off or be put off, to postpone or be postponed, to defer or be deferred.

পিছিলা *a.* (poet. & obs.) postern ('পিছিলা ঘাটে সে নায়').

পিছু var. of **পাছু**। **পিছু হটা** *v.* to fall back; to back out; to retreat, to beat a retreat.

পিছে *prep.* at the back of; on the back of; towards the back of. □ *adv.* backwards; towards or in the past. **পিছে পিছে** on the back of, at one's heels, following, pursuing.

পিজবোর্ড *n.* pasteboard.

পিঞ্জন *n.* act of opening out the fibres of cotton, wool, etc.; teasing; an apparatus for teasing.

পিঞ্জর *n.* a cage; the ribs; the thorax. **পিঞ্জরাবদ্ধ** *a.* incaged, encaged. **পিঞ্জরাবদ্ধ করা** *v.* to incage, to encage.

পিঞ্জিকা *n.* a skein or roll or wisp of carded cotton.

পিট pop. var. of **পিঠ**। **~টান** *n.* act of going off or departing quietly; fleeing, flight; act of beating a retreat. **পিটটান দেওয়া** *v.* to go off or depart quietly; to flee, to decamp, to take to one's heels; to show a clean pair of heels; to beat a retreat.

পিটন same as **পিটানি** (see **পিটা**)।

পিটনা *n.* a small cudgel for ramming the roof or the floor of a building, a rammer.

পিটপিট *int.* expressing : twitching as of the eye, flickering as of a lamp, peevishness, fastidiousness or mania for cleanliness. **পিটপিট করা, পিটপিটানো** *v.* (of the eye etc.) to twitch, to bat (an eyelid); (of a lamp etc.) to flicker; to behave peevishly or fastidiously; to show a mania for cleanliness. **পিটপিটানি** *n.* twitching as of the eye; flickering as of a lamp; peevishness; fastidiousness; a mania for cleanliness. **পিটপিটে** *a.* peevish; fastidious; over-scrupulous; stickler; stricken with a mania for cleanliness.

পিটা, পিটানো *v.* to strike, to beat (লোহা পিটানো) ; to pound, to batter, to ram (ছাদ পিটা) ; to whip up or switch, to thrash (ঝোপ পিটানো). □ *a.* beaten; rammed; thrashed; shaped by beating, wrought (পিটা লোহা). **পিটাই, পিটানি,** (pop.) **পিটুনি** *n.* act of beating or ramming or thrashing; a drubbing (পিটুনি খাওয়া). **পিটুনি পুলিশ** punitive police. **পিটুনি কর** বা **জরিমানা** punitive tax, punitive fine.

পিটালি *n.* a paste made of pounded rice, used as a cooking ingredient.

পিটিশন *n.* a petition. **পিটিশন করা** *v.* to petition. **~কারী** *n.* a petitioner.

পিটুনি see **পিটা**।

পিটুলি pop. var. of **পিটালি**।

পিঠ *n.* the back; the rear; immediate succession (পিঠে পিঠে) ; a surface or face (এপিঠ ওপিঠ) ; (in a game of cards) a trick. **পিঠ চাপড়ানো** *v.* to pat on the back; to drum one's back lightly, (idio.) to encourage patronizingly or with an air of superiority. **পিঠের চামড়া তোলা** *v.* to flog severely. **পিঠে পিঠে** back to back; on the back of; immediately succeeding in birth, born next.

পিঠা *n.* a sweet pie, a kind of cake.

পিঠাপিঠি *adv.* & *a.* same as **পিঠে পিঠে** (see **পিঠ**).

পিঠালি var. of **পিটালি**।

পিঠে coll. form of **পিঠা**।

পিড়া, পিড়ি, পিড়ে variants of **পিঁড়ি**।

পিণ্ড *n.* a lump; a conglomerated mass; (loos.) anything ball-shaped, a ball; food offering to the manes of forefathers; a lump of food; the body (as a conglomerated mass of পঞ্চভূত or the five elements). **~খর্জুর,** (coll.) **পিণ্ডে খেজুর** *n.* dates preserved in lumps, lump-dates. **~দ, ~দাতা** *a.* scripturally authorized to give food-offering to the manes; giving food-offering to the manes; providing with food. □ *n.* such a man. *fem.* **পিণ্ডদা, পিণ্ডদাত্রী**। **~দান** *n.* the sacrament of food-offering to the manes. **পিণ্ডদান করা** *v.* to offer food to the manes. **~লোপ** *n.* extinction or absence of persons or descendants authorized to offer food to one's manes; extinction of one's line of descent. **~শরীর** *n.* the body (as a conglomerated mass of পঞ্চভূত or five elements).

পিণ্ডাকার, পিণ্ডাকৃতি *a.* shaped like a lump; round and lumpish.

পিণ্ডিত *a.* shaped into a lump, conglomerated; conglomerate.

পিণ্ডীভূত *a.* conglomerate.
পিণ্ডীভূত দানা conglomerate crystal.
পিণ্ডে খেজুর *n.* dates preserved in lumps, lump-dates.
পিতঃ *int.* O father (cp. abba).
পিতল *n.* brass. **পিতলের কারিগর** *n.* a brazier.
পিতা *n.* father. **~মহ** *n.* one's father's father or uncle, a grandfather or a grand-uncle; an appellation of Brahma (ব্রহ্মা). **~মহী** *n. fem.* one's father's mother or aunt, a grandmother or a grand-aunt.
পিতুঃস্বসা same as **পিতৃস্বসা** (see **পিতৃ**).
পিতৃ *n.* (chiefly used as a *pfx.*) father. **~আজ্ঞা** *n.* father's command. **~ঋণ** *n.* one's obligation to one's father, filial obligation; debt incurred by one's father (esp. that which should be paid off by children). **~কর্ম** same as **পিতৃকৃত্য**। **~কল্প** *a.* father-like, fatherly. □ *n.* same as **~কৃত্য**। **~কার্য** same as **~কৃত্য**। **~কুল** *n.* one's father's line, spearside. **~কৃত্য, ~ক্রিয়া** *n.* obsequial rites performed in honour of the manes of one's father and forefathers. **~গণ** *n.* (myth.) heavenly sages (collectively) from whom the human race has evolved; manes of the forefathers of mankind or of an individual; dead ancestors or forbears or forefathers. **~গৃহ** *n.* father's house or family. **~ঘাতক, ~ঘাতী, ~ঘ্ন** same as **পিতৃহন্তা**। **~তর্পণ** *n.* water-offering to the manes of one's forefather, (cp.) libation. **~তুল্য** *a.* father-like, fatherly. **~ত্ব** *n.* paternity, fatherhood. **~দত্ত** *a.* given or transmitted by one's father; (rare) given to one's father. **~দায়** *n.* the solemn obligation of performing the obsequial rites of one's deceased father. **পিতৃদায়গ্রস্ত হওয়া** *v.* to be under the solemn obligation of performing the obsequial rites of one's deceased father. **~দেব** *n.* father looked upon as a deity (used as a term of respect). **~ধন** *n.* patrimony. **পিতৃধনসংক্রান্ত** *a.* patrimonial. **~পক্ষ** *n.* the dark fortnight immediately preceding the bright fortnight of the month of Aswin (আশ্বিন) ; one's father's side, spearside. **~পুরুষ** *n.* an ancestor, a forefather. **~বিয়োগ** *n.* death or bereavement of one's father. **~ব্য** *n.* a brother of one's father, an uncle. **পিতৃব্যপুত্র** *n.* son of a paternal uncle, a cousin. **~ভক্ত** *a.* devoted or loyal to or fond of one's father. **~ভক্তি** *n.* devotion to or fondness for one's father, filial piety. **~মাতৃদায়** *n.* the solemn obligation of performing the obsequial rites of one's deceased parents. **~মাতৃহীন** *a.* bereft of parents, orphan. **পিতৃমেধ, পিতৃযজ্ঞ** same as **পিতৃকৃত্য** or **পিতৃতর্পণ**। **~যান** *n.* the route for the journey of the manes to the lunar heaven or the region of the moon for settling there. **~রিষ্টি** *n.* (astrol.) the location of the zodiacal signs in one's horoscope indicating loss of one's father. **~লোক** *n.* the region of the moon where the manes dwell, the lunar heaven. **~শোক** *n.* grief or mourning for one's deceased father. **~শ্রাদ্ধ** *n.* obsequies of one's deceased father. **~স্বসা** *n.* a father's sister, an aunt. **~সম** same as **পিতৃতুল্য**। **~সেবা** *n.* act of attending upon or serving one's father devotedly. **~স্থানীয়** *a.* deserving to be respected as one's father. **~হত্যা** *n.* parricide, patricide. **~হত্যামূলক** *a.* patricidal. **~হন্তা** *a.* guilty of parricide or patricide. □ *n.* a parricide or patricide. *fem.* **~হন্ত্রী**। **~হীন** *a.* fatherless. *fem.* **পিতৃহীনা**।
পিত্ত *n.* bile, gall. **পিত্ত পড়া** *v.* to lose appetite because of abstinence from food when hungry. **পিত্ত জ্বলা** *v.* to have one's ill-humour roused, to burn or boil with indignation, to get cross or peered. **~কোষ** *n.* the gall-bladder. **~ঘ্ন** *a.* antibilious. **~জ্বর** *n.* bilious fever. **~নাশ** *n.* abominable perversion or corruption (from the fact that a fish tastes bitter if its gallbladder is burst open and its body smeared with bile). **~নালি** *n.* biliary ducts. **~নাশক** *a.* antibilious. **~পাথর, ~পাথুরি** *n.* gall stone, biliary stone. **~বিকার** *n.* (med.) biliary or bilious trouble or disorder. **~রক্ত** *n.* plethora. **~রক্ষা** *n.* appeasement of hunger by taking a small quantity of food; (sarcas.) a

mere show of gratification. **পিত্তরক্ষা করা** *v.* to appease one's hunger by taking a small quantity of food; (sarcas.) to make one content or be content with a mere show of fulfilment of one's desire. **~শূল** *n.* biliary colic.

পিত্তল *n.* brass. **~নির্মিত** *a.* made of brass, brazen. **~ফলক** *n.* a brass-plate.

পিত্তাতিসার *n.* (med.) bilious or biliary diarrhoea.

পিত্তাশয় *n.* the gall-bladder,

পিত্তি coll. var. of **পিত্ত**।

পিত্যেশ pop. corrup. of **প্রত্যাশা**।

পিত্রালয় *n.* father's house (esp. of a married woman).

পিত্র্য same as **পৈতৃক**।

পিদিম coll. corrup. of **প্রদীপ**।

পিধান *n.* a case, a sheath (as of a sword); a lid; a covering.

পিন *n.* a pin. **পিন আটকানো, পিনে আটকানো** *v.* to pin.

পিনদ্ধ *a.* tied, fastened (esp. to one's body); put on, worn.

পিনাক *n.* the bow of Shiva (শিব) ; a bow-shaped musical instrument of Shiva; a trident (esp. that of Shiva). **~পাণি, পিনাকী** *n.* Shiva (শিব), who carries a পিনাক in his hand.

পিনাল কোড *n.* the penal code.

পিনাস, (coll.) **পিনেস** *n.* a fetid discharge from the nostrils, ozaena; the pinnance.

পিন্ডারি *n.* a band of mercenary freebooters who operated in India till 1817, the Pindaris.

পিন্ডি coll.from of **পিন্ড**। **পিন্ডি চটকানো** *v.* to crush the lumps of food-offerings to the manes of forefathers; (fig.) to revile, to abuse severely.

পিন্ধন *n.* (poet. & obs.) act of putting on or wearing.

পিন্ধা *v.* (obs.) to put on, to wear. **পিন্ধাওল** *v.* to dress (one) in.

পিপাসা *n.* thirst; (fig.) eager desire. **পিপাসা পাওয়া** *v.* to feel thirsty. **পিপাসা মেটানো, পিপাসা দূর করা** *v.* to quench or slake one's thirst; (fig.) to satisfy one's desire. **পিপাসার্ত, পিপাসিত, পিপাসী, পিপাসু** *a.* thirsty; (fig.) eagerly desirous (of.) *fem.* **পিপাসার্তা, পিপাসিতা, পিপাসিনী**।

পিপীলিকা *n.* the ant.

পিপুল var. of **পিঁপুল**।

পিপে *n.* a cask, a barrel, a coop.

পিপ্পল same as **অশ্বত্থ**।

পিপ্পলি, পিপ্পলী *n.* a small pungent seed of the pepper genus used in medicine; long pepper; its plant.

পিয় poet. corrup. of **প্রিয়** and **প্রিয়া**।

পিয়ন *n.* a postman, a liveried messenger, a footman, a peon.

পিয়া same as **পিয়**।

পিয়াজ *n.* onion. **পিয়াজি** *n.* a kind of chop made of minced onion; light purple colour; effrontery, sauciness; impudent waggery. □ *a.* of light purple colour.

পিয়াদা *n.* an armed footman; a liveried messenger; a process-server; a bailiff; (in chess) a pawn.

পিয়ানো[১] *v.* (poet.) to make one drink, to cause to drink; to suckle.

পিয়ানো[২] *n.* a piano.

পিয়ার, পিয়ারা, পিয়ারী obs. forms of **পেয়ার, পেয়ারা** and **পেয়ারি** respectively.

পিয়াল *n.* a kind of nut-tree; its nut or seed.

পিয়ালা obs. form of **পেয়ালা**।

পিয়াস, পিয়াসা, পিয়াসী, পিয়াসু poet. forms of **পিপাসা, পিপাসী** and **পিপাসু** respectively.

পির *n.* a muslim saint.

পিরান *n.* a loose outer garment usu. worn by men.

পিরামিড *n.* a pyramid.

পিরিচ *n.* a saucer.

পিরিত, পিরিতি, পিরীত, পিরীতি *n.* love, amour; affection; attachment; secret or illicit love.

পিল[১] *n.* a pill (of medicine).

পিল[২] *n.* the elephant; (in chess) the bishop.

পিল করা *v.* (in certain games) to send (a ball or marble) into the pocket; to pocket (গাব্বু পিল করা).

পিলখানা *n.* a stable for housing elephants.

পিলপা *n.* a thick pillar. **~গাড়ি** *n.* act of building or fixing or planting a pillar to mark out the boundaries.

পিলপিল *int.* expressing: a swarming crowd. **পিলপিল করা** *v.* to swarm. **পিলপিল করে বেরোনো** to come out swarmingly.

পিলপে coll. form of **পিলপা**।

পিলসুজ *n.* a lamp-stand.

পিলু *n.* an Indian musical mode.

পিলে[1] pop. form of **প্লীহা**।

পিলে[2] correl. of **ছেলে** (ছেলেপিলে).

পিশাচ *n.* a necrophagous evil spirit, a ghoul; (fig.) a man of vile or cruel or nauseating or abominable nature. *fem.* **পিশাচী,** (inc.) **পিশাচিনী**। **~তত্ত্ব** *n.* demonology. **~সিদ্ধ** *a.* one who has made a ghoul one's slave by means of rigorous ascetic practices. *fem.* **~সিদ্ধা**।

পিশিত *n.* flesh; raw meat.

পিশুন *a.* scandal-mongering, talebearing; malicious; cruel.

পিষণ *n.* pulping; pressing; squeezing; kneading; crushing; grinding, pulverization; pressure; oppression.

পিষা, পেষা *v.* to render into a paste by crushing, to crush to powder, to pound, to pulp; to press; to squeeze; to knead; to crush; to grind, to pulverize; to oppress. **পিষাই, পেষাই** *n.* cost or charge of grinding; pulping; pressing; squeezing; kneading; crushing (to powder); pounding, grinding, pulverization. **পিষাই করা , পেষাই করা** *v.* same as **পিষা**। **পিষানো, পেষানো** *v.* to cause to pulp or press or squeeze or knead or crush or grind or pulverize.

পিষ্ট *a.* pulped; pressed, squeezed; crushed; ground, pulverized; oppressed.

পিষ্টক *n.* a kind of cake or sweet pie.

পিসতুতো *a.* born of a sister of one's father or father-in-law.

পিসতুতো ভাই বা বোন a cousin.

পিসবোর্ড *n.* pasteboard.

পিসশাশুড়ি *n. fem.* a sister of one's father-in-law.

পিসশ্বশুর *n.* the husband of a sister of one's father-in-law.

পিসা obs. form of **পিসে**।

পিসি *n.* a father's sister.

পিসে *n.* the husband of a sister of one's father.

পিস্তল *n.* a pistol.

পিহিত *a.* sheathed, encased.

পীঠ *n.* a low wooden seat on which one may sit in a squatting position; an altar; a seat or a resort (esp. of a deity); a holy place; (myth.) any of the fifty-one holy places where fell the pieces cut off from the body of Sati (সতী), the wife of Shiva (শিব) ; an institution or a place regarded with some sanctity (বিদ্যাপীঠ).

পীড়ক *a.* oppressing, persecuting, tormenting; forcing; insisting, pressing, chastising; accepting esp. in marriage (পাণিপীড়ক). □ *n.* an oppressor, a persecutor, a tormentor; one who forces or insists (on) or presses; a chastiser; one who accepts esp. in marriage.

পীড়ন *n.* oppression, persecution, torment; forcing; insistence, pressure; chastisement; acceptance esp. in marriage (পাণিপীড়ন). **পীড়ন করা** *v.* to press, to persecute, to torment; to force; to insist, to chastise; to accept esp. in marriage.

পীড়া *n.* trouble, pain, suffering, distress, affliction (মনঃপীড়া) ; a disease, an ailment, a disorder (পেটের পীড়া). **পীড়া দেওয়া** *v.* to afflict, to distress.

পীড়াগ্রস্ত *a.* ailing, sick, diseased.

পীড়াজনক, পীড়াদায়ক *a.* distressing, causing illness.

পীড়াপীড়ি *n.* repeated insistence or importunities or forcing. **পীড়াপীড়ি করা** *v.* to insist (on) or importune or force repeatedly, to pester, to press for.

পীড়িত *a.* sick, ill, ailing; diseased; afflicted; distressed, oppressed. *fem.* **পীড়িতা**।

পীড্যমান *a.* in the state of being oppressed or persecuted.

পীত[1] *a.* (of a drink) drunk, swallowed.

পীত[2] *n.* the yellow colour. □ *a.* yellow. **~চন্দন** *n.* yellow sandalwood or a paste made of it. **~জ্বর** *n.* yellow fever. **~ধড়া** *n.* a piece of loin-cloth dyed in yellow esp. one such as worn by Krishna (কৃষ্ণ). **~বাস, পীতাম্বর** *n.* a yellow loin-cloth; Krishna (কৃষ্ণ). □ *a.* wearing a yellow loin-cloth.

পীতাভ *a.* yellowish.

পীন *a.* plump, pleasantly fat and

rounded, ~পয়োধর *n.* a woman's plump breasts.

পীনস *n.* ozaena.

পীনোন্নত *a.* plump and jutting out. **~পয়োধর** a woman's plump and prominent breasts.

পীবর *a.* plump; corpulent, burly; well-developed; sturdy. *fem.* **পীবরা, পীবরী**।

পীযূষ *n.* nectar, ambrosia.

পীর rejected spell. of **পির**।

পীরিত, পীরিতি alt. spellings of **পিরিত** and **পিরিতি** respectively.

পুং[১] abbr. of **পুনশ্চ** (cp. p.s.)

পুং[২] in comp. used as a *pfx.* masculine, male, he-. **~কেশর** *n.* (bot.) a stamen. **~গব** alt. spell. of **পুঙ্গব**। **~জননকোষ** *n.* (bot.) a male gamete. **~দণ্ড** *n.* (bot.) a filament. **~বৎস** *n.* a bull-calf; a steer, a bullock. **~বাচক** *a.* (esp. in gr.) masculine. **~ভাব** *n.* masculinity (esp. of a woman); manliness, virility. **~ভাবাপন্ন** *a.* (of a woman) of masculine type, tomboyish. **~লিঙ্গ** *n.* (gr.) the masculine gender; the male genitals; the penis. ☐ *a.* (gr.) masculine. **~শ্চলী** *n.* a harlot; (rare) a tomboy. **~শ্চিহ্ন** *n.* the sign of masculinity; the male genitals. **~সবন** *n.* a sacrament performed on the third month of pregnancy out of desire of having a male child. **~স্কোকিল** *n.* a male cuckoo. **~স্তবক** *n.* (bot.) androecium. **~স্ত্ব** *n.* masculine semen; masculinity, virility, manhood; state of being a male.

পুঁই *n.* bassella, the Indian spinach, a creeper used as a pot-herb. **পুঁইয়ে, পুঁয়ে** *a.* creeping; very slender (পুঁইয়ে সাপ). **পুঁইয়ে পাওয়া, পুঁয়ে পাওয়া** *v.* to be attacked with rickets. **পুঁইয়ে-পাওয়া, পুঁয়ে-পাওয়া** *a.* affected with rickets, rickety.

পুঁচকে *a.* tiny.

পুঁছা alt. form of **পোঁছা**[২]।

পুঁজ *n.* purulent matter formed in boils, ulcer, wound etc. **পুঁজ হওয়া, পুঁজ জমা** *v.* to suppurate. **পুঁজ বার হওয়া** *v.* to discharge pus, to secrete pus.

পুঁজি *n.* money saved up; cash in hand; capital money, capital; savings; resources; possessions, belongings; an accumulated heap, an accumulation. **~পাটা** *n.* one's movable and immovable possessions or assets or property; savings. **~বাদ** *n.* capitalism. **~বাদী** *a.* capitalist, capitalistic. ☐ *n.* a capitalist.

পুঁটলি *n.* a small bundle or baggage.

পুঁটি *n.* a tiny fresh-water fish. **পুঁটিমাছের প্রাণ** (fig.) a short-lived or frail person; a weakling; a very narrow-minded person. **পুঁটিমাছের ফরফরানি** bragging of a man of little or no importance.

পুঁটুলি var. of **পুঁটলি**।

পুঁটে *n.* the ends of a kind of bangle; a kind of button.

পুঁতা older var. of **পোঁতা**[২]।

পুঁতি *n.* a kind of small pearl-shaped ball of glass with a small hole through it, bead. **পুঁতির মালা** a string of these balls, a string or necklace of beads.

পুঁথি *n.* a book; an ancient manuscript. **পুঁথি বাড়ানো** *v.* to lengthen out unnecessarily. **~গত** *a.* contained in or available in books only; bookish. **পুঁথিগত বিদ্যা** book-learning. **~পত্র** *n.* books and papers. **~শালা** *n.* a library; a museum or a repository of ancient manuscript.

পুকুর *n.* a pond, a tank, a pool. **পুকুর কাটা** *v.* to excavate a pond. **পুকুর ঝালানো** *v.* to dredge a tank. **পুকুর প্রতিষ্ঠা করা** *v.* to perform solemn rites before putting a newly excavated pond to use. **~চুরি** *n.* an unbelievably tremendous fraud.

পুঙ্খ *n.* the bottom part of an arrow. **পুঙ্খানুপুঙ্খ** *a.* thorough; thorough-going; minute; detailed; minutely searching or scrutinizing. **পুঙ্খানুপুঙ্খ ভাবে** *adv.* minutely, thoroughly, in every detail.

পুঙ্গব *n.* the ox; the bull; (as a *sfx.*) the best or greatest specimen (নরপুঙ্গব, নৃপপুঙ্গব).

পুচ্ছ *n.* the tail; the posteriors; the back part; the rear. **~হীন** *a.* tailless.

পুছ *n.* interrogation, questioning; inquiry.

পুছা, পোছা *v.* to ask, to inquire, to question, to interrogate; to pay heed to, to attach importance to (তাকে কেউ পোছে না).

পুজুরি dial. corrup. of **পুজারি** (see **পুজা**).

পুঞ্জ *n.* an accumulation, a collection, a heap, a pile, a mass, a multitude; a crowd. ~মেঘ *n.* see under মেঘ। **পুঞ্জিত, পুঞ্জীভূত** *a.* accumulated, collected, piled up; amassed; crowded, thronged. **পুঞ্জীকৃত** *a.* that which has been accumulated or collected or piled up or amassed.

পুঞ্জীগণিতক *n.* capital accounts.

পুট[1] *n.* the part of the body lying between the top extremity of the spine and the armpit; the length of this part. ~হাতা *n.* the measurement of length from the top extremity of the spine to the wrist.

পুট[2] *n.* a container, a vessel, a cup (পর্ণপুট) ; anything with which something is held or caught or seized or covered (কক্ষপুট) ; a crucible for boiling medicinal herbs etc. (পুটপাক).

পুটিং *n.* putty. **পুটিং করা, পুটিং দেওয়া** *v.* to putty.

পুটিত *a.* boiled in a crucible; covered; strung (as a garland); kneaded.

পুটুলি var. of পুঁটুলি।

পুডিং *n.* pudding.

পুড়ন *n.* burning; scalding, scorching; calcination; incineration; inflammation; state of becoming very hot, affliction.

পুড়া older form of পোড়া।

পুড়ুনি pop. var. of পোড়ানি (see পোড়া).

পুণ্ডরীক *n.* the white lotus. **পুণ্ডরীকাক্ষ** *n.* one with eyes as white as a pair of white lotuses; Vishnu (বিষ্ণু) or Krishna (কৃষ্ণ).

পুণ্ড্র, পুণ্ড্রক *n.* sugarcane; a sectarian mark on the forehead; an ancient race of Bengal.

পুণ্য *n.* virtue, piety. □ *a.* (used as a *pfx.*) holy, sacred; virtuous, pious. ~কর্ম *n.* an act of piety or virtue. ~কর্মা *a.* one who does or has done acts of piety or virtue. ~কাল *n.* a holy tide. ~কীর্তি *a.* celebrated for piety or virtuousness. ~ক্ষয় *n.* decay or waning of the strength of one's piety or virtue. ~ক্ষেত্র, ~তীর্থ *n.* a holy place; a place of pilgrimage. ~তিথি *n.* an auspicious lunar day for rituals; an auspicious day or time. ~তোয়া *a. fem.* (of rivers) containing holy water. ~দ *a.* adding to one's piety or virtue; holy. *fem.* পুণ্যদা। ~দর্শন *a.* one whose sight adds to another's piety or virtue. ~ধাম *n.* a sacred or holy abode; heaven. ~ফল *n.* the reward of or return for one's piety or virtue. ~ফলে *adv.* in return for acquired or accumulated virtue or merit. ~বতী *fem.* of পুণ্যবান। ~বল *n.* the strength or force of one's piety or virtue. ~বলে *adv.* by dint of the force of acquired merit or virtue. ~বান *a.* pious, virtuous; holy. ~ভূমি *n.* a holy land. ~যোগ *n.* (astrol.) an auspicious conjunction of stars or an auspicious time for performing solemn rites. ~লব্ধ *a.* obtained or earned by dint of one's piety or virtuousness. ~লাভ *n.* attainment or earning of piety or virtue. ~লোক *n.* a holy sphere or region; heaven; a pious or holy man. ~লোভ *n.* earnest desire for attaining or earning piety or virtue. ~লোভী *a.* earnestly desirous of earning piety or virtue. ~শীল *a.* given to performing acts of piety or virtue. *fem.* ~শীলা। ~শ্লোক *a.* celebrated for piety or virtuousness; virtuous; holy. ~সঞ্চয় *n.* accumulation of piety or virtue. ~স্নান *n.* holy bath; taking bath on a holy day or in a sacred river.

পুণ্যাত্মা *a.* pious, virtuous; holy.

পুণ্যাহ *n.* an auspicious day for performing solemn rites.

পুণ্যি coll. form of পুণ্য। ~পুকুর *n.* a vow observed by young unmarried girls.

পুত coll. corrup. of পুত্র।

পুতলি *n.* a puppet, a doll, a marionette; a favourite or pet (স্নেহের পুতলি) ; the pupil of the eye, the apple of the eye (নয়নপুতলি).

পুতী, পুতি coll. forms of পুত্রী।

পুতুপুতু *int.* expressing: excessive carefulness or attention or fondling. **পুতুপুতু করা** *v.* to take care of or attend on overmuch, to fondle overmuch.

পুতুল *n.* a doll, a puppet, a marionette; an instrument in another's hand; one who acts just as another tells him, a cat's-paw, an idol. ~খেলা *n.* a children's (esp.

girls') play in which an imaginary house-hold is built up with puppets as its members; (fig.) a meaningless action, a children's play; a triviality. ~নাচ *n.* a puppet-show, a puppet-play. পুতুল-নাচিয়ে *n.* a puppet-player. ~পুজো *n.* (sarcas.) idolatry. **(পরের) হাতের পুতুল** a puppet in another's hand, a cat's-paw.

পুত্তল *n.* a jack-straw, an effigy; a puppet, a doll, a marionette.

পুত্তলি[১] *n.* a pupa.

পুত্তলি[২], **পুত্তলী, পুত্তলিকা** variants of **পুত্তল**। **পুত্তলিপূজা** *n.* idolatry.

পুত্তিকা *n.* the white ant; the bee.

পুত্র *n.* a son; (in affectionate address) one who may be regarded as a son. ~কলত্র *n.* son and wife. ~কাম *a.* desirous of having a son. *fem.* ~কামা। ~পৌত্র *n.* son and grandson. ~পৌত্রাদি *n.* future generations, posterity. ~পৌত্রাদিক্রমে *adv.* from one generation to another, in successive generations. ~বতী *fem.* of **পুত্রবান**। ~বৎ *a.* & *adv.* like a son. ~বৎসল *a.* fond of or affectionate towards sons. ~বধূ *n.* son's wife, daughter-in-law. ~বান *a.* having a son or sons. ~বাৎসল্য *n.* love or affection for sons. ~রত্ন *n.* jewel of a son, a worthy or remarkable son. ~শোক *n.* grief caused by the death of a son; the feeling of bereavement at the loss of a son. ~সন্তান *n.* male child. ~হীন *a.* sonless. **পুত্রার্থী** *a.* desirous of having or wishing to have a son. **পুত্রার্থে** *adv.* with a view to getting a son. **পুত্রার্থে ক্রিয়তে ভার্যা** marriage only with a view to getting a son. **পুত্রিকা** *n.* a daughter; a foster-daughter; a doll, a puppet. **পুত্রী** *n.* a daughter; (in affectionate address) one who may be regarded as a daughter. **পুত্রীয়** *a.* of or for a son. **পুত্রেষ্টি, পুত্রেষ্টিকা** *n.* an oblation performed for the purpose of getting a son.

পুথি var. of **পুঁথি**।

পুদিনা *n.* spearmint, mint.

পুনঃ, (poet.) **পুন** *adv.* again; over again; once more. **পুনঃপুনঃ** *adv.* again and again, over and over again, repeatedly. **পুনঃপ্রবেশ** *n.* re-entry; entering again. **পুনঃপ্রাপ্ত** *a.* regained; recovered. **পুনঃপ্রাপ্তি** *n.* regaining; recovery. **পুনঃপ্রেরণ করা** *v.* to send again; to send back. **পুনঃপ্রেরিত** *a.* sent again; sent back. **পুনঃশিলীভবন** *n.* regelation. **পুনঃসংস্কার** *n.* renovation. **পুনঃসংস্কার করা** *v.* to restore to good condition, to renovate. **পুনঃস্থাপন** *n.* re-installation. **পুনঃস্থাপন করা** v. to re-install. **পুনঃস্থাপিত** *a.* re-installed. **পুনরধিকার** *n.* reoccupation, recapture. **পুনরধিকার করা** *v.* to reoccupy, to retake, to recapture. **পুনরধিকৃত** *a.* reoccupied, retaken, recaptured. **পুনরপি** *adv.* once more, once again. **পুনরর্পণ** *n.* act of giving again or giving back, return; restitution, restoration. **পুনরর্পণ করা** *v.* to give again; to give back, to return; to restitute, to restore. **পুনরাগত** *a.* returned, come back. **পুনরাগমন** *n.* return. **পুনরাগমন করা** *v.* to come back, to return. **পুনরাবর্ত, পুনরাবর্তন** *n.* revolving, revolution; return; rebirth. **পুনরাবর্তন করা** *v.* to revolve; to return; to be born again. **পুনরাবির্ভাব** *n.* reappearance; rebirth; **পুনরাবির্ভূত** *a.* reappeared; reborn. **পুনরাবৃত্ত** *a.* revolved; returned; recited; read over again; repeated; reborn. **পুনরাবৃত্তি** *n.* revolving, revolution; return; recitation, recital; a second reading; repetition, rebirth. **পুনরাবৃত্তি করা** *v.* to revolve; to return; to recite; to read again; to repeat; to be born again. **পুনরায়** same as **পুনঃ**। **পুনরাহূত** *a.* called again; recalled. **পুনরাহ্বান** *n.* a calling again; recall. **পুনরাহ্বান করা** *v.* to call again; to recall. **পুনরীক্ষণ** *n.* a review. **পুনরুক্ত** *a.* uttered again, repeated. **পুনরুক্তি** *n.* repetition, reiteration, reiterance; (rhet.) tautology. **পুনরুক্তি করা** *v.* to say or utter again, to repeat. **পুনরুক্তিদোষ** *n.* (rhet.) tautology. **পুনরুজ্জীবন** *n.* reanimation; revival; resuscitation. **পুনরুজ্জীবিত** *a.* reanimated; revived; resuscitated; brought back to life. **পুনরুজ্জীবিত করা** *v.* to reanimate; to revive; to resuscitate; to bring back to life. **পুনরুত্থান** *n.* act of rising again; reawakening; (Christ.) resurrection. **পুনরুত্থান করা** *v.* to rise again; to reawaken; (Christ.) to be resurrected.

পুনরুৎপত্তি same as পুনরুদ্ভব। পুনরুদ্দীপন *n.* re-animation; re-awakening; revival; rejuvenation. পুনরুদ্দীপ্ত, (loos.) পুনরুদ্দীপিত *a.* re-animated; re-awakened; revived; rejuvenated. পুনরুদ্ধার *n.* recovery; regaining; retrieval. পুনরুদ্ধার করা *v.* to recover; to regain or retrieve. পুনরুদ্ভব *n.* recurrence; regeneration; re-birth. পুনরুদ্ভূত *a.* recurred; regenerated; re-born. পুনরুল্লেখ *n.* repetition, recapitulation, restatement. পুনরুল্লেখ করা *v.* to repeat, to recapitulate, to restate; to say or mention again. পুনর্গঠন *n.* reconstruction; reorganization. পুনর্গঠিত *a.* reconstructed; reorganized. পুনর্জন্ম *n.* a new lease of life; reanimation; re-birth. পুনর্জাত *a.* reborn. পুনর্জীবন *n.* restoration to life; a new lease of life, a new life. পুনর্জীবিত *a.* restored to life; one who has got a new lease of life. পুনর্দখল *n.* recapture; re-occupation. পুনর্দখল করা *v.* to recapture or re-occupy. পুনর্নব *n.* finger-nail. পুনর্নবা *n.* a kind of spinach, the hog-weed. পুনর্নিবেশ *n.* a feed-back. পুনর্নির্বাচন *n.* re-election. পুনর্নির্বাচন করা *v.* to re-elect. পুনর্নির্বাচিত *a.* re-elected. পুনর্নির্মাণ *n.* reconstruction, re-building. পুনর্নির্মাণ করা *v.* to reconstruct, to re-build. পুনর্বসতি same as পুনর্বাসন। পুনর্বসু *n.* (astr.) the seventh of the twenty-seven zodiacal stars according to Hindu astronomy. পুনর্বার same as পুনঃ। পুনর্বাসন *n.* rehabilitation. পুনর্বিচার *n.* reconsideration; retrial, review, reappraisal, rehearing. পুনর্বিচার করা *v.* to reconsider; to review. পুনর্বিচারপ্রার্থী *n.* an appellant. পুনর্বিবাহ *n.* a second marriage; a remarriage. পুনর্ভূ *a. fem.* (of a woman) married again after being widowed or married with a man other than the person to whom one was betrothed. পুনর্মিলন *n.* re-union; reconciliation. পুনর্মিলিত *a.* reunited; reconciled. পুনর্মূষিক ভব (lit.) be reverted to a mouse; (fig.) be reverted to a former or original (esp. a very inferior) state. পুনর্যাত্রা *n.* a setting out on a journey for the second time, a second march; a return journey; (myth.) the return journey of Juggernaut (জগন্নাথ) in his chariot (see রথযাত্রা). পুনশ্চ *adv.* once again; once more. □ *n.* postscript. পুনস্থাপন, পুনস্থাপিত pop. spellings of পুনঃস্থাপন, পুনঃস্থাপিত।

পুনকে *a.* very small, tiny, wee.

পুন্নাগ *n.* the white lotus, the white lily; a kind of flower-plant, the nagakeshara (নাগকেশর).

পুন্নামনরক *n.* a region of hell called Put (পুৎ) to which a sonless person is condemned.

পুব coll. form of পূর্ব।

পুবাল, পুবালি, পুবে *a.* coming or blowing from the east, eastern.

পুর[1] *n.* relishing ingredients put into an article of food, stuffing.

পুর[2] *n.* a house, a dwelling-house, an abode (নন্দপুর) ; a city, a town, a village (হস্তিনাপুর). ~দ্বার *n.* the gate of a city or a house. ~নারী *n. fem.* a woman usually keeping to the zenana; a housewife; a female member (esp. a married one) of a family. ~ন্দর *n.* a name of Indra (ইন্দ্র), the king of gods. ~স্ত্রী, ~স্ত্রি *n.* a housewife; a married woman having her husband and children living. ~বাসী *a.* inhabiting a town or a village; living in a family. □ *n.* a citizen, townsman, a villager; a member or inmate of a family. *fem.* ~বাসিনী। ~রক্ষক *n.* a warder or warden of a house; a city guard. ~ললনা *n.* same as পুরনারী। ~শাসক *n.* a presidency magistrate. ~স্ত্রী same as পুরনারী।

পুরঃসর *a.* advanced. □ *in comp.* (used as a *sfx.*) having in front of, having first made or done (প্রণামপুরঃসর = having made obeisance).

পুরঞ্জন *n.* the soul, life.

পুরতঃ *adv.* in front, before; formerly.

পুরনো alt. spell. of পুরোনো।

পুরন্ত *a.* plump; well-developed; complete; full-grown.

পুরব poet. form of পূর্ব।

পুরবী alt. spell. of পূরবী।

পুরশ্চরণ *n.* worship of a deity with a view to attaining some end.

পুরস্কার *n.* a reward; a prize; remuneration; meed; cordial reception, welcome

('বসাইলা আসনে তারে করি পুরস্কার') ; honour, felicitation. **পুরস্কার দেওয়া** *v.* to reward.

পুরস্ক্রিয়া *n.* rewarding; act of awarding a prize; act of remunerating; cordial reception; honouring, felicitation.

পুরস্কৃত *a.* rewarded; remunerated; cordially received; honoured, felicitated. **পুরস্কৃত করা** *v.* to reward.

পুরা[1] *adv.* before, formerly, in the past, in ancient times.

পুরা[2] *a.* (for.) entire, whole, complete, full; replete (পুরা কলসি). □ *adv.* full, fully (পুরা পাঁচ হাত) ; completely, thoroughly (পুরা জানা).

পুরা[3], **পোরা** *v.* to fill (কলসিতে জল পুরছে) ; to stuff (ব্যাগে কাপড় পুরছে) ; to thrust in, to enter (মুখে পোরা) ; to put into, to confine (জেলে পোরা), to conceal inside; to be filled (with) (ছেলেপুলেতে ঘর পুরেছে) ; to blow or sound as a wind-instrument ('সবে পোরে সিঙ্গা বেনু') ; to be satisfied or realized or attained (আশা পুরেছে) ; to be completed or accomplished (কাজ পুরেছে).

পুরাকাল *n.* ancient times.

পুরাঙ্গনা same as **পুরনারী** (see **পুর**[2]).

পুরাণ *n.* a myth or mythology (esp. of Hindus). □ *a.* ancient; primordial (পুরাণ পুরুষ). **~কর্তা, ~কার** *n.* an author of a mythology. **~পুরুষ** *n.* God. **~প্রসিদ্ধি** *n.* mention in the Puranas or mythology; long-standing fame.

পুরাতত্ত্ব *n.* archaeology; antiquities; ancient history. **~জ্ঞ, ~বিদ** *a.* versed in archaeology or antiquities or ancient history. □ *n.* an archaeologist; an antiquary, an antiquarian; one versed in ancient history.

পুরাতন *a.* ancient; old; aged; backdated, out-of-date (পুরাতন ফ্যাশন) ; long-standing (পুরাতন প্রথা) ; experienced (পুরাতন কর্মচারী) ; inveterate (পুরাতন পাপী) ; chronic (পুরাতন রোগ). *fem.* **পুরাতনী** । **পুরাতন কর্মচারী** an old hand.

পুরাদস্তুর *adv.* to the fullest extent; completely; thoroughly, in a downright manner. □ *a.* complete; downright; thorough, out-and-out, thorough-going.

পুরাধ্যক্ষ *n.* a governor of a city; a warden of a house.

পুরানো[1] *a.* old; ancient; aged; backdated (পুরানো রীতি).

পুরানো[2] *v.* to fulfil, to satisfy; to fill.

পুরাপুরি *a.* complete; thorough; full, entire; downright. □ *adv.* completely; thoroughly; fully, entirely; in a downright manner; in extenso.

পুরাবিৎ, পুরাবৃত্ত same as **পুরাতত্ত্ববিদ** and **পুরাতত্ত্ব** respectively.

পুরি *n.* a kind of small and thin saucer-shaped brown bread fried in clarified butter.

পুরিয়া *n.* a tiny packet; a dose of medicine or other articles in a tiny packet; an Indian musical mode.

পুরী[1] rej. spell. of **পুরি** ।

পুরী[2] *n.* a house, a palace, a residence (রাজপুরী, ইন্দ্রপুরী) ; a city; a title of certain ascetics (ঈশ্বরপুরী).

পুরীষ *n.* faeces, excrement, stool; ordure, dung, droppings. **পুরীষোৎসর্গ** *n.* evacuation of ordure on something or somebody.

পুরু *a.* thick; fat; having a specific number of folds (সাতপুরু কাপড়).

পুরুত coll. form of **পুরোহিত** ।

পুরুষ *n.* man; a man; a male creature; a manly man, a he-man (সে খাঁটি পুরুষ) ; (phil. & theol.) the soul (পুরুষ ও প্রকৃতি) ; God; a generation (অধস্তন পাঁচ পুরুষ) ; (gr.) person (**উত্তম পুরুষ** = the first person; **মধ্যম পুরুষ** = the second person; **প্রথম পুরুষ** = the third person). □ *in comp.* male, he (পুরুষ জন্তু). **পরমপুরুষ** *n.* a superman; God, the Absolute. **পুরুষকার** *n.* manliness, prowess; intelligence; manly effort. **পুরুষজাতীয়** *a.* male; masculine. **~ত্ব** *n.* masculinity; manhood; manliness, virility; vigour; masculine sexual power. **পুরুষত্ববর্জিত, পুরুষত্ববিহীন, পুরুষত্বরহিত, পুরুষত্বশূন্য, পুরুষত্বহীন** *a.* lacking in masculine sexual power, impotent; unmanly; effeminate; lacking in vigour; faint-hearted. **পুরুষত্বহানি** *n.* loss of masculine sexual power, impotency. **~-পরম্পরা** *n.* succession of generations, lineal succession, heredity. **~পরম্পরাক্রমে** *adv.* from generation to generation, hereditarily. ~-পরম্পরাগত *a.* coming down from generation to generation; inherited; hereditary; traditional. ~পুঙ্গব *n.* a high specimen of humanity; a great man; a big man. ~প্রধান *n.* chief amongst men; (when attributed to God) Supreme. ~ব্যাঘ্র *n.* a tiger of a man. ~মানুষ *n.* a man; a male; a manly man. ~শার্দুল same as পুরুষব্যাঘ্র। ~শ্রেষ্ঠ same as ~প্রধান। ~সিংহ *n.* a lion amongst men. ~সুলভ *a.* common to or befitting a man; masculine. পুরুষাঙ্গ *n.* the male sex-organ, the penis. পুরুষাধম *n.* the basest or vilest of men; a dirty fellow; a rascal; an extremely cowardly man. পুরুষানুক্রম same as পুরুষ-পরম্পরা। পুরুষানুক্রমিক same as পুরুষ-পরম্পরাগত। পুরুষার্থ *n.* religious or spiritual attainment, earning of wealth, realization of desires and attainment of salvation: these four manly pursuits of life; happiness, bliss, salvation, beatitude. পুরুষালি *n.* masculinity; manliness, virility; (of a woman or a girl) tomboyishness. □ *a.* masculine; manly, virile; (of a woman or girl) tomboyish. পুরুষোচিত *a.* proper for a man; becoming or befitting a man; manly. পুরুষোত্তম *n.* an excellent man; a superman; the Supreme Being, God, Vishnu (বিষ্ণু).

পুরুষ্টু *a.* (coll.) well-developed, plum.

পুরো coll. form of পুরা[২]।

পুরোগ, পুরোগামী *a.* going before in point of time or place, preceding, leading; pioneering. পুরোগত *a.* gone before in point of time or place.

পুরোডাশ *n.* thick saucer-shaped bread.

পুরোধা *n.* a priest; a pioneer, avant garde.

পুরোনো *a.* old; ancient; backdated.

পুরোপুরি pop. form of পুরাপুরি।

পুরোবর্তী *a.* lying in front; preceding; advanced; apical.

পুরোভাগ *n.* the first part or share; the front. সৈন্যবাহিনীর পুরোভাগ the vanguard.

পুরোভূমি *n.* the foreground.

পুরোযায়ী *a.* preceding; leading; inaugurating or founding.

পুরোহিত *n.* a priest.

পুল *n.* a bridge (as on a river).

পুলক *n.* horripilation or gooseflesh (usu. caused by a delightful feeling or sensation); a thrill (of joy or delight); delight or joy. ~কন্টকিত, পুলকিত *a.* horripilated in delight; (greatly) delighted. পুলকোচ্ছ্বাস *n.* an outburst of delight.

পুলটিস *n.* a poultice.

পুলি[১] *n.* Port Blair in the Andamans.

পুলি[২] *n.* a kind of sweet roll.

পুলিন *n.* the part of a sandy beach or bank up to which the high-water mark reaches; (loos.) a sand-bank, a beach, shoal.

পুলিন্দা *n.* a packet or bundle or parcel (esp. a small one).

পুলিপিঠে same as পুলি[২]।

পুলিপোলাও *n.* deportation to Port Blair; (loos.) deportation, transportation.

পুলিশ, পুলিস *n.* the police; a policeman; a police constable.

-পুলে correl. of ছেলে (ছেলেপুলে).

পুষা, পোষা *v.* to bring up; to cherish (মনে আশা পুষছে); to nourish; to feed; to maintain, to support (পরিজনদের পোষা); to rear; to keep, to breed, to fancy (বাঁদর পোষা, পাখি পোষা).

পুষ্কর *n.* the lotus; water; cloud; the tip of an elephant's trunk; a holy lake near Ajmir.

পুষ্করিণী *n.* a pond, a tank, a pool.

পুষ্ট *a.* nourished; brought up; bred; developed; grown up; plump; fat; adiposed; fattened; mature; ripe; cherished. পুষ্ট-তাড়িত *n.* (phys.) positive electricity. পুষ্টাঙ্গ *a.* well-developed; fat; fattened. পুষ্টি *n.* nourishment; upbringing; breeding; development; growth; plumpness; fatness; adiposity; fattening; maturity; thorough ripeness; nutrition; cherishment. পুষ্টিকর, পুষ্টিজনক, পুষ্টিসাধক *a.* nutritious; nourishing. পুষ্টিসাধন *n.* nutrition; nourishment. পুষ্টিসাধন করা *v.* to nourish.

পুষ্প *n.* flower; blossom; menstrual flux; an eye-disease. ~ক, ~করথ *n.* the name of Kuvera's (কুবের) chariot capable of flying through the air at a great speed. ~করণ্ডক *n.* a flower-basket. ~কীট *a.* a flower-worm. ~কেতন, ~কেতু *n.* one whose banner is made of flowers; Madan (মদন) the god of love. ~গুচ্ছ *n.* a bunch of flowers. পুষ্প চয়ন করা *v.* to pluck or cull flowers. ~দণ্ড *n.* (bot.) a peduncle. ~ধনু *n.* a bow made of flowers; one holding such a bow; Madan (মদন) the god of love. ~দল *n.* a petal. ~ধন্বা *n.* one holding a bow of flowers; Madan (মদন) the god of love. ~নির্যাস *n.* essence of flower. ~পত্র *n.* a petal; flowers and leaves; (bot.) floral leaves. ~পত্রবিন্যাস *n.* (bot.) prefloration. ~পল্লব *n.* a twig with flowers; flowers and leaves. ~পাত্র *n.* a saucer for holding flowers (esp. one used in a religious service). ~পুট *n.* (bot.) a calyx. ~প্রতীক *n.* a floral diagram. ~বতী *a.* in menstruation, menstruating, menstruous. ~বাটিকা, ~বাটী *n.* a flower garden (esp. one with a summer-house); a garden-house. ~বাণ *n.* an arrow made of flowers; one using such arrows; Madan (মদন) the god of love. ~বিন্যাস *n.* (bot.) inflorescence. ~বৃন্ত *n.* a flower-stalk. ~বৃন্তিকা *n.* (bot.) a pedicel. ~বৃষ্টি *n.* a shower of flowers. ~ভূষণ *n.* an ornament made of flowers, a floral ornament. ~মঞ্জরী *n.* a flower-bud; a flower-stalk. ~মালা, ~মাল্য *n.* a garland of flowers, a flower-wreath. ~মুকুট *n.* a chaplet of flowers. ~মুকুল *n.* a flower-bud. ~রজঃ *n.* pollen. ~রস *n.* flower-juice, honey. ~রাগ *n.* topaz. ~রেণু *n.* pollen. ~শর same as পুষ্পবাণ। ~শয্যা *n.* a bed of flowers. ~সংকেত *n.* (bot.) a floral formula. ~সার *n.* essence of flower. ~সৌরভ *n.* aroma or fragrance of a flower. ~স্তবক *n.* a cluster or bunch of flowers, a bouquet; a wreath. ~হীন, ~শূন্য *a.* divested of flowers; flowerless. পুষ্পাগম *n.* florescence or its season. পুষ্পাগম-কাল *n.* the time of florescence; the season of flowers, the spring. পুষ্পাজীব *a.* dealing in flowers and flower-wreaths; making flower-wreaths professionally. □ *n.* a florist; a professional maker of flower-wreaths. পুষ্পাঞ্জলি *n.* an offering of a handful of flowers to a deity. পুষ্পাঞ্জলি দেওয়া *v.* to offer a handful of flowers in devotion or worship. পুষ্পাধার *n.* a flower-vase; a flower-pot. পুষ্পাভরণ, পুষ্পালংকার same as পুষ্পভূষণ। পুষ্পাসব same as পুষ্পমধু। পুষ্পিকা *n.* (bot.) a floret; the tartar of teeth; the concluding couplet or stanza of poem containing the author's name. পুষ্পিত *a.* in flower, blossomed. পুষ্পিতা *a. fem.* in flower, blossomed; in menstruation. পুষ্পেষু *n.* (the Hindu) god of love, (cp.) Cupid (মদন). পুষ্পোদ্গম same as পুষ্পাগম। পুষ্পোদ্যান *n.* a flower-garden.

পুষ্যা *n.* (astr.) the eighth of the twenty-seven stars according to Hindu astronomy.

পুষ্যি coll. form of পোষ্য।

পুস্তক *n.* a book. ~বিক্রেতা *n.* a book-seller. ~বিপণি *n.* a book-shop. ~ব্যবসায় *n.* book-trade. ~ব্যবসায়ী *n.* a book-seller. ~স্থ *a.* contained or written in a book. পুস্তকাগার *n.* a library. সাধারণ পুস্তাকাগার a public library. পুস্তকালয় *n.* a book-shop; a (rare) library. পুস্তকের দোকান a book-shop.

পুস্তনি, পুস্তানি *n.* (in book-binding) a fly leaf.

পুস্তবিকলন *n.* book-debit.

পুস্তা, পুস্তান variants of পোস্তা।

পুস্তিকা, পুস্তী *n.* a booklet; a pamphlet.

পূজক *a.* employed in worshipping. □ *n.* a worshipper, a devotee; a priest; a votary.

পূজন *n.* worship. পূজনীয় same as পূজ্য। *fem.* পূজনীয়া।

পূজয়িতা same as পূজক। *fem.* পূজয়িত্রী।

পূজা *n.* worship; adoration; devotion; reverence; cordial reception; glorification. □ *v.* poet. form of পূজা করা। পূজা করা *v.* to worship; to adore; to revere; to accord cordial reception to, to welcome; to glorify. পূজা দেওয়া *v.* to offer worship (to a deity); to offer presents in homage. পূজা পাওয়া *v.* to be worshipped or adored or revered or received cordially or welcomed. ~পার্বণ *n.* religious and social festivals; festive occasions. পূজাবকাশ *n.* vacation during a holy season, the puja (পূজা) holidays or vacation. পূজারি *a.* employed in worshipping; acting as a professional priest. □ *n.* a worshipper; a devotee; a votary; a priest. *fem.* পূজারিনি, (rej.) পূজারিণী। পূজাই same as পূজ্য। পূজাহ্নিক *n.* the daily religious service.

পূজিত *a.* worshipped; adored; revered; cordially received, welcomed; glorified, *fem.* পূজিতা।

পূজোপহার *n.* a gift or present offered during a holy festival, a puja (পূজা) gift or present.

পূজ্য *a.* worthy of worship or reverence or honour; worshipful; reverend; honourable; venerable. *fem.* পূজ্যা। ~পাদ *n.* one whose feet are worthy of worship or adoration, having worshipful feet; most reverend or adorable or venerable.

পূত *a.* holy, sacred, sanctified, pure. ~স্থান *n.* a sacred or holy place.

পূতাত্মা *a.* pure-souled; pure-hearted; holy; pious, virtuous.

পূতি *n.* stench, fetid smell. □ *a.* fetid (পূতিগন্ধ); rotten, putrid (পূতিমাংস).

পূতোদক *n.* holy water.

পূপ *n.* a sweet pie or cake. ~কার *n.* a baker. ~শালা *n.* a bakery.

পূব, পূবাল, পূবালি, পূবে rej. spellings of পুব, পুবাল, পুবালি, পুবে respectively.

পূয *n.* purulent matter formed in an ulcer, wound, boil etc.; pus. পূয জমা, পূয হওয়া *v.* to suppurate. পূয ঝরা *v.* to discharge or secrete pus.

পূর[1] alt. spell. of পুর[1]।

পূর[2] *n.* fulfilment; filling; completion; a mass of water; a stream.

পূরক *a.* fulfilling; filling; completing; (geom.) complementary; (arith. & alg.) multiplying. □ *n.* (arith.) a multiplier; (geom.) a complementary angle, a complement (also পূরক কোণ) ; act of breathing in yoga (যোগ).

পূরণ *n.* fulfilment (বাসনাপূরণ) ; filling (উদরপূরণ) ; repletion; completion (কালপূরণ) ; solution (সমস্যাপূরণ) ; compensation (ক্ষতিপূরণ) ; increase; (arith. & alg.) multiplication. পূরণ করা *v.* to fulfil; to fill, to complete; to solve; to compensate; to increase; (arith. & alg.) to multiply. ~বাচক *a.* (arith.) ordinal.

পূরণীয় *a.* to be fulfilled or filled or completed or solved.

পূরব rej. spell. of পুরব।

পূরবী *n.* an Indian Musical mode.

পূরয়িতা *a.* & *n.* one who fulfils or fills. *fem.* পূরয়িত্রী।

পূরা alt. spell. of পুরা[2,3]।

পূরিকা var. of পূরী।

পূরিত *a.* thoroughly filled, replete, filled; fulfilled; completed; solved; compensated; multiplied.

পূরী rej. spell. of পুরি।

পূর্ণ *a.* thoroughly filled, replete; full, whole; total; complete, perfect (পূর্ণ সুখ) ; fulfilled, gratified, realized; completed, completely passed (কাল পূর্ণ হওয়া) ; accomplished (সাধ পূর্ণ হওয়া) ; nature; fully grown. পূর্ণ করা *v.* to fill, to make full to the brim; to replete; to complete; to fulfil; to pass completely; to accomplish. ~কাম *a.* one whose desire has been fulfilled. ~কাল *a.* full-time. ~কুম্ভ *n.* a pitcher completely filled (esp. with water). ~গর্ভা *a. fem.* in the advanced or last stage of pregnancy, nearing travail. ~গ্রাস *n.* (astr.) total eclipse. ~চন্দ্র *n.* the full-moon, the hunter's moon. ~চ্ছেদ *n.* (gr.) a full stop. পূর্ণচ্ছেদ পড়া *v.* (fig.) to terminate or be closed for good. ~তা, ~ত্ব *n.* repleteness, fulness; completeness; fulfilment; completion; accomplishment; maturity; full growth. ~পাত্র *n.* a full cup, a full dish, a full plate, a full vessel. ~বয়স *n.* full age, maturity. ~বয়স্ক *a.* full-aged, grown up, major, adult. *fem.* ~বয়স্কা। পূর্ণবয়স্ক হওয়া *v.* to come of age, to attain majority. ~বিকশিত *a.* full-blown; fully manifested. ~বিকাশ *n.* full blowing; full manifestation. ~বেগ *n.* full speed, full tilt. ~বেগে *adv.* at full speed, in full career, at full tilt. ~ব্রহ্ম *n.* the Absolute Being, God. ~মন্ত্রী *n.* a cabinet minister (in charge of a full portfolio). ~মাত্রা *n.* the fullest measure or extent; (of medicines) a full dose. ~মাত্রায় *adv.* to the fullest measure or extent; entirely; wholly; thoroughly; in a downright manner. ~মাসী same as পৌর্ণমাসী। ~যুবক *n.* a full-grown young man. *fem.* ~যুবতী। ~সংখ্যা *a.* (arith.) an integer, a whole number. **পূর্ণা** *fem.* of **পূর্ণ**। **পূর্ণাঙ্গ** *a.* having all the limbs; complete in all parts; thorough; fully grown or developed. **পূর্ণাঙ্গতা** *n.* completeness in all parts; thoroughness; full growth or development. **পূর্ণানন্দ** *n.* full delight or joy; an appellation of God. **পূর্ণাবতার** *n.* a perfect incarnation; an appellation of Nrishingha (নৃসিংহ), Rama (রাম) and Krishna (কৃষ্ণ). **পূর্ণাবয়ব** same as **পূর্ণাঙ্গ**। **পূর্ণাভিলাষ** same as **পূর্ণকাম**। **পূর্ণায়ত** *a.* fully wide or widened or expanded. **পূর্ণায়ু** *a.* enjoying full longevity or long lease of life, long-lived. **পূর্ণাহুতি** *n.* the final offering; the burnt offering with which a sacrifice is concluded, the concluding (burnt) offering; (fig.) completion of self-sacrifice. **পূর্ণাহুতি দেওয়া** *v.* to offer the concluding (burnt) offering; (fig.) to complete, to sacrifice oneself.

পূর্ণক *n.* characteristic of a logarithm.

পূর্ণিমা *n.* the full-moon. ~নিশি *n.* a full-moon night. **পূর্ণিমার চাঁদ** the hunter's moon, the full-moon.

পূর্ণেন্দু *n.* the hunter's moon, the full-moon.

পূর্ণোপমা *n.* (rhet.) a sustained simile.

পূর্ত *n.* public works. ~বিভাগ *n.* the Public Works Department.

পূর্তি *n.* act of filling, repletion; completion; compensation. **পূর্তি-অধিদেয়, পূর্তি-ভাতা** *n.* a compensatory allowance.

পূর্ব *n.* the east; precedence in time or place (পূর্বকথিত) ; front; the past (পূর্বে দ্রাবিড়রা এ দেশে বাস করত). □ *a.* first; senior in age; past, former, preceding; eastern. **-পূর্বক** *in comp.* having in advance; having first made or done (প্রণামপূর্বক) ; with (প্রীতিপূর্বক). ~কথিত *a.* aforesaid. ~কায় *n.* the upper part of the body. ~কাল *n.* the past; ancient times; former times. ~কালিক, ~কালীন *a.* of the past, past; of ancient times, ancient; former times, former. ~কৃত *a.* previously or formerly done; done beforehand; done in anticipation. ~গামী *a.* going east or eastwards; going before, preceding; previous; antecedent. *fem.* ~গামিনী। ~জ *a.* born before, elder. □ *n.* an elder brother. ~জা *a. fem.* of **পূর্বজ**। □ *n. fem.* an elder sister. ~জন্ম *n.* a previous or former birth. ~জন্মার্জিত *a.* acquired during a former or previous birth. ~জীবন *n.* a previous or former birth; the past life; early life (cp. উত্তরজীবন). ~জ্ঞান *n.* past experiences; knowledge acquired during a former birth; anticipation. ~তন *a.* former; previous; past. ~দক্ষিণ *n.* south-east. □ *a.* south-eastern. ~দিক *n.* the east. ~দৃষ্ট *a.* previously seen; anticipated; foreseen. ~দৃষ্টি *n.* foresight. ~দেশ *n.* an eastern country or region, the east, the orient. ~দেশীয় *a.* of an eastern country or region; (rare) oriental. ~ধারণা *n.* preconception, preconceived notion. ~নিরীক্ষিত *a.* preaudited. ~নিরূপিত *a.* predestined; foreordained. ~পক্ষ *n.* a complaint; a plaint; (log.) a question, a problem for debate or discussion, the first part of an argument, a proposition. ~পরিকল্পনা *n.* preplanning. ~পরিকল্পিত *a.* preplanned. ~পরিচয় *n.* previous acquaintance. ~পরিচিত *a.* acquainted from before, formerly or already known. *fem.* ~পরিচিতা। ~পরিচিতি *n.* previous acquaintance. ~পুরুষ *n.* an ancestor, a forefather; a former generation. ~প্রচলিত *a.* formerly current or prevalent, current or prevalent in the past, previously in vogue. ~ফল্গুনী *n.* (astrol.) the eleventh of the twenty-seven stars according to Hindu astronomy. ~বঙ্গ Eastern Bengal, East Bengal. ~বৎ *adv.* as before. □ *a.* (log.) a priori. ~বর্ণিত *a.* described or narrated before, aforementioned, aforesaid. ~বর্তিতা *n.* precedence; antecedence; priority; seniority; fore-existence. ~বর্তী *a.* preceding; antecedent; prior; senior; fore-existent; previous; former. *fem.* ~বর্তিনী। ~বাদ *n.* a complaint. ~বাদী *n.* a complainant. ~ভাগ *n.* the forepart; the front; the eastern part. ~ভাদ্রপদ, ~ভাদ্রপদা *n.* (astrol.) the twenty-fifth of the twenty-seven zodiacal stars according to Hindu astronomy. ~ভাব *n.* the former or original state or condition. ~ভাষ *n.* preface, a foreword. ~মত *n.* the former opinion. ~মীমাংসা *n.* a philosophical treatise by Jaimini the ancient sage; philosophical doctrine of Jaimini and his followers. ~রঙ্গ *n.* the prologue (of a drama); a prelude. ~রাগ *n.* amorous attraction felt even before acquaintance with the lover; (inc.) courtship. ~রাত্র *n.* the first part or quarter of a night; early night; (loos.) the previous or last night. ~রাত্রি *n.* last night; the previous night. ~রাশি *n.* (math.) antecedent. ~লক্ষণ *n.* a presage; a foreboding. পূর্বলক্ষণ প্রকাশ করা *v.* to presage; to forebode. ~সংস্কার *n.* a notion or idea or impression or habit formed during a former birth or in the past. পূর্বাচল, পূর্বাদ্রি *n.* an imaginary eastern mountain from behind which the sun is believed to rise daily. পূর্বাদেশ *n.* a previous order. পূর্বাদেশ প্রত্যাহার করা to rescind a previous order. পূর্বাধিকার *n.* possession or right obtained earlier; priority; the right or claim of the first-born, primogeniture; former right or claim. পূর্বানুবৃত্তি *n.* continuation (of some account already begun). পূর্বাপর *a.* (also. *adv.*) from beginning to end, alpha and omega, thorough. পূর্বাপর বিবেচনা করা to consider the connected line of events, to consider the pros and cons of a proposal, to look before and after. পূর্বাপরবিরোধ *n.* inconsistency of acts or contexts of different times. পূর্বাপর-বৃত্ত *n.* (astr.) a prime vertical. পূর্বাপেক্ষা *adv.* than before. পূর্বাবধি *adv.* from before; since the beginning. পূর্বাবস্থা *n.* the former or previous or past state or condition. পূর্বাভাষ *n.* a presage; (dero.) a foreboding; a preface, a foreword; forecast (আবহাওয়ার পূর্বাভাষ). পূর্বাভাষ দেওয়া *v.* to presage; (dero.) to forebode. পূর্বাভ্যাস *n.* a previous or former habit or practice. পূর্বার্ধ *n.* the first half; the eastern half; (geog.) the eastern hemisphere. পূর্বাশা *n.* the east. পূর্বাষাঢ়া *n.* (astrol.) the twentieth of the twenty-seven stars according to Hindu astronomy. পূর্বাহ্ণ *n.* the first part or quarter of the day-time; (loos.) the forenoon. পূর্বাহ্ণিক *a.* of the first part or quarter of the daytime; to be done during the first part or quarter of the day-time. পূর্বিতা *n.* priority, precedence. পূর্বে *adv.* formerly, previously, before; in the past; in the front; in the east. পূর্বোক্ত *a.* aforesaid; mentioned before or above. পূর্বোক্তি *n.* a previous statement; a prefatory remark or utterance. পূর্বোত্তর *n.* the north-east. পূর্বোদ্ধৃত *a.* quoted before or above.

পূষা *n.* the sun.

পৃক্ত *a.* adjoining, contiguous, attached; associated; incorporated; united; admixed; saturated; related; connected, concerned.

পৃথক *a.* separate; different; separated; segregated; moved or lying aside; differentiated; alienated, estranged. □ *adv.* separately; severally, differently; apart. পৃথক করা *v.* to separate; to differentiate; to dissociate; to segregate; to alienate, to estrange; to remove apart. ~ত্ব *n.* separateness; distinction; difference; individuality. পৃথক পৃথক, ~ভাবে *adv.* separately; individually. ~করণ, পৃথকীকরণ *n.* separation; differentiation; dissociation; segregation; alienation, estrangement; act of removing apart. ~কৃত, পৃথকীকৃত *a.* separated; differentiated; dissociated; segregated; alienated, estranged, removed apart.

পৃথগন্ন *a.* (of a family) split up or divided into two or more units all having separate messing arrangements, separated.

পৃথগাত্মা *a.* individual; self-conscious.

পৃথগ্বিধ *a.* of a different kind; different; diverse, various, manifold.

পৃথগ্ভূত *a.* separated; differentiated; dissociated; segregated; alienated, estranged, removed apart.

পৃথিবী *n.* the earth, the world. ~তল *n.* the surface of the earth, the earth's crust or its outer part. ~পতি, ~পাল *n.* a king; an emperor. ~ব্যাপী, ~ময় *a.* extending all over the world; world-wide. **~মণ্ডল** *n.* the orb of the earth; the whole world.

পৃথু, পৃথুল *a.* extensive; wide; great; magnanimous; bulky, fat, heavy; muscular, robust. **পৃথুস্কন্ধ** *a.* with muscular and robust shoulders.

পৃথ্বী *n.* the earth, the world.

পৃষ্ঠ *n.* the back (of a human being or any other creature); the rear; the region of the back; the back part, the rear part; the hind part; surface, a face; (bot.) the dorsal surface. **ঘূর্ণপৃষ্ঠ** *n.* the surface of revolution. **~টান** *n.* (phys.) surface tension. **~তল** *n.* surface. **~দেশ** same as **পৃষ্ঠ**। **~পোষক** *n.* one who stands at the back to give support; a supporter; an upholder; a patron; a customer; a client. **~পোষকতা** *n.* support; patronization. **পৃষ্ঠপোষকতা করা** *v.* to support; to uphold; to patronize. **~পোষণ** *n.* act of standing at the back to give support; act of supporting or upholding; patronization. **~প্রদর্শন** *n.* fleeing, flight. **পৃষ্ঠপ্রদর্শন করা** *v.* to flee, to take to one's heels, to run away. **~প্রবাহ** *n.* (geog.) a surface drift. **~বংশ** *n.* the backbone, the spinal or vertebral column, the spine. **~ব্রণ** *n.* a dorsal carbuncle. **~ভঙ্গ** *n.* act of fleeing (esp. after a defeat). **~রক্ষক** *n.* a bodyguard. **পৃষ্ঠরক্ষা করা** *v.* to protect or guard the rear; to act as a bodyguard to. **~লেখ** *n.* an endorsement.

পৃষ্ঠা *n.* a page (of a book). **পৃষ্ঠাঙ্ক** *n.* page-number.

পৃষ্ঠোপরি *adv.* on the back (of).

পেঁকো *a.* full of slime or silt, like slime or silt, slimy, silty, miry.

পেঁচি *fem.* of **প্যাঁচা**।

পেঁচো coll. corrup. of **পঞ্চানন্দ**। **পেঁচোয় পাওয়া** *v.* to be affected with tetanus or rickets.

পেঁজা, পেঁটরা, পেঁড়া variants of **পিঁজা, পেটরা** and **পেড়া**[১] respectively.

পেঁদানি, পেঁদানো alt. spellings of **প্যাঁদানি** and **প্যাঁদানো** respectively.

পেঁপে *n.* the papaw, the pawpaw, the papaya.

পেঁয়াজ, পেঁয়াজি pop. variants of **পিয়াজ** and **পিয়াজি** respectively.

পেখন *n.* (obs. & poet.) seeing.

পেখম *n.* a peacock's plumage or tail esp. when expanded or spread out like a fan at the time of dancing. **পেখম ধরা, পেখম ফোলানো** *v.* (of a peacock) to expand or distend one's plumage or tail (when dancing); (fig.) to be beside oneself with joy, to be foolishly ostentatious in dress, to be vainglorious, to peacock.

পেখা *v.* (poet. & obs.) to see.

পেচক *n.* (for.) the owl. *fem.* **পেচকী**। **~শাবক** *n.* an owlet.

পেচ্ছাপ, পেছন, পেছপা, পেছু coll. forms of **প্রস্রাব, পিছন, পিছপা** (see **পিছ**) and **পাছু** respectively.

-পেজি *a. sfx.* having a specific number of pages (আটপেজি ফর্মা).

পেজোমি *n.* baseness; roguishness, roguery, knavishness, knavery; mischiefmongering. **পেজোমি করা** *v.* to commit an act of roguery or knavery; to make a mischief.

পেট *n.* the belly; the abdomen; the stomach; the womb (পেটের ছেলে) ; the inside, the hold (জাহাজের পেট) ; the loins (পেটে কাপড় থাকে না) ; (vul.) pregnancy (পেট হওয়া) ; the inmost part of one's heart (পেটের কথা) ; subsistence, livelihood (পেট চালানো). **খালি পেট** empty stomach. **ভরা পেট** full stomach. **পেট আঁটা** *v.* to get constipated, to have costiveness. **পেট ওঠা** *v.* to have one's belly distended after a hearty meal. **পেট কামড়ানো** *v.* to have a gnawing pain in the stomach; to have stomach-pain. **পেট কামড়ানি** *n.* a gnawing pain in the stomach; stomach pain, gripes. **পেট খসা** *v.* to have an abortion, to miscarry. **পেট খসানো** *v.* to cause an abortion (esp. unlawfully). **~খারাপ** *n.* a disorder of the stomach. **পেট খারাপ হওয়া** *v.* to have or to suffer from a stomach upset or disorder. **~গরম** *n.* dyspepsia, indigestion. **পেট চলা** *v.* to procure one's minimum or normal food or appease one's hunger (esp. daily); to make both ends meet. **পেট চালানো** *v.* to earn just enough to provide the bare necessities of life, to earn a living or subsistence wage.

পেট চিনচিন করা *v.* to feel a pinching sensation in the stomach esp. caused by extreme hunger. পেট চুঁইচুঁই করা *v.* to have a suppressed groaning noise in the stomach caused by hunger. পেট জ্বলা *v.* to have a burning sensation in the stomach. পেট ডাকা *v.* to have a rumbling noise in the belly as caused by diarrhoea or indigestion, to have collywobbles. পেট ধরা *v.* to be cured of diarrhoea or loose motions. পেট নরম হওয়া *v.* to have somewhat loose motions. পেট নামানো *v.* to have loose motions, to have diarrhoea; to purge (one's bowels). পেট ফাঁপা, পেট ফোলা *v.* to have one's belly distended owing to the accumulation of gas, to be affected with flatulence or tympanites. পেট বড় হওয়া *v.* to have the belly distended esp. on account of pregnancy. পেট ব্যথা *n.* stomach-pain, belly-ache. পেট ভরা *v.* to have one's hunger fully satisfied. পেট ভরে খাওয়া *v.* to eat one's fill. পেট ভরে খাওয়ানো *v.* to give one a full meal or full feed. ~ভাতা *n.* food given in lieu of wages, □ *adv.* for food in lieu of wages. পেট মরা *v.* to lose appetite esp. owing to want of sufficient food. ~মোটা *a.* pot-bellied. ~রোগা *a.* weak in digestive power; dyspeptic. ~সর্বস্ব *a.* one who loves nothing but a good fare; given to gourmandising; gluttonous, voracious. ~সর্বস্ব ব্যক্তি a. belly-god. পেট হওয়া *v.* (vul.) to become pregnant, to be big with child, to conceive, to be in the family way. পেটে আসা *v.* to be formed in the womb, to be conceived. পেটে এক মুখে আর insincere or hypocritical talk; double-facedness. পেটে খিদে মুখে লাজ concealment of one's eager desire on account of bashfulness. পেটে খেলে পিঠে সয় (fig.) troubles are sufferable when they bring in profits, trouble is patiently borne if it is paying; the mule will not grudge its load if there is the prospect of a good feed. পেটে তলানো *v.* to be accepted in one's stomach. পেটে থাকা *v.* to be accepted in one's stomach; (of a person) to be able to keep counsel or keep a secret (তার পেটে কথা থাকে না). পেটে ধরা *v.* to carry in one's womb, to conceive or bear. পেটে পেটে kept to oneself, kept concealed (পেটে পেটে কথা, পেটে পেটে শয়তানি). পেটে বোমা মারলেও কিছু বার না হওয়া (fig.) to be utterly lacking in education; completely illiterate. পেটে মারা *v.* to kill or weaken or subdue one by starving; to deprive one of one's means of livelihood or subsistence. পেটের অসুখ same as পেটখারাপ and পেটের গোলমাল। পেটের কথা the secret of one's heart; a secret intention. পেটের গোলমাল bowels complaint, stomach trouble. পেটের চিন্তা bread problem, worries about a living. পেটের জ্বালা, পেটের দায় smarts of hunger. পেটের দায়ে impelled or urged by the sting of hunger or poverty. পেটের ভাত চাল হওয়া (fig.) to be bewildered with fear or worry. পেটের ভিতর হাত-পা সেঁধনো (fig.) to become nonplussed with fear, to feel a cold wave running down one's spine. পেটের শত্রু a child who causes grief to its mother. পেটে সওয়া *v.* to be accepted in one's stomach.

পেটক *n.* a wicker-basket; a portmanteau, a trunk, a suit-case; a chest.

পেটন, পেটনি pop. variants of পিটন।

পেটভাতা, পেটমোটা see পেট।

পেটরা same as পেটক।

পেটরোগা, পেটসর্বস্ব see পেট।

পেটা pop. var. of পিটা।

পেটি[1] *n.* a waist-band, a belt, a girdle; the breast or middle part of a fish (পেটির মাছ).

পেটি[2] *n.* a basket; a chest.

পেটিকা, পেটী pop. variants of পেটক।

পেটুক *a.* gluttonous, voracious, fond of eating. পেটুক লোক *n.* a glutton, a gourmand, a belly-god.

পেটেন্ট *n.* a patent. □ *a.* protected by a patent, patent; (fig.) monotonous, trite (পেটেন্ট পরিহাস).

পেটেল *n.* the headman of a village; a leader; a faithful supporter or follower.

পেটো[1] *a.* made of jute; related to jute; trading jute (পেটো সাহেব).

পেটো[2] *n.* the rind of a banana tree; a style of braiding hair over one's brow.

পেটো[3] *n.* (coll.) a hand-bomb; a hand-grenade.

পেটোয়া *a.* obedient, faithfully following; cringing; patronized; favourite; dependent.

পেট্রল *n.* petrol.

পেড়া[1] same as **পেটক**।

পেড়া[2] *n.* a kind of sweetmeat made by solidifying cow-milk.

পেন্টলুন, পেন্টালুন rej. spellings of **প্যান্টালুন**।

পেতনি *n.* a female spirit; (sarcas.) an extremely ugly or dirty woman, a hag or a slut. **পেতনির আলো** will-o'-the-wisp.

পেতল *n.* (dial.) brass.

পেন[1] *n.* a fountain-pen.

পেন[2] *n.* pain, inflammation (বুকের পেন) ; labour-pain, travail (পোয়াতির পেন ওঠা).

পেনশন *n.* a pension. **~ভোগী** *n.* a pensioner.

পেনসিল *n.* a pencil.

পেনেট *n.* the circular pedestal of the sacred phallic sign.

পেন্ডুলাম *n.* a pendulum.

পেয় *a.* drinkable. □ *n.* anything drinkable; a drink.

পেয়াজ *n.* onion.

পেয়াদা pop. form of **পিয়াদা**।

পেয়ার[1] *n.* (in card-playing) a marriage or a pair, one of a marriage or pair.

পেয়ার[2] *n.* caress, fondling; affection; love. **পেয়ার করা** *v.* to caress, to fondle; to treat with affection; to love. **পেয়ারের দোস্ত** বা **বন্ধু** a close or bosom friend, a chum.

পেয়ারা *n.* the guava.

পেয়ারি *n. fem.* a favourite; a lover, a sweetheart; Radha (রাধা) the sweetheart of Krishna (কৃষ্ণ).

পেয়ালা *n.* a drinking cup, a goblet.

-পেয়ে *sfx.* footed, legged, -ped (চারপেয়ে = four-footed, four-legged, quadruped).

পেয়ে বসা *v.* to get advantage; to catch one on the hip.

পেরনো coll. form of **পার হওয়া**।

পেরু *n.* the turkey.

পেরুভীয় *a.* Peruvian.

পেরেক *n.* a nail, a wire-nail, a spike.

পেলব *a.* very soft or delicate; gentle; graceful; slim, slender; frail; light; lightsome. **~তা** *n.* pleasant softness or delicateness; gentleness; grace; slimness, slenderness; frailty; lightness, lightsomeness.

পেলা *n.* a gift or reward given to an artiste at a function; a prop.

পেল্লায় *a.* huge, enormous; monstrous, gigantic; tremendous.

পেশ *n.* act of presenting or placing before. **পেশ করা** *v.* to present or place before; to submit; to put up; to table.

পেশওয়াজ alt. spell. of **পেশোয়াজ**।

পেশকার *n.* a bench-clerk. **পেশকারি** *n.* bench-clerkship.

পেশল *a.* beautiful, charming; (inc. but pop.) muscular, thewy, robust; brawny.

পেশা *n.* a profession, a trade, a calling; (fig.) a practice, a habit. **~দার** *a.* professional. **~দারি** *n.* professionalism. □ *a.* professional.

পেশি, পেশী *n.* a muscle, a tendon; a sheath of a sword, a scabbard. **পেশীয়** *a.* relating to muscles, muscular. **~বহুল** *a.* muscular, brawny, thewy, robust, lusty. **~শক্তি** *n.* power of the muscles; physical strength. **~ সঞ্চালন** *n.* flexing or movement of muscles.

পেশোয়া *n.* a Maratha peshwa.

পেশোয়াজ *n.* a kind of baggy breeches worn by Muslim women or dancing-girls.

পেষক *a.* & *n.* one who or that which pulps or grinds or presses.

পেষণ *n.* pressing; grinding; crushing; kneading, squeezing; pulverization; oppression.

পেষণদন্ত *n.* a grinder, a molar tooth.

পেষণযন্ত্র *n.* a grinding stone.

পেষণি, পেষণী *n.* a mortar and a pestle; a grindstone, a mill-stone.

পেষল alt. spell. of **পেশল**।

পেষা pop. var. of **পিষা**। **~ই** *n.* same as **পেষণ**।

পেস্তা *n.* pistachio.

পৈছা, পৈঠা, পৈতা alt. spellings of **পইছা, পইঠা** and **পইতা** respectively.

পৈতামহ *a.* relating to a paternal grandfather.

পৈতৃক *a.* paternal, ancestral (পৈতৃক ভিটা, পৈতৃক সম্পত্তি) ; hereditary (পৈতৃক রোগ).

পৈত্তিক, পৈত্ত *a.* bilious, biliary.

পৈত্র, পৈত্র্য variants of **পৈতৃক** ।

পৈশাচ *a.* ghoulish. □ *n.* a form of marriage by force or artfulness. **পৈশাচিক** *a.* ghoulish; (fig.) nefarious, extremely obnoxious. *fem.* **পৈশাচিকী** । **পৈশাচিকতা** *n.* ghoulishness; (fig.) nefariousness, extreme obnoxiousness, fiendlike conduct. **পৈশাচী** *a. fem.* of **পৈশাচ** ।

পৈশুন, পৈশুন্য *n.* scandal-mongering, talebearing; malice, cruelty; villainy.

পো¹ contr. of **পোয়া** ।

পো² *n.* (vul.) a son or a male descendant (ঘোষের পো).

পোঁ *int.* denoting : a long and unchanging noise or note as of flute (শানাইয়ের পোঁ). **পোঁ করে** in a trice, in a jiffy, instantly, very quickly. **পোঁ ধরা** *v.* to give out a long and unchanging note or sound (as by a flute); (sarcas.) to cringe or fawn (upon), to support blindly and insistently. **পোঁ-ধরা** *a.* cringing, fawning.

পোঁচ *n.* a coating. **পোঁচ দেওয়া** *v.* to apply a coating (to), to coat. **পোঁচড়া, পোঁচলা** *n.* a coating; a brush for whitewashing made of jute fibres.

পোঁছ *n.* an instance or act of mopping or swabbing (ঝাড়পোঁছ).

পোঁছা¹ *n.* the tail of a fish and the region near about it; the part of the hand from the wrist to fingertips.

পোঁছা² *v.* to mop, to swab, to wipe; to rub out, to erase. **~নো** *v.* to cause to mop or swab or wipe or rub or erase.

পোঁটলা *n.* a bundle or baggage.

পোঁটা *n.* entrails, intestines, the gut (মাছের পোঁটা) ; (a drop of) nasal catarrh or mucus, (vul.) snot (নাকের পোঁটা) ; (dero.) a little boy, a kiddy.

পোঁত *n.* the length of the part of anything buried or implanted underground.

পোঁতা¹ var. or **পোতা¹** ।

পোঁতা² *v.* to plant (গাছ পোঁতা) ; to drive into (পেরেক পোঁতা) ; to bury, to inter. **~নো** *v.* to cause to plant or drive into or sow or bury.

পোঁদ *n.* (vul.) the anus; (vul.) the posteriors, the buttocks, the hips.

পোকা, (dial.) **পোক** *n.* an insect, a worm, a moth, a beetle. **পোকায়-খাওয়া** *a.* worm-eaten, moth-eaten. **~মাকড়** *n.* worms and insects.

পোক্ত *a.* strong, firm; durable; lasting; experienced, accustomed; seasoned.

পোখরাজ *n.* topaz.

পোগণ্ড *n.* a child between the age of five and fifteen; a cripple.

পোছা pop. var. of **পুছা** ।

পোট *n.* friendly terms; agreement; love. **পোট খাওয়া** *v.* to be on friendly terms (with); to agree (with); to be in love (with).

পোটলা var. of **পোঁটলা** ।

পোড় *n.* a spell of burning or scalding or singeing; affliction, distress; a severe ordeal. **পোড় খাওয়া** *v.* to get burnt or scalded or singed. **পোড়-খাওয়া** *a.* burnt, scalded, singed; passed through an affliction or distress or a severe ordeal.

পোড়া *v.* to burn; to be scalded or singed or calcined; scorched or incinerated; to inflame; to become very hot (জ্বরে গা পোড়ে) ; □ *a.* burnt; scalded; scorched; inflamed; incinerated; calcined; greatly heated. **~নি** *n.* affliction; distress. **~নো** *v.* to burn or scald or scorch or calcine or inflame. **পোড়া কপাল** hard luck, bad luck; (int.) ah me! **পোড়াকপালি** *fem.* unlucky, unfortunate. *mas.* **পোড়াকপালে** । **পোড়ারমুখি** *a.* & *n.* accursed (one), unfortunate; hateful (one); wicked.

পোড়ামাটি *n.* burnt or scorched earth. **পোড়া মাটির কাজ** terracotta; brownish-red earthen ware or art objects of this material.

পোড়েন *n.* woof.

পোড়ো alt. spell. of **পড়ো¹,²** ।

পোত *n.* a boat, a ship, a vessel (অর্ণবপোত, খপোত). **পোত চালানো** *v.* to captain (a ship); to pilot (an air-ship or ship). **~চালক** *n.* (of a ship) a captain; (of an airship) a pilot. **~-নিযুক্তক** *n.* shipping agent.

পোতা¹ *n.* plinth (of a house).

পোতা² *n.* (dial.) a son's son, a grandson.

পোতাধিপাল *n.* shipping master.

পোতাধ্যক্ষ *n.* a captain or master of a ship; (rare) a pilot of an aeroplane.

পোতারোহী *a.* sailing in a ship. □ *n.* a passenger of a ship.

পোতাশ্রয় *n.* a harbour, a haven.

পোদ *n.* a socially depressed caste amongst Hindus.

পোদ্দার *n.* a professional examiner of the genuineness of coins; a money-changer; a pawn-broker; a banker, a money-lender. **পোদ্দারি** *n.* the profession of a coin-examiner or money-changer or pawn-broker or banker or money-lender; (sarcas.) display of false authority or power. **পরের ধনে পোদ্দারি** see **পর**[3] ।

পোনা *n.* young of fish (esp. of a larger one like trout etc.). **~মাছ** *n.* a fish of the species of rui (রুই), katla (কাতলা), mrigel (মৃগেল) etc.

পোনি *n.* a pony, a tattoo.

পোয়া *n.* a fourth part, a quarter; one-fourth of a seer (সের) ; half-a-mile. □ *a.* one-fourth, quarter. **চারপোয়া** *a.* complete, full. **~বারো** *n.* a particular throw at dice; (sarcas.) an extraordinary piece of luck, success in everything, a run of luck, a lucky hit.

পোয়াতি *a.* pregnant (পোয়াতি বউ) ; recently delivered of a child (প্রসবের পরে পোয়াতি সুস্থ আছে). □ *n.* a pregnant woman; a woman recently delivered of a child. **পোয়াতি হওয়া** to conceive, to be in the family way.

পোয়ানো coll. form of **পোহানো** ।

পোয়াল *n.* straw.

পোরা pop. var. of **পুরা**[3] ।

পোর্টম্যানটো *n.* a portmanteau.

পোল pop. var. of **পুল** ।

পোলা *n.* (vul. & dial.) a son.

পোলাও *n.* a highly spiced dish of rice and meat boiled in clarified butter, pilau.

পোলো[1] alt. spell. **পলো** ।

পোলো[2] *n.* polo.

পোশাক *n.* dress, garment, clothes; apparel; outfit. **পোশাক ছাড়া, পোশাক খোলা** *v.* to undress oneself. **পোশাক ছাড়ানো, পোশাক খোলানো** *v.* to cause to undress. **পোশাক পরা** *v.* to dress oneself, to put on one's dress. **পোশাক-পরা** *a.* dressed (in.) **পোশাক পরানো** *v.* to dress. **পোশাকি** *a.* befitting fashionable society, fashionable (পোশাকি কথাবার্তা) ; official (পোশাকি নাম) ; elegant, refined (পোশাকি ভাষা) ; worn on formal or festive occasions (পোশাকি জামাকাপড়) ; merely formal, insincere, hypocritical (পোশাকি ভদ্রতা).

পোষ[1] coll. corrup. of **পউষ** ।

পোষ[2] *n.* taming, domestication; act of bringing under one's control, subdual. **পোষ-মানা** *a.* tame, domesticated; brought under control, subdued; habituated to obedience. **পোষ মানা** *v.* to become tame or domesticated; to come under control, to be subdued; to be habituated to obedience; (of a horse) to be broken. **পোষ মানানো** *v.* to tame, to domesticate; to bring under one's control, to subdue; to habituate to obedience; to break (as a horse).

পোষক *a.* cherishing; nourishing; aiding; upholding; supporting; countenancing or abetting. □ *n.* one who or that which cherishes or nourishes; an aider; an upholder; a supporter; a countenancer or abettor. **~তা** *n.* aiding; upholding, support, countenancing, abetment. **পোষকতা করা** *v.* to aid; to uphold, to support; to countenance, to abet. **পোষক স্তর** (bot. & zoo.) tapetum.

পোষড়া (coll.) same as **পউষপার্বণ** (see **পউষ**).

পোষণ *n.* upbringing; feeding; maintenance (পরিবার-পোষণ) ; cherishment; nourishment; act of supporting. **পোষণ করা** *v.* to bring up; to maintain; to cherish; to nourish; to support. **পোষণীয়** var. of **পোষ্য** ।

পোষা *v.* pop. var. of **পুষা** । □ *a.* tame, domesticated; pet; obediently following. **পোষা কুকুর** an obedient dog; a servilely obedient follower.

পোষাক, পোষাকি rej. spellings of **পোশাক** and **পোশাকি** respectively.

পোষানো *v.* to be sufficient for, to serve one's purpose, to suffice (এ টাকায় পোষাবে না) ; to agree with, to pull on well with (তার সঙ্গে আমার পোষাবে না) ; to cause to bring up or rear; to pay for or compensate (লোকসান পোষানো) ; to be able to bear or tolerate (এ শরীরে এত খাটুনি পোষায় না). **পোষানি** *n.* act of making another rear one's domestic animals.

পোষ্টা *a.* one who or that which brings up or rears or nourishes.

পোষ্টাই *a.* nutritious, nourishing. □ *n.* nutrition, nourishment.

পোষ্য *a.* worthy of being brought up or fed or maintained or cherished or nourished or supported; dependent for maintenance. *n.* **~পুত্র** *n.* an adopted son. **~বর্গ** *n. pl.* one's dependants (esp. those who live in the same family).

পোস্ট[1] *n.* the postal system, post; mail (আজকের পোস্টের চিঠি) ; an office or appointment, a post (ক্লার্কের পোস্ট).

পোস্ট[2] *n.* a pillar, a post (ল্যাম্প-পোস্ট).

পোস্ট-অফিস *n.* a post-office.

পোস্টকার্ড *n.* a post-card.

পোস্ট-গ্র্যাজুয়েট *a.* post-graduate.

পোস্টমাস্টার *n.* a postmaster.

পোস্টাপিস *n.* a post-office.

পোস্ত[1], **পোস্তদানা** *n.* mawseed, poppyseed.

পোস্তা, (coll.) **পোস্ত**[2] *n.* a joint (মেরে পোস্তা ওড়ানো) ; a central or wholesale market (আলুপোস্তা) ; masonry construction for strengthening a wall, embankment etc.

পোহানো *v.* to dawn, to end (রাত পোহানো), to bask (রোদ পোহানো) ; to warm up oneself (আগুন পোহানো) ; to suffer or undergo (ঝামেলা পোহানো).

পৌঁছ *n.* reach (পৌঁছ না মেলা) ; arrival (পৌঁছ খবর = news of arrival.)

পৌঁছা *v.* to arrive at, to reach (বাড়ি পৌঁছাল, হাত পৌঁছেছে) ; to come within reach; to come to hand (চিঠি পৌঁছায়). **~নো** *v.* to arrive at, to reach; to come within reach; to come to hand; to escort; to convey or carry (to); to bring to hand.

পৌগণ্ড same as **পোগণ্ড** ৷

পৌণ্ড্র var. of **পুণ্ড্র** ৷

পৌত্তলিক *a.* idolatrous. □ *n.* an idolater. **পৌত্তলিকতা** *n.* idolatry.

পৌত্র *n.* a son's or nephew's son, a grandson. *fem.* **পৌত্রী** a son's or nephew's daughter, a grand-daughter.

পৌনঃপুনিক *a.* recurring. **পৌনঃপুনিক দশমিক** recurring decimal. **পৌনঃপুনিকতা, পৌনঃপুন্য** *n.* recurrence; recurrency.

পৌনে *a.* three quarters of, three-fourths (পৌনে এক দিন) ; a quarter to (পৌনে বারোটা).

পৌর *a.* living in a particular city or house; relating to a city, urban, municipal; relating to house, indoor; civic. **পৌর-অধিকার** *n.* civic rights. **~কর** *n.* municipal tax. **পৌর চিকিৎসক** civil surgeon. **~জন** *n.* citizens; inmates (of a house). **~নিগম** *n.* municipal corporation. **~পদ** *n.* citizenship. **~পিতা** *n.* a chairman or a mayor (*fem.* a mayoress). **~প্রতিষ্ঠান** *n.* same as **পৌরসংঘ** ৷ **~বর্গ** same as **পৌরজন** ৷ **~বিজ্ঞান** *n.* civics. **~মুখ্য** *n.* an alderman (of a municipal corporation). **~সংঘ** *n.* a municipality. **~সংঘ-করণিক** *n.* a municipal clerk. **~সংঘ-বিচারক** *n.* a municipal magistrate. **~সভা** *n.* a municipal corporation. **~স্ত্রী** same as **পুরনারী** (see **পুর**[2]).

পৌরব *a.* descending from King Puru (পুরু).

পৌরাঙ্গনা same as **পুরনারী** (see **পুর**[2]).

পৌরাণিক *a.* pertaining to or versed in Hindu puranas (পুরাণ) or mythology, mythical; mythological; ancient. **পৌরাণিক কাহিনি** a mythological or Puranic tale or episode; a legend. **পৌরাণিক চরিত্র** a mythological character; a Puranic character. **পৌরাণিক নাটক** a mythological drama.

পৌরুষ same as **পুরুষত্ব** (see **পুরুষ**).

পৌরুষেয় *a.* (rare) pertaining to a man, masculine; man-made.

পৌরোহিত্য *n.* the office or profession of a priest, priesthood; presidentship, presidency (সভার পৌরোহিত্য). **পৌরোহিত্য করা** *v.* to act as a priest; to preside over (a meeting); to lead (as a movement).

পৌর্ণমাসী *n.* the full-moon.

পৌর্ব *a.* past; of the east, eastern. **~দেহিক, ~দৈহিক** *a.* relating to the body of a previous; of a previous birth.

পৌর্বাপর্য *n.* due order or succession; sequence.

পৌর্বাহিক *a.* relating to the previous day.

পৌর্বাহ্নিক *a.* relating to or due to be done in the first part or quarter of the day or in the forenoon.

পৌর্বী *fem.* of **পৌর্ব**।

পৌলস্ত্য *n.* of the sons of Pulastya (পুলস্ত্য) the sage; Kuvera, Ravana, Kumbhakarna, Bibhisana.

পৌলোমী *n.* a daughter of Puloma (পুলোমা), Sachi, Indra's queen.

পৌষ *n.* Paus, the ninth month of the Bengali calendar from mid December to mid January. **~পার্বণ** *n.* the festival of preparing and offering sweet pies made of new rice on the last day of the month of Paus. **~সংক্রান্তি** *n.* the last day of the month of Paus. **পৌষালি** *a.* relating to or grown in or performed in the month of Paus.

পৌষ্টিক *a.* nutritious, nutritive; alimentary. **~তন্ত্র** *n.* alimentary system. **পৌষ্টিক নালি** the alimentary canal.

প্যাঁকাটি coll. corrup. of **পাকাটি**।

প্যাঁক *int.* denoting the cry of the duck, quack. **প্যাঁকপ্যাঁক** *int.* quack! quack!

প্যাঁচ *n.* a spiral bend or coil or twist (স্ক্রুর প্যাঁচ, স্ক্রুতে প্যাঁচ দেওয়া) ; a screw (প্যাঁচ আঁটা) ; a tricky or shrewd turn (কথার প্যাঁচ) ; an intrigue or machination, entanglement, predicament (প্যাঁচে ফেলা) ; a difficult problem, an intricate or perplexing situation, false position, quandary, cleft stick (প্যাঁচে পড়া) ; complication, intricacy (ব্যাপারটায় বড় প্যাঁচ) ; mutual entwining (ঘুড়ির প্যাঁচ) ; a tangle (সুতোর বান্ডিলটায় প্যাঁচ লেগেছে) ; (in wrestling etc.) a style of holding; a tricky move (কুস্তির প্যাঁচ).

প্যাঁচা *n.* the owl; (sarcas.) an extremely ugly-looking man or boy. **প্যাঁচার ডাক** howling, hooting, screeching. **প্যাঁচা ডাকে** an owl; howls or hoots or screeches. **প্যাঁচার বাচ্চা** an owlet; (sarcas. –both *masc.* & *fem.*) an extremely ugly-looking person. **প্যাঁচার বাসা** an owlery. *fem.* **পেঁচি**।

প্যাঁচানো *v.* to twist or wring spirally, to screw; to writhe; to make intricate deliberately; to complicate; to entangle; to involve (তাকে এ ব্যাপারে প্যাঁচাচ্ছ কেন) ; to employ a shrewd or tricky turn in one's speech. ☐ *a.* twisted or wrung spirally; spiral; intricate, complicated; entangled; tortuous, full of angularity (প্যাঁচানো মন) ; having shrewd or tricky turns (প্যাঁচানো কথাবার্তা).

প্যাঁচালো same as **প্যাঁচানো** (*a.*).

প্যাঁটরা var. of **পেটরা**।

প্যাঁড়া var. of **পেড়া**।

প্যাঁদানি *n.* (infor.) belabouring or slogging, drubbing. **প্যাঁদানো** *v.* to belabour or slog, or drub; to beat up.

প্যাকবন্দি *a.* packed in a box, container etc.

প্যাকিং *n.* packing; a package, a packet.

প্যাচ প্যাচ *int.* denoting the noise caused by going along or wading through a slimy or miry place (প্যাচ প্যাচ করে চলা). **প্যাচপেচে** *a.* giving out or resembling the aforesaid noise; slimy or miry.

প্যাডেল *n.* a paddle; paddling. **প্যাডেল করা** *v.* to paddle.

প্যানপ্যান *int.* denoting the noise of complaining or imploring whimperingly or whiningly. **প্যানপ্যান করা, প্যানপ্যানানো** *v.* to complain or implore whimperingly or whiningly. **প্যানপেনে** *a.* given to complaining or imploring whimperingly or whiningly; whimpering or whining.

প্যান্ট, প্যানট, *n.* pantaloons; shorts. (ফুল) **প্যান্ট** *n.* trousers. **হাফপ্যান্ট** *n.* shorts.

প্যান্টালুন *n.* pantaloons, trousers; shorts.

প্যান্ডাল, প্যান্ডেল *n.* a canopy, a temporary shed erected for social or religious festivals.

প্যারাশুট *n.* parachute.

প্যালা *n.* a prop; reward or help given to an artiste or somebody.

প্যাসেঞ্জার *n.* a passenger. ☐ *a.* meant for carrying passengers.

প্র- *pfx.* denoting excellence, celebrity, abundance, excess, intensity, extensiveness, inception etc.

প্রকট *a.* clearly revealed or exposed; manifest, obvious, evident, clear. **~ন** *n.* clear revelation or exposition, manifestation. **প্রকটিত** *a.* clearly revealed or exposed.

প্রকম্প *n.* a severe tremor or quake. **~ন** *n.*

severe trembling, shaking or quaking. **প্রকম্পিত** *a.* severely shaken or trembling or quaking. **প্রকম্পিত করা** *v.* to cause to tremble or quake severely. **প্রকম্পিত হওয়া** *v.* to tremble or quake severely.

প্রকরণ *n.* a chapter or a part of a book; a process, a procedure; (self-sufficient) part of a process or procedure; technique; a context; a discourse. **~গত** *a.* technical; procedural; contextual.

প্রকর্ষ *n.* excellence; superiority; amelioration, development.

প্রকল্প *n.* hypothesis. **প্রকল্পিত** *a.* hypothetical; imagined.

প্রকাণ্ড *a.* huge, colossal, enormous, monstrous, gigantic, stupendous. □ *n.* a trunk of a tree. **~কায়** *a.* enormous in size, of great bulk, gigantic, monstrous, huge.

প্রকাম *a.* enough, sufficient.

প্রকার *n.* class, kind, sort, type, species, genus, variety (বহুপ্রকার খাদ্য) ; mode, method, way, manner, procedure, process, means (কী প্রকারে). **কী কী প্রকারে, কোন প্রকারে** by what means, in which way, how. **কোনো না কোনো প্রকারে** by some means or other, somehow; by hook or by crook.

প্রকারণ *n.* variation. **নিরন্তর প্রকারণ** (bot.) continuous variation. **সান্তর প্রকারণ** (bot.) discontinuous variation.

প্রকারান্তর *n.* another or a different sort or mode or way or method or means. **প্রকারান্তরে** *adv.* in or by another or a different method or way; in other words; indirectly; (dero) insinuatingly.

প্রকাশ *n.* revelation, exposition (রহস্য প্রকাশ, অর্থপ্রকাশ) ; demonstration, display, expression (দুঃখ প্রকাশ) ; suggestion, prognostication; appearance (আত্মপ্রকাশ) ; rise (সূর্যের প্রকাশ) ; efflorescence, blooming (ফুলের প্রকাশ) ; publication (গ্রন্থপ্রকাশ) ; disclosure, divulgation, divulging (গুপ্তকথা প্রকাশ) ; □ *a.* revealed, transpired; (journ.) stated (প্রকাশ যে = it is stated that). **প্রকাশ করা** *v.* to reveal, to expose; to demonstrate, to display, to express; to suggest, to prognosticate; to cause to appear or rise or bloom; to declare, to announce; to publish; to disclose, to divulge. **প্রকাশ পাওয়া, প্রকাশ হওয়া** *v.* to be revealed or exposed; to transpire; to come to light; to appear; to rise; to bloom; to be published. **প্রকাশক** *a.* revealing, exposing; demonstrating, displaying, expressing; suggesting; prognosticating; causing to appear or rise or bloom; declaring, announcing; publishing; disclosing, divulging. □ *n.* a revealer, an exposer; a demonstrator, a displayer, one who or that which expresses or suggests; a prognosticator; one who or that which causes to appear or rise or bloom; a declarer, an announcer; one who discloses and divulges; a publisher (esp. of books). *fem.* **প্রকাশিকা**। **প্রকাশক সংঘ** *n.* publishers' association or guild. **প্রকাশন, প্রকাশনা** *n.* publication (of books). **~নালয়** *n.* a publishing house. **~নীয়** *a.* that which can be or is to be revealed or demonstrated or published or disclosed; worth publishing. **~মান** *a.* appearing, rising, blooming; in the state of being revealed or published. **~যোগ্য** *a.* fit to be published; fit to be made public or open. **প্রকাশিত** *a.* revealed, exposed; transpired; demonstrated, displayed, expressed; suggested, prognosticated; risen, bloomed; declared, announced; published; disclosed, divulged; (journ.) stated. **প্রকাশিতব্য** *a.* that which is to be revealed or published; fit for or worthy of publication. **প্রকাশ্য** *n.* that which can be or is to be or will be revealed or demonstrated or suggested or announced or published; under publication; soon to be made known (ক্রমশ প্রকাশ্য) ; open to the public (প্রকাশ্য অধিবেশন) ; public (প্রকাশ্য স্থান) ; open (প্রকাশ্য আলোচনা). **প্রকাশ্য দিবালোকে** in broad daylight. **প্রকাশ্যে, প্রকাশ্যত** *adv.* publicly, into the open.

প্রকীর্ণ *a.* scattered or strewn or spread about; scattered or strewn or spread far and wide; various.

প্রকীর্তন *n.* wide celebrity; publicity (নামযশ প্রকীর্তন).

প্রকীর্তি *n.* great fame, wide celebrity.

প্রকীর্তিত *a.* greatly famed or famous or renowned, widely celebrated.

প্রকুপিত *a.* deeply enraged or angered, incensed, infuriated; excited. *fem.* **প্রকুপিতা**।

প্রকৃত *a.* true, real; genuine, pure; actual; right, correct; veritable (প্রকৃত বদমাশ). **~পক্ষে, ~প্রস্তাবে** *adv.* in fact; actually; really, truly. **~রূপে** *adv.* really; rightly.

প্রকৃতার্থ *n.* true significance, real meaning; inner significance.

প্রকৃতি *n.* nature (শান্তপ্রকৃতি) ; behaviour, habit, instinct (অসৎপ্রকৃতি) ; natural qualities, nature (বস্তুপ্রকৃতি) ; the external world, nature; the power that creates and regulates the world, Nature; the primordial female energy; (phil.) illusion, maya; people or subjects; (gr.) a root word. **~গত** *a.* pertaining to one's nature; instinctive, habitual; pertaining to physical nature, natural. **~জ, ~জাত** *a.* natural; inborn, innate, inherent, native; instinctive. **~দত্ত** *a.* given by nature, natural; innate. **~পুঞ্জ** *n. pl.* people or subjects. **~পূজা** *n.* nature-worship, animism. **~বাদ** *n.* naturalism, materialism; (gr.) consideration of the root-meaning of words, use of words in the root-meaning only, purism. **~বাদী** *a.* naturalistic, materialistic; (gr.) puristic. □ *n.* a naturalist, a materialist; (gr.) a purist. **~বিজ্ঞান** *n.* physics; natural science; natural philosophy. **~বিজ্ঞানী** *n.* a naturalist; a physicist. **~বিরুদ্ধ** *a.* contrary to nature. **~স্থ** *a.* in one's natural or normal state; come to one's senses; recovered. **প্রকৃতিস্থ হওয়া** *v.* to come to one's senses; to regain one's mental balance; to recover.

প্রকৃষ্ট *a.* best, excellent (প্রকৃষ্ট উপায়) ; most auspicious or favourable or suitable (প্রকৃষ্ট সময়). *fem.* **প্রকৃষ্টা**। **~তা** *n.* the state of being the best, excellence; auspiciousness, suitability.

প্রকোপ *n.* virulence, severity (জ্বরের প্রকোপ) ; excess (পিত্তের প্রকোপ) ; violent outbreak (কলেরার প্রকোপ) ; great anger, rage; great excitement. **~ন** *n.* excitation, excitement; provocation; enragement. **প্রকোপিত** *a.* excited; provoked; enraged; (of a disease etc.) grown virulent, aggravated; (of an epidemic etc.) violently broken out. **প্রকোপিত হওয়া** *v.* to be excited or provoked or enraged; to grow virulent, to aggravate; to break out violently.

প্রকোষ্ঠ *n.* the part of the hand from the elbow to the wrist, the fore-arm; a room, a cabin, a compartment; a room near the gate.

প্রকৌশল *n.* technique; procedure.

প্রক্রম *n.* beginning, commencement.

প্রক্রয় *n.* chartering.

প্রক্রান্ত *a.* begun, commenced; surpassed.

প্রক্বণ *n.* sound of a lute or a vina (বীণা).

প্রক্রিয়া *n.* a process, a procedure, a mode, a method.

প্রক্রীত *a.* chartered.

প্রক্ষালন *n.* washing. **প্রক্ষালন করা** *v.* to wash.

প্রক্ষালিত *a.* washed.

প্রক্ষিপ্ত *a.* flung, thrown, cast; placed within or inside; interpolated. **প্রক্ষিপ্তাংশ** *n.* an interpolated part, an interpolation.

প্রক্ষুব্ধ *a.* impassioned; agitated; excited.

প্রক্ষেপ, প্রক্ষেপণ *n.* flinging or casting, a throw; act or an instance of placing inside or within; an interpolation. **প্রক্ষেপক** *a.* flinging, casting, throwing, placing inside or within; interpolating. □ *n.* a thrower; one who places inside or within; an interpolator. **প্রক্ষেপ করা** *v.* to hurl, to throw; to interpolate.

প্রক্ষোভ *n.* emotion; impulse; an outburst of passion.

প্রখর *a.* very sharp or cutting; very acute or keen (প্রখর বুদ্ধি) ; severe (প্রখর তাপ) ; harsh (প্রখর বাক্য) ; very strict (প্রখর শাসন). *fem.* **প্রখরা**। **~তা** *n.* great sharpness or keenness; severity; harshness; excessive strictness.

প্রখ্যাত *a.* famous, renowned, celebrated. **~নামা** *a.* one whose name is famous.

প্রগণ্ড *n.* the upper arm.

প্রগত *a.* departed; past; gone, gone off; uplifted.

প্রগতি *n.* progress, advancement; (arith.) a progression.

প্রগতিবাদ *n.* theory of progress. **প্রগতিবাদী** *a.* progressive. □ *n.* advocate or champion or supporter or votary of progress. **প্রগতিশীল** *a.* progressive; modern. **প্রগতিশীলতা** *n.* progressive outlook, progressiveness; modernity.

প্রগল্ভ *a.* boastful, bragging; voluble; impertinent, saucy, impudent; unhesitating; smart; intrepid, bold; speaking unhesitatingly or smartly. **প্রগল্ভা** *a. fem.* of **প্রগল্ভ**। □ *n.* a very sportive and wanton young woman. **~তা** *n.* boasting; bragging; volubility; impertinence, sauciness, impudence; absence of hesitation; smartness; intrepidity; unhesitating or smart talk.

প্রগাতা *n.* a singer of Vedic hymns; a reciter of Vedic prayers; a singer or announcer.

প্রগাঢ় *a.* very thick or deep or dense; very severe; profound. **~তা** *n.* great thickness or depth or density; great severity; profundity.

প্রগ্রাহ্য *a.* (law) cognizable.

প্রচণ্ড *a.* furious, fierce, terrible; formidable; violent, severe. **~তা** *n.* furiousness, fierceness; terribleness; formidability; severity.

প্রচয় *n.* culling; collection; accumulation; a multitude; increase; multiplication.

প্রচল *a.* current. □ *n.* a convention. **~ন** *n.* act of bringing into practice, introduction usage, practice; currency. **প্রচলন করা** *v.* to bring into practice or currency; to introduce. **প্রচলন হওয়া** *v.* to be introduced or practised; to gain currency. **প্রচলিত** *a.* introduced; current, in vogue or prevailing taste; customary.

প্রচায় var. of **প্রচয়**।

প্রচার *n.* introduction; currency; announcement, proclamation; circulation; propaganda, publicity; preaching; disclosure; publication. **প্রচার করা** *v.* to introduce; to give currency (to); to announce, to proclaim; to circulate; to propagate; to give publicity to, to publicize; to preach; to disclose; to publish; to make public. **প্রচার হওয়া** *v.* to be introduced; to gain currency; to be announced or proclaimed or circulated or propagated; to get publicity; to be preached or disclosed or published; to become public. **প্রচারক** *a.* introducing; giving currency (to); announcing; circulating; giving publicity to; preaching; disclosing; publishing. □ *n.* an introducer; one who gives currency (to); an announcer, a proclaimer; a circulator; a missionary; a propagandist, a publicist; a preacher; a discloser; a publisher. **প্রচারণ** *n.* same as **প্রচার** and—a communique. **প্রচারণা** same as **প্রচার**। **প্রচার-অধিকর্তা** *n.* director of publicity. **~পত্র** *n.* a pamphlet; a propaganda magazine. **~মাধ্যম** *n.* medium for publicity; mass media. **~যন্ত্র** *n.* same as **প্রচারমাধ্যম**। **প্রচারিত** *a.* introduced; that which has gained currency, current; announced, proclaimed; circulated; propagated; publicized; preached; disclosed; published.

প্রচুর *a.* great in amount or degree or number; plentiful, abundant; profuse; ample; numerous; enough; sufficient. **প্রচুর পরিমাণে** *adv.* in abundance or in abundant quantity.

প্রচেতা *a.* having a mind never to be perturbed; wise. □ *n.* Varuna (বরুণ) the Water-god.

প্রচেষ্টা *n.* (repeated or unflagging) effort, endeavour, application, persistent attempt.

প্রচ্ছদ, প্রচ্ছদপট *n.* a cover or a jacket (esp. of a book).

প্রচ্ছন্ন *a.* covered; hidden, concealed; secret; invisible; (esp. in bot.) latent. **~তা** *n.* covertness; concealment; secrecy; invisibility; latency; coverture, disguise. **~বেশে** *adv.* in disguise, incognito. **~ভাবে** *adv.* covertly; secretly; invisibly; stealthily; latently.

প্রচ্ছাদন *n.* a cover; a thin wrapper for the upper body. **প্রচ্ছাদিত** *a.* covered, wrapped.

প্রচ্ছায় *n.* deep shade; a deeply shady place. **প্রচ্ছায়া** *n.* (phys.) umbra.

প্রজন *n.* breeding (of cattle).

প্রজনন *n.* begetting, progeniture, generation; procreation; child-bearing; (of animals) breeding. **প্রজনিকা** *n. fem.* begetter; mother.

প্রজন্ম *n.* a (certain) generation. **নতুন প্রজন্ম** the new generation. **পরবর্তী প্রজন্ম** the next generation.

প্রজা *n.* created beings, creatures; offspring, progeny, a descendant; citizens collectively, the people; a citizen; a tenant, a ryot; a subject; the public. **~তন্ত্র** *n.* a republic. **~তন্ত্রী** *a.* republican. **~পতি** *n.* (myth.) the creator or protector of all living creatures; Brahma (ব্রহ্মা) ; any one of the ten sons of Brahma (ব্রহ্মা) ; the butterfly. **প্রজাপতির নির্বন্ধ** an ordinance or regulation of the creator or protector of living creatures; (loos.) predestination in marriage. **~পালক** *n.* a ruler, a king. **~পালন** *n.* act of protecting or ruling the people. **প্রজাপালন করা** *v.* to rule over and look after the people. **~পীড়ক** *a.* oppressive, tyrannical. □ *n.* an oppressor; a tyrant. **~পীড়ন** *n.* oppression of subjects, tyranny. **~বতী** *a. fem.* having children or offspring. **~বর্গ** *n.* the whole body of subjects or citizens, the people; the tenantry. **~বিলি** *n.* act or system of leasing out land and houses on fixed rents and terms. **~বৃদ্ধি** *n.* multiplication of a race; increase or growth of population. **~রঞ্জন** *n.* endeavour to please the people or subjects. □ *a.* devoted to please the people or subjects. **~শক্তি** *n.* (pol.) the power of the people of a state, the popular power. **~স্বত্ব** *n.* the right of a subject (to land); the right of the people (to land). **~হিত** *n.* the wellbeing or good of the subjects.

প্রজাত *a.* produced, grown. *fem.* **প্রজাতা** ।

প্রজাতি *n.* species.

প্রজ্ঞ *a.* wise, sagacious; knowing.

প্রজ্ঞপ্তি *n.* a communication; a notice.

প্রজ্ঞা *n.* superior understanding or intelligence, profound wisdom; knowledge about philosophical reality. **~চক্ষু** *n.* eyes having superhuman or rare power of attaining knowledge; power to attain knowledge about philosophical reality. □ *a.* having superhumanly or uncommonly knowing eyes; endowed with philosophical insight into the ultimate reality. **~ত** *a.* well-known or widely known; famous. **~ন** *n.* especial or superior knowledge; knowledge about philosophical reality; a sign, a token; a hint. **~পক** *n.* a propagandist; a publicity man, a publicity officer. **~পন** *n.* propaganda; publicity; notification; a communique. **~পারমিতা** *n.* culmination of knowledge; highest knowledge; (in Buddhism) the goddess of knowledge. **~বান** *a.* endowed with the knowledge about philosophical reality; profoundly wise.

প্রজ্বলন *n.* act of burning strongly; flaming; enkindling, lighting; (fig.) excitation or rousing.

প্রজ্বলিত *a.* strongly burning, flaming; enkindled, lighted; (fig.) excited or roused. **প্রজ্বলিত হওয়া** *v.* to burn strongly; to be aflame or ablaze; to be enkindled or lighted; (fig.) to be excited or roused.

প্রজ্বালন *n.* act of causing to burn strongly; inflaming; enkindling, ignition, lighting; (fig.) act of exciting or rousing.

প্রজ্বালিত *a.* caused to burn strongly; inflamed; enkindled, ignited, lighted; (fig.) excited or roused. **প্রজ্বালিত করা** *v.* to cause to burn strongly; to inflame; to enkindle, to ignite, to light; (fig.) to excite or rouse.

প্রণত *a.* bowed or bent or lying prostrate in obeisance; stooping, bent, inclined. *fem.* **প্রণতা** । **প্রণত হওয়া** *v.* to bow or bend or lie prostrate in obeisance; to stoop, to bend, to incline. **প্রণতি** *n.* bowing or bending or lying prostrate in obeisance; stooping or bending, inclination.

প্রণব same as ওঁ ।

প্রণম্য *a.* one who is to be or fit to be saluted by bowing or bending to touch the feet.

প্রণয় *n.* love; amour; affection; attachment; friendship; amicable relation, good terms. **~গাথা** *n.* a love-lyric, a romantic ballad. **~গীতি** *n.* a lovesong, a love-lyric, an amorous ditty. **~ঘটিত** *a.* amatory, amorous. **~পত্র** *n.* a loveletter, a billet-doux. **~পাত্র** *n.* an object of love; a lover. **~পীড়িত** *a.* love-sick; lovelorn. **~বন্ধন** *n.* the ties of love; a love-knot, a lover's knot. **~ভাজন** *n.* same as **প্রণয়পাত্র**। □ *a.* worthy of being loved; beloved. **~লিপি** same as **প্রণয়পত্র**। **~লীলা** *n.* a lover's sport, an amorous sport; (pop.) a love-affair (esp. a secret one), an affaire de coeur. **~সম্ভাষণ** *n.* amorous talk. **প্রণয়াকাঙ্ক্ষা** *n.* a longing for love, desire for love. **প্রণয়াকাঙ্ক্ষী** *a.* longing for or desirous of love. **প্রণয়ানুরাগ** *n.* love or passion (for). **প্রণয়ানুরাগী** *a.* enamoured of. *fem.* **প্রণয়ানুরাগিণী**। **প্রণয়াসক্ত** *a.* in love with; smitten with love (for). **প্রণয়াস্পদ** same as **প্রণয়ভাজন**।

প্রণয়ন *n.* act of making; composition (গ্রন্থপ্রণয়ন), compilation; creation (সৃষ্টিপ্রণয়ন) ; act of drawing up (আইন প্রণয়ন). **প্রণয়ন করা** *v.* to make; to compose, to compile; to create; to draw up.

প্রণয়ী *n.* a lover; a gallant. □ *a.* given to loving; amorous. **প্রণয়িনী** *n. fem.* a sweetheart, a lady-love; a mistress. □ *a. fem.* of **প্রণয়ী**।

প্রণাম *n.* act of making obeisance by lying prostrate or bending and touching one's feet (cp. kowtow). **প্রণাম করা** *v.* to lie prostrate or bend and touch one's feet in obeisance. **প্রণামী** *n.* a present or money given at the time of making obeisance (গুরুপ্রণামী).

প্রণালী *n.* a drain; an aqueduct; (geog.) a strait, a channel; a procedure, a mode, a method, a system. **~বদ্ধ** *a.* methodical, systematic. **প্রণালীবদ্ধ করা** *v.* to systematize.

প্রণাশ *n.* annihilation, destruction, extinction; death. **প্রনষ্ট** *a.* annihilated, destroyed.

প্রণিধান *n.* close attention; profound meditation; deep consideration; earnest application or employment. **প্রণিধান করা** *v.* to pay close attention to; to meditate deeply; to consider deeply; to apply or employ earnestly (to). **~যোগ্য** *a.* deserving close attention or deep consideration.

প্রণিধি *n.* a spy; an emissary; a guide (কন্যাপ্রণিধি) ; close attention; meditation; deep consideration; earnest application; solicitation.

প্রণিপাত same as **প্রণাম**।

প্রণিয়ম *n.* regulation.

প্রণীত *a.* made; composed; compiled; created; drawn up; (of books etc) written.

প্রণেতা *n.* a maker; a composer; a compiler; a creator; one who draws up. *fem.* **প্রণেত্রী**।

প্রণোদন *n.* incitement, instigation; inducement, encouragement.

প্রণোদিত *a.* incited, induced; encouraged. **প্রণোদিত করা** *v.* to incite, to instigate; to induce, to encourage.

প্রতত *a.* wide; widespread; extended; expanded.

প্রতপ্ত *a.* very much heated or hot or angered or excited.

প্রতর্ক *n.* doubt; hesitation; assumption; supposition; consideration.

প্রতান *n.* (of creepers etc.) tension; a tendril.

প্রতাপ *n.* might, power; prowess; domineering influence; heat. **~শালী, প্রতাপান্বিত, প্রতাপী** *a.* mighty, powerful; domineeringly influential; (of the sun etc.) strongly burning or shining.

প্রতারক *n.* a cheat; a swindler, a sharper; an imposter, a deceiver; a beguiler; a chicaner.

প্রতারণা, প্রতারণ *n.* cheating; deception, chicanery; a deceit; a swindle, a fraud; hoodwinking; beguilement. **প্রতারণা করা** *v.* to cheat; to deceive; to swindle; to impose upon; to hoodwink; to beguile. **প্রতারণামূলক** *a.* fraudulent; deceitful.

প্রতারিত *a.* cheated; deceived; swindled; beguiled. *fem.* **প্রতারিতা**।

প্রতি¹ *prep.* towards (গৃহের প্রতি) ; to (পুত্রের প্রতি) ; regarding, concerning (ফুলের প্রতি আকর্ষণ).

প্রতি[2] *pfx.* denoting every, each; substituting, deputizing, vice-; counter-, re-, proximity, neighbourhood (প্রতিবাসী) ; contrary, anti-; similar, exact (প্রতিমূর্তি) ; equal (প্রতিযোগিতা).

প্রতিকরণীয় same as **প্রতিকার্য**।

প্রতি-আক্রমণ *n.* a counter-attack.

প্রতিকর্তা *a.* redressing; remedying, avenging; preventing; counteracting. □ *n.* a redresser; an avenger; a preventer; a counteractor.

প্রতিকর্ম *n.* redress; remedying; avenging; prevention; counteraction; dressing, toilet.

প্রতিকল্প *n.* a substitute. **প্রতিকল্পন** *n.* substitution.

প্রতিকার *n.* redress; remedy; revenge; prevention; counteraction. **প্রতিকার করা** *v.* to redress; to remedy; to avenge; to prevent; to counteract.

প্রতিকার্য *a.* redressible; remediable; that which can be or is to be avenged or counteracted; preventible.

প্রতিকূল *a.* opposed; contrary; hostile, malignant; adverse; unfavourable. **~তা** *n.* opposition; contrariety; antagonism, hostility, malignancy; adverseness, disfavour. **প্রতিকূলতা করা** *v.* to oppose; to be hostile to; to antagonize. **প্রতিকূলাচরণ** *n.* opposition; antagonism, hostility. **প্রতিকূলে** *prep.* against.

প্রতিকৃত *a.* redressed; remedied; avenged; prevented; counteracted.

প্রতিকৃতি *n.* a portrait; an image.

প্রতিক্রম *n.* inverse or reverse order.

প্রতিক্রিয়া *n.* a reaction; a response; an anti-progressive act or conduct; a swingback; counteraction. **~শীল** *a.* (pol.) anti-progressive, reactionary; (rare) responsive, reactive. **~শীলতা** *n.* the quality or state of being reactionary; obscurantism; opposition to progressiveness. **প্রতিক্রিয়াশীল হওয়া** *v.* to react; to be reactionary. **প্রতিক্রিয়াশীল ব্যক্তি** a reactionary.

প্রতিক্ষণ *adv.* every moment; always.

প্রতিক্ষিপ্ত *a.* rebounded. **প্রতিক্ষিপ্ত হওয়া** *v.* to rebound.

প্রতিক্ষেপণ *n.* act of throwing back or rebounding. **প্রতিক্ষেপণ করা** *v.* to throw back, to rebound.

প্রতিগমন *n.* return. **প্রতিগমন করা** *v.* to go back, to return, to recede.

প্রতিগামী *a.* returning; receding.

প্রতিগৃহীত *a.* accepted.

প্রতিগ্রহ *n.* acceptance of a gift; acceptance; a gift, a present; a promise, a pledge; (astrol.) a malignant planet or star. **প্রতিগ্রহণ** *n.* acceptance of a gift; acceptance. **প্রতিগ্রহণীয়** *a.* acceptable.

প্রতিগ্রাহ *n.* acceptance, acceptance of a gift. **প্রতিগ্রাহিত** *a.* caused to accept a gift. **প্রতিগ্রাহী** *a.* accepting a gift.

প্রতিগ্রাহ্য *a.* acceptable.

প্রতিঘাত *n.* a counter-stroke, a counter-blow. **প্রতিঘাত হানা** *v.* to deal (one) a counter-blow. **প্রতিঘাতন** *n.* act of killing. **প্রতিঘাতী** *a.* killing. *fem.* **প্রতিঘাতিনী**।

প্রতিচিত্র *a.* a blue print. **~মুদ্রক** *n.* a blue printer.

প্রতিচ্ছায়া *n.* a reflection; a shadow; an image, a likeness; resemblance, likeness.

প্রতিজিহ্বা *n.* uvula.

প্রতিজ্ঞা *n.* a solemn resolve or declaration; a vow; a promise, a pledge; (geom.) a theorem or a problem or a proposition. **প্রতিজ্ঞা করা** *v.* to resolve or declare solemnly; to promise. **প্রতিজ্ঞাত** *a.* resolved; promised; accepted; proposed. **~পত্র** *n.* a written promise or agreement, a bond; a written confession. **~পালন** *n.* act of keeping a promise. **প্রতিজ্ঞাপালন করা** *v.* to keep a promise. **~বদ্ধ** *a.* bound by a promise, under a pledge. **~ভঙ্গ** *n.* a breach of promise. **প্রতিজ্ঞাভঙ্গ করা** *v.* to break a promise. **~ভঙ্গকারী** *a.* promise-breaking. □ *n.* a promise-breaker.

প্রতিদত্ত *a.* given in return or exchange; required; returned.

প্রতিদান *n.* a gift or payment in return of another; exchange; requital, requite; retribution; repayment; revenge. **প্রতিদান দেওয়া** *v.* to give in return or exchange; to requite, to retribute; to repay; to take revenge upon. **~হীন** *a.* unrequiting.

প্রতিদিন *adv.* everyday, daily; per diem,

each day (প্রতিদিন কত মজুরি) ; day by day.

প্রতিদিষ্ট *a.* overruled.

প্রতিদেয় *a.* that which is to be or can be given in return or exchange; requitable, retributable.

প্রতিদ্বন্দ্ব, প্রতিদ্বন্দ্বিতা *n.* mutual hostility or strife; rivalry; competition. **প্রতিদ্বন্দ্বিতা করা** *v.* to fight or contend with; to rival; to vie or compete with. **প্রতিদ্বন্দ্বিতামূলক** *a.* competitive. **প্রতিদ্বন্দ্বী** *a.* contending; rivalling; competing; hostile. □ *n.* a contender; a rival; a competitor; an adversary. *fem.* **প্রতিদ্বন্দ্বিনী** ।

প্রতিধ্বনি *n.* an echo, a reverberation. **প্রতিধ্বনি করা** *v.* to echo, to reverberate. **প্রতিধ্বনিত** *a.* echoed, reverberated, resounded.

প্রতিনমস্কার *n.* salutation in reply to a salutation.

প্রতিনিধি *n.* a deputy; an agent; a representative; a delegate; a substitute; a proxy. **রাজপ্রতিনিধি** *n.* a viceroy. **প্রতিনিধিত্ব** *n.* office or tenure of a deputy or agent or representative or substitute. **প্রতিনিধিত্ব করা** *v.* to deputize; to act as an agent of; to represent; to act as a delegate or substitute or proxy of. **~বর্গ** *n.* a delegation, a deputation, body of representatives. **~সভা** *n.* a meeting of delegates or deputies or representatives.

প্রতিনিবর্তন *n.* return; refraining or desistance.

প্রতিনিবৃত্ত *a.* returned; having refrained or desisted (from). **প্রতিনিবৃত্ত হওয়া** *v.* to return (from); to refrain or desist (from). **প্রতিনিবৃত্তি** same as **প্রতিনিবর্তন** ।

প্রতিনিয়ত *adv.* every moment, constantly, always.

প্রতিনির্দেশ *n.* cross-reference.

প্রতিপক্ষ *n.* the hostile party; the opposite party, the opposition; the opponent; an enemy; a rival; (in law) a defendant. **প্রতিপক্ষীয়** *a.* of the opposite side or party or camp, of the contending side or camp.

প্রতিপত্তি *n.* honour; good standing; dominating or powerful influence; influence; power; (rare) proof. **~শালী, ~শীল, ~সম্পন্ন** *a.* enjoying honour; well-established; having domineering influence; influential; powerful.

প্রতিপত্র *n.* a counterfoil.

প্রতিপদ *n.* the first lunar day of a month.

প্রতিপদে *adv.* at every step; constantly.

প্রতিপন্ন *a.* ascertained; corroborated, confirmed; verified; proved, substantiated. **প্রতিপন্ন করা** *v.* to prove, to substantiate.

প্রতিপাদ *a.* antipodal. **~স্থান** *n.* (geog.) the antipodes.

প্রতিপাদক *a.* ascertaining; corroborating, confirming; verifying; proving, substantiating; performing.

প্রতিপাদন *n.* ascertainment; corroboration, confirmation; verification; proving, substantiation; accomplishment, performance. **প্রতিপাদন করা** *v.* to ascertain; to corroborate, to confirm; to verify; to prove, to substantiate; to accomplish, to perform. **প্রতিপাদনীয়** same as **প্রতিপাদ্য** ।

প্রতিপাদিকা *fem.* of **প্রতিপাদক** ।

প্রতিপাদিত *a.* ascertained; corroborated, confirmed; verified; proved, substantiated; accomplished, performed.

প্রতিপাদ্য *a.* to be ascertained or corroborated or confirmed or verified or proved or substantiated or accomplished or performed; ascertainable; confirmable; verifiable; provable; accomplishable, performable.

প্রতিপালক *a.* bringing up, rearing, fostering; feeding, maintaining; keeping, observing; complying, obeying; protecting, looking after the well-being of. □ *n.* one who brings up, a rearer, a fosterer; a feeder, a maintainer; a keeper, an observer; one who complies (with) or obeys; a protector, a guardian.

প্রতিপালন *n.* upbringing; rearing; fostering (সন্তান-প্রতিপালন) ; feeding; maintenance (পরিজন-প্রতিপালন) ; keeping, observance (প্রতিশ্রুতি-প্রতিপালন) ; act of obeying, compliance (আদেশ-প্রতিপালন) ; protection, act of looking after the well-being of (প্রজা-প্রতিপালন). **প্রতিপালন করা** *v.* to bring up; to rear; to foster; to feed, to maintain; to keep, to observe; to comply with, to obey; to protect, to look after the well-being of. **প্রতিপালনীয়** same as **প্রতিপাল্য**।

প্রতিপালিকা *fem.* of **প্রতিপালক**।

প্রতিপালিত *a.* brought up; reared; fostered; fed; maintained; observed; complied with, obeyed; protected, taken care of. *fem.* **প্রতিপালিতা**।

প্রতিপাল্য *a.* worthy of being brought up or reared or fostered or fed or maintained or kept or observed or complied with or obeyed or protected or taken care of.

প্রতিপোষক *a.* corroborative, bearing out; supporting; aiding.

প্রতিপোষণ *n.* corroboration, act of bearing out; act of supporting or aiding.

প্রতিপ্রভ *a.* (phys. & bot.) fluorescent. **প্রতিপ্রভা** *n.* fluorescence.

প্রতিপ্রশ্ন *n.* a counter-question.

প্রতিফল *n.* retributory punishment, retribution, requite, requital; relation, revenge; (loos.) punishment. **উপযুক্ত প্রতিফল** just retribution. **প্রতিফল দেওয়া** *v.* to mete out retributory punishment (to); to take revenge upon; to punish. **প্রতিফল পাওয়া** *v.* to suffer the consequences; to be punished.

প্রতিফলন *n.* reflection (as in a mirror). **প্রতিফলন কোণ** *n.* (phys.) angle of reflection. **প্রতিফলিত** *a.* reflected. **প্রতিফলিত করা** *v.* to reflect. **প্রতিফলিত হওয়া** *v.* to reflect.

প্রতিবচন same as **প্রতিবাক্য**।

প্রতিবন্ধ *n.* an obstacle, a hindrance; a frustration. □ *a.* hindered, obstructed; frustrated. **প্রতিবন্ধক** *a.* obstructing, hindering; opposing. □ *n.* an obstacle. **প্রতিবন্ধকতা** same as **প্রতিবন্ধ** (*n.*). **প্রতিবন্ধী** *a.* obstructed; obstructing; suffering from physical or mental disability, (inc.but pop.) handicapped.

প্রতিবর্ণীকরণ *n.* transliteration; transcribing in the character or script of another language. **প্রতিবর্ণীকৃত** *a.* transliterated.

প্রতিবর্তন *n.* obversion.

প্রতিবল *a.* equally strong or powerful. □ *n.* a hostile army or forces.

প্রতিবস্তূপমা *n.* (rhet.) a parallel simile.

প্রতিবাক্য *n.* an answer, a reply; a retort; an adverse comment.

প্রতিবাত *a.* windward. **প্রতিবাতে** *adv.* windwards.

প্রতিবাদ *n.* a counter-plea, a counter-argument; a protest; a counter. **প্রতিবাদ করা** *v.* to put forth a counter-plea or counter-argument; to protest. **~সভা** *n.* a protest meeting. **প্রতিবাদী** *a.* pleading against; pleading in reply; protesting; opposing, contending (against). □ *n.* (in law) a defendant, a respondent. *fem.* **প্রতিবাদিনী**।

প্রতিবাসী *a.* living or residing in the neighbourhood. □ *n.* a neighbour. *fem.* **প্রতিবাসিনী**।

প্রতিবিধান *n.* a counter-action or counter-measure; remedy, redress; revenge. **প্রতিবিধান করা** *v.* to take measures against; to remedy, to redress; to avenge.

প্রতিবিধিৎসা *n.* desire of taking measures against or remedying or redressing; revengefulness. **প্রতিবিধিৎসু** *a.* desirous of taking measures against or remedying or redressing; revengeful; avenging.

প্রতিবিধেয় *a.* remediable, redressable.

প্রতিবিপ্লব *n.* a counter-revolution. **প্রতিবিপ্লবী** *a.* counter-revolutionary.

প্রতিবিম্ব *n.* a reflected image, a reflection, an image. **প্রতিবিম্বন** *n.* act of being reflected, reflection. **প্রতিবিম্বিত** *a.* reflected.

প্রতিবিষ *n.* an anti-toxin; an antidote.

প্রতিবিহিত *a.* remedied, redressed, righted, avenged.

প্রতিবেদন *n.* a petition of complaint; a report.

প্রতিবেশ *n.* dwelling-houses in the neighbourhood; environs, surroundings; environment. **প্রতিবেশী** same as **প্রতিবাসী**। *fem.* **প্রতিবেশিনী**।

প্রতিবোধ, প্রতিবোধন *n.* manifestation, revelation; awakening; consolation. **প্রতিবোধিত** *a.* manifested, revealed; awakened; consoled.

প্রতিভা *n.* keen intelligence; presence of mind; inventive or creative faculty; genius; glow; brilliance. **~বান** same as **প্রতিভাধর**।

প্রতিভাত *a.* brightly appearing, shiningly visible; manifest, clearly revealed; clearly known; lighted; reflected.

প্রতিভাধর, প্রতিভাশালী, প্রতিভাসম্পন্ন *a.* keenly intelligent; endowed with exceptional inventive or creative faculty; endowed with genius. **প্রতিভাধর ব্যক্তি** a man of genius, a genius.

প্রতিভার *n.* counter-balance.

প্রতিভাষ *n.* an answer, a reply.

প্রতিভাস *n.* radiance, illumination; manifestation; revelation. **প্রতিভাসিত** *a.* radiant; manifested or revealed.

প্রতিভূ *n.* a representative, a deputy, an agent, a substitute; a hostage.

প্রতিভূতি-পত্র *n.* bail-bond.

প্রতিম *a.* (*in. comp.* used as a *sfx.*) like, resembling, equal to.

প্রতিমা *n.* an icon, an image; an idol. **~চূর্ণকারী** *a.* iconoclastic. □ *n.* an iconoclast. **~চূর্ণন** iconoclasm. **~নিরঞ্জন, ~বিসর্জন** *n.* the ceremonial immersion of an idol. **~পূজক** *n.* an idolater, an iconolater, an image-worshipper. □ *a.* idolatrous. **~পূজা** *n.* idolatry, iconolatry, image-worship. **~পূজাবিরোধী** *a.* opposed to image-worship; iconoclastic. **~শিল্প** *n.* the art of making images. **~শিল্পী** *n.* the artist who makes an image.

প্রতিমান *n.* a model, a pattern; (phys.) balancing, a weight. **প্রতিমান করা** *v.* (phys.) to balance.

প্রতিমুখ *n.* a direction towards one; front. □ *a.* (mech.) unlike; (bot.) opposite; facing. **প্রতিমুখে** *prep.* in the direction of.

প্রতিমুহূর্ত *adv.* every moment; always.

প্রতিমূর্তি *n.* an image, an icon, a portrait, a likeness; an exactly similar figure or appearance.

প্রতিযোগ *n.* antipathy; enmity, hostility; quarrel; rivalry; competition. **প্রতিযোগিতা** *n.* rivalry; competition; vying. **প্রতিযোগিতা করা** *v.* to compete or vie (with). **প্রতিযোগিতামূলক, প্রতিযোগিতাপূর্ণ** *a.* competitive. **প্রতিযোগী** *a.* rivalling; competing; vying; (geom.) conjugate. □ *n.* a rival; a competitor. *fem.* **প্রতিযোগিনী**।

প্রতিযোজন *n.* (bot.) adaptation.

প্রতিযোদ্ধা *n.* an opponent in duelling, an antagonist, a rival.

প্রতিরক্ষা *n.* defence. **প্রতিরক্ষা-মন্ত্রক** *n.* the ministry of defence.

প্রতিরুদ্ধ *a.* prevented; checked, resisted; obstructed; opposed; blockaded; stopped. **প্রতিরুদ্ধ করা** same as **প্রতিরোধ করা**।

প্রতিরূপ *n.* an image, a likeness; an exactly similar figure or appearance; a reflected image, a reflection, likeness, resemblance. □ *a.* similar; like, exactly resembling.

প্রতিরোধ *n.* prevention; check, resistance; obstruction; opposition; an obstacle, a blockade; stoppage. **প্রতিরোধ করা** *v.* to prevent; to check, to resist; to obstruct; to oppose; to blockade; to stop. **প্রতিরোধক, প্রতিরোধী** *a.* preventive; resistant; resisting; obstructive; obstructing; opposing; blockading; stopping. **~শক্তি** *n.* the power of or capacity for resistance or opposition. **প্রতিরোধিত** *a.* obstructed, resisted; opposed; stopped; prevented.

প্রতিলিপি *n.* a replica, a facsimile, a transcript, a copy.

প্রতিলেখ *n.* act of copying; transcription; a transcript, a copy. **প্রতিলেখক** *n.* a copyist. **প্রতিলেখন** *n.* copying.

প্রতিলোম *n.* reverse, inverse. **প্রতিলোম বিবাহ** marriage of a high-caste bride with a low-caste bridegroom. **প্রতিলোমজ** *a.* born of a low-caste father and a high-caste mother.

প্রতিশব্দ *n.* a synonym; an echo.

প্রতিশয়, প্রতিশয়ন *n.* a persistent squatting at the temple of a deity for divine favour or boon. **প্রতিশয়িত** *a.* thus squatting.

প্রতিশোধ *n.* revenge; requital; retaliation. **প্রতিশোধ নেওয়া** *v.* to requite; to retaliate; to take revenge (upon); to pay (a person) in his own coin, to give tit for tat, to avenge.

প্রতিশ্রুত *a.* promised, pledged; promise-bound; covenanted. **প্রতিশ্রুত হওয়া** *v.* to pledge oneself, to commit oneself by a promise. **প্রতিশ্রুতি** *n.* a promise, a pledge; a covenant. **প্রতিশ্রুতি ভঙ্গ** *n.* breach of or withdrawal from a promise or contract or pledge.

প্রতিষেধ *n.* prohibition, forbiddance; prevention; an antidote; therapeutics; a therapeutical drug. **প্রতিষিদ্ধ** *a.* prohibited, forbidden. **প্রতিষেধক** *a.* prohibitive; preventive; prophylactic, therapeutical, antidotal. □ *n.* a therapeutical or antidotal drug; an antidote, a prophylactic.

প্রতিষ্ঠা *n.* setting up, establishment, foundation (বিদ্যালয়-প্রতিষ্ঠা, বংশপ্রতিষ্ঠা) ; solemn dedication, consecration (পুকুর প্রতিষ্ঠা) ; installation (বিগ্রহপ্রতিষ্ঠা) ; observance (of a vow etc.); settling down, habilitation; good footing or standing, fame, reputation (প্রতিষ্ঠালাভ). **প্রতিষ্ঠা করা** *v.* to set up, to establish, to found; to dedicate solemnly, to consecrate; to instal; to make one settle down. **প্রতিষ্ঠা পাওয়া** *v.* to gain a good footing or standing; to earn fame or reputation. **প্রতিষ্ঠাতা** *n.* an establisher, a founder; a dedicator; one who instals or causes to settle down. *fem.* **প্রতিষ্ঠাত্রী** । **~ধিকার** *n.* goodwill (as of a business firm). **প্রতিষ্ঠান** *n.* an institute, an institution, an establishment. **~পক** *n.* same as **প্রতিষ্ঠাতা** । **~পন** *n.* setting up, establishment, foundation; solemn dedication, consecration; installation; settling down, habilitation. **~পয়িতা** same as **প্রতিষ্ঠাতা** । *fem.* **~পয়িত্রী** । **~পিত** *a.* set up, established, founded; solemnly dedicated, consecrated; installed; settled down, habilitated. **~বান** *a.* having a good footing or standing; famous, reputed.

প্রতিষ্ঠিত same as **প্রতিষ্ঠাপিত** (see **প্রতিষ্ঠা**). and—well-established; reputed, famous. **প্রতিষ্ঠিত করা** same as **প্রতিষ্ঠা করা** (see **প্রতিষ্ঠা**) and—to cause to have a good footing or standing; to make famous or reputed.

প্রতিসংহার *n.* withholding (of weapons etc.); warding off. **প্রতিসংহার করা** *v.* to hold back, to withhold; to ward off, to stave off.

প্রতিসংহৃত *a.* (of weapons etc.) held back, withheld; warded off.

প্রতিসম *a.* symmetrical. **প্রতিসাম্য** symmetry.

প্রতিসরণ *n.* (phys.) refraction. **প্রতিসরণ করা** *v.* to refract. **প্রতিসরণ কোণ** angle of refraction. **প্রতিসরণীয়** *a.* refrangible.

প্রতিসরাঙ্ক *n.* (phys.) refracting index.

প্রতিসর্গ *n.* (myth.) expansion of the creation after the original one, the secondary creation; universal dissolution.

প্রতিসারণ *n.* removal; withdrawal. **প্রতিসারণ করা** *v.* to remove; to draw or lead away, to withdraw.

প্রতিসারিত *a.* removed; led away.

প্রতিসারী *a.* going in an opposite direction; refracting; going against.

প্রতিসৃত *a.* (phys.) refracted.

প্রতিস্পর্ধা *n.* audacity, arrogance; defiance; challenge; spirit of challenge. **প্রতিস্পর্ধী** *a.* arrogant, audacious; challenging; emulative.

প্রতিস্বাক্ষর *n.* countersignature. **প্রতিস্বাক্ষরিত** *a.* countersigned.

প্রতিহত *a.* checked, prevented; repelled, staved off; obstructed; hurt in return; hurt; **প্রতিহত করা** *v.* to check, to prevent; to repel, to repulse, to stave off, to beat back, to obstruct.

প্রতিহনন *n.* act of killing a slayer.

প্রতিহন্তা *a.* & *n.* one who kills a slayer. *fem.* **প্রতিহন্ত্রী** ।

প্রতিহার *n.* a gate or a door; a doorkeeper, a gateman, a porter (*fem.* porteress portress), a janitor (*fem.* janitrix, janitress); an armed guard stationed at a door or a gate, act of giving up, abandonment, avoidance; a race of ancient India. **প্রতিহারী** *n.* an armed guard stationed at a door or a gate; a doorkeeper, a gateman, a porter. *fem.* **প্রতিহারিণী** ।

প্রতিহার্য *a.* that which should be given up or abandoned or avoided.

প্রতিহিংসা *n.* revenge, retaliation. **প্রতিহিংসা গ্রহণ করা** *v.* to take revenge (upon), to retaliate, to avenge. **~পরায়ণ** *a.* vindictive, revengeful, retaliative. **প্রতিহিংসিত** *a.* one upon whom revenge has been taken.

প্রতীক *n.* a symbol; a sign. **~বাদ, ~তা** *n.* symbolism. **প্রতীক ধর্মঘট** a token strike. **প্রতীকী** *a.* symbolic, symbolical. **প্রতীকিতা** *n.* symbolism.

প্রতীক্ষমাণ *a.* waiting for, awaiting; expecting, expectant. *fem.* **প্রতীক্ষমাণা**।

প্রতীক্ষা *n.* act of waiting for, awaiting; expectation. **প্রতীক্ষা করা** *v.* to wait for, to await; to expect. **~লয়** *n.* a waitingroom.

প্রতীক্ষিত *a.* awaited; expected.

প্রতীক্ষ্যমাণ *a.* one being waited for; that is being waited for.

প্রতীচী *n.* the west; the western world, the western hemisphere, the Occident.

প্রতীচীন, প্রতীচ্য *a.* of the west or of the western world, western, occidental.

প্রতীত *a.* realized, understood, cognized; having formed a notion; believing, convinced. **প্রতীতি** *n.* realization, understanding, cognition; a notion, an impression; a belief, a conviction.

প্রতীপ *a.* (geom.) vertically opposite; opposite or negative. □ *n.* (rhet.) a reversed simile. **~কোণ** *n.* (geom.) a vertically opposite angle. **~গতি** *n.* retrogression; (astr.) retrograde motion. **প্রতীপ চাপ** (phys.) negative pressure. **প্রতীপ স্রোত** (geog.) an anti-current.

প্রতীয়মান *a.* that which is being or capable of being realized or cognized or known; suggested (প্রতীয়মান সূর্য), (loos.) evident or visible. **প্রতীয়মান হওয়া** *v.* to appear, to wear the look of; to seem; to be evident, to be manifest.

প্রতীহার, প্রতীহারী alt. spellings of **প্রতিহার** and **প্রতিহারী** respectively.

প্রতুল *n.* abundance, plenty; prosperity, richness. □ *a.* abundant, plentiful.

প্রত্ন *n.* ancient, old, **~তত্ত্ব, ~বিদ্যা** *n.* archaeology. **~তত্ত্ববিৎ, ~বিদ** *n.* archaeologist; an antiquary, an antiquarian. **~তত্ত্বীয়, ~তাত্ত্বিক** *a.* archaeological; antiquarian.

প্রত্নজীববিদ্যা *n.* palaeontology. **প্রত্নোদ্ভিদবিদ্যা** *n.* palaeo-botany. **প্রত্নপ্রাণীবিদ্যা** *n.* palaeozoology.

প্রত্যক্‌চৈতন্য *n.* subconscious, subconsciousness.

প্রত্যক্ষ *a.* perceptible by senses; perceptible, visible, apparent; manifest, evident, clear; direct (প্রত্যক্ষ করা). □ *n.* senseperception; perception; a percept. **প্রত্যক্ষ করা** *v.* to perceive by senses; to perceive directly; to see, to visualize. **প্রত্যক্ষ উক্তি** (gr.) direct speech or narration. **প্রত্যক্ষ দিগন্ত** the visible or apparent horizon. **প্রত্যক্ষ ফল** direct or immediate result or consequence; (loos.) visible consequence. **~কর** *n.* a direct tax. **~কারী** same as **প্রত্যক্ষদর্শী**। **~গোচর** *a.* directly perceptible; visible; perceptible by senses. **~জ্ঞান** *n.* direct knowledge. **প্রত্যক্ষত** *adv.* apparently. **~দর্শন** *n.* direct perception, visualization, act of seeing with one's own eyes. **~দর্শী** *a.* directly perceiving, visualizing, seeing with one's own eyes. □ *n.* an eye-witness. **~প্রমাণ** *n.* visible evidence, direct proof. **~বাদ** *n.* materialism; positivism. **~বাদী** *a.* materialistic; positivistic. □ *n.* a materialist; a positivist. **প্রত্যক্ষ সাক্ষ্য** direct evidence. **প্রত্যক্ষী** same as **প্রত্যক্ষদর্শী**। **প্রত্যক্ষীকরণ** *n.* visualization, witnessing; perception; sense-perception. **প্রত্যক্ষীকৃত** *a.* seen with one's own eyes, directly seen, witnessed; perceived; perceived by senses. **প্রত্যক্ষীভূত** *a.* visible; directly seen; perceived or perceivable by senses.

প্রত্যগাত্মা *n.* the Supreme Being, God; the human soul endowed with the knowledge about theological and philosophical reality.

প্রত্যঙ্গ *n.* a subsidiary or minor limb, an appendage; (fig.) a small component or subsidiary part.

প্রত্যন্ত *a.* lying on or adjoining the border, bordering (on), contiguous, neighbouring. □ *n.* the border; the frontier region, the frontier; (in the Puranas) the land of Mlechhas (ম্লেচ্ছ). **~পর্বত** *n.* a hillock beside a mountain. **~প্রদেশ** *n.* a neighbouring country; the frontier; outskirts. **~বাসী** *a.* dwelling on the outskirts of a town or village or country; dwelling on a frontier.

প্রত্যবায় *n.* sin; vice; harm. **প্রত্যবায়ী** *a.* sinful; vicious; harmful.

প্রত্যবেক্ষণ *n.* enquiry; scrutiny; research; supervision.

প্রত্যভিজ্ঞা, প্রত্যভিজ্ঞান *n.* recognition.

প্রত্যভিবাদ, প্রত্যভিবাদন *n.* a salute or salutation in return. **প্রত্যভিবাদন করা** *v.* to salute in return, to return a salute.

প্রত্যভিযোগ *n.* a countercharge. **প্রত্যভিযোগ করা** *v.* to bring a countercharge.

প্রত্যয় *n.* trust; belief; confidence; conviction; firm impression or notion; (gr.) an inflection. **প্রত্যয় করা** *v.* to believe, to trust, to have confidence (in). **~জনক, ~যোগ্য** *a.* trustworthy, believable, worthy of belief, credible; convincing. **প্রত্যয়িত** *a.* trusty. **প্রত্যয়ী** *a.* believing; trusting; confident.

প্রত্যর্থী *n.* (in law) a contestant, a defendant, an opponent, an opposite party; an accused.

প্রত্যর্পণ *n.* giving back, return, repayment; restoration. **প্রত্যর্পণ করা** *v.* to give back, to return, to repay; to restore (to). **প্রত্যর্পিত** *a.* given back, returned, repaid; restored.

প্রত্যহ *adv.* everyday; daily; day by day; per diem.

প্রত্যাকর্ষণ *n.* counter-attraction.

প্রত্যাখ্যাত *a.* rejected, refused; discarded; disallowed; unentertained; (rare) neglected, slighted.

প্রত্যাখ্যান *n.* rejection, refusal; discardment; disallowance, refusal of permission; refusal to entertain; (rare) neglect, slight. **প্রত্যাখ্যান করা** *v.* to refuse to accept, to reject, to refuse; to discard; to disallow, to refuse permission; to refuse to entertain, to disappoint; (rare) to neglect, to slight.

প্রত্যাগত *a.* come-back, returned; (mech.) recoiled. **প্রত্যাগতি** *n.* return movement; return; (mech.) recoil.

প্রত্যাগমন *n.* a come-back; coming back; return. **প্রত্যাগমন করা** *v.* to come back, to return; (mech.) to recoil.

প্রত্যাঘাত *n.* a counterblow. **প্রত্যাঘাত করা** *v.* to deal a counterblow, to strike back.

প্রত্যাদিষ্ট *a.* divinely commanded or inspired; voided, repealed.

প্রত্যাদেশ *n.* a divine command or inspiration, a commandment; a divine announcement, an oracle; nullification, voidance, repeal.

প্রত্যানয়ন *n.* bringing back; act of bringing again. **প্রত্যানয়ন করা** *v.* to bring back; to bring again.

প্রত্যানীত *a.* brought back; brought again.

প্রত্যাবর্তন *n.* coming or going back, return. **প্রত্যাবর্তন করা** *v.* to come or go back, to return.

প্রত্যাবাসন *n.* repatriation. **প্রত্যাবাসন সাহায্য** *n.* repatriation benefit. **প্রত্যাবাসিত** *a.* repatriated.

প্রত্যাবৃত্ত *a.* come or gone back, returned. *fem.* **প্রত্যাবৃত্তা।** **প্রত্যাবৃত্ত হওয়া** *v.* to come or go back, to return.

প্রত্যায়ন *n.* attestation. **প্রত্যায়িত** *a.* attested.

প্রত্যালীঢ় *n.* the kneeling posture of an archer whilst shooting with his right leg doubled in the front and the left stretched out at the back.

প্রত্যাশা *n.* hope; longing; prospect; expectation; awaiting. **প্রত্যাশা করা** *v.* to hope or long (for); to expect; to await. **প্রত্যাশিত** *a.* hoped; longed for; prospective; expected; awaited. **প্রত্যাশী** *a.* hoping or longing for; expectant; awaiting.

প্রত্যাসন্ন *a.* very near, contiguous; that which is round the corner; imminent, impending.

প্রত্যাহত *a.* beaten back, repulsed, warded off, staved off; prevented; obstructed, resisted; frustrated; foiled.

প্রত্যাহরণ, প্রত্যাহার *n.* withdrawal; retraction; revocation; repeal; (phil.) abstraction. **প্রত্যাহরণ করা, প্রত্যাহার করা** *v.* to withdraw; to retract; to revoke, to rescind; to repeal.

প্রত্যাহৃত *a.* withdrawn; retracted; revoked, rescinded; repealed.

প্রত্যুক্তি *n.* an answer, a reply; a retort.

প্রত্যুত *con.* & *adv.* on the contrary, rather.

প্রত্যুৎপন্ন *a.* produced on the spur of the moment, extemporaneous; very prompt. **~মতি** *n.* presence of mind, ready wit. □ *a.* endowed with presence of mind, ready-witted. **~মতিত্ব** *n.* ready-wittedness; presence of mind.

প্রত্যুত্তর *n.* a retort, rejoinder. **প্রত্যুত্তর করা** *v.* to retort, to answer back.

প্রত্যুদাহরণ *n.* counter-example; a counter-precedent.

প্রত্যুদ্গমন, প্রত্যুদ্গম *n.* going forward or advancing in order to receive a visitor on the way; seeing off a respected visitor. **প্রত্যুদ্গমন করা** *v.* to go forward in order to receive a visitor on the way; to see off.

প্রত্যুপকার *n.* a good turn in return. **প্রত্যুপকার করা** *v.* to do (one) a good turn in return. **প্রত্যুপকর্তা, প্রত্যুপকারী** *a.* & *n.* one who does (one) a good turn in return. **প্রত্যুপকৃত** *n.* benefited in return.

প্রত্যুষ, প্রত্যূষ *n.* the dawn; daybreak; the morning. **প্রত্যুষে** *adv.* at dawn or daybreak, early in the morning.

প্রত্যেক *a.* each, every. □ *pro.* each, everyone. **প্রত্যেক লোকের, প্রত্যেকের** *a.* of each, of everybody.

প্রথম *a.* first; primitive (প্রথম যুগ) ; of the beginning, inceptive (প্রথমাবস্থা) ; most important, chief (প্রথম কথা) ; eldest (প্রথম পুত্র) ; foremost (প্রথম সারি) ; best (পরীক্ষায় প্রথম শ্রেণিতে প্রথম). *fem.* **প্রথমা**। **(পরীক্ষায়) প্রথম হওয়া** *v.* to come or stand first or to top the list (in an examination). **প্রথমত** *adv.* at first; firstly, in the first place, first. **~দর্শন** *n.* the first meeting. **প্রথমদর্শনে প্রণয়** love at first sight. **~পাদ** *n.* the first quarter. **~পুরুষ** *n.* (gr.) the third person. **~বয়স** *n.* the early age; the early youth. **প্রথম বিশ্বযুদ্ধ** the First World War. **প্রথমে** *adv.* at first; in the first place, first; in the beginning; in front, before all. **প্রথমাংশ** *n.* the first or early part. **প্রথমোক্ত** *n.* the one first spoken of or referred to first; former.

প্রথা *n.* usage, custom, practice; system, method. **~গত** *a.* customary. **~নুগ** *a.* in accordance with custom; customary; conventional. **~নুগত্য** *n.* loyalty or faithfulness to custom or convention. **~নুসারে** *adv.* according to the custom or practice or system, customarily. **~মতো** *adv.* according to or in accordance with custom or convention; conventionally.

প্রথিত *a.* famous, celebrated. **~নামা** *a.* one whose name is famous; renowned; widely famous. **~যশা** *a.* widely famous, renowned.

-প্রদ *sfx.* denotes giving (সুখপ্রদ).

প্রদক্ষিণ *n.* (ori. & ritually) clockwise circumambulation round an object; act of going around something. **প্রদক্ষিণ করা** *v.* to circumambulate in a clockwise manner around something; to go round something.

প্রদত্ত *a.* given; bestowed; conferred.

প্রদমিত *a.* subdued; restrained; suppressed.

প্রদর *n.* leucorrhoea.

প্রদর্শক *a.* showing; exhibiting; displaying; demonstrating. □ *n.* one who shows; one who shows one round, a guide; an exhibitor, a displayer; a demonstrator.

প্রদর্শন *n.* act of showing or showing round or exhibiting or displaying or demonstrating; act of seeing or observing thoroughly or minutely or carefully. **প্রদর্শন করা** *v.* to see or observe thoroughly or minutely or carefully. **প্রদর্শন করানো** *v.* to show; to show one round; to exhibit; to display; to demonstrate. **প্রদর্শনী** *n.* a public show, an exhibition.

প্রদর্শমালা *n.* a museum.

প্রদর্শিকা *fem.* of **প্রদর্শক**।

প্রদর্শিত *a.* shown; shown round; exhibited; displayed; demonstrated; clearly shown.

-প্রদা *fem.* of **-প্রদ**।

প্রদাতা var. of **প্রদায়ক**। *fem.* **প্রদাত্রী**।

প্রদান *n.* giving; bestowal; conferring; yielding; imparting. **প্রদান করা** *v.* to give; to bestow; to confer; to yield; to impart.

প্রদায়ক, প্রদায়ী *a.* giving; bestowing; conferring; yielding; imparting. *fem.* **প্রদায়িকা, প্রদায়িনী**।

প্রদাহ *n.* distress, affliction (মর্মপ্রদাহ) ; burning pain, inflammation (ফোড়ার প্রদাহ). **প্রদাহী** *a.* distressful, afflicting; causing inflammation, inflammatory.

প্রদীপ *n.* a lamp, a light; (fig.) one who

illuminates or glorifies (কুলপ্রদীপ). **প্রদীপন** *n.* act of illuminating or exciting; lighting of lamps.

প্রদীপ্ত *a.* illuminated, enkindled; brightly burning, blazing; shining; excited. **প্রদীপ্ত করা** *v.* to illuminate, to enkindle; to excite. **প্রদীপ্তি** *n.* illumination; bright glow; lustre; excitement.

প্রদৃপ্ত *a.* very proud or haughty or arrogant or vulgarly self-assertive or vigorous.

প্রদেয় *a.* that which is to be or can be given.

প্রদেশ *n.* a province; a state; a country; a region; a part.

প্রদোষ, প্রদোষকাল *n.* evening; nightfall, evening twilight; night. **প্রদোষান্ধকার** *n.* the gloom of the evening.

প্রদ্যোত *n.* glow; shine; a ray.

প্রধান *a.* chief, main, principal; prime; most important; leading, foremost; pre-eminent; predominant. □ *in comp.* (used as a *sfx.*) dominated by or chiefly characterized by (শীতপ্রধান). □ *n.* a chief; a headman; a leader; a royal counsellor; God; the primordial female energy. *fem.* **প্রধানা** । **প্রধান অক্ষ** the principal axis. **প্রধান অতিথি** the chief guest. **প্রধান আরক্ষিক** the head constable. **প্রধান করণিক** the head clerk. **প্রধান কর্মসচিব** the Chief Secretary. **প্রধান চরিত্র** the principal or chief or the focal character. **প্রধানত** *adv.* chiefly, mainly, principally, pre-eminently, predominantly. **প্রধানতা** *n.* primeness; supremacy; pre-eminence, predominance. **প্রধান বিচারপতি** the Chief Justice. **~মন্ত্রী** *n.* the Prime Minister. **~মূল** (bot.) the tap root. **~শিক্ষক** the headmaster. *fem.* **~শিক্ষিকা** the headmistress. **প্রধান সেনাপতি** the Commander-in-Chief.

প্রধাবন *n.* act of running rapidly, a quick run; a quick race.

প্রধাবিত *a.* running or caused to be running rapidly. **প্রধাবিত করা** *v.* to cause to run rapidly. **প্রধাবিত হওয়া** *v.* to run rapidly.

প্রধূমিত *a.* caused to emit smoke profusely; (of anger etc.) caused to be fuming; (fig.) angered. *fem.* **প্রধূমিতা** । **প্রধূমিত করা** *v.* to cause to emit smoke profusely; to fume. **প্রধূমিত হওয়া** *v.* to be emitting smoke profusely; to fume.

প্রধ্বংস *n.* annihilation, destruction. **প্রধ্বংসী** *a.* annihilating, destructive.

প্রনষ্ট *a.* utterly lost or ruined or destroyed. **প্রণাশ** *n.* destruction, annihilation.

প্রপঞ্চ *n.* extent; illusion, *maya*; delusion; phenomenal reality; the world; the worldly life; an error or mistake; untruth; falsehood; a collection, a multitude. **~ময়** *a.* full of illusions; illusory. **প্রপঞ্চিত** *a.* extensive; extended; illusive; illusory; erroneous.

প্রপা *n.* a place where drinking water is available or distributed, (cp.) a watering-place.

প্রপাত *n.* fall (of water etc.); a waterfall, a cascade, a cataract. **~রেখা** *n.* a fall line.

প্রপান same as **প্রপা** ।

প্রপিতামহ *n.* a great-grandfather (on one's father's side). *fem.* **প্রপিতামহী** a great-grandmother (on one's father's side).

প্রপূরণ *n.* filling up completely.

প্রপূরিত *a.* completely filled up.

প্রপৌত্র *n.* a grandson of one's son or nephew, a great-grandson. *fem.* **প্রপৌত্রী** *n.* a grand-daughter of one's son or nephew, a great-granddaughter.

প্রফুল্ল, (inc.) **প্রফুল্লিত** *a.* fully blossomed, full-blown, blooming, (প্রফুল্ল কমল); cheerful, gay (প্রফুল্ল বদন); happy; shining, bright. **প্রফুল্লচিত্ত** *a.* having a happy or cheerful heart. **প্রফুল্লচিত্তে** *adv.* with a happy or cheerful heart. **প্রফুল্লতা** *n.* cheerfulness; gaiety; happiness. **প্রফুল্লনয়ন** *a.* brighteyed. **প্রফুল্ল বদন** *n.* a cheerful face. **প্রফুল্লবদন** *a.* having a cheeful or happy or bright face. **প্রফুল্লভাবে** *adv.* cheerfully. **প্রফুল্লহৃদয়** same as **প্রফুল্লচিত্ত** ।

প্রফেসর *n.* a professor. **প্রফেসরি** *n.* professorship. **প্রফেসরি করা** *v.* to work as a professor.

প্রবক্তা *n.* a spokesman; one who is fluent or eloquent in speech. □ *a.* eloquent or fluent in speech.

প্রবচন *n.* an adage, a proverb; an apophthegm, apothegm; a popular or oftquoted saying; (rare) amplification.

প্রবঞ্চক *n.* a cheat, a swindler, an imposter, a deceiver; a beguiler.

প্রবঞ্চনা *n.* cheating; deception; deceit; swindle; fraud;beguilement. **প্রবঞ্চনা করা** *v.* to cheat; to deceive; to swindle; to impose upon; to hoodwink; to beguile. **~মূলক** *a.* fraudulent; deceitful.

প্রবঞ্চিত *a.* cheated; deceived; swindled; beguiled. *fem.* **প্রবঞ্চিতা** ।

প্রবণ *a.* inclined or sloping (প্রবণভূমি) ; inclined to, prone to, tending to (ভাবপ্রবণ) ; attached or addicted to, given to (চৌর্যপ্রবণ) ; eager to, ready to; proficient in. **~ভূমি** *n.* an escarpment; a declivity. **~তা** *n.* inclination, propensity, declivity; tendency, disposition; attachment, addiction; eagerness, readiness; proficiency.

প্রবন্ধ *n.* an essay, an article; a dissertation; a treatise; sequence; a trick, a stratagem ('যতেক প্রবন্ধ করে নিশাচরগণে'). **~কার** *n.* an essayist.

প্রবর *a.* (chiefly used as a *sfx.*) best, excellent (ধার্মিকপ্রবর). □ *n.* a line of descent, descent; the originating saint of a line of descent. **প্রবর সমিতি** select committee.

প্রবর্তক *a.* introducing, bringing into use or currency; inaugurating, starting; founding, establishing; employing, initiating. □ *n.* an introducer, one who introduces or brings (something) into use; an inaugurator; a pioneer; a founder; an employer, an initiator.

প্রবর্তন *n.* bringing into use, introduction; inauguration, start, inception; establishment; employment, initiation. **প্রবর্তন করা** *v.* to bring into use or currency, to introduce; to inaugurate, to start, to begin; to found, to establish; to employ, to initiate. **প্রবর্তনা** *n.* initiation; incitement; inducement; inspiration. **প্রবর্তনা করা** বা **দেওয়া** *v.* to initiate; to incite; to induce; to inspire.

প্রবর্তয়িতা *n.* an initiator; an inciter; an inducer. *fem.* **প্রবর্তয়িত্রী** ।

প্রবর্তিত *a.* brought into use, introduced; inaugurated, started, commenced; established, founded; employed, initiated, induced.

প্রবর্ধন *n.* increase, augmentation; growth. **প্রবর্ধক** *a.* causing growth or increase or development.

প্রবল *a.* very strong or powerful, mighty (প্রবল শত্রু, প্রবল ঝড়) ; severe, intense, excessive (প্রবল দুঃখ, প্রবল তাপ) ; predominant (বাক্যই প্রবল). *fem.* **প্রবলা** । **প্রবল ঝড়** violent storm. **প্রবল দুঃখ** acute or intense or great sorrow. **প্রবল পশ্চিমা (বায়ু)** brave west winds. **~তা** *n.* great strength or power; severity; intensity; predominance. **~পরাক্রম, ~পরাক্রান্ত, ~প্রতাপ** *a.* extremely powerful or mighty, mightily influential. **প্রবল বারিপাত** heavy shower or downpour.

প্রবসন *n.* emigration.

প্রবসিত *a.* emigrated.

প্রবহ *n.* a current, a flow (as of air or a stream). **~ণ** *n.* flow or flowing; blow or blowing. **~শীল, ~মান** *a.* flowing or blowing. **~মানতা** *n.* flow or flowing movement; stream (সময়ের প্রবহমানতা).

প্রবাদ *n.* a proverb, an adage; hearsay (জনপ্রবাদ). **প্রবাদ আছে যে** there is a saying that, it is said that. **~বাক্য** *n.* a proverb.

প্রবাল *n.* coral; a young shoot, a sprout; a new tree-leaf. **~কীট** *n.* the polyp, polype. **~দ্বীপ** *n.* a coral island. **~প্রাচীর** *n.* a coral reef, a barrier reef.

প্রবাস *n.* a spell of staying abroad; a foreign land. **~ন** *n.* sending abroad; banishment; (inc.) emigration. **~নপাল** *n.* the protector of emigrants. **প্রবাসিত** *a.* sent abroad; banished; (inc.) emigrated. **প্রবাসী** *a.* & *n.* one who is living abroad. *fem.* **প্রবাসিনী** ।

প্রবাহ *n.* a stream, a current, a flow (as of a river or air); a series, a train (ঘটনাপ্রবাহ, চিন্তাপ্রবাহ) ; (fig.) continuous onward movement (জীবনপ্রবাহ). **প্রবাহিণী** *a.* flowing. □ *n.* a river, a stream. **প্রবাহিত** *a.* (of a river) flowing, streaming; (of air, wind etc.) blowing; (fig.) passing or continuously moving onward. *fem.* **প্রবাহিতা** । **প্রবাহিত হওয়া** *v.* to flow, to stream; to blow; (fig.) to pass, to move onward continuously (সময় বা জীবন প্রবাহিত হওয়া). **প্রবাহী** *a.* flowing. **প্রবাহী ঋণ** floating debt. **প্রবাহী পরিসম্পৎ** floating assets.

প্রবিধান *n.* regulation.

প্রবিষ্ট *a.* entered. *fem.* **প্রবিষ্টা**। **প্রবিষ্ট হওয়া** *v.* to enter.

প্রবীণ *a.* elderly; aged, old; wise, judicious; well-experienced; skilful; delighted or consoled ('দুঃখী দেখে দ্রবীণ প্রবীণ চিত হয়'). **প্রবীণা** *a. fem.* elderly or aged. □ *n.* an elderly or aged woman. **প্রবীণতা, প্রবীণত্ব** *n.* elderliness; agedness, oldness; wisdom, judiciousness; well-experiencedness; skilfulness.

প্রবুদ্ধ *a.* enlightened; awakened or activized (প্রবুদ্ধ ভারত) ; inspired with wisdom; very wise.

প্রবৃত্ত *a.* engaged in, occupied with; induced to; undertaken or commenced. **প্রবৃত্ত করা** *v.* to set (one) to; to induce. **প্রবৃত্ত হওয়া** *v.* to set about, to be engaged in; to commence. **প্রবৃত্তি** *n.* act or state of being engaged in or occupied with or initiated to, engagement, occupation, initiation; inclination, tendency; desire; propensity; taste, appetite (আহারের প্রবৃত্তি নেই). **প্রবৃত্তি মার্গ** *n.* worldly life (as a way to salvation).

প্রবৃদ্ধ *a.* very old; overgrown; expanded; (geom.) reflex (**প্রবৃদ্ধকোণ** = a reflex angle).

প্রবেশ *n.* entrance, entry; admission (কলেজে প্রবেশ) ; right or power or freedom of entrance; access. **প্রবেশ করা** *v.* to come or go in or into, to enter, to be admitted into. **প্রবেশ করানো** *v.* to cause to enter, to enter, to admit into; to usher; to drive or thrust into (দেহে তরবারি প্রবেশ করানো). **প্রবেশ নিষেধ** entrance prohibited; no entrance, no admission, no admittance, no entry. **প্রবেশক** *a.* entering. □ *n.* an enterer. **~দ্বার** *n.* a gate; an entrance. **প্রবেশন** *n.* entering, entrance; act of being admitted into, admission; act of causing to enter. **~পত্র** *n.* entry permit; admit card. **~পথ** *n.* a gateway; an entrance. **~মূল্য** *n.* entry fee or admission fee. **প্রবেশলাভ করা** *v.* to be able to enter; to be admitted into. **প্রবেশা** poet. form of **প্রবেশ করা**। **প্রবেশাধিকার** *n.* right or freedom of entrance or admission, entry; access. **প্রবেশানুমতি** *n.* permission to enter or be admitted into, admittance. **প্রবেশিকা** *a. fem.* entering. □ *n. fem.* a primary textbook (ব্যাকরণ-প্রবেশিকা) ; a ticket, a pass. **প্রবেশিকা পরীক্ষা** *n.* the entrance examination (also; the matriculation examination). **প্রবেশিত** *a.* caused to enter; admitted (into); ushered. **প্রবেশ্য** *a.* enterable; permeable (**প্রবেশ্য শিলা** = permeable rock).

প্রবেষ্টা *n.* an enterer.

প্রবোধ *n.* consolation, solace; knowledge, enlightenment; manifestation; awakening. **প্রবোধ দেওয়া** *v.* to console, to solace. **প্রবোধ পাওয়া** *v.* to get consolation. **প্রবোধ মানা** *v.* to yield to consolation; to be consoled; to be amenable to consolation. **প্রবোধ না মানা** *v.* to be disconsolate. **প্রবোধন** *n.* consoling; awakening; enlightening. **প্রবোধিত** *a.* consoled; enlightened; awakened.

প্রব্রজ্যা *n.* wandering asceticism. **প্রব্রজ্যা নেওয়া** *v.* to take to wandering asceticism. **প্রব্রাজক** same as **পরিব্রাজক**।

-প্রভ in *comp.* (used as a *sfx.*) glowing like (অনলপ্রভ) ; glowing or shining (সুপ্রভ) ; resembling in splendour or glory (দেবপ্রভ) ; like.

প্রভঞ্জন *n.* a storm; a violent gust of wind; wind.

প্রভব *n.* cause; source; origin; influence; (phys.) generative cause.

প্রভা *n.* glow, radiance; a ray; lustre, brilliance, splendour, brightness. **~কর** *n.* the sun. **~কীট** *n.* the glow-worm. **~বান** *a.* radiant, glowing, shining; luminous. *fem.* **~বতী**। **~ময়** *a.* radiant, lustrous, luminous, refulgent.

প্রভাত *n.* morning; daybreak. **প্রভাত হওয়া** *v.* to dawn. **এখন প্রভাত** it is morning. **~কাল** *n.* the morning-time, morning. **~ফেরি** *n.* singing awakening songs in procession through the streets of a town or village. **~রাগ** *n.* the morning glow. **প্রভাত হয়েছে** it is dawn. **প্রভাতী, প্রভাতি** *a.* of the morning. □ *n.* a morning song or glorification, a matin. **প্রভাতে মেঘডম্বরঃ** (fig.) great cry but little wool.

প্রভাব *n.* authority, power, dominance; influence. **প্রভাব বিস্তার করা** *v.* to extend one's influence; to exert one's influence (upon); to bear upon. **~শালী, ~সম্পন্ন** *a.* influential. *fem.* **~শালিনী, ~সম্পন্না**। **প্রভাবান্বিত** *a.* influenced; (rare) endowed with the power of influencing. **প্রভাবিত** *a.* influenced. **প্রভাবিত করা** *v.* to influence.

প্রভু *n.* a master, a lord; an overlord; an employer; a husband; an owner; a king; God; a superman; a holy or very reverend man. **প্রভুতা, প্রভুত্ব** *n.* mastery, authority; predominance; overlordship, supremacy; ownership; sovereignty, rule. **প্রভুত্ব করা** *v.* to lord it over; to rule, to govern. **~ব্যঞ্জক** *a.* imperious; authoritative; peremptory; domineering; bossy. **~পত্নী** *n. fem.* a mistress. **~পরায়ণ** same as **প্রভুভক্ত**। **~পাদ** *n.* a title of honour affixed to the names of the religious teachers of Vaishnavas (বৈষ্ণব). **~ভক্ত** *a.* devoted or faithful to one's master; loyal. **~ভক্তি** *n.* devotion or faithfulness to one's master; loyalty. **~শক্তি** *n.* governmental power or authority, ruling power; domination, dominance; authority; influence.

প্রভূত *a.* profuse, much, abundant, plentiful; (rare) grown or evolved.

প্রভৃতি *con.* et cetera, and the rest, et al, and so on.

প্রভেদ *n.* distinction, difference; discrimination. **প্রভেদ করা** *v.* to differentiate; to distinguish; to discriminate; to separate. **প্রভেদক** *a.* differential.

প্রমত্ত *a.* inebriate, drunk, intoxicated, tipsy; beside oneself; infatuated, besotted; reckless; frenzied. *fem.* **প্রমত্তা**। **~তা** *n.* inebriety, inebriation, drunkenness, intoxication, tipsiness; the state of being beside oneself; infatuation, besottedness; recklessness; frenzy.

প্রমথ *n.* one of the demi-gods attending on Shiva (শিব).

প্রমথন *n.* act of trampling or routing or subduing or killing.

প্রমথিত *a.* trampled; routed; subdued; killed.

প্রমথেশ *n.* the lord of Pramathas (প্রমথ) ; Shiva (শিব).

প্রমদা *n.* a charming woman; a woman.

প্রমা *n.* true or positive knowledge; truth; conviction.

প্রমাই corrup. of **পরমায়ু**।

প্রমাণ *n.* proof; evidence; testimony; witness; a precedent; authority; conviction. □ *a.* of the standard size (প্রমাণ শার্ট) ; standard প্রমাণ মাপ) ; (esp. in phys.) normal (প্রমাণ প্রেষ) ; equivalent to, resembling (পর্বতপ্রমাণ). **প্রমাণ করা** *v.* to prove; to demonstrate; to substantiate. **প্রমাণ দেওয়া** *v.* to give evidence or proof (of); to prove; to demonstrate; to testify. **প্রমাণ হওয়া** *v.* to be proved. **~ক** *n.* a voucher. **~গ্রন্থ** *n.* an authoritative book. **~পঞ্জি** *n.* a bibliography. **~পত্র** *n.* a document; a written warrant or affidavit; a voucher; a receipt; a certificate; testimonial. **~বাক্য** *n.* an authoritative saying; a citation of precedents. **~সই** *a.* of full measure; up to the mark. **~সাপেক্ষ** *a.* subject to proof. **~সিদ্ধ** *a.* established by evidences, proved. **প্রমাণাভাব** *n.* want of evidence or proof. **প্রমাণিত, প্রমাণীকৃত** *a.* proved; demonstrated; substantiated.

প্রমাতা *a.* & *n.* one who proves or demonstrates or substantiates or testifies.

প্রমাতামহ *n.* the grandfather or a granduncle of one's mother, a maternal greatgrandfather. *fem.* **প্রমাতামহী** the grandmother or a grandaunt of one's mother, a maternal great-grandmother.

প্রমাথী *a.* trampling; routing; subduing; killing. *fem.* **প্রমাথিনী**।

প্রমাদ *n.* inadvertence, carelessness; an error; confusion; oblivion; intoxication; frenzy; a calamity, a terrible danger or distress (প্রমাদে পড়া). **~বশত, ~বশে** *adv.* inadvertently; by mistake, through carelessness; erroneously. **~শূন্য** *a.* free from error.

প্রমারা *n.* primero.

প্রমিত *a.* sure; ascertained; proved; measured; (esp. in phys.) standardized; (as a *sfx.*) measuring (চারহাত প্রমিত). **প্রমিত করা** *v.* to ascertain; to prove; to standardize. **প্রমিত দ্রব** (phys.) a standard solution. **~করণ** *n.* (phys.) standardization. **প্রমিতি** *n.* measure, true or positive knowledge, truth; conviction; proof.

প্রমীলা *n.* drowsiness; a female character of the Mahabharata; (fig.) a spirited and domineering woman (প্রমীলাদের দেশে) ; (cp.) an Amazon.

প্রমুখ *a.* (used as a *sfx.*) headed by, beginning with (কালিদাস প্রমুখ কবিগণ).

প্রমুখাৎ *adv.* from the mouth of; by word of one's mouth; verbally from.

প্রমেয় *a.* measurable; mensurable; (alg.) commensurable; provable; ascertainable.

প্রমেহ *n.* gonorrhoea.

প্রমোদ *n.* joy, delight; merriment; hilarity; enjoyment; pleasure; recreation; an entertainment; luxury. **~ক** *a.* gladdening; pleasing; entertaining. **~কানন** *n.* a pleasure-garden. **~গৃহ** *n.* a pleasure-house, a recreation-room, a recreation-hall. **~ন** *n.* act of gladdening or pleasing or entertaining. □ *in comp.* (used as a *sfx.*) giving delight or pleasure to, entertaining (চিত্তপ্রমোদন). **~ভ্রমণ** *n.* a pleasure-trip; promenade. **প্রমোদভ্রমণ করা** *v.* to be on a pleasure-tirp; to promenade. **প্রমোদিত** *a.* delighted; pleased; recreated, entertained. **প্রমোদোদ্যান** *n.* a pleasure-garden.

প্রযত্ন *n.* repeated or thorough endeavour or effort, perseverance. **প্রযত্ন করা** *v.* to persevere. **~সহকারে** *adv.* perseveringly; thoroughly; carefully.

প্রযুক্ত *a.* employed; applied, used. □ *prep.* for the sake of, owing to, due to, caused by, actuated by (ভয়প্রযুক্ত). **প্রযুক্তি** *n.* employment; application; a technique. **প্রযুক্তিবিদ্যা** *n.* technology. **প্রযুক্তিবিদ্যাগত** *a.* technological.

প্রযুজ্যমান *a.* in the state of being applied.

প্রযোক্তা *n.* an employer; an applier; a performer.

প্রযোজক *a.* same as **প্রয়োজক** । □ *n.* a producer esp. of motion pictures; a film producer.

প্রযোজ্য *a.* applicable. **~তা** *n.* applicability.

প্রয়াণ *n.* departure; (fig.) death. **প্রয়াণ করা** *v.* to depart; (fig.) to die.

প্রয়াত *a.* departed; deceased, passed away, dead and gone.

প্রয়াস *n.* an effort, an endeavour; a hard effort; toil; a desire. **প্রয়াস করা** *v.* to endeavour; to try or endeavour hard; to toil; to desire. **প্রয়াস পাওয়া** *v.* to endeavour; to make a hard attempt, to make a sincere and earnest effort; to toil. **প্রয়াসী** *a.* endeavouring; toiling hard; desirous.

প্রয়োগ *n.* employment; application; use or usage; mention; a precedent, an example; an instance. **প্রয়োগ করা** *v.* to employ; to apply; to use. **~দোষ** *n.* misapplication, wrong or unjust use. **~বাদ** *n.* (phil.) pragmatism. **~বাদী** *a.* pragmatist. **~বিন্দু** *n.* (phys.) a point of application. **~শালা** *n.* a laboratory. **প্রায়োগিক** *a.* (phil.) empirical.

প্রয়োজক *a.* employing; applying; using; performing; introducing; inaugurating or founding. **প্রয়োজক ক্রিয়া** causative verb.

প্রয়োজন *n.* necessity, need; purpose, object, end; motive; cause, occasion; use. **প্রয়োজনাতিরিক্ত, প্রয়োজনাতীত** *a.* more than what is necessary; more than enough; superfluous; unnecessary, redundant. **প্রয়োজনানুরূপ** *a.* satisfying needs, just enough to meet (one's) requirement, adequate, sufficient. **প্রয়োজনীয়** *a.* necessary, needful; serviceable, useful. **প্রয়োজনীয়তা** *n.* necessity, need; serviceability, usefulness.

প্ররোচক *a.* (usu. dero.) inducing, instigating, persuading, inciting. □ *n.* an inducer, an instigator, (law) abettor, a persuader, an inciter, an agent provocateur.

প্ররোচন, প্ররোচনা *n.* (usu. dero.) inducement, instigation, abetment, persuasion, incitement. **প্ররোচনা দেওয়া** same as **প্ররোচিত করা** (see **প্ররোচিত**). **প্ররোচনাদায়ক** *a.* same as **প্ররোচক** (*a.*).

প্ররোচিত *a.* (usu. dero.) induced, instigated, persuaded, incited. **প্ররোচিত করা** *v.* to induce, to instigate, to persuade, to incite.

প্ররোহ *n.* a bud; a shoot, a sprout; a scion; (bot.) an offset.

প্রলপন *n.* raving; delirium; incoherent utterance.

প্রলপিত *a.* raved; uttered in delirium; incoherently uttered.

প্রলম্ব *n.* an aerial root or a branch of a tree; anything creeping or hanging. **প্রলম্বন** *n.* creeping; hanging, suspension; prolongation. **~বিন্দু** *n.* (phys.) a point of suspension. **প্রলম্বিত** *a.* hanging, suspended; pendent; prolonged; creeping. **প্রলম্বিত করা** *v.* to hang, to suspend; to prolong.

প্রলয়, প্রলয়কাণ্ড *n.* universal dissolution or annihilation; a complete or very extensive destruction or holocaust; (fig.) a terrible disturbance or affray. **প্রলয়কাল** *n.* the time of universal dissolution or annihilation. **প্রলয়ংকর** *a.* causing universal dissolution; causing a complete or very extensive destruction; (fig.) terribly disturbing. **প্রলয়নাচন, প্রলয়নৃত্য** *n.* the cataclysmal dance of Lord Siva as described in the Puranas. **প্রলয়পয়োধি** *n.* the ocean of universal cataclysm or deluge. **প্রলয়লীলা** *n.* same as **প্রলয়কাণ্ড**।

প্রলাপ *n.* raving; delirium; incoherent utterance. **প্রলাপ বকা** *v.* to rave; to utter delirium; to talk incoherently. **প্রলাপী** *a.* raving; delirious; incoherently talking. *fem.* **প্রলাপিনী**। **প্রলাপোক্তি** same as **প্রলাপ**।

প্রলিপ্ত *a.* coated or smeared (with); involved or implicated (in); engaged or employed (in).

প্রলুব্ধ *a.* greatly allured or tempted; extremely greedy. *fem.* **প্রলুব্ধা**। **~তা** *n.* the state of being greatly allured or tempted; extreme greed.

প্রলেপ *n.* a coating; an ointment; act of coating or smearing. **প্রলেপ দেওয়া** *v.* to apply a coating or an ointment (to); to coat or smear (with). **প্রলেপক** *a.* coating; smearing. **প্রলেপন** *n.* coating or smearing. **প্রলেপন করা** *v.* to coat; to smear.

প্রলোভ *n.* very strong greed.

প্রলোভন *n.* allurement, temptation, enticement; a tempting object. **প্রলোভন দেখানো** *v.* to bring an allurement (to); to entice, to try to allure or tempt.

প্রলোভিত *a.* allured, tempted, enticed. **প্রলোভিত করা** *v.* to allure, to tempt, to entice. **প্রলোভিত করে নিয়ে যাওয়া** *v.* to entice away.

প্রশংসক *n.* one who speaks highly of, a praiser, an admirer.

প্রশংসন *n.* act of praising, commendation, extolment, admiration. **প্রশংসনীয়** *a.* praiseworthy, commendable, laudable, admirable.

প্রশংসা *n.* praise, commendation extolment, laudation, admiration, eulogy, applause; fame. **প্রশংসা করা** *v.* to praise, to commend, to extol, to laud, to admire, to eulogize, to applaud. **~পত্র** *n.* a certificate of merit; a written address of honour or felicitation. **~বাক্য, ~বাদ** *n.* a compliment; a eulogy. **~ভাজন** *n.* an object of praise; a praiseworthy person. **~মূলক** *a.* commendatory, laudatory, eulogistic. **~র্হ** *a.* praiseworthy, commendable, laudable. **~সূচক** same as **প্রশংসামূলক**।

প্রশংসিত *a.* praised, extolled, admired, eulogized, applauded.

প্রশমন, প্রশম *n.* allayment, soothing; stopping, dissuasion; restraining or resisting; quelling; (phys.) neutralization; mitigation; pacification. **প্রশমন করা** *v.* to allay or alleviate, to soothe; to stop, to dissuade; to check, to restrain, to resist; to subdue, to quell; (phys.) to neutralize; to mitigate, to make less severe; to pacify. **প্রশমলবণ** *n.* (chiefly in chem.) neutral salt. **প্রশমিত** *a.* allayed, alleviated, soothed; stopped, dissuaded; checked, restrained, resisted; subdued, quelled; (phys.) neutralized; mitigated; pacified. **প্রশমিত করা** same as **প্রশমন করা**।

প্রশস্ত *a.* praiseworthy, commendable; best, excellent; most suitable, fittest (প্রশস্ত উপায়) ; auspicious (প্রশস্ত সময়) ; magnanimous, liberal (প্রশস্ত হৃদয়) ;

wide, broad (চারহাত পরিমাণ প্রশস্ত) ; spacious, roomy (প্রশস্ত কক্ষ). **~তা** *n.* praiseworthiness; excellence; suitability; fitness; auspiciousness; magnanimity, liberality; width, breadth; spacious.

প্রশস্তি *n.* praise; a short laudatory hymn : a eulogium, a panegyric.

প্রশস্য *a.* praiseworthy, commendable, laudable.

প্রশাখা *n.* a branchlet; an offshoot.

প্রশান্ত *a.* very calm or quiet or peaceful; tranquil; unperturbed; unruffled. **~চিত্ত** *a.* enjoying peace or tranquillity at heart, composed, sedate, unagitated. **~বদন** *a.* having a tranquil or calm face or appearance. **প্রশান্ত মহাসাগর** the Pacific Ocean, the Pacific. **~মূর্তি** *a.* having a tranquil or calm or composed appearance. **~হৃদয়** same as **প্রশান্তচিত্ত**। **প্রশান্তি** *n.* perfect calm or quiet or peace, tranquillity.

প্রশাসক *n.* administrator.

প্রশাসন *n.* administration. **প্রশাসনিক** *a.* administrative. **প্রশাসন-আধিকারিক** *n.* administrative officer. **প্রশাসনিক কৃত্য** administrative function. **প্রশাসন-কৃত্যক** *n.* administrative service.

প্রশিক্ষণ *n.* training. **~প্রাপ্ত** *a.* trained.

প্রশিষ্য *n.* a disciple's disciple; a pupil's pupil. *fem.* **প্রশিষ্যা**।

প্রশ্ন *n.* a question; a query; interrogation; inquiry; a point at issue; a problem (বাঁচার প্রশ্ন) ; a disputed point. **প্রশ্ন করা** *v.* to question; to ask; to inquire; to interrogate; to set questions (as for examinees). **~কর্তা** *n.* a questioner; an inquirer; an interrogator; one who sets questions (as for examinees); a papersetter. *fem.* **প্রশ্নকর্ত্রী**। **~পত্র** *n.* a set of questions for the examinees, a paper. **~বাণ** *n.* questions that pierce or hurt like shafts or darts or arrows or missiles, questions piercing as a shaft, embarrassing or piercing questions. **প্রশ্নবাণে জর্জরিত করা** to ask too many or volleys of troublesome questions, to heckle. **~বোধক** *a.* denoting or signifying a question. **~বোধক চিহ্ন** *n.* note or sign of interrogation. **~মালা** *n.* a set of questions; (loos.) an exercise (for students). **প্রশ্নোত্তর** *n.* a question and its answer; a catechism. **প্রশ্নোত্তরী** *n.* a catechism.

প্রশ্বাস *n.* inhalation.

প্রশ্রয় *n.* indulgence, latitude, pampering; over-affection.; (rare) politeness. **প্রশ্রয় দেওয়া** *v.* to give (one) indulgence or latitude, to indulge, to pamper; to treat with over-affection. **~দাতা** *n.* one who gives indulgence, an indulger. **~দান** *v.* act of giving indulgence, indulgence. **~প্রাপ্ত** *a.* indulged, pampered.

প্রসক্ত *a.* greatly inclined or attached to, enamoured of; greatly addicted to. **প্রসক্তি** *n.* great inclination for or attachment or addiction to.

প্রসঙ্গ *n.* a subject for or under discussion; a topic for discussion, narration (রামায়ণ-প্রসঙ্গ) ; context (প্রসঙ্গ বর্ণনা). **প্রসঙ্গ উল্লেখপূর্বক** with reference to the context. **~ক্রমে, প্রসঙ্গত** *adv.* in course of discussion, incidentally, by the by, by the way. **প্রসঙ্গ তোলা** *v.* to refer to. **প্রসঙ্গান্তর** *n.* another topic, a different topic.

প্রসন্ন *a.* satisfied, pleased; delighted, glad, happy; gracious, propitious, favourable; clear, limpid, transparent (প্রসন্নসলিলা) ; calm and happy, complacent, bright (প্রসন্ন বদন). *fem.* **প্রসন্না**। **~তা** *n.* satisfied or pleased state; complacence, complacency; delightedness, gladness, happiness; graciousness, propitiousness, favourableness; clarity, limpidity, transparence; brightness. **প্রসন্ন হওয়া** *v.* to be pleased, to smile upon.

প্রসব *n.* act of bringing forth (a child or young), parturition, delivery; childbirth; production; creation; birth. **প্রসব করা** *v.* to bring forth; to give birth; (often facet.) to produce. **প্রসব করানো** *v.* to deliver of a child or young. **~দ্বার** *n.* the passage of childbirth; the valva. **প্রসব হওয়া** *v.* to be delivered of a child or young. **~বেদনা** *n.* lobour-pain, travail. **প্রসব বেদনা ওঠা** *v.* to be in travail, to be in labour. **প্রসবিতা, প্রসবী** *a.* giving birth to; producing □ *n.* a father, a progenitor; a producer. **প্রসবিত্রী, প্রসবিনী** *a. fem.* bringing forth; producing. □ *n. fem.* a mother, a progenitress; a (female) producer.

প্রসর *n.* act of going, movement; speed; expanse, extent, range, **উষ্ণতার প্রসর** (geog.) the range of temperature. **প্রসরণ** *n.* strolling; encompassment of enemy forces; expansion, extension; expanse, extent, range.

প্রসাদ *n.* grace, favour, propitiousness (ঈশ্বরপ্রসাদ) ; food-offering to a deity (this is taken by devotees after the sacrifice) ; remains of food taken by a superior or venerable person (গুরুর প্রসাদ) ; complacency; (of lit. composition) lucidity, clarity, perspicuity (also **প্রসাদগুণ). প্রসাদ পাওয়া** *v.* to enjoy the grace of; to partake of the food offered to a deity or of the remains of food taken by a superior person. **প্রসাদ নেওয়া** *v.* to partake of the food offered to a deity or of the remains of food taken by a superior person. **প্রসাদন** *n.* act of pleasing, propitiation. **~প্রার্থী** *a. & n.* one who asks for or seeks a favour; one desirous of partaking of the food offered to a deity or of the remains of food taken by a superior person. *fem.* **~প্রার্থিনী। প্রসাদাৎ** *adv.* through the grace or favour of. **প্রসাদিত** propitiated. **প্রসাদী** *a.* (of a food etc.) offered to a deity or partaken of by a superior person.

প্রসাধক *a. &n.* one who dresses or does another's toilet; one who embellishes or decorates, a decorator.

প্রসাধন *n.* dressing, toilet, toilette; embellishment, decoration. **প্রসাধন করা** *v.* to dress (usu. oneself); to make (one's) toilet ; to embellish; to decorate. **প্রসাধনী** *n.* a comb; a toilet article, toiletry, a cosmetic.

প্রসাধিকা *fem.* of **প্রসাধক।**

প্রসাধিত *a.* dressed; toileted; embellished; decorated.

প্রসার *n.* width; expanse; extent; expansion (বাণিজ্যের প্রসার) ; spread (শিক্ষার প্রসার). **প্রসারণ** *n.* act of stretching (out); extension; expansion; spreading; spread; (phys.) dilatation, dilation. **প্রসারণ করা** *v.* to stretch (out); to extend; to expand; to spread; (phys.) to dilate. **প্রসারাঙ্ক** *n.* (phys.) the co-efficient of expansion or dilation. **প্রসারিত** *a.* stretched (out); extended; expanded; spread (out). **প্রসারী** *a.* extending; expanding; expansive; extensive; wide. **সুদূর-প্রসারী** *a.* far-reaching, widely extended, far-flung (সুদূরপ্রসারী সাম্রাজ্য).

প্রসার্য *a.* stretchy; extensible; expansible. **~মাণ** *a.* in the process of being stretched (out) or expanded.

প্রসিদ্ধ *a.* famous, renowned, celebrated, well-known, reputed, (dero.) notorious. *fem.* **প্রসিদ্ধা। প্রসিদ্ধি** *n.* fame, renown, celebrity, reputation.

প্রসীদ *v.* be pleased (প্রসীদ হে দেবী).

প্রসুপ্ত *a.* soundly sleeping. **প্রসুপ্ত থাকা** *v.* to sleep soundly, to be fast asleep. **প্রসুপ্তি** *n.* sound sleep.

প্রসূ *n.* (chiefly used as a *sfx.* and in an adjectival sense) mother, progenitress. □ *a.* producing (স্বর্ণপ্রসূ = auriferous).

প্রসূত *a.* produced (of); resulted (from), evolved (out of); born (of); brought forth (by), begotten (by). **প্রসূতা, প্রসূতি** *n. fem.* a mother, progenitress; a woman recently delivered of a child; a (female) producer; (loos.) a woman in travail or a parturient woman. **প্রসূতিতন্ত্র** *n.* midwifery. **প্রসূতি সদন** *n.* maternity home; a maternity hospital.

প্রসূন *n.* a flower; a fruit; a bud, a blossom.

প্রসৃত *a.* emerged; widened, expanded, extended. **প্রসৃত হওয়া** *v.* to emerge (from); to widen. **প্রসৃতি** *n.* expansion, extension.

প্রস্ত *n.* a set (এক প্রস্ত বাসন) ; a wad (এক প্রস্ত নোট) ; a suite (এক প্রস্ত পোশাক) ; a spell (এক প্রস্ত ধমক)।

প্রস্তর *n.* stone; rock; pebble; fossil; a jewel. **~তুল্য** *a.* stone-like, stony; (fig.) very hard, motionless, unfeeling. **~নির্মিত** *a.* made of stone, stony. **~ফলক** *n.* a stone slab. **~ময়** *a.* stony, rocky; made of stone. **~মূর্তি** *n.* a stone statue.

~মূর্তিবৎ *a.* statuesque; (fig.) motionless or unperturbed. ~যুগ *n.* the Stone Age. প্রস্তরীভূত *a.* petrified; fossilized.

প্রস্তাব *n.* context; a proposal; a subject for or under discussion, a topic; a discourse; a motion; (of a book) a chapter, a section. **প্রস্তাব করা** *v.* to propose; to put up a proposal; to move a motion; to name (as a candidate for election). **প্রস্তাব তোলা** *v.* to raise a topic; to move a proposal or motion; to propose. **প্রস্তাবক** *n.* a proposer; a mover (of a motion). **প্রস্তাবনা** *n.* a proposal; commencement; (of a drama etc.) a prologue. **প্রস্তাবিত** *n.* proposed; raised or moved (as a topic); under discussion.

প্রস্তার same as **প্রসার**।

প্রস্তুত *a.* made; manufactured, formed; prepared, ready. **প্রস্তুত করা** *v.* to make, to manufacture, to form; to prepare, to make ready. **প্রস্তুত হওয়া** *v.* to be made or manufactured or formed; to get ready. **প্রস্তুতি** *n.* making; manufacture, formation; preparation, readiness.

প্রস্থ[1] var. of **প্রস্ত**।

প্রস্থ[2] *n.* width, breadth; expanse, extent; level ground, a plain (ইন্দ্রপ্রস্থ) ; a tableland, a plateau. **~চ্ছেদ** *n.* (math.) a cross-section.

প্রস্থান *n.* act of going off or setting out, departure; act of going out; (in drama) exit. **প্রস্থান করা** *v.* to go off; to set out; to depart; to go out. **প্রস্থানোদ্যত** *a.* on the point of departing or going out, ready to go. **প্রস্থানোদ্যোগ** *n.* preparation for departure.

প্রস্থিত *a.* gone off; set out; departed; gone out.

প্রস্ফুট, প্রস্ফুটিত *a.* full-blown, in (full) bloom; thoroughly manifested or revealed or unfolded. *fem.* **প্রস্ফুটিতা**। **প্রস্ফুটন** *n.* act of blooming fully; full bloom; thorough manifestation or revelation.

প্রস্ফুরণ *n.* slight vibration or tremor; phosphorescence; effervescence. **~শীল** *a.* slightly vibrating or trembling; phosphorescent; effervescent. **প্রস্ফুরিত** *a.* slightly vibrated or trembled; phosphoresced; effervesced. **প্রস্ফুরিত হওয়া** *v.* to vibrate or tremble slightly; to phosphoresce; to effervesce.

প্রস্বাপন *a.* soporific, opiate.

প্রস্রব *n.* an oozing.

প্রস্রবণ *n.* a fountain, a spring; oozing. **অন্তঃপ্রস্রবণ** *n.* (geog.) an underground spring. **উপরিপ্রস্রবণ** *n.* (geog.) a surface spring. **উষ্ণপ্রস্রবণ** *n.* a hot spring, a geyser. **ধাতব প্রস্রবণ** (geog.) a mineral spring. **সবিরাম প্রস্রবণ** (geog.) an intermittent spring.

প্রস্রাব *n.* urine; urination. **প্রস্রাব করা** *v.* to pass urine or water, to make water, to urinate; (coll.) to pee. **প্রস্রাবের পীড়া** *a* urinary disease or trouble.

প্রস্রুত *a.* oozed or trickled or dripped (from). **প্রস্রুত হওয়া** *v.* to ooze or trickle or drip (from).

প্রহত *a.* hurt; wounded; beaten, struck (as a drum).

প্রহর *n.* a measure of time equal to three hours. **প্রহর গোনা** (fig.) to pass time in idleness, to laze; to wait in anxiety or patiently; to bide one's time. **প্রহরার্ধ** *n.* time equal to one and half hours.

প্রহরণ *n.* a weapon (usu. one wielded by the hand, that is, not a missile); beating or striking.

প্রহরা *n.* watching or guarding; a watch, a watchman, a watcher, a sentinel, a sentry, a guard, a guardsman. **প্রহরা দেওয়া** *v.* to watch, to guard, to sentinel. **~ধীন** *a.* one who is under watch; guarded, watched. **~রত** *a.* engaged in watching or guarding or keeping watch.

প্রহরী *n.* a guard, a watchman, a watcher, a guardsman.

প্রহর্তা *n.* a person who beats or strikes.

প্রহসন *n.* a farce; a joke, a banter.

প্রহার *n.* a beating or striking; a blow, a stroke; (dial.) trouble or punishment. **প্রহার করা** *v.* to beat; to strike. **প্রহার দেওয়া** *v.* to give one a thrashing or licking. **~ক, ~কর্তা** *a.* & *n.* one who beats or strikes. *fem.* **~কর্ত্রী**।

প্রহৃত *a.* beaten, smitten; struck.

প্রহৃষ্ট *a.* very much delighted, very glad or happy. **~চিত্ত** *a.* very glad or happy at heart.

প্রহেলিকা *n.* a riddle, an enigma, a puzzle, a mystery. **~ময়** *a.* enigmatic, riddling, puzzling, mysterious.

প্রহ্লাদ *n.* (myth.) an Asura (অসুর) prince who was very much devoted to Vishnu (বিষ্ণু). **দৈত্যকুলে প্রহ্লাদ** (fig.) a saint amongst infidels.

প্রাংশু *a.* tall; high, lofty (প্রাংশু বৃক্ষ) ; hefty (প্রাংশুদেহ) ; long (প্রাংশুভুজ).

প্রাক্ *pfx.* denoting : prior, pre, eastern. **~কলন** *n.* an estimate. **~কলনিক** *n.* an estimator.

প্রাকাম্য *n.* (ascetical) power of moving or enjoying at will.

প্রাকার *n.* a wall; a bulwark; a rampart; a parapet. **~বেষ্টিত** *a.* surrounded by a wall.

প্রাকৃত *a.* natural, physical, unrefined, pertaining to the populace, (cp.) plebeian; traditional; commonplace, usual, general; base, mean; vulgar. □ *n.* the Prakrit language (usu. **প্রাকৃতভাষা**).

প্রাকৃতিক *a.* natural; physical; inorganic. **প্রাকৃতিক দৃশ্য** a natural scenery. **প্রাকৃতিক নিয়ম** a law of nature, a physical law. **প্রাকৃতিক নির্বাচন** (sc.) natural selection. **প্রাকৃতিক বিজ্ঞান** natural science; physical science; physics. **প্রাকৃতিক বিপর্যয়** natural calamity. **প্রাকৃতিক ভূগোল** physical geography. **প্রাকৃতিক মানচিত্র** a physical map.

প্রাক্কাল *n.* previous or former or preceding time; (pop.) immediately preceding time; eve. **প্রাক্কালিক, প্রাক্কালীন** *a.* former, previous. **প্রাক্কালে** *adv.* before; (pop.) on the eve of.

প্রাক্তন *a.* previous; former; (rare) of a previous birth, earned or acquired or done in a previous birth. □ *n.* (rare) destiny, fate; consequence of an act done in a previous birth (এ দুঃখ তার প্রাক্তন).

প্রাখর্য same as **প্রখরতা** (see **প্রখর**).

প্রাগ্জ্যোতিষ *n.* the ancient name of Kamrup or its inhabitants.

প্রাগভাব *n.* (phil.) non-existence of an object prior to its being brought into existence.

প্রাগল্‌ভ্য *n.* same as **প্রগল্‌ভতা** (see **প্রগল্‌ভ**), and shamelessness of women in love-affairs.

প্রাগাধুনিক *a.* pre-modern.

প্রাগুক্ত *a.* aforesaid; aforementioned.

প্রাগৈতিহাসিক *a.* pre-historic.

প্রাগ্রসর *a.* going ahead; prospering, developing; forerunner.

প্রাঙ্গণ *n.* a courtyard, a compound.

প্রাঙ্মুখ *a.* facing eastwards.

প্রাচী *n.* the east; the eastern hemisphere; the eastern world, the Orient.

প্রাচীন *a.* old; ancient; antique; aged; out-of-date; old-fashioned, antiquated. *fem.* **প্রাচীনা** I **প্রাচীনতা, প্রাচীনত্ব** *n.* oldness; ancientness; antiqueness; agedness; old-fashionedness, antiquatedness.

প্রাচীর *n.* a wall; a rampart; a parapet. **~চিত্র** *n.* wallpainting, a drawing on the wall. **~পত্র** *n.* a wallpaper, a wall magazine. **~বেষ্টিত** *a.* enclosed with a wall, walled (প্রাচীরবেষ্টিত নগর).

প্রাচুর্য *n.* plenty, abundance; affluence, milk and honey; profusion; amplitude; numerousness; sufficiency.

প্রাচ্য *a.* eastern, oriental. □ *n.* same as **প্রাচী** I **~দেশ** *n.* an oriental or eastern country.

প্রাজন *n.* a truncheon for driving cattle.

প্রাজাপত্য *n.* the usual Hindu form of marriage. □ *a.* relating to Prajapati (প্রজাপতি) the creator or protector of living beings.

প্রাজ্ঞ *a.* learned; wise, prudent. *fem.* **প্রাজ্ঞা** I **~তা** *n.* learning, wisdom; prudence.

প্রাঞ্জল *a.* easily understood, lucid, perspicuous; precise; clear, transparent. **~তা** *n.* lucidity, perspicuity, precision, preciseness; clarity, clearness, transparence.

প্রাণ *n.* life; the first of the five vital airs (namely, প্রাণ অপান সমান উদান and ব্যান) or these five airs collectively; life-breath; breath; heart, earnest desire ('প্রাণ চায় চক্ষু না চায়') ; vitality, vigour, vivacity (কাজে প্রাণ নেই) ; (in endearment) an extremely beloved person. **প্রাণ ওষ্ঠাগত হওয়া** *v.* (rare) to feel like dying; (fig. & pop.) to be extremely harassed or troubled or irritated. **প্রাণ খোলা** *v.* to open one's heart, to speak out one's heart. **প্রাণ থাকা** *v.* to remain alive. **প্রাণ দেওয়া** same as **প্রাণদান করা**। **প্রাণ নেওয়া** *v.* to kill; to torture almost to the point of killing. **প্রাণ পাওয়া** same as **প্রাণলাভ করা**। **প্রাণ বাঁচা** same as **প্রাণরক্ষা হওয়া**। **প্রাণ বাঁচানো** same as **প্রাণরক্ষা করা**। **প্রাণ বার করা** *v.* to make one out of breath, to exasperate beyond endurance. **প্রাণ বার হওয়া, প্রাণ যাওয়া** *v.* to breathe one's last; to become out of breath; to be exasperated. **প্রাণ নেওয়া** *v.* to take one's life; to kill. **প্রাণ হারানো** *v.* to lose one's life, to die; to be killed. **~কৃষ্ণ** *n.* Krishna (কৃষ্ণ) who is regarded by a devotee or a lover as dear as life; (fig.) a favourite or lover as dear as one's life. **~খোলা** *a.* open-hearted, frank, candid, hearty. **~গত** *a.* lying in one's heart of hearts; inmost; sincere. **~গতিক** *a.* concerning one's life or living; bodily, physical. **~ঘাতী** *a.* life-killing; murderous; deadly, fatal. **~চঞ্চল** *a.* lively, sprightly, vivacious. **~চাঞ্চল্য** *n.* liveliness, vivaciousness, sprightliness. **~ত্যাগ** *n.* death. **প্রাণত্যাগ করা** *v.* to die. **~দ** *a.* life-giving; animating, invigorating; resuscitant; life-saving. **~দণ্ড** *n.* death sentence, a lifer, capital punishment. **প্রাণদণ্ড দেওয়া** *v.* to sentence (one) to death, to award capital punishment. **প্রাণদা** *fem.* of **~দ**। **~দাতা** *n.* a giver of life; an animator, an invigorator; a resuscitant, a resuscitator. *fem.* **প্রাণদাত্রী**। **~দান** *n.* infusion of life (into); animation; invigoration; resuscitation; saving of life. **~দান করা** *v.* to infuse life (into); to give life (to); to animate, to invigorate; to give back one's life, to resuscitate; to save one's life; to sacrifice one's life, to give up one's life. **~দায়ক** same as **প্রাণদ**। *fem.* **প্রাণদায়িকা**। **~ধারণ** *n.* act of living; sustenance of oneself. **প্রাণধারণ করা** *v.* to live; to sustain oneself. **~নাথ** same as **প্রাণেশ্বর**। **~নাশ** same as **প্রাণবধ**। **~নাশক** same as **প্রাণঘাতী**। **~পণ** *n.* resolve of doing something even at the cost of one's life. **~পণে** *adv.* staking one's life, even at the cost of one's life. **~পতি** same as **প্রাণেশ্বর**। **~পাখি** *n.* the bird of life imprisoned in the cage of the body; life; life-breath. **প্রাণপাত করা** *v.* to wreck or lay down or sacrifice one's life; to strain all one's energies. **~পূর্ণ** same as **প্রাণবন্ত**। **~প্রতিম** *a.* resembling life; as dear as life. **~প্রতিমা** *n.* the idol of one's life; a woman or girl as dear as one's life. **~প্রতিষ্ঠা** *n.* the rite of investing an idol with life, (cp.) consecration; infusion of life (into), activization (as of an organization). **প্রাণ প্রতিষ্ঠা করা** *v.* (eccl.) to invest (an idol) with life, to consecrate; to infuse life into (an organization); to activize. **~প্রদ** same as **প্রাণদ**। **~প্রিয়** *a.* as dear as life; an object of deep affection; dearer than life. **~বঁধু** *n.* a lover as dear as one's life, a sweetheart. **~বধ** *n.* killing or slaying, manslaughter. **প্রাণবধ করা** *v.* to kill, to slay, to take a life. **~বন্ত** *a.* living, alive; animate; lively; vivacious. sprightly; cordial, genial; volatile, active. **~বন্ততা** *n.* the state of being alive or living; animation; liveliness, vivacity, sprightliness; cordiality, geniality, volatility, fullness of activity. **~বল্লভ** same as **প্রাণেশ্বর**। **~বান** same as **প্রাণচঞ্চল**। **~বায়ু** *n.* life-breath; the first of the five vital airs (namely প্রাণ, অপান, সমান, উদান and ব্যান) or all these airs collectively. **প্রাণবায়ু বার হওয়া** *v.* to breathe one's last, to die. **~বিয়োগ** *n.* death. **প্রাণবিয়োগ হওয়া** *v.* to die. **~বিসর্জন** *n.* sacrifice of one's life. **প্রাণবিসর্জন দেওয়া** *v.* to sacrifice one's life. **~ভয়** *n.* fear of losing one's life, fear of life. **~ভয়ে** *adv.* for fear of life. **~ময়** *a.* same as **প্রাণবন্ত,** and also—the sole object of one's life. *fem.* **প্রাণময়ী**। **প্রাণময় কোষ** (Hindu phil.) the life-cell of the body. **প্রাণরক্ষা করা** *v.* to save one's life; to sustain. **প্রাণরক্ষা হওয়া** *v.* to be saved from death; to be saved; to sustain oneself. **~লাভ** *n.* act of coming or coming back to life. **প্রাণলাভ করা** *v.* to come or come back to life. **~শূন্য** *a.* lifeless; inanimate; lacking in liveliness or vivacity or sprightliness, dull, lacking in cordiality or geniality, cold, inactive, lethargic;

callous. ~সংকট same as প্রাণসংশয়। ~সংশয় *n.* possibility of losing one's life, risk or hazard or peril of one's life. ~সংহার same as প্রাণবধ। ~সখা *n.* a bosom friend. ~সঞ্চার same as প্রাণদান। ~সম *a.* equal to life. ~হন্তা *n.* a slayer, a killer; a murderer (*fem.* a murderess). *fem.* ~হন্ত্রী। ~হর, ~হারক, ~হারী same as প্রাণঘাতী। *fem.* ~হরা, ~হারিকা, ~হারিণী। ~হীন same as প্রাণশূন্য। প্রাণাত্যয় *n.* destruction or loss of life, death; time of death or of loss of life. প্রাণাধিক *a.* dearer than one's life. *fem.* প্রাণাধিকা। প্রাণান্ত *n.* termination of life, death. প্রাণান্তকর *a.* causing death or termination of life; (fig.) extremely toilsome or causing extreme suffering. প্রাণান্ত পরিচ্ছেদ *n.* that which ends in or extends up to death; (fig.) extreme toil or suffering . প্রাণান্ত-পরিশ্রম *n.* extremely toilsome work, hard toil (likely to cost a person his life.) প্রাণেশ, প্রাণেশ্বর *n.* the lord of one's life; a husband; a lover. প্রাণেশ্বরী *n. fem.* the mistress of one's life; a wife; a ladylove, a sweetheart. প্রাণোৎসর্গ *n.* sacrifice of one's life. প্রাণোৎসর্গ করা *v.* to sacrifice one's life.

প্রাণায়াম *n.* breath-control as prescribed in the yoga system.

প্রাণী *n.* a living being, a creature, an animal; a human being, a person (বাড়িতে দুটি মাত্র প্রাণী). প্রাণীকুল *n.* the animal kingdom; fauna. প্রাণীজগৎ *n.* the animal kingdom, the animal world. প্রাণীতত্ত্ব, প্রাণীবিজ্ঞান, প্রাণীবিদ্যা *n.* zoology. প্রাণীতত্ত্বজ্ঞ, প্রাণীবিজ্ঞানী, প্রাণীবিদ্যাবিদ *n.* a zoologist. প্রাণীতত্ত্বীয় *a.* zoological. প্রাণীহিংসা *n.* killing of animals; (rare) cruelty to animals.

প্রাত, প্রাতঃ *n.* morning; the early morning; (fig.) inception, beginning. প্রাতঃকর্ম same as প্রাতঃকৃত্য। প্রাতঃকাল *n.* morning; the early morning. প্রাতঃকালীন *a.* of or for or in the morning, morning. প্রাতঃকালীন সংগীত a morning song, a matin. প্রাতঃকৃত্য, প্রাতঃক্রিয়া *n.* the routine morning duties of evacuation of bowels, personal washing, religious prayer etc. প্রাতঃনমস্কার *n.* the morning salutation, good morning. প্রাতঃপ্রণাম *n.* the morning obeisance done by touching the feet of a respected person. প্রাতঃভ্রমণ, প্রাতর্ভ্রমণ *n.* morning walk. প্রাতঃসন্ধ্যা *n.* the morning meditation or devotion; morning prayers. প্রাতঃসমীর, প্রাতঃসমীরণ *n.* the morning breeze. প্রাতঃস্নান *n.* bath at sunrise; the morning ablution or bath. প্রাতঃস্মরণীয় *a.* (lit.) one whose name should be recalled or uttered on waking in the morning; (fig.) of immortal fame, ever memorable.

প্রাতরাশ, প্রাতর্ভোজন *n.* the first meal of the day, the morning meal, breakfast. প্রাতর্ভোজন করা *v.* to take the morning meal or the first meal of the day, to breakfast.

প্রাতর্বাক্য *n.* the first words uttered on waking in the morning.

প্রাতর্ভোজন see প্রাতরাশ।

প্রাতিকূল্য *n.* same as প্রতিকূলতা (see প্রতিকূল)।

প্রাতিজনিক *a.* personal. প্রাতিজনিক খতিয়ান personal ledger account.

প্রাতিপদিক *n.* (gr.) an uninflected noun or adjective; a root noun or root adjective. □*a.* (gr.) uninflected.

প্রাতিভাসিক *a.* apparent but not real or actual, seemingly real.

প্রাতিষ্ঠানিক *a.* institutional; organizational; of or about the establishment.

প্রাতিস্বিক *a.* individual; characteristic; personal.

প্রাত্যহিক *a.* daily, diurnal. *fem.* প্রাত্যহিকী।

প্রাথমিক *a.* relating to inception or beginning, initial; early, primitive; primary. প্রাথমিক পুস্তক a primer. প্রাথমিক বিদ্যালয় a primary school. প্রাথমিক শিক্ষা primary education.

প্রাদি *n.* (in Sanskrit gr.) প্র পরা অপ সম নি অব অনু নির্ দুর্ বি অভি অধি সু উৎ পরি প্রতি অপি অতি উপ আ : these twenty prefixes collectively. প্রাদিসমাস *n.* (gr.) a system of forming compound words by adding any one of the aforesaid prefixes.

প্রাদুর্ভাব *n.* appearance; manifestation; serious or terrible outbreak (দুর্ভিক্ষের প্রাদুর্ভাব) ; extensive and terrible prevalence or excess (রোগের বা মশার

প্রাদুর্ভাব) ; (dero.) act of coming into power or importance.

প্রাদুর্ভূত *a.* manifested; seriously or terribly broken out; extensively and terribly prevalent, existing in a large number. **প্রাদুর্ভূত হওয়া** *v.* to appear; to become manifest; to break out seriously or terribly and usu. extensively (রোগ প্রাদুর্ভূত হওয়া).

প্রাদেশিক *a.* provincial (প্রাদেশিক স্বায়ত্তশাসন). **প্রাদেশিকতা** *n.* provincialism; parochialism; insularity.

প্রাধান্য *n.* primeness; supremacy, prominence, pre-eminence, predominance, **প্রাধান্য স্থাপন** বা **বিস্তার করা** *v.* to establish sway; to predominate, to domineer, to lord it over. **প্রাধান্য পাওয়া** *v.* to gain supremacy or prominence; to become predominant.

প্রাধিকার *n.* authority. **প্রাধিকারিক** *n.* a special officer.

প্রাধিকৃত *a.* authorized.

প্রান্ত *n.* an extremity, an end; a tip; a border, a margin; a brim; a rim; the outskirts (নগরপ্রান্ত). **~গ্রাবরেখা** *v.* (geog.) the terminal moraine. **~বর্তী, ~স্থ, ~স্থিত** *a.* lying or situated in or on or at the border; terminal; marginal; bordering. **~স্পর্শী** *a.* (bot.) valvate. **প্রান্তিক, প্রান্তীয়** *a.* lying or situated in or on or at the border; terminal; (esp. in bot.) marginal; bordering; (arith.) extreme. **প্রান্তিক উপযোগিতা** marginal utility. **বহুপ্রান্তীয়** *a.* parietal. **প্রান্ত্য** *a.* (esp. in phys.) terminal; marginal.

প্রান্তগ্রাবরেখা, প্রান্তবর্তী see **প্রান্ত**।

প্রান্তর *n.* a prairie, a wilderness, a waste, a vast expanse of arid land; a large tract of grass-land.

প্রান্তস্থ, প্রান্তস্থিত, প্রান্তস্পর্শী, প্রান্তিক, প্রান্তীয়, প্রান্ত্য see **প্রান্ত**।

প্রাপক *n.* a delivery-man; a person who receives (something), a recipient.

প্রাপণ *n.* giving delivery or receiving. **প্রাপণীয়** *a.* obtainable; to be or fit to be obtained.

প্রাপিত *a.* received or delivered through some agency.

প্রাপ্ত *a.* obtained, got; received; found; acquired, gained, attained, learnt (শিক্ষাপ্রাপ্ত) ; informed of (সংবাদপ্রাপ্ত). **প্রাপ্ত হওয়া** *v.* to obtain, to get; to receive, to be given; to find, to come across; to acquire, to gain; to attain; to learn; to be informed. **~কাল** *a.* on the point of death, dying; having attained the fullness of age. **~বয়স্ক** *a.* one who has attained majority, of age, adult, grown-up. **~ব্য** *a.* same as **প্রাপ্য** (*a.*). **~যৌবন** *a.* adult. *fem.* **~যৌবনা**।

প্রাপ্তি *n.* obtaining or getting; receipt; act of finding; acquirement, acquisition, gaining, attainment; act of learning; income, earnings; (often facet.) profit. **~যোগ** *n.* (hum.) run of luck, unexpected gain or an occasion for some gain. **~যোগ্য** *a.* same as **প্রাপ্য** (*a.*) **~সংবাদ** *n.* news of receipt. **~স্থান** *n.* a place from which something may be had. **~স্বীকার** *n.* acknowledgement of receipt.

প্রাপ্য *a.* obtainable; receivable; acquirable, attainable; to be paid, due (প্রাপ্য অর্থ). □ *n.* due.

প্রাবন্ধিক *n.* an essayist.

প্রাবরণ *n.* a thin and large scarf; a covering, a cover.

প্রাবল্য *n.* same as **প্রবলতা** (see **প্রবল**).

প্রাবীণ্য *n.* same as **প্রবীণতা** (see **প্রবীণ**).

প্রাবৃট, প্রাবৃষা *n.* the rainy season, the rains. **প্রাবৃষিক, প্রাবৃষ্য** *a.* of the rainy season.

প্রাবেশিক *a.* pertaining to entrance or admission. **প্রাবেশিক পরীক্ষা** an admission test.

প্রাভাতিক *a.* of the morning.

প্রামাণিক *a.* authoritative, authentic. **~তা** *n.* authoritativeness, authenticity.

প্রামাণ্য *n.* authoritativeness, authenticity. □ *a.* same as **প্রামাণিক**।

প্রায়¹ *adv.* usually (এমনই তো প্রায় ঘটে) ; frequently, every now and then, often (সে প্রায় এখানে আসে).

প্রায়² *a.* (chiefly used in comp. as a *sfx.*) resembling, like (গতপ্রায়) ; nearing, about, nearly, a little less than (প্রায় প্রতিদিন, প্রায় লাখ টাকা).

প্রায়³ *n.* death by starvation, desire to die of starvation or fasting (প্রায়োপবেশন) ; overmuchness.

প্রায়শ, (ori.) **প্রায়শঃ** *adv.* usually; often, frequently.

প্রায়শ্চিত্ত, (coll. corrup.) **প্রায়শ্চিত্তি** *n.* expiation, atonement, penance; the sacrament of penance. **প্রায়শ্চিত্ত করা** *v.* to expiate, to atone (for), to do penance. **প্রায়শ্চিত্তমূলক** *a.* expiatory.

প্রাযুক্তিক *n.* a technologist.

প্রায়োগজ *a.* same as **প্রায়োগিক**।

প্রায়োগিক *a.* (phil.) pragmatic, empirical; technical.

প্রায়োপবিষ্ট *a.* seated fasting till death; (loos.) on hunger strike.

প্রারব্ধ *a.* commenced, started; taken on hand, undertaken (প্রারব্ধ কর্ম). □ *n.* destiny, fate; the consequences of activities of a previous birth, which have begun to take effect ('ভোগদ্বারা প্রারব্ধের ক্ষয়')।

প্রারম্ভ *n.* beginning, commencement, outset, inception. **প্রারম্ভিক** *a.* of the beginning, initial.

প্রার্থনা, প্রার্থন *n.* a prayer (secular or religious); act of asking for, solicitaion ; supplication; application. **প্রার্থনা করা** *v.* to pray; to say one's prayer; to ask for, to solicit; to supplicate; to apply (for); to petition. **প্রার্থনা পূর্ণ করা** to grant a prayer.

প্রার্থনীয়, প্রার্থয়িতব্য *a.* worth praying or asking or applying for.

প্রার্থয়িতা same as **প্রার্থী**। *fem.* **প্রার্থয়িত্রী**।

প্রার্থিত *a.* prayed for, asked for; applied for; desired.

প্রার্থিনী *fem.* of **প্রার্থী**।

প্রার্থী *a.* praying for, asking for; applying for; desiring. □ *n.* one who prays for or asks for; an applicant; a candidate; a desirer.

প্রাশন *n.* act of eating; initiation to eating (অন্নপ্রাশন).

প্রাস *n.* an ancient missile.

প্রাসঙ্গিক *a.* contextual; relevant, pertinent.

প্রাসাদ *n.* a royal residence, a palace; a large building, an edifice. **~কুক্কুট** *n.* the pigeon. **~প্রহরী** *n.* a palace-guard.

প্রাহসনিক *a.* farcical; satirical; comic or comical.

প্রাহ্ণ *n.* the first part or quarter of the day; (loos.) forenoon.

প্রিন্টার *n.* a printer.

প্রিন্সিপাল *n.* a principal (of an institution).

প্রিভি কাউন্সিল *n.* the Privy Council (of Great Britain).

প্রিয় *n.* a beloved person; a lover; a darling; (chiefly in address) a husband; a friend. □ *a.* dear; beloved; favourite (প্রিয় বস্তু) ; pleasant. **প্রিয়ংবদ** *a.* fair-spoken, sweet-tongued. *fem.* **প্রিয়ংবদা**। **~কারক, ~কারী** *a.* doing agreeable things, causing pleasure by one's actions. *fem.* **~কারিণী**। **~চিকীর্ষা** *n.* desire of doing things agreeable to another, desire to do a good turn (to), benevolence. **~চিকীর্ষু** *a.* desirous of doing things agreeable to another, desirous of doing a good turn (to), benevolent. **~জন** *n.* a beloved person; a favourite; a kinsman or relative; a friend. **~তম** *a.* *super.* of **প্রিয়** । □ *n.* a most beloved person; a lover; a darling; a husband. *fem.* **~তমা**। **~তর** *a.* *compar.* of **প্রিয়** (*a.*). **~দর্শন** *a.* good-looking, handsome, comely. *fem.* **~দর্শনা**। **~দর্শী** *a.* treating everybody with love or affection. *fem.* **~দর্শিনী**। **~পাত্র** *n.* a favourite, a beloved person *fem.* **~পাত্রী**। **~বচন, ~বাক্য** *n.* pleasant or sweet words; adulatory words. **~বাদী** same as **প্রিয়ংবদ**। *fem.* **প্রিয়বাদিনী**। **~বিয়োগ** *n.* loss or death of a dear one, bereavement. **~বিরহ** *n.* separation from one's lover or dear one. **~ভাষণ** *n.* pleasant or sweet speech; adulatory speech. **~ভাষী** same as **প্রিয়ংবদ**। *fem.* **~ভাষিণী**। **~সখ,** (pop.) **~সখা** *n.* a dear or bosom friend; a boon companion. *fem.* **~সখী**। **~সমাগম** *n.* union or re-union with a dear one or dear ones; visit of dear ones. **প্রিয়া** *a.* *fem.* of **প্রিয়**। □ *n.* *fem,* a lady-love, a sweetheart; a darling; (chiefly in address) a wife.

প্রিয়ঙ্গু *n.* a sweet-smelling evergreen creeper, *Aglaia roxburghiana*.

প্রীণন *n.* act of pleasing; (loos.) adulation.

প্রীত *a.* pleased, satisfied; delighted, gladdened. □ *n.* (obs. & poet.) love or love affair. ('কুলকলঙ্কিনী হইনু করিয়া প্রীত') ; act of pleasing, pleasure ('শ্রীরামের প্রীতে ভাই মুখে বল হরি').

প্রীতি *n.* pleasure, satisfaction; delight, joy: love; affection; attachment; fondness; friendliness; amicability; amiability; favour (উপরওয়ালার প্রীতি). **প্রীতি অর্জন করা** *v.* to earn the favour of; to be pleased or satisfied or delighted. **~উপহার** *n.* a complimentary gift or present; a gift or token of love. **~কর** *a.* pleasing, pleasant; delightful; agreeable. **~পূর্ণ** *a.* loving; affectionate; friendly; amicable; amiable; cordial. **~ভরে** *adv.* lovingly; affectionately; in a friendly spirit; amiably; cordially; with delight. **~ভাজন** *n.* one deserving love or affection or friendship; a favourite. **~ভোজ, ~ভোজন** *n.* a feast or feasting. **~সম্ভাষণ** *n.* a cordial or friendly greeting. **~সম্মেলন** *n.* a friendly or cordial meeting or assembly or gathering. **~সূচক** *a.* expressing pleasure or delight; cordial; friendly.

প্রীয়মাণ *a.* in the state of being pleased or satisfied or delighted.

প্রুফ *n.* (print.) a proof or a proof-sheet. **প্রুফ তোলা** *v.* to pull a proof. **প্রুফ দেখা, প্রুফ সংশোধন করা** *v.* to read or correct a proof, to proof-read, to proof-correct. **~রিডার** *n.* a proof-reader. **~রিডিং, ~সংশোধন** *n.* proof-reading. **~সংশোধক** *n.* a proof-corrector, a proof-reader.

প্রেক্ষক *n.* a spectator; an onlooker; one of the audience.

প্রেক্ষণ *n.* act of seeing or looking on or watching; (loos.) act of seeing and hearing. **প্রেক্ষণিকা** *n.* an exhibition. **প্রেক্ষণীয়** *a.* worth seeing or watching; (loos.) worth seeing and hearing; capable of being seen and heard.

প্রেক্ষা *n.* seeing or viewing or watching; observation; review; act of seeing or (loos.) seeing and hearing a dramatic or musical performance or a dance. **~গার, ~গৃহ** *n.* a theatre-hall, a theatre; an opera-house; a music-hall; a gallery; (loos.) an auditorium; an observatory.

প্রেক্ষিকা *fem.* of **প্রেক্ষক** ।

প্রেক্ষিত *a.* seen; watched; observed; (loos.) seen and heard.

প্রেত *n.* an evil spirit, a goblin, a ghoul; a ghost; the spirit or ghost of a dead person. **~কর্ম, ~কার্য, ~কৃত্য, ~ক্রিয়া** *n.* funeral rites; obsequial rites. **~তত্ত্ব** *n.* spiritism, spiritualism. **~তত্ত্ববিদ** *n.* a spiritist, a spiritualist. **~তর্পণ** *n.* offering of water to the spirit of a deceased person. **~দেহ** *n.* a ghost (of a dead person), an apparition. **~নদী** *n.* (myth.) the river Baitarini (বৈতরণী) which the soul of the dead has to cross, (cp.) the Styx. **~পক্ষ** *n.* the dark lunar fortnight ending with the Mahalaya (মহালয়া). **~পিণ্ড** *n.* lump of food offered to the spirit of a deceased person. **~ভূমি** *n.* a burial ground, a cremation ground. **~পুরী** *n.* the abode of the dead, the spirit-world, (cp.) Hades. **~মূর্তি** *n.* a ghost, an apparition. **~যোনি** *n.* an evil spirit, a goblin, a ghoul. **~লোক** same as **প্রেতপুরী** । **প্রেতাত্মা** *n.* the soul or spirit of a dead person, a ghost, a spirit. **প্রেতাশৌচ** *n.* impurity of one's body caused by carrying a dead person. **প্রেতিনী** *n. fem.* a female evil spirit, a female goblin or ghoul.

প্রেপ্সু *a.* desirous of getting or obtaining.

প্রেম *n.* love, amour; universal love (জীবে প্রেম) ; affection; attachment; friendliness, amicability; cordiality; devotion (ঈশ্বরপ্রেম). **প্রেম করা, প্রেম দেওয়া** *v.* to make love; to treat with love or affection, to love, to court. **প্রেমে পড়া** *v.* to fall in love (with.) **~ডোর** *n.* a bond or string of (mutual) love or affection. **~দৃষ্টি** *n.* an amorous or lustful look or glance, a fond look. **~পত্র** *n.* a love-letter, a billet-doux. **~পাত্র** *n.* a person of love; a beloved one. **~পীড়িত** *a.* lovesick, love-lorn. **~পূর্ণ** *a.* full of love, loving; affectionate; full of devotion. **~প্রতিমা** *n.* an idol or image or embodiment of love. **~বন্ধন** *n.* the tie of (mutual) love or affection. **~বাণ** *n.* a love-shaft, a Cupid's shaft. **~বারি** *n.* tears of devotion or love. **~ভক্তি** *n.* loving devotion. **~ভিক্ষা** *n.* begging for love; wooing, courting. **প্রেমভিক্ষা করা** *v.*

to beg for (the) love (of); to woo, to court. ~ময় same as প্রেমপূর্ণ। *fem.* ~ময়ী। ~মুগ্ধ *a.* passionately in love, fascinated by love. ~লীলা *n.* amorous sports; dalliance; a love-affair, an affaire de coeur. ~শর same as প্রেমবাণ। ~সংগীত *n.* a love-song. ~হীন *a.* loveless, having no love. **প্রেমাকাঙ্ক্ষা** *n.* a longing for love. **প্রেমাকাঙ্ক্ষী** *a.* longing for love. *fem.* **প্রেমাকাঙ্ক্ষিণী**। **প্রেমানন্দ** *n.* joy or delight of love or devotion. **প্রেমানল** *n.* fire of love, burning passion. **প্রেমাবেগ** *n.* emotion or urge of love. **প্রেমামৃত** *n.* the ambrosia or nectar of love. **প্রেমার্দ্র** *a.* softened with love. **প্রেমালাপ** *n.* amorous conversation; a wooing. **প্রেমালাপ করা** *v.* to be engaged in amorous conversation, to woo. **প্রেমালিঙ্গন** *n.* an amatory or affectionate embrace. **প্রেমাশ্রু** same as প্রেমবারি। **প্রেমাসক্ত** *a.* having great amorous or devotional attachment (to). **প্রেমিক** *a.* given to love, loving; affectionate; devoted. □ *n.* a lover, a sweetheart; an affectionate man; a devotee. *fem.* **প্রেমিকা**। **প্রেমী** *a.* given to love, loving; devoted, attached.

প্রেয় *a.* desired; dear; to one's liking, agreeable.

প্রেয়সী *a. fem.* most beloved, dearest. □ *n.* a lady-love, a sweet-heart, a mistress; a wife.

প্রেরক *a.* sending, dispatching (despatching); transmitting; remitting. □ *n.* a sender, a despatcher; a transmitter; a remitter.

প্রেরণ *n.* act of sending, dispatch, transmission; remittance. **প্রেরণ করা** *v.* to send, to dispatch; to transmit; to remit.

প্রেরণা *n.* an urge; an inspiration. **প্রেরণা দেওয়া** *v.* to urge, to impel; to inspire. ~প্রাপ্ত *a.* urged; inspired.

প্রেরয়িতা same as প্রেরক। *fem.* **প্রেরয়িত্রী**।

প্রেরিত *a.* sent, dispatched; transmitted.

প্রেষ *n.* (mech. & phys.) pressure. ~ক্রম, ~নতি *n.* pressure-gradient. ~বেদন *n.* pressure-sensation.

প্রেষণ, প্রেষণা *n.* sending, dispatch; transmission; remittance; act of sending by performing solemn rites; inspiration. **প্রেষণী** *n. fem.* (obs.) a female go-between in a love affair. **প্রেষণীয়** *a.* to be sent or dispatched or transmitted or remitted.

প্রেষবর্ধক *n.* (phys.) a booster.

প্রেষিত *a.* sent, dispatched; transmitted; remitted; solemnly sent; dependent. *fem.* **প্রেষিতা**।

প্রেষ্য *a.* fit to be sent or transmitted or remitted. □ *n.* a servant, a foot-man; a messenger. *fem.* **প্রেষ্যা**।

প্রেস *n.* a printing-house, a press.

প্রেসক্রিপশন *n.* a prescription (of a physician).

প্রৈষ *a.* of dispatch or transmission; of postal transmission, postal.

প্রোক্ত *a.* authoritatively spoken or announced (ঋষিপ্রোক্ত).

প্রোটিন *n.* protein. **প্রোটিনসংশ্লেষ** *n.* protein synthesis.

প্রোত *a.* strung on thread; inlaid; woven (ওতপ্রোত).

প্রোৎসাহ *n.* great zeal or effort, ardour; great incitement or encouragement; a great incentive or stimulus. **প্রোৎসাহিত** *a.* greatly incited or encouraged. *fem.* **প্রোৎসাহিতা**।

প্রোৎসুক *a.* very much eager; ardent.

প্রোথিত *a.* planted or driven into; (rare) sowed; buried, interred. **প্রোথিত করা** *v.* to plant or drive into; (rare) to sow; to bury; to inter.

প্রোন্নত *a.* very high; highly developed, prosperous; highly advanced.

প্রোবেট *n.* (in law) a probate.

প্রোষিত *a.* gone abroad. ~পত্নীক, ~ভার্য *n.* a man pining on account of separation from his wife who has gone abroad. ~ভর্তৃকা *n.* a woman pining on account of separation from her husband who has gone abroad, (cp.) a grass widow.

প্রৌঢ় *a.* middle-aged; elderly. ~তা, ~ত্ব *n.* the age between youth and old age; elderliness.

প্রৌঢ়া *fem.* of প্রৌঢ়।

প্রৌঢ়ি *n.* energy; capacity, capability; ardour; zeal; talent.

প্র্যাকটিস *n.* repeated performance as a means of acquiring skill, practice; the exercise of a profession, a professional man's business, practice. **প্র্যাকটিস করা** *v.* to practise (হারমোনিয়াম বা ডাক্তারি প্র্যাকটিস করা).

প্লক্ষ *n.* one of the seven mythological islands; the fig tree.

প্লব *n.* leaping or hopping; swimming; floating; a raft, a float. **~কেন্দ্র** *n.* the centre of buoyancy. **~তা** *n.* buoyancy. **~ন** *n.* swimming; floating; buoyancy; act of going by leaps, hopping. **~মান** *a.* floating, buoyant. **~শক্তি** *n.* buoyancy.

প্লাগ *n.* a plug.

প্লানচেট see **প্ল্যানচেট**।

প্লাবক *a.* & *n.* one who or that which floods.

প্লাবন *n.* a flood, a deluge. **~পীড়িত** flood-stricken (বন্যাপীড়িত more usual).

প্লাবিত *a.* flooded; overflowed; inundated; streaming with (অশ্রুপ্লাবিত চোখ) ; drenched or steeped in (অশ্রুপ্লাবিত বদনে). **প্লাবিত করা** *v.* to flood; to overflow; to inundate; to cause to stream with; to drench or steep (in). **প্লাবিতা** *a. fem.* of **প্লাবিত** । □ *n.* (phys.) buoyance.

প্লাবিনী *fem.* of **প্লাবী** ।

প্লাবী *a.* flooding; inundating; overflowing; causing to stream with; drenching or steeping (in).

প্লাস[1] *n.* (math.) plus, the plus sign.

প্লাস[2] *n.* pliers.

প্লাসটার, প্লাস্টার *n.* a plaster.

প্লিডার *n.* a pleader. **প্লিডারি** *n.* the profession of a pleader. **প্লিডারি করা** *v.* to practise as a pleader.

প্লীহা *n.* the spleen; morbid enlargement of the spleen (also **প্লীহা বৃদ্ধি**). **~রোগ** *n.* enlargement of the spleen. **~ভঙ্গ** *n.* rupture of the spleen.

প্লুত *n.* (gr.) an extra-long vowel or sound; a protracted sound; a leap or hop; a (horse's) gallop. □ *a.* flooded, inundated; thoroughly drenched or steeped. **~গতি** *n.* a leaping or hopping movement; a gallop. □ *a.* going leapingly or hoppingly; galloping.

প্লেগ *n.* a deadly epidemic or pestilence, the plague.

প্লেট *n.* a plate, a saucer.

প্লেন[1] *a.* plane, flat; plain. **প্লেন করা** *v.* to plane; to smooth, to make plane.

প্লেন[2] *a.* plain, simple, ordinary.

প্লেন[3] *n.* an aeroplane, a plane.

প্ল্যাকার্ড *n.* a placard.

প্ল্যাটফর্ম *n.* a railway platform; a dais, a platform.

প্ল্যান *n.* a plan, an outline sketch; a scheme. **প্ল্যান করা** *v.* to draw an outline sketch of; to scheme, to plan.

প্ল্যানচেট *n.* planchette.

প্ল্যাসটার corrup. of **প্লাসটার** ।

ফ *n.* the twenty-second consonant of the Bengali alphabet.

ফইজত, (rej.) **ফইজৎ** *n.* bad reputation, a stigma; reproach, reprimand; a quarrel, a brawl; an affray. **ফইজত করা** *v.* to rebuke; to quarrel; to kick up a row.

ফকফকে *a.* very clean; very fair-complexioned.

ফকরে মালা see **ফকির।**

ফকির *n.* (Mus.) a mendicant ascetic, a fakir. **আমির ও ফকির** the rich and the poor. **ফকিরি** *n.* the state of a fakir; the attitude of renunciation. **ফকিরে মালা, ফকরে মালা** A fakir's rosary, a fakir's beadstring.

ফক্কড় *n.* a wag; a saucy fellow; a trickster; a knave. **ফক্কড়ি** *n.* waggery, sauciness; trickery; knavery. **ফক্কড়ি করা** *n.* to jest waggishly; to behave saucily with; to play a trick on.

ফক্করি coll. form of **ফক্কড়ি** (see **ফক্কড়**).

ফক্কা *a.* empty; unsubstantial.

ফক্কিকা *n.* a hoax; a quibble, an enigma, a riddle. **ফক্কিকার, ফক্কিকারি** *n.* act of hoaxing or hoodwinking.

ফঙ্গবানি, ফঙ্গবেনে *a.* brittle; fragile; frail.

ফচকে *a.* garrulous; drollish, waggish; saucy; tricksy; knavish; flippant, frivolous. **~মি** *n.* garrulity; drollery, waggery, sauciness; trickery; knavery; fippancy, frivolity. **ফচকেমি করা** *v.* to be garrulous or droll or waggish ; to behave saucily; to play a trick on; to be flippant or frivolous.

ফচ ফচ *int.* denoting : disgusting and useless prattling. **ফচ ফচ করা** *v.* to prattle uselessly and disgustingly.

ফজর *n.* (Mus.) the dawn; early morning.

ফজলি *n.* the largest species or variety of mango (grown in Malda).

ফট *int.* denoting : a popping sound (ফট করে ছিপি খোলা) ; a snapping sound. **ফটফট** *int.* denoting : repeated popping or snapping sounds. □ *adv.* with popping or snapping sounds.

ফটক *n.* the main gate; (loos.) a portico.

ফটকা, ফটকাবাজি *n.* (comm.) speculation in the share market. **ফটকাবাজার** *n.* the share market.

ফটকিরি *n.* alum.

ফটাফট *adv.* very quickly; in a jiffy.

ফটিক *n.* crystal, quartz. □ *a.* crystal clear, transparent. **ফটিক জল** *n.* rain-water; a species of bird, the iora.

ফটোগ্রাফ *pop.* corrup. of **ফোটোগ্রাফ।**

ফড়ফড় *int.* denoting : buzzing or fluttering of wings (as of insects); ostensible bustling or fussing; voluble or wordy display of one's importance. **ফড়ফড় করা** *v.* to flutter one's wings; to bustle or fuss ostensibly; to talk volubly to display one's importance. **ফড়ফড়ানি** *n.* buzzing or fluttering of wings; ostensible bustling or fussing; wordy display of one's importance.

ফড়িং *n.* the grasshopper. **ফড়িঙ্গা** *n.* a saltatory insect, the cricket. same as **ঝিঁঝিঁ।**

ফড়ে *n.* one of a class of traders purchasing commodities from the original producers and selling them to wholesalers; (loos.) a middleman. **~মি** *n.* typical behaviour of a middleman; (fig.) deceit (esp. in business), double-dealing.

ফণা, *n.* the expanded hood of a serpent; a hood. **ফণা ধরা** *v.* to expand one's hood. **~ধর** *n.* a species of snake capable of expanding its hood, the hooded snake; the snake (generally), the serpent.

ফণী *n.* the snake, the serpent. *fem.* **ফণিনী।** **~ন্দ্র, ~শ্বর** *n.* the king of snakes; the lord of snakes.

ফণীমনসা *n.* prickly pear, a small wild herb akin to cactus.

ফতুয়া *n.* a kind of loose cotton waistcoat.

ফতুর *a.* having all one's money exhausted; pauperized, penniless, (sl.,) broke. **ফতুর হওয়া** *v.* to have all one's money wasted; to be a broke; to be pauperized or penniless.

ফতে *n.* accomplishment or success (কাজ ফতে = accomplishment of or success in work); conquest or victory (কেল্লা ফতে = conquest of a fort; (fig.) a grand success; লড়াই ফতে = victory in war).

ফতো, ফোতো *a.* parasitic; without means; foppish. **ফতো নবাব, ফতো বাবু** a resourceless person who vainly affects affluence or practises dandyism; a fop.

ফতোয়া *n.* (Mus.) a mandate, a decree (esp. one conforming to Islamic laws). **ফতোয়া দেওয়া, ফতোয়া জারি করা** *v.* to issue a mandate or decree; to pass orders.

ফন্দি *n.* a scheme, a plot, an intrigue, a device; a stratagem; a secret intention. **ফন্দি আঁটা, ফন্দি করা** *v.* to devise a scheme or plan or stratagem, to plot, to intrigue. **ফন্দি খাটানো** *v.* to apply or effect a scheme or stratagem. **~ফিকির** *n.* shifts and subterfuges, tricky devices or ways and means. **~বাজ** *a.* (of a person) intriguing, scheming; full of intrigues.

ফপরদালাল alt. spell. of **ফোঁপরদালাল**।

ফয়তা *n.* (Mus.) a solemn prayer for salvation of the spirit of the dead. **ফয়তা পড়া** *v.* to pray solemnly for salvation of the spirit of the dead.

ফয়দা pop. corrup. of **ফায়দা**।

ফয়সালা *n.* judgment, a decree; adjudgment, an adjudication; settlement. **ফয়সালা করা** *v.* to pronounce or pass judgment, to decree; to adjudge, to adjudicate; to settle.

ফরজ *n.* (Mus.) a divine commandment.

ফরদা alt. spell. of **ফর্দা**।

ফরফর *int.* denoting: fluttering noise as made by the repeated and rapid movement of a thin article in air (পত্াকাটা ফরফর করছে) ; rapid and repeated bustle of a small article or its noise (পুঁটিমাছ ফরফর করে) ; restlessness or bustling (মেয়েটা ফরফর করছে). **ফরফর করা** *v.* to flutter rapidly; to bustle (esp. to display one's importance). **ফরফরানি** *n.* fluttering, flutter; bustling (esp. to display one's importance); bustle.

ফরমা *n.* (print.) a form, a forme, a format.

ফরমাইশ var. of **ফরমায়েশ** aud **ফরমাশ**।

ফরমান *n.* a decree (esp. a royal one), firman; an edict.

ফরমানো *v.* to issue an order; to requisition.

ফরমাশ, ফরমায়েশ *n.* an order; an order for supply, requisition. **ফরমাশ করা, ফরমাশ দেওয়া** *v.* to order; to place an order (with), to requisition. **ফরমাশ খাটা** *v.* to carry out orders (as by a servant). **ফরমায়েশি** *a.* ordered for, requisitioned; to order; requisitionary; made to order.

ফরসা *a.* fair-complexioned (ফরসা মেয়ে) ; fair, bright (ফরসা রং) ; clean or washed (ফরসা জামা) ; clear or cloudless (ফরসা আকাশ) ; brightened with daylight ('রাত পোহাল, ফরসা হল') ; exhausted (গুদাম ফরসা) ; desolated (কলেরায় গ্রাম ফরসা) ; bereft of good promise or prospect, blank (ভবিষ্যৎ ফরসা) ; accomplished, executed (কাজ ফরসা) ; lost (আশা-ভরসা ফরসা)।

ফরসি, *n.* a flat-bottomed hubble-bubble with a short and nonflexible smoking-tube.

ফরাকত *n.* separation; divorce, divorcement; seclusion; an open space; leisure or interval.

ফরাশ, ফরাস *n.* any covering for the floor or bed such as a durrie or a carpet or a similar thing; a servant whose duty is to make beds, light lamps, dust furniture etc.

ফরাসি *a.* French. □ *n.* a French; the French language, French.

ফরিয়াদ *n.* a legal complaint, a plaint; an action at law, a suit, a complaint. **ফরিয়াদি** *n.* a complainant, a prosecutor (esp. in a civil suit).

ফর্দ *n.* a list, a roll; an inventory, a catalogue; an estimate or a list of expenditure (বাজারের ফর্দ) ; a piece (এক ফর্দ কাগজ)।

ফর্দা *a.* open, uncovered (ফর্দা জায়গা) ; extensive (ফর্দা মাঠ). **~ফাঁই** *a.* torn asunder; tattered.

ফর্মা, ফর্সা alt. spellings of **ফরমা** and **ফরসা** respectively.

ফল *n.* a fruit; a product (শ্রমের ফল) ; an

effect (উপদেশের ফল) ; action (ওষুধের ফল) ; profit, gain, benefit (এ কাজে ফল নেই) ; result (খেলার ফল, পরীক্ষার ফল) ; result or answer of a mathematical sum (গুণফল) ; findings (ভাগ্য গণনার ফল) ; judgment or decree (মামলার ফল) ; success (বহু চেষ্টায় ফললাভ) ; due reward or punishment, consequence (পুণ্যের বা পাপের ফল). **ফল দেওয়া** same as **ফলদান করা**। **ফল ধরা** *v.* to fructuate. **ফল পাওয়া** *v.* to get fruits (as from a tree); to get good result; to suffer or take the consequences; to be profited. **ফল ভোগা** same as **ফলভোগ করা**। **~ওয়ালা** *n.* a fruit-dealer or fruit-seller, a fruiterer. *fem.* **~ওয়ালি** a fruiteress. **~কথা** *n.* the long and the short (of it); sum and substance, the gist; the last word, the conclusion. **~কর** *n.* a fruit-tax; a fruit-garden. □ *a.* yielding fruits, fructiferous (ফলকর গাছ = a fruit-tree); productive; fertile; effectual, efficacious, effective, fruitful. **~ত** *adv.* on the whole, roughly; consequently; in fact, indeed. **~ত্বক** *n.* (bot.) a pericarp. **~দ** *a.* same as **ফলকর** *(a.)*. **~দর্শিতা** *n.* foresight; prudence. **~দর্শী** *a.* having foresight, foreseeing; prudent. **ফলদান করা** *v.* to yield fruits; to be effective; to give a fruit offering to a deity. **~দায়ক** same as **ফলদ**। **~পাকান্ত** *a.* (of plants) that which dies when its fruits ripen. **~প্রদ, ~প্রসূ** *a.* same as **ফলকর** (*a.*). **~প্রাপ্তি** *n.* attainment of good or desired result; act of suffering or taking the consequences; profiting or being profited. **~বতী** *fem.* of **ফলবান**। **ফলবান** *a.* same **ফলকর** *(a.)*. **~বিক্রেতা** same as **ফলওয়ালা**। **~ভাগী** *a.* enjoying or suffering with others the consequences. *fem.* **ফলভাগিনী**। **ফলভুক** *a.* fruit-eating, frugivorous. **ফলভোগ করা** *v.* to suffer or take the consequences, to enjoy or suffer the effect. **~ভোগী** *a.* suffering or taking the consequences, enjoying or suffering the effect. **~মূল** *n.* fruits and roots. **~মূলাহারী** *a.* living on fruits and roots. **~লাভ** same as **ফলপ্রাপ্তি**। **~শূন্য** same as **ফলহীন**। **~শ্রুতি** *n.* narration of the effect of an act of piety or act of hearing this narration; the beneficial effect of listening to or reading the Vedas; (in lit. crit.) effect on the mind caused by reading a particular class of literature; (pop.) results, outcome. **~সিদ্ধি** *n.* same as **ফলপ্রাপ্তি**। **~হীন** *a.* unfructiferous; fruitless; (lit. & fig.) unproductive; ineffective; sterile; vain; useless; abortive; unprofitable. **ফলের বাগান** an orchard.

ফলক *n.* a blade (as of a sword); a tapering flat end or head (তিরের ফলক) ; a plate (তাম্রফলক) ; a slab (প্রস্তরফলক) ; a plank, a board (কাষ্ঠফলক) ; a shield; the bone of the forehead. **ফলকাকার** *a.* (bot.) foliaceous.

ফলন *n.* produce; outturn (এবার ফলন ভালো) ; origin, birth, production; occurrence; coming true.

ফলনা *n.* so-and-so.

ফলন্ত *a.* fructuous; fructiferous; fruitful; productive; fertile; bearing fruits.

ফলসা *n.* a kind of berry.

ফলা[১] *n.* a blade (অস্ত্রের ফলা) ; a thin and tapering end or head (তিরের ফলা) ; the system of forming compound or conjunct letters of two (or more) consonants (য-ফলা, র-ফলা) ; any of the consonantal symbols added to another letter (such as. ্য, ্র).

ফলা[২] *v.* to fructuate, to bear fruit (গাছটা ফলেছে) ; to grow (আম ফলেছে, ধান ফলেছে) ; to come true (কথা ফলা) ; to follow as a consequence (কর্মের ফল ফলা). □ *a.* (chiefly used as a *sfx.*) fructuating (দোফলা)।

ফলাও *a.* extensive (ফলাও কারবার) ; profuse (ফলাও ভোজ) ; exaggerated or magnified (ফলাও বর্ণনা). **ফলাও করা** *v.* to exaggerate or magnify. **ফলাও করে** *adv.* exaggeratingly magnifying; glibly.

ফলাকাঙ্ক্ষা *n.* desire for success. **ফলাকাঙ্ক্ষা করা** *v.* to desire success. **ফলাকাঙ্ক্ষী** *a.* desirous of success.

ফলাগম *n.* fructuation; the time of fructuation; attainment of success. **ফলাগম হওয়া** *v.* to fructuate; (of an action) to succeed.

ফলানো *v.* to fructify (আমগাছে জাম ফলানো) ;

to grow (ধান ফলানো) ; to exaggerate or magnify (লেখায় রং ফলানো) ; (facet.) to assert oneself (নে, আর ফলাসনি)।

ফলান্বেষণ *n.* search for fruits; desire for success. **ফলান্বেষণ করা** *v.* to search for fruits; to seek success.

ফলান্বেষী *a.* searching for fruits; seeking success.

ফলাফল *n.* good and bad effect or outcome of an action, consequences; success or failure; result, upshot.

ফলার *n.* a meal consisting of vegetarian food other than rice; act of eating such a meal. **ফলার করা** *v.* to take such a meal. **ফলারে** *a.* given to eating such meals.

ফলার্থী *a.* same as **ফলাকাঙ্ক্ষী** (see **ফলাকাঙ্ক্ষা**)।

ফলাশী *a.* frugivorous; feeding on fruits.

ফলাহার *n.* act of eating fruit; a meal consisting of articles of vegetarian food other than rice or act of taking such a meal. **ফলাহারী** *a.* frugivorous; subsisting on fruits only.

ফলি var. of **ফলুই**।

ফলিত *a.* proved true; applied, practical (ফলিত রসায়ন, ফলিত বিজ্ঞান). **~জ্যোতিষ** *n.* astrology. **~বিজ্ঞান** *n.* applied science.

ফলিতার্থ *n.* purport., import, gist, substance.

ফলুই *n.* a species of fresh water fish having silvery colour.

ফলে same as **ফলত**।

ফলোৎপত্তি *n.* fructuation; production or yield of fruits; attainment of success; issue of result or consequences.

ফলোৎপাদন *n.* act of growing or bearing fruits. **ফলোৎপাদন করা** *v.* to grow or bear fruits.

ফলোদয় *n.* fructuation; attainment of success, effectuation; getting proper results.

ফল্গু *n.* a subterranean river at Gaya. **~ধারা** *n.* the undercurrent flow of the Phalgoo (ফল্গু) ; (fig.) an undercurrent of any feeling.

ফল্গুনী *n.* the twin stars (namely, the পূর্বফল্গুনী and the উত্তরফল্গুনী) as described in Hindu astronomy.

ফষ্টিনষ্টি *n.* light banter; drollery; flippant witticism. **ফষ্টিনষ্টি করা** *v.* to practise light banter or drollery or flippant witticism.

ফস *int.* denoting : unguardedness, abruptness; swiftness etc.

ফসকা *a.* slack, loose. **~গেরো** *n.* a loose knot.

ফসকানো *v.* to slip (পা ফসকানো) ; to miss (শিকার ফসকানো, চাকরি বা সুযোগ ফসকানো).

ফসফরাস *n.* phosphorus.

ফসল *n.* harvest, crop; (fig.) effect. **ফসলের সময়** harvesting season or time, harvest. **ফসলি** *a.* relating to harvest or crop; calculated from the harvest-time. ☐ *n.* an era introduced by Akbar the Mughal emperor.

ফাইন *n.* a money-penalty, a fine. **ফাইন করা** *v.* to fine. **ফাইন দেওয়া** *v.* to pay a fine.

ফাইফরমাশ *n.* odd jobs or errands. **ফাইফরমাশ খাটা** *v.* to carry out odd jobs, to run on small errands.

ফাইল *n.* a cover for keeping papers; a rasping file, a file. **ফাইল করা** *v.* to put (papers) in a file or to submit (as an application), to file. **ফাইল ঘষা** *v.* to scrape or smooth with a file, to file.

ফাউ *n.* an extra or anything obtained gratis.

ফাউনটেন-পেন, ফাউন্টেন পেন *n.* a fountain-pen.

ফাও var. of **ফাউ**।

ফাঁক *n.* an intervening space, a gap (দুটি লাইনে অনেক ফাঁক) ; an opening, a hole, a chink, a fissure, an aperture (দেওয়ালের ফাঁক) ; a loophole (আইনের ফাঁক) ; open space (ফাঁকে বেড়ানো) ; void (ঘরে আর ফাঁক নেই) ; vacuum, vacuity (বোতলটায় আর ফাঁক নেই) ; leisure, respite, relief (এ কাজে চা খাওয়ার ফাঁকও নেই) ; opportunity (এই ফাঁকে ঘুমিয়ে নাও) ; a hiding or aloofness (ফাঁকে-ফাঁকে থাকা) ; omission (নেমন্তন্ন থেকে ফাঁকে পড়লাম) ; fault or failing; shortcoming, omission (মুসাবিদায় অনেক ফাঁক আছে) ; offbeat in an Indian musical measure (তিন তাল এক ফাঁক). **ফাঁক করা** *v.* to open (মুখ বা

দরজা ফাঁক করা) ; to part (ঠোঁট ফাঁক করা) ; to widen the gap (পা ফাঁক করা) ; to misappropriate, to defalcate (তহবিল ফাঁক করা) ; to exhaust, to consume (পকেট বা ভাঁড়ার ফাঁক করা). **ফাঁক হওয়া** *v.* to open; to part; to move apart; to be misappropriated or defalcated; to be exhausted or consumed. **~তাল,** (dial.) **তাল্লা** *n.* an accidental piece of luck, a fluke. **ফাঁক ফাঁক** *a.* sparse. **ফাঁকে ফাঁকে** *adv.* during leisure hours, at intervals; keeping aloof or apart; in hiding.

ফাঁকা *a.* uncovered, open (ফাঁকা জায়গা) ; desolate (ফাঁকা বাড়ি) ; empty (ফাঁকা হাত) ; blank (বন্দুকের ফাঁকা আওয়াজ) ; vain, unsubstantial, false, hollow, empty, evasive (ফাঁকা কথা). □ *n.* an open space (ফাঁকায় যাওয়া). **ফাঁকা আওয়াজ** a blank shot (of a gun.); (fig.) vain bragging or bullying or intimidation. **ফাঁকা ফাঁকা** *a.* almost empty or desolate.

ফাঁকি *n.* deception, evasion, eye-wash, hoodwinking; a hoax (শুভঙ্করের ফাঁকি) ; a fraud; a fallacy, sophistry (ন্যায়ের ফাঁকি) ; a quibble; secret or unnoticeable neglect (কাজে ফাঁকি). **ফাঁকি দেওয়া** *v.* to deceive, to evade, to hoodwink; to hoax; to cheat; to quibble; to give the slip; to neglect unnoticeably or slyly. **ফাঁকিতে পড়া** *v.* to be deceived or cheated; to be omitted (যার দাবি সবার আগে তাকেই ফাঁকি ?). **~ঝুকি** *n.* deception, evasion, eye-wash; neglect or perfunctoriness (ফাঁকিঝুকি দিয়ে কাজ). **~বাজ** *a.* deceitful, evasive; neglectful though undetected, slyly neglectful; shirking. **~বাজি** *n.* practice of deception or evasion; eye-wash; hoax; a fallacy; a sophistry; a quibble; sly neglectfulness; shirking. **ফাঁকিবাজি করা** same as **ফাঁকি দেওয়া**।

ফাঁড়া *n.* probability of some danger or even death according to astrology. **ফাঁড়া কাটানো** *v.* to get out of a danger or a risk of death.

ফাঁড়ি *n.* an outpost; a police outpost (also **পুলিস-ফাঁড়ি**). **~দার** *n.* one in charge of an outpost esp. of a police outpost.

ফাঁদ *n.* a trap, a snare, a pitfall; (fig.) an intrigue, a clique, a plot; (of bangles, nose-rings etc.) diameter. **ফাঁদ পাতা** *v.* to set or lay a trap; (fig.) to engineer an intrigue, to lay a plot. **ফাঁদে পড়া** *v.* to get into a trap or pitfall; (fig.) to get involved in an intrigue; to be caught in the toils. **ফাঁদে ফেলা** *v.* to entrap, to get one into a trap or pitfall; (fig.) to involve one in an intrigue.

ফাঁদা *v.* to lay the foundation of; to embark on, to start constructing (বাড়ি ফাঁদা) ; to start; to set up (ব্যাবসা ফাঁদা) ; to expand (দোকানখানা সে বেশ ফেঁদে ফেলেছে) ; to settle down firmly (পাড়ায় সে ফেঁদে বসেছে) ; to devise, to form (মতলব ফাঁদা), to lay (ফাঁদ ফাঁদা).

ফাঁদালো *a.* having a large diameter or opening (ফাঁদালো বালা).

ফাঁপ *n.* swelling; inflation; distension; flatulence (পেটের ফাঁপ). **ফাঁপ ধরা** *v.* to swell; to inflate; to distend; to become flatulent.

ফাঁপর *n.* a perplexing difficulty, an embarrassment, a scrape (ফাঁপরে পড়া). □ *a.* got into an embarrassing situation or into a tight corner.

ফাঁপা *v.* to swell, to inflate, to distend; to become flatulent; to flourish, to prosper (লোকটা ফেঁপে উঠেছে). □ *a.* hollow; swelled, inflated, distended; flatulent. **ফাঁপানো** *v.* to inflate; to swell; to extol exaggeratedly, to puff up. □ *a.* inflated; swelled.

ফাঁস[১] *n.* divulgation (of secrets). **ফাঁস করা** *v.* to divulge. **ফাঁস হওয়া** *v.*to leak out; to get divulged.

ফাঁস[২] *n.* a noose; a slip-knot, a loop; a rope for hanging criminals, a halter; strangling; death by hanging. **ফাঁস দেওয়া** *v.* to strangle.

ফাঁসা *v.* to be torn (কাপড় ফাঁসা) ; to get detached, to come away (হাঁড়ির তলা ফাঁসা) ; to miscarry, to fail (বিয়ের সম্বন্ধ ফাঁসা) ; to be divulged, to come to light (ষড়যন্ত্র ফাঁসা) ; (dero.) to get involved, to get into a scrape (লোকটি ফাঁসল). **ফাঁসানো** *v.* to tear, to rend; to detach, to cause to come away; to let down, to foil; to divulge, to bring to light; (dero.) to involve, to implicate in, to get one into a scrape. **ফেঁসে যাওয়া** *v.* to be divulged, to get known; to be involved, to get into a scrape.

ফাঁসি *n.* death or killing or suicide by hanging; strangling; a sentence of death by hanging; a rope for hanging, a halter; (rare) a noose, a slip-knot. **ফাঁসি দেওয়া** *v.* to hang; to strangle; to sentence to death by hanging. **ফাঁসি যাওয়া** *v.* to be hanged. **ফাঁসির আসামি** a convict sentenced to death by hanging. **ফাঁসির দড়ি** a rope for hanging, a halter. **~কাঠ** *n.* gallows. **ফাঁসির মঞ্চ** the hanging platform; the scaffold.

ফাঁসুড়ে *n.* a highwayman who strangles travellers and robs them; a hangman.

ফাগ, (poet.) **ফাগু** *n.* red powder which Hindus throw at one another during the Holi (হোলি) festival.

ফাগুন coll. corrup. of **ফাল্গুন**।

ফাগুয়া poet. & dial. var. of **ফাগ**।

ফাজলামি, ফাজলামো *n.* extreme talkativeness; sauciness, pertness; flippancy; waggery.

ফাজিল *a.* extremely talkative; saucy; pert; flippant; waggish; excess, surplus. □ *n.* excess expenditure; a. saucy or waggish person.

ফাট *n.* a crack, a chink, a fissure. **ফাট ধরা** *v.* to form a crack; to crack, to split, to break into chinks.

ফটক *n.* the main gate; (loos.) a portico; a guard-room or guard-house, a jail or gaol; imprisonment, jailing. **ফটক হওয়া** *v.* to be sentenced to imprisonment; to be jailed.

ফাটকা (com.) *n.* speculation in the share market. **~বাজার** *n.* the share market. **~বাজি** same as **ফাটকা**।

ফাটল *n.*, a crack, a fissure, a crevice.

ফাটা *v.* to break into chinks, to crack, to split, to rend; to chap (হাত বা পা ফাটা) ; to burst; to explode; (of a boil etc.) to burst open. □ *a.* cracked, split, rent; chapped; unlucky, unfortunate (ফাটা বরাত = bad luck). **ফাটানো** *v.* to crack, to split, to rend; to burst; to explode; to burst open. **~ফাটি** *n.* a scuffle with shedding of blood by both sides; a stiff affray; a rowdy quarrel.

ফাড়া *v.* to tear, to rend; to cleave. **ফাড়ানো** *v.* to cause to tear or rend or cleave or split.

ফাতনা *n.* the float of a fishing line.

ফানুস, ফানুশ *n.* a paper-balloon; a lampshade made of paper.

ফানেল *n.* a funnel.

ফান্দ var. of **ফাঁদ**।

ফায়দা *n.* good result; benefit; profit.

ফারকত, ফারখত *n.* a deed of relinquishment; a written acquittance; a written consent of divorcement or dissolution of marriage.

ফারসি *a.* Persian. □ *n.* the Persian language, Persian.

ফারাক *n.* difference; distance; discrepancy; separation.

ফার্ম[১] *n.* a business organization, a firm.

ফার্ম[২] *n.* a farm.

ফার্স্ট *a.* first. **ফার্স্ট হওয়া** to stand first, to come first, to secure the topmost position, to top the list.

ফাল *n.* a ploughshare, a coulter.

ফালতু, (dial.) **ফালতো** *a.* additional, surplus, extra; spare; unnecessary; useless; unsubstantial; nonsensical.

ফালা *n.* a long slice or strip. **ফালা করা, ফালা দেওয়া** *v.* to cut into long slices; to tear into long strips. **ফালা-ফালা** *a.* cut into long slices; torn into long strips; tattered. **ফালা-ফালা করা** *v.* to cut into long slices; to tear into long strips; to tear to shreds; to tatter.

ফালি *n.* a small slice or strip. **ফালি করা, ফালি দেওয়া** *v.* to cut into small slices; to tear into small strips. **ফালি-ফালি** *a.* cut into small slices; torn into small strips; tattered. □ *adv.* strip by strip.

ফাল্গুন *n.* the eleventh month of the Bengali calendar (from the middle of February to the middle of March). **ফাল্গুনি** *n.* one born in Phalgun (ফাল্গুন). □ *a.* of or relating to the month of Phalgun.

ফাস্ট *a.* & *adv.* fast (ঘড়িটা ফাস্ট, তোমার ঘড়ি ফাস্ট চলছে).

ফি১ *n.* a fee; charge or payment; subscription.

ফি২ *a.* every, each, per (ফি বছর).

ফিক *n.* a spasm caused by a sudden contraction of muscles; neuralgia, a stitch. □ *int.* denoting a sudden smile with a short catch of breath (ফিক করে হাসা). **ফিক ধরা** *v.* to have a stitch in one's sides. **ফিক ফিক** *int.* denoting giggling. **~ব্যথা** same as **ফিক** (*n.*).

ফিকির *n.* a clever means (ফিকির করা) ; a device, an intrigue; an opportunity, a pretext (এই ফিকিরে সে চম্পট দিল) ; an attempt to obtain, a search (কাজের ফিকির) ; a purpose (কোন ফিকিরে ঘুরছ). **ফিকির করা** *v.* to devise a clever or tricky means.

ফিকে *a.* dim (ফিকে আলো) ; pale, dull, faded (ফিকে রং) ; insipid, flat, vapid (ফিকে বর্ণনা) ; watery, thin (ফিকে দুধ).

ফিঙে, ফিঙা, ফিঙ্গাক, *n.* a species of fork-tailed passerine bird, the drongo; a small Y-shaped piece of wood; a sling, a catapult.

ফিচলেমি, (dial.) **ফিচলেমো** *n.* trickery; knavery; waggery.

ফিচেল *a.* sly, knavish, waggish.

ফিট১ *n.* a fainting fit. **ফিট পড়া, ফিট হওয়া** *v.* to faint.

ফিট২ *a.* fit; fitting; pieced together, fitted; well-dressed, thorough (ফিট বাবু). **ফিট করা** *v.* to piece together or adjust, to fit; to declare one competent or fit (ডাক্তার তাকে ফিট করে তুলেছেন)।

ফিটকিরি coll. form of **ফটকিরি**।

ফিটন *n.* a phaeton.

ফিটফাট *a.* neat and clean, spick and span (ফিটফাট সাজসজ্জা) ; thoroughly washed and well-dressed, spruce (ফিটফাট লোক)।

ফিতা, (coll.) **ফিতে** *n.* a tape; a ribbon, a riband, **চুল-বাঁধা ফিতে** a fillet. **লাল ফিতে** a red tape; (fig) rigid formality or intricate official routine, red-tape. **লাল ফিতের কারবার** (fig.) red-tapism. **~ওয়ালা, ~বিক্রেতা** *n.* a haberdasher. **ফিতে কাটা** (fig.) *v.* to inaugurate; to inaugurate by cutting the tape. **~ক্রিমি** *n.* a tapeworm.

ফিনকি *n.* a spark (as of fire); a thin jet or spray (as of any fluid). **ফিনকি দিয়ে বার হওয়া** (of blood etc.) to spurt out, to come out in a sudden spurt.

ফিনফিনে *a.* (of cloth etc.) very fine.

ফিনাইল *n.* phenyl.

ফিনিক *n.* glow, shine (জ্যোৎস্নার ফিনিক)।

ফিরতি *a.* returning, return (ফিরতি ডাক = return mail). □ *n.* what has been returned or saved, surplus, balance (পাঁচ টাকার ফিরতি) ; return journey, return (ফিরতি পথে). □ *adv.* at the time of return.

ফিরা, (coll.) **ফেরা** *v.* to come or go back, to return; to be returned or saved as balance etc. (পাঁচ টাকা থেকে দু-টাকা ফিরেছে) ; to turn (বাড়ির দিকে ফিরছে) ; to turn back or round (ফিরে তাকানো) ; to take a good turn, to improve (অবস্থা ফেরা) ; to become apathetic to, to turn away from (মন ফেরা) ; to wander, to roam, to loiter (পথে পথে ফেরা) ; to return disappointed (দরজা থেকে ফেরা). **ফিরানো, ফেরানো** *v.* to bring or send back, to cause to return; to save as balance etc; to cause to turn, to save as balance etc.; to cause to turn, to turn; to turn one back or round; to cause to take a good turn, to improve; to turn one from (মন ফিরানো) ; to send back disappointed; to return or change (তেলটা দোকানদারকে ফিরিয়ে দেব) ; to apply anew or to apply (কলি ফেরানো) ; to retract or withdraw (কথা ফিরানো) ; to ward off, to fend off, to parry (আঘাত ফিরানো).

ফিরি var. of **ফেরি**।

ফিরিঙ্গি *n.* a European; an Anglo-Indian.

ফিরিস্তি *n.* a list; a descriptive list; (loos.) a description. **কাজের ফিরিস্তি দেওয়া** to render an account of jobs done.

ফিরে *a.* next (ফিরে বার). □ *adv.* again, afresh (ফিরে বলা).

ফিরোজা *n.* turquoise; the blue colour of or as of turquoise.

ফিলটার *n.* a filter; filtering or filtration. **ফিলটার করা** *v.* to filter or filtrate. **ফিলটার কাগজ** *n.* filter-paper.

ফিলম, ফিল্ম *n.* a photographic film; a motion picture; a film. **ফিলম তোলা** *v.* to make a motion picture of, to film. **ফিলম-স্টার** *n.* a film-star.

ফিলহাল *adv.* recently (more usu. **হালফিল).**

ফিসফিস *int.* denoting : a whisper. **ফিসফিস করা** *v.* to whisper. **ফিসফিসানি** *n.* a whisper; a whispering noise.

ফুঃ *int.* pooh.

ফুঁ, ফুঁক *n.* a whiff, a puff; whiffing, puffing. **ফুঁ দেওয়া, ফুঁক দেওয়া** *v.* to whiff, to puff.

ফুঁকা, ফোঁকা *v.* to blow or play (as a wind-instrument) or smoke (as a cigarette) with puffs, to puff; to squander (সম্পত্তি ফুঁকে দেওয়া).

ফুঁড়া, ফোঁড়া *v.* to pierce; to penetrate; to probe. **ফোঁড়াফুঁড়ি** *n.* piercing at numerous places; repeated piercing; (facet.) medical injection.

ফুঁপান, ফোঁপানো *v.* to whimper, to sob; (inc.) to growl suppressedly in anger. **ফুঁপানি, ফোঁপানি** *n.* a whimper, a sob, a suppressed angry growl.

ফুঁয়ে ওড়ানো *v.* (fig.) to treat with utter neglect or contempt; to pooh-pooh; to give no importance; not to care a straw.

ফুঁসা, ফুঁসানো *v.* to hiss; to growl suppressedly in anger; to fume.

ফুকরানো *v.* to call or proclaim aloud ('নকীব ফুকরায়') ; to shout; to weep or lament aloud, to wail. **ফুকরে কাঁদা** *v.* to cry in a loud voice, to wail, to lament. see also **ডুকরানো।**

ফুকা, ফোকা *n.* the malpractice of blowing in air through the generative organ of a milch cow in order to obtain a larger quantity of milk. **ফুকা দেওয়া** v. to blow in air through the generative organ of a milch cow.

ফুকারা poet. form of **ফুকরানো।**

ফুকো coll. corrup. of **ফুকা।**

ফুঙ্গি *n.* a Buddhist friar or priest (esp. of Burma).

ফুচকা *n.* a crisp ball made of puffed wheat filled with mashed potato and tamarind juice with spices, phuchka.

ফুট১ *n.* an English measure of length (=12 inches), a foot.

ফুট২ *n.* a bubble or bubbles of liquid caused by boiling; effervescence caused by boiling, boiling state; frying and bursting open as a result of frying. **ফুট কাটা** *v.* to gasp for breath (পুঁটিমাছ ডাঙায় উঠে ফুট কাটে) ; to make an annoying or pungent or sarcastic comment, to make funny remarks; to poke fun at. **ফুট ধরা** *v.* to effervesce or rise in bubbles as a result of boiling; to burst open as a result of frying.

ফুটকড়াই, ফুটকলাই *n.* fried peas, parched peas.

ফুটকি *n.* a minute speckle, a dot.

ফুটন *n.* blooming or blowing or blossoming; boiling **ফুটন্ত জল)** ; rise or appearance; opening; effervescence or rising in bubbles by being boiled; act of bursting open as a result of frying; boiling; expression; piercing.

ফুটন্ত *a.* boiling; blooming, blossoming; blossomed; effervescing or rising in bubbles as a result of frying.

ফুটপাথ, ফুটপাত *n.* a footpath; a pavement; a sidewalk.

ফুটফুট১ *a.* having numerous dots or minute speckles.

ফুটফুট২ *int.* denoting: clearness, transparency, brightness, tidiness etc. **ফুটফুটে** *a.* very fair-complexioned and goodlooking (ফুটফুটে মেয়ে) ; very bright, silvery white (ফুটফুটে জ্যোৎস্না) ; very neat and tidy.

ফুটবল *n.* football; the game of football. **ফুটবল খেলা** *v.* to play football. **ফুটবল খেলোয়াড়** *n.* a footballer.

ফুটরুল *n.* a footrule.

ফুটা১, (coll.) ফুটো *n.* a hole; a crack; a crevice; a pore; a leak. □ *a.* porous; leaky. **ফুটো করা** *v.* to bore. **ফুটো হওয়া** *v.* to spring a leak.

ফুটা২, ফোটা *v.* to bloom, to blossom, to blow (ফুল ফোটা) ; to rise or become visible (তারা ফুটছে) ; to appear, to spread (জ্যোৎস্না ফুটেছে) ; to open (চক্ষু ফোটা) ; (fig.) to be able to look to one's own interests, to effervesce or rise in bubbles as a result of boiling (জল ফোটা) ; to burst open after frying (খই ফোটা) ; to be boiled or cooked (ভাতটা ভালো ফোটেনি) ; to be expressed (রং

ফোটা) ; to be uttered intelligibly (কথা ফুটেছে) ; to be unfolded, become distinct or manifest (চরিত্র ফুটে উঠেছে) ; to be pierced (কাঁটা ফোটা).

ফুটানি *n.* ostentatious or vain display or self-assertion; bragging, tall talk; vanity. **ফুটানি করা** *v.* to make an ostentatious display; to brag, to talk big; to indulge in vanity.

ফুটানো, ফোটানো *v.* to cause to bloom or blossom or blow; to cause to rise or appear or spread; to open; to cause to effervesce or rise in bubbles as a result of boiling; to boil or cook; to cause to burst open by frying; to express; to cause to utter intelligibly; to unfold, to make distinct or manifest; to pierce.

ফুটি *n.* a variety of melon. **~ফাটা** *a.* thoroughly burst, burst or rent asunder.

ফুটুনি coll. corrup. of **ফুটানি**।

ফুটো coll. form of **ফুটা**[১]।

ফুড়ুক, ফুড়ুৎ *int.* denoting: sudden flying away (ফুড়ুৎ করে উড়ে যাওয়া). **ফুড়ুক-ফুড়ুক, ফুড়ুৎ-ফুড়ুৎ** *int.* denoting: repeated flying for short spells; repeated bubbling noise caused by smoking a hookah.

ফুৎকার *n.* a whiff, a puff; whiffing, puffing; (rare) a whisper. **ফুৎকার দেওয়া** *v.* to whiff, to puff.

ফুৎশিখা *n.* a blow-pipe flame.

ফুরন *n.* piecework.

ফুরফুর *int.* denoting: gentle blowing of the wind; mild fluttering of light things (such as a flag, paper or hair) in the wind. **ফুরফুরে** *a.* gently blowing; fluttering.

ফুরসত *n.* leisure; respite.

ফুরসুত corrup. of **ফুরসত**।

ফুরানো *v.* to terminate, to end (দিন ফুরানো, পথ ফুরানো) ; to conclude, to close (গল্প ফুরানো) ; to be spent or exhausted or consumed (টাকা বা শক্তি বা খাবার ফুরানো) ; to cease to exist, to be lost (আশা ফুরানো).

ফুর্তি *n.* delight, merry-making; enjoyment; agility (শরীরে ফুর্তি নেই). **~বাজ** *a.* given to jollity, jovial, merry, jolly.

ফুল[১] *a.* of the full measure, standard (ফুলশার্ট) ; of or costing the full price, full (ফুলটিকিট).

ফুল[২] *n.* a flower, a blossom; a floral design (ফুলদার) ; the placenta. **ফুল তোলা** *v.* to pluck or pick or cull flowers; to embroider a floral design. **ফুল দেওয়া** *v.* to worship (a deity) with flower-offering. **ফুল ধরা** *v.* to flower, to be in blossom. **ফুল না পড়া** retention of the placenta. **ফুল পাড়া** *v.* to pluck or pick or cull flowers. **ফুলের ঘায়ে মূর্ছা যাওয়া** (fig.) to lose patience over a trifle, to display over-sensitiveness. **ফুলের সাজি** a flower-basket. **~ওয়ালা** *n.* a florist. *fem.* **~ওয়ালি** a flower-girl. **~কপি** *n.* the cauliflower. **~কাটা** same as **ফুলদার**। **~কারি** *n.* ornamental or decorated needlework, embroidery (with floral designs). **~খড়ি** *n.* writing chalk. **~ঝুরি** *n.* a firework emitting starlike sparks. **~ডোর, ~মালা** *n.* flower garland. **~তোলা** same as **ফুলদার**। **~দানি, ~দান** *n.* a flower-vase. **~দার** *a.* embroidered with floral designs, floriated, floreated. **~ধনু** *n.* Madan (মদন) the god of love, (cp.) Cupid; the Cupid's bow. **ফুল পড়া** *n.* ejection of the placenta. **~বাগান** *n.* a flower-garden. **~বাণ** *n.* Madan (মদন) the god of love, (cp.) Cupid; Cupid's shaft. **~বাতাসা** *n.* a kind of light and hollow sweet drop made of sugarcandy or treacle. **~শয্যা** *n.* (lit.) a bed of flowers, a flower-strewn bed; the Hindu ceremony on the third night of the marriage when the bridegroom and the bride are to sleep on a bed of flowers. **~শর** same as **ফুলবাণ**। **~হার** same as **ফুলডোর**।

ফুলকা for. but less used form of **ফুলকো**।

ফুলকি *n.* a spark.

ফুলকো *n.* a gill (of fish), a branchia. □ *a.* thin, hollow and inflated (ফুলকো লুচি).

ফুলন *n.* swelling; inflation, distension; (fig.) the state of being puffed up; (fig.) flourishing.

ফুলবাবু *n.* a thorough dandy or fop, a petit-maitre.

ফুলস্ক্যাপ *a.* foolscap.

ফুলা *v.* to swell; to be inflated, to distend; (fig.) to be puffed up; (fig.) to flourish. □ *n.* a swelling. □ *a.* swelled up; inflated, distended. **ফুলানো** *v.* to swell; to inflate, to distend; to pout (ঠোঁট ফুলানো) ; (fig.) to puff up; (fig.) to cause to flourish.

ফুলিয়ে ফাঁপিয়ে *adv.* exaggeratedly; in an inflated or puffed-up manner.

ফুলুরি *n.* a kind of cake made of powdered pigeon-pea or gram.

ফুলে ফেঁপে ওঠা *v.* to become inflated or distended; to become puffed up; to swell up; to become exceedingly rich.

ফুলেল *a.* perfumed with the essence of flower (ফুলেল তেল) ; full of flowers (ফুলেল ফাগুনে).

ফুল্ল *a.* blown, blooming, full-blown (ফুল্লকুসুম) ; thoroughly manifest or revealed (ফুল্ল জ্যোৎস্না) ; highly delighted or cheerful (ফুল্লনয়ন) ; sweetly smiling. □ *n.* a flower. **~কুসুমদাম** *n.* a garland of full-blown flowers. **~দাম** *n.* a wreath of flowers. **ফুল্লাধর** *n.* smiling lips. **ফুল্লারবিন্দ** *n.* a fullblown lotus.

ফুসকুড়ি *n.* a vesicle; a pimple, (med.) a pustule.

ফুসফুস *n.* the lung. **ফুসফুস-ধমনী** *n.* the pulmonary artery. **ফুসফুস-প্রদাহ** *n.* inflammation of the lungs; pneumonia. **ফুসফুসীয়** *a.* pulmonary. **ফুসফুসীয় সংবহন** pulmonary circulation.

ফুসমন্তর *n.* an imaginary secret incantation to entice or evade, cajolement to entice or evade (ফুসমন্তরে ভোলা) ; (dero.) secret counsel or instigation; an imaginary esoteric incantation endowing one with supernatural power.

ফুসলানো *v.* to instigate; to entice, to seduce; to cajole, to coax. **ফুসলে নিয়ে যাওয়া** *v.* to entice away. **ফুসলানি** *n.* instigation; enticement, seduction; cajolement, coaxing.

ফুস্কুড়ি alt. spell. of **ফুসকুড়ি** ।

ফেউ *n.* the jackal; a mad or rabid jackal; a kind of jackal which pursues tigers howlingly. **ফেউ লাগা** *v.* (of a tiger) to be pursued by howling jackals; (fig.) to be pestered by taunting pursuers; (fig.) to be doggedly pursued or harassed by a sleuth or detective.

ফেঁকড়া, ফেঁকড়ি *n.* a branchlet, a twig, a sprig, an offshoot; (fig.) a branch or offshoot or derivative of anything; (fig.) an incidental trouble or hindrance; (fig.) an objection. **ফেঁকড়া তোলা** *v.* to raise an objection. **ফেঁকড়া বাঁধানো** *v.* to cause trouble or hindrance or obstacle. **ফেঁকড়া বার হওয়া** *v.* to branch, out, to branch off.

ফেঁশো, ফেঁসো *n.* downy fibre of jute or yarn.

ফেঁসে যাওয়া v. see. **ফাঁসা** ।

ফেকাশে rej. spell. of **ফ্যাকাশে** ।

ফেকো, ফেকুয়া *n.* frothy spittle that comes out of the mouth whilst talking (usually caused by a long-continued fast or overmuch talking).

ফেচাং rej. spell. of **ফ্যাচাং** ।

ফেচফেচ rej. spell. of **ফ্যাচফ্যাচ** ।

ফেটা *n.* a turban; a puttee; a bandage.

ফেটানো *v.* to beat up into froth, to whisk.

ফেটি, ফেট্টি *n.* a small turban; a puttee; a bandage; a skein or reel of thread.

ফেন, ফেনা *n.* foam; froth; scum; lather (সাবানের ফেনা). **ফেন গালা** *v.* to strain off water from boiled rice. **সমুদ্রফেন** *n.* meerschaum, petrified sea-scum. **~নিভ** *a.* foam-like, foamy; frothy. **ফেনানো** *v.* to stir up into foam or froth; (fig.) to pad or amplify or exaggerate. **ফেনায়মান** *a.* rising in foam, foaming. **ফেনায়িত** *a.* stirred up into foam or froth, foaming, frothy; padded, amplified, exaggerated.

ফেনি *n.* a hollow sweet drop made of treacle or sugar (also **ফেনিবাতাসা**) ; a kind of sweet made of sugar.

ফেনিল *a.* foamy; frothy; foaming.

ফেনিবাতাসা see **ফেনি** ।

ফেব্রুআরি, ফেব্রুয়ারি *n.* February.

ফের *n.* a trouble, a danger; a peril (ফেরে পড়া = to get into a scrape); a risk (টাকার ফের) ; purpose or course (কাজের ফের) ; consequence (কর্মের ফের) ; vicissitude, malignity (ভাগ্যের ফের) ; change (রকমফের) ; reverse (অবস্থার ফের) ; a witty turn (কথার ফের) ; a circuit, a circuitous fold (কাপড়ের ফের). □ *adv.* again.

ফেরত *n.* act of giving or sending back,

return; redirection; repayment. □ *a.* given or sent back, returned; redirected; returned as unaccepted, refused (ফেরত চিঠি) ; immediately coming back (ফেরত ডাক = return mail); returning from (অফিস ফেরত) ; returned from (বিলাত-ফেরত = England-returned). **ফেরত আনা** *v.* to bring back. **ফেরত আসা** *v.* to come back; to come back unaccepted; to be returned to sender. **ফেরত দেওয়া** *v.* to send or give back, to return; to repay; to refuse to accept, to refuse; to redirect. **ফেরত নেওয়া** *v.* to take back; to withdraw, to retract. **ফেরত পাঠানো** *v.* to send back, to return; to refuse to accept, to refuse; to redirect. **~যোগ্য** *a.* that which can be or should be returned, returnable. **ফেরতা** *a.* returning or returned from. □ *n.* encompassment, folding or doubling (ফেরতা দেওয়া কাপড়) ; transfer (হাতফেরতা) ; recurrence, repetition (তালফেরতা). □ *adv.* at the time of return, on the way back (অফিসফেরতা). **ফেরতা দেওয়া** *v.* to wear a cloth by doubling or folding it.

ফেরা, ফেরানো pop. variants of **ফিরা** and **ফিরানো** respectively.

ফেরার, ফেরারি *a.* absconding. **ফেরার হওয়া** *v.* to abscond. **ফেরারি লোক বা আসামি** an absconder.

ফেরি *n.* pedlary, huckstery; (loos.) hawking. **ফেরি করা** *v.* to huckster; (loos.) to hawk. **~ওয়ালা** *n.* a pedlar, a huckster; (loos.) a hawker. *fem.* **~ওয়ালি** a hucksteress, a huckstress. **ফেরিওয়ালার মাল, ফেরির মাল** the wares of a pedlar, pedlary.

ফেরিশতা *n.* (Mus.) an angel.

ফেরু *n.* the jackal. **~পাল** *n.* a pack of jackals.

ফেরেববাজি, *n.* deception, cheating, fraud, swindling. **ফেরেববাজ** *a.* deceitful, fraudulent. □ *n.* a cheat, a deceitful person.

ফেরেশতা same as **ফেরিশতা**।

ফেল *a.* failed, plucked; unsuccessful (পরীক্ষায় ফেল) ; ceased to work or operate (হার্ট ফেল) ; run insolvent (ব্যাঙ্ক ফেল) ; missed because of lateness (ট্রেন ফেল). **ফেল করা** *v.* to fail; to get ploughed or plucked; to cease working; to stop; to miss. **ফেল করানো** *v.* to pronounce (one) unsuccessful; to fail a candidate. **ফেল পড়া** *v.* to become insolvent, to be bankrupt; to be exhausted. **ফেল হওয়া** *v.* to fail; to get ploughed or plucked; to cease working; to become insolvent; to stop; to miss, to be missed; to be exhausted.

ফেলনা *a.* fit to be cast away or rejected; negligible, insignificant; unworthy of attention.

ফেলা *v.* to let fall, to drop (চোখের পাতা ফেলা, ফোঁটা ফেলা) ; to throw, to fling, to cast (ডাস্টবিনে ময়লা ফেলা) ; to place, to put (মাটিতে পা ফেলা) ; to leave, to leave unused or uneaten (মাছটা ফেললে—খেলে না) ; to abandon, to desert (স্ত্রীকে ফেলে যাওয়া) ; to invest (ব্যাবসায় টাকা ফেলা) ; to spend (বাড়ির পিছনে টাকা ফেলা) ; to dissipate, to waste (বাজে ব্যাপারে টাকা ফেলা) ; to involve, to put (one) in (বিপদে ফেলা) ; to disobey or disregard (গুরুজনের কথা ফেলা) ; to propose (এখানে বিয়ের কথা ফেলো) ; to reject (এ প্রস্তাব ফেলা অনুচিত) ; to fix (তারিখ ফেলা) ; to write, to put down; to expel, to eject (নিশ্বাস ফেলা) ; (in comp. verbs) to finish up (খেয়ে ফেলা) ; to commit suddenly (বলে ফেলা). **~ছড়া, ~ফেলি** *n.* act of scattering away wastefully or negligently; dissipation, squandering; making large discount or allowance (ফেলাছড়া করে ধরলেও অনেক). **ফেলে আসা দিন** the bygone days, the past days, the yester years. **ফেলে রাখা** *v.* to put off, to postpone (কাজ ফেলে রাখা).

ফেসাদ rej. spell. of **ফ্যাসাদ**।

ফৈজত, alt. spell of **ফইজত**।

ফোঁকা pop. var. of **ফুঁকা**।

ফোঁটা *n.* a small roundish mark or a sectarian mark put on the forehead (সিঁদুরের বা চন্দনের ফোঁটা) ; a drop or blob of any liquid (বৃষ্টির ফোঁটা) ; a globular mark, a point; a pip on playing-cards; a point obtained in some card-games. **এক ফোঁটা** *a.* very small, tiny, a little, scanty. **অনভ্যাসের ফোঁটা** luxury or pleasure one is not used to. **ফোঁটা ফোঁটা পড়া** to drip. **এক ফোঁটা মেয়ে** a mere slip of a girl.

ফোঁড় *n.* a bore; a perforation; a stitch. **এ ফোঁড় ও ফোঁড়** pierced or piercing all through.

ফোঁড়া pop. var. of **ফুঁড়া**।

ফোঁপরদালাল *n.* an uncalled-for meddler, a busy body. **ফোঁপরদালালি** *n.* uncalled-for meddling; officiousness.

ফোঁপরা, ফোঁপর *a.* full of holes, honey-combed; hollow; containing nothing, empty. □ *n.* the vegetating seed within a coconut.

ফোঁপানি, ফোঁপানো pop. variants of **ফুঁপানি** and **ফুঁপানো** respectively.

ফোঁস *int.* denoting: a sudden deep sigh of suppressed grief etc.; a hiss of a snake; a sudden angry growl. **ফোঁস করা** *v.* to heave suddenly a deep sigh of suppressed grief etc.; to hiss; to growl angrily and suddenly, to snarl out. **~ফোঁস** *int.* denoting: repeated deep sighs of suppressed grief etc.; repeated hissing; repeated angry growls. **ফোঁসফোঁস করা, ফোঁসফোঁসানো** *v.* to heave repeatedly deep sighs of suppressed grief etc.; to weep profusely, to blubber; (of snakes) to hiss repeatedly; to make angry growls continuously. **~ফোঁসানি** *n.* repeated deep sighs of suppressed grief etc.; blubbering, profuse weeping; repeated hissing; continuous angry growls.

ফোঁসা, ফোঁসানি, ফোঁসানো pop. variants of **ফুঁসা, ফুঁসানি, ফুঁসানো** respectively.

ফোকর *n.* a hole, a small hole; a crevice, a niche; a cell.

ফোকলা *a.* one whose teeth have all fallen away, toothless.

ফোকাস *n.* focus. **অসৎ ফোকাস** (phys.) virtual focus. **সৎ ফোকাস** (phys.) real focus. **ফোকাস দূরত্ব** *n.* (phys.) focal length. **ফোকাস বিন্দু** *n.* (phys.) focal point.

ফোটা pop. var. of **ফুটা**[২]।

ফোটানো pop. var. of **ফুটানো**।

ফোটো, ফোটোগ্রাফ *n.* a photograph. **ফোটো তোলা** *v.* to take a photograph or snapshot of. **ফোটোগ্রাফি** *n.* photography.

ফোড়ন *n.* spices singed or fried and then mixed with any cooked dish to make the latter palatable; (fig. & usu. facet.) a remark or comment thrown in. **ফোড়ন কাটা** *v.* to throw in a remark or comment. **ফোড়ন দেওয়া** *v.* to add or mix singed or fried spices for amelioration of palatableness; (fig.) to throw in or interpose a remark or comment.

ফোড়া *n.* a furuncle, a boil; an abscess. **ফোড়া পেকেছে** *v.* the boil has suppurated or come to a head. **ফোড়া ফেটেছে** *v.* the boil has opened. **ফোড়া বসে গেছে** *v.* the boil has subsided.

ফোতো pop. spell. of **ফতো**।

ফোন *n.* phone, telephone. **ফোন করা** *v.* to ring (one) up, to telephone. **ফোন নম্বর** *n.* a telephone number.

ফোনোগ্রাফ *n.* a phonograph, a record-player.

ফোপরদালাল alt. spell. of **ফোঁপরদালাল**।

ফোমেনট, ফোমেন্ট *n.* fomentation. **ফোমেনট করা** বা **দেওয়া** *v.* to foment.

ফোয়ারা *n.* a fountain, a spring; an artificial fountain; a jet.

ফোরম্যান *n.* a foreman.

ফোলা *v.* pop. var. of **ফুলা** (*v.*).

ফোসকা *n.* a blister; a vesicle. **ফোসকা পড়া** *v.* to develop a blister. **ফোসকা ফেটেছে** *n.* the blister has burst open.

ফৌজ *n.* an army. **আজাদ হিন্দ ফৌজ** (hist.) the Indian National Army. **~দার** *n.* an army commander; a commissioner of police; an officer-in-charge of the police; a district magistrate or a divisional commissioner; a provincial governor. **~দারি** *a.* criminal. □ *n.* a criminal lawsuit or case. **ফৌজদারি আদালত** a criminal court. **ফৌজি** *a.* military.

ফ্যাঁকড়া alt. spell. of **ফেঁকড়া**।

ফ্যাকাশে *a.* pale; wan; anaemic; dim (ফ্যাকাশে আলো).

ফ্যাচফ্যাচ *int.* denoting: disgusting talkativeness or remonstrance. **ফ্যাচফ্যাচ করা** *v.* to indulge in disgusting talkativeness.

ফ্যাচাং *n.* an incidental trouble, a fix; a botheration. **ফ্যাচাং বাধানো** *v.* to raise an objection, to cause a hindrance; to create an unexpected trouble.

ফ্যা ফ্যা *int.* denoting: continuous prattling; continuous useless solicitation; continuous useless search.

ফ্যালফ্যাল *int.* denoting: bewildered gaze. **ফ্যালফ্যাল করে তাকানো** *v.* to look confusedly.

ফ্যাশান, ফ্যাশন *n.* fashion; vogue; style or mode; fashionableness or stylishness.

ফ্যাসাদ *n.* trouble; difficulty; a fix; a quarrel. **ফ্যাসাদে** *a.* troublesome, fond of creating troubles. **ফ্যাসাদে পড়া** *v.* to become involved in a trouble, to get into a trouble, to get into a scrape. **ফ্যাসাদ বাধানো** *v.* to create trouble or difficulty.

ফ্রক *n.* a frock (esp. for girls).

ফ্রি *a.* free. **ফ্রিতে পাওয়া** *v.* to obtain free of cost.

ফ্রেম *n.* a frame.

ফ্লাস্ক *n.* a thermos flask, a thermos; a flask.

ফ্ল্যানেল *n.* flannel.

ফ্ল্যাট *n.* a self-contained storey or floor of a building, a flat; a flatboat; a floating dock. □ *a.* lying or laid fully on one's back (ফ্ল্যাট হওয়া) ; (fig.) utterly dejected.

ব

ব *n.* the twenty-third letter of the Bengali alphabet.

বই[1] *n.* the root of a kind of arum.

বই[2] *n.* a book; a register. **বইয়ের পোকা** (lit. & fig.) a bookworm. **~পত্র** *n.* books and similar other things. **বই বাঁধানো** *v.* to bind books; to get books bound. **~মেলা** *n.* a book fair.

বই[3] *prep.* without, except, other than (তোমা বই জানি না).

বইকি *int.* & *adv.* of course (অতি ভোজনে শরীরের ক্ষতি হয় বইকি). □ *int.* denoting: denial, disbelief etc. (তা বইকি).

বইঠা *n.* a scull.

বউ *n.* wife; a daughter-in-law; a brother's wife, a sister-in-law; a married woman esp. one who usually keeps to a gynaeceum (usu. **ঘরের বউ**) ; a housewife; a newly-married wife (বউভাত). **বউ-কথা-কও** *n.* the Indian nightingale. **বউ-কাটকি** *n.* a woman given to torturing her daughter-in-law. **~ড়ি** *n.* a young wife; a childwife. **~দিদি,** (coll.) **~দি** *n.* an elder brother's wife, a sister-in-law. **~ভাত** same as **পাকস্পর্শ** (see **পাক[2]**). **~মা** *n.* a son's wife, a daughter-in-law; a younger brother's wife, a sister-in-law. **~মানুষ** *n.* a married woman usually keeping to a gynaeceum; a newly-married woman.

বউনি *n.* the first (cash.) sale or earning of the day.

বউল *n.* a bud, a blossom. **বউল ধরা** *v.* to put forth buds, to bud, to be in blossom.

বউলি *n.* an earring or eardrop (বীরবউলি).

বওয়া coll. corrup. of **বহা**। **আমার বয়ে গেছে** I do not care a hang. **বয়ে-যাওয়া ছেলে** a spoilt child.

বওয়াটে dial. corrup. of **বখাটে**।

বংশ[1] *n.* the bamboo; the backbone, the spine. **~দণ্ড** *n.* a bamboo-staff, a bamboo-stick; (fig.) stinkard. **~পত্র** *n.* bamboo-leaf. **~লোচন** *n.* tabasheer, tabashir. **~শলাকা** *n.* a slender (and often short) slip of bamboo.

বংশ[2] *n.* a race; a family; lineage; pedigree; posterity; offspring, children. **বংশে বাতি দেওয়া** (fig.) to continue a line of descent (as by a descendant). **~ক্ষয়, ~নাশ** *n.* loss, end or extinction of a family or race. **~গত** *a.* hereditary. **~গতি** *n.* heredity. **~গৌরব** *n.* family prestige or pride; the glory of a family. **~জ** *a.* born of a particular family; of good lineage; born of a kulin (কুলীন) family which has been socially lowered by matrimonial alliance with an inferior family. **~তালিকা** *n.* a genealogical table, a family tree; a genealogy. **~তিলক** *n.* one who is the gem or the crowning glory of a family; the most remarkable member of a family. **~ধর** *n.* a descendant; a scion. **~পরম্পরা** same as **বংশানুক্রম**। **~পরিচয়** *n.* the family identity; the genealogy. **~বৃদ্ধি** *n.* increase or multiplication of a race or family, growth in family size; procreation; breeding. **বংশবৃদ্ধি করা** *v.* to increase or multiply one's race or family; to procreate; to breed. **~বৈশিষ্ট্য** *n.* a family characteristic. **~মর্যাদা** *n.* family prestige. **~রক্ষা** *n.* saving one's family or race; protection of one's family. **~লতা** same as **বংশতালিকা**। **~লোপ** same as **বংশক্ষয়**।

বংশাঙ্কুর *n.* a bamboo shoot.

বংশানুক্রম *n.* a regular line of descent or succession; heredity. **বংশানুক্রমিক** *a.* hereditary. **বংশানুক্রমে** *adv.* from generation to generation; hereditarily.

বংশানুচরিত *n.* a genealogical history or register; a genealogy.

বংশাবতংস *n.* (fig.) one who is the ornament or glory of one's family.

বংশাবলি *n.* a genealogy; a genealogical table, a family tree.

বংশী *n.* a flute or pipe made of bamboo, a reed; a flute, a pipe. **~তট** *n.* the bank of the Jamuna at Brindaban where Krishna (কৃষ্ণ) played his flute. **~ধর, ~ধারী, ~বদন** *n.* a fluter, a flutist, a piper; Krishna (কৃষ্ণ). ~বট *n.* a banyan tree at Brindaban under which Krishna (কৃষ্ণ) played his flute. ~রব, ~ধ্বনি *n.* the note of a flute.

বংশীয় *a.* born of a particular family or race; pertaining to a family or race; familial.

বংশোদ্ভব *a.* same as **বংশজ**।

বঁইচি *n.* a kind of small juicy berry, (cp.) gooseberry or bramble.

বঁটি *n.* a kind of large knife fixed almost at right angle in a piece of wood on which one sits whilst cutting fish, vegetables etc. ~ঝাঁপ *n.* the practice of throwing oneself from above upon aforesaid knives during the feast of charak (চড়ক).

বঁড়শি var. **বড়শি**।

বঁদে alt. spell. of **বোঁদে**।

বঁধু, বঁধুয়া *n.* (poet.) a friend; a lover, a sweetheart; a gallant; (cp.) a winsome marrow.

বক *n.* a species of long-necked white bird, the stork; (cp.) the egret, the heron, the crane; a kind of heron-shaped flower. **বক দেখানো** *v.* to taunt by cupping one's palms almost in the shape of a heron. ~ঠুঁটো *n.* a species of river fish with a long and slender beak. ~ধার্মিক *a.* feigning or simulating virtuousness or piety, sanctimonious; hypocritical. ~বৃত্তি *n.* feigned virtuousness or piety, sanctimony; hypocrisy, dissimulation. ~যন্ত্র *n.* a flask with a long bentback neck used in distillation, a retort, a still; stethoscope.

বকঠুঁটো, বকধার্মিক see **বক**।

বকনা *n. fem.* a young cow that has not yet calved, a heifer.

বকবক *int.* denoting: intolerable prattling or chattering; overmuch talking. **বকবক করা** *v.* to prattle or chatter disgustingly; to talk overmuch.

বকবকম *int.* denoting: the cooing of the pigeon or any similar noise.

বকবকানি *n.* intolerable prattling; meaningless jabber or chatter; overmuch talking.

বকবৃত্তি see **বক**।

বকমকাঠ *n.* a kind of tree or its timber.

বকযন্ত্র see **বক**।

বকরা *n.* the he-goat, the billy-goat; the goat.

বকরি *n.* the she-goat, the nanny-goat; the goat.

বকরিদ *n.* a Muslim festival commemorating Ibrahim's (cp. Abraham) sacrifice of his own son to God.

বকলম *n.* the name of an illiterate person signed by another; (loos.) act of signing for another.

বকলস *n.* a buckle. **বকলস আঁটা** *v.* to buckle.

বকশি *a.* high government official of the Muslim regime in India whose chief duty was to act as a paymaster.

বকশিশ *n.* a reward; a tip. **বকশিশ দেওয়া** *v.* to reward; to tip.

বকা[1] *v.* to indulge in garrulity; to prattle, to talk overmuch; to scold, to chide.

বকা[2]**, বকাট, বকাটে** variants **বখা, বখাট** and **বখাটে** respectively.

বকাণ্ডপ্রত্যাশা *n.* a hope as vain as the expectation of a heron to obtain an egg of a bull, a vain hope.

বকানো *v.* to cause to talk overmuch.

বকাবকি *n.* a debate; an altercation; a scolding. **বকাবকি করা** *v.* to debate, to argue; to altercate, to bandy words; to scold; to chide.

বকামি var. of **বখামি** (see **বখা**).

বকুনি *n.* scolding, chiding; garrulity, prattling. **বকুনি খাওয়া** *v.* to be scolded or chid or rebuked. **বকুনি দেওয়া** *v.* to scold, to chide, to rebuke.

বকুল *n. Mimusops elengi*, a large evergreen flower-tree; its sweet-scented flower.

বকেয়া[1] *n.* a kind of hem-stitch which may be undone easily.

বকেয়া[2] *a.* still unpaid or undone; outstanding. □ *n.* arrears, arrearage. **বকেয়া বাকি** arrears or arrearage of the last year.

বক্কাল *n.* a medicinal tree-bark.

বক্তব্য *a.* to be said; worth saying; under discussion; discussible. □ *n.* one's say; a subject or context or discussion.

বক্তা *a.* lecturing; speaking; having the gift of the gab, eloquent. □ *n.* a speaker, a lecturer; an orator. **বক্তার** *a.* eloquent; made eloquent by divine inspiration; garrulous. □ *n.* such a person.

বক্তৃতা *n.* a speech, a lecture; a prattling; eloquence; (facet.) a rigmarole. **বক্তৃতা করা, বক্তৃতা দেওয়া** *v.* to deliver a speech, to speak, to lecture; to prattle; to indulge in a rigmarole. **বক্তৃতা থামাও, বক্তৃতা রাখো** stop talking, stop your harangue or garrulity. **~শক্তি** *n.* speaking power.

বক্ত্র *n.* the mouth.

বক্র *a.* bent, curved, tortuous; oblique; squint; crooked; (chiefly astrol.) antipatheitc. □ *n.* a bend, a turn. **~গতি** *a.* having a curved or sinuous or tortuous motion. **~গামী** *a.* curvedly or sinuously or tortuously moving crooked. **~চ্ছেদ** *n.* (geom.) an oblique section. **~তা** *n.* curvedness; sinuosity; obliqueness; squintness; curvature; crookedness, (chiefly astrol.) antipathy. **বক্রতা-কেন্দ্র** *n.* (phys.) a centre of curvature. **~দৃষ্টি** *a.* squint-eyed, cock-eyed; looking askance; squinting. **~নাস** *a.* having a curved or aquiline nose. **~পৃষ্ঠ** *a.* convex; arch-backed . **~রেখা** *n.* curved line, a curve. **~শিরাল** *a.* (bot.) curviveined. **~সংঘাত** *n.* (mech.) an oblique impact. **বক্রাংশুরেখা** *n.* (phys.) a caustic curve. **বক্রাংশুস্পর্শ** *n.* (phys.) causticity.

বক্রিমা same as **বক্রতা** (see **বক্র**).

বক্রী *a.* curved; tortuous, sinuous; (chiefly astrol.) antipathetic. **~করণ** *n.* curvation. **~কৃত** *a.* curved. **~ভূত** *a.* curved; turned antipathetic.

বক্রোক্তি *n.* (rhet.) a figure of speech akin to pun and erotesis; (loos.) a sarcasm; a sarcastic utterance.

বক্ষ *n.* the breast, the bosom; the chest; (fig.) the heart. **বক্ষঃস্থ** *a.* lying on the breast or chest or in the heart. **বক্ষঃস্থল** *n.* the region of the chest. **~স্পন্দন** *n.* palpitation or throbbing of the heart.

বক্ষ্যমাণ *a.* to be spoken of hereafter; (loos.) under discussion.

বক্সী rej. spell. of **বকশি** ।

বখরা *n.* a share. **বখরা করা** *v.* to divide into shares, to share, to apportion. **বখরা দেওয়া** *v.* to give a share, to share. **বখরা পাওয়া** *v.* to get a share, to share. **বখরা নেওয়া** *v.* to take a share, to share. **~দার** *n.* a sharer, a shareholder, a partner.

বখশিশ alt. spell. of **বকশিশ** ।

বখা *v.* to be spoilt by bad association; to sow one's wild oats; to go to the bad. □ *a.* spoilt by bad association; dissipated; gone to the bad; (euph.) saucy. **বখাটে** *a.* same as **বখা** (*a.*). **বখানো** *v.* to make one sow one's wild oats, to cause to go to the bad, to deprave. **বখামি, বখামো** *n.* dissipation, depravity; (euph.) sauciness.

বখিল *a.* miserly, parsimonious, stingy, niggardly.

বখেড়া *n.* a hindrance; a trouble, a quarrel, dispute.

বখেয়া var. of **বকেয়া**[1] ।

বগ dial. corrup. of **বক** ।

বগয়রহ var. of **গয়রহ** ।

বগল *n.* the armpit; the flank; neighbourhood, proximity. **বগলদাবা করা** *v.* to carry or conceal under one's armpit; (fig.) to appropriate secretly to oneself; (fig.) to take possession of or to bring under one's control. **বগল বাজানো** *v.* to rap one's armpit by putting a palm in it as a mark of mad delight; (fig.) to rejoice madly. **বগলে** *adv.* in the armpit; near, beside.

বগলা *n.* one of the ten manifestations of Goddess Durga (দুর্গা).

বগলি *n.* a purse made of cloth or woven with thread.

বগা *n.* (sarcas. or dero.) the egret, the heron, the crane; anything as unshapely as the egret (কাগাবগা).

বগি[1] *n.* a hooded buggy.

বগি[2] *n.* railway carriage, (cp.) a bogie.

বগি[3] *n.* a high-rimmed metal dish (also **বগিথালা**).

বঙ্ক, বঙ্কা *a.* (poet. & obs.) bent, curved, hunchbacked.

বঙ্কিম *a.* bent; curved; slightly bent; squint; oblique (বঙ্কিম চাহনি). **~বিহারী** *n.* Krishna (কৃষ্ণ).

বঙ্গ, বঙ্গদেশ *n.* Bengal; the ancient name

of East Bengal. ~জ *a.* born or produced in Bengal. □ *n.* a section of kayasthas (কায়স্থ) of Bengal (also **বঙ্গজ কায়স্থ**). ~দেশীয় same as **বঙ্গীয়**। ~ভাষা *n.* Bengali. ~বিভাগ, ~ভঙ্গ *n.* the partition of Bengal. **বঙ্গাধিপ** same as **বঙ্গেশ্বর**। **বঙ্গানুবাদ** *n.* translation or rendering into Bengali. **বঙ্গাব্দ** *n.* the Bengali era (counted from 693 A.D.). **বঙ্গীয়** *a.* of Bengal; born or produced in Bengal; Bengali. **বঙ্গেশ্বর** *n.* a king of Bengal.

বচ *n.* the sweet-flag.

বচন *n.* speech; utterance; a saying, an adage, an apophthegm, a maxim; (gr.) number (**একবচন** = the singular number; **দ্বিবচন** = the dual number; **বহুবচন** = the plural number). ~বাগীশ *a.* having the gift of the gab; eloquent, very talkative. ~বিন্যাস *n.* art or mode of speaking; eloquence; arrangement of words or speech. **বচনসর্বস্ব ব্যক্তি** a person of mere words, a wind-bag. **বচনীয়** *a.* speakable; blamable.

বচসা *n.* altercation; a brawl. **বচসা করা** *v.* to altercate, to wrangle, to bandy words; to brawl.

বছর, বচ্ছর coll. forms of **বৎসর**। ~ভর *adv.* throughout the year, all the year round.

বজরা *n.* a large pleasure or state boat; a man-of-war; a barge.

বজায় *a.* in force or intact or in position. **বজায় থাকা** *v.* to be in force or intact or in position. **বজায় রাখা** *v.* to keep up, to keep going, to maintain.

বজ্জাত *a.* (lit. & rare) base-born; wicked; naughty; mischievous. **বজ্জাতি** *n.* wickedness; naughtiness; mischievousness, mischief-making.

বজ্র *n.* thunderbolt, thunder; the weapon of Indra (ইন্দ্র) the king of gods; (loos.) lightning; (astrol.) a cross-sign (×) on the palm or sole of a person; diamond. **বজ্র আঁটুনি ফসকা গেরো** the more laws, the more flaws; (cp.) summum jus summum injustitia. ~কঠিন, ~কঠোর *a.* extremely hard, adamantine. ~কীট *n.* the pangolin. ~গম্ভীর *a.* deep and loud as thunderclap. **বজ্রগম্ভীর স্বরে** in a voice as deep as thunder, in a thunderous voice. ~গুণন *n.* (alg.) cross-multiplication. ~তুল্য *a.* adamantine; fatally severe; thunderous. ~ধর same as **বজ্রপাণি**। ~ধ্বনি, ~নাদ, ~নির্ঘোষ *n.* thunderclap; thunder-peal; (fig.) a voice or noise as deep and loud as thunderclap. ~পাণি *n.* one whose weapon is thunder, the thunderer; Indra (ইন্দ্র) the king of gods. ~পাত *n.* a crash of thunder; thunderbolt. ~বহ *n.* (phys.) a lightning conductor. ~বারক *n.* (phys.) a lightning arrester. **বজ্রাগ্নি** *n.* lightning. **বজ্রাঘাত** *n.* a thunder-stroke; (fig.) a sudden and fatal calamity. **বজ্রাহত** *a.* thunder-struck.

বঞ্চক *a.* & *n.* a deceiver; a swindler; one who deprives (another).

বঞ্চনা, বঞ্চন *n.* deception; deceit; fraudulence; a fraud; deprivation. **বঞ্চনা করা** *v.* to deceive; to defraud; to deprive (of.). **বঞ্চনাপূর্বক** *adv.* deceitfully; fraudulently; craftily. **বঞ্চনাময়** *a.* deceptive; illusory.

বঞ্চা *v.* (poet.) to deceive, to beguile; (poet.) to deprive (of); (poet.) to spend or pass ('সুখে বঞ্চিবে দিন') ; (poet.) to live, to lead one's life.

বঞ্চিত *a.* deceived; beguiled, defrauded; deprived. *fem.* **বঞ্চিতা**।

বট *n.* the banyan tree. ~পত্র *n.* a banyan leaf. ~মূল *n.* the base or foot of a banyan tree.

বটকেরা, বটখেরা *n.* banter, taunt.

বটঠাকুর *n.* an elder brother of one's husband.

বটতলা *n.* the foot of the banyan tree; Grub Street.

বটা *v.* to be (সে চালাক বটে).

বটিকা, বটী *n.* a pill, a globule.

বটু, বটুক *n.* (obs.) a Brahmin lad.

বটুয়া *n.* a small purselike bag made of cloth.

বটে *int.* just so (তাই বটে) ; exactly (বটেই তো) ; is it (বটে, এমন কথা ?) ; well (কী বলছ বটে) ; (sarcas.) no doubt (বীরেরাই পালায় বটে) ; take care (বটে রে). **বটে বটে** oh yes, just so, there you are.

বটের *n.* a species of small partridge akin to the quail.

বডিস *n.* a bodice; bra.

বড়, বড়ো *a.* large, big; high, tall, lofty; long; lengthy; fat; loud; excessive; severe; magnanimous, great; respectable, noble; older; elder; eldest; senior in position; rich, aristocratic; most important, principal, chief; leading; eminent; highly contested. □ *adv.* very thoroughly (বড় মন্দ). □ *int.* denoting: slight contempt (চাকরি তো বড়) ; amazement (বড়ো যে এলে). **বড়ো করা** *v.* to make one flourish; to extol usu. unduly; to enlarge (as a photograph); to lengthen (as a story); to expand (রাজ্য বড়ো করা), to increase (নামযশ বড় করা) ; to magnify, to exaggerate (বড় করে দেখা বা বলা) ; to elevate or edify (চরিত্র বড়ো করা) ; to liberalize (মন বা হাত বড় করা) ; to make louder, to raise (গলা বড় করা) ; to dilate (চোখ বড় করা) ; to heighten (আশা বড় করা) ; to bring up (ছেলে বড়ো করা). **বড় দেখানো** *v.* to look large or big; to loom large; to magnify. **বড় হওয়া** *v.* to grow up; to come of age; to flourish; to be expanded; to be edified; to be liberalized; to be glorified (মুখ বড় হওয়া). **বড় একটা না** not much, not at all; hardly; rarely; seldom; once in a blue moon. **বড় কথা** the most important word, chief words; tall-talk. **~কর্তা** *n.* a master or head of a family; the chief or boss of an organization; a headman. **~কুটুম্ব, ~কুটুম** *n.* a wife's brother, a brother-in-law. **বড় খেলা** a highly contested match; a big or important match; a great game. **বড় গলা** loud voice (বড় গলায় গান) ; proud or arrogant tone (বড় গলায় ঘোষণা). **বড় গল্প** a long story. **বড় গাছে নৌকা বাঁধা** (fig.) to resort to a great patron. **বড় ঘর** a large or spacious room; a hall; a high or aristocratic or noble family. **বড় জোর** at most, at best. **বড় জ্বালা** a great or severe affliction. **বড় ঝড়** a great or violent storm. **~ত্ব** *n.* seniority in age or position; greatness; magnanimity. **বড় দরের লোক** a man of high status. **~দাদা,** (coll.) **~দা** *n.* the eldest brother. **বড় দাম** a high or exorbitant price. **~দিদি,** (coll.) **~দি** *n. fem.* the eldest sister. **~দিন** *n.* (astr.) the winter solstice; (pop.) the Christmas Day. **বড় দুঃখ** deep or intense sorrow. **বড় দুর্দিন** terribly hard times. **বড় পেট** a large belly; voracious appetite; (fig.) exorbitant demand or tremendous greed. **বড় বড় বানরের বড় বড় পেট** (fig.) the more one has, the more one demands; the wealthier a man, the greater is his demand. **বড় বই** an enormous book, a fat volume; (fig.) magnum opus. **বড় বংশ** a high or respectable or noble family. **~বাবু** *n.* a head clerk; the seniormost male member of a family. **বড় বোন** *n. fem.* an elder sister,the eldest sister. **বড় ব্যাপার** a great affair. **বড় ভাই** *n.* an elder brother, a big brother, the eldest brother. **বড় মোকদ্দমা** a big or leading case. **বড় মজা** a great fun. **বড় মন** a magnanimous heart; a high mind; a master mind; an optimistic outlook. **~মানষি** *n.* ostentatious display or wealthiness or riches. **~মানুষ** *n.* a rich man; a great man. **বড় মুখ** elated or proud in speech (বড় মুখে বলা) ; nourishing a great hope (বড় মুখ নিয়ে আসা) ; dignified countenance; prestige; renown. **বড় মুখ ছোট হওয়া** to feel disgraced; to be put out of countenance. **~রানি** *n.* the chief queen (of a king who has several wives). **বড় লড়াই** a hard fight; a great battle. **~লাট** see **লাট২**। **~লোক** same as **বড়মানুষ**। **বড়লোকি** same as **বড়মানষি**। **বড় শরিক** the senior partner of an estate. **বড় শিকার** a big game; big game hunting. **বড় শীত** severe cold. **বড় সাহেব** *n.* the senior partner of a firm; the boss of an office. **বড় হাজরি** see **হাজরি**।

বড়বা *n.* (myth.) a sea-horse vomiting fire constantly; the mare. **~গ্নি, ~নল** *n.* the fire vomited by the aforesaid sea-horse.

বড়শি, বঁড়শি *n.* a fish-hook.

বড়া *n.* a kind of cake fried in oil (ডালের বড়া, ডিমের বড়া) ; a cake-like juicy sweet-meat (তালের বড়া).

বড়াই১ *n.* boast, bragging. **বড়াই করা** *v.* to boast, to brag.

বড়াই২, বড়ায়ি *n.* an old woman named Yogamaya (যোগমায়া) who acted as a go-between in the affaire de coeur of Radha (রাধা) and Krishna (কৃষ্ণ) ; a decrepit old woman; a great grandmother.

বড়ি *n.* a pill, a globule; a tablet, a ball (কালির বড়ি) ; a small conical ball made of the paste of pigeon-pea and dried in the sun (this ball is eaten after being fried or cooked).

বড়ু *n.* (obs.) a son of a Brahmin.

বড়ে, বোড়ে *n.* (in chess) a pawn. **বড়ের চাল** (in chess) the move of a pawn; (fig.) a very unassuming and yet a danger-spelling move.

বড়ো alt. spell. of **বড়** ।

বড্ড emphatic form of **বড়** ।

বণিক *n.* a merchant, a trader; a banian ; a vaishya or trader by caste.

বণিকসংঘ *n.* a corporation or association of the traders; a guild.

বণিকসভা *n.* chamber of commerce, association of traders or merchants.

বণিগ্‌বৃত্তি *n.* trade; traffic; trading; commercial spirit, commercialism.

বণ্টক *n.* a distributor, one who apportions or divides.

বণ্টন *n.* distribution; apportionment, division. **বণ্টন করা** *v.* to distribute; to apportion, to divide.

বণ্টিত *a.* distributed; apportioned, divided.

-বৎ *sfx.* denoting: equivalent to, resembling, like, as (পিতৃবৎ).

বৎস *n.* the young of the cow (or of any animal), a calf; (in affectionate address) a dear boy.

বৎসতর *n.* a bull-calf; a steer. *fem.* **বৎসতরী** a cow-calf; a heifer.

বৎসর *n.* a year; an era. **বৎসরান্তে** *adv.* at the end of a year; at year-ending.

বৎসল *a.* (used as a *sfx.*) affectionate, loving. *fem.* **বৎসলা** । **বৎসলতা** *n.* affectionateness, affection, love.

বৎসা *n.* (rare) (in affectionate address) a dear girl.

বৎসাদনী *n.* a medicinal plant, *Menispermum glabrum.*

বতারিখ *adv.* date by date; datewise.

-বতী *fem.* of **-বান্‌** ।

বত্রিশ *n.* & *a.* thirty-two.

বদ *a.* bad; evil, wicked; offensive (বদ গন্ধ) ; peevish (বদমেজাজ) ; infected, contaminated, defiled (বদরক্ত). **~খদ** *a.* ugly; troublesome or unmanageable or unwieldy. **~খেয়াল** *a.* wicked inclination or desire; evil intention or design; perverse propensity. **~জবান** *n.* abusive or filthy language. **বদজবান করা** *v.* to use abusive or filthy language. **~জাত** same as **বজ্জাত** । **~নাম** *n.* discredit; bad reputation; infamy; calumny. **বদনাম করা** *v.* to calumniate; to slander; to speak ill of. **~বু, ~বো** *n.* bad or foul smell, stink. **~ভ্যাস** *n.* bad or evil habit; indecent habit. **~মতলব** *n.* evil design, evil purpose. **~মেজাজ** *n.* illhumour, bad temper; petulance, peevishness. **~মেজাজি** *a.* ill-humoured, bad-tempered; petulant, peevish, cross-grained. **~রসিকতা** *n.* base or unrefined or indecent or vulgar humour or joke. **~রাগী** *a.* short-tempered, choleric. **~হজম** *n.* indigestion; dyspepsia.

বদন *n.* face, countenance; mouth; appearance. **~কমল** *n.* a lotus-like face; a face conceived as a lotus. **~ভরে** *adv.* with full-throated ease. **~মণ্ডল** *n.* face, countenance.

বদনা *n.* a kind of small pitcher with a slender spout.

বদমাশ, বদমাইশ, বদমায়েশ *a.* wicked; roguish, mischievous; profligate; (in affection) naughty. **বদমাশি, বদমায়েশি** *n.* wickedness; roguery, mischief; profligacy; naughtiness. **বদমাশি করা** *v.* to indulge in wickedness or roguery or profligacy; to be naughty.

বদর[১] *n.* the full moon; a Muslim saint (whose name is uttered by boatsmen to ensure a safe voyage).

বদর[২], বদরিকা, বদরী *n.* jujube.

বদল *n.* exchange (মালবদল) ; barter; substitution; change, alteration (ভোলবদল) ; transfer (অফিস বদল). **বদল করা** *v.* to exchange; to barter; to substitute; to change, to alter; to transfer. **বদলা** *n.* a thing or person seized or killed in retaliation; requital, retaliation; a substitute. **বদলা নেওয়া** *v.* to seize or kill in retaliation; to requite, to retaliate; to accept a substitute. **বদলানো** same as **বদল করা**। **বদলা-বদলি** *n.* exchange; change; mutual transfer. **বদলি** *a.* substituting; given or taken in exchange; bartered; substituted; transferred. □ *n.* substitution; a substitute; transfer; change. **বদলি করা** same as **বদল করা**। **বদলে** *adv.* in exchange of, in lieu of, in place of, instead, instead of.

বদান্য *a.* generous, bountiful, munificent, liberal, charitable. **~তা** *n.* generosity, bounty, munificence, liberality, charity.

বদ্ধ *a.* tied, bound, fastened; bound by an obligation (প্রতিজ্ঞাবদ্ধ) ; interwoven, dressed, put up (বদ্ধকবরী) ; shut, closed (বদ্ধদ্বার) ; confined, imprisoned, encaged (বদ্ধসিংহ) ; entrapped, ensnared (বদ্ধ মৃগ) ; caught in (পাশবদ্ধ) ; clasped (আলিঙ্গনে বদ্ধ) ; restrained, arrested (বদ্ধ স্রোত) ; stagnant (বদ্ধ জল) ; joined together (বদ্ধপাণি, একতাবদ্ধ) ; placed, put, arrayed, well-ordered (শ্রেণিবদ্ধ) ; firm (বদ্ধমূল) ; deep-rooted, deep-seated (বদ্ধ ধারণা) ; downright, thorough, confirmed, stark (বদ্ধ পাগল) ; (arith.) concrete (বদ্ধসংখ্যা). **~দৃষ্টি** *n.* a fixed or steadfast look, a gaze. **~পরিকর** *n.* firmly resolved; determined; resolute; girdled. **বদ্ধ পরিকর হওয়া** *v.* to be firmly resolved; to gird up one's loins, to gird oneself up. **বদ্ধ পাগল** crazy to the extreme. **~মুষ্টি** *a.* having closed or clenched one's palm; (fig.) close-fisted, niggardly, miserly. **~মূল** *a.* deep-rooted, deep-seated. **বদ্ধাঞ্জলি হওয়া** *v.* to fold or join one's palms. **বদ্ধাধান** *n.* (phys.) a bounded charge.

বদ্বীপ *n.* a delta. **~শীর্ষ** *n.* head of the delta.

বধ *n.* killing, slaughter. **বধ করা** *v.* to kill, to slay; to slaughter. **~কর্তা** *n.* a killer, a slayer; a slaughterer. *fem.* **~কর্ত্রী**। **~দণ্ড** *n.* capital punishment. **~স্থলী, ~স্থান** *n.* a place of execution or slaughter; a slaughter-house. **বধার্থ** *adv.* for killing or slaughter. **বধার্হ** same as **বধ্য**।

বধির *a.* deaf; (fig.) refusing to listen. **বধির করা** *v.* to deafen. **বধির হওয়া** *v.* to become deaf; (fig.) to turn a deaf ear (to). **বধিরতা, বধিরত্ব** *n.* deafness.

বধূ *n.* a wife; a newly married woman; a bride; a married woman; a daughter-in-law (usu. **বধূমাতা**). **~জন** *n.* a married woman esp. one whose husband is alive. **~বরণ** *n.* ceremoniously welcoming a bride or a daughter-in-law. **~মাতা** *n.* the daughter-in law. **~হত্যা** *n.* killing or murder of a married woman (usu.) in the husband's or father-in-law's house.

বধোদ্যত *a.* on the point of killing or slaying or slaughtering, ready to kill.

বধ্য *a.* (fit.) to be killed or slain or slaughtered. **~পাল** *n.* the supervisor of an execution. **~ভূমি** *n.* a place of execution or slaughter.

বন *n.* a forest, a jungle, a wood; an arbour, a bower, a grove. **~কপোত** *n.* the wood-pigeon, the cushat. **~কর** *n.* forest revenue; a forest cess. **~কর্মী** *n.* a forester; a worker in the forest department. **~কুক্কুট** *n.* the wild-fowl; the jungle-fowl; the wood-cock. **~কৃত্যক** *n.* forest service. **~গোলাপ** *n.* the briar, the briar-rose; the sweet briar. **~চর, ~চারী** *a.* living in a forest; wild; silvan. **~জ** *a.* forest-grown. **~জঙ্গল** *n.* thickets, underwood; woodlands. **~দেবতা** *n.* a wood-god, a silvan . *fem.* **বনদেবী**। **~পথ** *n.* a forest path, a jungle path. **~পরি** *n.* a wood-nymph, a dryad. **~পাল** *n.* a conservator of forests. **~ফুল** *n.* a wild flower. **~বাদাড়** same as **বনজঙ্গল**। **~বাস** *n.* living in a forest; banishment to the forest. **বনবাসে দেওয়া, বনবাসে পাঠানো** *v.* to banish or exile (one) to the forest. **বনবাসে যাওয়া** *v.* to go to live in a forest as a punishment; to be exiled to the forest. **~বাসী** *a.* & *n.* living in a forest, a forest dweller. *fem.* **~বাসিনী**। **~বিড়াল** *n.* the wild-cat; the tiger-cat, the bush-cat, the serval; the cougar, the puma. *fem.* **বনবিড়ালী**। **~বিহার** *n.* wandering in a forest (for pleasure etc.). **~বিহারী** *a.* roving in forests and groves esp. for pleasure. □ *n.* Krishna (কৃষ্ণ). **~বৃক্ষ** *n.* a forest-tree, a dryad. **~ভোজ, ~ভোজন** *n.* a picnic. **~মধু** *n.* wood-honey. **~মল্লিকা** *n.* the wild jasmine. ~মহোৎসব *n.* the festival of tree plantation. ~মানুষ *n.* any anthropoid ape such as the gorilla, the chimpanzee etc. ~মালা *n.* a garland of wild flowers. ~মালী *n.* one wearing a garland of wild flowers; Krishna (কৃষ্ণ). ~মোরগ same as বনকুক্কুট। ~রক্ষক *n.* a forest-ranger. ~রক্ষী *n.* a forest-guard. ~শূকর *n.* a wild hog. ~শ্রী *n.* the beauty of the forest; the forest; the beautiful forest. ~স্থ, ~স্থিত *a.* of a forest; situated in a forest; forest-grown, wild; silvan (বনস্থ জীবন). ~হংসী *n.* the wild-duck; the wild-goose.

বনবন[১] *n.* bonbon.

বনবন[২] *int.* denoting: a swift whirling motion. **বনবন করে ঘোরা** *v.* to rotate or whirl swiftly.

বনস্পতি *n.* a tree that bears fruit apparently without blossoms (such as, the fig tree); a very large tree.

বনা *v.* to get on together, to agree; to be on good terms (তাদের বনে না) ; to be reduced to or to be proved (বোকা বনা).

বনাত *n.* broad-cloth; baize.

বনানী *n.* a great forest; an extensive forest.

বনানো *v.* to cause to get on together, to cause to agree.

বনান্ত *n.* the outskirts or end of a forest.

বনান্তর *n.* another forest.

বনাবনি *n.* mutual agreement, amity, concurrence, concord.

বনাম *prep.* versus.

বনিতা *n.* a woman; a wife.

বনিবনা same as **বনাবনি**।

বনিয়াদ *n.* foundation, base, groundwork. **বনিয়াদি** *a.* traditional; traditionally aristocratic or noble (বনিয়াদি বংশ) ; basic (বনিয়াদি শিক্ষা).

বনীকরণ *n.* afforestation.

বনেচর same as **বনচর** (see **বন**).

বনেদ, বনেদি coll. forms of **বনিয়াদ** and **বনিয়াদি** respectively.

বনোয়ারি *n.* one wearing a garland of wild flowers; an appellation of Krishna (কৃষ্ণ).

-বন্ত *sfx.* denoting: possession or endowment (লক্ষ্মীবন্ত, রূপবন্ত).

বন্দক *a.* singing in adoration, hymning; extolling; saluting; worshipping. □ *n.* one who sings in praise, a hymnist; one who extols; one who salutes; a worshipper, a votary; one employed to glorify (esp. a prince) in songs (usu. at fixed hours and on particular occasions).

বন্দন, বন্দনা *n.* singing in adoration, hymning; a song of praise, a hymn; extolment; salutation; a salute; worship, adoration. **বন্দনা করা** *v.* to sing in adoration, to hymn; to extol, to salute; to worship, to adore. **বন্দনীয়** *a.* worthy of being glorified in songs; deserving obeisance; worshipful, adorable. *fem.* **বন্দনীয়া**।

বন্দর *n.* a port. ~পাল *n.* an overseer of the port, port commissioner. **মুক্ত বন্দর** a free port.

বন্দা (poet.) same as **বন্দনা করা** (see **বন্দনা**).

বন্দি *a.* imprisoned; confined; captivated. □ *n.* a prisoner; a captive. **বন্দি করা** *v.* to imprison; to capture, to take one prisoner.

বন্দিগৃহ same as **বন্দিশালা**।

বন্দিত *a.* glorified in songs, hymned; lauded, extolled; saluted; worshipped, adored. *fem.* **বন্দিতা**।

বন্দিত্ব, বন্দিদশা imprisonment, duress(e), confinement, captivity.

বন্দিনী *fem.* of **বন্দী[২]**।

বন্দিপাল *n.* a jailor, a jailer, a gaoler.

বন্দিমুক্তি *n.* release or liberation of prisoners.

বন্দিশালা *n.* a prison, a jail, a gaol; a guard-house, a guard-room.

বন্দিশ *n.* (in music) style; style of composition.

বন্দী[১] same as **বন্দক**।

বন্দী[২] *a.* alt. spell. of **বন্দি**।

বন্দুক *n.* a gun, a rifle, a bundook, a musket, a matchlock; a pistol, a revolver. ~ধারী *a.* armed with or carrying a gun or rifle. **বন্দুকধারী লোক** a gunman; a musketeer, a rifleman.

বন্দেগি *n.* (Mus.) humble salutation. **বন্দেগি জনাব** I humbly salute you, sir; I bow to thee, sir.

বন্দেজ *n.* arrangement; apportionment; distribution; allotment. **বন্দেজ করা** *v.* to arrange; to apportion; to distribute; to allot.

বন্দে মাতরম্ *v.* I salute thee, Mother. □ *n.* the first two words or (loos.) the title of the national song of India, Bandemataram.

বন্দোবস্ত *n.* arrangement; preparation; provision; settlement; land settlement; tenure (জমির বন্দোবস্ত) ; a contract. **বন্দোবস্ত করা** *n.* to make arrangements; to make preparations (for); to provide for; to settle; to make a contract (with). **বন্দোবস্ত দেওয়া** *v.* to have tenure (of land etc.) settled on oneself. **চিরস্থায়ী বন্দোবস্ত** (hist.) The Permanent Settlement.

বন্দ্য same as **বন্দনীয়**। **~বংশ** *n.* an adorable or noble family; Bandyopadhyay or Banerji family.

বন্ধ *n.* any device for binding or fastening (কোমরবন্ধ) ; a tie, a bond, bondage (প্রেমবন্ধ) ; a clasp, an embrace (ভুজবন্ধ) ; an obstacle (স্রোতোবন্ধ) ; construction (সেতুবন্ধ) ; composition (ছন্দবন্ধ) ; restraint or stoppage (ইন্দ্রিয়বন্ধ). □ *a.* shut, closed (বন্ধ জানালা, বন্ধ অফিস) ; stopped, ceased, discontinued (কথাবার্তা বন্ধ) ; obstructed, confined, shut in (কারাগারে বন্ধ). **বন্ধ করা** *v.* to shut, to close; to stop, to cease, to discontinue; to obstruct; to confine, to shut in. **গ্রীষ্মের বন্ধ** the summar vacation. **পূজার বন্ধ** the Puja holidays, the Puja vacation.

বন্ধ্ *n.* a strike, a cease-work movement; closure.

বন্ধক *n.* pawning, mortgage, hypothecation; a pawn, a pledge. **বন্ধক দেওয়া** *v.* to pawn, to pledge, to mortgage, tō hypothecate. **বন্ধক রাখা** *v.* to lend money taking something in pawn or mortgage. **~গ্রহীতা** *n.* a pawnbroker; a pawnee; a mortgagee. **~দাতা** *n.* a pawner; a mortgager. **~পত্র** *n.* same as **বন্ধকি দলিল**। **বন্ধকি** *a.* of pawning or mortgage or hypothecation (বন্ধকি দলিল = a mortgage deed); carrying on pawnbroking (বন্ধকি দোকান = a pawnshop); pawned, mortgaged, hypothecated (বন্ধকি সম্পত্তি). **বন্ধকি কারবার** a pawnbroker's business. **বন্ধকি দোকান** a pawnshop.

বন্ধন *n.* binding, fastening, tying; tethering; a tie, a bondage (বন্ধনমোচন) ; clasping or embracing, a clasp or embrace (ভুজবন্ধন) ; obstruction, an obstacle (স্রোতোবন্ধন) ; restraint, stoppage; confinement (কারাবন্ধন) ; composition (কবরীবন্ধন) ; construction (সেতুবন্ধন) ; unification (হৃদয়ে হৃদয়ে বন্ধন). **বন্ধন করা** *v.* to bind, to tie, to fasten; to tether; to clasp, to embrace; to obstruct, to restrain, to stop; to confine, to shut in; to unite. **~গ্রন্থি** *n.* a knot. **~দশা** *n.* captivity; imprisonment, incarceration. **~ফলক** *n.* a splint. **~মুক্তি** *n.* freedom from bondage or captivity. **~রজ্জু** *n.* a rope for tying or fastening, a tether. **~স্তম্ভ** *n.* a tying post. **~হীন** *a.* without ties or fetters; untied; unfettered; uncontrolled; unrestrained. **বন্ধনী** *n.* any device to bind or fasten, a tie, a band, a ligament; (print. & math.) a bracket. **বন্ধনীভুক্ত** *a.* bracketed.

বন্ধু *n.* a friend; a well-wisher; a benefactor, a patron; an ally; a comrade; an associate; a lover. **~তা, ~ত্ব** *n.* friendship; amity; alliance. **বন্ধুত্ব করা** *v.* to make friends with. **বন্ধুত্বপূর্ণ** *a.* friendly; amicable. **~নি** *n. fem.* a female friend; a friend's wife. **~প্রীতি** *n.* love or affection toward a friend. **~বর** *n.* close or intimate friend; an affectionate way of addressing or referring to a friend. **~বান্ধব** *n.* friends and relations. **~বিচ্ছেদ** *n.* estrangement or separation from friends; estrangement or separation from a friend. **~সুলভ** *a.* friendly. **~হীন** *a.* friendless.

বন্ধুর *a.* uneven, rugged; rough. **~তা** *n.* unevenness, ruggedness; roughness.

বন্ধুলি *n.* a variety of crimson flower or its plant.

বন্ধ্য *a.* fit to be bound or tied; unproductive, barren, sterile; childless. *fem.* **বন্ধ্যা**। **~তা, ~ত্ব** *n.* fitness for being bound or tied; unproductivity, barrenness, sterility; childlessness.

বন্য *a.* grown or growing or dwelling or

roving in the forest, wild; of the forest, silvan; unfit for civilized society; uncivilized; savage.

বন্যা[১] *fem.* of **বন্য**।

বন্যা[২] *n.* a flood; an inundation; a deluge. **বন্যার জল** floodwater. **~পীড়িত** *a.* flood-stricken. **~প্লাবিত** *a.* flooded. **~বিধ্বস্ত** *a.* devastated by the flood; flood-stricken.

বপক *n.* a sower; a planter.

বপন *n.* sowing; planting, plantation. **বপন করা** *v.* to sow; to plant. **~যন্ত্র** *n.* a sowing-machine.

বপা *n.* (poet.) to sow or plant.

বপু *n.* the body. **~ষ্মান** *a.* heavy-bodied, burly, corpulent, hefty. *fem.* **~ষ্মতী**।

বপ্তা same as **বপক**।

বপ্র *n.* ground; a field; a wall; a rampart; **~ক্রীড়া** *n.* act of digging earth with the horn or trunk (as by a bull or an elephant).

বমন *n.* vomiting; belching or ejecting (as by a volcano). **বমন করা** *v.* to vomit, to spew, to spue; to belch, to eject violently. **বমনেচ্ছা** *n.* nausea. **বমনোদ্রেক** *n.* nausea, retching. **বমনোদ্রেককর** *a.* nauseous, nauseating; vomitive; emetic. **বমনোদ্রেককর ওষুধ** an emetic.

বমাল *adv.* together with the stolen or looted thing (বমাল ধরা পড়া).

বমি *n.* vomited matter, vomit, spew, spue. **গা বমি-বমি করা** *v.* to have nausea. **বমিত** *a.* vomited; violently ejected (as by a volcano).

বম্বেটে alt. spell. of **বোম্বেটে**।

বয় *n.* a servant or serving-lad (esp. one employed in a hotel etc.)

বয়ঃ *n.* age; longevity or lifetime; youth or majority. **~ক্রম** *n.* age. **~প্রাপ্ত, ~স্থ** *a.* one who has attained youth or (loos.) marriageable age; of age, grown-up. *fem.* **~প্রাপ্তা, ~স্থা**। **বয়ঃপ্রাপ্ত পুরুষ** বা **স্ত্রীলোক** an adult, a major. **~সন্ধি** *n.* adolescence. **~সীমা** *n.* age-limit.

বয়কট *n.* boycott; (social or political) refusal. **বয়কট করা** *v.* to boycott.

বয়ড়া coll. corrup. of **বহেড়া**।

বয়ন[১] *n.* (poet. & obs.) the face.

বয়ন[২] *n.* weaving; knitting. **বয়ন করা** *v.* to weave; to knit. **~বিদ্যা** *n.* the art of weaving. **~যন্ত্র** *n.* a weaving machine; the loom. **~শিল্প** *n.* the weaving industry. **~শিল্পী** *n.* a weaver.

বয়নামা *n.* a sale certificate; a deed of sale.

বয়লার *n.* a boiler.

বয়স *n.* age; agedness (বয়স ঢাকা পড়া); youth or majority. **বয়স হওয়া** *v.* to come of age; to grow old, to become aged. **বয়সের গাছ পাথর নেই** (fig.) hoary with age. **বয়সের ধর্ম** the natural property or tendency of age. **~কাল** *n.* youth; majority, adulthood; one's greener days. **~-ফোঁড়া** *n.* an acne. **বয়সা** *n.* breaking or cracking of voice on attaining adolescence. **বয়সী** *a.* of a particular age (বালকবয়সী); equal in age (আমার বয়সী); advanced in age, aged, old. **বয়সোচিত** *a.* right and proper for one's age, befitting one's age, natural to a particular age.

-বয়স্ক[১] *sfx.* of a particular age, aged, old (তিন বৎসর বয়স্ক = three years old; aged three years).

বয়স্ক[২], বয়স্থ, বয়স্বী same as **বয়ঃস্থ** (see **বয়ঃ**). *fem.* **বয়স্কা, বয়স্থা, বয়স্বিনী**। **বয়স্কশিক্ষা** *n.* adult education.

বয়স্য *n.* a friend of the same age; a boon companion; an intimate attendant or flatterer. *fem.* **বয়স্যা**।

বয়া *n.* a buoy; a life-buoy.

বয়াটে corrup. of **বখাটে** (see **বখা**).

বয়ান[১] var. of **বয়ন[১]**।

বয়ান[২] *n.* a narration; a description.

বয়ান[৩] *n.* face, countenance ('হসিত বয়ানে চাহে মেঘপানে').

বয়াম *n.* a jar (usu. with a detachable lid and made of porcelain or glass).

বয়েত *n.* a couplet (esp. one in Arabic or Persian or Urdu).

বয়েস coll. corrup. of **বয়স**।

বয়োগুণ *n.* tendencies or propensities natural to a particular age.

বয়োজ্যেষ্ঠ *a.* older, elder; elderly.

বয়োধর্ম *n.* same as **বয়োগুণ**।

বয়োতীত *a.* past youth, past the prime of life.

বয়োবন্ধ *n.* age-bar.

বয়োবৃদ্ধ *a.* advanced in age, aged, old;

older. *fem.* **বয়োবৃদ্ধা** । **বয়োবৃদ্ধি** *n.* increase of age. **বয়োবৃদ্ধির সঙ্গে সঙ্গে** with the increase of age, as one grows old.

বর *n.* a desire granted by a deity or a superior person, a boon; a benison, a benediction, a blessing; a bridegroom; a husband. □ *a.* desired; greatest, most distinguished (নৃপবর) ; excellent, splendid, fine (বরতনু). **বর দেওয়া** *v.* to grant a boon. **বর পাওয়া** *v.* to obtain a boon. **বরের ঘরের মাসি কনের ঘরের পিসি** (fig.) one who hunts with the hound and runs with the hare. **~কনে** *n. pl.* the bride and the groom. **~কর্তা** *n.* the head of the bridegroom's party. **~দ** *a.* granting a boon; benedictory. **~দা** *a. fem.* of **বরদ** । □ *n.* Goddess Durga (দুর্গা). **~দাতা** *a.* & *n.* one who grants a boon. *fem.* **~দাত্রী** । **বরদান করা** *v.* to grant a boon. **~দান** *n.* act of granting a boon or prayer. **~পক্ষ** *n.* the bridegroom's party. **~পণ** *n.* a dowry in cash paid by the bride's parents or party to the bridegroom. **~পুত্র** *n.* a minion (esp. of a deity), a darling, a favourite. **~প্রদ** same as **বরদ** । *fem.* **~প্রদা** । **~বর্ণিনী** *n.* an excellent woman; a woman of peerless beauty. **~মাল্য** *n.* a garland of flower which the bride puts ceremonially round the neck of the bridegroom whilst accepting him as her husband; a garland of highest honour. **~যাত্রী, ~যাত্র** *n.* one who accompanies a bridegroom to a wedding.

বরং *adv.* rather, in preference.

বরকন্দাজ *n.* a footman or follower carrying a fire-arm.

বরখাস্ত *a.* removed from service, dismissed; cashiered. **বরখাস্ত করা** *v.* to remove from service, to dismiss; to cashier.

বরগা[1] *n.* a rafter (কড়ি-বরগা).

বরগা[2] *n.* a temporary lease of land on condition that a fixed portion of crop will be paid as revenue. **~দার** *n.* a lessee holding a piece of land under the aforesaid condition, a sharecropper.

বরজ[1] poet. corrup. of **ব্রজ** ।

বরজ[2] *n.* a plantation or (loos.) a plant of betel-leaves.

বরঞ্চ *adv.* rather, preferably.

বরণ[1] rej. spell. of **বরন** ।

বরণ[2] *n.* devotional or respectful or cordial (and esp. ceremonial) reception or acceptance or nomination or election, welcome (প্রতিমাবরণ, গুরুবরণ, বধূবরণ, সভাপতিপদে বরণ) ; submissive or deliberate acceptance (দুর্ভাগ্যবরণ) ; appointment, employment. **বরণ করা** *v.* to receive or accept or nominate or elect devotionally or respectfully or cordially (and esp. ceremonially), to welcome; to accept submissively or voluntarily; to appoint, to employ. **~ডালা** *n.* a wicker-tray holding articles with which one is received ceremonially. **~পত্র** *n.* a warrant. **বরণীয়** *a.* fit to be received or accepted or nominated or elected devotionally or respectfully or cordially (and esp. ceremonially), fit to be welcomed; fit to be accepted submissively or voluntarily; adorable; venerable; acceptable. *fem.* **বরণীয়া** ।

বরদার *n.* a bearer, a carrier (আসাবরদার = a mace-bearer); one who carries out, a complier (হুকুমবরদার).

বরদাস্ত *n.* bearing or enduring, act of brooking; toleration; patience. □ *a.* endured, tolerated, borne (বরদাস্ত হয় না). **বরদাস্ত করা** *v.* to bear, to bear with; to endure, to brook; to tolerate.

বরন *n.* (poet. form of **বর্ণ**) colour; complexion.

বরফ *n.* snow; ice. **~জল** *n.* ice-water. **~তুল্য** *a.* icy.

বরফট্টাই *n.* bragging, tall talk; ostentatious display or show. **বরফট্টাই করা** *v.* to brag; to make an ostentatious show.

বরফি *n.* a kind of rhomb-shaped sweetmeat made of condensed cowmilk.

বরবটি *n.* a variety of kidney bean, *Vigna sinensis*; cow pea.

বরবাদ *a.* utterly spoilt or wasted; cast away; (loos.) rejected. **বরবাদ করা** *v.* to cast away; (loos.) to reject; (rare) to spoil or waste.

বরয়িতা *n.* one who receives or accepts or nominates or elects devotionally or respectfully or cordially (and esp.

ceremonially), a welcomer; one who accepts submissively or voluntarily. *fem.* বরয়িত্রী ।

বরষ, বরষণ, বরষা, বরা[১] poet. forms of **বর্ষ, বর্ষণ, বর্ষা**[১]**, বর্ষা**[২] and **বরণ করা** (see **বরণ**[২]) respectively.

বরা[২] *n.* the boar, the hog.

বরাঙ্গ *n.* the best part of the body; the head. □ *a.* fine-limbed.

বরাঙ্গনা *n.* an excellent lady.

বরাঙ্গা, বরাঙ্গী, (erron.) **বরাঙ্গিনী** *a. fem.* fine-limbed. □ *n.* a fine-limbed or beautiful woman.

বরাত *n.* charge, commission (কাজের বরাত) ; order (often *pl.*); necessity or business (এদিকে একটু বরাত ছিল) ; authority to represent, assignment; order (to supply goods); fate, luck (মন্দ বরাত). **বরাত দেওয়া** *v.* to entrust a charge, to commission; to authorize or assign. **~চিঠি** *n.* a letter of authority or assignment; (comm.) a bill of exchange. **~গুণে** *adv.* by virtue of good luck. **~জোরে** *adv.* through good luck, through a stroke of luck. **বরাতি** *a.* (of a task) entrusted.

বরাদ্দ *n.* fixation, allotment; estimate, budget; ration (বরাদ্দ-অনুযায়ী বণ্টন). □ *a.* fixed, allotted; estimated; rationed. **বরাদ্দ করা** *v.* to fix beforehand, to allot; to estimate; to ration.

বরানুগমন *n.* act of accompanying a bridegroom to a wedding.

বরাবর *adv.* always or each time (বরাবর ভুল করা) ; all through, all along (বরাবর জঙ্গালের ভিতর দিয়ে) ; straightway (বরাবর উত্তরে যাও). □ *prep.* to, towards, near, along (নদী বরাবর). □ *a.* equivalent or similar to ('সুধা বিষে বরাবর'). **বরাবরেষু** *prep.* to, addressed to (used in Bengali letterwriting).

বরাভয় *n.* a particular sign made with fingers indicating grant of desire and assurance of safety.

বরাভরণ *n.* dress and ornaments given as gifts to a bridegroom by the bride's party.

বরারোহা *a. fem.* having well-shaped and well-developed hips.

বরাসন *n.* a seat for the bridegroom at a wedding; a seat of honour; highest seat; a dignified or beautiful seat.

বরাহ *n.* the boar, the hog; the third incarnation of Vishnu (বিষ্ণু) when he slew Bara (বরা) the demon. *fem.* **বরাহী** the sow.

বরিখ, বরিখন, বরিখা, বরিষ, বরিষন, বরিষা poet. corruptions of **বর্ষ, বর্ষণ, বর্ষা, বর্ষ, বর্ষণ** and **বর্ষা** respectively.

বরিষ্ঠ *a.* best; greatest; most honourable; chief; seniormost; (loos.) senior. *fem.* **বরিষ্ঠা** । **বরিষ্ঠ সেবক** a staff nurse.

বরীয়সী *fem.* of **বরীয়ান** ।

বরীয়ান *a.* better; greater; more honourable; senior.

বরুণ *n.* (myth.) the Hindu seagod (cp. Neptune Poseidon).

বরেণ্য *a.* honourable; best; desirable; deserving honourable or cordial reception or welcome. *fem.* **বরেণ্যা** ।

বরেন্দ্র, বরেন্দ্রভূমি *n.* ancient Gauda (গৌড়) or North Bengal.

বর্গ *n.* a class, a tribe, a genus, a species (প্রাণীবর্গ) ; a collection, an aggregate (বন্ধুবর্গ) ; (math.) the product of a quantity multiplied by itself, square (বর্গমূল) ; (gr.) any one of the five groups into which Bengali consonantal stops (that is, the letters from ক্ to ম্) are classified (ক্-বর্গ, চ্-বর্গ, ট্-বর্গ, ত্-বর্গ, প্-বর্গ) ; a chapter or section of a book; (theol.) any one of the four principal pursuits of life (see চতুর্বর্গ). **~ক্ষেত্র** *n.* a square area, a square. **~ঘন** *n.* (math.) the square of a cube. **~ফল** *n.* square. **~মূল** *n.* (math.) the square root. **বর্গমূল নির্ণয় করা বা বার করা** *v.* to find the square root of.

বর্গা alt. spell. of **বরগা** ।

বর্গি *n.* (hist.) the Maratha cavalry notorious for their free-booting inroads.

বর্গীয়, বর্গ্য *a.* of a class, tribal, generic, specific; (math.) relating to a square; (gr.) of or classified into the groups of the Bengali stops. **বর্গীয় বর্ণ** (gr.) any one of the twenty five consonantal stops of the Bengali alphabet.

বর্জন *n.* act of giving up; abandonment; disownment (স্ত্রী-পুত্র বর্জন) ; boycott

(বিদেশি দ্রব্য বর্জন). **বর্জন করা** *v.* to give up; to abandon; to disown; to boycott. **বর্জনীয়** *a.* fit to be given up or abandoned or disowned or boycotted. *fem.* **বর্জনীয়া**।

বর্জাইস *n.* (print.) bourgeois.

বর্জিত *a.* given up; abandoned; disowned; boycotted; omitted, left out ('নি'-বর্জিত) ; deprived of, devoid of (সুখবর্জিত). *fem.* **বর্জিতা**।

বর্জ্য *a.* same as **বর্জনীয়**।

বর্ণ *n.* colour; complexion; a race; a letter of the alphabet (স্বরবর্ণ) ; any one of the four Hindu castes (চতুর্বর্ণ). **~চোরা** *a.* (chiefly of mangoes) of a deceptive colour; (fig.) hypocritical. **বর্ণচোরা আম** see **আম**[৪]। **~জ্ঞান** *n.* knowledge of the alphabet; literacy. **~জ্ঞানহীন** *a.* illiterate. **~জ্যেষ্ঠ** *n.* a Brahmin. *fem.* **~জ্যেষ্ঠা**। **~দৃক** *n.* a chromoscope. **~পরিচয়** *n.* same as **~জ্ঞান**। **~বিদ্বেষ** *n.* hatred towards other (usu. lower) castes. **~বিপর্যয়** *n.* metathesis. **~বিশ্লেষণ** *n.* analysis or separation of the letters of a word. **বর্ণবিশ্লেষণ করা** *v.* to analyse or separate the letters of a word. **~বৈচিত্র্য** *n.* variety of colour. **~মণ্ডল** *n.* the alphabet. **~রেখাচ্ছটা** *n.* (phys.) line of spectrum. **~শ্রেষ্ঠ** *n.* a Brahmin. ☐ *a.* belonging to the highest caste. *fem.* **~শ্রেষ্ঠা**। **~সঙ্কর** *a.* hybrid, half-bred; mongrel, crossbred. ☐ *n.* a hybrid, a half-caste, a half-breed; a mongrel; a cross-breed. **~সাম্য** *n.* resemblance or symmetry in colour. **~হীন** *a.* colourless; pale.

বর্ণন, বর্ণনা *n.* description; narration; delineation; depiction; a statement; colouration. **বর্ণনা করা** *v.* to describe; to narrate; to delineate; to depict; to colour, to paint. **বর্ণনা দেওয়া** *v.* to give an account (of). **বর্ণনাকুশল** *a.* proficient in describing or narrating or delineating or colouring or painting. **বর্ণনাতীত** *a.* indescribable. **বর্ণনাতীত হওয়া** *v.* to be indescribable, to beggar or defeat description. **বর্ণনাপত্র** *n.* a written statement describing or narrating something. **বর্ণনীয়** *n.* to be described or narrated; describable.

বর্ণানুক্রম *n.* the alphabetical order. **বর্ণানুক্রমিক** *a.* arranged alphabetically. **বর্ণানুক্রমে** *adv.* in the alphabetical order, alphabetically.

বর্ণান্ধ *a.* colour-blind.

বর্ণাপেরণ *n.* (phys.) chromatic aberration.

বর্ণালি, বর্ণালী *n.* (phys.) a spectrum. **শুদ্ধ বর্ণালি** a pure spectrum. **শোষণবর্ণালি** *n.* spectrum absorption. **সৌরবর্ণালি** *n.* a solar spectrum. **বর্ণালিগত, বর্ণালিবিষয়ক** *a.* spectroscopic. **বর্ণালিবিশ্লেষণ** *n.* spectrum analysis. **বর্ণালিবীক্ষণ** *n.* a spectroscope. **সমক্ষবর্ণালিবীক্ষণ** *a.* direct vision spectroscope. **বর্ণালিমাপক** *n.* a spectrometer. **বর্ণালি-লিখন** *n.* spectrography. **বর্ণালি-লেখ** *n.* a spectrograph. **বর্ণালি-লেখী** *a.* spectrographic.

বর্ণাশুদ্ধি *n.* misspelling, spelling mistake.

বর্ণাশ্রম *n.* the four stages of the life of a Hindu as enjoined in the Vedas (see **চতুরাশ্রম**). **~ধর্ম** *n.* duties of the aforesaid four stages of life.

বর্ণিত *a.* described; narrated; delineated; stated; depicted; painted, portrayed.

বর্ণীয় *a.* relating to colour; (phys.) chromatic.

বর্ণে বর্ণে *adv.* word for word; completely, totally; to the letter.

বর্তন *n.* a utensil, a vessel; livelihood, occupation.

বর্তনী *n.* (phys.) a circuit. **খণ্ডিত বর্তনী** an open circuit. **সংহত বর্তনী** a closed circuit. **বর্তনী-ছেদক** *n.* a circuit-breaker. **বর্তনীপ্রবাহ** *n.* a circuit-current.

বর্তমান *n.* the present time, the present; current times, modern times; (gr.) the present tense. ☐ *a.* present (opp. absent); of the present, present; present day, current, modern; now existing or living or alive. **বর্তমান থাকা** *v.* to be present; to be existing or living or alive (now). **বর্তমান কাল** same as **বর্তমান** (*n.*). **~কালীন** *a.* present-day, current; occurring or being done when one is present or alive. **বর্তমানতা, বর্তমানত্ব** *n.* presence; existence; state of being alive. **বর্তমানে** *adv.* at present; when one is living or alive or present (পিতা বর্তমানে).

বর্তা, বর্তানো *v.* to devolve on (পিতার গুণ

পুত্রে বর্তায়) ; to keep going (বেঁচেবর্তে থাকা) ; to be kept going or be gratified (এ চাকরি পেলে সে বর্তে যাবে).

বর্তিকা *n.* a lamp; a wick of a lamp; a brush (esp. of a painter).

-বর্তিনী *fem.* of **-বর্তী** ।

বর্তিষ্ণু *a.* durable, lasting; stable.

-বর্তী *a.* (used as a *sfx.*) present, located (অগ্রবর্তী) ; amenable to (বশবর্তী).

বর্তুল *a.* spherical. □ *n.* a sphere; a ball; a spherical solid iron projectile used in games, a shot. **~নিক্ষেপ** *n.* putting the shot.

বর্তুলাকার *a.* spherical, round, circular.

বর্ত্ম *n.* a road, a path, a way; a set of rules of conduct or moral practice; (fig.) a means.

বর্ধক *a.* causing or promoting increase or growth or development or improvement or prosperity or expansion, augmentative, multiplicative.

বর্ধন *n.* increase, augmentation, multiplication, growth, development, expansion. □ *a.* same as **বর্ধক** (গৌরববর্ধন কার্য). **বর্ধন করা** *v.* to increase, to augment, to multiply, to enhance; to develop, to expand. **~ক্ষম** *a.* capable of being increased or augmented or multiplied or grown or developed or expanded. **~শীল** *a.* in a state of increase or augmentation or enhancement or development or expansion, growing, thriving, prosperous. **বর্ধনাঙ্ক** *n.* (phys.) power (of a lens).

বর্ধমান same as **বর্ধনশীল** (see **বর্ধন**).

বর্ধিত *a.* increased, augmented, multiplied, enhanced; grown; developed, expanded; accelerated (বর্ধিত বেগ). **বর্ধিত করা** same as **বর্ধন করা** (see **বর্ধন**).

বর্ধিষ্ণু same as **বর্ধনশীল** (see **বর্ধন**).

বর্না, বর্নানো *v.* (poet.) to describe, to narrate, to delineate, to depict.

বর্বর *n.* one of an uncivilised human race; a barbarian; a boorish fellow; a rude or ignorant or stupid or beastly or cruel man. □ *a.* uncivilized, barbarous, barbaric; boorish; rude; ignorant, stupid, beastly, atrocious, heinous (বর্বর হত্যা). **বর্বরতা** *n.* lack of civilization, barbarity, barbarism; boorishness; rudeness; ignorance, stupidity; beastliness; atrocity. **বর্বরোচিত** *a.* barbarous; atrocious; heinous; beastly; uncivilized.

বর্ম *n.* a coat of mail, an armour, a mail.

বর্মা *n.* Burmah. □ *a.* Burmese (বর্মা চুরুট).

বর্মি *n.* a Burmese, a Burman. □ *a.* Burmese.

বর্শা *n.* a spear, a lance; a pike. **~দণ্ড** *n.* the shaft of a spear; a pikestaff. **তিমি ধরার বর্শা** *n.* a harpoon. **~ধারী** *a.* armed with a spear or lance or pike. □ *n.* a spearman; a pikeman. **~ফলক** *n.* a spearhead. **~বিদ্ধ** *a.* pierced with a spear, speared, harpooned.

বর্ষ *n.* a year; (myth.) any one of the nine divisions of Jambu (জম্বু) or Asia; rain; cloud; shower or fall (তুষারবর্ষ). **~কাল** *n.* a period of one year; a full calendar year. **~জীবী** *a.* lasting or living for a year only; annual. **বর্ষজীবী উদ্ভিদ** an annual plant, an annual. **~প্রবেশ** *n.* New Year's Day (chiefly according to the Bengali calendar). **~বলয়** *n.* (bot.) the annual ring. **~মান** *n.* rain-gauge.

বর্ষকাল, বর্ষজীবী see **বর্ষ** ।

বর্ষণ *n.* rainfall; rain (বর্ষণহীন মেঘ) ; raining; act of falling down in a stream; showering; a shower; act of scattering or sprinkling or dispersing upon (আতরবর্ষণ, কিরণবর্ষণ) ; (fig.) gracious bestowal (আশীর্বাদবর্ষণ, ধন্যবাদবর্ষণ, উপহারবর্ষণ). **বর্ষণ করা** *v.* to rain upon, to shower, to scatter or sprinkle or disperse upon; to bestow graciously (upon). **~মুখর** *a.* vibrant with the patter of rain. **~শীল** *a.* disposed to rain; raining. **বর্ষণোন্মুখ** *a.* on the point of coming down as rain; on the point of raining; (fig.) on the point of weeping, tearful (বর্ষণোন্মুখ আঁখি).

বর্ষপ্রবেশ, বর্ষবলয় see **বর্ষ** ।

বর্ষা *n.* the rainy season, the rains; rain; rainfall. □ *v.* poet. form of **বর্ষণ করা** (see **বর্ষণ**). **~কালীন** *a.* happening during the rainy season; rainy. **~গম** *n.* the break of the monsoon. **~তি**[1] *n.* an unbrella; a raincoat, a mackintosh, a waterproof. **~তি**[2] *a.* grown in the rainy season. □ *n.* a room on the roof. **বর্ষাত্যয়**

n. termination of rain or of the rainy season, autumn. **~ধৌত** *a.* washed by rain. **~বসান** *n.* same as **বর্ষাত্যয়**।

-বর্ষিণী *fem.* of **-বর্ষী**।

বর্ষিষ্ঠ *a.* oldest; eldest; very old, burdened with age.

-বর্ষী *a.* (used as a *sfx.*) raining, showering, scattering, sprinkling, dispersing (আলোকবর্ষী).

-বর্ষীয় *a.* (used as a *sfx.*) of the age of, aged (ষোড়শবর্ষীয়). *fem.* **-বর্ষীয়া**।

বর্ষীয়সী *fem.* of **বর্ষীয়ান**।

বর্ষীয়ান *a.* older; elder; elderly; very old.

বর্ষোপল *n.* hail-stone.

বল[১] *n.* a ball; a playing ball; a football. **বল করা, বল দেওয়া** *v.* (in cricket) to bowl. **বল খেলা** *v.* to play football. **বলখেলা** *n.* the game of football. **বলবেয়ারিং** *n.* ball-bearings.

বল[২] *n.* power, might; force; strength; ability; energy; an armed force; a man or piece in chess; support or help; a supporter or helper. **~কর, ~কারক** *a.* strengthening, invigorating, (med.) tonic. **~ক্ষয়** *n.* loss or decay of strength; loss or decrease of soldiers or men (of an army etc.). (in chess) loss of pieces. **~ক্ষয়কর** *a.* weakening; causing loss of strength; causing loss of soldiers or men; (in chess) loss of pieces or men. **~গর্ব** same as **বলদর্প**। **~গর্বিত** same as **বলদৃপ্ত**। **~তুল্যাঙ্ক** *n.* (phys.) a mechanical equivalent (of heat.) **~ত্রিভুজ** *n.* a triangle of forces. **~দর্প** *n.* pride of strength or power. **~দায়ক** *a.* strengthening; invigorating; energizing. **~দৃপ্ত** *a.* proud of strength or power, conceited with strength or power. **~পূর্বক** *adv.* by force; by violence. **~প্রদ** same as **বলকর**। **বল প্রদান করা** *v.* to strengthen or invigorate. **~প্রয়োগ** *n.* exercise or application or use of force or violence. **বলপ্রয়োগ করা** *v.* to apply force; to force. **~প্রয়োগে** *adv.* by force; by violence. **~বৎ** *a.* operative, in force, intact. **বলবৎ করা** *v.* to put (a law etc.) into force. **~বতী** *fem.* of **~বান**। **~বত্তর** *a.* stronger; more forceful. **~বত্তা** *n.* powerfulness; (rare) forcefulness; possession of strength. **~বন্ত** same as **বলবান**। **~বর্ধক** *a.* invigorating. **~বর্ধন** *n.* increase of strength or power; invigoration; acceleration of force. ☐ *a.* causing increase of strength or power; invigorating, (med.) tonic; accelerating the force of. **বলবর্ধন করা** *v.* to increase strength or power; to invigorate, (med.) to tone up; to accelerate the force of. **~বান** *a.* strong; powerful robust, sturdy. **~বিদ্যা** *n.* mechanics. **~বিন্যাস** *n.* arraying of troops; arraying of pieces in chess. **~ভরসা** *n.* strength and support; support and prop. **~শালিতা** same as **বলবত্তা**। **~শালী** same as **বলবান**। *fem.* **~শালিনী**। **~শূন্য** same as **~হীন**। **~শ্রেণি** *n.* (phys.) system of forces. **~সামান্তরিক** *n.* (mech.) a parrallelogram of forces. **~সাম্য, বলস্থিতি** *n.* (phys.) equilibrium of forces. **~হীন** *a.* devoid of strength, weak; powerless, infirm; impotent. *fem.* **~হীনা**।

বলক *n.* swelling up of milk by boiling. **বলকা** *a.* swelled up by boiling (এক বলকা দুধ = milk swelled up but once by boiling).

বল-খেলা see **বল**[১]।

বলদ[১] *n.* the bull, the bullock; the ox.

বলদ[২] same as **বলপ্রদ** (see **বল**[২]). *fem.* **বলদা**।

বলন[১] *n.* speaking or narrating.

বলন[২] *n.* growth; increase; (bot.) nutation.

বল-নাচ *n.* ball-dance. **বল-নাচ নাচা** *v.* to take part in a ball.

বলবেয়ারিং see **বল**[১]।

বলয় *n.* an ornament for the wrist, a bangle, a bracelet; an annulus, a circular region, a sphere; an orb or orbit; a belt (শান্তবলয়). **~গ্রাস** *n.* (astr.) an annular eclipse. **বলয়াকার, বলয়াঙ্কিত** *a.* ring-shaped, circular, annular. **বলয়িত** *a.* encircled, enclosed, surrounded (সাগর-বলয়িত = sea girt); having a ring; ring-shaped, circular, annular. **বলয়ী** *a.* (bot.–of roots etc.) annulated.

বলা *v.* to say; to deliver a lecture, to speak; to mention (ও কথা আর বোলো না) ; to inform; to tell (এ খবর কাউকে

বোলো না) ; to permit (ডাক্তার ভাত খেতে বলেছে) ; to order or request, to ask (আসতে বলো) ; to counsel or advise (কী করি বল) ; to invite, to call (বিয়েতে কাউকে বলিনি) ; to speak out, to express (মনের কথা বলা) ; to narrate, to relate (গল্প বলা) ; to rubuke or censure ; to consider (ধন বল, মান বল, সবই দুদিনের).

বলাই corrup. of **বলরাম**—Balai.

বলাক *n.* a kind of small goose capable of flying high. *fem.* **বলাকা**। **বলাকা** *n.* a flight of geese.

বলা-কওয়া *n.* earnest solicitation or request (অনেক বলা-কওয়ার পর রাজি হওয়া) ; without any mention even (বলা-কওয়া নেই, একটা কাজ করে বসল).

বলাৎকার *n.* doing forcibly; act of forcing, violence, outrage; forcible outrage of modesty or chastity, rape, ravishment. **বলাৎকার করা** *v.* to do forcibly; to force, to outrage; to outrage one's modesty or chastity forcibly, to rape, to ravish.

বলাধান *n.* infusion of strength, invigoration. **বলাধান করা** *v.* to infuse strength (into), to strengthen, to invigorate.

বলাধিক্য *n.* excess or abundance or increase of strength or forces.

বলাধ্যক্ষ *n.* the commander of an army; a commander-in-chief.

বলানো *v.* to make one say or speak or tell or confess or divulge.

বলান্বিত *a.* powerful; strong; having armed forces or soldiers.

বলাবল *n.* ability and disability; strength and weakness.

বলাবলি *n.* conversation; talk; talking; discussion; repeated requests. **বলাবলি করা** *v.* to converse; to discuss; to request repeatedly.

বলি[১] *n.* a line or folding of the skin (ত্রিবলি) ; a wrinkle of the skin; a protrusion of the large intestine as in piles.

বলি[২] *n.* a sacrifice; sacrificing, sacrifice, immolation; a sacrificial beast, a victim; (fig.) one subjected to forcible death or suffering; a victim. **বলি দেওয়া** *v.* to immolate, to sacrifice; to victimize.

বলিত *a.* marked with lines of folding of the skin, furrowed; wrinkled, wrinkly.

বলিদান *n.* immolation, sacrifice. **বলিদান দেওয়া** *v.* to immolate, to sacrifice; to victimize.

বলিভুক *n.* the crow or any other bird, subsisting on orts of a meal.

বলিয়ে *a.* having good speaking power, eloquent; having the gift of the gab. **বলিয়ে-কইয়ে** *a.* having the gift of good talking, eloquent.

বলিষ্ঠ *a.* robust, stout, sturdy, burly; vigorous, forceful (বলিষ্ঠ রচনা), **~কায়** *a.* having a strong-built body, burly. **~তা** *n.* robustness, stoutness, sturdiness; vigour.

বলিহারি *a.* (iron.) excellent (বলিহারি বুদ্ধি). □ *adv.* rendered speechless, dumbfounded (বলিহারি যাই). □ *int.* excellent, bravo.

বলী[১] alt. spell. of **বলি**[১]।

বলী[২] *a.* full of strength, powerful, strong; heroic, valorous.

বলীবর্দ *n.* the ox; the bull.

বলীয়ান *a.* very strong or powerful.

বলে *v.* says; speaks; talks. □ *adv. & conj.* because, as, on the plea of, owing to (মা বকেছেন বলে খাবে না ?). □ *adv.* shortly, presently (বৃষ্টি এল বলে).

বল্কল, বল্ক *n.* the rind of a tree, bark. **বল্কলধারী** *a.* wearing bark (instead of a loincloth). *fem.* **বল্কলধারিণী**।

বল্গা, বগ্গা *n.* the mouthpiece of a bridle, bit; rein. **বল্গা আঁটা** *v.* (lit. & fig.) to bit. **বল্গা-হরিণ** *n.* the reindeer. **~হীন** *a.* reinless.

বল্মীক, বল্মিক *n.* an ant-hill.

বল্লব *n.* a milkman; a cook.

বল্লভ *n.* a husband; a lover, a sweet-heart; a favourite. *fem.* **বল্লভা,** (inc.) **বল্লভী**।

বল্লম same as **বর্শা**।

বল্লরি, বল্লরী *n.* a spike; a creeper.

বল্লা *n.* (dial.) the wasp.

বল্লালি *a.* relating to king Ballal Sen. **বল্লালি প্রথা** the order of nobility of certain families as introduced by Ballal Sen.

বল্লি, বল্লী *n.* a creeper.

বশ *n.* will, order, command, control, hold, authority, domination (বশে থাকা) ;

influence (মোহবশে). □ *a.* subject to another's will or command; subjugated; controlled; influenced; charmed (জাদুতে বশ) ; obedient; submissive; very much fond (of) and obedient (to) (বাচ্চাটি তার ভারি বশ). **বশ করা, বশে আনা** *v.* to bring under control; to tame; to break (as a horse); to win over; to influence; to charm. **বশ হওয়া, বশে আসা** *v.* to be brought under control; to be tamed or won over or influenced or charmed. **বশংবদ** *a.* obedient; submissive; at one's beck and call. **~ত** *adv.* on account of, owing to, because of. **~তা** *n.* subjection to another's will or command; subordination; subjection; state of being controlled or influenced or charmed; obedience; submissiveness, submission; great fondness and obedience. **~বর্তী** *a.* obedient; attached or addicted (to); influenced (by). *fem.* **~বর্তিনী, ~বর্তিতা** *n.* obedience, attachment or addiction; the state of being influenced (by).

বশিতা, বশিত্ব *n.* perfect continence (which is one of the eight divine graces of Shiva), attainable by men through asceticism); the power to control or charm everybody.

বশী *a.* perfectly continent; free, independent; (erron.) dependent.

বশীকরণ *n.* act of bringing under one's control, enslavement by enchantment or mesmerism or incantation; enchantment, hypnotization; a weird process to bring somebody under one's control. **বশীকরণ করা** *v.* to bring somebody under one's control (esp. by means of some mysterious and weird process); to enchant. **বশীকরণ-মন্ত্র** *n.* incantation believed to possess occult power of bringing others under control.

বশীকৃত *a.* brought under control; subjugated; tamed; enchanted; made obedient. *fem.* **বশীকৃতা** ।

বশীভূত *a.* brought under control; attached or addicted to; enchanted; fond of and obedient to. *fem.* **বশীভূতা** ।

বশ্য *a.* controllable; tamable; subduable; subjugated; dependent; obedient; submissive; attached or addicted (to); influenced (by). *fem.* **বশ্যা** । **~তা** *n.* dependence; obedience; submissiveness; attachment or addiction; the state of being influenced (by); loyalty. **বশ্যতা স্বীকার করা** *v.* to surrender; to give in; to accept the suzerainty of; to yield (to).

বসতি, (coll.) **বসত** *n.* residing or dwelling; residence, habitation; a dwelling-house, a residence, a habitation (জনবসতি) ; a colony; (loos.) a locality. **বসতি করা** *v.* to dwell, to reside; to set up or build one's residence or dwelling-house; to colonize, to settle. **বসতি স্থাপন করা** *v.* to set up one's residence; to colonize, to settle. **বসতবাড়ি, বসতবাটি** *n.* a dwelling-house; a homestead.

বসন *n.* cloth; a loincloth, a wearing cloth; dress. **~ভূষণ** *n.* clothings and ornaments, dress and ornaments. **বসনাঞ্চল, ~প্রান্ত** *n.* the hem or corner of a cloth.

বসন্ত *n.* the spring season, spring, the springtime; pox, small-pox, chicken-pox; an Indian musical mode. **~কাল** *n.* the spring season, the spring time, spring. **~কালীন** *a.* of spring; vernal. **~দূত** *n.* the messenger of spring; the cuckoo. **~পঞ্চমী** *n.* the fifth lunar day of the light fortnight of Magh (মাঘ) when Goddess Saraswati (সরস্বতী) is worshipped. **~বায়ু** *n.* vernal breeze, the south wind. **~সখ** *n.* the friend of spring; the cuckoo. **~সখা** *n.* one attended upon by Spring; Madana (মদন) the Hindu god of love. **বসন্তের কোকিল** (fig.) a fair-weather friend. **বসন্তোৎসব** *n.* the spring festival; the festival of holi (হোলি).

বসবাস *n.* residing or dwelling permanently, settling down. **বসবাস করা** *v.* to reside or dwell permanently, to settle down.

বসা[১] *n.* a substance found in adipose tissue, fat; marrow; grease.

বসা[২] *v.* to sit, to take one's seat; to be installed (গদিতে বসা) ; to be established or founded (গ্রামে গ্রামে স্কুল বসা) ; to start, to commence (আমাদের স্কুল এগারোটায় বসে) ; to freeze, to congeal, to solidify (দই বসা) ; to accumulate or settle (বুকে সর্দি বসা) ; to fit (মাথায় টুপি বসা) ; to be imposed or levied (ট্যাকস বসা) ; to enter (পেরেক বসা) ; to pierce (ছুরি বসা, দাঁত বসা) ; to stick or to get stuck (কাদায় গাড়ির চাকা বসা) ; to be imprinted (দাগ বসা) ; to be soaked (in) (গায়ে জল বসা) ; to be applied closely, to be attracted (মন বসা) ; to be wizened, to look haggard (চোখমুখ বসা) ; to become hoarse (স্বর বসা) ; to wait (তুমি একটু বসো) ; to come to stay or reside (প্রজা বা ভাড়াটে বসা) ; to be engaged in (বিচারে বসা) ; to do or commit something suddenly (করে বসা, বলে বসা). □ *a.* seated; frozen, congealed, solidified; wizened, haggard; hoarsened; sunken; depressed (বসা জমি) ; requiring much sitting, sedentary (বসা কাজ) ; unemployed (তার সব ছেলেই বসা). **বসানো** *v.* to cause to sit, to seat; to establish or found; to cause to congeal, to congeal, to freeze, to solidify; to impose or levy; to drive into, to enter; to pierce with; to imprint; to cause to be soaked (in); to apply closely; to cause to stay or reside; to engage; to set or stud with, to inlay (আংটিতে পাথর বসানো) ; to place or put (উনুনে হাঁড়ি বসানো) ; to implant, to deal (চড় বসানো). **একেবারে মায়ের মুখ বসানো** to be the image of one's mother. **বসার ঘর** a sitting room; a drawing room. **বসে থাকা** *v.* to be sitting; to remain sitting; to wait (for); to be unemployed; to be without work; to pass time in laziness, to laze. **বসে পড়া** *v.* to sit down; to be utterly disappointed (ফেল করে সে বসে পড়ল) ; to be ruined utterly (মামলায় হেরে সে বসে পড়ল). **বসে বসে** *adv.* by waiting for a long time (বসে বসে বেলা গেল) ; in an unemployed state, doing nothing; idly (বসে বসে খাওয়া). **বসে যাওয়া** *v.* (of land etc.) to sink, to become depressed; to be ruined; to desist or rest (আর খেলিস না—বসে যা) ; to stop (বাধা পড়েছে—বসে যাও).

বসু *n.* one of a class of demigods; wealth, riches. **~ধা** *n.* the earth. **~ধারা** *n.* an auspicious symbol painted on the inner wall of a room by Hindus at wedding etc. **বসুন্ধরা, ~মতী** *n.* the earth (often personified as mother-earth).

বস্তা *n.* a sack, a large bag; a bale. **~পচা** *a.* rotted or spoilt by being packed in a sack for a long time; (fig.) hackneyed. banal, trite. **~বন্দি** *a.* packed in a bale or sack.

বস্তি[1] *n.* quarters for the poor people (কুলি-বস্তি) ; a slum esp. one consisting of cutcha huts. **~বাসী** *n.* a slum-dweller, inhabitant of a slum.

বস্তি[2], **বস্তী** *n.* the abdomen; the bladder. **~শোধন** *n.* a diuretic.

বস্তু *n.* a thing, a material; subject-matter (usu. বিষয়বস্তু) ; substance (তোমার শরীরে বস্তু নেই) ; truth; (phil.) matter; (phys.) mass. **~গত** *a.* relating to a thing or matter. **~গত মান** intrinsic value. **~জগৎ** *n.* the material world, the world of matter. **বস্তুত** *adv.* in fact, indeed, really. **~তত্ত্ব** *n.* physics. **~তত্ত্ববিদ** *n.* a physicist. **~তন্ত্র** *n.* realism. **~তন্ত্রী, ~তন্ত্রীয়, ~তান্ত্রিক** *a.* realistic, materialistic. **~নিষ্ঠ** *a.* realistic; objective. **~নিষ্ঠা** *n.* realism; objectiveness. **~বাদ** *n.* realism; materialism. **~বাদী** *a.* & *n.* realist; materialist.

বস্ত্র *n.* cloth; loincloth; clothing, dress. **~গৃহ** *n.* a tent; a pavilion. **~হরণ** *n.* divestiture of clothes (esp. of the loincloth); denudation; stealing of (another's) clothes or loincloth. **~হীন** *a.* having no cloth or clothing to cover the body; naked, unclad. **বস্ত্রাঞ্চল** *n.* the hem or corner of a loincloth. **বস্ত্রাবাস** *n.* a tent; a pavilion. **বস্ত্রাবৃত** *a.* clothed; wrapped or covered by a cloth; draped. **বস্ত্রালংকার** *n.* clothes and ornaments. **বস্ত্রালয়** *n.* a cloth shop.

বহ *a.* (used as a *sfx.*) carrying, bearing, conveying (বার্তাবহ, গন্ধবহ) ; complying with (আজ্ঞাবহ).

বহতা *a.* flowing (বহতা নদী).

বহন *n.* carrying, bearing, conveying (যাত্রীবহন, সংবাদবহন) ; enduring, suffering (দুঃখবহন) ; flowing. **বহন করা** *v.* to carry, to bear, to convey; to endure or suffer. **~যোগ্য, বহনীয়** *a.* carriageable; bearable; conveyable; portable.

বহমান *a.* flowing, running (বহমান নদী) ; carrying; bearing, conveying.

বহর *n.* a collection or multitude (পোত বহর) ; a fleet (মিরবহর) ; width, breadth (বহরে বড়) ; ostentatious show, glamour (রূপের বহর, কাজের বহর).

বহা *v.* to bear, to carry, to endure or suffer; to flow, to run; to elapse, to pass (সময় বহা) ; to keep active, to keep up (শরীর বহে না).

বহানো *v.* to cause to bear or carry or convey or flow or run.

বহাল *a.* appointed, employed (চাকরিতে বহাল) ; installed, continuing in (পদে বহাল) ; (still) in force or effective (বহাল আদেশ বা চুক্তি) ; hale, healthy (বহাল তবিয়ত). **বহাল করা** *v.* to appoint, to employ; to instal; to bring in force, to make effective. **বহাল থাকা** *v.* to continue in; to be in force. **বহাল রাখা** *v.* to let (one) continue in; to keep in force; to keep up, to maintain (ঠাট বহাল রাখা). **বহাল তবিয়তে** in good or sound or perfect health.

বহি obs. form of **বই**[২] ।

বহিঃ *n.* outside, the exterior. □ *a.* outer, exterior, external. **~কর্ণ** *n.* the external ear, the auricle. **~কোণ** *n.* (geom.) an external or exterior angle. **~প্রকাশ** *n.* expression, external expression. **~প্রকোষ্ঠ** *n.* a room at the side of a house. **~প্রকোষ্ঠাস্থি** *n.* the outer bone of the forearm, the radius. **~প্রকোষ্ঠাস্থিগত** *a.* radial. **~শত্রু** *n.* external enemy; enemy from without. **~শুল্ক** *n.* customs duty. **~সমুদ্র** *n.* the high sea. **~স্থ** *a.* external; exterior; outer.

বহিত্র *n.* a ship, a boat, a vessel; a scull; an oar.

বহিরঙ্গ *a.* external; outer; superficial; unrelated. □ *n.* an external limb.

বহিরাগত *a.* emerged, issued out; coming from outside; foreign; adventitious.

বহিরাগমন *n.* issuing out or issuing forth, emergence.

বহিরাবরণ *n.* an outer covering; an outside coating; a shell, a crust, a slough, a rind.

বহিরিন্দ্রিয় *n.* any one of the five sense organs, namely, the eye, the ear, the nose, the tongue, the skin.

বহির্গত *a.* gone or come out, issued forth; emerged. **বহির্গত হওয়া** *v.* to go or come out, to issue, to issue forth; to emerge.

বহির্গমন *n.* act of issuing forth, emergence; act of going out. **বহির্গমন করা** *v.* to issue forth, to emerge; to go out.

বহির্গামী *a.* issuing forth, emerging; going out; outgoing.

বহির্গ্রহ *n.* (astr.) a superior planet.

বহির্জগৎ *n.* the outer or external world; the visible or phenomenal world; the material world.

বহির্জনিষ্ণু *a.* (bot.) exogenous.

বহির্দেশ same as **বহির্ভাগ** ।

বহির্দ্বার *n.* the front-door (of a building); the gate, the main gate, (as of a town, village or building).

বহির্দ্বিখণ্ডক *n.* (geom.) an external bisector.

বহির্বাটি *n.* an outhouse; a parlour or drawing-room.

বহির্বাণিজ্য *n.* foreign trade, external trade; export.

বহির্বাস *n.* a thin scarf or wrapper for the upper body; an outer-garment.

বহির্বিশ্ব same as **বহির্জগৎ** ।

বহির্বৃত্ত *n.* (geom.) an ex-circle.

বহির্ভাগ *n.* an outer or external or exterior portion; outskirts (as of a village or town).

বহির্ভূত *a.* issued forth, emerged; lying outside or beyond (দেশবহির্ভূত) ; beyond the range of (দৃষ্টিবহির্ভূত) ; contravening (বিধিবহির্ভূত).

বহির্মুখ *a.* facing outwards; (physiol.) outcarrying, efferent (বহির্মুখ নার্ভ) ; (bot.) extrose; wordly-minded; (chiefly phil.) extrovert. *fem.* **বহির্মুখী** । **বহির্মুখ ব্যক্তি** a worldly-minded man, an extravert, an extrovert. **~তা** *n.* the state of facing outside; the state of being efferent; extroversion; worldly-mindedness.

বহির্লিখিত *a.* (geom.) escribed.

বহিশ্চর্ম *n.* epidermis, cuticle.

বহিষ্করণ, বহিষ্কার *n.* expulsion; removal; ejectment, banishment; extraction;

drainage. বহিষ্করণ করা, বহিষ্কার করা *v.* to drive out, to expel; to remove; to eject; to banish; to extract; to drain; to draw out.

বহিষ্কৃত *a.* driven out, expelled; removed; ejected, banished; extracted; drained.

বহিষ্ক্রান্ত *a.* gone or come out, issued forth.

বহিস্ত্বক *n.* epidermis, cuticle.

বহিস্থ same as বহিঃস্থ (see বহিঃ).

বহু১ (obs.) a wife.

বহু২ *v.* (poet. & obs.) blows, let blow ('মলয় পবন বহু মন্দা').

বহু৩ *a.* many, numerous; much, manifold, diverse; profuse, abundant; long; more than one, poly-, multi-. ~কষ্টে *adv.* with great difficulty. ~কাল *n.* a long time. বহুকাল ধরে for a long time, for long. বহুকাল পরে after a long time. বহু কাল পূর্বে long ago. ~কালব্যাপী *a.* long continued or long-lasting; very old. ~কেলে *a.* very old, antique. ~কেশর *a.* (bot.) polyandrous. ~কোষ্ঠ *a.* (bot.) multilocular. ~ক্ষণ *n.* a long while, a long time. ~গর্ভপত্রী *a.* (bot.) polycarpellary. ~গুচ্ছ *a.* (bot.) polyadelphous. ~গুণ *a.* multiplied many times; many times over; many more, much more. ~জাতিক *a.* multinational. ~জ্ঞ *a.* polymathic, having varied or vast experience. বহুজ্ঞ ব্যক্তি a polymath; a man of varied or vast experience. ~তর *a.* many more; too many; too much; diverse, various; manifold; many, numerous; much, profuse. ~তল *a.* multi-storeyed. ~তলক *n.* (geom.) a polyhedron. ~তা same as বহুত্ব। ~ত্ব *n.* numerousness; muchness; profusion, abundance; excessiveness; diversity. ~ত্র *adv.* at or in many or diverse places. ~দর্শিতা *n.* varied or wide or vast experience. ~দর্শী *a.* having seen much; having varied experience or vast experience. *fem.* ~দর্শিনী। ~দূর *a.* very far, far-away, far-off, distant. □ *adv.* very far, far off, far away, at a great distance. □ *n.* a great distance, a far cry. ~দূরবর্তী *a.* far-off, remote. ~ধা *adv.* in many and diverse modes or methods or ways or directions or parts; diversely; many times. ~পতিত্ব *n.* polyandry. ~পত্নীক *a.* having many wives, ploygamous. ~পদ *a.* (alg.) polynomial; (zoo.) polypod. ~পদ প্রাণী a ploypod, a multiped. বহুপার্শ্বীয় *a.* (bot.) multiparous; multilateral. ~প্রসবিনী *a. fem.* bearing many children; prolific; fertile. ~প্রান্তীয় *a.* parietal. ~ফলকপত্র *n.* (bot.) a compound leaf. ~বচন see বচন। ~বর্ষজীবী *a.* (bot.) perennial; (of man) long-lived. ~বল্লভ *n.* one beloved of many women; Krishna (কৃষ্ণ). *fem.* ~বল্লভা a woman beloved of many men; a flirt; a prostitute. ~বিধ *a.* of many and diverse sorts. ~বিবাহ polygamy. ~বিবাহকারী *a.* polygamous. □ *n.* a polygamist. ~বিবাহকারিণী *a.* polyandrous. □ *n.* a polyandrist. ~বিস্তীর্ণ *a.* spread over a wide or large area, far-flung. ~বীজপত্রী (bot.) *a.* polycotyledon. ~ব্যয়সাধ্য *a.* very expensive or costly. ~ব্যয়ে *adv.* at a great cost or expense. ~ব্রীহি *n.* (gr.) mode of forming compound words (a compound word formed by this mode gives a meaning which neither of the constituent words implies). ~ভর্তৃক *a.* having many husbands. ~ভাগ, ~ভাগ্য *a.* very fortunate. □ *n.* a great fortune. ~ভাষিতা *n.* speaking many languages; garrulity, talkativeness. ~ভাষী *a.* speaking many languages, polyglottic; garrulous, talkative. বহুভাষী ব্যক্তি a polyglot; a garrulous or talkative person. ~ভুজ *a.* (geom.) polygonal; (bio.) polypous. □ *n.* a polygon; a polyp. ~ভুজক্ষেত্র *n.* (geom.) a polygon. ~ভ্রূণবীজতা *n.* (bot.) polyembryony. ~ভ্রূণবীজী *a.* (bot.) polyembryonic. ~মত *a.* highly esteemed; greatly honoured. ~মান *n.* high esteem; great honour. ~মানাস্পদ *a.* highly esteemed or revered. ~মুখ *a.* multifaced; multifarious; multiplex (বহুমুখ টেলিগ্রাফ) ; (of a school or co-operative society) multipurpose. *fem.* ~মুখী। ~মূত্র *n.* diabetes. ~মূত্রগত *a.* diabetic. ~মূত্রপীড়িত *a.* diabetic. ~মূর্তি *a.* multiform. ~মূল্য *a.* very costly; very precious. ~যৌগিক *a.* (bot.)

decompound. ~রাশিক *n.* (arith.) the double rule of three. ~রূপ[1] *a.* diverse multifarious. ~রূপ[2], বহুরূপী *a.* assuming different forms; polymorphic, multiform. □ *n.* the chameleon; an itinerant showman who amuses people by assuming various forms. *fem. a.* ~রূপিণী। ~রূপতা *a.* polymorphism. ~শ *adv.* many times, many a time and oft; in a great measure, to a great extent. ~শাখ *a.* having many branches. ~শাস্ত্রজ্ঞ *a.* polymathic. বহুশাস্ত্রজ্ঞ ব্যক্তি a polymath. ~শিরাল *a.* (bot.) multicostate. ~শ্রুত *a.* profoundly or vastly learned, erudite, well-versed in many disciplines. ~স্বামিক *a.* having to serve many masters; having many owners.

বহুড়ি *n.* (obs.) a newly married woman, a childwife.

বহুত *a.* much or many. বহুত আচ্ছা *int.* very good, excellent.

বহুল *a.* much, profuse, abundant, plentiful. ~পরিমাণে *adv.* in a great or large measure, profusely. ~তা, ~ত্ব *n.* muchness, profusion, abundance. plenty. বহুলীকরণ *n.* multiplication. বহুলীকৃত *a.* multiplied.

বহেড়া *n.* the beleric myrobalan.

বহ্নি *n.* fire. ~জ্বালা *n.* a flame; glow or heat of fire. ~মান *a.* flaming, blazing. ~শিখা *n.* a tongue of fire, a flame. ~সংস্কার *n.* cremation of a dead body.

বহ্বাড়ম্বর *n.* excessive pomp or éclat; great fuss.

বহ্বারম্ভ *n.* a grand or fussy preparation. বহ্বারম্ভে লঘুক্রিয়া much cry but little wool.

বা[1] var. of বাঃ।

বা[2] *con.* or. □ *adv.* possibly, perhaps (হবেও বা) ; alternatively (তুমিই বা গেলে) ; used to emphasize a question (হবেই বা না কেন ?).

বাই[1] *n.* a title affixed to the names of Marathi or Rajput women.

বাই[2] *n.* neurosis; a mania (শুচিবাই) ; a strong hobby, a crotchet, a craze (খেলা দেখার বাই).

বাই[3], বাইওয়ালি *n. fem.* a professional dancing-girl and songstress.

বাইচ, বাইচখেলা *n.* a boat-race, a regatta.

বাইজি same as বাই[3]।

বাইন var. of বান[1] and বায়েন।

বাইনাচ *n.* the dance of a professional dancing girl.

বাইবেল *n.* the Bible.

বাইরে coll. form of বাহিরে and বাহির।

বাইল *n.* a stalked leaf of the coconut-tree, palm-tree, etc.; a leaf of a door esp. of a folding door.

বাইশ *n.* & *a.* twenty-two. বাইশে *n.* the twenty-second day of a month, the twenty-second. □ *a.* twenty-second.

বাইস[1] *n.* a (carpenter's) chisel.

বাইস[2] *n.* a gripping tool, a vice.

বাইসিকল, বাইসিকেল, বাইসাইকেল *n.* a bicyle, a cycle. বাইসিকলে চড়া *v.* to ride a bicycle. বাইসিকলে চড়ে যাওয়া *v.* to cycle. বাইসিকল-আরোহী *n.* a cyclist.

বাঈ[1] rej. spell. of বাই[1]।

বাঈ[2] rej. spell. of বাই[3]।

বাউটি *n.* a kind of bracelet.

বাউন্ডুলে *a.* regarding nobody or nothing as one's own; Bohemian, vagabond. □ *n.* a vagabond; a tramp.

বাউরা *a.* mad, insane.

বাউরি *n.* a lowly Hindu caste; a member of this caste.

বাউল *n.* one of a class of Hindu stoical devotees singing songs in a special mode illustrating their doctrine; their song or mode of singing.

বাওয়া[1] *v.* to row; to steer, to propel; to paddle; to pass over; to cover; to go or ply or move along (পথ বেয়ে যাওয়া) ; to climb up or down (সিঁড়ি বেয়ে নামা).

বাওয়া[2] *a.* not containing any embryo, barren, addle (বাওয়া ডিম = an addle egg, a wind-bag).

বাংলা[1] *n.* Bengal, the land or state of Bengal; the Bengali language. □ *a.* written in Bengali (বাংলা বই) ; relating or pertaining to or of Bengal or of Bengali (বাংলা সাহিত্য).

বাংলা[2], বাংলো *n.* a bungalow.

বাঃ *int.* denoting : an exclamation in praise, wonder, taunt, disgust etc., ah, (cp. bah).

বাঁ, (dial.) বাঁও[1] *a.* & *n.* left. বাঁ-হাতি *a.*

lying on the left; left-handed; directed towards the left, anti-clockwise. **বাঁ-হাতের ব্যাপার** (iron.) act of accepting bribes.

বাঁও২ *n.* a fathom.

বাঁওড় *n.* the bend of a river where the current is obstructed, (cp.) an eddy, a whirlpool.

বাঁওয়া *a.* (dial.) left-handed.

বাঁক *n.* curvature; a curve; a bend, a turn (as of a road or river); a piece of long and bent pole borne on one's shoulder for carrying loads fastened to its ends. **~নল** *n.* a blowpipe; a u-tube; (bot.) a bent tube. **~মল** *n.* a kind of twisted bangle for the ankle.

বাঁকা *v.* to bend, to curve (রেখাটি বেঁকেছে) ; to turn (পথটি এখানে বেঁকেছে) ; to become reluctant or unfavourable or ungracious or antipathetic (কর্তা বেঁকেছেন). □ *a.* bent, curved (বাঁকা বাঁশ) ; stopping, hunched (বাঁকা পিঠ) ; slanting, aslant (খুঁটিখানা বাঁকা) ; winding, tortuous, sinuous, spiral, roundabout (বাঁকা পথ) ; furtive, squint, oblique (বাঁকা চাহনি) ; cynical or unfriendly (বাঁকা দৃষ্টিভঙ্গি) ; crooked (বাঁকা মন) ; rude, harsh (বাঁকা কথা) ; insinuating; sly (বাঁকা উক্তি) ; reluctant, unfavourable, antipathetic. **~চোরা** *a.* having many curves and twists; not straightforward, crooked (বাঁকাচোরা কথা). **বাঁকানো** *v.* to bend; to make reluctant or unfavourable or antipathetic. **বেঁকে বসা** *v.* to be placed or fixed slantingly; to become reluctant or unfavourable or antipathetic; to revise or retract one's previous opinion, desire, resolve etc., to refuse to fall in with or accede to.

বাঁখারি var. of **বাখারি**।

বাঁচন *n.* living, keeping alive, subsisting; resuscitation, revival; rescue or relief; state of remaining unimpaired, freedom from involvement.

বাঁচা *v.* to live, to keep alive; to subsist (বাঙালি ভাতে বাঁচে) ; to get back life, to be resuscitated, to revive (বিশল্যকরণীর গুণে লক্ষ্মণ বাঁচলেন) ; to be saved or rescued or relieved; to remain unimpaired, to be kept up or maintained or protected (স্বাস্থ্য বাঁচা, মান বাঁচা) ; to escape, avoid or to be spared (লোকসান বাঁচা, খরচ বাঁচা) ; to become surplus (ভোজের শেষে অনেক সন্দেশ বেঁচেছে). **বাঁচানো** *v.* to give back life, to resuscitate, to revive; to save or rescue or relieve; to keep up, to maintain, to protect; to escape, to save, to cut, to curtail (খরচা বাঁচানো) ; to save from being consumed (খাবার বাঁচানো) ; to carry on, to maintain (চাকরি বাঁচানো). **কারও পরে বেঁচে থাকা** to outlive a person. **কিছুর পরে** বা **কিছু এড়িয়ে বেঁচে থাকা** to survive something.

বাঁচোয়া *n.* rescue, relief, escape; safety; (rare) protection of life;

বাঁজা, বাঁঝা *a.* (of a woman) barren, sterile, unproductive.

বাঁট১ *n.* an udder, a teat, a dug.

বাঁট২ *n.* a haft, a handle.

বাঁটওয়ারা alt. spell. of **বাটোয়ারা**।

বাঁটকুল *n.* a dumpy, a very short man, a short-statured man; a man of short height. □ *a.* short. see also **বেঁটে**।

বাঁটন *n.* dividing, apportionment, allotment; distribution.

বাঁটা *v.* to divide; to share out, to apportion, to allot; to distribute. **বাঁটানো** *v.* to cause to divide or apportion or allot or distribute.

বাঁটুল *n.* a small ball (usu. of iron and used as a missile); (iron.) a short and fat man, a dumpy.

বাঁটোয়ারা var. of **বাটোয়ারা**।

বাঁদর *n.* the monkey; the ape; (dero.) a mischievous person. *fem.* **বাঁদরি**। **~মুখো** *a.* having a face as ugly as that of a monkey. *fem.* **বাঁদরমুখি**। **বাঁদরামি, বাঁদরামো** *n.* mischievousness; a monkey-trick; monkeyism. **বাঁদুরে** *a.* monkeyish.

বাঁদরলাঠি *n.* the drumstick tree, *Cassia fistula*.

বাঁদিপোতা *n.* a chequered cloth having multi-coloured stripes.

বাঁদি *n.* maidservant, a handmaid; a woman slave.

বাঁধ *n.* a dam; a breakwater, a bulwark; (geog.) a dyke. **বাঁধ দেওয়া** *v.* to dam. (fig.) to restrain. **বাঁধ নির্মাণ করা, বাঁধ বাঁধা**

v. to build a dam or breakwater or dyke.

বাঁধন *n.* binding or fastening; a tie, a knot (বাঁধন খুলে দাও) ; damming; obstruction; stopping or parking (as of a vehicle); restraining or appeasement (as of one's mind); composition; formation; construction, building, setting up; turning, attunement; unification; reduction or rendering; compactness (কথার বাঁধন). **~হারা** *a.* free, unbridled, unrestrained. **বাঁধনি** *n.* binding or fastening; a tie, a knot; due arrangement, methodicalness, order (কাজের বাঁধনি) ; compactness.

বাঁধা[1] *n.* pawning or mortgaging. □ *a.* pawned, pledged, mortgaged. **বাঁধা দেওয়া** *v.* to pawn, to pledge; to mortgage. **বাঁধা রাখা** *v.* to give or take in pledge.

বাঁধা[2] *v.* to bind, to tie, to fasten; to obstruct (স্রোত বাঁধা) ; to dam (খাল বাঁধা) ; to stop or park (গাড়ি বাঁধা) ; to restrain or appease (মন বাঁধা) ; to compose (গান বাঁধা) ; to form, to do (খোঁপা বাঁধা) ; to build or set up (ঘর বাঁধা) ; to attune (বীণা বাঁধা) ; to unite (প্রাণে প্রাণে বাঁধা) ; to be reduced to or rendered into, to turn into (জমাট বাঁধা, দান বাঁধা). □ *a.* bound; tied, fastened, obstructed; dammed; composed; formed, done; built, set up; attuned; routine (বাঁধা কাজ) ; regular (বাঁধা খদ্দের) ; stock (বাঁধা গৎ) ; rigid (বাঁধা নিয়ম) ; fixed (বাঁধা মাইনে) ; brick-built or stone-built, pucka (বাঁধা ঘাট). **বাঁধাই** *n.* binding or cost of binding esp. a book; enframing or cost of enframing (as a picture). **~কপি** *n.* cabbage. **বাঁধা গৎ** a stock phrase; a rigid rule or system. **~ছাদা** *n.* rolling up and tying as a baggage. **বাঁধাছাদা করা** *v.* to pack. **~ধরা** *a.* fixed; rigid; routine; stock; monotonous, trite. **~বুলি** *n.* a catchphrase, a catchword, a slogan. **বাঁধানো** *v.* to bind (as a book); to enframe (as a picture); to fix or manufacture artificial ones (দাঁত বাঁধানো) ; to inlay (হিরে দিয়ে বাঁধানো) ; to plate (সোনা দিয়ে বাঁধানো) ; to pave, to macadamize (রাস্তা বাঁধানো) ; to build with stone or brick (ঘাট বাঁধানো) ; to dam (খাল বাঁধানো) ; to cause to compose (গান বাঁধানো) ; to cause to build or set up (ঘর বাঁধানো) ; to cause to attune (বীণা বাঁধানো) ; to reduce to or render into (জমাট বাঁধানো). □ *a.* bound; enframed; artificial (বাঁধানো দাঁত = a set of artificial teeth, denture); inlaid; plated; paved, macadamized; brick-built or stone-built, pukka; dammed; built or set up. **~বাঁধি** *a.* fixed, hard and fast, unalterable. □ *n.* a rigid rule or system; strictness.

বাঁধুনি var. of **বাঁধনি** (see **বাঁধন**).

বাঁয়া *n.* a small semi-circular musical instrument of percussion played along with the tabla (তবলা). **ঢাকের বাঁয়া** (fig. & derisively) a useless accompaniment, a mere nothing; someone else's ditto.

বাঁশ *n.* the bamboo. **বাঁশ দেওয়া** (sl.)to take the wind out of one's sails; to ruin. **বুকে বাঁশ দেওয়া** to make a person lie at full length in between two bamboo-poles and then roll the poles oppressively as a punishment; (fig.) to torment severely. **বাঁশের চেয়ে কঞ্চি দড়** (fig.) the chip is harder than the old block, the greenhorn is tougher than the veteran. **বাঁশ বনে ডোম কানা** (fig.) one cannot see the wood for the trees. **~গাড়ি** *n.* (law) planting a bamboo-pole in the ground of an estate as a sign of taking possession of it. **~ঝাড়** *n.* a bamboo-clump.

বাঁশি, বাঁশরি *n.* a flute made of a kind of slender bamboo, a reed; a flute, a pipe. **বাঁশি বাজানো** *v.* to play on a flute, to pipe.

বাঁশিওয়ালা, বাঁশুরিয়া *n.* a flutist, a fluter, a piper.

বাক্ *n.* speech, language; learning; the organ of speech. **~চাতুরি, ~চাতুর্য** *n.* cleverness of speech; gift of the gab; artful or wheedling language, a quibble. **~চাপল্য** *n.* flippancy in speech; flippant speech; loquacity, talkativeness. **~ছল** *n.* artfulness or wheedlesomeness of speech; equivocation; a quibble. **~জাল** same as

বাগ্‌জাল। ~পটু same as বাগ্‌বিদগ্ধ। ~পটুতা, ~পটুত্ব same as বাগ্‌বৈদগ্ধ্য। ~পারুষ্য *n.* rudeness of speech; insulting words. ~প্রণালী *n.* mode of speaking; an idiom. ~প্রপঞ্চ *n.* elaborate speech; eloquence. ~রোধ inc. but pop. var. of বাগ্‌রোধ। ~শক্তি *n.* power or faculty of speaking. ~শক্তিরহিত, ~শক্তিহীন *a.* dumb; unable to speak; rendered speechless; dumbfounded. ~সংযম *n.* exercise of restraint in speech, sparingness in use of words, reticence, taciturnity. ~সর্বস্ব *a.* excelling only in words and incapable of action. বাক্‌সর্বস্ব ব্যক্তি a person of mere words, a wind-bag. ~সিদ্ধ *a.* having the power to utter infallible words. *fem.* ~সিদ্ধা। ~স্ফূর্তি *n.* utterance of words. ~স্বাধীনতা *n.* freedom of speech.

বাকল, (dial.) **বাকলা** *n.* rind of a tree, bark.

বাকস *n.* a medicinal plant, *Justicia gandrussa.*

বাক্‌সো same as **বাক্স**।

বাকি *a.* remaining (বাকি জীবন) ; outstanding (বাকি কাজ) ; unrealized or unpaid, overdue (বাকি পাওনা). □ *n.* the remainder, the balance; arrears (বাকি শোধ) ; credit (বাকিতে বেচা). **বাকি পড়া** *v.* to fall into arrears, to be overdue. **বাকি খাজনা** arrears of rent. **বাকি জায়** a list of unrealized rent or revenue. ~তে *adv.* in arrears; on credit (বাকিতে জিনিস কেনা). ~বকেয়া *n.* dues. **বাকি রাখা** *v.* to keep arrears; to default; to keep unpaid.

বাক্য *n.* speech, language; (gr.) a sentence; an expression; a saying. ~জ্বালা *n.* tormenting language, a talking-to. **বাক্যদান করা** *v.* to give one's word, to promise. ~বাগীশ *a.* having the gift of the gab; eloquent; voluble, glib, talkative, garrulous; excelling in words but incapable of action. ~বাণ *n.* (lit.) a shaft of words; piercing words. ~বিন্যাস *n.* (gr.) syntax; (loos.) skilful use of words, praiseworthy oration. ~বিশারদ same as **বাক্যবাগীশ**। ~ব্যয় *n.* speaking, talking. **বাক্যব্যয় করা** *v.* to speak, to talk. **বৃথা বাক্যব্যয় করা** *v.* to talk in vain; to throw away words. **বিনা বাক্যব্যয়ে** *adv.* without using a word, without speaking a word. ~স্ফূর্তি *n.* utterance of words. ~হারা, ~হীন *a.* speechless; dumb; mum. **বাক্যার্থ** *n.* the meaning of a sentence. **বাক্যালাপ** *n.* conversation (বাক্যালাপে মগ্ন) ; speaking terms (তাদের বাক্যালাপ নেই = they are not on speaking terms). **বাক্যালাপ করা** *v.* to converse; to talk together (usu. familiarly); to speak with.

বাক্স, বাক্‌সো *n.* a box; a case. ~জাত, ~বন্দি *a.* kept into a box. **বাক্সজাত করা, বাক্সবন্দি করা** *v.* to put into a box, to box.

বাখান *n.* praise, eulogy; description.

বাখানা *v.* (poet.) to narrate or describe or delineate or praise.

বাখারি *n.* a piece of split bamboo, a bamboo-slip.

বাখারি চুন *n.* unslaked lime, quick-lime.

বাগ[1] *n.* a garden (গোলাপবাগ).

বাগ[2] *n.* bridle (বাগডোর) ; control (বাগে পাওয়া) ; device or mode (কাজের বাগ) ; opportunity or advantage (বাগ পেয়ে) ; (dial.) a way or route (সে কোন বাগে গেল ?). **বাগ মানানো, বাগে আনা** *v.* to bring under control.

বাগ্‌জাল *n.* a web or mesh or trap of words; wheedling language; rigmarole; circumlocution; grandiloquence. **বাগ্‌জাল বিস্তার করা** *v.* to weave a web or set a trap of words; to speak wheedlingly; to circumlocute.

বাগডম্বর same as **বাগাড়ম্বর**।

বাগড়া *n.* (coll.) an obstacle, a hindrance, a hitch. **বাগড়া দেওয়া** *v.* to create a hitch, to hinder; to make a bottleneck; to take the wind out of one's sails.

বাগডোর *n.* rein.

বাগ্‌দত্তা *a. fem.* betrothed; affianced. □ *n. fem.* a betrothed girl.

বাগদা, বাগদা-চিংড়ি *n.* the prawn.

বাগ্‌দান *n.* betrothal; giving word; making a promise.

বাগদি *n.* a lowly Hindu caste; one of this caste. *fem.* **বাগদিনি**।

বাগ্‌দেবী *n.* Saraswati, the goddess of speech.

বাগ্‌ধারা *n.* a manner or mode of using words in speech, an idiom. ~গত *a.* idiomatic..

বাগ্‌বহুল *a.* verbose, full of words, having too many words; prolix. **বাগ্‌বাহুল্য** *n.* verbosity; prolixity.

বাগ্‌বিতণ্ডা *n.* altercation, wrangling; a hot dispute.

বাগ্‌বিদগ্ধ *a.* clever or apt in speech; eloquent. **বাগ্‌বৈদগ্ধ্য** *n.* eloquence.

বাগ্‌যন্ত্র *n.* the larynx.

বাগ্‌যুদ্ধ same as **বাগ্‌বিতণ্ডা**।

বাগাড়ম্বর *n.* grandiloquence; tall talk; verbiage. **বাগাড়ম্বর করা** *v.* to speak grandiloquently; to talk big; to brag; to speak verbosely.

বাগান *n.* a garden; a pleasure-ground; a grove. **আমবাগান** *n.* a mango-grove. **কলাবাগান** *n.* a clump of plantain trees. **নারকেল বাগান** *n.* a coconut-grove. **ফলবাগান** *n.* an orchard. **ফুলবাগান** *n.* a flower garden, a flower-bed. **সবজিবাগান** *n.* a kitchen garden. **বাগান করা** *v.* to garden. **বাগানে কাজ করা** *v.* to garden. **বাগানের কাজ** gardening.

বাগানো *v.* to bring under control; to break (বদমেজাজি ঘোড়াকে বাগানো) ; to manage, to obtain (চাকরি বাগানো, টাকা বাগানো) ; to manage to have performed or executed or done (কাজ বাগানো) ; to wangle (ছুটি বাগানো) ; to flourish (তেড়ি বাগানো) ; to defalcate or misappropriate (তবিল থেকে বাগানো).

বাগি *n.* bubo.

বাগিচা *n.* a small garden.

বাগিন্দ্রিয় *n.* the organ of speech.

বাগী alt. spell. of **বাগি**।

বাগীশ, বাগীশ্বর *n.* an eloquent man; a fluent speaker; an orator; (*fem.* an oratress, an oratrix). **বাগীশ্বরী** *fem.* of **বাগীশ**। □ *n.* Saraswati (সরস্বতী) the goddess of speech.

বাগুরা *n.* (obs.) a net, a snare. **বাগুরাবদ্ধ** *a.* caught in a trap or snare.

বাগ্মী *a.* having eloquence or oratorial power. □ *n.* a good or eloquent speaker; an orator. **বাগ্মিতা** *n.* eloquence; oratory.

বাঘ *n.* the tiger; (loos.) the panther, the leopard. *fem.* **বাঘিনি** the tigress. **বাঘে গোরুতে এক ঘাটে জল খাওয়া** (fig.) a very powerful administration under which even traditional antagonists behave as friends. **বাঘের ঘরে ঘোগের বাসা** (lit.) a tiger-wolf taking-up its abode in a tiger's lair; (fig.) a weakling settling in the lair of its deadly enemy. **বাঘের বাচ্ছা** a tiger's cub. **বাঘের মাসি** the cat. **~ছড়ি, ~ছাল** *n.* the skin of a tiger. **~নখ** *n.* a tiger's nail; an ornamental pendant for the neck; an aromatic substance; (hist.) a nail-like weapon worn by Shivaji as handgloves. **~বন্দি** *n.* an indoor game akin to fox and geese. **বাঘা** *n.* (dero.) the tiger, a tigerling (গোবাঘা) ; (affec.) a traditional name of a dog. □ *a.* very large (বাঘা মাছ) ; very powerful (বাঘা শাসন) ; very efficient (বাঘা কেরানি, বাঘা খেলোয়াড়) ; extremely sour (বাঘা তেঁতুল) ; commanding submission from others, very imposing (বাঘা লোক). **বাঘাম্বর** *n.* a piece of tiger's skin worn as loincloth.

বাঙ্‌নিষ্ঠ *a.* true to one's word, one who keeps his word or promise.

বাঙ্‌নিষ্পত্তি *n.* utterance of words. **বাঙ্‌নিষ্পত্তি করা** *v.* to utter or speak.

বাঙলা var. of **বাংলা**[1]।

বাঙাল *n.* a native of East Bengal; (iron.) an unrefined rustic. □ *a.* of East Bengal (বাঙাল প্রথা) ; born in East Bengal. *fem. n.* **বাঙালিনি, বাঙালনি**।

বাঙালি *n.* a native of Bengal, a Bengali. □ *a.* of Bengalis or of Bengal.

বাঙালে *a.* (usu. dero.) like a Bengali of the East, like or about an East Bengali.

বাঙ্গালা arch. form of **বাংলা**[1]।

বাঙ্ময় *a.* full of words, wordy; composed of words, worded. **বাঙ্ময়ী** *a. fem.* of **বাঙ্ময়**। □ *n.* Saraswati (সরস্বতী) the goddess of speech.

বাচ coll. corrup. of **বাইচ**।

বাচক[1] *a.* signifying, denoting.

বাচক[2] *n.* (coll.) prohibition or prejudice; (coll.) abstinence.

বাচন *n.* speaking; narration; utterance; a saying; reading; expounding, explanation. **বাচনিক** *a.* verbal, oral; in word.

বাচবিচার coll. form of **বাছবিচার**।

বাচস্পতি *n.* an eloquent speaker; an orator; a learned man.

বাচস্পত্য *n.* eloquence; erudition.

বাচাল *a.* talkative, garrulous; voluble. **বাচালতা** *n.* talkativeness, garrulity; volubility.

বাচ্চা, বাচ্ছা *n.* a young child, an infant; (sl.) a kid; offspring (লোকটা মানুষের বাচ্চা নয়) ; the young of a beast. □ *a.* young, infant (বাচ্চা ছেলে, বাচ্চা কুকুর). **বাচ্চাকাচ্চা** *n. pl.* young or infant children, little ones; kiddies.

বাচ্য *a.* to be spoken or uttered; speakable, utterable ; fit to be regarded as, namable (পদবাচ্য). □ *n.* (gr.) voice. **বাচ্যার্থ** *n.* actual or simple (and not figurative) meaning or sense of a word or sentence, the primary or original meaning (of a word etc.).

বাছন, বাছনি[১] *n.* same as **বাছাই** (*n.*).

বাছনি[২] milder form of **বাছা**[২] ।

বাছবিচার *n.* discrimination or choice (usu. meticulous or over-cautious one); prejudicial abstinence or avoidance. **বাছবিচার করা** *v.* to choose meticulously or over-cautiously; to abstain from, to avoid; to be prejudiced against. **বাছবিচার না করে, বিনা বাছবিচারে** without discrimination, indiscriminately.

বাছা[১] *n.* (in affectionate address) a son or a daughter or a person deserving to be treated as such (cp. My child.)

বাছা[২] *v.* to choose, to select; to pick and choose; to sort out or separate (ভালোমন্দ বাছা, খুদ বাছা) ; to eliminate unwanted elements from (চাল বাছা) ; to pick and eliminate or kill (উকুন বাছা). □ *a.* chosen, selected; sorted; freed from unwanted elements; choice, select (বাছা বাছা লোক = chosen or selected persons).

বাছাই *n.* choosing, choice, selection; picking and choosing; sorting or separating; elimination of unwanted elements. □ *a.* same as **বাছা**[২] (*a*). **বাছাই করা** same as **বাছা**[২] ।

বাছাধন *n. masc.* same as **বাছা**[১] ।

বাছুর *n.* the young of the cow, the calf. **বাছুর বিয়ানো** *v.* to calve. **বাছুরের মাংস** *n.* veal.

বাজ[১] *n.* thunderbolt, thunder; (loos.) lightning.

বাজ[২] *n.* the hawk; the falcon.

-বাজ[৩] *sfx.* denoting : skilled, given to, full of etc. (ফন্দিবাজ, স্ফূর্তিবাজ).

বাজখাঁই *a.* (of voice) very harsh and loud, strident (বাজখাঁই গলা).

বাজন *n.* the state of being played or beaten or sounded or rung (as a musical instrument, bell, coin etc.); the sound of beating or playing on a musical instrument, a bell etc. **~দার, বাজনাদার, বাজনাওয়ালা** *n.* an instrumentalist (esp. a professional one). **বাজনা** *n.* act or sound of playing on a musical instrument; music; a musical instrument.

বাজবৈরি, বাজবহরি *n.* a species or variety of large falcons; the eagle (?).

বাজরা[১] *n.* bulrush-millet, millet.

বাজরা[২] *n.* a wicker-hamper.

বাজা *v.* to sound or be sounded (মোটরের হর্ন বাজা) ; to ring or be rung, to toll (ঘণ্টা বাজা) ; to be played on (বীণা বাজা) ; to be beaten (ঢাক বাজা) ; to strike (ঘড়ি বাজা, তিনটে বাজা) ; to be announced by a sound (প্রহর বাজা) ; to be felt (হাতে বাজা) ; to jar on (কানে বাজা) ; to smart or pain (মনে বাজা). **ঘড়ি বাজে** the clock chimes or strikes. **ঘড়িতে একটা বাজে** the clock strikes one, it is one o'clock. **স্কুলের ঘণ্টা বাজে** the school-bell goes.

বাজানো *v.* to sound; to ring, to toll; to play on (as a musical instrument), to beat (as an instrument of percussion); to clink (as coins); to try to discover the inclinations, thoughts etc. of, to sound (লোকটাকে বাজিয়ে দেখা). **বাজিয়ে দেখা** *v.* to try or sound (somebody).

বাজার *n.* a market; a fair (রথের বাজার) ; goods or stores esp. for cooking purchased from the market (বাজারটা রাখলে কোথায় ?). **বাজার করা** *v.* to visit the market for buying things (esp. daily necessaries or stores), to shop. **বাজার বসেছে** the market has opened for the day; a new market has opened. **গরম বাজার** (comm.) boom. **চড়া বাজার** dear market. **নরম বাজার** (comm.) slump. **বাজার চড়া** market is up. **~দর** *n.* market price, the current price. **বাজার নরম** market is down; demand is slack. **বাজারে** *a.* selling or dealing at a market; (of a woman) taken to harlotry. **বাজারে মেয়েমানুষ** a prostitute. **বাজারে লোক** a market-man, a marketer.

-বাজি[1] *sfx.* denoting : practice, propensity, repleteness etc. (ফন্দিবাজি).

বাজি[2] *n.* magic, jugglery, legerdemain (ভোজবাজি) ; a feat (দড়াবাজি, মুখবাজি) ; a game, a turn, a spell, a bout (এক বাজি তাস বা দাবা) ; fireworks; a wager; a stake; (fig.) one's existence and activities in this world ('এবার বাজি ভোর'). **বাজি জেতা** *v.* to win a stake. **বাজি ধরা** *v.* to lay a wager; to stake. **বাজি পোড়ানো** *v.* to make a display of fire-works. **বাজি রাখা** *v.* to bet. **বাজি হারা** *v.* to lose a stake.

বাজিকর *n.* a juggler, a magician; (rare) an acrobat.

বাজিমাত *n.* (in chess) checkmate; complete victory or triumph in a game or anything.

বাজিয়ে *a.* skilled in playing on a musical instrument. □ *n.* an instrumentalist.

বাজী *n.* the horse; an arrow.

বাজীকরণ *n.* an aphrodisiac process or drug, an aphrodisiac.

বাজু *n.* an ornament for the arm, an armlet (also **বাজুবন্ধ**) the arm; a side; a side-post of a door or a cot.

বাজে *a.* inferior or trashy (বাজে মাল) ; insignificant, contemptible, worthless, good-for-nothing (বাজে লোক) ; false, unsubstantial, idle (বাজে কথা) ; useless, unnecessary (বাজে খাটুনি) ; undesirable, unwanted (বাজে ঝামেলা) ; extra or incidental (বাজে খরচ, বাজে আদায়). **~মার্কা** *a.* of inferior make or brand; inferior; insignificant.

বাজেয়াপ্ত *a.* confiscated, forfeited; foreclosed. **বাজেয়াপ্ত করা** *v.* to confiscate, to forfeit; to foreclose. **~করণ** *n.* confiscation, forfeiture; foreclosure.

বাঞ্ছন obs. *in comp.* (used as a *sfx.*) desired (by) (দেবেন্দ্রবাঞ্ছন).

বাঞ্ছনীয় *a.* desirable; agreeable.

বাঞ্ছা *n.* a desire, a longing; a wish. **বাঞ্ছা করা** *v.* to desire or long or wish (for). **~কল্পতরু** *n.* (myth.) a wishing-tree of heaven; one who grants all desires of supplicants.

বাঞ্ছিত *a.* desired, longed-for, wished-for. *fem.* **বাঞ্ছিতা** ।

বাট[1] *n.* (usu. poet.) a path, a road.

বাট[2] *n.* ingot, bullion.

বাটখারা *n.* a mass of metal adjusted to a standard and used in weighing or in calculating weight, a weight.

বাটন *n.* turning into paste by rolling something on a flat mortar with a pestle. **বাটনা** *n.* spices turned thus into paste; a quantity of spices to be rolled thus.

বাটপাড় *n.* a highwayman; a robber; a swindler. **বাটপাড়ি** *n.* highway robbery; robbery; swindling. **চোরের উপর বাটপাড়ি** (fig.) a swindler robs a thief.

বাটা[1] var. of **বাট্টা** ।

বাটা[2] *n.* a variety of small silvery-white fresh-water fish.

বাটা[3] *n.* a kind of metal tray (esp. one for holding betel-leaves).

বাটা[4] *n.* a Hindu rite of offering dishes of food to a son-in-law.

বাটা[5] *v.* to turn into paste by rolling (spices etc.) on a flat mortar with a pestle. □ *a.* (spices etc.) thus reduced to or turned into paste (বাটা মশলা).

বাটালি *n.* a chisel.

বাটি *n.* a hemispheroidal cup without handles. **বাটি চালা** *v.* to set a cup chasing a culprit by means of occult incantations. **এক বাটি** a cup (of); a cupful (of).

বাটিকা *n.* a small house; (loos.) a house (উদ্যানবাটিকা).

বাটুল var. of **বাঁটুল** ।

বাটোয়ারা *n.* apportionment; division; partition.

বাট্টা *n.* (comm.) a discount. **আসল বাট্টা** true discount.

বাড় *n.* growth, development (গাছের বাড়) ; increase (বেতনের বাড়) ; aggravation (রোগের বাড়) ; audacity. **বাড় বাড়া** to grow audacious, to become intolerably haughty, to be high and mighty.

বাড়ই *n.* a carpenter, a joiner.

বাড়তি *n.* growth or development or increase or aggravation or flourish (বাড়তির মুখে). □ *a.* surplus (বাড়তি মাল) ; extra (বাড়তি রোজগার) ; excessive, in excess (বাড়তি লাভ = excess profit).

বাড়ন[1] same as **বাড়** ।

বাড়ন[2] *n.* a besom, a broom.

বাড়ন্ত *a.* inclined to grow or develop, growing (বাড়ন্ত গড়ন) ; flourishing (বাড়ন্ত অবস্থা) ; (iron.) exhausted, deficit (ঘরে চাল বাড়ন্ত).

বাড়বাড়ন্ত *n.* great or growing prosperity; (iron.) bluster; lofty show.

বাড়ব *a.* (myth.) relating to a sea-horse vomiting fire constantly. □ *n.* fire vomited by the aforesaid sea-horse (usu. **বাড়বানল**).

বাড়া[1] *v.* to proceed, to go. **আগে বাড়া** *v.* to go forward or ahead, to advance.

বাড়া[2] *v.* to grow up, to develop (গাছ বাড়া) ; to increase (লোক বাড়া) ; to augment (বিপদ বাড়া) ; to be expanded (রাজ্য বাড়া) ; to aggravate (রোগ বাড়া) ; to flourish, to thrive (ধনসম্পদ বাড়া) ; to mend or sharpen (পেনসিল বাড়া) ; to grow audacious (বদমাশটা বড় বেড়েছে) ; to serve on a dinner-plate (ভাত বাড়া). □ *a.* mended; served on a dinner-plate; more or greater than ('সে মাটি মায়ের বাড়া'). **বাড়ানো** *v.* to develop; to increase; to multiply (বংশ বাড়ানো) ; to augment; to expand; to aggravate; to cause to mend or sharpen; to stretch; to extend, to crane (হাত বাড়ানো, গলা বাড়ানো) ; to cause to serve on a dinner-plate; to exalt or extol unduly or give undue importance to (অযোগ্য লোককে বাড়ানো) ; to exaggerate (বাড়িয়ে লেখা) ; to over-indulge (ছেলেটাকে সে বাড়িয়েছে) ; to enhance falsely (বয়স বাড়ানো). **~বাড়ি** *n.* excess; immoderation; intemperance; overmuchness; aggravation (রোগের বাড়াবাড়ি). **বাড়াবাড়ি করা** *v.* to go beyond the limit. **বাড়াবাড়ি হওয়া** *v.* to be aggravated; to be in excess. **বাড়া ভাতে ছাই দেওয়া** *v.* (fig.) to frustrate or foil somebody's hopes or plans almost at the point of success.

বাড়ি[1] *n.* a stroke, a hit (লাঠির বাড়ি) ; a staff, a stick, a cudgel (পাচনবাড়ি). **বাড়ি দেওয়া, বাড়ি মারা** *v.* to deal (one) a blow, to strike, to hit.

বাড়ি[2] *n.* a house; a building; a dwelling-house, an abode; a residence; a home. **~ওয়ালা** *n.* the owner of a house (esp. of tenanted one), (cp.) a landlord (*fem.* a landlady). *fem.* **বাড়িওয়ালি,** (coll.) **বাড়িউলি** । **~ঘর** *n.* homestead; houses and buildings; habitations. **~ভাড়া** *n.* house-rent; rent of a dwelling house. **~মুখো** *a.* & *adv.* homeward; home-bound. **যমের বাড়ি** (fig.) death's door.

বাণ *n.* an arrow, a shaft, a dart. **বাণ ছোড়া** *v.* to shoot an arrow. **~বিদ্ধ** *a.* pierced with an arrow. **~লিঙ্গ** *n.* a phallic symbol of Shiva.

বাণিজ্য *a.* trade, commerce, traffic. **বাণিজ্য করা** *v.* to trade, to traffic. **বাণিজ্য কর** *n.* a commercial tax. **~কেন্দ্র** *n.* a trade centre. **~তরি** *n.* a merchant ship, a merchantman. **~পোত** same as **বাণিজ্যতরি** । **~মন্ত্রক** *n.* the Ministry of Commerce. **~মন্ত্রী** *n.* a Minister of Commerce. **বাণিজ্য সামগ্রী** *n.* merchandise; ware, commodity; stock-in trade, requisites for a trade. **বাণিজ্যিক** *a.* commercial.

বাণী *n.* word; speech; a message; a maxim, an apophthegm; Saraswati (সরস্বতী) the goddess of speech.

বাণ্ডিল alt. spell. of **বানডিল** or **বাণ্ডিল** ।

বাত[1] *n.* word, speech (লম্বা বাত) ; news, information ('পুছে বাত').

বাত[2] *n.* wind; air; rheumatism; rheum. **~কর্ম** *n.* farting; a fart. **~গহ্বর** *n.* an air-pocket. **~গ্রস্ত** *a.* rheumatic. **~চক্র** *n.* windmill. **~ঘ্ন** *a.* curing rheumatism or lymphatic disorders. **~জ, ~জনিত** *a.* rheumatic. **~জ্বর** *n.* rheumatic fever. **~পৈত্তিক** *a.* rheumatic and biliary. **~বেদনা** *n.* rheumatic pain. **~ব্যাধি** *n.* rheumatism. **~ব্যাধিগ্রস্ত** *a.* rheumatic. **~রক্ত** *n.* a kind of blood-poisoning. **~রোগ** *n.* rheumatism. **~রোগগ্রস্ত** *a.* rheumatic. **~শূল** *n.* neuralgia. **~শোষক** *n.* (bot.) an aspirator.

বাতলানো *v.* to suggest; to point out; to devise. □ *a.* suggested; devised.

বাৎসরিক *a.* annual, yearly; taking place or happening annually. □ *n.* an annual rite or religious performance.

বাৎসল্য *n.* affection; love; parental love, philoprogenitveness; the sentiment of parental love.

বাতা *n.* a slip of bamboo or wood esp. one used in roofing, a lath, a slat.

বাতানুকূল *a.* air-conditioned. **বাতানুকূলতা** *n.* air-conditioning.

বাতান্দোলিত *a.* agitated or moved or tossed by wind.

বাতান্বিত *a.* aerated. **বাতান্বিত পানীয়** aerated water, (loos.) mineral water.

বাতাপি dial. corrup. of **বাতাবি**।

বাতাবকাশ *n.* an air space.

বাতাবরণ *n.* environment, surroundings, atmosphere.

বাতাবর্ত *n.* a whirlwind; a cyclone.

বাতাবি *n.* the shaddock, the pompelmoose, the pomelo (also **বাতাবি লেবু**).

বাতায়ন *n.* a window; a ventilator.

বাতাস *n.* air; wind; a gust of wind; fanning; (usu. dero.) influence or touch (নাস্তিকের বাতাস). **বাতাস করা** *v.* to fan. **বাতাস খাওয়া** *v.* to enjoy fanning; to cool oneself with fanning; to take the air. **বাতাস দেওয়া** *v.* to fan; (fig.) to kindle or encourage (ঝগড়ায় বাতাস দেওয়া). **বাতাস পাওয়া** *v.* to get air; (of boats etc.) to get favourable wind; (usu. dero.) to be influenced by. **বাতাস লাগা** *v.* to get air or (of boats etc.) wind; (usu. dero.) to be influenced by; to be possessed by an evil spirit. **বাতাসে ওড়া** *v.* to fly in air; (fig.) to move light-heartedly or airily. **বাতাসে ভর করে চলা** *v.* (fig.) to move as swiftly as the wind; (fig.) to move very lightly; (fig.) to move light-heartedly.

তাসা *n.* a kind of light convex sweet drop of sugar or molasses.

তাহত *a.* wind-beaten, wind-stricken; (rare) wind-bound.

তি *n.* a lamp, a light; a candle; a stick or rod (গালার বাতি).

তিক *n.* neurosis; a mania; a strong hobby, a crotchet, a craze (খেলা দেখার বাতিক). **~গ্রস্ত** *a.* neurotic; maniac; crotchety. **~গ্রস্ত ব্যক্তি** a neurotic; a crotchety man.

বাতিদান *n.* a lampstand; a candle-stick.

বাতিল *a.* forsaken or disowned; rejected; (law) void, set aside; annulled, rescinded; cancelled. **বাতিল করা** *v.* to forsake or disown; to reject; (law) to void, to set aside; to annul, to rescind; to cancel.

বাতিস্তম্ভ *n.* a lightpost, a lamppost.

বাতুল *a.* neurotic; mad, insane; crazy. **বাতুলতা** *n.* neurosis; madness, insanity; craziness.

বাত্যা *n.* a strong wind, a gale, a storm. **~পীড়িত** *a.* storm-stricken, storm-beaten. **~বিক্ষুব্ধ** *a.* storm-tossed; tempestuous (as the sea), agitated by stormy wind.

বাথান *n.* a cowhouse, a cattle-shed; a grazing ground, a pasture.

বাথুয়া, বেথো *n.* a variety of spinach.

বাদ[১] *n.* an obstacle, a hindrance; opposition. **বাদ সাধা** *v.* to obstruct, to hinder; to get in the way of; to oppose; to foil.

বাদ[২] *n.* an utterance (সাধুবাদ) ; an argument (বাদপ্রতিবাদ) ; a complaint or charge (বাদী) ; a dispute or brawl (বাদবিসংবাদ) ; (log.) correct judgment; a doctrine, an ism, a theory (সাম্যবাদ). **~প্রতিবাদ** *n.* argument, dispute, verbal dispute; altercation. **~বিতণ্ডা** *n.* wrangling, altercation; dispute; quarrel.

বাদ[৩] *n.* exception; omission; exclusion; exemption; deduction; subtraction; (comm.) a discount. □ *prep.* same as **বাদে** (*prep.*). **বাদ দেওয়া** *v.* to except; to omit; to exclude; to exempt; to deduct; to subtract; to discount. **বাদ পড়া, বাদ যাওয়া, বাদ হওয়া** *v.* to be excepted or omitted or excluded or exempted or subtracted or discounted.

বাদক *n.* an instrumentalist. **~সম্প্রদায়** *n.* a musical band.

বাদন *n.* act of playing on a musical instrument.

বাদপ্রতিবাদ see **বাদ**[২]।

বাদবাকি *a.* remaining.

বাদবিতণ্ডা see **বাদ**[২]।

বাদবিসংবাদ same as **বাদবিতণ্ডা**।

বাদল, (poet.) **বাদর,** (coll.) **বাদলা**[1] *n.* rain; a rainy day. **বাদল-মেঘ** *n.* nimbus.

বাদলা[2] *a.* of rain; of the rainy season ; rain-soaked; (loos.) moist; born or found in the rainy season (বাদলা পোকা) ; rainy (বাদলা দিন).

বাদলা[3] *n.* gold-thread or silver-thread (বাদলার কাজ).

বাদলে var. of **বাদুলে**।

বাদশা *n.* same as **বাদশাহ**। **কুঁড়ের বাদশা** a prince of idlers, an extremely lazy fellow.

বাদশাহ *n.* (Mus.) a great king or an emperor, badshah a padshah; the king of playing-cards. **~জাদা** *n.* a son of a badshah. *fem.* **~জাদি** a daughter of a badshah. **বাদশাহি** *n.* the office or reign or dominion of a badshah; a life as full of milk and honey or as pompous as that of a badshah. □ *a.* of or like a badshah; princely; imperial; majestic.

বাদসাদ *n.* partial discount or deduction or allowance.

বাদা *n.* an extensive marsh or fen; a wooded region.

বাদাড় *n.* a jungle; a wild tract of land full of thickets.

বাদানুবাদ same as **বাদপ্রতিবাদ**।

বাদাম[1] *n.* a sail ('রাধার নামে বাদাম').

বাদাম[2] *n.* nut, almond. **বাদামের খোলা** a nutshell.

বাদামি *a.* almond-coloured, brown; almond-shaped; almond-like.

বাদিত *a.* (chiefly of musical instruments) sounded, played on.

বাদিতা *sfx.* denoting : habit of speaking (সত্যবাদিতা) ; obedience to or practice of an ism (বাস্তববাদিতা).

বাদিত্র *n.* a musical instrument.

বাদিনী *fem.* of **বাদী**[2]।

বাদী[1] *n.* the principal note of a musical mode.

বাদী[2] *sfx.* denoting : speaking or accustomed to speak (সত্যবাদী) ; obedient to or practising an ism, -ist, -istic (সাম্যবাদী). □ *n.* a plaintiff or a complainant. **~-প্রতিবাদী** *n.* complainant and defendant.

বাদুড় *n.* a flying mammal, the bat; the flying-fox.

বাদুলে *a.* same as **বাদলা**[2]।

বাদে *prep.* except, without (সে বাদে সবাই) ; after (দুদিন বাদে). □ *adv.* afterwards, later on (বাদে এসো = come later).

বাদ্য *n.* instrumental music; a musical instrument. **~কর** *n.* an instrumentalist. **~করদল** *n.* a musical band; a concert party. **~ধ্বনি** *n.* sound of instrumental music. **~ভাণ্ড** *n.* musical instruments collectively; a set of musical instruments. **~যন্ত্র** *n.* a musical instrument.

বাদ্যি coll. form of **বাদ্য**।

বাধ var. of **বাদ**[1]।

বাধক *a.* obstructive; hindering. □ secondary amenorrhœa.

বাধা *v.* to stick (কাঁটায় কাপড় বাধা) ; to be obstructed or opposed (ধর্মে বাধে) ; to come to happen, to ensue or begin (লড়াই বাধা) ; to find it difficult or impossible (বুঝতে বাধে). □ *n.* an obstacle, a hindrance, an impediment; a hitch; a prohibition; prevention; obstruction; resistance; a trouble. **বাধা দেওয়া** *v.* to obstruct, to hinder, to impede; to resist; to prevent; to oppose. **বাধা পাওয়া** *v.* to be obstructed or hindered or impeded or resisted or prevented. **~জনক, ~দায়ক** *a.* obstructive, resistive; resistant; prohibitive, preventive. **~দান** *n.* obstructing, impeding; resisting; preventing; obstruction; resistance; prevention. **~নিষেধ** *n.* prohibition; hindrance; impediment; prevention. **~নো** *v.* to cause to stick; to bring about; to initiate, to start, to involve, to set (লড়াই বাধানো). **~প্রাপ্ত** *a.* obstructed; impeded; hindered; frustrated; resisted; prevented **~বন্ধ** *n.* hindrance, impediment; obstruction; obstacle. **~বন্ধহারা, ~বন্ধহীন** *a.* having no obstacles or hindrances without any impediment; unimpeded unobstructed. **~বিঘ্ন** *n.* impediments obstacles, obstructions, snags. **~হীন** same as **বাধাবন্ধহীন**।

বাধিত *a.* obstructed; prevented; resisted subdued; obliged, thankful, beholden (বাধিত থাকা বা হওয়া). **বাধিত করা** *v.* to oblige.

বাধোবাধো *a.* on the point of commencing or ensuing or breaking out (লড়াই বাধোবাধো) ; uneasy or hesitating (বাধোবাধো গলায়). **বাধোবাধো ঠেকা** to be in two minds, to be embarrassed, to hesitate to do or act, to be in a state of indecision.

বাধ্য *a.* preventible, resistible; obedient, obsequious, docile (বাধ্য ছেলে) ; amenable (সুযুক্তির বাধ্য) ; obliged (কর্তব্য পালনে বাধ্য) ; compelled or sure (to) (হার মানতে বাধ্য). **বাধ্য করা** *v.* to compel. **বাধ্য হয়ে** being compelled, under obligation or compulsion. **~তা** *n.* obedience, obsequiousness, docility; amenability; obligation; compulsion. **বাধ্যতাজনক, বাধ্যতামূলক** *a.* compulsory; obligatory; imperative. **~বাধকতা** *n.* mutual obligations; strictness; rigidity.

ান[1] *n.* the eel, (cp.) the lamprey.

ান[2] *n.* a flood, a deluge; a kind of tidal wave, a bore, an eagre (গঙ্গার বান) ; (fig.) a great flourish (আনন্দের বান). **বান ডাকা** *v.* to rise in flood, to be in flood or deluge; to rise in bore or eagre; (fig.) to flourish greatly. **বানে ভেসে যাওয়া** *v.* to be swept off or carried off in a flood; to be overflooded.

ান[3], (rej.) **বান্** *sfx.* denoting : possession, qualification etc. (গুণবান, বেগবান).

নচাল *a.* having the bottom ripped open (নৌকো বানচাল হওয়া) ; foiled, capsized, bungled (ফন্দি বানচাল হওয়া). **বানচাল হওয়া** *v.* to have the bottom ripped open; to fail, to be bungled, to miscarry, to end in a fiasco.

নডিল *n.* a bundle.

নতেল *n.* essential oil, etherial oil.

নপ্রস্থ *n.* the third stage of life according to the Vedas when a man advanced in years should leave his home and hearth and go to the forest to pass the remaining days of his life in spiritual meditation.

নর (for.) *n.* the monkey; the ape. *fem.* **বানরী** । **~তুল্য** *a.* monkeyish; apish.

নান *n.* spelling (of a word), orthography. **বানান করা** *v.* to spell. **~সমস্যা** *n.* the problem of orthography.

বানানো *v.* to make; to create; to construct or build; to compose (কবিতা বানানো) ; to manufacture (ঘড়ি বানানো) ; to produce or beget (ছেলে বানানো) ; to coin or mint (টাকা বানানো) ; to draw up (দলিল বানানো) ; to found, to set up (স্কুল বানানো) ; to form (শব্দ বানানো) ; to organize (দল বানানো) ; to cause to appear as (মানুষকে ভেড়া বানানো) ; to turn or render into (বোকা বানানো) ; to dress (as meat, fish etc.); to cook (কোরমা বানানো) ; to concoct or fabricate (মামলা বানানো) ; to get one up, to prepare (সাক্ষী বানানো) ; to invent, to devise (অজুহাত বানানো). □ *a.* artificial (বানানো পাহাড়) ; faked, counterfeit, forged (বানানো দলিল) ; got-up (বানানো মামলা, বানানো সাক্ষী).

বানি *n.* making charge (esp. for ornaments and dress).

বানিয়া *n.* a trader; a tradesman; a shopkeeper; (dero.) a very commercial-minded man, a commercialist; one guided only by profit and loss motive.

বানুরে *a.* monkeyish; apish; very mischievous.

বান্ডিল alt. spell. of **বানডিল** ।

বান্দর dial. corrup. of **বানর** ।

বান্দা *n.* a slave; a servant; an obedient or devoted person; (iron.) a man (সহজ বান্দা নয়). *fem.* **বান্দি, বাঁদি** a slave-woman; a maid-servant; an obedient or devoted woman.

বান্ধব *n.* a kinsman; a relation; a friend; an ally. *fem.* **বান্ধবী** a kinswoman; a woman relation; a lady friend; a girl friend.

বান্ধুলি corrup. of **বন্ধুলী** ।

বাপ[1] *n.* sowing; weaving.

বাপ[2] *n.* a father; (in affectionate address) a son or a person deserving to be treated as a son. **বাপকা বেটা, বাপের বেটা** a chip of the old block. **বাপকা বেটা সেপাইকা ঘোড়া, কুছ নেহি তো থোড়া থোড়া** (fig.) a son must inherit some qualities at least of his father. **বাপ তোলা** *v.* to abuse one by calling names of one's father. **বাপের জন্মে বা বয়সে** (fig.) at any time, ever. **কারও বাপের সাধ্য নেই**

(fig.) not within anybody's capacity, nobody is able to do, no one, not even one's sire has the grit or ability (to do).

বাপ৩, বাপরে, বাপস *int.* denoting: fright, amazement etc; O my God! O my!

বাপক *n.* one who causes to sow or weave; a sower; a weaver.

বাপ-ঠাকুরদাদা, বাপদাদা *n. pl.* ancestors, forefathers.

বাপতা coll. var. of **বাফতা**।

বাপধন *n.* (usu. facet.) a dear son.

বাপন *n.* act of causing to sow or weave or shave or tonsure; sowing; weaving; shaving or tonsuring.

বাপস see **বাপ৩**।

বাপান্ত *n.* abusing one by calling names of one's father. **বাপান্ত করা** same as **বাপ তোলা** (see **বাপ২**)।

বাপি১ alt. spell. of **বাপী**।

বাপী২ *n.* (in endearment) father; son.

বাপিত *a.* sown; woven; shaved or tonsured.

বাপী *n.* a large pond or tank or pool or artificial lake.

বাপু *int. & n.* a term for addressing a child or a junior person (in affection or disgust), my boy, my girl; an expression emphasizing disgust, amazement, interrogation etc. (একি জ্বালা বাপু, বাপুরে, কী হল বাপু).

বাপের জন্মে *adv.* never in my life (বাপের জন্মে শুনিনি).

বাফতা *n.* taffeta, taffety.

বাবদ *prep.* on account of. □ *n.* an account. **এই বাবদ** on this account, on account of this. **কীসের বাবদ** on what account. **কোন বাবদ** in which account; on what account.

বাবরি *n.* a mass of long and curling hair flowing down to a person's neck, a mane. **বাবরি-কাটা** *a.* maned, having a mane.

বাবলা *n.* the accacia, the bablah, the babul, Acacia arabica. **বাবলার আঠা** *n.* gum of accacia.

বাবা১ var. of **বাবাঃ**।

বাবা২ *n.* a father, (coll.) dad. □ *int.* same as **বাপু**। **বাবাজি** *n.* a reverend father; a title applied to ascetics esp. to the Vaishnav ascetics; a term for addressing a son or a junior person. **~জীবন** *n.* a term for addressing a son-in-law or a son or a junior person.

বাবাঃ *int.* denoting: fright, amazement etc.

বাবাজি, বাবাজীবন see **বাবা২**।

বাবু *n.* a title affixed to the name of a gentleman, Mr (হরিবাবু) ; a clerk (হেড অফিসের বড়বাবু) ; a Baboo, a babu; a male member of a family (ঘোষেদের মেজোবাবু) ; a proprietor; a master, an employer; an officer; a landlord; (in endearment) a husband, a father, a son a junior person; a gentleman; a fop, a dandy. □ *a.* given to luxury; dainty fastidious; foppish; lazy. **বাবু চাকর** a dandy of a servant; a dainty servant; a lazy servant. **~গিরি, ~য়ানা** *n.* indulgence in luxury; daintiness, fastidiousness, foppishness, foppery, dandyism. **~জি, ~মশাই** *n.* a respectful term for addressing a man.

বাবুই *n.* the weaver bird, the widow bird. **বাবুই তুলসী** *n.* a kind of wild basil.

বাবুর্চি *n.* (Mus.) a cook or chef. **~খানা** *n.* a cookhouse, a kitchen.

বাম১ var. of **বাঁও**।

বাম২ *n.* the left; Shiva (শিব). □ *a.* left (বামপার্শ্ব) ; antipathetic (বিধি বাম) beautiful (বামলোচনা).

বামন১ *n.* the fifth incarnation of Vishnu (বিষ্ণু) in the shape of a dwarf; a dwarf, a durgan.

বামন২ *n.* a Brahman; a Brahman priest or cook. *fem.* **বামনি**। **বামন গেল ঘর তো লাঙল তুলে ধর** (fig.) when the master is away servants neglect their work. **বামনের গো** (fig.) a person or a thing that yields maximum benefit at the minimum cost. **~ঠাকুর** *n.* a Brahman priest or cook. *fem.* **~ঠাকরুন** a female Brahman cook. **বামনাই** *n.* (dero.) practice of a Brahman or an exhibition of this.

বামপন্থী *n. & a.* (in pol.) a leftist; leftist.

বামা *n.* a beautiful woman; a woman.

বামাক্ষী *n.* a fair-eyed woman.

বামাচার *n.* a religious practice, prescribed in Tantrism, to be performed by a ma in collaboration with a woman. **বামাচারী** *n.* a follower of this practice.

বামাবর্ত, বামাবর্তী *a.* sinistrose; counter-clockwise; sinistral.

বামাল pop. corrup. of **বমাল**।

বামুন pop. var. of **বামন**[২]।

বামেতর *a.* right.

বামোরু *n.* a woman with elegant thighs.

বায় corrup. of **বায়ু** and **বায়ুতে**।

বায়না[১] *n.* an insistent and unreasonable or capricious demand; pretext, an excuse.

ায়না[২] *n.* earnest money. **বায়না করা** *v.* to deposit or advance earnest money.

ায়নাক্কা *n.* a detailed description, details; fastidiousness or capriciousness or unreasonable insistence about details; a pretext, an excuse.

ায়নানামা, বায়নাপত্র *n.* a conditional agreement of bargain drawn up on payment of earnest money.

ায়ব, বায়বীয়, বায়ব্য *a.* aerial, atmospheric; ethereal; etherial; aerobic; airy; pneumatic; gaseous; aerological; relating to the wind. **বায়ব অবরোহ, বায়ব মূল** (bot.) an aerial root. **বায়ব প্রতিসরণ** (astr.) atmospheric refraction. **বায়বীয়াকার** *a.* aeriform.

য়স *n.* the crow. *fem.* **বায়সী**।

য়ু *n.* air; wind; breeze; the atmosphere, sky; (Hindu phil.) any of the five vital airs; (Hindu med.) a vital humour; flatulence; neurosis. **অধিগ্রাহ্য বায়ু** complement air. **অধিত্যাজ্য বায়ু** supplemental air. **অশুদ্ধ বায়ু** impure air. **আদ্যবায়ু** *n.* supplemental air. **আয়নবায়ু** *n.* trade-wind. **দূষিত বায়ু** vitiated air. **নিয়তবায়ু** *n.* constant wind. **প্রত্যায়ন-বায়ু** *n.* anti-trade wind. **প্রবাহী বায়ু** tidal air. **প্রেষগ্রাহ্য বায়ু** complemental air. **বিশুদ্ধ বায়ু** fresh air. **মুক্তবায়ু** *n.* open air. **শিষ্টবায়ু** residual air. **~কোণ** *n.* the north-west. **~কোষ** *n.* an airbladder; an air-cell. **~গতিবিদ্যা** *n.* aerodynamics. **~গর্ভ** *n.* an air-core. **~গহ্বর** *n.* an air-pocket. **~গ্রস্ত** *a.* neurotic; a bit touched; (rare) flatulent. **~চলাচল, ~চলন** *n.* ventilation. **~চাপ** *n.* (phys.) atmospheric pressure. **~চোষক** *n.* (phys.) an aspirator. **~চ্ছেদ** *n.* air-gap. **~জীবী** *a.* (esp. bot.) aerobic. **~তত্ত্ব** *n.* pneumatics. **~তরঙ্গ** *n.* a wind wave; a current of air. **~তাড়িত** *a.* wind-driven. **~দেবতা** *n.* the wind-god. **~ধারকত্ব** *n.* (chem.) vital capacity. **~নিয়ন্ত্রিত** *a.* airconditioned. **~নিষ্কাশনযন্ত্র** *n.* an airpump. **~পথ** *n.* the airway. **~পরাগিত** *a.* (bot.) wind-pollinated. **~পরিবর্তন** *n.* a change of air. **বায়ুপরিবর্তন করা** *v.* to go to a new region to have a change of air. **~প্রবাহ** *n.* a stream of air, an air current; a gust of wind. **~প্রেষ** *n.* (phys.) atmospheric pressure. **~প্রেষক** *n.* an air-compressor. **~প্রেষদৃক** *n.* a baroscope. **~প্রেষলিক** *n.* a barograph. **~বেগ** *n.* velocity or speed of wind. **~বেগমাপক** *n.* (phys.) an anemometer. **~বেগে** *adv.* as speedily or swiftly as the wind. **~ভক্ষণ** *n.* (lit.) act of eating nothing but air; act of going without food, fasting. **~মণ্ডল** *n.* the atmosphere. **~মণ্ডলীয়** *a.* atmospheric. **~মান** *n.* an aerometer; a barometer. **~মানবিদ্যা** *n.* aerometry. **~যান** *n.* an aircraft. **~যুদ্ধ, আকাশযুদ্ধ** *n.* aerial battle. **~রন্ধ্র** *n.* an air-pore; an air-space. **~রোগ** *n.* neurosis; flatulence. **~রোগী** *n.* a neurotic; a patient of flatulency. **~রোধী** *a.* airtight. **~সঞ্চালন** *n.* ventilation. **~সেনা** *n.* Air Force. **বায়ুসেবন করা** *v.* to take the air, to have an airing. **~সেবনার্থে** *a.* & *adv.* for an airing; for purpose of taking fresh air. **~স্তর** *n.* any one of the different layers of air. **~স্থলী** *n.* an air-bladder.

বায়েন *n.* a player on a musical instrument of percussion.

বায়োস্কোপ *n.* cinema, bioscope.

বার[১] coll. form of **বাহির**।

বার[২] *n.* a royal court, a durbar; (of princes etc.) a sitting or presence in a court ('বার দিয়া বসিয়াছে বীরসিংহ রায়'); an appearance before applicants or visitors or in public esp. in state (জমিদার বা গুরু আজ বার দেবেন).

বার[৩] *n.* a day (রবিবার); a fixed or allotted day (হাটবার); a day of the week (আজ কী বার); an occasion, a time (দুবার); a turn (দেখি তোমার বারে কেমন খেলো).

বারই[১] *n.* dial. corrup. of **বারুজীবী**।

বারইয়ারি, বারোয়ারি *a.* performed by the public for the public, public; joint, combined. □ *n.* a public function organized by the public.

বারংবার *adv.* again and again, time and again, repeatedly.

বারক *a.* prohibitive; prohibitory; preventive; resistive.

বারকোশ *n.* a large wooden tray.

বারণ[১] *n.* the elephant.

বারণ[২] *n.* prohibition; prevention; resistance. **বারণ করা** *v.* to prohibit; to prevent; to resist. **বারণীয়** *a.* capable of being prohibited; preventible; resistible. **বারণোপায়** *n.* a preventive measure.

বারতা poet. corrup. of **বার্তা** ।

বারদরিয়া *n.* the open ocean, high seas.

বারনারী same as **বারাঙ্গনা** ।

বারফটকা *a.* given to dissipated frolicking away from one's dwelling-place; given to absenteeism.

বারফট্টাই *n.* bragging; ridiculous ostentatiousness, pomposity. **বারফট্টাই করা** *v.* to brag; to indulge in pompous display.

বারবনিতা same as **বারাঙ্গনা** ।

বারবরদার *n.* a porter; a traveller's luggage-carrying attendant. **বারবরদারি** *n.* porterage; service of a traveller's luggage-carrying attendant.

বারবার same as **বারংবার** ।

বারবিলাসিনী same as **বারাঙ্গনা** ।

বারবেলা *n.* (astrol.) a part of the day regarded as inauspicious for undertaking any important work (religious or other).

বারব্রত *n.* holy rites.

বারভুঁইয়া, বারভুঞা see **ভুঁইয়া** (under **ভুঁই**).

বারমাসী, বারমাস্যা older forms of **বারোমাসী** and **বারোমাস্যা** respectively.

বারমুখো same as **বারফটকা** ।

বারমুখ্যা *n.* a leading prostitute; (loos.) a courtezan.

বারয়িতা *n.* a prohibiter, a prohibitor; a preventer. *fem.* **বারয়িত্রী** ।

বারশিঙ্গা, বারশিঙা *n.* a kind of deer having six branches in either of its two horns.

বারা *v.* (poet.) to prohibit; to prevent; to ward off; to resist.

বারাঙ্গনা *n.* a public woman, a harlot, a prostitute, a whore.

বারাণ্ডা dial. corrup. of **বারান্দা** ।

বারান্তর *n.* another time, a different occasion. **বারান্তরে** *adv.* at another time; on a different occasion.

বারান্দা *n.* a (roofed or open) portico or corridor, a veranda, a verandah; a balcony.

বারি *n.* water. **~দ** *n.* cloud. **~ধারা** *n.* a shower or stream or torrent of rain. **~ধি, ~নিধি** *n.* the sea; the ocean. **~পাত** *n.* rainfall; a shower of rain. **~প্রবাহ** *n.* a stream or current of water. **~বাহ** *n.* cloud. **~মণ্ডল** *n.* the hydrosphere. **~রাশি** *n.* a mass of water (esp. of a sea or a river).

বারিত *a.* prohibited; prevented; warded off; resisted; (chiefly law) barred (তামাদিদোষে বারিত = barred by limitation).

বারীন্দ্র, বারীশ *n.* the ocean.

বারুই coll. corrup. of **বারই**[১], **বারই**[২] ।

বারুজীবী *n.* a Hindu caste occupied in growing and selling betel-leaves; one of this caste.

বারুণী *n.* a variety of wine; wine; the west; a bathing festival held on the eve of the fourteenth lunar day of the dark fortnight of Chaitra (চৈত্র) ; the wife of the sea god (cp. Tethys).

বারুদ *n.* gunpowder, powder. **~খানা** *n.* room for storing gunpowder, a magazine.

বারেক *adv.* (chiefly poet.) once, only once, but for once.

বারেন্দ্র *n.* a native of ancient Gauda (গৌড়) or North Bengal; one of a class of Bengali Brahmans.

বারে বারে *adv.* off and on; frequently, time and again.

বারো *n.* & *a.* twelve. **বারো হাত কাঁকুড়ের তেরো হাত বীচি** an instance of unseemly overmuchness. **~ই** *n.* the twelfth day of a month. **বারো মাস ত্রিশ দিন** *adv.* every day; throughout the year. **বারো মাসে তেরো পার্বণ** overnumerousness of religious festivities.

বারোমাসী, বারোমাস্যা *n.* the versified account of the weal and woe (usu.) told by a woman; the tale of weal and woe

বারোমেসে *a.* grown or occurring throughout the year; perpetual.

বারোয়াঁ, বারোঁয়া *n.* an Indian musical mode.

বারোয়ারি pop. form of **বারইয়ারি** ।

বার্ণিক *n.* a copyist; a writer; a printer.

বার্তা *n.* news, information; a message; a report; a dispatch. **~জীবী** *n.* a journalist.

বার্তাকু, বার্তাকী *n.* the brinjal, eggplant, aubergine.

বার্তাবহ *n.* a messenger; a courier.

বার্ধক *n.* superannuation.

বার্ধক্য *n.* old age, the vale of years; decrepitude. **~গ্রস্ত** *a.* old, decrepit.

বার্ধক্যতত্ত্ব, বার্ধক্যবিদ্যা *n.* the study of the problems of old age; gerontology.

বার্নিশ *n.* varnish. **বার্নিশ করা** *v.* to varnish.

বার্লি *n.* barley.

বার্ষিক *a.* yearly, annual. □ *n.* an annual grant or pension; an annuity; (loos.) an annual publication or issue (esp. of a periodical). **বার্ষিক গতি** annual motion, revolution (as opp. to rotation). **বার্ষিক লম্বন** annual parallax. **বার্ষিক বৃত্তি** annuity. **বার্ষিকী** *n.* a religious rite to be performed annually; an anniversary (মৃত্যু-বার্ষিকী) ; an annual publication or issue (esp. of a periodical).

বাল *n.* a male child, a boy; (*in comp.*) a child. **~ক্রীড়া** *n.* boyish sport; a child's play. **~খিল্য** *n.* (myth.) any one of the sixty thousand ascetics who were not more than a thumb in height; a Lilliputian, a midget, a pygmy. **~চর্যা** *n.* bringing up children. **~চাপল্য** *n.* childish flippancy or frolicsomeness. **~বাচ্চা** *n.* young or infant children, (sl.) kiddies, **~বিধবা** *n.* a child-widow. **~বৈধব্য** *n.* widowhood at a very early age. **~ভাষিত** *n.* the utterance of a child-like talk or prattle; (fig.) an utterance of no importance, babble. **~রোগ** *n.* a children's disease; an infantile disease, (med.) pediatric diseases. **~শশী** *n.* the moon of the second lunar night of a light fortnight. **~সুলভ** *a.* childlike, childish. **~সূর্য** *n.* the newly-risen sun; the rising sun.

বালক *n.* a boy, a male child; a tyro (রাজনীতিতে সে বালক) ; a greenhorn. **~কাল** *n.* childhood days, boyhood. **~তা, ~ত্ব** *n.* boyhood. **~বয়স** same as **বালককাল** । **~ভৃত্য** *n.* a boy-servant; a page. **~সুলভ, বালকোচিত** *a.* boyish; childish.

বালতি *n.* a pail; a pailful (এক বালতি জল).

বাল্ব *n.* an electric bulb.

বালসানো *v.* (of a child) to catch cold or become ill.

বালা[১] *n. fem.* a female child; a girl; a young woman; a daughter.

বালা[২] *n.* a bangle for the wrist.

বালাই *n.* an evil, a harm; a pest. □ *int.* an utterance to revoke a former utterance or to counteract a possible harm. (cp.) God forbid (বালাই, তুমি কেন মরবে ?). **বালাই নিয়ে মরা** to die taking away with oneself all harm that may occur to another. **বালাই ষাট** same as **বালাই** (*int.*).

বালাখানা *n.* a building with two or more stories; a room in an upper story.

বালাপোশ, (rej.) **বালাপোষ** *n.* a kind of linen wrapper stuffed with cotton.

বালাম *n.* a superior variety of rice; a boat for carrying this rice.

বালামচি *n.* horse-hair.

বালার্ক *n.* the newly-risen sun.

বালি *n.* sand; gravel; grit. **বালি ধরানো** *v.* (in building construction) to plaster. **~পূর্ণ, ~ময়** *a.* sandy; full of sand. **বালির বাঁধ** (fig.) an ineffectual action or measure (বালির বাঁধ দিয়ে দুঃখ ঠেকানো) ; (fig.) a transitory object, a deceptive foundation ('বড়র পীরিতি বালির বাঁধ'). **বালির প্রাসাদ** (fig.) a house of cards; a very transitory or deceptive foundation.

বালিকা *n. fem.* a female child, a girl; a young woman. **~বধূ** *n.* a child-wife. **~বয়স** *n.* girlhood. **~সুলভ** *a.* girlish; childish.

বালিঘড়ি *n.* a sand-glass.

বালিয়াড়ি *n.* a dune, a sand-hill.

বালিশ *n.* a pillow or a bolster.

বালু, বালুকা *n.* sand; gravel; grit. **বালুকাতট** *n.* a sand-band. **বালুকাময়** *a.* sandy, full of sand. **বালুচর** *n.* a sand-bed. **বালুঝড়** *n.* a sand-storm; a simoom, a simoon. **বালুশিলা** *n.* sandstone.

বালেন্দু *n.* the moon of second lunar night of the light fortnight; (geog.) the crescent. **~শৃঙ্গ** *n.* (geog.) horns of the crescent.

বাল্য *n.* age up to one's sixteenth birth day; boyhood or girlhood, childhood, infancy. **~কাল** *n.* childhood, infancy. **~প্রণয়, ~প্রেম** *n.* calf-love; childhood friendship. **~বন্ধু** *n.* a friend of one's childhood days. **~বিধবা** same as **বালবিধবা** । see **বাল** । **~বিবাহ** *n.* early marriage, child-marriage. **~শিক্ষা** *n.* child education; primary education. **~সখা** same as **বাল্যবন্ধু** । **~সঙ্গী, ~সহচর** *n.* a companion of one's childhood days. **বাল্যাবস্থা** *n.* childhood.

বাশুলি *n.* a female deity of Bengal identified with Chandi (চণ্ডী).

বাষট্টি *n.* & *a.* sixty-two.

বাষ্প *n.* vapour; steam; smoke; tears (বাষ্পপূর্ণ নয়ন) ; (fig.) faintest knowledge or appearance, ghost (সম্ভাবনার বাষ্পও নেই = there is not the ghost of a chance). **বাষ্প হওয়া** *v.* to be vaporized; to evaporate. **~চালিত** *a.* steam-driven. **~টান** *n.* (phys.) vapour-tension. **~দাহ** *n.* scald. **~পোত** *n.* a steam-vessel, a steamship, a steamer. **~মান** *n.* a hygrometer; a gasometer. **~মোচন** *n.* weeping; (bot.) transpiration. **~যান, ~শকট** *n.* a stream-driven vehicle; a railway train. **~স্নান** *n.* a vapour bath. **বাষ্পাকার** *a.* in the form of vapour, vaporous. **বাষ্পাকুল** *a.* filled with or steaming with tears. **বাষ্পাকুল নয়ন** tearful eyes, steaming eyes; (sl.) piping eyes. **বাষ্পীকরণ, বাষ্পীভবন** *n.* vaporization; evaporation. **বাষ্পীকৃত, বাষ্পীভূত** *a.* vaporized; evaporated. **বাষ্পীয়** *a.* relating to steam or vapour; vapoury; vaporous; steam-driven. **বাষ্পীয়যান, বাষ্পীয়শকট** same as **বাষ্পযান** ।

বাস১ *n.* an omnibus, a bus.

বাস২ *n.* smell (good or bad).

বাস৩ *n.* a dwelling-place, an abode; home; a habitation (মানুষের বাস দেখা যায় না) ; a habitat; staying, stay, residence (বিদেশবাস) ; cloth (পট্টবাস) ; clothing, garment, habiliments. **বাস করা** *v.* to live; to dwell; to abide, to reside; to stay.

বাস্ var. of **ব্যস** ।

বাসক১ same as **বাসা২** ।

বাসক২ *n.* a bedchamber, a bedroom. **~শয়ন** *n.* a bed in the bedchamber. **~সজ্জা, বাসসজ্জা** *n.* a woman who tidies up her bedchamber and dresses herself to receive her expected lover.

বাসকক্ষ *n.* a bedroom, a bedchamber; (cp.) a living-room.

বাসগৃহ *n.* a dwelling-house.

বাসন১ *n.* perfuming; incensing.

বাসন২ *n.* a vessel or container; a utensil. **~কোসন** *n. pl.* utensils collectively.

বাসনা১ *n.* a dried bark or spathe of the banana and other plants.

বাসনা২ *n.* desire, longing; wish; intention. **বাসনা করা বা হওয়া** *v.* to desire, to long (for); to wish; to intend. **~কুল** *a.* seized or overwhelmed with passion or desire.

বাসন্ত, বাসন্তিক *a.* of spring or springtime, vernal. **বাসন্তী** *a. fem.* vernal; light orange-coloured (বাসন্তীবাস পরা). □ *n.* Goddess Durga (দুর্গা). **বাসন্তীপূজা** *n.* a spring-festival when Goddess Durga is worshipped.

বাসব *n.* Indra (ইন্দ্র) the king of gods.

বাসভবন *n.* a dwelling-house; a residence.

বাসভূমি *n.* place or country of residence; home country; motherland.

বাসযোগ্য *a.* habitable.

বাসর১ *n.* a day (জন্মবাসর) ; a day of the week or a gathering on a particular day (রবিবাসর).

বাসর২, বাসরঘর *n.* a bride-chamber. **বাসরশয্যা** *n.* bridal bed.

বাসরীয় *a.* pertaining to a (particular) day (রবিবাসরীয়).

বাসসজ্জা see **বাসক২** ।

বাসস্থান *n.* a dwelling-place, an abode; a residence; a habitat.

বাসা১ *v.* to deem or feel (বেসেছি ভালো).

বাসা২ *n.* a medicinal plant, *Justicia gandrussa.* **বাসারিষ্ট** *n.* extract of *Justicia gandrussa.*

বাসা৩ *n.* a dwelling-house; a dwelling-place; a lodging-house; a rented or temporary residence; a habitat or a nest; (dero.) a haunt, a den (চোরের বাসা, দুর্নীতির বাসা). ~ড়িয়া, ~ড়ে *n.* a lodger. ~বাড়ি *n.* a rented lodging-house.

বাসি *a.* washed; placed for washing; not washed or cleansed since morning (বাসি মুখ, বাসি ঘর) ; stale, not fresh (বাসি দুধ, বাসি খবর) ; used or made or collected etc. overnight (বাসি কাপড় বা ভাত বা মাল বা জল). **বাসি করা** *v.* to wash (কাপড় বাসি করা). **বাসি বিয়ে** solemnities to be performed on the morning following the wedding night. **বাসি মড়া** the body of a person dead overnight.

বাসিত *a.* perfumed; scented.

-বাসিনী *fem.* of **-বাসী**[2] ।

বাসিন্দা *n.* an inhabitant, a native; a resident, an inmate; a dweller.

বাসী[1] alt. spell. of **বাসি** ।

-বাসী[2] *sfx.* denoting: inhabiting, dwelling, residing (দেশবাসী).

বাসুকি *n.* (myth.) the snake-king.

বাসুদেব *n.* Krishna (কৃষ্ণ) the son of Vasudeva (বসুদেব).

বাসুলী alt. spell. of **বাশুলি** ।

বাস var. of **ব্যস** ।

বাস্তব *a.* true, genuine; real; factual; actual; objective; material; materialistic. □ *n.* truth; reality; (phys.) an objective. **বাস্তব তথ্য** facts. **~তা** *n.* trueness, genuineness; reality; factuality; actuality; objectivity; materiality. **~বাদ** *n.* realism; objectivism; materialism. **~বাদী** *a.* realistic; objectivistic; materialistic. □ *n.* a realist; an objectivist; a materialist.

বাস্তবিক *a.* true, real, actual; sure. □ *adv.* indeed, really. **~পক্ষে** *adv.* as a matter of fact.

বাস্তব্য *a.* habitable. **~বিদ্যা** *n.* (bio.) ecology.

বাস্তু *n.* a dwelling-place; a dwelling; a dwelling-house; a piece of land on which a dwelling-house stands, a homestead; (also **বাস্তুভিটা**) ; a permanent and usually ancestral homestead (also **বাস্তুগৃহ**) ; buildings. **~কর্ম** *n.* building-construction; public works. **~কার** *n.* a civil engineer. **~কৃত্যক** *n.* the engineering service. **~ঘুঘু** *n.* (fig.) a vile person who resides irremovably in a family and brings it to ruin. **~দেবতা, ~পুরুষ** *n.* the guardian or tutelar deity of a homestead or family. **~ভিটা** *n.* homestead. **~সংস্থান** *n.* provision for dwelling. **~সাপ** *n.* a snake living in a house for a long time and without harming anybody. **~হারা** *a.* displaced from a homestead. □ *n.* a displaced person.

-বাহ *sfx.* denoting: carrying, bearing, conveying (ভারবাহ).

বাহক *a.* carrying, bearing, conveying. □ *n.* a carrier, a bearer (বাহক মারফত) ; a porter; (rare) a conveyance.

বাহন *n.* a riding animal, a mount; a vehicle; a medium (শিক্ষার বাহন) ; (iron.) a faithful follower; (dial.) rowing. □ *sfx.* denoting: mounting on (মহিষবাহন).

বাহবা, বাহা[1] variants of **বাঃ** ।

বাহা[2] *v.* the High Bengali form of **বাওয়া**[2] ।

বাহাত্তর *n.* & *a.* seventy-two. **বাহাত্তুরে** *a.* (lit. & rare) aged seventy-two years; (pop. & facet.) senile. **বাহাত্তুরে ধরা, বাহাত্তুরে পাওয়া** *v.* to be stricken with senility.

বাহাদুর *a.* performing a great feat; working wonders; skilful; valorous, brave; creditable, praiseworthy. □ *n.* a title of honour (রায়বাহাদুর). **বাহাদুরি** *n.* performance of a great feat; an achievement; skilfulness; a display of skill; valour, bravery; praiseworthiness; credit; (dero.) bravado. **বাহাদুরি করা** *v.* to brag; to make a display of skill or bravery. **বাহাদুরি দেওয়া** *v.* to give credit. **বাহাদুরি দেখানো** *v.* to make a show of skill or courage. **বাহাদুরি কাঠ** *n.* the trunk of the sal (শাল) and similar large trees; the timber of the aforesaid trunk.

বাহানা var. of **বায়না**[1] ।

বাহান্ন *n.* & *a.* fifty-two. **যাহা বাহান্ন তাহা তিপ্পান্ন** (fig.) when scores have been lost, what does it matter to lose a little more; the difference is too small to merit serious attention.

বাহার *n.* a beautiful show or exhibition; an ostentatious display; glamour; beauty; an Indian musical mode. **বাহারে, বাহারি** *a.*

having a beautiful show; showy, ostentatious; glamorous; beautiful.

বাহিকা *fem.* of **বাহক** ।

বাহিত *a.* rowed, steered; propelled; paddled; driven; carried, borne; conveyed; transported; caused to flow. *fem.* **বাহিতা** ।

-বাহিনী[1] *fem.* of **বাহী** ।

বাহিনী[2] *n.* (ori.) a division of army comprising 81 elephant-riders, 81 charioteers, 243 horsemen and 405 footsoldiers; an army, a battalion; a river, a stream.

বাহির (High Beng.) *n.* outside, exterior. □ *a.* external, exterior; outer; faraway; gone or lying beyond (শাসনের বাহির). **বাহির করা** *v.* to bring out; to draw out; to extract (রস বাহির করা) ; to drain out (ময়লা জল বাহির করা) ; to let out, to cause to flow out (রক্ত বাহির করা) ; to unsheathe (as a sword); to find out (ভুল বাহির করা) ; to expose; to expel; to cause to elope with oneself (বউ বাহির করা) ; to publish (a book or examination-result); to expose, to put an end to ; to invent or devise (যন্ত্র বা উপায় বা ফ্যাশন বাহির করা). **বাহির হওয়া** *v.* to go or come out, to emerge; to germinate, to sprout (অঙ্কুর বাহির হওয়া) ; to be drained out; to flow out; to be found out or exposed or detected (খুঁত বাহির হওয়া) ; to be published; to be revealed, to appear in public (আসল মূর্তি বাহির হওয়া) ; to be invented or devised; to become famous; (of women) to leave one's home and take to harlotry. **~সমুদ্র** *n.* high seas. **বাহিরানো** poet. form of **বাহির হওয়া** । **বাহিরে** *adv.* outside; abroad, away from home. □ *prep.* more than, other than, outside (ঘরের বাহিরে = out of doors); beyond (নাগালের বাহিরে).

-বাহী var. of **বাহ** ।

বাহু *n.* the arm; (pop.) the hand; (geom.) a side, an arm.

বাহুত্র, বাহুত্রাণ *n.* an armour for the arm, an arm-plate.

বাহুবন্ধন *n.* a hug; an embrace.

বাহুবল *n.* physical strength. **~দৃপ্ত** *a.* proud of physical stregnth or vigour.

বাহুমূল *n.* the armpit.

বাহুযুদ্ধ *n.* wrestling; a scuffle.

বাহুল্য *n.* numerousness or muchness; excess; superfluity. **বলাই বাহুল্য (যে)** (it) is needless to say (that); it goes without saying (that). **~বর্জিত** *a.* shorn of excesses or superfluities. **~বোধে** considering it superfluous or unnecessary.

বাহ্বাস্ফোট *n.* slapping of one's arms as a mark of parading one's strength or abilities (as done by a wrestler).

বাহ্য[1] var. of **বাহ্যে** ।

বাহ্য[2] *a.* portable, bearable.

বাহ্য[3] *a.* external; exterior; outer; meterial; visible but unreal or superficial (এহ বাহ্য). **~জগৎ** *n.* the material world. **~জ্ঞান** *n.* knowledge or consciousness about external or surrounding objects; sense-perception; consciousness. **~জ্ঞানরহিত, ~জ্ঞানশূন্য** *a.* (so dazed as to be) deprived of consciousness about external or surrounding objects; deprived of sense-perception or consciousness; stupefied; rapt; frantic; beside oneself. **~ত** *adv.* externally; outwardly; superficially. **~দৃশ্য** *n.* external or outward view or form. **~বস্তু** *n.* a visible or material object.

বাহ্যিক *a.* external; outward; material; visible but unreal or superficial.

বাহ্যে *n.* faeces, excrement, stool; evacuation of the bowels. **বাহ্যে করা** *v.* to evacuate one's bowels, to ease or relieve nature. **বাহ্যে করানো** *v.* to purge another's bowels. **বাহ্যে পাওয়া** *v.* to have a disposition to evacuate. **বাহ্যে যাওয়া** *v.* to go for the purpose of evacuation.

বাহ্যেন্দ্রিয় *n.* the eye, the ear, the nose, the tongue, the skin; any one of these five external sense-organs.

বি- *pfx.* denoting: opposition or antipathy, anti- (বিপক্ষ) ; lack, non-, un- (বিকল) ; badness or wrongness, mis-, in- (বিপথ) ; speciality or uncommonness (বিখ্যাত) etc.

বিউনি dial. var. of **বিনুনি** ।

বিউলি *n.* a variety of husked pigeon-pea.

বি এ B.A.

বি এল B.L.

বি এসসি B. Sc.

বিংশ *a.* twenty; twentieth. **~তি** *n.* & *a.* twenty. **বিংশতিতম** *a.* twentieth. *fem.* **বিংশতিতমী**।

বিঁড়া, বিঁড়ে dial. corruptions of **বিড়া**।

বিঁধ *n.* a bore, a perforation, a hole. **বিঁধা, বেঁধা** *v.* to be pierced or pricked; to pierce or prick; to perforate, to bore (কান বেঁধা). **বিঁধানো** *v.* to pierce; to prick; to perforate, to bore; to cause to be pierced or pricked or bored.

বিকচ[১] *a.* hairless; bald.

বিকচ[২] *a.* blooming; gleaming ('করুণাকিরণে বিকচ নয়ান').

বিকট *a.* huge and hideous, monstrous. **~দর্শন** *a.* monstrous-looking, of a frightful appearance. **~মূর্তি, বিকটাকার** *a.* monstrously shaped.

বিকনো var. of **বিকানো**।

বি কম B. Com.

বিকম্পিত *a.* trembling, rudely shaken.

বিকর্তন *n.* the sun.

বিকর্ষণ *n.* a pull in the opposite direction; (sc.) repulsion.

বিকর্ষী *a.* pulling in the opposite direction; (sc.) repulsive.

বিকল *a.* lacking in or crippled of a part or limb (বিকলাঙ্গ) ; worn-out or exhausted or disabled (বিকল শরীর) ; impaired or ruined (বিকল স্বাস্থ্য) ; out of order; out of service (বিকল যন্ত্র) ; confused or overwhelmed with worries etc.. harried (বিকল প্রাণ). **বিকল করা** *v.* (rare) to cripple; to exhaust or fatigue; to disable; to impair or ruin; to put out of order; to confuse or overwhelm, to harry, to harrow. **~তা, ~ত্ব** *n.* crippledom; exhaustion; disability; impairment, ruin; unserviceable or disordered or breakdown state; overwhelmed or confused or harried state.

বিকলা *n.* a measure of time (= ১/৬০ কলা), a second.

বিকলাঙ্গ *a.* crippled, physically handicapped; having defective limbs; disabled; (loos.) deformed. **বিকলাঙ্গ লোক** a cripple.

বিকলেন্দ্রিয় *a.* having a crippled sense organ; deformed; crippled.

বিকল্প *n.* an alternative concept; an alternative; a substitute; doubt; (gr.) a variant or a doublet; (phil.) fancy. **বিকল্প প্রমাণ** alternative proof. **বিকল্পে** *adv.* alternatively; as a substitute.

বিকশিত *a.* manifested (বিকশিত মহিমা) ; displayed, exhibited (বিকশিত দন্ত) ; arisen, cropped up (বিকশিত ভাব) ; developed (বিকশিত বুদ্ধি) ; opened or widened (বিকশিত নেত্র) ; blown, blooming (বিকশিত পুষ্প). **বিকশিত করা** *v.* to manifest; to display, to exhibit, to show; to cause to rise or crop up; to develop; to open or widen; to cause to bloom. **বিকশিত হওয়া** *v.* to be revealed or exhibited; to arise, to crop up; to develop; to open or widen; to bloom.

বিকানো *v.* to be sold, to sell (সস্তায় বিকানো) ; (fig.) to give away (দেশের কাজে জীবন বিকানো) ; to be accepted, received warmly or with honour (নামে বিকানো). □ *a.* sold; (fig.) given away.

বিকার *n.* deviation from the natural or normal state; perversion, perversity (রুচি বিকার) ; corruption (চরিত্রবিকার) ; decomposition (শবদেহের বিকার) ; aberration, derangement (মনের বিকার) ; (loos.) aversion or apathy (নেতৃত্বের প্রতি বিকার) ; morbidity (যৌনবিকার) ; delirium (জ্বরবিকার) ; a converted or altered form (স্বর্ণের বিকার হল অলংকার). **জ্বরবিকার** see **জ্বর**। **বিকারক** *n.* (sc.) a reagent. **বিকারক রশ্মি** *n.* (phys.) actinic rays. **~গ্রস্ত** *a.* perverted; corrupted; (loos.) averse or apathetic; morbid; delirious. **~তত্ত্ব** *n.* pathology. **~তাত্ত্বিক** *a.* pathological. □ *n.* a pathologist. **~প্রাপ্ত** *a.* changed; converted; decomposed.

বিকার্য *a.* changeable; prone to change (usu. for the worse).

বিকাল, বিকালবেলা *n.* the afternoon.

বিকাশ, বিকাশন *n.* a manifestation; display, exhibition; act of cropping up or arising; development; opening or widening; blooming. **বিকাশ পাওয়া** same as **বিকশিত হওয়া** (see **বিকশিত**). **বিকাশোন্মুখ** *a.* on the point of being manifested or exhibited; on the point of cropping up or arising; about to arise or develop; on the point of development; on the point of opening or widening or blooming.

বিকি *n.* sale. **~কিনি** *n.* buying and selling; traffic, trafficking.

বিকিরণ *n.* diffusion, dispersal, dispersion (as of light or rays); radiation (as of the sun). **বিকিরণ করা** *v.* to diffuse, to disperse.

বিকীর্ণ *a.* diffused, dispersed. **বিকীর্ণ করা** same as **বিকিরণ করা**। **বিকীর্ণ তাপ** radiated or diffused heat.

বিকীর্যমাণ *a.* in a state of diffusion or radiation.

বিকুলি a correl. of **আকুলি**।

বিকৃত *a.* perverted; corrupted, vitiated; decomposed (বিকৃত শব) ; morbid (বিকৃত মন) ; deranged; deformed (বিকৃত অঙ্গ) ; disfigured (বিকৃত চেহারা) ; monstrous or revolting (বিকৃত মূর্তি). **বিকৃত করা** *v.* to pervert; to corrupt, to vitiate; to deprave; to decompose; to affect with morbidity; to derange; to disfigure; to make unnatural (as voice). **~কণ্ঠ** *n.* unnatural or affected voice; hoarse voice; gruff voice. □ *a.* speaking in an unnatural or affected voice (esp. to conceal one's natural voice); speaking in a hoarse or in a gruff voice. **~চরিত্র** *a.* corrupted or vitiated in character, depraved. **~বুদ্ধি** *a.* perverted in thoughts, evil-minded, wrong-headed. **~মস্তিষ্ক** *a.* mentally deranged, insane; crazy. **~রুচি** *a.* perverted in taste. □ *n.* a perverted taste. **~স্বভাব** *a.* perverted in nature, peevish. **~স্বর** same as **বিকৃতকণ্ঠ**। **বিকৃতি** *n.* perversion; corruption, vitiation; decomposition, morbidity; derangement; deformity; disfigurement, disfiguration.

বিকেন্দ্রণ *n.* decentralization.

বিকেন্দ্রিত *a.* decentralized. **বিকেন্দ্রিত করা** *v.* to decentralize. **বিকেন্দ্রীকরণ** same as **বিকেন্দ্রণ**। **বিকেন্দ্রীকৃত** same as **বিকেন্দ্রিত**।

বিক্রম *n.* strength, power, might; valour; prowess. **~শালী, বিক্রমী** *a.* strong, powerful, mighty; valorous.

বিক্রয় *n.* selling, sale. **বিক্রয় করা** *v.* to sell. **বিক্রয়ার্থ** *adv.* on sale, for sale. **~কর্তা** *n.* a seller. *fem.* **~কর্ত্রী**। **~মূল্য** *n.* selling price, sale price. **~যোগ্য** *a.* salable, saleable; marketable. **বিক্রয়িক, বিক্রয়ী** same as **বিক্রেতা**। **~লব্ধ** *a.* obtained from sale, sale proceeds. **~সাধ্য** *a.* saleable; marketable.

বিক্রান্ত same as **বিক্রমশালী** (see **বিক্রম**).

বিক্রি coll. form of **বিক্রয়**।

বিক্রিয়া *n.* morbid reaction (চিত্তবিক্রিয়া) ; (sc.) reaction.

বিক্রীড়িত *n.* various sports and frolics, gambol.

বিক্রীত *a.* sold.

বিক্রেতা *n.* a seller; a vender, a vendor, a salesman. *fem.* **বিক্রেত্রী**।

বিক্রেয় *a.* salable, saleable; marketable; meant for selling. **বিক্রেয় দ্রব্য** goods on sale, goods for sale.

বিক্ষত *a.* (usu. correl. of **ক্ষত**) severely wounded or ulcerated.

বিক্ষিপ্ত *a.* scattered, dispersed, strewn; distracted (বিক্ষিপ্ত চিত্ত বা মন). **~চিত্ত** *a.* mentally disturbed.

বিক্ষুব্ধ *a.* offended, mortified, aggrieved; agitated.

বিক্ষেপ *n.* act of throwing about or scattering; dispersion; flinging or casting or shooting (শরবিক্ষেপ) ; distraction (মানসিক বিক্ষেপ). **বিক্ষেপণ** *n.* (sc.) scattering.

বিক্ষোভ *n.* offended state, mortification, grief; agitation; (pol.) movement provoked by discontent, unrest (গণবিক্ষোভ = popular unrest). **~কারী** *a.* & *n.* an agitator, one who agitates; a demonstrator, one who demonstrates. **~প্রদর্শন** *n.* demonstration, agitation. **বিক্ষোভ প্রদর্শন করা** *v.* (pol.) to demonstrate; to agitate; to organize demonstration.

বিখণ্ডিত *a.* cut or split, divided; refuted.

বিখাউজ *n.* eczema.

বিখ্যাত *a.* famous, renowned, celebrated. **বিখ্যাতি** *n.* fame, renown, celebrity.

বিগড়ানো *v.* to corrupt or spoil or to be corrupted or spoilt, to send or go to the bad (ছেলে বিগড়ানো) ; to deprave or be depraved (চরিত্র বিগড়ানো) ; to confuse or be confused (বুদ্ধি বিগড়ানো) ; to put or go out of order (কল বিগড়ানো) ; to make or become disloyal or hostile or unfriendly or refractory (প্রজা বা সাক্ষী

বা বন্ধু বা ঘোড়া বিগড়ানো) ; to upset or be upset (মন বিগড়ানো). **মত বিগড়ানো** *v.* to change one's mind.

বিগত *a.* departed; passed by, gone by; past; dead. **বিগত হওয়া** *v.* to depart; to pass by, to pass away. **~প্রাণ** *a.* dead. **~যৌবন** *a.* past one's prime or youth. *fem.* **~যৌবনা** past one's prime. **~শ্রী** *a.* passed or fallen from one's glory or splendour; one who has lost one's beauty. **~স্পৃহা** *a.* one who has lost inclination or interest or appetite, rendered apathetic; one who has controlled or given up one's desires or cravings or longings.

বিগর্হিত *a.* abominable, detestable; forbidden (শাস্ত্রবিগর্হিত) ; disgraceful.

বিগলন *n.* melting; (chem.) smelting.

বিগলিত *a.* thoroughly melted; smelted; exuded; (of dress, bun of hair etc.) dishevelled; thoroughly decomposed or putrefied (বিগলিত শব) ; (fig.) softened or moved (with compassion, grief etc.). *fem.* **বিগলিতা** । **বিগলিত করা** *v.* to melt thoroughly; to smelt; to cause to exude; to decompose or putrefy thoroughly; (fig.) to soften or move (with compassion, grief etc.).

বিগুণ *a.* divested of good qualities; corrupted; hostile.

বিগ্রহ *n.* an image of a deity, an idol; body; a war, a battle; a quarrel, a strife; (gr.) the words by which a compound word is expounded (usu. **বিগ্রহবাক্য**).

বিঘটন *n.* separation into different component parts, analysis; dissolution; destruction; (loos.) a mishap.

বিঘটিত *a.* separated into different component parts, analysed; dissolved; destroyed.

বিঘত *n.* the space from the end of the thumb to the end of the little finger when fingers are extended, a span. **~প্রমাণ** *a.* equal to a span, about nine inches in length.

বিঘা *n.* a measure of flat area (= 6400 sq. cubits = $^1/_3$ or 0.33 acre approx). **বিঘাকালি** *n.* (arith.) square-measure in terms of bighas (বিঘা).

বিঘূর্ণন *n.* (High Beng.) thorough revolution; wild or dreadful rolling (অক্ষিবিঘূর্ণন) ; reeling (মস্তকবিঘূর্ণন).

বিঘূর্ণিত *a.* thoroughly revolved; wildly or dreadfully rolling (বিঘূর্ণিত নেত্র) ; reeling (বিঘূর্ণিত মস্তক). **বিঘূর্ণিত করা** *v.* to revolve thoroughly; to roll dreadfully; to reel. **মস্তক বিঘূর্ণিত করা** *v.* to make one giddy; to bewilder; (fig.) to infatuate with success, to turn one's head.

বিঘোর corrup. of **বেঘোর** ।

বিঘোষিত *a.* extensively announced or proclaimed. **বিঘোষিত করা** *v.* to announce or proclaim extensively.

বিঘ্ন *n.* an obstacle or impediment; a hindrance; a hitch; harm, woe. **বিঘ্ন উৎপাদন** বা **সৃষ্টি করা** *v.* to create a hitch or impediment. **~কর** *a.* obstructive, hindering, impeding; creating a hitch. **~কারী** *a.* & *n.* one who impedes or creates a hitch or trouble. **~নাশক, ~নাশন, ~বিনাশন, ~হর, ~হারী** *a.* removing obstacles or impediments or harms or woes. **~পূর্ণ, ~ময়** *a.* full of obstacles or impediments; with so many obstacles or hitches. **বিঘ্নিত** *a.* hindered, impeded, obstructed.

বিচক্ষণ *a.* judicious, discreet; wise; experienced; farsighted; expert, adroit. **~তা** *n.* judiciousness, discreetness; discretion; prudence; wisdom; experience; experiencedness; farsightedness; expertness, adroitness.

বিচঞ্চল *a.* greatly agitated.

বিচরণ *n.* roaming, wandering, loitering; a ramble. **বিচরণ করা** *v.* to ramble, to wander, to loiter. **~কারী** *a.* wandering, roaming; one who wanders or roams or rambles. **~শীল** *a.* same as **বিচরণকারী** ।

বিচরা (poet.) same as **বিচরণ করা** ।

বিচর্চিকা *n.* herpes, scabies, itch, eczema etc.; any skin disease.

বিচলন *n.* agitation, perturbation; swerving, straying.

বিচলিত, বিচল *a.* agitated, perturbed; swerving, deviation, straying, strayed (ধর্মপথ থেকে বিচলিত) ; wavering. **বিচলিত করা** *v.* to agitate, to perturb; to cause to swerve or stray or waver. **বিচলিত হওয়া**

v. to be agitated or moved; to deviate or swerve. *fem.* **বিচলিতা, বিচলা**।

বিচার *n.* consideration, deliberation; argument; discussion; decision; inference; a (judicial) trial; judgment, finding. **কাজির বিচার** (derog.) mockery or travesty of justice. **বিচার করা** *v.* to consider, to deliberate; to argue; to discuss; to decide; to infer; to try (judicially); to judge. **~ক, ~কর্তা** *n.* a judge; a justice. *fem.* **~কর্ত্রী**। **বিচারকমণ্ডলী** *n.* the judges; The Bench. **বিচার করণিক** *n.* a judicial clerk. **~কার্য** *n.* trial; judgment. **~ক্ষম** *a.* able or authorized to judge. **~ক্ষমতা** *n.* ability to judge; competence or authority to judge. **~ণীয়** same as **বিচার্য**। **~দেয়ক** *n.* courtfee. **~পতি** *n.* a judge; a justice. **~পদ্ধতি, ~ব্যবস্থা** *n.* the judicial system; the legal procedure. **~বিবেচনা** *n.* deliberation, consideration; proper or due consideration. **~বিভাগ** *n.* the judiciary; the judges of a state collectively. **~ফল** *n.* finding, judgment, verdict. **~বিভ্রাট** *n.* miscarriage of justice, a travesty of justice. **~বিহীন, ~শূন্য** *a.* lacking in judgment, unjust; inconsiderate; indiscriminate. **বিচারা** poet. form of **বিচার করা**। **বিচারাধীন** *a.* under investigation; on trial; sub judice, under judicial consideration. **বিচারালয়** *n.* a court of justice, a law-court, a court. **বিচারাসন** *n.* a judgment-seat, the bench. **বিচারিত** *a.* considered, deliberated; argued; discussed; decided, adjudged; inferred; (judicially) tried; judged, adjudicated. **বিচারী** *a.* one who considers or judges (সুবিচারী).

বিচার্য *a.* that which is to be or can be judged or tried or considered; under consideration or trial.

বিচালি *n.* paddy-straw, paddy-hay.

বিচি *n.* a stone or seed of a fruit. **বিচিগজগজে** *a.* full of seeds.

বিচিকিচ্ছি *a.* extremely ugly; odd-looking; very unpleasant (বিচিকিচ্ছি ব্যাপার); very troublesome (বিচিকিচ্ছি কাজ বা অঙ্ক). **বিচিকিচ্ছি অবস্থায় ফেলা** *v.* to put (one) in a false position or embarrassing situation.

বিচিত্র *a.* multi-coloured, many-coloured; variegated, motley; variedly painted (বিচিত্র চিত্র); full of variety or diversity or vicissitudes (বিচিত্র জগৎ বা জীবন); multifarious (বিচিত্র ক্রিয়াকলাপ); amazing, wonderful (বিচিত্র লীলা, বিচিত্র প্রতিভা); queer, strange (বিচিত্র প্রাণী); beautiful (বিচিত্র শোভা). *fem.* **বিচিত্রা**। **~তা** *n.* variety; strangeness, queerness. **এটা বিচিত্র নয় (যে)** it is no wonder (that). **~বর্ণ** *a.* multi-coloured, variegated. **বিচিত্রানুষ্ঠান** *n.* a musical entertainment; variety entertainment; a soiree. **বিচিত্রিত** *a.* variegated; variously painted. *fem.* **বিচিত্রিতা**।

বিচূর্ণ *a.* thoroughly pounded; pulverized, triturated; completely broken or fractured, broken or fractured at several places (বিচূর্ণ অস্থি). □ *n.* a fine powder. **বিচূর্ণ করা** *v.* to pound thoroughly; to pulverize, to triturate; to break completely or at several places. **~ন** *n.* thorough pounding; pulverization, trituration; act of breaking completely or at several places. **বিচূর্ণিত** *a.* same as **বিচূর্ণ** (*a.*) **বিচূর্ণীভবন** *n.* (geog.) weathering.

বিচেতন *a.* unconscious, senseless.

বিচেষ্ট, বিচেষ্টিত *a.* making no effort, unendeavouring; desisting from. **বিচেষ্ট বা বিচেষ্টিত হওয়া** *v.* to give up efforts; to desist from.

বিচ্ছিন্ন *a.* separated; torn or broken away; detached; isolated; estranged; stray or sporadic. *fem.* **বিচ্ছিন্না**। **বিচ্ছিন্ন করা** *v.* to separate; to tear or break away; to detach; to isolate; to estrange; to alienate. **বিচ্ছিন্নতা** *n.* separation; detachment; isolation; secession; estrangement; alienation; lack of compactness, strayness. **বিচ্ছিন্নতাবাদ** *n.* separatism; disintegration. **বিচ্ছিন্নতাবাদী** *n.* & *a.* separatist; a separatist.

বিচ্ছিরি coll. corrup. of **বিশ্রী**।

বিচ্ছু *n.* the scorpion; (fig.) a very clever but naughty and mischievous person; (ছেলেটা একটা বিচ্ছু). □ *a.* (fig.) very clever but mischievous (বিচ্ছু ছেলে).

বিচ্ছুরণ *n.* (ori. & obs.) smearing or painting; (pop.) dispersion (as of rays); radiation (as of light); emanation.

বিচ্ছুরিত *a.* (ori. & obs.) smeared or painted; (pop.) dispersed (as rays); radiated (as light), scattered. **বিচ্ছুরিত করা** *v.* to disperse; to radiate; to cause to emanate or scatter.

বিচ্ছেদ *n.* separation; estrangement; discord, disintegration, dissension; difference; an interval; intermission (জ্বরবিচ্ছেদ). **বিচ্ছেদ-নিয়ম** *n.* (alg.) the law of distribution. **~বেদনা** *n.* the pang of separation, the woes of estrangement. **~মূলক** *a.* separatist; alienating; dissenting; disintegrating.

বিচ্যুত *a.* detached; fallen off, shed; separated; estranged; deviating or strayed from. *fem.* **বিচ্যুতা** । **বিচ্যুত হওয়া** *v.* to be detached or shed or separated or estranged; to turn away, to deviate or stray; to fail to observe or execute. **বিচ্যুতি** *n.* detachment; shedding; separation; estrangement; deviation, straying, dereliction.

বিছা *n.* the scorpion; a kind of broad necklace (usu. বিছাহার).

বিছানা *n.* a bed. **বিছানা করা, বিছানা পাতা** *v.* to make a bed. **বিছানা নেওয়া** *v.* to keep one's bed; take to one's bed, take to bed; to be ill.

বিছানো *v.* to spread (মাদুর বিছানো) ; to scatter or strew or lay (কাঁকর বিছানো).

বিছুটি *n.* a variety of nettle.

বিজকুড়ি *n.* pimple-like eruption or rash.

বিজড়িত *a.* intertwined; entangled; involved in; begone (দুঃখবিজড়িত = woebegone); beset with (মেঘবিজড়িত) ; embarrassed or encumbered or involved (দেনায় বিজড়িত). **বিজড়িত করা** *n.* to intertwine; to entangle; to involve (in); to beset (with); to embarrass or encumber (with.).

বিজন *a.* lonely, solitary, desolate.

বিজন্মা *a.* bastard, illegitimate.

বিজবিজ *int.* denoting: repugnant crowding as of worms (পোকা বিজবিজ করছে).

বিজয় *n.* victory, triumph; conquest (ভারতবিজয়) ; subdual or vanquishment (দানববিজয়) ; success (কর্মে বিজয়লাভ) ; (obs.) act of going. **~অভিযান** *n.* a march for victory, a march for conquests; a victory march. **~কেতন** *n.* the banner of victory. **~গর্ব** *n.* pride of victory. **~দৃপ্ত** *a.* proud of victory, flushed with victory; triumphant. **~লক্ষ্মী** *n.* the goddess of victory (cp. Minerva). **বিজয়লাভ করা** *v.* to be victorious or successful. **~স্তম্ভ** *n.* monument commemorating a victory, a victory pillar or column. **বিজয়া** *n.* Goddess Durga (দুর্গা) ; a female companion of Durga; the day on which the image of Durga is immersed (usu. **বিজয়াদশমী**). **বিজয়া সংগীত** *n.* any one of the songs about Durga's going to her husband's house leaving her paternal home. **বিজয়ী** *a.* victorious, triumphant; conquering; vanquishing. □ *n.* a victor; a conqueror; a vanquisher. *fem.* **বিজয়িনী** । **বিজয়োৎসব** *n.* celebration of victory; exultation for victory or success, triumph. **বিজয়োৎসব করা** *v.* to celebrate a victory. **বিজয়োন্মত্ত** *a.* beside oneself with joy for victory or success, madly rejoicing on account of victory or success. **বিজয়োল্লসিত** *a.* triumphant, exultant. **বিজয়োল্লাস** *n.* exultation for victory or success, triumph.

বিজলি, বিজলী *n.* lightning; electricity. **~তার** *n.* electric wire. **~পাখা** *n.* an electric fan. **~বাতি** *n.* an electric light or lamp.

বিজাতি *n.* a different race or caste; a hostile race.

বিজাতীয় *a.* pertaining to a different nation or race (বিজাতীয় বেশভূষা) ; heterogeneous (বিজাতীয় ভেদ) ; very strong, terrible, deadly (বিজাতীয় আক্রোশ).

বিজারণ *n.* reduction.

বিজিগীষা *n.* desire for attaining victory or success.

বিজিগীষু *a.* desirous of victory or success.

বিজিত *a.* defeated, vanquished; conquered; subdued. *fem.* **বিজিতা** ।

বিজিতেন্দ্রীয় *a.* (of one) who has mastered passions, having control over desires and passions, self-controlled.

বিজুরি, বিজুলি poet. corruptions of **বিজলি** ।

বিজৃম্ভণ *n.* yawning; a yawn.

বিজেতা same as **বিজয়ী** । *fem.* **বিজেত্রী** ।

বিজেয় *a.* capable of being defeated, vanquishable; conquerable.

বিজোড় *a.* odd, uneven; separated from the partner, unpaired, uncoupled; disjoined. **বিজোড় সংখ্যা** an odd number.

বিজ্ঞ *a.* learned, erudite; wise; experienced; expert; judicious, prudent. **~তা, ~ত্ব** *n.* erudition, learning; wisdom; experience; expertness; judiciousness, prudence.

বিজ্ঞপ্তি *n.* a notice, a circular; a bill; a placard; an advertisement or a notification.

বিজ্ঞা *fem.* of **বিজ্ঞ**।

বিজ্ঞাত *a.* well-informed, au fait; well-known; distinguished, famous.

বিজ্ঞান *n.* science. **~চর্চা, বিজ্ঞানানুশীলন** *n.* cultivation of science. **~বিদ, ~বেত্তা, বিজ্ঞানী** *a.* versed in science. □ *n.* a scientist.

বিজ্ঞাপন *n.* notification, announcement; a notice, a circular, a bill, a placard, an official bulletin, an advertisement; petitioning, supplication; a petition. **বিজ্ঞাপন দেওয়া** *n.* to advertise; to notify, to announce; to bill. **~দাতা** *n.* an advertiser. *fem.* **~দাত্রী**। **বিজ্ঞাপনীয়** *a.* fit to be notified or announced or advertised; fit to be petitioned for.

বিজ্ঞাপিত *a.* notified, announced; circulated, proclaimed; billed, advertised; petitioned, supplicated.

বিজ্ঞেয় *a.* that which is to be learned thoroughly or particularly.

বিট[১] *n.* a round or course (as of postman or watchman); a beat.

বিট[২] *n.* a bulbous plant, beet.

বিটকেল *a.* hideous or monstrous (বিটকেল মূর্তি) ; abominable or repulsive (বিটকেল গন্ধ) ; very ludicrous or queer (বিটকেল ব্যাপার) ; given to playing antics or cracking practical jokes; of a queer sort (বিটকেল লোক). **বিটকেলমি** *n.* practice of playing antics or cracking practical jokes.

বিটঙ্ক *n.* a pigeon-house, a dovecote; a trap for catching brids, a fowling-net.

বিটনুন, বিটলবণ *n.* a black variety of salt.

বিটপ *n.* a branch (of a tree); a twig; a school. **বিটপী** *n.* a tree.

বিটপালং *n.* a variety of spinach of the goosefoot family.

বিটলবণ see **বিটনুন**।

বিটলে *a.* knavish, roughish. **বিটলেমি** *n.* knavery, roguery.

বিটা *n.* beta. **বিটা-কণা** *n.* beta-particles. **বিটা-রশ্মি** *n.* beta-rays.

বিটেল var. of **বিটলে**।

বিড়ঙ্গ *n.* a medicinal plant or its fruit; wise, experienced.

বিড়বিড় *int.* denoting : muttering, mumbling. **বিড়বিড় করা** to mutter or mumble. **বিড়বিড়ানি** *n.* muttering, mumbling.

বিড়ম্বনা *n.* deception, (loos.) mockery or irony (ভাগ্যবিড়ম্বনা) ; unnecessary trouble or harassment (চাকরির জন্য চেষ্টা বিড়ম্বনা মাত্র).

বিড়ম্বিত *a.* deceived, (loos.) mocked; unnecessarily troubled or harassed.

বিড়া *n.* a coil of straw or cloth used as a pedestal for placing cooking-urns, pitchers etc. and also for wearing as a headgear; (of beetle-leaves etc.) a small roll, a bundle.

বিড়াল *n.* the cat. *fem.* **বিড়ালী** the she-cat. **বিড়ালের ভাগ্যে শিকে ছেঁড়া** (fig.) an undeserving person comes in for a windfall; unexpected success. **~ছানা** *n.* a kitten, a catling. **~জাতীয়** *a.* feline. **~তপস্বী** *n.* (fig.) a rogue feigning piety, a sanctimonious rogue, a hypocrite. **~তুল্য** *a* cat-like, feline. **বিড়ালাক্ষী** *a.* cat-eyed.

বিড়ি *n.* a kind of slender cigarette rolled in a tree-leaf.

বিড়ে coll. corrup. of **বিড়া**।

-বিৎ *(for.) sfx.* versed, au fait, cognizant, -ist (শাস্ত্রবিৎ, বিজ্ঞানবিৎ).

বিতং *n.* (obs.) details.

বিতংস *n.* a noose or rope for fastening birds, beasts etc.

বিতণ্ডা *n.* unnecessary argument; sophistical debate; (phil.) sophistry.

বিতত *a.* extended, expanded, spread out, outstretched; tense; pervaded. **বিততি** *n.* extent, expanse, stretch; tension; pervasion.

বিতথ, বিতথ্য *a.* untrue, false; futile, vain.

বিতরণ *n.* act of giving away; distribution. **বিতরণ করা** *v.* to give away, to distribute. ~কেন্দ্র *n.* a distributing centre.

বিতরা poet. form of **বিতরণ করা**।

বিতরিত *a.* given away; distributed.

বিতর্ক *n.* deliberation; a debate; argument, reasoning; wrangling, a dispute; doubt. **~ণীয়** *a.* debatable; arguable; disputable. **বিতর্কিকা** *n.* a debate; a debating forum. **বিতর্কিত** *a.* deliberated upon; debated; argued, reasoned; disputed; doubted.

বিতল *n.* (myth.) the second of seven underworlds.

বিতস্তা *n.* the river Jhelum.

বিতস্তি *n.* the space from the end of the thumb to the end of the little finger when fingers are extended, a span.

বিতাড়িত *a.* turned out; expelled. **বিতাড়িত করা** *v.* to turn out; to expel.

বিতান *n.* a structure in a garden for sitting in, a summer-house (লতাবিতান) ; a canopy, an awning; a tent; a pavilion; tension, stretch.

বিতিকিচ্ছি, বিতিকিচ্চি variants of **বিচিকিচ্ছি**।

বিতৃষ্ণ *a.* (ori.) not thirsty; disinterested; callous; averse to, apathetic; disgusted (with). **বিতৃষ্ণা** *n.* disinterestedness; callousness; aversion, apathy; disgust.

বিত্ত *n.* wealth, riches; property. **~বান, ~শালী** *a.* wealthy, rich. *fem.* **~শালিনী**। **বিত্ত সঞ্চয় করা** *v.* to amass wealth or riches. **~হীন** *a.* poor, indigent. □ *n.* (pol.) a have-not.

বিথর *n.* a tier, a layer (থরে-বিথরে).

বিথারা *v.* (poet.) to stretch out.

-বিদ *sfx.* var. of **-বিৎ**।

বিদকুটে var. of **বিদঘুটে**।

বিদগ্ধ *a.* witty; having the qualification of a connoisseur; learned; cultured; intelligent; skilful; clever. **বিদগ্ধা** *a. fem.* of **বিদগ্ধ**। □ *n.* (rhet.) a witty lady-love. **বিদগ্ধ-সমাজ** *n.* the intelligentsia; a learned society; a body of connoisseurs.

বিদঘুটে *a.* queer and ugly; troublesome; complicated (বিদঘুটে অঙ্ক).

বিদরা *v.* (poet.) to rend or split.

বিদল *a.* having no petal, apetalous; not belonging to one's party. □ *n.* pigeon-pea, dal.

বিদলন *n.* a thorough trampling or thrashing; thorough vanquishment, rout; extreme oppression.

বিদলিত *a.* thoroughly trampled or thrashed; routed; extremely oppressed. **বিদলিত করা** *v.* to trample or thrash thoroughly; to rout; to oppress extremely.

বিদায়[১] *n.* a gift or present, anything given in charity (ব্রাহ্মণবিদায়, কাঙালবিদায়).

বিদায়[২] *n.* removal, expulsion (আপদ বিদায়) ; permission for departure, leave (বিদায় চাওয়া) ; formal parting, farewell (তার বিদায়ের পর) ; separation, parting (চিরবিদায়) ; retirement from service. □ *int.* farewell, adieu, good-bye. **~কালীন** *a.* relating to the time of parting; relating to farewell, valedictory (বিদায়কালীন ভাষণ). **বিদায় করা** *v.* to remove, to expel, to dismiss. **বিদায় চাওয়া** *v.* to ask leave for departure. **বিদায় দেওয়া** *v.* to give one leave to depart; to see one off; to cause to retire from service, to retire. **বিদায় নেওয়া** *v.* to depart, to take leave; to part; to bid farewell; to retire from service. **বিদায় হওয়া** *v.* to depart, to be off.

বিদায়ী *a.* departing, leaving; taking leave; retiring from service; outgoing (বিদায়ী সভাপতি) ; valedictory.

বিদারক *a.* splitting, rending; cleaving; piercing; causing to burst. **হৃদয়-বিদারক** *a.* heart-rending.

বিদারণ *a.* splitting or rending or cleaving or piercing; act of causing to burst.

বিদারা *v.* (poet.) same as **বিদীর্ণ করা**।

বিদারিত same as **বিদীর্ণ**।

বিদারী same as **বিদারক**।

বিদিক *n.* (rare) a point intermediate between two cardinal ones of the compass; (pop.) an opposite or wrong direction (দিগ্বিদিক).

বিদিত *a.* known (বিদিত বিষয়) ; celebrated, famed (জগতে বিদিত) ; acquainted, informed, cognizant, au fait (বিদিত থাকা). **ভুবনবিদিত** *a.* of worldwide fame, renowned.

বিদীর্ণ *a.* split, rent; cleft; pierced; burst. **বিদীর্ণ করা** *v.* to split, to rend; to cleave; to pierce; to cause to burst.

বিদুর *n.* a character of the Mahabharata. **বিদুরের খুদ** an extremely small offering given in deep devotion, (cp.) a widow's mite.

বিদুষী *a. fem.* learned, erudite. □ *n. fem.* a learned woman.

বিদূর *a.* remote (বিদূর সম্পর্ক). □ *n.* a remote place (দূরে-বিদূরে).

বিদূরিত *a.* driven away; removed; expelled.

বিদূষক *n.* (in dramas) a clown, a jester, a buffoon.

বিদে *n.* a harrow, a rake. **বিদে দেওয়া** *v.* to harrow, to rake.

বিদেশ *n.* a foreign land or country. **~জ, ~জাত** *a.* grown or produced in a foreign land, exotic, foreign. **~ভ্রমণ** *n.* travels abroad. **~বাস** *n.* staying or living in a foreign country, living abroad. **~যাত্রা** *n.* starting on a journey abroad. **~স্থ** *a.* of a foreign land, foreign. **বিদেশাগত** *a.* coming from or imported from a foreign land. **বিদেশি** *a.* foreign, exotic, (arch.) outlandish, alien. □ *n.* a foreigner; an alien. *fem.* **বিদেশিনি**। **বিদেশি পুঁজি** foreign capital. **বিদেশি মুদ্রা** foreign currency. **বিদেশীয়** *a.* same as **বিদেশি** (*a*). **বিদেশে** *adv.* in or to a foreign land, abroad.

বিদেহ[1] *n.* modern Mithila (মিথিলা).

বিদেহ[2] *a.* bodiless, incorporeal. *fem.* **বিদেহা,** (inc.) **বিদেহী**।

বিদ্ধ *a.* pierced; pricked; perforated; bored. **বিদ্ধ করা** *v.* to pierce; to prick; to perforate; to bore. **~পত্র** *n.* (bot.) a perfoliated leaf.

বিদ্বজ্জন same as **বিদ্বান** (*n.*).

বিদ্বৎকল্প *a.* appearing to be learned (though not really so); near learned, just short of being learned.

বিদ্বৎকুল, বিদ্বৎসমাজ the learned society; the intelligentsia. **বিদ্বৎকুলতিলক** *n.* (fig.) a great savant.

বিদ্বান *a.* learned; erudite. □ *n.* a learned or erudite man, a savant, a scholar.

বিদ্বিষ্ট *a.* held in malice, maligned; envied; grudged.

বিদ্বেষ *n.* malice, malignity; envy; grudge; animosity, animus. **বিদ্বেষ করা** *v.* to bear malice (against), to malign; to envy; to grudge; to treat with animosity. **~পরায়ণ** same as **বিদ্বেষী**। **~প্রসূত** *a.* caused or generated by malice or malevolence. **~বুদ্ধি** *n.* malicious or envious or spiteful disposition. **~বুদ্ধি-প্রণোদিত, ~বুদ্ধিপ্রসূত** *a.* actuated by malicious or envious or spiteful inclination or disposition. **~ভাজন** *n.* an object of malice or envy or animosity. **~মূলক** *a.* malicious; malevolent; actuated by malice or malignity; spiteful. **বিদ্বেষানল** *n.* extreme malice, great malice. **বিদ্বেষী, বিদ্বেষ্টা** *a.* malicious, malignant; envious; grudging; full of animosity.

বিদ্যমান *a.* existent; present; in esse; alive, living. **~তা** *n.* existence; presence; state of being alive.

বিদ্যা *n.* learning; erudition; scholarship; skill; a subject of study (সর্ববিদ্যা-বিশারদ) ; a science (পদার্থবিদ্যা) ; an art (জাদুবিদ্যা, চুরিবিদ্যা) ; philosophy. **বিদ্যার জাহাজ** a prodigy of learning; (cp.) a walking encyclopaedia. **বিদ্যার বহর** (facet.) range of knowledge, extent of learning. **~গম** *n.* acquirement of learning. **~চর্চা** *n.* culture or cultivation of learning; practice of learning; acquisition of knowledge. **~দাতা** *n.* a teacher; a preceptor (*fem.* a preceptress), a guru. *fem.* **~দাত্রী**। **~দান** *n.* imparting of knowledge or learning. **বিদ্যাদান করা** *v.* to teach; to impart learning gratuitously. **~দেবী** *n.* Saraswati (সরস্বতী) the goddess of learning. **~ধন** *n.* knowledge conceived as wealth. **~ধর** *n.* one of an order of demi-gods famous for their personal beauty and skill in music. *fem.* **~ধরী**। **~নিধি** *n.* an ocean of learning : a title conferred on a scholar. **বিদ্যানুরাগ** *n.* love of learning, attachment to learning. **বিদ্যানুরাগী** *a.* fond of or attached to learning. *fem.* **বিদ্যানুরাগিণী**। **বিদ্যানুশীলন** same as **~চর্চা**। **বিদ্যানুশীলন করা** *v.* to cultivate learning or a science; to study. **~পীঠ** *n.* a centre of learning; an academy; a school. **~বতী** *fem.* of **বিদ্যাবান**। **~বত্তা** *n.* possession of learning, scholarship. **~বল** *n.*

power or force of learning. ~বান *a.* learned. ~বিনোদ *n.* delight of Goddess Saraswati (সরস্বতী) : a title conferred on a scholar. ~বিশারদ *a.* vastly learned. ☐ *n.* a title conferred on a scholar. ~ব্যবসায়ী *a.* & *n.* one who teaches professionally. ~ভূষণ *n.* an ornament of learning : a title conferred on a scholar. **বিদ্যাভ্যাস** same as **বিদ্যাচর্চা**। **বিদ্যাভ্যাস করা** *v.* to learn an art or science; to study; to learn one's lessons. ~মন্দির, **বিদ্যায়তন** *n.* a temple of learning; a school. ~রত্ন *n.* a jewel of learning : a title conferred on a scholar. **বিদ্যারম্ভ** *n.* initiation into one's studies (esp. with religious solemnities). **বিদ্যারম্ভ করা** *v.* to commence one's studies (esp. with religious solemnities). **বিদ্যার্জন** same as **বিদ্যালাভ**। **বিদ্যার্থী** *a.* desirous of acquiring learning; (loos.) engaged in studies. ☐ *n.* one who is desirous of acquiring learning; (loos.) a student, a scholar, a pupil, *fem.* **বিদ্যার্থিনী**। ~লব্ধ *a.* gained or earned by learning. ~লয় *n.* a school; an academy; (rare) a college; an institution; an institute; a seminary. **বিদ্যালয়ের ছুটির দিন** a school holiday. **বিদ্যালয়ের ছুটির সময়** closing time of a school; school vacation. **বিদ্যালয়ের সময়** school time; school hours. ~লাভ *n.* acquisition of learning; act of receiving education. **বিদ্যালাভ করা** *v.* to acquire learning; to receive education, to have one's education. ~শিক্ষা *n.* learning; act of receiving education. **বিদ্যাশিক্ষা করা** *v.* to learn; to receive education. ~শূন্য *a.* unlearned, uneducated; ignorant. ~সাগর same as **বিদ্যানিধি**। ~হীন same as **বিদ্যাশূন্য**। *fem.* **বিদ্যাহীনা**।

বিদ্যুৎ *n.* lightning; electricity. ~গর্ভ *a.* impregnated with electricity; charged with electricity. ~প্রবাহ *n.* an electric current. ~প্রভ *a.* as dazzlingly bright as a flash of lightning. *fem.* ~প্রভা। ~স্পন্দন, ~স্ফুরণ *n.* electric vibration. ~স্পৃষ্ট *a.* struck by lightning. ~স্ফুলিঙ্গ *n.* an electric spark. **বিদ্যুদ্দাম** *n.* a flash of lightning; a garland-like series of lightning flashes. **বিদ্যুদ্বর্ষী** *a.* discharging electricity. **বিদ্যুদ্বেগ** *n.* lightning speed. **বিদ্যুদ্বেগে** *adv.* as speedily as lightning. **বিদ্যুন্মালা** same as **বিদ্যুদ্দাম**। **বিদ্যুল্লতা** *n.* a streak of lightning.

বিদ্যোৎসাহী *a.* encouraging or patronizing promotion of learning or spread of education. *fem.* **বিদ্যোৎসাহিনী**। **বিদ্যোৎসাহিনী সভা** a society for promotion or spread of learning or education.

বিদ্যোপার্জন same as **বিদ্যালাভ**। see **বিদ্যা**।

বিদ্রব *n.* fleeing, flight; melting or being melted; dissolving; thaw.

বিদ্রাবণ *n.* turning into liquid, liquefaction. **বিদ্রাবিত** *a.* liquefied.

বিদ্রুপ, (rej.) **বিদ্রূপ** *n.* persiflage, banter; taunt, ridicule; sarcasm; irony. **বিদ্রুপ করা** *v.* to banter; to taunt, to ridicule; to scoff at; to jeer. **বিদ্রুপাত্মক** *a.* bantering; taunting; sarcastic; ironical.

বিদ্রুম *n.* ruby; coral; a young shoot.

বিদ্রোহ *n.* revolt, rebellion, insurrection, insurgence, insurgency; (loos.) treason; a coup, a coup d'état; mutiny. **বিদ্রোহ করা** *v.* to rise in rebellion, to revolt, to rebel, to mutiny. **বিদ্রোহাচরণ করা** *v.* to revolt; to become hostile or disloyal. **বিদ্রোহাত্মক,** ~মূলক *a.* rebellious; mutinous; insurgent; recalcitrant. **বিদ্রোহী** *a.* rebellious, insurgent; mutinous; hostile; disloyal. ☐ *n.* a rebel, an insurgent; a disloyal person. (loos.) a traitor. *fem.* **বিদ্রোহিণী**।

-বিধ *sfx.* sort, kind, type etc. (বহুবিধ = of many kinds.)

বিধবা *n. fem.* a widow. **বিধবা করা** *v.* to bereave of a husband, to widow. ~বিবাহ *n.* widow marriage.

বিধর্মা, বিধর্মী *a.* professing a different religion or creed; heretic. ☐ *n.* one professing a different religion; a heretic; an infidel.

বিধা *n.* sort, kind, variety, type; manner, mode; arrangement (সুবিধা).

বিধাতা *n.* a director, a controller, a regulator (ভাগ্যবিধাতা) ; God; Providence; Brahma (ব্রহ্মা). ~পুরুষ *n.* Providence personified (who is believed to write down the future of a newborn baby on its forehead).

বিধাতৃদত্ত *a.* God-gifted, God-given; bestowed by Providence.

বিধান *n.* a scriptural prescript or ruling; a prescript, a ruling (সভাপতির বিধান) ; a prescription (পথ্যবিধান) ; provision, arrangement (আনন্দবিধান) ; legislation; a law; a rule; a system (নববিধান). **বিধান দেওয়া** *v.* to prescribe; to issue a ruling, to rule. **~কর্তা** *n.* a director (*fem.* directress, directrix), a regulator, a controller; a law-giver; a legislator. *fem.* **~কর্ত্রী** । **~তন্ত্র** *n.* a code of laws; a system of legislation. **বিধান-পরিষদ** *n.* a legislative council. **~শাস্ত্র** *n.* jurisprudence, law. **~সংসদ** *n.* the Parliament. **~সংহিতা** *n.* a treatise on jurisprudence, a law-book. **~সভা** *n.* a legislative assembly.

বিধানিক *a.* legislative. **বিধানিক ক্ষমতা** legislative power. **বিধানিক প্রণালী** legislative procedure.

বিধায় *prep.* (leg.) on account of, because of, owing to, for (অসুস্থতা বিধায়).

বিধায়ক, বিধায়ী *a.* legislating; enacting; directing, controlling, regulating; issuing a rule; prescribing; making provision or arrangements for; causing to happen, bringing about. □ *n.* a member of a legislative assembly, an MLA. *fem.* **বিধায়িকা, বিধায়িনী** ।

বিধি *n.* a prescript, an edict; a prescription; a rule; a regulation; a law, an act; a means; a procedure; a method; a system; destiny, fate; God, Providence; Brahma (ব্রহ্মা). **বিধি-আধিকারিক** *n.* law officer. **~জ্ঞ** *a.* conversant with laws or rules; versed in scriptures. **~নির্দেশক** *n.* legal remembrancer. **~নির্দিষ্ট** *a.* regulated or prescribed or determined by rules or regulations. **~নিষেধ** *n.* restrictions or inhibitions. **~প্রয়োগ** *n.* application of a rule or law. **~বদ্ধ** *a.* regulated; enacted, codified; in keeping with form or established mode, formal. **বিধিবদ্ধ করা** *v.* to enact, to codify. **~বিড়ম্বনা** *n.* deception by fate; irony of fate. **~বিড়ম্বিত** *a.* beguiled by fate; suffered or suffering from irony of fate. **~বিরুদ্ধ** *a.* unlawful; irregular; informal. **~বিহিত** *a.* lawful; law-abiding; regular; formal. **~ভঙ্গ** *n.* breaking the rules or regulations; infringement or violation of a rule or law. **~মতো** *a.* in keeping with scriptural prescripts or edicts or rules; in keeping with rules or laws; just, rightful (বিধিমতো শাস্তি) ; (loos.) adequate; formal; (loos.) utmost (বিধিমতো চেষ্টা). **~লিপি** *n.* the prescript of Providence; destiny, fate. **~সংগত, ~সম্মত** *a.* in keeping with scriptural prescripts or edicts or rules; lawful, rightful; formal.

বিধিৎসা *n.* desire to make provision or arrangements for, desire to provide for.

বিধিৎসু *a.* desirous of making provision or arrangements for.

বিধু *n.* the moon.

বিধুত *a.* set trembling; shaken; vibrated. **বিধুত করা** *v.* to set trembling; to shake; to vibrate.

বিধুনন *n.* act of causing to tremble; shaking; vibration.

বিধুনিত same as **বিধুত** ।

বিধুবদন, বিধুমুখ *a.* moon-faced. *fem.* **বিধুবদনা, বিধুমুখী** ।

বিধুর *a.* afflicted (বিরহবিধুর) ; frightened; bewildered; overwhelmed, redolent of, surcharged with (গন্ধবিধুর) ; beside oneself with (আনন্দবিধুর). *fem.* **বিধুরা** । **~তা** *n.* affliction; fright; bewilderment; overwhelmed state, state of being beside oneself.

বিধূত, বিধূনন, বিধূনিত alt. spellings of **বিধুত, বিধুনন** and **বিধুনিত** respectively.

বিধৃত *a.* firmly caught or seized or arrested; grasped, realized, preserved; embalmed.

বিধেয় *a.* lawful, rightful; proper; that should be done or undertaken; predicable. □ *n.* (gr. & log.) a predicate; (phil.) a predicable.

বিধেয়ক *n.* a draft of a proposed law, a bill.

বিধৌত *a.* washed well, profusely washed.

বিধ্বংস *n.* complete ruin or destruction; devastation; demolition; **বিধ্বংসী** *a.* thoroughly ruining or destroying; devastating; demolishing.

বিধ্বস্ত *a.* utterly ruined or destroyed; devastated; demolished; (of an army etc.) routed. **বিধ্বস্ত করা** *v.* to ruin or destroy completely; to devastate; to demolish; to rout.

বিন *n.* a leguminous plant or its seed, bean.

বিনত *a.* stooping; bowed (in salutation); modest, demure; meek; submissive; polite; disciplined.

বিনতা১ *fem.* of **বিনত**।

বিনতা২ *n. fem.* (myth.) a wife of Kashyap the sage. **~নন্দন** *n.* a son of Binata (বিনতা); Aruna (অরুণ) the chariot-driver of the Sun-god; Garuda (গরুড়) the prince of birds.

বিনতি *n.* stooping; bowing (in salutation); modesty, demureness, submissiveness; politeness; discipline.

বিননি var. of **বিনুনি**।

বিনম্র *a.* very modest or demure or meek or submissive or polite or disciplined; bowing down in submission or politeness. *fem.* **বিনম্রা**। **~তা** *n.* great modesty or demureness or meekness or politeness or discipline; a bow or stooping in submission or politeness; great discipline.

বিনয় *n.* modesty; demureness : meekness, submissiveness; submission; solicitation; education or training; discipline. **বিনয়ন** *n.* educating or training; disciplining; removal. **~পূর্বক** *adv.* with humble submission. **~সহকারে** same as **বিনয়পূর্বক**। **বিনয়াবনত** *a.* bowing down in submission or politeness. *fem.* **বিনয়াবনতা**। **বিনয়ী** *a.* modest, demure; meek, submissive; disciplined.

বিনশ্বর *a.* perishable, destructible.

বিনষ্ট *a.* destroyed; perished; killed; ruined (বিনষ্ট রাজ্য); wrecked (বিনষ্ট পোত); lost or wasted (বিনষ্ট সম্পদ); corrupted, depraved (বিনষ্ট চরিত্র); spoiled (বিনষ্ট সুযোগ, বিনষ্ট খাদ্য).

বিনষ্টি *n.* destruction; ruin; extinction; (pop. & coll.) misuse, waste.

বিনা *prep.* except, without, save, but; excluding.

বিনানো *v.* to plait (hair) in a pigtail, to queue, to tress; to intertwine into the shape (as of a pigtail); to narrate or fabricate at length, to spin out (বিনিয়ে বলা বা কাঁদা).

বিনামা *n.* shoe; boot; slipper.

বিনায়ক *n.* a leader of the people; Ganesha (গণেশ) the god of the people; a teacher; a disciplinarian.

বিনাশ *n.* destruction; ruin; wreck; loss or waste; death; extinction; extermination; ravishment (সতীত্ববিনাশ); corruption, depravation (চরিত্রবিনাশ). **বিনাশ করা** *v.* to destroy; to ruin, to wreck; to waste; to kill; to exterminate; to ravish; to corrupt, to deprave. **বিনাশক** *a.* destructive; ruinous; wrecking; wasting; killing; exterminatory; ravishing; corruptive, depraving. □ *n.* a destroyer; a ruiner; a wrecker; a waster; a killer; an exterminator; a ravisher; a corrupter. **বিনাশন** *n.* destruction; ruination; wrecking; wasting; killing; extermination. □ *a.* (used chiefly as a *sfx.*) same as **বিনাশক** (*a.*). **~ধর্মী** *a.* destructive; exterminative. **~শীল** *a.* of a destructive or exterminative nature, destructive. **~সাধক** *a.* same as **বিনাশক** (*a.*). **~সাধন** *n.* same as **বিনাশন** (*n.*). **~প্রাপ্ত, বিনাশিত** same as **বিনষ্ট**। **বিনাশী** *a.* perishable; mortal; destructible; destructive; ruinous; killing; ravishing; depraving. *fem.* **বিনাশিনী** (not in the first three senses). **বিনাশোন্মুখ** *a.* about to perish; about to die, on deathbed, moribund; about to be destroyed or ruined.

বিনি coll. corrup. of **বিনা**।

বিনিঃসরণ *n.* emergence, act of coming or issuing out.

বিনিঃসৃত *a.* emerged, issued out. **বিনিঃসৃত হওয়া** *v.* to emerge, to come out, to issue out.

বিনিদ্র *a.* sleepless, wakeful (বিনিদ্র রজনী); vigilant.

বিনিন্দিত *a.* (used chiefly as a *sfx.*) reproached, put to shame (মৃণালবিনিন্দিত = reproaching or abashing even a lotus-stalk).

বিনিবৃত্ত *a.* restrained; prevented; checked; desisted.

বিনিময় *n.* exchange; barter; return;

requital, recompense; substitution. **বিনিময় করা** *v.* to exchange; to barter. **বিনিময়ে দেওয়া** *v.* to give in exchange (for) or in lieu (of); to give in return (for), to requite, to recompense. **বিনিময়-নিয়ম** *n.* (alg.) the commutative law. **বিনিময়-হার** *n.* the rate of exchange.

বিনিমেয় *a.* exchangeable; (esp. of coins) convertible.

বিনিয়ন্ত্রণ *n.* decontrol. **বিনিয়ন্ত্রণ করা** *v.* to decontrol.

বিনিয়ন্ত্রিত *a.* decontrolled.

বিনিযুক্ত *a.* appointed; commissioned; sent; entrusted with; (of money) invested. **বিনিযুক্তক** *n.* the Minister in charge of appointments.

বিনিয়ে *adv.* elaborately, verbosely, in so many words; ingratiatingly (ইনিয়ে-বিনিয়ে).

বিনিয়োগ *n.* appointment, commission; sending; entrusting; investment (of money in business). **বিনিয়োগ করা** *v.* to appoint, to commission; to send; to entrust (with); to invest, to lay out.

বিনিয়োজিত same as **বিনিযুক্ত**।

বিনির্গত *a.* what has emerged, come out, issued forth. **বিনির্গত হওয়া** *v.* to emerge, to come out, to issue forth.

বিনির্গম, বিনির্গমন *n.* coming out or issuing forth, emergence.

বিনির্ণয় *n.* ascertainment; award (of arbitration etc.)

বিনির্ণীত *a.* ascertained; awarded (by arbitration, tribunals etc.).

বিনির্দেশ *n.* ruling.

বিনিশ্চয় *n.* convincing or conclusive decision ('চর্যাচর্য-বিনিশ্চয়'). **বিনিশ্চিত** *a.* firmly or deliberately decided or concluded.

বিনীত *a.* modest, demure; meek, submissive; docile; polite; desciplined. *fem.* **বিনীতা**। **~ভাবে** *adv.* humbly, politely.

বিনু obs. poet. corrup. of **বিনা**।

বিনুনি *n.* a queue, a tress, a pigtail; act or manner of interwining into a queue or into a similar shape.

বিনে poet. corrup. of **বিনা**।

বিনেতা *n.* a controller, a director; a teacher; a discipliner. *fem.* **বিনেত্রী**।

বিনেয় *a.* tractable, docile.

বিনোদ *n.* act of making pleasant; pleasure; pleasant sport or diversion. □ *a.* pleasant; beautiful; good-looking.

বিনোদন *n.* making pleasant; act of giving pleasure, entertainment or gratification (চিত্তবিনোদন); removal, relaxation (শ্রমবিনোদন). **বিনোদনমূলক** *a.* entertaining, relating to entertainment. **বিনোদিত** *a.* made pleasant; entertained or gratified. **বিনোদিয়া** *a.* (obs. & poet.) pleasant, charming, beautiful. **বিনোদী** *a.* making pleasant; pleasurable, pleasant; entertaining or gratifying. **বিনোদিনী** *a. fem.* of বিনোদী beautiful, pleasant; □ *n.* Shriradhika.

বিন্তি *n.* a kind of card-game; (in some card-game) a tierce.

বিন্দু *n.* a drop (জলবিন্দু) ; a dot, a point (দশমিক বিন্দু) ; a small roundish mark; ('ললাটে সিন্দূর বিন্দু') ; (geom.) a point; a particle, a whit, an iota (একবিন্দু দুঃখ). **~বিসর্গ** *n.* (ori.) the alphabetical letters ং and ঃ ; (fig.) a particle, a whit, an iota; (fig.) the faintest hint, an inkling. **বিন্দুবিসর্গ জানা** *v.* to have the faintest knowledge (of). **~মাত্র না** not even to the smallest extent or amount; not a whit, not a jot or title.

বিন্ধা poet. corrup. of **বিদ্ধ করা**।

বিন্ধ্য *n.* the Vindhyas. **~বাসিনী** *a. fem.* dwelling on the Vindhyas. □ *n.* Goddess Durga (দুর্গা). *masc. a.* **বিন্ধ্যবাসী**।

বিন্ধ্যাচল *n.* the Vindhya mountains.

বিন্যস্ত *a.* placed in an orderly manner; arrayed (বিন্যস্ত সৈন্যবাহিনী) ; placed (ঘনবিন্যস্ত) ; artistically or neatly dressed or composed (বিন্যস্ত কবরী) ; applied in an orderly or artistic manner (বিন্যস্ত শব্দসমূহ). **বিন্যস্ত করা** *v.* to lay or place in an orderly manner; to array; to place; to dress or arrange artistically or neatly; to apply in an orderly or artistic manner.

বিন্যাস *n.* placing in an orderly manner; arraying or an array; artistic or neat dressing or arrangement (কেশবিন্যাস, বেশবিন্যাস) ; orderly or artistic application (শব্দবিন্যাস) ; (loos.) narration or fabrication at length, elaboration

(বিন্যাসসহকারে বলা) ; (math.) permutation.

বিপক্ষ *n.* a rival or opponent or opposite party; enemy forces; an opponent, a rival; an antagonist; an adversary, an enemy. **বিপক্ষতা** *n.* rivalry; opposition; antagonism; hostility, enmity. **~দল** *n.* a rival party; enemy forces. **বিপক্ষীয়** *a.* of a rival party or the enemy forces. **বিপক্ষে** *prep.* against; on the opposite side.

বিপজ্জনক *a.* dangerous, hazardous, perilous, risky.

বিপণন *n.* act of putting (goods) on the market for sale, marketing.

বিপণি, বিপণী *n.* a shop; a sales emporium; a market.

বিপৎ same as **বিপদ**। **~কাল** *n.* time of danger or crisis, a critical time.

বিপত্তারিণী *n.* a (Hindu) goddess; the goddess who keeps or saves from trouble or danger.

বিপত্তি *n.* a danger, a hazard; a trouble; a disaster; a mishap; adversity; a sharp turn in one's affairs. **~কর** *a.* causing danger or trouble or disaster or adversity. **~নাশন** *a.* remedying or counteracting dangers or troubles or disaster or adversity.

বিপত্নীক *a.* one whose wife is dead. **বিপত্নীক ব্যক্তি** a widower.

বিপথ *n.* a wrong or bad way; (fig.) an evil course of conduct. **বিপথে যাওয়া** *v.* to go astray; (chiefly astr.) to aberrate; (fig.) to go to the bad. **~গামী** *a.* gone astray; (chiefly astr.) aberrated; (fig.) gone to the bad; abandoned. *fem.* **বিপথগামিনী**।

বিপদ *n.* a danger; a mishap, a disaster; a difficulty, a trouble; adversity. **বিপদে পড়া** *v.* to run or fall into a danger, to be involved in a danger. **বিপদে ফেলা** *v.* to involve in a danger, to endanger, to imperil. **বিপদাপদ** *n. pl.* dangers and difficulties. **বিপদাপন্ন** *a.* endangered, imperilled. **বিপদুদ্ধার করা** *v.* to rescue or deliver from danger. **~কাল** *n.* time of danger, a critical time. **~গ্রস্ত** same as **বিপন্ন**। **~চিহ্ন** *n.* danger signal. **~বহুল** *a.* fraught with dangers and difficulties. **~বার্তা** *n.* a warning. **~ভঞ্জন** *a.* removing or counteracting dangers and difficulties. **~সংকুল** same as **~বহুল**।

বিপদ্দশা *n.* a crisis, a danger; difficulties; adversity.

বিপন্ন *a.* involved in danger or difficulty, endangered, imperilled; embarrassed. *fem.* **বিপন্না**।

বিপন্মুক্ত *a.* relieved of or rescued or freed from danger or difficulty, out of the wood. **বিপন্মুক্ত করা** *v.* to release or rascue from danger or difficulty, to bring out of the wood. **বিপন্মুক্তি** *n.* rescue or release from danger or difficulty.

বিপরীত *a.* opposite; contrary; contradictory; opposing, contending; counteracting; unfavourable, adverse (বিপরীত ভাগ্য) ; (loos.) hideous, monstrous (বিপরীত মূর্তি) ; unusual, odd, strange (বিপরীত কর্ম) ; (phys.) inverted; (phys. & math.) reciprocal; (geom.) converse. **বিপরীত করণী** (alg.) conjugate surd. **বিপরীত ক্রিয়া** (alg.) an invertendo. **বিপরীত প্রতিজ্ঞা** (geom.) a converse proposition. **বিপরীত প্রতিবিম্ব** (phys.) an inverted image. **বিপরীত শব্দ** opposite word, antonym. **বিপরীত শ্রেণি** (alg.) a harmonic series. **~কারী** *a.* hostile, inimical; counteracting; disobeying. **~ভাবে** *adv.* in reverse order; in the opposite manner.

বিপরীতার্থক *a.* opposite in meaning. **বিপরীতার্থক শব্দ** *n.* a word opposite in meaning, an opposite word, an antonym.

বিপর্যয়, (obs.) **বিপর্যায়** *n.* topsy-turvy; disorder; an upheaval; an upset; a disaster; a reverse; destruction; a rout; inversion (ক্রম-বিপর্যয় = inversion of order); a violent quarrel or incident. **বিপর্যয় ঘটানো** *v.* to cause an upheaval or upset or disaster or rout or inversion; to cause serious disruption. **বিপর্যয় কাণ্ড** a monstrous incident or affair.

বিপর্যস্ত *a.* topsy-turvy, topsy-turvied; disorderly; thrown into confusion; upset; destroyed; routed; inverted; utterly embarrassed. **বিপর্যস্ত করা** *v.* to topsy-turvy; to put into disorder, to disorder; to throw into confusion; to upset; to disrupt; to convulse; to destroy; to rout; to invert; to embarrass utterly.

বিপর্যাস *n.* (gr.) an inversion, reversal of the order.

বিপল *n.* a measure of time (= ১/৬০ পল = ২/৫ second).

বিপাক *n.* a bad or ugly consequence (কর্মবিপাক) ; a trouble, a danger (দৈববিপাক) ; digestion; (bio.) metabolism. **বিপাকীয়** *a.* metabolic. **বিপাকে পড়া** *v.* to fall or run into a trouble or danger, to be in a predicament. **বিপাকে ফেলা** *v.* to throw or put somebody into trouble or danger, to cause trouble or danger; to put someone into a scrape.

বিপিতা *n.* a step-father.

বিপিন *n.* a forest; a grove. **~বিহারী** *a.* frequenting groves for pleasure. □ *n.* Krishna (কৃষ্ণ).

বিপুল *a.* huge (বিপুলকায়) ; extensive, vast (বিপুল সমুদ্র) ; great in number or amount or degree (বিপুল সংখ্যা বা রাশি বা সম্পত্তি) ; very deep or great ; extremely severe; magnanimous (বিপুল হৃদয়). *fem.* **বিপুলা** । **বিপুলতা** *n.* hugeness; extensiveness; vastness; greatness in number or amount or degree; great depth; extreme severity; magnanimity.

বিপ্র *n.* a Brahman.

বিপ্রকর্ষ *n.* (gr.) anaptyxis, vowel insertion.

বিপ্রকর্ষণ *n.* driving away to a remote place; repelling, repulsion.

বিপ্রতীপ *a.* vertically opposite. **বিপ্রতীপ কোণ** (geom.) a vertically opposite angle.

বিপ্রযুক্ত *a.* separated, severed, detached, disunited, disjointed.

বিপ্রলব্ধ *a.* disappointed; deceived. **বিপ্রলব্ধা** *a. fem.* of **বিপ্রলব্ধ** । □ *n.* (rhet.) a lady-love who goes to a secret tryst but is disappointed by the absence of her lover.

বিপ্রলম্ভ *n.* disappointment; deception; quarrel; wrangling; failure of union or estrangement of lovers esp. at a tryst.

বিপ্লব *n.* a radical and very quick change, a revolution; a revolt, a rebellion, an insurrection; an upheaval, an uprising; a terrible disturbance. **অন্তর্বিপ্লব** *n.* an internal strife; a civil war. **প্রতিবিপ্লব** *n.* a counter-revolution. **বিপ্লব ঘটানো** *v.* to cause or bring about a revolution; to revolutionize (বিজ্ঞানজগতে বিপ্লব ঘটানো). **~পন্থী** *a.* revolutionary. □ *n.* a revolutionary. **~বাদ** *n.* revolutionism. **~বাদী** *a.* revolutionary. □ *n.* a revolutionist. **বিপ্লবাত্মক** *a.* revolutionary. **বিপ্লবী** *a.* revolutionary. □ *n.* a revolutionary, a revolutionist.

বিপ্লুত *a.* upset, thrown into confusion; raided, routed; troubled; bewildered, overwhelmed (ভয়বিপ্লুত) ; streaming with (অশ্রুবিপ্লুত).

বিফল *a.* fruitless, unsuccessful, vain, futile, abortive, unavailing, inefficacious, ineffective; useless. **বিফল করা** *v.* to baffle, to foil, to frustrate. **বিফল হওয়া** *v.* to abort, to be of no avail; to be foiled; to become unsuccessful, to fail. **বিফলতা** *n.* failure, futility, fruitlessness; uselessness. **~প্রযত্ন** *a.* failed in one's attempt, baffled. **বিফলীকরণ** *n.* baffling or foiling. **বিফলীকৃত** *a.* baffled, foiled. **বিফলীভূত** *a.* baffled, foiled, frustrated. **বিফলে** *adv.* in vain; in case of failure.

বিবক্ষা *n.* desire for saying, intended import.

বিবক্ষিত *a.* desired to be said.

বিবক্ষু *a.* desirous of saying.

বিবৎসা *a. fem.* (of a cow) bereaved of or separated from one's calf.

বিবদমান *a.* engaged in a quarrel, contending.

বিবমিষা *n.* inclination to vomit; nausea.

বিবর *n.* a hole, a cave; a cavity (মুখবিবর) ; a crevice.

বিবরণ *n.* a description; a statement, an account; recounting, narration; a narrative. **বিবরণ দেওয়া** *v.* to give an account of. **বিবরণী** *n.* a written report, an account.

বিবরা *v.* (poet.) to narrate or relate, to recount at length.

বিবর্জন *n.* abandonment, renunciation, rejection; quitting.

বিবর্জিত *a.* completely abandoned or rejected; renounced. *fem.* **বিবর্জিতা** ।

বিবর্ণ *a.* discoloured; pale; wan; glum. *fem.* **বিবর্ণা** । **~তা** *n.* discoloration; paleness; wanness; glumness.

বিবর্ত *n.* rotation, revolution; change; transformation; a changed or developed state; presence or existence in a particular manner; (phil.) illusory existence; illusion, *maya*. **বিবর্তন** *n.* rotation, revolution; act of moving back, return; change, transformation; evolution. **বিবর্তনবাদ** *n.* the theory of evolution. **~বাদ** *n.* (phil.) the doctrine of illusion or *maya*. **বিবর্তিত** *a.* rotated, revolved; moved back, returned; changed, transformed.

বিবর্ধক *a.* magnifying; amplifying (ধ্বনি-বিবর্ধক যন্ত্র = an amplifier). **বিবর্ধক কাচ** a magnifying lens.

বিবর্ধন *n.* thorough development, evolution; thorough enlargement or augmentation; (phys.) magnification; amplification.

বিবর্ধিত *a.* thoroughly developed or enlarged or augmented (phys.); magnified; amplified. **বিবর্ধিত করা** *v.* to develop or enlarge or augment thoroughly; to magnify; to amplify.

বিবশ *a.* benumbed; stupefied or overwhelmed; fatigued; utterly helpless; inconsolable; divested of selfcontrol, beside oneself with; (ori.) beyond control. *fem.* **বিবশা** । **~তা** *n.* numbness; stupefaction, insensateness.

বিবসন, বিবস্ত্র *a.* unclothed, undressed, naked. *fem.* **বিবসনা, বিবস্ত্রা** ।

বিবস্বান *n.* the sun or the sungod (cp. Sol.)

বিবাগী *a.* indifferent to worldly interests or pleasure; stoical; one who has renounced domestic ties or has left one's home for good. **বিবাগী হওয়া** *v.* to renounce worldly pleasures or interests; to go out into the world by renouncing worldy ties.

বিবাচক *n.* censor. **বিবাচক-পর্ষদ** *n.* board of censors. **বিবাচন** *n.* censorship.

বিবাদ *n.* a quarrel, a brawl; altercation; a dispute; a conflict; strife, hostility; a fight; an action at law, litigation; a breach of friendly relation. **বিবাদ করা** *v.* to quarrel, to brawl; to altercate; to dispute; to fight; to fight at law; to sever friendly relation. **~প্রিয়** *a.* quarrelsome; factious; litigious. **~বিসংবাদ** *n.* quarrels or brawls; disputes. **~সূচি** *n.* cause list. **বিবাদী** *a.* concerning a quarrel or dispute; under dispute (বিবাদী সম্পত্তি) ; contending; contesting; litigant; opposing, hostile. □ *n.* a contestant; a litigant; an opponent; the opposite party; the defendant (as opposed to the plaintiff); a note opposing the principal note of a musical mode. *fem.* **বিবাদিনী** (not in the musical sense).

বিবাহ *n.* marriage, wedding, bridal, nuptials. **বিবাহ করা** *v.* to marry, to wed. **বিবাহ দেওয়া** *v.* to marry, to give in marriage (to), to wed. **~বিচ্ছেদ** *n.* the legal dissolution of marriage, divorce. **বিবাহবিচ্ছেদ করা** *v.* to dissolve a marriage; to divorce. **~বিচ্ছেদকারী** *n.* a divorcee. **~ভোজ** *n.* a marriage feast, a bridal. **~যোগ্য** *a.* marriageable. *fem.* **~যোগ্যা** । **~সভা** *n.* the venue of a wedding ceremony. **বিবাহার্থী** *a.* willing or ready to marry. **বিবাহিত** *a.* married. *fem.* **বিবাহিতা** । **বিবাহোৎসব** *n.* a wedding ceremony and festivity, nuptials.

বিবি *n. fem.* a Musalman or European lady; (Mus.) a wife; a foppish and ease-loving woman; (of playing-cards) the queen. □ *a. fem.* foppish and ease-loving (বিবি বউ).

বিবিক্ত *a.* detached; isolated; secluded; alone; lonely, solitary; auspicious.

বিবিজান *n. fem.* (Mus.) a term of endearment to address one's wife; a European lady or a foppish and ease-loving woman.

বিবিধ *a.* of many and different kinds, sundry, diverse, various; miscellaneous. **~পত্রী** *a.* (bot.) heterophily.

বিবিয়ানা *n.* the style of living in ease and foppishness (as of a European lady); adoption of this style by a non-European woman.

বিবুধ *n.* a learned man; a deity.

বিবৃত *a.* stated; narrated; explained; revealed; expanded. **বিবৃত করা** *v.* to state; to narrate, to relate; to explain; to reveal; to expand. **বিবৃতি** *n.* a statement; narration; explanation; exposition; revelation; expansion. **বিবৃতি দেওয়া** to make a statement.

বিবৃত্ত *a.* turned about, revolved; returned.

বিবেক *n.* conscience; judgment, discretion; knowledge about reality, spiritual or metaphysical knowledge. **~চালিত, ~তাড়িত** *a.* impelled or goaded by conscience. **~দংশন** *n.* the sting of conscience. **~পীড়িত** *a.* conscience-smitten. **~বুদ্ধি** *n.* conscientiousness; (loos.) conscience; (loos.) judgment, discretion. **~বুদ্ধিসম্পন্ন** *a.* conscientious. **~শূন্য, ~হীন** *a.* lacking in conscience or conscientiousness; unscrupulous; devoid of judgment or discretionary power. **বিবেকী** *a.* conscientious.

বিবেচক *a.* thoughtful; discreet; judicious, prudent; considerate.

বিবেচনা *n.* deliberation; discretion; judiciousness, prudence; considerateness; thoughtful opinion (আমার বিবেচনায় = in my opinion, to my mind, according to me). **বিবেচনা করা** *v.* to consider; to deliberate; to judge; to think. **বিবেচনাধীন** *a.* under consideration. **~শক্তি** *n.* power of deliberation; discretion; power of judgment. **বিবেচনা-সাপেক্ষ** *a.* subject to consideration, under consideration.

বিবেচনীয় same as **বিবেচ্য**।

বিবেচিত *a.* deliberated; considered; judged; thought.

বিবেচ্য *a.* that which is to be considered or judged; worthy of consideration; under consideration.

বিব্রত *a.* embarrassed; encumbered. **বিব্রত করা** *v.* to embarrass; to encumber.

বিভক্ত *a.* divided; parted; partitioned; apportioned. **বিভক্ত করা** *v.* to divide; to part; to partition; to apportion.

বিভক্তি *n.* (gr.) a case-ending (also = **শব্দবিভক্তি**) or a verb-inflection. (usu. **ক্রিয়াবিভক্তি**).

বিভঙ্গ *n.* method; plan or design or draft outline of a work.

বিভজনীয় same as **বিভাজ্য**।

বিভজ্যমান *a.* that which is being divided or partitioned or apportioned.

বিভব *n.* wealth, riches, property; power; greatness; magnanimity; godhead, divinity; godliness; sanctifying grace, unction. **~শালী** *a.* wealthy, rich; powerful; great; magnanimous; unctuous. *fem.* **~শালিনী**।

বিভা *n.* glow; lustre; shine; a ray, a beam; light; beauty.

বিভাকর *n.* the sun.

বিভাগ *n.* division; partition : apportionment; distribution; a division (of a country etc.); a part, a portion, a section; department (বিচারবিভাগ). **বিভাগ করা** *v.* to divide; to partition; to apportion; to distribute. **বিভাগী** *a.* fissile. **বিভাগী-ছত্রাক** *n.* a fission fungus. **বিভাগী-শৈবাল** *n.* a fission alga. **বিভাগীয়** *a.* divisional, sectional; departmental (**বিভাগীয় কর্তা** = the departmental head, **বিভাগীয় বিপণি** = a departmental store).

বিভাজক *a.* dividing (বিভাজক গিরিশ্রেণি) ; parting; partitioning; apportioning; distributing. □ *n.* one who divides, a divider; (math.) a divisor.

বিভাজন *n.* a division; parting; partition; apportionment; distribution; (mech.) resolution of velocity. **পরমাণু-বিভাজন** *n.* splitting of atoms. **বিভাজিত** *a.* divided; separated.

বিভাজিকা *fem.* of **বিভাজক**।

বিভাজ্য *a.* to be divided or partitioned or apportioned or distributed, dividable; (math.) divisible. □ *n.* (math.) a dividend. **~তা** *n.* state of being dividable; (math.) divisibility.

বিভাব *n.* (rhet.) that element in the reading matter, which excites magnanimity, sorrow, surprise, resentment, terror, love, mirth, disgust or quietism; an excitant or determinant; a person in whom any of the aforesaid emotions resides.

বিভাবনা *n.* deliberation; perception; (rhet.) an effect without cause.

বিভাবরী *n.* the night.

বিভাবসু *n.* the sun.

বিভাবিত *a.* deliberated, felt, perceived; absorbed in a feeling ('গোরাভাবে বিভাবিত').

বিভাষা *n.* a foreign language; an alternative; a dialect.

বিভাস *n.* an Indian musical mode.

বিভাসিত *a.* lighted; illuminated; revealed.

বিভিন্ন *a.* of different kinds; diverse, various; of a different kind, different (বিভিন্ন লোকের). **বিভিন্ন পথে যাওয়া** *v.* to go severally. **~তা** *n.* diversity, variety; difference. **বিভিন্নার্থ** *n.* various or different meanings. **বিভিন্নার্থক** *a.* having or bearing various meanings.

বিভীতক, বিভীতকী *n.* the beleric myrobalan.

বিভীষণ *a.* extremely terrible. □ *n.* a character of the Ramayana; (fig.) a traitor to one's own family or country, a quisling, a fish-columnist. **বিভীষণ-বাহিনী** *n.* the fifth column.

বিভীষিকা *n.* intimidation; threat; terrible fear or panic; horror; a frightful sight (esp. a phantasmal one); a frightful hallucination. **~ময়** *a.* full of frightful sights or hallucinations; horrible.

বিভু *n.* God. **~ত্ব** *n.* Godhead. **~প্রেম** *n.* devotion to God.

বিভুঁই *n.* a foreign land (বিদেশ-বিভুঁই).

বিভূতি *n.* Godhead; godhead, divinity; special powers of Shiva (শিব) ; sanctifying grace, unction; prosperity; riches, wealth; ashes. **~ভূষণ** *n.* one who smears one's body with ashes; Shiva (শিব).

বিভূষণ *n.* an ornament; beauty; grace. □ *a.* unornamented; unadorned. *fem. a.* বিভূষণা।

বিভূষিত *a.* ornamented; adorned; embellished. *fem.* **বিভূষিতা**।

বিভেদ *n.* difference; differentiation; splitting up into factions, disintegration; separation, division. **বিভেদ করা** *v.* to differentiate. **বিভেদ সৃষ্টি করা** *v.* to create dissension or disunity. **~পন্থা** *n.* dissension; separatism; factionalism. see also **বিচ্ছিন্নতাবাদ**। **~মূলক** *a.* disintegrating; separatist. **বিভেদ সৃষ্টিকারী** *a.* one who or that which creates dissension or separatism or factionalism or disintegration. **কলাবিভেদ** *n.* (bot.) differentiation of tissues.

বিভেদক *a.* that which divides; that which creates a difference or dissension; that which separates; divisive; separating. □ *n.* a divisor; that which divides; a separator.

বিভোর, বিভোল same as **বিহ্বল**।

বিভ্রম *n.* illusion; delusion; doubt; a blunder, an error; folly or distraction caused by erotism; sport or enjoyment (esp. amorous).

বিভ্রাট *n.* a crisis, a danger; a difficulty, a trouble; turmoil, disorder, confusion; a mishap.

বিভ্রান্ত *a.* stricken with illusion or delusion; distracted; nonplussed; doubting, doubtful; blundering; stricken with erotic folly or distraction. **বিভ্রান্ত করা** *v.* to blur with illusion; to delude; to distract; to nonplus; to fill with doubt; to cause to blunder; to strike with erotic folly or distraction. **বিভ্রান্তি** *n.* illusion; confusion; delusion; distraction; nonplus; doubt; a blunder, an error; erotic folly or distraction. **বিভ্রান্তিকর** *a.* confusing; distracting; illusive.

বিম *n.* (in house-building etc.) a beam.

বিমথিত *a.* churned; oppressed; subdued.

বিমনা *a.* absent-minded; inattentive; worried; morose.

বিমর্দ, বিমর্দন *n.* pressing; grinding; rubbing; crushing; destroying or killing; routing. **বিমর্দন করা** *v.* to press; to grind; to rub; to crush, to destroy, to kill; to rout. **বিমর্দিত** *a.* pressed; ground; rubbed; crushed, destroyed, killed; routed.

বিমর্শ, বিমর্শন *n.* consideration, deliberation, discussion.

বিমর্ষ *n.* (rare) discontent. □ *a.* sad, morose, glum; melancholy. **~তা** *n.* sadness, moroseness, glumness; melancholy. **~ণ** *n.* displeasure; sadness.

বিমল *a.* clean, clear; pellucid; transparent; pure; holy; unblemished, immaculate. *fem.* **বিমলা**। **~চরিত্র** *a.* having an immaculate character. **~চিত্ত, ~হৃদয়** *a.* pure-hearted; holy-hearted. **বিমলাত্মা** *a.* pure-souled. **বিমলানন্দ** *n.* immaculate or unadulterated joy or delight.

বিমা *n.* insurance. **বিমা করা** *v.* to insure. **বিমার কিস্তি** an insurance premium. **বিমার**

দালাল an insurance agent. অগ্নিবিমা *n.* fire-insurance. জাহাজি বিমা marine insurance. জীবনবিমা *n.* life insurance. ~কারী *n.* the insured (বিমাকারী ব্যক্তি) or the insurer (বিমা প্রতিষ্ঠান). ~পত্র *n.* an insurance policy.

বিমাতা *n.* a step-mother.

বিমাতৃসুলভ *a.* like a step-mother; stepmotherly; (fig.) neglectful.

বিমান *n.* a chariot or other vehicle capable of moving in the air; an aircraft, an aeroplane; a seven-storied building; (loos.) the sky. **~আক্রমণ** *n.* an air raid. **~ঘাঁটি** *n.* an aerodrome. **~চলন** *n.* aviation. **~চালক** *n.* a pilot, an aviator. **~চারী** *a.* moving in the sky or air; aerial, ethereal; aviating. □ *n.* one capable of moving in the sky or air; an aerial or ethereal being; an aviator. *fem.* **~চারিণী**। **বিমান ডাক** *n.* air-mail. **~ধ্বংসী** *a.* anti-aircraft. **~পথ** *n.* airway. **~পরিবহণ** *n.* air-transport. **~বন্দর** *n.* an airport. **~বাহিনী** *n.* the Air Force. **~বিদ্যা** *n.* aeronautics. **~যুদ্ধ** *n.* an aerial battle. **বিমানাঙ্গন** *n.* an airfield.

বিমিশ্র *a.* mixed; adulterated; (bot.) polygamous. **বিমিশ্র প্রক্রিয়া** (arith.) alligation.

বিমুক্ত *a.* completely freed or liberated; released; relieved or cured; one who has attained salvation or beatitude; untied, loosened (বিমুক্ত কেশ) ; disengaged, discharged (বিমুক্ত শর).

বিমুখ *a.* averse, disinclined, disinterested, apathetic (বিষয়বিমুখ, কর্মবিমুখ) ; turned away from; adverse, unfavourable (ভাগ্য বিমুখ) ; displeased (দেবতা বিমুখ). **বিমুখ করা** *v.* to make one averse or disinclined or disinterested or apathetic (to), to cause to turn away (from); to make one adverse or unfavourable; to displease; to refuse or disappoint; to avert, to ward off (an attack etc.). **~তা** *n.* aversion, disinclination, lack of interest, apathy, adverseness, hostility; displeasure; disappointment.

বিমুগ্ধ *a.* thoroughly fascinated or infatuated or enamoured (of) or enchanted; utterly bewildered or confounded. *fem.* **বিমুগ্ধা**। **~তা** *n.* complete fascination or infatuation or enchantment; utter bewilderment.

বিমূঢ় *a.* incapable of discriminating; utterly stupid or ignorant; thoroughly fascinated or infatuated or bewitched; bewildered, confounded, stupefied. **~তা** *n.* incapability of discriminating; utter stupidity or ignorance; complete fascination or infatuation or bewitchment; bewilderment, confusion, stupefaction.

বিমূর্ত *a.* formless, unbodied; abstract (বিমূর্ত ভাব).

বিমৃশ্যকারী *a.* given to acting after careful deliberation; prudently or discreetly acting. **বিমৃশ্যকারিতা** *n.* practice of acting after careful deliberation; practice of acting prudently or discreetly.

বিমোচন *n.* act of letting loose; release; liberation, deliverance; relieving, relief (সংকট বিমোচন) ; dispelling or removal or cure (দুঃখবিমোচন, ব্যাধিবিমোচন) ; discharge (শরবিমোচন).

বিমোচিত *a.* let loose; released, freed; liberated, delivered; relieved; dispelled, removed or cured; discharged.

বিমোহ *n.* inertia; lethargy; stupid infatuation. **~ন** *n.* act of fascinating or infatuating. □ *a.* fascinating, infatuating. **বিমোহিত** *a.* fascinated, infatuated. **বিমোহিত করা** *v.* to fascinate, to infatuate, to bewitch.

বিম্ব[১] *n.* a bubble (অম্বু-বিম্ব) ; a reflection, a shadow; (geom.) an image; an object reflected; the disc or halo of the sun, moon and other planets. **বিম্বিত** *a.* reflected.

বিম্ব[২] *n.* a fruit of a pleasant red colour. **বিম্বাধর, বিম্বোষ্ঠ, বিম্বৌষ্ঠ** *n.* a lip as beautifully red as the bimba (বিম্ব) fruit. □ *a.* having such lips. *fem. a* **বিম্বাধরা, বিম্বোষ্ঠা, বিম্বৌষ্ঠী**।

বিযুক্ত, বিযুত *a.* detached, disjointed, separated, disconnected; (math.) subtracted. □ *prep.* minus. **বিযুক্ত করা** *v.* to detach, to disjoin, to separate, to disconnect.

বিয়ন্ত *a.* recently delivered of a child or

(in case of a beast) of a young (বিয়ন্ত বউ, বিয়ন্ত গাভি).

বিয়া obs. & dial. form of **বিবাহ**।

বিয়াকুল poet. corrup. of **ব্যাকুল**।

বিয়ানো *v.* to bring forth (a child or a young one), to give birth to. □ *n.* act or an instance of bringing forth.

বিয়াল্লিশ *n.* & *a.* forty-two.

বিয়ে coll. form of **বিবাহ**। **তার বিয়ের ফুল ফুটেছে** he or she is soon to get married. **~পাগলা** *a.* yearning or longing madly for marriage.

বিয়েন coll. corrup. of **বিয়ানো** (*n.*).

বিয়োগ *n.* separation or estrangement (বন্ধুবিয়োগ) ; death or bereavement (পিতৃবিয়োগ) ; absence or want; (math.) subtraction. **বিয়োগ করা** *v.* (math.) to subtract. **~ফল** *n.* (math.) the result of subtraction. difference. **~বিধুর** *a.* suffering from or afflicted with the pangs of separation or estrangement or bereavement. *fem.* **~বিধুরা**। **~ব্যথা** *n.* pain or pang of separation or estrangement or bereavement. **বিয়োগান্ত** *a.* ending unhappily or in separation of lovers, tragic (**বিয়োগান্ত নাটক** = a tragedy); ending in death, disaster, estrangement etc. (বিয়োগান্ত ব্যাপার).

বিয়োজক *n.* (gr.) a disjunctive.

বিয়োজন *n.* detachment, disjoining, disconnection; separation.

বিয়োজিত *a.* detached, disjointed, disconnected; separated.

বিরক্ত *a.* having no attachment (to); disinterested, averse; displeased, irritated, vexed, chagrined, disgusted. **বিরক্ত করা** *v.* to displease, to irritate, to vex, to chagrin, to disgust. **বিরক্তি** *n.* lack of attachment, displeasure, irritation, vexation, chagrin, disgust. **বিরক্তিকর, বিরক্তিজনক** *a.* irritating, vexatious, disgusting; bothersome.

বিরচন *n.* writing or composing; building, construction; forming or making (কবরীবিরচন).

বিরচিত *a.* written, composed; built, constructed; formed, made.

বিরজা *n.* (Vaishnava myth.) a river which the souls of the dead have to cross in order to reach Baikuntha (বৈকুণ্ঠ) the blissful abode of Vishnu (বিষ্ণু). **~ধাম** *n.* Puri in Orissa.

বিরত *a.* discontinued; dissuaded; (loos.) prevented; desisting or abstaining from (ভোগবিরত). *fem.* **বিরতা**। **বিরত করা** *v.* to cause to leave off, to dissuade; (loos.) to prevent; to cause to abstain from. **বিরত হওয়া** *v.* to desist (from); to discontinue, to leave off; to abstain (from). **বিরতি** *n.* desistance; abstinence; cessation; termination; pause; recess; interval.

বিরল *a.* sparse, thinly scattered or placed (বিরলদন্ত) ; very thinly frequented or inhabited by (জনবিরল) ; rare (বিরল ঘটনা). □ *n.* a secluded or lonely place, solitude. **বিরলকেশ** *a.* thin-haired; bald-headed, almost without hair on one's head. **~তা** *n.* sparseness : rareness, rarity. **~বসতি** *a.* thinly populated. **বিরলে** *adv.* in seclusion.

বিরস *a.* having no or little juice; sapless, dry; dull, insipid; dispirited, displeased, sullen, glum (বিরস বদন). **~তা** *n.* want of juice or sap; dullness, insipidity, dispiritedness, displeasure, sullenness, glumness. **বিরস বদন** *n.* a glum face; a gloomy face.

বিরহ *n.* absence or want; separation or estrangement esp. from one's lover (বন্ধুবিরহ). **বিরহিণী** *fem.* of **বিরহী**। **বিরহিত** *a.* devoid or destitute of (সুখবিরহিত) ; wanting in (কর্মবিরহিত) ; separated or estranged from; disjointed, detached; freed from (বন্ধনবিরহিত). *fem.* **বিরহিতা**। **বিরহী** *a.* separated or estranged from one's lover. **বিরহে** *adv.* in the absence of, away from (প্রিয়ার বিরহে).

বিরাগ *n.* want of attachment; lack of interest; aversion; displeasure; chagrin. **~ভাজন** *n.* an object of displeasure. □ *a.* causing displeasure or chagrin. **বিরাগভাজন হওয়া** *v.* to incur displeasure. **বিরাগী** *a.* having no attachment (to); disinterested; averse; displeased, chagrined. *fem.* **বিরাগিনী**।

বিরাজ *n.* graceful or conspicuous presence or existence. বিরাজ **করা,** (poet.)

বিরাজা *v.* to exist or be present gracefully or conspicuously; to exist, to be present. **~মান, বিরাজিত** *a.* gracefully or conspicuously existent or present; existent or present. *fem.* **~মানা, বিরাজিতা**।

বিরাট *n.* the Omnipresent, God. □ *a.* very great or vast or huge. **~ত্ব** *n.* extreme greatness or vastness or hugeness.

বিরানব্বই, (coll.) **বিরানব্বুই** *n.* & *a.* ninety-two.

বিরাম *n.* cessation; pause; intermission; interval; respite, leisure, rest. **~চিহ্ন** *n.* (gr.) a punctuation mark. **~হীন** *a.* ceaseless, non-stop, incessant : unending.

বিরাশি *n.* & *a.* eighty-two.

বিরিঞ্চি *n.* Brahma (ব্রহ্মা).

বিরিয়ানি *n.* a pilau-like preparation.

বিরুদ্ধ *a.* adverse, unfavourable ; hostile, inimical; antipathetic; obverse; contradictory; contrary; opposed. **~তা** *n.* adverseness, unfavourableness; hostility, enmity; antipathy; obverseness; contradiction; contrariety; opposition. **বিরুদ্ধ তড়িচ্চালক বল** (phys.) back electromotive force. **~বাদিতা** *n.* hostility; opposition; antipathy. **~বাদী** *a.* opposed; of the opposite side or camp. **বিরুদ্ধ-সমালোচনা** *n.* animadversion; unfavourable criticism. **বিরুদ্ধ সমালোচনা করা** *v.* to animadvert; to censure; to criticize unfavourably. **বিরুদ্ধাচার** *n.* a practice in opposition to usage; opposition. **বিরুদ্ধাচরণ** *n.* opposition; hostility. **বিরুদ্ধাচরণ করা** *v.* to oppose; to act in hostility, to be hostile (to); to go against. **বিরুদ্ধাচারী** *a.* indulging in practices in opposition to usage; opposing; hostile. *fem.* **বিরুদ্ধাচারিণী**। **বিরুদ্ধে** *adv.* against; in opposition to; in the teeth of.

বিরূপ *a.* ugly-looking, ugly; adverse, unfavourable; displeased. **বিরূপ প্রণালী** (log.) the method of difference. **~তা** *n.* ugliness; adverseness, disfavour; displeasure.

বিরূপাক্ষ *n.* one with eyes beyond the measure of beauty; Shiva (শিব).

বিরেচক *a.* aperient, aperitive, purgative. □ *n.* a purgative.

বিরেচন *n.* evacuation of the intestines, purgation.

বিরোচন *n.* the sun; the sun-god; a mythological demon or titan.

বিরোধ *n.* enmity, hostility; a quarrel, a dispute, a contention, a difference; a war; strife; disagreement; disharmony; mutual opposition or contradiction; antipathy; incongruity, dissimilarity. **বিরোধ করা** *v.* to quarrel; to oppose. **~মূলক** *a.* opposing; antagonistic. **বিরোধাভাস** *n.* (rhet.) a figure of speech in which things apparently contradictory exist side by side (cp. oxymoron, epigram). **বিরোধিতা** *n.* hostility, enmity; rivalry; opposition; antagonism; disagreement; antipathy. **বিরোধী** *a.* hostile, inimical; contending; rival; opposing; opponent; antagonistic; disagreeing; adverse. **বিরোধী পক্ষ** an opposite or hostile or rival party; an opponent; (in legislature) the opposition.

বিল[1] *n.* a hole, a pore; a cavity; a cave; a fen; a marsh.

বিল[2] *n.* a bill. **বিল করা** *v.* to make out a bill. **বিল পাস করা** *v.* to pass a bill. **বিল মেটানো** *v.* to pay off a bill, to foot the bill.

বিলকুল *adv.* entirely, wholly: unreservedly, outright; thoroughly, completely; altogether.

বিলক্ষণ *a.* (obs.) different; (rare) uncommon, unusual; great, large, enormous (বিলক্ষণ ভিড়) ; much; considerable. □ *adv.* thoroughly (বিলক্ষণ জানি) ; to a great extent (বিলক্ষণ খাওয়া, বিলক্ষণ বড়). □ *int.* excellent, fine, all right, surely, of course.

বিলপন *n.* lamentation, wailing.

বিলপমান *a.* engaged in lamentation, lamenting, wailing, bewailing.

বিলপা poet. form of **বিলাপ করা**।

বিলম্ব *n.* delay; lateness; procrastination; lingering. **বিলম্ব করা** *v.* to delay; to be late; to procrastinate; to linger, to tarry. **বিলম্ব করানো** *v.* to delay; to retard. **বিলম্বন** *n.* delaying; lingering; procrastination; retardation; act of hanging, suspension. **~শুল্ক** *n.* demurrage. **বিলম্বিত** *a.* delayed; late; retarded; hanging, suspended. **বিলম্বিত লয়** (Ind. mus.) slow measure (as opp. to **দ্রুতলয়** = fast measure). **বিলম্বী** *a.* delaying; making late; lingering; procrastinating; hanging, suspending. **বিলম্বে** *adv.* late. **অতি বিলম্বে** very late, after the fair.

বিলয় *n.* dissolution; extinction. **~বিন্দু** *n.* (phys.) a vanishing point.

বিলসা *v.* (poet.) to enjoy, to sport, to exist or be present gracefully ('দ্যুলোকে ভূলোকে বিলসিছ').

বিলসিত *a.* enjoyed; sported; dallied; beautified; adorned.

বিলাত[1] *n.* (of bills etc.) non-realization. **~-বাকি** *n.* outstanding or unrealized dues or bills, arrears.

বিলাত[2] *n.* England or Europe and also America; (loos.) a western country overseas. **~ফেরত, ~ফেরতা** *a.* returned from England or Europe, England-returned, Europe-returned, foreign-returned.

বিলাতি *a.* of or exported from England or Europe or a foreign country; English; European; foreign. **বিলাতি আমড়া** the hog-plum. **বিলাতি কাপড়** English or foreign textile materials or piecegoods. **বিলাতি কুমড়ো** a sweetish variety of pumpkin. **বিলাতি বেগুন** the tomato, the love-apple. **~য়ানা** (dero.) adoption or imitation of English or European style in daily life and conduct, anglomania, (journ.) Englishness, Europeanism.

বিলানো *v.* to give away or distribute (esp. in charity).

বিলাপ *n.* lament; lamentation, wailing. **বিলাপ করা,** (poet.) **বিলাপা** *v.* to lament, to wail or bewail. **বিলাপী** *a.* lamenting, wailing or bewailing. *fem.* **বিলাপিনী** ।

বিলাস *n.* enjoyment of milk and honey; luxury, daintiness and foppery; sport, recreation, pastime; amorous sport, dalliance; wantonness; an assumed artistic gesture or pose. **~কানন** *n.* a pleasure-garden. **~কুঞ্জ** *n.* a pleasure-grove. **~তরণী** *n.* a pleasure-boat. **~দ্রব্য, ~সামগ্রী** *n.* luxury goods. **~পরায়ণ, ~প্রিয়** same as **বিলাসী** । **~ব্যসন** *n.* luxury or daintiness; luxurious life. **~ভবন** *n.* a pleasure-house; a house for wanton frolics. **~মত্ত** *a.* lost in luxury or wanton frolics. **বিলাসিতা** *n.* enjoyment of milk and honey, luxury; daintiness and foppishness; indulgence in unnecessary or wasteful pleasure. **বিলাসী** *a.* given to enjoying milk and honey, luxurious; dainty and foppish; fond of sport or pastime; given to amorous sports or dalliance; wanton, sensual. *fem.* **বিলাসিনী** ।

বিলি *n.* distribution (টাকা বিলি) ; allotment, assignment (কাজ বিলি) ; act of handing over under specific terms and conditions, settlement (জমি বিলি) ; delivery (চিঠি বিলি). **বিলি করা** *v.* to distribute; to allot; to settle (land); to deliver.

বিলিতি, বিলেত coll. variants of **বিলাতি** and **বিলাত** respectively.

বিলিবন্দোবস্ত, বিলিব্যবস্থা, (coll.) **বিলিবন্দেজ** *n.* orderly arrangement and distribution or allotment.

বিলীন *a.* dissolved; faded away or vanished; gone to extinction; absorbed; destroyed.

বিলীয়মান *a.* in the state of being dissolved; evanescent, fading away, vanishing; in the state of being absorbed or destroyed.

বিলুণ্ঠিত *a.* rolling about, wallowing; plundered or robbed. *fem.* **বিলুণ্ঠিতা** । **বিলুণ্ঠিত হওয়া** *v.* to roll about, to wallow; to be plundered or robbed.

বিলুপ্ত *a.* faded away, vanished; extinct; destroyed, annihilated; abolished.

বিলেপ, বিলেপন *n.* smearing or anointing or painting; any substance to smear or anoint or paint with; an ointment, a balm, a salve, a paint, a plaster etc. **বিলেপন করা** *v.* to smear or anoint or paint.

বিলোকন *n.* seeing or viewing or looking eagerly or wistfully; observation.

বিলোকিত *a.* eagerly or wistfully seen or viewed; observed.

বিলোচন *n.* seeing or viewing or looking eagerly; the eye; one having ill-shaped or monstrous eyes; Shiva (শিব).

বিলোপ, বিলোপন *n.* extinction; fadeaway; disappearance; destruction or annihilation; death; abolition. **বিলোপ করা,**

বিলোপসাধন করা *v.* to cause to disappear; to destroy or annihilate; to kill; to abolish. **বিলোপ হওয়া, বিলোপপ্রাপ্ত হওয়া** *v.* to go to extinction, to become extinct; to fade away, to disappear; to be destroyed or annihilated; to die; to be abolished.

বিলোম *a.* hostile; inverse. **~কেন্দ্র** *n.* a centre of inversion. **~ক্রিয়া** *n.* inversion. **~বিধি** *n.* rule of inversion. **~ব্যাসার্ধ** *n.* a radius of inversion.

বিলোমাঙ্ক *n.* constant of inversion.

বিলোল *a.* quickly moving (বিলোল কটাক্ষ) ; greedy or wistful (বিলোল দৃষ্টি) ; dishevelled (বিলোল বেশবাস).

বিল্ব *n.* a kind of shell-fruit; the marmelos. **~পত্র** *n.* a leaf of the bel (বেল) tree. **~স্তনী** *n. fem.* having breasts as round and beautiful as a pair of bel (বেল) fruits.

বিল্লি *n. inf.* the cat.

বিশ *n.* & *a.* twenty.

বিশদ *a.* clear; elaborate; detailed (বিশদ বিবরণ) ; elucidated; white; clean. **বিশদ করা** *v.* to clarify; to elucidate. **~ভাবে** *adv.* in detail, elaborately.

বিশল্যকরণী (Ramayana) an all-healing plant, (cp.) the valerian.

বিশাই coll. corrup. of **বিশ্বকর্মা** (see **বিশ্ব**).

বিশাখা *n. fem.* the sixteenth of the twenty-seven stars according to Hindu astronomy.

বিশারদ *a.* learned, erudite; wise; well-versed; skilled, expert.

বিশাল *a.* very large, huge; vast, extensive; magnanimous. **~তা** *n.* hugeness; vastness; magnanimity; expanse. **~হৃদয়** *a.* large-hearted, magnanimous. **বিশালাক্ষ** *a.* large-eyed. **বিশালাক্ষী** *a. fem.* of **বিশালাক্ষ** । □ *n.* Goddess Durga (দুর্গা).

বিশিখ *n.* an arrow, a shaft.

বিশিষ্ট *a.* especial (বিশিষ্ট আসন) ; conspicuous, remarkable (বিশিষ্ট ভদ্রলোক) ; important or distinguished (বিশিষ্ট ব্যক্তি) ; prominent (বিশিষ্ট কবি) ; specific, peculiar, characteristic (বিশিষ্ট লক্ষণ) ; possessing (লেজবিশিষ্ট) ; containing (মগজবিশিষ্ট). *fem.* **বিশিষ্টা** । **~তা** *n.* speciality; conspicuousness or remarkability; importance; distinction; prominence; peculiarity, a characteristic; possession.

বিশীর্ণ *a.* extremely shrivelled or lean and thin or withered, wizened. *fem.* **বিশীর্ণা** । **~তা** *n.* state of being extremely shrivelled or lean and thin or withered or wizened. **~বদন** *a.* wizen-faced.

বিশুদ্ধ *a.* very pure and clean; holy, sacred; perfectly faultless or unblemished, immaculate; unadulterated, genuine, pure (বিশুদ্ধ ঘৃত) ; raw (বিশুদ্ধ কোহল) ; unmixed (বিশুদ্ধ শান্তি) ; refined (বিশুদ্ধ সোনা) ; innocent (বিশুদ্ধ আমোদ) ; correct, accurate (বিশুদ্ধ অঙ্কফল). **বিশুদ্ধ-চরিত্র** *a.* of pure or immaculate character. **~তা** *n.* perfect purity or cleanness; holiness, sacredness; immaculateness; genuineness; purity; state of being unmixed; innocence; correctness, accuracy. **বিশুদ্ধাত্মা** *a.* pure-souled. **বিশুদ্ধি** *n.* same as **বিশুদ্ধতা,** and esp. purification or sanctification.

বিশুষ্ক *a.* very dry; wizened (বিশুষ্ক দৃষ্টি) ; glum, morose (বিশুষ্ক মুখ). **~তা** *n.* extreme dryness; state of being wizened, glumness, moroseness.

বিশৃঙ্খল *a.* disorderly, confused, undisciplined; wayward, wild. **বিশৃঙ্খল করা** *v.* to disorder, to throw into confusion, to make a mess (of). **~তা, বিশৃঙ্খলা** *n.* disorderliness, disorder, confusion; indiscipline; waywardness, wildness.

বিশে *n.* the twentieth day of a month, the twentieth. □ *a.* (of the days of a month) twentieth.

বিশেষ *n.* excess or excellence; difference, distinction, discrimination; a sort, a kind, a type (জীববিশেষ) ; variety or novelty; (phil.) individuality or an individual. □ *a.* superior; different; extraordinary, especial (বিশেষ বাধা, বিশেষ ঘটনা) ; remarkable (বিশেষ উৎসাহ) ; specific (বিশেষ দর) ; peculiar or characteristic (বিশেষ লক্ষণ) ; particular (বিশেষ কাজ) ; (log.) predicating of part of the class denoted by the subject, particular; (phil.) individual. **বিশেষ করা** *v.* to differentiate; to distinguish; to particularize; to specify.

বিশেষজ্ঞ *a.* having especial knowledge, specialized; expert; especially versed (in). □ *n.* a specialist; an expert. **~তা** *n.* expertise; expert knowledge.

বিশেষত *adv.* especially; particularly; chiefly; moreover.

বিশেষণ *n.* attribution; an attribute; a peculiarity or characteristic; (gr.) the adjective. **ক্রিয়া-বিশেষণ** *n.* an adverb. **বিশেষণের বিশেষণ** (gr.) an adverb. **বিশেষণীয়** *a.* attributable; distinguishable; adjectival.

বিশেষত্ব same as **বৈশিষ্ট্য**। **~হীন** *a.* without any speciality or peculiarity; without any distinction; ordinary, commonplace.

বিশেষিত *a.* attributed; specified, distinguished; (gr.) qualified (as by an adjective).

বিশেষোক্তি *n.* (rhet.) a figure of speech in which a cause is mentioned as not producing the usual result (cp. paradox).

বিশেষ্য *n.* (gr.) the noun, the substantive.

বিশোধক *a.* purifying; sanctifying; refining; rectifying, corrective, corrigent; amending.

বিশোধন *n.* purification; sanctification; refinement; cleansing; rectification, correction; amendment. **বিশোধনীয়** same as **বিশোধ্য**।

বিশোধিত *a.* purified; sanctified; refined; cleansed; rectified, corrected; amended.

বিশোধ্য *a.* purifiable; sanctifiable; refinable; cleansable; rectifiable, correctible, corrigible (usu. not incorrigible); amendable.

বিশোষণ *n.* drying up, absorbing, absorption. **বিশোষিত** *a.* absorbed.

বিশ্ব *n.* the world, the earth; the universe. □ *a.* all; entire, whole. **~কর্মা** *n.* (myth.) the heavenly architect (cp. Vulcan). **~কোষ** *n.* an encyclopaedia, a cyclopaedia. **~চরাচর** *n.* the entire universe mobile and immobile. **~জন** *n.* all people of the world; mankind. **~জননী** *n.* the mother of the universe; Goddess Durga (দুর্গা). **~জনীন** *a.* universal; philanthropic. **~জনীনতা** *n.* universality; philanthropy. **~জিৎ** *n.* conqueror of the world. **~নাথ** *n.* God; Shiva (শিব). **~নিখিল** same as **বিশ্বসংসার**। **~নিন্দুক** *a.* (given to) decrying the whole world, decrying everything and everybody in the world; (loos.) censorious; cynical. **~পরিক্রমা** *n.* going or walking round the world, travelling round the world. **~পা, ~পাতা, ~পালক** *n.* the preserver of the world; God. **~পিতা** *n.* the father of the world; God. **~প্রীতি, ~প্রেম** *n.* universal love; philanthropy. **~প্রেমিক** *a.* loving the whole universe; philanthropic. □ *n.* one who loves the whole universe; a philanthropist, a philanthrope. **~বন্দিত** *a.* world famous, universally acclaimed. **~বাসী** *a.* inhabiting the world; cosmopolitan. □ *n.* same as **~জন**। **~বিখ্যাত** *a.* world-famous. **~বিদ্যালয়** *n.* a university. **~বিধাতা** *n.* the creator of the world, God. **~বিমোহন, ~বিমোহী** *a.* charming or bewitching the whole world. *fem.* **~বিমোহিনী**। **~বিশ্রুত** same as **~বিখ্যাত**। **~ব্যাপী** *a.* world-wide. **~ব্রহ্মাণ্ড** *n.* the whole universe. **~ভ্রাতৃত্ব, ~মানবতা** *n.* international brotherhood, internationalism. **~মৈত্রী** *n.* universal or international friendship or amity. **~ম্ভর** *n.* one who sustains the world; God; Narayana (নারায়ণ). **~ম্ভরা** *n. fem.* She who sustains all creatures; Mother Earth; the earth. **~যুদ্ধ** *n.* a world war. **~রূপ** *n.* the body in which the entire universe is reflected or exhibited; one whose form is represented by the entire universe; Narayana (নারায়ণ). **~শান্তি** *n.* world peace. **~সংসার** *n.* the whole universe. **~সংসারে** *adv.* in the whole universe; all over the world. **~সাহিত্য** *n.* the literature of the world, world literature. **~সৃষ্টি** *n.* the creation of the world. **~স্রষ্টা** *n.* the Creator of the world, God.

বিশ্বস্ত *a.* faithful; trusty, trustworthy, reliable, true; bonafide; believing; trusting, trustful, relying; confident. *fem.* **বিশ্বস্তা**। **~তা** *n.* trustworthiness; sincerity, bona fides. **~সূত্রে** *adv.* from a reliable source.

বিশ্বাস *n.* belief, faith; trust, reliance; confidence; a religious faith; a notion.

বিশ্বাস করা *v.* to believe, to put faith in; to trust, to rely (on), to confide in; to have a notion (that), to think. **বিশ্বাস করে বলা** *v.* to confide in. **~ঘাতক, ~ঘাতী** *a.* treacherous; traitorous; betraying. □ *n.* a traitor (*fem.* a traitress); a betrayer. *fem.* **~ঘাতিকা, ~ঘাতিনী** । **~ঘাতকতা** *n.* treachery; betrayal. **বিশ্বাসঘাতকতা করা** *v.* to commit treachery; to betray; to play one false. **বিশ্বাসঘাতকতা করে ধরিয়ে দেওয়া** *v.* to betray. **~পাত্র** *n.* a reliable or trustworthy person, a confidant (*fem.* a confidante). *fem.* **~পাত্রী** । **~ভঙ্গ** *n.* breach of trust; perfidy; treachery. **~ভাজন** *n.* same as **~পাত্র** । □ *a.* trustworthy; reliable. **~যোগ্য** *a.* believable, credible; trustworthy, reliable. **~হন্তা** same as **~ঘাতক** । *fem.* **~হন্ত্রী** ।

বিশ্বাসী same as **বিশ্বস্ত** ।

বিশ্বাস্য *a.* believable, credible; trustworthy, reliable.

বিশ্বেশ্বর *n.* God; Shiva (শিব). *fem.* **বিশ্বেশ্বরী** same as **আদ্যাশক্তি** (see **আদ্যা**).

বিশ্রব্ধ *a.* confidential (বিশ্রব্ধ আলাপ) ; profound (বিশ্রব্ধ জ্ঞান) ; very intimate (বিশ্রব্ধ বন্ধু) ; tranquil; fearless.

বিশ্রম্ভ *n.* a lovers' quarrel; love, amour, trust, confidence; unrestrained enjoyment; free love. **বিশ্রম্ভালাপ** *n.* a lovers' tête-a-tête; a confidential talk, a tête-a tête.

বিশ্রান্ত *a.* refreshed, recreated; one who has had rest; desisted; fatigued. **বিশ্রান্তি** same as **বিশ্রাম** ।

বিশ্রাম *n.* rest, repose; temporary desistance or cessation of labour; an interval. **বিশ্রাম করা, বিশ্রাম নেওয়া** *v.* to take rest, to repose; desist from work or labour (permanently or temporarily). **বিশ্রাম দেওয়া** *v.* to give rest; to release from or relieve of work or labour (permanently or temporarily), to rest. **~কাল** *n.* a time for rest or repose; an interval.

বিশ্রী *a.* ugly, ill-shaped; shameful (বিশ্রী পরাজয়) ; detestable, nasty (বিশ্রী ব্যাপার, বিশ্রী লোক) ; indecent, obscene (বিশ্রী কথা) ; unwieldy (বিশ্রী বোঝা) ; bad (বিশ্রী খাবার) ; uncivil, rude (বিশ্রী আচরণ) ; regrettable (বিশ্রী দুর্ঘটনা) ; awkward (বিশ্রী অবস্থা). **বিশ্রী অবস্থায় ফেলা** *v.* to put one in a false or an awkward position.

বিশ্রুত *a.* celebrated, famous.

বিশ্লিষ্ট *a.* disunited, detached, disjointed; separated; analysed. **বিশ্লিষ্ট করা** *v.* to disunite, to detach, to disjoin; to separate; to analyse.

বিশ্লেষ *n.* separation; disjoining; analysis; manifestation. **বিশ্লেষক** *a.* analysing. □ *n.* analyser. **বিশ্লেষণ** *n.* analysis. **বিশ্লেষণ করা** *v.* to analyse. **বিশ্লেষণাত্মক** *a.* analytical.

বিষ *n.* poison; venom; (fig.) an extremely detestable person or thing (দু-চোখের বিষ) ; (fig.) envy, malice, suspicion etc.; anything that corrupts or consumes the mind, canker (usu. **মনের বিষ**). **বিষ খাওয়া** *v.* to take poison (esp. in order to commit suicide). **বিষ খাওয়ানো** *v.* to cause to take poison, to poison (esp. in order to kill). **বিষ ঢোকা** *v.* to be infected with poison, to become poisoned; (fig.) to become malicious, envious, suspicious etc. **বিষ ঢোকানো** *v.* to infuse or infect with poison, to poison; (fig.) to make malicious, envious, suspicious etc. **বিষ দেওয়া** *v.* to administer poison, to poison (esp. in order to kill). **বিষ মারা** *v.* to take out the poison of; (fig.) to render powerless. **~কন্যা** *n. fem.* a girl or woman whose association or contact causes death to a person. **~কাঁটালি** *n.* belladonna. **~কুম্ভ** *n.* a pitcher containing poison; (fig.) a repository of malice or envy or jealousy. **বিষকুম্ভ পয়োমুখ** (fig.) very sweet-tongued but venomous or malicious at heart, (cp), a suave hangman. **~ক্রিয়া** *n.* action of poisoning; (fig.) a very harmful or perverse reaction (এ উপদেশে বিষক্রিয়া হবে). **~ঘটিত** *a.* of or caused by poison or poisoning; toxic, toxical. **~ঘ্ন** *a.* antidotal; antitoxic. **বিষঘ্ন ওষুধ বা পদার্থ** an antidote; an antitoxin. **~জ্বর** *n.* septic fever. **বিষণ** *n.* infection of poison, poisoning; inflammation. **~তুল্য** *a.* as virulent or killing as poison, venomlike; (fig.) unbearable or insufferable (বিষতুল্য বচন).

~দশন *n.* a poison-fang. **~দংশন** *n.* a venomous bite. **~দন্ত, ~দাঁত** *n.* a poison-fang. **বিষদাঁত ভাঙা** *v.* to extract the poison-fangs (as of a venomous snake); (fig.) to remove the source of harm or to disarm; to render powerless or harmless. **~দিগ্ধ** *a.* smeared with poison, poisonous; (fig.) spiteful or heart-rending (বিষদিগ্ধ বচন). **~দুষ্ট** *a.* infected with poison, poisonous; venomous. **~দৃষ্টি** *n.* a spiteful or malicious glance; (fig.) extreme disfavour (উপরওয়ালার বিষদৃষ্টি). **বিষদৃষ্টিতে পড়া** *v.* (fig.) to incur (one's) extreme displeasure. **~ধর** *a.* venomous. □ *n.* a (venomous or non-venomous) snake. **~নজর, ~নয়ন** same as **~দৃষ্টি**। **~নাশক** same as **বিষঘ্ন**। **~পান** *n.* drinking or taking poison. **~প্রয়োগ** *n.* administration of poison, act of poisoning (esp. in order to kill). **~ফোঁড়া** *n.* a septic boil or sore, a malignant tumour or carbuncle, a furunculus orientalis. **~বৎ** same as **~তুল্য**। **বিষবৎ পরিত্যাজ্য** to be shunned like poison. **~বিজ্ঞান, ~বিদ্যা** *n.* toxicology. **~বিদ্যাগত** *a.* toxicological. **~বিজ্ঞানী, ~বিদ্যাবিৎ** *a.* versed in toxicology. □ *n.* a toxicologist. **~বৃক্ষ** *n.* a tree yielding poisonous fruits; a poison-tree; (fig.) an object which a man nourishes to kill or to ruin himself. **~বৈদ্য** *n.* a healer of poisoning cases (esp. those caused by snake-bites). **~ভক্ষণ** *n.* taking poison (esp. in order to kill oneself). **~ময়** *a.* poisonous, venomous; (fig.) extremely distressing, bitter (বিষময় জীবন বা বচন). **~মিশ্রিত** *a.* mixed with poison; poisonous. **~হর** *a.* antidotal; antitoxic. *fem.* **~হরা**। **~হরী** *n.* Manasa (মনসা) the Goddess of snakes.

বিষণ্ণ *a.* sorrowful, sad, morose, glum, melancholy, depressed; gloomy, darkened (বিষণ্ণ আকাশ). *fem.* **বিষণ্ণা**। **~চিত্ত** *a.* sad at heart; down-hearted; down in the mouth, low-spirited. **~তা** *n.* sorrowfulness, sadness, moroseness, melancholy, depression; paleness; gloominess, gloom, darkness. **~দৃষ্টি** *n.* a sorrowful glance, a sad or sullen look. **~নয়ন, ~নেত্র** *n.* sad eyes. **~প্রকৃতি** *a.* of a melancholy temperament; hypochondriac. **~বদন, ~মুখ** *a.* having a sorrowful countenance, dejected. *fem.* **~বদনা, ~মুখী**।

বিষম *a.* severe; insufferable, unbearable (বিষম তাপ) ; deadly, terrible (বিষম আক্রোশ বা বিপদ) ; extraordinary (বিষম কাণ্ড) ; very intricate or complicated (বিষম ঝামেলা) ; violent (বিষম ঝগড়া) ; acute (রোগের বিষম অবস্থা) ; rash (বিষম সাহস) ; not level, uneven, undulating (বিষম ক্ষেত্র) ; unequal (বিষম বস্তুদ্বয়) ; (arith.) odd (বিষম রাশি). □ *n.* sudden choking and hiccups whilst eating or drinking. **বিষম কোণ** (geom.) an acute or obtuse angle. **~কোণী** *a.* acute or obtuse-angled. **বিষম গতি** (phys. & astr.) variable motion. **বিষম চতুর্ভুজ** (geom.) a trapezium. **বিষম ত্রিভুজ** (geom.) a scalene triangle, a scalene. **~দৃক** *a.* (phys.) astigmatic. **~দৃষ্টি** *n.* (phys.) astigmatism. **বিষম-পরিণতি** *n.* (bot.) dichogamy. **~পৃষ্ঠ** *a.* (bot.) bifacial; (geog.) having an uneven or undulating surface. **বিষম বেগ** terrible speed; (phys.) variable velocity. **বিষমভুজ তুলা** a steelyard.

বিষয় *n.* an object of sense-perception, a perceptible object; an object; a thing for enjoyment, earthly enjoyment or interests; worldly possessions; a property, an estate; (rare) domain, territory, a district; a topic, subject-matter, a theme; a cause (দুঃখের বিষয়) ; what relates to or concerns (এ ব্যাপার তারই বিষয়). □ *prep.* same as **বিষয়ে**। **বিষয়-আশয়** *n.* property and riches. **বিষয়ক** *sfx.* denoting : concerning, relating to, about. **~কর্ম** *n.* earning one's living; management of an estate. **~তৃষ্ণা** *n.* thirst for property and riches or for worldly pleasures and enjoyments. **~বাসনা** *n.* desire for property and riches or for worldly pleasures and enjoyments. **~বিতৃষ্ণ, ~বিমুখ** *a.* averse to property and riches or to worldly pleasures and enjoyments; stoical. **~বিতৃষ্ণা, ~বিমুখতা** *n.* aversion to property and riches or to worldly pleasures and enjoyments. **~বুদ্ধি** *n.* shrewd tact for management of an estate or for maintenance of domestic economy; worldly wisdom. **~বৈরাগ্য** same as **~বিতৃষ্ণা**। **~লালসা** *n.* greed for property and riches or for worldly pleasures and enjoyments. **~সূচি,** (rej.) **~সূচী** *n.* agenda; a table of contents serially arranged. **বিষয়ানুরাগ, বিষয়াসক্তি** *n.* attachment to property and riches or to worldly pleasures and enjoyments. **বিষয়ানুরাগী, বিষয়াসক্ত** *a.* attached to property and riches or to worldly pleasures and enjoyments. *fem.* **বিষয়ানুরাগিণী**। **বিষয়ান্তর** *n.* another topic; a different topic. **বিষয়ী** *a.* attached to worldly riches and pleasures; possessing property; possessing an estate, landed. **বিষয়ীভূত** *a.* included in the domain or jurisdiction of (আইনের বিষয়ীভূত) ; included in the agenda (আলোচনার বিষয়ীভূত). **বিষয়ে** *prep.* concerning, relating to, regarding, about.

বিষাক্ত *a.* smeared with or containing poison, poisonous; venomous (বিষাক্ত সাপ) ; malignantly septic (বিষাক্ত ঘা) ; malignant (বিষাক্ত ফোড়া) ; spiteful or acrimonious (বিষাক্ত বচন) ; bitter (বিষাক্ত সম্পর্ক). **বিষাক্ত করা** *v.* (of a wound etc.) to cause sepsis, to make malignant or septic; (of relation, mind etc.) to embitter.

বিষাণ *n.* a horn (of a beast); a wind instrument made of or shaped like a horn, a horn; a tusk.

বিষাদ *n.* low spirits, dejection; melancholy; sorrow, sadness; grief. **~গ্রস্ত, বিষাদিত, বিষাদী** *a.* low-spirited, dejected, down-hearted, down in the mouth; melancholy; sorrowful, sad; full of grief. *fem.* **~গ্রস্তা, বিষাদিতা, বিষাদিনী**।

বিষানো *v.* to make or become poisonous; to be inflamed (as a wound, boil etc.); (loos.) to make or grow septic (as a wound), to cause to suppurate or to suppurate (as a boil, wound etc.); (fig.) to embitter or be embittered (মন বিষানো). **বিষিয়ে তোলা, বিষিয়ে দেওয়া** same as **বিষানো**।

বিষুব *n.* the equinox. **~বৃত্ত** *n.* the equinoctial circle, the equinoctial, the equator. **~রেখা** *n.* the equinoctial line, equinoctial, the equator. **~লম্ব** *n.* (astr.) the declination. **~সংক্রান্তি** same as **বিষুব**। **বিষুবীয়** *a.* equinoctial.

বিষ্কম্ভক *n.* (in a drama) opening lines of an act in which an actor or actress narrates an incident not exhibited on the stage.

বিষ্টি *n.* (coll. form of **বৃষ্টি**) rain, a shower.

বিষ্টু coll. corrup. of **বিষ্ণু**।

বিষ্ঠা *n.* faeces, stool, excreta; (of beasts, birds, etc.) dung, excrement(s).

বিষ্ণু *n.* the second person of the Hindu Trinity who sustains the creation; Narayana (নারায়ণ), Hari (হরি). **~প্রিয়া** *n.* Goddess Lakshmi (লক্ষ্মী) the wife of Vishnu (বিষ্ণু). **~লোক** *n.* the abode of Lord Vishnu.

বিসংবাদ *n.* strife, a quarrel; discord; disagreement; a dispute. **বিসংবাদী** *a.* quarrelling; discordant; disputatious.

বিসকুট alt. spell. of **বিস্কুট**।

বিসদৃশ *a.* dissimilar; unequal; contradictory, contrary; hostile; incompatible; irrelevant; grotesque or odd (বিসদৃশ মূর্তি) ; unbecoming.

বিসমিল্লা, বিসমিল্লাহ *n.* (Mus.) an invocation of Allah whilst starting a work. **বিসমিল্লায় গলদ** (fig.) a mistake at the very beginning, an erroneous start.

বিসরণ *n.* (chiefly in phys.) deviation. **বিসরণ-কোণ** *n.* an angle of deviation. **গরিষ্ঠ বা বরিষ্ঠ বিসরণ-কোণ** the angle of maximum deviation. **লঘিষ্ঠ বিসরণ-কোণ** the angle of minimum deviation.

বিসর্গ *n.* a Bengali spirant or the letter resembling it (ঃ). **বিসর্গ-সন্ধি** see **সন্ধি**।

বিসর্জন *n.* giving up or renouncing; abandonment; renouncing, renouncement; renunciation; relinquishment; sacrifice (জীবনবিসর্জন) ; loss (বন্ধুবিসর্জন) ; waste or impairment (স্বাস্থ্যবিসর্জন) ; immersion esp. with solemnities (প্রতিমাবিসর্জন) ; immersion of the image of a deity (বিসর্জনের বাদ্য). **বিসর্জন করা, বিসর্জন দেওয়া** *v.* to give up; to abandon to relinquish; to sacrifice; to lose; to waste or impair; to immerse esp. with solemnities. **বিসর্জনীয়** *a.* to be given up or abandoned or relinquished or sacrificed or lost or wasted or impaired or immersed.

বিসর্জা poet. form of **বিসর্জন করা**।

বিসর্জিত *a.* given up, abandoned; renounced; relinquished; sacrificed; lost; wasted or impaired; immersed esp. with solemnities. *fem.* **বিসর্জিতা**।

বিসর্প *n.* erysipelas.

বিসর্প, বিসর্পণ *n.* act of moving slowly; creeping; sliding; spreading; pervading or diffusing. **বিসর্পিত** *a.* spread; diffused. **বিসর্পী** *a.* slowly moving; creeping; sliding; spreading; pervading; diffusive. *fem.* **বিসর্পিণী**।

বিসূচিকা *n.* cholera.

বিস্কুট *n.* biscuit.

বিসৃত *a.* extended, spread out.

বিসৃষ্ট *a.* thrown; abandoned, renounced, given up; sent or sent away.

বিস্তর *a.* many or much; too many or too much. □ *n.* a lot, plenty.

বিস্তার *n.* stretching; stretch; tension; extension; extent; expansion; expanse; spread, amplification; width, breadth. **বিস্তার করা** *v.* to stretch; to extend; to expand; to spread; to amplify; to widen. **বিস্তারিত** same as **বিস্তৃত**। **বিস্তারী** *a.* spreading, extending.

বিস্তার্য *a.* tensible, tensile; extendible, extensible, extensile; expansible; expansile; capable of being spread (out) or amplified or widened. **~তা** *n.* tensility, tensibility; extensibility.

বিস্তীর্ণ *a.* spread out; extensive; expansive; pervasive, vast.

বিস্তৃত *a.* stretched out, extended; expanded; spread out; amplified; widened; detailed (বিস্তৃত বর্ণনা). **বিস্তৃত করা** *v.* to stretch out; to expand; to spread out; to amplify; to widen. **বিস্তৃতি** same as **বিস্তার**।

বিস্ফারিত *a.* widened; enlarged; trembling, trembled, shaken. **~নেত্রে** *adv.* with eyes opened wide, looking widely.

বিস্ফুরিত *a.* trembling; trembled, shaken, flickering or sparkling; (of lips) pouting or pouted. **বিস্ফুরিতাধর** *a.* having trembling lips.

বিস্ফোট, বিস্ফোটক *n.* a boil, a furuncle; a malignant boil or follicle.

বিস্ফোরক *a.* explosive. □ *n.* an explosive.

বিস্ফোরণ *n.* explosion. **বিস্ফোরণ ঘটা** বা **হওয়া** *v.* to explode.

বিস্বন *n.* an earsplitting noise; sound; (phon.) a variant sound, an allophone. **~ভেদ** (phon.) *n.* allophonic variation.

বিস্বাদ *a.* distasteful; tasteless, insipid; vapid; (fig.) dull or disgusting.

বিস্ময় *n.* wonder, astonishment, amazement, surprise; marvel. **~কর, ~জনক** *a.* wonderful, marvellous; astonishing, amazing, surprising. **~চিহ্ন** *n.* (gr.) the note of admiration or exclamation (!). **~বিস্ফারিত** *a.* (of eyes) widened with amazement. **~বিহ্বল** *a.* beside oneself with wonder; astounded. **~মগ্ন** *a.* lost in wonder or amazement. **বিস্ময়ান্বিত, বিস্ময়াপন্ন** same as **বিস্মিত**। **বিস্ময়াবহ** same as **বিস্ময়কর**। **বিস্ময়াবিষ্ট, বিস্ময়াভিভূত** same as **বিস্ময়বিহ্বল**। **বিস্ময়োৎপাদক, বিস্ময়োৎপাদী** *a.* wonder-arousing; wonderful. **বিস্ময়োৎপাদন করা** *v.* to arouse wonder; to strike one with wonder. **বিস্ময়োৎফুল্ল** *a.* elated with wonder.

বিস্মরণ *n.* forgetting; oblivion. **বিস্মরণ হওয়া** *v.* to forget. **~শীল** *a.* forgetful, oblivious. **বিস্মরণীয়** *a.* forgettable.

বিস্মিত *a.* astonished; amazed, surprised. *fem.* **বিস্মিতা**। **বিস্মিত করা** *v.* to astonish; to amaze, to surprise. **বিস্মিত হওয়া** *v.* to wonder, to marvel; to be astonished or amazed or surprised. **~ভাবে** *adv.* wonderingly; with astonishment.

বিস্মৃত *a.* one who has forgotten; forgotten, off one's chump, unremembered. *fem.* **বিস্মৃতা**। **বিস্মৃত হওয়া** *v.* to fall into oblivion; to forget. **বিস্মৃতি** *n.* forgetfulness, forgetting; loss of memory; oblivion. **বিস্মৃতির অতলে, বিস্মৃতির অতল তলে** in the abyss of oblivion.

বিস্রস্ত *a.* fallen; slipped off (বিস্রস্ত বসন) ; dishevelled (বিস্রস্ত কেশ).

বিহগ, বিহঙ্গ, বিহঙ্গম *n.* the bird. *fem.* **বিহগী, বিহঙ্গী, বিহঙ্গমী**। **বিহঙ্গমা** *n.* a kind of telltale or tattler birds mentioned in folktales.

বিহনে *prep.* (poet.) without, in absence of.

বিহরণ *n.* sporting or frolicking; amorous frolicking, dalliance; promenading.

বিহরা poet. form of **বিহার করা** ।

বিহান *n.* (obs.) morning, daybreak, dawn.

বিহার *n.* sport or frolic; dalliance; amorous frolic; promenading; a pleasure trip; a promenade; a pleasure ground; a Buddhist or Jaina monastery or convent. **বিহার করা** *v.* to sport or frolic; to indulge in amorous frolics, to dally; to promenade.

বিহারি *n.* a man from Bihar, a Bihari. □ *a.* of or about Bihar.

বিহারী *a.* sporting or frolicking; indulging in amorous frolics, dallying; promenading. *fem.* **বিহারিণী** ।

বিহিত *a.* (pronun. : বিহিতো) conforming to the established or prescribed mode or form, formal; prescribed; proper, just; done, performed. □ *n.* (pronun. : বিহিৎ) (loos.) a remedy, redress, reparation. **বিহিত করা** *v.* to enact; to prescribe; (loos.) to remedy, to redress, to repair; to right. **বিহিতক** *n.* a legislative enactment, an act. **~কাল** *n.* auspicious or proper time.

বিহীন *a.* devoid of; deprived of, divested of; separated from.

বিহ্বল *a.* overwhelmed; beside oneself; bewildered. *fem.* **বিহ্বলা** । **বিহ্বল করা** *v.* to overwhelm; to make one beside oneself; to bewilder. **~তা** *n.* overwhelmed state; state of being beside oneself; daze; bewilderment.

বীক্ষণ *n.* careful observation.

বীক্ষমাণ *a.* engaged in careful observation.

বীক্ষিত *a.* carefully observed.

বীক্ষ্যমাণ *a.* under careful observation.

বীচি[1] *n.* a stone or pip or seed (of fruits); a testis (*pl.* testes), a testicle.

বীচি[2] (*for.*) *n.* a wave; a billow; a ripple; a ray, a beam. **~বিক্ষুব্ধ, ~বিক্ষোভিত** *a.* agitated with waves; wavy; billowy. **~ভঙ্গ** *n.* rising in waves. **~মালা** *n.* a succession of waves, a garland of waves; a garland of rays. **~মালী** *n.* the sun.

বীজ *n.* a stone or pip (of fruits); seed (for sowing); germ (of disease); semen, seed; a cause; a root-cause (কলহের বীজ). **অসস্যল-বীজ** (bot.) albuminous seed. **বীজ-অন্তস্ত্বক** *n.* (bot.) tegumen. **~কোষ** *n.* a seed-vessel, the ovary of a flower. **~কোষধারী** *a.* leguminous. **~গুটি** *n.* (bot.) a spore. **~ঘ্ন** *a.* disinfectant. **বীজঘ্ন পদার্থ** a disinfectant. **~তলা** *n.* a piece of nursery ground, a seed-bed, a seed-plot. **বীজত্বক** *n.* (bot.) a seed-coat. **~দূষণ** *n.* sepsis. **~দূষিত** *a.* septic. **~ধান** *n.* seed-paddy. **~বপন** *n.* sowing seeds. **বীজবপন করা** *v.* to sow seeds. **~বহিস্ত্বক** *n.* (bot.) testa. **~বারক** *a.* antiseptic. **বীজবারক পদার্থ** an antiseptic. **~মন্ত্র** *n.* a mystic word or words to be recited silently by a devotee. **~হীন** *a.* seedless; (bot.) aspermous. **বীজাঙ্কুর** *n.* a seedplant, a seedling.

বীজগণিত *n.* algebra. **বীজগাণিতিক** *a.* algebraic, algebraical. □ *n.* an algebraist.

বীজন *n.* fanning. **বীজন করা** *v.* to fan.

বীজিত *a.* fanned.

বীট[1] rej. spell. of **বিট**[2] ।

বীট[2], **বীটপালং**, **বীন** rej. spellings of **বিট**, **বিটপালং** and **বিন** respectively.

বীণা *n.* a kind of musical heptachord, a vina. **~দণ্ড** *n.* the top part of a vina to be held with the hand. **~নিন্দিত, ~বিনিন্দিত** *a.* putting to shame even the charming melody of a lyre, excelling even the sound of a vina in sweetness. *fem.* **~নিন্দিতা, ~বিনিন্দিতা** । **~পাণি** *n.* one who holds a vina in one's hand; Goddess Saraswati (সরস্বতী). **~বাদক** *n.* a vina-player. **~বাদন** *n.* playing on a vina.

বীতংস alt. spell. of **বিতংস** ।

বীতকাম *a.* freed from desire or all desires, past all desires.

বীতনিদ্র *a.* sleepless; wakeful; awake.

বীতরাগ *a.* having lost interest (in) or attachment (to), disaffected; apathetic disgusted.

বীতশঙ্ক *a.* freed from fear; dauntless fearless.

বীতশোক *a.* relieved of grief; past all grief.

বীতশ্রদ্ধ *a.* having lost one's faith (in) or reverence (for); disgusted. **বীতশ্রদ্ধ হওয়া** *v.* to be disgusted.

বীতস্পৃহ *a.* disinclined; callous; apathetical; indifferent (to worldly desires etc.).

বীথি, বীথিকা, বীথী *n.* a row, a line (তরুবীথি, পণ্যবীথি) ; an avenue, a vista.

বীন *n.* var. of **বীণা**। **~কার, ~বাদক** *n.* a vina-player.

বীপ্সা *n.* frequent repetition or occurrence, frequency. **~ব্যঞ্জক, ~সূচক** *a.* frequentative. **~সূচক শব্দ** (gr.) a frequentative.

বীভৎস *a.* extremely abominable or repulsive or loathsome; horribly or outrageously shaped, monstrous. **~তা** *n.* extreme abominableness or repulsiveness or loathsomeness; monstrosity. **~রস** *n.* (rhet.) a description inspiring repulsion in the mind of a reader or hearer.

বীম rej. spell. of **বিম**।

বীমা rej. spell. of **বিমা**।

বীর *a.* valiant, valorous; heroic; skilled in warfare; spirited. □ *n.* a valiant person; a heroic person, a hero; a skilled warrior; a spirited person; a great person (কর্মবীর). **~চূড়ামণি** *n.* the greatest of heroes. **~জননী** *n.* the mother of a hero. **~জায়া** *n.* the wife of a hero. **~ত্ব** *n.* valour; heroism. **বীরত্বপূর্ণ** *a.* valorous; heroic. **বীরত্বব্যঞ্জক** *a.* indicating valour or heroism ; valorous, heroic. **~দর্প** *n.* a hero's challenge; a heroic assertion or declaration. **~নারী** same as **বীরাঙ্গনা**। **~প্রসবিনী, ~প্রসূ** *a. fem.* giving birth to a hero or heroes; (of a country etc.) producing heroes. **~বর** *n.* a great hero. **~বৌলি** *n.* an earring worn by a hero (or generically by men). **~ভোগ্যা** *a. fem.* enjoyable only by heroes. **বীরভোগ্যা বসুন্ধরা** it is for the brave to conquer and enjoy the earth. **~মাতা** *n.* a hero's mother; a heroic mother. **~রস** *n.* (rhet.) a description that inspires heroism in the mind of a reader or hearer. **~শ্রেষ্ঠ** *a.* the greatest among heroic men. □ *n.* a most valiant man. **বীরা** *a. fem.* of **বীর** (*a.*). □ *n.* a woman having both husband and son; a kind of wine. **বীরাঙ্গনা** *n.* a heroic woman; a hero's wife. **বীরাচার** *n.* a system of worship according to Tantrism. **বীরাচারী** *a.* one who has adopted this system. **বীরাসন** *n.* a particular posture of sitting on one's haunches whilst practising **বীরাচার**। **বীরেশ্বর** *n.* the greatest hero; Shiva (শিব).

বীর্য *n.* heroism; prowess, valour, might, vigour, strength; spiritedness, spirit; (of an adult male) semen. **~বত্তা** *n.* heroism; valorousness, prowess, mightiness, vigorousness; spiritedness. **~বন্ত, ~বান, ~শালী** *a.* heroic; valorous, mighty, vigorous; spirited. *fem.* **~বতী, ~শালিনী**। **~হানি** *n.* loss of prowess or valour or strength or vigour; loss of seminal fluid; (med.) spermatorrhoea. **~হীন** *a.* lacking heroism or prowess or valour or vigour or power or spiritedness; impotent.

বুঁদ *a.* besotted (নেশায় বুঁদ) ; absorbed, engrossed (চিন্তায় বুঁদ).

বুঁদিয়া, ori. but now obs. var. of **বোঁদে**।

বুক[১] *n.* the chest, the breast; the measure of the chest; (fig.) the heart, the bosom. **বুক চাপড়ানো** *v.* to beat or slap one's own breast in order to express grief. **~জল** *n.* chest-high water. **~জ্বালা** *n.* burning pain in chest owing to acidity; heart-burn. **বুক ঠোকা** *v.* to strike one's own breast in order to parade one's courage. **বুক ঠুকে লাগা** *v.* to undertake or commence something slapdash. **বুক ঢিপঢিপ করা** same as **বুক দুরদুর করা**। **বুক দশ হাত হওয়া** same as **বুক ফুলে ওঠা**। **বুক দিয়ে পড়া** *v.* to set about with might and main; to come to help with might and main; to persevere doggedly. **বুক দুরদুর করা** to have palpitation, to feel nervous. **~ফাটা** *a.* heart-rending, extremely doleful or pathetic. **বুক ফাটা** *v.* to feel one's heart to be rending (with grief, longing etc.). **বুক ফাটে তো মুখ ফোটে না** although one is extremely eager to speak out one's mind, the tongue obstinately keeps mum. **বুক ফুলে ওঠা** *v.* to be puffed up.

বুক ফোলানো *v.* (lit.) to expand one's chest; (fig.) to be puffed up. **বুক বাঁধা** *v.* to be patient and courageous in danger or difficulty, to take heart. **বুক বাড়া** *v.* to grow audacious. **বুক ভাঙা** *v.* to break one's heart; to be heart-broken. **~ভাঙা** *a.* heart-breaking, extremely painful; broken-hearted. **বুক শুকানো** *v.* to have one's heart in one's mouth. **বুকে ঢেঁকির পাড় পড়া** to be stricken with extreme inward agitation on account of fear or malice. **বুকে বসে দাড়ি ওপড়ানো** to harm one who provides food and shelter. **বুকে বাঁশ দেওয়া** see **বাঁশ**। **বুকের ছাতি, বুকের পাটা** expanse or measure of one's chest; (fig.) daring, pluck, courage. **বুকের রক্ত চোষা** to send one slowly to death by means of oppression. **বুকের রক্ত দেওয়া** (fig.) to spend one's lifeblood for; (fig.) to sacrifice one's life. **বুকে হাঁটা** to crawl. **বুকে হাত দিয়ে বলা** to say sincerely, to say or utter in keeping with the dictates of one's conscience; to say or utter with courage or sincerity.

বুক২ *n.* reservation in advance, booking (থিয়েটারের সিট বুক করা) ; railway-booking (মাল বুক করা). **বুক করা** *v.* to book (seats etc.); to book (goods) by rail. **~কিপিং** *n.* book-keeping. **~পোস্ট** *n.* book-post. **বুকপোস্ট করা** *v.* to send by book-post. **~শেলফ** *n.* a book-shelf.

বুকড়ি *a.* coarse (বুকড়ি চাল).

বুকনি *n.* a particle; affected witty talk or remarks; tall talk; ludicrous mixture of a foreign language with one's own. **বুকনি ঝাড়া** *v.* (*infor.*) to indulge in witty talk or remarks affectedly ; talk big; to mix a foreign language ludicrously with one's own.

বুজকুড়ি *n.* a bubble; effervescence. **বুজকুড়ি দেওয়া** *v.* to rise in small bubbles.

বুজরুক *a.* pretentious, pretending, charlatanic; quackish. □ *n.* a charlatan, a quack; an impostor. **বুজরুকি** *n.* pretension, charlatanism, quackery.

বুজা, বোজা *v.* to shut or close (চক্ষু বুজেছে) ; to be filled up (গর্ত বোজা). □ *a.* shut or closed; filled up. **বুজানো** *v.* to shut or close; to fill up.

বুঝ *n.* consolation ; gumption; mutual understanding or agreement; explanation or manipulation (হিসাবের বুঝ) ; **বুঝ থাকা** *v.* to have mutual understanding or agreement. **বুঝ দেওয়া** *v.* to console or comfort; to explain or manipulate (accounts). **বুঝ মানা** *v.* to agree to be consoled, to accept consolation. **~সুঝ** *n.* gumption and patience.

বুঝা see **বোঝা**১ ।

বুঝি *adv.* denoting : probability, doubt, interrogation etc. তাই বুঝি is it so? **তোমার চোখে বুঝি ঘুম নেই** can't you sleep, eh?

বুট১ *n.* chick-pea, gram.

বুট২ *n.* a boot. **বুট পরা** *v.* to put on or wear boots. **বুট খোলা** *v.* to pull off boots.

বুটি *n.* diaper. **বুটি তোলা** *v.* to diaper. **~দার** *a.* diapered.

বুড়া১ *v.* to sink, to be submerged, to be immersed. **~নো** *v.* to drown, to submerge, to immerse; to dip (জলে পা বুড়ানো).

বুড়া২ older var. of **বুড়ো**।

বুড়ি১ *n.* (obs.) a unit of counting by twenties. **~কিয়া** *n.* a table of enumeration by twenties.

বুড়ি২ *a.* (*fem.* of **বুড়ো**) old, aged. □ *n.* an old woman. **পাকা বুড়ি** (facet.) a little girl behaving like a grown-up or elderly woman. **~পনা** *n.* comically elderly conduct of a little girl.

বুড়িয়ে যাওয়া same as **বুড়ো হওয়া**।

বুড়ো *a.* old, aged (বুড়ো লোক) ; very old, ancient (বুড়ো বট) ; overmature, overdeveloped (বুড়ো পাঁঠা) ; prematurely grown-up; purely (বুড়ো খোকা) ; precocious. □ *n.* an old man. **বুড়ো হওয়া** *v.* to grow old; to grow old prematurely; to become a veteran (মিস্ত্রিগিরিতে বুড়ো হওয়া). **বুড়ো বুড়ো** ludicrously elderly (বুড়ো বুড়ো চালচলন) ; precocious (বুড়ো বুড়ো কথা).

বুড়োটে *a.* grown old prematurely; oldish; precocious.

বুড়োপনা, বুড়োমি *n.* comically elderly conduct of a young person esp. of a child; precocity.

বুদ্ধ *a.* awakened; enlightened; wise. □ *n.* Gautama Buddha; the ninth incarnation of Vishnu (বিষ্ণু). **~ত্ব** *n.* supreme enlightenment or wisdom (esp. what Buddha attained).

বুদ্ধি *n.* understanding; discernment, judgment; gumption; sagacity; intelligence; intellect; talent; counsel, advice; a device or scheme; propensity, tendency (পাপবুদ্ধি). **বুদ্ধি করা** *v.* to plan, to scheme; to consult or confer with. **বুদ্ধি খাটানো** *v.* to apply tact and ingenuity, to have recourse to a contrivance. **বুদ্ধি দেওয়া** *v.* to advise, to counsel. **বুদ্ধি নেওয়া** *v.* to take counsel or advice of. **বুদ্ধি হারানো** *v.* to be at one's wit's end ; to lose one's senses; to become rash or injudicious. **বুদ্ধির ঢেঁকি** (fig.) an utterly foolish or stupid person, a dunce. **~গম্য** *a.* comprehensible; intelligible; conceivable. **~জীবী** *a.* earning one's livelihood by means of one's intellect; (loos.) intellectual. □ *n.* an intellectual. **বুদ্ধিজীবী সম্প্রদায়** the intelligentsia. **~দাতা** *n.* an adviser, a counsellor. *fem.* **~দাত্রী**। **~নাশ** same as **~ভ্রংশ**। **~বিকাশ** *n.* growth of intelligence or understanding. **~বৃত্তি** *n.* the faculty of understanding, intellect; sense, wit; reasoning, discernment, judgment. **~বৃত্তিমূলক** *a.* intellectual; rational. **~ভ্রংশ** *n.* loss or impairment of intellect, mental unhingement; folly; bewilderment; mental distraction; loss or corruption of senses. **~ভ্রষ্ট** *a.* mentally unhinged; one with intellect impaired; bewildered; mentally distracted; out of one's senses; foolish, stupid. **~মতী** *fem.* of **বুদ্ধিমান**। **~মত্তা** *n.* intellectuality; intelligence; talent; sagacity. **~মান** *a.* intelligent; talented; sagacious; shrewd; intellectual. **~হীন** *a.* unintelligent; stupid, foolish. *fem.* **~হীনা**। **~হীনতা** *n.* stupidity, foolishness; a folly. **বুদ্ধীন্দ্রিয়** *n.* the organ of cognition, the mind, a sense-organ.

বুদ্বুদ *n.* a bubble. **বুদ্বুদ ওঠা** *v.* to effervesce. **বুদ্বুদন** *n.* effervescence.

বুধ *n.* the planet Mercury (also **বুধগ্রহ**) ; Wednesday (usu. **বুধবার**) ; a learned or wise man (also **বুধজন**).

বুনট *n.* texture or grain (of cloth); weaving; woven fabric.

বুনন *n.* sowing; weaving; knitting. **বুননি** alt. form of **বুনানি** (see **বুনা**).

বুনা, var. of **বোনা**। **বুনানি** *n.* texture or grain (of cloth); weaving or knitting.

বুনিয়াদ var. of **বনিয়াদ**।

বুনো *a.* grown or produced in the forest, wild; born or living in the forest, savage, of the woods, arboreal; uncivilized, churlish (বুনো লোক, বুনো কথাবার্তা) ; (dero.) aboriginal. □ *n.* (dero.) an aboriginal.

বুভুক্ষা *n.* craving for food; hunger. **বুভুক্ষিত, বুভুক্ষু** *a.* hungry.

বুরুজ *n.* a bastion; a rampart; a dome; a kind of card-playing.

বুরুল *n.* a unit of measure, a digit (= 1 inch approx.).

বুরুশ *n.* a brush. **বুরুশ করা, বুরুশ দিয়ে ঝাড়া, বুরুশ লাগানো** *v.* to brush.

বুর্জোয়া *n.* a bourgeois; the bourgeoisie; the well-to-do class or a person belonging to it. □ *a.* bourgeois; well-to-do.

বুলবুল, বুলবুলি *n.* a bird of the *Pycnonotus* genus, the bulbul.

বুলানো *v.* to pass one's hand or a brush or a pen etc. lightly over something. **চোখ বুলানো** *v.* to eye cursorily. **তুলি বুলানো** *v.* to touch lightly with a paint-brush, to brush.

বুলি *n.* speech, language, a word or phrase or lingo or jargon (ইংরেজি বুলি) ; babble or prattle (as of a child or bird); a crammed speech; a maxim; a slogan. **বুলি আওড়ানো** *v.* to babble or prattle; to utter a crammed speech or a maxim or a slogan; to talk jargon; to use cliches (esp. of foreign origin) in one's speech. **বুলি ঝাড়া** *v.* same as **বুলি আওড়ানো** (except in the first sense). **বাঁধা বুলি** *n.* cant, a cliche.

বৃংহণ, বৃংহিত *n.* the call of the elephant.

বৃক *n.* the wolf; pancreatin, the pancreatic juice; (loos.) hunger. **বৃকোদর** *n.* one with as voracious an appetite as that of a wolf; Bhima of the Mahabharata.

বৃক্ক *n.* the kidney. **বৃক্কাকার** *n.* kidney-shaped, reniform.

বৃক্ষ *n.* a tree; a plant. **~কাণ্ড** *n.* a tree-trunk. **বৃক্ষচ্ছায়** *n.* extensive shade of rows of trees. **~চ্ছায়া** *n.* shade of a tree, tree-shade. **~তল** *n.* the foot of a tree. **~তলে** *adv.* under or underneath the tree. **~নির্যাস** *n.* exudation of a tree. **~বাটিকা** *n.* a garden-house. **~ময়** *a.* abounding in trees, woody. **~মূল** *n.* a tree-root; the foot of a tree; a tree-stump. **~রোপণ** *n.* planting trees. **বৃক্ষরোপণ করা** *v.* to plant a tree or trees. **বৃক্ষহীন** *a.* treeless. **বৃক্ষাগ্র** *n.* tree-top. **বৃক্ষান্তরাল** *n.* a place screened from the view by a tree or trees. **বৃক্ষারূঢ়** *a.* mounted or perched on a tree. **বৃক্ষোপাসনা** *n.* tree-worship.

বৃত *a.* respectfully or honourably received or chosen or appointed (সভাপতিরূপে বৃত) ; ordained (পুরোহিতপদে বৃত) ; covered. **~বিশোষণ, ~শোষণ** *n.* (phys. & bot.) selective absorption. **বৃতি** *n.* respectful or honourable reception or appointment; ordainment, ordination; covering; a fence, an enclosure; (bot.) a calyx. **বৃতিনল** *n.* (bot.) a calyx-tube. **বৃতিসদৃশ** *a.* (bot.) sepaloid.

বৃত্ত *n.* (chiefly in geom.) a circle; a sphere; character or conduct (দুর্বৃত্ত) ; (pros.) a system of versification (মাত্রাবৃত্ত). □ *a.* employed; accustomed; born. **গুরুবৃত্ত** *n.* (geog.) the Great Circle. **লঘুবৃত্ত** *n.* (geog.) the Small Circle. **~কলা** *n.* (geom.) a sector. **বৃত্তসমবর্তিত আলোক** circularly polarized light. **বৃত্তাংশ** *n.* the segment of a circle. **বৃত্তাকার** *a.* rotund; circular.

বৃত্তান্ত *n.* an account or details, facts (of an incident); news, tidings, information; a tale, a story.

বৃত্তি *n.* faculty (চিত্তবৃত্তি) ; nature or propensity (নীচবৃত্তি) ; conduct (বকবৃত্তি) ; a calling, a vocation, a profession, a trade (চৌর্যবৃত্তি) ; a regular money allowance, a stipend, a scholarship; narration; elucidation, explanation (সূত্রের বৃত্তি), recountal. **~জীবী** *a.* one who lives by engaging oneself in a vocation or profession; engaged in a profession. **বৃত্তি দান করা** *v.* to give or award or endow a stipend or scholarship. **~প্রশিক্ষণ** *n.* vocational training. **~প্রাপ্ত** *a.* recipient of a scholarship. **বৃত্তিপ্রাপ্ত ছাত্র** *n.* a scholar; a scholarship-holder. **~মূলক** *a.* vocational. **~শিক্ষা** *n.* vocational education.

বৃত্তীয় *a.* of or like a circle, circular; spherical. **বৃত্তীয় মান** circular measure.

বৃত্রারি *n.* the enemy of Britra (বৃত্র) the demon : an appellation of Indra (ইন্দ্র) the king of gods.

বৃথা *a.* futile, abortive, ineffectual, fruitless; useless (বৃথা বাক্যব্যয়) ; purposeless (বৃথা ভ্রমণ). □ *adv.* in vain; to no purpose; uselessly.

বৃদ্ধ *a.* aged, old; older; senior or veteran or grown-up or advanced or experienced (বয়োবৃদ্ধ, জ্ঞানবৃদ্ধ) ; ancient (বৃদ্ধ বট) ; lucky; enlarged or extended (প্রবৃদ্ধ). □ *n.* an old man. **~ত্ব, ~তা** *n.* agedness, oldness; old age; elderliness. **~প্রপিতামহ** *n.* a paternal great-great-grandfather. *fem.* **~প্রপিতামহী** a paternal great-great-grandmother. **~প্রমাতামহ** *n.* a maternal great-great-grandfather. *fem.* **~প্রমাতামহী** a maternal great-great-grandmother.

বৃদ্ধা *fem.* of **বৃদ্ধ**।

বৃদ্ধাঙ্গুলি *n.* the thumb; the big toe, the great toe.

বৃদ্ধাঙ্গুষ্ঠ *n.* the thumb; the big toe. **বৃদ্ধাঙ্গুষ্ঠ দেখানো** *v.* (iron. or joc.) to show the thumb to indicate deception, hood-winking or befooling.

বৃদ্ধাবস্থা same as **বৃদ্ধত্ব** (see **বৃদ্ধ**).

বৃদ্ধি *n.* augmentation, increase; growth; development; enlargement; rise (মূল্যবৃদ্ধি) ; advancement (জাতির শিক্ষাবৃদ্ধি) ; flourish; (bot.) accrescence; interest on money (চক্রবৃদ্ধি) ; usury. **বৃদ্ধি পাওয়া** *v.* to augment, to increase; to grow up; to develop; to be enlarged, to enlarge; to rise; to advance; to flourish; (bot.) to accrete. **~কর** *a.* promoting or helping growth. **~কাল** *n.* the period of growth. **মুখ্য বৃদ্ধিকাল** (bot.) the grand period of growth. **~জ** *a.* concerning growth. **বৃদ্ধিজ চলন** (bot.) a growth movement. **~জীবী** *n.* a usurer. **~দশা** *n.* (bot.) a phase of growth. **~প্রাপ্ত** *a.* enlarged; grown; grown outsize. **~বিস্তার** *n.* (bot.) distribution of growth. **~হার** *n.*

(bot.) the rate of growth. **~শীল** *a.* augmentating, increasing; growing; developing; enlarging; rising; advancing; flourishing; (bot.) accrescent. **~শ্রাদ্ধ** *n.* an obsequial rite in honour of manes (usu. performed on the eve of a marriage-ceremony etc.).

বৃন্ত *n.* (bot.) a stalk; a nipple. **~চ্যুত** *a.* (bot.) detached or nipped from the stalk. **~মধ্যক** *a.* (bot.) interpetiolar.

বৃন্দ *n.* a thousand millions; the total number; a large number, a multitude. **~গান** *n.* a group music, a chorus. **~বাদন, বাদ্যবৃন্দ** *n.* a concert.

বৃশ্চিক *n.* the scorpion; (astrol.) the Scorpio (usu. **বৃশ্চিকরাশি**). **~দংশন** *n.* the sting of a scorpion; (fig.) utter mortification.

বৃষ *n.* the ox; the bull; (astrol.) the Taurus; (as a *sfx.*) the best specimen (নরবৃষ). **~কাষ্ঠ** *n.* a wooden stake to which are fastened the bulls of the Brisotsarga (বৃষোৎসর্গ) ceremony. **~ধ্বজ** *n.* one who is marked by one's bull; Shiva (শিব). **~বাহন** *n.* one who mounts on a bull; Shiva (শিব). **~ভ** same as **বৃষ** (except in the astrological sense). **~রাশি** *n.* (astrol.) the Taurus. **~স্কন্ধ** *a.* bull-necked; very strong.

বৃষল *n.* a Shudra (শূদ্র) ; a sinner. *fem.* **বৃষলী** a Shudra (শূদ্র) woman; an adulteress or a profligate woman.

বৃষোৎসর্গ *n.* an obsequial ceremony in which four bulls are set free to move at liberty for the rest of their lives.

বৃষ্টি *n.* rain; rain-water; a shower (শরবৃষ্টি) ; **বৃষ্টি পড়া, বৃষ্টি হওয়া** *v.* to rain. **বৃষ্টি পড়ে** *v.* it rains. **বৃষ্টিচ্ছায়** *n.* (geog.) rain-shadow. **~জল** *n.* rain-water. **~পাত** *n.* rainfall; (meteor.) precipitation. **~বাদল** *n.* rains. **বৃষ্টিবাদলের দিন** *n.* a rainy day. **~বিন্দু** *n.* a rain-drop. **~মান, ~মাপক** *n.* a rain-gauge, a pluviometer. **বৃষ্টি সম্বন্ধীয়** *a.* pluvial. **~স্নাত** *a.* drenched or soaked in rain. **~হীন** *a.* rainless.

বৃষ্য *a.* invigorating; stimulant. □ *n.* an aphrodisiac; a stimulant.

বৃহৎ *a.* huge, big, large; extensive, vast; tall, high; long, important; complicated, big (বৃহৎ ব্যাপার) ; magnanimous (বৃহৎ হৃদয়) ; pompous (বৃহৎ কাণ্ড). **~কায়** *a.* big-bodied, gigantic, huge, colossal, bulky.

বৃহতী *fem.* of **বৃহৎ**।

বৃহত্তম *super.* of **বৃহৎ**।

বৃহত্তর *compar.* of **বৃহৎ**।

বৃহত্ত্ব *n.* largeness, bigness; greatness.

বৃহদন্ত্র *n.* (anat.) large intestines.

বৃহদাকার *a.* large in shape, big, enormous, huge, colossal.

বৃহস্পতি *n.* (myth.) the preceptor of gods; (astr.) the Jupiter; Thursday (usu. **বৃহস্পতিবার**). **একাদশে** (or **একাদশ**) **বৃহস্পতি** (astrol.) a very auspicious conjunction of stars in one's life. **বুদ্ধিতে বৃহস্পতি** a Brihaspati (বৃহস্পতি) in intelligence, a very intelligent person. **বৃহস্পতির বারবেলা** (astrol.) a part of Thursday considered utterly inauspicious for any work.

বে- *pfx.* denoting : absence, lack, negation, perversion etc.

বেঅকুফ, বেঅকুব *a.* foolish, stupid, silly. **বেঅকুফি, বেঅকুবি** *n.* foolishness, stupidity, silliness; a folly.

বেআইনি *a.* unlawful; illegal; lawless; outlawed or proscribed (বেআইনি পুস্তক), banned. **বেআইনি করা** *v.* to prohibit by law, to interdict or outlaw, to proscribe; to ban; to do something unlawful. **বেআইনি জনসমাগম** an unlawful assembly. **বেআইনিভাবে** *adv.* illegally, unlawfully.

বেআক্কেল *a.* foolish, stupid, silly; devoid of common sense. **বেআক্কেলে** pop. var. of **বেআক্কেল**।

বেআদব *a.* unmannerly; impudent. **বেআদবি** *n.* unmannerlines; impudence.

বেআন্দাজ, বেআন্দাজি *a.* not properly guessed or estimated or aimed; unestimated; beyond estimate; extravagant (বেআন্দাজি খরচ).

বেআবরু *a.* (of a woman) not keeping to the inner apartments; shamefully or indecorously exposed to public view; disgraced; (of a woman) having one's modesty outraged.

বেইজ্জত *a.* disgraced; insulted; put out of countenance; (of a woman) having one's modesty or chastity outraged.

□ *n.* disgrace; insult; state of being put out of countenance; outrage of modesty or chastity. **বেইজ্জত করা** *v.* to disgrace, to put to shame, to drag in the mud; to outrage the modesty of. **বেইজ্জতি** *n.* same as **বেইজ্জত** (*n.*).

বেইমান *a.* perfidious, unfaithful, false; (loos.) false to one's religious faith (esp. to Islam). **বেইমানি** *n.* perfidy.

বেউড়বাঁশ *n.* a thorny variety of bamboo.

বেএক্তিয়ার *a.* beyond jurisdiction, ultra vires; out of one's control.

বেওক্ত *a.* untimely.

বেওজর *a.* admitting no excuse or protest (বেওজর হুকুম). □ *adv.* without excuse or protest (বেওজর খাটা).

বেওয়া *n.* a childless widow.

বেওয়ারিশ *a.* ownerless; unclaimed; heirless; derelict.

বেঁটে *a.* dwarfish, short-statured. **~খাটো, ~খেঁটে** *a.* dumpy.

বেঁড়ে *a.* dock-tailed; tailless; (facet.) dwarfish (বেঁড়ে শয়তান).

বেঁধা pop. var. of **বিঁধা**।

বেঁয়ো *a.* lefthanded.

বেকসুর *a.* guiltless, innocent. **বেকসুর খালাস** acquittal on account of being found not guilty, clean acquittal. **বেকসুর খালাস হওয়া** to be acquitted on being found not guilty.

বেকানুন *a.* illegal.

বেকায়দা *a.* not amenable to any expedient; unwieldy; disadvantageous, awakward. □ *n.* an awakward situation, a tight corner. **বেকায়দায় ফেলা** *v.* to bring or throw into an awkward situation or a tight corner.

বেকার *a.* unemployed (বেকার অবস্থা, বেকার লোক) ; unoccupied, without work (বেকার সময়) ; useless (বেকার পরিশ্রম). **~ত্ব** *n.* unemployment; worklessness, occupationless. **~সমস্যা** *n.* the unemployment problem.

বেকুব, বেকুবি pop. variants of **বেঅকুফ, বেঅকুফি**।

বেখাপ, বেখাপ্পা *a.* unfitting; disproportionate; irrelevant, inappropriate; inconsistent; incompatible or awkward (বেখাপ অবস্থা).

বেখেয়াল *a.* without attention or intent, inattentive; absent-minded. □ *n.* inattention; absent-mindedness.

বেগ[1] *n.* (Mus.) the title of a Mughal or Turkish governor or landowner or noble man, beg, bey.

বেগ[2] *n.* speedy gait, rapidity, swiftness; speed, velocity (esp. in phys.) momentum, impetus; current, flow; desire to evacuate bowels or urinate; trouble or toil (টাকা আদায় করতে বেগ পেতে হয়েছে) ; severity, virulence (জ্বরের বেগ). **বেগ দেওয়া** *v.* to give trouble, to put to difficulty or inconvenience.

বেগতিক *n.* a helpless or unfavourable or awkward situation; a danger or difficulty; a tight corner. □ *a.* helpless or unfavourable; critical or difficult; awkward.

বেগত্রিভুজ *n.* a triangle of velocities.

বেগনি var. of **বেগুনি**।

বেগনিয়ামক *n.* a speed-governor.

বেগবতী *fem.* of **বেগবান**।

বেগবান *a.* fast-moving, speedy, swift; having a great velocity; sped up; having a strong current, flowing rapidly.

বেগবৃদ্ধি *n.* acceleration of speed, speed-up.

বেগম *n.* (Mus.) a queen; a lady (married or unmarried).

বেগমাপক *a.* measuring speed. **~যন্ত্র** speedometer.

বেগর *prep.* without, except.

বেগানা *a.* unknown; one whose identity is not known.

বেগার *n.* corvee. **বেগার খাটা** *v.* to work without wages, to render service gratis under pressure. **~ঠেলা** *a.* reluctantly and negligently done under duress.

বেগারে *a.* available for or rendering corvee service.

বেগার্ত *a.* extremely speedy; (fig.) utterly irresistible (বেগার্ত হৃদয়).

বেগুন *n.* the brinjal; the eggfruit or egg-apple; the egg-plant. **বেগুনি** *a.* purple, violet. □ *n.* the purple or violet colour; a fried snack prepared by dipping slices of brinjal in a thin paste of pulse-powder.

বেগোছ *a.* disorderly; disadvantageous, awkward. □ *n.* disorder; disadvantage; an awkward situation; a tight corner.

বেঘোর *n.* an utterly helpless situation (বেঘোরে মরা) ; absence of sensibility, torpor (বেঘোরে ঘুমানো).

বেঙ্গমা alt. spell. of **ব্যাঙ্গমা** *fem.* **বেঙ্গমি**।

বেচা *v.* to sell. □ *a.* sold. **~কেনা** *n.* buying and selling; traffic, trade. **বেচাকেনা করা** *v.* to trade or traffic (in), to buy and sell. **বেচানো** *v.* to cause to sell.

বেচারা, বেচারি *n.* a helpless or wretched or pitiable person; a harmless or innocent person.

বেচাল *a.* misbehaving; dissolute; refractory; difficult (বেচাল অবস্থা). □ *n.* misbehaviour, misdemeanour; dissoluteness; refractoriness; a difficulty.

বেজন্মা *a.* bastard, illegitimate.

বেজাত *n.* a different caste; a degenerated caste. □ *a.* degenerated in caste; bastard, illegitimate.

বেজায় *a.* much or many; excessive; tremendous. □ *adv.* very much; excessively; tremendously.

বেজায়গা *n.* a bad or wrong place; an improper place.

বেজার *a.* disgusted; displeased; sulky. **বেজার হয়ে** with a bad grace.

বেজি *n.* the mongoose, the ichneumon.

বেজিত *a.* worried, anxious (cp. **উদ্বেজিত**).

বেজুত *n.* a tight corner; a disadvantage; indisposition (শরীরের বেজুত). □ *a.* (of situation) disadvantageous; (of health) indisposed.

বেঞ্চ, বেঞ্চি *n.* a bench, a form.

বেটা *n.* a son; (in affection) an infant boy or a younger man : (dero.) a fellow, a bugger. □ *in comp.* (used as a *pfx.*) male, he-. □ *n. fem.* **বেটি** a daughter; (in affection) an infant girl or a younger woman. **বেটাছেলে** (vul.) *n.* a male person, a male. **বেটাচ্ছেলে, বেটার ছেলে** *n.* a term of colourless abuse, a bugger.

বেটাইম *n.* improper time. □ *a.* untimely.

বেটাছেলে, বেটাচ্ছেলে, see **বেটা**।

বেঠিক *a.* erroneous, incorrect, wrong; improper; uncertain.

বেডৌল *a.* ill-shaped, misshaped (বেডৌল পোশাক) ; ugly (বেডৌল মূর্তি).

বেড় *n.* encirclement; circumference; girth. **বেড় দেওয়া** *v.* to surround, to enclose, to encircle.

বেড়া *v.* same as **বেড় দেওয়া**। □ *a.* enclosing, surrounding (বেড়া আগুন, বেড়াজাল) ; enclosed, surrounded (বেড়া জায়গা). □ *n.* a fence; an enclosure; any object to enclose with.

বেড়ানো *v.* to walk (for pleasure or exercise), to stroll, to promenade; to go on an excursion or tour.

বেড়াজাল *n.* a kind of fishing net that brings the fish within an enclosure.

বেড়াল coll. var. of **বিড়াল**।

বেড়ি *n.* a shackle or chain (কোমরের বেড়ি) ; fetters, (poet.) gyves; a kind of tongs for gripping cooking utensils (হাতবেড়ি). **বেড়ি পরানো** *v.* to shackle; to fetter, (poet.) to gyve.

বেড়ে *int.* (coll.) excellent, fine; bravo.

বেড়েন *n.* cudgelling, drubbing, clubbing, flagellation (গোবেড়েন).

বেড়েলা *n.* a kind of shrub (growing by roadside), *Sida cordifolia.*

বেঢপ, (dial.) **বেঢক** *a.* unfitting; ugly; ill-shaped, misshapen; awkward.

বেঢ়া *v.* (poet. & obs.) to encircle; to encompass, to beset.

বেণি, বেণী *n.* a braid, a plait; pigtail; a tress; a stream (ত্রিবেণী). **বেণি বাঁধা** *v.* to tress; to braid, to plait. **~বদ্ধ** *a.* tressed. **~সংহার** *n.* braiding or plaiting the hair; tressing the hair into a plait.

বেণু *n.* a kind of thin bamboo of which flutes are made, a reed (বেণুকুঞ্জ) ; a flute made of this bamboo, a pipe. **~ধ্বনি, ~রব** *n.* the note of a bamboo-flute. **~বাদক** *n.* a player of a bamboo-flute.

বেত *n.* cane; rattan, ratan; a ferule; a stroke of ferule. **বেত মারা, বেতানো** *v.* to cane; to flagellate. **বেত লাগানো** *v.* to beat with a cane, to cane; to fit or mend with cane or strips of cane (as a chair). **বেতের চেয়ার** a cane-chair. **বেতের ছড়ি** a walking-stick made of cane, a rattan, a cane. **বেতের ঝুড়ি** a wicker-basket.

বেতন *n.* pay, a salary, wages. **~ক্রম** *n.* a scale of pay. **~দেয়ক** *n.* a pay-bill, an acquittance-roll. **~ভুক, ~ভোগী** *a.* salaried.

বেতমিজ *a.* uncivil; arrogant; impudent.

বেতর *a.* indisposed (বেতর শরীর) ; fuddled, sottish, besotted (নেশায় বেতর) ; embarrassed, off one's guard (জেরায় বেতর) ; dissimilar.

বেতরিবত *a.* uneducated; ill-bred, unmannerly.

বেতস *n.* the cane-plant; the rattan-plant; a variety of thin cane of which flutes are made. **~পত্র** *n.* a leaf of the cane-plant.

বেতানো see **বেত** ।

বেতার[১] *a.* tasteless, insipid; distasteful; (fig.) uninteresting, dull.

বেতার[২] *a.* wireless. □ *n.* the radio; wireless telegraphy. **বেতারে ঘোষণা করা** *v.* to broadcast. **~ঘোষণা** *n.* a broadcast; a radio announcement. **~বার্তা** *n.* a wireless telegram or message; radio news. **~যন্ত্র** *n.* a radio.

বেতাল[১] *n.* (mus.) a breach of measure. □ *a.* same as **বেতালা** ।

বেতাল[২] *n.* (myth.) a dead body possessed by a ghost. **~সিদ্ধ** *a.* having absolute domination over a ghost possessing a dead body.

বেতালা *a.* (of music) failing in measure, (of a musician) failing to maintain measure; (fig.) upset; confounded; confusing (বেতালা অবস্থা) ; (fig.) wayward or outlandish (বেতালা লোক).

বেতো *n.* rheumatic. **বেতো ঘোড়া** a weary horse, a jade.

বেত্তা *a.* (used as a *sfx.*) versed in.

বেত্র *n.* the cane-plant, cane, rattan, ratan (বেত্রকুঞ্জ) ; a cane, a ferule (বেত্রাঘাত). **~দণ্ড** *n.* a cane, a ferule; a flagellum; a sentence of or punishment by caning or whipping. **~ধর, ~ধারী** *a.* carrying a cane or rattan (esp. attributed to a guard). *fem.* **~ধারিণী, ~বতী** । **বেত্রাঘাত** *n.* a stroke with a cane; caning, flagellation. **বেত্রাঘাত করা** *v.* to cane; to flagellate, to whip. **বেত্রাসন** *n.* a cane seat, a rattan chair. **বেত্রাহত** *a.* caned, whipped. **বেত্রাহত কুকুরের মতো** like a dog which has been whipped, (cp.) with the tail between the legs.

বেথুয়া, বেথো *n.* a variety of spinach.

বেদ *n.* any one of the four Vedas, a Veda.

বেদখল *a.* (of a man) dispossessed, ousted, ejected; (of lands) put out of possession (of an occupier), not taken possession of (esp. by the owner), taken possession of unlawfully and often forcibly (as by an intruder). **বেদখল করা** *v.* to take possession of unlawfully (and esp. forcibly). **বেদখল থাকা** *v.* to remain unoccupied. **বেদখল হওয়া** *v.* to pass out of possession of; to be taken possession of unlawfully (and esp. forcibly). **বেদখলি** *a.* taken possession of unlawfully (and often forcibly).

বেদচতুষ্টয় *n.* the four Vedas (namely, ঋক্, সাম, যজুঃ, অথর্ব).

বেদচর্চা *n.* the study of the Vedas.

বেদজ্ঞ *a.* versed in the Vedas.

বেদজ্ঞান *n.* knowledge of the Vedas.

বেদন *n.* feeling, sensation; perception; pain; marriage; a gift.

বেদনা *n.* feeling; pain, ache; affliction; grief, sorrow; mental agony. **বেদনা করা** *v.* to pain, to ache. **বেদনা দেওয়া** *v.* to pain; to inflict pain on; to grieve; to agonize mentally. **বেদনা পাওয়া** *v.* to be pained; to feel pain; to be grieved. **~জনক, ~দায়ক** *a.* painful; grievous; agonizing; pitiable; sad. **~বোধ** *n.* feeling of pain. **~র্ত** *a.* afflicted; pained; agonized; aggrieved. **~হীন** *a.* painless, unaching.

বেদনিন্দক *n.* a disparager or rejector of the teachings of the Vedas; an atheist.

বেদনীয় *a.* capable of being felt; perceivable; cognizable.

বেদবাক্য *n.* a quotation from the Vedas; (coll.) an absolute or inviolable truth or command, (cp.) gospel truth.

বেদবিৎ *a.* versed in the Vedas.

বেদবেদাঙ্গ *n.* the Vedas and their branches or subsidiary parts (see **বেদাঙ্গ**).

বেদব্যাস *n.* Vyasa (ব্যাস) the author of the Mahabharata.

বেদম *a.* out of breath, breathless (ছুটে ছুটে

বেদম, বেদম ছুট) ; giving or taking no respite even to breathe (বেদম মার বা ভোজন). □ *adv.* out of breath, breathlessly; without respite even to breathe.

বেদমন্ত্র *n.* the prescribed mantras or incantations or sanctions of the Vedas.

বেদমাতা same as **গায়ত্রী**।

বেদরকারি *a.* unnecessary.

বেদল *n.* a different or hostile party or side. **বেদলীয়** *a.* of or belonging to a different or hostile party; hostile.

বেদসম্মত *a.* conforming to the Vedas.

বেদস্তুর *a.* contrary to rule or practice, unconventional.

বেদাঁড়া *a.* irregular ; unusual.

বেদাঙ্গ *n.* any one of the six branches of the Vedas (namely শিক্ষা, কল্প, ব্যাকরণ, নিরুক্ত, ছন্দ, জ্যোতিষ).

বেদাধ্যাপন, বেদাধ্যাপনা *n.* teaching the Vedas.

বেদাধ্যায়ী *a.* one studying the Vedas. □ *n.* one who studies the Vedas.

বেদানা *n.* the best variety of pomegranate.

বেদানুশীলন same as **বেদচর্চা** and **বেদাভ্যাস**।

বেদান্ত *n.* the Vedanta, the Upanishad; a theological treatise by Vyasa (ব্যাস). **~বাদ** *n.* the doctrine contained in the Vedanta. **বেদান্তবাদী** same as **বৈদান্তিক**।

বেদাভ্যাস *n.* study of the Vedas.

বেদি, বেদিকা *n.* an altar; a pulpit; a dais, a platform.

বেদিত *a.* submitted or represented to one for one's information.

বেদিতব্য var. of **বেদ্য**।

বেদী alt. spell. of **বেদি**।

বেদুইন *n.* a bedouin, a beduin.

বেদে *n.* one of a gypsy tribe of India. *fem.* **বেদেনি**।

বেদ্য *a.* to be learnt; knowable.

বেধ *n.* depth; thickness; a bore; boring, piercing, perforation.

বেধক *a.* & *n.* one who or that which bores or pierces or perforates.

বেধড়ক *a.* measureless, excessive. □ *adv.* exceedingly; violently; mercilessly (বেধড়ক ঠ্যাঙাল).

বেধন *n.* boring, piercing; perforation. **বেধনী, বেধনিকা** *n.* an instrument for boring; a drill, an auger; an awl.

বেধিত *a.* bored; pierced; perforated.

বেধ্য *a.* that which is to be or can be bored or pierced.

বেনজির *a.* without a precedent, without an example, unexampled; unparalleled.

বেনা *n.* verbena. **বেনার মূল** vertiver, cuscus. **বেনাবনে মুক্তো ছড়ানো** (fig.) to cast pearls before swine, to scatter seed amidst thorns.

বেনাম *n.* one's name used by another; a pseudonym. □ *a.* same as **বেনামা**। **বেনাম করা** *v.* to transfer (a property) to another only nominally (chiefly in order to evade liabilities). **বেনামে করা** *v.* to do (something) under another's name. **বেনামে লেখা** *v.* to write under a pseudonym. **~দার** *n.* a person to whom a property has been transferred only nominally. **বেনামা, বেনামি** *a.* transferred to another only nominally; anonymous or pseudonymous (বেনামা লেখা, বেনামি চিঠি) ; nameless (বেনামি বন্দর).

বেনারসি *a.* made in Banaras (বেনারসি সিল্ক) ; made of Banaras silk (বেনারসি শাড়ি). □ *n.* a woman's sari (cloth) made of Banaras silk.

বেনিয়ম *n.* illegality; irregularity; unlawfulness; violation of the rule. **বেনিয়ম করা** *v.* to break the rule, to violate the rule; to perpetrate an irregularity.

বেনিয়া coll. corrup. of **বানিয়া**।

বেনিয়ান *n.* a broker or financier; a kind of loose jacket or undergarment; a banian, a banyan.

বেনে coll. corrup. of **বানিয়া**।

বেনো *a.* produced or borne by flood. **বেনো জল** floodwater.

বেপছন্দ *a.* not liked, not to one's liking, disapproved.

বেপথু, বেপন *n.* trembling; tremour; quake, shake; shiver; thrill.

বেপমান *a.* trembling; quaking; shivering; feeling a thrill.

বেপরদা *a.* exposed; using no covering or yashmak (বেপরদা শরীর) ; not keeping to the inner apartments (বেপরদা মেয়েমানুষ). □ *n.* (mus.) a wrong scale.

বেপরোয়া *a.* fearing or heeding nothing or nobody; (loos.) reckless or desperate, devil-may-care. **বেপরোয়া লোক** an absolutely dauntless or heedless man; a desperado.

বেপর্দা alt. spell. of **বেপরদা** ।

বেপাত্তা *a.* without news of whereabouts, one whose whereabouts are unknown.

বেপোট *a.* out of place, out of the way; inconsistent; inappropriate; disadvantageous.

বেফাঁস *a.* divulged; uttered off guard, imprudently uttered (বেফাঁস কথা) ; unrestrained, loose, free (বেফাঁস মুখ).

বেফায়দা *a.* futile, vain; purposeless; useless.

বেবন্দোবস্ত *a.* disorderly; not properly managed; (of lands) not settled on. □ *n.* disorderliness; disorder.

বেবাক *a.* entire, whole; all.

বেমক্কা *a.* unbecoming; irrelevant; inappropriate; sudden (বেমক্কা মার). □ *adv.* suddenly or unreasonably (বেমক্কা মেরে বসল).

বেমানান *a.* unfitting; unbecoming; irrelevant; inappropriate; ill-matched; incompatible; awkward.

বেমালুম *a.* unperceivable, unperceived; stealthy. □ *adv.* imperceptibly; stealthily.

বেমেরামত *n.* disrepair, unrepair. □ *a.* wanting in repair, unrepaired.

বেয়াই coll. var. of **বেহাই** ।

বেয়াকুল poet. corrup. of **ব্যাকুল** ।

বেয়াড়া *a.* odd-looking; ungainly; awkward (বেয়াড়া অবস্থা) ; refractory or selfwilled (বেয়াড়া ছেলে) ; queer, odd, outlandish, difficult (বেয়াড়া প্রশ্ন).

বেয়াদপ, বেয়াদপি variants of **বেআদব** and **বেআদবি** respectively.

বেয়ান coll. var. of **বেহান** ।

বেয়ারা *n.* a carrier, a messenger, a bearer; an orderly.

বেয়ারিং *a.* sent by post with postage unpaid or underpaid.

বেয়াল্লিশ coll. var. of **বিয়াল্লিশ** ।

বের *a.* coll. corrup. of **বাহির** (*a.*).

বেরং *n.* a spoilt colour; a different colour; (in card-playing) a suit other than the trump.

বেরনো alt. spell. of **বেরোনো** ।

বেরসিক *a.* devoid of sense of humour; devoid of appreciative power; witless; (loos.) prosaic.

বেরাদর *n.* a brother; a friend; a kinsman, a relative.

বেরাল var. of **বেড়াল** ।

বেরিবেরি *n.* beriberi.

বেরিয়ে coll. var. of **বাহির হয়ে** । **বেরিয়ে পড়া** *v.* to get out (of); to set out on a journey; to come to light. **বেরিয়ে যাওয়া** *v.* to get out (of); to quit (a place), to depart; to out-strip; to set out on a journey, to go out-of-doors; to be exposed or to be adequately punished for (লম্বা কথা বেরিয়ে যাওয়া).

বেরোনো v. to go or get out, to come out; to be out; to be published (পরীক্ষার ফল বেরিয়েছে) ; to emerge.

বেল[1] *n.* a kind of sweet-smelling flower, the Arabian Jasmine, *Jasminum Sambac*.

বেল[2] *n.* a large bundle, a bale.

বেল[3] *n.* diapered lace.

বেল[4] *n.* the marmelos, the wood-apple. **বেল পাকলে কাকের কী** (fig.) it makes no difference for the blind when a circus-party comes to the city. **বেলের মোরব্বা** marmelos jam or jelly. **~শুঁঠ** *n.* pieces of dried wood-apple.

বেল[5] *n.* a bell. **বেল পড়ছে, বেল বাজছে** *v.* the bell goes.

বেল[6] *n.* bail. **বেল দেওয়া** *v.* to accept or admit to or allow bail (as by a magistrate). **বেল পাওয়া** *v.* to be allowed bail. **বেল হওয়া** *v.* to go or give or stand bail (for). **বেলে খালাস করা** *v.* to bail one out. **বেলে থাকা** *v.* to be on bail.

বেলওয়ারি alt. spell. of **বেলোয়ারি** ।

বেলচা *n.* a shovel.

বেল্ট্ *n.* a belt.

বেলদার[1] *n.* a digger.

বেলদার[2] *a.* fitted with a diapered lace (বেলদার টুপি).

বেলন, বেলনা *n.* rolling (esp. chapaties) with a roller; a rolling-pin; a cylindrical roller to roll chapaties; a cylinder.

বেলনাকার *a.* cylindrical.

বেলমোক্তা *adv.* all told, in all.

বেলা[1] same as **বেল[1]** ।

বেলা[২] *n.* the sea-shore, the coast, the sea-bank, the sea-beach; the full tide and ebb tide of the sea.

বেলা[৩] *v.* to roll (as chapaties with a roller). □ *a.* rolled.

বেলা[৪] *n.* a time of day (and not of night) (বেলা বারোটা) ; daytime (বেলাশেষ) ; advance of the morning (বেলা বাড়া) ; delay (esp. made in the morning) (বেলা করা) ; length, duration (জীবনের বেলা) ; time, specified time (খাওয়ার বেলা) ; turn (তোমার বেলা) ; an opportunity, an advantageous point of time (এইবেলা).

বেলানিল *n.* sea-breeze.

বেলাবসান *n.* close the day, evening; (late) afternoon.

বেলাবেলি *adv.* when there is still daylight; with daylight still there.

বেলাভূমি *n.* sea-beach, coastland.

বেলামুখ *n.* the beach-head.

বেলি var. of **বেল**[১] and **বেলা**[৪] ।

বেলিফ *n.* a bailiff.

বেলুন[১] *n.* a roller for rolling chapaties; a cylinder.

বেলুন[২] *n.* a balloon.

বেলে *a.* sandy. □ *n.* a kind of fish that likes to lie amidst sand. **~পাথর** *n.* sandstone.

বেলেল্লা *a.* wayward; boisterous; shameless, brazen-faced; lascivious, dissolute; rowdy. **~গিরি, ~পনা** *n.* waywardness; boisterousness; lasciviousness; rowdyism.

বেলোয়ারি *a.* made of cutglass (বেলোয়ারি ঝাড়) or bevelled glass (বেলোয়ারি চুড়ি). **বেলোয়ারি বাসন** glassware.

বেল্লিক *a.* lascivious, misbehaved; impudent; brazen-faced.

বেশ[১] *a.* excellent, fine, nice (বেশ ছেলে) ; too much, thorough (বেশ ভিজে) ; large in amount, measure or degree (বেশ টাকা, বেশ খাটুনি, বেশ ভার) ; well-to-do (বেশ অবস্থা). □ *adv.* excellently, nicely (বেশ নাচে) ; too much, thoroughly (বেশ ভিজেছে) ; to or in a large amount, measure or degree (বেশ খেতে পারে) ; very (বেশ ভালো). □ *int.* all right, good. **বেশ কম** considerably less.

বেশ[২] *n.* a dress, a garment; a garb, a guise. **বীরের বেশে** dressed like a hero, in the guise of a hero. **~কার** *n.* one who helps another in dressing and toilet, a dresser; one who decorates an idol, a decorator. **বেশধারণ করা** *v.* to dress, to put on an appearance or a guise. **~ধারী** *a.* dressed or guised (as). *fem.* **বেশধারিণী** । **~বিন্যাস** *n.* dressing (esp. meticulously or carefully); dressing and makeup. **~ভূষা** *n.* clothing and ornaments; dressing and toilet. **~ভূষাপরায়ণ** *a.* fond of fine dress, ornaments and toilet; dandified. *fem.* **~ভূষাপরায়ণা** ।

বেশর *n.* an ornament for the nose, (cp.) a nose-bob.

বেশরম *a.* shameless, brazen-faced.

বেশি *n.* excess (কমবেশি). □ *a.* in excess (বেশি হওয়া) ; many (বেশি লোক) ; much (বেশি দুধ). □ *adv.* excessively, much (বেশি হাসা). **বেশির ভাগ** the greater part or portion or number (বেশির ভাগ খাবার বা টাকা) ; for the most part. **বেশির ভাগ লোক** the majority; most people.

বেশী[২] *a.* (used as a *sfx.*) same as **বেশধারী** (see **বেশ**[২]). *fem.* **বেশিনী** ।

বেশুমার *a.* innumerable, countless.

বেশ্যা *n.* a prostitute, a harlot, a whore. **~গিরি, ~বৃত্তি** *n.* prostitution, harlotry. **বেশ্যালয়** *n.* a brothel, a whore-house, a house of ill-fame. **~সক্ত** *a.* habitually visiting or given to visiting prostitutes. **বেশ্যাসক্ত ব্যক্তি** a whore-monger.

বেষ্ট *n.* a fence, an enclosure; a circumference. **বেষ্টক** *a.* that which or one who surrounds; enclosing, surrounding, encircling; circumambient. **বেষ্টন** *n.* enclosing or surrounding; a wall (esp. one encompassing something); a fence, an enclosure; girth, circumference. **বেষ্টন করা** *v.* to enclose, to surround; to hem in. **বেষ্টনী** *n.* anything that encloses; a fence, an enclosure; a cordon; a wall; girth, circumference.

বেষ্টিত *a.* surrounded, hemmed in, encompassed, cordoned.

বেসন, (coll.) **বেসম** *n.* powdered pulse, pulse-meal.

বেসর alt. spell of **বেশর**।

বেসরকারি *a.* non-official, unofficial; not belonging to the government; private, personal.

বেসাত *n.* wares; merchandise. **বেসাতি** *n.* wares; merchandise; trading; a shopkeeper; a trader. **বেসাতি করা** *v.* to trade, to traffic.

বেসামরিক *a.* non-military, civil.

বেসামাল *a.* unable to restrain or check; divested of self-restraint; unrestrained; unguarded; disorderly; embarrassed.

বেসুদি *a.* without interest, bearing no interest, interest-free.

বেসুর, বেসুরো *a.* not in keeping with the tune or musical note (বেসুরো বাজনা) ; incapable of maintaining the tune, given to uttering false notes (বেসুরো গায়ক) ; discordant or uproarious or grating on ears (বেসুরো কোলাহল).

বেহদ্দ *a.* extreme; out-and-out, thorough (বেহদ্দ বদমাশ) ; boundless (বেহদ্দ শয়তানি). **বেহদ্দ বেহায়া** shameless to the core.

বেহাই *n.* the father-in-law or an uncle-in-law of a son or daughter.

বেহাগ *n.* an Indian musical mode.

বেহাত *a.* passed out of one's hand or possession or control; gone into another's hand or possession or control.

বেহান *n.* (*fem.* of **বেহাই**) the mother-in-law or an aunt-in-law of a son or daughter.

বেহায়া *a.* shameless, brazen-faced, browless.

বেহারা falsely elegant form of **বেয়ারা**।

বেহারি *a.* of Bihar. □ *n.* a native of Bihar.

বেহাল *a.* worn-out; disorganised; in total disarray; in a wretched condition.

বেহালা *n.* a violin, a fiddle. **বেহালার ছড়** a fiddlestick, a violin bow. **~বাদক** *n.* a fiddler, a violinist.

বেহিসাব *a.* unestimated, inestimable; unrestrained; improvident; incautious; uneconomical; extravagant. □ *n.* absence of estimate or economy; improvidence; lack of caution; extravagance. **বেহিসাবি** *a.* unrestrained; uneconomical; incautious; extravagant (বেহিসাবি খরচ).

বেহুঁশ *a.* unmindful; heedless; careless; senseless; not in one's proper senses; fainted, swooned.

বেহুদা *a.* unjust; unnecessary, useless. □ *adv.* unjustly; unnecessarily, uselessly, for nothing.

বেহেড *a.* having one's head turned; arrogant; bereft of common sense; bereft of power of thinking; thoughtless; off one's head (বেহেড মাতাল) ; besotted, sottish (নেশায় বেহেড).

বেহেশ্‌ত্‌, বেহেস্ত *n.* heaven.

বৈ rej. spell. of **বই**[২] & **বই**[৩]।

বৈকল্পিক *a.* alternative, variant.

বৈকল্য same as **বিকলতা** (see **বিকল**)।

বৈকাল *n.* the afternoon, the close of the day. **বৈকালিক, বৈকালীন** *a.* of the afternoon, afternoon. *fem.* **বৈকালিকী**। **বৈকালী** *n.* the evening food-offering to a deity.

বৈকুণ্ঠ *n.* the celestial abode of Vishnu (also **বৈকুণ্ঠধাম, বৈকণ্ঠপুরী**). **~নাথ, ~পতি** *n.* Vishnu (বিষ্ণু).

বৈকৃত *a.* perverted. **~কাম** *n.* a sex pervert; (psy.) a pervert.

বৈক্লব্য *n.* distress; mental prostration or unrest; embarrassment.

বৈগুণ্য *n.* lack of good quality; defect; hostility (গ্রহবৈগুণ্য).

বৈচিত্র্য *n.* multi-colouredness; variegation; variety or diversity or vicissitude; multifariousness; wonderfulness; queerness. **~পূর্ণ** *a.* variegated; diverse; multifarious; having variety or diversity. **~হীন** *a.* without variety or diversity; monotonous; drab.

বৈজয়ন্ত *n.* the capital or the palace or the flag of Indra (ইন্দ্র) the king of gods. **বৈজয়ন্তী** *n. fem.* a flag, a banner, a multi-coloured garland.

বৈজিক *a.* of seed; algebraical (বৈজিক রাশি = algebraical quantity); radical; seminal.

বৈজ্ঞানিক *a.* scientific (বৈজ্ঞানিক গবেষণা) ; versed in science. □ *n.* (loos.) a scientist.

বৈঠক *n.* a club, an assembly, a majlis; a conference, a meeting; a sitting; a hookahstand; a system of physical exercise by repeated sitting down and standing up alternately. **~খানা** *n.* a drawing-room, a parlour, a salon; a lounge. **বৈঠকি** *a.* suitable for an assembly or party (বৈঠকি গান বা গল্প).

বৈঠা alt. spell. of **বইঠা**।

বৈড়াল *a.* feline. **~ব্রত** *n.* (fig.) simulated holiness, sanctimony. **~ব্রতী** *n.* a hypocrite; hypocrisy.

বৈতনিক *a.* salaried; stipendiary; wageearning; not honorary.

বৈতরণী *n.* (myth.) a river which the spirits of the dead have to cross in order to reach the abode of the dead, (cp.) the Styx. **বৈতরণীর মাঝি** *n.* the ferryman across the Baitarani (বৈতরণী), (cp.) Charon.

বৈতানিক *a.* sacrificial. □ *n.* burnt-offering.

বৈতাল, বৈতালিক *n.* one employed to glorify (esp. a prince) in songs (usu. at fixed hours).

বৈদগ্ধ, বৈদগ্ধ্য *n.* wit; witticism; connoisseurship; erudition; learning; cleverness; adeptness.

বৈদর্ভ *a.* of Bidarbha (বিদর্ভ), a province of India. *fem.* **বৈদর্ভী**। **বৈদর্ভী রীতি** *a* style of literary composition in which compound words are avoided as far as practicable and great attention is paid to sweetness of diction.

বৈদান্তিক *a.* Vedantic. □ *n.* a Vedantic philosopher or scholar; a believer in the Vedanta doctrine; a Vedantist.

বৈদিক *a.* Vedic. □ *n.* one of a class of Brahmans; a Vedist.

বৈদূর্য *n.* chrysoberyl, cat's eye, lapis lazuli.

বৈদেশিক *a.* foreign; external; (arch.) outlandish; exotic; alien. **বৈদেশিক বাণিজ্য** *n.* foreign trade.

বৈদেহ *a.* of Bideha (বিদেহ) or Mithila (মিথিলা), a province of ancient India. **বৈদেহী** *a. fem.* of **বৈদেহ**। □ *n.* Sita (সীতা) of the Ramayana.

বৈদ্য *n.* a physician; a healer; one of an upper-class Hindu caste. **বৈদ্যক** same as **বৈদ্যশাস্ত্র**। **~নাথ** *n.* Shiva (শিব) (whose image is installed at Deoghar). **~শালা** *n.* a clinic ; a hospital. **~শাস্ত্র** same as **আয়ুর্বেদ**। **~সংকট** *n.* miscarriage of treatment on account of being treated by numerous physicians simultaneously.

বৈদ্যুতিক *a.* electric, electrical; electrically operated. **বৈদ্যুতিক বাতি** *n.* an electric lamp or light.

বৈধ *a.* lawful, legal; just; formal. **বৈধ ক্রিয়া** lawful act or rite. **বৈধ অধিকার** legal or lawful or just right.

বৈধব্য *n.* widowhood. **~বাস** *n.* widow's weeds.

বৈধর্ম্য *n.* difference in religious creed, religious difference; heresy, heterodoxy; difference in nature or function; difference.

বৈনতেয় same as **বিনতানন্দন** (see **বিনতা**[২]).

বৈনাশিক *a.* destructive, ruinous; cataclysmic.

বৈপরীত্য *n.* oppositeness, contrast (বর্ণ-বৈপরীত্য) ; contrariety; opposition; antipathy; adversity; an upset; a disaster.

বৈপিত্র, বৈপিত্রেয় *a.* born of the same mother and of a step-father (**বৈপিত্র ভ্রাতা** = a half-brother); of a step-father (বৈপিত্র সম্পত্তি). *fem.* **বৈপিত্রী, বৈপিত্রেয়ী**।

বৈপ্লবিক *a.* revolutionary; causing or effecting a radical change; radical; total (বৈপ্লবিক পরিবর্তন).

বৈবস্বত *a.* solar (বৈবস্বত মন্বন্তর = the solar dissolution). □ *n.* God Sani (শনি) ; Yama (যম) the god of death.

বৈবাহিক *a.* matrimonial; nuptial. □ *n.* the father-in-law or an uncle-in-law of a son or daughter. *fem. n.* **বৈবাহিকী,** (loos. & pop.) **বৈবাহিকা** the mother-in-law or aunt-in-law of a son or daughter.

বৈভব *n.* Godhead; divinity; sanctifying grace, unction; glory; wealth, riches. **~শালী** *a.* endowed with divinity or unction or glory; wealthy, rich, opulent.

বৈভাষিক *a.* alternative, variant.

বৈমাত্র, বৈমাত্রেয় *a.* born of a step-mother (**বৈমাত্র ভ্রাতা** = a step-brother); of a step-mother. *fem.* **বৈমাত্রী, বৈমাত্রেয়ী**।

বৈমানিক *a.* aeronautical. □ *n.* an airman, an aeronaut, an aviator.

বৈমুখ corrup. of **বিমুখ**। *fem.* **বৈমুখী**।

বৈমুখ্য same as **বিমুখতা** (see **বিমুখ**).

বৈয়ক্তিক *a.* personal.

বৈয়াকরণ *a.* grammatical; versed in grammar. □ *n.* a grammarian. **বৈয়াকরণিক** *n.* a grammarian.

বৈয়াঘ্র *a.* relating to the tiger.

বৈয়াসকী, বৈয়াসিকী *n.* a treatise on scriptural law compiled by Vyasa.

বৈর *n.* hostility, enmity. **~নির্যাতন** *n.* persecution of an enemy. **বৈরনির্যাতন করা** *v.* to persecute an enemy. **~ভাব** *n.* hostility; enmity. **~সাধন** *n.* hostility, enmity.

বৈরাগ var. of **বৈরাগ্য** ।

বৈরাগী *a.* apathetic to worldly interests, (cp.) stoical. □ *n.* (loos.) a Vaishnava anchorite.

বৈরাগ্য *n.* apathy towards worldly interests; stoicism; philosophical or spiritual consciousness. **বৈরাগ্যোদয়** *n.* access of philosophical or spiritual consciousness (in one's mind); awakening of the spirit of renunciation.

বৈরিতা *n.* enmity, hostility; malice.

বৈরী *a.* hostile, inimical; malicious : adverse, unfavourable. □ *n.* an enemy, a foe, an adversary. **~ভাবাপন্ন** *a.* hostile, inimical; adverse.

বৈলক্ষণ্য *n.* a changed state; change; difference; uncommonness.

বৈশাখ *n.* the first month of the Bengali calendar (from the middle of April to the middle of May). **বৈশাখী** *a.* of Baisakh (বৈশাখী পূর্ণিমা). **বৈশাখী ঝড়** a northwester or nor'-wester.

বৈশিষ্ট্য *n.* speciality; importance or distinction; prominence; a peculiarity, a characteristic. **~রেখা** *n.* (phys.) a characteristic curve.

বৈশেষিক *n.* a system of philosophy propounded by Kanada (কণাদ).

বৈশ্বানর *n.* fire; the god of fire, Agni (অগ্নি).

বৈশ্য *n.* a member of the third caste amongst Hindus. *fem.* **বৈশ্যা** । **~বৃত্তি** *n.* trade; the profession of a trader; business as a profession.

বৈষম্য *n.* dissimilarity; inequality; difference. **~মূলক** *a.* discriminatory, differential. **বৈষম্যমূলক আচরণ** differential or unfair treatment.

বৈষয়িক *a.* relating to property or wealth or earthly possessions or personal affairs; material, worldly.

বৈষ্ণব *a.* relating to Vishnu (বিষ্ণু) ; worshipping Vishnu; following the teachings of Chaitanya. □ *n.* a worshipper of Vishnu; a follower of Chaitanya, a Vaishnava; a Vaishnava mendicant. *fem.* **বৈষ্ণবী** । **~ধর্ম** *n.* the Vaishnava cult or religion; Vaishnavism.

বৈসাদৃশ্য *n.* dissimilarity; inequality, disparity; difference.

বোঁ *int.* expressing : a whirring sound as caused by quick revolution, flight etc. **বোঁ করে** with a whir, whirringly; very swiftly; dartingly.

বোঁচকা *n.* a small bundle tied up in a piece of cloth, a pack. **বোঁচকাবুঁচকি** *n.* luggage. **বোঁচকাবুঁচকিসমেত** bag and baggage.

বোঁচা *a.* having one's nose cut off, noseless; snub-nosed; truncated.

বোঁটা *n.* a leaf-stalk; a petiole; a leaf; a leaf-base; a nipple, a teat.

বোঁদে *n.* a kind of small globular sweetmeat made of powdered pigeon-pea dipped in liquefied sugar; bundia, bonde.

বোকা *a.* stupid, foolish, silly. □ *n.* a stupid or silly person, a dunce, a fool, a simpleton. **~চণ্ডী, ~রাম** *a.* grossly stupid. □ *n.* a grossly stupid person. **~পাঁঠা** *n.* an over-grown billygoat; (fig.) an utter-fool. **~মি** *n.* stupidity, foolishness; a folly.

বোচকা var. of **বোঁচকা** ।

বোজা, বোজানো pop. variants of **বুজা** and **বুজানো** respectively.

বোঝা[1] *v.* to understand, to comprehend; to sound (মন বোঝার চেষ্টা). **~নো** *v.* to make one understand or comprehend; to explain; to comfort or console.

বোঝা[2] *n.* a burden, a load. **বোঝাই** *n.* loading; filling or repleting, repletion. □ *a.* loaded; loaded to the full (বোঝাই নৌকা) ; filled or replete (with) (পুঁজে বোঝাই) ; burdened (with) (দুঃখে বোঝাই). **বোঝাই করা** *v.* to load; to load to the full; to burden; to fill or replete (with).

বোঝাই-করা *a.* loaded, packed or loaded to the full. **বোঝা-টানা** *a.* load-carrying. **বোঝা-টানা ঘোড়া** a pack-horse. **বোঝা-টানা জানোয়ার** a beast of burden, a pack-animal.

বোঝাপড়া *n.* an understanding; a compromise; a mutual agreement; confrontation (বিপক্ষ দলের সঙ্গে শেষ বোঝাপড়া).

বোঝাপড়া করা *v.* to come to terms, to come to or arrive at an understanding.

বোট *n.* a boat.

বোটকা *a.* resembling the body odour of a billy-goat, goatish.

বোটে *n.* (coll.) a scull.

বোড়া *n.* a kind of venomous snake; the viper.

বোড়ে alt. spell. of **বড়ে**।

বোতল *n.* a bottle. **বোতলে ভরা, বোতলে পোরা** *v.* to bottle.

বোতাম *n.* a button. **বোতাম পরানো** বা **লাগানো** *v.* to button; to fit with buttons; to sew a button into. **বোতামের ঘর** বা **ঘাট** *n.* a button-hole.

বোদমাটি *n.* a kind of black earth or soil.

বোদা *n.* distasteful, tasteless, insipid; (loos.) rather offensive (বোদা গন্ধ) ; (fig.) uninteresting, dull (বোদা লেখা), witless (বোদা লোক).

বোদ্ধা *a.* able to understand or comprehend or appreciate, knowing, knowledgeable.

বোধ *n.* knowledge; cognition; intellect; intelligence; perception; feeling; appreciation; consciousness; consolation; a notion or surmise. **বোধ করা** *v.* to feel; to perceive; to have a notion, to surmise. **বোধ থাকা** *v.* to have wisdom or cognition or intellect or intelligence or perception or feeling or appreciation or consciousness. **বোধ মানা** *v.* to be amenable to consolation. **বোধ হওয়া** *v.* to seem or appear (to be). **বোধ হয়** perhaps. **বোধক** *a.* signifying, indicative (of); imparting knowledge; arousing feeling or consciousness; enlightening. **~গম্য** *a.* intelligible; perceivable; comprehensible; knowable. **বোধন** *n.* inparting knowledge; arousal of feeling or consciousness; enlightenment; awakening; ceremonial awakening of Goddess Durga (দুর্গা) on the sixth lunar day immediately preceding the time of her autumnal worship; an inspiration. **~য়িতা** same as **বোধক**। *fem.* **~য়িত্রী**। **~শক্তি** *n.* power of understanding or feeling; power of appreciation; perception; comprehension; intellect; sensation. **~শক্তিহীন** *a.* devoid of power of understanding or feeling or appreciation; insensible; stupid; dull. **~শক্তিহীনতা** *n.* lack of the power of understanding. **~শোধ** *n.* common sense. **~হীন** *a.* incapable of understanding or feeling or appreciating or perceiving; stupid; dull. **বোধাতীত** *a.* unintelligible; imperceptible; incomprehensible; unknowable; beyond cognition. **বোধি** *n.* a kind of spiritual meditation or trance; knowledge about philosophical reality, final or supreme knowledge; the banian tree at Gaya under which Buddha sat in meditation and attained final knowledge (usu. **বোধিদ্রুম, বোধিবৃক্ষ**). **বোধিসত্ত্ব** *n.* a person whose very essence is knowledge; an incarnation of Gautam (গৌতম) immediately preceding his birth as Buddha. **বোধিকা** *fem.* of **বোধক**। □ *n.* a helpbook. **বোধিনী** same as **বোধিকা** (*n.*). **বোধের বাইরে** *adv.* beyond one's knowledge or comprehension; beyond one's ken. **বোধোদয়** *n.* enlightenment. **বোধ্য** *a.* intelligbile; perceivable; comprehensible; knowable.

বোন *n.* a sister. **~ঝি** *n.* a sister's daughter, a niece. **~পো** *n.* a sister's son, a nephew.

বোনা *v.* to sow; to weave or knit. □ *a.* sown; woven; knitted.

বোনাই *n.* a sister's husband, a brother-in-law.

বোবা *a.* dumb; speechless; mute; (fig.) inexpressible (বোবা ব্যথা).

বোম[1] coll. form of **বোমা**।

বোম[2] *n.* the yoke of a vehicle.

বোমা *n.* a bomb. **বোমা ছোঁড়া, বোমা ছুঁড়ে মারা, বোমা মারা** *v.* to bomb. **~প্রতিরোধী** *a.* bombproof. **~বর্ষণ** *n.* bombing. **বোমাবর্ষণ করা** *v.* to bomb. **~রু** *a.* employed in bombing. **বোমারু বিমান** *n.* bomber.

বোম্বাই *n.* Bombay. □ *a.* grown or produced in Bombay (বোম্বাই ছিট) ; largeshaped (বোম্বাই আখ) ; of a superior quality (বোম্বাই আম).

বোম্বেটে *n.* a pirate, a buccaneer; a dare-devil; a terrible person. **~গিরি** *n.* piracy, buccaneering; indulgence in dare-devil activities.

বোয়াল *n.* a kind of large fish akin to the flounder.

বোরকা, বোরখা *n.* a yashmak.

বোরা[১] *n.* a sack, a gunny-bag; a sackful (দুই বোরা ধান).

বোরা[২] *n.* a community of Mussalmans (usu. of Surat).

বোরো *n.* a kind of inferior paddy.

বোর্ড *n.* a board.

বোল[১] coll. corrup. of **বউল**।

বোল[২] *n.* speech, language; a word; a note or call (as of birds); a sound; babbling noise (শিশুর বোল) ; (mus.) a symbolic sound (তবলার বোল) ; musical notation.

বোলচাল *n.* speech and conduct; pertness and glibness; blustering; affected speech and air; suspiciously shrewd speech and conduct.

বোলটু *n.* a bolt. **বোলটু পরানো, বোলটু লাগানো** *v.* to fit with a bolt.

বোলতা *n.* the wasp, the hornet.

বোলবোলা *n.* fame and power, predominance.

বোল্টু alt. spell. of **বোলটু**।

বোষ্টম coll. form of **বৈষ্ণব**।

বৌ, বৌ-কথা-কও, বৌ-কাঁটকি, বৌদি, বৌদিদি alt. spellings of **বউ, বউ-কথা-কও, বউ-কাঁটকি, বউদি** and **বউদিদি** respectively.

বৌদ্ধ *a.* Buddhist, Buddhistic. □ *n.* a Buddhist. **~চক্র** *n.* the Buddhist cross or wheel. **~ধর্ম** *n.* Buddhism. **~ধর্মাবলম্বী** *a.* Buddhist. □ *n.* a Buddhist.

বৌভাত, বৌমা, বৌ-মানুষ alt. spellings of **বউভাত, বউমা** and **বউমানুষ** respectively.

বৌলি alt. spell. of **বউলি**।

ব্যক্ত *a.* expressed, revealed, exposed; uttered, said; disclosed; divulged; manifest. **ব্যক্ত করা** *v.* to express, to reveal, to expose; to utter, to say; to disclose, to divulge; to manifest. **ব্যক্ত হওয়া** *v.* to be revealed or expressed or manifest.

ব্যক্তি *n.* a person (usu. masc.) a man; (phil.) an invidual or individuality; manifestation. **~ক, ~গত** *a.* (both *masc.* & *fem.*) personal, private; individual. **ব্যক্তিগত জামিন** personal security. **~তন্ত্র, ~বাদ** *n.* (pol.) individualism. **~তা** *n.* individuality. **~তান্ত্রিক** *a.* individualistic. **ব্যক্তিত্ব** *n.* personality. **ব্যক্তিত্বব্যঞ্জক** *a.* expressing or indicating personality. **ব্যক্তিত্বশালী** *a.* having personality or individuality. **~বাদী** *a.* individualistic. □ *n.* an individualist. **~স্বাধীনতা** *n.* individualism.

ব্যক্তীকৃত *a.* expressed; revealed; manifested.

ব্যগ্র *a.* eager; earnest; excited; anxious; inquisitive, curious. **~তা** *n.* eagerness; earnestness; excitement; anxiety; curiosity.

ব্যঙ্গ *n.* mockery, taunt, ridicule; irony, sarcasm. **ব্যঙ্গ করা** *v.* to mock, to taunt, to ridicule, to jeer (at). **~কবিতা** *n.* a satire; a parody. **~কাব্য** *n.* satire. **~চিত্র** *n.* a cartoon. **~প্রিয়** *a.* given to taunting; satirical; given to sardonic merriment; jocose. **ব্যঙ্গোক্তি** *n.* a taunting remark or utterance, an ironical comment; an insinuation.

ব্যঙ্গ্য *a.* figurative, metaphorical; covert, implied. **ব্যঙ্গ্যার্থ** *n.* figurative or suggested meaning, suggestion, covert hint, implication; (rhet.) implied or suggested meaning transcending the primary sense of words, indirect meaning, obliquity.

ব্যজন *n.* fanning; a fan. **ব্যজন করা** *v.* to fan. **ব্যজনী** *n.* a fan.

ব্যঞ্জক *a.* expressing, signifying, indicative (of); suggesting, implying.

ব্যঞ্জন *n.* a cooked dish of vegetables or fish or meat, any spicy dish of cooked food; expressing, expression; a characteristic sign; (gr.) a consonant (usu. **ব্যঞ্জনবর্ণ**). **~সন্ধি** see **সন্ধি**। **ব্যঞ্জনা** *n.* (rhet.) suggestion, a gesture; a secondary meaning transcending the primary meaning of words; expressing, expression. **ব্যঞ্জনাপূর্ণ, ব্যঞ্জনাময়** *a.* suggestive; full of suggestiveness; full of implications. **ব্যঞ্জনান্ত** *a.* (gr.) ending with a consonant or a consonantal sound. **ব্যঞ্জনান্ত শব্দ** a word that ends with a consonant. **ব্যঞ্জিত** *a.* indicated, suggested; expressed.

ব্যতিক্রম *n.* infringement, violation, contravention (রীতির ব্যতিক্রম) ; exception. **ব্যতিক্রম করা** *v.* to infringe, to violate, to contravene. **ব্যতিক্রমী** *a.* discriminating; (loos.) exceptional; extraordinary.

ব্যতিব্যস্ত *a.* fretfully busy (নানা কাজে ব্যতিব্যস্ত) ; embarrassed (প্রশ্নবাণে ব্যতিব্যস্ত) ; harassed or harried (পুলিশের তাড়ায় ব্যতিব্যস্ত) ; very much irritated or disturbed (গোলমালে ব্যতিব্যস্ত). **ব্যতিব্যস্ত করা** *v.* to harass or harry; to irritate or disturb or pester very much.

ব্যতিরিক্ত *a.* other than, excepting, omitting; additional, extra.

ব্যতিরেক *n.* absence; lack; omission, exclusion; exception; distinction; difference; (rhet.) a figure of speech marked with excess of the subject over the object of comparison. **ব্যতিরেকে** *prep.* excluding, without, except, besides, in addition to.

ব্যতিহার *n.* exchange, barter; interchange; reciprocity. **ব্যতিহার-বহুব্রীহি** *n.* (gr.) a system of compounding correlative words (e. g. হাতাহাতি).

ব্যতীত *a.* passed away. □ *prep.* except, without, save, excluding.

ব্যতীপাত *n.* a disaster; a natural calamity (such as, earthquake); (astrol.) an astral conjunction portending a natural calamity.

ব্যত্যয় same as **ব্যতিক্রম** ।

ব্যথা *n.* pain, ache; affliction, distress (মর্মব্যথা) ; labour-pain, labour, travail. **ব্যথা ওঠা** *v.* to be in travail, to labour. **ব্যথা করা** *v.* to pain, to ache. **ব্যথা দেওয়া** v. to give pain, to pain; to afflict, to distress; to offend. **মনে ব্যথা দেওয়া** to tread on one's corns. **ব্যথা পাওয়া** *v.* to feel pain; to be pained or afflicted or distressed or offended. **~তুর** *n.* afflicted; distressed. **~নিবারক** *n.* painkiller, analgesic drug. **ব্যথিত** *a.* pained; afflicted, distressed; offended. **ব্যথী** *a.* feeling pain (সমব্যথী). *fem.* **ব্যথিনী** ।

ব্যপদেশ *n.* a pretext, a pretence, a plea; (loos.) necessity, exigency (কার্যব্যপদেশে = in course of work).

ব্যবকলন *n.* (math.) subtraction, deduction. **ব্যবকলন করা** *v.* to subtract, to deduct.

ব্যবচ্ছিন্ন *a.* dissected.

ব্যবচ্ছেদ *n.* dissection. **ব্যবচ্ছেদ করা** *v.* to dissect. **ব্যবচ্ছেদাগার** *n.* dissection room.

ব্যবধান *n.* intervening distance, distance; a location screened from the view; a screen; estrangement (দুই বন্ধুর মধ্যে সৃষ্ট ব্যবধান) ; stand-offishness, aloofness. **সুদূর ব্যবধান** a far cry.

ব্যবসায়, ব্যাবসা *n.* a profession, a calling, a vocation; trade, business, traffic, commerce. **ব্যাবসা করা** *v.* to be engaged in trade or commerce; to trade (in), to traffic (in), to deal (in). **ব্যবসায়ী, ব্যাবসাদার** *a.* engaged in business or commerce; trading or trafficking or dealing (in); commercial; mercantile; businesslike; commercial in spirit or temperament. □ *n.* a trader, a merchant, a tradesman, a trafficker, a dealer; a man in business; one who is commercial in spirit or temperament; one skilled in worldly affairs; one keenly alive to one's own interests. **ব্যাবসা-বাণিজ্য** *n.* trade and commerce. **ব্যবসায়ী প্রতিষ্ঠান** a mercantile firm. **ব্যবসায়ী-সংঘ** *n.* a traders' guild; a mercantile corporation; a chamber of commerce.

ব্যবসিত *a.* endeavouring; persevering; ascertained.

ব্যবস্থা *n.* arrangement; preparation; procurement (মূলধনের ব্যবস্থা) ; provision (ভবিষ্যতের ব্যবস্থা) ; prescription or direction (শাস্ত্রীয় ব্যবস্থা) ; a law, a statute, a rule; legislation; order, system (এ সংসারে কোনো ব্যবস্থা নেই) ; settlement (ঝগড়ার ব্যবস্থা). **ব্যবস্থা করা** *v.* to arrange (for); to make preparations for; to procure; to provide for; to prescribe or direct; to settle. **ব্যবস্থা দেওয়া** *v.* to prescribe; to direct; to enjoin. **ব্যবস্থা হওয়া** *v.* to be arranged or prepared for or procured or provided for or prescribed or directed; to be settled. **~পক** *a.* legislative; law-giving; regulative; prescribing or directing, prescriptive; arranging for; preparative; founding, instituting. □ *n.* a legislator; a law-giver; a regulator; a prescriber or director; one who makes arrangements or preparations (for); a founder. **ব্যবস্থাপক পরিষৎ** *a* legislative council. **ব্যবস্থাপক সভা** a legislative assembly. **~পত্র** *n.* a prescription; a prescript; a directive. **~পন** *n.* legislation; enactment; law-making; regulation; arrangement; preparation; prescription or direction; founding, institution. **~পনা** *n.* arrangement; preparation; organisation. **ব্যবস্থা-পরিষৎ** *n.* a legislative council. **~পিত** *a.* legislated; enacted; regulated; prescribed or directed; arranged (for); founded, instituted. **~শাস্ত্র** *n.* jurisprudence, the law; a law-book; the Smriti (স্মৃতি) or the code of ancient Hindu laws. **ব্যবস্থিত** same as **ব্যবস্থাপিত**। **ব্যবস্থিত-চিত্ত** *a.* of settled mind, calm and composed, of unruffled temperament; determined.

ব্যবহার *n.* behaviour, demeanour, conduct; treatment of others (বন্ধুর প্রতি ব্যবহার) ; law, jurisprudence; a lawsuit; a work for earning one's living (ব্যবহারোদ্দেশে) ; commerce, trade; custom, practice, usage; application or use (ওষুধ-ব্যবহার, টুপি-ব্যবহার). **ব্যবহার করা** *v.* to behave; to treat (a person), to behave towards; to apply, to use. **ব্যবহার থাকা** *v.* to be in use (এখন এর তেমন ব্যবহার নেই). **ব্যবহার হওয়া** *v.* to be applied or used; to be in use. **~করণিক** *n.* a bench-clerk. **~গত** *a.* pertaining to one's behaviour; customary; practical. **~জীবী** *n.* a lawyer; a pleader, an advocate, a barrister, an attorney, a solicitor. **~জ্ঞ** *a.* versed in law or jurisprudence. **~দর্শন** *n.* jurisprudence; science and art of trying a lawsuit. **~দর্শী** *n.* a judge; a juror; a jurist. **~দেশক** *n.* an attorney-at-law, an attorney; a solicitor. **~বিধি** *n.* code of laws, jurisprudence, the law; direction or rules for use or application. **~যোগ্য** *a.* fit to be used or applied; useful, serviceable. **~শাস্ত্র** *n.* jurisprudence. **~শাস্ত্রজ্ঞ** *a.* versed in jurisprudence. □ *n.* a jurist. **~সংহিতা** *n.* a compendium or collection of laws. **ব্যবহারজীব** same as **ব্যবহারজীবী**। **ব্যবহারিক, ব্যাবহারিক** *a.* applied (ব্যাবহারিক রসায়ন) ; practical (ব্যাবহারিক জ্যামিতি) ; experimental (ব্যবহারিক বিজ্ঞান) ; legal or judicial; pertaining to daily routine duties for earning one's living; customary; (phil.) materialistic; pragmatic.

ব্যবহার্য *a.* fit to be used or applied, useful, serviceable; that which is to be used or applied.

ব্যবহিত *a.* lying at a distance, lying apart; drawn apart, removed; screened off; covered.

ব্যবহৃত *a.* used; applied.

ব্যভিচার *n.* contrary or unlawful conduct or action; transgression; (rare) exception; unlawful sexual intercourse, adultery or fornication or incest. **ব্যভিচার করা** *v.* to behave or act contrarily or unlawfully : to transgress; to commit adultery or incest. **ব্যভিচারী** *a.* behaving or acting contrarily or unlawfully; transgressing; adulterous or incestuous. □ *n.* one who behaves or acts contrarily or unlawfully; a transgressor; an adulterer (*fem.* ব্যভিচারিণী = adulteress) or fornicator.

ব্যয় *n.* expenditure, expense; (loos.) cost; consumption (শক্তিব্যয়) ; waste or loss (জীবনব্যয়) ; use or application (বুদ্ধিব্যয়) ; passing (সময়ব্যয়). **ব্যয় করা** *v.* to expend, to spend, to consume; to waste; to use or apply; to pass. **ব্যয় হওয়া** *v.* to be expended or spent or consumed or wasted or be used or applied or passed. **~কুণ্ঠ** *a.* stingy, niggardly, closefisted; miserly; parsimonious. **ব্যয়কুণ্ঠ ব্যক্তি** a niggard; a miser. **~কুণ্ঠতা** *n.* stinginess, niggardliness, closefistedness; miserliness. **ব্যয়ন** *n.* disbursement. **~নাধিকারিক** *n.* a disbursing officer. **~বরাদ্দ** *n.* allotted expenditure. **~বহুল** *a.* expensive, costly. **~বাহুল্য** *n.* prodigality; extravagance;

expensiveness, costliness. ~বিহীন *a.* inexpensive; involving no expenditure, free. ~লাঘব *n.* cutting the expenditure short, curtailment of expenditure; reducing the expenditure. ~শীল *a.* prodigal; spendthrift, lavish, extravagant. **ব্যয়শীল ব্যক্তি** a prodigal; a spendthrift. ~শীলতা *n.* lavishness, extravagance. ~শূন্য same as ~বিহীন। ~সাধ্য, ~সাপেক্ষ *a.* expensive, costly. ~হ্রাস same as **ব্যয়লাঘব**। **ব্যয়িত** *a.* spent, disbursed; used up. **ব্যয়ী** *a.* one who spends; spendthrift, extravagant, prodigal, lavish.

ব্যর্থ *a.* futile, abortive, unavailing, vain; useless; unsuccessful. **ব্যর্থ করা** *v.* to baffle, to foil. **ব্যর্থ হওয়া** *v.* to abort, to be of no avail; to be foiled; to fail. ~তা *n.* futility, failure. ~কাম *a.* foiled, baffled, frustrated, unsuccessful, of one who has failed to achieve the desired object. **ব্যর্থ চেষ্টা** *n.* futile or abortive attempt; unsuccessful attempt. ~মনোরথ *a.* foiled or baffled; frustrated; unable or unsuccessful to fulfil one's object.

ব্যষ্টি *n.* individuality; the individual as opposed to a collection.

ব্যস্, বাস *int.* enough, no more, stop it (ব্যস্ ব্যস্, এবার থামো) ; presently, thereupon (ব্যস্, লড়াই বেধে গেল).

ব্যসন *n.* indulgence in vices; addiction to wine and other intoxicants; a sin; a vice; dissipation; a danger; a calamity; an evil or harm; grief, sorrow. **ব্যসনাসক্ত** *a.* addicted to vices; dissolute, given to dissipation.

ব্যস্ত *a.* eager; excited; impatient; anxious; worried; hurrying or hurried, bustling; engaged, employed; busy; distracted or perplexed; scattered; diffused; inverse. **ব্যস্ত করা** *v.* to make one hurry (esp. unduly); to make one bustle; to make one eager or impatient or anxious; to excite. **ব্যস্ত থাকা** *v.* to be engaged (in); to be busy (with). **ব্যস্ত রাখা** *v.* to keep one engaged (in) or busy (with). ~-অনুপাত *n.* (arith.) an inverse ratio. ~-অনুরূপ *a.* (geom.) inversely similar. ~তা *n.* eagerness; excitement; impatience; anxiety; worry; hurry, bustle; busyness, business; distraction, perplexity; scattered state; diffusion; inversion. ~বাগীশ *a.* fussy. ~সমস্ত *a.* flurried, bustling. ~সমস্ত হয়ে helter-skelter. **ব্যস্তালোক** *n.* (phys.) diffused light.

ব্যাং *n.* a frog; a toad. **ব্যাঙাচি** *n.* a tadpole. **ব্যাঙের ছাতা** *n.* toadstool; a mushroom.

ব্যাংক *n.* the bank; an institution for the keeping, lending, exchanging etc. of money. **ব্যাংক করণিক** *n.* a bank clerk. **ব্যাংকের বই** *n.* a bank passbook. **ব্যাংক ম্যানেজার** a bank manager or agent.

ব্যাঁকা coll. var. of **বাঁকা**।

ব্যাকটেরিয়া *n.* (in *pl.*) bacteria; (in *sing.*) a bacterium.

ব্যাকরণ, ব্যাকরণশাস্ত্র *n.* grammar. **ব্যাকরণগত** *a.* grammatical. **ব্যাকরণবিদ, ব্যাকরণশাস্ত্রজ্ঞ** *a.* versed in grammar. □ *n.* a grammarian.

ব্যাকুল, ব্যাকুলিত *a.* extremely eager or anxious or impatient or worried or curious or inquisitive or perplexed. *fem.* **ব্যাকুলা, ব্যাকুলিতা**। **ব্যাকুলতা** *n.* extreme eagerness or anxiety or impatience or worry or curiosity or perplexity. **ব্যাকুলচিত্ত** *a.* mentally disturbed or agitated.

ব্যাখ্যা *n.* explanation; interpretation; a detailed narration or description (usu. attended with comments); a commentary; an annotation. **ব্যাখ্যা করা** *v.* to explain; to expound; to interpret; to account for. ~কর্তা, ~কারী *n.* an explainer, an expounder; an annotator; a commentator; an interpreter. ~গ্রন্থ *n.* a book of notes, a commentary, an annotation; a crib, a key. ~ত *a.* explained, expounded; interpreted; accounted for. ~ন *n.* explanation; exposition; interpretation; a commentary. ~তা same as **ব্যাখ্যাকর্তা**। ~মূলক *a.* explanatory, expositional.

ব্যাখ্যেয় *a.* that which is to be or can be explained; explainable.

ব্যাগ *n.* a bag.

ব্যাঘাত *n.* a hindrance; an obstacle; interruption. **ব্যাঘাত করা** *v.* to hinder; to obstruct; to interrupt. **ব্যাঘাত সৃষ্টি করা** *v.* to put hindrance to, to interrupt; to put a damper on; to stand in the way. **ব্যাঘাতক** *a.* hindering; obstructive; interruptive.

ব্যাঘ্র *n.* the tiger; (as a *sfx.*) the best or strongest specimen (নরব্যাঘ্র). *fem.* **ব্যাঘ্রী** the tigress. **~তুল্য** *a.* tigerish; tigery, tigrine, tigroid. **~শাবক** *n.* a whelp of a tiger.

ব্যাঙ alt. spell. of **ব্যাং**। **ব্যাঙাচি, ব্যাঙের ছাতা** see **ব্যাং**।

ব্যাঙ্ক alt. spell. of **ব্যাংক**।

ব্যাঙ্গমা *n.* a kind of telltale or tattler birds mentioned in folk tales. *fem.* **ব্যাঙ্গমি**।

ব্যাজ[1] *n.* a badge.

ব্যাজ[2] *n.* a pretext, a pretence, simulation, deceit; a hindrance; interest for money; interest, use; delay. **~স্তুতি** *n.* false praise or eulogy; (rhet.) a figure of speech consisting of praise in garb of censure or censure in garb of praise, (cp.) irony, sarcasm.

ব্যাজার[1] alt. spell. of **বেজার**।

ব্যাজার[2] *n.* a badger, a dark-grey furry animal usu, going about at night.

ব্যাজোক্তি *n.* deceitful utterance; (rhet.) a figure of speech consisting of an attempt to conceal something by means of a pretence.

ব্যাট *n.* a circket-bat, a bat; a tennis-racket or a badminton-racket. **ব্যাট করা** *v.* to bat. **~বল** *n.* (the game of) cricket.

ব্যাটা alt. spell. of **বেটা**।

ব্যাত্ত *a.* expanded; opened; gaping.

ব্যাদড়া same as **বেয়াড়া**।

ব্যাদত্ত var. of **ব্যাত্ত**।

ব্যাদান *n.* expanding or opening or gaping. **ব্যাদান করা** *v.* to expand; to open; to gape.

ব্যাদিত inc. but pop. var. of **ব্যাত্ত**।

ব্যাধ *n.* a hunter or a fowler (by caste or profession). **~বৃত্তি** *n.* hunting; fowling.

ব্যাধি *n.* a disease, an ailment, a malady, a morbidity.

ব্যাধিগ্রস্ত, ব্যাধিত *a.* diseased, ailing; ill.

ব্যাধিনী *n. fem.* a hunter's or fowler's wife; a female of the hunting or fowling cast; (rare) a huntress.

ব্যাধিমন্দির *n.* (lit.) a shrine of diseases; (fig.) the body.

ব্যাধিমুক্ত *a.* cured of a disease, free from disease; healthy. **ব্যাধিমুক্ত করা** *v.* to cure one of a disease. **ব্যাধিমুক্তি** *n.* recovery from illness, cure of a disease.

ব্যাধিযুক্ত same as **ব্যাধিগ্রস্ত**।

ব্যাধিশূন্য, ব্যাধিহীন *a.* free from disease; healthy.

ব্যান *n.* one of the five vital airs of a living body.

ব্যান্ড *n.* a musical band; bandmusic; a strap for fastening, a band (ঘড়ির ব্যান্ড). **~মাসটার** *n.* a bandmaster.

ব্যাপক *a.* widespread, extensive, farreaching; pervading; pervasive, comprehensive; prevalent, rife. **(রোগাদি) ব্যাপক আকারে দেখা দেওয়া** to break out in an epidemic form.

ব্যাপন *n.* spreading or extending far and wide; pervasion; prevalence; (bot.) diffusion, covering.

ব্যাপা *v.* to spread or extend far and wide; to pervade; to prevail over.

ব্যাপাদন *n.* killing.

ব্যাপাদিত *a.* killed.

ব্যাপার *n.* an incident, a happening, an occurrence; a ceremony, a function (বিবাহ ব্যাপার) ; an affair, a matter (সর্বব্যাপারে) ; trade, commerce. **ব্যাপার কী** what's the matter? **~স্যাপার** *n.* happenings; goings-on; matter, business (ব্যাপারস্যাপার ভালো ঠেকছে না) ; behaviour; system, working. **ব্যাপারী** *n.* a trader, a dealer, a trafficker, a merchant.

ব্যাপিকা *a. fem.* pert and flippant; tomboyish.

ব্যাপিনী *fem.* of **ব্যাপী**।

ব্যাপী *a.* (used as a *sfx.*) extending over, pervading.

ব্যাপৃত *a.* engaged or occupied in, busy with *fem.* **ব্যাপৃতা**।

ব্যাপ্ত *a.* extending or spreading over; pervaded; diffused; covered or beset or filled (with). **ব্যাপ্তি** *n.* extension, spread; extent; pervasion, diffusion; covering or besetment, filling. **ব্যাপ্তিশীল** *a.* expansive; pervasive; diffusive.

ব্যাবর্তন, ব্যাবর্ত *n.* a coming or bringing

back, return; rotation; (sc.) torsion. **ব্যাবর্ত-তুলা** *n.* a torsion-balance. **ব্যাবর্ত-শির** *n.* a torsion-head. **ব্যাবর্তিত** *a.* returned; returning; rotated; rotating; twisted.

ব্যাবসা see **ব্যবসায়**।

ব্যাবৃত্তি *n.* retreat; turning backwards.

ব্যাভার *n.* (coll.) a gift, a present given for the sake of formality; coll. from of **ব্যবহার**।

ব্যাম *n.* a fathom.

ব্যামিশ্র *a.* (bot.) polygamous.

ব্যামো *n.* (coll.) an illness, a disease, an ailment.

ব্যামোহ *n.* ignorance; stupefaction; perplexity; infatuation.

ব্যায়রাম older var. of **ব্যারাম**।

ব্যায়াম *n.* physical exercise, exercise; gymnastics. **ব্যায়াম করা** *v.* to take (physical) exercise, to exercise. **খালিহাতে বা শুধু হাতে ব্যায়াম** free-hand exercise. **~কারী** *n.* one who takes physical exercise; a gymnast. **~কুশল** *a.* skilled in gymnastics. **~কুশলী** *n.* a skilled gymnast; a gymnast. **~ক্রীড়া** *n.* gymnastics. **~বীর** *n.* same as **~কুশলী**। **~শালা** *n.* a gymnasium. **~শিক্ষক** *n.* a physical instructor. **~শিক্ষা** *n.* physical training. **~সংক্রান্ত** *a.* relating to physical exercise, gymnastical, gymnastic. **ব্যায়ামাগার** *n.* same as **~শালা**।

ব্যারাম *n.* a disease, an ailment, a malady.

ব্যারিস্টার *n.* a barrister. **পশারহীন ব্যারিস্টার** *a* briefless barrister. **ব্যারিস্টারি** *n.* work of a barrister. **ব্যারিস্টারি করা** *v.* to practise as a barrister or counsel.

ব্যারোমিটার *n.* a barometer.

ব্যাল *n.* the snake; a beast of prey.

ব্যালোল *a.* quickly moving, restless, greedy or wistful (ব্যালোল দৃষ্টি)।

ব্যাস *n.* a diameter or its measure; width, breadth; expanse; Vyasa, the author of the Mahabharata. **~কূট** *n.* any one of the obscure passages of Vyasa's (ব্যাস) writings; an obscure composition. **~বাক্য** *n.* (gr.) formal words used in expounding a compound word. **ব্যাসার্ধ** *n.* a radius (*pl.*: radii).

ব্যাসার্ধ *n.* radius.

ব্যাসিলি *n.* (as pl.) bacilli; (as *sing.)* a bacillus. **~ঘটিত, ~সংক্রান্ত** *a.* bacillary, bacillar.

ব্যাহত *a.* obstructed, prevented; frustrated, foiled. **ব্যাহত করা** *v.* to obstruct; to thwart; to prevent; to frustrate; to foil.

ব্যাহৃতি *n.* utterance.

ব্যুৎক্রম *n.* inversion or violation of an order; an inverted order; an exception; an irregularity. **ব্যুৎক্রমে** *adv.* in an inverted order.

ব্যুৎপত্তি *n.* knowledge, learning (গণিতে ব্যুৎপত্তি) ; proficiency (অস্ত্রচালনায় ব্যুৎপত্তি) ; (gr.) derivation and original signification of words, etymology. **~গত** *a.* derivative, etymological.

ব্যুৎপন্ন *a.* erudite, learned; proficient; (gr.) originated or derived.

ব্যুৎপাদক *a.* imparting knowledge; productive of proficiency; (gr.) causing to be derived from oneself, originating. *fem.* **ব্যুৎপাদিকা**। **ব্যুৎপাদক শব্দ** (gr.) a root-word.

ব্যুৎপাদিত *a.* endowed with knowledge, made proficient; (gr.) etymologically derived.

ব্যূঢ় *a.* married; wide or broad (ব্যূঢ় বক্ষঃস্থল) ; (of a line of battle) arrayed; (of soldiers) lined up. **ব্যূঢ়োরস্ক** *a.* broad-breasted, broad-chested.

ব্যূহ *n.* a line of battle. **ব্যূহ স্থাপন করা** *v.* to array or form a line of battle, to line up; to align (troops). **ব্যূহ ভেদ করা** to break through a line of battle. **ব্যূহিত** *a.* (of soldiers) lined up; (of a line of battle) arrayed.

ব্যোম *n.* the sky, the air; ether; (fig.) a hoax. **~চর, ~চারী** *a.* (capable of) moving in the sky or air, ethereal; playing in the air. □ *n.* an aeronaut, an aviator. *fem.* **~চারিণী**। **~মণ্ডল** *n.* the region of the sky, the sky, the firmament, the atmosphere. **~যাত্রা** *n.* aerial navigation, aviation, a flight. **~যাত্রী** *n.* an aeronaut; an astronaut; a balloonist, an aviator; an airman; an air-passenger. **~যান** *n.* a balloon; an aeroplane.

ব্রঙ্কাইটিস *n.* bronchitis.

ব্রজ *n.* a pasture, esp. for cows; a path; a village near Mathura where Krishna (কৃষ্ণ) passed his childhood, (also ব্রজধাম)। **~কিশোর** *n.* the young lad of Braja (ব্রজ) ; Krishna (কৃষ্ণ) । **~কিশোরী** *n. fem.* Radha (রাধা) the sweetheart of Krishna. **~বিহারী** *n.* Krishna (কৃষ্ণ) who sported in Braja (ব্রজ). **~বুলি** *n.* a kind of mixed language used originally by Vidyapati in his poems. **~ভাষা** *n.* a branch of Hindi. **~লীলা** *n.* activities of Krishna (কৃষ্ণ) in Braja. **ব্রজাঙ্গনা** *n.* any one of the milkmaids of Braja (ব্রজ) who were enamoured of Krishna (কৃষ্ণ). **ব্রজেশ্বর** *n.* Krishna (কৃষ্ণ) the lord of Braja (ব্রজ). **ব্রজেশ্বরী** same as **ব্রজকিশোরী** ।

ব্রজ্যা *n.* wandering; travelling.

ব্রণ *n.* a boil, a tumour; an acne; an ulcer, a sore.

ব্রত *n.* a vow (religious or secular); practice of ascetical austerities in order to attain something (বিদ্যালাভের ব্রত) ; firm resolve attended with untiring endeavour (অর্থোপার্জনের ব্রত) ; penance (চান্দ্রায়ণব্রত). □ *a.* (used as a *sfx.)* undertaking or observing a vow (পুণ্যব্রত). **ব্রত আচরণ** বা **পালন করা** *v.* to observe a vow. **ব্রত উদ্‌যাপন করা** *v.* to fulfil a vow. **~কথা** *n.* holy or religious story, sacred story that is listened to as a penance. **ব্রত গ্রহণ** বা **ধারণ করা, ব্রত নেওয়া** *v.* to take a vow; to start practising certain religious rites.

ব্রতচারী *a.* observing a vow; undergoing ascetical austerities or penance. □ *n.* a kind of folk-dance. *fem. a.* **ব্রতচারিণী** ।

ব্রততী, ব্রততি *n.* a creeper.

ব্রতধারী same as **ব্রতচারী** ।

ব্রতভঙ্গ *n.* breach of a vow.

ব্রতী *a.* observing a vow; engaged or employed (in) (যুদ্ধব্রতী) ; initiated into. *fem.* **ব্রতিনী** ।

ব্রহ্ম১ *n.* Burma (also **ব্রহ্মদেশ**).**~বাসী** *a.* Burmese. □ *n.* a Burmese, a Burman. *fem.* **ব্রহ্মবাসিনী** ।

ব্রহ্ম২ *n.* the Absolute Being, God; a Brahman, a Brahmin. **~চর্য** *n.* a mode of life marked with devoted study of the Vedas and other scriptures and books of knowledge and with complete abstinence from sexual and secular pleasures. **~চর্যাশ্রম** *n.* the first stage of life (up to the age of 16) according to the Vedic Hindus when one has to practise brahmacharya (ব্রহ্মচর্য). **~চারী** *n.* one practising brahmacharya (ব্রহ্মচর্য) ; a Brahmin boy staying at the residence of the guru to receive his eduction, having undergone the sacrament of being invested with the holy sacrificial thread; one practising abstinence from sexual or other worldly pleasures and preparing to join an order of hermits. *fem.* **চারিণী** । **~জ্ঞ** *a.* one who has attained knowledge about God. **~জ্ঞান** *n.* knowledge about God. **~জ্ঞানী** *a.* having knowledge about God; following Brahmoism. □ *n.* one who has attained knowledge about God; a Brahmo. **~ণ্য** *a.* relating to God or to Brahmans. □ *n.* the superhuman power obtained through one's knowledge of God; uncommon spiritual power characteristic of Brahmans; Narayana (নারায়ণ) (usu. ব্রহ্মণ্যদেব). **~তালু** *n.* the crown of the head, the palate. **~তেজ** *n.* uncommon power of a Brahman. **~ত্ব** *n.* Godhead; divinity. **~ত্র** *n.* a piece of rent-free land given away to a Brahman. **~দৈত্য** *n.* an anthropophagous ghost of a Brahman; a demoniac ghost of a Brahman; a Brahman demon. **~পিশাচ** *n.* a necrophagous ghost of a Brahman, a Brahman ghoul. **~বাদী** *a.* (capable of) expounding mysteries about God; engaged in studying the Vedas; having knowledge about God; versed in or following Vedantic philosophy. □ *n.* such a person. *fem.* **~বাদিনী** । **~বিৎ** same as **ব্রহ্মজ্ঞ** । **~বিদ্যা** *n.* a branch of learning imparting knowledge about God. **~বৈবর্ত** *n.* one of the eighteen puranas (পুরাণ). **~ময়** *a.* pervaded by the presence of God. **~মীমাংসা** *n.* the second part of the Vedanta treating of the nature and attributes of God. **~রন্ধ্র** *n.* the central pore of the palate. **~লোক** *n.* the abode of Brahma (ব্রহ্মা) ; the highest one of the seven mythological heavens. **~শাপ** *n.* a curse of or put by a Brahman. **~সংহিতা** *n.* a Vaishnava scripture. **~সংগীত** *n.* a song of devotion to God. **~সূত্র** *n.* the holy sacrificial thread worn by Brahmans; any one of the aphorisms of the Vedanta composed by Vyasa (ব্যাস). **~স্ব** *n.* property or possessions of a Brahman. **ব্রহ্মস্বাপহরণ করা** *v.* to rob or misappropriate the property of a Brahman. **~স্বরূপ** *n.* true nature and attributes of God. **~হত্যা** *n.* slaying of a Brahman.

ব্রহ্মডাঙা *n.* the first person of the Hindu Trinity entrusted with the task of creation, Brahma.

ব্রহ্মাণী *n.fem.* the wife of Brahma.

ব্রহ্মাণ্ড *n.* the universe, the world, the creation.

ব্রহ্মাস্ত্র *n.* an ancient divine missile which could never be warded off.

ব্রহ্মোত্তর same as **ব্রহ্মত্র** (see **ব্রহ্ম**)[২] ।

ব্রাত্য *a.* degenerated; failed in observing one's vow or in religious rites, (loos.) outcast.

ব্রাশ *n.* a brush. **ব্রাশ করা** *v.* to brush.

ব্রাহ্ম *a.* relating to Brahma (ব্রহ্ম) or God; endowed with knowledge about God. □ *n.* a Brahmo, a Brahmoist. **~ধর্ম** *n.* Brahmoism. **~বিবাহ** *n.* act of inviting a bridegroom versed in scriptures and marrying him to a bride with due obeisance; marriage (by registration) in accordance with the rules of the Brahmo Samaj. **~সমাজ** *n.* the Brahmo Samaj **~মুহূর্ত** *n.* the period of forty-eighth minute immediately preceding sunrise.

ব্রাহ্মণ *n.* a Brahman, a Brahmin; a Brahman priest; a part of the Vedas treating of religious rites. **~ত্ব** same as **ব্রাহ্মণ্য**। **~পণ্ডিত** *n.* a Brahman scholar.**~সভা** *n.* a council of Brahmans for theological and social discussion and arbitration. **~সমাজ** *n.* the community of the Brahmans. **ব্রাহ্মণী** *n.* a Brahman's wife; a female Brahman, **ব্রাহ্মণ্য** *n.* the state of being a Brahman; characteristics and especial powers of Brahmans; the peculiar functions and duties of Brahmans (also **ব্রাহ্মণ্যধর্ম**) ; the community of Brahmans.

ব্রাহ্মিকা *n.* a female Brahmo.

ব্রাহ্মিশাক *n. Bacopa monnieri*, a herb used chiefly as medicine.

ব্রাহ্মী *n fem.* an ancient script or alphabet, Brahmi.

ব্রিজ *n.* a structure spanning a river, road etc., a bridge; a kind of card game, bridge.

ব্রিটিশ *a.* British. □ *n.* a Briton, a Britisher.

ব্রীড়া *n.* bashfulness, shyness, coyness. **~নত, ~বনত** *a.* hanging down one's head in coyness.

ব্রীড়িত *a.* shy; bashful.

ব্রীহি *n.* paddy crop of the rainy season; paddy (আশুব্রীহি) ।

ব্রেক *n.* a brake (of vehicle or machine). **ব্রেক কষা** *v.* to put on the brake (to), to brake, (fig.) to slow down.

ব্রোচ *n.* a brooch.

ব্র্যাকেট *n.* a small shelf fastened to a wall, a bracket; (loos) a niche or alcove; (in print, & math. –usu. *pl.*) parentheses (sing. parenthesis), brackets.

ব্র্যানডি, ব্র্যান্ডি *n.* brandy.

ব্লক *n.* a connected group of houses rooms villages etc., a block.

ব্লটিং পেপার *n.* blotting paper.

ব্লাউজ *n.* blouse.

ব্লাড ব্যাংক *n.* a bloodbank where blood is collected and stored.

ব্ল্যাকবোর্ড *n.* a blackboard.

ভ *n.* the twenty-fourth consonant of the Bengali alphabet.

ভইসা, ভঁইসা, ভয়সা *a.* made of buffalo-milk (ভইসা ঘি) ; drawn by the buffalo (ভইসাগাড়ি).

ভক্ত *a.* devoted (to); worshipping; reverent; worshipful; devout; strongly attached or addicted (to), fond or enamoured (of) (কবিতার ভক্ত, সুরার ভক্ত) ; having profound admiration for, admirer of (রবীন্দ্রভক্ত) ; yielding to the control or authority of, submissive or docile (শক্তের ভক্ত) ; obedient (to) (পিতৃভক্ত) ; faithfully following or pursuing (জিশুর ভক্ত, নীতির ভক্ত). □ *n.* a devotee; a votary, a worshipper; a devout person; one having strong attachment or addiction; a fan; an obedient person; a faithful follower or observer. **~প্রাণ** *a.* having a devout heart. **~বৎসল** *a.* graciously affectionate to votaries or devout persons or followers. **~বিটেল** *n.* one simulating devoutness, a sanctimonious person. **~শ্রেষ্ঠ, ভক্তাগ্রগণ্য** *a.* best or foremost amongst votaries or devout persons. **ভক্তাধীন** *a.* graciously obedient to votaries or devout persons (that is, always fulfilling their desires).

ভক্তি *n.* devotion; worship; devoutness, piety; profound admiration; strong attachment or addiction; obedience; trust or faith or reliance; inclination or relish or appetite (খাবারে ভক্তি) ; earnest pursuit, devotion (পড়াশোনায় ভক্তি). **ভক্তি করা** *v.* to be devoted to; to worship; to admire profoundly; to follow faithfully; to have trust or faith (in); to rely; to have inclination or relish or appetite (for); to be earnest (in), to pursue earnestly. **~গ্রন্থ** *n.* a devotional book. **~চিহ্ন** *n.* a mark or sign of devotion. **~তত্ত্ব** *n.* the doctrine or cult of or a treatise on devotion or devoutness or piety. **~পথ** *n.* devotion (without knowledge or practice) as the only means of attaining salvation, the path of devotionalism. **~পরায়ণ** *a.* devoted (to); worshipful; devout; strongly attached or addicted (to); having profound admiration (for); reverent; having trust or faith (in), reliant; having inclination or relish or appetite (for); earnest, earnestly pursuing. *fem.* **~পরায়ণা** । **~পরায়ণতা** *n.* devotion; worshipfulness; devoutness; strong attachment or addiction; profound admiration; earnestness, earnest pursuit, **~পূর্বক** *adv.* with devotion; reverentially; with trust or faith or reliance; willingly or with pleasure (ভক্তিপূর্বক খাওয়া বা নেওয়া) ; earnestly (ভক্তিপূর্বক পড়াশোনা করা). **~প্লুতচিত্ত** *n.* mind steeped in piety. **~বাদ** *n.* the doctrine holding that salvation is attainable by means of devotion only (without knowledge and practice); devotionalism. **~বাদী** *a.* devotionistic, devotionalistic. □ *n.* a devotionist, a devotionalist. **~ভরে** same as **ভক্তিপূর্বক** । **~ভাজন** *n.* a reverend or venerable or adorable person or object. □ *a.* reverend; venerable; adorable. **~ভাব** *n.* devout or worshipful or devoted or reverential disposition of mind. **~ভাবে** *adv.* devoutly; worshipfully; devotedly; devotionally; reverentially. **~মান** same as **~পরায়ণ** । *fem.* **~মতী** । **~মার্গ** same as **~পথ** । **~মূলক** *a.* devotional. **~যোগ** *n.* worship of God or effort to attain beatitude by means of devotion only (irrespective of knowledge or practice). **~রস** *n.* (rhet.) the sentiment of devotion. **~শীল** same as **~পরায়ণ** । *fem.* **~শীলা** । **~শূন্য, ~হীন** *a.* devoid of devotion or devoutness; irreverent; having no attachment (to); having no trust or faith (in), unreliant; having no inclination or relish or appetite (for); devoid of earnestness or willingness.

ভক *int.* expressing; the noise of sudden emission of smoke, smell etc., or ejection of phlegm.

ভক্ষক *a.* eating; feeding on (বায়ুভক্ষক) ;

(fig.) spoiling or depraving (বুদ্ধিভক্ষক), killing (সন্তানভক্ষক). □ *n.* an eater; one who feeds on; (fig.) a spoiler, a vitiator, a killer. **যে রক্ষক সেই ভক্ষক** law-makers are law-breakers.

ভক্ষণ *n.* act of eating or consuming. **ভক্ষণ করা** *v.* to eat, to consume. **ভক্ষণীয়** *a.* edible, eatable; to be eaten. □ *n.* an edible, an eatable; that which is to be eaten.

ভক্ষিত *a.* eaten; eaten up, consumed.

ভক্ষ্য same as **ভক্ষণীয়**। **ভক্ষ্যাবশেষ** *n.* leavings of food after eating, orts. **ভক্ষ্যাভক্ষ্য** *a.* & *n.* edible and inedible (thing).

ভগ *n.* the six divine graces collectively, namely, riches, vigour, fame, beauty, knowledge and renunciation; godhead, divinity; glory; fortune, good luck; beauty (সুভগ) ; the vagina; the anus (ভগন্দর).

ভগন্দর *n.* anal fistula.

ভগবতী *a. fem.* endowed with six divine graces (see **ভগ**) ; reverend, venerable. □ Goddess Durga (দুর্গা).

ভগবদারাধনা *n.* worship of God.

ভগবদ্গীতা *n.* a part of the Mahabharata epitomizing the teaching of the Upanishad (abbr. **গীতা**).

ভগবদ্দত্ত *a.* God-given.

ভগবদ্ভক্ত *a.* devoted to God, god-fearing; devout, pious. **ভগবদ্ভক্তি** *n.* devotion to God; devoutness, piety.

ভগবন্ *n.* voc. O God; O Reverend Sir, Your Reverence.

ভগবান *a.* endowed with the six divine graces (see **ভগ**) ; reverend, venerable, adorable. □ *n.* God.

ভগাঙ্কুর *n.* the clitoris.

ভগিনী *n. fem.* a sister; a cousin-sister. **~পতি** *n.* a sister's husband or a cousin-sister's husband, a brother-in-law.

ভগোল *n.* the zodiac.

ভগ্ন *a.* broken; fractured (ভগ্ন অস্থি) ; severed, detached (ভগ্নশাখ) ; pulverized (ভগ্ন শস্য) ; curved, stooping, hunched (ভগ্নপৃষ্ঠ) ; dilapidated (ভগ্নমন্দির) ; demolished (ভগ্নকুটির) ; impaired, ruined, shattered (ভগ্নস্বাস্থ্য) ; ungratified, unentertained (ভগ্নমনোরথ) ; depressed or dejected; defeated or routed (ভগ্নবাহিনী) ; hoarse, husky (ভগ্নস্বর) ; (arith.) fractional (ভগ্নসংখ্যা). **~কণ্ঠে** *adv.* in a broken or husky voice, hoarsely. **~গৃহ** *n.* a dilapidated house; (fig.) a house in utter disorder or confusion. **~চিত্ত** *a.* same as **~হৃদয়**। **~দশা** *n.* broken or dilapidated or ruined state, a state of decay. **~দূত** *n.* a messenger or a soldier bringing the news of defeat from the battlefield; (fig.) a person bringing bad or disheartening news. **~দেহ** *a.* having one's health run down or impaired or shattered. **~প্রায়** *a.* threatening to fall, tottering. **~মনোরথ** *a.* disappointed; balked, baulked. **~স্তূপ** *n.* a heap of broken-down remains, ruins. **~স্বাস্থ্য** *a.* with or in run-down or broken health. □ *n.* broken or run-down health. **~হৃদয়** *a.* broken-hearted; dejected. **ভগ্নাংশ** *n.* a broken-away part, a fraction; (arith.) a fraction. **ভগ্নাঙ্ক** *n.* (arith.) a fraction. **ভগ্নাবশিষ্ট** *a.* lying or remaining in or as ruins. **ভগ্নাবশেষ** *n.* broken-down remains, ruins; relics. **ভগ্নাবস্থা** *n.* broken-down or ruined or dilapidated state, a state of ruin or decay. **ভগ্নাবস্থ** *a.* broken-down, in ruins, dilapidated. **ভগ্নাশ** *a.* disappointed, despondent.

ভগ্নী pop. var. of **ভগিনী**।

ভগ্নোৎসাহ, ভগ্নোদ্যম *a.* repulsed in one's effort, disappointed, disheatened, depressed, balked, baulked; discouraged.

ভঙ্গ *n.* breaking or splitting (ধনুর্ভঙ্গ) ; fracture, rupture (অস্থিভঙ্গ) ; breach (বিশ্বাসভঙ্গ) ; violation, infringement (আইনভঙ্গ) ; non-observance, non-compliance (প্রতিশ্রুতিভঙ্গ) ; discontinuance, break (অনশনভঙ্গ) ; severance (সম্পর্কভঙ্গ) ; estrangement (বন্ধুত্ব ভঙ্গ) ; impairment (স্বাস্থ্যভঙ্গ) ; loss (আশাভঙ্গ) ; disbandment (দলভঙ্গ) ; dispersal (ছত্রভঙ্গ) ; (esp. of pol. parties) disintegration; dissolution ; termination, close (সভাভঙ্গ) ; a fold or contraction. (ত্রিভঙ্গ) ; crack (স্বরভঙ্গ) ; act or manner of rolling or dancing (তরঙ্গভঙ্গ) ; style or shape (ভ্রূভঙ্গ) ; suspension, break (যাত্রাভঙ্গ) ; act of fleeing away, flight, retreat (রণে ভঙ্গ) ; rout (শত্রুসৈন্য-ভঙ্গ) ; removal (সন্দেহভঙ্গ) ; interruption, break (তালভঙ্গ, নিদ্রাভঙ্গ) ; obstruction, an obstacle, a drawback ('এত ভঙ্গ বঙ্গদেশ') ; discouragement (মনোভঙ্গ) ; composition (কবরীভঙ্গ) ; a wave. **ভঙ্গ দেওয়া** *v.* to take to flight, to beat a retreat, to flee or withdraw as defeated (রণে বা বিতর্কে ভঙ্গ দেওয়া). **~কুলীন** *n.* a kulin (কুলীন) family or a member of it failing to observe the social (esp. matrimonial) restrictions enjoined on kulins. **~পয়ার** *n.* (pros.) a variety of payar (পয়ার) in which the second line of each of the four-line stanzas is merely the repetition of the first. **~প্রবণ** *a.* brittle, fragile; frail. **~প্রবণতা** *n.* brittleness.

ভঙ্গা *n.* leaves and shoots of hemp, bhang.

ভঙ্গি, ভঙ্গিমা *n.* a fashion (চুল বাঁধার ভঙ্গি) ; a distinction of style (রচনাভঙ্গি) ; manner (কাজ করার ভঙ্গি) ; shape or form (গঠনভঙ্গি) ; a pose, a posture (নৃত্যের ভঙ্গি) ; manner or attitude (তার কথার ভঙ্গিটি আপত্তিকর) ; elegance (শ্লেষের ভঙ্গি) ; attitudinization (আর ভঙ্গি করিস না) ; a wrinkle or fold or contraction (ভ্রূভঙ্গি). **ভঙ্গি করা** *v.* to attitudinize.

ভঙ্গিল *a.* brittle, fragile; frail; having folds; produced by folding processes.

ভঙ্গিল পর্বত a folded mountain, a fold mountain.

ভঙ্গুর *a.* brittle, fragile; frail; transitory or mortal (ভঙ্গুর জীবন). **~তা** *n.* brittleness, fragility; frailty; transitoriness, transience; mortality.

ভজকট *n.* a hitch; a trouble; a difficulty; a predicament.

ভজন *n.* glorification of a deity (esp. in devotional songs); worship, adoration; serving (রাজাকে ভজন) ; (mus.) a kind of devotional song, a devotional hymn. **~পূজন** *n.* prayer and worship. **~ভাজন** *n.* (fig.) act of persuading by flattery, coaxing and cajoling. **ভজনা** *n.* worship, adoration; serving; flattery, adulation. **ভজনা করা** *v.* to worship, to adore; to serve; to flatter, to adulate. **ভজনালয়** *n.* a house of worship; a shrine; a temple, a synagogue, a church, a mosque.

ভজা *v.* same as **ভজনা করা** (see **ভজন**). □ *a.* worshipping, devoted to (কর্তাভজা). **~নো** *v.* to cause to worship or adore or serve or to accept cordially or flatter or adulate; (chiefly dero.) to coax.

ভঞ্জক same as **ভঞ্জন** (*a.*).

ভঞ্জন *n.* breaking or splitting; removal, dispelling. □ *a.* (used as a *sfx.*) breaking or splitting or removing or dispelling (বিপদভঞ্জন হরি). **ভঞ্জন করা** *v.* to break, to split; to remove, to dispel.

ভঞ্জা poet. form of **ভঞ্জন করা**।

ভট্‌ভট্‌ *int.* indicating: repeated noise of forceful bursting of bubbles or emission of air, gas etc. **ভট্‌ভটি** *n.* (facet.) a motorscooter, an auto-scooter, a scooter, an auto-cycle; a boat driven by motor generator.

ভট্ট *n.* one of a class of heralds professionally singing or reciting family panegyrics; a panegyrist; a learned man, a scholar, a pundit; a teacher, a master. **~পল্লি** *n.* a village or locality inhabited by a large number of pundits. **ভট্টাচার্য** *n.* a title of some Brahmans. **ভট্টারক** *n.* a learned man, a scholar, a king, a prince; the sun. **পরমভট্টারক** *n.* a title of honour applied to a king, His Majesty or Your Majesty.

ভড় *n.* a kind of large freight boat with sails, a barge.

ভড়ং, ভড়ক *n.* ostentatious show or airs intended to parade one's importance or to keep up appearances; ostentatious show or airs.

ভড়কানো *v.* to beat a retreat or to halt on account of being scared; to be scared and confused (as of a witness); to stop by scaring, to scare away, to take fright; to scare and confuse. **ভড়কানি** *n.* scaring; scaring away.

ভড় ভড় *int.* denoting: the noise of rapid emission of something loose; the noise of rapid effervescence.

ভণা alt. spell. of **ভনা**।

ভণিত *a.* said or told (by). □ *n.* saying or telling. **ভণিতা** *n.* the mention of the name of the author in the opening or concluding lines of a poem or other literary compositions; (sarcas.) a commencement of a narrative with great eclat.

ভণ্ড *a.* feigning, pretentious; dissimulating, dissembling; hypocritical; deceitful; sanctimonious. □ *n.* a pretender; a quack, a charlatan; a dessimulator, a dissembler; a hypocrite, an imposter; a deceiver; a cheat; a sanctimonious person. **~তা, ~ত্ব** same as **ভণ্ডামি** । **ভণ্ডন** *n.* deception; cheating. **ভণ্ডানো** *v.* (chiefly poet.) to deceive, to cheat, to hoodwink. **ভণ্ডামি** *n.* pretension, feigning; charlatanism, quackery; dissembling; imposture, hypocrisy; deceit; sanctimony.

ভণ্ডুল *a.* foiled, baffled; spoiled. **ভণ্ডুল করা** *v.* to foil, to baffle; to spoil.

ভদন্ত *n.* a term for addressing a venerable (Buddhist) ascetic.

ভদ্র *a.* polished or elegant in taste or demeanour; (rare) civilized; courteous; polite; well-behaved, mannerly; amiable; suave; belonging to polished or high society; gentle, auspicious, propitious, salutary; honest, chaste. □ *n.* weal; welfare; Shiva (শিব). **ভদ্র আচরণ** gentlemanly conduct; good manners. **~কালী** *n.* a manifestation of Goddess Durga (দুর্গা). **~তা** *n.* polished or elegant taste or demeanour; courtesy, politeness; amiability; suavity; gentility; auspiciousness, propitiousness, salutariness; honesty, chastity; formality. **ভদ্রতা করা** *v.* to treat one courteously, to be formal with; to be suave. **ভদ্রতার অনুরোধে, ভদ্রতার খাতিরে** for courtesy's sake, for the sake of formalities. **ভদ্রতাচরণ** *n.* courteous or polite deportment or conduct, courtesy. **ভদ্রতাবিরুদ্ধ** *a.* discourteous, impolite, uncivil. **ভদ্রতামূলক** *a.* pertaining to courtesy, formal. **~মহিলা** *n. fem.* a gentle woman; a lady. **~লোক** *n.* a gentleman; a courteous or amiable man; an honest man. **ভদ্রলোকের এক কথা** (fig.) a gentleman or an honest man is always true to his words or promise. **~সন্তান** *n.* one coming of a respectable family; a gentleman. **~সমাজ** *n.* society of cultured or decent people. **~স্থ** *a.* (coll.) in the state of a gentlemen; gentlemanlike. **ভদ্রা** *a. fem.* of **ভদ্র** (*a.*). □ *n.* (astr. & astrol.) the second, seventh or twelfth day of a lunar fortnight (these days are considered inauspicious. **ভদ্রা পড়া** *v.* (dial.) to be obstructed or hindered; to have an impediment or a hitch or a set-back. **ভদ্রাভদ্র** *n.* good and evil; respectable and disreputable. **ভদ্রেশ্বর** *n.* a manifestation of Shiva (শিব). **ভদ্রোচিত** *a.* gentlemanlike, gentlemanly; polite, courteous; gentle.

ভদ্রাসন *n.* homestead.

ভনভন *int.* indicating: a humming or buzzing sound (as of bees, flies etc.). **ভনভন করা** *v.* to hum; to buzz. **ভনভনানি** *n.* hum; buzzing noise. **ভনভনে** *a.* buzzing.

ভনা *v.* (poet.) to narrate.

ভব *n.* essence, existence, ease; birth, origination; attainment; the material or mundane world, the earth, the universe; God; Shiva (শিব) ; weal, welfare. **~কারণ** *n.* the Creator, the First Cause, God. **~কারা** *n.* the world conceived as a prison for created beings, the prison of earth. **~ঘুরে** *a.* (lit.) roving all over the world, leading a wandering life; vagabond. □ *n.* a vagabond. **~ঘুরেমি** *n.* vagabondism, vagabondage. **~তারণ** *a.* delivering from earthly life; giving salvation. **~তারিণী** *a. fem.* of **~তারণ** । □ *n.* Goddess Durga (দুর্গা). **~ধব** *n.* the Lord of the universe, God. **~পার** *n.* deliverance from the earthly life. **~পারাবার** same as **ভবার্ণব** । **~বন্ধন** *n.* the bondage or bond of earthly life; earthly attachment (and also responsibilities). **~ভয়** *n.* the fears of mortal existence. **~ভয়তারণ, ~ভয়বারণ** *a.* & *n.* (one) who delivers or protects from the evils of earthly life. **~ভার** *n.* the burden of the world (esp. as borne by God); the burden of earthly life (as borne by mortals). **~লীলা** *n.* one's activities upon the earth, activities of one's mortal life. **ভবলীলা সাঙ্গ করা** *v.* to die. **~লোক, ~সংসার** *n.* the world; earthly life. **~সমুদ্র, ~সাগর, ~সিন্ধু** same as **ভবার্ণব**। **ভবের খেলা** same as **ভবলীলা**।

ভবদীয় *a.* your, yours.

ভবন[১] *n.* act of becoming, act of being reduced to (ঘনীভবন = condensation; বাষ্পীভবন = evaporation).

ভবন[২] *n.* a dwelling-house, a residence; a home; a house; a mansion. **~শিখী** *n.* a domesticated pea-fowl.

ভবানী *n.* Goddess Durga (দুর্গা) the wife of Bhaba (ভব).

ভবার্ণব *n.* the world conceived as an ocean, the ocean of the world.

ভবিতব্য *a.* inevitable. □ *n.* the inevitable; (loos.) destiny. **~তা** *n.* inevitability; (loos.) destiny.

ভবিষ্ণু *a.* sure to happen or crop up or be born.

ভবিষ্য *a.* future; posterior. **~নিধি** *n.* Provident Fund. **~পুরাণ** *n.* one of the eighteen puranas (পুরাণ). **~সূচনা** *n.* presage.

ভবিষ্যৎ *a.* future; posterior; later. □ *n.* the future; futurity; (loos.) destiny; consequence (এর ভবিষ্যৎ হল বিচ্ছেদ) ; future condition (তার ভবিষ্যৎ খারাপ) ; promise of future prosperity (ভবিষ্যৎ খোয়ানো). **~কাল** (gr.) the future tense. **ভবিষ্যতে** *adv.* in future. **ভবিষ্যদ্দ্রষ্টা** *n.* a person having the faculty to see into the future, a seer, a prophet.

ভবিষ্যদ্বক্তা *n.* a predictor; a sooth-sayer; a prophet.

ভবিষ্যদ্বাক্য, ভবিষ্যদ্বাণী *n.* a prediction; a prophecy. **ভবিষ্যদ্বাণী করা** to predict; to prophesy.

ভবিষ্যনিধি, ভবিষ্যপুরাণ, ভবিষ্যসূচনা see **ভবিষ্য**।

ভবী *n.* (ori. *fem.* but now also *masc.*) a pertinacious person. **ভবী ভোলবার নয়** (fig.) a pertinacious person will not give up his or her pursuit.

ভবেশ *n.* Lord Shiva; God Shiva.

ভব্য *a.* well-behaved, mannerly; gentle, quiet; polite, courteous; polished in taste or manners; honest; benefactory; auspicious; that which is to happen. **~তা** *n.* good behaviour; gentleness, quietness; politeness, courtesy; polished taste or manners; honesty; benefaction; auspiciousness; a sure contingency; necessity or certainty. **ভব্যা** *fem.* of **ভব্য**। **ভব্যিযুক্ত** *a.* (dial.) well-behaved; gentle, quiet, (sarcas.) genteel.

ভয় *n.* fear, dread, awe, terror; fright, consternation, dismay; horror; alarm, apprehension; panic; threat. **ভয় করা** *v.* to fear; to be afraid of. **ভয় খাওয়া** *v.* to be frightened, to get or have a fright; to fear. **ভয় খাওয়ানো** *v.* to frighten, to give a fright. **ভয় দেখানো** *v.* to threaten, to frighten, to hold out threats. **ভয় পাওয়া** same as **ভয় খাওয়া**। **ভয় পাওয়ানো, ভয় পাইয়ে দেওয়া** same as **ভয় খাওয়ানো**। **ভয় ভাঙা** *v.* to be freed from fear; to free from fear, to dispel fear. **ভয় হওয়া** *v.* to be stricken with fear. **ভয়ে জড়সড় হওয়া** *v.* to crouch in fear; to be numbed or stupefied with fright. **ভয়ে-ভয়ে** *adv.* timidly, timorously, fearfully. **ভয়ংকর** *a.* awful, terrific, fearful, terrible, dreadful, frightful; horrible; severe (ভয়ংকর রোদ) ; monstrous (ভয়ংকর মূর্তি) ; fierce (ভয়ংকর যুদ্ধ) ; tremendous (ভয়ংকর লোভ). *fem. a.* **ভয়ংকরী**। **~কাতর, ~কাতুরে** *a.* panicky; timid. **~তরাসে** *a.* (dial.) panicky; timid. **~ত্রাতা** *a.* & *n.* one who delivers from fear. **~দ, ~প্রদ** *a.* awe-inspiring, frightening, terrific, dreadful, fearful. *fem.* **~দা, ~প্রদা**। **~প্রদর্শন** *n.* act of threatening. **ভয়প্রদর্শন করা** *v.* to threaten. **~প্রাপ্ত** *a.* alarmed; frightened. **~বিহ্বল** *a.* terror-stricken, panic-stricken, overwhelmed or bewildered with fear. **~হীন** *a.* fearless, dauntless, intrepid.

ভয়ঙ্কর alt. spell. of **ভয়ংকর**।

ভয়সা same as **ভইসা**।

ভয়াকুল, ভয়াতুর same as **ভয়ার্ত**।

ভয়ানক same as **ভয়ংকর** (see **ভয়**).

ভয়াবহ same as **ভয়ংকর** (see **ভয়**).

ভয়াভিভূত *a.* overwhelmed with fear.

ভয়ার্ত *a.* stricken with fear, frightened; terror-stricken.

ভয়াল same as **ভয়ংকর** (see **ভয়**).

-ভর[১] var. of **-ভোর[১]**।

ভর[২] *n.* weight, pressure (ভর সওয়া) ; dependence or reliance (ভাগ্যের উপর

ভর) ; impulse of some emotion (শ্রদ্ধাভরে) ; a support or prop (লাঠির ভর) ; domination or possession or influence (পেতনির ভর, সরস্বতীর ভর) ; (phys.) mass. □ *a.* whole, entire (ভররাত) ; full, fully stuffed, replete (ভরপেট) ; measuring, amounting to (পোয়াভর). **ভর হওয়া** *v.* to be possessed. **শ্রদ্ধাভরে** *adv.* respectfully. **সাহসভরে** *adv.* boldly.

ভরকেন্দ্র *n.* (geom.) a centroid.

ভরণ *n.* filling or stuffing; supporting or maintaining, feeding; a salary, wages. **~পোষণ** *n.* feeding and clothing and sheltering, maintaining or supporting. **ভরণপোষণ করা** *v.* to provide with food and clothing and shelter, to maintain or support. **~পোষণের উপায়** *n.* means of maintaining, subsistence.

ভরণী *n.* the second of the twenty-seven stars according to Hindu astronomy.

ভরত, ভরতপাখি *n.* the skylark.

ভরতি *a.* filled, stuffed, replete, full; admitted into (কলেজে ভরতি). □ *n.* filling, repletion; admission. **ভরতি করা** *v.* to fill, to stuff, to replete; to admit (into).

ভরদুপুর *n.* far into the midday.

ভরদ্বাজ *n.* the skylark.

ভরন *n.* an inferior metal obtained from an alloy of coper, zinc and tin.

ভরপুর *a.* completely filled or saturated (with) (আনন্দে বা গন্ধে ভরপুর). □ *adv.* to the full (ভরপুর খাওয়া).

ভরপেট *a.* capable of filling the belly thoroughly (ভরপেট খাবার). □ *adv.* to one's bellyful (ভরপেট খাওয়া).

ভরবেগ *n.* (mech.) momentum.

ভরসন্ধ্যা *n.* full evening; advanced evening; far into the evening.

ভরসা *n.* reliance, confidence, trust; faith; a prop, support; a shelter, a refuge; hope, expectation; strength or dependence (কোন ভরসায় চাকরি ছাড়লে). **ভরসা করা** *v.* to rely on; to hope, to expect;to depend on. **ভরসা থাকা** *v.* to have reliance on or confidence; to have a hope, to have expectation. **ভরসা দেওয়া** *v.* to promise support or help; to encourage; to assure.

ভরা *v.* to fill; to stuff; to pack in; to enclose (খামে চিঠি ভরা) ; to load (জাহাজে মাল ভরা) ; to charge (with) (বন্দুকে গুলি ভরা) ; to be filled or stuffed (with), to be replete (with) (বৃষ্টির জলে পুকুর ভরা) ; to diffuse or be diffused ('ব্যথায় ভুবন ভরিছে') ; (fig.) to be thoroughly pleased or satisfied (গান শুনে মন ভরল). □ *n.* a (fully) loaded boat or vessel. □ *a.* filled; stuffed; full, replete; charged; loaded; brimming (ভরা নদী, ভরা পেয়ালা) ; mature, full (ভরা যৌবন) ; advanced (ভরা সাঁঝ) ; (fig.) pensive, thoughtful (বসে আছি ভরা মনে). **~ট** *n.* act of filling up completely; earthwork in filling. □ *a.* thoroughly filled up. **~ডুবি** *n.* sinking of a (fully) loaded boat or vessel; (fig.) utter ruin. **~নো** *v.* to cause to fill or stuff or pack in or enclose or load or charge with or diffuse or fill up completely or (fig.) satisfy thoroughly. **~ভরতি** *a.* full to the brim, filled to the brim.

ভরি *n.* a unit of weight equal to 180 grains or a little over 11 grams.

ভরো ভরো *a.* about to be filled up; nearly filled to the brim.

ভর্জন *n.* frying in oil, fat etc.

ভর্জিত *a.* fried in oil, fat etc.

ভর্ৎসক *a.* & *n.* one who rebukes or reproaches or censures.

ভর্ৎসনা *n.* scolding, rebuke; reproach; reprimand; censure. **ভর্ৎসনা করা** *v.* to chide, to scold, to rebuke; to reproach; to reprimand; to censure. **ভর্ৎসনীয়** *a.* blamable, censurable, condemnable; reprehensible.

ভর্ৎসিত *a.* scolded, rebuked; reproached; reprimanded; censured. *fem.* **ভর্ৎসিতা**।

ভর্তা *n.* a husband; a king; an overlord; a master; an employer; one responsible for maintenance, a maintainer.

ভর্তি alt. spell. of **ভরতি**।

ভর্তৃদারক *n.* a son of a king, a prince. *fem.* **ভর্তৃদারিকা** a princess.

ভর্ত্রী *n. fem.* a wife; a queen; a mistress; a female maintainer.

ভল্ল *n.* a spear-like missile, a spear, a lance.

ভল্লাত, ভল্লাতক *n.* a kind of nut-bearing plant or its nut, the gall-nut (?), the anacardium (?).

ভল্লুক *n.* the bear. *fem.* **ভল্লুকী**।

ভসকা, ভস্কা *a.* not sticking together, loose; watery; tasteless.

ভসভস *int.* expressing : noise of repeated emission of air.

ভস্ত্রা *n.* a blacksmith's bellows; a large leathern bag for carrying water.

ভস্ম *n.* ash, ashes; cinder; calx; remains of human body when burnt, ashes. **ভস্ম করা** *v.* to reduce or burn to ashes; to calcine. **~সাৎ** *a.* reduced or burnt to ashes. **~স্তূপ** *n.* an ash-heap. **ভস্মাচ্ছন্ন, ভস্মাচ্ছাদিত** same as **ভস্মাবৃত**। **ভস্মাধার** *n.* a vase for holding ashes of the dead, an urn; an ash-bucket, an ash-can; an ash-tray. **ভস্মাবশেষ** *n.* remains of anything burnt; remains of the human body when burnt; ashes. **ভস্মাবৃত** *a.* covered or smeared with ashes; (fig.) concealed or disguised (ভস্মাবৃত রূপ). **ভস্মীকরণ** *n.* reducing or burning to ashes; calcination. **ভস্মীকৃত, ভস্মীভূত** *a.* reduced or burnt to ashes; calcined; (fig.) utterly destroyed.

ভা *n.* glow, radiance, shine, lustre; light; a beam, a ray.

ভাই *n.* a brother; a cousin-brother, a cousin; (chiefly voc.) a grandson or grand-nephew, a friend; (voc.) a gentleman (সরে দাঁড়ান ভাই). **ভাইঝি** *n.* a brother's daughter, a niece. **ভাইঝি-জামাই** *n.* a niece's husband. **~দ্বিতীয়া** same as **~ফোঁটা**। **~পো** *n.* a brother's son, a nephew. **~ফোঁটা** *n.* the ceremony of **ভ্রাতৃদ্বিতীয়া** (see **ভ্রাতৃ**). **~বন্ধু, ~বেরাদর** *n.* kinsfolk and friends, one's own people.

ভাউলিয়া, ভাউলে *n.* a house-boat.

ভাও *n.* geneal condition or tendency, trend; price; rate.

ভাং *n.* leaves and shoots of hemp, bhang.

ভাংচি *n.* secret dissuasion; act of alienating someone secretly; intrigue that induces one to break away from or to be estranged from. **ভাংচি দেওয়া** *v.* to dissuade or to alienate by secret intrigue; to cause a split.

ভাংটা *n.* (dial.) small coins, change.

ভাঁওতা *n.* a hoax; a bluff; deception. **ভাঁওতা দেওয়া** *v.* to hoax; to bluff; to deceive. **~বাজ** *n.* a hoaxer; a bluffer; a deceiver. **~বাজি** *n.* hoaxing; bluffing; deceiving.

ভাঁজ *n.* a fold; a crease (জামার ভাঁজ) ; a plait (সিঁথির ভাঁজ). **ভাঁজ করা** *v.* to fold; to crease; to plait. **ভাঁজ হওয়া** *v.* to fold. **~-করা** *a.* folded. **~হীন** *a.* foldless, without a fold.

ভাঁজা *v.* to fold, to plait; (mus.) to hum or utter esp. to practise (সুর ভাঁজা) ; to move or brandish or wave (মুগুর ভাঁজা) ; to exercise with (ডাম্বেল ভাঁজা) ; to shuffle (as playing cards); (usu. dero.) to excogitate, to devise, to scheme (ফন্দি ভাঁজা).

ভাঁটা[1] var. of **ভাটা**।

ভাঁটা[2] *n.* a discus, a quoit.

ভাঁটি var. of **ভাটি**।

ভাঁটুই *n.* burdock.

ভাঁড়[1] *n.* a small earthen pot.

ভাঁড়[2] *n.* a case for containing barber's implements.

ভাঁড়[3] *n.* a court-jester, a fool; a buffoon; a clown; a droll; a witty person, a wit.

ভাঁড়[4] *n.* a store, a storeroom, a storehouse. **ভাঁড়ে ভবানী** utter emptiness in store, a completely exhausted store; (fig.) utter indigence.

ভাঁড়ানো *v.* to deceive, to hoodwink, to bamboozle; to assume a false name, appellation etc. suppressing what is true or authentic (নাম ভাঁড়ানো, পরিচয় ভাঁড়ানো).

ভাঁড়াভাঁড়ি *n.* repeated or mutual deception.

ভাঁড়ামি, ভাঁড়ামো *n.* jesting, foolery, waggery; buffoonery; clownery; drollery; witticism.

ভাঁড়ার, ভাঁড়ারি coll. variants of **ভাণ্ডার** and **ভাণ্ডারী** respectively.

-ভাক *a.* (used as a *sfx.*) sharing.

ভাক্ত *a.* minor, secondary, unimportant; simulating, hypocritical (ভাক্ত বৈষ্ণব) ; false (ভাক্ত কথা).

ভাগ[1] poet. corrup. of **ভাগ্য**।

ভাগ[2] *n.* sharing out, apportionment; partition (দেশ ভাগ) ; (esp. in math.) division; a piece, a fragment (শতভাগে

পরিণত) ; a share, a portion (সম্পত্তিতে আমার ভাগ) ; a division of time (দিবাভাগ) ; a region, a part (নিম্নভাগ). **ভাগ করা** *v.* to share out, to apportion; to partition; (esp. in math.) to divide. **ভাগ দেওয়া** *v.* to give a share or portion; to allow to participate in (কাজের ভাগ দেওয়া) ; (in math.) to divide. **ভাগ নেওয়া** *v.* to take a share, to share; to participate in. **ভাগ পাওয়া** *v.* to get a share; to be allowed to participate in. **ভাগের মা গঙ্গা পায় না** (fig.) no work can be well-executed if the workers do not work jointly; what belongs to all belongs to none. **~চাষি** *n.* a share-cropper. **~ধেয়** *a.* entitled to a share (esp. as an heir or inheritor). □ *n.* a share; revenue; fortune, fate. **~ফল** *n.* (math.) a quotient. **~বাটোয়ারা** *n.* sharing out, apportionment. **~শেষ** *n.* (math.) the remainder (in a sum of division). **~হর** *a.* taking a share, sharing. **~হার** *n.* sharing, act of taking a share; (math.) a method of division.

ভাগনা, ভাগনি, ভাগনে corruptions of **ভাগিনেয়, ভাগিনেয়ী,** and **ভাগিনেয়** respectively.

ভাগবত *a.* relating to God; divine; reverencing God, God-fearing, devoted to Vishnu (বিষ্ণু) (often affixed to the names of saintly or reverend persons). □ *n.* one of the Puranas (পুরাণ).

ভাগা[1] *n.* one of the equal parts of a thing, a lot (মাছের ভাগা).

ভাগা[2] *v.* to flee, to take to one's heels, to slip away.

ভাগাড় *n.* a waste land for depositing dead bodies of animals; a carrion-depot.

ভাগানো *v.* to put to flight, to drive away, to chase away.

ভাগাভাগি *n.* mutuality; reciprocity; swapping; sharing out; apportionment or partition or allotment amongst partners.

ভাগিনা coll. var. of **ভাগিনেয়**।

ভাগিনেয় *n.* (of a man) a sister's son; (of a woman) a son of one's husband's sister, a nephew. *fem.* **ভাগিনেয়ী** a niece.

ভাগী[1] *a.* (poet.) fortunate. □ *n.* (poet.) fortune.

ভাগী[2] *a.* receiving (upon oneself), a sharer, partaking of, participating in.

ভাগী[3] *a.* sharing, entitled to or enjoying a share (of) (সম্পত্তির ভাগী). □ *n.* a sharer, a shareholder.

ভাগীদার *n.* a sharer, a shareholder.

ভাগীরথী *n.* a name of the Ganges; a tributary of the Ganges.

ভাগ্য *n.* fate, fortune, luck, destiny; chance; good fortune, good luck. **~ক্রমে** *adv.* fortunately, luckily; by chance. **~গণনা** *n.* fortune-telling. **ভাগ্যগণনা করা** *v.* to foretell or tell one's fortune. **~গণনাকারী** *n.* a fortune-teller, an astrologer. **~গুণে** *adv.* by dint of one's good fortune; (often ironically) as one's fate would have it; because of one's ill fate. **~চক্র** *n.* the wheel of fortune; ever-changeful fortune. **~দেবতা** *n.* the god or goddess of fortune or destiny, Destiny, (cp.) the Fates. *fem.* **~দেবী**। **~দোষে** *adv.* through bad luck, unfortunately, as ill luck would have it. **~নিয়ন্তা** same as **~বিধাতা**। **~পরীক্ষা** *n.* a trial of luck. **ভাগ্য পরীক্ষা করা** *v.* to try one's luck. **~পুরুষ** same as **~বিধাতা**। **~ফল** *n.* one's destiny; astrological reading of one's fortune. **~বতী** *fem.* of **~বান**। **~বন্ত** same as **~বান**। **~বল** *n.* strength of one's good fortune; fortune's favour. **~বাদী** *n.* a fatalist. **~বান** *a.* fortunate, lucky. **~বিড়ম্বনা** *n.* bad or ill luck; misfortune; reverses of fate. **~বিধাতা** *n.* the divine ordainer of fortune or destiny, Destiny. *fem.* **~বিধাত্রী**। **~বিপর্যয়** *n.* reverses of fortune; reversal of fortune; misfortune. **~মন্ত** same as **~বান**। **~লিখন, ~লিপি** *n.* one's foreordained fortune (esp. as supposed to have been written on one's forehead by the god of destiny). **~হীন** *a.* unfortunate, luckless, ill-fated, unlucky. *fem.* **~হীনা**।

ভাগ্যি *n.* dial. corrup. of **ভাগ্য**। □ *int.* expressing : it is fortunate that, luckily (ভাগ্যি তুমি এলে). **ভাগ্যিস** *int.* same as **ভাগ্যি** (*int.*). **ভাগ্যোদয়** *n.* dawning of one's good fortune.

ভাঙ alt. spellings of **ভাং**।

ভাঙচি alt. spell. of **ভাংচি**।

ভাঙচুর *n.* breakage; rampage.

ভাঙটা alt. spell. of **ভাংটা**।
ভাঙড় *n.* a bhang-addict, Shiva (শিব).
ভাঙন[1] *n.* a species of flat fish, (cp.) the salmon.
ভাঙন[2] *n.* breaking, act of breaking up; act of coming off (নদীর পাড়ের ভাঙন) ; act of bringing down banks (নদীতে ভাঙন) ; disunion, breach, rift (সংসারে ভাঙন) ; disintegration (দলে ভাঙন) ; deterioration (বন্ধুত্বে ভাঙন) ; beginning of downfall (জমিদারিতে ভাঙন). **ভাঙন ধরা** *v.* to begin to come off or crumble down; to begin to bring down banks; to start disintegrating or cracking or disuniting.
ভাঙা *v.* to break or be broken, to split or be split; to fracture or be fractured; to grind (পাথর ভাঙা, গম ভাঙা) ; to pull down or come off, to demolish or to crumble down, to erode (বাড়ি ভাঙা, কুল ভাঙা) ; to open (প্যাকেট ভাঙা) ; to impair, to deteriorate (স্বাস্থ্য ভাঙা) ; to debase or be debased (কুল ভাঙা) ; to spoil or be spoiled ; to weaken or be weakened, to discourage or be discouraged (মন ভাঙা) ; to remove or be removed, to dispel or be dispelled (মান ভাঙা, ভয় ভাঙা) ; to dissolve or be dissolved, to disband (সৈন্যবাহিনী ভাঙা) ; to disintegrate or be disintegrated (দল ভাঙা) ; to break off negotiations etc. (সম্বন্ধ ভাঙা) ; to sever or be severed; to estrange or be estranged (বন্ধুত্ব ভাঙা) ; to sow dissension or disunion (ঘর ভাঙা) ; to disclose or divulge (সে কথাটা ভাঙেনি) ; to elaborate (ভেঙে বলা) ; to make or become hoarse (গলা ভাঙা) ; to walk, to traverse (পথ ভাঙা) ; to wade through (জল ভাঙা, জলা ভাঙা). □ *a.* broken, split; (fractured; ground; pulled down, demolished or impaired; deteriorated; debased; weakened, discouraged; dissolved; disintegrated; broken up; severed, estranged; rent with disunion; breached, hoarsened. **ভাঙা কপাল** ill fate, bad luck. **ভাঙা কপাল জোড়া লাগা** (fig.) to thrive again after a downfall; to retrieve one's fortunes. **ভেঙে বলা** *v.* to say in detail. **~চোরা** *a.* broken and unserviceable (ভাঙাচোরা বাসন) ; dilapidated (ভাঙাচোরা বাড়ি). **~নি** *n.* small coins, change; act of prejudicing (one) secretly against (কানভাঙানি). □ *a. fem.* given to intrigues, sowing dissension (ঘরভাঙানি বউ) ; prejudicing (one) secretly against (মনভাঙানি কথা). *a. masc.* **ভাঙানে**। **~নো** *v.* to cause to break or split or grind or pull down or open or debase or spoil or weaken or discourage or remove or dispel or disintegrate or break up or sever or estrange or produce breach, dissension etc. or walk or traverse or wade through; to change (as a coin or currency note); to cash (as a cheque). **ভাঙা-ভাঙা** *a.* almost broken; scattered or rent here and there (ভাঙা-ভাঙা মেঘ) ; broken (ভাঙা-ভাঙা হিন্দি) ; half-articulate, babbling (ভাঙা-ভাঙা বোল). **ভাঙাভাঙি** *n.* disruption, dissension; disintegration; prejudicing against; discouragement; repeated breaking or split.
ভাচিত্র *n.* a photograph. **~কর** *n.* a photographer, a photoman.
ভাজ *n.* a brother's wife, a sister-in-law.
ভাজক *a.* dividing. □ *n.* a divisor.
ভাজন[1] *n.* a receptacle (স্নেহভাজন).
ভাজন[2] *n.* dividing, division; frying.
ভাজনা *a.* used in frying. **~খোলা** *n.* a frying vessel (usu. a concave one); a frying pan).
ভাজা *v.* to fry; to roast; to parch; to scorch. □ *a.* fried; roasted; parched; scorched. □ *n.* a dish of anything fried. **~নো** *v.* to cause to fry or roast or parch or scorch. **ভাজা-ভাজা** *a.* almost fried, (fig.) extremely irritated or chafed. **~ভুজি** *n. pl.* fried snacks.
ভাজিত *a.* (esp. in math.) divided; apportioned; partitioned.
ভাজ্য *a.* dividable, divisible. □ *n.* (math.) a dividend.
ভাট *n.* one of a class of heralds versed in genealogies; a professional singer of eulogies.
ভাটক *n.* rent; hire; charges, fare, freight, wages; cost.
ভাটা, ভাটি[1] *n.* ebb, ebb-tide; the ebbward direction of a stream; downstream direction; downward direction; (fig.) decline. **ভাটা পড়া বা লাগা** *v.* to begin to

ebb; to ebb; (fig.) to begin to decline, to decline.

ভাটি[2] *n.* a kiln (for burning bricks etc.); a washerman's trough for boiling dirty clothes; a still; a vat; a distillery. **~খানা** *n.* a distillery; a liquor-shop.

ভাটিয়ালি *n.* an Indian musical mode ori. sung by boatmen. **ভাটিয়ালি গান** a song sung in the aforesaid mode, (cp.) a boat-song.

ভাড়া *n.* rent; hire (গাড়িভাড়া) ; charges, fare; freight (রেলভাড়া) ; wages (কুলিভাড়া). □ *a.* rented; hired; hackney (ভাড়া গাড়ি). **ভাড়া করা** *v.* to rent (বাড়ি ভাড়া করা) ; to hire (গাড়ি ভাড়া করা) ; to book (থিয়েটারের সিট ভাড়া করা). **ভাড়া খাটা** *v.* to be let out for hire. **ভাড়া দেওয়া** *v.* to let out for a rent, to rent; to put out to hire, to hire; to pay rent, hire, charges, fare, freight or wages. **ভাড়া পাওয়া** *v.* to obtain the use or service of by paying rent, hire, charges, fare, freight or wages. **ভাড়া নেওয়া** same as **ভাড়া করা**। **ভাড়াটিয়া,** (coll.) **ভাড়াটে** *a.* rented or tenanted; let out for hire; hackney; hired; mercenary (ভাড়াটে গুন্ডা). □ *n.* a tenant of a rented house; a hireling. **ভাড়াটে গাড়ি** a hackney-carriage, a hackney-coach. **ভাড়াটে সৈন্য** *n.* hired soldier; mercenary. **ভাড়াটে বাড়ি** *n.* a rented house.

ভাণ্ড *n.* a vessel, a receptacle; a pot; a small earthen pot; a pitcher; a jar; a chest, a box, a case; capital money, capital; stock.

ভাণ্ডার *n.* a store, a storehouse, a store-room; a treasury; a fund; a granary; a garner; a coffer. **~-করণিক** *n.* a store-clerk. **ভাণ্ডারে রাখা, ভাণ্ডারজাত করা** *v.* to store; to garner. **ভাণ্ডার পূর্ণ করা** *v.* to fill one's coffer. **~-সহায়ক** *n.* a depot assistant. **ভাণ্ডারী** *n.* a storekeeper; a treasurer.

ভাত *n.* boiled rice; the Hindu sacrament of letting a child eat rice for the first time (also **মুখে ভাত**). **~-কাপড়** *n.* food and clothing; (loos.) maintenance. **ভাত ছড়ালে কাকের অভাব হয় না** (fig.) be liberal with your purse and they will be liberal with support and flattery. **ভাত বাড়া** *v.* to serve rice.

ভাতা *n.* (ori.) ration-money; money paid in addition to salary, an allowance.

ভাতার *n.* (sl.) a husband. **~পুত** *n.* (sl.) husband and son.

ভাতি *n.* lustre, radiance; glow.

ভাতুড়ি *n.* slough.

ভাতুড়িয়া, ভাতুড়ে *a.* dependant on others for maintenance.

ভাতুয়া *a.* subsisting chiefly on rice, rice-eating; (fig.) feeble, cowardly.

ভাতে *a.* boiled along with rice (আলু ভাতে) ; cooked by keeping in the heat of boiled rice (মাছ ভাতে). □ *n.* any article of food thus boiled (**ভাতেভাত** = such articles of food and boiled rice).

ভাদর, ভাদ্দর corrup. of **ভাদ্র**।

ভাদুরে, ভাদ্দুরে *a.* of the month of Bhadra (ভাদ্র).

ভাদ্দরবউ coll. var. of **ভাদ্রবধূ**।

ভাদ্র, ভাদ্রপদ *n.* the fifth month of the Bengali calendar (from the middle of August to the middle of September).

ভাদ্রবধূ *n.* a brother's (usu. a younger brother's) wife, a sister-in-law.

ভান[1] *n.* glow, radiance; lustre; beauty; notion; knowledge.

ভান[2] *n.* a pretence, a pretext; feigning, dissimulation.

ভানা *v.* to husk (as rice); to grind, to mill (as corn, wheat etc.) **~নো** *v.* to cause to husk or grind or mill. **ধান-ভানা কল** a husking machine; a rice-mill.

ভানু *n.* the sun; a ray, a beam; grace, beauty. **~মতী** *a. fem.* graceful, beautiful. □ *n. fem.* (myth.) a celebrated female juggler. **ভানুমতীর খেলা বা খেল** amazing jugglery or magic; jugglery, magic.

ভাপ, ভাপরা *n.* steam; vapour; heat; fomentation; vapour-bath. **ভাপ বা ভাপরা দেওয়া** *v.* to foment; to treat with or apply a vapour-bath.

ভাপসা *a.* sultry (ভাপসা আবহাওয়া) ; musty (ভাপসা গন্ধ). **~নো** *v.* to become sultry; to swelter; to give out a musty odour.

ভাপা, ভাপানো *a.* manufactured or cooked by application of vapour (ভাপানো দই, ভাপানো মাংস).

ভাব *n.* birth, origination; existence, presence, essence, esse; shape (নবভাবে

প্রকাশ) ; intention; state, condition (মিশ্রভাব, তীব্রভাব) ; mental state, mood (ভাবান্তর) ; nature (তার ভাবখানা ওই) ; love, attachment, friendship, amity (দুজনের বেজায় ভাব) ; acquaintance (তার সঙ্গে অনেক লোকের ভাব) ; manner, mode (এভাবে চলবে) ; inner significance, implication, an idea (কবিতার ভাব) ; an abstract idea or thought, imagination (ভাবলোক) ; meditation, cogitation (ভাবমগ্ন) ; reverie, ecstasy (ঠাকুর ভাবে বিভোর) ; emotion, an outburst of emotion (ভাবোদ্দীপন) ; (amongst children) amity, peace (আড়ি-ভাব). **ভাব করা** *v.* to establish friendship with; to make friends with; to make acquaintance with; (amongst children) to be on amicable terms with, to make peace with. **ভাব জাগা, ভাব লাগা** *v.* to be affected with an emotion or idea; to be under the spell of a reverie or ecstasy. **ভাব হওয়া** *v.* to become friendly with; to be acquainted with; (amongst children) to be at peace with. **~গত** *a.* relating to inner significance or to the underlying idea; ideological; abstract. **~গতিক** *n.* intention and activities; attitude and bearing; manner, mode. **~গম্ভীর** *a.* full of weighty or solemn ideas; inspiring solemn ideas; grave and thoughtful. **~গর্ভ** *a.* impregnated with (deep) thoughts, thoughtful; having a deep meaning or significance; pregnant with ideas, imaginative. **~গ্রাহী** *a.* capable of grasping the inner significance or the underlying idea; appreciative; capable of reading the inmost thoughts; omniscient. **~জগৎ** *n.* the world of imagination. **~তরঙ্গ** *n.* a thought-wave. **~ধারা** *n.* a trend of thought, a line of thinking. **~পূর্ণ** same as **~গর্ভ**। **~প্রবণ** *a.* emotional; sentimental; maudlin. **~প্রবণতা** *n.* emotionalism; sentimentalism, sentimentality; maudlinism. **~বাচক** *a.* (chiefly in gr.) abstract (**ভাববাচক বিশেষ্য** = an abstract noun). **~বাচ্য** *n.* (gr.) the impersonal voice. **~বাদ** *n.* idealism. **~বাদী** *a.* idealistic; idealist. □ *n.* an idealist. **~বিলাসী** *a.* given to abstract speculation, visionary, idealistic. **~বিহ্বল** *a.* overwhelmed with emotion or ecstasy. **~ব্যঞ্জক** *a.* signifying a thought. **~ভঙ্গি** same as **~গতিক**। **~মূর্তি** *n.* an image; (loos.) the image of something; an ideated or ideal or imaginary shape or form or concept; a symbol of personification of an idea. **~লেশহীন** *a.* utterly blank or expressionless. **~শুদ্ধি** *n.* purity of idea or thought. **~শূন্য, ~হীন** *a.* blank, expressionless. **~সূচক** same as **~ব্যঞ্জক**।

ভাবন *n.* thinking, cogitation; meditation; invention; production; creation; a creator.

ভাবনা *n.* thought; cogitation; reflection, contemplation; worry, anxiety; repeated pulverization and purification or rectification of medicines etc.; saturation; infusion. **ভাবনা করা, ভাবনায় পড়া** *v.* to worry, to be worried.

ভাবা *v.* to think, to cogitate; to contemplate, to reflect; to conceive, to imagine; to consider, to judge; to regard, to take (one) for; to intend or resolve (কী ভেবে পড়া ছাড়লে) ; to contrive, to devise (উপায় ভাবা) ; to suppose or guess (বৃষ্টি হবে ভাবছ ?) ; to worry (for) (রোগা ছেলের জন্য ভাবা). **ভেবেচিন্তে** upon careful consideration.

ভাবাত্মক *a.* impregnated with ideas or thoughts; imaginative, abstract; full of significance.

ভাবানুগ *a.* natural, following the dictates of one's nature or thought.

ভাবানুষঙ্গ *n.* association of ideas.

ভাবানো *v.* to cause to think or worry; to worry (ওকে আর ভাবিয়ো না) ; to cause anxiety (এই ব্যাপারটাই তাকে ভাবাচ্ছে).

ভাবান্তর *n.* another state of mind or mood; change of mental state or mood.

ভাবান্বিত *a.* worried, anxious.

ভাবাবিষ্ট *a.* lost in ecstasy or reverie or thought; overwhelmed with emotion.

ভাবাবেশ *n.* absorption in ecstasy or reverie or thought; the state of being overwhelmed with emotion; excitation of an idea or emotion.

ভাবার্থ *n.* inner significance; purport, gist, substance.

ভাবালু same as **ভাবপ্রবণ** and **ভাববিহ্বল**।

ভাবিত *a.* conceived, thought of, contemplated; worried; purified, rectified, saturated; infused.

ভাবিনী *n.* a charming woman who is the embodiment of an idea or concept ('ভাবের ভাবিনী রাধা') ; (dero. or facet.) an emotional or wanton woman; a woman.

ভাবী *a.* future (ভাবী কাল, ভাবী ঘটনা) ; would-be (ভাবী রাজা). **~কাল** *n.* the future.

ভাবুক *a.* capable of or given to thinking or imagining, thoughtful or imaginative; capable of appreciation, appreciative; capable of forming original concepts, conceptive. **~তা** *n.* thoughtfulness; contemplativeness; imaginativeness; appreciativeness.

ভাবোচ্ছ্বাস *n.* an outburst of emotion or thought or ecstasy.

ভাবোদয় *a.* dawning of a thought or idea (in one's mind), birth of an idea; inspiration; setting in of an emotion.

ভাবোদ্দীপক *a.* thought-inspiring, thought-provoking; awakening ideas or emotions.

ভাবোদ্দীপন *n.* awakening of a thought or an idea or an emotion.

ভাবোদ্রেক *n.* awakening of an emotion or an idea or a thought.

ভাবোন্মত্ত *a.* beside oneself with emotion or ecstasy or reverie or with an idea.

ভাবোন্মাদ *n.* the state of being beside oneself with emotion or ecstasy or reverie or with an idea.

ভাবোন্মেষ same as **ভাবোদয়**।

ভাব্য *a.* thinkable, ponderable; considerable; that which will happen; inevitable.

ভাম *n.* the civet-cat.

ভামিনী *n.* a peevish woman, a shrew; a woman.

ভায় *v.* (poet.) to shine; (poet.) to exist or be present gracefully; to appear to be pleasing or likable.

ভায়রা, ভায়রাভাই *n.* the husband of one's wife's sister, a brother-in-law.

ভায়া *n.* (in familiar addressing) a brother, a friend, a comrade.

ভার *n.* gravity, heaviness, weight; load, burden, pressure (ঋণভার) ; responsibility, encumbrance (সংসারভার) charge, trust (কর্মভার) ; collection, a heap, clump (কেশভার) ; a bamboo pole borne on one'e shoulders for carrying loads hanging from its either extremities (ভারে-ভারে দই) ; a weight put on a scalepan to bring it into equipoise with the other scalepan. □ *a.* heavy, weighty, burdensome, unbearable, intolerable, burdensome, unbearable, intolerably miserable (জীবন ভার হওয়া) ; difficult (দেখা পাওয়া ভার) ; indisposed, feeling sick (দেহ ভার ঠেকা) ; affected with huff, sulky (মন ভার). **ভার করা** *v.* to darken with huff or to sulk (মুখ ভার করা) ; to become indisposed or sick. **ভার চাপানো, ভার দেওয়া** *v.* to load: to burden; to put a weight (as on a scalepan); to encumber; to entrust (one) with the charge of. **ভার নেওয়া** *v.* to carry burden or weight; to be loaded; to undertake a charge. **ভার বওয়া** *v.* to carry burden or weight; to shoulder a charge.**~কেন্দ্র** *n.* (mech.) the centre of gravity. **~গ্রস্ত** *a.* burdened, encumbered. **~বাহ, ~বাহক, ~বাহী** *a.* carrying load or weight. **ভারবাহী ঘোড়া** a pack-horse, a draught horse, a sumpter, **ভারবাহী পশু** a pack-animal, a beast of burden, a draught animal. **~মধ্য, ~মধ্যবিন্দু** same as **~কেন্দ্র**। **~শঙ্কু** *n.* a lever. **~সহ** *a.* capable of bearing or withstanding load or pressure. **~সাম্য** *n.* (chiefly pol.) balance of power; equilibrium. **~হীন** *a.* not heavy, light; not loaded; unburdened; unencumbered; having no charge; weightless (on account of absence of gravity)

ভারই *n.* the skylark; the quail.

ভারত *n.* India (formerly including Pakistan), the Republic of India, the Indian Union; a son or descendant of King Bharata (ভরত) ; the Mahabharata. **~নাট্যম** *n.* Bharat Natyam, an Indian classical dance form. **~বর্ষ** same as **ভারত** excepting the last two meanings. **~বর্ষীয়** *a.* of or dwelling in India, Indian. **~বাসী** *a.* living in India, Indian.

□ *n.* an Indian. ~**মহাসাগর** *n.* the Indian Ocean. ~**মাতা** *n.* India personified as the common mother of all Indians; Mother India. ~**রত্ন** *n.* a jewel of India; the title of highest honour conferred upon eminent citizens by the President of India. ~**রাষ্ট্র** *n.* the Republic of India, the Indian Union. ~**সন্তান** *n.* a child of the Indian soil, an Indian. ~**সভা** *n.* Indian Association. ~**সরকার** *n.* the Government of India, the Indian Government. **ভারতের সংবিধান** the Constitution of India.

ভারতী *n.* Saraswati (সরস্বতী) the Goddess of speech; speech.

ভারতীয় *a.* Indian. **ভারতীয় করা** *v.* to Indianize. **পশ্চিম-ভারতীয় দ্বীপপুঞ্জ** the West Indies. **পূর্ব-ভারতীয় দ্বীপপুঞ্জ** the East Indies. ~**করণ** *n.* Indianization. ~**য়তা** *n.* the state of being Indian; Indianness.

ভারপ্রাপ্ত *a.* entrusted with charge or responsibility of, in charge. **ভারপ্রাপ্ত আধিকারিক** an officer-in-charge.

ভারা *n.* a scaffold. **ভারা বাঁধা** *v.* to build or erect a scaffold.

ভারাক্রান্ত *a.* embarrassed with heavy load or burden; encumbered; afflicted (with worries, misery etc.).

ভারার্পণ *n.* commitment of a charge, entrustment of a charge. **ভারার্পণ করা** *v.* to commit a charge, to entrust (one) with a charge.

ভারার্পিত *a.* entrusted with a charge.

ভারিক্কি, ভারিক্কে *a.* grave, serious, not light; having a condescending or patronizing or bossy air. **ভারিক্কি ধরনের বা প্রকৃতির লোক** a man making a strong impression because of size, character, appearance etc., a man of imposing personality.

ভারিভুরি *n.* ostentatious show, pomp; bragging, vanity, pretence.

ভারী[1] *a.* heavy, weighty; large and heavy (ভারী দেহ) ; difficult, hard, serious (ভারী কাজ) ; inportant (ভারী লোক) ; having an important or grave air (ভারী চালচলন) ; great (ভারী আনন্দ বা দুঃখ) ; (sarcas.) nice (ভারী কথা) ; (sarcas.) too much (ভারী পড়া পড়ছে) ; afflicted, saddened, glum, sullen, morose (ভারী মন) ; gloomy (ভারী আবহাওয়া) ; (fig.) full of or abounding in money (ভারী পকেট). □ *n.* one who carries a load; a water-carrier, a bhisti.

ভারী[2] *adv.* very, extremely; too much or excessively (ভারী সুন্দর, ভারী মন্দ). □ *a.* great, excessive (ভারী মজা).

ভারুই *n.* the skylark; the quail.

ভার্যা *n.* wife.

ভাল *n.* the forehead; fate.

ভালাই *n.* welfare, weal; good, wellbeing.

ভালুক pop. coll. var. of **ভল্লুক**।

ভালো *a.* good; fair; excellent; auspicious (ভালো দিন) ; suitable (ভালো সময়) ; beneficial, wholesome (ভালো উপদেশ) ; helpful, useful, serviceable (ভালো ওষুধ, ভালো যন্ত্র) ; healthy, whole, sound (ভালো শরীর) ; recovered from illness; cured; rectified, corrected, redeemed, reclaimed, improved; flourished; honest (ভালো লোক) ; genuine (ভালো টাকা) ; innocent, harmless (ভালো মানুষ) ; proper; quiet, gentle; becoming, fitting; proficient (অঙ্কে ভালো) ; efficient (ভালো কর্মী) ; a large number of (সভায় ভালো লোক হবে) ; plentiful, sufficient (এ বছর ভালো বৃষ্টি হবে) ; true, official, not used in familiarity (তোমার ভালো নাম কী) ; great (ভালো যশ). □ *adv.* well; to or in a large number or amount or degree (সভায় লোক ভালো আসবে, সে ভালো খেতে পারে). □ *n.* good, weal, welfare, prosperity (পরের ভালো) ; right (ভালোমন্দ-বিচার). □ *int.* all right (ভালো, তাই হোক) ; well (ভালো, কী বলছ ?). **ভালো করা** *v.* to do well (না গিয়ে ভালো করেছ) ; to do good (to); to do one a good turn; to cure, to heal; to rectify or reclaim; to improve; to console or stimulate (মন ভালো করা). **ভালো করে** *adv.* well; carefully; minutely; meticulously; properly; at ease (ভালো করে শোয়া) ; soundly (ভালো করে মারা). **ভালো খাওয়া** *v.* to be accustomed to eat (and drink) choice things; to eat well; to be capable of eating much; to eat much. **ভালো চলা** *v.* (of vehicles, business-organizations, domestic or other establishments) to run well, to run smoothly; to have sufficient means for subsistence or for other purposes. **ভালো থাকা** *v.* to be in good health, to be well; to be happy; to be cosy and comfortable (মায়ের কোলে শিশুরা ভালো থাকে) ; to live in prosperity (ধনীর মেয়ে বিয়ে করে সে আছে ভালো) ; to live honestly (চোরটা এবার থেকে ভালো থাকবে) ; to be in good condition (রোদে দিলে গরম জামাকাপড় ভালো থাকে) ; to be quiet or gentle (কোঁতকা খেলে দুর্বৃত্তেরা ভালো থাকে). **ভালো দেখানো** *v.* to look well; to look beautiful; to look healthy; to look honest; to appear as becoming or befitting. **ভালো বলা** *v.* to speak well; to speak well of, to approve; to praise, to laud; to give good counsel, to advise well. **ভালো লাগা** *v.* to be to one's liking; to appear good to one; to taste or sound or seem well. **ভালো হওয়া** *v.* to recover from illness, to come round; to be cured; to be beneficial or profitable; to do good to (এতে তোমার ভালো হবে) ; to be corrected or reclaimed; to be good (ছেলেটি ভালো হবে) ; to improve or flourish (অবস্থা ভালো হওয়া) ; to prosper, to be prosperous (তোমার ভালো হোক) ; to assemble or come in a large number. **ভালো আপদ** an expression denoting: disgust, trouble etc.; what a pest! **ভালো কথা**[1] good counsel; profitable or moral advice. **ভালো কথা**[2] by the way (ভালো কথা, তুমি কি কাল যাবে ?). **ভালো ঘর** a respectable or marriageable family. **ভালো জ্বালা** same as **ভালো আপদ**। **ভালো থাকা** *v.* to be well,to get on well; to have good time. **ভালো থেকো** *v.* have a good time. **ভালো মনে** *adv.* sincerly; open-heartedly. **ভালোমন্দ** *n.*. good and bad; right and wrong; accident, mishap, death etc. (ভালোমন্দ ঘটা) ; choice articles of food. **ভালো মানুষ** *n.* a good man, a good soul; (derog.) a weak-minded person, a simpleton. **ভালো মানুষ সাজা** *v.* to pretend to be a good man; to pretend to be innocent. **ভালোমানুষি** *n.* honest and blameless conduct; (derog.) pretence of honesty and innocence. **ভালোয় ভালোয়** *adv.* safely, in safety; without let or hindrance.

ভালোবাসা *v.* to love, to be amorous towards; to have attachment or affection or fondness for; to like. □ *n.* love; attachment; amity, friendliness; friendship; affection; reverence; devotion; fondness; liking.

ভালোমনে ভালোমন্দ, ভালোয়-ভালোয় see **ভালো**।

ভাশুর *n.* an elder brother or cousin-brother of one's husband, a brother-in-law. **~ঝি** *n.* a daughter of such a brother-in-law. **~পো** *n.* a son of an aforesaid brother-in-law.

ভাষ, ভাষণ *n.* speech; utterance; a talk; a lecture; a statement. **ভাষক** *n.* a speaker; a lecturer. **ভাষণ দেওয়া** *v.* to speak; to give a talk; to deliver a lecture; to give a statement.

ভাষা *n.* speech; language; a dialect; mother-tongue, vernacular; an expression, a significant hint (বোবা ভাষা, আকাশের ভাষা) ; mode of speaking (রূঢ় ভাষা) ; (now obs.) any Indian language other than Sanskrit ('প্রেমদাস রচিল ভাষায়'). **স্পষ্ট ভাষায়** in plain or clear language, plainly, frankly; categorically. **~জ্ঞান** *n.* knowledge in or of a language; knowledge as to how to use a language properly. **~তত্ত্ব** *n.* philology; linguistics. **~তত্ত্বজ্ঞ, ~তত্ত্ববিদ** *n.* a philologist; a linguist. □ *a.* versed in philology or linguistics. **ভাষাতীত** *a.* not describable in language, beyond speech or language; inexplicable. **~ন্তর** *n.* another language; rendering into another language, translation. **ভাষান্তরিক** *n.* a translator, an interpreter. **ভাষান্তরিত** *a.* translated. **ভাষান্তরিত করা** *v.* to translate. **~বিজ্ঞান** same as **ভাষাতত্ত্ব**। **~বিজ্ঞানী** same as **ভাষাতত্ত্বজ্ঞ**।

ভাষিক *a.* relating to language; linguistic.

ভাষিণী *fem.* of **ভাষী**।

ভাষিত *a.* spoken, said; uttered; narrated; stated.

ভাষী *a.* (used as a *sfx.*) speaking (হিন্দিভাষী, মন্দভাষী).

ভাষ্য *n.* an explanation; a commentary; annotation, gloss. **ভাষ্য করা** *v.* to explain; to make a commentary of; to annotate; to gloss. **~কার** *n.* an explainer; a commentator; an annotator; a glosser, a glossarist.

ভাস[1] *n.* the vulture; the cock.

ভাস[2] *n.* glow, radiance, tinge.

ভাস[3] *n.* a Sanskrit playwright of ancient India.

ভাসন্ত, (loos. but pop.) **ভাসমান**[1] *a.* floating, natant, drifting.

ভাসমান[2] *a.* glowing, radiant; having a graceful appearance, showing-off.

ভাসা *v.* to float, to drift; to swim; to be buoyant; to be flooded (with) (বন্যায় দেশ ভাসা) ; to rise or strike or appear in, to occur to (মনে ভাসা) ; (fig.) to be overflowing. **ভাসান** *n.* immersion (as of an image of a deity); a kind of folk-song celebrating activities of some deities (মনসার ভাসান). **ভাসা-ভাসা** *a.* shallow, superficial. **ভাসা-ভাসা জ্ঞান** index-learning, skin-deep or superficial knowledge. **ভাসানো** *v.* to cause to float; to float; to levitate, to set adrift; to flood or overflow.

ভাসুর alt. spell. of **ভাশুর** ।

ভাস্কর *n.* the sun; a sculptor.

ভাস্কর্য *n.* sculpture.

ভাস্বতী *fem.* of **ভাস্বান** ।

ভাস্বর, ভাস্বান *a.* luminous; radiant; bright; (phys.) incandescent. **ভাস্বর দীপ** an incandescent lamp.

ভিক্ষা *n.* begging; earnest request or prayer, solicitation; importuning; alms; a dole; a charitable or gracious gift. **ভিক্ষা করা** *v.* to beg; to live by begging; to request or pray earnestly (for), to solicit (for); to importune. **ভিক্ষা দেওয়া** *v.* to give alms; to dole; to give or grant (something) charitably or condescendingly. **~চর্যা** *n.* same as **~বৃত্তি** । **~জীবী** *a.* living by begging, living on alms, mendicant. *fem.* **~জীবিনী** । **~ন্ন** *n.* food obtained by begging. **~পাত্র** *n.* an alms-dish, a beggar's bowl, (cp.) a clack-dish. **~বৃত্তি** *n.* begging, mendicancy. **~ভাণ্ড** same as **~পাত্র** । **~র্থী** *a.* & *n.* one who asks or prays for alms. *fem.* **ভিক্ষার্থিনী** । **~লব্ধ** *a.* obtained by begging. **ভিক্ষার চাল কাঁড়া আর আঁকড়া** beggars can't be choosers.

ভিক্ষিত *a.* begged; obtained by begging.

ভিক্ষু *n.* a Buddhist mendicant friar; a mendicant friar; a beggar-man.

ভিক্ষুক *n.* a beggar, a mendicant, a beggar-man, an alms-man; a humble petitioner. **~রমণী** *n.* an alms-woman, a beggar-woman. **~সম্প্রদায়** *n.* the beggardom.

ভিক্ষুণী *n. fem.* a Buddhist mendicant nun; a mendicant nun; a beggar-woman.

ভিখ *n.* (coll.) alms. **ভিখ মাগা** same as **ভিক্ষা করা** (see **ভিক্ষা**). **গেঁয়ো যোগী ভিখ পায় না** (fig.) a prophet is never honoured in his own country; (cp.) familiarity breeds contempt.

ভিখারি, (coll.) **ভিখিরি** same as **ভিক্ষুক** । *fem.* **ভিখারিনি** । **পথের ভিখারি** a street beggar; (fig.) an utterly resourceless and indigent person.

ভিজা, ভেজা *v.* to get wet; to soak with water or any other liquid; to soften by being steeped in water or any other liquid; (fig.) to soften emotionally (মন ভেজা). □ *a.* wet; soaked with or steeped in water etc.; containing water or vapour, damp, hydrous, vapoury (ভেজা বাতাস). **~নো** *v.* to make wet; to soak with or steep in water etc.; to soften by steeping in water etc.

ভিজিট *n.* a physician's fee for a professional call or visit.

ভিজে *a.* coll corrup. of **ভিজা** (*a.*). **ভিজে বেড়াল** (fig.) a terrible rogue appearing to be perfectly innocent and harmless, a wolf in sheep's skin.

ভিটা, (coll.) **ভিটে** *n.* the piece of ground on which a dwelling-house (esp. an ancestral one) rests; foundation; homestead. **ভিটা-ছাড়া** *a.* ejected or ousted from one's homestead; displaced from one's country. **ভিটা-ছাড়া লোক** *a.* displaced person. **~মাটি** same as **ভিটা** । **ভিটেমাটি উচ্ছন্ন করা, ভিটেমাটি চাটি করা** *v.* to raze one's homestead to the ground.

ভিটামিন *n.* vitamin.

ভিটে coll. form of **ভিটা** ।

ভিড় *n.* a crowd; throng; concourse; a mob; the rabble; multitude; rush (কাজের ভিড়). **ভিড় করা** *v.* to crowd; to throng; to rush (in) (মাথায় চিন্তা ভিড় করা). **ভিড় ঠেলা** *v.* to force one's way through a crowd.

ভিত *n.* foundation, base; plinth; a wall;

direction, side, a point of the compass (চারিভিতে).

ভিতর *n.* the interior, the inside; the midst, the middle; the inmost part (মনের ভিতরটা খাঁ-খাঁ করছে). □ *prep.* & *adv.* in, within, into, inside; in the midst of, amidst. □ *a.* inner. **ভিতরের কথা, ভিতরের খবর** a secret, inside information. **ভিতরের ব্যাপার** a secret; an internal affair. **~দিক** *n.* the inside; the inward direction or portion. **~বাড়ি** *n.* the inner apartments of a residential building; the gynaeceum, the seraglio. **~-বাহির** *n.* the inside and outside; ins and outs. **ভিতর-ভিতর** *adv.* inwardly; at heart; secretly, surreptitiously; under the counter. **~মহল** same as ভিতরবাড়ি। **ভিতরে** *prep.* & *adv.* same as ভিতর (*prep.* & *adv.*). **ভিতরে-ভিতরে** same as ভিতর-ভিতর।

ভিতু *a.* timid; cowardly; faint-hearted, chicken-hearted. **ভীতুর ডিম** (joc.) an utter coward; a person who is easily frightened or scared; a scare-cat.

ভিত্তি *n.* foundation, base; plinth; a wall; basis, ground, cause. **~প্রস্তর** *n.* the foundation-stone. **~মূল** *n.* the bottom of a foundation; base; plinth. **ভিত্তি স্থাপন করা** *v.* to lay the foundation of. **~হীন** *a.* groundless, baseless, causeless.

ভিদ্যমান *a.* in the state of being pierced or penetrated.

ভিন corrup. of ভিন্ন। **~দেশ** *n.* another country; a foreign land.

ভিন্দিপাল *n.* an ancient missile.

ভিন্ন *a.* other, different, separate; separated; isolated; segregated; estranged; parted; partitioned; split, torn, rent, severed, broken, fractured. □ *prep.* except, without, other than. **~জাতীয়** *a.* of a different race or nation; of a different kind or sort; heterogeneous. **~তা** *n.* otherness, difference. **ভিন্ন ধাতুর লোক** a man cast in a different mould. **~প্রকার** *a.* of a different kind or sort; heterogeneous. **~মত** *n.* a different opinion. □ *a.* disagreeing in opinion, dissenting. **~মতাবলম্বী** *a.* dissentient; holding a different opinion. □ *n.* a dissenter. *fem.* **~মতাবলম্বিনী**। **~রুচি** *a.* differing or disagreeing in taste or choice. □ *n.* difference of taste; different taste. **ভিন্নার্থ** *n.* a different meaning. □ *a.* conveying a different meaning or purport. **ভিন্নার্থক** *a.* same as **ভিন্নার্থ** (*a.*).

ভিমরুল *n.* the hornet. **ভিমরুলের চাক** hornet's nest. **ভিমরুলের চাকে খোঁচা দেওয়া** (lit. & fig.) to bring a hornet's nest about one's ears, to stir up a hornet's nest.

ভিয়ান, (coll.) **ভিয়েন** *n.* act of making sweetmeat, confectionery. **ভিয়েন করা** *v.* to prepare sweetmeat, to confect. **~ঘর** *n.* a room for making sweetmeat, a confectionary.

ভিরকুটি *n.* a frown; a grimace. **ভিরকুটি করা** *v.* to frown; to grimace.

ভিরমি *n.* sudden dizziness or daze; fainting; a swoon. **ভিরমি খাওয়া, ভিরমি লাগা** *v.* to be affected with sudden dizziness or vertigo, to be dazed suddenly; to faint, to swoon.

ভিল *n.* one of an aboriginal non-Aryan tribe of India.

ভিষক *n.* a physician.

ভিসা *n.* a visa.

ভিস্তি *n.* a leather bag for carrying water, a water-bag; a water-carrier, a bhisty. **~ওয়ালা** *n.* a bhisty.

ভীড় rej. spell. of ভিড়।

ভীত *a.* frightened, alarmed; afraid. *fem.* **ভীতা**। **ভীত করা** *v.* to frighten, to alarm. **~চিত্ত** *a.* timid, timorous; faint-hearted. **ভীতি** *n.* fear, fright, dread, terror, alarm. **ভীতিকর, ভীতিজনক, ভীতিপ্রদ** *a.* fearful, frightful, dreadful; terrible, horrible; alarming; threatening, menacing. **ভীতিপ্রদর্শক** *a.* threatening. □ *n.* one who threatens or frightens, a threatener. **ভীতিপ্রদর্শন** *n.* threatening or menacing; a threat, menace. **ভীতিপ্রদর্শন করা** *v.* to threaten, to menace. **ভীতিবিহ্বল** *a.* beside oneself with fright; seized with utter fright; terror-stricken. **ভীতু** & **ভীতুর ডিম** see **ভীতু**।

ভীম *a.* terrible, terrific, horrible; awful; tremendous. □ *n.* the second son of King Pandu (পাণ্ডু).

ভীমকর্মা *a.* doing terrible things.

ভীমদর্শন *a.* having a horrible or awe-inspiring appearance; awesome.

ভীমনাদ *n.* a terrific or an awe-inspiring sound or noise.

ভীমপরাক্রম *a.* awfully mighty or vigorous.

ভীমপলশ্রী, (coll.) **ভীমপলাশি** *n.* an Indian musical mode.

ভীমবিক্রম same as **ভীমপরাক্রম**। **ভীমবিক্রমে** *adv.* with aweful might; with awe-inspiring valour.

ভীমবেগ *n.* a terrible or tremendous speed.

ভীমরথী, (coll.) **ভীমরতি** *n.* senility, dotage. **ভীমরতিগ্রস্ত** *a.* senile.

ভীমরুল alt. spell. of **ভিমরুল**।

ভীমা *fem.* of **ভীম**।

ভীরু *a.* timid; cowardly, dastardly. **ভীরু ব্যক্তি** a timid person, a faint-heart; a coward, a dastard, a poltroon. **~চিত্ত** *a.* faint-hearted, chicken-hearted, timid; cowardly. **~তা** *n.* timidness, faint-heartedness; cowardice, poltroonery. **~স্বভাব** *a.* timid or timorous or cowardly by nature.

ভীল alt. spell. of **ভিল**।

ভীষণ *a.* terrible, horrible, terrific, awful; tremendous, severe (ভীষণ গরম) ; formidable (ভীষণ শত্রু) ; monstrous (ভীষণ মূর্তি). *fem.* **ভীষণা**। **~তা** *n.* terribleness, awfulness; tremendousness, severity; formidability; monstrosity. **~দর্শন** *a.* having a horrible appearance. **ভীষণাকার** *a.* having a monstrous form. **ভীষিত** *a.* frightened; scared.

ভীষ্ম *a.* terrible. □ *n.* a character of the Mahabharata.**ভীষ্মের প্রতিজ্ঞা** an unalterable or resolute vow or pledge; a firm resolve.

ভুঁই *n.* ground; a place; agricultural land, a field; land (জল থেকে ভুঁইয়ে ওঠা) ; a country (বিভুঁই) **~চাঁপা** *n.* a kind of fragrant flower. **ভুঁইঞা** alt. spell. of **ভুঁইয়া**। **~ফোঁড়** *a.* upstart. □ *n.* an upstart; a parvenu; mushroom. **~মালী** *n.* one of the Hindu sweeper community. **~য়া** *n.* (hist.) any one of the twelve (feudal) princes governing Bengal during the Mughal regime; a landowner.

ভুঁড়ি *n.* (usu. facet.) a pot-belly; (facet.) the belly. **ভুঁড়ি হওয়া** *v.* to grow pot-bellied.

ভুঁড়ো *a.* pot-bellied, abdominous.

ভুদো var. of **ভোঁদা**।

ভুক *sfx.* eating, subsisting on (পিপীলিকাভুক).

ভুক্ত *a.* eaten; enjoyed; suffered or experienced; enjoyed as one's property; included or incorporated (গ্রন্থভুক্ত, রাজ্যভুক্ত). **~ভোগী** *a.* having had similar suffering or experience in the past. **ভুক্তাবশিষ্ট, ভুক্তাবশেষ** *a.* (of food and drink) left from a meal. □ *n.* leavings of a meal, orts. **ভুক্তি** *n.* eating; enjoyment; possession as one's own; inclusion, incorporation, comprisal; an ancient administrative division of land, a district.

ভুখ *n.* hunger. **~মিছিল, ভুখামিছিল** *n.* a hunger march. **ভুখা** *a.* hungry. **ভুখা ভগবান** the hungry mass; the proletariat, the have-nots.

ভুজ *n.* the arm; the hand; (geom.) an arm (of an angle), a side (of a triangle, rectangle, polygon etc.); (math.) an abscissa.

ভুজংভাজাং *var.* of **ভুজুংভাজুং**।

ভুজগ, ভুজঙ্গ, ভুজঙ্গম *n.* the snake. *fem.* **ভুজগী, ভুজঙ্গী, ভুজঙ্গামী,** (pop.) **ভুজঙ্গিনী**। **ভুজঙ্গপ্রয়াত** *n.* a metre of Sanskrit poetry.

ভুজপাশ, ভুজবন্ধন *n.* the snare or clasp of one's arms; an embrace; (in wrestling etc.) a hug. **ভুজপাশে বা ভুজবন্ধনে বাঁধা** *n.* to clasp with the arms; to embrace; to hug.

ভুজবল *n.* the strength of one's arms; physical strength; might, prowess.

ভুজা *n.* parched corn eaten as snacks.

ভুজাংশ *n.* a celestial longitude.

ভুজিয়া same as **ভুজা**।

ভুজুংভাজুং *n.* false or flimsy arguments or allurements or consolation; cajolery.

ভুঞ্জা (poet.) *v.* to eat; to enjoy; to enjoy as one's property; to enjoy sexually; to suffer or undergo.

ভুঞ্জিত (poet.) *a.* eaten; enjoyed; enjoyed as one's property; enjoyed sexually; suffered or undergone.

ভুটভাট *int.* denoting: grumbling noise in the abdomen.

ভুটানি *a.* of or relating to Bhutan; Bhutanese. □ *n.* a Bhutanese, one who speaks the Bhutanese language.

ভুটিয়া same as **ভুটানি** ।

ভুট্টা *n.* maize, mealies.

ভুড়ভুড় *int.* denoting: noise of effervescence. **ভুড়ভুড় করা** *v.* to effervesce. **ভুড়ভুড়ানি, ভুড়ভুড়ি** *n.* effervescence.

ভুতি, ভুতুড়ি same as **ভুশুড়ি** ।

ভুনিখিচুড়ি *n.* a kind of hotchpotch cooked by frying rice and pigeon-pea very slightly in ghee.

ভুবঃ *n.* (myth.) the second of the seven heavens; the ethereal region, the sky, the firmament.

ভুবন *n.* (myth.) the seven heavens and seven underworlds; the universe; the world, the earth. **~বিখ্যাত** *a.* worldfamous. **~বিজয়ী** *a.* world-conquering. **~বিদিত** *a* known all over the world. **~ব্যাপী** *a.* worldwide; universal. **~-ভুলানো** *a.* enchanting the whole world, holding the world under a spell. **~ময়** *a.* all over the world, all around the world; ubiquitous. **~মনোমোহিনী** *a. fem.* captivating the minds of all people of the world. **~মোহন** *a.* fascinating the whole world. *fem.* **~মোহিনী** । **ভুবনেশ্বর** *n.* the lord of the universe; Shiva (শিব) esp. whose image is installed at Bhubaneswar; God. *fem.* **ভুবনেশ্বরী** one of the ten manifestations of Goddess Durga (দুর্গা).

ভুবর্লোক same as **ভুবঃ** ।

ভুয়া, (coll.) **ভুয়ো** *a.* unsubstantial, hollow, empty; false.

ভুরভুর *int.* denoting: diffusion with fragrance or perfume.

ভুরু *n.* the eyebrow.

ভুরো *n.* a kind of unrefined and coarse sugar.

ভুল *n.* an error, a mistake, a blunder; an omission; oblivion; delirium (ভুল বকা). □ *a.* erroneous, incorrect, wrong. **ভুল করা** *v.* to err; to blunder; to commit or make a mistake; to mistake (লোক বা পথ ভুল করা) ; to be guilty of omission; to forget. **ভুল ভাঙা** *v.* to be disillusioned. **ভুল হওয়া** *v.* to be wrong or incorrect; to be mistaken or omitted or forgotten. **~চুক, ~ভ্রান্তি** *n..pl.* errors and omissions. **ঠিকে ভুল** an error in addition; (loos.) an error in fundamentals. **ভুলা, ভোলা, ভুল করা** *v.* to mistake, to err, to blunder; to forget; to omit; to be relieved of (দুঃখ ভোলা); to be indifferent or callous to (কর্তব্য ভোলা) ; to be charmed or bewitched (সুন্দর মুখ দেখে ভোলা) ; to be enticed or deceived or tempted (প্রলোভনে ভোলা) ; to be cajoled (স্তোকবাক্যে ভোলা) ; to be wheedled (খেলা দিলে ছেলেটা ভোলে) ; to be consoled (গান শুনলে তাপিত হৃদয় ভুলবে). **ভুলানো** *v.* to cause to err or mistake or forget or omit; to relieve of; to charm, to bewitch; to entice; to deceive, to tempt; to cajole; to wheedle; to console. □ *a.* causing to err or mistake or forget or omit; relieving of; charming, bewitching; enticing, deceiving, tempting; cajoling; wheedling; consoling, **ভুলানি, ভুলুনি** *a.* & *fem.* one who charms or bewitches or entices or tempts or cajoles or wheedles. *masc.* **ভুলানে** । **ভুলুনে, ভুলো** *a.* apt to err, forgetful, oblivious. **ভুলের মাশুল দেওয়া** to pay for one's mistake or thoughtless act or folly.

ভুশ *int.* denoting: noise of springing up from under water, mire etc.

ভুশুড়ি *n.* the inedible pulp within a jackfruit or any other fruit. **ভুশুড়ি ভাঙা** *v.* to surfeit oneself, to gormandize. **গল্পের ভুশুড়ি ভাঙা** *v.* to go on telling stories one after another.

ভুশুন্ডি coll. corrup. of **ভূশণ্ডী** ।

ভুষা rej. spell. of **ভুসা** ।

ভুষি alt. spell. of **ভুসি** ।

ভুষ্টিনাশ *n.* total or gross waste (টাকার ভুষ্টিনাশ) ; utter bungling (কাজের ভুষ্টিনাশ) ; complete ruin or destruction (শত্রুর ভুষ্টিনাশ).

ভুসা *n.* soot; collyrium. **~কালি** *n.* ink made of soot; lampblack.

ভুসি *n.* chaff, husk,bran. **~মাল** *n.* cereals; refuse, waste matter. **ভুসিমালের খরিদ্দার** a buyer or customer of cereals; (fig. & dero.) a contemptible customer. **ভুসিমালের ব্যাপারি** a corn-dealer, a corn-merchant.

ভুসো coll. var. of **ভুসা**।

ভূ *n.* the earth, the world; land; ground. **~কম্প, ~কম্পন** *n.* earthquake. **~কম্পবিদ্যা** *n.* seismography, seismology. **~কম্পলিক** *n.* a seismograph. **~কর্ণ** *n.* a radius of the equator. **~কেন্দ্র** *n.* the centre of the earth. **~কেন্দ্রীয়** *a.* (astr.) geocentric. **~খণ্ড** *n.* a division or part of the earth, a region; a part of the landed portion of the earth; a country. **~গর্ভ** *n.* the bowels or inside of the earth; a subterranean region. **~গর্ভস্থ, ~গর্ভস্থিত** *a.* lying in the bowels of the earth; underground; subterranean. **ভূগর্ভস্থ রেলপথ** an underground railway, a tube-railway. **~গহ্বর** *n.* an underground cavity or hole; (geog.) a cavern; an underground chamber, a subterranean, a subterrene. **~গহ্বরবাসী** *a.* dwelling underground. □ *n.* a dweller in an undergorund cell, (cp.) a basement dweller, a subterranean. **~গোলক** *n.* a sphere representing the earth, a globe; the earth, the globe. **~চর** *a.* living or moving on land, terrestrial. **~চিত্র** *n.* a map. **~চিত্রাবলি** *n.* atlas. **~চুম্বকত্ব** *n.* (phys.) terrestrial magnetism. **~চ্ছায়া** *n.* the shadow of the earth; darkness. **~তত্ত্ব, ~তত্ত্ববিদ্যা** *n.* geology. **~তত্ত্ববিদ, ~তাত্ত্বিক** *n.* a geologist. **~তত্ত্বীয়** *a.* geological. **~তল** *n.* the surface of the earth; the face or floor of the earth; the nether world, Hades; ground. **~তলশায়ী** same as **~শায়ী**। *fem.* **~তলশায়িনী**। **~তলস্থ** *a.* terrestrial; earthly. **~তাত্ত্বিক** *n.* a geologist. **~ত্বক** *n.* (geog. & geol.) the crust of the earth. **~দান** *n.* gift of land (usu. by the rich for the benefit of the poor); the name of a movement by Vinoba Bhave to inspire big landholders to part with some parcels of land as a gesture of good will. **~নিম্ন** *n.* the region underground. □ *a.* underground. **ভূনিম্ন তার** an underground cable. **~পতিত** *a.* fallen on or to the ground; dropped or thrown or flung into the ground. **~পতিত হওয়া** *v.* to fall on or to the ground; to prostrate oneself on the ground. **~পরিধি** *n.* circumference of the earth. **~পাত** *n.* (geog.) a landship, landslide. **ভূপাতিত করা** *v.* to pull down or fell to the ground; to knock to the ground; to floor. **~পৃষ্ঠ** *n.* the surface of the earth. **~প্রদক্ষিণ** *n.* travel round the world; circumnavigation. **~প্রদক্ষিণ করা** *v.* to ambulate or travel round the earth; to rotate round the earth; (geog.) to circumnavigate. **~প্রকৃতি** *n.* (geog.) configuration of land. **~বলয়** *n.* the equator. **~বিষুব** *n.* the equator. **~বিষুবরেখা** *n.* the equatorial line, the equator. **~বিদ্যা** *n.* geology. **~বিদ্যাগত** *a.* geological. **~বিদ্যাবিদ** *n.* a geologist. **~বৃত্ত** *n.* the equatorial circle, the equator. **~ভাগ** same as **~খণ্ড**। **~ভার** *n.* the burden of sins committed by mankind; the burden of the earth; the burdensome charge of administering and protecting the earth. **~ভৃৎ** *n.* a mountain; a hill; a king. **~লুণ্ঠিত** *a.* rolling or wallowing on the ground; fallen to the ground; prostrated on the ground. *fem.* **~লুণ্ঠিতা**। **ভূলুণ্ঠিত হওয়া** *v.* to roll or wallow on the ground; to fall to the ground; to prostrate oneself on the ground. **~লোক** *n.* the earth. **~শয্যা** *n.* use of bare ground as one's bed. **~শায়িত, ~শায়ী** *a.* laid or lying upon the bare ground; fallen to or prostrated on the ground; knocked to the ground, floored. *fem.* **~শায়িতা, ~শায়িনী**। **~সংস্থান** *n.* topography. **~সম্পত্তি** *n.* landed property, real estate, demesne. **~স্তর** *n.* (geog. & geol.) a stratum of the earth. **~স্পন্দ** *n.* (geog.) an earth-tremor. **~স্বর্গ** *n.* an earthly paradise, a paradise on earth; Kashmir.

ভূঃ *n.* (myth.) the first of the seven regions.

ভূগোল, ভূগোলবিদ্যা *n.* geography.

ভূত *n.* one of a class of supernatural beings who attend on Shiva (শিব), (cp.) genii; a ghost; an evil spirit; a bogey; a goblin; a spectre, an apparition; a creature (সর্বভূত) ; any one of the five constituent elements (namely, earth, water, heat, air and space). □ *a.* past, gone by; (as *sfx.*) reduced to (প্রস্তরীভূত). □ *n.* the past (ভূত-ভবিষ্যৎ). **ভূত ছাড়ানো, ভূত ছাড়া,**

ভূত তাড়ানো *v.* to exorcise. ভূত দেখা *v.* to see an apparition; (fig.) to be frightened suddenly. ভূত নামানো same as ভূত ছাড়ানো, and (as by spiritualists) to call up ghosts in order to obtain messages from them. ভূতে ধরা, ভূতে পাওয়া *v.* to be possessed by an evil spirit, to be possessed. ভূতের ওঝা an exorciser. ভূতের নাচ devil's dance; (fig.) devil of a mess, the devil and all. ভূতের বাপের শ্রাদ্ধ (fig.) great and gross waste or extravagance. ভূতের বেগার, ভূতের বোঝা (fig.) profitless toil or venture. ভূতের রোজা an exorciser. ঘাড়ে ভূত চাপা (fig.) to be seized with an evil influence or company or practice or intention; to be possessed; to be obsessed. সরষের মধ্যে ভূত (fig.) virus in the antidote. ~কাল *n.* days gone by, the past; (gr.) the past tense. ~গ্রস্ত *a.* possessed by an evil spirit, possessed; (fig.) working or moving mechanically as if possessed; dazed. *fem.* ~গ্রস্তা। ~তত্ত্ব *n.* demonology. ~তত্ত্ববিদ *n.* proficient or versed in demonology. ~নাথ *n.* Shiva (শিব). ~পক্ষ *n.* the dark lunar fortnight. ~পূর্ব *a.* former, erstwhile, previous, late, (arch.) whilom. ~প্রেত *n.* evil spirits collectively, ghosts and spirits collectively. ~বলি same as ভূতযজ্ঞ। ~ভবিষ্যৎ *n.* the past and the future. ~ভাবন *n.* the creator and protector of all living beings; Shiva (শিব). ~ভোজন *n.* (often joc.) same as ~যজ্ঞ। ~যজ্ঞ *n.* the ceremonial feeding of all living beings by a householder. ~যোনি *n.* existence in the shape of a ghost after one's death. ভূতযোনি প্রাপ্ত হওয়া to become a ghost after one's death. ~শুদ্ধি *n.* purification of the elemental or mortal body. ~সঞ্চার *n.* inhabitation of a ghost. ভূতসঞ্চার হওয়া *v.* to be inhabited or possessed by a ghost or devil or evil spirit. ভূতাত্মা *n.* the elemental body; the human body; Brahma (ব্রহ্মা) or Vishnu (বিষ্ণু). ভূতাবিষ্ট same as ভূতগ্রস্ত। ভূতাবেশ *n.* possession by a ghost or evil spirit.

ভূতি *n.* eight supernal or divine powers (such as অণিমা, মহিমা, লঘিমা, প্রাপ্তি, প্রাকাম্য, ঈশিতা, বশিতা, কামাবশায়িতা); birth, origination.

ভূতুড়ে, ভূতুড়িয়া *a.* relating to ghosts (ভূতুড়ে কাহিনি = a ghost-story); done by ghosts, ghostly (ভূতুড়ে কাণ্ড = a ghostly affair): haunted by ghosts (ভূতুড়ে বাড়ি = a haunted house); ghost-like, haggard (ভূতুড়ে চেহারা), eerie, eery, weird, uncanny (ভূতুড়ে আবহাওয়া).

ভূধর *n.* a mountain, a hill.

ভূপ, ভূপতি, ভূপাল *n.* a king.

ভূপালি *n.* an Indian musical mode.

ভূভারত *n.* India and the rest of the world; the whole world.

ভূমণ্ডল *n.* the earth as a spherical body, the earth, the globe.

ভূমধ্য *n.* the centre of the earth; the bowels or inside of the earth. ভূমধ্যসাগর *n.* the Mediterranean Sea. ভূমধ্যসাগরীয় *a.* Mediterranean.

ভূমা *n.* the Omnipresent; the Supreme Being; God; sublimity; plurality; diversity. □ *a.* most abundant or numerous. ভূমানন্দ *n.* most abundant delight; the greatest or sublime joy; ecstasy; joy in a sense of vastness.

ভূমি *n.* the earth; the surface of the earth; soil; ground; floor; agricultural land, land, a field, a place, a site (রণভূমি); a country (জন্মভূমি); a repertory or receptacle (বিশ্বাসভূমি); (geom.) a base. ~কম্প, ~খণ্ড, ~গর্ভ same as ভূকম্প, ভূখণ্ড and ভূগর্ভ respectively (see ভূ). ~গ্রহ *n.* land acquisition. ভূমিগ্রহ-আধিকারিক *n.* land acquisition officer. ভূমিগ্রহ-সমাহর্তা *n.* a Land Acquisition Collector. ~জ *a.* grown out of the earth; earth-born; holding tenancy of land in lieu of menial services. ভূমিজ প্রজা (hist.) a villein. ~তল *n.* the surface of the earth; ground; floor. ~দান *n.* a grant of land. ~রাজস্ব *n.* land revenue. ~রেখা *n.* base line. ~লেখা *n.* land records. ~শয্যা, ~শায়িত, ~শায়ী same as ভূশয্যা, ভূশায়িত and ভূশায়ী respectively (see ভূ). ভূমিষ্ঠ হওয়া *v.* to fall to the ground; to prostrate oneself on the ground (ভূমিষ্ঠ হয়ে প্রণাম); to be born. ~সাৎ *a.* fallen to the ground; razed to the ground. ভূমিসাৎ করা

v. to pull down to the ground; to raze to the ground. ভূমিসাৎ হওয়া *v.* to fall to the ground; to be razed to the ground. ~সুত *n.* the Mars. ~স্থ, ~স্থিত *a.* lying or situated on the ground.

ভূমিকা *n.* a preface, a preamble, an introductory talk preceding a speech or action; a prologue; a presage; assumption of a dress or disguise; transfiguration; a role, a part. ভূমিকা গ্রহণ করা *v.* to take up a role; to take up the role of, to act as.

ভূম্যধিকারী same as ভূস্বামী।

ভূয়ঃ, (pop.) ভূয় *adv.* again and again, repeatedly. □ *a.* repeated. ভূয়সী *a.* repeated; profuse, copious (ভূয়সী প্রশংসা). ভূয়িষ্ঠ *a.* most abundant or numerous; great many; very much. ভূয়োদর্শন, ভূয়োদর্শিতা *n.* experience gathered by repeated direct perception or contact; wide experience. ভূয়োদর্শনজনিত *a.* born of long and wide experience. ভূয়োভূয়ঃ, (pop.) ভূয়োভূয় same as ভূয়ঃ।

ভূরি *a.* large in amount or number; abundant, profuse, copious, much; excessive, numerous, many. ~ভোজন *n.* a hearty meal; surfeit.

ভূর্জ *n.* the birch. ~পত্র *n.* the birch; the bark of the birch (formerly used in lieu of paper).

ভূশণ্ডি, ভূশণ্ডী *n.* (myth.) a crow living through ages; (ridi.) a very old person with out-of-date notions and often acting as a wet blanket on the joviality of youngsters; (cp.) a killjoy.

ভূষণ *n.* an ornament; a dress; ornamentation; dressing; personal embellishment; decoration; one who or that which adds to the beauty or glory (বিদ্বান দেশের ভূষণ = a learned man is the ornament of his country). ~প্রিয়া *a. fem.* fond of ornaments.

ভূষণ্ডী alt. spell. of ভূশণ্ডি।

ভূষা[1] var. of ভূষণ।

ভূষা[2] rej. spell. of ভুসা।

ভূষিত *a.* ornamented; dressed; decorated, adorned. *fem.* ভূষিতা। ভূষিত করা *v.* to adorn with ornaments, to ornament; to dress; to decorate, to adorn.

ভূস্বামী *n.* a landowner; a landlord, a zeminder; a king. *fem.* ভূস্বামিনী a female landowner; a landowner's wife; a queen.

ভৃগু *n.* a table-land, a plateau; a stiff cliff, a precipice.

ভৃঙ্গ *n.* the bumble-bee; the bee; the drongo. ~রোল *n.* the hornet.

ভৃঙ্গার *n.* a pitcher or jug with a spout, a ewer, (cp.) a flagon.

ভৃঙ্গারিকা, ভৃঙ্গারী *n.* a kind of insect, the cricket.

ভৃঙ্গি, ভৃঙ্গী *n.* one of the two chief attendants of Shiva (শিব).

ভৃত *a.* salaried or wage-earning; replete, full. ভৃতক *a.* salaried or wage-earning. □ *n.* a salary; wages. ভৃতি *n.* salary; wages; maintenance; feeding; filling. ভৃতিভুক *a.* salaried or wage-earning. ভৃতিভুক সম্প্রদায় the salariat, the salaried class.

ভৃত্য *n.* a servant; a salaried employee; a domestic servant.

ভেউভেউ *int.* denoting: noise of loud blubbering; a dog's yelling bark, bowvow.

ভেংচানো alt. spell. of ভ্যাংচানো।

ভেংচি *n.* a grimace, a grin. ভেংচি কাটা same as ভ্যাংচানো।

ভেঁপু *n.* a kind of wind-instrument; a bugle, a trumpet; a honk, a horn, a hoot (মোটরের ভেঁপু). ভেঁপু বাজানো *v.* to blow the aforesaid wind-instrument, to bugle, to trumpet; to honk, to hoot, to horn.

ভেক[1] var. of ভেখ।

ভেক[2] *n.* the frog.

ভেকা, (coll.) ভেকো *a.* confused, bewildered, stupefied. ভেকো লাগা *v.* to get confused, to be stupefied.

ভেখ *n.* asceticism, ascesis; Vaishnava asceticism; the garb of an ascetic esp. of a Vaishnava ascetic; disguise; simulation. ভেখ ধরা *v.* to take to asceticism esp. Vaishnava asceticism; to put on the garb of an ascetic esp. of a Vaishnava ascetic (also ভেখ নেওয়া) ; to assume a disguise; to simulate. ~ধারী *n.* an ascetic; a Vaishnava ascetic; a disguised person; a hypocrite.

ভেঙানো alt. spell. of ভ্যাঙানো।

ভেজা, ভেজানো[1] pop. variants of **ভিজা** and **ভিজানো** respectively.

ভেজানো[2] *v.* to close lightly (a door, window. etc.) without bolting, to close.

ভেজাল *n.* an adulterant; adulteration; (coll.) a trouble, a pest (উটকো ভেজাল). □ *a.* adulterated; spurious. **ভেজাল দেওয়া** বা **মেশানো** *v.* to adulterate. **ভেজাল বাধানো** *v.* to cause or create trouble; to tangle. **ভেজাল মেটানো** *v.* to put an end to doubts, difficulties etc. by supplying a solution.

ভেট *n.* a tribute (paid to a prince) or a complimentary gift or present (paid to a superior person) esp. during an interview (ভেট দেওয়া) ; a short visit, a call; a meeting; an interview. **ভেট করা** *v.* to call on, to visit; to meet; to interview.

ভেটকি *n.* a species of large flatfish found in rivers.

ভেটা poet. form of **ভেট করা**।

ভেটেরাখানা *n.* an inn; a place full of confused uproar (cp. bedlam).

ভেড়া[1] *v.* to come to or arrive (তরী কূলে ভিড়েছে) ; to come to the coast or bank (নৌকা ভেড়া) ; to ally or associate with (দলে ভেড়া)।

ভেড়া[2] *n.* the ram (masc.), the sheep (*neut.*); a fool. **পোষা ভেড়া** a cosset. **ভেড়ার গোয়াল** a sheep-fold. **ভেড়ার গোয়ালে আগুন লেগেছে** (facet.) a bad singer has started his musical baaing. **ভেড়ার ঠ্যাং** a sheep shank. **ভেড়ার ডাক** bleat, baa. **ভেড়ার পাল** a flock of sheep. **ভেড়ার মাংস** sheep's flesh; (when taken as food) mutton. **ভেড়ার লোম** sheep's wool. **ভেড়া চরানোর মাঠ** a sheep-run.

ভেড়াকান্ত *n.* (fig.) an utter fool.

ভেড়ানো var. of **ভিড়ানো** (see **ভিড়া**)।

ভেড়ি[1] *n.* an embankment, a dam; an embanked low land used as a fishery, a fishery dam. **ভেড়ি বাঁধা** *v.* to embank, to dam. **~ওয়ালা** *n.* an owner of a fishery dam.

ভেড়ি[2] *n. fem.* the ewe.

ভেড়ুয়া, (coll.) **ভেড়ো** *a.* as dastardly or silly as a sheep; henpecked; accompanying a professional dancing girl with instrumental music. □ *n.* such a man.

ভেতো pop. var. of **ভাতুয়া**।

ভেদ *n.* piercing; cleavage, split; difference; dissimilarity; disagreement, dissension; hostility; disunity; estrangement; antagonism, quarrel; separation; differentiation, discrimination; penetration (ব্যূহভেদ) ; disintegration; exposition, expounding, deciphering (অর্থভেদ) ; change, alteration (বুদ্ধিভেদ) ; a kind, a sort (রূপভেদ) ; looseness of bowels, diarrhoea. **ভেদ করা** *v.* to pierce, to cleave, to split; to differentiate, to discriminate; to penetrate; to expose, to expound, to decipher. **ভেদ জন্মানো** *v.* to sow dissension or discord; to disintegrate; to estrange. **~ক** *a.* one who or that which pierces or cleaves or splits or disintegrates or differentiates or discriminates or penetrates. **~জ্ঞান** *n.* perception of difference; discrimination; partiality. **~ন** piercing; cleaving; splitting; penetration. **~নীয়** *a.* capable of being pierced or cleft or split or penetrated, pregnable, vulnerable. **~নীতি** *n.* the policy of discrimination. **~বমি** *n.* diarrhoea attended with vomitting; cholera. **~বুদ্ধি** same as **~জ্ঞান**। **ভেদাভেদ** *n.* discriminatory treatment; discrimination; sense of meum and tuum (mine and thine). **ভেদিত** *a.* pierced; cleaved, split. **ভেদী** same as **ভেদক**। **ভেদ্য** same as **ভেদনীয়**।

ভেন্ডার *n.* a vendor.

ভেপসা alt. spell. of **ভ্যাপসা**।

ভেবড়ানো *v.* to be confounded or stupefied with fear, amazement etc.

ভেবা, ভেবাচেকা alt. spellings of **ভ্যাবা** and **ভ্যাবাচ্যাকা** respectively.

ভেরি, ভেরী *n.* a drum; a kettledrum.

ভেরেন্ডা *n.* the castor-oil plant, *Ricinus communis.* **ভেরেন্ডা ভাজা** (fig.) idling, to while away time; to remain idle or unemployed.

ভেল[1] (obs. & poet.) became or happened ('দশদিশ ভেল নিরদ্বন্দ্বা').

ভেল[2] *a.* spurious, counterfeit.

ভেলকি, ভেলকিবাজি *n.* magic, jugglery; hocus-pocus, conjuring; illusion. **ভেলকি দেখানো** *v.* to exhibit a magical show, to juggle, to conjure. **ভেলকি লাগা** *v.* to be dazed with a conjuring trick, to be spellbound or conjured; to be filled with illusions. **ভেলকি লাগানো** *v.* to put a spell on, to conjure; to delude. **ভেলকিওয়ালা** *n.* a magician, a juggler, a conjuror.

ভেলা *n.* a raft, a float, a coracle.

ভেল্কি alt. spell. of **ভেলকি** ।

ভেষজ *n.* a medicine; a drug; medical science; medicine. **~কর্ম** *n.* pharmacy; preparation and dispensing of drugs. **~বিদ্যা** *n.* medical science; medicine. **ভেষজালয়** *n.* a dispensary; a medical store, a drug-store, a pharmacy. **ভেষজী** *n.* pharmacist.

ভেস্তা *a.* upset or spoilt or foiled. **ভেস্তে যাওয়া** *v.* to fail, to come to naught. **ভেস্তানো** *v.* to upset or spoil or foil; to be upset or spoilt or foiled.

ভৈরব *n.* a manifestation of Shiva (শিব) ; an Indian musical mode. □ *a.* terrible or tremendous. **ভৈরবী** *n. fem.* one of the ten manifestations of Goddess Durga (দুর্গা) ; a famale ascetic worshipping Shiva (শিব) ; an Indian musical mode; a turbulent woman, (cp.) a termagant, (cp.) an Amazon. **ভৈরবীচক্র** *n.* a Tantrist drinking party.

ভৈষজ্য, ভৈষজ variants of **ভেষজ** । **ভৈষজবিদ্যা** *n.* pharmacology.

ভোঁ[1] *int.* ho, hoa, hullo.

ভোঁ[2] pop. corrup. of **ভোম** ।

ভোঁ[3] *int.* expressing: noise of the movement of wind, of running apace, of whistle etc. □ *n.* a whistle, a siren etc. (কারখানার ভোঁ). **ভোঁ দেওয়া** *v.* to whistle.

ভোঁতা *a.* blunt (ভোঁতা ছুরি) ; dull (ভোঁতা বুদ্ধি). **ভোঁতা করা** *v.* to blunt, to dull, to take away the edge of.

ভোঁদড় *n.* the otter, the civet-cat.

ভোঁদা *a.* corpulent; dull-witted, dunderheaded, imbecile.

ভোঁ-দৌড় *n.* a very swift or quick run, a break-neck run.

ভোঁ-ভোঁ *int.* denoting: dizziness (মাথা ভোঁ-ভোঁ) ; emptiness (পকেট ভোঁ-ভোঁ) ; great swiftness, whiz (ভোঁ-ভোঁ দৌড়) ; buzzing noise (কানামাছি ভোঁ-ভোঁ) ; repetition of ভোঁ sound. **ভোঁ-ভোঁ করা** to be filled with a ringing or humming sound (আমার কান ভোঁ-ভোঁ করছে = my ears are ringing).

ভোঁসভোঁস *int.* denoting: noise of deep and loud breathing (ভোঁসভোঁস করে ঘুমানো) ; heavy **ফোঁস** sound.

ভোক্তব্য *a.* edible, eatable; enjoyable; (facet.) sufferable.

ভোক্তা *a.* eating; enjoying. □ *n.* an eater; an enjoyer; *fem.* **ভোক্ত্রী** ।

ভোগ *n.* enjoying, enjoyment; suffering or sustaining; sufferance; act of possessing and using as one's own, appropriation; sensual or earthly pleasures; an object of enjoyment or an article of food; food-offering made to a deity; an affliction, a trouble (দুঃখ ভোগ). **ভোগ করা** *v.* to enjoy; to suffer or sustain; to suffer from; to possess and use as one's own; to enjoy sensual or earthly pleasures. **ভোগ দেওয়া** *v.* to make food and entertainments to a deity, to offer food-offering. **~তৃষ্ণা** *n.* thirst for sensual or earthly pleasures. **~দেহ** *n.* the subtle body to which a mortal being is reduced after death to enjoy or suffer the consequences of its earthly activities. **~বাসনা** same as **~লালসা** । **~বিলাস** *n.* sensual or earthly pleasures and luxury, (cp.) milk and honey. **~বিলাসী** *a.* enjoying sensual or earthly pleasures and luxury. **~লালসা** *n.* craving for sensual or earthly pleasures. **~স্বত্ব** *n.* occupancy right. **~সুখ** same as **~বিলাস** ।

ভোগবতী *n.* (myth.) the name of the Ganges as flowing in the nether world.

ভোগা[1] *n.* cheating or swindling; deceiving or hoaxing. **ভোগা দেওয়া** *v.* to cheat, to swindle; to deceive, to hoax.

ভোগা[2], ভোগ *v.* to suffer, to undergo, to sustain (যন্ত্রণা ভোগ) ; to suffer from (জ্বরে ভুগছে) ; to be afflicted or troubled or harassed or punished (দুর্বুদ্ধির জন্য ভোগা). **ভোগানো** *v.* to cause to suffer or undergo; to cause to suffer from; to afflict or trouble or harass or punish; to give persistent or protracted trouble (এ জ্বর ভোগাবে). **ভোগানি** *n.* suffering; affliction; trouble, harassment.

ভোগাকাঙ্ক্ষা same as **ভোগলালসা** and **ভোগাভিলাষ**।

ভোগানে *a.* causing suffering or harassment or trouble, irksome (ভোগানে মামলা).

ভোগান্ত, (coll.) **ভোগান্তি** *n.* extreme suffering or harassment or trouble. **ভোগান্ত** বা **ভোগান্তি হওয়া** *v.* to suffer or be troubled extremely.

ভোগাভিলাষ *n.* craving for sensual pleasures.

ভোগাসক্ত *a.* attached to sensual or earthly pleasures.

ভোগী *a.* & *n.* one who enjoys; one who suffers or sustains; one who possesses and uses something as one's own; one who enjoys sensual or earthly pleasures; one nourished with milk and honey.

ভোগৈশ্বর্য same as **ভোগবিলাস** (see **ভোগ**).

ভোগ্য *a.* enjoyable. *fem.* **ভোগ্যা** enjoyable; fit for sexual intercourse.

ভোজ *n.* a feast; a banquet; a meal; a repast. **ভোজ দেওয়া** *v.* to give or hold a feast; to entertain at a feast or dinner. **নৈশভোজ, সান্ধ্যভোজ** *n.* supper; dinner. **মধ্যাহ্নভোজ** *n.* lunch, luncheon. **ভোজের পোশাক** *n.* a dinner-suit.

ভোজন *n.* eating; feeding (কাঙালি ভোজন) ; a feast (বনভোজন) ; an article of food, food (কুভোজন). **ভোজন করা** *v.* to eat. **ভোজন করানো** *v.* to feed. **ভোজনং যত্রতত্র শয়নং হট্টমন্দিরে** practice of living a wild life in which one has no settled place for eating or sleeping, (cp.) Bohemianism, vagabondage. **~দক্ষিণা** *n.* a honorarium paid by a host to a Brahman for the latter's condescending to eat the food offered by the former. **~পটু** *a.* capable of eating voraciously, voracious. **~পাত্র** *n.* a dinner-plate. **~বিলাস** *n.* gourmandise, indulgence in good eating; gluttony, voraciousness. **~বিলাসী** *a.* gourmand, voracious. **ভোজনবিলাসী ব্যক্তি** a gourmand; a glutton. **~শালা, ভোজনাগার** *n.* a dining-room, a dining-hall; an eating-house; a hotel, a restaurant. **ভোজনাবশিষ্ট, ভোজনাবশেষ** same as **ভুক্তাবশিষ্ট**। **ভোজনালয়** *n.* an eating-house, a restaurant, a hotel.

ভোজপুরি *a.* born or grown in Bhojpur; of Bhojpur.

ভোজবাজি, ভোজবিদ্যা *n.* magic; jugglery, hocus-pocus, conjuring; illusion (সংসার এক ভোজবাজি). **ভোজবাজিকর** *n.* a juggler, a magician, a cojurer.

ভোজয়িতা *a.* & *n.* one who feeds. *fem.* **ভোজয়িত্রী**।

ভোজালি *n.* a dagger.

ভোজী *a.* (used as a *sfx.*) eating, feeding on (তৃণভোজী). *fem.* **ভোজিনী**।

ভোজোৎসব *n.* a feast; a banquet. **ভোজোৎসব-সম্বন্ধীয়** *a.* festal, festive.

ভোজ্য *a.* eatable, edible. □ *n.* an article of food, an eatable; food; food offering to the manes of ancestors. **~তেল** *n.* edible oil.

ভোট[1] *n.* Bhutan. □ *a.* Bhutanese.

ভোট[2] *n.* vote; franchise; election. **ভোট দেওয়া** *v.* to cast votes; to vote. **ভোট নেওয়া** *v.* to take votes; to put to vote. **ভোটে দাঁড় করানো** *v.* to nominate for election. **ভোটে দাঁড়ানো** *v.* to stand for or face election; to be elected. **ভোটে দেওয়া** *v.* to put to vote. **ভোটে দেওয়ার জন্য বলা** *v.* to call for a division. **~ক্ষেত্র** *n.* a constituency. **~গণনা** *n.* counting of votes. **~গ্রহণ** *n.* polling. **~পত্র** *n.* a ballot-paper. **~স্থান** *n.* a polling booth, a polling station. **ভোটার, ~দাতা** *n.* a voter.

ভোম *a.* stupefied, besotted, fuddled (নেশায় ভোম).

ভোমর[1] *n.* a drill, an auger.

ভোমর[2], ভোমরা pop. var. of **ভ্রমর**।

ভোমা *n.* a fool, a stupid person.

ভোর[1] *sfx.* denoting: continuing all through (দিনভোর) ; amounting (to) or measuring (তোলাভোর) etc.

ভোর[2] *a.* engrossed (চিন্তায় ভোর) ; stupefied, fuddled (নেশায় ভোর).

ভোর[3] *n.* morning, dawn, daybreak; termination, end (নিশিভোর) ; (fig.) awakening, dawning (নবজীবনের ভোরে). **ভোর করা** *v.* to pass the night (esp. without sleep); to spend or pass (রাত্রি ভোর করা). **~রাত** *n.* the early hours of dawn; the last hour or hours of the night. **ভোর হওয়া** *v.* to dawn. **ভোরে** *adv.* at dawn, at daybreak.

ভোরাই *n.* a morning song or hymn, a matin, (cp.) Matins.

ভোল[১] corrup. of **ভোর**[২]।

ভোল[২] *n.* a dress, a guise; a disguise; appearance. **ভোল ফেরানো** বা **বদলানো** *v.* to change one's dress; to improve one's appearance; (fig.) to improve one's social or financial condition.

ভোলা[১] see **ভুলা**।

ভোলা[২] *a.* forgetful, oblivious; forgotten. □ *n.* a forgetful person; Shiva (শিব).

ভোলানাথ *n.* (fig.) an utterly forgetful person; Shiva (শিব).

ভোলানি coll. var. of **ভুলানি**। *masc.* **ভোলানে**।

ভোলানো pop. var. of **ভুলানো**।

ভোল্টীয় *a.* (sc.) voltaic (ভোল্টীয় বিদ্যুৎ).

ভৌগোলিক *a.* geographical.

ভৌত *a.* elemental; material; physical. **~ধর্ম** *n.* a physical property. **~বিজ্ঞান** *n.* physical science.

ভৌতিক *a.* pertaining to or caused by apparitions, ghostly; elemental, material, physical, natural; astral. **ভৌতিক কাণ্ড** a ghostly affair. **ভৌতিক গল্প** a ghost-story. **ভৌতিক দেহ** the elemental body, the mortal frame; an astral body; a ghost. **ভৌতিক নিয়ম** the physical law, the law of nature. **ভৌতিক পদার্থ** a material thing. **ভৌতিক বিদ্যা** demonology. **ভৌতিক ব্যাপার** same as **ভৌতিক কাণ্ড**। **ভৌতিক স্তর** (theos.) the astral plane.

ভৌম *n.* the Mars. □ *a.* earthly, terrestrial; born out of earth. **ভৌম দূরবীক্ষণ** field glass. **ভৌম পুষ্পদণ্ড** scape.

ভৌমিক *n.* a landowner, a landlord; a fedual prince.

ভৌমী *a. fem.* **ভৌম** (*a.*).

ভ্যা *int.* denoting: bleating; baa; loud weeping (ভ্যা করে কাঁদা)

ভ্যাংচানো *v.* to make faces (at), to grimace, to grin (at).

ভ্যাঙানো same as **ভ্যাংচানো**।

ভ্যাজরভ্যাজর *n.* continuous and useless babbling; prattle.

ভ্যানতারা *n.* useless and disgusting murmuring or talk or prattle; useless or irrelevant talk; prolixity.

ভ্যানভ্যান *int.* denoting: buzzing noise (of flies, mosquitoes etc.); noise of continuous complaint.

ভ্যাপসা coll. var. of **ভাপসা**।

ভ্যাবা *a.* confounded, bewildered; grossly foolish. **~চ্যাকা** *n.* bewilderment; confusion. **ভ্যাবাচ্যাকা খাওয়া** *v.* to be bewildered or confounded or perplexed or puzzled or to be at ones wit's end. **~গঙ্গারাম** *n.* a dumbfounded or totally confused and bewildered person; a dullard; a fat-head.

ভ্যালা *int.* (ridi.) fine, nice. □ (joc) *a.* fomidable (ভ্যালা বিপদ).

ভ্রংশ, ভ্রংশন *n.* detachment; fall; downfall; deviation; a casting off (জাতিভ্রংশ); deprivation, loss (বুদ্ধিভ্রংশ); (phys.) displacement. **ভ্রংশ-হার** *n.* (phys.) the rate of displacement. **ভ্রংশিত** *a.* detached; fallen; downfallen; deviated; cast off; deprived of; (phys.) displaced.

ভ্রম *n.* an error; a mistake; a blunder; an omission; oblivion; illusion; a whirl; a whirlpool; whirlwind. **ভ্রম হওয়া** *v.* to be mistaken; to be guilty of omission. **ভ্রমে পড়া** *v.* to fall into an error; to be mistaken; to be confounded. **ভ্রমনিরসন করা** *v.* to remove a wrong notion (of); disillusion; to correct or rectify an error, to amend; to emend. **~ক্রমে** *adv.* same as **ভ্রমবশত**। **~প্রবণ** *a.* fallible. **~প্রবণতা** *n.* fallibility. **~প্রমাদ** *n. pl.* errors and omissions. **~বশত** *adv.* through a mistake or wrong notion. **~সংশোধন করা** same as **ভ্রমনিরসন করা**। **~সংকুল** *a.* full of errors, erroneous; full of wrong notions.

ভ্রমণ *n.* travel, journey (দেশভ্রমণ); ambulation, walking (প্রাতর্ভ্রমণ); revolution, rotation, whirl. **ভ্রমণ করা** *v.* to travel; to itinerate; to ambulate, to walk; to revolve, to rotate, to whirl. **~কারী** *n.* a traveller; an ambulator, a walker, a peregrinator. *fem.* **~কারিণী**। **~বৃত্তান্ত** *n.* an account of journey, travels, (cp.) travelogue. **~শীল** *a.* itinerant. **ভ্রমন্ত** *a.* travelling. **ভ্রমমাণ** *a.* travelling, journeying; itinerant.

ভ্রমর *n.* the hornet; the bumble-bee; the bee. *fem.* **ভ্রমরী**। **~কৃষ্ণ** *a.* as (beautifully) black as the bumble-bee; glossy and deep black. **~গুঞ্জন** *n.* the humming or buzzing of bumble-bees or bees.

ভ্রমরা alt. form of **ভোমরা** (see **ভোমর).**

ভ্রমাত্মক *a.* erroneous; illusive, illusory.

ভ্রমান্ধ *a.* blinded with errors or illusions.

ভ্রমি, ভ্রমী *n.* a whirlpool, an edy.

ভ্রমিযন্ত্র *n.* a drill, an auger.

ভ্রষ্ট *a.* detached; fallen; downfallen; cast off; deprived of; deviated, strayed; strayed from the rightful path; corrupted; vitiated in character, depraved. *fem.* **ভ্রষ্টা** । **~চরিত্র** *a.* characterless; depraved. *fem.* **~চরিত্রা** । **~তা** *n.* detached or fallen or downfallen or cast off state; deprivation; deviation; corruption; depravity. **ভ্রষ্টাচারণ, ভ্রষ্টাচার** *n.* a wicked or depraved practice; corruption; wrong-doing; depravity. **ভ্রষ্টাচারী** *a.* given to wrong-doing or depravity.

ভ্রাতা *n.* a brother; a cousin-brother, a cousin.

ভ্রাতুষ্পুত্র *n.* a brother's son, a nephew. *fem.* **ভ্রাতুষ্পুত্রী** *n.* a brother's daughter, a niece.

ভ্রাতৃ *n.* (used as a *pfx.*) a brother. **~ঘাতক** *n.* a fratricide. **~ঘাতী** *a.* fratricidal. **~জায়া** *n.* a brother's wife, a sister-in-law. **~ত্ব** *n.* the state of being a brother; fraternity, brotherhood. **~দ্বিতীয়া** *n.* the second lunar day of the bright fortnight in the month of Kartik (কার্তিক) when is held the Hindu ceremony of marking brother's foreheads by their sisters with sandalwood-paste. **~প্রেম** *n.* fraternal or brotherly love. **~বৎ** *a.* & *adv.* like a brother. **~বৎসল** *a.* affectionate towards one's brothers, full of fraternal love. *fem.* **~বৎসলা** । **~বধ** *n.* fratricide. **~বধূ** same as **~জায়া** । **~ভাব** *n.* brotherly feeling, brotherliness. **~স্নেহ** *n.* brotherly love. **~হত্যা** *n.* fratricide. **~হত্যাকারী** *a.* fratricidal. □ *n.* a fratricide.

ভ্রাত্রীয় *a.* brotherly, fraternal.

ভ্রান্ত *a.* erroneous; erring, mistaken; having a false notion; under an illusion; deluded; illusive; illusory. **~বিশ্বাস** *n.* a wrong or false or mistaken belief or notion; an illusion. **ভ্রান্ত ব্যাখ্যা** *n.* a false or incorrect explanation. **ভ্রান্তি** *n.* an error; a mistake; a false notion; illusion; delusion. **ভ্রান্তিকর, ভ্রান্তিজনক** *a.* causing error; illusive; delusive. **ভ্রান্তিবশত, ভ্রান্তিবশে** *adv.* by mistake. **ভ্রান্তিমান** *a.* erroneous; mistaken. □ *n.* (rhet.) a figure of speech marked by illusion. **ভ্রান্তিমূলক** *a.* erroneous; illusory; delusive.

ভ্রামর *a.* of or like the bee or bumble-bee. *fem.* **ভ্রামরী** ।

ভ্রাম্যমাণ *a.* that which is being made to travel or rotate; that which is being circulated; (pop.) itinerant, travelling (ভ্রাম্যমাণ বিক্রেতা) ; (pop.) circulating (ভ্রাম্যমাণ পাঠাগার) ; mobile (ভ্রাম্যমাণ ডাকঘর, হাসপাতাল ইত্যাদি). □ *n.* (inc.) a traveller (ভ্রাম্যমাণের দিনপঞ্জিকা).

ভ্রূ' *n* the eyebrow. **~কুঞ্চন, ~কুটি, ~কুটী** *n.* a frown. **ভ্রূকুটি করা** *v.* to frown. **ভ্রূকুটিকুটিল** *a.* (of looks or eyes) frowning. **ভ্রূক্ষেপ** *n.* act of casting one's eyes neglectfully or cursorily; (fig.) slightest heed. **ভ্রূক্ষেপ না করা** *v.* to refuse to look at even cursorily; (fig.) to take no heed of, to ignore completely. **~ধনু** *n.* the arch of the eyebrows. **~বিলাস** *n.* a pleasant knitting of one's brows, a charming frown; a lustful frown. **~ভঙ্গ, ~ভঙ্গি** same as **~কুঞ্চন** । **~মধ্য** *n.* space between the two eyebrows. **~লতা** *n.* the eyebrows as beautiful as creepers. **~লেখা** *n.* the hachures. **~সংকেত** *n.* a beckoning (esp. a stealthy one) by moving the eyebrows.

ভ্রূণ *n.* a foetus, an embryo. **~সম্বন্ধীয়** *a.* foetal. **~হত্যা** *n.* foeticide. **ভ্রূণহত্যা করা** *v.* to destroy a foetus; to cause an unlawful abortion.

ম *n.* the twenty-fifth consonant of the Bengali alphabet.

মই *n.* a ladder (usu. one made of bamboo and rope); a harrow. **মই দেওয়া** *v.* to harrow (a field).

মউ, মৌ *n.* honey. **মউ-আলু** *n.* sweet yam. **~চাক, ~মাছির চাক** *n.* a honeycomb; a beehive. **~মাছি** *n.* the bee. **মউমাছির রানি** a queen-bee. **~মাছি পালন** *n.* bee-keeping, apiculture. **~লোভী** *a.* fond of honey.

মউজ alt. spell. of **মৌজ**।

মউড় *n.* a tiara made of sola.

মউতাত alt. spell. of **মৌতাত**।

মউনি *n.* a churn, a churning-staff.

মউরলা alt. spell. of **মৌরলা**।

মউরি alt. spell. of **মৌরি**।

মওলবি, মওলানা variants of **মৌলবি** and **মৌলানা** respectively.

মকদ্দমা *n.* a lawsuit, a case, a process; an affair (বিয়েটা একদিনের মকদ্দমা) ; a dispute. **মকদ্দমা আনা** *v.* to bring a lawsuit (against); to proceed (against). **মকদ্দমা করা** *v.* to bring or file a lawsuit; to proceed (against); to conduct a case; to plead in a case; to try or judge a case; to enter into litigation. **মকদ্দমা তোলা** *v.* to bring up a case for trial.

মকমক *int.* denoting: the croaking of the frog. □ *n.* the croak. **মকমক করা** *v.* to croak.

মকর *n.* a mythological aquatic animal; (astrol.) the Capricorn. **~কেতন, ~কেতু** *n.* the Hindu God of love whose flag bears the symbol of the mythological makar (মকর). **~ক্রান্তি** *n.* the winter solstice. **~ক্রান্তিবৃত্ত** *n.* the tropic of Capricorn. **~ধ্বজ** *n.* a medicinal sublimate of mercury, sulphur and gold. **~বাহিনী** *a. fem.* riding on the mythological makar (মকর). □ *n.* Goddess Ganga (গঙ্গা). **~মণ্ডল** *n.* the tropic of Capricorn. **~রাশি** *n.* (astrol.) the Capricorn. **~সংক্রান্তি** *n.* (astr.) the transition of the sun from the Sagittarius to the Capricornus; (pop.) the winter solstice.

মকরন্দ *n.* the nectar or honey of a flower.

মকররি pop. corrup. of **মুকররি**।

মকরীয় *a.* of the Capricorn; of the tropic of Capricorn. **মকরীয় শান্তবলয়** (geog.) the calms of Capricorn.

মকশো *n.* practice; practice by tracing; repeated practising. **মকশো করা** *v.* to practise.

মকাই *n.* maize.

মকান *n.* a house, a dwelling house.

ম-কার *n.* a word beginning with ম। **পঞ্চ ম-কার** see **পঞ্চ**।

মকুব, মকুফ *n.* remission; condonation; exemption. **মকুব করা** *v.* to remit; to condone; to exempt.

মক্কা *n.* maize.

মক্কেল *n.* a client (of a pleader, barrister, attorney etc.) **~হীন** *a.* (of a legal practitioner) briefless.

মক্তব *n.* a Muslim primary school.

মক্স rej. spell. of **মকশো**।

মখমল *n.* velvet. **মখমলি** *a.* made of velvet; velvety (মখমলি আকাশ).

মগ[1] *n.* a mug.

মগ[2] *n.* a native of Arakan or Burma. **মগের মুলুক** Arakan; Burma; (fig.) a lawless country.

মগজ *n.* brains; intelligence; the intellect or the pate; memory.

মগজি *n.* ornamental border or hem (of a frock, shirt etc.).

মগডাল *n.* the topmost branch of a tree.

মগরা *a.* proud; haughty; audacious; cunning. **মগরামি** *n.* haughtiness, audacity; cunning.

মগ্ন, (poet.) **মগন** *a.* drowned; sunken; submerged; engrossed, absorbed (ধ্যানমগ্ন) ; overwhelmed (শোকমগ্ন) ; latent, dormant (মগ্নচৈতন্য). **মগ্নতা** *n.* sunkenness; submerged state; engrossment. *fem.* **মগ্না**। **মগ্নচড়া** *n.* a shoal. **মগ্নচৈতন্য** *n.* (psy.) the subconscious. **মগ্নশৈল** *n.* a submarine rock.

মঘা *n.* the tenth of the twenty-seven stars according to the Hindu astronomy.

মঙ্গল *n.* well-being, weal, welfare, good, benefit; the Mars; Tuesday; a kind of Bengali epic poems about popular deities (usu. **মঙ্গলকাব্য**). **মঙ্গল করা** *v.* to do good to. **~কর** *a.* auspicious, propitious; doing good. **~কামনা** *n.* good wishes. **~কামী** *a.* well-wishing. **মঙ্গলকামী ব্যক্তি** a well-wisher. **~কারী** *a.* & *n.* one who does good to others. *fem.* **~কারিণী**। **~গীত** *n.* a song narrating the glory of a deity. **~গ্রহ** *n.* the Mars. **~ঘট** *n.* a consecrated pitcher placed in a house to win divine favour. **~চণ্ডী** *n.* a manifestation of Goddess Durga (দুর্গা). **~জনক, ~দায়ক** same as **~কর**। *fem.* **~দায়িকা**। **~বার** *n.* Tuesday. **~ময়** *a.* benign, benignant, gracious, doing good, auspicious. □ *n.* God. *fem.* **~ময়ী**। **~সংবাদ, ~সমাচার** *n.* news of well-being; good news; (Christ.) gospel. **~সূত্র** *n.* a sacred or consecrated thread or string worn on the neck by woman. **মঙ্গলা** *n.* Goddess Durga (দুর্গা). **মঙ্গলাকর** *n.* a mine of good. **মঙ্গলাকাঙ্ক্ষা** same as **~কামনা**। **মঙ্গলাকাঙ্ক্ষী** same as **~কামী**। *fem.* **মঙ্গলাকাঙ্ক্ষিণী**। **মঙ্গলাচারণ, মঙ্গলাচার** *n.* a prayer, to obtain divine benison on the eve of commencing work or in the beginning of a drama, poem etc.; any rite performed for the welfare of the votary. **মঙ্গলামঙ্গল** *n.* good and evil, weal and woe. **মঙ্গলারতি** *n.* the ceremonial waving of lights before an idol. **মঙ্গলার্থে** *adv.* for the good or welfare of. **মঙ্গল্য** var. of **মাঙ্গলিক**।

মঙ্গোল, মঙ্গোলীয় *n.* a Mongol. □ *a.* Mongol, Mongolian, Mongoloid. **মঙ্গোলয়েড** *n.* a Mongoloid. □ *a.* Mongoloid.

মচ *int.* denoting: a sharp snapping noise. **মচমচ** *int.* denoting: repeated snapping noise. **মচমচে** *a.* crisp (মচমচে মুড়ি).

মচকানো *v.* to sprain or be sprained; to twist. **মচকানি** *n.* sprain; twist. **ভাঙে তবু মচকায় না** would rather break than bend.

মচ্ছব coll. corrup. of **মহোৎসব**।

মছলন্দ corrup. of **মসলন্দ**।

মজদুর variant of **মজুর**।

মজবুত *a.* firm; stiff, fast; strong, hard; lasting, durable.

মজলিশ *n.* a sitting, a meeting, a gathering; a party (চায়ের মজলিশ) ; an association, a society, a club. **মজলিশি** *a.* of or fit for a party or assembly; capable of brightening up a gathering or party with pleasant talk or bearing.

মজা[১] *v.* to be drowned; to lose oneself (in) (প্রেমে মজা, নেশায় মজা) ; to be charmed (with) or won over (by) (কথায় মজা) ; to silt up (পুকুর মজা) ; to be pickled thoroughly or overmuch (আচার মজা) ; to mature or ripen thoroughly (কাঁঠাল মজেনি) ; to be greatly endangered or utterly ruined (ব্যাঙ্ক ফেল পড়ায় সে মজল). □ *a.* silted up or dried up thoroughly or overmuch, matured or ripened. □ *n.* the delicious leavings of certain fruits from which juice has been extracted (তালের মজা).

মজা[২] *n.* pleasure; enjoyment; comfort and luxury (মজায় থাকা) ; sport, frolic; fun; banter, joke; a funny or pleasant affair or object. **মজা করা** *v.* to make fun (of); to make a song of; to pull one's leg; to indulge in pleasures and frolics. **মজা টের পাওয়া** *v.* to feel the weight or brunt of adventure or danger or difficulty; to feel the pinch of; to feel the evil consequences; to be punished, to have to kiss the rod. **মজা টের পাওয়ানো, মজা দেখানো** *v.* to drag one into a danger or trouble as a punishment; to punish; to teach one a lesson; to make one feel the evil consequences of. **মজা দেখা** *v.* to take delight in other's trouble; to view other's trouble with secret joy. **মজা মারা, মজা লোটা** *v.* to enjoy; to indulge in pleasures and frolics; to enjoy undue benefit from something; to live amidst pleasure and luxury. **মজার গল্প** a funny or amusing story.

মজাদার *a.* funny; amusing; delicious, palatable (মজাদার খাবার).

মজানো *v.* to drown; to cause to lose oneself (in); to charm, to win over; to silt up; to pickle thoroughly; to cause to mature or ripen thoroughly, to bring disgrace on (কুল মজানো) ; to endanger greatly or ruin utterly overmuch.

মজুদ, মজুত *a.* stored up; hoarded; reserved; in reserve for future use, reserve; still existing (আমার শক্তি এখনও মজুদ) ; ready to hand, at beck and call (হুকুম তামিলের জন্য মজুত আছি). **মজুদ তহবিল** reserve fund; reserve capital. **~দার** *n.* a hoarder. **~দারি** *n.* hoarding.

মজুর *n.* a labourer, a workman, a worker. *fem.* **মজুরনি**। **~সরদার** *n.* a foreman of a gang, a gangsman, a ganger. **মজুরের দল** a band of labourers; a gang. **মজুরি** *n.* labour cost or charges; wages of a labourer; labour work. **মজুরি করা** *v.* to work as a labourer.

মজ্জন *n.* sinking or being drowned.

মজ্জমান *a.* in the state of being drowned, sinking. *fem.* **মজ্জমানা**।

মজ্জা *n.* marrow, bone-marrow; pith; (physio.) core. **~গত** *a.* pertaining to marrow; inherent or inveterate. **~গহ্বর** *n.* a pith cavity.

মঝু *pro. a.* (poet. & obs.) my.

মঞ্চ *n.* a platform, a dais; a rostrum; a scaffold; the stage or theatre. **~নির্দেশন, ~নির্দেশনা** *n.* stage direction. **~ভাষণ** *n.* a platform speech. **~শিল্প** *n.* stagecraft; stage play. **~শিল্পী** *n.* a stage-player; a stage-decorator. **~সজ্জা** *n.* stage-decoration. **মঞ্চস্থ করা** *v.* to stage (a drama), to enact; (rare) to place on a platform. **মঞ্চাভিনয়** *n.* stage-acting; acting in a drama.

মঞ্জন *n.* cleansing (as teeth) by rubbing, brushing, etc.; an article for cleansing with (দন্তমঞ্জন).

মঞ্জরা *v.* (poet.) to blossom or sprout ('অশোক রোমাঞ্চিত মঞ্জরিয়া').

মঞ্জরি *n.* a young shoot or twig with new leaves (আম্রমঞ্জরি) ; a shoot; a sprout; a spike (পুষ্পমঞ্জরি) ; an ear (শস্যমঞ্জরি) ; a flower-spike (বকুলমঞ্জরি). **~দণ্ড** *n.* (bot.) a rachis. **~পত্র** *n.* (bot.) a bract.

মঞ্জরিত *a.* blossomed, budded, flowered; sprouted. **মঞ্জরিত হওয়া** *v.* to blossom, to bud, to flower; to sprout.

মঞ্জিল *n.* a palace; a magnificent building, a mansion.

মঞ্জীর *n.* an anklet with small jingling bells.

মঞ্জু *a.* beautiful, graceful, lovely; delicate; pleasant; sweet. **~কেশী** *a. fem.* having beautiful hair. **~ভাষিণী** *a. fem.* suave in speech, honey-mouthed, fair-spoken. **~ল** *a.* same as **মঞ্জু**। □ *n.* a flower-grove; a grove; a bower. **~শ্রী** delicate or charming grace or beauty; one possessing such grace or beauty; name of a Jain goddess. **~হাসিনী** *a. fem.* sweet-smiling.

মঞ্জুর *a.* sanctioned, approved, granted; permitted; accepted, admitted (আপিল মঞ্জুর হওয়া). **মঞ্জুর করা** *v.* to sanction, to approve; to grant; to permit; to accept, to admit.

মঞ্জুরি *a.* sanctioning, approving, permitting, accepting (মঞ্জুরি দস্তখত). **মঞ্জুরি কমিশন** grants commission.

মঞ্জুরিত inc. var. of **মঞ্জরিত**।

মঞ্জুষা *n.* a box, a chest, a casket.

মট, মট্ *int.* denoting: a snapping noise as caused by the splitting or twisting of anything hard. **মট্ করে** *adv.* with a cracking or snapping sound. **মট্মট্** *int.* denoting repeated **মট্** sound.

মটকা *n.* a coarse variety of tusser; the topmost (and also central) part of the surface of a thatched roof (cp. loft); feigned sleep; a large earthen barrel or cask. **মটকা মারা** *v.* to close up or block the opening at the centre of a thatched roof; to pretend sleep, to pretend to be sleeping.

মটকানো *v.* to twist (as a finger) or break (as a twig) with a snapping noise. **আঙুল মটকানো** *v.* to snap one's finger.

মটকি *n.* a large earthen barrel or cask.

মটন *n.* mutton. **~চপ** *n.* a mutton-chop.

মটর১ var. of **মোটর**।

মটর২ *n.* pea. **~কলাই,** (dial.) **~কড়াই** *n.* pea. **~ডাল** *n.* husked (ripened) pea-seeds used as dal. **~দানা** *n.* a grain or seed of pea; a necklace or a girdle studded with small balls resembling seeds of pea. **~মালা** *n.* a necklace studded with small balls resembling pea-seeds. **~শাক** *n.* pea-plant eaten as spinach. **~শুঁটি** *n.* a pea-pod, a peascod, a pease-cod, a pea-cod.

মটাৎ *int.* same as **মট্**।

মঠ *n.* a monastery or a nunnery, a convent; an abbey; a shrine, a temple; an academy; a sweetmeat made of congealed sugar shaped like a temple. **~ধারী, মঠাধিকারী, মঠাধ্যক্ষ** *n.* a head of a monastery or convent, an abbot. *fem.* **~ধারিণী** an abbess.

মড়ক *n.* a pestilence, a plague; (of cattle, beasts and birds) a murrain; widespread death (মাছের মড়ক). **মড়ক লেগেছে** a pestilence or a murrain has broken out; death is taking a heavy toll of lives. **~খোলা** *n.* a place for cremating or depositing (usu. neglectfully) people killed by a pestilence.

মড়মড় *int.* denoting noise of crashing of a hard substance.

মড়া *n.* a dead body, a corpse. **মড়া নিয়ে যাওয়া,** (contemp.) **মড়া ফেলা** *v.* to carry a corpse to the crematorium or graveyard. **মড়ার উপর খাঁড়ার ঘা দেওয়া** *v.* to strike a man when he is down; to add insult to injury; (cp.) flog a dead horse. **~খেকো** *n.* a ghoul, a ghost.

মড়িঘর *n.* a morgue.

মড়িপোড়া *a.* taking part in cremating the dead bodies of unrelated persons. □ *n.* such a Brahman (considered an outcast).

মড়ুঞ্চে *a.* stillborn; giving birth to stillborn babies (মড়ুঞ্চে পোয়াতি).

মণ rej. spell. of **মন**[1]।

মণি *n.* a precious stone, a jewel, a gem; (fig.) a precious object or treasure (খোকামণি); (fig.) a glorious person (রঘুমণি). **~ক** *n.* (geog.) mineral. **~কাঞ্চন** *n.* a jewel and gold; (fig.) combination or union of two very precious things. **~কাঞ্চনযোগ** *n.* an excellent union: (astrol.) a very auspicious conjunction of stars. **~কার** *n.* a jeweller, a lapidary. **~কোঠা** *n.* a room the floor and walls of which are set with gems. **~খচিত** *a.* inlaid with jewels. **~বন্ধ** *n.* the wrist. **~ভাণ্ডার** *n.* a jewel-house, (cp.) treasure-house or treasure-trove. **~মণ্ডিত** *a.* set or studded or adorned with gems. **~ময়** full of gems; made of gems; set or studded or adorned with gems. **~মাণিক্য** same as **~রত্ন**। **~মালা** *n.* a necklace set with gems. **~রত্ন** *n. pl.* gems and jewels, jewellery. **~হার** same as **~মালা**। **~হারা ফণী** (fig.) one who is fretfully aggrieved on account of losing one's most precious treasure or beloved person.

মণিপুরি *a.* of or produced in or born in Manipur. □ *n.* a native of Manipur.

মণিহারী rej. spell. of **মনিহারি**।

মণ্ড *n.* gruel; starch; pulp; paste.

মণ্ডন *n.* ornamentation; embellishment; decoration; toilet; overlaying or studding; an ornament.

মণ্ডপ *n.* a roofed or otherwise covered terrace or place usu. with four sides open; a pavilion.

মণ্ডল *n.* a circular or spherical area; a sphere, a circle, a ring, an orb, a globe (ভূমণ্ডল, দিঙ্মণ্ডল); an area; a region (নক্ষত্রমণ্ডল); an empire, a vast territory or kingdom; a country; a district, a village, a locality, a zone (বজ্রমণ্ডল); a community (প্রজামণ্ডল); an assemblage, a congregation (মন্ত্রিমণ্ডল, ভক্তমন্ডল); (geom.) a group; a village headman; a headman, a leader. **~পট্ট** *n.* (phys.) a zone plate. **মন্ডল পরিদর্শক** *n.* a circle inspector. **মণ্ডলাকার** *a.* circular, spherical, round, globular. **মণ্ডলী** *n.* a collection, a multitude; a community; an assemblage; a congregation; a circle (মণ্ডলী করে বসা). **মণ্ডলীকৃত** *a.* formed into a circle or coil. **মণ্ডলেশ্বর** *n.* a paramount ruler (esp. of a vast territory); an emperor.

মণ্ডা[1] alt. spell. of **মন্ডা**[1]।

মণ্ডা[2] see **মন্ডা**[2]।

মণ্ডিত *a.* ornamented; embellished; decorated (with). *fem.* **মণ্ডিতা**। **মণ্ডিত করা** *v.* to ornament; to embellish; to decorate; to dress; to overlay or stud (with).

মণ্ডূক *n.* the frog. *fem.* **মণ্ডূকী**।

মত[1] alt. spell. of **মতো**।

মত[2] *n.* an opinion, a view; consent; a theory; a doctrine, an ism; a tenet; a creed, a religion; a method, a principle; a mode or means. **মত করা** *v.* to agree (to); to intend. **মত করানো** *v.* to persuade. **মত দেওয়া** *v.* to consent to, to agree to; to give one's consent; to acquiesce; to pass one's opinion, to opine. **মত নেওয়া** *v.* to take or invite one's consent or opinion. **মত পাওয়া** *v.* to obtain one's consent or approval. **নানা মুনির নানা মত** (fig.) many minds many views; no two wise men agree. **যত মত তত পথ** as many tenets, as many ways to salvation. **~দান** *n.* giving one's opinion or consent; expressing one's views; casting one's vote. **~দ্বৈধ** same as **~বিরোধ**। **~পরিবর্তন** *n.* change of opinion. **~পার্থক্য** *n.* difference of opinion or views. **~বাদ** *n.* a theory; a doctrine; a tenet. **~বাদী** *a.* adhering to a particular theory or doctrine or tenet. **~বিরোধ, ~ভেদ, মতানৈক্য** *n.* difference of opinion; disagreement; dissension. **মতান্তর** *n.* difference of opinion, dissension; a different or contrary opinion or view or doctrine or theory. **মতান্তরে** *adv.* in or according to another view. **মতাবলম্বন করা** *v.* to accept or adhere to or profess an opinion or view or doctrine or theory or tenet or religion. **মতাবলম্বী** *a. & n.* one who accepts or adheres to or follows or professes a particular opinion or view or doctrine or theory or religion. *fem.* **মতাবলম্বিনী**। **মতামত** *n.* views for and against.

মৎকর্তৃক *adv.* by me.

মৎকুণ *n.* the bug.

মৎকৃত *n.* done or performed by me.

মৎপ্রণীত *a.* written or compiled or composed by me.

মতলব *n.* intention, purpose, design; a plan, a stratagem, an artifice, a wile. **মতলব আঁটা** *v.* to think out a plan, to scheme, to plan. **মতলব করা বা ভাঁজা** *v.* to contrive a stratagem; to intend, to design. **~বাজ, মতলবি** *a.* designing, scheming, artful, crafty, wily; self-devoted.

মৎসর *n.* envy, malice, spite; malevolence. ☐ *a.* envious, malicious, spiteful; malevolent; base, mean.

মৎস্য *n.* fish; the first of the ten incarnations of Vishnu (বিষ্ণু) ; (astrol.) the Pisces; an ancient state of India. **~করণ্ডিকা** *n.* a fish-creel. **~গন্ধা** *n. fem.* a woman or girl from whose body a fish-like smell emanates. **~ঘণ্ট** *n.* a highly seasoned dish of fish, fish-grill. **~জাত** *n.*(geog.) fishery products. **~জীবী** *n.* a fisherman, a fisher (*fem* : a fisherwoman, a fish-wife). **~ন্যায়** var. of **মাৎস্যন্যায়**। **~ব্যবসায়** *n.* the trade or profession of catching and selling fish. **~ব্যবসায়ী** *n.* a fishdealer, a fishmonger; a fisherman. **~ভোজী** *a.* same as **মৎস্যাশী**। **~রঙ্গ** *n.* the kingfisher, the halcyon. **মৎস্যাশী** *a.* fish-eating, piscivorous.

মতি[১] *n.* intelligence, intellect; mentality; memory; attention; devotion; inclination, propensity; desire. **~গতি** *n.* intentions and activities; card up one's sleeve. **~চ্ছন্ন** *a.* evil-minded, wicked; froward; wayward; foolish; out of one's mind, not in one's right mind. ☐ *n.* loss of good judgment; evil-mindedness; wickedness; frowardness; waywardness; a folly. **~ভ্রংশ, ~ভ্রম, ~ভ্রান্তি** *n.* loss of memory; loss of intellect or judgment; a lapse of judgment; an aberration; a mistake, an error; delusion. **~ভ্রষ্ট, ~ভ্রান্ত** *a.* demented; bereft of one's intellect or judgment; off one's head; forgetful, oblivious; committing a mistake or error, erring; deluded. **~মত্তা** *n.* sagacity, wisdom; intelligence; discreetness. **~মান** *a.* sagacious, wise; intelligent; discreet. **~স্থিরতা, ~স্থৈর্য** *n.* firmness of mind or resolve; mental equipoise. **~হীন** *a.* same as **~চ্ছন্ন** (*a.*). and—lacking in attention or devotion or inclination or intention.

মতি[২]**, মতিচুর, মতিয়া** inc. spellings of **মোতি, মোতিচুর,** and **মোতিয়া** respectively.

মতিহারি *a.* grown in Matihari. ☐ *n.* tobacco growing in Matihari.

মতো *a.* like, as, similar to (ফুলের মতো) ; according to or in keeping with (কথামতো) ; suiting or satisfying (মনের মতো) ; becoming or befitting (রাজার মতো আচরণ). ☐ *prep.* for (আজকের মতো, জন্মের মতো).

মত্ত *a.* intoxicated, sottish, drunk;

drunken; maddened, frenzied; mad; must; musty (মত্ত হস্তী = a must elephant, an elephant in a state of frenzy or run amok); maddened by rage or excitement; greatly proud of (ধনমত্ত) ; beside oneself with (আনন্দে মত্ত) ; absorbedly engaged in (গানে মত্ত) ; addicted to or indulging in (বিলাসে মত্ত). *fem.* **মত্তা**। **~তা** *n.* intoxicated state, intoxication; sottishness, drunkenness; frenzy; madness; must; highly enraged or excited state; great elation; the state of being beside oneself; absorbing preoccupation; addiction.

মথন *n.* churning; stirring; trampling; routing; crushing. **মথন করা** *v.* to churn, to stir; to trample; to rout, to crush.

মথনী *n.* butter; the churning rod.

মথা poet. form of **মথন করা**।

মথিত *a.* churned; stirred; trampled; routed; crushed. **মথিত করা** same as **মথন করা** (see **মথন**).

মদ *n.* vanity, pride; arrogance; intoxication; frenzy; infatuation; great joy or elation; musk; wine; intoxicating juice (মহুয়ার মদ) ; a watery exudation from the cheeks, temple etc. of an elephant in rut. **মদ খাওয়া** *v.* to drink wine, to drink. **~খোর** *a.* addicted to drinking wine. **মদখোর লোক** a drunkard. **~গর্ব** *n.* insane vanity or pride or arrogance. **~গর্বিত, ~গর্বী** *a.* mad with vanity or pride or arrogance. *fem.* **~গর্বিতা**। **~মত্ত** *a.* raving on account of being drunk; mad with vanity; (of an elephant) in rut. *fem.* **~মত্তা**। **মদমত্ত হাতি** an elephant in rut; a must elephant.

মদ্‌গুর old elegant form of **মাগুর**।

মদত *n.* aid, help, assistance; cooperation. **মদত দেওয়া** *v.* to aid, to help, to assist; to cooperate with.

মদন *n.* the Hindu god of love (cp. Cupid, Eros); amorous or sexual desire, eroticism. **~গোপাল** *n.* a cupid's minion; Krishna (কৃষ্ণ). **~পীড়িত** *a.* stricken with love or sexual desire, lovesick. *fem.* **~পীড়িতা**। **~বাণ** *n.* the shaft of Madana (মদন),(cp.) Cupid's shaft; (fig.) an erotogenous object. **~বাণপীড়িত** same as **~পীড়িত**। *fem.* **~বাণপীড়িতা**। **~মোহন** *n.* one who infatuates even Madana (মদন) ; Krishna (কৃষ্ণ). **মদনোৎসব** *n.* a spring festival held in honour of Madana (মদন) ; the festival of holi (হোলি).

মদাতঙ্ক, মদাত্যয় *n. delirium tremens.*

মদান্ধ *a.* blind with vanity.

মদালস *a.* feeling lethargic at the termination of a drunken bout; made indolent by incitation of sexual or amorous desire. *fem.* **মদালসা**।

মদির *a.* intoxicating; besotting; infatuating. **~তা** *n.* intoxication; drunkenness; infatuation. **মদিরা** *n.* rich wine (cp. Madeira). **মদিরাক্ষী, মদিরেক্ষণা** *n. fem.* a woman with eyes pleasantly dilated with or as with drunkeness; a woman having beautiful eyes. **মদিরাগৃহ** *n.* an ale-house, a grog-shop.

মদীয় *prop.* & *a.* my, mine.

মদো *a.* of or pertaining to wine (মদো গন্ধ) ; addicted to wine (মদো মাতাল). **~মাতাল লোক** a boozer, a drunkard.

মদোদ্ধত *a.* highly conceited or arrogant or haughty, stuck-up, puffed up.

মদোন্মত্ত same as **মদমত্ত** (see **মদ**). *fem.* **মদোন্মত্তা**।

মদোমাতাল see **মদো**।

মদ্দ, মদ্দা, মদ্দানি coll. variants of **মর্দ, মর্দা** and **মর্দানি** respectively.

মদ্য *n.* wine. **~প, ~পায়ী** *a.* addicted to drinking wine. ☐ *n.* a drunkard; a boozer. **~বিক্রেতা** *n.* a vintner, a wine merchant. **মদ্যাসক্তি** *n.* addiction to wine; addiction to drinking; booziness.

মদ্র *n.* the ancient name of the Punjab and some adjoining districts.

মধু *n.* honey; anything sweet; sweet juice; nectar; wine; the month of Chaitra (চৈত্র) ; spring; (fig.) sweetness or charm ('গোকুলে মধু ফুরায়ে গেল') ; opportunity of income esp. of extra or illegal income (এ চাকরিতে মধু নেই) ; money, wealth (কাপ্তানের মধু ফুরিয়ে গেছে). ☐ *a.* sweet-tasting, delicious; sweet, pleasing; full of honey or sweet juice. **~ক** *n.* liquorice. **~কণ্ঠ** *a.* sweet-voiced. **~কর** *n.* the bee, the black-bee.

fem. ~করী। ~কোষ *n.* a honeycomb; the testicle (of a goat, sheep etc.). ~গন্ধ, ~গন্ধি *a.* very sweet-scented or sweet-smelling. ~চক্র *n.* a honeycomb, a bee-hive. ~চন্দ্র, ~চন্দ্রমা, ~চন্দ্রিকা *n.* honeymoon. ~চন্দ্র যাপন করা *v.* to honeymoon. ~জ *n.* beeswax. ~নিশি *n.* the wedding night; a vernal or spring night; a very pleasant night. ~প *n.* the bee; the black-bee. ~পর্ক *n.* an oblation of honey, clarified butter, milk, curd and sugar all mixed together. মধুপর্কের বাটি a small bowl or cup or container for the above mixture for oblation; (fig.) anything small, brittle or tending to flop. ~পায়ী *n.* the bee; the black-bee. ~পূর্ণ *a.* full of honey; full of sweet juice; very delicious; very sweet or charming. ~বন *n.* a pleasant grove in Brindaban. ~বর্ষী *a.* showering honey; (fig.) very sweet or pleasing. ~ভাষী *a.* sweet-speaking, honey-tongued. ~মক্ষিকা *n.* the bee, the black-bee. ~ময় same as মধুপূর্ণ। ~মালতী *n.* a kind of creeper, (cp.) the honeysuckle. ~মাস *n.* the month of Chaitra (চৈত্র). ~মেহ *n.* diabetes. ~যামিনী *n.* a spring night; a very pleasant night; honeymoon. মধুযামিনী যাপন করা *v.* to honeymoon. ~রস *n.* sweet juice; sweetness. ~রাতি *n.* a spring night; a very pleasant night. ~লিট, ~লিহ, ~লেহ *n.* the bee, the black-bee. ~লুব্ধ, ~লোভী, ~লোলুপ *a.* avid of or fond of honey or sweet juice. ~স্বর *a.* sweet-voiced.

মধুর *a.* very sweet, honeyed; sweet; delicious; pleasant. *fem.* মধুরা। ~তা, ~ত্ব *n.* great sweetness; deliciousness; pleasantness. ~ভাষিণী *a.* *fem.* honey-tongued; soft-spoken. *masc.* ~ভাষী। ~প্রকৃতি, ~স্বভাব *a.* sweet-tempered. ~স্বর *a.* sweet-voiced. মধুরাম্ল *n.* an acid; acid. □ *a.* acid. মধুরালাপ *n.* pleasant or friendly conversation; (poet.) amorous conversation. মধুরিমা *a.* (great) sweetness; pleasantness.

মধূত্থ *n.* beeswax. ~বর্তিকা *n.* wax candle.

মধূৎসব same as মদনোৎসব। .

মধ্য *n.* the middle; the centre; the waist; the inside or interior; midst; interval. □ *a.* middle, central, mid; interior, inside; intervening, interim, mean; middling, mediocre; medium. মধ্য উষ্ণতা mean temperature. ~ক *a.* (arith.) mean. □ *n.* (arith.) a mean. ~কর্ণ *n.* the middle ear, (loos.) the tympanum. ~কাল *n.* (astr.) the meantime. ~কোণ *n.* (astr.) the mean anomaly. ~ক্ষীণা *a. fem.* having a slender waist. ~গ *a.* of the middling state, mean. *fem.* ~গা। ~গমন *n.* (astr.) culmination. ~চ্ছদা *n.* (physio.) the diaphragm. ~তল *n.* (astr.) the meridian plane. ~ত্বক *n.* (bot.) mesocarp. ~দিন *n.* (arch.) midday, noon. ~দেশ *n.* the middle or central part; the waist; the interior or inside; Central India. ~পদলোপী *n.* (gr.) a mode of framing compound words by deleting the word in the middle of other two. ~পর্দা, ~পরদা *n.* the middle lamella. ~পন্থা *n.* the middle course; the golden mean. ~পন্থী *a.* & *n.* moderate, (a person) avoiding extremes and following or pursuing the middle course or the golden mean. ~প্রাচ্য *n.* the Middle East; countries of the Middle East. ~বয়স্ক *a.* middle-aged. *fem.* মধ্যবয়স্কা। ~বর্তিতা *n.* the state of being in the middle; the state of being inside; intermediacy; intervention; mediation. ~বর্তী *a.* situated or stationed in the middle or inside or in the midst; intermediate; intervening; medial; mediating. *fem.* ~বর্তিনী। ~বর্তী নিযুক্তক a handling agent. মধ্যবর্তী হওয়া *v.* to lie in or go into the middle; to intervene; to mediate. ~বিত্ত *a.* middleclass, bourgeois. মধ্যবিত্ত-মনোবৃত্তি *n.* middleclass mentality; (esp. pol.) petty bourgeois mentality. মধ্যবিত্ত-সম্প্রদায় *n.* the middle class, the bourgeoisie. ~বিধ *a.* middling, mediocre. ~বিন্দু *n.* the centre. ~ভারত *n.* Central India. ~মণি *n.* a jewel at the centre of anything; (fig.) the most glorious or precious or prominent person or thing. ~মান *n.* an Indian musical measure. ~যুগ *n.* the Middle Ages. ~যুগীয় *a.* mediaeval. ~রাত্র *n.* midnight. ~রাত্রে *adv.* at midnight, at dead of night. ~রেখা *n.* (geog. & astr.)

the meridian; (geom.) a median. **মধ্যশিক্ষা পর্ষৎ** The Board of Secondary Education. **~শিরা** *n.* (bot.) the midrib. **~স্থ** *a.* of the interior or inside; inner; lying inside or in the interior; lying in the midst; intermediate, medial; intervening; mediating; intermediary. □ *n.* a mediator; an arbitrator, an arbiter; an intermediary, a middleman, a go-between. *fem.* **~স্থা**। **মধ্যস্থ ন্যায়ালয়** an arbitral tribunal. **~স্থতা** *n.* mediation; arbitration. **মধ্যস্থতা করা** *v.* to mediate; to arbitrate. **~স্থল** *n.* the middle; the centre; the inside, the interior; the midst. **~স্থিত** *a.* lying inside or in the interior; lying in the midst.

মধ্যন্দিন *n.* midday, noon.

মধ্যম *a.* middle; second in order of seniority or age (মধ্যমভ্রাতা = the second brother; মধ্যমপুত্র = the second son); (rare) intermediate, medial; middling, mediocre, moderate. □ *n.* the waist (সুমধ্যমা) ; (mus.) the major fourth of the C-scale. **~পন্থা** *n.* the middle course; (pol.) moderateness, moderatism. **~পন্থী** *a.* following the middle course; (pol.) moderate. **~বয়স্ক** *a.* middle-aged. *fem.* **~বয়স্কা**। **মধ্যমা** *n.* the middle finger; (geom.) a median. □ *a. fem.* second in order of seniority or age. **মধ্যমাঙ্গুলি** *n.* the middle finger.

মধ্যা, মধ্যাঙ্গুলি *n.* the middle finger.

মধ্যাহ্ন *n.* midday, noon. **~কালীন** *a.* of or at noon, midday, noonday, noontide; meridional. **~ক্রিয়া** *n.* any one of the scriptural or other midday duties; midday meal, luncheon, lunch. **~ভোজন** *n.* midday meal, luncheon, lunch. **মধ্যাহ্নভোজন করা** *v.* to take one's midday meal, to lunch. **~সূর্য** *n.* the midday sun, the meridian sun.

মধ্যাবস্থা *n.* mediocrity; the middle or middling state.

মধ্যে *prep.* in the middle, at the centre; in, into, within, inside; in between (ইতিমধ্যে) ; before the termination or commencement of, by (সপ্তাহমধ্যে,সন্ধ্যার মধ্যে) ; amidst, in the midst of, amongst or between. □ *adv.* some time back (মধ্যে একবার বলেছিলাম). **মধ্যে মধ্যে** *adv.* from time to time, occasionally, now and then; few and far between; sparsely.

মধ্যোচ্চগমন *n.* (astr.) upper culmination.

মধ্যোন্নতি *n.* (astr.) the meridian altitude.

মন[১] *n.* a measure of weight (=40 seers or about 82 lbs.), a maund. **~কষা** *n.* the system of calculating weight in terms of maunds, seers etc. **~কে** *adv.* for each maund, each maund; in every or each maund.

মন[২] *n.* mind; heart; mental state, mood; mentality; feeling; consideration; memory; inclination, desire; attraction, attachment, interest; attention; earnestness, devotion; sincerity; choice; resolve, decision. **মন আসা** same as **মন লাগা**। **মন ওঠা** *v.* to be satisfied or pleased. **মন করা** *v.* to resolve, to make up one's mind; to have a mind; to agree, to condescend (আপনি মন করলে চাকরিটা হবে). **মন কাড়া** *v.* to captivate the mind, to capture the fancy of; to win one's heart. **মন কেমন করা** *v.* to be uneasy in mind; to be worried. **মন খারাপ করা** see **খারাপ**। **মন খারাপ হওয়া** *v.* to be out of hearts; to be out of humour; to be saddened. **মন খোলা, মন খুলে বলা** *v.* to speak one's mind; to open one's heart; to break one's mind. **মন গলা** *v.* to soften (towards), to melt. **মন গলানো** *v.* to melt one's heart. **মন চাওয়া** *v.* to be inclined to; to agree to. **মন ছোটো হওয়া** *v.* to become small-minded; to feel small; to be stricken with a sense of inferiority; to become ungenerous or niggardly; to lose heart, to become dejected. **মন ছোটা** *v.* to be stricken with an impetuous inclination towards or desire for; to be greatly attracted. **মন জানা** *v.* to learn or know one's mind. **মন জোগানো** *v.* to comply with one's orders or desires; to act to please another; to humour; to flatter. **মন টলা** *v.* to become perturbed or worried; to be in two minds, to waver; to be of two minds; to soften emotionally, to melt. **মন টানা** *v.* to attract; to incline; to have a mind. **মন**

থাকা *v.* to have a desire for; to be inclined towards; to have interest in; to be attentive to. মন থেকে *adv.* sincerely; from the bottom of one's heart; by or out of one's imagination; (rare) from memory. মন দমা *v.* to become disheartened or discouraged. মন দেওয়া *v.* to apply one's mind to, to mind; to be earnest (মন দিয়ে কাজ করা) ; to pay attention or heed to; to fall in love with. মন পাওয়া *v.* to be able to please another; to win one's favour or love; to win the heart of. মনপ্রাণ দিয়ে চেষ্টা করা *v.* to try heart and soul. মন বসা same as মন লাগা। মন বিষানো *v.* to embitter or poison one's mind. মন ভাঙা *v.* to be disheartened or discouraged; to be broken-hearted or heart-broken. মন ভাঙানো *v.* to dishearten or discourage; to break one's heart; to prejudice one's mind (against), to earwig. মন ভোলানো *v.* to charm or captivate one's mind: to attract or please greatly; to win one's heart; to infatuate; to melt one's heart; to cajole; to take one's mind off (something). মন মাতানো *v.* to make one beside oneself with delight; to delight or please greatly. মন মানা *v.* to be consoled; to agree to accept at heart; to agree or consent to. মন রাখা same as মন জোগানো। মন লাগা v. to have a liking or inclination for; to have interest in; to have earnestness in. মন লাগানো *v.* to apply one's mind to, to attend to earnestly. মন সরা *v.* to have a desire for, to be willing (to). মন হওয়া *v.* to be inclined; to have half a mind; to become consented. মন হারানো *v.* to lose oneself; to lose one's heart; to be infatuated, to be greatly enamoured (of). মনে ওঠা *v.* to rise in one's mind, to occur to or strike one (ফন্দি মনে ওঠা) ; to be recollected (স্মৃতি মনে ওঠা). মনে করা *v.* to call to mind, to recollect; to resolve, to decide; to have a mind; to have half a mind; to feel; to suppose; to count, to regard, to consider, to think. মনে জাগা same as মনে ওঠা। মনে জানা *v.* to know or feel at heart. মনে থাকা *v.* to be remembered, to be retained in one's memory. মনে দাগ কাটা *v.* to impress one's mind indelibly; to bring home to; to make an imprint on one's mind; to occupy one's memory permanently. মনে ধরা *v.* to be to one's liking or choice; to be after one's heart. মনে নেওয়া *v.* to feel; to supose; to consider or think seriously. মনে পড়া *v.* to remember; to be recollected. মনে পুষে রাখা *v.* to nourish or cherish secretly at heart. মনে রাখা *v.* to remember; to bear or to keep in mind. মনে লাগা *v.* to be to one's liking, to be up to one's choice; to impress one's mind favourably; to be shocked or pained at heart; to feel or suppose. মনে স্থান দেওয়া to cherish or keep alive in one's heart. মনে হওয়া *v.* to feel; to suppose; to consider, to think; to count, to regard; to come to recollect; to appear; to seem. মনের আগুন mental anguish, heart-grief. মনের কথা one's secret thoughts and feelings and intentions, one's mind. মনের কালি the gloom of one's mind; sorrow, grief; ill-feeling; malice; concealed vice. মনের গোল doubt; hesitation. মনের জোর a strong will; moral courage; self-confidence; morale. মনের ঝাল a grudge. মনের ঝাল মেটানো *v.* to feed one's grudge. মনের বিষ concealed envy or malice; canker of the mind. মনের ব্যথা mental anguish, heart's pang. মনের মতো same as মনোমতো। মনের ময়লা same as মনের কালি। মনের মানুষ a person after one's own heart; a favourite; a minion; a lover. মনের মিল amicability; agreement, accord.

মনঃ ori. spell. of মন[২]। ~কল্পিত *a.* imagined; fancied; imaginary; fanciful; fantastic; fictitious. ~কষ্ট *n.* mental anguish, heartache, heart's pang; wounded feelings, mortification. মনঃকষ্ট দেওয়া *v.* to give pain to one's heart; to shock one's heart; to grieve, to sadden. মনঃকষ্ট পাওয়া *v.* to be stricken with mental anguish; to have one's feeling wounded, to be offended or mortified. ~ক্ষুণ্ণ *a.* shocked at heart; grieved; saddened;

disappointed; mortified; offended. ~পীড়া same as ~কষ্ট। ~পূত a. to one's liking or choice, after one's own heart; acceptable to; approved by. ~প্রাণ n. heart and soul. মনঃপ্রাণ দিয়ে চেষ্টা করা v. to try heart and soul. ~শিলা n. realgar, arsenic monosulphide. ~সমীক্ষক n. a psycho-analyst. ~সমীক্ষণ, ~সমীক্ষা n. psycho-analysis. মনঃসমীক্ষণ করা v. to psycho-analyse. ~সমীক্ষামূলক a. psycho-analytic (al). মনঃসংযোগ করা v. to apply one's mind (closely) to; to be attentive to, to concentrate (on). ~স্থ a. lying in the mind, mental; determined, resolved, decided; intended. মনঃস্থ করা v. to make up one's mind, to resolve, to decide, to intend. ~স্থৈর্য n. mental calm or equilibrium or placidity; firmness of the mind; firmness or fixity of decision.

মনকষা see মন[১]।

মনকষাকষি n. strained relations; mutual ill-feelings; bad blood. মনকষাকষি করা v. to strain one's relations with; to fall out with.

মনকে see মন[১]।

মনক্কা n. raisin.

মনখোলা a. open-hearted, hearty, frank, above-board; outspoken.

মন-গড়া same as মনঃকল্পিত।

মনচোর, (in endearment) মনচোরা n. a captivator of another's mind.

মনছাল same as মনঃশিলা।

মন-ঢালা a. whole-hearted.

মন-দেওয়া-নেওয়া n. mutual love-making; courtship.

মনন n. thinking, cogitation; guessing, supposition, surmise; deciding, resolution; conceiving, conception; a notion. মনন করা v. to think, to cogitate; to guess, to suppose, to surmise; to decide, to resolve; to conceive; to form a notion. ~শীল a. thoughtful; intellectual.

মনপবন n. (dial.) secret inclinations and intentions, one's mind. মনপবনের দাঁড় (in folk-tales) an oar by means of which a boat can be driven at any speed and in any directions as one desires.

মনপ্রাণ n. heart and soul.

মনমরা a. down-hearted, morose, low-spirited, vapoury, (*sl.*) browned off; dejected, melancholy.

মনরক্ষা n. compliance with one's orders or desires; acting or working to please another; humouring or flattering. মনরক্ষা করা v. to comply with one's orders or desires or wishes; to act to please another; to humour; to flatter.

মনশ্চক্ষু n. the mind's eye; imagination; insight.

মনশ্চাঞ্চল্য n. mental agitation or unrest; worry, anxiety, concern.

মনসবদার n. (hist.) one of a class of army commanders serving in lieu of a jaghir. মনসবদারি n. office of the aforesaid arny commanders.

মনসা n. (myth.) the Hindu Snake-Goddess; a kind of plant. ~মঙ্গল cult poetry concerning Goddess Manasa (মনসা).

মনসিজ n. Madana (মদন) the god of love.

মনস্কাম, মনস্কামনা same as মনোরথ।

মনস্তত্ত্ব n. psychology. মনস্তাত্ত্বিক a. psychological. □ n. a psychologist.

মনস্তাপ same as মনঃকষ্ট।

মনস্তুষ্টি n. mental satisfaction or pleasure; heart's content; (loos.) adulation. ~কর a. pleasing, satisfying; gratifying.

মনস্থ pop. spell. of মনঃস্থ (see মনঃ).

মনস্বী a. endowed with mental calm or peace; magnanimous, large-minded, large-hearted; great-hearted; (loos.) possessing sharp intellect. *fem.* মনস্বিনী। মনস্বিতা n. possession of mental calm or peace; magnanimity, large-mindedness; (loos.) possession of sharp intellect; sharpwittedness.

মনাক্কা n. raisin.

মনান্তর n. strained relations; bad blood; a quarrel; disagreement in opinion, dissension.

মনাসিব pop. var. of মুনাসিব।

মনি-অর্ডার n. a money-order. মনি-অর্ডার করা v. to send by money order. মনি-অর্ডারযোগে, মনি-অর্ডার করে *adv.* by money-order.

মনিব n. master (*fem.* : a mistress); an employer. *fem.* মনিবানি।

মনিব্যাগ *n.* a money-bag, a wallet, a purse.

মনিহারি *a.* dealing in stationery goods, cosmetics, fancy-goods, etc.; (loos.) stationery.

মনীষা *n.* sharp intellect; genius; sagacity. **মনীষী** *a.* possessing sharp intellect; endowed with genius; sagacious. □ *n.* a man of sharp intellect; a man of genius; a sagacious man; a sage.

মনু *n.* (myth.) any one of the fourteen sons of Brahma (ব্রহ্মা) ; the fourteenth Manu (মনু) regarded as the father and first law-giver of mankind.

মনুজ *n.* man; a man. **মনুজেন্দ্র** *n.* a king, a monarch.

মনুষ্য *n.* man; mankind, humankind; a human being; a man. *fem.* **মনুষী** womankind; a woman. **~কণ্ঠ** *n.* the human voice. **~কৃত** *a.* made or done by man; man-made. **~চরিত্র** *n.* the human character; (rare) a biography. **~জন্ম** *n.* birth as a human creature; the human life. **~ত্ব** *n.* humanness, humanity. **মনুষ্যত্বপূর্ণ** *a.* full of humaneness or humanity, humane. **মনুষ্যত্বহীন** *a.* devoid of humanity or human quality; inhuman; barbarous. **~ধর্ম** *n.* the moral and social duties of man; the religion of man; humanity. **~বর্জিত** *a.* man-forsaken; uninhabited; desolate. **~বসতি** *n.* a human habitation. **~মূর্তি** *n.* a figure of a man; a human being; a statue. **~হীন** *a.* desolate, not inhabited by man. **মনুষ্যাবাস** *n.* a human habitation; a human settlement; a town, a city, a village; a dwelling-house. **মনুষ্যেতর** *a.* belonging to a lower species than the human being; of a lower order, lower (মনুষ্যেতর প্রাণী). **মনুষ্যোচিত** *a.* befitting or becoming a man; humane.

মনুসংহিতা, মনুস্মৃতি *n.* a code of laws drawn up by Manu (মনু).

মনোগত *a.* seated in the mind or at heart, inward. **মনোগত ভাব** intention.

মনোগ্রাহী *a.* pleasant; agreeable; attractive.

মনোজ *a.* born in the mind; born of the mind □ *n.* the god of Love (who dwells in the mind); Cupid.

মনোজগৎ *n.* the sphere or realm of the mind; the realm of imagination or of ideas and thoughts; the realm of fancy.

মনোজ্ঞ *a.* captivating, attractive, pleasant, charming.

মনোদুঃখ same as **মনঃকষ্ট** ৷

মনোনয়ন *n.* selection; nomination; choosing; choice. **মনোনয়ন করা** *v.* to select; to nominate; to choose.

মনোনিবেশ *n.* (earnest) application of the mind; (close) attention. **মনোনিবেশ করা** *v.* to apply one's mind (earnestly or closely) to; to pay close attention to; to employ oneself intently or diligently in.

মনোনীত *a.* selected; nominated; chosen. *fem.* **মনোনীতা** ৷ **মনোনীত করা** same as **মনোনয়ন করা** ৷

মনোনেত্র *n.* same as **মানসনেত্র** see **মানস** ৷

মনোবল *n.* strength of mind; moral courage; self-confidence.

মনোবাঞ্ছা, মনোবাসনা same as **মনস্কাম** ৷

মনোবিকার *n.* aberration of the mind; mental distraction; mental neurosis; mental perversion.

মনোবিজ্ঞান, মনোবিদ্যা *n.* psychology. **মনোবিদ্যাগত** *a.* psychological. **মনোবিজ্ঞানী** *n.* a psychologist.

মনোবিবাদ same as **মন-কষাকষি** ৷

মনোবৃত্তি *n.* the faculty of the mind; mentality (গোলামি মনোবৃত্তি) ৷

মনোবেদনা, মনোব্যথা same as **মনঃকষ্ট** ৷

মনোব্যাধি *n.* a mental disease; psychoneurosis; psychosis. **~গ্রস্ত** *a.* mentally diseased; psychoneurotic; psychotic. **মনোব্যাধির চিকিৎসক** a psychiatrist. **মনোব্যাধির চিকিৎসা** psychiatry.

মনোভঙ্গ *n.* disappointment; despondency; dejection; discouragement.

মনোভাব *n.* one's secret thoughts and feelings, one's mind; mental state; attitude; predisposition.

মনোভার *n.* the burden of one's mind, heaviness of one's heart (that is, grief, huff etc.); mental distress.

মনোমতো *a.* to one's liking or choice, after one's own heart.

মনোমদ *a.* vanity, false pride.

মনোমধ্যে *adv.* in one's mind, at heart, inwardly.

মনোমন্দির *n.* the mind imagined as a temple.

মনোময় *a.* formed or conceived by the mind, mental; imagined; analogous to or identified with the mind. **মনোময় কোষ** (Hindu phil.) the third vessel of the individual soul.

মনোমালিন্য same as **মন-কষাকষি**।

মনোমুগ্ধকর, মনোমোহন *a.* captivating, fascinating, charming; very beautiful. *fem.* **মনোমোহিনী**।

মনোযোগ *n.* attention; heed; intentness. **মনোযোগ দেওয়া** *v.* to pay attention to; to pay heed to; to apply one's mind or oneself intently to. **~হীন** *a.* inattentive; heedless. **~হীনতা** *n.* inattention; inattentiveness; heedlessness. **মনোযোগী** *a.* attentive; heedful; intent. **মনোযোগিতা** *n.* attentiveness; attention.

মনোরঞ্জক *a.* entertaining the mind, pleasant; adulatory; flattering.

মনোরঞ্জন *n.* entertainment of the mind; diversion, recreation; act of pleasing; adulation. **মনোরঞ্জন করা** *v.* to entertain the mind of; to divert, to recreate, to amuse; to please; to adulate; to humour. **মনোরঞ্জিনী** *a. fem.* providing mental entertainment; diverting, recreating, amusing; pleasing; pleasant; adulatory.

মনোরথ *n.* heart's desire; desire; (secret) intention. **~পূরণ, ~সিদ্ধি** *n.* fulfilment of one's heart's desire or (secret) intention.

মনোরম *a.* pleasing to the mind, fascinating; pleasant, delightful; beautiful. *fem.* **মনোরমা**।

মনোরাজ্য same as **মনোজগৎ**।

মনোলোভা *a. fem.* alluring; fascinating; very beautiful.

মনোহর *a.* captivating; charming; very pleasant; lovely; very beautiful. **মনোহরণ** *n.* fascination; enchantment; attraction. □ *a.* attractive; fascinating, enchanting (মনোহরণ বেশ). **মনোহরণ করা** *v.* to captivate the mind. **মনোহরশাহি** *n.* a mode of kirtan (কীর্তন) songs. **মনোহরা** *a. fem.* of **মনোহর**। □ *n.* a variety of sweetmeat.

মনোহারী[1] same as **মনোহর**। **মনোহারিত্ব** *n.* power of captivating the mind; charm; loveliness; great beauty.

মনোহারী[2] rej. var. of **মনিহারি**।

মন্ডা[1] *n.* a sweet blob.

মন্ডা[2] *n.* poet. form of **মন্ডিত করা**।

-মন্ত same as **-বন্ত**।

মন্তব্য *n.* a remark; a comment. **মন্তব্য করা** *v.* to pass a remark, to remark; to make comments, to comment.

মন্ত্র, (coll.) **মন্তর** *n.* a portion of the Vedas containing sacred hymns; any one of the aforesaid hymns, a mantra; a mystic (and esoteric) word or words recited in prayer to God or a deity (শিবমন্ত্র, মন্ত্রজপ) ; a magical formula, a spell, an incantation (বশীকরণমন্ত্র) ; a principle, a motto (অহিংসামন্ত্র) ; counsel, advice; conference; decision, resolve; a design, a plan. **মন্ত্র দেওয়া** *v.* to initiate one into the worship of a deity by teaching one the prescribed mystic and esoteric word or words of prayer; to give counsel; to instigate. **মন্ত্র নেওয়া** *v.* to be initiated into the worship of a deity by learning (from a guru) the prescribed mystic and esoteric word or words of prayer; to be initiated into (দেশসেবার মন্ত্র নেওয়া) ; to take counsel. **~ক** *n.* ministry. **~কুশল** *a.* skilled in giving counsel. **~গুপ্তি** *n.* act of keeping counsel; act of keeping a resolve or design or plan secret. **মন্ত্রগুপ্তি-আইন** *n.* Official Secrets Act. **~গৃহ** *n.* a private room for consultation; a privy-council (in the ori. sense), a cabinet; a council-chamber. **মন্ত্র গ্রহণ করা** same as **মন্ত্র নেওয়া**। **~জ্ঞ** *a.* capable of counselling; conversant with the counsel or design of (esp. of an adversary). **~তন্ত্র** *n. pl.* mantras and incantations collectively; (dero.) spells. **~দাতা** *n.* (also *a.*) a guru or spiritual guide who initiates one into the worship of a deity by teaching one the prescribed mystic and esoteric words of prayer; an initiator (*fem.* an initiatrix); a counsellor. *fem.* **~দাত্রী**। **~দান করা** same as **মন্ত্র দেওয়া**। **~পাঠ** *n.* recital of Vedic mantras; recital of the prescribed mystic word or words of prayer; recital of incantations, incantation. ~পূত *a.* sanctified by means of uttering the prescribed mystic word or words of prayer (মন্ত্রপূত ঘট) ; protected or endowed with protective power by means of incantation (মন্ত্রপূত শরীর, মন্ত্রপূত কবচ). **~বল** *n.* the force of the prescribed mystic word or words of prayer; the power or force of incantation. **~বিদ** *a.* same as **~জ্ঞ** । □ *n.* a counsellor; a minister. **~ভবন** same as **~গৃহ** । **~ভেদ** *n.* discovery of a counsel or design (esp. of an adversary). **~মুগ্ধ** *a.* spell-bound. *fem.* **~মুগ্ধা** । **~শক্তি** same as **~বল** । **~শিষ্য** *n.* a disciple of a guru who has taught the former the prescribed mystic word or words to be recited in prayer to a deity; an initiated disciple; (fig.) an ardent follower. *fem.* **~শিষ্যা** । **~সাধন** *n.* regular recital of incantations or of the prescribed prayer in order to realize an end. **~সিদ্ধ** *a.* succeeded in attaining an end by means of regular recital of incantations or of the prescribed prayer; attained sucess in devotion through mantras. **~সিদ্ধি** *n.* attainment of an end by means of regular recital of incantations or of the prescribed prayer; attainment of success in devotion through mantras.

মন্ত্রণ, মন্ত্রণা *n.* (usu. private) discussion, conference; consultation; counsel, advice; designing; a design; instigation; an intrigue. **মন্ত্রণা করা** *v.* to discuss or confer (usu. in private); to consult; to design, to play; to intrigue. **মন্ত্রণাগৃহ** *n.* a private room or house for consultation; privy-council, a cabinet; a council chamber. **মন্ত্রণাদাতা** *n.* an adviser; a counsellor; an instigator. *fem.* **মন্ত্রণাদাত্রী** । **মন্ত্রণাপরিষদ** *n.* advisory council. **মন্ত্রণাভবন** same as **মন্ত্রণাগৃহ** ।

মন্ত্রিত্ব *n.* office of a minister or a counsellor of state, ministry.

মন্ত্রিপরিষৎ *n.* ministers collectively, the ministry, the cabinet.

মন্ত্রিবর *n.* (in courtesy) a great minister, (cp.) the hon'ble minister.

মন্ত্রিমণ্ডলী, মন্ত্রিসভা same as **মন্ত্রিপরিষৎ** ।

মন্ত্রী *n.* a counsellor of state, a minister, a cabinet-member; an advisor, a counsellor; (dero.) an instigator. **উপমন্ত্রী** *n.* a deputy minister. **প্রধানমন্ত্রী** *n.* a prime minister. **মুখ্যমন্ত্রী** *n.* a chief minister. **রাষ্ট্রমন্ত্রী** *n.* a minister of state.

মন্থ *n.* churning; a churning-stick; a beverage of pulverized barley or pulses.

মন্থন *n.* churning; stirring; agitating, agitation; trampling; destroying,. destruction. **মন্থন করা** *v.* to churn; to stir, to agitate; to trample; to destroy. **~দণ্ড** *n.* a churning-stick. **~পাত্র, ~ভাণ্ড** *n.* a churning-pot, (cp.) a churn. **~রজ্জু** *n.* a rope to which a churning-stick is fitted during the process of churning, a churning-rope. **মন্থনী** *n.* a churning-stick; a churningpot; a churn.

মন্থর *a.* slow; slack; sluggish, slothful; inert; slow-moving. **মন্থর হওয়া** *v.* to become slow; to slacken. **~গতি** *a.* slow-moving. □ *n.* slow motion. **~তা** *n.* slowness; slackness; sluggishness, sloth; inertia; slow movement or motion. **মন্থরা** *n.* a female character of the Ramayana; an instigating or intriguing woman.

মন্থী *a.* (chiefly used as *sfx.*) churning; stirring; agitating; trampling, destroying.

মন্দ *a.* slow; slow-moving, gentle; sluggish; slack; dim; bad, evil; wicked, vile; inferior; unfavourable, adverse; ill, impaired; indisposed (শরীরটা আজ মন্দ) ; indigent, poor (মন্দ অবস্থার লোক) ; impoverished; deteriorated (কারবার মন্দ) ; harsh, rude; scanty, small, poor (বেতন বড়ো মন্দ) ; small in number or quantity or degree (বয়স মন্দ নয়) ; ugly; dull, weak. □ *n.* harm, injury. **মন্দ করা** *v.* to do harm to, to cause injury to. **মন্দ আচরণ** misbehaviour, misconduct; ill-treatment. **মন্দ কথা** reproachful words; harsh or rude words; abusive or filthy language; an obscene word; a calumny; bad report. **মন্দ কাজ** a wicked deed; a misdeed; a disgraceful act. **~গতি** *a.* slow-moving; slow. □ *n.* slowness. **~গমন, ~গামী** same as **~গতি** । *fem.*

~গমনা, ~গামিনী। মন্দ চালচলন evil ways. ~তা, ~ত্ব *n.* slowness; slow motion; sluggishness; dimness; badness; wickedness, vileness; inferiority; unfavourableness, adverseness; illness, impaired state; indisposition; indigence, poverty; impoverishment; deterioration; harshness, rudeness; scantiness, smallness in number or quantity or degree; ugliness; dullness; weakness. ~ন *n.* (mech.) retardation. মন্দ নয় not bad, moderate; (sarcas.) fine, nice. মন্দ ফল bad result; evil consequence. ~বায়ু same as মন্দানিল। ~বুদ্ধি *a.* having evil or foul design; wicked, vile, ill-natured; dull-headed. মন্দ ব্যবহার same as মন্দ আচরণ। ~ভাগ, ~ভাগ্য *a.* ill-fated, unfortunate, unlucky. *fem.* ~ভাগা, ~ভাগ্যা, (loos.) ~ভাগিনী। ~মতি same as ~বুদ্ধি। মন্দ মন্দ *adv.* slowly, gently. মন্দ সময় bad times, hard times. ~সমীরণ same as মন্দানিল। ~স্রোত *n.* slow current. ~হাস্য *n.* a gentle laugh, a smile. ~হিল্লোল *n.* gentle waves. মন্দের ভালো rather tolerable in the midst of a world of evils; not bad.

মন্দর *n.* a mythological mountain.

মন্দা *a.* abated; (comm.) seized with depression, slumped. □ *n.* abatement; (comm.) depression, a slump; (poet. & obs.) a wicked person.

মন্দাকিনী *n.* (myth.) the name of the Ganges as flowing in heaven.

মন্দাক্রান্তা *n.* a metre of Sanskrit poetry.

মন্দাগ্নি *n.* loss of appetite; (inc.) indigestion or dyspepsia.

মন্দানিল *n.* a breeze; a mild and sweet wind.

মন্দার *n.* (myth.) a celestial tree or its flower; the coral tree. ~মালিকা *n.* a wreath or garland of mythological mandar (মন্দার) flowers.

মন্দির *n.* a temple; a shrine; a house of worship; a house (বিদ্যামন্দির) ; a room, a chamber (শয়নমন্দির) ; an abode (শরীর হল ব্যাধিমন্দির).

মন্দিরা *n.* a kind of small cup-shaped cymbals.

মন্দীভূত *a.* slowed down; retarded; dimmed; abated; (comm.) slumped. মন্দীভূত করা বা হওয়া *v.* to slow down; to retard; to dim; to abate; to cause a slump or to slump.

মন্দুরা *n.* stable; mat.

মন্দ্র *n.* a grave sonorous voice, (cp.) barytone; a kind of tom-tom. □ *a.* grave and sonorous, barytone. ~সপ্তক *n.* (mus.) the middle octave.

মন্বন্তর *n.* (myth.) the term of office of any one of the mythological Manus (মনু) covering a period of 3067200000 years; (pop.) a great and devastating famine (পঞ্চাশের মন্বন্তর).

মন্মথ *n.* (myth.) the Hindu god of love (cp. Cupid, Eros). ~শরাহত *a.* wounded with the shafts of love; love-sick.

মফস্সল, মফস্বল *n.* localities outside great towns or headquarters (cp. an outstation), mofussil.

মবলগ *a.* total, round; cash. মবলগ শ টাকা a round sum of one hundred rupees. মবলগ টাকা cash money. মবলগে *adv.* in all; on the whole.

মম (poet.) *prop. a.* my, mine.

মমতা, মমত্ব *n.* considering a person or thing as one's own; attachment; affection; love; feeling of kinship; (loos.) compassion, pity. ~পূর্ণ, ~ময় *a.* full of attachment; affectionate; loving; (loos.) compassionate, kind. *fem.* ~ময়ী। ~হীন *a.* devoid of attachment or affection, without or deviod of pity or compassion, unkind. *fem.* ~হীনা।

মমি *n.* a mummy (as of Egypt).

-ময় *sfx.* denoting: full of, made of, containing, abounding in etc. (স্বর্ণময়) ;-ful, -ous, -some, -y etc., pervading, -wide (রাজ্যময়). *fem.* -ময়ী।

ময়দা *n.* flour. ~কল *n.* a flourmill. ময়দা মাখা v. to knead flour.

ময়দান *n.* an open plain, an esplanade; a parade-ground, a maidan.

ময়না[1] *n.* a bird of the starling family, the myna, the hill mynah, *Gracula religiosa.*

ময়না[2], **ময়না তদন্ত** *n.* post-mortem examination, autopsy.

ময়রা *n.* a confectioner. *fem.* ময়রানি।

~গিরি *n.* confectionery. **ময়রার দোকান** a confectionery.

ময়লা *n.* excrement, faeces, stool, dung; refuse; filth, soil, dirt; gloom, melancholy; angularity, crookedness (মনের ময়লা). □ *a.* filthy; dirty, soiled; (of complexion) dark; not bright or clear, clouded, overcast (ময়লা আকাশ) ; glum, melancholy (ময়লা মুখ) ; crooked (ময়লা মন). **ময়লা করা** *v.* to soil. **ময়লার গাড়ি** a scavenger's cart or van or train, a night-soil cart. **~টে** *a.* slightly soiled; appearing to be soiled; (of complexion) darkish; slightly clouded or overcast; slightly glum.

ময়ান *n.* ghee mixed with dough for leavening. **ময়ান দেওয়া** *v.* to leaven (ghee to).

ময়াল *n.* the Indian python.

ময়ূখ *n.* a ray, a beam; lustre, glow. **~মালী** *n.* the sun.

ময়ূর *n.* the peacock. **~কণ্ঠী** *a.* peacock-blue. □ *n.* a peacock-blue sari or shawl. **~চূড়া, ~শিখা** *n.* peacock's crest. **~পঙ্খি** *n.* a boat shaped like a peacock. **~পাখা** *n.* a hand-fan made of the feathers of a peacock's tail. **~পুচ্ছ** *n.* the peacock's tail or feather. **~শাবক** *n.* a pea-chick. **ময়ূরী** *n. fem.* the pea-hen.

মর *a.* mortal; perishable. **~জগৎ** *n.* the perishable or mortal world; the earth. **~জীবন** *n.* mortal life. **~দেহ** *n.* the perishable body, the mortal frame. **~মানব** *n.* mortal man, a mortal.

মরক obs. var. of **মড়ক**।

মরকত *n.* emerald. **~কুঞ্জ** *n.* emerald bower. **~বর্ণ** *a.* emerald-green.

মরচে *n.* rust. **মরচে ধরা, মরচে পড়া** *v.* to contact rust, to rust.

মরজি *n.* will, desire, pleasure, sweet will. **যদি তোমার মরজি হয়** if you please, if you would. **যেমন তোমার মরজি** as you please. **~মাফিক** *a.* & *adv.* as or when one pleases.

মরণ *n.* death; decease; demise. **মরণ আর কী** it's death indeed; an expression of shame or mild rebuke; (cp.) hell. **~কামড়** *n.* the last and severest bite of a creature struggling against death; a dying person's last and most desperate attempt. **~কাল** *n.* the time of death, dying moments. **মরণকালে হরিনাম** (fig.) fruitless repentance for one's wickedness when one is dying, (cp.) death-bed repentance; (fig.) futile effort at the eleventh hour when almost all is lost. **~দশা** *n.* the last stage; the last gasp; utter ruin. □ *int.* same as **মরণ আর কী**। **মরণদশায় ধরা** *v.* to be in the state of ruining oneself; seized with a passion that would ruin oneself. **মরণবাড় বাড়া** *v.* to become excessively vainglorious or haughty only to bring about one's fall. **~শীল** *a.* mortal. **~শীলতা** *n.* mortality. **~হীন** *a.* deathless, immortal. **মরণাপন্ন** *a.* in the clutches of death, dying; moribund. *fem.* **মরণাপন্না**। **মরণাপন্নতা** *n.* the dying condition; the last gasp; the last stage. **মরণাশৌচ** *n.* personal impurity caused by the death of a relative. **মরণোন্মুখ** *a.* about to die, at death's door, dying, moribund.

মরত poet. corrup. of **মর্ত**।

মরদ *n.* a man, a male; a male animal; a manly man; a heroic man; a young man; (vul.) a husband. **মরদকা বাত হাতিকা দাঁত** a heroic man's irrevocable pledge or word is unfailingly dependable as ivory which never slumps or falls in price.

মরম poet. corrup. of **মর্ম**।

মরমর[1] alt. spell. of **মর্মর[2]**।

মরমর[2] *a.* about to die, dying; moribund; as if dying. Also **মরোমরো**।

মরমি *a.* cognizant or appreciative of the spirit of anything; mystic (মরমি কবি) ; sympathetic (মরমি বন্ধু).

মরমিয়া *a.* trying to probe into the spirit of religion etc. disregarding forms; pertaining to the transcendental mysteries about God (মরমিয়া তত্ত্ব) ; mystic, mystical (মরমিয়া কবি).

মরশুম, মরসুম *n.* a season; the time of the year for anything, a tide; opportune time of some continuance. **পূজার মরশুম** the Puja season. **বড়দিনের মরশুম** Christmas-tide. **শীতের মরশুম** the winter season, winter-time. **মরশুমি** *a.* seasonal. **মরশুমি ফুল** a season flower.

মরা[1] *n.* alloy (পানমরা). □ *a.* alloyed (মরা সোনা).

মরা² *v.* to die; (of trees etc.) to wither; to be ruined (চাকরি গেলে মরবে) ; to be extremely troubled or afflicted (ভেবে মরা) ; to be strongly seized with (লজ্জায় মরা) ; to suffer or be punished (বদমাশি করলে মরবে) ; to dry up, to silt up (নদী মরা) ; to be allayed, to abate (ব্যথা মরা) ; to decrease (তেজ মরা) ; to weaken (পেট মরা) ; to be spiritless (অভাবে মরে থাকা) ; to be out (বাতাসে আলো গেল মরে). □ *a.* dead; withered; dried up, silted up; allayed, abated; decreased; weak or weakened; utterly spiritless; extinct; dim. **অনাহারে মরা** *v.* to die of hunger, to starve; to famish. **মরমে মরা** *v.* to be extremely mortified or ashamed. **মরতে মরতে বাঁচা** *v.* to come back from the jaws of death. **মরে বাঁচা** *v.* to be relieved from suffering by death. **মরে মরে** impairing one's health utterly; with utmost strain and difficulty. **জীয়ন্তে মরা** more dead than alive. **মরা নাড়ি, মরা পেট** stomach weakened on account of continued under-feeding.

মরাই *n.* a large corn-bin made of mat, cane etc.

মরাকটাল *n.* ebb; low tide.

মরাকান্না *n.* (lit.) loud wailing on account of bereavement; (fig. & pop.) intolerably loud wailing.

মরাঠি var. of **মারাঠি**।

মরামাস *n.* dandruff, scurf.

মরাল *n.* the gander (*fem.* the goose); the swan. **মরালী**। **~গামিনী** *a. fem.* having a gait as graceful as that of the swan. **~নিন্দিত** *a.* excelling even the swan in beauty. **~শাবক, ~শিশু** *n.* a gosling, a cygnet.

মরা-হাজা *a.* tottery; very feeble. **মরেহেজে যাওয়া** *v.* to die out, to become extinct.

মরিচ *n.* black pepper, pepper; (dial.) capsicum, chillies.

মরিচা falsely elegant var. of **মরচে**।

মরি-মরি *int.* an expression of profound admiration etc.; (cp.) ripping.

মরিয়া *a.* desperate, (cp.) devil-may-care. **মরিয়া লোক** a desperado. **মরিয়া হয়ে** *adv.* desperately, in desperation.

মরীচি *n.* a ray, a beam. **~কা** *n.* a mirage; (fig.) an illusion. **~মালী** *n.* one wearing a garland of rays; the sun.

মরু, মরুভূ, মরুভূমি *n.* a desert; a wilderness; (fig.) a place or thing stuffed with afflictions. **মরুঝঞ্ঝা, মরুঝটিকা, মরুঝড়** *n.* a simoom, a simoon. **মরুময়** *a.* desert (মরুময় অঞ্চল) ; full of deserts (মরুময় দেশ) ; (fig.) full of unbearable afflictions. **মরুযাত্রী** *n.* a desert-traveller. **মরুযাত্রীর দল** *n.* a caravan. **মরুসাগর** *n.* the Dead-Sea. **মরুস্থল, মরুস্থলী** *n.* a desert.

মরুৎ, মরুত *n.* one of the five constituent elements (see **ভূত**) ; wind; air.

মরুমায়া same as **মরীচিকা**।

মরূদ্যান *n.* an oasis.

মর্কট *n.* the smallest species of the monkey, the monkey; (contemp.) a man of stunted growth. *fem.* **মর্কটী**।

মর্গ *n.* a morgue.

মর্গেজ corrup. of **মর্টগেজ**।

মর্জি alt. spell.of **মরজি**।

মর্টগেজ *n.* a mortgage. **~দেওয়া** *v.* to mortgage; to hypothecate. **~গ্রাহী** *n.* a mortgagee. **~দাতা** *n.* a mortgager.

মর্ত alt. spell. of **মর্ত্য**।

মর্তমান *n.* a variety of banana originally grown in Martaban.

মর্ত্য *n.* the mortal world, the earth, the world (also **মর্ত্যধাম, মর্ত্যভূমি, মর্ত্যলোক**) ; man, mankind; a mortal, a human being. □ *a.* mortal. **~লীলা** *n.* one's activities whilst living upon the earth.

মর্দ var. of **মরদ**।

মর্দন *n.* trampling; thrashing; pounding; grinding; kneading; massaging; subduing. □ *a.* (used as a *sfx.*) trampling or subduing (অরতিমর্দন). **মর্দন করা** *v.* to trample; to thrash; to pound, to grind; to knead; to massage; to subdue.

মর্দা *a.* male. □ *n.* a male creature. **মর্দানা** *n.* a man (esp. a grown-up one); □ *a.* male; manly. **মর্দানি¹** *n.* (dero.) manliness or masculinity. **মর্দানি²** *n. fem.* a tomboy, a hoyden. □ *a.* tomboyish, hoydenish (মর্দানি মেয়ে). **মর্দানি করা** *v.* to make an exhibition of manly vigour; to bravado; (of women) to behave in a masculine or mannish manner, to romp vigorously.

মর্দিত *a.* trampled; thrashed; pounded, ground; kneaded; massaged; subdued. **মর্দিত করা** same as **মর্দন করা**।

মর্দিনী *a. fem.* of **মর্দন** (*a.*).

মর্ম *n.* the part of the body which is the seat of vital airs; the heart; the core of the heart; inmost feelings or convictions; the heart of heart(s), the inmost heart; essence; implications, (inner) significance; gist; underlying truth; motive (কাজের মর্ম) ; mystery (মর্মোদ্ধার). **মর্ম জানা** বা **বোঝা** *v.* to know or grasp the implication or (inner) significance (of); to know one's inner feelings or convictions, to know one's heart; (dero.) to learn one's secret intentions, to fathom one's heart. **মর্মে আঘাত করা** *v.* to wound one's inmost feelings, to cut to the quick; to move one deeply; to give a home thrust. **এই মর্মে** to this effect. **মর্মে মর্মে** with all one's heart, thoroughly and deeply. **~কথা** *n.* inmost feelings or convictions, heart of hearts; mystery; underlying implication; gist, essence. **মর্মগ্রহণ করা** *v.* to comprehend or grasp the implication or (inner) significance (of). **~গ্রাহী** *a.* comprehending or grasping the implication or (inner) significance; capable of realizing one's inner feelings or convictions, sympathetic. **~ঘাতী** *a.* cutting to the quick, heart-striking. *fem.* **~ঘাতিনী**। **~জ্ঞ** *a.* cognizant of the implication or (inner) significance; cognizant of the value of; conversant with one's inner feelings or convictions. **~জ্বালা, ~দাহ** *n.* secret grudge or envy or grief or agony, heart-burning. **~দাহী** *a.* wounding one's feelings deeply, cutting to the quick; extremely agonizing. **~তুদ** same as **~বিদারী**। **~পীড়া** *n.* heart-ache; mental affliction or suffering; mortification; (rare) heart-burning. **~পীড়িত** *a.* grieved at heart; mortified. *fem.* **~পীড়িতা**। **~বিদারী** *a.* heart-rending; cutting to the quick; extremely pathetic (মমবিদারী দৃশ্য). **~বেদনা, ~ব্যথা** *n.* heart-ache, heart-grief; mortification. **মর্মভেদ করা** *v.* to drive into the heart, to strike the heart; (pop.) to comprehend the implication or (inner) significance (of); (loos.) to fish out one's secret intentions or designs; to fathom one's heart. **~ভেদী** *a.* driving into the heart, heart-striking, heart-rending. **~যন্ত্রণা** same as **~পীড়া**। **~স্থল** *n.* the core of the heart; the most vital or delicate part of the heart; (cp.) the quick; the heart. **~স্পর্শী** *a.* touching the inmost feelings, touching, pathetic; impressive; cutting to the quick. **মর্মাঘাত** *n.* a shock to one's heart or feelings; a home thrust; a very grievous hurt; a death-blow. **মর্মান্তিক** *a.* heart-breaking, heart-rending, cutting to the quick; piteous, pathetic; very grievous or fatal. **মর্মাবগত** same as **~জ্ঞ** **মর্মাবধারণ করা** same as **মর্মগ্রহণ করা**। **মর্মার্থ** *n.* underlying implication; inner significance, gist. **মর্মাহত** *a.* mortified; terribly sorry or aggrieved; wounded at heart; anguished.

মর্মর[১] *n.* marble.

মর্মর[২] *n.* rustle. **মর্মর করা** *v.* to rustle. **~ধ্বনি** *n.* a rustling noise, rustle. **মর্মরিত** *a.* rustling. **মর্মরিত হওয়া** *v.* to be rustling; to rustle.

মর্মোদ্ঘাটন, মর্মোদ্ধার, মর্মোদ্ভেদ *n.* elicitation or exposition of the underlying truth or (inner) significance or mystery. **মর্মোদ্ঘাটন করা** *v.* to elicit or bring out the underlying truth or (inner) significance or mystery (of); to find the sense or meaning of; to reveal the secret of, to puzzle out.

মর্যাদা *n.* dignity, honour; prestige; respect, preferential treatment, cordial reception (অতিথির মর্যাদা) ; good name, reputation; recognition, place or position (গুণীজনের মর্যাদা) ; decorum, grace (মর্যাদাপূর্ণ আচরণ) ; ceremonial form or etiquette (স্ব স্ব মর্যাদানুসারে দরবারে উপবেশন) ; status (প্রথম শ্রেণির ম্যাজিস্ট্রেটের মর্যাদা) ; a (complimentary) fee or tribute (কুলীনের মর্যাদা) ; value, worth, importance (প্রতিশ্রুতির মর্যাদা). **মর্যাদা দেওয়া** *v.* to attach importance to; to recognize the worth of; to receive or treat cordially; to pay heed to; to obey (আইনকে মর্যাদা দেওয়া) ; to pay respect to;

to give the status of. **মর্যাদা নষ্ট করা** *v.* to defame; to attaint; to disgrace; to dishonour; to impair the dignity or prestige or importance of; to cheapen. **~পূর্ণ** *a.* dignified; conforming to the rules of decorum; decent, graceful; respectful. **~শালী** *a.* dignified; having importance, respectable. **~হানি** *n.* defamation; attaint; disgrace; dishonour; indignity; loss of dignity or prestige; loss of importance. **মর্যাদাহানি করা** same as **মর্যাদা নষ্ট করা**। **~হানিকর** *a.* damaging, defamatory; humiliating.

মর্ষ, মর্ষণ *n.* forbearance, toleration; forgiveness; destruction.

মল[1] *n.* a bangle for the ankle.

মল[2] *n.* filth; soil; liquid filth or soil; any morbid secretion from the body; faeces, excrement, stool, (of inferior creatures) dung; a stain, a sullying mark, tarnish; a stigma; gloom, melancholy, angularity, crookedness (চিত্তমল); rust; verdigris; a sin, a vice. **মলত্যাগ করা** *v.* (of human beings) to ease oneself, to evacuate the bowel, to defecate, to pass stool, to stool; (of inferior creatures) to void excrement, to dung. **~দূষিত** *a.* fouled, filthy, foul. **~দ্বার** *n.* the anus. **মলনালী** *n.* the rectum. **~বাহী** *a.* carrying filth and soil (মলবাহী নালা); carrying stool or excrement (মলবাহী অন্ত্র). **~ভাণ্ড** *n.* the large intestine, the colon. **~ময়** *a.* full of dirt and filth. **~যুক্ত** *a.* soiled, dirty. **~শোধনাশয়** *n.* a septic tank. **মলাধার** *n.* the colon, the large intestine; the container for faeces or excrement. **মলাশয়** *n.* the colon; the large intestine.

মলন *n.* trampling; rubbing; scrubbing; massaging; threshing, thrashing.

মলম *n.* an ointment, an unguent; a balm.

মলমল *n.* a fine cotton fabric.

মলমাস *n.* (Hindu astr.) an intercalary month; (astrol.) an inauspicious month for marriage, etc.

মলয় *n.* a mountain range in South India, the Western Ghats (also মলয়গিরি, মলয়াচল); the ancient name of Malabar or of the Malay Peninsula; the south wind or vernal breeze; (cp.) zephyr (also **মলয়পবন, মলয়বায়ু, মলয়মারুত, মলয়সমীর, মলয়সমীরণ, মলয়ানিল**). **~জ** *a.* grown on the Malaya (মলয়) mountains. ☐ *n.* sandal-wood, sandal; the south wind; the vernal breeze. **মলয়জশীতল** *a.* cooled by the south wind.

মলা[1] obs. var. of **মল**[2]।

মলা[2] *v.* to trample; to rub; to scrub; to thresh; to thrash.

মলাই *n.* trampling; rubbing; scrubbing; massaging; threshing, thrashing.

মলাট *n.* a cover of a book, a back (cp. paper-back); a jacket of a book.

মলাশয় *n.* the colon.

মলিদা *n.* a fine and soft woollen fabric; a shawl made of this fabric.

মলিন *a.* dirty, unclean; soiled; tarnished; dark (মলিন গাত্রবর্ণ); dim; dull; overcast, gloomy (মলিন আকাশ); glum; sorrowful, sad (মলিন মুখ). *fem.* **মলিনা**। **~তা, ~ত্ব, মলিনিমা** *n.* dirtiness, uncleanliness; soiled or tarnished state; darkness; dimness; dullness; gloominess; gloom; glumness; sadness. **মলিনীকৃত** *a.* made dirty or soiled.

মল্ল *n.* a wrestler; an athlete; a champion. **~ক্রীড়া** *n.* wrestling; athletics. **মল্লক্রীড়া করা** *v.* to wrestle; to take part in athletics. **~প্রতিযোগিতা** *n.* a wrestling contest; an athletic tournament. **~বিদ্যা** *n.* the art of wrestling. **~বেশ** *n.* a wrestler's garb or uniform; (fig.) **~ভূমি** *n.* a wrestling ground or a venue for athletic tournaments, an arena. **~যুদ্ধ** *n.* wrestling. **মল্লযুদ্ধ করা** *v.* to wrestle. **~যোদ্ধা** *n.* wrestler.

মল্লার *n.* an Indian musical mode of the rainy season.

মল্লিকা *n.* a variety of jasmine.

মশক[1] *n.* a large leathern bag for carrying water.

মশক[2] *n.* the mosquito. **~দংশন** *n.* mosquito-bite. **~সংকুল** *a.* mosquito-infested.

মশকরা *n.* banter; joke, fun; buffoonery. **মশকরা করা** *v.* to joke, to cut a joke, to poke fun (at), to make fun (of); to play the buffoon.

মশগুল *a.* engrossed, absorbed, rapt, thoroughly occupied.

মশ মশ *int.* suggesting: the sound caused by the twisting of tanned hide as of boots; squeaking noise of new shoes etc. **মশ মশ করে চলা** (fig.) to strut.

মশলা *n.* spices; ingredients; materials (গল্পের মশলা); mortar (গাঁথনির মশলা). **~দার** *a.* spicy. **মশলা মেশানো** *v.* to mix spices or mortar.

মশা *n.* the mosquito. **ডাঁশ মশা** *n.* the gnat. **মশা মারতে কামান দাগা** (fig.) to crush a butterfly on a wheel.

মশাই var. of **মশায়**।

মশান *n.* a crematorium (esp. a vast one); an official place for infliction of capital punishment.

মশায় coll. corrup. of **মহাশয়** (esp. used as a polite term of address). **মশায়-মশায় করা** *v.* to curry favour.

মশারি *n.* a mosquito curtain, a mosquito net. **মশারি খাটানো** *v.* to rig up a mosquito curtain.

মশাল *n.* a torch; a flambeau; a link. **মশালচি** *n.* a torch-bearer; a linkman, a linkboy.

মসগুল alt. spell. of **মশগুল**।

মসজিদ *n.* a mosque, a masjid.

মসনদ *n.* a throne; (fig.) a seat of public office. **মসনদি** *a.* royal, regal; governmental, official; vested with official power.

মসলন্দ *n.* a very finely-woven mat.

মসলা rej. spell. of **মশলা**।

মসলিন *n.* a very fine and soft cotton fabric, muslin.

মসল্লা dial. var. of **মশলা**।

মসি, মসী *n.* ink; soot; a dark stain or spot. **~কার** *n.* one who inks, an inker, (loos.) an inkman. **~কৃষ্ণ** *a.* black as ink or soot, deep black. **~চিহ্নিত** *a.* marked with ink; having a dark stain or spot. **~তুল্য, ~বৎ** *a.* inky, black as ink; very black. **~নিন্দিত** *a.* even blacker than ink or soot. **~ময়** *a.* sooty, smudgy; smudged; inky; very black; extremely dark. **~মাখা, ~লিপ্ত** *a.* smeared with ink or soot; very black or dark. **~লাঞ্ছিত** same as **~নিন্দিত**।

মসিজীবী *n.* one who earn's one's living by writing books, pamphlets, articles etc.; a writer; a scribe; a journalist; an office-clerk, (coll.) a pen-pusher.

মসিনা *n.* linseed; flaxen. **~তেল** *n.* linseed-oil.

মসিপাত্র, মসিধান *n.* an inkpot, an inkhorn.

মসুর, মসূর, (coll.) **মসুরি** *n.* lentil.

মসূরিকা, মসূরী *n.* small-pox, variola.

মসৃণ *a.* perfectly plain, even, smooth; sleek; slippery, (bot.) glabrous; soothing (মসৃণ রং); soft (মসৃণ আকাশ); bland (মসৃণ কথাবার্তা) unobstructed, easy (যশের পথ মসৃণ নয়). **~তা** *n.* perfect plainness, evenness, smoothness; sleekness; slipperiness; (bot.) glabrousness; soothingness; softness; blandness; freedom from impediments, freeness, easiness.

মস্করা rej. spell. of **মশকরা**।

মস্ত *n.* the head (ছিন্নমস্তা). □ *a.* high, tall, lofty; very large or big, huge; very broad or long; vast extensive; big (মস্ত মামলা); great (মস্ত বীর); eminent (মস্ত লোক); very distinguished, very influential or powerful; very rich or opulent; elevated, noble (মস্ত আদর্শ); of great value (মস্ত কথা); very important (মস্ত প্রশ্ন); very difficult (মস্ত দায়িত্ব); very serious (মস্ত বিপদ); too much (মস্ত জ্বালা); (iron.) scanty, poor (মস্ত দরদ). □ *adv.* very (মস্ত বড়ো).

মস্তক *n.* (high. & for.) the head; the cranium, the skull, the brain; the top, the summit, the crest (হিমালয়ের মস্তক); the topmost or foremost position (মন্ত্রিসভার মস্তকে ছিলেন জওহরলাল). **মস্তক ছেদন করা** *v.* to decapitate, to behead; to truncate. **~চ্যুত** *a.* fallen from or slipped off the head or top. **~বিশিষ্ট** *a.* having a head, cephalous; headed (বহুমস্তকবিশিষ্ট = hydraheaded). **~ব্যবচ্ছেদ** *n.* cephalotomy. **~সংক্রান্ত** *a.* cephalic. **~হীন, ~শূন্য** *a.* headless; acephalous; truncated. **~শূল** *n.* headache, migraine. **মস্তকাবরণ** *n.* a covering for the head; a head-dress; a turban; a helmet; a cap; a veil. **মস্তকাভরণ** *n.* an ornament for the head. **মস্তকোপরি** *adv.* on or over the head. **মস্তকোর্ধ্বে** *adv.* over the head, overhead.

মস্তান *n.* a rowdy acting officiously as the leader of a locality. **মস্তানি[১]** *n.* rowdyism. **মস্তানি[২]** *n. fem.* a turbulent female of questionable morals; a rowdy harlot.

মস্তিষ্ক *n.* the encephalon; matter within the encephalon, brains; intellect, intelligence, brain. **মস্তিষ্ক খাটানো** *v.* to apply or tax one's brains. **মস্তিষ্ক বিকৃত করা** *v.* to drive crazy, to madden, to run crazy, to go mad; to puzzle or be puzzled; to irritate or fret; to derange one's brains. **মস্তিষ্কের কাজ** *n.* the function of the brain; an intellectual work, a brainy job. **মস্তিষ্ক আলোড়ন করা** *v.* to rack one's brains. **মস্তিষ্ক চালানো** same as **মস্তিষ্ক খাটানো**। **~প্রদাহ** *n.* brain-fever, cephalitis, cerebritis. **~বিকৃতি** *n.* mental derangement, insanity; brain-sickness; (pop.) loss of understanding or intelligence, folly, (cp.) brain-storm. **মস্তিষ্কবিজ্ঞান** *n.* cerebrology. **মস্তিষ্কবিজ্ঞানী** *n.* a cerebrologist. **মস্তিষ্কশূন্য, মস্তিষ্কহীন** *a.* lacking in intelligence, slow in understanding, dull-headed; stupid.

মস্যাধার *n.* an inkpot, an inkhorn; an ink-bottle.

মহকুমা *n.* a subdivision of a district. **~শাসক, ~হাকিম** *n.* a subdivisional officer, (contr.) an S.D.O. **~সংক্রান্ত** *a.* subdivisional.

মহড়া *n.* the front; a position at the front or in the front-line; (fig.) lead (কাজের মহড়া) ; rehearsal (অভিনয়ের মহড়া). **মহড়া দেওয়া** *v.* to rehearse (a dramatic performance). **মহড়া নেওয়া** *v.* to take position in the front and resist or repulse the advance party of the enemy forces; to confront, to face defiantly; to resist or repulse; to bear the brunt (of).

মহতী *fem.* of **মহৎ**।

মহৎ *a.* large, vast, extensive; (rare) best; high-minded, noble; excellent, sublime (মহৎ সাহিত্য) ; great, monstrous (মহৎ ভয়) ; elevated, high (মহৎ পদ). *compar.* **মহত্তর ;** *super.* **মহত্তম**। **মহত্ত্ব** *n.* (rare) largeness, vastness; high-mindedness, nobleness, nobility; excellence, sublimity; greatness.

মহত্তম, মহত্তর, মহত্ত্ব see **মহৎ**।

মহদাশয় *a.* high-minded, noble-natured, magnanimous, generous.

মহদাশ্রয় *n.* a shelter or refuge offered by a noble person; dependence upon great persons.

মহনীয় *a.* worshipful, adorable; venerable; honourable.

মহন্ত *n.* a head of a monastery, convent, temple etc.; (cp.) an abbot.

মহফিল *n.* a sitting or soiree of music, a musical soiree.

মহম্মদি *a.* Mohammedan, Muslim. □ *n.* a Mohammedan.

মহরত *n.* ceremonial beginning or renewal; opening ceremony.

মহরম *n.* the Muslim festival of Muharam; the first month of the Muslim calendar.

মহর্ষি *n.* a great sage or saint.

মহর্লোক *n.* (myth.) fourth amongst the seven heavens.

মহল *n.* a residence (রাজমহল) ; a house or building (রংমহল) ; the self-contained portion or annexe of a building (অন্দরমহল) ; a taluk or estate (খাসমহল) ; a society (মেয়েমহল).

-মহলা[১] *a.* having a particular number of self-contained portions or parts of a building (সাতমহলা বাড়ি).

-মহলা[২] *n.* rehearsal (of a dramatic performance); practice (নাচের মহলা) ; demonstration (বিদ্যাবুদ্ধির মহলা). **মহলা দেওয়া** *v.* to rehearse; to practise; to give a demonstration of.

মহল্লা *n.* part or quarter of a town, a ward.

মহা[১] *a.* (coll.) terrible or formidable (মহা শত্রু) ; excessive or exuberant (মহা ফুর্তি) ; large (মহাশোল).

মহা[২] *in comp.* used as a *pfx.* implying all the meanings of **মহৎ, মহান** and **মহতী**। **~কবি** *n.* a great poet; an epic poet. **~করণ** *n.* the secretariat (of the government); the secretariat building or buildings. **~কর্ষ** *n.* (phys.) gravitation. **~কর্ষাঙ্ক** *n.* gravitation constant. **~কর্ষীয়** *a.* gravitational. **মহাকর্ষীয় একক** a gravitational unit. **~কাব্য** *n.* (ori.) a narrative poem consisting of more than eight cantos depicting the whole life of a hero born of a god or born with divine grace in him; (pop.) an epic; (rare) great poetry or a great poem. **~কাব্যীয়** *a.* epical, epic. **~কায়** *a.* having a huge body; huge, monstrous, colossal. **~কাল** *n.* (myth.) a terribly destructive manifestation of Shiva (শিব); eternity; time to come, the future. *fem.* **~কালী** a terribly destructive manifestation of Goddess Durga (দুর্গা). **~কাশ** *n.* (sc.) the firmament beyond the solar region, the stellar sky, the outer space; (pop.) the vast endless sky. **~কাশচারণা** *n.* space-travel. **~কাশচারী** *n.* a spaceman, an astronaut. *fem.* **~কাশচারিণী** a spacewoman. **~কাশযান** *n.* a spacecraft. **~গুরু** *n.* any one of the most venerable persons, namely, father, mother, the religious initiator and husband. **~জন** *n.* a very virtuous or great man; an illustrious man; a great merchant or stockist or wholesaler; a creditor; a usurer, a money lender; any one of the mediaeval poets who composed kirtan (কীর্তন) songs about Radha (রাধা) and Krishna (কৃষ্ণ). **~জনি** *n.* usury, money-lending. □ *a.* relating to usury or money-lending; usurious. **মহাজনি করা** *v.* to practise usury, to act as a money-lender. **মহাজনি-কারবার** *n.* money-lending business; banking. **~জাগতিক** *a.* cosmic. **~জাগতিক রশ্মি** cosmic ray. **~জ্ঞান** *n.* knowledge about reality, the final knowledge; the occult knowledge by dint of which a dead man can be brought back to life. **~জ্ঞানী** *n.* (ori.) possessing knowledge about ultimate reality; profoundly wise. **~ঢ্য** *a.* very rich or wealthy. **~তপা** *a.* & *n.* one who has practised or is still practising severest ascetical austerities. **~তেজ** *n.* great spirit or vigour; great heat. **~তেজস্বী, ~তেজা** *a.* highly spirited or vigorous. *fem.* **~তেজস্বিনী**। **~ত্মা** *a.* high-souled; very high-minded or noble. □ *n.* an appellation of Gandhi, the great leader of India. **~দেব** *n.* a great god; Shiva (শিব). *fem.* **~দেবী** a great goddess; Goddess Durga (দুর্গা); a title of a chief queen. **~দেশ** *n.* a continent; (rare) a great or noble country. **~দেশীয়** *a.* continental. **~দ্যুতি** *a.* of great splendour, very bright or radiant or effulgent. **~দ্রাবক** *n.* sulphuric acid. **~ধনবান, ~ধনী** *a.* very wealthy or rich. **~ধমনী** *n.* the aorta. **~ধর্মাধিকরণ** *n.* the High Court. **~নগর, ~নগরী** *n.* a great city; a metropolis, a capital. **~নগরীয়** *a.* metropolitan. **~নট** *n.* a great dancer or actor. **~নন্দ** *n.* great or exhilarating joy or delight. **~নবমী** *n.* the ninth lunar day of the light fortnight of the month of Aswin (আশ্বিন) or Kartik (কার্তিক) which is the fourth day of the autumnal worship of Goddess Durga (দুর্গা). **~নাগরিক** *n.* the mayor; (rare) a great citizen. **~নাদ** *n.* a terrible or very loud sound or report or roar. **~নিদ্রা** *n.* sleep that knows no breaking; death. **~নির্বাণ** *n.* (Buddhism) cessation of individual existence, nirvana; the death of Buddha. **~নিশা** *n.* midnight, night far advanced, the dead of night, the dead hours of the night. **মহানুভব, মহানুভাব** *a.* highminded, magnanimous, large-hearted. **মহানুভবতা** *n.* high-mindedness. **~পদ্ম** *n.* & *a.* hundred billion. **~পাতক** *n.* a deadly sin. **~পাতকী** *a.* guilty of one or more deadly sins. **~পাত্র** *n.* the chief counsellor of a state, the prime minister; (loos.) a court-counsellor or courtier of the highest rank. **~পাপ** same as **~পাতক**। **~পাপিষ্ঠ, ~পাপী** same as **~পাতকী**। *fem.* **~পাপিষ্ঠা, ~পাপিনী**। **~পুরুষ** *n.* a man with supernatural powers; a saint who has attained knowledge about God and reality and power to look upon the world dispassionately; a high-souled man; a superman. **~পূজা** *n.* a solemn worship. **~প্রভু** *n.* a great master or saint or prophet; an appellaton of Chaitanya (চৈতন্য). **~প্রয়াণ** *n.* voluntary journey to court one's death; death. **~প্রয়াণ করা** *v.* to set out voluntarily to court one's death; to die. **~প্রলয়** *n.* complete dissolution of the universe; a universal cataclysm. **~প্রসাদ** *n.* a part of the food-offering to Jagannath at Puri taken by devotees as a mark of the deity's grace; the highest divine grace; offering or altarage to deities; meat-offering to a deity. **~প্রস্থান** same as **মহাপ্রয়াণ**। **~প্রাণ** *a.* large-hearted, magnanimous; (gr.) aspirate. □ *n.* (gr.) an aspirate. **~প্রাণতা** *n.* large-heartedness, magnanimity; (gr.) aspiration. **~প্রাণী** *n.* life conceived as having an existence independent of the body, (cp.) atman, the soul. **~বল** *a.* very powerful; strong, mighty. **~বাক্য** *n.* a saying of a great man, a great saying or maxim. **~বাহু** *a.* having very long and mighty arms; very strong, mighty. **~বিক্রম** *a.* possessing great prowess or valour. **~বিদ্যা** *n.* any one of the ten manifestations of Goddess Durga (দুর্গা) ; (facet.) the art of stealing. **~বিদ্যালয়** *n.* a college. **~বিষুব** *n.* the vernal equinox. **~বিষুবরেখা** *n.* the line of the vernal equinox. **~বিষুবসংক্রান্তি** *n.* the transition of the sun in the Aries; the day of the aforesaid transition. **~বীর** *n.* a great hero; the great Jaina preacher. **~বৈদ্য** *n.* a great or chief physician; (sarcas.) a charlatan, a quack. **~বোধি** *n.* an embodiment of the highest or final knowledge; an appellation of Gautama Buddha; highest or final knowledge. **~ব্যবহারদেশক** *n.* attorney-general. **~ব্যাধি** same as **~রোগ**। **~ভাগ** *a.* very lucky or fortunate; high-minded, magnanimous, noble-minded; endowed with noble human qualities. **~ভাব** *n.* the ecstatic state caused by profundity of love, devotion etc. **~ভুজ** same as **~বাহু**। **~মণ্ডল** *n.* a great guild or association or concourse. **~মতি,** **~মনা** *a.* high-minded, magnanimous; high-souled. **~মন্ত্র** *n.* a great mantra or incantation; very sacred words of initiation (দেশসেবার মহামন্ত্র). **~মন্ত্রী** *n.* the prime minister; (euph.) a great minister. **~মহিম,** **~মহিমান্বিত** *a.* highly glorious or majestic, most excellent. *fem.* **~মহিমান্বিতা**। **~মহোপাধ্যায়** *n.* a teacher of great teachers or scholars; an official title given to distinguished Sanskrit scholars. **~মাংস** *n.* human flesh taken as food, human meat. **~মাত্য** *n.* the prime minister. **~মাত্র** *n.* the prime minister; the chief courtier; the chief executive of the government. **~মান্য** *a.* highly venerable or honourable. **~মান্য পোপ** His Holiness the Pope (whilst addressing the Pope: Your Holiness). **~মায়া** *n.* (phil.) illusion, the material world or nature; Goddess Durga (দুর্গা). **~মায়াচ্ছন্ন** *a.* overwhelmed with or enveloped in (divine) illusion; self-obliviously enmeshed in worldly affairs. **~মারী** *n.* a devastating epidemic, a pestilence, a plague. **~মারী কাণ্ড** (usu. facet.) a great affair, a tumultuous affair. **~মারী-পীড়িত** pestilence-stricken. **~মুনি** *n.* a great ascetic or sage. **~মূল্য** *a.* of great value; very costly, dear. **~যশা** *a.* very famous, highly and widely celebrated or renowned. **~যাত্রা** same as **~প্রয়াণ**। **~যান** *n.* one of the two communities of the Buddhists (cp. **হীনযান**). **~যুদ্ধ** *n.* a great war; (loos.) a world war. **~যোদ্ধা** *n.* a great warrior, a great soldier. **~যোগী** *n.* a great ascetic. **~রণ্য** *n.* a large and dense forest. **~রথ,** (inc.) **~রথী** *n.* (ori.) one who commands a host of charioted fighters; (loos.) a great warrior fighting from on a chariot. **~রণ** *n.* a great war or battle. **~রাজ** *n.* a great king; an emperor; a great ascetic. **~রাজা** *n.* a government title awarded to the feudal princes, zamindars, rich citizens etc. of India during the British regime, a maharaja. **~রাজাধিরাজ** *n.* a king of kings, an emperor; a title conferred on a big landowner during the British regime. **~রাজ্ঞী** *n. fem.* the wife of a great king; a great queen; an empress. **~রানা,** (*rej.*) **~রাণা** *n.* the title of the rulers of Udaipur (or Chitore). **~রানি** *n.* the wife of a great king, a great queen; an empress; the wife of a maharana (মহারানা) ; the wife of a maharaja. **~রাত্রি** *n.* midnight; a solemn night (কালীপূজার মহারাত্রি) ; a terrible night (মৃত্যুর মহারাত্রি). **~রাষ্ট্রীয়** *a.* of Maharashtra, Maharashtrian. **~রুদ্র** *n.* an awesome manifestation of Shiva (শিব). **~রোগ** *n.* an almost incurable and (usu.

obnoxious) disease; leprosy; an inveterately bad habit or mannerism. ~র্ঘ, ~র্ঘ্য *a.* precious; costly; high-priced, dear. **মহার্ণব** *n.* an ocean; a great sea. **মহার্হ** same as ~র্ঘ। ~লয়া *n.* the new-moon day immediately preceding the autumnal worship of Goddess Durga (দুর্গা). ~শক্তি Goddess Durga (দুর্গা) ; great strength or power or prowess. ~শক্তিধর, ~শক্তিশালী *a.* having great strength or power or prowess. *fem.* ~শক্তিশালিনী। ~শঙ্খ *n.* a dead man's skull; an enormous conch. □ *n.* & *a.* thousand billions. ~শয় *a.* high-minded, magnanimous; high-souled. □ *n.* a term of courtesy affixed to the name of a gentleman, (cp.) Mr. (*fem.* Mrs.), Sir (*fem.* Madam). *fem.* ~শয়া। ~শূন্য same as ~কাশ। ~ষ্টমী *n.* the eighth lunar day of the light fortnight of the month of Aswin (আশ্বিন) or Kartik (কার্তিক) which is the third day of autumnal worship of Goddess Durga (দুর্গা). ~সংকট *n.* a great crisis. ~সত্ত্ব *a.* having great strength; very noble or magnanimous; high-souled. ~সভা *n.* great meeting or association; a (representative) legislative assembly, a parliament; a congress. ~সমারোহে *adv.* with much pomp and grandeur. ~সমুদ্র, ~সাগর *n.* an ocean. **আটলানটিক বা অতলান্তিক মহাসাগর** the Atlantic (Ocean). **উত্তর মহাসাগর** the Arctic Ocean. **দক্ষিণ মহাসাগর** the Antarctic Ocean. **প্রশান্ত মহাসাগর** the Pacific (Ocean). **ভারত মহাসাগর** the Indian Ocean. ~সাগরীয় *a.* oceanic. ~সামন্ত *n.* a commander-in-chief; a great general. ~সিন্ধু same as ~সমুদ্র। ~সুযোগ *n.* the best chance, the greatest chance. ~সুখ *n.* a great pleasure. ~স্থবির *n.* one belonging to the highest order of Buddhist monks.

মহান *masc.* of **মহৎ**।

মহান্ত var. of **মহন্ত**।

মহাফেজ *n.* a record-keeper (esp. a government record-keeper). ~খানা *n.* a record-room, archive. **জাতীয় মহাফেজখানা** the National Archive.

মহাভারত *n.* the Mahabharata, the greatest epic of the world. **মহাভারত অশুদ্ধ হওয়া** (fig.) occurrence of a serious fault or lapse, (cp.) profanation of the Bible. **মহাভারত আরম্ভ করা** (fig.) to begin an intolerably long harangue; (fig.) to make a long introduction.

মহাল rej. form of **মহল**।

মহি alt. spell. of **মহী**।

মহিমময় *a.* glorious; majestic; exalted; dignified. *fem.* **মহিমময়ী**।

মহিমা *n.* divine grace or power; glory; majesty; exaltedness, dignity; charm, influence (টাকার মহিমা). ~কীর্তন করা *v.* to sing or narrate the glory of. **মহিমান্বিত** same as ~ময়। *fem.* **মহিমান্বিতা**। ~ব্যঞ্জক *a.* expressive of grace or glory or majesty or exaltedness or dignity or power.

মহিমার্ণব *n.* one regarded as an ocean of grace or glory or majesty or exaltedness or dignity or power.

মহিলা *n.* a lady, a gentlewoman; a woman. **মহিলা সংঘ** *n.* a women's club or association. **মহিলা সমাজ** *n.* womenfolk, women's society.

মহিষ *n.* the buffalo. ~ধ্বজ, ~বাহন *n.* appellations of Yama (যম), the god of death. ~মর্দিনী *n. fem.* (myth.) Goddess Durga (দুর্গা) who slew the demon Mahisa (মহিষ) ; (fig.) a terrible female warrior, (cp.) an amazon; (facet.) a termagant.

মহিষাসুর *n.* (myth.) Mahisa (মহিষ) the demon. ~মর্দিনী same as **মহিষমর্দিনী**।

মহিষী *n.* a queen; the chief queen of a king; a female buffalo.

মহী *n.* the earth.

মহীতল *n.* the surface of the earth; the ground; the earth.

মহীধর *n.* a mountain; a hill.

মহীন্দ্র, মহীপতি, মহীপাল *n.* a king.

মহীমণ্ডল *n.* the earth, the entire earth.

মহীয়ান *a.* very glorified or majestic or exalted or noble.

মহীরুহ *n.* a tree (esp. a big one); a plant.

মহীলতা *n.* an earthworm.

মহুয়া *n.* a kind of butter-tree or its seed or flower, the mahua. **মহুয়ার মউ, মহুয়ার মধু** the honey of mahua flower; a fat obtained from mahua seeds, mahua butter.

মহেন্দ্র *n.* Indra (ইন্দ্র), the king of gods, Indra the Great; a mythological mountain range identified with the Eastern Ghats. **~পুরী, ~ভবন** *n.* the city or residence of Mahendra (মহেন্দ্র). **মহেন্দ্রাণী** *n. fem.* Sachi (শচী), the wife of Mahendra (মহেন্দ্র).

মহেশ, মহেশ্বর *n.* Shiva (শিব), the god of gods. **মহেশপুরী** *n.* Kailasa (কৈলাস), the city or abode of Mahesha (মহেশ). **মহেশী, মহেশ্বরী** *n. fem.* Goddess Durga (দুর্গা), the wife of Mahesha (মহেশ).

মহেষ্বাস *a.* having great skill in archery. □ *n.* a great archer.

মহোৎসব *n.* a solemn or grand festival; a grand gala; a great communion of Vaishnavas singing kirtan (কীর্তন) songs and eating together.

মহোৎসাহ *n.* great enthusiasm or energy or zeal. **মহোৎসাহী** *n.* greatly enthusiastic or energetic or zealous. **মহোৎসাহে** *adv.* with great enthusiasm or zeal.

মহোদধি *n.* an ocean; a (great) sea.

মহোদয় *a.* very generous or high-minded or high-souled; highly prosperous or opulent; greatly elevated or exalted. *fem.* **মহোদয়া** ।

মহোদ্যম same as **মহোৎসাহ** ।

মহোন্নত *a.* highly elevated or exalted; very lofty; greatly flourishing or prosperous. **মহোন্নতি** *n.* great elevation or exaltedness or height or altitude or flourish or prosperity or progress.

মহোপকার *n.* a great good turn, great benefit or service. **মহোপকারক, মহোপকারী** *a.* very beneficial or serviceable; very benevolent; highly benign. □ *n.* a great benefactor.

মহৌষধ *n.* a great or infallible medicine; (cp.) panacea.

মহৌষধি *n.* any phosphorescent shrub or creeper; the common grass, (cp.) the bent grass; any plant having high medicinal quality.

মা[১] *n.* (mus.) the major fourth of the 'C'-scale.

মা[২] *n.* mother; (coll.) mom, mamma, mama, ma; (of beasts) dam. **মায়ের জাত** womenfolk, womanhood, womankind. **মায়ের দয়া** (fig.) small pox or chicken pox.

মাই *n.* the mammary gland, the mamma (pl. mammae); milk of the mammae; (dial. & sl.) breasts. **মাই খাওয়া** *v.* to suck one's mother's breast. **মাই খাওয়ানো** *v.* to give suck to, to suckle. **মাই ছাড়ানো** *v.* to wean (a baby). **মাইয়ের বোঁটা** the mamilla, the teat, the nipple.

মাইক, মাইক্রোফোন *n.* a microphone, a mike.

মাইনর *a.* underage. □ *n.* an underage person, a minor.

মাইনে *n.* monthly salary or wage. **মাস মাইনে** same as **মাইনে** ।

মাইপোষ *n.* a sucking-bottle, a feeding-bottle.

মাইফেল *n.* a party revelling in music and dance.

মাইয়া dial. var. of **মেয়ে** ।

মাইরি *int.* by Maria or Mary (used as an oath).

মাইল *n.* a mile. **~পোস্ট** *n.* a mile-stone, a mile-post.

মাউই, মাউই-মা, মাঐ, মাঐ-মা *n.* a mother-in-law or aunt-in-law of a brother or sister or cousin.

মাওবাদ *n.* the doctrine or theory of Mao ze-dong, Maoism.

মাংস *n.* flesh; meat. **গোমাংস** *n.* beef. **ছাগমাংস** *n.* goat's meat. **পাখির মাংস** *n.* fowl. **বাছুরের মাংস** *n.* veal. **মুরগির মাংস** *n.* fowl, (loos.) chicken. **মেষমাংস** *n.* mutton. **শুয়োরের মাংস** *n.* pork. **হরিণের মাংস** *n.* venison. **মাংসের দোকান** a meat-shop, a butcher's shop, a shamble, a butchery. **মাংসের বাজার** a meat-market; a flesh-market. **~তুল্য** *a.* flesh-like; meaty. **~পেশি** *n.* muscle. **~বিক্রেতা** *n.* a meat-seller, a butcher. **~বৃদ্ধি** *n.* growth of flesh; accumulation of fat; adiposity. **~ল** *a.* fleshy, plump, fatty, adipose. **মাংসাশী** *a.* meat-eating; carnivorous.

মাকড়, মাকড়সা *n.* the spider; an arachnid. **মাকড়সার জাল** a spider-web, a cobweb; gossamer.

মাকড়ি *n.* a variety of earring.

মাকনা *n.* young elephant whose tusks have not yet been cut.

মাকাল *n.* a lovely-looking fruit with offensive-smelling inedible pulp, (cp.) the colocynth; (fig.) a very handsome but worthless person.

মাকু *n.* a shuttle (of weavers).

মাকুন্দ *a.* & *n.* one who, though of age, has not yet grown one's beard.

মাক্ষিক *a.* relating to bees or flies. □ *n.* honey; pyrites (স্বর্ণমাক্ষিক).

মাখন, (dial.) **মাখম** *n.* butter. **মাখন তোলা** *v.* to skim butter or milk. **মাখন দাগানো** *v.* to clarify butter by boiling. **মাখন মাখানো** *v.* to butter. **মাখনতোলা দুধ** butter-milk. **মাখন-দাগানো ঘি** clarified butter. **~বিক্রেতা** *n.* a butter-seller. *fem.* **~বিক্রেত্রী** a butter-wife, a butter-woman. **~-মাখানো** *a.* buttered, buttery.

মাখা *v.* to smear, to dab, to daub, to coat (রং মাখা) ; to knead (ময়দা মাখা) ; to mix with spices etc. in order to make something ready for cooking, to lard (মাংস মাখা) ; to mix with curry etc. to make something ready for eating, (cp.) to sauce (ভাত মাখা). **মাখানো** *v.* to cause to smear or dab or coat or knead or lard. **~মাখি** *n.* mutual or repeated smearing (রং মাখামাখি) ; frequent social communication, intimacy, act of mixing freely with, close association (পুলিশের সঙ্গে মাখামাখি). **মাখামাখি করা** *v.* to smear mutually or repeatedly, to indulge in frequent social communication with, to form an intimacy with, to mix freely with.

মাগ *n.* (sl.) a wife.

মাগধ *a.* of or relating to Magadha, Magadhan. **মাগধী** *n.* Magadhi, the Prakritic language which is considered the source of Hindi and Bengali. **অর্ধমাগধী** *n.* a kind of Magadhi (মাগধী) corrupted with mixture of several Prakritic dialects.

মাগন *n.* begging or praying.

মাগনা *a.* obtained by begging. □ *a.* & *adv.* cost-free, free, gratis (মাগনা জিনিস, মাগনা খাটা).

মাগা *v.* to beg; to ask for; to solicit; to pray for.

মাগি *n.* (sl.) a woman; (sl.) a prostitute. **~বাড়ি** *n.* (sl.) a brothel. **~মিনসে** *n. pl.* (sl.) wife and husband; man and wife, a couple.

মাগুর *n.* a species of fresh-water barbel, (cp.) the catfish.

মাগ্‌গি *a.* exorbitantly high in price, dear. **~গণ্ডা** *n.* dearness and scarcity. **~গণ্ডার দিন** বা **বাজার** days of high price and scarcity. **~ভাতা** *n.* dearness allowance.

মা-গোঁসাই *n.* the wife of a religious preceptor, a religious preceptress; (facet) a very harmless, innocent and ineffective person.

মাঘ *n.* the tenth month of the Bengali calendar (from the middle of January to the middle of February). **মাঘী** *a.* of the month of Magha (মাঘ). □ *n.* the fullmoon day in the month of Magha (also **মাঘী পূর্ণিমা**). **মাঘোৎসব** *n.* a religious festival observed by the Brahmo Samaj in the month of Magha (মাঘ).

মাঙন var. of **মাগন**।

মাঙ্গলিক, মাঙ্গল্য *n.* scripturally auspicious things such as mango-twigs, sandal etc.. well-being, weal, welfare. □ *a.* suspicious, propitious. **মাঙ্গলিক দ্রব্য** same as **মাঙ্গলিক** (*n*).

মাচা, মাচান *n.* a platform, a dais; a shelf; a scaffold; a stage; a shooting-platform usu. up a tree, a machan.

মাছ *n.* fish. **মাছ ধরা** *v.* to catch fish, to fish. **নদীর মাছ** a river fish, a fresh -water fish. **নোনা মাছ** salted fish. **নোনা জলের মাছ** a salt-water fish. **পুকুরের মাছ** a fish reared in a pond. **শুঁটকি মাছ** dried fish. **সমুদ্রের মাছ** a marine fish. **মাছের কাঁটা** a fish-bone. **মাছের ঘেরি** fishery. **মাছের চাষ** pisciculture. **মাছের ঝুড়ি** a fish-creel. **মাছের ডিম** spawn (of fish). **মাছের পুকুর** a fish-pond, a fish-stew, a stew-pond, a piscina. **মাছের বাজার** a fish-market. **মাছের ভেড়ি** a fishy dam, a fishery. **~ওয়ালা** *n.* fishmonger; (loos.) a fisherman. *fem.* **~ওয়ালি** *n.* a fishwife, a fish-woman; (loos.) a fisherwoman. **মাছধরা জাহাজ** a trawler. **মাছধরা জাল** a fishing net. **মাছধরা নৌকা** a fishing boat; a trawler. **~ভাজা** *n.* fried fish, fishfry.

মাছরাঙা *n.* the kingfisher.

মাছি *n.* the fly; the sight-hole of a gun.

~মারা *a.* fly-killing (মাছিমারা ওষুধ) ; (contemp.) blindly copying or transcribing without exercising discretion (মাছিমারা কেরানি). **মাছিমারা ওষুধ** a fly-bane.

মাছুয়া *a.* of fish, piscine (মাছুয়া গন্ধ) ; fishing, piscatorial, piscatory (মাছুয়া জাতি) ; fish-selling (মাছুয়া বাজার). □ *n.* a fishmonger or fisherman, a fisher. coll. form **মেছো**। *fem. n.* **মাছুয়ানি** a fish-wife, a fish-woman, a fisher-woman.

মাজ *n.* (bot.) pith within a stem.

মাজন *n.* scouring or scrubbing; act of cleansing (as teeth) by rubbing, brushing etc.; a cleansing substance. **দাঁতের মাজন** a dentifrice, a toothpowder, a toothpaste.

মাজা[১] *n.* the waist, the loins.

মাজা[২] *v.* to scour or scrub; to cleanse (as teeth) by rubbing, brushing etc.; to polish (as gold ornaments). □ *a.* scoured or scurbbed; cleansed by rubbing, brushing etc.; polished; employed or used in scouring or scrubbing. □ *n.* same as **মাজন**। **বাসন-মাজা চাকর** a scullion. **বাসন-মাজা ঝি** a scullerymaid. ~**ঘষা** *n.* meticulous scouring scrubbing or polishing; meticulous cleansing and dressing (রূপের মাজাঘষা) ; meticulous training and practice (গায়কদের মাজাঘষা) ; meticulous correction and modification, careful chiselling (লেখার বা ছবির মাজাঘষা). **মাজানো** *v.* to cause to scour or scrub or cleanse or polish.

মাজুফল *n.* the gall-nut. **মাজুফলের রস** gallic acid.

মাঝ *n.* the middle, the centre; the inside or interior; the midst or company (পুরুষের মাঝে) ; the bottom of one's heart (আমার মাঝে). □ *a.* middle, half (মাঝপথ). **মাঝ থেকে** from the middle or centre or inside or interior or midst; from the bottom of one's heart; being innocently or unnecessarily involved (তোমরা করলে চুরি আর মাঝ থেকে সে খেল মার). ~**খান** same as **মাঝ** (*n.*). ~**খানে** same as **মাঝে**। ~**দরিয়া** *n.* mid-stream; mid-ocean, mid-sea. ~**নদী** *n.* mid-river, mid-stream. ~**নদীতে** *adv.* half way into the river. **মাঝে** *adv.* meanwhile, in the meantime. **মাঝেমধ্যে, মাঝেমাঝে** *adv.* off and on, from time to time, at times.

মাঝামাঝি *a.* almost middle or central; middling, moderate (মাঝামাঝি অবস্থা). □ *adv.* almost in or to the middle or centre; almost halfway; almost half (মাঝামাঝি করা).

মাঝার *n.* (poet.) same as **মাঝ**।

মাঝারি *a.* middling, moderate, of medium grade, quality, size etc.

মাঝি *n.* a helmsman, a steersman; a boatswain; a boatman; (amongst Santal people) a headman or a husband. ~**গিরি** *n.* the profession of a helmsman or steersman or boatswain or boatman. ~**মাল্লা** *n.* a helmsman and his subordinate boatmen; boatmen; a boatswain and his subordinate sailors. ~**য়ান** *n. fem.* (amongst Santal people) the wife of a headman or a wife.

মাঝে, মাঝেমাঝে see **মাঝ**।

মাঞ্জা *n.* a glue made of powdered glass etc. for coating the string by which a kite is flown.

মাটকলাই *n.* groundnut, monkey-nut, earth-nut.

মাটকোঠা *n.* a mud-built house consisting of two or more stories.

মাটাপালাম *n.* a coarse borderless white fabric or loincloth.

মাটাম *n.* a try-square, a trying-square. ~**সই** *a.* placed or set at right angle, perpendicular.

মাটি *n.* earth; clay; soil; dust or dirt; the ground, the floor; landed property, land; the surface of the earth; the earth, the world; foothold. **মাটি করা** *v.* to spoil, to ruin; to impair. **মাটি কামড়ে (পড়ে) থাকা** (fig.) to keep lying to the ground immovable and motionlessly with all one's might and main (as by a wrestler); to persist doggedly. **মাটি দেওয়া** *v.* to bury, to inter. **মাটি মাড়ানো** *v.* (coll.) to come or visit. **মাটি হওয়া** *v.* to be spoiled. **পায়ের তলার মাটি সরে যাওয়া** (fig.) to lose one's foothold, to be utterly deprived of support, (cp.) to cut the grass from under one's feet. **মাটির**

দর dirt cheap. মাটির বাসন earthenware; crockery. মাটির দরে বিক্রি করা to sell for a mere trifle. মাটির মানুষ a very gentle and forbearing and honest man perfectly free from crookedness. বিলাতি মাটি cement. বেলেমাটি sandy soil.

মাটো *a.* lacklustre, dull (মাটো রং) ; uninteresting (মাটো খেলা) ; not thorough or compact (মাটো কাজ).

মাঠ *n.* a field, a maidan; a tract of agricultural land, land; a grazing ground, a pasture; an extensive open space (মাঠে মাঠে ঘোরা) ; a playing-field, a playground, a ground. **মাঠে মারা যাওয়া** (fig.) to be utterly lost or wasted. **~ঘাট** *n.* every place.

মাঠা *n.* cream (of milk); butter; whey, buttermilk. **মাঠা তোলা** *v.* to skim the butter. **মাঠা-তোলা দুধ** skim-milk, skimmed milk.

মাঠাকরুন *n.* mother, madam (used in politely addressing a lady).

মাঠাম var. of **মাটাম**।

মাড় *n.* (liquefied) starch extracted from rice etc. by boiling or used in the laundry as a stiffener. **মাড় দেওয়া** *v.* to starch.

মাড়া *v.* to pound (ওষুধ মাড়া) ; to thresh (as corn); to tread or trample. **মাড়াই** *n.* threshing. **মাড়ানো** *v.* to tread or trample.

মাড়ি pop. var. of **মাঢ়ী**।

মাঢ়ী *n.* (anat.) the gum. **মাঢ়ীর দাঁত** a cheek-tooth, a molar tooth.

মাণবক *n.* a (male) child; a manikin, a dwarf.

মাণিক rej. spell. of **মানিক**।

মাণিক্য *a.* ruby; (loos.) a gem.

মাত[1] *a.* thoroughly maddened or overwhelmed (নেশায় মাত) or charmed or captivated (গানে মাত, আসর মাত) or replete or pervaded (গন্ধে মাত). **মাত করা** *v.* to madden or overwhelm or charm or captivate or replete or pervade thoroughly.

মাত[2] *n.* (in chess) checkmating; act of defeating thoroughly (প্রতিপক্ষকে মাত করা) ; act of winning outright (বাজি মাত করা). □ *a.* checkmated; completely defeated. **মাত করা** *v.* to checkmate; to defeat thoroughly; to win outright.

মাতঃ, (pop.) **মাত[3]** *n.* (voc.) O mother.

মাতগুড় *n.* drossy molasses, treacle.

মাতঙ্গ *n.* the elephant. *fem.* **মাতঙ্গী,** (loos.) **মাতঙ্গিনী** the female elephant; (myth.) one of the ten manifestations of Goddess Durga (দুর্গা).

মাতন *n.* maddened state ; act of running amuck; frenzy; madness; (of elephants etc.) must; state of being beside oneself; absorption; feverish enthusiasm; excitement; revelry; a revel-rout; fermentation.

মাতব্বর *n.* a leader, a headman; a distinguished or influential man, a man of position. □ *a.* leading, distinguished, influential. **মাতব্বরি** *n.* (dero.) bossing; posing as a distinguished or influential or important man.

মাতলামি, মাতলামো *n.* drunken revel or revelry, riotous drunkenness.

মাৎসর্য *n.* envy, malice, spite; grudge, malevolence.

মাৎস্য *a.* piscine. □ *n.* one of the Puranas. **~ন্যায়** *n.* the principle that larger fishes will devour or gobble up the smaller ones; (pol.) a lawless or chaotic state in which the strong oppresses the weak.

মাতা[1] *n.* mother. **~পিতা** *n. pl.* parents. **~পিতৃহীন** *a.* parentless, orphan. *fem.* **~পিতৃহীনা**। **~মহ** *n.* the father or an uncle of one's mother, a maternal grandfather. *fem.* **~মহী** the mother or an aunt of one's mother, a maternal grandmother.

মাতা[2] *v.* to go mad; (of elephants etc.) to be seized with must, to be in must; to run amuck; to be frenzied or maddened; to be beside onelself, to be overwhelmed with; to be absorbed (in); to become feverishly enthusiastic; to be greatly excited; to indulge in a revel-rout; to rise and swell by the action of fermentation, to ferment.

মাতানো *v.* to send one mad; (of elephants etc.) to cause to be in must; to send one amuck; to madden; to overwhelm; to cause to be absorbed (in); to excite greatly; to cause to indulge in a revel-rout; to delight greatly; to ferment.

□ *a.* maddening, highly delightful (মনমাতানো গন্ধ).

মাতাপিতা, মাতাপিতৃহীন, মাতামহ, মাতামহী see **মাতা**[১] ।

মাতামাতি *n.* drunken revelry; great excitement; feverish activities or enthusiasm; revelry; romping naughtiness.

মাতাল *a.* intoxicated with wine, drunk, drunken; sozzled; addicted to drinking wine esp. to excess; infatuated, beside oneself; saturated. □ *n.* a drunk person; a boozer, a drunkard.

মাতুঃষ্বসা, মাতুঃস্বসা *n.* a mother's sister or cousin-sister, a maternal aunt.

মাতুল *n.* a mother's brother or cousin-brother, a maternal uncle. *fem.* **মাতুলানী, মাতুলী** the wife of a maternal uncle. **মাতুলালয়** *n.* the home or residence of a maternal uncle.

মাতৃ *n.* (in comp.) mother. **~ক** *a.* maternal; motherly; treated or fostered as by one's mother, mothered (নদীমাতৃক দেশ). **~কল্প** same as **~তুল্য** । **~কা** *n.* any one of a group of sixteen female deities; mother; one's mother's mother; a nurse; any one of the alphabetical letters; a matron. **~কুল** *n.* the mother's line, the distaff side. **~গণ** *n.* the eight divine female powers. **~ঘাতক, ~ঘাতী** *a.* guilty of or relating to matricide, matricidal. **~তুল্য, ~তুল্যা** *a.* deserving to be treated as one's mother; behaving as one's mother; motherly. **~দায়** *n.* the responsibility of performing the obsequies of one's deceased mother; (loos.) one's mother's death. **~দায়গ্রস্ত** *a.* charged with the onus of performing the obsequies of one's deceased mother; (loos.) in mourning for one's lately deceased mother. **~দুগ্ধ** *n.* mother's milk. **~পক্ষ** same as **~কুল** । **~পূজা** *n.* act of serving or adoring one's mother. **~বৎ** *adv.* (also *a.*) like one's mother. **মাতৃবৎ পরদারেষু** one should look upon another's wife as one's mother. **~বিয়োগ** *n.* mother's death. **~ভক্ত** *a.* devoted or deeply attached to one's mother. **~ভক্তি** *n.* devotion to one's mother. **~ভাষা** *n.* mother-tongue; vernacular. **~ভূমি** *n.* motherland, native land, mother-country. **~রিষ্টি** *n.* an inauspicious conjunction of planets in one's horoscope foreboding danger to one's mother's life. **~শাসন** *n.* matriarchy. **~শাসিত** *a.* matriarchal. **~শ্রাদ্ধ** *n.* the obsequies of one's deceased mother. **~ষ্বসা** same as **মাতুঃষ্বসা** । **~ষ্বস্রীয়, ~ষ্বস্রেয়** *n.* a son of one's mother's sister or cousin-sister. **~ষ্বস্রীয়া, ~ষ্বস্রেয়া** a daughter of one's mother's sister or cousin-sister. **~সম, ~সমা** same as **~তুল্য** । **~সেবা** same as **~পূজা** । **~স্তন্য** *n.* mother's milk. **~স্তব, ~স্তোত্র** *n.* a hymn or incantation of the sublime female energy associated with the work of creation; a hymn or incantation of any female deity; a devotional hymn offered to one's mother. **~হত্যা** *n.* matricide. **~হত্যাকারী** same as **~ঘাতক** । *fem.* **~হত্যাকারিণী** । **~হন্তা** *n.* a matricide. *fem.* **~হন্ত্রী** । **~হীন** *a.* motherless. *fem.* **~হীনা** ।

মাতোয়ারা, (rare) **মাতোয়ালা** *a.* rapt (in); beside oneself (with); besotted, drunken.

মাত্র (ori.) *n.* amount, measure, total. □ *adv.* only, merely (মাত্র দু-সের দুধ) ; just (এইমাত্র). □ *con.* as soon as (আমি আসামাত্র সে চেঁচিয়ে উঠল). □ *prep.* only for (ক্ষণমাত্র). □ *a.* every (মনুষ্যমাত্র অসুখী) ; mere (সে বালক মাত্র).

মাত্রা *n.* amount, measure, degree (শীতের মাত্রা) ; a dose (ওষুধের মাত্রা) ; limit (মাত্রাহীন লোভ) ; a horizontal straight line put over the consonants and some vowels of the Bengali alphabet; either of the measures long and short into which the letters of the alphabet are grouped; (pros.) a unit for measuring syllables (esp. in Sanskrit verses); a unit of division in Indian musical measure; (math.) dimension; (phys.) mass; (phys.) a unit of measure. **মাত্রা ছাড়ানো** *v.* to go beyond the limit of (decency etc.). **~জ্ঞান, ~বোধ** *n.* sense of proportion. **~তত্ত্ব** *n.* (med.) posology. **~বৃত্ত** *n.* (pros.) a system of metrical measure depending on differentiating alphabetical letters into long and short. **~হীন** *a.* limitless, boundless.

মাত্রিক *a.* (used as a *sfx.*) (gr. & *pros.*)

measured as long or short (দীর্ঘমাত্রিক, লঘুমাত্রিক) ; (mus.) consisting of a particular number of units of musical measure (ত্রিমাত্রিক তাল).

মাথট *n.* poll-tax; a capital levy.

মাথা *n.* the head; top, summit, crest (পাহাড়ের মাথা) ; tip (আঙুলের মাথা) ; end, extremity (পেনসিলের মাথা) ; a bend, a corner (চৌমাথা) ; prow (of a boat); brain, intellect (অঙ্কে বেশ মাথা) ; a headman, a chief, a leader (গাঁয়ের মাথা) ; an adviser, a counsellor (সব কূটবুদ্ধির মাথা তিনি). □ *int.* denoting: nothing (মাথা করবে). **মাথা আঁচড়ানো** *v.* to comb one's hair. **মাথা উঁচু করা** same as **মাথা তোলা**। **মাথা উড়ানো** *v.* to cut off one's head, to behead. **মাথা কাটা যাওয়া** *v.* (fig.) to be greatly ashamed; to be shamefully disgraced. **মাথা কোটা** *v.* to strike one's head (esp. repeatedly) against the floor or wall as a violent expression of huff, grief etc. **মাথা খাও** *int.* (used as an oath) you will eat my head if you will or will not do this, (cp.) for the love of me, beshrew me. **মাথা খাওয়া** *v.* (fig.) to ruin; to spoil; (fig.) to deprave. **মাথা খারাপ করা** *v.* (fig.) to chafe, to fret, to lose one's head. **মাথা খেলা** *v.* to have aptitude for (অঙ্কে মাথা খেলে). **মাথা খেলানো** *v.* (fig.) to strive to think out; to apply one's mind. **মাথা খোঁড়া** same as **মাথা কোটা**। **মাথা গরম করা** *v.* (fig.) to get angry. **মাথা গরম হওয়া** *v.* (fig.) to get angry; (fig.) to lose one's head; to have one's head turned; to feel giddy. **মাথা গলানো** *v.* to enter or pass or force one's head through; to interfere with, to poke one's nose into. **মাথা গুঁড়ো করা** *v.* to break one's skull; to dash one's brains out, to brain. **মাথা গুনতি করা** *v.* (fig.) to count the number of persons, to count the heads. **মাথা গুলিয়ে দেওয়া** *v.* (fig.) to nonplus, to bewilder, to confound. **মাথা গুলিয়ে যাওয়া** *v.* (fig.) to be nonplussed or confounded. **মাথা গোঁজা** *v.* (fig.) to take shelter somehow or with difficulty. **মাথা ঘষা** *v.* (women's) washing the head with soap or shampoo. **মাথা ঘামানো** see **ঘামানো**। **মাথা ঘোরা** *v.* to feel dizzy or giddy; (fig.) to have one's head turned. **মাথা ঘোরানো** *v.* to make one feel dizzy or giddy; (fig.) to turn one's head. **মাথা চাড়া দেওয়া** *v.* (fig.) to flourish, to thrive; (fig.) to assert oneself; (fig.) to rise in revolt. **মাথা চালা** *v.* to apply one's brain; (fig.) to cogitate. **মাথা চুলকানো** *v.* to scratch one's head as a mark of confusion or inability to think out something. **মাথা ঠান্ডা করা** *v.* (fig.) to cool down, to cool down one's anger or temper. **মাথা ঠান্ডা রাখা** *v.* (fig.) to keep one's head; to remain cool-headed or calm; (fig.) to keep one's countenance. **মাথা তোলা** *v.* to raise one's head; to look up; (fig.) to flourish, to thrive; (fig.) to assert oneself; (fig.) to hold one's head; (fig.) to rise in revolt. **মাথা দেওয়া** *v.* (fig.) to sacrifice one's life; (fig.) to bother; (fig.) to pay attention to. **মাথা ধরা** *v.* to have a headache. **মাথা নেওয়া** *v.* (fig.) to behead. **মাথা নোয়ানো** *v.* (fig.) to yield (to), to acknowledge the superiority or authority (of). **মাথা পেতে নেওয়া** *v.* (fig.) to accept tamely. **মাথা বাঁধা দেওয়া, মাথা বিকানো** *v.* (fig.) to enslave oneself (to), to sell one's soul (to); (fig.) to be over head and ears (দেনায় মাথা বিকানো). **মাথা মাটি হওয়া** *v.* (fig.) to impair or waste one's intelligence or intellect; (fig.) to become dull-headed or stupid. **মাথা হেঁট করা** *v.* to hang down one's head in shame; (fig.) to yield (to), to acknowledge the superiority or authority (of), to humiliate oneself. **মাথা হেঁট হওয়া** *v.* (fig.) to lose face, to be disgraced; (fig.) to be put to shame, to be put out of countenance. **মাথায় ওঠা** same as **মাথায় চড়া**। **মাথায় করা** *v.* (fig.) to honour very highly; (fig.) to fill with uproar. (চেঁচিয়ে বাড়ি মাথায় করা). **মাথায় কাপড় দেওয়া** *v.* to veil one's head with a portion of one's loincloth (as done by oriental women). **মাথায় খুন চড়া (চাপা)** *v.* to become extremely angry; to get furious, to fly into a towering rage. **মাথায় ঘোল ঢালা** (fig.) to humiliate (a person). **মাথায় চড়া** *v.* (path.) to go up in the brain (বায়ু মাথায় চড়া) ; (fig.) to take liberties (with) or become audacious (being encouraged by indulgence). **মাথায় ঢোকা** *v.* to be comprehensible to, to be understood by; to be seized with a notion or fancy; to be stricken with (মাথায় ভয় ঢোকা) ; to have a brain-wave (মাথায় নতুন আইডিয়া ঢোকা). **মাথায় তোলা** *v.* to give excessive indulgence; to give undue importance; to honour greatly (তাঁকে আমরা মাথায় তুলে রেখেছি). **মাথায় রাখা** *v.* (fig.) to treat with great adoration or respect or cordiality or care; (fig.) to abide by or observe with great devotion or care. **মাথার উপর কেউ না থাকা** *v.* to have no guardian. **মাথার ঘাম পায়ে ফেলা** v. (fig.) to sweat and drudge. **মাথার ঠাকুর** (fig.) a very venerable or dear person. **মাথার ঠিক না থাকা** *v.* (fig.) to be nonplussed or confounded; (fig.) to lose one's head. **মাথার তালু** top of the head, the crown. **মাথার দিব্যি** a self-imprecatory oath. **মাথা নেই তার মাথা ব্যথা** (fig.) much ado about nothing. **~ওয়ালা** *a.* brainy, intelligent. **~-কামড়ানি** *n.* same as **মাথাব্যথা**। **~-খারাপ** *a.* crack-brained; nutty; demented, crazy; lunatic. **মাথা-খারাপ লোক** a crack-brain; a nutty person; a lunatic. **~গরম** *a.* short-tempered. **মাথা ধরা** *n.* headache. **~পাগলা** same as **~খারাপ**। **~পিছু, ~প্রতি** *adv.* per capita. **~ব্যথা** *n.* headache; (fig.) worry; (fig.) concern; (fig.) responsibility. **~ভারী** *a.* top-heavy. **~মুন্ডু** *n.* head or tail (মাথামুন্ডু বুঝতে না পারা = unable to make head or tail). **~মোটা** dull-headed.

মাথাল *n.* a kind of improvised wicker-umbrella; the top of a pillar, a capital.

মাথালো *a.* brainy, intelligent.

মাথি *n.* the pith within the stem of the coconut-tree, date-tree etc.

মাথুর *a.* of Mathura (মথুরা) in India. □ *n.* a cycle of songs ventilating the sorrow of the people of Brindaban caused by Krishna's (কৃষ্ণ) departure to Mathura; song of this cycle.

মাদক *a.* intoxicating, inebriant (মাদক দ্রব্য). □ *n.* an intoxicant, an inebriant, a drug. **মাদক গ্রহণ** বা **সেবন করা** *v.* to take drug esp. narcotics habitually, to drug; to drug oneself. **~তা** *n.* intoxicating property or power. **~বর্জন** *n.* abstention from drug-taking; prohibition. **মাদকবর্জন করা** *v.* to abstain from drug-taking. **~সেবন** *n.* drug-addiction. **~সেবী** *a.* addicted to drugs esp. narcotics. □ *n.* a drug-addict, a drug-fiend.

মাদল *n.* a kind of tom-tom played on by the Santal (সাঁওতাল) people.

মাদার *n.* the coral tree.

মাদি *a.*(esp. of inferior creatures) female, (cp.) she- (মাদি কুকুর).

মাদুর *n.* a mat. **~কাঠি** *n.* dried stalk of a kind of grass used in weaving mats.

মাদুলি *n.* an amulet (usu. shaped like a tom-tom).

মাদৃশ *a.* like me; like myself. *fem.* **মাদৃশী**।

মাদ্রাজি *a.* of Madras (মাদ্রাজ). □ *n.* a native of Madras.

মাদ্রাসা *n.* a madrasa, a madrasah.

মাধব *a.* relating to honey; honeyed. □ *n.* Krishna (কৃষ্ণ) or Vishnu (বিষ্ণু). **মাধবী, মাধবিকা, মাধবীলতা** *n.* an evergreen creeper, (cp.) the myrtle. **মাধবীকুঞ্জ** *n.* a myrtle-bower.

মাধুকরী *n.* act of begging from door to door like the bee gathering honey from flower to flower.

মাধুরিমা inc. variant of **মধুরিমা**।

মাধুরী, মাধুর্য *n.* sweetness; deliciousness; pleasantness; beauty; (rhet.) elegance of style.

মাধ্বী *a.* kind of wine produced from honey; honey. **~ক** *n.* same as **মাধ্বী**।

মাধ্যন্দিন *a.* of midday or noon. **~রেখা** *n.* (astr. & geog.) the meridian.

মাধ্যম *n.* a medium.

মাধ্যমিক *a.* of the second stage or standard; middling; secondary. **মাধ্যমিক শিক্ষা** secondary education.

মাধ্যাকর্ষণ *n.* (sc.) gravitation or gravity. **মাধ্যাকর্ষণ-সূত্র** *n.* the law of gravitation.

মাধ্যাহ্নিক *a.* of noon or midday; meridian. *fem.* **মাধ্যাহ্নিকী**। **~ক্রিয়া** *n.* midday rites.

মাধ্যিক *n.* (bot.) a median.

মান[১] *n.* a unit or instrument of measure or weight, a measure; measuring or weighing; a unit of Indian musical measure; (math.) value; (alg.) degree; a standard. ~নির্ধারণ *n.* standardization.

মান২ *n.* honour, respect; cordial reception; fame; dignity; pride; (dero.) vanity. **মান দেওয়া** *v.* to treat with honour or deference. **মান রাখা** *v.* to do honour to, to respect, to heed; to do the honours (to); to save one's face.

মান৩ *n.* huff caused by undesirable behaviour of a beloved person; tiff, sulks, pique. **মান করা** *v.* to be in a huff, to huff, to sulk. **মান ভরে** *adv.* in a fit of pique or resentment. **মান ভাঙানো** *v.* to win over or placate a beloved who is in a huff.

মান৪, মানকচু *n.* the arum.

মানকলি *n.* a quarrel between husband and wife; a lover's quarrel.

মানচিত্র *n.* a map; a chart. **মানচিত্র অভিক্ষেপ** *n.* (geog.) stereographic projection. **~কার, ~কর** *n.* a cartographer. **~বিদ্যা** *n.* cartography, chartography. **মানচিত্রাঙ্কন** *n.* map-drawing. **মানচিত্রাবলি** *n.* maps; a book of maps, an atlas.

মানত *n.* a promise to offer a particular sacrifice to a deity on fulfilment of a prayer, a vow.

মানদ *a.* bestowing or conferring honour upon; fetching honour to.

মানদণ্ড *n.* a measuring rod, a measure; a standard or unit of measurement.

মানদা *fem.* of **মানদ**।

মানন, মাননা *n.* honouring or respecting; cordial reception; obeying; believing; acknowledgement, owing admission; heading; observance; act of calling on or appealing to or citing; act of promising to offer in sacrifice, vowing.

মাননীয় *a.* honourable; venerable; respectable. *fem.* **মাননীয়া**। **মাননীয়েষু** *adv.* to an honourable person (used as a polite mode of addressing a letter). *fem.* **মাননীয়াসু**।

মানপত্র *n.* an address of honour, a written felicitation.

মানব *n.* mankind, man; a man; a human being, a person. □ *a.* relating to or drawn up by Manu (মনু) the law-giver (মানব-ধর্মশাস্ত্র). *fem. n.* **মানবী** woman-kind; a woman. **মানবক** pop. spell. of **মাণবক**। **~চরিত্র** *n.* human nature or character. **~জাতি** *n.* mankind, humankind, the human race. **~জীবন** *n.* the human life, the life of man. **~তা, ~ত্ব** *n.* humanity. **মানবতাবাদ** *n.* humanism. **~ধর্ম** *n.* the religion of man; humanity. **~প্রকৃতি** *n.* human nature. **~লীলা** *n.* activities of a human being whilst existing upon the earth; existence as a human being. **মানবলীলা সংবরণ করা** *v.* to die, to breathe one's last. **~সমাজ** *n.* human world, mankind; the human society. **~হীন** *a.* having no human dweller, depopulated, desolate. **~হৃদয়** *n.* man's heart, the human heart; humane feelings. **মানবিক** *a.* human; humane. **মানবিক বিদ্যা** the humanities. **মানবীয়** *a.* human; humane. **মানবোচিত** *a.* befitting a human being, humane; (loos.) human.

মানবিন্দু *n.* (phys.) any of the fixed points (of a thermometer).

মানবী, মানবীয়, মানবোচিত see **মানব**।

মনভঙ্গ, মানভঞ্জন *n.* allaying of one's huff. **মানভঞ্জন করা** *v.* to allay one's huff. **মানভঞ্জন-পালা** *n.* a group of songs written about the soothing of Radha's (রাধা) huff by Krishna (কৃষ্ণ).

মানমন্দির *n.* an observatory.

মানময়ী *n. fem.* huffy; touchy.

মানমর্যাদা *n.* honour and dignity. **মানমর্যাদা রক্ষা করা** *v.* to keep up or maintain (one's) prestige.

মানস *n.* the mind; desire, intention, purpose. □ *a.* mental; inward; concealed in the mind; imaginary or fancied. **মানস করা** *v.* to desire, to intend, to purpose. **~কন্যা** *n.* a daughter born to one out of one's mind or fancy. **~তা** *n.* mentality. **~নেত্র** *n.* the mind's eye, the inward eye; imagination or fancy. **~পট** *n.* the canvas of the mind; imagination or fancy. **~পুত্র** *n.* a son born to one out of one's mind or fancy. **~প্রতিমা** *n.* an image conceived in the mind, a mental image. **~বিজ্ঞান** *n.* mental science. **~রাজ্য** *n.* the realm of fancy or imagination. **~সিদ্ধি** *n.* fulfilment of a desire or intention; attainment of an end. **~সুন্দরী, মানসী** *n.*

fem. the graceful woman of one's imagination.

মানসম্ভ্রম *n.* honour and prestige or modesty.

মানসাঙ্ক *n.* a mathematical sum to be worked out mentally.

মানসিক *a.* mental (মানসিক ব্যাধি) ; imaginary or fancied (মানসিক ভয়). □ *n.* a sacrifice or offering promised to a deity on condition that one's prayer be granted. **মানসিক করা** *v.* to promise a sacrifice or offering to a deity on condition that a prayer be granted. **মানসিক দেওয়া** *v.* to offer a promised sacrifice to a deity on fulfilment of a prayer.

মানসী *a. fem.* conceived by the mind, fancied (মানসী প্রতিমা). □ *n. fem.* a woman or sweet-heart of one's fancy (কবি মানসী).

মানহানি *n.* defamation; a libel. **মানহানি করা** *v.* to defame; to libel. **~কর** *a.* defamatory; libellous. **মানহানির মোকদ্দমা** a defamation case; a libel suit.

মানা[১] *n.* prohibition, forbidding. **মানা করা** v. to prohibit, to forbid.

মানা[২] *n.* to honour, to show respect to, to revere (গুরুজনকে মানা) ; to believe in (ভূতপ্রেত মানা) ; to regard, to count (ভাগ্য বলে মানা) ; to acknowledge, to admit, to own (অপরাধ মানা) ; to acknowledge the authority of (রাজাকে মানা) ; to obey, to abide by (উপদেশ মানা) ; to observe (শাস্ত্রীয় নিয়ম মানা) ; to heed (বাধা মানা) ; to accept, to yield to (সান্ত্বনা মানা) ; to call on or cite (সাক্ষী মানা).

মানান *n.* fittingness; becomingness; propriety; decorousness, decorum; beauty. □ *a.* fitting; becoming; decorous.

মানানসই *a.* same as **মানান** (*a.*).

মানানো[১] *v.* to cause to honour or revere or believe in or regard or count or acknowledge or own or obey or observe or heed or accept or yield to or call on.

মানানো[২] *v.* to befit, to become; to suit; to fit.

মানিক *n.* ruby; a jewel; (fig.) a precious object, an object of joy or hope. **~জোড়** *n.* a variety of egrets usually moving in pairs; (fig.–often dero.) a pair of inseparable friends or associates.

মানী *a.* honoured, respected; respectable, honourable; having prestige or dignity; particular about one's own prestige or dignity; egotistic; vainglorious; touchy. *fem.* **মানিনী** in all the senses of **মানী,** and esp.–one who often sulks on account of amorous quarrel; huffy.

মানুষ *n.* the human race, man; a man; a human being (male or female), a person; a grown-up person, an adult; proper human being (তোরা মানুষ হ). **মানুষ করা** *v.* to rear, to bring up (ছেলে মানুষ করা) ; to train one to be a proper man. **মানুষ হওয়া** *v.* to be brought up; to grow up, to become an adult; to grow up into a proper man. **~খেকো** *a.* maneating. □ *n.* a maneater. **~জন** *n.* men, people (মানুষজন দেখছি না). **মানুষের মতো মানুষ** a proper man; a great or eminent person; a man of worth; an ideal man. **মানুষিক** *a.* human. **মানুষী** *a.* human. □ *n.* a woman; womankind.

মানে *n.* meaning,interpretation, import, significance, implication; motive, purpose, cause (আন্দোলনের মানে) ; utility (জমি পতিত রাখার মানে কী ?). **মানে করা** *v.* to interpret; to expound; to explain. **মানে বোঝা** *v.* to comprehend the meaning or motive or intention or utility of. **মানে বোঝানো** *v.* to mean, to signify; to imply; to explain the meaning of. **মানে হওয়া** *v.* to serve a purpose; to be of any use; to convey a meaning.

মানে-বই *n.* a book of explanatory notes; a help-book, a key.

মানে-মানে *adv.* whilst one's prestige or dignity is still unimpaired.

মানোয়ার *n.* a man-of-war; a battleship, a warship. **মানোয়ারি** *a.* serving on board a warship, employed in the navy, naval; used in war.

মান্দাস *n.* a raft, a float.

মান্দ্য *n.* lack of natural urge, dearth, loss, decrease, dullness (ক্ষুধামান্দ্য) ; impairment (অগ্নিমান্দ্য) ; slowness; sloth; inertia.

মান্ধাতা *n.* a mythological king. **মান্ধাতার**

আমল time immemorial, time out of mind.

মান্য *a.* same as **মাননীয়** । □ *n.* honour, respect, cordial reception (মান্য করা); a gift of honour, a complimentary present (মান্য দেওয়া) ; compliance, observance. *fem. a.* **মান্যা** । **মান্য করা** *v.* to honour, to respect, to accord cordial reception (to); to comply with, to observe. **~গণ্য** *a.* respectable and important. **~বর** *a.* highly honourable or venerable or respectable. **~বরেষু** *adv.* to a highly respectable person (used as a polite mode of addressing a letter).

মাপ[1] *n.* pardon, excuse; remission; exemption. **মাপ করা** *v.* to pardon, to forgive, to excuse; to remit, to exempt.

মাপ[2] *n.* measure; dimension; measurement. **মাপ নেওয়া** *v.* to take measurements of, to measure. **মাপে হওয়া** *v.* to be of a particular measure or size, to measure; to fit in measurements. **~কাঠি, ~কাটি** *n.* a measuring-rod; a measure; a standard. **~জোখ, ~জোক** *n.* measurements; measurement; surveying. **মাপজোখ করা** *v.* to measure minutely; to survey. **~দড়ি** *n.* measuring rope or tape. **~সই** *a.* & *adv.* conforming to particular measurements. **~ক** *a.* measuring or weighing. □ *n.* a measure; a weigher. **~ন** *n.* measuring or weighing or sounding. **~দণ্ড** *n.* a measuring-rod. **~যন্ত্র** *n.* a weighing-machine. **~রজ্জু** *n.* a sounding-line, a plumb-line. **মাপনী** *n.* (geom.) a ruler, a scale.

মাপা *v.* to measure; to weigh; to survey (জমি মাপা) ; to measure the depth of, to sound; (fig.) to try to assess the importance or weight of. □ *a.* measured; weighed; surveyed; sounded; restrained, controlled, restricted (মাপা কথা, মাপা খাওয়া). **~জোখা, ~জোকা** *a.* conforming accurately to a particular measure, measured; restrained, controlled, restricted. □ *n.* measuring or surveying. **মাপানো** *v.* to cause to measure or weigh or survey or sound.

মাফ var. of **মাপ**[1] ।

মাফলার *n.* a scarf, a muffler; a comforter.

মাফিক *a.* like ; conforming to (রুচিমাফিক).

মাভৈঃ *v. imp.* (used as *int.*) don't fear, be not afraid. □ *a.* expelling fear (মাভৈঃ বাণী).

মামড়ি *n.* an encrustation, a scab. **মামড়ি পড়া** *v.* to develop a scab, to scab.

মামদো *n.* a ghost of a Mussalman. **~বাজি** *n.* (fig.) boastful and threatening behaviour, bluff, bluster.

মা-মরা *a.* motherless.

মামলা same as **মোকদ্দমা** । **~বাজ** *a.* litigious; barratrous. **~বাজি** *n.* litigiousness; barratry.

মামা *n.* a brother or cousin-brother of one's mother, a maternal uncle, an uncle. **~তো** *a.* descended from one's maternal uncle, avuncular. **মামাতো ভাই বা বোন** a cousin. **~শ্বশুর** *n.* a maternal uncle of one's husband or wife, an uncle-in-law.

মামি *n. fem.* the wife of a maternal uncle, an aunt. **~শাশুড়ি** *fem.* the wife of a maternal uncle of one's husband or wife, an aunt-in-law.

মামু (affectionate or facet.) corrup. of **মামা** ।

মামুলি *a.* hackneyed, trite, banal, stock; conventional, traditional, traditionally or conventionally fixed (মামুলি স্বত্ব) ; most ordinary, negligible, paltry (মামুলি ব্যাপার).

মায় *prep.* together with, inclusive of, with, even.

মায়া *n.* (theol.) illusion, the material world, physical or phenomenal nature, *maya;* delusion; infatuation, fascination; affection, attachment; tenderness; compassion; magic, jugglery; black magic, sorcery; deceit, a beguiling trick, chicanery; disguise. **মায়া করা** *v.* to think or treat with affection, to be attached to; to be reluctant to lose (টাকার বা চাকরির মায়া করা). **মায়ায় ভোলা** *v.* to be duped by attachment or sorcery or illusion or by a beguiling trick. **~কানন** *n.* a garden or grove created by sorcery, an enchanted garden. **~কান্না** *n.* insincere sorrow, crocodile tears. **~ঘোর** *n.* influence or spell of illusion or delusion or infatuation or enchantment. **~জাল** *n.* a cobweb or network or spell of illusion or delusion or attachment or infatuation or enchantment. ~জীবী *n.* a magician, a juggler; a conjurer. ~ডোর *n.* a string or bond of attachment or infatuation. **মায়াত্মক** *a.* illusory; delusive; enchanted; hypocritical; disguised. ~দণ্ড *n.* a magician's or conjurer's wand. ~দর্পণ same as ~মুকুর। ~ধারী *a.* concealing one's identity by casting a spell of illusion; hypocritical; disguised. ~পাশ same as ~জাল। ~বদ্ধ *a.* strongly held under illusion; greatly attached or infatuated or enchanted. ~বন্ধন *n.* the bond or tie of illusion or attachment or infatuation or enchantment. ~বলে *adv.* magically; by trickery or beguiling trick; by a spell of delusion or beguiling trick. ~বশ *a.* subject to attachment or affection or infatuation, fondly attached. ~বাদ *n.* (phil. & theol.) illusionism. ~বাদী a. (phil. & theol.) illusionistic. □ *n.* an illusionist. ~বিদ্যা *n.* jugglery, magic; conjury; sorcery, black magic. ~বী *a.* practising deceit, deceitful; practising sorcery; warranting affection, infatuating, enchanting (মায়াবী সৌন্দর্য). □ *n.* an enchanter (*fem.* an enchantress), a sorcerer (*fem.* a sorceress); a wizard (*fem.* a witch); a conjurer. *fem.* ~বিনী। ~মমতা *n. pl.* affection and compassion; love and attachment; (cp.) a soft spot (for). ~ময় *a.* illusive; delusive; infatuating; bewitching, enchanting; deceptive. *fem.* ~ময়ী। ~মুকুর *n.* a magic mirror. ~মুক্ত *a.* freed from attachment or affection; disillusioned; disenchanted. ~মৃগ *n.* (Ramayana) a stag appearing to be made of gold, which tempted Sita and led her to be kidnapped by Ravana; (fig.) a perilous illusion or temptation. ~মোহ same as ~ঘোর। ~রজ্জু same as ~ডোর। ~রাজ্য *n.* a land created by sorcery; a realm of infatuation or enchantment. ~হীন *a.* devoid of tenderness or compassion.

মায়িক *a.* magical; illusive; infatuating; enchanting.

মায়ের দয়া see **মা**[২]।

মার[১] *n.* death, destruction (সত্যের মার নেই) ; loss (টাকা মার খাওয়া বা যাওয়া). **মার যাওয়া** *v.* to be lost.

মার[২] *n.* the Hindu god of love (cp. Eros, Cupid); and evil spirit who tried to tempt Buddha (cp. Satan); killing or slaying.

মার[৩] *n.* beating or striking or thrashing or flogging. **মার খাওয়া** *v.* to be beaten up or flogged. **মার দেওয়া** *a.* to beat, to flog. ~কাট *n.* fighting and bloodshed; tumultuous brawl or affray; feverish haste and fuss; higgling. □ *adv.* & *a.* at best. ~কুটে *a.* given to beating on slightest pretext. ~খেকো *a.* one who is often flogged. ~ধর *n.* beating or flogging; beating and arresting (as by the police). ~পিট *n.* mutual fighting; fray; an affray, a riot; beating or flogging (esp. excessive). ~মার কাটকাট *n.* same as কাট। □ *a.* tumultuous, noisily violent, turbulent. ~মুখো *a.* about to strike or hurt; aggressive; frightening, threatening, menacing. *fem.* ~মুখী। ~মূর্তি *a.* about to strike or hurt; having an aggressive or menacing appearance. □ *n.* aggressive or menacing appearance.

মারওয়াড়ি var. of **মারোয়াড়ি**।

মারক *n.* a pestilence, a plague. □ *a.* destructive; pestilential.

মারণ *n.* killing, slaughter; destroying, destruction; an occult rite performed to cause one's death (মারণমন্ত্র) ; calcination (of metals). **মারণাস্ত্র** *n.* a weapon of destruction. **মারিত** *a.* killed; destroyed.

মারপিট see **মার**[৩]।

মারপ্যাঁচ *n.* shrewd or trappy trick (খেলার মারপ্যাঁচ) ; a shrewd or tricky twist or turn (কথার মারপ্যাঁচ) ; quibbling, equivocation.

মারফত *prep.* per, through, by. **দূত মারফত** through a messenger.

মারবাড়ি older var. of **মারোয়াড়ি**।

মারবেল *n.* marble; a little hard ball (ori. made of marble) used by boys in play, a marble. **মারবেল-পাহাড়** *n.* a marble rock.

মারমার কাটকাট see **মার**[৩]।

মারহাট্টা older var. of **মারাঠা**।

মারা *v.* to kill; to strike, to hit (বল মারা) ; to beat, to flog; to drive in, to pierce (ছুরি মারা = to stab); to strike with (চাবুক মারা) ; to deal (ঘুসি মারা = to deal one a blow); to afflict or distress (কথায় মারা) ; to ruin (চুরিটায় আমাকে মেরেছে) ; to destroy, to exterminate, to eradicate (বিষ মারা) ; to dry or dehydrate (রস মারা) ; to implant, to drive in (পেরেক মারা) ; to affix (টিকিট মারা) ; to sew up (তালি মারা) ; to paste (লেবেল মারা) ; to close up, to fill up (ফাঁক মারা) ; to rob, to pick (পকেট মারা) ; to obtain by unfair means, to misappropriate, to defalcate (টাকা মারা) ; to win or earn esp. by a fluke (লটারি মারা) ; to deprive of (অন্ন মারা, রুজি মারা) ; to cause to lose (জাত মারা) ; (inf.) to eat or gobble (ভাত মারা) ; to shout (হাঁক মারা) ; to give out, to emit (জেল্লা মারা) ; to block, to obstruct (পথ মারা) ; to blunt, to dull (ধার মারা, কোণ মারা) ; to tuck (মালকোঁচা মারা) ; (inf.) to score (গোল মারা) ; to adopt, to have recourse to, to exhibit (চাল মারা). **চাল মারা** see **চাল**[৩]। **মারা পড়া, মারা যাওয়া** *v.* to be killed; to die; to be lost (বহু টাকা মারা গেছে)।

মারাঠি *n.* a Marathi, a Maharashtrian; the Marathi language. □ *a.* Marathi; of Maratha or Maharashtra.

মারাত্মক *a.* deadly; fatal; terrific; unappeasable, incapable of being assuaged (মারাত্মক শোক).

মারামারি *n.* a scuffle; an affray; mutual fighting; hard higgling. **মারামারি করা** *v.* to scuffle; to fight mutually.

মারী, মারি *n.* pestilence, a plague; smallpox. **~গুটিকা** *n.* a pustule or vesicle of small-pox.

মারুত *n.* the wind, air. **মারুতি** *n.* a son of the wind-god.

মারোয়াড়ি *a.* of Marwar. *n.* a native of Marwar, a Marwari; the language of Marwar, Marwari.

মার্কসবাদ *n.* Marxism, the theory of Karl Marx.

মার্কসবাদী *n.* a Marxist. □ *a.* Marxist, Marxian.

মার্কা *n.* a mark, a sign, a brand. **মার্কা দেওয়া** *v.* to put a mark on, to mark; to brand. **~মারা** *a.* marked; branded (মার্কামারা চোর) ; notorious.

মার্কিন *n.* the United States of America, (contr.) U.S.A.; America; a citizen of the U.S.A.; an American; a coarse white fabric. □ *a.* of the U.S.A. or relating to the American.

মার্কেট *n.* a market. **মার্কেটিং** *n.* marketing; shopping. **মার্কেটিং করা** v. to visit a market for shopping, to market; to shop.

মার্গ *n.* a way, a path, a road (রাজমার্গ) ; a route; a means; a mode or means of attaining salvation (ভক্তিমার্গ) ; the anus; (mus.) the classical mode. **~সংগীত** *n.* classical music.

মার্চ *n.* the third month of the English calendar, March.

মার্জন *n.* scouring or scrubbing; cleansing (as of teeth) by rubbing, brushing etc.; rubbing; polishing (as of gold ornaments); freeing from sin, fault etc. chastening, absolution; chiselling. **মার্জনা** same as **মার্জন,** and–forgiving; pardon. **মার্জনা করা** *v.* to forgive, to pardon; to scour or scrub; to cleanse; to rub; to polish; to free from sin, fault etc., to chasten, to absolve; to chisel. **মার্জনাহীন** *a.* unforgiving; relentless. **মার্জনী** *n.* any implement for scrubbing or scouring or cleansing or rubbing with, a besom, a broom, a brush, a towel, a napkin etc.

মার্জার *n.* the cat; (mas.) the tomcat; any feline beast (জল-মার্জার). *fem.* **মার্জারী, মার্জারিকা** the female cat, the she-cat, (cp.) the pussy-cat.

মার্জিত *a.* scoured or scrubbed; cleansed; rubbed; polished; freed from sin, fault etc., chastened, absolved; refined (মার্জিত আচরণ, মার্জিত রুচি) ; elegant, chaste (মার্জিত ভাষা) ; chiselled or polished (রচনা মার্জিত করা) ; cultured (মার্জিত বুদ্ধি). **মার্জিত করা** same as **মার্জনা করা**।

মার্তণ্ড *n.* the sun. **~তাপ** *n.* the heat of the sun.

মার্বেল alt. spell of **মারবেল**।

মাল১ *n.* (sl.) wine, booze. **মাল টানা** *v.* (sl.) to drink wine, to booze.

মাল২ *n.* an Indian tribe; a member of this tribe; a snake-charmer; a healer (esp. one knowing occult methods) of poisonous snakebites (also **মালবৈদ্য**).

মাল৩ *n.* merchandise, wares (দোকানের মাল) ; goods; wealth, riches, property; revenue, rent; land-holding rented directly from the government. **~কড়ি** *n.* money, fund; the wherewithal. **~ক্রোক** *n.* distraint. **মালক্রোক করা** *v.* to distrain. **মালক্রোকি পরোয়ানা** a distraint warrant. **~খানা** *n.* a godown or store esp. for keeping valuable articles; room or building where revenue is received; a treasury. **মাল খালাস করা** *v.* to unload. **~গাড়ি** *n.* a luggage-van; a waggon; a goods-train. **~গুজার, ~গুজারদার** *n.* one who pays revenue (esp. directly to the government); a zamindar. **~গুজারি** *n.* land revenue. **~গুদাম** *n.* a godown; a store-house; a storeroom; a warehouse. **~জমি** *n.* a land-holding rented directly from the government. **~জামিন** *n.* security for goods or property. **~জাহাজ, ~নৌকা** *n.* a cargo-boat, a cargo-steamer. **~দার** *a.* wealthy, rich, moneyed. **~পত্র** *n. pl.* goods collectively; goods and chattels; luggage. **~বাহী** *a.* carrying goods, cargo etc. **~বাহী জাহাজ** same as **মালজাহাজ**। **~বোঝাই** *a.* loaded; (of ships) laden. **~বোঝাই করা** *v.* to load; (of ships) to lade. **~মশলা** *n. pl.* ingredients; materials.

মালকোঁচা *n.* loincloth worn by tucking it tightly between one's legs like a suspenser. **মালকোঁচা আঁটা বা দেওয়া বা মারা** *v.* to tuck one's loincloth tightly between one's legs like a suspenser.

মালকোশ, মালকোষ *n.* Malkosh; an Indian musical mode.

মালঝাঁপ *n.* a metre of Bengali versification.

মালঞ্চ *n.* a flower-garden.

মালতী *n.* a kind of jasmine or its plant. **~ফল** *n.* nutmeg.

মালপোয়া, মালপো *n.* a saucer-shaped sweetmeat made of flour or rice-powder fried in ghee or oil and then (sometimes) dipped in sugarjuice.

মালবৈদ্য see **মাল**৩ ।

মালভূমি *n.* plateau, a table-land.

মালশা *n.* a small earthen basin.

মালশাট *n.* loincloth worn by tucking it tightly between one's legs like a suspenser; bragging or vaunting (as by a fighter); slapping of one's arms etc. as one gets ready to attack. **মালশাট মারা** *v.* to tuck one's loincloth tightly between one's legs like a suspenser; to brag or vaunt; to slap one's arms etc. as one gets ready to attack.

মালসা alt. spell. of **মালশা** ।

মালা১ *n.* a fisherman by caste.

মালা২ *n.* a coconut-shell; a coconut-shell cut into the shape of a tumbler.

মালা৩ *n.* a nceklace; a chaplet or circlet; a garland; a string (জপমালা) ; a series, a row, a line (ঊর্মিমালা, পর্বতমালা). **মালা গাঁথা** *v.* to form into a wreath, to wreathe. **মালা জপা** *v.* to tell one's beads.

মালাই *n.* film or cream of milk.

মালাইচাকি *n.* the knee-pan, the knee-cap, the patella.

মালাই-বরফ *n.* ice-cream.

মালাকর, মালাকার *n.* a maker and seller of garlands (esp. by caste); a florist; gardener.

মালাচন্দন *n.* garlands and sandal-paste with which an adorable or honourable person is received. **মালাচন্দন দেওয়া** *v.* to receive with garlands and sandal-paste; (fig.) to receive with honour.

মালাবদল *n.* exchange of garlands or necklaces (as done by the couple at a wedding); marriage; marriage of Vaishnavas (which demands no other ceremony than the exchange of basil-necklaces by the couple). **মালাবদল করা** *v.* to exchange garlands or necklaces; to marry; to marry in the Vaishnava way.

মালাবারি *a.* of Malabar in India. □ *n.* a native of Malabar.

মালিক *n.* a proprietor (*fem.* a proprietress, a proprietrix), an owner; a master (*fem.* mistress), a lord. **~হীন** *a.* ownerless; derelict.

মালিকা dim. of **মালা**[৩] ।

মালিকানা, মালিকি *n.* ownership, proprietary; proprietorship; a right to possession, title; a fee, rent etc. to be paid to a proprietor, proprietary dues, a royalty. □ *a.* proprietary, proprietorial; relating to the title. **মালিকানা স্বত্ব** proprietary right.

মালিনী *fem.* of **মালী** (*n.* & *a.*).

মালিন্য same as **মলিনতা** (see **মলিন**).

মালিশ *n.* rubbing or massaging; an unguent, oil etc. for rubbing or massaging. **মালিশ করা** *v.* to rub or massage.

মালী *n.* same as **মালাকর** । □ *a.* wearing a garland or wreath (বনমালী).

মালুম *n.* feeling, perception, sensation. **মালুম করা বা পাওয়া** *v.* to feel, to perceive, to sense. **মালুম হওয়া** *v.* to be felt or perceived or sensed.

মালুমকাঠ *n.* a mast (of a ship).

মালো coll. var. of **মালা**[১] ।

মালোপমা *n.* (rhet.) multiple similes stringed together.

মাল্য *n.* a necklace; a chaplet or circlet; a string; a garland; a series, a row, a line. **~বান** *a.* wearing a garland; □ *n.* a mythological mountain. *fem. a.* **~বতী** । **~দান** *n.* the placing of a garland (round somebody's neck); garlanding.

মাল্লা *n.* an oarsman; a sailor or seaman of the lowest rank, a sailor or boatman by caste.

মাশুল *n.* duty, tax, customs; fare, freight; charge, price.

মাষ[১], **মাষকলাই** *n.* a kind of dal or pulse.

মাষ[২], **মাষা** *n.* a unit of weight for jewellers (= 18 or 15 grs.) or for apothecaries (9 grs. approx.).

মাষ্টার alt. spell. of **মাস্টার** ।

মাস[১] coll. corrup. of **মাংস** ।

মাস[২] *n.* a month. **মাসে, মাসে-মাসে** *adv.* every month. □ *a.* monthly (মাসে দশ টাকা আয়).

মাসকাবার *n.* close of a calendar month; (comm.) month-closing accounts. **মাসকাবারি** *a.* required at the close of a month; sufficient for a month; monthly.

মাসতুতো *a.* descended from a sister or a cousin-sister of one's mother or mother-in-law, avuncular, cousinly. **মাসতুতো ভাই, মাসতুতো বোন** a cousin.

মাসপয়লা *n.* the first day of a month; calends.

মাসবৃদ্ধি *n.* an intercalary month.

মাসভর *adv.* throughout the month.

মাসমাইনে *n.* monthly wages; a monthly salary.

মাসশাশুড়ি *n. fem.* a sister or a cousin-sister of one's mother-in-law, an aunt-in-law.

মাসশ্বশুর *n.* the husband of a **মাসশাশুড়ি**, an uncle-in-law.

মাসহরা, মাসহারা variants of **মাসোহারা** ।

মাসান্ত *n.* the last day of a month or near about it. **মাসান্তিক** *a.* of or about the end of a month, that which happens at the end of a month.

মাসি *n.* a sister or a cousin-sister of one's mother, an aunt.

মাসিক *a.* monthly. □ *n.* monthly obsequies; a monthly journal, a monthly; the menses, monthlies, periods.

মাসী older spell. of **মাসি** ।

মাসুল alt. spell. of **মাশুল** ।

মাসোহারা *n.* a monthly (monetary) allowance or stipend.

মাস্টার *n.* a teacher, a tutor, a trainer; a man in charge, a chief executive, a master (পোস্টমাস্টার). **মাস্টারি** *n.* act or profession of teaching or training.

মাস্তুল *n.* a mast (of a ship).

মাহাত্ম্য *n.* high-mindedness, nobility; excellence, sublimity; greatness, divine grace or power; glory, majesty; (loos.) charm or influence (টাকার মাহাত্ম্য, স্থানমাহাত্ম্য).

মাহিনা older var. of **মাইনে** ।

মাহিষ্য *n.* a caste amongst Hindus; a member of this caste.

মাহুত *n.* a keeper and driver of an elephant, a mahout.

মাহেন্দ্রক্ষণ *n.* (astrol.) the most auspicious conjunction of stars for commencing any work.

মিউ *int.* expressing: the cry of a cat, mew. **মিউমিউ** *int.* expressing: repeated mewing. **মিউমিউ করা** *v.* to mew repeatedly; to mew.

মিউনিসিপ্যাল *a.* municipal. **মিউনিসিপ্যালিটি** *n.* a municipality.

মিউমিউ see **মিউ**।

মিছরি sugar-candy. **মিছরির ছুরি** (fig.) a sweet verbal stab, words apparently sweet but meant to sting or deride. **মিছরির পানা** *n.* a cold drink or cordial made of sugar-candy.

মিছা corrup. of **মিথ্যা**। **~মিছি** *adv.* same as **মিথ্যা** (*adv.*).

মিছিমিছি *adv.* (coll.) for nothing, in vain, meaninglessly, uselessly. □ *a.* false; useless, meaningless.

মিছিল *n.* a procession.

মিছে coll. var. of **মিছা**।

মিজরাব *n.* a kind of thimble (made of wire) used by instrumentalists, (cp.) plectrum.

মিঞা alt. spell. of **মিয়া**।

মিট *n.* (book-keeping) balancing; paying off; act of making up, compounding; settlement or compromise. **মিট করা** *v.* to balance (an account); to pay off (a bill); to make up, to compound (a loss); to settle or compromise (a dispute). **মিট হওয়া** *v.* to be balanced or paid off or made up or compounded or settled or compromised. **~মাট** *n.* compromise; settlement. **মিটমাট করা** *v.* to compromise; to settle up (a difference, dispute etc.). **মিটমাট হওয়া** *v.* to be compromised or settled up.

মিটা, মেটা *v.* to be accomplished or finished (কাজ মেটা) ; to be removed or relieved (দুঃখ মিটেছে) ; to be settled or compromised (বিবাদ মিটল) ; to be satisfied or fulfilled (সাধ মেটানো) ; to be paid off (পাওনা মেটা) ; to be compensated or compounded (লোকসান মেটা) ; (book-keeping) to be balanced.

মিটমিট *int.* expressing: dim, flickering or almost dying state (as of a light); blinking (as of eyes). **মিটমিট করা** *v.* to flicker dimly; to blink. **মিটমিটে** *a.* dimly flickering; dim; blinking; (fig.) simulating or hypocritical. **মিটেমিটে ডান, মিটমিটে শয়তান** a witch or a rogue dissembling as an honest and simple soul; (fig.) a wolf in a sheepskin.

মিটানো *v.* to accomplish or finish; to remove or relieve; to settle or compromise; to satisfy or fulfil; to pay off; to compensate or compound; (book-keeping) to balance.

মিটার১ *n.* a meter (ইলেকট্রিকের মিটার, ট্যাকসির মিটার).

মিটার২ *n.* a unit of measuring length, a metre.

মিটার৩ *n.* a verse rhythm, fixed arrangement of accented and unaccented syllables, metre.

মিটিমিটি *adv.* flickering dimly (মিটিমিটি জ্বলা) ; blinkingly (মিটিমিটি চাওয়া). □ *a.* dimly flickering, dim; blinking. **মিটিমিটি করা** *v.* to flicker dimly; to blink.

মিটিং *n.* meeting.

মিঠা, (coll.) **মিঠে** *a.* sweet, delicious, palatable; melodious; suave, bland; pleasant; capable of producing a sweet and soft effect (সেতারির মিঠে হাত, ভাটিয়ালির মিঠে সুর) ; charming; fresh (মিঠে জল).

মিঠাই *n.* sweetmeat. **~ওয়ালা** *n.* a confectioner. **মিঠাইয়ের দোকান** a sweetmeat-shop, a confectionary.

মিঠেকড়া *a.* (of tobacco) moderately strong; (of words) suave yet cutting to the quick.

মিড় *n.* (mus.) sweet and pleasant rolling from one note to another.

মিত *a.* temperate; moderate; restricted; abstemious.

মিতকনে, মিতবর same as **নিতকনে** and **নিতবর** respectively.

মিতবাক same as **মিতভাষী**।

মিতব্যয়, মিতব্যয়িতা *n.* frugality, thrift, economy. **মিতব্যয়ী** *a.* frugal, thrifty, economical.

মিতভাষী *a.* economical in speech, taciturn; reticent, reserved. *fem.* **মিতভাষিণী**। **মিতভাষিতা** *n.* economy of speech, taciturnity; reticence, reservedness.

মিতভোজন same as **মিতাহার**।

মিতভোজী same as **মিতাহারী**।

মিতা *n.* friend; a born companion; an ally; a namesake.

মিতাক্ষর var. of **মিত্রাক্ষর**।

মিতাক্ষরা *n.* an ancient Hindu treatise on the law and rules of inheritance.

মিতাচার *n.* temperance, abstemiousness. **মিতাচারী** *a.* temperate, abstemious. *fem.* **মিতাচারিণী**। **মিতাচারিতা** *n.* same as **মিতাচার**।

মিতালি *n.* friendship; boon companionship; alliance.

মিতাশন, মিতাহার *n.* temperance in food and drink, abstemiousness. **মিতাশী, মিতাহারী** *a.* abstemious, temperate.

মিতি *n.* measure, measurement, -metry (জ্যামিতি) ; knowledge.

মিতে coll. var. of **মিতা**।

মিত্র *n.* a friend; a boon companion; an ally; the sun. **~তা, ~ত্ব** *n.* friendship; boon companionship; alliance. **~দ্রোহ** *n.* hostility or treachery to one's friend or ally or party. **~দ্রোহী** *a.* hostile or treacherous to one's friend or ally or party. *fem.* **~দ্রোহিণী**। **~ভেদ** *n.* estrangement of friends of allies, (chiefly pol.) disintegration of a party. **~লাভ** *n.* act or an instance of obtaining a new friend.

মিত্রা *fem.* of **মিত্র**।

মিত্রাক্ষর *n.* the rhymed verse, verse with end-rhyme.

মিথুন *n.* a male and a female, a couple, a pair; (astr. & astrol.) the Twins, the Gemini (also **মিথুনরাশি**).

মিথ্যা *n.* a lie; falsehood, untruth. □ *a.* untrue, false; imaginary, fanciful; got-up (মিথ্যা মামলা) ; baseless, unsubstantial (মিথ্যা ভয়) ; causeless, unprovoked (মিথ্যা রাগ) ; affected or feigned (মিথ্যা ঘুম) ; futile, vain (মিথ্যা চেষ্টা) ; useless, bootless (মিথ্যা কাজ). □ *adv.* for nothing; in vain. **মিথ্যা কথা** a lie. **মিথ্যা কথা বলা** to tell a lie. **~চরণ, ~চার** *n.* treacherous behaviour, false play, falsehood; treachery, pretension, dissimulation, hypocrisy. **~চারী** *a.* behaving treacherously, given to false play; pretentious, dissimulating, hypocritical. *fem.* **~চারিণী**। **~জ্ঞান, মিথ্যা ধারণা** *n.* a false or wrong notion or impression or idea. **মিথ্যাপবাদ** *n.* false blame or aspersion or calumny; a scandal. **~বর্ণন** *n.* misrepresentation; a false account. **~বাক্য** *n.* a lie. **~বাদ, ~ভাষণ** *n.* a lie; untruthfulness. **~বাদিতা, ~ভাষিতা** *n.* untruthfulness. **~বাদী, ~ভাষী** *a.* untruthful, lying. □ *n.* a liar. *fem.* **~বাদিনী, ~ভাষিণী**। **~সাক্ষী** *n.* a false witness; a tutored witness; a perjurer. **~সাক্ষ্য** *n.* false witness; tutored witness; perjury. **মিথ্যাসাক্ষ্য দেওয়া** *v.* to give false evidence; to bear false witness to; to perjure. **মিথ্যার জাহাজ বা ঝুড়ি** a ship (or ship-load) or basket of lies; (fig.) one given to telling innumerable lies unscrupulously. **মিথ্যার তোড় বা স্রোত** a spate of lies.

মিথ্যুক *a.* given to telling lies, untruthful. □ *n.* a liar.

মিথ্যে coll. form of **মিথ্যা**।

মিনতি *n.* a humble prayer or an earnest request; supplication, entreaty, solicitation. **মিনতি করা** *v.* to pray humbly; to request earnestly; to supplicate, to entreat, to solicit. **~পূর্ণ** *a.* full of humble prayer or earnest request; supplicatory, full of entreaties, solicitous.

মিনমিন *int.* denoting: act of mumbling or speaking faintly or hesitatingly; faintness; weakness; timidity. **মিনমিনে** *a.* mumbling or speaking faintly or hesitatingly; faint; weak; faint-hearted.

মিনসে *n.* (vul. in abuse or endearment) a grown-up man, a man; a husband.

মিনা, মিনে *n.* enamel; enamelling. **মিনা করা** *v.* to enamel. **মিনে-করা** *a.* enamelled.

মিনার *n.* a tower, a minar; a turret. **মসজিদের মিনার** a minaret.

মিনি[1] *a. & prep.* without, except, lacking in, sans (মিনিসুতোর মালা).

মিনি[2] *a.* small or minor (মিনিস্কার্ট, মিনিবাস). □ *n.* the small form of a thing; a minibus.

মিনিট *n.* the sixtieth part of an hour or of a degree, a minute; a moment. **মিনিটে মিনিটে** *adv.* every minute, every moment; repeatedly; at short intervals.

মিনি-মাগনা *a.* cost-free.

মিনে coll. var. of **মিনা**।

মিয়নো var. of **মিয়ানো**।

মিয়া, মিয়াসাহেব *n.* (Mus.) an appellation of courtesy affixed to the name of a man, (cp.) Mr,. Sir.

মিয়াদ older var. of **মেয়াদ**।

মিয়ানো *v.* to lose crispness (মুড়ি মিয়ানো) ; to lose energy or vigour, to become limp or flaccid (সে মিইয়ে পড়েছে, উৎসাহ মিয়ানো). □ *a.* bereft of crispness; bereft of energy or vigour, limp, flaccid.

মিরগেল coll. var. of **মৃগেল** ।

মিরজাই *n.* a waist-coat or vest with cotton padding inside.

মিরবহর *n.* an admiral.

মিরমুনশি *n.* chief clerk, head clerk; chief secretary.

মিরাস *n.* land held under hereditary title; the right of hereditary occupation. **মিরাস-ইজারা** *n.* lease or settlement of land to be enjoyed hereditarily.

মিল[1] *n.* a manufactory, a factory, a mill.

মিল[2] *n.* union; combination; addition; concord, harmony, agreement (মতের মিল) ; unison (সুরের মিল) ; balancing (হিসাবের মিল) ; similarity, likeness (চেহারার মিল) ; friendly terms; good terms; reconciliation, reconcilement (বিরোধীদের মিল) ; fitting (জোড়ের মুখে মিল) ; (pros.) rhyme (কবিতার মিল). **মিল করা** *v.* to unite; to combine; to add (up); to harmonize; to balance; to reconcile; to fit; (pros.) to put into rhyme, to rhyme. **মিল দেওয়া** *v.* to add; (pros.) to find out a rhyme for, to rhyme. **মিল হওয়া** *v.* to be in harmony, to agree; to be reconciled; to be balanced, to tally; to be fitting, to fit; (pros.) to be in rhyme, to rhyme. **~মিলাও, ~মিশ** *n.* good terms, friendly terms; amicability. **~যুক্ত** *a.* rhyming; rhymed; **~হীন** *a.* unrhymed, without rhyme.

মিলন *n.* union; combination; unity; alliance; reconciliation, reconcilement; meeting; meeting or union of lovers; sexual union; wedding, bridal (মিলন-বাসর). **মিলন করা, মিলন ঘটানো** *v.* to unite; to combine; to reconcile; to cause to meet; to cause to meet sexually or amorously; to wed, to marry. **~স্থান** *n.* a meeting-place; a tryst. **মিলনান্ত, মিলনান্তক** *a.* ending in union; ending happily. **মিলনান্তক নাটক** *a.* comedy. **মিলনোৎসব** *n.* a conference or assembly; a social gathering.

মিলমিলা, মিলমিলে *n.* measles.

মিলা, মেলা *v.* to meet together; to meet; to assemble; to get on or pull on together (ভাইয়ে ভাইয়ে মেলে না) ; to fit (জোড় মেলা) ; to agree, to correspond; to mix well or perfectly; to agree with the given result (অঙ্ক মিলেছে) ; to be balanced, to tally (হিসাব মেলা) ; (pros.) to rhyme; to be available (বাজারে মাছ মেলে না) ; to be procured or obtained (চাকরি মেলা). **মিলানো** *v.* to cause to meet together, to bring together; to cause to meet; to assemble; to fit; to cause to agree or correspond; to mix well or perfectly; to cause to agree with the given result; to balance, to tally; to compare (অঙ্কের ফল মিলানো) ; (pros.) to rhyme; to make available; to procure. **মেলামেশা** *n.* social intercourse; intimate association, familiarity. **মেলামেশা করা** *v.* to communicate socially; to make free with.

মিলিত *a.* united; combined; joint; joined; assembled; mixed; procured; met. **মিলিত করা** *v.* to unite; to combine; to join; to assemble; to mix; to cause to meet.

মিশ[1] *a.* inky, as dark as ink; very dark. **~মিশ** *int.* expressing: inky blackness or darkness. **~মিশে** *a.* as dark as ink; pitch-dark, very dark.

মিশ[2] *n.* mixing, mixture; blending; unison, agreement, harmony, accord. **মিশ খাওয়া** *v.* to be mixed or blended; to agree, to accord. **মিশ খাওয়ানো** *v.* to mix; to blend; to cause to agree, to reconcile; to harmonize.

মিশন *n.* a religious mission; a mission. **মিশনারি** *a.* missionary. □ *n.* a missionary.

মিশমিশ, মিশমিশে see **মিশ**[1] ।

মিশর *n.* Egypt. **মিশরীয়** *a.* of or pertaining to Egypt, Egyptian. □ *n.* an Egyptian.

মিশা, মেশা *v.* to mingle, to be mixed or blended; to get mixed; to be united or conjoined; to meet; to fall or run or flow into (নদী সাগরে মেশে) ; to be incorporated or amalgamated or integrated with; to merge into (ভারতের

সঙ্গে মিশেছে) ; to unite; to associate; to keep company with (কুসংসর্গে মিশছে) ; to fit (জোড় মেশা) ; to agree (কালোর পাশে নীল মিশবে না). **মিশানো** *v.* to mix, to blend, to mingle; to conjoin; to incorporate or amalgamate; to cause to merge into; to unite; to cause to associate with; to fit. **মেশামিশি** *n.* acquaintance; association; social communication; intimacy; familiarity. **মেশামিশি করা** *v.* to cultivate one's acquaintance or friendship; to associate with; to communicate or intercourse socially; to be intimate with; to make free with. **মিশাল,** (coll.) **মিশেল** *n.* mixture or blending; adulteration. □ *a.* mixed or blended; adulterate. **মিশাল করা** বা **দেওয়া** *v.* to mix or blend; to adulterate. **মিশালি** *a.* miscellaneous (পাঁচমিশালি).

মিশি *n.* a dentrifrice made of roasted tobacco and copperas.

মিশুক *a.* sociable, companionable.

মিশেল, মিশেলি coll. variants of **মিশাল** & **মিশেলি** respectively. see **মিশা** ।

মিশ্র *a.* mixed, blended; united; hybrid (মিশ্র জাতি) ; (math. & sc.) compound (মিশ্রভগ্নাংশ, মিশ্রযোগ). □ *n.* a mixture; (sc.) a compound. **~ক** *n.* a compounder; an ingredient of a compound. **মিশ্রকবিদ্যা** *n.* the art of compounding medicines. **~পদার্থ** *n.* a mixture; (sc.) a compound. **~বর্ণ** *a.* variegated. **~সুর** *n.* (mus.) a hybrid tune or mode. **~ধাতু** *n.* an alloy.

মিশ্রণ *n.* mixing, blending, compounding, mixture, composition; hybridization; union; unification; amalgamation; adulteration. **~বিধি** *n.* process of mixing or compounding or blending. **মিশ্রণীয়** *a.* miscible.

মিশ্রিত *a.* mixed, blended; compounded; hybridized; amalgamated; adulterated. **মিশ্রিত করা** *v.* to mix, to blend; to compound; to hybridize; to amalgamate; to adulterate.

মিষ্ট, (coll.) **মিষ্টি** *a.* sweet; delicious; pleasing, pleasant. □ *n.* sweetmeat, sweets. **মিষ্টতা, মিষ্টত্ব** *n.* sweetness; deliciousness; pleasantness. **মিষ্টভাষী** *a.* fair-spoken, honey-tongued. *fem.* **মিষ্টভাষিণী** । **মিষ্টিমুখ** *n.* a light repast of sweets (মিষ্টিমুখ করা to take a light repast of sweets); sweet or pleasant speech (মিষ্টি মুখে বলা to say sweetly or gently or suavely). **মিষ্টান্ন** *n.* sweetmeat, sweets; a sweet food prepared by boiling rice in milk; (cp.) frumenty. **মিষ্টালাপী** same as **মিষ্টভাষী** ।

মিস *n. fem.* Miss.

মিসি rej. spell. of **মিশি** ।

মিসিবাবা *n. fem.* (used by domestic servants) missy.

মিসেস *n. fem.* Mrs. Mistress.

মিস্টার *n.* Mr, Mister.

মিস্ত্রি *n.* a mechanic, an artisan, a smith; a machine foreman; a skilled or chief mechanic or artisan.

মিহি *a.* fine; fine-spun (মিহি কাপড়) ; contralto (মিহি সুর) ; effeminate and soft (মিহি গলা) ; very small (মিহিদানা) ; finely pulverized (মিহিগুঁড়ো) ; delicate, subtle (মিহি কারুকাজ).

মিহিদানা *n.* a kind of sweetmeat consisting of very small globules.

মিহির *n.* the sun.

মীড় rej. spell. of **মিড়** ।

মীন *n.* fish; (astrol.) the Fishes, the Pisces (usu. **মীনরাশি**) ; (myth.) the first of the ten incarnations of Vishnu (বিষ্ণু). **~কেতন, ~ধ্বজ** *n.* one whose standard bears the sign of a fish; Madan (মদন) the Hindu love-god. **~পোষ** *n.* pisciculture. **মীনাক্ষ** *a.* having piscine eyes. **মীনাক্ষী** *a. fem.* of **মীনাক্ষ** । □ a female deity of Deccan.

মীমাংসক *a.* & *n.* one who solves or decides or determines or settles or arbitrates. □ *n.* one versed in Mimansa (মীমাংসা) system of philosophy. **মীমাংসনীয়** *a.* (of a dispute or controversy) to be resolved, resolvable.

মীমাংসা *n.* solution (of a problem etc.), decision; determination (of truths etc.); act of clearing up or settling (of complication, doubt etc.); disposal (of an affair etc.); arbitration or compounding (of a dispute etc.); compromise: a philosophical treatise compiled by Jaimini (also **মীমাংসাদর্শন**). **মীমাংসা করা** *v.*

to solve, to decide; to determine; to clear up; to settle; to dispose of; to arbitrate; to effect a compromise, to compound.

মীমাংসিত *a.* solved, decided; determined; settled; arbitrated, compromised.

মুকতি poet. corrup. of **মুক্তি** ।

মুকররি *a.* (of land) held on payment of fixed rent.

মুকাবিলা older var. of **মোকাবিলা** ।

মুকুট *n.* a crown, a diadem, a coronet. **মুকুট পরা** *v.* to put on or wear a crown. **মুকুট পরানো** *v.* to crown. **মুকুট-পরা** *a.* diademed.

মুকুতা poet. corrup. of **মুক্তা** ।

মুকুন্দ *n.* one who gives salvation; Vishnu (বিষ্ণু).

মুকুর *n.* a mirror, a looking-glass, a speculum.

মুকুল *n.* a bud, a blossom. **মুকুলা** *v.* (poet.) to bud, to blossom, to effloresce, to flower; (of flowers) to bloom, to blow; (fig.) to become manifest, to be in bloom. **মুকুলাবরণ** *n.* (bot.) a bud-scale. **মুকুলিত** *a.* budded, blossoming, efforescent, flowering; blooming; (fig.) manifested, in bloom. *fem.* **মুকুলিতা** । **মুকুলোদগম** *n.* blossoming, budding.

মুক্ত *a.* having attained salvation, freed from earthly bondage or ties or attachments (মুক্ত পুরুষ) ; dispassionate, unaffected, unprejudiced, free (মুক্ত মন) ; liberal, bountiful; released, freed (কারামুক্ত) ; extricated (বিপদমুক্ত) ; acquitted, freed, discharged (দায়মুক্ত) ; loosened (বন্ধনমুক্ত) ; cured of, recovered from (রোগমুক্ত) ; unbolted (মুক্তদ্বার) ; unobstructed, open, free (মুক্তধারা, মুক্তবায়ু) ; unrestricted; untied, unfastened, bare (মুক্তকৃপাণ) ; delivered from or of (গর্ভমুক্ত) ; rescued; liberated; relieved of (ভয়মুক্ত) ; removed, cleared. **মুক্ত করা** *v.* to give salvation, to free from earthly bondage; to free (from); to release; to extricate; to acquit; to discharge; to loosen; to cure of; to open, to unbolt; to free from obstacles or restrictions; to untie, to unfasten; to unsheathe; to deliver from or of; to rescue; to liberate; to relieve (of); (loos.) to remove, to clear. **~কচ্ছ** *a.* one with the portion of the loincloth hanging loose instead of remaining tucked at the back of the waist between one's legs; (fig.) hurrying excessively and ludicrously, (cp.) having the tail between the legs. **~কণ্ঠে** *adv.* in a loud voice; speaking freely or unhesitatingly. **~কেশী** *a. fem.* having one's hair hanging loose. □ *n.* Goddess Kali (কালী). **মুক্ত ছন্দ** (pros.) free verse. **মুক্ত নগরী** an undefended or open city; liberated city. **~পুরুষ** *n.* (loos.) a man freed from obstacles or hindrances. **মুক্ত বন্দর** a free port. **~বেণি** *a.* having hair not tied up in a chignon. □ *n.* the confluence of Tribeni (ত্রিবেণি) at Allahabad. **~হস্ত** *a.* open-handed; munificent, generous. **~হস্তে** *adv.* in an open-handed manner, liberally.

মুক্তা *n.* a pearl. **~খচিত** *a.* set or studded or inlaid with pearls. **~গর্ভ** *a.* containing pearls, pearly. **~তুল্য** *a.* pearl-like, pearly. **~ফল** *n.* pearl; camphor. **~বলি, ~বলী** *n.* a collection or string of pearls. **~মালা, ~হার** *n.* a string of pearls; a pearl-necklace. **~শুক্তি** *n.* a pearl-oyster.

মুক্তি *n.* (theol.) salvation, nirvana; freedom from earthly attachments; release; extrication, deliverance; discharge (জ্যা-মুক্তি) ; acquittal; loosening; recovery (রোগমুক্তি) ; unbolting, opening; freedom from obstruction or restrictions; unsheathing (কোষমুক্তি) ; delivery from or of (গর্ভমুক্তি) ; rescue; liberation; relief (ভয়মুক্তি) ; emancipation (নারীজাতির মুক্তি) ; end or termination (গ্রহণমুক্তি). **মুক্তি দেওয়া** same as **মুক্ত করা** (see **মুক্ত**) except in the last sense. **মুক্তি পাওয়া** *v.* to attain salvation; to gain freedom; to be set free, to be released or freed; to be extricated; to be discharged; to be acquitted; to be loosened, to be let loose; to be cured, to recover; to be unbolted; to be freed from obstruction or restrictions; to be unsheathed; to be delivered from or of; to be rescued; to be liberated; to become independent or free; to be emancipated. ~দ, ~দাতা *a.* & *n.* one who gives salvation or frees or releases or extricates or acquits or lets loose or cures or rescues or liberates or relieves or emancipates. *fem.* ~দা, দাত্রী। ~দান *n.* giving salvation; freeing; releasing; extrication or deliverance; acquittal; curing; rescuing; liberating; relieving; emancipating. ~নামা, ~পত্র *n.* a deed of release; a deed of reconveyance; a passport; a permit. ~পণ *n.* ransom. ~ফৌজ, ~সেনা *n.* an army of liberation; the Salvation Army. ~যুদ্ধ *n.* a war of liberation. ~লাভ *n.* attainment of salvation; attainment of freedom; release; extrication or deliverance; acquittal; recovery; rescue; liberation, relief. ~স্নান *n.* ceremonial bathing (esp. in a river) on termination of an eclipse.

মুক্তো coll. var. of **মুক্তা**।

মুখ *n.* the face; the mouth; countenance, appearance(s) (লোকের কাছে মুখ থাকা) ; gift of the gab, oratorical skill, eloquence (উকিলটির মুখ নেই) ; acrimonious speech, sharp or caustic tongue (তার বড়ো মুখ হয়েছে) ; speech, language, mode of speaking (দুর্মুখ) ; an entrance (গুহামুখ) ; an opening (ফোঁড়ার মুখ) ; an outlet; an outfall (নদীমুখ) ; a tip, a point (ছুঁচের মুখ) ; an end, an extremity, a head (রাস্তার মুখ) ; outset, beginning (উন্নতির মুখ) ; direction (গৃহমুখে). **মুখ উজ্জ্বল করা** *v.* to bring glory or credit to, to glorify. **মুখ করা** *v.* to scold (esp. peevishly). **মুখ কুটকুট্ করা** same as **মুখ চুলকানো** (see চুলকানো). **মুখ খারাপ করা** *v.* to utter foul or filthy or abusive words. **মুখ খিঁচানো** *v.* to make faces (at); to mouth; to scold. **মুখ খোলা** *v.* to begin to speak, to open one's mouth. **মুখ গোঁজ করা** *v.* to pull a long face; to be down in the mouth. **মুখ চলা** *v.* to be eating or speaking or scolding. **মুখ চাওয়া** *v.* to be dependent (on a person); to be considerate about or partial to (a person). **মুখ চুন করা** *v.* to become pale (on account of fear, shame etc.). **মুখ ছোটো করা** *v.* to discountenance; to discredit; to disgrace. **মুখ টিপে হাসা** *v.* to smile in a jocular or an oblique or a sly manner, to smirk. **মুখ তুলতে না পারা** *v.* to be highly abashed, to be put out of countenance. **মুখ তুলে চাওয়া, মুখ তোলা** *v.* to look up; (fig.) to smile on. **মুখ থাকা** *v.* to have one's face saved, to have appearances kept up. **মুখ থুবড়ে পড়া** *v.* to fall on one's face. **মুখ দেখা** *v.* to see ceremonially the face of a person (esp. of a bride) for the first time. **মুখ দেখাতে না পারা** same as **মুখ তুলতে না পারা**। **মুখ দেখানো** *v.* to show one's face, to put in an appearance. **মুখ নষ্ট করা** *v.* to speak or plead in vain. **মুখ নষ্ট হওয়া** *v.* to have one's advice or request turned down. **মুখ পোড়ানো** *v.* to disgrace, to scandalize. **মুখ ফসকানো** *v.* (of words, remarks etc.) to slip off one's tongue. **মুখ ফেরানো** *v.* to turn away or look in another direction (in disgust, displeasure etc.); (fig.) to become unfavourable or hostile to. **মুখ ফোটা** *v.* to begin to speak (esp. for the first time); to utter. **মুখ ফোলানো** *v.* to pout one's lips; to pull a long face. **মুখ বন্ধ করা** *v.* to stop one's mouth, to silence or be silent. **মুখ বাঁকানো** *v.* to turn up one's nose (in displeasure, abhorrence etc.); to make a wry face. **মুখ বোজা** *v.* to stop one's mouth, to become reticent or uncommunicative. **মুখ ভার** (বা **ভারী**) করা same as **মুখ গোঁজ করা**। **মুখ ভেংচানো** same as **ভেংচানো**। **মুখ মারা** *v.* to put out of countenance; to disgrace; to silence; to deprive one of one's appetite by feeding one with a highly palatable dish. **মুখ রাখা** *v.* to save one's face; to keep up appearances. **মুখ লুকানো** *v.* to hide one's face. **মুখ শুকানো** *v.* to look pale. **মুখ সামলানো** *v.* to speak guardedly; to forbear speaking unreservedly; to observe restraint in speech; to hold one's tongue. **মুখ সেলাই করে দেওয়া** *v.* to sew up or seal one's lips, to silence. **মুখ হওয়া** *v.* to learn to take liberties in speech; to be unrestrained in speech; to form a habit of scolding; (of a boil, etc.) to open. **মুখে আনা** *v.* to utter. **মুখে**

আসা *v.* to occur to one to speak; to desire to utter; to be capable of being uttered; to be uttered. **মুখে খই ফোটা** *v.* to be chattering excessively, to have a long tongue; to be eloquent. **মুখে জল আসা** *v.* to have one's mouth watering. **মুখে দেওয়া** *v.* to eat. **মুখে ফুল-চন্দন পড়া** *v.* (used as a good wish) to have one's tongue blessed for having made a desirable or favourable or successful prophecy. **মুখে ভাত** *n.* the Hindu custom of a child's eating rice for the first time. **মুখে-মুখে** *adv.* orally; viva voce; extemporarily, off-hand, impromptu; defiantly to one's face, in retort (মুখে মুখে জবাব) ; transmitted orally from one person to another (মুখে মুখে প্রচারিত). **মুখের উপর** to one's face; defying openly. **মুখের কথা** (fig.) a very easy job; (fig.) an oral promise, word of mouth. **মুখের ছাঁদ** cut of one's jib. **মুখের তোড়** fluency of speech. **মুখের ভয়ে** in fear of bitter scolding, in fear of sharp or caustic tongue. **মুখের মতো** fitting. **কোন মুখে সেখানে যাবে** have you the face to go there ? **~আলগা** *a.* incapable of keeping a secret, given to divulging secrets; having no control over one's tongue; having a long tongue. **~কমল** *n.* a face conceived as a lotus, a lotus-face. **~চন্দ্র** *n.* moonface. **~চন্দ্রিকা** *n.* the ceremonial viewing of each other's face by a bride and a bridegroom at a Hindu wedding. **~চাপা** *a.* tongue-tied, uncommunicative. **~চুন** *n.* clear sign of discomfiture, fear etc. on one's face; abashed look. **~চোরা** *a.* bashful, shy; tongue-tied. **~চ্ছটা, ~চ্ছবি** *n.* the glamour or beauty of a face. **~ঝামটা, ~নাড়া** *n.* scolding, mouthing. **মুখ ঝামটা** বা **মুখ নাড়া দেওয়া** *v.* to scold, to mouth, to snarl at. **~নিঃসৃত, ~নির্গত** *a.* issuing or emerging or emerged from one's mouth or face. **~পত্র** *n.* a preface, a preamble, an introduction; a journal representing an organization or association. **~পদ্ম** same as **~কমল**। **~পাত** *n.* the opening or top plait of a folded cloth; the cover or jacket of a book; the front; the outward show; commencement, inception, inauguration. **~পাত্র** *n.* a spokesman; a leader (esp. of a deputation). **~পোড়া** *n.* (in abuses) a disgraceful or scandalous person; (in affection) a mischievous person; a kind of monkey, the langur (হনুমান). *fem.* **মুখপুড়ি** (in the first two senses only). **~ফোড়** *a.* (impertinently) outspoken. **~বন্ধ** *n.* an introduction, a preface. **মুখ ব্যাদান করা** *v.* to gape, to open one's mouth wide. **~ভঙ্গি** *n.* a wry face or mouth; a grimace. **মুখভঙ্গি করা** same as **ভেংচানো**। **~মণ্ডল** *n.* the face. **~মিষ্টি** *n.* sweet or suave language. □ *a.* fair-spoken, sweet-tongued. **মুখরক্ষা করা** *v.* to save one's face; to keep up appearances. **~রুচি** same as **~চ্ছটা**। **~রোচক** *a.* pleasant to the taste, tasty, palatable; appetizing. **মুখরোচক কথা** pleasant or palatable or flattering speech. **~লাবণ্য** same as **~চ্ছটা**। **~শশী** same as **~চন্দ্র**। **~শুদ্ধি** *n.* deodorization of the mouth by chewing betel-leaves etc. after taking meals. **~শ্রী** *n.* the beauty or grace of the face. **~সর্বস্ব** *a.* efficient in tall talk (but not in action). **মুখসর্বস্ব ব্যক্তি** a prattler, a gasbag.

মুখটি[১] corrup. of **মুখোপাধ্যায়**।

মুখটি[২] *n.* a lid, a cap, a cork, a stopper (as of a bottle etc.).

মুখর *a.* garrulous, talkative, long-tongued; acrimonious in speech, mouthy, sharp-tongued; shrewish, quarrelsome; noisy (মুখর নূপুর) ; resounded or resounding or reverberating; loud; voluble; clamorous. **মুখরা** *a. fem.* clamorous, loud-tongued, shrewish. □ *n.* a termagant, a vixen. **মুখরিত** *a.* resounded; resounding; giving out a noise, full of noise.

মুখস্থ *a.* committed to memory, got by heart, memorized, lying in or within the mouth. **মুখস্থ করা** *v.* to commit to memory, to get by heart, to memorize; to cram. **মুখস্থ বলা** *v.* to commit from memory. **~বিদ্যা** *n.* the art of cramming; knowledge confined to memory work.

-মুখা older var. of **-মুখো**।

মুখাকৃতি *n.* the cut or appearance of the face, aspect, countenance, visage, facial features.

মুখাগ্নি *n.* fire applied to the mouth of the dead at cremation; act of singeing the mouth of the dead at cremation. **মুখাগ্নি করা** *v.* to singe the mouth of the dead at cremation.

মুখাচ্ছাদন *n.* a cover or veil for the face, a face-cover; (of a corpse) a face-cloth.

মুখানি poet. contr. of **মুখখানি**।

মুখানো *v.* to wait in eager expectation, to crane one's neck in eagerness or expectation. □ *a.* having craned one's neck in eagerness or expectation.

মুখাপেক্ষা *n.* dependence upon another for anything.

মুখাপেক্ষী *a.* dependent upon, hanging on. *fem.* **মুখাপেক্ষিণী**। **মুখাপেক্ষী হওয়া** *v.* to depend upon, to hang on. **মুখাপেক্ষী ব্যক্তি** a dependant, a hanger-on. **মুখাপেক্ষিতা** *n.* dependence, act of hanging on.

মুখাবয়ব same as **মুখাকৃতি**।

মুখামৃত *n.* spittle, saliva; (fig.) a nectarine wise saying of a saintly person or great man.

মুখি *n.* a sprout or eye of the arum.

মুখিয়ে থাকা same as **মুখানো** (*v.*)

-মুখী *fem.* of **-মুখো**।

মুখুজ্জে coll. contr. of **মুখোপাধ্যায়**।

মুখো *sfx.* denoting: having a particular face, faced (পোড়ারমুখো) ; facing (উত্তরমুখো) ; towards (ঘরমুখো).

মুখোমুখি *adv.* & *prep.* face to face with; facing one another; vis-a-vis (শত্রুর মুখোমুখি). □ *a.* facing one another; face to face, confronting each other. **মুখোমুখি হওয়া** *v.* to come face to face with, to confront, to face, to fly in face of. **মুখোমুখি লড়াই** a battle royal.

মুখোশ *n.* a false face, a mask; (fig.) dissimulation, hypocrisy, disguise. **মুখোশ পরা** *v.* to masquerade, to mask; (fig.) to dissimulate, to disguise oneself. **মুখোশ পরানো** *v.* to mask; (fig.) to disguise.

মুখ্য *a.* chief, principal, main; pre-eminent; foremost, prime; original; major. **মুখ্য আধিকারিক** the chief officer. **~কর্ম** *n.* (gr.) a direct object. **~ক্রিয়া** *n.* a primary action; (gr.) a principal verb. **মুখ্য জোয়ার** high tide, flow tide. **~তল** *n.* the principal plane. **মুখ্য নিরীক্ষক** the chief auditor. **মুখ্য নির্বাহক** the chief executive officer. **মুখ্য ন্যায়াধীশ** chief judge. **~মন্ত্রী** *n.* the chief minister.

মুগ *n.* a kind of pigeon-pea.

মুগধ poet. corrup. of **মুগ্ধ**।

মুগা *n.* a kind of silkworm; a kind of coarse silk spun by the aforesaid silkworms.

মুগুর *n.* a mallet, a club, a cudgel; a rammer; hammer.

মুগ্ধ *a.* fascinated; enchanted, bewitched; highly attracted, captivated; spellbound; engrossed, absorbed (ধ্যানমুগ্ধ) ; entranced (আবেশমুগ্ধ) ; foolishly doting (স্নেহমুগ্ধ) ; enamoured of; foolish or ignorant (মুগ্ধবোধ) ; simple, naive (মুগ্ধস্বভাব). *fem.* **মুগ্ধা**। **মুগ্ধ করা** *v.* to fascinate; to enchant, to bewitch; to attract highly, to captivate; to engross or absorb; to entrance.

মুঘল var. of **মোগল**।

মুচকানো *v.* to sprain or cause to sprain, to be wricked or to wrick (পা মুচকেছে).

মুচকি *a.* half-expressed by the turning up of lips, (cp.) smirky (মুচকি হাসি).

মুচকে হাসা to turn up one's lips in a derisive or suppressed smile, (cp.) to smirk.

মুচড়ানো *v.* to contort; to wring, to twist, to wriggle; to wrench.

মুচমুচ, মুচমুচে softer variants of **মচমচ** and **মচমচে** respectively.

মুচলেকা *n.* (in law) a recognizance, a bond. **মুচলেকা দেওয়া** *v.* to enter into a recognizance, to furnish a bond.

মুচি[১] *n.* a crucible; a tiny saucer-shaped earthen vessel; a green coconut (recently grown) within which there is no water and no kernel).

মুচি[২] *n.* a worker in animal skin, a shoemaker, a cobbler, a cordwainer, a tanner.

মুচুকুন্দ *n.* a variety of champak flowers.

মুছা, মোছা *v.* to wipe; to mop, to swab; to rub out, to obliterate, to efface, to expunge (দাগ মোছা). **~নো** *v.* to cause to wipe or mop or swab or rub out or obliterate or efface or expunge.

মুজরা, (coll.) **মুজরো** *n.* a professional demonstration of singing or dancing (মুজরো করা) ; an engagement or call for the aforesaid demonstration (মুজরো পাওয়া) ; a discount or rebate.

মুজরিম *n.* a criminal.

মুঞ্জ *n.* a kind of grass from which cords are made.

মুঞ্জরন *n.* blossoming; sprouting.

মুঞ্জরা, মুঞ্জরিত, মুঞ্জরি variants of **মঞ্জরা, মঞ্জরিত** and **মঞ্জরি** respectively.

মুটে *n.* a porter. **মুটে-মজুর** *n.* labourers collectively; labourers as a class; (usu. derog.) a menial or low-grade worker.

মুঠ, মুঠা, মুঠি, মুঠো coll. forms of **মুষ্টি**। **মুঠোমুঠো** *a.* many handfuls (of); numerous, huge; of a great number, numerous; much, many (মুঠোমুঠো টাকা, মুঠোমুঠো ফুল).

মুড়কি *n.* parched paddy coated with boiled sugar or molasses.

মুড়া[1] older var. of **মুড়ো**[1] ।

মুড়া[2], **মোড়া** *v.* to cover, to wrap; to enclose (খামে চিঠি মোড়া) ; to fold (বিছানা মোড়া) ; to double up (হাঁটু মুড়ে বসা) ; to contort or twist or bend (দেহ মোড়া) ; to ravel in, to wind round (আঙুলে সুতো মোড়া).

মুড়া[3], **মোড়া** *v.* to pollard, to lop; to eat off the top (of) (ছাগলে গাছ মুড়েছে) ; to shave (মাথা মোড়া).

মুড়ানো, মুড়োনো *a.* pollarded, lopped; shaven. □ *v.* to pollard or cause to pollard, to lop or cause to lop; to shave or cause to shave.

মুড়ি[1] *n.* a kind of food made by parching rice on hot sand.

মুড়ি[2] *n.* the severed head of a goat, fish etc,; a counterfoil (চেকমুড়ি). **মুড়ি ঘণ্ট** *n.* a highly seasoned dish prepared with the head of fish or of a goat, sheep, etc.

মুড়ি[3] *n.* a folded edge or hem of cloth etc.; covering or wrapping. **মুড়ি দেওয়া** *v.* to hem; to cover or wrap oneself (কাঁথা মুড়ি দেওয়া). **মুড়ি-সেলাই** *n.* a hemstitch, a hem. **মুড়ি-সেলাই দেওয়া বা করা** *v.* to hem-stitch, to hem.

মুড়ো[1] *n.* the head of a fish; tip or corner (কাপড়ের মুড়ো) ; an end or extremity (ঘরের এ মুড়ো থেকে ও মুড়ো)।

মুড়ো[2] *a.* pollarded or lopped (মুড়ো গাছ) ; worn-out or decayed (মুড়ো ঝাঁটা)।

মুণ্ড, (coll.) **মুন্ডু** *n.* the head. **মুন্ডু ঘুরে যাওয়া** *v.* to be dazed (by astonishment, fear, worry etc.); to be infatuated, to have one's head turned (রূপ দেখে তার মুন্ডু ঘুরে গেল). **মুণ্ডচ্ছেদ করা, মুণ্ডচ্ছেদন করা** *v.* to behead, to decapitate. **মুণ্ডন** *n.* shaving, a shave; cutting or cropping. **মুণ্ডন করা** *v.* to shave; to cut or crop. **মুণ্ডপাত করা** *v.* to behead; (fig.) to ruin; to shower abuse on. **মুণ্ডমালা** *n.* a string or wreath of severed human heads. **মুণ্ডমালিনী** *a. fem.* wearing a wreath of severed human heads. □ Goddess Kali (কালী). **মুণ্ডাকার** *a.* shaped like a head; (bot.) capitate. **মুণ্ডি** *n.* a sweet drop steeped in sugar syrup (রসমুন্ডি). **মুণ্ডিত** *a.* shaven; cropped; pollarded, lopped. **মুণ্ডিত করা** *v.* to shave; to crop; to pollard, to lop. **মুণ্ডিতকেশ, মুণ্ডিতমস্তক** *a.* shaven-headed.

মুত *n.* (coll. & now vul.) urine.

মুতসুদ্দি *n.* a deputy or agent; a commercial agent, a banian.

মুতা, মোতা (vul.) *v.* to urinate, to make or pass water, to piss, to micturate. **মুতানো, মোতানো** *v.* to cause to urinate.

মুতাবেক *adv.* in accordance with, according to; in compliance with.

মুথা, (coll.) **মুথো** *n.* a kind of grass with aromatic roots.

মুদা, মোদা *v.* to close, to shut (আঁখি মোদা).

মুদারা *n.* (mus.) the scale of the medium tone, (cp.) barytone.

মুদি *n.* a grocer. **~খানা** *n.* a grocer's shop.

মুদিত[1] *a.* delighted, pleased.

মুদিত[2] *a.* closed, shut. **মুদিত করা** *v.* to close, to shut.

মুদগর *n.* a mallet, a club, a cudgel; a rammer; a hammer.

মুদ্দত *n.* time limit, fixed or stipulated time; deadline.

মুদ্দতি *a.* continuing or enforced for a fixed period; periodical; temporary.

মুদ্দাফরাশ, মুদ্দোফারাশ coll. corruptions of **মুর্দাফরাশ** (see **মুর্দা**).

মুদ্রক *n.* a printer.

মুদ্রণ *n.* printing; stamping; impression. মুদ্রণ করা *v.* to print; to stamp; to impress. মুদ্রণ নিবন্ধ press register. মুদ্রণ-নিবন্ধক *n.* press registrar. ~প্রমাদ *n.* printing mistake. মুদ্রণ-শোধক *n.* press corrector, proof-reader. মুদ্রণ-শোধন *n.* press correction, proof-reading. মুদ্রণীয় *a.* printable, worth printing.

মুদ্রলিখ *n.* a typewriter. মুদ্রলেখক *n.* a typist.

মুদ্রা *n.* a coin; a rupee; money, wealth; a seal, a signet, a stamp; any one of the peculiar signs made with fingers during prayer; any pose or gesture of dancing; a (ludicrous) mannerism (মুদ্রাদোষ). ~কর *n.* a printer. মুদ্রাকর-প্রমাদ *n.* a printing mistake. ~কার *a.* nummular. ~ক্ষর *n.* a printing type. ~ঙ্কন *n.* stamping or impressing or sealing. ~ঙ্কিত *a.* stamped, impressed, sealed. মুদ্রাঙ্কিত করা *v.* to stamp, to impress, to seal. ~দোষ *n.* a (ludicrous) mannerism. ~বিজ্ঞান *n.* numismatics. ~বিজ্ঞানী *n.* a numismatist. ~মান *n.* (econ.) money standard. ~মূল্য *n.* value of a coin or currency. ~ মূল্যহ্রাস *n.* depreciation or devaluation of a coin or currency. ~যন্ত্র *n.* a printing machine. ~লিপি *n.* a lithograph. মুদ্রাশঙ্খ *n.* litharge. ~স্ফীতি *n.* (econ.) inflation of money currency, inflation.

মুদ্রিত *a.* stamped, impressed, sealed; printed; shut, closed. মুদ্রিত করা *v.* to stamp, to impress, to seal; to print; to shut, to close. মুদ্রিত নয়নে *adv.* with closed eyes.

মুনশি *n.* a clerk, a scrivener, a scribe; a secretary; an Urdu teacher; a munshi. ~য়ানা *n.* erudition; skill in drafting or composition; calligraphy; skill; virtuosity. খাসমুনশি *n.* a private secretary.

মুনসেফ *n.* an officer trying suits at the lowest civil court, a munsiff. মুনসেফি *n.* the office of a munsiff. □ *a.* relating to a munsiff (মুনসেফি আদালত).

মুনাফা *n.* profit. মুনাফা লোটা *v.* to profiteer. ~খোর, ~বাজ *a.* given to profiteering. □ *n.* a profiteer. ~খোরি, ~বাজি *n.* profiteering.

মুনাসিব *a.* to one's liking or choice, agreeable to; fit, worthy.

মুনি *n.* a sage practising ascetical meditation (usu. in solitude), a hermit; a sage or an ascetic. মুনির আশ্রম a hermitage. ~বাক্য *n.* saying or utterance of a sage. নানা মুনির নানা মত many men many minds, sages differ.

মুনিব var. of মনিব।

মুনিবর *n.* a chief hermit; (hon.) a highly respectable sage.

মুনিয়া *n.* munia, a tiny Indian bird.

মুনিশ, মুনিষ *n.* a farm-hand.

মুনীন্দ্র *n.* a chief hermit.

মুন্সি rej. spell. of মুনশি।

মুন্সেফ alt. spell. of মুনসেফ।

মুফত *adv.* & *a.* cost-free, gratuitous; without remuneration, gratis. মুফতে *adv.* cost-free; gratuitously; free of cost.

মুফতি *n.* (Mus.) an expounder of Mohammedan laws, a mufti; the civilian dress of one who wears a uniform, mufti.

মুমুক্ষা *n.* desire for salvation.

মুমুক্ষু *a.* desirous of salvation.

মুমূর্ষু *a.* (ori. but rare) desirous of dying; (pop.) about to die, dying, moribund. মুমূর্ষু দশা dying state. মুমূর্ষাবস্থায় *adv.* in a dying state; on the point of death.

মুয়াজ্জিন *n.* (Mus.) one who announces the hours of prayer from a minaret, a muezzin.

মুরগা var. of মোরগ।

মুরগি *n.* (as *fem.*) the hen; (as neut.) a fowl, a chicken. মুরগির ছানা a chick, a chicken.

মুরছা, মুরছিত poet. corruptions of মূর্ছা and মূর্ছিত respectively.

মুরজ *n.* an instrument of percussion resembling a tom tom.

মুরতি poet. corrup. of মূর্তি।

মুরদ, মুরোদ *n.* ability; power; strength.

মুরলি, মুরলী *n.* a flute, a pipe.

মুরারি *n.* Krishna (কৃষ্ণ), who killed Mura (মুর) the demon.

মুরি *n.* a sewer, a gutter; a drain.

মুরিদ *n.* (Mus.) a devout person.

মুরুব্বি *n.* a guardian; a patron; a leader.

মুরব্বির জোর the support or patronage of a guardian or patron. **~গিরি, ~য়ানা** *n.* guardianship; patronage. **মুরব্বিগিরি করা** *v.* to assume officiously the post or role of a guardian; to assume the air of a guardian.

মুর্গি rej. spell. of **মুরগি**।

মুলতান *n.* an Indian musical mode.

মুলতানি *a.* of Multan. □ *n.* Multan the Indian musical mode.

মুলতুবি *a.* postponed, adjourned; deferred (মুলতুবি পাওনা); held in abeyance (মুলতুবি আইন). **মুলতুবি রাখা বা করা** *v.* to postpone, to adjourn; to defer; to put or hold in abeyance.

মুলা older var. of **মুলো**।

মুলাকাত older var. of **মোলাকাত**।

মুলুক *n.* a country; a kingdom; native land, motherland.

মুলো *n.* the radish.

মুল্লুক var. of **মুলুক**।

মুশকিল *n.* a difficulty, a trouble, a fix; a hitch, a rub. **মুশকিল বেধেছে** there is a difficulty or trouble or fix or hitch. **মুশকিলে পড়া** *v.* to run into a difficulty or trouble or fix. **মুশকিল আসান** removal of difficulty or trouble.

মুশকো জোয়ান *n.* (usu. (dero.) a strong and robust person.

মুষড়ানো *v.* to become downhearted or depressed or discouraged. **মুষড়ে পড়া** same as **মুষড়ানো**।

মুষল *n.* a mallet, a club; a rammer; a pestle (esp. of a husking-tree which is operated in the seesaw manner or of a mortar). **~ধারা** *n.* torrential downpour. **মুষলধারে বৃষ্টি পড়া** to rain cats and dogs, to rain in torrents.

মুষ্ক *n.* the scrotum. **~গ্রন্থি** *n.* the testicles. **মুষ্কচ্ছেদন করা** *v.* to castrate. **ছিন্নমুষ্ক** *a.* castrated.

মুষ্টি *n.* cupped palm of the hand; a handful; a fist; a handle, a haft, a hilt; firm hold, grip. **~গত** *a.* gripped; firmly held or controlled; clenched. **~প্রহার** same as **মুষ্ট্যাঘাত**। **~বদ্ধ** *a.* having a hand or hands closed or clenched; (of a hand) closed or clenched. **~ভিক্ষা** *n.* a handful of rice or other cereals given in charity. **~মেয়** *a.* only a handful of, a little or a few. **~যুদ্ধ** *n.* boxing; buffeting. **মুষ্টিযুদ্ধ করা** *v.* to engage in a boxing contest. **~যোগ** *n.* a quack remedy or medicine. **~যোদ্ধা** *n.* a boxer, a pugilist. **মুষ্ট্যাঘাত** *n.* a fisticuff, a box, a buffet. **মুষ্ট্যাঘাত করা** *v.* to box, to buffet.

মুসম্মত *n.* (Mus.) an appellation affixed to the names of Muslim women, (cp.) Miss, Mrs.

মুসলমান, মুসলিম *n.* a Mussulman, a Muslim. □ *a.* Mohammedan, Muslim. **মুসলমানধর্ম** *n.* Islam, Mohammedanism. **মুসলমানি** *n.* a Mohammedan female, a Muslim woman; the Muslim mode of life or fashion and practices; the Muslim custom of circumcision. □ *a.* Mohammedan.

মুসা *n.* Moses.

মুসাফির *n.* a wayfarer; a traveller; a traveller in foreign lands. **~খানা** *n.* an inn; a caravanserai.

মুসাবিদা *n.* a draft (of a document, writing etc.). **মুসাবিদা করা** *v.* to draft.

মুসুরি *n.* lentil.

মুস্কিল rej. spell. of **মুশকিল**।

মুহম্মদ var. of **মহম্মদ**।

মুহুরি[1] *n.* a sewer, a gutter, a drain; a strainer covering the mouth of a drain; a nut of a bolt; the measure of the cuff or ankle of garments.

মুহুরি[2] *n.* a clerk or scrivener. **~গিরি** *n.* clerkship.

মুহুর্মুহু *adv.* (also *a.*) again and again; repeatedly; with little or no respite.

মুহূর্ত *n.* a division of time (=48 minutes); a point of time, a moment, a while; a very short time. **এই মুহূর্তে** at this moment; just now; immediately, at once. **~কাল** *n.* a moment, a while. **~মধ্যে** *adv.* in a moment, in an instant, in two ticks, in a trice, in a jiffy. **~মাত্র** *adv.* only for a moment or while. □ *n.* only a moment.

মুহ্যমান *a.* stunned; stupefied; benumbed; extremely afflicted (শোকে মুহ্যমান)।

মূক *a.* dumb; mute; dumbfounded, speechless (বিস্ময়ে মূক হওয়া). **~-বধির** *a.* deaf and dumb. **মূক-বধির ব্যক্তি** a deaf-mute.

মূঢ় *a.* moving under an illusion; infatuated; stupid; ignorant; indiscreet; mentally obsessed. **~তা** *n.* ignorance; stupidity; bewilderment; indiscretion.

মূত্র *n.* urine. **~কৃচ্ছ্র** *n.* painful micturition, strangury. **মূত্রত্যাগ করা** *v.* to urinate, to make or pass water, to piss; to micturate. **~ধানী** *n.* a urinal; a piss-pot. **~নালি** *n.* the urethra. **মূত্রনালি-প্রদাহ** urethritis. **~নিঃসরণ** *n.* discharge of urine; urination. **~নিরোধ** *n.* retention of urine. **~বর্ধক** *a.* diuretic. **মূত্রবর্ধক-ওষুধ** a diuretic. **~মেহ** *n.* painful micturition; diabetes. **মূত্রাধার, মূত্রাশয়** *n.* (anat.) the bladder.

মূরতি alt. spell. of **মুরতি**।

মূর্খ *a.* stupid, foolish; uneducated, illiterate; ignorant; inexperienced. □ *n.* a stupid person, a fool, an idiot, a dunce; an uneducated or illiterate person; an inexperienced person, a greenhorn. **~তা** *n.* stupidity, foolishness; a folly; lack of education, illiteracy; ignorance; inexperience. **মূর্খতা প্রকাশ করা** *v.* to betray one's stupidity or ignorance. **~তাসূচক** *a.* betraying or indicative of stupidity or gross ignorance.

মূর্ছনা *n.* (mus.) a gradual modulation or rise and fall of voice; (mus.) a sweet tremor of voice.

মূর্ছা *n.* a fainting fit, a swoon; (med.) a syncope. □ *v.* same as **মূর্ছা যাওয়া**। **মূর্ছা যাওয়া** *v.* to faint, to swoon. **~গত, ~প্রাপ্ত** *a.* fainted, swooned; lying unconscious. **~বায়ু, ~রোগ** *n.* epilepsy; syncope. **~বায়ুগ্রস্ত** *a.* epileptic; syncopic, syncoptic. **~ভঙ্গ** *n.* regaining of consciousness from a fainting fit.

মূর্ছিত *a.* fainted, swooned. **মূর্ছিত হওয়া** *v.* to faint, to swoon.

মূর্ত *a.* corporeal, embodied, personized; incarnate; concrete; material; (phys.) real; (fig.) palpable, tangible, visible, manifest. **মূর্ত করা** *v.* to embody; to personize; to incarnate; to concretize; to make visible or tangible or manifest. **মূর্ত হওয়া** *v.* to assume a form; to be incarnated; to become palpable or tangible or visible or manifest.

মূর্তি *n.* a body; an incarnation; an embodiment; an image; a form, a shape, a figure, an appearance. **মূর্তি ধারণ করা, মূর্তি পরিগ্রহ করা** *v.* to assume a material body or form; to be incarnated; to assume a particular appearance; to personate. **~পূজক** *n.* an idolator (*fem.* an idolatress), an imageworshipper. **~পূজা** *n.* idolatry, imageworship. **~মান,** (loos.) **~মন্ত** *a.* embodied; incarnate; personized; personified; manifest, visible; (dero.) downright or mischievous. *fem.* **~মতী**। **মূর্তিমান শয়তান** the very embodiment of devil or satan.

মূর্ধন্য *a.* (gr.) cerebral. □ *n.* (gr.) a retroflex or cerebral letter , a cerebral.

মূর্ধা *n.* the head. **মূর্ধাভিষিক্ত** *a.* enthroned by being sprinkled with holy water on one's head.

মূর্বা, মুর্বী *n.* the bow-string hemp.

মূল *n.* a root; an esculent root, a bulbous plant, a bulb; beginning; origin; a cause or source of origin; (of money) capital or principal (সুদেমূলে) ; foundation, base, basis (অমূলক) ; the basal or embedded part of anything, the foot (বৃক্ষমূল) ; (math.) a factor of a quantity, root. □ *a.* first, original; fundamental; basic; primary; principal; chief, main; real; (of invested money etc.) capital or principal. **অবরোহ মূল** (bot.) a hanging root. **অস্থানিক মূল** (bot.) an adventitious root. **প্রধান মূল, মুখ্য মূল** (bot.) a tap root. **মূল উপাদান** an essential element. **মূল একক** a fundamental unit. **-মূলক** *sfx.* caused by, originating from (ভ্রান্তিমূলক বিশ্বাস) ; (inc.) causing or exhibiting (দুঃখমূলক ব্যাপার). **~কর্ম** *n.* the original or principal work. **~কারণ** *n.* the first or primary or original cause; the root-cause; the real cause. **~কেন্দ্র** *n.* the principal centre; headquarters; (comm.) the head office; (geom.) the radical centre. **~গত** *a.* basic, fundamental; radical. **মূল গায়েন** the leading singer of a chorus. **~গ্রন্থ** *n.* the original text or manuscript, (cp.) the source-book. **~চ্ছেদ, ~চ্ছেদন** same as **মূলোচ্ছেদ**। **~জ** *a.* originating from the root, radical. **মূলজ প্রেষ** *n.*

(bot.) the root-pressure. **~জীবী** *n.* (bot.) a root-parasite. **~ত** same as **মূলে**। **~তত্ত্ব** *n.* the first or primary principle; the basic or fundamental truth. **~ত্র** *n.* (bot.) a root-cap. **~দ** *a.* (alg.) rational. □ *n.* (alg.) a rational quantity, a rational. **~ধন** *n.* capital or principal (invested). **~ধর্ম** *n.* the fundamental properties. **~নীতি** *n.* the fundamental or basic or primary principle. **~প্রকৃতি** *n.* the original or elemental nature; (theol.) same as **আদ্যাশক্তি**। **~ভিত্তি** *n.* the foundation, the groundwork; inauguration; the primary or principal ground or basis. **~মন্ত্র** *n.* an esoteric word or words uttered inwardly at prayer; the guiding principle; firm resolve (জীবনের মূলমন্ত্র). **~রশ্মি** *n.* (phys.) a direct ray. **~রোম** *n.* (bot.) a root-hair. **~শিকড়** (chiefly bot.) the main root. **~সূত্র** *n.* the fundamental rule or principle. **মূলে** *adv.* at the root or base; in the beginning, originally; primarily; basically, fundamentally; at all. **মূলে ভুল করা** to get hold of the wrong end of the stick.

মূলা[১] rej. var. of **মূলো**।

মূলা[২] *n.* the nineteenth of the twenty-seven stars of Hindu astronomy.

মূলাকর্ষণ *n.* a pull by the root. **মূলাকর্ষণ করা** *v.* to pull by the root.

মূলাধার *n.* the real cause.

মূলানুগ *a.* following or in accordance with base or root or etymology; etymological; fundamental.

মূলীভূত *a.* causing origination; lying at the root; serving as the first or primary cause.

মূলে see **মূল[২]**।

মূলোচ্ছেদ, মূলোৎপাটন *n.* extirpation, eradication; (fig.) complete destruction. **মূলোচ্ছেদ করা, মূলোৎপাটন করা** *v.* to uproot, to root out, to extirpate, to eradicate; (fig.) to pay for; to destroy completely or thoroughly.

মূল্য *n.* price; rate; cost; value, worth; charge; wages, fee, remuneration; hire-charge, hire; freight. **মূল্য দেওয়া** *v.* to pay the price of; to remunerate; (fig.) to appreciate or recognize the value or worth of. **~জ্ঞাপন** *n.* quotation (of prices). **~নির্ধারক, ~নিরূপক** *a.* appraising; evaluating. □ *n.* an appraiser; an evaluator. **মূল্যনির্ধারণ** বা **নিরূপণ করা** *v.* to appraise; to evaluate. **~পত্র** (পাওনা সম্বন্ধে) *n.* a bill. **~বান** *a.* valuable, costly, precious. **~বৃদ্ধি** *n.* increase or rise in price, appreciation. **~বেদন** *n.* quotation of price or charge. **~বেদনপত্র** *n.* a tender. **~বোধ** *n.* idea or sense of values. **~হীন** *a.* valueless; worthless; (fig.) futile or useless. **~হ্রাস** *n.* fall in price or value, depreciation. **মূল্যানুসারে** *adv.* according to value or price, ad valorem. **মূল্যায়ন** *n.* assessment; evaluation. **মূল্যায়ন করা** *v.* to assess or estimate the price or value of; to appraise; to evaluate.

মূষা[১] *n.* a crucible.

মূষা[২], মূষিক *n.* the rat; the mouse (*pl.* mice).

মৃগ *n.* the deer; the stag; the antelope; ground game; a beast, an animal. **কস্তুরীমৃগ** *n.* the musk-deer. **কৃষ্ণসার-মৃগ** *n.* the black antelope. **চিত্রমৃগ** *n.* the spotted deer. **শাখামৃগ** *n.* the monkey. **~চর্ম** *n.* deer-skin; animal skin. **~তৃষা, ~তৃষ্ণা, ~তৃষ্ণিকা** *n.* a mirage. **~নয়না** *a. fem.* having eyes like those of a deer. **~নাভি** *n.* musk. **~মদ** *n.* musk. **~য়া** *n.* hunting (esp. of big games). **মৃগয়া করা** *v.* to hunt. **মৃগয়া করতে যাওয়া** *v.* to go out hunting. **মৃগয়াকারী** *n.* a hunter, a huntsman. **~রাজ** same as **মৃগেন্দ্র**। **~লোচনা** same as **~নয়না**। **~শিরা, ~শীর্ষ** *n.* the fifth of the twenty-seven stars according to Hindu astronomy. **~শিশু** *n.* a fawn. **~শৃঙ্গ** *n.* the horn of a buck. **মৃগাক্ষী** same as **~নয়না**। *masc.* **মৃগাক্ষ**। **মৃগাঙ্ক** *n.* one who bears the sign of a deer; the moon. **মৃগাঙ্কমৌলি, মৃগাঙ্কশেখর** *n.* one who bears the moon on one's forehead as a crown; Shiva (শিব). **মৃগাজিন** *n.* a deer-skin; an animal skin. **মৃগাজীব** *n.* a professional hunter. **মৃগী** *n.* (as *fem.*) the doe, the female beast (শাখামৃগী) ; (as *neut.*) epilepsy. **মৃগেন্দ্র** *n.* the king of beasts; the lion.

মৃগেল *n.* a species of large fresh-water fish with reddish eyes.

মৃণাল *n.* a stalk of the lotus or water-lily; the white esculent root of the lotus. **~নিন্দিত** *a.* excelling even a lotus stalk in beauty or delicateness. **~ভুজ** *n.* an arm as delicate as a lotus-stalk. **মৃণালিনী** *n.* a clump of the lotus or water-lily; (loos.) the lotus or the water-lily.

মৃত *a.* dead, deceased, defunct; lifeless; inanimate. **~কল্প, ~প্রায়, ~বৎ** *a.* almost or nearly dead, dying, moribund. **~দার** *a. masc.* one whose wife is dead. **মৃতদার ব্যক্তি** a widower. **~দেহ** *n.* a dead body; corpse (of a human being); carcass (of an animal). **~বৎসা** *a. fem.* (usually) giving birth to still-born babies. **~সঞ্জীবনী** *a.* capable of bringing back the dead to life. □ *n.* anything (esp. a medicine) capable of bringing back the dead to life. **মৃতাশৌচ** *n.* personal impurity caused by the death of a blood-relation.

মৃৎ *n.* earth, clay. **~কাণ্ডজ** *n.* (bot.) a radical leaf. **মৃৎক্ষয় রোধ** *n.* prevention of soil erosion. **~পাত্র** *n.* an earthen pot or vessel, an earthenware. **~পিণ্ড** *n.* a lump of clay or earth, a clod of earth. **~শিল্প** *n.* the potter's art, pottery; clay-modelling. **~সংরক্ষণ** *n.* soil-conservation.

মৃত্তিকা *n.* earth; clay, mud; soil; the ground; the earth; the world. **বাহিত মৃত্তিকা** (geog.) transported soil. **~গঠিত, ~নির্মিত** same as **মৃন্ময়** । **~গর্ভ** *n.* the bowels or inside of the earth; an underground place, the underground. **~পাত্র, ~ভাণ্ড** same as **মৃৎপাত্র** (see **মৃৎ**). **~ভোজন** *n.* geophagy. **~ভোজী** *a.* geophagous.

মৃত্যু *n.* death, decease, demise; loss of life; Yama (যম) the Hindu god of death. **~কামনা** *n.* desire of death; death-wish. **মৃত্যুকামনা করা** *v.* to desire to die; to desire another's death. **~কামী** *a.* desirous of dying; desirous of another's death. **~কাল** *n.* the time of death; the dying moment. **~কালীন** *a.* pertaining to the time of death or to the dying moments. **মৃত্যুকালীন এজাহার** a dying statement or declaration. **মৃত্যুকালে হরিনাম** deathbed repentance. **~গ্রাস** *n.* the jaws of death. **মৃত্যুগ্রাসে পতিত হওয়া** *v.* to fall into the jaws of death; to die; to be killed. **~চিহ্ন** *n.* same as **~লক্ষণ** । **মৃত্যুঞ্জয়** *a.* one who has conquered death; deathless, immortal. □ *n.* Shiva (শিব). **মৃত্যুঞ্জয়ী** *a.* loos. var. of **মৃত্যুঞ্জয়** (*a.*). **~তুল্য** *a.* death-like, deathly. **~দণ্ড** *n.* death-sentence, capital punishment. **মৃত্যুদণ্ড দেওয়া** *v.* to sentence to death, to award capital punishment (to). **মৃত্যুদণ্ডে দণ্ডিত হওয়া** *v.* to be sentenced to death. **~ভয়** *n.* the fear of death. **~মুখ** same as **~গ্রাস** । **~যন্ত্রণা** *n.* death-agony, death-throe. **~লক্ষণ** *n.* a sign of death or being dead. **~শয্যা** *n.* deathbed. **~শোক, ~জনিত শোক** *n.* sorrow caused by (some one's) death, grief caused by death. **~হীন** *a.* deathless, immortal; everlasting.

মৃদঙ্গ *n.* an instrument of percussion shaped almost like a tom-tom.

মৃদু *a.* soft, supple, delicate; slight, gentle; not heavy, light; slow; dim, tender; not loud, low; temperate (মৃদু তাপ) ; mild, meek, effeminate (মৃদু স্বভাব) ; noiseless, stealthy (মৃদু চরণে) ; not sharp or keen (মৃদু ধার, মৃদু বুদ্ধি). **~তা** *n.* softness; gentleness; mildness, tenderness. **~গতি** same as **~গামী** । **~গতিতে** *adv.* with a slow or gentle motion, moving gently. **~গমনা** same as **~গামিনী** । **~গম্ভীর** *a.* low and deep, rumbling (মৃদুগম্ভীর স্বর বা ধ্বনি). **~গামী** *a.* slowly going or moving; softly or stealthily going or moving. *fem.* **~গামিনী** । **~জল** (chem.) soft water. **~পবন, ~বায়ু** *n.* a gentle breeze, (naut.) a cat's-paw. **~ভাষী** *a.* soft-spoken. **~মন্দ** *a.* gently and pleasantly moving (মৃদুমন্দ বাতাস) ; low and sweet (মৃদুমন্দ ধ্বনি) ; slow; (iron.) light but sharp (মৃদুমন্দ আঘাত) □ *adv.* moving gently and pleasantly; gently and pleasantly; in a low and sweet manner; slowly; (iron.) lightly but sharply. **~রোমশ** *a.* (bot.) downy. **~স্পর্শ** *a.* soft to the touch. □ *n.* gentle touch. **~স্বভাব** *a.* of a gentle nature. □ *n.* gentle nature. **~স্বর** *n.* low voice. **~স্বরে** *adv.* in a low voice, in a whisper.

মৃদুল *a.* soft; tender; slow; light, noiseless. *fem.* **মৃদুলা** ।

মৃদুভাণ্ড same as **মৃৎপাত্র**।

মৃন্ময় *a.* made of earth or clay, earthen, clayey; mud-built (মৃন্ময় কুটির). *fem.* **মৃন্ময়ী**। **মৃন্ময় তলানি** (geog.) terrigenous deposit. **~পাত্র** same as **মৃৎপাত্র**। **~মূর্তি** *n.* a clay-model; an image made of clay. **~শিল্প** same as **মৃৎশিল্প**।

মে *n.* (the month of) May. **মে দিবস** *n.* May Day.

মেও, মেউ variants of **মিউ**।

মেওয়া *n.* a collective name of several nutritious fruits namely pomegranates, grapes, raisins, almonds etc.; any nutritious fruit. **~ওয়ালা** *n.* a fruit-seller, a fruiteret. *fem.* **~ওয়ালি** a fruiteress.

মেকদার *n.* measure.

মেকি *a.* counterfeit, spurious; faked, forged; artificial; false (মেকি কথা) ; dissimulating, impersonating (মেকি লোক)।

মেখলা *n.* an ornamental girdle; (rare) a sword-guard or sword-belt.

মেঘ *n.* cloud. **মেঘ করা** *v.* to cloud; to look cloudy; to become somewhat cloudy. **মেঘ কেটেছে** *v.* clouds have dispersed or lifted. **মেঘ জমা** *v.* to cloud. **মেঘ হওয়া** *v.* to cloud. **অলক-মেঘ** *n.* the cirrus. **অলকাস্তর-মেঘ** *n.* the cirro-stratus. **আস্তর-মেঘ** *n.* the stratus. **ঝঞ্ঝামেঘ,** (coll.) **ঝড়োমেঘ** *n.* the nimbus. **পুঞ্জমেঘ** *n.* the cumulus. **পুঞ্জালক-মেঘ** *n.* the cirro-cumulus. **ভাঙামেঘ** scattered clouds. **রাঙা মেঘ, সিঁদুরে মেঘ** a cirmson-coloured cloud which presages a storm. **~খণ্ড** *n.* a cloudlet. **~গর্জন** *n.* the roar or rumble of clouds; a clap of thunder. **~জাল** *n.* cumulated clouds. **~ডম্বর** *n.* cumulation of clouds; the roar or rumble of clouds; a clap of thunder. **মেঘডম্বর শাড়ি** a sari (শাড়ি) having the colour of the nimbus, a dark blue sari. **~নাদ** *n.* the roar or rumble of clouds; one who roars like rumbling clouds. **~নির্ঘোষ** same as **~গর্জন**। **~মণ্ডিত** *a.* overcast with clouds, cloudy; cloud-topped, (poet.) cloud-capt. **~মন্দ্র** *n.* the rumble of clouds. **~মন্দ্রস্বর** *n.* a voice resembling the rumble of clouds. **~ময়** *a.* full of clouds, cloudy, clouded. **~মল্লার** *n.* megh-mallar, an Indian musical mode. **~মালা** *n.* a string or series of clouds. **~মেদুর** *a.* rendered cool or pleasantly shadowy for being overcast with clouds. **~লা** *a.* overcast with clouds, cloudy. **মেঘাগম** *n.* the break or advent of the monsoon; the rainy season. **মেঘাচ্ছন্ন** *a.* thickly overcast with clouds, thickly clouded. **মেঘাড়ম্বর** same as **~ডম্বর**। **মেঘাত্যয়** *n.* the autumn. **মেঘে মেঘে বেলা হওয়া** *v.* (fig.) to become aged; grow old over the years.

মেচেতা *n.* freckles; lentigo. **মেচেতা পড়া** *v.* to be freckled.

মেছুনি *n. fem.* a fishwife; a fishwoman, a fisher-woman.

মেছুয়া *n.* a fishmonger or a fisherman. □ *a.* relating to fish (মেছুয়া গন্ধ) ; where fish is sold or auctioned or caught; piscivorous, fish-eating (মেছুয়া কুমির). **~ঘেরি** *n.* a place for catching fish, a fishery. **~বাজার** *n.* a fish-market. **~হাটা** *n.* a retail market for selling consignments of fish by auction; (fig.) a noisy place.

মেছেতা var. of **মেচেতা**।

মেছো pop. var. of **মেছুয়া**।

মেজ[1] *n.* a table; a desk.

মেজ[2] *n.* second-born (মেজছেলে) ; second in order of age or seniority (মেজকর্তা, মেজসাহেব)।

মেজরাব pop. corrup. of **মিজরাব**।

মেজমেজ rej. spell. of **ম্যাজম্যাজ**।

মেজাজ *n.* mood (of the mind); the habitual frame of mind, temperament; a fit of ill-humour or rage, temper. **মেজাজ খারাপ থাকা** *v.* to be out of humour. **মেজাজ খারাপ হওয়া** *v.* to run out of humour; to be in temper. **মেজাজ দেখানো** *v.* (usu. dero.) to show temper. **মেজাজ ভালো থাকা** *v.* to be in good humour. **মেজাজ ভালো হওয়া** *v.* to recover one's good humour. **খারাপ মেজাজ** ill humour. **খিট্‌খিটে মেজাজ** billious or peevish temperament. **খোশমেজাজ** see **খোশ**। **বদমেজাজ** see **বদ**। **ভালো মেজাজ** good humour. **রুক্ষ মেজাজ** choleric or haughty temperament. **হাসিখুশি মেজাজ** jolly or jovial temperament. **মেজাজি** *a.* having a particular or typical temperament (বদমেজাজি),

vainglorious, haughty; stylish (মেজাজি খেলা) ; in lofty or hot temper or mood.

মেজে, মেঝে *n.* the floor.

মেজো var. of **মেজ**[২] ।

মেট *n.* a ganger or gangsman; (naut.) a mate; (in India) a prisoner appointed task-master of fellow-prisoners, a mate.

মেটা pop. var. of **মিটা** ।

মেটুলি, মেটে[১] *n.* the liver of a goat, sheep etc. taken as food.

মেটে[২] *a.* made of clay or earth (মেটে পুতুল) ; mud-built (মেটে ঘর) ; plastered with clay or terra-cotta (দোমেটে) ; of earthy complexion, mud-coloured. **মেটে সাপ** a non-venomous mud-coloured snake.

মেঠাই coll. var. of **মিঠাই** ।

মেঠো *a.* pertaining to a field; befitting an open field; unparliamentary or demagogic (মেঠো বক্তৃতা) ; rustic or boorish (মেঠো আচরণ). **মেঠো পথ** a path through an open field formed by frequent movement of people. **মেঠো সুর** a rural tune.

মেড়া *n.* a ram proficient in fighting, a fighting-ram; the ram; (fig.) a blockhead, a dunce.

মেডেল *n.* a medal. **~ধারী, মেডেল-পাওয়া** *a.* medalled. **মেডেল-পাওয়া লোক** a medallist.

মেড়ো *n.* (contem.) a native of Marwar, a Marwari; (contemp.) an up-country-man of India.

মেঢ্র *n.* a ram; penis. **~ত্বক** *n.* prepuce, foreskin.

মেথর *n.* a cleanser of filth and nightsoil; a scavenger, a sweeper. *fem.* **মেথরানি** । **~গিরি** *n.* the profession of the aforesaid cleanser or sweeper; scavenging.

মেথি *n.* the fenugreek plant or its seed.

মেদ *n.* fat; marrow. **~জ** *a.* produced from fat. **~বৃদ্ধি** *n.* growth of fat, corpulence, obesity.

মেদা, মেদামারা *a.* effeminate; lacking in vigour or energy, spiritless. □ *n.* a milksop, a ninny, a sissy, a spiritless person.

মেদি coll. corrup. of **মেহেদি** ।

মেদিনী *n.* the earth, the world.

মেদুর *a.* plesantly soft or smooth; glib, unctuous; verdant, green.

মেধ *n.* a religious sacrifice, an oblation (অশ্বমেধ).

মেধা *n.* intellect; power of remembrance, (good) memory. **~বী** *a.* intelligent; gifted; endowed with a good memory or parts. *fem.* **~বিনী** ।

মেধ্য *a.* sacrificial; sacred.

মেনি *n.* (in endearment) a puss, a pussy-cat. **~মুখো** *a.* bashful, shy; effeminate (esp. in speech).

মেম *n.* a European woman. **~সাহেব, ~সাব** *n.* a European woman, a mem-sahib; a courteous form of addressing a lady of high social standing (esp. an anglicized one) used by servants etc.

-মেয় *a.* measurable, mensurable, countable, estimable (অমেয়, পরিমেয়) ; conjecturable; cognizable.

মেয়াদ *n.* due or appointed or prescribed time or duration (মেয়াদ ফুরানো) ; a sight (বিলের মেয়াদ) ; a term or period; a sentence to imprisonment (ছমাসের মেয়াদ হয়েছে). **মেয়াদ খাটা** *v.* to serve a term of imprisonment. **মেয়াদ ফুরিয়েছে** *v.* the term is over; the allotted span of life has expired. **মেয়াদ হওয়া** *v.* to be sentenced to imprisonment. **মেয়াদি** *a.* continuing for a time; periodic.

মেয়ে *n.* a daughter; a little girl, a girl; a woman. □ *a.* female, she (মেয়েবিড়াল) ; effeminate. **~ছেলে** (usu. considered ind.) *n.* same as **মেয়েমানুষ** । **~-মর্দ,** (coll.) **~-মদ্দ** *n. pl.* men and women; husband and wife. **~মর্দানি** *n.* a termagant, an Amazon; (cp.) a tomboy. **~মানুষ** *n.* a woman; womankind. **~মুখো** *a.* (of men) effeminate or timid in speech (and also in activity). **মেয়েলি** *a.* of women, feminine, womanly; effeminate, womanish (মেয়েলি ভাব). **~লোক** *n.* a woman.

মেরজাই *n.* a kind of waistcoat.

মেরাপ *n.* a temporary shed built of straw and bamboo-poles.

মেরামত *n.* repair, mending, reconditioning. **মেরামত করা** *v.* to repair, to mend, to recondition. **মেরামত হওয়া** *v.* to be repaired or mended or reconditioned.

মেরামতি *n.* cost or charges of repairing or mending or reconditioning. ☐ *a.* of repairing or mending or reconditioning.

মেরু *n.* either of the two ends of the earth's axis, a pole; the backbone, the spine; an axis. **সুমেরু** *n.* the North Pole. **~চুম্বকমাত্রা** *n.* (phys.) the pole-strength. **~জ্যোতি** same as **~প্রভা**। **~প্রদেশ** *n.* a polar region. **~প্রভা** *n.* the polar lights; aurora polaris (eg. aurora australis, aurora borealis). **~রেখা** *n.* the earth's axis; an axis. **উপাক্ষমেরুরেখা** *n.* the earth's axis minor. **পরাক্ষমেরুরেখা** *n.* the earth's axis major.

মেরুদণ্ড *n.* the backbone, the spine, the vertebral column; (fig.) strength or firmness of character. **~হীন** *a.* having no backbone, spineless, invertebrate; (fig.) lacking in strength of character. **মেরুদণ্ডহীন প্রাণীবর্গ** *n. pl.* the Invertebrata. **মেরুদণ্ডী** *a.* having a backbone or spine, vertebrate. **মেরুদণ্ডী প্রাণীবর্গ** *n. pl.* the Vertebrata.

মেরুন *n.* the brownish crimson colour. ☐ *a.* brownish crimson.

মেল[১] *n.* the letter-conveying post, the mail; any vehicle carrying the mail. ☐ *a.* carrying the mail (মেলভ্যান).

মেল[২] *n.* union; unity; an assemblage, a gathering; mating (esp. of domestic animals); (loos.) the heredity of a family considered for matrimonial purposes.

মেলা[১] *a.* great in number or quantity or expanse; numerous or abundant or extensive.

মেলা[২] *n.* a fair (রথের মেলা) ; a temporary exhibition (স্বদেশী শিল্পমেলা) ; an assemblage, a concourse (লোকের মেলা) ; a society (পণ্ডিতের মেলা).

মেলা[৩] *v.* to open (চোখ মেলা) ; to spread out (রোদে কাপড় মেলা).

মেলা[৪], **মেলানো**[১] pop. variants of **মিলা** and **মিলানো** respectively.

মেলানি *n.* meeting or union; a crowd; a society or association; parting, farewell; farewell greetings; a parting gift, a present, a gift.

মেলানো[২] *v.* (pron. ম্যালানো) to cause to open or spread out.

মেলামেশা *n.* intimancy; association; close relationship.

মেশা, মেশানো pop. variants of **মিশা** and **মিশানো** respectively.

মেশামিশি *n.* close association; free mixing; intimacy; familiarity; social communication.

মেশিন *n.* a machine.

মেষ *n.* (as *masc.*) the ram; (as *neut.*) the sheep; (astrol.) the Aries, the Ram. *fem.* **মেষী** the ewe. **~তুল্য, ~বৎ** *a.* sheepish. **~পাল** *n.* a flock of sheep; a shepherd (*fem.* : a shepherdess). **~পালক** *n.* a shepherd. **~পালন** *n.* tending of sheep. **~মাংস** *n.* mutton. **~শাবক** *n.* a lamb, a yeanling.

মেস *n.* an establishment for a number of persons taking their meals (and often living) together, a mess. **~বাড়ি** *n.* a mess-building, a mess.

মেসো *n.* the husband of one's mother's sister or cousin-sister, an uncle.

মেহ *n.* gleet; gonorrhoea.

মেহগনি *n.* mahogany.

মেহনত *n.* physical or manual labour, toil; (fig.) laborious effort or endeavour. **মেহনত করা** *v.* to labour, to toil; (fig.) to work or endeavour laboriously. **মেহনতি** *a.* engaged in manual labouring, toiling.

মেহেদি *n.* the henna.

মেহেরবান *a.* kind, benevolent; merciful. **মেহেরবানি** *n.* kindness; benevolence; mercy; graciousness. **মেহেরবানি করে** *adv.* kindly, please; graciously.

মৈত্র *a.* same as **মৈত্রেয়**। ☐ *n.* same as **মৈত্রী**। **মৈত্রী, মৈত্র্য** *n.* alliance; friendship; amity; an alliance or treaty; cooperation. **মৈত্রেয়** *a.* relating to allies or friends.

মৈথিল *a.* of or inhabiting Mithila. **মৈথিলী** *n.* the language of Mithila; a woman of Mithila.

মৈথুন *n.* sexual intercourse, copulation, cohabitation, coitus.

মৈনাক *n.* a mythological mountain.

মোকদ্দমা var. of **মকদ্দমা**।

মোকররি var. of **মুকররি**।

মোকাবিলা *n.* confronting, encountering; settlement of disputes by meeting face to face; settlement in presence of all concerned. **মোকাবিলা করা** *v.* to encounter or confront or try to settle disputes by sitting face to face; to brave.

মোকাম *n.* a residence, a dwelling house; a trading-station; a station; an address.

মোক্তার *n.* a mukhtar; a legally appointed representative, an attorney. **~নামা** *n.* a power-of-attorney. **মোক্তারি** *n.* mukhtarship. **মোক্তারি করা** *v.* to practise as a mukhtar.

মোক্ষ *n.* (theol.) release from the world or from the influence of nature, eternal emancipation, final beatitude, *nirvana,* salvation of the soul; rescue; death; release (গ্রহণমোক্ষ). **~ণ** *n.* freeing or rescuing or releasing or discharging, emancipation from bondage, redemption, bleeding or letting or shedding or removing or wiping. **মোক্ষণ করা** *v.* to free, to rescue, to release; to discharge; to bleed, to let blood; to shed; to remove; to wipe. **~দ** *a.* giving final beatitude or salvation of the soul, redeeming the soul. *fem.* **~দা** । **~দাতা** *a.* same as **মোক্ষদ** । □ *n.* a giver of eternal emancipation, a redeemer of the soul. *fem.* **~দাত্রী** । **~দায়ক** same as **মোক্ষদ** । *fem.* **~দায়িকা, ~দায়িনী** । **~ধাম** *n.* the abode of the blessed dead, heaven, (cp.) Elysium. **মোক্ষলাভ করা** *v.* to attain eternal salvation or bliss.

মোক্ষম *a.* unfailing; irrefutable; formidable; undeniable; terrible; fatal.

মোগল *n.* a Moghul. □ *a.* Moghul. **মোগলাই** *a.* pertaining to Moghuls; current amongst Moghuls.

মোচ *n.* a nib (of a pen); a point (of a pencil); a moustache. **মোচে তা দেওয়া** to twist moustache to make it curl.

মোচড় *n.* a contortion; a wring, a twist, a wriggle; a wrench; (fig.) constraint, pressure. **মোচড় দেওয়া** *v.* to contort; to wring, to twist, to wriggle; to wrench; (fig.) to constrain, to put (undue) pressure. **মোচড়ানো** *v.* to twist; to contort; to wring; to wriggle. **মোচড়া-মুচড়ি** *n.* repeated contortion or wringing or twisting or wriggling or wrenching; (fig.) persistent solicitation or higgling. **মোচড়ামুচড়ি করা** *v.* to contort or wring or twist or wriggle or wrench; (fig.) to solicit or higgle persistently.

মোচন *n.* releasing or loosening or opening or removing or dispelling or discharging or shooting (শরমোচন) or shedding (পত্রমোচন, অশ্রুমোচন) or (loos.) wiping. **মোচন করা** *v.* to set free, to release, to loosen, to unloose; to open, to remove; to dispel; to discharge or shoot; to shed; (loos.) to wipe. **মোচন-নিযুক্তক** *n.* a clearing agent.

মোচা *n.* a cone of the banana. **মোচাকার** *a.* conical.

মোছা, মোছানো pop. variants of **মুছা** and **মুছানো** respectively.

মোজা *n.* stockings; socks; hose. **গরম মোজা** woollen socks. **ফুল মোজা** *n.* socks that come up to the knee. **হাত-মোজা** *n.* gloves. **হাফ-মোজা** *n.* socks that come only up to the calf. **মোজা-পরা** *a.* stockinged, hosed. **মোজা-বিক্রেতা** *n.* a hosier.

মোট[1] *n.* a total, an aggregate, a sum total. □ *a.* total, aggregate; principal, chief, essential. **মোট কথা** the sum and substance, the long and the short of it. **মোট দেওয়া** *v.* to add up, to total. **মোটের উপর** on the whole; generally, on an average.

মোট[2] *n.* a load, a burden; a bundle; luggage. **~ঘাট** *n. pl.* different items of luggage. **~ঘাট সমেত** bag and baggage. **~বাহক** *n.* a porter.

মোটর *n.* a motor; a motor car. **~গাড়ি** *n.* a motor car. **মোটরগাড়ি চালানো** *v.* to drive a motor car; to motor. **ভাড়াটে মোটরগাড়ি** a hired motor car or a taxicab. **ভাড়াটে মোটরগাড়ির আড্ডা** a taxi-stand. **মোটরগাড়ির চালক, মোটরচালক** a motor driver; a motorist. **মোটর-মিস্ত্রি** *n.* a motor mechanic.

মোটা *a.* fat, corpulent, fatty, adipose, bulky; voluminous (মোটা বই) ; thick, coarse (মোটা কাপড়, মোটা চাল) ; grave or hoarse (মোটা স্বর) ; dull (মোটা বুদ্ধি) ; heavy (মোটা খরচ) ; large (মোটা আয়) ; high or handsome (মোটা মাইনে) ; plain, simple ; gross, rough, ordinary, pedestrian (চিত্রাদিতে মোটা কাজ). **মোটা ভাত-কাপড়** plain living. **~নো** *v.* to grow fat, to fatten, to put on weight or flesh. **~মাথা** *n.* a dullard, a fathead. □ *a.* fat-headed, stupid. **~মুটি** *a.* roughly or grossly estimating (মোটামুটি একমাস) ; rough (মোটামুটি হিসাব) ; doing away with formalities, summary (মোটামুটি বিচার) ; cursory (মোটামুটি পাঠ) ; moderate, middling (মোটামুটি অবস্থা). □ *adv.* roughly; grossly; summarily; cursorily; moderately; on the whole. **~সোটা** *a.* burly; stout and strong.

মোটে *adv.* in total, in all, altogether; only now, just now; at all; only. **মোটেই** *adv.* at all.

মোড় *n.* a turn, a bend, a crossing (রাস্তার মোড়)।

মোড়ক *n.* a packet; a tiny packet containing a dose of medicine; a carton, a paper cover.

মোড়ল *n.* a village headman; (facet.) a leader; the foreman of a group of workmen.

মোড়লি *n.* the position and function of the headman; (sarcas.) unnecessary bossing, overbearing or masterful manner.

মোড়া[১] *n.* a wicker stool.

মোড়া[২], মোড়ানো, মোতাবেক variants of **মুড়া[২], মুড়া[৩], মুড়ানো[২], মুড়ানো[৩],** and **মুতাবেক** respectively.

মোড়ামুড়ি *n.* repeated contortion or twisting or bending; (fig.) chaffering, higgling and haggling.

মোতায়েন *a.* stationed, posted; posted on guard; ready at hand for action. **মোতায়েন করা** বা **রাখা** *v.* to station, to post; to post on guard; to keep ready at hand (or in readiness) for action.

মোতি *n.* pearl.

মোতিচুর same as **মিহিদানা**।

মোতিম same as **মোতি**।

মোতিয়া *n.* a kind of small sweet-scented flower.

মোদক *n.* a ball-shaped sweetmeat (usu. made of posset); an invigorating (and also intoxicating) drug made of hemp-leaves; a confectioner.

মোদিত *a.* filled with fragrance; perfumed; delighted; cheerful.

মোদের poet. or dial. var. of **আমাদের**।

মোদ্দা *a.* chief, main, gross. □ *adv.* on the whole, after all, in short (মোদ্দা যাওয়া চাই)। □ *con.* but (যাই কর, মোদ্দা চাকরি ছেড়ো না)। **মোদ্দা কথা** the long and the short (of it), the sum and substance; the chief thing.

মোনা *n.* the pestle of a foot-driven husking-tree.

মোম *n.* beeswax. **মোম মাখানো** *v.* to wax. **~জামা, ~ঢাল** *n.* waxcloth. **~বাতি** *n.* a waxcandle. **~বাতিদান** *n.* a candlestick. **~বাতি বিক্রেতা** *n.* a wax-chandler. **মোমের কাগজ** wax-paper. **মোমের পুতুল** a wax-doll.

মোয় poet. var. of **আমাকে**।

মোয়া *n.* a sweetened ball of parched or fried rice etc. **ছেলের হাতে মোয়া** (fig.) a thing very easily obtainable.

মোর poet. or dial. var. of **আমার**।

মোরগ *n.* (as *masc.*) the cock; (as *neut.*) a fowl, a chicken. **মোরগের ঝুঁটি** *n.* a cock's comb, a cockscomb. **মোরগের ডাক** crow, cock- a-doodle. **~ফুল** *n.* the cock's-comb, the yellow-rattle, *Celosia cristata.*

মোরচা, মোর্চা *n.* a combination or coalition of different parties or groups; an alliance.

মোরব্বা *n.* sweetened fruit conserve, fruit jelly, jam.

মোরা poet. or dial. var. of **আমরা**।

মোরে poet. or dial. var. of **আমাকে**।

মোলাকাত *n.* an interview, a meeting. **মোলাকাত করা** *v.* to meet, to pay one a visit.

মোলায়েম *a.* soft and smooth (মোলায়েম জিনিস) ; tender, suave (মোলায়েম কথা).

মোল্লা *n.* (Mus.) a Muslim theologian or priest or teacher, a mullah, a mollah. **~গিরি** *n.* the profession or office of a mullah. **~তন্ত্র** *n.* government by or predominantly influenced by mullahs (cp. mollahcracy). **মোল্লার দৌড় মসজিদ পর্যন্ত** (dero.) one with restricted knowledge cannot go beyond the range of one's learning, a churchman becomes a fish out of water outside the church, the utmost reach of one's tether.

মোষ *n.* (coll.) a buffalo. **মোষের গাড়ি** a buffalo-drawn cart, a buffalo cart.

মোষড়ানো var. of **মুষড়ানো**।

মোসম্মত var. of **মুসম্মত**।

মোসাহেব *n.* a fawning or cringing attendant; a fawner, a toady; a flatterer. **মোসাহেবি** *n.* fawning, toadyism; flattery, adulation. **মোসাহেবি করা** *v.* to fawn upon as a sycophant; to toady; to fawn upon; to flatter.

মোহ *n.* (theol.) ignorance about reality; illusion; ignorance; mental obsession; infatuation; fascination; deep attachment, dotage; a fainting fit, a swoon; enchantment, bewitchment. **মোহ নিরসন করা** *v.* to dispel illusion or infatuation or enchantment. **~গ্রস্ত** *a.* affected with an illusion; ignorant; mentally obsessed; deluded; infatuated; fascinated or fondly attached; doting; fainted, swooned; enchanted, bewitched; stupefied. **~ঘোর** *n.* a spell of illusion or ignorance or mental obsession or infatuation or fainting fit or enchantment. **~জনক** *a.* illusive; causing mental obsession; infatuating; fascinating; causing to faint; enchanting, bewitching. **~জাল** same as **~পাশ**। **~তিমির** same as **~ঘোর**। **~নিদ্রা** *n.* stupor or hypnosis or trance caused by illusion; infatuation; a fainting fit. **~পাশ** *n.* the mesh of illusion or infatuation or enchantment. **~বদ্ধ** *a.* caught in the mesh or snare of illusion or infatuation or enchantment. **~বন্ধ, ~বন্ধন** *n.* the bondage of illusion or infatuation or enchantment. **~ভঙ্গ** *n.* recovery from illusion or infatuation or enchantment or from a fainting fit, disillusionment, disenchantment. **~মদ** *n.* pride caused by illusion or ignorance. **~মন্ত্র** *n.* an incantation to enchant; a magic spell. **~ময়** *a.* illusive, illusory; infatuating; enchanting. **~মুগ্ধ** *a.* captivated by illusion; infatuated; fascinated; fondly attached, doting; enchanted, bewitched, spellbound. **~মুদ্গর** *n.* a book of verse by Shankaracharya intending to dispel illusion; a cudgel dispelling illusion or ignorance or infatuation.

মোহন *n.* enchantment, bewitchment; infatuation, fascination. □ *a.* infatuating, fascinating (গোপীমোহন); charming (মোহন বেণু). **~চূড়া** *n.* an attractive or charming bun of hair put up on the crown of one's head. **~ভোগ** *n.* a kind of porridge made by boiling corn-flour in milk. **~মালা** *n.* a variety of gold necklace. **~মূর্তি** *n.* a fascinating figure.

মোহনা var. of **মোহানা**।

মোহনিয়া var. of **মোহন** (*a.*).

মোহন্ত var. of **মহন্ত**।

মোহম্মদি var. of **মহম্মদি**।

মোহর *n.* an obsolete gold coin of India and Persia, a mohur; a seal, a stamp.

মোহরত rej. spell. of **মহরত**।

মোহরম rej. var. of **মহরম**।

মোহানা *n.* (of a water-reservoir, pond etc.) a conduit, a channel; (of a river) a mouth, an estuary.

মোহান্ত var. of **মহন্ত**।

মোহান্ধকার same as **মোহঘোর**।

মোহিত *a.* enmeshed in illusion; fascinated; infatuated; beside oneself; swooned; enchanted, charmed; hypnotized. **মোহিত করা** *v.* to enmesh in illusion; to fascinate; to infatuate; to cause to swoon; to enchant, to charm, to hypnotize.

মোহিনী *a. fem.* enchanting, bewitching; charming; infatuating; possessing bewitching personal charm. □ *n. fem.* (myth.) an exquisitely bewitching figure of a woman assumed by Vishnu (বিষ্ণু) to delude asuras (অসুর); a woman of bewitching beauty or personal charm; witchcraft or sorcery (usu. **মোহিনীবিদ্যা**); hypnotism, mesmerism (also **মোহিনীবিদ্যা**). **মোহিনী মায়া** *n.* an enchanting illusion. **~শক্তি** *n.* the power of enchanting or bewitching; hypnotic power.

মোহ্যমান *a.* stunned; stupefied; benumbed; extremely afflicted (শোকে মোহ্যমান). *fem.* **মোহ্যমানা**।

মৌ *n.* honey.

মৌক্তিক *n.* a pearl; nacre.

মৌখিক *a.* verbal; oral, viva voce; lipdeep (মৌখিক ভালোবাসা); windy (মৌখিক বড়াই). **মৌখিক চুক্তি** verbal agreement or contract. **মৌখিক পরীক্ষা** an oral examination, a viva voce test.

মৌচাক *n.* a beehive, a honeycomb.

মৌজ *n.* pleasant stupor caused by drugging, besottedness (আফিমের মৌজ); comfort, ease; pleasure, relish. **মৌজ করা** *v.* to drug oneself to enjoy a pleasant stupor; to sit or lie comfortably or at ease; to relax (খাওয়ার পর মৌজ করা); to do something with relish (মৌজ করে খাওয়া). **মৌজ করে বসা** *v.* to sit easy or cosily or comfortably, (cp.) to be at home.

মৌজা *n.* a village; a group or block of villages regarded as an administrative unit (cp. a county).

মৌটুসি *n.* a very tiny bird sucking the honey of flowers, the sunbird.

মৌতাত *n.* extreme craving for liquor or drugs at routine hours as felt by inveterate drunkards and drug-addicts; act of drinking wine or taking drugs at routine hours; pleasant stupor caused by drugging or drinking. **মৌতাত করা** *v.* to drink wine or take drugs at the fixed hour. **মৌতাত ছুটে যাওয়া** *v.* to have one's pleasant drugstupor or besottedness disturbed. **মৌতাতের সময়** a fixed hour for taking drugs or drinking wine.

মৌন *n.* abstention from speech; reticence. □ *a.* (inc. but pop.) same as **মৌনী**। **মৌন ত্যাগ করা, মৌন ভঙ্গ করা** *v.* to break silence (esp. after the completion of a vow of abstaining from speech). **~ব্রত** *n.* a vow of abstaining from speech. **~ব্রতী** *a.* abstaining from speech under a vow. **~ভাব** *n.* reticence, silence. **মৌনভাব ধারণ করা** *v.* to keep silent. **~সম্মতি** *n.* silent assent; tacit assent or consent; consent implied by silence. **~স্বভাব** *a.* habitually reserved in speech, typically parsimonious in speaking, taciturn. **মৌনাবলম্বন করা** *v.* to undertake a vow of abstaining from speech; to keep silent. **মৌনী** *a.* abstaining from speech under a vow; silent, reticent; speechless or dumbfounded (বিস্ময়ে মৌনী); mute (মৌনী প্রকৃতি).

মৌমাছি *n.* the bee. **~পালন** *n.* bee-keeping, apiculture.

মৌরলা *n.* a species of very small and delicious fish.

মৌরি *n.* fennel; aniseed. **মৌরির জল** *n.* aqua anetha.

মৌরুসি *a.* ancestral, hereditary; enjoyable (মৌরুসি সম্পত্তি) or settled hereditarily (মৌরুসি পাট্টা). **মৌরুসি স্বত্ব** hereditary right.

মৌর্বী *n.* a bowstring (esp. one made of the bowstring hemp).

মৌর্য *n.* the Maurya dynasty.

মৌল *a.* relating to or originating from the root, radical; original; primary, fundamental, basic; (sc.) elemental. □ *n.* (sc.) an element. **মৌল নীতি** a basic or fundamental principle. **মৌল পদার্থ** (sc.) an element. **মৌল শিক্ষা** basic education.

মৌলবি *n.* (Mus.) a Mohammedan scholar or teacher.

মৌলানা *n.* (Mus.) a Mohammedan scholar or teacher or an order higher than that of maulabis (মৌলবি)।

মৌলি *n.* a crown, diadem; the head or forehead; hair done in a bun on the crown of the head.

মৌলিক *a.* pertaining to or originating from the root, radical; primitive, aboriginal; fundamental, basic, primary (মৌলিক নীতি বা শিক্ষা); prime (মৌলিক সংখ্যা); original (মৌলিক রচনা বা চিন্তা); (sc.) elementary; a Hindu surname. **মৌলিক পদার্থ** (sc.) an element. **মৌলিক সংখ্যা** (math.) a prime number. **~তা** *n.* originality.

মৌসুম *n.* a season; a fixed time or period of the year for occurrence or performance of something, a tide; the monsoon; the rainy season, the rains. **মৌসুমি** *a.* seasonal (মৌসুমি ফুল); periodical (মৌসুমি ভ্রমণ); monsoonal (মৌসুমি বাতাস). **~বায়ু** the monsoon.

ম্যাও var. of **মিউ**। **ম্যাও ধরা** *v.* to bell the cat; to bear the brunt; to face the music or difficulties boldly.

ম্যাগাজিন *n.* a periodical publication, a magazine.

ম্যাচ[1] *n.* a formal contest or game, a match (ফুটবল-ম্যাচ)।

ম্যাচ[2] *n.* a match-box, matches.

ম্যাজম্যাজ *int.* denoting: a feeling of physical uneasiness or indisposition or indolence. **ম্যাজম্যাজ করা** *v.* to feel physically indisposed or uneasy or sluggish.

ম্যাজিক *n.* magic. **ম্যাজিক-লণ্ঠন** *n.* magic lantern.

ম্যাজিসট্রেট, ম্যাজিস্ট্রেট *n.* a magistrate.

ম্যাজিসিয়ান *n.* a magician.

ম্যাজেনটা, ম্যাজেন্টা *n.* magenta.

ম্যাড়ম্যাড় *int.* expressing: lack of brightness, dullness. **ম্যাড়মেড়ে** *a.* dull in colour, lacklustre, mat, matt; dull.

ম্যানেজার *n.* a manager (*fem.* : a manageress). **ম্যানেজারি** *n.* managership. **ম্যানেজারি করা** *v.* to act as a manager; to manage.

ম্যাপ *n.* an atlas; a map. **ম্যাপ দেখা** *v.* to read a map. **ম্যাপ রচনা করা** *v.* to draw a map.

ম্যালেরিয়া *n.* malaria. **~ঘটিত** *a.* malarial. **~জ্বর** *n.* malarial fever. **ম্যালেরিয়া বিশেষজ্ঞ** *n.* malariologist.

ম্রিয়মাণ *a.* (ori.) dying, moribund; (pop.) glum, melancholy, deeply distressed, sorrowful. *fem.* **ম্রিয়মাণা**।

ম্লান *a.* pale; haggard, emaciated, shrivelled; dim; lacklustre, mat, matt; dull; cheerless, glum, sorrowful; darkened, gloomy; fatigued, without; (fig.) reduced, humbled, tarnished (গৌরব ম্লান হওয়া). **~তা, ~ত্ব, ম্লানিমা** *n.* paleness; haggardness; dimness; dullness; glumness, sadness; gloominess, fatigued state. **~মুখে** *adv.* with a sad or gloomy face. **ম্লানায়মান** *a.* getting pale or haggard or dim or dull or glum or gloomy.

ম্লায়মান *a.* darkening.

ম্লেচ্ছ *n.* a non-Aryan tribe of ancient India; a member of this tribe; a Greek settler of India; (loos. but pop.) a non-Hindu; the ancient Mlechchhas (ম্লেচ্ছ). □ *a.* non-Hindu or anti-Hindu; wicked, sinful, given to unscriptural practices. **~দেশ** *n.* the part of India inhabited by the ancient Mlechchhas (ম্লেচ্ছ). **ম্লেচ্ছাচার** *n.* the customs and practices of Mlechchhas (ম্লেচ্ছ) ; non-Hindu or unscriptural or evil customs and practices. **ম্লেচ্ছাচারী** *a.* adopting the customs and practices of Mlechchhas; given to non-Hindu or unscriptural or evil practices.

য *n.* the twenty-sixth consonant of the Bengali alphabet.

যই rej. spell. of **জই**।

যক coll. corrup. of **যক্ষ**। **যক দেওয়া** *v.* to inter ceremonially a living child together with all one's riches so that the ghost of the child may guard the riches; (sl.—facet.) to cheat one of one's money. **যকের ধন** riches guarded by a ghost; (fig.) (piled and closely guarded) riches of an extremely miserly person.

যকৃৎ *n.* the liver.

যকৃৎকোষ *n.* hepatic cyst.

যকৃৎপ্রদাহ *n.* hepatitis.

যক্ষ *n.* (myth.) one of a class of demigods; a ghost appointed to guard a treasure hidden underground; (iron.) an extremely miserly man. **~পুরী** *n.* (myth.) the city of Kuvera (কুবের). **~রাজ** *n.* Kuvera (কুবের) the king of Yakshas (যক্ষ).

যক্ষিণী *fem.* of **যক্ষ**।

যক্ষ্মা *n.* phthisis; tuberculosis, pulmonary consumption.

যখন *adv.* & *con.* when; whilst; whereas; because, as, since. **~ই** *adv.* & *con.* whenever, as soon (as), no sooner (than). **~কার** *a.* of a particular or specified time. **যখনকার যা তখনকার তা** (fig.) every work has its own time, everything must be done in its own proper time. **~তখন** *adv.* in time or out of time; in season or out of season; (much too) frequently (and often vexatiously); at any hour or time. **যখন যেমন তখন তেমন** suitable for the occasion; seasonable, (cp.) do in Rome as the Romans do.

যজন *n.* worshipping, worship; act of offering in sacrifice, sacrifice. **~যাজন** *n.* act of worshipping on behalf of one's own self as well as on behalf of others, priestcraft.

যজমান *n.* one on whose behalf a priest worships, a sheep of a priest.

যজুঃ, (pop.) **যজু, যজুর্বেদ** *n.* the Yajurveda. **যজুর্বেদীয়** *a.* of or conforming to the Yajurveda.

যজ্ঞ *n.* a Vedic sacrifice; a religious sacrifice, an oblation, a sacrifice; a burnt-offering; (fig.) a great and pompous affair or ceremony. **~কর্ম** *n.* sacrificial rite. **~কুণ্ড** *n.* a pit in which the sacrificial fire is made. **~ডুমুর** *n.* a variety of large figs. **~ধূম** *n.* the smoke of sacrificial fire. **~পশু** *n.* a sacrificial beast, a victim. **~পাত্র, ~স্থালী** *n.* a sacrificial vessel. **~বেদি** *n.* a sacrificial altar, an altar. **~ভূমি, ~শালা, ~স্থল, ~স্থান** *n.* a place of sacrifice. **~সূত্র** same as **উপবীত**। **যজ্ঞাগ্নি, যজ্ঞানল** *n.* the sacrificial fire. **যজ্ঞীয়** *a.* sacrificial. **যজ্ঞেশ্বর** *n.* the lord of religious sacrifices; Vishnu (বিষ্ণু). **যজ্ঞোপবীত** same as **উপবীত**।

যৎ[১] *n.* an Indian musical measure.

যৎ[২] *a.* what; whatever, whatsoever; all whatever. **~কালে** *adv.* & *con.* at the time when; when, whilst. **~কিঞ্চিৎ, ~সামান্য** *a.* (also *pro.*) (the little) whatever; the little; (only) a little. **~পরোনাস্তি** *a.* extreme, utmost.

যত *pro.* & *adv.* & *con.* as many or as much (যত এল তত গেল) ; all whatsoever (যত নষ্টের গোড়া) ; the more, the more (যত দেখবে, তত মজবে). **~ই** emphatic form of **যত**। **~কাল** *adv.* & *con.* as long (as), so long. **~কিছু** *pro.* & *a.* whatever, whatsoever. **~ক্ষণ** same as **~কাল**। **যতক্ষণ না** until, till. **~খানি** *adv.* & *con.* as much (as); as long (as); as far (as); as many (as). **~গুলি, ~গুলো** *adv.* & *con.* as many (as). **~টা** same as **~খানি**। **~দিন** *adv.* & *con.* as many days (as); as long (as); so long. **~দূর** *adv.* & *con.* as far (as). **~বার** *adv.* & *con.* as many times (as); as often (as). **যত নষ্টের গোড়া** the root of all evils or mischiefs. **যত বড়ো মুখ নয় তত বড়ো কথা** (fig.) an audacious utterance or remark.

যতন poet. corrup. of **যত্ন**।

যতি[1] *n.* (now rare) an ascetic; a hermit; a widow (ব্রাহ্মণের যতি).

যতি[2] *n.* (gr.) a stop; (pros.) a pause, a caesura. **~চিহ্ন** *n.* (gr.) a punctuation mark. **~পাত, ~ভঙ্গ** *n.* (pros.) a metrical fault or breach.

যতেক *a.* & *con.* (poet.) as much or as many, all whatever.

যত্ন *n.* laborious or zealous effort; careful or earnest attention, care; nursing; cordial or warm reception (অতিথিকে যত্ন) ; zeal; labour, toil. **যত্ন-আত্তি** *n.* cordial and warm reception, cordial treatment; care; earnest attention. **যত্ন করা, যত্ন নেওয়া** *v.* to endeavour laboriously or zealously; to attend to carefully, to take care of; to nurse; to receive cordially or warmly; to be zealous; to labour, to toil. **~পূর্বক, ~সহকারে** *adv.* with laborious or zealous endeavour; with careful or earnest attendance; carefully; zealously; laboriously. **~বান, ~শীল** *a.* laboriously or zealously endeavouring; carefully or earnestly attending to; careful; zealous; laborious, *fem.* **~বতী, ~শীলা** ৷

যত্র *adv.* & *con* in whichever place or subject; wherever; as much (as). **~তত্র** *adv.* here and there; anywhere and everywhere; everywhere. **যত্র আয় তত্র ব্যয়** spending all or whatever one earns.

যথা *adv.* as; as for instance, as for example, namely; as much; to the utmost degree, amount or number; in accordance with; where or in which. □ *a.* proper, fitting, right. **~কর্তব্য** *adv.* & *a.* in accordance with one's duty; as one's duty demands or warrants. **~কালে** *adv.* at the proper or right or suitable or due time; in time; in good time, betimes; seasonably; in due course. **~ক্রমে** *adv.* in regular or due order or succession; respectively. **~তথ** *a.* accurate; actual; true; real. **~তথা** same as **যত্রতত্র** (see **যত্র**). **~দিষ্ট** *a.* complying with or obedient to the order. **~নিয়মে** *adv.* in accordance with the rule or law or formalities. **যথানুপূর্ব** *a.* conforming to the regular or due order or succession or sequence. **~পূর্ব** *a.* & *adv.* as before. **~পূর্বং তথা পরং** no change in the condition or state; (derog.) as bad as ever. **~বৎ** *a.* & *adv.* according to the rule or law or formalities; as before; without change. **~বিধি** same as **~নিয়ম** ৷ **~বিহিত** *a.* & *adv.* as is prescribed or due. **যথাভিপ্রেত, যথাভিমত** *n.* & *adv.* according to one's desire, as one pleases. **~য়** *adv.* where, wherein. **~যথ** *a.* & *adv.* according to the due order or succession or sequence. □ *a.* accurate; exact; correct; right; just; true; fit. □ *adv.* accurately; exactly; correctly; rightly; justly; truly; fittingly, fitly (also **যথাযথভাবে**). **~যোগ্য** same as **যথোচিত** ৷ **~রীতি** *a.* & *adv.* as is usual or customary, according to usage or custom or practice. **~রুচি** *a.* & *adv.* according to one's inclination or taste or choice. **~শক্তি** *a.* & *adv.* to the best of one's abilities, as much as one can. **~শাস্ত্র** *a.* & *adv.* conforming to the scriptures or scriptural prescriptions. **~সময়ে** same as **~কালে** ৷ **~সম্ভব** *adv.* as far as or as much as or as many as possible. **~সর্বস্ব** *n.* whatever one possesses, one's entire possessions. **~সাধ্য** same as **~শক্তি** ৷ **যথাসাধ্য চেষ্টা করা** to try one's best or utmost. **~স্থান** *n.* the right or proper or fixed or appointed place.

যথার্থ *a.* right; correct; accurate; exact; genuine; authentic; true; actual; proper.

যথেচ্ছ, (rare) **যথেচ্ছা** *a.* & *adv.* as one desires or pleases or chooses or likes.**যথেচ্ছাচার** *n.* wilfulness; waywardness; indiscipline; reckless conduct. **যথেচ্ছাচারী** *a.* wilful; wayward; wanton; lacking in discipline; wild. *fem.* **যথেচ্ছাচারিণী** ৷

যথেষ্ট *adv.* & *a.* as much or as many as one desires. □ *a.* enough, sufficient; abundant; profuse.

যথোচিত, যথোপযুক্ত *a.* proper; fit; as one deserves; as is due to one; fitting; just. **যথোপযুক্তরূপে** *adv.* in a befitting manner.

যথোপযোগী *a.* fit, suitable; proper, becoming.

যদবধি *adv.* & *con.* up to which time, till when; from which time, since when.

যদি *con.* if, provided; that, in case, lest; when, since (একান্ত যদি যাবে তো এখনই যাও). **যদিই** *adv.* & *con.* if perforce; even if. **যদিও, যদিচ** *adv.* & *con.* although, even though. **যদি না** if not. **যদি বা** if, in case; since; if perforce; or if.

যদু *n.* (myth.) a king of ancient India. **~কুলপতি, ~নাথ, ~পতি** *n.* the chief of the Yadavas (যাদব). **~বংশ** *n.* Yadava (যাদব) clan founded by King Yadu (যদু). **~মধু** *n. pl.* (also *sing.*) (dero.) men in the street, Tom Dick or Harry.

যদৃচ্ছা *n.* one's own desire or will; free will; one's pleasure; fortuity; effortlessness. **~ক্রমে** *adv.* according to one's own desire or will or free-will; at pleasure; freely. **~লব্ধ** *a.* obtained by chance; fortuitous; obtained without effort.

যদ্দিন coll. contr. of **যতদিন**।

যদ্ভবিষ্য *a.* (lit.) depending on future; relying on fate, fatalistic. □ *n.* an unenterprising person who relies on fate or chance and is heedless of the present.

যদ্যপি *adv.* & *con.* even if, if perforce; although, even though.

যন্ত্র, (coll. corrup.) **যন্তর** *n.* a machine, a device; a tool, an implement; an apparatus; an instrument (বাদ্যযন্ত্র) ; an organ (শ্বাস যন্ত্র) ; instrumental music; (fig.) one who is used as a tool of another, a cat's paw, **যন্ত্রের ন্যায়** like a machine or an automaton or robot. **যন্ত্রকৌশল** *n.* mechanism; mechanical device. **যন্ত্রচালক** *n.* a machineman, an operator. **যন্ত্রচালনা** *n.* operation of a machine. **যন্ত্রনির্মাতা** *n.* a machinist, a mechanician, a mechanist; a tool-maker, **যন্ত্রপাতি** *n.* machinery; tools and implements. **যন্ত্রবিজ্ঞান** same as **যন্ত্রবিদ্যা**। **যন্ত্রবিৎ, যন্ত্রবিদ** *n.* a mechanician, a mechanist, a machinist, a mechanical engineer. **যন্ত্রবিদ্যা** *n.* mechanics, mechanical engineering. **যন্ত্রশালা** *n.* a room or building where machines are operated, a machineroom; a machine-shop; a toolhouse. **যন্ত্রশিল্পী** *n.* a mechanic; a mechanical engineer; (mus.) an instrumentalist. **যন্ত্রসংগীত** *n.* instrumental music.

যন্ত্রণা *n.* pain, pang; agony; affliction, suffering; anguish; torment, torture; a trouble, a pest. **যন্ত্রণা দেওয়া** *v.* to pain; to agonize; to afflict; to torment; to torture. **যন্ত্রণা পাওয়া** *v.* to be pained or agonized; to be afflicted, to suffer; to be tormented or tortured. **~কর, ~জনক, ~দায়ক** *a.* painful; agonising; afflicting; tormenting, torturing; troublesome, pestering.

যন্ত্রাংশ *n.* part or parts of a machine; machinery.

যন্ত্রী *n.* a machineman, an operator; an instrumentalist; a conspirator, an intriguer, a plotter, a machinator, a wire-puller; (fig.) a director.

যব১ *adv.* & *con.* (obs.) when.

যব২ *n.* barley; (astrol.) a mark on the thumb shaped like a barley grain (usu. **যবচিহ্ন**) ; a unit of lineal measure (1/4 inch).

যবক্ষার *n.* carbonate of potash; (inc.) nitre. **~জান** *n.* nitrogen.

যবদ্বীপ *n.* Java. **~বাসী** *a.* inhabiting Java. □ *n.* a Javanese, a Javan. **যবদ্বীপীয়** *a.* Javan, Javanese.

যবন *n.* an Ionian Greek; a Greek; a non-Hindu; (inc. but pop.) a Muslim.

যবনানী *n. pl.* scripts of the (Ionian) Greek settlers of ancient India.

যবনিকা *n.* a screen, a curtain; a drop-curtain, a drop-scene, a drop. **যবনিকা উত্তোলন করা** *v.* to draw the curtain; to raise the drop; (fig.) to reveal, to disclose. **~পতন, ~পাত** *n.* drop of a curtain between the acts or at the end of a play; (fig.) termination or shelving (of an affair). **যবনিকার অন্তরালে** behind the curtain, in camera.

যবনী *fem.* of **যবন**।

যবসুরা *n.* malt liquor.

যবস্থব var. of **জবুথবু**।

যবাগূ *n.* a gruel made of barley; (med.) a malt extract.

যবুথবু alt. spell. of **জবুথবু**।

যবে *adv.* & *con.* when.

যবোদর *n.* a lineal measure (1/8 inch).

যম১ *n.* restraint, continence; concentration of the mind in service of or in meditation on God.

যম২ *n.* the Hindu God of death (cp. Pluto.); (fig.) death (যম ঘনানো) ; an annihilator, a destroyer, an antidote (ম্যালেরিয়ার যম). **যমে ধরা** *v.* to die; to be at death's door, to be in the jaws of death; to be seized with a ruinous intention; to undertake a death-dealing venture. **যমের অরুচি** even repugnant to Yama (যম) or death; an utterly repugnant person. **যমের বাড়ি** same as **যমালয়**। **~জয়ী** *a.* one who has conquered death; immortal; deathless. **~জাঙ্গাল** *n.* the Milky Way, the Galaxy. **~দণ্ড** *n.* the sceptre of Yama (যম) ; Death's rod; (fig.) death-like mortification. **~দূত** *n.* a messenger of Yama (যম) ; a summoner of death; (fig.) a person of horrible or forbidding appearance, a messenger carrying a horrible message. **~দ্বার** *n.* the court of Yama (যম) ; death's door, gates of death or hell; (fig.) death. **যমদ্বারে (যমের দুয়ারে) যাওয়া** *v.* to die, to meet one's death; to be killed. **~দ্বিতীয়া** same as **ভ্রাতৃদ্বিতীয়া** (see **ভ্রাতৃ**). **~নী** *n. fem.* the wife of Yama (যম). **~পুকুর** *n.* a vow observed by unmarried Hindu girls. **~পুরী** same as **যমালয়**। **~যন্ত্রণা** *n.* death-agony; (fig.) deathly or terrible affliction. **~রাজ** *n.* King Yama (যম) the lord of death.

যমক *a.* twin-born, twin; (bot.) connate. ☐ *n.* a twin, twins; a connate leaf; (rhet.) analogue, pun.

যমজ *a.* twin-born, twin.

যমল *a.* paired, in pair. **যমল-গান** *n.* a duet song, a duet.

যমানিকা, যমানী *n.* caraway, carum, ptychotis.

যমালয় *n.* the city or abode of Yama (যম) or death; hell. **যমালয়ে পাঠানো বা দেওয়া** *v.* to send to the jaws of death; to kill. **যমালয়ে যাওয়া** *v.* to die; to be killed; to go to hell; to be condemned to hell; to be damned.

যমুনা *n.* Jamuna, a river of India; the name of Yama's (যম) sister.

যশ, যশঃ *n.* fame, renown, celebrity, good name, (good) reputation, credit. **যশ গাওয়া, যশঃকীর্তন করা, যশঃখ্যাপন করা** *v.* to celebrate one's fame, to sing one's praise; to glorify; to extol, to eulogize. **যশস্কর** *a.* bringing fame or renown; creditable. **যশস্কামনা, যশাকাঙ্ক্ষা** *n.* desire for fame or glory. **যশঃস্তম্ভ** *n.* the monument of fame or glory. **যশস্বী** *a.* famous, renowned, celebrated, reputed. *fem.* **যশস্বিনী**। **যশোগাথা, যশোগান, যশোগীতি** *n.* a song of praise. **যশোগান গাওয়া** same as **যশঃকীর্তন করা**। **যশোভাগ্য** *n.* luck or destiny to earn fame. **যশোদ** *a.* same as **যশস্কর**। ☐ *n.* mercury, quick-silver. **যশোদা** *a. fem.* of **যশোদ**। ☐ *n. fem.* Krishna's (কৃষ্ণ) foster-mother. **যশোদাদুলাল, যশোদানন্দন** *n.* the son of Yashoda (যশোদা) ; Krishna (কৃষ্ণ). **যশোমণ্ডিত** *a.* crowned with fame or glory. **যশোমতী** *n. fem.* same as **যশোদা** (*n.*). **যশোরাশি** *n.* great fame; wide celebrity; honours in plenty. **যশোরেখা** *n.* (palmistry) the line of fame. **যশোলাভ করা** *v.* to earn fame; to attain glory. **যশোলিপ্সা** *n.* greed of fame. **যশোলিপ্সু** *a.* greedy of fame. **যশোহানি** *n.* loss of fame or reputation; disgrace, infamy; discredit.

যশদ *n.* zinc.

যশোদা, যশোমতী, যশোলাভ see **যশ**।

যষ্টি *n.* a stick; a staff; a walking-stick; a rod; a wand (জাদুযষ্টি) ; a crutch (খঞ্জের যষ্টি) ; a prop (অন্ধের যষ্টি) ; a twig. **যষ্টিপ্রহার করা** *v.* to cudgel, to flagellate. **~মধু** *n.* liquorice.

যা১ var. of **যাও** used in contempt or familiarity. **ওই যা, গেল যা** an exclamation of mild regret or disgust.

যা২ *pro. relat.* what, which, that (যা গেছে তা যাক). **যা-কিছু** *pro.* whatever; something; everything. **যা থাকে বরাতে** come what may. **যা-হোক** however; anything (যা-হোক একটা কিছু).

যাই হোক however.

যাওয়া *v.* to go; to move (স্থানান্তরে যাওয়া) ; to proceed or advance (তুমি যাও, আমি আসছি) ; to walk; to start ('গো' বললেই যাবে) ; to leave or depart (ট্রেন এখনি যাবে) ; to come to an end, to end, to terminate or be terminated (চাকরি যাওয়া) ; to elapse, to pass (দিন যাওয়া) ; to be destroyed, to perish, to be lost

(জীবন যাওয়া, চোখের নজর যাওয়া, রাজ্য যাওয়া) ; to be spent (টাকা যাওয়া) ; to work (শরীর বা ঘড়ি ঠিক যাচ্ছে না) ; to last (জামাটা এক বছর যাবে) ; to suffice for (এ টাকায় দু-মাস যাবে) ; to stay or stop by (এদিকটা একবার দেখে যেয়ো) ; to accomplish an action (মরে যাওয়া) ; to be accomplished or to take place (চুরি যাওয়া) ; to go on, to continue (থেমো না, বলে যাও) ; to pass off (জ্বর যাওয়া) ; to be directed (তার দিকে দৃষ্টি যাওয়া) ; to be inclined (মন যাওয়া). **অস্ত যাওয়া** *v.* (of the sun, moon, stars etc.) to set. **এসে যাওয়া** *v.* to be of consequence, to matter. **নেমে যাওয়া** *v.* to get down, to descend; to be demoted or degraded; to be abated or decreased. **পড়ে যাওয়া** *v.* to fall down, to drop; to go on reading. **বেড়াতে যাওয়া** *v.* to go for a walk or stroll; to go to visit (a place); to make a pleasure-trip to. **যাওয়া-আসা** *n.* come-and-go; frequenting; intercourse. **যেতে বসা** *v.* to be on the point of being ruined or destroyed or lost.

যাঁতা rej. spell. of **জাঁতা**।

যাঁতি rej. spell. of **জাঁতি**।

যাঁহা *adv. & con.* where; just as, as soon as (also **যাঁহাতক**).

যাগ same as **যজ্ঞ**।

যাচক *n.* one who asks or prays (for), a petitioner; a beggar, a mendicant; a volunteer.

যাচন[1] same as **যাচাই** (see **যাচা**[2]).

যাচন[2], **যাচনা** *n.* act of asking (for), prayer, petition; begging; solicitation; volunteering. **যাচনা করা** *v.* to ask or pray (for); to beg; to solicit; to volunteer, to offer. **যাচিত** *a.* asked or prayed for; begged; solicited.

যাচা[1] same as **যাচনা করা**।

যাচা[2] *v.* to determine or estimate the price or worth of (a thing) by investigation or comparison. **~ই** *n.* act of determining or estimating the price or worth of (a thing) by investigation or comparison, test to find the quality (of). **~নো** *v.* to cause to determine or estimate the price or worth of (a thing) by investigation or comparison; to determine or estimate the price or worth of (a thing) by investigation or comparison.

যাচ্ছেতাই *a.* (ety. but not used) whatever one pleases; (pop.) utterly bad or ugly or worthless.

যাচঞা same as **যাচনা**।

যাজক *n.* a priest; a clergyman, a cleric. **~তন্ত্র** *n.* hierocracy. **~তা, ~বৃত্তি** *n.* priestship, priesthood; clericity. **যাজক-সম্প্রদায়** *n.* the priestly or clerical order, the priesthood, the clergy.

যাজন *n.* act of conducting a religious service in the capacity of a priest or clergyman. **যাজন করা** *v.* to conduct a religious service (as by a priest). **~বৃত্তি** *n.* the profession of the priest or the clergy, priestship, priesthood, clericity; a stipend or allowance given to a priest or clergyman, (cp.) a benefice. **যাজনিক** *a.* priestly, clerical; ecclesiastical.

যাজিকা *n. fem.* a priestess, a clergywoman.

যাজ্ঞসেনী *n.* the daughter of King Yajnasena (যজ্ঞসেন) ; Draupadi (দ্রৌপদী) of the Mahabharata.

যাজ্ঞিক *n.* one who performs a religious sacrifice; a priest; a ritualist. □ *a.* sacrificial, ritual.

যাঠা alt. spell. of **জাঠা**।

যাতনা same as **যন্ত্রণা**।

যা-তা *pro.* any indefinite thing bad or undersirable (যা-তা বলা). □ *a.* inferior, worthless (যা-তা কাপড়) ; messed up, messy (যা-তা অবস্থা) ; whimsical or wayward (যা-তা চিন্তা).

যাতায়াত *n.* come-and-go; frequentation; movement, plying (ট্রেন-যাতায়াত) ; traffic (লোক-যাতায়াত). **যাতায়াত করা** *v.* to come and go; to frequent; to move, to ply. **যাতায়াত-খরচ** *n.* travelling expenses or allowance. **যাতায়াতের পথ** a thoroughfare.

যাত্রা *n.* going; setting out on a journey; commencement of a journey (যাত্রা শুভ) ; a solemn ceremony performed on the eve of a journey in order to make the journey favourable (usu. **যাত্রানুষ্ঠান**) ; movement, a journey or voyage or flight; leaving, departure

(ট্রেনের যাত্রার সময়) ; (chiefly in Christ.) exodus; passing, career (জীবনযাত্রা) ; maintenance (সংসারযাত্রা) ; a religious ceremony, a festival (দোলযাত্রা) ; an open-air (usu. rural) opera or dramatic performance (যাত্রাগান) ; a time, an occasion. (এ যাত্রা বেঁচে গেলাম). **যাত্রা করা** *v.* to set out on a journey, to set out for; to start on a journey; to leave, to depart; to perform a solemn ceremony on the eve of a journey to make the journey favourable; to act in an oper-air opera; to stage an open-air opera or drama. **যাত্রার অধিকারী** *n.* the proprietor (who is also the manager and chief director) of an open-air opera or dramatic party. **যাত্রার দল** an open-air opera or dramatic party. **যাত্রার প্রাক্কালে** on the eve of departure. **এ যাত্রা** on this occasion, this time. **~গান** *n.* an open-air opera or drama; an open-air opera performance; a song contained in an open-air opera. **~পুস্তক** *n.* (Christ.) the Exodus. **যাত্রিণী** *fem.* of **যাত্রী**। **যাত্রীবাহী** *a.* carrying passengers. **যাত্রীবাহী জাহাজ** a passenger-ship. **যাত্রী** *a.* carrying or transporting passengers (যাত্রীনৌকা). □ *n.* a goer; a traveller, a passenger.

যাথাযথ্য *n.* correctness; propriety; exactness, exactitude.

যাথার্থ্য *n.* rightness; correctness; accuracy; reality; genuineness, authenticity; trueness; veracity; truth; actuality; propriety; exactness, exactitude.

যাদব *a.* descended from King Yadu (যদু). □ *n.* a descendant of King Yadu; Krishna (কৃষ্ণ). **যাদবী** *a. fem.* of **যাদব**। □ *n.* a Yadava (যাদব) female. **~বংশ** *n.* a clan descending from King Yadu (যদু).

যাদু rej. spell. of **জাদু**।

যাদৃশ, যাদৃক *a.* & *con.* such, as. *fem.* **যাদৃশী**। **যাদৃশী ভাবনা যস্য সিদ্ধির্ভবতি তাদৃশী** as one contemplates, so one gains; like thought, like success.

যান *n.* a vehicle, a conveyance, a carriage (অশ্বযান) ; a way, a route (পিতৃযান) ; a way of worship (হীনযান). **~বাহন** *n.* transport, conveyance. **~শালা** *n.* garage.

যান্ত্রিক *a.* pertaining to machines, mechanical; versed in machines or mechanical engineering or machine operating. □ *n.* a mechanic; a mechanical engineer; a machineman, an operator. **যান্ত্রিক গোলযোগ** mechanical disorder or defect.

যাপক *a.* & *n.* one who spends or passes (time).

যাপন *n.* spending or passing (time). **যাপন করা** *v.* to spend, to pass.

যাপা same as **যাপন করা**।

যাপিত *a.* (of time etc.) spent, passed.

যাপ্য *a.* (of time etc.) that which is to be or can be spent or passed; (of an action etc.) warranting animadversion or reflection, blamable; reprehensible; (of an affair etc.) deserving to be screened or kept concealed; incapable of being radically redressed or remedied or cured (যাপ্য রোগ).

যাবক *n.* lac-dye. **যাবক-রেখা** *n.* a line along the border of the foot of a woman painted with lac-dye.

যাবচ্চন্দ্রদিবাকর *adv.* as long as the sun and the moon will exist; eternally, perpetually, for ever.

যাবজ্জীবন *adv.* as long as one's life lasts, for life. □ *a.* life-long. **যাবজ্জীবন কারাদণ্ড** imprisonment for life, a life-term, a life sentence.

যাবৎ *adv.* & *con.* as long (as). □ *con.* till, until; during, for. □ *a.* all, entire, whatever.

যাবতীয় *a.* all, one and all, whatever.

যাবনিকা *a.* of Ionian Greeks; Greek; non-Hindu; (inc. but pop.) Muslim.

যাম *n.* a division of the hours of the day (=3 hours approx.). **~ঘোষ** *n.* the jackal (as it howls at every third hour).

যামিনী *n. fem.* the night. **~নাথ** *n.* the moon. **~যোগে** *adv.* by night; at night.

যাম্য *a.* southern. **যাম্যোত্তরবৃত্ত** *n.* (geog.) the meridian circle.

যায় *n.* a list, an inventory, a catalogue; account, sake (কীসের যায়ে).

যায়-যায় *a.* & *adv.* on the point of going; on the point of dying or collapsing (যায় যায় অবস্থা).

যাযাবর *a.* wandering without a settled

home, vagrant; nomadic, gypsy. **যাযাবর জাতি** *n.* nomads; gypsies, wandering tribes. **যাযাবর পাখি** a bird of passage, a migratory bird.

যার coll. contr. of **যাহার**। **~পরনাই** *a.* extreme. □ *adv.* extremely.

যাহা older form of **যা**[২]।

যিনি *pro.* who (used in respect).

যিশু, জিশু *n.* Jesus (Christ).

যুঁই alt. spell. of **জুঁই**।

যুকতি, যুকুতি poet. var. of **যুক্তি**।

যুক্ত *a.* joined; united, federated, amalgamated; attached or adjoining; joint; (chiefly gr.) compound; possessing, invested with (শ্রীযুক্ত) ; containing (দোষযুক্ত, ঘৃতযুক্ত) ; seized or stricken or affected with (ক্রোধযুক্ত) ; employed or engaged (কর্মে যুক্ত) ; attached or fitted or yoked (ঘানিতে যুক্ত) ; conforming to (যুক্তিযুক্ত) ; (math.) added. □ *prep.* & *n.* plus (৬ যুক্ত ১৭). **~কর** *n.* folded hands. □ *a.* with folded hands. **যুক্ত করা** *v.* to join, to unite. **যুক্ত কর্মসচিব** a joint secretary. **~দল** *a.* (bot.) gamopetalous. **যুক্ত প্রচেষ্টা** a joint or united effort. **~প্রদেশ** *n.* the United Provinces (in India). **~বেণি** *n.* the confluence of the Ganges, the Jamuna and the Saraswati near Allahabad. **~রাজ্য** *n.* the United Kingdom (of Great Britain and Ireland). **~রাষ্ট্র** *n.* the United States (of America); a federal state. **~রাষ্ট্রীয় বিচারালয়** a federal court. **~শাসন** *n.* joint government; dual government; joint magistracy. **~স্বাক্ষর** joint signature.

যুক্তা *a. fem.* of **যুক্ত** (*a.*).

যুক্তাক্ষর *n.* (gr.) a compound or conjunct letter.

যুক্তি *n.* joining, union, unification, federation, amalgamation; (rare) juncture, junction, a cause, a reason; argument or judgment; logic; deliberation; consultation; counsel, advice; a plan, a scheme. **যুক্তি আঁটা, যুক্তি করা** *v.* to consult, to confer; to intrigue together; to deliberate on; to plan, to scheme. **~দাতা** *n.* a counsellor, an adviser. *fem.* **~দাত্রী**। **যুক্তি দেওয়া** *v.* to give counsel, to advise. **যুক্তি দেখানো** *v.* to show cause; to argue, to adduce reason. **যুক্তি নেওয়া** *v.* to take counsel or advice. **~পূর্বক** *adv.* having planned (that); after conferring (with); with due deliberation; supported by reasons. **যুক্তি প্রদর্শন করা** same as **যুক্তি দেখানো**। **~বাদী** *a.* rationalistic, freethinking; amenable to reason, reasonable; (loos.) rational. **যুক্তিবাদী লোক** a rationalist, a freethinker; a reasonable person. **~বিরুদ্ধ** *a.* unreasonable; irrational. **~যুক্ত, ~সংগত, ~সম্মত, ~সহ** *a.* conforming to or supported by reason, reasonable;logical; advisable. **~শাস্ত্র** *n.* logic. **~শূন্য, ~হীন** *a.* unreasonable, irrational; groundless, causeless.

যুগ *n.* a period of twelve years; any one of the four mythological aeons or ages (namely সত্য, ত্রেতা, দ্বাপর and কলি) ; an aeon; an age; an era; an epoch; times (যুগের হাওয়া) ; (fig.) a great length of time (চুল বাঁধতেই এক যুগ গেল) ; a yoke; a pair (পদযুগ) ; a unit of lineal measure equal to four cubits. **~ক্ষয়** same as **যুগান্ত**। **~ধর্ম** *n.* the spirit of the times or age, zeitgeist; the trend of the times or age; (loos.) characteristics of the age or times. **~ধর্মপালন** *n.* adopting or following the trends of the age. **~স্কন্ধ** *n.* the pole to which a yoke is fixed; (fig.) the person who represents the spirit of an age. **~প্রবর্তক** *n.* the maker of an age or epoch. **~সন্ধি** *n.* transition of an age. **~সন্ধিকাল** *n.* the transition period. **~সন্ধিকালীন** *a.* transitional. **যুগান্ত** *n.* the end of an age; a universal dissolution causing the world to be created anew; a great radical revolution bringing in a new era. **যুগান্তকারী** *a.* epoch-making. **যুগান্তর** *n.* a different age; a new age; an epoch-making revolution. **যুগাবতার** *n.* the divine incarnation of the age; an epoch-making divine incarnation; the greatest teacher or preceptor of the age. **যুগোপযোগী** *a.* fitting the age or times; suitable to or befitting the age; obedient to the age or times; time-befitting.

যুগপৎ *a.* simultaneous. □ *adv.* simultaneously.

যুগল *n.* a pair, a couple, a brace (নয়নযুগল) ; a yoke, a team (অশ্বযুগল) ; a pair of married or betrothed persons or of lovers; a male and a female paired together (হংসযুগল). **~মূর্তি** *n.* a picture of Radha (রাধা) and Krishna (কৃষ্ণ) united together in love; a picture of a divine pair (হরগৌরীর যুগলমূর্তি).

যুগি *n.* a Hindu caste originally employed in weaving; a member of this caste.

যুগ্ম *n.* a pair, a couple. □ *a.* joint (যুগ্মসম্পাদক) ; (math.) even (যুগ্ম সংখ্যা).

যুগ্যি dial. corrup. of **যোগ্য**।

যুঝা, যোঝা *v.* to fight; to contend or vie (with); to struggle (against.) **~নো** *v.* to cause to fight or contend or struggle. **~যুঝি** *n.* mutual or repeated fight or contest or vying or struggle.

যুটি *n.* a pair, a couple, a brace; one of a pair, a partner (টেনিসে লিয়েন্ডারের যুটি ভূপতি).

যুত[1] alt. spellings of **জুত**।

যুত[2] *a.* possessing, invested with (শ্রীযুত).

যুতি *n.* addition; union.

যুদ্ধ *n.* a war, a battle, a fight; an engagement, an encounter, a combat; a tournament, a contest; struggle (অনেক যুদ্ধ করে সনেটটি লিখেছি). **যুদ্ধ করা** *v.* to fight, to battle, to war; to wage war; to encounter, to combat; to contend; to struggle, to strive hard. **যুদ্ধে নামা** *v.* to join the war; to declare war. **এলোমেলো যুদ্ধ** a skirmish. **হাতাহাতি যুদ্ধ** a battle-royal. **~ঋণ** *n.* a war-debt or war-loan. **~কালীন** *a.* wartime. **~কুশল** *a.* skilled in warfare; warlike, military, martial. **~কৌশল** *n.* military tactics; art of warfare; strategics. **~ক্ষেত্র** *n.* a battlefield. **~জয়** *n.* victory in war, victory. **~জয়ী** *a.* victorious in war, victorious. **যুদ্ধজয়ী ব্যক্তি** *n.* a victor in war, a victor, a victorious person. **~জাহাজ** *n.* warship, a man-of-war, a battleship. **~নাদ** *n.* a war-cry. **যুদ্ধং দেহি ভাব** bellicosity, militancy; pugnacity. **~নিপুণ** same as **~কুশল**। **~নীতি** *n.* rules and regulations of war; tactics of war; war policy. **~পটু** same as **~কুশল**। **~প্রিয়** *a.* bellicose, warlike. **~বন্দি** *n.* prisoner of war. **~বাজ** *a.* bellicose; encouraging war. **যুদ্ধবাজ ব্যক্তি** *n.* a warmonger, (cp.) a hawk. **~বিগ্রহ** *n.* hostilities and warfare. **~বিদ্যা** *n.* art of warfare; military tactics, strategics. **~বিধ্বস্ত** *a.* wartorn. **~বিভাগ** *n.* the War Department, the Defence Department; the War Office. **~বিরতি** *n.* truce, armistice, the cessation or stopping of fighting for a time, cease fire. **~বিশারদ** same as **~কুশল**। **~যাত্রা** *n.* a military expedition; a going out to war. **~রীতি** same as **~নীতি**। **~শান্তি, ~শেষ** *n.* end or cessation of war or hostilities, peace, armistice. **~সজ্জা** *n.* equipage for war; armament; a military dress, (cp.) a battledress. **~সাধ** *n.* desire to fight. **~স্থল** *n.* a battlefield. **যুদ্ধাবসান** same as **~শান্তি**। **যুদ্ধার্থ** *adv.* for war, to fight. **যুদ্ধার্থী** *a.* desirous of fighting; on the point of fighting; militant. **যুদ্ধোদ্যম** *n.* preparation for war. **যুদ্ধোন্মত্ত** *a.* war-neurotic; frenziedly fighting. **যুদ্ধোন্মাদ** *a.* crazy for war; bellicose; war-neurotic. □ *n.* craze for war, (cp.) bellicosity; war-neurosis. **যুদ্ধোন্মুখ** *a.* ready for war, on the war-path. **যুদ্ধোপকরণ** *n.* war materials, requisites for war; arms and amunition.

যুধিষ্ঠির্ *a.* capable of retaining mental calm during war. □ *n.* Yudhishthira, the eldest son of Pandu (পাণ্ডু).

যুধ্যমান *a.* engaged in fighting, belligerent.

যুবক, যুবতি, যুবতী, যুবজানি see **যুবা**।

যুবরাজ *n.* a crown prince. **ইংল্যান্ডের যুবরাজ** the Prince of Wales. **ফ্রান্সের যুবরাজ** the Dauphin. **রাশিয়ার যুবরাজ** the Tsarevich, the Czarevich.

যুবসমাজ *n.* the youth, the community of young people.

যুবসম্প্রদায় *n.* the community of young people, the youth collectively.

যুবসম্মেলন *n.* a youth conference.

যুবা, যুবক *a.* one who has attained youth; (loos.) grown-up; young. □ *n.* a young man, a youth. *fem.* **যুবতী, যুবতি**। **যুবজানি** *n.* the husband of a young woman. **যুবাকাল, যুবাবয়স** *n.* youth, young age; (of animals) calf-time.

যুযুৎসা *n.* desire for fighting or war, bellicosity; pugnacity.

যুযুৎসু *a.* desirous of fighting or war, bellicose; pugnacious.

যুঁই rej. spell. of **জুঁই**।

যূথ *n.* a flock, a herd, a pack, a flight, a swarm. **~চর, ~চারী** *a.* gregarious. **~পতি** *n.* the leading beast of a flock or herd. **~ভ্রষ্ট** *a.* strayed from the flock or herd. **যূথভ্রষ্ট পশু** a strayling, astray.

যূথিকা, যূথী *n.* a kind of jasmine.

যূপ *n.* a wooden framework to which the neck of a sacrificial victim is fixed at the time of immolation (also **যূপকাষ্ঠ**). **~কাষ্ঠ** same as **যূপ**।

যূষ *n.* decoction, broth, soup.

যে *rel. pro. & con.* who, which, that. □ *con.* that (বলছি যে আজ বাড়ি যাব). □ *a.* that which (যে ছোকরা, যে বিষয়). □ *int.* expressing doubt or uncertainty (কী যে হবে) ; cause (বেলা যে গেল, বাড়ি চলো) ; interrogation or inquiry (খেললি না যে) ; reproof (মিথ্যা বললি যে) ; drawing of attention or attachment of importance (দুঃখে বুক ফাটে যে) ; amazement (অত পড়ে ফেল করল যে) ; disgust (আবার বৃষ্টি এল যে) ; warning (ছুটে চলো—ট্রেন ছাড়ল যে) ; acceptance (যে আজ্ঞা). **যে অবধি** since when; up to which time, till when. **যে আজ্ঞা** all right, sir; as you please, sir; that's right, sir. **যে কটি** all the small number that, the few. **যে কারণে** for which reason, wherefore, why. **যে কালে** whilst, when. **যে কে সেই** *pro. & a.* as before, the same. **যে কেউ** whoever; anybody; any one. **যে কোনোজন, যে কোনোটি** any one. **যে কোনো স্থানে** anywhere; anywhere and everywhere; everywhere. **যেটুকু** *pro. a. & con.* all the small amount or degree or extent that, the little. **যে দিন** the day which or when; which day. **যে পর্যন্ত** up to which; up to which time; till. **যে যে** all who; all which. **যে সে** *pro.* any man in the street, Tom Dick or Harry; anybody whoever; anybody and everybody; anybody; everybody. □ *a.* ordinary, commonplace, humdrum.

যেই *adv. & con.* just when, just as, as soon as. □ *a.* which (যেইদিন). □ *pro.* whoever (যেই বলুক না কেন, শুনো না). **যেইমাত্র...সেইমাত্র** just when, just as, as soon as.

যেখান *n.* which place; whichever place. **~কার** *a.* of which particular place; of a particular place. **যেখানে** *adv. & con.* where; wherever. **যেখানে-সেখানে** *adv.* anywhere and everywhere; everywhere; all over the shop.

যেতে বসা see **যাওয়া**।

যেথা *n.* same as **যেখান**। □ *adv. & con.* same as **যেখানে**। **~কার, ~য়, যেথা-সেথা** same as **যেখানকার, যেখানে** and **যেখানে-সেখানে** respectively.

যেন *adv. & con.* as, like; as if; so that; that (প্রার্থনা করি যেন সুখী হও) ; taking care that (টাকা হারায় না যেন) ; accepting that or supposing that (তাই যেন হল) ; I am failing to recollect just now (কী যেন নাম). **কী যেন তাকে বল** what do you call him or her. **কী যেন তার নাম** what's his (or her or its) name. **যেন-তেন প্রকারে, যেন-তেন প্রকারেণ** somehow; by hook or by crook, by fair means or foul; negligently or perfunctorily.

যেবা *pro.* whoever; whichever.

যেমতি, যেমত (poet.) *adv. a. & con,* as, like, as like.

যেমন *a. & con.* as like; for instance, for example. □ *adv. & con.* as much or as like, as; just as, as soon as. □ *int.* expressing mild surprise or contradiction or contempt (তুমিও যেমন). **যেমনই** *a. & con.* as, like. □ *adv. & con.* same as **যেমন** (*adv. & con.*) **যেমন-তেমন** *a.* of any sort or kind; trifling, of a sort. **যেমন-তেমন করে** *adv.* in a haphazard manner, in a random or slipshod or designless fashion. **যেমনি** var. of **যেমনই**। **যেমন কর্ম তেমন ফল** as one has brewed, so one will drink; as you sow, so you reap; rightly served.

যেরূপ *a. con. & int.* same as **যেমন** (*a. con. & int.*). □ *adv. & con.* as much or as like, as.

যেহেতু *con.* because, since, as.

যৈছন, যৈছে *adv. & con.* (obs.) as much or as like, as.

যো১ rej. spell. of **জো**।

যো২ *pro.* (obs. & poet.) who. □ *a.* as. **যো হুকুম** as you command (indicating cringing obedience).

যোক্ত *n.* a halter; resource, provision (চাকরির যোক্ত নেই) ; facility or convenience (কাজে যোক্ত নেই).

যোগ *n.* union; mixture, blending; relation; connection, association; contact; cooperation, concert (একযোগে) ; act of joining with; yoga (যোগে বসা) ; an expedient or means; a medium (ডাকযোগে) ; a vehicle or a route (বিমানযোগে, শূন্যযোগে) ; a path or method for spiritual attainments (ভক্তিযোগ) ; a time (রজনীযোগে) ; (astr. & astrol.) a conjunction of stars and planets (বিস্কুম্ভযোগ) ; (astrol.) an auspicious time (বিবাহের যোগ) ; (astrol.) a probability of occurrence (মৃত্যুযোগ) ; a remedy, a medicine (মুষ্টিযোগ) ; food, repast (জলযোগ) ; facility or chance (লাভের যোগ) ; application or employment (মনোযোগ) ; (math.) addition; (math.) the plus sign. **যোগ করা** *v.* to unite; to mix, to blend; to practise yoga; to add. **যোগ দেওয়া** *v.* to unite; to associate with ; to participate; to report as for duty; to take up an employment, to join; to add. **~ক্রিয়া** *n.* (alg.) componendo. **~ক্ষেম** *n.* attainment or acquisition of unattained things and preservation of what is attained. **~দান** *n.* participation, taking part; attending. **যোগদান করা** *v.* to be associated with; to side with, to join (with); to take part in, to participate; to report for duty; to take up an employment, to join. **~নিদ্রা** *n.* self-absorbed trance of a divine person (বিষ্ণুর যোগনিদ্রা) ; a yogic trance (যোগনিদ্রামগ্ন তপস্বী). **~ফল** *n.* (arith.) result of addition, sum; (phys.) summation. **~বল** *n.* spiritual power derived from yogic practice or meditation. **~বাহী** *a.* uniting; connecting; acting as a medium; helping to maintain contact; (chem.) catalytic. **~ব্যায়াম** *n.* yoga; yogic exercise for physical and mental health. **~ভঙ্গ** *n.* break or interruption of yogic meditation; a failing in yogic practice or meditation. **~ভ্রষ্ট** *a.* interrupted or foiled in yogic practice or meditation; lured away or fallen from spiritual heights attained by means of yoga. **~মায়া** *n.* (Hindu theol.) the all-prevading illusory energy of godhead; Goddess Durga (দুর্গা). **~মার্গ** *n.* the yogic path of spiritual attainments or salvation. **~রূঢ়** *a.* (gr.) formed by compounding two or more words and implying a special meaning (যোগরূঢ় শব্দ). **~শাস্ত্র** *n.* the yogic scriptures; a book on yogic practice. **~সাজশ** *n.* undesirable or unfair or criminal collaboration; a conspiracy. **~সাজশে** *adv.* in collusion with. **~সাধন** *n.* unification; mixture; blending; joining; practice of yoga. **~সাধনা** *n.* practice of yoga. **~সিদ্ধ** *a.* successful in acquiring spiritual attainments or salvation through yogic practice; attained through yogic practice. **~সিদ্ধি** *n.* success in yogic practice; spiritual or other attainments or salvation obtained through yogic practice. **~সূত্র** *n.* connexion; correlation.

যোগাকর্ষণ *n.* molecular attraction; cohesion; gravity.

যোগাড় rej. spell. of **জোগাড়**।

যোগান rej. spell. of **জোগান**।

যোগাভ্যাস *n.* practice of yoga.

যোগাযোগ *n.* communion; unity, consistency (প্রারম্ভের সঙ্গে উপসংহারের যোগাযোগ) ; relation, connection, association; intercourse; contact, touch; communication, contact (তার সঙ্গে আমার বহুদিন যোগাযোগ নেই) ; co-operation (পরস্পর যোগাযোগে কার্যসাধন). **যোগাযোগ রক্ষা করা** *v.* to maintain contact (with); to maintain means of communication (with). **যোগাযোগ স্থাপন করা** *v.* to establish contact (with); to set up means of communication (with).

যোগারূঢ় *a.* absorbed in or successful in yogic meditation.

যোগালিয়া, (coll.) **যোগালে** *n.* an assistant, a helper; a hodman.

যোগাসন *n.* a posture of sitting or a seat

for yogic meditation; the posture of yogic exercise.

যোগাসীন *a.* seated in yogic meditation. *fem.* **যোগাসীনা**।

যোগিনী *n. fem.* (myth.) any one of the sixty-four female attendants of Goddess Durga (দুর্গা) ; a female ascetic or yogi; a woman who practises ardently (কর্মযোগিনী) ; (astr. & astrol.) a particular conjunction of stars (পশ্চিমে যোগিনী).

যোগী *n.* a yogi; an ascetic; one who practises ardently (কর্মযোগী). **যোগীন্দ্র, যোগীশ্বর** *n.* the greatest yogi or the lord of yogis; Shiva (শিব).

যোগীবেশ *n.* the conventional garb of an ascetic or yogi.

যোগে *adv.* by, with, through (ডাকযোগে, নৌকাযোগে).

যোগ্য *a.* worthy, fit, deserving; becoming (রাজার যোগ্য) ; proper, right; condign (যোগ্য শাস্তি) ; merited (যোগ্য পুরস্কার) ; eligible; competent, able, efficient. *fem.* **যোগ্যা**। **পাঠযোগ্য** *a.* readable, worth reading. **~তা** *n.* worthiness, fitness; worth merit; eligibility; competency, ability. **যোগ্যতানুসারে** *adv.* in order of merit. **যোগ্যতাপত্র** *n.* a certificate of competency.

যোজক *n.* (geog.) an isthmus. □ *a.* joining, linking; uniting.

যোজন *n.* joining or linking; unification; mixing or blending; employment (সৈন্যযোজন) ; application (শব্দযোজন) ; investment (as of money); fixation, implantation (ধনুকে শরযোজন) ; a measure of distance usu. about five miles, a yojana. **~গন্ধ** *n.* musk. **যোজনা** same as **যোজন** except in the last sense, and–*n.* planning or a plan (চতুর্থ যোজনা).

যোজিত *a.* joined, linked; unified; mixed, blended; employed, applied; invested; fixed, implanted.

যোজ্যতা *n.* valency.

যোঝা see **যুঝা**।

যোট rej. spell. of **জোট**।

যোটক *n.* union; combination; combination or agreement for matrimonial purposes (রাজযোটক) ; a pair; one of a pair. **যোটক মেলা** *v.* to be found agreeable or to combine well for matrimonial purpose; to be supplied with a pair, to be paired.

যোড়, যোড়া, যোড়ানো, যোত, যোতা rej. spellings of **জোড়, জোড়া, জোড়ানো, জোত,** and **জোতা** respectively.

যোত্র var. of **যোক্ত্র**।

যোদ্ধা *n.* a fighter, a warrior, a soldier.

যোদ্ধাজাতি *n.* a warlike or martial race.

যোদ্ধৃবর্গ *n.* warriors or soldiers collectively, fighting personnel.

যোদ্ধৃবেশ *n.* the dress or attire of a soldier; the military dress.

যোধ *n.* a battle, a fight, a war; a warrior, a soldier, a fighter.

যোনি *n.* the female genital passage, the vagina; a place of origin, a source (কমলযোনি) ; birth or racial origin (দেবযোনি).

যোয়ান[1] rej. spell. of **জোয়ান**[3]।

যোয়ান[2] *n.* caraway, carum, ptychotis.

যোয়াল alt. spell. of **জোয়াল**।

যৌক্তিক *a.* reasonable; logical, advisable. **~তা** *n.* resonableness; logicality; advisability.

যৌগ *n.* (chem.) a compound.

যৌগিক *a.* compound, composite; complex; mixed; (gr.) derivative; a yogic. **যৌগিক অণুবীক্ষণ** a compound microscope. **যৌগিক অর্থ** (gr.) the derivative meaning (of a word). **যৌগিক কাচ** a compound lens. **যৌগিক ক্রিয়া** a yogic performance; (gr.) a compound verb (e. g. করে ফেলা, বসে পড়া) (cp.) a verb phrase. **যৌগিক পদার্থ** a compound substance, a compound. **যৌগিক পন্থা** the yogic system or method. **যৌগিক বাক্য** (gr.) a compound sentence. **যৌগিক শব্দ** (gr.) a derivative; (loos.) a compound word, a compound. **যৌগিক সংখ্যা** (arith.) a mixed or complex number.

যৌতুক *n.* a dowry; a portion; a present or gift given at the time of certain sacramental ceremonies. **যৌতুক দেওয়া** *v.* to bestow a dowry upon, to dower, to give a present. **~প্রথা** *n.* the dowry system. **~হীন** *a.* portionless.

যৌথ *a.* united, combined; joint. **যৌথ কারবার** a joint stock company. **যৌথ চেষ্টা**

united or combined effort. যৌথ পরিবার a joint family. যৌথ স্বাক্ষর joint signature.

যৌন *a.* vaginal; biogenetic; sexual (যৌনসংগম) ; venereal (যৌনব্যাধি)। কর্মী *n.* a sex worker. ~তা *n.* sexuality. ~ক্ষমতা *n.* sexual power. ~দুর্বলতা *n.* sexual debility; impotence. ~রোগ *n.* sexual disease; syphilis or gonorrhoea. ~সংগম *n.* sexual union, copulation, sexual intercourse.

যৌবন *n.* youth; calf-time; youthfulness. ~কণ্টক *n.* an acne. ~কাল *n.* youth; calf-time; grown-up stage. ~প্রাপ্ত *a.* one who has attained youth. *fem.* ~প্রাপ্তা। ~প্রাপ্তি *n.* attainment of youth, coming of age. ~বতী *a. fem.* young; youthful. ~ভার *n.* development of the body on attainment of youth; the excitement of youthful passions. ~লক্ষণ *n.* the marks on or the development of the body indicating attainment of youth. ~শ্রী *n.* physical grace acquired on attainment of youth. ~সম্পন্ন *a.* full of youth; youthful; one who has attained youth. *fem.* ~সম্পন্না। ~সুলভ *a.* usual for youth, youthful. যৌবনাবস্থা same as যৌবনকাল।

যৌবরাজ্য *n.* the office or post of a crown prince. যৌবরাজ্যে অভিষিক্ত করা, যৌবরাজ্য প্রদান করা *v.* to instal as a crown prince.

র *n.* the twenty-seventh consonant of the Bengali alphabet.

রওনা *n.* setting out, setting out on a journey; departure; despatch (ডাক রওনা করে দেওয়া). **রওনা হওয়া** *v.* to set out, to set out on a journey; to depart. **রওনা করানো** *v.* to see off, to despatch; to arrange for one's journey.

রওয়া coll. corrup. of **রহা** ।

রওয়ানা older var. of **রওনা** ।

রং, রঙ *n.* colour, hue; dye; paint; complexion; (of playing cards) a suit or one of a suit or the trump-suit or a trump; exaggeration. **রং করা** *v.* to put colour on, to paint, to colour; to dye. **রং চড়ানো** *v.* to put colour on, to colour; to exaggerate. **রং হওয়া** *v.* to take on colour, to colour. **~চং** *n.* variegation in colouring; gaudiness. **~চঙা, ~চঙে** *a.* variegated in colours; gaudy. **~ঢং** *n.* fun and frolics; drollery; frolicking. **~দার** same as **রংচঙা** । **রংবেরং, রঙবেরঙ** *a.* variegated in colours; diverse. **রঙানো** *v.* to dye; to colour; to paint, see also **রাঙানো** ।

রংমহল *n.* a pleasure house; a place for entertainment; a theatre hall.

রংরুট *n.* a recruit.

রক[1] pop. var. of **রোয়াক** ।

রক[2] *n.* the gigantic roc bird of legends, the roc, the rok, the ruc.

রকম *n.* a variety, a sort, a kind; manner, fashion style, way; characteristic or habit (লোকটার রকমই ওই). □ *adv.* nearly or approximately, about (চার আনা রকম অংশ). **রকম রকম, রকমারি, রকমওয়ারি** *a.* of or in various sorts of fashions, various; assorted; different (রকম রকম লোক, রকম রকম রুচি). **রকমসকম** *n. pl.* (usu. dero.) ways, gestures or movements; symptoms (রোগীর রকমসকম).

রক্ত *n.* blood. □ *a.* blood-red, sanguine, red; dyed in red; (of eyes) bloodshot or reddened; inclined or attached (বিরক্ত, অনুরক্ত). **রক্ত গরম থাকা** *v.* to retain blood-heat, to be still alive; (fig.) to be still young or in vigour. **রক্ত জমাট করা** *v.* to curdle one's blood, to make one's blood freeze. **রক্ত জল করা** *v.* (lit.) to liquefy one's blood; (fig.) to work hard to the impairment of one's health. **রক্ত ঝরা** *v.* to bleed. **রক্ত দেওয়া** *v.* to donate one's blood (as to a blood-bank or a sick person); to transfuse blood (to the veins of a sick person); (fig.) to shed or spill one's own blood (দেশের জন্য রক্ত দেওয়া). **রক্ত নেওয়া** *v.* (med.) to draw one's blood for bacteriological examination. **রক্ত পড়া** *v.* to bleed. **রক্ত বন্ধ করা** *v.* to stop bleeding. **রক্ত হওয়া** *v.* to gain blood. **রক্তের অক্ষরে লেখা** (fig.) *a.* written in blood; containing the history of a great many losses of life or a massacre. □ *v.* (fig.) to shed one's own blood for. **রক্তের দামে কেনা** *a.* blood-bought. **রক্তের নেশা** same as **রক্তপিপাসা** । **রক্তের সম্পর্ক, রক্তের সম্বন্ধ** blood-relationship. **রক্ত-আঁখি** same as **রক্তচক্ষু** । **~কণিকা** *n.* a blood corpuscle. **লোহিত রক্তকণিকা** a red (blood) corpuscle. **শ্বেত রক্তকণিকা** a white (blood) corpuscle. **~কন্দল** *n.* the coral. **~কমল** *n.* the red lotus. **~করবী** *n.* the red oleander. **~কাঞ্চন** *n.* the mountain ebony. **~কুমুদ** *n.* the red lotus. **~ক্ষয়** *n.* loss of blood; bloodshed; (fig.) great impairment of health and energy. **~ক্ষয়ী** *a.* causing or involving loss of blood; causing or involving bloodshed, sanguinary; (fig.) causing great impairment of health and energy. **~ক্ষরণ** *n.* blood-letting, surgical drawing off of some of a patient's blood. **~গঙ্গা** *n.* a river of blood; a pool of blood caused by a heavy haemorrhage (মাথা ফেটে রক্তগঙ্গা) ; a great massacre, blood-bath (দাঙ্গায় রক্তগঙ্গা). **রক্ত-গরম** *a.* easily irritable or angered, hot-blooded; hot-headed, hot-brained. **~চক্ষু** *n.* blood shot eye(s);an angry look. □ *a.* having reddish eyes; bloody-eyed. **~চন্দন** *n.*

the red sandalwood. ~চাপ *n.* blood pressure. ~চোষা *a.* blood-sucking. □ *n.* a deadly blood-sucking lizard; (fig.) an exorbitant extortioner; a bloodsucker, a vampire. ~চোষা বাদুড় the vampire-bat. ~জবা *n.* the red chinarose. ~জিহ্ব *a.* having a ruddy or bloodred tongue. ~তঞ্চন *n.* clotting or congealing of blood. ~দান *n.* donation of one's blood (as to a blood-bank or a sick person); blood-transfusion; (fig.) act of shedding one's own blood, blood-sacrifice. ~দুষ্টি, ~দোষ *n.* blood-poisoning, pyaemia. ~নদী same as রক্তগঙ্গা। ~নয়ন same as রক্তচক্ষু। ~নিশান *n.* a red flag. রক্তপ *a.* blood-sucking. ~পদ্ম *n.* the red lotus. ~পাত *n.* bloodshed; haemorrhage. রক্তপাত করা *v.* to shed or spill blood. রক্তপাত হওয়া *v.* to bleed. ~পাতহীন *a.* bloodless; without bloodshed. রক্ত পান করা *v.* to suck or drink (another's) blood; (fig.) to extort exorbitantly. ~পায়ী *a.* bloodsucking. রক্তপায়ী বাদুড় the vampire-bat. ~পিণ্ড *n.* a lump of clotted or congealed blood; (fig.) an embryo. ~পিত্ত *n.* (med.) haemorrhage from the liver. ~পিপাসা *n.* thirst for blood. ~পিপাসু *a.* bloodthirsty. ~প্রদর *n.* (med.) a kind of leucorrhoea causing haemorrhage. ~বৎ *n.* blood-like; blood-red. ~বমন *n.* blood-vomiting; (med.) haematemesis. রক্তবমন করা *v.* to vomit blood. ~বর্ণ *a.* blood-red; ruddy; crimson. □ *n.* blood-red-colour; crimson colour. ~বসন *n.* red-coloured or crimson-coloured cloth. □ *a.* wearing a red coloured or crimson-coloured cloth. *fem. a.* রক্তবসনা। রক্তবসনা নারী a woman in red or crimson. ~বাহ *n.* a blood-vessel; a vein. ~বাহী *a.* blood-carrying. ~বিকার same as রক্তদুষ্টি। ~বিন্দু *n.* a drop of blood. ~বীজ *n.* (myth.) a demon each drop of whose blood, as soon as it fell to the ground, would instantly create a new demon equal to him; the pomegranate. রক্তবীজের ঝাড় (fig. & dero.) a family or collection which cannot be thoroughly exterminated. ~বৃদ্ধি *n.* increase of blood in the body. ~বেগুনি, ~বেগনি *a.* & *n.* violet, purple. ~ভাণ্ডার *n.* a blood-bank. ~মস্তু *n.* plasma; serum. ~মাংস *n.* flesh and blood composing one's body; flesh and blood. রক্তমাংসের শরীর the human body or the mortal frame (which is susceptible to pain). রক্তমাংসের সম্পর্ক blood-relationship. ~মোক্ষক *a.* blood-letting. ~মোক্ষণ *n.* blood-letting. রক্তমোক্ষণ করা *v.* to bleed (as a patient), to let another's blood. ~রঞ্জিত *a.* blood-stained; dyed in red. ~রস *n.* plasma. ~রাগ *n.* a crimson glow or colour. ~রাগমণি *n.* the onyx. ~রেখা *n.* a streak of blood; a streak of crimson light or colour. ~লোচন same as রক্তচক্ষু। ~শূন্য same as রক্তহীন। ~শোধক *a.* purifying or rectifying blood. ~শোষক same as রক্তচোষা। রক্তশোষণ করা *v.* to suck another's blood; (fig.) to extort exorbitantly. ~সংবহন, ~সঞ্চলন, ~সঞ্চালন *n.* circulation of blood. ~সঞ্চার *n.* blood-transfusion. ~স্নান *n.* (fig.) a great massacre, blood-bath. ~স্রাব *n.* haemorrhage. ~স্রোত *n.* a stream or flow of blood. ~হীন *a.* bloodless; anaemic; pale. ~হীনতা *n.* bloodlessness; anaemia; paleness. রক্তাক্ত *a.* smeared with blood; blood-stained (রক্তাক্ত বসন) ; bleeding (রক্তাক্ত দেহ) ; dyed or painted in crimson, crimson (রক্তাক্ত আকাশ). রক্তাতিসার *n.* blood-dysentery; bacillary dysentery; the bloody flux. রক্তাধিক্য *n.* (med.) plethora. রক্তাভ *a.* having a crimson glow, crimson; ruddy. রক্তাভাব *n.* blood-starvation. রক্তাম্বর same as রক্তবসন। রক্তারক্তি *n.* profuse bloodshed; mutual bloodshed; profuse haemorrhage. রক্তাল্পতা *n.* anaemia. রক্তিম *a.* reddish; crimson, blood-red, ruddy; reddened; flushed (e. g. flushed cheeks). রক্তিমা *n.* redness; red or crimson glow; ruddiness or a flush. রক্তোৎপল *n.* the red lotus. রক্তোপল *n.* ochre, red chalk.

রক্ষ, (ori.) রক্ষঃ *n.* (myth.) one of an anthropophagous race of India, a rakshas(a); an anthropophagite; a demon, a goblin. রক্ষঃকুল *n.* the rakshasa race. **রক্ষঃপুরী** *n.* Lanka, the city of rakshasas.

রক্ষক *n.* a protector; a defender; a guard, a guardsman; a guardian; a rescuer, a saviour; a preserver; a caretaker, a keeper; a maintainer; a depositor; a custodian.

রক্ষণ *n.* same as **রক্ষা** (*n.*). □ *a.* (used as a *sfx.*) protecting, defending, guarding (রাক্ষসকুলরক্ষণ). **~শীল** *a.* obscurantist; conservative. **রক্ষণাবেক্ষণ** *n.* supervision; care, custody, guarding. **রক্ষণাবেক্ষণ করা** *v.* to look after, to take care of; to supervise; to guard. **রক্ষণাবেক্ষণাধীন** *a.* in one's care or custody, under one's tutelage or guardianship. **রক্ষণীয়** *a.* that which is to be or can be protected or defended or guarded or rescued or preserved or observed or taken care of or maintained or deposited. *fem.* **রক্ষণীয়া**।

রক্ষা *n.* protection; defence; guarding; rescue, saving; preservation; observance, act of abiding by; act of taking care of, keeping; maintenance, upkeep, retention; depositing. □ *v.* poet. form of **রক্ষা করা**। **রক্ষা করা** *v.* to protect; to defend; to guard; to rescue; to save; to preserve; to observe, to keep; to look after, to take care of, to keep, to tend; to maintain, to keep up, to retain; to deposit. **প্রতিজ্ঞা রক্ষা করা** to keep or fulfil one's promise. **রক্ষা নেই** no escape. **~কবচ** *n.* an amulet believed to have occult power to safeguard the wearer; safeguard (সংখ্যালঘুদের জন্য রক্ষাকবচ). **~কর্তা** *n.* same as **রক্ষক**। *fem.* **~কর্ত্রী**। **~কালী** *n.* a manifestation of Goddess Kali (কালী).

ক্ষাবন্ধন same as **রাখিবন্ধন**।

ক্ষিগৃহ *n.* a guard-room.

ক্ষিণী *fem.* of **রক্ষী**।

ক্ষিত *a.* protected; defended; guarded; rescued, preserved; observed; taken care of; tended; maintained, kept up; deposited. **রক্ষিতা** *fem.* of **রক্ষিত**। □ *n.* a kept woman; a mistress, a concubine.

ক্ষী *n.* a guard, a guardsman.

ক্ষীবর্গ, রক্ষীসৈন্য *n.* the defence army; household troops, guards.

রক্ষোরাজ *n.* a king of rakshasas.

রগ *n.* the flat portion of either side of the head above the cheekbone, the temple. **রগ টিপ টিপ করা** *v.* to have a morbid throbbing of temples. **রগ ঘেঁসে** grazing the temple. **~চটা** *a.* quick-tempered.

রগড় *n.* fun; a practical joke; drollery. **রগড় করা** *v.* to make fun (of); to play a practical joke. **রগড় দেখা** *v.* to see or enjoy fun; (fig.) to take delight in another's trouble, misfortune etc.

রগড়ানো *v.* to rub; to massage; to curry; to chafe, to fret.

রগড়ারগড়ি *n.* mutual or repeated rubbing or currying or chafing or fretting or importunating or higgling.

রগরগে *a.* (of colour) bright; too deep and bright red.

রগুড়ে, রগড়িয়া *a.* given to making fun or playing jokes; given to drollery, drollish; funny, jocular, droll.

রঘু *n.* a great mythological king. **~কুল** *n.* the dynasty or line of King Raghu (রঘু). **~কুলপতি, ~নাথ, ~পতি** *n.* a patriarch or king of the line of Raghu (রঘু). **~নন্দন** *n.* a descendant of Raghu (রঘু). **~বংশ** same as **রঘুকুল**। **~বর** *n.* the best man of the line of Raghu (রঘু). **~মণি** *n.* the jewel of the line of Raghu (রঘু).

রঙ alt. spell. of **রং**।

রঙমহল alt. spell. of **রংমহল**।

রঙিন *a.* coloured; dyed; dapple, variegated; colourful.

রঙ্কু *n.* a kind of deer.

রঙ্গ *n.* fun; drollery; a practical joke, jest, banter; frolic; an entertaining show. **রঙ্গ করা** *v.* to poke fun at; to make fun (of), to make a song (of); to stage a comic show; to droll. **রঙ্গ দেখা** *v.* to see or enjoy fun; (fig.) to take delight in another's trouble, misfortune etc. **রঙ্গ দেখানো** *v.* to give an entertaining show; (fig.) to make one suffer for, to make one pay for, to punish deservedly, to pay one off.

রঙ্গক *n.* a pigment.

রঙ্গচিত্র *n.* a cartoon.

রঙ্গন *n.* painting; the ixora.

রঙ্গপ্রিয় *a.* fond of making fun or cracking

jokes, jocular; given to drollery, drollish; fond of fun and frolics, frolicsome.

রঙ্গভুমি *n.* a battlefield; a place of public contest, an arena; a wrestling ground; a theatre.

রঙ্গমঞ্চ *n.* the stage.

রঙ্গমহল rej. var. of **রংমহল**।

রঙ্গরস *n.* fun and frolics; wit and humour.

রঙ্গশালা *n.* a theatre.

রঙ্গস্থল same as **রঙ্গভুমি**।

-রঙ্গা *sfx.* indicating: possession of a colour or colours (তেরঙ্গা).

রঙ্গালয় *n.* a theatre.

রঙ্গিণী *a. fem.* jocular; gay, frolicsome; sportive; taking frenzied delight in (রণরঙ্গিণী) ; (loos.) wanton.

রঙ্গিন rej. var. of **রঙিন**।

রঙ্গিলা[1] same as **রঙ্গপ্রিয়**।

রঙ্গিলা[2] *a. fem.* coloured; dyed; dappled, variegated; red (রঙ্গিলা শাড়ি) ; brown (রঙ্গিলা গাই).

রচক same as **রচয়িতা**।

রচন *n.* building; formation; creation; making; composition.

রচনা *n.* building, construction; formation; creation; making; composition; a literary composition; an essay. **রচনা করা** *v.* to build, to construct; to form; to create; to make; to compose, to write (প্রবন্ধ বা পুস্তক রচনা করা). **কেশ-রচনা** *n.* hairdo. **কেশ রচনা করা** *v.* to do up or dress one's hair. **~কৌশল** *n.* method or style of building or making or of composition. **~নৈপুণ্য** *n.* skill in building or making or in composition. **~পদ্ধতি, ~প্রণালী** same as **~কৌশল**। **~শৈলী** *n.* style (esp.literary style). **~বলি** *n.* writings, literary or other works; collected writings. **~ভঙ্গি, ~রীতি** same as **~কৌশল**।

রচয়িতা *n.* a builder, a constructor; a creator, a maker; a composer; an author, a writer. *fem.* **রচয়িত্রী**।

রচা same as **রচনা করা**।

রচিত *a.* built; created; made; composed; written.

রজ, রজঃ *n.* dust; (bot.) pollen; the menstrual flow; (phil. & theol.) the second of the three natural qualities of creatures, the quality characterized by activeness and spiritedness (usu. **রজোগুণ**).

রজক *n.* a washerman. *fem.* **রজকী, রজকিনী** a washer-woman.

রজত *n.* silver. **~কান্তি** *a.* as beautifully white as silver. **রজত-জয়ন্তী** see **জয়ন্তী**। **~ধবল, ~শুভ্র** *a.* silver-white. **~বর্ণ** *a.* silver-coloured, silvery. **~মুদ্রা** *n.* a silver coin. **~মূল্য** *n.* price paid in silver coins. **রজতাঙ্গুরীয়** *n.* a silver-ring.

রজন *n.* rosin; resin; gamboge.

রজনী *n.* the night. **~কান্ত, ~নাথ** *n.* the moon. **~গন্ধা** *n.* the tuberose. **~যোগে** *adv.* at night,by night.

রজস্বলা *a. fem.* in menses.

রজোগুণ see **রজ**।

রজোদর্শন *n.* the first appearance of menses.

রজোবন্ধ *n.* menopause; cessation of menses; change of life.

রজ্জু *n.* rope, cord, string, cable. **~পথ** *n.* a ropeway. **~বদ্ধ** *a.* fastened with a rope, roped, corded, stringed. **~ভ্রম** *n.* the fallacy of mistaking (snakes etc.) for a rope.

রঞ্জক[1] *n.* gunpowder. **~ঘর** *n.* the magazine of a gun; a touch-hole.

রঞ্জক[2] *a.* used in dyeing or colouring; pleasing, gratifying, delightful. □ *n.* a dye, a paint, a colouring substance; a dyer. **~দ্রব্য, ~পদার্থ** *n.* a dye, a paint, a colouring substance; a pigment.

রঞ্জন *n.* dyeing; colouring, colouration; pleasing or entertaining, gratification. □ *a.* entertaining, pleasing, gratifying (মনোরঞ্জন). **~প্রণালী** *n.* the process of dyeing or colouring. **~বিদ্যা** *n.* art of dyeing or colouring; art of pleasing.

রঞ্জনরশ্মি *n.* Rontgen rays; X-rays.

রঞ্জনী *a. fem.* of **রঞ্জন** (*a.*).

রঞ্জা *v.* (poet.) to dye; to colour; to please.

রঞ্জিকা *fem.* of **রঞ্জক**[2]।

রঞ্জিত *a.* dyed; coloured; entertained. **রঞ্জিত করা** *v.* to dye; to colour.

রঞ্জিনী var. of **রঞ্জনী**।

রটন, রটনা *n.* circulation of a report, rumour, etc.; publicity; announcement; a scandalous report. **রটনা করা** *v.* to circulate, to give publicity to; to announce.

রটা *v.* to be in circulation, to circulate; to be made public. **রটানো** *v.* to circulate; to make public. **যা রটে তার কিছু বটে** (fig.) there is some truth in a rumour. **রটিত** *a.* circulated, made public, noised abroad, reported.

রড *n.* a rod (esp. one of metal).

রড় *n.* (obs.) a run to flee. **রড় দেওয়া** *v.* to start off running to flee, to be on the run, to bolt away.

রণ *n.* a war, a battle, a fight, a combat; a noise, a sound. **~কামী** *a.* desiring to fight; belligerent; militant. **~কুঠার** *n.* a battle-axe. **~কুশল, ~কৌশল, ~ক্ষেত্র** same as **যুদ্ধকুশল, যুদ্ধকৌশল** and **যুদ্ধক্ষেত্র** respectively. **~চণ্ডী** see **চণ্ডী**। **~চাতুর্য** *n.* planning and skilful movement of troops in a battle, efficient manoevring of army etc. **~জয়, ~জয়ী** same as **যুদ্ধজয়** and **যুদ্ধজয়ী** respectively. **~জিৎ** *a.* ever victorious in battles. **~ঢক্কা** same as **~ভেরী**। **~তরি** same as **যুদ্ধজাহাজ**। **~ন** *n.* act of making sounds; twanging (as of a bow); tingling (as of a stringed instrument). **~নাদ** *n.* a war cry. **~নিপুণ** same as **যুদ্ধকুশল**। **~নীতি** *n.* the art of planning an operation in war, war strategy or tactics. **~নৃত্য** *n.* a war-dance. **~নৈপুণ্য** *n.* skill in war or warfare or fighting. **~পাণ্ডিত্য** same as **~নৈপুণ্য**। **~পোত** same as **~তরি**। **~প্রিয়** *a.* fond of fighting or war; belligerent. **~বাদ্য** *n.* war-music; military band. **~বেশ** *n.* fighting attire; military dress; (fig.) belligerent approach. **~ভূমি** *n.* a battlefield. **~ভেরী** *n.* a war-drum, a kettledrum. **~মত্ত** same as **যুদ্ধোন্মত্ত**। **~যাত্রা** same as **যুদ্ধযাত্রা**। **~রঙ্গিণী** *a. fem.* taking delight in fighting □ *n. fem.* a woman fond of war or fighting. **~রণ, ~রণি** *n.* a twang (as of a bow); a tingling sound (as of a stringed instrument). **রণরণ করা** *v.* to twang; to tingle. **~সজ্জা, ~সাজ** same as **যুদ্ধসজ্জা**। **~স্থল, রণাঙ্গন** *n.* a battlefield. **~হুঙ্কার** *n.* war cry, battle cry. **রণিত** *a.* sounded; resounded; twanged; tingled, tingling. **রণিত করা, রণিত হওয়া** *v.* to sound; to resound; to twang; to tingle. **রণে ভঙ্গ দেওয়া** *v.* to retreat or flee from the battlefield; to cease fighting; to acknowledge defeat and retreat. **রণোন্মাদনা** *n.* extreme love of war, warmongering; a passion for war.

রত *a.* engaged in, employed in (পাঠরত) ; devoted to, attached to, addicted to (ভোগরত).

রতন coll. & poet. var. of **রত্ন**। **~চুড়** *n.* an ornament for the wrist, palms and fingers. **রতনে রতন চেনে** (fig.) one can pick up one's like easily.

রতি[১] *n.* the smallest measure of weight in India (=1.875 grains); (fig.) a very small amount.

রতি[২] *n.* the wife and consort of the Hindu love-god; sexual intercourse, copulation (also **রতিক্রিয়া**) ; (fig.) love, attachment; (rhet.) intent absorption of the mind.

রত্তি coll. var. of **রতি**[১] । □ *a.* vary small or tiny (একরত্তি ছেলে).

রত্ন *n.* a jewel, a gem; (fig.) the best specimen of a class (কন্যারত্ন). **~খচিত** *a.* studded or inlaid with a gem or gems. **~গর্ভ** *a.* impregnated with gems. **~গর্ভা** *a. fem.* (often sarcas.) giving birth to excellent children. **~জীবী** *n.* a jeweller; a lapidary. **~দ্বীপ** *n.* the coral island; treasure island. **~প্রসবিনী, ~প্রসবিত্রী, ~প্রসূ** *a. fem.* yielding gems; impregnated with gems; (fig.) giving birth to excellent children. **~বণিক** *n.* a dealer in gems or jewellery, a jeweller. **~ভাণ্ডার** *n.* a treasure of jewels. **~মণ্ডিত** *a.* bedecked with jewels, bejewelled. **~ময়** *a.* made of gems; gemmy. *fem.* **~ময়ী**। **~রাজি** *n.* gems, jewels; jewellery. **~সিংহাসন** *n.* throne studded or bedecked with jewels. **রত্নাকর** *n.* a mine or quarry of gems; the sea, the ocean. **রত্নাবলি** *n.* gems, jewels; a jewel necklace. **রত্নাভরণ, রত্নালংকার** *n.* a jewel ornament.

রথ *n.* a chariot; the chariot of Jagannatha; the festival of Jagannatha going in a chariot for a sea-bath; a car, a carriage, a vehicle. **রথ টানা** *v.* to draw the chariot of Jagannatha (by his devotees on the occasion of his going for a sea-bath). **রথ দেখা ও কলা বেচা** (fig.) to kill two birds with one stone. **রথের মেলা** a fair held on the occasion of the festival of Jagannatha going in a chariot for a sea-bath. **~চক্র** *n.* a wheel of a chariot or (rare) of a carriage. **~চালক, ~বাহক** *n.* a charioteer; (rare) a car-driver, a carman. **~যাত্রা** *n.* the Hindu festival of Jagannatha going in a chariot for a sea-bath. **রথাঙ্গ** same as **~চক্র**। **রথারূঢ়** *a.* riding in or mounted on a chariot or any vehicle; charioted. *fem.* **রথারূঢ়া**। **রথারোহণ করা** *v.* to board a chariot or any vehicle. **রথারোহী** *a.* riding in a chariot or any vehicle. ☐ *n.* a charioteer; a rider or passenger of any vehicle. *fem.* **রথারোহিণী**। **রথী** *n.* a charioteer; (hist.) a famous hero who fights riding in a chariot; a (famous or valorous) warrior; (fig.) a hero.

রথো *a.* trashy (রথো মাল) ; good-for-nothing, worthless (রথো লোক).

রদ[১] *a.* nullified, revoked, repealed, stayed. ☐ *n.* nullification, revocation. repeal (আইনরদ) ; stay (নিলামরদ). **রদ করা** *v.* to nullify, to revoke, to repeal, to stay. **রদের হুকুম** stay order.

রদ[২], রদন *n.* a tooth.

রদবদল *n.* additions and alterations; a reshuffle (মন্ত্রিসভার রদবদল).

রদ্দা *n.* a stroke with the arm on the nape of another's neck. **রদ্দা দেওয়া, রদ্দা মারা** *v.* to strike the nape of another's neck with one's arm.

রদ্দি *a.* trashy (রদ্দি মাল = rotten stuff); worthless, good-for-nothing (রদ্দি লোক).

রন্ধন, রন্ধনকার্য, রন্ধনক্রিয়া *n.* cooking; cookery. **রন্ধন করা** *v.* to cook. **রন্ধনগৃহ, রন্ধনশালা, রন্ধনাগার** *n.* a cookhouse, a kitchen. **রন্ধনপাত্র** *n.* a cooking utensil.

রন্ধিত *a.* cooked; (rare) dressed.

রন্ধ্র *n.* a hole; a pore, a cavity; a bore (as of a gun); a fault, an offence; an opening caused by a failing; (astrol.) the eighth house of the zodiac. **~ক** *n.* a borer. **~ক্যামেরা** *n.* a pin-hole camera. **~গত** *a.* entered into the hole. **~গত শনি** (astrol.) location of the Saturn in the eighth zodiacal house of one's horoscope causing one's destruction. **রন্ধ্রীয়** *a.* porous.

রপ্ত *a.* habituated, accustomed; acclimatized; thoroughly learnt or mastered. **রপ্ত করা** *v.* to be habituated or accustomed to; to be acclimatized to; to learn thoroughly. **রপ্তে রপ্তে** *adv.* gradually, slowly, by degrees.

রপ্তানি *n.* export. ☐ *a.* exported. **রপ্তানি করা** *v.* to export. **রপ্তানি বাণিজ্য** *n.* export trade; foreign trade. **রপ্তানি শুল্ক'** *n.* export duty.

রফা *n.* an amicable settlement, compromise; destruction (দফা-রফা). **রফা করা** *v.* to come to terms with, to make a compromise; to settle amicably. **~নামা** *n.* a deed of compromise.

রব *n.* a sound, a noise; a rumour. **রব উঠেছে** a rumour is in the air, there is a rumour. **রব করা** *v.* to make a noise.

রবরবা *n.* height of power and prestige.

রবাব *n.* a stringed musical instrument akin to the vina.

রবার *n.* india-rubber.

রবাহূত *a.* one who has come uninvited at a feast on hearing a report of it; one who has come uninvited (and is unwelcome).

রবি *n.* the sun; the sungod. **~কর** *n.* sunray, sunbeam; sunlight, sunshine. **~করোজ্জ্বল** *a.* brightened with sunrays; sunshiny, sunny. **~খন্দ** *n.* the spring crop (namely, wheat, barley etc.). **~চ্ছবি** *n.* sun's radiance. **~বর্ষ** *n.* the solar year. **~বার, ~বাসর** *n.* Sunday. **~মণ্ডল** *n.* the orb of the sun. **~মার্গ** *n.* the ecliptic. **~রশ্মি** same as **~কর**। **~শস্য** *n.* rabicrop (harvested in spring).

রবিউল-আউয়ল *n.* the third month of the Muslim calendar.

রবীন্দ্রসংগীত *n.* the song composed by Rabindranath Tagore, Tagore song.

রভস *n.* a strong upsurge of emotion; deep sorrow or grief; great delight, hilarity.

রমজান *n.* the ninth month of the Muslim calendar, Ramad(h)an.

রমণ *n.* sport; enjoyment; amorous dalliance; sexual intercourse, coition; a lover or husband (রাধামরণ). **রমণ করা** *v.* to indulge in sports or enjoyment; to dally amorously; to have sexual intercourse with.

রমণী *n.* a beautiful woman; a woman; a wife. **~মোহন পুরুষ** a lady-killer; a man who captures the fancy of a woman or casts a magic spell on her. **~রত্ন** *n.* a jewel of a woman, an ideal woman. **~সুলভ** *a.* womanly, feminine. **~সুলভ লাবণ্য** feminine grace, womanly grace or beauty.

রমণীয় *a.* delightful; beautiful, pleasant.

রমরমা *n.* abundance, plenty; affluence; pomp, éclat, splendour. □ *a.* affluent, plentiful; bountiful (রমারমা ব্যাবসা).

রমা[১] poet. var. of **রমণ করা**।

রমা[২] *n. fem.* Goddess Lakshmi (লক্ষ্মী) ; a lady-love, a sweetheart; a beautiful woman. **~কান্ত, ~নাথ, ~পতি, রমেশ** *n.* Vishnu (বিষ্ণু), the husband of Goddess Lakshmi.

রমিত *a.* sexually enjoyed; dallied (esp. amorously); sported with; made pleasant. *fem.* **রমিতা**।

রমেশ see **রমা**[২]।

রম্বস *n.* (geom.) a rhombus.

রম্ভা *n.* (myth.) one of the nymphs of Paradise; the banana, the plantain; the banana-tree.

রম্ভোরু *n.* a woman having thighs as well-shaped as banana-trees.

রম্য same as **রমণীয়**। *fem.* **রম্যা**। **~রচনা** *n.* personal (and usu. humorous) essay; (loos.) belles lettres.

রয়ানি *n.* the singing of the mythological story of Manasa (মনসা).

রলা *n.* a cylindrical piece of a treestump.

রশনা alt. spell. of **রসনা**[১], **রসনা**[২]।

রশারশি *n.* strings of various sizes taken collectively, cordage.

রশি *n.* cord, rope.

রশুন *n.* garlic.

রশ্মি *n.* a ray, a beam; a cord, a string, a rope; a bridle; eyelash. **নভোরশ্মি, মহাজাগতিক রশ্মি** cosmic rays. **~গুচ্ছ** *n.* a bundle of rays. **রশ্মীয়** *a.* radial. **রশ্মীয় কেন্দ্র** (phys.) the optical centre.

রস *n.* savour, flavour, taste; a liquid solution of anything hard (চিনির রস) ; a syrup; juice; exudation (খেজুররস) ; morbid exudation (ঘায়ের রস) ; sap (রসহীন কাঠ) ; essence (অন্নরস) ; lymph or mucus or phlegm (দেহে রসাধিক্য) ; semen; (poet.) strong attachment or love; (rhet.) sentiment expressed or flavour contained in a writing (শৃঙ্গার রস) ; (Vaishnavism) a way of worship (বাৎসল্যরস) ; inner or true significance, purport (কাব্যরস) ; charm; interest; sense of humour (লোকটি রসহীন) ; fun, banter, wit and humour; delight, hilarity, enjoyment, pleasure (রসে মাতা) ; (sl.) vanity or audacity; monetary resources, money; quicksilver, mercury. **রস করা** *v.* to make fun (of); to banter; to make a liquid solution of. **রস নামা** *v.* to become swollen with drospy. **রস পাওয়া** *v.* to find interest in. **রস ফুরানো** *v.* to run out of funds. **রস হওয়া** *v.* to become juicy; (sl.) to become vain or audacious. **~করা** *n.* a sweet and juicy drop made of the kernel of coconut. **~কর্পূর** *n.* mercury perchloride. **~কলি** *n.* a streak of mud painted on the bridge of the nose by a Vaishnava. **~কস, ~কষ** *n.* charm and sweetness. **~কসহীন** *a.* dry and outspoken (রসকসহীন কথাবার্তা) ; bald (রসকসহীন রচনা). **~গর্ভ** same as **রসাত্মক**। **~গোল্লা** *n.* a sweet and juicy drop made of posset and farina. **~গ্রহণ** *n.* appreciation. **রসগ্রহণ করা** *v.* to taste; (rhet.) to appreciate the flavour of. **~গ্রাহী** *a.* capable of appreciation, appreciative; receptive. **~ঘন** *n.* (rhet.) flavoury; full of concentrated flavour. **~জ্ঞ** *a.* appreciative of the inner or true significance, capable of appreciation; well-versed in, having connoisseurship in, au fait. *fem.* **~জ্ঞা**। **রসজ্ঞ ব্যক্তি** one capable of appreciation; a connoisseur. **~জ্ঞান** *n.* capability of appreciation; sense of humour. **~পূর্ণ** *a.* juicy, succulent; sapful, sappy; full of wit and humour. **~বড়া** *n.* a sweet and juicy drop made of pulped pigeon-pea. **~বতী** *a. fem.* full of wit and humour, intelligent and witty. **~বাত** *n.* rheumatic affection in the joints attended with swelling. **~বেত্তা** same as **~জ্ঞ**। **~বোধ** same as **~জ্ঞান**। **~ভঙ্গ** *n.* interruption of a spicy topic; interruption of enjoyment (usu. by coarseness). **~ময়** a. juicy; full of wit and humour; full of flavour. *fem.* **~ময়ী**। **~রচনা** *n.* witty or humorous writing. **~রাজ** *n.* the most witty and humorous man; Krishna (কৃষ্ণ) ; stibnite; antimony; quicksilver, mercury. **~শালা** *n.* a chemical laboratory or workshop. **~শাস্ত্র** *n.* poetics. **~সিন্দূর** *n.* cinnabar. **~স্থ** *a.* stricken with excess of phlegm or lymph or mucus. **~স্ফীত** *a.* (bot.) turgid. **~স্ফীতি** *n.* (bot.) turgidity, turgescence. **~স্রাব** *n.* (bot.) exudation. **~হীন** *a.* sapless; dry; dull; uninteresting.

রসদ *n.* provisions, rations (esp. of an army); food; (fig.) means or monetary resources (স্ফূর্তির রসদ).

রসনা[1] *n.* the tonuge; the palate. **রসনাগ্র** *n.* the tip of the tongue.

রসনা[2] *n.* an ornament worn round the waist; girdle.

রসনেন্দ্রিয় *n.* the sense-organ of taste, taste; (loos.) the tongue.

রসা *a.* juicy, succulent (রসা কাঁঠাল) ; slightly putrefied or rotten or decomposed (রসা মাছ). □ *n.* gravy (of meat or fish). □ *v.* to become juicy or sappy; to soften (মাটি রসেছে) ; to be stricken with excess of lymph or phlegm in the body (চোখ-মুখ রসেছে) ; to become slightly putrefied or rotten.

রসাঞ্জন *n.* stibnite; antimony; regulus.

রসাতল *n.* (myth.) the lowest of the seven underworlds. **রসাতলে দেওয়া** *v.* (fig.) to ruin or destroy utterly. **রসাতলে যাওয়া** *v.* (fig.) to be ruined or destroyed utterly.

রসাত্মক *a.* (rare) juicy; sappy; humorous, witty; (rhet.) flavoury.

রসাধিক্য *n.* (morbid) excess of phlegm or lymph or mucus in the body.

রসান *n.* a polishing stone, a stone for rubbing gold etc; (fig.) a spicy or pert remark.

রসানো *v.* to make juicy; to wet; (fig.) to make interesting by adding spicy or savoury comments (রসিয়ে বলা) ; (fig.) to make deep appeal to or to steep in sentiment (মন রসানো). □ *n.* act of steeping in juice; wetting; act of polishing gold etc.

রসাভাস *n.* (rhet.) a defect characterized by semblance of flavours or introduction of opposed flavour.

রসায়ন *n.* a medicine prolonging life and curing disease, an elixir; chemistry. **~বিদ** *a.* versed in chemistry. □ *n.* one versed in chemistry, an expert in chemistry; a chemist. **~বিদ্যা, ~শাস্ত্র** *n.* chemistry. **রসায়নাগার** *n.* a chemical laboratory. **রসায়নী** *a.* pertaining to chemistry (রসায়নী বিদ্যা) ; versed in chemistry.

রসাল *n.* the mango tree or its fruit.

রসালাপ *n.* a humorous or witty or amorous conversation. **রসালাপ করা** *v.* to be engaged in humorous or witty or amorous conversation.

রসালো *a.* juicy, succulent; tasteful, delicious; sappy; humorous, witty; entertaining (রসালো আলাপ) ; (rhet.) savoury (রসালো লেখা).

রসাস্বাদ, রসাস্বাদন same as **রসগ্রহণ**।

রসিক *a.* capable of comprehending the inner or true significance or the flavour (of), appreciative (কাব্যরসিক) ; versed in the art of love-making (রসিক নাগর) ; witty, humorous; jocose (রসিক লোক). *fem.* **রসিকা**। **~তা** *n.* a humorous or amorous frolic; a joke, a jest.

রসিদ *n.* a receipt. **রসিদ কাটা** *v.* to write out a receipt.

রসুই *n.* cooking. **রসুই করা** *v.* to cook. **~ঘর** *n.* a kitchen. **~য়ে** same as **রসুয়ে**।

রসুন[1] *n.* garlic.

রসুন[2] *v. imper.* please wait or stop.

রসুয়ে *a.* employed in cooking professionally. **রসুয়ে-বামুন** a brahmin cook.

রসুল *n.* (Mus.) a prophet.

রসেন্দ্র *n.* mercury.

রসোত্তীর্ণ *a.* (rhet.) having the intended flavour effectively established; acceptable as a work of art.

রসোদগার *n.* (Vaishnava lit.) recollection of the flavour of a union.

রহমত *n.* (Mus.) mercy, grace, kindness, benignancy.

রহমান *a.* (Mus.) merciful, graceful, kind, benignant.

রহস্য *n.* a mystery; a secret; a riddle; pleasantry, a joke; fun. **রহস্য করা** *v.* to make fun; to joke; to poke fun at, to crack a joke at. **রহস্য করে, রহস্যচ্ছলে** *adv.* by way of joke; jokingly. **রহস্যভেদ করা** *v.* to discover or solve a mystery, to puzzle out a mystery; to probe; to find out or expose a secret. **~ভেদী** *a.* (capable of or engaged in) discovering or solving a mystery; (loos.) capable of discovering the mysteries of crimes and detecting criminals. **~ময়** *a.* mysterious; occult; secret; hard to comprehend. **রহস্যাবৃত** *a.* veiled or shrouded in mystery; mysterious; occult; secret. **রহস্যালাপ** *n.* confidential talk; secret conference; humorous or witty or amorous conversation; a joke. **রহস্যালাপ করা** *v.* to talk confidentially; to confer secretly; to be engaged in a humorous or witty or amorous conversation; to joke. **রহস্যোদ্ঘাটন** same as **~ভেদ**।

রহা same as **থাকা**।

রহিত *a.* lacking in, devoid of, destitute of (কাণ্ডজ্ঞানরহিত) ; repealed, withdrawn, abolished; stayed, held over, postponed; stopped, discontinued. **রহিত করা** *v.* to repeal, to withdraw, to abolish, to annul, to abrogate, to revoke (আইন রহিত করা) ; to stay, to hold over, to postpone (নিলাম রহিত করা) ; to stop, to discontinue (প্রথা রহিত করা).

-রা১ *sfx.* indicating plurality, -s or -es (ছেলেরা).

রা২ *n.* a word or sound of the mouth, an utterance. **রা করা, রা কাড়া, রা সরা** *v.* to make a (or any) sound by the mouth; to utter a (or any) word; to respond. **সাত চড়ে রা না করা** not to utter a word or complain or protest even when repeatedly slapped or hit.

রাই১ *n.* mustard.

রাই২ corrup. of **রাধিকা**।

রাইকিশোরী *n.* young Radhika (রাধিকা).

রাইসরিষা *n.* rapeseed; mustard.

রাইফেল *n.* a rifle.

রাইয়ত older var. of **রায়ত**।

রাং১ *n.* a shank of any animal taken as food; the hough, the ham.

রাং২ *n.* tin.

রাংচিতা *n.* lead-wort.

রাংঝাল *n.* soldering with tin and lead, solder. **রাংঝাল করা** *v.* to solder with tin and lead, to solder.

রাংতা *n.* tinsel, tinfoil.

রাংমিস্ত্রি *n.* a tinker.

রাঁড় *a.* a widow; a prostitute; a concubine. **রাঁড়ের বাড়ি** a brothel.

রাঁড়া *n.* an unproductive or barren tree.

রাঁড়ি *n.* (vulg.) a widow.

রাঁদা variation of **র‍্যাঁদা**।

রাঁধনি১ *n.* a variety of parsley.

রাঁধনি২, রাঁধুনি *n. fem.* (also *masc.*) a (professional) cook. **রাঁধুনি বামুন** a Brahmin cook.

রাঁধা *v.* to cook. □ *a.* cooked. □ *n.* cooking. **রাঁধানো** *v.* to cause to cook or be cooked. **রাঁধাবাড়া** *n.* cooking and serving at table.

রাঁধুনি pop. var. of **রাঁধনি**।

রাকা *n.* the full moon setting in the small hours of the morning (usu. **রাকাশশী**) ; the night of such a full moon.

রাক্ষস *n.* (myth.) one of a non-Aryan anthropophagous race of India, a rakshas(a); a cannibal; (facet.) a glutton. **রাক্ষস-বিবাহ** *n.* a system of marriage in which the bridegroom abducts the bride or marries her by force. **রাক্ষসী** *n. fem.* of **রাক্ষস**। □ *a.* relating to rakshasas (রাক্ষসী মায়া). **রাক্ষসী বেলা** the terminal $^1/_5$th part of the daytime. **রাক্ষুসে** *a.* of or like a rakshas; monstrously severe or great (রাক্ষুসে খিদে) ; huge, gigantic, monstrous (রাক্ষুসে মুলো).

রাখা *v.* to place, to lay, to keep; to shelter; to protect, to guard; to preserve; to save; to rescue; to put into; to deposit; to keep for sale (এ দোকানে খারাপ মাল রাখে না) ; to maintain or grow on one's person (টিকি রাখা) ; to keep up, to maintain (ঠাট রাখা) ; to pawn or receive as a pawn (গয়না রেখে টাকা নেওয়া বা দেওয়া) ; to engage, to employ (চাকর রাখা) ; to rear or tame (গোরু রাখা, কুকুর

রাখা) ; to look after, to tend, to herd (দুজন রাখাল ঘোষেদের গোরু রাখে) ; to adopt (বন্ধ্যা নারীটি একটি ছেলে রেখেছে) ; to maintain for one's enjoyment, to keep (বেশ্যা রাখা) ; to set apart (অতিথির জন্য খাবার রাখা) ; to store (বছরের খোরাক রাখা) ; to put by, to set by, to lay by (টাকা রাখা) ; to refrain from mentioning or uttering (তার কথা রাখো—ঢের শুনেছি) ; to heed, to pay heed to, to obey, to comply with (অনুরোধ রাখা) ; to fulfil, to observe (প্রতিশ্রুতি রাখা) ; to leave (বউ রেখে কোথায় যাবে) ; to leave behind (কলমটা ঘরে রেখে এসেছি) ; to stop, to pull up, to park (গাড়ি এখানে রাখো) ; to cherish (মনে আশা রাখা) ; to bear (মনে রাখা) ; to buy (বাটিটা ফেরিওয়ালার কাছ থেকে রেখেছি) ; to take settlement of (জমি রাখা) ; to give (নাম রাখা) ; to gratify, to please (মন রাখা). **আটকে রাখা** same as **আটকানো** (*v.*). **কথা রাখা** *v.* to comply with or obey or accede to another's request; to keep one's promise or word. **করে রাখা** *v.* to have done or completed something beforehand. **চোখ রাখা** *v.* to keep an eye over, to watch. **জমিয়ে রাখা** *v.* to lay by, to save up; to store up; to accumulate, to pile up. **ধরে রাখা** *v.* to shut up; to detain; to hold back; to store up. **ফেলে রাখা** *v.* to put off. **মান রাখা** *v.* to show due respect to. **সাজিয়ে রাখা** *v.* to keep in order; to arrange in order; to display in order. **রেখে যাওয়া** *n.* to leave behind.

রাখাল *n.* a cowherd; a herdsman. **রাখাল-বালক** *n.* a cowboy. **রাখালি** *n.* the profession or wages of a cowherd or herdsman. **রাখালি গান** a pastoral song, a pastoral, a bucolic. **রাখালিয়া** *a.* of cowherds or herdsmen; pastoral.

রাখি *n.* a piece of thread which one ties round the wrist of another in order to safeguard the latter from all evils. **~পূর্ণিমা** *n.* the full moon day of the month of Shravan (শ্রাবণ) when a rakhi is tied round the wrist of another. **~বন্ধন** *n.* act or the festival of tying a rakhi (রাখি) round the wrist of another.

রাগ¹ *n.* a dye, a paint, a colour, a hue; a red hue or colour or tinge; love, affection (পূর্বরাগ) ; attachment, inclination; anger, passion, rage. **রাগ করা** same as **রাগা**। **রাগ দেখানো** *v.* to show temper. **রাগ হওয়া** *v.* to be angry. **~ত** *a.* angry, angered. **~তভাবে** *adv.* angrily; with a show of rage. **রাগা** *v.* to get or grow angry. **রাগানো** *v.* to anger; to irritate. **রাগান্ধ** *a.* blinded with rage. **রাগান্বিত** *a.* angered, angry. **রাগী** *a.* easily angered, quick-tempered, short-tempered, sulky, wrathful.

রাগ² *n.* any one of the six principal modes of Indian classical music; raga, a mode of Indian classical music. **রাগিণী** *n.* (mus.) any one of the thirty-six modes of Indian music secondary to the six ragas (রাগ) ; a musical mode or tune; a song. **~প্রধান** *a.* (of modes in Indian music) based on classical modes.

রাঘব *n.* a descendant of King Raghu (রঘু) ; Rama (রাম) of the Ramayana. **~প্রিয়া, ~বাঞ্ছা** *n.* Sita (সীতা) the wife of Rama (রাম) of the Ramayana. **~বোয়াল** a monstrously large sheatfish; a man of high social standing who is a virulent extortioner of people; a leading criminal (who generally manages to escape punishment). **রাঘবারি** *n.* Ravana (রাবণ) the enemy of Rama (রাম) of the Ramayana.

রাঙ, রাঙচিতা, রাঙঝাল, রাঙতা alt. spellings of **রাং, রাংচিতা, রাংঝাল** and **রাংতা** respectively.

রাঙা *a.* red, scarlet, crimson; fair-complexioned; flushed (লজ্জায় রাঙা) ; an elder, but (generally) lower in the scale of seniority (রাঙাদিদি). □ *v.* to become red or crimson, to redden; to become bright, to brighten; to flush. **~নো** *v.* to redden; to dye; to brighten; to cause to flush. **~বাস** *n.* a cloth dyed in red ochre; a scarlet cloth. **~মুলো** *n.* the red radish; (fig.) a handsome but worthless man.

রাজ¹ contr. of **রাজমিস্ত্রি**।

রাজ² *n.* a state or government.

-রাজ³ *sfx.* denoting: a king (গ্রিকরাজ) ; an excellent specimen (গজরাজ).

রাজ⁴ *pfx.* denoting: a king; government;

excellent, best. ~কন্যা *n.* a princess. ~কবি *n.* a court-poet; a poet-laureate. ~কর same as রাজস্ব। ~কর্ম, ~কার্য *n.* the office and duties of a king; a royal duty; a state affair; government service, public service. ~কর্মচারী *n.* an officer or servant of the state, a government officer; a public servant. ~কীয় *a.* royal, regal; kingly, princely; (fig.) magnificent. ~কুমার *n.* a king's son, a prince. *fem.* ~কুমারী a princess. ~কুল *n.* a royal line or family, a dynasty. ~কুলোদ্ভব *a.* born of a royal family, princely-born. ~কোষ *n.* a royal or government treasury, a treasury. ~ক্ষমা *n.* amnesty. ~গুরু *n.* a spiritual guide of a king or of a royal family. ~গৃহ *n.* a king's palace or city. ~চক্রবর্তী *n.* a sovereign king, a suzerain; a king of kings, an emperor. ~চিহ্ন *n.* a mark on one's person indicating that one is a king or will become a king; royal insignia. ~চ্ছত্র, (pop.) ~ছত্র *n.* an umbrella which is officially held over the head of a king. ~টিকা *n.* a holy mark painted on the forehead of a king at coronation. ~তক্ত same as রাজাসন। ~তন্ত্র *n.* monarchy; state administrative policy. ~ত্ব *n.* a kingdom, a realm; a state; a domain; reign, rule; predominance. রাজত্ব করা *v.* to reign, to rule, to govern; (fig.) to domineer, to dominate. রাজত্বকাল *n.* the time of one's reign, reign. ~দণ্ড *n.* a sceptre; a punishment inflicted by a king or by a law-court; (astrol.) a visible vertical line on one's forehead indicating the possibility of one's becoming a king. ~দত্ত *a.* given or conferred by a king or government. রাজদত্ত সম্মান a royal honour, a government honour, an official honour. ~দম্পতি, ~দম্পতী *n.* a royal couple. ~দরবার same as ~সভা। ~দর্শন *n.* an interview with a king; a visit to a king, seeing or meeting a king. ~দূত *n.* an ambassador (*fem* : an ambassadress); an envoy; a royal courier. ~দ্বারে *adv.* before a king; in a royal court; in a court of justice. ~দ্রোহ, ~দ্রোহিতা *n.* a revolt against the king or established authority, insurrection, insurgence, high treason; sedition. ~দ্রোহী *a.* insurgent; treasonous; seditious. □ *n.* an insurgent; a rebel against the king or established authority. *fem.* ~দ্রোহিণী। ~ধর্ম *n.* duties of a king, royal office. ~ধানী *n.* the capital of a country or state; a metropolis. ~নন্দন same as ~কুমার। *fem.* ~নন্দিনী। ~নামা *n.* the genealogical tree or chronology or a chronicle of a royal line or dynasty. ~নীতি *n.* politics; statecraft; (loos.) diplomacy. ~নীতিক *a.* political; (rare) diplomatic. □ *n.* a politician. ~নীতিজ্ঞ *a.* versed in politics; (loos.) versed in statesmanship or diplomacy. রাজনীতিজ্ঞ ব্যক্তি a politician; a statesman; a diplomat. ~নৈতিক pop. var. রাজনীতিক। ~পট্ট *n.* the seat of a king, a throne; kingship; a royal or government charter; a kind of black jewel. ~পথ *n.* a public thoroughfare, a highway; a main road (of a city). ~পদ *n.* the office of a king, kingship. ~পরিচ্ছদ *n.* royal robes. ~পাট same as ~পট্ট। ~পুত্র same as ~কুমার। *fem.* ~পুত্রী। ~পুরী *n.* the residence or palace of a king; the capital city of a king; (fig.) a magnificent building or city or residence. ~পুরুষ *n.* a king's officer; a government officer. ~প্রমুখ *n.* a government title given to the leading feudal chief of India, vested with powers similar to that of a governor. ~প্রসাদ *n.* royal favour or grace; government favour. ~প্রাসাদ *n.* a royal residence, a palace. ~বংশ same as ~কুল। ~বংশী *n.* a lowly Hindu caste chiefly of North Bengal; a member of this caste. ~বংশীয় *a.* dynastic; born of a royal family, of royal blood. *fem.* ~বংশীয়া। ~বন্দি *n.* a political prisoner. ~বাড়ি same as ~প্রাসাদ। ~বিধি *n.* a royal statute; a law. ~বিপ্লব *n.* a political revolution; a coup d'état. ~বেশ *n.* royal robes or attire. ~বৈদ্য *n.* physician to a king or queen; a prince of physicians. ~ভক্ত *a.* devoted to one's sovereign or state government, loyal. রাজভক্ত ব্যক্তি a loyalist. ~তন্ত্রবাদী *n.*

a royalist. ~ভক্তি n. loyalty. ~ভবন n. a king's residence or palace; a government house. ~ভয় n. fear of being punished by a king or a court of justice. ~ভাষা n. the king's language; the state language. ~ভৃত্য n. a king's servant; a servant of a royal household; a king's officer or man. ~ভোগ n. an article of food or a thing fit for a king; a sweet and juicy drop made of posset bigger than a রসগোল্লা। ~ভোগ্য a. fit to be eaten or used or enjoyed by a king or a prince. ~মজুর n. a mason's labourer, a hodman : (loos.) a mason. ~মন্ত্রী n. a king's counsellor, a minister of state, a cabinet member. ~মহিষী n. the chief queen of a king; queen-consort. ~মাতা n. a king's mother; a queen-mother. ~মার্গ same as ~পথ। ~মিস্ত্রি same as ~মজুর। ~মুকুট n. a royal crown or diadem; (fig.) kingship. ~যোগ n. a system of yoga in which action predominates. ~যোগ্য a. fit for a king, princely. ~যোটক n. (astrol.) the most auspicious union of planets (as found in the horoscopes of the bride and the bridegroom); (fig.) the most suitable union; the most advantageous coincidence. ~রক্ত n. royal blood. ~রাজ n. a king of kings. ~রাজড়া n. princes and princelings or princely persons; (usu. dero.) very important or wealthy or affluent persons. ~রাজেশ্বর n. a king of kings, an emperor. *fem.* ~রাজেশ্বরী an empress. ~রানি same as ~মহিষী। ~র্ষি n. a king who leads an ascetical life, a royal ascetic or sage. ~লক্ষ্মী n. the female deity safeguarding a kingdom and looking after its welfare. ~শক্তি n. the administrative power of a king or government. ~শয্যা, ~শয়ন n. a king's bed, a royal bed; a princely bed; a magnificent bed. ~শাসন n. a king's rule; punishment inflicted by a king. ~শ্রী same as ~লক্ষ্মী। ~সংস্করণ n. a deluxe edition (of a book). ~সদন same as ~প্রাসাদ। ~সন্নিধান n. royal presence; a royal court. ~সভা n. a royal court, a court, a durbar. ~সম্পদ n. royal treasure or riches, princely treasure or riches. ~সরকার n. a monarch's government or court. ~সাক্ষী n. (law) an approver. ~সিংহাসন n. a throne; (fig.) kingship. ~সূয় (যজ্ঞ) n. a sacrifice performed by a monarch in order to establish his suzerainty or supremacy over other kings. ~সেবা n. attendance on a monarch; king's or queen's service; (rare) government service, public service. ~স্ব n. tax or rent or revenue payable to a monarch or to the government, revenue. রাজস্বঘটিত, রাজস্ব-সংক্রান্ত a. fiscal, financial. রাজস্ব-পর্ষৎ n. the Board of Revenue. রাজস্বসচিব n. a finance minister, a finance member, a finance secretary. ~হংস n. the gander; the swan. *fem.* ~হংসী n. the goose (*pl.* geese). ~হত্যা n. regicide. ~হন্তা n. a regicide. *fem.* ~হন্ত্রী। ~হস্তী n. an elephant on which a monarch rides; an elephant fit to carry a monarch; an excellent elephant. *fem.* ~হস্তিনী। ~হাঁস coll. corrup. of রাজহংস। রাজহাঁসের বাচ্চা a gosling.

রাজগি n. kingship; a kingdom.

রাজন্য n. a feudal or tributary prince; member of a royal family.

রাজপুত n. a Rajput. *fem.* রাজপুতানি a Rajput woman.

রাজসিক a. endowed with রজোগুণ ; majestic; princely; magnificent.

রাজা১ v. (poet.) to exist or be present esp. gracefully (রাজে, রাজো).

রাজা২ n. a king, a monarch, a prince; a ruler; (in British India) a government title of honour; (chess) the king; (fig.) a man of a magnificent and towering personality. রাজা করা v. to make one king; (often sarcas.) to make one very wealthy or great. রাজা-উজির n. (lit.) a king and his prime minister; (fig.) very wealthy and influential men. রাজা-উজির মারা v. (fig. & dero.) to tell cock-and-bull stories about one's own capabilities and importance. রাজাজ্ঞা, রাজাদেশ n. a royal command or decree or mandate. রাজাধিকার n. a royal prerogative; a monarch's territory. রাজাধিরাজ n. a king of kings, a suzerain, an emperor.

রাজানুকম্পা, রাজানুগ্রহ *n.* royal favour or grace or mercy; favour or grace or mercy shown by the government. **রাজানুচর** *n.* a monarch's servant or follower or attendant. **রাজান্তঃপুর** *n.* the inner apartments of a monarch's residence; a royal gynaeceum. **রাজাবলি** *n.* a genealogical tree of a dynasty. **রাজাভরণ** *n.* royal ornament or emblem, regalia. **রাজাসন** *n.* royal seat, a throne; (fig.) kingship.

রাজি[১] *a.* agreed, consenting; agreeing, ready. **রাজি করা** *v.* to make one agree. **রাজি হওয়া** *v.* to agree, to consent.

রাজি[২] *n.* (used as a *sfx.*) a row, a line, a range (তরুরাজি, রোমরাজি, গিরিরাজি) ; a collection (পত্ররাজি).

রাজিনামা *n.* a letter or deed of consent; (in law) a joint petition of rival parties consenting to compromise.

রাজীব *n.* the lotus. **~লোচন** *a.* lotus-eyed; beautifully blue-eyed.

রাজেন্দ্র *n.* a great king; a suzerain; an emperor. *fem.* **রাজেন্দ্রাণী** the chief queen of a great king or suzerain; an empress.

রাজ্ঞী *n.* a queen; a queen-consort.

রাজ্য *n.* a state; a kingdom, a realm, a domain, a territory; reign, rule; (fig.)—(in the sense of immensity) a country, the earth, the universe (তার বুকে রাজ্যের ব্যথা). **~খণ্ড** *n.* a portion of a state or kingdom or country; a state; a kingdom, a country. **~চ্যুত** *a.* dispossessed of or driven from one's kingdom; dethroned, deposed. **~চ্যুত করা** *v.* to deprive of or remove from one's kingdom; to dethrone, to depose. **~চ্যুতি** *n.* dispossession of or removal from one's kingdom; dethronement. **~পাল** *n.* (in free India) the title of the governor of a state. **~পালন** same as **~শাসন**। **~ভার** *n.* the burden of governing a state. **রাজ্য ভোগ করা** *v.* to enjoy sovereignty. **~ভ্রংশ** same as **~চ্যুতি**। **~ভ্রষ্ট** same as **~চ্যুত**। **~রক্ষা করা** *v.* to defend or protect a state. **~লাভ** *n.* getting or acquiring a kingdom or becoming a king; getting the throne. **~লোভ** *n.* greed for the throne; greed for expansion of one's territory. **~লোভী** *a.* greedy of the throne; greedy of expanding one's territory. **~শাসন** *n.* administration of a state or kingdom. **~শাসন করা** *v.* to govern or rule a state or kingdom. **~সরকার** *n.* a state government (in free India). **~সীমা** *n.* the boundary or extent of a kingdom. **~হারা** same as **~চ্যুত**। **রাজ্যাধিকারী, রাজ্যাধিপতি** *n.* the lord or ruler of a state. **রাজ্যাপহরণ করা** *v.* to usurp a throne; to capture or acquire or take possession of another realm or country unlawfully. **রাজ্যাপহারক, রাজ্যাপহারী** *n.* & *a.* one who usurps a throne; one who captures or acquires or takes possession of another's realm or country unlawfully. **রাজ্যাভিলাষ** *n.* desire for a kingdom; ambition to rule; desire for expanding one's territory. **রাজ্যাভিলাষী** *a.* desirous of a kingdom; having ambition to rule; desirous of expanding one's territory. **রাজ্যাভিষিক্ত করা** *v.* to invest one with kingship, to crown one king, to enthrone. **রাজ্যাভিষেক** *n.* coronation of a monarch. **রাজ্যেশ্বর** *n.* a king. *fem.* **রাজ্যেশ্বরী** a queen.

রাঢ় *n.* the ancient name of the part of Bengal lying on the western bank of the Ganges. **রাঢ়ী, রাঢ়ীয়** *a.* of Rarha (রাঢ়).

রাণা rej. spell. of **রানা[১], রানা[২]**।

রাণী rej. spell. of **রানি**।

রাণ্ডী var. of **রাঁড়ি**।

রাত *n.* (coll.) night. **রাত কাটানো** *v.* to spend or pass a night. **রাত জাগা** *v.* to stay up far into the night, to sit up late, to take late hours. **রাত জেগে কাজ করা** to sit up and work late at night, to burn the midnight oil. **~কানা** same as **রাত্র্যন্ধ**। **~দিন** *adv.* day and night; always; ceaselessly. **~ভর, ~ভোর** *adv.* all night long, nightlong. **রাতের অন্ধকারে** *adv.* in the darkness of night, under cover of the dark night. **রাতের বেলায়** *adv.* at night.

রাতারাতি *adv.* overnight; whilst there is still night; (fig.) within a very short time (রাতারাতি ধনী হওয়া).

রাতি, রাতিয়া poet. corruptions of **রাত্রি**।

রাতুল *a.* blood-red, red, crimson.
-রাত্র *in comp.* (used as a *sfx.*) denoting: night (অহোরাত্র).
রাত্রি *n.* night; night-time, night-tide (also **রাত্রিকাল**) ; (fig.) obscurity (জীবনের রাত্রি নামা). **রাত্রি হয়েছে** *v.* it is night. **রাত্রি ভোর হওয়া** *v.* to dawn. **~কালীন** *a.* nightly, nocturnal. **~কালে** *adv.* by night, at night. **~চর, ~ঞ্চর** *a.* active by night; nightfaring. *fem.* **~চরী, ~ঞ্চরী** । **~জাগরণ করা** *v.* to keep awake by night. **~বাস** *n.* passing the night; night-rest; night-attire, night-clothes, night-dress, night-gear, a night-gown, a nighty, a nightie. **~বেলা , ~যোগে** *adv.* by night, at night.
রাত্র্যন্ধ *a.* night-blind, nyctalopic. **রাত্র্যন্ধ ব্যক্তি** a nyctalops. **~তা** *n.* night-blindness, nyctalopia.
রাধা, রাধিকা *n.* (myth.) the lady-love of Krishna (কৃষ্ণ). **রাধাকান্ত, রাধানাথ, রাধামাধব, রাধারমণ** *n.* Krishna, the lord of Radha (রাধা). **রাধাকৃষ্ণ** *n.* Radha (রাধা) and Krishna (কৃষ্ণ). **রাধাবল্লভি** *n.* a small saucer-shaped pancake made of kneaded flour stuffed with spicy paste of pigeon-pea. **রাধাষ্টমী** *n.* the eighth lunar day of the bright fortnight of the month of Bhadra (ভাদ্র), the birth-day of Radha (রাধা). **রাধিকারঞ্জন, রাধিকারমণ** same as **রাধাকান্ত** ।
রাধাচক্র *n.* a merry-go-round.
রাধাপদ্ম *n.* the sunflower.
রাধেকৃষ্ণ, রাধেমাধব *n.* Radha (রাধা) and Krishna (কৃষ্ণ). □ *int.* expressing: abhorrence, disgust etc.
রাধেয় *n.* a son or foster-son or nursling of Radha (রাধা), generally used of Karna (কর্ণ) in the Mahabharata.
রানা[1] *n.* the title of the rulers of Udaypur.
রানা[2] *n.* a balustrade or a raised terrance on either side of the flight of steps of a pond.
রানার *n.* a (postal) runner.
রানি *n.* a queen.
রান্না *n.* cooking. **রান্না করা** *v.* to cook. **~ঘর** *n.* a kitchen. **~বান্না, ~বাড়া** *n.* act of cooking and serving out meals.
রাব *n.* a kind of refuse or inferior treacle.
রাবড়ি *n.* a sweetmeat prepared by condensing films of milk. **গুলাবি রাবড়ি** macaroni.
রাবণ *n.* Ravana, the arch-villain of the Ramayana. **রাবণের চিতা** (fig.) unquenchable fire; (fig.) ceaseless affliction. **রাবণারি** *n.* an enemy of Ravana.
রাবণি *n.* a son of Ravana.
রাবিশ *n.* rubbish. □ *a.* trashy.
রাম *n.* the seventh incarnation of Vishnu (বিষ্ণু), the hero of the Ramayana. □ *a.* good looking; beautiful. □ *pfx.* large, big (রামছাগল, রামশালিক) ; extremely, utterly (রাম কুঁড়ে). □ *sfx.* a glaring specimen (বোকারাম). **রাম না হতে রামায়ণ** (fig.) occurrence or fancying of an incident when there is not even the ghost of its cause in view, (cp.) putting the cart before the horse. **না রাম না গঙ্গা** (fig.) neither this nor that. **সেই রামও নেই সেই অযোধ্যাও নেই** (fig.) O the times ! O the manners ! **রাম কহ, রাম বল, রামঃ** int. expressing: abhorrence, slight etc. **~কেলি** *n.* an Indian musical mode. **~খড়ি** *n.* a kind of red-tinged writing-chalk. **~চন্দ্র** *n.* same as **রাম** । □ *int.* same as **রামঃ** । **~দা** *n.* a kind of large chopper (used in beheading animals etc.). **~ধনু, ~ধনুক** *n.* the rainbow. **~ধুন** *n.* a song in glory of Rama (রাম). **~নবমী** *n.* the ninth lunar day of the bright fortnight of the month of Chaitra (চৈত্র) ; the birthday of Rama (রাম). **~পাখি** *n.* (facet.) the cock or hen, the fowl. **~রাজত্ব, ~রাজ্য** *n.* the reign or rule or realm of Rama (রাম) ; (fig.) an ideal realm or rule, (sarcas.) unrestrained predominance or monopoly. **রাম রাম** *int.* expressing: abhorrence, disgust etc.; phew; an expession of salutation in courtesy among upcountrymen. **~লীলা** *n.* the life and activities of Rama (রাম) ; an opera illustrating the life and activities of Rama (রাম). **~শিঙা,** (coll.) **~শিঙে** *n.* a funnel-shaped wind instrument or mouthpiece made of a buffalo's horn. **~শ্যাম** same as **রামাশ্যামা** ।
রামা *n. fem.* a beautiful woman; a lady-love, a sweetheart.
রামাইত var. of **রামায়েত** ।

রামায়ণকার *n.* the author of the Ramayana.

রামায়েত *n.* a Vaishnava sect.

রামাশ্যামা *n.* any man in the street, Tom and Tim, Tom Dick or Harry.

রায়[1] *n.* a judicial pronouncement, a judgment, a verdict. **রায় দেওয়া** *v.* to deliver or pronounce a judgment.

রায়[2] *n.* a king, a prince; a title of zemindars or important persons. □ *a.* large, big; long (রায়বাঁশ). **~বেঁশে** *n.* one proficient in fighting with staffs; a kind of dance with staffs. **~বাঘিনি** *n. fem.* (fig.) an extremely terrible woman, a termagant, a virago. **~বাহাদুর, ~রায়ান, ~সাহেব** *n.* different official titles once conferred on important citizens.

রায়ত *n.* a tenant of a piece of agricultural land, a ryot; a raiyat. **রায়তি** *a.* relating to ryots; (of agricultural land) settled permamently and hereditarily on a ryot; raiyatwari.

রাশ[1] *n.* the reins, the bridle. **রাশ আলগা করা** *v.* (lit. & fig.) to give rein to, to give the reins to. **রাশ টানা** *v.* to draw rein, to pull up; to restrain or bring under control, to give little freedom to.

রাশ[2] *n.* a heap, a pile; (astrol.) the birth-sign; nature, temperament. **~নাম** *n.* a name according to one's astrological birth-sign. **~-পাতলা, ~-হালকা** *a.* flippant, frivolous. **~ভারী** *a.* reserved in speech and manner, grave; imposing.

রাশি *n.* a heap, a pile; a collection; (math.) a number, a quantity; (astrol.) any one of the twelve signs of the zodiac. **রাশি রাশি** heaps of. **~চক্র** *n.* (geog. & astrol.) the zodiac. **~ভোগকাল** *n.* (astrol.) the time taken by a planetary body in passing through a sign of the zodiac.

রাশীকৃত *a.* piled up, heaped up; collected, amassed, accumulated.

রাষ্ট্র *n.* a state, a kingdom; a country. □ *a.* widely circulated or proclaimed (esp. all over a state or country). **রাষ্ট্র করা** *v.* to circulate or to noise abroad or proclaim widely. **~দূত** *n.* an ambassador (*fem.* an ambassadress). **~নায়ক** *n.* a ruler or popular leader of a state. **~নিযুক্তক** *n.* a charge d' affaires. **~নিয়োগাধিকার** *n.* the Public Service Commission. **~নীতি, ~নৈতিক** variants of **রাজনীতি** and **রাজনৈতিক** (see **রাজ**[4]). **~পতি** *n.* the president of a state; the president of the Republic of India. **~পুঞ্জ** *n.* a group or a union of states; (loos.) the United Nations. **~প্রধান** *n.* the head of a state. **~বিজ্ঞান** *n.* Political Science. **~বিপ্লব** *n.* a civil strife; a revolution. **~ভাষা** *n.* state language. **~মণ্ডল** *n.* a commonwealth. **~মন্ত্রী** *n.* a minister of state. **~সঙ্ঘ, ~সংঘ** *n.* the United Nations Organization. **রাষ্ট্রাধীন** within the jurisdiction or control or a state; *a.* territorial. **রাষ্ট্রায়ত্ত** *a.* nationalized. **রাষ্ট্রায়ত্ত করা** *v.* to nationalize. **রাষ্ট্রিক, রাষ্ট্রীয়** *a.* pertaining to a state or country; national; territorial. **রাষ্ট্রীয়করণ** *n.* nationalization.

রাস[1] older var. of **রাশ**[1]।

রাস[2], **রাসযাত্রা, রাসলীলা** *n.* the festival of dancing of Krishna (কৃষ্ণ) and Radha (রাধা) on রাসপূর্ণিমা। **রাসপূর্ণিমা** *n.* the full moon night of the month of Kartik (কার্তিক). **রাসবিহারী** *n.* Krishna (কৃষ্ণ). **রাসমঞ্চ, রাসমণ্ডপ, রাসমণ্ডল** *n.* the platform on which the festival of rasa (রাস) is held. **রাসোৎসব** same as **রাস**।

রাসন *a.* gustatory.

রাসভ *n.* the he-ass; the ass. *fem.* **রাসভী** the she-ass. **~নাদ** *n.* braying, hee-haw. **~নিন্দিত** *a.* putting even the ass to shame, worse than the ass. **~নিন্দিত কণ্ঠ** *n.* a voice the harshness of which would put even the ass to shame. **~বৎ** *a.* like an ass, ass-like.

রাসায়নিক *a.* of chemistry, chemical; versed in chemistry. □ *n.* one versed in chemistry, a chemist. **রাসায়নিক আসক্তি** chemical affinity. **রাসায়নিক দ্রব্য** a chemical. **রাসায়নিক পরীক্ষা** chemical examination.

রাসোৎসব see **রাস**[2]।

রাস্তা *n.* a road, a thoroughfare, a way. **রাস্তার ধার** the roadside, the wayside. **সদর রাস্তা** an open way, a highway. **সরকারি রাস্তা** a public road, a highway.

রাম্না *n.* a kind of orchid. **রাম্না গোত্রীয়** *a.* orchidaceous, orchideous.

রাহা *n.* a road, a way, a highway; a means (সুরাহা). **~খরচ** *n.* travelling expenses. **~জান** *n.* a highwayman. **~জানি** *n.* highway robbery.

রাহি *n.* a traveller.

রাহিত্য *n.* want, lack; absence.

রাহু *n.* (myth.) a truncated demon; (astrol.) the ascending node; (fig.) an enemy or one who causes ruin or an evil influence. **রাহুর দশা** (astrol.) the phase of the influence of the ascending node as indicated by one's horoscope; (fig.) a period marked with calumny, want, misfortune, misery etc. **~গ্রস্ত** *a.* (astrol.) eclipsed; (fig.) illfated; (fig.) fallen into obscurity, obscured; (fig.) fallen under the influence of an evil person or of one who causes ruin.

রি *n.* (mus.) the second note in the natural scale, D.

রিং *n.* a ring, a small hoop.

রিক্‌থ *n.* share, one's share of money or property.

রিক্ত *a.* empty; devoid of, destitute of; extremely poor, indigent, penniless. **রিক্ত করা** *v.* to empty. **~তা** *n.* emptiness; destitution. **~হস্ত** *a.* empty-handed; fundless, broke, penniless. **রিক্তা** *a. fem.* of **রিক্ত** । □ *n.* (astrol.) the fourth, ninth and fourteenth lunar days of a fortnight.

রিকশ, রিকশা *n.* a jinricksha(w), a ricksha(w).

রিঠা[1], (coll.) **রিঠে**[1] *n.* the soap berry; the soapnut.

রিঠা[2], **রিঠে**[2] *n.* a kind of small scaleless fish.

রিনিঝিনি, রিনঝিন *int.* denoting: a jingling sound.

রিপিট *n.* a rivet; rivetting. **রিপিট করা** *v.* to rivet.

রিপু[1] pop. corrup. of **রিফু** ।

রিপু[2] *n.* an enemy, an adversary; any one of the six inherent vices or cardinal passions of man, namely, sex passion, anger, greed, infatuation, vanity and envy (collectively called **ষড়্‌রিপু**). **~জয়, ~দমন** *n.* conquest of an enemy; subdual of one's inherent vices. **~দমন করা** *v.* to subdue passions or inherent vices. **~জয়ী** *a.* one who has vanquished one's enemies or subdued one's cardinal passions or inherent vices. **~পরতন্ত্র, ~পরবশ, ~বশ** *a.* giving oneself up to one's cardinal passions or inherent vices.

রিপোর্ট *n.* a statement of facts (খবরের কাগজের রিপোর্ট), a written statement of the result of an investigation (রক্তপরীক্ষার রিপোর্ট, পুলিশ রিপোর্ট), a report; an accusation or adverse report (তোমার নামে রিপোর্ট). **রিপোর্ট করা** *v.* to report; to report against.

রিফু *n.* darning. **রিফু করা** *v.* to darn. **~কর্ম** *n.* darning.

রিভলবার *n.* a revolver.

রিমঝিম, রিমিঝিমি *int.* expressing: a pattering sound as of rain falling.

রিরংসা *n.* desire for sexual intercourse; sex appetite; lust.

রি রি *int.* expressing: a physical sensation of anger, abhorrence etc.

রিল *n.* a reel.

রিষ *n.* envy, malice; grudge.

রিষ্ট, রিষ্টি *n.* a sin; woe; misfortune; (astro.) evil planetary aspect or influence; (rare) weal.

রিসালা *n.* a cavalry. **~দার, রিসালদার** *n.* the commander of a cavalry, a risaldar.

রিস্টওয়াচ *n.* a wrist-watch.

রিহার্সাল *n.* rehearsal of a dramatic performance. **রিহার্সাল দেওয়া** বা **দেওয়ানো** *v.* to rehearse.

রীত dial. corrup. of. **রীতি** ।

রীতি *n.* method, mode; custom, usage, practice, convention, rule; nature, habit; style, manner; way, fashion, go (যুগের রীতি). **~ক্রমে** same as **রীত্যনুসারে** । **রীতিনীতি** *n. pl.* manners and customs. **~বিরুদ্ধ** *a.* contrary to custom or usage, unconventional, informal; contrary to one's nature or habit; contrary to a particular style or manner or way or fashion, going against the current. **~মতো** *adv.* in keeping with custom or usage or convention or form; (pop.) considerably, thoroughly, soundly (রীতিমতো বড়োলোক). **~সংগত, ~সম্মত** *a.* in keeping with custom or usage; customary.

রীত্যনুসারে *adv.* as usual; in keeping with the custom or practice or rule or form, customarily, conventionally, formally.

রীল rej. spell. of **রিল**।

রুই[১] *n.* a kind of very delicious fresh water fish, (cp.) the trout.

রুই[২] *n.* the white ant.

রুইতন *n.* (of playing-cards) a diamond or the suit of diamond.

রুক্ষ *a.* rough; dry; harsh; rude; haughty; angry; hard (রুক্ষমাটি) ; uneven, rugged (রুক্ষ পথ). **~ভাবে** *adv.* rudely, harshly, roughly. **~ভাষী** *a.* rough-spoken. **~স্বভাব** *a.* haughty, arrogant; peevish, cross-grained.

রুখা[১], **রোখা** *v.* to get angry, to fly up in a passion; to be on the point of attacking, to be aggressive or affronting; to arrest the motion of, to stop (গাড়ি রোখা) ; to intercept, to obstruct, to check, to oppose the onset of (শত্রুকে রোখা).

রুখা[২], **রুখু, রুখো** *a.* dry; devoid of anything liquid such as curry or condiment (রুখু ভাত) ; devoid of oil, not sleek, dry (রুখো চুল, রুখো মাথা) ; not provided with food, without board (রুখু মাইনের চাকর).

রুগ্ণ *a.* sick, ill; diseased; sickly; emaciated or debilitated. *fem.* **রুগ্ণা**।

রুগি, রুগী coll. var. of **রোগী**।

রুচা *v.* to be agreeable to one's taste or liking.

রুচি *n.* beauty, lustre, glow (তনুরুচি) ; taste, choice, liking (কুরুচি) ; good taste; relish, inclination, propensity (আহারের রুচি, খেলায় রুচি) ; desire for food, appetite. **~কর** *a.* appetizing; tasteful; savoury; pleasant; (loos.) decent or elegant. **~বাগীশ** *a.* (usu. sarcas.) over-careful about good taste and decorum, fastidious; overnice; puritanical. **~বিরুদ্ধ** *a.* contrary to one's taste or liking; indecent; indecorous; inelegant. **~ভেদে** *adv.* according to different tastes, according to difference in taste or liking. **~র** *a.* decorous; beautiful; elegant; bright. *fem.* **রুচিরা**।

রুজি *n.* livelihood, living. **রুজি রোজগার করা** *v.* to earn one's livelihood, to earn a living.

রুজু[১] *a.* submitted, preferred; brought before a court, filed. **রুজু করা** *v.* to submit, to prefer; to bring before a court, to file (মামলা রুজু করা).

রুজু[২] *a.* straight; facing.

রুজু-রুজু *a.* facing or confronting one another.

রুটি *n.* a kind of thin saucer-shaped bread; bread. **রুটি গড়া** *v.* to make bread (by kneading, rolling and baking). **রুটি বেলা** *v.* to roll bread (into the shape of a saucer). **রুটি সেঁকা** *v.* to bake bread. **~ওয়ালা** *n.* a baker. **রুটির কারখানা** a bakery.

রুটিন *n.* a routine. **~বাঁধা** *a.* fixed by a routine, rigidly fixed or regular, routine (রুটিন-বাঁধা কাজ) ; (fig.) monotonous (রুটিন-বাঁধা জীবন).

রুদ্ধ *a.* shut, closed, bolted; confined; incarcerated; suppressed (রুদ্ধ ক্রন্দন) ; choked; suspended (রুদ্ধ স্পন্দন) ; motionless (রুদ্ধ বাতাস) ; obstructed, blockaded (রুদ্ধ প্রবাহ) ; intercepted, arrested, prevented. **রুদ্ধ করা** *v.* to shut, to close, to bolt, to confine; to incarcerate; to suppress; to choke;to suspend; to make motionless; to obstruct, to blockade; to intercept, to arrest; to prevent. **~কক্ষ** *n.* a closed room. **রুদ্ধকক্ষে সভা** বা **আলোচনা** a closed-door meeting, a meeting or conference in camera. **~কণ্ঠ** *a.* having one's voice choked. **~কণ্ঠে** *adv.* with a choked voice. **~গতি** *a.* having one's motion arrested; stopped; obstructed or blockaded. **~তাপ** *a.* (phys.) adiabatic. **~দ্বার** *a.* having the door or doors closed, close-door. **~দ্বার আলোচনা** a closed-door conference, a conference in camera. **~শ্বাস** *a.* breathless, with bated breath; out of breath. **~শ্বাসে** *adv.* with bated breath, breathlessly.

রুদ্র *n.* the manifestation of Shiva (শিব) as a destroyer. □ *a.* furious, terrible; destructive.

রুদ্রাক্ষ *n.* a kind of dried fruit which is used as a bead. **~মালা** *n.* a rosary composed of these fruits.

রুদ্রাণী *n.* (*fem.* of **রুদ্র**) shiva's (শিব) wife, Goddess Durga (দুর্গা).

রুধা, রোধা *v.* to shut, to close, to bolt; to suppress (ক্রন্দন রোধা) ; to choke (শ্বাস রোধা) ; to arrest (গতি রুধবে) ; to stop, to make motionless (বাতাস রোধা) ; to obstruct, to blockade (পথ রোধা) ; to hinder (উন্নতি রুধবে) ; to prevent, to intercept, to ward off (শত্রু রোধা) ; to restrain, to check (মন রোধা).

রুধির *n.* blood; (fig.) one's money. **রুধির পান করা** বা **শোষণ করা** *v.* to suck or drink another's blood; (fig.) to extract money oppressively from, to extort. **~ধারা** *n.* stream of blood. **~পায়ী** *a.* blood-sucking; (fig.) given to exacting money oppressively; extortionary. **~রঞ্জিত** *a.* smeared with blood, bloody. **~স্নান** *n.* (lit. & fig.) blood-bath. **~স্রোত** a stream of blood. **রুধিরাক্ত** same as **~রঞ্জিত**। **রুধিরাপ্লুত** *a.* drenched with blood, bloody.

রুনুঝুনু, রুনুরুনু, রুনঝুন, রুনরুন *int.* denoting: a sweet jingling sound as of the bells of a dancer's anklets.

রুপা, (coll.) **রুপো** *n.* silver, argent. **রুপোর চাকতি** (facet.) a silver coin, a rupee. **রূপালি, রুপোলি** *a.* silver-coloured, silvery, silver-white; argentine.

রুবাইয়াত *n.* a collection of Arabic or Persian quatrains, Rubaiyat.

রুমাল *n.* handkerchief, (coll.) hanky.

রুল[১] *n.* a strip for ruling lines, a ruler; a baton, a truncheon (পুলিশের রুলের গুঁতো) ; a straight line printed or drawn; a strip of metal for printing straight lines or to space out lines; a law; a precedent (রুল দেখানো) ; ruling. **রুল করা** *v.* to mark with straight lines, to rule; to make a law. **রুল জারি করা** *v.* to give or issue a ruling, to rule. **রুল টানা** *v.* to mark with straight lines, to rule. **রুল দেওয়া** *v.* to give or issue a ruling, to rule; (print.) to insert a metal rule.

রুলি *n.* a bangle for the wrist.

রুষিত, রুষ্ট *a.* angered, enraged; angry. *fem.* **রুষিতা, রুষ্টা**। **রুষ্ট করা** *v.* to anger, to enrage. **রুষ্ট হওয়া** *v.* to get angry, to be enraged, to fly up in a passion.

রুহিতন var. of **রুইতন**।

রূঢ় *a.* (gr.) expressing a conventional meaning not supported by etymology or derivation (রূঢ় শব্দ) ; (gr.) conventional and not supported by etymology or derivation (রূঢ় অর্থ) ; (pop.) rough, harsh, rude, haughty (রূঢ় ভাষা, রূঢ় আচরণ). **রূঢ় পদার্থ** an element. **~তা** *n.* roughness, harshness, rudeness, haughtiness.

রূঢ়ি *n.* origination, emergence; fame; (gr.) power of conveying a conventional meaning not supportable by etymology or derivation.

রূপ *n.* form, body, figure; shape, appearance; build; beauty, grace; mode, manner, fashion, type, kind, sort (এরূপ, সেরূপ) ; complexion, colour, hue; nature, habit; (gr.) conjugation (ধাতুরূপ), declension (শব্দরূপ) ; (phil.) a concept. **রূপে** *adv.* in form; in beauty (রূপে লক্ষ্মী). **রূপের ডালি** (fig.) an uncommonly beautiful person. **রূপের ধুচুনি** (fig. & sarcas.) an utterly ugly person. **রূপক** *n.* (rhet.) a figure of speech akin to metaphor and allegory. **রূপক-অর্থ** *n.* figurative meaning. **~কথা** *n.* a folktale; a legend, a fairy tale. **রূপক-কাহিনি** *n.* an allegorical tale or story, an allegory. **রূপক-বাক্য** *n.* a metaphorical or allegorical expression. **~কার** *n.* a moulder; an artist; a dresser (esp. of actors and actresses). **~গুণ** *n. pl.* beauty and merits. **~চাঁদ** *n.* (sl. & facet.) a silver coin, a rupee; money. **~জ** *a.* originating from or caused by beauty. **~তত্ত্ব** *n.* (ling.) morphology; aesthetics. **~তৃষ্ণা** *n.* thirst for beauty. **~দক্ষ** *a.* adept in assuming disguises; (of an actor or actress) proficient in using make-up; (of an artist) proficient in shaping or moulding. **~দস্তা** *n.* pewter, white metal, German silver. **রূপ ধারণ করা** *v.* to assume the disguise of, to disguise oneself as; to assume the person of a dramatic character; to impersonate; to appear as. **~ধারী** *a.* assuming the form or shape of; disguised as; impersonating; appearing as. *fem.* **~ধারিণী**। **~বতী** *fem.* of **~বন্ত**। **~বন্ত, ~বান** *a.* handsome, beautiful. **~মাধুরী, ~মাধুর্য** *n.* charm of beauty. **~মুগ্ধ, ~মোহিত** *a.* infatuated with beauty. *fem.* **~মুগ্ধা, ~মোহিতা**। **~যৌবন** *n. pl.* youth and beauty. **~যৌবনসম্পন্ন** *a.* full of youth and beauty, young and handsome. *fem.* **~যৌবনসম্পন্না**। **~রাশি** *n. pl.* personal beauty or grace or charm. **~লাবণ্য** *n.* charm of personal beauty. **~সী** *a. fem.* handsome, beautiful. □ *n. fem.* a beautiful woman.

রূপা rej. spell. of **রুপা**।

রূপান্তর *n.* a different form or shape; translation; transformation; (geog.) metamorphosis. **রূপান্তর করা, রূপান্তর ঘটানো** *v.* to render or change into a new form or shape; to translate; to transform; (geog.) to metamorphose. **রূপান্তরিত** *a.* rendered or changed into a new form or shape; transformed; (geog.) metamorphic. **রূপান্তরিত করা** same as **রূপান্তর করা**।

রূপায়ণ *n.* embodiment; shaping or forming; dramatic impersonation; act of giving a concrete shape; narrration, depiction.

রূপায়িত *a.* embodied; shaped; (of a dramatic character) impersonated; invested with a concrete shape; narrated, depicted.

রূপালী rej. spell. of **রুপালি**।

রূপী[1] *n.* a kind of ruddy-faced monkey, the ape.

রূপী[2] *sfx.* denoting: assuming a particular form or shape (নররূপী) ; assuming a dress or disguise (বহুরূপী).

রূপোপজীবিনী *n.* a prostitute.

রূপ্য *n.* silver. **রূপ্যাধ্যক্ষ** *n.* mint-master.

রে[1] var. of **রি**।

রে[2] *int.* expressing: a call to draw attention (esp. in contempt or affection), ho, hoa, hey; surprise, pain, sorrow etc.; oh, ah.

রেউচিনি *n.* rhubarb.

রেওয়া *n.* an annual balance-sheet.

রেওয়াজ *n.* custom, usage; practice; fashion; vogue; practice of music. **রেওয়াজ করা** *v.* to practise; to practise music. **রেওয়াজ থাকা** *v.* to be in vogue or fashion; to be the practice of; to be in practice. **রেওয়াজ হওয়া** *v.* to come into fashion or vogue.

রেঁদা see **র‍্যাঁদা**।

রেক *n.* a wicker container for measuring grain (its capacity is usually about one seer).

রেকাব[1] *n.* a stirrup.

রেকাব[2]**, রেকাবি** *n.* a small saucer or plate.

রেখক *n.* tracer.

রেখন *n.* cross.

রেখা *n.* a line; a streak; a stripe; a stria (pl. striae); a furrow; a row; a faint sign, a thin line (গোঁফের রেখা) ; (phys.) rulings. **রেখা টানা** *v.* to draw a line. **~কার** *a.* linear. **~গণিত** *n.* geometry. **~ঙ্কন** *n.* drawing of lines, lineation. **~ঙ্কিত** *a.* lineate, lineated; striated; striped; furrowed. **~চিত্র** *n.* a line-drawing; a rough sketch. **রেখাপাত করা** *v.* to draw a line; to make an impression (as on one's mind), to impress.

রেখিত *a.* crossed. **রেখিত চেক** a crossed cheque.

রেচক *a.* purgative, laxative, aperient; (bot.) excretory. □ *n.* a purgative, a laxative, an aperient.

রেচন *n.* evacuation of bowels, purging, purgation; (bot.) excretion. **রেচন করা** বা **করানো** *v.* to evacuate bowels, to purge. **~তন্ত্র** *n.* the excretory system. **~যন্ত্র** *n.* an excretory organ.

রেজগি, রেজকি *n.* any coin less than a rupee in value; small coin, change.

রেজাই *n.* a quilt; a kind of wrapper stuffed with carded cotton.

রেজিস্ট্রি, রেজিস্টারি *n.* registry, registration; a register. □ *a.* registered. **রেজিস্ট্রি করা** *v.* to register. **রেজিস্ট্রি অফিস** *n.* a registry office, a registry. **রেজিস্ট্রি-খাতা, রেজিস্ট্রি-বই** *n.* a register.

রেট *n.* price or cost, rate; speed (এই রেটে চললে পৌঁছানো যাবে না).

রেঞ্চ *n.* a wrench.

রেড়ি *n.* a euphorbiaceous plant or its

seed, *Ricinus communis*. **রেড়ির তেল** castor-oil.

রেডি *a.* ready. **রেডি করা** বা **করানো** *v.* to make ready. **রেডি হওয়া** *v.* to get ready.

রেডিয়াম *n.* radium.

রেডিয়ো *n.* radio, a radio set.

রেণু *n.* dust; powder; pollen; a minute particle or grain.

রেত pop. corrup. of **রেতি**।

রেতঃ *n.* semen. **~পাত** *n.* emission of seminal fluid.

রেতি *n.* a (carpenter's) file or rasp.

রেফ *n.* (́) this sign on Bengali consonant letters to indicate a preceding-r sound; an upright antenna or hair on heads of some creatures (দ্বিরেফ).

রেফারি *n.* a referee.

রেবতী *n.* the last of the twenty-seven stars according to Hindu astronomy.

রেবা *n.* the river Rabi.

রেয়াজ coll. var. of **রেওয়াজ**।

রেয়াত *n.* exemption; a show of respect; favour. **রেয়াত করা** *v.* to exempt; to respect; to favour.

রেয়ো *a.* arrived uninvited on hearing the report of a feast; uninvited. **~ভাট** *n.* a beggar arrived uninvited on the report of a feast.

রেল[1] *n.* a rail; a railway train or carriage (also **রেলগাড়ি**) ; a railway line, a railline (usu. **রেললাইন**) ; railings. **রেল-এনজিন** *n.* a railway engine. **~চালক** *n.* a railway engine-driver. **~পথ** *n.* railroad, railway. **~স্টেশন** *n.* railway station.

রেলিং *n.* railings.

রেশ *n.* a lingering faint resonance of a sound or note gradually dying out; a feeling that lingers faintly before dying out completely.

রেশম *n.* silk. **~কীট** *n.* silk-worm. **~গুটি** *n.* cocoon. **রেশমি** *a.* made of silk, silken, silk.

রেষারেষি *n.* mutual envy or malice or grudge; mutual rivalry.

রেস *n.* a contest of speed, a race; a horse-race; a race-meeting. **রেস দেওয়া** *v.* to contend in speed, to race. **রেসের ঘোড়া** a racehorse, a racer.

রেসালা corrup. of **রিসালা**।

রেসুড়ে *n.* a racing man, a racegoer; a race-addict.

রেস্ত *n.* capital, funds; wherewithal; provision of money, shift. **~শূন্য** *a.* having no capital; out of funds; shiftless.

রেস্তোরাঁ *n.* a restaurant.

রেহাই *n.* exemption; escape; acquittal. **রেহাই দেওয়া** *v.* to exempt; to let go unpunished; to acquit. **রেহাই পাওয়া** *v.* to be exempted (from); to escape; to be allowed to go unpunished; to be acquitted.

রেহান *n.* mortgage; pawn. **রেহান দেওয়া** *v.* to mortgage; to pawn. **~বন্ধ** *a.* mortgaged; in pawn, at pawn. **রেহানাবদ্ধ** same as **~বন্ধ**।

রৈখিক *a.* linear; lineal, lineate.

রোঁদ *n.* a prescribed circuit (as of a constable), a round, a beat. **রোঁদে বার হওয়া** *v.* to go on a round, to patrol.

রোঁয়া *n.* wool; fur; hair.

রোক *n.* cash purchase, cash and carry; ready money, cash. □ *a.* ready (রোক টাকা = ready money). **~ঋণ** *n.* cash credit. **~থোক** *adv.* in ready money, in hard cash, cash down. **~শোধ** *n.* cash payment (of a bill etc.) **~স্থিতি** *n.* cash-balance.

রোকড় *n.* an account of cash, a cash account; ready money, cash; cash-book (রোকড়ে ওঠা) ; jewellery; gold and silver ornaments. **রোকড়ের দোকান** a jeweller's shop.

রোকা *n.* a short letter or note, a chit.

রোখ *n.* a stubborn resolve or desire; spiritedness; growth (গাছের রোখ). **রোখ চাপা** *v.* to be seized with a strong resolve or desire. **রোখ দেখানো** *v.* to exhibit spiritedness (usu.. affected or impotent). **রোখা, রোখালো** *a.* of strong resolve; stubborn; spirited; exuberantly growing (রোখালো গাছ).

রোগ *n.* a disease, an ailment; morbidity; (fig.) an incorrigible bad practice or addiction, a vice (মিথ্যা বলা তার রোগ). **রোগ সারা** *v.* to recover from a disease, to be cured of a disease; to come round; (fig.) to be freed from a vice. **রোগ হওয়া, রোগে পড়া, রোগে ধরা** *v.* to fall ill, to be attacked with a disease; (fig.) to become a victim to a vice. **রোগে ভোগা** *v.* to suffer from an illness. **~ক্লিষ্ট** *a.* disease-stricken, sick. **~গ্রস্ত** *a.* diseased, ailing, sick. **~জনক** *a.* causing disease; unwholesome; (bot.) pathogenic. **~জীবাণু** *n.* a virus, a bacterium (pl. bacteria), a bacillus (pl. bacilli). **~জীর্ণ** *a.* worn-out or run down by disease. **~নিদান** *n.* the cause of a disease. **~নিদানতত্ত্ব** *n.* pathology. **~মুক্ত** *a.* cured of or recovered from a disease; free from disease (রোগমুক্ত থাকা). **রোগমুক্ত করা** *v.* to cure of a disease; to bring round. **রোগমুক্ত হওয়া** *v.* to recover from a disease; to come round. **~মুক্তি** *n.* recovery from a disease. **~যন্ত্রণা** *n.* the agonies of a disease. **~লক্ষণ** *n.* a symptom of a disease. **~শয্যা** *n.* a sick-bed. **~শান্তি** same as **~মুক্তি**। **~শোক** *n. pl.* disease and bereavement. **রোগা** *a.* diseased, ill, sick; sickly; lean, delicate; debilitated, emaciated. **রোগা হওয়া** *v.* to grow thin or thinner, to become emaciated; to lose flesh. **রোগাক্রান্ত** *a.* attacked with a disease, diseased, ill. **রোগাটে** *a.* somewhat lean; gaunt; slim. **রোগাতঙ্ক** *n.* pathophobia. **রোগা-পটকা** *a.* lean and feeble. **রোগার্ত** *a.* afflicted with disease or ailment. **রোগী** *a.* suffering from a disease; ailing, sick, ill. □ *n.* a sick man, a patient. *fem.* **রোগিণী**। **রোগের চিকিৎসা** treatment of a disease. **রোগের যন্ত্রণা** same as **~যন্ত্রণা**। **রোগোপশম** *n.* healing or cure of a disease; abatement of a disease.

রোচক *a.* tasteful, pleasant to the taste; delicious, palatable; dainty.

রোচনা *n.* same as **গোরোচনা**।

রোচা pop. var. of **রুচা**।

রোজ *n.* a date (কোন রোজ) ; a day of the month (সাতই রোজ) ; a day (তিন রোজ) ; daily wages (দু-টাকা রোজে) ; daily supply (রোজের দুধ). □ *a.* daily, everyday. **রোজ করা** *v.* to arrange for the daily supply (of). **রোজ-রোজ** *adv.* daily, every day. **~কার** *a.* of everyday, daily (রোজকার কর্তব্য). **রোজ-কেয়ামত** *n.* the Day of Judgment (according to scriptures). **~গার** *n.* earning; income. **রোজগার করা** *v.* to earn. **~গারি,** (coll.) **~গেরে** *a.* one who earns, earning. **~নামচা** *n.* a diary, a journal.

রোজা[1] same as **ওঝা**।

রোজা[2] *n.* holy fasting of Muslims from sunrise to sundown during the month of Ramadan (রমজান). **রোজা করা, রোজা রাখা** *v.* to keep this fast.

রোটিকা *n.* a slice of bread.

রোদ coll. form of **রৌদ্র**। **রোদ পোহানো** v. to enjoy the sun; to bask in the sun. **রোদে দেওয়া** *v.* (of clothes etc.) to lay or spread out in the sun to dry. **রোদে পোড়া** *v.* to expose oneself in the scorching sun, to become parched or scorched in the sun.

রোদন *n.* weeping or crying (esp. loudly), wailing. **রোদন করা** *v.* to weep or cry (esp. loudly), to wail. **~শীল** *a.* given to weeping or crying or wailing, lachrymose.

রোদ্দুর coll. corrup. of **রৌদ্র**।

রোধ, রোধন *n.* obstruction, blockade; hindrance; resistance. **রোধ করা** *v.* to obstruct, to block, to blockade; to hinder; to resist. **রোধক** *a.* obstructive, blocking, hindering; resistant. **রোধ-কুণ্ডলী** *n.* (phys.) a resistance coil. **রোধ-থার্মোমিটার** *n.* (phys.) a resistance thermometer. **রোধা** pop. form of **রুধা**। **রোধাঙ্ক** *n.* (phys.) specific resistance. **রোধিত** *a.* obstructed; blocked; blockaded; hindered; resisted. **রোধী** same as **রোধক**। *fem.* **রোধিনী**।

রোপণ *n.* plantation; sowing. **রোপণ করা** *v.* to plant; to sow. **~যন্ত্র** *n.* a sowing-machine. **রোপনীয়** *a.* to be planted or sowed. **রোপা** *v.* to plant; to sow. **রোপিত** *a.* planted; sown, sowed.

রোবাইয়াৎ var. of **রুবাইয়াত**।

রোম *n.* hair (chiefly of the body); wool; fur.

রোমক var. of **রোমান**।

রোমকূপ *n.* a pore of the skin of the body.

রোমন্থ, রোমন্থন *n.* rumination. **রোমন্থন করা** *v.* to ruminate, to chew the cud. **রোমন্থক** *n.* a ruminant.

রোমশ *a.* hairy; woolly; furry; shaggy.

রোমহর্ষ same as **রোমাঞ্চ**। **রোমহর্ষণ** *n.* same as **রোমাঞ্চ**। □ *a.* same as **রোমাঞ্চকর**।

রোমাঞ্চ *n.* horripilation, gooseflesh; thrill. **~কর** *a.* horripilant; thrilling; (loos.) horrible. **রোমাঞ্চিত** *a.* horripilated; thrilled

রোমান *a.* Roman. □ *n.* a Roman.

রোমাবলি *n.* a collection of hair; hair (collectively).

রোমীয় var. of **রোমান**।

রোমোদ্‌গম, রোমোদ্ভেদ *n.* sprouting or growth of hair.

রোয়া[1] *n.* a juicy seed-vessel of any fruit, a replum, a legume, a pod.

রোয়া[2] *v.* to sow, to plant (ধান রোয়া). □ *a.* sown or planted, that which has been sown or planted. **~নো** *v.* to cause to sow or plant.

রোয়াক *n.* a raised terrace in the front part of a building.

রোয়েদাদ *n.* an award of a share; an award. **সাম্প্রদায়িক রোয়েদাদ** a communal award.

রোরুদ্যমান *a.* in a state of weeping or wailing continually, bitterly or loudly. *fem.* **রোরুদ্যমানা**।

রোল *n.* a suppressed noise; a sound, a noise, an outcry, a cry.

রোলার *n.* a roller. **রোলার দেওয়া** *v.* to beat or flatten with a roller, to roll, to use a roller.

রোশনচৌকি *n.* a symphony or serenade of sanai (সানাই) and other instruments.

রোশনাই, রোশনি *n.* light; illumination; lustre.

রোষ same as **ক্রোধ**। **~কষায়িত** *a.* reddened with anger. **~কষায়িতলোচনে** *adv.* with eyes reddened with anger. **~দীপ্ত** *a.* inflamed with passion, burning with rage. **~শান্তি** same as **ক্রোধশান্তি**। **রোষাগ্নি, রোষানল** same as **ক্রোধাগ্নি**। **রোষান্বিত, রোষাবিষ্ট** same as **রুষ্ট**। *fem.* **রোষান্বিতা**।

রোষাবিষ্ট, রোষিত same as **রুষ্ট**। **রোষোন্মত্ত** *a.* mad with anger or rage, furious.

রোসো *v.* (imper.) wait.

রোস্ট *n.* roast.

রোহ, রোহণ *n.* act of riding or mounting or climbing.

রোহিণী *n.* (astr. & astrol.) the fourth of the twenty-seven stars of Hindu astronomy; (myth.) the name of the wife of the moon-god; a nine-year old unmarried girl (রোহিণী দান).

রোহিত, রোহিতক *n.* a variety of fresh water fish, the trout.

রৌদ্র *n.* sunshine, the sun. □ *a.* terrible, dreadful. **রৌদ্র উঠেছে** *v.* the sun is up. **রৌদ্র পোহানো** *v.* to bask in the sun; to take a sun-bath. **রৌদ্রে দেওয়া** *v.* to expose to the sun's rays, to spread in the sun to dry, to sun. **~দগ্ধ** *a.* sunburnt. **~দর্শন** *a.* fierce-looking, of a formidable appearance. **~পক্ব** *a.* sun-baked, sunned. **~রস** *n.* (rhet.) the emotion of rage. **~সেবন করা** same as **রৌদ্র পোহানো**। **~স্নান** sun-bath. **~স্নান করা** *v.* to sunbathe. **রৌদ্রোজ্জ্বল** *a.* shining in the sunlight, brightened with sunshine, sunclad.

রৌপ্য *n.* silver, argent. **~জয়ন্তী** see **জয়ন্তী**। **~নির্মিত** *a.* made of silver, silvern. **~ময়** *a.* full of silver, silvery; made of silver, silvern. **~মুদ্রা** *n.* a silver coin. **~মুদ্রাসমূহ** *n. pl.* silvers. **~মূল্যে** *adv.* in exchange of silver; in exchange of silvers or money. **রৌপ্যালংকার** *n.* a silver ornament; (in pl.) silvers.

রৌরব *n.* (Hindu myth.) a terrible hell.

র‍্যাঁদা *n.* a carpenter's plane.

র‍্যাপার *n.* a woollen wrapper.

র‍্যালা *n.* (coll.) a show of vanity or superiority, showing-off; boastful manner of speaking, bragging.

ল *n.* the twenty-eighth consonant of the Bengali alphabet.

লওয়া older. var. of **নেওয়া** ।

লংকা *n.* capsicum, chillies, red pepper. **~বাটা** *n.* paste of chillies prepared by pounding them with water. **~মরিচ** same as **লংকা** ।

লংক্লথ *n.* long-cloth.

লক আউট *n.* lock-out, closure declared by the owners of factories etc.

লকলক *int.* expressing: lolling (as of the tongue); dangling or brandishing (as of a cane); flashing (as of a flame of fire). **লকলকে** *a.* lolling; dangling; flashing.

লকট *n.* the loquat tree, loquat.

লকার *n.* a locker; safe-deposit vault of a bank etc for depositing customers' valuables.

লকেট *n.* a locket.

লক্কা *n.* a kind of beautiful fan-tailed pigeons; (sarcas.) a fop, a dandy.

লক্ষ[1] alt. spell. of **লক্ষ্য** । **লক্ষ করা** *v.* to notice, to observe; to note; to aim at; to cast a look or glance.

লক্ষ[2] *n.* & *a.* one hundred thousand, lakh, lac. □ *a.* numerous, countless (লক্ষবার বলেছি). **লক্ষ লক্ষ** innumerable, countless.

লক্ষণ *n.* a sign, a mark; an indication; a symptom; a characteristic, a trait; an omen, a presage, a prognostic. **~গীত** *n.* a song that describes the chief features of a raga or musical mode. **~যুক্ত** *a.* characterized by or possessing a sign or mark or indication or symptom or characteristic or omen; indicative of; presaging. **লক্ষণা** *n.* (rhet.) imposition of a second meaning when the primary one is barred, (loos.) metonymy or metaphor or synecdoche. **লক্ষণাক্রান্ত** same as **~যুক্ত** । **লক্ষণাত্মক** *a.* relating to signs or marks; symptomatic; characteristic. **লক্ষণীয়** *a.* noticeable; remarkable, noteworthy; perceptible; prominent.

লক্ষপতি *n.* a man worth a hundred thousand rupees or more, (loos.) a millionaire; a very wealthy man.

লক্ষাধিক *a.* more than a hundred thousand or lakh.

লক্ষিত *a.* noticed, seen, observed, espied; perceived; aimed at; implied, signified. **লক্ষিতার্থ** the second meaning given to a word when the primary meaning is barred.

লক্ষ্মী *n. fem.* the Hindu goddess of wealth and prosperity; fortune; beauty; grace. □ *a. fem.* & *masc.* well-behaved and good-natured. **লক্ষ্মীর বরপুত্র** Fortune's favourite. **লক্ষ্মীর ভাণ্ডার** an inexhaustible store. **~ছাড়া** *a.* bereft of grace and prosperity; wretched; uncouth; scoundrelly, wicked. *fem.* **~ছাড়ি** । **~ছাড়া, ~ছাড়া লোক** *n.* a scapegrace, a wretch, a scoundrel. **~প্যাঁচা** *n.* a kind of whitish owl on which Goddess Lakshmi rides. **~বন্ত, ~মন্ত** *a.* prosperous, rich, wealthly; auspicious or graceful (লক্ষ্মীবন্ত চেহারা). **~বার** *n.* the day of the week when the Goddess Lakshmi is worshipped, (usu.) Thursday. **~শ্রী** *n.* graceful signs or marks of prosperity or auspiciousness; grace or beauty resembling that of Goddess Lakshmi (লক্ষ্মী). **~স্বরূপিণী** *a.* resembling Goddess Lakshmi (লক্ষ্মী) in beauty and merits; appearing as Lakshmi incarnate.

লক্ষ্য *a.* noticeable, observable; noteworthy, remarkable; intended; aimed at. □ *n.* intention; aim, goal; a target; a look or glance. **লক্ষ্য করা** same as **লক্ষ করা** । **লক্ষ্য রাখা** *v.* to keep watch, to be on the watch. **~চ্যুত** same as **~ভ্রষ্ট** । **লক্ষ্যবেধ বা লক্ষ্যভেদ করা** *v.* to hit a mark or bull's-eye. **~বেধী, ~ভেদী** *a.* capable of hitting a mark. □ *n.* a marksman. **~ভ্রষ্ট** *a.* failing to hit the target, missing the mark; erratic; (fig.) beside the mark. **~ভ্রষ্ট হওয়া** *v.* to miss the mark. **~স্থল** *n.* mark, target. **~হীন** *a.* aimless. **লক্ষ্মীকৃত** *a.* observed, watched.

লখা corrup. of **লক্ষ করা**।

লগন poet. corrup. of **লগ্ন**। **~সা** *n.* the days or the season in which auspicious moments occur.

লগবগে *a.* flexible, supple, pliant; unsteady, swaying to and fro; tottering; flimsy.

লগা, লগি *n.* a pole of bamboo etc. esp. one for propelling a boat, a punt-pole; a pole with a hook fixed to one end for plucking fruits, flowers etc. **লগি ঠেলা** *v.* to punt.

লগুড় *n.* a heavy stick, a cudgel, a mallet, a club. **লগুড়াঘাত করা** *v.* to beat with a club or a cudgel. **লগুড়াহত** *a.* cudgelled, beaten with a stick, bastinadoed.

লগ্ন[১] *a.* attached or adhering or leaning to (কণ্ঠলগ্ন, দেহলগ্ন).

লগ্ন[২] *n.* (astrol.) the rising-time of any zodiacal sign or the time of the sun's transition to a zodiacal sign; (astrol.) a suitable or auspicious time or moment (বিয়ের লগ্ন) ; a point of time (মরণলগ্ন). **~পত্র** *n.* a written marriage-contract fixing astrologically the time of marriage. **~ভ্রষ্ট** *a.* failing to commence one's work within the astrologically appointed hours; (fig.) one who has missed the opportune moment.

লগ্না *fem.* of **লগ্ন**[২]।

লগ্নি *n.* investment (of money) in business enterprise; usury. **লগ্নি করা** *v.* to invest, to lay out; to lend at interest. **~করণ** *n.* investing, investment.

লঘিমা *n.* a yogic attainment that enables one to make one's body light or subtle at pleasure; absence of heaviness, lightness.

লঘিষ্ঠ *a.* lightest; smallest; minimum; lowest; least; very light or small. **লঘিষ্ঠ সাধারণ গুণিতক,** (সংক্ষেপে) **ল. সা. গু** (math.) the least common multiple, (abbr.) L.C.M.

লঘীয়ান *a.* less heavy, lighter; smaller; lower; very light or small. *fem.* **লঘীয়সী**।

লঘু *a.* not heavy, light; easily digestible and moderate; not serious, venial; small; frivolous, easy, carefree; swift or nimble yet noiseless; easily understood, easy, light (লঘুপাঠ) ; low, vile, inferior; contemptible; slighted; worthless, trivial; subtle; liquid, watery; (gr.) short. **~কায়** *a.* light-bodied; slim-bodied; short-statured. **~গামী** *a.* nimbly and yet noiselessly moving; light-moving. **~গুণক** *n.* (math.) reduction factor. **~চিত্ত, ~চেতা** *a.* light-headed; light-hearted; flippant, frivolous. **~জ্ঞান** *n.* disregard, contempt; slight. **~জ্ঞান করা** *v.* to think lighty of; to treat with contempt; to slight, to look down upon. **~নির্মাণ** *n.* minor works. **~পথ্য** *n.* light diet, (cp.) sick diet.**~পাক** *a.* easily digested or digestible, light. **~পাচ্য** *a.* easily digestible. **লঘু পাপ** a venial sin; a trivial offence. **লঘুপাপে গুরুদণ্ড** heavy punishment for a venial or trivial offence. **~পায়ে** *adv.* light-footedly. **~প্রকৃতি** same as **~চিত্ত**। **~বন্ধনী** *n.* the sign of parenthesis, the first bracket. **~বৃত্ত** *n.* a small circle. **~ভাবে** *adv.* lightly. **~ভোজন** *n.* a light and easily digestible meal. **~মস্তিষ্ক** *a.* light-headed; incapable of serious thinking; dull-headed. □ *n.* the cerebellum. **~সংগীত** *n.* light music. **~স্বর** *n.* a low or soft voice, (gr.) a short vowel. **~হস্ত** *a.* light-handed; dexterous.

লঘুলিপিক *n.* a stenographer.

লঘূকরণ *n.* lightening; simplification; (math.) reduction; (chem.) dilution; attenuation; commutation.

লঘূকৃত *a.* lightened; simplified; (math.) reduced; (chem.) diluted; attenuated; commuted.

লঙ্কা[১] alt. spell. of **লংকা**।

লঙ্কা[২] *n.* Ceylon; modern Sri Lanka. **~কাণ্ড** *n.* a canto of the Ramayana narrating the capture of Lanka (লঙ্কা) by Rama (রাম) ; (fig.) a tumultuous affray or brawl. **~দাহন** *n.* the burning of Lanka (লঙ্কা) by Hanuman (হনুমান). **~ধিপতি, ~পতি** *n.* the king of Lanka (লঙ্কা).

লঙ্কেশ *n.* the king of Lanka.

লঙ্গ *n.* (dial.) clove.

লঙ্গরখানা *n.* a place where cooked food is

distributed in charity to a number of persons.

লঙ্ঘন *n.* fasting; crossing; passing or leaping or scaling over; dereliction, non-observance; transgression; violation, infringement; non-compliance, non-abidance. **লঙ্ঘন করা** *v.* to cross; to pass or leap or scale over; to fail to perform; to transgress; to violate, to infringe; not to comply with, not to abide by, to disobey. **লঙ্ঘন দেওয়া** *v.* to keep fasting, to go without food.

লঙ্ঘা poet. form of **লঙ্ঘন করা**।

লঙ্ঘিত *a.* crossed; passed over; leapt over, scaled over; not observed; transgressed; violated, infringed; not complied with, not abided by.

লছমি corrup. of **লক্ষ্মী**।

লজ্‌ঝড় *a.* good-for-nothing (লজ্‌ঝড় লোক); worthless, trashy (লজ্‌ঝড় জিনিস); broken and unserviceable; unwieldy, unmanageable, troublesome (লজ্‌ঝড় বোঝা বা কাজ).

লজেঞ্চুস *n.* lozenge.

লজ্জত *n.* that part of the body which flushes in bashfulness, the face; glorious flush of chastity.

লজ্জমান *a.* feeling abashed; abashed, flushed. *fem.* **লজ্জমানা**।

লজ্জা *n.* bashfulness; modesty; shame; hesitation; diffidence; disgrace. **লজ্জা দেওয়া** *v.* to put to shame, to shame; to put out of countenance, to discountenance, to abash. **লজ্জা পাওয়া** *v.* to be ashamed; to feel shame; to be discountenanced or abashed. **লজ্জা বোধ করা** *v.* to feel shame; to feel diffident. **লজ্জার কথা, লজ্জার বিষয়** a disgraceful affair, a shameful matter, a disgrace, a shame. **লজ্জায় কুঁকড়ে যাওয়া** *v.* to shrink in shame. **লজ্জায় লাল** flushed with shame, to become red from shame. **~কর, ~জনক** *a.* shameful, disgraceful. **~জনিত** *a.* born of bashfulness or modesty or sense of delicacy. **~নত** same as **লজ্জাবনত**। **~নম্র** *a.* slightly bowed down with bashfulness; coy. **~ন্বিত** same as **লজ্জিত**। **~বতী** *fem.* of **লজ্জাবান**। **লজ্জাবতী লতা** the mimosa. **~বনত** *a.* having one's face hanging down in bashfulness or shame; stooping low in bashfulness or shame. **লজ্জাবনত মুখে** with a shame-faced look. **~বান** *a.* shy, bashful; coy; modest. **~বিহীন** same as **লজ্জাহীন**। **~বোধ** *n.* feeling of shame; sense of disgrace. **~শীল** *a.* bashful; coy; shy; modest. *fem.* **~শীলা**। **~শূন্য, ~হীন** *a.* shameless; brazen-faced; impudent; immodest. *fem.* **~শূন্য, ~হীনা**।

লজ্জিত *a.* ashamed; put to shame; abashed. *fem.* **লজ্জিতা**।

লটকানো *v.* to hang (ফাঁসিতে লটকানো); to hang up (দেওয়ালে লটকানো); to post (a bill, placard, poster etc.).

লটপট *int.* expressing: the state of flapping loosely. **লটপটে** *a.* hanging loosely; flapping loosely.

লটবহর *n.* luggage, baggage, outfit, kit.

লটরপটর *n.* the state of flapping or hanging loosely; (loos.) flirting, flirtation; debauchery.

লটারি *n.* a lottery, a raffle.

লড় *n.* (obs.) running or bolting, a bolt. **লড় দেওয়া** *v.* to bolt off, to take a run; to take to one's heels.

লড়া *v.* to fight; to encounter; to wrestle; to contend, to vie. **লড়াই** *n.* a fight, an encounter, an engagement; a battle, a war; a wrestling encounter or match; contention, vying. **~ইয়ে** almost obs. var. of **লড়িয়ে**। **~কু** *a.* fond of or in the habit of fighting, pugnacious. **~নো** *v.* to cause to fight or contend or vie; to set by the ears. **~লড়ি** *n.* mutual or repeated fight or quarrel or contention or vying; a scuffle or skirmish.

লড়িয়ে, লড়ুয়ে *a.* skilled in or given to fighting, bellicose; military. **লড়ুয়ে মনোবৃত্তি** fighting spirit. **লড়ুয়ে মোরগ** a gamecock, a fighting-cock.

লড্ডু, লড্ডুক *n.* a sweet drop.

লন্ঠন *n.* a lantern.

লতা *n.* a creeper. **~কুঞ্জ, ~গৃহ, ~মণ্ডপ** *n.* a retreat shaded with creepers, an arbour, a bower. **~নিয়া, ~নে** *a.* creeping. **~নো** *v.* (of a creeper) to creep along or up; to stretch or extend along or up. **~পাতা** *n.* creepers and herbs; spinach. **~প্রতান**

n. tendril. ~য়িত *a.* grown along the ground or on supports as a creeper, creeping along or up; stretching or extending along or up.

লতি *n.* the lobe of the ear.

লতিকা *n.* a small creeper; a creeper.

লন্ডভন্ড *int.* expressing: utter disruption or confusion or disorder or rout. লন্ডভন্ড হওয়া *v.* to be utterly disrupted or confused or routed.

লপটানো *v.* to entwine; to be entangled or involved (in).

লপ্‌সি *n.* gruel (of rice, dal etc).

লপেটা *n.* a kind of vamped slippers.

লপ্ত *n.* a stretch. এক লপ্তে at a stretch.

লব *n.* (math.) a numerator; a minute division or fracton of time; very small amount or fraction.

লবঙ্গ *n.* clove; the clove-tree. ~লতা, ~লতিকা *n.* a creeper bearing fragrant flowers, (cp.) the clove-pink; a kind of sweet pastry; (fig.) a modest and charming female.

লব্‌জ *n.* speech; language; a dialect; a mode of speaking; an idiom.

লবডঙ্কা *n.* (hum.) nothing, cipher, zero; a mare's nest.

লবণ *n.* salt. ~খনি *n.* salt-mine. ~ছাড়া *a.* (of food) salt-free. ~জল *n.* salt-water. saline water. ~পোড়া *a.* (of food) overmixed with salt, over-salted. ~সমুদ্র *n.* (myth.) the sea containing salt-water. লবণাক্ত *a.* smeared or oversmeared with salt; containing salt (usu. to excess); saltish, salted; salty; saline. লবণাম্বুধি *n.* (myth.) the sea containing salt-water; a sea, an ocean.

লবনচুষ vul. corrup. of লজেঞ্চুস।

লবেজান *a.* feeling like dying; extremely distressed or harassed.

লব্জ variant of লব্‌জ।

লব্ধ *a.* obtained; attained; gained; earned; acquired. *fem.* লব্ধা। ~কাম *a.* having one's desire fulfilled; having attained one's end; gratified. ~গুণ *n.* (bot.) acquired character. ~প্রতিষ্ঠ *a.* famous, one who has earned fame; established. ~বিদ্যা *a.* learned; wise.

লব্ধি *n.* attainment; gains; acquirements; acquisition. ~নির্ণয় *n.* (mech.—of velocity) composition.

লভ্য *a.* obtainable; attainable; acquirable; gainable; available; procurable; capable of being earned as profit. □ *n.* gains; profit. লভ্যাংশ *n.* a share of profit; the part of income regarded as profit.

লম্পট *a.* lascivious, licentious, libertine, debauched, profligate, lewd; wanton. □ *n.* a libertine, a profligate, a debauchee.

লম্ফ[1] *n.* lamp esp. a small kerosene lamp.

লম্ফ[2] *n.* a leap, a spring, a jump, a bound. লম্ফ দেওয়া *v.* to leap, to spring, to jump, to bound. এক লম্ফে at a leap. লম্ফে লম্ফে by leaps and bounds. ~ঝম্প *n.* continuous or repeated skipping or leaping; (fig.) excessive haste or fuss or ado or bragging. ~ন *n.* leaping or springing or jumping or bounding.

লম্ব *a.* hanging, pendent; vertically hanging; upright; vertical, plumb; perpendicular; (geom.) orthogonal; straight; (geog.) orthographic(al). □ *n.* a perpendicular. ~অভিক্ষেপ *n.* (geog.) orthographic projection, orthography; (geom.) orthogonal projection. ~কর্ণ *a.* long-eared. □ *n.* a traditional name for the ass, the goat, the rabbit etc. ~চ্ছেদ *n.* (geom.) a normal section. ~ন *n.* the state of being hung; (phys. & astr.) parallax. লম্বন-পদ্ধতি *n.* (phys.) parallax method. ~বিন্দু *n.* (geom.) an orthocentre. ~বৃত্ত *n.* (astr.) a vertical circle. ~মান *a.* hanging, suspended, pendent; dependent. ~সূত্র *n.* (mech.) a plumb-line.

লম্বরদার *n.* a leader of tenants entrusted with the charge of collecting revenue from other tenants.

লম্বা *a.* tall; lofty; long; long-continued; lengthy; (fig.) prostrate; (fig.) boastful or grandiloquent. □ *n.* length. লম্বা করা *v.* to lengthen; to expand; (fig.) to lay prostrate on the ground by beating. লম্বা দেওয়া *v.* to decamp; to run away, to flee, to take to one's heels. লম্বা হওয়া *v.*

to lie prostrate; to grow in length, to become long. **লম্বা কথা** boastful or grandiloquent talk, tall talk, big talk. **লম্বা চাল** excessive pomp or eclat esp. that which is displayed beyond one's means. **~ই** *n.* length; the measure of length. **লম্বাই-চওড়াই** *n.* length and breadth; the measure of length and breadth; bragging, boastful or grandiloquent talk (লম্বাই-চওড়াই মারা). **লম্বাংশ** *n.* polar distance. **~টে** slightly tall, tallish; longish. **লম্বায়** *adv.* in length, lengthwise. **~লম্বি** *adv.* lengthwise, lengthways.

লম্বিত *a.* hanging, pendent, suspended; dangling; oscillating. **লম্বিত বেণী** dangling pigtail.

লম্বে *adv.* in length.

লম্বোদর *a.* pot-bellied, corpulent. □ *n.* God Ganesha (গণেশ).

লয় *n.* dissolution or fusion into a greater esse; merging, fusion; dissolution; destruction; universal dissolution or annihilation; (mus.) tempo. **লয়ে আনা** *v.* (coll.) to bring under control; to compel someone to behave properly; to bring someone to his senses.

ললনা *n.* a woman; a gentlewoman, a lady; a wife.

ললাট *n.* the forehead, the front; the temple; fate; luck; destiny. **~ভূষণ** *n.* an ornament for the forehead. **~রেখা** *n.* a line on the forehead (esp. one indicating one's destiny). **~লিখন, ~লিপি** *n.* one's destiny as indicated by the lines on one's forehead. **ললাটিকা** *n.* a holy mark of sandal-paste, clay etc. put on the forehead; an ornament for the forehead.

ললাম *n.* ornament; a mark (of sandal wood paste etc.) on one's forehead.

ললিত *a.* beautitful, pleasant, charming; (of speech) suave, bland. □ *n.* dance or artistic gestures of women; pleasure and enjoyment; an Indian musical mode. **~কলা** *n.* (collec.) fine arts; (distr.) any branch of fine arts. *fem. a.* **ললিতা** ।

লশকর *n.* a soldier; a naval soldier; a sailor; armed forces.

লশুন var. of **রসুন** ।

লসসি *n.* milk-shake; yoghurt.

লসিকা *n.* lymph. **~তন্তুবৃদ্ধি** *n.* lymphatic growth. **~য়নী** *a.* lymphatic.

লস্কর alt. spell. of **লশকর** ।

লহনা *n.* dues, amount outstanding.

লহমা *n.* a minute fraction of time, a short while, a moment.

লহর *n.* a wave; a watercourse, a channel; a row or coil.

লহরি, লহরী *n.* a wave.

লহু[1] *n.* (obs. & poet.) blood.

লহু[2] *a.* (obs. & poet.) mild, gentle (লহুলহু হাস).

লা[1] pop. corrup. of **লাক্ষা**[1] ।

লা[2] *n.* (dial.) a boat.

লা[3] *int.* (used in familiarity or contempt by women amongst themselves) hullo, ei, oi, I say etc.

লাইন *n.* a line; a system (কাজের লাইন). **লাইন দেওয়া, লাইন বাঁধা** *v.* to line up, to stand in a queue, to queue up. **লাইন-বাঁধা** *a.* lined-up.

লাইনিং *n.* lining (as of a coat).

লাইফবেলট, লাইফবেল্ট *n.* a life-belt.

লাইফবোট *n.* a life-boat.

লাইব্রেরি *n.* a library. **~য়ান** *n.* a librarian.

লাইসেনস, লাইসেন্স *n.* a licence. **~বিহীন** *a.* unlicensed.

লাউ *n.* the bottle-gourd. **লাউয়ের খোলা** calabash. **~ডগা** *n.* the tender upper end of the bottle-gourd plant; a kind of very slender and non-venomous green snake. **~মাচা** *n.* a scaffold or trellis made of bamboo and twigs along which a bottle-gourd plant creeps up.

লাক্ষণিক *a.* symptomatic; figurative, metaphorical; symbolical; versed in soothsaying; oracular. **লাক্ষণিক অর্থ** same as **লক্ষিতার্থ** (see **লক্ষিত**).

লাক্ষা *n.* lac, shellac. **~কীট** *n.* an insect producing lac. **~রস** *n.* lac dye.

লাক্ষিক *a.* dyed with lac, lacquered.

লাখ coll. var. of **লক্ষ**[2] । **লাখ কথার এক কথা** (fig.) an utterance or saying of imcomparable or immeasurable worth. **লাখে লাখে** *adv.* in countless number, in great number.

লাখেরাজ *n.* rent-free. **লাখেরাজ জমি** a freehold.

লাখো-লাখো *a.* in lakhs, many lakhs of; innumerable, countless.

লাগ *n.* reach; contact; touch; contiguity; nearness. **~সই** *a.* appropriate, fitting, suitable.

লাগা *v.* to contact, to touch (গায়ে হাওয়া লাগা) ; to be smeared or soiled with (কাদা লাগা) ; to be attached or affixed; to catch (আগুন লাগা) ; to touch at, to stop at (তীরে জাহাজ লাগা) ; to stop or park (গাড়ি লাগা) ; to join (চাকরিতে লাগা) ; to begin, to start, to commence (গ্রহণ লাগা) ; to form (ভিড় লাগা) ; to be engaged in, to set to (খেতে লাগা) ; to be felt (as) (ভালো লাগা, গরম লাগা) ; to feel pain (আমার লাগছে) ; to be felt as painful (ফোড়াটায় লাগছে) ; to fit or suit, to be appropriate (শব্দটা ওখানে লাগবে না) ; to be considered equal, to compete with (ধ্রুপদের কাছে কি অন্য গান লাগে) ; to require, to need (দু-দিন লাগবে) ; to cost (একশো টাকা লেগেছে) ; to work (ওষুধটা লেগেছে) ; to come true (ভবিষ্যৎবাণী লেগেছে) ; to begin to quarrel (দু-পক্ষে লেগেছে) ; to be held (এখানে মেলা লাগবে) ; to pester, to tease (তার পিছনে লেগো না) ; to pursue, to chase, to hound, to follow, to shadow (পিছনে পুলিশ লেগেছে) ; to be attracted (কাজে মন লাগা) ; to pierce (বুকে তির লাগা) ; to strike, to hit (ঘুসি লাগা, চোট লাগা) ; to stick (গলায় কাঁটা লাগা) ; to fall under the evil influence of (এঁড়ে লাগা, শনি লাগা) ; to be seized with (ভিরমি লাগা). **লেগে থাকা** *v.* to stick; to pursue doggedly or resolutely.

লাগাও *a.* adjoining, lying side by side, contiguous.

লাগাড় *n.* continuity, stretch. □ *a.* continuous (লাগাড় বকবকানি).

লাগানো *v.* to attach, to affix; to apply, to set (আগুন লাগানো) ; to paint or smear or wash with (রং লাগানো) ; to touch (গায়ে গা লাগানো) ; to expose to (রোদ লাগানো) ; to bring to, to stop at (ঘাটে নৌকা লাগানো) ; to employ, to engage, to set to (কাজে লোক লাগানো, পড়ায় মন লাগানো) ; to apply, to use (বেত লাগানো) ; to involve (in), to set (to) (ঝগড়া লাগানো) ; to require, to need, to take, to spend (সময় লাগানো) ; to cost (খরচ লাগানো) ; to invest, to lay out (ব্যবসায়ে টাকা লাগানো) ; to rouse (মনে ভয় লাগানো) ; to cause to be seized with (ভিরমি লাগানো) ; to hit, to strike (মনে লাগানো, গাছে ঢিল লাগানো) ; to report (against) maliciously and secretly, to earwig, to calumniate (কারও নামে লাগানো). **লাগানি-ভাঙানি** *n.* malicious and secret report against a person, earwigging.

লাগাম *n.* a bridle; reins. **লাগাম পরানো** *v.* to bridle, to bit; (fig.) to restrain, to curb. **লাগাম কামড়ানো** to champ the bit. **~ছাড়া** *a.* unbridled; (fig.) unrestrained or (over-) free.

লাগায়েত var. of **নাগাদ**।

লাগি, লাগিয়া *prep.* (poet.) for, for the sake of, on account of.

লাগোয়া var. of **লাগাও**।

লাগেজ *n.* luggage. **লাগেজ করা** *v.* to book a luggage.

লাঘব *n.* decrease, reduction; meiosis; underestimation; lightness, levity; humiliation; promptness, quickness, dexterity (হস্তলাঘব). **লাঘব করা** *v.* to decrease, to reduce; to make light of, to reduce the weight of; to humiliate.

লাঙল *n.* a plough. **লাঙল চষা, লাঙল দেওয়া** *v.* to plough. **লাঙলের ফাল** a ploughshare. **~দণ্ড** *n.* the shaft of a plough. **~রেখা** *n.* a furrow.

লাঙুল, লাঙ্গুল *n.* a tail (of beasts.) **~হীন** *a.* tailless, anurous, anourous.

লাচাড়ি *n.* a Bengali poetical metre suitable for dancing; a song composed in this metre.

লাচার *a.* helpless, resourceless.

লাজ[1] corrup. of **লজ্জা**। **~লজ্জা** *n.* bashfulness; shame; coyness. **~লজ্জাহীন** *a.* shameless; coyless; unabashed.

লাজ[2] *n.* parched rice. **~বর্ষণ করা** *v.* to shower parched rice.

লা-জবাব *a.* unparalleled, incomparable; unanswering, silent.

লাজুক *a.* bashful, shy; coy; modest; diffident.

লাঞ্ছন *n.* a stain, a spot; a sign; an emblem; a flag; painting.

লাঞ্ছনা *n.* reproach, reprimand; disgrace, insult; persecution; harassment. **লাঞ্ছনা করা** *v.* to reproach, to reprimand; to disgrace, to insult; to persecute; to harass.

লাঞ্ছিত *a.* reproached, reprimanded; disgraced; insulted; persecuted; harassed; stained, spotted, bearing a particular sign or emblem or flag; painted.

লাট১ *n.* a parcel of land (chiefly agricultural) marked out for administrative purpose or a set of things offered together for sale, a lot. **~বন্দি** *a.* divided into lots.

লাট২ *a.* (of clothes) having the crease spoiled, ruffled, crumpled (also **লাট-ভাঙা**) ; prostrate on the ground. **লাট খাওয়া** *v.* (of paper-kites) to behave awkwardly and refuse to keep flying. **মেরে লাট করা** *v.* to knock (one) senseless or reeling to the ground by beating. **লাটে ওঠা** *v.* to go to the dogs; to fizzle, to flop, to come a cropper.

লাট৩ *n.* a governor (বাংলার লাট) ; a governor-general (usu. **বড়োলাট**) ; a commander-in-chief (usu. **জঙ্গিলাট**) ; (usu. hum.) *a.* a lord (লাট-বেলাট). **ছোটোলাট** *n.* a lieutenant-governor; a provincial governor.

লাট৪ *n.* a pillar (অশোকলাট).

লাট-বেলাট *n. pl.* (sarcas.) lords and nobles, big people.

লাট-ভাঙা see **লাট২**।

লাটসাহেব same as **লাট৩**।

লাটাই var. of **নাটাই**।

লাটিম, লাট্টু *n.* a top. **লাটিম ঘুরানো** to spin a top.

লাঠালাঠি *n.* fighting with sticks or staffs; a serious quarrel. **লাঠালাঠি করা** *v.* to fight one another with sticks or staffs; to quarrel seriously.

লাঠি *n.* a stick, a staff. **~খেলা** *n.* an exhibition fight with sticks. **লাঠি খেলা** *v.* to fight with sticks as an exhibition; to practise fighting with sticks. **~পেটা করা** *v.* to beat or belabour with a stick. **~বাজি করা** *v.* to fight or persecute with sticks. **~য়াল** *n.* a (skilled) figther with sticks. **~য়ালি** *n.* skill in, or the profession of, fighting with sticks.

লাডু dial. var. of **নাড়ু**।

লাথি, (dial.) **লাথ** *n.* a kick. **লাথি খাওয়া** *v.* to be kicked; to receive a kick. **লাথি মারা** *v.* to kick.

লাদ, লাদা, লাদি variants of **নাদ১, নাদা** and **নাদি** respectively.

লাফ *n.* a leap, a jump, a bound, a skip. **লাফ দেওয়া, লাফ মারা** *v.* to take a leap, to jump; to skip. **লাফে লাফে** by leaps and bounds. **লাফানো** *v.* to jump, to leap, to bound; to skip; to fret. □ *n.* jumping, leaping, bounding, skipping; fretting. **লাফানে** *a.* given to jumping or leaping; frisking; fretful. **লাফালাফি** *n.* frisking, gambolling; flouncing, fuss. **লাফালাফি করা** *v.* to frisk, to gambol; to flounce; to fuss.

লাব *n.* a kind of small brid of the quail family.

লাবণ *a.* saline; saltish.

লাবণ্য, (poet.) **লাবনি, লাবণি** *n.* physical grace or charm. **লাবণ্যময়** *a.* having a graceful or charming figure; (of a figure) graceful, charming. *fem.* **লাবণ্যময়ী**।

লাভ *n.* profit; income; gain; utility; attainment (বন্ধুলাভ). **লাভ করা** *v.* to make a profit; to earn; to gain, to attain. **লাভ হওয়া** *v.* to come or to turn out as a profit or income; to be profitable; to be of utility; to be attained. **~কর, ~জনক** *a.* profitable, gainful; lucrative. **~লোকসান, লাভালাভ** *n.* profit and loss; gain and loss.

লামা১ *n.* a Buddhist priest in Tibet, a lama.

লামা২ *n.* a South American animal, the llama.

লাম্পট্য *n.* lasciviousness, libertinism, debauchery, profligacy, lewdness; wantonness.

লায়েক *a.* grown-up, of full age; able, fit, competent; (dero.) grown-up enough to be a litertine.

লাল১ var. of **লালা**।

লাল২ *a.* & *n.* red. □ *a.* reddened; flushed. **লাল করা** *v.* to redden; to dye or paint red. ~ফিতে *n.* (fig.) official delay; redtapism. লাল বাতি জ্বালা to go into liquidation. লাল হওয়া *v.* to redden; to flush; (fig.) to flourish; to become rich.

লালচে *a.* reddish.

লালন *n.* act of bringing up carefully; carefully rearing or tending; fond cherishing (আশা-লালন). লালন করা *v.* to bring up carefully; to rear or tend carefully; to cherish fondly. লালন-পালন করা *v.* to nourish and bring up; to rear.

লালস[১] *a.* greedy, covetous; eagerly desirous or longing; lustful.

লালসা, (coll. corrup). লালস[২] *n.* greed, covetousness, avidity; eager desire or longing; lust.

লালা *n.* saliva; spittle, slaver. লালা ঝরা বা ঝরানো *v.* to salivate, to slaver. ~য়িত *a.* seized with eager greed; coveting; yearning for; hankering after. *fem.* ~য়িতা। ~য়িত হওয়া *v.* to be seized with eager desire; to covet; to yearn for; to hanker after. ~স্রাব *n.* salivation; slavering, drivelling.

লালিত *a.* carefully brought up; carefully reared or tended; fondly cherished. ~পালিত *a.* carefully nourished and brought up.

লালিত্য *n.* beauty; sweetness, charm; (of speech) suavity.

লালিমা *n.* red tint or glow.

লাশ *n.* a human carcass, a corpse, a dead body.

লাস্য, লাস *n.* a woman's dance; artistic or amorous gestures and postures of women. লাস্যময়ী *a. fem.* given to dancing; having artistic or amorous gestures and postures.

লিক, লিকি *n.* a young of a louse; the egg of a louse, a nit.

লিকলিক *int.* expreesing: great slenderness or thinness.লিকলিকে *a.* very slender or thin.

লিখন *n.* writing; composing; drawing or tracing; a piece of writing; a letter, a note, a chit; a script, manuscript. ~প্রণালী, ~ভঙ্গি *n.* style or mode of writing or composing.

লিখিত *a.* written (লিখিত জবানবন্দি = written deposition); composed; not verbal or oral.

লিখিতব্য *a.* to be written.

লিখিয়ে *n.* a writer; an author.

লিঙ্গ *n.* the penis; the phallus esp. of Shiva (শিব) ; sex; (gr.) the gender. ~পূজা *n.* phallicism, phallism, phallic worship. ~মূর্তি *n.* a phallic image. ~শরীর *n.* a phantasmal or subtle body. লিঙ্গায়েত *n.* a community worshipping the phallus of Shiva (শিব).

লিচু *n.* litchi or leechee, *Litchi chinensis.*

লিটার *n.* a litre.

লিপি *n.* a letter, an epistle, a missive; a note; a writing (ভাগ্যলিপি) ; an inscription (অনুশাসন-লিপি) ; a script or alphabet (ব্রাহ্মীলিপি). ~কর *n.* a writer, a scribe; a copyist; a penman; an amanuensis; a composer of a letter. লিপিকর-প্রমাদ *n.* a slip of the pen; an error committed by the copyist. ~কা *n.* a short letter, a chit or note; a letter. ~কার same as ~কর। ~কৌশল *n.* penmanship, the art or style of writing. ~চাতুর্য *n.* dexterity in writing or composing. লিপিবদ্ধ বা লিপিভুক্ত করা *v.* to place on record, to record; to write or include in a letter, book etc. ~বিদ্যা *n.* penmanship; calligraphy; the art of composing letters.

লিপ্ত *a.* smeared or daubed with; soiled with; involved or implicated in; engaged or employed in; joined together; (bio.) webbed. ~পাদ *a.* webfooted.

লিপ্যন্তর *n.* transliteration. লিপ্যন্তর করা *v.* to transliterate.

লিপ্সা *n.* eager desire to obtain; yearning; avidity. লিপ্সা করা *v.* to yearn or long for.

লিপ্সু *a.* yearning or longing for; avid.

লিভার *n.* the liver. লিভারের দোষ disorder or complaint or trouble of the liver.

লিরিক *n.* a lyric.

লিস্ট, (coll.) লিস্টি *n.* list, a roll, an inventory. লিস্ট করা *v.* to make a list of. লিস্টিভুক্ত *a.* enlisted.

লীঢ় *a.* licked; tasted.

লীন *a.* dissolved or fused into a greater

esse (ব্রহ্মে লীন) ; merged, fused; dissolved; disappeared; clinging to (কণ্ঠলীন). *fem.* **লীনা** । **~তাপ** n. (phys.) latent heat.

লীয়মান *a.* vanishing, disappearing, fading, melting, dissolving, evanescing.

লীলা *n.* sport; pleasure; dalliance; activities (কৃষ্ণের লীলা) ; (sarcas.) undesirable activities (নেতাদের লীলা) ; significant but unintelligible work or sport (বিধাতার লীলা). **~কমল** *n.* a lotus carried in the hand playfully; a toy lotus. **~কলহ** *n.* a lover's quarrel; a mock quarrel. **~কানন** *n.* a pleasure garden. **~কুঞ্জ** *n.* a pleasure grove. **~ক্ষেত্র** *n.* a field of activities; a venue of sports. **~খেলা** same as **লীলা** । **লীলাখেলা সাঙ্গ করা** *v.* (usu. sarcas.) to die; (iron–usu. of a criminal) to give up one's activities and surrender. **~চঞ্চল** *a.* frequently moving in playfulness; sweetly frolicsome. **~বতী** same as **~ময়ী** । **~ভূমি** same as **~ক্ষেত্র** । **~ময়** *a.* sweetly playful or sportive; given to sweet dalliance; attitudinizing; one whose activities, though significant, are not easily intelligible. *fem.* **~ময়ী** । **~য়িত** *a.* having assumed a beautiful pose or posture, attitudinized; full of delicate movements.

লু *n.* a very hot wave of summer wind that blows sometimes in a tropical region or in a desert; simoom.

লুই *n.* a kind of very soft woollen wrapper.

লুকানো *v.* to go into hiding, to hide; to remain invisible; to put out of sight, to hide, to conceal. □ *a.* hidden, concealed..

লুকোচুরি *n.* hide-and-seek; (fig.) an attempt to conceal, dodging. **লুকোচুরি খেলা** *v.* to play at hide-and-seek; (fig.) to try to conceal, to dodge.

লুক্কায়িত *a.* gone into hiding; hidden; concealed; disappeared. *fem.* **লুক্কায়িতা** । **লুক্কায়িত হওয়া** *v.* to go into hiding, to hide; to disappear.

লুঙ্গি, লুঙি *n.* a long (usu. stitched) loincloth worn by men, a lungi.

লুচি *n.* a kind of small and thin saucershaped bread fried in ghee.

লুচ্চা *a.* vulgarly lewd or wanton; lowly vulgar, caddish. □ *n.* a vulgar libertine; a cad. **~মি** *n.* vulgar lewdness; caddishness.

লুট *n.* plunder, loot; robbery, dacoity; reckless misappropriation; act of scattering something before a crowd to be picked up (হরির লুট) ; enjoyment in a great measure. **লুট করা** v. to plunder, to loot; to rob; to misappropriate recklessly; to enjoy in a great measure (মজা লুট করা). **লুটের মাল** booty, plunder, spoil. **~তরাজ, ~পাট** *n.* extensive plundering, pillage, sack. **লুটতরাজ বা লুটপাট করা** *v.* to plunder; to pillage, to sack.

লুটা *v.* to plunder, to loot; to rob; to misappropriate recklessly; to enjoy in a great measure; to roll esp. on the gorund (ভূমিতে লুটায়) ; to welter, to sprawl, to wallow. also **লোটা** *v.* (মজা লোটা).

লুটানো *v.* to roll or cause to roll esp. on the ground; to welter or sprawl or wallow; to cause to welter or sprawl or wallow.

লুটেরা *n.* one who loots, a plunderer, a robber.

লুটোপুটি *n.* rolling esp. on the ground; weltering, sprawling, wallowing. **লুটোপুটি খাওয়া** *v.* to roll esp. on the ground; to sprawl, to wallow.

লুঠেরা var. of **লুটেরা** ।

লুণ্ঠক *n.* a plunderer; a pillager; a robber; a thief; one who misappropriates recklessly; one who enjoys in a great measure.

লুণ্ঠন *n.* loot, plunder, robbing, robbery; pillage, sack; reckless misappropriation; enjoyment in a great measure. **লুণ্ঠন করা** same as **লুটা** ।

লুণ্ঠিত *a.* looted, plundered; robbed; pillaged, sacked; recklessly misappropriated; enjoyed in a great measure; rolling esp. on the ground, sprawling, *fem.* **লুণ্ঠিতা** ।

লুপ্ত *a.* no longer existing, extinct; defunct; abolished; gone out of currency or practice, obsolete; destroyed; covered, wrapped, extinct; (of species etc.)

that has disappeared or vanished; invisible; hidden, concealed; (bot.) abortive; (gr.) elided. **অধুনালুপ্ত আইন** a law now defunct. **~প্রায়** *a.* obsolescent; almost extinct or defunct or destroyed or covered or invisible or hidden or (bot.) abortive. **লুপ্তাঙ্গ** *n.* (bot.) an abortive organ. **লুপ্তোদ্ধার** *n.* recovery or reclamation of a thing lost or destroyed or ruined; discovery of a hidden or secret thing.

লুব্ধ, (poet.) **লুবধ** *a.* greedy, avid, covetous; tempted, allured, enticed. *fem.* **লুব্ধা** । **লুব্ধ করা** *v.* to tempt, to allure; to entice. **লুব্ধক** *n.* a hunter; a fowler; a lecher; (astr.) the Sirius, the Dogstar. **~দৃষ্টি** *a.* greedy looking. **লুব্ধ দৃষ্টি** *n.* greedy looks. **~প্রকৃতি** *a.* of a greedy nature, covetous.

লূতা *n.* the spider, an arachnid. **~তন্তু** *n.* cobweb; gossamer. **~তন্তুবৎ** *a.* gossamery, light as gossamer; (fig.) flimsy.

লেই *n.* glue; any glutinous substance or preparation.

লেংচা, লেংচানো, লেংটা, লেংড়া[1] rej. spellings of **ল্যাংচা, ল্যাংচানো, ল্যাংটা** and **ল্যাংড়া** respectively.

লেংটি, লেঙটি *n.* a small threadbare or loincloth.

লেংড়া[2] see **ল্যাংড়া**[2] ।

লেকচার *n.* a lecture; (sarcas.) a harangue. **লেকচার দেওয়া** *v.* to lecture; (sarcas.) to harangue. **লেকচার শোনা** *v.* to attend a lecture.

লেখ *n.* a piece of writing; an epistle, a letter; a graph.

লেখক *n.* a writer; a scribe; an author (*fem.* an authoress).

লেখন var. of **লিখন** ।

লেখনী *n.* anything to write with; a pen, a pencil, a painter's brush, a hair-pencil etc. **লেখনী চালনা করা** *v.* to write (esp. books.). **~প্রসূত** *a.* coming out of or produced by the pen.

লেখনীয় same as **লেখ্য** ।

লেখা *v.* to write; to compose (as a book); to write; to draw or describe or trace. □ *n.* same as **লিখন** । □ *a.* written; composed; drawn or traced. **~জোখা** *n.* accounts. **~নো** *v.* to cause to write or compose or write to or draw or trace; to teach one how to write. **~পড়া** *n.* reading and writing; education; studies; an agreement in black and white; a legally registered agreement. **লেখাপড়া করা** *v.* to read and write; to receive education; to study; to enter into or draw up a written agreement; to execute a legally registered agreement. **লেখালিখি করা** *v.* to write (repeatedly) to one another; to send in repeated correspondence; to do some writing; to make repeated representation in writing.

লেখিকা *fem.* of **লেখক** ।

লেখ্য *a.* that which is to be or can be written; used in writing only, written (লেখ্য ভাষা). □ *n.* anything written; an epistle, a letter; a script; a manuscript; a drawing, a painting, a picture, a sketch; a deed, a document, a record. **লেখ্য-নিবন্ধক** *n.* the Registrar of Assurances. **~পত্র** *n.* a deed, a document. **~প্রাপক** *n.* record finder. **~রক্ষক** *n.* a record-keeper. **লেখ্যাগার** *n.* record room. **লেখ্যোপকরণ** *n.* writing material, such as ink, pen, paper etc.

লেচি *n.* a lump of dough to be rolled and then fried or baked.

লেজ, ল্যাজ *n.* a tail; the hind-part of anything, the rump, the rear (সৈন্যবাহিনীর লেজ). **জাহাজের বা নৌকার লেজ** the stern. **লেজ গুটানো** *v.* (fig.) to turn tail, to run away with tail between the legs. **লেজ মাড়ানো** *v.* (fig.) to twist one's tail, to annoy. **লেজ মোটা হওয়া** to be puffed up or overbearing or bumptious or conceited. **লেজে খেলানো** *v.* (fig.) to harass one by giving false hopes or by keeping in suspense. **~কাটা শিয়াল** (sarcas.) a disgraced person endeavouring in vain to keep up appearance. **লেজা** *n.* the tail of a fish; the hind part of anything. **লেজামুড়ো** *n.* (fig.) anything in its entirety, alpha and omega. **লেজুড়** *n.* a tail; the rump, the rear; what is attached or affixed to the rear end;

(sarcas.) degrees or titles (তার নামের অনেকগুলি লেজুড়).

লেট *n.* delay. □ *a.* late. **লেট করা** *v.* to be late; to procrastinate.

লেটার-বক্স *n.* a letter-box; a pillar-box.

লেঠা see **ল্যাঠা**।

লেডিকেনি *n.* a kind of sweet drop made by frying posset.

লেতি, লেত্তি *n.* a piece of string for spinning a top.

লেদাড়ু, লেদাড়ে *a.* lazy; not smart; unenterprising.

লেনদেন, লেনাদেনা *n.* act of giving and taking; transaction; exchange; bargain; payment and repayment.

লেপ[১] *n.* quilt stuffed with cotton used as a wrap during sleep. **লেপের ওয়াড়** a quilt case.

লেপ[২] *n.* a layer of paint etc., a coat, a coating, a wash (মাটির লেপ) ; anything to coat or smear with.

লেপক *n.* one who applies a coating or wash; one who smears.

লেপচা *n.* a Himalayan race; a member of this race, a Lepcha.

লেপটানো *v.* to wrap round oneself; to cling to; to be involved or implicated in; to coat or smear.

লেপন *n.* coating or smearing. **লেপন করা** *v.* to coat, to wash, to smear.

লেপা *v.* same as **লেপন করা**। □ *a.* coated, washed, smeared. **~নো** *v.* to cause to coat or wash or smear.

লেপাফা, লেফাফা *n.* an envelope, a cover, a wrapper. **~দোরস্ত, ~দুরস্ত** *a.* outwardly or formally meticulous (but actually insincere and faulty).

লেবু[১] *n.* the lemon; the lime.

লেবু[২] *a.* (infor.) good-for-nothing; unpractical; stupid.

লেবেল *n.* a label. **লেবেল আঁটা** *v.* to label. **লেবেল-আঁটা** *a.* lebelled.

লেলাখ্যাপা var. of **নেলা খ্যাপা** & **ন্যালাখ্যাপা**।

লেলানো *v.* to incite (as a dog) to attack, to set on, to set upon.

লেলিহান *a.* repeatedly licking; blazing. fluttering (লেলিহান শিখা).

লেশ *n.* an iota, a jot, a bit; trace, shadow. **~মাত্র** *a.* (chiefly used in the negative) even an iota or bit of, even the faintest trace or shadow of.

লেস *n.* an ornamental fabric, a lace. **লেস পরানো** *n.* to decorate with a lace, to lace, to enlace.

লেহ, লেহন *n.* licking or lapping. **লেহন করা** *v.* to lick, to lap. **লেহনকারী, লেহী** *a.* & *n.* one who or that which licks or laps. **লেহ্য** *a.* (of food) to be eaten or taken by licking or lapping.

লৈখিক *a.* relating to or used in writing; not spoken or oral, written; (alg.) graphical; (rare) literary.

লৈঙ্গ, লৈঙ্গিক *a.* relating to the penis, penial; sexual.

লো var. of **লা**[৩]।

লোক *n.* a person, a human being; the public; mankind; a world, a sphere (ভূলোক) ; a region or abode (বিষ্ণুলোক). **লোক হাসানো** *v.* to be an object of public ridicule. **লোকে বলে** people say; they say; it is said. **~কাহিনি, ~কথা** *n.* a folktale, a folklore. **~গণক** *n.* a census enumerator. **~গণনা** *n.* census. **~গাথা** *n.* a ballad. **~চক্ষুতে** *adv.* in the eyes of the people or of the public. **~চক্ষুর সমক্ষে** publicly; openly. **~চরিত্র** *n.* human nature. **~জন** *n. pl.* people at large; one's followers or supporters or associates; retinue, suite, a train of followers. **~জানাজানি** *n.* public exposure, publicity. **~ত্রয়** (usu. **ত্রিলোক**) *n.* the three worlds (heaven, earth and the nether world). **~দেখানো** *a.* falsely exhibiting or displaying in presence of others, falsely demonstrative. **~নাট্য** *n.* folk drama. **~নিন্দা** same as **লোকাপবাদ**। **~নৃত্য** *n.* folk-dance. **~পরম্পরা** *n.* succession of generations; transmission from generation to generation of people or from man to man. **~পরম্পরাগত** *a.* transmitted or handed down from generation to generation of people, traditional; ciculated or transmitted from man to man. **~পাল** *n.* a king; (myth.) any one of the eight presiding deities of the eight corners of the universe; (in modern times) a Vigilance or Anticorruption Officer independent of the executive. **~প্রবাদ** *n.*

hearsay; (loos.) a rumour. **~প্রিয়** *a.* popular. **~প্রিয়তা** *n.* popularity. **~বল** *n.* the strength of one's supporters or followers; one's supporters or associates or followers collectively. **~বসতি** *n.* human habitation, settlement. **~বিশ্রুত** *a.* well-known to the people; famous, renowned, celebrated. **~ব্যবহার** same as **লোকাচার**। **~ভাষা** *n.* dialect, the language of the common people. **~মুখে** *adv.* from other people, from other people's mouth (লোকমুখে শুনেছি). **~রঞ্জন** folk-entertainment. **~লজ্জা** *n.* fear of looking small to the people, fear of public disgrace. **~লশকর** *n.* retinue, suite. **~লীলা** *n.* worldly activities. **~লৌকিকতা** *n.* social formalities; social amenities. **~শাসন** *n.* public administration. **~শিক্ষা** *n.* mass education. **~সংখ্যা** *n.* population. **~সংগীত** *n.* a folk-song. **~সমাকীর্ণ** same as **জনাকীর্ণ**। **~সমাগম** *n.* gathering or collection of people; gathering. **~সমাজ** *n.* human society; the public. **~সাহিত্য** *n.* folk literature. **~সেবক** *n.* a social welfare worker. **~সেবা** *n.* social (welfare) service. **~হিত** *n.* public welfare; public good. **~হিতকর** *n.* beneficial to the public; promoting the well-being of the people. **~হিতকর কার্য** a public welfare work or service. **~হিতব্রত** *a.* a vow to do public good, dedication to public service; devotion to public welfare work. **~হিতৈষণা** *n.* benevolence; (loos.) philanthropy. **~হিতৈষী** *a.* benevolent; (loos.) philanthropic. *fem.* **~হিতৈষিণী**।

লোকসান *n.* loss; damage, harm. **লোকসান করা** *v.* to damage, to harm; to cause or suffer a loss. **লোকসান দেওয়া** *v.* to suffer or incur a loss, to lose.

লোকাকীর্ণ same as **জনাকীর্ণ**।

লোকাচার *n.* a popular practice, a custom, a usage; customs and usages collectively. **লোকাচারের বিরুদ্ধে** *a.* contrary to popular practice, opposed to prevailing custom or usage.

লোকাতীত *a.* extramundane; superhuman; miraculous; extraordinary; supernatural.

লোকান্তর *n.* another world; the world where one goes after one's death, the next world, the beyond, the hereafter; (loos.) death (তাঁর লোকান্তরের পর). **~প্রাপ্ত, লোকান্তরিত** *a.* diceased, dead. **~প্রাপ্ত বা লোকান্তরিত হওয়া** *v.* to die. **~গমন, ~প্রাপ্তি** *n.* death.

লোকাপবাদ *n.* public censure; public scandal; infamy; obloquy.

লোকাভাব *n.* want of men; want of workers; thin population.

লোকায়ত *a.* secular (লোকায়ত সরকার).

লোকারণ্য *n.* a vast crowd of people; a great concourse of people. **(লোকে) লোকারণ্য হওয়া** *v.* to teem with a vast multitude of people.

লোকাল বোর্ড *n.* a local board.

লোকালয় *n.* human habitation; a human settlement or colony; a town, a village; (fig.) the human society.

লোকেশ *n.* god; the king.

লোকোত্তর same as **লোকাতীত**।

লোচন *n.* the eye. **~রঞ্জন** *a.* pleasing to the eye.

লোচ্চা pop. var. of **লুচ্চা**।

লোটন *n.* the tumbler pigeon, the tumbler (also **লোটন পায়রা**) ; a bun dressed so as to hang loosely.

লোটা[1] *n.* a metal pot.

লোটা[2], **লোটানো, লোড়া** pop. variants of **লুটা, লুটানো, নোড়া**।

লোধ্র, লোধ *n.* a kind of tree. **লোধ্ররেণু** *n.* a cosmetic powder prepared from the bark of this tree.

লোনা *a.* salty; saltish; saline; salted (লোনা মাছ). □ *n.* a damaging coating on walls etc. caused by moisture or damp; excess of salinity in soil, water or air (লোনায় স্বাস্থ্যহানি). **লোনায় ধরা** *v.* to be affected with a damaging coating caused by damp.

লোপ *n.* destruction; abolition; extinction; disppearance; concealment; (gr.) elision. **লোপ করা** *v.* to destroy; to abolish; to conceal, to hide. **লোপ পাওয়া, লোপ হওয়া** *v.* to be destroyed or abolished; to become extinct or obsolete; to disappear or vanish; to be concealed; (gr.) to be elided. **~প্রাপ্ত** same as **লুপ্ত**।

লোপাট *a.* thoroughly plundered or sacked; utterly destroyed; completely disappeared or hidden or concealed; carried off to a hiding-place without leaving any trace (লাস লোপাট). **লোপাট করা** *v.* to plunder or sack thoroughly; to destroy utterly; to hide or conceal thoroughly; to carry off to a hiding-place without leaving any trace.

লোফা *v.* to catch or take hold of a thing in the air, to take hold of a thing before it touches the ground; (fig.) to accept or receive eagerly. **লোফালুফি করা** *v.* to take or hold catches; to catch repeatedly; throwing and catching.

লোবান *n.* benzoin.

লোভ *n.* greed, avidity, covetousness; strong desire or inclination; strong desire to appropriate to oneself what belongs to others; thirst for worldly possessions; avarice, cupidity; allurement, enticement, temptation. **লোভ করা** *v.* to be greedy of, to covet, to have a strong desire or inclination for; to desire strongly to appropriate to oneself what belongs to others; to be thirsty of worldly possessions. **লোভ জন্মানো** *v.* to make one greedy. **লোভ দেখানো** *v.* to tempt, to allure. **লোভে পড়া** *v.* to fall into a temptation; to become greedy of. **লোভে পাপ, পাপে মৃত্যু** (fig.) temptation leads to sin and sin to death; (fig.) avarice leads to vice and vice to death. **লোভ সংবরণ করা** to check or control one's greed or tempatation. **~জনক** same as **লোভনীয়**। **~ন** *n.* act of tempting or alluring, enticement. □ *a.* same as **লোভনীয়**। **~নীয়** *a.* covetable; tempting, alluring; lucrative (লোভনীয় চাকরি) ; attractive, charming (লোভনীয় চেহারা). **লোভাতুর, লোভার্ত** *a.* stricken with (extreme) greed; greatly tempted; very much eager. *fem.* **লোভাতুরা, লোভার্তা**। **লোভী** *a.* greedy, avid, covetous; strongly desirous of or inclined to; strongly desirous of appropriating to oneself what belongs to others; greedy of worldly possessions; avaricious; easily tempted or allured.

লোম, লোমকূপ variants of **রোম** and **রোমকূপ** respectively.

লোমনাশক *a.* depilatory.

লোম-ফোঁড়া *n.* a boil in a hair follicle.

লোমশ, লোমহর্ষণ, লোমাবলি, লোমোদগম, লোমোদ্ভেদ variants of **রোমশ, রোমহর্ষণ, রোমাবলি, রোমোদগম** and **রোমোদ্ভেদ** respectively.

লোর *n.* (poet.) tears.

লোল *a.* restless, frequently moving (লোল কটাক্ষ) ; lolling; greedy or thirsty or extremely eager, wistful (লোল দৃষ্টি) ; loose or loosened. **~চর্ম** *a.* one whose skin hangs loosely on account of age. **~জিহ্ব** *a.* greedily lolling one's tongue; fluttering, blazing (লোলজিহ্ব অগ্নি).

লোলা *n.* the tongue (esp. which is greedy of food).

লোলুপ *a.* stricken with extreme greed; greatly tempted; very much eager; greedy, avid.

লোষ্ট্র *n.* a roundish small lump of earth; a small roundish stone or brickbat. **~বৎ** *adv.* & *a.* like a clod of earth; as valueless as a lump of earth.

লোহ *n.* iron; metal; blood; tears.

লোহা *n.* iron. **লোহার কারখানা** an iron foundry; a smithy. **লোহার জিনিস** hardware. **আকরিক লোহা** iron-ore. **ঢালাই লোহা** cast iron. **নরম লোহা** soft iron, pig-iron. **পেটা লোহা** wrought iron. **~চুর** *n.* iron filings; pulverized iron, iron dust; iron rust. **~র** *n.* a blacksmith. **~লক্কড়** *n.* iron and wood and similar substances and things made of them.

লোহিত *a.* & *n.* red. **~ক** *n.* (astr.) the Mars; ruby; spinel; spinel-ruby. **লোহিত-সাগর** *n.* the Red Sea.

লোহু, লৌ *n.* blood.

লৌকিক *a.* human; popular, public; social; worldly, earthly; formal; customary. **~তা** *n.* formality; a formal gift given to one esp. on a ceremonial occasion. **লৌকিকতা (রক্ষা) করা** *v.* to comply with formalities whilst dealing with one; to give or send a formal present.

লৌহ *n.* iron; steel. **~কার** *n.* a blacksmith. **~ঘটিত** *a.* ferrous; chalybeate. **~চূর্ণ** *n.* iron filings; pulverized iron, iron dust;

iron rust. ~নির্মিত *a.* made of iron or steel. ~বর্ত্ম *n.* a railway; a tramway. ~ময় *a.* made of iron or steel; full of iron. ~শৃঙ্খল *n.* iron chains, fetters.

ল্যাং *n.* the leg, the shank; causing to stumble by pushing one's leg into anothers. **ল্যাং দেওয়া, ল্যাং মারা** *v.* to cause to stumble or fall by pushing one's leg into another's; to trip; (sl.) to betray.

ল্যাংচা *n.* a kind of sweetmeat made of posset.

ল্যাংচানো *v.* to limp.

ল্যাংটা, (coll.) **ন্যাংটো** *a.* naked, nude. **ল্যাংটার নেই বাটপাড়ের ভয়** a destitute needn't be afraid of a swindler.

ল্যাংড়া[1] *n.* an excellent species of mango.

ল্যাংড়া[2] *a.* lame. □ *n.* a lame person.

ল্যাংবোট *n.* a longboat; (inc. but pop.) a slow-moving cargo-boat; (sarcas.) a constant companion or follower esp. one who impedes movement or progress; a drag, an encumbrance.

ল্যাঙট, ল্যাঙ্গট *n.* a tiny loincloth worn by Indian wrestlers and ascetics.

ল্যাজ, ল্যাজা alt. spellings of **লেজ** and **লেজা**।

ল্যাঠা *n.* trouble, difficulty; fix; a species of small and soft fish.

ল্যাম্প *n.* a lamp.

শ১ *n.* the thirtieth consonant of the Bengali alphabet.
শ২ coll. contr. of **শত** ।
শংকর alt. spell. of **শঙ্কর** ।
শংসন, শংসা *n.* praise, compliment. **শংসাপত্র** *n.* a certificate; a testimonial.
শংসিত *a.* praised, complimented.
শক *n.* the Scythian race; a Scythian; an era introduced in 78 A.D. (also শকাব্দ) ; any year (বাংলা শক).
শকট *n.* a vehicle, a carriage, a cart, a car. **গো-শকট** *n.* a bullock-cart; a hackery. **বাষ্পীয় শকট** a railway train. **~চালক** *n.* a carter, a driver, a carman; a coachman.
শকটিকা *n.* a small or toy car.
শকড়ি *n.* & *a.* that which has come in contact with cooked food or with the leavings of one's meal.
শকতি poet. corrup. of **শক্তি** ।
শকদ্বীপ *n.* Scythia.
শকরখন্দ *n.* the sweet potato, the yam.
শকল *n.* a portion, a part, a piece; a scale of fish; (bot.) bast. **~তন্তু** *n.* bast fibre.
শকাব্দ see **শক** ।
শকার-বকার *n.* filthy words beginning with শ and ব ; filthy revilings or abusive language.
শকারি *n.* the enemy or subduer of the Shakas (শক).
শকুন *n.* the vulture; an omen. **~জ্ঞ** *a.* versed in augury.
শকুনি *n.* the vulture; a character of the Mahabharata; (fig.) a relative who, by giving evil counsel, leads a family to ruin.
শকুন্ত *n.* the bird; the vulture. **~লা** *n. fem.* one who has been protected by a bird.
শক্ত১ *a.* capable, able, fit for work (শক্তসমর্থ = hardy); strong, powerful; efficient; hard to win over or deceive (শক্ত ব্যবসায়ী).
শক্ত২ *a.* hard, not soft; strong; stiff, obdurate; durable, tight; firm, steady; stubborn; severe, rigorous; strict; rigid; strenuous; niggardly, stingy (খরচের বেলায় সে শক্ত) ; harsh (শক্ত কথা) ; excruciating (শক্ত ব্যথা) ; difficult. **শক্ত ঘানি** (fig.) a very hard taskmaster; (fig.) a hard nut to crack; a very obdurate man. **শক্ত পাল্লায় পড়া** to have to deal with a person who is more than one's match, to catch a tartar. **শক্তের ভক্ত নরমের যম** (fig.) one who flatters a strong opponent but tyrannizes over a weak one, a jackal in Brobdingang playing the lion in Lilliput.
শক্তি *n.* power; strength, might; force; vigour; capacity; capability; potency (as of homoeopathic medicines); (phys.) energy; a state influential in international affairs, a power; (Hindu. myth.) the female principle taking part in the work of creation, Sakti, Shakti, a female deity; Goddess Durga (দুর্গা) ; an ancient missile. **~ক্ষয়** *n.* loss of power or strength or energy; (of an army) loss of men. **~ধর** *a.* powerful, strong. **শক্তি প্রয়োগ করা** *v.* to apply force. **~বর্গ** *n. pl.* states influential in international affairs or taking part in a war, powers. **~মত্তা, ~শালিতা** *n.* powerfulness, strength; forcefulness; possession of full vigour. **~মান, ~শালী** *a.* powerful, strong; forceful; vigorous; nervous (শক্তিশালী গদ্য). *fem.* **~মতী, ~শালিনী** । **~শেল** *n.* a dreadful or deadly mythological missile. **~সঞ্চয়** *n.* accumulation of strength or power; accumulation or preservation of energy. **শক্তি সঞ্চার করা** *v.* to infuse strength in; to invigorate; to energize. **~সামর্থ্য** *n.* power and capabilities. **~সাম্য** *n.* balance of power. **~হীন** *a.* powerless; weak; impotent. *fem.* **~হীনা** । **~হীনতা** *n.* powerlessness; weakness; impotence.
শক্তু *n.* a kind of farina made by grinding pulses, pulse-meal.
শক্য *a.* capable of being done. **~তা** *n.* practicability, feasibility; capability.
শক্র *n.* Indra (ইন্দ্র) the king of gods.
শখ *n.* a capricious inclination or liking;

a fancy; a hobby; a pursuit for amusement (শখের চাকরি) ; one's own accord or choice. **শখ করা** *v.* to incline to or choose or pursue capriciously or for amusement; to undertake or invite or choose voluntarily (শখ করে বিপদ ডাকা).

শঙ্কর *n.* Shiva (শিব) ; a species of sea-fish. *fem.* **শঙ্করী** Goddess Durga (দুর্গা).

শঙ্কা *n.* fear, dread, terror; alarm; misgiving; perturbation. **শঙ্কা করা** *v.* to fear, to apprehend; to have a misgiving. **~কুল** *a.* perturbed; full of misgiving; greatly frightened. *fem.* **~কুলা** । **~ন্বিত** same as **শঙ্কিত** । *fem.* **~ন্বিতা** । **~শূন্য** *a.* fearless; free from misgivings. **~হর, ~হরণ** *a.* one who or that which expels fear or misgiving. *fem.* **~হরা** । **~হীন** same as **~শূন্য** । *fem.* **~হীনা** ।

শঙ্কিত *a.* frightened, alarmed; afraid; seized with a misgiving; perturbed; fearful, timorous.

শঙ্কু *n.* a long pin of wood or metal; a probe; a prod; a skewer; a wedge; a peg, a stake; a gnomon; (chiefly in conics) a cone.

শঙ্খ *n.* the conch; a conchshell (esp. one that is sounded by blowing); a conchbangle. □ *n.* & *a.* billion (100,000,0000,000). **~চক্রগদাপদ্মধারী** *a.* carrying a conch-shell, a discus, a mace and a lotus. □ *n.* an appellation of God Narayana. **~চিল** *n.* a species of white-breasted kite. **~চূড়** *n.* the king-cobra. **~চূর্ণ** *n.* conchshell powder. **~চূর্ণী** see **শঙ্খিনী** । **~ধ্বনি, ~নাদ** *n.* the sound of blowing a conchshell. **~ধ্বনি করা, ~নাদ করা** *v.* to blow a conchshell. **~বণিক** *n.* a dealer and worker in articles of conchshells. **~বলয়** *n.* a bangle for the wrist made of conchshell. **~বিষ** *n.* white arsenic, ratsbane. **শঙ্খিনী** *n.* a woman of the third of four sexual categories; the evil spirit of a woman who has died when her husband is still alive, a female ghoul (also **শঙ্খচূর্ণী**).

শচি, শচী *n.* the wife of Indra (ইন্দ্র) the king of gods.

শজনে *n.* a kitchen plant, the horse-raddish. **~খাড়া** *n.* the edible stem or stalk of this plant.

শজারু *n.* the porcupine.

শজিনা for. var. of **শজনে** ।

শটকা, শটকান, শটকে variants of **সটকা, সটকান** and **শতকিয়া** respectively.

শটন *n.* rotting, decomposition, putrefaction.

শটি, শটী *n.* zedoary. **শটি ফুড** *n.* pulverized zedoary taken as food.

শঠ *a.* deceitful; swindling; knavish; sly; crooked. □ *n.* a knave, a crook. **~তা, শঠতাচরণ** *n.* deceit; swindling; knavery, chicanery; false play; sharp practice; slyness; crookedness. **শঠতা করা** *v.* to chicane, to deceive, to play false. **শঠে শাঠ্যং** an eye for an eye; a blow for a blow.

শণ *n.* hemp (plant or fibre); flax (plant or fibre). **শণে তৈরি** *a.* hempen; flaxen. **শণের নুড়ি** (lit.) a sheaf of fibres of flax; (fig.) grey hair.

শত *n.* & *a.* hundred. □ *a.* many or innumerable. **প্রতি শত** per cent. **শতক** *a.* having a number of hundreds; hundred. □ *n.* a hundred; an aggregate of one hundred similar things (সদ্ভাবশতক) ; a century. **~করা** *a.* & *adv.* per cent. **শতকরা হার, শতকরা হিসাব** percentage. **~কিয়া** *n.* a table of numbers up to 100. **~কোটি** *n.* & *a.* hundred crore. □ *a.* countless, innumerable. **~খণ্ড** *n.* a hundred pieces. □ *a.* reduced or torn to hundred pieces; reduced or torn to pieces; tattered. **~গুণ** *n.* a hundred times. □ *a.* hundred times of; a hundred times. □ *adv.* to or by hundred times; a hundred times; many or countless times, in or to a great degree or extent, far. **~গুণে** *adv.* same as **~গুণ** (*adv.*). **~গ্রন্থি** *a.* patched at hundred places; tattered. **~ঘ্নী** *n.* a mythological missile which could kill a hundred persons at one stroke. **~চ্ছিন্ন** *a.* torn at hundred places; tattered. **~তম** *a.* hundredth. *fem.* **~তমী** । **~দল** *n.* a hundred-petalled or many-petalled object; the lotus. **~দ্রু** *n.* the river Sutlej. **~ধা** *adv.* in or to a hundred divisions; a hundred times as much; hundredfold; in or to numerous divisions. **~ধার** *a.* having a hundred ends or edges or streams. **~ধারে** *adv.* in hundred streams, in innumerable streams. **~পদী** *n.* the centipede; the scorpion; the earwig. **~বর্ষজীবী** same as **শতায়ু**। **~বার্ষিক** *a.* centennial. **শতবার্ষিক উৎসব** the centenary. **~ভিষা** *n.* the twenty-fourth of the twenty-seven stars according to Hindu astronomy. **~মারী** *n.* (sarcas.) a bad physician who has killed a hundred patients, a charlatan, a quacksalver, a quack. **~মুখ** *a.* having one hundred mouths or outlets; (fig.) voluble, glib. **~মুখী** *n.* (hum.) a besom. **~মুখে** *adv.* glibly; in multifarious ways. **~মূলী** *n.* asparagus. **~রূপা** *a.* having many colours or shapes. **~শ** *adv.* by hundreds; hundredfold; hundred times over; over and over again. **~সহস্র** *n.* & *a.* hundred thousand. □ *a.* many, innumerable.

শতরঞ্জ, শতরঞ্চ *n.* chess.

শতরঞ্জি, শতরঞ্চি *n.* a durrie, a carpet.

শতাংশ *n.* one hundred parts; (pop.) one hundredth part.

শতাব্দ, শতাব্দী *n.* a century.

শতায়ু *a.* living for a hundred years. **শতায়ু ব্যক্তি** *a.* centenarian.

শতেক *a.* one hundred; many hundreds; many, innumerable; nearly or approximately a hundred. **~খোয়ারি** *n. fem.* (in vulgar reviling) a cursed woman who has seen the death of a hundred near ones.

শত্রু, (corrup.) **শত্তুর** *n.* an enemy, an adversary, a foe; an opponent. **শত্রুর মুখে ছাই** woe unto my enemies. **~ঘ্ন** *a.* of one who kills one's enemies. □ *n.* the youngest brother of Rama (রাম). **~জয়ী, ~জিৎ, ~প্তয়ী** *a.* victorious over enemies. **~তা** *n.* enmity, hostility, antagonism, animosity. **শত্রুতাচরণ** *n.* hostile conduct, animosity. **শত্রুতাচরণ করা** *v.* to be hostile to, to behave hostilely with. **~পক্ষ** *n.* the enemy party, the opponent. **~মিত্রভেদ** *n.* discrimination between one's enemies and friends. **~সংকুল** *a.* full of enemies.

শনশন *int.* expressing: the noise caused by the speedy flight of the wind, arrow etc.

শনাক্ত *n.* identification. **শনাক্ত করা** *v.* to identify.

শনি *n.* (myth.) a deity who is the son of the sun-god; the Saturn; Saturday (usu. **শনিবার**) ; (fig.) one who ruins utterly. **শনির দশা** (astrol.) the influence of Saturn; (fig.) the state of utter distress or ruin. **শনির দৃষ্টি** (astrol.) the aspect of Saturn; (fig.) state of utter distress or ruin. **~বলয়** *n.* the ring of Saturn.

শনৈঃ, (pop.) **শনৈ** *adv.* gradually, by and by, little by little; slowly. **শনৈঃ শনৈঃ** same as **শনৈঃ**।

শনৈশ্চর *n.* (myth.) a deity who is the son of the sun-god; Saturn.

শপ *n.* a finely woven large mat.

শপথ *n.* an oath, a swearing; a vow; a promise. **শপথ করা** *v.* to take an oath, to swear; to vow; to promise. **শপথ করানো** *v.* to cause to take an oath, to cause to swear or vow or promise. **শপথ করে, ~পূর্বক** *adv.* on oath, with an oath. **~পত্র** *n.* an affidavit. **~প্রমাণক** *n.* a Commissioner of affidavits.

শপাং, শপাৎ *int.* expressing: the noise of a quick and forceful stroke as of a whip; the swishing noise.

শপাশপ *int.* expressing: repeated **শপাৎ** sound; the noise of gulping any thin food greedily and quickly.

শফরী alt. spell. of **সফরী**।

শব, শবদেহ *n.* a dead body, a corpse. **শবদাহ, শবদাহন** *n.* cremation. **শবদাহ করা** *v.* to burn a dead body, to cremate. **শবদাহক** *n.* one who cremates, a cremator. **শবদাহনচুল্লি** *n.* a cremator; an incinerator. **শবদাহস্থান** *n.* a crematorium. **শবপরীক্ষা** *n.* post-mortem; autopsy. **শবপরীক্ষা করা** *v.* to make a post-mortem of, to autopsy. **শবব্যবচ্ছেদ করা** *v.* to dissect a dead body. **শবযাত্রা** *n.* a funeral procession. **শবযান** *n.* a bier. **শবসৎকার** *n.* obsequies, funeral rites; cremation. **শবসৎকার করা** *v.* to perform the obsequies of; to cremate. **শবসাধনা** *n.* a form of mystical rite or religious meditation performed by sitting upon a dead body in a crematorium usu. on a new-moon night; (fig.) a dreadful endeavour to achieve something. **শবাকার** *a.* corpse-like; looking like a corpse. **শবাগার** *n.* a morgue. **শবাচ্ছাদন-বস্ত্র** *n.* shroud; a winding-sheet; dead-clothes. **শবাধার** *n.* a bier. **শবানুগমন করা** *v.* to follow a corpse to the funeral place. **শবানুগামী, শবানুযাত্রী** *n.* one who follows a corpse to the funeral place, a mourner. **শবাসন** *n.* a posture of yogic exercise in which one lies still with the face up. **শবাসনা** *a. fem.* mounted upon a corpse. □ *n.* Goddess Kali (কালী).

শবর *n.* an ancient non-Aryan hunting community of India; a member of this community; a hunter. *fem.* **শবরী** ।

শবল *a.* dappled, variegated; brindled. *fem.* **শবলা, শবলী** ।

শবেবরাত *n.* a Muslim festival.

শব্দ *n.* a sound; a noise; a cry or call (পাখির শব্দ, কুকুরের শব্দ) ; a word. **শব্দ করা** *v.* to make a sound or noise; to cry or call. **~কর, ~কারী** *a.* making a sound or noise; crying or calling. **~কোষ** *n.* a lexicon; a dictionary. **~তত্ত্ব** *n.* philology. **~তরঙ্গ** *n.* a sound-wave. **~তাত্ত্বিক** *a.* philological. □ *n.* a philologist. **~দ্বৈত** *n.* reduplication of words. **~প্রকরণ** *n.* orthography. **~বহ** *a.* conveying sounds or sound-waves. **~বিন্যাস** *n.* arrangement of words; (gr.) syntax. **~বেধী** var. of **~ভেদী** । **~ব্রহ্ম** *n.* the Supreme Being consisting of sound only (cp. Logos); the Vedas. **~ভাণ্ডার** *n.* the treasure of words; the total corpus of words of a language. **~ভেদী** *a.* capable of hitting the target by merely hearing the sound made by it. **~যোজনা** *n.* adding or supplementing words. **~ময়** *a.* full of sound; noisy; word. **~শক্তি** *n.* different imports of a word; the capacity of words for conveying significance, power of words. **~শাস্ত্র** *n.* the science of words; grammar; philology; branches of learning collectively. **~হীন** *a.* soundless; noiseless; speechless; silent. **শব্দাতীত** *a.* beyond words; not expressible in words. **শব্দায়মান** *a.* in the state of making sounds, sounding; resounding. **শব্দার্থ** *n.* the meaning of a word, a word-meaning. **শব্দালংকার** *n.* any one of the figures of speech based on sound, such as, alliteration, onomatopoeia etc. **শব্দিত** *a.* sounded; filled with sound; resounded.

শম *n.* cessation, desistance; alleviation, mitigation; mental (and also sensual) restraint or calm; subsidence or conquest of desire.

শমন[১] alt. spell. of **সমন** ।

শমন[২] *n.* Yama (যম) the god of death; death. **~দ্বার** *n.* death's door. **~ভবন, ~সদন** *n.* the abode of death; the Hades; death's door. **শমনসদনে যাওয়া** *v.* to die. **শমনসদনে প্রেরণ করা** *v.* to kill; to send (one) to one's death.

শমি *n.* a kind of tree the *Acacia suma.*

শমিত *a.* allayed; subsided; repressed, restrained; calmed; quelled.

শমী alt. spell. of **শমি** ।

শমীধান্য *n.* any leguminous grain, pulse, bean etc.

শম্বর *n.* a kind of antelope with branched horns; a mythological demon. **শম্বরারি** *n.* the enemy or slayer of Shambar (শম্বর) the demon; Madana (মদন) the Hindu love-god.

শম্বুক, শম্বূক *n.* the snail. **~গতি** *n.* snail-like pace or movement; (fig.) procrastination, sluggishness, slowness. □ *a.* snail-paced; snail-slow; sluggish, slow.

শম্ভু *n.* Shiva (শিব).

শয্যা *n.* a bed; bedding; a couch or cot. **শয্যা তোলা** *v.* to put up or put away a bed. **শয্যা পাতা** *v.* to make a bed. **শয্যা নেওয়া** *v.* to become bedridden; to lie down. **~কণ্টকী,** (loos.) **~কণ্টক** *n.* a malady in which one feels as if one's bed is a bed of thorns. **~গত** same as **~শায়ী** । **~চ্ছাদন, ~চ্ছাদনী** *n.* a bedspread, a coverlet, a bedcover; a bedsheet. **~পার্শ্ব** *n.* bedside. **~প্রান্ত** *n.* the end of a bed. **শয্যা রচনা করা** *v.* to make a bed. **~শায়ী** *a.* bedridden, bedfast; lying down. *fem.* **~শায়িনী** । **~সঙ্গী, ~সহচর** *n.* a bedfellow; a husband; a paramour (*fem.* **~সঙ্গিনী, ~সহচরী** a concubine, a paramour).

শয়তান *n.* Satan, the Devil; a very wicked person, a rogue, a devil; (in endearment) a naughty fellow. **শয়তানি**[1] *n.* extreme wickedness, roguery, devilishness, devilry; (in endearment) mischievousness. **শয়তানি**[2] *n. fem.* of **শয়তান**। **শয়তানি করা** *v.* to do damage or harm to, to play the devil (with). □ Satanic; devilish; (in endearment) mischievous.

শয়ন *n.* lying down; sleep; a bed. **শয়ন করা** *v.* to lie down; to go to sleep; to sleep. **~কক্ষ, ~গৃহ, ~মন্দির, শয়নাগার** *n.* a bedroom, a bedchamber. **~কাল** *n.* bedtime.

শয়ান, শয়িত *a.* lying down; lying at length, (loos.) prostrate; sleeping, asleep. *fem.* **শয়ানা, শয়িতা**। **শয়ানরেখা** *n.* (bot.) a horizontal line.

শর *n.* an arrow, a shaft, a dart; a reed. **~ক্ষেপ** বা **~ক্ষেপণ** বা **~নিক্ষেপ করা** *v.* to shoot an arrow. **~জাল** *n.* a meshy shower of arrows. **~বন** *n.* a reed-hedge. **~বর্ষণ** *n.* a shower of arrows. **~বর্ষণ করা** *v.* to shower arrows (upon). **~বিদ্ধ** *a.* pierced or hit with an arrow. **~বৃষ্টি** *n.* a shower of arrows. **~ব্য** *n.* a target for arrow-shooting; a target. **~শয্যা** *n.* a number of arrows pierced through one's body in such a manner as to form a makeshift bed above the ground. **~সন্ধান করা** *v.* to plant an arrow on one's bow; to shoot an arrow; to aim an arrow (at). **শরাঘাত** *n.* a stroke of an arrow; a wound caused by an arrow. **শরাঘাত করা** *v.* to strike or wound with an arrow. **শরাভ্যাস** *n.* a practice of archery. **শরাভ্যাস করা** *v.* to practise archery. **শরারোপণ করা** *v.* to plant an arrow on a bow. **শরাসন** *n.* a bow (for shooting arrows). **শরাহত** *a.* struck or wounded with an arrow.

শরচ্চন্দ্র *n.* the autumnal moon.

শরণ *n.* a shelter, a refuge; recourse; (rare) a resort, a retreat, a house; a shelterer; a protector. **শরণ নেওয়া** *v.* to take shelter; to come or go for a shelter or refuge; to have recourse to. **শরণাগত, শরণাপন্ন** *a.* one who has come for shelter. □ *n.* a refugee. *fem.* **শরণাগতা, শরণাপন্না**। **শরণার্থী** *a.* seeking shelter or refuge. □ *n.* a refugee. **শরণ্য** *a.* giving or capable of giving shelter or protection; worthy of being sheltered or protected.

শরৎ, শরৎকাল *n.* autumn. **শরৎকালীন** *a.* autumnal.

শরদ same as **সরোদ**।

শরদিন্দু *n.* the autumnal moon. **~নিভাননা** *a. fem.* having a face resembling the autumnal moon (in brightness and beauty).

শরবত *n.* a sweet drink, a beverage, a cordial, sharbat.

শরবতি *n.* a bigger variety of lemon.

শরভ *n.* a kind of deer or antelope; a mythological octopod stronger even than the lion; a young elephant; a kind of corn-pest; the locust; the grasshopper.

শরম *n.* shame; bashfulness; coyness, modesty. **শরম করা, শরম লাগা** *v.* to feel or think shame; to be ashamed; to be abashed.

শরা *n.* a shallow earthen plate.

শরাব *n.* wine.

শরিক *n.* a joint-owner; a coparcener; a sharer, a partner; an associate. **শরিকান, শরিকানা** *n.* share of a joint owner or partner; a share; a part; (loos.) joint-ownership, coparcenery, partnership. **শরিকানি, শরিকি** *a.* jointly owned, coparcenery. **শরিকি সংঘর্ষ** *n.* strife or quarrel among partners.

শরিফ *a.* magnanimous, highminded, noble (শরিফ আদমি); holy, sacred (কোরানশরিফ, মক্কাশরিফ).

শরিয়ত *n.* the Islamic scripture or law.

শরীর *n.* the body; the physique; **~গত** *a.* lying within the body; of the body; bodily, physical. **~গ্রন্থি** *n.* a bone-joint. **~জ** *a.* produced or emerged from the body; (loos.) lying within the body (শরীরজ ব্যাধি); (loos.) of the body (শরীরজ ব্যাপার); bodily; physical. **শরীর ধারণ করা** *v.* to assume a body or form or shape; to take one's birth in the world. **~পাত** *n.* impairment or loss of health; death. **শরীরপাত করা** *v.* to impair one's health; to sacrifice one's life, to die. ~স্থ *a.* lying within the body; bodily, physical. **শরীরী** *a.* having a body; embodied; corporeal. *fem.* **শরীরিণী**।

শর্করা *n.* sugar; gravel, grit, rubble; (med.) concretion, calculus. **~বৎ** *a.* granular; gravelly, gritty; sugary. **~মিশ্রিত** *a.* sugared.

শর্ত *n.* a condition, a stipulation; an agreement. **শর্ত করা** *v.* to make an agreement or stipulation. **এই শর্তে** on this condition. **বিনা শর্তে** without condition, unconditionally. **~হীন** *a.* unconditional, unqualified. **শর্তাধীন** *a.* conditional.

শর্ব *n.* Shiva (শিব).

শর্বরী *n.* night.

শর্বাণী *n. fem.* the wife of Sharba (শর্ব) ; Goddess Durga (দুর্গা).

শর্মা *n.* a common surname of Brahmins (বিষ্ণুশর্মা) ; (in vaunts etc.) I, I the speaker, myself (এই শর্মা).

শলভ *n.* a kind of corn-pest; the grasshopper; the locust.

শলা, শলাকা *n.* a long pin or stick of metal or wood; (med.) a probe; a skewer.

শলি *n.* a dry measure of corn.

শল্ক *n.* a scale (esp. of fish); bark (of trees). **~বৎ** *a.* scaly.

শল্য *n.* a long pin or stick of metal or wood; (med.) a probe; a thorn; a fishbone; a sharp-pointed mythological missile; an arrow; an arrowhead, (fig.) cause of affliction or displeasure of the heart. **~চিকিৎসক** *n.* a surgeon. **~চিকিৎসা** *n.* surgery; a surgical operation. **~তন্ত্র**, **~বিদ্যা** *n.* surgery. **শল্যোদ্ধার করা** *v.* to extract a thorn, arrow etc. (from a body); (fig.) to remove a cause of affliction or displeasure from the heart.

শল্লকী *n.* the porcupine.

শশ, শশক *n.* the hare; the rabbit; the cony. **শশধর** *n.* the moon. **শশবিষাণ, শশশৃঙ্গ** *n.* (lit.) a hare's horn; an absurdity, a mare's nest. **শশব্যস্ত** *a.* frantically hurrying (esp. through fear). **শশব্যস্তে** *adv.* hurrying frantically.

শশা *n.* the cucumber.

শশাঙ্ক *n.* the lunar crescent, a digit of the moon. **~শেখর** same as **শশীভূষণ**।

শশী *n.* the moon.

শশীকর *n.* moonbeam; moonlight, moonshine.

শশীকলা *n.* a digit of the moon.

শশীপ্রভা *n.* moonlight, moonbeam.

শশীভূষণ *n.* one who has the moon as an ornament; Shiva (শিব).

শশীমুখী *n. fem.* one who has a face resembling the moon (in beauty).

শশীশেখর same as **শশীভূষণ**।

শষ্প *n.* young or tender grass. **~শয্যা** *n.* bed of grass. **শষ্পাবৃত** *a.* covered with tender grass.

শসা alt. spell. of **শশা**।

শস্তা alt. spell. of **সস্তা**।

শস্ত্র *n.* a weapon which is to be wielded by the hand and not thrown (e.g. a sword); a weapon; an iron tool for handicrafts; a surgical instrument or knife. **~চিকিৎসক** *n.* a surgeon. **~চিকিৎসা** *n.* surgery. **~জীবী** same as **শস্ত্রাজীব**। **~ত্যাগ** *n.* act of laying down or relinquishing one's arms. **~ধর, ~ধারী, ~পাণি** *a.* bearing arms, armed. **~বিদ্যা** *n.* the art and science of using weapons. **শস্ত্রাগার** *n.* an armoury; an arsenal. **শস্ত্রাজীব** *a.* earning one's livelihood as a professional soldier. □ *n.* a soldier.

শস্প alt. spell. of **শষ্প**।

শস্য *n.* corn, grain; (loos.) cereals; crop; harvest; kernel (of fruits), pulp; (bot.) albumen. **~ক্ষেত্র** *n.* a corn-field. **শস্য পেষণ করা** *v.* to grind corn; to husk. **শস্যপেষণ-যন্ত্র** *n.* a corn-mill; a husking-machine. **~ভাণ্ডার** *n.* a granary. **~ভোজী** *a.* feeding on corn, graminivorous; (of cornpests) destroying crop by eating it up. **~মঞ্জরি** *n.* a corn-stalk. **~ল** *a.* abounding in corn; (of fruits) full of kernel, pulpy; (bot.) albuminous. **~শালী** *a.* abounding in corn. *fem.* **~শালিনী**। **~শ্যামল** *a.* green with plentiful corn. *fem.* **~শ্যামলা**। **শস্য সংগ্রহ করা** *v.* to harvest; to procure corn esp. cereals. **শস্যসংগ্রহের কাল** harvest time, harvest. **শস্যাগার** *n.* a granary; a grange. **শস্যাধার** *n.* a corn-bin.

শহর *n.* a town; a city. **~কোতোয়াল** *n.* the

chief of city police. ~তলি *n.* outskirts of a town or city, a suburb. ~স্থ *a.* of or living in a town or city; urban.

শহিদ *n.* a martyr. **শহিদ হওয়া** *v.* to be martyred. ~ত্ব *n.* martyrdom.

শহুরে *a.* of or living in a town or city, urban; townish; cockney. **শহুরে জীবন** town-life, urbanity. **শহুরে হাওয়া** (usu. dero.) influence of a town or city, urbanity. ~পনা *n.* (dero.) urbanity, townishness; affected cockneyish behaviour or speech.

শা pop. contr. of **শাহ্**।

শাংকর alt. spell. of **শাঙ্কর**।

শাঁ, শাঁই *int.* expressing: a fizzing or swishing or hissing sound. **শাঁ-শাঁ, শাঁই-শাঁই** *int.* expressing: repetition of this sound; great speed.

শাঁখ, শাঁক *n.* the conch; a conchshell, a conch. **শাঁখ বাজানো** *v.* to blow a conchshell or a conch. **শাঁখের করাত** a saw for cutting conchshells (this saw cuts bothways), a conch-cutter; (fig.) any object the presence and absence of which are equally painful, something which cuts bothways; a dilemma. **শাঁক আলু, শাঁখ-আলু, শাঁকালু, শাঁখালু** *n.* a white esculent fruit shaped almost like a conchshell. **শাঁকচুন্নি, শাঁকচুর্ণী** corruptions of **শঙ্খচূর্ণী**। **শাঁখা** *n.* a bangle for the wrist made of conchshell, a conch-bangle. **শাঁখারি** *n.* a Hindu caste working and dealing in articles made of conchshells; a member of this caste; a worker or dealer in articles of conchshells.

শাঁস *n.* kernel, pulp; pith; core; marrow; (fig.) solid worth, substance (মগজে শাঁস নেই) ; (fig.) wealth, riches (লোকটার শাঁস ফুরিয়েছে). **শাঁসালো** *a.* abounding in kernel, pulpy, pithy; marrowy; (fig.) full of solid worth, substantial; (fig.) wealthy.

শাক *n.* any edible herb or creeper, spinach, spinage. **শাক দিয়ে মাছ ঢাকা** (fig.) a ludicrous and futile attempt at concealing a detestable offence. ~ভাত same as **শাকান্ন**। ~পাতা *n. pl.* edible herbs, creepers and leaves collectively; (fig.) extremely poor food. ~সবজি *n.* edible herbs, creepers, fruits and roots collectively; vegetables, greens. ~সবজির খেত a kitchen garden. **শাকান্ন** *n.* (lit.) a dish of only rice and spinach; (fig.) very poor or simple food. **শাকাহারী** *n.* a person subsisting on lean vegetarian diet.

শাকুন *a.* of birds, avian. ~বিৎ *n.* an augur. ~বিদ্যা *n.* augury. **শাকুনিক** *n.* a fowler; an augur.

শাক্ত *a.* devoted to or worshipping Sakti or the female principle of creation. □ *n.* a worshipper of Sakti, a Sakta, a Shakta. ~পদাবলি *n.* (*pl.*) poems or lyric poems in adoration of Sakti, the Goddess of creation or Goddess Kali.

শাক্য *n.* a Kshatriya clan. ~মুনি, ~সিংহ *n.* Gautama Buddha.

শাখা *n.* a branch of a tree, a bough; a ramus (*pl.* rami); a section, a part, a subordinate division, a branch; an offshoot. ~কন্টক *n.* a thorn. ~কলম *n.* (bot.) a cutting. ~চ্যুত *a.* fallen or detached from a branch or bough. ~নদী *n.* a tributary. **শাখান্তরাল** *n.* a position screened off by the branches of a tree. ~প্রশাখা *n. pl.* branches and twigs (of a tree); rami and ramuli; ramifications, sections and sub-sections; offshoots large and small. ~বিন্যাস *n.* (bot.) branching, ramification. ~মৃগ *n.* a ramal animal; the monkey; the ape.

শাখী *a.* having branches, branched, ramose. □ *n.* a tree.

শাগরেদ *n.* a disciple, a pupil; a trainee; a follower; a novice. **শাগরেদি** *n.* discipleship, pupilage, noviciate, novitiate, novicehood. **শাগরেদি করা** *v.* to act as a disciple or pupil or trainee or follower or novice.

শাঙন poet. corrup. of **শ্রাবণ**।

শাঙ্কর *a.* of Shankar (শঙ্কর) or Shiva (শিব) ; made or propounded by Shankaracharya (শাঙ্কর ভাষ্য).

শাজাদা, শাজাদি coll. corruptions of **শাহ্জাদা** and **শাহ্জাদি** (see **শাহ্**).

শাটিন *n.* satin.

শাঠ্য same as **শঠতা** (see **শঠ**).

শাড়ি *n.* an Indian woman's loincloth, the sari.

শাণ *n.* a whetstone; a grindstone; (also শাণ-পাথর) ; whetting; edge, sharpness; **শাণ দেওয়া** *v.* to whet, to sharpen; (fig.) to stimulate; (fig.) to make poignant. **~ওয়ালা** *n.* a whetter, a sharpener. **~পাথর** *n.* a whetstone. **শাণিত** *a.* whetted, sharpened (শাণিত তরবারি) ; sharp; (fig.) stimulated (শাণিত ক্ষুধা) ; (fig.) poignant, cutting to the quick (শাণিত তিরস্কার).

শাতন *n.* act of cutting off. **শাতন করা** *v.* to cut off; to clip (পক্ষশাতন করা).

শাদি *n.* (Mus.) marriage. **শাদি করা** *v.* to marry, to wed.

শান[১] alt. spell. of **শাণ**।

শান[২] *n.* a paved or cemented floor. **শান বাঁধানো** *v.* to pave.

শানা, শানানো[১] *v.* to be satisfied or gratified (তার অল্পে শানায় না).

শানানো[২] *v.* to whet, to sharpen; (fig.) to stimulate; (fig.) to make poignant.

শান্ত *a.* peaceful, quiet, tranquil; satisfied, gratified; appeased, pacified, calmed, quietened; composed; allayed; calm; gentle, mild. **শান্ত করা** *v.* to satisfy; to gratify; to appease, to pacify, to calm; to quieten. **~চিত্ত, ~চেতা** *a.* having a calm or quiet disposition; mild-tempered. **~দান্ত** *a.* mild and temperate. **~প্রকৃতি** *a.* gentle-natured; having a calm disposition. **~বলয়** *n.* (geog.) a belt or region of calms. **~ভাব** *n.* mental calm or tranquillity. **~মূর্তি** *a.* having a tranquil appearance. **~রস** *n.* (rhet.) the tranquil or calm sentiment. **~শিষ্ট** *a.* gentle and polite. **~স্বভাব** same as **~প্রকৃতি**।

শান্তি *n.* peace, tranquillity, calm, quietude; removal (আপদশান্তি) ; control (ক্রোধের শান্তি) ; satisfaction, gratification (ক্ষুধার শান্তি) ; pacification, appeasement; alleviation; freedom from disturbances, peace; termination or cessation (যুদ্ধশান্তি) ; termination of hostility or war; weal, welfare, wellbeing. **~জল** *n.* holy sacrificial water sprinkled upon votaries to ward off evils. **~নিকেতন** *n.* an abode of peace. **~পুরি** *a.* produced at Shantipur in Bengal. □ *n.* a very fine handloom cloth produced at Shantipur. **~পুরে** *a.* of Shantipur in Bengal; produced at Shantipur; current at or used at Shantipur (শান্তিপুরে বুলি); born or living at Shantipur. **~পূর্ণ** *a.* peaceful; calm; tranquil; quiet. **~প্রিয়** *a.* peace-loving. **~বিধায়ক** *a.* pacifying, pacifactory; peace-making. □ *n.* a peace-maker. **~ভঙ্গ** *n.* breach of peace. **~ভঙ্গ করা** *v.* to disturb the peace of; to create disturbance; to disturb. **~ভঙ্গকারী** *a.* disturbing the peace; creating disturbances; disturbing. *fem.* **~ভঙ্গকারিণী**। **~ময়** same as **~পূর্ণ**। *fem.* **~ময়ী**। **~রক্ষক** *n.* a defender of the peace; a policeman. **শান্তিরক্ষা করা** *v.* to maintain peace. **শান্তি স্থাপন করা** *v.* to make peace (with); to bring to a peaceful state. **~স্বস্ত্যয়ন** *n.* religious worship or service performed to ward off evils.

শাপ *n.* a curse, a malison, imprecation. **শাপ দেওয়া** *v.* to curse, to imprecate. **~গ্রস্ত** *a.* lying under a curse; cursed, accursed. *fem.* **~গ্রস্তা**। **~ভ্রষ্ট** *a.* fallen or expelled (esp. from heaven) by a curse. *fem.* **~ভ্রষ্টা**। **~মুক্ত** *a.* freed from a curse. **~মুক্তি, ~মোচন** *n.* release from a curse. **শাপমোচন করা** *v.* to release from a curse, to set free from a curse. **~শাপান্ত** *n.* (rare) a curse and release from it; (pop.) severe and repeated cursing. **শাপা** same as **শাপ দেওয়া**। **শাপান্ত** *n.* termination of a curse; release from a curse; (loos.) a spell of severe cursing.

শাবক, শাব *n.* a young of a bird or beast. **কুক্কুটশাবক** *n.* a chicken, a chick, a cockerel. **কুকুরশাবক** *n.* a puppy. **নেকড়েশাবক** *n.* a whelp of a wolf, a wolf-cub. **মেষশাবক** *n.* a lamb.

শাবল *n.* a crowbar.

শাবান *n.* the eighth month of the Muslim calendar.

শাবাশ *int.* bravo, well done, excellent.

শাব্দ *a.* relating to sounds or words; acoustic; phonetical; philological.

শাব্দিক *a.* same as **শাব্দ** । □ *n.* one versed in acoustics; a phonetician; a philologist; a grammarian; a lexicographer.

শামলা[1] *a.* (ori. *fem.*) of greenish black colour or complexion.

শামলা[2] *n.* a kind of official turban (উকিলের শামলা).

শামা[1] *n.* a lamp. **~দান** *n.* a portable lampstand, a lampad.

শামা[2], শামি *n.* an iron ferrule or covering (of a mace, stick etc.).

শামিকাবাব *n.* a kind of dry meat-chip.

শামিয়ানা *n.* an awning, a canopy; a canopied place.

শামিল *a.* equivalent or similar (to); almost the same (as) (মরার শামিল) ; participating or included (in) (আন্দোলনে শামিল).

শামুক *n.* the snail. **শামুক-চুন** *n.* shell-lime. **শামুকের খোলা** a shell of a snail.

শায়ক *n.* an arrow, a shaft, a dart.

শায়িত *a.* lying down; laid down; prostrate; lying or fallen flat; knocked down. *fem.* **শায়িতা** ।

শায়িনী *fem.* of **শায়ী** ।

শায়ী *a.* (used as a *sfx.*) lying or resting (on) (শয্যাশায়ী, ভূতলশায়ী) ; fallen (in) (রণশায়ী).

শায়ের *n.* a short lyric poem (usu. composed in Urdu or Hindi), a Sayer.

শায়েস্তা *a.* punished; subdued; chastened; corrected, rectified. **শায়েস্তা করা** *v.* to punish; to subdue; to chasten; to correct, to rectify.

শারঙ্গা *n.* a stringed musical instrument akin to a violin. **শারঙ্গী** *n.* the aforesaid instrument; one who plays on this instrument.

শারদ, শারদীয় *a.* autumnal. *fem.* **শারদী, শারদীয়া** । **শারদা** *n.* Goddess Durga (দুর্গা) ; Goddess Saraswati (সরস্বতী) ; a kind of vina.

শারি, শারিকা, শারী *n. fem.* the female **শালিক** ; (pop.) the female **শুক** ; a gaming die.

শারীর, শারীরিক *a.* bodily, physical; physiological; anatomical; corporal; **শারীরিক অবস্থা** state of the body, health. **শারীরিক দণ্ড বা শাস্তি** corporal punishment. **শারীরিক পরিশ্রম** physical labour. **শারীরতত্ত্ব, শারীরবিধান, শারীরবৃত্ত, শারীরবৃত্তি** *n.* physiology. **শারীরস্থান** *n.* anatomy.

শার্ঙ্গ *a.* of horns; made of horn. □ *n.* a (shooting) bow made of horn. **~ধর, ~পাণি, শার্ঙ্গী** *n.* one armed with a hornmade bow; Vishnu (বিষ্ণু).

শার্ট *n.* a shirt. **ফুল শার্ট** *n.* a long shirt, a shirt of usual length. **হাউই-শার্ট** *n.* a Hawaii shirt, a bush-shirt. **হাফ-শার্ট** *n.* a shirt of short length and usually with sleeves up to the elbows.

শার্দূল *n.* the tiger; (as a *sfx.*) an excellent or best specimen (নরশার্দূল). *fem.* **শার্দূলী** । **~বিক্রীড়িত** *n.* a Sanskrit poetical metre.

শার্শি, শার্সি pop. variants of **শাসি** ।

শাল[1] coll. corrrup. of **শালা[1]** ।

শাল[2] *n.* a shawl.

শাল[3] *n.* a large pike for impalement of criminals; (fig.) a heart-rending affliction or grief.

শাল[4] *n.* a large gregarious tree, the sal, the *Shorea robusta*; its timber; a large tubular river-fish.

শালগম *n.* turnip.

শালগ্রাম, শালগ্রাম-শিলা *n.* a black-geode worshipped as the symbol of Vishnu (বিষ্ণু).

শালতি *n.* a dugout made of the trunk of a sal tree.

শালনির্যাস *n.* resin.

শালপ্রাংশু *a.* as tall as a sal tree.

শালা[1] *n.* (used as a *sfx.*) a house, a building (অতিথিশালা), a room, a hall (রন্ধনশালা) ; an establishment (পাঠশালা) ; a shed, a construction (গো-শালা, অশ্বশালা) ; a workshop (কামারশালা) ; a store, a repertory (পশুশালা, রত্নশালা).

শালা[2] *n.* a brother or a cousin brother of one's wife, a brother-in-law; (in vul. familiarity) a fellow (cp. a jolly dog); (often) an epithet of abuse.

শালাজ, শালাবউ *n.* a wife of a brother-in-law, a sister-in-law.

শালি[1] *n.* the autumnal paddy (শালিধান) ।

শালি[2] *n. fem.* a sister or cousin sister of one's wife, a sister-in-law; (in vul. abuse) a woman (cp. a jolly bitch); often an epithet of abuse.

শালিক *n.* a kind of small yellow-beaked singing bird of the myna group, the house myna.

শালিধান্য, (coll.) **শালিধান** same as **শালি**[1] ।

-শালিনী *fem.* of **-শালী**[2] ।

শালী[1] rej. spell. of **শালি**[1] ।

-শালী[2] *a.* (used as a *sfx.*) possessing (বিভবশালী).

শালীন *a.* observant of the rules of decorum, decorous; decent; modest; polite, courteous. **~তা** *n.* decorum; decency; modesty; politeness, courtesy.

শালু *n.* a kind of red-coloured cotton fabric.

শালুক *n.* a stalk of the waterlily.

শাল্মলি, শাল্মলী *n.* the silk-cotton tree; a mythological island.

শাশুড়ি *n.* a mother-in-law; an aunt-in-law.

শাশ্বত *a.* eternal; everlasting, perpetual; immortal. *fem.* **শাশ্বতী** ।

শাসক *n.* a subduer; a ruler, a governor; an administrator (*fem.* administratrix); a controller, a repressor; one who enjoins; a discipliner, a chastiser, a chastener. **জেলা-শাসক** *n.* a district magistrate. **~মণ্ডলী** *n.* the governing body, the administrative body, the administration; the government. **~সম্প্রদায়** *n.* the ruling class.

শাসন *n.* subdual; rule; management (জমিদারি শাসন) ; government or administration (of a state); reign; control or repression (ইন্দ্রিয়শাসন) ; direction, dictation, enjoinment (শাস্ত্রের শাসন) ; an edict, a commandment (তাম্রশাসন), disciplining, chastisement, punishment (ছেলেকে শাসন) ; jurisdiction (শাসনাধীন). **শাসন করা** *v.* to subdue; to rule, to govern, to manage; to administer; to reign; to control or repress; to command; to discipline, to chastise, to chasten, to punish. **শাসনে আনা** *v.* to subdue; to subjugate; to bring under control; to bring into submission. **~কর্তা** same as **শাসক**। *fem.* **~কর্ত্রী**। **~কৃত্যক** *n.* administrative service. **~তন্ত্র** *n.* a form of government; constitution (of a state). **~তান্ত্রিক** *a.* relating to the form of government; constitutional. **~প্রণালী** *n.* a system of government. **~যন্ত্র** *n.* government machinery. **শাসনাধীন** *a.* under rule (of); governed (by); under jurisdiction (of); politically dependent (on another state), under domination (of). **শাসনিক** *a.* administrative; governmental; jurisdictional. **শাসনীয়** same as **শাস্য** ।

শাসানো *v.* to threaten. **শাসানি** *n.* threatening, a threat.

শাসি *n.* a window pane; a sash.

শাসিকা *fem.* of **শাসক** ।

শাসিত *a.* subdued; ruled, governed; managed; administered; controlled, repressed; disciplined, chastised, chastened, punished. **শাসিতা** *a. fem.* of **শাসিত** । □ *n.* an administrator; a teacher.

শাস্তা *n.* a ruler; a teacher, a preceptor; Gautama Buddha.

শাস্তি *n.* punishment; a sentence (ভুল শাস্তি) ; (fig.) severe affliction. **শাস্তি দেওয়া** *v.* to punish; to sentence; (fig.) to afflict. **শাস্তি পাওয়া** *v.* to be punished or sentenced; (fig.) to be afflicted. **~বিধান** *n.* infliction of punishment or penalty, administering punishment. **~ব্যবস্থা** *n.* punitive measures; provision for punishment. **~মূলক** *a.* punitive.

শাস্ত্র *n.* Hindu scriptures; any scripture; a treatise; an art or science. **~কার** *n.* an author of a Hindu scripture or any scripture or of a treatise. **~চর্চা করা** same as **শাস্ত্রানুশীলন করা** । **~জ্ঞ** *a.* versed in scriptures. **~জ্ঞান** *n.* scriptural knowledge. **~জ্ঞানী, ~দর্শী** same as **~জ্ঞ** । **~নিন্দা** *n.* denunciation of scriptures. **~নিষিদ্ধ** *a.* forbidden by scriptures; unscriptural. **~পারদর্শী** *a.* thoroughly versed in scriptures. **~বচন** *n.* a scriptural teaching; a gospel truth. **~বহির্ভূত** *a.* not contained in scriptures; unscriptural. **~বিদ** same as **~জ্ঞ** । **~বিধান, ~বিধি** *n.* a scriptural prescription or injunction; holy rite, a sacred ritual. **~বিরুদ্ধ** *a.* unscriptural. **~বিহিত** *a.* enjoined or prescribed by scriptures. **~ব্যাখ্যা** *n.* exposition or explanation of the teachings of scriptures. **~সংগত, ~সম্মত** same as **~বিহিত** ।

~সিদ্ধ *a.* confirmed by scriptures, lawful. শাস্ত্রানুমত, শাস্ত্রানুমোদিত same as শাস্ত্রবিহিত। শাস্ত্রানুযায়ী *a.* obedient to scriptures, scriptural. ☐ *adv.* same as শাস্ত্রানুসারে। শাস্ত্রানুশীলন *n.* study of scriptures. শাস্ত্রানুশীলন করা *v.* to study scriptures. শাস্ত্রানুসারে *adv.* in accordance with scriptures, obeying scriptures, scripturally. শাস্ত্রার্থ *n.* significance or (true) meaning of scriptural saying. শাস্ত্রালাপ *n.* scriptural discussion or talk. শাস্ত্রালাপ করা *v.* to discuss (or talk about) scriptures; (loos.) to discuss any technical subject. শাস্ত্রালোচনা *n.* discussion about or study of scriptures. শাস্ত্রালোচনা করা *v.* to discuss or study scriptures; (loos.) to discuss any technical subject. শাস্ত্রী *a.* versed in scriptures. ☐ *n* a title given to men versed in scriptures. শাস্ত্রীয় *a.* scriptural. শাস্ত্রীয় বচন a scriptural saying; a gospel truth. শাস্ত্রীয় সংগীত classical music. শাস্ত্রোক্ত *a.* sanctioned by the holy writ; mentioned in scriptures.

শাস্য *a.* governable; adiministrable; controllable; repressible; disciplinable; chastisable; punishable.

শাহ, শাহ্ *n.* the title of the king of Persia, the Shah; a (Muslim) king. ~জাদা *n.* (Mus.) a son of a king, a prince. ~জাদি *n. fem.* a daughter of a king, a princess.

শাহানশাহ্ *n.* (Mus.) a king of kings, an emperor; a great king.

শাহানা *n.* an Indian musical mode.

শাহি *a.* (Mus.) royal (শাহি বাগ).

শিউরানো coll. corrup. of শিহরানো।

শিউলি[1] pop. var. of শেফালি।

শিউলি[2] *n.* a man whose profession it is to incise the date-palm in order to obtain its juice.

শিং *n.* a horn. শিং নাড়া *v.* to wave one's horn threatening to butt or gore; (fig.) to become audaciously aggressive.

শিংশপা same as শিশু[1]।

শিক *n.* a thin metal rod; a window-bar (usu.) made of iron; a spit, a skewer.

শিককাবাব *n.* meat with spices roasted on a skewer.

শিকড় *n.* (bot.) root. শিকড় গাড়া *v.* to root, to strike root, to take root; (fig.) to be firmly established.

শিকনি *n.* nasal mucus. শিকনি ঝাড়া *v.* to blow one's nose. (তোমার) শিকনি পড়ছে (your) nose runs.

শিকল, (coll.) শিকলি *n.* a chain; fetters, shackles. শিকল আঁটা বা পরানো, শিকলে বাঁধা *v.* to chain, to enchain, to put in chains; to fetter, to shackle. শিকলের আংটা বা কড়া a link.

শিকা, (coll.) শিকে *n.* a reticulated bag made of strings or wires, kept hanging usually from the wall. শিকে ছেঁড়া *v.* (fig.) to gain by a lucky stroke, to win by a fluke. শিকেয় ওঠা *v.* (fig.) to be set aside, to be shelved. শিকেয় তোলা *v.* (fig.) to set aside, to shelve up.

শিকার *n.* hunting, venery; a hunted beast or bird, a prey; game. শিকার করা *v.* to hunt. শিকারে যাওয়া *v.* to go out hunting. শিকারি *n.* a hunter, a huntsman, a venerer. ☐ *a.* hunting. শিকারি কুকুর a hunting dog. শিকারি পশু বা পাখি a beast or bird of prey. পাখিশিকারি *n.* a fowler.

শিকে coll. var. of শিকা।

শিক্ষক *n.* a teacher; a tutor (*fem.* tutoress, tutress); a professor; a trainer, an instructor (*fem.* instructress); a preceptor (*fem.* preceptress). ~তা *n.* teachership; tutorage, tutorship; professorship; the profession of a teacher. শিক্ষকতা করা *v.* to work or act as a teacher, to teach. ~সমিতি *n.* a teachers' council.

শিক্ষণ *n.* act of learning, study; teaching or training; instruction. ~তত্ত্ব *n.* educational theory. শিক্ষণ-শিক্ষা *n.* teacher's training. শিক্ষণীয় *a.* to be learnt or taught.

শিক্ষয়িতা *n.* a teacher. *fem.* শিক্ষয়িত্রী।

শিক্ষা *n.* learning; study; practice; education; teaching, instruction; a precept; a moral; a lesson; training; (sarcas.) a bitter lesson, punishment. শিক্ষা করা *v.* to learn; to study; to practise. শিক্ষা দেওয়া *v.* to teach; to educate; to school; to instruct; to train; (sarcas.) to reprove or punish severely, to teach one a lesson. শিক্ষা পাওয়া *v.* to receive instruction or training or education; (sarcas.)

to receive reproof or punishment, to be taught a lesson. উচ্চশিক্ষা *n.* higher education. উচ্চমাধ্যমিকশিক্ষা higher secondary education. কলেজি শিক্ষা college education. কারিগরি শিক্ষা technical training. ~অধিকর্তা *n.* the Director of Public Instruction, the Director of Education. ~গুরু *n.* a teacher; a trainer, an instructor; a preceptor, a guru; an initiator. ~গ্রহণ করা *v.* to receive education or training or instruction. ~দাতা same as শিক্ষক। *fem.* ~দাত্রী। ~দান করা same as শিক্ষা দেওয়া। ~দীক্ষা *n.* secular and regular education and training; education and culture. ~ধিকার the Education Directorate. ~ধীন *a.* under training, apprenticed; receiving education; studying (under), being taught (by). ~নবিশ *n.* an apprentice; an understudy; a novice, a probationer. ~নবিশি *n.* apprenticeship; noviciate, novitiate. ~নবিশি করা *v.* to serve apprenticeship; to study under. ~পর্ষৎ *n.* an education board. ~পীঠ *n.* a seat of learning. ~প্রণালী *n.* a system or method of education or teaching or training. ~প্রদ *a.* educative; didactic; instructive. ~প্রাপ্ত *a.* trained; educated. ~বিভাগ *n.* the Education Department. ~বিস্তার *n.* spread of education. ~বিস্তার করা *v.* to spread education. ~ব্রতী *n.* an educationist; one who has dedicated his life to the cause of education. ~মন্ত্রক *n.* the Ministry of Education. ~মন্ত্রী *n.* the Minister of Education. ~মূলক *a.* educational. ~র্থী *a.* desirous of learning; seeking education or instruction or training. □ *n.* a learner; a student, a pupil; an apprentice, an understudy, a novice; a trainee. ~লাভ করা same as শিক্ষা পাওয়া। ~সংস্কার *n.* educational reforms. ~সচিব *n.* an education secretary. ~সমিতি *n.* a council of education. ~সম্বন্ধীয় *a.* educational.

শিক্ষিকা *fem.* of শিক্ষক।

শিক্ষিত *a.* educated; instructed; trained. *fem.* শিক্ষিতা। ~সম্প্রদায় *n.* the educated class; the intelligentsia.

শিখ *n.* Sikhs; a Sikh.

শিখণ্ড, শিখণ্ডক *n.* a peacock's tail; a tuft of hair on the head maintained uncut as by Brahmans. শিখণ্ডী *n.* the peacock; a character of the Mahabharata; (fig.) one from behind whose cover some misdeed is done.

শিখর *n.* top; apex, vertex; summit; crest; a mountain-peak, a peak.

শিখা[1] *n.* top, crest, summit; a tuft of hair on the head maintained uncut as by Brahmans; a flame; a beam (জ্যোতিঃশিখা).

শিখা[2] see শেখা।

শিখিনী *n.* the peahen.

শিখিপুচ্ছ *n.* a peacock's tail.

শিখী *n.* the peacock.

শিঙ alt. spell. of শিং।

শিঙা, শিঙ্গা *n.* a horn for blowing; a trumpet. শিঙা ফোঁকা *v.* (*sl.*) to die, (cp.) to kick the bucket, to give up the ghost.

শিঙাড়া *n.* a kind of stuffed snack shaped almost like a fruit of the water-chestnut.

শিঙার *n.* the dress or dressing of lovers going to meet.

শিঙি, শিঙ্গি *n.* a scaleless and slender fresh-water fish akin to the barbel.

শিঙ্গার var. of শিঙার।

শিঞ্জন, শিঞ্জিত[1] *n.* the sound of the dancer's anklets or similar things.

শিঞ্জিত[2] *a.* resounding (with); jingling (with).

শিঞ্জিনী *n.* an anklet that makes jingling noise (usu. by dancers).

শিটা, (corrup.) শিটে *n.* dregs, dross, feculence, sediment.

শিতি *n.* & *a.* white; black or blue. ~কণ্ঠ *n.* one with a blue-coloured neck; Shiva (শিব) ; the peacock.

শিথান *n.* the place or position at the head of a person lying; a pillow.

শিথিল same as শ্লথ। ~তা *n.* looseness, slackness; slowness; laxity, laziness; absence of earnestness. ~প্রযত্ন *a.* lacking in earnestness or carefulness in one's work or endeavour, negligently working.

শিন্নি coll. corrup. of শিরনি।

শিব *n.* good, weal, well-being; one of the

three principal Hindu gods, Shiva. □ *a.* good, beneficial; auspicious. **শিব গড়তে বাঁদর গড়া** (fig.) to do evil in one's attempt to do something good. **~চতুর্দশী** *n.* the fourteenth lunar day of the month of Phalgoon (ফাল্গুন) when Shiva is worshipped. **~জ্ঞান** *n.* the conception that all is good (যাত্রায় শিবজ্ঞান). **~ত্ব** *n.* the state of Shiva. **শিবত্বপ্রাপ্তি** *n.* death. **~নেত্র** *n.* the upturned eyes of Shiva; one with such eyes (eyes become so upturned on the eve of one's death). **~বাহন** *n.* the bull. **~রাত্রি** *n.* the night of **~চতুর্দশী**। **শিবরাত্রির সলতে** (fig.) the only son or the sole surviving descendant. **~লিঙ্গ** *n.* a phallic symbol of Shiva. **~লোক** *n.* the abode of Shiva.

শিবা *n.* the vixen; (loos.) the fox.

শিবানী *n.* Goddess Durga (দুর্গা) the wife of Shiva (শিব).

শিবালয় *n.* the abode of Shiva; a temple of Shiva (শিব).

শিবিকা *n.* a palanquine, a litter, a doolie, a sedan, a sedan-chair. **~রোহী** *a.* going in a palanquin or sedan. *fem.* **~রোহিণী**।

শিবির *n.* camp; a camp; a tent; encampment. **শিবির স্থাপন করা** *v.* to pitch a tent or tents; to encamp.

শিম *n.* the kidney-bean; the bean.

শিমুল *n.* the silk-cotton plant. **শিমুল তুলো** *n.* slik-cotton, kapok.

শিম্ব, শিম্বা, শিম্বি, শিম্বিকা *n.* the kidney-bean or its plant; the bean, the legume; a pod.

শিয়র *n.* the place or position at the head of a person lying; (fig.) imminence (শিয়রে শমন).

শিয়া *n.* the Shiah sect; a Shiah.

শিয়াকুল *n.* a wild-thorny plant or its berry; *zigyplus oenoplia.*

শিয়াল *n.* the jackal; the fox (*fem.* vixen). **~কাঁটা** *n.* a wild thorny plant, *agremone mexicana.* **~ফাঁকি** *n.* hoodwinking. **শিয়ালের যুক্তি** a mischievous counsel or plan.

শির[1] same as **শিরা**।

শিরঃ, (pop.) **শির**[2] *n.* the head; the cranium; crest; top; summit; the apex, vertex. **শিরে সংক্রান্তি** (fig.) an imminent danger. **শিরঃকম্প, শিরঃকম্পন** *n.* vertigo, dizziness; a nod. **শিরঃকোণ** *n.* (geom.) a vertical angle. **শিরঃপীড়া** *n.* headache; cephalitis.

শিরদাঁড়া same as **মেরুদণ্ড** (see **মেরু**).

শিরনি *n.* an oblation of sweets offered to deities or to the spirits of deceased holy persons.

শিরপ্যাচ, (inc.) **শিরপ্যাঁচ** *n.* a bejewelled or embroidered turban; a tiara.

শিরশির *int.* expressing a tingling or thrilling or uncanny sensation. **শিরশিরানি** *n.* such a sensation.

শিরশ্ছেদ, শিরশ্ছেদন *n.* decapitation, beheading. **শিরশ্ছেদ করা, শিরশ্ছেদন করা** *v.* to decapitate, to behead.

শিরস্ত্র, শিরস্ত্রাণ *n.* a cover of armour for the head, a helmet; a headdress; a turban; a cap; a hat.

শিরা *n.* a vein, a vena, a nerve, a tendon; (rare) the artery; (bot.) a costa. **~বিন্যাস** *n.* venation. **শিরাল** *a.* having prominent veins, venose; veined; (bot.) costate.

শিরিস alt. spell. of **সিরিশ**।

শিরীষ *n.* the rain-tree; its flower.

শিরোদেশ *a.* the region of the head; the head, the crown; top.

শিরোধার্য *a.* to be borne on the head; to be obeyed or be complied with; to be accepted with reverence. **শিরোধার্য করা** *v.* to bear on one's head; to obey or accept submissively or with reverence.

শিরোপা *n.* a turban of honour awarded by a prince etc.; a reward.

শিরোভূষণ *n.* an ornament for the head; (fig.) an object of glory or reverence, a glorious or reverend person, an excellent person.

শিরোমণি, শিরোরত্ন *n.* a jewel for the head; a title given to Sanskrit scholars; (fig.) an object of glory or reverence, a glorious or reverend person, an excellent person.

শিরোনাম *n.* the superscription of a letter; the heading (as of an essay).

শিরোরুহ *n.* hair growing on one's head.

শিল *n.* a stone slab or flat mortar for grinding spices (শিলনোড়া) ; hailstone, hail; a flat stone for sharpening tools, (cp.) a grindstone. **~নোড়া** *n.* the mortar and the pestle. শিল পড়া *v.* to hail. শিল পড়ছে it hails.

শিলা *n.* stone; rock; hailstone, hail. ~জতু *n.* bitumen; asphalt; benzoin. ~তল *n.* a floor paved with stone. ~পট্ট *n.* a stone slab. ~বর্ষণ, ~বৃষ্টি *n.* hailstorm. ~ময় *a.* made of stone; stony; rocky. ~মূর্তি *n.* a stone statue. ~রস *n.* storax; benzoin. ~লিপি *n.* a rock inscription.

শিলীভূত *a.* fossilized; petrified.

শিলীমুখ *n.* an arrow; the bee, the bumble-bee, the wasp.

শিল্প *n.* artistry; a work of art; a craft, a handicraft; arts and crafts; a technical art; an industry; fine arts. শিল্প অধিকর্তা *n.* the Director of Industries. ~কর্ম *n.* a work of art; a handicraft; artistry. ~কলা *n.* fine arts. ~কলাবিৎ *a.* versed in fine arts. ~কার same as শিল্পী। ~কুশল *a.* skilled in handicraft or in artistic work. ~কৌশল, ~নৈপুণ্য *n.* artistic skill; artistry; the method or technique of a work of art; technical skill. ~জাত *a.* manufactured, industrial. ~প্রদর্শনী *n.* an art exhibition; an industrial exhibition. ~বিদ্যা *n.* a technical or industrial art; a craft; a handicraft; a fine art. ~বিদ্যালয় *n.* an industrial or technical school; a school of fine arts, an art school. ~বিধি *n.* an industrial act; a rule of art. ~মন্ত্রক *n.* the ministry of industry. ~যন্ত্র *n.* a machine. ~যান্ত্রিক *n.* an industrial engineer. ~যোজন *a.* industrialization. ~শালা *n.* a workshop, a manufactory; a smithy; a studio, an atelier; a museum of arts and crafts. শিল্পায়ন *n.* industrialisation. শিল্পালয় *n.* an art institute. শিল্পিক *a.* artistic. শিল্পী *n.* an artist, a fine artist; an artisan; a handicraftsman (*fem.* handicraftswoman); (rare) an industrial or technical worker.

শিশমহল *n.* a house made of glass or largely of glass, a glass-house.

শিশি *n.* a phial made of glass.

শিশির *n.* dew; frost. ~কণা *n.* a dewdrop. ~ধৌত *a.* washed with dew. ~পাত *n.* dewfall. ~বিন্দু *n.* a dewdrop. ~স্নাত *a.* bathed in dew. ~সিক্ত *a.* drenched in or wet with dew. শিশিরাঙ্ক *a.* (phys.) dew-point.

শিশু[1] *n.* gregarious tree, the *Dulbergia sisoo*, its timber.

শিশু[2] *n.* an infant, a baby, a child; a young (ছাগশিশু). □ *a.* infant. ~কন্যা *n. fem.* an infant daughter, a baby daughter. ~কাল *n.* infancy, babyhood, childhood. ~ত্ব *n.* infancy. ~পাঠ *n.* a juvenile reader. ~পাঠ্য *a.* (of books) intended for or fit for juvenile readers. ~পালন *n.* childcare; bringing up and rearing of children. ~পুত্র *n.* an infant son, a baby son. ~প্রকৃতি *a.* childlike; simple as a child. □ *n.* childlike nature or simplicity. ~মার *n.* the porpoise; the dolphin; (astr.) the Cynosure. ~শিক্ষা *n.* child education; juvenile education. ~সন্তান *n.* an infant child, a baby child. ~সাহিত্য *n.* juvenile literature, children's literature. ~সাহিত্যিক *n.* an author of juvenile literature. ~সুলভ *a.* childlike, natural for a child; simple, innocent. ~হত্যা *n.* infanticide. ~হত্যাকারী *n.* an infanticide.

শিশুক same as শুশুক।

শিশ্ন *n.* the penis. শিশ্নোদরপরায়ণ *a.* given to too much eating and carnal or sensual pleasure.

শিষ *n.* an ear of corn; a cornstalk; a flower-spike; a flame.

শিষ্ট *a.* gentle, civil; polite, courteous, well-behaved, mannerly; good-natured; righteous; educated; elegant, chaste (শিষ্ট ভাষা). ~তা *n.* politeness, courteousness; civility; refinement, decorum; righteousness. ~বায়ু *n.* residual air. শিষ্ট ব্যবহার same as শিষ্টাচার। শিষ্ট সম্ভাষণ *n.* polite or courteous address. শিষ্টাচার, শিষ্টাচরণ *n.* etiquette; civility, courtesy; polite or amiable behaviour. শিষ্টাচারবিরুদ্ধ *a.* in contrast with or opposed to good manners. শিষ্টাচারী *a.* observant of the rules of etiquette; civil, courteous; well-behaved; amiable.

শিষ্য *n.* a pupil; a disciple; a (devoted) follower. *fem.* শিষ্যা। ~ত্ব *n.* pupilage; discipleship.

শিস, শিস্ *n.* a whistling sound made by contracting one's lips, a whistle; a sweet short note (as of birds). শিস দেওয়া *v.* to whistle.

শিহরন *n.* a thrill; a shiver or shudder; horripilation.

শিহরা, শিহরানো *v.* to have a thrill; to horripilate, to have goose-flesh; to shiver or shudder.

শিহরিত *a.* thrilled; horripilating; shivering or shuddering.

শীকর *n.* a very fine particle of rain flying in air; a drop of water.

শীঘ্র, (coll. corrup.) **শিগ্‌গির, শিগ্‌গিরি** *adv.* quickly, promptly, swiftly. □ *a.* quick, prompt, swift. **শীঘ্রকারী** *a.* prompt in action, prompt. **শীঘ্রগামী** *a.* fast-moving, swift, fast.

শীত *n.* winter; cold, chill; feeling of chilliness or cold. □ *a.* cold; cool; fit for winter (শীতবস্ত্র). **শীত করা, শীত ধরা, শীত লাগা** *v.* to feel cold; to shiver with cold. **শীত কাটানো** *v.* to winter. **শীতে কাঁপা** *v.* to shiver with cold. **শীত কেটেছে** to be relieved of the sensation of cold, winter is at an end. **শীত পড়েছে** winter has set in. **আজ শীত পড়েছে** it is cold today. **~কাঁটা** *n.* goose-flesh caused by (sudden) sensation of cold. **~কাতরতা** *n.* over-sensitiveness to cold; affliction caused by cold. **~কাতুরে** *a.* over-sensitive to cold. **~কাল** *n.* the winter season, wintertime, winter, cold weather. **~কালীন** *a.* of winter, winter, wintry. **~ক** *n.* a refrigerator. **~তাপনিয়ন্ত্রিত** *a.* air-conditioned. **~ন** *n.* refrigeration. **~প্রধান** *a.* characterized by predominance of cold. **~প্রধান দেশ** a cold country. **~বস্ত্র** *n.* warm clothes; winter garment; woollen clothes.

শীতল *a.* cold; chilly; cool; soothing (শীতল বায়ু) ; soothed, warmed up (প্রাণ শীতল) ; □ *n.* the evening food-offering to a deity. **শীতল করা** *v.* to make cold; to cool; to soothe, to assuage. **~পাটি** *n.* a mat very soothing and cool to lie upon. **~স্পর্শ** *a.* cold to the touch; (fig.) soothing. **শীতলা** *n.* the presiding female deity of small-pox, chicken-pox, measles etc. **~খোলা, শীতলাতলা** *n.* a place for public worship of Goddess Shitala (শীতলা). **শীতলীকরণ** *n.* making cool, cooling. **শীতলীভবন** *n.* getting cool, cooling.

শীতাংশু *n.* the moon.

শীতাগম *n.* advent of cold or winter.

শীতাধিক্য *n.* excess of cold.

শীতাতপ *n.* winter and summer; cold and heat. **~নিয়ন্ত্রিত** *a.* air-conditioned.

শীতার্ত *a.* stricken with cold; shivering with cold; over-sensitive to cold.

শীতোষ্ণ *a.* both hot and cold; tepid. **~বলয়** *n.* (geog.) the temperate zone.

শীৎকার *n.* hissing sound (indicating sudden sensation of pleasure).

শীধু *n.* honey; a kind of alcoholic drink made from sugar-cane juice.

শীর্ণ *a.* lean, thin; emaciated. *fem.* **শীর্ণা**। **~কায়** *a.* lean-bodied. **~তা** *n.* thinness, leanness.

শীর্ষ *n.* the head; top, apex, summit; tip; the highest or the first or the most distinguished place (also **শীর্ষস্থান**) ; (geom.) a vertex (of an angle etc.). **~ক** *a.* (used as a *sfx.*) having a particular title, entitled, styled; headed. **~কোণ** *n.* (geom.) a vertical angle. **~স্থ** *a.* situated on the top or on the head. **পরীক্ষায় শীর্ষস্থান অধিকার করা** to stand or come first in an examination. **~স্থানীয়** *a.* highest, first; most distinguished, chief, topmost.

শীল *n.* nature; natural disposition; character; conduct, behaviour, manners; practice. □ *a.* (used as a *sfx.*) natured, disposed to (দয়াশীল) ; practising (দানশীল). *fem. a.* **শীলা**। **~পত্র** *n.* a character-certificate. **~ব্রত** *a.* practising virtues, virtuous.

শুঁকা *v.* to smell. □ *a.* smelled, smelt. **শুঁকানো** *v.* to cause to smell.

শুঁটকি *a.* (of fish) preserved by seasoning and drying in the sun; emaciated and shrivelled up (শুঁটকি চেহারা). □ *n.* dried and seasoned fish.

শুঁটি *n.* a legume, a pod.

শুঁঠ *n.* dried ginger.

শুঁড় *n.* a proboscis, a trunk (as of the elephant); a snout (as of the tortoise); (facet.—of human beings) the mouth including the neck; an antenna, a feeler (as of an insect). **শুঁড় বাড়ানো** *v.* to stretch out one's proboscis or trunk or snout or antenna; (facet.—of human beings) to crane one's neck.

শুঁড়ি[১] *a.* very narrow (শুঁড়ি পথ).

শুঁড়ি[২] *n.* a wine-seller, a vintner; a distiller, a brewer; a publican, a taverner. **শুঁড়ির দোকান, ~খানা** *n.* a wine-shop, a grog-shop; a public house, a tavern, ale-house (old name). **শুঁড়ির সাক্ষী মাতাল** one offender bears out another, (cp.) birds of the same feather flock together.

শুঁয়া, (coll.) **শুঁয়ো** *n.* an antenna, a feeler; an awn (যবের শুঁয়া). **~পোকা** *n.* the caterpillar; the chrysalis.

শুক *n.* the popinjay, the parrot.

শুকতারা *n.* the vesper; (astr.) Venus.

শুকতো alt. spell of **শুক্ত।**

শুকনো same as **শুষ্ক। শুকনো কথায় চিঁড়ে ভেজে না** (fig.) mere words cannot accomplish a thing, mere words cannot butter bread, (cp.) fine words butter no parsnips.

শুকানো *v.* to free or be freed from moisture, water etc., to dry (কাপড় শুকানো) ; to sun or be sunned (ধান শুকানো) ; to wither or be withered (ফুল শুকানো) ; to emaciate or be emaciated (ছেলেটা শুকিয়ে যাচ্ছে) ; to heal or be healed (ঘা শুকানো).

শুক্ত, শুক্তনি *n.* a dish of bitters, bitters-curry.

শুক্তি, শুক্তিকা *n.* nacre, abalone, ear-shell, oyster. **শুক্তি-বীজ** *n.* pearl.

শুক্র *n.* (astr.) the Venus; the vesper; sperm, semen; the preceptor of daityas (দৈত্য) (usu. **শুক্রাচার্য**). **~তারল্য** *n.* spermatorrhoea, involuntary seminal discharge. **~বার, ~বাসর** *n.* Friday. **শুক্রাণু** *n.* spermatozoid.

শুক্ল *n.* the white colour. □ *a.* white, hoary, grey (শুক্ল কেশ) ; bright, light; clean, clear; fair; pure. *fem. a.* **শুক্লা। ~তা** *n.* whiteness. **~তিথি** *n.* any lunar day of the bright fortnight. **~পক্ষ** *n.* the bright fortnight.

শুখা *a.* dry; exclusive of bed and board (শুখা মাইনের কাজ). □ *n.* drought (হাজাশুখা) ; roasted or sunned tobacco used as quids or in bidis (বিড়ি).

শুঙ্গা, শুঙ্গা same as **শুঁয়া।**

শুচি *a.* pure; clean, immaculate; sanctified; holy; virtuous; white. **~তা** *n.* purity; cleanliness; immaculateness; sanctity; holiness; virtuousness; whiteness. **আপাতশুচিতা** a show of purity or sanctity or virtuousness or cleanliness; sanctimony. **~বাই, ~বায়ু** *n.* a hysterical mania for cleanliness and sanctity. **~বায়ুগ্রস্ত** *a.* suffering from a hysterical mania for cleanliness and sanctity. **~ব্রত** *a.* practising sanctity and virtue; virtuous and holy. **~শুভ্র** *a.* bright with sanctity or virtuousness. **~স্মিত** *a.* having a pure or bright smile. *fem.* **~স্মিতা।**

শুজনি *n.* a diapered bedcover.

শুণ্ড *n.* a proboscis, a trunk (as of the elephant); a snout (as of the tortoise).

শুণ্ডী same as **শুঁড়ি[২] ।**

শুদ্ধ *a.* faultless; flawless; immaculate; clean; pure; purified; rectified, holy, sacred; sanctified, consecrated; virtuous; chaste; genuine; unadulterated; correct, right (অঙ্কটি শুদ্ধ) ; mere, only (শুদ্ধ দুঃখ). □ *adv.* only, merely (শুদ্ধ একবস্ত্রে). **শুদ্ধ করা** *v.* to clean; to purify; to sanctify, to consecrate; to rectify, to correct; to amend. **~তা** *n.* correctness; flawlessness, faultlessness; purity; sacredness, holiness; chastity; genuineness. **শুদ্ধ বর্ণালি** (phys.) a pure spectrum. **~চিত্ত, ~মতি** *a.* chaste or virtuous in mind, pure-hearted. **~লেখ** *n.* a fair copy. **~সত্ত্ব** *a.* pure-souled. **শুদ্ধাচার** *n.* practice of virtue or sanctity; virtuousness; sanctity; cleanliness. □ *a.* practising virtue or sanctity or cleanliness. **শুদ্ধাচারিতা** same as **শুদ্ধাচার** (*n.*). **শুদ্ধাচারী** *a.* same as **শুদ্ধাচার** (*a.*). *fem.* **শুদ্ধাচারিণী। শুদ্ধাশুদ্ধ** *a.* holy and profane; pure and impure; right and wrong; correct and incorrect. **শুদ্ধি** *n.* purification; purgation; sanctification, consecration; rectification, correction, amendment; reformation; purity; cleanliness; chastity; correctness; reclamation from evil, untouchability, social inferiority etc. **শুদ্ধিপত্র** *n.* list of errors attached to a book, errata, corrigenda.

শুধা[১] *v.* to repay, to pay back.

শুধা[2], **শুধানো** *v.* to ask, to inquire.

শুধু *a.* empty (শুধু হাতে) ; bare (শুধু চোখে) ; mere, only (শুধু জল). □ *adv.* merely, simply, only (শুধু হাসছে). **শুধু শুধু** *adv.* for nothing (শুধু শুধু মার খাওয়া) ; in vain (শুধু শুধু চেষ্টা করা).

শুনশান *a.* without a noise, completely silent. □ *n.* complete silence.

শুনানি *n.* (law) a hearing.

শুনানো *v.* to make one hear; to inform; to cause to pay heed to; to sting with words, to revile, to give a person a piece of one's mind (কথা শুনিয়ে দিয়েছে). **গল্প শুনানো** *v.* to tell one a story. **গান শুনানো** *v.* to sing (one) a song.

শুভ *n.* weal, well-being, (the) good. □ *a.* doing good, beneficial, benefactory; auspicious; favourable; promising. *fem. a.* **শুভা**। **শুভংকর,** (inc.) **~কর** same as **~ঙ্কর**। **~কর্ম, ~কার্য** *n.* an auspicious work; a solemn or religious rite or function or ceremony. **~ক্ষণ** *n.* an auspicious or favourable moment or time; an opportunity, a chance. **~গ্রহ** *n.* (astrol.) an auspicious or favourable planet or star. **~ঙ্কর** *a.* doing good, beneficial, benefactory. **~ঙ্করী** *a. fem.* of **~ঙ্কর**। □ *n.* a system of arithmetical calculation introduced by Shubhankar. **~দ, ~দায়ক** same as **~ঙ্কর**। *fem.* **~দা**। **~দৃষ্টি** *n.* an auspicious or favourable or kind look or (astrol.) aspect; the solemn rite of the bride and bridegroom looking at each other at a Hindu wedding. **~ফল** *n.* a happy result or outcome. **~লক্ষণ** *n.* an auspicious sign or mark or omen. **~লগ্ন** *n.* an auspicious moment. **~সংবাদ** *n.* good news. **শুভাকাঙ্ক্ষা** *n.* well-wishing. **শুভাকাঙ্ক্ষী** *a.* well-wishing. □ *n.* a well-wisher. *fem.* **শুভাকাঙ্ক্ষিণী**। **শুভাগমন** *n.* an auspicious coming; a kind visit, a welcome visit. **শুভানুধ্যান** same as **শুভাকাঙ্ক্ষা**। **শুভানুধ্যায়ী** same as **শুভাকাঙ্ক্ষী**। *fem.* **শুভানুধ্যায়িনী**। **শুভানুষ্ঠান** *n.* an auspicious or solemn function or ceremony. **শুভার্থী** same as **শুভাকাঙ্ক্ষী**। *fem.* **শুভার্থিনী**। **শুভাশীর্বাদ** *n.* kind blessing or benediction. **শুভাশুভ** *n.* weal and woe; good and evil. **শুভেচ্ছা** *n.* well-wishes, good wishes.

শুভ্র *a.* white; grey, hoary (শুভ্র কেশ) ; incandescent, bright (শুভ্র আলোক) ; (fig.) pure, unblemished, chaste, virtuous (শুভ্র মন). *fem.* **শুভ্রা**। **শুভ্রতা** *n.* whiteness; (fig.) purity.

শুমার *n.* counting, enumeration (**আদমশুমার** = census); calculation; estimate.

শুয়ার, (coll.) **শুয়োর** same as **শূকর**। **শুয়োরের খোঁয়াড়** a pigsty, a swinesty, a piggery, a swinery. **শুয়োরের গোঁ** stupid obstinacy, pigheadedness. **শুয়োরের পাল** a flock of swine.

শুরু *n.* commencement, beginning; start; inception. **শুরু করা** বা **হওয়া** *v.* to commence, to begin; to start. **শুরু থেকে শেষ** from beginning to end.

শুরুয়া *n.* soup.

শুলফা, (coll.) **শুলফো** *n.* dill.

শুল্ক *n.* duty on import or export, customs; tax, toll; a marriage-portion, a dowry; price. **~শালা** *n.* the customs house. **শুল্কাধীন** *a.* bonded. **শুল্কাধীন পণ্যাগার** bonded warehouse.

শুশনি *n.* cress(es).

শুশুক *n.* the porpoise, the dolphin.

শুশ্রূষা *n.* nursing (of the sick). **শুশ্রূষা করা** *v.* to nurse. **~কারী** *n.* a male nurse. □ *a.* nursing. *fem.* **~কারিণী** *n.* a nurse; a (nursing) sister.

শুষা same as **শোষণ করা**।

শুষির alt. spell. of **সুষির**।

শুষ্ক *a.* dry (শুষ্ক বস্ত্র) ; withered (শুষ্ক পুষ্প) ; sapless, pithless (শুষ্ক কাষ্ঠ) ; dull, uninteresting, pointless (শুষ্ক তর্ক) ; pale (শুষ্ক মুখ) ; parched (শুষ্ক কণ্ঠ) ; harsh (শুষ্ক স্বর) ; vapoury or empty or insipid (শুষ্ক বাক্য) ; merely formal (শুষ্ক ভদ্রতা). **~তা** *n.* dryness.

শূক *n.* a beard of corn, an awn; the chrysalis. **~কীট** *n.* the caterpillar; the chrysalis. **~ঘ্ন** *a.* larvicide. **~ধান্য** *n.* awned rice.

শূকর *n.* the hog, the boar, the swine. *fem.* **শূকরী** the sow. **বন্যশূকর** *n.* the wild boar. **~ছানা, ~শাবক** *n.* the pig. **~পালক** *n.* a swineherd. **শূকরের মাংস** pork, ham.

শূদ্র *n.* the lowest of the four Hindu castes, Shudras; a shudra. **শূদ্রা** *a. fem.* a female shudra. **শূদ্রাণী** *n. fem.* a female shudra; a shudra's wife. **শূদ্রী** *n. fem.* a shudra's wife.

শূন *a.* poet, corrup. of **শূন্য** ।

শূন্য *n.* (math.) zero; cipher; nothing; the sky; an open or empty place, space, (the) void; inexistence; absence. □ *a.* destitute of, devoid of (জনশূন্য, বুদ্ধিশূন্য) ; vacant; empty; stoical, indifferent. □ *in comp.* (used as a *sfx.*) -less (গৃহশূন্য = homeless). **~কুম্ভ** *n.* an empty pitcher; (fig.—dero.) a man of no worth or substance, a man of straw. **~ক্রান্তি-রেখা** *n.* (astr.) the aclinic line. **~গর্ভ** *a.* containing nothing within, empty; hollow; (fig.) unsubstantial or insincere (শূন্যগর্ভ কথা = empty words). **~তা** *n.* vacancy; emptiness; stoicism, indifference. **~দৃষ্টি** *n.* a vacant or blank look. **~পথ** an aerial route. **~পানে** *adv.* towards the sky. **~বাদ** *n.* the Buddhist doctrine which holds that the world has evolved out of nothing and will pass into nothing; atheism, nihilism. **~বাদী** *a.* Buddhistic, Buddhist; atheistical, atheistic; nihilistic. □ *n.* a Buddhist; an atheist; a nihilist. **শূন্য মন** *n.* a vacant or unoccupied mind; an indifferent or stocial mind. **~মনে** *adv.* in a vacant mood. **~মার্গ** *n.* aerial path; passage through the air. **~যাত্রা** *n.* a flight. **~স্থান** *n.* empty or vacant space; a blank; a gap. **~হস্ত** *a.* empty-handed; financially hard up, broke; not carrying any weapon. **~হস্তে** *adv.* empty-handedly; without (having any) money; without carrying any weapon. **~হাত** same as **~হস্ত** । **~করণ** *n.* act of making empty; evacuation. **শূন্যীকৃত** *a.* emptied; evacuated.

শূপকার *n.* (loos.) a cook.

শূর *a.* valiant; heroic. □ *n.* a valiant man or fighter; a hero. **শূরোচিত** *a.* befitting a hero.

শূর্প *n.* a wicker-work platter or tray for winnowing.

শূল *n.* a stake for impaling a criminal; a trident; a pike; a skewer, a spit; pain, inflammation (দন্তশূল) ; colic. **শূলে দেওয়া, শূলে চড়ানো** *v.* to impale (as a criminal). **~ঘ্ন** *a.* curing inflammation or colic. **~পক্ক** *a.* skewered or spitted and roasted. **~পাণি** *n.* one holding a trident in one's hand; Shiva (শিব). **~বিদ্ধ** *a.* pierced with a trident or pike; spitted, skewered. **~বেদনা, ~ব্যথা** *n.* colic pain. **শূলাগ্র** *n.* pikehead; the point of a trident or stake. **শূলানি** *n.* pain, ache, inflammation; (coll.) itching. **শূলানো** *v.* to become painful, to ache, to inflame; (coll.) to have an itching for (পিঠ বা মুখ শূলানো). **শূলী** same as **~পাণি** । **শূল্য** *a.* roasted on a spit or skewer (শূল্য মাংস).

শৃগাল *n.* the jackal, *fem.* **শৃগালী** ।

শৃঙ্খল *n.* a chain; fetters, irons; rule, system, arrangement, due order; restraint or discipline. **শৃঙ্খল-নিয়ম** *n.* (math.) chain rule. **শৃঙ্খলা** *n.* method, system; due succession or order, sequence; arrangement, orderliness; restraint or discipline. **শৃঙ্খলাবদ্ধ** *a.* chained, fettered; methodical, systematic; orderly; disciplined. **শৃঙ্খলাহীন** *a.* disorderly; confused; undisciplined; immethodical, unmethodical, unsystematic; haphazard. **শৃঙ্খলিত** *a.* chained, fettered.

শৃঙ্গ *n.* a horn; an antler; a peak; summit; a wind-instrument ori. made of horn, a horn. **ক্ষুদ্র শৃঙ্গ** a cornicle. **~ধ্বনি** *n.* the sound of a (musical) horn.

শৃঙ্গাকার *a.* corniform.

শৃঙ্গার *n.* (rhet.) the sentiment relating to sexual union or intercourse (usu. **শৃঙ্গাররস**) ; the erotic sentiment; sexual intercourse, coition; toilet and dressing (of a woman preparing herself to meet her lover or of an elephant, an idol etc.).

শৃঙ্গী *a.* horned; corniculate. □ *n.* a horned beast.

শেওড়া, শ্যাওড়া *n.* a kind of wild tree.

শেওলা, শ্যাওলা pop. corrup. of **শৈবাল** ।

শেঁকো alt. spell. of **সেঁকো** ।

শেখ *n.* (Mus.) a Sheik(h).

শেখর *n.* a crown, a diadem, a coronet; a chaplet; a peak, a crest, a summit.

শেখা *v.* to learn; to study; to practise; to undergo training. □ *n.* learning; studying. □ *a.* that which has been learnt or studied or practised. **শিখানো, ~নো** *v.* to teach; to educate; to train; to instruct. □ *a.* that which has been taught; tutored, instructed. **শেখানো সাক্ষী** a tutored or primed witness.

শেজ[1] *n.* a bed.

শেজ[2] *n.* a lamp within a chimney, a lantern.

শেঠ *n.* an upcountry merchant.

শেফালি, শেফালী, শেফালিকা *n.* the horsinghar, a white fragrant autumnal flower; its tree.

শেমিজ *n.* a chemise.

শেয়াকুল, শেয়ান, শেয়ানা, শেয়াল, variants of **শিয়াকুল, সেয়ান, সেয়ানা** and **শিয়াল** respectively.

শেরওয়ানি *n.* a kind of long coat worn by men.

শের *n.* the tiger; the lion.

শেল *n.* a sharp-pointed mythological missile. **~সম** *a.* like the aforesaid missile; as painful or fatal as a stroke of the aforesaid missile. **বুকে শেলসম বাজা** to cut (a person) to the heart.

শেষ *n.* (myth.) a king of snakes; end, termination; close; conclusion, finish; completion; ruin or destruction or death (শত্রুর শেষ দেখা) ; the rear, the backside, the back-end, the rearmost or backmost part or position (সবার শেষে) ; the last or lowest position or place (সব শেষে) ; remainder, balance; settlement, solution (তর্কের শেষ). □ *a.* last; concluding; ultimate; final; lowest; rearmost; remaining. **শেষ করা** *v.* to finish, to complete, to end, to conclude; to ruin or destroy or kill, to do (one) in. **শেষ হওয়া** *v.* to be finished or concluded; to end, to conclude; to close; to be ruined or destroyed or killed. **শেষ অবস্থা, শেষ দশা** *n.* the last or final stage; the end; the dying stage. **~কালে** *adv.* at last, in the end. **~পাদ** *n.* the last quarter. **শেষ বিচার** *n.* the Last Judgment, Doom. **শেষ বিচারের দিন** the Judgment-day, Doomsday. **শেষ বিচারক** *n.* the Final Judge. **~ভাগ** *n.* the last part; the remaining portion. **~মুহূর্ত** *n.* the last moment, the eleventh hour. **~যাত্রা** *n.* the last journey; death. **~রক্ষা** *n.* that which saves the situation at the last moment, happy ending of a situation which seems hopeless. **~রাত, ~রাত্রি** *n.* the last part of the night; small hours. **শেষাবস্থা** same as **শেষ অবস্থা।** **শেষাশেষি** *adv.* at the last moment, at the eleventh hour; at last, in the end, at long last; ultimately; finally. **শেষে** *adv.* in the end; in conclusion; towards the close; ultimately, finally; at last; last (সে শেষে এল). **শেষোক্ত** *a.* mentioned last of all; last-named.

শেহালা poet. corrup. of **শ্যাওলা।**

শৈত্য *n.* coldness, cold; chilliness, chill; frigidity; humidity.

শৈথিল্য *n.* looseness, flaccidity; dishevelled or blowsy state; slackness; laxness; tiredness, fatigue; slowness, tardiness; absence of earnestness or carefulness.

শৈব *a.* of or worshipping Shiva (শিব). □ *n.* a Hindu community worshipping Shiva (শিব) ; a member of this community.

শৈবলিনী *n.* a river.

শৈবাল *n.* lichen, moss; alga (pl. algae).

শৈল *n.* a mountain; a rock; a hill. **~জ** *a.* born of or grown on a mountain or a hill; mountainous or hilly. **~জা** *a. fem.* of **শৈলজ।** □ *n.* same as **~সুতা।** **~জায়া** *n.* Menaka (মেনকা) the wife of the Himalayas. **~তত্ত্ব** *n.* petrology; petrography. **~ময়** *a.* mountainous or hilly. **~শিরা** *n.* a ridge. **~সুতা** *n.* daughter of a mountain; Goddess Durga (দুর্গা), the daughter of the Himalayas.

শৈলান্তরীপ *n.* a promontory.

শৈলী *n.* style (রচনাশৈলী).

শৈলেন্দ্র *n.* the lord or king of mountains; the Himalayas.

শৈলেয় *a.* hill-grown. □ *n.* a fragrant resin, benzoin, storax.

শৈলোৎক্ষেপ-বৃষ্টি *n.* (geog.) relief-rain.

শৈশব, শৈশবকাল, শৈশবাবস্থা *n.* infancy, babyhood; childhood; childhood days. **শৈশবকালীন** *a.* of infancy or childhood days; infantile. **শৈশবকালোচিত** *a.* proper for infancy or childhood; child-like; babyish or childish. **শৈশবসঙ্গী** *n.* a companion or friend of one's childhood.

শৈশবস্মৃতি *n.* reminiscence(s) of one's childhood days. শৈশবাবধি *adv.* from or since childhood.

শোঁ *int.* expressing: a swishing or whirring or whizzing sound.

শোঁকা, শোঁকানো pop. variants of **শুঁকা** and **শুঁকানো** respectively.

শোঁ-শোঁ *int.* expressing: repeated or continuous whizzing sound.

শোক *n.* mourning or grief. **শোক করা** *v.* to mourn, to grieve (for). **~গাথা, ~গীতি** *n.* an elegy; a dirge. **~গ্রস্ত** *a.* bereaved; grief-stricken. **~চিহ্ন** *n.* a sign or token of mourning. **~জনক** *a.* mournful; woeful, distressing, sad, lamentable. **~যাত্রা** *n.* a funeral procession. **~সংগীত** *n.* an elegy; a dirge. **~সন্তপ্ত** *a.* afflicted with grief, grief-stricken. **~সভা** *n.* a condolence meeting. **~সাগর** *n.* an ocean of grief. **~সূচক** *a.* indicating grief or mourning. **শোকাকুল** *a.* beside oneself with grief, overwhelmed with grief. **শোকাগ্নি** same as **শোকানল**। **শোকাচ্ছন্ন** *a.* beset or overwhelmed with grief. **শোকাতুর** same as **শোকার্ত**। **শোকানল** *n.* the burning fire of grief. **শোকাবহ** same as **~জনক**। **শোকাবিষ্ট** same as **শোকাচ্ছন্ন**। **শোকাবেগ** *n.* outburst of grief. **শোকাভিভূত** same as **শোকাচ্ছন্ন**। **শোকার্ত** *a.* grief-stricken. **শোকোচ্ছ্বাস** same as **শোকাবেগ**।

শোচন, শোচনা *n.* mourning or grieving; lamentation; repentance; regret. **শোচনীয়** *a.* mournful; grievous; woeful; lamentable; sad; regrettable; sorry (শোচনীয় অবস্থা = a sorry plight); miserable.

শোণিত *n.* blood. **~ধারা** *n.* a stream or flow of blood; (loos.) blood-circulation. **~কণা, ~কণিকা** *n.* a small drop of blood; (anat.) a blood-corpuscle. **~পাত** *n.* bloodshed; haemorrhage. **শোণিতপায়ী প্রাণী** a blood-sucker. **~পিপাসা** *n.* bloodthirstiness. **~পিপাসু** *a.* bloodthirsty. **~প্রবাহ** same as **~ধারা**। **~মোক্ষণ** *n.* (med.) blood-letting. **~রঞ্জিত** *a.* smeared with blood, bloodstained, bloodbespotted, bloody. **~শিরা** *n.* a vein; an artery. **~শোষণ** *n.* act of sucking in others' blood; (fig.) extortion. **~স্নান** *n.* blood-bath. **~স্রাব** *n.* haemorrhage. **শোণিতাক্ত** same as **~রঞ্জিত**।

শোণিমা *n.* red glow or tinge; flush.

শোথ *n.* dropsy. **শোথ নামা** *v.* to have dropsical swelling.

শোধ *n.* repayment; payment, acquittance, clearing off (dues); revenge, vengeance, retaliation. **শোধ করা** *v.* to repay; to pay. **শোধ তোলা** same as **শোধ নেওয়া**। **শোধ দেওয়া** *v.* to pay back, to repay; to pay; to take revenge (upon), to avenge; to retaliate. **শোধ নেওয়া** *v.* to take revenge (on, upon), to avenge; to retaliate. **শোধ যাওয়া** *v.* to be repaid or paid. **~বোধ** *n.* settling or balancing of accounts; (fig.) having one's revenge on somebody, squaring up with somebody; final settlement. **শোধ্য** *a.* repayable.

শোধক *a.* purifying; sanctifying; consecratory; cleansing, refining; rectifying; corrective; reformative; repaying; paying.

শোধন *n.* purification; sanctification, consecration; clearing or refining; rectification; amendment, correction; revision; reclamation; reformation; repayment; payment; acquittance. **শোধন করা** *v.* to purify; to sanctify, to consecrate; to cleanse or refine; to rectify; to amend, to correct; to revise; to reform. **শোধনী** *a. fem.* same as **শোধক**। **শোধনীয়** *a.* to be or capable of being purified or sanctified or consecrated or cleansed or refined or rectified or corrected or reformed or repaid or paid.

শোধরানো *v.* to rectify or be rectified; to correct or be corrected; to mind one's ways.

শোধা pop. var. of **শুধা**।

শোধাক্ষম *a.* insolvent. **শোধাক্ষমতা** *n.* insolvency.

শোধিত *a.* purified; sanctified, consecrated; cleansed, refined; rectified (শোধিত কোহল); amended, corrected; revised; reclaimed; reformed; repaid; paid.

শোনা *v.* to hear; to listen (to); to obey (কথা শোনা); to comply with; to pay heed to. □ *a.* that which has been heard or listened to; heard or learnt from others (শোনা কথা). **~নো** *v.* to make one hear; to inform or tell; to cause to obey; to cause to pay heed to. **গান শোনানো** *v.* to sing (one) a song. **~মাত্র** *adv.* immediately on hearing, directly upon hearing.

শোভন *a.* beautiful, lovely; comely, debonair; graceful; elegant; decorous; decent; becoming. *fem.* **শোভনা** । **শোভনীয়** *a.* becoming.

শোভমান *a.* existing or being present beautifully; looking beautiful or decorous. *fem.* **শোভমানা** ।

শোভা *n.* beauty; beautiful show; glamour. **শোভা করা** *v.* to beautify; to embellish; to adorn; to grace. **শোভা পাওয়া** *v.* to exist or be present beautifully; to look beautiful or decorous; to behove or become. **শোভা হওয়া** *v.* to look beautiful or decorous; to have a beautiful show; to be adorned or graced. **~কর** *a.* beautifying; adorning; decorating; giving grace to; giving glamour to. **~ময়** *a.* beautiful; graceful; having a beautiful show; glamorous. *fem.* **~ময়ী** । **~যাত্রা** *n.* a procession. **শোভাযাত্রা করে যাওয়া** *v.* to go in a procession. **শোভাযাত্রা বার করা** *v.* to take out a procession. **~যাত্রী** *n.* a processionist. **~শূন্য, ~হীন** *a.* having no beauty; having no beautiful show.

শোভিত *a.* beautifully existing; beautified; embellished; decked; adorned; decorated; graced.

শোভী *a.* beautifying; adorning; adding grace to. *fem.* **শোভিনী** ।

শোফার *n.* a chauffeur (*fem.* a chauffeuse).

শোয়া *v.* to lie down, to go to bed; to sleep. **শুয়ে পড়া** *v.* to lie down; to go to bed; to lie prostrate. **~নো** *v.* to cause to lie down; to lay down; to force to lie prostrate; to cause to succumb. **~বসা** *n.* (fig.) deportment, bearing; (fig.) act of living with another as neighbours or in the same society; (fig.) social intercourse. **~বসা করা** *v.* to live with another as neighbours or in the same society; to have social intercourse with.

শোর *n.* a loud (and confused) noise, an uproar. **শোর তোলা** *v.* to raise an uproar. **~গোল** *n.* an uproarious noise; hue and cry; clamour.

শোরা *n.* nitre, salt-petre. **~ঘটিত** *a.* nitric.

শোল *n.* a large tubular fish.

শোলা *n.* spongewood, hat-plant, sola. **শোলার কাজ** *n.* sola work, artistry with spongewood or sola. **শোলার টুপি** *n.* a sola hat.

শোষ *n.* dryness; juiceless or sapless state; (med.) consumption; (med.) sinus. □ *a.* dried up within (শোষ মূলো).

শোষ-কাগজ *n.* blotting-paper.

শোষক *a.* absorbing; drying up; sucking in; (fig.) extorting. □ *n.* an absorber; a sucker; (fig.) an extortioner, sponger.

শোষণ *n.* absorption; act of drying up; suction; (fig.) extortion. **শোষণ করা** *v.* to absorb; to dry up; to suck in; (fig.) to extort.

শোষা same as **শোষণ করা** ।

শোষিত *a.* absorbed; dried up; sucked in; (fig.) subjected to extortion.

শোহরত *n.* announcement, proclamation. **ঢোল-শহরত** *n.* proclamation by beat of drums.

শোহিনী *n.* an Indian musical mode.

শৌখিন *a.* given to niceties; given to luxury, luxurious; having refined or delicate taste; dainty; fancy (শৌখিন জিনিস = fancy goods). **~তা** *n.* luxuriousness; inclination to niceties; possession of refined or delicate taste; daintiness.

শৌচ, শৌচকর্ম, শৌচক্রিয়া *n.* purity; sanctity; scriptural cleansing or purification of one's body and mind; washing or cleansing of one's posteriors after evacuation of bowels. **শৌচ করা** *v.* to wash or cleanse one's posteriors after evacuation of bowels; to cleanse or purify scripturally one's body and mind; to sanctify. **শৌচাগার** *n.* a latrine, a lavatory, a toilet.

শৌণ্ড *a.* drunken, inebriate, intoxicated; greatly addicted or habituated to

(পানশৌণ্ড) ; celebrated (দানশৌণ্ড). **শৌণ্ডিক, শৌণ্ডী** same as **শুঁড়ি**[২] । **শৌণ্ডিকালয়** same as **শুঁড়িখানা**।

শৌর্য *n.* valour, prowess; heroism; strength and courage. **~শালী** *a.* valorous, valiant; heroic; strong and courageous. *fem.* **~শালিনী**।

শ্ব *n.* the dog. **~দন্ত** *n.* a canine tooth. **~বৃত্তি** *n.* dog-like behaviour, doggishness; servitude, servility; mean or cringing flattery.

শ্বশুর *n.* a father-in-law; an uncle-in-law. **~ঘর** *n.* a woman's father-in-law's house, a husband's house. **~বাড়ি, শ্বশুরালয়** *n.* a man's or woman's father-in-law's house.

শ্বশ্রু *n.* a mother-in-law; an aunt-in-law.

শ্বসন *n.* breathing, respiration; (loos.) inhalation. **কৃত্রিম শ্বসন** artificial respiration.

শ্বা, শ্বাদন্ত variants of **শ্ব** and **শ্বদন্ত** respectively.

শ্বাপদ *n.* any carnivorous ferocious beast of prey; (loos.) a wild beast. **~সংকুল, ~সমাকীর্ণ** *a.* infested with ferocious beasts of prey.

শ্বাস *n.* breathing, respiration; breath; asthma; asthmatic spasm; the last gasp. **শ্বাস ওঠা** *v.* to be in the last gasp; to be attacked with a spell of asthmatic spasm. **শ্বাস ছাড়া** *v.* to breathe out, to exhale. **শ্বাস নেওয়া** *v.* to breathe in, to inhale. **দুর্গন্ধ শ্বাস** *n.* foul breath; (med.) halitosis. **শ্বাসকষ্ট** *n.* breathing trouble; laboured breathing, dyspnoea; laboured breathing of a dying person. **~কেন্দ্র** *n.* (anat.) the respiratory centre. **~ক্রিয়া** *n.* breathing, respiration. **~গ্রহণ** *n.* inhalation. **~গ্রহণ করা** same as **শ্বাস নেওয়া**। **~ত্যাগ** *n.* exhalation. **~ত্যাগ করা** same as **শ্বাস ছাড়া**। **~নালী** *n.* (anat.) the windpipe, the trachea. **~প্রশ্বাস** *n.* breathing, respiration. **~যন্ত্র** *n.* (anat.) the respiratory organ, lungs. **~রোগ** *n.* any disease characterized by breathing trouble, such as, asthma, bronchitis etc. **~রোধ** *n.* suffocation or choking; bated breath. **~রোধ করা** *v.* to suffocate; to choke; to make breathless. **~রোধ হওয়া** *v.* to be suffocated or choked; to become breathless. **~রোধক** *a.* suffocating, choking. **শ্বাসারি** *n.* a medicine or cure for breathing trouble.

শ্বেত *n.* the white colour. □ *a.* white; (of hair) grey. **~কায়** *a.* white complexioned. **~কুষ্ঠ** *n.* leucoderma. **~চর্ম** *a.* white-skinned, white-complexioned. **~দ্বীপ** *n.* a mythological island, the island of the moon; (often facet.) the British Isles. **~পাথর, ~প্রস্তর** *n.* marble. **~প্রদর** *n.* leucorrhoea, whites. **~রক্ত কণিকা** a white corpuscle. **~শ্মশ্রু** *a.* greybearded. **~সর্ষপ** *n.* white mustard, *Brassica alba.* **~সার** *n.* starch. **অযুক্ত শ্বেতসার** (bot.) simple starch. **~হস্তী** *n.* (lit. & fig.) a white elephant. **শ্বেতাঙ্গ** *a.* one whose complexion is white. □ *n.* the white man, a European or an American. **শ্বেতাভ** *a.* having a slightly white glow or tinge, whitish; (loos.) incandescent. **শ্বেতি, শ্বেতী** *n.* leucoderma.

শ্মশান, শ্মশানপুরী, শ্মশানভূমি *n.* a crematorium, a crematory, a cremation-ground; (fig.) a deserted and cheerless place, house etc. **শ্মশানে পরিণত করা** *v.* to turn into or reduce to a cheerless desert. **শ্মশানকালী** *n.* Goddess Kali (কালী), the presiding deity of crematoria. **শ্মশানচারী** *a.* roaming or living in crematoria. *fem.* **শ্মশানচারিণী**। **শ্মশানবন্ধু** *n.* one who accompanies or carries a dead body to the crematorium. **শ্মশানবাসী** *a.* living in crematoria. *fem.* **শ্মশানবাসিনী**। **শ্মশানবৈরাগ্য** *n.* the perception of transitoriness of the world, with which the mind of a visitor to a crematorium becomes imbued for a while; (fig.) sham distaste or aversion for the world just before death.

শ্মশ্রু *n.* beard (of man's face). **~মণ্ডিত** *a.* covered with beard, bearded. **~ল** *a.* covered with beard, bearded. **~শূন্য, ~হীন** *a.* beardless. **~শোভিত** *a.* bedecked with beard, bearded.

শ্যাওলা *n.* lichen, moss; alga.

শ্যাম *a.* cloud-coloured; dark blue; bottle-green; green; dark-coloured; jet black;

having a dark yet very sweet complexion, (cp.) brunet (*fem.* brunette). ☐ *n.* Krishna (কৃষ্ণ). **শ্যাম রাখি কি কুল রাখি** to have to choose between one's lover and infamy on the one hand and one's husband and good name on the other; (fig.) to be between the horns of a dilemma. **~কান্তি** *a.* having a dark yet very sweet complexion. **~বর্ণ** *n.* cloud-like colour; dark blue or bottle-green colour; green or dark colour; jet black colour; dark yet very sweet complexion. ☐ *a.* same as **শ্যাম** (*a.*). **~ল,** (poet.) **~র** *a.* same as **শ্যাম** (*a.*). *fem.* **শ্যামলা**। **শ্যামলা বসুন্ধরা** the (mother) earth green with crops and vegetation. **~লতা, ~লিমা** *n.* the state of having cloud-like or dark blue or bottle-green or green or dark colour or a dark yet very sweet complexion. **~লী** *a.* (loos.) *fem.* of **~ল**। ☐ *n.* a pet name for a dark-coloured cow. **~সুন্দর** *n.* Krishna (কৃষ্ণ) ; a small bird of the munia family, the black-headed munia. **~ক, শ্যামা**[1] variants of **শ্যামাক**। **শ্যামা**[2] *a. fem.* of **শ্যাম** (*a.*). ☐ *n.* (rhet.) an uncommonly beautiful woman having a dazzlingly bright cream-coloured complexion, who is very pleasant to touch; Goddess Kali (কালী) ; a song-bird of the thrush-family, the shama; an evergreen creeper. **শ্যামাক** *n.* a kind of wild paddy. **শ্যামাঙ্গ** *a.* dark-complexioned. *fem.* **শ্যামাঙ্গা, শ্যামাঙ্গী, শ্যামাঙ্গিনী**। **শ্যামাপোকা** *n.* a green-coloured winged insect found in late autumn. **শ্যামায়মান** *a.* getting dark, darkening, getting or becoming bottle-green, or green.

শ্যালক same as **শালা**[2]।

শ্যালাজ same as **শালাজ**।

শ্যালিকা, শ্যালী same as **শালী**[2]। **শ্যালীপতি** same as **ভায়রা**।

শ্যেন *n.* the hawk, the falcon; the eagle, *fem.* **শ্যেনী**। **~চক্ষু, ~দৃষ্টি** *a.* hawk-eyed, falcon-eyed; eagle-eyed. **শ্যেন দৃষ্টিতে লক্ষ করা** to watch with a piercing or keen eye, to watch like a hawk.

শ্রদ্ধা *n.* love and respect, admiration, reverence; esteem; confidence, faith (নেতার প্রতি শ্রদ্ধা) ; devotion (সশ্রদ্ধ পূজা) ; inclination, desire (খাবারে শ্রদ্ধা). **শ্রদ্ধা করা** *v.* to love and respect, to admire, to revere, to esteem; to have confidence or faith in. **~ন্বিত, ~বান, ~লু, ~শীল** *a.* respectful, having faith or confidence in, faithful. **~ভাজন, ~স্পদ** *n.* an object of reverence, a reverend person. *fem.* **~স্পদা**। **~ভাজনেষু, ~স্পদেষু** to you or him as the reverend one (a form of addressing a reverend person in a letter).

শ্রদ্ধেয় *a.* reverend, venerable. *fem.* **শ্রদ্ধেয়া**।

শ্রবণ *n.* hearing; listening (to); audition; the ear. **শ্রবণ করা** *v.* to hear; to listen (to); give an audition. **~গোচর** *a.* coming within the range of hearing, audible. **~পথ** *n.* the ear; hearing. **~বহির্ভূত** same as **শ্রবণাতীত**। **~বিবর** *n.* the ear-hole. **~মধুর** *a.* sweet to hear. **~যোগ্য** *a.* worth listening to, fit to hear; audible. **~সুখকর** *a.* pleasing to the ear. **শ্রবণা** *n.* the twenty-second of the twenty-seven stars according to Hindu astronomy. **শ্রবণাতীত** *a.* incapable of being heard, inaudible. **শ্রবণীয়** same as **শ্রব্য**। **শ্রবণেন্দ্রিয়** *n.* the organ of hearing, the ear.

শ্রব্য *a.* fit to hear; audible; intended to be heard (**শ্রব্য কাব্য** = a poem intended to be heard, not seen i.e., excluding drama). **~তা** *n.* audibility.

শ্রম *n.* labour, toil; physical or manual labour; diligence, assiduity, industry (শ্রম বিনা লেখাপড়া হয় না) ; exertion, fatigue; rigour (সশ্রম কারাদণ্ড). **শ্রম করা** *v.* to labour, to toil; to do physical or manual labour; to apply oneself diligently or assiduously; to exert oneself; to undergo rigours. **উৎপাদক শ্রম** productive labour. **~কাতর** *a.* reluctant to toil, grudging labour; lazy. **~জ** *n.* produced by toil or industry. **~জনক** *a.* toilsome, strenuous, fatiguing. **~জল** *n.* perspiration (caused by toil), sweat. **~জীবী** *a.* earning one's livelihood by manual labour. ☐ *n.* same as **শ্রমিক**। **~ণ** *n.* a Buddhist mendicant, ascetic. *fem.* **~ণা**। **~বণ্টন, ~বিভাগ** *n.* (econ.) division of labour. **~বিমুখ** same as **~কাতর**। **~মন্ত্রক**

n. the Ministry of Labour. ~মহাধ্যক্ষ *n.* Labour Commissioner. ~লভ্য *a.* obtainable by effort or application. ~লব্ধ *a.* earned by toil or industry. ~শিল্প *n.* an industry. ~শীল, ~সহিষ্ণু *a.* devoted to labour, laborious, painstaking, hardy, industrious, diligent, assiduous. ~শীলতা *n.* industry, diligence, assiduity. ~সাধ্য *a.* involving labour; laborious, toilsome; strenuous; attainable by hard work. শ্রম স্বীকার করা *v.* to take pains. শ্রমাপনোদন করা *v.* to allay or remove fatigue; to refresh, to freshen up. শ্রমিক *n.* a manual labourer, a labourer; a workman, an industrial worker. শ্রমিক-আন্দোলন *n.* labour movement. শ্রমিক-গোলযোগ *n.* labour unrest; labour trouble. শ্রমিকদল *n.* a gang of labourers; (pol.) the Labour Party. শ্রমিক-সংঘ *n.* a trade union. শ্রমোপজীবী same as শ্রমজীবী। *fem.* শ্রমোপজীবিনী।

শ্রাদ্ধ *n.* a respectful and well-wishing offering to the manes, obsequies, sraddha; (sarcas.) extravagant use or spending, waste; (কথার শ্রাদ্ধ, টাকার শ্রাদ্ধ) ; (rather vul.) tremendous persecution or utter ruin; vituperation; (sl.) an undesirable affair. শ্রাদ্ধ করা *v.* to perform one's sraddha ceremony; (sarcas.) to use or spend extravagantly; to waste, (rather vul.) to persecute tremendously or ruin utterly; to revile. শ্রাদ্ধ খাওয়া *v.* to partake of the feast given on the occasion of a sraddha ceremony. শ্রাদ্ধ গড়াবে *v.* (sl.) the (undesirable) affair will go a long way. ~কার্য, ~ক্রিয়া *n.* (performance of) obsequies or sraddha. ~শান্তি *n.* sraddha and similar other rites so that the manes enjoy blessed peace.

শ্রান্ত *a.* fatigued, tired, wearied, exhausted. শ্রান্ত করা *v.* to fatigue, to tire, to weary, to exhaust. শ্রান্ত হওয়া *v.* to be tired or fatigued, to get tired; to be wearied or exhausted. ~ক্লান্ত *a.* extremely tired or exhausted. ~দেহ *a.* having a tired or exhausted body. শ্রান্তি *n.* fatigue, weariness, tiredness, exhaustion. শ্রান্তি বোধ করা *v.* to feel tired or exhausted. শ্রান্তিকর, শ্রান্তিজনক *a.* fatiguing, tiring, wearisome; laborious. শ্রান্তিহর *a.* removing or allaying weariness or exhaustion or fatigue; refreshing. শ্রান্তিহীন *a.* untiring, tireless.

শ্রাবণ[1] *n.* the fourth month of the Bengali calendar. ধারা-শ্রাবণ *n.* Shrabana (শ্রাবণ) the month of incessant rain or ceaseless downpour.

শ্রাবণ[2] *a.* auditory.

শ্রাব্য var. of শ্রব্য।

শ্রী *n.* Goddess Lakshmi (লক্ষ্মী) ; Goddess Saraswati (সরস্বতী) ; wealth, riches; affluence, prosperity; good luck, fortune; beauty, grace (মুখশ্রী) ; appearance; style, manner, attitude (কথার শ্রী) ; an appellation affixed to the name of a holy person dead or living or to that of a sacred thing or place (শ্রীসত্যেন্দ্র বসু, শ্রীচৈতন্য, শ্রীখোল, শ্রীক্ষেত্র) ; an Indian musical mode. ~করকমল *n.* a lotus-like auspicious hand. ~করকমলেষু to your or his lotus-like auspicious hand (a form of addressing a person politely in a letter). ~ক্ষেত্র *n.* Puri in Orissa. ~খণ্ড *n.* sandalwood. ~ঘর *n.* (sarcas.) a prison, a gaol, a jail. ~ঘরবাস *a.* imprisonment, incarceration. ~চরণ *n.* an auspicious foot. ~চরণেষু to your or his auspicious feet (a form of addressing a venerable person in a letter). ~চরণকমল *n.* a lotus-like auspicious foot. ~চরণকমলেষু same as ~চরণেষু। ~পঞ্চমী *n.* the fifth lunar day of the bright fortnight of the month of Magh (মাঘ) when Goddess Saraswati is worshipped. ~ফল *n.* the wood-apple. ~বৎস *n.* the clockwise circle of hair on the bosom of Vishnu (বিষ্ণু). ~বৎস লাঞ্ছন *n.* Vishnu (বিষ্ণু). ~বৃদ্ধি *n.* increase of wealth; prosperity; advancement, improvement. ~বৃদ্ধি লাভ করা *v.* to have one's wealth increased; to prosper, to thrive; to advance, to improve. ~বৃদ্ধিসাধন করা *v.* to cause to prosper or thrive; to promote prosperity or wealth; to cause to advance, to improve. ~ভ্রষ্ট *a.* fallen from or bereft of prosperity; deprived of beauty or grace or glamour; dilapidated; ruined.

~মণ্ডিত *a.* beautified; beautiful; graceful. **~মতী** *a. fem.* of **শ্রীমান** । ☐ *n.* a beautiful woman or girl; a young woman; Radha (রাধা). **~মৎ** *a.* gracious or glorious usu. affixed to the name of a saintly man or to that of a sacred book (শ্রীমদ্‌রামানুজ, শ্রীমদ্ভাগবত). **~মন্ত** *a.* fortunate, prosperous; wealthy, affluent. **~মান** *a.* beautiful, graceful, fortunate, wealthy, affluent (usu. affixed to the name of a junior person). **~মুখ** *n.* an auspicious face. **~যুক্ত, ~যুত** same as **শ্রীমান** (usu. affixed to the name of a senior or respectable man). *fem.* **~যুক্তা** । **~ল** same as **~যুক্ত** (usu. affixed to the name of an especially respectable or adorable man). **~শূন্য, ~হীন** *a.* deprived of grace or beauty or prosperity; ugly; wretched.

শ্রুত *a.* heard; famous, celebrated. **~কীর্তি** *a.* one whose deeds or feats have become widely famous. **~ধর, ~লিখন, ~লিপি, ~লেখক** same as **শ্রুতিধর, শ্রুতিলিখন, শ্রুতিলিপি, শ্রুতিলেখক** (see **শ্রুতি**).

শ্রুতি *n.* hearing; audition; the ear; hearsay (জনশ্রুতি) ; a myth; a legend; mythology; legends collectively; the Vedas; (mus.) a subtle note that is heard at the time of changing the voice from one note to another, (cp.) a quarter-tone. **~কটু, ~কঠোর** *a.* grating on ears, harsh to hear, grating, jarring; cacophonous, cacophonic. **~গোচর** *a.* coming within the range of hearing, audible. **~নাট্য** *n.* a drama that is enjoyed not by seeing it acted but by listening to it. **~ধর** *a.* capable of remembering whatever one hears. ☐ *n.* such a person. **~পথ** *n.* the ear-hole; the range of hearing, earshot. **~মধুর** *a.* sweet to hear. **~মূল** *n.* the root or base of the ear. **~লিখন** *n.* act of writing to dictation; shorthand writing, stenography. **~লিপি** *n.* a script written to dictation or by shorthand. **~লেখক** *n.* a writer taking dictation; a shorthand writer, a stenographer. **~সুখকর** *a.* pleasant to hear.

শ্রেণি, শ্রেণী *n.* a line, a row, a range; a series (সংখ্যাশ্রেণি) ; a community, a class (ধনিকশ্রেণি) ; a collection, a herd, a flock, a swarm (হস্তিশ্রেণি, পিপীলিকাশ্রেণি) ; a school or college class, a class, a form (ষষ্ঠ শ্রেণি, বি. এ. শ্রেণি) ; a division (তিন শ্রেণিতে বিভক্ত) ; (phys.) a grade. **~ফল** *n.* sum of series. **~বদ্ধ, ~বিন্যস্ত** *a.* arranged in a line or row, aligned, arrayed; (esp. in bot.) classified. **~বন্ধ, ~বিন্যাস** *n.* alignment, arrayment; classification. **~বন্ধ-পদ্ধতি, ~বন্ধ-প্রণালী** *n.* the system of alignment or arrayment or (chiefly in bot.) classification. **~বন্ধসূত্র** *n.* principles of classification. **~বিভাগ** *n.* classification; division into castes or communities or classes or groups. **~ভুক্ত** *a.* included in a particular line or class.

শ্রেয় *n.* good; weal; welfare; benefit; virtue; religion; final salvation, beatitude. ☐ *a.* good; beneficial; auspicious; proper; best, excellent; (pop.) preferable, better, superior. **~সী** *fem.* of **শ্রেয়ান** । **~স্কর** *a.* doing good (to), beneficial. *fem.* **~স্করী** । **শ্রেয়ান** *a.* better; superior; more beneficial; (loos.) good, excellent, beneficial. **শ্রেয়োলাভ** *n.* attainment of good or virtue or final salvation.

শ্রেষ্ঠ *a.* greatest; chief, principal; best, excellent; (pop.) greater or better, superior. *fem.* **শ্রেষ্ঠা** । **~তা, ~ত্ব** *n.* the state of being the greatest or chief or best or excellent; superiority or pre-eminence.

শ্রেষ্ঠী *n.* a merchant prince; a merchant; a banker; an opulent man.

শ্রোণি, শ্রোণী *n.* the hip, the buttocks, the loins, the posteriors.

শ্রোতব্য *a.* to be heard, proper to hear.

শ্রোতা *n.* a hearer; a listener.

শ্রোতৃবর্গ, শ্রোতৃমণ্ডলী *n.* the audience.

শ্রোত্র *n.* the ear; the Vedas.

শ্রোত্রিয় *n.* a Brahman versed in the Vedas; a class of Brahmans who are not kulins (কুলীন) ; a Brahman of this class.

শ্রোত্রী *fem.* of **শ্রোতা** ।

শ্রৌত *a.* enjoined or sanctioned in the Vedas, Vedic.

শ্লথ *a.* loose, flaccid (শ্লথ চর্ম) ; dishevelled (শ্লথ কবরী) ; blowsy (শ্লথ বেশবাস) ;

slack, loose, loosened, slackened, relaxed (শ্লথ বন্ধন) ; not strict, lax (শ্লথ শাসন) ; tired, worn-out, fatigued (শ্লথ দেহ) ; slow, tardy, slowed down, retarded (শ্লথগতি) ; not earnest or careful (সে পড়াশোনায় বড়ো শ্লথ).

শ্লাঘনীয়, শ্লাঘ্য *a.* praiseworthy, laudable, commendable; desirable.

শ্লাঘা *n.* praise, laudation, commendation, eulogy; self-praise.

শ্লিষ্ট *a.* connected, joined; attached; related; embraced; (rhet. & gr.) containing a pun, equivocal. **~প্রয়োগ** *n.* equivocation.

শ্লীপদ *n.* elephantiasis.

শ্লীল *a.* courteous, polite; modest; decent. **~তা** *n.* courtesy, politeness; modesty; decency. **শ্লীলতাহানি** *n.* violation of modesty, outraging the modesty (of a woman).

শ্লেট rej. spell. of **স্লেট** ৷

শ্লেষ *n.* (rhet.) pun; (loos.) a ridicule hinted artfully, an irony, an insinuation. **শ্লেষ করা** *v.* to direct an ironical remark (at or against); to insinuate (against). **শ্লেষোক্তি** *n.* an ironical or insinuating or quibbling remark.

শ্লেষ্মা *n.* nasal mucus, catarrh, rheum; mucus; phlegm. **বুকে শ্লেষ্মা জমা** *v.* to have congestion in one's chest. **শ্লেষ্মা ঝরা** *v.* to have one's nose running. **~ঘটিত** same as **শ্লৈষ্মিক** ৷ **~প্রধান** *a.* having predominance of phlegm, phlegmatic.

শ্লৈষ্মিক *a.* mucous; catarrhal, rheumatic; phlegmatic. **শৈষ্মিক ঝিল্লী** the mucous membrane.

শ্লোক *n.* a couplet, a distich, a verse, a poem; fame, renown (পুণ্যশ্লোক). **~বদ্ধ, শ্লোকাত্মক** *a.* versified.

ষ *n.* the thirty-first consonant of the Bengali alphabet.

ষট্ *n.* & *a* (used as a *pfx.*) six. **ষট্‌ক** *n.* a hexad; a sextet (te), a sestet. **~কর্ম** *n.* the six performances of a Brahman as enjoined by the scriptures. **~কোণ** *n.* a hexagon. **~চত্বারিংশ** *a.* forty-six. **~চত্বারিংশৎ** *n.* & *a.* forty-six. **~চত্বারিংশত্তম** *a.* forty-sixth. *fem.* **~চত্বারিংশত্তমী**। **~ত্রিংশ** *a.* thirty-six. **~ত্রিংশৎ** *n.* & *a.* thirty-six. **~ত্রিংশত্তম** *a.* thirty-sixth. *fem.* **~ত্রিংশত্তমী**। **~পঞ্চাশ** *a.* fifty-six. **~পঞ্চাশৎ** *n.* & *a.* fifty-six. **~পঞ্চাশত্তম** *a.* fifty-sixth. *fem.* **~পঞ্চাশত্তমী**। **~পদ** *a.* hexapod. □ *n.* the bumble-bee. *fem.* **~পদী**। **~ষষ্ট** *a.* sixty-six. **~ষষ্টি** *n.* & *a.* sixty-six. **~ষষ্টিতম** *a.* sixty-sixth. *fem.* **~ষষ্টিতমী**। **~সপ্ততি** *n.* & *a.* seventy-six. **~সপ্ততিতম** *a.* seventy-sixth. *fem.* **~সপ্ততিতমী**।

ষড়্ঋতু *n.* the six seasons, namely, summer, the rains, autumn, late autumn, winter and spring.

ষড়্গুণ *a.* multiplied by six, six times.

ষড়ঙ্গ *n.* the six limbs of a body, namely the head, the two hands or arms, the waist, the two legs or feet; the six Vedangas; six limbs or branches.

ষড়্জ *n.* (mus.) the first note of the natural major scale, C.

ষড়্দর্শন *n.* the six systems of Hindu philosophy.

ষড়্ধা *a.* of six kinds or manners; six times. □ *adv.* in six kinds or manners; six times.

ষড়্বিংশ *a.* twenty-six. **~তি** *n.* & *a.* twenty-six. **ষড়্বিংশতিতম** *a.* twenty-sixth. *fem.* **ষড়্বিংশতিতমী**।

ষড়্বিধ *a.* of six kinds; sixfold.

ষড়যন্ত্র *n.* a conspiracy, a secret plot, an intrigue. **ষড়যন্ত্র করা** *v.* to conspire, to plot, to intrigue. **~কারী** *n.* a conspirator, a plotter, an intriguer.

ষড়্রিপু see **রিপু**[২]।

ষড়্রস *n.* six kinds of flavour or taste or tang (viz. sweet, sour, salt, pungent, astringent, bitter).

ষড়শীতি *n.* & *a.* eighty-six. **~তম** *a.* eighty-sixth. *fem.* **~তমী**।

ষড়ানন *n.* one having six faces; (myth.) Kartikeya the commandar of the heavenly host.

ষণ্ড *n.* the bull, the ox; a eunuch. **ষণ্ডা** *a.* as obstinate and hefty as a bull; bull-headed; robust, hefty. **ষণ্ডামর্ক,** (erron.) **ষণ্ডামার্ক** *n.* (myth.) Sanda (ষণ্ড) and Amarka (অমর্ক), two roguish and godless teachers; (pop.) a very obstinate and robust rogue, a rowdy, a ruffian.

ষন্নবতি *n.* & *a.* ninety-six. **~তম** *a.* ninety-sixth. *fem.* **~তমী**।

ষণ্মাস *n.* (a period of) consecutive six months, a half-year.

ষত্ব *n.* (gr.) the use of ষ (esp. in place of শ, স). **~বিধান, ~বিধি** *n.* (gr.) the rules governing the use of ষ (esp. in place শ, স).

ষত্বণত্বজ্ঞান *n.* (lit.) knowledge of the right use of the letters ষ and ণ; (fig.) commom sense.

ষষ্টি *n.* & *a.* sixty. **~তম** a. sixtieth. *fem.* **~তমী**।

ষষ্ঠ *a.* sixth. **ষষ্ঠাংশ** *n.* a sixth part, one-sixth. **ষষ্ঠী** *a. fem.* of **ষষ্ঠ**। □ *n. fem.* a female deity who protects human babies; (gr.) the sixth case-ending; the sixth day of a lunar fortnight; the sixth day of the lunar fortnight when the ceremony of awakening Goddess Durga (দুর্গা) is held for her annual worship. **ষষ্ঠীর কৃপা** obtaining a child through the grace of Goddess Sasthi (ষষ্ঠী); the grace of Goddess Sasthi; being blessed with many children. **ষষ্ঠীতৎপুরুষ** *n.* (gr.) a system of forming compounds in which the first word actually drops the sixth case-ending. **ষষ্ঠীবাটা** *n.* a ceremonial gift sent to a son-in-law on the eve of জামাইষষ্ঠী (see জামাই). **ষষ্ঠীবুড়ি** *n.* Goddess Sasthi (ষষ্ঠী).

ষাঁড় *n.* the bull, the ox. **ষাঁড়ের গোঁ** bull-like obstinacy, bull-headedness. **ষাঁড়া-ষাঁড়ি** *n.*

a fight between two bulls. ষাঁড়া-ষাঁড়ির বান the tidal wave of the Ganges (which roars like two bellowing bulls engaged in fighting each other).

ষাট[1] *int.* May Goddess Sasthi (ষষ্ঠী) be with you for your safety.

ষাট[2] *n.* & *a.* sixty.

ষাণ্মাসিক *a.* six-monthly, half-yearly.

ষেট, ষেটে corrup. of ষষ্ঠী the goddess of children. ষেটের (কোলের) বাছা a favoured child of Goddess Sasthi (ষষ্ঠী) ; said of a child in way of blessing. ষেটেরা *n.* a ceremony performed on the sixth day of a child's birth.

ষোড়শ *n.* sixteen; a Hindu system of performing a sraddha ceremony in which sixteen different articles are given away. □ *a.* sixteen; sixteenth. ষোড়শাংশ *n.* a sixteenth part; one-sixteenth. ষোড়শী *a. fem.* sixteenth; sixteen years old. □ *n. fem.* one of the ten manifestations of Goddess Durga (দুর্গা) ; a sixteen year old woman. ষোড়শোপচার *n.* sixteen different articles required for a perfect worship. ষোড়শোপচারে *adv.* with all the necessary sixteen articles; (fig.) thoroughly; sumptuously.

ষোলো *n.* & *a.* sixteen. ষোলো-আনা *n.* sixteen anna, one rupee. □ *a.* total, entire, whole. □ *adv.* entirely, wholly, completely, thoroughly. ষোলো-কলা *n.* the sixteen digits of the moon. ষোলো-কলা পূর্ণ হওয়া *v.* (sarcas.) to be thoroughly fulfilled; to meet with complete disaster, to be utterly ruined.

ষ্ঠীবন *n.* spitting.

স[1] *n.* the thirty-second consonant of the Bengali alphabet.

স[2] *pfx.* indicating: together with, attended by (সচন্দন, সভৃত্য) ; of the same (সগোত্র, সতীর্থ).

সই[1] corrup. of **সখী** and **সহি** ৷

-সই[2] *sfx.* indicating: able to (টেকসই): -able, -ible; conforming to (পছন্দসই) ; up to (বুকসই).

সই[3] capable of hitting the mark, possessing marksmanship (হাতসই).

সই[4] *n.* a signature; an impression or mark given as a substitute for signature (ঢেরাসই, টিপসই). **সই করা, সই দেওয়া** *v.* to sign; to put an impression or mark as a substitute for signature. **তাই সই** let it be.

সইস *n.* a groom or a mounted attendant, a syce, a sice, a saice.

সওগাত *n.* a present, a gift.

সওদা *n.* purchase; trade; merchandise, wares; articles pruchased. **সওদা করা** *v.* to purchase, to buy, **~গর** *n.* a merchant; a merchant prince. **~গরি** *n.* the profession of a merchant, trading, commerce. ☐ *a.* mercantile, commercial. **~গরি করা** *v.* to work as a merchant, to follow the occupation of a trader; to trade. **~গরি আপিস** a mercantile firm, a merchant office. **~পত্র** *n.* purchases.

সওয়া[1] pop. var. of **সহা** ৷

সওয়া[2] *n.* & *a.* one and one-fourth, one and a quarter. **সওয়া ঘণ্টা** an hour and a quarter. **সওয়া তিন** three and a quarter. **সওয়া তিনটে বাজে** it is a quarter past three o'clock.

সওয়ানো pop. var. of **সহানো** ৷

সওয়ার *n.* a rider, (cp.) a sowar. ☐ *a.* riding, mounted. **সওয়ারি** *n.* a vehicle, a carriage; a mount; a passenger. **সওয়ারি হওয়া** *v.* to ride, to mount; to board a vehicle.

সওয়াল *n.* a question, an inquiry; (in law—loos.) pleading on behalf of the plaintiff, argument. **সওয়াল করা** *v.* to question, to inquire; to plead or argue on behalf of the plaintiff. **সওয়াল জবাব** *n.* questions and answers; (in law) argument and counter-argument, pleading and replication.

সং *n.* a clown, a bumpkin; a masque; a farce; a grotesque spectacle.

সংকট *n.* a crucial danger; a great difficulty; a very knotty problem; a critical situation, a tight corner; a crux; great intricacy; a very narrow path, a gorge (usu. **গিরিসংকট**). **~কাল** *n.* a critical time; hard times; a crisis. **সংকটাপন্ন** *a.* greatly endangered; faced with a great difficulty. **সংকটাবস্থা** *n.* a critical situation, a tight corner.

সংকর *n.* a half-breed, a half-caste; a mongrel; a hybrid; a mixture of heterogeneous things. ☐ *a.* half-bred; mongrel; crossbred, hybrid. **সংকরীকরণ** *n.* hybridization.

সংকর্ষণ *n.* a forceful pull; attraction; ploughing, cultivation.

সংকলক same as **সংকলয়িতা** ৷

সংকলন *n.* collection; culling; compilation; (math.) addition. **সংকলন করা** *v.* to collect; to cull; to compile; (math.) to add. **~গ্রন্থ** *n.* a compilation.

সংকলয়িতা *n.* a collector; a compiler; an adder. *fem.* **সংকলয়িত্রী** ৷

সংকলিত *a.* collected; culled; compiled; added.

সংকল্প *n.* a resolve, a determination; a (strong) desire; a solemn vow to do something (taken esp. on the eve of a religious worship); resolution. **সংকল্প করা** *v.* to resolve; to determine, to make up one's mind; to take a solemn vow to do something (esp. on the eve of a religious ceremony the purpose for which it is intended). **সংকল্প-বিকল্প** *n.* desire and doubt; certainty and uncertainty; hesitation. **~সাধন করা** *v.* to fulfil a resolve; to attain a desire; to give effect to a resolution. **সংকল্পিত** *a.* determined, resolved; purposed intended; passed or adopted as a resolution.

সংকাশ *a.* (used as a *sfx.*) like, similar to, resembling (আদিত্যসংকাশ).

সংকীর্ণ *a.* narrow; not spacious, small; illiberal, ungenerous. (সংকীর্ণ হৃদয়). **~চিত্ত, ~চেতা, ~মনা** *a.* narrow-minded, small-minded. **~তা** *n.* narrowness; smallness; illiberality.

সংকীর্তন *n.* singing in praise, singing the glory (of); singing in praise of God or a deity; a song in praise of God or a deity; a hymn. **সংকীর্তন করা** *v.* to sing in praise (of), to glorify in songs; to sing in praise of God or a deity; to hymn. **সংকীর্তিত** *a.* celebrated in songs; thoroughly narrated or extolled.

সংকুচিত *a.* curtailed; reduced; contracted; shrivelled; (phys.) compressed; closed or narrowed or shut; cowered (ভয়ে সংকুচিত); diffident, hesitating or hesitant. **সংকুচিত করা** *v.* to curtail or reduce or contract or shrivel; to compress; to close or shut or narrow; to cower. **সংকুচিত হওয়া** *v.* to be curtailed or reduced; to contract or shrivel; to get compressed; to draw back or to shrink; to cower or hesitate.

সংকুল *a.* (used as a *sfx.*) full of; crowded with, abounding in; infested with (শ্বাপদসংকুল).

সংকুলান *n.* sufficiency for meeting a need. **সংকুলান হওয়া** *v.* to be sufficient (for), to suffice (for).

সংকেত *n.* a beckoning, a beck, a gesture; a hint; a sign; a signal; a presage; a clue; a rule; a secret tryst for lovers.

সংকেত করা *v.* to beckon, to sign, to gesticulate. **সংকেত দেওয়া** *v.* to give a hint, to hint (at); to presage. **সংকেতে** *adv.* by means of gesticulation, by a sign; by hints or by suggestions; briefly.

সংকোচ *n.* contraction; curtailment (ব্যয় সংকোচ); hesitation, diffidence. **সংকোচ করা** *v.* to contract; to curtail, to cut down; to hesitate. **সংকোচ বোধ করা** *v.* to feel hesitation. **মরণ সংকোচ** *n.* rigor mortis. **সংকোচক** *a.* contracting; curtailing; astringent. **সংকোচন** *n.* contraction, curtailment; shutting; (phys.) compression. **সংকোচনশীল** *a.* contractile. **সংকোচনীয়** *a.* contractible. **সংকোচশূন্য, সংকোচহীন** *a.* unhesitating; unabashed; unscrupulous; shameless; smart, free.

সংক্রম, সংক্রমণ *n.* act of entering and settling down; transit, transition; (astr.) transition from one zodiacal sign to another; (of diseases etc.) infection, contagion; (of a practice, a virtue, a vice etc.) transmission esp. by contiguity or association. **সংক্রমণ করা** *v.* to enter and settle down; to transit; (astr.) to make a transit or pass from one zodiacal sign to another; to infect; to be transmitted (into) esp. by contiguity or association. **সংক্রমণিকা** *n.* a gallery. **সংক্রমিত** *a.* that which has entered and settled down; transited; (astr.) transited from one zodiacal sign to another; infected; transmitted. **সংক্রমিত হওয়া** *v.* to enter and settle down; (astr.) to pass or make a transit from one zodiacal sign to another; (of diseases) to infect; (of patients) to be infected; to be transmitted into; to be influenced by, to acquire (as a practice).

সংক্রান্ত *a.* (used as a *prep.*) of, relating to, pertaining to, concerning, regarding, as regards (তৎসংক্রান্ত).

সংক্রান্তি *n.* (astr.—of the sun and planets) transit or passage from one zodiacal sign to another; the last day of a Bengali month.

সংক্রামক *a.* infectious, contagious.

সংক্রামিত var. of **সংক্রমিত**।

সংক্ষিপ্ত *a.* summarized, condensed; shortened, abridged; abbreviated; curtailed; reduced; brief, short. **সংক্ষিপ্ত করা** same as **সংক্ষেপ করা**। **সংক্ষিপ্ত বিচার** *n.* a summary trial. **~সার** *n.* a summary, an abstract, a précis, a synopsis.

সংক্ষুব্ধ *a.* very much aggrieved or mortified or concerned or troubled or perturbed; (of seas etc.) extremely disturbed or agitated.

সংক্ষেপ *n.* summarization; condensation; shortening, abridgement; abbreviation;

curtailment; reduction; a summary, an abstract, a precis, a synopsis. **সংক্ষেপ করা** *v.* to summarize, to condense; to shorten, to abridge; to abbreviate; to curtail; to reduce. **~ণ** same as **সংক্ষেপ,** except in the last sense. **সংক্ষেপত, সংক্ষেপে** *adv.* in brief, in short, briefly. **সংক্ষেপিত** var. of **সংক্ষিপ্ত।**

সংক্ষোভ *n.* great aggrievement or mortification or concern or trouble or perturbation; (of seas etc.) great disturbance or agitation.

সংখ্যক *a.* (used as a *sfx.*) numbering; amounting to (শতসংখ্যক).

সংখ্যা *n.* enumeration, counting; a number; a numeral; (math.) a figure; reckoning, estimation. **সংখ্যা করা** *v.* to enumerate, to count; to reckon, to estimate. **সংখ্যা হওয়া** *v.* to be (capable of being) enumerated or counted or numbered. **~গণনা** *n.* enumeration; counting. **~গরিষ্ঠ** *a.* largest in number; (loos.) enjoying a majority. **~গুরু** *a.* large in number; larger in number; enjoying a majority. **সংখ্যাগরিষ্ঠ সম্প্রদায়** the majority community. **সংখ্যা-জ্যোতিষ** *n.* numerology. **~ত** *a.* numbered, counted, enumerated; calculated; reckoned. **সংখ্যাতীত** *a.* countless, innumerable, numberless. **~ন** *n.* enumeration, counting; numbering; calculation. **সংখ্যানুপাতে** *adv.* in proportion to number. **~পাত** *n.* act of writing down a number. **~বাচক** *a.* denoting numbers, numeral. **~মান** *n.* measure. **~মাপন** *n.* measurement. **সংখ্যায়ক** *n.* an enumerator, a calculator. **~লঘিষ্ঠ** *a.* smallest in number. **~লঘু, ~ল্প** *a.* small in number; smaller in number. **সংখ্যালঘু (বা সংখ্যালঘিষ্ঠ) সম্প্রদায়** the minority community.

সংখ্যেয় *a.* countable, calculable, enumerable.

সংগঠক *n.* an organizer.

সংগঠন *n.* formation into an organic whole; organization; an organized body, an organization. **সংগঠন করা** *v.* to organize.

সংগঠিত *a.* organized. **সংগঠিত করা** *v.* to organize.

সংগত[1] *a.* consistent (with); conforming (to); reasonable, proper, just. **সংগতি** *n.* consistency; unity; justness; propriety; (loos.) riches, wealth. **সংগতিসম্পন্ন** *a.* rich, well-to-do; moneyed. **সংগতিহীন** *a.* poor; broke; resourceless; inconsistent.

সংগত[2] (pron. শংগোৎ) *n.* musical accompaniment esp. by playing on the tabla. **সংগত করা** *v.* to accompany by playing on the tabla.

সংগম *n.* union; sexual intercourse, copulation; a confluence (ত্রিবেণীসংগম); a concourse (জনসংগম).

সংগমন *n.* concurrence.

সংগর *n.* parole.

সংগামী *a.* concurrent.

সংগীত *n.* a song; music. **জাতীয় সংগীত** *n.* a national song or anthem. **প্রভাতসংগীত** *n.* a morning song, a matin. **যন্ত্রসংগীত** *n.* instrumental music. **~জ্ঞ** *a.* versed in music. □ *a.* musician. **~প্রিয়** *a.* fond of music. **~বিদ্যা** *n.* the art of music. **~শালা** *n.* a music school **~শাস্ত্র** *n.* the art or science of music. **সংগীতানুরাগ** *n.* love for music. **সংগীতানুরাগী** *a.* fond of music. **সংগীতানুষ্ঠান** *a.* fond of music. *n.* a musical soiree, a musical performance.

সংগৃহীত *a.* collected, raised (সংগৃহীত চাঁদা বা লোক) ; compiled (সংগৃহীত কবিতাবলি) ; culled (সংগৃহীত ফুল).

সংগোপন *n.* thorough concealment; complete secrecy or privacy. **সংগোপনে** *adv.* in complete concealment or secrecy or privacy; secretly; unobservedly. **সংগোপিত** *a.* concealed or secret.

সংগ্রহ, সংগ্রহণ *n.* gathering, raising, collection; amount (esp. of money) collected; compilation; a collection, (গল্পসংগ্রহ) an anthology; (কবিতাসংগ্রহ) culling (পুষ্পসংগ্রহ). **সংগ্রহ করা** *v.* to gather, to raise, to collect; to compile; to cull.

সংগ্রহীতা var. of **সংগ্রাহক।** *fem.* **সংগ্রহীত্রী।**

সংগ্রাম *n.* a war; a battle: a fight; a conflict; a combat, an encounter; a struggle (জীবনসংগ্রাম). **সংগ্রাম করা** *v.* to engage in a war or battle; to fight; to combat, to encounter; to struggle. **~শীল, সংগ্রামী** *a.* given to fighting, never shy of fighting or struggling, fighting, combative. সংগ্রামী মনোবৃত্তি fighting spirit; the will to struggle.

সংগ্রাহক *n.* a gatherer, a raiser, a collector; a compiler; a culler. *fem.* **সংগ্রাহিকা** ।

সংঘ *n.* an association of persons; a body, a party, an organisation; a club; a guild; the Buddhist monastic society. ~**বদ্ধ** *a.* united; incorporated.

সংঘটন *n.* assemblage; occurrence; happening. **সংঘটিত** *a.* assembled, brought together; brought about. **সংঘটিত হওয়া** *v.* to occur, to be brought about, to take place.

সংঘর্ষ, সংঘর্ষণ *n.* a rubbing against each other; friction; collision; concussion; a clash. ~**জনিত** *a.* caused by collision or friction.

সংঘাত *n.* collision, clash; impact.

সংঘারাম *n.* a Buddhist monastery.

সংচিতি *n.* reserve.

সংচূর্ণন *n.* trituration.

সংচূর্ণিত *a.* triturated. **সংচূর্ণিত করা** *v.* to triturate.

সংজ্ঞা *n.* consciousness; an appellation, a name, a designation; (log.) connotation; (esp. in geom.) definition. **সংজ্ঞা দেওয়া** *v.* to give one a name or appellation, to name or designate. **সংজ্ঞা পাওয়া** *v.* to recover consciousness. **সংজ্ঞা হারানো** *v.* to lose consciousness, to swoon, to faint. ~**ন** *n.* consciousness; clear and thorough knowledge or perception. ~**নাশ** *n.* loss of consciousness, fainting. ~**নাশক** *a.* rendering unconscious or senseless. ~**বাচক** *a.* appellative; (gr.) proper. ~**বাচক বিশেষ্য** (gr.) the proper noun. ~**র্থ** *n.* technical meaning; definition. ~**লোপ** same as ~**নাশ** । ~**হীন** *a.* unconscious, senseless. **সংজ্ঞিত** *a.* appellated; defined.

সংনমন *n.* compression.

সংনমিত *a.* compressed.

সংনম্য *a.* compressible.

সংনির্ণয় *n.* judgment.

সংনির্ণীত *a.* adjudged.

সংপরিবর্তন *n.* modification.

সংপৃক্ত *a.* closely connected; (chiefly bot.) saturated. **সংপৃক্তি** *n.* close connection; saturation.

সংপৃষ্ট *a.* challenged.

সংপ্রশ্ন *n.* challenge (made by a sentry).

সংবৎ *n.* the era introduced by king Vikramaditya or Shalibahana in 56 B. C.; an era; a calendar year. **সংবৎসর** *n.* a whole year; a whole calendar year.

সংবদন *n.* tally.

সংবরণ *n.* restraint, checking; prevention; covering; concealment; putting on or wearing in a proper way; dressing or tying (as of tresses) in a proper way. **সংবরণ করা** *v.* to restrain, to check; to prevent; to cover; to conceal; to put on or wear properly; to dress or tie properly.

সংবরা (poet.) same as **সংবরণ করা** ।

সংবর্ত *n.* total annihilation or dissolution or cataclysm, (cp.) deluge, the cloud that appears to destroy the world.

সংবর্ধক *a* & *n.* one who or that which promotes growth or development or increase; one who receives respectfully or felicitates or pays a tribute of respect.

সংবর্ধন, সংবর্ধনা *n.* thorough growth or development or increase; respectful reception; felicitation; a tribute of respect. **সংবর্ধনা করা** *v.* to accord a respectful reception; to felicitate; to pay (one) a tribute of respect.

সংবর্ধিত *a.* thoroughly grown or developed or increased; accorded with a respectful reception; felicitated; one to whom a tribute of respect has been paid. *fem.* **সংবর্ধিতা** ।

সংবলিত *a.* containing; bearing; attended by; mixed with.

সংবহন *n.* circulation (রক্তসংবহন).

সংবাদ *n.* news; information; a message, a report; a story, a narrative (সর্পযজ্ঞ সংবাদ) meeting and conversation (সখী সংবাদ). ~**দাতা** *n.* a press reporter or newspaper correspondent. ~**পত্র** *n.* a newspaper. **সংবাদপত্র বিক্রেতা** *n.* a newsman. ~**পত্রসেবী** *n.* a journalist. **সংবাদ প্রতিষ্ঠান, সংবাদ সরবরাহ-প্রতিষ্ঠান** *n.* a news agency. ~**বাহক** *n.* a messenger; a courier. **সংবাদবাহক পারাবত** a carrier pigeon.

সংবাদী *n.* (mus.) a note accessorial or subsidiary to the principal one.

সংবাহ, সংবাহন *n.* act of carrying (loads); circulation (রক্তসংবাহন); massaging, massage; currying (as of a horse). **সংবাহন করা** *v.* to carry (loads); to circulate; to massage; to curry. **সংবাহক** *a.* load-carrying; circulating; massaging; currying. □ *n.* one who carries (loads); a porter; that which circulates; a massagist, a masseur (*fem.* masseuse); a currier. *fem.* **সংবাহিকা**। **সংবাহাগার** *n.* massage clinic. **সংবাহিত** *a.* carried; circulated; massaged; curried.

সংবিগ্ন *a.* worried; concerned, disturbed; agitated, frightened.

সংবিৎ *n.* consciousness. **সংবিৎ পাওয়া** *v.* to regain or recover consciousness. **সংবিৎ হারানো** *v.* to lose consciousness, to faint, to swoon.

সংবিদা *n.* an agreement; a deed of agreement.

সংবিদিত *a.* known; informed.

সংবিধান *n.* arrangement; prescription; the constitution of a state (ভারতের সংবিধান) **সংবিধান সভা** *n.* a constituent assembly. **~বহির্ভূত** *a.* unconstitutional.

সংবিধি *n.* statute. **~বদ্ধ** *a.* statutory.

সংবীত, সংবৃত *a.* covered; concealed; hidden, secret; contracted.

সংবেগ *n.* worry; anxiety; agitation; feeling of nervousness.

সংবেদ, সংবেদন, সংবেদনা *n.* sensation; susceptibility. **সংবেদনশীল** *a.* sensitive; susceptible, sensory, sensorial. **সংবেদ-নার্ভ** *n.* a sensory nerve. **সংবেদনশীলতা** *n.* sensitiveness, sensitivity. **সংবেদ্য** *a.* perceptible by senses, sensible; knowable.

সংবেশক *n.* hypnotist, a mesmerist.

সংবেশন *n.* hypnosis; hypnotism, mesmerism.

সংবেশিত *a.* hypnotized, mesmerized. **সংবেশিত করা** *v.* to hypnotize, to mesmerize.

সংভরণ *n.* supply and rationing; rationing. **~পত্র** *n.* a ration card.

সংমিশ্রণ *n.* thorough admixture.

সংযত *a.* regulated, disciplined; self-restrained, continent; temperate, moderate, sparing; prevented, repulsed; restrained, checked, curbed; subdued, controlled; demure; modest, gentle (সংযত আচরণ). **সংযত করা** *v.* to regulate, to discipline, to restrict; to temper, to moderate; to prevent; to repulse; to restrain, to check, to curb; to subdue, to control. **~চিত্ত** *a.* one who has controlled one's mind; one whose mind is tranquil or collected; self-restrained; temperate, abstemious. **~বাক** *a.* sparing or reserve in speech; reticent. **সংযতাহার** *a.* sparing or temperate in food and drink. **সংযতেন্দ্রিয়** *n.* one who has subdued one's passions, continent.

সংযম *n.* regulatedness, discipline; self-restraint, continence, temperance, sparingness; (বাকসংযম) ; restraint, check, curb; (বেগসংযম) ; subdual, control (ইন্দ্রিয়সংযম); demureness, modesty, gentleness, politeness (আচরণে সংযম) ; fast and other rites observed on the eve of a holy occasion (শিবরাত্রির সংযম). **সংযম করা** same as **সংযত করা,** and esp. to observe fast and other rites on the eve of a holy occasion. **সংযমন** *n.* regularization, disciplining; act of restraining oneself, act of making oneself continent; tempering, moderation; restraining or curbing; subduing or controlling. **সংযমিত** *a.* regulated or disciplined; tempered; prevented or repulsed; restrained or curbed; subdued or controlled. **সংযমী** *a.* practising self-control or discipline, continent, self-restrained; temperate, moderate, sparing, reserved; abstemious; demure, modest, gentle.

সংযাত্রিক *n.* processionist. **~দল** *n.* a procession.

সংযাত্রী *a.* going in a procession; voyaging. □ *n.* a processionist; a voyager.

সংযুক্ত, সংযুত *a.* joined, linked; attached; admixed; united; amalgamated; federated, federal; connected; joint. **সংযুক্তি, সংযুতি** same as **সংযোজন**।

সংযোগ *n.* joining, linking; a junction; attachment; admixture; union, amalgamation; connection; contact; association, company; intercourse, communication; liaison; close application (মনঃসংযোগ)।

~সাধন করা *v.* to join; to link; to unite. ~স্থাপন করা *v.* to establish connection, to contact, to get into touch (with). সংযোগাধিকারিক *n.* a liaison officer.

সংযোজক *a.* one who or that which joins or attaches or admixes or unites or amalgamates or adds; (gr.) copulative. সংযোজক অব্যয় (gr.) a copulative conjunction.

সংযোজন, সংযোজনা *n.* joining or linking; attachment; admixture; unification; amalgamation; addition. সংযোজন করা *v.* to join, to link; to attach; to admix; to unify; to amalgamate; to add.

সংযোজিত *a.* joined, linked; attached; admixed; unified; amalgamated; added.

সংরক্ষক *n.* a conserver, a conservator (*fem.* conservatrix); a preserver; a protector (*fem.* protectress, protectrix); a guard; a defender; a guardian, a custodian; a curator; one who arranges for reservation.

সংরক্ষণ, সংরক্ষা *n.* conservation; preservation; protection; guarding; defence; act of looking after, safe-keeping, safeguard; custody; reservation. সংরক্ষণ করা *v.* to conserve; to preserve; to protect; to guard; to defend; to reserve. ধর্ম সংরক্ষণ *n.* defence of faith. বাণিজ্যসংরক্ষণ *n.* protectionism. শক্তিসংরক্ষণ *n.* conservation of energy. সতীত্বসংরক্ষণ *n.* preservation of chastity. ~শীল *a.* (esp. pol.) conservative. সংরক্ষণীয় *a.* conservable; preservable; defendable, defensible; guardable; reservable. সংরক্ষণাগার *n.* a conservatory; a preservatory; a safe depository.

সংরক্ষিত *a.* conserved; preserved; protected; guarded; defended; safeguarded; reserved (সংরক্ষিত আসন).

সংরুদ্ধ *a.* obstructed, hindered; confined; besieged.

সংলগ্ন *a.* adjoining; (গৃহসংলগ্ন) ; clinging to (কণ্ঠসংলগ্ন) ; fixed or attached to; adhering to. সংলগ্ন হওয়া *v.* to adjoin; to cling to; to be fixed or attached to; to adhere to.

সংলাপ *n.* conversation; dialogue.

সংশপ্তক *n.* (myth.) an indomitable soldier (or divine origin) who fights for victory with his life, (cp.) a myrmidon.

সংশয় *n.* suspicion; doubt; hesitation; fear or concern, apprehension; uncertainty; (loos.) scepticism. ~কর, ~জনক *a.* doubtful, suspicious; uncertain. সংশয়াকুল *a.* greatly troubled by suspicion or doubt or hesitation; greatly afraid (of) or concerned (about) or apprehensive (of); (loos.) very much sceptic. সংশয়ান্বিত, সংশয়াপন্ন, সংশয়াবিষ্ট, সংশয়িত *a.* seized with suspicion or doubt, suspicious, hesitating; afraid. concerned, apprehensive; uncertain; (loos.) sceptical. সংশয়ী *a.* given to suspicion, suspicious; inclined to doubt; given to fear or apprehension; sceptical by nature.

সংশিত *a.* accomplished, performed; completed; determined, resolved, ~ব্রত *a.* faithful to one's vows.

সংশোধক *n.* a (thorough) purifier or reformer or rectifier or amender or corrector or reviser; a reclaimer from evil ways.

সংশোধন *n.* (thorough) purification or reformation or rectification or amendment or correction or revision. সংশোধন করা *v.* to purify; to reform; to rectify; to amend, to correct; (esp. in law & pol.) to revise. ~বাদ *n.* (pol.) revisionism. ~বাদী *n.* a revisionist. সংশোধনাগার *n.* a reformatory; (euph.) a house of correction, a jail. সংশোধনীয় *a.* reformable; rectifiable; amendable; corrigible; revisable.

সংশোধিত *a.* purified; reformed; rectified; amended; corrected; revised.

সংশ্লিষ্ট *a.* united; adhering, attached; involved in; associating with; related or connected (with), included in or component (সংশ্লিষ্ট বিভাগ).

সংশ্লেষ *n.* union; adhesion; attachment; involvement; association; relation, connection; componency; synthesis (সালোকসংশ্লেষ = photo-synthesis); (bot.) conjugation. ~ণ *n.* synthesis.

সংসক্ত *a.* attached; cohering, coherent; adhering; (phys.) tenacious; adjoining;

connected, related. **সংসক্ত হওয়া** *v.* to cohere. **সংসক্তি** *n.* attachment; cohesion, coherence; adherence; adjacency; connection; relation; (phys.) chemical affinity.

সংসদ *n.* an association, an assembly; a council; a parliament; the Indian Parliament. **~সচিব** *a.* a parliamentary secretary. **~সদস্য** *n.* a member of the Parliament, an M. P. **সংসদীয়** *a.* parliamentary. **সংসদীয় গণতন্ত্র** parliamentary democracy.

সংসর্গ *n.* association, company, fellowship; connection, relation, intercourse; sexual intercourse, cohabitation. **সংসর্গ করা** *v.* to associate with, to mix with. **সংসর্গ ছাড়া** *v.* to give up company, to dissociate oneself (from). **~দোষ** *n.* vices or evils of (bad) association or company. **সংসর্গাভাব** *n.* (log.) universal negation.

সংসার *n.* the world, the earth; a region; earthly life; domestic life; a family; earthly attachment and interests; (loos. of men only) marriage ('কর্তার দুই সংসার') ; (loos.) a wife. **সংসার করা** *v.* to lead domestic life; to manage domestic affairs (also সংসার চালানো) ; (of women) to act as one's housewife, to live with (রমা স্বামীর সংসার করে না) ; (loos.—of men) to marry. **সংসার পাতা** *v.* to set up a household esp. by marrying. **সংসার ত্যাগ করা** *v.* to renounce the world. **~ত্যাগী** *a.* one who has renounced the world. **~ধর্ম** *n.* domestic life or duties, family life or duties. **~বন্ধন** *n.* worldly attachment and interests, earthly bonds or ties; attachment to the family; kindred bonds or ties. **~বাসনা** *n.* desire to lead domestic life; desire to set up a household esp. by marrying; desire for earthly enjoyments. **~যাত্রা** *n.* earthly life; livelihood, daily life (সংসারযাত্রা নির্বাহ করা); domestic life. **~লীলা** *n.* earthly life; mortal life; human life. **~সুখ** *n.* earthly pleasures or happiness of domestic life. **সংসারাশ্রম** *n.* same as **গার্হস্থ্য** (*n.*) **সংসারাশ্রমে প্রবেশ করা** *v.* to start to live the life of a householder esp. by marrying; to enter the world, to settle down to married life, to marry and settle down. **সংসারী** *a.* leading a family life; secular. **সংসারী লোক** a family man. **ঘোর সংসারী** very much domesticated; deeply concerned with family and worldly interests; engrossed in earthly pleasures and interests.

সংসিদ্ধ *a.* perfectly successful; thoroughly accomplished; instinctive, natural, innate. **সংসিদ্ধি** *n.* perfect success; thorough accomplishment.

সংসৃষ্ট *a.* associated, related, affiliated, connected (with).

সংস্করণ *n.* (obs.) correction or revision; (pop.) an edition (of a book etc.).

সংস্কার *n.* purification; the sacrament of purification or reclamation; a sacrament (দশবিধসংস্কার) ; cleansing; dressing (কেশসংস্কার) ; reformation, reforms; mending, repair; correction, amendment (ভ্রমসংস্কার) ; revision (গ্রন্থসংস্কার) ; an irrational belief or notion, a stock notion; a prejudice or superstition; an impression (on the mind); innate knowledge or feeling, intuition, instinct (পূর্বজন্মের সংস্কার). **সংস্কার করা** *v.* to purify; to purify or reclaim sacramentally; to cleanse; to dress, to reform; to mend, to repair; to correct, to amend; to revise. **অন্ধ সংস্কার** *n.* a blind or irrational notion, a prejudice. **গৃহ সংস্কার** *n.* house-repair; (daily) cleansing of a house. **বেশ সংস্কার** *n.* tidying up of one's dress; dressing. **সংস্কারক** *n.* a purifier; a sacramental purifier or reclaimer; a cleaner; a dresser; a reformer; a mender, a repairer, a repairman; a corrector, an amender; a reviser. **~সাধন করা** same as **সংস্কার করা**। **~বদ্ধ** *a.* bound by stock notions or superstitions or prejudices or instincts. **~বর্জিত, ~হীন** *a.* (rare) not having received any sacrament; free from superstition or prejudice or stock notions. **~বাদ** *n.* the doctrine that the world may be made better by human effort, meliorism. **~বিমুখ** *a.* averse to reforms; conservative.

সংস্কারাচ্ছন্ন *a.* thoroughly dominated by or blinded by superstitions or prejudices or stock notions.

সংস্কৃত *a.* purified; one who has received a sacrament; cleansed; dressed; reformed; mended, repaired; corrected; revised; refined or elegant. □ *n.* Sanskrit. **~ঘেঁষা** *a.* Sanskritised. **~জ্ঞ** *a.* versed in Sanskrit. **সংস্কৃতি** *n.* culture.

সংস্থা *n.* (rare) position, location, situation; a society; an association; a club; a guild; an establishment.

সংস্থান *n.* orderly placing or arrangement; construction, formation, shape, structure, build; provision (ভবিষ্যতের সংস্থান). **আহারের সংস্থান** subsistence; provision of food.

সংস্থাপক *n.* an establisher, a founder.

সংস্থাপন *n.* establishment, foundation, **সংস্থাপন করা** *v.* to establish, to found, to set up.

সংস্থাপয়িতা same as **সংস্থাপক**। *fem.* **সংস্থাপয়িত্রী**।

সংস্থাপিকা *fem.* of **সংস্থাপক**।

সংস্থাপিত *a.* established, founded.

সংস্থিত *a.* placed or laid esp. in an orderly manner; arranged; stationed. **সংস্থিতি** *n.* the state of being placed or laid esp. in an orderly manner; arrangement; the state of being stationed.

সংস্পর্শ *n.* close touch or contact; connection, concern; association. **সংস্পর্শে আসা** *v.* to come in contact with; to get in touch with. **সংস্পর্শে থাকা** *v.* to associate with; to have connection with.

সংস্পৃষ্ট *a.* touched; contacted; touching.

সংস্রব *n.* relation, connection, concern; association, company. **সংস্রব এড়ানো** *v.* to avoid the company of. **সংস্রব থাকা** *v.* to have connection with. **সংস্রব রাখা** *v.* to associate with; to keep connection with. **সংস্রবে আসা** *v.* to come in contact with. **সংস্রবে থাকা** *v.* to have connection with; to associate with. **~হীন** *a.* having no connection or concern with; having nothing to do with.

সংহত *a.* thoroughly united or integrated or organized; (loos.) mobilized; compact; very firm. **সংহত করা** *v.* to unite or organize (into a compact body); to mobilize. **সংহত বর্তনী** a closed circuit. **সংহতি** *n.* complete union or integration or organization; mobilization; compactness; great firmness; (phys.) molecular attracting; (phys.) agglomeration. **সংহতি নষ্ট করা** *v.* to disintegrate, to cause disintegration.

সংহরণ *n.* killing; destruction; withdrawal, retraction, revocation; contraction. **সংহরণ করা** *v.* to kill, to slay; to destroy; to withdraw, to retract, to revoke; to contract.

সংহর্তা *n.* a killer, a slayer; a destroyer; a withdrawer. *fem.* **সংহর্ত্রী**।

সংহার *n.* killing, slaughter; destruction; end, termination, close, finish (উপসংহার) ; withdrawal, retraction, revocation (বাক্যসংহার, শরসংহার) ; contraction, collecting; act of dressing up (বেণীসংহার). **সংহার করা,** (poet.) **সংহারা** *v.* to kill, to slay; to destroy. **সংহারক** *a.* killing, slaying; destroying, destructive. □ *n.* a killer, a slayer; a destroyer. **সংহারমূর্তি** *n.* image or embodiment of annihilation or destruction; a formidable form. **সংহারী** *a.* (used as a *sfx.*) same as **সংহারক** *(a.). fem.* **সংহারিণী**।

সংহিতা *n.* a collection of writings, an anthology; a sacred book containing the entire body of Vedic incantations; the sacred code of Hindu laws entitled 'Smriti' (স্মৃতি) ; a code of laws; a code. **~কার** *n.* a compiler of a code; a lawgiver. **~বদ্ধ** *a.* condified.

সংহৃত *a.* collected; accumulated; killed or destroyed; withdrawn or retracted; contracted or shrunk; abridged.

সঁপা same as **সমর্পণ করা**।

সকড়ি same as **এঁটো**।

সকণ্টক *a.* having thorns, thorny.

সকরকন্দ rej. spell. of **শকরকন্দ**।

সকরুণ *a.* compassionate, kind; pitiable; pathetic; woeful, doleful.

সকর্মক *a.* (gr.) transitive. **সকর্মক ক্রিয়া** (gr.) a transitive verb.

সকল *a.* all; entire, whole. □ *pro.* all, everybody. □ *sfx.* denoting: plurality (বন্ধুসকল). **সকলেই** *pro.* one and all.

সকলের প্রিয় loved by all, favourite with everyone.

সকাণ্ড *a.* (bot.) having a stem, stemmed; (bot.) caulescent.

সকাতর same as **কাতর** except in the last sense. **সকাতরে** *a.* distressfully, sorrowfully, plaintively; very solicitously; very intently.

সকাম *a.* attended with or actuated by a desire or purpose, purposeful (সকাম কর্ম) ; lustful (সকাম দৃষ্টি). **~ধর্ম** *n.* religion practised with an end in view, purposeful piety; act of practising religion with a motive.

সকাল *n.* the morning or the dawn; hurry, haste. **সকাল হওয়া** *v.* to dawn.

সকাল সকাল *adv.* betimes, early, soon, quickly. **সকালে** *adv.* in the morning; at dawn, at daybreak; early, betimes.

সকাশ *n.* nearness, proximity; presence, company. **রাজসকাশে** *adv.* before or near the king, in the royal presence.

সকুণ্ডল *a.* having earrings; adorned with earrings; together with earrings (সকুণ্ডল কর্ণচ্ছেদন).

সকোপে *adv.* angrily.

সকৌতুক *a.* full of fun or amusement, funny, amusing, droll (সকৌতুক হাস্য) ; amused (সকৌতুক দৃষ্টি) ; amusedly inquisitive (সকৌতুক প্রশ্ন). **সকৌতুকে** *adv.* amusedly.

সক্তু *n.* the flour of fried barley or gram.

সক্রিয় *a.* engaged in or given to or capable of action, active (সক্রিয় থাকা) ; practical, active (সক্রিয় সাহায্য). **~তা** *n.* activeness.

সক্রোধে *adv.* same as **সকোপে**।

সক্ষম *a.* competent, capable; able, ablebodied, active (বৃদ্ধ এখনও সক্ষম).

সক্ষমতা *n.* competency, capability; ableness, ability, activeness.

সখ rej. spell. of **শখ**।

সখা *n.* a friend; a bosom or intimate friend, a confidant (*fem.* confidante); a well-wisher; a companion; a boon companion.

সখী *fem.* of **সখা**। **~ভাব** *n.* behaviour like a confidante; a system of Vaishnava worship in which the devotee regards himself or herself as a confidante of Krishna (কৃষ্ণ).

সখেদে *adv.* lamentingly; sorrowfully; with regrets, regretfully.

সখ্য *n.* (close) friendship or companionship; alliance. **সখ্য স্থাপন করা** *v.* to make friends with; to enter into alliance with.

সগর্ব *a.* proud, haughty. **সগর্বে** *adv.* proudly, haughtily.

সগর্ভা *a.* pregnant, big with child, in the family way.

সগুণ *a.* having qualities or attributes; possessing three primal qualities, namely সত্ত্ব, রজঃ and তমঃ ; (of a bow) having a string, stringed.

সগোত্র *a.* agnate; kindred; homogeneous. ☐ *n.* an agnate; a kinsman (*fem.* kinswoman). *fem* **সগোত্রা**। **~বিবাহ** *n.* endogamous marriage.

সগৌরবে *adv.* creditably; gloriously: honourably.

সঘন[১] *a.* clouded, cloudy.

সঘন[২] *a.* repeated or ceaseless (সঘন শব্দ). **সঘনে** *adv.* repeatedly or ceaselessly.

সঘর *n.* a family of equal social standing for matrimonial purpose.

সঙ alt. spell. of **সং**।

সঙিন, সঙীন alt. spellings of **সঙ্গিন**।

সঙ্গ *n.* company, association. **সঙ্গ করা** *v.* to associate with. **সঙ্গ দেওয়া** *v.* to give one company. **সঙ্গ পাওয়া** *v.* to come in contact of; to enjoy the company of.

সঙ্গগুণ *n.* good influence or merits of company or association; (sarcas.) vices of evil company (সঙ্গগুণে নষ্ট).

সঙ্গত, সঙ্গতি *alt.* spellings of **সংগত** and **সংগতি** respectively.

সঙ্গদোষ *n.* vices of evil company, vices contracted from bad company.

সঙ্গম alt. spell of **সংগম**।

সঙ্গরোধ *n.* quarantine.

সঙ্গিন *n.* a bayonet. ☐ *a.* serious, dangerous, critical (অবস্থা সঙ্গিন).

সঙ্গিনী *fem.* of **সঙ্গী**।

সঙ্গী *n.* a companion; a comrade; an associate or an accomplice.

সঙ্গীত alt. spell. of **সংগীত**।

সঙ্গীন rej. spell. of **সঙ্গিন**।

সঙ্গে *prep.* in the company of; in possession of; together with, along with; (in comparison) with (তার সঙ্গে তুলনা). **সঙ্গে সঙ্গে** *adv.* (always) in the company of (সঙ্গে সঙ্গে থাকা) ; (always) in one's possession (সঙ্গে সঙ্গে রাখা) ; as soon as, no sooner than (সে যাওয়ার সঙ্গে সঙ্গে বৃষ্টি নামল).

সঙ্গোপন, সঙ্গোপিত, সঙ্ঘ, সঙ্ঘটন, সঙ্ঘটিত, সঙ্ঘবদ্ধ, সঙ্ঘর্ষ, সঙ্ঘাত, সঙ্ঘারাম, সঙ্ঘৃষ্ট, alt. spellings of **সংগোপন, সংগোপিত, সংঘ, সংঘটন, সংঘটিত, সংঘবদ্ধ, সংঘর্ষ, সংঘাত, সংঘারাম** and **সংঘৃষ্ট** respectively.

সচকিত *a.* startled, alarmed, alerted; on the alert; timid.

সচন্দন *a.* together with sandal wood paste (সচন্দন পুষ্পাঞ্জলি).

সচরাচর *adv.* usually, commonly, often; customarily.

সচল *a.* moving; capable of moving; mobile; locomotive; effective; (fig.) active; current. **সচল করা** *v.* to put or set in motion.

সচিত্র *a.* containing pictorial illustrations, illustrated.

সচিব *n.* a minister; a counsellor; a companion; a secretary.

সচেতক *n.* (in parliamentary politics) a whip. **মুখ্য সচেতক** chief whip.

সচেতন *a.* animate, sentient; living; conscious; vigilant, alert. **সচেতন করা** *v.* to make conscious, to make alert. **সচেতন থাকা** *v.* to be on the alert; (cp.) to be on one's guard.

সচেষ্ট *a.* effortful; endeavouring, trying; zealous, eager, earnest; exerting.

সচ্চরিত্র *a.* having a good character, morally excellent, chaste, virtuous. *fem.* **সচ্চরিত্রা**। **~তা** *n.* moral excellence, chastity, virtuousness.

সচ্চিদানন্দ *a.* eternal and omniscient and ever blissful. □ *n.* God.

সচ্চিন্তা *a.* a good thought.

সচ্ছল *a.* well-to-do, well-off; solvent. **সচ্ছলতা** *n.* well-to-do or well-off state; solvency.

সচ্ছিদ্র *a.* containing a hole or holes, porose, porous; perforated.

সজনি *n. fem.* a confidante; a lady-love, a sweetheart.

সজল *a.* containing water, watery; containing rain (সজল মেঘ) ; tearful; wet, moist. **~নয়নে** *adv.* with tearful eyes; with eyes swimming in tears.

সজাগ *a.* wakeful; vigilant; on the alert; (of sleep) easily broken. **সজাগ থাকা** *v.* to be wakeful or vigilant or on the alert.

সজাতি *a.* of the same nationality; agnate; kindred; homogeneous. □ *n.* such a person. **সজাতীয়** *a.* same as **সজাতি** *(a.).*

সজারু alt. spell. of **শজারু**।

সজিনা alt. spell. of **শজিনা**।

সজীব *a.* living, alive; animate; vivacious; invigorated; rejuvenated. **সজীব করা** *v.* to animate; to vivify; to invigorate; to rejuvenate.

সজোর *a.* forceful, forcible; violent; high; loud; strong.

সজোরে *adv.* forcefully; forcibly; violently; (rare) emphatically.

সজ্জন *n.* a virtuous man; an honest man; (pop.) an amiable man. □ *a.* (pop.) amiable.

সজ্জা *n.* dress; decoration; furnishings, fittings and furniture; equipment, outfit, accoutrements; preparatory arrangements; preparation; arraying (as of troops). **~কক্ষ, ~গৃহ** *n.* a dressing-room; a greenroom.

সজ্জিত *a.* dressed; decorated; adorned; furnished; equipped; prepared; (esp. of troops) arrayed. *fem.* **সজ্জিতা**। **সজ্জিত করা** *v.* to dress; to decorate; to furnish; to equip, to fit out, to accoutre; to prepare; to array.

সজ্জীকরণ *n.* dressing; decoration, adornment; furnishing; equipping, equipment; accoutrement; preparation; arrayment (of troops).

সজ্জীকৃত same as **সজ্জিত**।

সজ্ঞানে *adv.* consciously; knowingly.

সঞ্চয় *n.* gathering, collection; saving; amassment, accumulation, storage; savings; a store, stock. **সঞ্চয় করা** *v.* to gather, to collect; to save; to amass, to accumulate, to store. **~কোষ** *n.* a secondary cell, a storage cell. **~জাত পর্বত** mountain of accumulation. **~ন** *n.* gathering, collection; saving; amassment, accumulation; compilation; selected or collected works or anthology; an anthology. **~শীল** *a.* in the habit of saving; thrifty, frugal. **~শীলতা** *n.* the habit of saving; thrift, frugality. **সঞ্চয়িতা** *n.* an anthologist; (loos.) selected works. **সঞ্চয়ী** *a.* given to saving; thrifty, frugal.

সঞ্চরণ *n.* movement; circulation; roaming; blowing. **সঞ্চরণ করা** *v.* to move; to circulate; to roam; to blow. **~শীল** *a.* given to or engaged in moving or circulating or roaming or blowing; mobile.

সঞ্চরমাণ *a.* on the move; in the state of moving or circulating or roaming or blowing.

সঞ্চরিত *a.* moved; circulated; roamed; blown. **সঞ্চরিত হওয়া** *v.* same as **সঞ্চরণ করা।**

সঞ্চলন *n.* movement; circulation; blowing; trembling; fluttering.

সঞ্চলিত *a.* moved; circulated; blown; trembling; fluttering. **সঞ্চলিত হওয়া** *v.* to move; to circulate; to blow; to tremble, to flutter.

সঞ্চায়ক *a.* accumulation. □ *n.* an accumulator. **সঞ্চায়ক ব্যাটারি** (phys.) a secondary battery, a storage battery.

সঞ্চার, সঞ্চারণ *n.* transition; (astr. & astrol.) transition from one zodiacal sign to another; transit; movement, motion; gait (পদসঞ্চার) ; pervasion, diffusion (আলোকসঞ্চার) ; accumulation, collection (মেঘসঞ্চার) ; appearance, oncoming, advent, beginning (যৌবনসঞ্চার) ; infusion (প্রাণসঞ্চার) ; transfusion (রক্তসঞ্চার) ; excitation, incitation, arousing (ভয়সঞ্চার). **সাহস সঞ্চার করা** *v.* to take courage. **সঞ্চারপথ** *n.* locus (*pl.* loci). **সঞ্চারিত** *a.* transited; (astr. & astrl.) transited to another zodiacal sign; moved; that which has pervaded or diffused; accumulated, collected; appeared; that which has come or begun; infused; transfused; excited, incited, roused. **সঞ্চারিত করা** *v.* to bring, to cause to set in or appear; to infuse, to transfuse; to excite, to incite, to rouse. **সঞ্চারিত হওয়া** *v.* to make a transit; (astr. & astrol) to make a transit to another zodiacal sign; to be in motion, to move; to pervade, to diffuse; to accumulate, to collect; to appear; to begin, to ensue; to be infused or transfused or incited or roused. **সঞ্চারী** *a.* in transit; moving, in motion; passing; evanescent; temporary; causing to move or pervade or diffuse or accumulate or collect or appear or ensue; oncoming; infusing; transfusing; excitant, inciting, rousing. □ *n.* (rhet.) the passing sentiment that is excited in the mind of a reader, a rhetorical accessory; (mus.) the third line or step of any of the Indian musical modes. *fem. a.* **সঞ্চারিণী।**

সঞ্চালন *n.* moving; waving; circulation. **সঞ্চালন করা** *v.* to move, to set in motion; to wave; to circulate.

সঞ্চালিত *a.* moved, set in motion; waved; circulated.

সঞ্চিত *a.* gathered, collected; saved; amassed, accumulated; hoarded, stored. **সঞ্চিতা** *n.* an anthology; selected works.

সঞ্জনন *n.* creation; production; generation; generating; producing.

সঞ্জাত *a.* born; produced, grown; sprung, evolved.

সঞ্জাব *n.* a border stitched to a piece of cloth or to the lower end of a mosquito net; a fringe; a lining.

সঞ্জীবন *a.* infusion of life, animation; restoration of life, reanimation. □ *a.* restoring life, reanimating; infusing life, animating. **সঞ্জীবনী** *a. fem.* of **সঞ্জীবন** *(a.).* □ *a.* an elixir restoring the dead to life (সঞ্জীবনী সুধা). **সঞ্জীবিত** *a.* restored to life; reanimalted; animated.

সট *int.* indicating: rapidity, quickness etc.

সটকা *n.* a long slender (and usu. flexible) pipe or tube attached to a hubble-bubble: the tobacco-smoke passes through this tube.

সটকান *n.* (pronun. সটকান্) decampment, stealthy escape, slip. **সটকান দেওয়া** *v.* to decamp, to escape stealthily.

সটকানো *v.* to decamp, to escape stealthily; to make good one's escape.

সটান *a.* lying straight ahead, horizontal, straight (সটান রাস্তা) ; lying at length (সটান হওয়া) ; perfectly erect ☐ *adv.* in a straight manner, straight ahead; lengthwise. flat; erectly; forthwith, straightway (সটান পাড়ি দেওয়া)।

সটীক *a.* containing explanatory notes, annotated, with a commentary.

সঠিক *a.* perfectly right or genuine : correct (সঠিক সংবাদ) ; accurate; exact. ☐ *adv.* quite correctly or accurately or exactly (সঠিক জানা). **~ভাবে** *adv.* correctly, properly; exactly, accurately.

সডাক *a.* inclusive of postage.

সড় *n.* (dero.) secret conference; (dero.) secret understanding or entente or arrangement; an intrigue, a plot, a conspiracy. **সড় করা** *v.* to confer secretly (with); to enter into a secret alliance or entente (with); to arrange secretly (with); to intrigue or conspire (with), to hatch a plot.

সড়ক *n.* a wide and long road; a highway; a street.

সড়কি *n.* a spear, a lance, a javelin. **~ওয়ালা** *n.* a spearman.

সড়সড় *int.* expressing: the quick gliding movement as of reptiles; slipperiness; an itching sensation (মারবার জন্য হাত সড়সড় করছে).

সড়াক, সড়াৎ *int.* expressing: sudden shooting fight as of reptiles.

সড়োগড়ো *a.* thoroughly mastered or learnt or accustomed or habituated; memorized. **সড়োগড়ো করা** *v.* to master or learn thoroughly; to get thoroughly accustomed (to) or habituated (with); to commit to memory, to memorize.

সৎ[১] *a.* having existence, in esse: omnipresent; eternal; real; honest, virtuous; good, excellent; solemn or charitable (সৎকর্ম). ☐ *n.* existence and nothing else; esse; God. **সৎ ফোকাস** (phys.) real focus.

সৎ[২] *a.* (used as a *pfx.*) related through another wife of one's husband or (mod. use) through another husband of one's wife, step; having one parent in common, half; related by another marriage, step-.

সৎ ছেলে *n.* a step-son. **সৎ-বোন** *n. fem.* a step-sister; a half-sister. **সৎ-ভাই** *n.* a step-brother; a half-brother. **সৎ-মা** *n.* a step-mother. **সৎ-মেয়ে** *n.* a step-daughter. **সৎ-শাশুড়ি** *n.* a step-mother-in-law.

সতত *adv.* always, ever, at all hours; ceaselessly, incessantly; perpetually.

সততা *n.* honesty, integrity; uprightness; goodness.

সৎপথ *n.* right or honest or virtuous course. **সৎপথাবলম্বী** *a.* taken to or following the right or virtuous course; virtuous, righteous.

সৎপরামর্শ *n.* good advise or counsel.

সৎপাত্র *n.* a just or honest person or bridegroom.

সতর, সতরঞ্চ (সতরঞ্চ), সতরঞ্চি (সতরঞ্চি) variants of **সতেরো, শতরঞ্চ** and **শতরঞ্চি**।

সতর্ক *a.* careful, alert, watchful, cautious. **সতর্ক করা** *v.* to warn, to caution. **সতর্ক থাকা** *v.* to be on the alert or one's guard, to be careful or cautious. **সতর্ক দৃষ্টি রাখা** *v.* to keep a careful watch or a watchful eye on. **সতর্কীকরণ** *n.* carefulness, alertness, cautiousness; watchfulness, vigilance.

সৎসঙ্গ *n.* (keeping) good company, association with good men.

সৎসাহস *n.* moral courage.

সৎস্বভাব *n.* goodness or honesty. ☐ *a.* goodnatured; honest; virtuous.

সতা same as **সতিন**। **সতাই** *n. fem.* a step-mother. **সতাতো** same as **সৎ**[২]।

সতিন *n. fem.* another wife of one's husband, a co-wife. **~কন্যা, ~পুত্র** same as **~ঝি** and **~পো** respectively. **সতিন-কাঁটা** *n.* a son or daughter of one's co-wife, who is regarded as one's thorn in the flesh. **~ঝি** *n.* a daughter of one's co-wife, a step-daughter. **~পো** *n.* a son of one's co-wife, a step-son.

সতী *n. fem.* (myth.) Sati, the daughter of Daksha and wife of Shiva (শিব); a wife intently devoted to her husband, a chaste or faithful wife; a widow who burns herself on her husband's pyre, a suttee, a sati. ☐ *a. fem.* (of a wife) intently devoted to one's husband, chaste. **~ত্ব** *n.* intent devotion of a wife to her husband, the chastity or faithfulness of a wife. **সতীত্বনাশ** *n.* violation of chastity; rape. **সতীত্বনাশ করা** *v.* to rape. **সতীত্বরক্ষা করা** *v.* preserve one's chastity. **~দাহ** *n.* the practice of widows burning themselves on their husbands' pyres, suttee, sati. **~পনা** *n.* (sarcas.) a show or affectation of chastity demonstrated by a wife; (sarcas.) pride of chastity or honesty (usu. false or overdone). **~লক্ষ্মী** *n.* a very chaste and pleasing wife who brings fortune to her husband. **~সাধ্বী** *n.* a perfectly chaste wife. **~সাবিত্রী** *a.* a wife as chaste and devoted as Sabitri (সাবিত্রী).

সতীন rej. spell. of **সতিন।**

সতীর্থ *n.* a pupil of the same teacher or institution at the same time; a class-fellow.

সতৃষ্ণ *a.* thirsty; (fig.) eager, yearning (for), wistful (সতৃষ্ণ দৃষ্টি). **~নয়নে** *adv.* with eager, yearning, wistful eyes.

সতেজ *a.* vigorous, spirited; animated; reinvigorated or resuscitated (রোগী সতেজ হয়েছে) ; (of trees and plants) luxuriant; emphatic. **সতেজে** *adv.* vigorously, spiritedly; animatedly; luxuriantly; emphatically.

সতেরো *n.* & *a.* seventeen. **~ই** *n.* the seventeenth day of a month, the seventeenth. ☐ *a.* (of the days of a month) seventeenth.

সত্তম *a.* (used as a *sfx.*) excellent, most virtuous (দ্বিজসত্তম).

সত্তর *n* & *a.* seventy.

সত্তা *n.* existence, entity, ens, esse; eternal existence (cp. eternality); origin or birth; excellence; honesty; integrity, goodness.

সত্ত্ব[১] *n.* juice, essence, extract, marrow; a preparation made of juice or essence or marrow.

সত্ত্ব[২] *n.* existence, presence; the primal quality of goodness or virtuousness and knowledge about reality; nature or instinct; soul; life; valour; courage; a creature, a being; a thing; wealth, riches; (loos.) juice or essence or a product of this. **সত্ত্বেও** *prep.* in spite of, notwithstanding, despite.

সত্বর *adv.* quickly, swiftly; fast. ☐ *a.* quick, swift; fast. **সত্বরে** *adv.* same as **সত্বর** *(adv.)*

সত্য *a.* real; true; genuine; right, correct. ☐ *n.* existence, entity, ens, esse; reality; truth; genuineness; an oath; a solemn vow; a promise; (myth.) the first of the four ages or aeons, the Golden Age. **সত্য করা** *v.* to take an oath; to take a solemn vow; to promise. **সত্য বলা** *v.* to speak the truth; to speak the right thing. **আপাতসত্য** *a.* true on the surface; verisimilar. ☐ *n.* verisimilar. **তিন সত্য** an oath or promise thrice uttered to make it inviolable. **সত্য কথা** truth. **সত্য কথা বলা** *v.* to speak the truth. **~কথন** *n.* act of speaking the truth, truthfulness. **~তা** *n.* truth; veracity; genuineness, authenticity. **~নারায়ণ** *n.* a Hindu deity. **~নিষ্ঠ, ~পরায়ণ** *a.* intently devoted to truth; true to one's word or vow. **~নিষ্ঠা, ~পরায়ণতা** *n.* intent devotion to truth; practice of keeping one's word or vow; integrity. **~পথ** *n.* the path of virtue, the right path; the correct means. **~পালন করা** *v.* to keep or fulfil one's promise or vow. **~পির** *n.* Satyanarayana (সত্যনারায়ণ) as worshipped by Muslims. **~প্রিয়** same as **সত্যানুরাগী।** **~বাদিতা** *n.* truthfulness. **~বাদী** *a.* truthful. *fem.* **~বাদিনী।** **~ব্রত** *a.* intently practising virtue and truthfulness. **~ভঙ্গ** *n.* breach of promise or vow or trust. **~যুগ** *n.* (myth.) the first of the four ages or aeons of the world, the Golden Age. **~সত্যই** *adv.* really; verily. **~সন্ধ** *a.* acceptant of truth; true to one's vow or promise. **সত্যাগ্রহ** *n.* earnest endeavour for the establishment of the reign of truth; (pop.) passive resistance or picketing or strike, satyagraha. **সত্যাগ্রহ করা** *v.* (pop.) to offer passive resistance or to strike. **সত্যাগ্রহী** *n.* a determined champion of truth or of the reign of truth; (pop.) one offering passive resistance or a picketer or a striker. **সত্যানুরাগ** *n.* love for or devotion to truth. **সত্যানুরাগী** *a.* truth-loving; devoted to truth. *fem.* **সত্যানুরাগিণী।** **সত্যানুসন্ধান করা** *v.*

to search for truth. **সত্যানুসন্ধায়ী** *a.* searching for truth. **সত্যান্বেষণ** *n.* search for truth. **সত্যান্বেষী** *a.* searching for truth. ☐ *n.* a seeker after truth. **সত্যাপন করা** *v.* to affirm; to take an oath. **সত্যাসত্য** *n.* truth and falsehood; the right and the wrong. ☐ *a.* true and false; right and wrong. **সত্যি** coll. form of **সত্য**। **সত্যিকার, সত্যিকারের** *a.* true; real; genuine.

সত্র *n.* a place or institution for charitable distribution of food, drink, clothing etc.; an almshouse; an oblation, a sacrifice.

সদ্গতি alt. spell. of **সদ্‌গতি**।

সদ্গুণ *n.* a good or noble quality; a virtue.

সদ্গুরু *n.* a good teacher, preceptor or instructor; a good religious preceptor.

সদন *n.* a residence, a dwelling-house; a house; presence (রাজসদন).

সদনুষ্ঠান *n.* performance of a solemn rite; a good or charitable deed or work.

সদন্তঃকরণ *n.* a good heart; a good purpose.

সদন্তঃকরণে *adv.* with a good heart, with a good purpose.

সদ্বাসনা *n.* good or honest wish.

সদ্বিম্ব *n.* (phys.) real image.

সদবুদ্ধি alt. spell. of **সদ্বুদ্ধি**।

সদভিপ্রায় same as **সদুদ্দেশ্য**।

সদম্ভ same as **সদর্প**।

সদয় *a.* kind; charitable; compassionate; merciful, benignant; gracious. **~চিত্ত** *a.* kind-hearted. **~ভাবে** *adv.* kindly, favourably.

সদর *n.* the principal city or the headquarters of a district; the outer portion or apartment of a residential building (also **সদর বাড়ি, সদর মহল**) ; the outer face of anything. ☐ *a.* of or situated in the headquarters of a district; principal, chief (সদর কাছারি); outer (সদর দরজা). **সদর-অন্দর নেই** (fig.) there is no privacy in anything here. **সদর কাছারি** the head office; headquarters. **সদর জমা** revenue to be paid to the government. **সদর দরজা** the main gate (of a building). **সদর দেওয়ানি আদালত** a chief civil court. **সদরআলা, সদরালা** *n.* a sub-judge. **সদর রাস্তা** main road.

সদর্থ *n.* a good meaning; the true or correct meaning. ☐ *a.* positive; having a good significance.

সদর্প *a.* proud, boastful, arrogant, haughty. **সদর্পে** *adv.* proudly, boastfully, arrogantly, haughtily.

সদলবলে *adv.* attended by one's friends and followers, attended by one's retinue; mustering strong. **সদলে** same as **সদলবলে**।

সদসৎ *a.* good and bad; right and wrong; existent and inexistent.

সদসদ্বিবেচনা *n.* discrimination between good and bad or between right and wrong.

সদস্য *n.* a member. *fem.* **সদস্যা**। **~তা** *n.* (loos.) membership.

সদা same as **সতত**।

সদাগর coll. corrup. of **সওদাগর**।

সদাচার *n.* good or virtuous practice; practice enjoined by the scriptures. **~পরায়ণ, সদাচারী** *a.* virtuous in practice.

সদাত্মা *a.* good-souled, honest, virtuous, righteous.

সদানন্দ *a.* ever cheerful. *n.* Shiva (শিব).

সদাব্রত *n.* a place or institution for charitable distribution of food and other things, an almshouse.

সদালাপ *n.* conversation on a good or pious or spiritual topic; (rare) amiable conversation. **সদালাপী** *a.* given to conversation on good or pious or spiritual topics; (pop) amiable in conversation.

সদাশয় *a.* noble-hearted, magnanimous; kind-hearted; amiable. **~তা** *n.* magnanimity, noble-mindedness; kind-heartedness.

সদাশিব *n.* Shiva. (শিব). ☐ *a.* very magnanimous and ever cheerful and content.

সদিচ্ছা *n.* a good or noble intention; well-wishing, **~প্রণোদিত** *a.* actuated by a good or noble intention; prompted by well-wishing.

সদুত্তর *n.* a good or honest reply; a correct or right or satisfactory answer.

সদুদ্দেশ্য *n.* a good or noble purpose or intention. **~পূর্ণ** *a.* well-meaning. **সদুদ্দেশ্যে**

adv. with a good or noble purpose or intention.

সদুপদেশ *n.* a good or wise advice or counsel; moral advice.

সদুপদেষ্টা *n.* a good or wise adviser; a moral instructor.

সদুপায় *n.* honest or virtuous or fair or good or suitable means.

সদৃশ *a.* (often used as a *prep.*) like; similar, resembling; identical; equal. **~কোণ** *a.* (geom.) equiangular. **~বিধান** *n.* homoeopathy.

সদ্গতি *n.* a happy journey after death; spiritual salvation, final beatitude; obsequies; cremation; (hum.) proper disposal. **সদ্গতি করা** *v.* to perform obsequies of; to cremate; (hum.) to dispose of. **সদ্গতি লাভ করা** *v.* to enjoy a happy journey after death; to attain final beatitude; to be properly cremated; (hum.) to be disposed of.

সদ্গোপ *n.* a Hindu caste (ori. the milkman class); a member of the caste.

সদ্বংশ *n.* a good or noble family. **~জাত** *a.* born in or descended from a good or noble family, well-born, nobly born, of noble descent, **সদ্বংশীয়** same as **~জাত**।

সদ্বক্তা *n.* an eloquent speaker, a good orator; (rare) one who says good things.

সদ্বিচার *n.* just or wise decision, justice, equity. **সদ্বিচারক** *n.* a good or wise or equitable judge.

সদ্বিবেচক *a.* gifted with judgment and penetration; sagacious; sane; judicious, discreet.

সদ্বিবেচনা *n.* judgment and penetration; sagacity; sanity, judiciousness, discretion, discreetness. **সদ্বিবেচনা করা** *v.* to think or judge or decide sagaciously or discreetly.

সদ্বুদ্ধি *n.* a good or virtuous design; good nature, goodness, good sense; right sort of intelligence.

সদ্ব্যবহার *n.* good behaviour; good or courteous treatment; proper use (সময়ের সদ্ব্যবহার). **সদ্ব্যবহার করা** *v.* to behave well, to behave oneself; to treat (one) well or courteously; to use well, to make good use of, to turn (something) to good account.

সদ্ব্যয় *n.* proper use (সময়ের সদ্ব্যয়); proper or useful spending (টাকার সদ্ব্যয়). **সদ্ব্যয় করা** *v.* to use properly; to spend properly or usefully.

সদ্ভাব *n.* friendship, amity; (rare) good behaviour ('সদ্ভাবশতক').

সদ্য *adv.* at once, forthwith; without delay, then and there; just, recently. **~ঃপাতী, ~পাতী** *a.* liable to fall as soon as rising ('অম্বুবিম্ব অম্বুমুখে সদ্যঃপাতী'); (of tree-leaves, flowers etc.) quickly deciduous; (fig.) very transitory or short-lived. **~ঃপ্রসূত, ~প্রসূত** *a.* very recently born, just born. **~ঃস্নাত, ~স্নাত** one who has taken one's bath just now. **সদ্য সদ্য** *adv.* immediately, at once; very recently, just. **সদ্যোজাত** *a.* just born; very recently born. **সদ্যোমৃত** *a.* just dead; recently dead.

সধবা *n. fem.* a married woman whose husband is alive, (cp) a feme covert. ☐ *a. fem.* having one's husband alive.

সধর্মা, সধর্মী *a.* possessing the same qualities or properties; following the same religion or trade.

সন *n.* a calendar year, an era.

সনদ, সনন্দ *n.* a deed of grant, a charter, a warrant, a sanad; a diploma, an academic certificate.

সনাক্ত rej. spell. of **শনাক্ত**।

সনাতন *a.* eternal, catholic; in vogue for a pretty long time, very old. (সনাতন প্রথা). **সনাতন ধর্ম** *n.* the eternal religion or form of worship, the catholic religion; (loos.) the very ancient form of Hinduism. Hindu religion and tradition. **সনাতনী** *a. fem.* of **সনাতন** *(a.).* ☐ *a. & n.* one who or that which follows **সনাতন ধর্ম**।

সনাথ *a.* having a master or overlord or protector or husband; possessing; accompanied by.

সনির্বন্ধ *a.* pertinaciously solictious, importunate. **সনির্বন্ধ অনুরোধ** earnest request or entreaty.

সনে poet. corrup. of **সঙ্গে**।

সনেট *n.* a sonnet.

সন্ত *n.* a saint, an ascetic.

সন্ততি *n.* offspring; descendants, progeny, posterity; a son or a daughter; a line of descent; sequence (ভাবসন্ততি) ; continuum.

সন্তপ্ত *a.* afflicted; aggrieved; heated; running a temperature. **সন্তপ্ত করা** *v.* to afflict, to distress; to grieve; to heat; to cause to run a temperature. **~হৃদয়ে** *adv.* with an afflicted or aggrieved heart.

সন্তরণ *n.* swimming; natation. **~কারী** *n.* a swimmer. *fem.* **~কারিণী**। **~দক্ষ, ~পটু** *a.* skilled in swimming; natatory; natatorial.

সন্তর্পণে *adv.* very cautiously or carefully; with circumspection.

সন্তান *n.* a son or a daughter, offspring; progeny; a descendant. **কন্যাসন্তান** *n. fem.* a daughter. **পুত্র সন্তান** *n.* a son. **~ধারণ করা** *v.* to carry a child in one's womb, to be big with child. **~পালন করা** *v.* to bring up or nurse a child. **~প্রসব** *n.* child-bearing; childbirth. **~প্রসব করা** *n.* to give birth to a child, to bear a child. **~বতী** *a. fem.* one who has borne a child, *masc.* **~বান** one to whom a child is born. **~বাৎসল্য** *n.* affection or love for children; philoprogenitiveness, **~সন্ততি** *n.* children; descendants. **~সম্ভবা** *a. fem.* pregnant. **~সম্ভাবনা** *n.* pregnancy. **~হীন** *a.* childless. *fem.* **~হীনা**। **সন্তানোচিত** *a.* becoming a son or daughter, filial. **সন্তানোৎপাদন করা** *v.* to beget a child, to procreate.

সন্তাপ *n.* great or severe heat; affliction, grief, mortification; bereavement; body temperature. **~ক্লিষ্ট, সন্তাপিত** same as **সন্তপ্ত**।

সন্তুষ্ট *a.* satisfied; gratified; pleased or propitiated; content or happy. **সন্তুষ্ট করা** *v.* to satisfy; to gratify; to please or propitiate; to make content or happy. **~চিত্তে** *adv.* with a contented heart, contentedly; happily. **সন্তুষ্টি** same as **সন্তোষ**।

সন্তোলন *n.* act of singeing lightly in oil or ghee.

সন্তোষ *n.* satisfaction; gratification; pleasure; propitiation; contentment or happiness. **সন্তোষ উৎপাদন করা বা প্রদান করা** same as **সন্তুষ্ট করা**। **~জনক** *a.* satisfactory. **~পূর্বক** *adv.* with satisfaction; with pleasure.

সন্ত্রস্ত *a.* greatly frightened or terrified or alarmed; panic-stricken; feverishly excited by the thought lest any faults should occur; awed.

সন্ত্রাস *n.* great fear or alarm, terror; panic. **সন্ত্রাসের রাজত্ব** a reign or terror. **~ক** *n.* a terrorist. **~বাদ** *n.* (pol.) terrorism. **~বাদী** *a.* pertaining to terrorism or terrorists. □ *n.* a terrorist. **সন্ত্রাসিত** *a.* greatly frightened or alarmed, terrified; (pol.) terrorized; panic-stricken.

সন্দংশ, সন্দংশিকা, সন্দংশী *n.* tongs, pincers, pliers, forceps etc.

সন্দর্ভ *n.* an essay, a treatise; a book; a collection or anthology.

সন্দর্শন *n.* minute or careful observation; supervision or inspection. **সন্দর্শন করা** *v.* to see or notice or observe minutely or carefully; to supervise or inspect.

সন্দিগ্ধ *a.* full of suspicion or inclined to suspect, suspicious; liable to suspicion, doubtful, suspected. **~চিত্ত, ~চেতা, ~মনা** *a.* having a suspicious mind; suspicious.

সন্দিহান *a.* seized with suspicion or doubt, suspicious, doubtful.

সন্দীপন *n.* enkindling; excitation, incitation, rousing. □ *a.* (*incomp.*) enkindling; inciting, rousing.

সন্দীপিত, সন্দীপ্ত *a.* enkindled, excited, incited, roused.

সন্দেশ *n.* news, information; a message, a report; order, command; a delicious sweetmeat made of posset. **~ওয়ালা** *n.* a manufacturer or seller of the aforesaid sweetmeat. **~বহ** *n.* a messenger, (cp.) a courier.

সন্দেহ *n.* doubt; suspicion. **সন্দেহ করা** *v.* to doubt; to suspect. **সন্দেহ নেই** no doubt, doubtlessly. **সন্দেহের অতীত** beyond doubt, above suspicion. **সন্দেহের পাত্র** a suspect. **সন্দেহের বিষয়** a matter of doubt. **সন্দেহের লেশ** a faint trace of doubt, a shadow of doubt. **~জনক** *a.* causing suspicion, suspicious; causing doubt, doubtful. **~জনকভাবে** *adv.* suspiciously.

~বাই, ~বাতিক *n.* propensity to suspect foul play, collusion etc.; a suspicious nature. ~বাদ *n.* scepticism. ~ভঞ্জন *n.* removal of doubt or suspicion or misgiving, resolution of doubt. **সন্দেহ ভঞ্জন বা নিরসন করা** *v.* to remove or resolve a doubt. ~স্থলে *adv.* in case of doubt or uncertainty. **সন্দেহাতীত** *a.* undoubted, indubitable. **সন্দেহের দোলা** vacillation caused by doubt. **সন্দেহের দোলায় দোলা** *v.* to vacillate on account of doubt.

সন্ধান *n.* search, quest, pursuit; research; discovery; trace; a mystery; a secret entrance ('সন্ধান লব বুঝিয়া') ; placing or planting or directing (শরসন্ধান) ; fermentation; joining. **সন্ধান করা** *v.* to search; to research; to discover; to trace or to try to trace; to place or plant (as an arrow on a bow); to ferment; to join. **সন্ধান নেওয়া** same as **সন্ধান করা।** **সন্ধান পাওয়া** *v.* to find or get a trace (of); to find out, to discover; to detect. **সন্ধান হওয়া** *v.* to be searched or traced; to be found out or discovered or detected. ~সূত্র *n.* a clue.

সন্ধানী, সন্ধানী *a.* engaged in searching; inquisitive; skilled in searching or detection. **সন্ধানী আলো** a searchlight.

সন্ধি *n.* union, unification; alliance, a treaty; a compact, a covenant; a joint (উরুসন্ধি) ; meeting or juncture (যুগসন্ধি) ; juncture of day and night (cp. twilight, gloaming); juncture of two lunar days; mystery, secrets (নারীর মায়ার সন্ধি) ; a tunnel, a (long) hole (সন্ধিপথ) ; (gr.) blending of the final sound of a word with the initial sound of the following word, sandhi (**স্বরসন্ধি**= blending of two vowel sounds; **ব্যঞ্জনসন্ধি** = blending of two consonantal sounds or of a consonantal sound with a vowel sound; **বিসর্গ সন্ধি** = blending of a বিসর্গ with a vowel or consonantal sound). **কপাট-সন্ধি** *n.* a hinge joint. **সন্ধি করা** *v.* to conclude a treaty; to enter into an alliance; to make a compact; to make peace; (gr.) to join by sandhi. ~ক্ষণ *n.* the juncture of two ages or periods or moments. ~ত *a.* joined; bound by a treaty; covenanted; fermented. ~পত্র *n.* a written covenant; a written agreement of peace. ~পূজা *n.* worship of Goddess Durga (দুর্গা) esp. in autumn at the juncture of the eighth and the ninth lunar day. ~প্রদাহ *n.* arthritis. ~বদ্ধ *a.* bound by a treaty or agreement; covenanted. ~বন্ধন *n.* a ligament, a nerve. ~বাত *n.* gout; (erron.) arthritis. ~বিগ্রহ *n.* war and peace. ~বিচ্ছেদ *n.* (gr.) disjoining of sandhi (সন্ধি). ~ভঙ্গ *n.* violation of a treaty or covenant; disruption of an alliance. ~স্থল *n.* juncture.

সন্ধিৎসা *n.* desire to know or enquire, curiosity, inquisitiveness.

সন্ধিৎসু *a.* curious, inquisitive.

সন্ধ্যা *n.* the juncture of day and night either at day break or nightfall, twilight; the evening, dusk, gloaming, nightfall (also **সন্ধ্যাবেলা**); the evening prayer to God or at any time of day or night (also **সন্ধ্যাহ্নিক**); time of performance (দু-সন্ধ্যা ভোজন) ; juncture of two ages, transition period; (fig.) beginning (কলির সন্ধ্যা) ; (fig.) the closing period, the close (জীবনসন্ধ্যা). **সন্ধ্যা করা** *v.* to say one's prayer (at any time of day) to be overtaken by evening (সে বাড়ি ফিরতে সন্ধ্যা করে). ~উপাসনা *n.* the evening prayer, vespers. ~কালীন *a.* of evening; evening. ~কালে *adv.* in the evening. ~গোধূলি *n.* evening twilight, gloaming, dusk, owl-light. ~তারা *n.* the evening star, the Vesper. ~দীপ *n.* an evening lamp. ~বন্দনা same as ~উপাসনা। ~রাগ, ~লোক same as ~গোধূলি।

সন্নত *a.* bowed down in obeisance; bent; inclined; humble, modest.

সন্নদ্ধ *a.* equipped with arms, armed; armoured; tightly fastened with cloth etc., well-tucked (সন্নদ্ধ বক্ষ) ; lined-up, aligned, arrayed, in close array (ঘনসন্নদ্ধ তরুরাজি).

সন্না *n.* small pincers or forceps.

সন্নিকট *adv. & prep.* very near or close to (গৃহসন্নিকট) ; in the presence of (নৃপসন্নিকট). □ *a.* very proximate or near; imminent, approaching (সন্নিকটমৃত্যু). **সন্নিকটে** *adv.* same as **সন্নিকট** *(adv.).*

সন্নিকর্ষ *n.* proximity, nearness. **সন্নিকর্ষণ** *n.* (math.) approximation.

সন্নিধান, সন্নিধি *n.* proximity, nearness, vicinity; presence (নৃপসন্নিধান) ; possession or custody (বন্ধুসন্নিধান টাকা). **সন্নিধানে** *adv.* near; in the presence of; in possession or custody of.

সন্নিপাত *n.* union; assemblage, collection; utter fall or ruin or destruction; (med.) a fever attended with morbidity of the three humours of the body; (loos.) typhoid.

সন্নিবদ্ধ *a.* firmly tied or shut; firmly set; strung together.

সন্নিবিষ্ট *a.* set in order; arrayed; entered into; inserted; intently occupied with.

সন্নিবেশ *n.* orderly placing; stationing (as of troops), arrayment; act of setting up or pitching (শিবির-সন্নিবেশ) ; assemblage; act of driving in, insertion. **সন্নিবেশিত** same as **সন্নিবিষ্ট** ।

-সন্নিভ (used as a *sfx*) similar to, looking like, equivalent to.

সন্নিযুক্ত *a.* confirmed. **সন্নিযুক্ত শল্যচিকিৎসক** a housesurgeon.

সন্নিয়োগ *n.* confirmation (in an office).

সন্নিহিত *a.* lying close to; adjoining, contiguous; proximate; approaching; (geom.) adjacent; (properly) placed; deposited. **সন্নিহিত কোণ** adjacent angle. **~মান** *n.* (geom.) close approximation.

সন্ন্যস্ত *a.* thrown; renounced, given up, deposited.

সন্ন্যাস *n.* asceticism; ascetic mendicancy; renouncement of the world; (med.) apoplexy. **সন্ন্যাস গ্রহণ করা** *v.* to take to asceticism or ascetic mendicancy. **সন্ন্যাসী** *n.* an ascetic; an ascetic mendicant. *fem.* **সন্ন্যাসিনী** । **অনেক সন্ন্যাসিতে গাজন নষ্ট** (fig.) too many cooks spoil the broth.

সন্মার্গ *n.* right path or way.

সপ *n.* a kind of large mat.

সপক্ষ *a.* siding with, partisan, favourable. **সপক্ষে** *adv.* in favour of, in support of. **সপক্ষতা করা** *v.* to support, to back.

সপত্ন *n.* an enemy; a rival.

সপত্নী *n. fem.* another wife of one's husband, co-wife. **~কন্যা** *n.* a step-daughter. **~পুত্র** *n.* a step-son.

সপত্নীক *a.* accompanied by wife; attended with wife. □ *adv.* with wife.

সপরিজন *a.* accompanied by or attended with one's family. □ *adv.* with one's family, en famille.

সপরিবারে *adv.* with one's family, en famille.

সপসপ *int.* indicating thorough wetness; sound of eating quickly (with a lisping noise); repeated whanging noise (সপসপ করে চাবুক মারা).

সপসপে *a.* wet, moist; damp; thoroughly wet; dripping wet.

সপাং, সপাৎ *int.* expressing : whanging noise (as caused by lashing or caning). **সপাৎ করে** *adv.* with a whang.

সপাদ *a.* footed, pedate, legged; one and a quarter of (সপাদ ধর্ম).

সপাসপ *adv.* very quickly and making a loud lisping noise (সপাসপ খাওয়া) ; with repeated whanging noise.

সাপিণ্ড *n.* a kinsman removed not before the seventh upward generation; (loos.) a near kinsman.

সাপিণ্ডীকরণ *n.* obsequial rites to be performed at the end of the first year of death; (hum.) utter destruction or undoing.

সপিনা *n.* a subpoena. **সপিনা জারি করা, সপিনা ধরানো, সপিনা পাঠানো** *v.* to subpoena. **সপিনা পাওয়া** *v.* to be subpoena'd.

সপুত্র *a.* having a son; accompanied by one's son. □ *adv.* with one's son.

সপুষ্পক উদ্ভিদ *n.* phanerogam.

সপেটা *n.* fruit of the Sapota.

সপ্ত *n* & *a.* Seven. **সপ্তক** *n.* a collection of seven; a heptad; the seven notes collectively of a musical scale (**সুরসপ্তক**). **~চত্বারিংশ** *a.* forty-seven. **~চত্বারিংশৎ** *n* & *a.* forty-seven. **~চত্বারিংশত্তম** *a.* forty-seventh. *fem.* **~চত্বারিংশত্তমী** । **~তি** *n* & *a.* seventy. **~তিতম** *a.* seventieth. *fem.* **~তিতমী** । **~ত্রিংশ** *a.* thirty-seven. **~ত্রিংশৎ** *n.* & *a.* thirty-seven. **~ত্রিংশত্তম** *a.* thirty-seventh. *fem.* **~ত্রিংশত্তমী** । **~দশ** *a.* seventeen; seventeenth. **~দশী** *a. fem.* of **~দশ** । □ *a. fem.* seventeen years old.

~দ্বীপ *n.* (Hindu myth.) the seven islands or divisions of the world. ~দ্বীপা *a. fem.* having seven islands; divided into seven islands or divisions. ~ধা *adv.* in seven parts or ways; by seven times. ~পদী *n.* the ceremony of going seven paces together performed by the bride and the bridegroom at a Hindu wedding; (pros.) a heptametre. ☐ *a.* seven-footed, heptapodic; (pros.) heptametrical. ~পাতাল *n.* (Hindu myth.) the seven underworlds. ~বিংশ *a.* twenty-seven. ~বিংশতি *n* & *a.* twenty-seven. ~বিংশতিতম *a.* twenty-seventh. *fem.* ~বিংশতিতমী। সপ্তম *a.* seventh. ~মী *a. fem.* of সপ্তম। ☐ *n.* the seventh day of a lunar fortnight. সপ্তমীপূজা *n.* autumnal worship of Goddess Durga (দুর্গা) on the seventh day of the lunar fortnight. ~যোজী *a.* (chem.) heptavalent. ~রথী *n.* the seven great charioteers of the Mahabharata. ~রথীবেষ্টিত *a.* surrounded by seven great charioteers of the Mahabharata; (fig.) surrounded by numerous opponents. ~র্ষি *n.* the seven great ancient sages of India; (astr.) the Plough; (astr.) the Great Bear, the Ursa Major (also সপ্তর্ষিমণ্ডল). ~লোক *n.* (Hindu myth.) the seven worlds. ~ষষ্টি *n.* & *a.* sixty-seven. ~ষষ্টিতম *a.* sixty-seventh. *fem.* ~ষষ্টিতমী। ~সপ্ততি *n* & *a.* seventy-seven. ~সপ্ততিতম *a.* seventy-seventh. *fem.* ~সপ্ততিতমী। ~সমুদ্র, ~সিন্ধু *n.* (Hindu myth.) the seven seas. ~সুর, ~স্বর *n.* (mus.) the seven notes of a scale. ~স্বরা *a.* (mus.) consisting of seven notes. ~স্বর্গ same as ~লোক। সপ্তা coll. contr. of সপ্তাহ। সপ্তাশীতি *n.* & *a.* eighty seven. সপ্তাশীতিতম *a.* eighty-seventh. *fem.* সপ্তাশীতিতমী। সপ্তাস্র *a.* heptagonal. ☐ *n.* (geom.) a heptagon. সপ্তাহ *n.* a calendar week; an aggregate of any consecutive seven days, a week. সপ্তাহকাল *n.* a period of seven days, a week. সপ্তাহকালমধ্যে *adv.* in a week's time, within seven days.

সপ্রতিবন্ধ *a.* conditional.

সপ্রতিভ *a.* having genius; unembarrassed; unhesitating; not to be embarrassed; smart, ready and alert to act, prompt and witty; having one's wits about one; having presence of mind.

সপ্রমাণ *a.* proved, vindicated. সপ্রমাণ করা *v.* to prove, to vindicate, to justify; to demonstrate.

সফর *n.* a travel; a journey; a tour. সফর করা *v.* to travel; to journey; to tour. সফরে বের হওয়া *v.* to go on a tour. ~সূচি *n.* tour programme.

সফরী *n.* a kind of tiny fish.

সফল *a.* fruitful, successful; efficacious, effective. সফল করা *v.* to make fruitful or successful; to make good; to attain, to achieve; to accomplish; to make effective, to carry through. সফল হওয়া *v.* to become fruitful; to be successful, to succeed; to succeed in attaining or accomplishing. ~কাম, ~মনোরথ *a.* successful in attaining or realizing one's desire or end. ~তা *n.* success; efficacy, effectiveness; success in attaining or accomplishing.

সফেদ *n.* the white colour, white. ☐ *a.* white.

সফেদা *n.* powdered rice; cornmeal; sapodilla, a kind of melon; white lead.

সফেন *a.* frothy; foamy; foaming; containing liquefied starch (সফেন অন্ন).

সব *a.* all, every, whole, entire. ☐ *pro.* everybody or everything, all; whatever one possesses, all.

সবংশে *adv.* with the entire family, en famille.

সবজান্তা *a.* professing to have knowledge of everything, all-knowing, know-all. সবজান্তা ব্যক্তি Mr Know-all.

সবজি *n.* green-stuff; vegetables. ~ওয়ালা *n.* a vegetable vender, a green grocer. ~বাগ, ~বাগান *n.* a vegetable garden, (cp.) a kitchen garden.

সবজে *a.* green. ~টে *a.* greenish.

সবরি *n.* a superior quality of banana.

সবর্ণ *a.* of the same caste; of the same class or kind, homogeneous; (gr.) belonging to the same phonetical group from the viewpoint of pronunciation; endogamous. ☐ *n.* one of the same caste or class or kind; (gr.) a letter of the alphabet belonging to the same phonetical group from the viewpoint of pronunciation. ~বিবাহ marriage within one's own caste, endogamy.

সবল *a*. strong; forceful; fit for work, able, invigorated (রোগী সবল হয়েছে). *fem*. **সবলা**। **সবলে** *adv*. forcefully.

সবস্ত্র *a*. together with wearing cloth; (rare) clothed.

সবসুদ্ধ *adv*. in all, all told; en bloc; bag and baggage, lock stock and barrel, with everything (সে সবসুদ্ধ চম্পট দিল).

সবাই *pro*. one and all; everyone, all.

সবাক *a*. talking. ~**চিত্র** *n*. a talking-film, a talking picture, a talkie.

সবাকার *var*. of **সবার**।

সবাত-শ্বসন *n*. (bot.) aerobic respiration.

সবাধ *a*. obstructed; restricted; constrained. **সবাধ গতি** (mech.) constrained motion.

সবান্ধব *a*. accompanied by one's friends and people. **সবান্ধবে** *adv*. with one's friends and people.

সবার *a*. of everybody, of all; owned or shared by all; common; public; universal.

সবিকল্প *a*. having an alternative; admitting of an alternative. **সবিকল্প জ্ঞান** realization of duality; awareness of distinction between the knower and the knowable or between adjective and substantive.

সবিতা *n*. the sun; the sun-god.

সবিতামণ্ডল *n*. the orb of the sun.

সবিনয় *a*. polite, modest; humble. **সবিনয় নিবেদন** *a*. humble submission. **সবিনয় প্রার্থনা** a humble prayer or request. ~**নিবেদনমিদং** it is humbly submitted that. **সবিনয়ে** *adv*. politely, modestly; humbly.

সবিরাম *a*. intermittent.

সবিশেষ *a*. detailed, elaborate (সবিশেষ বর্ণনা) ; uncommon, unusual (সবিশেষ ভদ্রলোক). ☐ *adv*. in detail, at length, elaborately; emphatically.

সবিস্তার *a*. fully extended (সবিস্তার প্রসারণ) ; detailed, elaborate (সবিস্তার বর্ণনা). ☐ *adv*. to the full extent; in detail, at length, elaborately (usu. **সবিস্তারে**).

সবিস্ময় *a*. astonished, amazed, surprised, wondering. **সবিস্ময়ে** *adv*. amazedly, wonderingly.

সবীজ *a*. having seeds, seeded. **সবীজ উদ্ভিদ** spermaphyta.

সবুজ *a* & *n*. green. ☐ *a*. young, tender-aged. ☐ *n*. a young person, a youth, (cp.) a greenhorn; young people collectively. **সবুজ কণিকা** *n*. (bot.) chlorophyll corpuscle. **সবুজাভ** same as **সবজেটে**। see **সবজে**।

সবুর *n*. patience; waiting or tarrying; delay. ☐ *int*. (used as an *imperat. v.*) have patience, hold on, wait. **সবুর করা** *v*. to have patience; to wait or tarry. **সবুরে মেওয়া ফলে** (fig.) patience has its reward, patience succeeds or pays.

সবৃত্তিক দূত *n*. a consul de carriere.

সবে[1] poet. var. of **সবাই**।

সবে[2] *adv*. just now or just then.

সবেবরাত alt. spell. of **শবেবরাত**।

সব্জি rej. spell. of **সবজি**।

সব্বাই emphatic form of **সবাই**।

সব্যসাচী *a*. ambidexter, ambidext(e)rous. ☐ *n*. an ambidexter; Arjuna of the Mahabharata.

সভয় *a*. afraid; fearful, timorous; timid. **সভয়ে** *adv*. with fear; fearfully, timorously; timidly.

সভর্তৃকা same as **সধবা** (*a*.).

সভা *n*. an assembly, a council; a committee; an association, a society, a club, a community (ব্রাহ্মণসভা) ; a conference, a meeting, an assemblage; an audience-chamber, a durbar (রাজসভা) ; a court (বিচারসভা). **সভা করা** *v*. to hold a meeting; to hold a court or durbar; to sit in a court or durbar. **সভা চলছে** *v*. the meeting is in progress, the meeting is under way. **সভা ডাকা** *v*. to convene a meeting. **সভা বসেছে** *v*. the meeting has commenced; the court has sat. **সভা ভাঙল** *v*. the meeting breaks up or ends; the court rises. **বণিকসভা** *n*. a chamber of commerce. **রাজ্যসভা** *n*. a legislative assembly; the Upper House of the Indian Parliament. **লোকসভা** *n*. a parliament; the Indian Parliament (the House of the People or the Lower House or

Chamber). **~কক্ষ** *n.* an assembly hall; a council-room; a meeting room; a committee-room. **~কবি** *n.* a court poet. **~গৃহ** same as **সভাকক্ষ** and **সভাভবন**। **~জন** *n.* a member of an assembly, council, court, association etc. or of the audience of a meeting; a courtier. **~তল** *n.* the venue or place of a meeting; the floor of an assembly house or hall (esp. of a legislative assembly). **~নেত্রী** *n. fem.* a woman president or chairperson of a meeting, assembly, association etc. **~পণ্ডিত** *n.* a Brahman scholar retained in a court, a court-pundit; a court-scholar. **~পতি** *n.* a president or chairman of a meeting, association etc.; the chairman of a legislative council; the speaker of a legislative assembly. **~পতিত্ব** *n.* presidentship, presidency; chairmanship; speakership. **~পতিত্ব করা** *v.* to preside (over). **~ভঙ্গ** *n.* the break-up or dissolution of a meeting; the rising of a court. *n.* **~ভবন** an assembly house, a council house; an association hall, a society house; a court house. **~রম্ভ** *n.* commencement of a meeting. **~সদ** *n.* a member of an assembly, council, committee, conference etc; a courtier; (law) an assessor. **~সমিতি** *n.* meetings and associations (collectively). **~সীন** *a.* sitting or seated at a meeting or in a court. **~স্থল** same as **~তল**।

সভ্য *n.* a member (of a club, association, assembly, parliament etc.). ☐ *a.* courteous, polite, civil, mannerly; refined; elegant; civilized. **সভ্য করা** *v.* to enrol as a member; to civilize. **সভ্য হওয়া** *v.* to be enrolled as a member; to be civilized; to become courteous or polite. **~জগৎ** same as **~সমাজ**। **~তা** *n.* courtesy, politeness, civility, mannerliness; culture, civilization. **সভ্যতাভিমানী** *n.* proud (often arrogantly) of one's refinement or culture or civilization. *fem.* **সভ্যতাভিমানিনী**। **~পদ** *n.* membership. **~পদ ত্যাগ করা** to resign or renounce membership. **~ভব্য** *a.* courteous and gentle (সভ্যভব্য মানুষ) ; passably refined or elegant (সভ্যভব্য পোশাক). **~সমাজ** *n.* refined or cultured society; civilized society; the civilized world.

সম *a.* equal; equivalent; similar, resembling (মৃত্যুসম) ; identical, same; uniform; straight; level flat; even, not odd (সমরাশি) ; impartial (সমদর্শী). ☐ *n.* (mus.) the terminal point of a measure.

সমকক্ষ *a.* of equal strength; equipotential; equally rivalling or contesting; evenly balanced; equal.

সমকাল *n.* the same time; the same age. **~কালবর্তী, সমকালিক, সমকালীন** *a.* contemporary, contemporaneous; coeval; simultaneous. **সমকালে** *adv.* at the same time; in the same age; simultaneously.

সমকেন্দ্রিক *a.* concentric.

সমকোণ *n.* (geon.) a right-angle. **সমকোণী, সমকৌণিক** *a.* right-angled. **সমকোণীয়** *a.* (geog.) orthogonal.

সমক্ষ *a.* lying before; visible; direct. **~দৃষ্টি** *n.* direct vision. **সমক্ষ বর্ণালিবীক্ষণ** direct vision spectroscope. **সমক্ষে** *adv.* before one's eyes; visible.

সমক্ষেত্র-অভিক্ষেপ *n.* an equal area projection.

সমগুণ, সমগুণসম্পন্ন *a.* of like virtue or quality or character. **সমগুণশ্রেঢ়ী** *n.* (math.) geometrical progression.

সমগ্র *a.* whole, entire; all; total; exhaustive; overall. **সমগ্র বিস্তার** overall width. **সমগ্র সূচি** an exhaustive list. **~ভাবে** *adv.* on the whole; entirely; thoroughly.

সমঘন *n.* (geom.) a regular solid.

সমচতুরস্র, সমচতুর্ভুজ *n.* (geom.) an equilateral tetragon; a square. ☐ *a.* square.

সমচ্ছেদ *n.* (phys.) a plane section.

সমজদার var. of **সমঝদার**।

সমজাতি, সমজাতীয় *a.* homogeneous, congeneric; congenetic.

সমঝদার *a.* capable of understanding or appreciating; (loos.) sympathetic or considerate. **সমঝদার লোক** a connoisseur. **সমঝদারি** *n.* capability of understanding or appreciating; sympathy or considerateness.

সমঝানো *v.* to understand; to appreciate; to feel; to deliberate; (loos.) to sympathize (with) or have consideration (for); (loos.) to be careful or cautious (সমঝে চলা) ; to make one understand or appreciate or feel; (sarcas.) to warn or scold or chastise.

সমঞ্জস *a.* perfectly proper; appropriate or just; fitting, well-balanced; consistent.

সমতল *a.* plain, level, smooth, flat. ☐ *n.* (geom.) a plain; a plane surface or figure, a plane.

সমতা *n.* equality; equivalence; similarity; identity, sameness; uniformity; straightness; levelness, flatness; impartiality.

সমতীত *a.* quite past or gone by.

সমতুল, (erron.) **সমতুল্য** *a.* equiponderate; comparable; equal, parallel; equipotential; equivalent.

সমত্বরণ *n.* uniform acceleration.

সমত্রিভুজ *n.* (geom.) an equilateral triangle.

সমদর্শন see **সমদর্শী** ৷

সমদর্শী *a.* impartial in consideration or treatment; equitable in dispensation of justice; impartial; equitable; fair-minded. *fem.* **সমদর্শিনী** ৷ **সমদর্শন, সমদর্শিতা** *n.* impartiality; equity; fair-mindedness.

সমদুঃখী *a.* sharing the same or having similar grief or affliction; sympathizing; sympathetic. *fem.* **সমদুঃখিনী** ৷

সমদূর, সমদূরবর্তী *a.* equidistant. **সমদূরবর্তিতা** *n.* equidistance.

সমদৃষ্টি *n.* impartial view; impartiality.

সমদ্বিবাহু, সমদ্বিভুজ *a.* (geom.) isosceles. **সমদ্বিবাহু ত্রিভুজ** an isosceles triangle.

সমধিক *a.* exceedingly great, excessive, exceeding, overmuch; considerable; many. ☐ *adv.* exceedingly, excessively, overmuch.

সমন *n.* a summons. **সমন জারি করা, সমন দেওয়া, সমন পাঠানো** *v.* to serve or issue a summons; to summon. **সমন ধরানো** *v.* to serve a summons.

সমন্বয় *n.* consistency; agreement; combination; synthesis; adjustment. **সমন্বয় করা** *v.* to bring into agreement; to bring about harmony or agreement; to make a synthesis of, to synthesize, to synthetize; to adjust. **~ন, ~বিধান, ~সাধন** *n.* act of bringing into agreement; act of bringing about harmony or agreement; unification; act of making a synthesis of; adjustment. **সমন্বয়িত** *a.* made consistent; unified; brought into agreement; synthesized; synthetized; adjusted.

সমন্বিত *a.* possessing; attended with; mixed with; full of.

সমপদস্থ *a.* equal in office or rank or status or dignity or authority.

সমপাঠী *n.* a class-fellow; a fellow-student. *fem.* **সমপাঠিনী** ৷ see also **সহপাঠি** ৷

সমপার্শ্বীয় *a.* (bot.) collateral.

সমপৃষ্ঠ same as **সমতল** (*a.*)

সমপ্রবাহ *n.* (phys.) a direct current.

সমপ্রেষ *n.* (phys.) uniform pressure. **সমপ্রেষরেখা** *n.* (geog.) an isobar.

সমবয়সী, সমবয়স্ক *a.* of the same or approximately the same age; contemporaneous, contemporary, coeval.

সমবর্ত-কোণ *n.* (phys.) the angle of polarization.

সমবর্তন *n.* (phys.) polarization.

সমবর্তাক্ষ *n.* (phys.) the axis of polarization.

সমবর্তিত *a.* polarized. **সমবর্তিত করা** *v.* to polarize.

সমবর্ষণ-রেখা *n.* (geog.) an isohyet.

সমবস্থ *a.* in or of the same or similar condition; in the same position or state as formerly, in status quo. **সমবস্থা** *n.* same or similar condition; unchanged position or state, status quo.

সমবায় *n.* an assemblage, an aggregate; combination; constant relation; co-operation. **সমবায় সমিতি** *n.* a co-operative society. **সমবায়ী** *a.* capable of combining; combined; co-operative; constantly related; component, constituent.

সমবাহু *a.* equilateral.

সমবিন্দু *a.* (geom.) concurrent.

সমবৃত্তি *a.* (bot.) analogous.

সমবেগ *n.* uniform velocity.

সমবেত *n.* assembled, collected; united; combined. **সমবেত করা** *v.* to bring together, to assemble. **সমবেত হওয়া** *v.* to come together, to assemble, to gather. **~ভাবে** *adv.* unitedly, in a body.

সমবেদনা, সমব্যথা *n.* sympathy; fellow-feeling; commiseration; compassion.

সমবেদী, সমব্যথী *a.* sympathetic; commiserative; compassionate. **সমবেদী কম্পন** *a.* sympathetic vibration.

সমভাব *n.* same or similar state of mind; same or similar state or condition or manner; similarity or sameness; equability. **সমভাবাপন্ন** *a.* having the same or similar state of mind; of the same or similar state or condition; similar or same; equable. **সমভাবাপন্ন জলবায়ু** equable climate. **সমভাবে** *adv.* in the same or similar way or manner; unchangingly; uniformly.

সমভিব্যাহারী *a.* (obs.) accompanying. *fem.* **সমভিব্যাহারিণী**।

সমভিব্যাহারে *adv.* (obs.) accompanied by or in the company of.

সমভূমি *a.* level, flat, plain; razed to the ground. **সমভূমি করা** *v.* to level; to raze to the ground.

সমমণ্ডল *n.* the temperate zone.

সমমতাবলম্বী *n & a.* of the same opinion; belonging to or believing in the same religion.

সমমাত্র *a.* (alg.) homogeneous.

সমমাত্রিক *a.* (pros.) consisting of feet of equal metres.

সমমালভূমি *n.* (geog.) a tableland, a plateau.

সমমুখ *a.* (mech.—of forces) like.

সমমূল্য *a.* of the same or equal price or value or rate; equivalent. **সমমূল্যে** *adv.* at the same or equal price or rate; at par.

সময় *n.* time; the time of the clock (দুটোর সময়) ; any particular time or part of day (সন্ধ্যার সময়) ; a point or period of time (সেই সময়) ; season; fixed or due time; working hours (স্কুলের সময়) ; an instance or time; suitable or opportune time; leisure; opportunity; state or condition; reign, regime, period, age; term of office; floruit; times (দুঃসময়) ; good days; the last gasp (বুড়োর সময় হয়েছে) ; longevity (সময় ফুরোলে সবাই মরবে) ; usage, practice, tradition, convention (কবিসময়প্রসিদ্ধি). **সময় করা** *v.* to make or find time (for), to find leisure (for); to fix time (for). **সময় বুঝে চলা** *v.* to accommodate oneself to the contemporary situation; to behave or move as a time-server; to live within one's present means. **সময় দেওয়া** *v.* to give or allow (one) time. **সময় দেখা** *v.* to read the time (of clocks etc.). **সময় নষ্ট করা** *v.* to waste time, to kill time; to lose an opportunity, to let go an opportunity. **সময় পাওয়া** *v.* to get or find time or leisure; to be given or allowed time. **সময় বলা** *v.* to tell the time (of clocks). **সময় হয়েছে** *v.* it is time; one's days are numbered. **অত্যল্প সময়ে** in no time. **কাজের সময়** the time for work; working hours. **প্রমাণ সময়** *n.* standard time. **বর্তমান সময়** present times. **বসন্তের সময়** springtime, the spring season, spring; in spring. **সন্ধ্যার সময়** evening time, evening; in evening. **স্থানীয় সময়** local time. **সময় সময়, সময়ে সময়ে** from time to time; at times; occasionally. **সময়ে ও অসময়ে** in season and out of season. **~ক্রমে** *adv.* in course of time. **সময় নিরূপণ করা** *v.* to ascertain the time (of); to fix the time (for). **~নিষ্ঠ** *a.* punctual. **~নিষ্ঠা** *n.* punctuality. **~মতো** same as **সময়ানুসারে**। **~রক্ষক** *n.* a time-keeper, (as of a factory). □ *a.* keeping time **~রেখা** *n.* a dateline. **~সারণি** *n.* time-table. **~সীমা** *n.* time limit; deadline. **~সেবক, ~সেবী** *n.* a time-server. □ *a.* time-serving. **সময়ানুসারে** *adv.* according to a particular or fixed time; according to the demand of the passing state or condition; according to the age or time. **সময়ান্তরে** *adv.* at another or some other time; (rare) after a time-lag. **সময়াভাব** *n.* want or paucity or shortage of time. **সময়োচিত, সময়োপযোগী** *a.* timely.

সমর *n.* a war, a battle, a fight. **~কৌশল** *n.* the art of planning operations in war, strategy. **~ক্ষেত্র, ~ভূমি** same as **যুদ্ধক্ষেত্র**। **~শায়ী** *a.* killed in a battle, fallen in a fight, killed in action. *fem.* **~শায়িনী**। **~সজ্জা, ~সাজ** *n.* battle-dress and arms and equipment (of any individual soldier); war equipment; preparation for war. ~স্থল, সমরাঙ্গন same as যুদ্ধক্ষেত্র। সমরানল n. war regarded as a widely devastating fire, fire or flames of war.

সমরাশি n. (arith.) an even number.

সমরূপ a. alike in form; homomorphic, homomorphous; homoeomorphic; alike in manner; uniform. ~তা n. uniformity.

সমরৈখিক a. collinear.

সমর্থ a. capable, able; competent; ablebodied; of full age and able to earn (সমর্থ ছেলে); of full age and fit for marriage (সমর্থ মেয়ে).

সমর্থক n. a seconder; a supporter; (dero.) a countenancer; a confirmer, a confirmator; a corroborator.

সমর্থন n. seconding (of a motion or nomination); support; (dero.) countenancing; confirmation; corroboration. সমর্থন করা v. to second; to support; to countenance; to confirm; to corroborate.

সমর্থা fem. of সমর্থ।

সমর্থিত a. seconded; supported; (dero.) countenanced; confirmed; corroborated. fem. সমর্থিতা।

সমর্পণ n. act of giving away; dedication; act of making over; act of committing to the charge or custody of; surrender. সমর্পণ করা v. to give away; to dedicate; to give; to make over; to commit to the charge or custody of; to yield up, to surrender. ~কারী a giver; a dedicator; one who makes over; one who commits to the charge or custody or; a yielder; a surrenderer. সমর্পণীয় a. that which can be or should be dedicated or made over or surrendered or committed to the charge (of). fem. ~কারিণী।

সমর্পা poet. form of সমর্পণ করা।

সমর্পিত a. given away; dedicated; given; made over; committed to the charge or custody of; yielded up, surrendered.

সমল a. dirty; filthy, foul.

সমলয় a. (phys.) synchronous. ☐ n. (phys.) synchronism. সমলয় করা v. (phys.) to synchronize.

সমশ্রেণি n. the same class or race or family or rank. ~ভুক্ত a. belonging to the same class or race or family or rank.

সমষ্টি n. a sum total, an aggregate; a total; the result of a sum of addition. ~করণ n. totalling; totalization; addition; (phys.) aggregation. ~গতভাবে adv. collectively.

সমসংযোগ n. (bot.) cohesion.

সমসত্ত্ব a. (bot.) homogeneous.

সমসাময়িক a. (erron. but pop.) contemporary, contemporaneous.

সমসূত্র n. (astr. & geog.) the prime vertical (circle); one and the same straight line (সমসূত্রে অবস্থান); one and the same string, bond etc. (সমসূত্রে গ্রথিত); one and the same means (সমসূত্রে জানা).

সমস্ত a. all, every; whole, entire; (gr.—of words) compounded. ~পদ n. (gr.) a compound word.

সমস্বরে adv. in one voice; unanimously.

সমস্যমান a. (gr.—of words) under the process of being compounded.

সমস্যা n. a problem; a question; a riddle, a poser, a puzzle; an intricate situation, a difficulty, a fix. সমস্যা পূরণ বা সমাধান করা v. to solve a problem; to propound a riddle, to riddle a riddle. ~পূর্ণ, ~মূলক a. problematic; replete with or full of problems; engimatic, riddling, puzzling; intricate, difficult. ~সংকুল same as ~পূর্ণ।

সমহার same as সমমূল্য।

সমা a. fem. of সম (a.).

সমাংশক a. (chem.) isomerous.

সমাংশে adv. in equal parts or portions or shares.

সমাকলন n. integral calculus.

সমাকীর্ণ a. widely and thoroughly bestrewn (with); pervaded (with); infested (with); full of.

সমাকুল a. greatly worried or distressed; full of misgivings; replete with, full of (গন্ধসমাকুল).

সমাকৃতি a. isomorphous.

সমাক্ষ a. co-axial. ~রেখা n. a parallel of latitude.

সমাখ্যাত a. celebrated, renowned, illustrious.

সমাগত a. arrived; assembled, gathered. সমাগত হওয়া v. to come, to arrive; to assemble, to gather.

সমাগম *n.* coming, arrival, assemblage; a gathering. **জনসমাগম** *n.* a concourse of people, a gathering; a crowd.

সমাঙ্গ *a.* regular.

সমাচার *n.* news, information, a message, a report.

সমাচ্ছন্ন *a.* thoroughly covered or enveloped or overcast; thoroughly overwhelmed or besotted.

সমাজ *n.* human society, society; any one of the divisions of biological history (পক্ষিসমাজ, পশুসমাজ) ; a community; a nation or race; a collective body of people having something in common, a class, a community (কবিসমাজ, বণিক সমাজ, শিক্ষিতসমাজ, নাগরিকসমাজ) ; an association; a gathering esp. a social one (সমাজে বসে খাওয়া). **সমাজে ঠেলা** *v.* to allot a lowly place in the society (to somebody). **সমাজ উন্নয়ন** *n.* social development, social upliftment. **~কল্যাণ** *n.* social welfare. **~চ্যুত করা** *v.* to cast (one) out of society, to ostracize, to boycott socially. **~চ্যুত ব্যক্তি** an outcast. **~চ্যুতি** *n.* expulsion from society, social boycott; social ostracism. **~তত্ত্ব** *n.* sociology. **~তন্ত্র** *n.* socialism. **~তন্ত্রী** *a.* socialistic, socialist. □ *n.* a socialist. **~তাত্ত্বিক** *a.* sociological. **~তান্ত্রিক** *a.* same as **সমাজতন্ত্রী** (*a.*) **~নীতি** *n.* social laws or principles; sociology; (rare) social ethics. **~পতি** *n.* the headman of a community. **~বদ্ধ** *a.* (of human beings) living in societies, social; (of inferior creatures) gregarious. **~বন্ধন** *n.* obligations of social life; bonds of society; mutual social relation , social ties. **~বহির্ভূত** *a.* outside the society, (cp.) extra-social; unsocial; socially outcast, ostracized. **~বিজ্ঞান, ~বিদ্যা** *n.* sociology. **~বিজ্ঞানী** *n.* a sociologist. **~বিধি** *n.* social law or rule. **~বিরুদ্ধ, ~বিরোধী** *a.* antisocial. **~শাসন** *n.* social laws and rules; the rule or authority of the society; administration of the society. **~শিক্ষা** *n.* social studies. **~সংস্কার** *n.* social reform. **~সংস্কার করা** *v.* to reform the society. **~সংস্কারক** *n.* a social reformer. **~হিতৈষণা** *n.* act of doing good to the society. **~হিতৈষী** *a.* endeavouring to do good to the society. □ *n.* a social welfare worker.

সমাদর *n.* very warm or cordial or respectful reception and careful treatment (as of a guest); felicitation (as of a hero); zealous reception (as of a commodity); passionate love or fondness (for). **সমাদর করা** *v.* to receive very warmly or cordially or respectfully and treat carefully; to felicitate; to receive zealously; to love passionately.

সমাদৃত *a.* very warmly or cordially or respectfully received and carefully treated; felicitated; zealously received; passionately loved.

সমাধা, সমাধান *n.* completion, accomplishment; termination, conclusion, end; settlement, decision; solution; propounding, riddling (ধাঁধার সমাধান). **সমাধা করা, সমাধান করা** *v.* to complete, to accomplish, to terminate, to conclude, to end; to settle, to decide; to solve, to puzzle out : to propound, to riddle.

সমাধি *n.* self-absorbed spiritual meditation during which the meditator loses his or her entity and becomes one with the Supreme Being; a reverie, a trance; a self-absorbed meditation; burial, interment, a grave, a sepulchral monument, a tomb, a mausoleum (also **সমাধিমন্দির**); (fig.) end. **~ক্ষেত্র** *n.* a burial-ground, a cemetery; (loos.) a grave. **~ভঙ্গ করা** *v.* to disturb or interrupt self-absorbed meditation; to give up self-absorbed meditation. **~মগ্ন** *a.* drowned or absorbed in profound meditation; tranced. **~স্তম্ভ** *n.* a tombstone. **~স্থ** same as **~মগ্ন,**— and buried. **সমাধিস্থ করা** *v.* to bury, to lay in the grave, to inter. **~স্থল, ~স্থান** same as **~ক্ষেত্র**।

সমাধ্যায়ী same as **সতীর্থ**।

সমান *a.* similar, alike; one and the same; identical; equal; uniform; unchanged, unchanging; impartial; straight; level, flat; (sl.) corrected by sound thrashing (পিটিয়ে সমান করা). □ *n.* one of the five vital airs. **সমান করা** *v.* to make similar or alike or identical; to equalize; to make uniform; to straighten; to level, to flatten; to dress (জমি সমান করা) ; to adjust or correct (ঘড়ি সমান করা) ; to put on properly (জামাকাপড় সমান করা) ; to correct by sound thrashing. **সমান-সমান** *n.* equivalent; equal; equalized; equal in strength; equally balanced; evenly contested; even; drawn (খেলা সমান-সমান) ; (in gambling) quits; neither more nor less; half-and-half (সমান-সমান ভাগ). **সমান-সমান দ্বন্দ্ব** *a.* Greek meeting a Greek. **সমানাধিকরণ** *a.* (of two or more objects) having the same abode or condition; (gr.) having the relation as between a noun and an adjective. **সমানাধিকার** *n.* equal rights and privileges for all.

সমানুপাত *n.* (math.) equal ratio, proportion. **সমানুপাতিক** *a.* (math.) proportionate or relating to proportion. **সমানুপাতিক প্রতিনিধিত্ব** proportional representation.

সমানে *adv.* ceaselessly, non-stop, incessantly; at a stretch.

সমানে-সমানে *a.* evenly contested. **সমানে-সমানে লড়াই** a Greek meeting a Greek.

সমান্তর *a.* (arith. & alg.—of numbers) equidistant (e.g. 3, 8, 13, 18); (geom.) parallel. **~তা** *n.* equidistance; parallelism. **~রেখা** *n.* a parallel line. **সমান্তর শ্রেণি** *n.* arithmetical progression; an arithmetic series.

সমান্তরাল *a.* (esp. in geom.) parallel. **সমান্তরাল ক্ষেত্র** a parallelogram. **সমান্তরাল রেখা** a parallel line. **সমান্তরাল সরলরেখা** a parallel straight line.

সমাপক *a.* completing; finishing; fulfilling.

সমাপতন *n.* (geom.) coincidence.

সমাপন *n.* completion; conclusion, ending, finishing, finish, close; fulfilment. **সমাপন করা** *v.* to complete; to conclude, to finish, to terminate, to close; to fulfil. **সমাপন হওয়া** *v.* to be completed or finished, to end, to close; to be fulfilled. **সমাপন সংগীত** *n.* a closing or concluding song.

সমাপিকা *a. fem.* of **সমাপক**। □ *a.* (gr.) finite. (**সমাপিকা ক্রিয়া** = a finite verb).

সমাপিত, সমাপ্ত *a.* completed; concluded, ended, finished, closed; fulfilled. **সমাপ্ত করা** বা **হওয়া** same as **সমাপন করা** বা **হওয়া**। **সমাপ্তি** same as **সমাপন**। **সমাপ্তি সংগীত** same as **সমাপন সংগীত**। **সমাপ্য** *a.* that which should be concluded or ended or finished.

সমাবতল *a.* (phys.) plano-concave.

সমাবরণ *n.* occultation.

সমাবর্তন *n.* return; the home-coming of a pupil after his long stay at his teacher's residence where he has completed his studies; a convocation (of a university or institution).

সমাবিষ্ট *a.* entirely occupied, engrossed; entered; possessed (as by an evil spirit); assembled, collected.

সমাবৃত *a.* thoroughly covered; concealed; enclosed or besieged; thickly encircled or accompanied (পরিজনসমাবৃত).

সমাবেশ *n.* assemblage (জনসমাবেশ) ; a gathering; intent attention, engrossment.

সমায়াত *a.* arrived, come.

সমাযোজন *n.* communication.

সমারূঢ় *a.* ceremonially or solemnly installed (upon) (সিংহাসনে সমারূঢ়) ; seated or mounted (upon); ascended.

সমারোহ *n.* pomp, grandeur, eclat; a thick crowd or grand assemblage (মেঘের সমারোহ). **সমারোহ করা** *v.* to give a display of pomp or grandeur; to make a splendid arrangement. **~পূর্ণ** *a.* pompous, full of grandeur or splendour or eclat. **~পূর্বক, সমারোহে** *adv.* pompously, ostentatiously; in a grandiose manner, in a grand way.

সমার্থ, সমার্থক *a.* synonymous. **সমার্থক শব্দ** a synonym. **~বোধক** same as **সমার্থক**। **~শব্দকোষ** *n.* a dictionary of synonyms, a thesaurus.

সমালোচক *n.* a critic, a reviewer; an animadverter, one who censures.

সমালোচন, সমালোচনা *n.* criticism, review; animadversion, censure. **সমালোচনা করা** *v.* to criticize, to review; to animadvert, to censure.

সমালোচিকা *fem.* of **সমালোচক**।

সমালোচিত *a.* criticized, reviewed ; animadverted, censured.

সমালোচ্য *a.* under review; open to criticism; censurable.

সমাস *n.* (gr.) compounding of two or more words into one. **সমাস করা** *v* . to compound two or more words into one. **সমাস ভাঙা** *v.* to resolve a compound word into components. **~বদ্ধ** *a.* compounded.

সমাসক্ত *a.* attached (to); addicted (to); deeply attentive or engrossed; joined.

সমাসন্ন *a.* that has come very near; imminent; approaching; impending.

সমাসীন *a.* solemnly or firmly seated or installed; seated, sitting.

সমাসোক্তি *n.* (rhet.) a figure of speech involving parallelism between the subject in hand and something understood (cp. personification, pathetic fallacy). (e.g. 'ঠকা ঠাঁই ঠাঁই কাঁদিছে নেহাই').

সমাহরণ *n.* gahering, collection. **সমাহরণ করা** *v.* to gather, to collect.

সমাহর্তা *n.* a collector; the chief official of a district who collects revenue and acts as a magistrate, a collector, *fem.* **সমাহর্ত্রী** ।

সমাহার *n.* collection; combination; abbreviation; summation; a multitude; (gr.) a system of compounding words, indicative of a number.

সমাহিত *a.* entirely occupied, engrossed; lost in meditation; placed; deposited; interred, buried. **সমাহিত করা** *v.* to bury, to inter.

সমাহৃত *a.* gathered, collected; combined.

সমিতি *n.* an association, a society; a club; a committee. **বণিক সমিতি** *n.* a chamber of commerce.

সমিৎ, সমিধ *n.* firewood, fuel; firewood for kindling a sacrificial fire.

সমিল *a.* (of poetry) with rhyme, rhymed.

সমীকরণ *n.* equalization; (alg.) equation; (arith.) reduction of fractions to a common denominator. **সমীকরণ করা** *v.* to equalize; (alg.) to equate; (arith.) to reduce (fractions) to a common denominator.

সমীকৃত *a.* equated. **সমীকৃত কাল** (arith.) equated time.

সমীক্ষণ *n.* thorough viewing or observation; investigation, search; scrutiny; deliberation.

সমীক্ষা same as **সমীক্ষণ,** and—truths (collectively or individually) expounded in the Sankhya philosophy.

সমীক্ষিত *a.* thoroughly viewed or observed; investigated, searched; researched; scrutinized, scanned; deliberated. **সমীক্ষ্যকারী** *a.* considering past results and taking precaution about consequences before taking any action, circumspect, discreet. *fem.* **সমীক্ষ্যকারিণী** । **সমীক্ষ্যকারিতা** *n.* consideration of past results and precaution about consequences before taking any action, circumspection.

সমীচীন *a.* just, reasonable; condign; proper; prudent, wise; expedient; right.

সমীপ *n.* proximity, nearness, vicinity; presence. **~বর্তী, ~স্থ** *a.* near, close to; approaching (ট্রেন স্টেশনের সমীপবর্তী হল). **সমীপে** *adv.* near, close to; in the presence of, before (রাজসমীপে).

সমীর, সমীরণ *n.* wind, air, breeze.

সমীহ *n.* show of respect; deference; hesitation caused by awe. **সমীহ করা** *v.* to pay respect to; to treat with deference; to look up to with awe and hesitation. **সমীহ না করা** *v.* not to pay respect to; to ignore.

সমুখ pop. var. of **সম্মুখ** ।

সমুচিত *a.* perfectly just or right or proper, condign (সমুচিত শাস্তি) ; adequate (সমুচিত পুরস্কার).

সমুচ্চ *a.* very high, lofty; elevated; exalted (সমুচ্চ পদ) ; very loud, vociferous (সমুচ্চ নাদ).

সমুচ্চয় *n.* a collection, a multitude. **পদসমুচ্চয়** *n.* all words collectively (as of a sentence); joining of words or sentences (as with a copulative).

সমুচ্ছেদ *n.* complete extirpation or eradication or extermination; destruction; ejection for good.

সমুজ্জ্বল *a.* very bright; radiant; brilliant, brightened; illuminated.

সমুৎপাটন *n.* pulling up, eradication, uprooting.

সমুৎপাটিত, সমুৎসাদিত *a.* completely extirpated or eradicated; destroyed; ejected for good.

সমুৎসুক *a.* very eager or curious.

সমুত্থান *n.* a rising up; great rise or flourishing; (Christ.) resurrection; an enterprise.

সমুত্থিত *a.* risen up; greatly flourished; (Christ.) risen from the dead. **সমুত্থিত হওয়া** *v.* to rise up; to flourish greatly; to rise from the dead.

সমুদয়, সমুদায় *a.* all; whole, entire; total. □ *n.* all persons or things; the entire thing or area.

সমুদ্দুর coll. var. of **সমুদ্র।**

সমুদ্ভব *n.* origination, origin; birth; evolvement; flourish.

সমুদ্ভাসিত *a.* flooded with light, illuminated; brightened.

সমুদ্ভূত *a.* originated; born; evolved.

সমুদ্যত *a.* about to, on the point of, perfectly ready or prepared; raised or lifted (সমুদ্যত খড়্গ).

সমুদ্র *n.* an ocean; a sea. **অকুল সমুদ্রে পড়া** *v.* (fig.) to be at sea, to be in great danger. **সমুদ্রে ঝাঁপ দেওয়া** *v.* (fig.) to brave or face a great danger. **সমুদ্র-উদ্ভিদ** *n.* a seaweed. **~গর্ভ** *n.* sea-bottom; the inside of the sea, the womb of the sea. **~গামী** *a.* sea-going; seafaring. **~জাত** *a.* sea-born. **~তট, ~তীর** *n.* sea-bank, seashore. **~পথ** *n.* sea-way, sea-route. **~পথে** *adv.* by sea. **~পৃষ্ঠ** *n.* the surface of the sea; sea-level. **~বহ্নি** *n.* submarine fire. **~বলয়াঙ্কিত** *a.* sea-girt. **~বায়ু** *n.* sea-breeze, sea-wind, sea-air. **~বাহিত** *a.* seaborne. **~বেলা** *n.* sea-beach, seashore, sea-bank. **~মন্থন** *n.* (Hindu myth.) the churning of the ocean by gods and demons. **~মেখলা** *a.* sea-girt. **~যাত্রা** *n.* a sea-voyage. **সমুদ্রযাত্রা করা** *v.* to make a sea-voyage, to go on a sea-voyage. **~যান** *n.* a sea-going vessel. **~যুদ্ধ** *n.* a sea-fight. **~স্নান** *n.* sea-bathing. **~স্রোত** *n.* ocean current.

সমুন্নত *a.* very high or lofty or elevated; (fig.) very exalted or dignified or noble.

সমুপস্থিত *a.* come close to; arrived; approaching; imminent.

সমুল্লেখ *n.* mention.

সমূল, সমূলক *a.* having a root; having a cause; having a foundation or basis, genuine (সমূলক ভয়). **সমূলে** *adv.* together with the root, root and branch, thoroughly, completely (সমূলে ধ্বংস).

সমূহ *n.* (chiefly used as a *sfx.* to indicate plurality) a multitude, total number (লোকসমূহ = the people, ব্যঘ্রসমূহ = tigers) □ *a.* many, much, numerous, great (সমূহ লোকসান) ; terrible, tremendous (সমূহ বিপদ).

সমৃদ্ধ *a.* thoroughly developed or grown up or flourishing; enriched; prosperous, affluent, wealthy, rich. *fem.* **সমৃদ্ধা।** **সমৃদ্ধি** *n.* splendid development or growth; enrichment; prosperity, affluence, wealthiness, richness. **সমৃদ্ধিশালী, সমৃদ্ধিসম্পন্ন** same as **সমৃদ্ধ।** *fem.* **সমৃদ্ধিশালিনী, সমৃদ্ধিসম্পন্না।**

সমেত *a.* together with, with; inclusive of, including.

সমোচ্ছ্বাস-রেখা *n.* co-tidal lines.

সমোত্তল *a.* (phys.) plano-convex.

সমোন্নতি-রেখা *n.* a contour line.

সমোষ্ণ-রেখা *n.* (geog.) the isotherm.

সম্পত্তি, সম্পদ *n.* wealth, riches, fortune; treasure; property, real estate; belongings, possessions; excellence (ভাবসম্পদ) ; glorious or proud acquisition (শিক্ষাই তার সম্পদ) ; pride or glory (তাজমহল দেশের সম্পদ). **সম্পত্তিশালী, সম্পদশালী** *a.* wealthy, rich; affluent; possessing a treasure; (pop.) owning a property. *fem.* **সম্পত্তিশালিনী, সম্পদশালিনী।**

সম্পন্ন *a.* performed, accomplished; completed; rich, wealthy, affluent, well-to-do (সম্পন্ন অবস্থা) ; endowed with, possessing (বুদ্ধিসম্পন্ন). *fem.* **সম্পন্না।**

সম্পর্ক *n.* relation; kinship; connection; concern; company, intercourse (দুষ্টের সঙ্গে সম্পর্ক). **সম্পর্ক রাখা** *v.* to maintain relation; to observe the formalities of kinship; to keep connection; to associate with, to keep company with. **সম্পর্ক স্থাপন করা** *v.* to enter into a relation or an alliance. **~শূন্য, ~হীন** *a.* unrelated; having no kinship (with), unconnected; having no concern (with); irrelevant.

সম্পর্কিত, সম্পর্কীয় *a.* related (with); having kinship (with); having affinity with; connected (with); concerned (with); relevant.

সম্পাত *n.* fall, drop (অশনিসম্পাত) ; incidence, a falling upon (আলোকসম্পাত) ; a stroke from above (অভিসম্পাত) ; occurrence (বিপদসম্পাত). **~বিন্দু** *n.* the point of incidence.

সম্পাদক *a.* performing, accomplishing, executive (**সম্পাদক সমিতি** = an executive committee); editing. ☐ *n.* a performer, an accomplisher; an executive; a secretary (সমিতির সম্পাদক) ; an editor (*fem.* editress). **সম্পাদকীয়** *a.* editorial. ☐ *n.* an editorial leader. **সম্পাদকীয় প্রবন্ধ** an editorial, a leader. **সম্পাদকীয় স্তম্ভ** an editorial column.

সম্পাদন, সম্পাদনা *n.* performance, accomplishment; editing. **সম্পাদন করা** *v.* to perform, to accomplish, to execute. **সম্পাদনা করা** *v.* to edit.

সম্পাদিকা *fem.* of **সম্পাদক** ।

সম্পাদিত *a.* performed, accomplished, executed; edited.

সম্পাদ্য *a.* to be performed or accomplished or executed. ☐ *n.* (geom.) a problem, (also **সম্পাদ্য প্রতিজ্ঞা**).

সম্পুট, সম্পুটক *n.* a small box, a casket; a screwed bag made of paper or tree-leaves, a cornet.

সম্পূরক *a.* completing; fulfilling; supplementing; supplemental; supplementary. **সম্পূরক কোণ** (geom.) a supplementary angle, a supplement.

সম্পূরণ *n.* completion; fulfilment; supplementation.

সম্পূর্ণ *a.* completed; finished; completely filled; complete, entire, whole, total; thorough; (dero.) downright ☐ *adv.* completely, entirely, wholly, totally; quite; thoroughly. **সম্পূর্ণ করা** *v.* to complete; to finish; to fill completely. **~তা** *n.* completion; fullness; completeness, entirety, wholeness, totality; thoroughness; perfection. **~রূপে** *adv.* same as **সম্পূর্ণ** (*adv.*)

সম্পৃক্ত *a.* related or connected (with); having concern (with), joined or united (with); saturated; inlaid. **সম্পৃক্তি** *n.* relation, connection; concern; joining, union; saturation; inlaying. **অতিসম্পৃক্তি** *n.* over-saturation.

সম্প্রচার *n.* wide circulation; broadcasting, broadcast. **সম্প্রচার-তরঙ্গ** *n.* (phys.) a broadcasting wave. **সম্প্রচার-কেন্দ্র** *n.* a broadcasting station. **সম্প্রচারিত** *a.* widely circulated; broadcast.

সম্প্রতি *adv.* now-a-days, in these days, at present, in present times; recently, lately, of late; just.

সম্প্রদাতা *a.* & *n.* one who gives or bestows or confers; one who gives away the bride ceremonially to the charge of the bridegroom.

সম্প্রদান *n.* giving; bestowal, conferment; act of giving away the bride ceremonially to the charge of the bridegroom; (gr.) the dative case (usu. **সম্প্রদানকারক**). **সম্প্রদান করা** *v.* to give; to bestow, to confer; to commit (the bride) ceremonially to the charge of (the bridegroom).

সম্প্রদায় *n.* a community, a sect; a society (কবিসম্প্রদায়) ; a brotherhood; a race (মানবসম্প্রদায়, পশুসম্প্রদায়) ; a company, a band (দস্যুসম্প্রদায়). **~ভুক্ত** *a.* belonging to a particular community or sect or society or brotherhood or race or band.

সম্প্রসার, সম্প্রসারণ *n.* expansion; extension; development. **সম্প্রসারণবাদ** *n.* expansionism. **সম্প্রসারণবাদী** *a.* expansionist. **সম্প্রসারণশীল** *a.* expanding, extending; expansive. **সম্প্রসারিত** *a.* expanded; extended; developed.

সম্প্রীতি *n.* love; amity; friendly terms (with); pleasure; delight.

সম্বৎ, সম্বৎসর alt. spellings of **সংবৎ** and **সংবৎসর** respectively.

সম্বদ্ধ *a.* firmly tied or joined or united; connected; related; having kinship with, affixed; affiliated; amalgamated. **সম্বদ্ধীকরণ** *n.* affiliation; amalgamation. **সম্বদ্ধীকৃত** *a.* affiliated; amalgamated.

সম্বন্ধ *n.* relation, connection; concern; intercourse; kinship, relationship, affinity; a marriage proposal or negotiation. **সম্বন্ধ করা** *n.* to negotiate a marriage; to make negotiations for a marriage. **সম্বন্ধ থাকা** *v.* to have connection or relation or concern or intercourse or kinship or relationship (with) **সম্বন্ধ রাখা** *v.* to keep connection with; to observe formalities of kinship or relationship. **রাসায়নিক সম্বন্ধ** chemical affinity. **~পদ** *n.* (gr.) a word in the possessive case, a genitive. **সম্বন্ধী** *a.* related (to), connected (with). □ *n.* wife's brother or cousin-brother (generally one older than the wife), a brother-in-law. **সম্বন্ধীয়** *a.* (used as a *prep.*) related to, concerning, regarding. **সম্বন্ধে** *prep.* concerning, regarding, about, as regards, as to.

সম্বরণ, সম্বরা[1] alt. spellings of **সংবরণ** and **সংবরা** respectively.

সম্বরা[2] *n.* spices singed in oil or ghee and mixed with any cooked dish by reboiling. **সম্বরা দেওয়া** *v.* to re-boil (a cooked dish) by mixing with spices singed in oil or ghee.

সম্বল *n.* money, provisions etc. for a journey; viaticum : a supply or resource of money etc.; a fund, capital money, capital; (total) savings; provision; resources; support, a prop. **সম্বল করা** *v.* to have recourse to, to resort to. **~শূন্য, ~হীন** same as **নিঃসম্বল।**

সম্বলিত, সম্বাদী alt. spellings of **সংবলিত** and **সংবাদী** respectively.

সম্বাধ same as **বাধা** (n.) and **ব্যাঘাত।**

সম্বুদ্ধ *a.* perfectly enlightened (esp. spiritually.) □ *n.* an appellation of Gautama Buddha.

সম্বোধন *n.* calling, accosting, address; a form of address; (gr.) the vocative case. **সম্বোধন করা** *v.* to accost, to address, to call. **~পদ** *n.* (gr.) a word in the vocative case. **সম্বোধিত** *a.* called; addressed.

সম্বোধা poet. form of **সম্বোধন করা।**

সম্বোধি *n.* perfect knowledge or consciousness (esp. of spiritual truths).

সম্বোধিত see **সম্বোধন।**

সম্ভব *n.* birth or origin (কুমারসম্ভব) ; (obs.) probability. □ *a.* born or originated (অযোনিসম্ভব) ; probable, likely (ঘটা সম্ভব) ; possible. **~ত** *adv.* probably, likely. **~পর** *a.* probable, likely; possible. **সম্ভবাতীত** *a.* beyond all probabilities; improbable, unlikely.

সম্ভাবনা *n.* probability, likelihood.

সম্ভাবনীয়, সম্ভাবিত, সম্ভাব্য *a.* probable, likely; contingent. **সম্ভাব্যতা** *n.* probability; likelihood.

সম্ভার *n.* a thing, an article; a load of things; a constituent material, an ingredient; a collection of things necessary to serve a particular purpose (পূজার সম্ভার) ; a collection, a heap (রত্নসম্ভার).

সম্ভাষণ, সম্ভাষ *n.* accosting, addressing; greeting, hail; conversation. **সম্ভাষণ করা,** (poet.) **সম্ভাষা** *v.* to accost, to address; to greet, to hail. **সম্ভাষিত** *a.* accosted, addressed; greeted, hailed.

সম্ভূত *a.* born; originated; produced; shot up, sprung; evolved; caused (অযত্নসম্ভূত). *fem.* **সম্ভূতা।**

সম্ভূয়সমুত্থান *n.* joint-stock business.

সম্ভোগ *n.* enjoyment; sexual intercourse. **সম্ভোগ করা** *v.* to enjoy; to have sexual intercourse with.

সম্ভ্রম *n.* honour, dignity, prestige; nobility; reverence mixed with awe and submission, deference; modesty. **সম্ভ্রম করা** *v.* to treat with reverence mixed with awe and submission, to treat deferentially. **~শালী** *a.* respectable, dignified; noble, *fem.* **~শালিনী।** **~হানি** *n.* dishonour; loss of prestige; indignity. **~হানি করা** *v.* to dishonour; to outrage the modesty of.

সম্ভ্রান্ত *a.* honoured; respectable; dignified; of noble birth, high-born, noble; aristocratic. **সম্ভ্রান্ত ব্যক্তি** an honoured or respectable or high-born person; an aristocrat. **~তন্ত্র** *n.* (pol.) government by aristocrats, aristocracy. **~বংশীয়** *a.* of a noble or aristocratic family; relating to the nobility; born in a noble family, high-born. *fem.* **~বংশীয়া।** **~সমাজ, ~সম্প্রদায়** *n.* the aristocracy, the nobility.

সম্মত *a.* consenting, agreeing, ready, willing, acquiescent; sanctioned or approved or permitted by conforming to (শাস্ত্রসম্মত) ; accepted, admitted, agreed upon (সর্ববাদীসম্মত). **সম্মত হওয়া** *v.* to agree, to consent, to give consent, to acquiesce. **সম্মতি** *n.* consent, assent, approval; acquiescence, willingness; sanction, approbation, permission; concurrence; conformation. **সম্মতি দেওয়া** *v.* to give consent; to permit. **সম্মতি পাওয়া** *v.* to get consent or permission (of).

সম্মান *n.* respectful and cordial reception; deferential treatment, deference; homage; reverence; honour, respect, dignity, prestige; credit. **সম্মান করা, সম্মান দেওয়া, সম্মান দেখানো** *v.* to receive cordially and with respect; to pay (one) deference or homage; to revere; to honour, to respect. **সম্মান নষ্ট করা** *v.* to dishonour, to disgrace; to discredit. **সম্মান পাওয়া** *v.* to be honoured. **সম্মান হারানো** *v.* to lose honour or credit or prestige. **~জনক** *a.* honourable; creditable. **~না** *n.* honouring; respectful felicitation. **~পূর্বক, ~পুরঃসর** *adv.* after showing respect, respectfully. **~ভাজন** same as **সম্মানার্হ**। **~লাভ** *n.* obtainment of honour or credit. **~হানি** *n.* loss of honour or credit or prestige, dishonour, discredit. **~হানি করা** *v.* to disparage, to lower (somebody) in the esteem of; to belittle; to dishonour. **সম্মানার্হ, সম্মানাস্পদ, সম্মানী** *a.* honourable; esteemable; respectable; venerable. **সম্মানিত** *a.* cordially or respectfully received; respectfully felicitated; honoured, respected; revered; honourable, respectable, venerable.

সম্মার্জন *n.* scouring or scrubbing; sweeping. **সম্মার্জনী** *n.* a scouring-brush, a scrubbing-brush; a broom, a besom; a mop, a swab.

সম্মিলন *n.* perfect union; amalgamation; junction; meeting; assemblage; a gathering esp. a social or cultural one; (pol.) a rally; (pol.—loos.) a conference. **সম্মিলনী** *n.* a society, an association; a club.

সম্মিলিত *a.* perfectly united; amalgamated; joined; meeting together; assembled; rallied. **~ভাবে** *adv.* unitedly; in a body.

সম্মুখ *n.* the forepart, the front. ☐ *a.* lying in the front; facing; anterior, frontal; facing one another. **~কোণ** *n.* (geom.) a subtended angle. **~গতি** *n.* the forward movement; progress; advance; progression. **~গামী** *a.* going forward; progressing, progressive. **~বর্তী** *a.* lying in front; facing; anterior; frontal; approaching. *fem.* **~বর্তিনী**। **~যুদ্ধ** *n.* a face-to-face fight; an open fight. **~সংগ্রাম** same as **~যুদ্ধ**। **~স্থ** same as **~বর্তী**। **সম্মুখীন হওয়া** *v.* to come face to face with; to confront; to approach; to encounter. **সম্মুখে** *adv.* in front of, before; in presence of.

সম্মেলক *a.* done or sung in chorus; sung in a group. ☐ *n.* a chorus. **~গান** *n.* a chorus, a song sung in chorus.

সম্মেলন *n.* a meeting; (loos.) a conference; assemblage, gathering; a gathering esp. a social or cultural one; (chiefly pol.) a rally.

সম্মোহ *n.* great or utter infatuation; hypnotization; hypnosis. **সম্মোহন** *n.* same as **সম্মোহ** ☐ *a.* infatuating; hypnotizing; hypnotic. *fem. a.* **সম্মোহিনী**। **সম্মোহিত** *a.* greatly or utterly infatuated; enchanted, charmed, hypnotized. **সম্মোহিত করা** *v.* to infatuate greatly or utterly; to hypnotize, to mesmerize.

সম্যক *adv.* in all respects; by all means; thoroughly; entirely, wholly; exhaustively; excellently; fitly. ☐ *a.* thorough, complete; entire, whole; exhaustive; excellent; fit; true.

সম্রাজ্ঞী *n. fem.* an express.

সম্রাট *n.* an emperor.

সয়তান, সয়তানি rej. spellings of **শয়তান** and **শয়তানি** respectively.

সযত্ন *a.* careful, meticulous; diligent; cordial (সযত্ন অভ্যর্থনা). **সযত্নে** *adv.* carefully, meticulously, with care; diligently; cordially.

সর *n.* a thin layer on milk or any other similar substance, film.

সরঃ *n.* a large pond; a lake.

সরকার *n.* a master; an owner; a ruler; the government; a collecting clerk; a purchasing clerk. **সরকারি** *a.* governmental;

public. □ *n.* office or post of a collecting or purchasing clerk. **সরকারি আদেশ** a government order. **সরকারি উকিল** a government pleader. **সরকারি চাকরি** government service. **সরকারি নিয়ন্ত্রণাধীন** under government control, government controlled. **সরকারি প্রতিবেদক** *n.* the public reporter. **সরকারি প্রতিবেদন** government report. **সরকারি বিদ্যালয়** a government school. **সরকারি ব্যবহারিক** a government counsel. **সরকারি রাস্তা** a highway, a public road.

সরগম *n.* the (Indian) musical octave.

সরগরম *a.* full of high spirits; full of enthusiasm and excitement; packed or crowded and noisy.

সরজমিন, সরেজমিন *n.* a scene of occurrence, the venue of an affair.

সরঞ্জাম *n.* things required for doing something; equipment; implements, appurtenances, accessories; paraphernalia.

সরট *n.* the chameleon.

সরণি, সরণী *n.* a road, a way, a path, a street; a route; an orbit (সূর্যসরণী) ; a method, a manner.

সরদার *n.* the chief man, a chief, a headman; a leader, a chieftain (*fem.* a chieftainess). *fem.* **সরদারনি। সরদার পড়ুয়া** *n.* a senior pupil assisting in school discipline and teaching, a monitor (*fem.* a monitress), a pupil-teacher. **সরদারি** *n.* chiefdom; leadership; chieftaincy. **সরদারি করা** *v.* to play the leader; (fig.) to behave in a masterful or overbearing manner.

সরপুরিয়া *n.* a kind of sweetmeat made of fried and stuffed nilk-film.

সরপোশ *n.* a small saucer for covering a tumbler, pitcher etc.

সরফরাজ *n.* a nawab of Bengal; (sarcas.) a very important man; a saucy fellow. **সরফরাজি** *n.* officiousness; untoward and intolerable bossing, overbearing manner; sauciness.

সরবত, সরবৎ rej. spellings of **শরবত।**

সরবরাহ *n.* supply; purveying; the amount supplied. **সরবরাহ করা** *v.* to supply; to purvey. **~কারী** *n.* a supplier; a purveyor.

সরভাজা *n.* a sweetmeat prepared by frying milk-film.

সরম rej. spell. of **শরম।**

সরল *a.* straight; candid, free from angularities, not crooked, guileless, naive; credulous; plain, unornate; free from complicacies, plain-sailing (সরল জীবন) ; honest, easy, simple (সরল প্রশ্ন). □ *n.* the sal tree; the deodar or any similar tree; (math.) simplification. **সরল করা** *v.* (esp. in math.) to simplify. **সরল অণুবীক্ষণ** (phys.) s simple microscope. **সরল দোলক** (phys.) a simple pendulum. **সরল দোলন** (phys.) simple harmonic motion. **~চিত্ত** *a.* simple-hearted. **~তা** *n.* candour, naivety, simplicity; plainness, unornateness, freedom from complicacies; honesty. **সরলতাপূর্ণ** *a.* candid, artless, naive, simple; plain, unornate; honest. **~প্রকৃতি** *a.* simple-natured, candid; not crooked; credulous. **~বর্গীয়** *a.* (bot.) coniferous. **~বিশ্বাসী** *a.* credulous **~মনা** *a.* same as **~চিত্ত। ~রেখা** *n.* a straight line. **~রৈখিক** *a.* formed of straight lines; rectilineal, rectilinear. **~রৈখিক ক্ষেত্র** *n.* (geom.) a rectilineal figure. **~স্বভাব** same as **~প্রকৃতি। হৃদয়, সরলান্তকরণ** *a.* simple-hearted. **সরলা** *a. fem.* of **সরল। সরলীকরণ** *n.* (chiefly in math.) simplification.

সরষে *n.* mustard seed. **সরষের ক্ষেত** mustard plot. **সরষের তেল** mustard oil. **ভিটেয় সরষে বোনা** (fig.) to ruin (someone) utterly by destroying one's homestead.

সরস *a.* same as **রসাল** (*a.*). *fem.* **সরসা।**

সরসিজ *n.* the water-lily, the lotus.

সরসী *n.* a large pond; a lake.

সরস্বতী *n.* the Hindu goddess of speech, learning, fine arts and wisdom (cp. Minerva); a title for proficiency in literature. **সরস্বতীর বরপুত্র** (lit.) a favoured son of Goddess Saraswati; (fig.) a man of great learning

সরহদ্দ *n.* perimeter, boundary, confines.

সরা১ alt. spell of **শরা।**

সরা২ *v.* to move, to stir; to move away, to withdraw; to move aside; to remove; to issue forth, to flow out, to come out (জল সরা, বাক্য সরা) ; to come in and go out, to pass (বাতাস সরা) ; (sl.) to die; to decamp, to slip away; to move facilely

(কলম সরা) ; to be willing or inclined (মন সরা) ; to be willing to work (হাত সরা).

সরাই *n.* an inn, a caravansarai. **~ওয়ালা** *n.* an innkeeper.

সরানো *v.* to take aside, to remove, to withdraw; to transfer; to recall or dismiss; to steal or defalcate. **সরিয়ে রাখা** *v.* to lay (something) aside, to keep for future use, to save.

সরাব rej. spell. of **শরাব** ।

সরাসরি *adv.* directly, straightway; straight ahead; in a cursory manner, summarily; outright. ☐ *a.* direct; straight; summary; outright. **সরাসরি বিচার** summary trial, summary justice.

সরিক, সরিকানা, সরিকানি alt. spellings of **শরিক, শরিকানা** and **শরিকানি** ।

সরিৎ *n.* a river, a stream.

সরিষা for. var. of **সরষে** ।

সরীসৃপ *n.* a reptile.

সরু *a.* of small girth or width, slender, delicate, thin; narrow; not coarse, fine; fine-spun; pointed (সরু ডগা) ; subtle, fine (সরু কাজ) ; treble, alto, tenor, soprano. **সরু গলা** a thin or longish neck; a treble voice, alto, tenor, soprano.

সরূপ *a.* similar in form or shape or appearance; resembling.

সরেজমিনে *adv.* right on the spot. **সরেজমিনে তদন্ত** investigation on the spot, local investigation.

সরেস *a.* best; excellent; superfine.

সরোজ *n.* the lotus; the lily. **সরোজিনী** *n.* a lotus clump; lotuses collectively; a pond full of lilies.

সরোদ *n.* sarod, a stringed musical instrument akin to the vina. **সরোদিয়া** *n.* one who plays on or is versed in playing on the aforesaid instrument.

সরোবর *n.* a large pond, a lake.

সরোরুহ *n.* lotus.

সরোষে *adv.* angrily, wrathfully.

সর্গ *n.* creation, origination; the physical nature, nature; (of a poetical work) a canto; any one of the three grand divisions of natural history (**প্রাণিসর্গ** = the animal kingdom).

সর্জ *n.* the sal tree.

সর্জন *n.* creation.

সর্জরস *n.* resin.

সর্জী, সর্জিকা *n.* fuller's earth.

সর্দার alt. spell. of **সরদার** ।

সর্দি *n.* catarrhal inflammation of the mucous membrane, nasal catarrh; cold. **সর্দি লাগা বা হওয়া** *v.* to catch cold. **~গরমি** *n.* sunstroke. **সর্দি ঝরছে** *v.* the nose runs.

সর্প *n.* the snake, the serpent. **সর্পে রজ্জুভ্রম** mistaking a rope for a snake; (fig.) glaring misconception or hallucination. **~দংশন** *n.* snakebite. **~দষ্ট** *a.* snakebit, bitten by a snake. **~ভুক** *a.* feeding on snakes (cp. serpentivorous).

সর্পাঘাত *n.* snakebite.

সর্পিণী *fem.* **সর্প** of and **সর্পী** (*a.*).

সর্পিল *a.* serpentine, winding, tortuous, zigzag, meandering (সর্পিল পথ, সর্পিল গতি) ; spiral (সর্পিল স্প্রিং).

সর্পী *a.* crawling, creeping, reptile, reptilian. ☐ *n. fem.* of **সর্প** ।

সর্ব *a.* all; whole, entire; complete, total, thorough; universal. ☐ *n.* Shiva (শিব). **সর্বংসহ** *a.* tolerating everything, allenduring, omnipotent. *fem.* **সর্বংসহা** । **~কালীন** *a.* of all times, all-time; working wholetime or covering whole time; wholetime. **~কালে** *adv.* in all times, ever. **~ক্ষণ** *n.* all time; the whole time, all the time. ☐ *adv.* every moment, always. **~গত** *a.* all-pervading; omnipresent. **~গুণাকর, ~গুণাধার** *n.* a container of all virtues or good qualities. ☐ *a.* (erron.) same as **~গুণান্বিত** । **~গুণান্বিত** *a.* endowed with all virtues or good qualities; all-good. **~গ্রাস** *n.* total eclipse; act of devouring or grabbing everything. **~গ্রাসী** *a.* all-devouring; all-grabbing. *fem.* **~গ্রাসিনী** । **~জনপ্রিয়** *a.* beloved of all, dear to all; universally popular. **~জনস্বীকৃত** *a.* universally or unanimously admitted or accepted. **~জনহিত** *n.* universal good, universal welfare; public good, public welfare. **~জনহিতকর** *a.* beneficial to all, good for all, universally good. **~জনীন** *a.* good for all, universally good; universal; public, common. **~জনীনতা** *n.* universality. **~জ্ঞ** *a.* all-knowing, omniscient.

সর্বজ্ঞতা *n.* omniscience. ~ত *adv.* in all respects; in everything; everywhere; in all ways; by all means; entirely, wholly; thoroughly. সর্বতোভাবে same as ~থা। ~ত্যাগী *a.* all-renouncing, all-sacrificing. *fem.* ~ত্যাগিনী। ~ত্র *adv.* everywhere; ever, in all times; in all directions; in all respects. ~গামী capable of or given to going or reaching everywhere. *fem.* সর্বত্রগামিনী। ~থা *adv.* in every way or manner, by all means; in all respects. ~দর্শী *a.* all-seeing. *fem.* ~দর্শিনী। ~দা *adv.* always, ever; in all times. ~দুঃখহর *a.* removing all sorrows or afflictions. *fem.* ~দুঃখহরা। ~দেশীয় *a.* pertaining to all countries, international, universal; country-wide. ~ধর্মসমন্বয় *n.* synthesis or harmonization of all religions. ~নাম *n.* (gr.) the pronoun. ~নাশ *n.* complete or total destruction; utter ruin; great harm; a great danger or calamity. সর্বনাশ করা *v.* to destroy completely or totally; to ruin utterly; to undo (a person); to cause a great harm or danger or calamity (to). সর্বনাশ হওয়া *v.* to be destroyed completely; to be ruined utterly; to be undone; to be harmed greatly; to be placed in a great danger or calamity. ~নাশা (loos.) *a.* same as ~নাশী (*a.*). □ *n.* (usu. in mild reproach) one who undoes a person by exposing him or her to shame; a shameless man. ~নাশী *a.* causing complete or total destruction; causing utter ruin; causing a great harm or danger or calamity to. □ *n.* *fem.* of ~নাশা। *fem a.* ~নাশিনী। ~নিয়ন্তা *n.* one who controls everything; the Supreme Ruler, God. *fem.* ~নিয়ন্ত্রী the controller of everything. ~নেশে coll. var. of ~নাশা। ~প্রকার *a.* of all kinds and varieties; omnigenous; all-round. ~প্রকারে *adv.* in every way; in all respects. ~প্রথম *a.* first, foremost. ~প্রধান *a.* chief of all, most distinguished; most important; pre-eminent; chief; sovereign, supreme. ~প্রিয় *a.* dear to everyone, beloved of all, popular with all, universally popular. ~বাদিসম্মত *a.* unanimously agreed or accepted, unanimous; universally agreed or accepted. ~বিধ same as ~প্রকার। ~বিষয়ে *adv.* in all matters; in everything; in all respects; in all subjects. ~বিষহর *a.* counteracting all poisons. ~বিষহর ওষুধ an antidote for all poisons, (cp.) the Venice treacle. ~ব্যাপী *a.* all-pervading; ubiquitous; ubiquitarian; omnipresent; (loos.) universal. *fem.* ~ব্যাপিনী। ~ব্যাপিতা *n.* the state of being all-pervading; ubiquity; omnipresence; (loos.) universality. ~ভুক *a.* omnivorous. ~ভূত *n.* all created beings. ~ভূতাত্মা *n.* the Soul that is present or inherent in all created beings. ~মঙ্গলা *n.* *fem.* one who is the cause or source of all good; Goddess Durga (দুর্গা). ~ময় *a.* all-pervading; ubiquitous; ubiquitarian; omnipresent; all in all (সর্বময় কর্তা) ; all-powerful, sovereign, supreme; omnipotent. *fem.* ~ময়ী। ~রোগহর *a.* counteracting or curing all diseases. ~রোগহর ওষুধ *n.* a cure-all, a panacea. ~লোক *n.* the whole universe; the whole world; all people of the world, everybody, all and sundry. ~শক্তি প্রয়োগ করা *v.* to apply total or utmost strength or power; to exert one's utmost; to apply all powers or forces. ~শক্তিমান *a.* all-powerful, almighty, omnipotent. ~শাস্ত্রজ্ঞ *a.* versed in all branches of learning or in all sciences or in all scriptures. ~শেষ *a.* last of all, ultimate. ~শেষে *adv.* last of all, at last. ~শ্রেষ্ঠ *a.* best of all; pre-eminent; highest; supreme. ~সমক্ষে *adv.* before everybody, in presence of all, in public, publicly, openly. ~সম *a.* equal in all respects, congruent. ~সময়, ~সময়ে *adv.* all times or hours; always, ever; every time. ~সম্মত *a.* unanimously approved or permitted or accepted or acknowledged. ~সম্মতিক্রমে *adv.* unanimously; with unanimous approval or support. ~সাকুল্যে *adv.* in all, in the aggregate, as a whole, collectively. ~সাধারণ *n.* the public, the people. ~সিদ্ধি *n.* attainment or realization of all desires or ends; complete success. ~স্ব *n.* whatever one possesses, one's total possessions, one's all. ~স্বহরণ *n.* robbing one of all one's belongings. ~স্বান্ত *a.* robbed of one's all belongings; utterly ruined. ~হিত same as ~জনহিত। সর্বাংশ *n.* all parts. সর্বাংশে *adv.* in every part; in all respects; completely, thoroughly; perfectly. সর্বাগ্র *a.* foremost; first; lying in the forefront. সর্বাগ্রে *adv.* in the foremost place; first of all, in the forefront. সর্বাঙ্গ *n.* the whole body; all limbs. সর্বাঙ্গসুন্দর *a.* beautiful in every limb; having a perfectly beautiful body; beautiful in all respects or in every part, perfectly beautiful. সর্বাঙ্গীণ *a.* covering the whole body, considering every limb; considering all aspects; thorough, comprehensive; total, complete. সর্বাঙ্গে *adv.* all over the body, all over; in every limb; in all parts; in all respects; thoroughly, completely, totally. সর্বাণী *n.* Goddess Durga the wife of Sarva (সর্ব). সর্বাত্মক *a.* all-pervading; comprehensive; total, complete; all out; supreme, sovereign. সর্বাদৃত *a.* well received by all, dear to all; universally popular. সর্বাধিক *a.* most of all, most, greatest, highest, largest; utmost. সর্বাধিনায়ক *n.* the supreme leader; the commander-in-chief. সর্বাধ্যক্ষ *n.* the director-general; (loos.) the managing director. সর্বান্তঃকরণে *adv.* whole-heartedly, with all one's heart, heart and soul, willingly and completely. সর্বাপেক্ষা *adv.* of all; beyond all; above all. সর্বাবয়ব same as সর্বাঙ্গ। সর্বাভরণ *n.* ornament for all the different limbs; all ornaments. সর্বার্থসাধক *a.* fulfilling all desires; realizing all ends; supplying all needs; (loos.) multipurpose (সর্বার্থসাধক সমবায় সমিতি বা বিদ্যালয়). *fem.* সর্বার্থসাধিকা। সর্বার্থসিদ্ধি *n.* same as সর্বসিদ্ধি। সর্বেশ্বর *n.* the lord or master of all; the supreme lord; God; Shiva (শিব). □ *a.* having sovereign authority over everybody; supreme; sovereign. সর্বেসর্বা *a.* all in all; invested with absolute authority; all-ruling; predominant. সর্বোচ্চ *a.* highest of all; most high, highest. সর্বোত্তম *a.* best, choicest, most excellent. সর্বোপরি *adv.* on the topmost place; uppermost; above all.

সর্ষপ *n.* mustard seed, rape-seed. সর্ষপ তৈল *n.* mustard-oil.

সলজ্জ *a.* abashed, ashamed; bashful, shy, modest, coy.

সলতে coll. var. of সলিতা।

সলমা *n.* diapers done with gold or silver thread.

সলা *n.* (dero. & usu. secret) conference, consultation, counsel (also সলা-পরামর্শ).

সলাজ corrup. of সলজ্জ।

সলি alt. spell. of শলি।

সলিতা *n.* a slender wick.

সলিল *n.* water. ~সমাধি *n.* a watery grave; drowning; loss or destruction by sinking; (fig.) utter loss, irrevocable loss.

সল্লকী *n.* the porcupine, the hedgehog.

সশঙ্ক, (pop.) **সশঙ্কিত** *a.* fearful, timorous; frightened, afraid; seized with a misgiving; timid. সশঙ্কে *adv.* fearfully, timorously; with a misgiving; timidly.

সশব্দ *a.* attended with a noise, sounding; attended with a loud noise; noisy; clamorous. সশব্দে *adv.* with a noise or sound; with a loud noise; noisily; clamorously.

সশরীরে *adv.* in the mortal body, alive (সশরীরে স্বর্গলাভ) ; in person, bodily (সশরীরে আগমন).

সশস্ত্র *a.* armed; in arms.

সশ্রদ্ধ *a.* respectful, deferential.

সশ্রম *a.* rigorous (সশ্রম কারাদণ্ড).

সসত্ত্বা *a. fem.* with child or young, pregnant. ~বস্থা *n.* pregnancy.

সসম্ভ্রম *a.* full of reverence mixed with awe and submission, deferential. সসম্ভ্রমে *adv.* with deference.

সসম্মান *a.* respectful; honourable. সসম্মানে *adv.* with respect; with honour, honourably; (academic) with honours (সসম্মানে বি.এ. পাস করা).

সসাগরা *a. fem.* consisting of or comprising oceans and seas (in addition to land), inclusive of oceans and seas. সসাগরা ধরণী the earth (or the landed portion of the earth) with all oceans and seas, the whole earth.

সসীম *a.* finite.

সসেমিরা *n.* stupefaction, bewilderment, nonplus, daze.

সসৈন্য *a.* attended with armed forces. **সসৈন্যে** *adv.* with armed forces.

সস্তা *a.* cheap. **সস্তার তিন অবস্থা** (fig.) cheap and nasty, a charger bought cheap turns a sorry nag.

সস্ত্রীক *a.* accompanied by one's wife, with wife.

সস্নেহ *a.* affectionate; loving. **সস্নেহে** *adv.* affectionately; lovingly, tenderly.

সস্মিত *a.* smiling. **~বদন** *n.* a smiling face. ☐ *a.* having a smiling face. *fem. a.* **~বদনা** । **~বদনে** *adv.* with a smiling face.

-সহ[১] *sfx.* expressing: capable of enduring, enduring; tolerable.

সহ[২] *prep.* together with, with. ☐ *a.* (used as a *pfx.*) acting together, co-; accompanying; having common interests, occupations, faiths etc.; associating; inherent; assisting, assistant, deputy, subjoint. **~অধিকর্তা** *n.* an assistant director. **~কর্মী** *n.* a co-worker, a colleague; an associate. **~কারী** *n.* a co-worker; an assistant. **~গ** *n.* (alg.) a co-efficient. **~গমন** *n.* act of going together; accompanying; act of dying together; act of burning oneself to death on one's husband's funeral pyre. **সহগমন করা** *v.* to go together; to accompany; to die together; to burn oneself to death on one's husband's funeral pyre. **~গামী** *a.* going together; accompanying; (rare) dying together or burning oneself to death on another's funeral pyre. *fem.* **~গামিনী** । **~গামী হওয়া** same as **সহগমন করা** । **~ঘটন** *n.* concurrence. **~ঘটমান** *a.* concurrent. **~চর, ~চারী** *a.* going together; accompanying; keeping company with; (gr.—of words) correlative. ☐ *n.* a companion; an associate; a friend; a confidant (*fem.* a confidante); an attendant, a follower. *fem.* **~চরী, ~চারিণী** । **~জাত** *a.* born at the same time; born of the same womb and (usu.) at the same time; twin; inborn; inherent, innate. **সহজাত অধিকার** birthright. **সহজাত সংস্কার** an instinct. **~দূত** *n.* an attache. **~ধর্মিণী** *n.. fem.* a wife associating with her husband in practice of virtues; (pop.) a wife. **~ধর্মী** *a.* following the same faith or religion; having common propensities or virtues or properties or functions. ☐ *n.* a co-religionist. **~পাঠী** *n.* a fellow-student, a class-fellow, a class-mate, *fem.* **~পাঠিনী** । **সহ-প্রধানশিক্ষক** *n.* an assistant headmaster. **সহ-প্রধানশিক্ষিকা** *fem.* an assistant headmistress, **~বাস** *n.* living or dwelling together; cohabitation. **সহবাস করা** *v.* to live or dwell together; to cohabit. **~ভাব** *n.* co-existence, concomitance. **~মরণ** *n.* dying together; burning oneself to death on one's husband's funeral pyre. **সহমরণে যাওয়া** *v.* to die together; to burn oneself to death on one's husband's funeral pyre. **~মর্মিতা** *n.* sympathy; empathy; compassion. **~মর্মী** *a.* sympathetic, compassionate. **~মৃতা** *a. fem.* one who has died with one's husband; one who has courted death by burning oneself on one's husband's funeral pyre. **~যাত্রী** *a.* going or travelling together; accompanying. ☐ *n.* a companion; a fellow-traveller. *fem.* **~যাত্রিণী** । **সহযাত্রী হওয়া** *v.* to go or travel or journey together; to accompany. **~যোগ, ~যোগিতা** *n.* act of associating; co-operation. **সহযোগিতা করা** *v.* to associate (with); to co-operate (with). **~যোগী** *a.* associating; co-operating. ☐ *n.* an associate; a co-worker, a colleague, a comrade; a co-operator. *fem.* **সহযোগী সম্পাদক** an associate editor. **~যোগে** *adv.* (used as prep.) together with; mixed with; with. **~যোজন** *n.* co-ordination. **~যোজিত** *a.* co-ordinated. **~যোদ্ধা** *n.* a fellow-soldier, a brother-at-arms. **~শিক্ষক** *n.* an assistant master (*fem.* an assistant mistress), an assistant teacher. *fem.* **~শিক্ষিকা** । **~সচিব** *n.* an assistant secretary. **~সমীকরণ** *n.* (alg.) simultaneous equation.

সহকার *n.* the mango tree; a mango twig **সহকার-শাখা** *n.* a mango twig; a bough of mango tree.

সহকারে *adv.* (used as a *prep.*) with (যত্নসহকারে = with care).

সহকারী *a.* assisting, assistant, sub-. □ *n.* an assistant. *fem.* **সহকারিণী**। **সহকারী প্রধানশিক্ষক** an assistant headmaster. **সহকারী সম্পাদক** an assistant editor; an assistant secretary.

সহজ *a.* inborn, innate, instinctive; natural, inherent; easy, not difficult or strenuous, simple; easily understood, plain; not crooked or tough, simple, plain (সহজ লোক). **~গম্য** *a.* easily accessible; (fig.) easy to understand. **~পাচ্য** *a.* easily digestible; easy to digest. **~প্রবৃত্তি** *n.* an instinct. **~বুদ্ধি** *n.* common sense; mother wit; (erron.) an instinct. **~বোধ্য** *a.* easily understood or comprehensible or intelligible. **~লভ্য** *a.* easily available or obtainable. **~সাধন** *n.* a form of worship in which a devotee acts according to the dictates of his or her instincts. **সহজিয়া** *n.* same as **~সাধন,** and—a Vaishnava or Buddhist community practising **~সাধন**। **সহজে** *a.* without difficulty, easily.

সহন *n.* enduring or suffering; toleration; patience. **~শীল** *a.* enduring; tolerant; patient. *fem.* **~শীলা**। **~শীলতা** *n.* endurance; tolerance; patience. **সহনীয়** *a.* bearable, endurable, sufferable; tolerable.

সহবত *n.* manners learnt in society; company, association, society; manners, good manners, courtesy.

সহর্ষ *a.* joyful; gleeful. **সহর্ষে** *adv.* joyfully; gleefully.

সহসা *adv.* suddenly; unexpectedly, all at once, all on a sudden, all of a sudden.

সহস্র *n* & *a.* thousand. □ *a.* innumerable, countless; many and diverse. **সহস্র সহস্র** thousands and thousands of, thousands of, many thousands, innumerable, countless. **~ক** *n.* a millennium. **~কর, ~কিরণ** *n.* one emitting countless rays; the sun. **~তম** *a.* thousandth. **~দল** *a.* thousand-petalled; having innumerable petals. **~ধা** *adv.* in a thousand ways; in countless ways; in manifold ways. **~ধারা** *n.* a cascade falling in innumerable streams; a fountain spouting in countless streams; a river flowing in a great many streams. **~পদ** *n.* the centipede, a myriapod. **~প্রকরণ** *a.* innumerable kinds of, many and diverse, manifold. **~বার** *adv.* countless times, many times, thousand times. **~লোচন** *a.* thousand-eyed, (cp.) Argus-eyed. □ *n.* Indra (ইন্দ্র), the king of gods. **~শীর্ষ** *a.* hydraheaded. **সহস্রার** *n.* lotus-shaped substance within the cranium.

সহা *v.* to bear; to suffer; to endure; to sustain; to be inured (to) (শীতগ্রীষ্ম সহা) ; to be acclimatized (আবহাওয়া সহা) ; to tolerate, to stand (অন্যায় সহা) ; to brook (অপমান সহা).

সহাধিকার ক্ষেত্র *n.* concurrent jurisdiction.

সহাধীক্ষক, সহাধ্যক্ষ *n.* an assistant superintendent.

সহাধ্যায়ী same as **সহপাঠী** (see **সহ**[২]).

সহানুভূতি *n.* sympathy; compassion; fellow-feeling. **~শীল** *a.* sympathetic or compassionate. **~সম্পন্ন** *a.* sympathetic; compassionate.

সহানো *v.* to cause to bear or suffer or endure or sustain; to inure; to acclimatize.

সহায় *n.* an aider; a helper; a patron; an assistant; a supporter; an ally; aid; help; patronization; assistant; support; a prop; a resource. **~ক** *a.* aiding; helping; patronizing; assisting; supporting; accessory; abetting; (gr.) auxiliary. **সহায়ক ক্রিয়া** (gr.) an auxiliary verb. **~তা** *n.* aid; help; patronization; assistance; support; abetment. **সহায়তা করা** *v.* to aid; to help; to patronize; to assist; to support; to abet. **সহায়তাকারী** same as **সহায়ক**। **~সম্বল** *n.* friends to turn to and resources to fall back on. **~সম্বলহীন** *a.* one without any resource or support; utterly helpless.

সহার্থ, সহার্থক same as **সমার্থ**।

সহাস্য *a.* smiling; laughing. **~বদনে, ~মুখে** *adv.* with a smiling face.

-সহি var. of **-সই**[২], **-সই**[৩], **-সই**[৪]।

সহিত (for. & high) *a.* & *prep.* accompanying, containing; with, together with, along with; accompanied by.

সহিষ্ণু *a.* having fortitude; stoical; patient,

enduring; tolerant. ~তা *n.* fortitude; patience, endurance; toleration, tolerance.

সহিস *n.* a syce, a groom.

সহৃদয় *a.* large-hearted, magnanimous; cordial (সহৃদয় অভ্যর্থনা); sincere and amiable (সহৃদয় কথাবার্তা) ; appreciative, appreciatory, sympathetic, considerate (সহৃদয় বিচার). *fem.* **সহৃদয়া** । ~তা *n.* large-heartedness, magnanimity; sympathy, compassion, kind-heartedness, amiability.

সহোদর *a.* born of the same mother. □ *n.* a brother born of the same mother, a brother. **সহোদরা** *a. fem.* of **সহোদর** (*a.*). □ *n.* a sister born of the same mother, a sister.

সহ্য *a.* endurable, bearable; tolerable; endured, suffered, tolerated (সহ্য হওয়া) ; acclimatized (আবহাওয়া সহ্য হওয়া). □ *n.* endurance, fortitude, tolerance (সহ্যের সীমা = the limit of one's patience, a limit to one's patience); the northern portion of the Western Ghat mountain range (usu. **সহ্যাদ্রি**). **সহ্য করা** *v.* to endure, to suffer, to bear; to tolerate, to brook, to put up with. ~**গুণ** *n.* the quality of bearing patiently, forbearance. **সহ্যাতীত** same as **অসহ্য** ।

সা *n.* (mus.) the first note of the gamut, C-major.

সাইকেল pop. var. of **বাইসিকল** ।

সাইজ *n.* size.

সাইনবোর্ড *n.* a sighboard.

সাইরেন *n.* a siren.

সাউ *n.* a merchant (by caste or profession); a moneylender.

সাউকারি *n.* pretence of honesty or innocence; assumed self-importance or pompousness.

সাং abbr. of **সাকিন** ।

সাংকেতিক *a.* symbolic, symbolical. □ *n.* (arith.) practice.

সাংখ্য *n.* a philosophical treatise written by Kapil; the Sankhya system of philosophy.

সাংখ্যিক *a.* numeral, figural.

সাংঘাতিক *a.* fatal; mortal; terrible; tremendous.

সাংবৎসর, সাংবৎসরিক *a.* continuing for a year; occurring every year; yearly, annual.

সাংবাদিক *a.* pertaining to news; journalistic. □ *n.* a journalist. **সাংবাদিকতা** *n.* journalism. **সাংবাদিকতা করা** *v.* to work as a journalist.

সাংসারিক *a.* domestic, familial; earthly, mundane, secular. **সাংসারিক জ্ঞান** worldly wisdom.

সাংস্কৃতিক *a.* cultural.

সাঁ, সাঁই[১] variants of **শাঁ** ।

সাঁই[২] *n.* a religious instructor or associate or preceptor; God.

সাঁইত্রিশ *n* & *a.* thirty-seven.

সাঁইসাঁই var. of **শাঁ-শাঁ** ।

সাঁওতাল *n.* an aboriginal tribe of India, Santals; a Santal.

সাঁকো *n.* a bridge; a culvert.

সাঁচা, সাঁচি, সাঁচ্চা variants of **সাচ্চা** ।

সাঁজ var. of **সাঁঝ** ।

সাঁজা *n.* rennet.

সাঁজাল *n.* fumigation by burning hay etc. in order to expel or repel mosquitoes.

সাঁজোয়া *n.* armour, a coat of mail. **সাঁজোয়া গাড়ি** *n.* an armoured car.

সাঁঝ coll. var. of **সন্ধ্যা** ।

সাঁঝাল alt. spell. of **সাঁজাল** ।

সাঁট *n.* brevity (সাঁটে সারা) ; a hint, a gesture (সাঁট বোঝা). **সাঁটে** *adv.* by hint, by a subtle insinuation; in short, in brief, briefly.

সাঁটা *v.* to fix or attach esp. tightly; to hold firmly, to grip (সেঁটে ধরা) ; (facet.) to gormandize, to gorge oneself with. ~**নো** *v.* to eat voraciously, to gorge oneself with, to eat greedily.

সাঁড়াশি *n.* tongs; forceps; pincers. **সাঁড়াশি-অভিযান** *n.* (mil.) a pincer-movement.

সাঁতরানো *v.* to swim.

সাঁতলানো *v.* to singe lightly with spices in oil, clarified butter or fat. □ *a.* singed.

সাঁতার *n.* swimming; natation. **সাঁতার কাটা, সাঁতার দেওয়া** *v.* to swim. **সাঁতার কাটার পুকুর** a swimming pool; (U. S.) a natatorium. **সাঁতার-জল** *n.* a mass of water so deep that one has to swim to keep oneself afloat. **সাঁতারু** *n.* a swimmer; an expert swimmer.

সাঁপি *n.* the roundish part at the front of the stocks into which the neck of a beast is put for immolation; a ferrule.

সাকরেদ alt. spell. of **শাগরেদ**।

সাকল্য *n.* entirety; totality; the total amount or number. **সাকল্যে** *adv.* in all.

সাকার *a.* having a form or body, bodied, corporeal. **সাকার-উপাসনা, সাকারোপাসনা** *n.* a form of worship in which deities are conceived as having forms; idolatry. **~বাদ** *n.* the doctrine that upholds **সাকারোপাসনা**। **সাকারোপাসক** *n.* an idolator. ☐ *a.* idolatrous.

সাকি *n.* a young lad or girl serving wine, a young tapster.

সাকিন *n.* a place of one's residence, address.

সাক্ষর *a.* literate. **সাক্ষরতা** *n.* literacy.

সাক্ষাৎ *a.* visible, bodied or incarnate (সাক্ষাৎ মৃত্যু) ; appearing in person (সাক্ষাৎ যম) ; resembling, equal to (মাতাপিতা সাক্ষাৎ দেবতা) ; direct. ☐ *n.* visibility in body, visible or perceptible presence (ঈশ্বরের সাক্ষাৎলাভ) ; a meeting, an interview (বন্ধুর সাক্ষাৎলাভ) ; presence (সাক্ষাতে বলা). **সাক্ষাৎ করা** *v.* to pay a visit to, to visit, to call on; to interview. **সাক্ষাৎ পাওয়া** *v.* to be able to meet (with); to have a meeting with; to happen to meet (with); to have an interview (with); (theol.) to be in communion (with). **~কার** *n.* meeting; interview. **~কারী** *n.* a visitor; an interviewee. *fem.* **~কারিণী**। **~প্রার্থী** *a* & *n.* one who asks for or seeks an interview (with). *fem.* **~প্রার্থিনী**। **~সম্বন্ধ** *n.* direct relation; outward or formal relation. **সাক্ষাতে** *adv.* in one's presence; face to face.

সাক্ষি pop. corrup. of **সাক্ষ্য**।

সাক্ষিগোপাল *n.* a holy place near Puri which Krishna (কৃষ্ণ) visited; (fig.) one rendered powerless and capable only of witnessing (other's misdeeds), a puppet.

সাক্ষী *n.* a witness; an eye-witness. **সাক্ষী পড়ানো** *v.* to prime or tutor a witness. **সাক্ষী মানা** *v.* to cite one as a witness; to call upon one as a witness. **সাক্ষীর কাঠগড়া** the witness-box. **সাক্ষীর জবানবন্দি** deposition of a witness or his examination in chief. **সাক্ষীর জেরা** cross-examination of a witness. **~সাবুদ** *n.* witness and evidence.

সাক্ষ্য *n.* witness, testimony, evidence; deposition. **সাক্ষ্য দেওয়া** *v.* to give evidence, to bear witness, to depose.

সাগর *n.* a sea; an ocean; a bay (বঙ্গোপসাগর). **~পার** *n.* seashore; the other shore or side of a sea. **~পারে** *adv.* on the seashore; beyond seas, abroad. **~মেখলা** a sea-girt. **~সংগম** *n.* the place where a river (esp. the Ganges) falls into a sea.

সাগু *n.* sago. **দুধসাগু** *n.* milk mixed with boiled sago. **~দানা** *n.* a grain of sago; sago.

সাগ্নিক same as **অগ্নিহোত্রী** (see **অগ্নি**).

সাগ্রহ *a.* eager, earnest; intent; wistful. **সাগ্রহে** *adv.* eagerly, earnestly, intently.

সাঙা *n.* a form of Hindu widow marriage where religious solemnities are more or less ignored.

সাঙাত *n.* (use. dero.) a friend, a companion; an accomplice.

সাঙ্কেতিক alt. spell. of **সাংকেতিক**।

সাঙ্খ্য alt. spell. of **সাংখ্য**।

সাঙ্গ *a.* bodied, corporeal; having all the limbs; complete in all part; completed, finished; ended. **সাঙ্গ করা** *v.* to complete, to finish; to end.

সাঙ্গপাঙ্গ erron. spell. of **সাঙ্গোপাঙ্গো**।

সাঙ্গরূপক *n.* (rhet.) prolonged or continued metaphor.

সাঙ্গোপাঙ্গ *a.* inclusive of all parts; attended by all friends and followers; attended by the whole retinue, in train. ☐ *n. pl.* friends and followers collectively; retinue, train.

সাঙ্ঘাতিক alt. spell. of **সাংঘাতিক**।

সাচ্চা *a.* true; genuine, real, pure; upright or righteous.

সাজ *n.* dress, raiment, garb; an ornament, a decorative article to be put on; equipment, outfit; make up; equipage; appurtenance; (dial.) rennet. **~গোজ** *n.* dressing; meticulous dressing. **~ঘর** *n.* a greenroom. **~ন্ত** *a.* embellishing, beautifying, decorative. **~শ** *n.* collusion (যোগসাজশে). ☐ *a.* (loos.) got-up

(সাজশ মামলা = a got-up case.) ~**সজ্জা** *n.* full dress; equipment, outfit; euipage; dressing; make-up; decoration; furniture and fittings. ~**সরঞ্জাম** *n.* equipment, outfit; equipage; appurtenance; furniture and fittings.

সাজা[1] *n.* punishment. **সাজা দেওয়া** *v.* to punish; to award a punishment. **সাজা পাওয়া** *v.* to be punished.

সাজা[2] *v.* to dress and embellish oneself; to be decorated; to assume a false dress or appearance, to disguise oneself, to pretend to be (সাধু সাজা) ; (of an actor or actress) to make up; to take up the role of (যাত্রায় কৃষ্ণ সাজা) ; to equip oneself (যুদ্ধের জন্য সাজা) ; to process (an intoxicant etc.) for inhaling or chewing (তামাক সাজা, পান সাজা) ; to behave, to become (তোমাকে সাজে না). ☐ *a.* appearing as, disguised, pretending; (of an intoxicant etc.) processed for inhaling or chewing.

সাজাত্য *n.* the state of being of the same nation or tribe or class; cognateness, kindredness; homogeneity.

সাজানো *v.* to dress and embellish; to decorate; to dress and lay artistically (বাগান সাজানো) ; to dress (another) so as to give a false appearance, to disguise, to cause to pretend to be; to dress (an actor or actress); to cause to take up the role of; to equip; (of a ship etc.) to fit out; to cause to process (an intoxicant etc.) for inhaling or chewing or smoking (কলকে সাজানো) ; to place in order (মালপত্র সাজানো) ; (of an army etc.) to array; to fabricate, to concoct, to cook, to get up (মামলা সাজানো). ☐ *a.* dressed and embellished; decorated, disguised; artistically laid and dressed; fabricated, got-up; concocted.

সাজি[1] *n.* a small high-rimmed and usually round wicker-tray.

সাজি[2], **সাজিমাটি** *n.* fuller's earth.

সাজো *a.* today's; fresh, recent; washed with fuller's earth within a few hours. (সাজো কাপড়). ☐ *adv.* recently, afresh (সাজো ভানা). ☐ *n.* same as ~**বাসি** । ~**বাসি** *n.* the system of washing clothes etc. with fuller's earth within a few hours; a washerman who washes clothes in the aforesaid system.

সাট[1] var. of **সাঁট** ।

সাট[2] *n.* (dero.) mutual understanding; collusion; a conspiracy.

সাটিন *n.* satin.

সাড় *n.* sensibility; sensitivity, sensation; feeling; perception; consciousness.

সাড়ম্বর *a.* pompous; ostentatious; showy. **সাড়ম্বরে** *adv.* pompously; ostentatiously.

সাড়া *n.* sound, noise; response, answer; reaction, response (উদ্ভিদের সাড়া) ; great animation or hubbub or noise, excitement (সাড়া পড়েছে) ; voice, speech or word (মুখে সাড়া নেই) ; sign of existence, throbbing (প্রাণের সাড়া). **সাড়া দেওয়া** *v.* to respond, to answer; to react or respond. ~**শব্দ** almost same as **সাড়া** ।

সাড়ি rej. spell. of **শাড়ি** ।

সাড়ে *a.* including also a half. **সাড়ে দশ** ten and a half. **সাড়ে দশটা** half past ten. **সাড়ে দশ টাকা** ten and a half rupees. **সাড়ে দশ মাইল** ten and a half miles, ten miles and a half. **সাড়ে বত্রিশ ভাজা** (fig.) a promiscuous mixture of different things; a medley; an assortment of different things.

সাত *n.* & *a.* seven. **সাত খুন মাফ** (fig.) condonation of every failing or offence, act of keeping one's eyes closed to all failings or offences of a particular person. esp. a favourite. **সাত চড়ে রা না বেরোনো** (fig.) the practice of taking every insult or oppression lying down, extreme meekness or inertia. **সাত নকলে আসল খাস্তা** (fig.) repeated imitation makes the original lose its identity. **সাত সমুদ্র তেরো নদীর পার** (in folk tales) a place where a human being can hardly go, (cp.) a place at the end of the world or beyond the corners of the world. **সাতেও নেই পাঁচেও নেই** (fig.) having no concern with, perfectly disinterested or aloof. **সাতই** *n.* the seventh day of a month, the seventh. ☐ *a.* (of the days of a month) seventh. ~**কাণ্ড** *a.* consisting of or divided into seven cantos; lengthy. ☐ *adv.* in detail, at great length

(সাতকাণ্ড বলা বা শোনা). **সাতকাণ্ড রামায়ণ** (fig.) a lengthy or detailed narrative or account. **~চল্লিশ** *n.* & *a.* forty-seven. **~জন্মে** *adv.* (ever) in the long past or future. **~তাড়াতাড়ি** *adv.* with an excessive haste, much too hastily. **~নরি** *a.* having seven tiers or strings (সাতনরি হার). **~নলা** *a.* seven-barrelled (সাতনলা বন্দুক). **~-পাঁচ** *a.* many and diverse. ☐ *adv.* about this and that. (সাত-পাঁচ ভাবা). **~পুরুষ** *n.* seven generations upwards or downwards; the long past or future. **~ষট্টি** *n* & *a.* sixty-seven. **~সকাল** *n.* very early morning. **~সতেরো** *n.* miscellany; a variety.

সাতা *n.* the seven of playing-cards.

সাতাত্তর *n.* & *a.* seventy-seven.

সাতানব্বই, (coll.) **সাতানব্বুই** *n.* & *a.* ninety-seven.

সাতান্ন *n.* & *a.* fifty-seven.

সাতাশ *n.* & *a.* twenty-seven.

সাতাশি *n.* & *a.* eighty-seven.

সাতাশে *n.* the twenty-seventh day of a month, the twenty-seventh. ☐ *a.* (of the days of a month) twenty-seventh.

সাতিশয় *a.* overmuch, excessive, exceeding; extreme. ☐ *adv.* overmuch, excessively, exceedingly; extremely.

সাতুই corrup. of **সাতই** (see **সাত**).

সাত্তা pop. var. of **সাতা**।

সাত্ত্বিক *a.* of or proceeding from or having **সত্ত্বগুণ** that is, goodness and purity (সাত্ত্বিক আচরণ, সাত্ত্বিক লোক) ; unconcerned about the consequence, dispassionate; pure; not actuated by any desire and unostentatious (সাত্ত্বিক পূজা বা দান). **সাত্ত্বিক আহার** plain and simple food; a simple fare. **~তা** *n.* purity in living, dispassionateness or unostentatiousness.

সাথ *n.* (dial.) company (সাথের লোক). ☐ *prep.* same as **সাথে**।

সাথি *n.* a companion; an associate.

সাথে *prep.* with, in company of.

সাদর *a.* cordial (সাদর অভ্যর্থনা). **সাদরে** *adv.* cordially, **~সম্ভাষণ** *n.* cordial address or reception.

সাদা *a.* white; grey; white-skinned (সাদা আদমি) ; free from angularities, candid, simple (সাদা মন) ; categorical, plain, unequivocal, downright (সাদা কথা) ; innocent (সাদা কাজ) ; having no coloured border or furbelow or flounce (সাদা ধুতি) ; unwritten, blank (সাদা কাগজ) ; unblurred; unintoxicated (সাদা চোখ). ☐ *n.* the white colour; the white-skinned people, the white race. **সই করা সাদা কাগজ** carte blanche. **সাদাকে কালো এবং কালোকে সাদা করা** (fig.) to misrepresent things or tell lies obviously and shamelessly, to lie in one's throat. **~চামড়া** *n.* white skin; the white-skinned people. **~টে** *a.* whitish. **সাদামাঠা, সাদামাটা, সাদাসিধা,** (coll.) **সাদাসিধে** *a.* free from angularities, candid, simple; simple-hearted, plain-living, ordinary; unostentatious, plain; categorical, unequivocal, downright, straight-cut; not crooked, honest; frank; straight; unornamented; bald, having no vicissitude, uninteresting; dull, drab. **~সাপটা** *a.* simple, plain; unostentatious.

সাদি[1] alt. spell. of **শাদি**।

সাদি[2] *n.* a horseman or horse-soldier; an elephant-rider or elephant-soldier.

সাদৃশ্য *n.* likeness; resemblance; similarity; affinity; equality; an image, a portrait.

সাধ *n.* desire; longing; fancy or choice (সাধের বস্তু) ; voluntary will, volition, pleasure, one's own accord (সাধ করে মৃত্যুবরণ) ; option; a ceremony for giving desired articles of food to a pregnant woman (সাধ দেওয়া বা সাধ খাওয়া). **সাধ করা** *v.* to desire; to long (for); to choose; to volunteer (for); to opt (for). **সাধ করে** *adv.* voluntarily; wilfully; willingly. **সাধ মিটিয়ে** *adv.* satisfying one's desire; to one's satisfaction.

সাধক *a.* austerely endeavouring to achieve an end; practising ascetic austerities; engaged in austere worship of God; performing or realizing; helping to perform or realize. ☐ *n.* an austere endeavourer; one who practises ascetic austerities; a worshipper of god; a worshipper, votary, a devotee.

সাধন *n.* austere endeavour; austere ascetic practice; worship of God; worship; performance, accomplishment; realization or attainment; a means, an instrument, a tool. **সাধন করা** *v.* to perform or accomplish or realize or attain esp. by dint of austere or arduous endeavour. **~পত্র** *n.* an instrument. **~প্রক্রিয়া** *n.* the mode of worship of God; the mode of accomplishment. **~ভজন** *n.* religious prayer or meditation and worship.

সাধনা *n.* same as **সাধন,** and—austere or arduous practice (সংগীত সাধনা) ; austerities; an object to attain for which an arduous endeavour is being made (আমাদের সাধের সাধনা) ; an austere vow or difficult goal (ভারতের সাধনা) ; importunity (সাধ্যসাধনা). **সাধন করা** *v.* to endeavour austerely or arduously; to be engaged in austere ascetic practice; to worship God; to practice austerely or arduously; (rare) to importunate.

সাধনী same as **সাধিত্র** ৷

সাধনীয় *a.* that for the accomplishment or attainment of which arduous endeavour should be made; to be performed or attained; worshipful, adorable.

সাধর্ম্য *n.* likeness, similarity, resemblance, mark or quality exactly alike.

সাধা *v.* to endeavour or practise austerely or arduously (মন্ত্র সাধা) ; to try to improve by practice (গলা সাধা) ; to accomplish (কাজ সাধা) ; to attain or realize ('সাধিতে মনের সাধ') ; to offer (ঘুস সাধা) ; to volunteer (সেধে বিপদে পড়া) ; to bring about, to put forward; to offer (বাদ সাধা) ; to try to pacify or appease (পায়ে ধরে সাধা) ; to importunate (না সাধলে সে আসবে না) ; (gr.) to derive (as a word). ☐ *a.* improved or chastened or prepared by practice (সাধা গলা) ; held out for acceptance, offered (সাধা ভাত).

সাধানো *v.* to cause to endeavour or practise austerely or arduously; to make one try to improve by practice; to cause to importunate.

সাধারণ *a.* ordinary, common, usual; banal, trite (সাধারণ লেখা) ; trifling, venial (সাধারণ অপরাধ) ; public (সাধারণ পাঠাগার) ; general (সাধারণ সভা) ; universal (সাধারণ মত) ; generic (বর্গের সাধারণ নাম) ; including all, at large (জনসাধারণ). ☐ *n.* the public, the people, the commonalty. *fem.* **সাধারণী** ৷ **সাধারণ কৃত্যক** *a.* general service. **সাধারণ ধর্ম** a general property or characteristic. **সাধারণ ভবিষ্যনিধি** the general provident fund. **সাধারণত** *adv.* ordinarily, usually, commonly; generally. **~তন্ত্র** *n.* a republic. **সাধারণতন্ত্র দিবস** *n.* the Republic Day. **~তন্ত্রবাদী, ~তন্ত্রী** *a.* republican. ☐ *n.* a republican. **~ভাবে** *adv.* generally, in general terms. **সাধারণ শিক্ষা** *n.* general education. **সাধারণ্য** *n.* general properties or characteristics; the public; the people, the commonality.

সাধাসাধি *n.* importunity. **সাধাসাধি করা** *v.* to importunate, to make repeated requests, to entreat.

সাধিকা *fem.* of **সাধক** ৷

সাধিত *a.* austerely or arduously endeavoured or practised; performed or accomplished; attained; proved; (gr.) derived. **সাধিত ধাতু** (gr.) a derivative verb, a derivative; (gr.) a derivative verb, a derivative. **সাধিত শব্দ** (gr.) a derivative.

সাধিত্র *n.* an instrument, a tool, an appliance.

সাধু *a.* pious, saintly, virtuous, righteous, honest; good, noble; elegant, chaste, polite, refined (সাধু ভাষা) ; proper, correct, appropriate, idiomatic (সাধুপ্রয়োগ). ☐ *n.* a saint, an ascetic, an anchorite; a merchant, a trader; a usurer; a money-lender. ☐ *int.* excellent (সাধু ! সাধু !). **সাধু অভিপ্রায়** honest or noble desire, honest intention. **সাধু সাবধান** (lit.) O merchant, beware of the swindler or thief, (cp.) caveat emptor; (fig.) beware of the danger. **~গিরি** *n.* a show of honesty or piety; simulation of piety or honesty or goodness, sanctimoniousness, sanctimony; (usu. facet.) act of leading the life of an ascetic. **~তা** *n.* saintliness, piousness, piety, virtuousness, righteousness, honesty, integrity; goodness, nobility. ~তাচারণ *n.* honest or upright or virtuous or good behaviour or dealing; practice of piety or virtue. ~বাদ *n.* applause, praise, approbation; thanksgiving. **সাধুবাদ দেওয়া** *v.* to applaud, to praise; to thank. ~ভাষা *n.* chaste or elegant or polished language (cp. **চলিতভাষা**). ~সঙ্গ *n.* association with saints and ascetics; company of saints and ascetics, good company. ~সম্মত *a.* virtuous, honest (সাধুসম্মত উপায়).

সাধে *adv.* of one's own accord, willingly ('সাধে কি আর বাবা বলে').

সাধ্বী *n. fem.* a virtuous or chaste woman; a faithful wife; (loos.) a female saint. ☐ *a. fem.* virtuous, chaste; faithful to one's husband.

সাধ্য *a.* within the range of one's capability (দুর্বলের সাধ্য নয়) ; capable of being done or accomplished or attained; curable; to be proved or deduced or inferred. ☐ *n.* (log.) a major term, an inference; (law) a point at issue; (pop.) capability, ability (সাধ্যের বাইরে). ~তা *n.* attainability; the range of one's capability; feasibility. ~পক্ষে *adv.* as much as one can do, to the best of one's ability. ~পাল *n.* a bailiff. ~বহির্ভূত same as **সাধ্যাতীত**। ~মতো, **সাধ্যানুরূপ, সাধ্যানুযায়ী** *a.* within the range of one's capability. ☐ *adv.* same as **সাধ্যপক্ষে**। **সাধ্যাতিরিক্ত, সাধ্যাতীত** *a.* beyond the range of one's capability. **সাধ্যানুসারে** same as **সাধ্যপক্ষে**। ~সাধনা *n.* repeated importunities.

সান alt. spell. of **শান**।

সানক, সানকি *n.* a plate or dish of china-clay or porcelain.

সানন্দ *a.* joyful; glad; happy; pleased. **সানন্দে** *adv.* joyfully, cheerfully; gladly; happily; with pleasure.

সানা[১] alt. spell. of **শানা**।

সানা[২] *v.* to knead.

সানাই *n.* a kind of wooden wind-instrument.

সানু *n.* a level area on the top of a mountain, a tableland, a plateau.

সানুকম্প *a.* compassionate.

সানুজ *a.* attended or accompanied by one's younger brother.

সানুদেশ same as **সানু**।

সানুনয় *a.* full of supplication or entreaty. **সানুনয় প্রার্থনা** a humble prayer. **সানুনয়ে** *adv.* supplicatingly, entreatingly.

সানুনাসিক *a.* nasal.

সানুরাগ *a.* full of love or attachment, loving.

সান্ত *a.* finite; limited.

সান্তর *a.* having space at intervals, sparse; rare; porous.

সান্তারা *n.* an orange-like fruit.

সান্ত্বনা *n.* consolation; solace. **সান্ত্বনা দেওয়া** *v.* to console, to solace. ~কারী, ~দাতা *a.* & *n.* one who consoles. *fem.* ~কারিণী, ~দাত্রী। ~দান *n.* (act of giving) consolation. ~দায়ক, ~প্রদ *a.* consolatory, consoling, solacing. ~বাক্য *n.* consolatory speech or words.

সান্ত্রি *n.* an armed guard or watchman; a soldier on guard, a sentry; (erron.) a policeman.

সান্দ্র *a.* dense, thick; (of liquids) concentrated, condensed, thick, viscid, viscous. ~তা *n.* density, thickness; viscosity. ~তাঙ্ক *n.* co-efficient of viscosity. **সান্দ্রতামাপক** *n.* a viscometer.

সান্ধ্য *a.* of evening. ~তারা, ~তারকা *n.* the evening-star, vesper. ~দীপ *n.* an evening-lamp. ~দৈনিক an evening newspaper, an evening news daily. ~পরিচ্ছদ *n.* evening-dress. ~বায়ু, ~সমীরণ *n.* evening-breeze. ~ভোজ *n.* a dinner; a supper. ~ভ্রমণ *n.* evening-walk. ~সংগীত *n.* evening song. ~সম্মিলনী, ~সম্মেলন *n.* an evening-party.

সান্নিধ্য *n.* proximity, closeness; presence, company (গুরুর সান্নিধ্য). **সান্নিধ্য এড়ানো** *v.* to avoid the company of; to give a wide berth to.

সান্নিপাতিক *a.* marked by disorder of three humours of the body, namely, blood, bile and phelgm. **সান্নিপাতিক জ্বর** typhoid, enteric fever.

সান্বয় *a.* containing rendering into prose with the grammatical connections shown or made explicit (সান্বয় ব্যাখ্যা).

সাপ *n.* a snake, a serpent; (fig.) a malicious person. **সাপও মরে, লাঠিও ভাঙে** (fig.) accomplishment of a difficult job without sustaining any loss or damage. **সাপ হয়ে কাটা আর রোজা হয়ে ঝাড়া** (fig.) to hunt with the hound and run with the hare. **সাপের ছুঁচো গেলা** (fig.) involvement in a nauseating or unpleasant affair which cannot now be shaken off. **সাপের পাঁচ-পা দেখা** (fig.) to get extremely audacious as if one has come into possession of some rare power. **সাপের হাঁচি বেদেয় চেনে** (fig.) a jeweller knows the shine of a gem.

সাপট *n.* loud bragging or bullying; a violent stroke (as with a tail).

সাপটা *a.* ordinary, drab (সাপটা রান্না) ; in lump, gross (সাপটা দর). □ *adv.* in lump and without discrimination (সাপটা কেনা).

সাপটানো same as **জাপটানো** ।

সাপিনি *fem.* of **সাপ** ।

সাপুড়িয়া, (coll.) **সাপুড়ে** *n.* a snake-charmer (by trade or caste.)

সাপেক্ষ *a.* depending or dependent (on), subject (to), governed by a particular stipulation. **সাপেক্ষানুমান** *n.* (log.) a mediate inference.

সাপ্তাহিক *a.* weekly. □ *n.* a weekly journal, a weekly.

সাফ *a.* cleansed; clean, clear; clear-cut, unequivocal; obvious, thorough; downright (সাফ মিথ্যা) ; perfect or traceless (সাফ খুন) ; empty or emptied (পকেট সাফ) ; freed of obstruction (পালাবার রাস্তা সাফ) ; completely destroyed or all dead (বংশ সাফ). □ *adv.* completely, thoroughly (সাফ উধাও). **সাফ করা** *v.* to cleanse; (facet.) to empty. **পকেট সাফ করা** (facet.) to pick one's pocket. **সাফ কথা** clear-cut words; final words. **সাফ কবালা** a deed of outright sale; a deed of conveyance. **সাফ জবাব** a straight answer; a sharp retort; (esp. in law) a complete denial.

সাফল্য *n.* success. **~মণ্ডিত** *a.* crowned with success; successful.

সাফাই *n.* cleansing; exculpation, an exonerative explanation; vindication of innocence. **সাফাই গাওয়া** *v.* to plead innocence, to plead not guilty. **সাফাই দেওয়া** *v.* to advance arguments to vindicate one's innocence. **সাফাই সাক্ষী** a witness vindicating the innocence of the accused.

সাব *pfx.* sub-.

সাব-ইনসপেকটর *n.* a sub-inspector.

সাব-এডিটর *n.* a sub-editor.

সাব-কমিটি *n.* a sub-committee.

সাবকাশ *a.* having leisure (for); with leisure or leave.

সাব-জজ *n.* a sub-judge.

সাবড়ানো same as **সাবাড় করা** ।

সাবধান *a.* careful, cautious, on one's guard, on the alert, heedful. □ *int.* be careful, take care, be on guard. **সাবধান করা** *v.* to caution, to warn. **সাবধানের মার নেই** (fig.) safe bind safe find. **সাবধানতা** *n.* carefulness, cautiousness, alertness, heedfulness. **সাবধানী** *a.* same as **সাবধান** (*a.*). **সাবধানে** *adv.* carefully, cautiously.

সাবন *n.* a solar day; a solar month. □ *a.* solar (সাবন মাস).

সাবয়ব *a.* having a body with limbs or constituent parts, corporeal.

সাব-রেজিস্ট্রার *n.* a sub-registrar.

সাবলীল *a.* effortless; easy; facile; artistic; artistically playful.

সাবাড় *a.* finished; thoroughly consumed or spent or (facet.) eaten up; utterly destroyed or ruined; killed or murdered, done in. **সাবাড় করা** *v.* to finish; to consume or spend thoroughly; (facet.) to eat up the whole amount of; to ruin or destroy utterly; to kill or murder, to do (one) in. **সাবড়ানো, সাবড়ে দেওয়া** same as **সাবাড় করা** ।

সাবান *n.* soap. **সাবান মাখা বা মাখানো** *v.* to soap. **একখণ্ড গোটা সাবান** a cake of soap. **এক চাকা গোটা সাবান** a soap-ball. **এক টুকরো সাবান** a piece of soap. **সাবানের ফেনা** suds, soap-suds, lather. **সাবানের কৌটো** *n.* a soap-case, a soap-dish. **~তুল্য** *a.* saponaceous, soapy.

সাবালক *a.* of age; adult. *fem.* **সাবালিকা** । **সাবালিকা হওয়া** *v.* to come of age; to attain adulthood, to reach majority. **~ত্ব** *n.* full age, majority; adulthood.

সাবাস alt. spell. of **শাবাশ**।

সাবিত্রী *n. fem.* a Vedic incantation recited at prayer; (myth.) Princess Sabitri who won back her husband from the clutches of Yama. **~ব্রত** *n.* a vow observed by Hindu married women.

সাবু pop. var. of **সাগু**।

সাবুদ *n.* evidence, proof. ☐ *a.* proved, vindicated (সাবুদ করা) ; (vul.) rectified, corrected (মারের চোটে সাবুদ). **সাবুদ করা** *v.* to prove, to vindicate; to rectify, to correct.

সাবেক *a.* old, ancient, past; former; previous; original, first. **সাবেকি** *a.* of old; old-fashioned, of old school (সাবেকি চালচলন) ; (cp.) dated.

সাব্যস্ত *a.* adjudged or adjudicated; decided; ascertained; resolved; fixed. **সাব্যস্ত করা** *v.* to adjudge or adjudicate; to decide; to ascertain; to resolve; to settle; to fix.

সাম *n.* the Sama Veda; any hymn or psalm of the Sama Veda. **~গান** *n.* a hymn of the Sama Veda.

সামগ্রিক *a.* total, entire, over-all (সামগ্রিক বিচার).

সামগ্রী *n.* (ori.) things collectively; (pop.) a thing, an article.

সামঞ্জস্য *n.* propriety, fitness; consistency, agreement; symmetry, harmony; mutual understanding, adjustment. **সামঞ্জস্য করা, সামঞ্জস্যবিধান করা** *v.* to bring into agreement; to harmonize; to adjust.

সামনা *n.* the front; the forepart; the surface usually presented, the face. **~সামনি** *a & adv.* facing each other; face-to-face with; in presence of.

সামনে *prep.* in front of, before, in the face of; opposite to, facing; on the face or surface of.

সামন্ত *n.* a feudal prince; a vassal; a leader; a commander; a chieftain; a headman. **~তন্ত্র** *n.* the feudal system. **~নৃপতি** *n.* a feudal prince. **~রাজ্য** *n.* a feudal state; a dependency.

সাময়িক *a.* periodic, periodical; temporary, passing, momentary; current (সাময়িক সংবাদ) ; published periodically. **সাময়িক উত্তেজনা** momentary excitement or impulse, heat or spur of the moment. **সাময়িক উত্তেজনাবশে** on the spur of moment, in the heat of the moment. **সাময়িক পত্রিকা** a journal published periodically, a periodical. **সাময়িকী** *n.* a current event or topic; (pop.) a journal of current topics.

সামরিক *a.* relating to war; military; martial, warlike. **সামরিক জাতি** a martial race. **সামরিক দণ্ডবিধি** martial law. **সামরিক বাহিনী** an armed force. **সামরিক বিচারালয়** a court martial. **সামরিক শক্তি** military strength. **সামরিক শিক্ষা** military training.

সামর্থ্য *n.* ability; capability; efficiency; strength, power. **~বাধ** *n.* efficiency-bar. **সামর্থ্যানুযায়ী** *adv.* according to one's ability or capability.

সামলানো *v.* to check, to restrain; to manage to keep in the proper place (কাপড় সামলানো) ; to protect, to guard, to keep safe; to manage; to surmount, to tide over (বিপদ সামলানো).

সামাজিক *a.* social; pertaining to social formalities, formal, ceremonious; sociable, companionable. **সামাজিকতা** *n.* sociableness; formalities; a formal gift. **সামাজিকতা করা** to do or perform social duties, to meet social obligations; to observe customary formalities; to bestow a gift on a ceremonial occasion.

সামান্তরিক *n.* a parallelogram. **সামান্তরিক-সূত্র** *n.* (mech.) the parallelogram of forces.

সামান্য *a.* ordinary, common, commonplace, banal, trite; generic; (esp. in log.) general; (pop.) trifling; insignificant; humble; very small in number or amount or degree. ☐ *n.* (log.) a genus; general or generic properties or characteristics. *fem. a.* **সামান্যা**। **সামান্য ধর্ম** a common or general or generic characteristic or property. **সামান্য ভগ্নাঙ্ক, সামান্য ভগ্নাংশ** vulgar fraction. **সামান্য লক্ষণ** a common or general or generic character or sign; a general definition. **সামান্য-লক্ষণা** *n.* intuition. **সামান্য সমীকরণ** *n.* (alg.) simple equation. **সামান্যীকরণ** *n.* generalization.

সামাল *int.* beware, be on guard, take care. **সামাল করা** *v.* to check; to manage;

to manage to keep in position or to keep safe or steady.

সামিয়ানা rej. spell. of **শামিয়ানা।**

সামিল rej. spell. of **শামিল।**

সামীপ্য *n.* proximity, nearness, contiguity; presence, company.

সামুদয়িক *a.* in entirety, entire; total; comprehensive; general.

সামুদ্র, সামুদ্রিক *a.* marine; oceanic; maritime; (of marks on one's person) helping to tell one's fortune (সামুদ্রিক লক্ষণ) ; astrological (সামুদ্রিক জ্যোতিষ). □ *n.* the art of telling one's fortune from the marks on one's person (cp. physiogmancy), (loos.) astrology or palmistry (usu. **সামুদ্রিক বিদ্যা**). **সামুদ্র জলবায়ু** maritime or oceanic climate. **সামুদ্রিক উদ্ভিদ** a seaweed; a seaplant. **সামুদ্রিক জাতি** a maritime race. **সামুদ্রিক জীব** a marine or maritime creature. **সামুদ্রিক তলানি** pelagic deposit. **সামুদ্রিক বাণিজ্য** seatrade, maritime trade.

সাম্প্রতিক *a.* of recent times, current, contemporary.

সাম্প্রদায়িক *a.* communal; sectarian. **সাম্প্রদায়িকতা** *n.* communalism; sectarianism. **সাম্প্রদায়িক দাঙ্গা** communal riot. **সাম্প্রদায়িক বাটোয়ারা** communal award.

সাম্মানিক *a.* honorary; (of a university study course) of or belonging to or relating to Honours degree.

সাম্য *n.* equality; similarity; similitude; equilibrium, equipoise, balance (শক্তিসাম্য) ; mental equilibrium; democracy, socialism, communism. **~কেন্দ্র** *n.* centre of similitude. **~বাদ** *n.* socialism; communism. **~বাদী** *a.* socialistic; communistic. □ *n.* a socialist; a communist. **~রক্ষা** *n.* maintenance of balance or equilibrium.

সাম্রাজ্য *n.* an empire. **~বাদ** *n.* imperialism. **~বাদী** *a.* imperialistic. □ *n.* an imperialist.

সায়[1] *n.* consent, assent (সায় দেওয়া).

সায়[2] *n.* termination. □ *a.* ended. **সায় করা** *v.* to end, to finish ('সে গান তোমার করো সায়').

সায়ংকাল *n.* the evening; the eventide. **সায়ংকালীন** *a.* of the evening; vespertinal, vespertine. **সায়ংকালীন প্রার্থনা** evening prayer.

সায়ংকৃত্য *n.* prayer and other things to be done in the evening; evening service, vespers.

সায়ংসন্ধ্যা *n.* evening prayer, (cp.) evensong.

সায়ক alt. spell. of **শায়ক।**

সায়ন *n.* (astr.) declination; the equinox.

সায়ন্তন same as **সায়ংকালীন।**

সায়বানা *n.* a canopy, an awning.

সায়র *n.* a sea; a large pond.

সায়া *n.* a petticoat. **ফাঁপানো সায়া** a hooped petticoat, a farthingale.

সায়াহ্ন *n.* the evening; evenfall. **~কাল** same as **সায়ংকাল।** **~কৃত্য** same as **সায়ংকৃত্য।**

সাযুজ্য *n.* (complete) unification; oneness; a form of final salvation which consists in the individual soul's complete absorption in the Supreme Soul, identification with God.

সায়ুধ *a.* armed. **সায়ুধ বাহিনী** armed battalion. **সায়ুধ রক্ষী** armed guard.

সায়েব pop. corrup. of **সাহেব।**

সায়েস্তা alt. spell. of **শায়েস্তা।**

সার *n.* the best or excellent part; duramen, heart-wood; sap (of a tree); film or cream (of milk); marrow (of bone); pith; essence; extract; inner significance, gist; substance, abstract; spirit, vigour, manure, fertilizer; (only) worth. (কথামাত্র সার). □ *a.* best, excellent; essential; real or true or inner. **সার করা** *v.* to have recourse to something on considering it the sole object of pursuit; to regard something as the best or sole object. **সার বোঝা** *v.* to regard something as the best or sole object; to form an unalterable and final conviction. **সার দেওয়া** *v.* to manure. **উদ্ভিজ্জ সার** vegetable manure. **খনিজ সার** mineral manure. **প্রাণিজ সার, প্রাণী-সার** animal manure. **মিশ্র সার** *n.* compost. **~কথা** (lit.) essential words; substance; gist; sum and substance. **~কুড়, ~গাদা, ~ডোবা** *n.* a dunghill, a manure-pit. **~গর্ভ** *a.* having an inner significance or import; rich in content; substantial. **~গ্রন্থ** *n.* a manual, a vade-mecum. **~নিবন্ধ** *n.* an abstract register. **~বত্তা** *n.* substantiality; real worth. **~বান** *a.* full of substance, substantial; rich in duramen, sappy; pithy; fertile. **~ভূত** *a.* abstracted into or reduced to substance only; (loos.) substantial; best, picked. **~মাটি** *n.* marl. **~শূন্য, ~হীন** *a.* pithless, sapless; unsubstantial. **~সংক্ষেপ** *n.* substance, summary; a precis; essence; see also **সারাংশ**। **~সংগ্রহ, ~সংকলন** *n.* collection or compilation of the substantial or best specimens or of the pick; an abstract; an anthology of the best things.

সারঙ্গা[1] see **সারঙ্গী[2]**।

সারঙ্গা[2] *n.* a variety of spotted deer.

সারঙ্গা, সারঙ্গী[1] *fem.* of **সারঙ্গা[2]**।

সারঙ্গী[2] *n.* a stringed instrument akin to the violin (usu. **সারঙ্গা**); one who plays on this instrument.

সারণি, সারণী *n.* a table. **সারণিত** *a.* tabled. **সারণীকরণ** *n.* tabling. **সারণীবদ্ধ** *a.* tabular. **সারণীভুক্ত** *a.* tabled.

সারথি *n.* a chariot-driver, a charioteer.

সারথ্য *n.* charioteering.

সারদা alt. spell. of **শারদা**।

সারবন্দি coll. form of **সারিবন্দি**।

সারমেয় *n.* the dog. *fem.* **সারমেয়ী** the bitch.

সারল্য same as **সরলতা** (see **সরল**).

সারস *n.* the stork. *fem.* **সারসী**।

সারসন *n.* a belt or girdle for men; a woman's ornamental girdle.

সারস্বত *a.* relating to Goddess Saraswati (সরস্বতী) ; learned. **~সমাজ** *n.* the learned people, the learned society; litterateurs collectively. **সারস্বতোৎসব** *n.* the festival of worshipping Goddess Saraswati.

সারা[1] *a.* extremely tired, fatigued, exhausted, harassed.

সারা[2] *v.* to hide, to conceal (টাকাগুলো সেরে রাখা) ; to finish, to accomplish (কাজ সারা) ; to kill, to destroy (দফা সারা) ; to ruin, to undo (জুয়ায় তাকে সারল) ; to mend, to repair (ঘড়ি সারা) ; to correct or rectify (দোষ সারা, ভুল সারা) ; to be corrected or rectified; to recover, to come round (রোগীটি সেরেছে) ; to cure, to heal (রোগ সারা) ; to be cured; to restore or improve (স্বাস্থ্য সারা) ; to be restored or improved. ☐ *a.* finished; mended, repaired; corrected.

সারা[3] *a.* entire, whole, all. **~ক্ষণ** *adv.* throughout the whole period; all day long. **~জীবন** throughout the whole of one's life, all life. **~দিন** all day long, all day. **সারা বছর** all the year round. **~বেলা** throughout the whole of the period or time; throughout the whole of the forenoon or afternoon. **~মাস** throughout the whole of the month. **~রাত** all night long.

সারাংশ *n.* substance, essence; abstract; gist; duramen; pith.

সারানো *v.* to mend or repair; to correct or rectify; to cure, to heal (রোগ সারানো) ; to restore or improve.

সারালো same as **সারবান** (see **সার**).

সারি[1] *n.* a kind of boatsong.

সারি[2] *n.* a row, a line; a range; a column; a series **~বন্দি** *a.* arranged in a row or line, aligned, alined; arrayed. **সারি-সারি** *adv.* in rows, in lines; serially.

সারি[3], সারিকা, সারিগামা, সারিন্দা variants of **শারি, শারিকা, সারেগামা** and **সারঙ্গা**।

সারূপ্য *n.* a form of final salvation consisting in the atttainment of God's personal grace in one's own person.

সারেং[1] pop. corrup. of **সারঙ্গ[1]**।

সারেং[2] *n.* a boatswain, a serang.

সারেগামা *n.* (mus.) the first four notes of the gamut, namely, cdef; musical notation, elementary lessons of music; (fig.) elementary knowledge.

সারেঙ্গি pop. form of **সারঙ্গী[2]**।

সারোদ্ধার *n.* extraction or elicitation of the true significance or inner meaning.

সার্কাস *n.* a circus-show; circus. **সার্কাস দেখানো** *v.* to take (someone) along to the circus; to hold a circus-show. **সার্কাস-খেলোয়াড়** *n.* a showman of a circus.

সার্জন *n.* a surgeon.

সার্জেন্ট, (corrup.) **সার্জেন** *n.* sergeant; a police-sergeant.

সার্টিফিকেট *n.* a certificate. **সার্টিফিকেট দেওয়া** *v.* to give (one) a certificate, to certify.

সার্থ *a.* moneyed, wealthy; significant, meaningful. ☐ *n.* a companion; a collection; a flock, a herd; a company;

merchants collectively; a company of merchants. সার্থক *a.* significant (esp. in arith.); successful; effective; useful; realized, gratified. সার্থকজন্মা *a.* successful in life. সার্থকতা *n.* (rare) significance; success; fruition; effectiveness; utility, use; realization; gratification. সার্থকনামা *a.* one who has fully justified one's name (esp. by one's attainments and deeds); famous. ~নিবন্ধক *n.* a registrar of firms. ~বাহ *n.* a company of merchants travelling together, a caravan of merchants; a merchant; a guide.

সার্ধ *a.* one and a half of.

সার্ব *a.* relating to all, universal. ~কালিক *a.* of all times; eternal; perpetual. ~জনীন same as সর্বজনীন (see সর্ব). ~জাতিক *a.* international; universal. ~জাতিক ভ্রাতৃত্ব international brotherhood. ~জাতিকতা *n.* internationalism. ~দেশিক same as সর্বদেশীয় (see সর্ব). ~ভৌম *n.* an emperor; a sovereign ruler, a sovereign; a title awarded to some Sanskrit pundits. ☐ *a.* worldwide; universal; having worldwide fame; (loos.) supreme, sovereign. ~রাষ্ট্রিক *a.* pertaining to all states; international; universal. ~লৌকিক *a.* universal.

সাল[1] alt. spell. of শাল[2], শাল[3], শাল[4] ।

সাল[2] *n.* an era; (pop.) hegira as current in Bengali, the Bengali era (comencing from 593 or 594 A.D.); a year.

সালগম *n.* turnip.

সালংকার, সালঙ্কার *a.* (of a person) embellished with ornaments, ornamented; (of language ornate. *fem.* সালংকারা, সালঙ্কারা ।

সালতামামি *n.* year-closing; the annual report or review; the annual accounts or balance-sheet.

সালতি alt. spell. of শালতি ।

সালন *n.* a very spicy and hot curry (usu.) of fish etc.

সালম-মিছরি *n.* salep.

সালসা *n.* an Ayurvedic (আয়ুর্বেদীয়) blood-purifying tonic (cp. sarsa); (loos.) an elixir.

সালাম alt. form of সেলাম ।

সালিক rej. spell. of শালিক ।

সালিয়ানা *n.* an annual grant or stipend or fee or rent. ☐ *a.* annual, yearly. ☐ *adv.* annually.

সালিশ *n.* an arbitrator (*fem.* an arbitratrix), an arbiter (*fem.* an arbitress); arbitration. সালিশের রায় arbitrament, arbitrement. সালিশি *n.* arbitration. ☐ *a.* arbitral; under arbitration.

সালু rej. spell. of শালু ।

সালুক rej. spell. of শালুক ।

সালোক্য *n.* a form of salvation that enables one to live with God in the same abode.

সালোয়ার *n.* a pyjama-like garment usu. worn by women.

সার্শি, সাশি *n.* a sash.

সাশ্রয় *n.* a cut in expenditure, a saving.

সাশ্রু *a.* with tears, tearful, full of tears. ~নয়নে *adv.* with tearful eyes.

সাষ্টাঙ্গ *a.* performed by touching the ground with one's eight limbs, namely, thighs, feet, hands, chest, head, eyes, sight and speech or tongue; lying at full length with the face to the ground. সাষ্টাঙ্গে *adv.* touching the ground with one's eight limbs; lying at full length with one's face to the ground.

সাহংকার *a.* full of pride or vanity; proud; conceited. সাহংকারে *adv.* proudly; conceitedly.

সাহচর্য *n.* companionship; company; cooperation, help.

সাহজিক *a.* natural; instinctive.

সাহস *n.* intrepidity; courage, bravery, boldness; daring; audacity. সাহস করা *v.* to dare, to venture; to make bold, to take or summon up courage. সাহসিক *a.* requiring or having courage, courageous, bold; daring; audacious. সাহসিকতা *n.* courage; courageousness; boldness; daring. সাহসী *a.* having courage, intrepid; courageous, brave, bold; daring. সাহসী হওয়া *v.* to be brave or courageous; to dare, to venture; to be audacious. *fem.* সাহসিনী ।

সাহানা alt. spell. of শাহানা ।

সাহায্য *n.* help, aid; assistance; support; backing, patronization; (dero.) abetment or collaboration; a gratuitous gift or donation. **সাহায্য করা** *v.* to help, to aid; to assist; to support; to back; to patronize; (dero.) to abet or collaborate; to give or donate gratuitously. **~কারক, ~কারী** *a.* helping, assisting; supporting; patronizing; helpful, conducive; (dero.) abetting or collaborating; ☐ *n.* a helper, an aider; an assistant; a supporter; a patron; (dero.) an abettor or collaborator. *fem.* **~কারিণী**। **সাহায্যদান করা** same as **সাহায্য করা**। **~প্রাপ্ত** *a.* in receipt of help or aid or assistance or support; aided. **~প্রাপ্ত বিদ্যালয়** a school in receipt of a grant-in-aid, an aided school. **~প্রার্থী** *a* & *n.* one who seeks help. *fem.* **~প্রার্থিনী**। **সাহায্যার্থ, সাহায্যার্থে** *adv.* in aid of; for help.

সাহিত্য *n.* literature; a book (ধর্মসাহিত্য) ; composition, writing (প্রচারসাহিত্য). **~কলা** *n.* the art of literary composition. **~ক্ষেত্র** *n.* field of literature. **~চর্চা** *n.* literary pursuit or discussion. **সাহিত্যচর্চা করা** *v.* to compose or study or cultivate literature. **~জগৎ** *n.* the literary world, the world of letters. **~বৃত্তি, ~ব্যবসায়** *n.* the literary profession. **~ব্যবসায়ী** *n.* same as **সাহিত্যিক** (*n.*). **~ভাণ্ডার** *n.* the store or repertory of literature. **~রথী** *n.* an eminent litterateur or writer. **~শিল্প** same as **~কলা**। **~সভা** *n.* a literary society or gathering; the literary world. **~সমাজ** *n.* the literary world, litterateurs collectively. **~সমালোচক** *n.* a critic of literature; a literary critic. **~সমালোচনা** *n.* literary criticism. **সাহিত্যসেবা করা** *v.* to pursue or compose or study or cultivate literature devotedly. **~সেবী** *a.* devoted to literature; devotedly pursuing or composing or studying or cultivating literature. ☐ *n.* a devotee of literature; a litterateur, a writer, an author. **সাহিত্যাকাশ** same as **~জগৎ**। **সাহিত্যাচার্য** *n.* one profoundly versed in literature; a connoisseur or a great teacher of literature; a great author or litterateur. **সাহিত্যানুশীলন** same as **~চর্চা**। **সাহিত্যালোচনা** *n.* literary discussion. **সাহিত্যালোচনা করা** *v.* to discuss literature. **সাহিত্যিক** *a.* literary (সাহিত্যিক বৈঠক) ; pursuing literature (সাহিত্যিক লোক). ☐ *n.* a litterateur, a man of letters, a writer, an author (*fem.* an authoress).

সাহু, সাহুকারি variants of **সাউ** and **সাউকারি** respectively.

সাহেব *n.* an appellation affixed to names of gentlemen, (cp.) Mr. (বাবুসাহেব, মৌলবিসাহেব) ; a proprietor or master or chief or boss (আপিসের বড়সাহেব) ; an Englishman or a European; one pretending to be an Englishman or European, a sham Englishman or European. **কালা সাহেব** (sarcas.) a dark-complexioned man adopting or assuming the dress and the style of living of an Englishman or European, a sham Englishman or European; an Anglo-Indian. **সাহেব সাজা** *v.* to adopt or assume the English or European dress and style of living (as by a non-English or non-European person). **সাহেব পাড়া** *n.* an English or European quarter in a town or village. **সাহেব-মেম** *n.* an Englishman and an Englishwoman; a European and a European woman; an English or European couple. **সাহেবি** *n.* the English or European dress or style of living as adopted by foreigners; Englishness or Europeanism (also **সাহেবিয়ানা**). ☐ *a.* like the English or Europeans; (rare) English or European.

সিংহ *n.* the lion; (astrol.) the Leo; (*in comp.*) the best or the most courageous specimen (পুরুষসিংহ). **~কেশর** *n.* lion's mane. **~তুল্য** *a.* lionlike, leonine. **~দ্বার** *n.* a gate, esp. a main gate, adorned with a figure of a lion; main gate. **~নাদ** *n.* lion's roar; war cry. **সিংহনাদ করা** *v.* to yell out a war cry. **~পুরুষ** *n.* a lion of a man; an exceptionally powerful and valiant man; a lionheart. **~বিক্রম** *n.* prowess like that of a lion; great prowess. **~বিবর** *n.* the den of a lion. **~রাশি** *n.* (astrol.) the Leo. **~শাবক, ~শিশু** *n.* a lion-cub, a lion's whelp, a lionet.

সিংহল *n* Ceylon, (at present) Sri Lanka. **সিংহলি** *a.* Ceylonese. ☐ *n.* a Ceylonese; the language of Ceylon, Ceylonese.

সিংহাবলোকন *n.* (fig.) looking behind on the past; review.

সিংহাসন *n.* a seat shaped like the figure of a lion; a throne. **সিংহাসন ত্যাগ করা** *v.* to abdicate the throne, to abdicate. **সিংহাসনে আরোহণ করা, সিংহাসনে বসা** *v.* to ascend the throne. **সিংহাসনে বসানো** *v.* to enthrone. **সিংহাসনচ্যুত করা** *v.* to dethrone; to depose. **~চ্যুত** *n.* dethronement; deposition. **~ত্যাগ** *n.* abdication. **সিংহাসনারূঢ়** *a.* seated on a throne; enthroned; reigning.

সিংহী, (loos.) **সিংহিনী** *n. fem.* the lioness.

সিঁড়ি *n.* a flight of steps, a staircase; a ladder.

সিঁথি *n.* parting of hair on one's head in opposite ways by combing. **সিঁথি কাটা** *v.* to part one's hair.

সিঁদ coll. corrup. of **সিঁধ**।

সিঁদুর *n.* (coll.) vermilion; mercuric sulphide; red lead. **সিঁদুরে মেঘ** cloud as red as vermilion; red cloud which presages a storm.

সিঁধ *n.* a hole made into a house by a burglar. **সিঁধ কাটা, সিঁধ দেওয়া** *v.* to break into a house by making a hole on the wall. **সিঁধ দিয়ে চুরি করা** *v.* to burglarize, (facet.) to burgle. **~কাটি, ~কাঠি** *n.* a burglar's tool or rod used in house-breaking. **~চুরি** *n.* burglary, house-breaking. **সিঁধেল চোর** a burglar, a house-breaker.

সিক, সিককাবাব alt. spellings of **শিক** and **শিককাবাব** respectively.

সিকতা *n.* sand; gravel; sandy soil. **~ময়** *a.* sandy; gravelly.

সিকা[1] alt. spell. of **শিকা**।

সিকা[2] *n.* same as **সিকি** (*n*).

সিকি, (coll.) **সিকে**[1] *n.* a coin valuing a quarter of a rupee, a four-anna bit; a fourth part. ☐ *a.* one-fourth of, a quarter of, quarter-. **সিকি অংশ** a fourth part.

সিকে[2] alt. spell. of **শিকে**।

সিক্কা *n.* an obsolete rupee-coin of India.

সিক্ত *a.* wet, moist; moistened; (fig.) tearful (সিক্ত নয়ন). **সিক্ত করা** *v.* to wet; to moisten.

সিকথ *n.* wax.

সিকনি alt. spell of **শিকনি**।

সিগারেট *n.* a cigarette. **সিগারেট খাওয়া** *v.* to smoke a cigarette.

সিঙ্গাড়া, সিঙাড়া alt. spellings of **শিঙাড়া**।

সিঙ্গাপুরি *a.* of or made in Singapur. ☐ *n.* a variety of banana.

সিঝা, সিজা *v.* to be boiled in water. **সিঝানো, সিজানো** *v.* to boil in water. ☐ *a.* boiled in water.

সিঞ্চন *n.* sprinkling; spraying; watering. **সিঞ্চন করা** *v.* to sprinkle; to spray; to water.

সিঞ্চা poet. form of **সিঞ্চন করা**।

সিঞ্চিত *a.* sprinkled; sprayed; soaked by sprinkling or spraying; watered. *fem.* **সিঞ্চিতা**।

সিটকানো *v.* to turn up or contract in abhorrence, disgust, contempt etc. (নাক সিটকানো).

সিটা alt. spell. of **শিটা**।

সিটি *n.* a whistling sound made by pressing two fingers on the tongue. **সিটি দেওয়া** *v.* to whistle.

সিত *a.* white; bright, light; grey. **~চন্দন** *n.* white sandal, *Santalum album*. **~পক্ষ** *n.* a bright fortnight. **সিতাংশু** *n.* the moon. **সিতি** *a.* white; blue; black or dark. **সিতিকণ্ঠ** *n.* a white-throated person or creature; Shiva (শিব) ; the peacock; the gallinule.

সিদ্ধ *a.* boiled; cooked by boiling; parboiled; boiled for sterilization or cleansing; (fig.) profusely sweating and utterly fatigued (as in heat or sultriness); accomplished, performed; realized, fulfilled, attained; successful; proficient, expert, skilled; having attained divine grace through austere religious practice; endowed with or possessing occult power; proved, substantiated; amenable to (যুক্তিসিদ্ধ). ☐ *n.* one of a class of demi-gods; an omniscient saint or man; boiled eatables. **সিদ্ধ করা** *v.* to boil; to cook by boiling, to parboil; to boil for sterilization or cleansing; (fig.) to cause to sweat profusely and be utterly fatigued; to accomplish, to perform; to fulfil, to gratify; to make one proficient or expert (in). **অর্ধসিদ্ধ,** (coll.) **আধ-সিদ্ধ** *a.* half-boiled. **সিদ্ধ চাল**

parboiled rice. ~কাম *a.* one who has realized one's end, one whose desire has been fulfilled. ~পীঠ *n.* a holy place where at least ten million immolations, one crore burnt-offerings and innumerable religious practices have taken place. ~পুরুষ *n.* a man who has attained divine grace through austere religious practice. ~মনোরথ same as সিদ্ধকাম। ~হস্ত *a.* thoroughly proficient or expert or skilled.

সিদ্ধাই *n.* divine grace or occult power obtained through austere religious practice.

সিদ্ধান্ত *n.* decision; conclusion; deduction; resolution; a Hindu astronomical treatise. **সিদ্ধান্ত করা** *v.* to decide; to conclude; to deduce; to resolve. **সিদ্ধান্তে উপনীত হওয়া** *v.* to come to a conclusion.

সিদ্ধান্ন *n.* parboiled rice; cooked rice.

সিদ্ধার্থ *a.* one who has realized one's end. ☐ *n.* the name of Gautama Buddha.

সিদ্ধি *n.* performance, accomplishment; realization, attainment; success; attainment of proficiency or skill or knowledge; attainment of divine grace; divine grace attainable through austere religious practice; spiritual salvation; leaves and shoots of hemp, bhang. **সিদ্ধি খাওয়া** *v.* to chew and swallow bhang; to drink a beverage of pulped bhang. **সিদ্ধি ঘোঁটা** *v.* to stir pulped bhang in milk, coconut-milk etc. in order to make a beverage. **সিদ্ধির শরবত** a beverage made by mixing pulped bhang with milk, coconut-milk etc. ~দ *a.* one who grants success or gratifies another's desire. ~দাতা *a.* same as সিদ্ধিদ ☐ *n.* Lord Ganesha (গণেশ). *fem. a.* **সিদ্ধিদাত্রী**। **সিদ্ধিলাভ করা** *v.* to succeed (in), to become successful; to attain proficiency or skill or knowledge; to attain divine grace through austere religious practice. **সিদ্ধেশ্বরী** *n. fem.* a Hindu goddess.

সিধা, (coll.) **সিধে** *a.* straight, not curved; lying continually onward (সিধা রাস্তা) ; shortest, not circuitous, direct (সবচেয়ে সিধে রাস্তা) ; easy, simple; straight (সিধে কথা) ; chastised or coerced. (গুঁতোর চোটে সিধে). ☐ *adv.* straight (সিধে চলা) ; at once, directly, straightway (বলামাত্র সিধে ছোটা). ☐ *n.* a gift of uncooked food arranged on a tray.

সিন *n.* a scene (of a drama); a painted scene put up on a stage; a scenery.

সিনা *n.* width of the chest; chest.

সিনান poet. corrup. of **স্নান**।

সিনেমা *n.* cinema, motion picture; a film; a cinema; a cinemahouse, a picture house, a picturepalace. **সিনেমা দেখা** *v.* to see a film; to go to pictures. **সিনেমা-ভক্ত** *n.* a film-fan. **সিনেমা-শিল্পী** *n.* a film-artist. **সিনেমা-স্টার** *n.* a film-star.

সিন্দুক *n.* a chest, a safe.

সিন্দুর *n.* mercuric sulphide, vermilion; red lead. **চীনা সিন্দুর** vermilion. **মেটে সিন্দুর** red lead.

সিন্ধি *a.* of Sindh; inhabiting or living in Sindh. ☐ *n.* a native of Sindh; the language of Sindh.

সিন্ধিয়া *n.* the title of the rulers of Gwalior, Sindhia.

সিন্ধু *n.* an ocean, a sea; the Indus (also **সিন্ধুনদ**); a province of Pakistan (usu **সিন্ধুপ্রদেশ**); an Indian musical mode. ~ঘোটক *n.* the walrus.

সিন্নি coll. corrup. of **শিরনি**।

সিপাই pop. var. of **সিপাহি**।

সিপাহসলার *n.* the commander-in chief.

সিপাহি *n.* a soldier; one holding the lowest rank in the Indian army, an Indian private, a sepoy; an armed guard; a constable.

সিম rej. spell. of **শিম**।

সিরকা alt. spell. of **সির্কা**।

সিরিশ, (rej.) **সিরিস** *n.* glue. ~কাগজ *n.* sand paper, glass-paper.

সির্কা *n.* vinegar (produced by fermenting molasses etc.)

সিল[1] *n.* the seal.

সিল[2] *n.* a seal; affixation of a seal. **সিল করা** *v.* to put a seal (on), to set a seal (to), to seal ~-করা *a.* sealed. ~মোহর *n.* a seal containing a name or any other sign.

সিস *n.* lead; a stick of blacklead within a pencil.

সিসা *n.* lead.

সিসৃক্ষা *n.* desire of creating.

সিসৃক্ষু *a.* desirous of creating.

সীতা *n.* a furrow; Sita (সীতা) the heroine of the Ramayana. ~পতি *n.* Rama, the husband of Sita. ~ভোগ *n.* a kind of sweetmeat.

সীধু alt. spell. of শীধু।

সীবন *n.* sewing; embroidery. সীবন করা *v.* to sew; (rare) to embroider. সীবন-শিল্প *n.* embroidery; (rare) art of sewing. সীবনী *n.* a needle; an awl; a perinium.

সীমন্ত *n.* the parting-line of hair of the head (esp. of a woman). সীমন্তিনী *n.* a woman whose husband is alive (esp. one who puts vermilion on the parting-line of the hair of one's head); a woman. সীমন্তিনী-শাসন *n.* (facet.) gynocracy, petticoat government. সীমন্তোন্নয়ন *n.* a Hindu sacrament received by a pregnant woman.

সীমা *n.* a boundary, a border; a frontier; limit (ধৈর্যের সীমা) ; end, termination (দুঃখের সীমা নেই) ; jurisdiction or holding (জমির সীমা). সীমা অতিক্রম করা *v.* to go beyond the limit (of), to go too far; to transgress. সীমানা *n.* bounding-lines; bounds, boundary, periphery; limit; end, termination; jurisdiction or holding. সীমা নির্ণয় করা *v.* to mark off or determine bounds (of), to demarcate, to demark, to delimit. সীমা নির্দেশ করা *v.* same as সীমা নির্ণয় করা। সীমান্ত *n.* a bounding-line, a border; a frontier. সীমান্ত-প্রদেশ *n.* a frontier province; frontiers. সীমান্তবাণিজ্য *n.* the frontier trade. সীমান্তরক্ষী *n.* frontier guard, border guard. সীমান্তরক্ষী বাহিনী border security force. ~-পরিসীমা *n.* end and measure. ~বদ্ধ *a.* confined within or restricted to limits, limited; restricted. ~রেখা *n.* border; borderline. ~সন্ধি *n.* the meeting-point of two boundary-lines (cp. a corner-stone). ~স্তম্ভ *n.* a boundary-post, a boundary-pillar. ~হীন *a.* limitless, unlimited, boundless, endless; infinite.

সীমিত *a.* limited. সীমিত সংঘ (comm.) a limited company.

সীল[১] and সীল[২] rej. spellings of সিল[১] and সিল[২] respectively.

সীস alt. spell of সিস।

সীসক, সিসা, (coll.) সিসে *n.* lead.

সু[১] *n.* an auspicious or beautiful or good person or thing.

সু[২] *pfx.* denoting : auspicious or beautiful, sweet, good, very, easy etc.

সুই, সুঁই *n.* a needle, an awl.

সুছাঁদ *a.* well-shaped.

সুঁটি rej. spell. of শুঁটি।

সুঁড়ি rej. spell. of শুঁড়ি।

সুঁদরি corrup. of সুন্দরী[২]।

সুঁদি *n.* the waterlily, the lotus.

সুকঠিন *a.* very difficult or hard or stiff or tough.

সুকণ্ঠ *a.* sweet-voiced, having a melodious voice. *fem.* সুকণ্ঠী।

সুকতলা alt. spell. of সুখতলা।

সুকর *a.* capable of being done or contrived easily, easy, simple.

সুকানি *n.* an oriental steersman or quartermaster of a steamer, seacunny.

সুকান্ত *a.* handsome, beautiful, of beautiful appearance.

সুকীর্তি *n.* wide or very valuable fame or renown.

সুকুমার *a.* very soft or tender; very young; very beautiful or graceful. *fem.* সুকুমারী। ~কলা same as সুকুমার শিল্প। সুকুমার বৃত্তি *n.* tender or fine attribute; fine sensibility; artistic bent of mind. ~মতি *a.* having a simple mind, innocent as a child, of a simple turn of mind; pure in heart. সুকুমার শিল্প *n.* fine arts. ~শিল্পী *n.* an artist; an artiste; a litterateur.

সুকৃত *a.* well-performed, well-done; well-built; virtuous; pious; doing good deeds. □ *n.* same as সুকৃতি। সুকৃতি *n.* a good act or deed; virtue, piety; religious practices; good, weal, , welfare; fortune, good luck. সুকৃতী same as সুকৃৎ।

সুকৃৎ *a.* observant of religious rules and prescriptions; virtuous, pious; fortunate.

সুকেশ *a.* having beautiful and luxuriant hair. *fem.* সুকেশা, সুকেশী, (loos.) সুকেশিনী।

সুকোমল *a.* very soft or tender.

সুকৌশলী *a.* very tricky or strategic or ingenious or skilful or artistic.

সুকৌশলে *adv.* by means of a nice trick or stratagem; by means of a fine artifice or device; very ingeniously or artistically; tactfully.

সুক্তা, (coll.), **সুক্ত,** (dial.) **সুক্তনি** *n.* a dish of bitter vegetables.

সুখ *n.* ease, comfort; contentment; happiness, joy; bliss. **সুখে থাকতে ভূতে কিলায়** (fig.) the folly of leaving a comfortable and peaceful situation for a troubled one; act of inviting unnecessary troubles. **সুখের পায়রা** (fig.) a person of happy-go-lucky temperament; a fair-weather friend. **~কর, ~জনক, ~দ, ~দায়ক** *a.* easeful, comfortable; giving contentment or pleasure or happiness or joy; happy, joyful, delightful, pleasant; blissful. **~দা, ~দায়িকা** । **~দুঃখ** *fem. n.* weal and woe, joy and sorrow, happiness and misery. **~বিধান করা** *v.* to provide for ease and comfort or for happiness. **~বোধ** same as **সুখানুভব** । **~ভাগী** *a.* partaking of or sharing another's joy or happiness. *fem.* **~ভাগিনী** । **সুখভোগ করা** *v.* to enjoy ease and comfort; to enjoy happiness or joy; to enjoy bliss. **~ভোগী** *a.* enjoying ease and comfort; enjoying happiness of joy; enjoying bliss and comfort; full of happiness or joy, happy, joyful; pleasant; blissful. **~ময়** *a.* full of ease and happiness. **~রবি** *n.* joy or happiness identified with the sun, the sun of joy or happiness. **~শয়ন, ~শয্যা** *n.* a comfortable bed, (cp.) a bed of down or of roses; a bed of pleasure. **~শান্তি** *n.* happiness and peace. **~শ্রাব্য** *a.* pleasant to hear; melodious and sweet or agreeable or pleasing to the ear. **~সংবাদ** *n.* (a piece of) happy news. **~সম্পদ** *n.* happiness and riches, milk and honey. **~সূর্য** same as **সুখরবি** । **~স্পর্শ** *a.* pleasant to the touch. **~স্বাচ্ছন্দ্য** *n.* happiness and ease, happiness and affluence, milk and honey. **~স্বপ্ন** *n.* a happy or pleasant dream. **~স্মৃতি** *n.* happy memory or recollection.

সুখেস্বাচ্ছন্দ্যে *adv.* in comfort and happiness.

সুখতলা *n.* a piece of soft leather placed inside a shoe, insole (of leather.)

সুখবর *n.* good news; happy news.

সুখাদ্য *n.* tasteful and nutritious food, delicious food, a delicacy.

সুখানুভব, সুখানুভূতি *n.* feeling of comfort or happiness. **সুখানুভব করা** *v.* to feel comfortable or happy.

সুখান্বেষণ *n.* search or quest for comfort or happiness, an endeavour to be comfortable or happy.

সুখান্বেষী *a.* searching for or seeking comfort or happiness.

সুখাবহ same as **সুখকর** (see **সুখ**).

সুখাসন *n.* a comfortable or pleasant seat.

সুখাসীন *a.* comfortably seated, seated at ease, *fem.* **সুখাসীনা** ।

সুখী *a.* happy; glad; comfortable; content; satisfied; enjoying milk and honey; given to luxury, luxurious; blessed.

সুখে *adv.* with ease, comfortably; contentedly; happily; gladly; in bliss.

সুখৈশ্বর্য *n.* happiness and riches.

সুখোৎপাদন *n.* production of happiness.

সুখোদয় *n.* the dawn or dawning of happiness of affluence.

সুখ্যাতি *n.* good reputation; fame; praise. **সুখ্যাতি করা** *v.* to praise.

সুগঠন *a.* well-shaped; fine-built; strong-built, □ *n.* good or fine shape.

সুগঠিত *a.* well-shaped; fine-built; strong-built; well-formed; well-constructed; well-organized.

সুগত *a.* having an excellent or majestic gait. □ *n.* an appellation of Gautama Buddha.

সুগন্ধ *n.* a sweet smell or fragrance or aroma. □ *a.* sweet-smelling, fragrant, aromatic. **~পূর্ণ, ~ময়** *a.* full of sweet smell, sweet-smelling, fragrant, aromatic. **সুগন্ধি** □ *n.* any substance made or used for the sake of its smell, a perfume; spinel. □ *a.* same as **সুগন্ধ** (*a.*) ।

সুগভীর *a.* very deep; profound.

সুগম *a.* easy to go over or traverse, easily accessible (সুগম পথ) ; easily obtainable; easy to learn or understand (সুগম সংগীত). **~তা** *n.* easy accessibility; easy obtainability; easy understandability.

সুগৃহীতনামা *a.* bearing a name the very utterance of which adds to one's piety.

সুগোল *n.* perfectly round; beautifully round or rotund; plump.

সুগ্রাহিতা *n.* sensitiveness.

সুগ্রাহী *a.* sensitive (সুগ্রাহী কাগজ).

সুচ *n.* a needle; an awl.

সুচতুর *a.* very cunning or sly; very clever or adroit. *fem.* **সুচতুরা** ।

সুচরিত, সুচরিত্র *n.* good character. ☐ *a.* good-charactered. *fem.* **সুচরিতা, সুচরিত্রা** । **সুচরিতেষু** to you or him of good character (a form of polite address in a letter) *fem.* **সুচরিতাসু** ।

সুচারু *a.* very beautiful; very neat. **রূপে** *adv.* beautifully, nicely; perfectly.

সুচিক্কণ *a.* very smooth and glossy.

সুচিত্রিত *a.* well-painted; well-decorated; well-described; nicely delineated.

সুচিন্তা *n.* a good or pious or high thought; pious or high thinking.

সুচিন্তিত *a.* carefully or judiciously considered, well-thought; well-thought-out, well-planned, well-devised. **সুচিন্তিত পরিকল্পনা** a well-thought-out plan.

সুচির *a.* very or too long, lasting for a long time ('সুচির শবরী'). ☐ *n.* a very long time. **~কালে** *adv.* in a very long time.

সুচেতা *a.* of a cheerful temperament, merry; happy and contented; careful, cautious.

সুছাঁদ *a.* well-shaped; artistically shaped; having an artistic style.

সুজন *n.* a good or honest or pious man, a good soul.

সুজনি rej. spell. of **শুজনি** ।

সুজলা *a. fem.* full of profuse or delicious water; well-innundated by rivers full of profuse or delicious water.

সুজাত *a.* well-born, nobly born; legitimately born. *fem.* **সুজাতা** ।

সুজি *n.* a coarse flour of wheat, (cp.) farina.

সুট[১] *n.* a suit (এক সুট পোশাক বা গয়না) ; a suit of European clothes. **সুট পরা** *v.* to put on a suit or a European dress. **~কেস** *n.* a suitcase. **সুট-পরা** *a.* wearing a suit; clothed in European dress.

সুঠাম *a.* well-shaped, shapely; having a well-shaped body; having an artistic pose or style; beautiful.

সুড়ঙ্গা of **সুরঙ্গ** ।

সুড়সুড় *int.* denoting : a tickling or titillating sensation. **সুড়সুড় করা** *v.* to tickle. **সুড়সুড়ি** *n.* a tickle; titillation. **সুড়সুড়ি দেওয়া** *v.* to tickle, to titillate.

সুডৌল *a.* well-shaped, shapely.

সুত *n.* a son. **~নির্বিশেষে** *adv.* making no difference between a son and others, like a son.

সুতনু *a.* graceful, handsome, beautiful, well-shaped. ☐ *n.* well-shaped or beautiful body. **সুতনুকা** *a.* & *n. fem.* of **সুতনু** ।

সুতন্বী *n. fem.* a woman possessing a beautifully slim body.

সুতপা *n.* an ascetic.

সুতপ্ত *a.* very hot or warm.

সুতরাং *con.* & *adv.* consequently, therefore, so, hence.

সুতলি *n.* a very thin thread or string; fibre of yarn; a wrapper of thin (cotton) thread.

সুতহিবুক *n.* (astrol.) a conjuction of stars and planets considered very auspicious for marriage.

সুতা *n. fem.* a daughter.

সুতার *a.* having a delicious taste. ☐ *n.* a delicious taste.

সুতি *a.* made of cotton thread or yarn. **~বস্ত্র** *n.* cotton fabric; cotton textile; cloth made of cotton.

সুতো *n.* thread; yarn; cotton-thread; a measure of length (= $^1/_4$ inch).

সুদ *n.* interest of loan, use, usury. **সুদ হওয়া** *v.* to accrue interest. **সুদ কষা** *v.* to find out or calculate interest. **সুদে খাটানো** *v.* to lay out or invest on interest. **সুদে ধার দেওয়া** to lend on interest. **সুদের সুদ, চক্রবৃদ্ধি সুদ** compound interest. **~খোর** *a.* living on usury, usurious. ☐ *n.* a usurer (*fem.* a usuress.) **~সমেত** with interest.

সুদক্ষ *a* very skilful or deft or proficient.

সুদর্শন *a.* good-looking, handsome; pleasing to the eye, lovely.. ☐ *n.* (myth.) the discus or quoit of Vishnu (বিষ্ণু) or Krishna (কৃষ্ণ), used to be hurled at enemies (also **সুদর্শনচক্র**). *fem. a.* **সুদর্শনা** ।

সুদি *a.* relating to usury, usurious. **~কারবার** *n.* usury.

সুদিন *n.* a good or favourable day; a time of prosperity, good times; (astrol.) an auspicious day or time.

সুদীর্ঘ *a.* very long; very long-continuing; very lengthy.

সুদুস্তর *a.* very difficult to cross over.

সুদূর *a.* far-off, very far or remote. **সুদূর ব্যবধান** very great distance, a far cry. **~পরাহত** *a.* hardly possible, likely once in a blue moon; foredoomed to failure.

সুদৃঢ় *a.* very firm or strong; very steady; absolutely unwavering.

সুদৃশ্য *a.* pleasing to the eye, lively, beautiful.

সুদ্ধ *adv.* & *prep.* together with, including (সবসুদ্ধ) ; even (রেসে তার বাড়িখানা সুদ্ধ গেছে).

সুধন্বা *a.* proficient in archery. □ *n.* a great archer.

সুধা[১] *n.* nectar, ambrosia; moonlight; lime. **সুধা ঢালা** *v.* to pour nectar; (fig.) to sweeten, to please, to flatter, to console. **সুধাংশু, ~কর** *n.* the moon. **~ধবল** *a.* white as moonlight. **~ধবলিত** *a.* treated with a lime-wash, whitewashed. **~পাত্র** *n.* a container or receptacle of nectar; a cup or goblet for drinking nectar, an ambrosial cup. **~বর্ষণ** বা **~বৃষ্টি করা** *v.* to shower or rain or sprinkle nectar; (of the moon) to scatter moonlight; (fig.) to please, to flatter, to console. **~বর্ষী** *a.* showering nectar; (fig.) pleasing or flattering or consoling. **~ভাণ্ড** same as **~পাত্র** । **~ময়** *a.* full of nectar; ambrosial, nectared; (fig.) very sweet or pleasing or flattering or consoling; (fig.—of a person) very well-behaved and charming. *fem.* **~ময়ী** । **~মাখা** *a.* filled with or soaked in nectar, nectarine; delicious; very sweet. **~সমুদ্র, ~সিন্ধু** *n.* (myth.) the sea of nectar, the ambrosial sea. **~সিক্ত** *a.* soaked with nectar; (fig.) very sweet or pleasant.

সুধী *n.* a learned or erudite man; a wise man. □ *a.* wise or judicious; learned, erudite.

সুধীর *a.* calm and composed, calm and collected; unperturbed, firm.

সুনজর *n.* good looks, good or kindly look; favourable look, favour. **সুনজরে থাকা** *v.* to be in the good books (of).

সুনয়না, (loos.) **সুনয়নী** *a. fem.* possessing beautiful eyes. *masc.* **সুনয়ন** ।

সুনাম *n.* good reputation, renown, fame; goodwill.

সুনিদ্রা *n.* good or sound or peaceful sleep.

সুনিপুণ *a.* very skilful or adroit; highly efficient or competent.

সুনিবিড় *a.* very deep, very dense or thick; very close or intimate (সুনিবিড় বন্ধুতা).

সুনিয়ন্ত্রিত *a.* well-controlled; well-governed; well-managed; well-regulated or well-restrained.

সুনিয়ম *n.* a good rule or law or principle; good management.

সুনির্দিষ্ট *a.* clearly or categorically or nicely defined or fixed.

সুনির্ধারিত *a.* firmly or categorically fixed or defined; well-defined.

সুনির্মল *a.* perfectly pure, immaculate; perfectly clear; pellucid, perfectly fresh.

সুনিশ্চয়, সুনিশ্চিত *a.* thoroughly certain or positive or sure or convincing; thoroughly assured or convinced. □ *adv.* certainly, positively, surely; convincingly; assuredly. **সুনিশ্চিতভাবে** same as **সুনিশ্চিত** (*adv.*).

সুনীতি *n.* a good or excellent principle; good morals.

সুনীল *a.* deep or dark blue; perfectly or flawlessly blue.

সুনেত্রা *a.* (*fem.*) one with beautiful eyes.

সুন্দ-উপসুন্দ *n. pl.* the two mythological demon brothers. **সুন্দ-উপসুন্দের লড়াই** (fig.) a relentless encounter, when Greek meets Greek.

সুন্দর *a.* beautiful, fine, nice, pretty; pleasant, lovely; goodlooking, handsome, fair; graceful, elegant; sweet (সুন্দর গান). **সুন্দর করা** *v.* to beautify, to embellish; to improve (হস্তাক্ষর সুন্দর করা).

সুন্দরী[১] *a. fem.* of **সুন্দর** □ *n.* a beautiful woman or girl.

সুন্দরী২ *n.* a kind of timber-tree grown in Sundarbans or its timber, *Heritiera sundari*, sundri.

সুন্নত *n.* circumcision. **সুন্নত করা** *v.* to circumcise.

সুন্নি *n.* a Muslim community (famous for its orthodoxy); a member of this community, a Sunni, a Sonnite, a Sunnite.

সুপ *n.* soup.

সুপক্ব *a.* thoroughly boiled; fully ripe; (facet.) well-experienced; (sarcas.) inveterately habituated or addicted; (sarcas.) grossly precocious.

সুপণ্ডিত *a.* well-versed; profoundly learned or erudite; well-educated.

সুপথ, সুপন্থা *n.* a good road; an honest or virtuous or conducive course or path or way or means.

সুপথ্য *n.* good or wholesome or hygienic food or diet.

সুপরামর্শ *n.* good advice or counsel.

সুপরিচিত *a.* well-known; widely known; famous.

সুপরিচালিত *a.* well-directed, well-managed.

সুপরিজ্ঞাত *a.* well-known; widely known.

সুপর্ণ *n.* the fowl; the chicken; Garuda, the mythical prince of birds.

সুপাচ্য *a.* easily digestible.

সুপাত্র *n.* a good or worthy or deserving or desirable person or claimant or bridegroom or match. *fem.* **সুপাত্রী** *n. fem.* a good or worthy or deserving or desirable female claimant or bride; an excellent bride.

সুপারি *n.* areca-nut, betel-nut; its tree, the Areca.

সুপারিশ *n.* recommendation. **সুপারিশ করা** *v.* to recommend. **সুপারিশ-পত্র** *n.* a letter of recommendation, a recommendation. **সুপারিশি** *a.* recommending, recommendatory.

সুপুত্র *n.* a good or excellent or worthy son. *fem.* **সুপুত্রী** a good or excellent or worthy daughter.

সুপুরি coll. corrup. of **সুপারি** ।

সুপুরুষ *n.* a handsome or well-built man. ☐ *a.* handsome or well-built.

সুপুষ্ট *a.* well-nourished, well-developed; plumb; adiposed.

সুপেয় *n.* a good drink. ☐ *a.* good for drinking; good as a drink.

সুপ্ত *a.* sleeping, asleep; (fig.) dormant; (fig.) latent; *fem.* **সুপ্তা** । **সুপ্ত আগ্নেয়গিরি** a dormant volcano. **সুপ্তি** *n.* sleep; (fig.) dormancy; (fig.) latency. **সুপ্তোত্থিত** *a.* risen from sleep, awake, awakened.

সুপ্রতিষ্ঠ, সুপ্রতিষ্ঠিত *a.* well-established, well-founded; firmly settled down; well-reputed, very famous; (mech.) stable.

সুপ্রভাত *n.* a fine morning; auspicious morning; (fig.) the dawn or dawning of fortune. ☐ *int.* good morning.

সুপ্রযুক্ত *a.* well-applied; very appropriately used.

সুপ্রয়োগ *n.* proper application, appropriate use, good or profitable utilization.

সুপ্রশস্ত *a.* very wide; very suitable or auspicious or broad.

সুপ্রসন্ন *a.* highly pleased or satisfied; extremely favourable or propitious; gracious or kind. **অদৃষ্ট সুপ্রসন্ন** in good luck, stars in the ascendant.

সুপ্রসব *n.* safe or smooth delivery (of a baby).

সুপ্রসিদ্ধ *a.* celebrated, renowned, illustrious.

সুপ্রাপ্য *a.* easily available.

সুফল *n.* good effect or result. **~দায়ক, ~প্রসূ** *a.* yielding good result, producing good effect.

সুফলা *a. fem.* yielding abundant fruits, abundantly or richly fructiferous or frugiferous; highly productive or fertile.

সুফি *n.* a Mohammedan community believing in pantheistic mysticism; a member of this community.

সুবক্তা *n.* a good speaker.

সুবচন *n.* salutary words or counsel; a good or wise saying; a maxim, an adage; sweet words; an epigram.

সুবচনী corrup. of **শুভচণ্ডী** ।

সুবদন *a.* having a beautiful or pretty face, fair-faced. *fem.* **সুবদনা,** (loos.) **সুবদনী** ।

সুবন্ত *a.* (Sans. gr.—of words) suffixed with or capable of being suffixed with case-endings. ~প্রকরণ *n.* the chapter on case-endings; declension.

সুবন্দোবস্ত *n.* good management or arrangement.

সুবর্ণ *n.* gold; a gold coin; (loos.) a mohur (মোহর). □ *a.* golden-coloured, golden. ~**খচিত** *a.* studded or set or inlaid with gold; (loos.) gold-centred (সুবর্ণখচিত পদক). ~**জয়ন্তী** see **জয়ন্তী**। ~**পদক** *n.* a gold-medal. **সুবর্ণপদকপ্রাপ্ত ব্যক্তি** *a.* gold-medallist. ~**প্রতিমা** same as **স্বর্ণপ্রতিমা**। ~**বণিক** *n.* a Hindu community originally trading in gold and carrying on banking business; a member of this community. ~**সুযোগ** *n.* a golden opportunity.

সুবহ *a.* easily or conveniently carried, portable. ~**তা** *n.* portability.

সুবা *n.* a province in Moghul India, a subah.

সুবাদ *n.* relation, connection. **এই সুবাদে** thus related or connected; owing to this; in this connection.

সুবাদার *n.* the governor of a subah, an Indian army officer holding a rank equivalent to that of a captain, a subahdar, a subadar. **সুবাদারি** *n.* subahadary, subahdarship.

সুবাস *n.* a sweet smell or odour; fragrance; aroma; perfume. **সুবাসিত** *a.* perfumed, scented. **সুবাসিত করা** *v.* to perfume, to scent. **সুবাসিত তেল** scented or perfumed oil.

সুবিখ্যাত *a.* very famous, renowned; well-reputed.

সুবিচার *n.* good or correct or impartial or wise judgment; justice, equity. **সুবিচার করা** *v.* to judge rightly or impartially or wisely; to mete out justice (to). **সুবিচারক** *n.* a good or impartial or wise judge.

সুবিজ্ঞাত *a.* well-known; reputed; famous.

সুবিদিত *a.* well-known; well-informed, au fait.

সুবিধা *n.* an excellent or favourable or advantageous means or circumstance; an advantage; an opportunity; convenience. **সুবিধা নেওয়া** *v.* to avail oneself of an opportunity or advantage; to take advantage of. ~**জনক** *a.* advantageous; opportune; convenient. ~**প্রাপ্ত** *a.* placed in an advantageous position; put to an advantage; having got an opportunity. ~**বাদ** *n.* opportunism. ~**বাদী** *n.* an opportunist. □ *a.* opportunist. ~**ভোগী** *a.* enjoying special privilege; privileged. ~**মতো** *adv.* conveniently; at one's convenience. **সুবিধা-সুযোগ** *n.* convenience and opportunity.

সুবিধি *n.* a good law or rule; (rare) a good remedy.

সুবিন্দু *n.* the zenith.

সুবিন্যস্ত *a.* well-arranged; well-arrayed; orderly; nicely laid out or displayed.

সুবিপুল, সুবিশাল *a.* very big or large, vast, gigantic, huge; immense.

সুবিমল *a.* wholly free from dirt or impurity; pure or faultless, immaculate; very clear.

সুবিস্তীর্ণ, সুবিস্তৃত *a.* well-spread; very extensive; vast; far-flung.

সুবুদ্ধি *a.* guided by or having good thoughts or inclinations or sense or discretion, sensible; conscientious; prudent. □ *n.* good thoughts or inclination or sense or discretion; conscientiousness; prudence.

সুবৃষ্টি *n.* good rain (that is, neither excessive nor scanty rain).

সুবে coll. corrup. of **সুবা**।

সুবেদী *a.* sensitive.

সুবেশ *n.* a fine dress; neatness of dress or dressing. □ *a.* well-dressed.

সুবোধ *a.* same as **সুবুদ্ধি** (*a.*)

সুবোধ্য *a.* easily understood, lucid; easily intelligible or comprehensible.

সুব্যক্ত *a.* clearly expressed; perfectly manifest.

সুব্যবস্থা *n.* good arrangement or management; good settlement; good provision. ~**যুক্ত** *a.* having good arrangement, with good arrangement.

সুব্রত *a.* one with a good vow; one who observes a vow religiously.

সুভক্ষ্য *a.* good to eat; (of food) pleasing to the palate, tasteful, fit for eating.

সুভগ *a.* fortunate; happy.

সুভদ্র *a.* very well-mannered.

সুভাষ *a.* one who speaks pleasantly. *fem.* **সুভাষিণী**।

সুভাষিত *a.* quite nicely or intelligibly or lucidly spoken. ☐ *n.* same as **সুবচন**।

সুভিক্ষ *a.* full of plentiful food.

সুমতি same as **সুবুদ্ধি। তোমার সুমতি হোক** may you come back to your senses, may good sense dawn on you.

সুমধুর *a.* very sweet or delicious; very melodious or dulcet; very pleasant.

সুমধ্যমা *a. fem.* having a delicately slender waist.

সুমনা *a.* wise; learned; large-hearted.

সুমন্ত্রণা *n.* good counsel or advice.

সুমন্দ *a.* sweet and slow (সুমন্দ গতি); sweetly and mildly blowing (সুমন্দ বায়ু).

সুমহান *a.* very great and noble; very magnificent; high-minded.

সুমার rej. spell. of **শুমার**।

সুমিষ্ট same as **সুমধুর**।

সুমীমাংসা *n.* a good or wise or correct or happy decision or settlement.

সুমীমাংসিত *a.* nicely or wisely or correctly or happily decided or settled.

সুমুখ coll. corrup. of **সম্মুখ**।

সুমেধা *a.* highly talented or intelligent.

সুমেরু *n.* a mythological mountain; the North Pole. **~প্রভা** *n.* Aurora Borealis. **~বৃত্ত** *n.* the Arctic Circle.

সুযুক্তি *n.* good counsel and advice; good reasoning or argument.

সুযোগ *n.* a favourable or convenient time, an opportunity; a chance. **সুযোগের প্রতীক্ষা করা** *v.* to bide one's opportunity or time. **~সন্ধানী** *a.* seeking an opportunity; opportunist. ☐ *n.* an opportunist.

সুযোগ্য *a.* quite or very worthy or competent or deserving.

সুয়ো *a. fem.* fortunate; dearly loved by one's husband.

সুর[১] *n.* voice; (mus.) tone, note, pitch, a strain, key. **সুর করা** *v.* to tune (as a musical instrument); to tune up; to set to music (গানে সুর করা); (often dero.) to modulate voice as in singing (সুর করে পড়া). **সুর দেওয়া** *v.* to set to music. **সুর বদলানো** *v.* to change the tune of (a musical instrument); to pass to another tune or pitch in singing; (fig.) to change one's tune, to sing to another tune; (fig.) to retract one's word. **সুর বাঁধা** *v.* to tune up; to adjust the strings etc. (of a musical instrument) to the right pitch. **সুর ভাঁজা** *v.* to hum a note or strain or tune. **~জ্ঞান, ~বোধ** *n.* ability to appreciate musical pitch. **~বোধহীন** *a.* tonedeaf. **~বাহার** *n.* a stringed musical instrument akin to the vina (**বীণা**). **~শিল্পী** *n.* versed in the art of music; an artiste. **~স্রষ্টা** *n.* a composer.

সুর[২] *n.* a god, a deity; the sun. **~কন্যা** *n.* a daughter of a god; a celestial female. **~গুরু** *n.* Brihaspati (বৃহস্পতি) the preceptor of gods. **~ধুনি, ~নদী** *n.* the Ganges as flowing in heaven under the name of **মন্দাকিনী**। **~পতি** same as **সুরেন্দ্র**। **~পুর, ~পুরী, ~লোক** *n.* the abode of gods. **~বালা** same as **সুরকন্যা**। **~রিপু** *n.* the enemy of gods; the demon. **~সুন্দরী** same as **সুরাঙ্গনা**।

সুরকি *n.* brick-dust.

সুরক্ষিত *a.* well-protected, well-guarded; well defended; well-preserved. *fem.* **সুরক্ষিতা**।

সুরঙ্গ, সুড়ঙ্গ *n.* a tunnel; a hole (as one made into a house by a burglar).

সুরত[১] *n.* sexual intercourse. **সুরতি** same as **সুরত**।

সুরত[২] *n.* appearance, form, shape; a means, an expedient. **~হাল** *n.* circumstance; condition; (law) a deposition; (pop.) an on-the-spot investigation.

সুরব *n.* a sweet or melodious noise or note or voice.

সুরবল্লী *n.* an astringent herb.

সুরভি[১] *n.* the name of the celestial wishing cow.

সুরভি[২] *n.* a sweet-smell, fragrance; an aroma; any substance made or used for the sake of its smell; a perfume. ☐ *a.* sweet-smelling, fragrant, armoatic; perfumed.

সুরভিত same as **সুবাসিত**।

সুরভী, সুরমা alt. spellings of **সুরভি**[২] and **সুর্মা**।

সুরম্য *a.* very pleasant or beautiful or magnificent (সুরম্য স্থান বা প্রাসাদ).

সুরসিক *a.* highly endowed with appreciative power; very witty; very humorous or jocose.

সুরা *n.* wine; alcohol; spirits. **~পাত্র** *n.* a decanter; a wine cup, a wine-glass. **সুরা পান করা** *v.* to drink wine, to drink; to tipple; to booze. **~পানাভ্যাস** *n.* drinking-habit **~পানোন্মত্ত** *a.* Sottish, besotted; drunk; drunken, boozed up, the worse for liquor. **~পানোন্মত্ততা** *n.* sottishness, besottedness, drunkenness. **~পায়ী** *a.* addicted to drinking, tipsy, bacchant; boozy. ☐ *n.* a drunkard, a bacchant; a tippler. **~রঞ্জিত** *a.* (of eyes) reddened on account of drinking. **~সার** *n.* alcohol. **নির্জল সুরাসার** absolute or pure alcohol. **বিশুদ্ধ** বা **শোভিত সুরাসার** rectified spirit.

সুরাঙ্গনা *n.* a heavenly courtesan.

সুরাসুর *n. pl.* gods and demons.

সুরাহা *n.* solution (সমস্যার সুরাহা) ; a good or adequate remedy (বিপদের সুরাহা) ; good arrangement or provision; an opportunity. **সুরাহা করা** *v.* to solve; to remedy; to make good arrangement or provision for; to provide for; to devise a good expedient or means.

সুরুক older var. of **সুলুক**।

সুরুচি *n.* good or refined taste, fine taste. **~সম্পন্ন** *a.* of refined taste or culture, of fine taste.

সুরুয়া rej. spell. of **শুরুয়া**।

সুরূপ *a.* handsome, beautiful; good-looking. *fem.* **সুরূপা**।

সুরেন্দ্র *n.* Indra (ইন্দ্র) the king of gods.

সুরেলা *a.* melodious, dulcet, musical.

সুরেশ্বর *n.* the lord of gods; Shiva (শিব) or Indra (ইন্দ্র). **সুরেশ্বরী** *n. fem.* Goddess Durga (দুর্গা) or Goddess Ganges (গঙ্গা).

সুর্তি[1] *n.* a lottery; a raffle. **~খেলা** *v.* to play at lottery; to have a game of lottery; to cast lots.

সুর্তি[2] *n.* a preparation of powdered tobacco taken with betal-leaves.

সুর্মা *n.* sulphate of antimony used as collyrium, kohl.

সুলক্ষণ *a.* bearing good or auspicious marks on one's person; having good or auspicious signs (সুলক্ষণ কাল). ☐ *n.* a good or auspicious mark or sign. *fem. a.* **সুলক্ষণা**। **সুলক্ষণাক্রান্ত** *a.* same as **সুলক্ষণ** (*a.*).

সুলতান *n.* a Muslim ruler, a sultan. *fem.* **সুলতানা** a sultana, a sultaness. **সুলতানি** *n.* sultanate ☐ *a.* sultanic.

সুলভ, সুলভ্য *a.* easily obtainable or available; cheap. **সুলভে** *adv.* cheaply.

সুললিত *a.* delicately soft or flexible; very pleasant or sweet or melodious or dulcet or musical.

সুলিখিত *a.* well-written; pleasant to read, perspicuous.

সুলুক *n.* a hole; a clue; secrets; (loos.) a weak point, a fault. **~সন্ধান** *n.* secrets; faults; clues; weak points.

সুলুপ *n.* a light boat, a sloop; a sloop-of-war.

সুলেখক *n.* a good writer or author, a writer remarkable for perspicuity. *fem.* **সুলেখিকা**।

সুলোচন *a.* having beautiful or fine eyes. *fem.* **সুলোচনা**।

সুশাসক *n.* a good or wise ruler.

সুশাসন *n.* good or wise government or rule.

সুশাসিত *a.* well-governed, wisely governed or ruled; well-controlled; well-restrained; well-disciplined.

সুশিক্ষা *n.* good or salutary education or training or advice.

সুশিক্ষিত *a.* well-educated; well-trained; well-advised.

সুশীতল *a.* very cool; very cold; very pleasant and cool.

সুশীল *a.* good-natured; well-behaved; having a good character; gentle. *fem.* **সুশীলা**।

সুশৃঙ্খল *a.* arranged or managed or controlled in an orderly fashion; orderly. **~ভাবে** *adv.* in good order, in an orderly manner. **সুশৃঙ্খলা** *n.* orderly arrangement or management or control; orderliness, order.

সুশোভন *a.* very beautiful or well-decorated or well-bedecked.

সুশোভিত *a.* very beautifully decorated or adorned or bedecked.

সুশ্রাব্য *a.* pleasing to the ear; sweet; melodious.

সুশ্রী *a.* of beautiful appearance, handsome, beautiful, comely, pretty.

সুষনি, সুসনি *n.* an edible aquatic spinach.

সুষম *a.* well-proportioned; well-balanced, balanced; beautiful. **সুষম খাদ্য** balanced diet.

সুষমা *n. fem.* sweet grace or beauty; any pleasing quality.

সুষির alt. spell. of **শুষির**।

সুষুপ্ত *a.* sleeping soundly, fast asleep.

সুষুপ্তি *n.* sound sleep.

সুষুম্না *n.* (Hindu med.) the middle one of the three arteries that pulsate at the wrist. **সুষুম্না কাণ্ড** *n.* the spinal cord.

সুষ্ঠু *a.* very nice; immaculate; smooth (সুষ্ঠু কাজ.)

সুসংবাদ *n.* a good news.

সুসংস্কৃত *a.* thoroughly repaired or rectified; well-refined; well-arranged; well-dressed; put on or worn in an orderly fashion; very refined and civil or polite.

সুসংহত *a.* well-integrated; well-assembled; compact.

সুসজ্জ, সুসজ্জিত *a.* well-dressed, well-equipped; well-decorated; well-furnished (সুসজ্জিত গৃহ).

সুসন্তান *n.* a worthy or good child.

সুসভ্য *a.* adequately or greatly civilized or refined.

সুসময় *n.* favourable or prosperous times, good days; a favourable or suitable moment.

সুসমাচার *n.* a good news; (Christ.) Gospel (মথিলিখিত সুসমাচার = the Gospel of St. Matthews.)

সুসম্পন্ন *a.* well-performed, well-executed. **সুসম্পন্ন করা** *v.* to perform or execute nicely or thoroughly.

সুসহ *a.* easy to bear or endure, tolerable.

সুসাধ্য *a.* easy to do or perform or execute or accomplish.

সুসার *n.* abundance, plenty; sufficiency, financial ease; ease.

সুস্থ *a.* sound of body, hale, healthy, free from disease (সুস্থ) ; in normal state, unperturbed, untroubled, calm, peaceful (সুস্থ মন, সুস্থ জীবন). **সুস্থ করা** *v.* to bring round; to cure; to bring to the normal state. **সুস্থ হওয়া** *v.* to come round; to recover; to get back to the normal state. **~দেহ, ~দেহী** *a.* sound of body, healthy, hale. **~চিত্ত** *a.* enjoying mental peace; sane; possessing mental equipoise. **~তা** *n.* soundness of body, healthiness; freedom from disease. **সুস্থ শরীরে** *adv.* in sound or good health, healthily.

সুস্থিত *a.* well-off; well-conditioned; well-placed or well-established (in life); (mech.) stable; enjoying mental equilibrium. **সুস্থিতি** *n.* equilibrium.

সুস্থির *a.* perfectly calm or composed; perfectly brought round; fully soothed; very steady; firmly settled or fixed or ascertained.

সুস্পষ্ট *a.* very clear, evident, explicit; thoroughly exposed or revealed, manifest; quite distinct. **~ভাবে** *adv.* very clearly; in unmistakable terms.

সুস্বন *n.* a sweet sound or note or melody.

সুস্বপ্ন *n.* a happy dream, a pleasant dream.

সুস্বর *n.* a sweet voice. ☐ *a.* sweet-voiced; melodious.

সুস্বাদ *n.* a pleasant or delicious taste (of food). ☐ *a.* very tasteful, delicious. **সুস্বাদু** *a.* same as **সুস্বাদ** (*a.*).

সুহাস *a.* pleasantly or charmingly smiling. *fem.* **সুহাসিনী**।

সুহৃদ, সুহৃৎ *n.* a friend; an ally; a well-wisher.

সুহৃদ্বর *n.* an excellent friend or ally or well-wisher.

সূক্ত *n.* any on of the complete Vedic incantations or verses or hymns or psalms; a wise or salutary saying, an apopthegm. **সূক্তি** *n.* a wise or salutary saying, an apopthegm.

সূক্ষ্ম *a.* fine; thin; narrow; acute; low-pitched, low; sharp, keen; pointed; accuminate; minutely scrutinizing, minute, hair-splitting; quite right or appropriate, just; subtle; delicately sensitive or susceptible, delicate; impalpable by senses; astral. **~কোণ** *n.* (geom.) an acute angle. **~কোণী** *a.* acute-angled. **~গ্রাহী** *a.* delicately sensitive or susceptible; delicate (সূক্ষ্মগ্রাহী যন্ত্র). **~তা** *n.* fineness; thinness; narrowness; lowness; sharpness, keenness;

pointedness; acuminateness; minuteness of scrutiny, minuteness; perfect appropriateness of justice; subtlety; delicate sensitiveness or susceptibility; delicateness; imperceptibility (by the senses); state of being astral. ~দর্শিতা *n.* keen-sightedness; insight; keen discernment; sagacity; minute and equitable judgment; scrutiny. ~দর্শী *a.* keen-sighted; endowed with insight or keen discernment; sagacious; judging minutely and with perfect equity; scrutinizing. *fem.* ~দর্শিনী। ~দৃষ্টি *n.* keen sight; insight; keen discernment; sagacity; minute and equitable judgement; scrutiny. ~দেহ *n.* a body not perceptible by senses; an astral body; (loos.) a ghost. ~দেহী *a.* having a body not perceptible by senses; having an astral body; (bio.) infusorial. **সূক্ষ্মদেহী জীবাণু** (bio.) *n.* an infusoria. ~বস্ত্র *n.* fine cloth. **অতি সূক্ষ্ম বস্ত্র** superfine cloth. ~বিচার *n.* minute and equitable judgment; hair-splitting scrutiny; fine discretion. ~বুদ্ধি *n.* keen intelligence; intellectual acumen. ☐ *a.* keenly intelligent. ~মান *n.* (geom.) close approximation. ~শরীর *n.* an astral body. **সূক্ষ্মাগ্র** *a.* sharp-pointed, acuminate. **সূক্ষ্মাতিসূক্ষ্ম** *a.* extremely fine or thin or keen or pointed or acuminate or scrutinizing or minute or subtle or delicate or impalpable, hairsplitting; (bio.) infusorial.

সূচক *a.* (chiefly used as *sfx.*) introducing; commencing; indicating, expressing; presaging; foreboding, ☐ *n.* (alg.) an index (*pl.* indices). **সূচক সংখ্যা** *n.* index number. ~সূত্র *n* (alg.) an exponential theorem.

সূচনা *n.* introduction; an introduction, a preface, a preamble; commencement; start, inception; indication, expression; presaging; a presage; foreboding. **সূচনা করা** *v.* to introduce, to make an introduction, to preface; to commence, to start; to indicate; to presage or forebode. **সূচিত** *a.* indicated; signified; implied.

সূচি, সূচী, সূচিকা *n.* a needle; an awl; an indicator (as of a measuring instrument or clock); a list, an inventory, a catalogue; a table of contents. **সূচিকর্ম, সূচিশিল্প** *n.* needlework; embroidery; (rare) tailoring. **সূচিজীবী** *n.* a tailor. **সূচিনিবন্ধ** *n.* index register. **সূচিপত্র** *n.* a table of contents, an index. **সূচিভেদ্য** *a.* capable of being pierced or perforated only with a needle; very compact, dense (সূচিভেদ্য অন্ধকার). **সূচিমুখ** *a.* having a point as thin and sharp as that of a needle, pin-pointed; acuminate.

সূচিকাভরণ *n.* a medicine in Ayurvedic pharmacopoea containing a minute quantity of snake-poison.

সূচ্যগ্র *n.* the point of a needle. ☐ *a.* not exceeding the point of a needle in thickness, magnitude, spaciousness etc.; an iota of ('সূচ্যগ্র মেদিনী'). ~পরিমাণ, ~পরিমিত *a.* same as **সূচ্যগ্র** (*a.*).

সূত *n.* an ancient Vaishya (বৈশ্য) community; a member of this community; an official singer of songs in praise of a prince, nobleman etc.; the Hindu community of carpenters; a carpenter.

সূতা rej. spell. of **সুতা**[2] ।

সূতিকা *n.* a woman recently delivered of a child; puerperal diarrhoea. ~গার, ~গৃহ *n.* a lying-in room. **জ্বর** *n.* puerperal fever.

সূত্র *n.* thread; yarn; fibre; a string; connection, a link (কর্মসূত্র) ; a tie, a bond (পরিণয়সূত্র) ; a series, a chain (চিন্তাসূত্র) ; a clue or trail (সন্ধানসূত্র) ; a brief hint or point (সমাধানের সূত্র) ; an aphorism (বেদান্তসূত্র) ; a rule, a law (ব্যাকরণের সূত্র) ; a summary introduction of a subject-matter, an argument; (of dramas etc.) a prologue; introduction, commencement, beginning; (alg.) a formula (*pl.* formulae, formulas). ~কার *n.* an aphoriser, an aphorist. ~কৃমি *n.* a thread-worm; (erron.) Ascaris. ~ধার *n.* a carpenter; a joiner; (in dramas) the chief actor who recites the prologue; (erron.—in a stage-play) a prompter. ~পাত *n.* commencement, beginning, start, inception. **সূত্রপাত করা বা হওয়া** *v.* to commence, to begin.

সূত্রাকার *a.* filiform.

সূদন *a.* (use as a *sfx.*) killing or slaying (মধুসূদন).

সূপ *n.* curry, soup; a curry of pigeon-pea. **~কার** *n.* a cook.

সূর *n.* the sun, the Sun-god, (cp.) Sol.

সূরি, সূরী *n.* a poet; a learned man, a scholar; a wise man.

সূর্প alt. spell. of **শূর্প**।

সূর্য *n.* the sun; the Sun-god. (cp.) Sol. **~কর, ~কিরণ** *n.* sunbeam; sunlight, sunshine. **~করোজ্জ্বল** *a.* sunbeamed, sunbeamy, sunshiny; sunny. **~কান্ত, ~কান্তমণি** *n.* flint-glass, burning-glass, cat's eye, aventurine felspar, sunstone. **~কেন্দ্রীয়** *a.* heliocentric. **~গ্রহণ** *n.* the solar eclipse. **~ঘড়ি** *n.* a sundial, a solarium. **~তেজ** *n.* the heat of the sun. **~পূজক** *n.* a heliolater, a sun-worshipper. **~পূজা** *n.* sun-worship, heliolatry. **~বংশ** *n.* an ancient dynasty descended from King Surya or from the Sun-god, the Surya dynasty. **~বংশধর** *n.* a descendant of the Surya dynasty. **~বংশীয়** *a* of the Surya dynasty. **~মুখী** *n.* the sunflower. **~রশ্মি** same as **সূর্যকর**। **~সারথি** *n.* (myth.) Aruna (অরুণ) the charioteer of the Sun-god. **~সিদ্ধান্ত** *n.* a Hindu treatise on astronomy. **সূর্যাবর্ত** *n.* the solar rotation; the rotation of the sun. **সূর্যাবর্তী** *a.* heliotropic. **সূর্যাবৃত্তি** *n.* heliotropism. **সূর্যালোক** *n.* sunlight; sunshine. **সূর্যাস্ত** *n.* sunset, sundown. **সূর্যাস্তকালে** *adv.* at sunset, at sundown. **সূর্যোদয়** *n.* sunrise. **সূর্যোদয়কালে** *adv.* at sunrise. **সূর্যোপাসক** same as **সূর্যপূজক**। **সূর্যোপাসনা** same as **সূর্যপূজা**।

সৃক্বণী *n.* the margin of lips, the corner of the mouth or of lips.

সৃজন *n.* creation; production, formation; designing; institution. **সৃজন করা** *v.* to create; to bring into existence; to make or produce or form; to design; to institute. **~কর্তা** *n.* a creator; a maker; a producer; a designer. *fem.* **~কর্ত্রী**। **সৃজনী** *a.* creative. **সৃজনীশক্তি** *n.* creative power or faculty.

সৃজা poet. form of **সৃজন করা**।

সৃজিত, সৃষ্ট *a.* created; made, produced, formed; designed; instituted. **সৃষ্টি** *n.* creation; making; production; designing; instituting; institution; a creation, a production; something made or instituted; the universe. **সৃষ্টি করা** same as **সৃজন করা**। **সৃষ্টিকর্তা** *n.* creator, maker; God. **সৃষ্টিকার্য** *n.* the work of creation, creation; the creation of the universe. **সৃষ্টিকৌশল, সৃষ্টিচাতুর্য** *n.* the art or the wonderful art of creation; the manner or method of creation. **সৃষ্টিক্ষমতা** *n.* the creative power or faculty. **সৃষ্টিছাড়া** *a.* not available anywhere in God's creation; unusual; bizarre, odd, outlandish, grotesque; eccentric; vagarish. **সৃষ্টিতত্ত্ব** *n.* cosmogony; cosmology. **সৃষ্টিনাশ করা** *v.* to destroy or dissolve the universe; to undo everything. **সৃষ্টিনাশা** *a.* (rare) causing universal dissolution; (pop.) undoing everything. **সৃষ্টিনৈপুণ্য** *n.* skill or deftness in creation or making. **সৃষ্টিবাদ** *n.* the doctrine of creation; cosmogony. **সৃষ্টিবৈচিত্র্য** *n.* (wonderful) diversity of the creation. **সৃষ্টিরক্ষা করা** *v.* to protect or preserve (and maintain) the world created by God. **সৃষ্টিলোপ করা** same as **সৃষ্টিনাশ করা**। **সৃষ্টিস্থিতিলয়** *n.* creation, preservation and dissolution (esp. of the universe).

সে *pro.* (*masc.*) he; (*fem.*) she, (*neut.*) it. □ *a.* that (সে লোক, সেদিন) ; past or ancient (সেকাল).

সেই *a.* that; that very. □ *pro.* that person or thing, that; that time. □ *adv.* after all (সেই তো মল খসালি) ; long ago (সেই গেলে). □ *con.* no sooner than, as, so (যেই এল, সেই গেল). **সেইখান, সেইজন** same as **সেখান, সেজন. সেই থেকে** from that time, thenceforth; from that (thing).

সেঁউতি[1] *n.* a bailing bucket or vessel, a bail, a bale.

সেঁওতি, সেঁউতি[2] *n.* a kind of indigenous white rose.

সেঁকো, সেঁকোবিষ *n.* arsenic.

সেঁজুতি *n.* an evening-lamp; a vesper-lamp.

সেঁতসেঁত, সেঁতসেঁতে alt. spellings of **স্যাঁতস্যাঁত** and **স্যাঁতসেঁতে** respectively.

সেঁধানো *v.* to enter, to go into; to cause to enter; to drive into.

সেক *n.* fomentation. **সেক দেওয়া** *v.* to foment.

সেকরা alt. spell. of **স্যাকরা** ।

সেকা *v.* to warm slowly in heat (আগুনে হাত সেকা) ; to bake (রুটি সেকা). □ *a.* baked.

সেকাল *n.* ancient times, the days of yore; past or bygone days, the past. **সেকাল ও একাল** the past and the present.

সেকেন্ড, সেকেনড *n.* a second (=$^1/_{60}$ minute). □ *a.* second. **সেকেন্ড হওয়া** *v.* to stand second. **এক সেকেন্ডে** in a second; in a trice.

সেকেন্দর, সেকেন্দার *n.* Alexander the Conqueror. **সেকেন্দরি, সেকেন্দারি** *a.* of King Secunder Sha. **সেকেন্দারি গজ** a lineal measure in which 1 yard is equal to 38 inches.

সেকেলে *a.* of ancient times; of the past; ancient; old; antiquated; old-fashioned; out of date; backdated. **সেকেলে লোক বা বস্তু** a back number.

সেখ erron. spell. of **শেখ** ।

সেখান *n.* that place. **সেখান থেকে** from that place, from there. **~কার** *a.* of that place. **সেখানে** *adv.* at or in or to that place, there.

সেগুন *n.* the teak; teak-wood.

সেচ, সেচন *n.* spraying or sprinkling or watering or baling; irrigation. **সেচন করা** *v.* same as **সেচা** (*v.*). **সেচকর** *n.* irrigation tax or cess. **সেচন-কৃত্যক** *n.* the Irrigation Service. **সেচনযন্ত্র** *n.* a sprinkling apparatus, a spray. **সেচনী** *n.* a spray, a sprinkling apparatus; a watering can; a bailing bucket or vessel, a bail, a bale. **সেচবিভাগ** *n.* the Irrigation Department. **সেচমন্ত্রক** *n.* the Ministry of Irrigation. **সেচমন্ত্রী** *n.* the Minister of Irrigation.

সেচা *v.* to spray or sprinkle; to water; to bail or bale out; to bail out water (partly or completely); to lift a small quantity from the bottom (সেচে তোলা) ; to dredge.

সেজ[1] *n.* a bed.

সেজ[2], সেজো *a.* third in order of birth, third-born (সেজো ভাই) ; third in order of seniority (সেজো সাহেব, সেজদা).

সেজন, (dial) **সেজনা** *n.* that person ; the Supreme Being, God.

সেজা, সেজানো, সেঝা, সেঝানো corruptions of **সিজা, সিজানো, সিঝা** and **সিঝানো** ।

সেট[1] *n.* a set (এক সেট বই) ; a suit (এক সেট পোশাক বা গয়না).

সেট[2] *a.* fixed in position or in required condition, set. **সেট করা** *v.* to set (বিভিন্ন অংশ সেট করা) ; to put something into proper position (হাত সেট করা).

সেতখানা *n.* a latrine, a lavatory.

সেতার *n.* a three-stringed (sometimes five-stringed with three additional strings in larger instruments) musical instrument. **~বাদক, সেতারি** *n.* one who plays the aforesaid musical instrument.

সেতু *n.* a bridge; a culvert; a causeway; a dam. **সেতু বাঁধা** *v.* to build a bridge (over); to bridge, to span. **~বন্ধ** *n.* a ridge of rocks extending from the southern extremity of India towards Sri Lanka, Adam's Bridge. **~মুখ** *n.* a bridgehead.

সেথা, সেথায় poet. or dial. variants of **সেখানে** ।

সেথো *n.* a traveller's professional companion and guide. **~গিরি** *n.* act of accompanying or guiding a traveller professionally.

সেনা *n.* an army, armed forces; a troop of soldiers; a soldier. **পশ্চাদ্‌বর্তী সেনা** the rear party of an army, the second echelon. **পুরোবর্তী সেনা** the advance party of an army, the vanguard; the advance guard. **সেনাধিকারিক** *n.* an army officer, a military officer. **~ধ্যক্ষ, ~নায়ক** *n.* an army commander, a general; the commander of a troop. **~নিবাস** *n.* army quarters, barracks; a cantonment; (loos.) a garrison. **সেনানিবেশ করা** *v* . to array or station soldiers esp. for a battle. **~নী** *n.* an army commander, a general; (pop.) the army; the soldiers. **~পতি** *n.* the commander-in-chief, an army commander, a general; the commander of a troop. **প্রধান সেনাপতি** the commander-in-chief. **~পতিত্ব** *n.* office of the commander-in-chief; generalship; command. **~পতিত্বে** *adv.* under one's command. **~বাস** same as

সেনানিবাস। ~ভঙ্গ *n.* a stampede, a debacle; defeat or retreat of an army. ~শিবির *n.* an army encampment; a cantonment.

সেপাই dial. corrup. of **সিপাই**।

সেপটেমবর, সেপ্টেম্বর *n.* September.

সেবক *a.* serving, waiting upon; nursing; worshipping, following. ☐ *n.* a servant, an attendant; a waiter (*fem.* waitress); a sick-nurse, a nurse; a worshipper, a votary; a follower. **~সমিতি** *n.* organization of social workers. **সেবকাধম** *n.* the humblest of servants.

সেবন *n.* eating or drinking or smoking (ঔষধসেবন, মদ্যসেবন, গঞ্জিকাসেবন) ; act of having or enjoying (বায়ুসেবন) ; worship, serving, waiting upon; nursing. **সেবন করা** *v.* to eat or drink or smoke, to have or enjoy, to take. **সেবনীয়** *a.* same as **সেব্য**।

সেবা *n.* serving, waiting upon; nursing; worship; eating or drinking or smoking or enjoying; (dial.) obeisance, salutation. ☐ *v.* poet. form of **সেবা করা**। **সেবা করা** *v.* to serve, to wait upon; to nurse; to worship; to eat or drink or smoke or have or enjoy; to take. **~ইত** *n.* a priest and beneficiary of a temple or a religious institution; a worshipper, a votary. **~দাসী** *n. fem.* a maiden dedicated to the service of a temple or a deity, (cp.) a nun; a woman who (usu. under a vow) serves an ascetic or a Vaishnava devotee or the head of a religious institution; (sarcas.) a concubine. **~ধর্ম** *n.* social service looked upon as a religion, the sacred task of serving others. **~য়ত, ~য়েত** variants of **সেবাইত**।

সেবিকা *fem.* of **সেবক**।

সেবিত *a.* served, waited upon; nursed; worshipped; eaten or drunk or smoked or enjoyed.

সেবী *a.* (used as a *sfx.*) one who serves or waits upon or nurses or worships; one who eats or drinks or smokes, addicted or habituated to; one who enjoys.

সেব্য *a.* to be eaten or drunk or smoked or enjoyed; worthy of being worshipped or served or nursed.

সেমই *n.* vermicelli.

সেমত, সেমতি *adv.* & *a.* (poet.) like that.

সেমুই var. of **সেমই**।

সেয়ান, সেয়ানা *a.* sly, shrewd; clever; feigning; of age, adult (মেয়ে সেয়ানা হয়েছে). **সেয়ানা পাগল** one feigning madness; one who has a method in one's madness. **সেয়ানে সেয়ানে কোলাকুলি** (fig.) diamond cuts diamond.

সের *n.* an obsolete Indian measure of weight (১/৪০ মন), a seer. **~কিয়া** *n.* the table of counting by seers. **~কে** *adv.* in each seer; for each seer.

সেরকশ *a.* obstinate, refractory.

সেরকিয়া, সেরকে see **সের**।

সেরা[১] *a.* best; excellent.

সেরা[২], **সেরি** *a.* (used as suffixes) weighing and holding or consuming a specific number of seers (সের).

সেরূপ *a.* of that form or kind. **সেরূপে** *adv.* in that manner or way.

সেরেফ *a* & *adv.* only; alone; mere or merely.

সেরেস্তা *n.* an office; a record-office. **~দার** *n.* an office superintendent; a headclerk, a chief clerk; a record-keeper.

সেলাই *n* sewing; seaming; a stitch or seam. **সেলাই করা** *v.* to sew; to seam; to stitch. **~কল** *n.* a sewing machine. **সেলাই খোলা** *v.* to unsew, to unstitch; to get unsewn. **সেলাইয়ের ফোঁড়** a stitch.

সেলাখানা *a.* an armoury, an arsenal.

সেলাম *n.* salutation, obeisance, a salute. **সেলাম করা** *v.* to salute, to make an obeisance; (iron.) to shun by showing feigned reverential awe. **সেলাম আলায়কুম, সেলাম আলেকুম** *int.* (Mus.) I salute you. **সেলামি** *n.* an irregular fee or present given to an owner, landlord, employer, boss etc. as a mark of obeisance (জমিদারের সেলামি) ; an illegal extra payment made to obtain something (বাড়িভাড়ার সেলামি).

সেলুন *n.* a barber's shop, a hair dresser's shop; a luxurious railway carriage or motor car used by dignitaries.

সেলেখানা, সেলেট variants of **সেলাখানা** and **স্লেট** respectively.

সেশন *n*. a session (কলেজের সেশন) ; (in law) sessions. **সেশনে পাঠানো** *v*. to commit to or send up to the sessions. **সেশন জজ** *n*. a sessions-judge.

সেহা *n*. entry showing payment of rent in a landlord's book. **সেহা করা** *v*. to enter or record rent-receipt.

সেহেতু *conj*. for that reason, that is why, because of that.

সৈকত *n*. the sandy beach of a sea, gulf, river etc.; sea-shore or beach.

সৈনাপত্য *n*. generalship, commandership; command (তাঁর সৈনাপত্যে দেশ জিতেছে).

সৈনিক *n*. a soldier; a fighter; an armed guard, a sentinel. **~জীবন** *n*. the life of a soldier; army life, military life. **~বৃত্তি** *n*. the profession of a soldier, military profession, soldiership. **সৈনিকবৃত্তি অবলম্বন করা** *v*. to become a soldier. **সৈনিকোচিত** *a*. soldier-like, soldierly, befitting a soldier.

সৈন্ধব *a*. marine; of or grown in sind or the Indus. □ *n*. sea-salt; marine salt; (loos.) rock-salt. **সৈন্ধব লবণ** same as **সৈন্ধব** (*n*.)

সৈন্য *n*. a soldier; an army; armed forces. **স্থায়ী সৈন্য** a standing army. **সৈন্য পরিচালনা করা** *v*. to command or lead or manoeuvre an army. **সৈন্য সমাবেশ করা** *v*. to station or array or mobilize armed forces. **~দল** *n*. an army; a regiment. **~যোজন** *n*. mobilization of an army. **~সামন্ত** *n*. armed forces and vassals. **সৈন্যাধ্যক্ষ** *n*. a commander of an army, a general; a commander-in-chief. the commander-in-chief. **সহকারী প্রধান সৈন্যাধ্যক্ষ** the second-in-command.

সৈয়দ *n*. a descendant of Imam Hossain, a sayyid, a sayid.

সৈরিন্ধ্রী, সৈরন্ধ্রী *n. fem*. a woman who lives away from her home and earns her livelihood by doing artistic work such as embroidery, hairdressing, etc.

সো *pro*. (poet. & obs.) he, she, it. □ *a*. (poet. & obs.) that.

সোঁ alt. spell. of **শোঁ**।

সোঁটা *n*. a thick stick or staff, a cudgel.

সোঁত vul. corrup. of **স্রোত**। **সোঁতা** *n*. a very thin stream.

সোঁদা *a*. smelling like dry earth wetted with rain-water.

সোঁদাল *n*. a kind of yellow flower or its plant, *Cursia fistula.*

সোচ্চার *a*. clamorous, vociferous.

সোজা *a*. straight, uncurved; lying straight in front of (নাক সোজা) ; lying continually onward; shortest, non-circuitous, direct; honest, upright, virtuous, free from angularities, simple; easy; unequivocal, plain (সোজা কথা) ; chastened or coerced (মারের চোটে সোজা). □ *adv*. straight ahead, continuously onward. **সোজা করা** *v*. to straighten; to chasten or coerce. **~সুজি** *adv*. by the straight or shortest route; straightly, straightway; diagonally; unequivocally, plainly, categorically, outspokenly.

সোডা *n*. soda; sodium carbonate; sodium bicarbonate; washing soda. **~ওয়াটার** *n*. soda-water; mineral water. **সোডা ওয়াটারের দোকান** *n*. a soda-fountain, a spa.

সোত var. of **সোঁত**।

সোৎকণ্ঠ *a*. anxious; eager.

সোৎসাহ *a*. zealous, ardent, enthusiastic. **সোৎসাহে** *adv*. zealously, ardently, with enthusiasm.

সোদর corrup. of **সহোদর**।

সোনা *n*. gold; a gold ornament; (in endearment) a precious treasure ('খোকা মোদের সোনা'). □ *a*. gold-coloured, golden, yellow; sweet, gentle-natured, brilliant (সোনা ছেলে). **কাঁচা সোনা, পাকা সোনা** unalloyed or pure gold. **কেলে সোনা** (in endearment) a dark-complexioned son; Krishna (কৃষ্ণ). **সোনায় সোহাগা** (fig.) a happy match, a most desirable union; (sarcas.) alliance of two vile persons. **সোনার কাঠি রুপোর কাঠি** (in folk-tales) means of keeping alive or killing; means of living or dying, life and death. **সোনার খনি** a gold-mine. **সোনার জল** gold ink; gold paint. **সোনার পাত** a gold-leaf. **সোনার পাথর বাটি** (fig.) an absurdity, a mare's nest. **সোনার বাট** gold bar. **সোনার বেনে** same as **সুবর্ণবণিক**। **সোনার সংসার** a happy and prosperous family. **~দানা** *n*. gold and things made of gold; (loos.) gold ornaments. ~ব্যাং *n.* a species of yellow frog, the golden frog. ~মুখ *n.* a fair and bright face; a happy face. □ *a.* having a fair and bright face. ~মুখ করে with an expression of delight or happiness. ~মুখী *a. fem.* of সোনামুখ। □ *n.* senna, sennapod. ~মুগ *n.* a variety of yellow pigeon-pea. ~লি *a.* gold-coloured, golden; gilded, gold-gilt; (fig.) very bright or happy (সোনালি দিন, সোনালি জীবন). সোনালি চুল golden hair. সোনালি চুলওয়ালা golden-haired. সোনালি চুলওয়ালা লোক a goldilocks. সোনালি জরি gold-thread. সোনালি মাছ a goldfish.

সোপকরণ, সোপচার *a.* with all articles of food and clothing required to be offered in religious worship.

সোপরদ্দ, সোপর্দ *n.* sending up or committing for trial. □ *a.* sent up or committed for trial.

সোপান *n.* a flight of steps, stairs; a staircase; a step; a ladder; an escalator. ~শ্রেণি, সোপানাবলি *n.* a flight of steps, stair.

সোম *n.* the moon; the moongod; Monday; the juice of wormwood. ~বার *n.* Monday. ~রস *n.* a beverage prepared from the juice of সোমলতা. ~রাজ *n.* wormwood. ~লতা *n.* (myth.) a kind of creeper whose growth is governed by the waxing and waning of the moon.

সোমত্ত *a. fem.* of age, grown up; one who has reached the marriageable age or the age of cohabitation.

সোমবার, সোমরস, সোমরাজ, সোমলতা see সোম।

সোয়াদ, সোয়ামি, সোয়ার, সোয়ারি corruptions of স্বাদ, স্বামী, সওয়ার and সওয়ারি respectively.

সোয়াস্তি *n.* (pop.) peace, ease, freedom from anxiety or concern, comfort, allayment.

সোয়েটার *n.* a sweater, a woolen jumper or pullover; a woolen jacket.

সোরগোল, সোরা rej. spellings of শোরগোল and শোরা respectively.

সোরাই *n.* a pitcher with a long and narrow neck, a flagon.

সোলা rej. spell of শোলা।

সোলে *n.* (chiefly in law) compromise. সোলে করা *v.* to compromise. ~নামা *n.* a deed of compromise.

সোসর *a.* (obs.) equal, like; equal in power or strength.

সোহম্‌, (pop.) সোহং I am He. সোহংবাদ *n.* the philosophical doctrine that identifies God with the individual soul.

সোহরৎ rej. spell. of শোহরত।

সোহাগ *n.* affection, love; caress, fondling; amorous caress. সোহাগ করা *v.* to treat with affection, to love; to caress, to fondle; to caress amorously. সোহাগি, সোহাগিনি *a. fem.* enjoying love of; beloved.

সোহাগা *n.* borax.

সোহিনী alt. spell. of শোহিনি।

সৌকর্য *n.* easiness or facility in doing or performing.

সৌকুমার্য *n.* great softness or tenderness; attractive youth or youngness; great beauty or grace.

সৌখিন rej. spell. of শৌখিন।

সৌগন্ধ, সৌগন্ধ্য *n.* a sweet smell, fragrance, aroma, perfume. সৌগন্ধিক *n.* a maker or seller of perfumes, a perfumer.

সৌজন্য *n.* courtesy, civility, good manners; (loos.) cordiality. সৌজন্য সাক্ষাৎ a courtesy meeting; a courtesy visit.

সৌদামিনী, (rare) সৌদামনী *n.* lightning.

সৌধ *n.* a large building, an edifice, a mansion. ~কিরীটিনী *a. fem.* adorned with numerous large buildings.

সৌন্দর্য *n.* beauty; loveliness; handsomeness; grace, elegance. ~বর্ধক *a.* enhancing or augmenting beauty, adding to charm or grace. ~মণ্ডিত *a.* covered with beauty; highly beautiful. ~শালী, ~সম্পন্ন *a.* beautiful; handsome; graceful. *fem.* ~শালিনী, ~সম্পন্না।

সৌপ্তিক *n.* a night-attack, a night battle.

সৌবীর *n.* an ancient state on the bank of the Indus.

সৌভাগ্য *n.* good luck, good furtune; prosperity. ~ক্রমে *adv.* by good luck, fortunately, luckily. ~বান, ~শালী *a.* fortunate; lucky; prosperous. *fem.* ~বতী, ~শালিনী। ~লক্ষ্মী *n. fem.* the presiding female deity of good fortune; good fortune personified. ~বশত *adv*. same as সৌভাগ্যক্রমে।

সৌভিক *n*. a conjuror, a wizard, an enchanter; magician.

সৌভ্রাত্র *n*. good terms amongst brothers; brotherly love; fraternity.

সৌমিত্র, সৌমিত্রি *n*. a son of Sumitra. (সুমিত্রা).

সৌম্য *a*. mentally calm or placid or balanced; beautiful, majestic, dignified, unruffled. ~দর্শন *a*. having a calm or placid appearance; good-looking, handsome; dignified, majestic; unruffled. ~ভাব *n*. mental calm or equilibrium; placidity. ~মূর্তি *a*. same as সৌম্যদর্শন। □ *n*. a calm or placid or unruffled appearance; a handsome figure.

সৌর *a*. solar; heliolatrous. ~কর *n*. a sunray; sunlight, sunshine. ~কলঙ্ক *n*. a sunspot. ~কাল *n*. solar time. ~জগৎ *a*. the solar region, the solar sphere, the solar system. ~দিন, ~দিবস *n*. (astr.) a solar day. ~বৎসর, ~বর্ষ *n*. (astr.) an astronomical or equinoctial or natural year, a solar year. ~বর্ণালি *n*. a solar spectrum. ~মণ্ডল same as সৌরজগৎ। ~মাস *n*. (astr.) a solar month.

সৌরভ *n*. a sweet smell or odour, fragrance, aroma.

সৌষ্ঠব *n*. beauty; decorum; grace; decoration; excellency; smoothness (কাজের সৌষ্ঠব) ; beautiful symmetry or shapeliness (অঙ্গসৌষ্ঠব).

সৌসাদৃশ্য *n*. nice or immaculate or close resemblance or similarity.

সৌহার্দ, সৌহার্দ্য, সৌহৃদ্য *n*. friendship; amity; fellow-feeling; cordiality. সৌহার্দপাশ, সৌহার্দবন্ধন *n*. tie or bond of friendship.

স্কন্দ *n*. Kartikeya (কার্তিকেয়).

স্কন্ধ *n*. the shoulder; (of a beast) neck; the trunk of the human body; a tree-trunk, a trunk; a section of a book, a chapter, a canto; an instalment; a part or division of an army. ~কাটা *a*. one with the head cut off; headless. □ *n*. a headless ghost. স্কন্ধে করা বা নেওয়া, স্কন্ধে বহন করা *v*. to take up upon one's shoulders; to carry upon one's shoulders; to shoulder. ~দেশ *n*. the region of the shoulder or (in case of a beast) the neck, shoulders.

স্কুটার *n*. a scooter.

স্কুল *n*. a school. স্কুল পালানো *v*. to play truant, to truant, to run away from school; to mooch. স্কুলে যাওয়া *v*. (in case of a student) to go to school; (in case of anybody who is not a student) to go to the school. স্কুলের ছুটি a school holiday. স্কুলের শিক্ষা school education. স্কুলের সময় school hours.

স্ক্রু *n*. a screw. স্ক্রু আঁটা *v*. to screw; to screw up. স্ক্রু খোলা *v*. to unscrew. মাথার স্ক্রু ঢিলা having some mental defect, with a screw loose.

স্খলন *n*. falling, a fall; shedding; act of coming off or getting detached, detachment; loosening; act of slipping off; act of losing one's footing, slipping; stumbling; a lapse, a mistake, an error; act of going astray, aberration; stuttering or mumbling; unguarded uttterance of undesirable things, a slip of the tongue.

স্খলিত *a*. fallen; shed; detached, come off; loosened; slipped off; slipped; stumbled; guilty of a lapse, mistaken; erred; erring; gone astray; aberrated; stuttering or mumbling; uttered unguardedly and unintentionally. স্খলিত হওয়া *v*. to fall; to be shed; to come off, to get detached, to get loose, to loosen; to slip off; to lose one's footing, to slip; to stumble; to go astray, to aberrate; to be uttered unguardedly and unintentionally; to slip from one's mouth. ~কণ্ঠ *a*. stuttering or mumbling. ~চরণ *a*. stumbled; stumbling. স্খলিতা *a*. *fem*. of স্খলিত। *n*. a fallen woman.

স্খালন (erron.) *n*. felling or shedding or detaching or loosening; removal or absolution (দোষস্খালন). স্খালন করা *v*. to fell; to shed; to detach; to loosen; to remove or absolve. See ক্ষালন।

স্টিম *n*. steam. অতিতাপিত স্টিম superheated steam. স্টিমার *n*. a steamer. স্টিমারঘাট *n*. a steamer-station, a wharf, a pier.

স্টুডিয়ো *n.* a studio.

স্টেশন *n.* a station.

স্ট্রিট *n.* a street; a road.

স্তন *n.* either of the mammary glands in women, a women's breast, the mamma (*pl.* mammae)

স্তনদুগ্ধ *n.* breast-milk.

স্তনন *n.* a sound, a noise; a cry of affliction, moaning; roaring; the rumbling of the cloud.

স্তনন্ধয় *a.* unweaned, suckling; infant. *fem.* **স্তনন্ধয়ী** ।

স্তনবৃন্ত *n.* a nipple, a teat.

স্তনভার *n.* the load of one's mammae; the burden of the breasts; fully developed breast.

স্তনাগ্র *n.* a nipple, a teat, a pap.

স্তনিত *a.* resounded; resounding; reverberated; filled with noise; sounded, ringing. □ *n.* the rumbling of the cloud. **সমুদ্র-স্তনিত** *a.* resounding with the roar of the sea. ('সমুদ্র স্তনিত পৃথ্বী'). □ *n.* the roaring of the waves.

স্তন্য *n.* breast-milk, mother's milk. **~জীবী** same as **স্তন্যপায়ী** । **~দাত্রী** *a.* suckling. □ *n.* a mother; a wet-nurse, **স্তন্যদান করা** *v.* to suckle. **স্তন্যপান করা** *v.* to suck. **~পায়ী** *a.* suckling; mammalian. **স্তন্যপায়ী প্রাণী** a mammal. **স্তন্যপায়ী প্রাণীবর্গ** the Mammalia. **স্তন্যপায়ী শিশু** a suckling.

স্তব *n.* singing in praise, hymnody; a song of praise, a hymn; glorification; eulogy; a eulogium, a eulogy. **স্তব করা** *v.* to sing in praise of, to hymn; to glorify; to eulogize.

স্তবক *n.* a bunch, a cluster; a bouquet; a collection; a stanza; a chapter (of a book).

স্তবগান *n.* a song of praise, a hymn.

স্তবপাঠ *n.* recital of a song of praise or of a hymn.

স্তবস্তুতি *n.* repeated singing in praise of; hymns collectively, hymnody; repeated glorification.

স্তব্ধ, স্তব্ধীভূত *a.* (rendered) motionless; stunned; stupefied, dazed; fallen or lying in a stupor; stiffened; stopped; calmed; calm.

স্তম্ভ *n.* a pillar, a post; a perpendicular section of a page or of a table, a column; stupor; motionlessness; stiffness; stagnancy; stagnation; stopping. **স্তম্ভক** *n.* a cylinder. **স্তম্ভন** *n.* stupefaction; act of causing to fall in a stupor; act of making motionless or stagnant; stiffening; stopping; act of making immobile or powerless by means of occult incantation etc. **স্তম্ভাকার** *a.* shaped like a pillar; columnal; cylindrical.

স্তম্ভিত *a.* stupefied; astounded; stunned; rendered motionless; stopped; brought to a standstill; made stagnant. *fem.* **স্তম্ভিতা** । **স্তম্ভিত হওয়া** *v.* to be struck dumb with amazement.

স্তর *n.* a layer; a stratum (*pl.* strata), a bed; a tier; a lamina (*pl.* laminae). **স্তরে স্তরে** layer by layer, in layers; in tiers. **স্তরে স্তরে স্থাপিত** stratified; tiered. **~নতি** *n.* the dip of strata. **~বিন্যাস** *n.* stratification. **~মেঘ** *n.* stratus. **স্তরায়ণ** *n.* stratification. **স্তরিত, স্তরীভূত** *a.* stratified; laminate(d). **স্তরিত বস্তু** a laminated core. **স্তরীভূত শিলা** (geog.) a stratified rock.

স্তাবক *n.* one who hymns or sings in praise of; a panegyrist; a eulogizer; a (cringing) flatterer, an adulator.

স্তিমিত *a.* motionless, immobile; fixed; unmoving; wet, moist, damp; (pop.) dim (স্তিমিত আলোক). **~নেত্রে** *adv.* with fixed looks, looking fixedly, gazingly.

স্তুত *a.* praised in a song or hymn; glorified; eulogized; flattered; propitiated. **স্তুতি** *n.* a song of praise, a hymn; singing in praise; glorification; a eulogy, a eulogium, an encomium (pl. encomia); eulogy; flattery; propitiation; a propitiatory speech. **স্তুতি করা** *v.* to sing in praise of, to hymn, to glorify; to eulogize; to flatter; to propitiate. **স্তুতি পাঠক** *n.* an encomiast. **স্তুতিপ্রিয়** *a.* fond of praise or adulation. **স্তুতিবাদ** *n.* an encomium, a eulogium, a eulogy; a laudatory speech.

স্তূপ *n.* a heap, a pile; a mound; a low hill (**বালির স্তূপ** = a dune); (in Buddhism) a stupa or tope. **স্তূপ করা, স্তূপাকার করা** *v.* to heap, to pile up. **~মেঘ** *n.* cumulus.

স্তুপাকার, স্তুপাকৃতি, স্তুপীকৃত *a.* collected in a heap, piled up.

স্তোক[1] *a.* little, a bit.

স্তোক[2] *n.* false or insincere consolation or assurance or promise. **~বাক্য** *n.* words containing false consolation or assurance or promise.

স্তোত্র *n.* a verse of praise (esp. of a deity), an encomium (*pl.* encomia). **স্তোত্র পাঠ করা** *v.* to recite hymn or a verse of praise. **~গাথা** *n.* a song of praise; a hymn.

স্ত্রী *n.* a wife; a married woman; a woman. □ *a.* (used as a *pfx.*) female, she- (স্ত্রী-পশু). **স্ত্রী-আচার** *n.* traditional rites performed at a wedding by women whose husbands are alive. **~গমন** *n.* sexual intercourse with one's wife or any other woman. **~চরিত্র** *n.* the nature and propensity of womankind, woman's nature. **~চিহ্ন** *n.* the vagina. **~জন্ম** *n.* birth as a woman. **~জাতি** *n.* womankind, the female sex, the fair sex. **~জাতীয়** *a.* feminine, female; feminal. **~ত্ব** *n.* womanly function and duties; womanly marks on one's person; womanhood; femineity, femininity. **~ত্যাগ করা** *v.* to desert or divorce a wife. **~দ্বেষী** *a.* misogynous, misogynistical. □ *n.* a misogynist. **~ধন** *n.* a woman's personal property; a dowry; a portion, dot. **~ধর্ম** *n.* menstruation, menses; womanly duties. **স্ত্রী পরিগ্রহ করা** *v.* to take a wife, to marry, to wive. **~পুরুষ** *n.* a man and a woman, male and female; husband and wife, man and wife, a couple. **~প্রত্যয়** *n.* (gr.) any inflection (used as a suffix) denoting feminine gender. **~বশ** *a.* uxorious, henpecked, **~বুদ্ধি** *n.* (usu. unwise) counsel of a woman. **~মূর্তি** *n.* a female figure. **~রত্ন** *n.* a jewel of a woman or wife. **~রোগ** *n.* a female disease. **~রোগ সম্বন্ধীয়** *a.* gynaecological. **~রোগ বিশেষজ্ঞ** *n.* a gynaecologist; a specialist in female diseases. **~লক্ষণ** *n.* any one of the characteristic signs of a female body. **~লিঙ্গ** *n.* (gr.) the feminine gender. **~লোক** *n.* a woman. **~শিক্ষা** *n.* female education. **~সংসর্গ, ~সহবাস** same as **~স্ত্রীগমন**। **সুলভ** *a.* womanly, feminine; womanish, effeminate. **~স্বভাব** *n.* womanly nature; effeminacy. **~স্বাধীনতা** *n.* freedom of women; female emancipation; (cp.) women's lib. **~হত্যা** *n.* murder of a wife or any woman. **~হরণ** *n.* abduction of women esp. for immoral purposes.

স্ত্রৈণ *n.* uxorious, henpecked.

-স্থ *sfx.* denoting: situated or located in; contained in; deposited in; arrived at, come of (বয়স্থ).

স্থগন *n.* cessation, stopping; postponement, suspension, adjournment; coming to a standstill.

স্থগিত *a.* ceased, stopped; discontinued; postponed, put off, suspended, adjourned; brought to a standstill.

স্থপতি *n.* an architect; a mason. **~বিদ্যা** *n.* architecture; masonry.

স্থবির *a.* decrepit; deprived of the power of movement or action, infirm. (স্থবির যুবক). □ *n.* a decrepit man; a Buddhist ascetic practising asceticism for more than ten years. **~ত্ব** *n.* decrepitude, infirmity (coming with age).

স্থল *n.* a place; a site; location, scene, venue; land; ground; condition, situation, circumstances, case (এরূপ স্থলে) ; stead, position, place (ভরসাস্থল) ; a container, a repository; a matter or object or point (তর্কস্থল). **~কমল** *n.* land-lily, (cp.) lily of the valley. **~গত** *a.* of or on the land, land; overland. **~চর** *a.* living or moving on land , terrestrial. **~পথ** *n.* a land-route. **~পথে** *adv.* by land, overland. **স্থলপদ্ম** same as **স্থলকমল**। **~বাণিজ্য** *n.* land-trade. **~বায়ু** *n.* land-breeze. **~বিশেষে** *adv.* in some cases; as the case may be; wherever apposite or appropriate. **~যুদ্ধ** *n.* land-fight. **~সংকট** *n.* an isthmus. **~সেনা, ~সৈন্য** *n.* land army. **স্থলাভিষিক্ত** *a.* placed in another's position or post; substituted; deputizing. **স্থলারবিন্দ** same as **স্থলকমল**। **স্থলী** *n.* a site, a place; a bag. a sac; a container, a repository. **স্থলীয়** *a.* of or on the land. land.

স্থাণু *n.* a peg; a pillar, a post; a stump; Shiva (শিব). □ *a.* immobile, motionless, stock-still. ~**বৎ** *a.* immobile or motionless like a pillar.

স্থান *n.* a place; a site; a region, a locality; a country; location, scene, venue; shelter; a repository, a container, a receptacle (ভরসাস্থান) ; situation, circumstances, case (এরূপ স্থানে) ; position, post; stead, place (তৎস্থানে) ; a holy place (কালীর স্থান) ; an abode, a habitat; space, room; scope; (phil.) space; (astrol.) a footing. **স্থানে স্থানে** here and there; at places; sporadically. ~**চ্যুত** *a.* displaced, dislocated; dislodged; removed. ~**চ্যুতি** *n.* displacement; dislocation; dislodgment; removal. **স্থানত্যাগ করা** *v.* to quit or leave a place, to remove. ~**বহুল** *a.* spacious, roomy, commodious. ~**বিবরণ** *n.* topography. ~**ভ্রষ্ট** same as **স্থানচ্যুত**। ~**মাহাত্ম্য** *n.* greatness or glory or sanctity of a place; influence of a place. ~**সংকুলান** *n.* provision of space; accommodation. **স্থানসংকুলান হওয়া** *v.* to be accommodated. **স্থানাঙ্ক** *n.* (math.) co-ordinates. **স্থানাঙ্ক পরিবর্তন** *n.* transformation of co-ordinates. **স্থানান্তর** *n.* another place. **স্থানান্তরে যাওয়া** *v.* to go to another place. to remove, to shift. **স্থানান্তরণ** *n.* removal or transfer to another place. **স্থানান্তরিত** *a.* removed to another place, shifted; transferred. **স্থানাপন্ন** *a* officiating. **স্থানাভাব** *n.* want of space or room or accommodation. **স্থানিক** *a.* local; regional. **স্থানীয়** *a.* local (স্থানীয় সময়) ; fit to be regarded as like (পিতৃস্থানীয়).

স্থাপক same as **স্থাপয়িতা**।

স্থাপত্য *n.* architecture; masonry; an architectural work. ~**শিল্পী** *n.* an architect; a mason. ~**সংক্রান্ত** *a.* architectural.

স্থাপন, স্থাপনা *n.* placing, putting; depositing; installation; (বিগ্রহস্থাপন) ; application; fixing (দৃষ্টিস্থাপন) ; settling (স্বস্থানে স্থাপন) ; establishment, setting up, founding an institution (মন্দির স্থাপন, ধর্মস্থাপন). **স্থাপন করা** *v.* to place, to put; to deposit; to instal; to apply; to settle; to establish, to set up, to found, to institute.

স্থাপয়িতা *n.* one who places or puts; one who instals; one who settles another; an establisher, a founder, an institutor. *fem.* **স্থাপয়িত্রী**।

স্থাপিত *a.* placed, deposited; installed; settled; established, set up, founded, instituted.

স্থাবর *a.* immovable; immobile. ~-**জঙ্গম** *n.* mobile and immobile world or beings, animate or inanimate world or beings. **স্থাবর ও অস্থাবর** movable and immovable, movables and immovables. **স্থাবর সম্পত্তি** immovable property, immovables, real estate.

স্থায়িতা, স্থায়িত্ব *n.* durability; permanence; unchangeability, fixity; perpetuity; immobility; stability.

স্থায়িভাব *n.* permanence; stability; (rhet.) any one of the permanent emotions that are expressed in poetry.

স্থায়ী *a.* lasting, durable; abiding; permanent; unalterable; everlasting, perpetual, immobile, firm, stable; fixed (স্থায়ী আমানত) ; standing (স্থায়ী আদেশ). ~**ভাবে** *adv.* stably; perpetually, permanently.

স্থাল, স্থালী *n.* a cooking pot or urn (esp. one made of clay); a plate or saucer (esp. one with a rim), a dish.

স্থিত *a.* located; remaining, staying, lying; existent, present; fixed, static, immobile, standstill; firm; unwavering. ~**ধি,** ~**প্রজ্ঞ** *a.* enjoying perpetual mental calm through philosophic contemplation and conviction. **স্থিতাবস্থা** *n.* a standstill; status quo. **স্থিতাবস্থা-চুক্তি** *n.* a standstill agreement. **স্থিতি** *n.* location; stay; position; existence, presence; fixity; stability; (in book-keeping) a balance. **স্থিতিকাল** *n.* duration. **স্থিতিপত্র** *n.* a balance-sheet. **স্থিতিবিদ্যা, স্থিতিবিজ্ঞান** *n.* statics. **স্থিতিশীল** *a.* lasting, durable; abiding; permanent; fixed; static; firm; stable. **স্থিতিস্থাপক** *a.* elastic. **স্থিতিস্থাপকতা** *n.* elasticity. **স্থিতীয়** *a.* statical. **স্থিতাধিকার** *n.* locus standi; recognized position.

স্থির *a.* motionless, stationary, still; permanent, perpetual, everlasting; firm, resolute; unperturbed, solid; steady;

calm, tranquil; fixed, settled; ascertained. □ *adv*. for certain; surely. **স্থির করা** *v*. to fix, to settle; to determine; to ascertain; to make steady. **~চিত্ত, ~চেতা** *a*. evenminded; single-minded; resolute; unwavering, firm. **~তা** *n*. motionlessness, stationariness; permanence; firmness; stolidness; steadiness, calmness, tranquillity; fixity; certainty. **~তারা** *n*. (astr.) a fixed star. **~দৃষ্টি** *n*. a fixed or steadfast look; a gaze. **~নিশ্চয়** *a*. firmly resolved; certain, sure; convinced. **~প্রতিজ্ঞ** *a*. firmly resolved, resolute, firm. **~প্রতিজ্ঞা** *n*. a firm resolve, resoluteness. **~বুদ্ধি, ~মতি** *a*. evenminded; staid. **~যৌবনা** *a. fem*. perpetually young, unaging, ageless. *masc*. **~যৌবন**। **~সিদ্ধান্ত** *n*. a firm resolve or decision; a conclusive finding or ascertainment. **স্থিরীকরণ** *n*. fixation, settling; decision; determination; ascertainment. **স্থিরীকৃত** *a*. fixed, settled; decided; determined; resolved; ascertained.

স্থূল *a*. fat, corpulent, bulky; flat, broad, snub; thick; coarse; dull; plain; not fine or subtle, naive, gross; approximate, rough; ordinary or banal or vulgar. **~কথা** *n*. the broad meaning; the substance; the long and the short (of it). **~কায়** *a*. heavy-bodied, hefty, corpulent, bulky, fat. **~কোণ** *n*. (geom.) an obtuse angle. **~কোণী** *a*. obtuse-angled. **~চর্ম** *a*. thick-skinned; insensitive, unfeeling. **~তা, ~ত্ব** *n*. fatness, corpulence, bulkiness; flatness, broadness; thickness; coarseness, dullness; plainness; naivety, grossness. **~দৃষ্টি** *n*. superficial observation; plain or superficial looks, plain eyes. **~দেহ** *n*. the material or gross body. the mortal frame. **~বুদ্ধি** *a*. dull-headed, thick-headed, dull-witted. **~বুদ্ধি ব্যক্তি** a dullard. **~মান** *n*. (geom.) rough approximation. **~শরীর** same as **স্থূলদেহ**। **স্থূলাঙ্গ** *a*. corpulent. **স্থূলোদর** *a*. pot-bellied, abdominous.

স্থৈতিক *a*. potential (স্থৈতিক শক্তি = potential energy).

স্থৈর্য *n*. firmness; stolidness, sang-froid; steadiness; calmness, tranquillity; patience.

স্থৌল্য same as **স্থূলতা**।

স্নাত *a*. bathed. **~ক** *n*. (ori.) a Brahman youth who has returned home from his guru's house after completion of his studies; a graduate. **~কোত্তর** *a*. postgraduate.

স্নান *n*. ablutions; bath. **স্নান করা** *v*. to take a bath, to bathe. **স্নান করানো** *v*. to cause to take a bath, to bathe. **আতপস্নান** *n*. sun-bath. **প্রাতঃস্নান** *n*. a bath taken early in the morning. **স্নানের ঘর** a bathroom. **~বস্ত্র** *n*. a piece of loincloth to be worn during a bath **~যাত্রা** *n*. the ceremony of Juggernaut's (জগন্নাথ) sallying out in procession for a bath. **স্নানাগার** *n*. a bathroom. **স্নানাহার** *n*. bathing and eating. **স্নানাহ্নিক** *n*. bathing and prescribed daily prayer to God. **স্নানীয়** *a*. fit for ceremonial ablutions. □ *n*. articles required for ceremonial ablution.

স্নায়বিক *a*. nerval; nervous. **স্নায়বিক দৌর্বল্য** nervous debility, neurasthenia.

স্নায়ু *n*. a sinew; a nerve. **~মণ্ডল** *n*. the nervous system. **~যুদ্ধ** *n*. a campaign to weaken an opponent by destroying his morale; the war of nerves. **~শূল** *n*. neuralgia, neuralgic pain.

স্নিগ্ধ *a*. oily, unctuous; smooth, glossy; loving, affectionate; cordial or charming; delightful to touch; pleasant, cooling, refreshing; cooled, calmed (স্নিগ্ধ হওয়া) ; sweet and soft (স্নিগ্ধ কণ্ঠ) ; tender (স্নিগ্ধ আলো). **~কান্তি** *a*. smooth-skinned; having a graceful bodily charm. **~জ্যোতি** *a*. having a tender lustre. **~তা** *n*. oiliness, greasiness, a soapy feel; smoothness, glossiness; softness; sweetness. **~দৃষ্টি** *n*. a pleasant look. **~শ্যামল** *a*. pleasantly green, verdant.

স্নেহ *n*. affection; love; tenderness; any fatty substance, fat (also **স্নেহপদার্থ**). **স্নেহ করা** *v*. to extend affection to, to love. **~দ্রব্য, ~পদার্থ** *n*. fatty or oily or greasy substance. **~পাত্র** *n*. same as **স্নেহভাজন** (*n*). *fem*. **~পাত্রী**। **~পুত্তলি, ~পুত্তলী** *n*. a doll or a very young object of affection or love. ~পরায়ণ, ~পূর্ণ, ~প্রবণ *a.* affectionate; loving. ~পালিত, ~পুষ্ট *a.* brought up with love and tenderness. ~বশে *adv.* impelled or moved by affection or love. ~ভাজন *n.* an object of affection or love, a beloved person. □ *a.* deserving affection or love. ~মমতা *n.* love and affection, deep attachment. ~ময়, ~শীল *a.* affectionate; loving. *fem.* ~ময়ী, ~শীলা। ~সঞ্চার *n.* infusion or upsurge of affection or love. ~সিক্ত *a.* drenched or softened with affection or love. ~শূন্য, ~হীন *a.* devoid of affection or love, unloving. ~স্পর্শ *n.* the touch of affection. স্নেহার্দ্র *a.* softened with affection or love. স্নেহালিঙ্গন *n.* an affectionate or loving embrace. স্নেহাশীর্বাদ *n.* affectionate blessing. স্নেহাস্পদ same as স্নেহভাজন।

স্পন্দ, স্পন্দন *n.* beating or throbbing (esp. at regular intervals), pulsation, palpitation; a beat; quivering; shaking or tremor (esp. mild); (mech.) vibration. নাড়ির স্পন্দন pulsebeat. নেত্রস্পন্দন *n.* quivering of eyelids. ~রহিত, ~হীন *a.* motionless; not beating; still. স্পন্দিত *a.* beating, throbbing, pulsating, palpitating; throbbed, pulsated, quivering; shaking, quaking; quivered; shaken, quaked; vibrating; vibrated. স্পন্দিত হওয়া *v.* to beat, to throb, to pulsate, to palpitate; to quiver; to shake; to vibrate.

স্পর্ধা *n.* courage or audacity to emulate or defy; emulation; daring to undertake a difficult task; daring; audacity; vaunting arrogance; rant and bluster. স্পর্ধা করা *v.* to emulate; to defy; to dare to undertake; to rant and bluster; to vaunt; to dare; to challenge. স্পর্ধিত, স্পর্ধী *a.* courageously or audaciously emulative or defiant; daring; ranting and blustering; arrogant; audacious.

স্পর্শ *n.* touch; contact. স্পর্শ করা *v.* to touch. স্পর্শক *a.* touching. □ *n.* (geom.) a tangent. ~কাতর *a.* very sensitive to touch; (fig.) touchy. ~কোণ *n.* an angle of contact. ~ক্রামক, ~ক্রামী *a.* contagious. ~জ্যা *n.* (geom.) a tangent. ~ন *n.* touching, touch. ~বর্ণ *n.* any one of the twenty-five consonants from ক to ম of the Bengali alphabet, a stop. ~বিন্দু *n.* point of contact. ~মণি *n.* the philosopher's stone. ~রেখা *n.* a tangent; a touch line. ~সুখ *n.* the pleasure of touch. স্পর্শানুভূতি *n.* perception by feeling; tactual perception. স্পর্শী *a.* touching; tangential; contagious; contacting. *fem.* স্পর্শিনী। স্পর্শিনীবল *n.* tangent force. স্পর্শিনীবেগ *n.* tangential velocity. স্পর্শেন্দ্রিয় *n.* the organ of touch, the skin.

স্পষ্ট *a.* clear; evident, manifest, obvious; express, explicit; positive, categorical; plain, outspoken. □ *adv.* clearly; evidently, manifestly, obviously; expressly, explicitly; positively; categorically; plainly, outspokenly. স্পষ্ট করা *v.* to clarify; to make clear or evident. স্পষ্টত *adv.* same as স্পষ্ট (*adv.*) ~বক্তা, ~বাদী, ~ভাষী *a.* plain-spoken, frank in speech, outspoken. □ *n.* an outspoken man. *fem.* ~বাদিনী, ~ভাষিণী। স্পষ্ট দিবালোকে in broad daylight. ~বাদিতা, ~ভাষিতা *n.* outspokenness, plain speaking; frankness in speech. স্পষ্টাক্ষরে *adv.* in distinctly legible letters (of the alphabet); in plain words, in clear terms. expressly, categorically. স্পষ্টাস্পষ্টি *a.* very clear, express, categorical; outspoken. □ *adv.* very clearly, expressly, categorically; outspokenly; quite plainly. স্পষ্টীকৃত *a.* made clear; clarified, elucidated. স্পষ্টোচ্চারণ *n.* frankness in speech, outspokenness; speaking frankly.

স্পৃশ্য *a.* tangible, tactile; touchable.

স্পৃষ্ট *a.* touched.

স্পৃহণীয় *a.* desirable; covetable; lik(e)able.

স্পৃহা *n.* desire, longing; liking; inclination (আহারে স্পৃহা). ~হীন *a.* free from all desires or longings.

স্ফটিক *n.* rock-crystal; crystal, quartz; glass. ~তুল্য *a.* crystal-like, crystalline. ~নির্মিত, ~ময় *a.* made of crystal; crystalline. ~স্তম্ভ *a.* a pillar of crystal, a crystalline column. স্ফটিকারি *a.* alum. স্ফটিকীভবন *n.* crystallisation.

স্ফাটিক *a.* made of crystal, crystalline.

স্ফার, স্ফারণ *n.* opening; manifestation; widening; expansion; width; expanse. **স্ফারিত** *a.* opened; manifested; widened; expanded.

স্ফীত *a.* swollen, bloated; inflated; expanded; augmented; flourished; puffed up. **স্ফীত হওয়া** *v.* to swell, to bloat; to be inflated; to be expanded, to expand; to be augmented; to prosper, to flourish; to be puffed up. **~কায়** *a.* fat-bodied, corpulent; inflated, swelled up, augmented. **স্ফীতি** *n.* swelling; bulging; inflation; expansion; augmentation; flourish; puffed-up state.

স্ফুট *a.* burst open; manifest, express, explicit, apparent (স্ফুট অর্থ) ; blown, bloomed, blooming (স্ফুট কুসুম) ; pierced, bored (দন্তস্ফুট). **~ন** *n.* bursting open; manifestation, expression, blooming; piercing, boring; boiling; effervescence. **~নাঙ্ক** *n.* the boiling-point. **~নোন্মুখ** *a.* on the point of bursting open or blooming or boiling. **স্ফুটিত** *a.* burst open; bloomed; blown; blooming; manifested, unfolded; pierced, bored; boiled.

স্ফুরণ *n.* quivering, trembling; glow, shine; glitter; incitement; awakening; expression, unfolding.

স্ফুরা poet. form of **স্ফুরিত হওয়া।**

স্ফুরিত *a.* quivered, trembled; quivering, trembling; glowing, shining; glittering; incited, awakened; expressed, manifested. **স্ফুরিত হওয়া** *v.* to quiver, to tremble; to glow, to shine; to glitter; to be incited or awakened; to be expressed or manifested. **স্ফুরিতাধর** *n.* quivering lips.

স্ফুলিঙ্গ *n.* a spark. **স্ফুলিঙ্গ ছড়ানো** *v.* to emit sparks, to spark. **স্ফুলিঙ্গ-মোক্ষণ** *n.* spark-discharge. **স্ফুলিঙ্গান্তর** *n.* a spark-gap.

স্ফূর্ত *a.* bloomed; revealed, unfolded, manifested; expressed; uttered. **স্ফূর্তি** *n.* blooming; revelation, unfolding, manifestation; expression; utterance; merriment; hilarity; joviality; sprightliness; amusement, fun; cheerful enthusiasm or energy. **স্ফূর্তি করা** *v.* to rejoice; to make merry; to revel. **স্ফূর্তি পাওয়া** *v.* to get delight; to feel invigorated or energized; to enjoy mirth or fun. **~জনক** *a.* cheering, exhilarating. **~ব্যঞ্জক** *a.* cheerful; merry; vivacious; sprightly. **~সহকারে** *adv.* cheerfully; merrily; vivaciously.

স্ফোট, স্ফোটক *n.* a boil; an abscess, a furuncle; a tumour; an acne, pimple; a pustule.

স্ফোটন *n.* act of causing to bloom; unfolding or revealing or expressing; splitting or cleaving or rending or boring or piercing. **স্ফোটনোন্মুখ** about to bloom. **স্ফোটনী** *n.* any tool for boring or piercing with, a gimlet, an auger, an awl, a needle.

স্ব *pro.* one's own self, self. (স্বকৃত) ☐ *n.* wealth, possessions (সর্বস্ব). ☐ *a.* one's own (স্বগৃহ). **স্ব স্ব** relating to each distributively, respective (স্ব স্ব কার্য). **স্ব স্ব প্রধান** each independent and self-sufficient; each considering himself or herself most important and slighting others.

স্বঃ *n.* heaven. (স্বর্গত).

স্বকপোলকল্পিত *a.* invented by one's own fancy.

স্বকর্ম, স্বকার্য *n.* one's own work or deed or duty or business.

স্বকাম *n.* narcissism.

স্বকীয় *a.* own; of one's own; personal; original (স্বকীয় ফন্দি) ; (math.) intrinsic. **~তা** *n.* originality.

স্বকৃত *a.* done by oneself, selfdone.

স্বখাত *a.* dug by oneself. **~সলিল** *n.* (fig.) consequences of one's own action or deed.

স্বগত *a.* (esp. in a drama) aside (to oneself.) **স্বগতোক্তি** soliloquy.

স্বগৃহ *n.* one's home or residence.

স্বগ্রাম *n.* one's native village or own village. **~বাসী** *n.* a co-villager.

স্বচক্ষে *adv.* with one's own eyes.

স্বচ্ছ *a.* transparent; translucent; pellucid; crystal-clear, crystalline; lucid. **~কাগজ** tracing paper. **~তা** *n.* transparency, clearness; lucidity, perspicuity. **~দৃষ্টি** *n.*

clear sight or vision. □ *a.* clear-sighted.

স্বচ্ছন্দ *a.* enjoying freedom of will or liberty of choice; free, independent; unrestrained; easy, at ease; comfortable; facile; spontaneous. □ *n.* one's own will, free will. **স্বচ্ছন্দ বোধ করা** *v.* to feel at ease, to feel comfortable. **~গতি** *a.* moving at ease; freely moving. □ *n.* easy or natural or free or unrestrained movement. **~চিত্তে** *adv.* with an easy heart; without demur, undermurringly. **~বিহার** *n.* free or unrestrained promenading or movement; rambling at pleasure. **স্বচ্ছান্দানুবর্তী** *a.* acting as one's heart dictates without considering outside influences, (cp.) self-poised. **স্বচ্ছন্দে** *adv.* freely; as one pleases; at pleasure; at ease, easily; facilely; undemurringly; with self-possession.

স্বচ্ছসলিলা *a. fem.* containing clear or transparent water. *masc.* **স্বচ্ছসলিল** ।

স্বজন *n.* one's own man; a kinsman (*fem.* a kinswoman), a relative; a relation; a member of one's own family or party; a friend; kith and kin. **স্বজনী** *fem.* of **স্বজন** in all senses, and—a confidante. **~ত্যাগ** *n.* disownment or desertion of one's own people. *n. & a.* one who has disowned or deserted one's own people. **~ত্যাগী** *n. & a.* one who has deserted or disowned one's own people. **~পোষণ** *n.* unduly favouring one's own people, nepotism.

স্বজাতি *n.* one's own race or nation or caste. **~দ্রোহ** *n.* hostility to or revolt against one's own race or nation or caste. **~দ্রোহী** *a.* hostile to or rebellious against one's own race or nation or caste. *fem.* **~দ্রোহিণী** । **~সুলভ** *a.* natural to one's caste or race or nation.

স্বজাতীয় *a.* belonging to one's own race or nation or caste or class.

স্বতঃ, (pop.) **স্বত** *adv.* by or of or in oneself or itself, (*in comp.*) self-; of one's own accord; spontaneously. **স্বতঃপ্রবৃত্ত** *a.* actuated or acting by oneself, self-acting; voluntary. **স্বতঃপ্রমাণ** *a.* self-evident; axiomatic. **স্বতঃসিদ্ধ** *a.* self-evident; axiomatic. □ *n.* a self-evident truth; (chiefly in geom.) an axiom. **স্বতঃস্ফূর্ত** *a.* spontaneous.

স্বতন্ত্র *a.* dependent on nobody but oneself, (cp.) self-guided; independent, free; separate; secluded; aloof; different or another (স্বতন্ত্র কথা); (anat.)sympathetic (স্বতন্ত্র নার্ভ). **স্বতন্ত্রা** *fem.* of **স্বতন্ত্র** in all senses, and—living apart from one's husband. **স্বতন্ত্রতা** *n.* same as **স্বাতন্ত্র্য** ।

স্বত্ব *n.* ownership; proprietary right, right to possession, right, title; lawful claim, claim. **স্বত্বের দলিল, ~পত্র** *n.* title-deed, a title. **স্বত্বের মামলা** a title-suit. **~ত্যাগ** *n.* relinquishment of right. **~ত্যাগপত্র** *n.* a deed of relinquishment. **~নিয়োগ** *n.* assignment. **~নিয়োগী** *n.* an assignee. **~নিরসন** *n.* expropriation. **~পত্র** *n.* a title-deed, a title. **স্বত্ববান** *a.* having a right or claim to; entitled. **~ভোগী** *a. & n.* a beneficiary. **~লোপ** *n.* abolition of right. **~লোপনীতি** *n.*(Ind. hist.) the Doctrine of Lapse. **~শূন্য** *a.* having no right or claim. **~সাব্যস্ত** *n.* establishment or determination of right or title. **স্বত্বসাব্যস্তের মামলা** a title-suit. **~স্বামিত্ব** *n.* right and ownership. **স্বত্বাধিকার** *n.* ownership and possession; proprietary right. **স্বত্বাধিকারী** *a.* rightfully owning or possessing. □ *n.* a proprietor (*fem.* a proprietress, proprietrix), an owner. *fem.* **স্বত্বাধিকারিণী** । **স্বত্বার্থন** *n.* act of putting forward one's claim, act of laying claim to. **স্বত্বার্থী** *n.* a claimant.

স্বদল same as **স্বপক্ষ** ।

স্বদেশ *n.* homeland, home, mother-country, motherland, native land. **~ত্যাগ** *n.* act of leaving one's native land, emigration; migration. **~ত্যাগী** *a.* one who has left one's native land; emigrating; migrating. □ *n.* such a person; an emigrant or a migrator. *fem.* **~ত্যাগিনী** । **~দ্রোহ** *n.* hostility to or revolt against one's native land. **~দ্রোহী** *n. & a.* hostile to or rebellious against one's native land. *fem.* **~দ্রোহিণী** । **~প্রেম, ~ভক্তি** *n.* patriotism. **~প্রেমিক, ~প্রেমী, ~ভক্ত** *n.* a patriot. □ *a.* patriotic. **~সেবক** *n.* a servant or devotee of one's native land. ~সেবা *n.* service of or devotion to one's native land. ~হিতৈষণা *n.* desire of doing good to one's native land. ~হিতৈষী *a.* desirous of doing good to one's native land. ☐ *n.* such a person. *fem.* ~হিতৈষিণী। স্বদেশানুরাগ *n.* attachment to one's native land; patriotism. ~স্বদেশানুরাগী *a.* attached to one's native land; patriotic. *fem.* স্বদেশানুরাগিণী। স্বদেশী *a.* of or made in one's native land; home-made, indigenous. ☐ *n.* (hist.) an Indian national movement favouring home industries and boycott of foreign goods, Swadeshi (also **স্বদেশী আন্দোলন**). **স্বদেশী করা** *v.* to participate in Swadeshi, **স্বদেশী শিল্প** home industry. **স্বদেশীয়** *a.* of or born in or made in one's native land.

স্বধর্ম *n.* one's own religion; the religion or the rites and duties or one's forefathers or race or class; characteristics or function of one's race or class; one's natural trade or calling. **স্বধর্মে নিধনং শ্রেয়ঃ পরধর্মো ভয়াবহঃ** it is better to be killed for one's faith than to embrace another religion, which latter action is terrible. ~চ্যুত,~ত্যাগী *a.* apostate. **স্বধর্মচ্যুত ব্যক্তি** an apostate. ~চ্যুতি, ~ত্যাগ *n.* apostasy. **স্বধর্মত্যাগ করা** *v.* to apostatize. ~পালক observing or defending one's religion. ☐ *n.* an observer or defender of one's religion. **স্বধর্মপালন করা** *v.* to observe or defend one's religion. ~পালনরত, ~রত *a.* engaged in observance or defence of one's religion; practising one's natural function or calling. ~ভ্রষ্ট same as ~চ্যুত।

স্বন *n.* sound; noise. ~ন *n.* sounding, ringing, sonance. ~বিদ্যা *n.* acoustics. ~মাপক *n.* a sonometer.

স্বনাম *n.* one's own name. **স্বনামে ও বেনামে** using one's own name and names of others; in one's real name and pseudonyms. ~ধন্য, ~প্রসিদ্ধ *a.* celebrated or known by one's own name; renowned, famous.

স্বনিত *a.* sounded; rung.

স্বপক্ষ *n.* one's own party or team. **স্বপক্ষীয়** *a.* of one's own party or team. *fem.* **স্বপক্ষীয়া**।

স্বপ্ন, (poet.) **স্বপন** *n.* a dream; (ori.) sleep; (fig.) fancy, a vision (আশার স্বপ্ন). **স্বপ্ন দেখা** *v.* to dream; to dream a dream; (fig.) to fancy, to vision. **স্বপ্ন ভাঙা** *v.* to awake from a dream; (fig.) to have one's fancy or fanciful hope or vision frittered away. **স্বপ্নেও না ভাবা** *v.* (fig.) not even to dream of. ~ঘোর same as **স্বপ্নাবেশ**। ~চারিতা *n.* somnambulism. ~চারী *a.* somnambulant. ☐ *n.* a somnambulist. *fem.* ~চারিণী। ~জগৎ *n.* dream-world; a dreamland. ~জাল *n.* the network of a dream or (fig.) vision. ~তত্ত্ব *n.* the science of dream, study and interpretation of dreams, oneirology. ~দর্শন *n.* dreaming; (fig.) visioning. ~দর্শী, ~দ্রষ্টা *a.* dreaming; (fig.) visionary. ☐ *n.* a dreamer; (fig.) a visionary. *fem.* ~দর্শিনী। ~দোষ *n.* (med.) involuntary emission of semen during sleep, nocturnal emission; (loos.) spermatorrhoea. ~প্রয়াণ *n.* somnambulism. ~বৎ *a.* dreamlike, dreamy; visionary; illusory. ~বিচার *n.* interpretation of dreams. ~ময় *a.* full of dreams, dreamy; formed or made in dreams. *fem.* ~ময়ী। ~রাজ্য, ~লোক same as ~জগৎ। ~লব্ধ same as **স্বপ্নাদ্য**। **স্বপ্নাতীত** *a.* undreamt-of; quite unexpected. **স্বপ্নাদিষ্ট** *a.* divinely commanded or inspired in a dream. **স্বপ্নাদেশ** *n.* a divine command or inspiration received in a dream. **স্বপ্নাদ্য** *a.* obtained in a dream. **স্বপ্নাবস্থা** *n.* the dreaming state. **স্বপ্নাবিষ্ট** *a.* obsessed in a dream or (fig.) vision; under the spell of a dream; deeply dreaming; dreamy. **স্বপ্নাবেশ** *n.* obsession caused by a dream or (fig.) vision; dreaminess; the spell of a dream. **স্বপ্নোত্থিত** *a.* awakened from a dream.

স্বপ্রকাশ *a.* self-manifested, self-revealed.

স্বপ্রচার *n.* self-advertisement, self-propaganda.

স্বপ্রণীত *a.* composed or compiled or written by oneself.

স্ববশ *a.* self-controlled; independent, free.

স্বভাব *n.* nature; a characteristic (innate or acquired); a natural quality, a property; character; instinct, disposition; conduct, behaviour; habit, practice; nature; original or normal or natural state. **স্বভাব যায় না মলে** one's nature does not change even at one's death. **~কবি** *n.* a poet by nature; a born poet, a poet of nature, a nature-poet. **~কুলীন** *n.* a member of a kulin (কুলীন) family whose familial characteristics have not been tarnished by undesirable matrimonial alliance or otherwise. **~কৃপণ** *a.* miserly or niggardly by nature. **~গত** same as **স্বাভাবিক**। **~গুণ** *n.* a natural or innate or habitual or characteristic or normal quality or function. **~চরিত্র** *n.* innate and acquired nature; character and conduct or practice. **~জ** *a.* originating from nature; natural; instinctive; habitual; abiogenetic; spontaneous. **~জাত** *a.* same as **স্বভাবজ**। **~ত** *adv.* naturally; by nature. **~দুর্বৃত্ত** *n.* a habitual offender; a born criminal. **~বিরুদ্ধ** *a.* unnatural; abnormal; contrary or opposed to one's nature. **~বর্ণনা** *n.* description of nature or phenomenal world. **~শোভা** *n.* a beautiful show of nature, natural beauty. **~সিদ্ধ, ~সংগত, ~সুলভ** *a.* natural; habitual. **~সুন্দর** *a.* beautiful by nature. **স্বভাবী** *a.* normal. **স্বভাবোক্তি** *n.* (rhet.) detailed poetical description of an object of nature; faithful transcript of life and nature.

স্বমত *n.* one's own or free opinion.

স্বয়ং *pro.* oneself, ownself, (*in comp.*) self. □ *adv.* personally; by oneself. **~ক্রিয়** *a.* automatic. **~ক্রিয়তা** *n.* automaticity, the quality of being automatic. **~চল** *a.* automobile. **~চল যান** an automobile. **~প্রবৃত্ত** *a.* self-engaged. **~বর** *n.* choosing of one's bridegroom oneself (esp. from amongst a number of invited suitors). **~বরা** *n. fem.* one who chooses one's bridegroom oneself (esp. from amongst a number of invited suitors). **~সম্পূর্ণ** *a.* self-sufficient (স্বয়ংসম্পূর্ণ ব্যক্তি) ; self-contained (স্বয়ংসম্পূর্ণ ফ্ল্যাট). **~সিদ্ধ** *a.* having realized one's end by one's own effort; self-proved, self-evident.

স্বয়ম্বর inc. spell. of **স্বয়ংবর**।

স্বয়ম্ভর *a.* self-fed, self-sustaining.

স্বয়ম্ভু, স্বয়ম্ভূ *a.* self-born; abiogenetic; born upon the earth of one's own accord.

স্বর *n.* voice; tone of voice; a musical note or pitch; tune; a vowel. **~কম্প** *n.* (*mus.*) a beat. **~কম্পন** *n.* modulation or tremor of voice. **~গ্রাম** *n.* (*mus.*) any recognized scale, gamut. **স্বরগ্রাম সাধা** *v.* (*mus.*) to run through a scale of notes. **~তন্ত্রী** *n.* the vocal chord. **~নিবেশ** *n.* (*mus.*) temperament; adjustment of tuning. **~বর্ণ** *n.* (gr.) a vowel. **~বদ্ধ** *a.* having one's voice choked. **~বৃত্ত** *n.* (pros.) a system of versification measured by the number of letters in each foot. **~ভক্তি** *n.* (gr.) vowel insertion. **~ভঙ্গ** *n.* morbid hoarseness of voice, aphonia. **~ভঙ্গি** *n.* modulation of voice; (mus.) intonation. **~মাধুর্য** *n.* sweetness of voice. **~মাপক** *n.* a sonometer. **~লহরী** *n.* waves or ripples of musical notes, wavy strain of music. **~লিপি** *n.* musical notation. **~সংগতি** *n.* (gr.) vowel harmony or mutation. **~সন্ধি** *n.* (gr.) the union or joining of the last vowel of a word with the initial vowel of the next word.

স্বরচিত *a.* composed or made or contrived or written by oneself.

স্বরাজ *n.* self-government, home rule, independence, swaraj.

স্বরাজ্য, স্বরাষ্ট্র *n.* one's own state; a self-governed or free state. **স্বরাষ্ট্রমন্ত্রক** *n.* the Ministry of Home Affairs. **স্বরাষ্ট্রমন্ত্রী** *n.* the Home Minister.

স্বরিত *n.* (*mus.*) a tone between the high and deep one and between the low and grave one, (cp.) tenor. □ *a.* voiced; uttered; sounded.

স্বরূপ *n.* nature; the natural or normal state or form; real or true nature or condition; similar or equal condition or form. □ *a.* like, similar. **~চিন্তা** *n.* meditation about oneself, introspection. **~নির্ণয়** *n.* determination of real character or nature; ascertainment of true form or state. ~লক্ষণ *n.* a characteristic. **স্বরূপত, স্বরূপে** *adv.* really, truly.

স্বর্গ *n.* the abode of God and gods and the blessed, heaven, Swarag, Svarga; (fig.) a place full of heavenly or supreme bliss (মাতৃভূমি আমার স্বর্গ) ; (fig.) supreme bliss or beatitude. **স্বর্গে বাতি দেওয়া** to set up a pole with a light suspended from its top enkindled in reverence to one's deceased forefathers; (fig.) to continue one's line of descent by procreation. **স্বর্গ হাতে পাওয়া** (fig.) to attain happiness and riches of all description; (fig.) to attain supreme happiness or joy. **স্বর্গে তোলা** *v.* (fig.) to extol in blatant advertisement, to puff up, to deify or elate, to flatter with false praise. **স্বর্গে যাওয়া** *v.* to go to heaven after death; to go or ascent to heaven; (euphem.) to die. **~গঙ্গা** *n.* the milky way, the Galaxy; the celestial river Mandakini (মন্দাকিনী). **~গত, ~ত** *a.* gone or ascended to heaven after death; (euphem.) dead. **~গমন** *n.* ascension to heaven; (euphem.) death. **~দ্বার** *n.* the gate of heaven; a Hindu holy place in Upper India. **~ধাম** *n.* heaven; a kind of indoor game. **~প্রাপ্তি** same as **~লাভ**। **~বাসী** *a.* residing in heaven. **~ভোগ** *n.* enjoyment of heaven or beatitude (after death). **~লাভ** *n.* attainment of heaven after death. **স্বর্গ লাভ করা** *v.* to attain heaven after death; (euphem.) to die. **~লোক** *n.* heaven, Swarga, Svarga. **~সুখ** *n.* heavenly bliss (esp. what is attainable after death), beatitude. **~স্থ** same as **স্বর্গীয়**। **স্বর্গাদপি** *adv.* even than heaven. **স্বর্গাধিপতি** *n.* the lord of heaven. **স্বর্গারূঢ়** same as **স্বর্গত**। **স্বর্গীয়** *a.* heavenly; divine, celestial; dead. **স্বর্গীয় পিতা** one's late or deceased father; heavenly father.

স্বর্ণ *n.* gold, aurum. **~কণা** *n.* a grain of gold. **~কমল** *n.* the red lotus. **~কার** *n.* a goldsmith (by caste or trade). **~খচিত** same as **সুবর্ণখচিত**। **~খনি** *n.* a goldmine; (fig.) a highly rewarding or profitable enterprise. **~পদ্ম** *n.* the red lotus. **~পত্র** *n.* a goldleaf; a gold-foil. **~প্রতিমা** *n.* a gold image, a golden image; (fig.) a very beautiful (female) figure or person. **~প্রসূ** *a.* auriferous ; (fig.) exceptionally fertile. **~বণিক** same as **সুবর্ণবণিক**। **~বর্ণ** *a.* having the colour of gold, gold-coloured, golden. **~ভূমি** *n.* an auriferous land; (fig.) a richly fertile land or soil. **~মণ্ডিত** *a.* gilded, gilt, aureated; gold-plaited. **~ময়** *a.* made of or full of gold, golden. **~মাক্ষিক** *n.* iron pyrites. **~মৃগ** same as **মায়ামৃগ**। **~রেণু** *n.* minute particles or grains of gold; gold dust. **~সিঁদুর** *n.* an Ayurvedic medicine containing mercury. **~সূত্র** *n.* gold thread; gold-wire. **স্বর্ণাক্ষর** *n.* a letter of gold. **স্বর্ণাক্ষরে লেখা** written in letters of gold. **স্বর্ণাঙ্গুরীয়, স্বর্ণাঙ্গুরীয়ক** *n.* a fingrring made of gold, a gold ring. **স্বর্ণাভরণ, স্বর্ণালংকার** *n.* a gold ornament.

স্বল্প *a.* very little; very few; only a little; only a few; a bit. **~তা** *n.* fewness. smallness, scantiness. **~ব্যয়ে** *adv.* at a low or small expense or cost; cheaply. **~ভাষী** *a.* speaking very little, parsimonious in speech; taciturn, reticent; reserved; curt, laconic. **স্বল্পায়ু** *a.* having a brief span of life, short-lived. **স্বল্পাহারী** *a.* subsisting on meagre or scanty meal or fare; abstemious.

স্বশাসন *n.* self-government, autonomy; self-control. **স্বশাসিত** *a.* self-governing, self-governed, autonomous; self-controlled.

স্বসা *n.* a sister; a cousin sister.

স্বস্তি *int.* be well, be in weal, (cp.) vale. □ *n.* a benedictory incantation; weal, good; contentment; (pop.) freedom from worry or anxiety, peace, relief (স্বস্তির নিশ্বাস) = a sigh of relief) **সুখের চেয়ে স্বস্তি ভালো** (fig.) peaceful poverty is better than worried affluence. **স্বস্তিক** *n.* a fylfot, a filfot, a swastika; a holy sign of fylfot painted with rice-paste etc.; the Buddhist cross; a posture of sitting in yogic practice (usu. **স্বস্তিকাসন**); a mansion with a portico or balcony in the front; a place where two roads intersect, a cross road. **~পাঠ, ~বাচন** *n.* recital or utterance of the benedictory incantation. ~বচন *n.* benedictory words or incantation. ~হীন *a.* peaceless, restless; having no respite, without respite, unrelieved.

স্বস্ত্যয়ন *n.* a religious service performed for fighting out evils, remission of sins, recovery from illness etc.

স্বস্থান *n.* one's own place; a place fixed for a particular person; one's residence or home.

স্বহস্ত *n.* one's own hand. স্বহস্তাক্ষর *n.* one's handwriting.

স্বাক্ষর *n.* a signature. স্বাক্ষর করা *v.* to sign. ~কারী *n.* a signatory. স্বাক্ষরিত *a.* signed.

স্বাগত *n.* auspicious coming or arrival, welcome; well-being, weal. স্বাগত জানানো *v.* to welcome. ~ভাষণ *n.* a welcome address. ~সম্ভাষণ *n.* act of receiving one cordially by inquiring after one's well-being.

স্বাচ্ছন্দ্য *n.* freedom of will or liberty of choice; freeness, freedom; ease; comfort; facileness, facility; spontaneity.

স্বাজাতিক *a.* relating to one's own countrymen or nation or race or caste; (loos.) nationalist. স্বাজাতিকতা, স্বাজাত্য *n.* (loos.) nationalism.

স্বাতন্ত্র্য *n.* dependence on nobody but oneself; independence, freedom; separateness; seclusion; aloofness.

স্বাতি, স্বাতী *n.* the fifteenth of the twenty-seven zodiacal stars according to Hindu astronomy.

স্বাদ *n.* taste; flavour, relish; good taste or flavour; gustation. ~গ্রহণ, ~ন *n.* act of tasting, gustation. ~গ্রাহী *a.* tasting. ~হীন *a.* tasteless, insipid, flavourless; flat.

স্বাদু *a.* tasty, tasteful, gustful; tasting sweet; delicious; sweet.

স্বাদেশিক *a.* of one's mother-country, national; patriotic; nationalistic. স্বাদেশিকতা *n.* patriotism; nationalism.

স্বাধিকার *n.* one's own right or territory or jurisdiction or privilege.

স্বাধীন *a.* independent; free; unrestrained, unrestricted. স্বাধীন করা *v.* to free; to liberate. স্বাধীন হওয়া *v.* to be free or independent. স্বাধীনতা *n.* independence; freedom. স্বাধীনতা দিবস *n.* the Independence Day. স্বাধীনভাবে *adv.* independently; freely.

স্বাধ্যায় *n.* study of the Vedas; studies. স্বাধ্যায়ী *n.* a student of the Vedas; a student.

স্বাবলম্বন, স্বাবলম্ব *n.* self-help; self-reliance; self-support; self-sufficiency. স্বাবলম্বী *a.* having recourse to self-help; self-reliant; self-supporting; self-sufficient.

স্বাভাবিক *a.* natural; characteristic; innate; instinctive, native; of the phenomenal world, normal; usual; spontaneous, not forced. স্বাভাবিকতা *n.* naturalness; normality; normalcy; usualness; spontaneity.

স্বামী *n.* a husband; a master; a lord; an employer; an overlord, a ruler; an owner, a proprietor; a title of saints or great ascetics (also স্বামিজি). স্বামিত্ব *n.* ownership, proprietorship; authority, rule. স্বামিনী *n. fem.* a mistress; a female employer or ruler; a proprietress. স্বামিহীন *a.* ownerless, masterless. স্বামিহীনা *a.* (of a woman) who has lost her husband, widowed.

স্বায়ত্ত *a.* self-possessed; self-controlled; self-governing. ~শাসন same as স্বশাসন। ~শাসিত same as স্বশাসিত।

স্বার্থ *n.* one's own interests, pleasure, welfare, etc.; self-interest. ~চিন্তা *n.* thoughts to devise means of realizing one's own interests, selfish thoughts, self-seeking. ~ত্যাগ *n.* self-sacrifice, self-denial. স্বার্থত্যাগ করা *v.* to sacrifice one's own interests. ~ত্যাগী *a.* self-sacrificing. ~পর, ~পরায়ণ *a.* selfish. ~পরতা, ~পরায়ণতা *n.* selfishness. ~বুদ্ধি *n.* a selfish motive or thought. ~বুদ্ধিপ্রণোদিত *a.* actuated or prompted by a selfish motive or thought. ~মগ্ন engulfed in thoughts of self-interest; absorbed in one's own affairs or interests. ~ময় *a.* full of selfishness. ~শূন্য, ~হীন *a.* unselfish; selfless; disinterested. ~সাধন, ~সিদ্ধি *n.* realization of one's own interests. স্বার্থান্ধ *a.* blinded with selfishness or self-interest, blindly or unscrupulously self-seeking.

স্বার্থান্বেষণ *n.* self-seeking. **স্বার্থান্বেষী** *a.* self-seeking. **স্বার্থান্বেষী ব্যক্তি** a self-seeker. **স্বার্থোন্মত্ত** *a.* madly self-seeking.

স্বাস্থ্য *n.* health; hygiene; happiness, peace. **পৌরস্বাস্থ্য** public health or hygiene. **দৈহিক স্বাস্থ্য** personal health or hygiene. **স্বাস্থ্য-অধিকর্তা** *n.* the Director of Public Health. **~কর** *a.* conducive to health, healthsome, healthful, healthy; salutary, salubrious. **স্বাস্থ্যকর স্থান** a health-resort, a health station. **~কৃত্যক** *n.* health services. **~পরিদর্শক** *n.* a sanitary inspector. **~প্রদ** same as **স্বাস্থ্যকর**। **~বিদ্যা** *n.* hygiene. **~বিধান** *n.* hygiene; measures for recovery or improvement of health; sanitation. **স্বাস্থ্যবিধান করা** *v.* to take measures for recovery or improvement of health. **~বিধি** *n.* science of or rules for healthy living; hygiene. **~ব্যবস্থা** *n.* sanitation. **~ভঙ্গ** *n.* ruin or wreck of health. **~মন্ত্রক** *n.* the Ministry of Health. **~মন্ত্রী** *n.* the Minister of Health. **~রক্ষা** *n.* preservation of health. **~লাভ** *n.* recovery of health. **~হানি** *n.* impairment of health. **~হীন** *a.* in ill-health, sickly. **স্বাস্থ্যান্বেষণ** *n.* search for health; attempt to recover health. **স্বাস্থ্যান্বেষী** *a.* searching for health; attempting to recover health, valetudinarian.

স্বাহা *n.* the wife of the sun-god. □ *int.* a word uttered whilst pouring ghee in the sacrificial fire.

স্বীকার *n.* acknowledgment, admission, admittance; confession; recognition, owning (বন্ধু বলে স্বীকার) ; acceptance (নিমন্ত্রণ স্বীকার) ; acquiescence, agreement, consent, assent, promise (দিতে স্বীকার) ; act of inviting upon oneself, courting (দুঃখস্বীকার) ; sustaining (ক্ষতিস্বীকার). **স্বীকার করা** *v.* to acknowledge, to admit; to confess; to recognize, to own; to accept; to acquiesce, to agree, to consent; to promise; to invite upon oneself, to court; to sustain. **স্বীকার হওয়া** *v.* to accept; to agree, to consent. **স্বীকারোক্তি** *n.* a confession.

স্বীকার্য *a.* acknowledgeable, admissible; to be recognized or admitted; fit to be confessed or owned; acceptable. □ *n.* (geom.) a postulate. **~রূপে** *adv.* admittedly.

স্বীকৃত *a.* acknowledged, admitted; confessed; recognized, owned; accepted; acquiesced, agreed, consented; promised. **স্বীকৃত বিষয়** an admitted fact; (geom.) a postulate. **স্বীকৃতি** *n.* acknowledgment, admission, admittance; confession, recognition, owning; acceptance; acquiescence, agreement, consent.

স্বীয় *a.* one's own, own.

স্বেচ্ছা *n.* one's own will, volition; free will; self-will. **~কৃত** *a.* voluntarily or wilfully done, voluntary, wilful. **~ক্রমে** *adv.* of one's own accord, voluntarily, wilfully; willingly. **~চার, ~চারিতা** *n.* wilfulness, self-will; waywardness, wantonness. **~চারী** *a.* wilful, self-willed; wayward, wanton. *fem.* **~চারিণী**। **স্বেচ্ছাধীন, স্বেচ্ছানুবর্তী** *a.* subject to one's free will (স্বেচ্ছাধীন কাজ) ; wilful, self-willed; wayward. (স্বেচ্ছাধীন ব্যক্তি). *fem.* **স্বেচ্ছাধীনা, স্বেচ্ছানুবর্তিনী**। **স্বেচ্ছানুবর্তিতা** same as **স্বেচ্ছাচার**। **~পূর্বক** same as **স্বেচ্ছাক্রমে**। **~প্রণোদিত** *a.* actuated or prompted by one's own will; wilful, deliberate. **~প্রদত্ত** *a.* voluntarily given. **~প্রবৃত্ত** *a.* employed by one's own will. **~মৃত্যু** *n.* (myth.) dying whenever one pleases to die; (pop.) voluntary or deliberate courting of death. **~সেবক** *n.* a volunteer. *fem.* **~সেবকা,** (pop.) **~সেবিকা**।

স্বেদ *n.* sweat, perspiration; vapour, steam. **~জ** *a.* born of or originating from sweat, perspiratory. **~জনক** *a.* causing or inducing sweat, perspiratory. **~জল, ~বারি** *n.* sweat, perspiration. **~বিন্দু** *n.* a bead of perspiration, a drop of sweat. **~সিক্ত, স্বেদাক্ত, স্বেদাপ্লুত, স্বেদার্দ্র** *a.* drenched or damp with sweat, sweaty, sweated.

স্বৈর *n.* act of doing as one pleases; waywardness; unrestrained exercise of one's will; arbitrariness; autocratic; despotism; freedom; dissoluteness. □ *a.* wayward, self-willed; arbitrary; despotic; free, unrestricted; dissolute.

~তন্ত্রী *a.* autocratic; arbitrary; despotic. ☐ *n.* an autocrat, a despot or an arbitrary ruler. ~তান্ত্রিক same as ~তন্ত্রী। ~শাসন *n.* despotic or arbitrary government; autocracy; despotism, tyranny. স্বৈরাচারী, স্বৈরিতা *n.* waywardness; dissoluteness; despotism, tyranny. ~তন্ত্র *n.* despotism, autocracy; (cp.) dictatorship. স্বৈরাচারী, স্বৈরী *a.* wayward; self-willed; dissolute, wild; despotic, tyrannical. স্বৈরিণী *a. fem.* of স্বৈরী। *n. fem.* a wayward or profligate woman.

স্বোপার্জিত *a.* self-acquired, earned or acquired by oneself; deliberately invited upon oneself.

স্মর *n.* Madana the Hindu god of love (cp. Cupid, Eros). ☐ *a.* remembering (জাতিস্মর).

স্মরণ *n.* remembrance, recollection; memory; reflection or meditation ('স্মরণ-বন্দন-পাদসেবন') ; remembering; silent or inward invocation in supplication (বিপদে বন্ধুকে স্মরণ) ; a request or summons to come (রাজা কর্তৃক ভৃত্যকে স্মরণ). স্মরণ করা *v.* to call; to mind, to recollect; to reflect or meditate; to invoke in supplication silently or inwardly; to request or summon to come. স্মরণ থাকা, স্মরণে থাকা *v.* to be borne in mind, to be remembered. স্মরণ হওয়া *v.* to occur to the mind, to be recollected or to reoccur or remember; to rise in one's memory. স্মরণ রাখা, স্মরণে রাখা *v.* to bear in mind, to remember. ~চিহ্ন *n.* a memento, a keepsake; a memorial. ~পট *n.* the canvas of memory. স্মরণপটে বা স্মরণপথে উদিত হওয়া same as স্মরণ হওয়া। ~পথ *n.* the way or course of memory. ~লিপি *n.* a reminder letter, a reminder; a memorandum. ~শক্তি *n.* the power of remembering things, the retentive capacity of mind, memory. ~শক্তিহীন *a.* lacking in memory; having poor memory. স্মরণাতীত *a.* incapable of being recollected; forgotten, immemorial. স্মরণাতীত কাল time immemorial, immemorial time, time out of mind. স্মরণার্থে *adv.* for reminding; for remembering. স্মরণিক *n.* a memorial; a remembrancer; a souvenir. *fem.* স্মরণিকা। স্মরণীয় *a.* fit to be remembered or recollected, memorable. স্মরণীয় বিষয়সমূহ memorable things or events, memorabilia.

স্মরা poet. form of স্মরণ করা।

স্মার *n.* a memo.

স্মারক *a.* causing to remember, reminding. ☐ *n.* a reminder. ~নিধি *n.* memorial fund. ~পত্র, ~লিপি *n.* a reminder; a memorandum; a memento.

স্মার্ত *a.* of or mentioned in or versed in the Smriti.

স্মিত *n.* a (light and sweet) smile. ☐ *a.* (lightly and sweetly) smiling; blooming (স্মিত যৌবন, স্মিত কুসুম). ~মুখে *adv.* with a smiling face.

স্মৃত *a.* recollected.

স্মৃতি *n.* inward recollection or reflection; remembrance; memory; meditation; a memento; a memorial; the holy law-book of the Hindus, the Smriti. ~কথা *n.* memoirs. ~চারণ *n.* reminiscence. ~চিহ্ন, ~নিদর্শন *n.* a memento; a memorial. ~পথ same as স্মরণপথ। ~বার্ষিকী *n.* an anniversary (esp. of a sad incident or death). ~বিভ্রম *n.* confusion or loss of memory. ~ভাণ্ডার *n.* memorial fund (শরৎ-স্মৃতি ভাণ্ডার). ~ভ্রংশ *n.* loss (esp. morbid loss) of memory; dementia; oblivion. ~ভ্রষ্ট *a.* one whose memory has been lost; suffering from dementia; forgotten. ~মন্দির *n.* a mausoleum; a cenotaph. স্মৃতিরক্ষা করা *v.* to commemorate. ~শক্তি same as স্মরণশক্তি। ~শাস্ত্র *n.* the holy law-book of the Hindus, the Smriti. ~স্তম্ভ *n.* a monumental pillar or column.

স্যন্দ *n.* going; velocity; oozing, exudation. স্যন্দী *a.* oozing, exuding; going.

স্যন্দন[1] *n.* (chem.) filtration.

স্যন্দন[2] *n.* going; velocity; (chem.) exudation; a chariot.

স্যমন্তক *n.* a mythological gem.

স্যমীক *n.* weevil; cloud.

স্যাঁতস্যাঁত *int.* expressing: dampness, moisture; wetness. স্যাঁতসেঁতে *a.* damp, moist; wet.

স্যাকরা *n*. a Hindu community of goldsmiths and silversmiths; a goldsmith or a silversmith. *fem*. **স্যাকরানি** ।

স্যাঙাত, স্যাঙ্গাত *n*. (usu. dero. or joc.) a bosom friend or companion; an accomplice.

স্যূত *a*. sewn, woven.

স্রংস, স্রংসন *n*. coming off or coming away or falling of. **স্রংস-উপত্যকা** *n*. a rift valley.

স্রক *n*. a flower-wreath, a garland; a necklace. **~চন্দন** *n*. a garland and sandal-paste.

স্রগ্ধর *a*. garlanded.

স্রবণ, স্রব *n*. exudation; oozing; flowing out; a spring, a fountain.

স্রষ্টা *n*. the Creator, God; Brahma (ব্রহ্মা) ; a creator.

স্রস্ত *a*. fallen off, come away or off, got detached.

স্রাব *n*. exudation; oozing; an outflow, a flow; discharge.

স্রুত *a*. exuded; oozed; distilled; flowed out. **স্রুতি** *n*. exudation; oozing; distillation; outflow.

স্রেফ var. of **সেরেফ** ।

স্রোত *n*. a stream (of water or any liquid); a current; a watercourse. **স্রোতে ভেসে যাওয়া** *v*. to drift down a stream, to drift away. **~স্বতী, ~স্বিনী** *n*. river, a stream. **স্রোতোবেগ** *n*. rush of current. **স্রোতোহীন** *a*. currentless; not flowing; stagnant.

স্লেট *n*. a slate (for writing on). **~পাথর** *n*. slate.

হ *n.* the thirty-third and last consonant of the Bengali alphabet.

হইচই *n.* a very loud uproar; fuss. **হইচই করা** *v.* to raise an uproar; to fuss noisily. **হইচই করে বেড়ানো** *v.* to gallivant, to gad about (noisily and cheerfully).

হইহই same as **হইচই**।

হওয়া *n.* being; happening, occurrence; birth; growth; production; collection, formation; accomplishment; performance; procurement; rendering; becoming; setting in; sufficing; the state of being in particular relation with; act of becoming one's own or one's property; fitting. □ *v.* to be; to come into existence, to be created; to happen, to occur, to take place (যুদ্ধ হওয়া) ; to be born; to grow (ধান হওয়া) ; to be produced or manufactured; to gather or collect; to form; to be earned or gained; to be acquired (তার টাকা হয়েছে = he has made money); to advance (বেলা হওয়া) ; to increase, to grow, to add to; to be finished or accomplished or performed; to be procured or obtained; to be rendered or turned into, to be reduced to; to become (রাজা হওয়া) ; to arrive (সময় হওয়া) ; to set in (সন্ধ্যা হওয়া) ; to extend over, to cover (দুদিন হল সে গেছে = it is two days since he went); to be seized or attacked with (ভয় বা জ্বর হওয়া) ; to fall (বৃষ্টি হওয়া) ; to be sufficient or adequate for, to suffice (এ টাকাতেই হবে) ; to bear a particular relation to (সে আমার কুটুম হয় = he is my relation); to become one's own or one's property (জমিটা তার হল) ; to fit (জামাটা গায়ে হবে না) ; to be likely to happen (তা হবে = it may be so, it may happen so). □ *a.* completed, finished; done; performed (হওয়া কাজ). **হয়ে আসা** *v.* to drop in temporarily (আসার পথে বাজারটা হয়ে এসো) ; to be about to terminate or end, to come near the close; to be in the last gasp, to be dying (তার হয়ে এসেছে).

হংস *n.* the drake; the gander, the swan; a greedless ascetic. **~গমনা, ~গামিনী** *a. fem.* walking (gracefully or with a slight waddle) like a duck. **~ডিম্ব** *n.* a duck's egg; (facet.) a cipher, a zero, a mere nothing. **~ধ্বনি**[1]**, ~নাদ** *n.* cackling. **~ধ্বনি**[2] *n.* an Indian musical mode. **~বাহন, ~রথ** *n.* one who rides a duck; Brahma (ব্রহ্ম). *n. fem.* **~বাহনা, ~বাহিনী** a female riding a duck; Goddess Saraswati (সরস্বতী). **~শাবক** *n.* a duckling. **হংসারূঢ়** *a.* seated on a goose or swan. **হংসী** *n. fem.* the duck; the goose.

হক *a.* rightful, just, right. □ *n.* rightful claim or title, right (হক আদায় করা, হকের ধন) ; just or right words (হক বলা).

হকচকানো *v.* to be nonplussed, to be taken aback; to be astounded or flabbergasted.

হকদার *n.* one having a rightful claim or title, a rightful claimant.

হকার *n.* a huckster, a pedlar; (loos.) a hawker. **খবরের কাগজের হকার** a newsman; a newsboy. **হকারি** *n.* huckstery, pedlary.

হকি *n.* hockey.

হকিকত *n.* (law) descriptive statement.

হকিম *n.* a physician practising the Islamic system of medicine; a hakim. **হকিমি** *a.* of a hakim. □ *n.* practice of Muslim system of medicine.

হকিয়ত *n.* proprietorship; right; claim; a title-suit.

হজ *n.* Mohammedan pilgrimage to Mecca and Medina, hadj, hajj. **হজ করা** *v.* to go on hadj.

হজম *n.* digestion; (iron.) misappropriation or appropriation to oneself by cunning (চাঁদার টাকা হজম) ; (idiom.) act of enduring tamely, pocketing, swallowing (অপমান হজম). **হজম করা** *v.* to digest; (iron.) to misappropriate or to appropriate to oneself by cunning; (idiom.)

to endure tamely, to take something lying down. **হজমি** *a.* digestive (হজমি গুলি = digestive pill).

হজযাত্রী *n.* a Muslim pilgrim to Mecca and Medina.

হজরত *n.* (Mus.) a lord, a master, a venerable or honourable person. **হজরত মোহম্মদ** the Prophet, the founder of Islam.

হট, হট্ *int.* indicating : suddenness, quickness, rashness etc. **হট করে** *adv.* hastily; suddenly; impetuously; abruptly.

হটা *v.* to move backwards or aside; to retreat; to evade an obligation or undertaking, to back out; to withdraw; to be defeated. **হটানো** *v.* to cause to move backwards or aside; to repel; to cause to retreat or back out or withdraw; to defeat.

হটিয়ে দেওয়া same as **হটানো**।

হট্ট *n.* a market. **~গোল** *n.* a confused uproar, a hullabaloo; rumpus; din. **~বিলাসিনী** *n.* a prostitute. **~মন্দির** *n.* (facet.) a hutted structure in a market used as a shop.

হঠ *n.* application of force, violation; retreat, withdrawal; defeat; indiscretion, imprudence; rashness.

হঠকারী *a.* rash, foolhardy, impetuous; indiscreet; obstinate. *fem.* **হঠকারিণী**। **হঠকারিতা** *n.* rashness; foolhardiness; impetuosity; indiscretion, obstinacy.

হঠযোগ *n.* a form of yogic practice or breath control by yogic means or prescribed poses.

হঠা, হঠানো variants of **হটা** and **হটানো**।

হঠাৎ *adv.* suddenly, all on a sudden, all of a sudden. **হঠাৎ নবাব** an upstart; (cp.) nouveau riche.

হড়কানো *v.* to get out of position accidentally; to lose one's footing; to slip; to glide; to slide. **হড়কানি** *n.* slipping or gliding or sliding.

হড়বড় *int.* indicating : great rapidity in talking, moving, doing etc. **হড়বড়ানো** *v.* to hurry overmuch in talking, walking, doing etc.; to fuss and hurry. **হড়বড়ে** *a & adv.* over-hasty; fussy and hasty.

হড়হড় *int.* indicating : slipperiness; rapidity; rattling noise; rumbling noise (পেট হড়হড় করা). **হড়হড় করা** *v.* to be slippery (to the touch). **হড়হড়ে** *a.* slippery.

হণ্ডা, হণ্ডিকা, হণ্ডী *n.* (now rare) an urn.

হত *a.* killed, slain; ruined, destroyed, spoiled, pulled down, impaired; lost, bereft of; frustrated, foiled; bad, wretched. **~কুচ্ছিত** *a.* (coll.) very ugly or uncouth; very mean or vile; very indecent. **~গৌরব** *a.* deprived of glory, shorn of glory; past all glory. **~চেতন, ~চৈতন্য, ~জ্ঞান** *a.* deprived of consciousness, unconscious; stupefied, utterly perplexed or confounded, flabbergasted. **~চ্ছাড়া** *a.* graceless; wretched; reckless and dissipated. **হতচ্ছাড়া লোক** a scapegrace; a wretch; a reckless and dissipated person; a rascal, a rogue, a scoundrel, a loafer. **~প্রায়** *a.* almost or nearly killed. **~বাক** *a.* speechless owing to amazement; dumb; dumbfounded. **~বীর্য** *a.* having lost one's vigour, rendered vigourless; weakened. **~বুদ্ধি, ~ভম্ব** *a.* stupefied, nonplussed, utterly perplexed or confounded, flabbergasted. **~ভাগা, ~ভাগ্য** *a.* unfortunate, illfated; wretched, miserable. *fem.* **~ভাগিনী, ~ভাগী**। **~মান** *a.* dishonoured; humbled; humiliated; slighted; disgraced. **~শ্রদ্ধ** *a.* having lost one's reverence for or faith in; disgusted, browned off. **~শ্রদ্ধা** *n.* irreverence; apathy; disregard; neglect; slight; disdain, despise. **~শ্রী** *a.* deprived or shorn of one's grace or beauty or prosperity or glory.

হতাদর *a.* not received with cordiality or warmth; neglected; slighted. □ *n.* lack of cordial or warm reception; neglect; slight.

হতাশ *a.* disappointed, crestfallen; dejected, down in the mouth, despondent. **হতাশ করা** *v.* to disappoint; to deject. **হতাশা** *n.* disappointment; dejection, despondence, despondency.

হতাশ্বাস *a.* having lost one's reliance (on) or faith (in); bereft of hope, hopeless, dejected, crestfallen, despondent.

হতাহত *a.* dead and wounded.

হতে *post.* from, since; of. same as থেকে।

হতোদ্যম same as **ভগ্নোদ্যম**।

হতোস্মি *int.* I am undone. **হা হতোহস্মি** see **হা-হতোস্মি**।

হত্যা *n.* killing, slaughter; massacre; murder; persistent squatting at the temple of a deity for obtaining divine favour. **হত্যা করা** *v.* to kill, to slay; to massacre (lit. & fig.); to murder. **হত্যা দেওয়া** *v.* to squat at the temple of a deity for obtaining divine favour; (fig.) to solicit doggedly. **~কাণ্ড** *n.* an instance of homicide; carnage; killing; a massacre; murder. **~কারী** *n.* a homicide; a murderer; a slayer, a killer. *fem.* **~কারিণী** *n.* murderess. **হত্যাপরাধ** *n.* the offence of homicide or murder; culpable homicide amounting to murder. **হত্যাপরাধী** *a.* guilty of homicide or murder. ☐ *n.* a homicide; a murderer (*fem.* a murderess). *fem.* **হত্যাপরাধিনী**।

হত্যে coll. corrup. of **হত্যা**।

হদিশ[1] *n.* information, trace, clue, first taste or glimpse (সুখের হদিশ) ; whereabouts (তার হদিশ কেউ জানে না) ; a means, a way (মুক্তির হদিশ).

হদিশ[2] *n.* the body of traditions about Mohammad the Prophet, the hadith; Muslim jurisprudence.

হদ্দ *n.* boundary or jurisdiction. ☐ *a.* extreme (হদ্দ মজা) ; not exceeding, in all (হদ্দ চার কাঠা). **~মুদ্দ** *a.* & *adv.* at the most; at best.

হনন *n.* killing, slaying, slaughter, murdering, murder. **হনন করা** *v.* to kill, to slay; to murder. **হননীয়** *a.* that which can be or is fit to be killed or slaughtered or slain.

হনহন *int.* indicating : walking or moving at a great speed. **হনহনিয়ে** *adv.* at a great speed, very fast; in hot haste.

হনু, হনূ *n.* the jaw or the jawbone, the mandible; the chin; (obs.) the Entellus; the langur. **হনুমান** *n.* the langur; a character of the Ramayana.

হন্টন *n.* (*facet.*) walking; walk.

হন্তদন্ত *a.* extremely hurried and anxious, in a nervous hurry or flurry; fussy.

হন্তব্য *a.* fit to be killed or slain; to be killed or slain.

হন্তা *n.* a killer, a slayer; a murderer (*fem.* a murderess). ☐ *a.* killing, slaying; murdering. **হন্তারক** *n.* a killer, a slayer; an obstructor; an obstacle. ☐ *a.* killing, slaying; obstructing.

হন্ত্রী *fem.* of **হন্তা**।

হন্দর *n.* (obs.) a hundred weight.

হন্য same as **হন্তব্য**। **~মান** *a.* in the state of being killed or destroyed. **হন্যমান শরীর** the body subject to death and destruction; the dying body.

হন্যে *a.* frantically rushing and looking for (হন্যে হয়ে খোঁজা) ; madly rushing to kill or beat or bite or attack, (cp.) running amok; frenzied; rabid (হন্যে কুকুর).

হপ্তা dial. corrup. of **সপ্তাহ**।

হবচন্দ্র *n.* an utterly stupid king of folk tales. **হবচন্দ্র রাজার গবচন্দ্র মন্ত্রী** a king and his minister, both utterly stupid; (fig.) a stupid person and his equally stupid counsellor.

হবন *n.* an oblation of fire; a fire-sacrifice; burnt-offering. **হবনী** *n.* a pit for making sacrificial fire.

হবা *n.* Eve.

হবি *n.* any article esp. ghee offered in fire-sacrifice, a burnt-offering; clarified butter, ghee; an oblation of fire, a fire-sacrifice. **হবিষ্য, হবিষ্যান্ন, হবিষ্যি** *n.* (rare) sunned rice boiled in ghee; (pop.) boiled sunned rice and ghee. **হবিষ্য করা** *v.* to eat (nothing but) boiled sunned rice and ghee. **হবিষ্যাশী** *a.* eating (nothing but) boiled sunned rice and ghee.

হবু *a.* to-be; would-be; future.

হবুচন্দ্র var. of **হবচন্দ্র**।

হব্য *n.* same as **হবি**। ☐ *a.* fit to be offered in fire-sacrifice, oblational.

হম var. of **হাম[2]**।

হম্বা var. of **হাম্বা**।

হম্বিতম্বি *n.* bluster, bullying; intimidation. **হম্বিতম্বি করা** *v.* to bully, to bluster; to intimidate; to breathe fire.

হ-য-ব-র-ল *n.* gibberish, abracadabra; disorder, messy condition.

হয়[1] *n.* the horse, the stallion.

হয়² *v.* the form of **হওয়া** in the present tense and third person. **হয়কে নয় করা** (fig.) to disprove what is true, to undo or unsettle a settled fact. **হয়-হয়** *a.* impending, imminent.

হয়³ *con.* either (হয় তুমি, নয় সে). **হয়..........নয়** either.......or.

হয়তো *adv.* perhaps, perchance; possibly; probably.

হয়রান *a.* harassed; fatigued; badgered. exasperated. **হয়রান করা** *v.* to harass; to fatigue; to badger, to exasperate. **হয়রানি** *n.* harassment; fatigue; exasperation.

হর *n.* Shiva (শিব) ; (math.) a denominator or divisor. □ *a.* killing; destroying; removing or allaying; taking away; carrying off; robbing; (math.) deducting or dividing.

হরকত *n.* obstacle, hindrance, impediment, obstruction, stumbling block.

হরকরা *n.* a messenger; a courier; a postal messenger, a runner; a postman.

হরগৌরী *n.* Shiva (শিব) and Durga (দুর্গা) ; the manifestation of Shiva and Durga in one body.

হরঘড়ি *adv.* every hour; always; often, every now and then.

হরণ *n.* carrying off, robbing, plunder, stealing, pilferage, lifting; abduction; removal, allayment; destruction or act of taking away; (math.) division. **হরণ করা** *v.* to carry off, to rob, to plunder, to steal, to pilfer, to lift; to abduct; to remove, to allay; to destroy or to take away; (math.) to divide. **হরণ-পূরণ** *n.* division and multiplication.

হরতন *n.* hearts (of playing-cards).

হরতাল *n.* stoppage of all work in protest throughout a wide area, hartal.

হরতুকি coll. var. of **হরীতকী** ।

হরদম *adv.* always; incessantly, continuously, non-stop; often, every now and then.

হরফ *n.* any letter of the alphabet, a character; (print.) a type. **হরফ-ঢালাই** *n.* typecasting. **হরফ ঢালাইয়ের কারখানা** a type-foundry.

হরবোলা *n.* one who mimics or is capable of mimicking various voices, sounds, notes etc., (cp.) a mimic.

হর-হর-বম্-বম্ *int.* a sound uttered in honour of Shiva (শিব).

হরষ, হরষিত poet. corruptions of **হর্ষ** and **হর্ষিত** respectively.

হরা¹ *a. fem.* of **হর** ।

হরা² poet. form of **হরণ করা** ।

হরি *n.* Narayana (নারায়ণ), Vishnu (বিষ্ণু), Krishna (কৃষ্ণ). □ *a.* yellow or auburn. **হরি ঘোষের গোয়াল** (lit.) the cowhouse of Hari Ghosh; (fig. & facet.) a place where noise and confusion reign; a pandemonium. **হরির লুট** scattering of বাতাসা, that is, sweet drops, in honour of Lord Hari for the congregation of devotees to pick up. **হরি হরি** O Hari! O Hari! (uttered to express amazement, disgust etc.) **~গুণগান** *n.* act of singing the glory of Lord Hari. **~চন্দন** see **চন্দন** । **~জন** *n.* (lit.) Lord Hari's people or flock; (pop.) the depressed classes amongst Hindus or a member of these classes. **~তাল** *n.* yellow orpiment. **~তাল-ভস্ম** *n.* the calx of yellow orpiment. **~ধ্বনি** *n.* a loud shouting of the name of Lord Hari. **~নাম করা** *v.* to utter (repeatedly) the name of Lord Hari in devotion. **~নামের ঝোলা বা ঝুলি** a bag to hold the rosary of beads which keep count of the number of times the name of Lord Hari is repeated by a devotee. **~নামের মালা** rosary of beads which keep count of the number of times the name of Lord Hari is uttered by a devotee. **~প্রেম** *n.* attachment or devotion to Lord Hari. **~বাসর** *n.* any eleventh lunar day of a fortnight which is a day of fast; (facet.) fasting. **~বাসর করা** *v.* (facet.) to go without food, to fast. **~বোল** *n & int.* a loud shouting of this word meaning "shout the name of Lord Hari". **~ভক্ত** *a.* devoted to or worshipping Lord Hari. □ *n.* a devotee of Lord Hari; a Vaishnava. **~ভক্তি** *n.* devotion to Lord Hari. **~ভক্তি উবে যাওয়া** *v.* (idiom.) to have one's high esteem or confidence lost. **~মটর** *n.* fast, fasting; going without food. **~মটর করা** *v.*

(facet.) to dine with Duke Humphrey or with Democritus, to enjoy Barmecide's feast, to tighten one's belt, to go without food. ~সংকীর্তন *n.* singing in chorus in praise of Lord Hari; a song thus sung. ~সভা *n.* an assembly to discuss the glory of Lord Hari. ~হর *n.* Lord Hari and Lord Hara or Shiva (শিব). ~হরাত্মা *a.* (usu. of two friends) inseparably united (like Lord Hari and Lord Hara in one body), (having) one soul and one mind, bosom.

হরিণ *n.* the buck, the stag, the deer (*pl.* deer); the antelope. *fem.* **হরিণী** the doe, the hind, the female deer or antelope. ~ছানা, ~শাবক, ~শিশু *n.* a fawn. ~নয়না, ~লোচনা, হরিণাক্ষী *a. fem.* fawn-eyed. ~বাড়ি *n.* a prison-house of ancient Calcutta; a prison, a gaol, a jail, a house of correction. **হরিণের মাংস** *n.* (as food) venison.

হরিৎ, হরিত *n.* the green colour; verdure. ☐ *a.* green; verdant. **হরিতাশ্ম** *n.* emerald; green vitriol; (erron. but pop.) blue vitriol.

হরিদ্বর্ণ *n* & *a.* green; yellow.

হরিদ্রা *n.* turmeric. ~বর্ণ *n.* & *a.* yellow. ~ভ *a.* yellowish.

হরিয়াল *n.* a species of yellow bird of the dove kind, the green pigeon.

হরিষ poet. corrup. of **হর্ষ**। **হরিষে-বিষাদ** *n.* a sudden onset of sorrow or calamity in the midst of joy or merry-making.

হরীতকী *n.* black myrobalan.

হরেক *a.* many and diverse; assorted; different (হরেক মত). ~রকম of various kinds; assorted.

হরেদরে *adv.* on the whole; on an average.

হর্তা *a* & *n.* one who carries off or robs or steals or abducts or removes or allays or destroys or kills. *fem.* **হর্ত্রী**। ~কর্তা *n.* a destroyer and builder; a killer and creator; (fig.) an absolute ruler, a dictator. ~কর্তাবিধাতা *n.* a destroyer, a killer and maintainer; a killer, creator and preserver; (fig.) an absolute ruler, a dictator.

হর্ম্য *n.* a large and beautiful building, an edifice, a mansion, a palace. ~তল *n.* the floor of any room of a mansion or palace. ~রাজি (for.) *n. pl.* large and grand mansions, palatial buildings.

হর্যক্ষ *n.* a lion.

হর্ষ *n.* joy, delight, pleasure; mirth; happiness; erection. (রোমহর্ষ) **হর্ষণ** *n.* same as **হর্ষ**। ☐ *a.* giving joy, joyful, delightful, delightsome, pleasant; causing to stand up, upright (লোমহর্ষণ). ~বিহ্বল *a.* beside oneself with joy. **হর্ষিত** *a.* gladdened, delighted, pleased. **হর্ষোচ্ছ্বাস** *n.* ecstasy, rapture, elation. **হর্ষোৎফুল্ল** *a.* blooming or beaming with joy or delight.

হল[১] *n.* gilding. **হল করা** *v.* to gild. ~করা *a.* gilded, gilt.

হল[২] *n.* the main room in a great house, a hall. Also **হলঘর**।

হল[৩] *n.* a plough. ~কর্ষণ করা, ~চালনা করা *v.* to plough, to till (land). ~চালক *n.* a ploughman, a tiller (of land), one who drives the plough. ~ধর, ~ভৃৎ same as **হলী**। ~ভৃতি *n.* agriculture, cultivation.

হলকা *n.* (obs.) a flock, a troop ('ষোড়শ হলকা হাতী') ; (pop.) a sudden hot wave (আগুনের হলকা).

হলদি *n.* (dial.) turmeric.

হলদে *a.* & *n.* yellow.

হলন্ত *a.* (gr.) ending with a (হল্ or হস্) sound or sign.; consonantal. ☐ *n.* a consonant; (gr.) the sublinear consonant sign (হল্ or হস্).

হলফ, হলপ *n.* a solemn swearing or oath. **হলফ করা** *v.* to swear, to take an oath. **ঈশ্বরের নামে হলফ করা** *v.* to swear by God. **হলফ করে বলা** *v.* to swear to. ~নামা *n.* an affidavit.

হলহল *int.*. indicating: overmuch looseness or slackness. **হলহলে** *a.* very loose or slack.

হলায়ুধ *n.* one using a plough as one's weapon; Balaram (বলরাম), the elder brother of Krishna (কৃষ্ণ).

হলাহল *n.* (myth.) a deadly poison.

হলী *n.* one equipped with a plough; a ploughman, a cultivator; Balaram (বলরাম) the elder brother of Krishna (কৃষ্ণ).

হলুদ *n.* turmeric; the yellow colour. □ *a.* yellow.

হল্য *a.* cultivable , arable. *fem.* **হল্যা** *n.* cultivated land.

হল্লা *n.* a riotous uproar or tumult, a hullabaloo; (sl.) a raid or chase by a posse of policemen. **হল্লা করা** *v.* to make a riotous uproar, to make a hullabaloo; to kick up a row.

হস্‌, হস্‌চিহ্ন *n.* (gr.) the sublinear sign of the consonant sound; ' ্ ' this sign.

হসন *n.* act of laughing or smiling; a laughter , a laugh; a smile.

হসন্ত var. of **হলন্ত**।

হসন্তিকা, হসন্তী *n.* a vessel for holding fire, a fire-pot, a fire-urn.

হসিত *a.* laughing; smiling; blooming.

হস্ত *n.* the hand; the forearm; the arm; the corresponding limb of beasts; a cubit. (দুই হস্তপরিমিত). **~কণ্ডূয়ন** *n.* (lit. but rare) the itching of the hand; (pop. & fig.) a strong desire to do something by the hand esp. to beat or write. **~কৌশল** *n.* artful use of the hand; (loos.) palming; sleight-of-hand. **~ক্ষেপ করা, ~ক্ষেপণ করা** *v.* to set one's hand to; to intervene, to interfere. **~গত** *a.* in one's possession, in hand, on hand; obtained; appropriated; received; seized. **~গত করা** *v.* to secure possession of, to get hold of; to get in hand or on hand; to appropriate; to seize. **~চালনা করা** *v.* to move one's hand; (facet.) to beat, to flog. **~চালিত** *a.* driven or run by the hand, hand-driven. **~চ্যুত** *a.* passed or slipped out of one's hand. **~চ্যুত হওয়া** *v.* to pass out of one's hand or possession or control; to slip out of one's hand. **~তল** *n.* the palm of one's hand. **~দ্বয়** *n.* the two hands, both hands. **~ধারণ করা** *v.* to hold one's hand. **~প্রসারণ করা** *v.* to stretch out or extend one's hand. **~মৈথুন** *n.* masturbation; self-abuse. **~রেখা** *n.* the line on the palm. **~রেখা পাঠ করা** *v.* to tell (one's) fortune from the lines on the palm. **~রেখা বিচার করা** *v.* to tell one's fortune by studying the lines on the palm. **~রেখাবিদ** *n.* a palmist. **~লাঘব করা** *v.* to palm. **~লিখিত** *a.* written by hand. **~লিখিত পুঁথি** a manuscript. **~লিপি, ~লেখ** *n.* handwriting; a manuscript. **~লিপি-বিশেষজ্ঞ** same as **হস্তাক্ষর-বিশেষজ্ঞ**। **~শিল্প** *n.* handicraft; handiwork. **~শিল্পী** *n.* a handicraftsman (*fem.* a handicraftswoman), an artisan. **হস্তাক্ষর** *n.* handwriting; calligraphy. **হস্তাক্ষর-বিশেষজ্ঞ** *n.* an expert in handwriting, a ch(e)irographist. **হস্তাঙ্গুলি** *n.* a finger. **হস্তান্তর** *n.* (rare) another or a different hand; (pop.) transfer to another's hand or possession or control; handing over; (law) conveyance; (rare) transfer to another hand. **হস্তান্তরের দলিল** a deed of conveyance. **হস্তান্তর করা** *v.* to transfer to another's hand or possession or control; to hand (something) over (to). **হস্তান্তরিত** *a.* transferred to another's hand or possession or control; handed over; (rare) transferred to another hand. **হস্তামলকবৎ** *a.* & *adv.* like a myrobalan placed on the palm of the hand; already in one's grasp. **হস্তার্পণ করা** *v.* to lay hands on; to set one's hand to; to interfere, to intervene.

হস্তবুদ *a.* accounts past and present; a descriptive rent-roll (of an estate) drawn up annually.

হস্তা *n.* the thirteenth of the twenty-seven zodiacal stars according to Hindu astornomy.

হস্তিদন্ত *n.* the elephant's tusk; ivory. **~খচিত** *a.* inlaid with ivory.

হস্তিনী *n. fem.* the female elephant, the cow-elephant; the worst of four types of women from the point of view of sexual union.

হস্তিপ, হস্তিপক *n.* the driver or keeper of an elephant.

হস্তিমদ *n.* a water secretion from the nostrils, eyes and penis of a must elephant.

হস্তিমূর্খ *a.* utterly stupid.

হস্তিশালা *n.* a stable for housing elephants.

হস্তিশুণ্ড *n.* the elephant's trunk.

হস্তী *n.* the elephant.

হা *int.* indicating : grief, suffering, amazement etc.; oh, ah, ha, alas.

হাই *n.* a yawn. **হাই তোলা** *v.* to yawn.

হাইফেন *n.* (gr.) a hyphen. **হাইফেন দেওয়া** *v.* to hyphen, to hyphenate.

হাউই, হাউইবাজি *n.* a rocket (for fireworks display).

হাউমাউ *n.* a loud or uproarious complaint attended with wailing; hue and cry. **হাউমাউ করা** *v.* to make a loud or uproarious complaint wailingly, to raise a hue and cry.

হাওড় *n.* an extensive marsh or quagmire or fen.

হাওদা *n.* a seat fixed on an elephant's back, a howdah, a haudah.

হাওয়া *n.* air; wind; breeze; climate; (fig.) contact or influence (দুষ্টের হাওয়া) ; (fig.) general tendency, trend (যুগের হাওয়া). **হাওয়া করা** *v.* to fan. **হাওয়া খাওয়া** *v.* to enjoy fanning; to have an airing; to air oneself; (sl.) to fast, to eat Barmecide's feast. **হাওয়া দেওয়া** *v.* to fan; (facet.) to decamp. **হাওয়া পাওয়া** *v.* to get air; (fig.) to get stimulus; (fig.) to come in contact (of) or to be influenced (by); (fig.) to sense. **হাওয়া বদল** *n.* a change of air; (lit. & fig.) a change of climate. **হাওয়া-বন্দুক** *n.* an air-gun. **হাওয়া লাগা** same as **হাওয়া পাওয়া** except the last meaning. **হাওয়া হওয়া** *v.* (facet.) to disappear, to vanish (into thin air); to decamp, to flee. **হাওয়া লাগানো** *v.* to air. **~অফিস** *n.* meteorological office. **~গাড়ি** *n.* a motor-car, a car.

হাওলা *n.* custody; charge. **হাওলা করা** *v.* to commit to the custody or charge of. **~জমি** *n.* a piece of land held under fixed terms and conditions. **~দার** *n.* one who holds an aforesaid piece of land.

হাওলাত *n.* borrowing; a debt; a loan. **হাওলাত করা** *v.* to borrow. **হাওলাত দেওয়া** *v.* to lend. **হাওলাত-বরাদ্দ** *n.* borrowing and fixing a future point of time for payment. **হাওলাতি** *a.* borrowed, taken on loan.

হাঁ[1] *n.* open mouth or expanse of open mouth or beak; a gape; an opening, an orifice (গর্তের হাঁ). **হাঁ করা** *v.* to stare with open mouth, to open one's mouth, to gape. **হাঁ হওয়া** *v.* to become wide open, to gape; to form a large hole in oneself. **হাঁ-হওয়া** *a.* gaping (such as wound).

হাঁ[2] *int. & adv.* indicating: acquiescence, affirmation, confirmation, presence, response etc., yes.

হাঁ[3]**, হাঁগা** *int.* used in addressing a person familiarly (হাঁগা মেয়ে).

হাঁউমাউ alt. spell. of **হাউমাউ**।

হাঁক *n.* a loud call or shout. **হাঁক দেওয়া, হাঁক পাড়া** *v.* to call or shout loudly, to bawl (to).

হাঁকডাক *n.* repeated loud calls or shouts; wide reputation of being wealthy and powerful. **হাঁকডাক পাড়া** *v.* to raise a hue and cry.

হাঁকড়ানো *v.* to brandish or move with an eclat (লাঠি বা ব্যাট হাঁকড়ানো) ; to drive very speedily or proudly (গাড়ি হাঁকড়ানো) ; to build with a great eclat (বাড়ি হাঁকড়ানো).

হাঁকপাক var. of **আঁকুপাঁকু**।

হাঁকা *v.* to call or announce or declare loudly.

হাঁকানো *v.* to drive away, to chase away; to drive proudly (গাড়ি হাঁকানো).

হাঁকাহাঁকি *n.* repeated loud calling or shouting. **হাঁকাহাঁকি করা** *v.* to call or shout loudly and repeatedly.

হাঁচা *v.* to sneeze. **~নো** *v.* to cause to sneeze.

হাঁচি *n.* a sneeze.

হাঁটকানো *v.* to rummage busily; to make a mess of in course of rummaging.

হাঁটা *v.* to walk. **~নো** *v.* to cause to walk; to teach one (esp. a baby) how to walk. **~পথ** *n.* a way to be covered by walking. **~হাঁটি** *n.* repeated walking; repeated visits on foot. **~হাঁটি করা** *v.* to go (to) or visit repeatedly on foot.

হাঁটু *n.* the knee. **হাঁটু গাড়া, হাঁটু পাতা** *v.* to kneel down, to be on one's knees. **এক হাঁটু জল** knee-deep water.

হাঁটুনি *n.* walking, ambulation.

হাঁড়ি *n.* an urn-shaped pot. **কেলে হাঁড়ি** an urn-shaped clay pot turned black on account of being used in cooking for a long time. **~কুড়ি** *n.* different pots and jars collectively; kitchen utensils. **হাঁড়ি ঠেলা** *v.* (fig.) to be burdened with the drudgery of cooking. **হাঁড়ির খবর** (fig.) the private affair; internal secrets or information.

হাঁড়িচাঁচা *n.* a bird akin to the magpie, the Indian tree-pie.

হাঁড়িয়া *n.* an inferior liquor distilled from fermented rice, rice-beer.

হাঁদা *a.* fat, corpulent; idiot, dull-witted. **~রাম** *n.* an idiot of idiots, a great idiot.

হাঁপ, হাঁফ *n.* laboured breathing; panting; asthmatic spasm. **হাঁপ ওঠা** same as **হাঁপ ধরা।** **হাঁপ ছাড়া** *v.* to expel a deep breath; (fig.) to breathe freely. **হাঁপ ছাড়ার অবকাশ** breathing-time, breathing-space, respite; a breather. **হাঁপ ধরা** *v.* to be out of breath; to pant, to breathe hard; to be seized with an asthmatic spasm. **হাঁপ ছেড়ে বাঁচা** *v.* (fig.) to breathe again, to heave a sigh of relief. **হাঁপানো** *v.* to pant; (fig.) to fidget. **হাঁপানি** *n.* panting; asthma. **হাঁপনি-রোগী** *n.* an asthmatic patient,

হাঁস *n.* the drake; (*fem.*) the duck; the gander; (*fem.*) the goose, swan. **হাঁস মারা ছটরা** duck-shot.

হাঁসকল *n.* a hasp; a latch.

হাঁসফাঁস *n.* laboured breathing; (fig.) fidget. **হাঁসফাঁস করা** *v.* to breathe with difficulty, to gasp for breath; to fidget.

হাঁসিয়া var. of **হাসিয়া।**

হাঁসুয়া *n.* a crescent-shaped knife with a haft.

হাঁসুলি *n.* a crescent necklace.

হাঁ-হাঁ *int.* used to prevent or interrupt suddenly.

হাকিক *n.* a kind of precious stone, cornelian.

হাকিম[১] pop. var. of **হকিম।**

হাকিম[২] *n.* a magistrate; a deputy magistrate; a judge; a ruler. **হাকিমি** *n.* magistracy. ☐ *a.* magisterial.

হাগা *v.* (*ind.*) to evacuate one's bowels, to ease or relieve nature; to have loose motions. **হাগানো** *v.* to evacuate another's bowels, to purge; to cause to have loose motions.

হাঘর *n.* (rare) a homeless person; (pop.) a low family. **হাঘরে** *a.* born of a low or indigent family.

হাঙর *n.* the shark; (fig.) an extortioner; (fig.) a sharper.

হাঙ্গামা, (corrup.) **হাঙ্গাম** *n.* a riot, an affray; a disturbance; a difficulty; a hitch; a raid, an inroad. **হাঙ্গামা করা, হাঙ্গামা বাধানো** *v.* to riot, to create a disturbance or difficulty, to brew trouble or mischief.

হাজত, হাজতখানা *n.* a guardroom for under-trial prisoners; a (police) lock-up; police custody.

হাজরি *n.* same as **হাজিরা** and—a European or English meal. **ছোট হাজরি** break-fast. **বড় হাজরি** lunch; dinner.

হাজা *v.* to rot or be spoilt by being drenched in water (esp. in rain-water) for a long time (ধান হাজা) ; to be affected with chilblain (পা হাজা). ☐ *n.* excessive rainfall or flood (হাজাশুখা) ; sore caused by excessive use of water, chilblain. **~মজা** *a.* (of a pond) shallow and miry.

হাজার *n & a.* thousand. **হাজার হাজার, হাজারে হাজারে** thousands of; countless; in countless number; in thousands. **হাজারে একটা** one in a thousand. **হাজার বললেও** even if repeated a thousand times or times without number. **হাজারি** *n.* a commander of a troop of thousand soldiers.

হাজাশুখা *n.* excessive rain or flood and drought.

হাজি *n.* a pious Muslim who has performed pilgrimage to Mecca and Madina, a haji.

হাজির *a.* appeared; present; attendant. **হাজির করা বা করানো** *v.* to bring (one) in presence (of), to make one appear, to present. **হাজির থাকা** *v.* to be in attendance; to attend; to be present. **হাজির হওয়া, হাজিরা দেওয়া** *v.* to put in an appearance, to appear; to attend; to be present. **হাজিরা, হাজিরি** *n.* attendance, appearance; presence. **হাজিরা-খাতা, হাজিরা-বই, হাজিরি-খাতা, হাজিরি-বই** *n.* an attendance register.

হাট *n.* a market (esp. one held on fixed days of the week); a fair; (fig.) a disturbingly noisy place (ঘর তো নয়—হাট) ;

(fig.) a concourse, an assemblage (বোকার হাট) ; (fig.) abundance, plenty (রূপের হাট). **হাট করা** *v.* to visit a market for buying and selling, to market; (fig.) to open fully or to open to public view (দরজা বা হৃদয় হাট করা). **হাট বসানো, হাট মেলানো** *v.* to establish a market; (fig.) to cause to assemble; to make a loud disturbing noise. **ভাঙা হাট** a market or fair on the point of closing for the day or for the term or for good; (fig.) anything disrupted or on the point of winding up. **~বার** *n.* a market-day. **হাটুরিয়া,** (coll.) **হাটুরে** *n.* a market-man (*fem.* a market-woman). □ *a.* carrying goods (and also people) to the market (হাটুরে নৌকা) ; going to the market for buying or selling, market-bound, marketing (হাটুরে লোক). **হাটে হাঁড়ি ভাঙা** to disclose or reveal one's guilt or wrongdoing in public, (cp.) to wash one's dirty linen in public.

হাড় *n.* bone. □ *a.* (used as a *pfx.*) to the bones, inveterate, utter. **হাড় কালি করা** *v.* (fig.) to exhaust or exasperate utterly (with toil or affliction); (fig.) to beat black and blue. **হাড় গুঁড়ো করা বা চূর্ণ করা** *v.* (fig.) to beat soundly, to belabour. **হাড় জুড়ানো** *v.* (fig.) to relieve or to feel relieved. **হাড় জ্বালানো** *v.* (fig.) to trouble or pester in the extreme. **হাড় ভাঙা, হাড়মাস আলাদা করা** same as **হাড় গুঁড়ো করা। হাড়ে বাতাস লাগা** *v.* (fig.) to feel relieved. **হাড়ে-মাসে জড়ানো** *v.* (fig.) to be inseparably connected. **~কাঠ, ~কাট** variants of **হাড়িকাঠ। ~কৃপণ** *a.* extremely miserly or niggardly; close-fisted. **হাড়কৃপণ লোক** a skinflint. **~গিলা,** (coll.) **~গিলে** *n.* the adjutant stork, the argala; (fig.) a long-necked long-legged thin person, (cp.) a bag of bones. **~গোড়** *n.* bones and ribs. **~জিরজিরে** *a.* (fig.) reduced to a skeleton, skinny. **~জ্বালানে** *a.* (fig.) troubling or pestering in the extreme. **~পাকা** *a.* (fig.) precocious to the bones. **~পাজি, ~বজ্জাত, ~বদমাশ** *a.* wicked to the bones. **~ভাঙা** *a.* (fig.) extremely toilsome or fatiguing, extremely strenuous. **~হদ্দ** *n.* all particulars or information. **~হাভাতে** *adv.* utterly indigent or wretched. **হাড়ে হাড়ে** *adv.* to the bones.

হাড়ি *n.* a scheduled caste amongst Hindus; a member of this caste.

হাড়িকাঠ, হাড়িকাট *n.* a wooden framework to which the neck of a sacrificial victim is fixed at the time of immolation.

হাডুডু, হাডু-ডুডু *n.* an Indian outdoor game, kabadi (কবাডি) ।

হাড্ডি *n.* (usu. facet.) bone. **~সার** *a.* reduced to a skeleton, very gaunt, skinny, skin and bone.

হাত *n.* the hand or the fore-arm or the arm; the corresponding limb of beasts; a cubit; (fig.) possession or control; (fig.) influence or manipulation, hand. **কাঁচা হাত** an inexperienced or unskilled worker, a raw or poor hand. **খালি হাত** an empty hand; an unornamented hand. **ছোট হাতের অক্ষর** a small letter (of the English alphabet). **পাকা হাত** a skilled or experienced worker, an old hand. **বড় হাতের অক্ষর** a capital letter (of the English alphabet). **হাত আসা** *v.* to develop the habit of. **হাত কচলানো** *v.* to wring one's hand (in order to express regret or to curry favour). **হাত করা** *v.* (fig.) to win (one) over or to bring under one's control or to bring into one's possession. **হাত কামড়ানো** *v.* (fig.) to squirm (lit. to bite one's hands) in disappointment or frustration. **হাত গোনা** *v.* to read one's hand or palm. **হাত গোটানো** *v.* (fig.) to take off one's hands, to cease participating in a work. **হাত চলা** *v.* to work quickly with one's hands, (fig.) to raise one's hand to strike (কথায় কথায় হাত চলে). **হাত চালানো** *v.* to quicken pace of work; to beat or belabour with one's hand, to cuff. **হাত জোড় করা** *v.* to fold one's hands; to apologize or solicit or salute with folded hands. **হাত জোড়া থাকা** *v.* to have one's hands full. **হাত তোলা** *v.* to beat with the hand, to lay hands on, to deal or strike a blow (to some one) with one's hand, to assault; to raise one's hand in order to vote for (or against) or to express one's assent, to raise one's hand (to support a person or a proposal). **হাত দিয়ে হাতি ঠেলা** (fig.) to accomplish a stupendous task by humble means. **হাত দেওয়া** *v.* to touch with one's hand to handle; to take in hand, to set one's hand to, to undertake; to intervene. **কপালে হাত দেওয়া** *v.* to become utterly dejected and stupefied at one's ill-luck. **হাত দেখা** *v.* to read one's hand or palm. **হাত ধরাধরি করে চলা** to walk hand in hand. **হাত পড়া** *v.* to be touched or handled; to be taken in hand, to be undertaken; to be interfered with. **হাত পাকানো** *v.* to get one's hands used to something by practice, to become skilled by practice. **হাত পাতা** *v.* to earnestly request or ask for (momentary) assistance or help, to beg. **হাত বোলানো** *v.* to pass one's hand lightly and often caressingly over anything. **গায়ে হাত বোলানো** *v.* (fig.) to win over or propitiate or pacify or console with adulatory words and caressing. **মাথায় হাত বোলানো** *v.* (facet.) to cheat by cajolery, to wheedle (something out of somebody), to wangle. **হাত মুঠো করা** *v.* to clench the fist. **হাতে করা** same as **হাতে নেওয়া**। **হাতে কলমে শেখা** *v.* to learn firsthand. **হাতেগোনা** *a.* only a handful, very few in number. **হাতে জল না গলা** (fig.) to be extremely close-fisted or miserly. **হাতে ধরা** *v.* (idiom.) to importunate or solicit very ardently. **হাতে নয় ভাতে মারা** *v.* (fig.) to subdue or weaken not by beating but by starving. **হাতে নেওয়া** *v.* to take or hold in one's hand; to take up or undertake. **হাতে পাওয়া** *v.* (fig.) to get under one's control. **হাতে পাঁজি মঙ্গলবার** (fig.) ready proof. **হাতে বেড়ি পড়া** *v.* (lit.) to be handcuffed; (fig.) to be arrested by the police on a criminal charge. **হাতে মাথা কাটা** *v.* (fig.) to become very haughty or to become very proud of one's power or authority. **হাতের ঢিল ছুড়ে দিলে আর ফেরে না** (fig.) a shot in the locker once thrown will not come back. **হাতের লক্ষ্মী পায়ে ঠেলা** *v.* (fig.) to throw away one's fortune. **~কড়ি, ~কড়া** *n.* a handcuff. **হাতকড়ি দেওয়া** বা **পরানো** *v.* to handcuff. **~করাত** *n.* a handsaw. **~কষা** *a.* stingy, niggardly, closefisted. **~কাটা** *a.* having one's arm or arms amputated; armless; (of shirts, blouses etc.), sleeveless. **~খরচ** *n.* pocket money. **~খালি** *a.* empty-handed; wearing no ornament in one's hands; having all one's money exhausted, broke; having no work on hand. **~খোলা** *a.* given to spending profusely, lavish; bountiful. **~চিঠি** *n.* a hand-note, a note or a sum of money borrowed; a chit; a short note or letter. **~ছাড়া** *a.* out of possession or control, lost, out of hand. **~ছানি** *n.* a beckoning with the hand. **~ছানি দেওয়া** *v.* to beckon with the hand. **~টান** *n.* stinginess; frugality; pilfering habit. **হাতড়ানো** *v.* to grope; to appropriate to oneself; to misappropriate. **~তালি** *n.* clapping of hands. **তালি দেওয়া** *v.* to clap one's hands. **~তোলা** *n.* a thing obtained out of another's favour; a charitable gift. **~ধরা** *a.* very obedient to. **হাত-পা বাঁধা** *a.* utterly helpless; inescapably bound to. **হাত-পা বেঁধে জলে ফেলা** *v.* (fig.) to throw or fling to the jaws of death whence escape is impossible; to consign to utter misery. **~বদল হওয়া** *v.* to change hands. **~বাক্স** *n.* a small box esp. for keeping money and other small valuables, a cash box, a handbox. **~বোমা** *n.* a hand-grenade. **~ভারী** *a.* close-fisted, stingy. **~মোজা** *n.* gloves. **~যশ** *n.* reputation for efficiency (esp. of physicians, lawyers, artisans etc.). **~ল** *n.* a handle. **~সই** *n.* good marksmanship. **~সাফাই** *n.* skill of the hand; sleight of hand; deftness in pilfering with the hand; the state of being light-fingered.

হাতা¹ *n.* limits; area, confines, precincts (বাড়ির হাতা)।

হাতা² *n.* a ladle; a sleeve (of a coat, shirt etc.). **হাত দিয়ে তোলা** *v.* to ladle out. **ফুলহাতা** *a.* having sleeves up to wrists. **হাফহাতা** *a.* having sleeves up to elbows only.

হাতানো *v.* to seize or to take possession of

(esp. by cunning); to appropriate to oneself; to misappropriate, to defalcate; to rummage with the hand; to handle.

হাতাহাতি *n.* a scuffle with hands, a hand-to-hand fight. ☐ *a.* hand-to-hand. **হাতাহাতি লড়াই** a battle-royal.

হাতি[1] *a.* (used as a *sfx.*) measuring so many cubits (দশহাতি ধুতি) ; directed towards the right or the left hand.

হাতি[2] *n.* the elephant; (fig.) a very corpulent or hefty or bulky or gigantic person. **হাতি পোষা** *v.* to keep an elephant; (fig.) to employ or keep somebody who entails tremendous expenditure for the employer or keeper. **হাতির খোরাক** an elephant's feed; (fig.) an enormous feed. **হাতির দাঁত** a tusk. **হাতির শুঁড়** a trunk.

হাতিয়ার *n.* a hand-weapon or handtool; a weapon; a tool. **~বন্দ** *a.* carrying arms on one's person, armed.

হাতিশাল *n.* a stable for housing elephants.

হাতিশুঁড় *n.* artichoke.

হাতুড়ি *n.* a hammer.

হাতুড়ে *a.* quacksalving, charlatanic. ☐ *n.* a quacksalver, a quack, a mountebank, a charlatan. **হাতুড়ে চিকিৎসক** a quack physician, a quack. **~গিরি** *n.* quackery, mountebankery, mountebankism, charlatanism.

হাতে *adv.* by hand; at hand; ready to hand; on hand. **হাতে-কলমে** *adv.* first-hand; by direct practice and training. **~খড়ি** *n.* the sacrament of initiation into one's studies, first lesson in writing to a child; (fig.) initiation into a work; commencement of apprenticeship or the initial stage of learning (a trade etc.). **~গড়া** *a.* handmade; (fig.) brought up or built (up) by oneself. **~নাতে** *adv.* in the very act of doing, red-handed. **হাতে স্বর্গ পাওয়া** to be blessed with an unexpected stroke of luck. **হাতে-হাতে** *adv.* from hand to hand; red-handed; directly; readily, promptly (হাতে-হাতে বিদায়) ৷

হাদিশ var. of **হদিশ**[2] ৷

হানা *v.* to drive (a weapon etc.), to strike with, to shoot (তির হানা) ; to cast, to dart (দৃষ্টি হানা) ; to flash (বিজলি হানা). ☐ *n.* an attack (শত্রুর হানা) ; a raid (পুলিশের হানা). ☐ *a.* haunted (by an evil spirit). **হানা দেওয়া** *v.* to raid; to haunt. **~দার** *n.* a raider. **~বাড়ি** *n.* a haunted house. **~হানি** *n.* mutual fighting, dash.

হানি *n.* destruction; loss, damage, impairment; a harm, an injury. **হানি করা** *v.* to destroy; to damage, to impair; to injure. **হানি নেই** (there is) no harm. **~কর** *a.* causing loss, destructive; damaging, impairing; harmful, injurious.

হাপর *n.* a furnace (esp. of a smith), a forge; bellows, a blower.

হাপিত্যেশ *n.* very greedy or eager expectation or longing; (erron.) regret or repentance. **হাপিত্যেশ করা** *v.* to long for or expect very greedily or eagerly; to regret or repent.

হাপুস[1] *a.* streaming with tears (হাপুস নয়নে কাঁদা).

হাপুস[2] *int.* indicating: the sound of eating noisily. **~হুপুস** *int.* indicating: quick repetition of the aforesaid sound.

হাফ *a.* half. **হাফ-আখড়াই** *n.* a kind of Bengali song-tournament. **হাফ-গেরস্ত** *n.* a demi-rep. **হাফ-টিকিট** *n.* a ticket (of railway, cinema, theatre etc.) issued at a concessional price to children, a concessional ticket. **হাফ-ডে** *n.* a half-holiday; work or wages for half the usual daily working hours, half time (also **হাফ-রোজ**).

হাব *n.* an artistic gesture or attitude or pose. **~ভাব** *n.* gestures and deportment; demeanour.

হাবলা *a.* dull-witted; idiotic.

হাবশি *n.* an Abyssinian; an African negro.

হাবা *a.* devoid of the power of speech, dumb; dull-witted, stupid, idiotic; boobyish. **হাবা লোক** a lubberly lout, a booby, a clodhopper, a dolt, a numskull, an idiot (also **হাবাগবা লোক**).

হাবিলদার *n.* an Indian sergeant, a havildar.

হাবুডুবু *n.* alternately rising above and going under water (as done by a drowning person), fidgety struggle of a drowning person to keep above water; (fig.) struggle to escape something, deep engrossment or involvement (কাজ বা দেনায় হাবুডুবু). **হাবুডুবু খাওয়া** *v.* to struggle with fidgetiness to keep afloat; (fig.) to be deeply engrossed, to be over head and ears.

হাবেলি *n.* a building; a residential house; a row or cluster of residential houses; huts, lines.

হাভাত, হাভাতে *n.* one without means of procuring one's daily food; (fig.) an utterly indigent or wretched person. □ *a.* having no means to procure one's daily food; utterly indigent or wretched.

হাম১ *n.* measles.

হাম২ *pro.* (obs. & poet.) I.

হামড়ি var. of **হুমড়ি**।

হামবড়া, হামবড় *a.* considering oneself the chief of all, self-important, self-conceited, egotistic(al); bumptious.

হামলা *n.* an attack; an assault; a raid; a riot; a row. **হামলা করা** *v.* to launch an attack or assault or raid (upon); to riot; to kick up a row.

হামলানো *v.* to low loudly for the calf (as by the cow).

হামা, হামাগুড়ি *n.* movement on all fours, crawling. **হামা টানা, হামাগুড়ি দেওয়া** *v.* to move on all fours, to crawl.

হামান *n.* an iron mortar. **~দিস্তা** *n.* mortar and pestle made of iron.

হামাম *n.* a bathing establishment, a Turkish bath, a hammam.

হামেশা *adv.* always; often.

হামেহাল same as **হামেশা**।

হাম্বা *int.* & *n.* the noise made by cows, low.

হাম্বির *n.* an Indian musical mode.

হায় *int..* expressing: regret, remorse, etc.; alas, ah. **হায় হায় করা** *v.* to utter repeatedly exclamations of regret, remorse etc.; (cp.) to beat the breast. **হায় রে কপাল** alack-a-day, alack.

হায়ন *n.* a calendar year, a year; an era.

হায়া *n.* bashfulness; modesty.

হার১ *n.* defeat. **~জিত** *n.* defeat and victory. **হার মানা, হার স্বীকার করা** *v.* to acknowledge defeat.

হার২ *n.* a necklace; a wreath; a string; (math.) division; (loos.) rate or proportion. **পরিবর্তহার** *n.* the rate of exchange. **হারে** *adv.* at the rate of. **শতকরা হার** rate per hundred, percentage.

হারকাত *n.* (in a game) the defeated team.

হারমোনিয়ম *n.* a harmonium.

হারা *v.* to be defeated; to lose (as in a game). □ *a.* (*in comp.*) having lost, deprived of, bereft of (গৃহহারা, সুখহারা), bereaved of, -less (মাতৃহারা = motherless).

হারানো *v.* to defeat, to vanquish; to lose, to miss (টাকা হারানো, সুযোগ হারানো) ; to be lost or missing. □ *a.* lost, missing. **~প্রাপ্তি** *n.* what has been lost and what has been found, lost and found. **হারানো সূত্র** *a.* missing link or clue.

হারাম *a.* any unholy or forbidden thing or creature according to Muslim scriptures; a boar, a swine. **~জাদা, ~জাদ** *n.* (abusively) a pig, a swine, a scoundrel. *fem.* **হারামজাদি**।

হারাহারি *a.* proportionate; average; pro rata.

হারি *n.* defeat, vanquishment.

হারিকেন *n.* a hurricane lantern.

-হারী *a.* (used as a *sfx.*) taking away, robbing; fascinating.

হারেম *n.* a harem.

হার্দিক *a* . relating to the heart; cordial; tender, affectionate.

হাল১ *n.* a helm, a rudder. **হাল ধরা** *v.* to steer.

হাল২ *n.* a plough; a metal hoop, a tire. **হাল চালানো, হাল দেওয়া** *v.* to plough, to till.

হাল৩ *n.* condition, state; circumstances. □ *a.* present, current; modern. **~খাতা** see **খাতা**। **~চাল** *n.* condition and symptoms; trend; attitude and gestures; character and conduct. **হাল ছেড়ে দেওয়া** to give up, to resign or surrender in despair. **হাল ধরা** to steer, to be at the helm of, to take the leadership. **~ফিল** *adv.* recently, lately, of late. **রাজার হাল** right royal condition; extremely happy state.

হালকা *a.* not heavy, light (হালকা ধাতু = light metal); of short weight; easily digested (হালকা খাবার = light meal); easy; mild; gently blowing (হালকা হাওয়া) ; unimportant, negligible, frivolous (হালকা ব্যাপার) ; airy (হালকা কথা) ; carefree (হালকা মন) ; light (in all the foregoing senses). **হালকা করা** *v.* to lighten; to reduce the amount of (কাজ হালকা করা) ; to disburden, to relieve (মন হালকা করা). **হালকাভাবে গ্রহণ করা** to take or treat lightly.

হালখাতা, হালচাল, হালফিল see **হাল**[3] ।

হালাক *a.* harassed or fatigued.

হালাল *a.* holy or permissible according to Mohammedan scriptures. ☐ *n.* the system of killing a beast by cutting its clavicle, as prescribed by Mohammedan scriptures.

হালি[1] *n.* a ploughman.

হালি[2] *n.* a helmsman, a steersman.

হালিয়া (now rare) *a.* one who ploughs; used in ploughing . ☐ *n.* a ploughman; bullock for the plough. see **হেলে**[1] ।

হালুইকর *n.* one who makes sweetmeats, a confectioner.

হালুম *int.* indicating: (facet.) the roar of a tiger.

হালুয়া *n.* a kind of porridge made by frying cornflour and then boiling it with sugar.

হাশিয়া *n.* the embroidered border of a woolen wrapper, shawl etc.

হাস *n.* a laugh; a smile.

হাসনুহানা, হাসনোহানা *n.* a species of very sweet-scented white flower that blooms in the evening, the night jasmine, *Cestrum noeturnum.*

হাসপাতাল *n.* a hospital.

হাসা *v.* to laugh; to smile; (fig.) to be illuminated, to brighten up (চন্দ্রলোকে নগরী হাসছে) ; to taunt, to ridicule, to deride (লোক হাসছে). **হাসানো** *v.* to make one laugh or smile; to cause to ridicule or deride; to be an object or butt of ridicule or derision (লোক হাসানো). **হাসাহাসি করা** *v.* to laugh over; to ridicule or deride; to continue to laugh; to upset the calmness of; to laugh together derisively. **হেসে উড়ানো, হেসে উড়িয়ে দেওয়া** *v.* to laugh away, to laugh, to scorn. **হেসে খেলে** *adv.* in an easy manner, in a happy-go-lucky manner; playfully. **হেসে হেসে** *adv.* smilingly.

হাসি *n.* a laugh; laughter; a smile; ridicule or derison; (fig.) brightness (চাঁদের হাসি). **হাসি পাওয়া** *v.* to feel inclined to smile; to feel inclined to smile a derisive smile, to feel inclined to laugh in one's sleeves. **হাসির পাত্র** an object or butt of ridicule or derision, a laughing-stock. **হাসির ব্যাপার** a ridiculous or ludicrous affair. **~কান্না** *n.* smiles and tears; tearful smiles; tears of joy; joy and sorrow mixed together; alternate joy and sorrow. **~খুশি** *n.* gaiety, liveliness, jollity, vivacity. ☐ *a.* gay, lively, jolly, cheerful, vivacious. **~ঠাট্টা, ~তামাশা** *n.* banter, badinage. **হাসিঠাট্টা করা, হাসিতামাশা করা** *v.* to enjoy a light and lively chat; to poke fun at, to make fun of, to pull one's leg. **~মুখ** *n.* a smiling face. **~মুখে** *adv.* with a smiling face; happily, gladly; ungrudgingly; willingly. **হাসির খোরাক** an object of ridicule, a laughing stock. **হাসির গল্প** *n.* a funny tale, a comic story, a humorous story. **~হাসি** *a.* smiling; bright; charming; pleasant.

হাসিনী *a. fem.* (used as a *sfx.*) smiling or laughing (মধুরহাসিনী).

হাসিল *a.* performed, accomplished; fulfilled, realized. **হাসিল করা** *v.* to perform, to accomplish; to have something fulfilled; to contrive, to realize.

হাস্য *n.* a laugh; laughter; a smile. **~কর, ~জনক** *a.* laughable, ridiculous; ludicrous, comical; farcial; humorous. **~কৌতুক, ~পরিহাস** *n.* wit and fun; pleasantry; buffoonery; banter, badinage; humour. **~ময়** *a.* smiling; pleasant; happy. *fem.* **~ময়ী** । **~মুখ** same as **হাসিমুখ** । **~রঞ্জিত** *a.* brightened with smile, beaming. **~রস** *n.* (rhet.) the sentiment of mirth, the comic. **~রসাত্মক** *a.* comical; humorous. **~রসাত্মক নাটক** a farce; a comedy. **~রসাভিনেতা** *n.* a comic actor, a comique. **~রসিক** *a.* witty; jocose; humorous. ☐ *n.* a witty or jocose person, a wit; a buffoon; a writer of comic stories, plays etc.; a humorist; a comic actor or singer, a comique. **হাস্যসংবরণ করা** *v.* to suppress or check laughter; to restrain the impulse to laugh. **হাস্যাস্পদ** same as **হাসির পাত্র** (see **হাসি**). **হাস্যোজ্জ্বল** *a.* brightened with smile, lit up with smile. **হাস্যোদ্দীপক, হাস্যোদ্রেককর** same as **হাস্যকর**।

হা-হতোস্মি *int.* alas, I am undone! alas, I am lost!

হাহা *int.* indicating: the noise of loud lamentation, grief, affliction etc.; emptiness, vacuity; desolation; the noise of guffaw. **হাহা করা** *v.* to lament or grieve or wail loudly; to be empty or desolate; to guffaw. **হাহা করে ওঠা** *v.* to burst into loud lamentation or wailing or into a guffaw. **~কার** *n.* loud lamentation or wailing. **~কার করা** *v.* to lament or bewail loudly.

হা-হুতাশ *n.* profound regret or repentance. **হা-হুতাশ করা** *v.* to regret or repent deeply.

হিং, হিঙ *n.* asafoetida.

হিং-টিং-ছট্ *n.* (sarcas.) meaningless gibberish resembling Sanskrit words in sound.

হিংসক *a.* given to killing or harming others; malevolent; malicious, spiteful; envious, jealous.

হিংসন, হিংসা *n.* killing, slaughter; malice; spite, malevolence; (loos.) envy, jealousy. **হিংসনীয়** *a.* that which is to be or ought to be killed; that which is to be or ought to be envied, enviable. **হিংসা করা** *v.* to kill, to slay; to harm; to malice; to envy, to be jealous of. **হিংসাত্মক** *a.* killing, slaying; malicious, spiteful, malevolent; envious. **হিংসাপরায়ণ** same as **হিংসক**।

হিংসিত *a.* killed, slain; harmed; maliced; (loos.) envied.

হিংসুক, হিংসুটে *a.* envious, jealous; spiteful, malicious.

হিংস্র, হিংস্রক *a.* cruel, ferocious; killing others; murderous. **হিংস্র পশু** a ferocious animal; a beast of prey. **হিংস্রতা** *n.* cruelty, ferocity, act of killing others.

হিঁচড়ানো *v.* to drag or graze forcefully; to trail along forcefully.

হিকমত *n.* power; might, strength; ability; efficiency.

হিক্কা *n.* a hiccup. **হিক্কা তোলা** *v.* to hiccup.

হিঙ্গু same as **হিং**।

হিঙ্গুল, হিঙ্গুলি *n.* the red sulphide or mercury, cinnabar; vermilion.

হিজড়া, (coll.) **হিজড়ে** *n.* a hermaphrodite; a eunuch.

হিজরি, হিজরা *n.* the Mohammedan era counted from 622 A.D., hegira, hejira, hijra.

হিজল *n.* a kind of tree, the Indian oak, the *Barringtonia acutangula.*

হিজলি-বাদাম *n.* cashew-nut.

হিজিবিজি *n.* an illegible and worthless or meaningless writing or drawing, a scribble, a scrawl. ☐ *a.* illegible and worthless or meaningless. **হিজিবিজি আঁকা** *v.* to scrawl. **হিজিবিজি লেখা** *v.* to scribble, to scrawl.

হিপ্তা, হিপ্তে corruptions of **হেলেঞ্চা**।

হিড় হিড় *int.* indicating : rapid and violent dragging along or falling down; the noise of such dragging or falling.

হিড়িক *n.* passing popular excitement or trend (বিটলেপনার হিড়িক) ; mad rush (দেশভ্রমণের হিড়িক) ; a great pressure (কাজের হিড়িক).

হিত *n.* good, benefit; well-being, weal, welfare. ☐ *a.* good, beneficial, salutary, wholesome. **হিতে বিপরীত** an attempt to do good resulting in a great harm. **হিত করা** same as **হিতসাধন করা**। **~কথা** same as **হিতোপদেশ**। **~কর** *a.* same as **হিত** (*a.*). *fem.* **হিতকরী**। **~কামনা** *n.* well-wishing. **হিতকামনা করা** *v.* to wish one good. **~কামী** *a.* well-wishing. **~কারী** *a.* same as **হিত** (*a.*). ☐ *n.* a benefactor. *fem.* **~কারিণী**। **~বাদী** *a.* telling beneficial or salutary words; giving beneficial advice or good counsel. *fem.* **~বাদিনী**। **~সাধন করা** *v.* to do good to; to benefit; to promote the well-being of. **হিতাকাঙ্ক্ষা** same as **হিতকামনা**। **হিতাকাঙ্ক্ষী, হিতার্থী** same as **হিতকামী**। *fem.* **হিতাকাঙ্ক্ষিণী**। **হিতার্থিনী**। **হিতাহিত** *n.* good and evil; right and wrong. **হিতাহিতজ্ঞান** *n.* knowledge of ascertaining or differentiating good and evil or right and wrong. হিতাহিত বিবেচনা করা *v.* to discriminate between good and evil or right and wrong. হিতৈষণা *n.* desire or disposition to do good (to); benevolence. হিতৈষী *a.* desirous of doing or disposed to do good (to.); benevolent. *fem.* হিতৈষিণী। হিতোপদেশ *n.* salutary or beneficial or good advice or teaching. হিতোপদেশক *a.* giving salutary or beneficial or good advice or teaching; didactic. হিতোপদেষ্টা *n.* & *a.* one who gives salutary or beneficial or good advice or teaching.

হিন্তাল same as হেঁতাল।

হিন্দি *n.* the Hindi language; Hindi.

হিন্দু *n.* a Hindu; Hindus (also হিন্দু জাতি); Hinduism (also হিন্দু ধর্ম) ☐ *a.* of Hinduism or Hindus, Hindu. ~ধর্মাবলম্বী *a.* Hindu. ~য়ানি *n.* (usu. sarcas.) practices and rites and sacraments of Hinduism. ~সমাজ *n.* the Hindu community or society.

হিন্দুস্থান *n.* Hindusthan, Hindosthan, India. হিন্দুস্থানি *a.* Indian; inhabiting Upper or Central India; of Hindusthan. ☐ *n.* the mixed dialect of Upper India, Hindusthani; an inhabitant of upper or central India.

হিন্দোল *n.* swinging; a swing; the festival of ঝুলন or swinging; an Indian musical mode.

হিবানামা *n.* (Mus.) a deed of gift.

হিব্রু *n.* the Hebrew race, Hebrews; a Hebrew (*fem.* Hebrewess), a Jew (*fem.* Jewess); the Hebrew language, Hebrew.

হিম *n* winter; snow; frost; dew; coldness, the cold; chill. ☐ *a.* cold; cool. হিম পড়ছে *v.* dew is collecting. ~ঋতু *n.* winter, (cp.) cold weather. ~গিরি *n.* the Himalayas. ~ঘর *n.* a cold store; cold storage. ~ঝঞ্ঝা *n.* a hail-storm; a blizzard. ~নিবারণ করা *v.* to ward off or prevent cold. ~বাহ *n.* a glacier. ~মণ্ডল *n.* (geog.) either of the frigid zones, a frigid zone. ~মিশ্র *n.* freezing mixture. ~রেখা *n.* the snow-line. ~শিলা *n.* hailstone; an iceberg. ~শীতল *a.* frigid; icy; ice-cold. ~শৈল *n.* an iceberg. ~সংহনন *n.* glaciation. ~সাগর *n.* a superior quality of mango; a kind of brain cooling medicinal oil. হিমাংশু *n.* the moon. হিমাগম *n.* advent of the cold season or of winter. হিমাঙ্ক *n.* freezing point. হিমাঙ্গ *n.* a body bereft of blood-heat (that is, in a state of collapse); a frozen body; a lifeless body. ☐ *a.* having any one of the aforesaid bodies. হিমাচল, হিমাদ্রি *n.* the Himalayas. হিমানি *n.* a collection or mass of snow or hoar frost; snow-ice; (loos.) ice. হিমায়ক *n.* a refrigerator. হিমায়ন *n.* refrigeration. হিমায়িত *a.* refrigerated. হিমায়িত করা *v.* to refrigerate. হিমালয় *n.* the Himalayas. হিমেল *a.* cold; very cold.

হিম্মত *n.* power, might; valour; courage; spiritedness, spirit.

হিমশিম *n.* extreme exhaustion or fatigue; trouble; bewilderment. হিমশিম খাওয়া *v.* to be almost fainting with exhaustion or fatigue or harassment; to cower in fear etc.; to be in deep waters or great difficulties.

হিয়া poet. corrup. of হৃদয়।

হিরণ *n.* gold. ~বরণ *a.* golden coloured.

হিরণ্ময় *a.* made of gold; golden-coloured; golden.

হিরণ্য *n.* gold. ~গর্ভ *a.* full of gold, auriferous. ☐ *n.* Brahma (ব্রহ্মা).

হিরাকস *n.* iron sulphate, green vitriol; copperas.

হিরে coll. form of হীরে। হিরের টুকরো (fig.) a very intelligent and promising person; a bright young person.

হিলোল poet. corrup. of হিল্লোল।

হিল্লে *n.* (discovery of) a means or method to work out or solve (অঙ্কের হিল্লে); (discovery of) a remedy (রোগের হিল্লে); disposal (কাজের হিল্লে); arrangement (মেয়ের বিয়ের হিল্লে); provision (ভবিষ্যতের হিল্লে); providing with an employment (বেকারের হিল্লে); settlement (বিবাদের হিল্লে); trace (চুরির হিল্লে).

হিল্লোল *n.* a wave; a swing; a wavy or swinging motion.

হিসসা, হিস্যা, (coll.) হিস্সে, হিস্যে *n.* a part allotted or owned or taken, a share.

হিস্‌সাদার *n.* a partner or share-holder or co-owner.

হিস্‌হিস্‌ *int.* indicating: repeated or continued hissing or fizzing sound. **হিস্‌হিস্‌ করা** *v.* to hiss, to fizz.

হিসাব, (coll.) **হিসেব** *n.* calculation; counting, reckoning; accounting; accounts; an estimate; rate; (fig.) consideration or deliberation; (fig.) explanation. **হিসাব করা** *v.* to calculate; (fig.) to consider or deliberate; (fig.) to take into account. **হিসাব চাওয়া** *v.* to ask for accounts or an estimate (of); (fig.) to demand an explanation, to call or bring to account. **হিসাব চুকানো, হিসাব মেটানো** *v.* to settle up accounts; to quit scores; to be quits; to cry quits; to close an account with. **হিসাব দেওয়া** *v.* to submit or tender accounts or an estimate; (fig.) to give an account. **হিসাব মেটানো** same as **হিসাব চুকানো**। **হিসাব রাখা** *v.* to keep accounts (of); (fig.) to be heedful of. **হিসাব হওয়া** *v.* to be calculated or counted or reckoned. **হিসাবে ধরা** *v.* to include in calculation or counting or reckoning or accounts or in an estimate. **কোন হিসাবে** on which account, at what rate; (fig.) on what ground or by what logic. **কোনো হিসাবেই না** on no account. **হিসাবের খাতা** an account-book. **হিসাব-কেতাব, হিসাব-কিতাব** *n.* detailed accounts; detailed or minute calculation; (fig.) detailed or minute consideration or deliberation. **~নবিশ** *n.* an accounts-clerk; (loos.) an accountant. **~নিকাশ** *n.* accounting; accounts; detailed reckoning; (fig.) an explanation. **হিসাব-পরীক্ষক** *n.* an auditor. **হিসাব-পরীক্ষা** *n.* audit. **হিসাব পরীক্ষা করা** *v.* to audit. **হিসাবি** *a.* of accounting or accounts; calculative; given to forethought, calculating; frugal, economical; cautious, circumspect.

হিস্টিরিয়া *n.* hysteria. **~গ্রস্ত** *a.* hysteric, hysterical.

হিহি *int.* indicating: violent shivering in cold; giggling noise. **হিহি করে কাঁপা** *v.* to shiver in cold. **হিহি করে হাসা** *v.* to giggle.

হীন *a.* devoid of; divested or deprived of; destitute of; lacking, bereaved of; -less (পাপহীন = sinless); base, mean; vile, hateful; lowly, depressed; inferior; lower (পদমর্যাদায় হীন) ; lowered, degraded; humiliated; humble; undignified; poor, indigent (হীন অবস্থা) ; miserable; decreased or diminished; dull, dim. **হীন করা** *v.* to debase; to lower, to degrade; to humiliate; to make poor or indigent. **~কর্মা** *a.* doing vile or hateful deeds; employed in a lowly or base work. **~চরিত্র** *a.* depraved; mean-natured. **~চেতা** *a.* mean-minded. **~জন্মা** *a.* low-born. **~জাতি** *a.* belonging to a lowly or depressed or vile caste or race. **~তা** *n.* privation, absence; lack; meanness; vileness, hatefulness; low state, depression; inferiority; humiliation; humility; indignity; poverty; misery; shortage. **হীনতাব্যঞ্জক** *a.* indicating meanness; disgraceful; undignified. **~প্রকৃতি;** a. mean-natured, of an ignoble character; small-minded. **~প্রভ** *a.* lack-lustre; dim. **~বল** *a.* weak; feeble; weakened, enfeebled. **~বুদ্ধি** *a.* having evil or vile thoughts. **~বৃত্তি** *n.* a vile or lowly occupation or calling. □ *a.* employed in a vile or lowly occupation. **~মতি, ~মনা** *a.* mean-minded; suffering from inferiority complex. **~মন্যতা, ~মানস** *n.* inferiority complex. **~যান** *n.* one of the two Buddhist sects. **হীনাবস্থ** *a.* poor, indigent; low-lived; in a miserable state. **হীনাবস্থা** *n.* poverty, indigence; a low life; a miserable or wretched state.

হীরক, হীরা *n.* diamond. **কাচ-কাটা হীরা** a glass cutter. **হীরার খনি** diamond ore, a diamond mine. **হীরার ধার** (fig.) great sharpness or keenness or acuteness of mind, intelligence etc. **পড়িলে ভেড়ার শৃঙ্গে ভাঙে হীরার ধার** keenness of mind is dulled in the company of fools. **হীরকচূর্ণ** *n.* diamond-dust, diamond-powder. **হীরকজয়ন্তী** *n.* diamond-jubilee; diamond anniversary.

হীরাকস rej. spell. of **হিরাকস**।

হীরামন *n.* (folk-tales) a traditional name of a talking popinjay.

হীরে rej. var. of **হিরে**।

হুইল *n.* a wheel; a fishing-rod having a wheel fixed to it for ravelling thread in and out.

হুংকার alt. spell. of **হুঙ্কার**।

হুঁ *int.* indicating: acknowledgment, acceptance, assent, consent, willingness, doubt etc.; yes, hmm.

হুঁকা, (coll.) **হুঁকো** *n.* a hookah, a hookah. **হুঁকাবরদার** *n.* a hookah bearer.

হুঁশ *n.* consciousness; sensibility; sensation; feeling or perception; good sense; cautiousness, caution. **হুঁশ হওয়া** *v.* to regain consciousness or sensibility or sensation or power of feeling or perception; to come to one's senses; to become cautious. **হুঁশিয়ার** *a.* cautious, circumspect, on the alert. **হুঁশিয়ারি** *n.* caution; cautioning; cautiousness.

হুক *n.* a hook. **~কৃমি** *n.* a hook-worm, ankylostoma.

হুকমত, হুকুমত *n.* authority; rule; government.

হুকুম *n.* an order; a command; an injunction; permission. **হুকুম করা** *v.* to order; to command; to enjoin. **হুকুম জারি করা** *v.* to issue an order or command or injunction. **হুকুম তামিল করা** বা **পালন করা** *v.* to carry out or execute an order, to comply with an order. **হুকুম দেওয়া** *v.* to give an order; to command; to issue an injunction; to give permission, to permit. **যো হুকুম** see **যো**[2]। **~দার** *int.* (in the army & police) who comes there; a call of challenge by a sentry. **~নামা** *n.* a written order, a writ of command; a warrant; a permit. **~বরদার** *n.* person who carries out order.

হুঙ্কার *n.* a roar; a menacing shout or cry. **হুঙ্কার ছাড়া, হুঙ্কার দেওয়া,** (poet.) **হুঙ্কারা** *v.* to roar; to utter a menacing shout or cry.

হুজুগ, হুজুক *n.* a passing popular excitement or trend; a fashion esp. a passing one; a rumour. **হুজুগ ছড়ানো** v. to spread a rumour. **হুজুগ তোলা** *v.* to raise a rumour. **হুজুগে মাতা** *v.* to participate (or involve oneself) madly in a passing popular excitement or trend. **হুজুগে** *a.* given to participating madly in a passing popular excitement or trend; given to accepting madly a passing fashion; given to indulging in rumours.

হুজুর *n.* a term for addressing a prince, a judge, a master etc.; Your Majesty, Your Highness, Your honour, My Lord, Your Excellency, Your Reverence, Sir etc.; a master, an honoured person; the presence of a prince, judge, master etc. (হুজুরে হাজির).

হুজ্জত *n.* altercation; a dispute; a hubbub, a row; a trouble, a quarrel. **হুজ্জত বাধানো** *v.* to raise a dispute; to create a row or trouble. **হুজ্জতি** *a.* given to create a row; troublesome; rowdyish; quarrelsome.

হুট করে *adv.* rashly or abruptly; hastily.

হুটপাট, হুটোপাটি *n.* noisy playing or frisking in sport. **হুটপাট করা** *v.* to play or gambol noisily.

হুড় *n.* a crowd; disorderly crowding and mutual shoving. **হুড় করা** *v.* to crowd and shove one another in a disorderly manner.

হুড়কা[1], **হুড়কো**[1] *a. fem.* afraid of cohabiting with one's husband; shunning one's husband's company.

হুড়কা[2], **হুড়কো**[2] *n.* a latch, a bolt. **হুড়কো আঁটা, হুড়কো দেওয়া** *v.* to latch, to bolt.

হুড়মুড় *int.* indicating: movement in a crowd shoving one another; sudden crumbling down of a large and heavy object. **হুড়মুড় করে ভেঙে পড়া** *v.* to crumble down noisily, to fall with a crash.

হুড়হুড় milder var. of **হড়হড়**।

হুড়া, (coll.) **হুড়ো** *n.* a shove, a push; (loos.) a cudgel. **হুড়ো লাগানো** v. to shove; to cudgel. **হুড়োহুড়ি** *n.* mutual shoving esp. in a crowd; noisy gambolling or playing. **হুড়োহুড়ি করা** *v.* to shove one another noisily; to gambol or play noisily.

হুড়ুম *int.* indicating : disorderly or sudden or noisy movement. **~দাড়ুম** *int.* indicating : repeated disorderly or noisy movement.

হুড়োহুড়ি see **হুড়া**।

হুতাশ[1] *n.* an expression of dejection.

worry, dismay etc. **হুতাশে** *adv.* through fright or dismay.

হুতাশ২, হুতাশন *n.* fire; the firegod; sacrificial fire.

হুতোম, (dial.) **হুতুম** *n.* the largest and ugliest species of owl.

হুদ্দো *n.* jurisdiction; precincts (of a building.)

হুনরি, হুনুরি *n.* one skilled in handicrafts. ☐ *a.* relating to handicrafts.

হুন্ডি *n.* a bill of exchange; a bank-draft; a note of hand. **হুন্ডি টাকা, হুন্ডি দেওয়া** *v.* to issue a bill of exchange. **হুন্ডি ভাঙানো** *v.* to cash a bill of exchange. **~গ্রাহক** *n.* a drawer. **~প্রেরক** *n.* a drawee.

হুপ্ *int.* indicating : the whooping cry of the monkey; the noise of sudden leaping; suddenness. **হুপ করে** suddenly (and rashly).

হুপিং কাশি *n.* whooping cough.

হুবহু *a.* identical; exactly similar. ☐ *adv.* exactly.

হুমকি *n.* a threat; intimidation. **হুমকি দেওয়া** *v.* to give a threatening, to threaten, to intimidate, to utter a threat.

হুমড়ি *n.* coming near to falling prone whilst walking or whilst attempting eagerly to approach somebody or get something; stumbling. **হুমড়ি খাওয়া** *v.* to come near to falling prone whilst walking or whilst attempting eagerly to approach somebody or get something; to stumble.

হুররে *int.* indicating a loud joyous clamour or shout.

হুরি *n.* a fairy.

হুল *n.* an antenna, a sting. **হুল ফোটানো, হুল বেঁধানো** *v.* to sting.

হুলস্থুল *n.* a tumultuous confusion, a great hubbub or commotion, a turmoil. **হুলস্থুল ব্যাপার** a tumultuous affair.

হুলাহুলি *n.* a commotion, a tumult; a sound made by Hindu women by moving their tongues within their mouths on festive occasions.

হুলিয়া *n.* a police circular containing the description of personal features of an absconding criminal and asking the public to help in his apprehension.

হুলু (also **হুলুধ্বনি, হুলুরব**), **হুলুস্থুলু** variants of **উলু, হুলস্থুল।**

হুলো, হুলো বেড়াল *n.* a tomcat.

হুল্লোড় *n.* a hubbub or tumult raised by a crowd; revelry.

হুশ, হুশিয়ার variants of **হুঁশ** and **হুঁশিয়ার** respectively.

হুস্ *int.* indicating : the noise of quick movement or emission. **হুস্-হুস্** *int.* indicating : repeated **হুস্** noise.

হুহু *int.* indicating : the noise made by a strong wind or by a powerful flame of fire; the state of affliction, dejection etc. (মন হুহু করা).

হূণ, (pop.) **হুন** *n.* Huns; a Hun.

হৃত *a.* robbed, looted, plundered; stolen. **~সর্বস্ব** *a.* robbed of everything, robbed of all one's possession; utterly ruined. **হৃতাধিকার** *a.* deprived of one's right or possession or office or privilege, dispossessed; ousted; dismissed, cashiered.

হৃৎ *n.* the heart. **~কন্দর** *n.* the inmost part of the heart, the bottom of one's heart, the bosom. **~কমল** same as **হৃদিপদ্ম।** **~কম্প, ~কম্পন** *n.* throbbing of the heart esp. in fear, palpitation; heartbeat. **~পিণ্ড** *n.* the heart. **~শূল** *n.* angina pectoris; (pop.) heartache. **~স্পন্দন** *n.* heartbeat.

হৃদয় *n.* the heart; the mind; the bosom. **~গ্রাহী** *a.* captivating the heart, very pleasant or charming. **হৃদয়ংগম করা** *v.* to feel deeply; to understand or grasp, to realize. **~জ** *a.* born of or originating from the heart. **~তন্ত্রী** *n.* the heartstring. **~দ্রবকর** *a.* melting the heart; pathetic, touching. **~পট** *n.* the heart conceived as a piece of canvas for painting. **~বল্লভ** *n.* a husband; a lover; a sweet-heart *fem.* **~বল্লভা** *a.* wife. **~বান** *a.* large-hearted, magnanimous; sympathetic; hearty. **~বিদারক, ~বিদারী, ~ভেদী** *a.* heart-rending; heart-breaking, pathetic; cutting to the quick. **~বেদনা, ~ব্যথা** *n.* heartache, grief, affliction; heart-burning, secret grudging. **~মন্দির** *n.* the heart conceived as a shrine; the sacred and secret abode of the heart. **~স্পর্শী** *a.*

touching or moving the heart; very appealing or pathetic. ~হীন *a.* heartless, extremely unfeeling; merciless. ~হীনতা *n.* heartlessness. হৃদয়াকাশ *n.* the heart conceived as the sky, the expanse of the heart. হৃদয়াবেগ *n.* emotion; excitement; outburst of emotion. হৃদয়াসন *n.* the heart conceived as a seat. হৃদয়েশ, হৃদয়েশ্বর *n.* the lord or master of one's heart; a lover; a husband. *n. fem.* হৃদয়েশ্বরী the mistress or lady of one's heart; a wife. হৃদয়োচ্ছ্বাস *n.* a great outburst of emotion, unrestrained outpouring of thought and feeling.

হৃদ্‌রোগ *n.* heart disease, cardiac complain, cardiac arrest; (cp.) coronary thrombosis.

হৃদি poet. form of হৃদয়। ~পট *n.* the canvas of the heart. ~পদ্ম *n.* the heart conceived as a lotus. ~পদ্মাসন *n.* the heart conceived as a lotus to sit upon, the seat of the heart-lotus.

হৃদ্গত *a.* lying in the inmost recesses of one's heart.

হৃদ্য *a.* captivating the heart, pleasant; dear to the heart; cordial; sincere, hearty; loving, amicable. ~তা *n.* pleasantness; cordiality; sincerity, heartiness; love; amicability.

হৃষীকেশ *n.* Vishnu (বিষ্ণু) ; Narayana (নারায়ণ) ; Krishna (কৃষ্ণ).

হৃষ্ট *v.* delighted, gladdened; glad, cheerful, joyful, happy; pleased. ~চিত্তে *adv.* with a happy mind; gladly, cheerfully, joyfully, happily. ~পুষ্ট *a.* cheerful and burly, buxom, happy and plump.

হে *int,* used in addressing or apostrophizing, O.

হেই *int.* (pop.) indicating : earnest solicitation or appeal.

হেঁইয়ো *int.* a call to exertion as in heaving, (cp.) heave ho.

হেঁচকা, হ্যাঁচকা *n.* a sudden tug or pull. □ *a.* sudden and forceful.

হেঁচকি same as হিক্কা।

হেঁচড়ানো pop. var. of হিঁচড়ানো।

হেঁজিপেঁজি *a.* most ordinary, of no importance, negligible. হেঁজিপেঁজি লোক a man in the street; (cp.) the rabble.

হেঁট *a.* bent down, bowing down (হেঁটমুণ্ড), bending down one's head, stooping (হেঁট হয়ে প্রণাম). □ *n.* the underneath, bottom (হেঁটে কাটা). লজ্জায় মাথা হেঁট করা to hang one's head from shame.

হেঁড়ে *a.* large and flat like an urn (হেঁড়ে মুখ) ; deep and harsh, croaking (হেঁড়ে গলা).

হেঁতাল *n.* a tree akin to the palm. হেঁতালের লাঠি a stick made of the timber of the aforesaid tree.

হেঁয়ালি *n.* a riddle, an enigma, a puzzle.

হেঁশেল *n.* a kitchen-room of a residential building, a kitchen.

হেঁসে pop. var. of হাঁসুলি and হাঁসুয়া।

হেঁসেল, হেঁসো, হেকমত variants of হেঁশেল, হাঁসিয়া, হিকমত।

হেড *n.* the head; intelligence, understanding. □ *a.* (*in. comp.*) chief, head. ~ক্লার্ক, ~বাবু *n.* a head clerk. ~মাস্টার *n.* a headmaster.

হেতু *n.* reason, cause; origin; the final cause; purpose; (log.) the argument for deduction; one of the five members of a syllogism in Indian logic. এই হেতু because of this, by this reason; by virtue of this; on account of this; for this purpose. ~বাদ *n.* act of showing cause; mention of the cause; argument, reasoning; the preamble of a law. ~বিদ্যা *n.* (phil.) teleology.

হেত্বাভাস *n.* a fallacy.

হেথা, হেথায় *adv.* (poet.) here.

হেদানো *v.* (sl.) to become extremely distressed for being separated from one's lover or from an object very much longed for, to desiderate.

হেদে *int.* (obs.) used in addressing, O.

হেন *a.* such, such like, like.

হেনস্তা, হেনস্থা *n.* slight, neglect; (coll.) distress; (coll.) harassment.

হেনা *n.* a very sweet-scented flower or its plant, the henna.

হেপা *n.* a troublesome burden or charge. হেপা পোহানো, হেপা সামলানো *v.* to bear a troublesome burden or execute a troublesome charge, (cp.) to bear the brunt of.

হেপাজত, হেফাজত *n.* custody, charge, care.

হেপাজতে দেওয়া *v.* to commit to the custody or charge or care of.

হেম *n.* gold □ *a.* (*in. comp.*) made of gold; golden. **~কান্তি** *a.* having golden lustre or complexion.

হেমন্ত *n.* the season occurring between autumn and winter comprising the months of Kartik (কার্তিক) and Agrahayana (অগ্রহায়ণ).

হেমাঙ্গ *a.* having a golden complexion; having a body made of gold. *fem.* **হেমাঙ্গী, হেমাঙ্গিনী।**

হেমাভ *a.* having a golden glow or radiance.

হেয় *a.* fit to be cast off; contemptible; despicable; slighted; base, vile; hateful; abject. **~জ্ঞান** *n.* contempt, slight; neglect. **~জ্ঞান করা** *v.* to regard as contemptible, to slight; to neglect; to belittle, to take a dim view of.

হেরফের *n.* alteration or modification esp. to a slight degree; (slight) difference; (accts.) manipulation (as in a balance sheet). **হেরফের করা** *v.* to alter or modify or differentiate (esp. slightly); (accts.) to manipulate.

হেরা *v.* (poet.) to behold, to see.

হেলা[1] *v.* to slant, to lean or incline to. □ *a.* slanting; leaning or inclining to. **হেলেদুলে** *adv.* swingingly sideways, swingingly, in waddling fashion.

হেলা[2] *n.* contempt, slight; disdain; neglect; ease. **হেলা করা** *v.* to treat with contempt, to slight; to despise; to neglect. **হেলায়** *adv.* with ease, without effort; through negligence or carelessness (হেলায় হারানো).

হেলান *n.* slanting, slant; leaning (দেওয়ালে হেলান দিয়ে বসা).

হেলানো *v.* to cause to slant or to lean or incline to. □ *a.* slanting, leaning or inclining to.

হেলাফেলা *n.* utter contempt or slight or disrespect or neglect. **হেলাফেলা করা** *v.* to slight or disrespect or neglect utterly. **হেলাফেলা করে** *adv.* without any effort; negligently.

হেলে[1] *a.* one who ploughs; used in ploughing (হেলে বলদ). □ *n.* a ploughman; a bullock for the plough.

হেলে[2] *n.* a species of small non-venomous snake.

হেলেঞ্চা *n.* a kind of water-cress, *Hingtsha repens.*

হেলেদুলে see **হেলা**[1]।

হেস্তনেস্ত *n.* finalization; final settlement. **হেস্তনেস্ত করা** *v.* to finalize; to settle finally; to see through.

হৈচৈ alt. spell. of **হইচই**।

হৈম[1] *a.* relating to the cold season or winter; cold; wintry.

হৈম[2] *a.* made of gold, golden; gold-coloured, aureated, golden; pertaining to gold, auric.

হৈমন্ত, হৈমন্তিক *a.* of the **হেমন্ত** season. *fem.* **হৈমন্তী।**

হৈমবত *a.* Himalayan. **হৈমবতী** *n.* Goddess Durga (দুর্গা).

হৈহৈ alt. spell. of **হইহই**।

হো *int.* ho, O; oh, ah.

হোঁচট *n.* a stumble. **হোঁচট খাওয়া** *v.* to stumble; to stumble over something.

হোঁতকা *a.* (dero.) corpulent; corpulent and dull-witted.

হোঁদল *a.* corpulent. **হোঁদল-কুতকুত** *n.* a corpulent and dark-complexioned man.

হোগলা, (dial.) **হোগল** *n.* bulrush, a species of aquatic grass chiefly used in building the walls of huts. **হোগলকুঁড়ি,** (corrup.) **হোঁগলগুঁড়ি** *n.* the pollen of the flowers of the aforesaid grass.

হোটেল *n.* a hotel; an inn; (loos.) an eating house. **~ওয়ালা** *n.* a hotel-keeper, a hotelier; an inn-keeper; (loos.) the owner or manager of an eating-house. *fem.* **হোটেলওয়ালি।**

হোতা *n.* a performer or a priest of a religious sacrifice.

হোত্র *n.* an oblation, a sacrifice. **হোত্রী** *fem.* of **হোতা। হোত্রীয়** *a.* relating to a religious sacrifice; sacrificial.

হোথা, হোথায় *adv.* (poet.) there.

হোম *n.* an oblation of fire into which ghee is poured. **~কুণ্ড** *n.* a pit for making a sacrificial fire. **~ধেনু** *n.* a cow whose milk is used in religious sacrifices. **~ভস্ম** *n.* the residual ashes of a sacrificial fire.

হোমরা-চোমরা *a.* (sarcas.) prominent and

influential and well-to-do, of high status or established social position. **হোমরা-চোমরা লোক** a big gun.

হোমাগ্নি, হোমানল *n.* a sacrificial fire.

হোমিয়োপ্যাথি *n.* homoeopathy.

হোরা *n.* (astrol.) an hour. **~বিজ্ঞান** *n.* astrology.

হোলি *n.* the Hindu feast of commemorating the throwing of red powder at one another by Krishna (কৃষ্ণ) and the milkmaids enamoured of him; the Hindu spring festival of spraying coloured water; the holi.

হোহো *int.* & *n.* the noise of a very loud laughter. **হোহো করে ওঠা** বা **হাসা** *v.* to burst into a very loud laughter, to guffaw.

হৌজ *n.* a large cistern or water reservoir.

হ্যাংলা *a.* repulsively greedy esp. of food. **~পনা, ~মি** *n.* repulsive greediness esp. of food.

হ্যাঁ var. of **হাঁ** ।

হ্যাঁচকা var. of **হেঁচকা** ।

হ্যাট *n.* a hat. **~ধারী** *a.* wearing a hat, hatted.

হ্যান্ডনোট *n.* a handwritten document of obligation to repay a loan , an IOU. **হ্যান্ডনোট কাটা** *v.* to write out or issue an IOU.

হ্যাদানো, হ্যাদে alt. spellings of **হেদানো** and **হেদে** respectively.

হ্যাপা *n.* a troublesome burden or charge. **হ্যাপা সামলানো** *v.* to bear a troublesome burden or execute a troublesome charge, to bear the brunt of.

হ্রদ *n.* a lake; a lagoon; a large pond. **~সংক্রান্ত** *a.* lacustrian.

হ্রস্ব *a.* short; small; dwarfish; low; low-pitched; small in amount, little; abbreviated; shortened; reduced; (gr.—of vowels) short. **~দীর্ঘজ্ঞান** *n.* (fig.) common sense, gumption, nous. **~স্বর** *n.* a short vowel. **হ্রস্বীকরণ** *n.* shortening; abbreviation; reduction.

হ্রাস *n.* diminution; decrease; shortening; reduction; curtailment; waning. **হ্রাস করা** *v.* to diminish; to decrease; to shorten; to reduce; to curtail. **হ্রাস পাওয়া, হ্রাস হওয়া** *v.* to be diminished, to diminish; to decrease; to be reduced or curtailed, to wane. **~প্রাপ্ত** *a.* diminished; decreased; reduced; abated; wanted. **~বৃদ্ধি** *n.* appreciation and depreciation, rise and fall (মূল্যের হ্রাসবৃদ্ধি) ; waning and waxing (চন্দ্রকলার হ্রাসবৃদ্ধি) ; aggravation and diminution (রোগের হ্রাসবৃদ্ধি).

হ্রী *n.* bashfulness, modesty. **~মান** *a.* modest, bashful. *fem.* **~মতী** ।

হ্রেষা, হ্রেষাধ্বনি *n.* the neighing of the horse, the neigh.

হ্লাদ, হ্লাদন *n.* delight, gladness, joy. **হ্লাদিত** *a.* delighted, gladdened; joyful. **হ্লাদিনী** *n.* (Vaishnav phil.) God; Radha (রাধা).

SPELLINGS TO NOTE

abacus
abhor, abhorred, abhorring, abhorrence
ageing or aging
agitator (not agitater)
airport, aircraft (but aerogramme, aerodrome, aeroplane)
alms, palm, psalm, calm
annihilate, annex, annoy, annul,
annual, annuity, anniversary
ascend, ascent
ascertain
assent (agreenent), assemble, associate
axel (of skating)
axillary
axle (of car wheels)

befit, befitting (but benefiting)
begin, beginning
biased, focused, focusing (or focussed, focussing)
biennial
bigot, bigoted
boycott
Brahman or brahman, buffalo, buffalos or buffaloes
buffet, buffeted, buffeting
burn, burned or burnt

centimetre (not cente-, not meter)
cerebellum (not - belum)
chameleon
channel
chronicle
chronometer
chrysanthemum
commit, committed, committing
compass (not - pas)
comprehensible
convener (not - or)
crystal, crystalline, crystallize
culinary (not - lli)

dairy (but diary)
dais
deceive, receive, seize, conceit, deceit
defeasible, defeasability
defence (not defense), defensible, defensive
define, definition (not - ation)
dig, digging
diarrohoea, pyorrhoea, homoeopathy
diphtheria, diphthong
discern, disciple, but decide, decision
discourteous
dissociate, dissent, dissatisfaction, disseminate, dissimilar, dissuade
dysentery
dyspepsia

eavesdrop, eavesdropping
ecclesiastical
edit, edited, editing, editor
effrontery
embarrass, embarrassing
entrepreneur
enuresis (not eneu-)
Eucharist
exacerbate
exaggerate
excel, but excelled, excellent

Fahrenheit
falcon
fallible
familiar, familiarity
Filipino, but Philippines
fluorescence, fluorescent
forego (go before), foregone conclusion
forgo (renounce)
frolic, frolicked, frolicking, but frolicsome

gallop, galloping
georgette
gipsy
glycerine
gorilla, but guerrilla
gregarious
grieve, grievous
grip, gripped, gripping
guillotine

haphazard
harass
heinous (not - neous)
hectare
hero, heroes
honour, honourable, but honorary, honorarium
hoof, hoofs (or hooves)
humour, humoured, but humorist, humorous
hyena (or hyaena)
hygiene

idiocy
idiosyncrasy, idiosyncratic
illegitimate
impermeable
imposter (or impostor)
impresario (not - ss -)
infallible
inasmuch as (not in as much)
in so far as (not insofar-)
in spite of (not inspite)
install (or instal), installation
instalment (not -ll -)
intelligentsia
irascible, iridescent
irrational, irrefutable, irreligious

joyful, joyfully
judgement (or judgment)

lachrymose
lackadaisical
lama (Buddhist monk), llama (A South American beast)
larynx (pl. larynges), laryngeal (not - gal)
legal, illegal
legible, illegible
level, levelled, levelling
licence (n), license or licence (v)
licentious

maintain, maintenance
manageable
manoevre
marriageable
mobile, mobility, immobile
monster, monstrosity, montrous
mouthful (pl. mouthfuls)
movable (or moveable)
mummy, mummification

narcissus, narcissism
needful, needfully
nowadays (not now-a-days)

occur, occurred, occurring, occurrence
oesophagus (not eso-)
oracle, oracular
orang - utan (less common spl. orang-outang)
oscillate (not - late)

panic, panicked, panicky
parallel, paralleled
postscript
potsherd
practice (n), practise (v)
precede, accede
prefer, preferred, preference
proceed
pursue, pursuit but persuade

quarrel, quarrelling, querulous

recur, recurred, recurring, recurrent
repair, reparation
repeat, repetition
reveal, revelation
rhetoric
rhinoceros
rhombus
rhyme
rhythm
roofs (not - ves)

satellite
separate (not -per-)
serviceable
stationary (static), stationery (writing materials etc sold at a shop)
submit, submitted, submitting

terrace
terrain
terrestrial

thermometer
threshold (but withhold)
traffic, trafficking
tyranny, tyrannical, tyrannise (or tyrannize)

vacillate, vacillation
vaccine
vacuum, vacuity, vacuous
viscera (pl), viscus(sing.)
viscid
viscous, viscosity or viscousness

Westminster (not -minister)
withhold
worry, worried, worrying

APPENDIX II

TITBITS OF ENGLISH GRAMMAR

(A) Use of prepositions :

will *abide by* (rules)
was *absorbed in* (studies)
shall *abstain from* (smoking)
will *accede to* (a proposal)
has *access to* (a minister's office)
was *accompanied by* (a friend)
have to *account for* (misconduct)
was *accused of* (misuse of money)
not *accustomed to* (hard work)
was *acquitted of* (charges)
is *adequate to* (one's needs)
was *admitted into* (Christianity)
was *admitted to* (an upper class)
is *adverse to* (one's interest)
has an *affection for* (children)
is *afflicted with* (a skin disease)
not *afraid of* (ghosts)
do not *agree with* (you)
do not *agree to* (your proposal)
was *alienated from* (his friends)
is *alive to* (the consequences)
not *amenable to* (reason)
is *angry with* (his friend)
am *annoyed with* (him)
is an *antidote against* (cholera)
his *anxiety for* (his friend's safety)
an *appeal to* (the Principal)
has an *aptitude for* (music)
will *arrive at* (the railway station)
will *attend upon* (a patient)
will *avail myself of* (this opportunity)
is *averse to* (music)
there is a *ban on* (an obscene book)
please *beware of* (dogs)
does not *believe in* (God)
life is *beset with* (problems)
is *blind to* (his son's faults)
got a *clue to* (the mystery)
please *concentrate on/upon* (your studies)
was *condemned to* (death)
will *confer with* (an assistant)
is *confident of* (success)
was *confined to* (bed)
am *convinced of* (his honesty)
must *cooperate with* (others)
was *cured of* (the disease)
he *deals in* (rice)
he *deals* (well) *with* (others)
he *despaired of* (success)
I *disagree with* (you)
had to *dispense with* (his help)
must *dispose of* (the work at hand)
was *divested of* (all his power)
will *dwell on/upon* (the subject of dowry)
no right to *encroach upon* (our jurisdiction)
is *entitled to* (membership)
was *entrusted with* (a hard task)
is *envious of* (his friend's success)
cows *feed on* (grass)
tries to *fight against* (corruption)
very much *fond of* (music)
very *good at* (playing chess)
was found *guilty of* (an offence)
does not *hanker after* (money)
no *hindrance to* (your entry)

was totally *ignorant of* (the incident)
was *indebted to* (him for his help)
was *indifferent to* (my advice)
hard work is *indispensable to* (success)
did not *indulge in* (luxury)
heavy penalty was *inflicted upon* (him)
they *inquired into* (the incident)
they *inquired of* him *about* (the matter)
do not *laugh at* (others' shortcomings)
have a *liking for* (painting)
did not *listen to* (my advice)
does not *long for* (wealth)
is thoroughly *negligent of* (duties)
was *overwhelmed with* (joy)
has a *passion for* (music)
he *plunged* headlong *into* (water)
he *prefers* (fiction) *to* (poetry)
will *preside over* (the meeting)
cannot *prevent* (him) *from* (entering the room)
he *prides* (himself) *on* (his capabilities)
had to *refrain from* (smoking)
does not *rely* (only) *on* (me)
he *repents of* (his misbehaviour)
do not *resort to* (physical force)
did not *respond to* (my appeal)
they *robbed* (him) *of* (all his money)
always *seeks for/after* (happiness)
is *short of* (funds)
do not *submit to* (brute force)
they *subsist on* (milk only)
no *sympathy for* (him)
no *taste for* (music)
please *think over* (my proposal)
am really *tired of* (attending calls)
was *true to* (his word)
not *used to* (such misbehaviour)
quite *versed in* (mathematics)
went there with a *view to* (protesting)
the nurse *waited upon* (the patient)
should *warn* (him) *against* (danger)
is *worthy of* (praise)
did not yield to (pressure or threat)

(B) Articles *a* or *an* :

1. *a* or *an* is used before a singular countable noun which denotes a class :
   A dog is a faithful animal (i. e. all dogs are so). A man has two legs. An ass brays.
2. *a* or *an* is used with a noun complement that includes a profession :
   She is a tall girl. He is a good player. My mother is an author.
3. *a* or *an* is used in numerical expressions :
   a dozen, a thousand, a crore.
4. *an* is sometimes used before a consonant letter that has the pronunciation of a vowel :
   an M.A, an STD, an LLB, an N.C.C, cadet.
5. *a* is used before u, eu, and ea if they are pronounced eu :
   a unit, a university, a useful thing, a unanimous resolution, a usage, a European, a ewe, a eulogy.
6. *a* is used before o when it is pronounced w :
   a one-rupee note, a one-day match, a one-to-one situation.

(C) The Definite Article—the

1. All nouns of which there is only one, take a *the* :
   the sun, the moon, the sky.
2. *The* is used before a noun that has become definite because of a former use of it :
   His house is not far from here. Can you see the top of the house?
3. *The* is used before a definite noun :
   the rear part of the house, the window of his room.
4. *The* is used before superlatives :
   the highest number, the tallest boy, the meanest man, the most ferocious animal, the longest journey.
5. *The* is used before *first, second, third* etc. :
   the first day at school, the Third Cricket Test Match, the second row.
6. *The* is used before singular nouns denoting a class :
   The cow gives us milk. The tiger has stripes. The lion prowls by night.

7. *The* is used before the names of seas, oceans, rivers, mountains etc. : The Himalayas, The Jamuna, The Arctic Ocean, The Indian Ocean
8. Ordinarily *The* is not used before the name of countries : India is now independent. The name of Burma has changed. But there are exceptions : The U.K., The U.S.A., The Netherlands.
9. *The* is not used before abstract nouns : Death must come some day. I do not fear death. But if they are used in a particular sense, the abstract noun will take a *the* : The death of Mother Teresa.

APPENDIX III

SCIENTIFIC NAMES OF INDIAN BIRDS

অসপ্রে (osprey)— *Pandion haliaetus*
আগ্গিন (singing bush lark)— *Mirafra javanica*
আবাবিল (swallow)— *Hirundo rustica*
ইগল (black eagle)— *Ictinaetus malayensis*
কসাই পাখি (grey shrike)— *Lanius excubitor*
কাক (house crow)— *Corvus splendens*
কাঠঠোকরা (roufus woodpecker)— *Micropternus brachyurus*
কাদা খোঁচা (common or Fantail snipe)— *Gollinago gallinago*
কানঠুঁটি (flamingo)— *Phoenicopterus roseus*
কাবাসি (black-headed cuckoo-shrike)— *Coracina melanoptera*
কায়েম (purple moorhen)— *Porphyrio porphyrio*
কারবানক (stone curlew)— *Burhinus oedicnemus*
কালিশামা/কালচিরি (Indian robin)— *Saxicoloides fulicata*
কালো দোচরা (black ibis)— *Pseudibis papillosa*
কুকা (crow-pheasant)— *Centropus sinensis*
কুরচি বক (little egret)— *Egretta garzetta*
কোঁচ বক (pond heron)— *Ardeola grayii*
কোকিল (koel)— *Eudynamys scolopacea*
খঞ্জন (large pied wagtail)— *Motacilla maderas patensis*
খঞ্জন (white wagtail)— *Motacilla alba*
খুন্তে বক (spoonbill)— *Platalea leucorodia*
খুরুলে প্যাঁচা (spotted owlet)— *Athene brama*
গগনবেড় (spotted billed pelican)— *Pelecanus philippensis*
গয়ার (snake bird, darter)— *Anhinga rufa*
গাইবক/গোবক (cattle egret)— *Bubulcus ibis*
গাংচিল (common tern)— *Sterna hirundo*
গাংশালিক (bank myna)— *Acridotheres ginginianus*
গোশালিক (pied myna)— *Sturnus contra*
ঘুঘু (ring dove)— *Streptopelia decaocto*
ঘুঘু (spotted dove)— *Streptopelia chinensis*
চড়াই (house sparrow)— *Passer domesticus*
চশমা পাখি/বাবুনা (white-eye)— *Zosterops palpebrosa*
চাকদোয়েল দ্র. নাচন
চাতক (pied crested cuckoo)— *Clamator jacobinus*
চিত্রদোয়েল (magpie robin)— *Copsychus saularis*
চিল (common pariah kite)— *Milvus migrans*
চোর পাখি (chestnutbellied nuthatch)— *Sitta castanea*
ছাতারে (jungle babbler)— *Turdoides striatus*
জংলি বটের (jungle bush quail)— *Perdicula asiatica*
জলপিপি (bronze-winged jacana)— *Metopidius indicus*
ঝুঁট শালিক (jungle myna)— *Acridotheres fuscus*

টিটিভ (red wattled lapwing)— *Vanellus indicus*
টিয়া (roseringed parakeet)— *Psittacula krameri*
টুনটুনি (tailor bird)— *Orthotomus sutorius*
ডাহুক (whitebreasted water hen)— *Amaurornis phoenicurus*
ডুবুরি (little grebe)— *Tachybaptus ruficollis,* (great crested grebe)— *Podiceps Cristatus*
তালচটক (ashy swallow-shrike)— *Artamus fuscus*
তালবাতাসি (palm swift)— *Cypsiurus parvus*
তিতির (black partridge)— *Francolinus francolinus*
তুরুম্‌তি দ্র. বাজ
তুলো ফুড়কি (ashy wren-warbler)— *Prinia socialis*
দাঁড়কাক (jungle crow)— *Corvus macrorhynchos*
দুধরাজ দ্র. শাহবুলবুল
দোয়েল দ্র. চিত্রদোয়েল
ধনেশ (Indian pied hornbill)— *Anthracoceros malabaricus (Malabar pied hornbill) Anthracoceros coronatus*
নাচন/চাকদোয়েল (white spotted fantail)— *Rhipidura albicollis*
নীলকণ্ঠ(Indian roller/blue jay)— *Coracias beghalensis*
পাওয়ে (grey-headed myna)— *Sturnus malabaricus*
পানকৌড়ি (little cormorant)— *Phalacrocorax niger*
পায়রা (pigeon)— *Columba livia*
পিট্টা (Indian pitta)— *Pitta brachyura*
পেলিকান দ্র গগনবেড়
প্যাঁচা দ্র খুরলে, লক্ষ্মী
ফটকা মাছরাঙা (pied kingfisher)— *ceryle rudis*
ফটিক জল (iora)— *Aegithinia tiphia*
ফিঙে (black drongo)— *Dicrurus adsimilis*
ফুটকি (wren warbler)— *Prinia subflava*
বটের (rain quail)— *Coturnix coromandelica*
বসন্ত বৌরি, বড়ো (blue-throated barbet)— *Megalaima asiatica*
বসন্ত বৌরি, ছোটো (crimson-breasted barbet)— *Megalaima haemacephala*
বাঁশপাতা (small green bee eater)— *Merops orientalis*
বাজ, তুরুম্‌তি (red headed merlin)— *Falco chicquera*
বাজ, শাহি (shaheen falcon)— *Falco peregrinus peregimator*
বাতাসি (house swift)— *Apus affinis*
বাবুই (baya weaver bird)— *Ploceus philippinus*
বুলবুল (redvented bulbul)— *Pycnonotus cafer*
কালোমাথা বুলবুল (black-headed bulbul)— *Pycnonotus atriceps*
বেনেবউ (blackheaded oriole)— *Oriolus xanthornus*
ভরত পাখি (small skylark)— *Alaunda gulgula*
ভীমরাজ (racket-tailed drongo)— *Dicrurus paradiseus*
ময়না (hill myna)— *Gracula religiosa*
ময়ূর (common peafowl)— *Pavo cristatus*
মাছরাঙা (small blue kingfisher)— *Alcedo Atthis*
মুরগি (fowl)— *Gallus domesticus; gallus bankiva*
মৌটুসি (maroon-breasted sunbird)— *Nectarinia lotenia*
মৌটুসি (purple-rumped sunbird)— *Nectarinia zeylonica*
রাজহাঁস (barheaded goose)— *Anser indicus*
রামগাঙরা (grey tit)— *Parus major*
লক্ষ্মী প্যাঁচা (barn owl)— *Tyto alba*
লাল মুনিয়া (red munia)— *Estrilda amandava*
লাল সহেলি (scarlet minivet)— *Pericrocotus flammeus*
শকুন (Bengal vulture)— *Gyps bengalensis*
শঙ্খচিল (brahmini kite)— *Haliastur indus*
শামুক খোল (openbill stork)— *Anastomus oscitans*
শালিক (Indian myna)— *Acridotheres tristis*
শাহবুলবুল / দুধরাজ (paradise flycatcher)— *Terpsiphone paradisi*

শাহিবাজ (shaheen falcon)— *Falco peregrinus preregrinator,* (peregrine falcon)— *Falco perigrinus*
শিকরে বাজ (shikra)— *Accipiter badius*
শ্যামসুন্দর (black-heaed munia)— *Lonchura malacca*
সাদা বক (large egret)— *Ardea alba*
সারস (sarus crane)— *Grus antigone*
হরিয়া (goldmantled chloropsis)— *Chloropsis cochinchinensis*
হরিয়াল (common green pigeon)— *Treron phoenicoptera*
হলদে পাখি, হলদে বেনেবউ (golden oriole)— *Oriolus oriolus*
হাড়িচাঁচা (treepie)— *Dendrocitta vagabunda*

APPENDIX IV

SCIENTIFIC NAMES OF INDIAN ANIMALS

ইঁদুর (mouse)— *Mus musculus*
উট (camel)— *Camelus dromedereius*
উদবিড়াল, ভোঁদড় (otter)— *Lutra lutra perspicallata*
উল্লুক (gibbon)— *Hylobates hoolock*
একশৃঙ্গ গণ্ডার (rhinoceros)— *Rhinoceros unicornis*
কাঠ বিড়াল (squirrel)— *Ratufa indica centralis*
কালো ভালুক (black bear)— *Selenarctos thibetanus*
কুকুর (dog)— *Canis familiaris*
কুমির (crocodile)— *Crocodilus palustris*
কৃষ্ণসার (blackbuck)— *Antolope cervicapra rupicapra*
খরগোশ (hare)— *Lepus nigricollis ruficaudatus*
খেঁকশিয়াল (fox)— *Vulpes bengalensis*
গন্ধগোকুল (civet)— *Viverricala malaccensis*
গয়াল (gayal)— *Bos frontalis*
গাধা (ass, donkey)— *Equus africanus*
গোরাল (goral)— *Naemor haedus goral hodgsoni*
গোরু (cow/ox)— *Bos indicus*
গৌর (gaur, Indian bison)— *Bos gaurus*
ঘড়িয়াল, মেছোকুমির (gharial)— *Garialis gangeticus*
ঘোড়া (horse)— *Equus cavallus*
চিতল হরিণ (chital)— *Axis axis*
চিতা (hunting leopard, cheetah)— *Acinonyx jubatus*
চিতাবাঘ (leopard)— *Panthera purdus fusca*
ছাগল (goat)— *Capra hircus*
ডোরাকাটা হাইনা (striped hyena)— *Hyaena hyaena*
নীলগাই (nilgai)— *Boselaphus tragocamelus*
নেকড়ে (wolf)— *Canis lupus pallipes*
বজ্রকীট/বনরুই (pangolin)— *Manis crassicaudata*
বনবিড়াল (wild cat)— *Felis chaus kutas*
বাঘ (tiger)— *Panthera tigris tigris*
বাদামি ভালুক (brown bear)— *Ursus arctos*
বাদুড় (bat)— *Pteropus medius*
বারশিঙ্গা (swamp deer)— *Cervus duvauceli*
বিড়াল (cat, domestic cat)— *Felis domesticus*
বুনোকুকুর (wild dog)— *Quon alpinus dukhunensis*
বুনো গাধা (wild ass)— *Equus hemionus khur*
বুনো মোষ (wild buffalo)— *Bubalus bubalus*
বুনো শুয়োর (wild boar)— *Sus scrofa cristatus*
বেজি (mongoose)— *Herpestes edwardsii nyula*
ভারতীয় ভালুক (Indian bear)— *Melursus ursinus ursinus*
ময়াল, অজগর (python)— *Python molurus*
মোষ (buffalo)— *Bos bubalus*
লাল পান্ডা (red panda)— *Ailurus fulgens fulgens*
লাল বাঁদর (rhesus monkey)— *Macaca mulatta*
লেমুর (lemur)— *Lemuroidac sp.*
শজারু (porcupine)— *Hystrix indica indica*

শম্বর হরিণ (sambar)— *Cervus unicolor niger*
শিয়াল (jackal)— *Canis aureus indicus*
সিংহ (lion)— *panthera leo persica*
হনুমান (langur)— *Prebytis entellus*
হাতি (elephant)— *Elephus maximus indicus*

APPENDIX V

SCIENTIFIC NAMES OF INDIAN PLANTS

অর্জুন— *Terminalia arjuna*
অতসী— *Crotalaria retusa.*
অড়হর— *Cajanus cajan*
অপরাজিতা— *Clitoria ternatea*
অশোক— *Saraca asoca, Saraca indica*
অশ্বগন্ধা— *Withania somnifera*
অশ্বত্থ— *Ficus religiosa*
আকন্দ— *Calotropis gigantea*
আকাশমণি— *Acacia auriculiformis*
আখ— *Saccharum officinarum*
আখরোট— *Juglans regia*
আঙুর— *Vitis vinifera*
আতা— *Annona squamosa*
আদা— *Zingiber officinale*
আনারস— *Ananus comosus*
আবলুস— *Disopyros ebenum*
আম— *Mangifera indica*
আমড়া (দেশি)— *Spondias pinnata*
আমড়া (বিলেতি)— *Spondias dulcis*
আমলকী— *Emblica officinalis*
আলু— *Solanum tuberosum*
আপেল— *Malus sylvestris, Pyrusmalus*
আঁশফল— *Euphoria longana*
আসশ্যাওড়া— *Glycosmis arborea*
উচ্ছে — *Momordica charantia*
এরন্ড— *Ricinus communis*
এলাচ (ছোটো)— *Elettaria cardamomum*
এলাচ (বড়ো)— *Amomum subulatum*
ওল— *Amorphophallus campanulatus*
কচু— *Colocasia esculenta*
কচুরিপানা— *Eichhornia crassipes*
কদম— *Anthocephalus indicus*
কন্টিকারি— *Solanum xanthocarpum*
কপি (ফুল)— *Brassica oleracea var. botrytis*
কপি (বাঁধা)— *Brassica oleracca var. capitata*
কয়েতবেল— *Limonia acidissima*
করবী— *Nerium indicum*
করমচা— *Carissa carandas*
কলকে— *Thevetia peruviana*
কলমি— *Ipomoea aquatica*
কলা— *Musa paradisiaca*
কাঁকরোল— *Momordica cochinchinensis*
কাঁকুড়— *Cuçumis melo*
কাঁঠাল— *Artocarpus heterophyllus*
কাজু— *Anacardium occidentale*
কাঞ্চন— *Bauhinia purpurea*
কার্পাস— *Gossypium herbaceum*
কামরাঙা— *Averrhoa carambola*
কামিনী— *Murraya paniculata*
কালমেঘ— *Andrographis paniculata*
কালোজাম— *Syzygium cumini*
কাশ— *Saccharum spontaneum*
কুঁচ— *Abrus precatorius*
কুরচি— *Holarrhena antidysenterica*
কুল— *Zizyphus jujuba, Zizyphus mauritiana*
কুলেখাড়া— *Hygrophila spinosa, Asteracantha longifolia*
কেয়া— *Pandanus tectorius*
কৃষ্ণকলি— *Mirabilis jalapa*
কৃষ্ণচূড়া— *Caesalpinia pulcherrima*
খেজুর, দেশি— *Phoenix sylvestris*
খেজুর, আরবীয়— *Phoenix dactylifera*
খেসারি— *Lathyrus sativus*
গন্ধরাজ— *Gardenia jasminoides*
গম— *Triticum aestivum*
গরান— *Ceriops roxburghiana*
গর্জন— *Dipterocarus alatus*
গাঁদা— *Tagetes patula*
গাঁদাল— *Paederia foetida*
গাজর— *Daucus carota*
গাব— *Diospyros embryopteris*
গুলঞ্চ— *Tinospora cordifolia*
গোলমরিচ— *Piper nigrum*
গোলাপ— *Rosa centifolia*
গোলাপজাম— *Syzygium jambos*
ঘৃতকুমারী— *Aloe barbadensis, Aloe vera*
চন্দন— *Santalum album*

চা— *Camellia sinensis*
চামেলি— *Jasminum grandiflorum*
ছাতিম— *Alstonia scholaris*
ছোলা— *Cicer arietinum*
জবা— *Hibiscus rosa-sinensis*
জয়ন্তী— *Sesbania aegyptiaca*
জলপাই— *Olea europaca*
জামরুল— *Syzygium malaccense*
জায়ফল— *Myristica fragrans*
জারুল— *Lagerstroemia flos-reginae, Lagerstroemia Speciosa*
জিয়ল— *Odina wodier*
জিরে— *Cuminum cyminum*
জুঁই— *Jasminum auriculatum*
জোয়ান— *Trachyspermum ammi, Carum copticum*
ঝাউ— *Casuarina equisetifolia*
ঝিঙে— *Luffa acutangula*
টগর— *Ervatamia divaricata*
টম্যাটো— *Lycopersicon lycopersicum*
ডালিম— *Punica granatum*
ঢ্যাঁড়শ— *Abelmoschus esculentus*
তমাল— *Cinnamomum tamala*
তরমুজ— *Citrullus lanatus*
তামাক— *Nicotiana tabacum*
তাল— *Borassus flabellifer*
তিল— *Sesamum indicum*
তিসি— *Linum usitatissimum*
তুঁত— *Morus alba*
তেঁতুল— *Tamarindus indica*
তুলসী— *Ocimum sanctum*
থানকুনি— *Centella asiatica*
দারচিনি— *Cinnamomum zeylanica*
দূর্বা— *Cynodon dactylon*
দেবদারু— *Polyalthia longifolia*
দেশি বাদাম— *Terminalia catappa*
দোপাটি— *Impatiens balsamina*
ধনে— *Coriandrum sativum*
ধান— *Oryza sativa*
ধুঁদুল— *Luffa cylindrica*
ধুতুরা— *Datura metel*
নয়নতারা— *Catharanthus roseus*
নাগকেশর— *Mesua ferrea*
নারকেল— *Cocos nucifera*
নিম— *Azadirachta indica*
নিশিন্দা— *Vitex negundo*
পটোল— *Trichosanthes dioica*
পদ্ম— *Nelumbo nucifera*
পলাশ— *Butea monosperma*
পাট— *Corchorus capsularis*
পান— *Piper betle*
পানিফল— *Trapa natans*
পারুল— *Stereospermum suaveolens*
পালং— *Spinacea oleracea*
পিপুল— *Piper longum*
পিয়াল— *Buchanania lanzan*
পুঁই— *Basella rubra*
পুনর্নবা— *Boerhaavia repens*
পেঁপে— *Carica papaya*
পেঁয়াজ— *Allium cepa*
পেয়ারা— *Psidium guajava*
ফণী মনসা— *Opuntia dillenii*
বঁইচি— *Flacourtia sepiaria*
বকফুল— *Sesbania grandiflora*
বকুল— *Mimusops elengi*
বচ— *Acorus calamus*
বট— *Ficus benghalensis*
বনচাঁড়াল— *Desmodium motorium, Desmodium gyrans*
বয়ড়া— *Terminalia belerica*
বরবটি— *Vigna sinensis*
বাঁশ— *Bambusa arundinacea*
বাজরা— *Pennisetum typhoides*
বাবলা— *Acacia nilotica, Acacia arabica*
বিছুটি— *Urtica dioica, Urtica urens*
বেগুন— *Salanum melongena*
বেল— *Aegle marmelos*
বেলফুল— *Jasminum sambac*
ব্রাহ্মি— *Bacopa monnieri*
ভুঁইচাপা— *Kaempferia rotunda*
ভুট্টা— *Zea mays*
ভৃঙ্গরাজ— *Wedelia calendulacea*
মটর— *Pisum sativum*
মসূর— *Lens culinaris*
মহুয়া— *Madhuca indica*
মাধবীলতা— *Hiptage benghalensis*
মানকচু— *Alocasia indica*
মুলো— *Raphanus sativus*
মেথি— *Trigonella foenum-graceum*
মৌরি— *Foeniculum vulgare*
যব— *Hordeum vulgare*
রজনীগন্ধা— *Polianthes tuberosa*
রশুন— *Allium sativum*
লঙ্কা— *Capsicum annuum*
লজ্জাবতী— *Mimosa pudica*
লবঙ্গ— *Syzygium aromaticum*
লাউ— *Legenaria vulgaris, Legenaria siceraria*

লিচু—*Litchi chinensis*
লেবু— *Citrus limon, Citrus medica*
শজনে— *Moringa oleifera*
শসা— *Cucumis sativus*
শণ— *Crotalaria juncea*
শাল— *Shorea robusta*
শালুক— *Nymphaea nouchali / Nymhaea rubra*
শিউলি— *Nyctanthes arbortristis*
শিম— *Dolichos lablab*
শিমুল— *Bombax ceiba*
শিরীষ— *Albizzia lebbeck*
শিশু— *Dalbergia sissoo*
শ্যাওড়া— *Streblus asper*
সবেদা— *Achras zapota*
সরষে— *Brassica nigra, Brassica campestris*
সুন্দরী— *Heritiera fomes, Heritiera minor*
সুপারি— *Areca catechu*
সূর্যমুখী— *Helianthus annuus*
সেগুন— *Tectona grandis*
স্থলপদ্ম— *Hibiscus mutabilis*
স্বর্ণলতা— *Cuscuta reflexa*
হরিতকী— *Terminalia chebula*
হলুদ— *Curcuma domestica, Curcuma longa*
হাতিশুঁড়— *Heliotropium indicum*
হাসনুহানা— *Cestrum nocturnum*
হিজল— *Barringtonia acutangula*
হিঞ্চে— *Enhydra fluctuans*

APPENDIX VI

THE SIGNS OF THE ZODIAC

মেষ— Aries
বৃষ— Tauras
মিথুন— Gemini
কর্কট— Cancer
সিংহ— Leo
কন্যা— Virgo
তুলা— Libra
বৃশ্চিক— Scorpio
ধনু— Sagittarius
মকর— Capricornus
কুম্ভ— Aquarius
মীন— Pisces

APPENDIX VII

COMMON ABBREVIATIONS

a.	adjective
AA	anti-aircraft
abbr.	abbreviation
ABLTC	Akhil Bhartiya Lok Tantrik Congress.
abs., abstr.	abstract
a/c	account
a/c no.	account number
AC	alternating current; Assistant Commissioner
AD.	Anno Domini (in the year of Our Lord)
ad., advt.	advertisement
ADB	Asian Development Bank
ADC	aide-de-camp
ad inf.	*ad infinitum* (to infinity)
adj.	adjective
adv.	adverb
AEC	Army Educational Corps
AEF	Allied Expeditionary Force
AI	Amnest International
AG	Adjutant-General Accountant General
agr.	agriculture
AIADMK	All India Anna Dravida Munnetra Kazhagam (দ্রাবিড় প্রগতি সংঘ)
AICC	All India Congress Committee

AID	Agency for International Development (USA)
AIDS	Acquired Immunodeficiency Syndrome
AIFB	All India Forward Bloc
AIFF	All-India Football Federation
AIIMS	All-India Institute of Medical Science
AIMIM	All India Majlis-eIttehadul Muslimeen
AINTUC	All-India Natinal Trade Union Congress
AIR	All-India Radio
AITUC	All-India Trade Union Congress
alg.	algebra
a.m.	ante meridiem (before noon)
amp.	ampere
AMICE	Associate Member of the Institute of Civil Engineers
anon.	anonymous
ANZAC	Australian and New Zealand Army Corps
AOPVs.	Advanced Offshore Patrol Vessels
AP	Associated Press
APEC	Asia-Pacific Economic Cooperation.
arch.	archaic
ARP	Air Raid Precautions
ASEAN	Association of South- East Asian Nations
Asst.	Assistant
ATM	automatic teller machine
a.t.s.	anti-tetanus (or tetanic) serum
ATS	Auxiliary Territorial Service
av.	average
BA	Bachelor of Arts
Bar.	Barrister
BARC	Bhava Atomic Research Centre
BASIC	Beginner's All-Purpose Symbolic Instruction Code.
BBC	British Broadcasting Corporation
BC	Before Christ
B.Com.	Bachelor of Commerce
BE	Bachelor of Engineering
Benelux.	Belgium Netherlands Luxemburg
BJD	Biju Janata Dal
BJP	Bharatiya Janata Party
BL	Bachelor of law
BOP	Balance of Payment
B. Pharm.	Bachelor of Pharmacy
B. Sc.	Bachelor of Science
BSE	Bombay Stock Exchange
BSF	Border Security Force
BSP	Bahujan Samaj Party
C.	Centigrade / Celsius
CA	Chartered Accountant
CAD	Computer-aided design
CAM	Computer-aided manufacturing
Cantab.	*Cantabrigiensis* (or Cambridge)
Caps.	Capitals, Capital letters
CBE	Commander of the British Empire
CBI	Central Bureau of Investigation
CD	Compact disc
CD-ROM	Compact disc read-only memory (for displaying stored data on computer screen)
CENTO	Central Treaty Organization
cf.	*confer* (compare)
chem.	Chemistry; chemical
CIA	Central Intelligence Agency (USA)
CID	Criminal Investigation Department
C-in-C	Commander-in-Chief
CII	Confederation of Indian Industries
CIL	Coal India Limited
CISF	Central Industrial Security Force

CIT	Calcutta Improvement Trust
CITU	Centre of Indian Trade Unions
CMC	Computer Maintenance Corporation; Calcutta Municipal Corporation
CMDA	Calcutta Metropolitan Development Authority
CND	Campaign for Nuclear Disarmament
CNN	Cable News Network
c/o	care of
CO	Commanding Officer
co., Co.	Company
COBOL	Common Business-Oriented Language
coll., colloq.	colloquial
Cominform	Communist Information Bureau
Comintern	Communist International
cp.	compare
CPC	Civil Procedure Code
CPI	Communist Party of India
CPI (M)	Communist Party of India (Marxist)
CPI (M-L)	Communist Party of India (Marxist-Leninist)
CRP	Central Reserve Police
Cr.PC	Criminal Procedure Code
CSCS	The Central Secretariat Clerical Service
CSIR	Council of Scientific and Industrial Research
CSS	Central Secretariat Service
CSSS	Central Secretariat Stenographers' Services
CTBT	Comprehensive Test Ban Treaty
CU	Calcutta University
CVO	Commander of the Royal Victorian Order
CWC	Central Warehousing Corporation; Congress Working Committee
DA	Dearness Allowance

DC	Deputy Commissioner; direct current
DC (D.D)	Deputy Commissioner (Detective Department)
DCM	Delhi Cloth Mills; Distinguished Conduct Medal
DDT	Dichloro-diphenyl-trichloroethane
dept.	department
dict.	dictionary
Div., div.,	Division, division
D Litt.	*Doctor Litterarum* (Doctor of Letters)
DLO	Dead Letter Office
DM	District Magistrate
DMK	Dravida Munnetra Kazhagam
DOS	Disk Operating System; digital operating system
D. Phil.	Doctor Philosophiae (Doctor of Philosophy)
Dr.	Doctor
D Sc.	Doctor of Science
DSO	Democratic Students' Organization
DSP	Deputy Superintendent of Police
DVC	Damodar Valley Corporation
ECG	Electrocardiogram (or -graph)
ECM	European Common Market
Ed.	Editor
ed.	Edited
EEC	European Economic Community
EEG	electro encephalogram
e.g.	*exempli gratia* (for example)
EPZs.	Export Processing Zones
E-mail	electronic mail
ESCAP	Economic and Social Commission for Asia and the Pacific
Esq.	Esquire
et. al.	*et alii* (and others)

etc.	*et cetera* (and so forth)
EU	European Union
FAO	Food and Agriculture Organization
FB	Forward Bloc
FBI	Federal Bureau of Investigation (USA)
FCI	Food Corporation of India
FIPB	Foreign Investment Promotion Board
ff.	following
FIFA	Federation of International Football Associations
fig.	figuratively
FM	frequency modulated
Fr.	French
FRCS	Fellow of the Royal College of Surgeons
FRS	Fellow of the Royal Society
GATT	General Agreement on Tariffs and Trade
GBE	Grand Cross of the British Empire
GCM	greatest common measure
GDP	Gross Domestic Product
Ger.	German
Gk	Greek
GMT	Greenwich Mean Time
GOC	General Officer Commanding
GOM	Grand Old Man
GPO	General Post Office
GSI	Geological Survey of India
HCF	highest common factor
HDFC	Housing Development Finance Corporation
HE	His (or Her) Excellency
HH	His (or Her) Highness
HIV	Human Immunodeficiency Virus
HMT	Hindusthan Machine Tools
h.p.	horse power
HMV	His Master's Voice
HQ	headquarters
HUDCO	Housing and Urban Development Corporation of India Ltd.
HVC	Himachal Vikas Congress
IA	Indian Airlines, Indian Army
IAF	Indian Air Force
IAS	Indian Administrative Service
ib., ibid.	*ibidem* (in the same place)
IBM	International Business Machines
IBRD	International Bank for Reconstruction and Development
ICBM	Inter-continental Ballistic Missile
ICC	International Cricket Council
ICE	Institute of Civil Engineers
ICI.	Imperial Chemical Industries
ICMR	Indian Council of Medical Research
ICS	Indian Civil Service
ICSSR	Indian Council of Social Science Research
ICICI	Industrial Credit and Investment Corporation of India
IDBI	Industrial Development Bank of India
i.e.	*id est* (that is)
IFA	Indian Football Association
IFS	Indian Forest Service
IGNOU	Indira Gandhi National Open University
IISc.	Indian Institute of Science
IIT	Indian Institute of Technology

ILO	International Labour Organization
IMA	Indian Medical Association
IMF	International Monetary Fund
IN	Indian Navy
INA	Indian National Army
INC	Indian National Congress
INS	Indian Naval Service
inc.	incorrect; incorporated
INSAT	Indian National Satellite
INTERPOL.	International Criminal Police Organisation
INTUC	Indian National Trade Union Congress
IOC	International Olympic Committee
IOU	I Owe You
IPA	International Phonetic Alphabet
IPC	Indian Penal Code
IPS	International Police Service
ISBN	International Standard Book Number
ISD	International Subscriber Dialling
ISI	(Bureau of) Indian Standards Institution; Indian Statistical Institute
IQ	Intelligence Quotient
ITO	International Trade Organization
JDU	Janata Dal United
JNU	Jawaharlal Nehru University
JP	Justice of the Peace
JPC	Joint Parliamentary Coimmittee
jr.	junior
KBE	Knight Commander of the British Empire
KC	King's Counsel
kg.	kilogram
KKK	Ku Klux Klan

km.	Kilometre
kw.	kilowatt
Lab.	labour; laboratory
lat.	latitude
Lat.	Latin
lb.	*libra* (pound)
lbw	leg before wicket
lc	lower case
LCM	least (or lowest) common multiple
lieut., Lt.	Lieutenant
LIC	Life Insurance Corporation of India
LLB	*Legum Baccalaureus* (Bachelor of Laws)
LLD	*Legum Doctor* (Doctor of Laws)
LMF	Licentiate of the Medical Faculty
Loc cit.	*Loco Citato* (Latin, in the place cited)
LSD	lisergic acid diethylomide
LTTE	Liberation of Tamil Tigers Elam
M	meridies (Latin, noon)
MA	Master of Arts
MB	*Medicinae Baccalaureus* (Bachelor of Medicine)
MBA	Master of Business Administration
MBBS	Bachelor of Medicine and Bachelor of Surgery
MBE	Member of the Order of the British Empire
MCC	Marylebone Cricket Club
MD	*Medicine Doctor* (Doctor of Medicine)
MDMK	Marumalarchi Dravida Munnetra Kazhagam
ME	Master of Engineering; Middle English;
memo	memorandum
Messrs.	Messieurs (gentlemen)
mg.	milligram
min.	minimum; minute
misc.	miscellaneous

MISA	Maintenance of Internal Security Act
MIT	Massachusetts Institute of Technology
MLA	Member of the Legislative Assembly
Mme.	Madame
MO	Medical Officer
m.o.	money order
MOU	Memorandum of Understanding
MP	Member of Parliament
m.p.h.	miles per hour
MRCP	Member of the Royal College of Physicians
MS	Master of Surgery
MSCP	Manipur State Congress Party
Mss, Ms.	manuscripts
NABARD	National Bank for Agriculture and Rural Development
NAI	National Archives of India
NASA	National Aeronautic Space Authority; National Aeronautics & Space Administration (USA)
NATO	North Atlantic Treaty Organization
naut.	nautical
NB	*nota bene* (note well)
NBT	National Book Trust
NCC	National Cadet Corps
NCDC	National Coal Development Corporations Ltd.
NCERT	National Council of Educational Research and Training
NCO	non-commissioned officer
NCSM	National Council of Science Museums
NET	National Eligibility Test
NGO	Non-Government Organization
NHRC	National Human Rights Commission
NIS	National Institute of Sports
NNP	Net National Product
no.	number, (pl. nos.)
NRI	non-resident Indian
NSE	National Stock Exchange
NSSO	National Sample Survey Organisation
NTC	National Textile Corporation
NTPC	National Thermal Power Corporation
OBC	other backward classes
OBE	Order of the British Empire
OECD	Organisation for Economic Co-operation and Development
obs.	obsolete
OED	Oxford English Dictionary
OGL	Open General Licence
OIC	Organisation of the Islamic Conference
OK	all correct
OM	Order of Merit
ONGC	Oil and Natural Gas Commission
OP	out of print
op. cit.	*opere citato* (in the work cited)
OPCW	Organization for the Prohibition of Chemical Weapons.
OPEC	Organisation of the Petroleum Exporting Countries
opp.	opposite
OT	Old Testament
OUP	Oxford University Press
OXFAM	Oxford Famine Relief
Oxon.	*Oxonia* (Oxford); *Oxoniensis* (of Oxford)
Oz	ounces
PEN	Poets, Playwrights, Editors, Essayists and Novelists

Penn.	Pennsylvania
per cent.	*per centum* (by the hundred)
pfx.	prefix
Ph. D.	*Philosophiae Doctor* (Doctor of Philosophy)
PIN	Postal Index Number
pl.	plural
PL 480	Public Law 480
PLO	Palestine Liberation Organization
p.m.	*post meridiem* (after-noon); *per mensem* (every month)
PM	Prime Minister
PMG	Post Master-General
PMK	Pattali Makkal Katchi
POW	prisoner of war
PRO	Public Relations Officer
pro tem.	*pro tempore* (Latin, For the time being)
PS	*post scriptum* (written after); police station
PTI	Press Trust of India
PTO	please turn over
PWD	Public Works Depart-ment
q.e.d.	quod erat demons-trandum (which was to be demonstrated or proved)
qr.	quarter
q.v.	*quod vide* (see it; lit. which see)
RA	Royal Academy
RADAR	Radio detecting and ranging
RAS	Royal Asiatic Society
RBI	Reserve Bank of India
ref.	reference
Rep.	representative; republic
Rev.	Reverend
RJD	Rashtriya Janata Dal
RMS	Railway Mail Service
r.p.m.	revolutions per minute
RSP	Revolutionary Socialist Party
RSVP	respondez s'il vous plait (reply, if you please)
Ry.	railway
SAARC	South-Asian Association for Regional Co-operation
SAD	Shiromani Akali Dal
SADM	Shiromani Akali Dal Maan
SAI	Sports Authority of India
SAIL	Steel Authority of India Limited
SC	Staff College; Supreme Court; Scheduled Classes
SCI	Shipping Corporation of India
SDBs.	Seaward Defence Boats
SDF	Sikkim Democratic Front
SDR	Special Drawing Rights
SEATO	South-East Asian Treaty Organization
SEBI	Securities and Exchange Board of India
sec.	second
seq.	*sequens* (following)
SIDO	Small Industries Development Organisation
SIDBI	Small Industries Development Bank of India
SJ	Society of Jesus
SLET	State-level Eligibility Test
Soc.	society
SOS	save our souls
SP	Samajwadi Party
Sp.	Spanish
SPCA	Society for the Preven-tion of Cruelty to Animals
SQC	Statistical Quality Control
SSI	Small Scale Industry
St.	Saint; street

ST	scheduled tribe
STC	State Trading Corporation
STD	Subscriber's Trunk Dialling
Syn.	Synonym, -ous
TA	Territorial Army
TB	tuberculosis
TDP	Telugu Desam Party
TIFR	Tata Institute of Fundamental Research
TISCO	Tata Iron and Steel Company
TMC	Trinamool Congress
TMC	Tamil Manila Congress
TNT	trinitroto luene (an explosive)
UAR	United Arab Republic
UGC	University Grants Commission
UK	United Kingdom
UNCTAD	United Nations Conference on Trade and Development
UNESCO	United Nations Educational Scientific and Cultural Organization
UNI	United News of India
UNICEF	United Nations International Children's Emergency Fund
UN	United Nations
UP	United Press; Uttar Pradesh; United Provinces
UPSC	Union Public Sevice Commission
USA	United States of America
USSR	Union of Soviet Socialist Republics
UTI	Unit Trust of India
VC	Vice Chancellor; Victoria Cross
vid.	*vide* (see)
viz.	*videlicet* (namely)
vol.	volume
VP	Vice President; Vice Principal
VS	Veterinary Surgeon
vs	versus
VSNL	Videsh Sanchar Nigam Limited
v.t.	Verb transitive
WEU	Western European Union
WFTU	World Federation of Trade Unions
WHO	World Health Organization
WIPO	World Intellectual Property Organisation
WTO	World Trade Organisation
WWF	World Wide Fund for Nature
YMCA	Young Men's Christian Association
ZSI	Zoological Survey of India

APPENDIX VIII

CONVERSION TABLE

Weight **Money Table**

[A]

1 tola, bhari	=	180 grains	=	11.664 grams
1 chhatak	=	900 grains	=	58.320 grams
16 chh (1 seer)	=	$2^1/_5$ pounds	=	933.000 grams
40 seers (1 maund)	=	$8^{22}/_7$ pounds	=	37.324 kilograms

[B]

16 drams (dr.)	=	1 ounce (oz.)
16 ounces (oz.)	=	1 pound (1b.)
14 pounds (1b.)	=	1 stone

Land Measure

[C]

1 chhatak	=	45 sq. ft.	=	4.18 sq. metre
16 chhataks (1 cottah)	=	720 sq. ft.	=	66.68 sq. metre
20 cottahs (1bigha)	=	0.33 acres	=	0.13 hectare
3 bighas (approx.)	=	1 acre		

Linear Measure

[D]

1 inch	=	2.5400 centimetres
1 foot	=	0.3048 metres
1 yard	=	0.9144 metre
1 mile	=	1.6093 kilometres
1 cubit (18 inches)	=	45.7200 centimetres

Metric System

[E] **Linear**

10 millimetres (mm.)	=	1 centimetre (cm.)		
10 centimetres (cm.)	=	1 decimetre (dm.)		
10 decimetres (dm.)	=	100 centimetres	=	1 metre (m.)
10 metres	=	1000 centimetres	=	1 decametre
10 decametres	=	100 metres	=	1 hectometre
10 hectometres	=	1000 metres	=	1 kilometre

[F] **Weight**

10 milligrams (mg.)	=	1 centigram (cg.)		
10 centigrams	=	1 decigram (dg.)		
10 decigrams	=	100 centigrams	=	1 gram (gm.)
10 grammes	=	1 decagram (dg.)		
10 decagrams	=	100 grams	=	1 hectogram (hg.)
10 hectograms	=	1000 grams	=	1 kilogram (kg.)
100 kilograms	=	1 quintal		
10 quintals	=	1000 kgs.	=	1 tonne

APPENDIX IX

BENGALI TERMINOLOGY OF ADMINISTRATION

Abrogation of Constitution	সংবিধান বাতিল
Absence	গরহাজিরা
Absentee	অনাবাসী
Absolute right	পূর্ণ স্বত্ব
Absolute title	পূর্ণ স্বত্বাধিকার
Abstract Form	সংক্ষিপ্ত নিদর্শ
Academic	শিক্ষাগত, কেতাবি
Academic Council	শিক্ষা সংসদ
Academic Session	শিক্ষাবর্ষ
Academy	পরিষৎ
Acceptor	প্রতিগ্রহীতা
Accession	সংযোজন, যোজনা, বৃদ্ধি, পরিগ্রহণ
Accessories	সরঞ্জাম
Accession Register	সংযোজন পঞ্জি
Accountant	হিসাবরক্ষক, গাণনিক
Accountant General	মহা-গাণনিক
Accounts Clerk	গণক করণিক
Accounts Officer	গণন আধিকারিক
Accredited	অধিকারপ্রাপ্ত, ক্ষমতাপ্রাপ্ত
Accrued interest	সঞ্চিত সুদ, জমা সুদ, অর্জিত সুদ, উপচিত সুদ
Accused	অভিযুক্ত, আসামি
Acknowledgment due (A/D)	প্রাপ্তিস্বীকার পত্র
Acquisition	অধিগ্রহণ, আহরণ, অর্জন
Acquaintance Book	বেতন বই
Acting	ভারপ্রাপ্ত, সাময়িক
Actionable Claim	নালিশযোগ্য দাবি, আদালতগ্রাহ্য দাবি
Actuary	গণনা বিশারদ, বিমা-গাণনিক, বিমা হিসাবনবিশ
A.D.C. (Aide-de-camp) to the Governor	রাজ্যপালের দেহরক্ষী / পার্শ্বচর
Additional Chief Engineer	অপর মুখ্য প্রযুক্তিবিদ
Additional Chief Secretary	অপর মুখ্য সচিব
Additional Director	অপর অধিকর্তা
Ad hoc	তদর্থক
Ad hoc Committee	তদর্থক সমিতি

Ad interim	অন্তর্বর্তী
Adjudicator	ন্যায়-নির্ণায়ক
Adjusted	সমন্বয়িত
adjustment	সমন্বয়ন
Administered Price	সরকার নির্ধারিত মূল্য
Administration	প্রশাসন, পরিচালনা
Administrative Officer	প্রশাসন আধিকারিক
Admiral	নৌ-সেনাপতি, অ্যাডমিরাল
Admiralty	প্রধান নৌ-সেনাপতির কার্যালয়, নৌ-সচিব সভা
Admiral, Vice	উপ নৌ-সেনাপতি
Admit to bail	জামিন মঞ্জুর করা
Ad-referendum	বিবেচনা সাপেক্ষ
Adult Franchise / Suffrage	বয়স্ক ভোটাধিকার
Adviser	উপদেষ্টা
Advisory Board	উপদেষ্টা পর্ষদ
Advocate General	মহা-অধিবক্তা
Affidavit	শপথ, হলফনামা
Affiliated to University	বিশ্ববিদ্যালয় অধিভুক্ত, বিশ্ববিদ্যালয় অনুমোদিত
Age-group	বয়োবর্গ, বয়োগোষ্ঠী
Agency	অনুসংগঠন, এজেন্সি
Agenda	আলোচ্য সূচি, কৃত্য-সূচি
Agricultural Co-operative Credit Society	কৃষি সমবায়-ঋণদান সমিতি
Agricultural Development Commissioner	কৃষি-বিকাশ মহাধ্যক্ষ
Agricultural Income Tax Officer	কৃষি আয়কর আধিকারিক
Aide-de-camp	এডিকং, দেহরক্ষী
Ambassador	রাষ্ট্রদূত, রাজদূত
Annexure	সংযোজনী, সংলাগ
Apartment	আবাসিকা, প্রকোষ্ঠ
Appellate Authority	আপিল কর্তৃপক্ষ, আপিল প্রাধিকারী
Application form	আবেদন নিদর্শ
Appointing authority	নিয়োগ অধিকারী
Apprentice-clerk	শিক্ষাধীন করণিক

Appropriate authority	যথাযোগ্য কর্তৃপক্ষ
Arbitrate award	মধ্যস্থতার রায়, রোয়েদাদ
Arbitrator	মধ্যস্থ, শালিশ
Area Headquarters	আঞ্চলিক সদর (দপ্তর)
Area Manager	অঞ্চল ব্যবস্থাপক / কর্মাধ্যক্ষ
Area Rationing Officer	স্থানিক সংবিভাগ আধিকারিক
Assembly Proceedings	বিধানসভার কার্যবিবরণ
Assessee	করদাতা, (কর) নির্ধারী
Assessment of resources	সংগতি নির্ধারণ
Assessor	(কর) নির্ধারক / নিরুপক
Assistant	সহ-, সহায়ক, সহকারী
At call	তলব মতো
Attache	সহদূত, অ্যাটাশে
Attached Officer	সংযুক্ত আধিকারিক
Attendence Register	হাজিরা খাতা
Attest	প্রত্যয়ন করা, সত্যায়ন করা
Attorney General	মহান্যায়বাদী
Auditor	নিরীক্ষক
Authenticate	প্রামাণিক করা
Authenticated	প্রামাণিক
Authorisation	অধিকার প্রদান
Authorised	অনুমোদিত, অধিকার প্রাপ্ত, প্রাধিকৃত
Autonomous	স্বশাসিত
Authority	কর্তৃত্ব, অধিকার, অধকারী, কর্তৃপক্ষ প্রাধিকারি ; সংস্থা
Back door policy	নেপথ্য কৌশল / নীতি
Backlog	জমে থাকা কাজ
Bail	জামিন
Bailiff	পেয়াদা, বেলিফ
Bailsman	জামিনদার
Ban	নিষেধাজ্ঞা, নিষেধ
Banned	নিষিদ্ধ
Basic education	মৌল শিক্ষা, বুনিয়াদি শিক্ষা
Beat Officer	বিট আধিকারিক
Bench Clerk	পেশকার
Bio-data	জীবনপঞ্জি
Birth Certificate	জাতক পত্র

B.D.O. (Block Development Officer)	ব্লক উন্নয়ন আধিকারিক
Board	পর্ষৎ, পর্ষদ
Board of Directors	পরিচালন পর্ষদ
Board of Secondary Education	মধ্যশিক্ষা পর্ষদ
Bond	মুচলেকা ; ঋণপত্র
Book transfer	জমা বদল
Budget	আয়ব্যয়ক
Buffer stock	আপৎকালীন মজুত
Bulletin	জ্ঞাপন পত্র
Cabinet	মন্ত্রী পরিষদ, মন্ত্রীসভা
Campaign	প্রচারাভিযান
Camp Office	শিবির কার্যালয়
Candidacy / Candidature	প্রার্থী হওয়া, প্রার্থীত্ব
Candidate	প্রার্থী, পদ-প্রার্থী, নির্বাচন-প্রার্থী
Capitation Fee	মাথট, মাথাপিছু দেয়
Carbon copy	কার্বন প্রতিলিপি
Card	পত্রী, কার্ড
Caretaker	অবধায়ক
Cash Register	রোকড় খাতা
Casting vote	নির্ণায়ক মত / ভোট
Casual leave	নৈমিত্তিক ছুটি
Caution money	জামানত
Ceiling	ঊর্ধ্বসীমা
Censor	বিবাচক, সেনসর
Central Bureau of Investigation	কেন্দ্রীয় তদন্ত ব্যুরো
Central Intelligence Department	কেন্দ্রীয় গোয়েন্দা বিভাগ
Certificate	শংসাপত্র, প্রমাণ পত্র
Certificate Officer	তলব আধিকারিক
Certificate of fitness	কার্যোপযোগ পত্র, ক্ষমত্বপত্র, যোগ্যতা পত্র
Certified copy	সুস্থতা পত্র, প্রত্যয়িত লিপি
Certify	প্রত্যয়ন করা, শংসা করা
Chairman / Chairperson	সভাপতি
Character Certificate	শীলপত্র, চরিত্রপত্র
Charge d'affair	সহদূত
Charge sheet	অভিযোগ পত্র
Chartered Accountant	সনদপ্রাপ্ত হিসাব পরীক্ষক

Checked and found to be correct	পরীক্ষান্তে নির্ভুল পাওয়া গেল
Check-list	নজর তালিকা, ঈক্ষা তালিকা
Check-post	নজর-ফাঁড়ি
Checking Officer	বীক্ষাধিকারিক
Chemical Engineer	রসায়ন প্রযুক্তিবিদ
Chief Conservator of Forests	মুখ্য বনপাল
Chief Executive	মুখ্য নির্বাহী
Chief Inspector of Smoke Nuisance	মুখ্য ধূমদূষণ পরিদর্শক
Chief Judge	মুখ্য বিচারক
Chief Justice	প্রধান বিচারপতি
Chief Medical Officer	মুখ্য চিকিৎসাধিকারি
Chief Metropolitan Magistrate	মুখ্য-মহানগর বিচারক
Chief Minister's Secretariat	মুখ্যমন্ত্রীর সচিবালয়
Chief reporter	মুখ্য প্রতিবেদক
Chief Whip	মুখ্য সচেতক
C.I.D. (Criminal Investigation Department)	গোয়েন্দা বিভাগ
Circle Inspector	মণ্ডল পরিদর্শক
Circuit House	সদর বাংলা, আবর্ত-ভবন
Circular	প্রচার বিজ্ঞপ্তি
Citizen, Naturalised	অধিকারপ্রাপ্ত নাগরিক
Civil Code	দেওয়ানি সংহিতা
Civil Court	দেওয়ানি আদালত
Civil Defence	অসামরিক প্রতিরক্ষা
Civil Engineer	বাস্তু প্রযুক্তিবিদ
Civil Marriage	আইনি বিবাহ
Civil Supplies Department	অসামরিক সরবরাহ বিভাগ
Claimant	স্বত্বার্থী, দাবিদার
Coalition Government	যৌথ সরকার
Code of Civil Procedure	দেওয়ানি কার্যবিধি
Code of Criminal Procedure	ফৌজদারি কার্যবিধি
Codified	বিধিবদ্ধ
Collector	সমাহর্তা
Collectorate	সমাহর্তালয়
Commissioner of Excise	অন্তঃশুল্ক মহাধ্যক্ষ
Commissioner of Income Tax	আয়কর মহাধ্যক্ষ
Commissioner of Police	আরক্ষা মহাধ্যক্ষ, নগরপাল
Committee	সমিতি, কমিটি
Communication Ministry	যোগাযোগ মন্ত্রক
Communiqué	ইস্তাহার, বিবৃতি
Community Development	সমষ্টি উন্নয়ন
Community Project	সমষ্টি প্রকল্প
Comptroller and Auditor General	মহা হিসাব-নিয়ামক ও (হিসাব) নিরীক্ষক
Confidential File	গোপন নথি
Constituent Assembly	গণপরিষদ
Consul-General	মহা-(বাণিজ্য) দূত
Consulate	উপদূতাবাস
Controller	নিয়ামক
Controller of Examination	পরিক্ষা-নিয়ামক
Convener	আহ্বায়ক
Convocation	সমাবর্তন
Cooperative Directorate	সমবায় অধিকার
Cooperative Housing Society	সমবায় আবাসন সমিতি
Co-opted	সহযোজিত
Copy	প্রতিলিপি, নকল, কপি
Corporate	নিগমবদ্ধ
Corporation	নিগম
Corporation, Municipal	পৌর-নিগম
Correspondence Clerk	পত্র-করণিক
Cost Accountant	ব্যয়-হিসাবরক্ষক
Council	পরিষদ, সংসদ
Councillor	পরিষদের সদস্য ; পৌর সভার সদস্য
Covering letter	পোষক পত্র, সহায়ক পত্র
Custody	অভিরক্ষা, জিম্মা, হেফাজত
Custom House	বহিঃশুল্ক ভবন
Dairy Development Officer	দোহ উন্নয়ন আধিকারিক
Deadline	সময়সীমা
Declaration	হলপ, ঘোষণা, ঘোষণাপত্র

Deed of agreement একরারনামা
Deemed University প্রতিম বিশ্ববিদ্যালয়, পরিগণ্য বিশ্ববিদ্যালয়
Delimitation Commission সীমানির্ধারণ-আয়োগ
Demi-official আধা সরকারি
Demophobia জনতাভীতি
Denationalisation বিরাষ্ট্রীয়করণ
Demurrage বিলম্ব শুল্ক, বিলম্বের খেসারত
Department বিভাগ
Deputation প্রতিনিয়োগ, ডেপুটেশন, প্রতিনিধিত্ব
Deputy উপ, প্রতিনিধি
Deputy Chairman উপ-সভাপতি
Detention নিরোধ, আটক
Detenue রাজবন্দি
Development উন্নয়ন, বিকাশ
Diarchy দ্বৈতশাসন
Diplomat কূটনীতিক
Directive নির্দেশপত্র
Directive Principles নির্দেশক-নীতিসমূহ
Director অধিকর্তা, পরিচালক
Directorate অধিকার, পরিদপ্তর
Directorate of Fisheries মৎস্য অধিকার
Disciplinary action শাস্তিমূলক ব্যবস্থা
Disposal নিষ্পত্তি, ব্যবস্থাপনা, বিলি ব্যবস্থা
Dispute বিবাদ
Dissent, note of ভিন্ন মন্তব্য
Dissident বিসংবাদী
District and Sessions Judge জেলা ও দায়রা বিচারক
District Gazetteer জেলা তথ্যকোষ
District Judge জেলা জজ
Division বিভাগ
Division (under the charge of Executive Engineer) ভুক্তি
Divisional Commissioner ভুক্তিপতি, বিভাগীয় কমিশনার
Division Bench খণ্ডপীঠ
Document of title স্বত্বপ্রমাণ দলিল
Documentation Officer তথ্য-সংরক্ষণ আধিকারিক
Dominion Status অধিরাজ্যের মর্যাদা
Duty Officer কর্মরত আধিকারিক

E.B. (efficiency bar) যোগ্যতাবিচার
Editorial Section সম্পাদকীয় উপশাখা
Election Commission নির্বাচন আয়োগ
Election Commissioner নির্বাচন মহাধ্যক্ষ
Electoral roll(s) নির্বাচক তালিকা
Electorate নির্বাচক মণ্ডলী
Electrical Engineer তড়িত প্রযুক্তিবিদ
Embassy দূতাবাস
Emergency আপৎকালীন ; জরুরি, সংকট, অত্যয়
Enclosure সংলগ্নী ; বেষ্টনী, বেড়া
Employment Exchange কর্মসংস্থান কেন্দ্র
Enclave ছিটমহল
Enforcement Branch নির্বহন শাখা
Establishment Clerk সংস্থা-করণিক
Estate duty সংস্থা কর
Estate Officer সংস্থা আধিকারিক
Estimate প্রাক্‌কলন, মূল্যানুমান
Estimatted আনুমানিক, প্রাক্‌কলিত, অনুমিত
European Common Market ইয়োরোপীয় অভিন্ন বাজার
Executive নির্বাহী, নির্বাহক
Executive Committee নির্বাহী সমিতি
Ex-officio পদসূত্রে, পদাধিকারে
Ex parte একতরফা
Extra judicial বিচার-বহির্ভূত
Extra legal আইন বহির্ভূত
Factories Act কারখানা আইন
Fact finding Committee তথ্যানুসন্ধান সমিতি
Faculty of Arts কলা অনুষদ
Fair price shop ন্যায্যমূল্যের দোকান
Feasibility report সম্ভাব্যতা প্রতিবেদন
Federation আমেল, ফেডারেশন
Field Manager ক্ষেত্রীয় ব্যবস্থাপক
Field Officer ক্ষেত্রীয় আধিকারিক
Field Worker ক্ষেত্রীয় কর্মী
File Copy নথি-প্রতিলিপি
Filing নথিভুক্তি, নথিভুক্তিকরণ, নথিবদ্ধকরণ
Final অন্তিম, চূড়ান্ত
Finance Commission অর্থ কমিশন আয়োগ
Finance Ministry অর্থ মন্ত্রক

Financier অর্থসংস্থানকারী
Finding সিদ্ধান্ত
First Information Report প্রথম এত্তেলা, এজাহার
Fiscal Policy রাজস্ব-নীতি
Forecasting Officer পূর্বাভাস আধিকারিক
Foreign Mission বৈদেশিক দূতাবাস
Foreign Secretary পররাষ্ট্র সচিব
Foreign Service পররাষ্ট্র কৃত্যক
Forest Guard বনরক্ষী
Forest Ranger বনরক্ষক
Form নিদর্শ, ফর্ম
Forme ফর্মা
Forum পীঠ, মঞ্চ
Freelance স্বাধীন, বিলগ্ন
Full Bench পূর্ণাসন, পূর্ণপীঠ
Functional কৃত্যগত, ব্যবহারিক
Functionary কৃত্যকারী, কর্মকর্তা
Fund তহবিল, নিধি
Fundamental মৌল, মৌলিক, মূল

Gazette রাজপত্র, গেজেট
Gazetted (রাজপত্রে) ঘোষিত
Gazetteer ভৌগোলিক নামসূচি, তথ্যকোষ, গেজেটিয়ার
General Council সাধারণ পরিষদ
General Diary নালিশনামা
General Manager মহাকর্মাধ্যক্ষ, ব্যবস্থাপক
General Secretary সাধারণ সম্পাদক
Governance শাসন
Governing Body পরিচালকবর্গ, শাসকবর্গ
Government Counsel সরকারি কৌসুলি
Government Undertaking সরকারি সংস্থা
Governor's Secretariat রাজ্যপালের সচিবালয়
Gradation list পর্যায় সূচি
Graded পর্যায়িত
Grand Trunk Road মহাপথ
Grant অনুদান, মঞ্জুরি
Grant-in-aid সহায়ক অনুদান
Ground Engineer ভূতল প্রযুক্তিবিদ
Guideline নিরিখ, নির্দেশিকা

Habeas Corpus সশরীর হাজিরা, বন্দি প্রত্যক্ষীকরণ
Handbill প্রচার পত্র, ইস্তাহার
Handbook সার পুস্তিকা
Handling agent মধ্যবর্তী নিযুতক
Hand note খত, হাতচিঠা
Hand-out জ্ঞাপনপত্র
Have-nots বিত্তহীন
Haves বিত্তবান
Head Clerk প্রধান করণিক
Head Jamadar সর্দার জমাদার
Head of a department বিভাগীয় প্রধান
Head Office প্রধান অফিস
Head of the Municipality পৌর প্রধান
Headquarters সদর দপ্তর
Health Assistant স্বাস্থ্য সহায়ক
Health Board স্বাস্থ্য পর্ষদ
Health Department স্বাস্থ্য বিভাগ
Health Officer স্বাস্থ্য আধিকারিক
Hegemony আধিপত্য, কর্তৃত্ব, নেতৃত্ব
Hereafter অতঃপর
Hereby এতদ্দ্বারা
Hereinafter অতঃপর
Herein এখানে
Herein before ইতিপূর্বে
Hereof এর, এ-সম্বন্ধে
Hereto এ পর্যন্ত
Hereupon এতে, এই কারণে
Herewith এতৎসহ, এইসঙ্গে
High Command শীর্ষাধিকার, হাউকমান্ড
High Commission প্র-মহাধ্যক্ষস্থান
Home Department স্বরাষ্ট্র বিভাগ
Home Ministry স্বরাষ্ট্র মন্ত্রক
Hon'ble মাননীয়
Honorary অবৈতনিক, সাম্মানিক
Honorary Magistrate অবৈতনিক ম্যাজিস্ট্রেট / শাসক
Honorary Secretary অবৈতনিক বা সাম্মানিক সম্পাদক
Housing Directorate আবাসন অধিকার
Hypothecated দায়বদ্ধ

Immigrant অভিবাসী
Immigration অভিবাসন
Imprest money অগ্রদত্ত (অর্থ)
imprint মুদ্রা বিজ্ঞপ্তি
Improvement Trust উন্নয়ন সংস্থা
Income Tax Investigation Department আয়কর তদন্ত বিভাগ
Income Tax Officer আয়কর আধিকারিক

Indian Administrative Service ভারতীয় প্রশাসন কৃত্যক
Industrial Complex শিল্প চত্বর
Industrial Estate শিল্প এলাকা, শিল্প মহাল
Inquiry Commission অনুসন্ধান আয়োগ
Inspector-General of Police মহা-আরক্ষা-পরিদর্শক
Inspector of Schools বিদ্যালয় পরিদর্শক
Intellectual বুদ্ধিজীবী, বৌদ্ধিক, মননশীল
Inter-departmental আন্তর্বিভাগীয়
Investigation তদন্ত, অনুসন্ধান
Issuing Officer প্রদানকারী আধিকারিক

Jail Warden কারাপ্রহরী
Jailor কারাধ্যক্ষ
Jamadar জমাদার
Joint Commission যুক্ত-আয়োগ
Joint Committee যুক্ত-সমিতি
Joint Director যুগ্ম-অধিকর্তা
Judicial Council ন্যায়-পরিষদ, বিচার পরিষদ
Jurist ব্যবহারশাস্ত্রজ্ঞ
Justice of Peace ন্যায়পাল

Keeper of Records মহাফেজ, দলিলরক্ষক

Labour Directorate শ্রম অধিকার
Labour Officer শ্রম আধিকারিক
Land Acquisition Officer ভূমিগ্রহ আধিকারিক
Law Agent আইন প্রতিনিধি
Law Officer আইন / বিধি আধিকারিক
Leap year অধিবর্ষ
Legal Adviser আইন উপদেষ্টা
Legal Remembrancer বিধি-নির্দেশক
Legislator বিধায়ক
Liaison সংযোগ, সম্পর্ক
Liaison Office সংযোগ কার্যালয়
Liaison Officer সংযোগ আধিকারিক
Librarian গ্রন্থগারিক
Licence অনুজ্ঞাপত্র
Licenced অনুজ্ঞাপ্রাপ্ত
Licencing Officer অনুজ্ঞা আধিকারিক
Lien পূর্বস্বত্ব
Liftman লিফট চালক
Line of action কর্মধারা, কর্মপদ্ধতি
Lingua-franca যোগাযোগের মুখ্য ভাষা
Liquidator অবলোপন আধিকারিক
Livestock Service পশুসম্পদ কৃত্যক
Directorate অধিকার
Local Government স্থানীয় শাসন
Locus Standi হস্তক্ষেপের অধিকার
Loud Speaker শব্দ বিবর্ধক

Maintenance Superintendent of Government Vehicles সরকারি যান রক্ষাধীক্ষক
Malafide অসদবুদ্ধিকৃত, অসদুদ্দেশ্য প্রণোদিত
Manager ব্যবস্থাপক, পরিচালক, কর্মাধ্যক্ষ
Managerial Staff ব্যবস্থাপক কর্মীবৃন্দ, পরিচালন কর্মীবৃন্দ
Managing Committee নির্বাহী সমিতি
Managing Director পরিচালন অধিকর্তা
Managing Editor নির্বাহী সম্পাদক
Mandamus পরমাদেশ, ম্যান্ডামাস
Master painter ওস্তাদ রংমিস্ত্রি
Master Plan মহাপরিকল্পনা
Mayor পুরপিতা, মেয়র
Meteorological Office আবহাওয়া অফিস
Migrant পরিযায়ী
Minister-in-charge ভারপ্রাপ্ত মন্ত্রী
Minister of State প্রতিমন্ত্রী
Ministry of Agriculture কৃষি মন্ত্রক
Ministry of Chemicals & Fertiliser রসায়ন ও সার মন্ত্রক
Ministry of Civil Aviation & Tourism অসামরিক বিমান চলাচল ও পর্যটন মন্ত্রক
Ministry of Civil Supplies, Consumer Affairs and Public Distribution System অসামরিক সরবরাহ, ভোগ্যপণ্য ও গণবন্টন মন্ত্রক
Ministry of Coal কয়লা মন্ত্রক
Ministry of Commerce বাণিজ্য মন্ত্রক
Ministry of Communications যোগাযোগ মন্ত্রক
Ministry of Defence প্রতিরক্ষা মন্ত্রক

Ministry of Environment and Forests	পরিবেশ ও বন মন্ত্রক
Ministry of External Affairs	বিদেশ মন্ত্রক
Ministry of Finance	অর্থ মন্ত্রক
Ministry of Food	খাদ্য মন্ত্রক
Ministry of Food Processing Industry	খাদ্য প্রক্রিয়াকরণ শিল্প মন্ত্রক
Ministry of Health & Family Welfare	স্বাস্থ্য ও পরিবার কল্যাণ মন্ত্রক
Minstry of Home Affairs	স্বরাষ্ট্র মন্ত্রক
Ministry of Human Resources Development	বিকাশ মন্ত্রক
Ministry of Industry	শিল্প মন্ত্রক
Ministry of Information & Broadcasting	তথ্য ও সম্প্রচার মন্ত্রক
Ministry of Labour	শ্রম মন্ত্রক
Ministry of Law, Justice & Company Affairs	আইন, বিচার ও কোম্পানি বিষয়ক মন্ত্রক
Ministry of Mines	খনি মন্ত্রক
Ministry of Non-Conventional Energy Source	অচিরাচরিত শক্তি-উৎস মন্ত্রক
Ministry of Parliamentary Affairs	পরিষদ বিষয়ক মন্ত্রক
Ministry of Personnel, Grievances and Pensions	কর্মীবর্গ, অভিযোগ ও পেনসন মন্ত্রক
Ministry of Petroleum and Natural Gas	পেট্রোলিয়াম ও প্রাকৃতিক গ্যাস মন্ত্রক
Ministry of Planning and Programme Implementation	উন্নয়ন ও কার্যক্রম রূপায়ণ মন্ত্রক
Ministry of Power	বিদ্যুৎ মন্ত্রক
Ministry of Railway	রেল মন্ত্রক
Ministry of Rural Areas and Employment	গ্রামাঞ্চল ও কর্মসংস্থান মন্ত্রক
Ministry of Science and Technology	বিজ্ঞান ও প্রযুক্তি মন্ত্রক
Ministry of Steel	ইস্পাত মন্ত্রক
Ministry of Surface Transport	ভূতল পরিবহন মন্ত্রক
Ministry of Textiles	বস্ত্রশিল্প মন্ত্রক
Ministry of Urban Affairs and Employment	শহরাঞ্চল ও কর্মসংস্থান মন্ত্রক
Ministry of Welfare	কল্যাণ মন্ত্রক
Ministry of Works and Housing	পূর্ত ও আবাসন মন্ত্রক
Monthly return	মাসিক হিসাব দাখিল
Municipal Corporation	পৌরনিগম
Municipality	পৌরসভা, পৌরসংঘ, নগর পালিকা
National Economic Council	জাতীয় অর্থ পরিষদ
Negotiable Instrument Act	হস্তান্তরযোগ্য লেখ্য আইন, সম্প্রদেয় পত্র আইন
Non-bailable offender	জামিন অযোগ্য অপরাধী
Non-collegiate	অবিদ্যায়তনিক
Non-Commissioned Officer	অবিশেষিত আধিকারিক
Non-judicial stamp	অনাবদালতি স্ট্যাম্প
Note	মন্তব্য
Notice	বিজ্ঞপ্তি, প্রজ্ঞাপন
Notice Board	বিজ্ঞপ্তি ফলক
Notified Area Authority	প্রজ্ঞাপিত অঞ্চল কর্তৃপক্ষ
O. C. (Officer-in-charge)	ভারপ্রাপ্ত আধিকারিক
Office	দপ্তর, করণ, কার্যালয়, কাছারি, অফিস ; পদ
Office-bearer	কর্মকর্তা
Official	সরকারি ; পদস্থ কর্মচারী
Official Secrets Act	মন্ত্রগুপ্তি আইন
Officiating	অস্থায়ী, ভারপ্রাপ্ত
On deputation	প্রতিনিযুক্ত
On probation	অবেক্ষাধীন
On study leave	শিক্ষাবকাশে, শিক্ষাছুটিতে
Onus	ভার (যেমন, প্রমানের ভার), দায়
On this understanding	এই মর্মে
Operating cost	চালন ব্যয়
Operation and maintenance	চালন ও রক্ষণাবেক্ষণ

Order	আদেশ ; ক্রম
Orderly	আর্দালি
Ordinance	অধ্যাদেশ
Organisation	সংগঠন, প্রতিষ্ঠান
Orientation	কোনো নির্দিষ্ট দিকে ফেরানো, অভিমুখ
Original	মূল, আসল
Outfit allowance—	উর্দি ভাতা
Outstanding Work	বাকি কাজ
Outward Register	নির্গম নিবন্ধ
Overheads	স্থির ব্যয়
Overhead charges / cost	স্থির ব্যয়
P.A (Personal Assistant)	ব্যক্তিগত / স্বকীয় সহায়ক
Package deal	গুচ্ছ প্রস্তাব, গুচ্ছ চুক্তি, সামগ্রিক চুক্তি
Panel	ক্রমসূচি, নাম তালিকা
Parameter	পরিশর্ত
Parliament	সংসদ
Parliamentarian	সাংসদ
Passport	ছাড়পত্র
Patent	কৃতি-স্বত্ব, অসপত্ন অধিকার
Pay-roll	বেতনপঞ্জি
Pay slip	বেতনপত্রী
Penal Code	দণ্ড সংহিতা
Pen-down strike	কলম-ধর্মঘট
Pen-man	লেখক, লিপিকুশল
Pension	অবসর বেতন, উত্তর বেতন, অবসর ভাতা / বৃত্তি
Pensioner	অবসরবেতনভোগী
Peon	চাপরাশি
Per head	মাথা পিছু
Per mensem	প্রতিমাসে
Persona grata	আস্থাভাজন
Personnel Department	কর্মচারী-বিষয়ক বিভাগ
Personnel Officer	কর্মচারী-বিষয়ক আধিকারিক
Pilot project	অগ্রণী প্রকল্প
Planning Commission	যোজনা আয়োগ
Police	আরক্ষা, পুলিশ
Police Outpost	(পুলিশ) ফাঁড়ি
Police Picket	পুলিশ প্রহরা
Police Station	থানা
Police Verification	পুলিশি যাচাই
Polling Agent	ভোট (গ্রহণ) প্রতিনিধি
Polling Booth	ভোট কেন্দ্র, ভোটঘর
Polling Officer	ভোটগ্রহণ আধিকারিক
Port Commissioner	বন্দরপাল, বন্দর মহাধ্যক্ষ
Port Folio	পত্রকোশ ; দপ্তর
Port Trust	বন্দর সংস্থা
Postman	ডাকহরকরা, ডাক-পিওন
Post Master	ডাকঘর-কর্তা
Post Master General	ডাক মহাধিকারিক
Power of Attorney	মোক্তারনামা, ওকালতনামা
Presidency Magistrate	প্রেসিডেন্সি বিচারক
Presiding Officer	ভোটকেন্দ্রের মুখ্য আধিকারিক
Press and Registration of Books Act	মুদ্রণ ও গ্রন্থনিবন্ধন আইন
Press Information Bureau	সংবাদ তথ্য কেন্দ্র
Press Releage	সংবাদ লিপি, সংবাদ সরবরাহ
Press Secretary	সংবাদ সচিব
Principal	অধ্যক্ষ ; প্রধান ; মুখ্য (বাণিজ্যে) মূলধন, আসল
Priority list	পূর্বিতা-সূচি, অগ্রাধিকার তালিকা
Private and Confidential	একান্ত ও গোপনীয়
Probate	ইস্টিপ্রমাণক
Probation	অবেক্ষা, শিক্ষানবিশি
Probationary	অবেক্ষাধীন, শিক্ষানবিশ
Probationer	অবেক্ষাধীন বা শিক্ষাধীন ব্যক্তি
Probation period	অবেক্ষকাল, শিক্ষানবিশকাল
Proforma	ছক
Proforma Invoice	চালানকল্প
Project	প্রকল্প
Project Officer	প্রকল্প আধিকারিক
Proper Channel	যথামাধ্যম
P.S. (Postscript)	পুনশ্চ
Public Administration	সরকারি প্রশাসন
Public Grievance	জন অভিযোগ
Public Notification	প্রকাশ্য বিজ্ঞপ্তি, প্রকাশ্য প্রজ্ঞাপন

Public Prosecutor	সরকারি অভিযোক্তা
Public Relations Officer	জনসংযোগ আধিকারিক
Public Service Commission	জন কৃত্যক আয়োগ
Public Utility Service	জনহিত কৃত্যক
Public Vehicles Department	জলযান বিভাগ
Public Welfare	জনকল্যাণ
Public Works Department	পূর্ত বিভাগ
Quarters	আবাস (যেমন Staff Quarters কর্মী আবাস)
Quotation	উদ্ধৃতি ; মূল্যজ্ঞাপন, দরপত্র
Ranger of Forests	বনরক্ষক
Receptionist	আপ্যায়ক / আপ্যায়িকা
Receipt Register	প্রাপ্তি খাতা, প্রাপ্তি নিবন্ধ
Record	লেখ্য, নথি
Recorder	নিবেশক, লিপিবদ্ধকারী
Record Keeper	নথি-রক্ষক, লেখ্য-রক্ষক
Record Office	দলিল আফিস, লেখ্য কার্যালয়
Record room	লেখ্যাগার, মহাফেজখানা
Recruiting Officer	নিয়োগ আধিকারিক
Rector	অধিশিক্ষক
Referendum	গণভোট
Regional council	আঞ্চলিক পরিষদ
Register	খাতা, নিবন্ধ ; নিবন্ধভুক্ত করা
Registrar (Co-operative Society)	নিবন্ধক (সমবায় সমিতি)
Registrar (High Court)	নিবন্ধক (প্রধান বিচারালয় বা মহাধর্মাধিকরণ)
Registrar (Home and other Departments)	করণাধ্যক্ষ
Relief Office	ত্রাণ কার্যালয়
Rent Controller	ভাড়া নিয়ামক
Reservation	সংরক্ষণ
Resolution	প্রস্তাব, সংকল্প
Restricted Holiday	সংরক্ষিত ছুটি, নিয়ন্ত্রিত ছুটি
Return	বিবরণী / দাখিলা

Revenue Board	রাজস্ব পর্ষদ
Roster-book	পালা-বই
Rotunda	গোল-ঘর, রোটান্ডা
Scam	আর্থিক প্রতারণা, জোচ্চুরি
Scheduled Caste	তফশিলী সম্প্রদায়
Scheduled Tribe	তফশিলী আদিবাসী
Scheme	পরিকল্পনা
Screening Board	বাছাই পর্ষদ
S.D.O (Sub-divisional Officer)	মহকুমা শাসক
Search-warrant	তল্লাশি পরোয়ানা
Secondary Education Board	মধ্য-শিক্ষা পর্ষদ
Secretarial	সচিবালয় সংক্রান্ত
Secretariat	মহাকরণ, সচিবালয়
Secretary	সচিব, সম্পাদক
Secretary General	মহাসচিব
Section	ধারা
Section Officer	শাখা আধিকারিক
Security Council	নিরাপত্তা পরিষদ
Select Committee	প্রবর সমিতি
Self-Government	স্বায়ত্তশাসন
Senate	অধিষদ, সিনেট
Senator	আধিষদিক, সিনেট সদস্য
Sergeant (Calcutta Police)	সার্জেণ্ট (কলকাতা পুলিশ)
Service, Administrative	প্রশাসনিক কৃত্যক
Service rules	কৃত্যক বিধি
Session, Academic	পাঠবর্ষ, শিক্ষাবর্ষ
Sessions Judge	দায়রা বিচারক
Settlement Officer	ভূ-বাসন আধিকারিক
Sheriff	শেরিফ
Shipping Agent	পোত নিযুক্তক
Shipping Corporation	পোত নিগম
Show cause notice	কারণ দর্শানোর বিজ্ঞপ্তি
Signatory	স্বাক্ষরকারী, সইদাতা
Sine die	অনির্দিষ্টকাল
Sine qua non	অপরিহার্য
Sitting	বৈঠক
Sitting member	বর্তমান সদস্য
Slip of pen	লিখন বা লিপি প্রমাদ
Small Industries Corporation	ক্ষুদ্র শিল্প নিগম
Small Scale Industry	ক্ষুদ্রায়তন শিল্প, ক্ষুদ্র শিল্প

Sole Distributor	একমাত্র পরিবেশক
Solicitor	ব্যবহারদেশক, সলিসিটর
Solicitor General	মহাব্যবহারদেশক
Speaker (of the Assembly)	অধ্যক্ষ
Specification	বিনির্দেশ, নির্দিষ্ট বিবরণ
Stamp duty	মুদ্রাঙ্ক শুল্ক
Stamp paper	মুদ্রাঙ্কিত কাগজ
Standard	আদর্শ, প্রমাণ, প্রমিত
Standing Committee	স্থায়ী সমিতি / কমিটি
State Transport	রাষ্ট্রীয় পরিবহন
Status quo	স্থিতাবস্থা
Stay order	স্থগিতাদেশ
Stearing Committee	পরিচালন সমিতি
Stop-gap	সাময়িকভাবে, অন্তর্বর্তীকালীন
Sub-Committee	উপ-সমিতি
Sub-division	মহকুমা, উপবিষয়
Sub-divisional Agricultural Officer	মহকুমা কৃষি আধিকারিক
Sub-divisional Judicial Magistrate	মহকুমা বিচারক ম্যাজিস্ট্রেট
Sub-editor	অবর সম্পাদক
Sub Judice	বিচারাধীন, বিচারাপেক্ষ
Subordinate	অধীন, অধস্তন
Subordinate Court	নিম্ন আদালত, অধস্তন আদালত
Suburb	শহরতলি, উপনগর
Suburban	শহরতলি, উপনগরীয়
Succession Certificate	উত্তরাধিকার পত্র
Summit Conference	শীর্ষ সম্মেলন
Suo motu	স্বতঃপ্রবৃত্ত
Superintendent	অধীক্ষক
Superintendent of Customs	বহিঃশুল্ক অধীক্ষক
Superintendent of Excise	অন্তঃশুল্ক অধীক্ষক, আবগারি শুল্ক অধীক্ষক
Superintendent of Police	আরক্ষাধ্যক্ষ, পুলিশ সুপার
Superintending Engineer	অধীক্ষক প্রযুক্তিবিদ বা ইঞ্জিনিয়ার
Supervisor	অবেক্ষক, তত্ত্বাবধায়ক
Supplement	ক্রোড়পত্র, পূরণ
Supreme Court	মহাধিকরণ, সর্বোচ্চ বিচারালয়, উচ্চতম ন্যায়ালয়
Symposium	আলোচনাচক্র
Table	সারণি, তালিকা
Tariff	মাশুল, শুল্ক
Task force	বিশেষ উদ্দেশ্যসাধক কর্মীগোষ্ঠী
Technical	প্রায়োগিক, কারিগরি
Technician	যন্ত্রবিদ
Technologist	প্রযুক্তিবিদ, প্রকৌশলী
Tenancy Act	প্রজাস্বত্ব আইন
Tender money	বায়না
Tender Notice	দরপত্র বিজ্ঞপ্তি
Term of Office	পদের মেয়াদ, কার্যকাল
Terms of reference	বিচার্য বিষয়, অনুসন্ধেয় বিষয়
Textbook Committee Secretary	পাঠ্যপুস্তক সমিতি সচিব
Through proper channel	যথাযথ মাধ্যম বরাবর, যথামাধ্যমে
Title page	নাম-পৃষ্ঠা, আখ্যাপত্র
Toll-bridge	পারানি সেতু
Toll-house	কুতঘর, পারানি-ঘর
Toll Station (forest)	কুতঘাঁটি
To whom it may concern	সংশ্লিষ্টের প্রতি, সংশ্লিষ্টের উদ্দেশ্যে
Trade Discount	বাণিজ্য বাটা
Traffic police	যান-আরক্ষী, যান-পুলিশ
Traffic signal	পরিযান সংকেত
Trainee	প্রশিক্ষাধীন, প্রশিক্ষার্থী
Trainer	প্রশিক্ষক
Transfer	বদলি, স্থানান্তরণ, হস্তান্তর
Transit Visa	ক্রান্তি ভিসা
Treasury	কোষাগার
Tribunal	ন্যায়পীঠ
True Copy	অবিকল প্রতিলিপি বা নকল
Trust	অছি, ন্যাসপাল
Trust-deed	অছি-দলিল
Trust fund	ন্যাস-নিধি
Trustee	অছি, ন্যাসরক্ষক
Type Copy	মুদ্রাক্ষরিত প্রতিলিপি, টাইপ করা কপি
Typewriter	মুদ্রলিখ, টাইপরাইটার
Typist	মুদ্রাক্ষরিক
Under certificate of posting	ডাক-প্রত্যয়িত
Urbanisation	নগরায়ণ
Vacancy	রিক্তি, শূন্যপদ

Vacant post	রিক্ত পদ, শূন্যপদ
Verify	প্রতিপাদন করা
Vested	বর্তিয়েছে এমন, নিহিত, কায়েমি, ন্যস্ত
Via media	মাধ্যমে
Vice-Chairman	সহ-সভাপতি
Vice-Chancellor	উপাচার্য
Vice-Principal	উপাধ্যক্ষ
Vice Versa	বিপরীতভাবে
Vigilence Commission	তদারকি আয়োগ বা কমিশন
Visa	ভিসা, প্রবাসাজ্ঞা
Visa, Transit	ক্রান্তি-ভিসা
Vote-on-account	আপাত ব্যয় মঞ্জুরি
Voucher	প্রমাণক, ভাউচার
Vox Populi	গণকণ্ঠ
Warden	অবধায়ক
Ward-master	কক্ষাধিপাল
Watch and Ward	পাহারা-টহলদারি
Week-day	কাজের দিন
West Bengal Sales Tax Act	পশ্চিমবঙ্গ বিক্রয়কর আইন
West Bengal State Profession Tax Act	পশ্চিমবঙ্গ রাজ্য বৃত্তিকর আইন
West Bengal Land Reforms Act	পশ্চিমবঙ্গ ভূমিসংস্কার আইন
Whip	সচেতক
Whip, Chief	মুখ্য সচেতক
Whispering Campaign	গুঞ্জন প্রচার
Working Committee	পরিচালন-সমিতি
Works Committee	কর্মসমিতি, কারখানা সমিতি
Writ	আজ্ঞালেখ, লেখ
Writers' Building	মহাকরণ
yours faithfully / yours sincerely	ভবদীয়
Youth Welfare Officer	যুব কল্যাণ-আধিকারিক
Zonal Office	আঞ্চলিক কার্যালয়

NOTES

NOTES

NOTES